Tolley's Tax Cases 2015

Thirty-ninth Edition

by Alan Dolton MA (Oxon)

Kevin Walton MA

Tolley®

Members of the LexisNexis Group worldwide

United Kingdom	LexisNexis, a Division of Reed Elsevier (UK) Ltd, 30 Farringdon Street, London EC4A 4HH and 9-10, St. Andrew Square, Edinburgh EH2 2AF
Australia	Reed International Books Australia Pty Ltd trading as LexisNexis, Chatswood, New South Wales
Austria	LexisNexis Verlag ARD Orac GmbH & Co KG, Vienna
Benelux	LexisNexis Benelux, Amsterdam
Canada	LexisNexis Canada, Markham, Ontario
China	LexisNexis China, Beijing and Shanghai
France	LexisNexis SA, Paris
Germany	LexisNexis Deutschland GmbH, Munster
Hong Kong	LexisNexis Hong Kong, Hong Kong
India	LexisNexis India, New Delhi
Italy	Giuffrè Editore, Milan
Japan	LexisNexis Japan, Tokyo
Malaysia	Malayan Law Journal Sdn Bhd, Kuala Lumpur
New Zealand	LexisNexis NZ Ltd, Wellington
Singapore	LexisNexis Singapore, Singapore
South Africa	LexisNexis, Durban
USA	LexisNexis, Dayton, Ohio

First published in 1976

Published by LexisNexis

A CIP Catalogue record for this book is available from the British Library.

ISBN for this volume: 9780754549451

Printed and bound in Great Britain by CPI William Clowes Limited, Beccles, Suffolk NR34 7TL

Visit LexisNexis at www.lexisnexis.co.uk

About This Book

This thirty-eighth edition of Tolley's Tax Cases contains entries for more than 3,500 cases, decided up to 1 January 2015, which are relevant to current tax legislation. The book is one of the Tolley annuals and is updated to 1 January each year. Where possible, 'postscripts' have been added where later decisions bear directly on relevant entries.

The coverage of tax cases includes income tax, corporation tax, capital gains tax, inheritance tax, national insurance contributions, petroleum revenue tax and stamp duty land tax. Certain estate duty cases relevant to current legislation are also included. Cases concerning value added tax are covered in the companion volume, Tolley's VAT Cases.

As usual, the book covers not only United Kingdom cases in the First-Tier Tribunal, Upper Tribunal, High Court (or Court of Session) and above, but also relevant decisions of the Privy Council, the Court of Justice of the European Communities, and the European Court of Human Rights, as well as Irish cases which turn on legislation similar to that of the UK. The book also contains summaries of Special Commissioners' decisions published from 1996 to 2009. There are comprehensive cross-references, and up to four reports are cited for each case to facilitate access.

In addition to a full alphabetical case index, there is a comprehensive subject index and tables of statutes and statutory instruments. There is also the usual survey of the decisions of the Courts and Tribunals in 2014. The overall significance of the year's decisions may be judged from the narrative survey.

The majority of tax cases relate to periods before the current legislation (including Taxes Management Act 1970, Taxation of Chargeable Gains Act 1992, Capital Allowances Act 2001, Income Tax (Earnings and Pensions) Act 2003, Income Tax (Trading and Other Income) Act 2005, Income Tax Act 2007, Corporation Tax Act 2009 and Corporation Tax Act 2010) came into force. References marked with an asterisk (*) are to legislation which has replaced that involved in the case summarised. See the note at the beginning of chapter 72 with regard to the Inheritance Tax Act 1984.

If it is desired to refer to a particular case, the parties to which are not known, or to cases dealing with a particular subject, the book provides three ways of obtaining the information required. Firstly, there is the Contents list at the beginning of the book, which lists the chapters and the main headings in them. The longer chapters are also headed by their own contents lists, which contain any subheadings as well as the main headings. Secondly, there is a table of statutes. The cases are listed by reference to current legislation where the legislation in force at the time of the case has been replaced. Thirdly, there is an extensive general subject index at the end of the book.

The summaries of cases reported in the Official Reports of Tax Cases are published with the permission of the Controller of Her Majesty's Stationery Office.

The original text and the first twelve editions of this book were written by the late Victor Grout CBE, LLB, formerly HM Senior Principal Inspector of Taxes, Inland Revenue Department, Somerset House.

Contents

Abbreviations and References

An asterisk (*) added to a statutory reference indicates that it has replaced, or is similar to, the relevant legislation involved in the case.

Abbreviations

ACT	Advance Corporation Tax
Adm Ct	Administrative Court
A-G	Attorney-General
BES	Business Expansion Scheme
CAA	Capital Allowances Act 2001
CA	Court of Appeal
CA(A)	Court of Appeal (Australia)
CCA	Court of Criminal Appeal
CCAB	Consultative Committee of Accountancy Bodies
CE	Court of Exchequer (Scotland) (Its jurisdiction is now exercised by the Court of Session)
Ch D	Chancery Division
CGT	Capital Gains Tax
CGTA	Capital Gains Tax Act 1979
CIR	Commissioners of Inland Revenue
CIRA	Customs and Inland Revenue Act
CJEC	Court of Justice of the European Communities
CJEU	Court of Justice of the European Union
col.	column
Comm Ct	Commercial Court
Commrs	General or Special Commissioners
CS	Court of Session (Scotland)
CT	Corporation Tax
CTA	Corporation Tax Act

CTT	Capital Transfer Tax
CTTA	Capital Transfer Tax Act 1984
DC	Divisional Court
EAT	Employment Appeal Tribunal
EC	European Community
ECHR	European Court of Human Rights
ED	Estate Duty
EEC	European Economic Community
EPD	Excess Profits Duty.
Ex D	Exchequer Division (now absorbed into Chancery Division)
Ex(I)	Exchequer Division (Ireland)
ex p.	ex parte
FA	Finance Act
F(No 2) A	Finance (No 2) Act
Fam D	Family Division
FC(A)	Federal Court (Australia)
FCA(HK)	Final Court of Appeal (Hong Kong)
FTC	Finance and Tax Chamber (of the First-Tier Tribunal)
FTT	First-Tier Tribunal
HC	High Court
HC(A)	High Court (Australia)
HC(I)	High Court (Ireland)
HCJ(S)	High Court of Justiciary (Scotland)
HL	House of Lords
HMRC	Commissioners of Her Majesty's Revenue & Customs
ICAEW	Institute of Chartered Accountants in England and Wales
ICTA	Income and Corporation Taxes Act
IHT	Inheritance Tax
IHTA	Inheritance Tax Act 1984
IRRA	Inland Revenue Regulation Act 1890
ITA	Income Tax Act

ITEPA	Income Tax (Earnings and Pensions) Act 2003
ITTOIA	Income Tax (Trading and Other Income) Act 2005
KB	King's Bench Division
LC	Lands Chamber (of the Upper Tribunal)
LGA	Local Government Act
LPA	Law of Property Act
LT	Lands Tribunal
MWA	Manchester Winter Assizes
NIQB	Northern Ireland Queen's Bench Division
NIRC	National Industrial Relations Court
NZSC	New Zealand Supreme Court
oao	on the application of
OTA	Oil Taxation Act 1975
PC	Privy Council
PCTA	Provisional Collection of Taxes Act 1968
PDA	Probate, Divorce and Admiralty Division
PRT	Petroleum Revenue Tax
QB	Queen's Bench Division
RC	Rolls Court
Reg	Regulation
RSC	Rules of the Supreme Court
s	Section
SC	Supreme Court
SC(I)	Supreme Court (Ireland)
Sch	Schedule
Sec	Section (of ICTA 1988)
SI	Statutory Instrument
SP	Inland Revenue Statement of Practice
Sp C	Special Commissioners
SPD	Supplementary Petroleum Duty
SRA	Solicitors' Regulation Authority
SSAA	Social Security Administration Act 1992

SSCBA	Social Security Contributions and Benefits Act 1992
SSCTFA	Social Security Contributions (Transfer of Functions, etc.) Act 1999
t/a	trading as
TC	Tax Chamber (First-Tier Tribunal)
TCC	Tax & Chancery Chamber (Upper Tribunal)
TCEA	Tribunals, Courts and Enforcement Act 2007
TCGA	Taxation of Chargeable Gains Act 1992
TIOPA	Taxation (International and Other Provisions) Act 1992
TMA	Taxes Management Act 1970
UKSC	United Kingdom Supreme Court
UKUT	United Kingdom Upper Tribunal
UT	Upper Tribunal
VATA	Value Added Tax Act 1994

References (*denotes a series accredited for citation in court)

AC	*Law Reports, Appeal Cases, (Incorporated Council of Law Reporting for England and Wales, 3, Stone Buildings, Lincoln's Inn WC2A 3XN).
All ER	*All England Law Reports, (Lexis Nexis, Lexis House, 30 Farringdon Street, London EC4A 4HH).
All ER (Comm)	*All England Law Reports (Commercial Cases), (Lexis Nexis, as above).
All ER (D)	All England Reporter Direct, (Lexis Nexis, as above).
All ER (EC)	*All England Law Reports: European Cases, (Lexis Nexis, as above).
ALR	Australian Law Reports.
ATC	*Annotated Tax Cases, (Gee & Co. (Publishers) Ltd., South Quay Plaza, 183 Marsh Wall, London E14 9FS) (ceased 1977).
Beav	*Beavan's Reports.

BCLC	Butterworths' Company Law Cases, (Lexis Nexis, as above).
BMLR	Butterworths' Medico-Legal Reports, (Lexis Nexis, as above).
BPIR	Bankruptcy and Personal Insolvency Reports (Jordan Publishing Ltd, 21 St Thomas Street, Bristol BS1 6JS).
BR(NS)	Bligh's Reports (New Series).
BTC	British Tax Cases, (CCH Editions Ltd., Telford Road, Bicester, Oxon OX6 0XD).
CBNS	Common Bench New Series Reports.
Ch	*Law Reports, Chancery Division.
CLR	Commonwealth Law Reports.
CMLR	Common Market Law Reports (European Law Centre, South Quay Plaza, 183 Marsh Wall, London E14 9FT).
Cr AR	Criminal Appeal Reports.
Crim LR	*Criminal Law Reports.
CSIH	*Court of Session, Inner House Cases.
CSOH	*Court of Session, Outer House Cases.
CTTL	*Capital Transfer Tax Leaflets, (Inland Revenue, Room 8, New Wing, Somerset House, Strand, London WC2R 1LB).
DLR	Dominion Law Reports.
E & E	Ellis & Ellis's Reports.
ECCD	European Commission Collection of Decisions.
ECDR	European Commission Decisions and Reports.
ECHR	European Court of Human Rights Reports
ECR	European Community Reports.
EG	Estates Gazette.
EHRR	European Human Rights Reports.
EWCA Civ	*England & Wales Court of Appeal Civil Cases.
EWCA Crim	*England Wales Court of Appeal Criminal Cases.
EWHC Admin	*England Wales High Court (Administrative Court).
Ex D	*Law Reports, Exchequer Division (see also below).
Fam D	*Law Reports, Family Division.
FCR	Federal Court Reports (Australia).

FLR	*Family Division Law Reports.
H & N	*Hurlstone and Norman's Reports.
ICR	Industrial Cases Reports.
IEHC	Irish High Court Decisions.
IESC	Supreme Court of Ireland Decisions.
IR	*Irish Reports, (Law Reporting Council, Law Library, Four Courts, Dublin).
ITC	*Irish Tax Cases, (Government Publications, 1 and 3, G.P.O. Arcade, Dublin 1).
ITLR	International Tax Law Reports, (Lexis Nexis, as above).
KB	*Law Reports, King's Bench Division.
LR Ex	*Law Reports, Exchequer Division.
LR Ind App	*Law Reports, Indian Appeals.
LTR	*Law Times Reports.
NZLR	New Zealand Law Reports.
OJ	Official Journal of the European Communities.
QBD	Queen's Bench Decisions
RVR	Rating and Valuation Reporter, (Rating Publishers Ltd, 180 Fleet Street, EC4A 2HG).
SC	Court of Session Cases.
SCLR	Scottish Civil Law Reports.
SFTD	Simon's First-Tier Tax Decisions, (Lexis Nexis, as above).
SLR	*Scottish Law Reporter.
SLT	*Scots Law Times.
Sp C	Special Commissioners' Decisions, (Tax Tribunals, 15-19 Bedford Avenue, London WC1B 3A5).
SSCD	Simon's Special Commissioners' Decisions, (Lexis Nexis, as above).
STC	*Simon's Tax Cases, (Lexis Nexis, as above).
STI	Simon's Tax Intelligence, (Lexis Nexis, as above).
SVC	Share Valuation Cases, (Lexis Nexis, as above).
SWTI	Simon's Weekly Tax Intelligence, (Lexis Nexis, as above).
TC	*Official Reports of Tax Cases, (The Stationery Office, P0 Box 276, London SW8 5DT).

TL	*Tax Case Leaflets, (The Stationery Office, as above).
TL(I)	Irish Tax Case Leaflets, (as ITC above).
TLR	*Times Law Reports (bound volumes).
TR	*Taxation Reports, (Gee & Co. (Publishers) Ltd., as above).
TVC	Tolley's VAT Cases, (Lexis Nexis, as above).
UKHL	*UK House of Lords.
UKPC	*UK Privy Council.
VTD	*VAT Tribunal Decisions, (Combined Tax Tribunal, 15/19 Bedford Avenue, London WC1B 3A5).
WLR	*Weekly Law Reports, (Incorporated Council of Law Reporting, as above).
WN	*Weekly Notes, (Incorporated Council of Law Reporting, as above).
WR	*Weekly Reporter.
WTLR	Wills and Trusts Law Reports.

The first number in the citation refers to the volume, and the second to the page, so that [1985] 1 All ER 15 means that the report is to be found on page fifteen of the first volume of the All England Law Reports for 1985. Where no volume number is given, only one volume was produced in that year. Some series, such as the ATC, have continuous volume numbers.

In English cases, Scottish and Northern Irish decisions (unless there is a difference of law between the countries) are generally followed but are not binding.

In the text, citation where appropriate is of the Official Reports of Tax Cases, Simon's Tax Cases, the official court judgment number (either the Law Reports or the Weekly Law Reports for cases before 2001), and the All England Law Reports. Only in default of these are other series referred to. For ECJ cases, the official case reference is given together with citations for the Common Market Law Reports, the European Community Reports, and (where appropriate) Simon's Tax Cases and the All England Reports.

Where legal decisions are very recent and in the lower courts, it must be remembered that they may be reversed on appeal. But references to the official Tax Cases ('*TC*') and to the Appeal Cases ('*AC*') may be taken as final.

Glossary of Latin & Old French Phrases

acte claire	so obvious as to leave no scope for any reasonable doubt.
causa causans	the immediate cause; the last link in the chain of causation.
causa sine qua non	an essential link in the chain of causation, but not the immediate cause.
certiorari	a writ commanding a lower court to certify a matter to the High Court.
eiusdem generis	of the same type.
estoppel	rule of evidence which stops a person from denying the truth of a statement previously made by him to, and relied on by, another person.
estoppel per rem judicatum	rule of evidence which stops a person from contesting an issue decided by the Court in previous litigation between the same parties.
ex gratia	voluntarily, without accepting legal liability.
ex parte	an application made to the court by one party without giving notice to the other party.
in re	in the matter of; concerning.
inter alia	among other things.
mandamus	a writ ordering the performance of a specific duty.
obiter dictum/obiter dicta	opinion(s) expressed by a judge in passing, on issues which do not form part of the essential reasoning of the decision in the case (and thus carry little authority as precedents).
per incuriam	where a court overlooks relevant authorities (so that the decision may be considered doubtful or unreliable).
prima facie	at first sight.
ratio decidendi	reason for deciding; the principle of law on which a case is decided.

re	in the matter of; concerning.
res judicata	an issue which a court has decided in an action between parties and cannot be questioned in a later action between the same parties.
sic	thus (used, for example, to show that a grammatical mistake was that of the original authority being cited, and is not a mistake made by the editor or typesetter).
sine die	indefinitely.
sub nomine	under the name of.
sui generis	of its own type.
ultra vires	outside the powers recognised by law as belonging to the person or body in question; without authority.

Survey of Leading Decisions in 2014

There follows a numerical analysis and outline narrative survey of the decisions reached in 2014 and included in this book. The numerical analysis is confined to decisions in UK courts, and thus excludes decisions of the Privy Council, ECJ and ECHR. 'Other' decisions are those in which HMRC were not a party and were neutral as to the outcome, or those which were not wholly or substantially in favour of either party. The figures in brackets are the averages of the corresponding figures for the years 2004–2013 inclusive.

Court	Number of decisions			
	TOTAL	For HMRC	For taxpayer	Others
First-Tier Tribunal (including Special Commissioners 2003–2009)	517 (197.6)	399 (140.2)	71 (37.6)	47 (19.8)
Upper Tribunal, High Court and Court of Session (Outer House)	39 (33.5)	21 (21.3)	14 (6.6)	4 (5.6)
Court of Appeal, CA(NI) and Court of Session (Inner House)	17 (13.1)	9 (8.1)	5 (3.1)	3 (1.9)
Supreme Court (including House of Lords 2003-2009)	2 (3.0)	– (1.8)	1 (1.1)	1 (0.1)
Total for all courts and tribunals (including Special Commissioners)	575 (247.2)	429 (171.4)	91 (48.4)	55 (27.4)

For several years the European Commission has been taking infraction proceedings against the United Kingdom (and other EU Member States) in its attempts to ensure a more harmonised VAT system. More recently it has begun to take similar steps in the field of direct tax, and it has taken such proceedings in three cases against the United Kingdom. In the case of *European Commission v United Kingdom (C-172/13)*, **25.25** EUROPEAN LAW, the Commission alleged that the UK had failed to fully implement the ECJ decision in *Marks & Spencer plc v Halsey*, **25.20** EUROPEAN LAW. Advocate-General Kokott delivered an Opinion emphatically rejecting the Commission's contentions, holding that 'the contested United Kingdom rules on group relief go even further than is required by European Union law in that they provide for cross-border relief in certain cases' and did not contravene the principle of freedom of establishment. However the ECJ found in favour of the Commission in the subsequent cases of *European Commission v United Kingdom*

(C-112/14), **25.96** EUROPEAN LAW, where it held that the provisions of *TCGA 1992, s 13* contravened *Article 63* of the TFEU, and *European Commission v United Kingdom (C-640/13)*, **25.155** EUROPEAN LAW, where it held that the provisions of *FA 2007, s 107* contravened *Article 4* of the *Treaty on European Union* (also known as the Maastricht Treaty, and not to be confused with the separate *Treaty on the Functioning of the European Union*).

In *Felixstowe Dock & Railway Co Ltd v HMRC*, **25.32** EUROPEAN LAW, the ECJ delivered a decision in favour of the company, holding that *Articles 49 and 54* of the TFEU 'must be interpreted as precluding legislation of a Member State under which it is possible for a resident company that is a member of a group to have transferred to it losses sustained by another resident company which belongs to a consortium where a "link company" which is a member of both the group and the consortium is also resident in that Member State, irrespective of the residence of the companies which hold, themselves or by means of intermediate companies, the capital of the link company and of the other companies concerned by the transfer of losses, whereas that legislation rules out such a possibility where the link company is established in another Member State'.

In *Göthlin v Sweden*, **31.11** HUMAN RIGHTS, the European Court of Human Rights held that the imprisonment of a trader who had removed an asset on which the tax authority had levied distraint, and had failed to comply with a subsequent court injunction, did not contravene the European Convention on Human Rights, holding that his imprisonment had been 'proportionate to the legitimate aim to induce him to fulfil his legal obligation to cooperate with the authorities and give them the necessary information about his property so that they could secure the payment of his tax debt'.

In *OAO Neftyanaka Kompaniya Yukos v Russia (No 2)*, **31.111** HUMAN RIGHTS, the ECHR awarded an oil company damages of €1,866,104,634, following the sale at auction of its principal assets. The ECHR has issued contrasting decisions on the principle of 'double jeopardy', where both civil and criminal proceedings are taken against the same person. The ECHR delivered judgments in favour of the tax authority in *Hakka v Finland*, **31.117** HUMAN RIGHTS, and *Pirttimaki v Finland*, **31.118** HUMAN RIGHTS, but delivered judgments in favour of the applicant in *Nykanen v Finland*, **31.119** HUMAN RIGHTS, and *Glantz v Finland*, **31.120** HUMAN RIGHTS.

The Supreme Court delivered an important judgment in favour of the appellant company in *Forde & McHugh Ltd v HMRC*, **73.55** NATIONAL INSURANCE CONTRIBUTIONS, holding that payments which a company had made to a funded unapproved retirement benefit scheme for the benefit of one of its directors were not 'earnings' of the director at the time of the payment. The Court held that any payments made out of the fund to the director would be deferred earnings, but the payments which the company made into the fund were not earnings.

In *HMRC v Marks & Spencer plc (No 4)*, **25.23** EUROPEAN LAW, the Supreme Court unanimously upheld the decision which the CA had reached in October 2011 (against which both sides had appealed).

Last year's edition of this survey commented on the controversial Ch D decision in *Mehjoo v Harben Barker*, **58.48** TAX PLANNING AND AVOIDANCE, observing that:

> " . . . at a time when judges in the Supreme Court and Court of Appeal have castigated some accountants for promoting tax avoidance schemes, Silber J took quite the opposite approach and held that the accountants had been negligent in failing to advise their client to adopt a specific avoidance scheme, even though that scheme was subsequently blocked by anti-avoidance legislation. Silber J's decision is also open to criticism in that he expressed the opinion that, although the appellant had been resident in the UK for many years, there had been little risk that the Revenue would contend that he had acquired an UK domicile of choice. It appears very difficult to reconcile this part of Silber J's decision with HMRC's successes in the similar cases of *Steiner v CIR*, **48.57** RESIDENCE, and *Furse v CIR*, **48.60** RESIDENCE. . . . "

And, as Peter Vaines subsequently observed in Tax Journal, "the Solicitors Regulation Authority has warned that solicitors could be censured and fined if they are involved in implementing schemes to reduce their client's liability to SDLT. By heeding this warning, it seems that solicitors risked being sued for professional negligence." Fortunately, as most commentators had hoped and anticipated, Silber J's decision was unanimously and emphatically reversed by the Court of Appeal, which held that the accountants had not been negligent. For a discussion of the case law relating to professional negligence in the light of the CA decision, see the article by Michael Thomas in Tax Journal, 7 November 2014. Incidentally Silber J's suggestion that "there had been little risk that the Revenue would contend that he had acquired an UK domicile of choice" now looks even more dubious in the light of the subsequent case of *Baron Wrottesley v HMRC*, **48.65** RESIDENCE, which is still awaiting a final decision, but where the appellant's claim not to be domiciled in the UK appears to be based on rather stronger ground than Mr Mehjoo's was.

In *Allison v Horner*, **58.41** TAX PLANNING AND AVOIDANCE, the CA upheld the QB decision that a woman who had persuaded an investor to enter a scheme relating to film production, and had advised him that it qualified for tax relief, had been guilty of fraudulent misrepresentation.

In *HMRC v Lloyds TSB Equipment (No 1) Ltd*, **8.103** CAPITAL ALLOWANCES, the CA remitted the case to the First-tier Tribunal to reconsider whether *CAA 2001, s 123(4)* applied to the transactions in question. In *Deutsche Bank Group Services (UK) Ltd v HMRC*, **22.308** EMPLOYMENT INCOME, the CA reversed the Upper Tribunal decision and held that, on the facts found by the First-tier Tribunal, the relevant arrangements met the requirements of *ITEPA 2003, s 429(4)*. In *Interfish Ltd v HMRC*, **63.227** TRADING PROFITS, the CA upheld the Upper Tribunal decision that a company was not entitled to a deduction for sponsorship payments which it had made to a rugby club.

In *HMRC v Lord Howard of Henderskelfe's Executors*, **71.118** CAPITAL GAINS TAX, the CA upheld the Upper Tribunal decision, which might at first sight seem to be counter-intuitive, that a valuable painting qualified as a wasting asset within the definition in *TCGA 1992, ss 44(1)*. Briggs LJ observed that the reference to 'plant and machinery' in what is now *TCGA 1992, s 44(1)(c)* had been introduced by *FA 1965* 'to prevent those disposing of plant and machinery from seeking to argue that, because it had a predictable life of more than 50 years, the computation of gains or losses on its disposal should admit the deduction of the full acquisition cost, rather than the written-down cost attributable to wasting assets'. Rimer LJ observed that the exemption for wasting assets, contained in what is now *TCGA 1992, s 45*, had been introduced by *FA 1968* and 'was probably not so much with a view to benefiting taxpayers with a new exemption on gains on the disposal of tangible movables as to foreclose their opportunity of achieving allowable losses on such disposals'.

In *Woodland Trust v Loring & Others (Smith's Executors)*, **72.211** INHERITANCE TAX, the CA unanimously upheld the generally accepted interpretation of IHTA 1984, s 8A, which provides that the value of a widow's nil-rate band may be increased by the amount of her late husband's unused nil-rate band. (The deceased had left a gift equal to her nil-rate band to her family, with the residue of her estate passing to a charity. The charity claimed that the provisions of *s 8A* should not apply, which would have increased the amount it received, at the expense of the deceased's family. As one online commentator observed, the case appears to show 'just how aggressive some charities have become in recent years in trying to maximise their income. Gone are the times when they were just grateful for any donations received.')

In *Sir AF Morrison v HMRC*, **71.121** CAPITAL GAINS TAX, the Court of Session reversed the Upper Tribunal decision, allowed the appellant's appeal in principle, and remitted the case to the First-tier Tribunal to reconsider the deductible amount. (Not untypically, the Court of Session released its decision in this somewhat complex case on 23 December, only two days before Christmas.)

The Ch D reached an interesting decision in *Routier & Venables (Coulter's Executors) v HMRC*, **72.28** INHERITANCE TAX, where Rose J held that a gift to a Jersey trust failed to qualify for exemption under *IHTA 1984, s 23(6)* because the words 'held on trust for charitable purposes' required 'not only that the charitable purposes be UK law charitable purposes but that the relevant trust be subject to the jurisdiction of the United Kingdom courts as well'. This decision is in line with the House of Lords decision in the 1955 case of *Camille & Henry Dreyfus Foundation Inc v CIR*, **9.99** CHARITIES. However, several commentators have observed that the decision in *Camille & Henry Dreyfus Foundation Inc* is inconsistent with the subsequent ECJ decisions in *Centro di Musicologia Walter Stauffer v Finanzamt München für Körperschaften*, **25.98** EUROPEAN LAW, and *Persche v Finanzamt Lüdenscheid*, **25.103** EUROPEAN LAW. HMRC have indicated (in their Inheritance Tax Manual at para IHTM11112) that they accept that this is the case with effect for gifts made on or after 27 January 2009 (the date of the *Persche* judgment) but not for gifts before that date. Rose J's decision does not discuss whether HMRC are correct in drawing the line at 27 January 2009, and it is not surprising that the executors have appealed to the CA.

In *HMRC v BPP University College of Professional Studies*, **4.110** APPEALS, Judge Mosedale took the somewhat draconian step of barring HMRC from an appeal for failing to comply with Tribunal directions. Not surprisingly, HMRC promptly appealed to the Upper Tribunal, which reversed her decision, holding that it had been 'outside the reasonable exercise of judicial discretion'.

In *HMRC v Ingenious Games Llp*, **4.116** APPEALS, the Upper Tribunal ordered three associated partnerships to disclose certain documents. Newey J held that it would be 'unfair and unjust' for the partnerships 'to be able to suppress or keep from the view of HMRC and the FTT relevant documents which may be harmful to their case'.

In *Vaccine Research Limited Partnership v HMRC*, **8.108** CAPITAL ALLOWANCES, where the members of a Jersey limited partnership had claimed research and development allowances, and loss relief, totalling more than £192,000,000, the Upper Tribunal upheld the First-tier decision that only £14,000,000 of the expenditure qualified for allowances.

In *Samadian v HMRC*, **63.207** TRADING PROFITS, the Upper Tribunal upheld the First-tier decision that a doctor was not entitled to a deduction for the cost of travelling between his home and two private hospitals where he worked. Arnold J held that the journeys between the doctor's home and the private hospitals were 'partly for the purpose of conducting his private practice at the hospitals and partly for the purpose of enabling him to maintain his home (the place where he lives and conducts his private life) at a location of his choosing'.

As was widely expected, the Upper Tribunal allowed HMRC's appeal in *HMRC v McLaren Racing Ltd*, **66.74** TRADING PROFITS, reversing a controversial decision by Judge Hellier and holding that the company was not entitled to deduct a fine of £32,000,000 which had been imposed by the FIA. The Upper Tribunal held that 'a deliberate activity which is contrary to contractual obligations and the rules and regulations governing the conduct of the trade, which is not an unavoidable consequence of carrying on a trade and which could lead to the destruction of the trade, is not an activity carried on in the course of that trade'.

In *Gilchrist v HMRC*, **72.216** INHERITANCE TAX, the Upper Tribunal upheld a notice of determination under *IHTA 1984, s 64*, distinguishing the earlier decision in *Howell & Morton v Trippier*, **56.107** SETTLEMENTS. David Richards J held that 'the scrip dividend shares and their proceeds of sale were, both for general trust purposes and for the purposes of IHT, capital of the settlement'.

The 2012 edition of this survey discussed the case of the case of *R (oao Lunn) v HMRC (and related application)*, **50.42** REVENUE ADMINISTRATION, where HMRC's Criminal Investigation Unit had begun a detailed investigation of an unqualified accountant, and formed the conclusion that he 'had systematically committed fraud'. Not surprisingly, HMRC have begun enquiries into the returns submitted by many of the accountant's clients. The first of these enquiries to give rise to a published Tribunal decision was *Sheard v HMRC*, **44.161** PENALTIES, where the appellant had transferred her business to a limited company, and HMRC had imposed a penalty at 15% on the basis that her return as a sole trader had understated her income and overclaimed her expenses. The appellant accepted that some of her income had been incorrectly credited to the company, but contended that her inaccuracies were attributable to her accountants. The First-tier Tribunal dismissed her appeal. Judge Walters held that the appellant 'should have noticed, and queried, and rejected, a reallocation of almost £30,000 of turnover (two-thirds of the total) from her sole trader activity in that year to a limited company acquired by her midway through the following tax year'. For a fuller discussion of this case, see the article by Mike Truman in Taxation, 23 October 2014.

The First-tier Tribunal decision in *Amah v HMRC (No 2)*, **61.54** TRADING INCOME, is of particular interest because Judge Cornwell-Kelly disapproved *obiter dicta* of Judge Radford in a previous appeal involving the same appellant (see **4.137** APPEALS). The appellant had carried on business as a freelance dispensing optician, but subsequently began working as a freelance locum optician. In granting an application for a late appeal against HM-RC's rejection of a claim to carry forward loss relief, Judge Radford simply needed to find that the appellant had an arguable case (as well as a reasonable excuse for the lateness of the appeal). However, Judge Radford appeared to go further than this, and to prejudge the merits of the appeal by expressing the view that the optician 'had continued in his trade as a self-employed dispensing optician throughout'. The substantive appeal was subsequently heard by Judge Cornwell-Kelly, who dismissed it, holding on the evidence that 'the facts very clearly indicate the cessation of one business activity and the commencement of another'.

Table of Statutes

This Table lists cases summarised in this book by reference to the provision(s) of the Taxes Acts underlying the decision, whether or not the provision is referred to in the summary. Where the relevant legislation pre-dates the Taxes Acts, the case is listed by reference to the equivalent provision in those Acts. Cases not turning on a provision of the Taxes Acts, but of interest in relation to them, are included where appropriate.

Table of Statutory Instruments

Table of Cases under Names of Parties

The table is referenced to the paragraph number. Cases are normally indexed under the name of both parties, except where the respondent is the CIR or HMRC, such cases being indexed under the name of the appellant only.

A

B

C

D

E

F

G

H

I

J

Ch D, [2000] All ER (D) 2137.

K

L

M

N

O

P

Q

R

S

T

U

V

W

X

Y

Z

1

Allowances and Tax Rates—Individuals

The cases in this chapter are arranged under the following headings.

GENERAL NOTE

There have been substantial changes to the system of personal allowances in recent years. The married couple's allowance was introduced for 1991/92 (see *ICTA 1988, s 257A*, introduced by *FA 1988*), replacing the 'higher personal allowance' which had previously been available to married men. This allowance was in turn abolished for 2000/01 (except where one partner was born on or before 5 April 1935). A new 'children's tax credit' was introduced for 2001/02 and 2002/03, but was withdrawn for 2003/04 and was replaced by a new 'child tax credit'. Although described as a 'tax credit', this is in fact a type of social security benefit, as is the 'working tax credit' which was also introduced with effect from 2003/04. For details of the changes, see Tolley's Income Tax.

Married Couple's Allowance (ITA 2007, ss 45, 46)

NOTE

The married couple's allowance was introduced for 1991/92 (see *ICTA 1988, s 257A*, introduced by *FA 1988*), replacing the 'higher personal allowance' which had previously been available to married men. This allowance was in turn abolished for 2000/01 (except where one partner was born on or before 5 April 1935). See *FA 1999, ss 31, 32*.

Marriage annulled

[1.1] An individual (D) married in 1921 and was allowed the higher personal allowance available to married men under the legislation then in force. The marriage was never consummated, and was declared null and void by a court decree in 1933. The Revenue issued additional assessments withdrawing the higher personal allowance for 1928/29 to 1932/33. D appealed. The Commissioners allowed his appeal, holding that the marriage subsisted until the decree of nullity. The KB upheld their decision. Lawrence J held that, applying the reasoning in *Anderton & Halstead Ltd v Birrell*, **63.243** TRADING PROFITS, 'it is not lawful for an additional assessment or an original assessment to be made by reference to facts which arise after the year of assessment'. Accordingly, the Revenue had no power to make an assessment 'with reference to the years 1928/29 and following by reason of facts which came into existence after those years'. *Dodworth v Dale*, KB 1936, 20 TC 285; [1936] 2 KB 503; [1936] 2 All ER 440.

Husband and wife living separately under same roof

[1.2] A couple had married in 1959. In 1982 the husband (H) declared his intention of seeking a divorce, which was granted in 1987. He claimed higher personal allowance for 1983/84 to 1986/87 inclusive. The Revenue rejected his claims, considering that in those years H and his wife were separated, so that higher personal allowance was not due. H appealed. The General Commissioners dismissed his appeal, finding that the couple had lived 'as separate households under the same roof', and holding that they were therefore separated in such circumstances that the separation was likely to be permanent. The Ch D upheld the Commissioners' decision as one of fact. On the evidence, H had not 'wholly maintained' his wife during the years in question. Applying *dicta* of Denning LJ in *Hopes v Hopes*, CA [1948] 2 All ER 920 (a case concerning divorce based on desertion), 'the husband who shuts himself up in one or two rooms of a house, and ceases to have anything to do with his wife, is living separately and apart from her as effectively as if they were separated by the outer door of a flat'. The Commissioners were also entitled to conclude that H's action in seeking a divorce confirmed that the *de facto* separation was likely to be permanent. Accordingly higher personal allowance was not due. *Holmes v Mitchell*, Ch D 1990, 63 TC 718; [1991] STC 25.

Polygamous marriage

[1.3] An individual (N), who was domiciled in Pakistan but resident in the UK from 1965, had married in 1968 at an English civil ceremony. The couple separated in 1969 and the marriage was dissolved by decree absolute in 1975. Meanwhile, N had married S in Pakistan at a Muslim ceremony. Thereafter he maintained S, but she remained in Pakistan until 1975. He claimed the higher personal allowance in respect of her for 1970/71 to 1975/76. The Revenue initially rejected the claim but the CA allowed N's appeal by consent. Having regard to the reference to 'deceased wife' in *ICTA 1970, s 12* (housekeeper allowance), and the position which would arise if a person had the misfortune to lose a wife twice in one year, the expression 'his wife' must be construed as 'a person being his wife'. *Nabi v Heaton*, CA 1983, 57 TC 292; [1983] STC 344; [1983] 1 WLR 626. (*Note. ICTA 1970, s 12* became *ICTA 1988, s 258*, which was repealed by *FA 1988, s 25*.)

Allowance claimed for 'common law wife'

[1.4] A man had cohabited with the same woman for eleven years without being legally married to her. He claimed higher personal allowance, contending that the word 'wife' should be read as including a common law wife. The Ch D held that he was not entitled to the allowance, holding that a 'wife' was a person with whom a taxpayer had entered into a marriage recognised by civil law, and did not include a common law wife. *Rignell v Andrews*, Ch D 1990, 63 TC 312; [1990] STC 410.

Married couples—other cases

[1.5] For other cases involving the assessment of married persons, see 37 MARRIED COUPLES.

Life assurance relief (ICTA 1988, s 266)

NOTE

See *ICTA 1988, s 266(3)(c)* for the withdrawal of the relief in respect of insurance policies issued after 13 March 1984. For a case concerning the *Income Tax (Life Assurance Premium Relief) Regulations 1978*, see *United Friendly Insurance plc v CIR*, **34.4** LIFE ASSURANCE. For a case concerning the certification of a qualifying policy under *ICTA 1988, s 267 and Sch 15*, see *R (oao Monarch Assurance plc) v CIR*, **34.5** LIFE ASSURANCE.

Definition of life assurance

[1.6] In a case concerning the provisions of *ITA 1853, s 54*, where the substantive issue has been clarified by subsequent legislation, Kennedy LJ defined life assurance as 'that in which one party agrees to pay a given sum upon the happening of a particular event contingent upon the duration of human life'. *Gould v Curtis*, CA 1913, 6 TC 293.

Premium advanced by insurer

[1.7] A life insurance policy provided that part of the premium could be met by an advance by the insurer on the security of the policy. The HL held (by a 5-1 majority, Lord James dissenting) that the part so advanced had not been paid for the purposes of life assurance relief. (The legislation at the time was *ITA 1853, s 54*. The relevant words of *ICTA 1988, ss 266, 273* are similar.) *Hunter v Attorney-General*, HL 1904, 5 TC 13; [1904] AC 161.

Premiums advanced and deducted on maturity

[1.8] An individual (H) took out an endowment insurance policy in 1911. It matured in 1930. £15 of each of the first seven annual premiums was advanced by the insurance company, and the £105 so advanced was deducted from the amount paid to H when the policy matured. H claimed life insurance relief for 1930/31 on the £105. The Special Commissioners rejected the claim, and H applied to the KB for an order of *mandamus* to reverse their decision. The KB dismissed his application, applying the HL decision in *Hunter v A-G*, **1.7** above, and holding that H had not paid the £105. *R v Special Commrs (ex p. Horner)*, KB 1932, 17 TC 362.

Insurance on joint lives

[1.9] Two directors of a company effected an insurance on their joint lives, bearing the premiums equally. One of them (W) claimed life insurance relief on his half share. The KB rejected the claim, holding that the insurance was not on W's life within the meaning of what is now *ICTA 1988, s 266(2)(b)*. *Wilson v Simpson*, KB 1926, 10 TC 753; [1926] 2 KB 500.

Reduction of premium on merger of insurance companies

[1.10] Following the merger of two life insurance companies, the premium on a life insurance policy was reduced by the application of a bonus. The KB upheld the Revenue's contention that life insurance relief was due only on the reduced premium. *Watkins v Hugh Jones*, KB 1928, 14 TC 94.

Life assurance policy—whether carried out in UK

[1.11] In a case concerning the meaning of the words 'United Kingdom policy' in the *Policyholders Protection Act 1975*, Lord Goff held that a policy which was effected in the UK as part of the carrying on of insurance business in the UK was necessarily carried out in the UK, unless the business of which the contract was a part had in the meantime been transferred to an insurer not carrying on insurance business in the UK. *Scher & Others v Policyholders Protection Board & Others*, HL [1993] 3 All ER 384. (*Note*. Although not a tax case, this is relevant in considering the provisions of *ICTA 1988, Sch 15*. For HMRC's interpretation of this decision, see Insurance Policyholder Taxation Manual, para IPTM1110.)

Life assurance policies—date on which effected

[1.12] A life insurance company (L) treated some of its policies as having been made on 13 March 1984, and therefore as being unaffected by the restriction in what is now *ICTA 1988, s 266(3)(c)* and as qualifying for tax relief. It reclaimed tax accordingly. Subsequently the Revenue formed the opinion that some of the relevant policies had not been effected until after 13 March 1984 and sought to recover the relevant amounts from L. L appealed, contending that all the policies in question had been made before midnight on 13 March 1984. The Special Commissioner upheld the Revenue's contention that a significant number of the contracts had not been completed at that time, holding that 'a unilateral act on the part of (L), not communicated to the policy proposers or their agents, cannot be construed as an action completing the contracts in question'. *Legal & General Assurance Society Ltd v CIR (and related appeal)*, Sp C [1996] SSCD 419 (Sp C 96).

Miscellaneous

Claimant bankrupt

[1.13] A trader was made bankrupt in 1921 and was discharged from bankruptcy in 1926. He claimed a repayment of tax for 1921/22 to 1925/26 inclusive, contending that he was entitled to personal allowance on the income from property sequestrated during his bankruptcy. The CS unanimously rejected the claim, holding that the income was the income of the trustee in bankruptcy and that neither the bankrupt nor the trustee was entitled to the relief. *CIR v Fleming*, CS 1928, 14 TC 78.

Allowances to non-residents

[1.14] A British subject (C) was resident and ordinarily resident abroad. He was life tenant of a share of the residuary estate under his father's will, subject to the payment of an annuity to C's mother. The trustees had not appropriated any of the investments of the estate to meet the annuity. The investments included UK government securities and overseas stocks and shares, the income on all of which was received by the trustees less tax. C claimed a repayment. In making the repayment, the Revenue treated the annuity as payable rateably out of the whole of the income of the estate. C appealed, contending that the annuity should be treated as payable out of the UK income. The CA unanimously rejected this contention and upheld the repayment made by the Revenue. Lord Hanworth observed that it would be 'a dangerous thing to appropriate particular securities to the payment of particular annuities, and the right course is to make the best use of the funds and to pay the annuities in full and not to give the particular annuitant the danger of losing a certain portion of his income by reason of the fact that the dividends derived from his securities are insufficient to meet the total sum which he has to receive'. *CIR v Crawshay*, CA 1935, 19 TC 715.

2

Annual Payments (ITA 2007, s 899)

The cases in this chapter are arranged under the following headings.

GENERAL NOTE

The treatment of annual payments (including annuities) is governed by several provisions of the Taxes Acts. The cases in this chapter are those in which the issue is whether a payment is or includes an annual payment within what is now ITA 2007, s 899. For cases where the issue is the liability to account for tax under what is now ITA 2007, ss 900–903, see **20** DEDUCTION OF TAX. For cases where the issue is whether an annual payment is chargeable to income tax on the recipient under ICTA 1988, s 18 or ITTOIA 2005, ss 683–686, see **39.22** to **39.41** MISCELLANEOUS INCOME. For annual payments treated as income of the payer under the settlements legislation, see **56** SETTLEMENTS.

There have been significant changes to the legislation governing annual payments, notably in FA 1988. The cases in this chapter should be read in the light of the changes in the legislation.

Whether payment deductible from total income

NOTE

See the General Note at the start of **30** HIGHER RATE LIABILITY as to the relevance of surtax cases in relation to that liability. See the cases noted at **30.33** *et seq*. HIGHER RATE LIABILITY as to the deduction of yearly interest in arriving at total income.

Insurance premiums paid under covenant

[2.1] An individual (H) appealed against a supertax assessment, contending that life insurance premiums which he paid under deed of covenant should be treated as annual payments deductible from his total income. The Special Commissioners rejected this contention and dismissed his appeal, holding that payments of life insurance premiums were not annual payments 'as they are in fact allocations of income to the formation of a capital fund'. The CA unanimously upheld their decision. Swinfen Eady MR held that the payments were not deductible as 'annual payments', since they were not 'in the nature of income payments'. *Earl Howe v CIR*, CA 1919, 7 TC 289; [1919] 2 KB 336.

(*Notes.* (1) This is considered to be a leading case on the definition of 'annual payments' for tax purposes. (2) *Obiter dicta* of Scrutton LJ were disapproved in the subsequent case of *R v Special Commrs (ex p. Shaftesbury Homes & Arethusa Training Ship)*, **2.16** below. (3) 'Supertax' was subsequently replaced by surtax in 1927. Surtax was in turn replaced by higher rate income tax in 1973.)

Percentage of profits carried to reserve under will trust

[2.2] A testator left the goodwill and assets of his business on trust for his two sons for life, on condition that they entered into partnership in order to carry on the business. The trustees required them to enter into an agreement under which 12% of the profits was to be set aside to form a reserve fund to meet any loss (and so preserve the assets). One of the sons claimed that the sum set aside was an annual payment charged on the partnership profits, so diminishing his income for supertax purposes. The Revenue rejected the claim on the grounds that the reserve fund was an application of the partnership profits. The KB allowed the son's appeal. Rowlatt J held that 'the remaindermen under the will are entitled to have this reserve fund maintained, and the necessary payments made to it', so that 'this 12% is an annual payment reserved or charged upon the net profits of the partnership'. *Stocker v CIR*, KB 1919, 7 TC 304; [1919] 2 KB 702.

Domestic employees remunerated by annual payments

[2.3] A wealthy taxpayer (W) covenanted to make certain annual payments to a number of his domestic employees. The payments, having regard to the surrounding circumstances, were, in substance but not in form, remuneration. W claimed that they should be treated as annual payments deductible from his total income. The HL held (by a 4-1 majority, Lord Atkin dissenting) that the payments were annual payments from which tax was deductible, and were allowable deductions in arriving at W's income for surtax. *Duke of Westminster v CIR*, HL 1935, 19 TC 490. (*Notes.* (1) The covenants would not now be effective for tax purposes, but the case remains an authority on the meaning of 'annual payment', and as an illustration of the courts' traditional inclination to consider form rather than substance. (2) Lord Tomlin's judgment includes the celebrated *dictum* that 'every man is entitled if he can to order his affairs so that the tax attaching under the appropriate *Acts* is less than it otherwise would be'. This *dictum* has frequently been discussed in subsequent cases, particularly in the light of the *Ramsay* principle (see **71.268** *et seq.* CAPITAL GAINS TAX). The extent to which Lord Tomlin's principle should be treated as applicable to complex tax avoidance schemes was questioned by Lord Roskill in *Furniss v Dawson*, **71.288** CAPITAL GAINS TAX. In the 1992 case of *Ensign Tankers (Leasing) Ltd v Stokes*, **59.85** TRADING INCOME, Lord Templeman stated that 'subsequent events have shown that though this *dictum* is accurate as far as tax mitigation is concerned it does not apply to tax avoidance'. For the distinction between tax mitigation and tax avoidance, see *New Zealand Commissioner of Inland Revenue v Challenge Corporation*, **58.12** TAX PLANNING AND AVOIDANCE. In *Ensign Tankers*, Lord Templeman also specifically approved Lord Atkin's dissenting judgment in the *Duke of Westminster* case. In the 1997 case of *CIR v McGuckian*, 3.64 ANTI-AVOIDANCE, Lord Steyn observed that while Lord Tomlin's words 'still point to a material consideration, namely the general liberty of the citizen to arrange his financial affairs as he thinks fit, they have ceased to be canonical as to the consequence of a tax avoidance scheme'. In the same case, Lord Cooke of Thorndon observed that the *Ramsay* principle was 'more natural and less extreme' than the majority decision in the *Duke of Westminster* case, and specifically refrained 'from speculating about whether a sharper focus on the concept of "wages" in the light of the statutory purpose and the circumstances of the case would or would not have led to a different result in the *Duke of Westminster* case'.)

Share of business profits payable as part of purchase price

[2.4] Following the death of a dentist, his assistant (R) purchased the business for £5,000 plus 25% of the net profits for the next ten years. R subsequently appealed against a surtax assessment, contending that these payments were annual payments which were deductible from his total income for surtax purposes. The CA unanimously rejected this contention and upheld the assessment, holding that the payments were instalments of capital and not annual payments. *CIR v Ramsay*, CA 1935, 20 TC 79.

[2.5] Following the death of a partner (P), the surviving partners agreed to purchase his share in the partnership, and paid his executors 50% of the profits for the next three years which would have been payable to P if he had continued to be a partner. They appealed against surtax assessments, contending that these payments should be treated as deductible from their total income. The KB rejected this contention and upheld the assessments, holding that the payments were instalments of capital and not annual payments. *CIR v Ledgard; CIR v Pyman*, KB 1937, 21 TC 129; [1937] 2 All ER 492.

[2.6] On the retirement of a partner (B), the remaining partners agreed to pay him a sum equal to $^1/_{14}$ 'of the net profits of the business for the three years ending 31 December 1937, 1938 and 1939, under deduction of Income Tax'. B died in 1937. In 1938 the partnership paid his representatives £2,389, representing, after deduction of tax, $^1/_{14}$ of the net profits for 1937. One of the remaining partners appealed against a surtax assessment, contending that his share of the gross amount represented by this payment should be allowed as a deduction. The Special Commissioners accepted this contention and allowed his appeal, and the CS unanimously upheld their decision. *CIR v Hogarth*, CS 1940, 23 TC 491.

Maintenance of wife confined to asylum

[2.7] A married woman was committed to an asylum, and her husband was appointed as receiver of her estate. He undertook to make up the deficiency between her income and the amount required for her maintenance. He appealed against surtax assessments, contending that the payments which he made were annual payments which should be deducted in computing his income for surtax. The Special Commissioners rejected this contention and dismissed his appeal, and the KB upheld their decision. The payments were not income of his wife and thus were not 'annual payments' for surtax purposes. *Watkins v CIR*, KB 1939, 22 TC 696; [1939] 2 KB 420; [1939] 3 All ER 165.

Payments to separated wife under verbal agreement

[2.8] Under a verbal agreement, a husband (P) paid a yearly allowance to his separated wife. The CA held that the agreement was legally binding, and that the allowance was deductible in computing P's income for surtax. *Peters' Executors v CIR*, CA 1941, 24 TC 45; [1941] 2 All ER 620.

Supplementary benefit payments by husband

[2.9] See *McBurnie v Tacey*, 36.12 MAINTENANCE PAYMENTS.

Alimony payments under foreign court order

[2.10] A Netherlands court ordered a man (B) to pay alimony to his former wife. B subsequently moved to the UK, and appealed against a surtax assessment, contending that he should be allowed to deduct these payments in computing his income. The Ch D rejected this contention and dismissed his appeal, holding that, to qualify as a deduction, an annual payment must be one from which UK tax could be deducted at source. *Bingham v CIR*, Ch D 1955, 36 TC 254; [1955] Ch 95; [1955] 3 All ER 321.

Annuity payable under obligation assumed under a will

[2.11] Under a will, shares were held in trust for the testator's son (B), subject to the payment of a free-of-tax annuity to his sister. B undertook the obligation to pay the annuity. The Revenue treated the annuity as an annual payment deductible in computing B's total income (so that his entitlement to earned income relief fell to be reduced under the legislation then in force). Bappealed, contending that the payment was a voluntary payment. The CA unanimously rejected this contention and dismissed his appeal, holding that the annuity was an annual payment. *Dealler v Bruce*, CA 1934, 19 TC 1.

Covenanted payments in discharge of capital liability

[2.12] In 1926 an individual (M) agreed to pay a company (G) £33,000. In 1930 he entered into a deed of covenant to pay G the £28,000 which he still owed under the agreement. He subsequently appealed against surtax assessments, contending that the payments under this covenant were annual payments which should be allowed as deductions. The CA unanimously rejected this contention, holding that the covenanted payments were of a capital nature and were not allowable deductions for surtax. *CIR v Mallaby-Deeley*, CA 1938, 23 TC 153; [1938] 4 All ER 818.

Payments to executors of deceased partner

[2.13] A partnership made payments to the executors of the deceased partner in respect of profits earned before the death. The surviving partners claimed that these payments were annual payments and should be deducted in computing their total income for surtax purposes. The CS unanimously held that the payments were not annual payments. *CIR v Hunter; CIR v Duncanson*, CS 1955, 36 TC 181. (*Note*. The payments were also held not to be an admissible deduction in computing the partnership profits—see *McCash & Hunter v CIR*, **62.26** TRADING PROFITS.)

Payments for capital sums—whether 'annual payments'

[2.14] Under a tax avoidance scheme, two individuals received sums from a registered charity in return for making five 'annual payments' to the charity. They claimed to deduct the amounts of the payments in computing their income for tax purposes. The Revenue raised assessments on the basis that the payments were not deductible as 'annual payments', since the scheme should be treated as a fiscal nullity under the principles laid down in *WT Ramsay Ltd v CIR*, **71.285** CAPITAL GAINS TAX. The HL upheld the assessments (reversing the decision of the CA and restoring that of the Special Commissioners). The claimants had not made annual payments within the meaning of *ICTA 1988*, because the steps taken under the scheme were self-cancelling. The schemes had no object or effect other than the manufacture of claims that the taxpayers had reduced their income. They had not reduced their actual income and had not been put to any capital expense other than the cost of the scheme. The HL specifically disapproved the earlier decision in *CIR v Plummer*, HL 1979, 54 TC 1; [1979] STC 793; [1979] 3 WLR 689; [1979] 3 All ER 775, on the grounds that it was inconsistent with the decision in the subsequent case of *WT Ramsay Ltd v CIR*. *Moodie v CIR & Sinnett*; *Sotnick v CIR & Edwards*, HL 1993, 65 TC 610; [1993] STC 188; [1993] 1 WLR 266; [1993] 2 All ER 49. (*Note*. See also *ITA 2007, s 904*.)

Avoidance scheme—purported 'manufactured overseas dividend'

[2.15] An individual (C) entered into a complex avoidance scheme, designed to obtain a tax deduction of more than £300,000 in respect of purported payments of 'manufactured overseas dividends' which he claimed to have made to a company. HMRC rejected the claim and the First-tier Tribunal dismissed C's appeal, applying the principles laid down in *Moodie v CIR & Sinnett*, **2.14** above, and *WT Ramsay Ltd v CIR*, **71.285** CAPITAL GAINS TAX. Judge Walters observed that the various transactions, which had taken place within a few days, were self-cancelling, and held that they were 'artificial steps which should be ignored'. Furthermore, applying the CA decision in *Earl Howe v CIR*, **2.1** above, 'only annual payments which are payable under deduction and retention of tax as between the payer and the payee can be allowed as deductions from the income of the payer for income tax purposes'. The Upper Tribunal unanimously upheld this decision, observing that 'it is apparent from the full and clear findings of fact that there were neither payments nor loan notes in a real or practical sense. Their purpose was not a commercial purpose, but exclusively a tax avoidance purpose.' The transactions had 'no practical significance beyond enabling the taxpayer to claim that the requirements of the legislative provisions had been complied with'. *A Chappell v HMRC*, UT [2014] UKUT 344 (TCC). (*Note*. See also now *ITA 2007, s 581A*, introduced by *FA 2008, Sch 23*.)

Whether an annual payment—appeals by charities

Bequest to charity of net profits of a business

[2.16] A business was bequeathed to trustees to carry it on and, subject to certain annuities, to pay the balance of the profits to a charity. The trustees were assessed on the business profits. The charity claimed repayment of the tax, contending that the amounts paid were 'annual payments' within what is now *ITA 2007, s 899*. The KB granted the claim and the CA unanimously upheld this decision. *R v Special Commrs (ex p. Shaftesbury Homes & Arethusa Training Ship)*, CA 1922, 8 TC 367; [1923] 1 KB 393.

Annual contributions to meet deficiencies of a charity

[2.17] Under the *Epping Forest Act 1878*, the Corporation of London was appointed as the Conservators of Epping Forest, and regulated and managed the forest. The Conservators were regarded as a separate entity from the Corporation, and as a charity. The Corporation was required to make contributions each year to meet any deficiencies in the income account of the Conservators. Until 1948/49 the Corporation made such payments in full, but for 1948/49 the Corporation deducted tax on the basis that the payment was an annual payment within what is now *ITA 2007, s 899*. The Conservators claimed repayment of the tax, but the Revenue rejected the claim, considering that the payment was not an annual payment since it was not 'pure income profit' within the definition propounded by Lord Greene in *Comiskey & Others v Hanbury (in re Hanbury)*, **2.36** below. The Special Commissioners allowed the Conservators' appeal, and the HL unanimously upheld their decision, holding that the contribution was an annual payment payable under deduction of tax. Lord Reid observed that the payments were 'made primarily to achieve a public benefit of a charitable nature'. *CIR v Corporation of London (as Conservators of Epping Forest)*, HL 1953, 34 TC 293; [1953] 1 WLR 625; [1953] 1 All ER 747.

Subscriptions to charity by covenant

[2.18] A registered charity allowed its members to use club, restaurant and bar facilities at its headquarters in London. Some of its members paid their subscriptions to it under deeds of covenant and deducted tax. The charity claimed repayment of the tax deducted. The Revenue rejected the claim and the CA unanimously dismissed the charity's appeal, holding that the payments were not 'annual payments', since the members received significant benefits in return for their subscriptions. *CIR v National Book League*, CA 1957, 37 TC

455; [1957] Ch 488; [1957] 2 All ER 644. (*Note.* The decision was approved by the HL in *Campbell v CIR*, **2.20** below, but *obiter dicta* of Lord Evershed were disapproved.)

[2.19] A registered charity organised a Festival of Arts, and allowed its members to book seats at reduced prices. Some of its members paid their subscriptions to it under deeds of covenant and deducted tax. The charity claimed repayment of the tax deducted. The Revenue rejected the claim and the Ch D dismissed the charity's appeal, applying the principles laid down in *CIR v National Book League*, **2.18** above, and holding that the payments were not 'annual payments'. *Taw & Torridge Festival Society Ltd v CIR*, Ch D 1959, 38 TC 603.

Covenanted payments related to acquisition of business of payer

[2.20] A charitable trust entered into an arrangement, intended to lead to the acquisition of a tutorial business carried on by a company (T), by which T covenanted to pay 80% of its trading profits to the trustees for seven years. It withheld tax from the payments and the trustees claimed a repayment. The Special Commissioners rejected the claim, and the HL unanimously upheld their decision, holding that the payments were applied for charitable purposes, but were not income in the hands of the trustees, because the trustees were contractually bound to return them to T and because the trustees received them as capital. (The HL unanimously disapproved *obiter dicta* of Lord Evershed in *CIR v National Book League*, **2.18** above.) *Campbell & Another v CIR*, HL 1968, 45 TC 427; [1970] AC 77; [1968] 3 All ER 588.

Rentcharges—whether annual payments or partly capital

[2.21] The Church Commissioners of England claimed repayment under *ITA 1952, s 447(1)(a)* of the tax deducted from certain payments to them of rentcharges within *ITA 1952, s 177* for 1959/60 to 1963/64 inclusive. (The payments were the subject of the decision in *CIR v Land Securities Investment Trust Ltd*, **63.43** TRADING PROFITS.) The Revenue rejected the claim, considering that the payments should be divided between an income element and a capital element. The Special Commissioners allowed the Church Commissioners' appeal and the HL unanimously upheld this decision, holding that the true legal nature of the bargain was that the Church Commissioners sold their reversions for ten annual payments of £96,000. *CIR v Church Commissioners for England*, HL 1976, 50 TC 516; [1976] STC 339; [1977] AC 329; [1976] 2 All ER 1037. (*Note.* Under the law in force at the time, rentcharges were payable under deduction of tax. Despite the subsequent changes in the legislation, the case is still an important authority on the distinction between capital and income with regard to annual payments.)

Repayment claims by recipients other than charities

Payment for education of child—whether annual payment

[2.22] A company (ICI) paid £27,000 per year, by covenant and under deduction of tax, to trustees, to be used for the education of specified children of staff employed outside the UK by some of its associated companies. ICI had power to vary the list of recipients. The trustees made payments into bank accounts in the names of the children. The Revenue rejected a repayment claim on behalf of one of the children, considering that the payments by the trustees were not 'pure income profit' within the definition propounded by Lord Greene in *Comiskey & Others v Hanbury (in re Hanbury)*, **2.36** below. The bank, into which the payment had been made, appealed on behalf of the child. The Ch D allowed the appeal, holding that the payments were income of the child and were within the definition of 'annual payments', so that the tax was repayable. (The Ch D also rejected the Revenue's contention that the payments should be deemed to be remuneration of the child's father.) *Barclays Bank Ltd v Naylor*, Ch D 1960, 39 TC 256; [1961] Ch 7; [1960] 3 All ER 173.

Payments for school fees of mentally handicapped boy

[2.23] The father of a mentally handicapped boy thought it desirable for the boy to attend a two-year residential course at an institution run by MENCAP, who required students to be sponsored by, and have their fees paid by, local authorities. Essex County Council agreed to sponsor the boy and to pay his fees if the father agreed in writing to reimburse the Council for the full amount of the fees. The boy's father entered into a covenant to make payments to the Council of amounts which would approximately equal the amount of fees payable, and in a covering letter to the Council indicated his intention to deduct basic rate tax from payments under the deed, stating that the tax would be recoverable from the Revenue, and agreeing to pay by cheque any amount by which the gross payments fell short of the fees. The Council claimed repayment of the tax deemed to have been deducted by the boy's father. The Revenue rejected the claim and the CA unanimously dismissed the Council's appeal. Dillon LJ held that the payments were not 'pure income profit' in the hands of the Council, as the covering letter from the boy's father to the Council had earmarked the net payments as for the purpose of meeting his son's fees. *Essex County Council v Ellam*, CA 1989, 61 TC 615; [1989] STC 317; [1989] 2 All ER 494. (*Note*. For the principle of 'pure income profit', see **2.36** below.)

Whether payer should account for tax

NOTE

For deduction of tax from interest payable, see **33.1** *et seq.* INTEREST PAYABLE.

Purchase price paid in instalments

[2.24] A mine was sold on terms whereby part of the purchase price was to be paid in equal half-yearly instalments over 40 years. It was held that tax was not deductible from the instalments. The words 'annual payments' in the legislation were *eiusdem generis* with rent, interest and annuities, and should not be construed as including instalments of capital payments. *Foley v Fletcher*, Ex D 1858, 3 H & N 769; 7 WR 141.

Assignment of lease for yearly amounts equivalent to rent

[2.25] An individual (C) held a leasehold interest in certain property, which was sub-let for £1,925 per annum. He assigned his interest to a company (P) in return for an immediate payment of £1,000 and yearly payments of £1,625 for the period of the lease. P deducted tax from the payments. C took proceedings against P, contending that P should have made the payments in full. The KB rejected this contention and gave judgment for P, holding that the yearly payments were an annuity from which tax was deductible. *Chadwick v Pearl Life Insurance Co*, KB 1905, 21 TLR 456; [1905] 2 KB 507.

Payment of debt by instalments

[2.26] Under a compromise agreement reached following bankruptcy proceedings, a debtor agreed to pay the creditor by instalments. The debtor deducted tax from the agreed payments. The creditor took proceedings in the KB, claiming that the debtor was not entitled to withhold tax. The CA gave judgment for the creditor, holding that the payments were capital payments rather than 'annual payments', and that the debtor was not entitled to withhold tax. *Dott v Brown*, CA [1936] 1 All ER 543.

Periodical payments in consideration for shares

[2.27] See *CIR v 36/49 Holdings Ltd*, **64.63** TRADING PROFITS.

Public annuity—whether capital element can be distinguished

[2.28] The Secretary of State for India acquired a railway, paying for it by an annuity rather than a lump sum. The annuity was for 48 years, payable half-yearly, of amounts calculated on the basis that the aggregate payments equalled the total of the value of the railway plus interest at 2.85% per annum on the unpaid balance of the value. The Secretary of State deducted tax from the whole of the first two payments, treating them as payments of a public annuity (within Schedule C under the legislation then in force). The annuity trustees brought an action against the Secretary of State. The CA gave judgment for the trustees, holding that tax was deductible only from the interest element in each payment. The HL unanimously upheld this decision. *Scoble & Others v Secretary of State for India*, HL 1903, 4 TC 618; [1903] AC 299. (*Note*. This is a leading case on the circumstances in which an 'annuity' may be divided between income and capital elements for tax purposes.)

[2.29] The decision in *Scoble v Secretary of State for India*, 2.28 above, was applied in the similar subsequent case of *East India Railway Co v Secretary of State for India (No 1)*, KB 1905, 21 TLR 606; [1905] 2 KB 413. The same acquisition was considered again in *East India Railway Co v Secretary of State for India (No 2)*, Ch D 1924, 40 TLR 241 where the Ch D held that certain deferred annuities could be distinguished from the ordinary annuities which were the subject of the previous decision, and that tax was deductible from the whole of them.

Payments to local authority to meet street repairs

[2.30] A local authority agreed to repair some privately-owned streets. The owners agreed to pay the corporation £600 p.a. for 20 years. They did not deduct tax from the first three payments, but deducted tax from the whole of the subsequent payments. The corporation took proceedings in the KB, contending that tax should not have been deducted and that it was entitled to payment in full. The KB held that tax was deductible only from the interest element in the payments. *Goole Corporation v Aire & Calder Navigation Trustees*, KB [1942] 2 All ER 276.

Payment of percentage of receipts for use of secret process

[2.31] A UK company (N) made payments to an individual (D) who was resident outside the UK, as consideration for the exclusive use of a secret process for 40 years. N deducted tax from the payments. D took proceedings in the KB, claiming that tax should not have been deducted. The KB rejected this contention and upheld the deduction of tax. *Delage v Nugget Polish Co Ltd*, KB 1905, 21 TLR 454.

Payments for use of patents

[2.32] See the cases noted at 20.34 to 20.36 DEDUCTION OF TAX.

Copyright royalties

[2.33] See *CIR v Longmans Green & Co Ltd*, 20.19 DEDUCTION OF TAX, and *Rye & Eyre v CIR*, 20.20 DEDUCTION OF TAX.

Overseas company guaranteeing dividends of UK company

[2.34] See *Aeolian Co Ltd v CIR*, 20.28 DEDUCTION OF TAX.

Payments under profit-sharing agreement

[2.35] A company (U) made payments to another company under a profit-sharing agreement, and deducted tax. The Revenue assessed U on the basis that the payments were 'annual payments within' what is now *ITA 2007, s 899*, and that U should have accounted for tax. U appealed, contending that the payments were not annual payments but were dividends within *ITA 1918*,

General Rule 20 so that, under the legislation then in force, it was not required to account for tax. The KB accepted this contention and allowed the appeal. *Utol Ltd v CIR*, KB 1943, 25 TC 517; [1944] 1 All ER 190. (*Note. General Rule 20* became *ITA 1952, s 184*, which was repealed by *FA 1965*.)

Payment for use of chattels

[2.36] In proceedings between the remaindermen under a settlement and the executor of the deceased life tenant, the executor was awarded £22,923 in respect of the remaindermen's use of certain chattels during the preceding eight years. The remaindermen claimed to deduct tax from the payment. The CA unanimously rejected this contention. Lord Greene MR held that, since the payment had the quality of recurrence, it was not 'pure income profit' and that tax was not deductible. *Comiskey & Others v Hanbury (in re Hanbury deceased)*, CA 1939, 38 TC 588; 20 ATC 333. (*Note. Obiter dicta* of Lord Greene were strongly criticised by Viscount Radcliffe in the 1964 case of *CIR v Frere*, 30.33 HIGHER RATE LIABILITY, where he commented that 'the conception of "pure income" as a significant category of income under the tax code is, I think, a recent discovery which might have surprised, for instance, the makers of the *Income Tax Act* of 1842'.)

Receipts from films following cancellation of employment

[2.37] A film company cancelled the contract of one of its employees, and agreed to pay him 'a sum equal to 60% of all moneys (if any) in excess of £110,000' received by the company or a subsidiary in respect of certain films. The company deducted tax from the payments. The employee took proceedings against the company, contending firstly that the payments were capital, and alternatively that they were employment income or professional income. The KB rejected the employee's contentions and gave judgment for the company, holding that the payments were 'annual payments' from which tax had been properly deducted. The CA unanimously upheld this decision. *Asher v London Film Productions Ltd*, CA 1943, 22 ATC 432; [1944] 1 KB 133; [1944] 1 All ER 77.

Yearly payments under will for rent collection

[2.38] See *Clapham's Trustees v Belton*, 20.30 DEDUCTION OF TAX.

Purchased annuity—determination of capital element

[2.39] See *Rose v Trigg*, 52.69 SAVINGS AND INVESTMENT INCOME.

Payment to divorced wife for maintenance of children

[2.40] See *Spencer v Robson*, 36.6 MAINTENANCE PAYMENTS.

Alimony payable to non-resident under overseas contract

[2.41] Following a divorce, the former husband (K) lived in the UK while his former wife lived in the USA. Under a deed executed in the USA, K agreed to pay alimony to her. He failed to make the agreed payments, and she took proceedings against him in the English High Court. He agreed to pay her the arrears of £6,000. He deducted tax from the payment. She threatened to take proceedings for the balance, and K applied to the QB for a declaration that he had satisfied the judgment. The QB held that he was not entitled to deduct tax. The relevant contract had been made in the USA, and his former wife's right to receive £6,000 under an American contract could not be diminished by English law. *Keiner v Keiner*, QB 1952, 34 TC 346; [1952] 1 All ER 643.

Payments out of capital of trust fund

[2.42] See *Williamson v Ough*, 39.29 MISCELLANEOUS INCOME; *Stevenson v Wishart*, 56.108 SETTLEMENTS, and the cases noted at 20.21 to 20.26 DEDUCTION OF TAX.

Annuities under will in excess of income of estate

[2.43] See *Trustees of Peirse-Duncombe Trust v CIR*, 20.27 DEDUCTION OF TAX.

Annual payments—whether 'free of tax'

General principles

NOTE

'Free of tax' is the convenient and commonly-used term for indicating a payment of an amount which, after tax, will produce the stipulated sum. Although over the years there have been more than forty reported cases where the issue was whether a particular wording in a will created a free-of-tax annuity, the pitfalls are now well known and cases of this type now rarely reach the courts. The broad rule is that general words not mentioning tax will not make a payment 'free of tax' without clear evidence of the testator's intention. Cases illustrating this principle are listed in the following paragraphs.

[2.44] A will had originally bequeathed a number of annuities 'clear of all deductions whatsoever, except income tax'. The testator subsequently executed a codicil to make the annuities 'free of legacy duty and every other deduction'. The CA held that the effect of the codicil was that the annuities were free of income tax. *Williams v Marson (in re Buckle)*, CA 1894, 1 Ch 286.

[2.45] In 1910 the Earl of Shrewsbury appointed two jointures of £1500 each to his wife 'clear of all deductions whatsoever for taxes or otherwise'. The Earl died in 1921. His trustees paid his widow the net sum of £2,250 in respect of the jointures, and deducted £750 in respect of income tax. The widow issued an originating summons, claiming that she should have been paid the gross amount of £3,000 free of income tax. The CA accepted this contention and allowed her appeal, holding that the jointures were free of income tax (but liable to supertax), and that the trustees were required to pay her £3,000 in respect of the jointures. *Countess of Shrewsbury v Earl of Shrewsbury (in re Shrewsbury Estate Acts)*, CA 1923, 40 TLR 16; [1924] 1 Ch 315. (*Note*. For a subsequent case concerning the surtax liability on the jointures, see *Countess of Shrewsbury & Talbot v CIR*, **2.52** below.)

[2.46] A deceased husband's will left his wife an annuity of 'such a sum in every year as after deduction of the income tax for the time being payable in respect thereof will leave a clear sum of £2,000'. His executors issued an originating summons to ascertain whether any deduction should be made in respect of supertax. The Ch D held that the £2,000 was free of income tax but was liable to supertax. Russell J observed that 'the testator did not intend that in addition to income tax being deducted, a proportion of the supertax payable by his wife in respect of her total income should also be deducted'. Accordingly, 'the annuity is to be paid free of income tax only, and there will be a declaration that the widow is not entitled to payment of any sum in respect of supertax'. *Selmes v Bates (in re Bates)*, Ch D 1924, 4 ATC 518; [1925] Ch 157. (*Notes*. (1) 'Supertax' was subsequently replaced by surtax in 1927. Surtax was in turn replaced by higher rate income tax in 1973. (2) The decision here was not followed by the CA in the subsequent case of *In re Reckitt; Reckitt v Reckitt*, **2.48** below, on the grounds that the will here provided a gift of a sum 'after deduction of' income tax, rather than 'a gift of an annuity free from income tax'. The CA held that an annuity 'free from income tax' would also have been free from surtax. For the position in Scotland, compare *Prentice's Trustees v Prentice*, **2.55** below.)

[2.47] A deceased husband's will left his wife an annuity of £12,000, free of income tax and supertax. Supertax was replaced by surtax in 1927. The Ch D held that the reference in the will to supertax also covered surtax. Bennett J observed that 'there is no real or substantial difference between supertax and surtax. Both taxes are taxes imposed upon individuals whose incomes are in excess of some standard sum to be raised or lowered annually by Parliament.' *Hulton v Midland Bank Executor & Trustee Co Ltd (in re Hulton)*, Ch D 1930, 9 ATC 570; [1931] 1 Ch 77.

[2.48] A deceased husband's will left his wife an annuity of £5,000, 'free of income tax'. The CA unanimously held that the annuity was also free of surtax. Lord Hanworth MR observed that 'surtax is in essence an additional income tax' and there was no indication in the will 'to restrict the words to income tax as known for so many years'. The decision in *Re Bates*, **2.46** above, was not followed, on the ground that the will there did not provide 'a gift of an annuity free from income tax, as in the present case' but was a gift of a sum 'after deduction' of income tax. *Reckitt v Reckitt (in re Reckitt)*, CA 1932, 11 ATC 429; [1932] 2 Ch 144. (*Note*. The decision here was distinguished (and implicitly disapproved) by the CS in the subsequent case of *Prentice's Trustees v Prentice*, **2.51** below.)

[2.49] A deceased husband's will directed that his trustees should account for the income tax payable upon annuities to his wife and daughters. The CS held that the trustees were also required to account for surtax on the annuities, but (by a 3-1 majority, Lord Murray dissenting) that the surtax to be accounted for was restricted to the liability that would have been payable if the annuities had been the only taxable income. Lord Hunter held that the testator had not 'intended to impose an unlimited burden on the residue of his estate which, in the event of his daughters marrying very wealthy husbands, might prevent his son and his son's children, who were to be interested in the residue, from deriving any benefit therefrom'. *Baird's Trustees v Baird*, CS 1933, 12 ATC 407.

[2.50] The decision in *Baird's Trustees v Baird*, **2.49** above, was distinguished in a subsequent Scottish case where the CS held that an annuity should be calculated on the basis that the recipient's supertax liability should be 'averaged or spread over the taxable income as a whole'. Lord Clyde held that the decision in *Baird* turned on the point 'that the direction to pay free of supertax was expressed in such a way as to point to the idea of a supertax limited in some way to the annuity alone. What was to be paid was supertax "upon" the annuity. Slight differences in words often make great differences in construction. Because the supertax of which the annuity was to be free was described as the supertax "upon" the annuity, the court which disposed of the case found itself in a position to entertain and to accept the idea of a notional supertax imposed at a notional rate or rates.' *Richmond's Trustees v Richmond*, CS 1935, 14 ATC 489. (*Note.* For another issue in this case, see **2.61** below.)

[2.51] A deceased husband's will left his wife an annuity of £5,000, 'free of all deductions including income tax and government duty'. The widow had a private income and was liable to surtax. The CS held that the trustees were not required to pay any of the surtax due on the annuity, approving the Ch D decision in *Re Bates*, **2.46** above, but distinguishing (and implicitly disapproving) the CA decision in *Re Reckitt*, **2.48** above. Lord Blackburn held that 'there is a very strong presumption in favour of the view that a testator who makes the bequest of an annuity "free of income tax" means no more than that his trustees are to pay the annuity free of the deductions for income tax which they would otherwise be entitled to make. If that presumption is justified, then the expression "free of income tax" should always be given its narrower meaning in the absence of words to indicate that the testator intended them to have the wider meaning'. *Prentice's Trustees v Prentice*, CS 1934, 13 ATC 612; [1935] SC 211.

[2.52] Following the decision in *Countess of Shrewsbury v Earl of Shrewsbury*, **2.45** above, the Revenue issued supertax and surtax assessments on the recipient of the jointures, in respect of the income tax on the gross amounts. The recipient appealed. The KB dismissed her appeals, holding that the annual jointures of £3000 should be treated as a net amount, after deduction of income tax. Accordingly the income tax due on the jointures formed part of the recipient's income for surtax purposes. *Countess of Shrewsbury & Talbot v CIR*, KB 1936, 20 TC 538; [1936] 2 KB 582; [1936] 2 All ER 101.

[2.53] As part of a divorce settlement, a husband (H) covenanted that he and his personal representatives should pay to trustees 'such a sum as after deduction of income tax at the standard rate for the time being in force and of every other tax on income for the time being in force shall leave a clear sum of £4,000' for his former wife. She subsequently married a very wealthy man, so that under the legislation then in force, the annuity gave rise to significant surtax liability. The trustees of the settlement issued an originating summons, claiming that the liability was to provide an annuity free of income tax but not free of surtax. The Ch D rejected this contention and the CA dismissed the trustees' appeal, holding that the annuity was given free of surtax and the representatives were bound to provide a sum sufficient to satisfy the surtax on the income. *Colledge v Horlick (in re Horlick's Settlement Trusts)*, CA 1938, 17 ATC 549; [1938] 4 All ER 602.

[2.54] A married couple divorced in 1936. The husband subsequently paid his former wife alimony of £8 per week. He died in 1947. His will left his former wife an annuity of £416, or of one-third of the income of his estate, whichever was the less. The CA held that the annuity was free of income tax, distinguishing *In re Hooper*, **2.55** below, and holding that the annuity should be treated as being 'paid in continuance of the alimony which the testator had been paying during his lifetime'. *In re Batley (No 1)*, CA 1951, 30 ATC 182; [1951] Ch 558. (*Note*. For subsequent proceedings in this case, see *Public Trustee v Hert (in re Batley) (No 2)*, **2.71** below.)

Annuities held not to be free of tax

[2.55] In the following cases, listed in chronological order, annuities were held not to be free of tax. *Abadam v Abadam 1864*, 10 LT 53; 33 Beav 475 (annuity under a will 'payable without any deduction whatsoever'); *Countess of Shrewsbury v Earl of Shrewsbury*, Ch D 1906, 22 TLR 598 (annuity under a separation agreement 'clear of all deductions'); *Machell v Parry (re Musgrave)*, **20.16** DEDUCTION OF TAX (annuities under a will to be paid 'without deduction'); *Farrer v Loveless (in re Loveless)*, Ch D 1918, 34 TLR 356; [1918] 2 Ch 1 (a 'clear annuity' under a will); *Re Shepherd*, CA 1920 unreported (annuity 'free of all deductions whatsoever'); *Public Trustee v Wells (in re Wells' Will Trusts)*, Ch D 1940, 19 ATC 158; [1940] Ch 411; [1940] 2 All ER 68 (annuity under a will 'free of all deductions'); *Belk v Best & Others (in re Best's Marriage Settlement)*, Ch D 1941, 20 ATC 235; [1942] Ch 77; [1941] 3 All ER 315 (annuity under a settlement of 'such a sum as shall after all deductions'); *CIR v Watson*, CS 1942, 25 TC 25 (annuity under a will payable out of 'the whole free residue of the year's income'); *Phillips v Steel (in re Hooper)*, Ch D [1944] Ch 171; [1944] 1 All ER 227 (annuity under a will 'to be paid free of all deductions whatsoever'); *Barclays Bank v Wright (in re Wright)*, Ch D 1952, 31 ATC 433; [1952] 2 All ER 698 (a bequest of 'net income of £10 per week').

Alimony paid under court order

[2.56] A divorce court order required a husband to pay his former wife alimony of '£120 per annum (free of tax)'. She claimed an income tax repayment, on the basis that the payments should be treated as being a net amount after deduction of tax. The Revenue rejected the claim, and she appealed. The Commissioners allowed her appeal and the KB upheld their decision, holding that she was entitled to the repayment claimed. *Spilsbury v Spofforth*, KB 1937, 21 TC 247; [1937] 4 All ER 487.

[2.57] The decision in *Spilsbury v Spofforth*, **2.56** above, was approved in a subsequent case in which a magistrate had made a maintenance order for £2 per week against a husband. Lord Merriman held that the order should have been expressed as being 'less tax', and that it was 'completely wrong' to provide for such a payment to be 'free of tax'. *Wallis v Wallis*, PDA [1941] 2 All ER 291.

[2.58] Following a divorce, a court order provided for the payment of maintenance of £52 per annum 'free of tax'. The husband paid this amount, but the wife issued a judgment summons requiring him to pay £52 grossed up at the standard rate of income tax. Tucker J granted judgment for the wife and the CA dismissed the husband's appeal, holding (by a 2–1 majority, Denning LJ dissenting) that the order required payment of an amount that would produce £52 after deduction of income tax, even though tax was not deductible under the legislation then in force. Morris LJ observed that, for the reasons explained in *Wallis v Wallis*, **2.57** above, it was undesirable 'that the order should have been made in the form in which it was made'. Furthermore, the order had failed to take account of the statutory provisions relating to 'small maintenance payments' *Jefferson v Jefferson*, CA 1955, 34 ATC 320; [1956] 1 All ER 31. (*Note.* At the relevant time, the taxation treatment of small maintenance payments was governed by *ITA 1952, ss 205–207*, deriving from *FA 1944, s 25*. These provisions became *ICTA 1988, s 351*, which was repealed by *FA 1988* for payments made after 5 April 1989.)

Whether annuitant may retain income tax repaid

[2.59] A deceased husband's will left his wife an annuity of £1,000 payable 'free of income tax'. She claimed the reliefs to which she was entitled, obtaining repayment of part of the tax deducted from the gross annuity. The Ch D held that she must account to the trustees of the will for a proportion of her repayment, representing the ratio of the net annuity to her total net income. *Le Fevre v Pettit (in re Pettit)*, Ch D 1922, 38 TLR 787; [1922] 2 Ch 765. (*Note.* The decision was approved by the CA in *Few v Byrne (in re Maclennan)*, **2.62** below.)

[2.60] A woman's will left two annuities which 'after deducting therefrom income tax thereon at the current rate for the time being, would amount to the clear yearly sum' of £350 and £60. The Revenue duly made an income tax repayment to one of the annuitants. The Ch D held that the annuitant could retain the tax repaid, distinguishing *In re Pettit*, **2.59** above, on the ground that the testatrix had 'not bequeathed the annuities free of income tax'. *Jones v Jones (in re Jones)*, Ch D 1933, 12 ATC 595; [1933] Ch 842.

[2.61] A deceased husband's will left his wife an annuity of £5000 'to be paid free of income tax and supertax which shall be borne by my trust estate'. She had some other income, and the Revenue issued assessments charging surtax on her. The trustees claimed that the amount of the annuity should be reduced to take account of the widow's personal allowances. The CS rejected this claim (by a 3-1 majority, Lord Fleming dissenting). Lord Clyde observed that 'the trustees have not paid any part of the tax on the widow's independent income. They cannot therefore claim repayment of what they have not paid, and could not be asked to pay. The widow alone is in a position to claim and receive repayment.' *Richmond's Trustees v Richmond*, CS 1935, 14 ATC 489. (*Note*. For another issue in this case, see **2.50** above.)

[2.62] A deed provided for two annuities, one to be paid 'after deduction of income tax but not surtax' and the other to be paid 'clear of income tax but not surtax'. The CA held that the trustees were entitled to take account of the annuitants' personal allowances and reliefs in computing the payments to be made, applying *In re Pettit*, **2.59** above, and distinguishing *In re Jones*, **2.60** above. *Few v Byrne (in re Maclennan)*, CA 1939, 18 ATC 121; [1939] Ch 150; [1939] 3 All ER 81.

[2.63] The Ch D reached a similar decision, also applying *In re Pettit*, **2.59** above, in a case where an annuity under a will was 'free of income tax at the current rate'. *Midland Bank Executor & Trustee Co Ltd v Eves (in re Eves)*, Ch D 1939, 18 ATC 401; [1939] Ch 969.

[2.64] In a Scottish case, a testator directed his trustees to pay his sister (K) the residuary income of his estate 'free of government duties and expense', and directed that if the income amounted to less than £1,000 in any year, K could require the trustees to pay her the difference out of the capital of the estate. The trustees applied to the CS for a determination as to whether they were required to pay the difference between £1,000 and the gross residuary income, or the difference between £1,000 and the net residuary income after deducting income tax. The CS held (by a 3-1 majority, Lord Fleming dissenting) that the trustees were required to pay the difference between £1,000 and the gross residuary income, applying *Richmond's Trustees v Richmond*, **2.61** above, and distinguishing *In re Maclennan*, **2.62** above. Lord Normand held that 'the expression "government duties" is not apt to cover income tax'. *Rowan's Trustees v Rowan*, CS 1939, 18 ATC 378; [1940] SC 30.

[2.65] An annuity of £700 under a will was payable 'free of death duties and all other taxes'. The annuitant claimed the reliefs to which she was entitled, obtaining repayment of part of the tax deducted from the gross annuity. The Ch D held that she must account to the trustees of the will for a proportion of her repayment, applying *In re Pettit*, **2.59** above, and distinguishing *In re Jones*, **2.60** above. *Neilson v King & Others (in re Jubb)*, Ch D 1941, 20 ATC 297.

[2.66] The decision in *Re Pettit*, **2.59** above, was also applied in a case where the annuity under a will was of such a sum as 'after deduction of income tax for the time being payable in respect thereof will leave a clear sum of £350'. Evershed J distinguished *In re Jones*, **2.60** above, and also held that, in applying *Re Pettit*, 'post-war credits' payable under *FA 1941* should be treated in the same way as other allowances and reliefs. *National Provincial Bank Ltd v Mackenzie (in re Tatham)*, Ch D 1944, 23 ATC 283; [1945] Ch 34; [1945] 1 All ER 29.

[2.67] The Ch D reached a similar decision, applying *In re Pettit*, **2.59** above, and *In re Eves*, **2.63** above, in a case where a will directed the payment of annuities 'free of all deductions whatsoever and free from income tax at the current rate for the time being deductible at source'. *Midland Bank Executor & Trustee Co Ltd v Williams (in re Williams)*, Ch D 1945, 24 ATC 199; [1945] Ch 320; [1945] 2 All ER 102.

[2.68] The decision in *Re Pettit*, **2.59** above, was applied in a case where annuities under a will were payable 'clear of income tax up to but not exceeding 5s 6d in the £ but not surtax'. The Ch D held that the annuitant should pay to the trustees a proportion of the repayments attributable to the annuities, in the ratio which 5s 6d bore to the standard rate of income tax. (At the relevant time, the standard rate of income tax was 50%, so that the annuitant was entitled to retain 45% of the repayments and had to pay 55% to the trustees.) The Ch D also held that post-war credits should be taken into account, applying *In re Tatham*, **2.66** above. *Jenks v Bates (in re Bates's Will Trusts)*, Ch D 1945, 24 ATC 300; [1946] Ch 83; [1945] 2 All ER 688.

[2.69] The decision in *Re Bates*, **2.68** above, was approved by the CA in a subsequent case where annuities under a will were payable 'without deduction of income tax up to a maximum of 5s in the £'. *Healey & Another v Arno & Others (in re Arno)*, CA 1946, 25 ATC 412; [1947] Ch 198; [1947] 1 All ER 64.

Whether annuitant must claim repayment

[2.70] Under a will, the widow of the testator received an annuity of £365 'clear of income tax'. This was her sole income. She was entitled to claim personal allowances, but would have been required to pay all the tax repayment to the trustees, applying the principles laid down by *Re Pettit*, **2.59** above. She refused to apply for a repayment. The trustees of her husband's will issued an originating summons, claiming that they were entitled to deduct from her annuity the sum which she was entitled to claim from the Revenue. The Ch D accepted this contention and gave judgment for the trustees. Bennett J observed that 'for some reason or other the widow has refused to make the claim upon the Commissioners of Inland Revenue which she is entitled to make. Whether this is from ignorance or stupidity or obstinacy on the part of the old lady I do not know'. However, the other beneficiaries should not 'suffer for it'. *Hickley v Kingcombe (in re Kingcombe)*, Ch D 1936, 15 ATC 37; [1936] Ch 566; [1936] 1 All ER 173.

[2.71] A deceased husband's will left his former wife an annuity of £416, or of one-third of the post-tax income of his estate, whichever was the less. She subsequently remarried. The trustee of the will issued an originating summons, claiming that the annuitant should be required to account to the trustee for any tax repayment which she received which was attributable to the annuity, applying the principles laid down by *Re Pettit*, **2.59** above. The CA held that where the annuitant received the full annuity of £416, she was required to exercise her statutory right to recover the tax reliefs in respect of her annuity (if necessary by applying to be separately assessed) and to reimburse the trustees accordingly. However, where the post-tax income of the estate was less than £1248, so that the annuitant received less than £416, she was not required to reimburse the trustees. *Public Trustee v Hert (in re Batley) (No 2)*, CA 1952, 31 ATC 410; [1952] Ch 781; [1952] 2 All ER 562.

'Free-of-tax' annuity—no tax liability

[2.72] Under a will, a beneficiary (C) was entitled to an annuity of £100 'free of all deductions including income tax'. The Revenue discovered that the trustees required C to pass any repayment of tax deemed to have been deducted to them. For 1939/40, C had no other income and no tax liability. She claimed a repayment but the Revenue rejected her claim, considering that there was no tax repayable, as her income of £100 was not liable to tax and payment of £100 gross would satisfy the requirements of the will. She appealed. The General Commissioners allowed her appeal (by a 2-1 majority) and the HL upheld their decision, holding (by a 3-2 majority, Lords Russell and Simonds dissenting) that repayment should be made on the basis that the income was £100 grossed up at the standard rate. Lord Maugham observed that 'a named annual sum cannot literally be given free from income tax, since the annuitant must normally pay income tax on his or her income'. However, the testator's intention 'could be achieved by the simple means of holding that the testator must have intended to give, in addition to the fixed annuity, such a sum as would enable the trustees in each year to discharge the income tax on the total amount of the fixed annuity and the additional sum'. *CIR v Cook*, HL 1945, 26 TC 489; [1946] AC 1; [1945] 2 All ER 377.

Amount of annuity where annuitant required to reimburse trustees

[2.73] Under the terms of a will, an annuitant was required to pay over to trustees part of the income tax recovered on claiming personal allowances (see **56.109** to **56.120** SETTLEMENTS for the relevant provisions). The Revenue issued an assessment on the basis that the amount paid to the trustees remained part of the annuitant's income for surtax purposes. The Special Commissioners allowed the annuitant's appeal and the KB upheld this decision, applying the decision in *Re Pettit*, **2.59** above. Croom-Johnson J held that since the annuitant was required to pay the amount to the trustees, she had received it as a trustee and 'it was not money to which she was beneficially entitled'. Accordingly it did not form part of her income. *CIR v Duncanson*, KB 1949, 31 TC 257; [1949] 2 All ER 846.

Whether loss relief to be taken into account

[2.74] An annuitant claimed loss relief for a trading loss under *ITA 1918, s 34* (similar to *ITA 2007, s 64*), and received a repayment accordingly. The bank which acted as trustee of the will claimed that the annuitant was required to pay most of the repayment to the bank, applying the principles in *Re Pettit*, **2.59** above. The Ch D gave judgment for the bank and the CA unanimously upheld this decision. Sir Raymond Evershed MR observed that 'it is not in law possible to make a gift of so much per annum "free of income tax"' and held that 'the purposes of the testator will have been satisfied' provided that 'the net sum specified by the testator is left in the hands of the beneficiary'. *Barclays Bank Ltd v Lyons (in re Lyons)*, CA 1951, 30 ATC 377; [1952] Ch 129; [1952] 1 All ER 34.

Application of TMA, s 106(2) to 'tax-free' annuities, etc

Interest 'free from income tax' under promissory note—whether void

[2.75] An individual (H) gave a former business partner a promissory note for £6,000, providing for the payment of interest at 10% 'free from income tax'. The Revenue issued a surtax assessment in which the £600 interest payable was allowed as a deduction in computing H's taxable income. H appealed, contending that the £600 should be treated as a net payment and that should be allowed a deduction for the grossed-up equivalent. The Ch D rejected this contention and upheld the assessment, holding that the promissory note was an agreement within what is now *TMA, s 106(2)*, and that the provision was void, so that only the £600 actually paid was allowable as a deduction. *CIR v Hartley*, Ch D 1956, 36 TC 348.

Payments under separation agreement

[2.76] Under a separation agreement, a husband agreed to pay his wife £35 per month 'free of income tax'. For 1955/56 to 1957/58, the husband was not resident in the UK and had no income chargeable to UK tax. The Revenue issued income tax assessments on the wife, charging tax on £420 for each year. For 1959/60, the husband was resident in the UK but his taxable income was only £366. The Revenue issued an assessment on the wife, charging tax on £74. She appealed against all four assessments, contending that the words "free of income tax" should 'be read as a form of shorthand for "such a sum as would after deduction of tax at the standard rate give £35"'. The HL unanimously allowed her appeal, holding that what is now *TMA, s 106(2)* did not apply to the agreement. Lord Reid held that the agreement should be construed as providing that the husband 'undertook that, in addition to paying these sums to her, he would pay any tax which might become due by reason of his making these payments'. *CIR v Ferguson*, HL 1969, 46 TC 1; [1970] AC 442; [1969] 1 All ER 1025. (*Note*. The HL explicitly refrained from deciding whether the principles laid down by *In re Pettit*, **2.59** above, would apply to any repayment obtained by the wife. Lord Reid observed that 'that is a matter purely between husband and wife and the husband is not a party to this appeal'. See *Stokes v Bennett*, **39.38** MISCELLANEOUS INCOME, for the recovery by the Revenue of tax deducted by non-residents.)

Agreement to pay remuneration 'without any deductions and taxes'

[2.77] See *Jaworski v Institution of Polish Engineers*, **42.89** PAY AS YOU EARN.

Annual payments—miscellaneous

ITA 2007, s 450(2)—payments ineligible for relief

[2.78] A corporation borrowed money for municipal undertakings such as gasworks and tramways which were profitable, and for sanitary works which were not. The effect of the *Leeds Corporation (General Powers) Act 1901* was that it was not permitted to mix the funds. It had insufficient money in its sanitary works fund to meet its interest liability, and thus paid some of the interest out of untaxed income (the municipal rates). The Revenue issued an assessment charging tax on the balance of the interest. The HL unanimously upheld the assessment. Lord Atkinson held that 'the corporation cannot retain for their own benefit the income tax they have deducted' because 'it was not legally payable out of the particular fund out of which it has in fact been paid'. *Sugden v Leeds Corporation*, HL 1913, 6 TC 211.

ITA 2007, s 450(3)—payments out of capital

[2.79] See *Central London Railway Co v CIR*, **20.4** DEDUCTION OF TAX, and *Chancery Lane Safe Deposit & Offices Co Ltd v CIR*, **20.5** DEDUCTION OF TAX.

ITA 2007, s 450(5)—payments reimbursed

[2.80] A borough council borrowed money to finance a housing scheme under the *Housing of the Working Classes Act 1890*. Its net expenditure on the scheme was reimbursed by the London County Council. The Revenue issued assessments to recover the tax which the council had deducted from the interest which it paid. The KB upheld the assessments. *Dickson v Hampstead Borough Council*, KB 1927, 11 TC 691.

[2.81] A corporation built a substantial number of houses under the *Housing of the Working Classes Act 1890*. In order to finance this, it issued housing bonds on which it paid interest. It deducted tax from the interest. However, its net expenditure was subsequently reimbursed by the Local Government Board under *Town Planning Act 1919, s 7*. The Revenue issued assessments to recover the tax which the corporation had deducted. The Special Commissioners upheld the assessments and the HL unanimously dismissed the corporation's appeal. *Corporation of Birmingham v CIR*, HL 1930, 15 TC 172.

[2.82] A corporation borrowed money to maintain and repair certain roads under the *Local Government Act 1929*. It was reimbursed by the county council under *LGA 1929, s 117(3)*. The Revenue issued assessments to recover the tax which the corporation had deducted from the interest which it paid. The Special Commissioners upheld the assessments, and the KB dismissed the corporation's appeal. *Scarborough Corporation v CIR*, KB 1947, 28 TC 147.

Annuity to reimburse tax

[2.83] Under a will, the testator's widow (M) received certain income and an annuity of such an amount as would reimburse the whole of her supertax and income tax liability above a certain level. The Revenue issued a supertax assessment on the basis that the amounts of tax which the trustees paid on behalf of M formed part of her total income for the year. The Special Commissioners upheld the assessment, and the KB dismissed M's appeal. *Meeking v CIR*, KB 1920, 7 TC 603. (*Note*. The supertax paid by the trustees was grossed up before inclusion in M's income liable to supertax, and was included in her income only for supertax purposes.)

Tax on annuity borne by estate—whether income of annuitant

[2.84] A testator had bequeathed his widow an annuity free of income tax and surtax, and directed that the estate must bear a specified proportion of the tax payable by the widow. The Revenue issued assessments on the basis held that the tax borne by the trustees should be treated as income of the annuitant for tax purposes. The CA unanimously upheld the assessments. *Lord Michelham's Trustees v CIR; Lady Michelham's Executors v CIR*, CA 1930, 15 TC 737.

Whether tax includes overseas tax

[2.85] Under the will of a testator domiciled in England, his widow was entitled to an annuity 'free of all taxes (including income tax) and duties'. Sixteen years after her husband's death, she became resident in Kenya. The trustees of her husband's will issued an originating summons, claiming that they were only required to pay the UK tax on the annuity, and were not required to pay any Kenyan tax. The Ch D accepted this contention and granted a declaration accordingly, holding that the provision in the will related only to UK taxes and duties and not to Kenyan tax, since the testator did not contemplate that his widow would live abroad. *Frazer v Hughes (re Frazer)*, Ch D 1941, 20 ATC 73.

Annuity under will—testator domiciled abroad

[2.86] A testator, domiciled in Ceylon but resident in the UK, directed his trustees to pay his widow an annuity of such a sum as 'after deduction of income tax' amounted to £2,000 sterling. For 1941/42 the trustees paid her £2,900 (of which £900 was specified as representing the tax liability). The Revenue issued an assessment on the widow, charging tax on £2,900. She appealed, contending that she was only taxable on £2,000. The General Commissioners accepted this contention and allowed her appeal, and the KB upheld their decision. Wrottesley J held that, since the testator had been domiciled in Ceylon and the bulk of his estate was there, his will should be read as referring to Ceylon income tax and not to UK income tax. *Havelock v Grant*, KB 1946, 27 TC 363.

Annual payments deducted in computing profits

[2.87] See *Moss Empires Ltd v CIR*, 20.9 DEDUCTION OF TAX.

Whether payments of remuneration annual payments

[2.88] See *Jaworski v Institution of Polish Engineers*, 42.89 PAY AS YOU EARN.

Payments towards operating deficit of news agency

[2.89] See *British Commonwealth International Newsfilm Agency v Mahany*, 64.70 TRADING PROFITS.

Copyright royalties—whether 'annual payments'

[2.90] See *Lawrence v CIR*, 9.104 CHARITIES.

Royalties—whether 'annual payments'

[2.91] See *Rank Xerox Ltd v Lane*, 71.27 CAPITAL GAINS TAX.

3

Anti-Avoidance

The cases in this chapter are arranged under the following headings.

GENERAL NOTE

The cases in this chapter are those turning on the application of the specialist anti-avoidance legislation in *ICTA 1988, ss 747-756*; *ITA 2007, ss 615–809*; *CTA 2010, ss 731–937* and *TIOPA 2010, ss 146–217*. There have been substantial changes to the legislation in recent years. The case summaries should be read in the light of these changes. For cases involving the application of the settlements legislation to prevent the avoidance of surtax or higher rate liability, see 56 SETTLEMENTS. With regard to the general approach of the courts to tax avoidance schemes, see 58 TAX PLANNING AND AVOIDANCE.

Manufactured interest (ITA 2007, ss 578–580)

Interaction of manufactured interest rules and accrued income rules

[3.1] See *HMRC v D'Arcy*, 3.2 below, and *Barnes v HMRC*, 3.5 below.

Accrued income profits (ITA 2007, ss 618–681)

Definition of transfer of securities

[3.2] A woman (D) entered into a tax avoidance scheme involving transactions in gilts, designed to create a tax deduction for a manufactured interest payment. The Revenue issued a closure notice on the basis that the deduction was not allowable: they subsequently accepted that the deduction was allowable but contended that D was taxable on an amount approximately equal to the deduction under the accrued income scheme. D appealed, contending that the effect of what is now *ITA 2007, s 620(3)* was that the sale and repurchase were both deemed to have taken place on the same day, so that the effect of what is now *s 675(1)* was that she should be deemed never to have held the securities for the purpose of the accrued income legislation. The Special Commissioner accepted this contention and allowed the appeal, and the Ch D upheld this decision. Henderson J held that 'the accrued income scheme does not throw up a charge to counterbalance the deduction admittedly available to (D) for her manufactured interest payment. But the accrued income scheme and the provisions relating to manufactured interest were enacted at different times and with different statutory purposes. They do not form part of a single unified code'. *HMRC v D'Arcy*, Ch D 2007, [2008] STC 1329: [2007] EWHC 163 (Ch). (*Note. ICTA 1988, Sch 23A* was subsequently amended by *FA 2004* to close the loophole which was exploited by this scheme.)

Variable interest rate

[3.3] A company (F) issued six loan notes to an associated company (P), which transferred them to another associated company (L), which sold them to a bank. The notes provided for a fixed interest of 7.43375% from issue to redemption, but also provided for interest to be paid on irregular days and in irregular amounts. The Revenue issued a notice of determination under *TMA, s 41* that the accrued interest was taxable on P and L. The companies appealed. The Special Commissioners reviewed the evidence in detail and dismissed the appeals, observing that the transactions were intended to realise a substantial capital gain which P could shelter by using capital losses within the group, and were designed to circumvent the 'accrued income' provisions . The Commissioners observed that the purpose of the legislation was 'to provide that where variable rate securities are transferred there is an income tax charge on the real commercial value of the interest transferred and not on the artificially deflated value'. The CA upheld the Commissioners' decision (by a 2-1 majority, Peter Gibson LJ dissenting). Under the terms of the notes, the actual rate of interest for the interest period ending 15 June 1995 was 0.8%; for the interest period ending on 15 September 1995 was 27.3%, and for the interest period ending on the maturity date was 7.4%. Sir Andrew Morritt observed that 'the rate at which interest is "carried" by these notes is different in each of the three periods which, according to the terms of issue, make up the period from issue to redemption'. Tuckey LJ observed that 'the variable interest regime seems to be the more appropriate regime for the taxation of these notes', since with a fixed interest security one would expect the amount of interest to be the same for the same period at any time from issue to redemption', whereas these notes provided for three 'interest periods' in which the interest would 'differ markedly depending upon the period in which it accrues. This therefore looks like a variable interest security'. *Cadbury Schweppes plc v Williams (No 2); Cadbury Schweppes Overseas Ltd v Williams*, CA 2006, [2007] STC 106; [2006] EWCA Civ 657. (*Note*. For a previous appeal by one of the companies, see **18.46** CORPORATION TAX.)

Price differential on sale and repurchase

[3.4] An Irish bank (B) had a wholly-owned UK subsidiary (H). In November 2000 B agreed to purchase some securities from a Cayman Islands company (C), and covenanted not to transfer the securities to anyone other than H. B and H entered into an agreement whereby B granted H a 'call option' on the securities and H granted B a 'put option' on the securities. (The effect of this was that either party could require the transfer of the securities from B to H.) H and C entered into an agreement whereby H granted C a 'call option' on the securities and C granted H a 'put option' on the securities. B received dividends totalling £3,617,322 on the securities, before exercising its 'put option' and transferring the securities to H in February 2001. Six days later H exercised its own 'put option' and transferred the securities to C, having received dividends totalling £358,151. In its tax return for the year ending March 2001, H claimed a deduction of £3,975,473 (ie the total of the dividends received by it and B). Following an enquiry, the Revenue issued an amendment rejecting the claim. H appealed, contending that *ICTA 1988, s 737A(5)* had the effect of deeming that H had paid a 'manufactured overseas dividend' of £3,975,473 to B; that what is now *ITA 2007, s 607* had the effect of deeming there to have been a payment of interest by C to B, and that B could not be taxed on this payment since it was resident outside the UK. The Special Commissioners accepted these contentions and allowed the appeal, observing that 'the legislation does not in every respect sit comfortably with repo transactions involving more than two parties'. The Commissioners held that *s 607* required 'the interest to be treated as arising to the interim holder, the maker of the deemed loan, which in the present case is (B)'. The Commissioners accepted that 'the result is bizarre' but held that there was 'no justification for seeking to construe (*s 607*) in any other way'. The CA unanimously upheld this decision. Lawrence Collins LJ held that the effect of the legislation was that the deemed payment of interest had to be treated as paid to B rather than to H. There was no 'legitimate process of interpretation which will solve the Revenue's problem'. *HMRC v Bank of Ireland Britain Holdings Ltd*, CA [2008] STC 398; [2008] EWCA Civ 58. (Note. *ICTA 1988, s 737A* was subsequently amended by *FA 2006, Sch 6* with the intention of reversing the effect of this decision with effect from 27 June 2006, and was repealed for agreements coming into force on or after 1 October 2007. See the HMRC Technical Note issued on 27 June 2006 regarding the *FA 2006* changes. See *FA 2007, Sch 13* for the current legislation.)

Interaction of accrued income rules and manufactured interest rules

[3.5] An individual (B) entered into a complex scheme, devised by a firm of tax advisers, which sought to take advantage of a perceived mismatch between the 'accrued income' legislation (originally contained in *ICTA 1988, s 710 et seq*) and the legislation governing the taxation of manufactured interest payments (originally contained in *ICTA 1988, Sch 23A* and subsequently re-enacted in *ITA 2007, ss 578-580*). He submitted a return claiming a deduction of £1,200,000. HMRC disallowed the claim, and B appealed. The First-tier Tribunal, Upper Tribunal and the CA unanimously dismissed his appeal. Sir Timothy Lloyd held that 'the scheme fails because the transaction undertaken fell within the definition of a stock-lending arrangement' (in *TCGA 1992, s 263B*), so that B failed to qualify for relief under the 'accrued income' legislation. Vos LJ and McFarlane LJ also upheld the Upper Tribunal decision that, even if the transfers of the securities had qualified for relief under the 'accrued income' legislation, B was not entitled to the relief he claimed under the manufactured interest provisions. Sir Timothy Lloyd did not express an opinion on this point. *N Barnes v HMRC*, CA [2014] EWCA Civ 31.

Transactions in securities (ITA 2007, ss 682–713; CTA 2010, ss 731–751)

Whether a 'tax advantage' (ITA 2007, s 687; CTA 2010, s 732)

Bonus issue followed by redemption—whether a tax advantage obtained

[3.6] The Revenue issued a notice under what is now *ITA 2007, s 695* relating to a bonus issue of debentures in 1953, which were redeemed in 1961. The HL upheld the notice (by a 3-2 majority, Lords Hodson and Morton dissenting), holding that the tax advantage was the avoidance of the tax which would have been borne if the reserves used for the bonus issue had been distributed by way of dividend, that the redemption was a transaction in securities and that it arose in connection with the 'distribution of profits' of the company. *CIR v Parker (and related appeals)*, HL 1966, 43 TC 396; [1966] AC 141; [1966] 1 All ER 399.

[3.7] A company had issued stock of £284,235. In 1959 it made a bonus issue of £189,490, of which £60,000 was paid out of a capital redemption reserve fund and £129,490 was paid out of accumulated profits. In 1960 it reduced its capital by £284,235, ie returning 60% of its capital to the stockholders. The Revenue issued a notice under what is now *ITA 2007, s 695* to a stockholder (H). The Special Commissioners upheld the notice with regard to 45.55% (i.e. $^{129490}/_{284235}$) of the payment. The CA unanimously upheld their decision, holding that H had received a tax advantage. *Hague v CIR*, CA 1968, 44 TC 619; [1968] 2 All ER 1252. (*Note.* Another point at issue in this case, relating to H's wife, is now of historical interest only, following the introduction of separate assessment for married couples. See Simon's Taxes, para D9.103.)

[3.8] The decision in *Hague v CIR*, 3.7 above, was applied in the similar subsequent cases of *CIR v Horrocks; CIR v Wainwright*, Ch D 1968, 44 TC 645; [1968] 3 All ER 296.

[3.9] A company made a bonus issue of redeemable preference shares in 1954. It redeemed the shares in June 1965. The Revenue issued a notice under what is now *ITA 2007, s 695*. The Special Commissioners upheld the notice, accepting that there were *bona fide* commercial reasons for the transactions, but holding that the appellant had failed to show that obtaining a tax advantage was not one of the main objects of the redemption. The Ch D upheld this decision as one of fact. *Hasloch v CIR*, Ch D 1971, 47 TC 50.

Purchase of shares by company from shareholder

[3.10] Two individuals each held 50% of the shares of a company (G), which had accumulated substantial profits and cash reserves, and also each held 50% of the shares of another company (M). They sold the shares in M to G for £121,000. The Revenue issued notices under what is now *ITA 2007, s 695*. The HL unanimously upheld the notices, holding that the vendors had received the £121,000 'in connection with the distribution of profits' of G and obtained a tax advantage. *CIR v Cleary; CIR v Perren*, HL 1967, 44 TC 399; [1968] AC 766; [1967] 2 All ER 48.

[3.11] The Revenue issued a notice under what is now *ITA 2007, s 695* to an accountant (B) who was the controlling shareholder of a company which purchased shares in five other companies from B and his wife for £25,000. The CA unanimously upheld the notice, holding that the transaction had not been carried out for *bona fide* commercial reasons and that B had received consideration representing the value of assets 'available by way of dividend', within *s 685*. *CIR v Brown*, CA 1971, 47 TC 217; [1971] 1 WLR 1495; [1971] 3 All ER 502.

[3.12] 38% of the shares in a manufacturing company (P) were held by its principal director (L). A further 47% of the shares were held by another company (H) which was controlled by L. In 2002/03 L sold his entire shareholding to H for £275,000. The sale qualified for retirement relief from CGT. The Revenue issued a notice under what is now *ITA 2007, s 695*, on the basis that a main object of the transaction had been to obtain a tax advantage. The Special Commissioner dismissed L's appeal, holding that although there were commercial reasons for the transaction, it had been carried out in order to obtain a tax advantage. On the evidence, P had funded H's purchase of L's shareholding so that L could obtain retirement relief. *TG Lloyd v HMRC*, Sp C [2008] SSCD 681 (Sp C 672).

[3.13] A married couple were the controlling shareholders of a family building company (P), which had significant assets. They wished to transfer the business to a new company which would ultimately be controlled by their sons, without the new company taking over any contingent liabilities for work carried out by P. In 2001 the couple sold their shares in P to a newly-incorporated company (S), in which they held non-voting preference shares while they and their elder son held ordinary shares. They also each received £50,000 cash. P's trade was then transferred to a wholly-owned subsidiary of S. The Revenue issued a notice under what is now *ITA 2007, s 695*. The couple appealed, contending that the transactions had been carried out for *bona fide* commercial reasons and did not have the obtaining of a tax advantage as a main object. The Special Commissioner dismissed their appeals, finding that the shares had been sold for *bona fide* commercial reasons but that 'one of the objects of the sale of the shares was to obtain a cash payment for the appellants which gave them a tax advantage'. *PA & Mrs M Snell v HMRC*, Sp C [2008] SSCD 1094 (Sp C 699).

Share exchange—whether 'in connection with' ensuing dividend

[3.14] Two individuals owned shares in a company (K) which held property which had the potential for development at a substantial profit. They entered into a series of complex transactions including the exchange of their shares in K for shares in another company (P) at a substantial premium followed by the payment of a substantial dividend by K to P. The Revenue issued notices under what is now *ITA 2007, s 695*, specifying this share exchange and dividend payment. The Ch D upheld the notices and consequential assessments. *Anysz v CIR; Manolescue v CIR*, Ch D 1977, 53 TC 601; [1978] STC 296.

Share exchange followed by interest-free loans—whether a tax advantage

[3.15] In an avoidance scheme, the initial stages of which were similar to that used in *Anysz v CIR*, **3.14** above, the scheme went a stage further in that the greater part of the development profit reached the shareholders as interest-free loans from a company which they subsequently acquired. The Revenue issued notices under what is now *ITA 2007, s 695* and consequential assessments. The HL unanimously upheld the notices and assessments, holding that the loan transactions were within the definition of 'transactions in securities' and that the shareholders had obtained a tax advantage 'by the receipts of the loans repayable to a company which they now control'. *Williams & Others v CIR*, HL 1980, 54 TC 257; [1980] STC 535; [1980] 3 All ER 321.

Sale of shares to employee share ownership trust

[3.16] In December 2003 a company (N) established a 'qualifying employee share ownership trust' within *FA 1989, s 67*. N's controlling shareholder (G) had a substantial loan account with N, which would give rise to a corporation tax liability under what is now *CTA 2010, s 455* unless it were repaid. G sold 15,750 shares to the trust for £630,000 (reducing his shareholding from 82.2% to 63.8%). HMRC subsequently issued a notice to G under *ITA 2007, s 698*. G appealed, contending that he had not sold the shares for the purpose of obtaining a 'tax advantage'. The First-Tier Tribunal reviewed the evidence in detail, rejected this contention, and dismissed G's appeal. Judge Wallace held that 'the relevant tax advantage was the receipt by the appellant of £630,000 as capital so that he did not pay income tax on it'. The Upper Tribunal upheld this decision. Warren J held that 'a tax advantage can be obtained in consequence of a transaction in securities notwithstanding (*a*) that another operation, which is not a transaction in securities, is a necessary ingredient and (*b*) that such other operation is not one which takes place "in consequence of " the transaction in securities'. *NP Grogan v HMRC*, UT 2010, [2011] STC 1. (*Note*. The Upper Tribunal rejected an application for leave to appeal against this decision—UT 22 November 2010 unreported.)

Avoidance scheme—computation of the amount of the advantage

[3.17] A company (C) owned property valued at £10 million, which it wished to sell. 70% of its shares were held by another company (L), the remaining 30% being held by the Church Commissioners. Under a complex scheme, designed to avoid tax by taking advantage of a loophole in *ICTA 1970, s 80(6)*, C sold the property for £9.8 million and subsequently declared abnormal dividends. Meanwhile, L had exchanged its shareholding in C for shares in a newly-formed company (J), and L's shareholders received interest-free loans from another company (N), which was sold to J by the promoters of the scheme. The Revenue issued assessments on the shareholders under what is now *ITA 2007, s 685*. The HL unanimously upheld the assessments in principle, holding that a tax advantage had arisen to the shareholders. However, the HL reduced the amount of the assessments, holding that since N had subsequently been charged to corporation tax, which could only be paid by repaying some of the loans, the amounts which they would have to repay to N should be excluded from the assessments. *Bird & Others v CIR (and related appeals)*, HL 1988, 61 TC 238; [1988] STC 312; [1988] 2 WLR 1237; [1988] 2 All ER 670.

Sale of shares—whether consideration for stock

[3.18] A company (W) had acquired a framed picture for £50 in the course of its business which included dealing in frames and pictures. The picture was later found to be worth about £130,000. Another company (K) wished to acquire the picture. W transferred its trading assets, other than the picture and some minor items, to an associated company. K then acquired the shares in W for £44,447 (the price reflecting the expected tax consequences of the transactions). The Revenue issued notices under what is now *ITA 2007, s 695* to the shareholders in W. The Ch D upheld the notices, holding that the consideration for the shares clearly represented the value of W's trading stock. The shareholders had obtained a tax advantage by avoiding the tax which would have been payable if W had sold the picture in the ordinary way and distributed the profits by way of dividend. *CIR v Wiggins (and associated appeals)*, Ch D 1978, 53 TC 639; [1979] STC 244; [1979] 1 WLR 325; [1979] 2 All ER 245.

Purchase shortly before redemption of debentures with interest in arrear

[3.19] A merchant bank (K), which dealt in securities, purchased some debentures for £305,101, on which no interest had been paid for more than 20 years. Three months later the debentures were repaid in full for £148,269 plus accrued interest of £113,779. In its tax computations K claimed a deduction for the fall in the value of the debentures. The Revenue issued a notice under what is now *CTA 2010, s 743* on the basis that these transactions had been undertaken in order to obtain a tax advantage and should be excluded from the computation of K's profits. The Special Commissioners allowed K's appeal, holding that the transactions had been undertaken for *bona fide* commercial reasons. The Ch D upheld their decision, holding that K had made 'a simple purchase of debenture stock' which was 'an ordinary commercial transaction'. *CIR v Kleinwort Benson Ltd*, Ch D 1968, 45 TC 369; [1969] 2 Ch 221; [1969] 2 All ER 737.

Forward dividend-strip

[3.20] In two forward dividend-stripping cases, the agreement for the sale of the shares in the company being stripped was before 5 April 1960 (the date on which the provisions in *FA 1960* which became what is now *ITA 2007, s 682 et seq.* came into force), but the dividends were paid after that date. In one of the cases, the purchase price was paid forthwith, but the vendor was required to deposit an equal amount with a bank to be released on payment of the dividends. The Revenue issued notices under what is now *ITA 2007, s 695*. The vendors appealed, contending that the relevant transactions had taken place before 5 April 1960. The HL unanimously rejected this contention and upheld the notices, holding that the agreements for the sale of the shares had not been implemented before that date. Furthermore, each payment of a dividend and of the corresponding instalment of the purchase price was a separate transaction. *Greenberg v CIR; CIR v Tunnicliffe*, HL 1971, 47 TC 240; [1972] AC 109; [1971] 3 All ER 136. (*Notes*. (1) Lord Reid's judgment includes the well-known observation that 'plain words are seldom adequate to anticipate and forestall the multiplicity of ingenious schemes which are constantly being devised to evade taxation. Parliament is very properly determined to prevent this kind of tax evasion, and if the courts find it impossible to give very wide meanings to general phrases, the only alternative may be for Parliament to do as some other countries have done, and introduce legislation of a more sweeping character, which will put the ordinary well-intentioned person at much greater risk than is created by a wide interpretation of such provisions as those which we are now considering'. (2) *Obiter dicta* of Lord Simon of Glaisdale, on the question of whether a dividend was a transaction in securities, were specifically disapproved by Lord Millett in the subsequent case of *Laird Group plc v CIR*, **3.23** below.)

Exempt approved pension scheme

[3.21] In 1984 a company (U). which acted as trustee of an exempt approved pension scheme within *ICTA 1988, s 592*, purchased 1,000 shares in a company (T) for £100,000. The pension scheme had previously lent substantial sums of money to T, and the shares carried a 'put option' enabling the pension scheme to require T's holding company to purchase the shares for 7.5% of T's net asset value. In 1987 T's holding company was taken over by an outside company (S). In 1988 U advised S that it was considering exercising its 'put option', and after negotiations it was agreed that T should repurchase the shares from the pension scheme for £2,662,750 (a sum which, with a tax credit of 33.33%, would equal 7.5% of T's net asset value). The share repurchase was treated as a dividend for tax purposes, and the tax credit attaching to this distribution was repaid to the pension scheme at its request. Subsequently the Revenue issued a notice to U under what is now *CTA 2010, s 743*, declaring that the result of the transaction was that a Schedule F assessment should be raised on the trustee of the pension scheme. The trustee appealed, contending that the dividend was not 'abnormal'. The Special Commissioner allowed the appeal but the Ch D reversed this decision and remitted the case to the Commissioner. Sir John Vinelott declined to follow the decision of Aldous J in *Sheppard & Another v CIR (No 2)*, Ch D 1993, 65 TC 724; [1993] STC 240, and held that charities and other exempt bodies should not be treated as outside the scope of the provisions. *CIR v Universities Superannuation Scheme Ltd*, Ch D 1996, 70 TC 193; [1997] STC 1. (*Note*. Although the decisions in *Sheppard & Another v CIR (No 2)* and *CIR v Universities Superannuation Scheme Ltd* were both by the Ch D, it is settled law that 'where there are conflicting decisions of courts of co-ordinate jurisdiction, the later decision is to be preferred if it is reached after full consideration of the earlier decision' (per Denning J in *Minister of Pensions v Higham*, KB [1948] 1 All ER 863).)

Whether a 'transaction in securities' (ITA 2007, s 684(2); CTA 2010, s 751)

Payment of dividend—whether a transaction in securities

[3.22] In the case noted at 3.20 above, Lord Simon of Glaisdale expressed the opinion that the payment of a dividend was a transaction in securities, within what is now *ITA 2007, s 684*, but Lord Wilberforce held that it was not 'necessary, or opportune, to decide whether the payment of a dividend, or the consequent payment to the taxpayer, was itself, separately, a transaction in securities'. *Greenberg v CIR; CIR v Tunnicliffe*, HL 1971, 47 TC 240; [1972] AC 109; [1971] 3 All ER 136. (*Note*. See now the subsequent HL decision in *Laird Group plc v CIR*, **3.23** below, in which Lord Millett specifically approved the reasoning of Lord Wilberforce and disapproved that of Lord Simon.)

[3.23] In June 1990 a public company (L) acquired the whole of the share capital of a private company (S). In December 1990 L received an abnormal dividend of £3,000,000 from S. L set this franked investment income against a large dividend payment to its shareholders. The Revenue issued a notice under what is now *CTA 2010, s 743*, on the basis that L had obtained a tax advantage as a result of the dividend from S, which was a transaction in securities and had not been paid for commercial reasons. L appealed, contending that the dividend should not be treated as a transaction in securities. The HL unanimously accepted this contention and allowed the appeal. Lord Millett held that 'by declaring a dividend, the directors effectively release funds due to the shareholders from their power to retain them in the business', and that whether the company was in liquidation or continuing to carry on business, 'the distribution of the undistributed profits of a company to the shareholders entitled thereto merely gives effect to the rights attached to the shares. The funds are released, in the one case from the liquidator's discretion to retain them for the purpose of the winding-up, and in the other from the directors' discretion to retain them for the purposes of the undertaking.' Accordingly the declaration and payment of a dividend was not a 'transaction in securities'. *Laird Group plc v CIR*, HL 2003, 74 TC 399; [2003] STC 1349; [2003] UKHL 54; [2003] 4 All ER 669.

Company reconstruction—liquidation of old company

[3.24] A family company, controlled by three brothers, had carried on business as clothing manufacturers. In 1958 it made a bonus issue of shares. In 1963 the shareholders agreed that the company should be liquidated. The liquidator distributed more than £70,000 to the shareholders. The Revenue issued notices under what is now *ITA 2007, s 695* to the shareholders on the basis that they had gained a tax advantage by receiving the company's profits through a bonus issue of shares rather than by payment of dividends. The shareholders appealed, contending that the notices were invalid because the liquidator had failed to hold a final meeting of the company, as required by *Companies Act 1948* (see now *Insolvency Act 1986, s 94*). The Special Commissioners rejected this contention and dismissed the appeals, finding that the company had been dissolved on 1 January 1965. The CA upheld their decision as one of fact. *Marks & Others v CIR*, CA [1973] STC 541.

[3.25] On 10 April 1964 a trading company, with substantial undistributed profits, went into voluntary liquidation. The controlling shareholder (J) held 75% of the shares. Immediately before the liquidation, the shareholders and the prospective liquidator had entered into an agreement, as a result of which the company's business and most of its assets were transferred to a dormant company which J owned, in consideration for loan notes in that company, and the remaining assets were distributed to J. The Revenue issued a notice under what is now *ITA 2007, s 695* to J, ruling that 75% of the undistributed income was to be treated as a net dividend to him for 1964/65. J appealed, accepting that he had obtained a tax advantage but contending that the notice was invalid because the advantage was not a consequence of a 'transaction in securities'. The HL unanimously rejected this contention and dismissed J's appeal, holding that the 'liquidation agreement' was a transaction in securities, since it altered the rights attached to the shares by substituting agreed valuations and a conventional mode of distribution for the statutory provisions governing a voluntary liquidation. *CIR v Joiner*, HL 1975, 50 TC 449; [1975] STC 657; [1975] 1 WLR 1701; [1975] 3 All ER 1050.

[3.26] A company, which had significant reserves of capital and revenue, was liquidated and its trade was transferred to a new company. The liquidator made a cash distribution to the shareholders. The Revenue issued a notice under what is now *ITA 2007, s 695*, since the shareholders had gained a tax advantage by receiving cash from the liquidator rather than a dividend. The husband of one of the shareholders appealed. The Ch D dismissed his appeal, applying the decision in *CIR v Joiner*, **3.25** above, and holding that the distribution in the liquidation was a transaction in securities. *Addy v CIR*, Ch D 1975, 51 TC 71; [1975] STC 601.

Whether transactions effected for commercial reasons (ITA 2007, s 685(2)(a); CTA 2010, s 734(2)(a))

[3.27] A company carried on business as coal merchants. A rival company made a take-over bid. Some of the directors wished to retain control of the company, and made a counter-offer, which was successful. To finance their purchase, they had to borrow money from a bank. In order to help them repay some of the loans, the company made a bonus issue of shares and subsequently repaid it. The Revenue issued notices under what is now *ITA 2007, s 695*. One of the directors appealed, contending that the transactions had been undertaken for commercial reasons and that any tax advantages were ancillary to this. The Special Commissioners accepted this contention and allowed his appeal, and the HL unanimously upheld their decision. Lord Upjohn observed that 'no commercial man in his senses is going to carry out commercial transactions except upon the footing of paying the smallest amount of tax involved'. *CIR v Brebner*, HL 1967, 43 TC 705; [1967] 2 AC 18; [1967] 1 All ER 779. (*Note*. The transactions in question took place before *FA 1965*. See now *CTA 2010, ss 1024–1027*.)

[3.28] A family company issued bonus preference shares in 1951 to avoid a possible loss of control to outside shareholders. They were replaced by redeemable shares in 1958 as a preliminary to a public flotation, and were redeemed in 1963. The Revenue issued notices under what is now *ITA 2007, s 695*. The shareholders appealed, contending that the transactions had been entered into for commercial reasons. The Special Commissioners accepted this contention and allowed the appeals, and the HL unanimously upheld their decision as one of fact. *CIR v Goodwin (and related appeal)*, HL 1976, 50 TC 583; [1976] STC 28; [1976] 1 WLR 191; [1976] 1 All ER 481. (*Note*. See the note following *CIR v Brebner*, **3.27** above.)

[3.29] A farmer (R) and his brother each held 37.4% of the shares of a family investment company (E). They also each held 50% of the shares of a company (H), whose only significant asset was a 20% holding in a public company (C) of which their father was managing director and in which E had a 32.6% holding. R wanted to raise cash to purchase an adjoining farm. His father wished to keep ownership of C within the family. Accordingly R and his brother sold their shares in H to E for £102,000 in cash. The Revenue issued notices under what is now *ITA 2007, s 695*. R appealed, contending that the shares had been fairly valued at £102,000 and the transactions had been carried out for commercial reasons. The Ch D accepted this contention and allowed his appeal. *Clark v CIR*, Ch D 1978, 52 TC 482; [1978] STC 614; [1979] 1 WLR 416; [1979] 1 All ER 385. (*Note*. For another issue in this case, relating to R's brother, see **3.32** below.)

[3.30] On 29 December 1992 a company (M), which was a member of a group, acquired from its parent company the share capital of four other subsidiary companies. On 30 December it received dividends from three of those companies. On 31 December the four companies sold their trades and assets to other companies in the group. M made a claim under *ICTA 1988, s 242* to set part of its trading losses against the surplus of franked investment income represented by the dividends and the accompanying tax credit. The Revenue rejected the claim and issued a notice under what is now *CTA 2010, s 743*. M appealed, contending that the transactions had been carried out for commercial reasons and did not have the obtaining of a tax advantage as a main object. The Special Commissioners accepted M's evidence and allowed its appeal, but the Revenue issued a notice under *ICTA 1988, s 705(2)*, requiring the appeal to be reheard by a tribunal constituted under *ICTA 1988, s 706* (see **3.42** below). The tribunal duly reheard the appeal and noted that it had been provided with 'a substantial amount of written material relevant to the issue that had not been disclosed to the Revenue and had not been produced as evidence before the Special Commissioners'. On the evidence, there were commercial reasons for the reorganisation of the two divisions within the group in question. However, 'the transactions did not simply produce the required reorganisation of the two divisions'. The purchase of the share capital of the four companies by M, and the dividends received by M, could not be explained rationally unless the requirement to obtain a tax advantage was taken into account, and 'would not have been carried out unless the obtaining of a tax advantage had been a main object'. Accordingly the tribunal dismissed M's appeal, holding that 'the obtaining of a tax advantage was a main reason, if not the main reason' for the transactions in question. *Marwood Homes Ltd v CIR (No 3)*, Tribunal 1998, [1999] SSCD 44.

'The ordinary course of making or managing investments' (ITA 2007, s 685(2)(b); CTA 2010, s 734(2)(b))

[3.31] A company purchased 1,900,000 of its shares from the trustees of its staff pension scheme. (The purchase was necessary to comply with the *Occupational Pension Schemes (Investment of Scheme's Resources) Regulations 1992*, which provided that an occupational pension scheme should not have more than 5% of its assets invested in employer-related investments.) The scheme submitted a claim for repayment of the tax credit attaching to the distribution. The Revenue repaid the amount claimed, but subsequently issued a notice under what is now *ITA 2007, s 695*. The trustees appealed, contending that the sale had been 'in the ordinary course of making or managing investments' and did not have the obtaining of a tax advantage as a main object. The Special Commissioners accepted this contention and allowed the appeal. Applying *dicta* of Lord Upjohn in *CIR v Brebner*, **3.27** above, 'the obtaining of a tax advantage was not the main object or one of the main objects of the trustees'. Furthermore, applying the Special Commissioners' decision in *Clark v CIR*, **3.29** above, the trustees had done what 'any prudent investor' would have done in the ordinary course of managing his investments. *Lewis v CIR*, Sp C [1999] SSCD 349 (Sp C 218).

[3.32] In the case noted at **3.29** above, a farmer (R) and his brother (C) each held 37.4% of the shares of a family investment company (E). R wished to raise cash to purchase an adjoining farm, and decided to sell his shares. C also sold his shares in order not to be left with an unmarketable minority holding. The Revenue issued a notice under what is now *ITA 2007, s 695*. The Special Commissioners allowed C's appeal, finding that C had sold his shares 'in the ordinary course of making or managing investments'. *Clark v CIR*, Sp C 1978, 52 TC 482; [1978] STC 614; [1979] 1 WLR 416; [1979] 1 All ER 385.

The prescribed circumstances (ITA 2007, ss 686–694; CTA 2010, ss 735–742)

Whether amount of dividend 'abnormal'

[3.33] In February and March 1996 the trustees of a pension scheme purchased a large number of shares in a public company (P). In May and June 1996 the trustees sold some of the shares back to P. Under the legislation then in force, most of the sale price was treated as a distribution by P, and the trustees were entitled to receive a tax credit. In 1999 the Revenue issued a notice under what is now *CTA 2010, s 743* in respect of these sales. The trustees appealed, contending that the statutory conditions were not satisfied, because they had not received 'an abnormal amount by way of dividend'. The Special Commissioners accepted this contention and allowed the appeal, holding that the amount of the qualifying distribution was 'fixed by the market' and was therefore 'normal'. The CA upheld their decision. Jonathan Parker LJ held that the amount in question did not substantially exceed 'a normal return on the consideration provided by the recipient for the relevant securities'. *Sema Group Pension Scheme Trustees (aka Omega Group Pension Scheme Trustees) v CIR*, CA 2002, 74 TC 593; [2003] STC 95; [2002] EWCA Civ 1857. (*Note. ICTA 1988, s 231* was subsequently amended by *FA 1998* to provide that tax credits are no longer claimable in such circumstances.)

ITA 2007, s 685—whether 'transaction whereby' satisfied

[3.34] Three shareholders owned and controlled a property-dealing company (C), and five other companies holding properties worth more than £1,000,000. A complex avoidance scheme was carried out comprising some 30 transactions extending over 12 months. The initial steps in the scheme were the acquisition of the shares in the five companies by E (a company associated with the advisers who devised the scheme) and the sale of the properties to C. Both these steps were taken in April 1969. The crucial step in the scheme was the declaration of abnormal dividends of £555,000 by the five companies in April 1970. The Revenue issued notices under what is now *ITA 2007, s 698*, and the shareholders appealed. The Special Commissioners allowed the appeals, finding that the sale and the dividend payments 'were separate transactions' and that the sale 'could have taken place without abnormal dividends ever having been paid'. Accordingly, the conditions of what is now *ITA 2007, s 685* were not satisfied. The HL upheld this decision as one of fact. *CIR v Garvin; CIR v Rose*, HL 1981, 55 TC 24; [1981] STC 344; [1981] 1 WLR 793.

[3.35] In a case in which a scheme similar to that in *CIR v Garvin*, 3.34 above, was used, an appeal against a notice under what is now *ITA 2007, s 698* and the consequential assessments was dismissed. The facts differed from *Garvin* in that the scheme was carried out in a period of two weeks and, on the evidence, it was certain that once it had been embarked on, the abnormal dividend would be declared. The Special Commissioners held that the relevant 'transaction' was the whole series of operations, and the Ch D upheld their decision. *Emery v CIR*, Ch D 1980, 54 TC 607; [1981] STC 150.

[3.36] A married couple owned a company (B1), with the husband (E) owning 51% of the shares. In 1998 the couple separated. In December 2000 the couple incorporated another company (B2), with E again owning 51% of the shares. In September 2001 E's wife transferred her shares in B2 (which had not yet traded) to E. In January 2002 B1 transferred its business to B2, and in February 2002 B1 went into members' voluntary liquidation. The liquidator made capital distributions to E and his wife. HMRC issued a notice under what is now *ITA 2007, s 698* on E, on the basis that he had received a tax advantage by reason of a transaction in securities. E appealed, contending that the obtaining of a tax advantage was not the main object, or one of the main objects, of the transactions. The First-tier Tribunal accepted this contention and allowed E's appeal, finding that B2 'was not set up with tax avoidance as its main or one of its main purposes'. On the evidence, the purpose of the transactions in question was 'to separate the personal and commercial interests' of E and his wife 'in a simple and commercially logical way given that they were separated and were divorcing'. The transactions were bona fide commercial transactions and were 'in the normal course of managing investments'. This was 'a straightforward liquidation of a company, which on its own generated the alleged tax advantage inherent in the capital gains treatment'. The liquidation of B1 'gave the divorcing wife what she wanted in terms of finality and cash' and was 'a commercially appropriate solution'. *AJ Ebsworth v HMRC*, FTT [2009] UKFTT 199 (TC); [2009] SFTD 602, TC00152.

[3.37] In May 2000 a company (T) with distributable reserves acquired a company (W) with negative reserves. On the same day T's controlling shareholder (B) acquired loan stock which W had issued. From May 2000 to 2002 T made loans to W, following which W repaid some of the loan stock. In February 2002 T's trade was hived down to W, which made further repayments of loan stock to B. HMRC issued assessments on B on the basis that he had received a tax advantage by reason of a transaction in securities. The First-tier Tribunal reviewed the evidence in detail and issued a decision in principle dismissing the appeal up to the amount of T's distributable reserves until the hive-down of its trade, but allowing the appeal in respect of any further profits made by W after the hive-down. Judge Avery Jones observed that 'on the hive-down there was a transfer of assets that represents the value of available assets of (T) corresponding to its distributable reserves up to the date of the hive-down'. The fact that assets had been lent by T to W, or transferred on the hive-down in consideration of a debt, did not prevent those assets from continuing to represent assets available for distribution by T by way of dividend. However assets representing profits made by W after the hive-down were not 'assets that would have been available to (T) for distribution by way of dividend'. *M Bamberg v HMRC*, FTT [2010] UKFTT 333 (TC); [2010] SFTD 1231, TC00618.

Notification procedure (ITA 2007, ss 695-700; CTA 2010, ss 743–747)

[3.38] A married couple made statutory declarations under what is now *ITA 2007, s 696*, and the Revenue informed them that they proposed to take further action under what is now *ITA 2007, s 697*. The couple then issued an originating summons against the members of the tribunal and the Board of Inland Revenue, claiming that they should be given an opportunity to see the Revenue counter-statement and to address argument to the tribunal. The members of the tribunal and the Board applied for the originating summons to be struck out as there was no reasonable cause of action. The Ch D accepted this contention and ordered the summons to be struck out, holding that the procedure under *s 697* did not include a hearing before the tribunal. The couple appealed to the HL, which unanimously dismissed their appeal, holding that the couple were not entitled to see the Board's counter-statement before the tribunal decided whether or not there was a *prima facie* case, and that although the tribunal had power to seek further comment from a taxpayer if it considered this appropriate, it must allow the Board to reply to any such comment. Lord Donovan observed that 'the decision of the tribunal is conclusive if it is adverse to the Commissioners though not so to the taxpayer'. *Wiseman & Another v Borneman & Others*, HL 1969, 45 TC 540; [1971] AC 297; [1969] 3 All ER 275.

[3.39] A tribunal had determined, in accordance with what is now *ITA 2007, s 697*, that there was a *prima facie* case for proceeding against an actor (H) who had entered into a complex series of transactions. H issued a writ seeking a declaration that the determination was null and void as the relevant documents had been considered by only three of the four persons appointed to the tribunal under what is now *ITA 2007, s 704*. The CA unanimously rejected his application and the HL unanimously dismissed his appeal, holding that *s 704* should be construed as meaning that the tribunal to which a particular case had been referred was to consist of the chairman and not fewer than two of the persons appointed by the Lord Chancellor. *Howard v Borneman & Others (No 2)*, HL 1975, 50 TC 322; [1975] STC 327; [1976] AC 301; [1975] 2 All ER 418.

[3.40] The tribunal determined under what is now *ITA 2007, s 697* that there was a *prima facie* case for proceeding against an individual (B). The Revenue subsequently issued a surtax assessment on B. He issued an originating summons against the Board of Inland Revenue and members of the tribunal, seeking a declaration that the tribunal's determination was a nullity. The Ch D rejected his contentions and dismissed the summons, and the CA unanimously dismissed his appeal. *Balen v CIR & Others*, CA 1978, 52 TC 406; [1978] STC 420; [1978] 2 All ER 1033. (*Note*. See now *ITA 2007, s 698(1)*.)

Action under ITA 2007, s 684—whether subject to judicial review

[3.41] See *R v CIR (ex p. Preston)*, 50.25 REVENUE ADMINISTRATION.

Appeals procedure (ITA 2007, s 705; CTA 2010, s 750)

Notice of requirement under ICTA 1988, s 705(2)

[3.42] Following the Special Commissioners' decision in the case noted at 3.30 above, the Revenue issued a notice under *ICTA 1988, s 705(2)*, requiring the appeal to be reheard by a tribunal constituted under *ICTA 1988, s 706*. The company applied to the tribunal for an order striking out the notice, contending that it was an abuse of process. The tribunal rejected this contention and dismissed the company's application. The Revenue's requirement for a rehearing had been in accordance with the rights granted to the Revenue by *ICTA 1988, s 705(2)*, and was not an abuse of process. *Marwood Homes Ltd v CIR (No 2)*, Tribunal [1998] SSCD 53.

Transfers of assets abroad (ITA 2007, ss 714–751)

General

Cases where the appellant was successful

Settlement of rents receivable under determinable lease

[3.43] In the case noted at 56.40 SETTLEMENTS, some properties abroad had been demised to a UK company, the rents to be paid to trustees resident in Paris. (The treatment of the rents in relation to the company was considered in *Union Cold Storage Co Ltd v Adamson*, 63.38 TRADING PROFITS.) The rents payable had been settled to the trustees to invest and accumulate the income (with wide powers to the settlors to direct how the rents were to be invested). The trust fund comprising the investments and accumulated income was to be divided into two parts, to be held on trust for the children and remoter issue of each of the settlors as either might appoint by deed or will. Power was reserved to each of them to appoint by will in favour of his widow, although one subsequently executed a deed relinquishing this power. In 1942 the Revenue issued assessments on the basis that what is now *ITA 2007, s 721* applied. The HL allowed the appeals against all the assessments, holding that the reference to a 'wife' in the relevant legislation did not include a widow and that the power to enjoy income was held jointly and therefore not acquired by an individual within *s 721*. *Lord Vestey's Executors & Vestey v CIR; Lord Vestey's Executors & Vestey v Colquhoun*, HL 1949, 31 TC 1; [1949] 1 All ER 1108. (*Note*. The relevant legislation is now *ITA 2007, s 714(4)*, which refers to a 'spouse' rather than a 'wife'.)

Transfer of assets abroad—whether for tax avoidance or tax mitigation

[3.44] From 1973 to 1987 an individual (W) and his wife were resident in Hong Kong, and neither resident nor ordinarily resident in the UK. In 1986 W retired and received a lump sum payment from his employer. He invested this in a single premium bond with a company resident in the Isle of Man. In exchange, the company issued him a number of insurance policies linked to the fund. In 1987 he returned to the UK and became both resident and ordinarily resident. On the maturity of some of the insurance policies issued by the Isle of Man company, he took out further single premium bonds with the same company, and in 1990 he added further investments to the first bond, in return for which the company issued three further insurance policies. Under the particular types of bond in question, the investor was entitled to nominate investments up to the value of the money transferred, and the value insured under the policies was linked to the performance of those investments. The Revenue issued assessments charging tax under what is now *ITA 2007, s 720*, on the basis that W and his wife had sought to avoid income tax by the transfer of assets abroad. They appealed, contending that the relevant transfers had not been made for the purpose of avoiding liability to taxation. The Special Commissioner allowed their appeals, and the HL upheld this decision as one of fact. Lord Nolan held that there was an important distinction between tax avoidance and tax mitigation, and that it would be absurd 'to describe as "tax avoidance" the acceptance of an offer of freedom from tax which

Parliament has deliberately made'. For the purposes of what is now *ITA 2007, Part 13*, tax avoidance should be construed as 'a course of action designed to conflict with or defeat the evident intention of Parliament'. Furthermore, the fact that W and his wife had the power to nominate the underlying investments was not sufficient reason to distinguish the case from the majority of similar cases where investors did not have such power, since W had 'no legal or equitable interest' in the underlying investments. *CIR v Willoughby & Another*, HL 1997, 70 TC 57; [1997] STC 995; [1997] 1 WLR 1071; [1997] 4 All ER 65. (*Notes.* (1) The HL also held that the 1986 transfer was outside the scope of *ICTA 1988, s 739* because W and his wife were not ordinarily resident in the UK at the time it was made. The decision on this point was overtaken by *FA 1997, s 81*, which introduced *ICTA 1988, s 739(1A)*, providing that, for income arising on or after 26 November 1996, *ICTA 1988, s 739* applied whatever the ordinary residence status of the individual when the transfer was made, and applied even if it was not shown that the avoiding of liability to income tax was 'one of the purposes for which the transfer was effected'. See now *ITA 2007, s 721(5)*. (2) For the Revenue's practice following this decision, see the Revenue Press Release dated 18 December 1997. With regard to the tax treatment of personal portfolio bonds, see also *ICTA 1988, s 553C*, introduced by *FA 1998, s 89*.)

Japanese citizen transferring money to Jersey

[3.45] A woman (B) was born in the UK, of an English father and a Japanese mother. In 1991/92 B's maternal grandfather (G), who was a Japanese citizen, transferred a large sum of money to the UK for the purpose of benefiting B. On the advice of a solicitor, and in order to avoid liability to IHT, G subsequently (in June 1992) established a discretionary settlement in Jersey and transferred the money from the UK to this settlement. G informed the trustee of the settlement that he wished B to be the principal beneficiary (and did not want the money to be used to benefit B's mother). G died in Japan two years later. The Revenue issued a 1992/93 assessment charging tax on B under what is now *ITA 2007, s 720*. B appealed, contending that *s 720* did not apply, since 'the avoidance of liability to taxation was neither the purpose nor one of the purposes for which the transfer or associated operations were effected'. The Special Commissioners accepted this contention and allowed B's appeal. Applying *dicta* of Lord Templeman in *New Zealand Commr of Inland Revenue v Challenge Corporation Ltd*, **58.12** TAX PLANNING AND AVOIDANCE, G's motives in transferring the money from the UK to Jersey were tax mitigation rather than tax avoidance. The Commissioners observed that, by virtue of *IHTA, s 157(1)*, if G had arranged for the funds to be left in the UK in the form of foreign currency, no IHT would have been payable. By virtue of *IHTA, s 6(1)*, property situated outside the UK was excluded property if the person beneficially entitled to it was domiciled outside the UK. The Commissioners held that there was no 'difference in principle between an action designed to take advantage of the provisions of *s 157* as against actions designed to take advantage of the provisions of *s 6*'. On the evidence, the Commissioners found that 'the tax implications of siting the trust in Jersey were a matter of indifference to (G)'. *Beneficiary v CIR*, Sp C [1999] SSCD 134 (Sp C 190).

Transfer of shareholding to Bermudan company—whether ITA 2007, s 739(4) applicable

[3.46] An individual (C), who was domiciled in the Republic of Ireland, owned 59% of the shares in a UK company (H), which in turn owned a company trading as a reinsurance broker. In 1982 C transferred his shareholding to a newly-formed Bermudan company (B). The Revenue issued assessments on C for 1993/94 to 1995/96 inclusive, charging tax under what is now *ITA 2007, s 720* in respect of dividends paid by H to B. C appealed, contending that the effect of what is now *ITA 2007, s 739(4)* was that *s 720* did not apply, since the transfer had been undertaken for *bona fide* commercial purposes. He gave evidence that he had wanted to establish a Bermudan holding company so that he could compete for business, and for experienced staff, in both the UK and the USA and 'did not want either London or the USA to be seen as the master with the other as servant'. The Special Commissioner (Dr. Avery Jones, sitting alone) accepted this contention and allowed the appeal, holding that *ITA 2007, s 739* imposed a subjective test and that, on the evidence, the Bermudan holding company had been set up for *bona fide* commercial purposes, rather than to avoid tax. Dr. Avery Jones specifically declined to follow the previous Commissioner's decision in *Carvill v CIR (No 1)*, **3.61** below, observing that he had 'had the benefit of hearing more witnesses' than the previous Commissioner. *Carvill v CIR (No 2)*, Sp C [2000] SSCD 143 (Sp C 233). (*Note*. For subsequent developments in this case, see **3.62** and **3.63** below. For an appeal against Schedule E assessments, see *Carvill v Frost*, **4.434** APPEALS.)

Cases where the assessment was upheld

Assets transferred to overseas company

[3.47] An individual (C) transferred UK investments to a Canadian company in return for shares and non-interest-bearing debentures (redeemable at a premium) in the company. These were then transferred to the trustees of discretionary trusts set up for the sole purpose of preventing C (who was 'drinking heavily' and 'incapable of managing his own affairs') from being able to deal with his assets himself. In the relevant year, the company paid no dividend and applied its income in redeeming some of the debentures. The Revenue assessed C's executors on the basis that the income of the company was deemed to be his under what is now *ITA 2007, s 721*. The CA unanimously upheld the assessment. *Cottingham's Executors v CIR*, CA 1938, 22 TC 344; [1938] 2 KB 689; [1938] 3 All ER 560.

[3.48] An individual (B) transferred assets to a Canadian company (D) in return for debentures in D, which were transferred to a trust to pay the redemption moneys to him for life. The Revenue assessed B's executors on the basis that D's income was deemed to be his under what is now *ITA 2007, s 721*. The KB upheld the assessments, holding that B had been entitled to receive a benefit out of D's income, and thus to have power to enjoy it. *Admiral Earl Beatty's Executors v CIR*, KB 1940, 23 TC 574.

[3.49] Two brothers transferred assets to separate Canadian companies in return for debentures in the companies. They subsequently exchanged their debentures. The KB upheld assessments under what is now *ITA 2007, s 720*, holding that the reciprocal gifts did not take the income outside the scope of the legislation. *Beatty v CIR (and related appeal)*, KB 1940, 23 TC 574.

[3.50] A UK resident transferred shares to a Canadian company which he controlled, receiving a series of promissory notes payable on demand. The Revenue assessed him on the company's income under what is now *ITA 2007, s 720*. The KB upheld the assessments, holding that he had power to enjoy the company's income. *Lee v CIR*, KB 1941, 24 TC 207.

[3.51] As a consequence of a series of complex transactions extending over a period of years, four Canadian companies acquired certain valuable assets previously held by an individual (W), and W became entitled to, *inter alia*, a series of promissory notes payable at intervals of three months. (The promissory notes were the subject of an earlier decision in *Lord Howard de Walden v Beck*, 52.52 SAVINGS AND INVESTMENT INCOME.) The Revenue assessed W on the basis that the income of the companies was deemed to be his by virtue of what is now *ITA 2007, s 721*. He appealed, contending that he only had 'power to enjoy' a small proportion of the income of the companies. The Special Commissioners rejected this contention and dismissed his appeals, and the KB and the CA upheld their decision. The effect of what is now *ITA 2007, s 723(2)(3)* was that W was deemed to have power to enjoy the entire income of the companies. Lord Greene MR observed that the provisions were 'intended to be an effective deterrent which will put a stop to practices which the legislature considers to be against the public interest' and 'it scarcely lies in the mouth of the taxpayer who plays with fire to complain of burnt fingers'. *Lord Howard de Walden v CIR*, CA 1941, 25 TC 121; [1942] 1 KB 389; [1942] 1 All ER 287.

[3.52] An individual (R) transferred some shares to a Kenyan company which he controlled. The company credited the cost of the shares to an account described as a loan account. The Revenue assessed R on the company's income under what is now *ITA 2007, s 720*. The KB upheld the assessment, holding that the effect of what is now *ITA 2007, s 723(2)* was that R was 'deemed to have power to enjoy' the company's income. *Ramsden v CIR*, Ch D 1957, 37 TC 619.

[3.53] In 1971 a building contractor arranged for the ownership of an industrial estate to be transferred to family settlements for his two young grand-daughters (B and N). B and N became entitled to the ownership of the land when they reached the age of 18 (in 1980 and 1982 respectively). On reaching the age of 18, they each assigned their interests in the land to Jersey companies, of which their parents were directors. The Revenue subsequently issued assessments on B and N, charging tax on the companies' income on the basis that the transfers had made for the purpose of avoiding UK tax. B and N appealed, contending that the transfers had been made at the instigation of their parents, to protect their assets 'from dissipation by unsuitable boyfriends or possible divorce'. The Special Commissioner upheld the assessments and dismissed the appeals, holding on the evidence that the assets had been transferred with the aim of avoiding future liability to capital transfer tax and the higher rates of income tax. *Mrs SA Burns v HMRC (and related appeal)*, Sp C [2009] SSCD 165 (Sp C 728).

[3.54] A married couple (Mr & Mrs S) owned three companies which provided residential care to the elderly, and owned the properties from which two of those companies traded. They each established settlements in the Isle of Man, which acquired the entire share capital of two newly-incorporated Isle of Man companies. They transferred the properties which they owned to the Isle of Man companies, so that the UK companies began paying rent to the Isle of Man companies. HMRC issued rulings that the dividends which the Isle of Man companies had paid out of profits accruing from the rents which they received in respect of the UK properties were taxable income of Mr & Mrs S by virtue of what is now *ITA 2007, s 720*. The First-tier Tribunal reviewed the evidence in detail and upheld HMRC's rulings in principle (subject to agreement as to the exact figures). *R & Mrs G Seesurrun v HMRC*, FTT [2014] UKFTT 783 (TC), TC03900.

Assets transferred to overseas trust

[3.55] An individual (B) transferred shares to trusts of a settlement established in Liechtenstein. B was excluded from benefiting from the trust in question, but the trustees were empowered to transfer the trust fund to another trust. The Revenue assessed B under what is now *ITA 2007, s 720* on the income from the shares. The Ch D upheld the assessments and the CA unanimously dismissed B's appeal. The provisions of the settlement could be exercised so as to confer upon B a 'power to enjoy income', within what is now *ITA 2007, s 722(1)*. Morritt LJ observed that 'the structure was more complicated and fiscally expensive than was necessary'. The 'obvious inference' was 'that the scheme was to preserve the income of the company in as fiscally beneficial an environment as possible'. Mance LJ observed that the purpose of the settlement was not 'to dispose of assets outright or finally, but to shelter them, hopefully in a tax-free environment, and to be able to recover them at some date in the future if so wished'. *CIR v Botnar*, CA 1999, 72 TC 205; [1999] STC 711. (*Note*. The Special Commissioners had upheld, in principle, the validity of assessments under the extended time limits on the basis that B had been guilty of 'fraudulent or negligent conduct'.)

Shares transferred abroad—dividends satisfied by debentures

[3.56] A UK resident transferred stock in a US company to two Canadian companies, the stock of which was indirectly held in trust for his children. The Revenue assessed him on the income of the Canadian companies under what is now *ITA 2007, s 720*. He appealed, contending that dividends on the US stock, satisfied by debentures redeemable at 30 days' notice, were capital rather than income. The KB rejected this contention and upheld the assessments, holding that the dividends were income. *Aykroyd v CIR*, KB 1942, 24 TC 515; [1942] 2 All ER 665.

Transfer of assets procured but not executed by person assessed

[3.57] In a case where the facts were complex, the HL upheld the CA decision that what is now *ITA 2007, ss 720, 721* applied to a transfer which had been procured but not executed by the person assessed, and applied where the transfer of assets was made to a person who was UK-resident at that time but not at the time when the relevant income arose. *Congreve & Congreve v CIR*, HL 1948, 30 TC 163; [1948] 1 All ER 948. (*Note*. *Dicta* of Lord Simonds on the scope of *ss 720, 721* were disapproved by a subsequent HL in the 1979 case of *Vestey & Others v CIR*, HL 1979, 54 TC 503; [1980] STC 10. The substantive decision in that case has been overtaken by changes in the legislation deriving from *FA 1981*.)

Rights under overseas contract of employment

[3.58] A surveyor (B), resident in the UK, set up a scheme whereby he became the sole employee of a Jersey company (D). He was to receive no salary until he was 70, but D was to provide him with financial assistance. He subsequently referred potential clients to D. The Revenue issued assessments under what is now *ITA 2007, s 720*. The Ch D upheld the assessments, holding that the employment contract conferred rights on D which were assets for the purposes of what is now *ITA 2007, s 717*. B received benefits out of a tax-free fund accumulated by D from its exploitation of his services, and he therefore had power to enjoy D's income by virtue of what is now *ITA 2007, s 723(3)*. *CIR v Brackett; Brackett v Chater*, Ch D 1986, 60 TC 134; [1986] STC 521. (*Note*. For another issue in this case, see **60.31** TRADING INCOME.)

Assets transferred abroad to avoid estate duty

[3.59] A UK resident appealed against assessments under what is now *ITA 2007, s 720*, contending that he had transferred assets abroad to avoid estate duty, and that this was outside the definition of 'taxation' in what is now *ITA 2007, s 739*. The Special Commissioners dismissed the appeals, holding that 'taxation' included estate duty. The CA upheld their decision. *Sassoon v CIR*, CA 1943, 25 TC 154.

Whether transfer of assets was to avoid taxation

[3.60] A UK resident (P) was assessed under what is now *ITA 2007, s 720* on the income of an Irish company. The Special Commissioners upheld the assessments, finding that P's father, who was resident in the Republic of Ireland, had transferred UK securities to the company to avoid UK taxation. The CA upheld their decision. *Philippi v CIR*, CA 1971, 47 TC 75; [1971] 1 WLR 1272; [1971] 3 All ER 61.

Transfer of shareholding to Bermudan company

[3.61] An individual (C), who was domiciled in Ireland, owned 59% of the shares in a UK company (H), which in turn owned a company trading as a reinsurance broker. In 1982 C transferred his shareholding to a newly-formed Bermudan company (B). The Revenue issued assessments for 1987/88 to 1992/93 inclusive, charging tax under what is now *ITA 2007, s 720* in respect of dividends paid by H to B. C appealed, contending that the transfer had been undertaken for *bona fide* commercial purposes and was 'not designed for the purpose of avoiding liability to taxation'. The Special Commissioner rejected this contention and dismissed C's appeal, observing that he did 'not accept all C's evidence 'at face value' and finding that C's memory of events was 'somewhat selective'. C appealed to the High Court, and made a preliminary application for the Stated Case to be amended. The Ch D rejected this application, and C subsequently withdrew his appeal and paid the tax assessed. *Carvill v CIR (No 1)*, Ch D 1995, 70 TC 126; [1996] STC 126.

(*Notes.* (1) For an appeal against subsequent assessments for 1993/94 to 1995/96, see **3.46** above. (2) For subsequent claims for restitution and judicial review, see **3.62** and **3.63** below.)

[3.62] The unsuccessful appellant (C) in the case noted at **3.61** above paid the assessed tax for 1987/88 to 1992/93 in 1995. In March 2000 a different Special Commissioner allowed his appeal against assessments for 1993/94 to 1995/96 inclusive (see **3.46** above). In 2001 C applied to the Ch D for repayment of the amounts paid for 1987/88 to 1992/93. The Ch D dismissed his application, holding that the decision with regard to the earlier assessments remained final and conclusive even though a different Commissioner had reached a different decision with regard to the later assessments. Hart J observed that the onus of proof was on the appellant, and that 'the doctrine of *res judicata* does not apply to the decision of Commissioners in relation to the amount of tax due in respect of one year of assessment so as to preclude either the taxpayer or the Revenue from contesting the self-same issue of fact or law on an appeal in relation to a different year of assessment'. *Carvill v CIR (No 3)*,Ch D [2002] STC 1167; [2002] EWHC 1488 (Ch).

[3.63] The unsuccessful applicant in the case noted at **3.60** above subsequently applied for judicial review of the Revenue's refusal to refund the tax in question, contending that the refusal was unfair. The QB reviewed the evidence in detail, rejected this contention, and dismissed the application. *R (oao Carvill) v CIR*, QB 2003, 74 TC 477; [2003] STC 1539; [2003] EWHC 1852 (Admin).

Assignment of dividends—application of Ramsay principle

[3.64] An individual (M), resident in Northern Ireland, entered into a complex and badly-documented series of transactions designed to extract cash from a company of which he was the controlling shareholder, and to avoid income tax liability on the amounts paid out by the company by receiving the proceeds as capital rather than income. His shares were transferred to non-resident trustees to be held for the benefit of him and his wife, and the trustees then sold the rights to substantial dividends which were expected to be declared. (The trustees received slightly less than the full amount of the dividends, the balance being retained by the company to which the rights had been sold.) The Revenue issued assessments on M for 1979/80 and 1980/81, charging tax under what is now *ITA 2007, s 720* on the amounts of the dividends (£400,000 for 1979/80 and £492,000 for 1980/81). M appealed against the assessments. He only produced photocopies of the deeds of assignment in evidence, the originals apparently having been destroyed by his solicitor. The Special Commissioner upheld the 1980/81 assessment, finding on the evidence that the relevant assignment had been backdated and that for that year, 'the assignment came into being after the declaration of the 1980 dividend, and the dividend belonged (at least for a while) to the trustee'. Accordingly, the payments received by the trustee were income rather than capital. However, the Commissioner allowed M's appeal against the 1979/80 assessment, considering that for that year the trustee had received capital payments rather than income payments. The HL unanimously allowed the Revenue's appeal against this decision and restored the 1979/80 assessment (while limiting the quantum of the assessment to the £396,000 which the trustee had actually received, rather than to the full amount of the dividend). Applying the principles laid down in *WT Ramsay Ltd v CIR*, **71.285** CAPITAL GAINS TAX, the assignment of the dividends 'was inserted for the sole purpose of gaining a tax advantage', and therefore fell to be disregarded. Notwithstanding the assignment, the payments were received as income rather than capital. (The HL also rejected M's contention that the transaction should have been assessed under what is now *ITA 2007, s 616* and that *s 720* did not therefore apply, holding that the effect of the *Ramsay* principle was that *s 616* did not apply.) The majority decision in *Duke of Westminster v CIR*, **2.3** ANNUAL PAYMENTS, was distinguished (and implicitly disapproved) in the judgments of Lord Steyn and Lord Cooke of Thorndon. Lord Steyn observed that while Lord Tomlin's words in that case 'still point to a material consideration, namely the general liberty of the citizen to arrange his financial affairs as he thinks fit, they have ceased to be canonical as to the consequence of a tax avoidance scheme'. Lord Cooke of Thorndon observed that the *Ramsay* principle was 'more natural and less extreme' than the majority decision in the *Duke of Westminster* case. *CIR v McGuckian*,HL 1997, 69 TC 1; [1997] STC 908; [1997] 1 WLR 991; [1997] 3 All ER 817. (*Notes.* (1) With regard to M's contention that the transaction should have been assessed under *s 616*, the CA had held that the court could deal with an assessment as if it had been made under another provision if 'the taxpayer had not laid its cards on the table and had in consequence misled the inspector of taxes', and held that the case 'affords an unedifying example of the lengths to which some tax advisers appear to feel justified in going to keep material facts and documents from the knowledge of the Revenue'. Since the HL allowed the Revenue's appeal on the interpretation of *s 720*, it did not consider M's cross-appeal against this decision. (2) The CA dismissed a cross-appeal by M, in relation to the 1980/81 assessment, on the grounds that he had failed to comply with the statutory time limit for transmitting the Stated Case—see **4.180** APPEALS.)

Assessment on shareholder born in Irish Republic

[3.65] A UK company had carried on a telephone betting business. It sold this business to a Gibraltar company. HMRC issued assessments on the three principal shareholders under what is now *ITA 2007, s 720*. The shareholders appealed. The First-tier Tribunal allowed the appeals by one of the shareholders (AF), who had not played an active part in the business and who had been born in the Irish Republic. Judge Raghavan held that the effect of the ECJ decision in *Gouvernement de la Communauté française et Gouvernement Wallon v Gouvernement Flamand*, **25.15** EUROPEAN LAW, was that AF was in a different position to the shareholders who had UK nationality. AF's Irish nationality 'meant that she did have European law rights of establishment and to move capital. As a non-UK Member State national these rights applied in relation to her ability to establish and move capital to Gibraltar. The UK anti-avoidance legislation which applied at the relevant time operated to restrict those rights, without justification, and was not proportionate. Applying a conforming interpretation to the UK legislation, the scope of the motive defence to the charge was widened, which meant it was able to be applied in relation to assessing the purpose for which the transfer took place in respect of (AF)'. (The Tribunal dismissed most of the appeals by the other shareholders, finding that they had transferred the business in order to avoid UK betting duty, but allowed appeals against one assessment which had been issued outside the statutory time limit on the grounds that the appellant had not been negligent, and allowed appeals against two more assessments on the grounds that they failed to meet the requirements of *TMA, s 29(5).) Mrs A Fisher v HMRC (and related appeals) (No 1)*, FTT [2014] UKFTT 804 (TC); [2014] SFTD 1341, TC03921.

Computation of income of overseas company

[3.66] A UK resident was assessed under what is now *ITA 2007, s 720* on the income of a Bahamas investment company. He appealed, contending that certain short-term gains of the company should not be treated as income and that management expenses which the company had incurred should be deducted in computing the income. The Special Commissioners rejected these contentions and upheld the assessments. The HL unanimously upheld their decision. *Lord Chetwode v CIR*, HL 1977, 51 TC 647; [1977] STC 64; [1977] 1 WLR 248; [1977] 1 All ER 638.

Failure to disclose profits within ITA 2007, s 720—conviction for cheating the revenue

[3.67] See *R v Dimsey*, 51.7 REVENUE PROSECUTIONS.

Associated operations (ITA 2007, s 719)

[3.68] A married woman had sold her interest in a Rhodesian mining partnership to a Rhodesian company for shares and non-interest-bearing debentures. The company paid no dividends but applied the whole of its profits in the redemption of its debentures. The Revenue assessed her husband under what is now *ITA 2007, s 720* on her share of the company's income from the partnership. The HL unanimously upheld the assessments, holding that the sale and the company's business were 'associated operations', within what is now *ITA 2007, s 719*. *Latilla v CIR*. HL 1943, 25 TC 107; [1943] AC 377; [1943] 1 All ER 265. (*Note.* Viscount Simon's judgment includes the observation that 'of recent years much ingenuity has been expended in certain quarters in attempting to devise methods of disposition of income by which those who were prepared to adopt them might enjoy the benefits of residence in this country while receiving the equivalent of such income, without sharing in the appropriate burden of British taxation. . . . There is, of course, no doubt that they are within their legal rights, but that is no reason why their efforts, or those of the professional gentlemen who assist them in the matter, should be regarded as a commendable exercise of ingenuity or as a discharge of the duties of good citizenship. On the contrary, one result of such methods, if they succeed, is, of course, to increase *pro tanto* the load of tax on the shoulders of the great body of good citizens who do not desire, or do not know how, to adopt these manoeuvres.')

[3.69] A testator died in 1882, leaving his estate to his six children in equal shares. The estate was not divided until 1933 when, by a deed of family arrangement, some of its investments and sinking fund policies were transferred to a UK investment company. In 1935, this company sold the policies and certain investments to a newly-formed Canadian company. The Revenue issued a surtax assessment on one of the beneficiaries under what is now *ITA 2007, s 720*. The CA unanimously upheld the assessment, holding that the 1933 and 1935 transactions were 'associated operations'. Scott LJ held that 'the interval during which the beneficiaries were thinking out their "associated operations" could not make any difference to the legal conclusion'. *Corbett's Executrices v CIR*, CA 1943, 25 TC 305; [1943] 2 All ER 218.

[3.70] In 1933, a married couple each sold investments to a Canadian company for shares and debentures. Subsequently, their daughter became entitled to a life interest in the shares and debentures, under a 1934 settlement with regard to those from her father, and under her mother's will with regard to the remainder. The Revenue assessed her on the income of the Canadian company under what is now *ITA 2007, s 720*. She appealed, contending that her mother's will was not an 'associated operation' within what is now *ITA 2007, s 719*. The Special Commissioners rejected this contention and dismissed her appeal, and the HL unanimously upheld their decision. Lord Cohen held that on the death of a testator, 'the assets affected are identified and the will is an operation effected by the testator in relation to the assets so ascertained'. If those assets 'included assets transferred or assets representing assets transferred, it necessarily follows that the will is an associated operation'. *Bambridge v CIR*, HL 1955, 36 TC 313; [1955] 1 WLR 1329; [1955] 3 All ER 812. (*Note*. The assessments were not on the transferor of the assets. The decision on this point was subsequently disapproved in *Vestey & Others v CIR*, HL 1979, 54 TC 503; [1980] STC 10, but the assessments would now appear to be authorised following the changes in the legislation deriving from *FA 1981*. The case remains an important authority on the definition of an 'associated operation'.)

Transfer of investments to Irish company—subsequent loan to transferee

[3.71] In 1948 an individual transferred investments to a company established in the Republic of Ireland, partly to avoid UK tax. He received shares in the company as consideration, and settled the shares on irrevocable trusts in favour of his children. In 1952 he lent the company £12,000 free of interest. The Revenue assessed him on the basis that the income of the company should be deemed to be his under what is now *ITA 2007, s 720*. The Ch D allowed his appeal, holding on the evidence that the transfer of the investments and the subsequent loan were not 'associated operations'. Upjohn J held that there was 'no connection whatever between the charge of transferred assets on the one hand and either the lending of the money or the right to receive payment on the other'. *Fynn v CIR*, Ch D 1957, 37 TC 629; [1958] 1 WLR 585; [1958] 1 All ER 270.

Power to obtain information (ITA 2007, s 748)

Whether notice under ITA 2007, s 748 valid

[3.72] The Revenue issued a notice under what is now *ITA 2007, s 748* on a Canadian bank, seeking particulars of certain sales of gilt-edged stocks carried out by its London branch on behalf of a Bahaman company. The bank took out a summons asking whether it was bound to furnish any, and if so which, of the particulars specified in the notice. The Ch D gave judgment for the Revenue, holding that the bank had not established that the sales were ordinary banking transactions within what is now *ITA 2007, s 750*, and that even if a notice were to contain an unauthorised question, the rest of the notice was not thereby invalidated. *Royal Bank of Canada v CIR*, Ch D 1971, 47 TC 565; [1972] Ch 665; [1972] 1 All ER 225.

[3.73] An individual (C) acted as the London representative of, and subsequently as the managing director of the English subsidiary of, a Bermudan bank which specialised in the formation or management of Bermudan companies, partnerships and settlements. In January 1972 the Revenue served a notice on him under what is now *ITA 2007, s 748*, requiring particulars of all transactions or operations in which he or his staff had acted for UK customers since 5 April 1965, relating to the formation or management of foreign companies, partnerships or settlements. He brought an action seeking a declaration that the notice was invalid, contending that the Board was not entitled to ask questions about unidentified transactions on behalf of unidentified principals and that the notice was unduly burdensome and oppressive. The QB rejected these contentions and dismissed his action, holding that the particulars requested were within the scope of *s 748*. Furthermore, the notice was not unduly burdensome or oppressive, since C should have kept the necessary records. Ackner J observed that C's task 'would now be a relatively light one if he had taken any steps to anticipate being required to give this information'. *Clinch v CIR*, QB 1973, 49 TC 52; [1973] STC 155; [1974] QB 76; [1973] 1 All ER 977.

Penalties for failure to comply with notices under ITA 2007, s 748

[3.74] See *Mankowitz v Special Commrs & CIR*, **44.366** PENALTIES.

Transactions in land (ITA 2007, ss 752–772; CTA 2010, ss 815–833)

Assessment of consideration contingently receivable in future

[3.75] A complex series of transactions was carried out in relation to land originally owned or contracted to be purchased by a large building company (C). As part of the transactions, two Guernsey companies acquired the land for £218,200, obtained planning permission, and sold it to C for £1,348,000 in March 1974. It was a condition of the sale that, should the land be nationalised or compulsorily acquired within five years, a proportion of the purchase price would be refunded, the proportion reducing each year. As security for this obligation, £1.1m of the purchase price was deposited with a Guernsey finance company, the deposit being released in instalments as the obligation reduced. At the same time, the finance company lent C £1.1m, secured on the land, to finance its purchase. The Revenue assessed C's controlling director (Y) for 1973/74 on the basis that he had provided the Guernsey companies with the opportunity to realise their gains from the sale of the land. Y appealed, contending that what is now *ITA 2007, s 752* did not apply because the transactions were at market value. The HL unanimously rejected this contention and held that the transactions were within *s 752*, but also held that, having regard to what is now *ITA 2007, s 768(2)*, the £1.1m could not be included in the assessment, which was reduced accordingly. (Viscount Dilhorne held that 'a gain is not realised until it can be effectively enjoyed or disposed of', and observed that Y would be liable under *s 752* in subsequent years as the instalments of the purchase price were released.) *Yuill v Wilson*, HL 1980, 52 TC 674; [1980] STC 460; [1980] 1 WLR 910; [1980] 3 All ER 7. (*Notes.* (1) For assessments relating to subsequent years, see *Yuill v Fletcher*, **3.76** below. (2) For a subsidiary issue in this case, see **4.199** APPEALS.)

Consideration payable in instalments—when gains 'realised'

[3.76] After the HL decision in *Yuill v Wilson*, **3.75** above, the Revenue raised assessments on Y for the four years 1976/77 to 1979/80 inclusive on the instalments of the purchase price due to be released in those years, the land having not been nationalised or compulsorily purchased. The assessments aggregated £1,092,256 but it was subsequently found that the timetable in the contracts had not been strictly adhered to and that amounts had been released before 1976/77. On appeal the Special Commissioners adjusted the assessments to an aggregate of £676,476, the instalments actually released in the four years. The CA dismissed Y's appeal against this decision. Applying *dicta* of Viscount Dilhorne in *Yuill v Wilson*, a gain was 'realised' within the meaning of what is now *ITA 2007, s 756(2)* only when it could be effectively enjoyed or disposed of. Accordingly the gains from the sale of the land were realised by the Guernsey companies only as and when the instalments became payable, and not by reference to the 1974 value of the companies' contingent contractual rights. It would be inconsistent with the legislation to value as money's worth consideration which is received in money; in any event the matter was concluded by the Special Commissioners' finding that, on the evidence offered, there was no market in which the companies could have found buyers for their rights to the £1.1m at commercially realistic prices. *Yuill v Fletcher*, CA 1984, 58 TC 145; [1984] STC 401.

Whether gain provided by person assessed

[3.77] In May 1973 an individual (S) bought property in London for £20,000. Shortly afterwards he contracted to sell the property for £25,000 to a Bahaman company (M). The contract provided that M could nominate another purchaser. The contract was completed in August, the property being transferred to a UK company for £33,500. £25,000 of this was paid to S, the balance of £8,500 being paid to M and two other Bahaman companies. The Revenue assessed S on the £8,500 under what is now *ITA 2007, s 752*. The Special Commissioner upheld the assessment, and the Ch D and the CA unanimously dismissed S's appeal against this decision. There was no evidence that the Bahaman companies did more than act as passive recipients of the £8,500. The onus was on S to show that the assessment was excessive. The Commissioner was entitled to conclude that the transactions were not normal trading transactions, but were transactions designed to avoid tax. *Sugarwhite v Budd*, CA 1988, 60 TC 679; [1988] STC 533.

Year in which gain realised

[3.78] A property developer (L) operated through a large group of companies. He owned 90.5% of the group equity, while W owned 4.5% and B owned 5%. L acquired and began to develop two sites, outside the group. Following representations by W and B, he agreed that they should receive respectively a 4.5% and 5% share in the two ventures, confirming the agreement in letters to W and B in which he said that the agreed shares of his interest in the property and its proceeds of disposal 'are held by me in trust for you absolutely'. L then carried out, in his own name, an avoidance scheme (using premiums payable by instalments) which resulted in the sale of the land to the group in March 1971 at a capital gain of more than £900,000. Of this, the respective shares of W and B were £41,395 and £45,995. L paid them £20,000 each in January 1971, and paid them the balance during 1971/72. The Revenue issued assessments on them for 1970/71, under what is now *ITA 2007, s 752*, on their shares of the gain. The Ch D dismissed their appeals, holding that the conditions of what is now *ITA 2007, s 756(1)(d)* were satisfied. W and B were 'concerned in' the scheme within the meaning of *ITA 2007, s 757(1)(c)** and therefore within the ambit of the legislation. The gain was realised in 1970/71, the year in which the land was sold to the group. *Winterton v Edwards; Byfield v Edwards*, Ch D 1979, 52 TC 655; [1980] STC 206; [1982] 2 All ER 56. (*Note.* The Commissioners also confirmed a similar assessment on L on his share of the gain. This was not taken to the High Court. His group had become insolvent in 1975.)

Whether notice under ITA 2007, s 771 invalid

[3.79] The Revenue issued notices under what is now *ITA 2007, s 771* to two companies and their directors. They began an action in the Ch D, seeking a declaration that the notices did not comply with the wording of *s 771*, were unreasonably burdensome and oppressive, and were invalid. The Ch D rejected these contentions and dismissed the action, and the CA unanimously upheld this decision. Buckley LJ observed that 'the person upon whom the notice is served is only required to answer it "to the best of his information, knowledge and belief" '. There was no evidence that 'the recipient of the notice would be likely to be unable to answer the questions put to him'. *Essex & Others v CIR & Grugan*, CA 1980, 53 TC 720; [1980] STC 378.

Sale of shares immediately after sale of land

[3.80] A property-dealing company (K) acquired a disused warehouse in 1969 for £30,000. Subsequently, planning permission became available for the property, making it very valuable. After negotiations, K sold the property to another company (M) for £1,900,000, and immediately afterwards K's shareholders sold their shares in K to an unrelated company (T). The Revenue issued assessments on K's former shareholders on the basis that they had received gains of a capital nature within what is now what is now *ITA 2007, s 752(2)*. The Ch D allowed their appeals against the assessments. Vinelott J held that the effect of what is now *s 766* was that sales of the shares of a property-dealing company, after it had sold its land as trading stock, were outside the scope of *s 752*. *Chilcott v CIR (and related appeals)*, Ch D 1981, 55 TC 446; [1982] STC 1. (*Notes*. (1) The Special Commissioners had also held that certain earlier transactions carried out by the same shareholders were within *s 752*. The shareholders did not appeal against this decision. (2) *Obiter dicta* of Vinelott J were not followed, and implicitly disapproved, by the CA in the subsequent case of *Page v Lowther*, 3.81 below.)

Transactions not specifically intended to avoid tax

[3.81] The trustees of an estate comprising four large houses leased the estate for 99 years to a development company (T) under an agreement whereby T would demolish the existing houses and build new leasehold houses and flats on the site, and the trustees would receive premiums calculated by reference to the sale price of the new houses and flats. The Revenue issued assessments on the trustees on the basis that the premiums which they received were liable to income tax under what is now *ITA 2007, s 752*. They appealed, contending that they had not entered into the transactions with the aim of avoiding tax. The CA unanimously dismissed the appeal, holding that the transactions were an 'arrangement' within what is now *ITA 2007, s 753(1)(b)*. *Page v Lowther*, CA 1983, 57 TC 199; [1983] STC 799.

Judicial review of assessments under ITA 2007, s 759(6)

[3.82] A Jersey company (N) had a UK subsidiary (S). In 1981, N purchased land in the UK for £325,000 which it later sold to S for £1,125,000. S then resold the land to an independent purchaser for £1,150,000. The Revenue assessed S's directors under what is now *ITA 2007, s 759(6)*, on the basis that they had directly or indirectly provided an opportunity for another person to realise a gain. They applied for judicial review to quash the assessments, contending that the inspector had made the assessments for the purpose of making enquiries about other individuals of a kind not authorised by the statutory powers of enquiry. The QB granted leave. Nolan J observed that there was no evidence that the applicants were 'beneficially entitled to the gain or to the property from whose disposal it arose'. Furthermore, certain observations in a letter from the Revenue seemed to be 'mistaken and indeed inexplicable'. *R v Inspector of Taxes (ex p. Kissane & Clarke)*, QB [1986] STC 152; [1986] 2 All ER 37.

Controlled foreign companies (ICTA 1988, ss 747–756)

NOTE.

ICTA 1988, ss 747-756 was repealed by *FA 2012* with effect for accounting periods beginning on or after 1 January 2013.

Assessments under ICTA 1988, s 747

[3.83] A UK company (B), which was a member of a UK group of companies, had a subsidiary company (S) which was incorporated and resident in the Netherlands. S received substantial amounts of interest from a company in the same group as B. These receipts were exempt from UK taxation under the UK/Netherlands Double Taxation Agreement (*SI 1980/1961*). In 1994 the Revenue served notices on the relevant UK companies in the group, identifying S as a controlled foreign company within *ICTA 1988, ss 747–756*. In 1995 the Revenue issued assessments on B, charging tax on an amount representing an apportioned share of S's profits, including the interest, under *ICTA 1988, s 747*. B appealed, contending that the amounts included in the assessments which were attributable to the interest should be treated as exempt from UK tax under the Double Taxation Agreement. The Special Commissioners rejected this contention and dismissed B's appeal, holding that the assessments were in accordance with *ICTA 1988, s 747(4)(a)* and that the exemption under the UK/Netherlands Agreement did not extend to the amounts assessed under *ICTA 1988, s 747*. The CA upheld this decision. The chargeable profits referred to in *ICTA 1988, s 747(4)(a)* had to be ascertained without reference to the UK/Netherlands Agreement. The 'chargeable profits' as defined by *ICTA 1988, s 747(6)(a)* were a notional sum which existed only as a measure of imputation. Millett LJ observed that 'where tax is charged on a conventional or notional sum which exists only as the product of a calculation, the fact that one of the elements in the calculation is measured by reference to an amount of exempted income does not make the exempted income the subject of the tax'. *Bricom Holdings Ltd v CIR*, CA 1997, 70 TC 272; [1997] STC 1179.

Requirements of ICTA 1988, s 748(3)

[3.84] The Revenue issued several directions to a company (ABTA), applying the CFC legislation of *ICTA 1988, s 747 et seq.* to the profits of two captive insurance companies for the periods from 1 July 1996 to 30 June 1999. ABTA appealed, contending that the effect of *ICTA 1988, s 748(3)* was that no apportionment should be made, since it was not 'one of the main reasons for the company's existence in that period to achieve a reduction in United Kingdom tax by a diversion of profits from the United Kingdom'. The Special Commissioners reviewed the evidence in detail, rejected this contention, and dismissed ABTA's appeal. The Commissioners held that the transactions satisfied the requirements of *ICTA 1988, s 748(3)(a)*, holding that the tax reductions which ABTA had actually achieved were 'an effect of the transaction' and were 'not one of the main purposes that ABTA was trying to achieve'. However, the Commissioners also held that ABTA failed to satisfy the requirements of *ICTA 1988, s 748(3)(b)*, observing that *ICTA 1988, s 748(3)(b)* 'accepts the genuineness of the transaction but considers whether the reason for the existence of non-resident entity (*sic*) was the reduction in tax caused by its being non-resident, and therefore concentrates on whether the same result could have been achieved using a UK-resident vehicle'. On the evidence, one of the main reasons why ABTA had chosen to use captive insurance companies, rather than an in-house fund, 'was to achieve the tax reduction by the diversion of profits between the existence of the captives and the other alternatives'. The Commissioners observed that 'a UK-resident captive would achieve exactly the same result but without the tax benefits'. *Association of British Travel Agents Ltd v CIR*, Sp C [2003] SSCD 194 (Sp C 359).

ICTA 1988, ss 747–756—whether valid under EC law

[3.85] The Revenue formed the opinion that a company (V), which had established a subsidiary company in Luxembourg, was liable to tax under the 'controlled foreign companies' legislation of *ICTA 1988, ss 747–756*. They issued a notice of enquiry under *FA 1998, Sch 18 para 24*. V subsequently applied to the Special Commissioners for a direction under *FA 1998, Sch 18 para 33*, contending that the notice was unreasonable because the relevant legislation contravened *Article 43EC* of the *EC Treaty*. Following the CJEC decision in *Cadbury Schweppes plc v CIR*, 25.33 EUROPEAN LAW, the Special Commissioners rejected this contention, holding (by the casting vote of the chairman) that *ICTA 1988, s 748(3)* could and should be construed in a way that was compatible with the *EC Treaty*. The CA unanimously upheld this decision. Sir Andrew Morritt observed that 'the obligation on the English courts to construe domestic legislation consistently with Community law is both broad and far-reaching'. The legislation should be construed on such a basis as to introduce an additional exception in respect of a controlled foreign company 'if it is, in that accounting period, actually established in another Member State of the EEA and carries on genuine economic activities there'. Longmore LJ held that 'the proposed insertion merely adds a further exemption which is allied to (although different from) the exemption granted to subsidiaries created or used without the motive of reducing the UK company's liability to tax. Any inquiry as to motive as originally envisaged by the Act, is likely to encompass the question whether the resulting CFC is an artificial arrangement; the proposed insertion merely makes clear that CFCs which are not artificial arrangements will be exempt from the provisions of *section 747(1)*'. This was 'permissible interpretation of the statute and not impermissible legislation by the court'. *HMRC v Vodafone 2*, CA [2009] STC 1480; [2009] EWCA Civ 446.

[3.86] See also *Cadbury Schweppes plc v CIR*, 25.33 EUROPEAN LAW, and *Test Claimants in the CFC and Dividend Group Litigation v CIR*, 25.34 EUROPEAN LAW.

Transactions between associated persons (TIOPA 2010, ss 146–217)

Shares held by trustees—whether common control

[3.87] A company (L) sold two ships to another company (N) at less than their market value. The majority of the ordinary shares of L were held by four trustees of a deed of provision, and nearly all those of N were held by three trustees of another deed of provision. The first-named trustee of each deed, entitled to exercise the voting rights attached to the shares, was the same person. The Revenue made a direction on the basis that both companies were under the same control . L appealed, contending that the two companies were not under the same control. The Special Commissioners accepted this contention and allowed the appeal, observing that 'since the two bodies of trustees were by no means identical and the respective trusts were not in favour of the same person, the wishes of the two bodies of trustees were not necessarily the same'. The CS unanimously upheld their decision. Lord Clyde held that the profits tax cases relating to 'controlling interest' (see **17.10** *et seq.* CONTROL OF COMPANIES) were of no assistance, since the statutory definition of 'control' was different from that of 'controlling interest'. He held that Parliament was dealing with 'a real association between two companies, not just the accidental association arising from what must often be a coincidence — namely, that the same individual is the first-named trustee in the register of two companies in respect of a majority holding of shares which may have no connection with one another at all'. *CIR v Lithgows Ltd*, CS 1960, 39 TC 270.

Adjustments to assessments

[3.88] The Revenue made a direction in a case involving three associated companies where assessments for several years were open. The companies applied for declarations that the direction was ineffective, contending that such a direction could only validate a new assessment, and could not validate an adjustment to an existing assessment. The Ch D rejected this contention and dismissed the applications, and the CA upheld this decision. *TMA, s 50(7)* enabled the Commissioners to increase an assessment, and it was clear that they were entitled to receive evidence which would lead to an increase in the assessment. The functions of an inspector at the hearing of an appeal were not restricted to what was expressly authorised by *TMA, s 50(3)*. As a party to an appeal concerning an assessment which might be increased, as well as reduced or extinguished, the inspector was entitled to ask the Commissioners to exercise any of the powers which Parliament had entrusted to them, and to adduce evidence in support of his application. The CA specifically disapproved *obiter dicta* of Lord Diplock in *White & Others v Vandervell Trustees Ltd & CIR*, HL 1970, 46 TC 341. *Glaxo Group Ltd & Others v CIR*, CA 1995, 68 TC 166; [1996] STC 191. (*Note. White & Others v Vandervell Trustees Ltd & CIR* was a case concerning provisions in *Rules of the Supreme Court 1965 (SI 1965/1776)* which have been superseded by the *Civil Procedure Rules 1998 (SI 1998/3132), part 19.*)

Originating summons

[3.89] The Revenue advised a UK company (B) that it intended to serve statutory notices in respect of transactions between B and a Singapore subsidiary. The transactions had taken place in years for which assessments were under appeal, and for which the time limits for raising further assessments had expired. B applied for a declaration that it should not be required to supply the information required, contending that any profits or income disclosed by such a notice would have to be the subject of a new assessment, and that since such an assessment would be out of time, the compiling of the information required by the notices would be burdensome, oppressive, and a waste of time. The Revenue applied to have the summons struck out, contending that the issue of the notices was within the exclusive jurisdiction of the Special Commissioners, and alternatively that even if the court had jurisdiction, it should not hear the summons since to do so would not resolve the issues which were the subject of the appeals. The Ch D rejected the Revenue's application, holding that the court had jurisdiction to hear the summons and that it was both convenient and economic for it to do so, since it might have the effect of saving B from having to compile a large quantity of information. Accordingly, the summons should be considered at a separate hearing, prior to the hearing of the appeals by the Commissioners. *Beecham Group plc v CIR*, Ch D 1992, 65 TC 219; [1992] STC 935. (*Note*. There was no further public hearing of the appeal.)

Interest-free loans to non-resident associated company

[3.90] Two UK subsidiaries of a US company made interest-free loans to another subsidiary which was resident in the US. The Revenue issued directions to the effect that, in computing the taxable profits of the UK companies, notional interest on the loans should be included as if they had been made at arm's length. The companies appealed against the directions and the relevant assessments. The Special Commissioners dismissed the appeals, holding that the loans constituted the 'giving of business facilities' and thus were within the scope of the legislation. *Ametalco UK v CIR (and related appeal)*, Sp C [1996] SSCD 399 (Sp C 94).

Loans by parent company to trustee to finance purchase of shares

[3.91] A company (W) executed a trust deed establishing a share option scheme. It made loans to the trustee, to enable the trustee to purchase shares and grant options to the employees of two subsidiary companies. The Revenue issued directions to W, with the effect of reducing W's excess management expenses and charges on income, available for surrender to its subsidiaries. The companies appealed. The Special Commissioners upheld the directions and assessments in principle (subject to agreement as to figures), holding that the transactions involved the giving of business facilities by W to the subsidiary companies and were within the scope of the legislation. *Waterloo plc v CIR (and related appeals)*, Sp C 2001, [2002] SSCD 95 (Sp C 301). (*Note*. For the Revenue's practice following this decision, see Revenue Tax Bulletin February 2003, pp 1002–1007.)

Transfer pricing—provision not at arm's length

[3.92] A UK company (DS) sold electrical goods by retail. It encouraged customers to purchase extended warranty agreements. The liability to customers was insured or reinsured by an associated Isle of Man company (DI). The Revenue formed the opinion that the transactions were within the scope of the transfer pricing legislation, and began an enquiry into DS's returns. The Revenue and DS referred the case to the Special Commissioners under *FA 1998, Sch 18 para 31A*. The Commissioners reviewed the evidence in detail and held that a provision 'had been made or imposed as between (DS) and (DI) by means of a transaction or series of transactions'. At the time of making or imposing that provision, 'the same person or persons was or were directly or indirectly participating in the management, control or capital of (DS) and (DI)'. The provision actually made or imposed differed from the arm's length provision which would have been made between independent enterprises, and conferred a potential advantage on DS in relation to UK taxation. The Commissioners adjourned the case for further consideration of the specific adjustment which 'should be made in computing for tax purposes (DS's) profits and losses if the arm's length provision had been made or imposed instead of the actual provision'. *DSG Retail Ltd v HMRC (and related appeals)*, Sp C [2009] SSCD 397; [2009] UKFTT 31 (TC), TC00001. (*Note*. The Commissioners also heard appeals relating to accounting periods from 1996 to 1999, concerning the application of *ICTA 1988, s 770* prior to its substitution by *FA 1998*. The Commissioners held that DS had given business facilities to DI, that DS and DI were under common control, and that the facilities had been given at a price 'which was less than the price at which they would have been expected to be given if the parties to the transactions had been independent persons dealing at arm's length.)

Other anti-avoidance legislation

Interpretation of FA 2003, s 195—companies acquiring own shares

[3.93] Three associated companies entered into a tax avoidance scheme, which they disclosed under the *Tax Avoidance Schemes (Prescribed Descriptions of Arrangements) Regulations 2006 (SI 2006/1543)*. One of the companies (BJ) issued a large quantity of shares, reacquired them later in the same month, and made a similar large issue of shares just under a year later. The scheme was intended to take advantage of a perceived loophole in *ICTA 1988, s 730A* (which has subsequently been repealed) by allowing one of the companies (BH) to claim a deduction for a deemed interest payment of £14,000,000 which it had made to BJ. HMRC issued a ruling that BJ was required to include the £14,000,000 in its profits chargeable to corporation tax. BJ appealed, contending that the effect of *FA 2003, s 195* was that it was deemed not to have acquired the shares in question. The First-tier Tribunal rejected this contention and dismissed the appeal. Judge Sinfield observed that *FA 2003, s 195(2)* 'is precisely drafted. It provides that the acquisition of the shares by the company is not to be treated as the acquisition of an asset. It does not say that, where a company buys its own shares, the transaction is not to be treated as an acquisition of shares. The effect of *section 195(2)* is that the shares acquired are not to be treated as assets of the acquirer, not that no shares are acquired.' *Biffa (Jersey) Ltd v HMRC*, FTT [2014] UKFTT 982 (TC), TC04094. (Note. At a subsequent hearing, the Tribunal ordered BJ to pay costs—[2015] UKFTT 0010 (TC), TC04222.)

FA 2004, s 306—whether 'notifiable arrangements'

[3.94] In 2005 a company (M) marketed a tax avoidance scheme, under which wealthy individuals formed a Jersey limited partnership to carry on a financial trade, and contributed capital equal to the tax loss which they wished to create. The Revenue formed the opinion that M had failed to notify the scheme as required by *FA 2004, s 308*. They laid an information before the Special Commissioners. M defended the proceedings, contending that the scheme fell outside the scope of *FA 2004, s 306(1)*, since it involved the purchase of a dividend, which was not within the definition of a 'financial product' in *Tax Avoidance Schemes (Information) Regulations 2004 (SI 2004/1863), reg 7*. The Special Commissioner accepted this contention, observing that 'the list of financial products is somewhat strange' but that it appeared that 'the Regulation is looking at the proximate cause of the expected tax advantage, which is not therefore from the inclusion of a share in the arrangements'. Accordingly the conditions of *reg 6(2)* were not satisfied, so that the scheme was not notifiable and there could be no penalty. *HMRC v Mercury Tax Group Ltd (No 2)*, Sp C [2009] SSCD 307 (Sp C 737). (*Notes.* (1) See now *Tax Avoidance Schemes (Prescribed Descriptions of Arrangements) Regulations 2006 (SI 2006/1543)*, which came into force on 1 August 2006. It appears from the decision that the company accepted that the scheme fell within the 2006 Regulations, and notified it in September 2006. (2) For a subsequent case involving this company, see **13.25** COMPANY LIQUIDATION AND RECEIVERSHIP.)

4

Appeals

The cases in this chapter are arranged under the following headings.

GENERAL NOTE.

During 2009, major changes took place to the tax appeal system. These changes, brought about by the *Tribunals, Courts and Enforcement Act 2007*, included the creation of a new two-tier tribunal structure. From 1 April 2009, appeals which were previously heard by the Special Commissioners or the General Commissioners are (in nearly all cases) now heard by the Tax Chamber of the First-tier Tribunal. Appeals from the First-tier Tribunal are to the Finance and Tax

Chamber of the Upper Tribunal. Exceptionally, some particularly complex or important appeals may start in the Upper Tribunal. Appeals from the Upper Tribunal are to the Court of Appeal.

For summaries of appeals against penalties, see **44** PENALTIES.

Appeals to Commissioners

General and miscellaneous

Whether appeal may be withdrawn

[4.1] The Revenue issued an estimated additional assessment on an individual (E). He appealed to the Special Commissioners, but later purported to withdraw his appeal. The Revenue were not satisfied that the assessment was adequate, and asked the Special Commissioners to hear and determine the appeal. E applied to the KB for a writ prohibiting the Commissioners from hearing the appeal. The KB rejected his application and the CA unanimously dismissed E's appeal against this decision. Lord Wright MR observed that the evidence suggested that 'the assessment ought to be something like ten times as much as the sum so far assessed on the appellant'. The Commissioners were 'assessing or estimating the amount which in the interests of the country at large the taxpayer ought to have to deal with as the basis on which he is to be taxed'. A notice of appeal was not 'merely an act from which the taxpayer can at his discretion at any time resile'. Once the appeal was under way, the appellant could not 'prevent the Commissioners from ascertaining and settling the sum to be assessed'. *R v Special Commrs (ex p. Elmhirst)*, CA 1935, 20 TC 381; [1936] 1 KB 487. (*Note.* See now *TMA, s 54(4)*. For a case concerning *s 54(4)*, see *Beach v Willesden Commrs*, **44.332** PENALTIES.)

Whether notice of hearing served

[4.2] The General Commissioners confirmed an assessment, in the absence of the appellant. He applied to the QB for an order to quash the determination, contending that he had not been served with formal notice of the hearing. The QB accepted his evidence 'on the balance of probabilities' and granted his application. *R v Tavistock Commrs (ex p. Adams) (No 1)*, QB 1969, 46 TC 154.

[4.3] In 1974 the Special Commissioners confirmed estimated assessments on a trader (M). The Revenue subsequently began bankruptcy proceedings, and in 1979 M applied for judicial review of the assessments. The QB rejected the application and he appealed to the CA, contending that he had not received proper notice of the meeting in 1974. The CA dismissed his appeal, finding that there was evidence that the notice was in M's possession the day after the meeting. *R v Special Commissioner (ex p. Moschi)*, CA [1981] STC 465.

Validity of Crown Office subpoenas

[4.4] The Special Commissioners confirmed assessments on an individual (S) following evidence given by witnesses attending on Crown Office subpoenas. S began proceedings against the Revenue, contending that the subpoenas were invalid and claiming damages. The QB dismissed the proceedings and the CA dismissed S's application for leave to appeal. *Soul v CIR*, CA 1962, 40 TC 506; [1963] 1 All ER 68.

'No case to answer' submission by appellant

[4.5] In an appeal before the Special Commissioners concerning legislation which is now obsolete, the Revenue opened the proceedings but the Commissioners held that the company had no case to answer. The Ch D remitted the case to the Commissioners, holding that the Revenue had discharged the onus of proof on the balance of probabilities. *CIR v White Bros Ltd*, Ch D 1956, 36 TC 587.

[4.6] See also *R v Special Commrs (ex p. Martin)*, **29.81** FURTHER ASSESSMENTS: LOSS OF TAX.

Appeal adjourned for agreement of figures

[4.7] In an Irish case, a Special Commissioner heard an appeal against an estimated assessment on a builder (W) for 1935/36. Wcontended that he had ceased trading in that year. The Commissioner agreed that it had, and adjourned the appeal for agreement of the figures. The inspector discovered new evidence, and at a subsequent hearing the Commissioner held that he was not satisfied that W had ceased trading in 1935/36. W applied for a court order to quash the second decision. The Court rejected the application, holding that there had been no determination of the appeal. *Whelan v Smidic*, HC(I) 1938, 2 ITC 188; [1938] IR 626.

[4.8] See also *Larner v Warrington*, **71.51** CAPITAL GAINS TAX.

Whether two appeals may be heard together

[4.9] The Revenue issued assessments, covering the years 1973/74 to 1986/87 inclusive, on two guest house proprietors (a man and woman who were not married but who lived together and had five children together). The Special Commissioners heard the proprietors' appeals together, reviewed the evidence in detail, and determined the appeals. The Ch D and the CA upheld the Commissioners' decision, rejecting the proprietors' contention that the appeals should not have been heard together. Peter Gibson LJ observed that 'it must be for Commissioners to decide whether it is appropriate, if the affairs of one taxpayer are connected with the affairs of another taxpayer, to have the two appeals heard at the same time, both from the viewpoint of economy as far as their own time is concerned and also so that one decision may not be taken inconsistently with another decision'. On the evidence, 'the Commissioners acted entirely properly when they directed that the appeals should be heard together'. *Johnson v Walden; King v Walden*, CA 1995, 68 TC 387; [1996] STC 382. (*Note.* For subsequent developments in this case, see **5.85** ASSESSMENTS and **29.42** FURTHER ASSESSMENTS: LOSS OF TAX.)

[4.10] In the case noted at **42.55** PAY AS YOU EARN, the Revenue issued determinations on a company (P) under the *Income Tax (PAYE) Regulations 2003, reg 80*. They also issued similar notices charging NIC under *SSCTFA 1999, s 8*. P appealed. The Revenue applied for the appeals to be heard together. P opposed the application but the Special Commissioner directed that the appeals should be heard together. *PA Holdings Ltd v HMRC*, Sp C [2008] SSCD 1185 (Sp C 707).

[4.11] HMRC issued rulings to two associated companies that the exercise of certain options to employees gave rise to a liability to national insurance contributions. Both companies appealed. HMRC applied for the appeals to be heard together. The First-tier Tribunal granted the application but the Upper Tribunal reversed this decision. Norris J noted that HMRC had already begun county court proceedings against one of the companies (GSI), and had stated that they intended to take similar proceedings against the other company (GSL). Both companies contended that the proceedings were outside the time limit provided by *Limitation Act 1980, s 9*. Norris J held that the hearing of GSL's appeal should be halted in order to permit the companies to raise their 'limitation arguments' in the county court. *Goldman Sachs Services Ltd v HMRC (aka Yellow v HMRC)*, UT [2009] UKUT 290 (TCC); [2010] STC 763. (*Note*. For an associated appeal, see **4.18** below.)

Preliminary point of law—application for separate hearing

[4.12] A company had been accepted as an investment trust, under what is now *CTA 2010, s 1158*, on the strength of certificates supplied by a leading accountancy firm. In 1996 the firm began to doubt the accuracy of the certificates, and communicated its concerns to the Revenue. The Revenue withdrew its approval of the company under what is now *CTA 2010, s 1159*, and issued corporation tax assessments. The company appealed, and requested the Special Commissioner to consider, as a separate issue, whether the Revenue had the power to withdraw approval under *s 1159*in the absence of fraudulent misrepresentation. The Commissioner rejected this request, holding that to determine the preliminary point as a separate matter would protract matters rather than shortening them. *Investment Trust v CIR*, Sp C [1998] SSCD 287 (Sp C 173). (*Note*. There was no public hearing of the substantive appeal.)

[4.13] An individual (W) appealed against an assessment under the 'settlements' legislation for 2000/01. His appeal was set down for hearing by the Special Commissioners, in accordance with *TMA, s 46B(4)*. His accountant applied for a preliminary hearing by the General Commissioners, to consider whether the Revenue had made a 'discovery' under *TMA, s 29*. The Special Commissioner dismissed the application *JA Walker v HMRC*, Sp C 2007, [2008] SSCD 130 (Sp C 626). (*Note*. The appeal was adjourned pending the HL decision in *Garnett v Jones (re Arctic Systems Ltd)*, **56.50** SETTLEMENTS.)

[4.14] The appellant in the case noted at **48.20** RESIDENCE applied for a preliminary hearing to consider whether the Revenue had made a 'discovery' under *TMA, s 29*. The Special Commissioner dismissed the application, applying the principles laid down by Lords Wilberforce and Scarman in *Tilling v Whiteman*, HL [1979] 2 WLR 401; [1980] AC 1; [1979] 1 All ER 737. *DW Hankinson v HMRC (No 1)*, Sp C 2007, [2008] SSCD 377 (Sp C 649). (*Note*. For other issues in this case, see **4.321** below and **5.25** ASSESSMENTS.)

[4.15] The Upper Tribunal reached a similar decision in *J Hargreaves v HMRC*, UT [2014] UKUT 395 (TCC).

[4.16] The First-tier Tribunal reached a similar decision in *D Healey v HMRC*, FTT [2014] UKFTT 889 (TC), TC04004.

[4.17] See also *Baron Wrottesley v HMRC*, **48.65** RESIDENCE.

[4.18] In the case noted at **73.73** NATIONAL INSURANCE CONTRIBUTIONS, the appellant company (GSI) applied for a preliminary hearing to determine whether it could be treated as the employer of the employees who had exercised the options. The First-tier Tribunal rejected the application but the Upper Tribunal reversed this decision. Norris J observed that the underlying issue was whether an associated company (GSL) was a 'foreign employer', with the result that GSI was the 'host employer'. He held that there should be a preliminary hearing which should be confined to the specific question of 'the presence of (GSL) in Great Britain'. *Goldman Sachs International v HMRC (No 1) (aka Blue v HMRC)*, UT 2009, [2010] STC 763; [2009] UKUT 290 (TCC). (*Notes.* (1) For the appeal by the associated company, see *Goldman Sachs Services Ltd v HMRC*, **4.11** above. (2) For another issue in this case, see **4.164** below.)

Whether Scottish courts can direct English Commissioners

[4.19] A company director who lived in Scotland applied to a Scottish court for a Notice of Suspension, complaining that English General Commissioners had confirmed an assessment on him and that he had not received notice of the appeal hearing. The CS rejected the application, holding that the Commissioners' decision could only be set aside by an order of an English court. *Rutherford v Lord Advocate*, CS 1931, 16 TC 145.

Delay in determining appeals

[4.20] In a Hong Kong case, an appellant sought an order of *certiorari* quashing determinations of two assessments, on the grounds that the appeals against the assessments, which were required to be dealt with within 'a reasonable time' had been left in abeyance, without being acknowledged, for more than three years, and she had been entitled to assume that the assessments had been abandoned. The PC rejected this contention and dismissed her appeals. Lord Slynn observed that 'if the Commissioner failed to act within a reasonable time, he could be compelled to act by an order of *mandamus*', and that it would be 'unfair to other taxpayers who need to shoulder the burden of government expenditure' if the Revenue were to be prevented from pursuing assessments because of a failure to act within a reasonable time. *Wang v Hong Kong Commissioner of Inland Revenue*, PC [1994] STC 753; [1994] 1 WLR 1286; [1995] 1 All ER 367.

Applications for review

[4.21] See *Phillips v Burrows*, **4.442** below; *Forbes v Director of the Assets Recovery Agency (No 2)*, **4.444** below; *Dunne v HMRC*, **46.20** PENSION SCHEMES; and *Siwek v CIR (No 2)*, **55.2** SELF-ASSESSMENT.

The right of appeal (TMA, s 31)

Scope of appeal against closure notice

[4.22] In the case noted at **8.79** CAPITAL ALLOWANCES, two limited liability partnerships claimed capital allowances in respect of capital expenditure on computer software. 75% of the purchase price of the software was funded by 'non-recourse loans', which were indirectly made available by the vendor of the software. HMRC rejected the claims on the grounds that the expenditure had been incurred 'with a view to granting to another person a right to use or otherwise deal with any of the software in question', within *CAA 2001, s 45(4)*. They issued closure notices, against which the partnerships appealed. At the hearing of the appeals, HMRC abandoned their original contention with regard to *s 45(4)*, but defended the closure notices on alternative grounds. The Ch D accepted the partnerships' contention that the right of appeal under *TMA, s 31(1)(b)* was 'confined to an appeal against any conclusions stated or amendments made by a closure notice', but the CA allowed HMRC's appeal against this decision (by a 2-1 majority, Arden LJ dissenting). Moses LJ held that the retention of *TMA, s 50*, following the introduction of self-assessment, was 'a powerful indication that Parliament did not intend to change the jurisdiction of the Commissioners in as dramatic a fashion as the introduction of a system of self-assessment might have suggested'. There was a public interest 'that taxpayers pay a correct amount of tax'. Parliament had not 'chosen to identify some legal principle defining the limitations on the scope and subject-matter of an enquiry and consequently an appeal'. It 'would be wrong for the court to attempt to do so. Any statement of principle is likely to condemn both taxpayer and the Revenue to too rigid a straitjacket. It might prevent a taxpayer from advancing a legitimate factual or legal argument which had hitherto escaped him or deprive, on the other hand, the public of the tax to which it is entitled'. The Supreme Court unanimously upheld this decision. Lord Walker held that 'in issuing a closure notice an officer is performing an important public function in which fairness to the taxpayer must be matched by a proper regard for the public interest in the recovery of the full amount of tax payable. In a case in which it is clear that only a single, specific point is in issue, that point should be identified in the closure notice. But if, as in the present case, the facts are complicated and have not been fully investigated, and if their analysis is controversial, the public interest may require the notice to be expressed in more general terms.' *HMRC v Tower Mcashback LLP1 (and cross-appeal)*, SC [2011] UKSC 19; 80 TC 641; [2011] STC 1143.

[4.23] In the case noted at **71.4** CAPITAL GAINS TAX, the Revenue had issued a closure notice and an amendment to a return on the basis that a sale of a share in a non-trading partnership was chargeable to income tax, but subsequently sought to defend the amendment on the basis that the sale was a capital gain which did not qualify for business taper relief. The Special Commissioner held that the Revenue were entitled to 'contend for other treatment' since 'the factual background is the payment of £500,000 pursuant to the agreement' and the alternative contentions were permissible as 'different arguments of law'. *CM Chappell v HMRC*, Sp C 2008, [2009] SSCD 11 (Sp C 717).

[4.24] See also *Orchid Properties v HMRC*, 4.108 below, and *Fidex Ltd v HMRC*, 4.109 below.

Partnerships—right of appeal

[4.25] See *Phillips v HMRC*, **41.54** PARTNERSHIP.

The notice of appeal (TMA, s 31A)

Whether notice of appeal must specify grounds of appeal

[4.26] In the case noted at **55.18** SELF-ASSESSMENT, an accountant sent a notice of appeal to the Special Commissioners, stating that 'due to the conduct of HMRC Officers we will not disclose the reasons for appeal'. The Revenue applied for a ruling that the notice of appeal was invalid, as it had failed to state the grounds of appeal, as required by *TMA, s 31A(5)*. The Commissioner accepted this contention, holding that the purported notice of appeal was invalid. *Jacques v HMRC (No 1)*, Sp C [2006] SSCD 40 (Sp C 513).

[4.27] The decision in *Jacques v HMRC (No 1)*, **4.26** above, was applied in the similar subsequent case of *Maincourse Ltd v HMRC*, FTT [2011] UKFTT 89 (TC), TC00966.

[4.28] See also *Westview Rail Ltd v HMRC*, **16.19** CONSTRUCTION INDUSTRY.

Late appeals

[4.29] In 1984 the Revenue rejected claims to interest relief under what is now *ICTA 1988, s 353*. In December 1989 the claimant applied to make a late appeal against the rejection of the claims. The Special Commissioner dismissed the application, holding that there was no reasonable excuse for the delay in making the application. *Orakpo v Lane*, Sp C 1995, [1996] SSCD 43 (Sp C 59).

[4.30] In 1997 the Revenue issued a loss determination under *TMA, s 41A*. In April 2001 the company applied to make a late appeal against the determination. The Special Commissioner dismissed the application, holding that there was no reasonable excuse for the delay in making it. *Consultants Ltd v HM Inspector of Taxes*, Sp C [2002] SSCD 162 (Sp C 307).

[4.31] See also *R v Special Commrs (ex p. Magill)*, **4.222** below; *R v Hastings & Bexhill Commrs (ex p. Goodacre)*, **4.223** below; *R (oao Browallia Cal Ltd) v City of London Commrs*, **4.224** below, and *R (oao Cook) v General Commissioners*, **4.225** below.

The parties to the appeal

Inspector present when Commissioners deliberating

[4.32] The KB set aside a decision by General Commissioners, and ordered a rehearing of the appeal, in a case where the Inspector had been present while the Commissioners were deliberating. The KB held that the Inspector had 'no more right to be present when the Commissioners are considering their determination' than any other party to an appeal. *R v Brixton Commrs (ex p. Lion Brewery Co Ltd)*, KB 1912, 6 TC 195.

Clerk to Commissioners discussing appeal with Revenue

[4.33] General Commissioners heard certain appeals, reserving their decision until after the hearing. They determined the appeals the following month. In the intervening period, the Clerk to the Commissioners had discussed the case with the Revenue representatives. The appellant became aware of this and applied for judicial review of the decision. The Revenue agreed that the determination should be set aside, and the QB made an order accordingly. (Costs were awarded to the appellant.) *R v Wokingham Commrs (ex p. Heron)*, QB 1984 STI 710.

Commissioners' meeting not attended by Clerk

[4.34] In a case where the substantive issue is no longer relevant, the CA unanimously held that a Commissioners' meeting had been properly constituted notwithstanding that the Clerk had failed to attend. *Venn v Franks*, CA 1958, 38 TC 175.

Commissioner and appellant potential trade competitors

[4.35] A butcher (R), who carried on business in Holyhead, appealed against several estimated assessments. One of the Commissioners hearing the appeal was a director of a company which owned a wholesale butcher's business in Holyhead. The Commissioners confirmed the assessments. Subsequently R applied to the QB for an order quashing the decision, contending that the Commissioner was a trade competitor and there was reasonable cause to fear that he might have been biased against him. The QB granted the application. Michael Davies J observed that knowledge of local matters and local taxpayers was in general an advantage for General Commissioners rather than a disqualification. However Holyhead was not a large community and 'any reasonable person would think it most unfortunate that one of the few butchers in that area should sit in a tax appeal involving another of the few butchers in the same area'. *R v Holyhead Commrs (ex p. Roberts)*, QB 1982, 56 TC 127.

Whether appellant may plead in writing

[4.36] In the case noted at 22.37 EMPLOYMENT INCOME, the appellant was abroad at the time the Special Commissioners heard the appeal, and was not represented. He had, however, sent in lengthy written pleadings to support his appeal. These were read to the Commissioners by the Revenue representative, and were taken into account in determining the appeal. *Caldicott v Varty*, Ch D 1976, 51 TC 403; [1976] STC 418; [1976] 3 All ER 329.

[4.37] A jewellery manufacturer (B) appealed against assessments for 1975/76 to 1981/82 inclusive. The appeals were listed for hearing by the Special Commissioners on a Monday. On the previous Friday B's accountants submitted a bundle of documents to the Commissioners on his behalf. B did not attend the hearing, but a junior employee of his accountants attended to read a prepared statement. The Commissioners refused to admit the statement, holding that there was 'no satisfactory explanation' for B's failure to attend the hearing, which 'meant that he could not be examined on any evidence which he might offer'. They determined the appeals for 1975/76 to 1978/79 inclusive. The CA unanimously upheld their decision, holding that a tribunal was not bound to read documents submitted by a litigant in person who failed to attend the hearing himself. Oliver LJ observed that 'the Commissioners are an investigatory body' and held that 'it is important that they should have the appellant before them'. *Banin v MacKinlay*, CA 1984, 58 TC 398; [1985] STC 144; [1985] 1 All ER 842.

Representation at hearing—definition of 'accountant'

[4.38] In the case noted at 52.57 SAVINGS AND INVESTMENT INCOME, the appellant asked to be represented by a qualified accountant (F) who had been suspended from membership of two accountancy bodies following his conviction for criminal offences relating to the falsification of documents and statements. The General Commissioners refused to hear F and the Ch D upheld their decision. *Cassell v Crutchfield (No 1)*, Ch D 1995, 69 TC 253; [1995] STC 663.

Witnesses and evidence

Whether appellant may demand to be examined on oath

[4.39] At a Special Commissioners' meeting, an appellant (F) declined to produce accounts and demanded to be put on oath to swear the accuracy of his return. The Commissioners refused to do so, and confirmed the assessment. F applied to the QB for an order requiring the Commissioners to state a Case. The QB rejected his application and the CA unanimously dismissed his appeal, holding that the Commissioners were under no obligation to put the appellant on oath. *R v Special Commrs (in re Fletcher)*, CA 1894, 3 TC 289.

False evidence given under oath—whether perjury

[4.40] The appellant in the case noted at 56.56 SETTLEMENTS gave evidence before the Special Commissioners that his sister had paid for certain shares. He was subsequently charged with, and convicted of, perjury in connection with this evidence. He appealed against his conviction. The CCA dismissed his appeal, holding that the Special Commissioners were a tribunal within the *Perjury Act 1911, s 1*, and that a person giving false evidence to them under oath could be convicted of perjury. *R v Hood-Barrs*, CCA [1943] KB 455; [1943] 1 All ER 665.

Evidence inconclusive—effect of TMA, s 50(6)

[4.41] A district warden (R), employed by a London Borough Council during the Second World War, appealed against assessments on receipts from local businesses for supervising firewatching. The Commissioners found that it was 'impossible for us to determine whether or not the assessments appealed against were excessive or inadequate in amount', and allowed R's appeal. The KB reversed their decision and restored the assessments. Macnaghten J held that, since the Commissioners had not been satisfied that the assessments were incorrect, the effect of what is now *TMA, s 50(6)* was that they were obliged to dismiss the appeal. *Eagles v Rose*, KB 1945, 26 TC 427.

Admissibility of evidence relating to other taxpayers

[4.42] In a Ceylon case, a bus company had appealed against estimated assessments. At the hearing the Revenue produced a document, based on the returns of seven other bus companies (the names of which were not disclosed), indicating a standard correlation between takings and expenditure on petrol. The tribunal accepted the document as evidence and determined the assessments. The PC upheld their decision, holding that there had been no breach of confidentiality and that the document had been properly and fairly used. Viscount Simon observed that the courts 'would strongly deprecate the production or use of such a document if it did in effect disclose information about other identified or identifiable taxpayers, but it is obvious that the document was prepared and produced not for this purpose but to help to show that the ratio above referred to between net profits as assessed and the cost of petrol and oil was a fairly constant ratio in many cases, and that in using the suggested ratio as a test the assessor, and the Commissioner after him, were not acting capriciously or at random'. *Gamini Bus Co Ltd v Colombo Income Tax Commr*, PC [1952] AC 571.

Admissibility of hearsay evidence

[4.43] In the case noted at 48.86 RESIDENCE, a company (F) claimed relief from tax under the UK/Barbados Double Tax Agreement. The Revenue rejected the claim, considering that F was not resident in Barbados. F appealed to the Special Commissioners, and tendered as evidence statements by its secretary that it was managed and controlled in Barbados, and by the Barbados Deputy Commissioner of Inland Revenue that it was resident there. The Special Commissioners declined to admit the evidence in question, holding that it was hearsay evidence, of which notice should have been given under the *Rules of the Supreme Court 1965* as then in force. The Ch D upheld their decision, holding that the Commissioners had been entitled to exercise their discretion not to admit the evidence. *Forth Investments Ltd v CIR*, Ch D 1976, 50 TC 617; [1976] STC 399. (*Note*. The *Rules of the Supreme Court 1965* have now been replaced by the *Civil Procedure Rules 1998 (SI 1998/3132)*, of which *rule 33* deals with the use of hearsay evidence.)

Expert evidence

[4.44] At the hearing of an appeal relating to a child allowance claim, an Inland Revenue officer gave evidence as to the procedure for issuing birth certificates in Pakistan. The claimant appealed to the Ch D, contending that this was expert evidence, of which prior notice should have been given under the *Rules of the Supreme Court 1965* as then in force. The Ch D accepted this contention and remitted the case to the Commissioners. *Khan v Edwards*, Ch D 1977, 53 TC 597; [1977] TR 143. (*Note*. The *Rules of the Supreme Court 1965* have now been replaced by the *Civil Procedure Rules 1998 (SI 1998/3132)*, of which *rule 35* deals with the use of expert evidence.)

[4.45] An individual (T) claimed allowances in respect of several children and relatives in the Yemen. The Revenue rejected the claim and he appealed. At the hearing, an expert witness gave evidence that some of the documents which T had produced in support of his claim were false. The General Commissioners dismissed T's appeal and the Ch D upheld their decision as one of fact. *Talib v Waterson*, Ch D [1980] STC 563.

Whether appellant bound by affidavit in other proceedings

[4.46] In 1975 an individual (W) received more than £900,000 from abroad, but did not declare this in his returns. In 1976 a Hong Kong company began legal action against him, and in interlocutory proceedings in this action he swore an affidavit that the amounts were his share of profits from speculative trading in commodities. The Revenue became aware of the affidavit and raised estimated assessments. W appealed, contending that the affidavit was inadmissible as evidence. The Commissioners rejected this contention and determined the appeals, and the Ch D upheld their decision. *Wicker v Fraser*, Ch D 1982, 55 TC 641; [1982] STC 505.

Potential witness abroad and unable to attend

[4.47] Two appellants applied to the High Court for a special examiner to take evidence, in support of their appeal, from a person resident abroad who was stated to be unable to travel to the UK. The CA rejected their application, holding that there was no jurisdiction to make the order applied for. *In re Leiserach & Another*, CA 1963, 42 TC 1. (*Note*. See now the *Civil Procedure Rules 1998 (SI 1998/3132), rule 34.13*.)

Potential witness in prison

[4.48] At the hearing of an appeal before the Commissioners, the appellant objected that he was at a disadvantage, since a potential witness was unable to attend because he was in prison. The Commissioners recorded in the Case Stated that 'we nevertheless decided to call upon the appellant to proceed in the absence of the witness and he agreed to do so'. The Ch D held that this was ambiguous, as it was not clear whether the appellant had continued against his will. The Ch D therefore remitted the case to the Commissioners for clarification of what had occurred before them. *Aspinall v Greenwood*, Ch D 1988, 60 TC 670; [1988] STC 609.

Application for witness summons

[4.49] In the case noted at 73.137 NATIONAL INSURANCE CONTRIBUTIONS, a company (T) provided the services of its principal director to another company (C), which in turn provided them to a large motor company (F). The Revenue applied for a witness summons to be issued to one of F's employees (B), who had provided information in writing about the arrangements between T and F. The Special Commissioner granted the application, observing that although B had already submitted written evidence, 'the documentary evidence may well be expanded and/or clarified by oral evidence'. *Tilbury Consulting Ltd v Gittins (No 1)*, Sp C 2003, [2004] SSCD 1 (Sp C 379).

[4.50] HMRC obtained information that a partnership had made 26 cash credits to an account with an Indian bank, and had exchanged approximately £250,000 in old £20 bank notes for the same amount in new bank notes. They formed the opinion that the partnership had understated its profits, and began an investigation into the partnership's affairs. They issued a notice to the partnership's bank under *TMA, s 20(3)*. The bank complied with this notice. The partnership became aware that HMRC had obtained information from its bank, and applied for the issue of witness summons to some of the bank personnel. The bank opposed the application on the grounds of public interest immunity, contending that the disclosure of some of the information sought by the partnership might reveal 'the identity, location, office or position' of its employees or officers connected with money laundering supervision arrangements, and might reveal its 'documents, systems, procedures or controls' connected with its money laundering supervision arrangements. The Special Commissioner held that a specific document which the partnership had requested could be 'disclosed in a redacted form without there being any real risk of serious prejudice to any important public interest', but declined to grant the partnership's applications for witnesses summonses requiring bank employees to give evidence at the hearing of its appeal. *Chemists v HMRC; Chemists v Bank plc*, Sp C [2009] SSCD 472; [2009] UKFTT 66 (TC), TC00007.

Attendance of HMRC officer as witness

[4.51] A subcontractor (H) claimed a deduction for subsistence expenses. HMRC considered that the amount claimed was excessive, and disallowed part of it. H appealed to the First-tier Tribunal, which reviewed the evidence and allowed the appeal in part. Judge Williams noted that 'HMRC had indicated to the appellant, in reply to correspondence, that the officer of Revenue and Customs who had made the decisions under appeal would attend as a witness at the hearing and would answer questions. Shortly before the hearing that officer was withdrawn as a witness. At the hearing the tribunal asked HMRC why this was so. Part of the answer was that the officer's senior managers had considered it to be in the interests of the officer's health and safety. This was because of statements made by the appellant in the correspondence leading to the hearing. While the tribunal in no way condones some of the comments made by the appellant in writing, the tribunal made it clear to the officer representing HMRC at the hearing that this was entirely unacceptable as a ground for not producing a witness. Such matters are entirely for the tribunal and those assisting the tribunal. All tribunals have arrangements in place to deal with any threat to personal safety and all tribunal judges are aware of them.' *G Huntley v HMRC*, FTT [2010] UKFTT 551 (TC), TC00804.

Admissibility of documents in evidence

[4.52] An appeal against estimated assessments was heard by a Special Commissioner. At the hearing, the appellant objected to the Revenue's use of computer-generated documents in evidence. The Special Commissioner held that the documents were admissible evidence. *Taylor v Cox (and related appeals)*, Sp C [1998] SSCD 179 (Sp C 163).

Commissioners' powers not to call character witness

[4.53] The Revenue rejected a claim to industrial buildings allowance, on the grounds that the claimant (W) had not made a written election within the statutory two-year time limit. W appealed, contending that his accountant (M) had posted the relevant notice of election in 1988, and producing a photocopy of a letter dated 1988 in evidence. The Revenue produced a notification from M dated 1990, and produced evidence from a Government chemist to suggest that the letter subsequently produced by W, although dated 1988, had been prepared on an inkjet printer after 1988. The General Commissioners dismissed the appeal, finding that they were not satisfied that M had posted the election in question in 1988. W appealed to the Ch D, contending that the Commissioners had acted wrongly by refusing to call M's rabbi to give evidence with regard to M's credibility. The Ch D rejected this contention and dismissed the appeal. Rattee J held that the Commissioners had been entitled to decide not to call the rabbi. *Walker v Smith*, Ch D 1999, 72 TC 447; [1999] STC 605. (*Note*. Compare *R v Patel*, **51.2** REVENUE PROSECUTIONS, where the CA held that the law of forgery was applicable to a false document put forward in support of a tax claim.)

Admissibility of Revenue capital statements as evidence

[4.54] The Revenue issued assessments on a car dealer (J). The Commissioners determined the assessments in accordance with capital statements put forward by the Revenue (except on two points on which the Commissioners accepted J's evidence). J appealed to the Ch D and also applied for an order that the case should be remitted to the Commissioners, contending that the capital statements were not lawful evidence. The Ch D and the CA unanimously dismissed both the appeal and the application, holding that the capital statements were admissible as evidence. *Johnson v Scott*, CA 1978, 52 TC 383; [1978] STC 476.

Use of local knowledge by Commissioners

[4.55] See *R v Holyhead Commrs (ex p. Roberts)*, **4.35** above, and *Forest Side Properties (Chingford) Ltd v Pearce*, **67.9** TRADING PROFITS.

Applications for adjournments

Appeal adjournment refused by Commissioners

[4.56] On the third hearing of an appeal against an estimated assessment, the General Commissioners refused the appellant's application for a further adjournment, and confirmed the assessment. The CS unanimously upheld their decision. Lord Clyde described the appeal as 'hopeless'. *Hamilton v CIR*, CS 1930, 16 TC 28.

[4.57] Similar decisions were reached in *Noble v Wilkinson (and related appeal)*, Ch D 1958, 38 TC 135; *Gault v CIR*, CS 1990, 63 TC 465; [1990] STC 612; *Fletcher & Fletcher v Harvey*, **29.39** FURTHER ASSESSMENTS: LOSS OF TAX; *Hawkins v Fuller*, **29.45** FURTHER ASSESSMENTS: LOSS OF TAX, and *Kilburn v Bedford*, **29.98** FURTHER ASSESSMENTS: LOSS OF TAX.

Appeal determined in absence of appellant

[4.58] The personal representative of a deceased taxpayer appealed against a notice of determination of inheritance tax. Between January and July 2002 the appeal was listed for hearing before the Special Commissioners on three occasions, but was adjourned each time at the request of the appellant. The appeal was relisted for August 2002. The appellant did not attend, but wrote to the Commissioners requesting a further adjournment on the grounds that she had not received papers from her solicitor. The Special Commissioner rejected this request and heard the appeal in the appellant's absence, dismissing the appeal and confirming the notice of determination. *Smith (Norcott's Personal Representative) v CIR*, Sp C [2002] SSCD 411 (Sp C 330).

Commissioners refusing adjournment—case remitted for rehearing

[4.59] Following an investigation on a company, the Revenue had made alternative assessments on the company and on its principal director and shareholder (R). The appeals were listed for hearing together in February 1967, and were adjourned because R had suffered a coronary thrombosis in December 1966. The appeals were relisted for June 1967. R's barrister applied for a further adjournment on the grounds that R had had an operation in May, and would be unable to travel for a further two or three months. The Commissioners rejected the application and heard the appeals in R's absence. The company's accountant gave evidence that its books were well kept and that there was nothing in the general pattern of its accounts to make him suspicious. The Commissioners determined income tax assessments on R, and profits tax and excess profits tax assessments on the company, on the basis that the company had received undeclared income which it had passed to R as undisclosed remuneration. R and the company appealed, contending that the Commissioners had acted unreasonably in refusing a further adjournment and in rejecting the accountant's evidence. The CA accepted this contention and allowed the company's appeal, holding that the assessments on the company should be discharged as the only admissible evidence given was that its accounts were correct. The CA also held that R's appeals against the income tax assessments should be remitted to a different panel of Commissioners for rehearing. *Rose v Humbles*; *Aldersgate Textiles Ltd v CIR*, CA 1971, 48 TC 103; [1972] 1 WLR 33; [1972] 1 All ER 314.

[4.60] Following a lengthy investigation, estimated assessments were made on a company, some of them under the extended time limits where there had been fraud or wilful default. The principal factual issue was the cash living expenses of a director of the company. At the hearing of the appeal, the director could not attend because of a heart condition and the company applied for an adjournment. The Revenue opposed the application on the grounds that the director was likely indefinitely to be unfit to attend a hearing. The Commissioners refused the application, found that there had been wilful default and determined the assessments on the basis of the Revenue figures. The company appealed to the Ch D, which remitted the case to be heard by different Commissioners, holding that the Commissioners had erred in not considering whether the director could have attended an adjourned hearing and in assuming that he would not recover. *Timings Tools Ltd v Mellersh*, Ch D 24 June 1981, 1981 STI 327.

[4.61] An individual (T), who had received substantial amounts of bank interest, delayed submitting his returns. The Revenue began proceedings to recover penalties and interest. The General Commissioners summoned T to appear before them in February 1987. His solicitor produced a medical certificate indicating that he was suffering from depression and was unfit to answer questions. The Commissioners adjourned the hearing until April, when a further certificate was produced indicating that T's condition remained unchanged. The Commissioners refused a further application for an adjournment, awarded penalties and granted interest certificates. T appealed against the penalties and began judicial review proceedings with regard to the grant of interest certificates. Morritt J allowed the appeal, granted an order of *certiorari*, and ordered a further hearing of the proceedings before the Special Commissioners, holding that the General Commissioners should have granted a further adjournment. *Thorne v Sevenoaks Commrs and Another; R v Sevenoaks Commrs (ex p. Thorne)*, Ch D & QB 1989, 62 TC 341; [1989] STC 560.

[4.62] An appeal against CGT assessments was originally listed for hearing in July 1988, but was adjourned to September at the appellant's request. The appellant did not attend the second hearing, but his agents sent a letter requesting an adjournment, contending that all the necessary information had been supplied to the Revenue, that the assessments should be reduced to nil, and that further enquiries could be dealt with by correspondence. The Commissioners refused a further adjournment and confirmed the assessments. The Ch D held that the Commissioners had acted unreasonably, and should either have granted a further adjournment or have considered the computations submitted by the appellant's agents. The determinations were set aside and the case was remitted for hearing by a different panel of Commissioners. *Packe v Johnson*, Ch D 1990, 63 TC 507; [1991] STC 1.

Jurisdiction of Commissioners

Appeal designated as 'lead case'

[4.63] In the case noted at **73.56** NATIONAL INSURANCE CONTRIBUTIONS, several companies had entered into arrangements, devised by an accountancy firm, whereby bonuses were paid to directors or employees in the form of antique gold coins located outside the UK. All the coins in question were purchased from the same broker. The companies did not account for Class 1 NIC on the bonuses. The Revenue issued rulings that NIC was due, and the companies appealed. The Revenue and the companies' accountants made a joint application for one of the appeals to be designated as the 'lead case'. The Commissioner granted the application. *EDI Services Ltd v HMRC (and related appeals)*, Sp C [2006] SSCD 60 (Sp C 515).

[4.64] The Special Commissioner made a similar direction in *Spectrum Computer Supplies Ltd v HMRC*, **73.57** NATIONAL INSURANCE CONTRIBUTIONS.

[4.65] Following the direction noted at **4.64** above, one of the companies (H) applied for a direction that it should be removed from the proceedings, but failed to attend the hearing of its application. The Commissioner dismissed the application, finding on the evidence that 'the facts of (H) are sufficiently similar to those of the lead case for me to reach a *prima facie* conclusion that (H) should remain bound by the outcome of the lead case proceedings'. *Halewood International Ltd v HMRC*, Sp C [2006] SSCD 650 (Sp C 556).

TMA, s 46B—questions to be determined by Special Commissioners

[4.66] See *Walker v HMRC*, 4.13 above.

TMA, Sch 3—whether directory or mandatory

[4.67] See *Murphy v Elders*, 4.82 below, and *CIR v Adams*, 44.85 PENALTIES.

Jurisdiction of Commissioners in relation to penalties

[4.68] See *R v Havering Commrs*, 44.86 PENALTIES, and *Toogood v Bristol Commrs*, 44.327 PENALTIES.

Jurisdiction of Commissioners contested

[4.69] Following an investigation, assessments were raised on the husband of a woman who owned a millinery business in Nuneaton, where the couple had lived until 1952 when they moved to Essex. The Nuneaton Commissioners determined the assessments and the husband appealed, contending that the Nuneaton Commissioners had no jurisdiction, and that the appeals should have been transferred to the Clacton Commissioners. The Ch D rejected this contention and dismissed the appeal, which Cross J described as 'hopeless'. *Sinsbury v Burgess*, Ch D 1968, 47 ATC 397.

[4.70] In the case noted at 29.35 FURTHER ASSESSMENTS: LOSS OF TAX, the Revenue raised assessments on a company which had its registered office in Northampton. The Northampton Commissioners determined the assessments. The company appealed to the CA, contending that the Commissioners had no jurisdiction because its principal place of business was outside Northampton. The CA unanimously rejected this contention and dismissed the appeal. *Frederick Lack Ltd v Doggett*, CA 1970, 46 TC 524.

[4.71] The Revenue issued an assessment to an individual (L) charging tax on his profit from a transaction in land. He appealed, and his appeal was listed for hearing came before the Tavistock Commissioners. They accepted his evidence that the transaction was implemented in Surrey, and decided that they had no jurisdiction. The appeal was accordingly listed for hearing by the Kingston Commissioners. L applied for an order to prohibit the Kingston Commissioners from determining the appeal. The QB rejected the application. Lord Widgery CJ observed that 'there are no grounds whatever why this court should say that the Kingston Commissioners lacked jurisdiction'. *R v Kingston & Elmbridge Commrs (ex p. Adams)*, QB 1972, 48 TC 75.

[4.72] An American corporation, with a head office and principal place of business in Surrey, appealed against corporation tax assessments. The appeals were partly heard by the St Pancras Commissioners without the question of jurisdiction having been raised. The corporation then applied to the QB for orders prohibiting the Commissioners from proceeding with the appeals or alternatively directing them to consider whether they had jurisdiction. The QB rejected the applications, holding that the question of jurisdiction was for the Commissioners to consider. *R v St Pancras Commrs (ex p. Church of Scientology of California) (and related application)*, QB 1973, 50 TC 365; [1973] STC 417.

[4.73] A doctor (P) issued a summons against General Commissioners, challenging their jurisdiction in hearing various appeals by him and the validity of precepts which they had issued. The QB dismissed the summons and the CA unanimously dismissed P's appeal, holding that he should have challenged the Commissioners' jurisdiction by demanding a Stated Case, and should have challenged the validity of the precepts by applying for a prerogative order to quash them. Buckley LJ observed that 'these proceedings are misconceived, no doubt due to the fact that the taxpayer has tried to deal with them on his own, without professional legal assistance, which often leads litigants into difficulties. If he wants to pursue these matters further, he would be very well advised to obtain legal advice and assistance.' *Parikh v Birmingham North Commrs*, CA [1976] STC 365.

The Commissioners' decision

Whether Commissioners bound by previous decision on same facts

[4.74] In a Northern Ireland case, a whiskey-distilling company had gone into voluntary liquidation in August 1920. The liquidator continued distilling until March 1921, and continued to sell stock after that date. The Revenue assessed the company for 1920/21 on the basis that the liquidator was carrying on the trade. The Special Commissioners upheld the assessment, but the Recorder of Belfast reversed their decision. Meanwhile the Revenue had made a similar assessment for 1921/22. The Commissioners allowed the company's appeal against this assessment, holding that they were bound by the Recorder's decision for 1920/21. The Revenue appealed, and the HL remitted the case to the Commissioners to rehear the appeal, holding that they were not bound by the Recorder's previous decision. *Edwards v 'Old Bushmills' Distillery Co Ltd*, HL 1926, 10 TC 285. (*Note.* The KB subsequently upheld the Recorder's decision—see **59.44** TRADING INCOME.)

[4.75] In 1918, the Special Commissioners heard appeals against super-tax assessments on the income of a person (M) who had been declared a lunatic under the *Lunacy Act 1890*. They allowed deductions for the 'lunacy percentage' paid to the Crown under the *Lunacy Act* and the remuneration paid to the administrator of M's estate. The Revenue did not appeal against the decision, and allowed the deductions for subsequent years. In 1928 the KB heard the similar case of *AB v Simpson*, **52.39** SAVINGS AND INVESTMENT INCOME, and held that the deductions in question were not allowable. Following this decision, the Revenue refused to allow the deductions for 1928/29. The Special Commissioners allowed an appeal by the administrator, holding that they were bound to follow the decision reached in 1918. The Revenue appealed to the CA which remitted the case to the Commissioners, holding that the Commissioners were not bound to follow their previous decision. Romer LJ held that 'the only thing that the Commissioners have jurisdiction to decide directly and as a substantive matter is the amount of the taxpayer's income for the year in question'. Their decision could not 'be conclusive in reference to the ascertainment of the taxpayer's income for any subsequent year of assessment'. *CIR v Sneath*, CA 1932, 17 TC 149; [1932] 2 KB 362. (*Notes.* (1) The decision here was approved and applied by the PC in the subsequent case of *Ranaweera v Ramachandran*, PC 1969, 45 TC 423; [1970] 2 WLR 500. (2) Following the *Mental Health Act 1959*, the term 'lunatic' is no longer officially used.)

[4.76] An individual appealed against assessments for 1935/36 to 1940/41 inclusive, contending that the assessability of the income in question was *res judicata* because of a previous Commissioners' decision in his favour in 1931. The Special Commissioners dismissed his appeal, and the KB and CA upheld their decision. Lord Greene MR observed that 'there is no such thing as *res judicata* in respect of the decisions of Income Tax Commissioners. They may or may not follow their previous decision; but they are not bound to because the subject-matter is a different year's tax and a different year's assessment and is not the same as the subject-matter of the previous ruling'. *Patuck v Lloyd*, CA 1944, 26 TC 284.

[4.77] In the case noted at **9.34** CHARITIES, the Ceylon Board of Review had granted a claim to charitable relief for 1949/50, but subsequently rejected a similar claim for 1950/51 to 1954/55. The trustees appealed, contending that the decision for 1949/50 estopped the Board from refusing the relief for later years. The Privy Council rejected this contention and dismissed the trustees' appeal. *Caffoor & Others (Abdul Gaffoor Trustees) v Colombo Income Tax Commr*, PC 1961, 40 ATC 93; [1961] AC 584; [1961] 2 All ER 436.

[4.78] See also *Bourke v P Lyster & Sons Ltd*, **4.235** below.

Commissioners' decision wrongly announced by Clerk

[4.79] General Commissioners determined an appeal against a company, but the Clerk erroneously announced the decision as being in the company's favour. The KB held that the decision as announced by the Clerk was not the decision of the Commissioners, and that the Commissioners were entitled to determine the relevant assessments in accordance with their actual decision. *R v Morleston & Litchurch General Commrs (ex p. GR Turner Ltd)*, KB 1951, 32 TC 335.

Whether Commissioners' proceedings conformed to natural justice

[4.80] Under a procedure which has since become obsolete, the Commissioners were required to give a certificate for repayment of tax in respect of a claim for loss relief under provisions corresponding to *ITA 2007, s 64*. A body of Commissioners issued such certificates, at a meeting at which the Revenue were not represented, in respect of losses for which no written claim and no computation had been submitted to the Revenue. The Revenue appealed to the CS, which quashed the certificates, holding that the Commissioners had departed from the fundamental principles of natural justice. The HL unanimously upheld the CS decision. *CIR v Hood Barrs*, HL 1961, 39 TC 683.

Assessment confirmed while taxpayer's agent temporarily absent

[4.81] General Commissioners confirmed an assessment on a company. The company's agent, a solicitor, had left the waiting room for a few minutes for professional purposes, returning two minutes after the Commissioners had determined the appeal. They refused to reconsider the appeal. The CS remitted the case to the Commissioners for a rehearing, holding that the Commissioners had acted unreasonably. *R & D McKerron Ltd v CIR*, CS 1979, 53 TC 28; [1979] STC 815.

Related appeals heard by different panels of Commissioners

[4.82] Following an investigation, the Revenue issued assessments on a company on the basis that it had made undisclosed profits, and assessments on its controlling director (M) on the basis that he had received undisclosed remuneration from it. Both M and the company appealed. The General Commissioners allowed the company's appeal, finding that the accounts were correct. A different panel of Commissioners heard M's appeal, found that wilful default had been established and determined the assessments accordingly. M appealed to the Ch D, contending that the decision on the company's appeal gave rise to estoppel *per rem judicatum*. The Ch D rejected this contention and dismissed the appeal, holding that the decision on the company's appeal was not binding on the Commissioners who heard M's appeal, since the questions and parties were different in each case. (The Ch D also held that *TMA, Sch 3* was directory rather than mandatory, applying *CIR v Adams*, 44.85 PENALTIES.) *Murphy v Elders*, Ch D 1973, 49 TC 135; [1974] STC 34.

Application to reopen appeals

[4.83] At the hearing of an appeal at which the appellant was not present or represented, the Commissioners determined assessments in accordance with figures which the taxpayer's accountant had put forward to the inspector. Subsequently the Revenue applied for an interest certificate under *TMA, s 70*. At the hearing of the application, the appellant attended and requested that the appeal should be reopened. The Commissioners rejected the appellant's request, and the QB and CA unanimously upheld their decision. *R v Epping & Harlow Commrs (ex p. Goldstraw)*, CA 1983, 57 TC 536; [1983] STC 693; [1983] 3 All ER 257.

[4.84] Appeals were listed for hearing by General Commissioners on 21 September 1982. On 20 September the appellant (L) was told by her accountant that the inspector had informed him that the hearing was to be adjourned and that she need not attend. However, the Commissioners did in fact hear and determine the appeals on 21 September, and on 27 September L received from the Clerk a letter enclosing the determination. The Commissioners refused to reopen the appeals. Subsequently the Revenue Solicitor agreed that an order should be made quashing the decision and remitting the appeals to a fresh body of Commissioners. The QB ordered accordingly. *R v O'Brien (ex p. Lissner)*, QB 15 October 1984, 1984 STI 710.

[4.85] An individual (D) appealed against assessments for 1999/2000 and 2000/01. In May 2006 the General Commissioners upheld the assessments. D lodged an application for the decision to be set aside. The General Commissioners rejected the application and D applied for judicial review. The QB rejected his application and the CA upheld this decision. Arden LJ observed that D 'had had plenty of time to meet the questions put forward by the Inland Revenue and satisfy them on all the questions on which they required to be satisfied. The Commissioners decided that, as he had not produced the accurate information, he had had enough time.' They had been 'entitled to come to what was essentially a discretionary decision'. *R (oao Dogar) v General Commrs*, CA [2009] EWCA Civ 152.

Appeal determined in principle before determination of figures

[4.86] The Revenue raised assessments on the basis that sums deposited in a bank account were undeclared business profits. The trader contended that the deposits were from relatives abroad. The Commissioners rejected this contention and held that they 'were not satisfied that the amounts were not trading income', leaving the assessments to be adjusted between the parties in accordance with 'our decision in principle as set out above'. The parties failed to agree figures, and at a further hearing to determine the amount of the assessments, the Commissioners refused to consider evidence of an alleged alternative source of the deposits. The trader subsequently applied for judicial review of their decision. The QB and CA rejected the application. *R v St Marylebone Commrs (ex p. Hay)*, CA 1983, 57 TC 59; [1983] STC 346.

Whether TMA, s 50(6) applicable

[4.87] Estimated corporation tax assessments on a company for 1979 and 1980 became final and conclusive. (The 1980 assessment was confirmed by the Commissioners in the absence of accounts, and the Commissioners refused the company's application to make a late appeal against the 1979 assessment.) The assessments took previous losses into account. Subsequently the company appealed against corporation tax assessments for 1981 and 1983, contending that it had been overcharged by the 1980 assessment, and that the losses could therefore be set against the later assessments by virtue of *TMA, s 50(6)*. The General Commissioners allowed the company's appeal but the Ch D reversed their decision. The 1979 and 1980 assessments had become final and could not be reopened. *TMA, s 50(6)* operated only on an appeal, and the only assessment to which it could apply was the 1980 assessment, which could not now be reopened. The appeals in question were against the 1981 and 1983 assessments. Accordingly the losses, for which relief had been given in the 1979 and 1980 assessments, were not available to be carried forward against the 1981 and later assessments. *Auckland v Pavh (International) Ltd*, Ch D 1992, 65 TC 99; [1992] STC 712.

Interaction of TMA, ss 50(6) and 95

[4.88] See *Morris & Morris v HMRC (No 3)*, 44.190 PENALTIES.

Determination of appeal—TMA, s 55(9)

[4.89] See *Re A Debtor*, 4.406 below.

Publication of Special Commissioners' decisions

[4.90] In the case noted at 74.8 PETROLEUM REVENUE TAX, a public company appealed to the Special Commissioners. The appeal was heard in private and was dismissed. The Presiding Special Commissioner decided that an anonymised report of the decision should be published. The company applied for only a brief report of the decision to be published, on the grounds that even an anonymised report would enable it to be identified by 'any reader of the decision who came from the same industry'. The Special Commissioner rejected the application, holding that the decision 'ought to be published' since it related 'to an issue which depends on the construction of a section that has not been before the courts before'. There were no 'trade secrets' involved, but the company wanted to protect its tax affairs 'from public knowledge'. The company's 'wish to preserve confidentiality' was 'not of sufficient merit' to warrant a decision not to publish a report. *Y Co Ltd v CIR*, Sp C [1996] SSCD 147 (Sp C 69). (*Note*. For cases where similar applications were rejected in relation to proceedings in the High Court, see *In re H*, **4.161** below, and *Treharne v Guinness Exports Ltd*, **4.165** below.)

Appeals to the First-tier Tribunal

Tribunal Procedure (First-tier Tribunal) (Tax Chamber) Rules (SI 2009/273)

SI 2009/273, rule 5—application for stay of proceedings

[4.91] An individual (S) claimed loss relief of more than £300,000 relating to alleged trading in biofuels and paper pulp. HMRC formed the opinion that the claimed loss was part of a tax avoidance scheme and that the promoters of the scheme may have committed a criminal offence. They began an enquiry into the scheme, and subsequently issued a closure notice amending S's self-assessment and rejecting his claim for loss relief. S appealed to the First-tier Tribunal. HMRC applied for the appeal proceedings to be stayed for six months, and for an extension of time to serve their Statement of Case, giving evidence that about 360 traders, and 19 limited liability partnerships, had made similar claims, and that tax of more than £40,000,000 was at stake. S opposed the application but the tribunal granted it. Judge Walters observed that S appeared to have shown 'a marked reluctance to provide the full information and documents' which HMRC wished to consider as part of their enquiry. The arguments in favour of staying the proceedings would have 'been much weaker if the appellant had, before the closure notice was issued, provided HMRC with as much relevant factual information as possible'. The tribunal also directed that the case should be categorised as 'complex', under *Tribunal Procedure (First-tier Tribunal) (Tax Chamber) Rules (SI 2009/273), rule 23(2)(d)*. *Swallow v HMRC*, FTT [2010] UKFTT 481 (TC), TC00742. (*Note*. HMRC also applied for the release of the decision to be delayed, on the grounds that its release may prejudice subsequent criminal proceedings. The tribunal rejected this contention and directed that the decision should be released in anonymised form. The tribunal specifically declined to follow the decision in the VAT case of *Global Active Technologies Ltd v HMRC*, [2006] VATDR 190 (VTD 19715), which HMRC had cited as an authority. Judge Walters observed that, in *V v C*, CA [2001] EWCA Civ 1509, the CA had been 'dismissive of the reality of the risks to a fair trial from related civil proceedings having been conducted and determined beforehand'.)

[4.92] HMRC issued a ruling that a company (P) should have accounted for national insurance contributions on substantial payments to an employee benefit trust. P appealed, and applied for the proceedings to be stayed pending the Upper Tribunal decision in *HMRC v Murray Group Holdings Ltd*, **42.53** PAY AS YOU EARN. HMRC opposed the application but the First-tier Tribunal granted it. Judge Herrington held that 'the further appeal proceedings in *Murray Group Holdings* will be of material assistance to the FTT in the present appeals. The reason for this is because that appeal will give rise to a binding decision on the FTT as to which of the two approaches articulated in the *Murray Group*'s majority and minority decisions is the correct legal approach. The principle derived from consideration of those issues will be fundamental to the way in which the FTT will need to approach the facts of these appeals.' *Peel Investments (UK) Ltd v HMRC (and related appeals)*, FTT [2013] UKFTT 404 (TC), TC02800.

SI 2009/273, rule 8—application to strike out appeal

[4.93] A pensioner (C) received pensions from three different former employers. For part of 2009/10 HMRC set his personal allowances against two of these sources, leading to an underpayment of tax. In November 2010 HMRC issued a tax calculation notice (P800) stating that there had been an underpayment of £808.60. C appealed to the First-tier Tribunal. HMRC applied to the tribunal for the appeal to be struck out under *SI 2009/273, rule 8*, contending that there was no right of appeal against a form P800. The tribunal rejected this application. Judge Redston held that it was arguable that a form P800 was a notice of assessment giving rise to a right of appeal under *TMA, s 31*, and directed that the case should be relisted for further hearing. *RE Clark v HMRC*, FTT [2011] UKFTT 302 (TC), TC01164. (*Note*. There was no further hearing of the appeal, which was settled by agreement. See now, however, the subsequent decision in *Prince v HMRC*, **4.94** below.)

[4.94] Judge Redston's decision in *RE Clark v HMRC*, **4.93** above, was not followed in a subsequent case in which three individuals sought to appeal against forms P800. The First-tier Tribunal accepted HMRC's application for the appeals to be struck out. Judge Bishopp held that the form P800 was 'a reconciliation of the taxpayer's PAYE record. It is not the result of the ordinary assessment process, by which — quite outside the PAYE system — a taxpayer's income, gains, allowances and reliefs are determined, a calculation of the tax is made, the calculation is notified to the taxpayer and (subject to appeal) the amount so calculated becomes payable; nor is it akin to the adjustment of a self-assessment return, by closure notice or discovery assessment.' Where an employee was aggrieved as to 'the manner in which the PAYE system is being applied to his affairs', the correct course was to appeal against a notice of coding, under *Income Tax (PAYE) Regulations 2003 (SI 2003/2682), regs 18, 19*. *M Prince v HMRC (and related appeals)*, FTT [2012] UKFTT 157 (TC); [2012] SFTD 786; TC01852.

[4.95] Judge Bishopp's decision in *Prince v HMRC*, **4.94** above, was applied in the similar subsequent cases of *P Hill v HMRC*, FTT [2012] UKFTT 612 (TC), TC02289; *I Hudson v HMRC*, FTT [2012] UKFTT 661 (TC), TC02332; *R Fleming v HMRC*, FTT [2013] UKFTT 197 (TC), TC02612; *C Flood v HMRC*, FTT [2013] UKFTT 251 (TC), TC02665, and *J Moyes v HMRC*, FTT [2014] UKFTT 1030 (TC), TC04126.

[4.96] Following the death of an accountant (T), his executor opted to use the form R27 rather than to submit a tax return giving details of T's income. After receiving the completed form R27, HMRC issued a calculation showing a small repayment due, which they duly made. T's executor sought to lodge an appeal, contending that the repayment was inadequate. HMRC applied for the appeal to be struck out on the grounds that the calculation was not an assessment and there was no right of appeal against it. The First-tier Tribunal accepted this contention and struck out the appeal, applying Judge Bishopp's decision in *Prince v HMRC*, **4.94** above. Judge Porter observed that the executor would have a statutory right of appeal if he filed a self-assessment return. *JG Taylor (J Taylor's Executor) v HMRC*, FTT [2013] UKFTT 483 (TC), TC02866.

[4.97] HMRC issued three determinations under *TMA, s 28C*. The recipient (B) submitted a notice of appeal. HMRC applied for the appeal to be struck out, contending that the Tribunal had no jurisdiction to hear an appeal against a determination under *s 28C*. The First-tier Tribunal accepted this contention and struck out the appeals. Judge Hellier held that 'the procedure envisaged by *section 28C* requires no right to appeal against the amounts in any determination'. He observed that 'a taxpayer has a remedy for incorrect amounts which he may pursue by submitting a return and self-assessment'. The Upper Tribunal upheld this decision. Judge Clark observed that B 'had a choice. If he had wanted to keep open the ability to question within the Tribunal appeals system the amounts of the tax stated by the determinations to be due, he needed to take the path labelled "submit self assessments". By deciding to follow the other path and allow the determinations to stand unchanged, he denied himself the opportunity of challenging on appeal the amounts of tax demanded as a result of those determinations.' *M Bartram v HMRC*, UT [2012] UKUT 184 (TCC); [2012] STC 2144.

[4.98] In 2007/08 an individual (C) received a large termination payment. He declared this on his return, but HMRC failed to include it in his 2007/08 assessment (which charged tax of less than £5,000). In 2010 they issued a further assessment charging tax on it. C appealed. HMRC applied for the appeal to be struck out, contending that since the assessment was based on information contained in HMRC's return, and had been made within the statutory time limit, C's appeal had no prospect of success. The First-tier Tribunal accepted this contention and struck out the appeal. *A Churchill v HMRC*, FTT [2012] UKFTT 656 (TC), TC02328.

[4.99] HMRC formed the opinion that an accountant's tax returns had substantially understated his income, and had omitted income from property transactions. They issued a notice under *FA 2008, Sch 36* requesting information and documents. The accountant failed to comply with the notice, and HMRC imposed penalties and issued amendments to his self-assessments. In 2010 the accountant appealed, contending that his records had been destroyed in a flood. Subsequently the First-tier Tribunal issued directions, which the accountant failed to comply with. In 2012 HMRC applied to the tribunal requesting the appeal to be struck out on the grounds that the accountant had failed to comply with the directions. Judge Scott granted the application, observing that the accountant had 'repeatedly failed to comply' with the tribunal's directions, and that in view of the accountant's conduct, the appeal against the amendments had 'no realistic prospect of success'. *C O'Brien v HMRC*, FTT [2012] UKFTT 581 (TC), TC02258.

[4.100] Judge Mure reached a similar decision in *D McKee v HMRC*, FTT [2014] UKFTT 806 (TC), TC03923.

[4.101] An architect (D) submitted his 2005/06 return within the statutory time limit. More than three years later, he submitted an amendment to the return, claiming a repayment. HMRC rejected the claim on the grounds that it had been made outside the statutory time limits. D appealed, and HMRC applied for the appeal to be struck out. The First-tier Tribunal granted HMRC's application. *PC Durkin (t/a Halifax Architects) v HMRC*, FTT [2012] UKFTT 706 (TC), TC02373.

[4.102] In May 2008 a couple claimed loss relief for 2005/06. HMRC rejected the claim on the grounds that it had been made outside the statutory time limits. The couple appealed, and HMRC applied for the appeal to be struck out. The First-tier Tribunal granted HMRC's application, applying the decision in *Durkin v HMRC*, **4.101** above. *BH & Mrs AB Chauhan v HMRC*, FTT [2014] UKFTT 851 (TC), TC03967.

[4.103] A couple lodged a notice of appeal with the Tribunal Centre, claiming that they had overpaid tax. The First-tier Tribunal struck out the appeal, finding that 'the dispute between the parties relates to payments and allocations of payments, rather than any dispute concerning the underlying taxation liabilities, all of which were agreed between the parties back in 2008. This tribunal has no general jurisdiction in relation to debt collection disputes between HMRC and taxpayers.' *M & Mrs J Ashley v HMRC*, FTT [2013] UKFTT 385 (TC), TC02782.

[4.104] In April 2013 a woman appealed against her 2013/14 notice of coding. In August 2013 HMRC sent her an explanation of the code, which was followed by further correspondence. In May 2014 HMRC applied for the appeal to be struck out on the ground that the code had expired. Judge Poole granted the application. *Ms P Stewart v HMRC*, FTT [2014] UKFTT 927 (TC), TC04040.

[4.105] See also *Allen v HMRC*, **24.9** ERROR OR MISTAKE RELIEF, and *Mrs P Sutton v HMRC*, **52.11** SAVINGS AND INVESTMENT INCOME.

SI 2009/273, rule 8—application to strike out part of appeal

[4.106] Following the CA decision in *R (oao Shiner) v HMRC*, **21.44** DOUBLE TAX RELIEF, HMRC issued closure notices and amendments to S's tax returns for 2005/06 to 2007/08. S appealed against the closure notices. HMRC applied to the First-tier Tribunal for part of the appeals to be struck out on the grounds that they were an attempt to relitigate matters which had been settled by the CA decision. Judge Kempster accepted this contention and granted HMRC's application, holding that the CA decision was a 'binding authority', so that 'any debate before this Tribunal on the point would be a foregone conclusion'. *I Shiner v HMRC (No 2) (and related application)*, FTT [2014] UKFTT 372 (TC), TC03505.

SI 2009/273, rule 8—application to strike out HMRC's case

[4.107] HMRC issued assessments on two brothers, charging tax on income from an overseas trust. They appealed to the First-tier Tribunal, and lodged an application under *SI 2009/273, rule 8* for HMRC's Statement of Case to be struck out. The First-tier Tribunal dismissed the application. *R & S Thomas v HMRC (No 3)*, FTT [2014] UKFTT 273 (TC), TC03412. (*Note*. For previous proceedings involving these appellants, see *R (oao HMRC) v Berkshire Commrs*, **29.124** FURTHER ASSESSMENTS: LOSS OF TAX; *R & S Thomas v HMRC (No 1)*, **55.23** SELF-ASSESSMENT, and *R & S Thomas v HMRC (No 2)*, **4.380** below. For subsequent developments in this case, see **4.111** below.)

SI 2009/273, rule 8—application to strike out part of HMRC's case

[4.108] A partnership acquired a property in 1996 and sold it in 2002. In its tax return it declared a capital gain on the sale, and claimed business asset taper relief. Following an enquiry into the return, HMRC issued an amendment to the partnership's self-assessment, charging income tax on the basis that the sale was part of the partnership's trading activities. The partnership appealed. In HMRC's Statement of Case for the hearing of the appeal, they included an alternative contention that, if the tribunal should find that the transaction was an investment activity, the sale did not qualify for business asset taper relief. The partnership applied for this part of the Case to be struck out, contending that this argument had not been referred to in HMRC's original closure notice. The First-tier Tribunal rejected the partnership's application, applying the principles laid down in *Chappell v HMRC*, **4.23** above. Judge Berner observed that 'although HMRC's conclusion and their amendments reflected the trading issue, the subject matter of the enquiry, and of the conclusion, was the purchase and sale of the property'. Accordingly, 'the purchase and sale is the scope of the appeal over which the Tribunal has jurisdiction. The arguments of HMRC as regards the calculation of a chargeable gain, in the event that their trading argument does not succeed, and the appropriate application of taper relief, is within the scope of the subject matter of the conclusion and the scope of the appeal. The consequence of HMRC's conclusion on the trading issue was not only an amendment of the partnership return to increase the trading profit; it also had the consequence of reducing the capital gains computation to zero. If the tribunal were to find for the appellant on the trading profits point, the result would be to restore the appellant's self-assessment for capital gains. Simply to restore the appellant's calculation, including the application of business asset taper relief, would not be consistent with the duty of the tribunal to determine the amount of tax payable.' *Orchid Properties v HMRC (No 1)*, FTT [2010] UKFTT 329 (TC), TC00614. (*Note*. For subsequent developments in this case, see **4.393** below.)

[4.109] In the case noted at **18.6** CORPORATION TAX, a company (F) entered into a complex scheme designed to produce a substantial loss for tax purposes. HMRC began an enquiry and issued a closure notice stating that the effect of *FA 1996, Sch 9 para 19A* was that the actual loss was very much less than F had claimed. F appealed. In HMRC's Statement of Case, they sought to defend the closure notice by virtue of *FA 1996, Sch 9 para 13* as well as of *para 19A*. F applied for this part of the Statement of Case to be struck out. The First-tier

Tribunal rejected the application and the Upper Tribunal dismissed F's appeal against this decision, applying the Supreme Court decision in *HMRC v Tower Mcashback LLP1*, 4.22 above. *Fidex Ltd v HMRC (No 1)*, UT [2014] UKUT 454 (TCC).

SI 2009/273, rule 8—application to bar HMRC from appeal

[4.110] In a VAT case, where the substantive issue has been superseded by *FA 2011*, the appellant company applied for HMRC to be barred from an appeal for persistently failing to comply with Tribunal directions. Judge Mosedale granted the application but the Upper Tribunal reversed her decision, holding that it had been 'outside the reasonable exercise of judicial discretion'. Judge Bishopp held that HMRC's failings were 'not so grave as to warrant a barring order'. *HMRC v BPP University College of Professional Studies v HMRC (No 1)*, UT [2014] UKUT 496 (TCC).

[4.111] Following the decision in *R & S Thomas v HMRC (No 3)*, 4.107 above, the appellants lodged an application for HMRC to be barred from the proceedings. The First-tier Tribunal dismissed the application. *R & S Thomas v HMRC (No 4)*, FTT [2014] UKFTT 640 (TC), TC03764.

SI 2009/273, rule 9—application by third party to be joined in appeal

[4.112] In the case noted at 3.65 ANTI-AVOIDANCE, which concerned the transfer of a business from the UK to Gibraltar, the Government of Gibraltar applied to be joined in the appeal. The First-tier Tribunal dismissed the application. Judge Raghavan held that the Government of Gibraltar did not have 'a sufficient interest in the proceedings between the appellants and HMRC to become a party to the proceedings'. *Mrs A Fisher v HMRC (and related appeals) (No 2)*, FTT [2014] UKFTT 805 (TC), TC03922.

SI 2009/273, rule 15—admissible evidence

[4.113] In the case noted at 59.108 TRADING INCOME, HMRC submitted a witness statement by a chartered accountant. The partnership applied for this statement to be excluded, contending that it was not 'reasonably required to resolve the proceedings', within *Civil Procedure Rules, rule 35*. The First-tier Tribunal rejected this contention and dismissed the application, holding that it should hear the accountant's evidence at the hearing of the appeal, and observing that the relevance of his evidence 'will not be fully apparent until we have heard the case fully presented by each side'. *Eclipse Film Partners No 35 Llp v HMRC (No 3)*, FTT [2011] UKFTT 401 (TC), TC01256.

[4.114] HMRC began an enquiry into the returns submitted by two Jersey partnerships. They formed the opinion that the partnerships had been established to implement a marketed tax avoidance scheme and were not carrying on any trade. They issued amendments to the partnership returns. The partnerships appealed, and submitted a witness statement by an accountant (S) who was employed as a consultant by the company which had promoted the scheme. HMRC applied for some paragraphs of S's witness statement to be excluded on the basis that they were expert evidence rather than evidence of a witness of fact. The First-tier Tribunal dismissed HMRC's application. Judge Sinfield accepted the companies' contention that S's evidence 'was not expert evidence but direct evidence of how the swaps and leasing markets worked based on his experience in banking'. Some of S's evidence was hearsay, but 'the Tribunal can and does accept hearsay evidence, although it will carry less weight than direct evidence'. *The Leasing No 1 Partnership v HMRC (and related appeal)*, FTT [2014] UKFTT 360 (TC), TC03495.

[4.115] Following the decision in *Foulser & Foulser v MacDougall*, **71.260** CAPITAL GAINS TAX, the case was remitted to the First-tier Tribunal to consider the amount of the assessment. After the beginning of the hearing, the appellants lodged an application that the tribunal should decline to admit further evidence from HMRC, since their tax adviser had been arrested on suspicion of cheating the public revenue and false accounting, and following his arrest, HMRC had obtained information relating to their tax affairs which they considered to be legally privileged. The First-tier Tribunal dismissed the application, holding that it did not have the jurisdiction to make the order sought. Judge Berner held that any allegation that 'prosecutors have been guilty of such serious misbehaviour that they ought not to be allowed to benefit to the defendant's detriment' would be a matter for the High Court. However, the Upper Tribunal remitted the case for rehearing. Morgan J expressed the view that Judge Berner appeared to have misunderstood one of the appellants' contentions. He held that the First-tier Tribunal had jurisdiction to determine the tax appeal under *TMA 1970*, and that if the information which HMRC had obtained had produced a risk of unfairness, it was for the First-tier Tribunal to make appropriate directions. *B & D Foulser v HMRC*, UT [2013] UKUT 38 (TCC); [2013] STC 917. (*Note.* For subsequent developments in this case, see **43.19** PAYMENT OF TAX.)

SI 2009/273, rule 16—application for disclosure

[4.116] Three associated limited liability partnerships claimed that they had incurred substantial trading losses, and that the partners were entitled to substantial tax relief against their other income. HMRC began an enquiry, and subsequently issued closure notices rejecting the claims on the basis that the partnerships' activities did not amount to trading. The partnerships appealed. HMRC requested the partnerships to disclose certain documents in accordance with *SI 2009/273, rule 16*. (HMRC accepted that as the partnerships had lodged appeals, it was no longer appropriate to adopt the procedure under *FA 2008, Sch 36 para 1*.) The Upper Tribunal ordered the partnerships to disclose the documents requested by HMRC. Newey J held that it would be 'unfair and unjust' for the partnerships 'to be able to suppress or keep from the view of HMRC and the FTT relevant documents which may be harmful to their case, as a consequence of the limitation on the extent of HMRC's inspection of documents during the investigatory stage as a result of a sensible co-operative approach to the conduct of the investigation which was agreed as being in the interests of both sides'. (However, Newey J rejected HMRC's application for a 'third party disclosure order' against a television company which had had some dealings with the partnerships.) *HMRC v Ingenious Games Llp (and related applications)*, UT [2014] UKUT 62 (TCC); [2014] STC 1416.

SI 2009/273, rule 16(4)—application for witness summons to be set aside

[4.117] A limited partnership (C), one of whose members was a company (G), submitted a return claiming that it had made a loss of £60,000,000. Following an enquiry, HMRC rejected the claim. C appealed, and applied for witness summonses to be issued to two of G's former directors (M and Y), who were resident in Jersey. M and Y applied for the summonses to be set aside under *SI 2009/273, rule 16(4)*, contending that C had failed to reply to questions which they had asked concerning the appeal, and 'had failed to make full disclosure to the Tribunal when applying for the issue of the summons'. Judge Mosedale accepted this contention and granted the applications, finding that 'only if the applicants had been provided with answers and still refused to give evidence should the Tribunal have been approached to issue a summons'. *Clavis Liberty Fund 1 Lp v HMRC*, FTT [2014] UKFTT 1077 (TC), TC04166.

SI 2009/273, rule 17—application for appeal to be reinstated

[4.118] In a case where the facts were broadly similar to *HMRC v Tower Mcashback LLP1*, **8.79** CAPITAL ALLOWANCES, a limited liability partnership appealed against a closure notice. Following correspondence, the partner who had lodged the appeal wrote to the Tribunal withdrawing it. Another partner subsequently applied for the appeal to be reinstated. The First-tier Tribunal rejected the application. Judge Sinfield held that the appeal 'would not have any reasonable prospect of success'. *Tower Mcashback 3 LLP v HMRC*, FTT [2014] UKFTT 1081 (TC), TC04170.

SI 2009/273, rule 19—proceedings without notice

[4.119] See *Dr AM Skelly v HMRC (and related applications)*, **49.108** RETURNS AND INFORMATION.

SI 2009/273, rule 32—application for appeal to be heard in private

[4.120] Applications for appeals to be heard in private were dismissed in *Consultant Services Group Ltd v HMRC*, FTT [2014] UKFTT 197 (TC), TC03337, and in *Mr A v HMRC*, **4.150** below.

SI 2009/273, rule 38—application for decision to be set aside

[4.121] In the case noted at **42.63** PAY AS YOU EARN, a Special Commissioner (sitting in London) upheld a determination under what is now *Income Tax (PAYE) Regulations 2003 (SI 2003/2682), reg 80* on the basis that a civil engineering contractor (W) was acting as an employer. W subsequently applied for the decision to be set aside, contending that he had requested that the case should be heard in Colchester (where his local General Commissioners had sat) and on a different date. Judge Wallace granted the application, observing that it was 'unfortunate' that the case had been heard while W's adviser (a retired accountant) was on holiday, and that it was not clear 'why the matter was listed in London'. He noted that 'the appeal involved a very substantial sum for a sole trader' and that this was 'the type of case where the inequality of arms is particularly unfortunate'. Furthermore, HMRC had failed to comply with the Management Directions, as they had failed to serve their skeleton argument on the appellant, which was 'particularly serious since the appellant had no professional representation'. Accordingly it was 'in the interests of justice that the decision should be set aside and that the appeal should be listed for rehearing by the First-tier Tribunal in Colchester'. *PJ Wright v HMRC (No 3)*, FTT [2009] SFTD 748; [2009] UKFTT 227 (TC), TC00177.

[4.122] In a case where a partnership had appealed against a penalty for failing to file a return, Judge Poole held that 'the function of the Tribunal is to provide efficient resolution of disputes between taxpayers and HMRC. Whilst some latitude may be allowed for taxpayers who are inexperienced in presenting their case, it would completely undermine the Tribunal's function if it were routinely to allow losing parties (whether taxpayers or HMRC) to relitigate appeals on the basis that they did not feel they had put sufficient evidence before the Tribunal when it first heard the appeal. Parties should be well aware that an appeal offers a one-off opportunity to put their case as best they can, not an opportunity to hope for successful outcome on the basis of minimal effort and then make a better second attempt if the first fails, possibly followed by an even better third attempt, and so on. To put it in layman's terms, an appellant must realise that the appeals system gives him one bite at the cherry unless a very good reason can be shown why he should have a second.' *D Fraser v HMRC*, FTT [2012] UKFTT 189 (TC), TC01884.

[4.123] In a case where the First-tier Tribunal had dismissed an appeal by an accountancy firm against a penalty (see **44.267** PENALTIES), the firm subsequently applied for the decision to be set aside. The tribunal dismissed the application. *Rennie Smith & Co v HMRC (No 2)*, FTT [2013] UKFTT 638 (TC), TC03023.

[4.124] A similar decision was reached in *Leggett Porter & Howard Executive Pension Fund v HMRC*, FTT [2014] UKFTT 933 (TC), TC04046.

[4.125] In one of the cases noted at **49.98** RETURNS AND INFORMATION, the First-tier Tribunal dismissed an appeal against a notice under *FA 2008, Sch 36 para 1*. The appellant failed to attend the hearing (which had been postponed twice), but subsequently applied for the decision to be set aside. The tribunal dismissed the application. Judge Sinfield observed that 'it is clearly not in the interests of justice to set aside a decision that was correctly decided simply because one of the parties is not present'. *Mrs P Lee v HMRC (No 2)*, FTT [2012] UKFTT 434 (TC), TC02116.

[4.126] In the case noted at **29.60** FURTHER ASSESSMENTS: LOSS OF TAX, the unsuccessful appellant subsequently applied to the First-tier Tribunal for Judge Nowlan's decision to be set aside. Judge Berner rejected his application. *P Daniel v HMRC (No 3)*, FTT [2014] UKFTT 916 (TC), TC04030.

[4.127] In the case noted at **44.80** PENALTIES, the First-tier Tribunal allowed an appeal against a penalty, finding that HMRC had not proved that the appellant had submitted a paper return before submitting an online return. HMRC subsequently lodged an application for the decision to be set aside. Judge Brannan rejected the application, applying the principles laid down by Judge Poole in *Fraser v HMRC*, **4.122** above. *T Rosenbaum's Executor v HMRC (No 2)*, FTT [2013] UKFTT 495 (TC), TC02884.

Late appeals

Application dismissed

[4.128] In 2007 a trader applied to make late appeals against an assessment for 2002/03, and amendments to self-assessments for 2003/04 and 2004/05. The First-tier Tribunal dismissed the application, holding that there was no 'reasonable excuse for bringing these appeals out of time'. (The tribunal also dismissed appeals against assessments for 1999/2000 and 2000/01, and an amendment to the trader's self-assessment for 2001/02. The tribunal was very critical of the trader's tax adviser, who was a former Inland Revenue employee, concluding that the trader 'may wish to review carefully the advice she has received from and the actings of her tax adviser'.) *Mrs M McCrae v HMRC*, FTT [2009] UKFTT 55 (TC); TC00034; TC00123.

[4.129] A similar decision was reached in a case where the First-tier Tribunal applied the principles laid down by Morgan J in the VAT case of *Data Select Ltd v HMRC*, UT [2012] UKUT 187 (TCC); [2012] STC 2195. *A McMullan v HMRC*, FTT [2013] UKFTT 640 (TC), TC03025.

[4.130] An application to lodge a late appeal, following an amendment to a partnership return, was dismissed in *Mrs AW Gibbs v HMRC*, FTT [2013] UKFTT 236 (TC), TC02650.

[4.131] Applications to lodge late appeals were also dismissed in *A MacDonald v HMRC*, FTT [2010] UKFTT 172 (TC), TC00476; *M Leliunga v HMRC*, FTT [2010] UKFTT 229 (TC), TC00530; *Mrs CA Spencer v HMRC*, FTT [2010] UKFTT 370 (TC), TC00652; *R Legg v HMRC*, FTT [2010] UKFTT 562 (TC), TC00813; *Park Property World Ltd v HMRC*, FTT [2010] UKFTT 617 (TC), TC00859; *M Zafar v HMRC*, FTT [2010] UKFTT 619 (TC), TC00861; *Martin & Gaynor O'Hearne Properties Ltd v HMRC*, FTT [2011] UKFTT 86 (TC), TC00963; *KP O'Brien v HMRC*, FTT [2011] UKFTT 103 (TC), TC00979; *G Sadiq v HMRC*, FTT [2011] UKFTT 144 (TC), TC01018; *A Ali v HMRC*, FTT [2011] UKFTT 180 (TC), TC01049; *A Rue v HMRC*, FTT [2011] UKFTT 205 (TC), TC01070; *KJ Carver v HMRC*, FTT [2011] UKFTT 323 (TC), TC01183; *J Harouni v HMRC*, FTT [2011] UKFTT 361 (TC), TC01216; *JS Digpal v HMRC*, FTT [2011] UKFTT 484 (TC), TC01331; *R Ali v HMRC*, FTT [2011] UKFTT 490 (TC), TC01337; *Mrs S Bohra v HMRC*, FTT [2011] UKFTT 531 (TC), TC01378; *Pen Associates Europe Ltd v HMRC*, FTT [2011] UKFTT 554 (TC), TC01399; *K Welch v HMRC*, FTT [2011] UKFTT 565 (TC), TC01410; *M Squire v HMRC*, FTT [2011] UKFTT 770 (TC), TC01607; *R Camps v HMRC*, FTT [2011] UKFTT 777 (TC), TC01611; *D Porter v HMRC*, FTT [2012] UKFTT 87 (TC), TC01783, *P MacGregor v HMRC*, FTT [2012] UKFTT 168 (TC), TC01864; *N Galvin v HMRC*, FTT [2012] UKFTT 280 (TC) TC01968; *Bansons v HMRC*, FTT [2012] UKFTT 396 (TC) TC02080; *Cristel Ltd v HMRC*, FTT [2012] UKFTT 400 (TC) TC02095; *P Wallace v HMRC (No 1)*, FTT [2012] UKFTT 433 (TC), TC02115; *S Bell v HMRC*, FTT [2012] UKFTT 534 (TC), TC02210; *Ellenwell Properties Ltd v HMRC*, FTT [2013] UKFTT 74 (TC), TC02492; *P Wallace v HMRC (No 2)*, FTT [2013] UKFTT 227 (TC), TC02641; *Kent County Council v HMRC*, FTT [2013] UKFTT 327 (TC), TC02730; *LA Davidson v HMRC*, FTT [2013] UKFTT 372 (TC), TC02771;

D McLoughlin v HMRC, FTT [2013] UKFTT 567 (TC), TC02956; *K Guthrie & N Walsh (t/a the Railway Tavern) v HMRC*, FTT [2013] UKFTT 592 (TC), TC02981; *F Bamgbopa v HMRC*, FTT [2013] UKFTT 664 (TC), TC03046; *MP Mandagie v HMRC*, FTT [2013] UKFTT 672 (TC), TC03054; *E Akinlade v HMRC*, FTT [2014] UKFTT 291 (TC), TC03430; *N Archer v HMRC*, FTT [2014] UKFTT 423 (TC), TC03552; *O O'Hara v Serious Organised Crime Agency*, FTT [2014] UKFTT 500 (TC), TC03627; *Miss J Lawford v HMRC*, FTT [2014] UKFTT 583 (TC), TC03707; *D Conquer v HMRC*, FTT [2014] UKFTT 612 (TC), TC03737; *Finchley United Services Club Ltd v HMRC*, FTT [2014] UKFTT 763 (TC), TC03883; *Somes Creation Ltd v HMRC*, FTT [2014] UKFTT 777 (TC), TC03895; *Upton Park Halal Meat & Poultry v HMRC (and related appeals)*, FTT [2014] UKFTT 784 (TC), TC03901; *EM Wilkins & KM Oldershaw (t/a Get Your Life Back) v HMRC*, FTT [2014] UKFTT 809 (TC), TC03926; *A Okubuto v HMRC*, FTT [2014] UKFTT 820 (TC), TC03937; *TC Chen v HMRC*, FTT [2014] UKFTT 848 (TC), TC03965; *M Howes v HMRC (No 2)*, FTT [2014] UKFTT 886 (TC), TC04001; *A Mathers v HMRC*, FTT [2014] UKFTT 893 (TC), TC04008; *A Palmiero v HMRC*, FTT [2014] UKFTT 922 (TC), TC04036; *G Santo v HMRC*, FTT [2014] UKFTT 961 (TC), TC04073; *A & Mrs F Pia v HMRC*, FTT [2014] UKFTT 1015 (TC), TC04111, and *C Burns v HMRC*, FTT [2014] UKFTT 1053 (TC), TC04146.

Application allowed

[4.132] The First-tier Tribunal allowed an application to lodge a late appeal in a case where a former publican (L) had suffered brain damage following a heart attack, and had been evicted from the public house which he ran. The tribunal observed that there was 'serious doubt' whether L had received some letters which HMRC had posted to him, and held that, in view of his medical history, 'it would be in the interests of justice to allow this application'. *G Lupson v HMRC*, FTT [2011] UKFTT 100 (TC), TC00976.

[4.133] A company (P) failed to respond to queries from HMRC concerning its tax return. In January 2009 HMRC issued an amendment to the return. In June 2009 P applied to lodge a late appeal against the amendment. HMRC opposed the application but the First-tier Tribunal granted it. Judge Brannan held that 'the prejudice to the appellant of being unable to advance an arguably meritorious appeal outweighed its dilatoriness and any prejudice to HMRC'. *Pytchley Ltd v HMRC*, FTT [2010] UKFTT 277 (TC), TC01139.

[4.134] An accountant (M) applied to lodge a late appeal against a surcharge notice. HMRC opposed the application but the First-tier Tribunal granted it. Judge Staker held that the case was 'very finely balanced', but observed that the appeal had only been 47 days late, and that M had a 'good record as a taxpayer'. *D Mond v HMRC*, FTT [2011] UKFTT 374 (TC), TC01229.

[4.135] The First-tier Tribunal granted an application to lodge a late appeal against a penalty in a case where the applicant stated that he had never received a letter which HMRC claimed to have sent on 4 June 2010, requiring him to file a return. Judge Geraint Jones observed that HMRC had 'not seen fit to exhibit a copy' of the letter which they claimed to have sent, and that it was possible that HMRC had not in fact sent it, or that it had been sent but 'went astray in the post'. On the evidence, HMRC had never told the applicant 'which kind of tax return he was required to complete'. *A Armstrong v HMRC*, FTT [2011] UKFTT 799 (TC), TC01635.

[4.136] HMRC began an enquiry into a partnership. In December 2008 they issued closure notices and amendments. In March 2012, following discussions with the HMRC Debt Management Unit, the partners applied for permission to lodge late appeals, contending that they had never received the closure notices and amendments. Judge Cannan accepted the partners' evidence and granted the applications. *Advance Consulting v HMRC (and related appeals)*, FTT [2012] UKFTT 567 (TC), TC02245.

[4.137] The appellant in the case noted at **61.54** TRADING INCOME had applied to lodge a late appeal against the rejection of his claim for loss relief. The First-tier Tribunal granted his application. Judge Radford found that he had been misinformed by HMRC and by his previous accountant, and 'had a reasonable excuse for making the late appeal'. *HL Amah v HMRC (No 1)*, FTT [2013] UKFTT 409 (TC), TC02805. (*Note*. Obiter dicta of Judge Radford were subsequently disapproved by Judge Cornwell-Kelly—see **61.54** TRADING INCOME.)

[4.138] The First-tier Tribunal granted an application to lodge a late appeal by a trader (M) who provided services to drivers who had been involved in road accidents, including introducing them to solicitors who would pursue claims on a 'no win no fee' basis. M had submitted returns on a cash basis, but HMRC had issued notices of amendment on the basis that his accounts should have been drawn up on an accruals basis. Judge Nowlan observed that there was a genuine dispute as to the correct basis on which M's accounts should have been prepared, and that 'because the accountant has persisted in the belief that the cash basis is the appropriate basis on which to recognise all receipts, and because all later accounts have been prepared on that basis, it is only by allowing the late appeal that the appellant has any chance of avoiding what will otherwise be the inequity of being taxed on £75,000 more income than it (*sic*) will ultimately have received'. *S Mahmood (t/a Elite Claims) v HMRC*, FTT [2013] UKFTT 518 (TC), TC02906.

[4.139] In March 2000 HMRC began an enquiry into the returns submitted by a hairdresser (D). D moved from the UK to Spain later that month. In May 2000 HMRC issued amendments to D's self-assessments for 1997/98 and 1998/99. D returned to the UK in 2012, and subsequently applied to lodge late appeals against the 1997/98 and 1998/99 amendments, contending that she had been unaware of the liability. The First-tier Tribunal granted her application. *Mrs CL Davison v HMRC*, FTT [2013] UKFTT 743 (TC), TC03121.

[4.140] In March 2013 HMRC issued a protective CGT assessment for 2006/07 on an individual (P) who had sold a property during that year. In May 2013 P's accountant submitted a revised calculation of the gain. HMRC did not treat this letter as an appeal. In August 2013 P formally applied to lodge a late appeal against the assessment. Judge Powell granted the application, holding that the letter which P's accountant had submitted in May 2013 should have been treated as an appeal, and observing that 'the appellant and his representative co-operated from the outset'. *C Patel v HMRC*, FTT [2014] UKFTT 668 (TC), TC03791.

Appeal sent by fax—whether valid

[4.141] HMRC began an enquiry into a company (G) which operated several retail pharmacies. On 23 July 2009 they issued 'jeopardy amendments' to G's self-assessments, increasing its tax liability by more than £1,000,000. On 21 August G's accountant sent HMRC a fax stating that he would 'be sending appeal and postponement applications to those amendments in due course'. The HMRC officer dealing with the case treated this as an expression of intention rather than a formal appeal. Subsequently HMRC began action to collect the debt, and G sent a further fax indicating that it was appealing against the amendments. HMRC treated this as an application to make a late appeal, and rejected it on the grounds that there was no reasonable excuse for the delay. G lodged an application with the First-tier Tribunal, contending firstly that the fax which it had sent on 21 August had been a valid notice of appeal (and was within the statutory time limit), and alternatively that it had a reasonable excuse for not having appealed with the statutory limit. The First-tier Tribunal accepted these contentions and allowed the applications, finding that 'the fax of 21 August 2009 was sufficient to amount to a valid appeal against the amendments made'. *Greenoaks Pharmacy Ltd v HMRC*, FTT [2011] UKFTT 254 (TC), TC01118.

Late notification of appeal to Tribunal—application of TMA, s 49G

[4.142] A company (G) claimed a deduction for a payment to an employee benefit trust. HMRC issued an assessment disallowing the claim. G's accountants appealed and requested a review. HMRC reviewed the assessment and upheld it in December 2011. G did not notify the First-tier Tribunal of its appeal, as required by *TMA, s 49G*. However, after further correspondence with HMRC, G sent an application to notify its appeal to the Tribunal in January 2014. Judge Brooks granted the application, observing that G appeared to have an arguable case, and had relied upon the accountants who had established the employee benefit trust and had corresponded with HMRC on its behalf, but had subsequently ceased to act for it. *Greenwich Investments Ltd v HMRC*, FTT [2014] UKFTT 822 (TC), TC03939.

Late notification of appeal to Tribunal—application of TMA, s 49H

[4.143] A trader (R) appealed against three discovery assessments and a closure notice. He appealed in April 2008, and the appeals were stood over. Following the replacement of the General Commissioners by the First-tier Tribunal with effect from April 2009, HMRC wrote to R offering a review of the assessments. R did not respond to HMRC's letter, but in April 2010 he applied to notify the appeals to the First-tier Tribunal under *TMA, s 49H*. Sir Stephen Oliver granted the application, observing that R's appeals had been lodged within the statutory time limit and that it was 'in the interests of the administration of justice that permission under *section 49H* should be given'. *DL Roberts v HMRC*, FTT [2011] UKFTT 385 (TC), TC01240.

[4.144] In February 2009 an employee (M) lodged an appeal against a notice from HMRC rejecting a claim to seafarers' earnings deduction. In April 2009 M moved to the USA, without informing HMRC. On 29 April 2009 HMRC wrote to M's UK address stating that, following the introduction of the new tribunal system, 'you have until 18 May 2009 to have requested either an independent review of your appeal by HMRC or have made an application directly to the Tribunal Service'. On 27 May 2009 HMRC again wrote to M's UK address, purporting to agree the appeal under *TMA, s 54*. In March 2012 M returned to the UK. In December 2012, M wrote to HMRC stating that he was appealing against the tax allegedly owed. HMRC treated this as an appeal against their letter of 27 May 2009, and declined to accept it. M then lodged an appeal with the First-tier Tribunal. Judge Ruthven Gemmell issued a direction under *TMA, s 49H(3)* that the substantive appeal should proceed. He observed that, although HMRC had offered a review under *TMA, s 49C*, M had not accepted this, and that HMRC had failed to make any further enquiries as to M's intentions. *I Menzies v HMRC*, FTT [2013] UKFTT 376 (TC), TC02775.

Miscellaneous

TMA, s 31—right of appeal against partnership assessments

[4.145] See *Mcashback Software 6 Llp v HMRC*, **41.55** PARTNERSHIPS.

Whether HMRC may cite pre-1995 Special Commissioners' decision

[4.146] In *Ardmore Construction Ltd v HMRC*, **33.12** INTEREST PAYABLE, HMRC cited an unpublished Special Commissioners' decision, dating from before 1995, as an authority. Judge Brooks observed that 'given that the judicial function of the Special Commissioners was originally derived from (*ITA 1842, ss 130, 131*), there must be thousands of unpublished decisions known by and available only to HMRC'. Applying the principles laid down by Lord Diplock in *Fothergill v Monarch Airlines Ltd*, HL [1981] AC 251, he held that it was inappropriate 'for HMRC to cite an unpublished decision of the Special Commissioners before the FTT'.

Application for stay of proceedings

[4.147] In 2009 the High Court made a 'freezing order' against two individuals who had been suspected of VAT fraud. In November 2010 the Serious Organised Crime Agency raised assessments under *POCA 2002, s 317*, charging income tax of more than £300,000 on each of them. They appealed, and applied for the appeals to be stayed pending the determination of the High Court proceedings against them. The First-tier Tribunal rejected this application. Judge Clark held that there was no justification for a stay of the proceedings. *ME & A Peries v SOCA*, FTT [2011] UKFTT 674 (TC), TC01516.

Application to amend grounds of appeal

[4.148] In the case noted at **71.81** CAPITAL GAINS TAX, an ccountant began business in 1981 and transferred his business to an associated company in 2003. HMRC issued an amendment to his self-assessment, increasing the CGT liability on the disposal, and he appealed, contending that the amendment understated the valuation of the goodwill of his business at March 1982. He subsequently applied to amend the grounds of appeal to include a contention that the valuation of the business at the date of disposal was excessive. HMRC opposed the application, but the First-tier Tribunal granted it. Judge Mosedale held that 'neither the delay nor extra costs are grounds on which leave to amend the grounds of appeal should be refused'. *GM Wildin v HMRC (No 1)*, FTT [2012] UKFTT 86 (TC), TC01782.

Application for decision to be anonymised

[4.149] In the case noted at 18.58 CORPORATION TAX, the appellant company applied for the decision to be anonymised. The First-tier Tribunal rejected this contention. Judge Barton held that the Tribunal Rules 'do not contain any specific provision relative to the publication of a decision', and held that 'it is not enough that a taxpayer wishes to conceal his private affairs from others'. *Reddleman Properties Ltd v HMRC*, FTT [2011] UKFTT 395 (TC), TC01250.

[4.150] A broadcaster submitted a tax return claiming that he had made a loss. HMRC discovered that the alleged loss resulted from the broadcaster's use of a tax avoidance scheme, and issued an amendment rejecting the claim. The broadcaster appealed, and made a preliminary application for the hearing to be in private and for the decision to be anonymised. The First-tier Tribunal rejected the application. Judge Bishopp observed that 'there is an obvious public interest in its being clear that the tax system is being operated even-handedly, an interest which would be compromised if hearings before this tribunal were in private save in the most compelling of circumstances'. *Mr A v HMRC*, FTT [2012] UKFTT 541 (TC); [2012] SFTD 1257, TC02217. (Note. For the substantive appeal, see 59.100 TRADING INCOME.)

[4.151] In *Mr & Mrs Chan v HMRC*, 75.26 STAMP DUTY LAND TAX, where HMRC had imposed a penalty on a solicitor (C) who had submitted an inaccurate SDLT return, Judge Mosedale rejected C's application for the decision to be anonymised, but noted that he would have the opportunity to appeal to the Upper Tribunal. She concluded that 'my decision on anonymity and/or my decision on the application for permission could be appealed, and in that sense they are not final'. She therefore agreed to 'anonymise this decision until the appeal process on both aspects of my decision is exhausted'. C did not appeal to the Upper Tribunal, and the Tribunal Centre subsequently republished the decision without anonymisation.

Appeals to the Upper Tribunal

Application for late appeal

[4.152] In a VAT case, the Upper Tribunal rejected an application by HMRC to lodge a late appeal. Judge Sinfield held that 'it would not be consistent with the need to ensure that appeals in the Upper Tribunal are conducted efficiently to allow HMRC to serve a notice of appeal almost two months after the time limit has expired'. *HMRC v McCarthy & Stone Developments Ltd*, UT [2014] UKUT 196 (TCC); [2014] STC 973. (*Note. Obiter dicta* of Judge Sinfield were subsequently disapproved by Judge Bishopp in *Leeds City Council v HMRC*, 4.453 below.)

[4.153] HMRC formed the opinion that a publican (F) had failed to operate PAYE on some payments to employees. In August 2009 they issued notices of determination. F did not appeal, and in October 2010 HMRC issued a statutory demand. Subsequently F applied to lodge a late appeal against the determinations. The First-tier Tribunal rejected the application but the Upper Tribunal remitted the case to a different judge for reconsideration. Judge Berner held that the First-tier Tribunal had 'directed its attention almost exclusively to the question whether (F) had a reasonable excuse for failing to make an appeal within the proper time limits', when it should also 'have considered the merits of the proposed appeal'. *D O'Flaherty v HMRC*, UT [2013] UKUT 161 (TCC); [2013] STC 1946.

Application for hearing to take place in private

[4.154] In *HMRC v Sir AF Morrison (and cross-appeal)*, **71.121** CAPITAL GAINS TAX, the Upper Tribunal rejected an application for its hearing of the appeals to take place in private. Lord Glennie held that 'the court will not depart from the principle of open justice simply to save one or other party from embarrassment'.

Judicial review application to Upper Tribunal—procedure

[4.155] In the case noted at **42.39** PAY AS YOU EARN, several associated companies appealed to the First-tier Tribunal and also applied to the Upper Tribunal for judicial review. The appropriate procedure was considered by Warren J and Judge Avery Jones, sitting as judges of both tribunals. The judges decided (by the casting vote of Warren J) that the tax appeal should be heard first in the First-tier Tribunal, with the judicial review proceedings being dealt with in the Upper Tribunal only in the light of the decision of the First-tier Tribunal. Accordingly, the tax appeal should be heard by the First-tier Tribunal, and the judicial review proceedings would be stayed until 28 days after the First-tier Tribunal decision. *Reed Employment plc v HMRC (No 2) (and related appeals)*, UT 2010, [2011] STC 695. (*Note*. At a subsequent hearing, the Upper Tribunal dismissed the companies' applications for judicial review, finding that the companies had been 'less than forthcoming' with HMRC—UT [2014] UKUT 160 (TCC).)

Appeals to the High Court and above

Stated Case procedure

NOTE

The Stated Case procedure applied to the Special Commissioners until 31 August 1994, and to the General Commissioners until they were replaced by the First-tier Tribunal with effect from 1 April 2009: see the note at the head of this chapter.

General principles

Commissioners refusing demand for Stated Case

[4.156] In a Scottish case, General Commissioners dismissed several appeals by a restaurant proprietor (R). He requested a Stated Case. The Commissioners rejected his request on the ground that no point of law was involved. R applied for judicial review. The CS granted his application, finding that the Commissioners had acted unreasonably, and ordered the Commissioners to produce a Stated Case. *Rouf (t/a The New Balaka Restaurant) v Dundee Commrs*, CS 2006, [2008] STC 1557; [2006] CSOH 195. (*Note.* For subsequent developments in this case, see *Rouf v HMRC*, **29.65** FURTHER ASSESSMENTS: LOSS OF TAX.)

[4.157] The Ch D reached a similar decision in *R (oao Coombes) v Guildford & Wotton Commrs*, QB [2006] EWHC 1483 (Admin). (*Note.* For subsequent developments in this case, see **71.163** CAPITAL GAINS TAX.)

[4.158] An individual (J) appealed against assessments for 1995/96 and 1996/97. In February 2009 the General Commissioners dismissed his appeals, and J requested a Stated Case. The Commissioners asked J to identify 'the question of law on which he required a case to be stated'. J refused to comply with this request. The Commissioners therefore refused to state a Case, and J applied for judicial review. The CS dismissed his application. Lord Bracadale observed that J had failed to provide any 'sensible explanation' for refusing to identify a question of law, and that 'relatively general questions of law could easily have been focused'. He specifically distinguished the 2006 decision in *Rouf (t/a The New Balaka Restaurant) v Dundee Commrs*, **4.156** above. *Jesner v Renfrew Commrs*, CS [2010] STC 1045; [2010] CSOH 23.

Whether successful party can demand Stated Case

[4.159] The Special Commissioners discharged an assessment but the appellant requested a Stated Case. The Ch D held that there were no grounds for appeal, and awarded costs to the Revenue. *Sharpey-Schafer v Venn*, Ch D 1955, 34 ATC 141; [1955] TR 143.

[4.160] In the case noted at **71.221** CAPITAL GAINS TAX, the Special Commissioner had dismissed an appeal. The appellant demanded a Stated Case. The Revenue also expressed dissatisfaction against the Commissioner's rejection of one of the Revenue's contentions, and lodged a cross-appeal against the Commissioner's decision. The CS held that it was unnecessary for the Revenue to demand a separate Stated Case. If the point of law in question was not dealt with on the Case demanded by the appellant, the Revenue should have invited the Commissioner to include an additional question related to the other contention. *Gordon v CIR (and cross-appeal)*, CS 1991, 64 TC 173; [1991] STC 174.

Whether respondent's name can be withheld

[4.161] A doctor appealed to the Special Commissioners against certain surtax assessments. The question was whether, for tax purposes, he was living with his wife (whom he had married secretly). The Commissioners allowed his appeal and the Revenue demanded a Case. The doctor applied for the case to be listed without disclosing his name. The Ch D rejected the application. Ungoed-Thomas J held that there was insufficient reason to override the 'fundamental requirement of publicity in our administration of justice', and specifically declined to follow the decision of McCardie J in *Southern v AB*, **59.72** TRADING INCOME. *In re H*, Ch D 1964, 42 TC 14.

[4.162] In the case noted at **22.236** EMPLOYMENT INCOME, the General Commissioners had allowed an appeal by a dermatologist (B), and HMRC appealed to the Ch D. The proceedings took place in open court, but B subsequently applied for the judgment to be anonymised. The Ch D rejected her application. Henderson J held that 'the principle of public justice is a very potent one' and that 'in tax cases the public interest generally requires the precise facts relevant to the decision to be a matter of public record, and not to be more or less heavily veiled by a process of redaction or anonymisation'. *HMRC v Banerjee (No 2)*, Ch D 2009, 80 TC 625; [2009] STC 1930; [2009] EWHC 1229 (Ch); [2009] 3 All ER 930.

Whether appellant's name can be withheld

[4.163] In the case noted at **25.95** EUROPEAN LAW, one of the appellant companies applied for the case to be listed without its name being disclosed. The case was listed in the Daily Cause Lists without the company's name being disclosed, but the Ch D rejected the company's request that its name should remain undisclosed on publication of the judgment. *NEC Semi-Conductors Ltd v CIR (and related appeals) (re ACT Class 3 Group Litigation Order)*, Ch D 2003, TL 3718; [2004] STC 489; 6 ITLR 416; [2003] EWHC 2813 (Ch).

[4.164] In the case noted at **4.18** above, the appellant company made a 'privacy application' to the Upper Tribunal. The case was listed in the Upper Tribunal's list of forthcoming hearings without the company's name being disclosed, but the tribunal rejected the company's request that its name should remain undisclosed on publication of the judgment. *Goldman Sachs International v HMRC (aka Blue v HMRC)*, UT 2009, [2010] STC 763; [2009] UKUT 290 (TCC).

Application to amend Stated Case

[4.165] The Commissioners allowed a company's appeal and the Revenue required the Commissioners to state a Case, which was duly stated and transmitted to the High Court. The company applied for an order remitting it to the Commissioners to amend it, considering that certain passages in it would be damaging if made public. The Ch D rejected the application. *Treharne v Guinness Exports Ltd*, Ch D 1967, 44 TC 161.

Whether Stated Case defective

[4.166] In the case noted at **61.3** TRADING INCOME, the appellant (N) applied by way of judicial review for an order to 'set aside and nullify' the Commissioner's decision, contending that the Stated Case was incomplete and criticising the Commissioner's conduct of the appeal. The QB rejected his application and the CA dismissed N's appeal, holding that the Commissioner had conducted the appeal correctly and that, with regard to the Stated Case, N should have made an application in the Ch D. *R v Special Commr (ex p.*

Napier), CA 1988, 61 TC 206; [1988] STC 573. (*Note.* The Ch D subsequently refused to remit the Case to the Commissioner—see **4.204** below. For an appeal against summary judgment, see **4.245** below.)

[4.167] General Commissioners dismissed an appeal in May 1989. The appellant (D) requested a Stated Case. In March 1990, having still not received a draft of the Case, he applied for an order directing the Commissioners to state a Case. On 20 April the appellant was sent a draft of the Case, which was transmitted to the High Court in August. In the meantime the hearing of D's application had been adjourned so that he could consider the draft Case. At the adjourned hearing D contended that the Stated Case was defective and that the Commissioners should be required to state a further Case. Vinelott J dismissed the application, holding that if the Case was inadequate, the appellant could apply to the Court to have it remitted to the Commissioners for amendment. However, the request for a Case to be stated had been complied with, and the application before the Court could not be treated as an application for remission. *Danquah v CIR*, Ch D 1990, 63 TC 526; [1990] STC 672.

[4.168] See also the cases noted at **4.198** to **4.204** below.

Whether Stated Case can be declared a nullity

[4.169] In the case noted at **39.47** MISCELLANEOUS INCOME, the appellant (W) applied for a declaration that the Stated Cases were a nullity, or alternatively that they should be remitted to the Commissioners for amendment. The QB rejected the application and the CA dismissed W's appeal, holding that the Cases could not be a nullity and that there were no grounds for remitting them. *Way v Underdown*, CA 1974, 49 TC 215; [1974] STC 11; [1974] 2 All ER 595.

[4.170] An individual (P) appealed against two assessments. The Commissioners upheld the larger assessment but allowed his appeal against the smaller assessment. Both sides appealed (although P failed to submit the Stated Case within the statutory time limit). P applied to strike out the Revenue's appeal, contending that the Case Stated for the Revenue disclosed 'no reasonable cause of action'. The Ch D rejected this contention and the CA unanimously dismissed P's appeal. *Petch v Gurney*, CA 1994, 66 TC 743; [1994] STC 689; [1994] 3 All ER 731.

Death of respondent after Case demanded

[4.171] General Commissioners allowed an appeal and the Revenue demanded a Stated Case. The respondent (W) died before it had been stated. A copy was served on W's executor. He refused to be made a party to the action. The KB held that the proceedings had begun when the Stated Case had been demanded, and ordered the case to proceed with the executor as respondent. *Smith v Williams*, KB 1921, 8 TC 321; [1922] 1 KB 158.

Death of Commissioner after Case demanded

[4.172] In the case noted at **63.217** TRADING PROFITS, the appellant (N) unsuccessfully contended that the Stated Case was invalid as it had been signed by only one of the two Commissioners who heard his appeal, the other having since died. The CA held that, if the Case was invalid, there could be no competent appeal to the courts. As N had proceeded with his appeal, he could not argue that the Case was invalid. *Norman v Golder*, CA 1944, 26 TC 293; [1945] 1 All ER 352. (*Note*. Various other contentions raised by N, who appeared in person, were also rejected.)

Retirement of Commissioner after Case demanded

[4.173] In the case noted at **66.18** TRADING PROFITS, the Stated Case was signed by one of the two Special Commissioners who heard it, the other having since retired. The Court required the retired Commissioner to sign the Case, before proceeding with the hearing. *O'Dwyer v Irish Exporters & Importers Ltd*, HC(I) 1942, 2 ITC 251; [1943] IR 176.

[4.174] In the case noted at **71.27** CAPITAL GAINS TAX, the Ch D remitted the Stated Case to the Commissioners. One of the Commissioners who had stated the Case had subsequently retired, and was re-appointed to enable him to act in the matter. *Rank Xerox Ltd v Lane*, Ch D 1977, 53 TC 185; [1977] STC 285; [1978] Ch 1; [1977] 3 All ER 593.

[4.175] In the case noted at **4.395** below, the appellant (who appeared in person) contended that the Stated Case was defective as it had not been signed by a Commissioner who had heard the application but had subsequently retired. The Ch D and CA unanimously rejected this contention and dismissed the appeal. *Parikh v Currie*, CA 1978, 52 TC 366; [1978] STC 473.

Evidence not referred to in Stated Case—whether admissible in High Court

[4.176] See *Thomas v Reynolds & Broomhead*, **8.65** CAPITAL ALLOWANCES, and the cases noted at **4.205** to **4.209** below.

Time limits

[4.177] General Commissioners determined an appeal and the Revenue demanded a Stated Case. The relevant tax district received it on 24 August. The Inspector there sent it to the Solicitor of Inland Revenue, who filed it in the High Court on 2 September. Under the law then in force, the time limit for transmitting a case to the High Court was seven days. The KB refused to hear the Revenue's appeal, as the Case had not been filed within the statutory time limit. *Grainger v Singer*, KB 1927, 11 TC 704; [1927] 2 KB 505.

[4.178] An appeal was struck out in a case where a company liquidator failed to transmit the Stated Case to the High Court within the 30-day time limit. *Valleybright Ltd (in voluntary liquidation) v Richardson*, Ch D 1984, 58 TC 290; [1985] STC 70.

[4.179] Similar decisions were reached in *Brassington v Guthrie*, Ch D 1991, 64 TC 435; [1992] STC 47; *Gurney v Spence*, Ch D 2001, [2002] STC 758, and *Petch v Gurney*, **4.170** above.

[4.180] The CA reached a similar decision in *CIR v McGuckian*, **3.64** ANTI-AVOIDANCE.

[4.181] A company expressed dissatisfaction with determinations by General Commissioners, and requested a Stated Case. The Commissioners sent the

Case to the company on 11 January 2002. The company received it on 14 January, but did not send it to the High Court until 12 February (and sent it by second-class post). The High Court received the Case on 15 February, and struck out the appeal on the grounds that the company had not transmitted it within the 30-day time limit. Blackburne J held that the requirement for the Case to be transmitted within 30 days meant that it had to be received by the High Court within 30 days. *New World Medical Ltd v Cormack*, Ch D [2002] STC 1245; [2002] EWHC 1787 (Ch).

[4.182] The decision in *New World Medical Ltd v Cormack*, **4.181** above, was applied in a similar subsequent case where Norris J observed that 'the interests of justice in achieving finality and in securing observance of the time limits laid down in the rules are weighty factors which come down in favour of refusing permission to extend time'. He held that 'whilst serious, the denial of the right of appeal has to be weighed against the position in which HMRC find themselves by reason of the delay. It is necessary for HMRC to manage their litigation and to undertake their tax collections in an organised way. A late appeal prejudices them in both respects, as is demonstrated by the fact that it was at about the time when HMRC sought to collect the tax that the deficiencies in the case stated and the appeal process came to light.' *Woodpecker Ltd v HMRC*, Ch D 2009, 80 TC 248; [2009] EWHC 3442 (Ch).

[4.183] A company expressed dissatisfaction with a determination by General Commissioners, and requested a Stated Case. The Commissioners sent the Case to the company in December 2004. The company did not send it to the High Court until February 2005. The Ch D struck out the appeal on the grounds that the company had not transmitted it within the 30-day time limit. *Significant Ltd v Farrel*, Ch D [2005] EWHC 3434 (Ch); [2006] STC 1626.

[4.184] The decision in *Significant Ltd v Farrel*, **4.183** above, was applied in the similar subsequent case of *Haven Healthcare (Southern) Ltd v York*, Ch D 2005, 77 TC 592; [2005] STC 1662; [2005] EWHC 2212.

Delay in paying fee

[4.185] In the case noted at **29.104** FURTHER ASSESSMENTS: LOSS OF TAX, the appellant requested a Stated Case within the 30-day time limit, but did not pay the requisite fee until more than three years later. The Commissioners stated the Case and the CA held that they were justified in doing so. *Anson v Hill*, CA 1968, 47 ATC 143.

Stated Case incomplete—whether transmitted in time

[4.186] In the case noted at **62.66** TRADING PROFITS, the company raised a preliminary objection that the inspector had not transmitted the Stated Case to the High Court in time. The case had been signed and sent to the inspector, but documents to be attached to it did not reach him until several months later. The CA held that the Stated Case was not complete until the documents had been attached to it (with the consequence that the preliminary objection failed). *CIR v Hugh T Barrie Ltd*, CA(NI) 1928, 12 TC 1223.

Appeal determined in principle—time limit for Stated Case

[4.187] In a development land tax case, the Commissioners had met on 15 February and 15 March 1978. The Revenue requested a Stated Case on 31 March. The appellant objected, contending that the appeal had been determined on 15 February so that the request for a Stated Case was outside the 30-day time limit. The Ch D rejected this contention, holding that the decision on 15 February was a decision in principle only, and the appeal had not been finally determined until the meeting on 15 March. *Furniss v Ford*, Ch D 1981, 55 TC 561; [1981] STC 641.

[4.188] A similar decision was reached in *Gibson v Stroud Commrs and Morgan*, Ch D 1989, 61 TC 645; [1989] STC 421. (*Note*. For the substantive appeal, see **71.73** CAPITAL GAINS TAX.)

Delay in sending copy of Stated Case to respondent

[4.189] In the case noted at **33.22** INTEREST PAYABLE, the Revenue did not notify the respondent that the case had been transmitted to the High Court until six days after its transmission. He contended that the Court had no jurisdiction to hear the Revenue's appeal. The Ch D rejected this contention, holding that the relevant provision was directory rather than mandatory and that the delay of six days was not unduly long. *Hughes v Viner*, Ch D 1985, 58 TC 437; [1985] STC 235; [1985] 3 All ER 40.

Whether time limit directory or mandatory

[4.190] In the case noted at **8.114** CAPITAL ALLOWANCES, the General Commissioners gave a decision in principle in favour of the appellant company (H) in February 1995. On 1 March 1995 the Revenue requested a Stated Case. On 13 April 1995 the Clerk to the Commissioners sent a draft Case to H. H sent representations to the Clerk in July 1995. In April 1996 the Commissioners formally determined the amounts of tax payable, and in May 1996 they signed the Case and it was transmitted to the court. H contended as a preliminary point that the court had no jurisdiction to hear the appeal, in view of the ten-month delay between the date on which it had sent representations to the Clerk and the date on which the Case had been signed. The CA rejected this contention, holding that it had jurisdiction to hear the appeal. The time limit did not begin to run until the determination of the assessments on 29 April 1996. Furthermore, the time limit was directory rather than mandatory, and it would be wrong for the Revenue to be penalised as a result of the General Commissioners' delay. *McKinney v Hagans Caravans (Manufacturing) Ltd*, CA(NI) 1997, TL 3531; [1997] STC 1023.

Time limit where single Case Stated covered three related appeals

[4.191] In a case where the substantive issue has been superseded by *FA 1989, s 115*, the Special Commissioner stated a single Case in relation to three related cross-appeals by the Revenue. The Revenue submitted the Case together with a fee of £15. However, when the Revenue applied to have the appeals set down for hearing, the companies lodged objections, contending that the action number allotted to the case related to the first-named company only and not to the other two companies, and that in respect of those other two companies, the Court had no jurisdiction to hear the appeals as the Revenue had not transmitted Cases within the required 30-day period. The Ch D held that it had jurisdiction to hear all the Revenue's cross-appeals. Although the Commissioner had only signed one document, it took effect as if he had stated three Cases. *Steele v Getty Oil Co (and related appeals)*, Ch D 1990, 63 TC 376; [1990] STC 434.

Remission of Case to the Commissioners

General

[4.192] There have been several cases in which the Court has not decided the appeal, returning the Stated Case to the Commissioners for further findings, and which have not come back to the Court. Normally such cases are of no general interest and not included in this book. In *Brimelow v Price*, **29.44** FURTHER ASSESSMENTS: LOSS OF TAX, a Case was remitted to the Commissioners to explain their finding of no wilful default. Other cases involving remissions to the Commissioners and points of general interest are noted below.

[4.193] In the case noted at **22.227** EMPLOYMENT INCOME, the Special Commissioners had dismissed five appeals. The appellants demanded Stated Cases. After receiving the draft Cases they suggested various amendments, which the Commissioners did not accept. The CS remitted the Cases to the Commissioners, holding that it was not clear from the Cases whether the purported facts set out therein were admitted, proved, found by the Commissioners or merely contended by the parties. The Commissioners should set out in the body of each case, in separate numbered paragraphs, the facts which they had found. *Fitzpatrick v CIR (and related appeals)*, CS 1990, TL 3263; [1991] STC 34. (*Note*. For a subsequent application by the appellants, see **4.194** below.)

[4.194] Following the remission of the Stated Cases in the appeals noted at **4.193** above, the Commissioners amended each of the Cases, and the amended Cases were set down for hearing in the Inner House of the CS. Eight weeks before the date of the hearing, the appellants petitioned for judicial review, contending that the Commissioners had failed to convene a hearing at which the appellants could have made submissions, and that the relevant facts were not fully set out in the Stated Cases. The Outer House of the CS dismissed the petition, holding that all the matters in question could be considered by the Inner House at the hearing of the substantive appeal. Since that hearing was only eight weeks away, it would not be appropriate to proceed by means of judicial review. *Fitzpatrick & Others v Lord Advocate*, CS 1991, TL 3322.

[4.195] In the case noted at **71.127** CAPITAL GAINS TAX, the Special Commissioner allowed the company's appeal and the Revenue requested a Stated Case. The company applied for the Case to be remitted to the Commissioner for further findings of fact, contending that the extent to which the Commissioner had accepted its evidence was not made clear in the Stated Case. The Ch D accepted this contention and remitted the Case to the Commissioner for further findings of fact, including clarification of what the Commissioner meant by the expression 'composite transaction'. *Whittles v Uniholdings Ltd*, Ch D 1993, 68 TC 528; [1993] STC 671. (*Note*. For a subsequent application by the company, see **4.196** below.)

[4.196] Following the remission of the Stated Case in the appeal noted at 4.195 above, the Commissioner made further findings of fact in accordance with the judge's directions. Before the appeal was reheard by the Ch D, the company applied for an order that the Case should be remitted to the Commissioner for a second time with a direction to hear further evidence. The Ch D accepted the application, observing that there was an apparent inconsistency between the findings of fact which the Commissioner had made in the original Stated Case (where he had described some currency transactions as 'part and parcel of a composite transaction') and his subsequent finding that 'the dollar loan and the forward contract were only part of a composite transaction in the sense that the company would not have entered into the one without entering into the other'. The Case was again remitted to the Commissioner with a direction that the company's managing director should be permitted to give further evidence. *Whittles v Uniholdings Ltd (No 2)*, Ch D 1993, 68 TC 528; [1993] STC 767.

[4.197] In the case noted at **8.52** CAPITAL ALLOWANCES, the Special Commissioner stated a Case which included no reference to certain evidence given at the hearing. The Revenue applied for the Case to be remitted to the Commissioner to include reference to this evidence, and the Ch D granted the application. Jacob J held that the evidence in question was material to a tenable argument and was not inconsistent with the Commissioner's findings of fact. *Bradley v London Electricity plc*, Ch D 1996, 70 TC 155; [1996] STC 231.

Case remitted to Commissioners by CA—remission disapproved by HL

[4.198] In the case noted at **65.50** TRADING PROFITS, the CA directed that the case should be remitted to the Commissioners, but the HL reversed their decision (by a 3-2 majority). Lord Denning held that 'the general rule of every appellate court is not to allow a new point to be raised except on a question of law which no evidence could alter'. *Evans Medical Supplies Ltd v Moriarty*, HL 1957, 37 TC 540; [1958] 1 WLR 66; [1957] 3 All ER 718.

[4.199] A similar decision was reached in the case noted at **3.75** ANTI-AVOIDANCE, where the CA remitted the case to the Commissioners, but the HL held that the remission was 'unnecessary and erroneous'. Lord Edmund-Davies held that 'the exercise of the power of remitter' called for 'a cautious approach'. *Yuill v Wilson*, HL 1980, 52 TC 674; [1980] STC 460; [1980] 1 WLR 910; [1980] 3 All ER 7.

Refusal of application for remission

[4.200] The Revenue began an investigation into a company (F), and made assessments outside the normal six-year time limit, on the basis that there had been fraud or wilful default. The Commissioners found that there had been wilful default, and confirmed the assessments. F demanded a Stated Case. After the Case had been stated, F applied for an order remitting it for amendment, contending that some of the evidence given on its behalf should have been included. The Ch D rejected the application. Applying the principles laid down by Lord Greene in *Royal Choral Society v CIR*, **9.11** CHARITIES, 'the Case should not simply set out the evidence given; what is of interest is the evidence accepted'. The CA unanimously dismissed F's appeal. *Fen Farming Co Ltd v Dunsford*, CA 1974, 49 TC 246; [1974] STC 373.

[4.201] Two companies applied for a Stated Case to be remitted to the Special Commissioners for amendment. The Ch D refused the application, holding that the findings of fact were a matter for the Commissioners. *Consolidated Goldfields plc v CIR; Gold Fields Mining & Industrial Ltd v CIR*, Ch D 1990, 63 TC 333; [1990] STC 357. (*Note*. The appeal was subsequently dismissed by consent. For a later appeal by one of the companies, see **8.75** CAPITAL ALLOWANCES.)

[4.202] The decision in *Consolidated Goldfields plc v CIR*, **4.201** above, was applied in the similar subsequent case of *Able (UK) Holdings Ltd v Skelton*, Ch D [2006] STC 1902; [2006] EWHC 1535 (Ch).

[4.203] The Special Commissioners confirmed assessments on income from furnished lettings after a hearing lasting 15 days. The Commissioners recorded in the Stated Case that they disbelieved the appellant's evidence and discounted some of the evidence given by witnesses whom he had called, considering that some of their evidence appeared to have been rehearsed. The appellant applied for the Case to be remitted for further findings of fact. The Ch D rejected the application and dismissed the appeal. In view of the length of the hearing, it could not be said that the Commissioners had erred in refusing to admit further evidence. *Zielinski v Pickering*, Ch D 1993, 68 TC 279; [1993] STC 418. (*Note*. A subsequent application for a late appeal against this decision was dismissed—see **4.228** below.)

[4.204] Applications for the remission of a Stated Case were also dismissed in *Carvill v CIR (No 1)*, **3.61** ANTI-AVOIDANCE; *Euro Fire Ltd v Davison*, **11.7** CLOSE COMPANIES; *Irving v Tesco Stores (Holdings) Ltd*, **18.69** CORPORATION TAX; *Hill v Davison*, **22.159** EMPLOYMENT INCOME; *McLeish v CIR*, **22.240** EMPLOYMENT INCOME; *Watson v Samson Bros*, **27.4** FARMING; *Verdon v Honour*, **29.5** FURTHER ASSESSMENTS: LOSS OF TAX; *Fletcher & Fletcher v Harvey*, **29.39** FURTHER ASSESSMENTS: LOSS OF TAX; *Hurley v Taylor*, **29.47** FURTHER ASSESSMENTS: LOSS OF TAX; *Wilcock v Frigate Investments Ltd*, **33.28** INTEREST PAYABLE; *Jeffries v Stevens*, **47.5** PROPERTY INCOME; *Napier v Griffiths*, **61.3** TRADING INCOME; *Watts v Hart*, **61.51** TRADING INCOME, and *Willson v Hooker*, **71.379** CAPITAL GAINS TAX.

Case remitted to Commissioners—whether appellant entitled to be heard

[4.205] In a case which turned on assessment provisions which have since been superseded, the Ch D remitted a case to the Commissioners for further findings of fact, but without admitting further evidence. Following the further findings, the Ch D decided the case in the appellant's favour and the CA upheld this decision. The CA also observed that natural justice required that the appellant should have been given an opportunity to make representations to the Commissioners. *Lack v Doggett*, CA 1970, 46 TC 497.

Case remitted to Commissioners—whether further evidence admissible

[4.206] In the case noted at **28.13** FOREIGN INCOME, the HL ordered the Stated Case to be remitted to the Commissioners. At the subsequent hearing, the appellant submitted further evidence as to United States law in support of his contentions. The Commissioners declined to examine the further evidence and confirmed the assessments. The CA upheld their action (by a 2-1 majority, Greer LJ dissenting). Russell LJ held that 'what was sent back to the Commissioners was the question of the investments representing the trust fund, not the question of the nature of (the appellant's) interest in the trust fund'. *Archer-Shee v Baker*, CA 1928, 15 TC 1.

[4.207] In the case noted at **65.1** TRADING PROFITS, the Ch D remitted the Stated Case to the Commissioners to adjust the 1945/46 assessment on the basis that the business had ceased in that year. The Commissioners called for new evidence on the value of the closing stock. The Ch D upheld the appellant's contention that the Commissioners had not been entitled to hear new evidence. Pennycuick J held that 'it is a well-established and salutary rule that parties to an appeal to the Court should not, in the absence of special circumstances, be enabled to go back to the Commissioners and call fresh evidence on issues which were raised in the original proceedings and as to which they had full opportunity of calling such evidence as they might be advised'. *Bradshaw v Blunden (No 2)*, Ch D 1960, 39 TC 73. (*Note.* The decision was approved by the HL in *Yuill v Wilson*, **3.75** ANTI-AVOIDANCE.)

[4.208] An appellant (P) contended that he was ordinarily resident in the Isle of Man. The Special Commissioners considered this contention at a preliminary hearing and, after hearing P's evidence and that of a witness, held that he was ordinarily resident in the UK. At a subsequent hearing P alleged that the witness's evidence had been untruthful. The Commissioners refused to reconsider this issue and determined the appeals on the basis that P was ordinarily resident in the UK. He appealed to the Ch D, and applied for the appeals to be reheard by a different panel of Commissioners. The Ch D rejected this contention and dismissed his appeal, applying the principles laid down in *Braddock v Tillotson's Newspapers Ltd*, KB [1949] 2 All ER 306; [1950] 1 KB 47, and holding that 'additional evidence merely directed towards the credit of a witness will in no circumstances be allowed'. *Potts v CIR*, Ch D 1982, 56 TC 25; [1982] STC 611.

[4.209] Two associated companies appealed against estimated assessments. At the hearing before the General Commissioners, the Revenue alleged that the companies had received payments of more than US$9m which had been diverted by their principal director (who had subsequently died). In their decision, the Commissioners stated that it was incumbent on the Revenue to prove fraud, and held that they had not done so. The Ch D allowed the Revenue's appeal and the CA upheld this decision. By stating that it was incumbent on the Revenue to prove fraud, the Commissioners had seriously misdirected themselves in law. Furthermore, it appeared that the companies' chief executive had given false evidence before the General Commissioners. The CA held (by a 2–1 majority, Mustill LJ dissenting) that this created special circumstances which, applying the principles laid down in *Meek v Fleming* (see the note below), justified a new hearing with the admission of fresh evidence. It was agreed that the case should be remitted to the Special Commissioners, rather than to the General Commissioners. *Brady v Group Lotus Car Companies plc and Lotus Cars Ltd*, CA 1987, 60 TC 359; [1987] STC 635; [1987] 3 All ER 1050. (*Note. Meek v Fleming*, CA [1961] 2 QB 366; [1961] 3 WLR 532; [1961] 3 All ER 148 was a case concerning an action against a police officer alleging false imprisonment and assault. Holroyd Pearce LJ held that 'where a party deliberately misleads the court in a material manner, and that deception has probably tipped the scale in his favour (or even, as I think, where it may reasonably have done so), it would be wrong to allow him to retain the judgment thus unfairly procured'.)

Case remitted to Special Commissioners—death of Commissioner

[4.210] In the case noted at **58.16** TAX PLANNING AND AVOIDANCE, the CA remitted the case to the Special Commissioners to determine the appeals on the basis that two documents relied upon by the appellants were shams and had no legal effect. One of the two Special Commissioners who had heard the original appeals subsequently died. One of the appellants subsequently applied for judicial review, contending that there should be a complete rehearing of the appeals by new Commissioners. The QB rejected this contention and dismissed the application. Evans-Lombe J held that the appeal could be concluded by the remaining Special Commissioner, or by a reconstituted panel of Special Commissioners. The provisions of *TMA, s 45(3)*, which provided for the continuation of proceedings with the consent of the parties, did not prevent the Presiding Special Commissioner from having the power to replace an incapacitated Commissioner. Evans-Lombe J observed that *TMA, s 45(3)* (which derived from *FA 1967*) 'was intended by the legislature as an enabling provision not a preventive one designed to restrict the jurisdiction of Commissioners in certain cases'. *R (oao Hitch) v Oliver & Everett (Special Commissioners)*, QB 2005, 77 TC 70; [2005] STC 474; [2005] EWHC 291 (Admin); [2005] 1 WLR 1651.

Admissibility of evidence

[4.211] At the Commissioners' hearing of the appeals which were the subject of *Amis v Colls*, **29.28** FURTHER ASSESSMENTS: LOSS OF TAX, the inspector admitted in cross-examination that he had received certain information from an informer. This was recorded in the Stated Case as admitted or proved. The appellant's solicitor subsequently discovered the informer and obtained from him a signed statement that he had supplied false information to the inspector. The appellant thereupon applied to the QB for an order quashing the Commissioners' determination. The QB rejected the application. Lord Parker CJ observed that there was 'no evidence at all' that the statement submitted by the appellant's solicitor was true, or that 'the statements originally made were false'. *R v Great Yarmouth Commrs (ex p. Amis)*, QB 1960, 39 TC 143.

[4.212] In an investigation case, General Commissioners determined assessments on a company director. He appealed, contending that the effect of the Commissioners' findings was that he had stolen money from the company and that such sums were not taxable income. The Ch D dismissed his appeal. Stamp J observed that the director's contention involved 'asking this Court to make a finding of fact which the Commissioners were not asked to make'. *Frowd v Whalley*, Ch D 1965, 42 TC 599.

[4.213] In the case noted at **61.48** TRADING INCOME, the appellant company (C) sought to put in affidavits to show, by evidence not in the Stated Case, that the Commissioners had misdirected themselves by assuming that it bore the burden of proof in the appeal. The Ch D held that evidence could not be filed in the High Court to supplement or contradict a Stated Case (and that the onus was on C to show that it had begun a new trade). *Cannon Industries Ltd v Edwards*, Ch D 1965, 42 TC 625; [1966] 1 WLR 580; [1966] 1 All ER 456.

[4.214] The Inland Revenue issued assessments charging tax on a married man on bank interest received by his wife, in accordance with the legislation then in force. The General Commissioners confirmed the assessments, and the husband appealed to the Ch D where, appearing in person, he produced a copy of a letter to an inspector of taxes which he contended was a claim for separate assessment under *ICTA 1970, s 38*. The letter had never been put before the General Commissioners and was not in the prescribed form. The Ch D dismissed his appeal, holding that the appellant could not submit new evidence and that there was no question of law for consideration in the High Court. The CA upheld this decision. *Hotter v Spackman*, CA 1982, 54 TC 774; [1982] STC 483. (*Note. ICTA 1970, s 38* became *ICTA 1988, s 283*, which ceased to have effect for 1990/91 and subsequent years of assessment, following the changes enacted by *FA 1988*.)

[4.215] In the case noted at **18.62** CORPORATION TAX, the company applied to the CA for leave to adduce as further evidence a note of a meeting with its accountants. The CA rejected the application, observing that the note of the meeting had been compiled unilaterally and its contents had not been communicated to the Revenue. Accordingly it could not be used as an aid to the construction of the letter in which the company had claimed group relief. *Farmer v Bankers Trust International Ltd*, CA 1991, 64 TC 1; [1991] STC 585.

[4.216] See also *Thomas v Reynolds & Broomhead*, **8.65** CAPITAL ALLOWANCES (where the Ch D refused to hear new evidence), and *Watson v Samson Bros*, **27.4** FARMING (where the Ch D refused to remit the case to the Commissioners for a further finding of fact).

Use of Hansard

[4.217] In *Pepper v Hart*, **22.171** EMPLOYMENT INCOME, the HL held that Hansard could be used as an aid to interpretation where 'legislation is ambiguous or obscure, or leads to an absurdity; the material relied upon consists of one or more statements by a Minister or other promoter of the Bill together if necessary with such other Parliamentary material as is necessary to understand such statements and their effect; and the statements relied upon are clear'. (The Lords also observed that this would not, as the Attorney-General had contended, contravene *Article 9* of the *Bill of Rights 1688*.)

[4.218] The principles laid down in *Pepper v Hart*, **22.171** EMPLOYMENT INCOME have been applied in several subsequent cases including *Griffin v Craig-Harvey*, **71.322** CAPITAL GAINS TAX; *Holland (Holland's Executor) v CIR*, **72.21** INHERITANCE TAX, and *Martin v Horsfall*, **72.66** INHERITANCE TAX.

[4.219] In a subsequent (non-tax) case, Lord Hoffmann held that 'it will be very rare indeed for an Act of Parliament to be construed by the courts as meaning something different from what it would be understood to mean by a member of the public who was aware of all the material forming the background to its enactment but who was not privy to what had been said by individual members (including Ministers) during the debates in one or other House of Parliament'. *Robinson v Secretary of State for Northern Ireland and Others*, HL [2002] UKHL 32; [2002] All ER (D) 364 (Jul).

[4.220] In another non-tax case, Lord Steyn held that 'if exceptionally there is found in Explanatory Notes a clear assurance by the executive to Parliament about the meaning of a clause, or the circumstances in which a power will or will not be used, that assurance may in principle be admitted against the executive in proceedings in which the executive places a contrary contention before a court'. However, it was impermissible 'to treat the wishes and desires of the Government about the scope of the statutory language as reflecting the will of Parliament. The aims of the Government in respect of the meaning of clauses as revealed in Explanatory Notes cannot be attributed to Parliament. The object is to see what is the intention expressed by the words enacted.' *R (oao Westminster City Council) v National Asylum Support Service*, HL [2002] UKHL 38; [2002] 4 All ER 654.

[4.221] In a VAT case, Norris J held that 'an internal note by one civil servant to another (which has not been referred to in Parliament in the process of enactment) is no more admissible in construing a statute than one contracting party's letter to his solicitor would be in construing a contract'. *HMRC v The Rank Group plc*, Ch D [2009] EWHC (Ch) 1244.

Late appeals

Refusal of late appeal—request for Stated Case

[4.222] In a Northern Ireland case, the Special Commissioners rejected an application to admit a late appeal, holding that the application had not been made 'without unreasonable delay', as required by *TMA, s 49(1)*. The applicant (M) requested the Commissioners to state a Case, which they declined to do, and then applied to the QB for judicial review. The QB rejected the application, holding that an application under *TMA, s 49(1)* was not an appeal, and that M had no right to require the Commissioners to state a case. There had been no error of law in the Commissioners' decision to reject the application. *R v Special Commissioners (ex p. Magill)*, QB (NI) 1979, 53 TC 135; [1981] STC 479.

Refusal of late appeal—whether Commissioners acting unreasonably

[4.223] An application to make a late appeal against several assessments was set down for hearing before General Commissioners. The hearing was arranged for 22 April, but the clerk did not send notification of this date to the applicant until 8 April. The applicant was staying in Portugal and did not receive the notification until 17 April (Good Friday). He telephoned his daughter in England, and she wrote a letter to the Commissioners requesting that the hearing be adjourned. The Commissioners refused this request and also refused the application for a late appeal. The applicant sought judicial review of the Commissioners' decision. Schiemann J held that the Commissioners had failed to give the applicant a fair opportunity to present his case, quashed the Commissioners' decisions and remitted the case to a differently constituted panel of Commissioners. *R v Hastings & Bexhill Commrs (ex p. Goodacre)*, QB 1994, 67 TC 126; [1994] STC 799.

[4.224] In December 2001 the Revenue rejected a loss claim by a company, and issued a notice of determination stating the amount of the loss as nil. In July 2002 the company lodged a late appeal against the determination. The Revenue referred this to the General Commissioners under *TMA, s 49*. The Commissioners rejected the company's application, holding that there was no reasonable excuse for the delay in lodging the appeal. The company applied for judicial review of the Commissioners' decision. The QB granted the application. Evans-Lombe J held that there was 'no relevant prejudice to the public finances if this appeal is allowed to be lodged out of time'. On the evidence, the Commissioners 'mistook the extent of the powers which they had to exercise'. He directed the Commissioners to hear the company's appeal against the determination. *R (oao Browallia Cal Ltd) v City of London Commrs*, QB 2003, 75 TC 686; [2004] STC 296; [2003] EWHC 2779 (Admin).

[4.225] An employer (C) failed to account for PAYE and NIC to the Revenue, who issued determinations under the *Income Tax (PAYE) Regulations*. C did not appeal, and the Revenue lodged a statutory demand and issued a bankruptcy petition. C then lodged a late appeal, which the Revenue referred to the General Commissioners under *TMA, s 49*. The Commissioners rejected the application, holding that there was no reasonable excuse for the delay in lodging the appeal. C applied for judicial review of the Commissioners' decision. At an initial hearing, Burton J granted this application, applying the principles laid down in *R (oao Browallia Cal Ltd) v City of London Commrs*, **4.224** above. The Commissioners reheard the case and again held that the conditions of *TMA, s 49(1)* had not been complied with. C again applied for judicial review. Dyson LJ rejected his application, holding that there was a 'public interest in these cases in achieving finality in litigation' and 'a public interest in promoting the policy that challenges to assessments by way of appeal should be brought within the short period specified by the statute'. *R (oao Cook) v Northampton General Commissioners*, QB [2009] STC 1212; [2009] EWHC 590 (Admin).

Commissioners allowing late appeal—whether decision unreasonable

[4.226] An employee (L) had worked on 'jack-up' drilling rigs. The Revenue had issued assessments on the basis that L was not entitled to foreign earnings deduction under the legislation then in force (see now *ITEPA 2003, s 379*), since the drilling units were not a 'ship', as required by *ITEPA 2003, s 384**. Following the CA decision in *Clark v Perks*, **22.287** EMPLOYMENT INCOME, L made a late claim for foreign earnings deduction. The Revenue accepted the claims for years within the statutory six-year time limit, but rejected the claims for 1991/92 to 1993/94, on the basis that the claims had been made outside the statutory time limit. L lodged late appeals against these three assessments, which the Revenue referred to the General Commissioners in accordance with *TMA, s 49(1)*. The Commissioners allowed the application, stating that L 'had a reasonable excuse for not bringing these appeals within the time limit'. The Revenue applied to the CS for judicial review of the Commissioners' decision, contending that it was *ultra vires* and unreasonable. Lord Drummond Young reviewed the evidence in detail and allowed the Revenue's application. He held that *TMA, s 49* should 'be viewed in the same context as other provisions designed to allow legal proceedings to be brought even though a time limit has expired. The central feature of such provisions is that they are exceptional in nature; the normal case is covered by the time limit, and particular reasons must be shown for disregarding that limit. The limit must be regarded as the judgment of the legislature as to the appropriate time within which proceedings must be brought in the normal case, and particular reasons must be shown if a claimant or appellant is to raise proceedings, or institute an appeal, beyond the period chosen by Parliament.' He observed that the effect of *TMA, s 33(2)* was that 'a taxpayer should not be able to obtain relief for an error or mistake if his return was made in accordance with the practice generally prevailing at the time' and that 'where an assessment is made in accordance with generally prevailing practice at the time of the relevant tax return, it cannot be reopened'. The General Commissioners had ignored that policy. Therefore, applying *dicta* of Lord Macfadyen in *SHBA Ltd v The Scottish Ministers*, CS [2002] SLT 1336, the Commissioners' decision was unreasonable and was 'one that no reasonable body of General Commissioners, properly directed on the law, could have reached'. *Advocate-General for Scotland v Aberdeen City Commrs*, CS 2005, 77 TC 391; [2006] STC 1218; [2005] CSOH 135.

Stated Case procedure—late appeals to High Court

[4.227] See the cases noted at **4.177** to **4.181** above.

Application to CA for late appeal against High Court decision

[4.228] In the case noted at **4.203** above, the unsuccessful appellant applied to the CA for an extension of time for appealing against the Ch D decision. The CA rejected the application, holding on the evidence that there was no chance of the appeal succeeding. *Zielinski v Pickering*, CA 1993, 68 TC 279.

[4.229] The CA reached a similar decision in the case noted at **44.329** PENALTIES, distinguishing the earlier decision in *Palata Investments Ltd & Others v Burt & Sinfield Ltd*, CA [1985] 1 WLR 942; [1985] 2 All ER 517. *Khan v Newport Commrs & CIR*, CA 1995, 70 TC 239.

'Res judicata'

Retrospective effect of court decisions

[4.230] Two individuals, L and H, were each entitled to an annuity 'free of income tax' under the will made in 1939 of a testator who died in 1940. In 1942, on an appeal to which H, but not L, was a party, the CA held that, for the purposes of the relevant legislation (modification of pre-war provisions for tax-free annuities), the governing date was the date of the will, with the result that H's annuity fell to be reduced. The appeal was not taken further, but in 1946, in a similar case (*Berkeley v Berkeley*, HL [1946] AC 555; [1946] 2 All ER 154) the HL held that the date of death of the testator was the governing date. H and L then applied to the court to determine whether their annuities should be paid in full. The Ch D held that for H the matter was *res judicata* and the reduction in his annuity must stand, but this was not the case for L. L's annuity was therefore payable in full and she could claim the full amount retrospectively. *Re Waring decd., Westminster Bank Ltd v Burton-Butler and Others*, Ch D [1948] Ch 221; [1948] 1 All ER 257.

[4.231] Between 1942 and 1945, a contractor paid royalties to a farmer for sand and gravel taken from his land, purporting to deduct tax under the authority of *FA 1934, s 21*. The farmer acquiesced in the deduction from the first payment but objected to later deductions. In 1948 the HL decision in *Russell v Scott*, 30 TC 375 (subsequently overtaken by *FA 1963*) made it clear that tax was not deductible. The KB held that the farmer was entitled to a refund of the tax where he had not acquiesced in its deduction, but not of the tax deducted from the first payment. *Gwyther v Boslymon Quarries Ltd*, KB [1950] 2 KB 59; [1950] 1 All ER 384.

Court decisions—effect on subsequent years

[4.232] See *Hood Barrs v CIR (No 3)*, **56.57** SETTLEMENTS.

Whether Revenue estopped on grounds of equity

[4.233] An Irish company appealed against its excess profits duty assessment for the year to 27 March 1915, objecting to its 'pre-war standard' by reference to which its excess profits liable to the duty were ascertained. After litigation, the appeal was determined by the Court of Appeal. Errors were discovered in the calculation of the standard, and in the assessment for the three years to March 1920 the Revenue used an amended standard. The company appealed, contending that the standard fixed for the year to March 1915 was binding for subsequent periods. The Irish Supreme Court held that the Revenue was free to correct the calculation of the standard. The matter was not *res judicata*, nor was the Revenue estopped on grounds of equity. *Bolands Ltd v CIR*, SC(I) 1925, 1 ITC 42; 4 ATC 526.

[4.234] In the case noted at **46.26** PENSION SCHEMES, a barrister sent a letter to the Revenue in 1995 with details of retirement annuity relief which she claimed to be available for carry-forward. A Revenue officer (apparently an executive officer below the grade of inspector) sent a fax acknowledging the letter without querying the barrister's computation. In 1996 the barrister claimed to carry forward the relief against her subsequent income. The Revenue rejected the claim on the basis that the barrister's computation did not comply with *ICTA 1988, s 655(1)(b)*. The barrister appealed, contending *inter alia* that the Revenue should be bound by the acknowledgment which they had faxed to her in 1995. The General Commissioners rejected this contention and dismissed her appeal, and the Ch D upheld their decision. Lewison J observed that *TMA, s 54* did not apply since the 1994/95 assessment had not been under appeal, and even if the 1994/95 appeal had been settled by agreement, such an agreement could not have committed the Revenue to agreeing the barrister's liability for any year other than 1994/95 itself. He observed that 'unless there is formal machinery which would enable the Commissioners to determine a formal claim to carry forward a specific sum, a *section 54* agreement cannot have that effect. The point is not that the legislation permits amounts to be carried forward. Rather, the point is whether the machinery for determining tax liability is limited to determining the amount of the taxpayer's liability for a particular year of assessment, or whether it extends to determining an amount due in a future year. Only in the latter case could a *section 54* agreement bind the Revenue for future years of assessment.' *Lonsdale v Braisby*, Ch D 2004, TL 3735; [2004] STC 1606; [2004] EWHC 1811 (Ch).

Decision purporting to govern subsequent assessments

[4.235] In an Irish case, a company appealed against an assessment for 1952/53. Included in the assessment was a bad debt recovery in the basis period, to the extent to which, with previous recoveries, it exceeded an allowance for doubtful debts which had been made in the 1940/41 assessment. The 1940/41 assessment had been determined on appeal by a Circuit Court judge who had stated in his decision that any recoveries would not be assessable. The HC(I) held that this statement had no binding effect with regard to the 1952/53 appeal. The jurisdiction of the Circuit Court judge in the 1940/41 appeal was limited to the determination of the appeal before him. *Bourke v P Lyster & Sons Ltd*, HC(I) 1958, 3 ITC 247.

Whether Revenue may invoke principle of 'issue estoppel'

[4.236] See *Carter Lauren Construction Ltd v HMRC*, **16.20** CONSTRUCTION INDUSTRY.

Estoppel 'per rem judicatum'

[4.237] See *Murphy v Elders*, **4.82** above; *CIR and HMRC v Test Claimants in the FII Group Litigation (No 4)*, **25.89** EUROPEAN LAW, and *Spens v CIR*, **56.100** SETTLEMENTS.

General and miscellaneous

The distinction between fact and law

[4.238] In the case noted at **59.29** TRADING INCOME, the House of Lords overturned a Commissioners' decision with regard to the definition of trading, where the Commissioners had expressed their conclusion as a finding of fact. Lord Radcliffe held that 'the Court can allow an appeal from the Commissioners' determination only if it is shown to be erroneous in point of law', but that the Court should intervene where 'the facts found are such that no person acting judicially and properly instructed as to the relevant law could have come to the determination under appeal' and where 'the true and only reasonable conclusion contradicts the determination'. In the same case, Viscount Simonds held that the Courts should only overturn a Commissioners' finding of fact 'if it appears that the Commissioners have acted without any evidence or upon a view of the facts which could not reasonably be entertained'. *Edwards v Bairstow & Harrison*, HL 1955, 36 TC 207; [1956] AC 14; [1955] 3 All ER 48. (*Note*. This is the leading case concerning when the Courts will disturb a finding of fact by Commissioners.)

[4.239] The principles laid down in *Edwards v Bairstow & Harrison*, **4.238** above, have been applied in a very large number of subsequent cases. In the interests of space, such decisions are not listed individually in this book. In *Ransom v Higgs*, **59.99** TRADING INCOME (where the HL reversed the Commissioners' decision), Lord Simon of Glaisdale held that 'where an appeal lies only on a point of law, the appellate tribunal ought only to interfere with a decision falling within "the no-man's land" of fact and degree if a plain error shows that the instance tribunal must have misdirected itself in law'. In *Furniss v Dawson*, **71.288** CAPITAL GAINS TAX, Lord Brightman held that the court 'can and should interfere with an inference of fact drawn by the fact-finding tribunal which cannot be justified by the primary facts'. But 'if the primary facts justify alternative inferences of fact', the court should not 'substitute its own preferred inference for the inference drawn by the fact-finding tribunal'.

Whether Scottish decisions should be followed by English courts

[4.240] In the case noted at **54.10** SCHEDULE E, the HL reversed the CA decision and in so doing overruled a Court of Session decision which the CA had followed. In the CA, Lord Evershed MR observed that although the CA was not bound to follow the decisions of the Court of Session, it ought to do so 'unless there are compelling reasons to the contrary'. In the HL, Lord Reid approved this approach, observing that 'it is undesirable that there should be conflicting decisions on revenue matters in Scotland and England'. *Abbott v Philbin*, HL 1960, 39 TC 82; [1961] AC 352; [1960] 2 All ER 763.

Whether an appeal to the High Court may be withdrawn

[4.241] In the case noted at **56.56** SETTLEMENTS, the Special Commissioners' decision governed surtax assessments on a settlor covering 1941/42 to 1953/54. It was to the settlor's advantage to accept the Commissioners' decision for 1947/48 onwards. The Ch D gave him leave to withdraw his appeals for these years. Upjohn J observed that the effect of the decision in *R v Special Commrs (ex p. Elmhirst)*, **4.1** above, was that 'a taxpayer who has given notice of appeal from the assessing Commissioners cannot withdraw it, as the Special Commissioners, being an administrative body, are bound to find the true figure of assessment'. However, when an appellant requested a Stated Case, he was 'entitled to ask the Special Commissioners to state a Case in respect only of the years which he chooses.' Accordingly he could 'before the case has been fully heard and argued, withdraw such years in respect of which he does not desire to appeal'. *Hood Barrs v CIR (No 3)*, Ch D 1959, 39 TC 209.

[4.242] However, in the case noted at **65.1** TRADING PROFITS, the Ch D refused leave to withdraw an appeal as it had already been the subject of a decision by the Court. *Bradshaw v Blunden (No 2)*, Ch D 1960, 39 TC 73.

Effect of difference of opinion by judges

[4.243] In the case noted at **62.66** TRADING PROFITS, the Revenue's appeal was heard by two judges in the KB(NI) who took opposite views of the disputed issue. After considering whether it was the practice for the junior judge to withdraw his judgment, the Court decided to make no order. The decision of the Recorder of Belfast (in favour of the company) therefore stood. The Revenue appealed to the CA, but the substantive issue was eventually settled by agreement. *CIR v Hugh T Barrie Ltd*, CA(NI) 1928, 12 TC 1223; [1928] KB(NI) 209. (*Note*. For a preliminary issue in this case, see **4.186** above.)

[4.244] In the case noted at **68.21** TRADING PROFITS, the Revenue's appeal against the CA decision was heard by four Law Lords. They were equally divided and, because of the equal division of opinion, the CA decision stood. *Smith v Lion Brewery Co Ltd*, HL 1910, 5 TC 568; [1911] AC 150. (*Note.* In the Supreme Court, it is now usual for five judges to hear appeals.)

Allegation of misconduct of appeal by Commissioners

[4.245] The appellant in the case noted at **61.3** TRADING INCOME appealed against summary judgment, seeking leave to defend on the grounds that there had been impropriety in the proceedings before the Commissioner. The CA dismissed his appeal, holding that the assessments could not be reopened and that the Revenue was entitled to summary judgment. *CIR v Napier*, CA [1993] STC 815.

Correctness of assessments challenged in collection proceedings

[4.246] See the cases noted at **43.4** to **43.9** PAYMENT OF TAX.

Whether Revenue can raise a new question of law

[4.247] In a case where the facts were unusual, the CA held that a settlement was not void for uncertainty (see **56.139** SETTLEMENTS) and that the undistributed income was not income of the settlor. Before the Commissioners, the Revenue had supported the assessments under appeal on the alternative grounds that the settlement was void or, if it was not void, that the undistributed income was within legislation in *ITA 1952* which was broadly similar to *ITTOIA 2005, ss 624–628*. The Commissioners had found for the Revenue on the second of these grounds. The settlor contended that the Revenue could not maintain its first contention, as it was not stated in the Case as an issue for the Court's opinion. The CA rejected this contention, holding that it was open to the Revenue 'to seek to uphold the decision in its favour on any ground of law available, including a ground decided against it by the Commissioners'. *Muir v CIR*, CA 1966, 43 TC 367; [1966] 1 WLR 1269; [1966] 3 All ER 38.

[4.248] See also *Kirby v Thorn EMI plc*, **71.28** CAPITAL GAINS TAX.

Vexatious litigant

[4.249] The unsuccessful appellant in the case noted at **4.270** below brought a series of unsuccessful High Court actions against the Revenue. On an application by the Attorney-General, the QB made an order under *Supreme Court of Judicature (Consolidation) Act 1925, s 51*, declaring him a vexatious litigant. *In re Soul*, QB 1964, 42 TC 164. (*Note.* The appellant had previously been convicted of fraud and sentenced to two years' imprisonment. For subsequent proceedings, see **4.250** below.)

Appellant bankrupt—refusal of trustee in bankruptcy to prosecute appeal

[4.250] Having lost two appeals in the High Court and given notice of appeal to the CA, an appellant was adjudicated bankrupt. His trustee in bankruptcy was unwilling to pursue the appeals, and the CA dismissed them. *Soul v CIR*, CA 1966, 43 TC 662. (*Note.* For subsequent proceedings, see **43.5** PAYMENT OF TAX.)

Application by Revenue for consent order

[4.251] General Commissioners had allowed a taxpayer's appeal. The Revenue demanded a Case which was duly stated and transmitted to the High Court but, after the appeal had been set down for hearing, the taxpayer decided not to oppose it. The Revenue applied for a consent order allowing its appeal and reversing the Commissioners' decision. The Ch D held that it had no power to make the order. Megarry J held that 'the law is a matter for decision by the Court after considering the case, and not for agreement between John Doe and Richard Roe, with the Court blindly giving its authority to whatever they have agreed'. Accordingly, 'the appeal thus remains in being, to be duly heard and determined.' He observed that, if the taxpayer did not wish 'to be involved in avoidable expense', he did not need to 'be represented or take part in the hearing of the appeal'. *Slaney v Kean*, Ch D 1969, 45 TC 415; [1970] Ch 243; [1970] 1 All ER 434. (*Note. Obiter dicta* of Megarry J were disapproved by Lord Donovan in the subsequent case of *Ranaweera v Ramachandran*, PC 1969, 45 TC 423; [1970] 2 WLR 500.)

[4.252] The decision in *Slaney v Kean*, **4.251** above, was not followed in a subsequent case where the parties came to an agreement after a case had been set down for hearing, and the Ch D ordered a stay of proceedings. *Toms v Sombreat Ltd*, Ch D 25 June 1979, 1979 STI 313.

Representation by unincorporated society

[4.253] At the hearing of *Animal Defence & Anti-Vivisection Society v CIR*, **9.42** CHARITIES, the society's president appeared to argue its case. The Ch D refused to hear her, holding that she was not a litigant and that an unincorporated society must be represented in the High Court by counsel. *Animal Defence & Anti-Vivisection Society v CIR*, Ch D 1950, 29 ATC 155.

Appeals dismissed by consent—application for reinstatement

[4.254] In the case noted at **3.21** ANTI-AVOIDANCE, the Ch D granted an application for reinstatement of an appeal, holding on the evidence that the appellant's solicitor had acted beyond his authority in agreeing to the dismissal of the appeals. *Sheppard v CIR (and cross-appeal)*, Ch D 1992, 65 TC 716; [1992] STC 460; [1992] 3 All ER 58. (*Note*. The appellant was ordered to pay half of the Revenue's costs concerning the application.)

Whether individual partner may appeal against partnership assessment

[4.255] A medical partnership appealed against assessments for 1976/77 to 1987/88 inclusive. The main points of contention were the deductibility of expenses incurred by the individual doctors. Before the hearing of the appeal, the inspector reached agreement on the figure of allowable expenditure with all the partners except for one (B) who had left the partnership. B attended the hearing of the appeal and contended that the amount of the expenditure which the inspector had agreed to allow the other partners was excessive. The Commissioners declined to hear B on the expenses claims of the other partners, and adjourned the hearing to enable the inspector and B to agree the level of B's expenses. At the resumed hearing, they determined the assessments in the figures contended for by the inspector, which reflected an agreed figure for B's expenses. B requested a Stated Case. The remaining partners applied to the

Ch D for a declaration that B was not the 'appellant', and that the Commissioners had no jurisdiction to state a Case. The Ch D granted the declaration, but the CA reversed this decision and directed that the case be relisted for rehearing. A person who was dissatisfied with a Commissioners' determination might declare his dissatisfaction to the Commissioners, regardless of whether the determination was in respect of an assessment on himself alone, or on himself jointly with others. B was entitled to declare his dissatisfaction and to lodge an appeal to the High Court. *Sutherland & Partners v Barnes (and related appeal)*, CA 1994, 66 TC 663; [1994] STC 387; [1994] 3 WLR 735; [1994] 4 All ER 1.

Case referred to ECJ—application for further direction

[4.256] The Special Commissioners referred the case noted at 25.33 EUROPEAN LAW to the ECJ for a ruling. After the ECJ had registered the case, the appellant companies applied for a direction that the Commissioners should clarify that some of the statements in the UK's written observations were 'unsubstantiated allegations'. The Commissioners declined to make the direction sought, but observed that 'the Court and the parties may be assisted by our clarifying in this decision how we, as the fact-finding and referring tribunal, now understand the difference between the parties over the facts'. *Cadbury Schweppes plc v CIR (No 2); Cadbury Schweppes Overseas Ltd v CIR (No 2)*, Sp C [2006] SSCD 35 (Sp C 512).

Applications for prerogative orders

Cases where the application was unsuccessful

Application for order of mandamus

[4.257] After General Commissioners had determined appeals against estimated assessments, the appellant applied for an order of *mandamus* directing the Commissioners to rehear the appeals. The KB dismissed his application, holding that the Commissioners' decision could not be questioned by way of *mandamus*. *R v Winchester Commrs*, KB 1922, 2 ATC 49.

[4.258] In an Irish case, an individual (S) claimed a repayment of tax under *ITA 1918, s 25* (see the note above 56.109 SETTLEMENTS). The Special Commissioners rejected the claim, and S applied for an order of *mandamus* requiring them to repay the tax, on the ground that they had misconstrued the law. The court rejected the application, holding that the Commissioners had been acting in a judicial and not an executive capacity and that their decision couldnot be altered by a prerogative order, even if they had misconstrued the law. *R v Special Commissioners (re Spain)*, HC(I) 1927, 1 ITC 227; [1934] IR 27.

[4.259] The Special Commissioners heard appeals against several assessments and gave a decision in principle in favour of the Revenue, adjourning the proceedings for the figures to be agreed. The appellant applied for an order of *mandamus* directing the Commissioners to determine the appeals 'according to law'. The QB dismissed the application, holding that the appellant should have proceeded by requesting a Stated Case. Lord Parker CJ described the application as 'wholly misconceived', and held that '*mandamus* only lies where a body charged with a public duty deliberately refuses to adjudicate at all, or directs its mind to the wrong question, or possibly acts without jurisdiction, as, for instance, if the so-called rules of natural justice were not complied with'. *R v Special Commrs (ex p. Philippi)*, QB 1966, 44 TC 31.

[4.260] See also *R v Special Commrs (ex p. Horner)*, **1.8** ALLOWANCES AND TAX RATES; *R v St Pancras Commrs (ex p. Church of Scientology)*, **4.72** above; *R v Special Commissioners (ex p. Carrimore Six Wheelers Ltd)*, **4.264** below; *R v HM Inspector of Taxes for Ashford & Others (ex p. Frost)*, **4.265** below; *R v Kensington Commrs (ex p. Wyner)*, **4.266** below; *R v Special Commrs (ex p. Headmasters' Conference)*, **9.46** CHARITIES; *R v Special Commrs (ex p. Rank's Trustees)*, **9.53** CHARITIES; *R v Holborn Commrs (ex p. Rind Settlement Trustees)*, **29.72** FURTHER ASSESSMENTS: LOSS OF TAX; *R v Walton Commissioners (ex p. Wilson)*, **42.3** PAY AS YOU EARN, and *R v CIR & Quinlan (ex p. Rossminster Ltd & Others)*, **49.63** RETURNS AND INFORMATION.

Application for writ of prohibition

[4.261] An individual born in Germany, who had owned property in London but had subsequently moved to South Africa, was assessed on his income from the London property. He applied for a writ to prohibit the General Commissioners from proceeding on the assessments, contending that they had no jurisdiction since he was not resident in the UK. The CA rejected this contention and dismissed his application, holding that the liability to assessment depended on questions of fact which it was for the Commissioners to determine. *R v St Marylebone Commrs (ex p. Schlesinger)*, CA 1928, 13 TC 746.

[4.262] The inspector for Launceston District issued an assessment to an individual (L) charging tax on his profit from a transaction in land. He applied for a prerogative order to quash the assessment, contending that the transaction was implemented in Surrey and the inspector could not assess a trade not carried on in his District. The CA rejected the application, holding that there was no such territorial limitation on an inspector's exercise of his powers under the Act. *R v Tavistock Commrs (ex p. Adams) (No 2)*, CA 1971, 48 TC 56. (*Note*. For subsequent developments in this case, see **4.71** above.)

[4.263] See also *R v Special Commrs (ex p. Elmhirst)*, **4.1** above; *R v St Pancras Commrs (ex p. Church of Scientology)*, **4.72** above; *R v Kensington Commrs (ex p. Aramayo)*, **5.19** ASSESSMENTS; *R v St Giles & St George Commrs (ex p. Hooper)*, **5.20** ASSESSMENTS; *R v Special Commrs (ex p. Rogers)*, **29.70** FURTHER ASSESSMENTS: LOSS OF TAX; *R v Havering Commrs (ex p. Knight)*, **44.86** PENALTIES, and *Stockler Charity (a firm) v HMRC (No 2)*, **44.187** PENALTIES.

Application for order of certiorari

[4.264] In the case noted at **24.2** ERROR OR MISTAKE RELIEF, the CA had rejected a company's claim that rental income which it had received should have been assessed under Schedule A rather than under Schedule D. The company subsequently made a similar claim in relation to other rents. Because of the previous decision, the Special Commissioners refused to state a Case. The company applied for orders of *certiorari* and *mandamus* to require the Commissioners to hear and determine the appeal. The CA rejected the application. *R v Special Commissioners (ex p. Carrimore Six Wheelers Ltd)*, CA 1947, 28 TC 422. (*Note*. The CA also rejected the company's contention that, because only two Commissioners were present at the meeting, the meeting was invalid.)

[4.265] In March 1971 notices of assessment, which did not state the date of issue, were sent to accountants acting for an executrix. The accountants lodged appeals. Subsequently the executrix complained that the assessments were defective, and in February 1972 the inspector issued a second set of notices covering the same years. After the time limit for appealing had expired, and at a time when the appeals against the original assessments had been listed for hearing by the local General Commissioners, the executrix submitted late appeals against the second set of assessments, with an election that the appeals should be heard by the Special Commissioners. The General Commissioners did not determine the appeals, and the Revenue suggested to the accountants acting for the executrix that a joint application should be made for the original appeals to be transferred from the General Commissioners to the Special Commissioners. The executrix did not respond to this, but applied for an order of *certiorari* to quash the original assessments, for an order prohibiting the General Commissioners from hearing the appeals, and alternatively for an order of *mandamus* directing the appeals against the second set of assessments to be transmitted to the Special Commissioners. The QB dismissed the applications, holding that the proper course was to adopt the Revenue's suggestion of arranging for the appeals to be transferred to the Special Commissioners. Lord Widgery CJ observed that 'where an equally convenient remedy exists, the discretionary powers represented by the prerogative orders are not as a matter of practice employed'. *R v HM Inspector of Taxes for Ashford & Others (ex p. Frost)*, QB [1973] STC 579.

[4.266] The Revenue addressed notices of assessment to the executors of a deceased person, at the deceased's last address. Appeals were lodged by accountants who had acted for the deceased. There was in fact only one executor (the son of the deceased), and he died before the appeals had been heard. His widow applied for an order of *certiorari* to quash the assessments, for an order prohibiting the Commissioners from hearing the appeals, and for an order of *mandamus* directing the inspector to issue valid notices. The CA rejected her application. Lord Widgery CJ observed that the fact that the typist had added an 's' at the end of the word executor 'could not conceivably render the assessment a nullity'. *R v Kensington Commrs (ex p. Wyner)*, CA 1974, 49 TC 571; [1974] STC 576.

[4.267] An application for an order of *certiorari* was also dismissed, on the grounds that the normal appeals procedure could have been used, in *R v Special Commrs (ex p. Morey)*, CA 1972, 49 TC 71

[4.268] See also *R v Tavistock Commrs (ex p. Adams) (No 1)*, **4.2** above; *R v Great Yarmouth Commrs (ex p. Amis)*, **4.211** above; *R v Special Commrs* *(ex p. Rogers)*, 29.70 FURTHER ASSESSMENTS: LOSS OF TAX; *R v Holborn Commrs (ex p. Rind Settlement Trustees)*, 29.72 FURTHER ASSESSMENTS: LOSS OF TAX; *R v Walton Commissioners (ex p. Wilson)*, 42.3 PAY AS YOU EARN; *R v CIR (ex p. Chisholm)*, 42.15 PAY AS YOU EARN; *R v CIR (ex p. Sims)*, 42.17 PAY AS YOU EARN; *R v CIR (ex p. Cook and Keys)*, 42.18 PAY AS YOU EARN, and *R v CIR & Quinlan (ex p. Rossminster Ltd & Others)*, 49.63 RETURNS AND INFORMATION.

Revenue revoking direction that dividend payable gross

[4.269] See *R v CIR (ex p. Camacq Corporation)*, 18.90 CORPORATION TAX.

Application for declaration

[4.270] General Commissioners had dismissed appeals against assessments on property income. The appellant began an action in the Ch D against another individual (M) and against the Revenue, applying for a declaration that the properties in question were owned by M rather than by him. The Ch D ordered that the action against the Revenue should be struck out, holding that the claim disclosed no reasonable cause of action and was an abuse of the process of the court. *Soul v Marchant & CIR*, Ch D 1962, 40 TC 508. (*Note*. For subsequent proceedings, see 4.249 and 4.250 above.)

[4.271] Two companies engaged in 'dividend-stripping' operations applied to the Ch D for the determination of two questions, the answers to which affected the success or failure of the operations. The Ch D struck the summons out and the CA dismissed the companies' appeals. Lord Denning held that the summons was 'an abuse of the process of the court'. *Argosam Finance Co Ltd v Oxby & CIR; FA & AB Ltd v Lupton*, CA 1964, 42 TC 86; [1965] Ch 390; [1964] 3 All ER 561. (*Note*. One of the companies subsequently appealed to the HL with regard to the substantive issue—see 59.56 TRADING INCOME.)

Application for declaration—whether High Court has jurisdiction

[4.272] Several large companies applied to the Ch D for a declaration that certain provisions of UK legislation, which denied group relief to UK companies in certain circumstances, contravened *Article 43EC* of the *EC Treaty* and the standard OECD Double Taxation Convention. The Ch D declined to make the declaration which the companies had requested. Park J held that 'issues of tax law which are disputed between taxpayers and the Revenue ought to be resolved on appeals to the Commissioners'. The HL upheld the Ch D decision (by a 3-2 majority, Lord Hope of Craighead and Lord Walker of Gestingthorpe dissenting). Lord Nicholls of Birkenhead held that 'these claims in the High Court are *prima facie* a misuse of the court's process. These claims cover the same ground in all respects as the appeals pending before the appeal commissioners. The remedy sought is co-extensive with adjudicating upon existing, open assessments. The essence of the High Court claims is that these assessments were wrong, that the court should so hold, and that the court should itself calculate the amounts which ought to have been assessed and order repayment of the overpaid excess. There could hardly be a more obvious example of seeking to sidestep the statutory procedure.' He observed that there was a 'distinction between obtaining the tax relief to which the claimant is entitled and obtaining damages for unlawful failure to make such relief available' but held that 'having claims in both classes is not a sufficient reason for a company declining to make a group relief claim in respect of accounting periods where this can still be done'. *Autologic Holdings plc & Others v CIR (re Claimants under Loss Relief Group Litigation Order)*, HL 2005, 77 TC 504; [2005] STC 1357; [2005] UKHL 54; [2005] 4 All ER 1141. (*Note*. For subsequent developments in this case, see *Claimants under Loss Relief Group Litigation Order v HMRC (No 2)*, **25.24** EUROPEAN LAW.)

Cases where the application was settled by agreement

Prerogative orders—jurisdiction of Divisional Courts

[4.273] An individual (E) applied to the QB for an order of *mandamus*, requiring the Special Commissioners to amend a Stated Case. In the event, E reached an agreement with the Revenue which made it unnecessary to remit the Case. However, Donaldson LJ observed that applications should normally be made to the Ch D as the specialised court in tax matters. The QB had residual jurisdiction over the supervision of such matters as the validity of, or errors in, the proceedings. *R v Special Commrs (ex p. Emery)*, QB 1980, 53 TC 555; [1980] STC 549.

Cases where the application was successful

Application for order of certiorari

[4.274] The Revenue issued a corporation tax assessment on a company (S) for the period from 1 February 1977 to 25 October 1977, on the basis that S's trade had ceased on the latter date. S appealed. The Revenue subsequently received information suggesting that S's trade had not ceased on 25 October 1977, and amended the terminal date of the assessment to 31 January 1978, without giving S notice of the proposed amendment. The Special Commissioner confirmed the assessment, and S applied to the QB for an order of *certiorari*. The QB granted the order. Nolan J held that 'it is axiomatic that a taxpayer must know the nature of the assessment which is being made upon him. It is equally axiomatic that if the nature of the assessment changes, the taxpayer must know of the change and of the reasons why it is made before it can be confirmed upon appeal.' *R v Ward; R v Special Commissioner (ex p. Stipplechoice Ltd) (No 3)*, QB 1988, 61 TC 391; [1989] STC 93. (*Note*. For subsequent developments in this case, see **5.111** ASSESSMENTS.)

Application for order of mandamus

[4.275] See *R v Special Commrs (ex p. Shaftesbury Homes & Arethusa Training Ship)*, **2.16** ANNUAL PAYMENTS; *Rouf (t/a The New Balaka Restaurant) v Dundee Commrs*, **4.156** above, and *R v Special Commrs (ex p. University College of North Wales)*, **9.6** CHARITIES.

Revenue application for order to quash Commissioners' decision

[4.276] See *R (oao HMRC) v Berkshire Commrs*, **29.124** FURTHER ASSESSMENTS: LOSS OF TAX.

Applications for judicial review

NOTE

Judicial review was introduced in 1977. It is now governed by *Civil Procedure Rules 1998 (SI 1998/3132), Sch 1, RSC Order 53*, and is the procedure for obtaining relief by way of prerogative order (i.e. an order of mandamus, prohibition or certiorari). For cases concerning prerogative orders, see **4.257** to **4.276** above. However, judicial review is not confined to such cases, and an applicant may obtain a declaration or injunction in any case where, in the opinion of the court, it would be 'just and convenient for the declaration or injunction to be granted'. See the judgment of Lord Scarman in *R v CIR & Another (ex p. Rossminster Ltd & Others)*, **49.63** RETURNS AND INFORMATION. For examples of cases where declarations were granted although prerogative orders were held not to be appropriate, see *R v Secretary of State for Transport (ex p. Factortame Ltd & Others) (No 3)*, **25.165** EUROPEAN LAW, and *R v Secretary of State for Employment (ex p. Equal Opportunities Commission)*, **25.170** EUROPEAN LAW. For a historical discussion of judicial review with regard to taxation, see 'Taxation: Judicial Review and Other Remedies' by Ian Saunders (John Wiley & Sons, 1996). For a discussion of judicial review in the context of appeals under the new tribunal system, see the CA decision in *R (oao Cart) v Upper Tribunal*, CA [2010] EWCA Civ 859.

Cases where the application was unsuccessful

Application for judicial review of Commissioners' decision

[4.277] The CA unanimously dismissed an application for judicial review of the General Commissioners' determination of an appeal against a CGT assessment. *Page v Daventry Commrs & Others*, CA [1980] STC 698.

[4.278] Applications for judicial review of the confirmation of estimated assessments by the General Commissioners were also dismissed in *R v Brentford Commrs (ex p. Chan & Others)*, QB 1985, 57 TC 651; [1986] STC 65; *R v Boston Commrs (ex p. CD Freehouses Co Ltd)*, QB 1989, 63 TC 45; [1990] STC 186, and *R (oao Bottomley) v Pontefract Commrs*, QB [2009] STC 2532; [2009] EWHC 1708 (Admin).

[4.279] See also *R (oao Carvill) v CIR*, **3.63** ANTI-AVOIDANCE; *R (oao Dogar) v General Commrs*, **4.85** above; *R v North London General Commrs (ex p. Nii-Amaa)*, **29.48** FURTHER ASSESSMENTS: LOSS OF TAX, and *R v Walton Commissioners (ex p. Wilson)*, **42.3** PAY AS YOU EARN.

Contractor failing to deduct tax from subcontractor

[4.280] See *R v Collector of Taxes (ex p. Robert Goodall (Builders) Ltd)*, **16.46** CONSTRUCTION INDUSTRY.

Employer failing to deduct tax under PAYE

[4.281] See *Reed Employment plc v HMRC*, **4.155** above, and *R v CIR (ex p. McVeigh)*, **42.16** PAY AS YOU EARN.

TCGA 1992, s 152(3)—Revenue refusing to extend three-year time limit

[4.282] See *R (oao Barnett) v CIR*, **71.226** CAPITAL GAINS TAX.

TCGA 1992, Sch 5B—Revenue refusing to extend three-year time limit

[4.283] See *R (oao Devine) v CIR*, 71.213 CAPITAL GAINS TAX.

FA 1998, Sch 18 para 24—Revenue enquiry into company tax return

[4.284] See *R (oao Spring Salmon & Seafood Ltd) v CIR*, 49.72 RETURNS AND INFORMATION.

FA 2000, Sch 12—application for judicial review

[4.285] See *R (oao Professional Contractors Group) v CIR*, 22.41 EMPLOYMENT INCOME.

FA 2004, s 320—application for judicial review

[4.286] See *Aegis Group of Companies v CIR*, 4.450 below.

FA 2008, s 58—application for judicial review

[4.287] See *R (oao Huitson) v HMRC*, 21.43 DOUBLE TAX RELIEF.

FA 2013, s 194—application for judicial review

[4.288] See *R (oao St Matthews West Ltd) v HM Treasury*, 75.27 STAMP DUTY LAND TAX.

Refusal of late appeal

[4.289] See *R v Special Commissioners (ex p. Magill)*, 4.222 above.

Rejection of loss claims

[4.290] See *R (oao De Silva) v HMRC (and related application)*, 35.4 LOSS RELIEF.

Alleged breach of confidentiality by senior HMRC official

[4.291] See *R (oao Ingenious Media Holdings plc) v HMRC (and related application)*, 50.15 REVENUE ADMINISTRATION.

Revenue resiling from 'forward tax agreement' with non-domiciliary

[4.292] See *Fayed & Others v Advocate-General for Scotland and CIR*, 50.26 REVENUE ADMINISTRATION.

Application for judicial review of Revenue investigation

[4.293] See *R (oao Fayed & Others) v CIR*, 50.27 REVENUE ADMINISTRATION.

Revenue refusing to implement alleged concessionary practice

[4.294] See *R v Inspector of Taxes (ex p. Brumfield & Others)*, 41.36 PARTNERSHIPS; *R v CIR (ex p. J Rothschild Holdings plc) (No 2)*, 50.30 REVENUE ADMINISTRATION; *R v CIR (ex p. SG Warburg & Co Ltd)*, 50.29 REVENUE ADMINISTRATION, and *R v Inspector of Taxes (ex p. Fulford-Dobson)*, 71.135 CAPITAL GAINS TAX.

Company allegedly misled by informal statements by Revenue officers

[4.295] See *R v CIR (ex p. MFK Underwriting Agencies Ltd & Others)*, 50.32 REVENUE ADMINISTRATION.

Withdrawal of assurance based on inadequate disclosure by company

[4.296] See *R v CIR (ex p. Matrix Securities Ltd)*, **50.33** REVENUE ADMINISTRATION.

Effect of delay in claim for judicial review

[4.297] In February 1982, General Commissioners determined appeals by a couple who traded in partnership. In 1984 the couple applied for judicial review of the Commissioners' decision. The QB dismissed the application, holding that there was no good reason for extending the statutory time limit. *R v Tavistock Commrs (ex p. Worth & Worth)*, QB 1985, 59 TC 116; [1985] STC 564.

[4.298] See also *R v Special Commissioner (ex p. Moschi)*, **4.3** above, and *R v HM Inspector of Taxes (ex p. Brumfield & Others*, **41.36** PARTNERSHIPS.

Application for judicial review relating to persons other than the applicant

[4.299] In the case noted at **71.194** CAPITAL GAINS TAX, the Special Commissioner held that a company director (W) was chargeable to CGT in respect of a disposal of loan notes. W applied for judicial review, contending that other taxpayers who had made similar disposals had not been required to pay CGT. The QB dismissed his application. Moses J held that 'the Revenue are under a duty, pursuant to (*IRRA 1890, ss 1, 13(1)*), to collect and cause to be collected every part of inland revenue'. There was 'no arguable unfairness in their pursuing that duty' even if it was alleged that they had failed to do so in relation to other taxpayers.' *R (oao Weston) v CIR*, QB 2004, 76 TC 207.

[4.300] See also *CIR v National Federation of Self-Employed and Small Businesses Ltd*, **50.23** REVENUE ADMINISTRATION.

Application for judicial review following Statement of Practice

[4.301] In 1989 a married couple sold shares to a German company. Four months later, the Inland Revenue published Statement of Practice SP 5/89. The husband realised that the effect of this was that if his wife had transferred her shares to him before the sale, they could have been treated as a single holding, with a higher deemed acquisition value. He applied by way of judicial review for a declaration that the shares should be valued as if his wife had transferred them to him. The QB dismissed the application. There had not been an inter-spouse transfer of the shares, and the Revenue had a duty to demand the tax actually due. *R v CIR (ex p. Kaye)*, QB 1992, 65 TC 82; [1992] STC 581.

HMRC accused of lenient settlement with large company

[4.302] See *R (oao UK Uncut Legal Action Ltd) v HMRC*, **50.24** REVENUE ADMINISTRATION.

Judicial review proceedings rendered abortive by retrospective legislation

[4.303] See *R v HM Treasury (ex p. Leeds Permanent Building Society)*, 4.408 below.

Application for judicial review of interest charge

[4.304] The QB dismissed an application for judicial review of an interest charge under *TMA, s 86*. Latham J held that the provisions of *s 86* did not raise any question of public law requiring judicial review. Furthermore, the words of *s 86* were clear and unambiguous, and interest ran from the date laid down by *TMA, s 86(3A)* even though the trade in question had ceased after the date on which the relevant assessment was issued, with the effect that the assessment (which was still under appeal on the date of cessation) fell to be computed on a current year basis rather than on a preceding year basis. *R v CIR (ex p. Barker & Beresford)*, QB 1994, 66 TC 654; [1994] STC 731.

[4.305] In *Segesta Ltd v HMRC*, **71.214** CAPITAL GAINS TAX, the Upper Tribunal held that an issue of shares failed to qualify for EIS reinvestment relief, so that the shareholder (O) was required to pay capital gains tax. O subsequently applied for judicial review of the decision to charge interest on the tax. The Upper Tribunal dismissed his application. Sales J observed that O 'had had the benefit for a very long period of obtaining the monies which he should have paid over by January 1998 in respect of his liability for tax'. The CA rejected O's application to appeal against this decision. Beatson LJ observed that 'Statute prescribes that interest should be charged as compensation for failure to pay tax in time. In this case, the interest of the state is in collecting tax and in ensuring that taxpayers do not have an incentive to pay late and do not gain an advantage as against other taxpayers in doing so.' *Oyston v HMRC*, CA [2013] EWCA Civ 1292.

Claim for exemption—application for judicial review

[4.306] In the case noted at **26.18** EXEMPT INCOME, the QB dismissed an application for judicial review of the Revenue's decision to issue assessments, holding that the applicant's claim to exemption should be determined by the Special Commissioners. *R v CIR (ex p. Caglar)*, QB 1995, 67 TC 335; [1995] STC 741. (*Note*. For the substantive appeal, see .)

[4.307] See also *Harley Development Inc v Hong Kong Commr of Inland Revenue*, **50.28** REVENUE ADMINISTRATION.

Withdrawal of approval of pension scheme

[4.308] See *R v CIR (ex p. Roux Waterside Inn Ltd)*, **46.8** PENSION SCHEMES, and *R (oao Mander) v CIR*, **46.9** PENSION SCHEMES.

Revenue action under ITA 2007, s 695

[4.309] In *R v CIR (ex p. Preston)*, **50.25** REVENUE ADMINISTRATION, the HL rejected an application for judicial review of a notice under what is now *ITA 2007, s 695*. Lord Templeman held that 'judicial review should not be granted where an alternative remedy is available' and that 'judicial review process should not be allowed to supplant the normal statutory appeal procedure'. Lord Scarman held that 'a remedy by way of judicial review is not to be made available where an alternative remedy exists' and that 'where Parliament has provided by statute appeal procedures, as in the taxing statutes, it will only be very rarely that the courts will allow the collateral process of judicial review to be used to attack an appealable decision'.

Application for judicial review of issue of assessments

[4.310] In a New Zealand case, the shareholders of two companies participated in tax avoidance schemes devised by an accountant. The Revenue issued assessments and the shareholders applied for judicial review. The New Zealand courts dismissed the applications, and the Privy Council dismissed appeals by the shareholders, holding that where there was a statutory appeal procedure, judicial review should only be granted in exceptional circumstances. There were no exceptional circumstances here. *O'Neil & Others v New Zealand Commissioner of Inland Revenue*, PC [2001] STC 742; [2001] UKPC 17; [2001] 1 WLR 1212.

Application by Revenue for judicial review of Commissioner's decision

[4.311] During the hearing of the appeal in *Major v Brodie & Another*, **33.26** INTEREST PAYABLE, an English Special Commissioner refused to permit the Revenue to introduce evidence of Scottish law. The Revenue applied for judicial review of the Commissioner's decision. The QB rejected the application, holding that if the Revenue considered that the Commissioner had erred in law, the correct procedure was to challenge the decision by way of Case Stated. *R v Special Commissioners (ex p. HM Inspector of Taxes)*, QB 29 June 1995, 1995 STI 1101. (*Note*. The Commissioner subsequently allowed both parties to submit evidence of Scottish law. For a discussion of the proceedings, see British Tax Review 1998, pp 666–671.)

Application for disclosure of Revenue documents

[4.312] See *R v CIR (ex p. Taylor) (Nos. 1 & 2)*, **49.31** and **49.32** RETURNS AND INFORMATION.

Application for judicial review of action under TMA, s 20

[4.313] See *R (oao Paulden Activities Ltd & Others) v HMRC*, **49.48** RETURNS AND INFORMATION.

Application for judicial review of action under TMA, s 20C

[4.314] See *R v CIR & Another (ex p. Rossminster Ltd & Others)*, **49.63** RETURNS AND INFORMATION.

Application for judicial review of enquiry under TMA, s 28A

[4.315] See *R (oao Golding) v General Commissioners*, **55.25** SELF-ASSESSMENT.

Application for judicial review of criminal prosecution

[4.316] See *R v CIR (ex p. Mead & Cook)*, **51.18** REVENUE PROSECUTIONS, and *R v CIR (ex p. Allen)*, **51.19** REVENUE PROSECUTIONS.

Application for judicial review of bill of indictment

[4.317] An individual (D) was charged with defrauding the Revenue. He indicated that he would not attend a committal hearing, contending that he was suffering from stress. The Crown applied for a bill of indictment. D sought leave to apply for judicial review of this decision. The QB dismissed his application, holding that the question of whether a bill of indictment was justified was a matter for consideration by the judge to whom the application for the bill was referred. *R v CIR (ex p. Dhesi)*, QB 1995, 67 TC 580.

TMA, s 20(8E)—failure to provide written summary of notices

[4.318] See *R v CIR (ex p. Continental Shipping Ltd & Atsiganos SA)*, **49.56** RETURNS AND INFORMATION.

Application for judicial review of notices under FA 2008, Sch 36

[4.319] See *R (oao Derrin Brother Properties Ltd) v HMRC*, **49.107** RETURNS AND INFORMATION.

Use of taxation to fund military expenditure

[4.320] A group of pacifists applied for judicial review of the Treasury's use of taxation to fund military expenditure. The QB rejected the application and the CA unanimously dismissed their appeal. *R (oao Boughton & Others) v HM Treasury*, CA [2006] EWCA Civ 504. (*Note*. See also *Cheney v Conn*, **5.2** ASSESSMENTS; the cases noted at **5.3** ASSESSMENTS, and *Hibbs v United Kingdom*, **31.64** HUMAN RIGHTS.)

Application for review of residence ruling

[4.321] In the case noted at **48.20** RESIDENCE, HMRC issued a ruling that an individual (H) was resident in the UK for 1998/99. He appealed, contending that he had been resident in the Netherlands for that year, and also applied for judicial review. The QB dismissed the application for judicial review, observing that the appeal had been set down for a ten-day hearing beginning on 19 October 2009, and holding that 'in a case of this nature, where the factual dispute relates to matters that occurred many years ago, it is strongly in the public interest that the tax appeal should be heard as soon as is reasonably practicable'. Accordingly the First-tier Tribunal should proceed to hear the appeal as arranged. *R (oao Hankinson) v HMRC*, QB [2009] STC 2158; [2009] EWHC 1774 (Admin). (*Note*. For a preliminary issue in this case, see **4.14** above.)

[4.322] The decision in *R (oao Hankinson) v HMRC*, **4.321** above, was unanimously approved by the CA in *P Daniel v HMRC (No 1)*, CA [2012] EWCA Civ 1741; [2013] STC 744. (*Note*. The substantive appeal was subsequently dismissed—see **29.60** FURTHER ASSESSMENTS: LOSS OF TAX.)

[4.323] The Revenue issued a ruling that two UK citizens, who had houses in both England and Belgium, were resident in the UK for 2001/02, and were therefore liable to pay capital gains tax. They applied for judicial review, contending that Revenue Pamphlet IR20 indicated that they would not be treated as resident in the UK, and that they therefore had a legitimate expectation that they would not be liable to CGT. The CA unanimously dismissed their application, and the Supreme Court upheld this decision (by a 4-1 majority, Lord Mance dissenting). Lord Wilson observed that parts of IR20 had been 'very poorly drafted' but held that it did not make any representation from which the claimants could have derived a legitimate expectation that they should be treated as non-resident. Lord Hope concluded that the appellants' contention 'that the Revenue had raised a legitimate expectation that their claim would be determined more favourably than the law and a proper construction of IR20 would indicate was simply not made out by the evidence'. *R (oao Davies & James) v HMRC*, SC [2011] UKSC 47; [2011] STC 2249; [2012] 1 All ER 1048.

[4.324] The Supreme Court reached a similar decision (also by a 4-1 majority, Lord Mance dissenting) in dismissing an application for judicial review of the decision noted at **48.18** RESIDENCE, which it heard with *R (oao Davies & James) v HMRC*, **4.323** above. *R (oao Gaines-Cooper) v HMRC*, SC [2011] UKSC 47; [2011] STC 2249; [2012] 1 All ER 1048.

HMRC seeking to set VAT repayment against income tax liability

[4.325] In his 2007/08 and 2008/09 returns, an individual (R) claimed that he had incurred substantial losses in 2009 and 2010, and sought to set this against his income tax liability for 2007/08. HMRC subsequently began an enquiry into R's 2008/09 return. They also began county court proceedings to collect unpaid tax for 2007/08. However these proceedings were stayed pending the decision in *HMRC v Cotter*, **35.51** LOSS RELIEF. In 2011 R submitted a VAT return claiming a substantial repayment. HMRC accepted that this repayment was due, but sought to set it against R's income tax liability under *FA 2008, s 130*. R applied for judicial review. The Upper Tribunal dismissed his application, applying the Supreme Court decision in *HMRC v Cotter*. *R (oao K Rouse) v HMRC (No 2)*, UT [2013] UKUT 615 (TCC); [2014] STC 230. (*Note*. See now *ITA 2007, s 128(5A)*, introduced by *FA 2009, s 68*.)

Jersey limited partnership—whether a partnership or a company

[4.326] See *R v CIR (ex p. Bishopp) (p.p. Pricewaterhouse Coopers); R v CIR (ex p. Allan) (p.p. Ernst & Young)*, **41.48** PARTNERSHIPS.

Cases where the application was successful

TMA, s 41—Special Commissioner authorising late assessment

[4.327] See *R v Special Commr, ex p. Stipplechoice Ltd (No 1)*, **29.75** FURTHER ASSESSMENTS: LOSS OF TAX.

Refusal of late appeals

[4.328] See *R v Hastings & Bexhill Commrs (ex p. Goodacre)*, **4.223** above, and *R (oao Browallia Cal Ltd) v City of London Commrs*, **4.224** above.

Refusal of tax certificate—procedural irregularity at hearing

[4.329] In a Northern Ireland case, a contractor (C) applied for a tax certificate under *ICTA 1988, s 561*. The Revenue rejected the application on the grounds that C had not complied with the requirements of *ICTA 1988,* *s 562*. C appealed, contending that the breaches were 'minor and technical', within *s 562(10)*. The General Commissioners rejected this contention and dismissed the appeal. C applied for judicial review, contending that there had been a procedural irregularity at the Commissioners' hearing, in that the Revenue had made a written submission to the Commissioners without giving him notice. The QB accepted this contention and directed that the appeal should be reheard by a different body of Commissioners. Weatherup J held that 'it is elementary that in any adversarial hearing the decision-maker should not receive from one party material that may be relevant to the decision and is not provided to the other party' and that 'it is an aspect of procedural fairness that there should be transparency in the process'. *R (oao Corr) v General Commissioners*, QB(NI) 2005, [2006] STC 709; [2005] NIQB 62.

Application for disclosure of Revenue documents in judicial review proceedings

[4.330] In the case noted at 50.29 REVENUE ADMINISTRATION, a company sought the disclosure of documents relating to the Revenue practice in applying *FA 1973, Sch 19 para 10* to share exchange transactions. The QB made an order limited to internal Revenue documents of a general nature, but excluding documents relating to individual and particular cases. The CA unanimously upheld this decision. *R v CIR (ex p. J Rothschild Holdings plc) (No 1) (and cross-appeal)*, CA 1987, 61 TC 178; [1987] STC 163.

Notices under TMA, s 20(3)—application for judicial review

[4.331] See *R v O'Kane & Clarke (ex p. Northern Bank Ltd)*, 49.31 RETURNS AND INFORMATION.

Revenue action under TMA, s 20C—application for judicial review

[4.332] See *R v CIR & Others (ex p. Kingston Smith)*, 49.65 RETURNS AND INFORMATION.

Accountant suspected of fraud—application for judicial review

[4.333] See *R (oao Lunn) v HMRC*, 50.42 REVENUE ADMINISTRATION.

Application for review of residence ruling

[4.334] A company had requested confirmation from an inspector that one of its subsidiaries was resident in the UK. The inspector gave the requested confirmation, but this was subsequently revoked by the Revenue, which took the view that the company had not made a full and proper disclosure of all relevant matters. The QB granted the company leave to apply for judicial review of the revocation, holding that the evidence showed that the company had an arguable case. *R v CIR (ex p. Howmet Corporation & Another)*, QB [1994] STC 413.

HMRC refusing claim for seafarers' earnings deduction

[4.335] HMRC rejected two claims for seafarers' earnings deduction. The claimants appealed, contending that a Revenue publication entitled 'Seafarers – Notes on Claims for 100% Foreign Earnings Deductions', which had originally been published in 1993 and was colloquially known as the 'Blue

Book', had given them a legitimate expectation that they would be entitled to the relief. The QB accepted this contention and allowed their applications. Wyn Williams J observed that both the 'Blue Book', and form S203(New), stated that a day would be treated as a day of absence from the UK if the claimant was outside the UK at the end of that day (ie even if he had only left the UK in the late evening). However, HMRC had subsequently formed the opinion that the Blue Book and the form S203(New) were misleading, and that days on which a claimant left the UK should only be treated as days of absence if the vessel was en route to an overseas port (rather than to another UK port). He held that 'a taxpayer is entitled to rely upon a statement made in a formal publication unless and until the statement is revoked, withdrawn or altered'. On the evidence, HMRC had not 'published any document which was aimed at eligible seafarers which suggested that the Blue Book was obsolete or redundant in any of the tax years with which this case is concerned'. The Blue Book had given the claimants a legitimate expectation that their claims to seafarers' earnings deduction would be allowed. *I Cameron v HMRC (and related application)*, QB [2012] EWHC 1174 (Admin); [2012] STC 1691.

HMRC withdrawing pension scheme approval

[4.336] In the case noted at **46.1** PENSION SCHEMES, HMRC withdrew their approval of a pension scheme. They subsequently sought to impose tax charges on the scheme members. Several of the members applied for judicial review, contending that the charges were unfair, since HMRC had previously included the scheme in a published list of recognised schemes, and this had given them a legitimate expectation that they could transfer their pension funds into the scheme. The QB accepted this contention and granted the applications. Charles J observed that HMRC had withdrawn similar charges in similar cases. *R (oao Gibson) v HMRC (and related applications)*, QB 20 June 2013 unreported. (*Note*. For HMRC's practice following this decision, see http://www.hmrc.gov.uk/pensionschemes/transfers-to-qrops.pdf. At the time of writing, no transcript of Charles J's decision is available.)

Revenue resiling from informal administrative procedure

[4.337] See *R v CIR (ex p. Unilever plc)*, **50.41** REVENUE ADMINISTRATION.

Appeals against estimated assessments

NOTE

The cases below are appeals to the courts against determinations of assessments which had been estimated because of the absence or inadequacy of accounts or information on behalf of the taxpayer. The cases exclude those where the assessments were made in connection with investigations, for which see **29** FURTHER ASSESSMENTS: LOSS OF TAX. Decisions by the Special Commissioners or the First-tier Tribunal on appeals against estimated assessments have not been summarised unless the decision appears to raise a point of general importance.

Precept not complied with

[4.338] The Revenue issued assessments on a trader (S) who had received certain from Austria. He appealed, and the Commissioners issued 'precepts' requiring further information. S failed to comply with the precepts, and the Commissioners determined the assessments on the basis of the information available. The CS unanimously upheld their decision. Lord Clyde observed that 'the Commissioners have given the appellant the fullest opportunity, by precept and invitation, to attend the meeting at which his case was to be heard'. However, 'instead of availing himself of that opportunity, the appellant preferred to take the position that the matters of fact in question were of exclusively Austrian interest, and would not be communicated by him to the Commissioners who were hearing his appeal'. There was 'no alternative except to treat as final the findings in fact which the Commissioners made in this Stated Case'. Lord Cullen observed that 'if, as would rather seem to be the case, the appellant has in his possession further information which would have thrown additional light on the position', but had 'chosen to withhold it, notwithstanding the request for its production made by the Commissioners, he has only himself to blame'. *Schulze v Bensted (No 2)*, CS 1922, 8 TC 259.

Accountant discredited—additional assessments

[4.339] A partnership's accounts were submitted by an accountant who was subsequently convicted of perjury. The Revenue made additional estimated assessments on the partnership. The Commissioners confirmed the assessments and the KB upheld their decision. *Tudor & Onions v Ducker*, KB 1924, 8 TC 591.

Accounts not produced

[4.340] A farming partnership appealed against an estimated assessment, but did not submit any accounts in support of the appeal. The Commissioners confirmed the assessment, and the KB upheld their decision. *H & C Stephenson v Waller*, KB 1927, 13 TC 318.

Uncertified accounts rejected

[4.341] A partnership which carried on an engineering business appealed against an estimated assessment, and produced accounts prepared by the senior partner, together with the original records. The Commissioners accepted the Revenue's contention that the assessment should be confirmed unless accounts audited by a qualified auditor were submitted within two months. The partnership appealed to the KB, which upheld the Commissioners' decision. *Hunt & Co v Joly*, KB 1928, 14 TC 165.

[4.342] A stockbroker (W) appealed against estimated assessments. He produced accounts which bore an accountant's certificate stating merely that had been 'prepared from the books of my client', but bore no certificate as to their accuracy. The Commissioners adjourned the appeal for six months to allow W to submit fully certified accounts. He failed to do so, and the Commissioners confirmed the assessments. The CA unanimously upheld their decision. *Wall v Cooper*, CA 1929, 14 TC 552.

Unsatisfactory accounts or figures rejected

[4.343] The Revenue issued an assessment on a sole trader, estimating his income as £400. He appealed and produced accounts prepared by a firm of solicitors, showing a profit of £233. The Revenue contended that the accounts were unreliable because 'a balancing figure had been used to represent drawings' and there was a book-keeping error of £10 in the treatment of depreciation. The Commissioners reduced the assessment to £345. The trader appealed. The CS held that there was no evidence in the Stated Case to support the Commissioners' determination, and remitted the case to them to reconsider the assessment. *Anderson v CIR*, CS 1933, 18 TC 320.

[4.344] A bookmaker (C) appealed against an estimated assessment of £500 on a bookmaker. The General Commissioners rejected C's accounts and increased the assessment to £2,000. The Ch D dismissed C's appeal, holding that there was evidence to support the increase. *Cain v Schofield*, Ch D 1953, 34 TC 362.

[4.345] A general dealer appealed against estimated assessments. At the hearing, he produced an incomplete statement of his profits. The General Commissioners found that he had not discharged the onus on him to show that the assessments were excessive, and confirmed them. The CS upheld their decision. *Moll v CIR*, CS 1955, 36 TC 384.

[4.346] General Commissioners determined an appeal against an estimated assessment on the basis of the inspector's figures, rather than those submitted by the trader. The Ch D upheld the Commissioners' decision. *Jacobs v Eavis*, Ch D 1956, 36 TC 576.

[4.347] A trader (H) who owned a sawmill appealed against estimated assessments. The Special Commissioners were not satisfied that H's accounts truly reflected the trading results of the sawmill, and confirmed the assessments. The CS upheld their decision. *Hood Barrs v CIR (No 4)*, CS 1967, 46 ATC 448.

[4.348] The Revenue considered that the accounts submitted by a car repairer were unsatisfactory. The Commissioners confirmed the assessments and the Ch D upheld their decision. *Cutmore v Leach*, Ch D 1981, 55 TC 602; [1982] STC 61.

[4.349] The Commissioners reduced estimated assessments on a self-employed market porter (B), who had not kept proper accounts. B appealed to the Ch D, contending that the assessments were still too high. The Ch D dismissed his appeal. *Branch v Smith*, Ch D 1984, [1985] STC 139.

[4.350] A decorator (B) appealed against estimated assessments for 1976/77 to 1982/83. The General Commissioners were not satisfied as to the accuracy of B's accounts and determined the appeals on the basis of their own estimates of his likely profits, confirming two assessments, slightly reducing one and increasing the remaining four. The Ch D upheld their decision. *Brittain v Gibb*, Ch D 1986, 59 TC 374; [1986] STC 418.

[4.351] The decision in *Brittain v Gibb*, 4.350 above, was applied in the similar case of *Mellor v Gurney*, Ch D 1994, 67 TC 216; [1994] STC 1025.

[4.352] A taxi driver appealed against estimated assessments. The General Commissioners did not accept his records as accurate and determined the assessments in reduced amounts. The Ch D upheld their decision. *Coy v Kime*, Ch D 1986, 59 TC 447; [1987] STC 114.

[4.353] The Ch D also upheld an estimated assessment on a taxi driver in *Adams v Hanson*, Ch D 1990, 63 TC 296; [1990] STC 374.

[4.354] A publican appealed against estimated assessments for 1973/74 to 1977/78 inclusive. His business records were poor and his accountant produced a capital statement, on the basis of which the assessments were too high for three years but slightly too low for the other two. The Commissioners increased the assessments to the amounts shown by the statement for those two years, and confirmed the other three assessments. The CA upheld their decision, holding that the Commissioners were entitled to look at each year separately and to take estimates into account. *Donnelly v Platten*, CA(NI) 1980, [1981] STC 504.

Onus on appellant to disprove assessment

[4.355] The Revenue issued an estimated additional assessment of £50,000 on a manufacturing company after discovering an increase of £22,920 in its capital account. The Commissioners confirmed the assessment, and the CA unanimously upheld their decision as one of fact. *T Haythornthwaite & Sons Ltd v Kelly*, CA 1927, 11 TC 657.

[4.356] A company's accounts showed a sum of £1,392 as capital introduced. The Revenue issued an assessment treating £1,300 of this as additional trading income. The Commissioners confirmed the assessment, and the CA unanimously upheld their decision as one of fact. *Stoneleigh Products Ltd v Dodd*, CA 1948, 30 TC 1.

[4.357] The Revenue issued estimated assessments for several years on a company which sold women's clothing, after discovering that a sale for £30 had been omitted from its books. The Commissioners confirmed the assessments subject to certain agreed amendments. The Ch D upheld their decision. *Rosette Franks (King Street) Ltd v Dick*, Ch D 1955, 36 TC 100.

[4.358] The Revenue issued estimated assessments for 1944/45 to 1956/57 inclusive on a garage proprietor who had repeatedly failed to supply information about his tax affairs. The General Commissioners confirmed the assessments, and the Ch D upheld their decision as one of fact. *Pierson v Belcher*, Ch D 1959, 38 TC 387.

[4.359] A freelance writer appealed against estimated assessments. The Commissioners reduced the assessments on his income from writing, but increased assessments on income from furnished lettings. The Ch D upheld their decision as one of fact. *Yoannou v Hall*, Ch D 1978, 53 TC 32; [1978] STC 600.

[4.360] A self-employed delivery driver (B) appealed against estimated assessments, and produced returns but no supporting accounts or records.

The Commissioners determined the appeals in amounts below the assessments but substantially above the amounts which B had declared. The Ch D upheld their decision as one of fact. *Bookey v Edwards*, Ch D 1981, 55 TC 486; [1982] STC 135.

[4.361] The Revenue issued estimated assessments charging tax on bank interest. The General Commissioners confirmed the assessments, and the CA unanimously upheld their decision as one of fact. *Eke v Knight*, CA 1977, 51 TC 121; [1977] STC 198.

[4.362] The Revenue issued an estimated assessment on a coin dealer (P). The Commissioners upheld the assessment and the Ch D dismissed P's appeal. *Phillimore v Heaton*, Ch D 1989, 61 TC 584; [1989] STC 374.

[4.363] The Revenue issued estimated assessments on a partnership which had operated three restaurants. The Special Commissioners upheld the assessments in principle, holding that 'the onus was on the appellants to show why the Revenue was wrong in assessing the unverified banking receipts for the periods in question as income from the only major identifiable source, namely Schedule D partnership income from their restaurant business'. *Sharifee & Others (t/a Café Flutist) v Wood*, Sp C [2004] SSCD 446 (Sp C 423).

[4.364] See also *Rouf v HMRC*, **29.65** FURTHER ASSESSMENTS: LOSS OF TAX, and the cases at **29.69** *et seq* FURTHER ASSESSMENTS: LOSS OF TAX.

Estimated assessment on bank interest

[4.365] A Rotary Club failed to submit returns. The inspector raised estimated assessments on bank interest in amounts somewhat in excess of figures notified to him by a bank. The club appealed, contending that the assessments were invalid as the inspector had known the true figures at the time he made the assessments, and therefore had not made them to the best of his judgment. The Special Commissioner rejected this contention and determined the assessments in agreed figures. The CA unanimously upheld this decision, holding that the inspector was entitled to consider the possibility that the club had received untaxed interest from other bank accounts in addition to the account of which he was aware. *Blackpool Marton Rotary Club v Martin*, CA 1989, 62 TC 686; [1990] STC 1. (*Note.* For another issue in this case, not taken to the CA, see **70.8** VOLUNTARY ASSOCIATIONS.)

First-tier Tribunal substantially allowing appeals

[4.366] In a Scottish case, a trader (C) carried on a business of repairing motor vehicles. HMRC began an enquiry into his return for 2006/07, which declared turnover of £42,777. They subsequently issued a closure notice amending his return to charge additional tax of £17,663 (on the basis that his turnover for the year had been more than £94,000), and also issued estimated assessments for 2004/05, 2005/06 and 2007/08, computed by applying the RPI to the estimated turnover for 2006/07. C appealed, contending that much of his income in 2006/07 had derived from gambling winnings. The First-tier Tribunal reviewed the evidence in detail and substantially allowed his appeal.

Judge Reid found that HMRC's estimate of C's turnover for 2006/07 was 'wholly unrealistic', since it suggested that 'there would have to have been a constant stream of motor vehicles passing through the appellant's premises fifty weeks a year and a production rate of six or seven vehicles every day'. He directed that the 2006/07 liability should be recomputed on the basis that C's turnover for the year had been £60,000. He also held that the estimated assessments for other years should be discharged, holding that the application of the RPI was not 'a legitimate way of proceeding' and observing that C's declared turnover for 2007/08 was £61,234, which was in line with the turnover as found by the tribunal for 2006/07. He commented that it was impossible to 'form any view as to the extent to which, if at all, the appellant has under-declared his turnover in these earlier years. This seems to distinguish the collection of cases on this general topic conveniently gathered together in Simon's Taxes.' *W Chapman v HMRC*, FTT [2011] UKFTT 756 (TC), TC01593.

Special Commissioners allowing appeal

[4.367] For a case in which the Special Commissioners allowed an appeal against estimated assessments, see *Gamble v Rowe*, 35.18 LOSS RELIEF.

Estimated capital gains tax assessment

[4.368] An appeal against an estimated CGT assessment was dismissed in *Horner v Madden*, Ch D 1995, 67 TC 434; [1995] STC 802.

Payment of tax pending appeal against estimated assessment

[4.369] See *Parikh v Currie*, 4.395 below.

Settling of appeals by agreement (TMA, s 54)

Whether appeal settled by agreement

[4.370] The Revenue issued CGT assessments to an individual (D), charging tax on the basis that a payment of £399,000 which he had received was consideration for the disposal of certain shares. D appealed, claiming that part of the payment was compensation for the loss of a directorship and was not consideration for the shares. The Revenue offered to treat £70,000 as compensation for the loss of the directorship. D did not agree to this figure, but at the hearing of the appeal, he contended that subsequent correspondence with the Revenue amounted to the agreement of the appeal, within *TMA, s 54*. The Special Commissioners rejected this contention and dismissed his appeal, holding that although the inspector had agreed in principle with the suggestion that the payment should be apportioned, there had been no agreement on figures, and thus no agreement of the appeal within *s 54*. The CA unanimously upheld this decision. Orr LJ held that, for an agreement to fall within *s 54*, it 'must be an agreement that the assessment is to be upheld or an agreement that it be discharged or an agreement that it is to be varied and, if it is an agreement to vary, it must specify what the varied amount of the assessment is to be or, at the very least, must provide the Commissioners with a basis from which the varied figure can be readily calculated. In the present case the agreement provided neither a figure nor any basis on which a figure could be calculated'. Accordingly, it 'was not an agreement falling within the section'. *Delbourgo v Field*, CA 1978, 52 TC 225; [1978] STC 234; [1978] 2 All ER 193.

[4.371] In November 1988 the Revenue issued an estimated 1987/88 CGT assessment to a company director (S), who had disposed of several loan notes for consideration of more than £3,000,000. S appealed. In May 1993 the Revenue issued an amended notice of assessment indicating no chargeable gains and no tax payable. The inspector subsequently wrote to S's accountants, stating that this notice had been issued because of information on file 'which suggests that there are substantial capital losses available for carry forward'. (The accountants subsequently ceased to act for S in relation to the appeal.) In November 1993 the inspector wrote to S, apologising for 'overlooking the fact that your loan notes had been redeemed' and for not including the gain in the amended notice. After further correspondence, the appeal was set down for hearing before the Special Commissioners, where S contended that the May 1993 notice had been an agreement, within *s 54*. The Special Commissioners rejected this contention and held that the appeal was still open. They were 'satisfied that (S) or his advisers knew after the receipt of this letter that the inspector had issued the amended notice in error, that error being that he had overlooked the disposal' of the loan notes. There had clearly been no *s 54* agreement before the issue of the amended notice, and the issue of that notice did 'not of itself change that fact'. The notice did not in itself constitute a *s 54* agreement. On the evidence, 'all the prior discussions with (S) and his agents had been on their part on the basis that (S) had a significant liability. At no time had (S) proposed that the liability should be treated as nil.' The issue of the notice was 'a unilateral act by the Revenue' which 'came out of the blue'. The purpose of *s 54* was 'to encourage settlement of disputes by discussion between the taxpayer and the Revenue. It is not its purpose to encourage unilateral generosity by the Revenue.' The Ch D and the CA unanimously upheld this decision. Jonathan Parker J held that the amended notice 'did not contain any offer capable of acceptance by the taxpayer so as to result in a *s 54* agreement'. Schiemann LJ observed that 'any citizen would be delighted to find that his tax liability was in truth nil. But in fact this taxpayer's liability was not nil and there is no reason to suppose that he thought it nil.' *Schuldenfrei v Hilton (aka Silver v HM Inspector of Taxes)*, CA 1999, 72 TC 167; [1999] STC 821.

[4.372] In the case noted at **71.341** CAPITAL GAINS TAX, an individual (R) had submitted a 1996/97 return indicating no tax due. In January 1998 the Revenue acknowledged the return and sent R a calculation of nil liability, based on the return. Subsequently the Revenue initiated an enquiry into the return and amended R's self-assessment under *TMA, s 28A*. R appealed, contending that the acknowledgement sent in January 1998 constituted an agreement under *TMA, s 54*. The Ch D rejected this contention and dismissed the appeal. Neuberger J observed that 'all that the inspector was doing was saying to the taxpayer: "On the basis of your figures this is your liability."' It was 'clear on the face of the relevant and current agreement that the inspector was not accepting the taxpayer's figures. She was simply stating the result of the taxpayer's entries.' Secondly, *TMA, s 9A(1)* gave the Revenue the right to enquire into a return. Thirdly, even if the acknowledgement sent by the Revenue could be held to be an agreement, it took place before there was any question of a notice of appeal, so that *s 54* had no application. *Rigby v Jayatilaka*, Ch D 2000, 72 TC 365; [2000] STC 179.

[4.373] In 2008 an individual (P) appealed against an assessment and an amendment to his self-assessment. He subsequently agreed the amount of the liability with HMRC. HMRC advised the Tribunal Centre that the appeals had been settled by agreement under *TMA, s 54*. In 2011 P applied for the appeal to be reinstated. The First-tier Tribunal rejected his application, finding that there had been an agreement under *s 54*, and that P had failed to repudiate it within the 30-day time limit provided by *s 54(2)*. *F Perera v HMRC*, FTT [2011] UKFTT 451 (TC), TC01303.

[4.374] A similar decision was reached in *C Thompson v HMRC (and related appeal)*, FTT [2014] UKFTT 826 (TC), TC03944.

[4.375] The Revenue issued income tax and surtax assessments on an individual (W). He appealed. Most of the appeals were determined by General Commissioners, and the other three were the subject of an agreement under *TMA, s 54(5)* between an inspector of taxes and an accountant who had been authorised to receive copies of assessments sent to W by a document dated nine months before the agreement. The Revenue began proceedings to recover the tax. W appealed against judgment and sought leave to defend the proceedings, contending that he had not given the accountant authority to enter into an agreement with the inspector on his behalf. The CA unanimously rejected this contention and dismissed W's appeal, finding that he had authorised the accountant to act on his behalf in his dealings with the Revenue, had apparently accepted for a substantial period of time that the accountant was corresponding with the Revenue on his behalf, and had not revoked the accountant's authority until more than two years after the determination of the assessments in question. *CIR v West*, CA 1991, 64 TC 196; [1991] STC 357.

[4.376] The decision in *CIR v West*, 4.375 above, was also applied in *K Marshom v HMRC*, FTT [2014] UKFTT 1027 (TC), TC04123, and in *CIR v Robinson*, 6.28 BANKRUPTCY.

[4.377] HMRC began an enquiry into the returns submitted by a sole trader (T). They issued estimated assessments and imposed penalties. T appealed. Following discussions, HMRC wrote to T's accountants offering to agree the appeals on the basis of a gross profit rate of 63%. T's accountants replied agreeing to this proposal but requesting that the penalties should be reduced. T subsequently applied to the First-tier Tribunal, requesting the reinstatement of the appeals. The tribunal accepted HMRC's contention that the appeals against the assessments had been settled by agreement under *TMA, s 54* and could not be reopened. However the tribunal accepted T's contention that the appeals against the penalties had not been agreed, and directed that they should be relisted for hearing. *F Tuncel v HMRC*, FTT [2014] UKFTT 171 (TC), TC03309.

[4.378] An individual (C) was made bankrupt in 1990. The Revenue accepted late appeals against assessments covering 1982/83 to 1990/91. In 1996 the appeals were settled by an agreement, under *TMA, s 54*, between the Revenue and C's trustee in bankruptcy. Later that year the trustee in bankruptcy paid a small dividend to all C's unsecured creditors, including the Revenue. C subsequently sought to have the appeals for 1988/89 and 1989/90 heard by a Special Commissioner. The Special Commissioner dismissed C's appeals, holding that the result of C's bankruptcy was that he had lost the right to pursue the appeals, and that the trustee in bankruptcy 'had sole responsibility for dealing with all these appeals'. The trustee had settled the appeals by agreement, within *TMA, s 54*, and 'the Special Commissioners have no jurisdiction to reopen appeals settled by the trustee in bankruptcy'. *Ahajot (Count Artsrunik) v Waller*, Sp C [2004] SSCD 151 (Sp C 395).

[4.379] A chartered accountant (M) entered into a series of transactions in 1997/98, intended to produce a capital loss. Following an enquiry, HMRC rejected his loss claim and amended his self-assessment to charge additional tax of £951,790. M appealed, and applied for postponement of the tax. The General Commissioners rejected the postponement application, and HMRC took county court proceedings to collect the tax. The Durham County Court gave judgment for HMRC, and in 2006 M was declared bankrupt. The trustee in bankruptcy decided not to proceed with the appeal against the closure notice, and admitted HMRC's claim. In 2010 M sought to have his appeal heard by the First-tier Tribunal. The First-tier Tribunal held that he had no 'locus standi' to pursue the appeal, as that right had vested in the trustee, who had agreed to settle the appeal, within *TMA, s 54(1)*. The Upper Tribunal upheld this decision. *D McNulty v HMRC*, UT [2012] UKUT 174 (TCC); [2012] STC 2110.

[4.380] In *R (oao HMRC) v Berkshire Commrs*, **29.124** FURTHER ASSESSMENTS: LOSS OF TAX, the QB upheld HMRC's contention that an agreement under *TMA, s 54*, signed in 2004 by two brothers who had carried on business in partnership, only covered the years from 1998/99 to 2001/02. Following the QB decision, HMRC issued further closure notices for 2002/03. The brothers appealed, contending as a preliminary point that, notwithstanding the QB decision, the issue of further notices was precluded by the previous agreement, and alternatively that the relevant liabilities had been settled by agreement at a meeting with HMRC in April 2012. The First-tier Tribunal rejected these contentions, holding that the QB decision was binding with regard to the scope of the 2004 agreement, and that the April 2012 meeting did not constitute an agreement of the appeals, within *s 54*. *R & S Thomas v HMRC (No 2)*, FTT [2013] UKFTT 203 (TC), TC02618. (*Note*. For subsequent proceedings in this case, see **4.107** above.)

[4.381] Following an enquiry into a return submitted by a sole trader (E), HMRC issued a notice of amendment directing that £19,400 which E had claimed as expenses should be included in his profits. E appealed, contending that the £19,400 had been paid to subcontractors who had carried out work on his computers. E attended a meeting with an HMRC officer (D) in January 2009. D formed the opinion that, at this meeting, E had agreed that the £19,400 should be included in his profits. E disagreed, and wrote to HMRC in February 2009 confirming his disagreement. E subsequently applied to the

First-tier Tribunal to have his appeal set down for hearing. HMRC opposed the application, contending that the appeal had already been agreed under *TMA, s 54*. The First-tier Tribunal rejected HMRC's contention, granted E's application, and allowed his appeal. Judge Radford found that E had never signed any agreement under *s 54*, and that E had paid the £19,400 for work on his computers. She also found that E 'was misled to a degree by (D) and was of the belief that the invoices had been accepted'. *J Edoh v HMRC*, FTT [2012] UKFTT 787 (TC), TC02438.

[4.382] See also *Jones v Mason Investments (Luton) Ltd*, **5.33** ASSESSMENTS; *Cansick (Murphy's Executor) v Hochstrasser*, **5.41** ASSESSMENTS, and *Foulser v HMRC*, **43.19** PAYMENT OF TAX.).

Extent of agreement based on mistaken view of the law

[4.383] In 1968 a company (S) entered into a sale and leaseback agreement in relation to its trading premises, which it had acquired before April 1965. In arriving at the gain/loss on the disposal, it elected that the basis value of the premises should be taken as their market value on 6 April 1965. In 1974 an inspector agreed with S's accountant that there was a loss of £100,125 available for carry-forward. Both had, however, failed to realise that what is now *TCGA 1992, Sch 2 para 17(2)* applied, so that there was neither a gain nor a loss. In 1976 the Revenue issued an estimated corporation tax assessment for the accounting period ending December 1975. S appealed. The appeal was settled by an agreement under *TMA, s 54(1)*, with £374 of the loss being allowed against a capital gain. In a subsequent letter, the inspector agreed that capital losses of £99,751 were still available to be carried forward. In its accounting period ending December 1981, S made a substantial gain, against which it claimed to set the balance of the loss. A different inspector reviewed the position, noticed the error made in 1974, and rejected the claim. The Ch D upheld his decision. Knox J held that the effect of an agreement under *TMA, s 54(1)*'can be no wider than the binding effect of a determination of Commissioners or an appeal from them'. He observed that 'there is no machinery provided for determination of the size of an allowable loss which both the taxpayer and the Crown agree is more than large enough to wipe out all chargeable gains in the relevant accounting period but upon which they disagree about the excess over those chargeable gains.' *Tod v South Essex Motors (Basildon) Ltd*, Ch D 1987, 60 TC 598; [1988] STC 392.

[4.384] In the case noted at **33.30** INTEREST PAYABLE, assessments for periods up to 31 March 1988 had been settled under *TMA, s 54*, and an inspector had agreed a figure of 'excess management expenses' available for carry-forward. Subsequently the Revenue formed the opinion that the payments in question were not allowable for tax purposes. The Ch D held that the agreement under *TMA, s 54* only covered the assessments which had been the subject of the relevant appeal, and did not bind the Revenue for subsequent years. The HL upheld this decision. Lord Hope held that 'an agreement made under *s 54* has no wider effect upon the position of either party than that which has been provided for by the statute'. *MacNiven v Westmoreland Investments Ltd*, HL 2001, 73 TC 1; [2001] STC 237; [2001] 2 WLR 377; [2001] 1 All ER 865. (*Note*. The HL found in favour of the company on the substantive issue.)

[4.385] In the case noted at **46.27** PENSION SCHEMES, Lewison J held that 'unless there is formal machinery which would enable the Commissioners to determine a formal claim to carry forward a specific sum, a *section 54* agreement cannot have that effect. The point is not that the legislation permits amounts to be carried forward. Rather, the point is whether the machinery for determining tax liability is limited to determining the amount of the taxpayer's liability for a particular year of assessment, or whether it extends to determining an amount due in a future year. Only in the latter case could a *section 54* agreement bind the Revenue for future years of assessment.' *Lonsdale v Braisby*, Ch D [2004] STC 1606; [2004] EWHC 1811 (Ch). (*Note*. For another issue in this case, see **4.234** above.)

[4.386] See also *Cansick v Hochstrasser*, **5.41** ASSESSMENTS.

Appeal settled by agreement—excess group relief given

[4.387] In November 1983 a company (B) appealed against a corporation tax assessment for its accounting period ending in September 1982. The appeal was settled by agreement under *TMA, s 54*, the profits being determined at £62,480,000. However, group relief of £3,550,000 was, in error, given twice in the computation. The error was discovered in November 1989, but B refused to agree to the rectification of the assessment, contending that it was incapable of amendment. The Revenue began proceedings before the General Commissioners. B applied for judicial review of the Revenue's decision, and the Revenue applied to the QB for a declaration that B's chargeable profits for the relevant accounting period were £66,030,000 rather than £62,480,000, and that the agreement under *TMA, s 54* should be rectified accordingly. The QB rejected B's application for judicial review and granted the declaration sought by the Revenue. The ordinary law of contract applied. The effect of an agreement under *TMA, s 54* was that it should be final and conclusive as regards the issues which it determined, but that did not prevent the court from considering whether all the conditions necessary to the formation of a proper contract had been satisfied. There was an implicit common understanding that group relief would be given once only against the gross taxable profits. The determination under *TMA, s 54* wrongly recorded that common intention. Accordingly, the excess group relief should be deleted from the assessment. *Richart v Bass Holdings Ltd; R v HMIT (ex p. Bass Holdings Ltd)*, QB 1992, TL 3354; [1993] STC 122.

Agreement under TMA, s 54 based on mistake of fact

[4.388] The Revenue issued a CGT assessment on an individual (F) who had disposed of some shares. The inspector wrote to the F's agents informing them that the valuation of the shares in question had been agreed by the Inland Revenue Shares Valuation Division ('SVD'), and inviting them to agree the open appeal under *TMA, s 54*. The agents did so. F subsequently sought to proceed with his appeal against the assessment, contending that he had not agreed to the valuation in his discussions with SVD, and that there had been no valid agreement under *s 54*. The Special Commissioner accepted F's evidence that he had not reached an agreement with SVD, and held that he was entitled to proceed with his appeal. *Fox v Rothwell*, Sp C [1995] SSCD 336 (Sp C 50).

Whether further assessment permissible

[4.389] See the cases noted at 5.75 to 5.86 ASSESSMENTS. In *Olin Energy Systems Ltd v Scorer*, 5.81 ASSESSMENTS, Fox LJ held that the purpose of *TMA, s 54* 'must be to protect the taxpayer by producing finality', and that Parliament 'must have contemplated that the taxpayer would be protected, even though the inspector made some error in his view of the facts or the law'. In *Gray v Matheson*, 5.82 ASSESSMENTS, Vinelott J held that further assessments were permissible when the agreement under *TMA, s 54* was based on returns or accounts containing figures which were subsequently shown to be incorrect.

Appeal settled by agreement—whether further enquiry permissible

[4.390] See *Easinghall Ltd v HMRC*, 55.29 SELF-ASSESSMENT.

Agreement under TMA, s 54—subsequent claim under TMA, s 33

[4.391] See *Eagerpath Ltd v Edwards*, 24.6 ERROR OR MISTAKE RELIEF, and *Thompson v CIR*, 24.7 ERROR OR MISTAKE RELIEF.

Validity of agreement disputed in collection proceedings

[4.392] See *CIR v Aken*, 43.9 PAYMENT OF TAX, and *R v HM Inspector of Taxes (ex p. Uchendu)*, 43.31 PAYMENT OF TAX.

Withdrawal of appeal—application of TMA, s 54(4)(a)

[4.393] In the case noted at 4.108 above, HMRC had originally contended that the appellant partnership (OP) had been trading, and that its returns had understated its profits by more than £1,000,000. HMRC had subsequently raised an alternative argument, accepting OP's contention that the relevant transactions were capital in nature but rejecting OP's contention that they qualified for business asset taper relief. The result of this would be that each of the six partners would have made a capital gain of £110,099, rather than £35,903 as declared in the partnership returns, and OP's total profit would be increased by £444,996 (ie an increase of £74,166 for each of the partners). In May 2011 HMRC issued an amended Statement of Case stating that they accepted OP's contention that it had not been trading and stating that 'the profit should be increased by £74,166'. In June 2011 OP's accountants sent an email to HMRC and the Tribunal Centre stating that OP 'wish to withdraw their appeal against the contention by HM Revenue & Customs that the partnership profit should be increased by £74,166'. In September 2011 HMRC issued amendments to the returns of each of the partners showing an increased profit of £74,166 for each partner. OP appealed against these amendments, contending that its original appeals had been determined by a binding agreement under *TMA, s 54*, by which the total partnership profit, rather than the profit for each partner, had been increased by £74,166. The First-tier Tribunal rejected this contention. Judge Sinfield observed that the email sent by OP's accountants 'stated that the appeal that was being withdrawn was against the contention by HMRC that the partnership profit should be increased by £74,166. This was an odd statement as there was no previous decision to that effect and (OP) had never appealed against any such decision. (OP)'s notice of appeal referred to a primary claim for an increase in profit of £1,146,102 and a secondary claim for £444,996.' He observed that it was 'very unlikely' that the accountants, 'who had computed the overall tax liability of £444,996 in the notice of appeal by multiplying HMRC's figure for the increase in profit per partner of £74,166 by the number of partners, did not realise that the amount of £74,166 in the amended statement of case was a simple error rather than a proposal to settle'. It appeared that OP 'was deliberately trying to take advantage of an obvious error in the statement of case which understated the tax in dispute'. Applying the CA decision in *Schuldenfrei v Hilton*, **4.371** above, there had been no agreement of the appeal under *s 54(1)*. By virtue of *TMA, s 54(4)*, the consequence of OP's withdrawal of the appeal was 'that the decision under appeal should be upheld without variation'. The appeal had been against HMRC's contention that the partnership's profit should be increased by £444,996. Judge Sinfield concluded that 'as a consequence of withdrawing the appeal in the absence of an agreement, (OP) has made itself liable to pay the tax due on the basis of HMRC's alternative argument with no opportunity to appeal against that decision'. *Orchid Properties v HMRC (No 2)*, FTT [2012] UKFTT 651 (TC), TC02323.

Application of TMA, s 54(4)(b)

[4.394] See *Beach v Willesden Commrs & CIR*, **44.332** PENALTIES.

Recovery of tax not postponed (TMA, s 55)

Application for postponement

[4.395] An appellant (P) applied for payment of tax to be postponed under *TMA, s 55*. The Special Commissioners rejected the application, finding that P had failed to submit evidence as to the amount of the relevant income. The Ch D and the CA unanimously upheld their decision. *Parikh v Currie*, CA 1978, 52 TC 366; [1978] STC 473. (*Notes*. (1) For another issue in this case, see **4.175** above. (2) The appellant appeared in person. Stamp LJ and Roskill LJ both described the appeal as 'hopeless'.)

[4.396] In the case noted at **43.8** PAYMENT OF TAX, a company, the registered office of which was in Scotland, applied for judicial review of a decision by a Special Commissioner, sitting in London, on an application under *TMA, s 55* for postponement of the tax charged by two corporation tax assessments. The

Revenue had taken proceedings in the CS to recover the tax in question, and applied to the QB for the judicial review proceedings to be stayed, contending that any such proceedings were proper to the CS rather than to the QB. The QB ordered a stay of the proceedings, holding that the proper forum for the resolution of the dispute between the parties was clearly the CS. MacPherson J held that 'as a matter of common sense and convenience', all activity in the case should be in Scotland. Costs were awarded to the Revenue. *R v Special Commr (ex p. RW Forsyth Ltd)*, QB 1986, 61 TC 7; [1986] STC 565; [1987] 1 All ER 1035.

[4.397] In December 2000 the Revenue issued a CT assessment charging tax of £36,872,466. On 8 January 2001 the company (P) appealed, and applied for postponement of the whole amount, stating in its application that it believed that it had no tax liability. On 12 January the Revenue wrote to P stating that the postponement application was not accepted. However, on 15 January the Revenue issued a form 64-5 indicating that the full amount of tax was agreed to be postponed. On 17 January the Revenue issued a replacement form 64-5 indicating that no tax was agreed to be postponed. The postponement application was heard by a Special Commissioner on 30 March. P contended firstly that the form 64-5 which the Revenue had issued on 15 January was an agreement of its postponement application, within *TMA, s 55(7)*, and secondly that the full amount of tax should be postponed. The Revenue gave evidence that the form had been issued in error, as a result of a computer operator pressing the wrong button, and that a replacement form had been issued as soon as the error had been realised. On the evidence submitted at the hearing, the Revenue accepted that £688,008 of the tax should be postponed, but contended that there were no grounds for postponing the balance of £36,184,458. The Special Commissioner accepted the Revenue's evidence and dismissed P's application, holding on the evidence that there were 'no reasonable grounds for believing that the appellant is overcharged to tax, other than by the sum of £688,008 as agreed'. Furthermore, in view of the wording of the letter which the Revenue had issued on 12 January, the form 64-5 which the Revenue had issued in error on 15 January did not constitute an agreement of the postponement application, within *TMA, s 55(7)*. P appealed to the Ch D, contending that the effect of the decision in *Bray v Best*, **54.20** SCHEDULE E, was that the whole of the tax should be postponed. Park J remitted the case to a different Special Commissioner for reconsideration of P's arguments on this issue. The Revenue appealed to the CA, contending that it had been unnecessary for Park J to remit the case, since he should himself have determined the validity of P's arguments concerning the effect of the decision in *Bray v Best*. The CA rejected this contention. Peter Gibson LJ held that Park J had been 'right not to usurp the functions of the Special Commissioner'. *Pumahaven Ltd v Williams (aka Sparrow Ltd v HM Inspector of Taxes)*, CA 2003, 75 TC 300; [2003] STC 890; [2003] EWCA Civ 700. (*Note*. P's contention, based on the decision in *Bray v Best*, was that because it did not hold the relevant source of income during the period assessed, there should be no tax liability. This principle was laid down by the HL in the 1921 case of *National Provident Institution v Brown*, **52.51** SAVINGS AND INVESTMENT INCOME, but was subsequently unanimously disapproved by the HL in the 2000 case of *The Centaur Clothes Group Ltd v Walker*, **18.60**

CORPORATION TAX: see in particular the leading judgment of Lord Hoffmann. However, the inspector who represented the Revenue before the Special Commissioner failed to make any reference to the decision in *Centaur Clothes Group Ltd v Walker*.)

[4.398] In the case noted at **22.317** EMPLOYMENT INCOME, the appellant (R) applied for payment of the tax charged to be postponed under *TMA, s 55*. The General Commissioners dismissed the postponement application and HMRC applied for summary judgment. The Ch D dismissed HMRC's application. Floyd J held that the Commissioners should have granted R's application for postponement. An application for summary judgment should only be granted where there was 'no real prospect of success in defending the claim'. This was not the case here. *HMRC v KA Rogers*, Ch D [2009] EWHC 3433 (Ch); [2010] STC 236.

[4.399] Four individuals appealed against amendments to their self-assessments for 2004/05. They applied under *TMA, s 55* for postponement of the tax due, contending that they had suffered losses in 2005/06 which would be available to be carried back against the tax assessed. HMRC rejected three of the postponement applications, considering that the applicants had not shown that they had incurred the losses which they had claimed. In the case of the fourth application, they agreed to postpone tax of £924,000 but refused to postpone the balance of £520,000. The First-tier Tribunal upheld HMRC's decisions, holding that the applicants had failed to show the 'amount believed to be overcharged to tax', as required by *TMA, s 55(3)*. *M Cox v HMRC (and related appeals)*, FTT [2010] UKFTT 51 (TC), TC00364.

[4.400] Following an enquiry, HMRC formed the opinion that an individual (G) had failed to declare tax due on certain income. They issued an amendment to G's return, charging additional tax of £112,500. G applied for payment of the additional tax to be postponed. HMRC rejected the application and the First-tier Tribunal dismissed G's appeal. *D Gradel v HMRC*, FTT [2010] UKFTT 325 (TC), TC00610.

[4.401] A company (B) purchased a farm. It decided to develop a golf course on the site, and received substantial payments in return for allowing material to be tipped on the site. HMRC issued an assessment charging tax on these payments. B appealed and applied for postponement of the tax charged by the assessments, contending that it had received the payments as agent for an associated partnership. HMRC opposed the postponement application but the tribunal granted it, expressing the view that 'there is evidence on which a tribunal could reasonably conclude that the company did not receive the tipping receipts in its own right'. *Blunts Farm Estate Ltd v HMRC*, FTT [2010] UKFTT 469 (TC), TC00731.

[4.402] HMRC issued protective assessments for the years 1989/90 to 2007/08, under *TMA, s 29*, on an individual (P) who had failed to declare income from a Jersey bank account. P appealed, and applied for postponement of the tax charged. The First-tier Tribunal allowed the postponement application for 1989/90 to 1995/96, but dismissed it for 1996/97 to 2007/08. *H Patel v HMRC*, FTT [2011] UKFTT 104 (TC), TC00980.

[4.403] The Serious Organised Crime Agency (subsequently replaced by the National Crime Agency) raised various assessments on a company director (D) and his estranged wife (F). They appealed, and applied for postponement of the tax charged. The First-tier Tribunal reviewed the evidence in detail and dismissed D's application, finding that there were no 'grounds for believing that he will successfully challenge' the disputed assessments, but allowed F's application, finding that she had a reasonable contention that she had been assessed on income which should have been assessed on D. *GH Dong v National Crime Agency (No 1)*, FTT [2014] UKFTT 128 (TC), TC03268. (*Note*. For subsequent developments in this case, see **4.405** below.)

[4.404] The Serious Organised Crime Agency (subsequently replaced by the National Crime Agency) issued assessments for 1996/97 to 2004/05 on a woman (H) whose husband had been imprisoned for money laundering and whose bank account showed substantial deposits. H appealed, and applied for postponement of the tax charged. The First-tier Tribunal granted her application for 1996/97 but dismissed it for 1997/98 to 2004/05 inclusive. *Mrs NS Haq v National Crime Agency*, FTT [2014] UKFTT 1104 (TC), TC04192.

Whether TMA, s 55(6A) valid

[4.405] Following the decision noted at **4.403** above, the unsuccessful applicant (D) applied for permission to appeal. Judge Mosedale observed that *TMA, s 55(6A)*, which had been introduced by the *Transfer of Tribunal Functions and Revenue and Customs Appeals Order 2009 (SI 2009/56), Sch 1 para 34(8)*, stated that there was no right of appeal against a decision of the First-tier Tribunal concerning a postponement application, and had 'removed the pre-existing right of appeal'. She held that this provision was *ultra vires* and unlawful, and declined to apply it. She granted D permission to appeal against the decision noted at **4.403** above. *GH Dong v National Crime Agency (No 2)*, FTT [2014] UKFTT 369 (TC), TC03502.

Determination of tax payable—effect of TMA, s 55(9)

[4.406] Appeals against estimated assessments came before General Commissioners in April 1991 and were adjourned until June 1991. The appellant (S) and his agent attended the first hearing but did not attend the subsequent hearing, and the Commissioners determined the appeals were determined by . Subsequently the Revenue issued a determination under *TMA, s 55(9)*, indicating the amount of tax payable in accordance with the Commissioners' determination of the appeal. However, S had left the address to which the determination was sent, and never received it. The Ch D held that, since notice of the total sums payable had not been given to S in accordance with *TMA, s 55(9)*, the tax had not become payable and there was no ground to found a statutory demand under *Insolvency Act 1986, s 268(1)(a)*. *Re A Debtor (No 1240/SD/91), Sinclair v CIR*, Ch D 1992, 65 TC 94; [1992] STC 771.

The award of costs

Applications by appellant

Cases where the application was unsuccessful

Costs of premature application for judicial review

[4.407] A Netherlands company (O) received royalties from a UK company (T). The Revenue instructed T to deduct tax from the payments. In April 1984 O applied for a direction that the payments should be made gross, since, by virtue of the Double Taxation Treaty between the UK and the Netherlands, the royalties were not subject to UK tax. On 18 June, without giving advance warning to the Revenue, O applied for judicial review. In July the Revenue accepted that the royalties were not subject to UK tax. O applied to the QB for the costs of its application for judicial review. The QB rejected the application, holding that O should have warned the Revenue of its intention to apply for judicial review, since this might have made the proceedings unnecessary. *R v CIR (ex p. Opman International UK)*, QB 1985, 59 TC 352; [1986] STC 18; [1986] 1 WLR 568; [1986] 1 All ER 328.

Proceedings rendered abortive by retrospective legislation

[4.408] Two building societies had made applications for judicial review of the validity of the *Income Tax (Building Societies) Regulations (SI 1986/482)*. However, these proceedings were rendered abortive by the enactment of *FA 1991, s 53*, which provided that the regulations should be retrospectively deemed to have been valid. Further proceedings were rendered abortive by *F(No 2)A 1992, s 64*. The societies applied for a payment of indemnity costs. The QB dismissed the applications, holding that, with regard to the proceedings which were rendered abortive by *FA 1991*, costs should be paid to the societies only on the standard basis (which the Treasury had conceded), and that, with regard to the subsequent proceedings, each side should bear its own costs. Neill LJ observed that, even in a case where there were good grounds for thinking that legislation had been introduced at the behest of a Government Department, 'it would need careful consideration before one came to the conclusion that an order for costs should be made against the Government Department', since the decision to change the law was the decision of Parliament. Furthermore, 'indemnity costs are a form of order which the court makes only in very exceptional circumstances', and it would be 'quite wrong to apply that unusual and draconian form of order in circumstances such as these'. Mantell J observed that 'if you take on a Government Department one of the inherent risks to which you have to have regard' was that 'halfway through you will find that the goal posts have moved'. *R v HM Treasury (ex p. Leeds Permanent Building Society); R v HM Treasury (ex p. National & Provincial Building Society)*, QB 12 May 1993, Times 28 May 1993. (*Note.* Following this decision, the societies made an unsuccessful application to the European Court of Human Rights—see **31.94** HUMAN RIGHTS.)

Successful appellant represented by 'tax adviser'—application for costs

[4.409] In the case noted at **68.134** TRADING PROFITS, the appellant had consulted a firm of tax advisers. Following the CA decision in his favour, he applied for costs incurred by the relevant partner (M), who was a member of the Chartered Institute of Taxation but not a solicitor. The Revenue objected to the claim on the grounds that M was not a solicitor or barrister, so that the appellant had to be treated as a 'litigant in person'. The CA accepted the Revenue's contentions that the appellant was not entitled to the amount claimed. Dyson LJ held that 'where a member of the Chartered Institute of Taxation instructs a barrister under the Licensed Access Scheme, the presence of the barrister does not prevent the party on whose behalf the barrister has been instructed from being a litigant in person'. Applying the principles laid down by Tuckey LJ in *United Building & Plumbing Contractors v Malkit Singh Kajila*, CA [2002] EWCA Civ 628, the appellant was 'not entitled to recover costs as a disbursement in respect of work done by (M) which would normally have been done by a solicitor who had been instructed to conduct the appeal. This means that the appellant is not entitled to recover for the cost of (M) providing general assistance to counsel in the conduct of the appeals.' *Agassi v Robinson (No 2)*, CA 2005, [2006] STC 580; [2005] EWCA Civ 1507; [2006] 1 All ER 900. (*Note.* The HL subsequently reversed the CA decision on the substantive appeal, and restored the Ch D decision which had been in favour of the Revenue.)

Successful appeal against estimated assessments

[4.410] In the case noted at **35.18** LOSS RELIEF, the Special Commissioner allowed appeals against estimated assessments, finding on the evidence that it was 'very improbable that the appellant made business profits, either of the amounts estimated in the assessments, or at all'. The Commissioner rejected the appellant's application for costs, holding that the Revenue had not acted 'wholly unreasonably', so that costs were not to be awarded. The Ch D upheld this decision. *Gamble v Rowe*, Ch D [1998] STC 1247.

Revenue withdrawing assessments before hearing

[4.411] The Revenue had issued several CGT assessments on an individual (C), who was the settlor of a Cayman Islands settlement and who occupied a house which was partly owned by the trustees of the settlement. C appealed, and the appeals were listed for hearing before a Special Commissioner on 20 September 1999. On 17 September the Revenue informed C's solicitors that they agreed that five of the assessments should be discharged and that the other two should be reduced. C refrained from entering into an agreement under *TMA, s 54*, and asked the Commissioner to make an award of costs. The Commissioner rejected the application, holding that the Revenue had not acted 'wholly unreasonably'. On the evidence, it was not until May 1999 that C's solicitors had provided information that C had received no benefit from his occupation of the property (because the costs of repair and insurance exceeded its annual value). The Revenue had then requested the District Valuer to reconsider his previous valuation, and there had been no unreasonable delay in doing this. Part of the reason for the delay in the valuer inspecting the property was that C had been away on holiday. *Carter v Hunt*, Sp C 1999, [2000] SSCD 17 (Sp C 220).

[4.412] An individual (H) had failed to submit tax returns, and HMRC had issued estimated assessments. Subsequently H submitted late returns showing very low income, and HMRC agreed to withdraw the assessments. H applied for costs. The First-tier Tribunal rejected his application, holding that HMRC had not acted unreasonably. *J Hannigan v HMRC*, FTT [2010] UKFTT 141 (TC), TC00447.

[4.413] The First-tier Tribunal reached similar decisions in *G Waller v HMRC*, FTT [2010] UKFTT 450 (TC), TC00715, and *T Maryan v HMRC*, FTT [2012] UKFTT 215 (TC), TC01910.

[4.414] HMRC issued a determination that a company (S) was required to pay national insurance contributions. S appealed, and HMRC subsequently withdrew the determination. S applied for costs of £4,993. HMRC offered to pay costs of £4,500. S rejected this offer. The First-tier Tribunal reviewed the evidence in detail and held that the hourly rate claimed by S's accountant (R) was excessive. Judge Herrington also found that S had acted unreasonably in refusing HMRC's offer, and in prolonging the correspondence in litigation. He held that 'no reasonable adviser, having been offered approximately 90% of the amount claimed against a background of real doubt as to whether a large proportion of the claim was recoverable in any event, would have advised against acceptance of such an offer'. S's unreasonable conduct had 'caused HMRC, at public expense, to incur further substantial costs'. Judge Herrington directed that S should pay costs of £12,611 to HMRC. He observed that '(S) and their adviser have been the authors of their own misfortune. (R), in particular, has had an unshakeable conviction in his own rectitude which has led to his inability to deal with the matter in a pragmatic fashion'. *Stomgrove Ltd v HMRC*, FTT [2014] UKFTT 169 (TC), TC03307.

[4.415] An individual (L) appealed against a CGT assessment, contending that it had been raised outside the statutory time limit and failed to meet the requirements of *TMA, s 29(5)*. After correspondence, HMRC withdrew the assessment, and L applied for costs. The First-tier Tribunal dismissed the application, holding that HMRC had not acted unreasonably. *P Letts v HMRC*, FTT [2014] UKFTT 709 (TC), TC03830.

HMRC agreeing to discharge assessments after adjournment of hearing

[4.416] A couple appealed against assessments for 1996/97 to 2005/06. The appeals were set down for hearing before the General Commissioners, but had not been heard when the Commissioners' jurisdiction was transferred to the First-tier Tribunal under the *Tribunals, Courts and Enforcement Act 2007*. The First-tier Tribunal began hearing the appeals in October 2009, but the hearing was adjourned. Following the adjournment, HMRC agreed to discharge the assessments. The couple applied for costs, but the tribunal rejected their application. Judge Mosedale held that the effect of *Transfer of Tribunal Functions and Revenue and Customs Appeals Order 2009 (SI 2009/56), Sch 3 para 7* was that the tribunal could not award costs in cases where the appeals were 'current proceedings' within *para 1(2)* of that *Order*. *B & VR Dines v HMRC*, FTT [2011] UKFTT 452 (TC), TC01304.

Revenue agreeing to reduce assessments shortly before hearing

[4.417] The Revenue began an enquiry into a bricklayer's returns, formed the opinion that his declared income was insufficient to meet his expenditure, and issued an assessment. The bricklayer appealed, and his accountant contended that the inspector had overestimated the relevant expenditure, which was within the declared income of the bricklayer and his wife. The Special Commissioner adjourned the appeals to enable the bricklayer to submit copies of his wife's bank statements. After he had done so, the Revenue agreed to settle the appeal by agreement under *TMA, s 54*. The bricklayer subsequently applied for costs. The Commissioner dismissed this application, holding that the Revenue had not acted 'wholly unreasonably'. *Conlon v Hewitt*, Sp C 2004, [2005] SSCD 46 (Sp C 436).

[4.418] HMRC began an enquiry into the return submitted by an individual (C), and subsequently issued an amendment, against which C appealed. On the day of the hearing, HMRC agreed to reduce the amount charged by the amendment. C applied for costs. The First-tier Tribunal rejected his application, holding that HMRC had not acted unreasonably, and the Upper Tribunal dismissed C's appeal against this decision. *GC Catana v HMRC*, UT [2012] UKUT 172 (TCC); [2012] STC 2138.

Appellant partly successful—application for costs

[4.419] In a case where an appeal against an assessment was partly successful, the appellant applied for costs. The Special Commissioner dismissed the application, finding that the Revenue had acted unreasonably, but observing that 'each party has succeeded in roughly equal amounts' and holding that this was not 'a case where costs should be awarded'. *McEwan v HMRC*, Sp C July 2005 (Sp C 488).

Application for costs by successful appellant

[4.420] The succesful appellant in the case noted at **22.286** EMPLOYMENT INCOME subsequently applied for costs. The Commissioners rejected the application, holding that the Revenue had not acted 'wholly unreasonably' and that, although there had been a delay in hearing the appeal, this delay 'was due as much to the appellant as to the Inland Revenue'. *Lavery v MacLeod*, Sp C [2003] SSCD 413 (Sp C 375).

[4.421] In *Vela-Castro & Others v Wilson (No 1)*, **71.229** CAPITAL GAINS TAX, the Special Commissioner held that the sale of goodwill qualified for rollover relief. The successful appellants subsequently applied for costs. The Commissioner dismissed this application, finding that HMRC had 'acted reasonably throughout the appeal proceedings'. *Kidney & Others v HMRC*, Sp C [2006] SSCD 660 (Sp C 558).

[4.422] In the case noted at **23.8** ENTERPRISE INVESTMENT SCHEME, the successful appellant company applied for costs. The Special Commissioner dismissed the application, finding that HMRC had 'acted wholly reasonably in connection with the hearing of the appeal'. *GC Trading Ltd v HMRC (No 2)*, Sp C [2008] SSCD 855 (Sp C 686).

[4.423] The successful appellant in the case noted at **44.430** PENALTIES applied for costs. The First-tier Tribunal dismissed his application, holding that HMRC had not acted unreasonably. *G Brown v HMRC (No 2)*, FTT [2014] UKFTT 984 (TC), TC04096.

Unsuccessful appellant applying for costs

[4.424] In the case noted at **22.168** EMPLOYMENT INCOME, the Revenue had initially sought to collect national insurance contributions as well as income tax. The Revenue subsequently withdrew their claims to national insurance contributions, and the Special Commissioners found in favour of the Revenue on the income tax appeals. The unsuccessful appellants applied for costs, contending that the Revenue had acted unreasonably in seeking to charge national insurance contributions. The Special Commissioner rejected this contention and dismissed the application. *Collins v Laing (No 2); X1 Software Ltd v Laing (No 2)*, Sp C [2005] SSCD 453 (Sp C 472).

[4.425] A company, which had unsuccessfully appealed to the Special Commissioners against notices of amendment charging tonnage tax, subsequently applied for costs. The First-tier Tribunal dismissed the application, holding that HMRC had not acted unreasonably. *Western Ferries (Clyde) Ltd v HMRC*, FTT [2011] UKFTT 541 (TC), TC01388.

Cases where the application was partly successful

[4.426] In the case noted at 25.22 EUROPEAN LAW, the appellant company (M) applied for the costs of its appeal to the Upper Tribunal. The Tribunal observed that it was not appropriate to award M the whole of its costs, since HMRC had been successful in relation to part of the period covered by the appeal. The Tribunal judged that M had been successful with regard to 75% of the appeal and HMRC had been successful with regard to 25%. Accordingly the Tribunal held that, in principle, HMRC should pay M 50% of its costs. The Tribunal also expressed concern that the amount claimed by M was grossly excessive. The Tribunal noted that M had claimed costs of £433,000, and expressed the view that 'this is a breathtaking amount for an appeal in circumstances where the Tribunal gave full and carefully reasoned decisions on all the issues in dispute, and where the arguments of both parties before us very substantially followed those put to the Tribunal. Although very large amounts of money are at stake, there must come a limit beyond which costs become disproportionate. This is a case where the Costs Judge will need to consider most carefully the question of proportionality under *CPR 44.4(2)(a)* as well as examining in depth the reasonableness of the time spent and work done. It is not immediately apparent to us how two Grade A solicitors could spend respectively 221.5 hours and 181.5 hours on this appeal — that is to say on this case since the time of the decisions of the Tribunal — at a cost of over £231,000 spending 90 and 98 hours on documents and 55 and 41 hours attending on clients. That does not take account of other members of the team, with one Grade B solicitor spending a total of 233.6 hours at a cost of £87,600.' The tribunal directed that there should be 'a detailed assessment' of the amounts which M had claimed. *Marks & Spencer plc v HMRC (No 2)*, UT [2010] UKUT 296 (TCC).

Successful appellant applying for indemnity costs

[4.427] Following the successful appeal noted at 29.128 FURTHER ASSESSMENTS: LOSS OF TAX, the appellant applied for costs to be awarded on the indemnity basis. The First-tier Tribunal rejected this application. Judge Berner held that this was 'not a case where it would be appropriate, or in the interests of justice, to award costs on an indemnity basis'. He directed that HMRC should make an interim payment of £650,000 towards the appellant's costs. *GP Curran v HMRC (No 2)*, FTT [2012] UKFTT 655 (TC), TC02327.

HMRC withdrawing assessments before hearing

[4.428] In May 2012 an individual (L) appealed against various assessments. In December 2012 he submitted a Statement of Case in support of his appeal. On 15 February 2013 HMRC agreed to withdraw the assessments. L subsequently applied for costs. Judge Poole found that HMRC had not acted unreasonably in defending the case prior to L's submission of additional information in December 2012. Since they required time to consider this information, he concluded that 'HMRC did not act unreasonably in defending or conducting the appeal up to 1 February 2013, but that they did so act for the period after that date until 15 February 2013'. He awarded L costs of £150. Judge Poole also observed that 'if it could be shown that an appellant was in possession of information or evidence that would have persuaded HMRC to withdraw its defence of an appeal, but for whatever reason that appellant withheld that information or evidence and as a result put HMRC to the unnecessary effort and expense of continuing with the appeal until a much later date, HMRC may well have a claim for their own costs in respect of the appellant's unreasonable conduct in doing so, even though the appeal itself is successful as a result of their withdrawal upon the eventual production of that information or evidence. In such circumstances, a wasted costs order might also be made against an adviser personally' (under *TCEA 2007, s 29(4)*). *PK Lam v HMRC*, FTT [2014] UKFTT 079 (TC), TC03219.

[4.429] In January 2012 HMRC issued estimated assessments on a farming partnership, covering the period from 1989/90 to 2007/08. They also imposed penalties. The partnership appealed. In November 2013, three days before the scheduled hearing of the appeal, HMRC withdrew the assessments and penalties. The partnership applied for costs. Judge Brooks held that HMRC had not acted unreasonably, finding that they 'took a pragmatic decision not to defend the appeal in a similar manner to an appellant who, after receiving advice from counsel, may decide to withdraw an appeal for commercial considerations'. However, HMRC had failed to comply with directions issued by the tribunal, and this had caused additional work for the partnership's accountants. He therefore ordered HMRC 'to pay the partnership's costs that have arisen as a result of the failure by HMRC to comply with the directions of the tribunal'. *JH & IM Ward v HMRC (and related appeals)*, FTT [2014] UKFTT 108 (TC), TC03248.

HMRC delay in settling case—whether unreasonable

[4.430] A company (S) claimed a deduction for sponsorship payments to a major rugby club. In May 2008 HMRC began an enquiry into S's return, and in March 2010 they issued a notice of amendment rejecting the claim on the grounds that the expenditure was not wholly and exclusively for the purpose of S's business. S appealed. In January 2012 HMRC decided not to contest the appeal. S applied for costs, contending that HMRC had acted unreasonably in not settling the case sooner. The First-tier Tribunal accepted this contention. Judge Raghavan observed that HMRC had received S's witness statements in June 2011, and held that HMRC should have settled the case within 28 days of receiving the witness statements. Accordingly he directed that HMRC should pay S's costs from 20 July 2011. *Southwest Communications Group Ltd v HMRC*, FTT [2012] UKFTT 701 (TC), TC02370.

[4.431] HMRC formed the opinion that a company director (E) had received underdeclared income from the company. In 2009 they issued discovery assessments. E appealed, contending that the sums were not remuneration. In 2012 HMRC issued a direction under *SI 2003/2682, reg 72*. E appealed against the direction. Following a directions hearing in 2013, E applied for an award of costs, contending that HMRC 'had failed to engage with the appellant in order to agree directions which might have obviated the need for a directions hearing'. Judge Cannan accepted this contention, finding that HMRC had 'seemed to be content just to sit back and let the appellant and the judge do all the work'. He held that 'the respondents' failure to engage amounted to unreasonableness for the purposes of *Rule 10(1)(b)*' (of *SI 2009/273*). *I Elder v HMRC*, FTT [2014] UKFTT 728 (TC), TC03849.

Cases where the application was successful

Costs awarded—cost of preparing Stated Case

[4.432] In two unrelated appeals, costs were awarded against the Revenue. The appellants included in their claims for costs expenses incurred in preparing and setting the draft Stated Case. The KB allowed the claims, but the Revenue objected to the expenses in question and appealed to the CA. The CA unanimously dismissed the Revenue's objections, holding that the expenses were allowable. *Lord Mayor, Alderman & Citizens of the City of Manchester v Sugden; Gresham Life Assurance Ltd v Bishop*, CA 1903, 4 TC 595; [1903] 2 KB 171.

Special Commissioners awarding costs to appellant

[4.433] In the case noted at **72.171** INHERITANCE TAX, the Special Commissioner held that the Revenue were not justified in seeking to impose a penalty on a solicitor who had submitted an estimated valuation in his capacity as an executor. The solicitor subsequently applied for costs. The Commissioner awarded costs to the solicitor, holding on the evidence that it was 'difficult to see what logical or rational basis the Revenue had for instituting proceedings', and that 'by proceeding as they did the Revenue had acted wholly unreasonably in connection with the hearing'. *Robertson v CIR (No 2)*, Sp C [2002] SSCD 242 (Sp C 313).

[4.434] In 1990 the Revenue issued assessments for 1983/84 to 1988/89 to an individual (C) who was resident in the UK but domiciled in the Republic of Ireland. C appealed, contending that the assessments were incorrect because his earnings related to duties performed outside the UK, so that they were outside the scope of Schedule E Case I (and were not taxable under Schedule

E Case III since the income had not been remitted to the UK). After prolonged correspondence, the appeals were transferred to the Special Commissioners in 2000. Following a hearing in December 2003, the Revenue agreed to withdraw the assessments. C applied for costs. The Commissioners granted this application, holding that the Revenue had acted 'wholly unreasonably', and that C should be awarded his costs from March 2000. The Revenue had had all the relevant information since early 2000, and the decision not to resist the appeals 'should have been taken nearly four years earlier'. The Commissioners also noted that the Revenue officers responsible for the assessments had failed to 'adhere to the guidelines in IH 2508'. The director of the Inland Revenue Special Compliance Office (M) had defended the assessments when it should have been clear that they were incorrect. M had failed to address 'the merits of the Inland Revenue's case under Schedule E'. C's solicitors had complained to the Chairman of the Board of Inland Revenue, and the Revenue should have reviewed the merits of their case in response to that complaint. Despite this, the Revenue had continued to defend the assessments. Furthermore, there had been excessive delay in listing the appeal for hearing. *Carvill v Frost*, Sp C 2004, [2005] SSCD 208 (Sp C 447).

[4.435] Following the decision reported at **4.434** above, the appellant applied for costs to be awarded on the indemnity basis, rather than on the standard basis. The Special Commissioners granted the application, holding that 'in all the circumstances of this case we are satisfied that the Inland Revenue's conduct was unreasonable to a sufficiently high degree to require us to make the costs award on the indemnity basis'. *Carvill v Frost (No 2)*, Sp C [2005] SSCD 422 (Sp C 468).

[4.436] A company applied for a CIS 5 tax certificate. The Revenue rejected the claim on the grounds that the company had not complied with *ICTA 1988, s 565(2A)*. The company appealed. The Revenue subsequently accepted that the company had complied with *s 565(2A)*, but rejected the application on the different grounds that the company had not complied with *s 565(3)*. The company also applied for costs, contending that the Revenue's handling of its application had been unreasonable. The Special Commissioner accepted this contention and awarded costs to the company, holding that the Revenue had 'acted wholly unreasonably in connection with the hearing in not producing their evidence about compliance and making a decision on it until the day before the hearing'. *Oriel Support Ltd v HMRC (No 2)*, Sp C [2007] SSCD 670 (Sp C 615). (*Note*. For a subsequent appeal by the same company, see **42.105** PAY AS YOU EARN.)

First-tier Tribunal awarding costs to appellant

[4.437] HMRC issued a discovery assessment, charging tax of £13,000, on the executors of a Lloyds underwriter. The executors appealed. Shortly before the hearing of the appeal, HMRC withdrew the assessment. The executors applied for costs. The First-tier Tribunal granted their application. Judge Nowlan found that 'the return in this case was made precisely in accordance with the guidelines published by HMRC as to how executors should prepare the last relevant return for the deceased "name" at Lloyds'. HMRC had failed to comply with their own guidelines in not opening an enquiry within the statutory period. He held that HMRC had acted unreasonably, so that the appellants were entitled to their costs. *Atkins' Executors v HMRC*, FTT [2011] UKFTT 468 (TC), TC01318.

[4.438] In a case where the facts are not fully set out in the decision, HMRC sought to collect tax from an employee rather than the employer, but the First-tier Tribunal allowed the employee's appeal. The employee subsequently applied for costs. The tribunal granted the application, holding that HMRC had acted unreasonably and directing that HMRC should pay 50% of the employee's costs. *N Deluca v HMRC*, FTT [2011] UKFTT 579 (TC), TC01422.

[4.439] HMRC imposed a penalty on a solicitor (B), but withdrew it shortly before the hearing after accepting that B had a reasonable excuse as his wife had been admitted to hospital. Judge Khan held that HMRC had acted unreasonably in failing to withdraw the penalty at an earlier stage, and awarded B costs of £180 (10 hours at £18 per hour). *NH Bogle v HMRC*, FTT [2014] UKFTT 201 (TC), TC03341.

Costs of application for judicial review

[4.440] A married couple were the sole directors of a small company (V) in the construction industry. In May 2007 the husband suffered a serious head injury, which required brain surgery. Following this, V failed to account for PAYE for the four months from May to August 2007. HMRC issued notices under *Income Tax (PAYE) Regulations 2003 (SI 2003/2682), reg 78(4)*, requiring payment of £83,967. In October 2007 they began county court proceedings to recover this amount. V paid the actual PAYE liability of £64,884, but declined to pay the balance. In May 2008 V applied for judicial review, and the county court proceedings were adjourned. In June 2008 HMRC withdrew the county court proceedings. V declined to withdraw the proceedings for judicial review, claiming that it was entitled to costs. The QB rejected this contention but the CA unanimously allowed V's appeal. Pill LJ observed that HMRC had 'persisted in their County Court claim until the judicial review proceedings had been commenced'. On the evidence, the 'insistence of HMRC in persisting with its claim for the deemed sum, and its complete lack of flexibility, was susceptible to challenge'. It 'was difficult to understand why HMRC had not exercised its discretion under Tax Bulletin 18 not to collect the full assessed amount'. Accordingly, it had not been 'an abuse of the process of the court or unreasonable for the appellants to resort to a public law claim in the prevailing circumstances. Despite the good sense and relevance of the equitable liability practice, HMRC had initiated, and despite all reasonable efforts by the appellants to settle for the sum actually due, persisted in their statutory claim for the amount deemed to be due. HMRC failed to respond to the appellants' proposals for over four months, notwithstanding reminders. They were then supplied with detailed and, it appears, scrupulous, calculations of the sum actually due but persisted in a claim for the sum deemed to be due under *regulation 78*.' V's decision to apply for judicial review had been reasonable. The CA awarded V costs of £6,000. *R (oao Valentines Homes & Construction Ltd) v HMRC*, CA [2010] STC 1208; [2010] EWCA Civ 345.

Applications by the Revenue

[4.441] In the case noted at 8.110 CAPITAL ALLOWANCES, the Revenue applied for costs. The Special Commissioner reviewed the evidence and found that the appellant had 'behaved unreasonably' and had 'waged a war of attrition against the Revenue for years', wasting 'weeks of Revenue time which could have been better employed'. However, the Commissioner (Mr. de Voil) observed that 'although on an objective test I suspect that the vast majority of reasonable men would say that the appellant has behaved unreasonably, on a subjective test the appellant believes that he is justified in acting as he does'. Furthermore, 'the *Regulations* require that, before making an award of costs, I should be of the opinion that the appellant has acted *wholly* unreasonably *in connection with the hearing*. The appellant has been unreasonable, but he has not been wholly unreasonable, and his unreasonableness is only connected with the hearing to a very minor extent.' Accordingly, the Commissioner declined to make an award of costs. *Salt v Young*, Sp C [1999] SSCD 249 (Sp C 205).

[4.442] An individual (P) had appealed against a number of estimated assessments. At a hearing in May 1998, he was represented by counsel, who requested an adjournment on the grounds that P was living in Portugal and was not fit to travel to the UK. The Commissioner granted an adjournment on terms whereby P was directed to deliver certain particulars and documents, including medical reports. He failed to comply with the direction. A further hearing took place in June 1998, which he did not attend, and at which he was not represented. A penalty of £2,500 was imposed. He again failed to attend a subsequent hearing in July 1998, and the Commissioner found that P had 'acted wholly unreasonably in connection with this hearing in not complying with the directions' issued in May 1998 and in failing to notify either the Revenue or the Special Commissioners that he did not intend to appear or to be represented. P applied to have this decision set aside. His application was set down for hearing in October 1998. P again failed to attend and was not represented. The Commissioner dismissed P's application and directed that he should pay the whole of the Revenue's costs. *Phillips v Burrows*, Sp C [2000] SSCD 112 (Sp C 229, 229A).

[4.443] In the case noted at 44.358 PENALTIES, a married couple who owed substantial amounts of tax had falsely claimed that they were not resident in the UK, and had failed to comply with a notice under *TMA, s 20(1)*, The Commissioner awarded costs against the couple, holding on the evidence that they had 'acted wholly unreasonably in connection with the hearing'. The Ch D upheld this decision and made a 'wasted costs' order against the couple's solicitors. Lightman J held that a solicitor would 'be liable to a wasted costs order if, exercising the objective professional judgment of a reasonably competent solicitor, he ought reasonably to have appreciated that the litigation in which he was acting constituted an abuse of process'. On the evidence, the appeal had been 'hopeless' and had been 'the last of a continuing series of actions and omissions' which had been 'designed to delay liability for and payment of capital gains tax in respect of the sale'. The order was 'justified and indeed required to discourage any continued abuse and to protect the integrity of the process in Revenue cases and appeals'. *Morris & Morris v Roberts (No*

2), Ch D 2005, 77 TC 204; [2006] STC 135; [2005] EWHC 1040 (Ch). (*Note.* For subsequent developments in this case, see **44.190** PENALTIES.)

[4.444] Following the decision noted at **29.17** FURTHER ASSESSMENTS: LOSS OF TAX, the appellant's accountant requested a formal review of the decision. However neither the appellant nor the accountant attended the review. The Special Commissioner upheld the previous decision and awarded costs to the Assets Recovery Agency, holding that the appellant and his accountant had 'acted wholly unreasonably in connection with the hearing'. *MP Forbes v Director of the Assets Recovery Agency (No 2)*, Sp C [2007] SSCD 653 (Sp C 613).

[4.445] A Netherlands company (N) reclaimed withholding tax in respect of royalties. The Revenue rejected the claim, and N appealed. After a preliminary hearing, N withdrew the appeal. The Revenue applied for costs, contending that N had 'continued to press the appeal even though it was clear it was hopeless'. The Special Commissioner expressed 'great sympathy' with the Revenue's application, but rejected it, finding that although the behaviour of N's representative had not been 'sensible, essentially reasonable or necessarily in the best interest of her clients', it had not been 'wholly unreasonable'. *Nightswood BV v HMRC*, Sp C 2007, [2008] SSCD 384 (Sp C 651).

[4.446] The Revenue issued assessments on the basis that a wealthy businessman (B) was resident in the UK. B appealed, contending that he was not resident in the UK. The Special Commissioner held a preliminary hearing in 2007, and the appeal was listed for a full hearing for 2008. On the first day of the hearing B's counsel informed the Commissioner that B had decided to withdraw his appeal. The Revenue applied for costs. The Special Commissioner granted the Revenue's application. The Commissioner observed that certain documents which B had submitted as evidence that he was not resident appeared to have been altered, and 'on the balance of probabilities' there seemed to be 'no other explanation' than that they had been 'deliberately doctored to mislead the respondent and the tribunal'. It appeared that B had withdrawn his appeal because he had realised that the Revenue were 'likely to prove that his evidence did not stand up'. Accordingly B had 'acted wholly unreasonably in connection with the hearing'. *Businessman v HMRC*, Sp C [2008] SSCD 1151 (Sp C 702).

[4.447] In a case where a company had withdrawn an appeal against an information notice two days before the hearing, HMRC applied for costs of £832 (5.7 hours at £146 per hour). Judge Mosedale granted the application, finding that 'the appellant's behaviour in both bringing and then maintaining this appeal until the last moment was unreasonable'. *RP Baker (Oxford) Ltd v HMRC*, FTT [2014] UKFTT 420 (TC), TC03549.

[4.448] An individual (M) appealed against a notice under *FA 2008, Sch 36*, contending that three documents which HMRC had requested were subject to legal professional privilege. However he withdrew his appeal shortly before the hearing. HMRC applied for an award of costs on the basis that M had acted unreasonably, because the effect of the Supreme Court decision in *R (oao Prudential plc) v Special Commissioner*, **49.35** RETURNS AND INFORMATION, was that the Tribunal would be bound to hold that the documents were not subject to legal professional privilege. The First-tier Tribunal accepted this contention and granted HMRC's application in principle. Judge McKenna directed that M should provide 'details of his financial circumstances' so that she could consider his ability to pay HMRC's costs, as required by *Tribunal Procedure (First-tier Tribunal) (Tax Chamber) Rules 2009, SI 2009/273, rule 10(5)*. *M Alimadadian v HMRC*, FTT [2014] UKFTT 641 (TC), TC03765.

[4.449] A company (T) appealed against a notice under *FA 2008, Sch 36*, contending that various documents which HMRC had requested were subject to legal professional privilege. However T withdrew its appeal shortly before the hearing. HMRC applied for an award of costs on the basis that T had acted unreasonably, because the effect of the Supreme Court decision in *R (oao Prudential plc) v Special Commissioner*, **49.35** RETURNS AND INFORMATION, was that the Tribunal would be bound to hold that the documents were not subject to legal professional privilege. The First-tier Tribunal accepted this contention and awarded HMRC costs of £1,598. Judge Sinfield held that '(T) and its adviser knew from the outset that the claim to legal privilege was groundless and the appeal did not have any reasonable prospect of success'. *Taylor Made Consulting Ltd v HMRC*, FTT [2014] UKFTT 903 (TC), TC04018.

Company withdrawing application for judicial review

[4.450] A group of companies began judicial review proceedings against the Revenue, challenging the validity of *FA 2004, s 320*. The group subsequently withdrew its application for judicial review. The Revenue applied for costs. The Ch D awarded the Revenue 85% of its costs. Park J held that the companies' application for judicial review had been misconceived. However, the award of costs would be reduced by 15% to take account of the Revenue's repeated failure to answer correspondence from the companies. *Aegis Group of Companies v CIR*, Ch D [2005] EWHC 1468 (Ch); [2006] STC 23.

Costs awarded against company's agent

[4.451] In proceedings following *Wilcock v Pinto & Co*, **60.21** TRADING INCOME, in which the decision was in favour of the Revenue, the CA held that the order for costs should be made against the company's UK agent. *Wilcock v Pinto & Co*, CA 1925, 10 TC 415; [1925] 1 KB 30.

Costs of appeal to Upper Tribunal

[4.452] Following the Upper Tribunal decision in *HMRC v Taylor & Haimendorf (No 2)*, **23.5** ENTERPRISE INVESTMENT SCHEME, HMRC applied for costs of £17,990, including a claim for £8,010 in respect of 38 hours' attendance on documents. The shareholders objected to HMRC's claims. The Upper Tribunal held that HMRC were entitled to reasonable costs but that the claim for £8,010 was excessive, and reduced the amount in question to £925 (representing five hours' work by a grade C lawyer and one hour by a grade A lawyer). The tribunal therefore awarded HMRC total costs of £10,905. *HMRC v Taylor; HMRC v Haimendorf*, UT March 2011, FTC/43/2010.

Late application for costs by HMRC

[4.453] In a VAT case, Judge Bishopp granted a late application for costs by HMRC. *Leeds City Council v HMRC*, UT [2014] UKUT 350 (TCC).

Revenue awarded costs of appeal to High Court

[4.454] Following the Ch D and CA decisions in the case noted at **25.21** EUROPEAN LAW, HMRC applied for costs. The Ch D directed that the appellant company (M) should pay HMRC's costs of the appeal to the Ch D, and that M should pay part of HMRC's costs of the appeal to the CA (those relating to M's French subsidiary, but not those relating to its German and Belgian subsidiaries). *HMRC v Marks & Spencer plc (No 1)*, Ch D [2010] STC 2575; [2010] EWHC 2215 (Ch).

Miscellaneous

Unsatisfactory evidence submitted by counsel for appellant

[4.455] In the case noted at **72.23** INHERITANCE TAX, Lightman J held that much of the affidavit evidence submitted by the counsel for the appellant failed to comply with the *Rules of the Supreme Court 1965* as then in force, and was inadmissible. Lightman J took the 'exceptional' course of granting an adjournment to enable the appellant to put in further admissible evidence, because 'on the evidence as it stood', the appellant's 'otherwise meritorious appeal would be likely to fail' and it did not appear right 'that the taxpayers should suffer this penalty for the default of their legal advisers in the preparation of the evidence'. After an adjournment the necessary further evidence was admitted and the appeal was allowed. Lightman J held that in the circumstances the appellants should pay all the costs up until the final affidavit containing the further evidence was received, and that there should be no order for costs thereafter. *Bennett & Others v CIR*, Ch D 21 December 1994 unreported. (*Notes*. (1) The substantive appeal is reported at [1995] STC 54. However this report is an edited version which does not include Lightman J's decision on costs. (2) The *Rules of the Supreme Court 1965* have now been replaced by the *Civil Procedure Rules 1998 (SI 1998/3132)*.)

Whether HMRC should share costs of unsuccessful appeal

[4.456] In the case noted at **59.108** TRADING INCOME, the appellant partnership had applied for a direction that HMRC should pay half the costs of preparing material for the hearing of the appeal. The First-tier Tribunal granted the direction, but subsequently dismissed the substantive appeal. HMRC appealed to the Upper Tribunal, contending that since the partnership had opted out of the 'costs-sharing regime' under *SI 2009/273, rule 10(1)(c)*, the First-tier Tribunal had exceeded its jurisdiction in ruling that it should pay half of the partnership's costs. The Upper Tribunal accepted this contention and allowed HMRC's appeal. Judge Berner held that the First-tier Tribunal had 'no power to direct the sharing of costs of complying with directions, except in exercise of its power to award wasted costs or in the case where a party or their representative has acted unreasonably in bringing, defending or conducting the proceedings. The only case where the FTT would have full power to order costs-sharing is in a case categorised as complex where the taxpayer had not opted out.' The partnership appealed to the CA, which unanimously upheld Judge Berner's decision. Moses LJ observed that, by opting out of the costs-sharing regime, the partnership had taken 'a particular view as to the risks it was prepared to face in pursuing the appeal'. *Eclipse Film Partners No 35 Llp v HMRC (No 5)*, CA [2014] EWCA Civ 184.

Costs—whether allowable in computing profits

[4.457] See the cases noted at **63.155** to **63.157** TRADING PROFITS, and *Spofforth & Prince v Golder*, **63.160** TRADING PROFITS.

5

Assessments

The cases in this chapter are arranged under the following headings.

GENERAL NOTE

The assessing procedure was radically amended with effect from 1996/97, with the introduction of self-assessment. The provisions are outlined in detail in Tolley's Income Tax. For cases concerning the question whether a loss of tax has been brought about 'careless or deliberately', within *TMA, s 29(4)*, see **29** FURTHER ASSESSMENTS: LOSS OF TAX. For appeals against estimated assessments, see **4.338** *et seq* APPEALS. For cases concerning the specific provisions relating to self-assessment, which took effect from 1996/97, see **55** SELF-ASSESSMENT. Despite the changes, many of the cases concerning the earlier case law, relating to *TMA, s 29 as originally enacted* and its precursors, may still be relevant to the current provisions. Such cases are summarised in this chapter.

The scope of the power of assessment

Validity of assessment

Whether any territorial limit on inspector's powers of assessment

[5.1] See *R v Tavistock Commrs (ex p. Adams) (No 2)*, **4.262** APPEALS, and *Bensoor v Devine*, **55.16** SELF-ASSESSMENT.

Effect of international law

[5.2] A farmer appealed against an assessment, contending that it was invalid under the *Geneva Conventions Act 1957* because taxation was used to fund nuclear weapons. The Ch D rejected this contention and dismissed his appeal. *Cheney v Conn*, Ch D 1967, 44 TC 217; [1968] 1 WLR 242; [1968] 1 All ER 779.

[5.3] See also *R (oao Boughton & Others) v HM Treasury*, **4.320** APPEALS; *C v United Kingdom*, **31.61** HUMAN RIGHTS; *Hibbs v United Kingdom*, **31.64**

HUMAN RIGHTS; *Gladders v Prior*, **43.39** PAYMENT OF TAX, and *Turton v Birdforth Commrs*, **44.187** PENALTIES.

Authority of Parliament disputed

[5.4] A former president of the National Association of Master Masons of Great Britain appealed against two income tax assessments, contending that the supreme authority in Great Britain was the Master Mason, and that he was therefore not subject to UK tax. The Ch D rejected this contention and dismissed his appeal. *Lloyd v Taylor*, Ch D 1970, 46 TC 539.

[5.5] The Revenue issued an assessment on an individual (H), charging tax on income from property. H appealed, contending that he was not bound by Acts passed by Parliament, as he had been denied the opportunity to stand for election to Parliament. The Ch D dismissed his appeal. *Hebden v Pepper*, Ch D [1988] STC 821.

[5.6] See also *Bell v HMRC*, **44.15** PENALTIES.

Validity of Act of Parliament disputed

[5.7] An architect appealed against an assessment which included Class 4 National Insurance Contributions, contending that the *Social Security Act 1975* was invalid. The CA unanimously rejected this contention and dismissed his appeal. *Martin v O'Sullivan*, CA 1984, 57 TC 709; [1984] STC 258.

Delay by Revenue in making assessments

[5.8] A taxpayer had made his returns promptly to the appropriate inspector of taxes, but the tax office had not passed the relevant information promptly to the Surtax Office. As a result, notices of the surtax assessments on him for the years 1965/66 to 1970/71 were not issued to him until January 1972. He appealed, contending that, because of the delay, the assessments were invalid. The Ch D rejected this contention and dismissed his appeal. *Hossack v CIR*, Ch D 1974, 49 TC 483; [1974] STC 262.

TMA, s 30—recovery of tax repaid

[5.9] A company (T) failed to submit returns for accounting periods ending 31 March and 30 September 1996. The Revenue issued estimated assessments, and T appealed. The General Commissioners dismissed the appeals and confirmed the assessments. Subsequently T submitted a return for the period ending 30 September 1998, claiming a large loss. Part of the loss was carried back to the period ending 30 September 1997, extinguishing the taxable profits for that period. This in turn meant that payments of advance corporation tax, which had previously been set against the profits for the period ending 30 September 1997, became available for set-off against the two previous periods. In setting the ACT against T's liability for the period ending 30 September 1996, an inspector incorrectly used figures given in a return which T had belatedly submitted, rather than the figures from the estimated assessment which the Commissioners had confirmed, and authorised a repayment accordingly. In April 1999, having realised this mistake, the Revenue issued an assessment under *TMA, s 30* to recover the incorrect repayment. T appealed, contending that the wording of *TMA, s 30* was permissive rather than mandatory, and that the Revenue should have exercised their discretion not to issue the assessment. The General Commissioners accepted this contention, but the Ch D allowed the Revenue's appeal and restored the assessment. Lloyd J observed that the assessments for the accounting periods ending in 1996 had 'not been altered in accordance with any express provision of the Taxes Acts', and held that 'the assessments confirmed by the General Commissioners on appeal stand good. It would be irrelevant, even if it were the case, that the profit figures on which these assessments are based are not the true figures'. The Commissioners had no jurisdiction to consider the Revenue's exercise of their discretion by way of review or appeal. Furthermore, the Commissioners had no material on which they could have found that the discretion was exercised wrongly or unreasonably. In the circumstances, the assessment which the Revenue had issued in April 1999 was 'binding and conclusive'. *Guthrie v Twickenham Film Studios Ltd*, Ch D 2002, 74 TC 733; [2002] STC 1374; [2002] EWHC (Ch) 1936.

Application of TMA, s 32—double assessment

[5.10] A married couple had bought and sold metals at various dates. The Revenue raised a capital gains tax assessment in respect of the transactions and alternative Sch D, Case I assessments on the basis that they were trading. The CGT assessment became final and the couple paid the tax charged (at the then CGT rate of 30%). They appealed against the income tax assessments and contended as a preliminary point that there had been double assessment within *TMA, s 32(1)*, and that the finalisation of the CGT assessment precluded the Revenue from contending that they had been trading. The General Commissioners accepted this contention and discharged the income tax assessments, without considering whether the couple had been trading. The Revenue appealed to the Ch D, which remitted the case to the Commissioners with an order to continue the hearing, holding that it was within the Revenue's power to raise alternative assessments to protect their position. The couple were not at risk of double taxation for, having regard to the repayment provisions of *TMA, s 32(1)*, they could reclaim the CGT paid if the income tax assessments were upheld. The CA unanimously upheld this decision. Lawton LJ held that there was no merit in the appeal, and that the Revenue could not be precluded or estopped from proceeding with income tax assessments. *Bye v Coren*, CA 1986, 60 TC 116; [1986] STC 393.

[5.11] See also *Salt v Fernandez (No 2)*, **53.19** SCHEDULE D.

Alternative assessments

[5.12] The Revenue formed the opinion that two individuals (M and H) had made substantial gains from transactions in land. They issued CGT assessments, plus alternative income tax assessments under Schedule D and under what is now*ITA 2007, s 752*. M and H only appealed against the Schedule D assessments, so that the other assessments became final. The Revenue began proceedings for the recovery of the tax payable under the *s 752* assessments. M and H resisted the action, contending that the assessments were invalid because they were cumulative, and that if the assessments were alternative, appeals against the Schedule D assessments should have the effect of suspending any liability under the others. The CS rejected these contentions, holding that the assessments were clearly to be regarded as alternative, none of which should be treated as prior to any of the others. The Revenue was fully entitled to make three separate assessments to tax. Double taxation would not be imposed, because the Revenue would only be entitled to payment of the tax found due under one of the three assessments. As there had been no appeal against the *s 752* assessments, the tax charged had become due and payable. *Lord Advocate v McKenna; Lord Advocate v Henderson*, CS 1989, 61 TC 688; [1989] STC 485.

[5.13] In a similar case where no appeals had been made against any of the three assessments, the Revenue initially issued a writ for the tax due on all three assessments, but subsequently amended its statement of claim to the tax due under what is now *ITA 2007, s 752* only. The Revenue obtained summary judgment and the defendant appealed, contending that the assessments were cumulative and should be treated as void. The CA rejected these contentions. The assessments were alternative rather than cumulative, and the Revenue was entitled to summary judgment in respect of the tax charged by the *s 752* assessment. *CIR v Wilkinson*, CA 1992, 65 TC 28; [1992] STC 454.

Assessability of income for year in which source not possessed

[5.14] In case concerning advance corporation tax (which was subsequently abolished from 6 April 1999 by *FA 1998, s 31*), Lord Hoffmann expressed the view that it was 'no longer true to say that liability to income tax depends upon the existence during the year of assessment of a source within the charge' and held that 'there is no longer any basis for assuming that income, or a person, can only be within the charge to corporation tax in a given year of assessment if the income is from or the person has a source of income within the charge to that tax'. Lord Hoffmann specifically declined to follow the majority decision in the 1921 case of *National Provident Institution v Brown*, **52.51** SAVINGS AND INVESTMENT INCOME. *Centaur Clothes Group Ltd v Walker*, HL 2000, 72 TC 379; [2000] STC 324; [2000] 1 WLR 799; [2000] 2 All ER 589. (*Note*. However, the 'source doctrine', as laid down by *National Provident Institution v Brown*, **52.51** SAVINGS AND INVESTMENT INCOME, was subsequently applied by the Ch D in the 2007 case of *HMRC v Bank of Ireland Britain Holdings Ltd*, **3.3** ANTI-AVOIDANCE, where counsel for HMRC apparently failed to draw the judge's attention to the HL decision in *Centaur Clothes Group Ltd v Walker*.)

Assessment on current year basis issued before end of year of assessment

[5.15] A UK resident (B) received income from the Republic of Ireland, which was assessed on a current year basis. In October 1986 the Revenue issued a 1986/87 assessment on this income. B appealed, contending that the assessment was premature and invalid. The Special Commissioners accepted this contention and allowed his appeal, and the Ch D upheld their decision. Hoffmann J held that 'the imposition of liability to tax on the full amount of the income arising in a year necessarily entails that the year has elapsed. Until then the profits in respect of which he is liable to tax will not exist and therefore no charge to tax can attach'. *Jones v O'Brien*, Ch D 1988, 60 TC 706; [1988] STC 615. (*Note*. The case was decided on the wording of *TMA,* *s 29* as originally enacted. *TMA, s 29* was subsequently amended by *FA 1988* to permit certain 'current year' assessments, and the amended legislation was in turn substituted by *FA 1994*, on the introduction of self-assessment. Despite the changes in the legislation, HMRC cite the case as authority for their view that 'it is not possible to anticipate a loss by claiming it before the end of the accounting period': see HMRC Business Income Manual, BIM85005.)

Assessability where taxpayer resident in UK for only part of year

[5.16] *FA 1968, s 41* imposed a tax (special charge) for 1967/68 on the investment income of an individual not domiciled in the UK if he was resident and ordinarily resident in that year and had been ordinarily resident throughout the nine preceding years. The Revenue issued an assessment on an individual (N), who had been resident and ordinarily resident in the UK from 1919 until 29 January 1968. N appealed, contending that he was not liable to the charge on income arising after he had ceased to be resident. The Special Commissioners rejected this contention and the Ch D dismissed N's appeal, holding that residence for part of a year was residence in that year. The income was to be calculated on an annual basis and there was no provision for restricting the charge to the income which arose before N's departure from the UK. *Neubergh v CIR*, Ch D 1977, 52 TC 79; [1978] STC 181.

[5.17] See also the cases noted at 53.30 to 53.32 SCHEDULE D—SUPERSEDED LEGISLATION.

Validity of assessment—other cases

[5.18] For cases concerning the validity of an assessment, where the dispute concerns the manner in which the assessment was issued, see 5.100 to 5.108 below.

Discovery (TMA, s 29(1))

NOTE

See the note at the beginning of this chapter with regard to the substitution of *TMA, s 29* by *FA 1994*.

General

[5.19] In a case where the substantive issue is no longer of importance, the KB held that 'discover' does not mean 'ascertain by legal evidence' but 'come to the conclusion' from the available information. *R v Kensington Commissioners (ex p. Aramayo)*, KB 1913, 6 TC 279.

[5.20] The Revenue received information suggesting that a company director had failed to declare income from a partnership. They issued assessments under the 'discovery' provisions. The director applied for a writ of prohibition. The KB rejected the application. Lord Reading CJ held that an inspector 'discovers' something if he 'honestly and *bona fide* after due care and diligence' comes to the conclusion on the information in his possession that a person is chargeable. If the person assessed is aggrieved, his remedy is by way of appeal. *R v St Giles & St George Commrs (ex p. Hooper)*, KB 1915, 7 TC 59; [1915] 3 KB 768. (*Note.* This case and *R v Kensington Commissioners (ex p. Aramayo)*, **5.19** above, relate to assessing procedures which are now obsolete but the relevant legislation, *TMA 1880, s 52*, is broadly similar to *TMA 1970, s 29*.)

[5.21] The Revenue had made assessments on an individual (B) by virtue of what is now *ITA 2007, s 698* in respect of the income of certain foreign companies. They subsequently issued additional assessments for the same years in respect of the income of another foreign company. B appealed, contending that there had been no discovery. The Ch D rejected this contention and upheld the assessments. *Earl Beatty v CIR*, Ch D 1953, 35 TC 30; [1953] 1 WLR 1090; [1953] 2 All ER 758.

[5.22] In July 1998 a woman (G) sold some shares in a limited company. Her accountants sent a tax computation (showing a capital loss) to the Revenue. In March 1999 the Inland Revenue Share Valuation Division wrote to G's accountants, requesting further information with regard to the valuation of the shares. In July 1999, without consulting her accountants, G submitted a form R40 claiming a small tax repayment, which was duly paid to her. In December 2000 the Revenue wrote to G stating that they wished to make some enquiries into her repayment claim. In May 2002 G's accountants wrote to the Inland Revenue Share Valuation Division indicating that they agreed the Revenue's valuation of the shares which G had sold, and agreed that the sale gave rise to a capital gain, rather than a capital loss. In July 2002 the Revenue issued G with a tax return for 1998/99. G did not submit this return, but did submit a form SA108 showing the capital gain as agreed by her accountants. In October 2002 the Revenue issued a CGT assessment on the gain, under the provisions of *TMA, s 29*. The Special Commissioner upheld the assessment and dismissed G's appeal. The Commissioner observed that the form R40 'is not a return', but was a claim, submitted 'in a form designed by the Inland Revenue to establish the correctness of information given in support of the claim'. G had failed to fulfil her 'obligation to complete and submit the self-assessment return form', and the Revenue were entitled to issue a 'discovery assessment' under *TMA, s 29(1)*. The Commissioner observed that 'as far as capital gains tax is concerned, the purpose of a discovery assessment is to ensure that any gains which have not been assessed are subjected to assessment'. Furthermore, the issue of an assessment under *s 29* did not require any finding of 'negligent conduct'. *Osborne v Dickinson*, Sp C 2003, [2004] SSCD 104 (Sp C 393).

[5.23] The decision in *Osborne v Dickinson*, **5.22** above, was applied in the similar subsequent case of *Henke v HMRC*, **71.324** CAPITAL GAINS TAX.

[5.24] The Revenue formed the opinion that a publican had underdeclared his profits. They issued an assessment under the 'discovery' provisions of *TMA, s 29*. The publican appealed, contending that the assessment was invalid because the Revenue had not issued a notice of enquiry under *TMA, s 9A*. The Special Commissioner rejected this contention and dismissed the appeal, holding that *TMA, ss 9A* and *29* were 'completely separate'. The Revenue could issue an assessment under *s 29* where they discovered a loss of tax, regardless of whether there had been an enquiry under *s 9A*. *Kennerley v HMRC*, Sp C [2007] SSCD 188 (Sp C 578).

[5.25] In the case noted at **48.20** RESIDENCE, HMRC issued a 'discovery' assessment charging CGT on a company director who had signed a tax return stating that he was 'employed abroad under a full-time working contract of employment'. The First-tier Tribunal upheld the assessment, finding that despite the statement in his return, H had spent less than half the year in the Netherlands, and that as a matter of law he had remained resident in the UK. The Tribunal also held that there had been a 'discovery', and that H's conduct in signing the return amounted to 'negligent conduct'. The Upper Tribunal and the CA unanimously upheld this decision. Lewison LJ held that the tribunal had been entitled to find that the conditions of *s 29* were satisfied, and that 'whether either or both the conditions are fulfilled is a question of objective fact to be decided in case of dispute by way of appeal'. *DW Hankinson v HMRC (No 3)*, CA [2011] EWCA Civ 1566; [2012] STC 485. (*Note*. The Supreme Court dismissed an application for leave to appeal against this decision.)

[5.26] HMRC received information indicating that a property developer (P) had claimed an excessive amount of relief under what is now *ITA 2007, s 131*. They issued a discovery assessment to recover the tax. The First-tier Tribunal dismissed P's appeal, holding that there had been a discovery within *TMA, s 29*. *R Price v HMRC*, FTT [2014] UKFTT 929 (TC), TC04042.

[5.27] Following an enquiry, HMRC formed the opinion that an employee (M) had substantially overclaimed expenses on his returns. They issued discovery assessments to recover the tax due. The First-tier Tribunal dismissed M's appeals. *F Medlicott v HMRC*, FTT [2014] UKFTT 945 (TC), TC04058.

[5.28] For cases where the First-tier Tribunal held that there had been no 'discovery', see *Howell v HMRC*, **41.66** PARTNERSHIPS, and *Bhadra (t/a Admirals Locums) v HMRC*, **61.18** TRADING INCOME.

Change of opinion by Revenue—whether a discovery

[5.29] An inspector of taxes reached the conclusion that trustees of a will were taxable on certain untaxed War Loan interest, and issued additional assessments under the 'discovery' provisions. A previous inspector had discussed the matter with the trustees, and agreed that there was no liability. It was accepted that the second inspector's conclusion was correct. The KB upheld the assessments, holding that there had been a 'discovery'. *Williams v Grundy's Trustees*, KB 1933, 18 TC 271; [1934] 1 KB 524.

[5.30] On the death of a partner (M), the partnership paid his trustees a sum which included a share of the accrued profits up to the date of death. The Revenue made a surtax assessment for the year in which M died, on the basis that he was not entitled to any share of the firm's profits for that year. They subsequently made an additional assessment to include M's share of the partnership profits. The CS unanimously upheld the assessment. Lord Normand held that the word 'discovery' covered 'just the kind of discovery which was made here, when the Special Commissioners found out that, by reason of a misapprehension of the legal position, certain of the profits chargeable to tax had been omitted from the first assessment'. *CIR v Mackinlay's Trustees*, CS 1938, 22 TC 305.

[5.31] The Special Commissioners' decision in *Osborne v Steel Barrel Co Ltd (No 1)*, **65.31** TRADING PROFITS, was reached in 1940, several years after the relevant transactions. The interval resulted in complications in arriving at the stock figures for years after the opening period. The Revenue reached an agreement with the company (S), but did not make the appropriate reduction in the accounts figure for opening stock for the 1939/40 assessment. The Revenue subsequently issued an additional assessment remedying the error, and S appealed, contending that there had been no discovery. The CA unanimously rejected this contention and upheld the assessment. *Steel Barrel Co Ltd v Osborne (No 2)*, CA 1948, 30 TC 73.

[5.32] Certain Schedule A assessments (under the pre-*FA 1963* Schedule A system) were found to be incorrect although all the relevant information had been in the possession of the inspector at the time. The Revenue issued additional assessments to correct the error. The CA unanimously upheld the assessments, holding that there had been a discovery. *Commercial Structures Ltd v Briggs*, CA 1948, 30 TC 477; [1948] 2 All ER 1041.

[5.33] In 1964 the Revenue issued assessments on a company (M) on the basis that it was trading as a property dealer. M appealed, contending that the assessments were invalid as the Revenue had previously issued assessments on its rental income. The Ch D upheld the assessments, holding that there had been a discovery (and that there had been no agreement within what is now *TMA, s 54* precluding the assessment). *Jones v Mason Investments (Luton) Ltd*, Ch D 1966, 43 TC 570.

[5.34] Between 1954 and 1962 an individual (P) acquired a number of houses, with sitting tenants at controlled rents. He sold the houses as they became vacant. The transactions were declared in his returns. No assessments were raised until 1965, when a new inspector formed the opinion that the transactions amounted to trading, and raised assessments for 1958/59 to 1963/64 inclusive. P appealed, contending that the inspector had not made any 'discovery'. The Commissioners rejected this contention and dismissed the appeal, and the CA upheld this decision. Lord Denning held that an inspector made a discovery 'not only when he finds out new facts which were not known to him or his predecessor', but also 'when he finds out that he or his predecessor got the law wrong and did not assess the income when it ought to have been'. *Parkin v Cattell*, CA 1971, 48 TC 462.

[5.35] In a case where HMRC formed the opinion that a company director had underdeclared his income, the First-tier Tribunal rejected the director's contention that there had not been a 'discovery'. Judge Scott held that 'a discovery can include a discovery that the law has been wrongly applied or that one is mistaken about the law', applying the principles laid down by Lord Denning in *Cenlon Finance Co Ltd v Ellwood*, **5.75** below. *MSK Yip v HMRC*, FTT [2014] UKFTT 865 (TC), TC03981.

[5.36] In an Irish case, a company (W), which operated a quarry and also manufactured concrete blocks and cement pipes, claimed a deducion for the estimated value of the sand and gravel extracted from its own land used in its manufacturing. The Revenue did not query the claim until 1966/67 when, on appeal, the Circuit Court judge held that the deduction was not permissible. W acquiesced in this decision but appealed against additional assessments for 1961/62 to 1965/66 withdrawing the deduction. The HC(I) upheld the assessments, rejecting W's contention that there had been no 'discovery'. *W Ltd v Wilson*, HC(I) 1974, TL(I) 110.

[5.37] See also *Brodie's Trustees v CIR*, **20.21** DEDUCTION OF TAX; *Stones v Hall*, **22.117** EMPLOYMENT INCOME; *British Sugar Manufacturers Ltd v Harris*, **63.126** TRADING PROFITS; and *Multipar Syndicate Ltd v Devitt*, **64.37** TRADING PROFITS.

Assessments issued during investigation—whether any discovery

[5.38] See *Young v Duthie*, **5.79** below, and *Scott & Scott (t/a Farthings Steak House) v McDonald*, **29.88** FURTHER ASSESSMENTS: LOSS OF TAX.

Whether assessment may take account of facts which arose subsequently

[5.39] See *Dodworth v Dale*, **1.1** ALLOWANCES AND TAX RATES, and *Anderton & Halstead Ltd v Birrell*, **63.243** TRADING PROFITS.

Additional assessments on incomplete information

[5.40] Following the death of a trader (M), his accountant informed the inspector that cash commissions had not been put through his books and a bank account had not been disclosed. The Revenue issued additional assessments on M's executrix. She appealed, contending that the inspector had made no discovery. The CS unanimously rejected this contention and dismissed her appeal. *McLuskey's Executrix v CIR*, CS 1955, 36 TC 163.

Whether more than one additional assessment permissible

[5.41] In 1948 the Revenue issued additional assessments on an innkeeper (M), charging tax on goods purchased for M's own consumption. The Commissioners allowed M's appeals. In 1955, following an investigation, the Revenue issued further additional assessments on the basis that M had underdeclared takings. M's executor appealed, contending *inter alia* that that what is now *TMA, s 29* permits the making of only one further assessment for any one year. The Ch D rejected this contention and upheld the assessments. *Cansick (Murphy's Executor) v Hochstrasser*, Ch D 1961, 40 TC 151.

[5.42] See also *Easinghall Ltd v HMRC*, **55.29** SELF-ASSESSMENT.

Further assessment while first assessment under appeal

[5.43] In January 1976 the Revenue issued an estimated assessment on profits of £100,000 on a company (D) for its accounting period to 31 March 1975. D appealed. Before the appeal had been heard, the Revenue received further information indicating that D's actual profits had been £172,751. In November 1977 the Revenue issued a further assessment on the balance of £72,751. D appealed again. General Commissioners heard both appeals in 1982 and determined the total profits to be £172,751. D appealed to the Ch D, contending that the second assessment was invalid and the Commissioners should have increased the first assessment to £172,751. This would have been to D's advantage because of the provisions of *TMA, s 86* (interest on overdue tax) as then in force. The Ch D rejected this contention, holding that the Revenue had been entitled to make a further assessment under *TMA, s 29*, notwithstanding that the first assessment was under appeal, and the Commissioners' correct course under *TMA, s 50(6)* was to confirm both assessments. *Duchy Maternity Ltd v Hodgson*, Ch D 1985, 59 TC 85; [1985] STC 764. (*Note*. The relevant provisions of *TMA, s 86* were amended by *FA 1982, s 69* in relation to notices of assessment issued after 30 July 1982.)

Further assessment to correct arithmetical error

[5.44] The Revenue issued an assessment on an employee (M) charging tax on income of £11,111. There was no dispute as to this figure but, because of an arithmetical error, the tax was understated by £315. The Revenue subsequently issued a further assessment to recover this £315. M's personal representatives appealed, contending that in discussions with M's accountant, leading up to the assessment, the Revenue had purported to rely on what is now *TMA, s 29(1)(c)*, and that the assessment should be discharged as there had been no excess relief within *s 29(1)(c)*. The Ch D rejected this contention and upheld the assessment. Scott J held that 'assessment to tax' covers 'all the various stages leading up to the calculation and statement of the tax payable'. An arithmetical error can be corrected under *s 29(1)(b)*, and the fact that the inspector had said that he was relying on *s 29(1)(c)* in making the assessment did not preclude him from defending it under *s 29(1)(b)*. *Vickerman v Mason's Personal Representatives*, Ch D 1984, 58 TC 39; [1984] STC 231; [1984] 2 All ER 1.

Practice generally prevailing (TMA, s 29(2))

[5.45] A woman (E) had submitted a return claiming business asset taper relief in respect of a disposal of land. HMRC formed the opinion that E was not entitled to the relief, because the partnership of which she was a member had not been carrying out the trade of farming, but had let the land under a conacre agreement. They issued a discovery assessment. E appealed, contending that her return had complied with the 'practice generally prevailing', so that the effect of *TMA, s 29(2)* was that the assessment was invalid. The First-tier Tribunal rejected this contention and dismissed E's appeal. Judge Tildesley observed that E had 'claimed business taper relief on the basis that the partnership's letting of the land in conacre was a trading activity despite the fact that the tenant farmed the land not the partnership'. To meet the requirements of *TMA, s 29(2)*, she would have to establish that 'the prevailing practice at the relevant time treated lettings in conacre where the owner did not farm the land as trading activities'. The evidence showed that conacre lettings were only treated as trading activities for tax purposes where the owner took an active involvement in the farming of the land. The fact that one previous Inspector had allowed relief which was not justified in law was not conclusive, since that Inspector 'had no involvement with the formulation of HMRC's policy on farming and conacre lettings'. *Mrs DN Evelyn v HMRC*, FTT [2011] UKFTT 121 (TC), TC00997.

[5.46] In the case noted at 64.9 TRADING PROFITS, the Special Commissioners held that *TMA, s 29(2)* did not apply to the case in question, since 'a practice generally prevailing has to be a practice, or agreement, or acceptance over a long period whereby the Revenue agreed or accepted a certain treatment of sums in particular circumstances'. *Rafferty v HMRC*, Sp C [2005] SSCD 484 (Sp C 475).

[5.47] See also *HMRC v Household Estate Agents Ltd*, 5.71 below.

Whether HMRC should have been aware of loss of tax (TMA, s 29(5))

[5.48] A company director (V) was liable to income tax on the value of a house. In his 1997/98 tax return, which he submitted in July 1998, he submitted a valuation of £100,000. In September 1998 the Revenue advised V that his return had been processed 'without any need for correction'. In October 1999 the company submitted a corporation tax return, and the Revenue subsequently formed the opinion that the value of the house had been more than £100,000. In June 2000 they issued a further assessment on the basis that the true value had been £145,000. V appealed, contending that the issue of a further assessment was not authorised by *TMA, s 29*. The CA unanimously rejected this contention and upheld the assessment, holding that *TMA, s 29(5)* did not prohibit the issue of the assessment. Auld LJ observed that it would frustrate the aims of the self-assessment scheme, ie 'simplicity and early finality of assessment to tax, to interpret *section 29(5)* so as to introduce an obligation on tax inspectors to conduct an intermediate and possibly time-consuming scrutiny' of returns 'when they do not disclose insufficiency, but only circumstances further investigation of which might or might not show it.' He held that 'the key to the scheme is that the inspector is shut out from making a discovery assessment under (*s 29*) only when the taxpayer or his representatives, in making a honest and accurate return or in responding to a *section 9A* enquiry, have clearly alerted him to the insufficiency of the assessment, not where the inspector may have some other information, not normally part of his checks, that might put the sufficiency of the assessment in question'. On the information available to them, the Revenue 'could not have been reasonably expected' to be aware that the valuation was inadequate. Chadwick LJ observed that 'the inspector could reasonably be expected to infer that information as to the value of the asset existed; but he could not reasonably be expected to infer that information as to a value in excess of £100,000 existed'. *Veltema v Langham*, CA 2004, 76 TC 259; [2004] STC 544; [2004] EWCA Civ 193. (*Note.* For the Revenue's practice following this decision, see the Revenue Guidance Note issued on 24 December 2004, reproduced at *2005 SWTI 12*.)

[5.49] In 1998/99 a woman (C) made substantial capital gains. On her tax return she declared that she had made a capital loss. The Revenue subsequently discovered that this alleged loss was attributable to a 'scheme' suggested by C's bank. In 2004 they issued an assessment to disallow the loss which C had claimed. C appealed, contending that the assessment had been made outside the statutory time limit. The Special Commissioner rejected this contention and dismissed the appeal, observing that the scheme had been intended to take advantage of the provisions of *TCGA, s 71(2)* by providing for a loss to be incurred by a UK resident while a corresponding gain accrued to trustees who were resident outside the UK, for non-resident UK beneficiaries. The Commissioner reviewed the evidence in detail and observed that it appeared that 'the scheme was not carried out as intended', that it involved entities which were 'connected' for the purpose of *TCGA, s 286*, and that the effect of *TCGA, s 18* was that C 'was not entitled to deduct the claimed allowable loss in determining her net chargeable gains in her 1998/99 return'. The fact that C had claimed a large 'round sum' loss in her tax return meant that 'an inspector could have been expected to have been aware that it was possible that there was an insufficiency but could not have been reasonably expected to conclude that it was probable that there was an insufficiency'. Accordingly the conditions of *TMA, s 29(5)* were satisfied and the assessment was not prohibited by *s 29(3)*. The Commissioner also held that *TMA, s 29* did not contravene the *Human Rights Act*, and that the relevant assessment had been made when the relevant Revenue officer 'authorised the entry of its amount into the computer'. *Mrs LF Corbally-Stourton v HMRC*, Sp C [2008] SSCD 907 (Sp C 692).

[5.50] An individual (S) used a similar avoidance scheme to that in *Corbally-Stourton v HMRC*, 5.49 above. HMRC issued a discovery assessment. S appealed, contending that the assessment had been made outside the statutory time limit. The First-tier Tribunal and the Upper Tribunal unanimously rejected this contention and dismissed S's appeal. Newey J held that 'the tax return might have alerted the hypothetical officer to the fact that (S) was seeking to take advantage of a tax scheme, but it did not contain enough information to make the officer aware of an "actual insufficiency" or to justify the making of an assessment'. *DS Sanderson v HMRC*, UT [2013] UKUT 623 (TCC); [2014] STC 915.

[5.51] An individual (G) submitted two returns in which he overclaimed foreign tax credits. When HMRC discovered this, they issued assessments to recover the tax due. G appealed, contending that the assessments had been issued outside the statutory time limit. The First-tier Tribunal rejected this contention and dismissed the appeals. Judge Coverdale held that the conditions of *TMA, s 29(5)* were satisfied. *K Gobie v HMRC*, FTT [2012] UKFTT 695 (TC), TC02364.

[5.52] A former army officer (S) purchased a yacht, which he hired to customers. In his tax returns he claimed that he was carrying on a yacht chartering business and that losses, derived from capital allowances, should be allowed against his other income. HMRC subsequently discovered that S had failed to meet the requirements of *ITA 2007, s 75*, and issued discovery assessments. The First-tier Tribunal dismissed S's appeal, holding that the conditions of *TMA, s 29(5)* were satisfied. *A Salmon v HMRC (No 2)*, FTT [2014] UKFTT 666 (TC), TC03789.

[5.53] In 1998 a woman invested £100,000 in an overseas bond. In 2002 she encashed the bond, realising a gain of £24,588. Although the bond was an overseas bond, she did not declare the gain on her tax return, stating 'tax treated as paid'. In 2005 HMRC issued an assessment under *TMA, s 29*. The First-tier Tribunal upheld the assessment, holding that HMRC could not have been expected to be aware that the return was incorrect. *Miss MM Anderson v HMRC*, FTT [2009] UKFTT 258 (TC), TC00206.

[5.54] In March 2008 a company (P) purchased some of its own shares from two of its directors. The directors subsequently submitted returns declaring capital gains on the sales. HMRC subsequently issued discovery assessments on the basis that because the sales were of shares in P, the transactions should have been treated as distributions and subject to income tax rather than capital gains tax. The directors appealed, contending that the assessments had been issued outside the statutory time limit. The First-tier Tribunal rejected this contention and dismissed the appeals, applying the principles laid down in *Veltema v Langham*, **5.48** above. *D & M Brown v HMRC*, FTT [2012] UKFTT 425 (TC), TC02107.

[5.55] The CA decision in *Veltema v Langham*, **5.48** above, was also applied in the subsequent case of *McQueen v HMRC*, **63.241** TRADING PROFITS, where the Special Commissioner held that expenditure on rally driving had not been adequately disclosed in a trader's tax returns, so that 'discovery' assessments had been issued within the statutory time limits.

[5.56] A similar decision, also applying the CA decision in *Veltema v Langham*, **5.48** above, was reached in a case where a company had incorrectly claimed deductions for goodwill. *Pennine Drilling & Grouting Services Ltd v HMRC*, FTT [2013] UKFTT 200 (TC), TC02615.

[5.57] The CA decision in *Veltema v Langham*, **5.48** above, was also applied in the subsequent case of *Agnew v HMRC*, **35.23** LOSS RELIEF, where the First-tier Tribunal allowed an appeal against an assessment for 2003/04, finding that in October 2004 the appellant had given an HMRC officer sufficient information to enable the officer to conclude that the trade had not been conducted on a commercial basis for 2003/04, while he had been ill and his wife had been looking after him. Accordingly the issue of the 2003/04 assessment had been precluded by *TMA, s 29(5)*. However, the appellant had not made it clear that the trade would continue to be conducted on a non-commercial basis for subsequent years, and the officer had warned the appellant that HMRC would review the 2004/05 accounts in due course to assess profitability. Accordingly the tribunal found that 'no officer of HMRC could have been reasonably expected, on the basis of the information made available to him before 31 January 2006, to be aware of the insufficiency in the appellant's self-assessment for the year 2004/05'.

[5.58] An individual (T) entered into an avoidance scheme of the type which was held to be ineffective in *Drummond v HMRC*, **71.84** CAPITAL GAINS TAX. HMRC issued an assessment under *TMA, s 29*. D appealed, contending that the assessment had been issued outside the statutory time limit. The First-tier Tribunal rejected this contention and dismissed the appeal, applying the CA decision in *Veltema v Langham*, **5.48** above, but the Upper Tribunal remitted the case for rehearing. *JS Tetley v HMRC*, UT June 2012 unreported. (*Note*. At the time of writing, no transcript of the Upper Tribunal decision is available, and there has been no further public hearing of the appeal.)

[5.59] In 2006/07 an individual (C) entered into an avoidance scheme which was broadly similar to that which was subsequently held to be ineffective in

Drummond v HMRC, **71.84** CAPITAL GAINS TAX. In July 2009 HMRC issued a discovery assessment under *TMA, s 29*. C appealed, contending that the assessment had been issued outside the statutory time limit. The First-tier Tribunal accepted this contention and allowed the appeal, distinguishing the CA decision in *Veltema v Langham*, **5.48** above. Judge Nowlan held that there had been a discovery within *TMA, s 29(1)*, but that the information provided with C's return was sufficient to show that 'no officer could have missed the point that an artificial tax avoidance scheme had been implemented'. Any officer reviewing the return 'should then have proceeded to seek some guidance from colleagues' and an enquiry should have begun before the closure of the 'enquiry window' on 31 January 2009. The Upper Tribunal upheld this decision. Norris J held that 'on the basis of the information made available to him before the closure of the enquiry window, an officer would have been reasonably expected to have been aware of the insufficiency of tax such as to justify an assessment'. Accordingly, the assessment was not authorised by *TMA, s 29(5)*. *HMRC v Dr M Charlton (and related appeals)*, UT [2012] UKUT 770 (TCC); [2013] STC 866.

[5.60] The decision in *HMRC v Dr M Charlton (and related appeals)*, **5.59** above, was distinguished in a subsequent case where the appellant (S) had, in 2000/01, entered into an avoidance scheme which was broadly similar to that which was subsequently held to be ineffective in *Drummond v HMRC*, **71.84** CAPITAL GAINS TAX. Judge Kempster observed that 'in *Charlton* the taxpayers' returns included the scheme reference number that had been allocated by HMRC when the tax avoidance scheme had been registered by the scheme promoters'. Furthermore, in the *Charlton* case, the Ch D decision in *Drummond* had been issued before the closure of the relevant enquiry window. In the present case, however, the decision in *Drummond* 'was still several years away when the enquiry window closed in January 2003', and 'the relevant law relating to the scheme adopted by (S) was of a degree of complexity such as to make it unreasonable for the officer to be aware of an insufficiency on the basis of the information contained in (S's) tax return'. *R Smith v HMRC*, FTT [2013] UKFTT 368 (TC), TC02768.

[5.61] Judge Reid reached a similar decision in the Scottish case of *N Pattullo v HMRC (No 2)*, FTT [2014] UKFTT 841 (TC); [2015] SFTD 24, TC03958. (*Note*. For a preliminary issue in this case, see **49.43** RETURNS AND INFORMATION.)

[5.62] The Upper Tribunal decision in *HMRC v Dr M Charlton (and related appeals)*, **5.59** above, was applied in a subsequent case where the appellant (F) had wrongly claimed taper relief on the redemption of certain loan notes. Judge Khan held that the information contained in F's return was sufficient to have enabled an HMRC officer to realise that the loan notes were qualifying corporate bonds and that F was not entitled to taper relief. *M Freeman v HMRC*, FTT [2013] UKFTT 496 (TC), TC02885.

[5.63] The Upper Tribunal decision in *HMRC v Dr M Charlton (and related appeals)*, **5.59** above, was also applied in a subsequent case where HMRC had discovered in 2007 that a company director had failed to declare car benefit on his tax returns, but did not issue discovery assessments until 2011. *M Ive v*

HMRC (and related appeal), FTT [2014] UKFTT 400 (TC), TC03529. (*Note*. Appeals by the company against determinations charging Class 1A NIC were dismissed.)

[5.64] A partnership operated a newsagents' business. In 2000 it took over a sub-post office. The senior partner (S) became the subpostmaster. In 2002 the partnership was incorporated. In 2004 the sub-post office was closed, and the Post Office paid S compensation. S's accountant treated the compensation payment as belonging to the company rather than to S, and submitted returns accordingly. In October 2006 HMRC issued discovery assessments on the basis that the compensation payment should have been treated as S's personal income, rather than as income of the company. S, and the company, appealed, contending firstly that the treatment in the accounts had been correct, and alternatively that the assessment was invalid because the relevant information had already been disclosed to HMRC before the 'enquiry window' had closed. The First-tier Tribunal rejected S's first contention, holding that the payment belonged to S personally and should have been declared in his personal return. However the tribunal accepted S's alternative contention and allowed the appeal, finding that the relevant information had been fully disclosed to HMRC, so that the discovery assessment was not authorised by *TMA, s 29(4)* or *(5)* and had been issued outside the statutory time limit. *M Singh v HMRC*, FTT [2011] UKFTT 707 (TC), TC01544.

[5.65] A married couple controlled a company (P) and were the only members of an unapproved retirement benefit scheme (M). P transferred certain property interests to M. When HMRC discovered this, they issued an assessment charging tax on the basis that the amounts transferred were employment income of the husband. He appealed, contending that his tax returns had noted that he had received certain benefits from P, so that the assessments had been issued outside the statutory time limits. The First-tier Tribunal rejected this contention and dismissed the appeal, holding that the assessments were authorised by *TMA, s 29(5)*. Judge Tildesley held that the relevant entries in the appellant's returns 'were carefully crafted disclosures seeking to pass through the initial checks carried out by HMRC but in no way meeting the test of clearly alerting an officer of the Board to an actual insufficiency. The entries fell far short of the requirement of a full and complete disclosure to justify an early finality of the assessments.' Accordingly, 'an officer of the Board could not have been reasonably expected on the basis of the appellant's disclosures before the expiry of the enquiry windows to be aware of the actual insufficiency in the tax assessments for 2004/05 and 2005/06'. *A Omar v HMRC*, FTT [2011] UKFTT 722 (TC), TC01559.

[5.66] In 1992 a life assurance company dismissed one of its directors (W). In 1998 he was awarded substantial damages against the company. He did not declare this on his 1998/99 tax return, but informed HMRC of the award at a meeting in April 2000. However HMRC did not issue an assessment until January 2005. The First-Tier Tribunal allowed W's appeal against the assessment, holding that the assessment failed to meet the requirements of *TMA, s 29(5)*. *A While v HMRC*, FTT [2012] UKFTT 58 (TC), TC01755.

[5.67] See also *Fisher v HMRC*, **3.65** ANTI-AVOIDANCE; *Letts v HMRC*, **4.415** APPEALS; *Macklin v HMRC*, **21.8** DOUBLE TAX RELIEF, and *Mrs R & Mrs S Thomas v HMRC*, **44.104** PENALTIES.

Amendments of partnership statements (TMA, s 30B)

[5.68] A limited liability partnership made losses on the purchase and resale of three commercial properties. It treated these as trading losses. HMRC issued a 'discovery amendment' for 2005/06 under *TMA, s 30B(1)*, reclassifying the losses as 'property losses' (so that the members of the partnership would not be able to set the losses against their general income). The partnership appealed, contending that the amendment was not authorised by *s 30B(1)*, since this only applied where profits had been omitted, or where 'an amount of profits so included is or has become insufficient', and did not apply in a situation where there had only been losses and there had not been any profits. The First-tier Tribunal accepted this contention and allowed the appeal. Judge Raghavan held that the reference to profits in *s 30B* could not be construed so as 'to cover negative amounts'. He also accepted the partnership's contention that the losses were trading losses, finding that 'the appellant's intention was to trade in the properties not hold onto them to earn rental income from them'. *Albermarle 4 Llp v HMRC*, FTT [2013] UKFTT 83 (TC); [2013] SFTD 664, TC02501.

[5.69] A limited partnership carried on business as a fund manager. In August 2005 it submitted its partnership statement for 2004/05, claiming a deduction for certain 'rebated fees', including fees which it had reimbursed to its partners as well as to external investors. In August 2008 HMRC amended the partnership statement on the basis that the fees rebated to partners were not allowable as deductions. The partnership appealed, contending firstly that it was entitled to a deduction for the fees, and alternatively that HMRC's amendment was outside the statutory time limit. The General Commissioners accepted both these contentions, and HMRC appealed to the CA. The CA unanimously held that the rebated fees were not allowable deductions, as they had not been wholly and exclusively for the purpose of the partnership's trade, applying the HL decision in *MacKinlay v Arthur Young McClelland Moores & Co*, **41.30** PARTNERSHIPS. However, the CA dismissed HMRC's appeal on the grounds that the amendment had been issued outside the statutory time limit. The effect of *TMA, s 30B(6)* was that the amendment was only valid if, at 31 January 2007, the relevant officer 'could not have been reasonably expected, on the basis of the information made available to him before that time' to be aware that the partnership statement was incorrect. On the evidence, the partnership had submitted the relevant information in a letter dated 30 March 2006. Sir Andrew Morritt held that the hypothetical HMRC officer should be assumed to have been aware of the decision in the *Arthur Young* case. Therefore the effect of the letter was that 'an officer of the Board could have been reasonably expected to be aware that the amount of the profits included in the partnership return was insufficient'. *HMRC v Lansdowne Partners Limited Partnership*, CA [2011] EWCA Civ 1578.

[5.70] See also *Stockler Charity v HMRC*, **29.84** FURTHER ASSESSMENTS: LOSS OF TAX.

Requirements of FA 1998, Sch 18

Assessment under FA 1998, Sch 18, para 41(1)

[5.71] A company (H) claimed a deduction for a payment of £60,000 to an employee benefit trust. The Revenue issued a 'discovery' assessment under *FA 1998, Sch 18, para 41* on the basis that the effect of what is now *CTA 2009, ss 1288, 1289*, as interpreted by the HL in *Dextra Accessories Ltd & Others v MacDonald*, 53.38 SCHEDULE D, was that the payment was not allowable as a deduction. H appealed, contending that the return had been made 'in accordance with the practice generally prevailing at the time when it was made', so that *Sch 18, para 45* applied. The Ch D rejected this contention and upheld the assessment. Henderson J observed that the claim was not in accordance with the guidance which the Revenue had published in the Inspector's Manual. Accordingly *Sch 18, para 45* did not apply. *HMRC v Household Estate Agents Ltd*, Ch D 2007, 78 TC 705; [2008] STC 2045; [2007] EWHC 1684 (Ch).

[5.72] The decision in *HMRC v Household Estate Agents Ltd*, 5.71 above, was applied in the similar subsequent case of *Boyer Allan Investment Services Ltd v HMRC*, FTT [2012] UKFTT 558 (TC); [2013] SFTD 73, TC02235.

Determination under FA 1998, Sch 18, para 41(2)

[5.73] A company (N) submitted a return claiming to have made a loss in 2005. HMRC formed the opinion that N had claimed deductions for substantial expenditure which was not wholly and exclusively for the purposes of its trade. In December 2011 they sent a letter to N's accountants purporting to disallow the deductions, and stating that they had made 'protective discovery assessments'. N appealed, contending as a preliminary issue that HMRC had not made a 'discovery determination' within *FA 1998, Sch 18, para 41(2)*, so that the losses remained available to carry forward. In June 2012 HMRC sent a letter, headed 'notice of determination', to N. The First-tier Tribunal allowed N's appeal against this determination, holding that it had been made outside the statutory time limit. Judge Sinfield rejected HMRC's contention that they had made a 'discovery determination' in December 2011, holding that the letter which HMRC had issued at that time 'did not have the appearance of an official record of a decision to make a determination in relation to a taxpayer but appeared to be part of the ongoing correspondence between HMRC and (N's) accountant in relation to the tax dispute. The only decision that the letter clearly recorded was the decision to issue protective assessments.' *Nijjar Dairies Ltd v HMRC*, FTT [2013] UKFTT 434 (TC), TC02828. (*Note*. An appeal against an information notice under *FA 2008, Sch 36 para 1* was dismissed.)

FA 1998, Sch 18 para 76—assessment to recover excessive group relief

[5.74] In December 2003 a company (M) claimed group relief of £999,000 for its accounting period ending December 2001 in respect of losses incurred by an associated US company. HMRC rejected the claim. In September 2007 HMRC issued an assessment under *FA 1998, Sch 18 para 76*. M appealed, contending that the assessment had been issued outside the statutory time limit. The First-tier Tribunal rejected this contention and dismissed the appeal, holding that the assessment had been made within the six-year time limit of *FA 1998, Sch 18 para 46*. *Morritt Properties (International) Ltd v HMRC*, FTT [2010] UKFTT 554 (TC); [2011] SFTD 186, TC00807.

The Cenlon principle

Appeal settled by agreement—whether additional assessment competent

[5.75] A company (C) appealed against assessments for 1953/54 and 1954/55, and submitted accounts and computations in which a capital dividend was excluded from the receipts. The accounts formed the basis period for the four years 1953/54 to 1956/57. The Revenue accepted the computations, settled the 1953/54 and 1954/55 appeals accordingly, and made an assessment for 1955/56, against which C did not appeal. A new inspector subsequently reviewed the position and considered that the capital dividend was taxable. He made additional assessments for the years 1953/54 to 1955/56 (and a first assessment for 1956/57) treating the dividend as a taxable receipt. C appealed. The Special Commissioners dismissed C's appeals against the assessments for 1955/56 and 1956/57, holding that the capital dividend was taxable and that there had been a discovery. The HL unanimously upheld their decision. Viscount Simonds held that there was 'no reason for saying that a discovery of undercharge can only arise where a new fact has been discovered. The words are apt to include any case in which for any reason it newly appears that the taxpayer has been undercharged, and the context supports rather than detracts from this interpretation'. However, C's appeals against the 1953/54 and 1954/55 assessments were allowed. The Special Commissioners held that, since the point in dispute had been agreed under what is now *TMA, s 54* for 1953/54 and 1954/55, it could not be reopened by the Revenue in additional assessments for those years. The CA unanimously upheld this decision. Upjohn LJ held that the Revenue could not use an additional assessment 'to relitigate the very point, and in this case the only point, that has been agreed between the parties'. The Revenue did not take the point to the HL. *Cenlon Finance Co Ltd v Ellwood (and related appeals)*, HL 1962, 40 TC 176; [1962] AC 782; [1962] 1 All ER 854. (*Notes*. (1) For the Revenue's practice following this decision, see Revenue Pamphlet IR 131, SP8/91, issued on 26 July 1991. HMRC consider that an agreement under *TMA, s 54* is not binding if an inspector has failed to notice an arithmetical error in a computation. (2) For the tax treatment of capital dividends, see now Simon's Taxes, para D7.330.)

[5.76] The Revenue made income tax and surtax assessments on an individual (K) in respect of his wife's income from an American trust. The assessments were on the basis of the net income remitted. K appealed, and the appeals were settled by agreement under what is now *TMA, s 54*. In 1958, following the decision in *CIR v Countess of Kenmare*, **56.54** SETTLEMENTS, K's accountants informed the Revenue that K's wife had a discretionary power over the capital of the fund as well as the income. The Revenue issued additional assessments for 1952/53 to 1956/57 on the basis that the liability should be on the full income of the trust. K appealed, contending that the effect of the decision in *Cenlon Finance Co Ltd v Ellwood*, **5.75** above, was that the assessments were invalid. The Special Commissioners rejected this contention and dismissed the appeal, holding that there had been a 'discovery' and that there had been no agreement on the question of whether the liability was on the full income. The Ch D upheld this decision. Wilberforce J held that the power to raise additional assessments was 'limited only to the extent that, where there has been an agreement as to a particular point, that particular point cannot be later reopened'. In this case, it was not until 1958 that the Revenue were informed 'that the discretion in the American settlement extended to capital as well as to income'. *Kidston v Aspinall*, Ch D 1963, 41 TC 371.

[5.77] In the case noted at **20.5** DEDUCTION OF TAX, the appellant company contended that an assessment under *ITA 1952, s 170* was barred by an agreement in writing under what is now *TMA, s 54* in respect of the original assessment for that year. The HL rejected this contention and upheld the further assessment, distinguishing *Cenlon Finance Co Ltd v Ellwood*, **5.75** above. Lord Wilberforce observed that the relevant agreement 'did not touch the matter now in dispute'. *Chancery Lane Safe Deposit & Offices Co Ltd v CIR*, HL 1965, 43 TC 83; [1966] AC 85; [1966] 1 All ER 1.

[5.78] A similar decision, also distinguishing *Cenlon Finance Co Ltd v Ellwood*, **5.75** above, was reached in the case noted at **65.36** TRADING PROFITS. The Ch D held that further assessments were valid since, at the time when the appeals against the first assessments had been settled by agreement, the question of whether the sale price of the land was substantially less than its market value had not been 'canvassed between the parties or agreed to be settled'. *Skinner v Berry Head Lands Ltd*, Ch D 1970, 46 TC 377; [1970] 1 WLR 1441; [1971] 1 All ER 222.

[5.79] A timber merchant traded from 1944 to 1953, when he transferred his business to a company. His appeals against assessments for 1945/46 to 1952/53 were settled by agreement under what is now *TMA, s 54*. In 1967, following an investigation, the Revenue issued further assessments for these years under what is now *TMA, s 36*. The Commissioners found that there had been fraud, and determined the appeals in accordance with the evidence. The Ch D upheld their decision. Megarry J held that 'where agreements have been reached upon a footing which the Inspector afterwards finds out to be untrue, there seems to me to be a plain case of "discovery"'. *Young v Duthie*, Ch D 1969, 45 TC 624.

[5.80] An appeal against an assessment for 1962/63 was settled by agreement, but the Revenue subsequently issued an additional assessment withdrawing an allowance made in the original assessment. The CA unanimously held that the additional assessment was invalid, applying the principles laid down in *Cenlon Finance Co Ltd v Ellwood*, **5.75** above. Russell LJ held that 'the precise question raised by the additional assessment' had been 'decided by the agreement leading to the amended assessment'. *Banning v Wright*, CA 1970, 48 TC 421. (*Notes*. (1) *Obiter dicta* of Sachs LJ were subsequently disapproved by Lawton LJ in *Olin Energy Systems Ltd v Scorer*, **5.81** below. (2) For another issue in this case, taken to the HL, see **47.9** PROPERTY INCOME.)

[5.81] A company had carried on a ship-chartering trade which ceased in 1967, and a manufacturing trade which continued after that date. For the year to 30 November 1968, the Revenue had issued a small estimated assessment. Following an appeal, accounts and computations had been sent in, in which the profits of the trade had been treated as covered by unused losses from previous years, created by interest on a loan from the company's parent. The figures were eventually agreed and the inspector issued a statement amending the assessment to £123,403 'less losses or charges treated as losses £123,403', reducing the tax payable to nil. There was no explicit reference to the treatment of the interest by either the accountants or the inspector. Subsequently a different inspector concluded that the losses had been wrongly deducted and issued a further assessment to withdraw the deduction. The company appealed, contending that the losses had been correctly deducted. The Ch D rejected this contention and held that the losses could not be set against the profits of the manufacturing trade (see **63.288** TRADING PROFITS). The company accepted this but appealed to the CA, contending that, as the appeal against the first assessment had been determined by agreement, the Revenue was precluded from making the further assessment. The CA accepted this contention and allowed the appeal (by a 2–1 majority, Kerr LJ dissenting). Fox LJ observed that 'the purpose of the section must be to protect the taxpayer by producing finality'. While 'the provision of misleading information, albeit honestly, by the taxpayer may give rise to different considerations', that proviso did not arise in this case. The HL unanimously upheld this decision, distinguishing *Chancery Lane Safe Deposit & Offices Co Ltd v CIR*, 5.77 above. Lord Keith of Kinkel held that the material which the company's accountants had submitted in their computation 'was sufficient to bring home to the mind of an ordinarily competent inspector' that they were claiming to have the carried-forward losses of the ship-chartering trade set against the profits of the manufacturing trade. He held that 'the situation must be viewed objectively, from the point of view of whether the inspector's agreement to the relevant computation, having regard to the surrounding circumstances including all the material known to be in his possession, was such as to lead a reasonable man to the conclusion that he had decided to admit the claim'. Here the question had to be answered in the affirmative. Lord Templeman observed that the case showed that the Revenue could not safely assume that the accounts 'complied with elementary rules of accountancy and tax law'. *Olin Energy Systems Ltd v Scorer*, HL 1985, 58 TC 592; [1985] STC 218; [1985] 1 WLR 490; [1985] 2 All ER 375. (*Note*. See the note following *Cenlon Finance Co Ltd*, **5.75** above.)

[5.82] Assessments on a publican and garage proprietor for 1984/85 to 1986/87 had been determined by agreement under *TMA, s 54* in accordance with the figures declared in his accounts to November 1985. Following receipt of his accounts for the period to November 1986, an inspector began an investigation into the publican's affairs, formed the opinion that the accounts for the two years to November 1984 had not declared the true profits, and raised further assessments for 1984/85 and 1985/86 under *TMA, s 29*. The publican appealed, accepting that his accounts had understated his profits, but contending that the agreement under *TMA, s 54* prevented the inspector from raising further assessments. The Ch D rejected this contention and upheld the assessments. The trading profits shown in the accounts for the year in question were incorrect. The issue of further assessments could not be barred by an agreement between the parties that was based on statements made by the proprietor as to his trading profits which were admittedly incorrect. *Gray v Matheson*, Ch D 1993, 65 TC 577; [1993] STC 178; [1993] 1 WLR 1130.

[5.83] A company's appeals against assessments for its accounting periods ending in 1991 and 1992 were settled by agreement under *TMA, s 54* in 1995. In 1997 and 1998 the Revenue made three directions under *ICTA 1988, s 770*, relating to an agreement for the payment of royalties by the company to its parent company. They raised further assessments accordingly. The company appealed, contending that the effect of the *s 54* agreement was that the Revenue were not entitled to raise further assessments. The Special Commissioners accepted this contention and allowed the appeal. The company's financial controller had taken care 'to conceal nothing from the Inland Revenue'. There had been ample information available to the inspector, and he had 'intended a final determination of the computations for the relevant years'. Accordingly, the Revenue were not entitled to reopen the matter by directions under *s 770*. *Newidgets Manufacturing Ltd v Jones*, Sp C [1999] SSCD 193 (Sp C 197). (*Note. ICTA 1988, s 770* was substituted by *FA 1998*. See now *TIOPA 2010, ss 146–217*.)

[5.84] A company (S) acquired the business of another company (P) on 31 December 1991. P had paid UK bank interest, and claimed this as a charge against income. In its return for its 1992 accounting period, S claimed relief as a charge on income for interest which had been accrued by P in 1991 but had been paid by S in 1992. Its appeal against an assessment for this accounting period was settled by agreement, under *TMA, s 54*, in 1994. In 1997 new accountants advised the Revenue that the bank interest which P and S had paid should have been treated as a trading expense, rather than a charge on income. In 1998 the Revenue issued a further assessment to S for the 1992 accounting period, as part of an enquiry into 'transfer pricing' which was not connected with the treatment of the bank interest. In 1999 S's new accountants asked for P's 1991 assessment to be reopened to allow the bank interest paid for that year as a trading expense. The Revenue rejected the claim, on the grounds that the relevant assessment had been settled in 1993, by agreement under *TMA, s 54*, and could not be reopened. S's accountants replied that they would accept that P's 1991 assessment could not be reopened if the Revenue would agree that the brought-forward figure was a charge on income in S's 1992 accounting period. The Revenue rejected this request, and sought to amend the further assessment which had been issued on S in 1998, to disallow the bank interest which had been treated as a charge for the 1992 accounting period. The Special Commissioner held that the Revenue was not entitled to increase the 1998 assessment to disallow the bank interest, because when the original assessment for that period was settled by agreement under *TMA, s 54*, the inspector must be 'taken to have agreed the deduction of the UK bank interest as a charge'. (The Commissioner also observed that, if the treatment of the bank interest had not been covered by the previous *s 54* agreement, the 1998 assessment could have been adjusted, since 'once an assessment is under appeal any other matter can be bolted onto the assessment until it is determined'.) *Sun Chemical Ltd v Smith*, Sp C [2002] SSCD 510 (Sp C 340).

Further assessments on undeclared income

[5.85] The Revenue issued assessments, covering the years 1973/74 to 1986/87 inclusive, on a guest house proprietor (K). K appealed. The Special Commissioners heard his appeals in 1991, reviewed the evidence in detail, and determined the appeals. K appealed to the CA, which heard his appeal in 1995 and upheld the Commissioners' decision (see **4.9** APPEALS). Meanwhile, also in 1995, the Revenue discovered that K had purchased a further property in 1983, which he had not disclosed to them. In 1996 they issued further assessments, covering 1977/78 to 1985/86 inclusive, to take account of the additional resources required to finance the purchase and running costs of this property. K appealed, contending *inter alia* that the effect of *TMA, s 46(2)* was that the Revenue were not entitled to raise further assessments. The Special Commissioners rejected this contention, holding that *s 46(2)* 'does not preclude the making of further assessments where further matters come to the notice of the Inland Revenue after a decision of the appeal commissioners'. On the evidence, K had supplied misleading information to the Revenue and the Special Commissioners. The Commissioners upheld the assessments in principle, reducing the total tax charged from £58,600 to £53,393. The Ch D upheld their decision. Jacob J observed that K's conduct clearly constituted 'wilful default or worse'. *King v Walden (No 2)*, Ch D 2001, 74 TC 45; [2001] STC 822; 3 ITLR 682. (*Note*. For another issue in this case, see **29.42** FURTHER ASSESSMENTS: LOSS OF TAX.)

Whether assessments precluded by agreement with SOCA

[5.86] See *Pepper v SOCA*, **29.24** FURTHER ASSESSMENTS: LOSS OF TAX.

The person assessable

Individual below age of majority—whether assessable personally

[5.87] A young jockey, who was below the age of majority (then 21 but subsequently reduced to 18) was assessed on his profits. He applied for a writ of prohibition to discharge the assessment, contending that, as he was below the age of majority, he could not be assessed personally. The CA unanimously rejected this contention and dismissed his application, holding that the provisions for the assessment of the trustee or guardian of a person below the age of majority, should there be one, were simply machinery provisions, and did not prevent the Revenue from assessing a person below the age of majority who did not have a trustee or guardian. *R v Newmarket Commissioners (ex p. Huxley)*, CA 1916, 7 TC 49; [1916] 1 KB 788.

Liability of guardian of child below age of majority

[5.88] An American citizen (F) died in 1906, having outlived his son. F's will established a trust, the beneficiaries being his three grandchildren, who were below the age of majority and lived with their mother (D). In 1907 D and her children moved to the UK. The trustees of F's will sent substantial remittances to D as guardian of the children. The Revenue issued an assessment on D, charging tax on the sums remitted. She appealed, contending that she could not be assessed as the money did not belong to her. The HL unanimously rejected this contention and dismissed her appeal. Earl Loreburn held that the payments were 'made in fulfilment of a testamentary disposition for the benefit of the children in the exercise of a discretion conferred by the will'. Lord Parker of Waddington held that it was 'enough that the guardian or other person should receive and have the direction and application on behalf of the owner of the profits and gains sought to be assessed'. *Drummond v Collins*, HL 1915, 6 TC 525; [1915] 2 AC 1011.

Payments to divorced parents for maintenance of children

[5.89] See the cases noted at 36.5 *et seq.* MAINTENANCE PAYMENTS.

Non-residents trading in UK—assessment of agents

[5.90] See the cases noted at 60.12 *et seq.* TRADING INCOME.

Notice of assessment sent to overseas address

[5.91] Two directors of a UK company lived in Paris. They failed to submit UK tax returns. The Revenue issued estimated supertax assessments to their Paris addresses by registered post. They appealed, contending that the assessments were invalid. The KB rejected this contention, holding that the assessments had been validly made. Rowlatt J observed that 'what the statute really directs is the mere service of a notice, and that is all it is. There is no international difficulty involved in serving a notice abroad.' *CIR v Huni (and related appeals)*, KB 1923, 8 TC 466; [1923] 2 KB 563. (*Note*. The decision was subsequently approved by the HL in *Whitney v CIR*, 5.92 below.)

Whether non-resident assessable in own name

[5.92] An American citizen received dividends from a UK company. He failed to submit UK tax returns. The Revenue issued estimated supertax assessments to his New York address by registered post. He appealed, contending that a non-resident could be assessed, if at all, only in the name of a trustee or agent and not in his own name. The Special Commissioners rejected this contention and dismissed his appeals, and the HL upheld their decision (by a 3-2 majority, Viscount Cave and Lord Phillimore dissenting). Lord Dunedin observed that 'once it is fixed that there is liability, it is antecedently highly improbable that the statute should not go on to make that liability effective. A statute is designed to be workable, and the interpretation thereof by a court should be to secure that object, unless crucial omission or clear direction makes that end unattainable.' *Whitney v CIR*, HL 1925, 10 TC 88; [1926] AC 37.

Assessment on trustee—application of TMA, s 114(1)

[5.93] An individual (M) purchased a large property for use as a Masonic temple. He subsequently transferred the property to a trust. The Revenue assessed him personally on certain trading profits arising from the property. He appealed, contending that the assessments were invalid. The Special Commissioners rejected this contention and upheld the assessments, holding that he was assessable as the person in receipt of the profits, and that any error in the form of the assessment was remedied by what is now *TMA, s 114(1)*. The CS unanimously upheld the Commissioners' decision. Lord Moncrieff observed that M was 'not only a trustee *ab initio* but was *ab initio* the sole trustee. As such trustee he necessarily ingathered and administered every penny of the revenue'. It could not 'affect the chargeability of the revenue whether the trust itself or the trustee be assessed'. *Martin v CIR*, CS 1938, 22 TC 330.

Wrong trustees assessed

[5.94] In the case noted at **71.146** CAPITAL GAINS TAX, an assessment on the trustees of a settlement was made on the wrong persons. The Ch D held that, in the circumstances, including previous correspondence between the parties as to the persons assessable, the defect was cured by *TMA, s 114(1)*. *Hart v Briscoe & Others*, Ch D 1977, 52 TC 53; [1978] STC 89; [1978] 2 WLR 832; [1978] 1 All ER 791.

Restaurant proprietor

[5.95] The Revenue issued an assessment on the owner of a restaurant. He appealed, contending that the profits of the restaurant accrued to his brother, who managed the restaurant (and who was an undischarged bankrupt). The Commissioners dismissed the appeal, finding that the appellant was the sole proprietor of the restaurant and that his brother was an employee. The CS upheld the Commissioners' decision. On the evidence, the appellant had failed to show that he had divested himself of the right to receive the profits of the restaurant, or that the profits accrued to someone other than himself. *Alongi v CIR*, CS 1991, 64 TC 304; [1991] STC 517.

Whether income taxable on company or director

[5.96] HMRC formed the opinion that a builder (J) had failed to account for tax on the profit on a construction contract. They issued an assessment charging tax accordingly. J appealed, contending that he had done the work on behalf of a company in which he owned a 50% shareholding. The First-Tier tribunal reviewed the evidence in detail, rejected this contention and dismissed the appeal, finding that J had carried out the work as a sole trader. *J Johnstone v HMRC*, FTT [2011] UKFTT 57 (TC), TC00935.

[5.97] A woman (H) agreed to provide consultancy services to a client through a newly-formed company (T). Much of the work was performed before T was incorporated. However the fee was subsequently paid into T's bank account. T included the fee in its accounts and paid the corporation tax. Subsequently HMRC formed the opinion that the income was taxable on H rather than on T, under *ITTOIA 2005, s 8*, and issued a protective discovery assessment. H appealed. The First-tier Tribunal allowed her appeal. Judge Reid held that 'the substance and commercial effect of the arrangements' was that H was never entitled to the income, and was not taxable on it. *Miss M Hepburn v HMRC*, FTT [2013] UKFTT 445 (TC), TC02837.

Whether income taxable on shareholder or wife

[5.98] A shareholder (R) only declared half of his dividend income on his return. HMRC issued discovery assessments, and R appealed, contending that the other half of the income should be treated as belonging to his wife. The First-tier Tribunal rejected this contention and dismissed his appeal. *P Rowe v HMRC*, FTT [2014] UKFTT 909 (TC), TC04023.

Disposal of land by members' club

[5.99] See *CIR v Worthing Rugby Football Club Trustees*, **70.9** VOLUNTARY ASSOCIATIONS.

The issue and form of the assessment

Whether assessment made before notice served

[5.100] An individual (H) died in September 1966. In 1970 the Revenue began an enquiry into his returns, and on 16 March 1970 an inspector issued further assessments on his administrators for the years 1960/61 to 1966/67. Notices of these assessments were sent to H's widow, who was one of the three administrators, but were returned to the tax office, and were reissued to H's son, who was also one of the administrators, on 7 April 1970. The administrators appealed, contending that the assessments were out of time, having been made after the end of 1969/70, the 'third year' of *TMA, s 40(1) as originally enacted*. The Special Commissioners rejected this contention, finding that the assessments had been made on 16 March 1970, within the prescribed time limit, and determined the assessments. The Ch D and the CA upheld their decision, holding that the making of an assessment did not depend on its being served. Fox LJ held that 'an assessment is different from and will be followed by the notice of assessment'. They were 'two wholly different things'. *Honig & Others (Honig's Administrators) v Sarsfield*, CA 1986, *59 TC 337*; [1986] STC 246. (*Note*. The Ch D also upheld the Commissioners' findings of wilful default and their determination of the appeals, as one for which there was ample evidence. This point was not taken to the CA.)

[5.101] In *Corbally-Stourton v HMRC*, **5.49** above, the Special Commissioner observed that 'in the days before widespread computer use, when an inspector made an assessment he did so by writing it in the assessment book'. He noted that 'no longer is an assessment book maintained. HMRC's practice now is that the relevant officer will write to the taxpayer indicating that an assessment is to be made and will key into HMRC's computers the amount of the assessment.' He held that an assessment had been made when the relevant Revenue officer 'authorised the entry of its amount into the computer'.

[5.102] See also *Thurgood v Slarke*, **29.69** FURTHER ASSESSMENTS: LOSS OF TAX.

Whether assessment valid if notice not served

[5.103] An assessment was made (by the General Commissioners under the procedure then in force) on a manager employed by a limited company. The notice of assessment was left at the company's head office (which he visited less than once a month). The company secretary failed to forward it to the employee. The Collector of Taxes sent requests for payment to both the company's address and the employee's home address, but received no response. The Collector subsequently levied distraint at the employee's home address. He claimed damages for wrongful distraint, contending that he had never received the original notice of assessment. The KB gave judgment for the employee. Bankes J observed that 'the object of the notice is to give the person charged an opportunity of challenging the correctness of the assessment by appealing against it'. What is now *TMA, s 115(1)* required the notice to be sent to the employee's 'usual or last known place of abode'. The company's head office was not 'in any real sense the plaintiff's place of abode, either from the business or domestic point of view'. Accordingly the assessment was invalid and the distraint was unlawful. *Berry v Farrow*, KB [1914] 1 KB 632.

Notice of assessment sent to an address abroad

[5.104] See *CIR v Huni* and *Whitney v CIR*, 5.94 and 5.95 above.

Whether assessment must specify tax payable

[5.105] In a case where the substantive issue has since been clarified by *TMA, s 50(8)*, the Ch D held that an assessment must include a statement of the amount of tax payable. *Hallamshire Industrial Finance Trust Ltd v CIR*, Ch D 1978, 53 TC 631; [1979] STC 237; [1979] 1 WLR 620; [1979] 2 All ER 433.

Effect of TMA, s 114

[5.106] In the case noted at **60.29** TRADING INCOME, the company contended as a subsidiary point that one of the assessments under appeal was invalid because of an error in the description of the profits assessed. Megarry J held that the error was cured by what is now *TMA, s 114*. The legislation does not 'provide an impervious cover for gross errors', and the likelihood of the recipient of the assessment being deceived or misled would be an important factor. Here the error was not so gross or misleading as to be incapable of cure under *s 114*. *Fleming v London Produce Co Ltd*, Ch D 1968, 44 TC 582; [1968] 1 WLR 1013; [1968] 2 All ER 975.

[5.107] In the case noted at 65.57 TRADING PROFITS, the First-tier Tribunal dismissed appeals by a company director (G). G appealed to the Upper Tribunal, contending that the notices of assessment were invalid because they did not give details of the statutory provisions under which they were raised. The Upper Tribunal rejected this contention and dismissed the appeal, holding that the notices of assessment were 'in substance and effect' in conformity with the Taxes Acts, and were therefore authorised by *TMA, s 114*. *PG Gunn v HMRC*, UT [2011] UKUT 59 (TCC); [2011] STC 1119.

Year of assessment wrongly described in assessment

[5.108] In the case noted at 71.290 CAPITAL GAINS TAX, an 1975/76 assessment on trustees had been incorrectly typed as one for 1974/75. The inspector realised the error too late for a fresh 1975/76 assessment to be made. He purported to 'vacate' the assessment, instructing the Collector not to demand the tax, but without informing the trustees. The CA held that the assessment was invalid. An inspector has no general powers to vacate an assessment once it has been served. The relevant fiscal year is an integral, fundamental part of the assessment and *TMA, s 114(1)* could not in any circumstances justify the treatment of an assessment made for one year as an assessment made for another year. The assessment stood as one for 1974/75 and the trustees' appeal against it was allowed. *Baylis v Gregory & Weare (Gregory's Trustees)*, CA 1987, 62 TC 1; [1987] STC 297.

Error in wording of penalty notice—effect of TMA 1970, s 114

[5.109] See *Mrs ME Pipe v HMRC*, 44.13 PENALTIES.

Whether assessment made by correct inspector

[5.110] A contractor appealed against an assessment under what is now *Regulation 14(1)* of the *Income Tax (Sub-Contractors in the Construction Industry) Regulations (SI 1993/743)*, contending that the assessment was invalid because the inspector who had signed the assessment had not himself made it. The CA rejected this contention and dismissed his appeal. It was not necessary for the assessment to be signed by the inspector whose decision it was to make it. The management inspector who had signed the assessment certificate had done so as an agent of the inspector who had been responsible for the case. The signing of the assessment certificate was 'a purely ministerial act' which did not require the exercise of any independent discretion. The assessment was 'made' by the inspector who had made the decision to assess. *Burford v Durkin*, CA 1990, 63 TC 645; [1991] STC 7.

Revision of period of assessment under ICTA 1988, s 12(8)

[5.111] In the case noted at 29.76 FURTHER ASSESSMENTS: LOSS OF TAX, the Revenue issued a late assessment on a company (S) for the period 1 February 1977 to 25 October 1977, as the inspector responsible for raising the assessment had formed the opinion that S had ceased to trade on 25 October

1977, when it sold a site which it had developed. Subsequently, after receiving further evidence, the Revenue accepted that S had continued to trade until after 31 January 1988, and sought to revise the terminal date of the assessment under what is now *ICTA 1988, s 12(8)*. S appealed, contending that the Revenue had no power to revise the terminal date. The Special Commissioner allowed the appeal, holding on the evidence that at the time when he made the assessment, the inspector had not been uncertain about the terminal date, so that the conditions for the application of *s 12(8)* were not satisfied. The CA upheld this decision, holding that the test for the application of *s 12(8)* was subjective rather than objective. On the evidence, the Commissioner had made a clear finding of fact that, at the time when he issued the assessment, the inspector had not been uncertain as to the terminal date. The fact that a reasonable inspector would or could have been doubtful as to the correct terminal date was not conclusive. Consequently the terminal date of the assessment in question could not be amended subsequently. Peter Gibson LJ observed that the Revenue 'must seek leave out of time if it wishes to raise a fresh assessment'. *Kelsall v Stipplechoice Ltd*, CA 1995, 67 TC 349; [1995] STC 681. (*Note*. For a preliminary issue in this case, see **4.274** APPEALS.)

6

Bankruptcy and Personal Insolvency

The cases in this chapter are arranged under the following headings.

Proof of tax by Revenue

Proof of tax on estimated assessment

[6.1] The Revenue issued an estimated assessment on an individual (C) who did not appeal and was subsequently made bankrupt. The Revenue lodged proof in respect of the unpaid tax, and C applied to the QB for the proof to be struck out. The QB rejected the application and gave judgment for the Revenue. Wright J held that the statutory mode of appeal must be followed, and that the court had no jurisdiction to reopen the amount of the assessment. *Calvert v Walker*, QB 1899, 4 TC 79; [1899] 2 QB 145.

[6.2] Assessments on a manufacturer (M) were confirmed in the case noted at 29.97 FURTHER ASSESSMENTS: LOSS OF TAX. M was subsequently adjudged bankrupt, and the Revenue lodged proof for the unpaid tax charged by the assessments. M's wife applied to the Ch D for the bankruptcy to be annulled, contending that the assessments had been excessive. The Ch D dismissed the application, applying *Calvert v Walker*, **6.1** above, and holding that the previous confirmation of the assessments was 'final and binding'. *Moschi v CIR*, Ch D 1953, 35 TC 92.

[6.3] A similar decision was reached in a subsequent case where Blackburne J observed that 'Parliament has provided a clear and exclusive machinery for considering appeals' and held that it was 'not open to the Bankruptcy Court to review the manner in which the assessment has been made, much less to investigate the merits of the assessment.' *Lam v CIR*, Ch D [2005] EWHC 592 (Ch); [2006] STC 893.

Application for judicial review of proof of debt

[6.4] An individual (S) was declared bankrupt in November 2006 after failing to pay PAYE and NIC for several years. S subsequently applied for judicial review of HMRC's proof of debt, contending that the amounts demanded were excessive. The Upper Tribunal dismissed his application. Warren J held that HMRC's decision to submit a proof of debt was not 'open to challenge'. The correct course of action would have been for S to have made an application under *Insolvency Act 1986, s 303*, challenging the trustee's decision to accept HMRC's proof. *R (oao Singh) v HMRC; R (oao Singh) v Rose*, UT [2010] STC 2020.

Statutory demands

Whether statutory demand may be set aside

[6.5] In September 1990 the Revenue obtained judgment in respect of £14,811 owed by a worker in the construction industry. In June 1991 the Revenue served a statutory demand on the debtor in respect of this sum, together with interest due under the judgment, and a further £23,269 claimed under what is now *regulation 8* of the *Income Tax (Sub-contractors in the Construction Industry) Regulations (SI 1993/743)*. The Revenue held about £24,000 in respect of deductions by contractors who had employed the debtor as a sub-contractor. The Registrar set aside the Revenue's demand under *rule 6.5(4)(d)* of the *Insolvency Rules (SI 1986/1925)*, considering that it would be wrong for the Revenue to proceed with a petition before the ultimate liability had been ascertained. The Revenue appealed to the Ch D, which reversed the registrar's decision. Where a statutory demand was based on a judgment, the court could not go behind the judgment in an application to set aside the statutory demand, nor could it adjourn the application to await the result of an application to set aside the statutory demand. Even if a statutory demand overstated the amount of the debt, that did not justify the setting aside of the demand. *Re A Debtor (No 657/SD/91), CIR v The Debtor*, Ch D 1992, 65 TC 127; [1992] STC 751.

[6.6] The Revenue served a statutory demand on a debtor in respect of tax, interest and national insurance contributions for 1986/87 to 1989/90 inclusive. The debtor applied for the statutory demand to be set aside. The Deputy Registrar dismissed this application and authorised the Revenue to present a bankruptcy petition. The debtor appealed, contending that he had made subsequent losses in 1991/92 which would be available for carry-back and reduce the amount of the debt. The Ch D dismissed the debtor's appeal, holding that the Deputy Registrar had not erred in law, and there was no reason to set aside the statutory demand. The fact that the debtor claimed to have made subsequent losses could not affect the tax due for 1986/87 and 1987/88 on which the demand was based. Harman J described some of the debtor's claims as 'entirely fanciful, erroneous and unsustainable'. *Re A Debtor (No 383/SD/92), Neely v CIR*, Ch D 1992, 66 TC 131.

[6.7] The Revenue served a statutory demand on a debtor in respect of tax, interest and national insurance contributions payable under assessments which had been confirmed by the Special Commissioners. The debtor appealed to the Ch D, contending that the demand should be set aside as the assessments were excessive. The Ch D dismissed the appeal, holding that the tax was payable and that the demand could not be set aside under *rule 6.5(4)* of the *Insolvency Rules 1986*. *Re A Debtor (No 960/SD/92), ex p. The Debtor v CIR*, Ch D 1993, 66 TC 268; [1993] STC 218.

[6.8] A similar decision was reached in *Chauhan v CIR*, Ch D [2004] EWHC 1304 (Ch); [2004] BPIR 862.

[6.9] The Revenue served a statutory demand in respect of unpaid capital gains tax and interest. The debtor applied to set aside the demand, contending that he could pay the liability if he were given time to realise some shares. The registrar dismissed the application and the Ch D upheld this decision, holding that there were no grounds for setting aside the demand. *Re A Debtor (No 415/SD/93), ex p. The Debtor v CIR*, Ch D 1993, [1994] 1 WLR 917; [1994] 2 All ER 168.

[6.10] The decision in *Re A Debtor (No 415/SD/93)*, **6.9** above, was applied in the similar subsequent case of *Re A Debtor (No 24 of 2000), Ch D 20 March 2001 unreported.*

[6.11] An application for a late appeal against a statutory demand was dismissed in *HMRC v Soor v CIR*, Ch D [2005] EWHC 3080 (Ch); [2006] BPIR 429.

[6.12] The Revenue obtained county court judgment against a debtor (C) in respect of unpaid capital gains tax and penalties. They subsequently issued a statutory demand. C applied for the demand to be set aside, contending that the United Kingdom Government had contravened international law by its military operations in Iraq, and that consequently he was entitled to withhold tax. The registrar rejected this contention and granted judgment for the Revenue, and the Ch D dismissed C's appeal against this decision. *Coverdale v HMRC*, Ch D [2006] EWHC 2244 (Ch).

[6.13] A trader failed to submit returns. The Revenue subsequently issued estimated assessments, which became final and conclusive in the absence of an appeal. The trader failed to pay the tax charged by the assessments, and the Revenue served a statutory demand. The trader applied for the demand to be set aside, contending that he had been suffering for depression. The district judge reviewed the evidence, including a medical report from the trader's doctor, and dismissed the application. The Ch D dismissed the trader's appeal. Lewison J observed that the trader's depression was not making it impossible for him to deal with paperwork, and that 'the fact remains that even those with mental problems must pay their tax'. *Owen v HMRC*, Ch D [2007] EWHC 395 (Ch).

Insolvency Act 1986

NOTE

For cases concerning corporate insolvency and the Insolvency Act 1986, see **13.1** to **13.12** COMPANY LIQUIDATION AND RECEIVERSHIP.

IA 1986, s 257—whether Revenue entitled to send proxy by fax

[6.14] In accordance with *Insolvency Act 1986, s 257*, a meeting of creditors was convened for 12 June 1995 to consider debtors' proposals for voluntary arrangements. On 9 June the Revenue sent a completed proxy form by first-class post, directing the chairman of the meeting to vote against the proposals. This form was delayed in the post and was not received until 13 June. In the meantime, the Revenue had sent a further copy of the proxy form by fax on the morning of the meeting. The chairman of the meeting received this fax but declined to act on the instructions. The Revenue issued originating applications seeking reversal of the chairman's decision to refuse to admit their debt for voting purposes, and revocation of the approval of the proposed voluntary arrangements. The Ch D granted the applications, holding that the faxed proxy form had been signed for the purposes of the *Insolvency Rules 1986 (SI 1986/1925)*. Laddie J observed that 'fax transmission is likely to be a more reliable and certainly is a more speedy method of communication than post' and held that creditors should not be required 'to convey their views to the chairman by the older, slower and less reliable form of communication'. *Re A Debtor (Nos. 2021 & 2022 of 1995), CIR v The Debtor*, Ch D 1995, [1996] 2 All ER 345.

Revenue application under Insolvency Act 1986, s 262

[6.15] The Revenue presented a bankruptcy petition concerning a debtor who had failed to pay substantial arrears of tax. The debtor submitted a proposal for an individual voluntary arrangement. The Revenue applied under *Insolvency Act 1986, s 262* for the arrangement to be revised or revoked. The Newcastle upon Tyne County Court rejected the application and the Revenue appealed to the Ch D. Ferris J allowed the Revenue's appeal, holding on the evidence that the proposed arrangement unfairly prejudiced the interests of the Inland Revenue. *Re A Debtor (No 101 of 1999)*, Ch D 10 July 2000 unreported.

[6.16] The chairman of a creditors' meeting approved a proposal for an individual voluntary arrangement relating to a debtor's affairs. The chairman informed the meeting that it did not appear that any claims could be made against the debtor under *Insolvency Act 1986, s 339* (relating to transactions at an undervalue). The Revenue applied under *Insolvency Act 1986, s 262* for the arrangement to be revoked, contending firstly that the chairman of the meeting had accepted a company as a voting creditor when it was not in fact a creditor and thus not entitled to vote; and, secondly, that the chairman's claim that *s 339* was inapplicable was inaccurate. The district judge accepted these contentions and revoked the arrangement. The Ch D upheld this decision, holding that the chairman's conduct showed 'a serious falling short of the standards to be expected of a competent insolvency practitioner'. *Fender v CIR*, Ch D [2003] BPIR 1304.

[6.17] HMRC had issued assessments charging tax of more than £4,000,000 on an individual (E) who had failed to submit returns. In February 2011 E was declared bankrupt. In March 2011 a meeting of E's creditors, at which HMRC were not represented, agreed an individual voluntary arrangement. In April 2011 HMRC issued an application to revoke the individual voluntary arrangement. The Ch D granted the application. Sir Andrew Morritt found that E had misrepresented the amount which he owed to HMRC, and held that 'the amount of an assessment is a debt and is both liquidated and ascertained'.

On the evidence, HMRC were E's major creditor and had been entitled to more than 50% of the votes at the meeting. *HMRC v Earley & Others*, Ch D [2011] EWHC 1783 (Ch).

Debtor failing to comply with individual voluntary arrangement

[6.18] A married couple had substantial debts, including unpaid income tax. They entered into individual voluntary arrangements with their creditors. However, they failed to pay their tax liabilities in accordance with the arrangements. At the request of the Revenue, the supervisor of the voluntary arrangements presented bankruptcy petitions against the couple. The district court found that the couple owed substantial amounts of tax, and made bankruptcy orders against them. They appealed to the Ch D. Blackburne J dismissed their appeals, holding that 'their default had been sufficiently substantial to justify the making of the bankruptcy orders against them'. *Kong & Kong v CIR*, Ch D 14 April 2005 unreported.

IA 1986, s 265—date on which debtor ceased business

[6.19] The proprietor of a nursing home incurred a tax liability of about £500,000. In January 1987 she went to live in Tenerife, and in May 1987 she sold the business as a going concern. In February 1991, the Revenue presented a bankruptcy petition against her, and in November 1991 the Registrar made a bankruptcy order against her. She appealed to the Ch D, contending that the court had no jurisdiction to make the order, since she had not carried on business within three years of the presentation of the petition. The Ch D dismissed her appeal, holding that, for the purposes of the *Insolvency Act 1986, s 265(1)*, the carrying on of a business continued until all debts incurred in the course of the business had been paid. These debts included the tax liability. *A Debtor (No 784 of 1991) v CIR & Official Receiver*, Ch D 1992, 64 TC 612; [1992] STC 549; [1992] 3 WLR 119; [1992] 3 All ER 376.

[6.20] An individual (W) did not appeal against, or pay the tax charged by, assessments on income from property dealing for 1977/78 to 1979/80. In 1991 the Revenue obtained judgment in the High Court, and in 1993 the Revenue petitioned to have W made bankrupt. W objected to the petition, contending that he had never carried on a business as a property dealer, and had not carried on business in England or Wales in the three years preceding the presentation of the petition, so that the conditions of *Insolvency Act 1986, s 265* were not satisfied. The Registrar dismissed W's notice of objection but the Ch D allowed W's appeal. Colyer J observed that the Revenue, as petitioning creditor, could have required W to attend the hearing before the Registrar for cross-examination, but had not done so. Colyer J held that 'the mere fact that an assessment had not been appealed (*sic*) was not conclusive as to the question whether the debtor had been trading'. *Wilkinson (A Debtor) v CIR*, Ch D 1994, 68 TC 157.

Insolvency Act 1986, s 267—validity of creditor's petition

[6.21] In 2001 the Revenue served a statutory demand on a debtor. His application to set that demand aside was dismissed, and he was adjudged bankrupt in 2002. He subsequently applied for the bankruptcy order to be set aside. The registrar rejected his application, and the Ch D dismissed his appeal, holding that the Revenue's petition had fulfilled the conditions of *Insolvency Act 1986, s 267*, and observing that the debtor was 'substantially insolvent'. The CA unanimously upheld this decision. *Ahmad v CIR*, CA 1 December 2004 unreported. (*Note*. For a preliminary issue in this case, see **6.37** below.)

[6.22] A similar decision was reached in *Harris v HMRC*, Ch D [2011] EWHC 3094 (Ch).

IA 1986, s 271(3)—application for annulment of bankruptcy order

[6.23] In June 2001 the Revenue issued a statutory demand for more than £170,000 of unpaid tax. In November 2002 the debtor was made bankrupt. He appealed to the Ch D under *Insolvency Act 1986, s 271(3)*, contending that the Revenue should have accepted an earlier offer of security. The Ch D rejected this contention and dismissed the appeal, holding on the evidence that the debtor had failed to provide information about the proposed security, and the Revenue were justified in refusing the offer. *Re A Debtor (No 435/SD/02), Egleton v CIR*, Ch D 27 February 2003 unreported. (*Note*. A subsequent application for the rescission of the bankruptcy order was also dismissed—see **6.30** below.)

[6.24] In June 2008 HMRC served statutory demands on two partners in a firm of solicitors, who had substantial tax liabilities dating back to 2003/04. The failed to pay the tax, and in September 2008 HMRC presented bankruptcy petitions. The hearing of the petitions was initially adjourned. In March 2009 the Solicitors' Regulation Authority (SRA) intervened in the solicitors' practices under *Solicitors Act 1974, s 35, Sch 1* on the grounds that it 'had reason to suspect dishonesty within the firm'. Following the SRA's intervention, the firm ceased to carry on business. In July 2009 bankruptcy orders were made against both solicitors. They appealed to the Ch D, contending that HMRC should have accepted an offer of security over certain properties which they owned. The Ch D rejected this contention, and dismissed the appeal. Henderson J observed that HMRC had adopted a policy 'not to accept security in the form of legal charges over land', on the grounds that they 'do not have the resources to act as mortgagees and to administer the sales of mortgaged property'. The solicitors had 'had plenty of time to raise money on the security of their properties'. On the evidence, HMRC were entitled to have concluded 'that the time for negotiation had passed and the interests of the Exchequer would be best served by pressing for bankruptcy orders to be made'. Furthermore, there were no grounds which would have justified a further adjournment of the bankruptcy petitions, since 'the discretion to adjourn should only be exercised if there is a reasonable prospect of the petition debt being paid in full within a reasonable period'. There had been a 'history of delay and broken promises', and there had been 'no reasonable prospect of payment in full being made within a reasonable time'. *AJ Ross v HMRC; DS*

Holmes v HMRC, Ch D [2010] STC 657; [2010] EWHC 13 (Ch); [2010] 2 All ER 126. (*Note.* The CA dismissed applications by the solicitors to appeal against this decision. Patten LJ held that it had been 'appropriate to take a fairly hard line and to accord priority to HMRC's undoubted prima facie right to obtain bankruptcy orders over protestations that a further adjournment might finally yield the payment in full which had so signally failed to materialise in the past.'—[2011] EWCA Civ 919.)

[6.25] Applications for annulment of bankruptcy orders were also dismissed in *Cullinane v CIR*, Ch D 1999, [2000] BPIR 996; *Shamash v CIR*, Ch D 2001, [2002] BPIR 189; *Verrall v CIR*, Ch D [2003] EWHC 3083 (Ch), [2004] BPIR 456; *Dickins v CIR*, Ch D [2004] EWHC 852 (Ch), [2004] BPIR 718; *Beresford v CIR*, Ch D 8 February 2005 unreported; *Worby v CIR*, Ch D [2005] EWHC 835 (Ch), [2005] BPIR 1249; *O'Callaghan v HMRC*, Ch D 14 December 2005 unreported; *Monks v HMRC*, Ch D 3 March 2006 unreported, and *Adeosun v HMRC*, Ch D [2011] EWHC 1577 (Ch).

[6.26] The Revenue served a statutory demand on an individual (L). He applied for the demand to be set aside, contending that he had paid £25,000 in respect of his personal liabilities, but that the Revenue had wrongly allocated this against the liabilities of a company which he controlled. The district judge rejected this contention and directed that L's application 'be struck out without a hearing'. The Revenue subsequently issued a bankruptcy petition. L's wife wrote to the court requesting an adjournment for 56 days, on the grounds that L was ill. The registrar rejected this request and made a bankruptcy order against L. The Ch D allowed L's appeal against this decision. Applying the principles laid down by Neuberger J in *Fox v Graham Newspaper Group Ltd*, Ch D 2001, Times 3.8.2001, 'where a litigant in person is seeking an adjournment for the first time, the court should be very careful indeed before concluding that it would be appropriate to proceed with the application or appeal in his absence. The court should only take such a course if it is satisfied either that it was right to grant the litigant the relief he sought or it is satisfied that the application or appeal was plainly hopeless.' On the evidence, this was 'plainly a case where the debtor should have been given an opportunity on the hearing of the petition to put forward the evidence that he wishes to put forward in relation to the allocation of the £25,000'. The registrar's decision not to adjourn the petition had been 'plainly mistaken'. The Ch D set aside the bankruptcy order and remitted the petition to the registrar. *CIR v Lee-Phipps*, Ch D [2003] BPIR 803.

IA 1986, s 306—vesting of bankrupt's estate in trustee

[6.27] See *Borchert v Cormack*, 46.23 PENSION SCHEMES.

IA 1986, s 375—application for rescission of bankruptcy order

[6.28] In June 1997 the Revenue presented a bankruptcy petition against a debtor (R). A bankruptcy order was subsequently made. In March 1998 R applied, under *Insolvency Act 1986, s 375(1)*, for rescission of the order, contending that he had arranged for payment of part of the debt and that he disputed the balance. A deputy registrar allowed the application but the Ch D reversed this decision and restored the bankruptcy order. *Insolvency Act 1986* established a precise statutory scheme setting out specific rules as to how a bankrupt could escape bankruptcy by the payment of debts. *Insolvency Act 1986, s 282(1)(b)* provided that a debtor had to make arrangements for the payment of all his debts, not just the judgment debts. The conditions of *s 282(1)(b)* could not be circumvented by invoking *s 375(1)*, except in 'exceptional circumstances'. The bankruptcy order here had been rightly made, and the deputy registrar had failed to appreciate the true relationship of *s 282(1)(b)* and *s 375(1)*. On the evidence, the provisions of *s 282(1)(b)* were not satisfied, and there were no exceptional circumstances justifying the exercise of discretion under *s 375(1)*. Accordingly, the bankruptcy order had to stand. *CIR v Robinson*, Ch D 26 November 1998 unreported. (*Note*. For another issue in this case, see **4.376** APPEALS.)

[6.29] A similar decision was reached in a case where a contractor (C) had failed to submit tax returns, and the Revenue had issued determinations under *TMA, s 28C*. C was declared bankrupt in 2003. In 2007 his trustee in bankruptcy applied for possession and sale of C's house. C applied for the bankruptcy order to be rescinded. The Ch D held that there were no grounds to justify the rescission of the order. Sir Andrew Morritt observed that an order for rescission would prejudice all of C's creditors, since there was no evidence that C 'could or would pay them'. *HMRC v Cassells*, Ch D 2008, [2009] STC 1047; [2008] EWHC 3180 (Ch).

[6.30] Applications for the rescission of bankruptcy orders were dismissed in *Egleton v CIR (No 2)*, Ch D [2003] EWHC 3226 (Ch), [2004] BPIR 476; *AJ Ross v HMRC (No 2)*, Ch D [2012] EWHC 1054 (Ch), and *Newsam v CIR*, **29.122** FURTHER ASSESSMENTS: LOSS OF TAX.

[6.31] In 2005 HMRC received an informant's letter suggesting that a woman (H) was carrying on a profitable business as a breeder of horses. Following this letter, HMRC issued determinations charging tax. H did not reply to various letters from HMRC, or pay the tax charged. In May 2008 HMRC served a statutory demand, and in August 2008 H was declared bankrupt. Following the bankruptcy, HMRC accepted that the determinations had been excessive and H applied for the bankruptcy order to be rescinded. The Ch D granted the application, finding on the evidence that H 'lacked mental capacity' and had 'suffered from a mental impairment that had a substantial and long term effect on her ability to carry out normal day-to-day activities'. *Haworth v Cartmel*, Ch D [2011] EWHC 36 (Ch); [2011] All ER (D) 23 (Mar).

Rescission of bankruptcy order—subsequent claim for damages

[6.32] A building contractor (W) failed to make tax returns for six successive years. Assessments on him became final and conclusive by virtue of *TMA, s 46(2)*. He did not pay the tax charged by the assessments, and was declared bankrupt in 1993. In 1999 the Revenue agreed to rescind the bankruptcy order under *Insolvency Act 1986, s 375(1)*. W then brought proceedings against the Revenue, contending that the bankruptcy proceedings had been instituted maliciously. The Ch D rejected this contention and dismissed the proceedings. Jacob J held that the bankruptcy proceedings had been 'properly launched', and that 'the accusations made against the Inland Revenue officials involved in the case were wholly a construct of (W's) mind. They bear no resemblance whatever to reality.' *Woodward v CIR*, Ch D 2001, 73 TC 516. (*Notes*. (1) For a preliminary issue in this case, see **50.17** REVENUE ADMINISTRATION. (2) The CA subsequently dismissed an application to appeal against this decision—see [2002] EWCA Civ 123.)

Insolvency Act 1986, s 423—application to set aside trust deed

[6.33] See *CIR v Hashmi & Ghauri*, **19.22** DECEASED PERSONS.

Miscellaneous

Undischarged bankrupt—whether assessable on earnings

[6.34] A trader was made bankrupt in 1948. In 1958/59 and 1959/60, while he was still an undischarged bankrupt, he worked as a waiter. The Revenue issued assessments charging tax on his earnings. He appealed, contending that as he was an undischarged bankrupt, the earnings did not belong to him. The General Commissioners rejected this contention and dismissed his appeal, and the CA upheld their decision. *Hibbert v Fysh*, CA 1962, 40 TC 305.

Penalties awarded during bankruptcy

[6.35] The Revenue began penalty proceedings under *TMA, ss 93, 95* against an individual (H) who owed substantial amounts of tax. While the proceedings were in progress, H successfully petitioned to be declared bankrupt. The Revenue were, apart from one trivial amount, the only creditor, and there were sufficient funds to cover the tax due. H's trustee in bankruptcy made an application to the Ch D, which held that any penalties awarded after the bankruptcy were provable debts, and that the penalties could only be compromised if H and the trustee both agreed. *Re Hurren (a bankrupt), The Trustee v CIR & Hurren*, Ch D 1982, 56 TC 494; [1982] STC 850; [1983] 1 WLR 183; [1982] 3 All ER 982. (*Note*. The Revenue was the only substantive creditor and it was stated that, in practice, the Revenue does not proceed for penalties in a bankruptcy where there are other creditors who cannot be paid in full.)

Limitation Act 1980—interaction of s 24 and s 37(2)

[6.36] In December 1999 the Revenue served a statutory demand relating to a judgment debt, comprising unpaid income tax, which was more than six years old. The debtor applied to have the demand set aside, contending that the judgment debt was statute-barred under *Limitation Act 1980, s 24*. The Ch D rejected this contention. Hart J held that the judgment did not extinguish 'the pre-existing liability of the debtor in respect of which the judgment had been entered'. Accordingly, the effect of *Limitation Act 1980, s 37(2)(a)* was that the Revenue 'were entitled to proceed against this debtor'. (However, Hart J allowed the debtor's appeal, holding on the evidence that the specific statutory demand in question did not fulfil 'the requirements of the statutory form'.) *Bruton v CIR (re A Debtor No 647 of 1999)*, Ch D 22 February 2000 unreported. (*Note. Limitation Act 1980, s 37(2)(a)* provides that it does not apply to any proceedings by the Crown for the recovery of any tax, duty or interest thereon.)

[6.37] The Ch D dismissed a debtor's appeal in a subsequent case where the debtor contended that a statutory demand for unpaid tax contravened the *Limitation Act 1980*. Evans-Lombe J observed that 'this contention appears to have overlooked the specific provisions of *s 37(2)* of the *Limitation Act 1980*, which excludes from the provisions of the Act claims for tax of this kind'. *Ahmad v CIR*, Ch D [2004] EWHC 2292 (Ch); [2005] BPIR 541. (*Note*. For another issue in this case, see **6.21** above.)

Bankruptcy—claim by bankrupt to personal allowance

[6.38] See *CIR v Fleming*, **1.13** ALLOWANCES AND TAX RATES.

Insolvent partnership—partners applying for administration order

[6.39] A solicitors' partnership, with two equity partners and four salaried partners, became insolvent, owing at least £1,700,000 to the Revenue and at least £700,000 to other creditors. The Revenue served bankruptcy petitions on the two equity partners and began a winding-up petition against the firm. The equity partners applied to the Ch D for an administration order, with provision for the immediate sale of the business and assets to two of the salaried partners. The Revenue opposed the application but the Ch D granted it, accepting the partnership's evidence that 'an immediate sale of the partnership business will achieve a better result for the partnership's creditors as a whole than would be likely if the partnership were to be wound up without first being in administration'. On the evidence, the Ch D observed that 'the proposed sale appears to be the only way of saving the jobs of the 50-odd employees of the partnership'. *DKLL Solicitors v HMRC*, Ch D [2007] EWHC 2067 (Ch).

Trustee continuing business of insolvent partnership

[6.40] See *Armitage v Moore*, **59.43** TRADING INCOME.

Tax chargeable on sales during bankruptcy

[6.41] See *In re McMeekin*, **71.370** CAPITAL GAINS TAX.

Trustee in bankruptcy declining to pursue appeal

[6.42] See *Soul v CIR*, **4.250** APPEALS.

Whether trustee in bankruptcy authorised to settle open appeals

[6.43] See *Ahajot v Waller*, 4.378 APPEALS.

7

Building Societies

The cases in this chapter are arranged under the following headings.

Income Tax (Building Societies) Regulations 1986

Whether regulations ultra vires

[7.1] The special arrangements for building societies in *ICTA 1970, s 343* were amended for 1986/87 onwards by *FA 1985, s 40*. The revised *s 343(1A)* enabled the Board to make new arrangements for 1986/87 onwards by statutory instrument. Following this, the *Income Tax (Building Societies) Regulations 1986 (SI 1986/482)* were made, the retrospective nature of which was explicitly confirmed by *FA 1986, s 47(1)*, which further amended *s 343(1A)*. *Regulation 11* was a transitional provision, which purported to treat interest and dividend payments from the end of the society's last accounting period ending in 1985/86 to the end of February 1986, as having been paid on various dates between March 1987 and March 1990 (dependent on when they were paid in 1985/86). The result in the case of the Woolwich Equitable Building Society, whose last accounting period ending in 1985/86 actually ended on 30 September 1985, was that interest and dividend payments in the five months to February 1986 were deemed to have been paid in March 1987 and March 1988, with the consequence that in the years 1986/87 and 1987/88 it would be required to account for tax on twenty-nine months' payments. It applied by way of judicial review for a declaration that *reg 11* was unlawful. The Ch D granted the declaration and the HL unanimously upheld this decision. Lord Oliver held that Parliament was entitled to take what was, on ordinary principles, the unusual course of seeking to tax more than one year's income in a single year of assessment. However, it had been admitted by the Revenue that *reg 11(4)* was invalid, because it sought to charge tax by reference to the rate of 30% which had applied for 1985/86, rather than the rate of 29% which Parliament had enacted for 1986/87. *Subsection (4)* was an integral part of *reg 11*, which, without that *subsection*, would have a quite different effect to that clearly intended by the draftsman. Accordingly, the invalidity of *subsection (4)* infected the whole of *reg 11*, with the result that the regulation was void and ineffective in its entirety. *R v CIR (ex p. Woolwich Equitable Building Society)*, HL 1990, 63 TC 589; [1990] STC 682; [1990] 1 WLR 1400; [1991] 4 All ER 92. (*Note*. The regulations were subsequently validated by *FA 1991, s 53*. For a case in which the validity of *FA 1991, s 53* was upheld, see *National & Provincial Building Society v United Kingdom*, **31.94** HUMAN RIGHTS. For an application for costs by two societies which had launched judicial review proceedings, see *R v HM Treasury* *(ex p. Leeds Permanent Building Society)*; *R v HM Treasury (ex p. National & Provincial Building Society)*, 4.408 APPEALS.)

[7.2] For a subsequent application by the company for payment of interest on the tax repaid to it following the QB decision reported at 7.1 above, see 32.4 INTEREST ON TAX OVERPAID.

Miscellaneous

Interest element in building society repayments

[7.3] See *Leeds Permanent Benefit Building Society v Mallandaine*, 52.3 SAVINGS AND INVESTMENT INCOME.

Merger of two building societies

[7.4] See *Northern Rock Building Society v Davies*, 61.63 TRADING INCOME.

Flotation of building society as public limited company

[7.5] See *Halifax plc v Davidson*, 63.30 TRADING PROFITS, and the cases noted at 63.31 TRADING PROFITS.

Valuation of conversion of society into limited company

[7.6] See *Ward, Cook & Buckingham (Cook's Executors) v CIR*, 72.121 INHERITANCE TAX.

Sale of houses—treatment of collateral security

[7.7] See *John Cronk & Sons Ltd v Harrison*, 68.40 TRADING PROFITS, and *Chibbett v Harold Brookfield & Son Ltd*, 68.41 TRADING PROFITS.

8

Capital Allowances

The cases in this chapter are arranged under the following headings.

GENERAL NOTE

The *Capital Allowances Act 2001* received Royal Assent on 22 March 2001. It was intended to codify the existing law and rewrite it in more modern English, as part of the Tax Law Rewrite Project. It also made some minor changes to the law regarding capital allowances. For a discussion of the principles underlying the revision, see the article by John Pearce in 'British Tax Review 2001', pp 359–381.

Agricultural buildings allowances

[8.1] The tenant of a sheep farm was resident in the USA. The only dwelling-house on the farm was occupied by the head shepherd. The tenant incurred expenditure on a new scullery. The Revenue only agreed to grant allowances on one-third of the expenditure, by virtue of what is now *CAA 2001, s 369(3)*. The tenant appealed, contending that, since he did not live in the house, it should not be treated as a farmhouse and the whole of the expenditure should be treated as qualifying for allowances. The Commissioners rejected this contention and dismissed the appeal, holding that the house was a 'farmhouse'. The CS upheld their decision as one of fact. Lord Carmont observed that a farmhouse did not 'cease to be the farmhouse merely because the person conducting the farm is not the farmer himself but a person to whom he delegates the duty of running the farm'. *Lindsay v CIR*, CS 1953, 34 TC 289.

[8.2] A father and son farmed in partnership, living in the farmhouse. On his marriage, the son moved to a new house built on the farm, the cost being borne by the partnership. The partnership claimed capital allowances on the whole of the expenditure, on the basis that the house was a cottage within the meaning of what is now *CAA 2001, s 361(1)*. The Revenue only agreed to grant allowances on one-third of the expenditure, considering that the house was a 'farmhouse' within what is now *CAA 2001, s 369(3)*. The Commissioners allowed the partnership's appeal, holding that the house was an 'agricultural cottage' rather than a 'farmhouse'. The CS upheld their decision as one of fact. Lord Clyde held that 'the pre-existing liability of the debtor in respect of which the judgment had been entered'. He observed that 'under the partnership agreement the son for whom it was built and who occupies it must give his whole time and attention to the business of the partnership'. Lord Guthrie observed that 'a partner who works on a farm is engaged in husbandry just as much as a labourer who works on the same farm. If the partner requires a residence on the farm in order to do his work, then the construction of his house is equally for the purposes of husbandry as the construction of a house for a hired servant.' *CIR v John M Whiteford & Son*, CS 1962, 40 TC 379.

[8.3] In June 1964 a farmer, who had incurred considerable capital expenditure qualifying for agricultural buildings allowances, conveyed the freehold in his farm to the trustees of a settlement for the benefit of his family. On the next day, as required under the terms of the settlement, the trustees leased it back to him for 40 years. The Revenue issued an assessment on the basis that the effect of these transactions was that the farmer had transferred 'the whole of his interest in the land in question', and was no longer entitled to allowances in respect of expenditure incurred before June 1964. He appealed, contending that he should be treated as having retained part of his original interest in the land, and continued to be entitled to the allowances. The Commissioners accepted this contention and allowed his appeal, and the Ch D upheld their decision. Megarry J held that the relevant legislation was 'intended to operate broadly', so that a right to allowances would only be lost 'if the result of a transaction is that the whole of a taxpayer's interest in the land has been transferred to another'. He observed that 'where the technicalities of English conveyancing and land law are brought into juxtaposition with a United Kingdom taxing Statute, I am encouraged to look at the realities at the expense of the technicalities. The taxpayer's interest has, *uno ictu*, been merely reduced from ownership of the freehold to ownership of a lease: the whole of his interest in the land has not therefore been transferred to another'. *Sargaison v Roberts*, Ch D 1969, 45 TC 612; [1969] 1 WLR 951; [1969] 3 All ER 1072. (*Note*. For the general rule as to what is the 'relevant interest' in relation to expenditure qualifying for agricultural buildings allowances, see now *CAA 2001, ss 364–368*.)

[8.4] In a case where the substantive issue has been overtaken by subsequent changes in the legislation, the members of a family farming partnership occupied a 20-room house, only two of the rooms being used for business purposes (neither of them being exclusively so used). The Revenue accepted that the house was within the definition of a 'farmhouse'. However, this concession was doubted by Lord Upjohn and Lord Donovan. Lord Upjohn observed that the question of whether a house was within the definition of a farmhouse 'must be judged in accordance with ordinary ideas of what is appropriate in size, content and layout, taken in conjunction with the farm buildings and the particular area of farmland being farmed'. *Korner & Others v CIR*, HL 1969, 45 TC 287. (*Note*. The substantive issue concerned the definition of 'farm land'. Following the HL decision on this point, the relevant legislation was amended by *FA 1969* to reverse the effect of the decision. See now *ITTOIA 2005, s 876(1)*.)

Industrial buildings allowances

Definition of 'industrial building or structure' (CAA 2001, s 271)

General principles

Definition of a 'structure'

[8.5] In a non-tax case in which a tilting furnace was held to be a structure, Denning LJ held that 'a structure is something of substantial size which is built up from component parts and intended to remain permanently on a permanent foundation; but it is still a structure even though some of its parts may be movable, as, for instance, about a pivot. Thus, a windmill or a turntable is a structure. A thing which is not permanently in one place is not a structure, but it may be "in the nature of a structure" if it has all the qualities of a structure, save that it is on occasion moved on or from its site.' *Cardiff Rating Authority v Guest Keen Baldwin's Iron and Steel Co Ltd*, CA 1948, [1949] 1 KB 385; [1949] 1 All ER 27.

[8.6] In a subsequent case where the CA held that a soda flash tower at an oil refinery was a structure, Denning LJ held that it was 'characteristic of a structure that it is built up of component parts on the site. But a thing may be in the nature of a structure, even if it is not built up on the site, but is brought there all in one piece'. *BP Refinery (Kent) Ltd v Walker*, CA [1957] 2 QB 305; [1957] 1 All ER 700.

Cases held to qualify for allowances

Electricity generating station

[8.7] The KB held that the power house of an electricity generating station was a single industrial building, and qualified for allowances. (The Revenue had contended that each internal section of the power house should be treated as a separate building, some of which would have failed to qualify for allowances under the legislation then in force.) *Lancashire Electric Power Co v Wilkinson*, KB 1947, 28 TC 427.

Drawing-office—whether within CAA 2001, s 277(1)(e)

[8.8] An engineering company claimed industrial buildings allowances on a drawing-office, which was predominantly used for the preparation of plans for the workshops. The Revenue rejected the claim on the basis that it was precluded by what is now *CAA 2001, s 277(1)(e)*. The Commissioners allowed the company's appeal and the CS upheld their decision, holding that the drawing-office was an industrial building and not an office for the purposes of *s 277(1)(e)*. Lord Cooper held that 'a drawing-office of this type' was no more an 'office' than a machine shop was a 'shop'. *CIR v Lambhill Ironworks Ltd*, CS 1950, 31 TC 393.

Building for packing coal for retail sale

[8.9] A co-operative society sold coal in paper bags. It constructed a separate building to screen and pack the coal. It claimed industrial buildings allowances on the building. The Revenue rejected the claim on the grounds that the building was ancillary to a retail shop, within what is now *CAA 2001, s 277(1)(b)*. The CS unanimously allowed the society's appeal, holding that the building was an industrial building and qualified for allowances. Lord Clyde held that 'the breaking of bulk coupled with the separating out of the dross by screening and the subsequent packaging of the coal into paper bags involves a "process"' within what is now *CAA 2001, s 274(1)(a)*. Furthermore, the building was not 'ancillary or subservient to the purpose of the retail shop where the product from the building may ultimately be sold', so that 'the purpose of the activity conducted in this building on the facts was the development of a substantial wholesale business.' *Kilmarnock Equitable Co-operative Society Ltd v CIR*, CS 1966, 42 TC 675. (*Note*. This case was distinguished in *Bestway (Holdings) Ltd v Luff*, **8.17** below, and *Sarsfield v Dixons Group plc*, **8.18** below.)

Warehouse

[8.10] A group of companies manufactured and sold shoes. The parent company (H) built a warehouse, which was used by one of its subsidiaries (J) to store shoes which the group sold. About one-third of the shoes had been manufactured by a member of the group (K) and not delivered to any purchaser; the rest had been purchased from other manufacturers. H claimed industrial buildings allowances on the warehouse. The Revenue rejected the claim but the CS allowed H's appeal and the HL unanimously upheld this decision. Lord Reid held that J's storage of the shoes which K manufactured was a qualifying trade within what is now *CAA 2001, s 274(1)(a)*. As these shoes were not stored in a separate part of the warehouse, the whole of the warehouse qualified for allowances. *Saxone Lilley & Skinner (Holdings) Ltd v CIR*, HL 1967, 44 TC 122; [1967] 1 WLR 501; [1967] 1 All ER 756. (*Note*. Following this decision, HMRC accept that IBA is due on the whole of a building in such circumstances except where qualifying use is less than 10% of the total use of the building—see Capital Allowances Manual, para CA32315.) The decision here was distinguished in the subsequent case of *HMRC v Maco Door & Window Hardware (UK) Ltd*, **8.15** below, on the grounds that J's only trade was that of storage.)

Laundry building in enterprise zone

[8.11] A syndicate installed a laundry building, to be used by an NHS Trust, in an enterprise zone. One of the investors (T) claimed tax relief on the basis that the building was a 'commercial building' within *CAA 2001, s 271(1)(b)(iv)*. HMRC rejected the claim and T appealed, contending that the NHS Trust which leased the building had arranged for two other health boards to use it, and that this was a trading relationship. The First-tier Tribunal accepted this contention and allowed T's appeal. Judge Mure held that 'the defraying of overheads and other expenses approximates to a profit motive in this context' and that 'the absence of an additional excess element of profit makes little difference'. The laundry activity conducted within the building was within the definition of a trade, and the building qualified as a commercial building. The Upper Tribunal upheld this decision as one of fact. *HMRC v D Thomson*, UT [2014] UKUT 360 (TCC).

Building housing computer used for industrial purposes

[8.12] In an Irish case, a building housing a computer was held to be an industrial building, as the computer was principally used for industrial rather than clerical purposes. *O'Conaill v Waterford Glass Ltd*, HC(I) 1982, TL(I) 122.

Bonded transit sheds

[8.13] In an Irish case, bonded transit sheds, which were used as a clearing house for goods unloaded from ships, were held to be industrial buildings in use for the purposes of a dock undertaking. *Patrick Monahan (Drogheda) Ltd v O'Connell*, HC(I) 1987, 3 ITR 661.

Cases held not to qualify for allowances

Warehouse

[8.14] A firm, which traded as selling agents for various manufacturers, claimed industrial buildings allowances on a warehouse under what is now *CAA 2001, s 274(1)(a)*. The KB rejected the claim, holding that allowances were not due since *s 274(1)(a)* only provided allowances for storage where the goods had 'not yet been delivered to any purchaser'. The firm had purchased the goods which it kept in the warehouse, and any storage was merely incidental to their resale. *Dale v Johnson Bros*, KB(NI) 1951, 32 TC 487.

[8.15] A company (M), which was a UK subsidiary of an Austrian company, claimed industrial buildings allowance on a warehouse. The warehouse was used to house goods such as doorlocks and doorhandles, which were manufactured by the Austrian company and stored in the warehouse while awaiting sale to wholesalers and to manufacturers of doors and windows in the UK. The Revenue rejected M's claim on the basis that M was not carrying on a qualifying trade, within what is now *CAA 2001, s 274*. M appealed, contending that it was carrying on a trade of 'storage', which qualified for allowances. The HL rejected this contention (by a 3-2 majority, Lord Scott of Foscote and Lord Mance dissenting). Lord Walker of Gestingthorpe observed that M was 'storing and selling goods which are its own property. Its trade is not storage. It is that of a merchant, buying goods and selling them on at a profit.' There was 'a clear and important distinction' between 'a trade and an activity undertaken in the course of a trade'. Lord Neuberger of Abbotsbury specifically disapproved the decision of Finlay J in *Crusabridge Investments Ltd v Casings International Ltd*, Ch D 1979, 54 TC 246. *HMRC v Maco Door & Window Hardware (UK) Ltd*, HL 2008, 79 TC 287; [2008] STC 2594; [2008] UKHL 54; [2008] 3 All ER 1020.

Inland warehouse for goods imported in containers

[8.16] A company (C) traded as a clothing wholesaler. 90% of its stock was imported, and kept in a warehouse in Manchester, which was occupied by a subsidiary company which carried on a storage business. C claimed industrial buildings allowances on the warehouse. The Revenue rejected the claim, and C appealed, contending that the goods were stored in the warehouse on their arrival in the UK. The CA rejected this contention and dismissed C's appeal, holding that when the goods reached the Manchester warehouse they were no longer in transit, so that the storage by the subsidiary was not a qualifying trade within what is now *CAA 2001, s 274(1)(a)*. Fox LJ held that 'there must be imported a requirement that the warehouse can, having regard to its location, be reasonably regarded in the normal course of its trade as providing a storage service in relation to a particular port (or ports or airport or airports) in the United Kingdom, for goods or materials on the occasion of their arrival by sea or air into such port or airport'. The allowance was 'given to encourage the provision of storage for goods which have just arrived in the United Kingdom and before their onward transit.' *Copol Clothing Ltd v Hindmarch*, CA 1983, 57 TC 575; [1984] STC 33; [1984] 1 WLR 411.

'Cash and carry' warehouses

[8.17] A group of companies operated cash-and-carry wholesale supermarkets, which were not open to the general public, but which were used by retail traders and caterers. The group appealed against corporation tax assessments, contending that the supermarkets qualified for industrial buildings allowances. The Special Commissioners rejected this contention and dismissed the appeal, and the Ch D upheld this decision. Since the group relied on the swift disposal of its stock, it was not carrying on a qualifying trade of storage within what is now *CAA 2001, s 274(1)(a)*. Lightman J held that 'storage' should be construed as meaning 'keeping in storage as a purpose and end in itself, and does not extend to such storage as is merely a necessary and transitory incident of the conduct of the business of a wholesale supermarket'. Accordingly, the warehouses did not qualify as industrial buildings. *Bestway (Holdings) Ltd v Luff*, Ch D 1998, 70 TC 512; [1998] STC 357. (*Notes.* (1) For HMRC's practice following this decision, see Capital Allowances Manual, para CA32224. (2) The decision was subsequently approved by the HL in *HMRC v Maco Door & Window Hardware (UK) Ltd*, **8.15** above.)

Warehouse—whether used for purposes ancillary to those of a retail shop

[8.18] Prior to May 1981, a warehouse had been used as a storage and distribution depot for goods prior to their delivery to retail shops, and it was accepted that the effect of what is now *CAA 2001, s 277(1)(b)* was that expenditure on the warehouse did not qualify for industrial buildings allowances. In May 1981 the business in question was transferred to another company in the same group, which carried on a distribution business. That company, and a third company in the group, claimed industrial buildings allowances on expenditure on the warehouse in their next accounting periods. The CA unanimously rejected the claim, holding that the warehouse was still in use for a purpose ancillary to the purposes of a retail shop, so that allowances were still precluded by *s 277(1)(b)*. On the evidence, the purpose of the warehouse was exclusively that of receiving, storing and distributing to the retail shops the goods which were necessary for those shops to operate. The use of the warehouse was necessarily subordinate and ancillary to the purpose of the retail shops. The fact that the warehouse was used for the purposes of a transport undertaking did not prevent it from falling within *s 277(1)(b)*. Accordingly, the warehouse did not qualify for industrial buildings allowance. *Sarsfield v Dixons Group plc (and related appeals)*, CA 1998, 71 TC 121; [1998] STC 938.

Warehouse—whether goods subjected to any process

[8.19] A company (F) purchased large quantities of electronic components, which it sold to customers in smaller quantities. It claimed industrial buildings allowances on the warehouse where the components were kept. HMRC rejected the claim on the basis that F was carrying on a trade of distribution so that the warehouse failed to qualify for allowances. F appealed, contending that it was subjecting the goods to a process. The First-tier Tribunal rejected this contention and dismissed the appeal. Judge Walters observed that 'the individual products are not subjected to a sufficiently substantial measure of uniformity of treatment or system of treatment to cause the system of operations conducted in the building to be a "process" in the relevant sense'. *Farnell Electronic Components Ltd v HMRC*, FTT [2011] UKFTT 597 (TC), TC01440.

[8.20] A group of companies which sold goods by mail order claimed industrial building allowances on two warehouses which were used to store goods. HMRC rejected the claims and the companies appealed, contending that they should be treated as subjecting the goods to a process. Both the First-tier Tribunal and the Upper Tribunal rejected this contention and dismissed the appeals. David Richards J held that 'the unpacking of goods received in large quantities, and their repackaging in parcels of smaller quantities, involving no treatment or adaptation of the goods in question', did not qualify as 'the subjection of those goods to a process'. *Next Distribution Ltd v HMRC (and related appeals)*, UT [2014] UKUT 227 (TCC); [2014] UKUT 2682.

Kennels

[8.21] A married couple provided quarantine facilities and transport services for dogs and cats brought into the UK from abroad. They claimed that the kennels qualified for industrial buildings allowance under what is now *CAA 2001, s 274(1)(a)*. The Ch D rejected this contention, applying the principles laid down in *Copol Clothing Ltd v Hindmarch*, **8.16** above. Sir Donald Nicholls VC observed that the quarantining of the animals was not part of the ordinary process of transportation, but was undertaken to satisfy a statutory requirement. *Carr v Sayer & Sayer*, Ch D 1992, 65 TC 15; [1992] STC 396. (*Note*. For another issue in this case, see **8.68** below.)

*Colliery houses—whether within CAA 2001, s 277(3)**

[8.22] The National Coal Board (NCB) claimed industrial buildings allowance in respect of dwelling-houses built for and occupied by the employees of a colliery. The Revenue rejected the claim by virtue of what is now *CAA 2001,* *s 277(1)*. The NCB appealed, contending that the buildings qualified for allowances by virtue of what is now *s 277(3)*, on the grounds that it was unlikely that the coal seams would be exhausted until about 2141, and that the houses would have little or no value at that time. The HL rejected this contention and dismissed the appeal, holding that the buildings did not qualify for allowances, since they were capable of use as dwellings by persons other than the colliery employees. Lord Morton observed that the purpose of *s 277(3)* was to grant allowances for houses which it would be impossible for the owners to sell or let if the mine were no longer worked, because they were too remote from any town or village. Lord Radcliffe observed that the value to be taken account of was 'value as affected by the circumstance of the closing of the mine; it is not value as affected by the normal physical decay of the building itself'. *CIR v National Coal Board*, HL 1957, 37 TC 264; [1958] AC 104; [1957] 3 WLR 61; [1957] 2 All ER 461.

Crematorium

[8.23] A company claimed industrial buildings allowances on a crematorium. The Ch D rejected the claim, holding that a crematorium was not a qualifying trade within what is now *CAA 2001, s 274(1)(a)*. Stamp J observed that human remains were not 'goods' or 'materials'. *Bourne v Norwich Crematorium Ltd*, Ch D 1967, 44 TC 164; [1967] 1 WLR 691; [1967] 2 All ER 576.

Administrative block in complex

[8.24] A company manufacturing pharmaceuticals carried on its business from blocks of buildings in a 53-acre site which was treated as a single unit for rating purposes. The blocks included an administrative block which cost less than 10% of the whole and was connected to a pharmaceutical block by a covered passage. The company claimed industrial buildings allowances on the whole unit. The Revenue rejected the claim for allowances on the administrative block, considering that it was a separate building and did not qualify as an industrial building. The Special Commissioners dismissed the company's appeal, finding that 'the administrative block was not sufficiently physically integrated with the other structural units within the layout'. The Ch D upheld their decision as one of fact. *Abbott Laboratories Ltd v Carmody*, Ch D 1968, 44 TC 569; [1968] 2 All ER 879.

Building used for making up wage packets

[8.25] A company claimed industrial buildings allowances on a building used for making up wage packets, and storing notes and coins. The Revenue rejected the claim on the basis that notes and coins were not 'goods'. The Ch D upheld the Revenue's ruling. Slade J held that 'a dealing with coins or notes simply as currency cannot constitute the subjection of goods to a process', within what is now *CAA 2001, s 274(1)(a)*. *Buckingham v Securitas Properties Ltd*, Ch D 1979, 53 TC 292; [1980] STC 166; [1980] 1 WLR 380.

Depots of plant hire contractor

[8.26] A company, which carried on a plant hire business, owned a number of depots at which it stored the equipment between hirings and carried out any necessary repair and maintenance work. It claimed industrial buildings allowances on the depots. The Revenue rejected the claim and the CA unanimously dismissed the company's appeal. Templeman LJ held that the equipment was not subjected to a 'process' within what is now *CAA 2001, s 274(1)(a)*, since the word 'process' connotes a substantial measure of uniformity or a system of treatment, whereas the company treated each item of equipment individually. *Vibroplant Ltd v Holland*, CA 1981, 54 TC 658; [1982] STC 164; [1982] 1 All ER 792.

Building used by bank for processing documents

[8.27] A banking company claimed industrial buildings allowances on a building which was used for processing cheques and other documents. The Revenue rejected the claim, and the CA unanimously dismissed the company's appeal, holding that the documents which were processed at the building were not within the definition of 'goods or materials' for the purposes of what is now *CAA 2001, s 274(1)(a)*. *Girobank plc v Clarke*, CA 1997, 70 TC 387; [1998] STC 182; [1998] 1 WLR 942; [1998] 4 All ER 312.

Miscellaneous

Relevant interest

[8.28] An individual (H) built a factory on land he held under a 99-year lease. He sub-let the factory to a company for a premium and a low rent for a term expiring three days before the head lease. The company claimed industrial buildings allowances on the factory. The Ch D rejected the claim. Plowman J held that the company did not become entitled to H's relevant interest in the factory for the purposes of what is now *CAA 2001, s 271(3)*. *Woods v RM Mallen (Engineering) Ltd*, Ch D 1969, 45 TC 619. (*Note*. For the Revenue's practice following this decision, see Capital Allowances Manual, para CA33020. For the current provisions regarding the 'relevant interest' for the purposes of industrial buildings allowances, see *CAA 2001, ss 286–291*.)

CAA 2001, s 272(1)—apportionment of part of price to land

[8.29] A syndicate purchased a retail warehouse at a cost of £1,131,735 and claimed industrial buildings allowances. The Revenue issued determinations on the basis that part of the expenditure was attributable to the land on which the warehouse stood, and, by virtue of what is now *CAA 2001, s 272(1)*, did not qualify for allowances. The syndicate appealed, contending that, even if part of the purchase price was attributable to land and an apportionment was required, the Revenue's determinations apportioned too much of the price to land. The Special Commissioner reviewed the evidence in detail and held that the disallowable element should be a proportion of the purchase price computed in accordance with the formula in *TCGA 1992, s 42(2)*, as proposed by the inspector. On the evidence, the Commissioner found that 37.51% of the purchase price (i.e. £424,527) was disallowable. The Ch D upheld the Commissioner's decision. Sir John Vinelott held that what is now *CAA 2001, s 272* required an apportionment of the purchase price and the formula in *TCGA 1992, s 42(2)*, which did 'no more than apply the principles of rateable apportionment where there is a part disposal', was appropriate in the circumstances of the case. *Bostock & Others v Totham*, Ch D 1997, 69 TC 356; [1997] STC 764.

Plant and machinery allowances

What comprises plant or machinery

NOTE

See now, for specific provisions concerning qualifying expenditure, *CAA 2001, ss 21–38*, deriving from *FA 1994*.

Cases held to constitute plant or machinery

Whether horse constitutes plant

[8.30] In a workmen's compensation case, the CA held that a horse was plant. Lord Esher MR observed that 'in many businesses horses and carts, wagons, or drays, seem to me to form the most material part of the plant: they are materials or instruments which the employer must use for the purpose of carrying on his business, and without which he could not carry it on at all.' Lindley LJ held that plant 'includes whatever apparatus is used by a business-man for carrying on his business—not his stock-in-trade, which he buys or makes for sale; but all goods and chattels, fixed or moveable, live or dead, which he keeps for permanent employment in his business'. *Yarmouth v France*, CA 1887, 19 QBD 647. (*Note*. This *dictum* has been applied in many subsequent cases. It was approved by the HL in *Hinton v Maden & Ireland Ltd*, 8.32 below.)

Hulk used for coal storage—whether plant

[8.31] In a case relating to a provision for wear and tear deductions for machinery or plant, which is now obsolete, the KB held that the hulk of an old sailing-ship, which was used for bunkering coal, was plant. *John Hall Junior & Co v Rickman*, KB [1906] 1 KB 311.

Knives and lasts used by shoe manufacturer

[8.32] A company (M) trading as shoe manufacturers used large numbers of knives and lasts on its machines. The knives and lasts had an average life of three years,and M claimed investment allowances under *FA 1954*. The HL allowed the claim, holding (by a 3–2 majority, Lords Keith and Denning dissenting) that the expenditure was capital expenditure and that the knives and lasts were plant. *Hinton v Maden & Ireland Ltd*, HL 1959, 38 TC 391; [1959] 1 WLR 875; [1959] 3 All ER 356.

Office partitions

[8.33] A company trading as shipping agents claimed capital allowances on movable office partitioning. The Commissioners allowed the claim, finding that the partitioning could be frequently moved, and holding that it was within the definition of 'plant'. The CA upheld the Commissioners' decision. Ormerod LJ observed that it was 'clear that the movable partitions were so adapted that the arrangements inside the building should be as flexible as possible to meet the changing demands of the trade'. Pearson LJ observed that 'the short question in this case is whether the partitioning is part of the premises in which the business is carried on, or part of the plant with which the business is carried on'. The Commissioners had been entitled to find that the partitioning was plant. *Jarrold v John Good & Sons Ltd*, CA 1962, 40 TC 681; [1963] 1 WLR 214; [1963] 1 All ER 141.

Dry dock

[8.34] A company (B) trading as shipbuilders and repairers constructed a 'dry dock' on the bank of the Clyde. The dock was intended to act like a hydraulic chamber, in which a variable volume of water could be used to lower a ship for inspection and repair and to raise it again to high-tide level so that it could sail away. B claimed capital allowances on the basis that the whole of the expenditure was on machinery or plant. The Revenue rejected the claim but the Special Commissioners allowed B's appeal, finding that the dock was 'not a mere shelter or home' but 'played an essential part in the operations which took place in getting a ship into the dock, holding it securely and then returning it to the river'. The HL upheld the Commissioners' decision (by a 3–2 majority, Lords Hodson and Upjohn dissenting), overruling the earlier decision of Finlay J in *Margrett v Lowestoft Water & Gas Co* (see 63.70 TRADING PROFITS). *CIR v Barclay Curle & Co Ltd*, HL 1969, 45 TC 221; [1969] 1 WLR 675; [1969] 1 All ER 732.

Swimming pools

[8.35] A company which operated a caravan park claimed capital allowances on the cost of constructing two swimming pools provided with an elaborate system for filtering, chlorinating and heating the water. The Revenue rejected the claim but the Special Commissioners allowed the company's appeal and the Ch D upheld their decision. Megarry J held that the pools were 'part of the means whereby the trade is carried on, and not merely the place at which it is carried on'. *Cooke v Beach Station Caravans Ltd*, Ch D 1974, 49 TC 514; [1974] STC 402; [1974] 1 WLR 1398; [1974] 3 All ER 159.

Artificial football pitches

[8.36] A company claimed capital allowances on the cost of constructing artificial football pitches, including the associated work on excavation, infilling, etc. The Revenue rejected the claim but the Special Commissioner allowed the company's appeal and the CS upheld this decision as one of fact. Lord Kirkwood held that the Commissioner 'was entitled to regard the synthetic carpet as a separate entity'. The pitches did not constitute a 'fixed structure', and were 'not merely part of the premises'. On the evidence, 'the relevant item of plant was the carpet, and the works underneath constituted the alteration of land for the purpose only of installing the plant'. Accordingly the expenditure qualified for capital allowances. *CIR v Anchor International Ltd*, CS 2004, 77 TC 38; [2005] STC 411.

Grain silos

[8.37] A company which imported and resold grain claimed plant and machinery allowances on two dockside concrete silos. The Revenue issued a ruling that the silos qualified for industrial buildings allowances but were not within the definition of 'plant'. The Special Commissioners allowed the company's appeal, finding that the silos performed the specific function of holding the grain in a position from which it could be conveniently delivered to purchasers, rather than merely storing it. The CA(NI) upheld their decision as one of fact. Lowry CJ observed that 'plant does not require to be mechanically active in its operation'. *Schofield v R & H Hall Ltd*, CA(NI) 1974, 49 TC 538; [1975] STC 353.

Law books

[8.38] A barrister claimed capital allowances on purchasing law books and law reports soon after he started practice. The CA allowed his claim, declining to follow the decision in *Daphne v Shaw*, KB 1926, 11 TC 256, and holding that a barrister's textbooks were 'plant' within the definition in *Yarmouth v France*, **8.30** above. *Munby v Furlong*, CA 1977, 50 TC 491; [1977] STC 232; [1976] 1 WLR 410; [1976] 1 All ER 753.

Gazebo in garden of public house

[8.39] A publican purchased a gazebo which she placed in the garden of the public house, to provide cover for customers who wished to smoke. She claimed capital allowances on the cost of the gazebo. HMRC rejected the claim on the basis that the gazebo had become part of the premises. The First-tier Tribunal allowed the publican's appeal, holding that the gazebo was 'plant' and observing that 'regarded as a whole it is more appropriate to call it apparatus than to call it premises'. *Mrs CA Andrew v HMRC*, FTT [2010] UKFTT 546 (TC); [2011] SFTD 145, TC00799.

Lighting and decor of licensed premises

[8.40] A brewery company (S) installed decor, murals, light fittings and electrical wiring in some hotels and public houses which it operated as part of its business. It claimed capital allowances on the basis that the expenditure was on plant. The 'decor and murals' included items affixed to the walls, but all were detachable. The Revenue rejected the claim, and S appealed, contending that the lighting and decor of each premises were carefully designed, having regard to the type of clientele it was desired to attract. The Special Commissioners accepted S's evidence and allowed the appeal (with the exception of the expenditure on electrical wiring). The Commissioners found that S's trade included the provision of accommodation in 'a situation which includes "atmosphere"—atmosphere judged in the light of the market which the premises are intended to serve', and held that the fittings and decor served a functional purpose in the trade. The HL upheld their decision. Lord Lowry observed that 'the creation of atmosphere is, for the purposes of his trade, an important function of the successful hotelier'. As a general test, 'something which becomes part of the premises, instead of merely embellishing them, is not plant, except in the rare case where the premises are themselves plant, like the dry dock in *CIR v Barclay Curle & Co Ltd*' (see **8.34** above). The disputed items here embellished the premises and did not become part of the premises. Accordingly, they constituted plant. *CIR v Scottish & Newcastle Breweries Ltd*, HL 1982, 55 TC 252; [1982] STC 296; [1982] 1 WLR 322; [1982] 2 All ER 230.

Decorative screens in windows of building society branches

[8.41] A building society claimed capital allowances on decorative screens which it installed in the windows of its branches. The screens showed the society's name and coat of arms. The Revenue rejected the claim but the Ch D allowed the society's appeal. Goulding J held that the screens were 'part of the apparatus employed in the commercial activities of the society's business'. They 'were not used as premises but were part of the means by which the relevant trade was carried out'. *Leeds Permanent Building Society v Proctor*, Ch D 1982, 56 TC 293; [1982] STC 821; [1982] 3 All ER 925.

Poultry house

[8.42] In an Irish case, a company which carried on the business of egg production incurred expenditure on a specially designed deep pit poultry house. The poultry house was held to be plant. *O'Srianain v Lakeview Ltd*, HC(I) 1984, TL(I) 125. (*Note*. The decision was questioned by Peter Gibson LJ in *Attwood v Anduff Car Wash Ltd*, **8.51** below.)

Grandstand at racecourse

[8.43] In an Irish case, the proprietors of a racecourse incurred expenditure on renovating the grandstand. The area of the stand was increased, the roof was replaced, and the terracing was altered. The Circuit Judge held that the grandstand constituted plant, so that part of the work qualified for capital allowances. The HC(I) upheld this decision in principle, holding that the provision of a stand was 'part of the means to get people to go to that racecourse for viewing horse races'. *O'Grady v Roscommon Race Committee*, HC(I) 6 November 1992 unreported. (*Note*. For another issue in this case, see **63.81** TRADING PROFITS.)

Control room to house security equipment

[8.44] A company carried on a business of installing, maintaining and monitoring intruder alarm systems. It constructed a control room to house security equipment. In its returns, it treated this expenditure as being on plant and machinery and as qualifying for capital allowances. HMRC issued amendments to disallow the allowances claimed, and the company appealed. The First-tier Tribunal allowed the appeal, holding on the evidence that 'the sums incurred on the construction of the control room' were 'incidental to the sums incurred on the acquisition of plant and machinery in the form of security equipment'. *B & E Security Systems Ltd v HMRC*, FTT [2010] UKFTT 146 (TC), TC00452.

Cases where the expenditure was apportioned

Wallpaper designs

[8.45] A company which manufactured wallpaper and fabrics used blocks, rollers and screens bearing the appropriate design. The designs were made either by the company's studio or by freelance artists. About one-half of them were used immediately, the rest being filed for possible use later. The company claimed investment allowances on the basis that the designs were plant. The Revenue rejected the claim but the Commissioners allowed the company's appeal, holding that the expenditure could be attributed to the blocks, rollers and screens, which were plant. The Ch D upheld their decision. *McVeigh v Arthur Sanderson & Sons Ltd*, Ch D 1968, 45 TC 273; [1969] 1 WLR 1143; [1969] 2 All ER 771. (*Note*. Cross J observed that it was arguable that, as some of the designs were 'never actually put on any block, screen or roller', a proportion of the expenditure should be disallowed. However, instead of proposing an apportionment, the Revenue had chosen to argue the case on the basis that 'not one penny of the design costs should be allowed'.)

Electrical installation

[8.46] A company (C) claimed capital allowances on the entire cost (£945,000) of the electrical installation for a new retail store. The Revenue accepted that about £360,000 was for plant (mainly standby systems, a public address system, and certain ancillary wiring). However, the Revenue rejected £480,000 of the claim (mainly the lighting and the wiring to and on each floor). The remaining £105,000 was for transformers, which were needed to convert current from the national grid to the requisite voltage, and the main switchboard. The Revenue proposed to apportion this between the allowable and disallowable items. C appealed, contending that the installation as a whole was a single item of plant. The Special Commissioners rejected this contention and dismissed the appeal, except that they held that the transformers (£50,000 of the £105,000) and certain minor items (costing £23,000 of the £480,000) were plant. They held that the switchboard was not plant. The CA upheld their decision, except with regard to the switchboard, which qualified as plant because its size and nature was dictated by the necessity to control the part of the installation which was agreed or held to be plant. The HL unanimously dismissed C's appeal. Lord Hailsham defined plant as 'the means by which a trade is carried on in an appropriately prepared setting' and held that 'the contrast is between the thing implanted, i.e. the plant, and the prepared setting into which it is placed'. On the evidence, the Commissioners were entitled to find that 'the multiplicity of components' in the installation precluded treating it as a single entity. Whether the individual components were plant was a question of fact and degree for the Commissioners. *Cole Bros Ltd v Phillips*, HL 1982, 55 TC 188; [1982] STC 307; [1982] 1 WLR 1450; [1982] 2 All ER 247.

Expenditure on modernising restaurants

[8.47] Two companies, which operated chains of restaurants, claimed capital allowances on the replacement of shopfronts, floor and wall tiles, murals, and lighting, and the installation of new water-tanks, staircases and raised floors. The Revenue rejected the claims. The Special Commissioners allowed the companies' appeals in part, holding that decorative items such as murals, decorative brickwork and wall panels were within the definition of 'plant', but that the shopfronts, tiles, water-tanks, staircases and raised floors were not plant since they were part of the premises or setting within which the trades were carried on. The Ch D upheld the Commissioners' decision in general, but held that certain expenditure on lighting by one of the companies qualified as expenditure on plant, since the Commissioners had found that this was specially installed to create an atmosphere of 'brightness and efficiency' in the restaurants. The CA dismissed the companies' appeals against this decision. Fox LJ observed that 'there is a well-established distinction, in general terms, between the premises in which the business is carried on and the plant with which the business is carried on. The premises are not plant.' *Wimpy International Ltd v Warland; Associated Restaurants Ltd v Warland*, CA 1988, 61 TC 51; [1989] STC 273.

Expenditure on converting buildings into public houses

[8.48] A company, which operated a large chain of public houses, incurred substantial expenditure in converting a dilapidated theatre, and two shops, into public houses. It claimed capital allowances on this expenditure. HMRC rejected much of the claim on the basis that various items of expenditure did not qualify as 'plant'. The company appealed. The Special Commissioners reviewed the evidence in detail and allowed the appeal in part, holding inter alia that decorative panelling did not qualify as plant because it was 'part of the premises'; that kitchen tiles also did not qualify as plant; that expenditure on a new drainage system qualified as plant, and that certain items of preliminary expenditure qualified for allowances under what is now *CAA 2001, s 25*. Following a further hearing by the First-tier Tribunal, both sides appealed to the Upper Tribunal, which dismissed the company's appeal and allowed HMRC's appeal in part, holding that expenditure on work in the toilet areas did not qualify for allowances. The Tribunal also held that certain preliminary expenditure should be apportioned, observing that 'apportionment of preliminaries between items which do, or do not, qualify for capital allowances is the only solution in relation to unattributable preliminaries, and may be the sensible solution where attribution is uneconomic'. *JD Wetherspoon plc v HMRC (and cross-appeal)*, UT [2012] UKUT 42 (TCC); [2012] STC 1450.

Platform and lighting erected in single-storey warehouse

[8.49] A company trading as wholesale merchants used a single-storey warehouse in which it erected a storage platform, made of chipboard on a steel grid supported by pillars and bolted to the ground for safety. The platform covered most of the warehouse floor area. The company claimed capital allowances on the platform and on additional lighting installed beneath the platform. The Revenue rejected the claim, considering that the platform was part of the premises. The company appealed, contending that it served a functional purpose in the business and constituted 'plant'. The Commissioners accepted this contention and allowed the company's appeal, holding that the platform was a 'movable temporary structure'. The Ch D upheld the Commissioners' decision with regard to the platform but reversed it with regard to the lighting. With regard to the platform, the Commissioners were entitled to reach the conclusion that it had not become part of the premises. However, the lighting had been installed to provide 'a general illumination' and was therefore not plant. *Hunt v Henry Quick Ltd*, Ch D 1992, 65 TC 108; [1992] STC 633.

[8.50] A similar decision was reached in a case which the Ch D heard with *Hunt v Henry Quick Ltd*, **8.49** above. *King v Bridisco Ltd*, Ch D 1992, 65 TC 108; [1992] STC 633.

Car wash site

[8.51] A company operated several car wash sites. Each site included a building, which incorporated the wash machines and control equipment, and surrounding tarmac areas which were used for circulation, queuing and parking of cars. The company claimed capital allowances on the basis that each site was to be treated as a single entity and as 'plant'. The Commissioners accepted this contention but the Ch D reversed this decision and remitted the case to them to consider the disputed items individually. The CA dismissed the company's appeal. On the evidence, the site on which the car wash business was operated, and the building in which the machinery was housed, functioned as the premises in which the business was carried on, rather than as 'apparatus functioning as plant'. *Attwood v Anduff Car Wash Ltd*, CA 1997, 69 TC 575; [1997] STC 1167.

Underground electrical substation

[8.52] An electricity company claimed capital allowances on the whole of its expenditure on an underground substation, contending that it constituted a single item of plant. The Special Commissioner allowed the company's claim but the Ch D reversed this decision. Blackburne J held that the structure of the substation functioned as the premises from which the company's trade was carried on, rather than the apparatus with which it was carried on. (The case was remitted to the Commissioner to determine the allowances due on particular components of the substation which the Revenue accepted as plant.) *Bradley v London Electricity plc*, Ch D 1996, 70 TC 155; [1996] STC 1054. (*Note*. For a preliminary issue in this case, see **4.197** APPEALS.)

Cases held not to constitute plant or machinery

Stallions

[8.53] A stud proprietor claimed capital allowances on two stallions. The KB rejected the claim. Rowlatt J held that a stallion did not diminish in value by reason of wear and tear and hence did not fall within the wording of the legislation then in force (*CIRA 1878, s 12*). *Earl of Derby v Aylmer*, KB 1915, 6 TC 665; [1915] 3 KB 374. (*Note*. For a case in which a horse was held to constitute plant, see *Yarmouth v France*, **8.30** above.)

Greyhounds

[8.54] In the case noted at **65.4** TRADING PROFITS, the KB held that greyhounds, kept by a company which organised greyhound race meetings, were not plant or machinery. *Abbott v Albion Greyhounds (Salford) Ltd*, KB 1945, 26 TC 390; [1945] 3 All ER 308.

Lighting

[8.55] In a war damage compensation case, a company contended that electric lighting in a tea-shop should be held to be 'plant'. The Ch D rejected this claim. Uthwatt J held that the lighting did not constitute plant because it was part of the 'general setting in which the business is carried on'. *J Lyons & Co Ltd v Attorney-General*, Ch D 1944, 170 LT 348; [1944] 1 All ER 477.

Wallpaper pattern books

[8.56] A company which sold wallpaper claimed capital allowances on its wallpaper pattern books. The Commissioners rejected the claim, holding that the books were not plant. The Ch D upheld their decision. Pennycuick J held that the expenditure on the books was revenue expenditure rather than capital expenditure, since they had a life of 'little more than two years'. *Rose & Co (Wallpapers & Paints) Ltd v Campbell*, Ch D 1967, 44 TC 500; [1968] 1 WLR 346; [1968] 1 All ER 405.

Prefabricated buildings

[8.57] A partnership which operated a school claimed capital allowances on prefabricated buildings for use as a laboratory and a gymnasium. The Revenue accepted that gymnasium equipment was plant, but rejected the rest of the claim. The General Commissioners dismissed the school's appeal, finding that the partnership had not produced evidence to justify any of the cost of the laboratory being attributed to specific items of equipment. The CA unanimously upheld the Commissioners' decision. *St. John's School (Mountford & Knibbs) v Ward*, CA 1974, 49 TC 524; [1975] STC 7.

Holiday cottages

[8.58] An accountant purchased a house and some adjacent land, and arranged for the construction of four cottages, to be let as holiday accommodation. She claimed capital allowances on stone floors, windows, on painting and decorating, and on the creation of an earth mound. HMRC rejected the claims and she appealed, contending that the whole site should be treated as plant. The First-tier Tribunal rejected this contention and dismissed her appeal, holding that 'neither the whole site nor any of the individual items can be classed as plant or machinery'. *Mrs ME McMillin v HMRC*, FTT [2011] UKFTT 65 (TC), TC00943.

Canopy at petrol station

[8.59] A company which operated a petrol station claimed capital allowances on a metal canopy which protected the service area. The Ch D rejected the claim. Brightman J held that the canopy was not plant, since it merely provided shelter and was not 'part of the means by which the operation of supplying petrol is performed'. *Dixon v Fitch's Garage Ltd*, Ch D 1975, 50 TC 509; [1975] STC 480; [1976] 1 WLR 215; [1975] 3 All ER 455.

Ship used as floating restaurant

[8.60] A company claimed capital allowances on the cost of purchasing and adapting an old ferry boat and barge for use as a floating restaurant. The Ch D rejected the claim, holding that the vessels were not plant, and the CA unanimously dismissed the company's appeal. Buckley LJ observed that the vessels were 'not part of the apparatus employed in the commercial activities of that business, but were the structure within which the business was carried on'. Shaw LJ held that 'a characteristic of plant appears to me to be that it is an adjunct to the carrying on of a business and not the essential site or core of the business itself'. Templeman LJ observed that there was 'a distinction between premises in which a business is carried on and the plant with which a business is carried on'. However, as a matter of law there was 'no distinction between a restaurant in the Thames and a fish and chip shop in Bethnal Green. Premises only become plant if they perform the function of plant.' *Benson v Yard Arm Club Ltd*, CA 1979, 53 TC 67; [1979] STC 266; [1979] 1 WLR 347; [1979] 2 All ER 336.

Building used as 'car valeting bay'

[8.61] A company (R) claimed capital allowances on the construction of a building used as a 'car valeting bay', where it applied glasscoat finishes and wax to new cars. HMRC rejected the claim and R appealed, contending that the building qualified as 'plant'. The First-tier Tribunal rejected this contention and dismissed the appeal. Judge Shipwright observed that the building was 'a workshop designed to allow glasscoat to be applied advantageously', and was 'a place of work which does not amount to plant'. *Rogate Services Ltd v HMRC*, FTT [2014] UKFTT 312 (TC), TC03449.

False ceilings

[8.62] A company which operated a restaurant business claimed capital allowances on false ceilings which were installed in parts of its premises open to the public, and were intended to conceal pipes and wiring. The Ch D rejected the claim, holding that the ceilings were not plant, since they merely provided a covering and had no 'functional element'. Fox J held that 'in determining whether something is plant, the test to be applied is a functional test; that is to say, does that thing perform a function in the actual carrying out of the trade?' *Hampton v Fortes Autogrill Ltd*, Ch D 1979, 53 TC 691; [1980] STC 80.

Grandstand at football ground

[8.63] In the case noted at **63.80** TRADING PROFITS, a football club replaced an unsafe grandstand at its ground and claimed that the new stand should be treated as plant and as qualifying for capital allowances. The Revenue accepted that the new seats were plant, but rejected the claim with regard to the construction of the stand. The Special Commissioners dismissed the club's appeal on this point, and the Ch D upheld their decision. Vinelott J held that the stand was 'the setting or place where, rather than the means by which, the trade is carried on'. *Brown v Burnley Football & Athletic Co Ltd*, Ch D 1980, 53 TC 357; [1980] STC 424; [1980] 3 All ER 244.

Furniture for flat above business premises

[8.64] In the case noted at **63.225** TRADING PROFITS, a surveyor claimed capital allowances on his expenditure on furnishing a flat above his business premises. The Commissioners rejected the claim and the Ch D upheld their decision. Walton J observed that 'the contents of the flat were not in any way used for the purposes of the trade'. *Mason v Tyson*, Ch D 1980, 53 TC 333; [1980] STC 284.

Inflatable tennis court cover

[8.65] Two partners carried on business as professional tennis coaches, in connection with which they used two tennis courts. To enable them to continue coaching during the winter months, they purchased a large polythene cover which, when inflated by air and tethered by cables attached to a concrete ring beam, covered the area of the two courts. It was erected from September to Easter and stored in a hut when taken down. They claimed capital allowances on the cover. The Ch D rejected the claim. Walton J held that, on the facts found by the Commissioners, the cover merely provided shelter for the business activities and did not 'play a part in the actual running of the business'. (The partners appeared in person and indicated that the cover did more than just provide shelter, but as such evidence was not in the Stated Case, Walton J held that he could 'pay no judicial attention' to them.) *Thomas v Reynolds & Broomhead*, Ch D 1987, 59 TC 502; [1987] STC 135.

Putting greens at golf course

[8.66] A company (F) which operated a golf course arranged for the construction of three new putting greens. It claimed capital allowances on the basis that the greens were 'plant'. The Revenue rejected the claim and the Special Commissioner dismissed F's appeal, holding that the greens were not 'plant', but were part of the premises where F carried on its trade. *Family Golf Centres Ltd v Thorne*, Sp C [1998] SSCD 106 (Sp C 150).

All-weather horse race track

[8.67] A company (L) claimed capital allowances on the construction of an all-weather track for horse racing. The Revenue rejected the claim and L appealed, contending that the track constituted 'plant'. The CA unanimously rejected this contention and dismissed the appeal. Mummery LJ held that the racetrack functioned 'as premises on which the trade of horse racing is carried on'. The effect of the all-weather track was 'to enlarge the area of the racecourse' which was available 'to function as premises, on which more frequent horse racing can take place'. *Lingfield Park 1991 Ltd v Shove*, CA 2004, 76 TC 363; [2004] STC 805; [2004] EWCA Civ 391.

Kennels

[8.68] A married couple provided quarantine facilities and transport services for dogs and cats brought into the UK from abroad. They constructed permanent quarantine kennels and temporary outdoor moveable kennels. The General Commissioners held that both types of kennels constituted plant. The Revenue accepted that the temporary kennels constituted plant, but appealed against the Commissioners' decision with regard to the permanent kennels. The Ch D held that the permanent kennels did not constitute plant, since they were purpose-built permanent buildings or structures and were 'the premises at which and in which the business was conducted'. Sir Donald Nicholls VC held that buildings which 'would not normally be regarded as plant, do not cease to be buildings and become plant simply because they are purpose-built for a particular trading activity'. Accordingly, capital allowances were not due in respect of any part of the expenditure on their construction. *Carr v Sayer & Sayer*, Ch D 1992, 65 TC 15; [1992] STC 396. (*Note*. The Ch D also held that the kennels did not qualify as industrial buildings—see **8.21** above.)

Glasshouse at garden centre

[8.69] A partnership which operated a garden centre incurred expenditure on the construction of a glasshouse, with panes which could be opened and shut to control ventilation. The partnership claimed capital allowances on the basis that the glasshouse constituted 'plant'. The Ch D rejected the claim, holding that the glasshouse was not within the definition of 'plant'. The CA unanimously rejected the partnership's appeal. Nourse LJ observed that the glasshouse was a fixed structure 'to which plants are brought already in a saleable condition'. The fact that it provided 'the function of nurturing and preserving the plants while they are there cannot transform it into something other than part of the premises in which the business is carried on'. *Gray v Seymours Garden Centre (Horticulture)*, CA 1995, 67 TC 401; [1995] STC 706.

Personal security (CAA 2001, s 33)

[8.70] A partnership which sold aquariums, fish and associated products incurred expenditure of £81,353 on erecting fencing around land which it owned. It claimed capital allowances on the expenditure. Following an enquiry, HMRC issued a closure notice rejecting the claim, and the partnership appealed, contending that the fencing should be treated as qualifying for allowances under *CAA 2001, s 33*. The First-tier Tribunal rejected this contention and dismissed the appeal, finding that 'what evidence there is leads directly to the only conclusion that the purpose in incurring the expenditure was to protect the land and the stock'. Accordingly the expenditure did not meet the requirements of *s 33*. *PD, J & LD Brockhouse (t/a A5 Aquatics) v HMRC*, FTT [2011] UKFTT 380 (TC), TC01235.

Employments and offices (CAA 2001, s 36)

CAA 2001, s 36—restriction on qualifying expenditure

[8.71] A vicar claimed capital allowances under what is now *CAA 2001, s 15(1)(i)* in respect of a slide projector and an overhead projector which he had bought so as to provide visual sermons in his church. The Ch D rejected the claim, holding that the equipment was not 'necessarily provided' for the purpose of the vicar's religious duties, as required by what is now *CAA 2001, s 36(2)*. Vinelott J held that *s 36(2)*, requiring that the plant or machinery was 'necessarily provided for use in the performance of the duties' of the employment or office, had to be interpreted as rigidly as the similar test under what is now *ITEPA 2003, s 336(1)*. He observed that it was 'impossible to suppose that the legislature intended that there should be a different test and that capital expenditure on the provision of equipment for use in the performance of the duties of an office or employment should be allowable although the revenue cost of maintaining it might not be'. On the evidence, the vicar could have performed his duties without the equipment. Accordingly the expenditure failed to qualify for allowances. *White v Higginbottom*, Ch D 1982, 57 TC 283; [1983] STC 143; [1983] 1 WLR 416.

Annual investment allowance qualifying expenditure (CAA 2001, s 38A)

Application of CAA 2001, s 38A(3)

[8.72] A farming partnership, comprising a married couple and a company of which they were the directors, claimed an annual investment allowance under *CAA 2001, s 38A*. HMRC rejected the claim on the basis that the partnership was not a 'qualifying person', as defined by *s 38A(3)*. The First-tier Tribunal dismissed the partnership's appeal against this decision. *Hoardweel Farm Partnership v HMRC*, FTT [2012] UKFTT 402 (TC), TC02097.

[8.73] The First-tier Tribunal reached a similar decision in the Scottish case of *Drilling Global Consultant Llp v HMRC*, FTT [2014] UKFTT 888 (TC), TC04003.

Trade discontinued in period in which expenditure incurred

[8.74] In July 2008 an engineer (K) purchased a new van. On 31 March 2009 he transferred his business to a company. In his 2008/09 return, he claimed an annual investment allowance on the purchase of the van. HMRC rejected the claim on the basis that he had discontinued his trade in the same period in which he acquired the van, so that the effect of *CAA 2001, s 38B, General Exclusion 1* was that no allowance was due. The First-tier Tribunal dismissed K's appeal against this decision. *DA Keyl v HMRC*, FTT [2014] UKFTT 493 (TC), TC03619.

First-year qualifying expenditure (CAA 2001, ss 39–51)

Whether leased machinery qualifying for first-year allowances

[8.75] A company (P) leased some machinery to another company (D). P's motive in leasing the machinery was to obtain 100% first-year allowances, and the lease included a clause providing for adjustment of the rent if 100% capital allowances were not available for the accounting period in which the expenditure was incurred. The Revenue rejected P's claim to allowances and the Special Commissioners dismissed P's appeal against this decision, holding that the transactions did not constitute a trade of leasing, since their 'paramount or sole motive or object' was 'to avoid an immediate burden to corporation tax'. Subsequently the Revenue agreed that P should receive 100% first-year allowances as a non-trading lessor, and P withdrew an appeal against the Special Commissioners' decision. However, since such allowances were only available against income from the particular source, rather than against P's total income, P demanded additional rent from D. The Ch D upheld P's claim. Carnwath J observed that there was 'no issue as to the reasonableness of the decision not to pursue the appeal to the High Court'. *Gold Fields Mining & Industrial Ltd v GKN (United Kingdom) plc & Another*, Ch D [1996] STC 173. (*Note.* Expenditure on the provision of plant or machinery for leasing, whether in the course of a trade or otherwise, is now generally excluded from being 'first-year qualifying expenditure' by *CAA 2001, s 46(2), General Exclusion 6*.)

[8.76] A company incurred expenditure on the provision of plant and machinery. This was used by a subsidiary company, which paid the parent company an annual charge, computed on the basis of the subsidiary company's turnover. The parent company claimed first-year allowances on the plant and machinery. The Revenue rejected the claim on the basis that the expenditure was 'on the provision of plant or machinery for leasing', so that the effect of what is now *CAA 2001, s 46(2), General Exclusion 6*was that first-year allowances were not due. The company appealed, contending that the plant and machinery had not been purchased 'for leasing'. The Special Commissioner rejected this contention and dismissed the appeal. *MF Freeman (Plant) Ltd v Jowett*, Sp C [2003] SSCD 423 (Sp C 376).

Hire of crane—whether within CAA 2001, s 46(2), General Exclusion 6

[8.77] In a non-tax case, a company hired a crane with an operator to another company to help in the construction of a new football stadium. The QB held that the relevant contract was a construction contract within the *Housing Grants, Construction and Regeneration Act 1996*, and was not simply the letting of plant on hire. *Baldwins Industrial Services plc v Barr Ltd*, QB 6 December 2002 unreported. (*Note.* Although this is not a tax case, HMRC regard it as establishing the principle that 'the supply of plant or machinery with an operator, by a business, is the provision of a service and not mere hire'. Accordingly such a supply is not excluded from being 'first-year qualifying expenditure' by *CAA 2001, s 46(2), General Exclusion 6*. See Revenue Interpretation RI 262, issued in August 2003.)

Excavation support equipment—CAA 2001, s 46(2), General Exclusion 6

[8.78] A company (M) claimed first-year allowances on excavation support equipment, which it hired out. HMRC rejected the claim on the basis that the expenditure was 'on the provision of plant or machinery for leasing', so that the effect of *CAA 2001, s 46(2), General Exclusion 6* was that first-year allowances were not due. M appealed, contending that the equipment had not been acquired for leasing, since it provided design services (through a subcontractor) as well as equipment. The First-tier Tribunal accepted this contention and allowed the appeal. Judge Cannan held that 'there can be circumstances where plant is supplied without labour but with other services and benefits such that the expenditure on such plant falls outside *General Exclusion 6*'. On the evidence, M was 'providing an overall service beyond the leasing of assets referred to in *General Exclusion 6*. It is analogous to a scaffolding firm hiring scaffolding but also providing something more, namely the labour to erect and dismantle the scaffolding'. *MGF (Trench Construction Systems) Ltd v HMRC*, FTT [2012] UKFTT 739 (TC); [2013] SFTD 281, TC02399.

Limited liability partnerships—claim for capital allowances on software

[8.79] Two limited liability partnerships claimed capital allowances in respect of capital expenditure on computer software. 75% of the purchase price of the software was funded by 'non-recourse loans', which were indirectly made available by the vendor of the software. HMRC rejected the claims on the grounds that the expenditure had been incurred 'with a view to granting to another person a right to use or otherwise deal with any of the software in question', within *CAA 2001, s 45(4)*. They issued closure notices, against which the partnerships appealed. At the hearing of the appeals, HMRC abandoned their original contention with regard to *s 45(4)*, but defended the closure notices on alternative grounds. The Supreme Court held that, on the facts found by the Special Commissioner, the partnerships were only entitled to 25% of the allowances which they had claimed, applying the 1992 decision in *Ensign Tankers (Leasing) Ltd v Stokes*, **8.100** below, and distinguishing the 2004 decision in *Mawson v Barclays Mercantile Business Finance Ltd*, **8.101** below. Lord Walker held that the composite transactions in this case 'did not, on a realistic appraisal of the facts, meet the test laid down by the Capital Allowances Act, which requires real expenditure for the real purpose of acquiring plant for use in a trade'. *HMRC v Tower Mcashback LLP1 (and cross-appeal)*, SC [2011] UKSC 19; 80 TC 641; [2011] STC 1143; [2011] 3 All ER 171. (*Note*. For another issue in this case, see **4.22** APPEALS.)

Cars, etc. (CAA 2001, ss 74–82)

Whether car 'of a type not commonly used as a private vehicle'

[8.80] *FA 1954* introduced investment allowances, but provided that such allowances were not due in respect of road vehicles, unless they were 'of a type not commonly used as private vehicles and unsuitable to be so used', or were 'provided wholly or mainly for hire to or for the carriage of members of the public in the ordinary course of a trade'. In two separate appeals, General Commissioners held that cars fitted with dual controls, and used for driving tuition, were 'of a type not commonly used as private vehicles and unsuitable to be so used', and thus qualified for allowances. The Ch D upheld the Commissioners' decisions. *Bourne v Auto School of Motoring (Norwich) Ltd*; *Coghlin v Tobin*, Ch D 1964, 42 TC 217.

Van

[8.81] A radio and TV dealer claimed an investment allowance on a mini-van, which was registered as a goods vehicle and used solely for business purposes. The Ch D rejected the claim, holding that the van was a vehicle of a type commonly used as a private vehicle and suitable to be so used. *Tapper v Eyre*, Ch D 1967, 43 TC 720; [1967] 1 WLR 1077; [1967] 2 All ER 636.

[8.82] An electrical contractor claimed an investment allowance on a 7-cwt van, licensed as a goods vehicle and used solely for business purposes, but not specially adapted in any way for use in the business. The Revenue rejected the claim and the Commissioners dismissed the contractor's appeal, holding that the van was a vehicle of a type commonly used as a private vehicle and suitable to be so used. The CS unanimously upheld their decision as one of fact. *Laing v CIR*, CS 1967, 44 TC 681.

[8.83] A TV rental company claimed investment allowances on mini-vans and Morris 1000 vans, all licensed as goods vehicles and used as such. The Revenue rejected the claim but the Special Commissioners allowed the company's appeal and the Ch D upheld their decision, holding that the vans were vehicles 'of a type not commonly used as a private vehicle and unsuitable to be so used'. Megarry J observed that 'it would seem to be a bizarre result if a purchaser of genuine trade vehicles for trade purposes were to be deprived of his allowance merely because the financial inducements of the purchase tax system had proved sufficiently great to tempt thousands of motorists to use for private purposes identical vehicles which, though unsuitable for those purposes, are nevertheless usable for them'. *Roberts v Granada TV Rental Ltd*, Ch D 1970, 46 TC 295; [1970] 1 WLR 889; [1970] 2 All ER 764.

[8.84] A company, which sold retail furniture on credit, claimed investment allowances on Austin A35 vans and Bedford 6-cwt vans, all licensed and used as goods vehicles. The Revenue rejected the claim but the Ch D allowed the company's appeal. Megarry J held that the only reasonable conclusion on the evidence was that the vans were vehicles 'of a type not commonly used as a private vehicle and unsuitable to be so used'. *S & U Stores Ltd v Gordon*, Ch D 1970, 46 TC 295; [1970] 1 WLR 889; [1970] 2 All ER 764. (*Note*. The Ch D heard the case with *Roberts v Granada TV Rental Ltd*, **8.83** above.)

Qualifying hire cars—CAA 2001, s 82

[8.85] A driving instructor claimed investment allowance (see **8.80** above) in respect of a car which was not specially adapted, but which was used for driving tuition, claiming that part of the amounts which she charged customers was for the hire of the vehicle. The Ch D rejected her claim. Buckley J held that 'the pupils never obtained any right or interest in the car which could be said to amount to a hiring'. *Frazer v Trebilcock*, Ch D 1964, 42 TC 217. (*Note*. The Ch D heard the case with *Bourne v Auto School of Motoring (Norwich) Ltd* and *Coghlin v Tobin*, **8.80** above.)

Fire officer's car

[8.86] See *Gurney v Richards*, **22.172** EMPLOYMENT INCOME.

CAA 2001, s 207(2)—reduction of allowances

[8.87] A farmer drove an Alvis car. It was accepted that six-sevenths of the use of the car was for business purposes and one-seventh for private purposes. The Revenue considered that the capital allowances should be abated by more than one-seventh to take into account 'personal choice' of the car. The Ch D allowed the farmer's appeal, holding that there was no evidence to justify any abatement. Danckwerts J held that the car did not appear 'to have been an extravagant purchase, having regard to the cost of a second-hand car of sufficiently recent vintage to be an economic proposition'. *Kempster v McKenzie*, Ch D 1952, 33 TC 193.

[8.88] A farming company purchased a Bentley for the use of its managing director, who was a substantial shareholder. On a mileage basis, eleven-twelfths of the use of the car was for business purposes and one-twelfth was for private purposes. The gross capital allowances were £1,749. The Commissioners held that this amount should be reduced by an abatement of £1,020 for personal choice and by a further £146 (i.e. one-twelfth of £1,749) for private mileage, reducing the allowance to £583. The Ch D upheld their decision. Vaisey J observed that the car in question 'was a most extravagant purchase' and had not been 'made entirely having regard to the requirements of the farming business'. *GH Chambers (Northiam Farms) Ltd v Watmough*, Ch D 1956, 36 TC 711; [1956] 1 WLR 1483; [1956] 3 All ER 485.

Fixtures (CAA 2001, ss 172–204)

Equipment leased to local authorities—whether 'belonging' to lessor

[8.89] Several associated companies leased items of equipment to local authorities. The equipment consisted mainly of central heating installed in council houses; other leases involved swimming pool equipment, crematorium equipment, a sheltered alarm system, car park lifts and boilers. The companies claimed capital allowances in respect of the equipment. The Revenue rejected the claims on the grounds that the equipment did not 'belong' to the lessors, as required by what is now *CAA 2001, s 11(4)*, and that the lessor and lessee could not make an election under what is now *CAA 2001, s 177*, since the expenditure in question had been incurred before 12 July 1984, when *FA 1985, s 59, Sch 17* (which introduced what is now *CAA 2001, s 177*) came into force. The HL held that the companies were never the owners of the equipment, either in law or in equity. The equipment had become fixtures, and thus the property of the local authorities, before the leases were entered into. Accordingly, the lessors were not entitled to allowances on expenditure incurred before 12 July 1984 on plant and machinery installed in premises owned and occupied by the local authorities. Furthermore, the companies did not hold any 'interest in land' within what is now *CAA 2001, s 175*. However, local authorities could enter into an election under what is now *CAA 2001, s 177*, even though they were not themselves liable to income or corporation tax, so that the companies would be entitled to allowances where the relevant expenditure was incurred after 11 July 1984. The HL held that the true determination of the question when the liability was incurred required a finding of fact in relation to each individual case. If it could be shown that in any case the company had given specific and unconditional approval to the purchase of the equipment by the authority, and the terms to be included in the lease schedule had been finally agreed, the company would have incurred the expenditure when the authority had purchased the equipment, because it would then have become liable to reimburse the authority. In any other case, liability would not have been incurred until the lease schedule had been completed. The HL therefore remitted the case to the Special Commissioners to determine the appeals accordingly. *Melluish v BMI (No 3) Ltd (and related appeals)*, HL 1995, 68 TC 1; [1995] STC 964; [1995] 3 WLR 630; [1995] 4 All ER 453. (*Notes*. (1) The legislation was subsequently amended by *FA 1997, Sch 16*, which was intended to reverse that part of this decision which gave allowances to equipment lessors on fixtures leased to persons not liable to tax. For the current legislation, see *CA 2001, ss 178, 179*. (2) For HMRC's interpretation of the effects of the decision, see Business Leasing Manual, para BLM32545.)

Railway land and fixtures leased by local authority to company

[8.90] A railway line in Somerset was closed by British Rail in 1971. In 1975 Somerset County Council purchased the freehold of the railway and leased it to a company. In 1989 the company paid a premium of £210,000 for a new lease. The company claimed writing-down allowances on the basis that £107,000 of this related to plant and machinery on the railway line. The Revenue rejected the claim and the Special Commissioner dismissed the company's appeal. Under what is now *CAA 2001, s 182(1)(cc)*, the company could only claim allowances if 'no person has previously become entitled to an allowance in respect of any capital expenditure incurred on the provision of the fixture'. It appeared that most of the fixtures in question had been installed before the railway was nationalised in 1948, so that the Great Western Railway (which operated the line before nationalisation) would have been entitled to claim allowances thereon. *West Somerset Railway plc v Chivers*, Sp C [1995] SSCD 1 (Sp C 1). (*Note. CAA 2001, s 182(1)(cc)* only applies where the purchaser acquired the interest in the relevant land before 24 July 1996: see *CAA 2001, Sch 3 para 35*.)

Purchase of care home—application of CAA 2001, s 185

[8.91] A partnership (G) purchased a care home in December 2003 for £650,000. In the purchase agreement, £597,500 was attributed to the property, while £40,000 was attributed to fixtures and fittings, and £12,500 was attributed to goodwill. G claimed capital allowances on the basis that £106,014 of the £597,500 was attributable to plant and machinery. HMRC rejected the claim and the First-tier Tribunal dismissed G's appeal. Judge Blewitt observed that it appeared that the vendors had been entitled to claim capital allowances in respect of the expenditure in question. G had produced no evidence to show that the vendors had not made such a claim. Therefore the effect of *CAA 2001, s 185(2)(b)* was that G was not entitled to the allowances claimed. *Tapsell Tapsell & Lester (t/a The Granleys) v HMRC*, FTT [2011] UKFTT 376 (TC), TC01231.

Automatic public conveniences, etc. leased to local authorities

[8.92] A company leased automatic public conveniences to local authorities. It also let on hire other items of street furniture such as bus shelters. It claimed capital allowances on the items. The Revenue rejected the claim on the basis that the items were fixtures, within what is now *CAA 2001, s 173(1)*. The Special Commissioner dismissed the company's appeal, holding that the items were fixtures rather than chattels. Furthermore, the company did not hold an interest in the relevant land at the time the items became fixtures, and the rights which the company obtained after the fixtures had been installed did not amount to a licence to occupy land. Accordingly, the items did not qualify for allowances. *JC Decaux (UK) Ltd v Francis*, Sp C [1996] SSCD 281 (Sp C 84). (*Note*. See now *CAA 2001, ss 177(1)(a)(ii), 179*, deriving from *FA 1997*.)

Anti-avoidance (CAA 2001, ss 213–233)

Sale and leaseback of film master negative

[8.93] A company, which traded in leasing equipment, purchased for £22 million a film that was to be made in the UK. It leased the master print of the film to a distribution company, associated with the vendor, for a twelve-year period. It entered into a similar agreement with another film company, and claimed capital allowances in respect of its expenditure on the two films. The Revenue rejected the claim, considering firstly that capital allowances were not due by virtue of what is now *CAA 2001, s 125*, and alternatively that the allowances were precluded by the anti-avoidance provision in what is now *CAA 2001, s 215*. The Ch D allowed the company's appeal, holding on the evidence that it could not reasonably be considered that the distribution agreements were entered into without regard to the interests of the distribution company, or for a non-commercial purpose. The fact that the lessees had not expected to make a profit out of the licences was not sufficient by itself to found the conclusion that the distribution agreements were not entered into in the ordinary course of the lessees' business. The films were used by the lessees for the purposes of a trade otherwise than for leasing, the distribution agreements not being leases but representing arrangements made by the lessees in the course of their trades for the exploitation of the films. Consequently the allowances were not prohibited by *s 125*. Since the transactions were not artificial, but were designed to make a profit, *s 215*did not apply. *Barclays Mercantile Industrial Finance Ltd v Melluish*, Ch D 1990, 63 TC 95; [1990] STC 314.

Miscellaneous

Renewals basis

[8.94] A railway company was allowed to deduct its expenditure on renewals of plant in computing its profits. It claimed that it should be allowed statutory wear and tear allowances (the precursors of modern capital allowances) in addition. The Special Commissioners rejected this contention and the Court upheld their decision. Lord Gifford observed that the company 'cannot get deduction for deterioration twice over'. *Caledonian Railway Co v Banks*, CE 1880, 1 TC 487.

Plant used by associated overseas company

[8.95] See *Union Cold Storage Co Ltd v Jones*, 63.221 TRADING PROFITS.

Interest on money borrowed to finance purchase of plant

[8.96] A company, formed to acquire and hire out an oil drilling rig, began trading in October 1971 when its rig was completed. It had borrowed substantial amounts to finance the construction of the rig and, prior to October 1971, had paid £495,000 for commitment fees and interest on its borrowing. It claimed capital allowances on this expenditure as part of the cost of the rig. The Revenue rejected the claim and the HL dismissed the company's appeal (by a 4–1 majority, Lord Salmon dissenting). Lord Wilberforce held that the fees 'were expenditure on the provision of money to be used on the provision of plant, but not expenditure on the provision of plant'. Therefore they were not within what is now *CAA 2001, s 11(4)*. Lord Hailsham observed that the legislation should be construed so as to 'provide the same allowance for the taxpayer who meets the cost of an oil rig out of his own accumulated resources, the taxpayer who meets the same cost by a debenture issue or an issue of shares to the public, and the taxpayer who simply borrows the money'. *Ben-Odeco Ltd v Powlson*, HL 1978, 52 TC 459; [1978] STC 460; [1978] 1 WLR 1093; [1978] 2 All ER 1111.

Contributions to sewage authority

[8.97] A company which operated a restaurant made a contribution to a sewage authority towards the cost of an extension to a public sewer, to connect it to the drains of the restaurant. It claimed capital allowances on the contribution. The Revenue rejected the claim and the CA unanimously dismissed the company's appeal. Lord Denning held that the sewage and drainage pipes were not plant, since they were 'part of the setting in which the business is carried on'. Stamp LJ observed that 'the presence of the pipe attached to the premises would not have been dictated by the nature of the particular trade there carried on'. *Bridge House (Reigate Hill) Ltd v Hinder*, CA 1971, 47 TC 182.

Exchange loss on repayment of loan linked with purchase of plant

[8.98] In 1973 a UK company (S) agreed to purchase plant from a Swiss company (B). Under the contract, 3,000,000 Swiss francs of the purchase price was payable in ten equal half-yearly instalments, beginning on the completion of the installation of the plant (which took place in 1974). B could not finance the construction out of its own resources, and a Swiss bank agreed to credit B with the 3,000,000 francs, while S agreed to make its ten half-yearly payments of 300,000 francs to the bank rather than to B. S made these payments for two years, during which time the pound depreciated against the Swiss franc, increasing the sterling cost to S of making the payments. By agreement with the bank, S paid off the balance of the 3,000,000 francs in 1976 and claimed capital allowances on the sterling equivalent of the payment. The Revenue only agreed to grant allowances on the sterling equivalent at 1974 prices, considering that the additional expenditure was attributable to the provision of finance and not to the provision of machinery. S appealed. The Special Commissioners allowed the appeal, finding that the balance of the 3,000,000 francs was 'directly connected' with the provision of the plant. The Ch D upheld their decision, holding that the disputed expenditure became payable in 1976 rather than in 1974, and qualified for allowances. *Van Arkadie v Sterling Coated Materials Ltd*, Ch D 1982, 56 TC 479; [1983] STC 95.

Payment to cancel option over plant

[8.99] In 1965 a company (IDC), engaged in exploration for oil and gas, acquired a drilling barge for the purposes of its trade, under an agreement whereby it gave the supplier of the barge an option to repurchase it. The barge increased in value, and in 1969 IDC paid the supplier more than £500,000 for the cancellation of the option. It claimed capital allowances on this payment. The Revenue rejected the claim and IDC appealed, contending that it was expenditure on the provision of the barge. The Special Commissioners accepted this contention, holding that the payment was capital expenditure rather than revenue expenditure, and that it qualified for writing-down allowances. The Ch D upheld this decision. Vinelott J observed that 'the expenditure was made to retain in IDC's ownership an asset which constituted at that time IDC's only substantial means of earning profits'. *Bolton v International Drilling Co Ltd*, Ch D 1982, 56 TC 449; [1983] STC 70. (*Note.* The Ch D also held that the expenditure qualified for an initial allowance under provisions in *CAA 1968* which have since been superseded.)

Cost of film production shared by company and limited partnership

[8.100] A company (E) became a partner in two limited partnerships, each set up to finance the production and exploitation of a feature film. It claimed relief for losses incurred by the partnerships, which arose from claims for capital allowances in respect of the expenditure incurred on production of the films. The first of the films cost $14 million, of which the partnership contributed $3,250,000, the balance being financed through payments from the production company, described as 'non-recourse loans', and repayable exclusively out of the receipts of the film. E claimed that the partnership was entitled to a first-year allowance in respect of the whole cost of the film. The Revenue rejected the claim, considering firstly that the partnerships were not trading (see **59.85** TRADING INCOME), secondly that in each case the plant (i.e. the master negative) did not belong to the partnership, and thirdly that, because 75% of the cost of the production was actually financed by the production company, the partnership had only incurred expenditure of $3,250,000 on the plant. The HL held that the plant belonged to the partnership, but that the partnership was only entitled to capital allowances in respect of expenditure of $3,250,000, rather than $14 million. The balance of $10,750,000 had been paid by the production company, and could not in any meaningful sense be categorised as a loan. It had been paid into a bank account in the partnership name not to finance the production of the film, but to enable the partnership to indulge in a tax avoidance scheme. The transactions had been structured so as to ensure that the production company paid the whole cost of the film exceeding $3,250,000, and that the partnership would not be liable for the cost of the film in excess of that amount. *Ensign Tankers (Leasing) Ltd v Stokes*, HL 1992, 64 TC 617; [1992] STC 226; [1992] 2 WLR 469; [1992] 2 All ER 275. (*Note*. Costs were awarded to the Revenue.)

UK finance company participating in leaseback scheme

[8.101] A UK finance company (B) agreed to purchase a pipeline, which was accepted as plant and machinery, from the Irish Gas Board for £91,000,000 and to lease the pipeline back to the Board for 31 years. The Board in turn subleased the pipeline to a UK subsidiary company (G). Arrangements were agreed whereby the whole of the purchase price paid by B was deposited with a Jersey company (D), so that it was not available for immediate use by the Board, but was ultimately paid by D to B's holding company. B claimed capital allowances on the £91,000,000. The Revenue rejected the claim on the basis that the money was not expenditure incurred on the acquisition of plant or machinery, within what is now *CAA 2001, s 11*. The CA allowed B's appeal and the HL unanimously upheld this decision, holding that the object of granting the allowance was 'to provide a tax equivalent to the normal accounting deduction from profits for the depreciation of machinery and plant used for the purposes of a trade'. Where the trade was finance leasing, 'this means that the capital expenditure should have been incurred to acquire the machinery or plant for the purpose of leasing it in the course of the trade.' These requirements were 'in the case of a finance lease concerned entirely with the acts and purposes of the lessor'. On the evidence, the purchase and leaseback were part of B's 'ordinary trade of finance leasing'. What subsequently happened to the purchase price did 'not affect the reality of the expenditure by (B) and its acquisition of the pipeline for the purposes of its finance leasing trade'. *Mawson v Barclays Mercantile Business Finance Ltd* *(aka ABC Ltd v M)*, HL 2004, 76 TC 446; [2005] STC 1; [2004] UKHL 51; [2005] 1 All ER 97. (*Note*. See now, however, *CAA 2001, ss 221–228*, largely deriving from *F(No 2) A 1997, s 46*.)

[8.102] A US company (C), which wished to raise finance, owned a large quantity of mechanical equipment, located in the USA. It assigned the equipment to a subsidiary company (L), which was incorporated in the US but resident in the UK. L entered into an agreement with a UK finance company (B), whereby B agreed to purchase the equipment for £165,800,000 and lease it back to L for slightly over 30 years, at an escalating rent. B claimed capital allowances on the £165,800,000. The Revenue rejected the claim, and the Ch D and CA unanimously dismissed B's appeal. Chadwick LJ held that the equipment was 'used otherwise than for a qualifying purpose', within what is now *CAA 2001, s 110(2)(c)(d)*, so that the expenditure did not qualify for allowances. For the purposes of *s 110(d)*, the relevant lease was the headlease, rather than the sub-lease. Chadwick LJ observed that the denial of allowances was 'a fiscal disincentive, calculated to discourage the owner from incurring expenditure in the provision of machinery or plant for leasing to a non-resident on the terms of a finance lease; or for leasing on the terms of a finance lease to a lessee who is not a non-resident if, at any time during the requisite period, the plant or machinery may be used for the purpose of being leased (by that, or a subsequent, lessee) to a non-resident'. That discouragement was removed if the non-resident lessee was to 'use the machinery or plant for the purposes of a trade, otherwise than for leasing, in circumstances in which, if he had bought the machinery or plant himself (instead of leasing it) he could have claimed a first-year allowance or treated his expenditure as qualifying expenditure'. In a multi-lease case, the owner could 'protect his allowances by appropriate restrictions in the finance lease which preclude sub-letting to a non-resident save on terms which would fall within the permitted leasing exemption'. *BMBF (No 24) Ltd v CIR (aka Delta Finance Newco v CIR)*, CA 2003, 79 TC 352; [2004] STC 97; [2003] EWCA Civ 1560.

UK finance company—lease of ship—CAA 2001, s 123

[8.103] A UK company (L), which carried on a trade of finance leasing, claimed capital allowances on expenditure on two ships, which were designed and built to ship liquefied natural gas from Norway to Spain and the USA. HMRC issued an amendment rejecting the claim, considering that the effect of *CAA 2001, s 123(4)* was that L was not entitled to the allowances it had claimed. The First-tier Tribunal allowed L's appeal but the CA unanimously remitted the case to the Tribunal to reconsider the application of the restriction imposed by *CAA 2001, s 123(4)*. Rimer LJ held that 'although the FTT was no doubt entitled to find that each transaction in the relevant series served a genuine commercial purpose, it does not follow that the obtaining of the capital allowances was incapable of also being a main object of the transactions, even if it was not the main object of the transactions. The FTT does not explain why it was not such a main object.' He observed that 'even if each of the transactions was entered into for a genuine commercial purpose, it may still be the case that a main object of structuring them in the way they were was to obtain the capital allowances', and that the facts set out by the FTT appeared to indicate that this had been the case. *HMRC v Lloyds TSB Equipment Leasing (No 1) Ltd*, CA [2014] EWCA Civ 1062; [2014] STC 2770.

Transfer of machinery between connected parties—disposal values

[8.104] A partnership ceased trading in 1994/95, and transferred its machinery to a company controlled by two of the partners, the value of the machinery being credited to their directors' accounts with the company. The Revenue issued assessments for the last three years of trading (1992/93 to 1994/95) computed under the legislation then in force. The Special Commissioner upheld the assessments, expressing the opinion that there was no sale (despite the agreement of the parties that there was) and holding *inter alia* that 'there was a disposal value for machinery transferred to the company even though no payment was received'. The partnership appealed to the Ch D, which remitted the case to the Commissioner for rehearing. Lightman J held that the agreed evidence showed that there had been a sale of the machinery, and directed that the Commissioner should reconsider the question of the disposal value. *Parmar & Others (t/a Ace Knitwear) v Woods*, Ch D 2002, 74 TC 562; [2002] STC 846; [2002] EWHC 1085 (Ch).

[8.105] Following the decision reported at 8.104 above, the Special Commissioner reheard the case and held that, when the value of the plant and machinery which was transferred to the company was placed to the credit of the directors' loan accounts with the company, this constituted payment to the partnership for the assets. *Parmar & Others (t/a Ace Knitwear) v Woods (No 2)*, Sp C [2003] SSCD 297 (Sp C 367).

Mineral extraction allowances

[8.106] In a Trinidad and Tobago case, a company provided certain specialist services in connection with the drilling and operation of oil wells. Among its services were the installation of a steel pipe which was inserted into the well and kept in position by a cement jacket. The company claimed capital allowances on the basis that it was carrying on a trade of working oil wells. The Revenue rejected the claim on the grounds that the company was not carrying on such a trade, and the PC dismissed the company's appeal. On the evidence, the activities which the company carried on were not sufficiently comprehensive to be described as the working of oil wells. (Lord Hoffmann observed, by way of analogy, that an electrical contractor may undertake work in the course of the construction of houses, but he was not carrying on a trade as a housebuilder.) *Trinidad Oilwell Service Ltd v Trinidad & Tobago Board of Inland Revenue*, PC [1999] STC 1034.

Research and development allowances

Whether expenditure incurred on behalf of claimant

[8.107] A UK company (G) was a subsidiary of a Norwegian partnership, another subsidiary of which (S) was a member of two syndicates holding oil exploration licences. The actual exploration was done by other members of the syndicates, but S was obliged to pay a proportion of the syndicate expenditure. G agreed to pay S's share of the syndicate costs in return for a share of the oil, and claimed capital allowances in respect of the expenditure. The Revenue rejected the claim, considering that the expenditure had not been 'directly undertaken' on behalf of G within the meaning of what is now *CAA 2001, s 439(1)*. The CA unanimously dismissed G's appeal. Kerr LJ held that 'the requirement that the research must be directly undertaken by or on behalf of the taxpayer claiming the allowance is intended to be restrictive in its effect and to denote a close and direct link between the claimant and the work undertaken'. Here the exploration was undertaken on behalf of the members of the syndicate, but it was not undertaken on behalf of G, which was not entitled to the allowances. *Gaspet Ltd v Elliss*, CA 1987, 60 TC 91; [1987] STC 362; [1987] 1 WLR 769.

[8.108] The members of a Jersey limited partnership claimed research and development allowances for expenditure on vaccine research and development. They claimed loss relief totalling more than £192,000,000. HMRC rejected the claims, accepting that a Jersey company (N), which was a member of the partnership, had paid a subcontractor (P) £14,000,000 on research and development, but considering that the partnership had not been trading and that the other partners were not entitled to the allowances which they had claimed. The partners appealed, contending that N had been working for the partnership as a contractor. The First-tier Tribunal reviewed the evidence in detail and allowed their appeals in part but rejected the majority of the partners' claims for relief. Judge Williams held that only the £14,000,000 which N had paid to P could in law 'be regarded as incurred on research and development'. The other sums which the partners had contributed to the partnership had not been spent on research and development, and thus did not qualify for allowances. Both sides appealed to the Upper Tribunal, which unanimously upheld the First-tier decision. *Vaccine Research Limited Partnership v HMRC (and related appeals)*, UT [2014] UKUT 389 (TCC). (*Note*. For a preliminary issue in this case, see 55.32 SELF-ASSESSMENT.)

Writer and publisher—whether entitled to research allowances

[8.109] A writer (S) had published a book about film technology, which he had written himself, and a booklet about the construction of plays, which had been written in 1911. He claimed research allowances in respect of a television, a videocassette recorder, a scanner and a tape streamer. The Revenue accepted that they qualified for allowances as plant or machinery but rejected the claim to research allowances. The Special Commissioner dismissed S's appeal, holding that all the research which S had carried out related to his work as an author, and that even if S were to be treated as carrying on a trade of publishing, he had not conducted any research relating to that trade. *Salt v Golding*, Sp C [1996] SSCD 269 (Sp C 81). (*Note*. For a subsequent case in which S was held to be carrying on a trade of publishing, see *Salt v Fernandez*, 59.91 TRADING INCOME.)

[8.110] Similar decisions, involving the same appellant, were reached in *Salt v Young*, 4.441 APPEALS, and *Salt v Buckley*, 63.231 TRADING PROFITS.

Miscellaneous

CAA 2001, s 563—apportionment of consideration

[8.111] A dentist decided to emigrate and sold his practice to another dentist. The first draft of the purchase agreement provided for the lease of the premises to be assigned and the goodwill to be sold for £450 and for the equipment to be taken over at a valuation of £1,445. However, to help the purchaser to obtain a bank loan, in the final agreement the amount attributed to the lease and goodwill was increased to £1,450, and the amount attributed to equipment was reduced to £445. The matter was referred to the Commissioners for an apportionment under what is now *CAA 2001, s 563*. The Commissioners held that the amount to be attributed to the equipment was £1,445, as in the draft. The vendor appealed, contending that the Commissioners should have been bound by the terms of the final agreement. The Ch D rejected this contention and dismissed the appeal. *Fitton v Gilders and Heaton*, Ch D 1955, 36 TC 233.

[8.112] A partnership sold its business to a company for £17,500. The sale agreement attributed £15,850 of this to the premises and £1,650 to plant and machinery which had a written-down value of £1,283. The Revenue considered that the agreement undervalued the plant and machinery, and issued an assessment on the basis that the value of the plant and machinery was £4,783, so that a balancing charge of £3,500 arose. The partnership appealed. The General Commissioners determined the assessment on the basis that the plant and machinery should be valued at £3,783. The Ch D and the CA unanimously upheld their decision as one of fact. *Wood & Another (t/a A Wood & Co) v Provan*, CA 1968, 44 TC 701. (*Note*. The CA also rejected a contention by the partnership that the case should be reheard by the Special Commissioners rather than the General Commissioners.)

CAA 2001, s 532—contributions

[8.113] A company incurred expenditure on plant and machinery, and subsequently received grants from the Northern Ireland Government. The company claimed capital allowances on the full amounts of the expenditure it had incurred. The Revenue issued assessments on the basis that the effect of what is now *CAA 2001, s 532* was that allowances were not due on the amounts of the grants. The CA dismissed the company's appeal, holding that the expenditure had been met by the grants 'either directly or indirectly', within the meaning of *s 532*. *Cyril Lord Carpets Ltd v Schofield*, CA(NI) 1966, 42 TC 637.

[8.114] A company which was developing a large caravan site in Northern Ireland received grants from the International Fund for Ireland (a fund which had been established by a treaty between the governments of the UK, the Republic of Ireland, and the USA). It spent the grants on the development of the site, and claimed capital allowances. The CA held that, to the extent that the expenditure was financed by the grants, it did not qualify for capital allowances, since the fund was a public body, within what is now *CAA 2001, s 532*. The CA held that the criteria for determining whether a body was a public body were '(*a*) the public source of the constitution of the body; (*b*) its performance of a public service for the wider good of the public; (*c*) the degree of public control and accountability; (*d*) the absence of profit for private citizens; and (*e*) public funding'. *McKinney v Hagans Caravans (Manufacturing) Ltd*, CA(NI) 1997, 69 TC 526; [1997] STC 1023. (*Note*. For a preliminary issue in this case, see **4.190** APPEALS.)

Wasting assets—withdrawal of a capital allowance

[8.115] See *Burman v Westminster Press Ltd*, **71.116** CAPITAL GAINS TAX.

9

Charities

The cases in this chapter are arranged under the following headings.

Definition of charity (CTA 2010, s 467)

Bodies held to be charities

General principles

[9.1] Lands were conveyed to trustees, to apply the rents in maintaining certain missionary establishments, a school for the children of ministers and missionaries, and certain other religious establishments. The trustees claimed a repayment of income tax on the grounds that the income was applied 'to charitable purposes', and qualified for exemption from income tax under what is now *ITA 2007, s 531*. The Revenue rejected the claim on the basis that 'charity' should be given its popular meaning of the relief of poverty. The treasurer of the trust appealed. The CA allowed the appeal, and the HL upheld this decision (by a 4–2 majority, Lord Halsbury and Lord Bramwell dissenting). Lord Macnaghten held that 'charity' should be held to comprise 'four principal divisions; trusts for the relief of poverty, trusts for the advancement of education, trusts for the advancement of religion, and trusts beneficial to the community and not falling under any of the preceding heads'. Such trusts did not cease to be charitable 'because incidentally they benefit the rich as well as the poor'. *Special Commrs v Pemsel*, HL 1891, 3 TC 53; [1891] AC 531. (*Note*. This is the leading case on the meaning of 'charitable purposes'. The principles laid down by Lord Macnaghten have been extensively applied in subsequent charity cases.)

Relief of poverty

Almshouse

[9.2] Trustees operated a home for 'ladies in reduced circumstances', aged 50 or over. Women were only admitted if they had an income of at least £25 p.a. The KB held that the home was within the definition of an 'almshouse' and was 'an institution the objects of which are entirely and absolutely charitable', and qualified for exemption from income tax under the legislation then in force. *Mary Clark Home Trustees v Anderson*, KB 1904, 5 TC 48; [1904] 2 KB

645. (*Note.* The term 'almshouse' does not appear in the current legislation, but it is considered that the home would still qualify as a 'charity'.)

Society for relief of widows and orphans of members

[9.3] A society of medical practitioners was established for the relief of widows and orphans of its members. Its income came partly from members' subscriptions but mainly from investments, donations and legacies. The Special Commissioners held that its income was applied to 'charitable purposes only', and the KB upheld their decision. *CIR v Society for the Relief of Widows and Orphans of Medical Men*, KB 1926, 11 TC 1.

Society for relief of disabled members and dependants

[9.4] A society of medical practitioners was established to help any member disabled by 'illness or accident or age', and the dependants of such members. More than 40% of its income came from members' subscriptions, with the remainder coming from donations, legacies and investments. The Special Commissioners held that its income was applied to 'charitable purposes only', and the KB upheld their decision. *CIR v Medical Charitable Society for the West Riding of Yorkshire*, KB 1926, 11 TC 1. (*Note.* The case was heard in the KB with *CIR v Society for the Relief of Widows and Orphans of Medical Men*, 9.3 above.)

Advancement of education

City of London School

[9.5] The City of London School was founded by the Corporation of London, which made annual payments towards its support. Although substantial fees were charged, the Corporation did not make, or seek to make, any profit. The CA held that the school was a 'public school' for the purposes of the legislation then in force. Lord Esher held that 'the object of this school is the education of a sufficiently large number of persons to enable us to say that that object is a public object' and that 'the mere fact of some money being paid by those who are interested in the persons to be educated in this school does not prevent this school from being a public school'. *Blake v Mayor, etc. of London*, CA 1887, 2 TC 209; 19 QBD 79. (*Note.* The term 'public school' no longer appears in *CTA 2010, s 466–517.*)

University college

[9.6] A university college claimed a repayment of income tax on the grounds that it was established 'for charitable purposes only', and qualified for exemption from income tax under the legislation then in force. The Revenue rejected the claim on the grounds that the college did not only provide education for the poor. The college applied to the KB for an order ordering the Revenue to grant the exemption. The KB granted the application and the CA unanimously upheld this decision, holding that a trust for the advancement of education does not require an element of poverty to be charitable. *R v Special Commrs (ex p. University College of North Wales)*, CA 1909, 5 TC 408.

Roman Catholic school

[9.7] A Roman Catholic school appealed against an income tax assessment, contending that it was a 'public school' and qualified for exemption under the legislation then in force. The KB accepted this contention and allowed the appeal. Rowlatt J distinguished his earlier decision in *Ackworth School v Betts*, 9.32 below, observing that in that case the proprietors had wished to keep the school 'essentially private', whereas the school here was intended for 'a very considerable section of the community'. *Cardinal Vaughan Memorial School Trustees v Ryall*, KB 1920, 7 TC 611.

Girls' Public Day School Trust

[9.8] The Girls' Public Day School Trust was established as a limited company, to provide 'public day schools for the education of girls of all classes'. It claimed that a school which it operated in Wimbledon was a 'public school' and qualified for exemption under the legislation then in force. The Revenue rejected the claim on the grounds that the school was not financed by voluntary donations and that the company's shareholders had a substantial interest in it. The General Commissioners allowed the company's appeal and the HL upheld their decision. Viscount Hailsham observed that there was 'an express finding of fact that the "sole object" of the council which carries on the school is to maintain the school at the highest level of efficiency'. Furthermore, 'the education provided is recognised by the Local Education Authority as being what is commonly described as a public school education. During all the material dates the school was largely maintained by public monies and in the view of the Board of Education the school satisfied the regulation which prohibits any Parliamentary grant to a school conducted for private profit.' *Ereaut v Girls' Public Day School Trust Ltd*, HL 1930, 15 TC 529; [1931] AC 12.

Woollen industry association

[9.9] A company, limited by guarantee, had been established to promote education, instruction and study in the woollen industry. The company established a technical college, at which instruction was given in the principles and practice of woollen manufacture. It appealed against an income tax assessment, contending that the college was a charity and qualified for exemption under the legislation then in force. The CS accepted this contention and allowed the company's appeal (by a 3–1 majority, Lord Blackburn dissenting). Lord Clyde held that 'instruction in the principles of a trade, and in the applications of science to its practice' was 'plainly educational'. *Scottish Woollen Technical College Galashiels v CIR*, CS 1926, 11 TC 139.

Musical association

[9.10] An association was formed to promote and conduct music festivals and other musical events in Scotland. It claimed that its investment income and its profits from its festivals qualified for exemption from tax. The Revenue rejected the claim and the association appealed, contending that it was a 'trust for the advancement of education' and therefore a charity. The Special Commissioners accepted this contention and allowed the appeal, and the CS upheld their decision as one of fact (by a 3–1 majority, Lord Blackburn dissenting).

Lord Sands observed that the question 'as to whether a particular charity answers to a general description is one in regard to which the Special Commissioners have wide experience. Their opinion upon such a matter in a borderline case ought not, therefore, to be lightly overruled.' *CIR v Glasgow Musical Festival Association*, CS 1926, 11 TC 154.

[9.11] The Royal Choral Society was formed 'to promote the practice and performance of choral works'. It claimed that it should be treated as exempt from income tax on its investment income and trading profits. The Revenue rejected the claim but the KB allowed the Society's appeal and the CA upheld this decision. Lord Greene MR held that 'a body of persons established for the purpose of raising the artistic taste of the country' was 'established for educational purposes'. *Royal Choral Society v CIR*, CA 1943, 25 TC 263; [1943] 2 All ER 101.

Institution of Civil Engineers

[9.12] The Institution of Civil Engineers was founded in 1818 'for the general advancement of mechanical science'. It claimed that it was a charity and entitled to exemption from income tax. The Revenue rejected the claim on the basis that one of its objectives was to benefit its members. The Institution appealed. The CA allowed the appeal, holding that the Institution was established 'for charitable purposes only'. Romer LJ held that 'the advantage to the members is not the purpose of the society, but merely an incidental consequence of the way in which it promotes science'. *Institution of Civil Engineers v CIR*, CA 1931, 16 TC 158; [1932] 1 KB 149.

Educational trust with incidental non-charitable benefits

[9.13] Shares in a company had been settled on a trust 'for charitable purposes in connection with the advancement of education and the relief of poverty'. The trustees were directed to provide an annual travelling scholarship for a student who had passed the final examination of the Incorporated Sales Management Association, to travel abroad to acquire 'experience in the commercial and selling methods used'. They also made payments to some of the company's employees for the education of their children. The trustees accepted that the latter payments were not for charitable purposes by virtue of the HL decision in *Oppenheim v Tobacco Securities Trust Co Ltd* (see **9.59** below), but claimed that the trust had an 'overall charitable intention' and qualified as a charity. The Revenue rejected the claim but the Ch D allowed the trustees' appeal, holding that, even though some of its income had been applied for non-charitable purposes, the trust had been established for charitable purposes and that the annual scholarship award was an application of its income for charitable purposes. *George Drexler Ofrex Foundation Trustees v CIR*, Ch D 1965, 42 TC 524; [1966] Ch 675; [1965] 3 All ER 529.

Publication of law reports

[9.14] A company, limited by guarantee, had been incorporated in 1870 to prepare and publish law reports, its profits not being distributable. In 1966 it applied for registration as a charity under the *Charities Act 1960*. The Charity Commissioners rejected the application, and the company appealed, contending that it was established 'for charitable purposes only'. The Ch D accepted this contention and allowed the appeal, and the CA upheld this decision. Sachs LJ observed that 'where the purpose of producing a book is to enable a specified subject, and a learned subject at that, to be studied', it was published for the advancement of education. Buckley LJ held that the company had a 'primary scholastic function of advancing and disseminating knowledge of the law', which was 'exclusively charitable'. *Incorporated Council of Law Reporting v Attorney-General*, CA 1971, 47 TC 321; [1972] Ch 73; [1971] 3 All ER 1029.

Students' union of medical college

[9.15] The Revenue issued a ruling that the students' union of a medical college (part of a university and attached to a teaching hospital) was not exclusively charitable, on the grounds that it existed for the benefit of its members. The college applied to the Ch D for a ruling that the union was a charity and was entitled to be registered under *Charities Act 1960*. The Ch D held that the union was established for charitable purposes, because its predominant object was 'to further the educational purposes of the medical college'. *London Hospital Medical College v CIR and Attorney-General*, Ch D 1976, 51 TC 365; [1976] 1 WLR 613; [1976] 2 All ER 113.

Football Association Youth Trust

[9.16] The Football Association established a trust to encourage pupils of schools and universities 'to play association football or other games or sports'. The Charity Commissioners registered the trust, but the Revenue appealed to the Ch D, contending that the objects of the trust were not exclusively charitable. The HL unanimously rejected this contention and held that the trust was entitled to registration as a charity. Lord Hailsham held that it would be wrong 'to confine the meaning of education to formal instruction in the classroom or even the playground'. On the evidence, the object of the trust was the advancement of physical education. *CIR v McMullen and Others (Football Association Youth Trust) and Attorney-General*, HL 1980, 54 TC 413; [1980] 2 WLR 416; [1980] 1 All ER 884.

Ethical Society

[9.17] The objects of an 'ethical society', established in 1824, included 'the study and dissemination of ethical principles and the cultivation of a rational religious sentiment'. It applied to the Ch D for a declaration that it was established for charitable purposes. The Ch D granted the declaration. Dillon J held that 'the study and dissemination of ethical principles' satisfied 'the criterion of charity as being for the advancement of education'. *Barralet & Others (South Place Ethical Society Trustees) v Attorney-General & CIR*, Ch D 1980, 54 TC 446; [1980] 1 WLR 1565; [1980] 3 All ER 918.

Furtherance of craftsmanship

[9.18] An association was formed to promote craftsmanship and public interest in it. Its main activities had been the conversion of two buildings for use as workshops by craftsmen. The Charity Commissioners registered it as a charity, but the Revenue appealed to the Ch D, contending that the objects of the association were not exclusively charitable. The Ch D rejected this contention and dismissed the Revenue's appeal. Fox J held that the purposes of the association were 'educational in a field of sufficient value to the public to be charitable'. Accordingly, the association was entitled to be registered as a charity. *CIR v White & Others (re Clerkenwell Green Association of Craftsmen)*, Ch D 1980, 55 TC 651.

Advancement of religion

Support of missionary work

[9.19] See *Special Commrs v Pemsel*, **9.1** above.

Baptist benevolent fund

[9.20] The Baptist Union of Ireland established a benevolent fund with the object of providing annuities for its members and their widows and orphans. The fund was financed partly by subscriptions from members but mainly by voluntary contributions. The company which acted as the trustee of the fund claimed that its investment income should be treated as exempt from income tax. The Revenue rejected the claim but the KB allowed the company's appeal. MacDermott J held that the fund was aimed 'at the advancement of religion through the benefits it confers on the Baptist ministry' and was 'sufficiently altruistic in character' to qualify as being established for charitable purposes only. *Baptist Union of Ireland (Northern) Corporation Ltd v CIR*, KB(NI) 1945, 26 TC 335.

Exclusive Brethren

[9.21] A trust owned property which was used as a meeting room by the Exclusive Brethren (formerly known as the Plymouth Brethren). The Charity Commissioners ruled that the trust was not entitled to registration as a charity. The trustees appealed. The Ch D allowed the appeal. Walton J held that the trust was established 'for religious purposes' and was entitled to be registered as a charity. *Holmes & Others v Attorney-General*, Ch D 11 February 1981, Times 12.2.1981.

Hospitals, etc

Nursing home

[9.22] An association was established in 1907 to provide nursing facilities in Peeblesshire to people who could not afford to pay the usual fees. It operated a nursing home and provided hospital treatment and nursing services at below commercial rates for its members (who were required to pay small annual subscriptions) and others. It claimed that its investment income should be treated as exempt from income tax. The Revenue rejected the claim but the Special Commissioners allowed the association's appeal, holding that the association was a charity. The CS upheld their decision as one of fact. Lord Clyde observed that 'a hospital erected entirely for the benefit of the poor is none the less solely directed to that purpose because, in order to provide it with some nucleus of revenue apart from voluntary subscriptions, it runs a special ward for paying patients'. The association had been formed 'to provide cheap first-class nursing for those who cannot afford it'. It remained charitable even though 'as an incident and adjunct of its operation, it also provides some services to persons who are perfectly well able to pay and actually pay a full price for them'. Lord Sands held that 'it is not fatal to the charitable character of an institution that the beneficiaries should pay for the benefits they get, always provided that they pay less than the market price of that benefit and that the difference is made up to them from benevolent sources'. *CIR v Peeblesshire Nursing Association*, CS 1926, 11 TC 335.

Convalescent home

[9.23] An unregistered friendly society was established for 'the relief of distressed members and the widows and orphans of members and the promotion of social intercourse and recreation'. It purchased a house which was used as a convalescent home, and conveyed it to trustees for the use of its members. It claimed that the convalescent home was a hospital, and exempt from tax under Schedule A under the legislation then in force. The Revenue rejected the claim but the KB allowed the society's appeal. Rowlatt J held that 'the mere circumstance that the number of recipients of the benefits of this place' was limited to members of the society did not prevent it from qualifying as a 'hospital'. *Grand Council of the Royal Antediluvian Order of Buffaloes v Owens*, KB 1927, 13 TC 176; [1928] 1 KB 446.

Other trusts 'beneficial to the community'

'Benevolent institutions'

[9.24] Under a Scottish will, funds were held on trust for the benefit of such charities 'or charitable or benevolent institutions' in Calcutta as the trustees thought fit. The trustees claimed exemption under what is now *ITA 2007, s 532*. The Revenue rejected the claim on the grounds that a 'benevolent institution' was not necessarily a charity. The CS allowed the trustees' appeal, holding that *Special Commrs v Pemsel*, **9.1** above, required the statutory words 'charitable purposes' to be interpreted under English law, but that Scottish law applied to the interpretation of Scottish trust deeds. Lord Clyde held that, under Scottish law, 'a Scottish deed which puts money in trust for "charitable or benevolent purposes" is neither more nor less than a trust for "charitable purposes" alone'. Lord Sands held that, in Scotland, 'a purpose which is benevolent is also charitable'. *Jackson's Trustees v Lord Advocate*, CS 1926, 10 TC 460.

Temperance café trust

[9.25] A will trust provided for a fund to be used to provide a 'Temperance Public House' in Falkirk, to provide its inhabitants 'with comfortable rooms where wholesome refreshments may be obtained, where they are free from the temptation of intoxicating liquors'. The Special Commissioners held that the trust was established 'for charitable purposes only', and the CS upheld their decision. Lord Sands held that 'the promotion of temperance is a charitable object'. *CIR v Falkirk Temperance Café Trust*, CS 1926, 11 TC 353. (*Note*. In the subsequent case of *Sir HJ Williams' Trustees v CIR*, **9.70** below, Lord Normand held that this decision rested 'on the ground that the predominant purpose of the trust was the moral improvement by means of temperance of the inhabitants of Falkirk, and the cafés and temperance hotel provided by the trust were so subordinated to the predominant purpose that it was possible to distinguish them from an ordinary commercial venture in catering and hotel-keeping'.)

Temperance canteens

[9.26] A trust was established to run a temperance canteen in Hereford. The trust deed provided that the profits from the canteen were to be invested or applied in running similar canteens or to promote temperance. The profits were in fact invested or paid to temperance organisations. The trust claimed relief on its trading profits and investment income. The Revenue rejected the claim but the Ch D allowed the trust's appeal. Harman J held that the trust deed showed that 'the object of these people was the promotion of temperance, and the furnishing and running of this canteen by voluntary help was their chosen means to that end'. *Trustees of the Dean Leigh Temperance Canteen v CIR*, Ch D 1958, 38 TC 315.

Holiday home

[9.27] A draper established a trust to provide a holiday home for persons in the drapery trade 'requiring temporary rest and change of air for the benefit of their health'. The Special Commissioners held that the trust was for 'charitable purposes only' and the CA upheld their decision. Lawrence LJ held that 'the expression "requiring temporary rest and change of air for the benefit of their health" implies that the trust is one for the relief of physical distress, and this takes it into the category of convalescent homes and takes it out of the category of mere holiday resorts'. *CIR v Roberts Marine Mansions Trustees*, CA 1927, 11 TC 425.

Agricultural society

[9.28] A society had been formed in 1837 for the 'general promotion of agriculture'. In 1925 it claimed that it was a charity and was exempt from tax on its investment income. The Revenue rejected the claim on the basis that the society had been formed to benefit its members. The society appealed, contending that it was established for 'purposes beneficial to the community'. The Special Commissioners accepted this contention and allowed the appeal, and the CA upheld their decision as one of fact. Atkin LJ held that a society formed for the purpose merely of benefiting its own members was not formed for a charitable purpose, and if it were a substantial part of a sociaty's object that it should benefit its members, it would not be established for a charitable purpose only. However, 'if the benefit given to its members is only given to them with a view of giving encouragement and carrying out the main purpose which is a charitable purpose', then 'the mere fact that you benefit the members in the course of promoting your charitable purpose would not prevent the establishment being for charitable purposes only'. Lawrence LJ observed that 'agriculture is an industry not merely beneficial to the community but vital to its welfare'. *CIR v Yorkshire Agricultural Society*, CA 1927, 13 TC 58; [1928] 1 KB 611.

Municipal recreation ground

[9.29] Under a will, the residue of the deceased's estate was paid to a town council 'for amenity purposes' in the town. The council invested the amount which it received, and applied the investment income towards the cost of a recreation ground. It claimed a repayment of income tax on this income. The Revenue rejected the claim and the council appealed. The Special Commissioners allowed the appeal, holding that the 'amenity purposes' had to be treated as 'charitable purposes'. The CS unanimously upheld their decision. *CIR v Tayport Town Council*, CS 1936, 20 TC 191.

Liberal newspaper

[9.30] In an Indian case, a trust was established under the will of a newspaper proprietor, to maintain the newspaper and continue its 'liberal policy'. The trustees appealed against an income tax assessment, contending that the income was exempt as the trust was a charity for an 'object of general public utility' (the relevant statutory test). The Privy Council accepted this contention and allowed the appeal, holding on the evidence that 'the object of the paper may fairly be described as "the object of supplying the province with an organ of educated public opinion"'. *Tribune Press Lahore (Trustees) v Income Tax Commr Punjab Lahore*, PC [1939] 3 All ER 469.

Crystal Palace

[9.31] Under the *Crystal Palace Act 1914*, a body of trustees were entrusted with the control and management of the Crystal Palace 'as a place of public resort and recreation' and for 'the promotion of industry, commerce and art'. The trustees applied to the Ch D for a declaration that the trust was established for 'the benefit of the public' and was of a charitable nature (for the purposes of the *Town and Country Planning Act 1947*). The Ch D granted the declaration. Danckwerts J observed that, throughout the *Crystal Palace Act 1914*, 'the note which is stressed is the provision of benefits to the public'. *Crystal Palace Trustees v Minister of Town and Country Planning*, Ch D 1950, [1951] Ch 132; [1950] 2 All ER 857.

Bodies held not to be charities

Educational bodies

Quaker school

[9.32] A school was founded by the Society of Friends and managed by members of the Society. Places in the school were reserved primarily for children of members. The school claimed that it was a 'public school' and was exempt from Schedule A tax under the legislation then in force. The Revenue rejected the claim and the KB dismissed the school's appeal, holding that it was not a 'public school' (and was also not a 'charity school' for the purposes of Inhabited House Duty). Rowlatt J held that 'the persons who founded this school wanted to avoid having a public school, they wanted to have a school which they should keep particularly under their own control'. *General Committee for Ackworth School v Betts*, KB 1915, 6 TC 642. (*Note*. The term 'public school' no longer appears in *CTA 2010, s 466–517*.)

School owned by company

[9.33] A company owned and operated a school with about 450 pupils. Almost all of the company's receipts arose from fees paid for pupils. The company claimed that it was a 'public school' and was exempt from Schedule A tax under the legislation then in force. The Revenue rejected the claim and the KB dismissed the company's appeal. Rowlatt J held that the school had 'no real permanent character' and 'continues to exist only at the corporate will of the members of this company'. It lacked the element of permanency which was 'part of the essentials of a public school'. *Birkenhead School Ltd v Dring*, KB 1926, 11 TC 273.

Educational trust with priority to grantor's family

[9.34] In a Ceylon case, the Board of Review held that a trust for education with priority to the grantor's family was not charitable. The Privy Council upheld this decision and dismissed the trustees' appeal. Lord Radcliffe held that if people, for whose benefit an educational trust was created, derived their title to their benefits 'as descendants of a named person or as employees of a named company, the trust must be regarded merely as a family trust, and not as one for the benefit of a section of the community'. *Caffoor & Others (Abdul Gaffoor Trustees) v Colombo Income Tax Commissioner*, PC 1961, 40 ATC 93; [1961] AC 584; [1961] 2 All ER 436. (*Note*. For another issue in this case, see 4.77 APPEALS.)

Educational trust—income applied for a limited class of beneficiaries

[9.35] A company (E) was established for the advancement of education (accepted as a charitable purpose). In practice, most of its income was applied towards the education of children of the employees or former employees of one particular trading company (M), although it also made some grants to educational institutions. It claimed that its income qualified for exemption. The Ch D rejected the claim in relation to the income applied for the benefit of M's employees or ex-employees, on the grounds that the application of E's income to the making of grants to the children of M's employees, without inviting applications from other possible beneficiaries, was not an application for charitable purposes only. The CA unanimously dismissed E's appeal. Lord Denning MR held that 'a trust is for the public benefit if it is for the benefit of the community or a section of the community. The inhabitants of a named place are a section of the community for this purpose, but the employees of a particular company or companies are not.' Accordingly, the money had not been applied for the public benefit. *CIR v Educational Grants Association Ltd*, CA 1967, 44 TC 93; [1967] Ch 993; [1967] 2 All ER 893.

Political and similar objects (including reform of the law)

Temperance Council

[9.36] An association was established with the object of effecting changes in the law relating to the sale of alcoholic drinks. It claimed that it was a charity and that its investment income should be treated as exempt from tax. The KB upheld the Revenue's rejection of the claim. Rowlatt J observed that the association 'was instituted mainly with the direct purpose to effect changes in the law'. This was a 'political purpose', and accordingly the association was not a charity. *CIR v Temperance Council of the Christian Churches of England and Wales*, KB 1926, 10 TC 748.

Anglo-Swedish Society

[9.37] An association was formed in 1918 with the object of promoting 'a closer and more sympathetic understanding between the English and Swedish peoples' by facilitating visits to England by Swedish journalists. It claimed that it was a charity and that its investment income should be treated as exempt from tax. The Revenue rejected the claim and the KB dismissed the association's appeal. Rowlatt J observed that 'not every trust for matters of public utility' was a charity. *Anglo-Swedish Society v CIR*, KB 1931, 16 TC 34.

Jewish resettlement

[9.38] A company was formed in 1907 with the primary object of acquiring land in Palestine, Syria and Turkey, to be settled by Jews. Most of the settlers came from eastern Europe. The company claimed that it was a charity and that its investment income should be treated as exempt from tax. The Revenue rejected the claim and the HL unanimously dismissed the company's appeal. Lord Thankerton held that the company could not be regarded as a 'trust for purposes beneficial to the community' (within the principles laid down in *Special Commrs v Pemsel*, **9.1** above) because ' "community" predicates the existence of some political or economic body settled in a particular territorial area'. On the evidence, 'the area here is an enormous area with no political or economic homogeneity between the various parts'. *Keren Kayemeth Le Jisroel Ltd v CIR*, HL 1932, 17 TC 27; [1932] AC 650.

Trust fund in memory of former Prime Minister

[9.39] In 1929 a trust was established to honour the memory of a former Prime Minister, and to preserve a historic building for use as an economic, social and political education centre. It claimed that it was a charity and that its income should be treated as exempt from tax. The Revenue rejected the claim and the KB dismissed the trust's appeal, holding that it was not charitable, as its primary object was a political or party one. Finlay J observed that 'it is impossible to hold that a trust which is simply a trust for the propagation of the political principles of a particular party is a good charitable trust'. On the evidence, the trust's premises were being used as 'an educational centre for the Conservative Party'. *Bonar Law Memorial Trust v CIR*, KB 1933, 17 TC 508.

Voluntary workers

[9.40] An association was formed in 1919, to enrol voluntary workers to carry on essential services in the event of strikes or lock-outs. During the general strike of 1926 it enrolled some 2,500 volunteers. The trustees of the association claimed that it was a charity and that its investment income should be treated as exempt from tax. The Revenue rejected the claim and the CS dismissed the trustees' appeal. Lord Normand observed that 'a trust which exists for the purpose of supporting the Government' had entered the political arena 'and has not even a remote resemblance to charity'. Lord Fleming observed that 'a body which has for its purpose the taking of a certain line of political action cannot be regarded as a charitable institution'. *Roll of Voluntary Workers (Trustees) v CIR*, CS 1941, 24 TC 320.

Anti-Vivisection Society

[9.41] The National Anti-Vivisection Society claimed that it was a charity and that its investment income should be exempt from tax under what is now *CTA 2010, s 486*. The Revenue rejected the claim and the HL dismissed the Society's appeal (by a 4–1 majority, Lord Porter dissenting). Lord Simonds held that 'a main object of the Society is political, and for that reason the Society is not established for charitable purposes only'. On the evidence found by the Commissioners, any 'public benefit in the direction of the advancement of morals' would be 'outweighed by the detriment to medical science and research and consequently to the public health which would result if the Society succeeded in achieving its object'. *CIR v National Anti-Vivisection Society*, HL 1947, 28 TC 311; [1948] AC 31; [1947] 2 All ER 217.

[9.42] The decision in *CIR v National Anti-Vivisection Society*, **9.41** above, was applied in the similar subsequent case of *Animal Defence & Anti-Vivisection Society v CIR*, Ch D 1950, 32 TC 55. (*Note*. See **4.253** APPEALS for a preliminary issue in this case.)

Trust for improvement of international relations

[9.43] In 1919 a married couple created a trust for the improvement of international relations. In 1962 the trustees applied to the Ch D for a ruling that the objects of the trust were charitable. The Ch D held that the objects were political and not charitable. Plowman J held that they were 'really no more than propaganda'. *Buxton & Others v Public Trustee & Others*, Ch D 1962, 41 TC 235. (*Note*. Plowman J also held that the trust was not validated by the *Charitable Trusts (Validation) Act 1954*, that the trust was void for perpetuity, and that the trust fund was held upon a resulting trust for the settlors or their personal representatives.)

Amnesty International

[9.44] Amnesty International was founded in 1961 with the object of securing worldwide observance of the United Nations' 1948 proclamation of the Universal Declaration of Human Rights. In 1977 it established a trust, which applied to the Charity Commissioners for registration as a charitable trust. The Commissioners rejected the application, and the trustees applied to the Ch D for a declaration that they were entitled to be registered. The Ch D dismissed the application. Slade J observed that the objects of the trust included the release of 'prisoners of conscience' and the abolition of capital and corporal punishment, and held that these objectives were political rather than charitable, applying the HL decision in *National Anti-Vivisection Society v CIR*, **9.41** above. *McGovern & Others v Attorney-General & CIR*, Ch D 1981, [1982] 1 Ch 321; [1982] 2 WLR 222; [1981] 3 All ER 493.

Trust for study of 'militarism and disarmament'

[9.45] The Charity Commissioners refused to register as charitable a trust which had the stated objective of 'the education of the public in the subject of militarism and disarmament'. The Ch D dismissed the trustees' appeal, holding on the evidence that the objectives of the trust were political, rather than charitable. The CA upheld this decision. Chadwick LJ observed that 'there are differing views as to how best to secure peace and avoid war'. On the evidence, the object of the trust was 'not to educate the public in the differing means of securing a state of peace and avoiding a state of war', but was to promote demilitarisation. *Southwood & Another v Attorney-General*, CA [2000] All ER (D) 886.

Professional associations

Headmasters' Conference

[9.46] The Headmasters' Conference was incorporated in 1909. It applied to the QB for an order ruling that it was a charity and that its income should be treated as exempt from tax. The KB dismissed the application, holding that it was not established for charitable purposes only. Shearman J observed that, under its Memorandum of Association, one of its purposes was 'to initiate and promote or oppose measures, legislative or administrative, in Parliament or elsewhere'. Furthermore, it was authorised to spend money 'in improving the status and position of the scholastic profession quite apart from the general interests of education'. *R v Special Commrs (ex p. Headmasters' Conference)*, KB 1925, 10 TC 73.

General Medical Council

[9.47] The General Medical Council was established by the *Medical Act 1858*, 'to enable persons requiring medical aid to distinguish qualified from unqualified practitioners'. It claimed that it was a charity and that its investment income should be exempt from tax under what is now *CTA 2010, s 486*. The Revenue rejected the claim and the CA dismissed the Council's appeal. Lord Hanworth MR observed that there was 'an advantage to the professional members of this Society, who are given the privilege of suing if they are members of this body of registered medical practitioners'. (Under the *Medical Act 1858*, unqualified practitioners were not allowed to take legal proceedings for unpaid fees.) It followed that the Council was partly formed for professional purposes, and was not established for charitable purposes only. *General Medical Council v CIR*, CA 1928, 13 TC 819.

Pharmaceutical Society of Ireland

[9.48] The Pharmaceutical Society of Ireland was formed by statute to hold examinations for persons wishing to be pharmaceutical chemists and to keep a register of those who were professionally qualified. It appealed against an income tax assessment, contending that it was a charity. The Special Commissioners rejected this contention and dismissed the appeal, and the HC(I) upheld this decision, holding that the Society was not a charity (and that its activities of conducting schools and examinations were trades). *Pharmaceutical Society of Ireland v CIR*, HC(I) 1937, 2 ITC 157; [1938] IR 202; 17 ATC 587.

Geologists' Association

[9.49] The Geologists' Association claimed that it was a charity and that its investment income should be exempt from tax under what is now *CTA 2010, s 486*. The Revenue rejected the claim and the Special Commissioners dismissed the association's appeal, holding that it was not established for charitable purposes only, since its main object was 'the combination of members for scientific purposes and mutual improvement and the giving and receiving of instruction among themselves'. The CA upheld this decision as one of fact. Russell LJ observed that 'the Commissioners have found as a fact that the main object that the main object of the association is the furtherance of the knowledge of geology among its members, and that any furtherance of education generally or for benefit of the public which accrues is an incidental by-product of the main object'. *Geologists' Association v CIR*, CA 1928, 14 TC 271.

Institution of Engineers

[9.50] An engineers' institution, federated to the Institute of Mining Engineers, claimed that it was a charity and that its investment income should be exempt from tax under what is now *CTA 2010, s 486*. The Revenue rejected the claim and the Special Commissioners dismissed the institution's appeal, holding that it was not established for charitable purposes only, since its main object was to increase its members' 'technical and professional knowledge'. The KB upheld this decision as one of fact. *Midland Counties Institution of Engineers v CIR*, KB 1928, 14 TC 285.

Nursing Council

[9.51] The General Nursing Council for Scotland was established in 1919 under an Act of Parliament to provide a scheme for the registration of nurses. It claimed that it was a charity and that its investment income should be exempt from tax under what is now *CTA 2010, s 486*. The Revenue rejected the claim and the CS dismissed the Council's appeal. Lord Sands held that 'the test must be whether the benefit of the funds for which exemption is sought' went 'exclusively to the service of educational or benevolent purposes, or whether, on the other hand, it does not in part go to the advancement of professional interest'. On the evidence, the Council's activities were partly for the benefit of its members. *General Nursing Council for Scotland v CIR*, CS 1929, 14 TC 645.

Merchant Navy officers

[9.52] A company was incorporated to provide a central representative body for the Merchant Navy service in relation to matters affecting the interests or status of its members. It claimed that it was a charity and that its investment income should be exempt from tax under what is now *CTA 2010, s 486*. The Revenue rejected the claim and the KB dismissed the company's appeal, holding that it was not established for charitable purposes only, since it was partly formed for the benefit of its members. *Honourable Company of Master Mariners v CIR*, KB 1932, 17 TC 298.

Religious trusts

[9.53] An individual (R) conveyed a large sum of money to trustees 'for the benefit of such persons, institutions or purposes' as he may appoint. In default of any such appointment, the deed provided that the funds would be held for the benefit of the Wesleyan Methodist Church. For 1917/18 to 1919/20, the whole of the income was applied to charitable purposes, in accordance with R's written instructions. The trustees claimed exemption under what is now *ITA 2007, s 532*. The Special Commissioners rejected the claim and the CA unanimously dismissed the trustees' appeal, holding that, because of the power of appointment in favour of non-charitable purposes, the trust was not established for charitable purposes only. *R v Special Commrs (ex p. Rank's Trustees)*, CA 1922, 8 TC 286.

[9.54] A trust was established in 1922 for the purposes 'of assisting and helping in the religious moral social and recreative life of those connected with the Presbyterian Church in the City of Londonderry'. The trustees claimed that the trust was a charity and should be exempt from Schedule A income tax. The Revenue rejected the claim and the trustees appealed. The Special Commissioners dismissed the appeal and the CA(NI) upheld their decision. Andrews LCJ held that the trust was not solely for the 'advancement of religion', and that the purposes of the trust did not conform 'to the requirements and essentials of a legal charity'. *Londonderry Presbyterian Church House Trustees v CIR*, CA(NI) 1946, 27 TC 431.

[9.55] The decision in *Trustees of the Londonderry Presbyterian Church House v CIR*, **9.54** above, was approved by the HL in a subsequent stamp duty case concerning properties held on trust 'for the promotion of the religious, social and physical well-being of persons resident in the County Boroughs of West Ham and Leyton', by 'the provision of facilities for religious services and instruction and for the social and physical training and recreation' of people resident in those boroughs who were 'members or likely to become members of the Methodist Church'. The HL held (by a 4–1 majority, Lord Reid dissenting) that the trusts were not 'established for charitable purposes only'. Viscount Simonds observed that 'the moral, social and physical well-being of the community or any part of it is a laudable object of benevolence and philanthropy, but its ambit is far too wide to include only objects which the law regards as charitable'. *Baddeley & Others (Trustees of the Newtown Trust) v CIR*, HL 1955, 35 TC 659.

[9.56] A property was held on trust for certain purposes which were accepted as charitable, and also generally 'for the promotion and aiding of the Roman Catholic Church in the district' in which the property was situated. The trustees claimed that the trust was a charity and should be exempt from Schedule A income tax. The Revenue rejected the claim and the CA unanimously dismissed the trustees' appeal. Jenkins LJ held that the trust was not established for charitable purposes only, since the purposes set out in the trust deed could include 'activities outside the scope of what is recognised by the law as religious charity'. *Ellis & Others v CIR*, CA 1949, 31 TC 178.

[9.57] A company limited by guarantee was incorporated in 1939 for 'the advancement of the Christian religion', particularly 'the principles of the Oxford Group Movement'. It claimed that it was a charity and that its investment income should be exempt from tax under what is now *CTA 2010, s 486*. The Revenue rejected the claim and the CA dismissed the company's appeal. Tucker LJ held that the company's objects 'extend far beyond purely religious activities, and permit or even require for their attainment activities which may be secular or political'. *The Oxford Group v CIR*, CA 1949, 31 TC 221; [1949] 2 All ER 537.

[9.58] Properties were held on trust for the Roman Catholic inhabitants of certain parishes for 'religious, educational and other parochial requirements of the said inhabitants'. The trustees claimed that the trust was a charity and should be exempt from Schedule A income tax. The Revenue rejected the claim and the QB(NI) dismissed the trustees' appeal, applying the CA decision in *Londonderry Presbyterian Church House Trustees v CIR*, 9.54 above. *Cookstown Roman Catholic Church Trustees v CIR*, QB(NI) 1953, 34 TC 350.

Trusts for employees

[9.59] A will directed the payment of certain sums 'to some organisation or charity' for the benefit of the employees of a firm. Questions arose concerning the construction of the will and a compromise was sanctioned by court order in 1919. The order directed the establishment of an 'employees' fund' and stipulated that its object should be limited to charitable purposes. The fund was set up and approved by the court in 1921. The trustees claimed a repayment of income tax for 1951/52 and 1952/53. The Revenue rejected the claim on the basis that, because the fund was to benefit the employees of a specific company, it was not a charity. The trustees appealed, contending that the effect of the 1921 court order was that the fund must be held to be charitable. The Ch D rejected this contention and dismissed the appeal. Applying the 1951 HL decision in *Oppenheim v Tobacco Securities Trust Co Ltd*, HL [1951] AC 297; [1951] 1 All ER 31, the fund was not a charity. Upjohn J observed that '30 years ago it was not always appreciated that in order to constitute a valid charitable trust it must be a public trust, and that if a trust is limited to the employees of a company, the personal nexus constituted by that common employment does not satisfy the necessary test'. Furthermore, the 1921 court decision did not give rise to any estoppel, and the trusts were not validated by the *Charitable Trusts (Validation) Act 1954*. *William Vernon & Sons Ltd Employees' Fund Trustees v CIR*, Ch D 1956, 36 TC 484; [1956] 1 WLR 1169; [1956] 3 All ER 14. (*Note. Oppenheim v Tobacco Securities Trust Co Ltd* was a non-tax case establishing that a class of beneficiaries under a trust is not a 'section of the public' if the only nexus among the members of the class is that they are employees of a particular employer. The rule in *Oppenheim* is modified if the trust is for the relief of poverty. Thus a trust for the benefit of the 'poor employees' of a particular company was held to be charitable in *Dingle v Turner*, HL [1972] AC 601; [1972] 1 All ER 878.)

Winding-up of employee share trust—charity as residuary beneficiary

[9.60] The trust deed of an employees' share scheme authorised the trustees to wind up the share scheme and to hold the net proceeds of the sale of the shares, and any other surplus funds, for the absolute benefit of a charity. Following negotiations for the sale of the share capital of the employing company, the share scheme was duly wound up and the shares held by the trust were repurchased by the company. The trustees claimed that the proceeds of the share repurchase were a qualifying distribution which was exempt from tax, and claimed repayment of the tax credit. The Revenue rejected the claim and the CS dismissed the trustees' appeal, holding that the proceeds of the sale of the shares were not income of a charity as and when they were received by the trustees, since the duties to be performed by the trustees in winding up the share scheme were conceived purely in the interests of the employing company, and the charity was in the position of a residuary beneficiary. *Guild & Others (William Muir (Bond 9) Ltd Employees' Share Scheme Trustees) v CIR*, CS 1993, 66 TC 1; [1993] STC 444.

Miscellaneous bodies

Simplified Spelling Society

[9.61] A trust was established for the benefit of the Simplified Spelling Society, or 'any other society or association having for its principal object the simplification of or improvement of English spelling or the English language'. The trustees claimed that the trust was a charity and that its investment income should be treated as exempt from tax. The Revenue rejected the claim and the KB dismissed the trustees' appeal. *Sir GB Hunter (1922) 'C' Trustees v CIR*, KB 1929, 14 TC 427.

Flying club

[9.62] A company (S), formed in 1928 with the objects of promoting aviation, organised a pageant, which made a profit. It claimed that it was a charity and that its income should be treated as exempt from tax. The Revenue rejected the claim and the Special Commissioners dismissed S's appeal, finding that it 'was formed for the promotion of flying by its members and was primarily a club'. The CS upheld this decision. Lord Morison observed that 'to argue that a flying club is entitled to the exemptions which the Statute gives to charitable institutions only appears to me to be absurd'. *Scottish Flying Club Ltd v CIR*, CS 1935, 20 TC 1.

Foxhound society

[9.63] In the case noted at **26.9** EXEMPT INCOME, the KB held that a society established to promote foxhound breeding was not a charity. Lawrence J held that 'the main purpose of the appellant society's activities is to benefit foxhunting, not to benefit the community'. *Peterborough Royal Foxhound Show Society v CIR*, KB 1936, 20 TC 249; [1936] 2 KB 497; [1936] 1 All ER 813.

Recreation ground used by company's employees

[9.64] In 1933 a trading company (E) conveyed a recreation ground to the National Playing Fields Association, to be held in trust for the benefit of E's employees (and, if not so required, for the benefit of the inhabitants of a certain borough). In the relevant years the recreation ground was used for the benefit of the employees, and the general public were only admitted by invitation. A trust, founded for purposes which were accepted as charitable, spent money on the improvement of the recreation ground, and claimed a repayment of income tax. The Revenue rejected the claim and the KB dismissed the trustees' appeal. Lawrence J held that the recreation ground was not being used for 'charitable purposes', since it was not available 'for the public at large'. *Wernher's Charitable Trust (Trustees) v CIR*, KB 1937, 21 TC 137; [1937] 2 All ER 488.

Industrial and provident society

[9.65] A registered industrial and provident society (H), with wide philanthropic objects, owned several houses which were let at economic rents. Its rules permitted it to pay dividends to its members. The trustees claimed that H was a charity and should be exempt from Schedule A income tax. The Revenue rejected the claim and the KB dismissed the trustees' appeal. Macnaghten J held that the trust was not charitable, since 'one of the purposes of the society is to pay dividends to its members out of its profits'. *Hugh's Settlement Ltd v CIR*, KB 1938, 22 TC 281; [1938] 4 All ER 516.

Foreign bondholders' corporation

[9.66] In 1898 a corporation was established by a private Act of Parliament, to protect the rights and interests of holders of public securities (particularly those of foreign and colonial securities issued in the UK). In 1941 it claimed that it was a charity and that its investment income should be treated as exempt from tax. The Revenue rejected the claim and the CA dismissed the corporation's appeal. Lord Greene MR observed that the object of the corporation was 'to enable a certain limited class of investor to protect, so far as possible, his investment, and to get his money back, or as much of it as can be extracted, from a reluctant foreign government'. This was not within the definition of 'charitable purposes'. *Corporation of Foreign Bondholders v CIR*, CA 1944, 26 TC 40; [1944] KB 403; [1944] 1 All ER 420.

Pig Marketing Board

[9.67] In 1933 a statutory body was established in Northern Ireland for regulating the marketing of pigs. It claimed that it was a charity and that its investment income should be treated as exempt from tax. The Revenue rejected the claim and the KB(NI) dismissed the board's appeal. MacDermott J held that the board was not established for charitable purposes only, since one of its purposes was 'the promotion of the interests of a particular commercial class'. *Pigs Marketing Board (Northern Ireland) v CIR*, KB(NI) 1945, 26 TC 319.

Mutual provident associations

[9.68] The Nuffield Foundation was established under a trust deed in 1943, for various purposes 'so far as the same are charitable purposes according to the law of England'. The trustee (N) made a grant of £25,500 from the Foundation's income to the trustees of a guarantee fund, which had been established with the object of promoting the formation of mutual insurance associations 'to assist the members thereof to meet expenditure necessitated by illness.' N claimed that the payment of £25,500 was made for charitable purposes, so that the Foundation was entitled to exemption from income tax on £51,000 of its income. The Revenue rejected the claim and the KB dismissed N's appeas. Wrottesley J held that 'the encouragement of thrift by means of mutual benefit societies is not a general charitable object'. The object of the guarantee fund was to encourage the promotion of mutual insurance associations, rather than simply 'to relieve sickness or promote health'. Accordingly, the fund was not established for charitable purposes only, and the payment by the Foundation did not qualify for exemption. *Lord Nuffield*

(Ordinary Trustee of the Nuffield Foundation) v CIR; Nuffield Provident Guarantee Fund v CIR, KB 1946, 28 TC 479.

Death benefit fund

[9.69] The Royal Naval and Royal Marine Officers' Association claimed that its death benefit fund was a charity, and that the fund's income should be exempt from income tax. The Ch D upheld the Revenue's rejection of the claim. Danckwerts J held that the fund was not charitable, as the Association's primary purpose was the provision of death benefits for its members. It was 'substantially a mutual benefit society, and not an altruistic charitable body'. *CIR v Royal Naval & Royal Marine Officers' Association*, Ch D 1955, 36 TC 187.

London Welsh Association

[9.70] A trust was established in 1937 for the purpose of establishing an institute and meeting place in London, to be used 'for the benefit of Welsh people'. It held several properties, some of which it let to tenants. The trustees claimed that the trust was a charity and should be exempt from Schedule A income tax. The Revenue rejected the claim and the Special Commissioners dismissed the trustees' appeal, holding that the trust was not a charity, since it could not be effectively distinguished from 'an ordinary social club'. The HL unanimously upheld their decision. *Sir HJ Williams' Trust v CIR*, HL 1947, 27 TC 409.

Drama company

[9.71] A non-profit-making company, limited by guarantee, was formed to produce, in association with what is now the Arts Council, plays which were considered to be 'of outstanding merit' but to be unlikely to be a commercial success. It appealed against income tax assessments, contending that its profits should be treated as exempt. The Special Commissioners rejected this contention and dismissed the appeal, holding that some of the objects set out in the company's Memorandum of Association were not charitable, so that the company failed to qualify for exemption. The CA unanimously upheld this decision. *Tennent Plays Ltd v CIR*, CA 1948, 30 TC 107; [1948] 1 All ER 506.

[9.72] A company limited by guarantee was formed in 1946 with wide objects including the production of 'classical, artistic, cultural and educational dramatic works'. It claimed that its profits should be treated as exempt. The Revenue rejected the claim and the Ch D dismissed the company's appeal. Upjohn J held that it was 'difficult to attach any real charitable concept to an artistic dramatic work'. *Associated Artists Ltd v CIR*, Ch D 1956, 36 TC 499; [1956] 1 WLR 752; [1956] 2 All ER 583.

Police sports association

[9.73] An association was formed in 1938 'to encourage all forms of athletic sports and general pastimes'. Membership was restricted to officers and former officers of the Glasgow Police Force. The association held an annual sports meeting to raise funds, and claimed that its profits from this qualified for exemption. The HL rejected the claim, holding (by a 4–1 majority, Lord Oaksey dissenting), that the association was not a charity. Lord Normand held that, although 'promoting the efficiency of the police forces' was a charitable purpose, the association's object of 'providing recreation to the members' was not charitable. Accordingly, the association was not established 'for charitable purposes only'. *CIR v Glasgow Police Athletic Association*, HL 1953, 34 TC 76; [1953] AC 380; [1953] 1 All ER 747.

'Sports Foundation' associated with football club

[9.74] Three individuals, one of whom was a solicitor, had lent significant sums of money to a local football club (W), which competed in the Southern League, and paid its first–team players expenses allowances of about £100 per week. In 2003 the three arranged for the formation of a trust (E) described as a 'sports foundation', of which they became trustees. E's stated objects conformed with the Recreational Charities Act 1958. The trustees asked W to repay £60,000 of the loans to E. On the following day E agreed to make a grant of £50,000 to W. Subsequently the trustees requested the remainder of their loans to be repaid to E, and claimed tax relief on the basis that these repayments constituted qualifying donations to charity. Initially the Revenue accepted the trustees' claims, but they subsequently issued assessments to recover the tax, considering firstly that the trustees had not actually made any qualifying donations, and secondly that although E's stated objects were charitable, in practice E did not qualify as a charity, since it had 'merely acted as a conduit for funds to the football club'. The Special Commissioner dismissed the trustees' appeals, holding that the effect of the *Recreational Charities Act 1958* was that for a club to qualify as a charity, 'it had to be open and available to all, regardless of ability, and the raison d'être of the club had to be that of providing a sporting facility for all. It was then acknowledged that sport was competitive so that clubs would often want to compete and to form teams, but the clear emphasis was that the team element had merely to be an incident of the provision of sport for all generally. The teams were there to foster the ambition of the members generally to improve and to join the teams.' However, a club that was 'principally designed to run a competitive football team (rather than just offer team games to foster the general aims of the club to promote sport equally for all) would not qualify as a charitable organisation'. W's principal object was 'to compete in outside leagues, and opportunities offered to the public were secondary'. Furthermore, although E's stated objects were charitable, in practice it 'had never acted as or been a charity' since its 'real and clear object was to filter the totality of donations that it received to the club in order to meet all the costs that had been met out of the directors' loans, and thus enable those loans to be repaid'. *PA Simpson & Others (Trustees of the East Berkshire Sports Foundation) v HMRC*, Sp C [2009] SSCD 226 (Sp C 732).

Town Council Entertainments Committee

[9.75] In 1942 a town council established an entertainments committee. This committee operated a public putting green and organised dances, sports and concerts. The Revenue issued assessments charging income tax on the profits, and the committee appealed, contending that it was a charity. The CS rejected this contention and dismissed the appeal. Lord Cooper held that it was impossible to 'describe as charitable an enterprise which carries on dances at a profit and applies the surplus in relieving the ratepayers of the cost of alterations to the Town Hall'. *Linlithgow Town Council Entertainments Committee v CIR*, CS 1953, 35 TC 84.

Fund for maintenance of historic building

[9.76] The Trades House of Glasgow and its constituent craft guilds owned a historic building, which they used for business and social purposes. They also frequently let the building to outside bodies on commercial terms. In 1966 the Trades House established a fund for the maintenance of the building. It claimed that the fund was a charity and that its income was exempt from tax. The Revenue rejected the claim and the Trades House appealed, contending that the maintenance and preservation of the building was a public benefit. The CS unanimously dismissed the appeal, holding that the fund was not a charity, since one of its purposes was to relieve the owners from part of the cost of maintaining the building. *Trades House of Glasgow v CIR*, CS 1969, 46 TC 178.

Citizens' Advice & Aid Service

[9.77] In a Guyana case, the Privy Council held that a Citizens' Advice & Aid Service was not established for charitable purposes only, applying the HL decision in *Baddeley & Others (Newtown Trust) v CIR*, **9.55** above. *D'Aguiar v Guyana Commissioner of Inland Revenue*, PC 1970, 49 ATC 33.

Training and Enterprise Council

[9.78] A Training and Enterprise Council appealed against assessments charging corporation tax on interest, contending that it was a charity and thus was exempt. The Revenue rejected the claim on the grounds that the Council was not established for charitable purposes only, since one of the objects set out in its Memorandum of Association was to promote 'the development of industry, commerce and enterprise'. The Ch D upheld the Revenue's rejection of the claim. Lightman J held that, although some of the Council's objects were charitable as being for the advancement of education, one of its main objects enabled the Council 'to promote the interests of individuals engaged in trade, commerce or enterprise and provide benefits and services to them'. The existence of these objects disqualified the Council from having charitable status. *CIR v Oldham Training & Enterprise Council*, Ch D 1996, 69 TC 231; [1996] STC 1218.

Trust for 'institutions operating for the public good'

[9.79] In a Cayman Islands case, a trust was established to pay income 'to any one or more religious, charitable or educational institution or institutions or any organisations or institutions operating for the public good'. The PC held that the purposes of the trust were 'not exclusively charitable'. Lord Browne-Wilkinson observed that 'general words are not to be artificially construed so as to be impliedly limited to charitable purposes only'. *Attorney-General of the Cayman Islands v Wahr-Hansen*, PC [2000] 3 WLR 869.

Company providing rented housing

[9.80] A company (H) was incorporated in 2001 to administer more than 12,000 properties in St Helens, which had been owned by the local borough council. It subsequently amended its Memorandum of Association, and was registered as a charity from December 2004. It appealed against corporation tax assessments for its accounting periods ending in March 2003 and 2004, contending that it should be treated as a charity for those periods even though it had not been registered as a charity until December 2004. The First-tier Tribunal rejected this contention and dismissed the appeal, observing that H's housing stock 'was not available to the community of St Helens at large' and finding that its principal aim had been to provide benefits for its existing tenants. The Upper Tribunal and the CA unanimously upheld this decision. Lloyd LJ held that H's objects were not limited 'to undertaking operations which are for the primary benefit of the community, to the exclusion of non-incidental benefit for individuals'. The provision 'of a housing stock available for occupation by tenants generally (rather than so as to relieve a charitable need)' did not qualify as a charitable purpose. Furthermore, 'the degree of individual benefit afforded by the provision of housing is so substantial that it cannot properly be regarded as subordinate to the public benefit of the availability of a stock of suitable housing. It is not sufficient that the operations of (H) should be required to be for the benefit of the community. They can qualify as such without being charitable. In order to be charitable the benefit provided must be of an appropriate kind, and this is not.' *Helena Partnerships Ltd (aka Helena Housing Ltd) v HMRC*, CA [2012] EWCA Civ 569; [2012] STC 1584; [2012] 4 All ER 111.

Trading by charities (ITA 2007, s 524; CTA 2010, s 478)

Colportage

[9.81] A society, founded for the diffusion of religious literature, sold books from shops in Edinburgh and Belfast and through 'colporteurs' who also acted as 'cottage missionaries'. The Edinburgh shop made a profit, but the colportage made a substantial loss. The Revenue issued an assessment charging income tax on the net profits from the shops. The society appealed, contending that the loss from the colportage should be set against the profits from the shops. The court rejected this contention and upheld the assessment, holding that the colportage was 'a charitable mission' and was not part of the society's trade of bookselling. *Religious Tract and Book Society of Scotland v Forbes*, CE 1896, 3 TC 415.

YMCA restaurant open to public

[9.82] The YMCA operated a restaurant which was open to the public. The Revenue issued an assessment charging income tax on the restaurant profits. The YMCA appealed, contending that the restaurant should be treated as an integral part of its other activities, and that it had made an overall loss. The KB upheld the assessment, applying the principles laid down in *Religious Tract and Book Society of Scotland v Forbes*, 9.81 above. *Grove v Young Men's Christian Association*, KB 1903, 4 TC 613.

Furnished letting of rooms for public use

[9.83] A hospital, which was accepted as being a charity, let a concert hall and a ballroom in an adjacent building for various forms of public entertainment. It also provided an attendant, who was required to ensure 'that no smoking or improper conduct is permitted at any entertainment or meeting'. The Revenue issued assessments taxing the profits as trading income. The hospital appealed, contending that the letting was not trading income, but was within Schedule A and exempt from income tax under the legislation then in force. The Special Commissioners rejected this contention and upheld the assessments, and the HL unanimously upheld their decision. Lord Birkenhead held that the letting was 'a business or a concern in the nature of business'. Accordingly the profits were within Schedule D rather than Schedule A, and did not qualify for exemption. *Governors of Rotunda Hospital Dublin v Coman*, HL 1920, 7 TC 517; [1921] 1 AC 1.

Hospital also operating private nursing home

[9.84] In an Irish case, a hospital, which was accepted as being a charity, also operated a private nursing home for fee-paying patients. The hospital and the nursing home were administered as one undertaking. The Revenue issued an assessment on the profits of the nursing home. The SC(I) upheld the assessment, holding that the operation of the nursing home amounted to carrying on a trade, and the fact that separate accounts were not kept was immaterial. (In the HC(I), Hanna J observed that 'the charity is for the sick poor' whereas the nursing home was 'for the sick rich'.) *Davis v Superioress Mater Misericordiae Hospital Dublin*, SC(I) 1933, 2 ITC 1; [1933] IR 503.

Convent school—whether nuns were 'beneficiaries of the charity'

[9.85] A convent operated a school. It claimed that its profits were exempt from income tax under what is now *CTA 2010, s 478*. The Revenue rejected the claim but the KB allowed the convent's appeal, holding that the nuns were 'beneficiaries of the charity', within what is now *CTA 2010, s 479(1)(b)*. Finlay J observed that the nuns were not simply teachers but had taken 'the vow of poverty' and were 'fed and clothed by the convent'. *Convent of the Blessed Sacrament Brighton v CIR*, KB 1933, 18 TC 76.

Weekly local dances

[9.86] A local committee of the British Legion organised weekly public dances, to raise money for the British Legion Remembrance Trust Fund. The Revenue assessed the profits under Schedule D Case I. The Legion appealed, contending firstly that the dances did not constitute a trade and alternatively that the profits should be treated as exempt under the legislation then in force. The Special Commissioners rejected these contentions and dismissed the appeal, and the CS upheld their decision as one of fact. *British Legion Peterhead Branch v CIR*, CS 1953, 35 TC 509. (*Note*. Lord Cooper observed that 'the enterprise was not conducted on an ordinary commercial basis' and that 'the actual receipts require to be considerably discounted'. For HMRC's practice following this decision, see Business Income Manual, BIM24475.)

Other cases

[9.87] See also *CIR v Glasgow Musical Association*, **9.10** above; *Royal Choral Society v CIR*, **9.11** above; *Dean Leigh Temperance Canteen Trustees v CIR*, **9.26** above, and *Pharmaceutical Society of Ireland v CIR*, **9.48** above.

Covenanted donations to charity

Whether covenant may be backdated

[9.88] Under a deed dated 3 February 1927, an individual (R) covenanted to make seven payments annually to a charity on 31 December each year 'during the term of the seven years from the 6 April 1926', the first payment to be made on 31 December 1926. In fact, the first payment was made on 4 February 1927. R withheld tax from his payments and the hostel claimed repayment. The Revenue rejected the claim on the grounds that the payments were for a period which could not exceed six years, so that the covenant was ineffective for tax purposes under the legislation then in force. The CA unanimously held that the covenant could not be backdated and that the hostel was not entitled to repayment. *CIR v The Hostel of St Luke (Trustees)*, CA 1930, 15 TC 682.

Whether deed may be rectified

[9.89] A company (R) executed a covenant in July 1988. The deed provided for the last payment to be made on 1 April 1991. Consequently the payments under the deed did not qualify as covenanted payments to charity, since the period for which they were payable did not exceed three years. R applied for an order to rectify the covenant so that the last payment would be made on 19 July 1991. The Ch D rejected the application and the CA dismissed R's appeal. Peter Gibson LJ held that the court would order rectification of a document if it was satisfied that it did not give effect to the true agreement of the parties and that there was an issue capable of being contested between the parties. However, an application had to be established by clear evidence, and the court could not rectify a document merely on the ground that it failed to achieve the desired fiscal objective. On the evidence, R had failed to establish to the required standard that the covenant had not given effect to the intentions of its financial controller. *Racal Group Services Ltd v Ashmore & Others*, CA 1995, 68 TC 86; [1995] STC 1151.

Application for rectification of deed of covenant

[9.90] An application for rectification of a deed of covenant was rejected in *Royal College of Veterinary Surgeons v Meldrum*, Sp C 1995, [1996] SSCD 54 (Sp C 60).

Assessments to recover gift aid relief

[9.91] From 2005 to 2008 a registered charity (S) reclaimed income tax of more than £200,000 in relation to purported 'gift aid' donations. HMRC subsequently formed the opinion that S was not entitled to the repayments, and issued assessments to recover the tax. S appealed, contending that the donations were genuine although the funds had been misappropriated by a company (D) which acted as a fundraiser. The First-tier Tribunal reviewed the evidence in detail and dismissed the appeal, finding that some of the alleged donors had specifically denied making any donations to S, and that S's company secretary was 'not a reliable witness', since many of his statements 'were inconsistent with each other or inconsistent with other evidence'. Judge Mosedale observed that 'it is improbable that individuals making generous gifts to a charity would pay the money to its fundraiser and not to an account in the name of the charity'. *Siri Ltd v HMRC*, FTT [2011] UKFTT 794 (TC), TC01630.

[9.92] A registered charity (OT) had two subsidiary companies, one of which operated a hotel. OT reclaimed gift aid relief in respect of donations which had been made to its two subsidiaries. When HMRC discovered this, they issued an assessment to recover the tax, on the basis that the payments had been made to the subsidiary companies, neither of which were charities, rather than to OT. The First-tier Tribunal upheld the assessment and dismissed OT's appeal. *Odyssey Tendercare Ltd v HMRC*, FTT [2012] UKFTT 539 (TC), TC02215.

Release of loans to charity—whether relief due

[9.93] Two individuals made loans to a charity's building fund. They subsequently wrote letters to the charity 'releasing' the loans and claimed relief under what is now *ITA 2007, s 414*. The Special Commissioner held that relief was not due, since the letters were not for consideration and were not under seal, and thus were 'mere promises, unenforceable at law, and incapable of amounting to gifts either of money or of anything else'. *Battle Baptist Church v CIR & Woodham*, Sp C [1995] SSCD 176 (Sp C 23).

Subscription to Masonic lodge—whether a 'qualifying donation'

[9.94] A freemason claimed that part of his subscriptions to his Masonic lodge should be treated as qualifying for gift aid relief. HMRC rejected his claim and he appealed. The First-tier Tribunal dismissed his appeal, holding that none of the subscription qualified for relief, since he had not made a gift to charity 'as an individual'. *W Osborne v HMRC*, FTT [2010] UKFTT 368 (TC), TC00650.

Variation of will in favour of charity

[9.95] The sole legatee under a will entered into a Deed of Variation, whereby £20,000 was bequeathed to a charity. The legatee claimed relief under what is now *ITA 2007, s 416*, and signed a form R190(SD) certifying that he had paid £26,666 (i.e. £20,000 grossed-up at 25%) to the charity. The charity claimed a repayment of £6,666, which the Revenue made. Subsequently the Revenue formed the opinion that the donation of £20,000 did not satisfy the requirements of *s 416* and thus was not a 'qualifying donation', on the basis that the legatee had saved inheritance tax of £8,000, and had therefore received a benefit in consequence of making it, so that the charity should not have received any repayment. They issued an assessment to recover the £6,666. The charity appealed, contending that the inheritance tax saving should not be treated as a benefit within *s 416(7)*. The Special Commissioner rejected this contention and dismissed the appeal, holding that since the legatee was 'the sole legatee or residuary beneficiary of the estate, he ultimately benefited from the inheritance tax saving'. Accordingly, the donation was not a qualifying donation within *s 416*. *St. Dunstan's v Major*, Sp C [1997] SSCD 212 (Sp C 127).

[9.96] The First-tier Tribunal reached a similar decision in *RM Harris v HMRC*, FTT [2010] UKFTT 385 (TC); [2010] SFTD 1159, TC00667.

ITA 2007, s 426(6)—election to carry back gift aid relief

[9.97] In 2005/06 a farmer (C) sold some of his assets. In August 2006 he submitted his 2005/06 tax return. In November 2006 he set up a charitable trust, and in January 2007 he made a substantial payment to the trustees. Later that month he submitted an amended 2005/06 tax return, claiming to carry back gift aid relief in respect of this payment against his income and gains for 2005/06. HMRC rejected the claim on the basis that the legislation specifically provided that such a claim could only be made in C's original return and could not be made in an amended return. The First-tier Tribunal dismissed C's appeal. Judge Hellier observed that 'common sense and fairness appear to be on the taxpayer's side', but held that the wording of the legislation was clear and unambiguous. The requirement that an election 'may not be made in an amendment to a return' might encourage 'delay in the delivery of returns', but this was 'not absurdity in the sense of a result wholly inconsistent with the aim of encouraging charitable giving. It is in the circumstances an odd stipulation and one for which no clear policy may be evident, but that is not the same as absurdity or repugnance.' *J Cameron v HMRC*, FTT [2010] SFTD 664; [2010] UKFTT 104 (TC), TC00415.

Miscellaneous matters

Whether trust established in UK

[9.98] A charitable trust was established under the will of a testator domiciled in Canada. Two of the three trustees were resident in the UK and the trustees claimed exemption from UK tax. The Revenue rejected the claim on the grounds that that exemption applied only to charitable trusts established in the UK, and that the trust in question was established outside the UK. The KB held that the trust was entitled to exemption. Lawrence J held that, although exemption only applied to trusts established in the UK, the trust in question was established in the UK. *CIR v Gull*, KB 1937, 21 TC 374; [1937] 4 All ER 290.

Overseas trusts

[9.99] A foundation for the advancement of chemistry, etc., incorporated in the USA, received income from UK royalties. It claimed a repayment of the tax deducted from this income. The Revenue rejected the claim and the foundation appealed. The HL unanimously dismissed the appeal. Lord Morton of Henryton held that relief for charities was 'limited to bodies of persons or trusts established in the United Kingdom'. *Camille & Henry Dreyfus Foundation Inc. v CIR*, HL 1955, 36 TC 126; [1956] AC 39; [1955] 3 All ER 97.

[9.100] The decision in *Camille & Henry Dreyfus Foundation Inc. v CIR*, 9.99 above, was applied in a subsequent case where the Special Commissioner held that trusts established in Guernsey and Jersey were 'not charitable for United Kingdom tax law'. *Civil Engineer v CIR*, Sp C 2001, [2002] SSCD 72 (Sp C 299). (*Note.* For another issue in this case, see **48.48** RESIDENCE, ORDINARY RESIDENCE AND DOMICILE.)

[9.101] The Ch D reached a similar decision, also applying *Camille & Henry Dreyfus Foundation Inc. v CIR*, **9.99** above, in *Routier & Venables (Coulter's Executors) v HMRC*, **72.28** INHERITANCE TAX.

Funds donated from one charity to another and accumulated

[9.102] Two companies (H and S), registered as charities, had been set up in tandem by a married couple. The main function of H was to raise funds for S. H donated its income and gains to S, and claimed relief from tax. The Revenue rejected the claim in relation to sums which S had retained, considering that, since S had not distributed the funds, they had not been applied for charitable purposes. The Special Commissioners allowed H's appeal and the CA upheld their decision. *CIR v Helen Slater Charitable Trust Ltd*, CA 1981, 55 TC 230; [1981] STC 471; [1981] 3 WLR 377; [1981] 3 All ER 98. (*Note.* See now, however, *CTA 2010, s 474*, deriving from *FA 1986*.)

Payments to charities—whether tax deductible

[9.103] See the cases noted at **2.16** *et seq.* ANNUAL PAYMENTS.

Non-charitable payments out of trust income—copyright royalties

[9.104] An individual assigned copyright royalties under a publishing agreement to trustees, directing them to make certain non-charitable payments and to apply any balance of the trust income for specified charitable purposes. The

Revenue issued assessments on the trustees, charging income tax on the net royalties under Schedule D Case VI. They appealed, contending that, because they had spent a proportion of the trust income for charitable purposes, they should be entitled to a repayment of the equivalent proportion of the tax. The KB rejected this contention and dismissed the appeal, holding that the income was not 'applicable to charitable purposes only'. *Lawrence & Others v CIR*, KB 1940, 23 TC 333.

ITA 2007, s 431—relief for gifts of shares to charities

[9.105] An individual (G) made two gifts of 118,750 shares in a company (C) to two major charities. He claimed relief of £237,500 under *ITA 2007, s 431*, on the basis that the shares had a market value of £1 each. HMRC issued an amendment to G's return, restricting the relief to £71,250 on the basis that the shares had a market value of 30p each. G appealed. The First-tier Tribunal reviewed the evidence in detail and allowed his appeal in part, holding that the shares should be valued at 35p each, so that the 'relievable amount' under *ITA 2007, s 434* was £83,125. *N Green v HMRC*, FTT [2014] UKFTT 396 (TC), TC03525.

[9.106] An individual (F) entered into a scheme designed to exploit the provisions in what is now *ITA 2007, s 431 et seq* providing for relief for gifts of shares to charity. He purchased securities with a market value of about £500,000 and transferred them to a charitable trust (S). In accordance with a previous agreement, S then transferred 99% of the value of the securities to a non-charitable trust (M) for the benefit of F and his family. F claimed relief under what is now *s 431*. HMRC rejected the claim on the basis that the effect of the Ramsay principle (see **58.6** TAX PLANNING AND AVOIDANCE) was that there was a single composite transaction under which F should be treated as having transferred 99% of the value of the securities to M rather than to S. The First-tier Tribunal dismissed F's appeal, applying the principles laid down by Lewison J in *Berry v HMRC*, **52.72** SAVINGS AND INVESTMENT INCOME. Judge Poole held that F had not 'disposed of the whole of the beneficial interest' in the securities to S. By the time he had disposed of the securities, there was 'an expectation' that an option would be exercised whereby S would end up with only 1% of the value of the securities, and 'there was no likelihood in practice of any other result'. Therefore 99% of the disposal made by F 'was to (M) via (S), and not to (S) itself'. Judge Poole observed that the transaction whereby S received 1% of the value of the securities 'was a fiercely-negotiated arm's length transaction. In exchange for the agreed 1% "turn" and other payment, (S) agreed to participate in the appellant's tax avoidance arrangements, allowing its charitable status to be used as the crucial heart of those arrangements. This may well open up other issues for (S), but such matters are beyond the scope of this appeal.' Neither the disposal of 99% of the value of the securities to M, or the disposal of 1% of the value of the securities to S, qualified for relief under what is now *s 431*. *W Ferguson v HMRC*, FTT [2014] UKFTT 433 (TC); [2014] SFTD 934, TC03562.

10

Claims to Relief or Repayment

The cases in this chapter are arranged under the following headings.

NOTE

See also 1 ALLOWANCES AND TAX RATES, 24 ERROR OR MISTAKE RELIEF, and 32 INTEREST ON OVERPAID TAX.

Time limits for claims

TMA 1970, s 43

[10.1] In a case concerning Schedule A provisions which have been superseded by subsequent changes in the legislation, the CS held (by a 2-1 majority, Lord Clyde dissenting) that the General Commissioners had no jurisdiction to extend the time limit laid down by what is now *TMA 1970, s 43*. *Bulkeley-Gavin v CIR*, CS 1965, 42 TC 320.

TMA 1970, Sch 1AB, para 3

[10.2] In 2011 a taxpayer (L) claimed a repayment of tax which had been deducted under PAYE in 2002/03. HMRC rejected the claim on the grounds that it had been made outside the statutory time limit, The First-tier Tribunal dismissed L's appeal against this decision. Judge Poole held that, since the claim had been made after March 2010, it was subject to the time limits laid down by *TMA 1970, Sch 1AB*. The claim was clearly outside the four-year time limit laid down by *Sch 1AB para 3(1)*. *A Lauricella v HMRC*, FTT [2012] UKFTT 542 (TC), TC02218.

[10.3] In 2012 a doctor (N) claimed relief under *TMA 1970, Sch 1AB* for 2006/07. HMRC rejected the claim on the grounds that N's 2006/07 return had been submitted online in February 2008, so that it was outside the time laid down by *Sch 1AB para 3*. The First-tier Tribunal dismissed N's appeal. Judge Porter held that the case fell within *Sch 1AB para 2(4)*, and observed that 'four years is more than enough time for her to have taken action, which she has chosen not to do'. *Dr O Nwisi v HMRC*, FTT [2013] UKFTT 733 (TC), TC03110.

[10.4] Judge Mure reached a similar decision in *J Bbosa v HMRC*, FTT [2014] UKFTT 694 (TC), TC03815.

[10.5] Judge Brooks reached a similar decision in *Dr V Raftopoulou v HMRC*, FTT [2014] UKFTT 818 (TC), TC03935.

Limitation Act 1980

[10.6] In the case noted at **25.18** EUROPEAN LAW, two groups of companies had claimed repayments of ACT on the basis that the UK legislation in force at the relevant time constituted discrimination contrary to what is now *Article 43EC* of the *EC Treaty*. The CJEC upheld this contention. One of the companies (H) had submitted a claim covering for the years 1989 to 1994, but had failed to make a subsequent claim covering a payment which it made in July 1995. In 2003 it applied to amend its claim to include this payment. The Ch D rejected the application. Park J held that the effect of the *Limitation Act 1980* was that the six-year time limit had expired, and the court had no discretion to permit an amendment of the claim. *Hoechst UK Ltd v CIR*, Ch D [2003] EWHC 1002 (Ch); [2004] STC 1486.

[10.7] Following the ECJ decision in *Metalgesellschaft Ltd & Others v CIR*, **25.18** EUROPEAN LAW, a UK subsidiary of a German company claimed a repayment of advance corporation tax which it had paid between 1993 and 1996. The Revenue agreed to repay the ACT which the company had paid within six years of the claim, but refused to repay the ACT which it had paid more than six years before, on the grounds that repayment was barred by *Limitation Act 1980, s 2*. The HL allowed the company's appeal (by a 4-1 majority, Lord Scott of Foscote dissenting). Lord Hope of Craighead held that, applying the principles laid down by Lord Goff in *Kleinwort Benson Ltd v Lincoln City Council*, HL [1998] 3 WLR 1095; [1998] 4 All ER 513, the right to recover payments made under a mistake of law 'extends to the payment of taxes made to the Revenue on the mistaken belief that they were due and payable'. Furthermore, 'the enrichment of a public authority because a payment was made to it in response to a demand in the mistaken belief that the law under which the demand was made was the law is no less unjust than an enrichment arising from a mistake of law in a private transaction'. Accordingly, the effect of *Limitation Act 1980, s 32(1)(c)* was that the limitation period had not begun until 8 March 2001 (the date of the ECJ decision in *Metalgesellschaft Ltd & Others v CIR*). *Deutsche Morgan Grenfell Group plc v HMRC (and cross-appeal)*, HL 2006, 78 TC 120; [2007] STC 1; [2006] UKHL 49; [2007] 1 All ER 449. (*Note.* See now, however, *FA 2004, s 320* and *FA 2007, s 107*. For a case concerning *FA 2004, s 320*, see *Europcar UK Ltd & Others v HMRC*, **10.9** below. For cases concerning *FA 2007, s 107*, see *Test Claimants in the FII Group Litigation v HMRC (No 3)*, **25.93** EUROPEAN LAW, and *European Commission v United Kingdom (No 3)*, **25.155** EUROPEAN LAW.)

[10.8] See also *Trustees of BT Pension Scheme v HMRC (and related appeals)*, **18.98** CORPORATION TAX.

Whether FA 2004, s 320 applicable

[10.9] In nineteen cases where the facts were broadly similar to those in *Deutsche Morgan Grenfell Group plc v HMRC*, **10.7** above, the companies had submitted claims for repayment of ACT under *Civil Procedure Rules 1998 (SI 1998/3132)* before 8 September 2003 (the date on which *FA 2004, s 320* came into force). However, the companies had subsequently amended the wording of their claims. The Ch D reviewed the evidence in detail and held that eighteen of the claims were unaffected by the restriction in *FA 2004, s 320*, since the claimants had previously indicated that the claims were based on the principle of mistake of law. However, the claim submitted by the remaining company (H) had been 'a remarkably obscure and uninformative document' which was 'inadequate to raise a case of mistake-based restitution'. On the evidence, H had not previously indicated that it was submitting a claim based on the principle of mistake of law, and the amendments which it had made after 8 September 2003 had amounted to the submission of a new claim, which fell within the restrictions imposed by *FA 2004, s 320*. Accordingly, H could not reclaim ACT which it had paid more than six years before the submission of its original claim in January 2001. *Europcar UK Ltd & Others v HMRC (re ACT Group Litigation)*, Ch D [2008] STC 2751; [2008] EWHC 1363 (Ch).

[10.10] Following the decision noted at **10.9** above, H appealed to the CA. While the appeal was pending, the Ch D gave judgment in *Test Claimants in the FII Group Litigation v HMRC*, **25.88** EUROPEAN LAW, holding that *FA 2004, s 320* contravened European law. Following this decision, H applied to the Ch D for an interim repayment. The Ch D granted the application. Henderson J ordered that H should receive an interim payment of the full amount claimed (approximately £505,000). *Heidelberg Graphic Equipment Ltd v HMRC (and related application)*, Ch D [2009] STC 2334; [2009] EWHC 870 (Ch).

Miscellaneous

Restitutionary claim under common law—TMA 1970, s 33(2A)

[10.11] See *Monro v HMRC*, **24.4** ERROR OR MISTAKE RELIEF.

Repayment claim—TMA 1970, Sch 1AB para 3

[10.12] A hairdresser (S) submitted a 2008/09 tax return showing taxable profits of £9,916. In 2011 she submitted a repayment claim, stating that she had overstated her turnover by £10,000. HMRC rejected the claim and the First-tier Tribunal dismissed S's appeal. Judge Poole observed that S had failed to produce 'any business records or any clear and satisfactory explanation of how the turnover was supposedly overstated in her original return'. *Ms J Simpson v HMRC*, FTT [2013] UKFTT 665 (TC), TC03047.

[10.13] A woman (S) submitted a 2005/06 tax return showing a substantial capital gain from a disposal of shares in a company, of which she had been the company secretary. In 2009 she wrote to HMRC claiming a refund and alleging that the transaction had been carried out by her former husband. HMRC rejected the claim and S appealed. The First-tier Tribunal dismissed her appeal. Judge Walters found on the balance of probabilities that S had been the beneficial owner of the shares. *Ms SN Sehgal v HMRC*, FTT [2013] UKFTT 673 (TC), TC03055.

[10.14] A financial adviser (M) claimed overpayment relief, contending that his accounts had failed to include a deduction for commission which he had paid to his son. HMRC rejected the claim and the First-tier Tribunal dismissed M's appeal, finding that he had failed to produce sufficient evidence to justify the claim. *BJ Melling v HMRC*, FTT [2014] UKFTT 008 (TC), TC03149.

[10.15] An individual (P) took proceedings in the Employment Tribunal against a company (W), claiming that he had not been paid £18,000. The Employment Tribunal gave judgment for P, but W did not comply with the judgment. P submitted a tax return for 2006/07, including the salary of £18,000 and claiming a repayment on the basis that W should be treated as having withheld tax of £5,400. HMRC rejected the claim and the First-tier Tribunal dismissed P's appeal. Judge Nowlan held that 'any claim for a repayment of tax for the year 2006/07 was not a proper claim since there was no evidence at all that any tax had ben paid or suffered'. *J Partridge v HMRC*, FTT [2014] UKFTT 828 (TC), TC03946.

[10.16] See also *Lauricella v HMRC*, **10.2** above.

Special relief—claim under TMA 1970, Sch 1AB para 3A

[10.17] In a Northern Ireland case, an individual (M) failed to submit returns for 2006/07 and 2007/08. In 2009 HMRC issued determinations. In July 2012 M submitted the returns, showing a lower tax liability. In August 2012 he submitted a claim for special relief under *TMA 1970, Sch 1AB*, stating that he had relied on his previous accountant to submit the returns, but that accountant had been in poor health (and had died in June 2012). HMRC rejected the claim but the First-tier Tribunal allowed M's appeal. Judge Rankin found that M had believed that his previous accountant was 'handling his affairs in a correct manner' and 'was unaware of his agent's serious medical condition'. He held that the conditions of *Sch 1AB, para 3A(4)* were satisfied. *W Maxwell v HMRC*, FTT [2013] UKFTT 459 (TC), TC02849. (*Note. Obiter dicta* of Judge Rankin were disapproved by Judge Redston in the subsequent case of *Currie v HMRC*, **10.18** below.)

[10.18] A self-employed barrister's clerk (C), who owned at least three properties, failed to submit returns for 2005/06 and 2006/07. HMRC issued determinations charging tax of £10,000 for each year. In 2012 C claimed special relief under *TMA 1970, Sch 1AB*, contending that the determinations were excessive. HMRC rejected the claims and the First-tier Tribunal dismissed C's appeal, holding that the determinations had been reasonable. Judge Redston observed that C had 'significant assets and does not keep proper books and records'. Accordingly it was not unreasonable for HMRC to enforce the determinations. *DF Currie v HMRC*, FTT [2014] UKFTT 882 (TC); [2015] SFTD 51, TC03997.

TMA 1970, Sch 1A—claims, etc. not included in returns

[10.19] See *Forthright (Wales) Ltd v Davies*, **23.10** ENTERPRISE INVESTMENT SCHEME.

TMA 1970, Sch 1B—claims for relief involving two or more years

[10.20] See *Norton v Thompson*, 35.3 LOSS RELIEF.

Incorrect repayment claim—validity of subsequent assessment

[10.21] See *Osborne v Dickinson*, 5.22 ASSESSMENT.

Tax deducted from payments to subcontractors

[10.22] See *Hudson Contract Services Ltd v HMRC (No 2)*, 16.55 CONSTRUCTION INDUSTRY.

Group relief—form of claim

[10.23] See *Gallic Leasing Ltd v Coburn*, 18.61 CORPORATION TAX, and *Farmer v Bankers Trust International Ltd*, 18.62 CORPORATION TAX.

Tax withheld from annual payments made in arrear

[10.24] See *CIR v Crawley & Others*, 20.47 DEDUCTION OF TAX.

Rent-a-Room relief (ITTOIA 2005, ss 784-802)

[10.25] A woman (W) submitted returns claiming rent-a-room relief under *ITTOIA 2005, s 784 et seq*. HMRC issued assessments, and imposed penalties under *TMA 1970, s 95*, on the basis that the income did not qualify for relief. W appealed. The First-tier Tribunal dismissed the appeal, finding that the property concerned was not W's only or main residence, as required by *ITTOIA 2005, s 786(1)*. *Ms M Woods v HMRC*, FTT [2011] UKFTT 663 (TC), TC01505.

11

Close Companies (CTA 2010, ss 438–465)

The cases in this chapter are arranged under the following headings.

Basic definitions (CTA 2010, ss 439–454)

CTA 2010, s 451—attribution of rights and powers of trustees

[11.1] A company (N) was controlled by trustees of a will trust, in which the deceased's widow (W) had a life interest. N was entitled to small companies' relief. The Revenue restricted the relief on the basis that N was an associated company of L, a company controlled by the trustees of a discretionary trust set up by W's late husband. The trustees of both the will trust and the discretionary trust were 'associates' of W, and the Revenue attributed the trustees' rights and powers to W under what is now *CTA 2010, s 451*, so that she was taken to have both companies under her control for the purposes of what is now *CTA 2010, s 450*. N applied for judicial review, contending that the Revenue had a discretion whether to exercise the power of attribution. The HL found in favour of the Revenue (reversing the decision of the CA and restoring that of the QB). Lord Scott of Foscote held that 'when the circumstances of a particular person are being examined in order to determine whether that person has control of a particular company, that person "shall be taken" to have control if any of the possible *subsection (6)* attributions give him or her control'. *R v CIR (ex p. Newfields Developments Ltd),* HL 2001, 73 TC 532; [2001] STC 901; [2001] 1 WLR 1111; [2001] 4 All ER 400.

[11.2] 71% of the shares in a company (G) were held by the same shareholder (D). In 1987 D and his wife established a settlement for the benefit of their three children. This settlement acquired 99% of the shares in another company (S). The Revenue issued corporation tax assessments on the basis that G and S were associated. The Special Commissioners upheld the assessments, holding that the effect of what is now *CTA 2010, s 448(1)* was that D, and the trustees of the settlement he had established, were 'associates'. Accordingly, by virtue of what is now *CTA 2010, s 451*, D was deemed to have control of S as well as of G, and the two companies were associated for the purposes of the legislation. The Ch D upheld the Commissioners' decision. *Gascoines Group Ltd & Others v HM Inspector of Taxes,* Ch D 2004, 76 TC 623; [2004] STC 844; [2004] EWHC 640 (Ch).

CTA 2010, s 448(1)—whether co-trustees are 'associates'

[11.3] A close company had borrowed money from one of its shareholders, who had subsequently died. His estate, including the shares in the company, had not been administered. There were three executors, one of whom was a participator in the company. The Ch D held that the effect of what is now *CTA 2010, s 448(1)* was that the other two executors were his associates, and the CA unanimously upheld this decision. Consequently, the interest which the company paid to the executors was, under the law in force at the time, a distribution and was not deductible as a charge on income. *Willingale v Islington Green Investment Co,* CA 1972, 48 TC 547; [1972] 1 WLR 1533; [1972] 3 All ER 849.

Charges to tax in connection with loans (CTA 2010, ss 455–464)

Failure to notify liability under CTA 2010, s 455

[11.4] A close company (E) received income from investments in property. Its controlling director was a married woman, and the company's consultancy work and rent collection were undertaken by her husband. The fees for such work were collected by the husband, and paid to E annually in arrear. The Revenue considered that the payments were a loan to an associate of a participator in E, and gave rise to a liability under what is now *CTA 2010, s 455*. In addition, the Revenue considered that E had been guilty of neglect in failing to notify its chargeability to tax under *s 455*, and charged interest accordingly. The General Commissioners held that E had been guilty of neglect, and confirmed the interest charges. E appealed, contending that there was no statutory requirement for it to notify liability under *s 455*. The Ch D rejected this contention and upheld the interest charges for the accounting periods ending in 1984 to 1986 inclusive, and the CA unanimously upheld this decision. *TMA 1970, s 109* applied the corporation tax provisions to tax under *s 455*. E was required to notify any liability under *s 455* in addition to notifying its chargeability to corporation tax. *Earlspring Properties Ltd v Guest,* CA 1995, 67 TC 259; [1995] STC 479. (*Notes.* (1) Interest charges for accounting periods ending in 1982 and 1983, where the loans had been repaid before the issue of the relevant assessments, were discharged by virtue of the provisions of *ICTA 1970, s 286(5)* as originally enacted. However, the relevant provision was amended by *FA 1986* with regard to loans or advances made after 18 March 1986, so that it appears that the interest charges would now be valid notwithstanding the repayment of the loans. (2) For another issue in this case, not taken to the CA, see **63.171** TRADING PROFITS.)

[11.5] A close company failed to notify chargeability under what is now *CTA 2010, s 455*, and the Revenue charged interest. The company appealed, contending that there was no statutory obligation to notify liability under *s 455*. The Ch D rejected this contention and upheld the interest charges, holding that the effect of *TMA 1970, s 109* was that a close company was obliged to notify the Revenue of its liability to tax in connection with loans to participators. *Joint v Bracken Developments Ltd,* Ch D 1994, 66 TC 560; [1994] STC 300.

[11.6] Appeals against determinations charging interest under *TMA 1970, s 88* on liability under what is now *CTA 2010, s 455* were dismissed in *Euro Fire Ltd v Davison,* CA 1999, 71 TC 535; [1999] STC 1050. (*Note.* Appeals against assessments under what is now *ITEPA 2003, s 175* were also dismissed—see **22.159** EMPLOYMENT INCOME.)

CTA 2010, s 455—assessments on undeclared profits

[11.7] The Revenue formed the opinion that a close company, which carried on a 'cash and carry' business, had underdeclared substantial amounts of takings. They issued estimated corporation tax assessments, and also issued assessments under what is now *CTA 2010, s 455*, on the basis that the underdeclared takings had been loaned or advanced to the directors. The Special Commissioners upheld the assessments and dismissed the company's appeals, finding on the evidence that there had been 'numerous "incidents" which enable us to infer that the company and its directors were committing fraud on the Inland Revenue on a massive scale' and that 'considerable loans were made to the directors in excess of the returns in the accounts'. *Khera's Emporium Ltd v Marshall (and related appeals),* Sp C [1998] SSCD 206 (Sp C 167). (*Note.* Appeals against determinations under *reg 49* of the *Income Tax (Employments) Regulations 1993 (SI 1993/744)*, charging tax on wages paid to employees from which PAYE had not been deducted, were also dismissed.)

[11.8] HMRC formed the opinion that a close company (P) had underdeclared its profits. They issued discovery assessments, and also issued assessments under what is now *CTA 2010, s 455*, on the basis that the underdeclared takings had been loaned or advanced to P's controlling director. The First-tier Tribunal reviewed the evidence in detail and upheld the assessments in principle, while reducing the amounts. Judge Barton found that the director's evidence was 'less than credible'. *Powerlaunch Ltd v HMRC*, FTT [2011] UKFTT 583 (TC), TC01426.

[11.9] HMRC issued assessments under what is now *CTA 2010, s 455* on a company which operated a lap-dancing club. The First-tier Tribunal upheld the assessments. Judge Mure observed that treating the additional takings as having been loaned to the directors, rather than as fees or dividends, produced 'a more favourable practical result' for the directors. *Risky Business Ltd v HMRC*, FTT [2012] UKFTT 751 (TC), TC02408.

[11.10] See also *Easow v HMRC*, **29.10** FRAUDULENT OR NEGLIGENT CONDUCT; *Cooksey v HMRC*, **29.66** FRAUDULENT OR NEGLIGENT CONDUCT; *Rhodes v HMRC*, **44.153** PENALTIES, and *TSD Design Development Engineering Ltd v HMRC*, **44.171** PENALTIES.

Money withdrawn from company account by director/shareholder

[11.11] In 2004 an unmarried couple (S and J) incorporated a company (M) to carry out construction work. J owned 51% of the shares, while S owned 49% of the shares and controlled M's finances. In 2008 S and J separated. S withdrew more than £110,000 from M's bank accounts. He also sold M's van and used the proceeds to buy a car which he registered in his own name. HMRC issued an amendment to M's self-assessment for the year ended March 2009, charging tax under *CTA 2010, s 455* on the amounts which S had withdrawn from M. The First-tier Tribunal dismissed M's appeal against this amendment. Judge Aleksander observed that the effect of the decision in *Bamford v ATA Advertising Ltd*, **63.150** TRADING PROFITS, was that M was not entitled to a deduction for the amounts which S had withdrawn. *Mirror Image Contracting Ltd v HMRC*, FTT [2012] UKFTT 679 (TC), TC02350.

Payment by service company of expenses of director's business

[11.12] The expenses of an estate agency were paid by a service company, of which the estate agent was the controlling director. The Revenue issued assessments under what is now *CTA 2010, s 455*, charging tax in respect of these payments. The company appealed, contending firstly that the service fees did not fall due for payment until such time as the company's accountants or auditors notified the company and the director of the final annual calculation of the charge, and secondly that there was no 'debt' within the meaning of *s 455*. The Special Commissioner rejected these contentions and dismissed the appeals, finding that 'the amount of the fee was initially and contractually agreed to be the amount of the relevant costs plus a mark-up of approximately one-ninth of the relevant costs'. On the evidence, a liability arose 'as soon as the service company incurs cost in providing the relevant services to the business'. The liability under *s 455* was not affected by the fact that, during the period covered by the assessments, the director and the company entered into a limited partnership agreement. The Ch D upheld this decision. Pumfrey J held that the words 'incurs a debt' in what is now *s 455(4)* covered 'the point in time at which the debtor became legally committed to some future expenditure, albeit unascertained'. Applying the principles laid down in *O'Driscoll v Manchester Insurance Committee*, CA [1915] 3 KB 499, it followed that the director had incurred a debt to the close company. *Andrew Grant Services Ltd v Watton (aka HCB Ltd v HM Inspector of Taxes)*, Ch D 1999, 71 TC 333; [1999] STC 330. (*Note*. An appeal by the director against assessments under what is now *ITEPA 2003, s 173* was also dismissed—see **22.154** EMPLOYMENT INCOME.)

Company operating 'employee participation scheme'—whether making loans to participators

[11.13] A company (AC) operated an 'employee participation scheme', designed to give shares to 'selected key employees'. Such employees entered into a 'facility agreement'. HMRC considered that the effect of the agreement was that the employees became indebted to the company. They issued assessments charging tax under what is now *CTA 2010, s 455*. AC appealed, contending that the effect of the HL decision in *Potts' Executors v CIR*, **56.69** SETTLEMENTS, was that it should not be treated as having made loans to the employees. The First-tier Tribunal rejected this contention and dismissed the appeals, finding that the effect of the agreement was that AC 'agreed with each employee to purchase shares on the employee's behalf from the trustee using the appellant's money, which money the employee agreed to repay at a later (uncertain) date'. Judge Mosedale observed that the tribunal should not 'give a strained and unnatural reading of "debt" to compensate for a wide definition of "participator" resulting in situations being caught by the anti-avoidance provision which may not have been the object of the anti-avoidance legislation'. The Upper Tribunal upheld this decision, unanimously declining to follow obiter dicta of Lord Simonds in *Potts' Executors v CIR*, on the grounds that Lord Simonds had adopted 'a literal approach to construction of the legislation', which had subsequently been rejected by the HL in *Barclays Mercantile Business Finance Ltd v Mawson*, **8.101** CAPITAL ALLOWANCES. The arrangements here constituted 'the making of loans to the employees', and the employees had incurred a debt to the company. *Aspect Capital Ltd v HMRC*, UT [2014] UKUT 81 (TCC); [2014] STC 1360.

Company director subscribing for shares and failing to pay

[11.14] In 2000 a US citizen (G) agreed to subscribe for a controlling shareholding in a UK company (R), paying in four annual instalments. G failed to make these payments. HMRC issued an assessment charging tax under what is now *CTA 2010, s 455*. R appealed, contending that *s 455* should not be treated as applying to a subscription for shares by someone who was not already a 'participator' in the company. Judge Connell accepted this contention and allowed the appeal, distinguishing the FTT decision in *Aspect Capital Ltd v HMRC*, **11.13** above, because that case concerned the grant of additional shares to existing participators, and holding that 'securing control of a close company is not within the contextual or purposive meaning of incurring a "debt"'. *RKW Ltd v HMRC*, FTT [2014] UKFTT 151 (TC), TC03289.

CTA 2010, s 456(1)—whether business 'includes the lending of money'

[11.15] In a non-tax case, Viscount Radcliffe held that '"the lending of money", to be part of the ordinary business of a company, must be what may be called a lending of money in general, in the sense, for example, that moneylending is part of the ordinary business of a registered moneylender or bank'. *Steen v Law*, PC [1963] AC 287; [1963] 3 All ER 770. (*Note*. For the Revenue's practice following this decision, see Revenue Tax Bulletin February 1992, p 14. They accepted that a single loan to a participator, even where it was made on commercial terms, would not of itself be evidence of the existence of a commercially constituted business of lending money.)

[11.16] In a Northern Ireland case, a close company (D) lent £30,000 to its chairman in 1997. The Revenue issued an assessment under what is now *CTA 2010, s 455*. D appealed, contending that the loan had been 'in the ordinary course of a business carried on by it which includes the lending of money'. The CA unanimously rejected this contention and upheld the assessment. Carswell LCJ held that the statutory phrase 'a business carried on by it which includes the lending of money' required 'a certain regularity of recurrence of such transactions'. D had made 'loans on some eight occasions over a period of 14 years to one associate of a participator'. This was not 'capable of amounting to a business'. The fact that the chairman 'did not seek or obtain any tax advantage from the transaction' was not conclusive. *Brennan v The Deanby Investment Co Ltd*, CA(NI) 2001, 73 TC 455; [2001] STC 536.

CTA 2010, s 456(5)—whether director worked full-time

[11.17] In a profits tax appeal, the issue was whether a company director (who was a 71-year old widow) was required to devote substantially the whole of her time to the company's service in more than half the relevant year. On the evidence she usually worked for a normal working day on each Tuesday, Thursday and Friday, and in the year she worked for 168 days out of a possible maximum 286 working days (counting Saturdays as half days) or 312 working days (counting Saturdays as whole days). The CA(NI) held that, in applying the legislation, intermittent periods could not be aggregated. Although she was rather more than a half-time 'working director' for the whole year, she was not a full-time 'working director' for more than half the year. *CIR v D Devine & Sons Ltd*, CA(NI) 1963, 41 TC 210. (*Note*. The relevant legislation, *FA 1937, Sch 4 para 11* as substituted by *FA 1952, s 34*, has no counterpart in current income tax legislation. However, the case may still be relevant with regard to *CTA 2010, s 456(5)* and *ITEPA 2003, s 67(3)*. HMRC cite the case as an authority in their Employment Income Manual, para EIM20202.)

Miscellaneous

Release from liability to repay loan

[11.18] See *Collins v Addies* and *Greenfield v Bains*, **52.66** SAVINGS AND INVESTMENT INCOME.

12

Company Distributions (CTA 2010, ss 997–1117)

The cases in this chapter are arranged under the following headings.

Taxation of distributions (CTA 2009, s 1258)

Interpretation of CTA 2009, s 1258

[12.1] In 1995 a company (C) purchased 89,700 of its own shares from another company (S). S appealed against a CT assessment for the relevant period, contending that the effect of what is now *CTA 2009, s 1258* was that the consideration should not be treated as chargeable to corporation tax. The Special Commissioners rejected this contention and dismissed the appeal, and the CA unanimously upheld the Commissioners' decision. Carnwath LJ held that *s 1258* should be construed as preventing the imposition of 'a tax which is directly charged on the dividends as such, rather than indirectly as part of the computation of a taxable amount'. *Strand Options & Futures Ltd v Vojak*, CA 2003, 76 TC 220; [2004] STC 64; [2003] EWCA Civ 1457. (*Note*. In the report in HMSO Tax Cases, the company is incorrectly referred to as 'Strand Futures & Options Ltd'. Companies House have confirmed that the company's correct name is 'Strand Options & Futures Ltd'.)

Definition of distributions (CTA 2010, ss 998–1028)

Whether and when distribution made

[12.2] A company (J) had lent more than £60,000 to its three directors. In 1966/67 it sold some surplus assets, and in August 1968 its annual general meeting approved draft accounts showing a capital distribution in place of the previous loans. The Revenue issued alternative assessments for 1967/68 and 1968/69 (under Schedule F in accordance with the legislation then in force) on the basis that J had made a distribution. J appealed, contending firstly that it had not made a distribution and alternatively that if it had done so, the distribution had occurred in 1966/67. The Special Commissioners rejected these contentions and upheld the 1968/69 assessment, finding that J had made a distribution in August 1968. The CS unanimously upheld their decision as one of fact. Lord Emslie held that the Commissioners 'were entitled to take the view that the date of the distribution could only be the date on which the company authorised the making of the distribution, which would not become due or payable at any earlier time'. *John Paterson (Motors) Ltd v CIR*, CS 1977, 52 TC 39; [1978] STC 59.

Company writing off loan and transferring property to shareholder

[12.3] See *Cassell v Crutchfield (No 2)*, 52.57 SAVINGS AND INVESTMENT INCOME.

Gifts by company to charity—CTA 2010, s 1020

[12.4] The controlling director of a company (N) died in 1999. Her executors established a charity (F), to which they transferred her shares in N. N subsequently agreed to make substantial donations to F, and claimed that these should be deducted in computing its profits. The Revenue rejected the claim on the basis that the payments were distributions 'in respect of shares' within what is now *CTA 2010, s 1000*. N appealed, contending that the payments fell within what is now *CTA 2010, s 1020*, and were exempt under what became *CTA 2010, s 1021*. The Special Commissioners accepted this contention and allowed the appeal, rejecting the Revenue's contention that *ss 1020, 1021* were limited to bilateral transactions, and holding that they 'applied to a transaction under which an asset (or a liability) was transferred without any *quid pro quo* moving to the company as well as to a bilateral transaction in which there is a transfer to, as well as by the company'. Accordingly the payments were within *s 1021*, and were deductible in computing N's profits. *Noved Investment Company v HMRC*, Sp C [2006] SSCD 120 (Sp C 521). (Note. See now *CTA 2010, s 1020(2A)*, introduced by *FA 2012* to replace *CTA 2010, s 1021* for distributions made on or after 17 July 2012.)

Payment of dividends from funds provided by parent company

[12.5] In 1989 a company (C) acquired another company (L) and its five subsidiaries. One of these subsidiaries (E) suffered significant losses and became 'technically insolvent', and the companies entered into a scheme designed to enable E and the other subsidiaries to carry back ACT against corporation tax which they had paid for previous years. The share capital of L and E was significantly increased by the issue of new shares to C and L respectively, and was then reduced to create reserves against which the companies' accumulated deficits could be offset. Three days after the reductions in capital, C made cash gifts to L's five subsidiaries, which then paid dividends, in amounts slightly smaller than the cash gifts, to L. L then paid a dividend to C, which was identical in amount to the dividends which it had received from the subsidiaries. The dividends paid by the subsidiaries to L gave rise to a liability to pay ACT of £3,110,666. The subsidiaries made claims to recover corporation tax of the same aggregate amount. C claimed the right to offset the franked investment income which it received from L in computing its liability to pay ACT on a dividend which it had paid to its shareholders. The Revenue issued an assessment on C, charging ACT of £3,110,666, on the basis that C was not entitled to treat the dividends paid by the subsidiaries to L, and by L to C, as franked investment income. C appealed. The Special Commissioners dismissed the appeal. On the evidence, there had been a single composite transaction within the scope of the principles laid down in *WT Ramsay Ltd v CIR*, 71.285 CAPITAL GAINS TAX. Although the scheme as a whole had commercial purposes, the gift of money by C to the five subsidiaries, and the subsequent dividend payments, 'were merely inserted steps which had no purpose apart from recovering ACT'. Accordingly, the payments in question were not 'distributions', and were not franked investment income in the hands of L or C. *Cedar plc v HM Inspector of Taxes (and related appeal)*, Sp C [1998] SSCD 78 (Sp C 155).

Purchase of own shares (CTA 2010, ss 1033–1048)

Whether purchase within CTA 2010, s 1033

[12.6] An individual (M) had been a director of a family company, in which he held a number of shares. He resigned his directorship in 1989. The company lent him £50,000. In 1995 the company purchased 2,747 of his shares, which had originally cost him £1 each. In consideration for the shares, the company wrote off the loan of £50,000. The Revenue issued an income tax assessment on the basis that the effect of the transaction was that the company had made a distribution (of £47,253 net, i.e. £59,066 gross). M appealed, contending that the payment should be treated as not giving rise to a distribution, on the grounds that it was capital expenditure and had been made for the purposes of benefiting the company's trade. The General Commissioners rejected these contentions and dismissed M's appeal, and the Ch D upheld their decision as one of fact. *Moody v Tyler*, Ch D 2000, 72 TC 536; [2000] STC 296. (*Note*. The appellant appeared in person.)

[12.7] In 1966 a married couple purchased the shares of a trading company. They continued to be the company's sole directors and shareholders until 2000, when their son (R) was appointed as a director and granted a share in the company. A property developer offered to purchase the company's premises. Following disagreements between R and his father, the company's accountant was asked 'to consider tax-efficient ways to allow (the couple) to retire from the business and to dispose of their shares without selling them outside the family'. In March 2001 the company purchased the couple's shares. They resigned their directorships on the following day. In the same month the company sold its existing premises to the property developer. Most of the sale price was used to pay R's parents for their shares, and the company continued to trade on a much smaller scale, from rented premises. The Revenue issued amendments to the couple's self-assessments on the basis that the payments by the company were distributions. The couple appealed, contending that the payments had been made for the purpose of benefiting the company's trade. The Special Commissioner reviewed the evidence in detail, rejected this contention, and dismissed the appeals. The Commissioner observed that the transactions did not benefit the company's trade, since the company had been left 'without permanent premises'. On the evidence, 'the purchase of the shares was not made wholly or mainly for the purpose of benefiting the trade but to facilitate (the couple's) retirement'. *Allum & Allum v Marsh*, Sp C 2004, [2005] SSCD 191 (Sp C 446). (*Note*. The Special Commissioner also held that payments of £30,000 to each of the couple were taxable emoluments, within what is now *ITEPA 2003, s 62*.)

[12.8] A company (T) was incorporated in 2002. In 2005 there was a disagreement between its shareholders, following which it was agreed that T would purchase the shareholding of its secretary (B). T made various payments to B without complying with the requirements of the *Companies Acts*. Following an enquiry, HMRC issued a formal decision that B had received a distribution of £120,000 from T in 2005/06. B appealed, contending that the agreement between T and B had contravened *Companies Act 1985, s 164*, and should be treated as void. The First-tier Tribunal accepted the latter contention and allowed B's appeal. Judge Poole held that T's acquisition of its shares from B should be treated as void, and that T (which had subsequently gone into administration) was entitled to recover the money which it had paid to B. *R Baker v HMRC*, FTT [2013] UKFTT 394 (TC), TC02790.

Requirements of CTA 2010, ss 1037, 1038

[12.9] A company had two major directors, each of whom owned about 47% of the shares in the company. One of the directors (S) wished to retire. It was agreed that the company should purchase his shares, with the aim of taking advantage of what is now *CTA 2010, s 1033* and ensuring that S would receive the proceeds as capital rather than income. However, as part of the transaction, the company issued 130,000 preference shares, which were purchased by S and his wife. The Revenue issued assessments on S and the company, on the basis that S's shareholding had not been 'substantially reduced', as required by what is now *CTA 2010, ss 1037, 1038*. S and the company appealed, contending that S should be treated as having 'substantially reduced' his shareholding, because he intended giving 100,000 of the preference shares to his daughter (who was over 18 and therefore not deemed to be an 'associate'). The Special Commissioner dismissed the appeals, finding that S had not relinquished ownership of the shares, and that 'his intention was to give his daughter the money when the shares were redeemed, but not to give her the shares themselves. In the meantime he has received the interest instalments, by cheques at six-monthly intervals, and has paid the amounts received into his own bank account'. On the evidence, 'he intended no more than that his daughter should benefit from the money which he received on redemption of the shares.' *Preston Meats Ltd v Hammond; Sharples v Hammond*, Sp C 2004, [2005] SSCD 90 (Sp C 435).

13

Company Liquidation and Receivership

The cases in this chapter are arranged under the following headings.

Insolvency Act 1986

NOTE

For cases concerning personal insolvency and the *Insolvency Act 1986*, see **6.14** to **6.33** BANKRUPTCY AND PERSONAL INSOLVENCY.

Company voluntary arrangement—Insolvency Act 1986, s 4(4)

[13.1] A football club suffered serious financial difficulties, and went into administration with assets of £230,000 and debts of £24,000,000 (including a debt of £525,000 to the Inland Revenue). In order to retain its membership of the Football League, it was required by the League to pay certain non-preferential creditors (employees and former employees) in full. The club's administrators proposed a voluntary arrangement whereby a prospective purchaser would pay these non-preferential creditors in full, the preferential creditors (including the Revenue) would be paid 30p in the £, and other non-preferential creditors would receive nothing. The arrangement was approved at a creditors' meeting, although the Revenue opposed it. The Revenue applied for a court order revoking or suspending the arrangement, contending that the payment of the non-preferential creditors contravened *Insolvency Act 1986, s 4(4)*. The Ch D rejected the Revenue's application and the CA dismissed the Revenue's appeal. Neuberger LJ observed that this was a 'rather unusual case' because nobody would be prepared to purchase the company's business 'without being satisfied that the club could continue to play in the League'. He observed that 'in the great majority of cases where a company in administration agrees to sell its undertaking to a purchaser, who undertakes to pay off some of the company's creditors, there will be a reduction in the consideration payable by the purchaser to reflect the fact that he has so undertaken. In such a case, unlike the present, it can fairly be said that, at least unless the creditors who are to be paid off are preferential creditors, that contract would potentially be unfair to the preferential creditors'. However, on the facts of this case, the payments did not contravene *Insolvency Act 1986, s 4(4)*. *CIR v Wimbledon Football Club Ltd*, CA [2004] EWCA Civ 655; [2004] All ER (D) 437 (May).

[13.2] A similar decision was reached in another case where a football club suffered financial difficulties and entered a company voluntary arrangement. HMRC applied for the arrangement to be set aside, contending that the rules of the Premier League and the Football League contravened the general principles of insolvency law by unfairly giving preferential treatment to 'football creditors'. The Ch D dismissed the application. Mann J observed that if the voluntary arrangement were set aside, 'the club would not have the means to trade into the new season' and there would be 'a very sizeable risk, if not a virtual inevitability, that the club will be expelled and forced into liquidation'. If that happened, the club 'would cease trading and would be likely to fall out of the leagues altogether. Registration of its players would be lost. The football creditors may or may not be paid by the Premier League (they probably would) but the moneys would certainly not flow for the benefit of the other unsecured creditors', so that 'the unsecured creditors would almost certainly be worse off than under the CVA'. Mann J concluded that 'there is no way in which worthwhile money is likely to flow into this insolvency, or in which asset values can be preserved other than via the CVA'. *HMRC v Portsmouth City Football Club Ltd*, Ch D [2010] EWHC 2013 (Ch).

Validity of Football League rules giving priority to 'football creditors'

[13.3] Following the decision in *HMRC v Portsmouth City Football Club Ltd*, 13.2 above, HMRC took court proceedings against the Football League, seeking a declaration that by giving priority to 'football creditors' over other creditors, the League's rules contravened the principles of insolvency law. The Ch D rejected this contention and dismissed HMRC's application. Sir David Richards held that HMRC had not shown that the League's rules automatically violated either the 'pari passu' principle or the 'anti-deprivation rule'. He held that the 'pari passu' principle only came into play where a company went into liquidation, and did not apply to an administration which did not result in a liquidation. The 'anti-deprivation' rule did apply to companies in administration, but the League rule requiring the transfer of a share where a member club went into administration did not automatically contravene it. *HMRC v The Football League Ltd*, Ch D [2012] EWHC 1372 (Ch).

Company administration—Insolvency Act 1986, s 19(5)

[13.4] Administration orders were made in respect of a number of associated companies. One of the companies continued to trade and to pay its employees. The administrators failed to pay PAYE and NIC deductions to the Revenue. The Revenue applied to the Ch D, which held that the administrators were required to pay these sums. The effect of *Insolvency Act 1986, s 19(5)* was that PAYE and primary Class 1 national insurance contributions enjoyed special priority over the general expenses of the administrators, since 'administrators should not be encouraged to fund an administration with the PAYE or NIC deductions they have made or will make from the salary roll'. The CA upheld this decision. Sir Richard Scott VC held that the special priority in *Insolvency Act 1986, s 19(5)(6)* attached to the gross sums payable before deductions and was not limited to the net liability to the employee. *CIR v Lawrence & Rolph (in re FJL Realisations Ltd)*, CA [2000] 1 BCLC 204.

Final meeting of company—Insolvency Act 1986, s 94

[13.5] See *Marks & Others*, 3.24 ANTI-AVOIDANCE.

Provisional liquidator—Insolvency Act 1986, s 135

[13.6] An individual was appointed provisional liquidator of a company, under *Insolvency Act 1986, s 135*, in September 1997. The liquidation was completed in March 1998 by the sale of the business as a going concern. The company had continued to trade, under the liquidator's supervision, in the interim period, and employed staff, in respect of which it was liable to pay PAYE and NIC. The liquidator applied to the Ch D for directions with regard to his liability to account for the PAYE and NIC, and to whether he could deduct his expenses. The Ch D held that the liquidator was under a duty to ensure that tax was accounted for, in its entirety, to the revenue authorities. This duty took priority to the liquidator's claim for expenses. *Re Grey Marlin Ltd*, Ch D [1999] 3 All ER 429.

Application by liquidator—Insolvency Act 1986, s 167

[13.7] A company (G) sold its assets in 2004 and ceased trading. In 2008 it went into liquidation. In 2009 HMRC submitted a proof of debt for unpaid corporation tax for 2003 and 2004. In 2010 G's liquidator began proceedings against G's two former directors, alleging misfeasance. In 2012 HMRC issued discovery assessments on G, charging further corporation tax in respect of the disposal of G's assets. The liquidator appealed against these assessments, but subsequently indicated that he had 'doubts as to the merits of the substantive appeals'. The directors requested that the appeals should be assigned to them, and the liquidator applied to the Ch D for directions under *Insolvency Act 1986, s 167(3)*. The Ch D held that the right to appeal could only be exercised by the liquidator and could not be assigned. *Williams v Glover & Pearson (re GP Aviation Group International Ltd)*, Ch D [2013] EWHC 1447 (Ch).

Floating charges—Insolvency Act 1986, s 176A

[13.8] Two associated companies had granted floating charges over their assets to a third company (H). In April 2006 the companies went into administration. The Revenue considered that the effect of *Insolvency Act 1986, s 176A(6)* was that the administrators held the 'prescribed part' of the companies' net profit for the benefit of the unsecured creditors, who should be paid that part in preference to H. The administrators applied to the Ch D for a ruling on the interpretation of *s 176A*. The Ch D upheld the Revenue's interpretation. Patten J observed that *Insolvency Act 1986, s 176A* had been inserted by *Enterprise Act 2002*, and had been intended 'to set aside a portion of the company's assets secured by the floating charge for the satisfaction of unsecured debts and to do so by restricting the right of the floating charge holder to have recourse to those assets to satisfy the debts due under the floating charge'. Accordingly H was 'not entitled to participate in the prescribed part in respect of any claim based on any shortfall in its security'.

Thorniley & Another v HMRC (re Airbase Services UK Ltd), Ch D [2008] EWHC 124 (Ch); [2008] All ER (D) 47 (Feb).

Unlawful dividend—Insolvency Act 1986, s 212

[13.9] In 1994 a company (L) sold a successful business for £10,000,000, giving rise to a chargeable gain of about £7,000,000 and a corporation tax liability of about £2,300,000. In 1995 L's shareholders sold their shares in L to a newly-formed company (C), in return for shares in C. L subsequently declared a dividend of £5,900,000 in favour of C, without making provision for the corporation tax liability. L also lodged a claim for rollover relief, relating to a leaseback arrangement entered into by a subsidiary company (M) which it had subsequently sold. In 1997 L went into creditors' voluntary liquidation. The Revenue rejected the claim for rollover relief and issued an assessment to recover the unpaid corporation tax from L. The Revenue applied under *Insolvency Act 1986, s 212* for an order that L's directors should pay £5,900,000 for misfeasance or breach of duty as directors, on the grounds that the dividend was unlawful under *Companies Act 1985, s 263*, and that in authorising and procuring it, the directors had acted in breach of their duty to the company and its creditors. The Ch D granted the Revenue's application. Etherton J observed that *Companies Act 1985, s 263* provided that a company should not make a distribution except out of profits available for the purpose. He held that, with regard to the leaseback transaction entered into by M, there was 'no real trading activity involved', and 'the only possible purpose of the transaction was tax mitigation. This was not a case of a transaction which had the characteristics of a genuine trading transaction. The entire transaction was coloured, both in terms of the intention of (M) and in terms of the contractual provisions, by the motive of tax mitigation.' The interim accounts which L's directors had produced failed to comply with the requirements of *Companies Act 1985, s 270*, since they failed to make proper provision for the charge to corporation tax on the sale of L's business. Etherton J observed that 'on any reasonable view, it was likely that the rollover relief claim would fail.' The dividend was unlawful under *Companies Act 1985, s 270(5)*, and the directors had acted in breach of their duties. *CIR v Richmond & Jones (re Loquitur Ltd)*, Ch D 2003, 75 TC 77; [2003] STC 1394; [2003] EWHC 999 (Ch).

Insolvency Act 1986, s 216—'prohibited names'

[13.10] A company became insolvent and went into liquidation. Its principal director (W) subsequently formed a second company with a very similar name. The Revenue applied to the Ch D for an order that the similarity of the company names fell within *Insolvency Act 1986, s 216*, and that the effect of *s 216(3)* was that W was prohibited from being a director of the second company without permission of the court. The Ch D accepted this contention and gave judgment for the Revenue. Laddie J observed that the companies were in 'adjacent fields of commerce', and held that it was 'likely or probable that the reasonable customer, or member of the public, who knows of these two companies' would associate them. *HMRC v Walsh*, Ch D [2005] EWHC 1304 (Ch); 2 BCLC 455.

Liability of company director for company's tax debts

[13.11] A company went into liquidation in January 1997. One of its directors (N) had also been the controlling director of a second company until December 1996, when he resigned and was succeeded by his son. He was reappointed a director in July 1997 and remained a director until that company went into liquidation in December 1997. The Revenue took proceedings against N, contending that, by virtue of *Insolvency Act 1986, ss 216, 217*, he was liable for the tax debts of both companies. The Ch D granted judgment for the Revenue, holding that the companies were associated within the meaning of *s 216*, and that N had been involved in the management of both companies at all material times. *CIR v Nash*, Ch D [2003] EWHC 686 (Ch); [2003] BPIR 1138.

[13.12] A company went into liquidation in June 2001. Its controlling director (B) acquired the company's assets and carried on a similar business as a sole trader. In September 2001 he incorporated a second company with a similar name, which carried on the business until it went into liquidation in September 2003. The Revenue took proceedings against B, contending that, by virtue of *Insolvency Act 1986, ss 216, 217*, he was liable for the tax debts of the second company. The Ch D granted judgment for the Revenue, applying the principles laid down in *HMRC v Walsh*, **13.10** above, and holding that the names of the two companies were so similar that there was a 'probability that members of the public, comparing the names in the relevant context, would associate the companies with each other'. *HMRC v Benton-Diggins*, Ch D [2006] EWHC 793 (Ch); [2006] 2 BCLC 255.

[13.13] HMRC took proceedings against a company director (B) under *Insolvency Act 1986, ss 216, 217*, seeking to recover tax and NIC which the company had failed to pay. The Ch D gave judgment for HMRC, and the CA dismissed B's application for leave to appeal against this decision. *Brotherston v HMRC*, CA [2014] EWCA Civ 219.

Whether individual acting as a de facto director

[13.14] A married couple each held 50% of the issued share capital in a company (P), which held 100% of the issued share capital of two subsidiary companies, which in turn were appointed to act as director and secretary of a further 42 companies. Although these companies were 'associated' within *ICTA 1988, s 13*, none of them accounted for the higher rate of corporation tax. HMRC issued assessments, which the companies failed to pay. They all went into administration in October 2004, and subsequently went into liquidation. HMRC, which was the only creditor, formed the opinion that the couple were *de facto* directors of the 42 companies and had acted in breach of their duties by causing the companies to pay substantial dividends without making provision for the higher rate of corporation tax. They took proceedings against the couple, seeking to make them liable for the unpaid tax. The Ch D reviewed the evidence in detail and gave judgment against the husband (H) but not against his wife, holding that H was a *de facto* director of the companies, but that his wife had not been shown to be a *de facto* director. The CA allowed H's appeal, holding that he had not been a *de facto* director of the companies. The Supreme Court upheld this decision (by a 3-2 majority, Lord Walker and Lord Clarke dissenting). Lord Hope held that, on the facts of this case, 'it has not been shown that (H) was acting as *de facto* director of the composite companies so as to make him responsible for the misuse of their assets'. Lord Collins held that 'there is no material to suggest that (H) was doing anything other than discharging his duties as the director of the corporate director of the composite companies. It does not follow from the fact that he was taking all the relevant decisions that he was part of the corporate governance of the composite companies or that he assumed fiduciary duties in respect of them. If he was a *de facto* director of the composite companies simply because he was the guiding mind behind their sole corporate director, than that would be so in the case of every company with a sole corporate director.' He commented that 'the proposed extension which is inherent in HMRC's case is a matter for the legislature and not for this court'. In a dissenting judgment, Lord Walker expressed concern that the majority decision would 'make it easier for risk-averse individuals to use artificial corporate structures in order to insulate themselves against responsibility to an insolvent company's unsecured creditors'. *HMRC v Holland (re Paycheck Services 3 Ltd and other companies)*, SC [2010] UKSC 51; [2011] STC 269; [2011] 1 All ER 430. (*Note*. See now *Companies Act 2006, s 155*, which provides that a company must have at least one director who is a 'natural person'.)

Miscellaneous

Assets distributed on liquidation—tax not accounted for

[13.15] The liquidators of a company realised the company's assets and distributed the proceeds to contributors, without paying income tax which had been assessed and which ranked as a preferential debt under the legislation then in force. The Attorney-General took proceedings against the liquidators. The Ch D held that the liquidators had been guilty of misapplication and misfeasance, and ordered them to pay the assessed tax to the Revenue with interest. *In re The Watchmakers' Alliance & Ernest Goode's Stores Ltd*, Ch D 1905, 5 TC 117.

[13.16] A company went into voluntary liquidation. The liquidators distributed most of the company's assets to its major shareholder (W), without accounting for tax. The Attorney-General applied for an order directing W to refund to the liquidator sufficient assets to pay the tax due. The Ch D granted the order, and the CA unanimously dismissed W's appeal. *In re Aidall Ltd*, CA 1932, 18 TC 617.

Tax chargeable on transactions during liquidation

[13.17] A company went into voluntary liquidation in 1925. The liquidator continued to trade, and drew remuneration from the company, but failed to pay tax on the company's profits while it was trading. The Attorney-General took proceedings against the liquidator to require him to refund the money which he should have set aside to pay the tax. The Ch D gave judgment for the Attorney-General. Maugham J held that tax charged on a company's trading profits while it was in voluntary liquidation formed part of the 'costs, charges and expenses incurred in the winding-up', and that, in a normal case, 'the whole of the expenses of the winding-up ought to be paid before the remuneration of the liquidator'. (However, Maugham J agreed to allow the remuneration for the period immediately after the liquidation to take priority, finding that at that time the liquidator had no way of knowing that the company's assets would be insufficient to meet the tax liability.) *In re Beni-Felkai Mining Co Ltd*, Ch D 1933, 18 TC 632; [1934] Ch 406.

[13.18] A liquidator sold the properties of a company which was in compulsory liquidation. The sales resulted in substantial corporation tax liability on the gains. The liquidator applied to the court for a ruling on whether this tax took priority over claims by other creditors. The Ch D held that the tax was a 'necessary disbursement' of the liquidator, and ranked ahead of the unsecured creditors. The CA unanimously upheld this decision. *In re Mesco Properties Ltd*, CA 1979, 54 TC 238; [1979] STC 788; [1980] 1 WLR 96; [1980] 1 All ER 117. (*Note*. The decision was unanimously approved by the HL in *Re Toshoku Finance UK plc*, **13.19** below.)

[13.19] T, which was a UK subsidiary of a Japanese company, was placed in creditors' voluntary liquidation. It had lent substantial sums of money to a Liechtenstein fellow-subsidiary (E), which was insolvent. The Revenue claimed corporation tax on deemed interest due from E, under the 'loan relationships' provisions of *FA 1996*, arising after the date of T's liquidation. T's liquidators applied to the court for a ruling as to whether they were required to discharge liability for corporation tax on deemed interest which had not in fact been received, in priority to other claims. The CA held that the liquidators were required to pay such tax in priority to other claims. The HL unanimously upheld this decision. Lord Hoffmann observed that 'the statute expressly enacts that a company is chargeable to corporation tax on profits or gains arising in the winding-up. It follows that the tax is a post-liquidation liability which the liquidator is bound to discharge and it is therefore a "necessary disbursement" within the meaning of the *Insolvency Rules*' *(SI 1986/1925)*. *Re Toshoku Finance UK plc, Kahn & Another v CIR*, HL [2002] STC 368; [2002] UKHL 6; [2002] 3 All ER 961.

Set-off of Crown debts

[13.20] An order was made for the compulsory winding-up of a company (C). At the date of winding-up, C owed £4,726 to the Inland Revenue and £951 to the DHSS. It was also owed £4,055 by Customs & Excise in respect of reclaimable input tax. Customs repaid £3,651 of this before becoming aware of the other Crown debts. They then requested the liquidator to set the amount repaid against the other Crown debts. The liquidator refused to comply with this request and Customs began proceedings for the recovery of the £3,651. The Ch D gave judgment for Customs, holding that the Crown was entitled to require a set-off and to recover the money which it had paid to the liquidator by mistake. *Re Cushla Ltd*, Ch D [1979] STC 615; [1979] 3 All ER 415.

Appeal against compulsory winding-up order

[13.21] In January 1993 a compulsory winding-up order was made against a company which owed tax to the Inland Revenue. The company appealed to the CA, contending that it had offered to pay its tax liability by instalments, had begun doing so, and had not been told that the instalments were unacceptable until October 1992. The CA unanimously dismissed the company's appeal, holding that the Revenue were not legally bound to accept the company's offer. *In re Selectmove Ltd*, CA 1993, 66 TC 552; [1995] STC 406; [1995] 1 WLR 474; [1995] 2 All ER 531.

Revenue proceeding against receiver and debenture-holder

[13.22] The debenture-holder of a company (C) appointed a receiver, but shortly afterwards revoked the appointment and accepted a payment from the receiver as settlement of his claim. At the time of the appointment, C owed tax to the Revenue which constituted a preferential debt under the legislation then in force. The Revenue proceeded against both the receiver and the debenture-holder to recover its preferential debt, and the Ch D granted judgment against both. Goff J held that 'once the receiver has collected assets, he is liable to the extent of those assets for any preferential debts of which he has notice'. The debenture-holder was also under a statutory duty to ensure that the preferential creditors received payment. *CIR v Goldblatt & Another*, Ch D 1971, 47 TC 483; [1972] Ch 498; [1972] 2 All ER 202.

Realisations during receivership

[13.23] In 1994 a company director (P) was charged with fraud, and a receiver was appointed to manage the companies which he had controlled. P was convicted of fraud, and the court made a confiscation order. In 2002 P applied for the restraint order to be discharged. The receiver applied to the court for directions as to whether she was required to account for tax on the realisations made during the receivership. Lightman J held that 'where there is a realisation by the receiver, the tax liability (whether for capital gains or income tax) should remain that of the defendant alone', so that the receiver was not taxable. *Dayman v CIR (re Piacentini)*, Ch D 2003, 75 TC 288; [2003] STC 924; [2003] EWHC 113 (Admin).

Proceedings under Company Directors Disqualification Act 1986

[13.24] An accountant and tax adviser (E) had been a director of a limited company which went into receivership with significant debts. The Secretary of State for Trade and Industry took proceedings against E under the *Company Directors Disqualification Act 1986*. In 2001 E gave an undertaking not to act as a company director for four and a half years. Following this, the ICAEW began disciplinary proceedings against E. E subsequently applied to the Ch D for the undertaking to be set aside, and the ICAEW halted its disciplinary proceedings pending the hearing of this application. The Ch D rejected E's application. Lightman J held that it would not be in the public interest 'to write out of history unattractive episodes in (E's) past. These episodes do cast a shadow and are inevitably of concern to the professional bodies of which (E) is a member, for those bodies must have a responsibility to maintain public confidence in their members and to protect the public. Whether and, if so, what action is required for these purposes in the light of the disqualification undertaking and attached schedule of admitted facts is a matter for them to decide'. The CA unanimously dismissed E's appeal against the Ch D decision. (Arden LJ observed that the disqualification period had expired, so that E was free to act as a company director, but that the significance of the case was that the ICAEW was now free to resume its disciplinary proceedings against E.) *Eastaway v Secretary of State for Trade and Industry*, CA [2007] EWCA Civ 425.

Voting rights of creditor—Insolvency Rules 1986, rule 2.38

[13.25] A company (M) went into administration in September 2009. The administrators subsequently submitted proposals to the company's creditors, including HMRC. HMRC opposed the proposals. However the administrator (K) who acted as chairman at the creditors' meeting ruled that HMRC only ranked as a creditor to the extent of £1,500,000, with the result that the proposals were carried. HMRC appealed to the CA, contending that K should have accepted them as creditors for more than £8,000,000, with the result that the proposals should have been defeated. The CA unanimously accepted this contention, allowed HMRC's appeal, and ordered that the administrators should summon a further meeting of creditors. Lord Neuberger MR observed that HMRC had 'serious concerns' about the conduct of M's directors, and had requested a representative of a major accountancy firm to act as joint liquidator. The administrators had failed 'to explain, even in general terms, the nature or detail of any argument upon which the company was relying to have the corporation tax determinations or assessments set aside'. They had 'simply denied liability for all but a small proportion of the claimed tax in the most general terms and failed to put forward any specific evidence or legal arguments as to why the whole or part of the sums claimed were not due, and they had failed to put forward any grounds in the notices of appeal and applications for stay in respect of payment of the tax, in circumstances where the statute required such grounds'. Accordingly, HMRC should have been accorded 'a level of votes which would have defeated the proposals as put to the meeting'. *HMRC v Maxwell; HMRC v Klempka*, CA [2010] EWCA Civ 1379. (*Note*. For a previous case involving the same company, see *HMRC v Mercury Tax Group Ltd (No 2)*, **3.94** ANTI-AVOIDANCE.)

Expenses of liquidation—Insolvency Rules 1986, rule 4.218

[13.26] A company went into liquidation in 1995. It had sufficient assets to pay preferential creditors a dividend of just under 44p in the £, leaving nothing for unsecured creditors. The liquidator formed the opinion that there were grounds for taking proceedings against the company's former directors. He proposed to recoup the costs of these proceedings out of the company's assets, under *Insolvency Rules 1986 (SI 1986/1925), rule 4.218*. The Revenue and three other preferential creditors refused to consent to the liquidator's proposal. The liquidator applied to the court for authority to use the company's funds in this way. The CA rejected the application, holding that there was insufficient evidence to justify this. Peter Gibson LJ observed that 'it is appropriate to be cautious where the court is asked to provide for the liquidator's costs out of the assets even if the litigation ultimately proves unsuccessful, particularly where the preferential creditors who would otherwise be paid a dividend oppose the use of the company's moneys for that purpose'. *Lewis v CIR and Others*, CA 2000, [2001] 3 All ER 499.

Charge over uncollected debts—whether a fixed or floating charge

[13.27] In a New Zealand case, a company had granted its bank a charge over its uncollected debts. The company subsequently went into receivership. The only assets available for distribution to creditors were the uncollected debts. The receivers took the view that the charge was a fixed charge, so that the proceeds were payable to the bank. The Revenue considered that the charge was a floating charge, so that the proceeds were payable to the company's employees and the Revenue, as preferential creditors. The CA found in favour of the Revenue, and the PC dismissed the receivers' appeal, holding that the charge was a floating charge. Lord Millett observed that the company had the 'freedom to deal with the charged assets without the consent of the holder of the charge'. Furthermore, 'the debenture was so drafted that the company was at liberty to turn the uncollected book debts to account by its own act. Taking the relevant assets to be the uncollected book debts, the company was left in control of the process by which the charged assets were extinguished and replaced by different assets which were not the subject of a fixed charge and were at the free disposal of the company. That is inconsistent with the nature of a fixed charge.' *Agnew & Bearsley v New Zealand Commissioner of Inland Revenue (re Brumark Investments Ltd)*, PC [2001] UKPC 28; [2001] WLR 454. (*Notes.* (1) The decision here was subsequently approved by the HL in the non-tax case of *National Westminster Bank plc v Spectrum Plus Ltd*, HL [2005] UKHL 41; [2005] 4 All ER 209, where the HL unanimously held that a debenture, which purported to grant a bank a fixed charge, only granted it a floating charge. (2) For the Revenue's practice following this decision, see the Inland Revenue Statement issued on 13 February 2002, and the joint HMRC/DTI statement issued on 6 September 2005.)

Distraint levied by Collector—subsequent liquidation of company

[13.28] See *Herbert Berry Associates Ltd v CIR*, 43.21 PAYMENT OF TAX, and *Brenner v HMRC (re Jet Support Centre Ltd)*, 43.22 PAYMENT OF TAX.

14

Compensation, etc.—'Gourley' Principle

The cases in this chapter are arranged under the following headings.

GENERAL NOTE

In quantifying compensation, etc. for a loss of income, the hypothetical tax on the lost income may be taken into account. Although this principle, established by *British Transport Commission v Gourley*, **14.1** below, does not enter directly into the assessment of tax liabilities, it is of interest to tax practitioners and cases illustrating it are included here. See also the cases noted at **15.1** *et seq.* COMPENSATION FOR LOSS OF EMPLOYMENT for the assessment of compensation receipts connected with employments; **52.5** *et seq.* SAVINGS AND INVESTMENT INCOME for the assessment of the interest element in compensation, and **66.1** *et seq.* TRADING PROFITS for the treatment of compensation payments in computing business profits. For a detailed discussion of the principle, see the article by Jolyon Maugham and Jonathan Peacock in the New Law Journal, 28 July 2000, pp 1153–1154.

House of Lords decisions

Railway accident

[14.1] A civil engineer was awarded damages against the British Transport Commission following injuries suffered in a railway accident. The award included an amount in respect of actual and prospective loss of earnings which was fixed at £37,720 without taking the tax position into account and at £6,695 after deducting the hypothetical income tax and surtax which would have been payable on the lost earnings. The HL held (by a 6-1 majority, Lord Keith of Avonholm dissenting) that the £6,695 (rather than the £37,720) should be included in the award. Earl Jowitt held that 'the broad general principle which should govern the assessment of damages in cases such as this is that the tribunal should award the injured party such a sum of money as will put him in the same position as he would have been in if he had not sustained the injuries', and that 'to ignore the tax element at the present day would be to act in a manner which is out of touch with reality'. *British Transport Commission v Gourley*, HL 1955, 34 ATC 305; [1956] AC 185; [1955] 3 All ER 796.

Damages following death of husband

[14.2] The QB awarded damages of £54,000 to a widow under the *Fatal Accidents Acts*, following the death of her husband in a car accident. The HL unanimously upheld the award. Lord Reid held that such an award should take into account the widow's potential liability to income tax on the interest arising from the capital awarded, and that in estimating this tax liability, any private income should be ignored. He observed that 'this case is in a sense *British Transport Commission v Gourley* in reverse, for that case instructs us that we must see what the plaintiff really lost taking account of taxation. There damages had to be reduced if taxation was taken into account. Here they have to be increased'. Lord Pearson observed that the widow should 'be awarded such a sum of damages as will produce annually over the relevant period an amount which, after deduction of income tax on the income element of her receipts, will yield the proper annual sum'. *Taylor v O'Connor*, HL 1970, [1971] AC 115; [1970] 1 All ER 365.

Compulsory purchase of premises

[14.3] In order to widen a road, acounty council made a compulsory purchase order against property owned by a company (W). W claimed compensation from the council. In awarding compensation, the Lands Tribunal included £11,600 for temporary disturbance of W's business (measured by reference to its estimated profits lost while it was finding new premises). The Revenue agreed that this compensation was not taxable. The council appealed, contending that the award should be reduced to take account of the tax that would have been paid on the profits. The HL unanimously accepted this contention, applying the principles laid down in *British Transport Commission v Gourley*, **14.1** above. *West Suffolk County Council v W Rought Ltd*, HL 1956, 35 ATC 315; [1957] AC 403; [1956] 3 All ER 216. (*Note.* The decision in this case was distinguished in the subsequent case of *Stoke-on-Trent City Council v Wood Mitchell & Co Ltd*, **14.13** below, where the CA held that a similar payment of compensation was liable to corporation tax, so that there was no reason to reduce the amount awarded.)

Damages awarded to Lloyd's underwriters against managing agent

[14.4] Several Lloyd's underwriters were awarded substantial damages against the company (G) which acted as their managing agent. G contended that the amount of the damages should be reduced in accordance with the principles laid down in *British Transport Commission v Gourley*, **14.1** above, firstly on the basis that the damages should be treated as non-taxable, and alternatively to take account of the fact that some of the underwriters might have secured tax relief on their losses at a higher rate of tax than the rate of tax payable. The HL rejected these contentions, holding that the damages would be taxable in the hands of the underwriters and that the amount of the damages should not be reduced. *Deeny & Others v Gooda Walker Ltd & Others*, HL 1996, 68 TC 458; [1996] STC 299; [1996] 1 WLR 426; [1996] 1 All ER 933.

Other cases

Lump sums in commutation of pensions

[14.5] A company went into voluntary liquidation, and its liquidator was required to pay lump sums in commutation of certain pensions. The Ch D held that the payments should be reduced to take account of the income tax which would have been charged on the pensions, applying the principles laid down by *British Transport Commission v Gourley*, **14.1** above. *In re Houghton Main Colliery Co Ltd*, Ch D 1956, 23 ATC 320; [1956] 1 WLR 1219; [1956] 3 All ER 300. (*Note. Obiter dicta* of Wynn-Parry J, with regard to the relevant computations, were disapproved by Orr LJ in the subsequent case of *Lyndale Fashion Manufacturers v Rich*, **14.12** below.)

Damages for breach of contract of sale

[14.6] An individual (M) agreed to sell certain shares to a purchaser (S), but failed to complete the contract. S claimed damages of the amount by which the market value of the shares at the time of the breach of the contract exceeded the contract price. M's representatives contended that the damages should be reduced on the basis that S might have been liable to income tax on any profit he might have made on re-selling the shares. The CS rejected this contention, holding that it was too remote to be taken into account. *Spencer v MacMillan's Trustees*, CS 1958, 37 ATC 388.

Compensation for prohibition on working minerals

[14.7] A company was awarded compensation for being prohibited from working minerals under a railway line. The QB held that the compensation should be reduced to take account of the tax that would have been due on the lost profits, applying the principles laid down in *British Transport Commission v Gourley*, **14.1** above. The compensation was by reference to the profits lost and not by reference to the value of the minerals. Phillimore J observed that 'inequality of compensation is inevitable when the incidence of tax is applied', and that 'the party required to compensate will always be lucky or unlucky dependent on the tax position of the person claiming damages or compensation'. *Thomas McGhie & Sons Ltd v British Transport Commission*, QB 1962, 41 ATC 144; [1963] 1 QB 125; [1962] 2 All ER 646.

Damages for loss of employment

[14.8] A company (G) terminated the appointment of its managing director. He sued G for breach of contract and was awarded compensation of £12,680. The CS held that the principles laid down in *British Transport Commission v Gourley*, **14.1** above, should be applied, but that allowance should be made for any actual tax liability on the compensation under what is now *ITEPA 2003, ss 401–416*. *Stewart v Glentaggart Ltd*, CS 1963, 42 ATC 318; [1963] SLT 119.

[14.9] An employee (P) was awarded damages of £1,200 for wrongful dismissal. The CA held (by a 2-1 majority, Sellers LJ dissenting) that the damages should be reduced to £820 in accordance with the principles in *British Transport Commission v Gourley*, **14.1** above, to take account of the tax which would have been deducted from P's earnings if he had not been dismissed, and of the unemployment benefit which he received following his dismissal. *Parsons v BNM Laboratories Ltd*, CA 1963, 42 ATC 200; [1964] 1 QB 95; [1963] 2 All ER 658.

[14.10] A company dismissed its managing director (B) in July 1962, following a change of ownership. B, who had worked for the company since 1922 (when he was aged 14), claimed damages for wrongful dismissal. The QB found that he was unlikely to find similar employment elsewhere, and awarded him damages of £26,948. In computing the award, the QB applied the principles laid down in *British Transport Commission v Gourley*, **14.1** above. The QB held that the hypothetical tax to be taken into account should be arrived at by spreading it over the period from July 1962 to March 1969. *Bold v Brough Nicholson & Hall Ltd*, QB 1963, [1964] 1 WLR 201; [1963] 3 All ER 849.

Calculation of tax where Gourley applies

[14.11] A commercial traveller was dismissed without reasonable notice and received compensation of £495 for lost earnings. The CA held that the principles laid down in *British Transport Commission v Gourley*, **14.1** above, applied and that the hypothetical tax should be calculated by assuming that the £495 was the top slice of the earned income for the relevant year. *Lyndale Fashion Manufacturers v Rich*, CA 1972, [1973] STC 32; [1973] 1 WLR 73; [1973] 1 All ER 33.

Damages for loss of earnings—treatment of tax refund

[14.12] An employee suffered an injury at work resulting in a period of absence. As a consequence, he obtained a refund of tax which had already been deducted from his earnings under PAYE. The QB held that this refund should be taken into account in arriving at the damages payable to him for loss of earnings. *Hartley v Sandholme Iron Co Ltd*, QB [1974] STC 434; [1975] QB 600; [1974] 3 All ER 475.

Compulsory purchase of premises

[14.13] The Lands Tribunal awarded a company (W) compensation of £12,228 for loss of profits following the compulsory acquisition of its premises. The council which had acquired the premises appealed to the CA, contending that the award should be reduced to take account of the hypothetical tax on the lost profits. The CA unanimously rejected this contention and dismissed the council's appeal, observing that the Revenue had taken the view that corporation tax would be chargeable on part of the compensation.

W was therefore entitled to the gross amount of £12,228. *Stoke-on-Trent City Council v Wood Mitchell & Co Ltd*, CA 1978, [1979] STC 197; [1980] 1 WLR 254; [1979] 2 All ER 65.

Damages for breach of trust

[14.14] Shares held in trust were sold at a loss. The beneficiaries of the trust took proceedings against the company which acted as trustee, claiming damages for breach of trust. The Ch D gave judgment for the beneficiaries, holding that they were entitled to damages and that their potential tax liability could not be taken into account in assessing the loss. Brightman J distinguished *British Transport Commission v Gourley*, **14.1** above, and held that the tax liability of individual beneficiaries 'does not enter into the picture because it arises not at the point of restitution to the trust estate but at the point of distribution of capital or income out of the trust estate'. *Bartlett & Others v Barclays Bank Trust Co Ltd (No 2)*, Ch D [1980] 2 WLR 430; [1980] 2 All ER 92.

[14.15] A singer, two companies which had employed him, and a lyricist took legal action against a music publisher (D) and a group of companies which he controlled. The Ch D held that D and his companies had been in breach of a fiduciary duty in retaining certain sums, which the plaintiffs were therefore entitled to recover. The Ch D also held that no deductions were to be made in respect of UK or other taxation, and that the defendants were also not entitled to make any tax deductions from any award of compound interest, applying the principles laid down in *Bartlett & Others v Barclays Bank*, **14.14** above. *John & Others v James & Others*, Ch D [1986] STC 352.

Compensation for revocation of drag racing licence

[14.16] A Borough Council revoked a licence granted to a company to conduct drag racing on a disused airfield. The company was awarded compensation, expressed to be for loss of profits, by the Lands Tribunal. The Tribunal considered that the compensation would not be subject to corporation tax and reduced the amount payable by the Council accordingly. The company was informed by the Revenue that the compensation would be liable to corporation tax, and therefore appealed to the CA against the decision of the Lands Tribunal to reduce the compensation. The CA held that the compensation was derived from the licence to conduct drag racing and that the licence was an asset within what is now *TCGA 1992, s 22(1)*. Consequently the compensation would be chargeable to corporation tax and the Tribunal was wrong to reduce the amount of the compensation. *Pennine Raceway Ltd v Kirklees Metropolitan Borough Council*, CA 1988, [1989] STC 122.

Repayment of sick pay following receipt of compensation

[14.17] An employee (F) suffered an accident at work, and received sick pay for twelve months. The employer subsequently paid him compensation for the injury, including the amount of the sick pay, calculated under the principles laid down in *British Transport Commission v Gourley*, **14.1** above. F repaid the net amount of sick pay that he had received. The employer claimed that F should also repay the tax and national insurance contributions that had been deducted. F refused to do so, and the employer obtained judgment in the County Court. The CA allowed F's appeal, holding that he was only obliged to repay the net amount that he had received, and was under no obligation to repay amounts which had been paid to the Inland Revenue or the DSS. *British Railways Board v Franklin*, CA [1993] STC 487.

Compensation payments recoverable under indemnity contract

[14.18] A company (C) owned an oil rig, which exploded. It had to pay compensation to the surviving victims and the relatives of those who died in the explosion. These payments were accepted as deductible expenses in computing C's taxable profits. C claimed to recover the compensation which it had paid from the company (L) which had built the rig, under an indemnity clause in the relevant contracts. The CS held that L was obliged to pay C compensation under the clauses, but that in computing the amount due, the reduction in C's tax liability, resulting from the payments, should be taken into account. *Caledonia North Sea Ltd v London Bridge Engineering Ltd*, CS [2000] SLT 1123. (*Note*. For a discussion of the decision, see British Tax Review 2001, pp 174–193.)

15

Compensation for Loss of Employment (ITEPA 2003, ss 401–416)

The cases in this chapter are arranged under the following headings.

Pre-1960 cases

NOTE.

The cases in this section relate to years before the introduction by *FA 1960* of the 'golden handshake' legislation (see now *ITEPA 2003, ss 401–416*). They remain relevant because of the exemption for the first £30,000 of such payments (see *ITEPA 2003, s 403(1)*).

Cases held to be taxable

'Compensation' on resignation provided for in service agreement

[15.1] Two directors of a company resigned and, under the terms of their appointment, were entitled to 'compensation' equal to their remuneration for their last five years of service. The Revenue issued assessments charging tax on the payments, and the directors appealed. The CA unanimously upheld the assessments, holding that the payments were emoluments and were taxable for the directors' final year of service. *Henry v Foster*, CA 1932, 16 TC 605. (*Note*. Compare *Hunter v Dewhurst*, **15.11** below. For a recent analysis of the distinction between the cases, see the judgment of Chadwick LJ in *EMI Group Electronics Ltd v Coldicott*, **15.25** below.)

[15.2] In 1944 a tobacco company entered into a new three-year service agreement with one of its employees (S). The agreement gave the company the right to terminate S's employment at the end of 1945 or 1946 on condition that it paid him £10,000 or £6,000 respectively as 'compensation for loss of office'. The company terminated the agreement at the end of 1945, and paid S £10,000 in accordance with the agreement. The Revenue issued an assessment charging tax on this, and S appealed. The CA unanimously upheld the assessment, holding that the payment was a taxable emolument. Sir Raymond

Evershed MR observed that S had got 'exactly what he was entitled to get under his contract of employment' *Dale v de Soissons*, CA 1950, 32 TC 118; [1950] 2 All ER 460.

Payment to director wishing to retire but remaining

[15.3] A director of a building company, who had played an important part in its development, wished to retire. After correspondence the company entered into a deed under which it paid him £45,000 in consideration of his undertaking not to resign. Thereafter he continued in office, receiving less than 30% of his previous salary, and devoting much less of his time to the company's business. The Revenue issued an assessment charging tax on the £45,000, and he appealed. The HL unanimously upheld the assessment, distinguishing *Hunter v Dewhurst*, **15.11** below, on the grounds that the payment in that case was made as compensation for the loss of a right to a future lump sum payment, whereas the payment here was made as an inducement to continue in office. *Prendergast v Cameron*, HL 1940, 23 TC 122; [1940] AC 549; [1940] 2 All ER 35.

Realisation of investments held in trust for employee

[15.4] In 1921 a company employed an accountant (R) under a complex and unusual service agreement, under which R was entitled, in addition to his normal salary, to the interest on investments made by trustees of specified amounts which the company paid to them each year. R resigned in September 1927 and the investments were transferred to him. The Revenue issued an assessment charging tax on the value of the investments, and he appealed. The CA unanimously upheld the assessments, holding that the value of the investments was taxable remuneration of 1927/28. *Edwards v Roberts*, CA 1935, 19 TC 618.

Managing director—compensation for reduction in salary

[15.5] In 1935 a company agreed to pay its managing director a salary of £15,000 pa. Two years later he resigned as managing director because of ill-health, but continued to act as an advisory director at a salary of £1,000 pa. The company paid him compensation of £75,000, and the Revenue issued an assessment charging tax on this. The KB upheld the assessment, applying the HL decision in *Wales v Tilley*, **15.8** below. *Wilson v Daniels*, KB 1943, 25 TC 473; [1943] 2 All ER 732. (*Note*. For the deductibility of the payment in computing the company's profits, see *Wilson v Nicholson Sons & Daniels Ltd*, **63.179** TRADING PROFITS.)

Compensation to company directors for surrender of certain rights

[15.6] An investment company (T) was registered in 1932. Its rules gave special rights to two of its directors. In 1939 T was converted into a public limited company. It paid the directors £10,000 each in return for relinquishing their rights under the previous rules. One of the directors appealed against an assessment on the £10,000. The Commissioners dismissed his appeal and the KB upheld their decision, applying the HL decision in *Wales v Tilley*, **15.8** below. *Leeland v Boarland*, KB 1945, 27 TC 71; [1946] 1 All ER 13.

Payments on cancellation of service agreement

[15.7] In May 1940 a company appointed a manager under a five-year contract, at a salary of £750 pa. In December 1940 it terminated his contract and agreed to pay him his agreed salary until the end of 1941. In March 1941 it paid him £687, representing the salary due for March to December 1941. The Revenue issued assessments for 1940/41 and 1941/42, charging tax on the total amounts which he had received from the company. He appealed, contending that the lump sum payment of £687 was not taxable. The Commissioners rejected this contention and upheld the assessments, and the KB upheld their decision. *Hofman v Wadman*, KB 1946, 27 TC 192.

Cases held to be partly taxable

Managing director—compensation for reduced salary and loss of pension

[15.8] In 1937 a company agreed to pay its managing director (T) a salary of £6,000 pa, and a pension of £4,000 pa for ten years after his retirement. In 1938 T entered into a revised agreement with the company, under which his salary was reduced to £2,000 pa and he relinquished his pension rights, in return for two payments of £20,000 each. The Revenue issued an assessment charging tax on the £40,000 which T received under this agreement, and he appealed. The HL held that he was taxable on the proportion of the £40,000 referable to the reduction in his salary, applying *Prendergast v Cameron*, **15.3** above, but not on the proportion representing the capitalisation of his pension, applying *Hunter v Dewhurst*, **15.11** below. The HL remitted the case to the Commissioners to apportion the £40,000 accordingly. *Wales v Tilley*, HL 1943, 25 TC 136; [1943] AC 386; [1943] 1 All ER 280.

Payments on cancellation of service agreement

[15.9] The proprietor of a public house employed a manager (C) under a contract which gave him a right to a fixed salary, plus 25% of the profits of the business, for a fixed period. Subsequently the proprietor sold the business, and paid C £2,000 in settlement of all 'past, present and future claims' under the contract. The Commissioners determined the relevant income tax assessments on the basis that £1,090 of the £2,000 was taxable, as being his 25% share of the business profits up to the termination of the agreement (and that the balance of £910 was not taxable). C appealed, contending that none of the £2,000 was taxable. The CA rejected this contention, but held that it was necessary to ascertain the total amount which he could have recovered as damages for breach of contract, and that he was taxable on a proportion of the £2,000 equal to the proportion which £1,090 bore to the total damages which he could have recovered (eg if the total recoverable damages were £2,180, he would be taxable on 50% of the £2,000). The CA therefore remitted the case to the Commissioners. *Carter v Wadman*, CA 1946, 28 TC 41.

Cases held not to be taxable

Payment to company secretary/liquidator on winding-up

[15.10] A company which had been formed in 1912 was voluntarily wound up in 1916. The company secretary (C), who had acted without remuneration, was appointed as liquidator. After discharging all liabilities, a surplus remained and the shareholders voted to give this equally to the chairman and to C, with their thanks for the services they had rendered the company. The Revenue issued an assessment on C charging tax on the payment which he had received. He appealed, contending that the payment was a voluntary gift and was not taxable under the legislation then in force. The CA accepted this contention and allowed his appeal (by a 2-1 majority, Atkin LJ dissenting). Younger LJ held that 'the personality of the appellant' was 'everything. His office or offices, as such, whatever they were, were relatively nothing. They may have been *conditio sine qua non*, but they were not *conditio causans*.' *Cowan v Seymour*, CA 1919, 7 TC 372; [1920] 1 KB 500. (*Note*. The attempt to draw a distinction between a '*conditio causans*' and a '*conditio sine qua non*' was strongly criticised by Lord Wright in the subsequent case of *Smith Hogg & Co Ltd v Black Sea & Baltic General Insurance Co Ltd*, HL [1940] AC 997; [1940] 3 All ER 405, and by Lord Simon of Glaisdale in *Brumby v Milner*, **22.76** EMPLOYMENT INCOME. Lord Simon observed that the attempt to draw such a distinction had 'been generally abandoned', and considered that the relevant issue should not 'be determined by outmoded and ambiguous concepts of causation couched in Latin'.)

Payment to director wishing to retire but remaining

[15.11] The chairman of a company wished to retire. On retirement, he would have been entitled to 'compensation' of £12,900, equal to his remuneration for his last five years of service. His co-directors wished to be able to continue to consult him, and he agreed to remain a director at a greatly reduced rate of remuneration. He waived his right to 'compensation' on final retirement, and was paid £12,900 in lieu. The Revenue issued an assessment charging tax on this, and he appealed. The HL allowed his appeal (by a 3–2 majority, Viscount Dunedin and Lord Macmillan dissenting), holding that the £12,900 was not taxable income. Lord Atkin held that 'a sum of money paid to obtain a release from a contingent liability under a contract of employment cannot be said to be received "under" the contract of employment, is not remuneration for services rendered or to be rendered under the contract of employment, and is not received "from" the contract of employment'. *Hunter v Dewhurst*, HL 1932, 16 TC 605. (*Note*. With regard to payments to directors of the company who retired, see *Henry v Foster*, **15.1** above. For a recent analysis of the distinction between the cases, see the judgment of Chadwick LJ in *EMI Group Electronics Ltd v Coldicott*, **15.25** below.)

Agreed damages on cancellation of service agreement

[15.12] In 1923 a company cancelled the service agreement of its general manager (D), which had several years to run. He began proceedings against the company, which were settled in 1928 by the company paying him 'agreed damages' of £57,250. The Revenue issued assessments on him for the years

1923/24 to 1926/27, dividing the £57,250 over the four years in accordance with provisions made in the company's accounts for 1923 to 1926 for the commission contingently payable to D. He appealed against the assessments. The KB allowed his appeal, holding that the £57,250 was a capital payment and was not taxable. *Du Cros v Ryall*, KB 1935, 19 TC 444.

Managing director giving up management of subsidiary

[15.13] A company's managing director agreed to manage the affairs of a subsidiary in return for a percentage of its profits. These profits were greater than had been anticipated, and after two years the company ended the arrangement and paid him £4,000 as compensation. The Revenue issued an assessment charging tax on this, and he appealed. The Special Commissioners allowed his appeal, holding that the payment was compensation rather than remuneration, and was not taxable. The KB upheld their decision, applying the principles laid down by Lord Atkin in *Hunter v Dewhurst*, **15.11** above. *Duff v Barlow*, KB 1941, 23 TC 633.

[15.14] In 1920 an insurance company appointed an experienced broker (H) as a director, under an agreement whereby he received 50% of the commission from connections which he introduced to the company. In 1939 the company appointed H as managing director, and paid him £30,000 as compensation for agreeing to give up his rights under the previous agreement. The Revenue issued an assessment charging tax on the £30,000, and H appealed. The KB allowed his appeal, holding that the £30,000 was not taxable. Atkinson J held that 'the £30,000 had nothing whatever to do with his remuneration as managing director'. *Hose v Warwick*, KB 1946, 27 TC 459.

Payment to college president on retirement

[15.15] In an Irish case, the president of a university college retired after 31 years' service. The governing body granted him, in addition to his maximum pension entitlement, an extra £1,000 'on account of a great number of services unrewarded, as expressed in a labour of lengthened overtime work during the past seven or more years, and the limited statutory pension to which he is entitled'. The Revenue issued an assessment charging tax on the £1,000, and he appealed. The Special Commissioner allowed his appeal, holding that the payment was a personal gift. The HC(I) upheld this decision (by a 2-1 majority, Martin Maguire J dissenting). *Mulvey v Coffey*, HC(I) 1942, 2 ITC 239; [1942] IR 277.

Payment to director following resignation on request

[15.16] In 1938 a company appointed a managing director (H) under a six-year contract. In 1943 the board of directors asked him to resign. The company paid him the remainder of the amount due under his contract. The Revenue issued an assessment charging tax on this, but the CA allowed H's appeal. Sir Raymond Evershed MR held that the payment was 'consideration for the abandonment altogether of (H's) contracted rights', and was not taxable remuneration. *Henley v Murray*, CA 1950, 31 TC 351; [1950] 1 All ER 908.

Payments on cancellation of service agreement

[15.17] In 1956 a company employed a consultant under a five-year contract, with a salary of £4,000 pa. After he had worked for just over 12 months, the company ended the contract and agreed to pay him £4,000 for the year following the termination and £2,000 for the year after that. The Revenue issued assessments charging tax on the payments, and he appealed. The Ch D allowed his appeal, holding that the payments were compensation for surrendering the employment and not taxable emoluments. Stamp J distinguished *Hofman v Wadman*, **15.7** above, on the grounds that the employer there retained the right to call on the employee to perform certain advisory services; *obiter dicta* of Macnaghten J in that case were not followed and were implicitly disapproved. *Clayton v Lavender*, Ch D 1965, 42 TC 607.

Post-1960 cases

Payments held to be within *ITEPA 2003, s 62*

Payments on cancellation of service agreement

[15.18] A company employed a director under a contract which provided for a deemed loss of office, with consequent entitlement to compensation, on certain specified events including the disposal of certain premises which the company traded from. The company subsequently ceased trading from the premises, and paid the director compensation. The Revenue issued an assessment charging tax on this. The Ch D upheld the assessment, holding that the compensation was paid in accordance with the director's contract, and was therefore taxable. *Williams v Simmonds*, Ch D 1981, 55 TC 17; [1981] STC 715.

[15.19] In 1995 a company gave one of its employees (D) notice of termination of his employment, and requested him not to attend the office. Under the terms of D's contract, the company was required to give 18 months' notice of termination or to continue to pay his salary in lieu of notice. Following negotiations, D accepted a lump sum of £75,000. The Revenue issued an assessment on this amount. D appealed, contending that it was chargeable under what is now *ITEPA 2003, s 401* rather than what is now *s 62*, so that the first £30,000 was free of tax under what is now *ITEPA 2003, s 403(1)*. The Ch D rejected this contention and upheld the assessment. Lloyd J held that the payment arose from D's contract of employment and was therefore an emolument from his employment. Accordingly the whole £75,000 was chargeable to tax. *Richardson v Delaney*, Ch D 2001, 74 TC 167; [2001] STC 1328.

[15.20] In September 2001 an employee (N) was told that she was being made redundant. She was contractually entitled to three months' notice. She was paid her salary for these three months, but was not required to attend her employer's office. The Revenue issued an amendment to her self-assessment charging tax on the salary which she received. She appealed, contending that the payments qualified for exemption under what is now *ITEPA 2003,* *s 403(1)*. The Special Commissioner rejected this contention and dismissed her appeal, finding that she had effectively been required to take 'garden leave' for three months and holding that her salary remained taxable. The Ch D upheld this decision. Park J held that 'the question of whether an employment is determined immediately (that is, without notice and in breach of contract), or whether it is terminated on notice and without a breach of contract, depends on the facts of the particular case. On the facts of this case the correct analysis is that (N's) employment terminated on the expiry of three months' notice'. *Ibe v McNally (aka Redundant Employee v McNally)*, Ch D 2005, TL 3760; [2005] STC 1426; [2005] EWHC 1551 (Ch).

Payment to director following retirement

[15.21] See *Allum & Allum v Marsh*, **12.7** COMPANY DISTRIBUTIONS.

Contractual payment following change of duties

[15.22] In 1991 the parent company of a group informed the managing director of one of the subsidiaries that it wished him to relinquish that post and become managing director of another company in the group. He agreed to the transfer on terms whereby he would receive a substantial redundancy payment if he were to leave the group before March 1993. He ceased employment in the group in October 1992, and received £187,800 in cash plus a car valued at £9,200. The Revenue issued an assessment charging tax on this £197,000. The director appealed, contending that the payment was a termination payment within whatis now *ITEPA 2003, s 401*, so that he was entitled to relief under *ITEPA 2003, s 403*. The Special Commissioner rejected this contention and dismissed his appeal, holding that the payment had been made under the terms of the 1991 agreement as an inducement to accept another post within the group. The right to the payment was 'bound up with the continued employment to such an extent' that it was an emolument from his employment with the group. *Antelope v Ellis*, Sp C [1995] SSCD 297 (Sp C 41).

Contractual bonus payment

[15.23] An individual (P) was employed by a company (H) which provided temporary staff for client companies, under contracts whereby the workers remained employees of H, rather than of its clients. H arranged for P to do some work for one of its clients (M), under a fixed-term contract. At the conclusion of the contract. P received a bonus of £30,000, in accordance with the terms of the contract. In his tax return, P treated this bonus as a redundancy payment within *ITEPA 2003, s 401*, so that he was entitled to relief under *ITEPA 2003, s 403*. HMRC issued a ruling that the payment did not qualify for exemption, and P appealed. The First-tier Tribunal dismissed his appeal, holding that the payment was a contractual bonus payment which was outside the scope of *ITEPA 2003, s 401*. *RLM Pratt v HMRC*, FTT [2010] UKFTT 151 (TC), TC00457.

Bonus payment received after retirement

[15.24] A senior civil servant (B) retired in April 2007. In December 2007 he received a bonus payment of £6,500, from which tax was deducted. In his tax return he claimed that this should be treated as a compensation payment within *ITEPA 2003, s 401*, qualifying for relief under *s 403*. HMRC issued a closure notice ruling that the payment constituted earnings within *s 62*, and did not qualify for relief. The First-tier Tribunal dismissed B's appeal against this decision. *P Bovey v HMRC*, FTT [2012] UKFTT 226 (TC), TC01920.

Payments in lieu of notice

[15.25] A company made payments in lieu of notice to two senior employees whom it had made redundant. It did not deduct tax from the payments. The Revenue issued determinations under the *Income Tax (Employments) Regulations*. The Special Commissioners upheld the determinations, finding that the payments were made in accordance with the relevant contracts and holding that they were emoluments rather than additional redundancy payments. The Ch D and the CA upheld this decision. Chadwick LJ held that 'a payment in lieu of notice, made in pursuance of a contractual provision, agreed at the outset of the employment, which enables the (employer) to terminate the employment on making that payment', was 'properly to be regarded as an emolument from that employment'. *EMI Group Electronics Ltd v Coldicott (aka Thorn EMI Electronics Ltd v Coldicott)*, CA 1999, 71 TC 455; [1999] STC 803; [2000] 1 WLR 540. (*Notes*. (1) The Revenue accepted that payments in lieu of notice to junior employees were not taxable emoluments, since the employees had no contractual right to them. (2) For the Revenue's current practice, see Revenue Tax Bulletin February 2003, pp 999–1001.)

[15.26] A company made more than 100 employees redundant, and made payments in lieu of notice. It did not deduct tax from the payments. The Revenue issued determinations under the *Income Tax (Employments) Regulations 1993, reg 49*, and the Ch D dismissed the company's appeal. Lightman J observed that the employees were entitled under their contracts to specified payments in lieu of notice. There was no variation or discharge of their contracts of employment, and the payments were made in accordance with the contracts 'in circumstances which their contracts expressly contemplated, namely payment in lieu of notice. An event contemplated and provided for in their contracts occurred triggering the clause in their contracts entitling them to payment and the payment must constitute emoluments from the employees' employment.' *SCA Packaging Ltd v HMRC*, Ch D [2007] STC 1640; [2007] EWHC 270 (Ch).

[15.27] A woman (C) began employment with a company in January 2005. In April 2005 the company asked her to leave. The company subsequently paid her £17,971, from which it deducted tax. In her 2005/06 self-assessment return, C treated this payment as non-taxable. HMRC issued a notice of amendment treating the payment as taxable, and C appealed. The First-tier Tribunal dismissed her appeal, applying the principles laid down in *EMI Group Electronics Ltd v Coldicott*, **15.25** above, and holding that the payment was a taxable emolument since it had been paid in accordance with C's contract of employment. *Ms L Cornell v HMRC*, FTT [2009] UKFTT 140 (TC), TC00108.

[15.28] An individual (G) began working for a company in 2002. In August 2004 he was made redundant, and was paid £76,872 in lieu of notice. In his tax return, he claimed a repayment on the basis that the first £30,000 of this was exempt from tax. HMRC issued an amendment charging tax on the basis that the payment had been made in accordance with G's contract of employment, and was therefore a taxable emolument which did not qualify for exemption. G appealed. The First-tier Tribunal dismissed his appeal, applying the principles laid down in *EMI Group Electronics Ltd v Coldicott*, **15.25** above, and *SCA Packaging Ltd v HMRC*, **15.26** above. *P Goldberg v HMRC*, FTT [2010] UKFTT 346 (TC), TC00628.

[15.29] A payment of £14,000 in lieu of notice was held to be a taxable emolument in *Ms J Howell v HMRC*, FTT [2010] UKFTT 584 (TC), TC00834.

[15.30] Similar decisions were reached in *A McDonald v HMRC*, FTT [2011] UKFTT 456 (TC), TC01308; *B Goldman v HMRC*, FTT [2012] UKFTT 313 (TC); [2012] SFTD 1048, TC01999; *G Hayward v HMRC*, FTT [2012] UKFTT 431 (TC), TC02113; *K Harrison v HMRC*, FTT [2012] UKFTT 737 (TC), TC02397, and *S Manley v HMRC*, FTT [2013] UKFTT 99 (TC), TC02517.

Fee paid to footballer as inducement to agree to transfer

[15.31] See *Shilton v Wilmshurst*, **22.81** EMPLOYMENT INCOME

Payments held to be within ITEPA 2003, s 401

Payments on cancellation of service agreement

[15.32] A company appointed a new managing director (R) in 2005. In July 2007 he ceased to be managing director and was given the title 'commercial director'. In January 2008 he left the company under an agreement by which he received a termination payment of £77,731. The company treated £30,000 of this as free of tax under *ITEPA 2003, s 403*, and deducted tax from the balance. R appealed, contending that a further £30,000 should be treated as non-taxable compensation for the loss of rights under the company's enterprise management incentive scheme. The First-tier Tribunal rejected this contention and dismissed his appeal. *G Reid v HMRC*, FTT [2012] UKFTT 182 (TC), TC01877.

[15.33] A Spanish citizen (G) began working for a Spanish company (S), which was a member of an international group, in 1991. In 2000 he was transferred to a UK company (SU) in the same group. In 2003 his employment was terminated. Following negotiations, SU paid G £694,783 as compensation. Following an enquiry, HMRC issued a ruling that part of this payment was taxable under *ITEPA 2003, s 62*. R appealed, contending that the whole of the payment should be treated as compensation for loss of employment, within *ITEPA 2003, s 401*, and as qualifying for relief for 'foreign service' under *ITEPA 2003, s 413*. The First-tier Tribunal accepted this contention and allowed R's appeal. *A Gomez Rubio v HMRC*, FTT [2012] UKFTT 361 (TC), TC02047.

[15.34] A payment under a 'compromise agreement', as compensation for the loss of share option rights, was also held to fall within *ITEPA 2003, s 401* in a case where the First-tier Tribunal specifically rejected the appellant's cpontention that part of the payment should be treated as capital rather than income. *IG Essack v HMRC*, FTT [2014] UKFTT 159 (TC), TC03297.

Voluntary redundancy

[15.35] An employee had a number of disputes with his employer concerning alleged racial discrimination against him. He and his employer entered into an agreement expressed as relating 'to the appellant's severance from the employer on grounds of voluntary redundancy'. Following this agreement, he took early retirement and received compensation totalling £180,000, of which £84,925 was taken in the form of a pension and £95,075 was paid as a lump sum, from which tax was deducted. He subsequently claimed a refund of the tax, contending that £65,684 of the lump sum payment should be treated as tax-free, and submitted a self-assessment return showing his taxable lump sum as nil. The Revenue rejected the claim and amended his self-assessment return accordingly. He appealed. The Special Commissioner dismissed his appeal, holding that 'in substance and reality the £180,000 (including the sum at issue in the appeal) was paid for the voluntary termination' and was taxable under what is now *ITEPA 2003, s 401*. *Appellant v HM Inspector of Taxes*, Sp C [2001] SSCD 21 (Sp C 268). (*Note*. The Commissioner also observed that, even if the £65,684 had been held to be outside the scope of *Is 401*, it would probably have been taxable under what is now *ITEPA 2003, s 225*.)

Payment to dismissed employee

[15.36] An individual (R) was dismissed from his employment in 1996. His contract of employment had provided that his employer 'may make a payment in lieu of notice to the employee'. He took proceedings against his former employer, claiming damages for unfair dismissal and breach of contract. The CA held that the contract had given the employer the discretion to make a payment in lieu of notice, but had not required it to do so, so that R's claim was for wrongful dismissal. *Rowley v Cerberus Software Ltd*, CA [2001] EWCA Civ 78. (*Note*. For the Revenue's practice following this decision, see Revenue Interpretation RI 249, reproduced in Tax Bulletin 63, February 2003. The Revenue accept that for tax purposes, the payment was a termination payment within what is now *ITEPA 2003, s 401*, rather than a taxable emolument, so that it qualified for relief under what is now *ITEPA 2003, s 403* and there was no liability to Class 1 NIC.)

Payments to redundant employees

[15.37] A manufacturing company made a large number of employees redundant. Following negotiations with the employees' union, it paid each employee £2,500 in recognition of any rights under the *Trade Union and Labour Relations (Consolidation) Act 1992*. The Revenue issued a determination under the *Income Tax (Employments) Regulations*. The company appealed, contending that the payments were covered by the exemption for payments up to £30,000 under what is now *ITEPA 2003, s 403*, so that it had not been required to deduct tax. The Special Commissioner accepted this contention and allowed the appeal, holding that the source of the employees' right to any award was the *Trade Union and Labour Relations (Consolidation) Act*, and 'not the employer and employee relationship'. *Mimtec Ltd v CIR*, Sp C [2001] SSCD 101 (Sp C 277).

[15.38] An individual (P) had been employed for many years by a group of companies which operated an employee incentive scheme known as a 'stock bonus plan'. In 1998 he was made redundant. In 2001 he received a disbursement of £64,726 under the 'stock bonus plan'. The Revenue issued a ruling that this was a taxable emolument. P appealed, contending that it should be treated as a termination payment under what is now *ITEPA 2003, s 401*. The Special Commissioner accepted this contention and allowed the appeal, holding on the evidence that the payment had been made in settlement of claims that P could have 'made in an action for breach of employment rights'. It was not simply 'satisfaction of an existing entitlement to remuneration earned during the period of employment'. Accordingly it was not an emolument from P's employment, but fell within *s 401*. *Porter v HMRC*, Sp C [2005] SSCD 803 (Sp C 501).

Compensation following 'constructive dismissal'

[15.39] A woman (C) began employment with a company in 1996. In 2003 her responsibilities were changed. She took the view that this amounted to 'constructive dismissal'. Her employers took the view that the circumstances did not amount to 'constructive dismissal', and that she had resigned. However, following negotiations, she was paid a lump sum representing three months' salary as a 'goodwill gesture'. HMRC issued an amendment to her self-assessment, charging tax on the basis that the payment was a taxable emolument. She appealed, contending that it was a compensation payment within *ITEPA 2003, s 401*, and qualified for the £30,000 exemption under *ITEPA 2003, s 403*. The First-Tier Tribunal accepted this contention and allowed her appeal, applying the principles laid down in *EMI Group Electronics Ltd v Coldicott*, **15.25** above, and accepting C's contention that the circumstances amounted to 'constructive dismissal'. *Dr J Clinton v HMRC*, FTT [2009] UKFTT 337 (TC), TC00278.

Compensation following termination of employment

[15.40] A city council had paid an employee (C) an allowance for using his car on council business. It terminated this contract and re-employed C without a car allowance. C appealed to an industrial tribunal, which held that the termination of his previous contract amounted to unfair dismissal, and ordered the council to pay compensation to C and to reinstate the car allowance. Subsequently the council agreed to make a compromise payment of £5,060 to C. The Revenue issued a notice of amendment, ruling that this was taxable. C appealed, contending that it was covered by the exemption for payments up to £30,000 under what is now *ITEPA 2003, s 403*. The General Commissioners accepted this contention and allowed his appeal, and the Ch D and CA upheld their decision. Peter Gibson LJ held that the payment was not an emolument of C's employment, but was made 'in connection with or in consequence of' the termination of that employment. *Wilson v Clayton*, CA 2004, 77 TC 1; [2005] STC 157; [2004] EWCA Civ 1657.

[15.41] A 'compromise payment' was also held to qualify for exemption under *ITEPA 2003, s 403* in *NJ Wood v HMRC*, FTT [2010] UKFTT 288 (TC), TC00577.

[15.42] A company (J) made an employee (M) redundant in March 2010. M received statutory redundancy pay of £10,640. He began proceedings against J, alleging unfair dismissal and age discrimination. J subsequently paid M £200,000 under a compromise agreement. M did not include this in his tax return. HMRC agreed to treat £60,000 of this payment as exempt, but issued an amendment charging tax on £140,000. The First-tier Tribunal dismissed M's appeal, and reduced the exemption under *ITEPA 2003, s 403* to £19,360 to take account of the previous payment of £10,640. Judge Redston held that HMRC's agreement to treat £60,000 as exempt was 'an unlawful concession' which was outside HMRC's powers. Applying the principles laid down by Lord Hoffmann in *R (oao Wilkinson) v CIR*, **31.77** HUMAN RIGHTS, *TMA 1970, s 1* could not be construed 'so widely as to enable the Commissioners to concede, by extra-statutory concession, an allowance which Parliament could have granted but did not grant'. While some of the payment may have represented compensation for injury to M's feelings, it was also paid in connection with the termination of his employment, and was taxable accordingly. *K Moorthy v HMRC*, FTT [2014] UKFTT 834 (TC), TC03952.

Compensation to subpostmaster on loss of office

[15.43] An individual (B) had been appointed as a subpostmaster in 2000. In 2005 the Post Office decided to close his office (along with a large number of similar post offices). The Post Office paid B £77,905 as compensation. B did not include this payment on his 2005/06 tax return. HMRC issued an amendment treating it as taxable under *ITEPA 2003, s 401* (subject to relief for the first £30,000 under *s 403*). B appealed, contending that he should be treated as a self-employed agent of the Post Office. The First-Tier Tribunal rejected this contention and dismissed his appeal, holding that a subpostmaster held an 'office' and the payment which B had received was taxable compensation for the loss of that office. *B Bimson v HMRC (No 2)*, FTT [2012] UKFTT 216 (TC), TC01911.

[15.44] Similar decisions were reached in *LS Uppal v HMRC*, FTT [2010] UKFTT 215 (TC), TC00516; *A Cude v HMRC*, FTT [2010] UKFTT 424 (TC), TC00693, *Mrs R Orme v HMRC*, FTT [2011] UKFTT 618 (TC), TC01460; *Mrs IO Owolabi v HMRC*, [2012] UKFTT 334 (TC), TC02020, and *Mrs BJ Panesar v HMRC*, [2012] UKFTT 688 (TC), TC02359.

[15.45] In a similar case, the Post Office paid a subpostmaster (P) compensation of £76,008. HMRC issued an assessment on the basis that £30,000 of this qualified for exemption under *ITEPA 2003, s 403*, but that the remainder was subject to tax. P appealed, contending that he should be allowed a deduction for a payment of £37,122 which he had made to his wife, who had worked for him. The First-tier Tribunal rejected this contention and dismissed his appeal, finding that P's wife had been a partner in the retail business which had operated in conjunction with the sub-post office, and had not been an employee. *HS Patel v HMRC*, FTT [2014] UKFTT 1101 (TC), TC04189.

Payment in respect of change to redundancy entitlement

[15.46] In 1973 an individual (C) began working for a company (B) which had a contractual redundancy scheme. In 1996 B decided to phase out its contractual redundancy scheme, and paid C £33,148 as compensation. B only deducted tax from £3,148 of this payment. In 2005 C was made redundant. He received a redundancy payment and a payment in lieu of notice. In his tax return, he treated £30,000 of the payment as exempt from tax under *ITEPA 2003, s 403(1)*. HMRC issued an amendment denying the exemption, on the grounds that the exemption had been exhausted by the payment which C had received in 1996. The First-Tier Tribunal allowed C's appeal but the Upper Tribunal reversed this decision and upheld HMRC's amendment, holding that 'a payment made to satisfy a contingent right to a redundancy payment will normally derive its character from the nature of the payment it replaces'. The payment made in 1996 had been made in return for C's agreement 'to a change in his contractual redundancy entitlements' and had fallen within what is now *ITEPA 2003, s 403*. *HMRC v KG Colquhoun*, UT [2010] UKUT 431 (TCC); [2011] STC 394. (Note. At a subsequent hearing, the Upper Tribunal awarded HMRC costs of £1,000—UT April 2011, FTC/36/2010.)

Payment under Employment Rights Act 1996

[15.47] A woman (T) had been employed as an auditor. Her employment was terminated in 2009. She applied to the Employment Tribunal for interim relief under *Employment Rights Act 1996, s 128*. She received monthly payments pending the hearing of her claim by the Employment Tribunal, which found that she had been unfairly dismissed. Her former employer subsequently agreed to pay her legal costs. In completing her 2009/10 tax return, she treated the interim relief payments which she had received as representing compensation for the loss of her employment (so that the first £30,000 was exempt from tax). HMRC issued a notice of amendment charging tax on the payments. The First-tier Tribunal allowed T's appeal, holding that T's employment had ended in 2009. Judge Poole observed that 'it was only as a result of the termination of her employment that she became entitled to claim interim relief. When that relief was granted, it did not have the effect of reinstating her employment, it merely entitled her to receive certain payments and other benefits equivalent to what she would have received if the employment had continued.' *ME Turullols v HMRC*, FTT [2014] UKFTT 672 (TC); [2014] SFTD 1099, TC03795.

Provision of car for former director

[15.48] The chairman of a limited company, which had a number of subsidiary companies, was not re-elected at the company's 1987 annual general meeting. At the next board meeting he was dismissed from all his executive posts within the group. He remained a non-executive director of some of the subsidiary companies until resigning in 1988 under an agreement whereby the company paid him £110,000, and was to provide him with a car for nine years. He appealed against an assessment for 1987/88, contending that the provision of the cars was outside the scope of *ITEPA 2003, s 403**. The Special Commissioner rejected his contention, holding that the operation of *s 403** was not 'limited to benefits which are convertible into money'. The amount of the benefit to be brought into charge 'should be calculated by reference to the value in money terms which would be placed by a reasonable person on the right to use a motor car taking into account the restrictions contained in the termination agreement'. *George v Ward*, Sp C [1995] SSCD 230 (Sp C 30). (*Note*. For the valuation of benefits, see *ITEPA 2003, s 415*, deriving from *ICTA 1988, s 148(6)*.)

Costs incurred in connection with terminal payments

[15.49] In 1976 a company dismissed its general manager (J), paying him three months' salary (£2,250) in lieu of notice. An industrial tribunal subsequently awarded him £5,200 for unfair dismissal. The Revenue issued an assessment charging tax on the award. (At the time, the exemption under what is now *ITEPA 2003, s 403* was £5,000.) J appealed, contending that he should be allowed a deduction of £1,300 for his legal expenses and £500 in respect of the expenses incurred in finding new employment. The Ch D rejected these contentions and upheld the assessment, holding that the wording of the legislation did not authorise any such deduction. *Warnett v Jones*, Ch D 1979, 53 TC 283; [1980] STC 131; [1980] 1 WLR 413.

Cases held to be partly taxable

Payments on cancellation of service agreement

[15.50] A company was dissatisfied with the performance of three of its directors, and invited them to resign. Following negotiations, the company and the directors entered into compromise agreements whereby the directors received termination payments, part of which was expressed to represent a return of pension contributions and part was expressed as compensation for the loss of share option rights. In their tax returns, the directors treated these payments as not taxable. The Revenue issued amendments charging tax on the payments, and the directors appealed. The Special Commissioner allowed the appeals in part, holding that the part of the payments representing returns of pension contributions and loss of share option rights fell within what is now *ITEPA 2003, s 401*. *Brander & Others v HMRC*, Sp C [2007] SSCD 582 (Sp C 610).

[15.51] A company made its sales director (J) redundant. It paid him compensation, which it treated as falling within *ITEPA 2003, s 401*. J appealed, contending that £30,000 of the compensation which he had received should be treated as non-taxable compensation for the loss of rights under the company's enterprise management incentive scheme. Judge Gort accepted this contention and allowed J's appeal, specifically declining to follow the earlier decision in *Reid v HMRC*, **15.32** above (which concerned the managing director of the same company). *I Johnson v HMRC*, FTT [2013] UKFTT 242 (TC), TC02656.

Compensation following 'constructive dismissal'

[15.52] In a Northern Ireland case, an individual (W) had been employed by a dairy company from 1979 until 1994. He subsequently received a severance payment of £63,500 from the company. He was also awarded £77,446 by a tribunal on the grounds that his loss of employment 'amounted to a constructive dismissal based on religious discrimination'. This included a payment of £12,500 in respect of 'injury to feelings'. The Revenue assessed both payments under what is now *ITEPA 2003, s 401*. W appealed, contending that the compensation awarded by the tribunal should not be taxable. The Special Commissioner reviewed the evidence and held that the £12,500 for 'injury to feelings' was not taxable, but that the balance of £64,946 was taxable under *s 401*. *Walker v Adams*, Sp C [2003] SSCD 269 (Sp C 344).

[15.53] In 2002 a senior bank employee resigned from his employment after being told that he would receive a written warning for 'breach of internal procedures'. In 2003 he claimed compensation on the grounds of unfair 'constructive dismissal'. The bank subsequently paid him £250,000 in compensation, and deducted tax as required by what are now the *Income Tax (PAYE) Regulations*. The employee objected to the deduction of tax. The Revenue issued a ruling that £10,000 of the payment was for 'injury to feelings' and was not taxable (applying the principles laid down in *Walker v Adams*, **15.52** above), but that the remaining £240,000 was taxable under what is now *ITEPA 2003, s 401*. The employee appealed, contending that only £50,000 should be treated as falling within *s 401*, and that the remaining £200,000 should not be taxed on the grounds that it represented compensation for loss of reputation and injury to feelings. The Special Commissioner rejected this contention and dismissed the appeal, holding that there was 'a direct link between the compensation and the termination of the appellant's employment'. On the evidence, the bank had conducted 'an investigation which followed transparent procedures into a complaint that the appellant had not met compliance regulations', and 'the compensation allocated to injury to feelings should be limited to a maximum of £10,000'. *Mr A v HMRC (No 2)*, Sp C [2009] SSCD 269 (Sp C 734).

Payment following racial discrimination

[15.54] An individual (C) was employed by a US bank in London. He subsequently began proceedings against the bank, claiming that he had been subjected to racial discrimination and harassment. He agreed a settlement whereby his employment was terminated, the bank paid him £500,000 (from which it deducted income tax), and he waived all legal claims against the bank. HMRC issued an amendment to his self-assessment, treating £28,000 of the £500,000 as non-taxable damages but treating the balance of £472,000 as taxable compensation for loss of his employment (subject to the £30,000 exemption under *ITEPA 2003, s 403*). C appealed, contending that only £18,000 of the payment should be treated as compensation for the loss of his employment, and that the balance of £482,000 should not be treated as taxable. The First-tier Tribunal reviewed the evidence in detail and allowed the appeal in part, holding that £165,000 of the payment was compensation for the loss of C's employment, and that the balance of £335,000 was not taxable. Judge Sadler found that C had been subjected to racial abuse, and that the New York courts had ordered the bank to pay substantial damages to some female employees following claims of sexual discrimination. He observed that C's claims 'might have resulted in his receiving damages payable under United States legislation had the matter been dealt with in the New York courts'. While a payment of £335,000 'might be seen as a large amount by way of settlement for non-pecuniary loss as a result of alleged discrimination and harassment', the case had to be viewed in the light of C's 'likely rights under United States legislation'. *CA Oti-Obihara v HMRC*, FTT [2010] UKFTT 568 (TC); [2011] SFTD 202, TC00819. (*Note. Obiter dicta* of Judge Sadler were disapproved by Judge Redston in the subsequent case of *Moorthy v HMRC*, **15.42** above.)

Cases held not to be taxable

Payment to former Army officer

[15.55] A former Army sergeant (C) applied for several 'non-regular permanent staff posts' without success. He left the Army in February 1994. In December 1994 he applied to the Army for redress, contending that he should have been appointed to a non-regular permanent staff post, and that he had been unfairly dismissed. In July 2001 the Army Board agreed that he should have been appointed to one of the posts for which he had applied, and in May 2005 they offered him more than £150,000 in compensation (which took account of C's loss of pension entitlement). The Army Board deducted tax at the basic rate (which was then 22%). HMRC amended C's self-assessment to tax the appropriate part of the award at the higher rate of 40%. C appealed, contending that the payment should not have been subject to tax. The Special Commissioner accepted this contention and allowed C's appeal, observing that C had left the Army of his own accord, some time after the failure of his applications for various posts had been rejected, and that he 'should have received compensation for the selection boards' failings even if he had stayed in the Army because the compensation was awarded for failings in the procedure leading to his not being offered posts which he was not offered while still in the Army's employment'. Accordingly the Commissioner held that there was no direct link 'between the payment of compensation and the termination of (C's) employment with the Army'. *TJ Crompton v HMRC*, Sp C [2009] SSCD 504; [2009] UKFTT 71 (TC), TC00012.

16

Construction Industry: Contractors and Subcontractors

The cases in this chapter are arranged under the following headings.

Construction industry scheme (FA 2004, ss 57–77)

FA 2004, s 58—definition of 'subcontractor'

[16.1] A company (L) failed to deduct tax from payments to two subcontractors falsely claiming to be directors of another company (B). The Revenue assessed L to recover the tax, and L appealed. The Commissioners dismissed the appeal, finding that they were not satisfied that L's directors had taken 'reasonable steps to satisfy themselves' that the two men 'were in fact genuine officers or representatives of (B)'. The Ch D upheld the Commissioners' decision as one of fact. *Ladkarn Ltd v McIntosh*, Ch D 1982, 56 TC 616; [1983] STC 113.

FA 2004, s 59—definition of 'contractor'

[16.2] A company (M) carried out construction work on two substantial properties. It failed to deduct tax from payments to subcontractors. The Revenue issued assessments to recover the tax. The company appealed, contending that it should not be treated as a 'contractor', within *ICTA 1988, s 560(2)(a)*. The General Commissioners rejected this contention and dismissed the appeal, and the Ch D upheld their decision. Sir Francis Ferris held that, on the evidence, M was 'a person carrying on a business which includes construction operations'. *Mundial Invest SA v Moore*, Ch D 2005, [2006] STC 412; [2005] EWHC 1735 (Ch).

[16.3] An individual (J), and a company which he controlled, owned several properties, which were let as investments. J arranged for his son (M) to organise some refurbishment work on the properties, paying him £200 per week and reimbursing all the expenditure which he incurred. HMRC formed the opinion that M was a contractor, and issued assessments charging tax under *ICTA 1988, s 559(4)* on sums which he had paid to subcontractors. M appealed, contending that he was acting as an agent for his father. The First-Tier Tribunal allowed his appeal. Judge Porter observed that 'the legislation makes it clear that a property business that acquires and disposes of buildings for capital gain or uses the buildings for rental is outside the scope of the Construction Industry Scheme, unless its expenditure on construction operations is sufficient for it to be treated as a "deemed contractor"'. On the evidence, the properties were investment properties and did not 'fall within the ambit of the construction industry scheme'. M was carrying out his father's instructions and supervising the work on his behalf. As an employee, he should have been paid under deduction of PAYE, but it appeared that he had 'paid the appropriate amount of tax'. (Judge Porter noted that it was 'unclear whether the workers had also paid an appropriate amount of tax'.) *M Buckingham v HMRC*, FTT [2010] UKFTT 593 (TC), TC00843.

FA 2004, s 61—deductions on account of tax

[16.4] In a Scottish case, a building company (C) was registered under the construction industry scheme. In March 2007 it engaged a firm (T) as a subcontractor, and did not deduct tax from the payments it made. HMRC issued an assessment to recover the tax due, and also imposed a penalty (at the rate of 10%) under *TMA, s 98A(4)*. C appealed, contending that one of T's partners had told one of its directors that T had gross payment status, and had produced a card which appeared to verify this. The First-Tier Tribunal accepted C's evidence and allowed its appeal. Judge Barton found that the document which T had produced 'may not have been authentic', but held that C's director had taken 'reasonable care' to comply with *FA 2004, s 61*, and that C's 'failure to deduct the tax was due to an error made in good faith'. *Croftport Ltd v HMRC*, FTT [2011] UKFTT 419 (TC), TC01272.

[16.5] A company (R) operated the construction industry scheme. HMRC discovered that, in accounting for tax under the scheme, it had failed to deduct tax from certain payments of expenses (principally travel and lodging expenses) to subcontractors. They issued determinations under *SI 2005/2045, reg 13* to recover the tax due. R appealed, contending that it had taken reasonable care to comply with *FA 2004, s 61*, and that its failure to make the relevant deductions was due to an error made in good faith. The First-tier Tribunal accepted R's evidence and allowed its appeal. *Refit Shopfitting Services Ltd v HMRC*, FTT [2013] UKFTT 42 (TC), TC02462.

[16.6] A company (F) operated the construction industry scheme. HMRC formed the opinion that, in accounting for tax under the scheme, it had overstated the amounts of the payments it made which represented the cost of materials, and had therefore not deducted sufficient tax from the payments it made to its contractors. They issued determinations under *SI 2005/2045, reg 13* to recover the tax. The First-tier Tribunal dismissed F's appeal against the determinations. Judge Poole observed that *FA 2004, s 61(1)* required a deduction to be made from all payments made to subcontractors, except for 'any part of the payment which is shown to represent the materials cost'. He held that 'the word "shown" in this context connotes the satisfactory demonstration by appropriate evidence of the relevant facts, in a way which can be properly evaluated not just by the contractor but also by HMRC and, if necessary, the tribunal'. F had failed to submit satisfactory evidence to displace the determinations. (The tribunal also dismissed an appeal against the cancellation of F's gross payment status.) *Flemming & Son Construction (West Midlands) Ltd v HMRC*, FTT [2012] UKFTT 205 (TC), TC01900.

[16.7] In 1991 an English accountant, who lived in the Isle of Man, incorporated a company (O). In 1999 O incorporated a subsidiary company (IM). IM began to carry on business in the UK, and to help construction workers to obtain work, but did not register under the construction industry scheme. In 2001 IM incorporated a UK subsidiary (IK), which applied for, and obtained, registration under the scheme. In 2007 HMRC began an enquiry into IK's returns. HMRC subsequently discovered that IK had made substantial payments to IM, and formed the opinion that these had been made for the supply of subcontract labour, and should have been treated as falling within the construction industry scheme. They issued determinations charging tax of more than £42,000,000, and issued a notice cancelling IK's gross payment status. IK appealed. The First-tier Tribunal reviewed the evidence in detail and dismissed the appeals. Judge Herrington found that IM 'performed a management role in relation to contracts for work entered into by the construction workers within the firms for whom they provided their services'. It acted 'as the construction worker's agent in remitting payments in respect of arrangements entered into by the construction worker for the provision of his services to third parties'. IK had been 'established purely to enable payments to be received gross and to replicate what was previously effected directly by construction firms and agencies with (IM) until it became clear that those entities required to deal with an entity that could receive gross payments'. IK was 'a mere conduit for the passing through of sums it received gross in respect of construction services provided by the construction workers to the construction firms concerned'. For the purposes of the construction industry scheme, IK was a contractor. The payments which it made to IM were 'contract payments', since IM was a 'nominated person' within *FA 2004, s 60(1)(c)*. Judge Herrington concluded that IM had been 'fully aware of the risk that the arrangements may not be compliant with the CIS but deliberately refrained from discussing it with HMRC'. Its actions were 'likely to have resulted in a shocking level of tax evasion and loss of the revenue to the Exchequer in respect of sums that should have been accounted for in respect of payments made to the construction workers'. *Island Contract Management (UK) Ltd v HMRC*, FTT [2013] UKFTT 207 (TC), TC02622.

[16.8] A married couple traded as building contractors, but failed to operate the construction industry scheme. HMRC issued notices of determination under *Income Tax (Construction Industry Scheme) Regulations 2005 (SI 2005/2045), reg 13*, to recover the tax which the couple should have deducted from the payments they made to the subcontractors who worked for them. The couple appealed, contending that they had not been aware of the scheme. The First-tier Tribunal dismissed their appeal. Judge Vellins observed that 'it is well established that ignorance of the law is not a defence'. *KG & Mrs HE Johnston (t/a Johnston Builders) v HMRC*, FTT [2010] UKFTT 212 (TC), TC00513.

[16.9] Determinations under what is now *SI 2005/2045, reg 13* were also upheld in *MJ Thomas v HMRC*, FTT [2010] UKFTT 567 (TC), TC00818;

Britannic Estates Ltd v HMRC, FTT [2014] UKFTT 974 (TC), TC04086, and *Hughes v HMRC*, **29.127** FURTHER ASSESSMENTS: LOSS OF TAX.

[16.10] Two brothers, who traded in partnership in the construction industry, failed to deduct tax from certain payments to subcontractors. HMRC issued determinations under *Income Tax (Construction Industry Scheme) Regulations 2005 (SI 2005/2045), reg 13*. The partnership appealed, contending that the subcontractors had accounted for the tax due on their income and that *SI 2005/2045, reg 9* applied. The First-tier Tribunal reviewed the evidence and allowed the appeal in part, finding that some of the subcontractors had made returns and paid the tax due, but that three of the subcontractors had not 'provided any assistance in resolving the dispute'. The tribunal therefore upheld the determinations with regard to the amounts paid to those three subcontractors. *G & A Hardwicke (t/a PVC Fascia Company) v HMRC*, FTT [2011] UKFTT 17 (TC), TC00894.

[16.11] HMRC discovered that an electrical contractor (W) had failed to deduct tax from payments he had made to two subcontractors, and issued a determination under *Income Tax (Construction Industry Scheme) Regulations 2005 (SI 2005/2045), reg 13*. W appealed, contending that the determination was excessive, and that the main contractor for whom he had worked had fraudulently overstated the amount which he had received and had passed on to his subcontractors). The First-tier Tribunal accepted this contention and reduced the amount charged by the determination. *R Winsor (t/a Winsor Electrical) v HMRC*, FTT [2012] UKFTT 668 (TC), TC02339.

[16.12] In a Scottish case, HMRC discovered that a company (J), which installed suspended ceilings, had failed to deduct tax from payments made to two companies which had acted as subcontractors. They issued determinations under *Income Tax (Construction Industry Scheme) Regulations 2005 (SI 2005/2045), reg 13*. J appealed, contending that it had taken reasonable care to comply with the regulations, as both the companies were controlled by a long-serving subcontractor (B) who had a tax certificate, and it had assumed that B's certificate would also cover the work done by the companies. The First-tier Tribunal allowed J's appeal, finding that 'this was the only error that (J) had made with its subcontractors over a seven-year period' and holding that J had taken 'reasonable care'. *J & M Interiors (Scotland) Ltd v HMRC*, FTT [2014] UKFTT 183 (TC), TC03323.

FA 2004, s 64—requirements for registration for gross payment

Requirements of FA 2004, Sch 11 para 8

[16.13] A married couple had traded in partnership, fixing cladding to the outside of concrete buildings. They had about 20 subcontractors, and had registered for gross payment under the construction industry scheme. In 2010 HMRC cancelled their registration on the grounds that during 2009 they had made three payments of tax (the balancing payment due on 31 January, and the payments on account due on 31 January and 31 July) more than 30 days late. The couple appealed, contending that they had made a loss during 2009 (following a claim for damages by a customer) which they had subsequently claimed to carry back to 2007/08, so that the payments they had been required to make were not in fact due and should be disregarded for the purposes of *FA 2004, Sch 11 para 8*. The First-Tier Tribunal accepted this contention and allowed the appeal. Judge Mosedale held that in view of the couple's loss relief claim, 'it is likely that they will have no tax to pay for some time to come' and in view of their good compliance record before 2009, there was no reason to expect that they would fail to meet future tax obligations. *A & P Noden v HMRC*, FTT [2011] UKFTT 214 (TC), TC01079.

Requirements of FA 2004, Sch 11 para 10

[16.14] A company carried on an agency business, similar to an employment agency, introducing subcontract labour to clients in the construction industry. It held a tax certificate under *ICTA 1988, s 561*. The Revenue rejected an application for the renewal of the certificate, considering firstly that the company's activities did not constitute 'the furnishing or arranging for the furnishing of labour in carrying out construction operations', within *FA 2004, Sch 11 para 10*, and secondly that the company had not complied with its tax obligations in the qualifying period. The company appealed, contending firstly that its activities were within *FA 2004, Sch 11 para 10*, and secondly that its failures were 'minor and technical', and should be ignored. The Special Commissioner reviewed the evidence in detail and accepted the company's first contention, holding that the company's activities were within *FA 2004, Sch 11 para 10*. However, the Commissioner rejected the company's second contention, holding that the failures were not 'minor and technical'. Accordingly the Commissioner dismissed the appeal. Both sides appealed to the Ch D, which upheld the Commissioner's decision. *Hudson Contract Services Ltd v HMRC (and cross-appeal)*, Ch D 2007, 78 TC 756; [2007] STC 1363; [2007] EWHC 73 (Ch). (*Note*. For subsequent developments in this case, see **16.55** below.)

[16.15] A company (G) provided 'a comprehensive administrative, compliance and company secretarial service for personal service companies'. About 65% of its business related to personal service companies in the construction industry. In 2003 it applied for a CIS 5 tax certificate, which was granted. In 2006 it applied to renew the certificate. HMRC rejected the application, considering firstly that G's activities did not constitute 'the furnishing or arranging for the furnishing of labour in carrying out construction operations', within *FA 2004, Sch 11 para 10*, and secondly that G had not complied with its tax obligations in the qualifying period. G appealed. The Special Commissioner reviewed the evidence in detail and dismissed the appeal, holding that G's business did include 'the furnishing or arranging for the furnishing of labour in carrying out construction operations'. However, in some cases G had failed to withhold tax from companies which did not hold CIS 4 certificates, so that it failed to met the compliance test of *Sch 11 para 12*. *Gabem Management Ltd v HMRC*, Sp C [2007] SSCD 247 (Sp C 586).

Requirements of FA 2004, Sch 11 para 12

[16.16] A company applied for 'gross payment status' within the construction industry scheme. HMRC rejected the application on the grounds that the company had failed the 'compliance test' laid down by *FA 2004, Sch 11, para 12*, in that it had not paid its corporation tax by the due date. The

First-Tier Tribunal dismissed the company's appeal against this decision. Judge Berner observed that 'gross payment status depends on the satisfaction of conditions, such as compliance with tax obligations. The possible commercial effect of failing to achieve such status through non-compliance cannot form the basis for an appeal against refusal.' *Bellwell Plant Ltd v HMRC*, FTT [2010] UKFTT 318 (TC), TC00605.

[16.17] Similar decisions were reached in *D Forsyth v HMRC*, FTT [2012] UKFTT 209 (TC), TC01904; *Dale Services Contracts Ltd v HMRC*, FTT [2012] UKFTT 299 (TC), TC01985; *Hudson Contract Services Ltd v HMRC*, **16.14** above, and *Gabem Management Ltd v HMRC*, **16.15** above.

Requirements of FA 2004, Sch 11 para 14

[16.18] A contractor (B) had registered for 'gross payment status' within the construction industry scheme. Under the self-assessment system, he was required to make a payment on account of tax due on 31 January 2007. He failed to make this payment until 23 April 2007. On 8 February 2008 HMRC cancelled his registration on the grounds that he had failed to meet his compliance obligations. The First-Tier Tribunal allowed B's appeal against this decision. Judge Walters observed that *FA 2004, Sch 11 para 14* provided that the 'qualifying period' for the purpose of the scheme was 'the period of twelve months ending with the date of the application in question'. In B's case, this was 'the period of 12 months ending with 8 February 2008'. 31 January 2007 did not fall within this 'qualifying period'. Judge Walters held that HMRC 'may not therefore rely on non-compliance with that obligation for the purposes of cancelling the appellant's registration for gross payment by a determination on 8 February 2008'. *T Bruns (t/a TK Fabrications) v HMRC*, FTT [2010] UKFTT 58 (TC), TC00371. (*Notes.* (1) HMRC were not represented at the hearing. HMRC reportedly take the view that the obligation is a continuing one, so that B's non-compliance continued from 31 January 2007 to 22 April 2007, ie that it continued into the qualifying period. In the absence of any representative from HMRC, Judge Walters did not specifically consider this argument. (2) *Obiter dicta* of Judge Walters were not followed, and were implicitly disapproved, by Judge Blewitt in the subsequent case of *Industrial Contracting Services Ltd v HMRC*, **16.23** below.)

FA 2004, s 66—cancellation of registration for gross payment

[16.19] A company (W) had registered for 'gross payment status' within the construction industry scheme. In 2008 HMRC cancelled its registration on the grounds that it had failed to satisfy the 'compliance test', in that its PAYE payments had been made consistently late, it had failed to pay its corporation tax, and had failed to submit its corporation tax return. The First-Tier Tribunal dismissed W's appeal against this decision. Judge Brooks observed that W had failed to specify its grounds of appeal. Applying the principles laid down in *Jacques v HMRC (No 1)*, **4.26** APPEALS, it followed that the appeal was invalid. *Westview Rail Ltd v HMRC*, FTT [2009] UKFTT 269 (TC), TC00215.

[16.20] A glazing contractor (G) had registered for 'gross payment status' within the construction industry scheme. In 2008 HMRC cancelled his registration on the grounds that he had failed to satisfy the 'compliance test', in that he had delayed paying his tax liabilities until well after the due date. G appealed. The First-Tier Tribunal dismissed his appeal, holding that there was no reasonable excuse for G's late payment of the tax due. *J Grosvenor v HMRC*, FTT [2009] UKFTT 283 (TC), TC00227.

[16.21] Both partners in a partnership had registered for 'gross payment status' within the construction industry scheme. In 2008 HMRC cancelled the registration of one of the partners (B) on the grounds that he had failed to satisfy the 'compliance test', in that he had delayed paying his tax liabilities until well after the due date. B appealed, contending that he had a reasonable excuse because he had been suffering financial difficulties. The First-Tier Tribunal dismissed his appeal, holding that 'an insufficiency of funds is not of itself a reasonable excuse'. *R Beard v HMRC*, FTT [2009] UKFTT 284 (TC), TC00228.

[16.22] Similar decisions were reached in *A Longworth & Sons Ltd v HMRC*, FTT [2009] UKFTT 286 (TC), TC00230; *D Munns v HMRC*, FTT [2009] UKFTT 290 (TC), TC00234; *Strongwork Construction Ltd v HMRC*, FTT [2009] UKFTT 292 (TC), TC00236; *Ductaire Fabrications Ltd v HMRC*, FTT [2009] UKFTT 350 (TC), TC00288; *Enderbey Properties Ltd v HMRC*, FTT [2010] UKFTT 85 (TC), TC00396; *E Chatterton v HMRC*, FTT [2010] UKFTT 147 (TC), TC00453; *GC Ware Electrics v HMRC*, FTT [2010] UKFTT 197 (TC), TC00499; *S Getty v HMRC*, FTT [2010] UKFTT 251 (TC), TC00546; *Mrs S Grayson v HMRC*, FTT [2010] UKFTT 252 (TC), TC00547; *T Pollard v HMRC*, FTT [2010] UKFTT 269 (TC), TC00563; *Eurotec Services v HMRC (and related appeal)*, FTT [2010] UKFTT 321 (TC), TC00608; *K1 Construction Ltd v HMRC*, FTT [2010] UKFTT 347 (TC), TC00629; *Glen Contract Services Ltd v HMRC*, FTT [2010] UKFTT 391 (TC), TC00673; *Desmond Magee & Sons v HMRC*, FTT [2010] UKFTT 456 (TC), TC00721; *D Williams v HMRC*, FTT [2010] UKFTT 508 (TC), TC00763; *AT McLeod v HMRC*, FTT [2010] UKFTT 542 (TC), TC00795; *GRD Systems v HMRC*, FTT November 2010 (TC00797); *S Jordan (t/a Steve Jordan Fencing) v HMRC*, FTT [2010] UKFTT 570 (TC), TC00821; *P Wright v HMRC*, FTT [2011] UKFTT 14 (TC), TC00891; *M McDowall v HMRC*, FTT [2011] UKFTT 28 (TC), TC00905; *BP Davies (t/a Davies Construction) v HMRC*, FTT [2011] UKFTT 77 (TC), TC00955; *W Begbie (t/a Ready Steady Labourers) v HMRC*, FTT [2011] UKFTT 184 (TC), TC01053; *N Bruce (t/a Norrie Bruce Plant Hire) v HMRC*, FTT [2011] UKFTT 241 (TC), TC01105; *Shaw Cleaning Service v HMRC*, FTT [2011] UKFTT 378 (TC), TC01233; *JJ Duffy v HMRC*, FTT [2011] UKFTT 405 (TC), TC01260; *FP McDermott v HMRC*, FTT [2011] UKFTT 477 (TC), TC01324; *Base Brickwork v HMRC*, FTT [2012] UKFTT 536 (TC), TC02212, and *East Midlands Contracting Ltd v HMRC*, FTT [2013] UKFTT 25 (TC), TC02445.

[16.23] A company, which was registered for 'gross payment status' within the construction industry scheme, made a payment of Class 1A NIC 20 days late. HMRC cancelled its registration. The company appealed, contending that the cancellation was disproportionate and unreasonable. The First-Tier Tribunal reviewed the evidence and the previous case law in detail, rejected this contention, and dismissed the appeal. Judge Blewitt specifically declined to follow *obiter dicta* of Judge Walters in *Bruns*, **16.18** above, which the company had cited as an authority. *Industrial Contracting Services Ltd v HMRC*, FTT [2011] UKFTT 290 (TC), TC01152.

[16.24] See also *Flemming & Son Construction (West Midlands) Ltd v HMRC*, **16.6** above.

[16.25] A carpenter (M), who used a number of subcontractors, had registered for 'gross payment status' within the construction industry scheme. In 2008 HMRC cancelled his registration on the grounds that he had made four tax payments after the due dates. M appealed, contending that he had a reasonable excuse because he had suffered cash-flow difficulties following a recession in the building industry. The First-Tier Tribunal accepted M's evidence and allowed his appeal, observing that M's main client was a large building company which had stopped building following a sudden change in the 'economic climate'. On the evidence, 'the drop in building work in the Corby area was sudden and severe'. Sir Stephen Oliver held that M had 'dealt in a fair and business-like way with the demands on his available cash resources' and 'came up to the required standards contemplated by the expression "reasonable excuse" in the context of the CIS'. *S Mutch v HMRC*, FTT [2009] UKFTT 288 (TC), TC00232.

[16.26] Similar decisions were reached in *Prior Roofing Ltd v HMRC*, FTT [2009] UKFTT 302 (TC), TC00246; *K Joseph-Lester (t/a Scaffold Access Services) v HMRC*, FTT [2011] UKFTT 114 (TC), TC00990; *A Kincaid (t/a AK Construction) v HMRC*, FTT [2011] UKFTT 225 (TC), TC01090; *PSR Control Systems Ltd v HMRC*, FTT [2012] UKFTT 478 (TC), TC02155, and *T Daniel v HMRC*, FTT [2013] UKFTT 136 (TC), TC02565.

[16.27] A similar decision was reached in a case where the tribunal allowed an appeal by a partnership which carried on business as carpet fitters. Judge Brannan observed that the cash-flow problems which the partnership had suffered in early 2009 'coincided almost exactly with one of the worst financial crises in this country's history'. *Connaught Contracts v HMRC*, FTT [2010] UKFTT 545 (TC), TC00798.

[16.28] A small construction company (C) had registered for 'gross payment status' within the construction industry scheme. In 2008 HMRC cancelled its registration on the grounds that it had made eight tax payments after the due dates. C appealed, contending that it had a reasonable excuse because in May 2007 the eight-year-old daughter of its company secretary had suffered a double fracture of her leg and had subsequently suffered serious illness, requiring treatment in hospital, before being diagnosed with epilepsy. The tribunal allowed C's appeal, observing that the secretary had difficulties 'balancing childcare with full-time work' and that three of the late payments had been made within 14 days of the due date. Judge Brooks held that C should 'be treated as complying with its obligations and as having satisfied the compliance test'. *Cormac Construction Ltd v HMRC*, FTT [2009] UKFTT 380 (TC), TC00315.

[16.29] A family partnership had registered for 'gross payment status' within the construction industry scheme. In 2009 HMRC cancelled its registration on the grounds that the partners had made several tax payments after the due dates. The partnership appealed, contending that the cancellation was unfair because the partners had previously made late payments without being warned that this would jeopardise the partnership's gross payment status, and that the partnership had suffered cash-flow problems because of late payment by two local authorities which were their major clients. The First-Tier Tribunal accepted this contention and allowed the appeal, observing that the local authorities were 'in breach of the public sector's obligation to pay invoices within the then 30 day time limit'. *Bannister Combined Services v HMRC*, FTT [2010] UKFTT 158 (TC), TC00463.

[16.30] A company (D) had registered for 'gross payment status' within the construction industry scheme. In 2008 HMRC cancelled its registration on the grounds that it had submitted four monthly returns, and had made several payments, after the due date. D appealed, contending that it had a reasonable excuse because it had relied on its company secretary. The First-Tier Tribunal accepted this contention and allowed the appeal, applying the principles laid down in *Rowland v HMRC*, **43.44** PAYMENT OF TAX. *Devon & Cornwall Surfacing Ltd v HMRC*, FTT [2010] UKFTT 199 (TC), TC00501.

[16.31] A partnership had registered for 'gross payment status' within the construction industry scheme. In 2009 HMRC cancelled its registration on the grounds that it had made two payments after the due date. The partnership appealed, contending that it had a reasonable excuse because it had relied on its general manager, who had worked for the partnership for 12 years but had subsequently been made redundant. The First-Tier Tribunal accepted this contention and allowed the appeal, applying the principles laid down in *Rowland v HMRC*, **43.44** PAYMENT OF TAX. *MR Harris Groundworks v HMRC*, FTT [2010] UKFTT 358 (TC), TC00640.

[16.32] A small family company had registered for 'gross payment status' within the construction industry scheme. In 2009 HMRC cancelled its registration on the grounds that it had made several PAYE payments after the due date. The company appealed, contending that it had a reasonable excuse because it had relied on a consultant, whom it had paid £60,000 pa, but had subsequently dispensed with his services after discovering that he had failed to arrange for the necessary payments. The First-Tier Tribunal accepted this contention and allowed the company's appeal, holding that it was reasonable for the company to have expected the consultant 'to ensure that it fully complied with its obligations especially as he was being paid £60,000 a year to do so'. Judge Brooks held that 'by relying on the consultant to undertake its administration, the company had a reasonable excuse for the late PAYE payments during the review period and should therefore be treated as having satisfied the compliance test'. *RW Westworth Ltd v HMRC*, FTT [2010] UKFTT 477 (TC), TC00738.

[16.33] A similar decision was reached in a case where the appellant company gave evidence that it had relied on its accountant. Judge Gandhi held that this constituted a reasonable excuse. *Thames Valley Renovations Ltd v HMRC*, FTT [2011] UKFTT 69 (TC), TC00947.

[16.34] A company (S) had registered for 'gross payment status' within the construction industry scheme. In 2010 HMRC cancelled its registration on the grounds that it had made several tax payments after the due date. S appealed, contending that if it lost its gross payment status, it would probably lose a contract worth £3,200,000 and would have to make many of its 100 employees redundant. The First-Tier Tribunal allowed the appeal. Judge Brooks held that the consequences of the withdrawal of gross payment status would be 'disproportionate to the late payment of tax'. *S Morris Groundwork Ltd v HMRC*, FTT [2010] UKFTT 585 (TC), TC00835.

[16.35] Judge Brooks reached a similar decision in a case where HMRC had cancelled the registration of a contractor who had been suffering cash-flow problems and had made one payment of tax after the due date. *A Wood (t/a Popeye) v HMRC*, FTT [2011] UKFTT 136 (TC), TC01010.

[16.36] A company (J) had registered for 'gross payment status' within the construction industry scheme. In 2011 HMRC cancelled its registration on the grounds that it had made several payments of PAYE after the due date. J appealed, contending that the cancellation was disproportionate and would prevent it from tendering it for contract work and cause it to cease trading. The First-tier Tribunal accepted this contention and allowed the appeal, holding that the tribunal's decision was supervisory rather than appellate, and finding that 'the decision to cancel the appellant's registration was made without taking into account the financial effect on the company'. Judge Cannan specifically declined to follow the Ch D decision in *Barnes v Hilton Main Construction Ltd*, Ch D 2005, 77 TC 255; [2005] STC 1532; [2005] EWHC 1355 (Ch) (which HMRC had cited as an authority), observing that 'the provisions for cancellation of an existing registration under *FA 2004* are quite different to the provisions for the grant of a certificate under *ICTA 1988*'. *JP Whitter (Waterwell Engineers) Ltd v HMRC (No 2)*, FTT [2012] UKFTT 639 (TC), TC02316. (*Note.* HMRC have appealed to the Upper Tribunal against this decision. The Upper Tribunal began hearing the appeal on 1 December 2014.)

[16.37] The decision in *JP Whitter (Waterwell Engineers) Ltd v HMRC (No 2)*, **16.36** above, was applied in the similar subsequent case of *John Kerr Roofing Contractors v HMRC*, FTT [2013] UKFTT 135 (TC), TC02564. (*Note.* HMRC have appealed to the Upper Tribunal against this decision.)

Determination under FA 2004, s 66(1)—whether valid

[16.38] In 2008 a contractor had registered for 'gross payment status' within the construction industry scheme. In January 2010 HMRC cancelled his registration on the grounds that he had failed to pay his tax liability by the due date. He appealed, contending that he had a reasonable excuse because of cashflow difficulties. The First-Tier Tribunal reviewed the evidence in detail and rejected this contention, finding that he 'could easily have paid the outstanding tax' but had 'simply failed to do so', so that there was no reasonable excuse within *FA 2004, Sch 11 para 4(4)*. However, the tribunal allowed the appeal on the grounds that HMRC had failed to exercise their discretion under *FA 2004, s 66(1)*. Judge Brannan held that 'in order to make a determination under *section 66(1)*, HMRC must exercise its discretion. If it does not exercise its discretion it has not made a determination for the purposes of the statute. The determination is invalid and has no effect.' *J Scofield v HMRC (No 2)*, FTT [2011] UKFTT 199 (TC); [2011] SFTD 560, TC01068. (*Note.* At a subsequent hearing, the tribunal rejected the appellant's application for costs—FTT [2012] UKFTT 673 (TC), TC02344.)

[16.39] In a subsequent case where the tribunal found that HMRC had failed to exercise their discretion in cancelling a partnership's registration, the tribunal remitted the case to HMRC to reconsider their decision in the light of the partnership's long-standing record of compliance. Judge Gort observed that 'there was no deliberate withholding of money, only a lack of understanding of how the partners should set about dealing with the loss of the relevant documents'. *BG & MA Saunders v HMRC*, FTT [2011] UKFTT 551 (TC), TC01396.

[16.40] The decision in *Scofield v HMRC (No 2)*, **16.38** above, was applied in a subsequent case where Judge Hellier observed that 'after we sought the parties' representations in relation to the *Scofield* decision, HMRC wrote to explain that they had now amended their procedures, but offered no new evidence in relation to this case'. *Piers Consulting Ltd v HMRC*, FTT [2011] UKFTT 613 (TC), TC01456.

[16.41] Judge Hellier reached a similar decision in *Cardiff Lift Company v HMRC*, FTT [2011] UKFTT 628 (TC); [2012] SFTD 85, TC01470.

Requirements of FA 2004, s 66(5)

[16.42] A partnership had registered for 'gross payment status' within the construction industry scheme. HMRC cancelled its registration on the grounds that one of the partners had failed to meet his compliance obligations. The partnership appealed. The First-Tier Tribunal allowed the appeal, finding that HMRC had carried out the 'compliance test' on 4 March 2009 but had failed to notify the partnership until 5 May 2009. Accordingly HMRC had failed to notify the partnership 'without delay', as required by *FA 2004, s 66(5)*. *Radford & Robinson v HMRC*, FTT [2010] UKFTT 31 (TC), TC00345.

[16.43] A couple who operated a plant hire business had registered for 'gross payment status' within the construction industry scheme. In May 2009 HMRC issued a form CIS 308 cancelling their registration on the grounds that they had made several tax payments late, and had failed to meet the 'compliance test'. The couple did not receive this notice, but subsequently discovered from a contractor that their registration had been cancelled. They appealed. The First-Tier Tribunal allowed the appeal, finding that 'HMRC was unable to produce a copy of the CIS 308 notification' and 'although there is a copy screen-print record of the CIS 308 being issued, there is no copy of the actual notice or any of the related correspondence'. Accordingly HMRC had not proved, on the balance of probabilities, that they had notified the partnership of the cancellation 'without delay', as required by *FA 2004, s 66(5)*. *P & Mrs T Ithell v HMRC*, FTT [2011] UKFTT 155 (TC), TC01029.

FA 2004, s 70—contractors' returns

[16.44] A partnership submitted CIS returns on a photocopy of the relevant form. HMRC imposed penalties on the basis that the photocopies did not satisfy the requirements of *SI 2005/2045, reg 4(1)*. The First-Tier Tribunal allowed the partnership's appeal. Judge Hellier observed that *reg 4(1)* provided that a return must be made 'in a document or format provided or approved by the Commissioners' (ie using the word 'or' rather than the word 'and'). He held that 'if HMRC provide a document to be used as a return that they must have approved its format. Thus the format of an original return is approved. That means that the format of a copy of that document is also approved. HMRC may not approve the document – the photocopy – but they must be taken to have approved its format. That means that the submission of a return on a document which is a photocopy of an original return is the making of a return within *Regulation 4(1)*.' *Scotts Glass & Glazing Services v HMRC*, FTT [2011] UKFTT 508 (TC), TC01355.

[16.45] See also *Bushell v HMRC*, 44.206 PENALTIES, and *Contour Business Interiors v HMRC*, 44.207 PENALTIES.

SI 2005/2045, reg 9—recovery from subcontractor

[16.46] A building contractor took on a subcontractor who presented a tax certificate which did not belong to him. The contractor paid the subcontractor without deduction of tax, and the Revenue issued an assessments to recover the tax. The Collector declined to make a direction under what is now *SI 2005/2045, reg 9*. The contractor applied for an order that the Collector should make a direction and for the assessments to be quashed. The QB rejected the application. On the facts of the case, the Collector had properly considered the question of whether the contractor had taken reasonable care to comply with the regulations, and was entitled to come to the conclusion that a direction was inappropriate. *R v Collector of Taxes (ex p. Robert Goodall (Builders) Ltd)*, QB 1988, 61 TC 219; [1989] STC 206.

[16.47] A contractor (H) failed to deduct tax from payments made to a subcontractor (F). H subsequently requested HMRC to make a direction under *Income Tax (Construction Industry Scheme) Regulations 2005 (SI 2005/2045), reg 9*. HMRC refused to make such a direction, and H appealed. The First-tier Tribunal dismissed his appeal, finding that he had failed to take 'reasonable care' to comply with the regulations. *S Hoskins v HMRC*, FTT [2011] UKFTT 284 (TC), TC01972.

[16.48] A company (P), which traded as an electrical contractor, failed to deduct tax from payments made to another company (C), which had worked for it as a subcontractor. P subsequently requested HMRC to make a direction under *Income Tax (Construction Industry Scheme) Regulations 2005 (SI 2005/2045), reg 9*. HMRC refused to make such a direction, and P appealed, contending that the failure to deduct tax was the result of an error by one of its staff, who had mistakenly recorded C as having a tax certificate when it did not. The First-tier Tribunal accepted P's evidence and allowed the appeal. Judge Aleksander observed that this was the first such mistake which P had made in ten years of operating the scheme, and held that 'the compliance systems to be expected of a substantial multi-national contractor with a large and sophisticated accounting department are very different from the systems to be adopted by a small business'. *PDF Electrical Ltd v HMRC*, FTT [2012] UKFTT 708 (TC), TC02375.

[16.49] A company (D) failed to deduct tax from several payments made to subcontractors. D subsequently requested HMRC to make a direction under *Income Tax (Construction Industry Scheme) Regulations 2005 (SI*

2005/2045), reg 9. HMRC refused to make such a direction, and D appealed, contending that its company secretary had mistakenly believed that the scheme only applied to payments made in respect of labour, and did not apply to payments made in respect the hire of plant. The First-tier Tribunal dismissed the appeal with regard to the majority of the payments, finding that the secretary had been careless in not being aware of the distinction between plant and materials, and holding that this did not constitute a reasonable excuse. However, the Tribunal allowed the appeal in respect of one payment of £4000, finding that the relevant invoice could have been interpreted as relating to materials rather than to plant. *Doocey North East Ltd v HMRC*, FTT [2014] UKFTT 863 (TC), TC03979.

[16.50] See also *Refit Shopfitting Services Ltd v HMRC*, **16.5** above, and *Hardwicke v HMRC*, **16.10** above.

Miscellaneous

Use of falsely completed forms 715—whether forgery

[16.51] Foremen working for a company in the construction industry falsely completed forms 715 in the names of various subcontractors. The foremen's supervisor was aware of this, but nevertheless transmitted the forms to the company's head office. He was convicted of forgery at a Crown Court, and sentenced to two years' imprisonment. He applied to the CA for leave to appeal against this decision. The CA unanimously rejected his application. *R v Hiscox*, CA 1978, 52 TC 497.

Misuse of payments made to foreman

[16.52] A foreman who received gross payments on behalf of each of three subcontractors in respect of work done was convicted of dishonestly obtaining money with the intention of permanently depriving the contractor thereof, by falsely representing that it was due to the subcontractors and that he was an agent authorised to receive it on their behalf. The QB reluctantly quashed the convictions, on the grounds that he had received a cheque rather than money, and that the contractor had not been deceived into handing over the cheques. The dishonesty did not start until the cheques were handled in a dishonest way. *Brady v CIR*, QB 1988, [1989] STC 178.

Misuse of stolen certificate and vouchers

[16.53] A stolen 714 certificate and form 715 vouchers were found in the possession of an individual (M). He was convicted of conspiracy to cheat the public revenue and appealed, contending, *inter alia*, that there was no common law offence of cheating the public revenue. The CA dismissed his appeal, applying the decisions in *R v Hudson*, **51.1** REVENUE PROSECUTIONS, and *R v Redford*, CA [1988] STC 845, and holding that there was a common law offence of cheating the public revenue. On the evidence, M had clearly intended to defraud the Revenue by misusing the certificate and vouchers. *R v Mulligan*, CA Criminal Division 1989, [1990] STC 220.

Delay in issuing tax certificate—contractor claiming damages

[16.54] In early 1999 a building contractor (M) transferred his business to a newly-formed company (N). In June 1999 N applied for a CIS 6 tax certificate. The Revenue did not issue the certificate until September 1999. Part of the delay was caused by a Revenue employee, who was 'unaware of the clear guidance in the CIS Manual' and did not appreciate that the Revenue would accept evidence of M's turnover in support of N's application. Part of the delay was caused by N failing to fully complete or sign the relevant forms, and part was caused by a Revenue employee who completed the forms on N's behalf, and incorrectly treated the application as relating to a CIS 4 registration card rather than to a CIS 6 tax certificate. Subsequently the Revenue paid N compensation of about £3,000. N took proceedings against the Revenue, contending that it had lost significant business because of the delay, and claiming damages of more than £400,000. The Ch D rejected the claim, holding that the Revenue did not owe any 'direct duty of care' to process applications for tax certificates quickly. N appealed to the CA, which allowed the appeal in part. Chadwick LJ held that 'the legislature did not intend to confer a private law right of action for damages' in a case where a certificate ought to have been issued, but was not. Parliament 'did not intend to impose a statutory duty to issue a certificate within an ascertainable time', since 'the time which the Revenue might properly require in order to determine whether the relevant conditions were satisfied could have been expected to vary from case to case and to be difficult to predict in any particular case'. and 'to require a certificate to be issued (or refused) within a specified time would have been to introduce a degree of inflexibility which was foreign to the legislative purpose.' However, on the evidence, an unidentified Revenue employee (X) had contributed to the delay by completing the application form which N had failed to complete, and treating it as an application for a CIS 4. That went 'beyond an administrative mistake made in the ordinary course of processing the application'. X had not simply been processing an application which had been made, but had effectively assumed 'an authority to make an application which had not been made'. In assuming that authority, X had assumed 'a duty of care' to N. *Neil Martin Ltd v HMRC*, CA 2007, 79 TC 60; [2007] STC 1802; [2007] EWCA Civ 1041. (*Note*. The CA only considered the preliminary legal issues, and did not consider whether the result of X's actions was that N was entitled to claim any further compensation from the Revenue.)

Repayment claim by agency

[16.55] A company (H) carried on an agency business, similar to an employment agency, introducing subcontract labour to clients in the construction industry. It claimed a substantial repayment of PAYE and NIC which it had deducted from amounts paid to its clients. The Ch D rejected the claim. Mackie J held that H had paid the money as agent for its clients, and was precluded from recovering payment without the specific authorisation of its clients. Furthermore, the General Commissioners had already made a finding of fact that H was acting as a payroll agent (see **16.14** above). Applying the principles laid down by Viscount Radcliffe in *Kok Hoong v Leong Cheong Kweng Mines Ltd*, PC 1963, [1964] 1 All ER 300, H could not 'start again on a basis it had abandoned before the General Commissioners'. *Hudson Contract Services Ltd v HMRC (No 2)*, Ch D [2007] EWHC 2561 (Ch).

Penalty for late submission of subcontractors' return

[16.56] See *Bysermaw Properties Ltd v HMRC*, **44.194** PENALTIES; the cases noted at **44.197** PENALTIES to **44.212** PENALTIES, and *Jonathan David Ltd v HMRC*, **44.282** PENALTIES.

17

Control of Companies

The cases in this chapter are arranged under the following headings.

General

Control for purposes of CTA 2010, s 1124

[17.1] See *CIR v Lithgows Ltd*, 3.87 ANTI-AVOIDANCE, and *Irving v Tesco Stores (Holdings) Ltd*, 18.69 CORPORATION TAX.

CTA 2010, s 450—definition of 'control'

[17.2] A company (C) held 40% of the share capital of another company (L). It had also lent money to L. This loan relationship was not part of C's trade, but C claimed a deduction for part of the debt owed by L, under the 'loan relationships' provisions. The Revenue rejected the claim on the basis that the effect of the loan relationship was that C had control of L. The Special Commissioner dismissed C's appeal, holding that C had control of L, within what is now *CTA 2010, s 450*, and was not entitled to a deduction for the debt owed by L. *Conlon Construction Ltd v Jarman*, Sp C 2003, [2004] SSCD 6 (Sp C 380).

[17.3] See also *Executive Benefit Services (UK) Ltd v HMRC*, 18.55 CORPORATION TAX.

CTA 2010, s 451—definition of 'control'

[17.4] See *R v CIR (ex p. Newfields Development Ltd)*, 11.1 CLOSE COMPANIES; *Gascoines Group Ltd & Others v HM Inspector of Taxes*, 11.2 CLOSE COMPANIES, and *Trend Properties Ltd v Crutchfield*, 18.9 CORPORATION TAX.

TCGA 1992, s 167(3)—control of company 'by virtue of holding assets'

[17.5] See *Foulser & Foulser v MacDougall*, 71.260 CAPITAL GAINS TAX.

CTA 2009, s 472—whether lender controlled borrower

[17.6] See *Fenlo Ltd v HMRC*, 18.9 CORPORATION TAX.

Control for purposes of IHTA 1984, s 269

[17.7] See *Walding & Others v CIR*, 72.219 INHERITANCE TAX, and *Walker's Executors v CIR*, 72.220 INHERITANCE TAX.

Whether shares held as trustee to be taken into account

[17.8] In an estate duty case, a company had an issued share capital of 8,350 shares. Until 1936 the company's founder (S) had held 4,750 of these shares. In 1936 he transferred 3,650 of these to a settlement of which he was the settlor and the first-named trustee. He retained the other 1,100 shares. The HL held (by a 4-1 majority, Lord Reid dissenting) that S had retained control of the company, applying the principles laid down in *J Bibby & Sons Ltd v CIR*, 17.14 below. Lord Denning held that, for the purpose of the relevant legislation, 'potential control by one person jointly with another is to be regarded as giving him control of the company', and that 'if he holds the joint holding in a fiduciary capacity only, it does not count. But if he holds it beneficially, or is himself the founder of the joint holding, having created it by his own disposition, then it counts as giving him control just as if he were a single owner.' *Barclays Bank Ltd v CIR*, HL [1960] 2 All ER 817.

Effect of management share with special rights

[17.9] In a case concerning legislation which has been superseded, five-twelfths of the ordinary shares of a company (H) were held by SN Ltd, five-twelfths by SC Ltd, and two-twelfths by B Ltd. There was also one 'management share' in H, which was jointly beneficially owned by SN Ltd and SC Ltd. It carried three times the total votes of all other shares, and SN Ltd, as the first registered holder, was entitled to exercise the voting rights. The Revenue issued surtax directions on the basis that SN Ltd alone controlled H. The Ch D upheld the directions. *CIR v Harton Coal Co Ltd*, Ch D 1960, 39 TC 174; [1960] Ch 563; [1960] 3 All ER 48.

Controlling interest

NOTE

There have been several cases turning on whether a 'controlling interest' was held in a company for the purposes of profits tax and other taxes which are now obsolete. The cases are noted in this section.

[17.10] A holder of 50% of a company's share capital, with a casting vote as chairman, was held to have a controlling interest in *CIR v BW Noble Ltd*, KB 1926, 12 TC 911. (*Note*. The decision was approved by the HL in *British-American Tobacco Co Ltd v CIR*, 17.12 below.)

[17.11] A majority of the shares of a company (C) were owned by another company (P), which in turn was owned by C's two directors. The CA unanimously held that they had a controlling interest in C. *CIR v FA Clark & Son Ltd*, CA 1941, 29 TC 49; [1941] 2 All ER 651.

[17.12] The HL reached a similar decision in a case involving the indirect ownership of eleven non-resident companies. Viscount Simon LC observed that 'the appellant company has, in respect of each of the foreign companies referred to in the Case, the control of the majority vote', and held that 'the owners of the majority of the voting power in a company are the persons who are in effective control of its affairs and fortunes'. *British-American Tobacco Co Ltd v CIR*, HL 1942, 29 TC 49; [1943] 1 All ER 13.

[17.13] 59% of the shares in a company (B) were owned by a Danish company (S). 30% of the shares in B were owned by one of its directors (E), who also held a majority of the shares in S. A further 10% of the shares in B were owned by another director. The Revenue issued profits tax assessments on the basis that B's directors had a 'controlling interest' in it (so that not all of the claimed directors' remuneration was deductible). The CA unanimously upheld the assessments. Lord Evershed held that 'where the registered shareholder is a body corporate you nevertheless may, and indeed must, for certain purposes look beyond the register; for since the company cannot itself speak you must find out with whose voice it must do so. You may therefore ask, who does control the body corporate by the necessary shareholding interest in it?' On the evidence, E 'controlled the Danish company in the sense that his was the voice with which the Danish company spoke in its capacity as registered shareholder'. *S Berendsen Ltd v CIR*, CA 1957, 37 TC 517; [1958] Ch 1; [1957] 2 All ER 612.

[17.14] A company's directors had a controlling interest in the company if shares which they held as trustees were taken into account, but not if such holdings were ignored. The Revenue issued an EPT assessment on the basis that the directors did not have a 'controlling interest' in the company. The company appealed, contending that the trustee shareholdings gave the directors a 'controlling interest' (thus entitling it to a greater allowance under provisions in *F(No 2) A 1939, s 13*). The CA accepted this contention and allowed the appeal, and the HL unanimously upheld this decision. Lord Russell of Killowen held that the words 'controlling interest' should be construed as 'controlling voting power' rather than as 'beneficial interest'. Lord Porter observed that 'the shares giving control are held by the directors not merely as trustees but also with some personal interest as well'. Lord Simonds held that 'those who by their votes can control the company do not the less control it because they may themselves be amenable to some external control'. Accordingly, the directors held a controlling interest in the company. *J Bibby & Sons Ltd v CIR*, HL 1945, 29 TC 167; [1945] 1 All ER 667.

[17.15] The decision in *J Bibby & Sons Ltd v CIR*, **17.14** above, was applied in a subsequent case in which shares held by directors as trustees were taken into account for the purpose of provisions in *ITA 1952* which have been superseded. Danckwerts LJ observed that the words 'persons interested in any shares' were 'exactly applicable to the position of a trustee who holds shares subject to a trust'. *CIR v Park Investments Ltd*, CA 1966, 43 TC 200.

[17.16] Four members of the same family each held 25% of the shares in a company (ML). ML had two directors, one of whom (MM) was one of the shareholders, the other director not being a family member and having no shares in the company. MM had the power to appoint himself as chairman of the directors and to preside at ML's general meetings. However, he did not exercise this power, and the chairman appointed at general meetings was one of the other shareholders, who was not a director of ML. The Revenue issued EPT assessments on the basis that ML's directors had a 'controlling interest' in ML. ML appealed, contending that it was controlled by the three shareholders who were not directors, and that the directors did not have a 'controlling interest' (thus entitling it to a greater deduction for directors' remuneration). The Special Commissioners accepted this contention and allowed ML's appeal, and the KB upheld their decision. *CIR v Monnick Ltd*, KB 1949, 29 TC 379.

[17.17] A company's directors held less than 25% of the shares in the company. However, more than 30% of the shares were owned by the elderly mother of one of the directors (M). She had executed a power of attorney in favour of M. The Revenue issued EPT assessments on the basis that the directors did not have a 'controlling interest' in the company. The company appealed, contending that the existence of the power of attorney gave the directors a 'controlling interest' (thus entitling it to a greater allowance under provisions in *F(No 2) A 1945, Sch 5*). The Ch D rejected this contention and upheld the assessments, and the CA unanimously upheld this decision. Tucker LJ held that the power of attorney was 'not effective to give to (M) a greater controlling interest than he had by virtue of the shares of which he was the registered holder'. *CIR v James Hodgkinson (Salford) Ltd*, CA 1949, 29 TC 395.

[17.18] More than half of a company's share capital was held by the trustees of the will of the former controlling director (B). Under the company's Articles of Association, the voting rights in respect of these shares resided in the trustee who was the first named in the company's register (B's widow), who was not a director of the company. However, in accordance with their powers under the Articles of Association, the trustees appointed another trustee (F) as 'governing director' of the company. The Revenue issued EPT assessments on the basis that the directors did not have a 'controlling interest' in the company. The company appealed, contending that the effect of the trustees' appointment was that F had a 'controlling interest'. The Special Commissioners rejected this contention and dismissed the appeal, and the CS unanimously upheld their decision. Lord Keith observed that F had 'practically absolute power' but that he did not have 'at any time a controlling interest in the company in the sense that at general meetings of the company he could control the company's affairs'. *John Shields & Co (Perth) Ltd v CIR*, CS 1950, 29 TC 475.

[17.19] A company's directors held about 49% of the shares in the company. A further 49% belonged to the estate of a deceased shareholder, one of whose executors was a director of the company. The shares were not registered in the executors' names. The Revenue issued EPT assessments on the basis that the directors did not have a 'controlling interest' in the company. The company appealed, contending that the executors' holding should be ignored and that the directors had a 'controlling interest'. The Special Commissioners rejected this contention and dismissed the appeal, and the High Court upheld their decision. Danckwerts J held that 'the executors are entitled to exercise the right of voting which the deceased holder of the shares would have been entitled to if he had been still alive'. *Joseph Appleby Ltd v CIR*, HC 1950, 29 TC 483.

[17.20] Half of the voting shares in a company (S) were held by its managing director. The other half were held by the trustees of a settlement. They were registered in the name of a bank which acted as custodian trustee under the *Public Trustee Act 1906, s 4*, but both the managing trustees were directors of S. S's Articles of Association did not provide for a casting vote; in the event of equal votes being cast, the decision was left to arbitration. The Revenue issued a profits tax assessment on the basis that S's directors had a 'controlling interest' in the company. The Special Commissioners allowed S's appeal and the CA unanimously upheld their decision, holding that the directors did not have a controlling interest, since the shares held in trust had to be treated as being held by the bank, which was 'not merely a nominee or bare trustee'. *CIR v Silverts Ltd*, CA 1951, 29 TC 491; [1951] Ch 521; [1951] 1 All ER 703. (*Note. Obiter dicta* of Sir Raymond Evershed were disapproved by the same judge in the subsequent case of *S Berendsen Ltd v CIR*, **17.13** above.)

Beneficial ownership of shares

[17.21] A UK company held all the common stock of a US company. Under wartime regulations, the stock was pledged as security for a loan from the US Government to the UK Government. For this purpose, blank transfers of the stock were deposited with a US corporation through which the loan was made, and powers of attorney appointing proxies were given. Dividends on the stock were received by the corporation and used to service the loan. The CA held that the UK company remained the beneficial owner of the stock (for excess profits tax purposes). The US corporation's interest in the stock was that of a mortgagee. *English Sewing Cotton Co Ltd v CIR*, CA 1947, 26 ATC 79.

[17.22] A company (PE) agreed to sell its shares in a wholly-owned subsidiary (PB) which had accumulated losses. Under the sale agreement, PE was required to purchase PB's assets and arrange for the discharge of its liabilities before the completion of the sale. PE subsequently acquired four leasehold properties from PB, and on the following day it transferred its shares in PB to the purchaser. The Revenue charged stamp duty on the transfer of the leasehold properties. PE appealed, contending that the transfer was exempt because it had been the beneficial owner of the shares in PB. The CA unanimously rejected this contention and dismissed the appeal, holding that the beneficial interest in the shares had become vested in the purchaser when the agreement for sale was signed. *Parway Estates Ltd v CIR*, CA 1958, 45 TC 135.

[17.23] OM Ltd held the shares in S Ltd. Both companies went into voluntary liquidation on the same date, the same person being appointed liquidator for both. The Ch D upheld profits tax assessments on both companies, holding that OM Ltd ceased to be the beneficial owner of the shares in S Ltd from the commencement of the winding-up. *CIR v Olive Mill Spinners Ltd (and related appeal)*, Ch D 1963, 41 TC 77; [1963] 1 WLR 712; [1963] 2 All ER 130.

[17.24] See also *J Sainsbury plc v O'Connor*, **18.64** CORPORATION TAX, and the cases noted at **18.79** *et seq.* CORPORATION TAX.

18

Corporation Tax

The cases in this chapter are arranged under the following headings.

NOTE

In general, cases relating to assessments on companies, whether to corporation tax or under the legislation before the introduction of corporation tax, are included under the appropriate heading elsewhere in this book where the relevant legislation is (or was) applicable to both individuals and companies, or there is (or was) similar legislation applicable to individuals. Accordingly, the cases in this chapter relate to provisions applicable to companies only, with no counterpart in the legislation applicable to individuals. For cases relating to close company matters, see 11 CLOSE COMPANIES. For claims to loss relief, see 35.34 *et seq* LOSS RELIEF.

Loan relationships (CTA 2009, ss 292–476)

Inter-company debt—whether a 'loan relationship'

[18.1] In 2004 a company (M) claimed a corporation tax deduction of £6,690,000 in relation to certain transactions with an associated company. HMRC rejected the claim and M appealed, contending that the transactions arose from 'transactions for the lending of money' which constituted a 'loan relationship' within what is now *CTA 2009, ss 302, 303*. The First-tier Tribunal rejected this contention and dismissed the appeal, observing that 'the companies had apparently not retained copies of their bank statements' and that 'it is hard to understand why this basic documentation was not available to explain the transactions'. On the evidence, M had failed to show that there had been a 'lending of money'. The Upper Tribunal and the CA unanimously upheld this decision as one of fact. Etherton LJ observed that 'no-one gave evidence for (M) who had any direct knowledge of the transactions. Nor did anyone give evidence who had actually drawn up the entries in the books and records of (M) and other group companies on which (M) relies. Nor did anyone give evidence about the way the group carried on business at the time of the transactions, with particular reference to the commercial relations and dealings between the companies within the group.' *MJP Media Services Ltd v HMRC*, CA [2012] EWCA Civ 1558; [2013] STC 2218.

CTA 2009, ss 335-347—continuity of treatment on transfers

[18.2] The parent company of a group subscribed for zero coupon loan notes in several group companies. Those loan notes were then transferred to an associated company (V) for shares issued with a nominal value equal to the then value of the loan notes, but at a premium, on terms that the premium would be paid up by capitalising profits arising on the loan notes and appropriating those sums to V's share premium account. HMRC issued an amendment to V's return, increasing its taxable profit by bringing the credit on the accrual of profits on the loan notes into account. The CA unanimously dismissed V's appeal. Gross LJ held that 'the "transaction" or "series of transactions" must be considered as a whole; it cannot be correct to look at a part only of any such transaction. It follows that the assignment to the appellant cannot be considered (and disregarded) without likewise considering (and disregarding) the appellant's agreement to capitalise the profits and transfer them to its share premium account.' Lewison LJ held that 'a transaction is (at least) a bilateral agreement. It makes no sense to disregard part of the transaction, when the statute clearly requires the whole transaction to be disregarded, except for very limited purposes.' *Vocalspruce Ltd v HMRC*, CA [2014] EWCA Civ 1302.

Funding bonds—effect of CTA 2009, s 413

[18.3] A company (F) had issued several 'funding bonds', within what is now *CTA 2009, s 413*, to other companies in its group. HMRC had treated these as being within the scope of the 'foreign exchange' legislation of *FA 1993*, so that a taxable gain had arisen on the bonds in the relevant accounting period. F appealed, contending that the effect of *s 413* was that the 'funding bonds' were income rather than capital for all tax purposes, and that the foreign exchange legislation did not apply. The Special Commissioners rejected this contention and dismissed the appeal. The Commissioners noted that *s 413* derived from *FA 1938, s 25*, and had been enacted to reverse the effect of the decision in *Cross v London & Provincial Trust Ltd*, CA 1938, 21 TC 705. They held that *s 413* 'only deals with what happens on the issue of the funding bonds on two dates, namely issue and redemption'. It did not deal with 'the tax treatment of any gains or losses which might arise in respect of the funding bonds between issue and redemption, either as chargeable gains or losses or exchange gains or losses', and did not apply to 'any event other than the issue and redemption of the funding bonds and, in particular, does not govern the taxation of any gains or losses made during the lifetime of the funding bonds'. Accordingly, *s 413* did not prevent the application of the 1993 legislation. *Finance Ltd v HM Inspector of Taxes (No 2)*, Sp C [2005] SSCD 407 (Sp C 466).

CTA 2009, s 441—unallowable purposes and tax relief schemes

[18.4] A company (P) held a large shareholding in another company (W). It wished to sell half of these shares. In an attempt to avoid the corporation tax which would become due on the sale, P sold the shares in March 2001 to a newly-acquired subsidiary (E). In April 2001 E sold those shares in the open market, realising a chargeable gain of £8,595,731. In November 2001 E incorporated three subsidiary companies. E and its subsidiaries then undertook a number of derivative transactions in an attempt to reduce or avoid the corporation tax due on the gain. As part of the scheme (which was devised by an accountancy firm), E sold one of the subsidiaries (Q) to an unconnected third party in 2002, and claimed a capital loss of £8,864,992 on the disposal. HMRC subsequently began enquiries into the transactions and issued closure notices to the effect that the gain on the shares in W was chargeable to corporation tax; that E was not entitled to the capital losses which it had claimed; and that two of E's subsidiaries were not entitled to the capital losses which they had claimed. The Upper Tribunal upheld the closure notices, holding that 'even if (E) can be said to have gained and lost on the 2001 derivative transactions, the "gains" and "losses" did not have the character of income'. Furthermore, the transactions were 'designed to achieve a "loss" or "gain" of fiscal significance without there ever being any prospect of a loss or gain having a commercial reality'. *Explainaway Ltd v HMRC (and related appeals)*, UT [2012] UKUT 362 (TCC); [2012] STC 2525.

[18.5] A UK company (H) was a subsidiary of another UK company (OI) which in turn was owned by a Jersey company (J). It borrowed £2,000,000 from a bank in order to pay a dividend of £1,999,500 to OI, which in turn declared a similar dividend which it paid to J. Four days later H borrowed £1,999,500 from J and used this to repay the bank. H agreed to pay J £2,150,000 after 363 days. The companies entered similar transactions in subsequent years, and H claimed a deduction for the difference between the amount it had borrowed from J and the amount repayable to J. HMRC issued a closure notice rejecting the claim on the basis that the transactions had had 'an unallowable purpose' within what is now *CTA 2009, s 441*. H appealed, contending that it had made a commercial decision to fund dividend payments by short-term loans. The First-tier Tribunal dismissed the appeal, observing that 'it is perfectly possible for a transaction to have a legal identity but not necessarily have a commercial purpose', and holding on the evidence that H had had a 'tax avoidance purpose' for entering the relevant transactions. *AH Field (Holdings) Ltd v HMRC*, FTT [2012] UKFTT 104 (TC); TL 3837, TC01800.

[18.6] In December 2004 a company (F) entered into a complex series of transactions designed to produce a substantial loss for tax purposes. At the end of its 2004 accounting year, F changed its accounting practice from UK GAAP to IFRS. Following this change, it claimed a deduction of €83,849,399 in its 2005 accounting period. HMRC rejected the claim on the basis that the claimed deduction was attributable to an 'unallowable purpose', within what is now *CTA 2009, s 441*. The Upper Tribunal upheld HMRC's rejection of the claim, holding that, on the basis of a just and reasonable apportionment, the debit in question 'was wholly attributable to an unallowable purpose of (F) in respect of the loan relationships represented by the relevant bonds', and should not be brought into account. *HMRC v Fidex Ltd (No 2) (and cross-appeal)*, UT [2014] UKUT 454 (TCC). (*Note*. For a preliminary issue in this case, see 4.109 APPEALS.)

[18.7] A group of companies entered into a tax avoidance scheme designed to achieve a loan relationship debit in the borrowing company (N) without incurring a tax charge in any other group company. A loan was structured to provide a return in the form of preference shares issued by N not to the lender (V) but to another company in the group (S). HMRC issued rulings that V was taxable under the 'loan relationship' provisions of *FA 1996, ss 80–105*, that S was taxable on its receipt of the preference shares under Schedule D Case VI, and that the effect of *FA 1996 Sch 9 para 13* was that N was not entitled to the loan relationship debit which it had claimed. The companies appealed. The First-tier Tribunal allowed the appeals by V and N, holding that the value of the shares issued by V to S did not form part of V's profits under *FA 1996, ss 80–105*, and that *FA 1996 Sch 9 para 13* did not apply to N's 'debtor relationship', so that no part of the debit on N's debtor relationship was prevented from being brought into account under *FA 1996, ss 80–105*. However the First-tier Tribunal dismissed the appeal by S, holding that its receipt of the shares was taxable income under Schedule D Case VI, because the source of that income was the loan agreement. *Versteegh Ltd v HMRC (and related appeals)*, FTT [2013] UKFTT 642 (TC); [2014] SFTD 547, TC03026. (*Notes*. (1) At a subsequent hearing, Judge Berner directed that HMRC should pay N's costs, but that V and S should pay the costs of their appeals. He observed that 'having regard to the litigation as a whole, and looking at the position in a realistic and commercially sensible way, the decisions of the Tribunal on the individual appeals had the overall consequence that the scheme failed, and the taxpayer groups did not succeed in their objectives. Looking at the matter overall, where the scheme would succeed only if there were both a deduction in the borrower and no taxable profit in either the lender or the share recipient, HMRC was the successful party by virtue of the single finding that the share recipient was taxable.'—FTT [2014] UKFTT 397 (TC), TC03526. (2) Both sides have appealed to the Upper Tribunal against the First-tier decision.)

Loan relationships—connected parties

[18.8] A company (T) lent £23,265 to another company (B). T's controlling shareholder (L) held a 50% shareholding in B, the remaining 50% being held by an accountant (K) who was in partnership with L. B did not repay the loan, and was subsequently struck off the Register of Companies. T claimed a deduction for the amount of the loan. The Revenue rejected the claim on the basis that T and B were connected. The Special Commissioner dismissed T's appeal, finding that L had control of T, that L and K were 'associates', and that L and K together had control of B. Accordingly the effect of what is now *CTA 2010, s 450* was that L should be treated as having control of B, so that T and B were connected. Therefore T was not entitled to the deduction. *Trend Properties Ltd v Crutchfield*, Sp C [2005] SSCD 534 (Sp C 478).

CTA 2009, s 472—definition of 'control'

[18.9] In 1992 a company (B) which was incorporated in the Bahamas lent £1,200,000 to a UK company (F), which had purchased two houses and converted them into a hotel. F entered into certain covenants with B. The hotel was unsuccessful, and F was unable to make the agreed interest payments. In 2002 B gave a notice of default and demanded immediate repayment of the loan. In 2003 B accepted £650,000 in full and final settlement, and released the remainder of the loan and interest. The Revenue issued a ruling that the amount released had to be brought into account in computing F's profits. F appealed, contending that the effect of the covenants it had entered into meant that it was effectively controlled by B, and that the amount released should not be brought into account. The Special Commissioner rejected this contention and dismissed the appeal, holding on the evidence that the covenants which F had entered into had not given B control of F for the purposes of what is now *CTA 2009, s 472*. The Commissioner observed that the covenants were 'restricted in their scope and negative in their nature. They are typical of those found in agreements governing highly geared secured loans, such as this. Their purpose is to protect the financial interests of the lender: to ensure that the lender's security package is protected, that value is not leached out of the borrower and that the lender is provided with reliable financial information so that it can monitor the loan.' Accordingly the amount of the released debt had to be brought into account for the purpose of computing F's taxable profits. *Fenlo Ltd v HMRC*, Sp C [2008] SSCD 1245 (Sp C 714).

Financial futures transactions

[18.10] See *HSBC Life (UK) Ltd v Stubbs (and related appeals)*, **34.6** LIFE ASSURANCE.

Manufactured interest payments

[18.11] A UK company (D) entered into a number of sale and repurchase 'repo' transactions with an Irish bank. It purchased gilts for £812,000,000 and resold them for £785,000,000, having received 'coupon' payments totalling £28,800,000. Accordingly, these transactions produced an economic and accounting profit of £1,800,000. However, in its tax return D did not include a credit entry for the £28,800,000 'coupon' which it had received, and claimed that it should be treated as having made a loss of £27,000,000. HMRC rejected the claim and issued an amendment to D's return. The Supreme Court unanimously dismissed D's appeal. Lord Walker held that 'the need for a symmetrical solution lies at the heart of this appeal'. The effect of the legislation was that the 'coupon' payments totalling £28,800,000 should be apportioned, and there should be both a credit and debit entry of £2,900,000. *DCC Holdings (UK) Ltd v HMRC*, SC [2010] UKSC 58; 80 TC 301; [2011] STC 326; [2011] 1 All ER 537. (*Note*. See now *FA 2009, Sch 30*. This was enacted with the intention of ensuring that 'tax treatment follows the treatment of the payments in company accounts prepared in accordance with GAAP': see the Ministerial Statement reproduced at *2009 SWTI 440*.)

Loan relationship—avoidance scheme—application of FRS 5

[18.12] In 2000 a company (GP) lent £300,000,000 to a subsidiary company (GB). GB issued GP with unsecured loan stock valued at £300,000,000, redeemable in 2004. In 2003 GP assigned its right to receive interest on the loan stock to another subsidiary company (GK) in return for preference shares which carried the right to a special dividend. GB paid loan interest to GK, which paid the special dividend to GP, which also retained the right to receive the repayment of the £300,000,000 loan. HMRC formed the opinion that the purpose of these arrangements, which had been devised by a large accountancy firm, was to take advantage of a perceived loophole in the 'loan relationship' provisions and to achieve a tax saving by allowing GB to claim a deduction for the interest payable without GP being taxed on the interest. HMRC issued amendments to GP's corporation tax returns, on the basis that generally accepted accounting principles (and particularly FRS 5) required GP to derecognise the loan principal to the extent needed to reflect its current value at the date of assignment, and to bring a sum equivalent to the difference between that amount and its face value into account as a loan relationship credit. (HMRC's amendment assessed the required credit as £20,453,476.) GP appealed. The First-tier Tribunal dismissed the appeal (subject to agreement as to figures), holding that GP's accounts had failed to recognise that, although its overall position was unchanged, the value of the loan had been diminished in exchange for an augmentation elsewhere. Accordingly the accounts in which GP continued to recognise the loan in full did not accurately reflect GP's own position. The effect of the assignment had been that GP 'no longer had the right to receive the interest; it had instead a more valuable subsidiary'. The transaction should have been 'properly reflected by partial derecognition of the loan, and an addition to the value of (GP's) investment in its subsidiaries'. GP had not been justified in departing from FRS 5. The tribunal noted that there was a possibility that this might eventually lead to double taxation, but observed that 'the transactions were a device for ensuring that relief for payment was not matched by taxation of the receipt; and the appellants have no evident difficulty with that outcome. It does not seem to us that they can legitimately complain if the scheme fails in its purpose and instead results in their paying tax twice.' The Upper Tribunal upheld this decision. Mann J held that the First-tier Tribunal had been entitled to find that 'derecognition was required in the circumstances of this case', and upheld HMRC's contention that 'there was a "realised profit" which arose on the repayment of the loan'. *Greene King plc v HMRC (and related appeal)*, UT [2014] UKUT 178 (TCC); [2014] STC 2439.

Derivative contracts (CTA 2009, ss 570-710)

Interest rate swaps

[18.13] A company (P) submitted a return claiming a non-trading loan relationship debit of £105,000,000, relating to two payments made at the inception of two 'swap' transactions which had taken place in that period.

for the amortisation of the goodwill which it had acquired from M. HMRC rejected the claim on the grounds that M and B had been 'related parties' at the time of the acquisition, so that the deduction was prohibited by what is now *CTA 2009, s 882(1)(b)*. The First-tier Tribunal dismissed B's appeal against this decision, finding that M had been a participator in B at the time when B acquired the goodwill from him. *Blenheims Estate & Asset Management Ltd v HMRC*, FTT [2013] UKFTT 290 (TC), TC02696.

Relief for employee share acquisitions (CTA 2009, ss 1001-1038B)

Interpretation of CTA 2009, s 1015

[18.21] In 2004, following a management buy-out, a UK company (B) granted its former company secretary (R), who lived in the USA, an option to subscribe for shares equal to 12.5% of B's issued share capital. In 2007 R exercised the option and sold the shares, realising a substantial gain. B claimed that the gain on the option qualified for relief from corporation tax under what is now *CTA 2009, s 1015*. HMRC rejected the claim on the grounds that the legislation required that the option must have been granted by reason of the grantee having been employed by the grantor, and although R had been B's company secretary, he had received no remuneration and the option had been granted as a consequence of the management buy-out. The First-tier Tribunal dismissed B's appeal against this decision. *Metso Paper Bender Forrest Ltd v HMRC (and related appeal)*, FTT [2013] UKFTT 674 (TC); [2014] SFTD 529, TC03056.

Investment companies (CTA 2009, s 1218)

NOTE

CTA 2009, s 1218 derives from *ICTA 1988, s 130*, which was amended by *FA 2004, s 38* to include a reference to a 'company with investment business', defined as 'any company whose business consists wholly *or partly* in the making of investments'. This differs from an 'investment company', which was defined as 'any company whose business consists wholly *or mainly* in the making of investments'. Cases relating to periods before the enactment of *FA 2004* should be read in the light of the changes to the legislation. Most of the rules applying to 'investment companies' now apply to the broader category of 'companies with investment business', so that the definition of an 'investment company' has reduced in importance. See Tolley's Corporation Tax for more details.

[18.22] A holding company appealed against assessments to excess profits duty, contending that it was not carrying on any business. The KB rejected this contention and upheld the assessments. Rowlatt J held that the company's principal business was 'the making of investments' and the fact that it was not 'turning over' its investments was not conclusive. *CIR v Tyre Investment Trust Ltd*, KB 1924, 12 TC 646.

[18.23] In an Irish case, a company had been formed to acquire a large family estate, with a view to its management and development, and a life interest in land in England. The SC(I) held that it was not within the definition of an investment company. *Howth Estate Co v Davis*, SC(I) 1935, 2 ITC 74.

[18.24] The decision in *Howth Estate Co v Davis*, **18.23** above, was applied in another Irish case, involving a family estate company. Part of the estate was sold, the proceeds being invested in Stock Exchange securities, but in the relevant year the bulk of the company's income was rental income from the estate. Teevan J observed that 'what has to be looked to is the nature of the operations or functions of the company. The search is not for a company making investments but for a company whose main business is the making of investments.' That involved 'the purpose of the operations as well as their nature'. *Casey v Monteagle Estate Co*, HC(I) 1960, 3 ITC 313; [1962] IR 406.

[18.25] In a case dealing with legislation which is now obsolete, a financial company was assessed on its profits from share-dealing. From 1933 to 1936, its trading profits greatly exceeded its investment income. For the 15 months to 31 March 1938, its trading loss was larger than its investment income. It went into voluntary liquidation on 1 April 1938. The HL held (by a 4-1 majority, Lord Russell of Killowen dissenting) that the company was not within the definition of an 'investment company'. Lord Porter observed that 'the company's activities were directed to earning profits from its dealings in stocks and shares, and not, except incidentally, to deriving income from the interest and dividends of the stocks and shares in which it dealt'. *FPH Finance Trust Ltd v CIR*, HL 1944, 26 TC 131; [1944] AC 285; [1944] 1 All ER 653.

[18.26] A company (T) was incorporated to administer an estate in Putney. It appealed against three assessments on investment income, contending that it was an investment company and was entitled to deduct management expenses from the interest. The Special Commissioner dismissed the appeal, holding that T 'was not incorporated for the purpose of turning the land to account for the purpose of profit nor for making distributions to its shareholders'. Its business was 'to manage and administer the property', rather than to make investments'. *Tintern Close Residents Society Ltd v Winter*, Sp C [1995] SSCD 57 (Sp C 7).

[18.27] Similar decisions were reached in the similar cases of *Greenwood Property Management Ltd v Winter*, Sp C [1995] SSCD 115 (Sp C 8); *Fairlawns Residents' Association Ltd v Winter*, Sp C [1995] SSCD 120 (Sp C 9); *100 Palace Gardens Terrace Ltd v Winter*, Sp C [1995] SSCD 126 (Sp C 10); *South Court Residents Ltd v Winter*, Sp C [1995] SSCD 131 (Sp C 11); *Fairburn Court Residents' Association Ltd v Winter*, Sp C [1995] SSCD 159 (Sp C 12); *Four Philbeach Gardens Management Co Ltd v Winter*, Sp C [1995] SSCD 165 (Sp C 13); *Wessex Court (Putney) Residents' Association Ltd v Winter*, Sp C [1995] SSCD 170 (Sp C 14); *No 36 Queens Gate Ltd v Winter*, Sp C [1995] SSCD 208 (Sp C 15); *12–14 Clifton Gardens (Management) Ltd v Winter*, Sp C [1995] SSCD 213 (Sp C 16); *3 Westgate Terrace Management Ltd v Winter*, Sp C [1995] SSCD 219 (Sp C 17); *Downings Management Ltd v Winter*, Sp C [1995] SSCD 224 (Sp C 18) and *White House Drive Residents Association Ltd v Worsley*, Sp C 1996, [1997] SSCD 63 (Sp C 108).

Housing Society—whether an investment company

[18.28] A company had been formed under the *Industrial and Provident Societies Act 1965* to acquire housing stock from a local authority. It claimed to carry forward its excess charges on income. The Revenue rejected the claim on the grounds that the company was not an 'investment company'. The Special Commissioner allowed the company's appeal and the Ch D upheld this decision. Lightman J held that 'the purpose and nature' of the company's business was 'that of holding investments in the form of the portfolio, and none the less so because in so doing its object is to fulfil the social purpose of providing affordable housing'. It had acquired the houses in order to produce a profitable return and was therefore an 'investment company'. Lightman J observed that it was 'difficult to conceive that the legislature can have intended that a body such as the society should be placed in respect of this form of tax relief in a disadvantageous position compared with that of a commercial company'. *Cook v Medway Housing Society Ltd*, Ch D 1996, 69 TC 319; [1997] STC 90.

Company hitherto an investment company—whether now dealing

[18.29] See *Halefield Securities Ltd v Thorpe*, 59.59 TRADING INCOME.

Property-owning company—whether carrying on a trade

[18.30] See *Webb v Conelee Properties Ltd*, 68.45 TRADING PROFITS.

Management expenses (CTA 2009, ss 1219–1231)

NOTE

CTA 2009, ss 1219–1223 derive from *ICTA 1988, s 75*, as substituted by *FA 2004, ss 38–40*. The changes made to the legislation in 2004 were intended to extend eligibility for the relief given by section 75 to all companies with investment business, and not just those within the historical definition of 'investment companies'. See the Inland Revenue consultative document 'Corporation Tax Reform: The Next Steps', issued on 10 December 2003.

Discount allowed by life assurance company

[18.31] See *North British & Mercantile Insurance Co v Easson*, 68.67 TRADING PROFITS.

British division of Canadian life assurance company

[18.32] See *Sun Life Assurance Co of Canada v Pearson*, 68.70 TRADING PROFITS.

Exchange loss on payment of interest

[18.33] The capital liability of an investment company included 4% and 6% Bearer Bonds, held largely abroad, the interest on which was payable in sterling in London or, at the bearer's option, in New York, Amsterdam or Frankfurt in local currency at fixed rates of exchange. Because of the exchange rates at the relevant period, the majority of the coupons were cashed in New York or Amsterdam and the company suffered an exchange loss of £67,932 in paying its interest. The KB held that the loss was not an expense of management. *Bennet v Underground Electric Railways Co of London Ltd*, KB 1923, 8 TC 475; [1923] 2 KB 535.

Application of legislation to investment companies

[18.34] An investment trust company claimed relief on its management expenses. The HL unanimously held that it was entitled to the relief it had claimed. *Simpson v The Grange Trust Ltd*, HL 1935, 19 TC 231; [1935] AC 422. (*Note.* There have been major subsequent changes to the legislation, but the case illustrates the principle that 'the rule applicable to life insurance companies, whereby relief is restricted to the amount of tax which would have been paid if the profit had been assessed under *CTA 2009, s 35*, does not apply to an investment-holding company'. See Simon's Taxes, para D7.310.)

Costs of debenture issue

[18.35] The Special Commissioners held that the expenses of an investment company in issuing debenture stock (to replace existing debentures and other indebtedness) were not expenses of management. The KB upheld their decision. Macnaghten J held that 'expenses incurred in the rearrangement of the loan capital of a company stand on the same footing as expenses incurred in raising loan capital. Neither expenses incurred in raising loan capital nor expenses incurred in rearranging loan capital in a manner more satisfactory to the company can in my opinion be regarded as expenses of the management of the business'. *London County Freehold & Leasehold Properties Ltd v Sweet*, KB 1942, 24 TC 412; [1942] 2 All ER 212.

Brokerage and stamp duty on investment changes

[18.36] The Special Commissioners held that brokerage and stamp duties incurred by an investment company on changes of its investments were not admissible as management expenses, since they formed 'an integral part' of the price of purchase and sale. The CA unanimously upheld their decision. Tucker LJ held that what is now *CTA 2009, ss 1219–1223* was concerned with 'the expenses of management, not expenses incurred by the management in carrying out the proper business of the company'. *Capital & National Trust Ltd v Golder*, CA 1949, 31 TC 265; [1949] 2 All ER 956.

[18.37] A life assurance society claimed that brokerage and stamp duties on changes of investments should be allowed as management expenses. The Special Commissioners rejected the claim and the HL upheld the Commissioners' decision (by a 4–1 majority, Lord Reid dissenting). Viscount Simonds held that 'the expense of purchasing an investment is not an expense of management' and that the relevant stamp duties were 'a part of the expenses of the particular purchase not of the expenses of management'. Lord Morton held that the expenses were 'so closely linked with the transaction of purchase that they may naturally be considered as items in the total cost of a purchase which has already been resolved upon by the management of the company, and not as expenses of management'. *Sun Life Assurance Society v Davidson*, HL 1957, 37 TC 330; [1958] AC 184; [1957] 2 All ER 760.

Payments to guarantor of loan stock capital

[18.38] A company was a member of a large international group, the ultimate parent of which was a German company. Its function was to raise money on the Stock Exchange with which to finance UK operations of the group. In 1975, it placed on the Stock Exchange a £15m issue of redeemable loan stock, the interest and principal of which was guaranteed by the German parent, into whose shares the stock was convertible after 1985. For reasons connected with the German tax code, the company was required to pay the parent 0.25% per annum on the stock outstanding. The Special Commissioners held that the commission payments were not management expenses. The CA unanimously upheld this decision. Dillon LJ held that the payments were part of the consideration for obtaining the guarantee and could not be severed from the cost of the issue of the loan stock. *Hoechst Finance Ltd v Gumbrell*, CA 1983, 56 TC 594; [1983] STC 150.

Excessive directors' remuneration

[18.39] For 1960/61, the surplus of an investment company was absorbed by directors' fees of £1,800. The Special Commissioners found that only £600 of this was allowable as an expense of management, since 'neither the company, nor its directors and shareholders, nor its auditor, ever consciously determined that the directors should be remunerated for their services and incidental expenses as directors by paying them £600 each; all concerned were simply minded to cause the company to dispose of substantially the whole of its profits' by paying directors' fees. The Ch D upheld the Commissioners' decision as one of fact. Plowman J held that they were entitled to investigate the true nature of the remuneration, and to apply the reasoning in *Copeman v William Flood & Sons Ltd*, **63.170** TRADING PROFITS. *LG Berry Investments Ltd v Attwooll*, Ch D 1964, 41 TC 547; [1964] 2 All ER 126.

Administration expenses

[18.40] As part of an unsuccessful 'dividend-stripping' operation (the subject of *Cooper v Sandiford Investments Ltd*, **59.55** TRADING INCOME) the shares of an investment company (F) were purchased by the company carrying out the 'dividend-stripping' operation (S). F paid S two sums of £1,000, each described as administration expenses. It submitted a repayment claim on the basis that the payments were management expenses. The Revenue rejected the claim, and the Special Commissioners dismissed F's appeal, finding that there was no evidence that S had provided any relevant services to F. The Ch D upheld the Commissioners' decision as one of fact. *Fragmap Developments Ltd v Cooper*, Ch D 1967, 44 TC 366.

Accountants' and solicitors' fees

[18.41] An investment company (H) held 50% of the share capital of a trading company (B). It had written letters of assurance to B's banks in connection with B's credit arrangements. B suffered financial difficulties and H was faced with a potential liability under its letters of assurance. It consulted solicitors concerning the extent of its liability, and commissioned accountants to make a report into B's affairs. It claimed relief for its accountants' and solicitors' fees as management expenses. The Revenue rejected the claim on the basis that the payments were capital expenditure. The Special Commissioner allowed H's appeal, holding that the payments were not capital expenditure, since they were not 'spent on assets or advantages of an enduring nature'. The payments were incurred in the course of H's management of its investments, and qualified for relief as management expenses. *Holdings Ltd v CIR*, Sp C [1997] SSCD 144 (Sp C 117).

Professional fees relating to prospective acquisition

[18.42] In an Irish case, a company incurred expenditure in preliminary investigations into the prospective acquisition of two subsidiary companies. It did not proceed with the acquisition, and claimed relief for the expenditure as management expenses. The SC(I) rejected the claim, holding that the expenditure was capital expenditure. Murphy J held that 'even allowing for the technical and artificial nature of fiscal legislation, it would require the clearest words to justify the inference that the legislature intended to arrive at taxable profits or income for an accounting period by deducting a capital payment from a revenue receipt'. *Hibernian Insurance Co Ltd v Macuimis*, SC(I) [2000] 2 IR 263.

[18.43] A company (C) incurred substantial expenditure in evaluating a projected acquisition of another company. It did not proceed with the acquisition, and claimed relief for the expenditure as management expenses. The Revenue rejected the claim, and C appealed. The Ch D allowed the appeal (reversing the decision of the Special Commissioners) and the CA upheld this decision. Carnwath LJ declined to follow the decision in *Hibernian Insurance Co Ltd v Macuimis*, **18.42** above, and held that the relevant activities 'were all part of the process of managerial decision-making'. He also held that capital expenditure was not excluded by the legislation as in force at the relevant time. *Atkinson v Camas plc*, CA 2004, 76 TC 641; [2004] STC 860; [2004] EWCA Civ 541; [2004] 1 WLR 2392. (*Note*. See now, however, *CTA 2009, s 1219(3)(a)*, deriving from *FA 2004, s 38*, which specifically states that expenses of a capital nature are excluded from deduction as management expenses.)

Professional fees relating to company privatisation

[18.44] In 1988 a company (D), which had several subsidiary companies and had previously been a private company, floated 25% of its shares on the Stock Exchange. The flotation was not a success and in 2000 D decided that its shares should be delisted and that it should revert to being a private company. It incurred costs of £433,574. It claimed a deduction for these as management expenses. HMRC rejected the claim, considering firstly that D was a trading company and was not an investment company, and alternatively that the expenses did not qualify as 'management expenses'. The Upper Tribunal dismissed D's appeal. Mann J held that D qualified as an 'investment company', but that the expenditure in question did not qualify as 'management expenses'. He observed that 'the principal motivation behind the delisting, and behind the board's support for the delisting, was concern for share price or share valuation, and the perceptions of third parties of the position of (D) in the market'. The expenditure had not been incurred 'in order to manage the business', but in order 'to improve the investments'. *Dawsongroup Ltd v HMRC*, UT 2010, 80 TC 270; [2010] STC 1906; [2010] EWHC 1061 (Ch).

Holding company guaranteeing rental payments by subsidiary

[18.45] A company (M) leased various properties, which it used as retail stores. M's holding company (H) guaranteed the rental payments which M was required to make under the leases. In 2008 M went into administration and H was required to make payments under the lease guarantee agreements. H claimed a deduction for these payments as management expenses. HMRC rejected the claim on the grounds that the payments did not qualify as management expenses, considering that they had been primarily expended for the purposes of M's retail business, rather than for the purposes of H's investment business. The First-tier Tribunal reviewed the evidence in detail and allowed H's appeal in part. Judge Short observed that 'the providing of a parent company guarantee is a common core task of a holding company' but held that 'this is essentially expenditure on the assets of the business' which 'falls on the wrong side of the line of deductible management expenses'. However, she also held that certain lump sum payments which H had made did qualify as management expenses, since H had made these payments 'to protect its own business and the impact on that business of being liable under these guarantee obligations'. *Howden Joinery Group plc v HMRC (and related appeal)*, FTT [2014] UKFTT 257 (TC); [2014] SFTD 1186, TC03396.

Whether expenditure to be 'spread' in accordance with FRS4

[18.46] In 1995 a holding company (C) incurred expenditure in respect of the issue of eurobonds and 'preferred securities', which qualified as management expenses under the legislation then in force. In C's accounts, the expenditure was 'spread' over the term of the securities, in accordance with Financial Reporting Standard 4. However, for corporation tax purposes, C claimed that the whole of the expenditure should be treated as deductible in its accounting period ending in December 1995. The Revenue rejected the claim on the basis that the accounting treatment should be followed, and the whole of the expenditure had not been incurred for the period ending in 1995. The Special Commissioner allowed C's appeal, holding that the period for which the costs of obtaining the finance was disbursed was the period when the finance was obtained. The Commissioner (Dr. Avery-Jones) held that FRS4 was concerned with the treatment of the loan as a whole, whereas *ICTA 1988* did not take a 'global view' of the loan. *Cadbury Schweppes plc v Williams (No 1)*, Sp C [2002] SSCD 115 (Sp C 302). (*Note.* For a subsequent appeal by the same company, see **3.3** ANTI-AVOIDANCE.)

Assessments on property dealing

[18.47] See *Jones v Mason Investments (Luton) Ltd*, **5.33** ASSESSMENTS.

Interaction with double tax relief

[18.48] See *Jones v Shell Petroleum Co Ltd*, **21.36** DOUBLE TAX RELIEF.

Maintenance expenditure by property-owning company

[18.49] In a case involving surveyors' fees paid by a property-owning company, the Special Commissioners held that expenses admissible as maintenance expenditure under *ITA 1918, s 33(1)* were not admissible as expenses of management, whether or not they had been included in a maintenance relief claim. The KB upheld their decision. *London & Northern Estates Co Ltd v Harris*, KB 1937, 21 TC 197; [1937] 3 All ER 252. (*Note. ITA 1918, s 33* dealt with 'maintenance' relief under the old Schedule A system, which was repealed by *FA 1963*.)

[18.50] A property company claimed that the cost of advertising empty accommodation in order to find new tenants should be allowed as management expenses. The KB rejected the claim, holding that the expenditure was an expense of management of the property and was not deductible as an expense of management of the company under what is now *CTA 2009, s 1219*. *Southern v Aldwych Property Trust Ltd*, KB 1940, 23 TC 707; [1940] 2 KB 266.

Manufactured dividends paid under stock loan agreement

[18.51] In 2003 a UK investment company (F) entered into an 'overseas securities lender's agreement' with a Netherlands bank (AB), which carried on business through a UK branch and was an 'approved UK intermediary' within *Income Tax (Manufactured Overseas Dividends) Regulations 1993 (SI 1993/2004), reg 2(1)*. Under the agreement, F became the legal and beneficial owner of certain preference shares in a Cayman Islands company (B) until 29 March 2004, and was required to pay a 'manufactured dividend' to AB in respect of any dividend paid on the shares during the currency of the loan. F subsequently entered into an agreement with B under which it agreed to subscribe for an identical batch of preference shares in B. F then sold the original shares in B to an Irish bank (AI) for £50,314,975. B paid dividends totalling £51,000,000 to AI, and F paid 'manufactured dividends' of the same amount to AB, in accordance with the loan agreement. F then transferred the second batch of shares in B to AB, thereby completing the loan agreement. F claimed a deduction of £51,000,000 as management expenses (which it surrendered to its parent company as group relief). HMRC issued an amendment to F's self-assessment to exclude the deduction, considering that the 'dividends' which B had paid were actually returns of capital and that the 'manufactured dividends' which F had paid did not qualify as management expenses. F appealed, contending that its sale of the shares to AI had been necessary to provide funds; that the transactions had given rise to a chargeable gain of £49,314,875, which it had declared on its return; that the dividends which B had paid were 'overseas dividends', and that the effect of *SI 1993/2004, reg 4(1)(c)* was that it was entitled to the deduction for management expenses which it had claimed. The First-tier Tribunal accepted these contentions and allowed the appeal, holding that the dividends were income rather than capital, applying the principles laid down by *Hill v Permanent Trustee Co of New South Wales*, **56.141** SETTLEMENTS, and that the transactions were not a 'sale and repurchase of securities'. The Upper Tribunal and the CA unanimously upheld this decision. Moses LJ held that 'the reality was the distribution of share premium as dividends, as (B) was free to do under Cayman Islands companies law. That mechanism establishes that the payments were income. The correct identification of the dividends as income, notwithstanding that they were paid out of share premium account, mirrors the situation in United Kingdom company law prior to 1948.' *HMRC v First Nationwide*, CA [2012] EWCA Civ 278; [2012] STC 1261.

Small profits rate (CTA 2010, ss 18–34)

Inclusion of non-resident companies in computation

[18.52] A company (J), which was resident in the UK but was the subsidiary of a Netherlands parent company, claimed small companies' relief . The Revenue issued an amendment to the claim on the grounds that the company was associated with its parent company and other companies resident in the Netherlands. J appealed, contending that the inclusion of companies resident outside the UK in the computation contravened *Article 43EC* of the *EC Treaty*. The Special Commissioner rejected this contention and dismissed J's appeal, holding that there was no restriction on the parent company's right to freedom of establishment, and no discrimination. *Jansen Nielsen Pilkes Ltd v Tomlinson*, Sp C [2004] SSCD 226 (Sp C 405).

[18.53] A company (S), which carried on business as an insurance broker, was a wholly-owned subsidiary of a UK company, most of whose share capital was owned by a company (G) which was resident in Liberia. S claimed marginal small companies' relief on the basis that it had two associated companies. HMRC rejected the claims on the basis that S had not provided sufficient information about G's ownership, and that it appeared that S might be associated with several overseas companies. S appealed. The First-tier Tribunal reviewed the evidence in detail and allowed the appeal. Judge Clark held that 'in order to show that the relevant conditions are met, the burden of proof falls on the taxpayer'. However, the standard of proof was 'the balance of probabilities', On the evidence, S had provided sufficient evidence 'to demonstrate that the possibility of the existence of any further associated companies beyond those covered by its claims can be discounted'. *Seascope Insurance Services Ltd v HMRC*, FTT [2011] UKFTT 828 (TC); [2012] SFTD 524, TC01664.

CTA 2010, s 25—whether company carrying on a business

[18.54] See the cases noted at 59.18 to 59.21 TRADING INCOME.

Inclusion of associated company in computation

[18.55] A company (E) claimed small companies' relief. HMRC restricted the claim on the basis that E's controlling shareholder (M) had made a substantial loan to another company (H), so that E and H were associated for the purposes of the legislation. The First-tier Tribunal dismissed E's appeal against this decision, finding that if H had been wound up, M would have received more than half of its assets. Therefore M was deemed to have control of H, so that H and E were 'associated companies'. *Executive Benefit Services (UK) Ltd v HMRC*, FTT [2010] UKFTT 550 (TC), TC00803.

[18.56] A company (G) claimed small companies' relief. HMRC rejected the claim on the basis that G had an associated company (E). The First-tier Tribunal dismissed G's appeal, finding that the issued capital of G and E was owned by the same seven family members, albeit in slightly different ratios, and that three of those seven had a 'controlling combination' in both companies. *Ghelanis Superstore & Cash & Carry Ltd v HMRC*, FTT [2014] UKFTT 111 (TC); [2014] SFTD 835, TC03251.

CTA 2010, s 34—close investment-holding companies

[18.57] In 1962 a close company (H) purchased a property for the purpose of a trade of photography. It ceased to carry on this trade in 1996, and began leasing the property. In 2007, after a dispute with the tenant, it sold the property. In its accounts for the year ending May 2008, H claimed that it was entitled to the benefit of the small companies' rate. HMRC rejected the claim on the basis that H was a 'close investment-holding company'. H appealed, contending that it intended to reinvest the sale proceeds in another property, so that it existed 'for the purpose of making investments in land', within what is now *CTA 2010, s 34(2)(b)*. The First-tier Tribunal accepted H's evidence and allowed its appeal. *Herts Photographic Bureau Ltd v HMRC*, FTT [2010] UKFTT 629 (TC), TC00868.

[18.58] A company (R) submitted a CT return claiming the benefit of the small companies' rate (subsequently renamed the 'small profits rate' in *CTA 2010*). HMRC issued an amendment charging tax at the full CT rate, on the basis that R was a 'close investment-holding company'. R appealed, contending that it existed 'for the purpose of making investments in land', within what is now *CTA 2010, s 34(2)(b)*. The First-tier Tribunal rejected this contention and dismissed the appeal, finding that most of R's income was rental income from an associated company, so that even though R's long-term intention may have been to derive most of its income from lettings to unconnected parties, it remained a close investment-holding company during the year in question. *Reddleman Properties Ltd v HMRC*, FTT [2011] UKFTT 395 (TC), TC01250. (*Note.* The tribunal also rejected the company's application for the decision to be anonymised—see **4.149** APPEALS.)

ICTA 1988, s 13AA—definition of 'first relevant amount'

[18.59] A company (H) submitted a CT return in which it claimed the benefit of the CT 'starting rate' under *ICTA 1988, s 13AA*. The Revenue amended H's self-assessment to take account of the fact that H had one associated company, so that the effect of *s 13AA(4)* was that the 'first relevant amount' was £5,000 (ie £10,000 divided by 2). H appealed, contending that the 'first relevant amount' should be construed as £10,001 (ie dividing £10,000 by one, and then adding the number of its associated companies). The Special Commissioner rejected this contention and dismissed H's appeal. The Commissioner held that the words '£10,000 divided by one plus the number of associated companies' should be construed 'in their context in accordance with the intention of Parliament'. He observed that H's contention was 'that Parliament has instructed taxpayers to divide £10,000 by one which is a pointless exercise always resulting in £10,000, and then add the number of associated companies resulting in a seemingly pointless increase of the £10,000 by 0.1% for every associated company giving rise to a trivial reduction in tax'. There was no reason 'why Parliament should have intended to do that', whereas the Revenue's interpretation of *s 13AA(4)* gave 'a rational result'. *Hallamshire Estates Ltd v Walford*, Sp C [2004] SSCD 330 (Sp C 412).

Group relief (CTA 2010, ss 97–188)

CROSS-REFERENCE

For the CGT provisions for transfers within a group of companies, see **71.266** *et seq.* CAPITAL GAINS TAX.

Surrender of relief

Claim made after surrendering company left group

[18.60] A company (C) had been a member of a large group. It left the group in December 1969, having made a loss in the period ended November 1969. It agreed to surrender this loss to another member of the group. Subsequently C began to make profits and the Revenue issued CT assessments. C appealed, contending that it should still be entitled to relief for the loss it had suffered in the period ending November 1969, and that its surrender of this relief had been invalid because it had left the group before the surrender. The Ch D rejected this contention and dismissed the appeal. Nourse J observed that group relief was available where 'the surrendering company and the claimant company are members of the same group throughout the whole of the surrendering company's accounting period to which the claim relates, and throughout the whole of the corresponding accounting period of the claimant company'. It was not also necessary 'that the two companies should still be members of the same group when the claim is made'. *AW Chapman Ltd v Hennessey*, Ch D 1981, 55 TC 516; [1982] STC 214.

Form of group relief claim

[18.61] A company (G) appealed against an assessment, stating as the grounds of appeal that 'profits will be covered by group relief'. G's accounts for the period were subsequently submitted, and showed the tax due of £167,000 as fully covered by group relief. No further particulars were submitted before the expiry of the two-year limit for making a claim. The Revenue refused to allow group relief on the grounds that G had merely indicated its intention to make a claim and had not actually made a claim within the time limit. The HL allowed G's appeal against this refusal. A claim had to be made by an identified claimant company to relief against identified or identifiable profits for an identified accounting period. However, the legislation as then in force did not indicate any order in which the surrender, claim and consent leading to allowance of group relief were to take place, and there appeared to be no reason why a company should not make a claim to group relief before it knew the extent of any available reliefs or whether the company to which they were available was willing to surrender them. The making of a claim served no other purpose than that of alerting the Revenue to the fact that reliefs were to be sought. (Lord Oliver observed that, if the making of claims in a generalised form proved inconvenient, the Revenue could exercise its powers under *TMA 1970, s 42(5)*.) *Gallic Leasing Ltd v Coburn*, HL 1991, 64 TC 399; [1991] STC 699; [1991] 1 WLR 1399; [1992] 1 All ER 336. (*Note*. See now, however, the form of claim rules prescribed by *FA 1998, Sch 18 paras 67, 68*.)

[18.62] In December 1975 a company (BTI) made group relief claims for the losses accruing to two other group companies (RL and BTH) to be set against its profits for its accounting period ending 31 December 1973. The amounts of the losses in question were specified in the claims. However BTI's profits had not yet been agreed, and in February 1976 BTI made a further claim in respect of the losses of another group company (OB). This claim was expressed to be provisional, as BTI considered that its profits would be covered by the relief already claimed from RL and BTH, and neither the amount of OB's losses nor the amount of relief required was specified in the claim. In August 1979, long after the expiry of the two-year time limit, BTI sought to withdraw the two earlier claims and substitute the third claim in its entirety. The Revenue refused to accede to this request, and the Ch D upheld their refusal, holding that a claim to group relief had to be made in terms that were comprehensible and understandable. BTI had claimed specific amounts in respect of the losses of RL and BTH before making a claim in respect of OB's losses. A claimant was tied to the order of priorities claimed within the statutory time limit. BTI could not, after the expiry of the time limit, abandon its two earlier claims and substitute a new one in their place. *Farmer v Bankers Trust International Ltd*, Ch D 1990, 64 TC 1; [1990] STC 564. (*Note*. For another issue in this case, see **4.215** APPEALS.)

Consortium relief (CTA 2010, s 151)

[18.63] ICI owned 49% of the shares of a holding company (H), which in turn owned 90% of the shares of 23 trading companies, only four of which were resident in the UK. (Six were resident elsewhere in the EC, and 13 were resident outside the EC.) One of the four UK-resident companies (C) had incurred trading losses, and ICI claimed consortium relief in respect of these losses. The Revenue rejected the claim, considering that, because most of H's subsidiaries were resident outside the UK, H did not qualify as a holding company for the purposes of the legislation. ICI appealed, contending firstly that the fact that it was itself resident in the UK was sufficient for it to qualify as a holding company, and alternatively that the restrictions imposed by what is now *CTA 2010, s 151(3)* were a breach of what is now *Article 43EC* of the *EC Treaty*. The HL rejected ICI's first contention, holding that the effect of *s 151(3)* was to restrict consortium relief in respect of holding companies to such companies whose business consisted wholly or mainly of the holding of shares in UK-resident trading subsidiaries. However, the HL directed that the case should be referred to the ECJ to consider ICI's alternative contention. The ECJ ruled that what is now *Article 43EC* should be interpreted as precluding a Member State from applying legislation which, in a case where a company established in that State belonged to a consortium which exercised the right of freedom of establishment in order to set up subsidiaries in other Member States, made a particular form of tax relief subject to the requirement that the holding company's business consisted wholly or mainly in the holding of shares in subsidiaries that were established in the Member State concerned. However, in circumstances such as those of ICI, where the majority of the subsidiary companies were established outside the EC, the difference of treatment was outside the scope of Community law, and the national court was not required to interpret the legislation in conformity with Community law, or to disapply it altogether. ICI requested that the case should be reheard by the HL, which upheld the Revenue's rejection of the company's claim. Lord Nolan held that 'in the circumstances of the present case, Community law presents no obstacle' to the application of the legislation. H did not qualify as a 'holding company', and ICI was not entitled to consortium tax relief. *Imperial Chemical Industries plc v Colmer*, HL 1999, 72 TC 1; [1999] STC 1089; [1999] 1 WLR 2035; [2000] 1 All ER 129.

[18.64] A UK company (S) and a Belgian company (G) agreed to set up and manage a subsidiary company (H) as a joint venture. Under the agreement 75% of H's share capital was held by S, the remaining 25% being held by G. An option agreement gave G the option to purchase, and S an option to require G to purchase, a further 5% of H's issued share capital after five years. The price payable by G was to be the paid-up value of the shareholding increased by annual interest and decreased by any dividend paid on them. Neither option was ever exercised and the option agreement was abandoned in 1985. S claimed group relief in respect of H's trading losses. The Revenue refused to allow relief, considering that so long as the option agreement was in force, the effect of what is now *CTA 2010, s 151(4)* was that H was not to be treated as a 75% subsidiary of S, and relief was not due. The Ch D allowed S's appeal, and the CA upheld this decision. Notwithstanding the option agreement and the restrictions attached to its shareholding by the principal agreement, S had remained the beneficial owner of the whole of its 75% shareholding. The legislation was concerned with arrangements affecting the rights attaching to shares, rather than arrangements affecting the ownership of shares. Accordingly, S was entitled to group relief in respect of H's losses throughout the period that the option agreement was in force. *J Sainsbury plc v O'Connor*, CA 1991, 64 TC 208; [1991] STC 318; [1991] 1 WLR 963. (*Note*. See now, however, *CTA 2010, s 174*.)

[18.65] A public company (B) acquired a large shareholding in a company (C) which carried on a reinsurance business and had incurred losses. Under the share purchase agreement, B was required to pay the vendor (T) an 'earn-out consideration' equal to any distribution made by C. One of B's subsidiaries (BI) subsequently claimed consortium relief in respect of losses incurred by C. HMRC rejected the claim on the grounds that B's contractual obligation to pay an 'earn-out consideration' to T affected its 'beneficial entitlement' to any distribution made by C. BI appealed. The Upper Tribunal allowed the appeal, holding that B's contractual obligations 'to pay earn-out consideration to (T) did not deprive (B) of "beneficial entitlement" to any distribution (actual or notional) made by (C)'. The Tribunal held, that for the purposes of the legislation dealing with consortium relief, '"beneficial entitlement" is a wider concept than "equitable ownership"'. *BUPA Insurance Ltd v HMRC*, UT [2014] UKUT 262 (TCC); [2014] STC 2615.

Arrangements for transfer of company (CTA 2010, ss 154–156)

[18.66] A ship-owning group had a prospective entitlement to capital allowances which was substantially greater than its current profits. It entered into a complex scheme with P, the parent company of another group, with the aim of enabling P to use part of the capital allowances as group relief. P agreed to pay M, the parent company of the ship-owning group, 87% of the tax saved by P's group. Under the scheme, the relief was surrendered to P by G, which had previously been a subsidiary of M, and which became a 75% subsidiary of P but was not controlled by P within the meaning of what is now *CTA 2010, s 1124*. The Revenue rejected the claim on the ground that, in the relevant period, the shareholders of P did not control G, and the shareholders of P and M considered together could control G but did not control P, so that arrangements were in existence under which, by virtue of what is now *CTA 2010, s 154*, both companies were not to be treated as members of the same group. P appealed. The Special Commissioners dismissed the appeal and the HL upheld their decision (by a 3-2 majority, Lords Wilberforce and Russell dissenting). Lord Bridge of Harwich held that for the purpose of *s 154*, 'arrangements' should be construed as including 'those arrangements which regulate the conduct of the affairs of either of the companies in accordance with the wishes of its controlling shareholders'. There was no reasonable construction of *s 154* which would exclude the particular facts of this case. *Pilkington Bros Ltd v CIR*, HL 1982, 55 TC 705; [1982] STC 103; [1982] 1 WLR 136; [1982] 1 All ER 715.

[18.67] Two companies (N and C) were both wholly-owned subsidiaries of a major public company (L). In 1987 L had granted an unrelated company (V) the right to purchase the share capital of another of its subsidiaries (G), which imported cars manufactured by V. C imported cars manufactured by a Spanish company in which V had a 75% shareholding, and the contract between L and V contained a clause intended to enable L to recover losses which C had made by providing for an extension of the import agreement until 1995 coupled with an option for the Spanish company to acquire C at that time. C made substantial losses in the year ending 30 September 1989. N claimed group relief in respect of these losses. The Revenue rejected the claim on the basis that the effect of the 1987 agreement was that there were arrangements by which V could obtain control of C, so that the effect of whati s now *CTA 2010, s 154* was that group relief was not due. N appealed, contending that the clause in question did not constitute arrangements by which V could obtain control of C within *s 154*. (By the time of the appeal, L had sold C to the Spanish company in December 1989.) The Special Commissioners allowed the appeal, holding that the contract was, in principle, within the definition of 'arrangements', but the relevant provisions could never have operated, because the projected extension of the import agreement would have been invalid under what is now *Article 81EC* of the *EC Treaty* and because the option was conditional on the Office of Fair Trading not making a reference to the Monopolies Commission. A material part of the 'arrangements' had no effect and accordingly V could not have obtained control of C by virtue of them. *Scottish & Universal Newspapers Ltd v Fisher*, Sp C [1996] SSCD 311 (Sp C 87).

'Arrangements' only existing for part of accounting period

[18.68] A company (L) granted to an unconnected company options to acquire the shares of a subsidiary company (M). The options lapsed five weeks after they were granted, and the shares in M remained the unfettered property of L for the rest of the year. M made a trading loss in the year, and L claimed group relief in respect of that loss. It was accepted that the options over M's shares were arrangements within what is now *CTA 2010, s 154*. The Revenue rejected L's claim to relief. L appealed, contending that M should only be treated as not being a member of the same group of companies as L for the five-week period during which the arrangements subsisted, and that the loss should be apportioned on a time basis between the 47 weeks during which M was to be treated as a group member and the five weeks during which it was not to be so treated. The Special Commissioner allowed L's appeal and the Ch D upheld this decision, holding that an apportionment should be permitted on a time basis, allowing relief for the part of M's losses that related to the period during which it was to be treated as a group member. *Shepherd v Law Land plc*, Ch D 1990, 63 TC 692; [1990] STC 795.

Definition of 'control' in CTA 2010, s 1124

[18.69] A holding company (T) entered into a complex scheme with the object of enabling it to claim as group relief the losses of R, a member of another group of companies (S). These losses mostly arose from capital allowances on a ship being constructed by a Japanese company. The scheme was designed both to escape what is now *CTA 2010, s 154* and to enable S to represent to the Japanese company that R was its subsidiary, within the meaning of the *Companies Act*. The Ch D held that T was not entitled to group relief, since it did not control R within the meaning of what is now *CTA 2010, s 1124*, either at board level or at the level of a company general meeting. *Irving v Tesco Stores (Holdings) Ltd*, Ch D 1982, 58 TC 1; [1982] STC 881.

Miscellaneous

Group relief provisions—whether valid under EC law

[18.70] See *Claimants under Loss Relief Group Litigation Order v HMRC (No 2)*, 25.24 EUROPEAN LAW; *Philips Electronics UK Ltd v HMRC*, 25.31 EUROPEAN LAW, and *Felixstowe Dock & Railway Co Ltd v HMRC (and related appeals)*, 25.32 EUROPEAN LAW.

Amount available for group relief

[18.71] In its accounting period ending in 1994, a company's charges on income exceeded its profits by more than £48,000,000. It also realised chargeable gains of slightly over £6,000,000, which were covered by allowable losses brought forward from previous periods. It claimed to surrender the £48,000,000 as group relief, without deducting the £6,000,000 of chargeable gains. The Revenue issued a determination that the chargeable gains had to be set against the amount available for surrender, so that the company could only surrender £42,000,000 rather than £48,000,000. The HL unanimously allowed the company's appeal. Lord Hoffmann held that in construing what is now *CTA 2010, s 105(5)*, 'losses' were 'losses allowed by way of relief against profits and not losses, such as allowable losses, deducted in the computation of profits'. *MEPC Holdings Ltd v Taylor*, HL 2003, 75 TC 632; [2004] STC 123; [2003] UKHL 70; [2004] 1 All ER 536.

Whether FA 1994, s 227A applicable

[18.72] See *Standfast Corporate Underwriters Ltd v HMRC*, 69.9 UNDERWRITERS.

CTA 2010, s 1119—definition of 'ordinary share capital'

[18.73] A company (S), limited by guarantee, claimed group relief. The Revenue rejected the claim on the grounds that the company did not have any ordinary share capital, and so was not a 75% subsidiary of any company and was not a member of a group. The company appealed, contending that the deposits of its founder members were 'issued share capital (by whatever name called)' and thus were ordinary share capital within what is now *CTA 2010, s 1119*, and that as not less than 75% of these deposits were owned directly or indirectly by a holding company of a trading group, it was therefore a member of the group and was entitled to claim group relief. The Special Commissioner rejected this contention and dismissed the appeal. It was accepted that a trading company, which was the principal member of the group in question, had made 38 of the 41 founder members' deposits in S, which had been established in 1945 as a mutual insurance company to provide insurance for the companies in the group. However, these deposits were not within the definition of 'issued share capital'. The phrase 'issued share capital (by whatever name called)' should be construed as meaning 'that part of the authorised share capital of a company as has been issued, whether or not it is called ordinary share capital'. As S did not have authorised share capital, it did not have any issued share capital. *South Shore Mutual Insurance Company Ltd v Blair*, Sp C [1999] SSCD 296 (Sp C 215).

[18.74] See also *Tilcon Ltd v Holland*, 18.92 below.

Late claim to group relief—application for judicial review

[18.75] Several associated companies, whose accounting periods were not identical, submitted claims to group relief in excessive amounts, because the relevant profits and losses had been time-apportioned incorrectly. The companies' accountants subsequently made a late claim for some of the relief to be set against the profits of another company in the group. HMRC rejected the claim on the basis that it had been made outside the statutory time limit. The companies applied for judicial review, contending that HMRC should have alerted them to the mistakes in the original claims more promptly, and that the rejection of the late claim was irrational. The QB rejected these contentions and dismissed the applications. Blair J held that 'in a commercial setting such as this, the responsibility for formulating a claim for group relief correctly must lie with the group. It was for the group to apportion losses in a way that maximised relief, not the Revenue'. He also observed that there was 'no reason in principle why the tax avoidance factor should not be taken into account in deciding whether to admit a late claim or not. In reaching its decision, HMRC must be entitled to take account of the fact that (for example) the relevant losses have not been incurred in the course of the group's trading activities, but have been acquired for the purpose of increasing the claim to group relief.' The CA unanimously upheld this decision. Arden LJ held that 'none of the passages in Code of Practice 14 relied on by the appellants imposed an obligation on HMRC to disclose a matter which had been spotted prior to the enquiry but which was not present to the minds of the officials of HMRC handling the affairs of the taxpayer during the enquiry. To hold otherwise would indeed without justification shift the responsibility for those errors from those who had caused the error, namely the taxpayer and its advisers, to HMRC.' *R (oao Bampton Group Ltd) v King (HMRC) (and related applications)*, CA [2012] EWCA Civ 1744; [2014] STC 56.

Disallowance of trading losses (CTA 2010, ss 673–676)

NOTE

For the Revenue's interpretation of what constitutes a 'major change in the nature or conduct of a trade or business', see HMRC Statement of Practice SP 10/91 (as revised and reissued on 22 April 1996).

Whether a major change in customers, etc.

[18.76] A company (P) manufactured and sold picture frames and mouldings, mainly to wholesalers. It ran into financial difficulties, and in 1976 its shares were acquired by a public company, which was the parent of a group of companies operating in the same field. At the change of ownership P had unused trading losses. It claimed relief for these under what is now *CTA 2010, s 45*. The Revenue rejected the claim on the basis that the change had resulted in most of P's sales being to distribution companies within the same group, and that this was a major change in customers, outlets or markets of the trade, within what is now *CTA 2010, s 673(4)(b)*. P appealed. The Special Commissioners allowed the appeal, finding that the companies within the group ordered P's products only to fulfil specific orders from customers, many of whom were wholesalers who had previously bought directly from P, and holding on the evidence that there had been no significant change in the manner of distributing the goods which P made. The CA(NI) upheld their decision as one of fact. Gibson LJ held that 'whether there has been a change in the conduct of the trade clearly imports a qualitative test because one is looking for a different type of conduct'. However, 'in judging whether the change is major, a different criterion should be applied. The obvious contrast is between changes which are major and those which are minor; that is to say, it is a question of degree, or a quantitative matter.' *Willis v Peeters Picture Frames Ltd*, CA(NI) 1982, 56 TC 436; [1983] STC 453.

Increase in turnover—whether a major change in conduct of trade

[18.77] A company (T) which operated a chain of retail shops changed its promotional policy, discontinuing the issue of trading stamps and reducing its prices. The change resulted in a substantial increase in its turnover, and it claimed stock relief in respect of its increased stock. The Revenue considered that there had been a major change in the conduct of T's trade, so that the relief had to be restricted. T appealed. The Special Commissioners allowed the appeal, holding that there had been no 'major' change in the conduct of the trade since the alteration had not been 'fundamental'. The Ch D remitted the case to the Commissioners, holding that they had misdirected themselves in law. Warner J held that the word 'major' should be construed as meaning something more than 'significant' but less than 'fundamental'. *Purchase v Tesco Stores Ltd*, Ch D 1984, 58 TC 46; [1984] STC 304. (*Note*. There was no further public hearing of the appeal.)

Change in purchasing policy

[18.78] A company (P) carried on the business of minting coins and medallions from precious metals, including gold. It purchased the entire stock of gold of its principal supplier, and also began to purchase gold directly from wholesalers. As a result, its stock increased from £26,000 to £352,000, and it claimed stock relief in respect of this. The Revenue rejected the claim, on the grounds that there had been a major change in the conduct of P's trade.

The Commissioners dismissed P's appeal, and the Ch D and the CA unanimously upheld their decision as one of fact. *Pobjoy Mint Ltd v Lane*, CA 1985, 58 TC 421; [1985] STC 314.

Loss carry-forward on company reconstructions (CTA 2010, ss 940A–953)

NOTE

The provisions of *CTA 2010, ss 940A–953* originally derive from the previous income tax provisions of *FA 1954, s 17*. The cases noted at **18.79** to **18.82** below are income tax cases under *FA 1954, s 17*. The cases should be read in the light of the subsequent changes in the legislation.

[18.79] On 31 March 1960, a company (S) accepted an offer from another company (B) for its shares in a subsidiary (W), which acted as an agent for a German company (D). The offer was subject to a condition that within a month a letter from D would be produced confirming that D would not terminate W's agency and that meanwhile W would not declare any dividend or bonus on its shares. D proved unwilling to provide the requested letter, but B made other satisfactory arrangements with D and informed S on 18 May 1960 that the contract had accordingly become unconditional. Meanwhile, on about 9 May, S transferred its trade to W. W claimed relief on S's unused losses. The Revenue rejected the claim on the basis that S had ceased to be the beneficial owner of its shares in W from the date of acceptance of the conditional offer. W appealed, contending that S had remained the beneficial owner until 18 May. The Special Commissioners rejected this contention and dismissed the appeal, and the CA unanimously upheld this decision. Lord Donovan held that 'if one finds, as here, that the company which made the losses, though still the legal owner of the shares, is bereft of the rights of selling or disposing or enjoying the fruits of these shares', it would be 'a misuse of language to say that it still remained the beneficial owner of these shares'. *Wood Preservation Ltd v Prior*, CA 1968, 45 TC 112; [1969] 1 All ER 364.

[18.80] A company (M) went into liquidation in December 1960 with substantial unused losses. Its liquidator continued its trade, and arranged for the formation of a new company (W), which was formed in 1961. M subscribed for 99 of the 100 shares in W, which acquired M's trade in January 1962. W appealed against an assessment for 1964/65, claiming relief for M's unused losses. The Revenue rejected the claim and W appealed, contending that from December 1960 to January 1962 M's trade should be treated as belonging to the secured and/or preferential creditors, and that W's shares were held in trust for the same people. The Ch D rejected this contention, holding that W was not entitled to relief. Cross J observed that there was 'no reason for saying that after the transfer the preferred creditors were the sole beneficial owners of the shares in the new company to the exclusion of the ordinary creditors and/or the shareholders in the old company'. *Pritchard v MH Builders (Wilmslow) Ltd*, Ch D 1968, 45 TC 360; [1969] 1 WLR 409; [1969] 2 All ER 670.

[18.81] A company (J) had incurred losses, and its bank had appointed a receiver. The receiver decided to sell J and entered into negotiations with a prospective purchaser (G). In February 1965 it was agreed that J should sell its business to a new company (T) in return for shares in T, and should then sell T to a subsidiary of G. The sale was completed in July 1965. T subsequently appealed against assessments on its profits, claiming relief for J's losses. The Revenue rejected the claim on the basis that the correspondence between J's receiver and G amounted to a binding contract to sell the shares in T, with the result that J was never their beneficial owner. T appealed, contending that the agreement made in February 1965 was only a conditional agreement, and that J had been the beneficial owner of its shares until July 1965. The Special Commissioners rejected this contention and dismissed the appeal, holding that there had been 'a binding contract' in February 1965. The Ch D upheld their decision, holding that there had been 'an unambiguous offer and 'a perfectly unqualified and unambiguous acceptance'. *JH & S Timber Ltd v Quirk*, Ch D 1972, 48 TC 595; [1973] STC 111.

[18.82] In June 1962, a compulsory winding-up order was made against a company (M). In January 1963, another company (C) acquired M's trade. M had been the legal and beneficial owner of the shares in C before the winding-up, and had remained the registered owner. C claimed relief on M's unused losses. The Revenue rejected the claim, and C appealed, contending firstly that the trade belonged to M immediately before and after the transfer as trustee for its creditors and contributors and was accordingly under the same beneficial ownership throughout, and alternatively that because M remained the legal owner of its assets and the beneficial ownership did not vest in any other person, it must be taken also to have remained the beneficial owner. The Ch D rejected these contentions and held that relief was not due, and the HL unanimously dismissed C's appeal. Lord Diplock held that there was 'a consistent line of judicial authority that upon going into liquidation a company ceases to be "beneficial owner" of its assets as that expression has been used as a term of legal art since 1874'. Furthermore, 'there has been a consistent use in taxing statutes of the expressions "beneficial owner" and "beneficial ownership" in relation to the proprietary interest of a company in its assets which started with the *Finance Act 1927*, where the context makes it clear that a company upon going into liquidation ceases to be "beneficial owner" of its assets as that expression is used in a taxing statute'. *Ayerst v C & K (Construction) Ltd*, HL 1975, 50 TC 651; [1975] STC 345; [1976] AC 167; [1975] 2 All ER 537.

[18.83] A Swiss company (M) began trading in the UK in 2001. It submitted corporation tax returns claiming loss relief. HMRC issued amendments disallowing the claims on the basis that the requirements of what is now *CTA 2010, ss 940A–953* were not satisfied. M appealed, contending as a preliminary point that the UK legislation contravened the EC Treaty. The First-tier Tribunal rejected this contention and dismissed the appeal. Judge Shipwright observed that 'it is hard to see, when transfers of trades and transfers of shares are each treated in the same way whether UK-incorporated or non-UK incorporated companies are involved, that there is a restriction which is discriminatory'. *Mindpearl AG v HMRC*, FTT [2011] UKFTT 555 (TC), TC01400.

Company reconstruction during receivership

[18.84] See *Wadsworth Morton Ltd v Jenkinson*, 61.27 TRADING INCOME.

Whether same trade carried on by subsidiary

[18.85] A company (R) was incorporated in 1906 to manufacture motor vehicles. In the course of time, it greatly expanded its activities to include, *inter alia*, the manufacture of aero engines. It ran into serious financial difficulties over the development of a particular engine (the RB 211) and a receiver was appointed in 1971. By that time, the business of the company was organised into six divisions, treated as one trade for tax purposes, of which by far the largest was that dealing with the RB 211 project. On 23 May 1971, the receiver transferred that division and three others to a Government-owned company (R1). On 19 June, he transferred the remaining two, concerned mainly with the manufacture of motor vehicles, to M, a subsidiary formed for the purpose. M claimed relief for R's unrelieved losses. The Special Commissioners rejected the claim, holding that the relative scale of the activities of the two companies indicated that M's trade was different from R's trade. The Ch D upheld their decision. Walton J observed that 'the losses of which (M) seeks to claim the benefit were incurred in a trade which, whatever it was, included the development of the RB 211 engine. That engine, after the splitting of the company, continued to be developed by (R1) and not by (M). Thus, if anybody could be said to be carrying on the same trade as that in which the losses were incurred, it would appear to be (R1) and not (M).' *Rolls Royce Motors Ltd v Bamford*, Ch D 1976, 51 TC 319; [1976] STC 162.

[18.86] A company (G) had carried on a garage business, which had made losses. A property company (E) wished to purchase the site from which G traded, but did not wish to purchase G's business. In January 1995 G transferred its trade to a subsidiary company (Y). Later the same morning, E purchased G's share capital, and another company (B) purchased Y's share capital and took over the trade. B subsequently claimed relief for the losses which G had incurred. The Revenue rejected the claim on the basis that the statutory conditions were not satisfied, as Y had never carried on the trade in question. The Special Commissioner dismissed B's appeal, finding that no transactions had been 'completed during the period of about 90 minutes when (Y) owned the business assets. No customers attended the premises during this period.' Since Y had not carried on the trade previously carried on by G, it followed that B was not entitled to the benefit of G's losses. *Barkers of Malton Ltd v HMRC*, Sp C [2008] SSCD 884 (Sp C 689).

Marketing company taking over trade of manufacturing company

[18.87] A company (M) manufactured jeans and casual clothing. It sold such goods to an associated company (J) which marketed them. M incurred trading losses and ceased trading in 1983. J took over its trade and assets. J claimed that it was entitled to relief for the losses incurred by M. The Ch D allowed the claim, holding that J was carrying on M's former trade even though the profits of that trade were no longer being separately realised. *Falmer Jeans Ltd v Rodin*, Ch D 1990, 63 TC 55; [1990] STC 270. (*Note*. See now *CTA 2010, s 951*.)

CTA 2010, s 945—relevant liabilities and assets

[18.88] In 2006 a company (H) acquired the business and assets of an associated company (E). In its subsequent tax return H claimed relief for trading losses which E had incurred. HMRC rejected the claim on the basis that E's relevant liabilities had exceeded its relevant assets, and that H had not assumed legal responsibility for E's liabilities, so that the effect of what is now *CTA 2010, s 945* was that H was not entitled to the relief claimed. H appealed, contending that it had in fact transferred funds to E to allow it to pay its creditors. The First-tier Tribunal dismissed the appeal, observing that H had chosen to procure the discharge of E's liabilities by making a loan, which was recorded as an asset in H's balance sheet. Judge Geraint Jones observed that 'it is questionable whether that was consistent with the directors' fiduciary duties to (H)'. He also observed that 'had this transaction been quite lawfully constructed appropriately, upon sound professional advice, the appropriate and desired outcome could have been achieved for the appellant'. However, as a matter of law, H had not given consideration for E's business by assuming or discharging E's liabilities. Accordingly H was not entitled to the relief claimed. *Houston Cox Interiors Ltd v HMRC*, FTT [2010] UKFTT 510 (TC), TC00765.

Miscellaneous matters

Accounts covering period of more than one year

[18.89] A property-dealing company, which had appealed against estimated assessments, made up a single set of accounts for the period from April 1968 to December 1973. The Revenue ascertained, by reference to the actual deals in each accounting period, that there had been profits in the first five accounting periods and a large loss in the last accounting period. (Since only a small part of the loss could be used against the profits of the preceding accounting periods, the tax payable exceeded that which would have been payable if the overall profit of the six years had been spread on a time-apportionment basis.) The Special Commissioners determined the appeal in accordance with the Revenue's figures. The company appealed to the Ch D, contending that the overall profit should have been apportioned on a time basis under what is now *CTA 2010, s 1172*. The Ch D rejected this contention and upheld the Commissioners' decision. Goulding J held that it was not obligatory for the Revenue to divide and apportion the profits of the period for which the accounts were made up, where a 'more accurate and a fairer estimate of profit or loss' of the chargeable periods was available. *Marshall Hus & Partners Ltd v Bolton*, Ch D 1980, 55 TC 539; [1981] STC 18.

Revenue revoking direction that dividend payable gross

[18.90] A US corporation (C) acquired about 70% of the shares in a British company and sought to acquire a further 20% which were held by an agent on behalf of the US Treasury. It was proposed that the company would declare a dividend on the shares, and that C would waive its right to the dividend. The dividend would be paid out of the capital resources which the company had built up before the US agent acquired its shares. The Revenue, on an application by the agent's solicitors, issued a direction to the company to pay the dividend gross. Subsequently the Revenue ascertained that the transaction was structured to ensure that the agent would receive $41 million, the minimum he was prepared to accept, for the shares. Some $8 million of this was attributable to the tax credit attached to the dividend. Since the dividend was paid out of profits arising before the acquisition of the shares by the agent, the tax credit would not have been available to other shareholders. Consequently the Revenue considered that the structure of the transaction represented an abuse of sovereign immunity, and revoked its authorisation for the dividend to be paid gross. C applied to the QB for an order quashing the Revenue's decision to revoke the authorisation. The QB rejected the application and the CA unanimously dismissed C's appeal, holding that the Revenue had good cause to revoke the authorisation. There was no binding rule requiring the Revenue to give consent to payment of a tax credit by a company direct to a foreign government. *R v CIR (ex p. Camacq Corporation and Another)*, CA 1989, 62 TC 651; [1989] STC 785; [1990] 1 WLR 191; [1990] 1 All ER 173.

Co-trustees—whether associates

[18.91] See *Willingale v Islington Green Investment Co*, **11.5** CLOSE COMPANIES.

Interpretation of 'ordinary share capital'

[18.92] A company claimed consortium relief and contended that its fixed rate preference shares should be taken into account in arriving at its holding of ordinary share capital in the surrendering company. The Ch D rejected this contention, holding that the way in which the contractual right of a preference shareholder was given effect did not affect the nature of that right and did not bring the preference shares within the definition of 'ordinary share capital'. *Tilcon Ltd v Holland*, Ch D 1981, 54 TC 464; [1981] STC 365.

Status of 'Gesellschaft mit beschränkter Haftung' (GmbH)

[18.93] In an appeal against an assessment under Schedule D Case V, the CA upheld the Revenue's contention that a German 'Gesellschaft mit beschränkter Haftung' (GmbH) was equivalent to an English limited company, rather than a partnership. *Ryall v Du Bois Co Ltd*, CA 1933, 18 TC 431.

Profits not specified in corporation tax assessment

[18.94] In 1973 the Revenue made an estimated assessment on a company for the year to 31 March 1973, showing chargeable profits of £8,000, made up of building society interest and dividends of £12,000 less charges of £4,000. The company appealed, and submitted accounts and a computation showing substantially higher profits, including capital gains and Schedule A income. However, for undisclosed reasons, the matter rested there for several years, neither side taking any action about the open appeal. It was eventually set down for hearing by the Special Commissioners in 1983. The company contended that, although *TMA 1970, s 50(7)* enabled the Commissioners to increase the amount of the income from a source specified in the assessment, it did not enable them to add income from a new source, and that the assessment should be discharged. The Commissioners rejected this contention and increased the assessment to figures agreed between the parties, i.e. Schedule A income of £10,463 and capital gains of £27,721 less management expenses and charges of £6,550. The Ch D upheld their decision. Vinelott J held that, in the case of a company, all chargeable income and chargeable gains for a given accounting period should 'be aggregated and included in a single assessment. An appeal against that assessment is an appeal against the profit chargeable to corporation tax shown in the assessment. Once the appeal is lodged, then the assessment is at large until determined by the Commissioners.' *Owton Fens Properties Ltd v Redden*, Ch D 1984, 58 TC 218; [1984] STC 618.

CTA 2009, s 931W—income taxed as trade profits

[18.95] See *Elsina Ltd v HMRC*, 44.157 PENALTIES.

Staffing costs—CTA 2009, s 1123

[18.96] A company (G) claimed that certain payments which it had made to an associated company (L) were 'staffing costs', within what is now *CTA 2009, s 1123*, and qualified for tax relief as expenditure on research and development. HMRC rejected the claim and G appealed, contending that the payments should be treated as emoluments of its controlling director (F). The General Commissioners dismissed G's appeal and the Ch D upheld their decision. Henderson J observed that 'the provisions form a detailed and meticulously drafted code, with a series of defined terms and composite expressions, and a large number of carefully delineated conditions, all of which have to be satisfied if the relief is to be available'. He held that 'a detailed and prescriptive code of this nature leaves little room for a purposive construction, and there is no substitute for going through the detailed conditions, one by one, to see if, on a fair reading, they are satisfied. It also needs to be remembered, in this context, that the relief is a generous one, which grants a deduction for notional expenditure which has not actually been incurred.' On the evidence, the payments in question were not 'emoluments paid by (G) to (F)'. *Gripple Ltd v HMRC*, Ch D [2010] STC 2283; [2010] EWHC 1609 (Ch).

Partnerships—CTA 2009, s 1263

[18.97] See *Altus Group (UK) Ltd v Baker Tilly Tax & Advisory Services Llp*, 58.50 TAX PLANNING AND AVOIDANCE.

Foreign income dividends

[18.98] Following the reference to the ECJ in *Test Claimants in the FII Group Litigation v CIR (No 1)*, **25.87** EUROPEAN LAW, but before the ECJ decision in that case, several pension funds took proceedings against the Revenue, claiming that the provisions of UK law which denied them tax credits in respect of foreign income dividends contravened EC law, and applying for the case to be referred to the ECJ. Park J rejected the application for the case to be referred to the ECJ, holding that the question of jurisdiction was purely one of UK law and would fall to be decided 'in the English courts and without any reference to the ECJ'. The application of the *Limitation Act 1980* was also purely an issue of national law and should be determined in the national courts. Park J held that 'the rules in the *Limitation Act 1980* to my mind plainly comply with the principles of equivalence and effectiveness', and that 'a six years limitation period is fully long enough to rule out any argument that the exercise of rights arising by virtue of Community law is practically impossible or excessively difficult'. *Trustees of BT Pension Scheme v HMRC (and related appeals) (No 1)*, Ch D 2005, [2006] STC 1685; [2005] EWHC 3088 (Ch).

[18.99] Following the decision noted at **18.98** above, the case was reheard by the First-tier Tribunal, which reviewed the evidence in detail and allowed the trustees' claims in part. The tribunal dismissed the majority of the claims on the grounds that they had been made outside the statutory time limit, but allowed the claims relating to foreign income dividends for 1997/98. The trustees appealed to the CA, which upheld the tribunal decision that *TMA 1970, s 43* applied to the claims and that many of them had been lodged outside the statutory time limit. *Trustees of BT Pension Scheme v HMRC (No 2)*, CA [2014] EWCA Civ 23; [2014] STC 1156. (*Note.* Both sides were given leave to apply for a further hearing to consider other issues in this case.)

[18.100] See also *Test Claimants in the FII Group Litigation v HMRC (No 2)*, 25.88 EUROPEAN LAW.

CTA 2010, s 330—oil activities—ring fence trades

[18.101] In 2006 a UK company (W) acquired a 29% interest in an oilfield near the Shetlands from its US parent company (P). In 2008 W left P's group, triggering a CGT liability under *TCGA 1992, s 179* (see **71.282** et seq) on the transfer of the interest in the oilfield. HMRC charged this to corporation tax at the 'ring fence' rate of 30%, and also sought to impose a 20% supplementary charge under what is now *CTA 2010, s 330*. W appealed, contending that it was not liable to the supplementary charge. The First-tier Tribunal rejected this contention and dismissed W's appeal. (Judge Mure upheld HMRC's contention that the effect of *FA 2012, s 182* had been 'simply to clarify rather than alter fundamentally the charging provisions'.) *Wintershall E & P Ltd v HMRC*, FTT [2014] UKFTT 318 (TC), TC03452.

Investment trust—withdrawal of approval under CTA 2010, s 1159

[18.102] See *Investment Trust v CIR*, 4.12 APPEALS.

19

Deceased Persons

The cases in this chapter are arranged under the following headings.

Income accrued before the date of death

Accrued interest on surrender of Victory Bonds

[19.1] In 1919 the Government issued 4% Victory Bonds on terms whereby they could be surrendered in satisfaction of estate duty for an amount equal to their par value plus accrued interest. An individual (F) purchased Bonds with a face value of £100,000. He died in 1925, and his executors surrendered the Bonds to pay some of his estate duty liability. The Revenue issued an assessment charging income tax on the accrued interest of £800. The Special Commissioners allowed the executors' appeal, holding that the amount representing accrued interest was not taxable income. The KB upheld this decision. *Monks v Fox's Executors*, KB 1927, 13 TC 171. (*Note*. This decision was distinguished in the subsequent case of *Mitchell v CIR*, **19.10** below. Megaw J held that the decision 'only establishes that no income tax should be paid on an apportioned amount of dividends on the bonds from the date of the last payment previous to the death till the date of transfer of the bonds, and has no application to interest arising after the date of transfer'.)

Interest accrued before, but receivable after, death

[19.2] An individual (R) died in 1925. Shortly after his death, his trustees received £2,000 in War Loan interest including the period before his death. The Revenue issued an assessment charging tax on this. The trustees appealed, contending that it should be treated as capital. The CS unanimously rejected this contention and upheld the assessment. Lord Clyde observed that 'monies which arise or accrue in the form of income to trustees, as administrators of the estate under their charge, are not simply passed on to the trust beneficiaries as their income. At the very least, there are administrative charges and expenses to be met which must be paid out of these monies; and in very many cases such monies never reach the hands of any trust beneficiary in the form of income at all.' Nevertheless the interest remained chargeable to income tax in the hands of the trustees. *Reid's Trustees v CIR*, CS 1929, 14 TC 512.

[19.3] A widow (H) died in 1929. Her executors subsequently received dividends and interest which had accrued before her death. They submitted a claim for repayment of income tax, contending that the dividends and interest should be treated as income of H. The CS unanimously rejected this contention. Lord Clyde observed that H could not be treated as 'the person receiving or entitled to' the income. Lord Blackburn observed that the executors had received the income 'as income of the trust estate, and not as income to which she was entitled during her life'. *CIR v Henderson's Executors*, CS 1931, 16 TC 282.

Accrued annuity to date of death of annuitant

[19.4] An individual (S) was entitled under a will to an annuity of £300, which was payable quarterly but accrued from day to day. S died in 1941, and his executor received the accrued annuity up to his death. He claimed repayment of the tax which had been deducted (and which would have been repayable if the accrued annuity had been S's income). The KB rejected the claim, applying the principles laid down in *CIR v Henderson's Executors*, **19.3** above. Macnaghten J held that, as the accrued annuity was not payable to S, it did not qualify as part of his income. *Bryan v Cassin (Scott's Executor)*, KB 1942, 24 TC 468; [1942] 2 All ER 262.

Accrued interest on death of life tenant of Guernsey settlement

[19.5] Under a Guernsey settlement, an individual (S) who lived in Guernsey was entitled to the interest on a holding of War Loan. Because he was resident in Guernsey, he was exempt from UK tax on this income. S died in 1937. His executor was resident in the UK. The Revenue issued an assessment on the executor, charging income tax on the accrued interest. He appealed, contending that because S had not been resident in the UK, the interest should be treated as exempt from UK income tax. The KB rejected this contention and dismissed his appeal. Lawrence J held that 'these sums were income of the executor' and, applying the decision in *CIR v Henderson's Executors*, **19.3** above, 'the executor cannot claim to enjoy the exemption which attached to (S)'. *Wood v Owen*, KB 1940, 23 TC 541; [1941] 1 KB 92.

Income from estates during administration (ITTOIA 2005, ss 649–682)

[19.6] A will, leaving the residue of the testator's estate to charity, was contested by next-of-kin. The proceedings were resolved by the charity making over one-third of the residuary estate to the next-of-kin. The proceedings delayed the division of the estate, and the executors received investment income under deduction of tax. The HL rejected the charity's claim to repayment of the tax deducted, holding that the charity had no interest in the testator's property prior to the residue being ascertained. The income of the estate was income of the executors and not income of the charity. Viscount Cave held that 'when the personal estate of a testator has been fully administered by his executors and the net residue ascertained, the residuary legatee is entitled to have the residue as so ascertained with any accrued income, transferred and paid to him; but until that time he has no property in any specific investment forming part of the estate or in the income from any such investment and both corpus and income are the property of the executors and are applicable by them as a fixed fund for the purposes of administration.' *R v Special Commrs (ex p. Dr Barnardo's Homes National Incorporated Association)*, HL 1921, 7 TC 646.

[19.7] The decision in *R v Special Commrs (ex p. Dr Barnardo's Homes)*, **19.6** above, was applied by the Privy Council in the Australian case of *Queensland Commr of Stamp Duties v Livingston*, PC [1964] 3 All ER 692.

[19.8] A testator's will directed that his estate should be divided when his youngest child reached the age of 25. This occurred in 1916, but the executors did not divide the estate until 1925. The Revenue issued supertax assessments on the legatees on the basis that the appropriate share of the estate income should be treated as their income for tax purposes. They appealed, contending that as the estate was still in the course of administration, none of the income was taxable on them. The KB accepted this contention and allowed their appeals. *Daw v CIR (and related appeals)*, KB 1928, 14 TC 58.

[19.9] In a supertax appeal, the CA held that the question of whether the residue of the estate had been ascertained was a question of fact for determination by the Commissioners. Lord Hanworth MR observed that the question was 'has the administration of the estate reached a point of ripeness at which you can infer an assent, at which you can infer that the residuary estate has been ascertained and that it is outstanding and not handed over merely for some other reason'. *CIR v Sir Aubrey Smith*, CA 1930, 15 TC 661; [1930] 1 KB 713. (*Note*. For HMRC's interpretation of this decision, see Capital Gains Manual, paras CG30700, CG30790 and CG30943.)

[19.10] The executors of a will had deposited Victory Bonds with the Revenue with a view to transferring them in payment of death duties. They received an allowance in respect of accrued interest to the date when the bonds were transferred. This allowance was set against interest on unpaid death duties in arriving at the residuary income to be paid to the beneficiaries under the will. The residuary income was included in surtax assessments on the beneficiaries. The husband of one of the beneficiaries appealed, contending that the accrued Victory Bond interest should be excluded from the computation of the residuary income. The Special Commissioners rejected this contention and dismissed his appeal, and the KB upheld their decision. *Mitchell v CIR*, KB(NI) 1933, 18 TC 108.

[19.11] An individual (G) died in 1934. His executors made up accounts to 5 April 1935, under which £13,600 was credited to G's daughter (C), who was a beneficiary under his will. However, the residuary account of the estate was not made up until May 1935. The Revenue issued a surtax assessment on C's husband (under the legislation then in force) for 1934/35, including the grossed-up equivalent of the £13,600. He appealed, contending that no income arose prior to the ascertainment of the residue of G's estate. The KB accepted this contention and allowed the appeal, and the CA unanimously upheld this decision, applying the principles laid down in *R v Special Commrs (ex p. Dr Barnardo's Homes)*, **19.6** above. Sir Wilfrid Greene MR held that 'during the period of administration, the income is the executors' income and nobody else's'. *Corbett v CIR*, CA 1937, 21 TC 448.

[19.12] In a case involving surtax assessments on certain residuary legatees, the date of ascertainment of the residue was in dispute. The KB upheld the Special Commissioners' decision as one of fact for which there was evidence, but the CA then approved a compromise which was agreed between the parties. *CIR v Pilkington (and related appeals)*, CA 1941, 24 TC 160.

[19.13] A married woman died in 1943, and her husband (S) became entitled to the residue of her estate. She had been life tenant under a trust and her executors received an amount representing her accrued net income as life tenant up to her death. The Revenue issued a surtax assessment on S, charging tax on the gross amount of this income. He appealed. The Special Commissioners dismissed his appeal and upheld the assessment, holding that the income was part of the income of the estate. The KB upheld this decision, applying the principles laid down in *Wood v Owen*, **19.5** above. *Stewart's Executors v CIR*, Ch D 1952, 33 TC 184.

[19.14] A widow received an annuity of £2,500 under her husband's will. He also left his residuary estate on trust for her. The Revenue issued surtax assessments on her income from the trust. She appealed, contending that the annuity should be treated as capital and that she should not be taxed on the residuary income. The Special Commissioners rejected these contentions, dismissed her appeal, and determined the assessments in accordance with the figures put forward by the Revenue. The Ch D and the CA unanimously upheld their decision. *Carlish v CIR*, CA 1958, 38 TC 37. (*Note*. The appellant appeared in person. .)

Other matters

Accumulated income payable to heir-at-law

[19.15] A testator who died domiciled in Scotland directed certain income to be accumulated. The period of accumulation exceeded 21 years, and further accumulation became unlawful. Under Scottish law, two-thirds of the income became payable to the heir-at-law, who was below the age of majority. His *curator bonis* claimed repayment of the tax charged. The Revenue rejected the claim, considering that the amounts received on behalf of the heir-at-law were capital, and the *curator* appealed. The CS unanimously allowed the appeal, holding that they were receipts of income. *Duncan v CIR*, CS 1931, 17 TC 1.

Revenue investigations and penalties

[19.16] See *Harrison v Willis Bros*, **29.85** FURTHER ASSESSMENTS: LOSS OF TAX, as to the liability of the executors of a deceased partner in relation to extended time limit assessments on the partnership. See *A-G v Midland Bank*, **29.120** FURTHER ASSESSMENTS: LOSS OF TAX, as to the liability of the executors if a taxpayer dies following a negotiated 'back duty' settlement. See also *Dawes v Wallington Commissioners*, **44.81** PENALTIES.

Loan repayments after death of moneylender

[19.17] See *Bennett v Ogston*, 52.17 SAVINGS AND INVESTMENT INCOME.

Periodical payments continuing after death

[19.18] See *Westminster Bank Ltd v Barford*, 39.39 MISCELLANEOUS INCOME.

Whether trader's personal representatives continue trading after death

[19.19] See the cases noted at 59.47 *et seq.* TRADING INCOME.

Appeal to High Court—death of taxpayer after Case demanded

[19.20] See *Smith v Williams*, 4.171 APPEALS.

IHTA, s 200(1)—transfer on death—person liable

[19.21] See *Perry v CIR*, 72.167 INHERITANCE TAX.

Insolvency Act 1986, s 423—application to set aside trust deed

[19.22] The Revenue were investigating the affairs of a deceased trader (G). G had made a trust deed transferring his beneficial interest in a property to his son, who was under the age of 18. The Revenue applied to the Ch D for the deed to be set aside under *Insolvency Act 1986, s 423*. Hart J granted the Revenue's application, finding that G had engaged in 'a persistent pattern of gross underdeclaration of profits over the years preceding that in which the disputed trust deed was executed'. In executing the deed, G 'had the intention of putting the property beyond the reach of his creditors'. Accordingly the trust deed should be set aside. The CA upheld this decision. On the evidence, the Ch D had been entitled to find that G had intended to put the property beyond the reach of the Revenue, and that that intention had been a significant factor in his decision to execute the deed. *CIR v Hashmi & Ghauri*, CA [2002] EWCA Civ 981; [2002] 2 BCLC 489.

Executors claiming relief under ITA 2007, s 131 and TCGA 1992

[19.23] An individual (L) subscribed for shares in two companies which subsequently became insolvent, and made a substantial loan to a third company. In May 2010 L was killed in a motoring accident. His executors submitted claims for relief under *ITA 2007, s 131* and *TCGA 1992, s 24* on the basis that the shares had become of negligible value by the date of L's death, and claimed relief under *TCGA 1992, s 253* in respect of the loan. HMRC accepted that the shares had become of negligible value but rejected the claims on the basis that any claim had to be made by the shareholder and could not be made posthumously by a shareholder's executors. The First-tier Tribunal allowed the executors' appeals against the rejection of the claims under *s 131* and *s 24*, but dismissed their appeal against the rejection of the claim under *s 253*. Judge Mosedale held that 'there is nothing any of the relevant Acts that expressly provides that personal representatives can, or cannot, make claims in respect of the deceased's chargeability which the deceased could have made had he lived to file his return'. Applying a purposive interpretation of *s 131* and *s 24*, 'the personal representatives of the deceased are treated as the deceased in so far as they are returning the deceased's own tax liability'. With regard to the claim under *TCGA 1992, s 253*, she held that the executors could make such a claim 'and could carry it forward against any future losses incurred by (L)'. However, since L had no tax liability for the period following his death, 'the tax benefit of the losses to which he was entitled can not be carried forward any further. In particular, they cannot be used to offset any gains incurred by the executors during the period of their executorship.' *PL Drown & Mrs RE Leadley (JJ Leadley's Executors) v HMRC*, FTT [2014] UKFTT 892 (TC), TC04007.

20

Deduction of Tax (ITA 2007, ss 847–987)

The cases in this chapter are arranged under the following headings.

GENERAL NOTE

The cases in this chapter relate to payments where the issue is the liability to account to HMRC for tax under what is now *ITA 2007, ss 847–987*. There have been substantial changes to the relevant legislation, and the summaries should be read in the light of these changes. *'Rule 21'* in the summaries is *ITA 1918, General Rule 21* (re-enacted as amended in *ITA 1952, s 170*) which was broadly similar to *ITA 2007, ss 899–901*. For a review of the origins of the legislation relating to the deduction of tax, see the judgment of Donovan LJ in *Grosvenor Place Estates Ltd v Roberts*, **39.23** MISCELLANEOUS INCOME. For cases relating to the liability of the recipient to account for tax under what is now *ITTOIA 2005, ss 683–686*, see **39.22** *et seq.* MISCELLANEOUS INCOME. See **16** CONSTRUCTION INDUSTRY: CONTRACTORS AND SUB-CONTRACTORS for deduction of tax from certain payments to sub-contractors and **42** PAY AS YOU EARN for deduction of tax under PAYE.

Whether payment from profits or gains brought into charge for tax

No assessable profits

[20.1] The profits of the Metropolitan Water Board (MWB) were taxed under Schedule A (under the law in force at the time) on the 'preceding year' basis. It also paid substantial annual interest from which it deducted tax. However, in 1921/22 it made a loss, with the result that there was no Schedule A assessment on its profits for 1922/23. MWB failed to hand over to the Revenue the tax which it had deducted from the interest it paid during 1922/23. The Revenue took proceedings to recover the tax due under *ITA 1918, General Rule 21*. The KB gave judgment for the Revenue, and MWB appealed, contending that, because the interest was met out of the actual profits which it had made in 1922/23 (which greatly exceeded the interest paid), it should be treated as having been wholly paid out of profits brought into charge to tax. The CA unanimously rejected this contention and dismissed the appeal. *A-G v Metropolitan Water Board*, CA 1927, 13 TC 294; [1928] 1 KB 833. (*Note*. Although the preceding year basis of assessment no longer applies, the case is still sometimes cited as an authority on the interpretation of what is now *ITA 2007, ss 899–901*. The actual decision was approved by a majority of the HL in the subsequent case of *Allchin v Corporation of South Shields*, **20.8** below, but *obiter dicta* of Lawrence LJ were disapproved.)

[20.2] A trading company (L) paid substantial debenture interest under deduction of tax. From 1923/24 to 1926/27 it made losses. The Revenue issued assessments under *ITA 1918, General Rule 21* to recover the tax which L had deducted from the interest it paid (less a small amount of interest it received). L appealed, contending that it should not be required to account for the tax because the interest should be treated as having been paid out of accumulated profits. The CA unanimously rejected this contention and dismissed the appeal. *Luipaard's Vlei Estate & Gold Mining Co Ltd v CIR*, CA 1930, 15 TC 573; [1930] 1 KB 593.

Profits covered by losses brought forward

[20.3] A company's trading profits for 1933/34 were covered by losses brought forward from earlier years. The Revenue issued an assessment under *ITA 1918, General Rule 21* to recover tax which the company had deducted from interest which it had paid. The company appealed, contending that the interest should be treated as having been paid out of 'profits or gains brought into charge for income tax'. The CA unanimously rejected this contention and dismissed the appeal, applying the principles laid down in *A-G v Metropolitan Water Board*, **20.1** above. *Trinidad Petroleum Development Co Ltd v CIR*, CA 1936, 21 TC 1; [1937] 1 KB 408; [1936] 3 All ER 801.

Interest charged to capital

[20.4] A railway company (C) paid debenture interest and charged it to capital in its accounts. Its trading income substantially exceeded the interest paid. The Revenue issued an assessment under *ITA 1918, General Rule 21* to recover tax which C had deducted from interest which it had paid. C appealed, contending that the interest should be treated as having been paid out of 'profits or gains brought into charge for income tax'. The HL unanimously rejected this contention and dismissed the appeal. Lord Macmillan observed that 'there was a deliberate decision to charge the sum in question against capital and not against revenue'. C had therefore 'prevented the diminution of the distribution fund', and could not 'claim to retain the tax deducted from their shareholders on paying them their dividends'. *Central London Railway Co v CIR (and related appeals)*, HL 1936, 20 TC 102; [1937] AC 77; [1936] 2 All ER 375.

[20.5] A company (C) borrowed money to finance the reconstruction of its premises, and charged part of the interest to capital in its accounts. The Revenue assessed this interest on C under *ITA 1952, s 170*. C appealed, contending that the interest should be treated as having been paid out of 'profits or gains brought into charge for income tax'. The HL rejected this contention and dismissed the appeals (by a 3-2 majority, Lords Reid and Upjohn dissenting). Lord Morris of Borth-y-Gest observed that 'if interest is charged to capital rather than to revenue, the dividend fund is *pro tanto* increased'. An interest payment could not 'in one and the same year be debited to capital', with the result that the dividend fund was enhanced, 'and also notionally be treated as debited to revenue so as to enable tax which is deducted to be retained'. *Chancery Lane Safe Deposit & Offices Co Ltd v CIR*, HL 1965, 43 TC 83; [1966] AC 85; [1966] 1 All ER 1. (*Note*. For another issue in this case, see 5.77 ASSESSMENTS.)

[20.6] The decision in *Chancery Lane Safe Deposit & Offices Co Ltd v CIR*, 20.5 above, was applied by the HL in the similar subsequent case of *Fitzleet Estates Ltd v Cherry*, HL 1977, 51 TC 708; [1977] STC 397; [1977] 1 WLR 1345; [1977] 3 All ER 966.

[20.7] A company (B) was assessed under *ITA 1952, s 170* on certain annual payments which it made under covenant in consideration for its acquisition of shares. Its profits exceeded the annual payments, but were less than the aggregate of the payments and dividends it paid. In its accounts, the payments were balanced by capital receipts from the sale of the shares. The Special Commissioners upheld the assessments, and the HL unanimously dismissed B's appeal. Lord Morris of Borth-y-Gest observed that the transactions which gave rise to this case 'seem to have an air of total unreality'. *B W Nobes & Co Ltd v CIR*, HL 1965, 43 TC 133; [1966] 1 WLR 111; [1966] 1 All ER 30.

Whether total income available to frank total annual payments

[20.8] Under the law in force at the time, a local authority's various activities were assessed separately. It paid annual interest under deduction of tax. The Revenue assessed it under *ITA 1918, General Rule 21*, charging tax on the basis that it was liable on the excess of the interest attributable to a particular undertaking over the assessable income of that undertaking. The authority appealed, contending that the assessment should be reduced to the excess of the aggregate interest over its aggregate income of the year. The Special Commissioners accepted this contention and allowed the appeal, and the HL unanimously upheld their decision, holding that the annual payments in a year were to be treated as notionally paid out of the total taxable income for the year. *Allchin v Corporation of South Shields*, HL 1943, 25 TC 445; [1943] AC 607; [1943] 2 All ER 352. (*Note*. The CS had reached a similar decision in *CIR v Ayr Town Council*, CS 1938, 22 TC 381. The substantive issue has been overtaken by *CTA 2010, s 984*, but the general principle remains of interest.)

Annual payments deducted in computing profits

[20.9] Two companies jointly guaranteed the payment of dividends at 7% by a third company for five years. One of the companies (M) claimed that the payments which it made under the guarantee should be treated as deductible in computing its profits, on the grounds that the guarantee was for trading purposes. The Special Commissioners allowed the deduction and the Revenue accepted the decision. The Revenue then assessed the payments under *ITA 1918, General Rule 21* on the ground that they were annual payments and that, having been deducted in computing M's profits, they were not payable out of profits or gains brought into charge to tax. M appealed, contending that the payments should not be treated as 'annual payments'. The Special Commissioners rejected this contention and dismissed the appeal, and the HL unanimously upheld their decision. Lord Macmillan held that 'the fact that the payments were contingent and variable in amount does not affect the character of the payments as annual payments'. *Moss Empires Ltd v CIR*, HL 1937, 21 TC 264; [1937] AC 785; [1937] 3 All ER 381.

[20.10] See also *Renfrew Town Council v CIR*, **39.28** MISCELLANEOUS INCOME; *Paterson Engineering Co Ltd v Duff*, **63.277** TRADING PROFITS, and *Gresham Life Assurance Co Ltd v A-G*, **68.62** TRADING PROFITS.

Liability for accumulated interest discharged

[20.11] A woman (B) had mortgaged her reversionary interest in a settlement, receiving £3,100 in return. The mortgage deed provided that B should pay the mortgagee (L) interest at 5.5% p.a. L died in 1920 and B died in 1933. She had not paid any interest since 1906, and L's trustees subsequently capitalised the unpaid interest. Early in 1940 the trustee of the settlement handed the whole of the settlement funds (£7,604) to L's trustees, without deducting tax. The Revenue assessed him under *ITA 1918, General Rule 21* on the basis that he should have deducted tax from the payment (except for the £3,100 originally advanced). The HL unanimously upheld the assessment, holding that the amount of the excess was interest (apart from £105 which was treated as representing costs incurred by L's trustees). Applying the principles laid down in *Paton (Fenton's Trustee) v CIR*, **33.15** INTEREST PAYABLE, the capitalisation of interest did not amount to payment. The HL also held that the trustee was the person 'by or through whom' the interest was paid. *CIR v Oswald (Trustee of the Cosier Settlement)*, HL 1945, 26 TC 435; [1945] AC 360; [1945] 1 All ER 641. (*Note*. The decision overruled *CIR v Lawrence Graham & Co*, CA 1937, 21 TC 158.)

Person 'by or through whom' payment made

[20.12] A solicitor (H) lent money to a builder (B). The loans were secured on houses which B built. When the houses were sold, H remitted the proceeds to B after deducting the interest (less tax) which was due to him as mortgagee. Tax on some of the interest fell to be accounted for under *ITA 1918, General Rule 21*. The Revenue assessed this on H as the person by or through whom the interest was paid. The Special Commissioners dismissed H's appeal and the KB upheld their decision. *Howells v CIR*, KB 1939, 22 TC 501; [1939] 2 KB 597; [1939] 3 All ER 144.

[20.13] See also *CIR v Oswald*, **20.11** above; *Rye & Eyre v CIR*, **20.20** below, and *Aeolian Co Ltd v CIR*, **20.28** below.

Failure to deduct

Attempt to recover tax by deduction from subsequent payments

[20.14] In one of the cases noted at 2.55 ANNUAL PAYMENTS, the Ch D held that an annuity described as 'clear of all deductions' under a separation agreement, which had hitherto been paid in full, was subject to deduction of tax. A dispute between the parties as to the amount of the arrears of the annuity went to arbitration. On a special case stated by the arbitrator, the CA held that tax could be deducted from the arrears but that the tax which had not been deducted from payments already made could not be recouped from the arrears. *Countess of Shrewsbury v Earl of Shrewsbury*, CA 1907, 23 TLR 224.

[20.15] Similar decisions have been made in several other cases relating to arrears of alimony including *Re Hatch, Hatch v Hatch*, Ch D [1919] 1 Ch 351; *Ord v Ord*, KB [1923] 2 KB 432; *Taylor v Taylor*, CA 1937, 16 ATC 218, [1938] 1 KB 320; *Brine v Brine*, KB 1943, 22 ATC 177; *Hemsworth v Hemsworth*, KB [1946] KB 431 and *Johnson v Johnson*, PDA 1946, 25 ATC 466.

[20.16] Under a will, annuities were to be paid 'without deduction'. At first the trustees paid them in full. They subsequently applied to the Ch D to determine whether they should have deducted income tax. The Ch D held that tax should have been deducted from the annuities, since 'without deduction' should be construed as 'without any deduction except that of income tax'. Neville J also held that the overpayment could be recouped from subsequent payments, since the practice of the court in administering estates was to make adjustments to allow for honest mistakes 'in order that the trustee may so far as possible be recouped the money which he has inadvisedly paid'. *Re Musgrave, Machell v Parry*, Ch D [1916] 2 Ch 417.

[20.17] Under the law in force prior to *FA 1963*, tax at the standard rate was deductible from the whole of rent payable under a 'long lease'. However, where the lease did not qualify as 'long', only the Schedule A tax on the annual value was deductible. A company (D) paid rent due under a long lease, but its assistant secretary mistakenly deducted only the Schedule A tax, which was less than tax at the standard rate on the full rent. On discovering the error, D began to recoup the overpayment from its subsequent payments of rent. The lessor (T) brought an action to recover the amounts which the company had withheld, and D counter-claimed for a refund of the overpayments. The QB gave judgment for D, holding that the mistake as to the length of the lease was one of fact and that T should repay the overpayments. Pilcher J observed that 'morally there are very few merits in the plaintiff's case'. *Turvey v Dentons (1923) Ltd*, QB 1952, [1953] 1 QB 218; [1952] 2 All ER 1025.

[20.18] A Jersey company (T) let premises to another company (P) under a lease which provided for quarterly payments of rent. P should have deducted tax from the payments, but failed to deduct tax from the first four. On realising this, P did not pay the fifth instalment, considering that it was entitled to set the amount which should have been deducted from the earlier payments against the amount of the subsequent payment. T issued a writ claiming payment of the unpaid rent. The Ch D gave judgment for T, holding that once a relevant payment was complete, the right to deduct was lost. Since four quarterly payments had been made, the first annual payment was complete. *Tenbry Investments Ltd v Peugeot Talbot Motor Co Ltd*, Ch D [1992] STC 791. (*Note*. See now *ITA 2007, s 971(4)(5)*, deriving from *FA 1995, s 40*.)

Copyright royalties

[20.19] A UK publishing company (L) acquired the right to produce and publish an English translation of a work by a French author (M). L paid 500,000 francs to M for the right to sell 28,000 copies. The agreement provided for further payments if more than 28,000 copies were sold. However, only 7,000 copies were sold. The Revenue issued an assessment on the basis that the payment of 500,000 francs was a payment of copyright royalties. L appealed, contending that it was a lump sum capital payment. The KB rejected this contention and upheld the assessment. Finlay J held that 'this was a licence and not a complete assignment of the copyright', and that the payment was 'in respect of royalties'. *CIR v Longmans Green & Co Ltd*, KB 1932, 17 TC 272.

[20.20] A UK resident (B) agreed to pay advance royalties of £300 for a licence to stage a London production of a play written by a French author. The production was unsuccessful and no further royalties were payable. B's solicitors failed to deduct tax from the £300. The Revenue issued an assessment to recover the tax from them. The Special Commissioners upheld the assessment and the HL unanimously dismissed the solicitors' appeal. Lord Atkin held that the solicitors were assessable since they were the persons through whom the £300 had been paid. *Rye & Eyre v CIR*, HL 1935, 19 TC 164; [1935] AC 274.

Payments out of capital of trust fund

[20.21] The trustees of a deceased person were directed to hold part of the estate on trust, to pay the income to his widow and to make payments out of capital if that was necessary in order to ensure a payment of not less than £4,000 in any year. The Revenue issued assessments charging tax on the payments out of capital, and the trustees appealed. The Special Commissioners dismissed the appeals, and the KB upheld their decision. Finlay J held that the payments were 'annual payments' notwithstanding the fact that they had been paid out of capital rather than income. Accordingly the trustees were required to deduct tax. *Brodie's Trustees v CIR*, KB 1933, 17 TC 432. (*Note*. 18 months before the assessments were made, the trustees' solicitor had been informed by an Inland Revenue officer that there would be no liability. The KB rejected the trustees' contention that there had been no 'discovery', as required by what is now *TMA 1970, s 29*. For cases concerning 'discovery', see **5.19** *et seq* ASSESSMENTS.)

[20.22] The trustees of a settlement made payments out of capital for the maintenance of the life tenant. They failed to deduct tax, and the Revenue issued assessments charging tax on the payments. The trustees appealed, contending that they should not be required to deduct tax. The Special Commissioners rejected this contention and dismissed the appeals, holding that the payments were taxable income from which tax should have been deducted. The KB upheld this decision. *Lindus & Hortin v CIR*, KB 1933, 17 TC 442.

[20.23] A testator directed in his will that £250 be paid each year to each of his two daughters out of the capital of the estate. The Revenue issued an assessment charging tax on the payments. The trustees appealed, contending that they should not be required to deduct tax because the payments had been made out of capital. The Special Commissioners rejected this contention and dismissed the appeal, holding that the payments were annuities from which tax was deductible. The KB upheld this decision. Wrottesley J held that 'the source from which the money is raised' was irrelevant, and that the payments were 'within the definition of an annuity'. *Jackson's Trustees v CIR*, KB 1942, 25 TC 13.

[20.24] Trustees of a will made discretionary payments to the life tenant, out of the capital of the residuary estate. The Revenue issued assessments on the basis that they were 'annual payments' from which tax was deductible. The trustees appealed (and the recipient appealed against surtax assessments). The Special Commissioners dismissed the appeals, and the CA unanimously upheld their decision. Lord Greene MR held that the fact that the payments 'were made out of capital is irrelevant'. *Cunard's Trustees v CIR; McPheeters v CIR*, CA 1945, 27 TC 122; [1946] 1 All ER 159.

[20.25] The trustees of a settlement were directed to pay the income to the settlor (M) during his life. If the income was below £6,500 'after deduction therefrom of income tax at the current rate', they were to meet the deficiency out of capital unless M directed to the contrary. The Revenue assessed the trustees on the grossed-up amounts of the sums paid to M out of capital. The trustees appealed, contending that tax was not deductible because the trustees should be treated as repaying M his own capital. The Special Commissioners rejected this contention and dismissed the appeal, and the CA upheld this decision, holding that M had ceased to be entitled to the capital when he executed the deed of settlement, so that he received the payments as income. The CA also held (by a 2–1 majority, Tucker LJ dissenting) that the sums should not be grossed up. *John Morant Settlement Trustees v CIR*, CA 1948, 30 TC 147; [1948] 1 All ER 732.

[20.26] Under a will, the residue was held on trust for the income to be paid to the widow for life, with power for the trustees to pay her £1,000 per annum out of the capital. £1,000 was paid to her out of the capital for each of five successive years prior to the ascertainment of the residue. The Revenue issued assessments on the trustees charging tax on the payments. The trustees appealed, contending that since the payments had been made before the administration of the estate was complete, they should not be required to deduct tax. The Special Commissioners rejected this contention and dismissed the appeal, and the Ch D upheld their decision. *Milne's Executors v CIR*, Ch D 1956, 37 TC 10.

Annuities under will in excess of trust income

[20.27] The income of a trust was insufficient to pay the annuities directed by the will. The trustees arranged loans in order to pay the annuities, and subsequently repaid the loans out of capital. They failed to account to the Revenue for tax on the annuities. The Revenue issued assessments on the trustees charging tax on the payments. The trustees appealed, contending that the payments should be treated as voluntary payments and that they should not be required to account for tax. The Special Commissioners rejected this contention and dismissed the appeal, and the Ch D upheld their decision. *Trustees of Peirse-Duncombe Trust v CIR*, KB 1940, 23 TC 199.

US company guaranteeing dividends of UK company

[20.28] An American company guaranteed the preference dividends of a UK company. In years for which the UK company had no profit, it paid the preference shareholders amounts equal to their net dividends and debited the gross amounts to the American company. The Revenue issued assessments on the basis that it should have deducted tax. The company appealed. The Special Commissioners dismissed the appeal and the KB upheld their decision. Lawrence J held that the gross amounts were annual payments, and that the UK company was required to deduct tax as the person by or through whom the payments were made. *Aeolian Co Ltd v CIR*, KB 1936, 20 TC 547; [1936] 2 All ER 219.

Application of ICTA 1988, s 821

[20.29] In 1937 a company (N) paid arrears of patent royalties within *ITA 1918, General Rule 21* in full before the Finance Bill had been enacted. It took proceedings in the KB under what is now *ICTA 1988, s 821(2)*, to recover from the recipients the tax which it had failed to deduct. The KB gave judgment for N. MacNaghten J held that *s 821(2)* applied to payments not made out of profits or gains brought into charge, notwithstanding that N could have deducted the tax under the authority of the *Provisional Collection of Taxes Act*. *Nesta Ltd v Wyatt & Another (Johnson's Executors)*, KB 1940, [1941] 1 KB 44; [1940] 4 All ER 217.

Yearly payments under will for rent collection

[20.30] A testator's will directed his trustees to pay £100 per year to his secretary in return for collecting certain rents. (The balance of the rents was paid to the testator's children.) The Revenue ruled that the payments were annual payments, and that tax was deductible under what is now *ITA 2007, s 900*. The General Commissioners dismissed the trustees' appeal, and the Ch D upheld their decision. *Clapham's Trustees v Belton*, Ch D 1956, 37 TC 26.

Failure to deduct tax under PAYE

[20.31] See *Bernard & Shaw Ltd v Shaw*, 42.85 PAY AS YOU EARN.

Purchased annuity—determination of capital element

[20.32] See *Rose v Trigg*, 52.69 SAVINGS AND INVESTMENT INCOME.

Periodical payments in consideration for shares

[20.33] See *CIR v 36/49 Holdings Ltd*, **64.63** TRADING PROFITS.

Patent royalties (ITA 2007, s 903)

[20.34] A French firm (S) had purchased a European patent licence from the American owner of the patents. A UK company (C) made an agreement with S, under which it made payments to the owner in return for being allowed to use the patents in the UK. The Revenue issued an assessment on C, charging tax on the payments under what is now *ITA 2007, s 903*. C appealed, contending that since the contract had been signed in France, it was outside the scope of UK tax. The Special Commissioners rejected this contention and dismissed the appeal, and the KB upheld their decision. *International Combustion Ltd v CIR*, KB 1932, 16 TC 532.

[20.35] A company (H) agreed to pay another company (D) £3,000 in instalments for a licence to use a patent for five years. H deducted tax from the payments. D took proceedings against H, claiming that the £3,000 was capital, and that H had not been entitled to withhold tax. The KB accepted this contention and gave judgment for D. *Desoutter Bros Ltd v JE Hanger & Co Ltd and Artificial Limb Makers Ltd*, KB 1936, 15 ATC 49; [1936] 1 All ER 535.

[20.36] A UK company (B) acquired a licence to use a French patent for ten years, in return for payment of £25,000 (£15,000 of which was payable on signing the agreement and the remaining £10,000 in two six-monthly instalments) and ten annual payments of £2,500 each, described as a 'royalty'. The Revenue issued assessments charging tax on all the payments, and B appealed. The Special Commissioners allowed the appeal in part, holding that the initial £25,000 was capital but that the remaining ten payments were not, and were subject to deduction of tax. The CA unanimously upheld the Commissioners' decision as one of fact. *CIR v British Salmson Aero Engines Ltd (and cross-appeal)*, CA 1938, 22 TC 29; [1938] 2 KB 482; [1937] 3 All ER 464.

Miscellaneous

Rectification of documents

[20.37] In certain circumstances, the courts will rectify documents if they do not embody the intention of the parties. This has arisen in a number of cases where the issue was the intention of the parties in relation to the deduction of tax. As they involve a question of general law and turn on their particular facts they are not summarised individually. They include *Burroughes v Abbott*, Ch D 1921, [1922] 1 Ch 86; *Jervis v Howle & Talke Colliery Co Ltd*, Ch D 1936, [1937] Ch 67; *Fredensen v Rothschild*, Ch D 1941, 20 ATC 1; *Van der Linde v Van der Linde*, Ch D [1947] Ch 306 and *Whiteside v Whiteside*, CA 1949, 28 ATC 479; [1950] Ch 65; [1949] 2 All ER 913.

[20.38] For other cases concerning rectification of documents, see *Racal Group Services Ltd v Ashmore & Others*, **9.89** CHARITIES; *Royal College of Veterinary Surgeons v Meldrum*, **9.90** CHARITIES; *Toronto-Dominion Bank v Oberoi & Others*, **47.10** PROPERTY INCOME, and the cases noted at **72.180** to **72.189** INHERITANCE TAX.

Payment by UK executors to resident of Kenya

[20.39] Under a contract made in the UK, K lent money to B. B agreed to pay interest at 8% p.a. Both K and B were resident in Kenya. B also had a house in the UK, where he stayed for two or three months each summer. He subsequently died. His executors, who were resident in the UK, paid interest to K without deducting tax. The Revenue assessed them on the basis that they should have deducted tax from the payments. The KB upheld the assessments. Finlay J observed that B had made an English will and had English executors, because 'a large part of his property was situate in England'. The executors were resident in the UK and had paid the debt from a source arising in the UK. *CIR v Viscount Broome's Executors*, KB 1935, 19 TC 667.

Payment by UK resident to Isle of Man bank

[20.40] See *Perrin v HMRC*, **33.11** INTEREST PAYABLE.

Annual payments made in arrears—deduction of tax

[20.41] In a Scottish case, a woman was owed alimony by her husband and sought to recover it from a debt owed to him by a tenant. The CS rejected her claim, holding that the tenant had no power to deduct tax. *Fletcher v Young*, CS 1936, 15 ATC 531.

Interest received by mortgagee

[20.42] A company went into liquidation. One of its shareholders (H) had mortgaged his shares. The liquidator paid the distribution in respect of these shares to the mortgagee (F). H wished to redeem the shares. F had accounted for tax from the interest payable to her. H applied to the Ch D, contending that F should not have accounted for tax. The Ch D and the CA unanimously rejected this contention. MacKinnon LJ held that F 'was not doing anything but that which she was bound to do'. *Hollis v Wingfield & Others*, CA 1940, 19 ATC 98; [1940] 1 All ER 531.

Payments in arrear—rate of tax applicable

[20.43] Instalments of a jointure and an annuity fell into arrear in 1936. They were paid several years later, when the rate of tax was significantly higher. The trustees asked the Ch D to determine whether tax should be deducted at the rate in force when the payments became due, or at the rate in force when the payments were actually made. The Ch D held that tax should be deducted at the rate in force when the payments became due, since the relevant years were those in which the jointure and annuity fell into arrear and ought to have been paid. *Re Sebright, Public Trustee v Sebright*, Ch D [1944] Ch 287.

Payments in arrear—year for which income of payee

[20.44] In 1971 an individual (P) covenanted to pay £5,000 a year to a charity for seven years. He did not make the promised payments for 1974-1976 until 1979-1982, when he paid them after deducting tax at the rate applicable when they fell due. In 1984 the charity trustees claimed repayment of the tax which P had deducted from these payments. The Revenue rejected the claim on the ground that the payments were income of the year in which they fell due, and the claim had been made outside the six-year time limit of *TMA 1970, s 43(1)*. The Ch D upheld the Revenue's refusal. Vinelott J held that the effect of the legislation was that, where an annual payment was made out of profits or gains brought into charge to tax, tax should be deducted at the rate in force when the payment became due, and that the payment formed part of the payee's total income for that year by reference to which the tax was deducted. Accordingly the repayment claim had been made outside the time limit of *s 43(1)*. *CIR v Crawley & Others*, Ch D 1986, 59 TC 728; [1987] STC 147.

Maintenance less tax set against debt

[20.45] A divorced woman was liable to pay £460 to her former husband for the former matrimonial home. Under a court order in 1957, the debt was to be set off against maintenance payable by her husband to her at the rate of £200 p.a. less tax. In 1960 she took proceedings against her husband, contending that the debt had been cleared and that he was in arrear with the maintenance payments. The husband defended the proceedings, contending that the amount of maintenance to be set off was the net amount of £115 p.a., i.e. £200 less the tax deductible, so that he was not in arrear with the payments (the standard rate of tax was then 42.5%). The CA unanimously accepted this contention and gave judgment for the husband. Harman LJ observed that the wife was 'no worse off because, owing to the amount of her income, she gets back practically the whole of the £85 from the Inland Revenue'. *Butler v Butler*, CA [1961] 1 All ER 810.

Sterling debentures—interest payable in foreign currency

[20.46] A UK company (R) had issued 7% sterling debentures, under terms whereby the holder could opt for payment in New York in dollars or in Amsterdam in florins at specified fixed rates of exchange. Because of a fall in the value of sterling, many holders exercised the option. R accounted for tax under *ITA 1918, General Rule 21* on the sterling amounts shown as payable on the interest warrants, rather than the sterling actually needed to satisfy the payment in dollars or florins. The Revenue issued an assessment on the basis that R should have accounted for tax on the sterling value of the actual payments made. The HL allowed R's appeal (by a 4–1 majority, Lord Russell of Killowen dissenting), holding that R was only required to account for tax on the sterling amounts shown on the warrants. *Rhokana Corporation Ltd v CIR*, HL 1938, 21 TC 551; [1938] AC 380; [1938] 2 All ER 51. (*Note*. The HL accepted that the excess of the amount received by the debenture-holder over the amount of the *Rule 21* assessment was income in his hands, but held that the onus was on the Revenue to collect the tax by assessment of the recipient if it could.)

Interest on foreign bonds paid by guarantor

[20.47] A Greek bank defaulted on sterling bearer bonds it had issued which carried interest payable in London. Another Greek bank, carrying on business at a London branch, assumed the responsibilities of a bank which had guaranteed the bonds and resumed the service of the bonds and interest coupons in England, deducting tax from the interest. A Channel Islands company, which held some of the bonds on behalf of non-residents, sued the bank for payment of the tax deducted, contending that the payments were income from securities outside the UK, and that tax was not deductible. The HL unanimously accepted this contention. Lord Hailsham of St Marylebone held that the source of the income was an obligation 'situated outside the United Kingdom'. *Westminster Bank Executor & Trustee Co (Channel Islands) Ltd v National Bank of Greece SA*, HL 1970, 46 TC 472; [1971] AC 945; [1971] 1 All ER 233.

Assessment of recipient where tax not deducted

[20.48] See *Quarter Sessions for the County of Glamorgan v Wilson*, 39.22 MISCELLANEOUS INCOME, and *Grosvenor Place Estates Ltd v Roberts*, 39.23 MISCELLANEOUS INCOME.

Assessment of recipient—whether tax deducted

[20.49] See *Postlethwaite v CIR*, 39.24 MISCELLANEOUS INCOME.

Whether overseas bank carrying on banking business in UK

[20.50] A company (H) had paid interest without deduction of tax to three banks outside the UK in seven consecutive quarterly periods from April 1980 to December 1981. The Revenue issued assessments on the basis that H should have deducted tax from the payments. H appealed, contending that it was not required to deduct tax because all three banks were carrying on a banking business in the UK. The Special Commissioner allowed its appeal as regards the payments to two of the banks but not as regards the payments to the third bank (S). The Ch D upheld the Commissioner's decision as one of fact. S was an Isle of Man company conducting a banking business there, but it had no banking premises or representative in the UK. Although it had made loans to at least 16 UK residents and had advertised in the UK for customers, this was not sufficient to amount to carrying on a *bona fide* banking business in the UK. An overseas company could carry on a business in the UK without a branch or agency there, but the characteristics of a banking business required that, in addition to lending, it took deposits. *Hafton Properties Ltd v McHugh*, Ch D 1986, 59 TC 420; [1987] STC 16.

Accrued interest debt assigned to company resident abroad

[20.51] A company (M), which had obtained substantial loans from a UK bank (N), became insolvent. N acquired its shares in 1984, and ceased charging interest in 1989. In 1990 N sold its shares in M, and assigned all the interest to a Channel Islands company for nominal consideration. In 1995 M made a payment of interest to the assignee, and failed to deduct tax. The Revenue issued an assessment on the basis that M should have deducted tax. M appealed, contending that since the debt had been assigned to a Channel Islands company, it should not be required to deduct tax. The Special Commissioner rejected this contention and dismissed the appeal. *Mistletoe Ltd v Flood; Appletree Group v Flood*, Sp C 2002, [2003] SSCD 66 (Sp C 351).

Application of ITA 2007, s 963 to non-residents

[20.52] See *Stokes v Bennett*, 39.38 MISCELLANEOUS INCOME.

21

Double Tax Relief

The cases in this chapter are arranged under the following headings.

Double taxation agreements (TIOPA 2010, ss 2–7)

General principles

Double Taxation Agreement—interaction with UK legislation

[21.1] In 1957 a company (C), which was resident in the Republic of Ireland, claimed repayment of tax under the 1926 UK/Ireland double taxation agreement (which has subsequently been superseded by the 1976 agreement). The Revenue rejected the claim on the grounds that the effect of *F(No 2) A 1955, s 4* was that no repayment was due. C appealed, contending that it was entitled to repayment under the 1926 agreement, which should be treated as overriding the subsequent UK legislation. The HL rejected this contention and dismissed the appeal. Viscount Simonds held that 'the company has no rights under any agreement. Its rights arise from the Act of Parliament which confirms the agreement and gives it the force of law'. Furthermore, 'neither comity nor rule of international law can be invoked to prevent a sovereign State from taking what steps it thinks fit to protect its own revenue laws from gross abuse or to save its own citizens from unjust discrimination in favour of foreigners'. *Collco Dealings Ltd v CIR*, HL 1961, 39 TC 509; [1961] 2 WLR 401; [1961] 1 All ER 762. (*Note*. The repayment claim arose from 'dividend-stripping' operations—see 58.4 TAX PLANNING AND AVOIDANCE. *F(No 2) A 1955, s 4* (which was intended to counter dividend-stripping) was subsequently superseded by *FA 1965* (which introduced Schedule F).)

[21.2] A Swiss bank claimed a payment of tax credits on dividends under *ICTA 1988, s 243*. The Revenue rejected the claim on the grounds that credits under *s 243* were only available to UK companies. The Special Commissioners dismissed the bank's appeal, holding that the bank's claim under *article 23* of the 1977 UK-Switzerland Double Tax Convention had not been incorporated into UK law under *ICTA 1988, s 788* (see now *TIOPA 2010, s 6*). The CA upheld the Commissioners' decision. Moses LJ observed that the bank was 'not seeking relief from anything; it has no liability. It seeks payment of a tax credit, in an amount calculated by reference to the distributions it has received. It is not seeking relief because there is no liability to an amount of tax which would otherwise be payable.' Arden LJ questioned whether the bank was entitled to a claim under the Convention, holding that 'inability to set franked investment income against distributions does not carry any consequences under *art 23*' and that 'a permanent establishment is not entitled to set an associated tax credit against its liability to tax or to the payment of the surplus of the tax credit over its liability to UK tax. It is hardly possible that the contracting states, having excluded permanent establishments from *art 10*, intended them to be able to claim to use the tax credit through *art 23*.' *HMRC v UBS AG*, CA [2007] STC 588; [2007] EWCA Civ 119; 9 ITLR 767.

UK/USA agreements

1946 Agreement—definition of 'a resident of' the UK

[21.3] A British peer (S) and his wife, an American citizen, lived in the UK. The Revenue issued an assessment charging tax on S's wife's American income. S appealed, contending that since his wife had disclaimed British citizenship, she was not 'a resident of the United Kingdom' for the purposes of a specific provision in the 1946 UK/USA double taxation convention as then in force, so that her American income qualified for exemption under that convention. The Ch D accepted this contention and allowed his appeal. *Lord Strathalmond v CIR*, Ch D 1972, 48 TC 537; [1972] 1 WLR 1511; [1972] 3 All ER 715. (*Note*. The decision turns on the detailed wording of the convention. The relevant words in this and the following case were omitted from the 1980 UK/USA agreement, but the case may remain relevant with regard to the interpretation of other similar agreements.)

1946 Agreement—definition of 'citizenship'

[21.4] A woman (R) who was born in the USA acquired British citizenship by marrying a British subject. She was resident in the UK when she died in 1969. Her husband claimed that her American income should be treated as exempt from UK tax. The Revenue rejected the claim and R's administrator appealed. The Special Commissioner dismissed the appeal and the Ch D upheld this decision. The 1946 UK/USA double taxation convention then in force provided that 'dividends and interest paid by a corporation of one Contracting Party shall be exempt from tax by the other Contracting Party', except where the recipient was a citizen of that other Contracting Party. Walton J held that this provision operated reciprocally, and distinguished the earlier decision in *Lord Strathalmond v CIR*, **21.3** above, on the grounds that the appellant's wife in that case had disclaimed British citizenship. *Avery Jones (Rowley's Administrator) v CIR*, Ch D 1976, 51 TC 443; [1976] STC 290; [1976] 2 All ER 898.

1975 Agreement—group relief

[21.5] Two companies (FC and FL) were resident in the UK. Their parent company (FM) was resident in the USA. FL incurred trading losses, which it claimed to surrender to FC. FC claimed group relief in respect of these losses. HMRC rejected the claim on the grounds that FM was resident in the USA. FC appealed, contending that the effect of the 'non-discrimination article' in the 1975 UK/USA double taxation agreement was that group relief was available between two UK resident directly-held 75% subsidiaries of a US parent company in circumstances where it would be available if the parent company were UK resident. The First-tier Tribunal accepted this contention and allowed the appeal, holding that 'on the facts of this appeal the difference in treatment is because the direct holding company is US rather than UK resident. No other ground for the difference in treatment can be shown. That is therefore discrimination prevented by the plain wording of the Treaty provision.' The Upper Tribunal and the CA unanimously upheld this decision. Rimer LJ held that 'the only reason for the difference in treatment' was that FM was resident in the USA. *HMRC v FCE Bank plc*, CA [2012] EWCA Civ 1290; [2013] STC 14; 15 ITLR 329. (*Note*. The Supreme Court dismissed HMRC's application for leave to appeal against this decision.)

1980 Agreement—scope of Article 1

[21.6] A US corporation (BD) had two unlimited subsidiary companies (BKP and BUK) which were both incorporated in the UK. Both BKP and BUK entered into forward contracts, as a result of which BKP made a substantial loss and BUK made a substantial profit. The transactions had no commercial purpose other than to produce a matching profit and loss, and were carried out for the purpose of taking advantage of the different treatment of the profit in US and UK tax law. BKP surrendered most of its loss as group relief, while BUK claimed that its UK tax liability should be extinguished by double taxation relief for US tax which BD had paid on the same profit. (The US taxed the profit in the hands of BD because for federal US income tax purposes BUK was classified as a 'disregarded entity'.) The Revenue rejected BUK's claim to double taxation relief, and BUK appealed, contending that the UK was required to give relief under Article 1 of the 1980 Double Taxation Agreement between the UK and the USA. The Special Commissioners rejected this contention and dismissed the appeal, and the CA unanimously upheld this decision. Arden LJ held that 'the primary purposes of the Treaty are, on the one hand, to eliminate double taxation and, on the other hand, to prevent the avoidance of taxation'. Accordingly, 'the Treaty should be interpreted to avoid the grant of double relief as well as to confer relief against double taxation'. *HMRC v Bayfine UK* , CA [2011] EWCA Civ 304; [2011] STC 717; 13 ITLR 747.

1980 Agreement—UK resident moving to USA

[21.7] A UK resident (S) terminated his employment in March 2000, and received a termination payment in April, from which UK tax was deducted at 23%. In October 2000 he left the UK to take up permanent residence in the USA. Subsequently the UK Revenue issued an assessment charging tax at 40% on part of the termination payment which S had received. S appealed, contending that the effect of the 1980 UK/USA Double Taxation Agreement was that he should not be charged further UK tax. The Special Commissioner rejected this contention and dismissed his appeal, holding that the effect of Article 15 of the Agreement was that the payment was taxable in the UK. *Squirrell v HMRC*, Sp C [2005] SSCD 717 (Sp C 493).

UK/USA 2001 Double Tax Convention, article 17(1)

[21.8] A UK resident (M) worked in the USA for the International Bank for Reconstruction and Development from 1976 to 1998, when he retired and returned to the UK. He received pension payments from the Bank. In July 2008 he claimed error or mistake relief on the basis that these payments should be treated as exempt from UK tax under Article 17(1) of the UK/USA Double Tax Convention 2001. In December 2008 HMRC rejected the claims. However, in April 2009 M submitted identical claims for 2003/04 and 2006/07, without referring to their previous rejection. A different HMRC officer accepted the claims and authorised a repayment. In March 2010 HMRC issued discovery assessments to recover the tax. The First-tier Tribunal dismissed M's appeal, holding that the Bank's pension plan was not 'established in the USA' for the purposes of the double taxation agreement, and that the discovery assessments were authorised by *TMA 1970, s 29*. Judge Walters held that the claim which M had made in April 2009 'was abusive, and the proper course, if (M) had decided that he wished to pursue the matter in the fact of HMRC's refusal of 10 December 2008, was to seek to bring an appeal out of time against that refusal'. *M Macklin v HMRC*, FTT [2013] UKFTT 554 (TC); [2014] SFTD 290; 16 ITLR 355, TC02943.

UK/USA 2001 Double Tax Convention, article 22(1)

[21.9] In 1996 a UK company (R) recruited a senior executive (H) from the USA. H resigned her employment in 2004. R made an ex gratia payment of £150,000, without deducting tax. The Revenue issued a determination charging tax on the payment. R and H appealed, contending that the payment was exempt from UK tax under Article 22(1) of the UK/USA Double Tax Convention 2001. The Special Commissioner accepted this contention and allowed the appeal, rejecting HMRC's contention that the payment constituted 'salaries, wages and other similar remuneration' within Article 14 of the Convention. *Resolute Management Services Ltd v HMRC; Mrs KA Haderlein v HMRC*, Sp C [2008] SSCD 1202 (Sp C 710).

Delaware limited liability company

[21.10] An individual (S), who was resident in the UK, helped to form a Delaware limited liability company (H). The US authorities charged tax on S's share of H's profits, treating H as a transparent entity. S claimed double taxation relief for the US tax. HMRC issued discovery assessments for 1997/98 to 1999/2000, and amendments to S's self-assessments for 2000/01 to 2003/04, on the basis that H should not be treated as transparent and that S was not entitled to double taxation relief. The Upper Tribunal upheld HMRC's assessments and amendments. Mann J held that S was not taxed on 'the same profits that were taxed in the United States', H was not transparent, and S was not entitled to double taxation relief under the US/UK Treaty. The CA unanimously dismissed S's appeal against this decision. Arden LJ held that 'the relevant test for determining whether a person is taxed on the same profits or income in both jurisdictions is whether the source of the profits or income in each jurisdiction is the same'. On the facts of this case, H's profits did not belong to its members and S had no 'proprietary right to the profits'. *Anson v HMRC (aka Swift v HMRC)*, CA [2013] EWCA Civ 63; [2013] STC 557.

Other agreements

UK/Hungary Agreement—definition of two-year time limit

[21.11] A Hungarian national (V) visited the UK from 21 January 1979 to 22 January 1981, and again from 19 February 1981 to 28 January 1982. On each occasion he took up an appointment as a research associate at a university. He claimed exemption from UK income tax for 1981/82 under the UK/Hungary Double Taxation Agreement, which provides that a Hungarian who visits the UK for a period not exceeding two years for university research should be exempted from UK tax on any remuneration from that research for a period not exceeding two years from the date he first visited the UK. The Special Commissioners allowed relief for 1981/82 but the Ch D reversed their decision, holding that V was not entitled to relief because he had already spent more than two years on university research in the UK. *CIR v Vas*, Ch D 1989, 63 TC 30; [1990] STC 137.

[21.12] A Hungarian national (D) arrived in the UK on 30 April 1989 to work as a university lecturer under a contract ending on 30 September 1990. Shortly before the end of this contract, he obtained a similar contract at the University of Ulster, beginning on 1 October 1990. He appealed against Schedule E assessments for 1989/90 to 1991/92, contending that he was entitled to relief under the UK/Hungary Double Taxation Agreement. The Revenue rejected the claim on the grounds that the exemption only applied where the visit was for a period 'not exceeding two years'. The Special Commissioner dismissed D's appeal. On the evidence, there had been a single visit to the UK which had exceeded two years. The fact that there had been a change of employer, and that D had spent one day in the Republic of Ireland before taking up duty in Ulster, did not mean that the two contracts could be treated as separate visits. *Devai v CIR*, Sp C 1996, [1997] SSCD 31 (Sp C 105).

UK/Germany Agreement—whether German nationality retained

[21.13] In two cases heard together, two individuals who had been born in Germany, but had emigrated to Britain in 1939 and had become naturalised British subjects, appealed against assessments on pensions from Germany, contending that, for the purposes of the Double Taxation Agreement between the UK and Germany, they had retained their German nationality. The Special Commissioners dismissed their appeals, holding that they had lost their German nationality, and the HL unanimously upheld this decision. Lord Cross of Chelsea held that English law refers the question whether a person is a national of another State to the municipal law of that State, and the appellants had not claimed German nationality under the provisions of the German Constitution as enacted in 1949. *Oppenheimer v Cattermole; Nothman v Cooper*, HL 1975, 50 TC 159; [1975] STC 91; [1976] AC 249; [1975] 1 All ER 538.

UK/Germany Agreement—effect of 'silent partnership'

[21.14] See *Memec plc v CIR*, 21.27 below.

UK/Ireland Agreement

[21.15] A former Inland Revenue officer (P) moved to the Irish Republic in 2004. In 2006 he began receiving a civil service pension. This was taxed in the UK, by virtue of Article 18(2) of the Double Taxation Agreement between the UK and the Irish Republic. In 2009 P appealed to the First-tier Tribunal, contending that Article 18(2) was unfairly discriminatory, that this contravened EU law, and that his liability to UK tax should be restricted to the tax that would have been borne by an Irish citizen in his circumstances. The tribunal rejected these contentions and dismissed his appeal. Judge Gammie observed that there was no double taxation, and that 'a Member State is not in breach of its Treaty obligations because it taxes differently and less favourably than some other Member State'. *K Percival v HMRC*, FTT [2013] UKFTT 240 (TC); [2014] SFTD 57, TC02654.

[21.16] See also *Wensleydale's Settlement Trustees v CIR*, 48.89 RESIDENCE.

UK/France Agreement—unpaid French tax

[21.17] A professional sportsman (S), domiciled in the UK, claimed double tax relief in respect of French tax which had not been paid or assessed, but which was potentially chargeable. The Revenue rejected the claim on the basis that no credit was due unless and until French tax had been paid. The Special Commissioners dismissed S's appeal against this decision. *Sportsman v CIR*, Sp C [1998] SSCD 289 (Sp C 174).

UK/Netherlands Agreement—restriction of tax credit

[21.18] See *Océ van Grinten NV v CIR*, 25.190 EUROPEAN LAW.

UK/Jersey Agreement—income from Jersey partnership

[21.19] A UK resident (P) claimed double tax relief in respect of his income from a Jersey partnership. The Revenue rejected the claim on the basis that the effect of what is now *ITTOIA 2005, s 858* was that relief was not due. The Special Commissioners dismissed P's appeal, observing that *s 858* derived from *F(No 2) A 1987* and had been enacted in order to clarify the law following previous litigation involving the same appellant (see *Padmore v CIR (No 1)*, CA 1989, 62 TC 352). The Commissioners observed that *s 858* 'clearly deals with the case of a United Kingdom resident partner in a non-resident partnership and states unambiguously that a tax treaty shall not affect any liability to tax in respect of the resident partner's share of any income or capital gains of the partnership'. It was abundantly clear 'that the legislature planned to overturn the decision of the Court of Appeal in *Padmore* for the future'. The Ch D upheld this decision. Applying the principles laid down by Lord Bingham in *R v Secretary of State for the Environment, Transport and the Regions (ex p. Spath Holme Ltd)*, HL 2000, [2001] WLR 15, 'the overriding aim of the court must always be to give effect to the intention of Parliament as expressed in the words used'. Lightman J observed that it was 'clear beyond question' that the legislature's purpose was to remove the exemption', and that 'the departure from the provisions of the Jersey Arrangement and the removal of the tax exemption were plainly and deliberately made'. *Padmore v CIR (No 2)*, Ch D 2001, 73 TC 470; [2001] STC 280; 3 ITLR 315.

UK/Yugoslav Agreement—income from employment in North Sea

[21.20] A Croatian (K) was employed on vessels in the North Sea, which were operated by a company resident in the UK. Tax was deducted from his remuneration under PAYE. He claimed a repayment, contending that he qualified for relief under the UK/Yugoslav Double Taxation Treaty. HMRC rejected his claim and the First-tier Tribunal dismissed his appeal. Judge Scott observed that K's employment 'was exercised in the United Kingdom', and was not taxed in Croatia. She held that double taxation relief was not available 'where a UK-based company, which has the benefit of the employee's services, has borne the costs of remuneration'. *T Kljun v HMRC*, FTT [2011] UKFTT 371 (TC), TC01226.

UK/Israel Agreement—income from UK pension

[21.21] An Israeli citizen (W) received a UK pension, which was not taxed in Israel. HMRC issued a ruling that it was taxable in the UK. W appealed, contending that it should be treated as exempt under Article XI of the UK/Israel Double Tax Treaty. The First-tier Tribunal rejected this contention and dismissed his appeal. Judge Berner observed that Article XI(2) of the Treaty provided that a pension 'derived from sources within the United Kingdom by an individual who is a resident of Israel and subject to Israel tax in respect thereof, shall be exempt from United Kingdom tax'. However W's pension was not subjected to Israeli tax, so it did not qualify for exemption from UK tax under this provision. *P Weiser v HMRC*, FTT [2012] UKFTT 501 (TC); [2012] SFTD 1381, TC02178.

UK/Barbados Agreement—proof of company residence

[21.22] See *Forth Investments Ltd v CIR*, 48.84 RESIDENCE.

UK/Mauritius Agreement

[21.23] See Smallwood *(Settlor of the Trevor Smallwood Trust) v HMRC*, 48.90 RESIDENCE.

UK/Switzerland Agreement—claim for tax credits on dividends

[21.24] See *HMRC v UBS AG*, 21.2 above.

Unilateral relief by UK (TIOPA 2010, ss 8–17)

Interpretation of TIOPA 2010, s 9

[21.25] A company operating a worldwide construction business made an overall trading loss, but suffered foreign tax in respect of trading profits in three overseas countries. It claimed double taxation relief, in respect of this foreign tax, against corporation tax attributable to non-trading income and capital gains. The Revenue rejected the claim and the Ch D dismissed the company's appeal. Hoffmann J held that under what is now *TIOPA 2010, s 9*, credit for foreign tax 'shall be allowed against any UK income tax or corporation tax computed by reference to *that* income'. The company here was not chargeable to any tax in respect of the income on which the foreign tax was charged. No relief was therefore due. *George Wimpey International Ltd v Rolfe*, Ch D 1989, 62 TC 597; [1989] STC 609.

Unilateral relief for Venezuelan tax

[21.26] A UK company (G) carried on business as petroleum and natural gas consultants. It entered into a contract with a Venezuelan company, requiring it to carry out a technical study for the rehabilitation of three Venezuelan oilfields. Under the contract it received $161,000 for work carried out in the UK and $48,300 for work carried out in Venezuela. The Venezuelan government levied tax on 90% of G's total receipts for the work. G claimed unilateral tax relief, which the Revenue refused to allow, considering that the Venezuelan tax was equivalent to a turnover tax rather than an income tax. The Special Commissioner allowed G's appeal in principle, holding that the Venezuelan tax corresponded to UK income tax or corporation tax, and directed that credit should be allowed against corporation tax attributable to $48,300. Both sides appealed to the Ch D. (G contended that relief should be available against the whole of the income under the contract, and not just against the $48,300 attributable to the work done in Venezuela.) The Ch D upheld the Commissioner's decision and dismissed both appeals. Scott J held that although the Venezuelan tax was computed on the basis that only 10% of gross income could be deductible as expenditure in computing profits, it was still expressed to be a tax on profits rather than a turnover tax. Accordingly it corresponded to UK income tax or corporation tax. Under what is now *TIOPA 2010, s 9*, unilateral relief was only due in respect of the income 'arising in' Venezuela. Of the income under the contract, only $48,300 was income arising in Venezuela. Accordingly credit could only be allowed against the corporation tax attributable to that $48,300. *Yates v GCA International Ltd (and cross-appeal)*, Ch D 1991, 64 TC 37; [1991] STC 157. (*Notes*. (1) For the Revenue's practice following this decision, see Revenue Pamphlet IR 131, SP 7/91, 26 July 1991. (2) The decision that relief should only be available against the income attributable to the work done in Venezuela was disapproved by the Special Commissioners and the Ch D in the subsequent case of *Legal & General Assurance Society Ltd v Thomas*, **21.40** below.)

Interpretation of 'dividend'

[21.27] A UK company (M) controlled a German company (G). In 1985 they entered into a 'stille gesellschaft' (a 'silent partnership' agreement) under German law, whereby M made a capital contribution to G and obtained a contractual right to 87.84% of the partnership profits. M claimed double taxation relief in respect of the payments which it received under the agreement. The Revenue rejected the claim on the grounds that the payments arose from the partnership agreement. M appealed, contending firstly that the source of the payments should be deemed to be G's trading subsidiaries, so that relief was due under the UK/Germany Double Taxation Agreement, and alternatively that the payments were dividends. The Special Commissioner rejected these contentions and dismissed the appeal, and the Ch D and CA unanimously upheld this decision. With regard to M's first contention, the source of the income was the partnership agreement. This agreement, unlike an English or Scottish partnership, could not be treated as transparent. With regard to M's alternative contention, the payments could not be treated as 'dividends', since the payments were not related to shares and the partnership was not a company. Accordingly, double taxation relief was not due. *Memec plc v CIR*, CA 1998, 71 TC 77; [1998] STC 754. (*Note*. For the Revenue's practice following this decision, see Revenue Tax Bulletin February 1999, p 627.)

Dividend from Guernsey company

[21.28] In 2003 a woman (B), who was resident in the UK, received a dividend of £25,000 from a Guernsey company. In her 2003/04 tax return, she claimed foreign tax credit relief of £6,250. Following an enquiry, HMRC rejected the claim, on the basis that 'unilateral relief is not due to a shareholder since the whole of it represents tax which the company would have borne if the dividend had not been paid'. B appealed, contending that the rejection of her claim contravened European law. The First-tier Tribunal rejected this contention and dismissed her appeal. *Ms V Buxton v HMRC*, FTT [2012] UKFTT 506 (TC); [2013] SFTD 1, TC02183.

Underlying tax (TIOPA 2010, ss 57–71)

[21.29] An individual (H) received in full a dividend on his holding of preference shares in an Indian company. The Indian company had paid the dividend partly out of dividends it received (less UK tax) on ordinary shares which it held in UK companies. The Revenue issued an assessment charging tax on the full amount of the dividend, and H appealed, contending that the assessment should be reduced to take account of the UK tax deducted from the dividends received by the UK company. The HL unanimously rejected this contention and upheld the assessment, holding that H was assessable on the full amount of the dividend. *Barnes v Hely-Hutchinson*, HL 1939, 22 TC 655; [1940] AC 81; [1939] 3 All ER 803.

[21.30] A Canadian company (C), not trading in the UK, paid dividends to UK shareholders, using a UK bank as its agent. The bank accounted for tax on the dividends. C claimed a repayment of some of this tax on the grounds that it represented tax which had been deducted from dividends it had received from UK companies and interest it had received from British banks. The Revenue rejected the claim and the HL unanimously dismissed C's appeal. Lord Macmillan observed that there was no double taxation, because 'the income of a foreign company and the income received from it in dividends by its British shareholders are not to any extent or effect one and the same income'. *Canadian Eagle Oil Co Ltd v R*, HL 1945, 27 TC 205; [1946] AC 119; [1945] 2 All ER 499. (*Note*. The case was heard in the HL with *Selection Trust Ltd v Devitt*, **21.31** below. The decision overruled *Gilbertson v Fergusson*, CA 1881, 1 TC 501. Its effect was subsequently modified by *FA 1946, s 31*. This became *ITA 1952, s 201*, which was repealed by *FA 1965*.)

[21.31] A UK company (S) dealing in, and holding, investments, claimed to exclude from its trading profits the proportion of dividends it received from an American company which were attributable to dividends received by that company from UK companies, from which UK tax had been deducted. The Revenue rejected the claim and the HL unanimously dismissed S's appeal. *Selection Trust Ltd v Devitt*, HL 1945, 27 TC 205; [1946] AC 119; [1945] 2 All ER 499. (*Note*. The case was heard in the HL with *Canadian Eagle Oil Co Ltd v R*, **21.30** above. See also the note following that case.)

[21.32] A company (B) received dividends from an Indian subsidiary. The dividends were grossed up under Indian law by an amount representing tax. This amount was subsequently repaid by the Indian authorities. B claimed unilateral relief in respect of the Indian tax underlying the dividends. The Revenue assessed B on the gross amount of the income and granted unilateral double tax relief on the basis that the amount of the refund should be deducted in arriving at the underlying tax. The Special Commissioners dismissed B's appeal, and the Ch D upheld their decision. *Brooke Bond & Co Ltd v Butter; Brooke Bond & Co Ltd v CIR*, Ch D 1962, 40 TC 342.

[21.33] In its return for the year ending 31 December 2004, a company (P) claimed credit for double tax relief of £21,103,383. HMRC issued a notice of amendment restricting the credit to the underlying tax which had actually been paid (£7,029,973). P appealed, contending that it should also be entitled to credit for the balance of £14,073,410. The First-tier Tribunal rejected this contention and dismissed P's appeal. Sir Stephen Oliver held that P's claim was 'unsound in law having regard to the strict wording of the computational rules' and was based on 'tax that has never been payable'. He also observed that P had entered into a scheme which 'was designed and implemented for no reason other than tax avoidance. It depended on the alchemy of turning share capital into distributable reserves almost overnight.' For such a claim to be effective, 'there has to be a payment that can properly and realistically be characterised as a dividend, and the claim must relate to foreign or UK tax borne on the relevant profits represented by the dividend'. On the facts here, there were 'neither profits on which tax was borne nor any payment that could realistically be classed as a dividend'. *Peninsular & Oriental Steam Navigation Company v HMRC*, FTT [2013] UKFTT 322 (TC), TC02725.

Underlying tax—amount of 'relevant profits'

[21.34] A company (B) was entitled to relief in respect of the foreign tax underlying dividends received from its subsidiaries in Canada and the USA. The Revenue computed the relief on the basis that the 'relevant profits' (see now *TIOPA 2010, s 59*) were the profits available for distribution as shown by the accounts of the company paying the dividend. B appealed, contending that the 'relevant profits' should be the profits as computed for the purposes of assessment to the foreign tax. (There was a substantial difference because of the treatment of depreciation.) The Special Commissioners rejected this contention and dismissed B's appeal, and the HL unanimously upheld this decision. Lord Wilberforce observed that the profits assessed could be more or less than the profits shown by the accounts, but B could not be treated as having a separate fund of untaxed profits. *Bowater Paper Corporation Ltd v Murgatroyd*, HL 1969, 46 TC 37; [1970] AC 266; [1969] 3 All ER 111.

Miscellaneous

Part of overseas tax repaid—exchange rate

[21.35] An author, resident in the UK, received income from the USA, from which tax had been deducted, in 1946 when the exchange rate was $4.03 to the £. Part of the tax was repaid in 1950 when, because of a devaluation of sterling, the rate was $2.80. She was entitled to credit for the tax under the relevant UK/USA double taxation convention. The Revenue granted relief on the basis that the amount of US tax ranking for credit was the original payment converted at $4.03 less the amount refunded converted at $2.80. The author appealed, contending that the refund should be converted at $4.03. The Special Commissioners accepted this contention and allowed her appeal, and the Ch D upheld their decision. Harman J held that 'the alteration in the rate of exchange is purely an outside circumstance which has nothing to do with the liability for tax'. *Greig v Ashton*, Ch D 1956, 36 TC 581; [1956] 1 WLR 1056; [1956] 3 All ER 123.

Management expenses and double taxation relief

[21.36] Two investment-holding companies were entitled to relief for their management expenses, the amount of which exceeded their UK income. They had substantial overseas income on which they had been given double tax relief at varying rates. The Revenue computed the relief on the basis that the management expenses should be set against the income on a pound for pound basis, with income charged at a higher rate relieved before income charged at a lower rate. The companies appealed, contending that the whole of the management expenses should be relieved at the standard rate. The HL unanimously rejected this contention and upheld the Revenue's computation. Lord Wilberforce observed that 'the repayment is not at any "rate" but is of a proportion of tax paid. No doubt when the proportion has been calculated it is possible to work out at what rate the repayment is made, but that is a very different thing from requiring the calculation to start with a rate.' *Jones v Shell Petroleum Co Ltd*; *Cropper v British Petroleum Co Ltd*, HL 1971, 47 TC 194; [1971] 1 WLR 786; [1971] 2 All ER 569. (*Note*. The appeal related to periods before the introduction of corporation tax and involved dividends within *ITA 1952, s 350*, which was later repealed by *FA 1965*.)

Treatment of loss from overseas operations

[21.37] A Malaysian company had a branch in Singapore, the profits from which were not liable to Malaysian income tax by virtue of a double taxation agreement between Malaysia and Singapore. In 1968, the Singapore branch made a substantial loss. The company claimed that this loss should be treated as available for set-off in computing its Malaysian income tax. The Malaysian tax authority rejected the claim on the basis that the effect of the agreement was that the loss was not available for set-off. The PC allowed the company's appeal, holding (by a 4-1 majority, Lord Russell of Killowen dissenting) that the loss remained available notwithstanding the agreement and the possibility that the loss might in the future reduce the Singapore tax liability. *Hock Heng Co v Malaysian Director-General of Inland Revenue*, PC [1979] STC 291; [1979] 2 WLR 788; [1980] AC 360.

TIOPA 2010, s 33—minimisation of foreign tax

[21.38] A company (H) claimed double taxation relief for US tax for 2000 and 2001. The claim arose from H being a member of two Delaware partnerships. The Revenue issued amendments to H's returns, denying the relief on the grounds that H had not taken 'all reasonable steps' to minimise the US tax, as required by what is now *TIOPA 2010, s 33*. H appealed. The Special Commissioners allowed the appeal, observing that 'in essence, this appeal is about the effect of the UK and the US analysing a transaction differently for tax purposes (for general law purposes, so far as we can tell, both the US and the UK are likely to respect the partnership character of the transactions). Seen from the UK, the appellant has entered into a US partnership that has paid tax in the US (because it has elected to be taxed as a corporation for US tax purposes) and is claiming double taxation relief for that tax. Seen from the US, the appellant is not a partner in the US partnership because of the agreement in place from the outset for the repurchase of the appellant's partnership interest'. The Commissioners held that, for the purpose of *s 33(2)*, 'the steps that might reasonably be taken do not include the entering into a completely different transaction, whether or not it has a similar economic effect. While the transaction entered into may have economic similarities to a loan it is not a loan but an investment in a US partnership, as it purports to be.' There were 'no other reasonable steps' open to H which 'would reduce the amount of US tax'. Accordingly, *s 33* did not restrict H's ability to claim relief. *Hill Samuel Investments Ltd v HMRC*, Sp C [2009] SSCD 315 (Sp C 738).

Application of TIOPA 2010, s 42

[21.39] An insurance company (C), which received foreign dividends, was entitled to have the foreign tax which it had paid on such dividends set against the UK tax otherwise chargeable on the income. However, if the foreign tax on any amount of relevant income exceeded the UK tax chargeable on that income, the surplus foreign tax was not available for relief against any other type of income, or against income of any other accounting period. C sought to minimise such consequences by allocating charges on income (such as loan interest) to UK profits, claiming that charges could be allocated to UK profits even where they exceeded the relevant amount of such profits, with the objective of increasing the amount of UK tax on foreign dividend income against which foreign tax might be set, and producing excess charges on income in respect of which loss relief might be claimed. The Revenue rejected the claim and the Commissioners dismissed C's appeal, holding that the right to allocate charges against income for the purposes of double tax relief was limited to 'the purpose of setting foreign tax against UK tax on the same profit'. The CA unanimously upheld this decision. Peter Gibson LJ held that double tax relief was not a 'relief from tax which reduces profits' for the purposes of what is now *CTA 2010, s 189*, but was 'a credit to be allowed against UK tax', within what is now *TIOPA 2010, s 42*. What is now *TIOPA 2010, s 42(3)* did not 'permit a company to allocate to profits a deduction greater than the amount necessary to reduce those profits to nothing'. *Commercial Union Assurance Co plc v Shaw*, CA 1998, 72 TC 101; [1999] STC 109. (*Note*. For another issue in this case, not taken to the CA, see **63.289** TRADING PROFITS.)

Computation of double taxation relief on trading income

[21.40] An insurance company (L) claimed double taxation relief in respect of income which had been taxed on a 'gross' basis overseas, but which formed part of its trading income, taxable in the UK under Schedule D Case I under the legislation then in force (and taxed under the 'I minus E' basis). The Revenue only agreed to allow relief for a proportion of the overseas tax (the proportion of the trading income which was overseas income). L appealed, contending that it should be entitled to relief in respect of the full amount of the overseas tax. The Special Commissioners accepted this contention, holding that although 'it might be expected that Parliament and the treaty negotiators would have wished to achieve' the restriction which the Revenue sought to impose, there was nothing in the legislation to justify such a restriction. Accordingly, credit was available for the full amount of the overseas tax 'against any corporation tax charged on the Case I profit in which the foreign income is a receipt, subject only to the limit of the maximum rate of credit'. The Commissioners also held that, in the case of an insurance company, double taxation relief should be computed separately for 'pension business' and that 'the part of the foreign income referable to the pension business will normally be credited against the tax on the profits of the pension business computed on Case I principles'. The Ch D upheld the Commissioners' decision. Evans-Lombe J held that 'the taxpayer should be entitled to credit, against the UK corporation tax thrown up by its computation, for foreign tax paid in the relevant period of assessment, such credit to be limited only so that the foreign tax cannot exceed the UK tax which would have been chargeable on that income'. He also held that 'foreign tax charged at source on foreign income attributable to pension business is to be creditable against that tax chargeable under that Case on the profits of the pension business'. *Legal & General Assurance Society Ltd v HMRC (aka Legal & General Assurance Society Ltd v Thomas (No 1))*, Ch D 2006, 78 TC 321; [2006] STC 1763; [2006] EWHC 1770 (Ch); 8 ITLR 1124. (*Notes*. (1) The legislation was subsequently amended by *FA 2000* and *FA 2005*. See now *TIOPA 2010, ss 42, 57(3)* and *99–104*. (2) For another issue in this case, see **34.1** LIFE ASSURANCE.)

Application of CTA 2010, s 54

[21.41] A Brazilian bank appealed against an assessment for its accounting period ending 31 December 1976, contending that it had made losses in the previous two accounting periods which should be set against the profits, and that the restriction in *FA 1976, s 50* (the predecessor of *CTA 2010, s 54*) did not apply, since the tax-exempt interest in question had been received before its enactment. The Ch D and the CA unanimously rejected this contention and upheld the assessment. Morritt LJ observed that the purpose of *FA 1976, s 50* was to prevent losses derived in the manner claimed from being set off against profits or income arising after 15 April 1976 (the date from which *FA 1976, s 50* took effect), notwithstanding the fact that the tax-exempt interest in question had been received before that date. *Boote v Banco do Brasil SA*, CA 1997, 69 TC 333; [1997] STC 327.

Joint venture company—whether CTA 2010, s 1122(4) applicable

[21.42] A company (E), resident in the Netherlands, had been established as a joint venture, 50% of its shares being owned by an Italian company and the remaining 50% being owned by members of a UK group. It had a wholly-owned UK subsidiary. The Revenue issued rulings that E was not entitled to tax credits on dividends paid to it by the subsidiary. The Ch D upheld the Revenue's rulings, and the CA dismissed E's appeal against this decision. On the evidence, E's shareholders were 'acting together to secure or exercise control' of the company, within what is now *CTA 2010, s 1122(4)*. Accordingly the effect of *SI 1980/1961, article 10(3)(d)* was that relief was not due. *Steele v EVC International NV*, CA 1996, 69 TC 88; [1996] STC 785.

FA 2008, s 58—application for judicial review

[21.43] An individual (H), who was resident in the UK, sought to avoid income tax by supplying his services to UK clients through an Isle of Man intermediary. He claimed double taxation relief under the UK/Isle of Man Double Taxation Agreement (although his income from the Isle of Man intermediary was not charged to tax in the Isle of Man). HMRC rejected his claims, and he appealed. While the appeals were pending, Parliament enacted *FA 2008, s 58*, with retrospective effect. H applied for judicial review, contending that *s 58* contravened the *European Convention on Human Rights*. The QB rejected this contention and dismissed his application. Kenneth Parker J observed that the arrangements which H had entered into 'had no genuine commercial purpose' and were 'artificial'. He also noted that *F(No 2) A 1987, s 62* had previously been enacted to counter a somewhat similar avoidance technique (see *Padmore v CIR (No 1)*, CA 1989, 62 TC 352) and had retrospective effect. He observed that this should have 'sent out a clear signal to taxpayers and their advisers that the legislature would be very likely to take effective and decisive steps to counter, even with retrospective measures, any attempt, through artificial arrangements, to take advantage of a double taxation agreement'. He held that Parliament had been entitled 'to legislate with retrospective effect, particularly in order to ensure a "fair balance" between the interests of the great body of resident taxpayers who paid income tax on their income from a trade or profession in the normal way, and the taxpayers, like the claimant, who had sought to exploit, by artificial arrangements, the DTA'. The CA unanimously upheld this decision. Mummery LJ held that the relevant provisions of *FA 2008* were proportionate and compatible with the Convention, and that 'the retrospective amendments were enacted pursuant to a justified fiscal policy that was within the State's area of appreciation and discretionary judgment in economic and social matters. The legislation achieves a fair balance between the interests of the general body of taxpayers and the right of the claimant to enjoyment of his possessions, without imposing an unreasonable economic burden on him. This outcome accords with the reasonable expectations of the taxation of residents in the State on the profits of their trade or profession. The legislation prevents the DTA tax relief provisions from being misused for a purpose different from their originally intended use. There has been no conduct on the part of the State fiscal authorities that has made the retrospective application of the amended legislation to his tax affairs an infringement of his Convention rights'. *R (oao Huitson) v HMRC*, CA [2011] EWCA Civ 893; [2011] STC 1860; 14 ITLR 90.

[21.44] In 2005 an individual (S), who was resident in the UK, had established a settlement, aimed at taking advantage of what he perceived as a loophole in the UK/Isle of Man Double Taxation Agreement. Subsequently Parliament enacted *FA 2008, s 58*, with retrospective effect. S applied for judicial review, contending that *s 58* was incompatible with the *EC Treaty* and with the *European Convention on Human Rights*. The CA unanimously rejected this contention, holding that *s 58* was proportionate and was compatible with the *Convention*. Mummery LJ also observed that, on the evidence, it did not appear that there had been any 'movement of capital' falling within *Article 56EC*. *R (oao Shiner) v HMRC*, CA [2011] EWCA Civ 892; [2011] STC 1878; 14 ITLR 113. (*Notes*. (1) The CA heard the case with *R (oao Huitson) v HMRC*, **21.43** above. (2) For subsequent developments in this case, see **4.105** APPEALS.)

Double taxation relief—difference in countries' tax rates

[21.45] See *Gilly & Gilly v Directeur des Services Fiscaux du Bas-Rhin*, **25.8** EUROPEAN LAW.

22

Employment Income

The cases in this chapter are arranged under the following headings.

GENERAL NOTE

From *ITA 1842* to *FA 1922*, income from 'public offices or employments' was assessed under Schedule E, but income from other employments was assessed under Schedule D. Following the HL decision in *Great Western Railway Co Ltd v Bater*, **22.23** below, *FA 1922* extended the scope of Schedule E to include employments which had previously been assessed under Schedule D, Case II. Employment income continued to be assessed under Schedule E until 5 April 2003. The *Income Tax (Earnings and Pensions) Act 2003* received Royal Assent on 6 March 2003. The previous provisions whereby income tax on employment and pension income was charged under Schedule E therefore no longer have effect for 2003/04 and subsequent years. For details, see Tolley's Income Tax. Most of the cases in this chapter were decided on the pre-2003 legislation, but appear to remain relevant to the current legislation. For cases concerning compensation for loss of employment, see **15** COMPENSATION FOR LOSS OF EMPLOYMENT. For cases concerning deduction of tax by employers, see **42** PAY AS YOU EARN.

Employment income: charge to tax (ITEPA 2003, ss 3–61)

Employment (ITEPA 2003, s 4)

ITEPA 2003, s 4(1)—'employment under a contract of service'

Cases held to constitute employment

[22.1] In an Irish case, a nun was employed as a teacher by her Religious Order, and was required to hand over her earnings to the Order. She appealed against assessments on her earnings, contending that she did not have an 'employment of profit'. The HC(I) rejected this contention and upheld the assessments, and the SC(I) unanimously upheld this decision. *Dolan v K*, SC(I) 1944, 2 ITC 280; [1944] IR 470.

[22.2] A married woman who was employed as a schoolteacher also received fees for teaching needlework and dressmaking at evening classes, under a separate agreement with the same education authority. Her husband appealed against assessments on these fees, contending that they did not arise from an employment, and should have been assessed under Schedule D. The Ch D rejected this contention and dismissed his appeal. *Fuge v McClelland*, Ch D 1956, 36 TC 571.

[22.3] An engineer (M) was appointed by a Borough Council to supervise the execution of sewerage works under the instructions of a firm of consultant engineers. The Council paid M a salary but declined to pay contributions under the *Local Government Superannuation Act* on the basis that he was not an employee. The QB allowed M's appeal, holding that he was employed under a contract of service rather than a contract for services, and was therefore an employee. Lord Parker CJ observed that 'superintendence and control cannot be the decisive test when one is dealing with a professional man or a man of some particular skill and experience'. *Morren v Swinton & Pendlebury Borough Council*, QB [1965] 1 WLR 576; [1965] 2 All ER 349.

[22.4] A professional dancer worked for a theatrical company under a contract which was in a standard form approved by the British Actors' Equity Association. The Revenue assessed him on the basis that he was an employee. He appealed, contending that he was self-employed and assessable under Schedule D. The Ch D rejected this contention and upheld the assessment. Pennycuick V-C held that 'virtually all the relevant factors point to this being a contract of service'. *Fall v Hitchen*, Ch D 1972, 49 TC 433; [1973] STC 66; [1973] 1 WLR 286; [1973] 1 All ER 368.

[22.5] In an Australian case, a company engaged lecturers to deliver 'weight-watchers' classes. The relevant contracts included a clause whereby the lecturers could arrange for substitute lecturers, approved by the company. The Privy Council held that the lecturers were employees. Lord Brandon held that 'a lecturer is tied hand and foot by the contract with regard to the manner in which she performs her work under it'. *Narich Property Ltd v Australian Commissioner of Payroll Tax*, PC [1984] ICR 286.

[22.6] A qualified dentist, domiciled in New Zealand, came to the UK in January 1975 to provide general dental services for the NHS. Initially he authorised the NHS to pay the prescribed fees for his work to the UK practice, and received an agreed proportion of the fees from the practice. However, with effect from April 1975 he entered into a verbal contract of employment with a Panamanian company in return for a fixed salary, while the company verbally agreed with the practice to supply his services to the practice in return for a proportion of the NHS fees and a management charge. The Revenue issued an assessment on the basis that he was self-employed. He appealed, contending that he was an employee of the Panamanian company (so that, under the legislation then in force, he should be assessed under Schedule E and was entitled to a 50% 'foreign earnings deduction'). The Special Commissioners accepted this contention and allowed his appeal, holding on the evidence that his arrangement with the Panamanian company was a contract of employment. The Ch D upheld their decision as one of fact. *Cooke v Blacklaws*, Ch D 1984, 58 TC 255; [1985] STC 1. (*Note.* The 50% 'foreign earnings deduction' was abolished by *FA 1984*.)

[22.7] A barrister received fees from lecturing to adult students. Initially the Revenue included these fees in his Schedule D assessments, but from 1976, when they comprised about one-third of his income, the Revenue decided that they arose from a contract of employment, and should be assessed under Schedule E under the legislation then in force. The barrister appealed, contending that the fees should be assessed under Schedule D. The Special Commissioners rejected this contention and dismissed his appeal, holding on the evidence that 'the language of the contractual documents points inescapably to the establishment of master and servant relationships'. The Ch D upheld their decision. *Sidey v Phillips*, Ch D 1986, 59 TC 458; [1987] STC 87.

[22.8] A professional singer (W), living in Sussex and assessed as a self-employed person, was appointed as a lecturer in music at a technical college in Liverpool. He was required to attend the college on four days each week during term-time. The Revenue assessed this as employment income, and W appealed, contending that it should be assessed under Schedule D. The General Commissioners dismissed his appeal, holding on the evidence that he was 'an employed person'. The Ch D upheld their decision as one of fact. *Walls v Sinnett*, Ch D 1986, 60 TC 150; [1987] STC 236.

[22.9] In a Hong Kong case, the Privy Council held that a stonemason working at a construction site was an employee rather than a subcontractor (reversing the decision of the Hong Kong courts). Lord Griffiths observed that 'the picture emerges of a skilled artisan earning his living by working for more than one employer as an employee and not as a small businessman venturing into business on his own account as an independent contractor with all its attendant risks. The applicant ran no risk whatever save that of being unable to find employment which is, of course, a risk faced by casual employees who move from one job to another'. *Lee Ting Sang v Chung Chi-Keung*, PC [1990] 2 WLR 1173.

[22.10] A share fisherman, who had worked on the same trawler from 2000 to 2009, had submitted tax returns indicating that he was self-employed, but subsequently formed the opinion that he should have been treated as an employee. He appealed against an assessment and an amendment which HMRC had issued on the basis that he was self-employed. The First-tier Tribunal allowed his appeal, distinguishing the 2002 decision in *Todd & Others v Adams & Chope*, 22.20 below. Judge Tildesley held that he had been 'employed under a contract of service'. *G Barney v HMRC*, FTT [2011] UKFTT 861 (TC), TC01695.

[22.11] A salesman (Y) had received commission from a company (S) which supplied windows and conservatories. HMRC issued assessments on the basis that Y was self-employed. He appealed, contending that he had been an employee of S. The First-tier Tribunal accepted this contention and allowed his appeal. *Y Yetis v HMRC*, FTT [2012] UKFTT 753 (TC), TC02410.

[22.12] See also *Andrews v King*, 42.40 PAY AS YOU EARN; *Stagecraft Ltd v Minister of National Insurance*, 73.21 NATIONAL INSURANCE CONTRIBUTIONS; *ITV Services Ltd v HMRC*, 73.22 NATIONAL INSURANCE CONTRIBUTIONS; *Whittaker v Minister of Pensions and National Insurance*, 73.23 NATIONAL INSURANCE CONTRIBUTIONS; *Vandyk v Minister of Pensions and National Insurance*, 73.24 NATIONAL INSURANCE CONTRIBUTIONS; *Greater London Council v Minister of Social Security*, 73.27 NATIONAL INSURANCE CONTRIBUTIONS; *Global Plant Ltd v Secretary of State for Health & Social Security*, 73.29 NATIONAL INSURANCE CONTRIBUTIONS; *Market Investigations Ltd v Minister of Social Security*, 73.30 NATIONAL INSURANCE CONTRI-

BUTIONS; *Benjamin & Collins v Minister of Pensions and National Insurance*, 73.31 NATIONAL INSURANCE CONTRIBUTIONS; *Performing Right Society Ltd v Mitchell & Booker (Palais de Danse) Ltd*, 73.33 NATIONAL INSURANCE CONTRIBUTIONS; *Amalgamated Engineering Union v Minister of Pensions and National Insurance*, 73.35 NATIONAL INSURANCE CONTRIBUTIONS; *Beloff v Pressdram Ltd & Another*, 73.36 NATIONAL INSURANCE CONTRIBUTIONS; *Ferguson v John Dawson & Partners (Contractors) Ltd*, 73.37 NATIONAL INSURANCE CONTRIBUTIONS; *Demibourne Ltd v HMRC*, 73.45 NATIONAL INSURANCE CONTRIBUTIONS, and *The Athenaeum Club v HMRC*, 73.47 NATIONAL INSURANCE CONTRIBUTIONS.

Cases held not to constitute employment

[22.13] In an Irish case, a taxpayer received 10% of certain rents under his father's will 'so long as (he) continues to manage and look after' the property. He was assessed on the basis that the amounts which he received were remuneration from an employment. He appealed, contending that the payments were conditional gifts under the will and did not arise from an employment. The SC(I) accepted this contention and allowed his appeal. *O'Reilly v Casey*, SC(I) 1942, 2 ITC 220; [1942] IR 378.

[22.14] A company (S) operated two 'gentlemen's entertainment clubs' in London. It arranged for young women to dance at the clubs, and treated them as self-employed. The dancers received payments from customers at the clubs, in the form of vouchers which S distributed. A dancer (Q), who had worked at one of the clubs from June 2007 to December 2008, took proceedings against S in the Employment Tribunal, contending that she had been an employee of S and had been unfairly dismissed. The Employment Appeal Tribunal held that Q had been an employee, but the CA unanimously allowed S's appeal, holding that Q had been self-employed. Elias LJ held that 'the club did not employ the dancers to dance', and that the dancers paid the club 'to be provided with an opportunity to earn money by dancing for the clients'. *Stringfellows Restaurants Ltd v NE Quashie*, CA [2012] EWCA Civ 1735.

[22.15] An insurance agent had worked for a company as an employee from 1971 to 1973, when he negotiated a new agreement under which he was treated as self-employed. In 1975 the company terminated the agreement. He made a claim for unfair dismissal under the *Trade Unions and Labour Relations Act*, contending that he had remained an employee despite the provisions of the 1973 agreement. The industrial tribunal rejected this contention and the CA dismissed his appeal, holding that he had been self-employed. Lord Denning MR observed that 'if the true relationship of the parties is that of master and servant under a contract of service, the parties cannot alter the truth of that relationship by putting a different label upon it'. However, 'if their relationship is ambiguous and is capable of being one or the other, then the parties can remove that ambiguity, by the very agreement itself which they make with one another. The agreement itself then becomes the best material from which to gather the true legal relationship between them.' *Massey v Crown Life Insurance Co*, CA 1977, [1978] 2 All ER 576.

[22.16] A company operated a banqueting business at a hotel. Two wine butlers and a barman, whom the company had treated as self-employed, lodged a claim with an industrial tribunal, contending that they should have been treated as employees with consequential rights under the *Employment Protection (Consolidation) Act 1978*. The industrial tribunal rejected the claim, holding that the workers were independent contractors rather than employees. The CA upheld this decision as one of fact (by a 2-1 majority, Ackner LJ dissenting). *O'Kelly & Others v Trusthouse Forte plc*, CA 1983, [1984] 1 QB 90; [1983] 3 All ER 456. (*Note*. For HMRC's interpretation of this decision, see Employment Status Manual, para ESM7100.)

[22.17] A freelance vision mixer (L), who worked on short-term contracts lasting for one or two days, was assessed as an employee. He appealed, contending that he was self-employed. The Special Commissioner accepted this contention and allowed his appeal, and the CA unanimously upheld this decision. The fact that L only provided his personal skills, and did not provide any equipment, did not necessarily lead to the conclusion that he was an employee. On the evidence, L was an independent contractor who worked for 20 or more production companies each year, and was not dependent upon any particular paymaster for the financial exploitation of his talents. The Commissioner was justified in concluding that he was in business on his own account. *Hall v Lorimer*, CA 1993, 66 TC 349; [1994] STC 23; [1994] 1 WLR 209; [1994] 1 All ER 250.

[22.18] A driver (T) had worked for a publishing company (E), but was made redundant in 1995. Later that year E re-engaged him on a self-employed basis. The Revenue continued to treat him as an employee, and T subsequently applied to the Industrial Tribunal for a ruling that he was an employee. E appealed to the CA, which held that T was self-employed. Peter Gibson LJ held that the right of substitution was inconsistent with employment, since 'where, as here, a person who works for another is not required to perform his services personally, then as a matter of law the relationship between the worker and the person for whom he works is not that of employee and employer'. On the terms of the contract, 'the only conclusion which (the Tribunal) could properly have reached was that this was a contract for services'. *Express & Echo Publications Ltd v Tanton*, CA [1999] ICR 693. (*Note*. Compare, however, the Privy Council decision in *Narich Property Ltd v Australian Commissioner of Payroll Tax*, **22.5** above, which was not cited in this case, and where the Privy Council held that lecturers were employees despite the existence of a substitution clause. *Obiter dicta* of Peter Gibson LJ with regard to the right of substitution were implicitly disapproved by Park J in the subsequent case of *Usetech Ltd v Young*, **73.128** NATIONAL INSURANCE CONTRIBUTIONS, on the grounds that they were inconsistent with the decision in *Narich Property Ltd v Australian Commissioner of Payroll Tax*.)

[22.19] In 1995 an employment agency arranged for a woman to work as a receptionist for a local company. In 1997 the company asked the agency to terminate her employment. She took proceedings against the agency, claiming that she had been unfairly dismissed. The CA unanimously rejected her claim, holding on the evidence that she had never been an employee of the agency. Longmore LJ held that 'mutuality of obligation and the requirement of control on the part of the potential employer are the irreducible minimum for the existence of a contract of employment'. *Johnson Underwood Ltd v Montgomery*, CA [2001] All ER (D) 101 (Mar). (*Note*. The tax treatment of agency workers is governed by *ITEPA 2003, ss 44–47*. However HMRC regard this as an important decision on the definition of a 'contract of employment'. For their interpretation of this decision, see Employment Status Manual, para ESM7240.)

[22.20] Several fishermen were drowned when a trawler capsized off the coast of Cornwall. Some of their dependants claimed damages from the owners of the trawler. The QB held that the fishermen were employees, and the owners of the trawler appealed. The CA unanimously allowed the appeal, holding on the evidence that the fishermen had been self-employed and had not been employees. *Todd & Others v Adams & Chope*, CA [2002] EWCA Civ 509. (*Note.* The fishermen had been treated as self-employed for tax purposes.)

[22.21] See also *Parade Park Hotel v HMRC*, **42.67** PAY AS YOU EARN; *Barnett v Brabyn*, **59.87** TRADING INCOME; *Chadwick v Pioneer Private Telephone Co Ltd*, **73.20** NATIONAL INSURANCE CONTRIBUTIONS; *Ready Mixed Concrete (South East) Ltd v Minister of Pensions & National Insurance*, **73.25** NATIONAL INSURANCE CONTRIBUTIONS; *Turnbull v HMRC*, **73.26** NATIONAL INSURANCE CONTRIBUTIONS; *Mitchell v HMRC*, **73.28** NATIONAL INSURANCE CONTRIBUTIONS; *Convery v HMRC*, **73.38** NATIONAL INSURANCE CONTRIBUTIONS; *Lewis (t/a MAL Scaffolding) & Others v HMRC*, **73.39** NATIONAL INSURANCE CONTRIBUTIONS; *Castle Construction (Chesterfield) Ltd v HMRC*, **73.40** NATIONAL INSURANCE CONTRIBUTIONS; *Bell v HMRC*, **73.41** NATIONAL INSURANCE CONTRIBUTIONS; *President of the Methodist Conference v Parfitt*, **73.42** NATIONAL INSURANCE CONTRIBUTIONS; *President of the Methodist Conference v Preston*, **73.43** NATIONAL INSURANCE CONTRIBUTIONS; *Davies v Presbyterian Church of Wales*, **73.44** NATIONAL INSURANCE CONTRIBUTIONS; *Slush Puppie Ltd v HMRC*, **73.46** NATIONAL INSURANCE CONTRIBUTIONS; *Gould v Minister of National Insurance*, **73.88** NATIONAL INSURANCE CONTRIBUTIONS, and *Argent v Minister of Social Security*, **73.89** NATIONAL INSURANCE CONTRIBUTIONS.

Offices and office-holders (ITEPA 2003, s 5)

Note. For HMRC's interpretation of what constitutes an office, see Employment Status Manual, para ESM2502.

College bursar

[22.22] The bursar of a college at Oxford University appealed against an assessment, contending that his earnings should be treated as exempt. The QB rejected this contention and upheld the assessment, holding that the bursar held an 'office'. *Langston v Glasson*, QB 1891, 3 TC 46.

Railway employees—definition of 'office'

[22.23] In a case concerning the assessment of employees of a railway company, where the substantive issue has been superseded by subsequent changes in the legislation, Rowlatt J defined an 'office' as a 'permanent, substantive position which had an existence independent from the person who filled it, which went on and was filled in succession by successive holders'. In the HL, Lord Atkinson specifically approved this definition. Lord Sumner observed that a railway clerk did not 'hold any office at all. He merely sits in one.' *Great Western Railway Company v Bater*, HL 1922, 8 TC 231. (*Note.* The definition has now been partly incorporated into *ITEPA 2003, s 5(3).*)

Secular priest acting as headmaster of school

[22.24] A congregation of secular priests (the Fathers of the Oratory) had established a school. One of the congregation was appointed as headmaster, and was voted a nominal salary, which he donated to the congregation. The Revenue assessed him on this under Schedule E. He appealed, contending that his service was gratuitous and that he had no legal right to the salary. The KB allowed his appeal, holding that his headmastership was not an 'office of profit'. *Reade v Brearley*, KB 1933, 17 TC 687.

Assistant curate—whether holding an 'office'

[22.25] See *Slaney v Starkey*, 22.55 below.

Part-time appointment of doctor—whether an 'office'

[22.26] A radiologist (R), who carried on a private practice in Rugby, also held a part-time appointment as a consultant with a regional hospital board. The Revenue issued assessments under Schedule E on the basis that the appointment was an 'office'. The Ch D upheld the assessment, holding that R was 'the holder of a public office'. The HL unanimously upheld this decision. (The HL also held that since the remuneration from the appointment was assessable under Schedule E, the expenses attributable to it could be deducted only in the Schedule E assessments in accordance with the Schedule E rules. Expenses relating to the appointment which were not deductible under Schedule E could not be allowed as deductions in the Schedule D assessments on R's private practice.) *Mitchell & Edon v Ross (and related appeals)*, HL 1961, 40 TC 11; [1962] AC 813; [1961] 3 All ER 49.

Short-term appointments by Department of Environment—whether an 'office'

[22.27] A civil engineer (C) acted from time to time as an inspector on behalf of the Department of the Environment in public local enquiries. The Revenue issued assessments charging tax on the fees from these appointments, on the basis that each appointment was an 'office'. C appealed, contending that the appointments were not 'offices' and that the income should be assessed under Schedule D. The Commissioners accepted this contention and allowed his appeal, and the HL upheld their decision (by a 3-2 majority, Lords Edmund-Davies and Bridge dissenting). Lord Wilberforce defined the word 'office' as connoting 'a post to which a person can be appointed, which he can vacate and to which a successor can be appointed'. *Edwards v Clinch*, HL 1981, 56 TC 367; [1981] STC 617; [1981] 3 WLR 707; [1981] 3 All ER 543.

Barrister's clerk—whether holding an office

[22.28] In 1985 a barrister's clerk (D), who had previously been accepted as an employee, entered into a new contract with each member of chambers under which he agreed to provide, at his own expense, each barrister with a 'full clerking service'. In return, he was to receive a specified percentage of each barrister's gross earnings. The Revenue issued assessments on the basis that, despite the form of the contracts, D continued to hold an office, so that his income was assessable under Schedule E. The Special Commissioners allowed D's appeal, holding that he was self-employed under a contract for services, and the Ch D upheld their decision. The post of barrister's clerk was a 'job description' rather than an office. *McMenamin v Diggles*, Ch D 1991, 64 TC 286; [1991] STC 419; [1991] 1 WLR 1249; [1991] 4 All ER 370.

Subpostmaster—whether holding an office

[22.29] See the cases noted at **15.43** to **15.45** COMPENSATION FOR LOSS OF EMPLOYMENT.

Taxable earnings: resident employees (ITEPA 2003, ss 14–19)

NOTE

See now *ITEPA 2003, s 15*, deriving from *ICTA 1988, s 202A*, which was inserted by *FA 1989* for 1989/90 and subsequent years.

Emoluments received after year in which earned

[22.30] An individual (F) was employed under a contract which stipulated that he would be paid monthly in arrears, on the 6th of each month. HMRC issued a ruling that the payment which he received on 6 April 2007 was taxable for 2007/08. F appealed, contending that it was taxable in 2006/07. The First-tier Tribunal rejected this contention and dismissed the appeal. Judge King held that the effect of *ITEPA 2003, s 18(1)* was that the payment was taxable when F became entitled to it, which was on 6 April 2007. *E Fountain v HMRC*, FTT [2011] UKFTT 570 (TC), TC01413.

Contractual obligation to repay bonus received in previous tax year

[22.31] In 2005 an employee (M) signed an agreement to remain with his employer (J) for five years, in return for a payment of £250,000. The agreement provided that if M left his employment within the five-year period, he would be required to repay a proportion of the bonus. The £250,000 was treated as taxable earnings of 2005/06. In December 2006 M resigned from his employment and became liable to repay J £162,500. J initially claimed that this amount should be deducted from his taxable earnings for 2005/06, but subsequently claimed that it should be treated as 'negative taxable income' for 2006/07. HMRC rejected the claims, and M appealed. The First-tier Tribunal allowed his appeal, holding that the full amount of £250,000 had been correctly treated as taxable income for 2005/06, but that the repayment of £162,500 was 'negative taxable income' for 2006/07, within *ITEPA 2003, s 11*. The Upper Tribunal upheld this decision. Warren J held that *s 11* 'was designed to articulate the operation of the existing legislation and practice rather than creating something new'. He observed that 'just as an amount received after the termination of an employment may still be earnings from that employment, and so chargeable as employment income, the same must be true in reverse of negative earnings, so that a payment by employee to employer after the employment had terminated can be taken into account' in calculating taxable earnings. *HMRC v Julian Martin*, UT [2014] UKUT 429 (TCC).

Period for which director's remuneration assessable

[22.32] A company made up its accounts to 30 June, and voted directors' remuneration after the end of the year. A director was assessed for 1942/43 on the remuneration voted to her for the period from 28 May 1942 (when her appointment began) to 30 June 1942, plus three-quarters of the remuneration voted to her for the year to 30 June 1943. She appealed, contending that the assessment should be restricted to the remuneration voted in 1942/43, i.e. the remuneration for the first period only. The Special Commissioners rejected this contention and dismissed her appeal, and the KB upheld their decision. *Dracup v Radcliffe*, KB 1946, 27 TC 188.

[22.33] A company director was voted remuneration of £37,625 in the year ending 30 June 1988 and more than £90,000 in the year ending 30 June 1989. The Revenue issued a 1988/89 assessment on remuneration of £80,315, computed on the 'earnings basis'. The director appealed, contending that he should only have been assessed on £37,625, on the non-statutory 'accounts basis'. The Special Commissioner rejected this contention and dismissed the appeal. *Malone v Quinn*, Sp C [2001] SSCD 63 (Sp C 273).

Housing allowance—year of assessment

[22.34] An individual (W) joined the Royal Ulster Constabulary in 1994. Certain promotional material, which had been supplied to him by the Northern Ireland Police Authority, indicated that he would be paid a housing allowance. However the Police Authority initially refused to pay him an allowance, on the grounds that there had been a change in the RUC conditions of service three days before he began his employment. Following negotiations between the Police Authority and the Police Federation, including a test case brought in the High Court by another officer, the Police Authority agreed to pay him the allowance in question, and made a payment of £6,124 in September 1997. £2,624 of this related to 1995/96 and £3,500 related to 1996/97. W did not include this payment on his 1997/98 tax return. The Revenue amended the return on the basis that the £6,124 was assessable for 1997/98, being the year of receipt. W appealed, contending that £2,624 was assessable for 1995/96 and £3,500 for 1996/97. The Special Commissioner rejected this contention and dismissed the appeal, holding that 'the assessability of an emolument for a particular year of assessment must be capable of being judged at the time, not later than immediately after the year in question'. On the evidence, W 'could not have demonstrated his entitlement to payments of housing allowance, in respect of the period prior to 6 April 1997, at the relevant time or times'. The Commissioner also observed that W's arguments rested on 'the proposition that he should have included appropriate amounts in his returns for the earlier years, at the time when the returns were due'. *White v CIR*, Sp C [2003] SSCD 161 (Sp C 357).

Non-resident or non-domiciled employees (ITEPA 2003, ss 20–41)

Non-resident employee—whether income remitted to UK

[22.35] An individual (P), whose main home was in Germany, worked in the UK from April 2006 to October 2008, during which time he was accepted as resident, but not ordinarily resident, in the UK. His fiancée (L) had lived in the UK since 2003, having arrived as a student. P's earnings for days when he was working in the UK were taxable under *ITEPA 2003, s 25*, and his earnings for days when he was working outside the UK were chargeable under *ITEPA 2003, s 26* (so that they were only taxable if they were remitted to the UK). P's salary was paid into a Guernsey bank account. In his 2007/08 tax return, P stated that he had earned £490,621 relating to duties outside the UK, and that only a small part of these earnings had been remitted to the UK. He therefore claimed a substantial repayment. HMRC began an enquiry, and ascertained that some of P's salary had been transferred from the Guernsey account to an Isle of Man account in the joint names of P and L. A debit card relating to this account had been used to draw cash from cash machines in the UK, and to purchase goods in the UK. HMRC issued an amendment to P's self-assessment, ruling that this money had been remitted to the UK and was therefore taxable under *s 26*. P appealed, contending that the money which had been transferred to the Isle of Man account was beneficially owned by L, and that he was not chargeable on the sums which L had withdrawn from the account. The First-tier Tribunal accepted P's evidence and allowed the appeal. Judge Herrington observed that the circumstances in which the Isle of Man account was opened as a joint account rather than solely in L's name were wholly plausible, since 'it would be difficult for a young student from overseas to be given an account immediately that allowed the use of an unrestricted debit card, as opposed to the account that (L) had with a restricted use debit card before she met (P)'. *KO Pflum v HMRC*, FTT [2012] UKFTT 365 (TC), TC02051. (*Note. ITEPA 2003, s 25* was repealed, and *ITEPA 2003, s 26* was amended, by *FA 2008* with effect from 2008/09.)

Duties abroad—whether a Crown appointment under ITEPA 2003, s 28

[22.36] A civil servant, whose duties were performed outside the UK, appealed against income tax assessments, contending that his employment was not 'of a public nature' for the purposes of what is now *ITEPA 2003, s 28(2)(a)* because he was in a 'subordinate position'. The General Commissioners rejected this contention and dismissed his appeals, and the Ch D upheld their decision. Megarry J observed that 'the duties described in the Case Stated are plainly of importance to the efficiency of an important branch of the public service' and that 'the language of the Act *prima facie* applies to all civil servants'. *Graham v White*, Ch D 1971, 48 TC 163; [1972] 1 WLR 874; [1972] 1 All ER 1159. (*Note.* The appellant appeared in person.)

[22.37] The Minister of Overseas Development assigned an employee to the Fijian Government, to act as a senior assessor in the Fijian Inland Revenue. His salary was paid by the UK Government, which was reimbursed by the Fijian Government. He appealed against an assessment charging UK income tax, contending that he was not paid 'out of the public revenue' for the purposes of what is now *ITEPA 2003, s 28(2)(b)*. The Special Commissioners rejected this contention and dismissed his appeal, observing that he 'was throughout the relevant year paid his salary out of moneys charged to the Consolidated Fund'. The Ch D upheld their decision. Brightman J held that 'the fact that the United Kingdom Government received partial recoupment at a later date from the Government of Fiji' was 'totally irrelevant', and observed that 'it was clearly stated in the terms and conditions of his appointment' that United Kingdom income tax 'would be deducted from his salary if he were assigned overseas'. *Caldicott v Varty*, Ch D 1976, 51 TC 403; [1976] STC 418; [1976] 3 All ER 329. (*Notes*. (1) The appellant appeared in person. (2) For another issue in this case, see **4.36** APPEALS.)

ITEPA 2003, s 38—earnings for period of absence from employment

[22.38] In a case where the substantive issue has been overtaken by subsequent changes in the legislation, an airline pilot performed most of his duties outside the UK. He claimed that a proportion of his emoluments for periods when he was not working should be treated as emoluments for duties performed outside the UK. The General Commissioners rejected this contention and dismissed his appeal, and the CA upheld their decision. It could not be proved that, but for his absence from his employment on rest days, holidays or sick leave, he would have performed duties outside the UK. Accordingly, by virtue of what is now *ITEPA 2003, s 38*, the emoluments for the periods of absence had to be treated as emoluments for duties performed in the UK. *Leonard v Blanchard*, CA 1993, 65 TC 589; [1993] STC 259.

ITEPA 2003, s 39—incidental duties

[22.39] In the case noted at **54.13** SCHEDULE E, Sir John Pennycuick V-C held that the words 'merely incidental to' were 'apt to denote an activity (here the performance of duties) which does not serve any independent purpose but is carried out in order to further some other purpose'. *Robson v Dixon*, Ch D 1972, 48 TC 527; [1972] 1 WLR 1493; [1972] 3 All ER 671. (*Note*. For the Revenue's interpretation of this decision, see Revenue Tax Bulletin April 2005, pp 1201, 1202.)

Agency workers (ITEPA 2003, ss 44–47)

[22.40] See the cases noted at **42.10** PAY AS YOU EARN to **42.14** PAY AS YOU EARN.

Personal service companies (ITEPA 2003, ss 48–61)

[22.41] A group of contractors applied for judicial review of the provisions introduced by *FA 2000, s 60, Sch 12* (see now *ITEPA 2003, ss 48–61*), contending that, by reclassifying contractors who worked through personal service companies as employees, the provisions were a breach of the *EC Treaty* and the European Convention on Human Rights. The QB reviewed the evidence in detail, rejected these contentions, and dismissed the application. Burton J held that the provisions did not amount to 'fundamental interference with (the) financial position' of the contractors affected, and that 'to subject service contractors to the common law of employment' did not interfere with their human rights. The CA unanimously upheld this decision. Robert Walker LJ held that the provisions did not constitute a 'state aid' within the meaning of *Article 87EC* of the *EC Treaty*. They also did not breach the provisions of the *EC Treaty* concerning freedom of movement or freedom to provide services. On the evidence, they did not involve a 'direct and demonstrable inhibition' on the establishment of a business within the UK, or on the provision of services without establishment. Genuine self-employed activities would not be affected and 'a business of providing employee-like services will be taxed as if there was a real employment situation'. *R v CIR (oao Professional Contractors Group Ltd and Others)*, CA 2001, 74 TC 393; [2002] STC 165; [2001] EWCA Civ 1945; 4 ITLR 483.

[22.42] See also *HMRC v Larkstar Data Ltd*, **42.46** PAY AS YOU EARN. For cases concerning the *Social Security Contributions (Intermediaries) Regulations 2000 (SI 2000/727)* (the NIC equivalent of *ITEPA 2003, ss 48–61*), see 73.125 *et seq*. NATIONAL INSURANCE CONTRIBUTIONS.

[22.43] For cases concerning the borderline between employment and self-employment, see 22.1 to 22.21 above.

Employment income: earnings and benefits treated as earnings (ITEPA 2003, ss 62–226)

Earnings (ITEPA 2003, s 62)

ITEPA 2003, s 62(2)(a)—definition of 'salary'

[22.44] In an 1892 bankruptcy case, the CA held that regular payments to an actor were a 'salary'. Fry LJ held that a 'salary' should have 'four characteristics – first, that it is paid for services rendered; secondly, that it is paid under some contract or appointment; thirdly, that it is computed by time; and fourthly, that it is payable at a fixed time'. *In re Shine, ex p. Shine*, CA [1892] 1 QB 522. (*Note.* In the subsequent case of *Greater London Council v Minister of Social Security*, 73.27 NATIONAL INSURANCE CONTRIBUTIONS, MacKenna J held that where the 'unit of time is a short period', there was a fifth characteristic, namely 'that the contract should provide for the recurrence of the sessions of work throughout the contract period, whether that period is fixed or indefinite'. HMRC regard these as the two leading cases on the definition of 'salary'. See the Revenue Press Release dated 26 June 2003.)

Part of gross salary set aside as 'thrift fund' contribution

[22.45] The Corporation of the City of Manchester deducted compulsory contributions to a 'thrift fund' from its employee' salaries. The Revenue issued assessments charging tax on the basis that these contributions formed part of the employees' salaries. Two of the employees appealed. The CA unanimously upheld the assessments, holding that the full amount of the gross salary was taxable remuneration. *Bell v Gribble*; *Hudson v Gribble*, CA 1903, 4 TC 522.

Part of salary credited to provident fund

[22.46] A percentage of the salaries of schoolteachers at an independent school was not paid directly to the schoolteachers, but was retained in a provident fund and paid to them with accumulated interest on retirement, subject to certain conditions. The Revenue issued assessments on the basis that the amounts so credited formed part of the teachers' salaries. One of the teachers appealed. The KB upheld the assessment. Channell J held that 'a sum receivable by way of salary or wages is not the less salary or wages taxable because for some reason or another the person who receives it has not got the full right to apply it just as he likes'. *Smyth v Stretton*, KB 1904, 5 TC 36.

Employer paying tax on employee's salary

[22.47] A railway company had agreed to pay the tax on its employees' salaries. The Revenue issued an assessment on the basis that the tax in question was part of the employees' income. The Special Commissioners upheld the assessment and the HL unanimously dismissed the company's appeal. Lord Dunedin held that 'the total emolument of the official is not only the cash salary but also the sum necessary to maintain that cash salary at its undiminished figure'. *North British Railway Company v Scott*, HL 1922, 8 TC 332; [1923] AC 37. (*Note.* The appeals were against assessments on the employer, under machinery for the assessment of railway employees which is now obsolete.)

[22.48] A shipping company habitually, but voluntarily, paid the tax on the salaries of its employees. The Revenue issued assessments on the basis that the tax paid was an assessable emolument. The company's accountant appealed. The General Commissioners dismissed his appeal and the HL unanimously upheld their decision. Viscount Cave LC observed that the fact 'that the payment is voluntary makes no difference'. *Hartland v Diggines*, HL 1926, 10 TC 247; [1926] AC 289.

Civil servant serving abroad—'colonial allowance'

[22.49] A civil servant held the position of deputy cashier in a naval base in Singapore. His salary included a 'colonial allowance' to meet the increased cost of living abroad. The Revenue issued assessments on the basis that the full salary, including the 'colonial allowance', was assessable on him. He appealed, contending that the 'colonial allowance' was not taxable income. The Special Commissioners rejected this contention, holding that the 'colonial allowance' was part of his salary, and the CA unanimously upheld their decision. *Robinson v Corry*, CA 1933, 18 TC 411; [1934] 1 KB 240. (*Notes.* (1) The CA also upheld the Commissioners' decision that he was not entitled to a deduction for the extra cost of living abroad. (2) The case also concerned the tax treatment of accommodation provided for the appellant, but the decision on this point was superseded by subsequent changes in the legislation: see now *ITEPA 2003, ss 97–113*.)

ITEPA 2003, s 62(2)(a)—definition of 'wages'

[22.50] In 1976 a company began paying its employees weekly wages of between £1 and £4, in gold sovereigns. The employees sold the sovereigns to the wife of one of the company's directors, for £1 per coin less than their cost to the employer. The Revenue issued assessments charging tax on the value of the sovereigns. One of the employees appealed, contending that, as the sovereigns were legal tender, he could only be assessed on the face value of the coins. The Special Commissioners rejected this contention and dismissed his appeal, holding that the sovereigns were being used 'as a commodity', rather than as currency. The Ch D upheld their decision. Browne-Wilkinson J held that the amount of the employee's emoluments 'was the amount for which he was able to realise, and indeed did realise, the sovereigns that he received'. Therefore 'the full value of the gold sovereigns is the proper amount which is taxable in his hands'. *Jenkins v Horn*, Ch D 1979, 52 TC 591; [1979] STC 446; [1979] 2 All ER 1141.

ITEPA 2003, s 62(2)(b)—'gratuity or other profit'

Christmas gift to minister

[22.51] A church congregation gave their minister a sum of £100 each Christmas, raised by voluntary subscription. The Revenue issued an assessment charging tax on this. The minister appealed, contending that it should not be treated as part of his income. The court rejected this contention and upheld the assessment. Lord Marshall held that the minister received the gift 'in respect of the discharge of his duties of that office'. *In re Strong*, CE 1878, 1 TC 207.

Grants to clergyman from Augmentation Fund

[22.52] A vicar applied for, and received, annual grants from the Queen Victoria Clergy Sustentation Fund. The Revenue issued assessments charging tax on these grants. The vicar appealed, contending that they should not be treated as part of his income. The CA rejected this contention and upheld the assessments. Sir Richard Collins MR observed that the grants were not simply a donation, 'but an augmentation of a benefice made under an organised system'. *Herbert v McQuade*, CA 1902, 4 TC 489; [1902] 2 KB 631.

[22.53] A Nonconformist minister applied for, and received, annual grants from a Ministers' Stipend Augmentation Fund, which took into account the amount of his income. The Revenue issued assessments charging tax on these grants. The minister appealed, contending that they were not 'income arising from his office'. The CA rejected this contention and upheld the assessments. Cozens-Hardy LJ observed that it was 'primarily not a personal gift but an augmentation of the stipend of the minister'. *Poynting v Faulkner*, CA 1905, 5 TC 145.

Easter offerings

[22.54] The Bishop of Chichester encouraged churchwardens and parishioners to give 'freewill offerings at Easter' to the parochial clergy. The Revenue issued assessments charging tax on these gifts. The Vicar of East Grinstead appealed against an assessment, contending that the gifts should not be treated as taxable income. The HL unanimously rejected this contention and dismissed the vicar's appeal. Lord Loreburn LC observed that 'where a sum of money is given to an incumbent substantially in respect of his services as an incumbent, it accrues to him by reason of his office. Here the sum of money was given in respect of those services.' *Cooper v Blakiston*, HL 1908, 5 TC 347; [1909] AC 104.

Voluntary collections for assistant curate

[22.55] A parish church arranged voluntary collections on Whit Sunday for its assistant curate. The Revenue issued assessments charging tax on these collections. The curate appealed, contending that he did not hold any 'office' within what is now *ITEPA 2003, s 5*, and that he should not be required to pay tax on the collections. The KB rejected these contentions and upheld the assessment, holding that he held an office within *s 5*, and that the collections were taxable income. *Slaney v Starkey*, KB 1931, 16 TC 45; [1931] 2 KB 148.

'Commission' to director for negotiating sale of branch

[22.56] An accountant acted as the secretary and director of a company. He negotiated the sale of a branch of the company, which paid him £1,000 'as commission for his services in negotiating the sale'. The Revenue issued an assessment charging tax on the £1,000. He appealed, contending that it was a voluntary gift and that tax should not be charged. The Commissioners rejected this contention and dismissed his appeal, and the KB upheld their decision. Rowlatt J held that the payment was 'remuneration for services', and was taxable. *Mudd v Collins*, KB 1925, 9 TC 297.

Payment to director for services abroad

[22.57] The chairman and director of a UK company received additional remuneration for 'extra services' to the company while on a long visit to China. He appealed against assessments charging tax on this remuneration. The Commissioners dismissed his appeal and the CA unanimously upheld their decision, holding that the sums he received were 'profits from the office or employment'. *Barson v Airey*, CA 1925, 10 TC 609.

Director's bonus described as 'gift'

[22.58] A company made increased profits in 1922, and the shareholders voted that the directors should receive a 'gift' of £2,000. The Revenue issued assessments charging tax on these payments, and the chairman appealed. The KB upheld the assessment, holding that the payment was 'extra remuneration' and was taxable. *Radcliffe v Holt*, KB 1927, 11 TC 621.

Long-service bonuses

[22.59] A company paid two of its employees bonuses after 25 years' service. The Revenue issued assessments charging tax on them. The employees appealed. The Commissioners dismissed the appeals and the KB upheld this decision, holding that the bonuses were 'remuneration for services rendered'. *Weston v Hearn; Carmouche v Hearn*, KB 1943, 25 TC 425; [1943] 2 All ER 421.

Taxi-driver's tips

[22.60] The Revenue issued an assessment on a driver who was employed by a taxi hire company, on the basis that tax should be charged on tips which the driver received. He appealed, contending that tax should not be charged on the tips. The KB rejected this contention and upheld the assessment, holding that the tips were taxable remuneration. Atkinson J held that 'tips received by a man as a reward for services rendered, voluntary gifts made by people other than the employers, are assessable to tax as part of the profits arising out of the employment if given in the ordinary way as a reward for services'. *Calvert v Wainwright*, KB 1947, 27 TC 475; [1947] 1 KB 526; [1947] 1 All ER 282.

Collections for professional cricketer

[22.61] A professional cricketer (D) was employed by a club in the Lancashire League, the rules of which provided for collections from spectators for good performances by professional players. During the 1951 season D received 11 such collections. The Revenue issued an assessment on the basis that these collections were taxable, and D appealed. The CA upheld the assessment, holding that the collections were taxable. Birkett LJ observed that 'the chief and decisive fact' was 'the contract of employment which had provided for these very collections to be made'. *Moorhouse v Dooland*, CA 1954, 36 TC 1; [1955] Ch 264; [1955] 1 All ER 93.

Christmas presents to huntsman

[22.62] A professional huntsman (W) received Christmas presents in cash from persons with whom he was in contact in the course of his employment. The Revenue issued assessments charging tax on these payments, and W appealed. The Special Commissioners dismissed his appeal, holding that the payments were assessable, and the CA upheld their decision. Jenkins LJ observed that there was 'a widespread custom in the hunts in most parts of the country' to give the huntsman 'presents of cash at Christmas'. Accordingly, they were received 'by virtue of his office or employment'. *Wright v Boyce*, CA 1958, 38 TC 160; [1958] 1 WLR 832; [1958] 2 All ER 703.

Voluntary payments by associations of Lloyd's Names

[22.63] During the late 1980s several Lloyd's underwriters suffered substantial losses, and subsequently formed associations to take legal proceedings against certain Lloyd's agents, insurers and actuaries. The litigation was settled in 1997. One of the associations made its chairman (M) a voluntary payment of £160,000. He also received a voluntary payment of £120,000 from another association, of which he had been deputy chairman. He did not include these payments on his 1997/98 tax return. The Revenue issued an amendment to his return, on the basis that the payments were taxable emoluments. The Special Commissioners dismissed M's appeal, finding that the payments 'were received in respect of the discharge of the duties of an office' and 'were in recognition of services rendered. They were not gifts in recognition of services or "peculiarly due" to personal qualities'. Accordingly, they were taxable. *McBride v Blackburn*, Sp C [2003] SSCD 139 (Sp C 356).

ITEPA 2003, s 62(2)(c)—definition of 'emolument of the employment'

Clothing allowance paid to police detective

[22.64] The Glasgow Police Force paid its detectives a clothing allowance in cash. They were required to buy clothing which was 'suitable for their duties'.

The Revenue issued assessments charging tax on these allowances. The CS upheld the assessments. *Fergusson v Noble*, CS 1919, 7 TC 176.

'Benefit' paid to footballer

[22.65] A footballer (H) played for Everton FC for more than ten years, but was then transferred to Preston. Everton paid him a 'benefit' of £650 in accordance with Football League rules. The Revenue issued an assessment charging tax on this. The KB upheld the assessment, holding that the payment was taxable remuneration from H's employment. *Davis v Harrison*, KB 1927, 11 TC 707.

[22.66] The KB reached a similar decision in three subsequent cases where Lawrence J observed that the payments 'are expected, are generally asked for and are usually accorded'. *Corbett v Duff (and associated appeals)*, KB 1941, 23 TC 763; [1941] 1 KB 730; [1941] 1 All ER 512.

Payment to company secretary

[22.67] The directors of a company agreed that its secretary should receive £2,000 for negotiating the sale of its works. The Revenue issued an assessment charging tax on the payment. The KB upheld the assessment. *Shipway v Skidmore*, KB 1932, 16 TC 748.

Payment on death of director

[22.68] A company's managing director (M) was employed under a contract which provided for a termination payment of £10,000. M died in 1934. The Revenue issued an assessment on his executors, charging tax on the payment. The CA unanimously upheld the assessment. *Allen & Murray (Murray's Executors) v Trehearne*, CA 1938, 22 TC 15.

Remuneration assigned

[22.69] The managing director of a mining company was entitled to 5% of the redemption proceeds of certain loan notes. He assigned these payments to a creditor in return for being released from the debt. The Revenue assessed him on these payments on the basis that they were emoluments of his directorship. The KB upheld the assessments. *Parkins v Warwick*, KB 1943, 25 TC 419.

Endowment insurance premiums

[22.70] An employer agreed to pay the premiums on an endowment policy for an employee. The Revenue issued assessments charging tax on the premiums. The KB upheld the assessments. *Richardson v Lyon*, KB 1943, 25 TC 497.

Payment for surrender of future commission

[22.71] A company paid its managing director £1,250 in return for surrendering his right to receive certain commission. The Revenue issued an assessment charging tax on the payment. The KB upheld the assessment. Atkinson J observed that 'the bonuses he would have received if they had been paid under the agreement would have been profits from his employment, and the mere fact that they agree on another form of remuneration does not alter its character'. *Bolam v Muller*, KB 1947, 28 TC 471.

[22.72] A Swedish company acquired a UK company (M). M's directors had been entitled to commission, related to profits. Two of them agreed to alterations in their contracts, whereby the provision for commission was removed; they each received a one-off payment of £6,000, and their salaries were substantially increased. The Revenue issued assessments charging tax on the payments of £6,000. The Ch D upheld the assessments, holding that the payments were taxable as compensation for the loss of future commission. *McGregor v Randall; McGregor v Gillett*, Ch D 1984, 58 TC 110; [1984] STC 223; [1984] 1 All ER 1092.

Lecture fees paid to hospital consultant

[22.73] A full-time consultant radiologist, employed at a teaching hospital, received fees for giving lectures at the hospital. The Revenue issued assessments charging tax on these fees. The CS unanimously upheld the assessments. *Lindsay v CIR*, CS 1964, 41 TC 661.

Signing-on fee to rugby footballer

[22.74] A rugby league club paid a signing-on fee of £500 (in two instalments) to a player who had previously been an amateur, under a contract whereby a proportionate part of the fee would be returnable if he did not continue to serve the club for a stipulated period. The Revenue issued assessments charging tax on the £500. The Ch D upheld the assessments, holding that the effect of the contract was that the payments were taxable. *Riley v Coglan*, Ch D 1967, 44 TC 481; [1967] 1 WLR 1300; [1968] 1 All ER 314.

Compensation to refuse collectors for loss of agreed rights

[22.75] A council allowed its refuse collectors to participate in a salvage scheme, under which they could sell salvageable materials from the refuse which they collected. The council decided to end the scheme. After strike action and negotiation with the appropriate trade union, it paid each of the collectors £450 as compensation. The Revenue issued assessments charging tax on the £450. One of the collectors appealed. The Ch D upheld the assessment, holding that the £450 was 'an emolument of his employment'. *Holland v Geoghegan*, Ch D 1972, 48 TC 482; [1972] 1 WLR 1473; [1972] 3 All ER 333.

Incentive scheme wound up and assets distributed among employees

[22.76] In 1963, a company lent £700,000 to trustees to acquire shares in the company and distribute the dividends among employees of the company and its subsidiaries. Following a merger in 1969, the scheme was wound up in 1971, and the balance of the trust fund was distributed among employees and pensioners who had qualified for the scheme. Two of the employees appealed against assessments on the distributions. The HL unanimously upheld the assessments, holding that the terminal payments could not be distinguished from the annual distributions, and were taxable emoluments. *Brumby v Milner; Day v Quick*, HL 1976, 51 TC 583; [1976] STC 534; [1976] 1 WLR 1096; [1976] 3 All ER 636.

Lump sum payment on withdrawal of company car

[22.77] In 1968 a company provided two of its employees with cars. In 1974 it withdrew the cars and offered each employee compensation, approximately equal to their second-hand value. The employees accepted the offers, and the Revenue assessed them on the compensation. The Ch D upheld the assessments, holding that the compensation was 'a perquisite of their employment'. *Bird v Martland*; *Bird v Allen*, Ch D 1982, 56 TC 89; [1982] STC 603.

Compensation to Government employee for loss of trade union rights

[22.78] Until 1983 the staff employed at the Government Communications Headquarters (GCHQ) had the right to join a trade union and to apply to an industrial tribunal under employment protection legislation. In 1983 the Government withdrew these rights. The staff affected were given the option of seeking a transfer elsewhere or of remaining in GCHQ and being paid compensation. An employee who was not a union member, and who opted to remain in GCHQ, received an *ex gratia* payment of £1,000. The Revenue issued an assessment charging tax on this, and she appealed. The CA unanimously dismissed her appeal. Neill LJ observed that the £1,000 'was paid because of the employment and because of the changes in the conditions of employment and for no other reason'. Accordingly it was a taxable emolument. *Hamblett v Godfrey*, CA 1986, 59 TC 694; [1987] STC 60; [1987] 1 WLR 357; [1987] 1 All ER 916.

School fees paid by employer

[22.79] A Hong Kong company paid school fees for the daughter of one of its employees direct to a UK boarding school. He was assessed on the basis that the fees constituted an emolument of his employment. The Privy Council upheld the assessment. Lord Templeman observed that the money was paid at the request of the employee, and was equivalent to money paid to the employee. A sum contracted to be paid by an employer for the benefit of an employee was within the definition of an emolument. *Glynn v Hong Kong Commr of Inland Revenue*, PC 1990, 63 TC 162; [1990] STC 227; [1990] 2 WLR 633.

Football club—avoidance scheme involving Jersey settlement

[22.80] A professional footballer (L) was resident in the UK but domiciled in Ireland. In 1979 his employer agreed to lend £266,000, free of interest, to the trustees of a Jersey settlement for the benefit of L. The trustees invested the £266,000. The Revenue raised assessments on the basis that the amount of the interest deriving from the loan was an emolument of L's employment. He appealed, contending that the income was not an emolument since the loan was repayable on demand. (It was accepted that the loan was not caught by what is now *ITEPA 2003, s 175*, since it was made to the trustees rather than to L.) The Ch D upheld the assessments. If an employer were to lend money to a bank on terms that interest would be paid to the employee until further order, that interest would be taxable as an emolument of the employment. The purpose and effect of the arrangement was to provide the taxpayer with income as long as he remained in his employment. *O'Leary v McKinlay*, Ch D 1990, 63 TC 729; [1991] STC 42.

Fee paid to footballer as inducement to agree to transfer

[22.81] A football club (N) agreed to transfer one of its players to another club (S). N paid the player £75,000. The Revenue issued an assessment charging tax. The player appealed, contending that the first £30,000 was exempt from tax under what is now *ITEPA 2003, s 403*. The HL unanimously rejected this contention and upheld the assessment, holding that an emolument arose from employment if it was provided as a reward or inducement for the employee to remain or become an employee. Inducements by third parties did not have to be referable to the performance of services by the employee under the contract of employment in order to be taxable as earnings within what is now *ITEPA 2003, s 62*. The payment by N was made to induce the taxpayer to become an employee of S. It was therefore an emolument from his employment with S, and was taxable accordingly. *Shilton v Wilmshurst*, HL 1991, 64 TC 78; [1991] STC 88; [1991] 2 WLR 530; [1991] 3 All ER 148.

Ex gratia payment from Department of Economic Development

[22.82] An employee of a government-owned, loss-making company waived his rights under a non-statutory redundancy scheme and accepted new employment in a new 'buy-out' company. He received an ex gratia payment of £5,806, £1,300 of which was paid by the new company with funds provided by the Department of Economic Development (DED), and £4,506 of which was paid directly by the DED. The Revenue included the £5,806 in his 1989/90 assessment. The Special Commissioner held that, while the £1,300 paid by the new company was taxable through being an inducement to enter into employment with that company, the £4,506 paid by the DED was not taxable, since it was neither an emolument from employment nor a benefit. The HL unanimously upheld this decision. The payment from the DED was not an inducement to the taxpayer to enter into an employment, but was compensation for loss of rights under the non-statutory redundancy scheme. A non-statutory redundancy payment did not fall within the definition of an emolument from employment, and a payment for the waiver of the right to such a payment must be treated similarly. *Mairs v Haughey*, HL 1993, 66 TC 273; [1993] STC 569; [1993] 3 WLR 393; [1993] 3 All ER 801. (*Note*. For the Revenue's practice following this decision, see SP 1/94, issued on 17 February 1994.)

Ex gratia lump sum payment from employer

[22.83] A company was suffering financial difficulties, and had failed to make agreed payments into an employees' pension scheme. It paid one of its employees (T) a lump sum of £11,953 as compensation. T did not include this payment on his tax return. HMRC issued an amendment charging tax on it and the First-tier Tribunal dismissed T's appeal, holding that the payment was an emolument of T's employment. *D Taylor v HMRC*, FTT [2011] UKFTT 209 (TC), TC01074. (*Note*. The tribunal allowed T's appeal against a penalty, finding that he had taken professional advice, and had not been negligent.)

Payments to employees on change of company ownership

[22.84] The directors of a trading company informed its employees that they would be made redundant, but would receive a supplementary redundancy payment in addition to their statutory entitlement. The company subsequently changed ownership, continued to trade on a smaller scale, and retained some of its employees. In accordance with a condition in the purchase agreement, the company paid these employees the amounts which had previously been agreed as supplementary redundancy payments. The Revenue issued assessments on the basis that the payments were taxable emoluments. The CS upheld the assessments. Ross LJ held that 'a payment to be made as a supplementary redundancy payment to employees whose services have been terminated is different in character from a payment which is to be made by employers to all existing employees irrespective of whether or not they are made redundant'. Since the payments were made to continuing employees, they could not be regarded as compensation for loss of employment. *Allan v CIR; Cullen v CIR*, CS 1994, 66 TC 681; [1994] STC 943.

[22.85] In an Irish case, a company (E) purchased the shares of another company (G). One of G's major shareholders (K) entered into a service agreement with E. K signed a letter stating that £250,000 of the sale price of his shares was paid as an inducement to enter into the service agreement. K continued to act as a director of one of G's subsidiaries, but did not take up employment with E. The Revenue assessed the £250,000 as an emolument. The SC(I) upheld the assessment, holding that the evidence indicated that E was satisfied to accept K's continued service with the subsidiary as 'compliance with the terms of his service agreement'. *O'Connell v Keleghan*, SC(I) [2001] IESC 42. (*Note.* For another issue in this case, see **71.336** CAPITAL GAINS TAX.)

Payment on transfer of employment

[22.86] A company (S) carried on a drinks distribution business. In 2006 it transferred that business to another company (K). The transfer fell within the *Transfer of Undertakings (Protection of Employment) Regulations 2006*. Some of the employees were concerned because K's pension scheme appeared to be less generous than S's pension scheme. Following negotiations, K made lump sum payments to the transferring employees. HMRC issued a ruling that K was liable to pay national insurance contributions on these payments, and amended the employees' returns on the basis that they were chargeable to income tax. K, and two of the employees, appealed. The First-tier Tribunal dismissed the appeals, and the CA unanimously upheld this decision. Mummery LJ held that the tribunal had been entitled to find that there had been 'a relevant connection or a link between the payments to the employees and their employment'. *Kuehne & Nagel Drinks Logistics Ltd v HMRC (and related appeals)*, CA [2012] EWCA Civ 34; [2012] STC 840.

Payment to manager retained on purchase of plant

[22.87] A company (S) purchased a chemical plant from another company (G). S wished to retain the services of the plant manager. G operated two share option schemes, and the manager was concerned that he would lose the tax advantages afforded to him by these schemes. After negotiations, S agreed to pay him £24,103, being the amount required to compensate him for the lost benefit grossed up at 40%. The Revenue assessed him on this amount. The Special Commissioner upheld the assessment, holding that the payment was 'part and parcel of the arrangements' which induced him to take up employment with S. It was therefore an emolument from his employment. *Teward v CIR*, Sp C [2001] SSCD 36 (Sp C 270).

Partnership business transferred to company—employee receiving shares

[22.88] A partnership had agreed that one of its employees (M) was entitled to 2.5% of the proceeds of the sale or dissolution of the partnership. The partnership transferred its business to a company, and M received shares in the company in accordance with the agreement. He did not declare this as taxable income in his return. The Revenue issued an amendment on the basis that the value of the shares was a taxable emolument. The Special Commissioner upheld the Revenue's amendment and dismissed M's appeal. *McLoughlin v HMRC*, Sp C [2006] SSCD 467 (Sp C 542).

Payment to accountant on taking up employment

[22.89] In 2001 an accountant (M) agreed to take up employment with a merchant bank. He received some 'restricted stock units', which he subsequently (in 2006/07) converted into common stock. HMRC issued an amendment to his 2006/07 tax return to charge income tax on the value of the stock. M appealed. The First-tier Tribunal dismissed his appeal, holding that the restricted stock was an inducement to enter into a contract of employment, which was taxable on its conversion as an emolument of that employment, within *ITEPA 2003, s 62(2)*. *B Macey v HMRC*, FTT [2010] UKFTT 533 (TC), TC00787.

[22.90] See also *Glantre Engineering Ltd v Goodhand*, **42.37** PAY AS YOU EARN.

Garage allowance to salesmen with company car

[22.91] See *Beecham Group Ltd v Fair*, **42.38** PAY AS YOU EARN.

Payments held not to be earnings

Grant from Augmentation Fund

[22.92] The General Commissioners held that a grant to a curate from a Curates' Augmentation Fund, in recognition of his 'faithful previous service', was not taxable under the legislation then in force. The QB upheld their decision. *Turner v Cuxson*, QB 1888, 2 TC 422; 22 QBD 150. (*Note*. Compare the subsequent cases of *Herbert v McQuade*, **22.52** above, and *Poynting v Faulkner*, **22.53** above.)

Gifts on account of poverty

[22.93] The Revenue issued an assessment on a clergyman (T), charging tax on gifts which he had received from church collections. The KB allowed T's appeal, holding that the gifts were not taxable on the grounds that they were not remuneration for services but were given because he was 'poorly off'. *Turton v Cooper*, KB 1905, 5 TC 138. (*Note*. Compare, however, the subsequent CA decision in *Poynting v Faulkner*, **22.53** above.)

Priest living at communal presbytery

[22.94] A priest (D), in charge of a Roman Catholic mission in Glasgow, lived at a communal presbytery house where the household expenses were met out of income of the mission. The Revenue issued an assessment charging tax on these expenses, and D appealed. The CS allowed his appeal. Lord Clyde held that 'the maintenance must be excluded from computation on the ground that it is neither money nor money's worth—that is, it is incapable of conversion into money by the recipient'. *Daly v CIR*, CS 1934, 18 TC 641.

Proceeds of benefit match of county cricketer

[22.95] In 1920 a county cricket club designated a match as a benefit match for one of its players (S). The net proceeds (gate money less expenses) of the match amounted to £939. The club temporarily invested this on S's behalf, and passed them to him in 1923. The Revenue assessed him on the £939 for 1920/21, and he appealed. The Commissioners allowed his appeal and the HL upheld their decision (by a 4-1 majority, Lord Atkinson dissenting), holding that the £939 was 'not remuneration for services, but a personal gift'. *Reed v Seymour*, HL 1927, 11 TC 625; [1927] AC 554. (*Note.* Compare, with regard to repeated collections for league cricketers, *Moorhouse v Dooland*, **22.61** above.)

Professional golfer—betting winnings on matches

[22.96] A professional golfer, employed by a golf club, habitually bet on private games of golf in which he played, and regularly won. The Revenue issued an assessment charging tax on his winnings, and he appealed, contending that they were not taxable. The Special Commissioners allowed his appeal and the KB upheld their decision. Lawrence J held that the winnings 'did not arise from his employment or vocation'. *Down v Compston*, KB 1937, 21 TC 60; [1937] 2 All ER 475.

Compensation for loss on sale of house on transfer

[22.97] A company (ICI) operated a housing scheme for employees whom it transferred from one part of the country to another. Two employees who were transferred made a loss on the sale of their houses, and ICI paid them compensation under the scheme. The Revenue assessed the compensation and the employees appealed. The Ch D allowed the appeals and the HL unanimously upheld their decision, holding that the compensation was not a taxable emolument. Lord Radcliffe observed that the test to be applied was 'contained in the statutory requirement that the payment, if it is to be the subject of assessment, must arise "from" the office or employment'. Although it was 'not sufficient to render a payment assessable that an employee would not have received it unless he had been an employee, it is assessable if it has been paid to him in return for acting as or being an employee'. Here the payment was not paid to the employee as wages, but in respect of his personal situation as a houseowner. *Hochstrasser v Mayes*; *Jennings v Kinder*, HL 1959, 38 TC 673; [1960] AC 376; [1959] 3 All ER 817. (*Notes.* (1) Viscount Simonds and Lord Cohen expressed the view that the case turned 'upon whether the fact of employment is the *causa causans* or only the *sine qua non*'. However, this reasoning was strongly criticised by Lord Simon of Glaisdale in the subsequent case of *Brumby v Milner*, **22.76** above. Lord Simon observed that the attempt to draw a distinction between a '*causa causans*' and a '*causa sine qua non*' had been disapproved by Lord Wright in *Smith Hogg & Co Ltd v Black Sea & Baltic General Insurance Co Ltd*, HL [1940] AC 997; [1940] 3 All ER 405, and had 'been generally abandoned'; and considered that the relevant issue should not 'be determined by outmoded and ambiguous concepts of causation couched in Latin'. (2) For HMRC's interpretation of this decision, see Employment Income Manual, para EIM00750.)

Signing-on fee to rugby footballer

[22.98] Three rugby football players received signing-on fees on joining Rugby League clubs as professionals. The Revenue issued assessments charging tax on them, and they appealed. The Special Commissioners allowed the appeals, holding that the payments were not taxable, since they were not in respect of services to be rendered to the players' new clubs, but were compensation for the loss of amateur status and of their rights to participate in Rugby Union (which was then restricted to amateurs) and amateur athletics. The CA unanimously upheld this decision. *Jarrold v Boustead (and related appeals)*, CA 1964, 41 TC 701; [1964] 1 WLR 1357; [1964] 3 All ER 76. (*Note*. For a subsequent case in which this decision was distinguished, see *Riley v Coglan*, 22.74 above.)

Electricity board—voluntary payment to engineer

[22.99] In 1962 the UK Atomic Energy Authority seconded one of its employees (M) to an electricity board to help with the construction of a nuclear power station. In July 1964 M left the UKAEA and became an employee of the board. In December 1964 the board paid him £1,000, stating that this was a gift to mark their appreciation of his work during his secondment. The Revenue issued an assessment charging tax on this, and he appealed. The General Commissioners allowed his appeal, holding that the payment was a gift or testimonial and was not a taxable emolument. The CS unanimously upheld their decision as one of fact. *CIR v Morris*, CS 1967, 44 TC 685. (*Note*. See now *ITEPA 2003, s 62(2)(b)*. It is arguable that the payment would now be taxable as a 'gratuity'. For HMRC's approach to the legislation, see Employment Income Manual, para EIM01460.)

Payment to bank employee on passing examination

[22.100] A bank expected its male clerks to take the examinations of the Institute of Bankers, and made cash awards to those who passed. The Revenue issued an assessment charging tax on one of the awards, and the employee appealed. The Commissioners allowed his appeal, holding that the awards were not remuneration for services and were not taxable. The Ch D upheld their decision as one of fact. *Ball v Johnson*, Ch D 1971, 47 TC 155.

Gift and prize awarded to footballer

[22.101] The Football Association paid a bonus of £1,000 to each of the 'squad' of 22 players from which the English team in the 1966 World Cup was selected. The team captain (M) also received £750 from a manufacturing company as an unsolicited prize for being adjudged the best player. The Revenue assessed these payments, and M appealed. The Ch D allowed his appeal. Brightman J held that the payments had 'the quality of a testimonial or accolade rather than the quality of remuneration for services rendered', and were not taxable. *Moore v Griffiths (and related appeal)*, Ch D 1972, 48 TC

338; [1972] 1 WLR 1024; [1972] 3 All ER 399. (*Note.* See now the note following *CIR v Morris*, **22.99** above.)

Transfer of cottage to company director

[22.102] An individual (B) obtained planning permission to construct three cottages. He arranged for a local building company (H) to carry out the work. The cottages were built during 2004. Under the agreement, B retained one of the cottages himself, transferred one of the other cottages to H, and transferred the third cottage to H's controlling director (T). T, who had separated from his wife shortly beforehand, lived in the cottage, but subsequently (in 2006) sold it to H. HMRC issued an amendment to T's self-assessment for 2004/05, treating the value of the cottage as an emolument of his employment with H. T appealed, contending that he had contributed personally to the cost of the construction, and that the transfer of the cottage was consideration for his financial contribution, rather than an emolument of his employment. The First-tier Tribunal accepted this contention and allowed his appeal, finding that T had 'contributed to the company one half of the development costs, including direct costs and a proportion of overheads applicable to the project, amounting to £105,000, from his private resources'. *DJ Thresh v HMRC*, FTT [2010] UKFTT 29 (TC), TC00343.

Payment of $2,000,000 to company director

[22.103] In 1985 a British citizen (C) became marketing director of a UK subsidiary of an American company (R), which was controlled by a wealthy married couple. The couple subsequently divorced, and the wife (D) acquired control of R. In 1994 C resigned his directorship, without receiving any compensation. He rejoined R in 1997, after D had sold her shares to another company (H). In 1998 D paid C $2,000,000. C did not declare this on his tax return. Subsequently, following an enquiry into undeclared bank interest, HMRC formed the opinion that the $2,000,000 had been an emolument from C's employment with R. C appealed, contending that it had been a personal gift from D, and was not taxable. The First-tier Tribunal accepted this contention and allowed the appeal. Judge Nowlan observed that D had made a profit of about $600,000,000 from the sale of her shares in R, and had chosen 'to make generous gratuitous payments to various people' who had supported her after her divorce and had contributed to R's success. He commented that 'if the lord of the manor is particularly fond of one of the household servants, and makes some gift for that reason, the receipts of this nature may very well not be emoluments'. The payment was wholly unexpected, and was completely disproportionate to C's salary. Accordingly it had not been an emolument. *C Collins v HMRC*, FTT [2012] UKFTT 411 (TC), TC02088.

Taxable Benefits: Expenses payments (ITEPA 2003, ss 70–72)

Attendance allowance to director

[22.104] A director of a benevolent fund received an allowance for attending directors' meetings. In 1935/36 he attended 74 such meetings. The Revenue assessed him on the allowance (allowing a 25% deduction for expenses), and he appealed. The Special Commissioners dismissed his appeal, and the KB upheld their decision. Lawrence J held that the director 'was a holder of an office of profit'. *Dingley v McNulty*, KB 1937, 21 TC 152.

Meals allowance when working abnormal hours

[22.105] A local government officer (D) was required to attend council meetings in the evenings. He received no additional remuneration for this, but could claim flat-rate allowances in respect of evening meals. The Revenue issued an assessment on the allowances. D appealed, contending firstly that the allowances were not taxable, and alternatively that the amount he actually spent on such meals should be allowed as a deduction. The Ch D rejected these contentions and upheld the assessment. Wynn-Parry J observed that it was accepted that Dwas not entitled to a deduction for any payment he made for lunch. He held that 'having regard to the term of his employment that when required he must stay late', there was no distinction 'between the nature of the interval for lunch and the interval for tea or the interval for dinner'. *Sanderson v Durbidge*, Ch D 1955, 36 TC 239; [1955] 1 WLR 1087; [1955] 3 All ER 154.

Travelling and subsistence allowances to MEPs

[22.106] See *Lord Bruce of Donington v Aspden*, 25.150 EUROPEAN LAW.

Taxable Benefits: Vouchers and credit-tokens (ITEPA 2003, ss 73–96)

[22.107] A company habitually gave £10 vouchers to its employees and pensioners at Christmas to be spent at shops of their choice. The Revenue issued assessments charging tax on the vouchers. Two of the employees appealed, contending that the vouchers were personal gifts and were not taxable under the legislation then in force. The Special Commissioners rejected this contention and dismissed their appeals, holding that 'the vouchers were made available in return for services rather than as gifts not constituting a reward for services'. The HL unanimously upheld this decision, holding that the £10 was a taxable emolument which arose from the employment. Lord Reid observed that 'this is a case of gifts regularly made by the employer'. Lord Morris of Borth-y-Gest observed that 'the vouchers were distributed by the employers in their capacity as employers and because they were employers: they were received by the employees in their capacity as employees and because they were employees'. *Laidler v Perry; Morgan v Perry*, HL 1965, 42 TC 351; [1966] AC 16; [1965] 2 All ER 121.

Taxable Benefits: Living accommodation (ITEPA 2003, ss 97–113)

Pre-1977 legislation

NOTE

The provisions of *ITEPA 2003, ss 97–113* originally derive from *FA 1977, ss 33, 33A*. The cases noted at **22.108** to **22.115** below relate to periods before the introduction of these provisions, but may still be relevant as illustrating points of general principle.

Deduction from salary in respect of board and lodging

[22.108] A married couple were employed by an asylum, which provided them with board, lodging, washing and uniform, for which certain amounts were deducted from their gross salaries. The Revenue issued assessments charging tax on the gross salaries. The couple appealed, contending that they should only be taxed on the net pay which they actually received. The KB rejected this contention and upheld the assessments. *Cordy v Gordon*, KB 1925, 9 TC 304; [1925] 2 KB 276.

[22.109] The decision in *Cordy v Gordon*, **22.108** above, was unanimously approved by the CA in the similar subsequent case of *Machon v McLoughlin*, CA 1926, 11 TC 83.

Company paying bills relating to house owned by director

[22.110] A company's managing director and controlling shareholder arranged for the company to pay his household rates, gas and electricity bills, and other household expenses. The Revenue assessed him on the amounts which the company paid. The KB upheld the assessment. Finlay J held that the payments were 'profits of his office of Managing Director'. *Nicoll v Austin*, KB 1935, 19 TC 531.

Lodging allowances to army personnel

[22.111] Two soldiers were allotted civilian billets in lieu of barracks accommodation, and were paid lodging allowances. The Revenue issued assessments charging tax on the lodging allowances, and the soldiers appealed. The Ch D upheld the assessments. Wynn-Parry J held that the allowances were taxable income, and that the actual cost of the soldiers' lodgings could not be allowed as a deduction. *Nagley v Spilsbury*; *Evans v Richardson*, Ch D 1957, 37 TC 178.

Company paying employee's rent

[22.112] In an Irish case, a company arranged with a local Council that the Council would provide houses to be let to the company's employees. The company paid the rent. One of the employees appealed against assessments in which the rent paid for him was treated as part of his emoluments. The HC(I) upheld the assessments. *Connolly v McNamara*, HC(I) 1960, 3 ITC 341.

Flat provided at reduced rent

[22.113] A company required a senior employee to move from Hertfordshire to London. It obtained a London flat for him at a rent of £500 pa, into which he and his family moved, paying the company a rent of £150 pa. The Revenue issued an assessment charging tax on the difference of £350. The Ch D upheld the assessment, holding that the £350 pa was a taxable emolument and was not allowable as a deduction. *McKie v Warner*, Ch D 1961, 40 TC 65; [1961] 1 WLR 1230; [1961] 3 All ER 348.

Repairs paid for by employer

[22.114] The managing director of a company (G) lived in a house which G owned. He paid rent to G, which paid for certain repairs to the house. The Revenue issued assessments charging tax on these amounts, and the director appealed. The QB(NI) upheld the assessments. *Doyle v Davison*, QB(NI) 1961, 40 TC 140.

Fuel and gardener's services paid for by employer

[22.115] A company which owned a paper mill required a manager (B) to live in a house, near to the mill, which it provided. The company paid for coal and electricity supplied to the house, and for a gardener. The Revenue issued assessments charging tax on these payments, and B appealed. The CA unanimously upheld the assessments. Pearson LJ held that the payments were taxable emoluments because they were made in connection with the provision of 'domestic or other services'. Although the manager was required to live in the house, the payments did not qualify as allowable deductions because they were made 'for the benefit of the persons living in the house' and not 'for the purpose of maintaining the fabric'. *Butter v Bennett*, CA 1962, 40 TC 402; [1963] Ch 185; [1962] 2 All ER 204.

Current legislation

NOTE

The provisions of *ITEPA 2003, ss 97–113* originally derive from *FA 1977, ss 33, 33A*.

Whether ITEPA 2003, s 99 applicable

[22.116] A nursery foreman (V) was provided with a bungalow, in which he lived rent-free. The Revenue assessed him in respect of the benefit of free accommodation. He appealed, contending that the accommodation was provided for the performance of his duties, so that the effect of what is now *ITEPA 2003, s 99* was that the benefit was not taxable. The Special Commissioners rejected this contention and dismissed his appeal, and the Ch D upheld their decision. Vinelott J held that on the evidence, V's employment was not an employment in which it was 'customary for employers to provide living accommodation' and it was not 'necessary for the proper performance of the duties' of his employment that he should live in the particular accommodation. The exceptions in *s 99* therefore did not apply. *Vertigan v Brady*, Ch D 1988, 60 TC 624; [1988] STC 91.

Farming company—directors' accommodation

[22.117] A married couple were directors of a farming company (C). They were assessed on the value of living accommodation and other benefits which C provided. They appealed, contending firstly that they had effectively paid rent and reimbursed other expenses by the provision of their services to C in managing the farm and certain investments, and alternatively that the expenses had been reimbursed by profits accruing to C from the investment of funds which they had lent to it. The Special Commissioner rejected these contentions and dismissed their appeals, and the Ch D upheld this decision. Warner J held that 'the provision of services in exchange for the provision of benefits in kind cannot be either the payment of rent or a making good of the cost to the company of providing the benefits in kind'. *Stones v Hall*, Ch D 1988, 60 TC 738; [1989] STC 138.

Company arranging funerals—accommodation for controlling director

[22.118] A company arranged funerals. Its controlling director was a married woman (C). Her husband was employed by the company as the funeral manager. They lived in residential accommodation belonging to the company and forming part of its business premises. HMRC issued amendments to C's self-assessments, charging tax on the accommodation (and on other benefits such as the provision of cars and petrol, and the payment of utility and telephone bills). C appealed. The General Commissioners reviewed the evidence in detail and upheld the amendments in principle, holding that the provision of living accommodation for C was a taxable benefit, as were 25% of the utilities bills, 20% of the landline telephone bills and 10% of the mobile telephone bills. The Ch D and CA upheld their decision. Patten LJ observed that the effect of C's shareholding was that she had a 'material interest in the company', and held that 'there is no detectable error of law in the reasoning of the General Commissioners'. *Collings v HMRC*, CA [2010] EWCA Civ 605.

'Shadow' director—liability to tax

[22.119] In the case noted at 51.8 REVENUE PROSECUTIONS, the HL held that a 'shadow director' was liable to tax on benefits including the free provision of living accommodation. Lord Hutton held that it was Parliament's intention that 'accommodation and benefits in kind received by a shadow director should be taxed in the same way as those received by a director'. The effect of what is now *ITEPA 2003, s 67(1)*was that 'a shadow director is taken to be a director'. Accordingly, 'it follows that living accommodation and benefits received by him should be treated as emoluments'. *R v Allen*, HL 2001, 74 TC 263; [2001] STC 1537; [2001] UKHL 45; [2001] 4 All ER 768.

Taxable Benefits: Cars, vans, etc. (ITEPA 2003, ss 114–172)

Deductions from pay for use of company car

[22.120] A company introduced a scheme whereby it allowed its employees the use of a car. It reduced the pay of such employees by a specified amount. The Revenue assessed the employees on the gross pay. One of them (B) appealed, contending that he should only be assessed on his net pay. The HL unanimously rejected this contention and upheld the assessment. Lord Morris of Borth-y-Gest held that the 'reduction' was in reality an agreed deduction from B's gross pay, rather than a reduction in his gross pay, and that 'on a true interpretation of the contractual arrangements the position was that the monetary wage to which (B) was entitled remained unaltered'. (Lord Reid found in favour of the Revenue on the alternative ground that B's right to use the car was a perquisite which he could have turned into money by surrendering it, and was therefore taxable.) *Heaton v Bell*, HL 1969, 46 TC 211; [1970] AC 728; [1969] 2 All ER 70.

Car benefits—whether taxable emoluments

[22.121] An accountant was provided by his employers with cars for his private use. He appealed against assessments on him for 1974/75 to 1977/78, which included amounts under the benefits legislation (see now *ITEPA 2003, s 114 et seq*). The Special Commissioners dismissed his appeal and the Ch D upheld their decision. *Wilson v Alexander*, Ch D [1986] STC 365.

Elddis Autostratus motorhome—whether a 'car'

[22.122] A company (C) purchased a Elddis Autostratus motorhome for the use of its managing director (M). The Revenue issued an amendment to M's self-assessment, requiring him to pay income tax on the car and car fuel benefit. They also issued a ruling that C was required to pay Class 1A national insurance contributions. C and M appealed, contending that the motorhome was not a 'car' for the purposes of the legislation. The Special Commissioner rejected this contention and dismissed the appeals, and the Ch D upheld this decision. Park J held that the motorhome was 'a mechanically propelled road vehicle' and was within the statutory definition of a 'car'. *Morris v HMRC; County Pharmacy Ltd v HMRC*; Ch D [2006] STC 1593; [2006] EWHC 1560 (Ch).

Land Rover Discovery—whether a 'car'

[22.123] A company provided a specially modified Land Rover Discovery for the use of one of its employees. He appealed against his notice of coding, contending that the result of the modifications was that the vehicle should be treated as a 'goods vehicle' within *ITEPA 2003, s 115(2)* and was not a car. The First-tier Tribunal rejected this contention and dismissed his appeal. *T Jones v HMRC*, FTT [2012] UKFTT 265 (TC), TC01958.

Fire officer's car equipped with flashing light and emergency equipment

[22.124] See *Gurney v Richards*, 22.172 below.

Joint ownership of cars—taxable benefit

[22.125] In August 1997 a company (H) purchased a second-hand Ferrari for £37,995. It sold a 5% share in the car to one of its directors (V) for £1,889. In December 1998 it sold the remaining 95% of the Ferrari to V for £20,000. In the same month it purchased a second-hand BMW for £37,500, and sold a 5% share in the BMW to V for £1,875. In 2002 it sold the remaining 95% of the BMW to V. V completed his tax returns on the basis that the joint ownership of the cars meant that the benefit provisions of what is now *ITEPA 2003, s 114 et seq* did not apply, and that he was chargeable under the more favourable provisions of what is now *ITEPA 2003, s 201 et seq*. The Revenue issued amendments to his self-assessments, charging tax under *s 114 et seq*. The Ch D upheld the amendments. Pumfrey J held that 'the words "made available (without any transfer of the property in it)" are not to be construed in a manner which has the result that the conferring of any interest upon the employee sufficient to give the employee an independent right to possess and use the asset is sufficient to prevent the car from being "made available"'. Furthermore, it was clear that *s 114* 'establishes a special regime for motor cars and that that regime should be applied as the words of the section can reasonably bear a meaning that encompasses the present case'. *Christensen v Vasili*, Ch D 2004, 76 TC 116; [2004] STC 935; [2004] EWHC 476 (Ch).

[22.126] The Ch D decision in *Christensen v Vasili*, **22.125** above, was applied in the similar subsequent case of *Samson Publishing Ltd v HMRC (and related appeals)*, FTT [2010] UKFTT 489 (TC), TC00749.

Cars made available to directors—whether within ITEPA 2003, s 114

[22.127] A company leased cars to two of its directors. HMRC issued assessments charging tax under *ITEPA 2003, s 114*. The directors appealed, contending that because they were charged for the use of the cars, the leases should not be treated as falling within *s 114(1)(a)*. The First-tier Tribunal rejected this contention and dismissed the appeals. The Tribunal also held that tax was chargeable on payments of 'mileage allowances' to the directors, observing that the cars were company vehicles within *ITEPA, s 236(2)*, so that the exemption in *s 229* did not apply. *A Whitby v HMRC (and related appeal)*, FTT [2009] UKFTT 311 (TC), TC00255.

[22.128] A group of companies leased cars to various employees. HMRC issued assessments charging tax under *ITEPA 2003, s 114*. The Upper Tribunal held that the leases were at arm's length and were excluded from *s 114* by virtue of *s 114(3) as originally enacted*. Rose J expressed the view that 'fair bargains are excluded from the regime for taxing benefits conferred on employees because there is no benefit which is properly subject to tax'. *HMRC v Apollo Fuels Ltd*, UT [2014] UKUT 95 (TCC); [2014] STC 1559. (*Note*. *ITEPA 2003, s 114(3)* has subsequently been repealed by *FA 2014, s 23*, with effect from 6 April 2014.)

[22.129] A family company (F) purchased two cars from a finance company under a hire-purchase agreement, and made them available to its controlling directors. HMRC issued a ruling that income tax was chargeable under *ITEPA 2003, s 114*. The First-tier Tribunal dismissed F's appeal. *Frank Hudson Transport Ltd v HMRC*, FTT [2010] UKFTT 503 (TC), TC00758. (*Note*. For another issue in this case, see **22.175** below.)

[22.130] A similar decision was reached in *V Baldorino v HMRC*, FTT [2012] UKFTT 70 (TC), TC01766.

[22.131] Two relatives (D and P) were the directors of a family company (L). They were also members, along with D's wife and son, of a partnership (C) which provided administrative services to L. C provided the partners with cars. HMRC issued assessments on the basis that the provision of these cars was a taxable benefit of the directors, within *ITEPA 2003, s 114*. L, and the directors and partners, appealed, contending that any benefit was received because of the partnership, and could not be attributed to the directorships which D and P held. The First-tier Tribunal rejected this contention and dismissed the appeals. Judge Sadler observed that the question was 'in what circumstances a car is to be regarded as made available by reason of a person's employment where it is made available to that person (or a member of his family) not by the employer but by a third party'. On the evidence, C 'would not have existed, commercially, but for the company, its only customer. There was no commercial rationale for C to provide cars to its partners, or for L to pay C 'an amount sufficient to enable (C) to recoup the capital costs of the cars and the car fuel it provided to its partners'. Accordingly, 'the cars in question were made available, and the car fuel benefit provided, to each of the individual appellants' by reason of the employment of D and P. *DJ Cooper v HMRC (and related appeals)*, FTT [2012] UKFTT 439 (TC), TC02120.

ITEPA 2003, s 116—whether car made available to director

[22.132] In 1998 a company (H) which carried on an antiques business purchased a Ferrari, which it sold in 2005. HMRC issued an assessment charging tax on the basis that the car had been made available to H's principal director (G). G appealed, contending that the Ferrari had been purchased for advertising purposes, and had not been made available to him, as he had other cars which he used for his private motoring. The First-tier Tribunal accepted G's evidence and allowed his appeal. *M Golding v HMRC*, FTT [2011] UKFTT 232 (TC), TC01097. (*Note*. HMRC did not appeal against this decision, but have stated that they consider that it 'does not set any precedent of any kind': see Taxation, 22 September 2011, p 27.)

ITEPA 2003, s 117—whether car available by reason of employment

[22.133] The principal director (G) of a company (P) separated from his wife (S) in 2009. S had previously been employed by P, and provided with a car. Following the separation she ceased to work for P but continued to be paid a salary of £12000 pa, and retained the car. HMRC issued an assessment on the basis that the car had been provided by virtue of her employment with P. S appealed, contending that the car had been provided for her by G under a court order requiring him to pay her maintenance. The First-tier Tribunal accepted this contention and allowed her appeal. Judge Connell held that the court order showed 'that the maintenance package agreed between (S) and (G) included the provision by him, not the company, of a vehicle, and that he would pay for the running costs of the vehicle'. He observed that 'maintenance payments under agreements or court orders made in the EU Member States since 15 March 1988 are generally outside the UK system'. He concluded that the use of the car was a benefit taxable on G, rather than on S. *Mrs S Gibson v HMRC*, FTT [2014] UKFTT 935 (TC), TC04048.

ITEPA 2003, s 118—whether car available for private use

[22.134] The director of a plant hire company (M) was responsible for the maintenance of M's plant at its premises and at various sites. He was required to be on call at any time and was sometimes called from his home to a site outside his normal working hours. M provided him with a car, and told him that he was 'not expected' to use it for private purposes. The Revenue assessed him on the cash equivalent of the benefit, and he appealed, contending that M required him to take the car home each night because of the risk of vandalism, and that he did not use the car privately. The Commissioners accepted his evidence and allowed his appeal, holding that the car had not been made available for his private use. The Ch D upheld their decision. Vinelott J held that the director's home was 'his working base' and, when travelling from home to M's premises or to a site, he was travelling in the performance of his duties. The evidence was sufficient to support the inference that the employer prohibited private use. *Gilbert v Hemsley*, Ch D 1981, 55 TC 419; [1981] STC 703.

ITEPA 2003, s 144—deduction for payments for private use

[22.135] An employee (Q) was provided with a car by his employer, but was required to pay for it. The Revenue issued assessments including car benefit, and Q appealed, contending that the payments which he made to insure the car should be deducted in computing the car benefit. The CS rejected this contention and upheld the assessments, holding that only payments made for the private use of a car could be deducted in computing the car benefit. The payments here were made for the insurance of the vehicle, rather than for the use of it. *CIR v Quigley*, CS 1995, 67 TC 535; [1995] STC 931.

[22.136] A company provided one of its directors with a car. He appealed against a charge to car benefit, contending that he had repaid the cost of using the car, as required by *ITEPA 2003, s 144(1)*. The First-tier Tribunal accepted his contention and allowed his appeal. Judge Geraint Jones specifically rejected HMRC's contention that *s 144* required that the sum that the employee was required to pay for any tax year in question must be paid within that tax year. He observed that the words 'the tax year in question' only appeared in *s 144(1)(a)* and did not also appear in *s 144(1)(b)*, so that a relevant payment was deductible even if it was made after the end of the tax year in question. *P Marshall v HMRC*, FTT [2013] UKFTT 46 (TC), TC02466.

ITEPA 2003, s 149—car fuel

[22.137] Two employees were provided with cars by their employers, and were allowed to use the cars for private motoring. They were also allowed to purchase petrol for his private motoring with a credit card provided by their employers. The Revenue issued assessments charging tax on the cost of the petrol to the employer The Ch D upheld the assessments. Scott J held that the employees became liable to pay for the petrol when it was put into their cars, and the employer's payment of the amounts due was a taxable emolument. *Richardson v Worrall; Westall v McDonald*, Ch D 1985, 58 TC 642; [1985] STC 693.

[22.138] A company director (L) was provided with a Porsche by his employer. HMRC issued amendments to his self-assessments, charging tax on car fuel benefit under *ITEPA 2003, s 149*. The First-tier Tribunal dismissed L's appeal, finding that he had paid for the fuel for the car for by the use of a company credit card and that he had not produced any records indicating that he had reimbursed the company for the cost of the fuel. *JB Little v HMRC*, FTT [2011] UKFTT 324 (TC), TC01184.

ITEPA 2003, s 151—fuel for private use reimbursed retrospectively

[22.139] A company provided two of its employees with cars, which it allowed them to use for private motoring. The employees submitted expenses claims for fuel, which the company paid. The Revenue discovered that the employees had reclaimed fuel for private motoring as well as for business mileage, and issued assessments charging tax on this. In 2005 the company asked the employees to repay the amounts which they had claimed for private motoring in 2002/3 and 2003/4. The employees did so, and the company and employees appealed against the assessments, contending that the effect of *ITEPA 2003, s 151* was that the assessments should be withdrawn. The Special Commissioner dismissed the appeals, observing that *s 151* required that the employee should repay the cost of providing the fuel 'in the tax year in question'. The employees here had not reimbursed the cost of the fuel until after the end of the tax year in question, so there were no grounds for discharging the assessments. *Impact Foiling Ltd v HMRC (and related appeals)*, Sp C [2006] SSCD 764 (Sp C 562).

ITEPA 2003, s 167—pooled cars

[22.140] HMRC issued a ruling that a company was required to pay Class 1A national insurance contributions in respect of two cars. The company appealed, contending that the cars were 'pooled cars', within *ITEPA 2003, s 167*. The First-tier Tribunal accepted this contention and allowed the appeal. The tribunal found that 'the cars were from time to time taken home overnight by employees particularly where they required these to start the next working day making a journey which would make more sense to start from their home rather than from the parking area for the cars'. However the tribunal held that this did not prevent the cars from qualifying as 'pooled cars', since they were normally kept at the company's premises and 'met the condition that pooled cars are not normally kept overnight on or near the residence of any of their employees'. *Industrial Doors (Scotland) Ltd v HMRC*, FTT [2010] UKFTT 282 (TC), TC00571.

[22.141] A company (N), which was controlled by a married couple, carried on a business of training hairdressers. The couple's home was N's registered office, and the husband (E) acted as the company secretary. HMRC issued a ruling that N was required to pay Class 1A national insurance contributions in respect of a car which E used. N appealed, contending that the car qualified as a pooled car, since it was also used by other employees and was not used privately, and that its place of business was its registered office, which was E's permanent workplace as well as his home. The First-tier Tribunal accepted N's evidence and allowed the appeal. *New Image Training Ltd v HMRC*, FTT [2012] UKFTT 469 (TC), TC02146.

[22.142] HMRC formed the opinion that a company had failed to declare car benefit in respect of two cars used by a company's managing director. They issued discovery assessments, and the director appealed, contending that the cars qualified as 'pooled cars', within *ITEPA 2003, s 167*. Judge Blewitt accepted the director's evidence and allowed his appeal. *GH Tahmosybayat v HMRC*, FTT [2014] UKFTT 571 (TC), TC03696. (*Note*. The case was heard with *Isocom Ltd v HMRC*, **29.6** FURTHER ASSESSMENTS: LOSS OF TAX.)

[22.143] HMRC issued a ruling that a company which operated a restaurant was required to pay Class 1A national insurance contributions in respect of a Jaguar car which was owned by the company and used by its controlling director (Y). The company appealed, contending that the car should be treated as a 'pooled car', within *ITEPA 2003, s 167*. The First-tier Tribunal rejected this contention and dismissed the appeal, finding that there was no evidence 'that the car had actually been driven by any person other than (Y)', so that the condition of *s 167(3)(a)* was not satisfied. The tribunal observed that 'given the nature of the car it was likely that there was some private use of it by (Y)' and that it appeared that the car was frequently kept overnight at Y's home, so that *s 167(3)(d)* was also not satisfied. *Yum Yum Ltd v HMRC*, FTT [2010] UKFTT 331 (TC), TC00616.

[22.144] A Land Rover, which was made available to a single employee, was held not to be a 'pooled car' in *P Erediauwa v HMRC*, FTT [2010] UKFTT 630 (TC), TC00869.

[22.145] A Mercedes Benz, which was made available to a company director, was held not to be a 'pooled car' in *Mrs A Ryan-Munden v HMRC*, FTT [2011] UKFTT 12 (TC), TC00889.

[22.146] A Porsche, which was made available to a company director, was held not to be a 'pooled car' in *D Munden v HMRC*, FTT [2013] UKFTT 427 (TC), TC02821.

[22.147] A retail partnership made an Astra car available for two of its employees, who were also the daughter and son-in-law of one of the partners. HMRC issued an assessment charging national insurance contributions, and imposing penalties. The partnership appealed, contending that the Astra should be treated as a pooled car, within *ITEPA 2003, s 167*. The First-tier Tribunal rejected this contention and dismissed the appeal. *Ahmed Brothers (t/a First Stop 2 Shop) v HMRC*, FTT [2012] UKFTT 545 (TC), TC02222.

[22.148] Similar decisions were reached in *McKenna Demolition Ltd v HMRC (and related appeal)*, 73.81 NATIONAL INSURANCE CONTRIBUTIONS; *Autowest Ltd v HMRC*, 73.82 NATIONAL INSURANCE CONTRIBUTIONS; *Time For Group Ltd v HMRC*, 73.82 NATIONAL INSURANCE CONTRIBUTIONS, and *Vinyl Designs Ltd v HMRC*, 73.82 NATIONAL INSURANCE CONTRIBUTIONS.

ITEPA 2003, s 169

[22.149] See *S Barnard Ltd v HMRC*, 73.84 NATIONAL INSURANCE CONTRIBUTIONS.

Taxable Benefits: Loans (ITEPA 2003, ss 173–191)

Loan to employee subsequently waived

[22.150] An assistant health visitor (G), employed by a county council, took a nine-month full-time course for training as a health visitor. The council lent her £637, paid in monthly instalments during the course, under an agreement whereby the obligation to return the loan would be waived if she worked for the council as a health visitor for 18 months after completing the course. She completed the course in July 1966, and continued to work as a health visitor for the authority until January 1968, when the loan was duly waived. The Revenue assessed the amount (on her husband in accordance with the legislation then in force). He appealed, contending that the loan was scholarship income within what is now *ITTOIA 2005, s 776* and was not a taxable emolument. The Ch D rejected this contention and upheld the assessment.

Plowman J held that the loan was not scholarship income, but was 'a reward for past services', and that the discharge of the obligation to repay it was a taxable emolument of G's employment for 1967/68. *Clayton v Gothorp*, Ch D 1971, 47 TC 168; [1971] 1 WLR 999; [1971] 2 All ER 1311.

Advance of salary on transfer of place of employment

[22.151] A civil servant (T) was required by his employers to move from Wigan to London. He received an advance of salary of £8,440, on which no interest was payable. The advance was repayable on demand in certain circumstances, but in fact was repaid by monthly instalments over a ten-year period. T appealed against an assessment on it, contending that the advance was not a loan for the purposes of what is now *ITEPA 2003, s 173*, as he derived no benefit from it. The Ch D rejected this contention and upheld the assessment. Peter Gibson J held that the true legal nature of the advance was a loan to T by his employer. The legislation did not require the finding of any advantage to T from the loan. *Williams v Todd*, Ch D 1988, 60 TC 727; [1988] STC 676.

Interest-free loan to assist employee to purchase house

[22.152] A company (S) made an interest-free payment of £10,200 to an employee (H) who had been transferred from Newark to Kent, to help him to buy a suitable house in Kent. It was agreed that the loan would be secured by a charge on the house and would be repayable if the property were sold or if H left S. It was also agreed that, when the charge was called in, S would receive the same proportion of the sale price or valuation as the loan bore to the purchase price. The Revenue issued an assessment for 1992/93 on the basis that the loan was within what is now *ITEPA 2003, s 173*. H appealed, contending that the loan was not taxable because the amount he would have to repay to S would not necessarily be the same as the £10,200 which S had paid. The Special Commissioner rejected this contention and dismissed the appeal. The payment to H was a loan, and could not be transmuted into something other than a loan merely because it could and would be discharged on the occurrence of one of two specific events by the tender of an amount which might be more or less than the amount borrowed. *Harvey v Williams*, Sp C [1995] SSCD 329 (Sp C 49).

[22.153] A similar decision was reached in a subsequent appeal by the same employee against assessments for 1993/94 to 1995/96. *Harvey v Williams (No 2)*, Sp C [1998] SSCD 215 (Sp C 168).

Beneficial loan from service company

[22.154] The expenses of an estate agency were paid by a service company, of which the estate agent (G) was the controlling director. The Revenue issued assessments charging tax in respect of these payments. G appealed, contending that the service fees did not fall due for payment until such time as the company's accountants or auditors notified the company and the director of the final annual calculation of the charge. The Special Commissioner rejected this contention, finding that 'the amount of the fee was initially and contractually agreed to be the amount of the relevant costs plus a mark-up of approximately one-ninth of the relevant costs'. The effect of the arrangements was that the service company was extending credit to G, and this credit was within the scope of what is now *ITEPA 2003, s 173(2)*. Accordingly, liability arose in respect of expenditure by the service company 'made in or towards the performance of the services to be provided to the business'. The liability was not affected by the fact that, during the period covered by the assessments, G and the company entered into a limited partnership agreement. The Ch D dismissed the director's appeal against this decision. Pumfrey J held that the words 'any form of credit' in *s 173(2)*should be construed widely and given their ordinary and natural meaning. On the evidence, the company's function 'was merely to provide an intermediary for the purpose of paying all the usual outgoings of the business', and accordingly G had received credit. With regard to the date at which the credit arose, Pumfrey J upheld the Revenue's contention that credit was extended from day to day. There were no grounds for treating the credit as being deferred until the date when the service company actually paid a particular supplier. *Grant v Watton (and cross-appeal) (aka Gold v HM Inspector of Taxes)*, Ch D 1999, 71 TC 333; [1999] STC 330. (*Note*. An appeal by the company against assessments under what is now *CTA 2010, s 455* was also dismissed—see **11.12** CLOSE COMPANIES.)

Bank employee receiving mortgage

[22.155] An employee of a major bank purchased a house with the aid of a mortgage from his employer, at a rate not available to the general public. HMRC issued a ruling that tax was due under *ITEPA 2003, ss 174, 175*. The employee appealed, contending that the 'official rate' applied by *s 175* was too high. The First-tier Tribunal dismissed his appeal. Judge Geraint Jones held that 'the appellant is caught in a situation where the amount of his benefit is calculated by reference to inflexible statutory rules, rather than by reference to the reality of the benefit actually obtained'. *J Flanagan v HMRC*, FTT [2012] UKFTT 484 (TC), TC02161.

[22.156] The decision in *Flanagan v HMRC*, **22.155** above, was approved and applied in the similar subsequent case of *PD Curtis v HMRC*, FTT [2014] UKFTT 165 (TC), TC03303.

[22.157] In a Scottish case, a bank provided one of its employees (EA) with a mortgage comprising two loans with different account numbers. One of the loans was for £35,000 and carried interest at the Bank of England base rate, while the other was for £105,000 and initially carried interest at 0.74% above the Bank of England base rate. The bank included these loans as a benefit on EA's P11D, but EA did not declare the loans on her tax return. When HMRC discovered this, they issued notices of amendment charging tax under *ITEPA 2003, s 175*. EA appealed, contending that the loan for £105,000 was on terms available to the general public, so that only the loan for £35,000 should be treated as giving rise to a taxable benefit. The First-tier Tribunal accepted this contention and allowed her appeal, finding that 'the loan of £105,000 was not an employment-related loan because it was a separate and distinct loan and was available to the general public'. *Mrs E Amri v HMRC*, FTT [2014] UKFTT 317 (TC), TC03451.

Beneficial loans to employees—ITEPA 2003, s 175

[22.158] A company (L) arranged for a company established in the British Virgin Islands to make loans available to its two directors and a senior employee (W), under arrangements described as 'discount loan agreements'. HMRC issued rulings that the loans (which were expressed to be for ten years) gave rise to liability to income tax under *ITEPA 2003, s 175*, and to Class 1A national insurance contributions. L and the borrowers appealed, contending that since the borrowers had been required to pay a sum described as a 'discount' at the end of the period of the loan, the arrangements were outside the scope of *s 175*. The First-tier Tribunal rejected this contention and dismissed the appeals. Judge Short observed that the directors' loans had in fact been 'rolled over' under revised arrangements, after the end of the original ten-year term of the loan, and that W had not repaid his loan until 14 years after the original agreement. Accordingly the directors could not 'be treated as having paid the interest since it has not actually, from their perspective, been discharged'. *Leeds Design Innovation Centre Ltd v HMRC (and related appeals)*, FTT [2014] UKFTT 009 (TC); [2014] SFTD 681, TC03150.

Loan by company to joint account of director and wife

[22.159] A company transferred a sum of money to a joint deposit account, held by one of its directors (H) and his wife. The result of the transfer was that H's director's loan account became overdrawn. The Revenue assessed H on the resulting benefit. The General Commissioners dismissed H's appeal and the CA upheld their decision, observing that the legislation applied to loans to relatives of employees as well as to loans to employees. *Hill v Davison*, CA 1999, 71 TC 535; [1999] STC 1050. (*Note.* Appeals against assessments under what is now *CTA 2010, s 455* were also dismissed—see **11.6** CLOSE COMPANIES.)

Avoidance scheme—loan by employer to employee

[22.160] HMRC discovered that a company (S) had made significant loans (in a depreciating currency) to an employee (B), without accounting for PAYE. They issued discovery assessments on B, on the basis that the loans fell within *ITEPA 2003, s 173*. The First-tier Tribunal dismissed B's appeals. Judge Gort observed that B was not 'a straightforward witness', and held that the loans were not genuine. S had intended 'that the amount of the effective repayments in sterling would be considerably less than the amount of sterling advanced to the scheme users', so that 'the difference was effectively waived or written off from the outset'. The financial benefit arising from this was an emolument, within *ITEPA 2003, s 188(1)(b)*. *P Boyle v HMRC*, FTT [2013] UKFTT 723 (TC), TC03103.

Income from loan by employer to trustees of settlement for employee

[22.161] See *O'Leary v McKinlay*, **22.80** above.

Taxable Benefits: Acquisitions of shares (ITEPA 2003, ss 192–197)

[22.162] The legislation which became *ITEPA 2003, ss 192–197* derived from *FA 1976*, and was repealed by *FA 2003*. The acquisition of securities at less than market value is now covered by *ITEPA 2003, ss 446Q–446W*. For cases concerning these provisions, see **22.312** to **22.320** below. Share options are now covered by *ITEPA 2003, ss 471–487*. For cases concerning these provisions, see **22.323** and **22.326** below.

Taxable Benefits: Residual liability (ITEPA 2003, ss 201–215)

Expenses of defending driving charge against director

[22.163] A company director was involved in an accident, in which a pedestrian was killed, while driving a company car on business. He was charged with causing death by dangerous driving. If he had been convicted, he would have been liable to be imprisoned. The company did not wish to be deprived of his services, and arranged for its solicitors to defend him and paid the cost of the defence. He was acquitted. The Revenue assessed the director on the basis that the amount paid by the company was a benefit, within what is now *ITEPA 2003, s 201*. The director appealed. The Special Commissioners dismissed his appeal and the HL unanimously upheld their decision. Lord Reid observed that the director 'knew and accepted what was being done on his behalf though he may not have realised how much it was costing'. Viscount Radcliffe observed that 'it does not reduce the value of a present to say that the recipient could not or would not have bought it for himself'. *Rendell v Went*, HL 1964, 41 TC 641; [1964] 1 WLR 650; [1964] 2 All ER 464.

Use of company yacht by directors

[22.164] In 1983 a married couple (Mr & Mrs R) established two companies (M and W). In 2001 M purchased two large yachts, which were chartered to customers and were also used by the directors for meetings with prospective clients. W, which operated a conference centre, purchased some expensive items of jewellery which Mrs R wore at important functions. It also purchased two antique clocks, one of which was kept in an office at the couple's home address. In 2007 HMRC began an enquiry into Mr & Mrs R and the companies. They subsequently issued assessments on the basis that the provision of the yacht, jewellery and clocks was a benefit for the directors which gave rise to a tax liability under *ITEPA 2003, s 201*. The directors appealed. The First-tier Tribunal upheld the assessments in principle, holding that 'given the very wide definition of "benefit" in the legislation, it must follow that the use of the yachts, jewellery and clocks by Mr & Mrs (R) are to be treated as such'. On the evidence, the couple were entitled to a deduction under *ITEPA 2003, s 365* in respect of the costs attributable to the yacht, but were not entitled to any such deduction in respect of the jewellery and clocks. *M & Mrs G Rockall v HMRC*, FTT [2014] UKFTT 643 (TC), TC03767.

Joint ownership of cars—taxable benefit

[22.165] See *Vasili v Christensen*, **22.125** above.

Provision of office accommodation in home of prospective employee

[22.166] In January 1991 a company based in Warwickshire made an offer of employment to an accountant who lived in London. The accountant accepted the offer, but did not wish to move to Warwickshire or to commute on a daily basis, and it was agreed that he would work from home and that the company would pay the cost of converting his loft into an office. The company spent more than £20,000 on this, making payment to the builders in March 1991 (although the actual work was not undertaken until July and August 1991). The accountant began his employment in May 1991. The Revenue included the amount of the expenditure in his 1991/92 assessment, as a benefit in kind within what is now *ITEPA 2003, s 201*. He appealed, contending that because the expenditure had been incurred in 1990/91, when he was not an employee of the company, it was not taxable under the legislation then in force. The Ch D rejected this contention and upheld the assessment. Jonathan Parker J held that, for the purposes of *s 201*, no benefit was provided until the benefit in question became 'available to be enjoyed by the taxpayer'. *Templeton v Jacobs*, Ch D 1996, 68 TC 735; [1996] STC 991; [1996] 1 WLR 1433.

'Shadow' director—whether within ITEPA 2003, s 201

[22.167] In the case noted at **51.8** REVENUE PROSECUTIONS, the HL held that a 'shadow director' was liable to tax on benefits within what is now *ITEPA 2003, s 201*. Lord Hutton held that it was Parliament's intention 'that accommodation and benefits in kind received by a shadow director should be taxed in the same way as those received by a director'. The effect of what is now *ITEPA 2003, s 67(1)* was that 'a shadow director is taken to be a director'. Accordingly, 'it follows that living accommodation and benefits received by him should be treated as emoluments'. *R v Allen*, HL 2001, 74 TC 263; [2001] STC 1537; [2001] UKHL 45; [2001] 4 All ER 768.

Company taking legal proceedings against minority shareholder

[22.168] 95% of the shares in a software company (X) were held by its managing director (C), the remaining 5% being held by another shareholder (L). C arranged for X to take legal proceedings against L, as a result of which C became the sole shareholder in X. C failed to declare these payments on his tax returns. The Revenue issued a 'discovery' assessment and amendments to C's self-assessments. C and X appealed, contending that the expenditure had been incurred in order to 'protect the company from a potentially disruptive employee and recalcitrant shareholder'. The Special Commissioner dismissed the appeals, finding that C had clearly obtained a benefit from the legal action and that this benefit was not simply incidental. Accordingly the legal costs had to be apportioned. (The Commissioner observed that 'there are no fixed rules or formulae about how an apportionment should be done. It is only required that the apportionment must be based on the facts of the case and lead to a result which is fair and reasonable.') *Collins v Laing; Xi Software Ltd v Laing*, Sp C 2004, [2005] SSCD 249 (Sp C 450). (*Note*. The appellants subsequently made an unsuccessful application for costs—see **4.424** APPEALS.)

Employee benefit trust allocating money to sub-funds

[22.169] An employee benefit trust received contributions from a number of associated companies. It allocated certain sums to sub-funds for the benefit of six employees, as a reward for past performance. The Revenue issued assessments on the basis that the allocation of a payment to a sub-fund was taxable, either as an emolument or as a taxable benefit. The employees appealed, contending that the allocation of a payment to a sub-fund was not a taxable emolument and that the legislation for the taxation of benefits only applied to actual benefits rather than to potential benefits. The Special Commissioners accepted this contention and allowed the appeals, finding that the employees were 'not free to do whatever they like with the sub-funds which are held on the trusts applicable to them'. The Commissioners observed that 'in order for the funds to be in the unfettered control of the six, the trustee must exercise its discretion and take the further action of appointing those funds absolutely to them as beneficiaries. The highest the case can be put is that the trustee is likely to comply with any reasonable request that is for the benefit of the beneficiaries, which is hardly surprising in the context of a trust established for the benefit of employees. This falls far short of saying that the trustee is a cipher.' *Caudwell & Others v MacDonald*, Sp C [2002] SSCD 413 (Sp C 331). (*Notes*. (1) The Commissioners heard the appeal with *Dextra Accessories Ltd & Others v MacDonald*, **53.38** SCHEDULE D. (2) The Commissioners also held that the *Ramsay* principle — see **58.6** TAX PLANNING AND AVOIDANCE — did not apply to the transactions.)

Employer buying shares from employee at above market value

[22.170] In 2001 a company (T) purchased the shareholding of another company (SE). One of SE's employees (S) took employment with T and exchanged his shares in SE for shares in T, which were valued at $47.245 each. T's shares subsequently declined in value. In 2002 S sold these shares back to T at the price which he had originally paid for them. Because T's shares had fallen in value, S received £1,533,391 more than he would have done if the shares had been priced at their market value. HMRC subsequently issued a closure notice amending S's return for 2002/03 by including the £1,533,391 as an emolument of his employment. S appealed to the First-tier Tribunal, which reviewed the evidence in detail and dismissed the appeal. The tribunal held that the transactions were not within the scope of the legislation which became *ITEPA 2003, ss 192–197*, but that the difference between the market value of the shares and the price which T paid S for them was taxable as a benefit within what is now *ITEPA 2003, s 201*. *JP Smith v HMRC*, FTT [2009] SFTD 731; [2009] UKFTT 210 (TC), TC00163.

ITEPA 2003, s 203—computation of cash equivalent of benefit

[22.171] Nine schoolteachers and the school bursar had their sons educated at concessionary reduced fees of approximately 20% of the standard fees. The reduced fees covered the direct costs attributable to each boy, but did not include any indirect costs. The boys occupied surplus places at the school and their education there was at the discretion of the school, rather than an entitlement. The Revenue raised assessments on the basis that, in computing the cash equivalent of the benefits, the overall running costs of the whole school should be apportioned pro rata to the concessionary places. The HL unanimously allowed the teachers' appeals, holding that only the marginal costs should be assessed. The wording of the relevant legislation was ambiguous. It derived from *FA 1976*, and, during the Parliamentary debates which preceded its enactment, the then Financial Secretary had clearly stated that the intention of the legislation was to assess such in-house benefits on the marginal cost to the employer, rather than on the average cost. Hansard could be used as an aid to interpretation where 'legislation is ambiguous or obscure, or leads to an absurdity; the material relied upon consists of one or more statements by a Minister or other promoter of the Bill together if necessary with such other Parliamentary material as is necessary to understand such statements and their effect; and the statements relied upon are clear'. In the light of these statements, the ambiguity should be resolved by construing the relevant legislation in such a way as to give effect to the intentions of Parliament. *Pepper v Hart & Others*, HL 1992, 65 TC 421; [1992] STC 898; [1992] 3 WLR 1032; [1993] 1 All ER 42. (*Note.* For the Revenue's practice following this decision, see the Revenue Press Release issued on 21 January 1993.)

Fire officer's car equipped with flashing light and emergency equipment

[22.172] A senior fire officer was provided by his employers with a saloon car fitted with a flashing light and other emergency equipment. He was required to be available for call to incidents at all times except when on leave. The Revenue assessed him to car benefit. When the appeal was heard by the High Court, his counsel contended that the vehicle was not a car within what is now *ITEPA 2003, s 115*. The Ch D accepted this contention, holding that the car was 'of a type not commonly used as a private vehicle and unsuitable to be so used', since it would be an offence for a vehicle equipped with a flashing light to be used on the public road other than for fire brigade or police purposes. The assessment could not be upheld under *s 114*, but since this point had not been raised before the Commissioners, the case was remitted to them to consider whether liability arose under the general provisions of what is now *ITEPA 2003, s 201 et seq*. *Gurney v Richards*, Ch D 1989, 62 TC 287; [1989] STC 682; [1989] 1 WLR 1180. (*Note.* There was no further public hearing of the appeal. It is understood that it was accepted that the benefit was taxable under the legislation then in force. See now, however, *ITEPA 2003, s 248A*, introduced by *FA 2004*. For a subsequent case concerning the taxable amount of such benefits, see *Kerr v Brown*, **22.173** below.)

[22.173] Two senior fire officers were provided by their employers with cars fitted with flashing blue lights and emergency equipment. They drove the cars between their homes and the fire brigade premises, but did not use them privately. The Revenue issued assessments on the basis that the provision of the cars was a taxable benefit within what is now *ITEPA 2003, s 201 et seq*. The assessments were computed by taking the annual value prescribed by what is now *ITEPA 2003, s 205*, adding the estimated cost of maintenance and fuel, multiplying the resulting figure by the mileage relating to journeys between the officers' homes and their brigade premises, and dividing it by the total number of miles travelled in the year. The officers appealed, contending firstly that there should be no taxable benefit since the cars were used exclusively for fire brigade purposes, and alternatively that the annual value should be reduced by excluding those days on which the cars were not available at all for private purposes. The Special Commissioners accepted the officers' alternative contention and directed that the amount of the assessments should be reduced by taking the prescribed annual value and deducting 'the same proportion as the aggregate number of the appellants' rest and leave days per year bears to the number of days in a year'. *Kerr v Brown; Boyd v Brown*, Sp C [2002] SSCD 434 (Sp C 333). (*Note*. See now, however, *ITEPA 2003, s 248A*, introduced by *FA 2004* with effect from 6 April 2004.)

[22.174] Following the decision reported at 22.173 above, the parties were unable to agree the quantification of the benefit and the case was again referred to the Special Commissioners 'for clarification in three respects'. The Commissioners held that, in the context of the rota systems worked by the officers, a 'day' should be defined 'as any unbroken period of 24 hours, whenever it commences'. Secondly, they held that 'for the purposes of the formula apportioning the standing costs of the vehicles, we would not exclude a day as a rest day (being a day on which the car was not available for the private use of the individual concerned) merely because a part of that rest day might have been spent in the vehicle commuting to and from home'. Finally, they held that 'only a complete rest or leave day should count in the formula as being a day on which the vehicle was not available for the individual's private use'. *Kerr v Brown; Boyd v Brown (No 2)*, Sp C May 2003 (Sp C 333A).

Executive box at football club

[22.175] A family company (F) hired an executive box at a League One football club. The son of F's controlling directors played for the club. HMRC issued a ruling that this was a benefit in kind for the directors, and that income tax was chargeable under *ITEPA 2003, s 203*. F appealed, contending that the box had been hired to entertain customers, and that the directors did not need to hire the box in order to see their son play, as they could have obtained free tickets from their son. The First-tier Tribunal accepted this contention and allowed F's appeal on this point, holding that the hire of the box was not a 'benefit in kind' for the directors. *Frank Hudson Transport Ltd v HMRC*, FTT [2010] UKFTT 503 (TC), TC00758. (*Note*. For another issue in this case, see 22.129 above.)

ITEPA 2003, s 212—scholarships to sons of director

[22.176] A company made payments to two sons of one of its directors (K) while they were at university. HMRC issued assessments on K, charging tax on the basis that the payments were taxable benefits. The First-tier Tribunal dismissed K's appeal, holding that the payments were taxable by virtue of *ITEPA 2003, s 212*. *S Kutcha v HMRC (and related appeal)*, FTT [2013] UKFTT 369 (TC), TC02769.

Payments treated as earnings (ITEPA 2003, ss 221–226)

ITEPA 2003, s 222—payments by employer on account of tax

[22.177] In a Scottish case, a company agreed to make bonus payments to three directors in rhodium as part of a scheme to avoid national insurance contributions. On the directors' instructions, the company immediately sold the rhodium, and subsequently credited the full sale proceeds to the directors' loan accounts. The Revenue issued assessments charging tax on the payments. The directors appealed, contending that, although the payments in question had been credited to their loan accounts, it was accepted that they could not draw the funds until the tax had been paid to the Revenue, so that they should be treated as having made good the tax due to their employer within 30 days, within *ICTA 1988, s 144A(1)(c)*. The Special Commissioner (Mr. Coutts, sitting alone) accepted the directors' evidence and allowed their appeals, stating that 'while perhaps in theory, monies in the directors' loan account were available to be drawn on by the directors, I have no hesitation in finding that this, in this particular case, would not and indeed could not have happened'. *Ferguson v CIR (and related appeals)*, Sp C 2000, [2001] SSCD 1 (Sp C 266). (*Notes*. (1) The relevant time limit under *ICTA 1988, s 144A(1)(c)* was 30 days. The corresponding time limit under *ITEPA 2003, s 222(1)(c)* was extended from 30 to 90 days by *FA 2003, s 144*. (2) For an English case in which a similar NIC avoidance scheme was held to be ineffective, see *NMB Holdings Ltd v Secretary of State for Social Security*, **58.11** TAX PLANNING AND AVOIDANCE.)

[22.178] In 2001 two company directors exercised share options which they had been granted, and realised substantial gains. One of the directors (C) declared the gain on his 2001/02 tax return, but the other (G) did not. In October 2003 the company paid the Class 1 national insurance contributions arising from the exercise of the options. In 2006 the Revenue issued an amendment to C's return, charging tax on the exercise of the options under what is now *ITEPA 2003, s 222*. They also issued a discovery assessment on G. Both directors appealed. The Special Commissioner dismissed their appeals and the Ch D and CA unanimously upheld this decision. Lloyd LJ observed that the directors had failed to reimburse the company within the statutory time limit. Accordingly they were liable to tax under *s 222*, which was 'clear and unambiguous in its terms'. *JE Chilcott v HMRC (and related appeal)*, CA [2010] EWCA Civ 1538; TL 3838; [2011] STC 456. (*Note*. The Supreme Court dismissed an application for leave to appeal against the CA decision.)

[22.179] On 28 October 2007 an employee (M) notified his employer (T) that he wished to exercise his rights under a share option scheme, under which he paid £7,636 for shares which had a market value of £111,579. The scheme rules provided that M was required to reimburse T for the PAYE due in respect of the option. However, T did not provide M with details of the amount due from him until 28 March 2008. T paid this in April 2008. Subsequently HMRC issued an assessment on M, charging tax under *ITEPA 2003, s 222* on the basis that he had failed to reimburse T within the statutory 90-day time limit. M appealed, contending that he had reimbursed T within a month of T informing him of the liability. The First-tier Tribunal allowed M's appeal, finding that the 'relevant date' for the purpose of *s 222(4)* was 28 March 2008, when T had informed M of the amount of the liability, rather than 28 October 2007, when M had informed T that he wished to exercise his option. Sir Stephen Oliver observed that *s 222* was 'penal in its effect' and that 'where it applies, it brings into charge to tax notional amounts that would otherwise have no place in the taxing system'. It had been introduced 'to prevent grossly abusive schemes designed to avoid PAYE'. There had been 'nothing remotely abusive' about T's share option scheme, but HMRC had 'conducted their PAYE investigation without apparently troubling to look at the scheme rules. Nor did the assessing officer nor did the officer who conducted the review. The result that, unless (M) had appealed, HMRC would have earned a substantial windfall gain at his expense.' He concluded that 'when Parliament introduced *section 222*, they expected it to be properly and carefully exercised', and that it should not be treated as 'mechanistic in its effect'. *B Manning v HMRC*, FTT [2013] UKFTT 252 (TC), TC02666.

ITEPA 2003, s 225—consideration for 'restrictive undertaking'

[22.180] See *RCI (Europe) Ltd v Woods*, **73.69** NATIONAL INSURANCE CONTRIBUTIONS, and *Kent Foods Ltd v HMRC*, **73.70** NATIONAL INSURANCE CONTRIBUTIONS.

Employment income: exemptions (ITEPA 2003, ss 227–326)

ITEPA 2003, s 229—mileage allowance paid to doctor

[22.181] A doctor carried on his practice from his home. He also held appointments as an obstetrician and an anaesthetist at a hospital 15 miles from his home, under which he was required to be on stand-by duty at certain times. He was telephoned when needed, and generally instructed hospital staff by telephone before driving to the hospital. He received a mileage allowance from the hospital, which covered only 10 miles of the journey each way. The Revenue assessed him on this allowance and he appealed, contending firstly that the allowance was not a taxable emolument, and alternatively, that if it were taxable, his travelling expenses should be allowed as a deduction. The HL allowed his appeal (by a 3-2 majority in respect of each of the contentions raised). The mileage allowance paid to him was a reimbursement of expenses incurred and did not form part of his emoluments. Furthermore, his duties began when he received a telephone call from the hospital, so that the amount by which his travelling expenses exceeded the amount reimbursed was allowable as a deduction. *Pook v Owen*, HL 1969, 45 TC 571; [1970] AC 244; [1969] 2 All ER 1. (*Note*. HMRC regard this as an 'exceptional case'. For their interpretation of this decision, see Employment Income Manual, para EIM32373.)

Mileage allowances paid by employment bureau

[22.182] See *Reed Employment plc v HMRC (No 4)*, **42.39** PAY AS YOU EARN.

Urologist—emergency call-out fees

[22.183] A urologist (W), based at an NHS hospital, undertook rotational appointments at other hospitals. In 2003/04 he received expenses of £3,416 to cover the amount by which his journey to these hospitals exceeded his journey to the hospital where he was based. In 2005/06 he received £633 to cover 'emergency call-out expenses'. He did not include either of these payments in his tax returns. HMRC issued amendments to his self-assessments charging tax on both amounts, and W appealed. The First-tier Tribunal dismissed his appeal for 2003/04, holding that these expenses were not 'relocation expenses' within *ITEPA 2003, s 287*, and did not qualify for exemption under *ITEPA 2003, ss 337-339*. However the tribunal allowed his appeal for 2005/06 in part, holding that the call-out expenses qualified for exemption to the amount of 40p per mile, in accordance with *ITEPA 2003, ss 229, 230* (so that £478 of the £633 qualified for exemption). *Dr M Wilkinson v HMRC*, FTT [2010] SFTD 1063; [2010] UKFTT 283 (TC), TC00572.

Allowances for use of private car in travelling

[22.184] A rent officer (P), employed by a local council, was required to travel by car in the course of his duties. He used his private car for this, and the council paid him amounts based on a scale agreed by the National Joint Council for Local Authority Services. In 1978/79 he received a lump sum of £220 (calculated by reference to 'standing charges' such as tax, insurance, depreciation and loss of interest), plus mileage allowances totalling £148. The mileage allowance was 11.4p per mile, of which 5.5p was calculated by reference to his 'running expenses' (petrol and repairs, etc.) and 5.9p by reference to the 'standing charges'. The Revenue assessed the allowances and P appealed. The Commissioners determined the appeal on the basis that the £368 was part of his emoluments, and that his allowable expenses were £64. The Ch D upheld this decision, distinguishing *Pook v Owen*, **22.181** above, on the grounds that the mileage allowance was not simply a reimbursement of expenses, but included a substantial contribution to the overhead costs of maintaining the car. *Perrons v Spackman*, Ch D 1981, 55 TC 403; [1981] STC 739; [1981] 1 WLR 1411.

[22.185] A schoolteacher voluntarily attended parents' evening meetings at her school. She was paid a mileage allowance for using her car to travel between her home and the school to attend the meetings. The Revenue assessed the allowance, and she appealed. The Commissioners allowed her appeal and the Ch D upheld their decision. Walton J held that the payment to her was not made as a remuneration or reward for acting as or being an employee, as it was not part of her duties to attend the meetings. Furthermore, even if she had been contractually required to attend them, the payment was a reimbursement of expenses and not an emolument. Walton J observed that 'the Crown spends so much time and effort persecuting minnows that it is small wonder it has no energy left to pursue the real sharks'. *Donnelly v Williamson*, Ch D 1981, 54 TC 636; [1982] STC 88.

Cars leased to employees—whether within ITEPA 2003, s 229

[22.186] See *Whitby v HMRC*, 22.127 above.

Reimbursement of training costs—whether exempt

[22.187] A woman who had been employed by an accountancy firm studied for an MBA, paying tuition fees of £18,000. After completing the course, she took up a position with a different employer, at a salary of £63,000 pa with a 'signing bonus' of £18,000. The Revenue issued an amendment to her self-assessment, treating the payment as taxable. She appealed, contending that although the payment had been described as a 'bonus', it was in fact reimbursement of her MBA tuition costs, and should be treated as exempt under what is now *ITEPA 2003, s 250*. The Special Commissioner accepted this contention and allowed her appeal, holding that the payment was within *s 250* and was not excluded by *s 253*. *Silva v Charnock*, Sp C [2002] SSCD 426 (Sp C 332).

ITEPA 2003, s 271—removal benefits

[22.188] In 2009/10 a company (B) recruited a new employee (F) to work in Berkshire. Since F lived in Sussex, B offered him a 'relocation package' and informed him that this would be exempt from tax under *ITEPA 2003, s 271*. However, on F's 2009/10 P11D, B declared taxable benefits of £4,498 in respect of temporary accommodation provided under the 'relocation package'. Meanwhile F had formed the opinion that B had misdescribed the nature of the work. B and F subsequently agreed that F's employment would terminate by mutual consent in October 2011, and that B would pay F compensation of £30,000, which was exempt from tax under *ITEPA 2003, s 403*. F submitted a repayment claim in respect of the relocation benefits and lodged an appeal to the First-tier Tribunal. Judge Aleksander found that the appeal was premature, because HMRC had requested further information from F and had not reached a formal decision on his claim. However Judge Aleksander observed that HMRC had contended that because F had never actually moved to Berkshire, but had lived in temporary accommodation, the benefits were taxable in full. He expressed the view that 'HMRC's submissions have considerable merit in cases where an employment continues, but the employee never permanently relocates. In such cases, the relocation benefit would be, in reality, a subsidy for long distance commuting.' However, he considered that the exemption should not be denied where an employee was planning to move, but died before doing so. In this case, he expressed the view that 'the relocation benefits provided by (B) to (F) would be eligible for tax relief from the start of (F's) employment until the date on which it became certain that (F's) employment with (B) was no longer permanent'. Any relocation benefits provided after that date would not qualify for exemption. *P Figg v HMRC*, FTT [2014] UKFTT 578 (TC), TC03703. (*Note*. F had also claimed tax relief for accountancy fees. The First-tier Tribunal held that these were not deductible, and also dismissed his appeals against surcharges and penalties.)

Employment income: deductions allowed from earnings (ITEPA 2003, ss 327–385)

General rule for deduction of expenses (ITEPA 2003, s 336)

Expenditure held not to be allowable

Domestic assistance

[22.189] A married couple were appointed as schoolteachers at the same school at a joint salary. They claimed a deduction for the wages of a domestic servant employed to carry out household duties while the wife was teaching at the school. The QB rejected the claim. *Bowers v Harding*, QB 1891, 3 TC 22; [1891] 1 QB 560.

[22.190] A widower paid £3 per week to his mother-in-law and a friend to look after his young children while he was at work. He claimed that part of this should be allowed as a deduction. The Ch D rejected his claim. *Halstead v Condon*, Ch D 1970, 46 TC 289.

Extra cost of living near work

[22.191] A water board employee was required to live in Central London, near his work. He appealed against an assessment, contending that he should be allowed a deduction of £55 to represent the additional costs of living near his work. The KB rejected this contention and upheld the assessment. Croom-Johnson J observed that 'it does not follow that, because you want to live in a particular way, therefore the additional expense is wholly, exclusively or necessarily incurred in the performance of your duties'. *Bolam v Barlow*, KB 1949, 31 TC 136.

[22.192] A tax consultant (B) was also Clerk to four Divisions of General Commissioners. In 1980 he gave up his consultancy and moved to Malta. He sold his previous UK residence and purchased a property in Dorset, primarily for use as an office in relation to his duties as Clerk, with the aid of a mortgage. He claimed that the mortgage interest should be allowed as a deduction from his emoluments. The Revenue rejected his claim and the Ch D dismissed his appeal. It had been B's personal choice to take out a loan at interest and to use that loan to purchase a property. The interest payments were not deductible. *Baird v Williams*, Ch D 1999, 71 TC 390; [1999] STC 635.

[22.193] An engineer, who had moved from Essex to Bath, appealed against income tax assessments, claiming a deduction for the additional cost of living in Bath. The Commissioners rejected the claim and dismissed his appeal, and the KB upheld their decision. *Collis v Hore (No 1)*, KB 1949, 31 TC 173.

[22.194] See also *McKie v Warner*, 22.113 above.

Army officer—'mess expenses'

[22.195] A Territorial Army officer (N) appealed against an assessment, claiming that he should be allowed a deduction for various 'mess expenses', including payments to a batman, the hire of camp furniture, and tickets to various dances. The Ch D rejected his claims and upheld the assessment (apart from a deduction of £6 for the cost of hotel accommodation when attending conferences and tactical exercises). Vaisey J noted that the Commissioners had found as a fact that the hotel expenses were 'necessarily, exclusively and wholly incurred' in the performance of N's duties, but held that 'as a precedent in other cases, it should be applied with very great caution. A hotel bill is certain to include charges for "extras" involving some measure of extravagance and personal indulgence as well as charges for necessaries'. *Lomax v Newton*, Ch D 1953, 34 TC 558; [1953] 1 WLR 1123; [1953] 2 All ER 801.

[22.196] A similar decision was reached in *Griffiths v Mockler*, Ch D 1953, 35 TC 135; [1953] 1 WLR 1123; [1953] 2 All ER 805.

Army personnel—cost of lodgings

[22.197] See *Nagley v Spilsbury*, **22.111** above.

Subsistence expenses

[22.198] An engineering firm required an employee to work away from home for long periods, and paid him a 'living allowance'. He appealed against an assessment on this, contending that an equivalent amount should be allowed as a deduction. The Ch D rejected this contention and upheld the assessment. *Elderkin v Hindmarsh*, Ch D 1988, 60 TC 651; [1988] STC 267.

[22.199] A travelling salesman appealed against income tax assessments, claiming that he should be allowed a deduction for 'subsistence'. The Special Commissioner rejected this contention and dismissed his appeal. *Bevins v McLeish*, Sp C [1995] SSCD 342 (Sp C 51).

[22.200] A claim for subsistence expenses was also rejected in *MP Goncalves v HMRC*, FTT [2011] UKFTT 545 (TC), TC01392.

[22.201] See also *Robinson v Corry*, **22.49** above; *Sanderson v Durbridge*, **22.105** above; *Phillips v Hamilton*, **22.265** below, and *Bennett v HMRC*, **22.266** below.

Legal costs

[22.202] The managing director of a company resigned and began legal proceedings against it, which were settled by agreement on the second day of the hearing. He claimed a deduction for his legal costs. The KB rejected his claim, holding that he had not been 'necessarily obliged' to incur the expenditure. *Eagles v Levy*, KB 1934, 19 TC 23.

[22.203] A Stock Exchange dealer (N) agreed to join a new employer. The Securities Association refused to re-register him pending an investigation into allegations by his previous employer, but subsequently accepted that the allegations were unfounded. N claimed that the legal costs which he had incurred should be allowed as a deduction. The Revenue rejected the claim and the Special Commissioner dismissed his appeal, holding that he had not incurred the expenditure 'in the performance of the duties' of the new employment, and had not been 'necessarily obliged' to incur the expenditure in question. *Nevis v CIR*, Sp C [2000] SSCD 144 (Sp C 281).

[22.204] A company (C) dismissed an employee (W). W began legal proceedings, claiming unfair dismissal. The Employment Appeal Tribunal awarded him compensation, but W appealed to the CA, contending that the amount of the award was inadequate. The CA dismissed his appeal and ordered him to pay C's costs. W claimed that his legal costs, including the costs which the CA had ordered him to pay, should be allowed as a deduction. HMRC rejected his claim and the First-tier Tribunal dismissed his appeal. *M Wardle v HMRC*, FTT [2013] UKFTT 599 (TC), TC02986.

Director guaranteeing company's debts

[22.205] A company, which was in financial difficulties, entered into a factoring agreement which required its directors to give personal guarantees for some of its debts. One of the directors (G) paid £10,925 under this agreement, and claimed that this, plus interest and legal costs, should be allowed as a deduction from his remuneration. The Revenue rejected the claim and the Special Commissioner dismissed G's appeal. *Guarantor v HMRC*, Sp C [2008] SSCD 1154 (Sp C 703).

Agency fee

[22.206] An employee obtained a post through an agency. He had to pay the agency a fee of £30 (5% of his first year's remuneration). He appealed against an assessment, contending that the £30 fee should be allowed as a deduction. The KB rejected this contention and dismissed his appeal. *Shortt v McIlgorm*, KB 1945, 26 TC 262; [1945] 1 All ER 391.

Expenses of seeking employment

[22.207] The Special Commissioner dismissed an appeal against an assessment charging tax on unemployment benefit, rejecting the appellant's contention that he should be allowed to deduct the costs of seeking new employment. *Harrop v Gilroy*, Sp C [1995] SSCD 294 (Sp C 39).

Educational expenses

[22.208] A student laboratory assistant was required to attend evening classes in preparation for a university degree. He appealed against an assessment, contending that his travelling expenses to the classes, and the cost of his textbooks, should be allowed as deductions. The KB rejected these contentions and upheld the assessment. Macnaghten J observed that 'few people sleep at the place where the duties of their office are performed, but it is well established that you cannot claim deduction for the expenses of getting from the place where you sleep to the place where you perform the duties. The expenses permitted to be deducted must be expenses incurred in the performance of the duties of the office.' *Blackwell v Mills*, KB 1945, 26 TC 468; [1945] 2 All ER 655.

[22.209] A headmaster claimed a deduction for the cost of attending a course of weekend lectures to improve his knowledge of history. The Ch D rejected his claim, holding that 'the payment for the course was not wholly, exclusively and necessarily incurred in the preparation of his own lectures or in the performance of his duties'. *Humbles v Brooks*, Ch D 1962, 40 TC 500.

Training expenses

[22.210] A trainee accountant (P) claimed a deduction for the cost of studying for an ACCA qualification. The Revenue rejected the claim and the Special Commissioner dismissed P's appeal, holding that the expenses were not 'incurred wholly, exclusively and necessarily in the performance of the duties of his employment'. *DW Perrin v HMRC*, Sp C [2008] SSCD 672 (Sp C 671).

[22.211] A pilot (E) claimed a deduction of more than £17,000 for the cost of training to qualify for his pilot's licence. HMRC accepted that exam fees paid to the Civil Aviation Authority were deductible, but rejected the majority of E's claim. The First-tier Tribunal dismissed E's appeal. Judge Barton observed that the expenses had been incurred before E began his employment. Since he 'was not in employment when these expenses were incurred, he is not entitled to any deduction'. *PE Edgar v HMRC*, FTT [2011] UKFTT 245 (TC), TC01109.

Reimbursement of training expenses

[22.212] Two airline pilots were provided with training at their employers' expense. Their contracts provided that, if they left their employment within three years, they would have to reimburse part of the cost of their training. They both resigned their employment within the three-year period, and subsequently made reimbursement payments as required by their contracts. They claimed that these should be allowed as deductions. The Revenue rejected the claims and the Special Commissioner dismissed the pilots' appeals, observing that the payment was required 'because of the termination of the contract', rather than in the performance of the employees' duties. *Hinsley v HMRC; Milsom v HMRC*; Sp C [2007] SSCD 63 (Sp C 569).

Examination fees

[22.213] A solicitor's clerk claimed a deduction for the Law Society examination fees. The Ch D held that the fees were not allowable deductions. Plowman J observed that he had incurred the expenditure 'not to benefit or fulfil an obligation to an employer but to benefit himself because he wanted to become a solicitor'. *Lupton v Potts*, Ch D 1969, 45 TC 643; [1969] 1 WLR 1749; [1969] 3 All ER 1083.

[22.214] A medical registrar claimed that examination fees, and other related expenses, should be allowed as a deduction from his earnings. The Ch D held that the fees and expenses were not allowable deductions. *HMRC v Decadt*, Ch D 2007, 79 TC 220; [2008] STC 1103.

Domestic expenses

[22.215] An insurance agent appealed against income tax assessments, contending that 20% of his expenditure on rent, rates, electricity, gas, coal and water should be allowed as a deduction. The Ch D rejected this contention and upheld the assessments. *Roskams v Bennett*, Ch D 1950, 32 TC 129.

[22.216] In the case noted at 22.252 below, a company director claimed a deduction for the cost of a record player and gramophone records 'for the purpose of providing a stimulus of good music while he worked'. The

General Commissioners rejected the claim and the CA unanimously upheld their decision. *Newlin v Woods*, CA 1966, 42 TC 649.

[22.217] A certified accountant (L), who was employed by an accountancy firm, claimed a deduction of £3,000 which she described as 'rent'. HMRC rejected the claim and she appealed, contending that this related to the use of her home as an office. The First-tier Tribunal dismissed her appeal. Judge Clark found that there was 'no evidence that keeping an office at her home was a requirement of (L's) employment', and held that the claim did not meet the requirements of *ITEPA 2003, s 336*. *Miss SH Ling v HMRC*, FTT [2011] UKFTT 793 (TC), TC01629. (*Note.* The accountant appeared in person. Various other claims, including a large claim for travelling expenses, were also rejected.)

Club subscriptions

[22.218] A bank paid for the manager of its Westminster branch to join two London clubs. He appealed against an assessment, contending that the subscriptions were allowable deductions as he had joined the clubs to meet potential customers. The CA unanimously dismissed his appeal. Donovan LJ observed that 'the test is not whether the employer imposes the expense but whether the duties do, in the sense that, irrespective of what the employer may prescribe, the duties cannot be performed without incurring the particular outlay'. *Brown v Bullock*, CA 1961, 40 TC 1; [1961] 1 WLR 1095; [1961] 3 All ER 129.

Telephone expenses

[22.219] A clerk employed in the NHS made business calls from his home telephone. His employer reimbursed the cost of these calls. He appealed against an assessment, claiming that his telephone rental should be also allowed as a deduction. The General Commissioners rejected this contention and dismissed his appeal, and the Ch D upheld their decision. Brightman J observed that 'it would be possible for a telephone service to charge no rental at all and to cover the cost of the telephone service entirely by way of a charge in respect of each individual call'. However, in this case, 'the private calls predominated by a large margin'. None of the rental could be allowed as a deduction. *Lucas v Cattell*, Ch D 1972, 48 TC 353.

[22.220] See also *Nolder v Walters*, **22.231** below, and *Hamerton v Overy*, 22.274 below.

Clothing

[22.221] A computer engineer appealed against an assessment, claiming a deduction of £50 for wear and tear to suits which he wore at work (as required by his employer). The Commissioners rejected his claim, and the Ch D upheld their decision. Goulding J held that 'if a taxpayer works in an occupation where ordinary civilian clothing is worn of the sort that is also worn off duty', the cost of the clothing was not 'wholly or exclusively incurred in the performance of the duties of the employment'. *Hillyer v Leeke*, Ch D 1976, 51 TC 90; [1976] STC 490. (*Note.* The decision was approved by the HL in *Mallalieu v Drummond*, **63.216** TRADING PROFITS.)

[22.222] The decision in *Hillyer v Leeke*, **22.221** above, was applied in the similar subsequent cases of *Woodcock v CIR (and related appeal)*, Ch D 1977, 51 TC 698; [1977] STC 405, and *Ward v Dunn*, Ch D 1978, 52 TC 517; [1979] STC 178.

[22.223] A television newsreader claimed deductions for the cost of purchasing and laundering the clothing which she wore while reading the news, and for the cost of having her hair done. HMRC rejected the claim and she appealed, contending that she did 'not need the clothes for warmth as it is warm inside the studios, and that she would be prepared to read the news without clothes and only wears the clothes because her employer requires it'. The First-tier Tribunal rejected this contention and dismissed her appeal. Judge Staker did 'not accept as realistic that she could perform her duties without wearing any clothes at all if she were not required by her employer to do so'. He observed that 'the clothing in this case is ordinary everyday clothing, there is nothing about the clothing that restricts the use of any particular outfit only to work, and the appellant has not established that there is any contractual requirement for the expenditure'. *Ms S Williams v HMRC*, FTT [2010] UKFTT 86 (TC), TC00397.

Dietary supplements

[22.224] A rugby player claimed a deduction for vitamin supplements, creatine and protein supplements. The Ch D held that the expenditure was not deductible. It was 'incurred in order to enable him to perform his duties', and not in the performance of the duties. *Ansell v Brown*, Ch D 2001, 73 TC 338; [2001] STC 1166. (*Note*. For HMRC's practice following this decision, see Employment Income Manual, para EIM32507.)

[22.225] The decision in *Ansell v Brown*, **22.224** above, was applied in the similar subsequent case of *JS Emms v HMRC*, Sp C [2008] SSCD 618 (Sp C 668).

Newspapers

[22.226] Five journalists received allowances from their employer to reimburse them for the cost of newspapers and periodicals which they purchased. The Revenue issued assessments on the allowances. The journalists appealed, accepting that the allowances were emoluments but contending that the expenditure had been incurred 'in the performance of the duties of the office or employment'. The HL rejected this claim and upheld the assessments (by a 4-1 majority, Lord Browne-Wilkinson dissenting). A journalist did not purchase and read newspapers in the performance of his duties, but for the purpose of ensuring that he would carry out his duties efficiently. *Smith v Abbott; Smith v Shuttleworth (and related appeals)*, HL 1994, 66 TC 407; [1994] STC 237; [1994] 1 WLR 306; [1994] 1 All ER 673. (*Note*. The case was heard in the HL with *Fitzpatrick v CIR (No 2)*, **22.227** below.)

[22.227] A similar decision was reached in a Scottish case which the HL heard with *Smith v Abbott & Others*, **22.226** above. *Fitzpatrick & Others v CIR (No 2)*, HL 1994, 66 TC 407; [1994] STC 237; [1994] 1 WLR 306; [1994] 1 All ER 673. (*Note*. For a preliminary issue in this case, see **4.193** and **4.194** APPEALS.)

[22.228] The decision in *Fitzpatrick & Others v CIR (No 2)*, 22.227 above, was applied in the subsequent case of *P Gamble v HMRC*, FTT [2010] UKFTT 564 (TC), TC00815.

Psychotherapy

[22.229] A psychiatrist (S) claimed a deduction in respect of psychotherapy sessions. The Revenue rejected the claim and the Special Commissioner dismissed S's appeal. *Snowdon v Charnock*, Sp C [2001] SSCD 152 (Sp C 282).

[22.230] A similar decision was reached in *Consultant Psychiatrist v HMRC*, Sp C [2006] SSCD 653 (Sp C 557).

Expenditure held to be partly allowable

Hotel expenses

[22.231] An aeroplane pilot was employed by a company operating from Croydon Airport. He was liable to be called for duty at any time, and when on duty was sometimes away from home overnight. He claimed deductions for the cost of travelling between his home and the airport, the cost of a telephone at his home (his duty calls were notified to him by telephone), and the amount by which his hotel expenses when he was away from home exceeded the flat-rate allowance paid to him by his employer. The KB upheld the Commissioners' decision that his hotel expenses were allowable deductions, but held that the cost of travelling between his home and the airport and the cost of a telephone were not deductible. *Nolder v Walters*, KB 1930, 15 TC 380.

Local councillor—expenditure on communications

[22.232] A London borough councillor (L) received allowances from the council totalling £11,500 pa, which were accepted as taxable. He claimed deductions of £2,006 in respect of the use of his home as an office, £1200 for expenditure on communications to his constituents, plus deductions for expenditure on childminding and on various subscriptions and publications. HMRC agreed to allow a deduction of £334 in respect of the use of one room in L's home as an office, but rejected the remainder of the claim. L appealed. The First-tier Tribunal allowed the claim for expenditure on communications, holding that 'the task of representing the community to the local authority demands that the councillor informs himself of the needs of the ward and informs the constituents of the council's plans and policies. Without communicating through newsletters and special street letters the councillor would be left with no effective means of carrying out his duties.' The tribunal observed that, if the newsletters had been partly for the purpose of promoting the political party to which L belonged, the cost would not have been allowable, but found that, on the evidence here, 'none of the newsletters and street letters had anything to do with elections and none seeks to canvass the votes of the recipients'. However, the tribunal rejected the remainder of L's claims. Sir Stephen Oliver observed that 'for tax purposes, child care expenditure is not allowable as a deduction in computing taxable earnings. This is because child care expenses are not dictated by the requirements of the job of being a councillor; instead they have to be incurred to meet the personal circumstances of the councillor'. The expenditure on subscriptions and publications was not allowable, applying the 1925 KB decision in *Simpson v Tate*, **22.271** below. *PA Lorber v HMRC (No 2)*, FTT [2011] UKFTT 110 (TC), TC00986. (*Note*. For other appeals by the same appellant, see **22.233** below, **37.3** MARRIED COUPLES and **56.35** SETTLEMENTS.)

Local councillor—domestic expenses

[22.233] Following the decision noted at **22.232** above, the councillor requested a review of the decision disallowing his claims relating to the use of his home as an office, plus expenditure on childminding and on various subscriptions and publications. The First-tier Tribunal reheard the appeal and upheld its earlier decision. Sir Stephen Oliver noted that HMRC had agreed to allow a deduction of £334 in respect of the use of L's home as an office, and held that he had produced no evidence to justify a larger deduction. *PA Lorber v HMRC (No 3)*, FTT [2012] UKFTT 492 (TC), TC02169.

Secretarial assistance to office-holder

[22.234] See *Evans v HMRC*, **44.116** PENALTIES.

Expenditure held to be allowable

Subscription to London clubs

[22.235] A company based in Northern Ireland paid subscriptions for its managing director to two London clubs, on the ground that it was cheaper for him to stay in the clubs than in hotels when he was visiting London on company business. He claimed a deduction for the subscriptions. The Special Commissioners accepted his claim, holding on the evidence that, in the unusual circumstances, the subscriptions were no more than a retaining fee paid to secure suitable inexpensive accommodation for the director on his visits to London. The CA unanimously upheld their decision, distinguishing *Brown v Bullock*, **22.218** above. Lord MacDermott CJ held that the Commissioners had been entitled to find that the director 'became a member and paid his subscriptions solely to obtain the accommodation and facilities he needed in the performance of his duties at a more reasonable cost than staying in appropriate hotels would involve'. Curran LJ held that 'if the duties cannot be performed without incurring the outlay in question, the possibility that the taxpayer may incidentally enjoy some personal benefit from such outlay does not prevent it from being wholly, exclusively and necessarily expended in the performance of the said duties'. *Elwood v Utitz*, CA(NI) 1965, 42 TC 482.

Attendance at dermatology courses and conferences

[22.236] A dermatologist (B), employed by an NHS trust, claimed deductions for the costs of attending various courses, conferences and meetings. HMRC issued amendments to B's self-assessments disallowing the claims. B appealed, contending that she was required to attend the courses as a condition of her employment, and that they took place within her normal working hours. The General Commissioners allowed her appeal (by a majority), finding that the expenses 'were all incurred wholly and exclusively and necessarily as an intrinsic part of the performance of her duties'. The Ch D upheld the Commissioners' decision as one of fact and the CA upheld this decision (by a 2-1 majority, Pitchford LJ dissenting). Rimer LJ held that 'the reason why (B) attended the courses and incurred the expense she did in doing so was because she was required to attend them as part of the duties of her employment and because if she did not do so, her employment would have been terminated'. Hooper LJ held that 'it does not follow from the fact that a taxpayer receives an incidental personal benefit from the expenditure, that the obtaining of the benefit necessarily becomes a "purpose" which defeats the "exclusivity" requirement'. *HMRC v Banerjee (No 1)*, CA 2010, 80 TC 205; [2010] STC 2318; [2010] EWCA Civ 843; [2011] All ER 985. (Note. For another issue in this case, not taken to the CA, see **4.162** APPEALS.)

Travel expenses (ITEPA 2003, ss 337–342)

Solicitor

[22.237] A solicitor, who lived and carried on business at Worcester, was appointed Clerk to the Justices at Bromyard (which is 14 miles from Worcester). He appealed against an assessment on his income from this post, claiming that his travelling expenses between the two places should be allowed as a deduction. The QB rejected the claim. Hawkins J observed that there was no difference between this case and the case of a man who worked in London but chose 'for his own convenience or pleasure' to live in Brighton, and commute by train. Such expenses were not 'necessarily incurred in the transaction of his business'. *Cook v Knott*, QB 1887, 2 TC 246. (*Note.* The decision was approved by the HL in *Ricketts v Colquhoun*, **22.245** below.)

Company directors

[22.238] A company reimbursed its directors their travelling expenses from their homes to the company's office. The Revenue issued an assessment charging tax on the payments. The QB upheld the assessment, applying the decision in *Cook v Knott*, **22.237** above. *Revell v Directors of Elworthy Bros & Co Ltd*, QB 1890, 3 TC 12.

[22.239] A company (T) was controlled by a married couple, who spent five months visiting Australia. T paid the cost of the trip. The Revenue issued an assessment on the husband (N) charging tax on this, and he appealed. The Special Commissioners held that £490 was allowable in respect of each director. The Ch D upheld their decision as one of fact with regard to the £490 attributable to N, but held that none of the expenses attributable to his wife were allowable. *Maclean v Trembath*, Ch D 1956, 36 TC 653; [1956] 1 WLR 437; [1956] 2 All ER 113.

[22.240] A managing director was paid 'lump sum' allowances to reimburse travelling expenses. The General Commissioners found that not all of these were deductible, and accepted an apportionment proposed by the Revenue (disallowing from £250 to £300 of the amounts claimed for each year). The CS upheld their decision as one of fact. *McLeish v CIR*, CS 1958, 38 TC 1.

[22.241] A married couple were directors of a family farming company. They visited the USA and Canada on an organised tour, at a cost of £791, which the husband paid personally. He appealed against an income tax assessment, claiming that £500 of the £791 should be allowed as a deduction. The Ch D rejected the claim and upheld the assessment. Ungoed-Thomas J held that 'a very substantial part was clearly spent both on sightseeing and on matters of general interest to farmers and not in the performance of duties as directors or director of the company at all'. *Thomson v White*, Ch D 1966, 43 TC 256.

[22.242] The controlling director of a family company claimed a deduction for expenses incurred in visiting a customer in London. The General Commissioners rejected the claim and the Ch D upheld their decision. *Smith v Fox*, Ch D 1989, 63 TC 304; [1989] STC 378.

[22.243] A computer consultant lived in Bedfordshire and also owned a flat in Croydon. He formed a limited company to provide his services to his former employer in Croydon. He claimed a deduction for the cost of travelling from Bedfordshire to Croydon each week. The Special Commissioner dismissed his appeal, holding that the travel had not been necessarily incurred in the course of his employment. The Ch D upheld this decision. *Miners v Atkinson*, Ch D 1995, 68 TC 629; [1997] STC 58.

Cost of maintaining motorcycle

[22.244] An employee took up a post in Bideford. He was unable to find accommodation in the town and rented a house three miles away. He purchased a motorcycle to travel to work and claimed a deduction for the cost of maintaining it. The KB rejected the claim. Rowlatt J held that the cost of travelling to the office was 'not an expense of carrying on an office'. *Andrews v Astley*, KB 1924, 8 TC 589.

Recorder of Portsmouth

[22.245] A barrister, who lived and practised in London, was appointed Recorder of Portsmouth. He appealed against an assessment on his income from this post, claiming a deduction for his travelling expenses between London and Portsmouth, for his Portsmouth hotel expenses, and for the cost of conveying his robes when attending the Quarter Sessions in Portsmouth. The Commissioners rejected the claim, and the HL unanimously upheld their decision. Viscount Cave observed that 'a man must eat and sleep somewhere', and held that 'if he elects to live away from his work so that he must find board and lodging away from home, that is by his own choice, and not by reason of any necessity arising out of his employment'. Lord Blanesburgh observed that the barrister had incurred the expenses in question 'because, for his own purposes, he chose to live in London'. *Ricketts v Colquhoun*, HL 1925, 10 TC 118; [1926] AC 1.

Aeroplane pilot

[22.246] See *Nolder v Walters*, 22.231 above.

Student laboratory assistant

[22.247] See *Blackwell v Mills*, 22.208 above.

Factory worker

[22.248] In 1942, a married woman, who had previously been 'fully occupied with household duties', was ordered to work at an ordnance factory. She appealed against assessments on her wages, claiming that her travelling expenses should be allowed as deductions. The KB rejected her claim. *Phillips v Emery*, KB 1945, 27 TC 90; [1946] 1 All ER 144.

Car expenses in excess of employer's allowance

[22.249] A civil servant (M), employed in the Inland Revenue Audit Division, claimed a deduction for the cost of using his car on Revenue business (in excess of the amount which the Revenue reimbursed him). The Special Commissioners rejected his claim and the Ch D upheld their decision. *Marsden v CIR*, Ch D 1965, 42 TC 326; [1965] 1 WLR 734; [1965] 2 All ER 364. (*Note.* M also claimed a deduction for the cost of repairing and cleaning the clothes which he wore on Revenue business. This was also rejected.)

[22.250] See also *Pook v Owen*, 22.181 above, and *Perrons v Spackman*, 22.184 above.

Cattle society secretary

[22.251] The secretary of a cattle society (R) lived 19 miles from R's office. He frequently visited local farmers in the course of his duties, and R required him to keep a car for this purpose. He normally used his car to travel to his office, so that he could use it to visit farmers, and claimed a deduction for the amount by which the cost of travelling by car between his home and office exceeded the rail fare. The Commissioners rejected his claim and the Ch D upheld their decision. *Burton v Rednall*, Ch D 1954, 35 TC 434.

Overseas travel

[22.252] A company's managing director claimed a deduction for the cost of a trip to Peru and Chile. The Revenue rejected the claim on the basis that the trip was a holiday. The CA dismissed the director's appeal. *Newlin v Woods*, CA 1966, 42 TC 649. (*Note.* For another issue in this case, see 22.216 above.)

[22.253] A county surveyor, while on leave, attended a conference in Tokyo. He claimed a deduction for his expenses, on the basis that he had made the visit because he was concerned that a proposed river bridge would lead to flooding. The Commissioners rejected his claim, holding that the expenditure was not 'wholly, exclusively and necessarily in the course of his duties'. The CA unanimously upheld their decision. *Owen v Burden*, CA 1971, 47 TC 476; [1972] 1 All ER 356.

Canadian director appointed by UK company

[22.254] A UK brewery group appointed the president of a Canadian brewery company as a director, with a 'special assignment' of helping the group to expand. He spent an average of between 50 and 85 days in the UK each year, but did most of his work outside the UK, by correspondence or telephone. He received no remuneration but was reimbursed his travelling expenses between Canada and the UK. The Revenue issued assessments charging tax on these payments. The HL allowed the director's appeal (by a 3-2 majority, Lord Wilberforce and Lord Simon of Glaisdale dissenting). Lord Reid held that 'the essential feature' of the case was that it 'was impossible for the companies which contracted with him to get the work done by anyone else'. The reimbursement of his expenses was an emolument, but the expenses were necessarily incurred in travelling in the performance of the duties of his office. Lord Morris of Borth-y-Gest held that, on the evidence, some of the director's duties were performed in Canada and some were performed in the UK. Accordingly, 'his journeys to and from the United Kingdom were made necessary by the very nature of his office or employment and of his assigned duties'. *Taylor v Provan*, HL 1974, 49 TC 579; [1974] STC 168; [1975] AC 194; [1974] 1 All ER 1201.

American taking employment in London

[22.255] In 2004 an American citizen (L) took up employment with Goldman Sachs in London. He rented a house in the UK, and claimed deductions for the rent, the costs of travel from the house to his office, and for 'subsistence expenses'. HMRC rejected the claim and L appealed, contending that since he had intended to return to the USA within two or three years, his office in London should be treated as a 'temporary workplace' for the purposes of *ITEPA 2003, s 339*. The First-tier Tribunal rejected this contention and dismissed L's appeal. Judge Radford held that the London office 'did not qualify as a temporary workplace and therefore the travel and subsistence expenses were not deductible'. *S Long v HMRC*, FTT [2012] UKFTT 148 (TC), TC01843.

Doctor's travelling expenses

[22.256] A doctor in general practice held three part-time hospital appointments. He claimed a deduction for expenses incurred in travelling to and between the hospitals at which he was employed, and for the cost of attending seminars abroad. The Special Commissioner held that the deductions claimed were not allowable, and the CA unanimously upheld this decision. The doctor's duties did not begin until he arrived at the hospitals, and he was not acting in the course of his duties when attending the seminars. *Parikh v Sleeman*, CA 1990, 63 TC 75; [1990] STC 233.

[22.257] An endocrinologist claimed a deduction for the cost of travelling to the hospital where he worked. HMRC rejected his claim and the First-tier Tribunal dismissed his appeal, finding that he 'had only one place of work, that being the hospital and therefore no expenses were incurred necessarily on travelling in the performance of the duties of the employment'. *Dr W Reiter v HMRC*, FTT [2010] UKFTT 299 (TC), TC00587.

[22.258] A surgical trainee, who had worked at six different hospitals during a six-year period, claimed a deduction for his travelling expenses. HMRC rejected his claim and the First-tier Tribunal dismissed his appeal. Judge Radford observed that 'each placement was a separate employment'. *T Sathesh-Kumar v HMRC*, FTT [2011] UKFTT 489 (TC), TC01336.

[22.259] See also *Pook v Owen*, **22.181** above; *Hamerton v Overy*, **22.219** above, and *Bhadra v Ellam*, **42.12** PAY AS YOU EARN.

NHS employee

[22.260] An employee of a NHS Trust claimed that the expenses of travelling from his home to Trust premises should be allowed as a deduction. The

Revenue rejected his claims and the Special Commissioner dismissed his appeal. The fact that he read Trust papers at home did not mean that his home was a base of his employment. *Knapp v Morton*, Sp C 1998, [1999] SSCD 13 (Sp C 177).

Civil servant working partly from home

[22.261] A DSS officer (E) lived in Kings Lynn and worked there (or on detached duty) until 1990, but was subsequently transferred to Leeds. He continued to live in Kings Lynn, travelling to and from Leeds each week. In 1996 the DSS introduced a 'homeworking' scheme, under which he was allowed to do some of his work from home. In his self-assessment returns for 1997/98 and 1998/99, E claimed a deduction for the expenses of travelling to and from Leeds, and for a sum in respect of the use of part of his home as an office. The Ch D held that the amounts claimed were not allowable. Patten J observed that the necessity of travelling to Leeds was dictated by E's 'choice of the place where he lives and not by the nature and the terms of the job itself'. The Leeds office was his 'permanent workplace' within *ITEPA 2003, s 339**, so that the costs of travelling to and from Leeds were 'ordinary commuting', the costs of which were prohibited by *ITEPA 2003, s 338**. Additionally, the costs of heating and lighting a workspace in his home were not 'wholly, exclusively and necessarily incurred in the performance of his duties', since they were 'equally attributable to the maintenance of his home as such'. *Kirkwood v Evans*, Ch D 2002, 74 TC 481; [2002] STC 231; [2002] EWHC 30(Ch); [2002] 1 WLR 1794.

[22.262] A Revenue officer (L) had worked for many years at Revenue offices within daily commuting distance of her home in Warwickshire. In 2000 she successfully applied for a post in London. She was allowed to work at the London office for two or three days each week, and from her home for two or three days each week. She claimed a deduction for the costs of travelling from Warwickshire to London. The Revenue rejected the claim on the basis that this expenditure was 'ordinary commuting', which was not deductible by virtue of *ITEPA 2003, s 338*, and the Special Commissioner dismissed L's appeal. *HP Lewis v HMRC*, Sp C [2008] SSCD 895 (Sp C 690).

Schoolteacher

[22.263] A supply teacher claimed a deduction for the costs of travelling between her home and the schools at which she worked. The Revenue rejected the claim and she appealed, contending that the expenses should be treated as allowable, because she used her home for marking work and preparing lessons. The Special Commissioner dismissed her appeal, accepting that she had a 'secondary place of work' at home but holding that the expenses were not allowable, because the location of her secondary place of work was dictated by her choice of where to live, rather than by the requirements of the job itself. *Warner v Prior*, Sp C [2003] SSCD 109 (Sp C 353).

[22.264] In an Irish case, a schoolteacher claimed a deduction for travelling expenses between his home and school. The HC(I) rejected his claim. *Phillips v Keane*, HC(I) 1925, 1 ITC 69; [1925] 2 IR 48.

Construction worker

[22.265] During 2000/01 a construction worker was employed by three different construction companies. He claimed that the cost of travelling from his home to the three sites, and a sum representing 'subsistence expenses', should be allowed as a deduction. The Revenue rejected his claim, and he appealed. The Special Commissioner dismissed his appeal, holding that each of the three sites was a 'permanent workplace' within what is now *ITEPA 2003, s 339(2)*, so that the travelling expenses were 'ordinary commuting' and were not allowable as a deduction by virtue of *s 338(2)*. *Phillips v Hamilton; Macken v Hamilton*, Sp C [2003] SSCD 286 (Sp C 366).

[22.266] A scaffolder (B), whose home was in Lancashire, was employed at various construction sites in the London area. He rented accommodation in London, returning to Lancashire at weekends. He claimed deductions in respect of the rented accommodation, subsistence and travel. HMRC issued notices of amendment rejecting the claims. The Special Commissioner upheld the notices and dismissed B's appeal. *SJ Bennett v HMRC*, Sp C [2007] SSCD 158 (Sp C 576).

[22.267] From September 2002 to June 2005 a miner (W), whose home was in Colwyn Bay, was employed at Heathrow Airport, working on the construction of a new terminal. He claimed deductions for his travelling expenses. HMRC rejected the claims and he appealed. The First-tier Tribunal reviewed the evidence in detail and allowed his appeal in part. Judge Berner held that from September 2002 to January 2004 Heathrow had not been W's 'permanent workplace', within *ITEPA 2003, s 338(3)*, so that his expenses were allowable. However, from January 2004 Heathrow had become W's 'permanent workplace', so that his expenses from January 2004 to June 2005 were not allowable. *M Williams v HMRC*, FTT [2012] UKFTT 378 (TC), TC02062.

[22.268] An employee, whose home was in Liverpool, worked on the construction of tunnels at various sites including Stratford, Croydon and Hindhead. He claimed deductions for his travelling expenses. The First-tier Tribunal allowed his appeal, holding that none of the sites at which he worked had constituted a 'permanent workplace', within *ITEPA 2003, s 338*. *C Wragg v HMRC*, FTT [2014] UKFTT 553 (TC), TC03679.

Employee based at power stations

[22.269] From March to October 2008 a company (G) employed a worker (R) under a 'retainer contract', under which he could be required to work at various sites. In November 2008 R agreed to work for G under a short-term contract which stipulated that he would be based at Brigg power station. In January 2009 R began working for G under another short-term contract which stipulated that he would be based at Medway power station. R claimed a deduction for the costs of travelling from his home to the various sites at which he had worked. HMRC agreed to allow a deduction while R was employed under a 'retainer contract', on the basis that the effect of that contract was that each of the sites was a 'temporary workplace', within *ITEPA 2003, s 339(3)*. However, HMRC rejected his claims for the periods when he was employed under a short-term contract, on the basis that each of these contracts stipulated that R should be based at a 'permanent workplace', within *ITEPA 2003, s 339(2)*. The First-tier Tribunal dismissed R's appeal against this decision. *N Ratcliffe v HMRC*, FTT [2013] UKFTT 420 (TC), TC02814.

Tax on car benefit

[22.270] A salesman (C) was provided with a car. For 1993/94, the car benefit was £2,030 and the tax thereon was £812. C appealed against an assessment, accepting that the £2,030 was assessable but contending that the £812 should be allowed as a deduction. The General Commissioners rejected this contention and dismissed his appeal, and the Ch D upheld their decision. *Clark v Bye*, Ch D 1996, 69 TC 305; [1997] STC 311.

Fees and subscriptions (ITEPA 2003, ss 343–345)

Subscriptions to professional societies

[22.271] A county medical officer claimed a deduction for the cost of subscriptions to four professional societies. The Special Commissioners found that it was customary for county medical officers to be members of the societies, but it was not a condition of his employment. The KB held that the deduction was not allowable. Rowlatt J held that the holder of a public office was not entitled 'to deduct any expenses which he incurs for the purpose of keeping himself fit for performing the duties of the office, such as subscriptions to professional societies, the cost of professional literature and other outgoings of that sort. If deductions of that kind were allowed in one case every professional office holder would claim to be entitled to deduct the payments made by him to every scientific society to which he happened to belong and the price which he paid for every professional publication, and there would be no end of it'. *Simpson v Tate*, KB 1925, 9 TC 314; [1925] 2 KB 214. (*Note.* The report at 9 TC 314 is an edited version which only includes two paragraphs of Rowlatt J's judgment. It omits the above quotation, which was subsequently cited with approval by Lord Templeman in *Smith v Abbott*, **22.226** above. The full judgment is reproduced in the report in [1925] 2 KB.)

[22.272] The decision in *Simpson v Tate*, **22.271** above, was applied by the First-tier Tribunal in the 2011 case of *Lorber v HMRC*, **22.232** above.

[22.273] An engineer, employed by the London County Council, appealed against an income tax assessment, contending that a subscription to the Institution of Civil Engineers should be allowed as a deduction. The KB rejected this contention and upheld the assessment. *Wales v Graham*, KB 1941, 24 TC 75.

[22.274] A doctor (H), employed as a consultant by a regional hospital board, claimed a deduction for a subscription to the Medical Defence Union. The Commissioners rejected his claim and the Ch D upheld their decision. *Hamerton v Overy*, Ch D 1954, 35 TC 73. (*Note.* H also claimed deductions for travelling expenses, telephone expenses, and 25% of the cost of employing a maid. These claims were also rejected.)

[22.275] The Professional Golfers' Association applied to HMRC to be approved under *ITEPA 2003, s 344* (so that its members would be entitled to tax relief on their subscriptions). HMRC rejected the claim and the First-tier Tribunal dismissed the PGA's appeal. Judge Poole held that the PGA's activities were not 'wholly or mainly directed' to objects within *ITEPA 2003, s 344(2)*. *The Professional Golfers' Association Ltd v HMRC*, FTT [2013] UKFTT 605 (TC), TC02992.

Retired doctor—subscription to General Medical Council

[22.276] A retired doctor received a civil service pension and had no other source of income. He paid an annual subscription of £80 to the General Medical Council, and claimed a deduction for this subscription. The Revenue rejected the claim and he appealed. The Special Commissioner dismissed his appeal, holding that the subscription was not deductible. *Singh v Williams*, Sp C [2000] SSCD 404 (Sp C 250).

Expenses of ministers of religion (ITEPA 2003, s 351)

Minister—voluntary contributions to stipend of assistant

[22.277] A minister (M) claimed a deduction for voluntary contributions which he made towards the stipend of his assistant minister. The court rejected his claim, holding that the payments were not 'necessarily' incurred in the performance of M's duties. *Lothian v Macrae*, CE 1884, 2 TC 65.

Minister—expenses of visiting congregation, etc

[22.278] The CS held that a minister could be allowed a deduction for his expenses of visiting members of his congregation and of attending church meetings, where these activities were part of his duty 'enjoined on him by his superiors'. *Charlton v CIR*, CS 1890, 27 SLR 647.

Minister—costs of arranging substitute during holidays

[22.279] A minister claimed a deduction for various expenses including the costs of applying for 'the augmentation of his stipend' and of arranging for a substitute minister while he went on holiday. The General Commissioners rejected these claims and the CE dismissed the minister's appeal. Lord Kinnear held that 'it is impossible to say that money paid by him in order to get somebody else to perform a part of his duty is an expense incurred by him in performing his duty himself'. *Jardine v Gillespie*, CE 1906, 5 TC 263.

Curate—expenses of transfer to another curacy

[22.280] A curate moved from Faversham to Edmonton, and incurred removal expenses of £42. He appealed against an income tax assessment, claiming that the removal expenses should be allowed as a deduction. The KB rejected the claim, holding that the expenses had been incurred in order to take up his duties, rather than in the performance of his duties. *Friedson v Glyn-Thomas*, KB 1922, 8 TC 302.

Rates and house duty on vicarage

[22.281] A vicar appealed against an assessment, contending that 12.5% of the rates and 'inhabited house duty' which he paid on the vicarage should be allowed as a deduction. The KB rejected this contention and upheld the assessment. *Butcher v Chitty*, KB 1925, 9 TC 301.

Opposition to Bill for compulsory purchase of rectory

[22.282] The Secretary of State for Air promoted a Bill for an extension to an aerodrome, which would have involved the acquisition of the site of a rectory. The rector of the parish opposed the Bill and succeeded in securing the inclusion in the Bill of a clause requiring the Secretary of State to provide an alternative rectory. He appealed against an assessment, contending that costs of £240 which he had incurred in this should be allowed as a deduction. The Commissioners accepted this contention and allowed his appeal, and the KB upheld their decision. Macnaghten J held that the rector 'had a duty to resist any attempt to eject him from that residence' and to oppose anything 'which would prevent his successor from following him in possession of the rectory house and grounds'. *Mitchell v Child*, KB 1942, 24 TC 511; [1942] 2 All ER 504.

Agency fees paid by entertainers (ITEPA 2003, s 352)

[22.283] Two television presenters claimed deductions under what is now *ITEPA 2003, s 352* in respect of fees which they paid to their agent. The Revenue rejected the claims on the basis that the couple were not within the definition of 'entertainers' in what is now *s 352A(4)*. The couple appealed, contending that they were 'theatrical artists' within *s 352A(4)*. The Special Commissioner (Mr. Nowlan) accepted this contention and allowed their appeal. He observed that the legislation derived from *FA 1990*, and that there did not appear to be 'any policy objective on the part of Parliament or HMRC that either is actually seeking to single out and catch a minute percentage of the working population in the invidious position of being exposed to pay agents fees of up to 17.5% of their salary with VAT on top, and then being unable to obtain a tax deduction for those fees'. It would be 'odd and unfair' to deny the presenters 'the tax deduction that they are claiming'. Although the statutory phrase 'theatrical artist' was ambiguous, there was 'no implicit requirement that the performance needs actually to be in the theatre. If an artist is performing on television, in a club or even in the street and the performance can be described as "theatrical", the fact that the performer may never have set foot in a theatre is irrelevant. "Theatrical" means "some sort of performance in the nature of that in the theatre".' Mr. Nowlan held that it was not 'necessary or appropriate in this decision to try to indicate whether various other presenters, game show hosts, and people such as newsreaders' would rank as 'theatrical artists'. However he went on to express the view that 'newsreaders and the weathermen on television are not "theatrical artists"'; that 'presenters of current affairs programmes' were 'neither entertainers nor theatrical artists'; that 'game show hosts can probably cross the line and be described as "theatrical performers"'; and that quiz show hosts were 'borderline'. *Madeley & Finnigan v HMRC*, Sp C [2006] SSCD 513 (Sp C 547).

Personal security assets and services (ITEPA 2003, s 377)

[22.284] A company incurred significant expenditure on providing security services for its chairman (H). The Revenue issued assessments charging tax on the basis that this was a taxable benefit. H appealed, contending that the expenditure qualified for relief under what is now *ITEPA 2003, s 377*, since he had received death threats from the IRA, so that there was a 'special threat' to his physical security arising from his employment. The Special Commissioners accepted this contention and allowed H's appeal, holding on the evidence that 'there was a special threat to the personal physical security of the appellant because the appellant was a potential terrorist target' and that 'the threat to the appellant arose wholly or mainly by virtue of his employment'. The Commissioners observed that 'by virtue of his prominence in business life in connection with which he maintained high profile political connections and friendships, he was a member of a very small group of people who are likely to be regarded as entitled to the deduction'. *Lord Hanson v Mansworth*, Sp C [2004] SSCD 288 (Sp C 410).

Deductions from seafarers' earnings (ITEPA 2003, ss 378–385)

ITEPA 2003, s 378—definition of 'qualifying day'

[22.285] In a case where the substantive issue has been overtaken by subsequent changes in the legislation, the Ch D upheld the Revenue's contention that a 'qualifying day' for the purposes of what is now *ITEPA 2003, s 378* was a calendar day, and thus did not include a day in which an employee worked abroad but returned to his home in the UK before midnight. *Hoye v Forsdyke*, Ch D 1981, 55 TC 281; [1981] STC 711; [1981] 1 WLR 1442. (*Note*. See also *ITEPA 2003, s 378(4)* and HMRC Employment Income Manual, para EIM33004.)

ITEPA 2003, s 385—definition of 'ship'

[22.286] In 1995/96 an individual (L) was employed on a mobile offshore drilling unit, in various locations off the West African coast. He claimed a foreign earnings deduction under the legislation then in force (see now *ITEPA 2003, s 379*). The Revenue rejected his claim on the basis that the drilling unit was not a 'ship', as required by what is now *s 384*. L appealed, contending that the drilling unit should be treated as a 'ship' for the purposes of the deduction. The Special Commissioners accepted this contention and allowed his appeal, holding that the fact that the drilling unit 'does not appear at first glance to be what a layman would describe as a ship' was not conclusive. The unit had undertaken several voyages during the year in question, including a voyage of 2,500 miles from Nigeria to Senegal. The Commissioners held that 'the rig was operating as a ship whilst in transit with the sole exception of the fact that it did not provide its own motive power'. *Lavery v MacLeod*, Sp C [2000] SSCD 118 (Sp C 230). (*Notes*. (1) The relevant legislation was amended by *FA 1998*, which introduced *ICTA 1988, s 192A*. The Revenue considered that the effect of *ICTA 1988, s 192A(3)* — the precursor of *ITEPA 2003, s 385* — was that the drilling unit would no longer qualify as a ship. See Revenue Tax Bulletin, February 2002, pp 913–915. The Revenue's interpretation of the amended legislation was upheld by the CS in *Palmer v HMRC*, **22.288** below. (2) For a subsequent application for costs, see **4.420** APPEALS.)

[22.287] An individual who was employed on a 'jack-up' drilling rig claimed foreign earnings deduction under the legislation then in force (see now *ITEPA 2003, s 379*). The Revenue rejected his claim on the basis that the drilling unit was not a 'ship', as required by what is now *ITEPA 2003, s 384*. He appealed, contending that the drilling rig should be treated as a 'ship' for the purposes of the deduction. The General Commissioners accepted this contention and allowed his appeal, holding that the rig qualified as a ship because 'it was capable of navigation, the motive power being the engines of the towing tugs with all aspects of navigation being controlled from on board the rig'. The CA upheld this decision as one of fact. Robert Walker LJ observed that the purpose of the legislation had been 'to accord more generous treatment to foreign earnings from employment as a seafarer, as compared with other foreign earnings'. He held that 'there is no obvious reason why engineers and others doing skilled and demanding work on a jack-up oil rig should not qualify for the same treatment'. *Clark v Perks (and related appeals)*, CA 2001, 74 TC 187; [2001] STC 1254. (*Note.* See now, however, the note following *Lavery v MacLeod*, **22.286** above, and the CS decision in *Palmer v HMRC*, **22.288** below.)

[22.288] In 1998/99 an individual (P) was employed on an offshore semi-submersible vessel, carrying out exploration for mineral resources. He claimed foreign earnings deduction under the legislation then in force (see now *ITEPA 2003, s 379*). The Revenue rejected his claim on the basis that the vessel was excluded from the definition of a 'ship' by what is now *ITEPA 2003, s 385*, since it was an 'offshore installation' within the meaning of the *Mineral Workings (Offshore Installations) Act 1971*. The General Commissioners dismissed P's appeal and the CS upheld their decision as one of fact. Lord Penrose observed that 'it is undoubtedly the case that different regulations classify structures in different ways according to their purpose, and on occasion depending on the department of government sponsoring their promulgation. But the regulatory point of reference in this case is clear and specific and nothing can turn on the possible application of provisions that have not been incorporated for tax purposes.' *Palmer v HMRC*, CS 2006, 77 TC 738; [2006] CSIH 8.

[22.289] From 1999 to 2004 an individual (L) was employed on a self-propelled oil drilling rig. He claimed foreign earnings deduction under the legislation then in force (see now *ITEPA 2003, s 379*). The Revenue rejected his claim for the period during which the rig was in use, and the period before the rig was brought into use, on the basis that it was an 'offshore installation' within the meaning of the *Mineral Workings (Offshore Installations) Act 1971*, and was therefore excluded from the definition of a 'ship' by what is now *ITEPA 2003, s 385*. (However the Revenue accepted that the rig was not an 'offshore installation' after it had been taken out of use, and therefore qualified as a ship for part of 2002/03.) The Special Commissioner dismissed L's appeal, applying the CS decision in *Palmer v HMRC*, **22.288** above. *JA Langley v HMRC*, Sp C 2007, [2008] SSCD 298 (Sp C 642).

[22.290] Five employees, who worked on a vessel in Brazilian territorial waters, claimed foreign earnings deduction for 2002/03 and 2003/04. The

Revenue rejected the claims on the basis that the vessel was 'a structure used while standing or stationed in relevant waters for the exploitation of mineral resources', within *Offshore Installation and Pipeline Works (Management and Administration) Regulations 1995 (SI 1995/738), reg 3*. Accordingly the effect of *ITEPA 2003, s 385* was that the employees were not entitled to the deduction. The employees appealed. The Special Commissioner dismissed the appeals, holding that the vessel was 'used for the exploitation of mineral resources, notwithstanding that the wells were killed or shut down while it was being used'. *KW Torr v HMRC (and related appeals)*, Sp C [2008] SSCD 772 (Sp C 679).

[22.291] An individual (G) was employed on a 'multipurpose platform supply vessel'. which provided accommodation for people constructing off-shore oil tanks. He claimed seafarers' earnings deduction for 2004/05 to 2006/07 inclusive. HMRC rejected the claim on the basis that the vessel was an 'offshore installation' and was not within the definition of a 'ship'. The Upper Tribunal dismissed G's appeal. Judge Bishopp held that the purpose of the legislation was 'to deny relief to those who are working on essentially fixed installations used, directly or indirectly, for mineral exploitation.' *G Gouldson v HMRC*, UT [2011] UKUT 238 (TCC); [2011] STC 1902.

[22.292] The decision in *Gouldson v HMRC*, **22.291** above, was applied in the similar subsequent case of *G Paterson v HMRC*, FTT [2012] UKFTT 446 (TC), TC02127.

[22.293] Three individuals, who worked on a 'semi-submersible self-erecting tender rig', which was anchored close to drilling platforms and used in connection with those platforms, claimed seafarers' earnings deduction. HMRC rejected the claims on the basis that the rig was an 'offshore installation' and did not qualify as a 'ship'. The First-tier Tribunal upheld HMRC's rulings and dismissed the employees' appeals. *T Wright v HMRC (and related appeals)*, FTT [2010] UKFTT 373 (TC), TC00655.

[22.294] Four employees, who worked on three vessels used for oil production, claimed foreign earnings deduction for 2002/03 and 2003/04. HMRC rejected the claims on the basis that for much of the relevant periods, the vessels were excluded from the definition of a 'ship' by what is now *ITEPA 2003, s 385*, since they were used as 'offshore installations' within *Offshore Installation and Pipeline Works (Management and Administration) Regulations 1995 (SI 1995/738), reg 3*. The employees appealed. The First-tier Tribunal reviewed the evidence in detail and allowed the appeals in part, holding *inter alia* that for part of the period in dispute, two of the vessels were excepted from being an 'offshore installation' by *SI 1995/738, reg 3(2)(d)*, since they were 'not being used for the exploitation of mineral resources by means of a well' but were 'used as a multi-purpose maintenance and construction support vessel', and qualified as ships. The tribunal also found that for most of the period in dispute, the third vessel had been taken out of use within *SI 1995/738, reg 3(2)(e)*, and was therefore not an 'offshore installation'. *D Spowage v HMRC (and related appeals)*, FTT [2009] SFTD 393; [2009] UKFTT 142 (TC), TC00110.

[22.295] In 2001/02 and 2002/03 an employee (D) worked on a multi-purpose vessel, which operated to the west of the Shetland Islands and on the

Norwegian Continental Shelf. He claimed seafarers' earnings deduction. HMRC rejected the claim on the basis that the vessel had been used as an 'offshore installation' within *Offshore Installation and Pipeline Works (Management and Administration) Regulations 1995 (SI 1995/738), reg 3*. The First-tier Tribunal allowed D's appeal, holding that the vessel had not been an 'offshore installation' because it had been 'moving around to such a high degree' that it had not been 'stationed'. *J Davies v HMRC*, FTT [2012] UKFTT 127 (TC), TC01822.

Employment income: income which is not earnings or share-related (ITEPA 2003, ss 386–416)

Payments to non-approved pension schemes (ITEPA 2003, ss 386–392)

NOTE.

ITEPA 2003, ss 386-392 was repealed by *FA 2004* with effect from 6 April 2006, subject to certain transitional provisions set out in *FA 2004, Sch 36*.

Transfers of shares to unapproved pension scheme

[22.296] A company transferred sixteen shareholdings in different quoted companies to a funded unapproved retirement benefits scheme, for the benefit of one of its directors. The director did not declare this on his tax return. The Revenue issued an amendment to his self-assessment, charging income tax on the value of the transferred shares (treating the total value as more than £145,000). The director appealed. The Special Commissioners upheld the Revenue's amendment and dismissed the director's appeal in principle (subject to agreement as to figures). The Commissioners observed that the statutory words 'as a matter of literal construction, connote no more than that a transfer of value is required'. There was no 'cogent policy reason for confining the charge to contributions made in money'. The legislation was 'apt to cover a transfer of value whether in the form of a monetary payment or of a payment in kind'. The Ch D and CA unanimously upheld the Commissioners' decision. Rimer LJ observed that the relevant legislation derived from *FA 1947, s 19*, which referred to funded schemes, and that it was 'difficult to discern any reason why Parliament should have been intended to limit the type of funding that *section 19(1)* had in mind to funding by cash payments'. *Irving v HMRC*, CA 2008, 79 TC 836; [2008] STC 597; [2008] EWCA Civ 6. (*Note*. Sedley LJ criticised the wording of the legislation, commenting that 'not for the first time, we have had to go to Bannockburn by way of Brighton Pier. This is not how legislation should be written.')

[22.297] The decision in *Irving v HMRC*, **22.296** above, was applied in the similar subsequent case of *M Allan v HMRC*, FTT [2013] UKFTT 142 (TC); [2013] SFTD 715, TC02540.

Transfer of property to unapproved pension scheme

[22.298] A company (H) established a funded unapproved retirement benefits scheme for the benefit of its controlling shareholder (M). In March 2005 H transferred two freehold properties, valued at £475,000, to the scheme. M failed to declare this on his tax return. When HMRC discovered this, they issued a discovery assessment charging tax under *ITEPA 2003, s 386*. The First-tier Tribunal upheld the assessment and dismissed M's appeal. Judge Cornwell-Kelly observed that '(M's) memory of events was poor and he appeared to attach, and at the time of the events in question to have attached, little importance either to exactitude or to compliance with his legal obligations'. *D McWhinnie v HMRC*, FTT [2013] UKFTT 588 (TC), TC02977.

[22.299] In 2006 a building company established a funded unapproved retirement benefits scheme for the benefit of its directors (who became trustees of the scheme), and transferred some land with development potential to the scheme. HMRC discovered that the directors had not declared this on their tax returns. HMRC issued closure notices amending the directors' self-assessments to include the value of the contributions. The directors appealed, contending that they were not taxable because no part of the land had been allocated to any specific individual. The First-tier Tribunal reviewed the evidence in detail and dismissed the appeals in principle (but slightly increased the amount charged on two of the directors, and slightly reduced the amount charged on another director). Judge Gammie held that there was 'no reason why a FURBS should have to operate on the basis that amounts paid by the employer to the trustees of the FURBS are always expressly attributed to a specific employee or specified employees'. There would be 'little sense in Parliament taxing specific contributions but leaving untaxed general funding'. *NS Philpott v HMRC (and related appeals)*, FTT [2014] UKFTT 853 (TC), TC03969.

Substitution of beneficiary under unapproved pension scheme

[22.300] In 2004 a company (P) established an unapproved Guernsey pension scheme for the benefit of its controlling director (MD). P transferred two properties to the scheme. MD failed to declare this on his returns, and HMRC issued amendments accordingly. In 2010 MD applied for relief under *ITEPA 2003, s 392*, contending that he was no longer a beneficiary under the scheme and that his brother (DD) had been substituted for him. HMRC rejected the claim. MD appealed, and applied for judicial review. The Upper Tribunal dismissed his appeal but allowed his claim for judicial review. David Richards LJ upheld HMRC's contention that there was no statutory right of appeal against the refusal of an application for relief under *ITEPA 2003, s 392*. However, he also held that the HMRC officer who had rejected MD's original claim had misinterpreted *s 392(1)*. There was no evidence that MD had been under any obligation to make any payment to DD, or that DD was under any obligation to reimburse MD for his generosity in transferring his rights under the scheme. *M Dhanak v HMRC (and cross-appeal)*, UT [2014] UKUT 68 (TCC); [2014] STC 1525.

Employer-financed retirement benefits (ITEPA 2003, ss 393–400)

[22.301] In 1997 a bank employee (S) signed an agreement that he would retire in January 2000. Although the bank continued to pay his salary during the intervening period, he was seconded to a charity. From January 2000 he received a pension, including medical benefit payments. These payments were treated as non-taxable until 5 April 2006. From 6 April 2006 the pension scheme treated them as taxable, following the changes to *ITEPA 2003* which were enacted by *FA 2004* with effect from 6 April 2006. S included the payments in his tax return for 2006/07, but in 2010 he submitted a repayment claim, contending that they were not taxable and that he had included them in his return in error. HMRC rejected his claim and S appealed, contending that his employment had terminated in 1997, so that the payments he received were 'excluded benefits' within *ITEPA 2003, s 393B(3)(d)* and the *Employer-Financed Retirement Benefits (Excluded Benefits for Tax Purposes) Regulations (SI 2007/3537)*. The First-tier Tribunal rejected this contention and dismissed S's appeal, holding that his employment had not terminated until January 2000, so that the payments were not 'excluded benefits'. *C Swingler v HMRC*, FTT [2011] UKFTT 242 (TC), TC01106.

[22.302] A company director (T) retired in February 2009, at the age of 66, at the request of his employer (G). G paid him £37,200. T did not include this as taxable income on his 2008/09 return. After an enquiry, HMRC issued an amendment to his self-assessment, charging tax on it. T appealed. The First-tier Tribunal dismissed his appeal, holding that the payment was a 'relevant benefit' which had been provided 'on or in anticipation of the retirement of an employee', within *ITEPA 2003, s 393B*, and was taxable accordingly. *DV Thomas v HMRC*, FTT [2013] UKFTT 43 (TC), TC02463.

[22.303] An employee (F) had been a member of a private healthcare scheme provided by his employer (N). F retired in 1995, but remained a member of N's healthcare scheme until 2009, when N offered him a lump sum payment if he agreed to leave the scheme. F accepted the offer and received a payment of £29,873. In his 2009/10 tax return, F treated this payment as a capital receipt. Following an enquiry, HMRC issued a closure notice ruling that the payment was chargeable to income tax as a 'relevant benefit' within *ITEPA 2003, s 393B*. The First-tier Tribunal upheld HMRC's ruling and dismissed F's appeal. *G Forsyth v HMRC*, FTT [2014] UKFTT 915 (TC), TC04029.

Payment from retirement benefit scheme on redundancy

[22.304] An employee (B) worked for a brewery company (Y) from 1979 to 2006, when he was made redundant at the age of 48. Y had operated a funded unapproved retirement benefit scheme, of which B had been a member. On his redundancy, B received shares from the scheme, which he immediately sold. He did not seek further employment, but decided to live off his savings. HMRC issued an assessment charging tax at the higher rate on the amount which B had received from the scheme. B appealed, contending that the receipt and redemption of the shares was a relevant benefit within *ITEPA 2003, s 393B* and qualified for transitional relief under *FA 2004, Sch 36*. The First-tier Tribunal accepted this contention and allowed B's appeal. Judge Powell found that B had 'firmly decided to retire during the redundancy process for good reasons connected with his specialist skills and the likelihood (or lack of it) that they would be attractive to other potential employers'. Although he had been forced to accept redundancy, 'he was also entitled to retire from employment'. *GF Ballard v HMRC*, FTT [2013] UKFTT 87 (TC), TC02505.

Payments and benefits on termination of employment, etc. (ITEPA 2003, ss 401–416)

[22.305] See 15 COMPENSATION FOR LOSS OF EMPLOYMENT.

Employment income: income and exemptions related to securities (ITEPA 2003, ss 417–554)

NOTE

There have been substantial changes in the legislation relating to share options and incentives in recent years. The cases in this section should be read in the light of the changes in the legislation.

General (ITEPA 2003, ss 417–421L)

ITEPA 2003, s 420—definition of 'securities'

[22.306] A company (L) which operated a pharmacy entered into a scheme intended to take advantage of the 'restricted securities' provisions of *ITEPA 2003, s 423* and pay its controlling director (F) £300,000 without accounting for PAYE or NIC. HMRC issued determinations charging PAYE and NIC on the basis that the scheme was ineffective, and the First-tier Tribunal dismissed L's appeal, specifically distinguishing the Upper Tribunal decision in *UBS AG v HMRC (No 2)*, 22.307 below. Judge Raghavan observed that 'whether the shares were "restricted securities" is not directly in point as the issue this case turns on is whether the award of bonus is to be regarded as falling within the "money" exclusion to *Part 7* in *s 420(5)(b)*, such that *Part 7* does not apply'. He held that, when the shares were awarded, 'realistically what (F) was getting was money. On that basis *Part 7* is not accessed.' The transaction was 'one which it was the intention of Parliament to exclude from the regime in *Part 7* by operation of the "money" exception', and the scheme amounted 'to a bonus of money rather than shares'. *LM Ferro Ltd v HMRC*, FTT [2013] UKFTT 463 (TC), TC02853.

Restricted securities (ITEPA 2003, ss 422–432)

[22.307] A bank entered into arrangements for certain bonuses, intended to be payable to identified individual employees, to be paid into a scheme and used to purchase interests in shares in a company resident outside the UK. HMRC issued determinations under *PAYE Regulations, reg 80* on the basis that the sums in question were 'earnings received by employees'. The bank appealed, contending that the shares received by the employees were 'restricted securities' within *ITEPA 2003, s 423*. The Upper Tribunal accepted this contention and allowed the appeal, holding that the words 'entitled to payment' in *ITEPA 2003, s 18(1)* should be confined to denoting 'a present right to present payment', rejecting HMRC's contention that they also included a right to a future payment. Henderson J held that 'Parliament's concern in *s 423(2)(c)* must have been to negate the depressing effect on market value which would otherwise be caused by the hypothetical acquisition of the relevant securities by the purchaser subject to the provision for transfer, reversion or forfeiture, and to ensure that if the employee were entitled to receive only the depressed market value of the securities, they would still be restricted securities'. He concluded that 'the scheme was technically sound and produced the fiscal results which it was planned to produce'. The CA unanimously upheld this decision. *HMRC v UBS AG*, CA [2014] EWCA Civ 452; [2014] STC 2278. (*Note*. The Supreme Court has granted HMRC's application for leave to appeal against this decision.)

[22.308] The CA reached a similar decision in a case which it heard with *HMRC v UBS AG (No 2)*, **22.307** above, involving a scheme with a similar intention, but devised by different professional advisers, in which the Upper Tribunal had held that the 'complex shareholding structure' of the relevant companies failed to meet the conditions of *ITEPA 2003, s 429*. The CA allowed the bank's appeal, holding on the facts found by the First-tier Tribunal that the requirements of *s 429(4)* were satisfied. *Deutsche Bank Group Services (UK) Ltd v HMRC*, CA [2014] EWCA Civ 452; [2014] STC 2278. (*Note*. The Supreme Court has granted HMRC's application for leave to appeal against this decision.)

[22.309] A company (T) entered into a tax avoidance scheme, devised by an accountancy firm, involving the award of restricted shares in a subsidiary company to its managing director (L), with the aim of paying him a substantial bonus without incurring any liability to PAYE or NIC. The subsidiary company was subsequently liquidated, and its assets were distributed to L. HMRC issued determinations charging PAYE and NIC. The First-tier Tribunal dismissed T's appeal, specifically distinguishing the Upper Tribunal decision in *UBS AG v HMRC (No 2)*, **22.307** above. Judge Kempster observed that the *UBS* case 'involved several hundred employees of multinational services companies', whereas in the present case there was 'a very close identity' between T and L, and it was L himself who had decided to implement the scheme. The only aim was to extract the 'surplus cash' from T, and the only rationale for the subsidiary company 'was to put money in and then strip it out again as soon as possible thereafter'. Applying the principles laid down in *WT Ramsay Ltd v CIR*, **71.285** CAPITAL GAINS TAX, the restricted securities and the subsidiary company should be disregarded, and 'the only coherent analysis of the transaction is that the surplus cash of the employer was paid to the relevant employees'. *Tower Radio Ltd v HMRC (and related appeal)*, FTT [2013] UKFTT 387 (TC); [2014] SFTD 377, TC02784.

[22.310] See also *LM Ferro Ltd v HMRC*, **22.306** above, and *Stratton v HMRC*, **44.154** PENALTIES.

Convertible securities (ITEPA 2003, ss 435-444)

[22.311] An individual (B) who had established a travel business transferred it to a limited company (V). In 2002/03 the shares in V were acquired by a newly-incorporated company (T) in a share exchange. B acquired 270,000 deferred shares in T at a cost of 2p per share. In 2005 these deferred shares were converted into ordinary shares. HMRC subsequently issued a ruling that this gave rise to a tax charge under *ITEPA 2003, ss 436-440*. B appealed, contending that HMRC's Employment-Related Securities Manual, para ERSM40040, indicated that HMRC would not impose such a charge where the shares had been acquired before 1 September 2003. The First-tier Tribunal dismissed the appeal. Judge Walters held that the conversion was within *s 436*, and that the Tribunal had no jurisdiction to consider whether HMRC should have applied the concession referred to at ERSM40040. Any challenge to HMRC's refusal to apply a concession would be a matter for judicial review. *M Bruce-Mitford v HMRC*, FTT [2014] UKFTT 954 (TC), TC04067.

Securities acquired for less than market value (ITEPA 2003, ss 446Q–446W)

Note. The cases noted at 22.312 to 22.320 below relate to periods before the enactment of this legislation, but may still remain useful as illustrating points of general principle.

Director's commission applied in taking up shares

[22.312] A company's managing director was entitled to commission of 2% of the company's turnover. This was credited to him in the company's accounts. To assist the company during a trade depression, he agreed to the credit being used to purchase new shares. He appealed against an assessment, contending that tax should not be charged on the commission which he received in shares rather than cash. The Commissioners rejected this contention and upheld the assessment, holding that the full amount of the commission credited to him was taxable income. The CA unanimously upheld this decision. *Parker v Chapman*, CA 1927, 13 TC 677. (*Note*. The appellant appeared in person.)

Shares allotted to directors at par

[22.313] A company gave its directors the privilege of taking shares in the company at their par value (which was considerably less than their market value). The Revenue assessed the managing director on the excess of the market value of the shares which he acquired over the price which he paid for them. The HL unanimously upheld the assessments. Lord Atkin observed that this was 'an immediate profit in the nature of money's worth received by the director as remuneration for his services'. *Weight v Salmon*, HL 1935, 19 TC 174.

Shares allotted to employees under incentive scheme

[22.314] Five employees of a brewery company were allowed to subscribe for shares in its holding company at their par value (which was considerably less than their market value). They agreed verbally (but not in writing) that they would not sell the shares without the directors' consent. The Revenue issued assessments charging tax on the excess of the market value of the shares which they acquired over the price which they paid for them. Two of the employees appealed. The KB upheld the assessments in principle, holding that the grant of the shares represented a taxable emolument, but remitted the case to the Commissioners to determine the taxable amount, taking into account the restrictions on resale. *Ede v Wilson*; *Ede v Cornwall*, KB 1945, 26 TC 381; [1945] 1 All ER 367.

Shares given to employees via trust

[22.315] In 1928 a company director transferred 2,000 shares in the company, to be held on trust for the benefit of employees selected by the directors, in order to give such employees 'an interest in the business in consideration of past or future services and with a view to the prosperity of the company'. In 1951, 250 of the shares were transferred to an employee (B) in accordance with these provisions. The Revenue issued an assessment charging tax on the value of the shares. B appealed, contending that the grant of the shares should be treated as a gift and not as taxable remuneration. The Ch D rejected this contention and upheld the assessment. *Patrick v Burrows*, Ch D 1954, 35 TC 138.

Gift of shares to directors

[22.316] The controlling director of a company died in 1936, leaving his shares to a family trust. In 1945 the trustees agreed to transfer some of the shares to two of the directors (who were not family members), on the death of the settlor's widow. The shares were duly transferred in 1953, and the Revenue issued assessments charging tax on the directors. The Special Commissioners allowed their appeals, holding on the evidence that the shares were gifts or testimonials, and were not taxable under the legislation then in force. The CA upheld their decision (by a 2-1 majority, Jenkins LJ dissenting). Sellers LJ observed that the directors 'from their long association with and their devotion to the company were well qualified to have some substantial stake and standing as shareholders of the company', and that the transfers 'created a more equitable distribution of the share capital'. *Bridges v Bearsley*; *Bridges v Hewitt*, CA 1957, 37 TC 289; [1957] 1 WLR 674; [1956] 3 All ER 789.

[22.317] In 1988 a UK company (SU), which was a subsidiary of an overseas company (SN), recruited a senior employee (R). R subsequently became SU's managing director, and in 1996 he became its chairman. In 2001 he was awarded a 9% shareholding in SN for a nominal consideration of $1 per share. He left SU in 2003 when part of its business was taken over by a competitor. HMRC subsequently issued an assessment on R, charging tax on the basis that the transfer of the shareholding in SN was an emolument deriving from his employment with SU. R appealed, contending that the transfer should be treated as a non-taxable gift or testimonial, applying the principles laid down by Sellers LJ in *Bridges v Bearsley*, **22.316** above. The First-tier Tribunal accepted this contention and allowed the appeal, finding that by the time of the transfer R had become an alcoholic, so that his value as an employee 'had greatly diminished and his contribution at that time was not worth the value of the shares in (SN) transferred to him'. Judge Brannan held that the transfer was 'in the nature of a testimonial' and that 'the employment or office was not the active or dominant cause of the transfer'. *KA Rogers v HMRC*, FTT [2011] UKFTT 167 (TC); [2011] SFTD 788, TC01036. (*Notes.* (1) For a preliminary issue in this case, see **4.398** APPEALS. (2) Judge Brannan's decision lays considerable emphasis on the distinction between a '*causa causans*' and a '*causa sine qua non*', applying *dicta* of Viscount Simonds in the 1959 case of *Hochstrasser v Mayes*, **22.97** above. Viscount Simonds' reasoning was subsequently strongly criticised by Lord Simon of Glaisdale in *Brumby v Milner*, **22.76** above. Lord Simon observed that the attempt to draw a distinction between a '*causa causans*' and a '*causa sine qua non*' had been disapproved by Lord Wright in *Smith Hogg & Co Ltd v Black Sea & Baltic General Insurance Co Ltd*, HL [1940] 3 All ER 405, and had 'been generally abandoned'; and considered that the relevant issue should not 'be determined by outmoded and ambiguous concepts of causation couched in Latin'. Judge Brannan's decision fails to refer to the HL decision in *Brumby v Milner*.)

Shares acquired on preferential terms and issued in instalments

[22.318] In October 1953, a company secretary elected, under an 'employee share purchase plan', to acquire 15 shares in the company, at 15% less than their market price at that time. The purchase price was to be paid in instalments, the shares being issued as the instalments were paid. Three of the shares were issued to him in 1953/54, and the remaining 12 were issued in 1954/55. The Revenue issued assessments for each of those years, charging tax on the excess of the market price of the shares when they were actually issued over the price he paid for them. He appealed, accepting that the acquisition gave rise to a tax liability for 1953/54, but contending that the taxable amount should be calculated by reference to the market price in October 1953. The Special Commissioners accepted this contention and adjusted the assessments accordingly, holding that the benefit arose in October 1953, when he elected to purchase the shares. The Ch D upheld the Commissioners' decision. *Bentley v Evans*, Ch D 1959, 39 TC 132.

Shares given to accountant on taking up post as company director

[22.319] The senior partner of a firm of accountants was asked to become joint managing director of a company (K). He agreed to do so on condition that he was given some shares in K. The controlling shareholder agreed to give him 4,000 shares, and he resigned his partnership and began working for K. The Revenue issued an assessment charging tax on the value of the shares as emoluments of his directorship. He appealed, contending that the shares were compensation for giving up his partnership, and were not a taxable emolument. The Commissioners accepted this contention and allowed his appeal, holding that the transfer of the shares 'was not something in the nature of a reward for his future services'. The Ch D upheld their decision. Megarry J observed that 'if a professional man is his middle years gives up his career and embarks on some quite different activity, he is most unlikely to be able to pick up his former profession as soon as his other activities end, for to a greater or less degree he will have grown rusty in his skills and knowledge, and will have ceased to be in close daily contact with his professional brethren'. *Pritchard v Arundale*, Ch D 1971, 47 TC 680; [1972] Ch 229; [1971] 3 All ER 1011.

Share issue—preferential shares for employees at below market price

[22.320] In 1969, a company (R) offered shares to the public at 25s each. It offered preferential shares at 20s each to its employees and employees of other companies in the same group. A director of one of R's subsidiary companies was allotted 5,000 preferential shares. The Revenue issued an assessment charging tax on the excess of the market price of the shares over the amount which he paid for them. The director appealed. The Special Commissioners upheld the assessment, finding that the shares were worth 24s each when the director acquired them, and holding that the acquisition of shares at below their market price was a taxable emolument. The HL unanimously upheld their decision. Lord Diplock observed that R's purpose in making the shares available 'was to encourage established employees of the company and of companies within the group to become shareholders in the parent company'. This was 'an advantage afforded to the taxpayer in return for acting as or being an employee'. *Tyrer v Smart*, HL 1978, 52 TC 533; [1979] STC 34; [1979] 1 WLR 113; [1979] 1 All ER 321.

Securities disposed of for more than market value (ITEPA 2003, ss 446X–446Z)

[22.321] A company's managing director (G) had been allotted a 6.63% shareholding in its holding company (B) under an agreement whereby, if B were sold to a third party, G would be entitled to one-third of any increase in B's value between the date of his share purchase and the date of disposal. In 2003 all the shares in B were purchased by an unconnected company (J) for £5,903,219. The effect of the earlier agreement was that £1,451,172 of this was allocated to G for his shares (so that he received substantially more per share than the other shareholders). HMRC issued a determination that G's shares had been sold for more than their market value, giving rise to a charge to income tax under *ITEPA 2003, ss 446X–446Z*, on which the company was required to account for PAYE. The Special Commissioner upheld the determination and dismissed the company's appeal, holding that 'to calculate the market value of each and every £1 ordinary share in (B), i.e. including (G's) shares', one simply 'takes the total paid by (J) for (B), namely £5,903,219,and divides that figure by the number of ordinary shares issued, 222,037. That results in a market value of £26.59 per share.' The CS and the Supreme Court dismissed the company's appeal against this decision. Lord Walker observed that the company was contending that, when J acquired the shares in B, each of G's shares 'had a market value about three times greater than each of the shares owned by the other shareholders. That would be a very surprising result.' When J purchased the shares, 'it was not concerned with the division of the sale price between the vendors'. G's entitlement to one-third of any increase in B's value had no value to a purchaser, but was personal to G. On the evidence, the Special Commissioner had been correct to find that G had disposed of his shares at a price which exceeded their market value. *Gray's Timber Products Ltd v HMRC (aka Company A v HMRC)*, SC 2010, 80 TC 96; [2010] STC 782; [2010] UKSC 4; [2010] 2 All ER 1.

Post-acquisition benefits from shares (ITEPA 2003, ss 447–450)

Dividends on shares allotted to employees—whether earned income

[22.322] A company made some of its shares available at par to selected employees under its Articles of Association. The Revenue issued assessments on the basis that dividends on these shares were investment income (and thus were liable to a 'special contribution' charged on investment income by *FA 1948*). One of the employees appealed, contending that the dividends should be treated as earned income. The Ch D accepted this contention and allowed his appeal. Danckwerts J held that the shares were 'attached to the office or employment', and thus qualified as 'earned income'. *Recknell v CIR*, Ch D 1952, 33 TC 201; [1952] 2 All ER 147.

Share options (ITEPA 2003, ss 471–484)

Exercise of share option

[22.323] In 1974 a bank employee (P) was granted an option to buy 960 shares in the bank under a share option scheme. The option was not exercisable until more than seven years had elapsed. In 1981/82 P exercised his rights under the scheme and realised a gain. He appealed against an assessment, contending that, since the original grant of the option had not been charged to tax, there should be no liability on the exercise of the option. The Ch D rejected this contention and upheld the assessment. *Ball v Phillips*, Ch D 1990, 63 TC 529; [1990] STC 675.

[22.324] The decision in *Ball v Phillips*, 22.323 above, was applied in a similar subsequent case where the Special Commissioner held that 'income tax is chargeable on the exercise of the right to acquire shares even when the shares are retained and not sold'. *Employee v HMRC*, Sp C [2008] SSCD 688 (Sp C 673). (*Note*. The appellant had failed to declare the gains on his return, and the Commissioner held that he had been guilty of 'negligent conduct' within *TMA, s 29(4)*—see **29.56** FURTHER ASSESSMENTS: LOSS OF TAX.)

[22.325] A company (B) had allocated one of its employees (P) units in an option scheme known as a 'capital accumulation plan'. In 2004 P left his employment but retained his rights under the scheme. B subsequently issued shares to P under the scheme. P submitted a self-assessment return claiming a refund of the tax that B had deducted under PAYE. HMRC began an enquiry, rejected the repayment claim, and issued a closure notice requiring P to pay further tax of £813,133. The First-tier Tribunal dismissed P's appeal. Judge McKenna held that the 'capital accumulation plan' units were employment-related securities options, within *ITEPA 2003, s 471*. The distribution of the shares to P was a chargeable event, within *ITEPA 2003, s 477(3)*. *M Phair v HMRC*, FTT [2013] UKFTT 349 (TC), TC02752.

Share option not exercisable for seven years

[22.326] Under a complex earnings-related savings scheme, in 1974/75 a bank employee (D) paid £1 for an option to acquire some shares in the bank at a prescribed price, agreed to be £147 less than the market value of the shares when the option was granted. The right to exercise the option did not mature for seven years and was contingent on certain conditions. The Revenue assessed the £147 for 1974/75. D appealed, contending that the option had no assessable value when it was granted. The Ch D rejected this contention and upheld the assessment, holding that the option had a monetary value, and was a taxable emolument of 1974/75. Vinelott J held that 'an option to acquire shares at less than the then market price, albeit after a period of time and, in broad terms, conditionally on remaining in the employment of a company in the group and maintaining the save-as-you-earn contract for seven years, must *prima facie* be taken to be a right of a kind which has a monetary value'. *Williamson v Dalton*, Ch D 1981, 55 TC 575; [1981] STC 753.

Date on which option assessable

[22.327] An individual (S) had been granted a number of share options in 1998. He was made redundant in July 1999. He rejoined another company in the same group in October 1999, but left in December 1999. He exercised his share options in January 2000 (and sold the shares in July 2000). He did not declare this option in his 1999/2000 tax return. The Revenue issued an assessment for 1999/2000 charging tax on the gains. S appealed, contending that he had assigned the options to a financial adviser (M) by a verbal agreement in July 1999, when they were worth significantly less. The Special Commissioner rejected this contention and dismissed the appeal, finding that the relevant agreement between S and M was undocumented and was not 'a legally binding contract'. Accordingly, S had not assigned the options in July 1999; he had exercised them for his own benefit in January 2000 and was taxable accordingly. *Sheikh v HMRC*, Sp C [2006] SSCD 49 (Sp C 514).

Payment for cancellation of share options

[22.328] Between 1992 and 1994 an employee (B) was granted a number of share options in the company which employed him. In April 1995 he was made redundant. He retained his share options until January 1997, when the company paid him £10,102 for the cancellation of the options. He did not include this payment on his 1996/97 tax return. The Revenue issued a notice of amendment charging tax on the payment. B appealed, contending that the payment should be treated as exempt from tax under what is now *ITEPA 2003, s 403*. The Special Commissioner rejected this contention and dismissed his appeal, holding that the payment was chargeable to tax under what is now *ITEPA 2003, s 477*. *Bluck v Salton*, Sp C [2003] SSCD 439 (Sp C 378); *Bluck v Salton (No 2)*, Sp C [2004] SSCD 177 (Sp C 400). (*Note*. The relevant legislation has subsequently been amended by *FA 2003*. For the Revenue's interpretation of this decision, see the Inland Revenue Statement issued on 13 November 2003.)

[22.329] An employee (R) was made redundant in 2007. She had been previously granted four share options. Following her redundancy, her employer failed to comply with the share option agreements and instead made her a cash payment. HMRC issued a ruling that this was a benefit in connection with a failure to acquire securities and was taxable under *ITEPA 2003, s 477*. R appealed, contending that an HMRC Guidance publication entitled 'Approved Company Securities Option Plans', issued in January 2008, indicated that the payment would not be taxable. The First-tier Tribunal dismissed her appeal. Sir Stephen Oliver observed that the HMRC publication was 'as illiterate and as potentially misleading as any official publication that we have come across'. However, the payment was clearly taxable under *s 477*. *Ms C Rawcliffe v HMRC*, FTT [2013] UKFTT 111 (TC), TC02529.

Share incentive plans (ITEPA 2003, ss 488–515)

[22.330] In 2005 a French bank with a branch in London made its branch manager (S) redundant. S received shares valued at £144,632, plus a cash payment of £56,863. The bank deducted tax at 20%. S submitted a tax return treating the payments as non-taxable and claiming a repayment. Following an enquiry, HMRC issued an amendment to S's self-assessment, charging tax on the payments. S appealed, contending that the shares should be treated as exempt from income tax under *ITEPA 2003, ss 488-515*. The First-tier Tribunal rejected his contention and dismissed his appeal. Judge Aleksander observed that 'the evidence that they were not tax-approved is overwhelming'. *L Sjumarken v HMRC*, FTT [2011] UKFTT 37 (TC), TC00914. (*Note*. The appellant appeared in person.)

Approved SAYE schemes (ITEPA 2003, ss 516–520)

Amendments to SAYE scheme

[22.331] A company (R) which operated two approved employees' share option schemes (an executive scheme and a SAYE scheme) proposed to merge with a Dutch company. Following the merger, companies which had previously been wholly-owned subsidiaries of R would no longer be controlled by R within the meaning of what is now *CTA 2010, s 1124*. R applied for the approval of proposed amendments to its share option schemes to cater for the consequences of that change of control, in particular to prevent the options becoming exercisable on the date of the change and lapsing if not then exercised within six months. The Revenue refused to approve the proposed amendments on the grounds that the effect of the alterations would be a difference in the rights held by option-holders, and that the new rights would not meet the statutory requirements (see now *ITEPA 2003, Sch 3* for SAYE schemes and *Sch 4* for CSOP schemes). The Special Commissioner allowed R's appeal in part, holding that the Revenue was entitled to refuse its approval to the alterations to the SAYE scheme, since a scheme which extended to a company of which the grantor did not have 'control' was not within the definition of a group scheme, but that the Revenue should not have refused approval to the alterations to the executive scheme, since the relevant alterations merely amounted to the removal of an existing right, rather than the creation of a new one. The CA unanimously upheld the Commissioner's decision, holding that there was a critical distinction between a person obtaining a right which he did not previously have and a person ceasing to have a right which he previously had. The elimination of one of the events on which the existing right would have been exercisable could not realistically be described as the obtaining of a new and different right to acquire scheme shares. Accordingly, existing option-holders had not obtained a new right. *CIR* *v Reed International plc*, CA 1995, 67 TC 552; [1995] STC 889. (*Note.* For HMRC's interpretation of this decision, see Employee Share Schemes Unit Guide, para ESSUM47960.)

Approved CSOP schemes (ITEPA 2003, ss 521–526)

Amendments to company share option scheme

[22.332] A company (B) operated employees' share option schemes which had been approved by the Revenue. In 1986 it applied to the Revenue for approval of proposed amendments to the schemes, so that it could make the acquisition of option shares dependent on the performance by the employees of tasks imposed after the grant of the option. The Revenue refused to approve the amendments, considering that any performance conditions should be imposed at the time the option was granted, rather than subsequently. The Special Commissioner allowed B's appeal against this refusal, and the Ch D upheld this decision. The validity of the option was not affected by the fact that the number of shares which the employee might be entitled to acquire could be governed not only by conditions set when the option was granted, but also by conditions subsequently imposed or varied in good faith as part of an incentive scheme. *CIR v Burton Group plc*, Ch D 1990, 63 TC 191; [1990] STC 242. (*Note.* For HMRC's interpretation of this decision, see Employment Shares Scheme Unit Guide, para ESSUM47950.)

[22.333] A company (E) operated a share option scheme which had been approved by the Revenue. Under the scheme, the options granted could not be exercised until nine years after the dates on which they were granted. Subsequently E sought approval for an amendment to the scheme to reduce the time limit from nine years to six years. The Revenue approved the amendment in relation to options to be granted in the future, but refused to approve the amendment in respect of existing options, since the price at which those options had been granted was very much less than the market value of the shares at the time of the proposed amendment. The Ch D upheld the Revenue's refusal to allow a retrospective amendment, holding that the legislation (see now *ITEPA 2003, s 521 et seq*) contemplated a right to acquire a specified number of shares at a specified price and within a specified time-span. The rights which the option-holders had obtained at the date when the original options were granted were not the same as the rights which they would have if effect were given to the proposed amendments. The Revenue had been entitled to refuse its approval to the proposed alteration. *CIR v Eurocopy plc*, Ch D 1991, 64 TC 370; [1991] STC 707.

[22.334] See also *CIR v Reed International plc*, 22.331 above.

Compensation for loss of rights under share option scheme

[22.335] A company director (E) was a member of a share option scheme, operated by the group of which the company which employed him was a subsidiary. In May 1986 there was a change in the ownership of the company, with the result that it ceased to be a member of the group and E's rights under the share option scheme lapsed. In September 1987 the group made him an ex gratia payment of £10,000. The Revenue issued an assessment charging tax on this payment, and E appealed. The General Commissioners allowed his appeal, finding that there was no relevant connection between the source of the payment and E's employment at the time the payment was made, and holding that the payment was neither an emolument from the employment nor a benefit provided by reason of that employment. The Ch D upheld the Commissioners' decision, applying the principles laid down in *Hochstrasser v Mayes*, **22.97** above, and *Abbott v Philbin*, **54.10** SCHEDULE E. The value realised on the exercise of share option rights was not to be treated as a taxable emolument. Accordingly, a payment made as compensation for the loss of such rights was also not a taxable emolument. *Wilcock v Eve*, Ch D 1994, 67 TC 223; [1995] STC 18.

23

Enterprise Investment Scheme (ITA 2007, ss 156–257)

The cases in this chapter are arranged under the following headings.

GENERAL NOTE

The Enterprise Investment Scheme (EIS) was introduced by *FA 1994*, reviving the legislation previously governing the Business Expansion Scheme (BES), which had been withdrawn for shares issued after 31 December 1993. The relevant legislation is now in *ITA 2007, ss 156–257*. See Tolley's Income Tax for details.

The investor (ITA 2007, ss 162–171)

ITA 2007, s 163—whether individual connected with company

[23.1] In April 1987 an individual (W) acquired 40,000 shares in a company. At that time there were a total of 40,002 shares in the company, so that W had a 99.995% shareholding. Further shares were issued in October 1987 and January 1988, reducing W's percentage shareholding to below 30%. In November 1987 W claimed BES relief in respect of his acquisition of shares. The Revenue rejected the claim on the basis that W was 'connected with' the company for the purposes of what is now *ITA 2007, s 163*, since his shareholding had exceeded 30% of the issued share capital during the 'relevant period'. W appealed, contending that he should be granted relief because his shareholding had not exceeded 30% of the issued share capital throughout the relevant period. The General Commissioners rejected this contention and dismissed his appeal, holding that *s 163* disqualified from relief a person who had been connected with the company at any time during the relevant period. The CA upheld the Commissioners' decision. *Wild v Cannavan*, CA 1997, 70 TC 554; [1997] STC 966.

ITA 2007, s 164—date on which shares issued

[23.2] Two banks issued shares in companies under schemes designed to make use of business expansion scheme relief linked to loans from the banks. The shares were allotted to applicants before 16 March 1993 (the date when the precursor of *ITA 2007, s 164* came into force), but the names of the shareholders' nominees were not entered into the Registers of Members until 2 April. The Revenue considered that the shares had not been issued before 16 March 1993, so that what is now *ITA 2007, s 164* applied and no relief was due. The banks issued originating summonses, seeking declarations that the shares were issued when there was a contractual obligation to enter the applicants in the register and for the applicants to accept the entries as being made on their behalf. The Ch D granted the declarations but the CA reversed this decision, and the HL dismissed the banks' appeals (by a 3-2 majority, Lords Jauncey and Woolf dissenting). There was a distinction between the allotment of a share and the issue of that share. The crucial date was when the name of a shareholder was entered in the company's Register of Members. On the evidence, the shares in question were not issued until 2 April, when they were registered. Accordingly, what is now *ITA 2007, s 170* applied to the shares and no relief was due. *National Westminster Bank plc v CIR; Barclays Bank plc v CIR*, HL 1994, 67 TC 1; [1994] STC 580; [1994] 3 WLR 159; [1994] 3 All ER 1.

ITA 2007, s 167—whether employee connected with company

[23.3] Three investors claimed EIS relief in respect of issues of shares in a company (TN). HMRC issued amendments to their self-assessments, ruling that the effect of what is now *ITA 2007, s 167* was that relief was not due, because the investors had been employees of another company (TO), which had previously carried on the same trade but had gone into receivership after making losses. The First-Tier Tribunal allowed the investors' appeals, holding that the investors qualified for relief under what is now *ITA 2007, s 169*. Judge Poole held that the question of whether there had been a previous connection or involvement 'should be tested at the time of the issue of eligible shares which is being considered'. At the time of that share issue, the trade was being carried on by TO, and TN 'had never carried on any trade'. *R Thomason v HMRC (and related appeals)*, FTT [2010] UKFTT 579 (TC), TC00829.

ITA 2007, s 170—persons interested in capital of company

[23.4] Seven individuals applied for shares in a company, each holding just under 15% of the issued share capital. They claimed BES relief. The Revenue rejected the claim on the basis that since they were associates of each other for the purposes of the relief, the effect of what is now *ITA 2007, s 170(9)* was that their shareholdings should be aggregated and thus exceeded the 30% limit of *s 170(1)*. The shareholders appealed, contending that the second part of *s 170(9)* should be construed as merely qualifying the first part of that *subsection*, and did not apply to *s 170(1)*. The CA rejected this contention and upheld the Revenue's rejection of the claim (by a 2–1 majority, Ward LJ dissenting). Mummery LJ held that as all the shareholders were associates of each other, none of them qualified for relief. *Cook v Billings & Others*, CA 2000, 73 TC 580; [2001] STC 16.

[23.5] Two individuals claimed EIS relief in respect of shares in a company (W). HMRC rejected their claims on the grounds that they were connected with W, since the effect of certain loans they had made was that they each held more than 30% of W's capital (aggregating loan and share capital for the purposes of the legislation). They appealed, contending that they should not be treated as 'connected' within the terms of the legislation, since they did not hold 30% of the company's issued share capital. The Upper Tribunal rejected this contention and upheld the assessments. Roth J held that the 30% threshold applied to a 'single, composite category' which included loan capital as well as share capital. He observed that 'depending upon the nominal value of his shareholding, an investor will have to take care as to the proportion that he advances of the company's total borrowing. The fact that this is not within his sole control, and that the amount of the company's total loan capital may fluctuate, is inherent in the use in the eligibility criterion of the concept of a proportion of total loan capital.' *HMRC v NRJ Taylor (and related appeal) (No 2)*, UT 2010, FTC/43/2010. (*Note.* The Upper Tribunal rejected the shareholders' application for leave to appeal against this decision—UT 4 March 2011 unreported. For the award of costs, see **4.452** APPEALS.)

General requirements (ITA 2007, ss 172–179)

ITA 2007, s 174—purpose of share issue

[23.6] An individual, who owned a reversionary interest in two properties, transferred the properties to a newly-incorporated company, receiving shares in the company as consideration. He claimed BES relief. The Ch D held that he was not entitled to relief, holding that the shares had not been issued 'for the purpose of raising money', as required by what is now *ITA 2007, s 174*. Hart J observed that 'what Parliament had in mind was the issue of shares for a money consideration, not the issue of shares for something which would be described as money's worth. The normal usage of the word "money" would not include real property'. *Thompson v Hart*, Ch D 2000, 72 TC 543; [2000] STC 381.

[23.7] A company issued loan notes, which it subsequently converted into ordinary shares. It applied for EIS certificates. The Revenue rejected the claim on the basis that the conversion shares had not been 'issued in order to raise money for the purpose of a qualifying business activity', as required by what is now *ITA 2007, s 174*. The Special Commissioner reviewed the evidence in detail and dismissed the company's appeal. The conversion of loan notes into shares had not been carried out 'in order to raise money', as required by *s 174*, and it appeared that the relevant funds had been transferred to a subsidiary company, rather than being used for the purpose of a qualifying trade. There had also been a 'return of value' to the subscribers, within *TCGA 1992, Sch 5B, para 13*. However, the Commissioner held that other issues of shares by the company did qualify for EIS relief, since the company was primarily a manufacturing company, and the fact that it leased some of the products which it manufactured did not prevent it from qualifying for relief. *Optos plc v HMRC*, Sp C [2006] SSCD 687 (Sp C 560).

[23.8] A company (GC) issued shares to its principal director (G) on 31 March 1999. In December 1999 and March 2001 GC lent some of the money raised by the share issue to a company (GL) controlled by G's wife. Also in March 2001 GC, which had previously been a holding company, acquired the trade of a subsidiary company which carried on an advertising business. GC applied for an EIS certificate in respect of the share issue. The Revenue rejected the claim on the grounds that the effect of the loans to GL was that the shares had not been 'issued in order to raise money for the purpose of a qualifying business activity', as required by what is now *ITA 2007, s 174*. GC appealed, contending that the loans had been on a short-term basis and repayable on demand, and 'were no different from putting the money on deposit at a bank'. The Special Commissioner accepted this contention and allowed the appeal, holding that the loans were 'the equivalent of a bank deposit', since GC 'had raised the money from the share issue and had to hold or "park" it until it was needed for the acquisition'. Accordingly 'the loans were a step in the wider purpose of acquiring the qualifying trade'. *GC Trading Ltd v HMRC (No 1)*, Sp C 2007, [2008] SSCD 178 (Sp C 630). (*Note.* The Special Commissioner rejected an application for costs—see **4.422** APPEALS.)

[23.9] See also *Domain Dynamics (Holdings) Ltd v HMRC*, **71.210** CAPITAL GAINS TAX, and *Harvey's Jersey Cream Ltd v HMRC*, **71.211** CAPITAL GAINS TAX.

ITA 2007, s 175—use of money raised

[23.10] In 1998 a company (F) submitted a form EIS1 to the Revenue, requesting authority to issue certificates to certain investors to enable them to claim EIS relief. The Revenue rejected the claim on the basis that part of the money invested had been used to pay dividends, and thus had not been used for a 'qualifying business activity', as required by what is now *ITA 2007, s 175*. F appealed, contending firstly that the refusal of the claim did not comply with what is now *ITA 2007, s 204*, and secondly that the money raised by the share issue should be treated as satisfying the conditions of *s 175*, since it was both raised and used for the purpose of a company which was carrying on a qualifying trade. The Special Commissioner rejected these contentions and dismissed the appeal, and the Ch D upheld this decision. The Commissioner held that the purpose of *s 204* was simply to provide that there should be a right of appeal against the refusal to give authority to issue a certificate and not to require the Inspector to adopt any particular procedure before he refused to do so. On the evidence, he noted that some of the dividends in question had been paid to employees, and held that since the employees had 'agreed to work for remuneration partly in the form of dividends', these dividends could be treated as being 'paid for the purpose of the trade'. However, significant dividends had also been paid to shareholders who were not employees. These dividends could not be treated as having been paid for the purposes of F's trade, so that the company failed to meet the conditions of *s 175*. Lightman J held that 'there is no reason why Parliament should have effectively required the inspector in every case, not simply to consider the application, but also to formally open an inquiry under (*TMA, Sch 1A*) in relation to each application that is submitted to him in order that he may later be in a position to issue a closure notice'. Furthermore, 'the payment of a significant part of the monies raised on payment of dividends to investors plainly was not and cannot have been employment of the monies raised for the purposes of (F's) qualifying trade'. Applying the principles laid down by Lord Davey in *Strong & Co of Romsey v Woodifield*, **66.70** TRADING PROFITS, 'a payment of dividends to investors is not made "for the purpose" of the trade or for the purpose of earning profit'. Lightman J also observed that he had 'some doubt whether payment by way of dividends to employees are in any different position in this regard from dividends paid to investors. If arrangements are made to pay employees in place of salary by way of dividends which do not attract national insurance, it should not too readily be assumed that payment of those dividends out of monies raised on a share issue such as the present will be in compliance with (*s 175*). That question does not however require to be decided on this appeal.' *Forthright (Wales) Ltd v Davies*, Ch D 2004, 76 TC 134; [2004] STC 875; [2004] EWHC 524 (Ch).

[23.11] An individual (R) claimed EIS relief in respect of money he had subscribed to a company (S), which operated two restaurants. HMRC rejected the claim on the basis that S had kept most of the money in an instant access account, so that 80% of the money subscribed had not been 'employed' in S's trade within the statutory qualifying twelve-month period. R and S appealed. The First-Tier Tribunal dismissed their appeals. Judge Nowlan observed that the legislation 'imposes a definite time period within which different percentages of the cash raised by a share issue must be employed in the trade, and they admit of no exception for the situation where the directors wanted to meet the test but were unable to do so'. The Upper Tribunal upheld this decision. Sales J held that the legislation 'requires the money actually to be used in some way for the purposes of carrying out the qualifying activity within the relevant one-year period'. *C Richards v HMRC (and related appeal)*, UT [2011] UKUT 440 (TCC); [2012] STC 174. (*Note. ITA 2007, s 175* has subsequently been amended by *FA 2009, s 27, Sch 8 para 7* to extend the qualifying period from 12 months to 24 months.)

[23.12] The Upper Tribunal decision in *Richards*, **23.11** above, was applied in a subsequent case where the First-tier Tribunal dismissed an appeal by a family company, holding that 'the company had not shown that the money raised by the share issue was committed or earmarked and therefore employed for a specific purpose within 12 months from the date of the investment as required by the legislation'. *Benson Partnership Ltd v HMRC*, FTT [2012] UKFTT 63 (TC), TC01760.

ITA 2007, s 179—definition of 'qualifying business activity'

[23.13] A company (F) carried on a business of providing financial market analysis. It incurred losses in its early years of trading, and raised further money by two issues of shares. It claimed enterprise investment scheme relief in respect of these share issues. The Revenue rejected F's forms EIS 1, on the basis that the money raised by the shares had been loaned to two wholly-owned subsidiaries (one of which was incorporated in the USA, and the other in Singapore), and that the share issue was not wholly for the purpose of a qualifying business activity, as required by what is now *ITA 2007, s 179*. F appealed, contending that it had 'decided to establish a presence in New York and Singapore in order to support its existing, mainly European, client base with a comprehensive analysis of the markets across the globe'. The Special Commissioner accepted F's evidence and allowed the appeal, holding on the evidence that 'it cannot realistically be said that the appellant had a separate purpose of raising money to invest in the subsidiaries for the purpose of saving the subsidiaries' businesses; the appellant is merely indirectly paying for the analysis that it needs'. Accordingly the money was 'raised wholly for the purpose of the appellant's qualifying business activity'. The Commissioner observed that 'if the subsidiaries had been carrying on business normally by selling their services to the appellant for a consideration (whether or not the arm's length price), any investment in the subsidiaries by way of loan could not qualify as being wholly (or even mainly) for the purpose of the appellant's trade carried on in the UK'. However, on the evidence, F was 'paying nothing for the services for which the subsidiaries were set up to provide, and making loans to the subsidiaries is the means by which the appellant obtains those services which it requires for the purpose of its trade'. *4Cast Ltd v Mitchell*, Sp C [2005] SSCD 280 (Sp C 455).

The issuing company (ITA 2007, ss 180–200)

ITA 2007, s 183(1)—interpretation of 'qualifying company'

[23.14] A company (H) was incorporated in 1999. In 2000 it made an issue of shares. The shareholders claimed relief under the EIS, and H began trading later that year. In 2001 H acquired the shares of a company (V) with a similar trade. Later that year H ceased trading and became a non-trading parent company. In 2003 the Revenue issued a notice withdrawing the tax relief on the grounds that H had not complied with the conditions of what is now *ITA 2007, s 183(1)*. H appealed, contending that the relevant conditions were satisfied because a 'relevant qualifying trade' had been carried on by a qualifying subsidiary (V) after it had ceased to carry on such a trade itself. The Ch D rejected this contention and upheld the Revenue's notice. Pumfrey J held that 'it is essential that on the date on which the shares are issued it must be possible to determine whether a qualifying business activity is being carried on: and this is only possible if the relevant company can be identified at this point'. Relief was only available 'in respect of money raised to be employed for the purpose of a qualifying business activity', and that condition had to be satisfied at the date of issue of the shares. V had not been a subsidiary of H at the date of issue of the shares, and so its trade was not a qualifying business activity on that date. *HMRC v Valentine Marketing Holdings Ltd*, Ch D 2006, TL 3788; [2007] STC 1631; [2006] EWHC 2820(Ch).

ITA 2007, s 189—qualifying trades

[23.15] A company (C) was incorporated in 1994. In June 1995 it agreed to supply printing, postage, stationery, technical accountancy and taxation literature, and the services of accounting and taxation staff to an accountancy firm (B). In July 1995 B's employees became employees of C. In order to avoid national insurance contributions, they were only paid nominal salaries, and also received shares in C and dividends in respect of those shares. C invoiced B quarterly for the provision of services, but B did not pay the invoices promptly. By July 1997 B owed C £288,548 in unpaid fees. In August 1997 C issued shares to five subscribers and raised £299,900. £262,375 of this was immediately applied in paying off debts. C applied to the Revenue for authority to certify that the issue of shares qualified for enterprise investment scheme relief. The Revenue rejected the application on the grounds that C was carrying on a trade of providing accountancy services, which was not a qualifying trade by virtue of what is now *ITA 2007, s 192(1)(f)*. C appealed, contending that it supplied staff, rather than accountancy services, and was therefore not excluded from the definition of a 'qualifying trade' by *s 192(1)(f)*. The Special Commissioner rejected this contention and dismissed the appeal, observing that the distinction which C sought to draw 'between the provision of the services of accountants and the provision of accountancy services is in fact a distinction without a difference'. B's clients would have detected no change in the relationship between themselves and B following the interposition of C in 1995. The same accountant would be dealing with their affairs in the same way. C was supplying the services of accountants to an accountancy firm. This had to be viewed as supplying accountancy services, and could not be viewed 'merely as the supply of a human being'. Accordingly the effect of what is now *ITA 2007, s 189* was that C's trade was not a qualifying trade. *Castleton Management Services Ltd v Kirkwood*, Sp C [2001] SSCD 95 (Sp C 276).

ITA 2007, s 192—whether company carrying on leasing trade

[23.16] See *Optos plc v HMRC*, 23.7 above.

Attribution of and claims for EIS relief (ITA 2007, ss 201–207)

ITA 2007, s 202—time limit for claims for relief

[23.17] In March 1993 a taxpayer (H) made an investment of £40,000 in a company which had begun trading two months previously. In January 1999 he claimed BES relief in respect of this investment. The Revenue rejected the claim on the basis that it had been made after the expiry of the time limit specified in *ICTA 1988, s 306(1)* as then in force. He subsequently claimed 'error or mistake' relief under *TMA, s 33*. The Revenue rejected this claim and he appealed. The Special Commissioner dismissed his appeal, holding that a 'return' for the purpose of *TMA, s 33* 'did not include a BES claim'. Accordingly, 'any error or mistake in the claim can only be remedied under (*TMA, s 42(8)*) by a supplementary claim within the time limit for the original claim'. *Howard v CIR*, Sp C [2002] SSCD 408 (Sp C 329). (*Note*. The time limit in *ICTA 1988, s 306(1)(b)* was increased to five years with effect from 1996/97: see now *ITA 2007, s 202*.)

ITA 2007, s 203—claims for relief

[23.18] An individual (M) subscribed for 931 shares in a company (V). He claimed EIS relief in respect of this investment. The Revenue rejected the claim on the grounds that V had not issued an EIS certificate in respect of this issue of shares. The Special Commissioner dismissed M's appeal against this decision. *M Ashley v HMRC*, Sp C 2007, [2008] SSCD 219 (Sp C 633).

ITA 2007, s 203—compliance certificates

[23.19] See *Forthright (Wales) Ltd v Davies*, 23.10 above.

Withdrawal or reduction of EIS relief (ITA 2007, ss 208–257)

ITA 2007, s 213—value received from company

[23.20] The controlling directors of a building company (C) incorporated six new companies and claimed BES relief. The purpose of all six companies was to provide rented housing, let on assured tenancies. C undertook building work for the new companies. Subsequently the Revenue issued assessments withdrawing the relief in respect of the BES companies, on the basis that C was connected with the BES companies within what is now *ITA 2007, s 993*, and that the directors' remuneration from C therefore fell within what is now *ITA 2007, s 213*. The directors appealed and applied for judicial review of the Revenue's decision to raise the assessments. The Ch D dismissed the application and upheld the assessments. Lawrence Collins J held that the effect of the application of *s 213* to connected persons was that 'relief may be reduced by value received from a connected company by the investor even if the value received has nothing whatever to do with the BES company'. The payments here were within *s 213*. With regard to the application for judicial review, he observed that there was nothing in the relevant Revenue publications 'which could have led to any expectation that the payments received by the taxpayers would be disregarded for BES relief purposes'. Furthermore, 'it would be absurd if the knowledge of an official dealing with the PAYE affairs of a company could be imputed for the purpose of fixing the Revenue with knowledge that it was connected with a BES company, and that relevant payments were being made to persons who were interested in the BES company'. *Fletcher v Thompson & Thompson; R (oao Thompson & Thompson) v Fletcher*, Ch D 2002, 74 TC 710; [2002] STC 1149; [2002] EWHC 1447 (Ch); [2002] EWHC 1448 (Admin).

Change of control of company—whether ITA 2007, s 247 applicable

[23.21] In 2010 several shareholders claimed EIS relief on the acquisition of shares in a new company (P). Another company (E), which had an AIM listing, subsequently acquired the shares in P under a share exchange whereby

P's shareholders received shares in E. HMRC issued a ruling that the effect of these transactions was that the shareholders were no longer entitled to EIS relief. Four of the shareholders appealed, contending that the transactions should be treated as falling within *ITA 2007, s 247*. The First-tier Tribunal rejected this contention and dismissed their appeals. Judge Nowlan held that *s 247* required that 'the company issuing the shares must be a company prior to the acquisition, in which the only issued shares are subscriber shares'. For this purpose, 'subscriber shares' had to be construed as 'the shares that are to be issued to those who subscribe to the Memorandum of association of the company on its initial formation'. The appellants' shares were not subscriber shares', and thus the result of the takeover was that they had forfeited their EIS relief. *A Finn v HMRC (and related appeals)*, FTT [2014] UKFTT 426 (TC), TC03555.

Miscellaneous

Losses on disposal of units in enterprise zone unit trust

[23.22] See *Smallwood v HMRC*, **71.107** CAPITAL GAINS TAX.

TCGA, Sch 5B—interaction with taper relief under TCGA, s 2A

[23.23] See *Daniels v HMRC*, **71.11** CAPITAL GAINS TAX, and *Stolkin v HMRC*, **71.12** CAPITAL GAINS TAX.

TCGA, Sch 5B para 1(2)—purpose of share issue

[23.24] See *Blackburn v HMRC*, **71.209** CAPITAL GAINS TAX; *Domain Dynamics (Holdings) Ltd v HMRC*, **71.210** CAPITAL GAINS TAX, and *Harvey's Jersey Cream Ltd v HMRC*, **71.211** CAPITAL GAINS TAX.

TCGA, Sch 5B para 1(3)—application for judicial review

[23.25] See *R (oao Devine) v CIR*, **71.213** CAPITAL GAINS TAX.

TCGA, Sch 5B para 13—'return of value' to subscribers

[23.26] See *Optos plc v HMRC*, **23.7** above; *Blackburn v HMRC*, **71.209** CAPITAL GAINS TAX; *Domain Dynamics (Holdings) Ltd v HMRC*, **71.210** CAPITAL GAINS TAX, and *Segesta Ltd v HMRC*, **71.214** CAPITAL GAINS TAX.

24

Error or Mistake Relief (TMA 1970, s 33)

The cases in this chapter are arranged under the following headings.

GENERAL NOTE

TMA 1970, s 33 was substituted by *FA 2009* with effect from 1 April 2010. The case summaries in this chapter should be read in the light of the changes to the legislation.

The requirements of TMA 1970, s 33(2A)

Return made on basis of 'practice generally prevailing'

[24.1] A company (R) had purchased wagons under hire-purchase agreements. The part of the payments which represented the cost of hire was allowed as a deduction in computing its profits. For several years the total hire element had been spread evenly over the period of the hire purchase agreement. As from 1929/30, following a decision by the Special Commissioners in another case, the Revenue agreed to apportion the hire element on an actuarial basis. R made an error or mistake claim for the years 1924/25 to 1928/29, for the allowance for those years to be recomputed accordingly. The Special Commissioners rejected the claim, accepting the Revenue's evidence that R had adopted the basis generally followed during those years, so that the effect of what is now *TMA 1970, s 33(4)* was that no relief was due. The KB dismissed R's appeal. Finlay J held that what was the generally prevailing practice in the relevant years was a pure question of fact, and no point of law in connection with the computation of profits arose within the meaning of *TMA 1970, s 33(2A)*. *Rose, Smith & Co Ltd v CIR*, KB 1933, 17 TC 586. (*Note*. The decision was subsequently approved by the CA in *Carrimore Six Wheelers Ltd v CIR*, 24.2 below.)

[24.2] A company (C) received rental income from an advertisement hoarding at its business premises. This income was within Schedule A under the legislation then in force. However, for convenience and with the agreement of the Revenue, it consistently included the rental income in its return of trading profits for assessment under Schedule D Case I, and was assessed accordingly. It subsequently claimed error or mistake relief, contending that the rental income should have been assessed under Schedule A. The Special Commissioners rejected the claim and the CA unanimously dismissed C's appeal, holding that the return had been made in according with the prevailing practice, and that there was no point of law in connection with the computation of profits. Lord Greene MR held that a 'deliberate wrong entry, made with full knowledge that it was a wrong entry,' could not be described as an 'error or mistake'. (The decision also turned on certain words in the relevant legislation at the time which have not survived.) *Carrimore Six Wheelers Ltd v CIR*, CA 1944, 26 TC 301; [1944] 2 All ER 503. (*Note*. For a subsequent application by the company, see *R v Special Commrs (ex p. Carrimore Six Wheelers Ltd)*, **4.264** APPEALS.)

[24.3] An engineer (C) had claimed a deduction for his actual motoring expenses. He subsequently made claims for error or mistake relief, contending that he should have been allowed a greater deduction under the 'fixed profit car scheme'. The Revenue rejected the claims, on the basis that the claims for years up to 1995/96 had been made outside the statutory limit, and that the return for 1996/97 had been computed 'in accordance with the practice generally prevailing at the time it was made', so that the effect of *TMA 1970, s 33(2A)* was that no relief was due. The Special Commissioner dismissed C's appeal. *Cook v Wood*, Sp C 2004, [2005] SSCD 267 (Sp C 451).

Restitutionary claim under common law for repayment of tax

[24.4] In 1998 and 1999 a taxpayer (M) made substantial capital gains by exercising a share option and subsequently selling some of the shares. He declared and paid CGT in accordance with the Revenue's published interpretation of the law. In December 2002 the CA held that the Revenue's practice was incorrect (see *Mansworth v Jelley*, **71.17** CAPITAL GAINS TAX). M subsequently made a claim for repayment of some of the CGT he had paid. The Revenue rejected the claim on the basis that the return had been made in accordance with the practice generally prevailing, so that the effect of *TMA 1970, s 33(2A)* was that no relief was due. M began an action in the Ch D, contending that he was entitled to a restitutionary claim under common law for recovery of money paid under a mistake of law. The Ch D rejected this claim, and the CA unanimously dismissed M's appeal. Arden LJ observed that the purpose of *s 33(2A)* was 'to protect public finances. If there was no control over claims for repayment, there would always be the risk that a very substantial amount of tax would become repayable as a result of developments in case law possibly many years after it had been spent.' Parliament had 'created a specific remedy with a limitation to exclude payments made under generally accepted practice. That limitation would be defeated if the court permitted an action to be brought at common law.' She also held that *TMA 1970, s 33* did not contravene the *European Convention on Human Rights*. *Monro v HMRC*, CA 2008, 79 TC 579; [2008] STC 1815; [2008] EWCA Civ 306.

The requirements of TMA 1970, s 33(4)

Whether a 'point of law' concerning computation of profits.

[24.5] Two companies had submitted returns and computations on the basis that certain transactions fell within Schedule D Case VI under the legislation then in force. In 1969 the Special Commissioners decided, in another case, that such transactions were not within Case VI. The Revenue did not appeal against that decision, and the companies subsequently claimed error or mistake relief. The Revenue rejected the claims and the CA unanimously dismissed the companies' appeals, applying the decisions in *Rose, Smith & Co Ltd v CIR*, **24.1** above, and *Carrimore Six Wheelers Ltd v CIR*, **24.2** above. Lowry CJ held that 'the mere fact that a point of law will or may, when decided, affect the *amount* of profits which a taxpayer is found, or deemed, to have earned does not, to my mind, turn that point into a point of law arising in connection with the *computation* of profits. For this to happen, the point for decision must itself relate to the method of computation.' *Arranmore Investment Co Ltd v CIR (and related appeal)*, CA(NI) 1973, 48 TC 623; [1973] STC 195.

Agreement under TMA 1970, s 54—subsequent claim under TMA 1970, s 33

[24.6] A company (E) appealed against a corporation tax assessment. The appeal was settled by agreement under *TMA 1970, s 54*. Under the agreement, E's interest payable was set against its trading profits. Subsequently, E submitted a claim for error or mistake relief under *TMA 1970, s 33*, asking for the interest payable to be set against its rental income rather than its trading profits (which would be covered by a claim for terminal loss relief following the cessation of the trade in question). The Revenue rejected the claim on the basis that the *s 54* agreement was final and conclusive, and there had been no 'error or mistake'. The Special Commissioner dismissed E's appeal, noting that E's accountants had treated the interest payable as a deduction from trading income, and that the Revenue had agreed the accountants' computation. The CA upheld this decision. Robert Walker LJ observed that, by virtue of *TMA 1970, s 33(4)*, neither an appellant nor the Revenue was entitled to appeal against a determination by a Special Commissioner of a claim under *TMA 1970, s 33*, except on a point of law arising in connection with the computation of profits. The question of whether the agreement under *TMA 1970, s 54* applied to the claim could not 'possibly be regarded as a question of law in connection with the computation of profits.' *Eagerpath Ltd v Edwards (a.k.a. Grafton Ltd v CIR)*, CA 2000, 73 TC 427; [2001] STC 26.

[24.7] The decision in *Eagerpath Ltd v Edwards*, **24.6** above, was applied in a subsequent case where the Revenue had issued Schedule D assessments on an accountant (T). The assessments had been settled by agreement under *TMA 1970, s 54*, but T subsequently sought to claim bad debt relief by making a claim under *TMA 1970, s 33*. The Revenue rejected his claim and the Special Commissioner dismissed his appeal, holding that the 'issue of bad debt relief' had been covered by the agreement under *section 54*. The Commissioner also held that T was not entitled to bad debt relief for the relevant years of assessment, so that there was no 'error or mistake' in the relevant returns. *Thompson v CIR*, Sp C [2005] SSCD 320 (Sp C 458).

Miscellaneous

Claim under TMA 1970, s 33 after agreement of self-assessment

[24.8] A subcontractor (W) purchased a car in February 1997 and a van in early 1998. He claimed 100% of the expenses relating to the van, and 75% of the expenses relating to the car, as deductible under Schedule D, Case I. In 1998 the Revenue opened an enquiry under *TMA 1970, s 9A*, into W's 1996/97 and 1997/98 returns. W, accompanied by his father, attended a meeting with two Revenue inspectors, who refused to allow any deduction for any expenses relating to W's car. Following the meeting, W signed an amendment to his self-assessment, withdrawing his claim for expenses relating to his car. In 1999 the Revenue opened an enquiry into W's 1998/99 return. W consulted an accountant, who estimated (on the basis of mileage records and petrol receipts) that the business use of W's car had been 72.6%. He submitted revised accounts for 1996/97 and 1997/98. The Revenue refused to reopen these years, on the basis that W's original self-assessments had been settled by agreement. W then submitted a claim for error or mistake relief. The Revenue rejected this claim on the same basis, and W appealed to the Special Commissioner, contending that he had been placed under duress when he attended the meeting with the two inspectors and withdrew his original claim to car expenses. The Special Commissioner allowed W's appeal, holding that 'an agreement reached, after an Inspector of Taxes had given notice under *section 9A* of the intention to enquire into the appellant's tax returns and before the issue of a completion notice under (*TMA 1970, s 28A(5)*) and the amendment of a self-assessment under *section 28A(3)* does not preclude a claim for error or mistake relief'. (The Commissioner also found on the evidence that there had not in fact been an agreement, observing that the inspectors who conducted the meeting with W had failed to comply with the guidelines laid down by the Revenue's Investigation Handbook. Although W was dyslexic and could not read well, they had wrongly refused to allow his father to use a tape recorder at the meeting. It appeared that, by the end of the meeting, W would have 'agreed to anything just to get it over. There was no meeting of minds; there was no consensus. Justice would appear to indicate that this is a case where a claim to error or mistake relief should be capable of being made.') *Wall v CIR*, Sp C [2002] SSCD 122 (Sp C 303).

Claim made outside statutory time limit

[24.9] In 1999/2000 a dentist formed the opinion that his accounts had overstated his profits, because of errors by his previous accountant. He submitted a claim for error or mistake relief. The Revenue accepted the claim for 1993/94 onwards, but rejected the claim for 1992/93 and earlier years on the grounds that it was outside the six-year time limit of *TMA 1970, s 33(1)* as then in force. In 2009 the dentist lodged an appeal to the First-tier Tribunal.

The tribunal struck out the appeal, holding that it had no jurisdiction under *SI 2009/273*. *G Allen v HMRC*, FTT [2011] UKFTT 26 (TC), TC00903.

Whether relief due where no formal assessment issued

[24.10] See *Woodcock v CIR*, 22.222 EMPLOYMENT INCOME.

Recovery of tax erroneously not deducted at source

[24.11] See the cases noted at 20.18 *et seq.* DEDUCTION OF TAX.

Exchange loss following fall in value of sterling

[24.12] See *Radio Pictures Ltd v CIR*, 63.311 TRADING PROFITS.

Claim to deduct wife's wages in computing business profits

[24.13] See *Abbott v CIR*, 63.175 TRADING PROFITS.

Unclaimed 'deposits' paid by customers

[24.14] See *Gower Chemicals Ltd v HMRC*, 64.65 TRADING PROFITS.

Partnership continuation election—whether within TMA 1970, s 33

[24.15] Following the retirement of one of the members of a partnership, the partners submitted an election that they should be taxed on a continuation basis. Subsequently they formed the opinion that the election had not been to their advantage. They submitted a claim for error or mistake relief under *TMA 1970, s 33*, and appealed against an assessment that had been issued in accordance with the election. The Revenue rejected the claim, and the Special Commissioner dismissed their appeal against the assessment and declined to state a Case for the High Court on the ground that the point raised in the appeal was not a point of law arising in connection with the computation of the partnership profits. One of the partners applied for judicial review of this decision. The QB dismissed the application, holding that it would be an abuse of the court's powers to require the Commissioner to state a Case on this matter. The continuation election had not been a return, and a mistaken election did not constitute an 'error in a return'. *R v Special Commrs (ex p. Tracy)*, QB 1995, 67 TC 547; [1996] STC 34.

CGT on sale of restaurant—whether TMA 1970, s 33 applicable

[24.16] In 1989 a married couple sold a restaurant to an unconnected company for cash of £77,500 and a quantity of shares. These shares included 45 shares in a company (F), which were valued in the contract at £77,590. The Revenue issued an estimated CGT assessment, and the husband (M) appealed.

In 1993 his accountants submitted a computation showing a chargeable gain of £72,851, which was agreed under *TMA 1970, s 54*. Subsequently he consulted new accountants. In April 1995 they submitted a claim that the shares in F had become worthless, within *TCGA 1992, s 24(2)*. In June 1995 they submitted an amended computation, omitting any reference to the sum of £77,590 attributed in the original contract to the shares in F, and showing the chargeable gain as £53,617. The Revenue treated this letter as a claim to error or mistake relief and accepted the computation. In December 1998 the accountants submitted a further amended computation, showing a chargeable gain of only £7,116, and omitting the sum of £77,500 paid in cash as well as the £77,590 attributed to the shares in F. The Revenue treated the letter as a further claim to error or mistake relief, but rejected the computation and therefore rejected the claim. The Special Commissioner dismissed M's appeal. On the evidence, there were no grounds for error or mistake relief. It was accepted that the shares in F had become of negligible value, but the computation which M's accountants had submitted in June 1995 excluded the consideration which had been attributed to those shares. Furthermore, the computation submitted in December 1998 was clearly inaccurate, as it omitted the cash sum of £77,500. On the evidence, the original assessment had been amended to the correct sum of £53,617, as stated in the computation submitted in June 1995. *Marsden v Gustar*, Sp C [2000] SSCD 371 (Sp C 246).

Employee—claim to deduct legal costs

[24.17] See *Nevis v CIR*, 22.203 EMPLOYMENT INCOME.

Late claim to BES relief—whether TMA 1970, s 33 applicable

[24.18] See *Howard v CIR*, 23.17 ENTERPRISE INVESTMENT SCHEME.

Claim to have capital payment allowed as trading expense

[24.19] See *Triage Services Ltd v HMRC*, 63.116 TRADING PROFITS.

Appellant claiming to have been employee

[24.20] An individual (T) began working as a salesman, for a Danish company (D), in 1994. T's contract stated that he was an employee. However D did not deduct tax from the payments which it made to him. In 2002, on the advice of an accountant, T submitted tax returns for 1996/97 to 2001/02 on the basis that he was self-employed. In 2003 T engaged a different accountant who considered that he should have been treated as an employee, and submitted a claim to error or mistake relief under *TMA 1970, s 33*. HMRC rejected the claim and the First-tier Tribunal dismissed T's appeal. Judge Powell observed that T had 'failed to deal with his tax affairs at all for years after he started work for the company'. It was likely that 'the PAYE liability would have exceeded the tax paid on the self-assessment returns'. Therefore it was 'just and reasonable to deny relief altogether'. The Upper Tribunal unanimously dismissed T's appeal, observing that the right of appeal in *TMA*

1970, s 33 was 'strongly circumscribed' and holding that there was no 'point of law arising in connection with the computation of (T's) income for the years in question'. *PG Tindale v HMRC*, UT [2014] UKUT 324 (TCC).

25

European Law

The cases in this chapter are arranged under the following headings.

Treaty on the Functioning of the European Union

NOTE

The first significant steps towards the present-day 'European Union' were taken in 1951, when the European Coal & Steel Community (ECSC) was established by the Treaty of Paris. This was followed by the establishment of the Council of Ministers and of the European Court of Justice. In 1957 the Treaties of Rome established the European Atomic Energy Community (EAEC) and the European Economic Community (EEC). The UK joined all three Communities with effect from 1 January 1973, following the *European Communities Act 1972*. In February 1992 the UK Government signed the Treaty on European Union (also known as the Maastricht Treaty), which made significant amendments to the EEC Treaty. These included changing the title of the Community from the 'European Economic Community' to the 'European Community', and changing the name of the Council from the 'Council of the European Communities' to the 'Council of the European Union'. The EC Treaty (originally the EEC Treaty) was further amended by the Treaty of Amsterdam which came into effect on 1 May 1999, and was substantially amended by the Treaty of Lisbon which came into effect on 1 December 2009, and renamed it as 'The Treaty on the Functioning of the European Union'. In accordance with the general practice of the UK courts (see, for example, the explanation in the judgment of Henderson J in *Prudential Assurance Co Ltd v HMRC (and related appeals) (No 2)*, **25.94** below), this chapter uses the abbreviation 'ECJ' to refer both to the Court of Justice of the European Union (as it has been since the entry into force of the Treaty of Lisbon on 1 December 2009) and to the Court of Justice of the European Communities (as it previously was). Most of the cases in this chapter relate to the interpretation of the Treaty on the Functioning of the European Union and its predecessors, deriving from the 1957 Treaty of Rome establishing the EEC. However the ECJ has also considered the compatibility of UK tax law with the Treaty on European Union (also known as the Maastricht Treaty): see **25.155** below.

Prohibition of discrimination (Article 18)

[25.1] A 'European School' was established in Oxfordshire, so that children of EC officials could be taught in their native language. The teaching staff were employed by their national authorities and seconded to the Schools. They received a salary from their national authority calculated by reference to the national scale, and in addition the school paid a 'European supplement' to bring their salary up to a standard established by EC regulations, and a 'differential allowance' calculated by reference to the level of domestic taxation. The UK Revenue considered that the amounts were liable to UK tax when paid to a UK national, and issued assessments on the headmaster of the Oxfordshire school (who was a UK citizen). He appealed, contending that the assessments were a breach of what is now *Article 18* of the TFEU (which prohibits discrimination on grounds of nationality). The Special Commissioners referred the matter to the ECJ, which held that neither what is now *Article 18* , nor the general principles of Community law, required a member state 'to exempt salaries of teachers at a European School situated on its territory from domestic taxation, where those teachers are nationals of that member state'. *Hurd v Jones*, ECJ Case C-44/84; [1986] STC 127; [1986] ECR 29; [1986] 3 WLR 189.

[25.2] A German citizen (S) made maintenance payments to his former spouse, who was resident in Austria. He claimed that he should be allowed a tax deduction for these payments. The tax authority rejected his claim, and he appealed, contending that this was a breach of what is now *Article 18* of the TFEU. The case was referred to the ECJ, which rejected S's claim, and held that the Treaty 'must be interpreted as not precluding a taxpayer resident in Germany from being unable, under national legislation such as that at issue in the main proceedings, to deduct from his taxable income in that Member State the maintenance paid to his former spouse resident in another Member State in which the maintenance is not taxable, where he would be entitled to do so if his former spouse were resident in Germany'. *Schempp v Finanzamt München V*, ECJ Case C-403/03; [2005] STC 1792.

Citizenship (Articles 20–24)

TFEU, Article 21—freedom of movement and residence

[25.3] Following an application by the European Commission, the ECJ held that, by maintaining in force fiscal provisions 'making entitlement to exemption from tax on capital gains arising from the transfer for valuable consideration of real property intended for the taxable person's own and permanent residence or for that of a member of his family subject to the condition that the gains realised should be reinvested in the purchase of real property situated in Portuguese territory', Portugal had failed to fulfil its obligations under what is now *Article 21* of the TFEU. *EC Commission v Portuguese Republic*, ECJ Case C-345/05; 26 October 2006 unreported.

[25.4] A Finnish pensioner (T) lived in Spain, although her pension remained taxable in Finland, where the authorities levied a withholding tax at the rate of 35%. If T had lived in Finland, her pension would have been taxed at

28.5%. She appealed, and her case was referred to the ECJ for a ruling as to whether the relevant Finnish legislation contravened what is now *Article 21* of the TFEU. The ECJ held that the Treaty 'precludes national legislation according to which the income tax on a retirement pension paid by an institution of the Member State concerned to a person residing in another Member State exceeds in certain cases the tax which would be payable if that person resided in the first Member State, where that pension constitutes all or nearly all of that person's income'. *Re Turpeinen*, ECJ Case C-520/04; [2008] STC 1.

[25.5] Under Polish law, health insurance contributions paid in Poland were deductible for income tax purposes, but health insurance contributions paid in other EU Member States were not. A German, who lived in Poland and paid health insurance contributions in Germany, appealed to the Polish courts, contending that this contravened the EC Treaty. The case was referred to the ECJ, which held that the Treaty 'precludes legislation of a Member State which makes the granting of a right to a reduction of income tax by the amount of health insurance contributions paid conditional on payment of those contributions in that Member State on the basis of national law and results in the refusal to grant such a tax advantage where the contributions liable to be deducted from the amount of income tax due in that Member State have been paid under the compulsory health insurance scheme of another Member State'. *Rüffler v Dyrektor Izby Skarbowej we Wrocławiu Ośrodek Zamiejscowy w Wałbrzychu*, ECJ Case C-544/07; [2009] STC 1464.

[25.6] Hungarian legislation provided that, for property tax purposes, a purchaser of residential property could deduct the value of another Hungarian residential property which was sold within 12 months of the purchase. This deduction was only available for sales of residential property in Hungary, and was not available for sales of residential property elsewhere in the EU. The European Commission took proceedings in the ECJ, contending that this was a breach of what is now *Article 21* of the TFEU. The ECJ rejected the Commission's contentions. *European Commission v Republic of Hungary*, ECJ Case C-253/09; 1 December 2011 unreported.

Workers (Articles 45–48)

TFEU, Article 45—freedom of movement

[25.7] A German national lived and worked in Luxembourg from 1973 until October 1983, when he moved to Germany. The Luxembourg income tax deducted from his salary in 1983 exceeded his liability for that year, and he claimed a repayment. The Luxembourg authority rejected his claim, and he appealed, contending that this was a breach of his right to freedom of movement under what is now *Article 45* of the TFEU. The case was referred to the ECJ, which held that *Article 45* precluded a member state 'from providing in its tax legislation that sums deducted by way of tax from the salaries and wages of employed persons who are nationals of a member state and are resident taxpayers for only part of the year because they take up residence in the country or leave it during the course of the tax year are to remain the property of the Treasury and are not repayable'. *Biehl v Administration des Contributions du Grand-Duché de Luxembourg*, ECJ Case C-175/88; [1991] STC 575.

[25.8] A married couple lived in France, near the border with Germany. The wife worked in Germany. Her employment income was taxed in both countries, but under a double taxation agreement (based on the OECD model), she was allowed double tax relief in France. This relief was given in terms of the French tax due, which was less than the tax which she suffered in Germany. The couple took appeal proceedings, contending that this was a breach of her right to freedom of movement under what is now *Article 45* of the TFEU. The case was referred to the ECJ, which rejected the couple's contentions, holding that *Article 45* did not preclude the application of a tax credit mechanism of the type laid down in the relevant double taxation agreement. The object of a bilateral agreement for the avoidance of double taxation was simply to prevent the same income from being taxed in each of the two contracting states. It was not to ensure that the tax to which a taxpayer was subject in one state was no higher than that to which he or she would have been subject in the other. *Gilly & Gilly v Directeur des Services Fiscaux du Bas-Rhin*, ECJ Case C-336/96; [1998] STC 1014; [1998] All ER (EC) 826.

[25.9] Under Luxembourg law, married couples were entitled to joint assessment only if they were both resident in Luxembourg. A Belgian national worked in Luxembourg and lived there from Mondays to Fridays, but spent weekends in Belgium with his wife, who did not work, and their children. The Luxembourg authorities taxed him as if he were a single person without dependants. He appealed, contending that this was a breach of what is now *Article 45* of the TFEU. The case was referred to the ECJ, which held that *Article 45* precluded national rules under which the joint assessment of a married couple was 'conditional on their both being resident on national territory and that tax advantage is denied to a worker who is resident in that State, where he/she receives almost the entire income of the household, and whose spouse is resident in another Member State'. *Zurstrassen v Administration des Contributions Directes*, ECJ Case C-87/99; [2001] STC 1102.

[25.10] In another Luxembourg case, the ECJ held that the Treaty 'is to be interpreted as precluding national legislation which does not entitle a Community national who is not resident in the Member State in which he receives income that constitutes the major part of his taxable income to request, for the purposes of determination of the tax rate applicable to the income so received, that negative rental income relating to property situated in another Member State which he does not himself occupy be taken into account, whilst a resident of the first State can request that such negative rental income be taken into account'. *État du Grand-Duché de Luxembourg v HU Lakebrink & K Peters-Lakebrink*, ECJ Case C-182/06; [2008] STC 2485.

[25.11] In a Netherlands case, the ECJ held that certain Netherlands legislation contravened what is now *Article 45* of the TFEU. The ECJ held that *Article 45* precluded rules 'whereby a taxpayer forfeits, in the calculation of the income tax payable by him in his State of residence, part of the tax-free amount of that income and of his personal tax advantages because, during the year in question, he also received income in another Member State which was taxed in that State without his personal and family circumstances being taken into account'. The ECJ also observed that 'Community law contains no specific requirement with regard to the way in which the State of residence must take into account the personal and family circumstances of a worker who, during a particular tax year, received income in that State and another Member State, except that the conditions governing the way in which the State of residence takes those circumstances into account must not constitute discrimination, either direct or indirect, on grounds of nationality, or an obstacle to the exercise of a fundamental freedom guaranteed by the EC Treaty'. *De Groot v Staatssecretaris van Financien*, ECJ Case C-385/00; [2004] STC 1346; 5 ITLR 711.

[25.12] In a German case, the ECJ held that what is now *Article 45* of the TFEU precluded national legislation 'which does not permit natural persons in receipt of income from employment in one Member State, and assessable to tax on their total income there, to have income losses relating to their own use of a private dwelling in another Member State taken into account for the purposes of determining the rate of taxation applicable to their income in the former state, whereas positive rental income relating to such a dwelling is taken into account'. *Ritter-Coulais & Ritter-Coulais v Finanzamt Germersheim*, ECJ Case C-152/03; [2006] STC 1111; [2006] All ER (EC) 613.

[25.13] In another German case, the ECJ held that what is now *Article 45* of the TFEU did not preclude national legislation 'according to which allowances such as those at issue in the main proceedings, granted to a civil servant of a Member State working in another Member State in order to compensate for a loss of purchasing power at the place of secondment, are not taken into account in determining the tax rate applicable in the first Member State to the other income of the taxpayer or of his spouse, whereas equivalent allowances granted to a civil servant of that other Member State working on the territory of the first Member State are taken into account for the purposes of determining that tax rate'. *Schulz-Delzers & Schulz v Finanzamt Stuttgart III*, ECJ Case C-240/10; [2011] STC 2144.

[25.14] In another German case, the ECJ held that *Article 45* of the TFEU 'must be interpreted as precluding national legislation of a Member State pursuant to which income received for employment activities by a taxpayer who is resident in that Member State and has unlimited tax liability is exempt from income tax if the employer is established in that Member State, but is not so exempt if that employer is established in another Member State'. *H & P Petersen v Finanzamt Ludwigshafen*, ECJ Case C-544/11; [2013] STC 1195.

[25.15] In a Belgian case, the ECJ held that a care insurance scheme contravened what is now *Article 45* of the TFEU, 'in so far as such limitation affects nationals of other Member States or nationals of the Member State concerned who have made use of their right to freedom of movement within the European Community'. However, the breach did not affect the rights of Belgian nationals who had 'never exercised their freedom to move within the European Community', since Community law 'cannot be applied to such purely internal situations'. Citizenship of the European Union was 'not intended to extend the material scope of the Treaty to internal situations which have no link with Community law'. *Gouvernement de la Communauté française et Gouvernement Wallon v Gouvernement Flamand*, ECJ Case C-212/06; [2008] 1 ECR 1683; [2009] All ER (EC) 187.

[25.16] An Estonian who lived in Finland received a small pension, which was charged to Estonian tax, although if he had still lived in Estonia, he would have received a personal allowance which would have extinguished the tax liability. He complained to the European Commission, which took proceedings in the ECJ, contending that the Estonian legislation contravened *Article 45* of the TFEU. The ECJ gave judgment for the Commission, holding that by excluding non-resident pensioners from benefiting from personal allowances, Estonia had failed to fulfil its obligations under *Article 45*. *European Commission v Republic of Estonia*, ECJ Case C-39/10; 10 May 2012 unreported.

Right of establishment (Articles 49–55)

Article 49—UK cases

[25.17] A UK company wished to emigrate to the Netherlands. Under *ICTA 1970, s 482(1)*, it was required to seek consent from the Treasury. The Treasury rejected the application, and the company took judicial review proceedings, seeking a declaration that it was entitled to transfer its residence to the Netherlands without Treasury consent. The QB referred the case to the ECJ, which held that neither the EC Treaty nor *EC Directive 73/148* gave a company the right to transfer its central management and control to another Member State. *R v HM Treasury & CIR (ex p. Daily Mail & General Trust plc)*, ECJ Case C-81/87; [1988] STC 787; [1988] ECR 5483; [1989] 1 All ER 328. (*Note*. The requirement to seek Treasury consent for a transfer of company residence was abolished by *FA 1988*.)

[25.18] Under the UK system of advance corporation tax (which was abolished from 6 April 1999—see the note preceding **18.50** CORPORATION TAX), a group income election under *ICTA 1988, s 247* was only available where both the subsidiary and the parent company were resident in the UK. The UK subsidiaries of two German companies claimed that this constituted discrimination, contrary to what is now *Article 49* of the TFEU, since it resulted in them suffering a cash-flow disadvantage in comparison with the subsidiaries of companies resident in the UK. The ECJ held that it was contrary to *Article 49* for the legislation of a Member State 'to afford companies resident in that Member State the possibility of benefiting from a taxation regime allowing them to pay dividends to their parent company without having to pay advance corporation tax where their parent company is also resident in that Member State but to deny them that possibility where their parent company has its seat in another Member State'. *Metalgesellschaft Ltd & Others v CIR*, ECJ Case C-397/98; *Hoechst AG v CIR*, ECJ Case C-410/98, TL 3686; [2001] STC 452; [2001] 2 WLR 1497; [2001] All ER (EC) 496. (*Note*. For subsequent applications by the claimant companies, see **10.6** CLAIMS TO RELIEF OR REPAYMENT and **32.5** INTEREST ON OVERPAID TAX.)

[25.19] Following the ECJ decision in *Metalgesellschaft Ltd & Others v CIR*, **25.18** above, several UK companies took proceedings against the Revenue, claiming that the UK's system of advance corporation tax, as in force from

1973 to 1999, contravened what is now *Article 49* of the TFEU. The Ch D referred the case to the ECJ, which held that the Treaty did 'not prevent a Member State, on a distribution of dividends by a company resident in that State, from granting companies receiving those dividends which are also resident in that State a tax credit equal to the fraction of the corporation tax paid on the distributed profits by the company making the distribution, when it does not grant such a tax credit to companies receiving such dividends which are resident in another Member State and are not subject to tax on dividends in the first State'. *Test Claimants in Class IV of the ACT Group Litigation (Pirelli UK plc, Essilor Ltd, Sony UK Ltd and BMW (GB) Ltd) v CIR*, ECJ Case C-374/04; [2007] STC 404; 9 ITLR 360; [2007] All ER (EC) 351. (*Note.* For subsequent proceedings involving the same claimants, see **25.28** below.)

[25.20] A UK company (M) established subsidiary companies in Belgium, France and Germany. These subsidiaries made losses. M claimed group relief on the basis that it should be entitled to set the losses which these companies made against its UK profits. The Revenue rejected the claim and M appealed, contending that the relevant provisions of the UK legislation, which prevented an EU-resident subsidiary trading outside the UK from surrendering losses to its ultimate UK parent, were a breach of what is now *Article 49* of the TFEU. The Ch D referred the case to the ECJ, which observed that Member States were entitled to prevent any possibility 'that losses would be used twice', and to avoid the possibility of losses being 'transferred to companies established in the Member States which apply the highest rates of taxation and in which the tax value of the losses is therefore the highest'. The ECJ concluded that the Treaty did not 'preclude provisions of a Member State which generally prevent a resident parent company from deducting from its taxable profits losses incurred in another Member State by a subsidiary established in that Member State although they allow it to deduct losses incurred by a resident subsidiary'. However, it was contrary to the Treaty 'to prevent the resident parent company from doing so where the non-resident subsidiary has exhausted the possibilities available in its State of residence of having the losses taken into account for the accounting period concerned by the claim for relief and also for previous accounting periods and where there are no possibilities for those losses to be taken into account in its State of residence for future periods'. *Marks & Spencer plc v Halsey*, ECJ Case C-446/03; [2006] STC 237; [2006] 2 WLR 250; [2006] All ER (EC) 255. (*Notes.* (1) See now *FA 2006, s 27, Sch 1* and *CTA 2010, ss 111–128*, which were intended to give effect to this decision. (2) For subsequent developments in this case, see **25.21** below. See also *Re Loss Relief Group Litigation*, **4.272** APPEALS.)

[25.21] Following the decision noted at **25.20** above, the case was referred back to the Ch D to consider M's specific claims. The Ch D held that M was not entitled to relief for the losses of its French subsidiary, and remitted the case to the Special Commissioners to hear further evidence with regard to the losses of the German and Belgian subsidiaries. The CA unanimously upheld this decision. Chadwick LJ held that the Revenue were entitled to require 'a notice from the non-resident surrendering company which confirms that it has exhausted the possibilities available in its state of residence of having the losses in respect of which the claim is made taken into account for the accounting period to which the claim relates or for previous accounting periods and that there is no possibility of those losses being taken into account in its state of residence for future periods, either by the surrendering company or by a third party'. The Revenue were also entitled to require 'appropriate evidence to support that notice'. *Marks & Spencer plc v Halsey (No 2)*, CA 2007, [2008] STC 526; [2007] EWCA Civ 117; 9 ITLR 739. (*Note*. At a subsequent hearing, costs were awarded to HMRC—see **4.454** APPEALS.)

[25.22] Following the decision noted at **25.21** above, the case was reheard by the First-tier Tribunal (which had succeeded the Special Commissioners with effect from April 2009). The Tribunal allowed M's appeals in principle, holding that at 20 March 2007, when M had made valid claims to group relief, there were no possibilities of the losses being taken into account in Germany or Belgium. With regard to the quantification of the losses, the Tribunal upheld M's contention that 'the no-possibilities test has to be applied to the local law losses, and the conversion of the losses to which the no-possibilities test applies is necessary to ensure that greater losses are not available than would be the case if the losses were incurred by a UK resident subsidiary'. When losses had been 'identified as no-possibilities losses', it was 'an unjustified restriction to prevent their relief because of different German and UK recognition rules'. HMRC appealed to the Upper Tribunal, which upheld the First-tier Tribunal decision in favour of M for the periods ending March 2000 to March 2002, and upheld the First-tier Tribunal's decision in favour of M with regard to the quantification of the losses. (However, the Upper Tribunal found in favour of HMRC for the periods ending March 1997 to 1999, holding that, 'in relation to the claims which were made in time, the no possibilities test was not satisfied at the date of the claims; later claims made were outside the relevant time limits, and (M) should not be allowed specially to make a claim outside those time limits'.) The CA unanimously upheld this decision, and both sides appealed to the Supreme Court, which held two separate hearings. At its first hearing, the Supreme Court unanimously upheld M's contention that it would be contrary to European law to preclude cross-border group relief 'where the claimant company has been able to show, on the basis of the circumstances known at the date when it makes its claim, that there has been no possibility of the losses in question being utilised in the Member State of the surrendering company in any accounting period prior to the date of the claim and no possibility of such utilisation in the accounting period in which the claim is made or in any future accounting periods'. *HMRC v Marks & Spencer plc (No 3) (and cross-appeal)*, SC [2013] UKSC 30; [2013] STC 1262; [2013] 3 All ER 835. (*Notes*. (1) For subsequent developments in this case, see **25.23** below. (2) For an application by the company for costs, see **4.426** APPEALS.)

[25.23] Following the decision noted at **25.22** above, the Supreme Court held a further hearing to consider three further issues in the case, and unanimously upheld the CA decision on all three points, upholding the manner in which M had computed its losses, but holding that some of M's claims (the 'pay and file claims', rather than the 'self-assessment claims') had been lodged outside the statutory time limits. *HMRC v Marks & Spencer plc (No 4) (and cross-appeal)*, SC [2014] UKSC 11; [2014] STC 819; [2014] 2 All ER 331.

[25.24] Following the CA decision in *HMRC v Marks & Spencer plc (No 3) (and cross-appeal)*, **25.22** above, 39 companies which had made claims for cross-border group relief applied to the Ch D for a direction that their claims should be referred to the ECJ. The Ch D rejected the applications. Henderson J observed that HMRC had appealed to the Supreme Court against the decision noted at **25.22** above, and held that the companies' application was 'both premature and (at best) procedurally questionable'. *Claimants under Loss Relief Group Litigation Order v HMRC (No 2)*, Ch D [2013] EWHC 205 (Ch).

[25.25] The European Commission began proceedings against the United Kingdom in the ECJ, seeking a declaration that the provisions of *CTA 2010, ss 111–128* failed to comply with the ECJ decision in *Marks & Spencer plc v Halsey*, **25.20** above. Advocate-General Kokott delivered an Opinion rejecting the Commission's contentions, holding that 'the contested United Kingdom rules on group relief go even further than is required by European Union law in that they provide for cross-border relief in certain cases' and did not contravene the principle of freedom of establishment. *European Commission v United Kingdom*, ECJ Case C-172/13; 23 October 2014 unreported.

[25.26] Two UK companies paid dividends to two Netherlands companies and an Italian company in the same group. The effect of the relevant double taxation agreements between the UK, the Netherlands and Italy was that when the Dutch and Italian companies received dividends from one of the UK companies, they received payments from the Revenue equal to 6.875% of the dividends. Following the ECJ decision in *Metalgesellschaft Ltd & Others v CIR*, **25.18** above, the UK companies claimed damages from the Revenue on the basis that the provisions of *ICTA 1988, s 247* contravened what is now *Article 49* of the TFEU. The HL remitted the case to the Ch D to consider whether, if a group income election had been available, 'the group would have elected to have the United Kingdom subsidiaries pay the dividends in question free of ACT or, instead, would have chosen that the United Kingdom subsidiaries should pay the dividends outside group income elections, thus enabling the overseas parents to receive convention tax credits'. Lord Nicholls of Birkenhead held that the relevant double taxation agreements had to be 'interpreted purposively'. Applying a purposive interpretation of the relevant agreements, 'if the UK-resident subsidiary of a parent resident in another member state of the European Union had paid a dividend to its parent while a group income election was in force, the parent would not have been entitled to a tax credit in respect of the dividend under double taxation conventions'. He observed that 'the loss sustained by the subsidiary cannot fairly be assessed in isolation. The commercial reality is that by not having the opportunity to make a group income election the group lost the opportunity to take advantage of a fiscal package: a package which affected the parent in one way and its subsidiary in a different way. In calculating the loss suffered by the group, that is, the parent and the subsidiary, regard must be had to both elements in the package. The effect on the parent must be considered as well as the effect on the subsidiary.' Accordingly, 'the amount of the convention tax credits received by the Dutch and Italian parent companies is to be taken into account in calculating the compensation payable'. The HL also held that ACT was not a 'withholding tax' for the purposes of the *EC Parent and Subsidiary Directive*. *Pirelli Cable Holding NV & Others v CIR (No 1)*, HL 2006, 77 TC 409;

[2006] STC 548; [2006] UKHL 4; [2006] 2 All ER 81. (*Note*. For subsequent developments in this case, see **25.27** below.)

[25.27] Following the HL decision reported at **25.26** above, the case was remitted to the Ch D, where one of the companies (P) raised a new contention that if it had made a group income election, the dividends paid to the non-resident companies would have been paid free of ACT. The Ch D rejected this contention, holding that if P had exercised a group income election, the non-resident companies would not have been entitled to a tax credit upon the subsequent payment of the mainstream corporation tax. The CA unanimously dismissed P's appeal against this decision. Moses LJ held that 'in circumstances in which the United Kingdom levies no tax on the dividend received by the parent resident in Italy, no obligation to eliminate any subsequent double taxation is imposed on the United Kingdom under Community law'. *Pirelli Cable Holding NV & Others v HMRC (No 2)*, CA 2008, 79 TC 232; [2008] STC 508; [2008] EWCA Civ 70.

[25.28] Following the CA decision in *Pirelli Cable Holding NV & Others v HMRC (No 2)*, **25.27** above, the case was again remitted to the Ch D to consider the factual question referred by the HL in the case noted at **25.26** above, ie whether, if a group income election had been available, 'the group would have elected to have the United Kingdom subsidiaries pay the dividends in question free of ACT or, instead, would have chosen that the United Kingdom subsidiaries should pay the dividends outside group income elections, thus enabling the overseas parents to receive convention tax credits'. The Ch D heard the case along with similar claims by two other groups of companies, in the context of the group litigation noted at **25.19** above. Henderson J reviewed the evidence in detail and rejected P's contentions, and the CA unanimously upheld this decision. Lord Neuberger MR held that the UK was not required 'to provide equivalent relief from economic double taxation for non-resident shareholders to that which it provides for resident shareholders, merely because it has been unwise enough to negotiate a DTC which charges income tax at 5% on outgoing dividends and then provides a partial tax credit which is amply sufficient to discharge that liability'. *Test Claimants in the ACT Group Litigation (Class 2 and Class 4) v HMRC (No 2)*, CA [2010] EWCA Civ 1480; [2011] STC 872. (*Note*. The Supreme Court rejected an application by the companies for leave to appeal against this decision.)

[25.29] Several UK companies applied to the Ch D for a declaration that *ICTA 1988, ss 209, 212, Sch 28AA*, which imposed restrictions on the deductibility of interest on loan finance granted by a parent company resident in another Member State, contravened what is now *Article 49* of the TFEU. The Ch D referred the case to the ECJ, which held that the Treaty precluded 'legislation of a Member State which restricts the ability of a resident company to deduct, for tax purposes, interest on loan finance granted by a direct or indirect parent company which is resident in another Member State or by a company which is resident in another Member State and is controlled by such a parent company, without imposing that restriction on a resident company which has been granted loan finance by a company which is also resident, unless, first, that legislation provides for a consideration of objective and verifiable elements which make it possible to identify the existence of a purely artificial arrangement, entered into for tax reasons alone, to be established and allows taxpayers to produce, if appropriate and without being subject to undue administrative constraints, evidence as to the commercial justification for the transaction in question and, secondly, where it is established that such an arrangement exists, such legislation treats that interest as a distribution only in so far as it exceeds what would have been agreed upon at arm's length'. However, what is now *Article 49* did not apply 'where that legislation applies to a situation in which a resident company is granted a loan by a company which is resident in another Member State or in a non-member country and which does not itself control the borrowing company and where each of those companies is controlled, directly or indirectly, by a common parent company which is resident in a non-member country. In the absence of Community legislation, it is for the domestic legal system of each Member State to designate the courts and tribunals having jurisdiction and to lay down the detailed procedural rules governing actions for safeguarding rights which individuals derive from Community law, including the classification of claims brought by injured parties before national courts and tribunals.' *Test Claimants in the 'Thin Cap' Group Litigation v CIR*, ECJ Case C-524/04; [2007] STC 906; 9 ITLR 877.

[25.30] Following the ECJ decision noted at **25.29** above, the case was referred back to the Ch D. Henderson J delivered a lengthy judgment, against which both sides appealed to the CA. The CA allowed HMRC's appeal (by a 2-1 majority, Arden LJ dissenting) and dismissed the claimants' cross-appeal. Stanley Burnton LJ expressed the opinion that it was 'difficult to reconcile' the ECJ judgment in the case noted at **25.29** above with the subsequent judgment in *Oy AA v Finland*, **25.70** below. He held that that case, together with the subsequent decision in *Société De Gestion Industrielle (SGI) v Belgian State*, **25.60** below, made it clear that 'the objectives of ensuring the balanced allocation between Member States of the power to tax, together with the prevention of tax avoidance, may justify legislation that would otherwise be an unlawful interference with the freedom of establishment'. He also held that 'the application of an arm's length test is appropriate and sufficient for this purpose. It is a proportionate measure to achieve those objectives.' Furthermore, the 'transactions in issue did not satisfy the arm's length test, and the UK thin cap legislation was appropriately and lawfully applied to them'. *Test Claimants in the 'Thin Cap' Group Litigation v HMRC (No 2)*, CA, [2011] EWCA Civ 127; [2011] STC 738. (*Note.* The Supreme Court rejected an application by the companies for leave to appeal against this decision.)

[25.31] A UK company (P) claimed consortium relief in respect of losses incurred by a UK branch of an associated Netherlands company. HMRC rejected the claim on the basis that the effect of *ICTA 1988, s 403D* and *s 406(2)* was that P was not entitled to relief for these losses. P appealed, contending that the UK legislation contravened EC law. The Upper Tribunal directed that the case should be referred to the ECJ for a ruling on the interpretation of what is now *Article 49* of the TFEU. The ECJ held that what is now *Article 49* 'must be interpreted as meaning that where, under the national legislation of a Member State, the possibility of transferring, by means of group relief and to a resident company, losses sustained by the permanent establishment in that Member State of a non-resident company is subject to a condition that those losses cannot be used for the purposes of foreign taxation, and where the transfer of losses sustained in that Member State by a resident company is not subject to any equivalent condition, such provisions constitute a restriction on the freedom of a non-resident company to establish itself in another Member State.' Such a restriction 'cannot be justified by overriding reasons in the public interest based on the objective of preventing the double use of losses or the objective of preserving a balanced allocation of the power to impose taxes between the Member States or by a combination of those two grounds.' *Philips Electronics UK Ltd v HMRC*, ECJ Case C-18/11; [2013] STC 41. (*Note.* See now the amendments to *CTA 2010, s 107* enacted by *FA 2013, s 30*.)

[25.32] Several members of a group of companies (with an ultimate Hong Kong parent) claimed group relief in respect of losses made by a UK company (HUK) through an intermediate holding company (HS) which was resident in Luxembourg. HMRC rejected the claim on the basis that the effect of *ICTA 1988, s 402(3B)* and *s 406(2)* was that the companies were not entitled to relief. The companies appealed, contending that the relevant UK provisions contravened EC law. The First-tier Tribunal referred the case to the ECJ for a ruling on whether *Articles 49* and *54* of the TFEU should be treated as precluding 'the requirement that the "link company" be either resident in the United Kingdom or carrying on a trade in the United Kingdom through a permanent establishment situated there'. The ECJ held that *Articles 49* and *54* of the TFEU 'must be interpreted as precluding legislation of a Member State under which it is possible for a resident company that is a member of a group to have transferred to it losses sustained by another resident company which belongs to a consortium where a "link company" which is a member of both the group and the consortium is also resident in that Member State, irrespective of the residence of the companies which hold, themselves or by means of intermediate companies, the capital of the link company and of the other companies concerned by the transfer of losses, whereas that legislation rules out such a possibility where the link company is established in another Member State'. *Felixstowe Dock & Railway Co Ltd v HMRC (and related appeals)*, ECJ Case C-80/12; [2014] STC 1489. (*Note.* Following the ECJ decision, the First-tier Tribunal issued a further decision, formally holding that *ICTA 1988, s 406(2)* had contravened European law—FTT [2014] UKFTT 452 (TC); [2014] SFTD 955, TC03579.)

[25.33] A UK company (C) had two subsidiaries resident in the Republic of Ireland, which were subject to a 10% rate of tax. The Revenue issued assessments on C on the basis that the 'controlled foreign companies' legislation of *ICTA 1988, ss 747–756* applied. C (and its parent company) appealed. The Special Commissioners referred the case to the ECJ, which held that the EC Treaty 'must be interpreted as precluding the inclusion in the tax base of a resident company established in a Member State of profits made by a CFC in another Member State, where those profits are subject in that State to a lower level of taxation than that applicable in the first State, unless such inclusion relates only to wholly artificial arrangements intended to escape the national tax normally payable. Accordingly, such a tax measure must not be applied where it is proven, on the basis of objective factors which are ascertainable by third parties, that despite the existence of tax motives that

CFC is actually established in the host Member State and carries on genuine economic activities there'. *Cadbury Schweppes plc v CIR; Cadbury Schweppes Overseas Ltd v CIR*, ECJ Case C-196/04; [2006] STC 1908; [2006] 3 WLR 890; [2007] All ER (EC) 153. (*Notes*. (1) For a preliminary issue in this case, see **4.256** APPEALS. (2) See now the changes implemented by *FA 2007, Sch 15*.)

[25.34] Following the ECJ decision in *Metalgesellschaft Ltd & Others v CIR*, **25.18** above, several UK companies took proceedings against the Revenue, claiming that the application of *ICTA 1988, ss 747–756* was a breach of the EC Treaty. The Ch D referred the case to the ECJ, which held that the Treaty 'must be interpreted as precluding the inclusion in the tax base of a resident company established in a Member State of profits made by a controlled foreign company in another Member State, where those profits are subject in that State to a lower level of taxation than that applicable in the first State, unless such inclusion relates only to wholly artificial arrangements intended to escape the national tax normally payable. Accordingly, such a tax measure must not be applied where it is proven, on the basis of objective factors which are ascertainable by third parties, that despite the existence of tax motives, that controlled foreign company is actually established in the host Member State and carries on genuine economic activities there.' *Test Claimants in the CFC and Dividend Group Litigation v CIR*, ECJ Case C-201/05; [2008] STC 1513. (*Note*. For subsequent developments in this case, see **25.94** below.)

[25.35] See also *Vodafone 2 v HMRC*, **3.85** ANTI-AVOIDANCE; *Re Loss Relief Group Litigation*, **4.272** APPEALS; *Jansen Nielsen Pilkes Ltd v Tomlinson*, **18.52** CORPORATION TAX; *Imperial Chemical Industries plc v Colmer*, **18.63** CORPORATION TAX; *Test Claimants in the FII Group Litigation v CIR*, **25.87** and **25.88** below; *R v CIR (ex p. Commerzbank AG)*, **32.1** INTEREST ON OVERPAID TAX and *Foulser & Foulser v MacDougall*, **71.260** CAPITAL GAINS TAX.

Article 49—German cases

[25.36] Under German law, married couples who lived in Germany enjoyed certain tax concessions which were not available to couples who lived outside Germany. A German dentist, who worked in Germany but lived with his wife in the Netherlands, appealed against tax assessments, contending that the relevant provisions were a breach of what is now *Article 49* of the TFEU. The case was referred to the ECJ, which held that *Article 49* did not 'preclude a member state from imposing on its nationals who carry on their professional activities within its territory and who earn all or almost all of their income there or possess all or almost all of their assets there a heavier tax burden if they do not reside in that state than if they do'. *Werner v Finanzamt Aachen-Innenstadt*, ECJ Case C-112/91; [1996] STC 961.

[25.37] An Austrian citizen (M) lived and worked in Germany. His wife lived in Austria, where she looked after their daughter and received benefit payments which were not subject to tax. The couple were not 'permanently separated'. M claimed that he and his wife should be jointly assessed under German income tax law. The tax authority rejected the claim on the basis that M's wife was not resident in Germany, and that M should be taxed as if he were unmarried. M appealed, and the case was referred to the ECJ, which held that what is now *Article 49* of the TFEU 'precludes a resident taxpayer from being refused, by the Member State of his residence, joint assessment to income tax with his spouse from whom he is not separated and who lives in another Member State'. *Finanzamt Dinslaken v Meindl*, ECJ Case C-329/05; [2007] STC 314.

[25.38] Under German law, companies with a permanent establishment in Germany, but with their seat in another Member State, could not benefit from certain tax concessions which were available to German companies. The ECJ held that the relevant provisions were a breach of what is now *Article 49* of the TFEU. *Compagnie de Saint-Gobain Zweigniederlassung Deutschland v Finanzamt Aachen-Innenstadt*, ECJ Case C-307/97; [2000] STC 854.

[25.39] A German company (L) claimed a deduction for losses incurred by a permanent establishment in Luxembourg. The tax authority rejected the claim and L appealed, contending that the relevant German law was a breach of what is now *Article 49* of the TFEU. The case was referred to the ECJ, which rejected L's contentions, holding that the Treaty 'does not preclude a situation in which a company established in a Member State cannot deduct from its tax base losses relating to a permanent establishment belonging to it and situated in another Member State, to the extent that, by virtue of a double taxation convention, the income of that establishment is taxed in the latter Member State where those losses can be taken into account in the taxation of the income of that permanent establishment in future accounting periods'. *Lidl Belgium GmbH & Co KG v Finanzamt Heilbronn*, ECJ Case C-414/06; [2008] STC 3229.

[25.40] German corporation tax legislation contained a provision requiring payment of interest on debts due from parent companies to be recategorised as a 'covert distribution of profits' when the relevant loan capital was 'more than three times the shareholder's proportional equity capital at any point in the financial year, save where the company limited by shares could have obtained the loan capital from a third party under otherwise similar circumstances or the loan capital constitutes borrowing to finance normal banking transactions'. The ECJ held that the EC Treaty precluded the measure in question. The ECJ observed that the relevant legislation 'does not have the specific purpose of preventing wholly artificial arrangements, designed to circumvent German tax legislation, but applies generally to any situation in which the parent company has its seat, for whatever reason, outside the Federal Republic of Germany'. *Lankhorst-Hohorst GmbH v Finanzamt Steinfurt*, ECJ Case C-324/00; [2003] STC 607; 5 ITLR 467. (*Note*. With regard to the UK, the Ch D subsequently made a Group Litigation Order covering related claims. See *Test Claimants in the 'Thin Cap' Group Litigation v CIR*, **25.29** above.)

[25.41] In another German case, the ECJ held that the EC Treaty precluded national legislation 'which, in the case of a branch of a company having its seat in another Member State, lays down a tax rate on the profits of that branch which is higher than that on the profits of a subsidiary of such a company where that subsidiary distributes its profits in full to its parent company'. *CLT-UFA SA v Finanzamt Köln-West*, ECJ Case C-253/03; [2007] STC 1303.

[25.42] In another German case, the ECJ held that where 'a parent company holds shares in a non-resident subsidiary which give it a definite influence over the decisions of that foreign subsidiary and allow it to determine its activities', what are now *Articles 49* and *54* of the TFEU 'preclude legislation of a Member State which restricts the right of a parent company which is resident in that State to deduct for tax purposes losses incurred by that company in respect of write-downs to the book value of its shareholdings in subsidiaries established in other Member States'. *Rewe Zentralfinanz eG v Finanzamt Köln-Mitte*, ECJ Case C-347/04; [2008] STC 2785.

[25.43] In another German case, the ECJ held that the EC Treaty 'must be interpreted as not precluding tax legislation of a Member State under which the income of a resident national derived from capital invested in an establishment which has its registered office in another Member State is, notwithstanding the existence of a double taxation convention concluded with the Member State in which the establishment has its registered office, not exempted from national income tax but is subject to national taxation against which the tax levied in the other Member State is set off'. *Columbus Container Services BVBA & Co v Finanzamt Bielefeld-Innenstadt*, ECJ Case C-298/05; [2008] STC 2554; 10 ITLR 366.

[25.44] A German company (D) set up a permanent establishment in Italy. The lira fell in value against the deutschmark, and D made a loss as a result. It sought to set this against its German profits. The tax authority rejected the claim, and D appealed. The case was referred to the ECJ, which held that it was contrary to what is now *Article 49* of the TFEU 'for a Member State to allow a currency loss to be deducted as operating expenditure in respect of an undertaking with a registered office in a Member State only in so far as its permanent establishment in another Member State does not make any tax-free profits'. *Deutsche Shell GmbH v Finanzamt für Großunternehmen in Hamburg*, ECJ Case C-293/06; [2008] STC 1721.

[25.45] In another German case, the ECJ held that the EC Treaty precluded legislation which, for the purposes of share valuation, treated a company's holding in a partnership established in another Member State as having 'a greater value than its holding in a partnership established in the Member State concerned'. *Heinrich Bauer Verlag Beteiligungs GmbH v Finanzamt für Großunternehmen in Hamburg*, ECJ Case C-360/06; 2 October 2008 unreported.

[25.46] See also *Finanzamt Hamburg Am Tierpark v Burda GmbH*, 25.189 below.

Article 49—Netherlands cases

[25.47] Under Netherlands law, self-employed taxpayers who were resident in the Netherlands were allowed tax relief for contributions to a pension reserve. However, such relief was not available to self-employed taxpayers who lived outside the Netherlands. A Belgian physiotherapist, who was a partner in a practice in the Netherlands, claimed tax relief on a pension contribution. The Netherlands inspector rejected the claim, and the case was referred to the ECJ, which held that the relevant provisions constituted discrimination which was contrary to the EC Treaty. *Wielockx v Inspecteur der Directe Belastingen*, ECJ Case C-80/94; [1995] STC 876.

[25.48] Under Netherlands law, taxpayers who were resident in the Netherlands were taxed at 13% on their lowest band of income, but taxpayers who lived outside the Netherlands were taxed at 25% on the same band. The controlling director of a Netherlands company lived in Belgium, and was taxed at 25% on his income from the company. He appealed, and the case was referred to the ECJ, which held that the relevant provisions constituted discrimination which was contrary to the EC Treaty. *Asscher v Staatssecretaris van Financien*, ECJ Case C-107/94; [1996] STC 1025.

[25.49] A US holding company (H) had subsidiaries in both Germany and the Netherlands. The German branch had a Netherlands branch, which it sold to the Netherlands company as part of a group reorganisation. The sale included some immovable property, on which the Netherlands authorities levied land transfer tax. If both companies had been resident in the Netherlands, the transfer would have been exempt from the tax. H appealed, contending that the charge to tax contravened what is now *Article 49* of the TFEU. The case was referred to the ECJ, which upheld H's contentions, holding that 'the rules regarding equality of treatment forbid not only overt discrimination by reason of nationality or, in the case of a company, its seat, but all covert forms of discrimination which, by the application of other criteria of differentiation, lead in fact to the same result'. *Halliburton Services BV v Staatssecretaris van Financiën*, ECJ Case C-1/93; [1994] 1 ECR 1137.

[25.50] In another Netherlands case, the ECJ held that what is now *Article 49* of the TFEU 'precludes a national provision which, when determining the tax on the profits of a parent company established in one Member State, makes the deductibility of costs in connection with that company's holding in the capital of a subsidiary established in another Member State subject to the condition that such costs be indirectly instrumental in making profits which are taxable in the Member State where the parent company is established'. *Bosal Holdings BV v Staatssecretaris van Financien*, ECJ Case C-168/01; [2003] STC 1483; 6 ITLR 105; [2003] All ER (EC) 959.

[25.51] Netherlands legislation provided for the taxation of latent increases in value of company holdings on the emigration of a substantial shareholder. The controlling shareholder of three Netherlands companies, emigrated to the UK. He appealed against a charge to income tax, contending that this legislation contravened the EC Treaty. The case was referred to the ECJ, which held that the Treaty 'must be interpreted as precluding a Member State from establishing a system for taxing increases in value in the case of a taxpayer's transferring his residence outside that Member State'. *N v Inspecteur van de Belastingdienst Oost/kantoor Almelo*, ECJ Case C-470/04; 7 September 2006 unreported.

[25.52] In another Netherlands case, the ECJ held that the EC Treaty did not 'preclude legislation of a Member State which makes it possible for a parent company to form a single tax entity with its resident subsidiary, but which prevents the formation of such a single tax entity with a non-resident subsidiary, in that the profits of that non-resident subsidiary are not subject to the fiscal legislation of that Member State'. *Re X Holding BV*, ECJ Case C-337/08; [2010] STC 941.

[25.53] In another Netherlands case, the ECJ held that *Article 49* of the TFEU did not preclude 'legislation of a Member State under which the amount of tax on unrealised capital gains relating to a company's assets is fixed definitively, without taking account of decreases or increases in value which may occur subsequently, at the time when the company, because of the transfer of its place of effective management to another Member State, ceases to obtain profits taxable in the former Member State; it makes no difference that the unrealised capital gains that are taxed relate to exchange rate gains which cannot be reflected in the host Member State under the tax system in force there'. However, *Article 49* did preclude 'legislation of a Member State which prescribes the immediate recovery of tax on unrealised capital gains relating to assets of a company transferring its place of effective management to another Member State at the very time of that transfer'. *National Grid Indus BV v Inspecteur van de Belastingdienst Rijnmond / kantoor Rotterdam*, ECJ Case C-371/10; [2012] STC 114.

[25.54] In another Netherlands case, the ECJ held that *Articles 49* and *54* of the TFEU 'must be interpreted as precluding legislation of a Member State under which a resident parent company can form a single tax entity with a resident sub-subsidiary where it holds that sub-subsidiary through one or more resident companies, but cannot where it holds that sub-subsidiary through non-resident companies which do not have a permanent establishment in that Member State'. *Inspecteur van de Belastingdienst/Noord/kantoor Groningen v SCA Group Holding BV*, ECJ Case C-39/13; [2014] STC 2107.

[25.55] In another Netherlands case, the ECJ held that *Articles 49* and *54* of the TFEU 'must be interpreted as precluding legislation of a Member State under which treatment as a single tax entity is granted to a resident parent company which holds resident subsidiaries, but is precluded for resident sister companies the common parent company of which neither has its seat in that Member State nor has a permanent establishment there'. *X AG v Inspecteur van de Belastingdienst Amsterdam (and related appeals)*, ECJ Case C-40/13; [2014] STC 2107.

Article 49—Belgian cases

[25.56] In a Belgian case, the ECJ held that what is now *Article 49* of the TFEU 'precludes legislation of a Member State under which a company incorporated under national law, having its seat in that Member State, may, for the purposes of corporation tax, deduct a loss incurred the previous year from the taxable profit for the current year only on the condition that that loss was not capable of being set off against the profit made during that same previous year by one of its permanent establishments situated in another Member State, when the loss, although set off, cannot be deducted from taxable income in either of the Member States concerned, whereas it would be deductible if the establishments of that company were situated exclusively in the Member State in which it has its seat'. *Algemene Maatschappij voor Investering en Dienstverlening NV v Belgium*, ECJ Case C-141/99; [2003] STC 356; 3 ITLR 201.

[25.57] In another Belgian case, the ECJ held that what is now *Article 49* of the TFEU precluded national legislation 'which lays down minimum tax bases only for non-resident taxpayers'. *Talotta v État Belge*, ECJ Case C-383/05; [2008] STC 3261.

[25.58] In another Belgian case, the ECJ held that what is now *Article 49* of the TFEU precluded national legislation 'under which interest payments made by a company resident in a Member State to a director which is a company established in another Member State are reclassified as dividends and are, on that basis, taxable, where, at the beginning of the taxable period, the total of the interest-bearing loans is higher than the paid-up capital plus taxed reserves, whereas, in the same circumstances, where those interest payments are made to a director which is a company established in the same Member State, those payments are not reclassified as dividends and are, on that basis, not taxable'. *NV Lammers & Van Cleef v Belgische Staat*, ECJ Case C-105/07; 17 January 2008 unreported.

[25.59] In another Belgian case, the ECJ held that the EC Treaty did not preclude national legislation 'which provides for the retention of tax at source on interest paid by a company resident in that Member State to a recipient company resident in another Member State, while exempting from that retention interest paid to a recipient company resident in the first Member State, the income of which is taxed in that Member State by way of corporation tax'. *État Belge SPF Finances v Truck Venter SA*, ECJ Case C-282/07; 22 December 2008 unreported.

[25.60] In another Belgian case, a company (S) contended that the Belgian transfer pricing legislation contravened what is now *Article 49* of the TFEU. The ECJ rejected S's contentions, holding that *Article 49* 'must be interpreted as not precluding, in principle, legislation of a Member State, such as that at issue in the main proceedings, under which a resident company is taxed in respect of an unusual or gratuitous advantage where the advantage has been granted to a company established in another Member State with which it has, directly or indirectly, a relationship of interdependence, whereas a resident company cannot be taxed on such an advantage where the advantage has been granted to another resident company with which it has such a relationship'. *Société De Gestion Industrielle (SGI) v État Belge*, ECJ Case C-311/08; 21 January 2010 unreported.

[25.61] In another Belgian case, the ECJ held that *Article 49* of the TFEU 'must be interpreted as precluding legislation of a Member State, such as the legislation at issue in the main proceedings, under which payments made by a resident taxpayer to a non-resident company for supplies or services are not to be regarded as deductible business expenses where the non-resident company is not subject, in the Member State of establishment, to tax on income or is subject, as regards the relevant income, to a tax regime which is appreciably more advantageous than the applicable regime in the former Member State, unless the taxpayer proves that such payments relate to genuine and proper transactions and do not exceed the normal limits, whereas, under the general rule, such payments are to be regarded as deductible business expenses if they are necessary for acquiring or retaining taxable income and if the taxpayer demonstrates the authenticity and amount of those expenses'. *Société d'investissement pour l'agriculture tropicale SA v État Belge*, ECJ Case C-318/10; [2012] STC 1988.

[25.62] The ECJ held that 'by maintaining different rules for the taxation of income from capital and movable property according to whether it is earned by resident investment companies or non-resident investment companies with no permanent establishment in Belgium', Belgium had failed to fulfil its obligations under *Article 49* of the TFEU. *European Commission v Belgium*, ECJ Case C-387/11; [2013] STC 587.

[25.63] In another Belgian case, the ECJ held that *Article 49* of the TFEU 'must be interpreted as precluding national legislation under which, for calculation of a deduction granted to a company subject to full tax liability in a Member State, the net value of the assets of a permanent establishment situated in another Member State is not taken into account when the profits of that permanent establishment are not taxable in the first Member State by virtue of a double taxation convention, whereas the assets attributed to a permanent establishment situated in the territory of the first Member State are taken into account for that purpose'. *Argenta Spaarbank NV v Belgische Staat*, ECJ Case C-350/11; [2013] STC 2097.

Article 49—other cases

[25.64] A French company (F) had a branch in Luxembourg. This branch declared a taxable profit in 1986, having declared no profit for the previous five years. F claimed that it should be entitled to apportion its total losses for that period and set a proportion of these against the branch's profit for 1986. The Luxembourg authorities rejected the claim on the basis that the losses 'were not economically linked to income received in Luxembourg'. F appealed and the case was referred to the ECJ, which held that the EC Treaty did not preclude a member state from making the carry-forward of losses 'subject to the condition that the losses must be economically related to the income earned by the taxpayer in that state, provided that resident taxpayers do not receive more favourable treatment'. Furthermore, a member state could require a non-resident taxpayer 'to demonstrate clearly and precisely that the amount of the losses which he claims to have incurred corresponds, under its domestic rules governing the calculation of income and losses which were applicable in the financial year concerned, to the amount of the losses actually incurred in that state'. *Futura Participations SA v Administrations des Contributions*, ECJ Case C-250/95; [1997] STC 1301.

[25.65] A Scottish bank had a branch in Greece. Under Greek law, the profits of this branch were taxed at 40%, although the profits of Greek banks could be taxed at only 35%. The bank appealed and the case was referred to the ECJ, which held that the EC Treaty precluded legislation 'which, in the case of companies having their seat in another Member State and carrying on business in the first Member State through a permanent establishment situated there, excludes the possibility, accorded only to companies having their seat in the first Member State, of benefiting from a lower rate of tax on profits, when there is no objective difference in the situation between those two categories of companies which could justify such a difference in treatment'. *Royal Bank of Scotland plc v Greek State*, ECJ Case C-311/97; [2000] STC 733.

[25.66] In a French case, the ECJ held that the EC Treaty precluded 'national legislation which, in imposing a liability to tax on dividends paid to a non-resident parent company and allowing resident parent companies almost full exemption from such tax, constitutes a discriminatory restriction on freedom of establishment', and national legislation which imposes, only as regards non-resident parent companies, a withholding tax on dividends paid by resident subsidiaries, even if a tax convention between the Member State in question and another Member State, authorising that withholding tax, provides for the tax due in that other State to be set off against the tax charged in accordance with the disputed system, whereas a parent company is unable to set off tax in that other Member State, in the manner provided for by that convention.' *Denkavit Internationaal BV v Ministre de l'Économie, des Finances et de l'Industrie (and related appeal)*, ECJ Case C-170/05; [2007] STC 452; 9 ITLR 560.

[25.67] In another French case, the ECJ held that what are now *Articles 49* and *63* of the TFEU 'preclude legislation of a Member State intended to eliminate economic double taxation of dividends, such as that at issue in the main proceedings, which allows a parent company to set off against the advance payment, for which it is liable when it redistributes to its shareholders dividends paid by its subsidiaries, the tax credit applied to the distribution of those dividends if they originate from a subsidiary established in that Member State, but does not offer that option if those dividends originate from a subsidiary established in another Member State, since, in that case, that legislation does not give entitlement to a tax credit applied to the distribution of those dividends by that subsidiary. Where a national tax regime such as that at issue in the main proceedings does not of itself lead to the passing on to a third party of the tax unduly paid by the person liable for that tax, EU law precludes a Member State refusing to reimburse sums paid by the parent company on the grounds either that such reimbursement would lead to the unjust enrichment of the parent company, or that the sum paid by the parent company does not constitute an accounting or tax charge for it but is set off against the total of the sums which may be redistributed to its shareholders.' However, the ECJ also held that 'the principles of equivalence and effectiveness do not preclude the reimbursement to a parent company of sums which ensure the application of the same tax regime to dividends distributed by its subsidiaries established in France and those distributed by the subsidiaries of that company established in other Member States, and subsequently redistributed by that parent company, being subject to the condition that the person liable for the tax furnish evidence which is in its sole possession and relating, with respect to each dividend concerned, in particular to the rate of taxation actually applied and the amount of tax actually paid on profits made by subsidiaries established in other Member States, whereas, with respect to subsidiaries established in France, that evidence, known to the administration, is not required. Production of that evidence may however be required only if it does not prove virtually impossible or excessively difficult to furnish evidence of payment of the tax by the subsidiaries established in the other Member States, in the light in particular of the provisions of the legislation of those Member States concerning the avoidance of double taxation, the recording of the corporation tax which must be paid and the retention of administrative documents. It is for the national court to determine whether those conditions are met in the case before the national court.' *Ministre du Budget, des Comptes publics et de la Fonction publique v Accor SA*, ECJ Case C-310/09; [2012] STC 438.

[25.68] In a Hungarian case, the ECJ held that what is now *Article 49* of the TFEU should 'be interpreted as not precluding legislation of a Member State under which a company incorporated under the law of that Member State may not transfer its seat to another Member State whilst retaining its status as a company governed by the law of the Member State of incorporation'. *Cartesio Oktató és Szolgáltató bt*, ECJ Case C-210/06; [2009] All ER (EC) 269.

[25.69] Portugal imposed an 'exit tax' on the unrealised capital gains of companies which ceased to be resident there. The European Commission took proceedings in the ECJ, seeking a declaration that the Portuguese legislation contravened what is now *Article 49* of the TFEU. The ECJ gave judgment in favour of the Commission, holding that, by prescribing 'the immediate taxation of unrealised capital gains relating to the assets concerned but not of unrealised capital gains resulting from purely national operations', Portugal had failed to fulfil its obligations under *Article 49*. *European Commission v Portuguese Republic*, ECJ Case C-38/10; 6 September 2012 unreported.

[25.70] In a Finnish case, the ECJ held that what is now *Article 49* of the TFEU did not preclude national legislation 'whereby a subsidiary resident in that Member State may not deduct an intra-group financial transfer which it makes in favour of its parent company from its taxable income unless that parent company has its establishment in that same Member State'. *Oy AA v Finland*, ECJ Case C-231/05; [2008] STC 991; [2007] All ER (EC) 1079.

[25.71] In another Finnish case, the ECJ held that the EC Treaty 'must be interpreted as precluding legislation of a Member State which exempts from withholding tax dividends distributed by a subsidiary resident in that State to a share company resident in that State, but charges withholding tax on similar dividends paid to a parent company in the form of an open-ended investment company (SICAV) resident in another Member State which has a legal form unknown in the law of the former State', and was exempt from income tax under the law of that other Member State. *Aberdeen Property Fininvest Alpha Oy v Finland*, ECJ Case C-303/07; [2009] STC 1945.

[25.72] In a French case, the ECJ held that a French law 'under which a French parent company can establish an integrated group with its sub-subsidiary only if it holds the sub-subsidiary through a French subsidiary and not through a subsidiary established in another member state, constitutes a restriction on freedom of establishment'. However, 'this restriction may be justified by the need to maintain the coherence of the tax system, if the exclusion is appropriate for prevention of a double deduction for losses, and does not go beyond what is necessary for the achievement of this objective'. It was for the national court to determine whether such a restriction was justified. *Papillon v Ministère du budget, des comptes publics et de la fonction publique*, ECJ Case C-418/07; [2009] STC 542; 11 ITLR 140.

[25.73] A Finnish company merged with a Swedish subsidiary and claimed that the losses of that subsidiary should be deductible from its profits taxed in

Finland. The Finnish tax authority rejected the claim and the company appealed. The case was referred to the ECJ for a ruling on the interpretation of *Article 49* of the TFEU. The ECJ held that *Article 49* did not 'preclude national legislation under which a parent company merging with a subsidiary established in another Member State, which has ceased activity, cannot deduct from its taxable income the losses incurred by that subsidiary in respect of the tax years prior to the merger, while that national legislation allows such a possibility when the merger is with a resident subsidiary'. However, such legislation would be 'incompatible with European Union law if it does not allow the parent company the possibility of showing that its non-resident subsidiary has exhausted the possibilities of taking those losses into account and that there is no possibility of their being taken into account in its State of residence in respect of future tax years either by itself or by a third party'. *Re A Oy*, ECJ Case C-123/11; [2013] STC 1960.

[25.74] A Danish bank (N) had established branches in Finland, Sweden and Norway. These branches made losses, which N set against its profits taxable in Denmark. N subsequently closed the branches and transferred their business to associated companies based outside Denmark. The tax authority sought to recover the loss relief, and N appealed, contending that the relevant Danish legislation contravened *Article 49* of the TFEU. The case was referred to the ECJ, which upheld N's contentions, holding that *Articles 49* and *54* 'preclude legislation of a Member State under which, in the event of transfer by a resident company to a non-resident company in the same group of a permanent establishment situated in another Member State or in another State that is party to the Agreement on the European Economic Area, the losses previously deducted in respect of the establishment transferred are reincorporated into the transferring company's taxable profit, in so far as the first Member State taxes both the profits made by that establishment before its transfer and those resulting from the gain made upon the transfer'. *Nordea Bank Danmark A/S v Skatteministeriet*, ECJ Case C-48/13; [2015] STC 34.

Article 51—exceptions to right of establishment

[25.75] A Dutch national held a legal diploma giving him the right to exercise the profession of *avocat* in Belgium, but was excluded from that profession on the grounds that he was not a Belgian national. He appealed, and the case was referred to the ECJ for guidance on the interpretation of what is now *Article 51* of the TFEU. The ECJ held that the exception to the right of freedom of establishment provided by what is now *Article 51* must be restricted to activities 'which in themselves involve a direct and specific connection with the exercise of official authority', and did not include 'activities such as consultation and legal assistance or the representation and defence of parties in court, even if the performance of these activities is compulsory or there is a legal monopoly in respect of it'. *Reyners v Belgian State*, ECJ Case 2/74; [1974] ECR 631.

Article 52—special treatment for foreign nationals

[25.76] The Italian tax authority issued an assessment charging tax on money which an Italian citizen (B) had won in casinos outside Italy, although winnings from casinos in Italy were not taxed. B appealed, contending that the

Italian legislation contravened the TFEU. The ECJ upheld B's contentions, rejecting the tax authority's claim that the legislation was authorised by what is now *Article 52* of the TFEU, and holding that *Article 52* 'must be interpreted as precluding legislation of a Member State which subjects winnings from games of chance obtained in casinos in other Member States to income tax and exempts similar income from that tax if it is obtained from casinos in its national territory'. *C Blanco v Agenzia delle Entrate Direzione Provinciale I di Roma*, ECJ Case C-344/13; 22 October 2014 unreported.

Services (Articles 56–62)

Article 56—freedom to provide services

[25.77] In a German case, the ECJ held that 'national measures liable to hinder or make less attractive the exercise of fundamental freedoms guaranteed by the Treaty must fulfil four conditions: they must be applied in a non-discriminatory manner; they must be justified by imperative requirements in the general interest; they must be suitable for securing the attainment of the objective which they pursue; and they must not go beyond what is necessary in order to attain it'. *Gebhard v Consiglio dell'Ordine degli Avvocati e procuratori di Milano*, ECJ Case C-55/94; [1995] 1 ECR 4165; [1996] 1 CMLR 603; [1996] All ER (EC) 189.

[25.78] Under Finnish legislation, contributions to pension schemes operated by Finnish insurance undertakings were deductible from taxable income, but contributions to such schemes operated by foreign insurers were not normally deductible. A doctor, who had moved from Germany to Finland, paid voluntary contributions to two German insurance institutions. The tax authority ruled that he was not entitled to deduct these contributions from his taxable income. He appealed, and the case was referred to the ECJ for a ruling on whether the relevant Finnish legislation was compatible with what is now *Article 56* of the TFEU. The ECJ ruled that what is now *Article 56* 'is to be interpreted as precluding a Member State's tax legislation from restricting or disallowing the deductibility for income tax purposes of contributions to voluntary pension schemes paid to pension providers in other Member States while allowing such contributions to be deducted when they are paid to institutions in the first-mentioned Member State, if that legislation does not at the same time preclude taxation of the pensions paid by the above mentioned pension providers'. *Re Danner*, ECJ Case C-136/00; [2002] STC 1283; 5 ITLR 119.

[25.79] In a case involving a resident of the Netherlands who had worked in Germany, the ECJ held that the EC Treaty precluded 'a national provision such as that at issue in the main proceedings which, as a general rule, takes into account gross income when taxing non-residents, without deducting business expenses, whereas residents are taxed on their net income, after deduction of those expenses. However, those articles of the Treaty do not preclude that same provision in so far as, as a general rule, it subjects the income of non-residents to a definitive tax at the uniform rate of 25%, deducted at source, whilst the income of residents is taxed according to a progressive table including a tax-free allowance, provided that the rate of 25% is not higher than that which would actually be applied to the person concerned, in accordance with the progressive table, in respect of net income increased by an amount corresponding to the tax-free allowance.' *Gerritse v Finanzamt Neukölln-Nord*, ECJ Case C-234/01; [2004] STC 1307; 5 ITLR 978.

[25.80] In a French case, the ECJ held that what is now *Article 56* of the TFEU 'precludes legislation of a Member State which restricts the benefit of a tax credit for research only to research carried out in that Member State'. *Laboratoires Fournier SA v Direction des verifications nationales et internationals*, ECJ Case C-39/04; [2006] STC 538.

[25.81] In a German case, the ECJ held that the EC Treaty did not preclude 'national legislation under which a procedure of retention of tax at source is applied to payments made to providers of services not resident in the Member State in which the services are provided, whereas payments made to providers of services resident in that Member State are not subject to such a retention'. *FKP Scorpio Konzertproduktionen GmbH v Finanzamt Hamburg-Eimsbüttel*, ECJ Case C-290/04; [2007] STC 1069.

[25.82] In a case concerning a Portuguese company which had carried on business in Germany, the ECJ held that what is now *Article 56* of the TFEU did not preclude national legislation which 'makes repayment of corporation tax deducted at source on the income of a taxpayer with restricted tax liability subject to the condition that the operating expenses in respect of which a deduction is claimed for that purpose by that taxpayer have a direct economic connection to the income received from activities pursued in the Member State concerned, on condition that all the costs that are inextricably linked to that activity are considered to have such a direct connection, irrespective of the place and time at which those costs were incurred'. *Centro Equestre da Lezí-ria Grande Lda v Bundesamt für Finanzen*, ECJ Case C-345/04; [2008] STC 2250; [2007] All ER (EC) 680.

[25.83] In a German case, the ECJ held that what is now *Article 56* of the TFEU 'must be interpreted as precluding legislation of a Member State which allows taxpayers to claim as special expenses conferring a right to a reduction in income tax the payment of school fees to certain private schools established in national territory, but generally excludes that possibility in relation to school fees paid to a private school established in another Member State'. *Schwarz & Gootjes-Schwarz v Finanzamt Bergisch Gladbach*, ECJ Case C-76/05; [2008] STC 1357.

[25.84] An Austrian company (J) claimed an 'investment premium' in respect of some lorries which it had hired to an associated company, which used them in Germany and other Member States. The tax authority rejected the claim on the grounds that the lorries were mainly used outside Austria. J appealed, contending that the relevant Austrian legislation contravened what is now *Article 56* of the TFEU. The ECJ accepted this contention, holding that *Article 56* 'precludes legislation of a Member State, such as that at issue in the main proceedings, pursuant to which undertakings which acquire tangible assets are refused the benefit of an investment premium solely because the assets in respect of which that premium is claimed, which are hired out for remuneration, are used primarily in other Member States'. *Jobra Vermogensverwal-*

tungs-Gesellschaft mbH v Finanzamt Amstetten Melk Scheibbs, ECJ Case C-330/07; [2008] All ER (D) 140 (Dec).

[25.85] In two Netherlands cases, the ECJ held that the EC Treaty 'must be interpreted as not precluding the application by a Member State, where savings balances and income from those balances are concealed from the tax authorities of that Member State and the latter have no evidence of their existence which would enable an investigation to be initiated, of a longer recovery period when the balances are held in another Member State than when they are held in the first Member State. The fact that that other Member State applies banking secrecy is not relevant in that regard.' *X v Staatssecretaris van Financiën*, ECJ Case C-155/08; *Passenheim van Schoot v Staatssecretaris van Financiën*, ECJ Case C-157/08; [2009] STC 2441; [2009] All ER (EC) 888.

[25.86] In an Italian case, the ECJ held that what is now *Article 56* of the TFEU 'must be interpreted as precluding national legislation which allows taxpayers to deduct from gross tax the costs of attending university courses provided by universities situated in that Member State but excludes generally that possibility for university tuition fees incurred at a university established in another Member State'. *E Zanotti v Agenzia delle Entrate – Ufficio Roma 2*, ECJ Case C-56/09; 20 May 2010 unreported.

Capital and payments (Articles 63–66)

Article 63—UK cases

[25.87] Several UK companies applied to the Ch D for a declaration that the UK corporation tax rules, under which dividends from UK companies were not taxed but dividends from companies resident in other EC member states were subject to tax, contravened the EC Treaty. The Ch D referred the case to the ECJ, which held that the Treaty 'must be interpreted as meaning that, where a Member State has a system for preventing or mitigating the imposition of a series of charges to tax or economic double taxation as regards dividends paid to residents by resident companies, it must treat dividends paid to residents by non-resident companies in the same way. What is now *Article 63* of the TFEU 'precludes legislation of a Member State which exempts from corporation tax dividends which a resident company receives from another resident company, where that State levies corporation tax on dividends which a resident company receives from a non-resident company in which it holds at least 10% of the voting rights, without granting the company receiving the dividends a tax credit for the tax actually paid by the company making the distribution in the State in which the latter is resident.' The ECJ also held that 'individuals should have an effective legal remedy enabling them to obtain reimbursement of the tax unlawfully levied on them and the amounts paid to that Member State or withheld by it directly against that tax'. *Test Claimants in the FII Group Litigation v CIR (No 1)*, ECJ Case C-446/04; [2007] STC 326; 9 ITLR 426.

[25.88] Following the ECJ decision noted at 25.87 above, the case was referred back to the Ch D. Henderson J delivered a lengthy judgment, against which both sides appealed, and the CA unanimously held that there should be a further reference to the ECJ. The ECJ observed that 'in the United Kingdom the effective level of taxation of the profits of resident companies is lower than the nominal rate of tax in the majority of cases. It follows that application of the imputation method to foreign-sourced dividends as prescribed by the legislation at issue in the main proceedings does not ensure a tax treatment equivalent to that resulting from application of the exemption method to nationally-sourced dividends.' The ECJ held that 'the difference in the tax treatment of the two categories of dividends is not justified by a relevant difference in situation. Therefore, legislation such as that at issue in the main proceedings constitutes a restriction on freedom of establishment and on capital movements.' Accordingly, '*Articles 49 TFEU* and *63 TFEU* must be interpreted as precluding legislation of a Member State which applies the exemption method to nationally-sourced dividends and the imputation method to foreign-sourced dividends if it is established, first, that the tax credit to which the company receiving the dividends is entitled under the imputation method is equivalent to the amount of tax actually paid on the profits underlying the distributed dividends and, second, that the effective level of taxation of company profits in the Member State concerned is generally lower than the prescribed nominal rate of tax'. The ECJ also held that 'European Union law must be interpreted as meaning that a parent company resident in a Member State, which in the context of a group taxation scheme, such as the group income election at issue in the main proceedings, has, in breach of the rules of European Union law, been compelled to pay advance corporation tax on the part of the profits from foreign-sourced dividends, may bring an action for repayment of that unduly levied tax in so far as it exceeds the additional corporation tax which the Member State in question was entitled to levy in order to make up for the lower nominal rate of tax to which the profits underlying the foreign-sourced dividends were subject compared with the nominal rate of tax applicable to the profits of the resident parent company. European Union law must be interpreted as meaning that a company that is resident in a Member State and has a shareholding in a company resident in a third country giving it definite influence over the decisions of the latter company and enabling it to determine its activities may rely upon *Article 63 TFEU* in order to call into question the consistency with that provision of legislation of that Member State which relates to the tax treatment of dividends originating in the third country and does not apply exclusively to situations in which the parent company exercises decisive influence over the company paying the dividends.' *Test Claimants in the FII Group Litigation v HMRC (No 2)*, ECJ Case C-35/11; [2013] STC 612. (*Note*. For HMRC's practice following the CA decision, see HMRC Brief 22/10, issued on 3 June 2010.)

[25.89] Following the decision in the case noted at 25.88 above, the Ch D held a further hearing and HMRC sought to make various amendments to their defence. Henderson J rejected the application and the CA unanimously dismissed HMRC's appeal. Gloster LJ held that 'the issue which HMRC wishes to raise has been conclusively determined against it by Henderson J and the Court of Appeal. Therefore HMRC is estopped *per rem judicatum* from raising the issue a second time'. *CIR and HMRC v Test Claimants in the FII Group Litigation (No 4)*, CA [2014] EWCA Civ 1214.

[25.90] Following the CA decision noted at 25.89 above, the Ch D held a further hearing and Henderson J delivered a lengthy decision, holding inter alia that 'the EU principle of effectiveness requires the claimants to be given a remedy under national law which reimburses the whole of the unlawfully levied ACT. They have to be compensated, in the sense of receiving restitution, for the loss which they sustained by the payment of that tax. Viewed from the claimants' perspective, their loss includes, at a minimum, the amounts of unlawful tax which they paid. Whether the Revenue were correspondingly enriched by the payments is irrelevant, because the remedy required by EU law is not a purely subtractive one. Accordingly, it must be contrary to EU law for the Revenue to contend that they are excused from making restitution of the unlawful tax on the basis that they were not enriched by its receipt.' He held that the claimants were entitled 'to restitution of the full amounts of the principal sums of unlawfully paid tax', together with 'restitution of the time value of the prematurely paid (or utilised) ACT, from the dates of payment until the dates of utilisation' and 'restitution of the time value of the amounts recoverable under each of the above headings, from the dates of payment (or the dates of utilisation of ACT payments in the second category) until the date when restitution is made'. *Test Claimants in the FII Group Litigation v HMRC (No 5)*, Ch D [2014] EWHC 4302 (Ch).

[25.91] Following the Ch D decision in the case noted at 25.88 above, two associated companies applied for an interim payment. The Ch D awarded an interim payment of £4,400,000, and HMRC appealed to the CA, which unanimously upheld the payment in principle but reduced it to £1,490,932. *HMRC v GKN Group (and related appeal)*, CA [2012] EWCA Civ 57; [2012] STC 953.

[25.92] Following the ECJ decision noted at 25.88 above, the companies in the case noted at 25.91 above lodged a further application, seeking a further interim payment of £3,350,000. The Ch D held that the companies were entitled to a further interim payment, but that the amount claimed was excessive, and awarded an interim payment of £2,750,000. *GKN Holdings plc v HMRC (and related application)*, Ch D [2013] EWHC 108 (Ch).

[25.93] In the case noted at 25.88 above, the CA had upheld HMRC's contention that the relevant ACT provisions could be interpreted in such a way as to be compatible with Community law. Arden LJ held that 'a conforming interpretation can be achieved simply by reading in words that make it clear that it is not just resident companies that can claim a credit under *section 231* but also other persons entitled to do so by Community law to the extent that they are so entitled'. The CA also upheld HMRC's contentions that English law provided a restitutionary remedy for such claims, as applied in *Woolwich Equitable Building Society v CIR*, 32.4 INTEREST ON OVERPAID TAX; that such claims were subject to a six-year limitation period; and that HMRC were not precluded from relying upon the curtailed limitation period for mistake-based claims introduced by *FA 2004, s 320* and retrospectively extended by *FA 2007, s 107*. The claimants appealed to the Supreme Court against these parts of the CA decision. The Supreme Court held that there should be a further reference to the ECJ to consider whether European law required only that a Member State must make available an adequate remedy which meets the principles of effectiveness and equivalence; or whether it required every remedy recognised in domestic law to be available so that a claimant could obtain the benefit of any special advantages that this may offer on the question of limitation, in which case *FA 2004, s 320* would contravene European law. (The Supreme Court also held that, by 2006, the claimants had acquired a legitimate expectation that their claims would not be rendered ineffective by the introduction of a retrospective limitation period, so that *FA 2007, s 107* was unlawful.) The ECJ gave judgment in favour of the claimants, holding that 'in a situation in which, under national law, taxpayers have a choice between two possible causes of action as regards the recovery of tax levied in breach of European Union law, one of which benefits from a longer limitation period, the principles of effectiveness, legal certainty and the protection of legitimate expectations preclude national legislation curtailing that limitation period without notice and retroactively'. *Test Claimants in the FII Group Litigation v HMRC (No 3)*, ECJ Case C-362/12; [2014] STC 638. (*Note. FA 2007, s 107* was subsequently amended by *FA 2014, s 299*.)

[25.94] A large insurance company, and two associated companies, took proceedings in the Ch D, contending that the UK rules on the taxation of dividends were a breach of what is now *Article 63* of the TFEU. At an initial hearing, Henderson J expressed the provisional view that the claims fell within the scope of *TMA, s 33*, but directed that the proceedings should be adjourned pending the ECJ decision in *Test Claimants in the FII Group Litigation v HMRC (No 2)*, 25.88 above. Following the ECJ decision in that case, Henderson J held a further hearing and delivered a lengthy judgment. He held, inter alia, that 'the test claimants have failed on the facts to prove their entitlement to a tax credit for the underlying tax actually paid; this failure involves no breach by the United Kingdom of the principle of effectiveness; and there is therefore no reason either to disapply the requirement of proof, or to grant a tax credit at the nominal rate as a proxy'. However, the UK was required 'to grant a credit at the nominal rate of corporation tax paid by the distributing company, quite separately from the credit for underlying tax actually paid'. The legislation should 'be construed in such a way as to grant a limited credit for foreign-sourced portfolio dividends of the amount needed to secure compliance with EU law'. ACT set against corporation tax which had been held to be unlawful must be repaid. Where repayments were due, interest should be paid on a compound basis. *Prudential Assurance Co Ltd v HMRC (and related appeal)*, Ch D [2013] EWHC 3249 (Ch); [2014] STC 1236.

[25.95] Following the ECJ decision in *Metalgesellschaft Ltd & Others v CIR*, 25.18 EUROPEAN LAW, several UK companies, which were subsidiaries of parent companies resident in the USA or Japan, claimed restitution for ACT which they had paid. The Revenue rejected the claim and the HL unanimously dismissed the companies' appeals. Lord Hoffmann observed that 'if a US parent were to interpose a UK resident holding company between itself and its UK-resident subsidiary, the control would remain in the US but there would be no objection to an election by the UK subsidiary and its immediate, UK-resident parent'. An election was 'a joint decision by two entities paying and receiving dividends that one rather than the other will be liable for ACT. This is not a concept which can meaningfully be applied when one of the entities is not liable for ACT at all'. *Boake Allen Ltd v HMRC; NEC Semi-Conductors Ltd v CIR (and related appeals) (re ACT Class 3 Group Litigation Order)*, HL [2007] STC 1265; [2007] UKHL 25; [2007] 3 All ER 605.

[25.96] The European Commission took proceedings against the UK in the ECJ, seeking a declaration that the provisions of *TCGA 1992, s 13*, which provided for a difference in treatment between domestic and cross-border activities with regard to the attribution of gains to participators in non-resident companies, contravened *Article 63* of the TFEU. The ECJ granted the declaration, holding that *s 13* was 'not confined specifically to targeting wholly artificial arrangements which do not reflect economic reality and are carried out for tax purposes alone, but also affects conduct whose economic reality cannot be disputed'. *European Commission v United Kingdom*, ECJ Case C-112/14; 13 November 2014 unreported.

[25.97] See also *Fisher v HMRC*, **3.65** ANTI-AVOIDANCE.

Article 63—German cases

[25.98] In a German case, the ECJ held that what is now *Article 63* of the TFEU 'must be interpreted as precluding a Member State which exempts from corporation tax rental income received in its territory by charitable foundations which, in principle, have unlimited tax liability if they are established in that Member State, from refusing to grant the same exemption in respect of similar income to a charitable foundation established under private law solely on the ground that, as it is established in another Member State, that foundation has only limited tax liability in its territory'. *Centro di Musicologia Walter Stauffer v Finanzamt München für Körperschaften*, ECJ Case C-386/04; [2008] STC 1439.

[25.99] In another German case, the ECJ held that the EC Treaty must 'be interpreted as precluding tax legislation under which, on a distribution of dividends by a capital company, a shareholder who is fully taxable in a Member State is entitled to a tax credit, calculated by reference to the corporation tax rate on the distributed profits, if the dividend-paying company is established in that same Member State but not if it is established in another Member State'. *Meilicke & Others v Finanzamt Bonn-Innenstadt (No 1)*, ECJ Case C-292/04; [2008] STC 2267; 9 ITLR 834.

[25.100] Following the decision noted at **25.99** above, the German court again referred the case to the ECJ for guidance regarding the amount of tax credit which the appellants could claim. The ECJ held that 'the calculation of the tax credit must be made in relation to the rate of corporation tax on the distributed profits applicable to the dividend-paying company according to the law of the Member State of establishment; however the amount to be imposed may not exceed the amount of the income tax to be paid on dividends received by the recipient shareholder in the Member State in which that shareholder is fully taxable'. The detailed provisions of the relevant German legislation contravened the EC Treaty, but 'the tax authorities of the Member State of taxation are entitled to require that shareholder to provide documentary evidence enabling them to ascertain, clearly and precisely, whether the conditions for obtaining a tax credit under national legislation are met without having to make an estimate of that tax credit'. National legislation should 'permit the offsetting of foreign corporation tax imposed on dividends paid by a capital company established in another Member State by submitting either a certificate relating to that tax in accordance with the legislation of the Member State in which the shareholder is fully taxable, or documentary evidence allowing the tax authorities of that Member State to determine, clearly and precisely, whether the conditions for obtaining that tax advantage were met. It is for the referring court to determine a reasonable period for the submission of such a certificate or documentary evidence'. *Meilicke & Others v Finanzamt Bonn-Innenstadt (No 2)*, ECJ Case C-262/09; [2013] STC 1494.

[25.101] In a German corporation tax case, the ECJ held that what is now *Article 63* of the TFEU must be interpreted as 'not precluding legislation of a Member State which excludes the reduction in value of shares as a result of the distribution of dividends from the basis of assessment for a resident taxpayer, where that taxpayer has acquired shares in a resident capital company from a non-resident shareholder, whereas, had the shares been acquired from a resident shareholder, such a reduction in value would have reduced the acquirer's basis of assessment. This applies in cases where such legislation does not exceed what is necessary to maintain a balanced allocation of the power to impose taxes between the Member States and to prevent wholly artificial arrangements which do not reflect economic reality and whose only purpose is unduly to obtain a tax advantage. It is for the national court to examine whether the legislation at issue in the main proceedings is limited to what is necessary in order to attain those objectives'. *Glaxo Wellcome GmbH & Co v Finanzamt München II*, ECJ Case C-182/08; [2010] STC 244.

[25.102] The European Commission applied to the ECJ for a declaration that 'by taxing dividends distributed to a company with its registered office in another Member State or in the European Economic Area more heavily in economic terms than dividends distributed to a company with its registered office in its territory', Germany had failed to fulfil its obligations under what is now *Article 63* of the TFEU. The ECJ granted the declaration. *EC Commission v Federal Republic of Germany*, ECJ Case C-284/09; [2011] STC 2392.

[25.103] A German taxpayer (P) claimed a deduction for a donation of goods to a Portuguese retirement home which was run by an organisation recognised as a charity under Portuguese law. The German tax authority rejected the claim on the grounds that the donee was not established in Germany. P appealed, contending that the German legislation contravened what is now *Article 63* of the TFEU. The case was referred to the ECJ, which upheld P's contentions, holding that *Article 63* precluded national legislation 'by virtue of which, as regards gifts made to bodies recognised as having charitable status, the benefit of a deduction for tax purposes is allowed only in respect of gifts made to bodies established in that Member State, without any possibility for the taxpayer to show that a gift made to a body established in another Member State satisfies the requirements imposed by that legislation for the grant of such a benefit'. *Persche v Finanzamt Lüdenscheid*, ECJ Case C-318/07; [2009] STC 586; [2009] All ER (EC) 673.

[25.104] In a German case concerning the sale of company shares, the ECJ held that what is now *Article 63* of the TFEU precluded national legislation 'by which the profits from a sale of shares in 2001 in a limited company established in another Member State are immediately taxable where the seller had held, either directly or indirectly, a share of at least 1% of the company's capital within the previous five years, whereas the profits from the sale of shares in 2001, in the same circumstances, in a limited company established in that first Member State subject to unlimited corporation tax were subject to tax only in the case of a substantial shareholding of at least 10%'. *Grønfeldt & Grønfeldt v Finanzamt Hamburg Am Tierpark*, ECJ Case C-436/06; 18 December 2007 unreported.

[25.105] In another German case, the ECJ held that what is now *Article 63* of the TFEU precluded national legislation 'which, for the purposes of calculating the tax on an inheritance consisting of assets situated in that State and agricultural land and forestry situated in another Member State, provides that account be taken of the fair market value of the assets in that other Member State, whereas a special valuation procedure exists for identical domestic assets, the results of which amount on average to only 10% of that fair market value, and reserves application of a tax-free amount to domestic agricultural land and forestry in relation to those assets and takes account of their remaining value in the amount of only 60% thereof'. *Jäger v Finanzamt Kusel-Landstuhl*, ECJ Case C-256/06; [2009] BTC 8112.

[25.106] In another German case, the ECJ held that what are now *Articles 63 to 65* of the TFEU 'must be interpreted as precluding legislation of a Member State relating to the calculation of inheritance tax which provides that, in the event of inheritance of immovable property in that State, in a case where, as in the main proceedings, the deceased and the heir had a permanent residence in a third country, such as the Swiss Confederation, at the time of the death, the tax-free allowance is less than the allowance which would have been applied if at least one of them had been resident in that Member State at that time'. *Y Welte v Finanzamt Welbert*, ECJ Case C-181/12; 17 October 2013 unreported.

[25.107] A German woman transferred some property to her two sons, under an agreement whereby each of the sons paid her an annuity of €1,000 per month. The sons received rental income from the property. One of the sons lived in Germany and was permitted to deduct the annuity payments from the rental income under German law. The other son (S) lived in Belgium and was not allowed to make a similar deduction. He appealed, and the case was referred to the ECJ for a ruling on whether the relevant German legislation contravened *Article 63* of the TFEU. The ECJ found in favour of S, holding that '*Article 63 TFEU* must be interpreted as precluding legislation of a Member State which, while allowing a resident taxpayer to deduct the annuities paid to a relative who transferred to him immovable property situated in the territory of that State from the rental income derived from that property, does not grant such a deduction to a non-resident taxpayer, in so far as the undertaking to pay those annuities results from the transfer of that property'. *U Schröder v Finanzamt Hameln*, ECJ Case C-450/09; [2011] STC 1248.

[25.108] A brother and sister had Spanish citizenship but lived in Germany. On the death of their father, they inherited a house in Spain, from which they received rental income. Under German law, this income received less favourable tax treatment than would have been the case if the house had been situated in Germany. They appealed, and the case was referred to the ECJ for rulings on what is now *Article 63* of the TFEU. The ECJ held that *Article 63* 'precludes income tax legislation of a Member State under which natural persons who are resident and liable to unlimited taxation are entitled to have losses from the letting or leasing of an immovable property deducted from the taxable amount in the year in which those losses arise, and the income from such property assessed on the basis of the application of the decreasing-balance method of depreciation, only if the property in question is situated on the territory of that Member State'. *Grundstücksgemeinschaft Busley-Cibrian v Finanzamt Stuttgart-Körperschaften*, ECJ Case C-35/08; 15 October 2009 unreported.

[25.109] German legislation restricted the amount of foreign withholding tax which could be set against German income tax liability relating to dividends distributed by companies established outside Germany. A couple who received dividends from several different countries appealed against notices of assessment, contending that the German legislation contravened *Article 63* of the TFEU. The case was referred to the ECJ, which held that *Article 63* 'must be interpreted as precluding rules of a Member State under which, in the context of a system aimed at limiting double taxation, where persons subject to unlimited tax liability pay on foreign income, in the State where that income originates, a tax equivalent to the income tax levied by the said Member State, the offsetting of that foreign tax against the amount of income tax levied in the said Member State is carried out by multiplying the amount of the tax due in respect of taxable income in the same Member State, including foreign income, by the proportion that that foreign income bears to total income, that latter sum not taking into account special expenditure or extraordinary costs such as costs relating to lifestyle or to personal and family circumstances'. *M & C Beker v Finanzamt Heilbronn*, ECJ Case C-168/11; [2013] STC 1334.

[25.110] In another German case, the ECJ held that *Article 63* of the TFEU 'cannot have the effect of requiring Member States to go beyond the cancelling of national income tax payable by a shareholder in respect of foreign-sourced dividends received and to reimburse a sum whose origin is in the tax system of another Member State'. It also held that *Article 63* 'must be interpreted as not precluding application of the exemption method to dividends distributed by companies resident in other Member States and in third States, when the imputation method is applied to dividends distributed by companies resident in the same Member State as the company receiving them and, if the latter company records losses, the imputation method results in the tax paid by the resident company that made the distribution being fully or partially refunded'. *Kronos International Inc v Finanzamt Leverkusen*, ECJ Case C-47/12; [2014] All ER (D) 137 (Sep).

Article 63—Belgian cases

[25.111] A Belgian decree, which authorised the contracting of a public loan with two German banks on the Eurobond market, stipulated that withholding tax on interest payable on the loan was to be waived, and that Belgian residents were not permitted to subscribe. The EC Commission applied for a declaration that, by prohibiting Belgian residents from acquiring securities under the loan, Belgium had failed to fulfil its obligations under what is now *Article 63* of the TFEU. The ECJ granted the declaration, holding that the free movement of capital was a fundamental freedom under the TFEU, and its prohibition could not be justified on the grounds of a general presumption of tax evasion or fraud. *EC Commission v Kingdom of Belgium*, ECJ Case C-478/98; [2000] STC 830.

[25.112] A Belgian couple received dividends from a French company. In accordance with French law, the amount of the dividend was grossed up by 50% (the 'avoir fiscal'), and a withholding tax of 15% was levied at source. Under Belgian legislation, the total of the dividend and the 'avoir fiscal', minus the withholding tax, was taxed at 25%. The couple appealed, contending that this contravened what is now *Article 63* of the TFEU. The case was referred to the ECJ, which rejected the couple's contentions, holding that *Article 63* 'does not preclude legislation of a Member State, such as Belgian tax legislation, which, in the context of tax on income, makes dividends from shares in companies established in the territory of that State and dividends from shares in companies established in another Member State subject to the same uniform rate of taxation, without providing for the possibility of setting off tax levied by deduction at source in that other Member State'. *Kerckhaert & Morres v Belgische Staat*, ECJ Case C-513/04; [2007] STC 1349; [2007] 1 WLR 1685.

[25.113] The decision in *Kerckhaert & Morres v Belgische Staat*, 25.112 above, was applied in a similar subsequent case in which the ECJ held that the Treaty did not preclude a bilateral tax convention 'under which dividends distributed by a company established in one Member State to a shareholder residing in another Member State are liable to be taxed in both Member States, and which does not provide that the Member State in which the shareholder resides is unconditionally obliged to prevent the resulting juridical double taxation'. *Damseaux v État Belge*, ECJ Case C-128/08; [2009] STC 2689.

[25.114] In another Belgian case, the ECJ held that the EC Treaty precluded national legislation concerning the assessment of inheritance and transfer duties payable in respect of immovable property 'which makes no provision for the deductibility of debts secured on such property where the person whose estate is being administered was residing, at the time of death, not in that State but in another Member State, whereas provision is made for such deductibility where that person was, at that time, residing in the first-mentioned Member State, in which the immovable property included in the estate is situated'. *Eckelkamp & Others v Belgische Staat*, ECJ Case C-11/07; 11 September 2008 unreported.

[25.115] A Belgian woman died in 2004, leaving her estate to a German religious organisation (M). The Belgian tax authorities imposed succession duties (broadly equivalent to inheritance tax) at 80%. If M had been established in Belgium, duties would have been charged at only 7%. M appealed, contending that the relevant legislation contravened what is now *Article 63* of the TFEU. The case was referred to the ECJ, which accepted M's contentions, holding that *Article 63* 'precludes legislation of a Member State which reserves application of succession duties at the reduced rate to non-profit-making bodies which have their centre of operations in that

Member State or in the Member State in which, at the time of death, the deceased actually resided or had his place of work, or in which he had previously actually resided or had his place of work'. *Missionswerk Werner Heukelbach eV v État Belge*, ECJ Case C-25/10; [2011] STC 985.

[25.116] In another Belgian case, the ECJ held that *Article 63* of the TFEU 'must be interpreted as precluding legislation of a Member State such as that at issue in the main proceedings which provides, as regards inheritance tax, for a limitation period of ten years for the valuation of registered shares in a company whose centre of effective management is established in another Member State, while the same limitation period is two years when the company's centre of effective management is in the first Member State'. *Halley & Others v Belgische Staat*, ECJ Case C-132/10; 15 September 2011 unreported.

Article 63—Swedish cases

[25.117] Swedish tax legislation provided that, where shares were transferred at undervalue to a wholly Swedish-owned company, capital gains tax was deferred. However, there was no such deferral where the transfer was to a non-Swedish company in which the transferor had a holding (whether directly or indirectly), or to a Swedish company in which a non-Swedish company had a holding. Two Swedish nationals wanted to transfer shares in a Swedish company to another company which was partly owned by a non-Swedish company. They applied to the Swedish courts for a ruling that the Swedish legislation contravened the EC Treaty. The case was referred to the ECJ, which held that what the Treaty precluded national legislation 'which excludes the transferor at undervalue of shares in companies from the benefit of deferral of tax due on capital gains made on those shares where the transfer is to a foreign legal person in which the transferor directly or indirectly has a holding which is not such as to give him definite influence over the decisions of that foreign legal person or allow him to determine its activities'. *X & Y v Riksskatteverket*, ECJ Case C-436/00; [2004] STC 1271; 5 ITLR 433.

[25.118] In another Swedish case, the ECJ held that what the EC Treaty precluded national legislation 'which provides that a payment in respect of a share repurchase to a non-resident shareholder in connection with a reduction in share capital is taxed as a dividend without there being a right to deduct the cost of acquisition of those shares, whereas the same payment made to a resident shareholder is taxed as a capital gain with a right to deduct the cost of acquisition'. *Bouanich v Skatteverket*, ECJ Case C-265/04; 8 ITLR 433.

[25.119] In another Swedish case, the ECJ held that the EC Treaty should 'be interpreted as not precluding the legislation of a Member State which provides that exemption from income tax in respect of dividends distributed in the form of shares in a subsidiary may be granted only if the company making the distribution is established in a State within the EEA or a State with which a taxation convention providing for the exchange of information has been concluded by the Member State imposing the tax, where that exemption is subject to conditions compliance with which can be verified by the competent authorities of that Member State only by obtaining information from the State of establishment of the distributing company'. *Skatterverket v A*, ECJ Case C-101/05; [2009] STC 405.

Article 63—Austrian cases

[25.120] In an Austrian case, the ECJ held that Austrian legislation which provided a reduced rate of income tax for shareholders who received income from capital of Austrian origin, while providing that income from capital originating in another Member State failed to qualify for the reduced rate, contravened what is now *Article 63* of the TFEU. *Lenz v Finanzlandesdirektion für Tirol*, ECJ Case C-315/02; [2004] All ER (D) 277 (Jul).

[25.121] In two other Austrian cases, which the ECJ heard together, the ECJ held that the Austrian legislation governing the taxation of dividends contravened *Article 63* of the TFEU. The Austrian legislation provided that portfolio dividends from companies established in non-EU States which were members of the EEA were only exempt if 'a comprehensive agreement for mutual assistance with regard to administrative matters and enforcement exists between the Member State and non-member State concerned'. The ECJ held that this contravened *Article 63*, since 'only the existence of an agreement for mutual assistance with regard to administrative matters proves necessary for the purpose of attaining the objectives of the legislation in question'. *Article 63* also precluded legislation which provided that portfolio dividends from companies established outside both the EU and EEA failed to qualify for either exemption or double tax credit. Additionally, *Article 63* precluded 'national legislation which grants resident companies the possibility of carrying losses suffered in a tax year forward to subsequent tax years and which prevents the economic double taxation of dividends by applying the exemption method to nationally-sourced dividends, whereas it applies the imputation method to dividends distributed by companies established in another Member State or in a non-member State, in so far as, when the imputation method is applied, such legislation does not allow the credit for the corporation tax paid in the State where the company distributing dividends is established to be carried forward to the following tax years if the recipient company has recorded an operating loss for the tax year in which it received the foreign-sourced dividends'. *Haribo Lakritzen Hans Riegel BetriebsgmbH v Finanzamt Linz*, ECJ Case C-436/08; *Österreichische Salinen AG v Finanzamt Linz*, ECJ Case C-437/08; [2011] STC 917.

Article 63—other cases

[25.122] Luxembourg legislation allowed tax relief for 'resident taxpayers who are natural persons and acquire shares representing cash contributions in fully-taxable resident capital companies', but denied such relief for the acquisition of shares in companies resident in other member States. The ECJ held that this contravened what is now *Article 63* of the TFEU. *Ministre des Finances v Weidert & Paulus*, ECJ Case C-242/03; [2005] STC 1241.

[25.123] Under Finnish legislation, dividends from Finnish companies attracted a tax credit, but dividends from companies established outside Finland did not. The ECJ held that this contravened what is now *Article 63* of the TFEU. *Manninen v Finland*, ECJ Case C-319/02; [2004] STC 1444; 7 ITLR 119; [2005] All ER (EC) 465.

[25.124] In another case regarding Finnish legislation, the ECJ held that 'by introducing and maintaining in force a scheme under which dividends paid to foreign pension funds are taxed in a discriminatory manner, the Republic of Finland has failed to fulfil its obligations under *Article 63*'of the TFEU. *European Commission v Republic of Finland*, ECJ Case C-342/10; [2013] STC 280.

[25.125] In another Finnish case, the ECJ held that *Articles 63* and *65* of the TFEU 'do not preclude national tax legislation such as that at issue in the main proceedings, which does not allow a taxpayer who resides in the Member State concerned and is fully liable to income tax there to deduct the losses arising on the transfer of immovable property situated in another Member State from the income from moveable assets which is taxable in the first Member State, although that would have been possible, on certain conditions, if the immovable property had been situated in the first Member State'. *Re K*, ECJ Case C-322/11; 7 November 2013 unreported.

[25.126] In a Netherlands case, the ECJ held that what is now *Article 63* of the TFEU did not 'preclude legislation under which a Member State denies non-resident taxpayers who hold the major part of their wealth in the State where they are resident entitlement to the allowances which it grants to resident taxpayers', and that it also did not 'preclude a rule laid down by a bilateral convention for the avoidance of double taxation such as the rule at issue in the main proceedings from not being extended, in a situation and in circumstances such as those in the main proceedings, to nationals of a Member State which is not party to that convention'. *D v Inspecteur van de Belastingdienst/Particulieren/Ondernemingen buitenland te Heerlen*, ECJ Case C-376/03; [2005] STC 1211; 7 ITLR 927; [2006] All ER (EC) 554.

[25.127] In another Netherlands case, the ECJ held that the EC Treaty 'must be interpreted as not precluding a law of a Member State under which a non-resident taxpayer who receives income in that State only from savings and investments and who is not insured under the social security system of that Member State cannot claim entitlement to tax credits in respect of national insurance, whereas a resident taxpayer who is insured under that social security system is entitled to those credits'. *Blanckaert v Inspecteur van de Belastingdienst/Particulieren/Ondernemingen buitenland te Heerlen*, ECJ Case C-512/03; [2005] STC 1574; 8 ITLR 146; [2006] All ER (EC) 587.

[25.128] In another Netherlands case, the ECJ held that what is now *Article 63* of the TFEU did not preclude national legislation 'by which the estate of a national of that Member State who dies within ten years of ceasing to reside in that Member State is to be taxed as if that national had continued to reside in that Member State, while enjoying relief in respect of inheritance taxes levied by other States'. *Van Hilten-van der Heijden v Inspecteur van de Belastingdienst/Particulieren/Ondernemingen buitenland te Heerlen*, ECJ Case C-513/03; [2008] STC 1245.

[25.129] In another Netherlands case, the ECJ held that the EC Treaty precluded national legislation which provided for a withholding tax on dividends distributed by a company established in that Member State to a company established in another Member State, 'while exempting from that tax the dividends paid to a company liable to corporation tax in the first Member State or which has a permanent establishment in that Member State which owns the shares in the company making the distribution'. *Amurta SGPS v Inspecteur van de Belastingdienst/Amsterdam*, ECJ Case C-379/05; [2008] STC 2851.

[25.130] In another Netherlands case, the ECJ held that the EC Treaty precluded national legislation 'concerning the assessment of inheritance duties and transfer duties payable in respect of an immovable property situated in a Member State, which, for the assessment of those duties, makes no provision for the deductibility of overendowment debts resulting from a testamentary parental partition inter vivos where the person whose estate is being administered was residing, at the time of death, not in that State but in another Member State, whereas provision is made for such deductibility where that person was residing, at the time of death, in the first-mentioned Member State, in which the immovable property included in the estate is situated, in so far as such rules apply a progressive rate of taxation and in so far as the combination of the failure to take into account such debts and that progressive rate could result in a greater tax burden for heirs who are not in a position to rely on such deductibility'. *DMMA Arens-Sikken v Staatssecretaris van Financiën*, ECJ Case C-43/07; 11 September 2008 unreported.

[25.131] In two Netherlands cases involving the tax treatment of dividends paid to companies established in the Netherlands Antilles, the ECJ held that 'European Union law must be interpreted as not precluding a tax measure of a Member State which restricts movements of capital between that Member State and its own overseas country and territory whilst pursuing the objective of combating tax avoidance in an effective and proportionate manner'. *X BV v Staatssecretaris van Financiën*, ECJ Case C-24/12; *TBG Ltd v Staatssecretaris van Financiën*, ECJ Case C-27/12; [2014] STC 2394.

[25.132] A Luxembourg company, which held property in France, was required to pay an annual capital tax of 3% of the value of those properties. It appealed, and the case was referred to the ECJ, which held that what is now *Article 63* of the TFEU precluded national legislation 'which exempts companies established in France from the tax on the commercial value of immovable property owned in France by legal persons, when, in respect of companies established in another Member State, it makes that exemption subject either to the existence of a convention on administrative assistance between the French Republic and that State for the purposes of combating tax avoidance and tax evasion or to the existence of a requirement in a treaty containing a clause prohibiting discrimination on grounds of nationality to the effect that those companies cannot be more heavily taxed than companies established in France, and which does not allow the company established in another Member State to supply evidence to establish the identity of the natural persons who are its shareholders'. *Européenne et Luxembourgeoise d'investissements SA v Directeur Général des impôts*, ECJ Case C-451/05; 11 October 2007 unreported.

[25.133] In 1998 a German woman inherited some property in Portugal. She sold it in 2003. The Portuguese tax authorities issued a capital gains tax assessment. She appealed, contending that the Portuguese legislation taxed her more heavily than would have been the case if she had been resident in Portugal, and that this contravened what is now *Article 63* of the TFEU. The case was referred to the ECJ, which held that *Article 63* precluded national legislation 'which subjects capital gains resulting from the transfer of immovable property situated in a Member State, in this case Portugal, where that transfer is made by a resident of another Member State, to a tax burden greater than that which would be applicable for the same type of transaction to capital gains realised by a resident of the State in which that immovable property is situated'. *EWI Hollmann v Fazenda Pública*, ECJ Case C-443/06; [2008] STC 1874.

[25.134] The EC Commission applied to the ECJ for a ruling that Italian tax legislation, which subjected the distribution of dividends to non-Italian companies (outgoing dividends) to tax treatment which was significantly less favourable than that applied to the distribution of dividends to Italian companies (domestic dividends), contravened what is now *Article 63* of the TFEU. The ECJ largely upheld the Commission's contentions, holding that 'by making dividends distributed to companies established in other Member States subject to a less favourable tax regime than that applied to dividends distributed to resident companies', Italy had failed to fulfil its obligations. *EC Commission v Italy*, ECJ Case C-540/07; 19 November 2009 unreported. (*Note*. Italy was ordered to pay 75% of the costs, and the Commission was ordered to pay 25%.)

[25.135] In a French case, the tax authority ruled that a company (P) which had its registered office in France could not benefit from an exemption from tax on immovable property, on the grounds that P's effective centre of management was in the British Virgin Islands. P appealed, contending that the relevant French legislation contravened *Article 63* of the TFEU. The case was referred to the ECJ, which rejected P's contentions, holding that *Article 63* did not preclude national legislation which 'exempts from the tax on the market value of immovable property located in the territory of a Member State of the European Union companies having their registered office in the territory of that State and makes entitlement to that exemption, for a company whose registered office is in an overseas country or territory, conditional either on the existence of a convention on administrative assistance to combat tax evasion and avoidance concluded between that Member State and that territory or on there being a requirement, under a treaty containing a clause prohibiting discrimination on grounds of nationality, that those legal persons are not to be taxed more heavily than companies established in the territory of that Member State'. *Prunus Sarl v Directeur des Services Fiscaux*, ECJ Case C-384/09; [2011] STC 1392.

[25.136] In another French case, the ECJ held that *Articles 63* and *65* of the TFEU 'must be interpreted as precluding the legislation of a Member State which provides for the taxation, by means of withholding tax, of nationally-sourced dividends when they are received by undertakings for collective investments in transferable securities resident in another State, whereas such dividends are exempt from tax when received by undertakings for collective investments in transferable securities resident in the Member State in question'. *Santander Asset Management SGIIC SA v Directeur des residents à l'étranger et des services généraux*, ECJ Case C-338/11; [2012] STC 1785.

[25.137] Portuguese legislation required people who were not resident in Portugal, but who received Portuguese income which required the submission of a tax return, to appoint a tax representative in Portugal. The European Commission took proceedings in the ECJ, seeking a declaration that this contravened what is now *Article 63* of the TFEU. The ECJ accepted this contention and held that Portugal had failed to fulfil its obligations under the Treaty. *EC Commission v Portuguese Republic*, ECJ Case C-267/09; 5 May 2011 unreported.

[25.138] The Portuguese 'thin capitalisation' legislation provided that, where a Portuguese company paid interest on part of an overall debt which was categorised as excessive, it was not deductible if it was paid to a lender established in a non-EU state, but was deductible if it was paid to an associated company which was resident in the EU, subject to certain provisos. A Portuguese company, which had claimed a deduction for interest paid to an associated US company, appealed against the disallowance of part of that interest, contending that the relevant Portuguese legislation breached what is now *Article 63* of the TFEU. The ECJ held that the Portuguese legislation did not meet 'the requirements of legal certainty' and therefore could not 'be considered to be proportionate to the objectives pursued'. More generally, the ECJ held that national rules of this type 'are precluded where, if the lending company established in a non-member country does not have a shareholding in the resident borrowing company, they nevertheless presume that the overall debt owed by the borrowing company forms part of an arrangement designed to avoid the tax normally payable or where they do not make it possible, at the outset, to determine their scope with sufficient precision'. *Itelcar – Automóveis de Aluguer Lda v Fazenda Pública*, ECJ Case C-282/12; 3 October 2013 unreported.

[25.139] In a Polish case, the ECJ held that *Article 63* of the TFEU 'must be interpreted as precluding tax legislation of a member state, such as that at issue in the main proceedings, under which dividends paid by companies established in that member state to an investment fund situated in a non-member state cannot qualify for a tax exemption, provided that that member state and the non-member state concerned are bound by an obligation under a convention on mutual administrative assistance which enables the national tax authorities to verify any information which may be transmitted by the investment fund'. *Emerging Markets Series of DFA Investment Trust Company v Dyrektor Izby Skarbowej w Bydgoszczy*, ECJ Case C-190/12; [2014] STC 1660.

Article 64—transitional provisions

[25.140] In an Austrian case, the ECJ held that what is now *Article 64* of the TFEU was 'without prejudice to the application by a Member State of legislation which existed on 31 December 1993 under which a shareholder in receipt of dividends from a company established in a non-member country, who holds two thirds of the share capital in that company, is taxed at the ordinary rate of income tax, whereas a shareholder in receipt of dividends from a resident company is taxed at a rate of half the average tax rate'. *Holböck v Finanzamt Salzburg-Land*, ECJ Case C-157/05; [2008] STC 92.

[25.141] In a Netherlands case, the ECJ held that the EC Treaty did not preclude national legislation 'which grants a concession to fiscal investment enterprises established in that Member State on account of tax deducted at source in another Member State from dividends received by those enterprises, and restricts that concession to the amount which a natural person resident in the first Member State could have had credited, on account of similar deductions, on the basis of a double taxation convention concluded with that other Member State‘ However, the Treaty precluded national legislation 'which grants a concession to fiscal investment enterprises established in that Member State on account of tax deducted at source in another Member State or third country from dividends received by those enterprises, and reduces that concession where and to the extent to which the shareholders of those enterprises are natural or legal persons resident or established in other Member States or in third countries, since such a reduction adversely affects all the shareholders of those enterprises without distinction. In that respect, whether the foreign shareholders of a fiscal investment enterprise are resident or established in a State with which the Member State of establishment of that enterprise has concluded a convention providing for reciprocal crediting of tax deducted at source from dividends is irrelevant.' A restriction was covered by what is now *Article 64* of the TFEU 'as being a restriction on the movement of capital involving direct investment in so far as it relates to investments of any kind undertaken by natural or legal persons and which serve to establish or maintain lasting and direct links between the persons providing the capital and the undertakings to which that capital is made available in order to carry out an economic activity.' *Staatssecretaris van Financiën v Orange European Smallcap Fund NV*, ECJ Case C-194/06; 20 May 2008 unreported.

State Aid (Article 107)

[25.142] The CA held that differential rates of insurance premium tax, introduced by *FA 1997*, constituted a 'state aid' within the meaning of what is now *Article 107* of the TFEU, and should therefore have been notified to the EC Commission. *R v Customs & Excise Commrs (ex p. Lunn Poly Ltd and Another)*, CA [1999] All ER (D) 208.

[25.143] The Spanish province of Guipuzcoa created tax concessions for investments in new fixed assets above a certain value. The EC Commission issued a provisional decision that the concessions constituted a 'state aid' within what is now *Article 107* of the TFEU. Guipuzcoa applied to the ECJ for annulment of the decision, contending that the measures should not be treated as an unlawful state aid, and that the Commission was misusing its powers. The ECJ rejected this contention and dismissed the application, observing that the Commission's decision was 'merely provisional', and holding that it was reasonable for the Commission to express 'the provisional view that the tax measures at issue, which *de facto* restrict the grant of the tax credit to undertakings with significant financial resources, offer an appreciable advantage to the beneficiaries of that tax concession in relation to their competitors'. *Territorio Historico de Guipuzcoa, Diputacion Foral de Guipuzcoa & Others v EC Commission*, ECJ Case T-269/99; [2002] All ER (D) 337 (Oct).

[25.144] A similar decision was reached in *Territorio Historico de Alava, Diputacion Foral de Alava & Others v EC Commission*, ECJ Case T-346/99; [2002] All ER (D) 338 (Oct).

[25.145] The Azores Regional Assembly introduced reduced rates of income tax and corporation tax. The EC Commission issued a decision that the reductions constituted a 'state aid' within what is now *Article 107* of the TFEU, and that, although the concessions were justified with regard to the majority of businesses, they were not justified in so far as they applied to financial services and 'intra-group services'. Portugal applied to the ECJ for annulment of the decision. The ECJ dismissed the application, holding that the Commission was justified in holding that 'in so far as their effects on the decision as to the place of establishment by undertakings in a group and the external effect on the local economy are insignificant, such activities do not contribute sufficiently to regional development to be declared compatible'. *Portuguese Republic v EC Commission*, ECJ Case C-88/03; [2007] STC 1032.

[25.146] In 2002 the Government of Gibraltar proposed certain reforms to its corporate tax legislation, under which certain companies would qualify as 'exempt companies' or 'qualifying companies'. In 2004 the European Commission issued a ruling that the proposals constituted a 'State aid', within what is now *Article 107* of the TFEU. The Court of First Instance annulled the ruling, but the Commission appealed to the ECJ, which reversed the CFI decision and upheld the Commission's ruling, holding that 'a measure by which the public authorities grant certain undertakings favourable tax treatment which, although not involving the transfer of State resources, places the recipients in a more favourable financial position than other taxpayers amounts to State aid'. The Gibraltar Government had not shown any justification for 'the selective advantages enjoyed by offshore companies' under the proposals. *European Commission v Government of Gibraltar (and related appeal)*, ECJ Case C-106/09; [2012] STC 305.

[25.147] In an Italian case, the ECJ held that tax exemptions for workers' co-operative societies constituted a state aid, within what is now *Article 107* of the TFEU, 'only in so far as all the requirements for the application of that provision are met'. In the case in question, it was for the national court 'to determine in particular whether the tax exemptions in question are selective and whether they may be justified by the nature or general scheme of the national tax system of which they form part, by establishing in particular whether the co-operative societies at issue in the main proceedings are in fact in a comparable situation to that of other operators in the form of profit-making legal entities and, if that is indeed the case, whether the more advantageous tax treatment enjoyed by those co-operative societies, first, forms an inherent part of the essential principles of the tax system applicable in the member State concerned and, second, complies with the principles of consistency and proportionality'. *Amministrazione delle Finanze v Paint Graphos Scarl (and related appeals)*, ECJ Case C-78/08; [2011] STC 2303.

[25.148] See also *R v A-G (ex p. Imperial Chemical Industries plc)*, **74.6** PETROLEUM REVENUE TAX.

[25.149] The provisions of *FA 2000, Sch 12* were held not to be a 'state aid' in *R v CIR (oao Professional Contractors Group)*, **22.41** EMPLOYMENT INCOME.

European Parliament (Article 232)

[25.150] A Member of the European Parliament received flat rate travelling and subsistence allowances for attending its meetings. In 1975/76 his allowances for travelling and subsistence exceeded his actual expenditure. The Revenue issued an assessment on the allowances, with a deduction for his expenses. He appealed, and the Special Commissioners referred the case to the ECJ to consider whether what is now *Article 232* of the TFEU, or the *Protocol on the Privileges and Immunities of the European Communities*, prohibited Member States from taxing the allowances. The ECJ held that, although the allowances were not *ipso facto* exempt from national taxes, Member States were 'bound to facilitate the achievement of the Communities' tasks and abstain from any measure which could jeopardise the attainment of the objectives of the treaty'. It was 'essential that each member of the Parliament should at all times be able to attend all the meetings and participate in all the activities of the Parliament and its organs without suffering financial loss, regardless of the member's place of residence, the location of his constituency and his available financial means'. It was for the European Parliament to decide what allowances should be made to its members for its proper functioning. The national revenue authorities were 'bound to respect the decision taken by the European Parliament to refund travel and subsistence expenses to its members on a lump-sum basis' and could not 'demand from a member of the European Parliament returns or vouchers for the actual travel and subsistence expenses incurred in the interests of the Parliament and reimbursed by it, as such a demand would be incompatible with this method of lump-sum reimbursement'. However, the allowances 'must not exceed reasonable limits consistent with the refund of travel and subsistence expenses. In so far as the lump sum fixed for the allowances is excessive and in reality constitutes in part disguised remuneration and not reimbursement of expenses, the Member States are entitled to charge such remuneration to national income tax'. The ECJ concluded that 'Community law prohibits the imposition of national tax on lump-sum payments made by the European Parliament to its members from Community funds by way of reimbursement of travel and subsistence expenses, unless it can be shown in accordance with Community law that such lump-sum reimbursement constitutes in part remuneration'. *Lord Bruce of Donington v Aspden*, ECJ Case 208/80; [1981] STC 761; [1981] ECR 2205; [1981] 3 CMLR 506.

Court of Justice (Articles 251–281)

TFEU, Article 267—whether case should be referred to ECJ

[25.151] In a 1974 case, concerning a dispute between French companies which produced champagne and two English companies which produced cider, the French companies requested the case to be referred to the ECJ under what is now *Article 267* of the TFEU. The QB refused to refer the case, and the CA unanimously upheld this decision. *HP Bulmer Ltd & Another v J Bollinger SA & Others*, CA [1974] Ch 401; [1974] 2 All ER 1226.

[25.152] In a 1980 case concerning the import of pornographic material, Lord Diplock stated that English judges should not 'be too ready to hold that, because the meaning of the English text (which is one of six of equal authority) seems plain to them, no question of interpretation can be involved'. *R v Henn & Darby*, HL 1980, [1981] AC 850; [1980] 2 All ER 166. (*Note*. This was the first case which the HL referred to the ECJ for a preliminary ruling.)

[25.153] In an Italian case, the ECJ held that a case should be referred to the ECJ under what is now *Article 267* of the TFEU unless the national court considered that the question was 'acte claire', i.e. that the correct application of Community law was 'so obvious as to leave no scope for any reasonable doubt as to the manner in which the question raised is to be resolved'. *Srl CILFIT and Lanificio di Gavardo SpA v Ministro della Sanita*, ECJ Case 283/81; [1982] ECR 3415; [1983] 1 CMLR 472.

[25.154] However, in a subsequent German case, Advocate-General Jacobs held that it was not 'appropriate, or indeed possible, for the Court to continue to respond fully to all references which, through the creativity of lawyers and judges, are couched in terms of interpretation, even though the reference might in a particular case be better characterised as concerning the application of the law rather than its interpretation'. *Wiener SI GmbH v Hauptzollamt Emmerich*, ECJ Case C-338/95; [1998] 1 CMLR 1110.

Treaty on European Union ('Maastricht Treaty')

[25.155] Following the HL decision in *Deutsche Morgan Grenfell Group plc v HMRC (and cross-appeal)*, **10.7** CLAIMS TO RELIEF OR REPAYMENT, Parliament enacted *FA 2007, s 107*. The European Commission applied to the ECJ for a ruling that this contravened *Article 4(3)* of the *Treaty on European Union* (also known as the Maastricht Treaty, and not to be confused with the separate *Treaty on the Functioning of the European Union*.) The ECJ delivered judgment in favour of the Commission, holding that by adopting *s 107* 'which curtailed, retroactively and without notice or transitional arrangements, the right of taxpayers to recover taxes levied in breach of EU law, the UK had failed to comply with its obligations under *Article 4(3)*'. *European Commission v United Kingdom*, ECJ Case C-640/13; 18 December 2014 unreported.

EC Directives

General principles

EC Directives—whether directly applicable

[25.156] In a German VAT case, the ECJ held that 'wherever the provisions of a directive appear, as far as their subject matter is concerned, to be unconditional and sufficiently precise', their provisions could 'be relied upon as against any national provision which is incompatible with the directive or in so far as the provisions define rights which individuals are able to assert against the State'. *Becker v Finanzamt Münster-Innenstadt*, ECJ Case C-8/81; [1982] ECR 53; [1982] 1 CMLR 499.

[25.157] In a case concerning unequal treatment of men and women by a health authority, the ECJ held that a directive could be relied on against a state authority acting as an employer. *Marshall v Southampton & South West Hampshire Health Authority*, ECJ Case C-152/84; [1986] ECR 723; [1986] 1 CMLR 688; [1986] 2 All ER 584.

[25.158] In a case concerning unequal treatment of men and women by a statutory corporation, the ECJ held that a directive was directly applicable against 'a body, whatever its legal form, which has been made responsible, pursuant to a measure adopted by the State, for providing a public service under the control of the State and has for that purpose special powers beyond those which result from the normal rules applicable in relations between individuals'. *Foster & Others v British Gas plc*, ECJ Case C-188/89; [1990] ECR 3313; [1990] 3 All ER 897.

[25.159] In an Italian case, the ECJ held that a Member State which had failed to implement the provisions of a directive could not rely on the terms of the directive against individuals. *Pubblico Ministero v Ratti*, ECJ Case 148/78; [1979] ECR 1629; [1980] 1 CMLR 96.

[25.160] In an Italian case concerning a consumer protection directive which not had been implemented in Italian law, the ECJ held that, since directives were not directly effective against private entities, consumers could not derive rights against traders from the directive. *Dori v Recreb Srl*, ECJ Case C-91/92; [1994] 1 ECR 3325; [1994] 1 CMLR 665; [1995] All ER (EC) 1.

Primacy of EC Directives over national legislation

[25.161] In a 1964 case, the ECJ held that 'the EEC Treaty has created its own legal system which, on the entry into force of the Treaty, became an integral part of the legal systems of the Member States and which their courts are bound to apply. By creating a Community of unlimited duration, having its own institutions, its own personality, its own legal capacity and capacity of representation on the international plane and, more particularly, real powers stemming from a limitation of sovereignty or a transfer of powers from the States to the Community, the Member States have limited their sovereign rights, albeit within limited fields, and have thus created a body of law which binds both their nationals and themselves.' The transfer by the Member States 'from their domestic legal system to the Community legal system of the rights and obligations arising under the Treaty carries with it a permanent limitation of their sovereign rights, against which a subsequent unilateral act incompatible with the concept of the Community cannot prevail'. *Costa v ENEL*, ECJ Case C-6/64; [1964] ECR 585; [1964] CMLR 425.

[25.162] In an Italian case, the ECJ held that 'a national court which is called upon, within the limits of its jurisdiction, to apply provisions of Community law, is under a duty to give full effect to those provisions, if necessary refusing of its own motion to apply any conflicting provision of national legislation, even if adopted subsequently, and it is not necessary for the court to request or await the prior setting aside of such provisions by legislative or other constitutional means'. *Amministrazione delle Finanze dello Stato v Simmenthal SpA*, ECJ Case C-106/77; [1978] ECR 629; [1978] 3 CMLR 263.

[25.163] In a 1990 UK case, concerning regulations issued under the *Merchant Shipping Act 1988*, the ECJ held that a national court was required to set aside a rule of national law which it considered was the sole obstacle preventing it from granting interim relief in a case concerning Community law. *Factortame Ltd & Others v Secretary of State for Transport (No 2)*, ECJ Case C-213/89; [1990] 1 ECR 2433; [1990] 3 CMLR 375; [1991] 1 All ER 70.

State liability to pay damages for failure to implement Directive

[25.164] In an Italian case, the ECJ held that the Italian government was liable to pay compensation to employees of an insolvent company, who had suffered financial loss through Italy's failure to implement a directive guaranteeing such employees their arrears of wages. *Francovich v Italian State*, ECJ Case C-6/90; [1991] 1 ECR 5357; [1993] 2 CMLR 66. (*Note.* For the procedure to be adopted in the UK in seeking to apply the principles laid down in this case, see *R v Secretary of State for Employment (ex p. Equal Opportunities Commission)*, **25.170** below.)

[25.165] The principles laid down in *Francovich v Italian State*, **25.164** above, were applied in two subsequent cases in which national legislation was held to be contrary to EC law. The ECJ ruled that 'the principle that Member States are obliged to make good damage caused to individuals by breaches of Community law attributable to the state is applicable where the national legislature was responsible for the breach in question'. *Brasserie du Pêcheur SA v Federal Republic of Germany; R v Secretary of State for Transport (ex p. Factortame Ltd & Others) (No 3)*, ECJ Cases C-46/93, C-48/93; [1996] 1 ECR 1029; [1996] 1 CMLR 889; [1996] 2 WLR 506; [1996] All ER (EC) 301.

[25.166] The decisions in *Brasserie du Pêcheur SA v Federal Republic of Germany; R v Secretary of State for Transport (ex p. Factortame Ltd & Others) (No 3)*, **25.165** above, were applied in the subsequent case of *R v Ministry of Agriculture, Fisheries & Food (ex p. Hedley Lomas (Ireland) Ltd)*, ECJ Case C-5/94; [1996] 1 ECR 2553; [1996] 2 CMLR 391; [1996] All ER (EC) 493.

[25.167] In a case concerning claims for compensation by German residents following the insolvency of two German tour operators, the ECJ held that 'failure to take any measure to transpose a directive in order to achieve the result it prescribes within the period laid down for that purpose constitutes *per se* a serious breach of Community law and consequently gives rise to a right of reparation for individuals suffering injury if the right prescribed by the directive entails the grant to individuals of rights whose content is identifiable, and a causal link exists between the breach of the state's obligation and the loss and damage suffered'. *Dillenkofer & Others v Federal Republic of Germany*, ECJ Case C-178/94, C-179/94; [1996] 1 ECR 4845; [1996] 3 CMLR 469; [1996] All ER (EC) 917.

[25.168] The decisions in *Brasserie du Pêcheur SA v Federal Republic of Germany; R v Secretary of State for Transport (ex p. Factortame Ltd & Others) (No 3)*, **25.165** above, were distinguished in a case in which the ECJ held that a breach of *Directive 90/435/EC* was not sufficiently serious to give rise to a claim to compensation. *R v HM Treasury (ex p. British*

Telecommunications plc), ECJ Case C-392/93; [1996] 1 ECR 1631; [1996] 2 CMLR 217; [1996] 3 WLR 303; [1996] All ER (EC) 401.

[25.169] A similar decision was reached in *Denkavit Internationaal BV & Others v Bundesamt für Finanzen*, 25.182 below.

Claims to compensation under Francovich principle—procedure

[25.170] In a case in which the HL held that certain provisions of the *Employment Protection (Consolidation) Act 1978* were incompatible with the EC Treaty, Lord Keith of Kinkel observed that 'if there is any individual who believes that he or she has a good claim to compensation under the *Francovich* principle, it is the Attorney-General who would be defendant in any proceedings directed to enforcing it'. *R v Secretary of State for Employment (ex p. Equal Opportunities Commission)*, HL [1994] 1 All ER 910.

Specific Directives

Council Directive 77/799/EEC—spontaneous exchange of information

[25.171] A Netherlands taxpayer (WN) claimed a deduction for maintenance payments which he made to his estranged wife in Spain. The Netherlands authorities informed him that they proposed to send information about these payments to the Spanish authorities in accordance with *Council Directive 77/799/EEC, article 4*. WN took proceedings against the authorities, and the case was referred to the ECJ, which held that *article 4(1)(a)* must be interpreted as meaning that it was not necessary for the 'loss of tax' referred to therein to be covered by an express measure on the part of the competent authority of another Member State. The effect of *article 4(1)(a)* was that a Member State was, without prior request, to forward information to the tax authorities of another Member State where it had grounds for supposing that, without that information, an unjustified saving in tax might exist or be granted in that other State. In that context, it was not necessary for that saving to amount to a large sum. The expression 'loss of tax' should be interpreted as referring to 'an unjustified saving of tax in another Member State'. *WN v Staatssecretaris van Financien*, ECJ Case C-420/98; [2001] STC 974; 2 ITLR 685.

Council Directive 88/361/EEC, article 1—movements of capital

[25.172] In a Netherlands case, the ECJ held that *Council Directive 88/361/EEC, article 1* precluded a legislative provision which made the grant of an exemption from income tax on dividends paid to shareholders subject to a condition that those dividends were paid by a company which was established in that Member State. The question of whether the person applying for exemption was an ordinary shareholder, or an employee holding shares under an employees' savings plan, was not material. *Staatssecretaris van Financien v Verkooijen*, ECJ Case C-35/98; [2002] STC 654; 2 ITLR 727.

Council Directive 90/434/EEC—definition of 'independent business'

[25.173] In a Danish case, the shareholders of a company applied to the tax authority for confirmation that a proposed transfer of the company's assets to a new company would qualify for tax exemption. The tax authority ruled that the transactions would qualify for exemption provided that certain specific conditions were met. The shareholders sought judicial review of the legality of the conditions, and the case was referred to the ECJ for a ruling on the interpretation of *Council Directive 90/434/EEC, article* 2. The ECJ ruled that *article 2(c)* must be interpreted as meaning that there was no transfer of assets 'where the terms of a transaction are such that the proceeds of a significant loan contracted by the transferring company remain with that company and the obligations arising from the loan are transferred to the company receiving the transfer'. It was for the national court to determine whether a transfer of assets involved an 'independent business' within the meaning of *article 2(i)*. For this purpose, an 'independent business' should be construed as 'an entity capable of functioning by its own means, where the future cash-flow requirements of the company receiving the transfer must be satisfied by a credit facility from a financial institution which insists, in particular, that the shareholders of the company receiving the transfer provide security in the form of shares representing the capital of that company'. *Anderson og Jenson ApS v Skatteministeriet*, ECJ Case C-43/00; [2004] STC 1115; 4 ITLR 523.

Council Directive 90/434/EEC, article 4—mergers or divisions

[25.174] A company claimed that the Italian legislation dealing with transfers of assets and share exchanges contravened *Article 4* of *Directive 90/434/EEC*. The ECJ rejected this contention. *3DI Srl v Agenzia delle Entrate Direzione Provinciale di Cremona*, ECJ Case C-207/11; 19 December 2012 unreported.

Council Directive 90/434/EEC, article 8—share exchanges

[25.175] In a Danish case concerning a corporate restructuring, an exchange of shares was followed by a dividend distribution. The Danish authorities sought to charge tax on the transactions. One of the shareholders appealed, contending that the exchange of shares was exempt under *Article 8(1)* of *Directive 90/434/EEC*. The case was referred to the ECJ, which held that '*Article 8(1)* of *Directive 90/434* precludes, in principle, the taxation of such an exchange of shares, unless national rules on abuse of rights, tax evasion or tax avoidance may be interpreted in accordance with *Article 11(1)(a)* of *Directive 90/434* and thus justify the taxation of that exchange'. *HM Kofoed v Skatteministeriet*, ECJ Case C-321/05; [2008] STC 1202.

[25.176] A German company transferred its controlling holding in a subsidiary to a French company in exchange for securities issued by the French company. The German tax authority sought to tax the capital gain arising, on the basis that the shares in the subsidiary should be valued at market value. The German company appealed, contending that they should be valued at 'book value'. The case was referred to the ECJ for a ruling on the interpretation of *Article 8* of *Directive 90/434/EEC*. The ECJ held that *Article 8(1)* and *(2)* 'precludes legislation of a Member State under which, in consequence of an exchange of shares, the shareholders of the acquired company are taxed on the capital gains arising from the transfer and the capital gain is deemed to correspond to the difference between the initial cost of acquiring the shares transferred and their market value, unless the acquiring company carries over the historical book value of the shares transferred in its own tax balance sheet'. *AT v Finanzamt Stuttgart-Körperschaften*, ECJ Case C-285/07; [2009] STC 1058.

Council Directive 90/434/EEC, article 11—principal objective of merger

[25.177] The sole shareholder and director of two private Netherlands companies planned to acquire the shares in a newly-created holding company in exchange for shares in the first two companies. She applied to the Netherlands tax authority to treat the proposed transaction as a 'merger by exchange of shares', and appealed against the rejection of her application. The case was referred to the ECJ for a ruling on the interpretation of *Council Directive 90/434/EEC*. The ECJ held that Member States could refuse to apply the provisions of *Council Directive 90/434/EEC* where a planned operation had tax evasion or avoidance as a principal objective, within *Article 11* of the *Directive*. In determining whether a planned operation had tax evasion or avoidance as a principal objective, the competent national authorities had to carry out a general examination of the operation in each particular case. For the purposes of *Article 11* of the *Directive*, 'valid commercial reasons' had to be interpreted as involving more than the attainment of a purely fiscal advantage such as the horizontal setting-off of losses. *Leur-Bloem v Inspecteur der Belastingdienst/Ondernemingen Amsterdam* 2, ECJ Case C-28/95; [1997] STC 1205; [1997] 1 ECR 4161; [1998] 2 WLR 27; [1997] All ER (EC) 738.

[25.178] In another Netherlands case, the ECJ held that *Article 11(1)(a)* of *Directive 90/434/EEC* 'is to be interpreted as meaning that the favourable arrangements which that directive introduces may not be withheld from a taxpayer who has sought, by way of a legal stratagem involving a company merger, to avoid the levying of a tax such as that at issue in the main proceedings, namely transaction tax, where that tax does not come within the scope of application of that directive'. *Modehuis A Zwijnenburg BV v Staatssecretaris van Financiën*, ECJ Case C-352/08; [2010] STC 1929.

[25.179] In a Portuguese case, the ECJ held that *Article 11(1)(a)* of *Directive 90/434/EEC* 'is to be interpreted as meaning that, in the case of a merger operation between two companies of the same group, the fact that, on the date of the merger operation, the acquired company does not carry out any activity, does not have any financial holdings and transfers to the acquiring company only substantial tax losses of undetermined origin, even though that operation has a positive effect in terms of cost structure savings for that group, may constitute a presumption that the operation has not been carried out for "valid commercial reasons" within the meaning of *Article 11(1)(a)*. It is incumbent on the national court to verify, in the light of all the circumstances of the dispute on which it is required to rule, whether the constituent elements of the presumption of tax evasion or avoidance, within the meaning of that provision, are present in the context of that dispute.' *Foggia – Sociedade Gestora de Participações Sociais SA v Secretário de Estado dos Assuntos Fiscais*, ECJ Case C-126/10; [2012] STC 219.

[25.180] In a Slovenian case, a company (P) proposed to transfer part of its business to a new company. It applied to the tax authority for confirmation that this qualified for the tax advantages conferred by *Directive 90/434/EEC*.

The tax authority rejected the application on the grounds that it had been lodged outside the relevant time limit. P appealed, and the case was referred to the ECJ for a ruling on the interpretation of *Article 11(1)(a)* of *Directive 90/434/EEC*. The ECJ held that *Article 11(1)(a)* 'must be interpreted as not precluding national legislation, such as that at issue in the main proceedings, under which the grant of the tax advantages applicable to a division in accordance with that directive is subject to the condition that the application relating to that operation is submitted within a specified period. However, it is for the national court to ascertain whether the details of the implementation of that period, and more particularly the determination of its starting-point of the period, are sufficiently precise, clear and foreseeable to enable taxpayers to ascertain their rights and to ensure that they are in a position to enjoy the tax advantages provided for by that directive.' *Pelati d.o.o v Republika Slovenija*, ECJ Case C-603/10; 18 October 2012 unreported.

[25.181] See also *Kofoed v Skatteministeriet*, 25.175 above.

Council Directive 90/435/EEC—exemption from withholding tax

[25.182] In implementing *Directive 90/435/EEC*, Germany took advantage of the derogation provided for in *Article 3(2)*, and refused to apply the exemption unless a one-year holding period had been completed before the distribution was made. Three Netherlands companies with German subsidiaries appealed against the refusal of exemption, contending that it was not necessary for the minimum period to have expired before the exemption could apply, provided that the parent company continued to hold the shares for the minimum period. The ECJ held that Member States were not obliged to grant the tax advantage provided for by *Article 5(1)* immediately, simply on the basis of an unilateral undertaking by the parent company to observe the minimum holding period. Member States were free to determine the detailed arrangements for ensuring that the minimum holding period was observed, and it was not for the Court to impose a particular arrangement on a Member State. The manner in which Germany had implemented the *Directive* did not give rise to any right to compensation. *Denkavit Internationaal BV & Others v Bundesamt für Finanzen*, ECJ Case C-283/94; [1996] STC 1445; [1996] 1 ECR 5063.

[25.183] In implementing *Directive 90/435/EEC*, France adopted the exemption method under *Article 4(1)*, and provided that net income from holdings giving entitlement to application of the tax regime for parent companies which was received by a parent company in the course of a financial year could be deducted from the net total profits of that company, after deduction of a proportion of costs and charges, fixed at 5% of the total revenue from the holdings, including tax credits. The effect of this provision was that the 5% in question was added back to the parent company's taxable income. A French bank took court proceedings against the tax authority, contending that the French provisions failed to comply with *Article 4* of the *Directive*. The case was referred to the ECJ, which rejected the bank's contentions, holding that 'the concept of "profits distributed by the subsidiary", within the meaning of the last sentence of *Article 4(2)* of *Directive 90/435/EEC*' was to be interpreted as 'not precluding legislation of a Member State which includes in those profits tax credits which have been granted in order to offset a withholding tax levied by the Member State of the subsidiary in the hands of the parent company'. *Banque Féderative du Crédit Mutuel v Ministre de l'Économie, des Finances et de l'Industrie*, ECJ Case C-27/07; [2008] STC 2192.

[25.184] In Belgium, dividends which a parent company received from subsidiaries resident elsewhere in the EC were included in the parent company's basis of assessment, and subsequently deducted therefrom only in so far as the parent company had taxable profits. A Belgian company (N) which had suffered losses appealed to the Belgian courts, contending that the relevant legislation contravened *Directive 90/435/EEC*. The case was referred to the ECJ, which upheld N's contentions, holding that *Article 4(1)* of *Council Directive 90/435/EEC* 'must be interpreted as precluding legislation of a Member State, such as that at issue in the main proceedings, which provides that dividends received by a parent company are to be included in its basis of assessment in order subsequently to be deducted from that basis in the amount of 95%, in so far as, for the tax period in question, the parent company has a positive profit balance after deduction of other exempted profits'. *Belgische Staat v NV Cobelfret*, ECJ Case C-138/07; [2009] STC 1107.

[25.185] In another Belgian case, the ECJ held that 'the concept of a holding in the capital of a company of another Member State', within *Article 3* of *Council Directive 90/435/EEC*, 'does not include the holding of shares in usufruct. However, in compliance with the freedoms of movement guaranteed by the EC Treaty, applicable to cross-border situations, when a Member State, in order to avoid double taxation of received dividends, exempts from tax both the dividends which a resident company receives from another resident company in which it holds shares with full title and those which a resident company receives from another resident company in which it holds shares in usufruct, that Member State must apply, for the purpose of exempting received dividends, the same treatment to dividends received from a company established in another Member State by a resident company holding shares with full title as that which it applies to such dividends received by a resident company which holds shares in usufruct'. *État Belge – SPF Finances v Les Vergers du Vieux Tauves SA* , ECJ Case C-48/07; 22 December 2008 unreported.

[25.186] In another Belgian case, a company (P) carried out a merger with two subsidiary companies, which transferred their assets to P and were dissolved without going into liquidation. P claimed that the way in which the resulting surplus was treated under Belgian legislation was a breach of *Article 4(1)* of *Directive 90/435/EEC*. The Bruges Court of First Instance ruled that P was not entitled to the credit which it had claimed, on the grounds that the transactions in question amounted to a liquidation of P's subsidiaries. P appealed to the Ghent Court of Appeal, which referred the case to the ECJ for a ruling on the interpretation of 'liquidation' in *Article 4(1)*. The ECJ issued a ruling in favour of P, holding that 'the dissolution of a company in the context of a merger by acquisition cannot be considered to be such a liquidation'. *Punch Graphix Prepress Belgium NV v Belgische Staat*, ECJ Case C-371/11; [2013] STC 603.

[25.187] In 1993 a Netherlands company (E) received dividends from a Portuguese subsidiary. The dividends were paid net of tax. Two types of Portuguese tax were deducted from the dividends: IRC (broadly equivalent to corporation tax) was levied at 15% and ISD (a 'succession and donation' tax) was levied at 5%. E appealed, contending that *Article 5(4)* of *Council Directive 90/435/EEC* only authorised the deduction of IRC at 15% and did not authorise the deduction of ISD. The case was referred to the ECJ, which upheld E's contentions, holding that the objective of *Council Directive 90/435/EEC* 'would be undermined if the Member States were permitted deliberately to deprive companies in other Member States of the benefit of the *Directive* by subjecting them to taxes having the same effect as a tax on income, even if the name given to the latter places them in the category of tax on assets'. Accordingly, *Article 5(4)* 'in so far as it limits to 15% and 10% the amount of the withholding tax on profits distributed by subsidiaries established in Portugal to their parent companies in other Member States, must be interpreted as meaning that that derogation relates not only to corporation tax but also to any taxation, of whatever nature or however described, which takes the form of a withholding tax on dividends distributed by such subsidiaries'. *Ministerio Publico v Epson Europe BV*, ECJ Case C-375/98; [2002] STC 739.

[25.188] A Greek company (AZ), which was a subsidiary of a Netherlands company, claimed a repayment of tax on profits which it had distributed to its parent company. The Greek tax authority rejected the claim, and AZ appealed, contending that the tax in question was a 'withholding tax', so that the refusal to repay it contravened *Council Directive 90/435/EEC*. The case was referred to the ECJ, which upheld AZ's contentions, holding that there was a withholding tax 'where national legislation provides that, in the event of distribution of profits by a subsidiary (a public limited company or equivalent company) to its parent company, in order to determine the taxable profits of the subsidiary its total net profits, including income which has been subject to special taxation entailing extinction of tax liability and non-taxable income, must be reincorporated into the basic taxable amount, when income falling within those two categories would not be taxable on the basis of the national legislation if they remained with the subsidiary and were not distributed to the parent company'. *Athinaiki Zithopiia AE v Ellinikio Dimosio (Greek State)*, ECJ Case C-294/99; [2002] STC 559; 4 ITLR 116.

[25.189] In a German case, the ECJ held that 'a provision of national law which, in relation to cases where profits are distributed by a subsidiary to its parent company, provides for the taxation of income and asset increases of the subsidiary which would not have been taxed if they had remained with the subsidiary and had not been distributed to the parent company does not constitute withholding tax within the meaning of *Article 5(1)*' of *Directive 90/435/EEC*. The ECJ also held that what is now *Article 43EC* of the *EC Treaty* must be interpreted as not precluding national legislation 'under which the taxation of profits distributed by a subsidiary resident in a Member State to its parent company is subject to the same corrective mechanism regardless of whether the parent company is resident in the same Member State or in another Member State even though – unlike a resident parent company – a non-resident parent company is not granted a tax credit by the Member State in which the subsidiary is resident'. *Finanzamt Hamburg Am Tierpark v Burda GmbH*, ECJ Case C-284/06; [2008] STC 2996.

[25.190] A UK company (OUK) paid dividends to its Netherlands parent company (ON). In accordance with *SI 1973/317*, OUK added an amount representing the appropriate tax credit, less 5% of the aggregate of the amount of the dividend and the amount of the tax credit, as provided by *Article 10* of the UK/Netherlands Double Taxation Agreement. ON claimed repayment from the UK Revenue of the 5% which had been withheld in accordance with the Agreement. The Revenue rejected the claim and ON appealed, contending that the relevant provision of the Agreement violated its rights under Community law. The Special Commissioner directed that the case should be referred to the ECJ, which held that, although the 5% charge amounted to a withholding tax on profits which a subsidiary distributed to its parent company, it did not amount to a withholding tax 'in so far as it is imposed on the tax credit to which that distribution of dividends confers entitlement in the United Kingdom'. Furthermore, even where the charge did amount to a withholding tax, it fell 'within a body of agreement-based provisions relating to the payment of tax credits to the recipients of dividends' which were 'designed thereby to mitigate double taxation'. Accordingly, its imposition was permitted by *Article 7(2)* of *Directive 90/435/EC*. *Océ van der Grinten NV v CIR*, ECJ Case C-58/01; [2003] STC 1248; 6 ITLR 137. (*Note*. *SI 1973/317* was revoked by *SI 1999/1927* with effect from 21 July 1999.)

[25.191] The Italian tax authorities levied withholding taxes on certain financial transfers by Italian subsidiaries to their Netherlands parent companies, which the tax authorities considered to be dividend distributions. The companies appealed, and the case was referred to the ECJ for rulings on the interpretation of *Directive 90/435/EEC*. The ECJ held that it was for the national courts 'to ascertain, in particular, whether the Italian tax authorities in practice waive, as a matter of course, the tax revenue from the adjustment surtax in the event of a dividend distribution by an Italian company to a Netherlands company, including where the adjustment surtax is not collected by those tax authorities but the amounts corresponding to that surtax are transferred directly by the Italian company to the Netherlands company. If there were found to be such a waiver, that transfer, when carried out, could be regarded as a distribution of profits.' The ECJ concluded that it appeared that 'a withholding tax such as that at issue in the cases in the main proceedings is not a withholding tax on distributed profits generally prohibited by *Article 5(1)*' of the Directive. However, 'if the referring court were to find that the "refund" of the "adjustment surtax" is not fiscal in nature, a withholding tax such as that at issue in the cases before it would be a withholding tax on distributed profits which is, as a rule, prohibited by *Article 5(1)*'. Furthermore, if the national court were to regard the tax at issue as falling within *Article 5(1)*, 'that withholding tax could be held to come within the scope of *Article 7(2)* of that directive only if, first, that convention contained provisions intended to eliminate or mitigate the economic double taxation of dividends and, secondly, the charging of that withholding tax did not cancel out the effects thereof, a matter which it would be for the referring court to assess'. *P Ferrero e SpA v Agenzia delle Entrate–Ufficio di Alba*, ECJ Case C-338/08; *General Beverage Europe BV v Agenzia delle Entrate–Ufficio di Torino 1*, ECJ Case C-339/08, 24 June 2010 unreported.

Council Directive 2003/49/EC—interest and royalty payments

[25.192] Under German legislation, interest payments were not fully deductible when determining the taxable profits of the company making the payment. A German subsidiary of a Netherlands company appealed, contending that this contravened *Directive 2003/49/EC*, and the case was referred to the ECJ. The ECJ rejected the company's contentions, holding that *Article 1(1)* of *Directive 2003/49/EC* 'must be interpreted as not precluding a provision of national tax law under which loan interest paid by a company established in one Member State to an associated company in another Member State is incorporated into the basis of assessment of the business tax payable by the former company'. *Scheuten Solar Technology GmbH v Finanzamt Gelsenkirchen-Süd*, ECJ Case C-397/09; [2011] STC 1622.

Miscellaneous

Application of ECJ decisions—whether retrospective

[25.193] In a Belgian case concerning what is now *Article 157* of the TFEU (which lays down the principle 'that men and women should receive equal pay for equal work'), the ECJ held that its decision could not have retrospective effect for periods prior to the date of the judgment, except with regard to those who had 'already brought legal proceedings or made an equivalent claim'. The ECJ observed that 'important considerations of legal certainty affecting all the interests involved, both public and private, make it impossible in principle to reopen the question as regards the past'. *Defrenne v SA Belge de Navigation Aerienne Sabena*, ECJ Case 43/75; [1976] ECR 455; [1976] 2 CMLR 98; [1981] 1 All ER 122.

[25.194] The decision in *Defrenne v Sabena*, 25.193 above, was applied in a subsequent case concerning occupational pension schemes. The ECJ held that 'overriding considerations of legal certainty preclude legal situations which have exhausted all their effects in the past from being called into question where that might upset retroactively the financial balance of many contracted-out pension schemes'. Accordingly, what is now *Article 157* of the TFEU 'may not be relied on in order to claim entitlement to a pension with effect from a date prior to that of this judgment, except in the case of workers or those claiming under them who have before that date initiated legal proceedings or raised an equivalent claim under the applicable national law'. *Barber v Guardian Royal Exchange Assurance Group*, ECJ Case 262/88; [1990] 1 ECR 1889; [1990] 2 CMLR 513; [1990] 2 All ER 660.

[25.195] The decisions in *Defrenne v Sabena*, **25.193** above, and *Barber v Guardian Royal Exchange Assurance Group*, **25.194** above, were distinguished in a case where a Danish employment levy was held to be incompatible with the *EC Sixth VAT Directive*. The ECJ held that, since the EC Commission had warned the Danish government that the levy in question appeared to be a breach of Community law, it was inappropriate to limit the temporal effect of the judgment. *Dansk Denkavit ApS & Others v Skatteministeriet*, ECJ Case C-200/90; [1992] 1 ECR 2217; [1994] 2 CMLR 377; [1994] STC 482.

[25.196] The decision in *Dansk Denkavit ApS & Others v Skatteministeriet*, 25.169 above, was applied in a subsequent case in which the ECJ held that 'the financial consequences which might ensue for a government owing to the unlawfulness of a tax have never justified in themselves limiting the effects of a judgment of the Court'. The ECJ observed that 'to limit the effects of a judgment solely on the basis of such considerations would considerably diminish the judicial protection of the rights which taxpayers have under Community fiscal legislation'. *Roders BV & Others v Inspecteur der Invoerrechten en Accijnzen*, ECJ Case C-367/93; [1995] 1 ECR 2229.

Validity of time limit imposed by national law

[25.197] In a German case, the ECJ held that 'the right conferred by Community law must be exercised before the national court in accordance with the conditions laid down by national rules' and that the imposition of time limits 'with regard to actions of a fiscal procedure is an application of the fundamental principle of legal certainty protecting both the taxpayer and the administration concerned'. *Rewe-Zentralfinanz eG & Rewe-Zentral AG v Landwirtschaftskammer für das Saarland*, ECJ Case C-33/76; [1976] ECR 1989; [1977] 1 CMLR 533.

[25.198] In a French case, the ECJ held that 'a national legislature may not, subsequent to a judgment of the Court from which it follows that certain legislation is incompatible with the EC Treaty, adopt a procedural rule which specifically reduces the possibilities of bringing proceedings for recovery of taxes which were wrongly levied under that legislation'. *Deville v Administration des Impôts*, ECJ Case 240/87; [1988] ECR 3513; [1989] 3 CMLR 611.

[25.199] In an Irish case, a national time limit for claiming a social security benefit was held to be invalid, since the time limit in question 'had the result of depriving the applicant of any opportunity whatever to rely on her right to equal treatment under the directive'. *Emmott v Minister for Social Welfare & Another*, ECJ Case C-208/90; [1991] 1 ECR 4269; [1991] 3 CMLR 894.

[25.200] The decision in *Emmott v Minister for Social Welfare & Another*, 25.199 above, was distinguished in a subsequent Netherlands case in which a national law, under which payment of arrears of benefits was restricted to a maximum period of twelve months, was held to be valid. *Steenhorst-Neerings v Bestuur van de Bedriffsvereniging voor Detailhandel, Ambachten en Huisvrouwen*, ECJ Case C-338/91; [1993] 1 ECR 5475; [1995] 3 CMLR 323.

[25.201] The decision in *Steenhorst-Neerings v Bestuur van de Bedriffsvereniging voor Detailhandel, Ambachten en Huisvrouwen*, 25.200 above, was applied in the similar subsequent case of *Johnson v Chief Adjudication Officer (No 2)*, ECJ Case C-410/92; [1994] 1 ECR 5483; [1994] 1 CMLR 725; [1995] All ER (EC) 258.

[25.202] In a Belgian case, a partnership had appealed against a charge to tax. During the proceedings, it sought to raise an alternative contention based on the EC Treaty. The Belgian Court of Appeal held that, under Belgian law, this contention could not be considered on the grounds that it had been raised outside the 60-day time limit laid down by the Belgian Tax Code, and referred the case to the ECJ to consider whether the relevant provision was compatible with Community law. The ECJ held that the time limit was invalid under Community law, and directed that the substantive question of whether the charge to tax was compatible with the *EC Treaty* should be considered by the Belgian court. *SCS Peterbroeck Van Campenhout & Cie v Belgium*, ECJ Case C-312/93; [1995] 1 ECR 4599; [1996] 1 CMLR 793; [1996] All ER (EC) 242.

[25.203] In a Danish case in which a five-year limitation period was held to be reasonable, the ECJ observed that 'the setting of reasonable limitation periods for bringing proceedings is compatible with Community law. Such periods cannot be regarded as rendering virtually impossible or excessively difficult the exercise of rights conferred by Community law, even if the expiry of those periods necessarily entails the dismissal, in whole or in part, of the action brought'. *Fantask A/S & Others v Industriministeriet*, ECJ Case C-188/95; [1998] 1 CMLR 473; [1998] All ER (EC) 1.

[25.204] In an Italian case, the ECJ held that 'the fact that the Court has given a preliminary ruling interpreting a provision of Community law without limiting the temporal effects of its judgment does not affect the right of a Member State to impose a time-limit under national law within which, on penalty of being barred, proceedings for repayment of charges levied in breach of that provision must be commenced. Community law does not prohibit a Member State from resisting actions for repayment of charges levied in breach of Community law by relying on a time-limit under national law of three years'. *Edilizia Industriale Siderurgica Srl v Ministero delle Finanze*, ECJ Case C-231/96; [1998] 1 ECR 4951.

[25.205] Similar decisions were reached in *Aprile Srl v Amministrazione delle Finanze dello Stato*, ECJ Case C-228/96; 17 November 1998 unreported and *Roquette Frères SA v Direction des Services Fiscaux du Pas-de-Calais*, ECJ Case C-88/99; [2000] All ER(D) 2008.

[25.206] In a Belgian VAT case, the ECJ held that 'in the absence of Community rules governing a matter, it is for the domestic legal system of each Member State to lay down the detailed procedural rules governing actions for safeguarding rights which individuals derive from the effect of Community law'. Furthermore, the position of the tax authorities could not 'be compared with that of a taxable person. The authorities do not have the information necessary to determine the amount of the tax chargeable and the deductions to be made until, at the earliest, the day when the return referred to in *Article 22(4)* of the *Sixth Directive* is made'. In the case of an inaccurate or incomplete return, it was 'only from that time that the authorities can start to recover the unpaid tax. Thus, the fact that the five-year limitation period begins to run as against the tax authorities on the date on which the return should in principle be made, whereas an individual may exercise his right to deduction only within a period of five years as from the date on which that right arose, is not such as to infringe the principle of equality.' *Société Financière d'Investissements SPRL (SFI) v Belgian State*, ECJ Case C-85/97; 19 November 1998 unreported.

Recovery of charges levied in breach of Community law

[25.207] In an Italian case, the ECJ held that the Italian government was not entitled to withhold repayment of charges which had been levied contrary to Community law. *Amministrazione delle Finanze dello Stato v San Giorgio SpA*, ECJ Case C-199/82; [1983] ECR 3513; [1985] 2 CMLR 658.

The principle of 'legal certainty'

[25.208] In a French case, the ECJ held that 'rules imposing charges on the taxpayer must be clear and precise so that he may know without ambiguity what are his rights and obligations and may take steps accordingly'. *Administration des Douanes v Société Anonyme Gondrand Freres*, ECJ Case C-169/80; [1981] ECR 1931.

Decision reached without reference to ECJ case law

[25.209] In a 1993 case, the CA held that 'the fact that a national court, in considering a case on the basis of national legislation implementing a directive but where the directive itself is not directly pleaded, did not refer to the relevant case law of the European Court on the directive, is a factor which contributes to a finding that the judgment is unreliable and should be quashed'. *Wren v Eastbourne Borough Council*, CA [1993] 3 CMLR 166.

Protocol on the Privileges and Immunities of the EC

[25.210] An official of the European Commission owned a house in the UK. He claimed mortgage interest relief at source, although the amount of his taxable income was less than the amount of interest which he paid. The Revenue rejected his claim, considering that he was not a 'qualifying borrower' because his income as a Commission official was exempt from UK tax. He appealed to the Special Commissioners, who referred the case to the ECJ for a ruling as to whether the *Protocol on the Privileges and Immunities of the European Communities* required the UK to grant officials of the EC the same subsidies that were paid to qualifying borrowers, determined in accordance with the relevant national provision. The ECJ answered the question in the negative, holding that the *Protocol* merely required that EC officials should be able to enjoy any tax advantage normally available to taxable persons, so as to prevent them from being subject to a greater tax burden. The appellant here was claiming a non-fiscal financial benefit, rather than relief from any fiscal charge. *Tither v CIR*, ECJ Case 333/88; [1990] 1 ECR 1133; [1990] STC 416.

[25.211] See also *Lord Bruce of Donington v Aspden*, 25.150 above.

Status of European Communities Act 1972

[25.212] In a non-tax case, Laws LJ held that 'Parliament cannot bind its successors by stipulating against repeal, wholly or partly, of the *European Communities Act*. It cannot stipulate as to the manner and form of any subsequent legislation. It cannot stipulate against implied repeal any more than it can stipulate against express repeal. Thus there is nothing in the *European Communities Act* which allows the Court of Justice, or any other institutions of the EU, to touch or qualify the conditions of Parliament's legislative supremacy in the United Kingdom. Not because the legislature chose not to allow it; because by our law it could not allow it. That being so, the legislative and judicial institutions of the EU cannot intrude upon those conditions. The British Parliament has not the authority to authorise any such thing. Being sovereign, it cannot abandon its sovereignty. Accordingly there are no circumstances in which the jurisprudence of the Court of Justice can elevate Community Law to a status within the corpus of English domestic law to which it could not aspire by any route of English law itself.' *Thoburn v Sunderland City Council (and related appeals)*, QB [2002] EWHC 195 (Admin).

26

Exempt Income

The cases in this chapter are arranged under the following headings.

Crown exemption

[26.1] The HL held that assize courts and police stations were for the use and service of the Crown, and were exempt from income tax under Schedule A under the law in force at the time. Lord Watson held that 'the purposes are all public purposes of that kind which, by the constitution of this country, fall within the province of government, and are committed to the Sovereign; so that the occupiers, though not perhaps strictly servants of the Sovereign, might be considered *in consimili casu*'. *Coomber v Berks Justices*, HL 1883, 2 TC 1; 9 App Cas 61.

[26.2] In a Scottish case, a burgh court was held to be a public court of justice occupied for Crown purposes (and hence exempt from tax under Schedule A under the law in force at the time). However, municipal offices did not qualify for exemption, and nor did public baths operated by a city council. *Adam v Maughan*, CE 1889, 2 TC 541.

[26.3] A Netherlands bank held a quantity of gold, which was located in London. In 1940 German troops invaded the Netherlands. Under the *Trading with the Enemy Act 1939*, custody of the gold was passed to the Custodian of Enemy Property, who sold the gold and invested the proceeds (accounting for tax on the income). Following the end of the Second World War, the proceeds were passed to the Administrator of Hungarian Property (on the grounds that the principal shareholder of the bank was a Hungarian). The bank subsequently took proceedings against the Administrator, claiming that it was entitled to the gross interest on the income derived from the proceeds, on the basis that the Custodian was entitled to exemption from income tax under the legislation then in force. The HL accepted this contention and gave judgment for the bank (by a 3-2 majority, Lords Morton and Keith dissenting). Lord Tucker held that the principle of Crown immunity 'extends at least to include all those officers of State and their subordinates who now perform, pursuant to statutory authority, functions of public government which were formerly the peculiar prerogatives of the Crown'. *Bank voor Handel en Scheepvaart NV v Administrator of Hungarian Property*, HL 1954, 35 TC 511.

Statutory exemptions

Exemption under local and private Acts of Parliament

[26.4] The Thames Conservancy Act 1894 provided that the Thames Conservators were 'exempt from all Parliamentary rates, taxes, assessments and payments whatsoever'. The Revenue issued assessments (under Schedule A under the law in force at the time) and the Conservators appealed, contending that this exemption extended to income tax. The Commissioners accepted this contention and allowed the appeal, and the KB upheld this decision. *Stewart v Conservators of River Thames*, KB 1908, 5 TC 297; [1908] 1 KB 893.

[26.5] The Revenue issued assessments (under Schedule A under the law in force at the time) on the proprietors of a ferry across the River Tamar. The proprietors appealed, contending that the ferry was exempt from 'Parliamentary' tax under an Act of 1790. The KB accepted this contention and allowed the appeal, and the CA unanimously upheld this decision. Applying the principles laid down by the HL in *Associated Newspapers Ltd v Corporation of the City of London*, HL [1916] 2 AC 429, the exemption extended to income tax, notwithstanding that it had not been imposed at the time. *Pole Carew & St. Levan v Craddock*, CA 1920, 7 TC 488; [1920] 3 KB 109.

[26.6] By a special Act of 1871, an annuity was granted to a member of the Royal Family 'free of all taxes and assessments and charges'. The Revenue issued assessments charging tax on the annuity. The KB discharged the assessments, holding that the effect of the 1871 Act was that the annuity was not liable to income tax or supertax. *Duke of Argyll v CIR*, KB 1913, 7 TC 225. (*Note.* At the relevant time, the provisions now contained in *ITA 2007, s 844* were then contained in *ITA 1842*. Scrutton J held that 'the Act of 1871 is in fact inconsistent with the earlier Act of 1842, and Parliament, as it is entitled to do, has to the extent of this particular annuitant repealed the Act of 1842'.)

[26.7] Under an Act of 1767, the tolls of local Drainage Commissioners were exempted from 'all taxes, rates, assessments or impositions'. The Revenue issued assessments charging tax on the tolls, on the basis that the exemption only applied to local taxation. The KB discharged the assessments, holding that the exemption extended to income tax. *Ancholme Drainage Commrs v Weldhen*, KB 1936, 20 TC 241; [1936] 1 All ER 759.

Trade union—CTA 2010, s 981

[26.8] A trade union claimed exemption under what is now *CTA 2010, s 981* for income used to provide legal assistance for its members. The Special Commissioners rejected the claim, holding that the benefits to members were not provident benefits. The QB dismissed the union's appeal, holding that whether or not the benefits were provident benefits, the claim failed because they were met out of the income of the general fund and not out of income applicable for provident purposes. *R v Special Commissioners (ex p. National Union of Railwaymen)*, QB 1966, 43 TC 445; [1967] 1 WLR 263; [1966] 2 All ER 759.

Agricultural societies—CTA 2010, s 989

[26.9] A society (P), which had been established to promote the interests of foxhound breeding, held an annual show. It appealed against assessments on its profits and on interest it received, claiming charitable exemption under what is now *CTA 2010, s 478*, or alternatively exemption under what is now *CTA 2010, s 989* on the profits of its show. The KB held that P was not established for charitable purposes only, but was entitled to exemption under *s 989* on the profits of its show. Lawrence J held that the breeding of foxhounds was within the definition of 'livestock breeding', since 'the words "live stock"' included 'all live animals and birds the breeding of which is regulated by man'. *Peterborough Royal Foxhound Show Society v CIR*, KB 1936, 20 TC 249; [1936] 2 KB 497; [1936] 1 All ER 813.

[26.10] In an Irish case, a committee which managed annual races was held not to be an agricultural society. *Ward Union Hunt Races Trustees v Hughes*, HC(I) 1937, 2 ITC 152.

[26.11] The Revenue issued an assessment on an association (C), which had been formed for the purposes of cultivating and encouraging the improvement and exhibition of cage birds. C appealed, contending that it was an agricultural society within what is now *CTA 2010, s 989*. The Special Commissioners accepted this contention and allowed the appeal, and the CS unanimously upheld this decision. *CIR v City of Glasgow Ornithological Association*, CS 1938, 21 TC 444.

ITTOIA 2005, s 731—damages for personal injury

[26.12] An individual (M) was made redundant in March 2002, having been on sick leave for the previous 18 months. From August 2001 he received monthly payments under a permanent health insurance policy taken out by his former employer. The Revenue issued an assessment for 2002/03, charging tax on these payments. M appealed, contending firstly that the payments should be treated as instalments of capital, and alternatively that they qualified for exemption under what is now *ITTOIA 2005, s 731*, because they were made to compensate a 'prospective personal injury claim related to work-related stress'. The Special Commissioner rejected these contentions and dismissed his appeal, holding on the evidence that the payments were not 'made in discharge of any claim for an amount (or estimated amount) of damages'. There was 'no agreement settling a claim for damages for personal injury whereby the damages consisted wholly or partly of the payments under the PHI policy'. *WAF Minto v HMRC*, Sp C 2007, [2008] SSCD 121 (Sp C 625).

ITTOIA 2005, s 751—interest on damages for personal injury

[26.13] A geologist (P) was kidnapped in Angola in 1998 and was never seen or heard from again. He had taken out a life insurance policy, and in 2002 the insurers paid his parents £100,000 under the policy, plus a further £36,425 which was described as interest. HMRC issued a ruling that the £36,425 was subject to income tax and chargeable on P's parents. P's parents appealed, contending firstly that it should be treated as exempt under what is now

ITTOIA 2005, s 751, and alternatively that they were not the 'person receiving or entitled to the interest', within what is now *ITTOIA 2005, s 371*. The Upper Tribunal rejected the first contention, holding that the payment failed to qualify for exemption under *s 751*, but allowed the parents' appeal on the grounds that they were not 'entitled to the interest' within *s 371*. *A & Mrs G Pope v HMRC*, UT [2012] UKUT 206 (TCC); [2012] STC 2255.

Scholarship income—ITTOIA 2005, s 776

[26.14] A married woman received payments from the Home Office to sponsor her training as a probation officer on a postgraduate course. The Revenue issued assessments (on her husband under the legislation then in force) charging the payments to income tax. The husband appealed, contending that the payments were not emoluments from his wife's employment, and were exempt as scholarship income by virtue of what is now *ITTOIA 2005, s 776*. The Special Commissioner accepted these contentions and allowed his appeal. The Revenue appealed to the CA, contending that the assessments were validated by what is now *ITEPA 2003, s 709*, since they had been made in accordance with established practice. The CA unanimously rejected this contention and upheld the Commissioner's decision. Nolan LJ held that *s 776* conferred an 'unqualified exemption' on the payments in question, and that *s 709* could not be treated as displacing this. *Walters v Tickner*, CA 1993, 66 TC 174; [1993] STC 624.

[26.15] In *Clayton v Gothorp*, 22.150 EMPLOYMENT INCOME, a loan to an employee on a sandwich course, which was waived on the completion of the course, was held not to be scholarship income.

[26.16] In a child allowance case, a taxpayer made payments under a deed of covenant to his son (R), who ws studying law at a university, and contended that these payments were income to which R was 'entitled as holder of an educational endowment'. The Ch D rejected this contention, holding that the deed of covenant could not be treated as an 'educational endowment'. *Gibbs v Randall*, Ch D 1980, 53 TC 513. (*Note*. For HMRC's interpretation of this decision, see Employment Income Manual, para EIM06220.)

Training allowances—ITEPA 2003, s 298

[26.17] An officer in the Civil Defence Corps received a 'training bounty' from a local authority. The Revenue issued an assessment charging tax on it. The officer appealed, contending that it should be treated as exempt under what is now *ITEPA 2003, s 298*. The Ch D rejected this contention and upheld the assessment. Stamp J held that the 'bounty' was not payable 'out of the public revenue', since the expression 'the public revenue' should be construed as referring to 'the public revenues of the Kingdom and not the receipts or revenues of a local authority'. Accordingly the 'bounty' did not qualify for the exemption. *Lush v Coles*, Ch D 1967, 44 TC 169; [1967] 1 WLR 685; [1967] 2 All ER 585.

Consuls and official agents—ITEPA 2003, ss 300, 301

[26.18] Following hostilities in 1974, part of Cyprus was occupied by Turkish forces. In 1983 an assembly elected by the inhabitants of this part of Cyprus made a unilateral declaration of independence under the name of the Turkish Republic of Northern Cyprus (TRNC). This declaration was not accepted by the United Nations. The TRNC established a diplomatic mission in London, but the UK government refused to grant it diplomatic recognition as a foreign state. The Revenue issued assessments charging tax on the salaries of the mission's officials. They appealed, contending that the salaries should have been treated as exempt under what is now *ITEPA 2003, ss 300, 301*. The Special Commissioners dismissed the appeals, holding that the TRNC was not a 'foreign state' for the purposes of *ss 300, 301*, since it was not recognised as such by the UK government, or by any other state apart from Turkey. (The Commissioners also held that the appellants were Commonwealth citizens as defined by *British Nationality Act 1981*.) *Caglar v Billingham (and related appeals)*, Sp C [1996] SSCD 150 (Sp C 70). (*Note*. For a preliminary issue in this case, see **4.306** APPEALS.)

Claim to exemption under Diplomatic Privileges Act 1964

[26.19] A woman (J), who was born and domiciled in the Philippines, came to the UK in April 1991. In June 1991 she took up employment as a cook at the Zambian High Commission in London, and in 1992 she began a similar job with the Namibian High Commission. She paid UK income tax on her earnings, but subsequently submitted a claim for repayment under *TMA, s 33*, claiming that her earnings were exempt from UK income tax under *Diplomatic Privileges Act 1964* and *article 37(3)* of the *Vienna Convention on Diplomatic Relations* (which provides exemption for 'members of the service staff' of a diplomatic mission who are not 'permanently resident in the receiving State'). The Revenue rejected her claim on the basis that the Namibian High Commission had not notified the Foreign and Commonwealth Office that J was a member of its mission staff (and also that J was permanently resident in the UK). J appealed, contending that she was a member of the staff of the mission and that she was not permanently resident in the UK because she intended to return to the Philippines. The Special Commissioner dismissed J's appeal, accepting that her intention was to return to the Philippines but holding that she was not entitled to exemption because she had 'not been notified as a member of a diplomatic mission in the United Kingdom'. The Commissioner also held that she was permanently resident in the UK, observing that the Namibian High Commission had notified the UK authorities that she was employed as 'locally engaged staff', which carried 'the connotation that she was presumed to be permanently resident here'. *Jimenez v CIR*, Sp C [2004] SSCD 371 (Sp C 419).

27

Farming, etc. (ICTA 1988, s 53; CTA 2009, s 36)

The cases in this chapter are arranged under the following headings.

Income tax cases

Grazing rights

[27.1] Two farmers occupied land under 'conacre' or 'agistment' agreements with the landowner. The farmers received income from letting grazing rights. The Revenue issued assessments charging income tax, and the KB dismissed the farmers' appeals. *McKenna v Herlihy; Woodburn v Herlihy*, KB(I) 1920, 7 TC 620.

Profits on sales of timber

[27.2] A farmer (T) made profits from the sale of trees on his farms. He had planted most, but not all, of the trees himself. The KB held that the profits arose from T's trade, and were taxable under Schedule D Case I under the legislation then in force. *Elmes v Trembath*, KB 1934, 19 TC 72.

Ploughing grants

[27.3] A dairy farmer (H) received grants under wartime legislation for ploughing up his pasture land. The Revenue issued an assessment charging tax on them. H appealed, contending that the grants were compensation for the destruction of a capital asset, and should not be charged to income tax. The Special Commissioners rejected this contention and dismissed his appeal, holding that the grants were receipts of H's trade. The KB upheld their decision. *Higgs v Wrightson*, KB 1944, 26 TC 73; [1944] 1 All ER 488.

Flood rehabilitation grants

[27.4] The Ministry of Agriculture paid grants to a farming partnership (S) to promote the rehabilitation of land on its farm which had been damaged by flooding. The grants exceeded the actual cost of rehabilitation. The Revenue issued assessments charging tax on them. The Commissioners allowed S's appeal, holding that the sums were paid to restore a capital asset and were not taxable. The Ch D upheld their decision as one of fact. *Watson v Samson Bros*, Ch D 1959, 38 TC 346.

Income from land let for grazing

[27.5] In a case concerning legislation which has subsequently been superseded, the CS held (by a 3-1 majority, Lord Moncrieff dissenting) that the owner of land let for grazing for a period of less than a year was occupying it wholly or mainly for the purposes of husbandry, and that the grazing rent was trading income. *CIR v Forsyth Grant*, CS 1943, 25 TC 369. (*Note.* For HMRC's interpretation of this decision, see Business Income Manual, BIM55065.)

Rent from farmland let on two-year lease

[27.6] A haulage contractor (B), who owned a farm, let 210 acres of farmland on a two-year lease. The Revenue issued an assessment charging income tax on the payments under the lease. B appealed, contending inter alia that part of this was capital, and that the balance was trading income and had been assessed under the wrong case of Schedule D. The General Commissioners rejected these contentions and dismissed his appeal, and the CA unanimously upheld their decision. *Bennion v Roper*, CA 1970, 46 TC 613. (*Note.* For HMRC's interpretation of this decision, see Business Income Manual, BIM55060.)

Orchard purchased with growing crop—computation of profits

[27.7] A fruit grower and salesman purchased for £5,500 a freehold cherry orchard including the growing crop, which was nearly ripe. The crop was subsequently picked and sold for £2,903, which he accepted as a trading receipt. He appealed against assessments to income tax and excess profits tax, contending that in computing his profits, he should be allowed a deduction of £2,500, being the estimated value of the growing crop at the time he purchased it. The KB rejected this contention, holding that none of the £5,500 could be deducted, since the trees were part of the land, so that the payment was capital expenditure. The CA unanimously upheld this decision. Jenkins LJ held that 'outlay on the purchase of an income-bearing asset is in the nature of capital outlay, and no part of the capital so laid out can, for income tax purposes, be set off as expenditure against income accruing from the asset in question'. *CIR v Pilcher (and related appeals)*, CA 1949, 31 TC 314; [1949] 2 All ER 1097.

Farmer—sale of growing crops

[27.8] A farmer (G) sold two farms with entry on 15 May 1950, under an agreement whereby the purchaser (D) should take over certain crops at a valuation to be made 'immediately before harvest'. G continued farming on other land, and in December 1950, after the crops had been harvested, he received £5,500 from D. The Revenue issued an assessment on the basis that this sum should be included in G's profits for the year ending 31 May 1950. He appealed, contending that it should be assessed for the year ending 31 May 1951. The CS unanimously accepted this contention and allowed his appeal. *Gunn v CIR*, CS 1955, 36 TC 93; [1955] SLT 266.

Unrelieved losses of farm sold by company

[27.9] A company (E) had operated a farm in Worcestershire for many years. In January 1956 it acquired a farm in Scotland, and in May 1956 it disposed of the Worcestershire farm. It claimed that the unrelieved losses and capital allowances of the Worcestershire farm could be set against the profits of the Scottish farm. The Revenue rejected the claim but the Commissioners allowed E's appeal and the Ch D upheld their decision. *Bispham v Eardiston Farming Co (1919) Ltd*, Ch D 1962, 40 TC 322; [1962] 1 WLR 616; [1962] 2 All ER 376.

ITA 2007, s 67—restriction on relief for farming

[27.10] See *M Howes v HMRC (No 1)*, 35.15 LOSS RELIEF, and *CJ & Mrs MA French v HMRC*, 35.16 LOSS RELIEF.

Farming losses—effect of ITA 2007, s 74

[27.11] See *Walsh & Walsh v Taylor*, 35.20 LOSS RELIEF.

Sale of turf

[27.12] A farming company (J) received payments from contractors for the right to remove turf from the farm. The Revenue issued assessments charging tax on them, and J appealed, contending that they were capital receipts and not chargeable to income tax. The Ch D rejected this contention and upheld the assessments. *Lowe v JW Ashmore Ltd*, Ch D 1970, 46 TC 597; [1971] Ch 545; [1971] 1 All ER 1057.

ITTOIA 2005, s 11—definition of 'woodlands'

[27.13] A farmer owned an area of land which was planted with coniferous trees, intended to be sold as Christmas trees. She appealed against income tax assessments, contending that the land was 'woodlands', within what is now *ITTOIA 2005, s 11* so that the profits were not trading income. The Special Commissioner rejected this contention and dismissed her appeal, and the Ch D upheld this decision. The land was not within the definition of woodlands, since it was covered in growing trees which resembled bushes rather than timber trees. *Jaggers (t/a Shide Trees) v Ellis*, Ch D 1997, 71 TC 164; [1997] STC 1417.

Co-operative society—whether carrying on business of husbandry

[27.14] A co-operative dairy society carried on a creamery with milk supplied by its members, all of whom were farmers. It appealed against an assessment to excess profits duty, contending that it was carrying on a business of husbandry (and thus was exempt from the duty). The KB rejected this contention and upheld the assessment. Kenny J held that 'husbandry presupposes a husbandman and a connection with land and production of crops or food in some shape'. *CIR v Cavan Central Co-operative Agricultural & Dairy Society Ltd*, KB(I) 1917, 12 TC 1.

Poultry farming—whether within definition of husbandry

[27.15] Poultry farming was held to be within the definition of 'husbandry' in *Lean & Dickson v Ball*, CS 1925, 10 TC 341; *Jones v Nuttall*, KB 1926, 10 TC 346 and *Reid v CIR*, CS 1947, 28 TC 451. (*Note*. These cases relate to legislation which has subsequently been superseded, under which farming was assessed to income tax under Schedule B. However, they remain relevant with regard to the definition of 'husbandry'.)

ITTOIA 2005, s 221—averaging of farmers' profits

[27.16] See *Donaghy v HMRC*, 65.60 TRADING PROFITS.

Agricultural land and buildings—capital allowances

[27.17] See the cases noted at 8.1 to 8.4 CAPITAL ALLOWANCES.

Farmers' cars—capital allowances

[27.18] See *Kempster v McKenzie*, 8.87 CAPITAL ALLOWANCES, and *GH Chambers (Northiam Farms) Ltd v Watmough*, 8.88 CAPITAL ALLOWANCES.

Farming partnerships—whether children members of partnership

[27.19] See the cases noted at 41.13 to 41.16 PARTNERSHIPS.

Joint crop growing—whether a partnership

[27.20] See *George Hall & Son v Platt*, 41.3 PARTNERSHIPS.

Death of farmer—whether trustee trading or realising assets

[27.21] See *Pattullo's Trustees v CIR*, 59.49 TRADING INCOME, and *CIR v Donaldson's Trustees*, 59.50 TRADING INCOME.

Stallion fees

[27.22] See the cases noted at 59.37 *et seq*. TRADING INCOME.

Premium under EC scheme to change to meat production

[27.23] See *White v G & M Davies Ltd*, 66.56 TRADING PROFITS and *CIR v W Andrew Biggar*, 66.57 TRADING PROFITS.

UK farmer visiting Australia—expenses not deductible

[27.24] See *Sargent v Eayrs*, 63.110 TRADING PROFITS.

Capital gains tax cases

Surrender of agricultural lease—whether any CGT liability

[27.25] See *Davis v Powell*, 71.45 CAPITAL GAINS TAX, and *Davis v Henderson*, 71.46 CAPITAL GAINS TAX.

Sale of milk quota—CGT liability

[27.26] See *Cottle v Coldicott*, 71.101 CAPITAL GAINS TAX.

Farmer—sale of land reflecting development value

[27.27] See *Watkins v Kidston*, 71.72 CAPITAL GAINS TAX.

Sale of farmland—whether farmer entitled to retirement relief

[27.28] See the cases noted at 71.239 *et seq.* CAPITAL GAINS TAX.

Inheritance tax cases

IHTA, s 115(2)—definition of 'agricultural property'

[27.29] See the cases noted at 72.82 to 72.89 INHERITANCE TAX.

IHTA, s 115(3)—valuation of agricultural property

[27.30] See *Lloyds TSB plc (Antrobus' Personal Representative) v Twiddy*, 72.90 INHERITANCE TAX.

Whether property 'occupied for the purposes of agriculture'

[27.31] See the cases noted at 72.91 to 72.93 INHERITANCE TAX.

Valuation of freehold interest in tenanted agricultural property

[27.32] See *Willett & Another v CIR*, 72.113 INHERITANCE TAX.

Renunciation of agricultural tenancy—valuation of transfer

[27.33] See *Baird's Executors v CIR*, 72.114 INHERITANCE TAX.

Valuation of interest in non-assignable agricultural tenancy

[27.34] See *Walton v CIR*, 72.115 INHERITANCE TAX.

28

Foreign Income (ITTOIA 2005, ss 829–845)

The cases in this chapter are arranged under the following headings.

Whether income has been remitted

Interest invested in bonds—remittance of proceeds

[28.1] A life assurance company (S) received interest from American securities. Under the legislation then in force, this was assessable on a remittance basis. It invested the interest in American bearer bonds. The bonds were sent to the UK for safe custody and were later realised, the proceeds being received in the UK. The Revenue issued assessments on the basis that the proceeds were taxable for the year in which the bonds were realised. The Commissioners upheld the assessments and the CS unanimously dismissed S's appeal. *Scottish Provident Institution v Farmer*, CS 1912, 6 TC 34.

Proceeds of selling investments

[28.2] The Revenue issued assessments to a US citizen, who was resident but not domiciled in the UK, charging income tax on the proceeds of sale of certain American investments, which had been remitted to a UK bank account. She appealed, contending that they were remittances of capital and were not chargeable to income tax. The Special Commissioners accepted her evidence and allowed her appeal, and the CA unanimously upheld their decision. *Kneen v Martin*, CA 1934, 19 TC 33; [1935] 1 KB 499.

Sums remitted from overdrawn foreign accounts

[28.3] A UK resident (F) was taxable on remittances of profits from plantations which he owned in Ceylon, which were managed by agents on his behalf. The Revenue issued assessments charging tax on sums which were remitted by the agents and credited to F's London bank account. He appealed, contending that they should be treated as remittances of capital, since his accounts in Ceylon had been consistently overdrawn. The Special Commissioners upheld the assessments, holding that the remittances were of income, and the CS unanimously upheld their decision. Lord Normand observed that the Commissioners were entitled to find that 'what was received in this country was not derived from some realisation of capital or from some capital account, but was in truth derived from the income arising from possessions in Ceylon'. *Fellowes-Gordon v CIR*, CS 1935, 19 TC 683.

Trust income paid to UK-resident children

[28.4] A UK resident (T) was the life tenant of a US trust, and was taxable on the trust income. She instructed the trustees to pay allowances to her children, all except one of whom were also resident in the UK, out of the income to which she was entitled. The Revenue issued assessments on the basis that the income was hers and had been remitted to the UK. T's executors appealed, contending that the income no longer belonged to her at the time when it was remitted. The Special Commissioners rejected this contention and upheld the assessments. The CA unanimously dismissed the executors' appeals, holding that T was entitled to the income in question and was taxable accordingly. *Timpson's Executors v Yerbury*, CA 1936, 20 TC 155; [1936] 1 KB 645.

Taxpayer's instructions not followed by bank

[28.5] A UK resident (D) had several separate bank accounts with a US bank. She instructed the bank to remit a sum of money from a fund made up of money which was taxable in the UK on the arising basis. Against her instructions, the bank remitted the money from an account which was only taxable in the UK on the remittance basis. Her husband's executors appealed against an assessment, contending that the remittance should be deemed to have been partly made from sources which had already been taxed on the arising basis, and partly from capital. The CS accepted this contention and allowed the appeal (by a 3-1 majority, Lord Morison dissenting). Lord Normand held that D was entitled 'to insist on exact fulfilment of her instructions and to require the bank to make any necessary correction in their bank entries'. *Duke of Roxburghe's Executors v CIR*, CS 1936, 20 TC 711; [1936] SC 863.

Draft on foreign bank posted abroad

[28.6] A US citizen, domiciled in the USA, was resident in the UK from February 1928. She made a voluntary allowance to her daughter, who was resident in the UK, by way of a banker's draft from her US income. The Revenue included this amount in an assessment on her for 1928/29, on the basis that it had been remitted to the UK. She appealed. The Special Commissioners allowed her appeal, holding that this was not taxable on her in the UK, since under Californian law, the sum had ceased to belong to her when the relevant banker's draft was posted in California to her daughter. The KB upheld this decision. Lawrence J distinguished the CA decision in *Timpson's Executors v Yerbury*, **28.4** above, on the grounds that in that case 'the mother could at any time before the actual receipt and encashment of the bill of exchange in question have stopped it', whereas in the present case, once the banker's draft had been purchased and posted, 'nothing could prevent the gift being completed or could prevent it coming into the hands of the donee'. *Carter v Sharon*, KB 1936, 20 TC 229; [1936] 1 All ER 720. (*Note*. The case also concerned the application of the 'preceding year' basis of assessment, which has subsequently been superseded.)

Draft on foreign bank handed to payee in London

[28.7] A UK resident (W) instructed an Indian bank to send him a draft for £10,000 in favour of a London hospital, debiting the cost to his Indian bank account. On receipt of the draft, he handed it to the hospital. The bank account had been built up from income from an Indian trade, and from the proceeds of sale of an Indian investment purchased out of the accumulated Indian income. It was agreed that £2,200 of the £10,000 came out of the Indian income which had borne UK tax. The Revenue issued an assessment charging income tax on the full amount. W appealed, contending firstly that the balance of £7,800 was capital, and alternatively that it was not taxable as his income because he was not entitled to it. The KB rejected these contentions and dismissed his appeal, holding that the balance was a remittance of income of an Indian possession and that W became entitled to it when it was received in the UK. Wrottesley J held that 'if a man resides here he cannot, by investing for the time being his income abroad, change its character vis-à-vis the income tax collector'. *Walsh v Randall*, KB 1940, 23 TC 55.

Overseas profits set against trading debt

[28.8] The partners of a London firm were also partners (with local merchants) in two overseas businesses, in Chile and Australia. They were entitled to shares of profits from the Australian firm. They instructed the Australian firm to credit the amounts in question to the Chilean firm, and then transfer the money to London, where it was set against a debt owed by the Chilean firm to the London firm. The Revenue assessed them on the basis that this was a remittance of the profits of the Australian firm. They appealed, contending that the money which was sent to London constituted the reduction of the debt owed by the Chilean firm, and was not a remittance of income. The Commissioners accepted this contention and allowed their appeal, and the CA upheld this decision. Lord Greene MR held that if the money 'had come direct from Australia to London, it would unquestionably have been a remittance of profits derived by London from Australia. In the course of its journey from Australia back to London its character had been entirely changed. It had been changed because it had passed into the ownership of Chile and become an asset belonging to Chile, and, when it came out from the ownership of Chile, it came out for the purpose, not of effecting a transfer from Australia to London of London's share in the Australian profits, but for the purpose of discharging a debt due from Chile to London'. *Timbrell v Lord Aldenham's Executors (and related appeals)*, CA 1947, 28 TC 293.

Compulsory sale of dollar balances to Government

[28.9] In an Irish case, a woman was compelled, under wartime emergency powers, to sell to the Ministry of Finance dollars to her credit in a New York bank, representing US income collected on her behalf by the bank. The Ministry credited the sterling equivalent to her account in an Irish bank. It was held that the US income had been remitted to Ireland. *O'Sullivan v O'Connor*, HC(I) 1947, 26 ATC 463.

Proceeds of sales of dollar cheques

[28.10] The life tenant under an American will trust was resident in the UK but domiciled in the USA. His income from the trust was paid in dollars into his account with a New York bank. He drew dollar cheques on the account in favour of a UK bank, which sold the dollars to the Bank of England, crediting the net sterling proceeds to his account with the UK bank. The HL unanimously held that the amounts so credited were remittances of his American income, and were chargeable to UK income tax. Lord Radcliffe observed that 'remittances payable in the United Kingdom' was a phrase 'capable of applying to the instrument employed to effect the transfer, to the credit arising from the transfer' and 'to the whole operation of remitting money to be paid here'. *Thomson v Moyse*, HL 1960, 39 TC 291; [1961] AC 967; [1960] 3 All ER 684.

Whether income 'received in the United Kingdom'—other cases

[28.11] There are several pre-1918 cases turning on whether there had been a remittance of income but where, under the law now in force, the income would be assessable on an arising basis. In the interests of space, such cases are not summarised individually in this book. The cases include *Standard Life Assurance Co v Allan*, CS 1901, 4 TC 446; *Gresham Life Assurance Society Ltd v Bishop*, HL 1902, 4 TC 464; *Scottish Provident Institution v Allan*, HL 1903, 4 TC 591; and *Scottish Widows' Fund Life Assurance Society v Farmer*, CS 1909, 5 TC 502.

Miscellaneous

Shares in overseas company resident in the UK

[28.12] A US subsidiary of a UK company (E), previously resident in the UK, ceased to be so resident at the end of 1916/17 with the result that, from 1917/18 onwards, E became liable to UK income tax on its dividends from the subsidiary. Under the law then in force, the assessment for any year was based on the average of the income of the three preceding years. The Revenue considered that dividends paid by the subsidiary before 1917/18 should be included in arriving at the average for the assessments for 1917/18 to 1919/20. The Special Commissioners allowed E's appeal and the HL upheld their decision (by a 4-1 majority, Lord Sumner dissenting), holding that shares in an overseas company resident in the UK were not overseas possessions. *Bradbury v English Sewing Cotton Co Ltd*, HL 1923, 8 TC 481; [1923] AC 744. (*Note.* The substantive issue is no longer relevant, but the case is of interest in illustrating the principle that the same income may not be subjected to tax twice without statutory authority.)

Beneficiary's liability on income of specific investments

[28.13] A married woman, resident in the UK, was the sole life tenant, under an American will trust, of a fund which consisted entirely of foreign possessions and securities. The Revenue issued assessments charging income tax on her husband (under the legislation then in force). He appealed, contending that the assessments should be confined to the income which was actually remitted. The HL upheld the assessments in principle (by a 3-2 majority, Viscount Sumner and Lord Blanesburgh dissenting). The majority of the HL held that the assessments should be on the basis that the income receivable by the beneficiary arose from the specific securities or possessions forming the fund. The case was remitted to the Commissioners to determine whether the income from the different sources was assessable under the arising basis or on the remittance basis. *Archer-Shee v Baker*, HL 1927, 11 TC 749; [1927] AC 844. (*Note*. For subsequent developments in this case, see *Archer-Shee v Baker (No 2)*, **4.206** APPEALS, and *Garland v Archer-Shee*, **28.14** below. The decision here was not followed in *Garland v Archer-Shee*, **28.14** below, on the basis that the majority of the HL had incorrectly assumed that New York trust law was similar to UK trust law.)

[28.14] The appellant in *Archer-Shee v Baker*, **28.13** above, appealed against similar assessments for subsequent years. He submitted evidence of the relevant New York law (which had not been submitted in the case noted at **28.13** above, and which the CA had declined to admit in *Archer-Shee v Baker (No 2)*, **4.206** APPEALS). The HL unanimously allowed his appeal, holding that, on the basis of the evidence of New York law, the life tenant 'had no right to any specific dividends or interest at all'. Her right under the will was 'only a chose in action available against the trustees'. Accordingly, under the legislation then in force, the liability was confined to the income remitted. *Garland v Archer-Shee*, HL 1930, 15 TC 693; [1931] AC 212.

Annuity payable under Australian will

[28.15] A woman (N), who was resident in the UK, was the life tenant of some property in Australia under her grandfather's will. The will provided for the payment of a specific annuity to another beneficiary (N's aunt), and for the trustees to receive remuneration. The Revenue issued assessments charging tax on N's income from the estate. She appealed, contending that she should only be assessed on the amounts remitted to the UK. The Special Commissioners rejected this contention and dismissed her appeal, holding that she was assessable on the whole of the income, subject to deductions for the trustees' remuneration and for the annuity. The KB upheld their decision. *Nelson v Adamson*, KB 1941, 24 TC 36; [1941] 2 KB 12; [1941] 2 All ER 44.

Alimony paid under Swedish court order

[28.16] A divorced woman, resident in Scotland, received alimony from her former husband, resident in Sweden, under a Swedish court order. The Revenue issued assessments charging tax on the alimony. The CS unanimously upheld the assessments, holding that the alimony was income, arising from a 'foreign possession', and was taxable in the UK. *CIR v Anderstrom*, CS 1927, 13 TC 482.

Annuity under Indian deed of separation

[28.17] A married woman (C) was separated from her husband and received from him an annuity, under an Indian deed of separation. The Revenue issued assessments charging income tax on the annuity, and C appealed. The Special Commissioners dismissed her appeal, holding that the annuity was 'income from a foreign possession', and the KB upheld their decision. *Chamney v Lewis*, KB 1932, 17 TC 318.

Income from Germany released after First World War

[28.18] German banks held certain foreign securities and possessions on behalf of a British subject (K) who was domiciled and ordinarily resident in the UK. During the 1914/18 War, the income was credited to him in his accounts with the banks. He died in 1916. Additionally, the banks transferred certain amounts to the 'Treuhander' (the German 'custodian of enemy property'), and did not thereafter earn interest. Compensation, calculated at 5% per annum on the amounts transferred, was paid after the Treaty of Versailles. The Revenue issued assessments on the basis that the relevant income arose when it was credited, and that the compensation was taxable income. K's executors appealed, contending that the relevant income had arisen when it was credited, that the Revenue had failed to issue assessments within the statutory time limits, and that the compensation was not income. The Special Commissioners accepted these contentions and allowed the executors' appeals, and the CA unanimously upheld their decision. *Simpson v Bonner Maurice Executors*, CA 1929, 14 TC 580.

Overseas pensions

[28.19] The Revenue issued an assessment charging tax on allowances received under the unapproved pension scheme of a Canadian company. The recipients appealed, contending that they were a return of superannuation contributions. The Ch D rejected this contention and upheld the assessments. *Bridges v Watterson; Bridges v Byrne*, Ch D 1952, 34 TC 47; [1952] 2 All ER 910. (*Note*. The payments were assessed under Schedule D Case V under the legislation then in force. They would now be 'foreign pension income' within *ITEPA 2003, ss 573–576*.)

[28.20] A British subject returned to the UK in 1978, after having worked for 20 years in the United States. He was entitled to a retirement benefit, payable monthly, from the US. The Revenue issued assessments charging tax on the pension, and he appealed. The Commissioners dismissed his appeal and the CA unanimously upheld their decision. *Aspin v Estill*, CA 1987, 60 TC 549; [1987] STC 723. (*Notes*. (1) The pension was assessed under Schedule D Case

V under the legislation then in force. It would now be 'foreign pension income' within *ITEPA 2003, ss 573–576*. (2) For another issue in this case, see **50.47** REVENUE ADMINISTRATION.)

[28.21] The decision in *Aspin v Estill*, 28.20 above, was applied in a similar subsequent case where a doctor and his wife, who were resident in the UK, appealed against assessments on retirement payments from the USA and France. The Special Commissioner dismissed their appeals and the CS upheld this decision. *Albon & Albon v CIR & Hinwood*, CS 1998, 71 TC 174; [1998] STC 1181.

Redundancy payments from former employer

[28.22] A UK citizen had worked in France for a French employer from 1975 to 1981, when he was made redundant at the age of 59. Under the redundancy agreement, he received regular payments from his former employer until reaching the age of 65, when he became entitled to a pension. Shortly after the redundancy, he returned to the UK. The Revenue issued assessments charging income tax on the payments. He appealed, contending that they should be treated as capital. The Special Commissioner rejected this contention and upheld the assessments, holding that the payments were income rather than capital. *Beveridge v Ellam*, Sp C 1995, [1996] SSCD 77 (Sp C 62).

Income from overseas trust

[28.23] A UK citizen (F) received a dividend of £159,559 from a Bahamian trust. F failed to declare this on his tax return, and HMRC issued an assessment charging tax on it. The First-tier Tribunal upheld the assessment and dismissed F's appeal. *J Frye v HMRC*, FTT [2012] UKFTT 221 (TC), TC01916.

ITTOIA 2005, s 838—expenses attributable to foreign income

[28.24] A UK resident purchased a flat in Gibraltar, with the aid of a loan from the Gibraltar branch of a UK bank. He let the flat through agents in Gibraltar and used the rental income to repay the loan. He appealed against an assessment on the rent, contending that the interest payable on the loan should be allowed as a deduction. The Ch D rejected this contention and upheld the assessment. *Ockendon v Mackley*, Ch D 1982, 56 TC 2; [1982] STC 513; [1982] 1 WLR 787.

29

Further Assessments: Loss of Tax (TMA, s 36)

The cases in this chapter are arranged under the following headings.

GENERAL NOTE

The cases in this chapter cover assessments made under the extended time limits provided by *TMA, s 36*. *TMA, s 36* has been substantially amended since its original enactment, when it referred to 'fraud, wilful default or neglect'. It was substantially amended by *FA 1989*, when the reference to 'fraud, wilful default or neglect' was replaced by a reference to 'fraudulent or negligent conduct'. It was also substantially amended by *FA 2008*, when the reference to 'fraudulent or negligent conduct' was replaced by a reference to a 'loss of tax brought about carelessly or deliberately'. The chapter includes assessments raised on the basis that a loss of tax has been 'brought about carelessly or deliberately by the taxpayer or a person acting on his behalf' (see *TMA, s 29(4)* as amended by *FA 2008*). The chapter also includes assessments involving criminal conduct, under the *Proceeds of Crime Act 2002*. For cases concerning penalties imposed in investigation or enquiry cases, see **44** PENALTIES. For cases concerning the Revenue's powers to obtain information, including the provisions of *TMA, ss 20–20D*, see **49** RETURNS AND INFORMATION. For cases concerning criminal prosecutions, see **51** REVENUE PROSECUTIONS.

Fraud

Definition of 'fraud'

[29.1] In a non-tax case, Lord Herschell held that 'fraud is proved when it is shown that a false representation has been made knowingly, or without belief in its truth, or recklessly, careless whether it be true or false'. Lord Bramwell held that 'a man who makes a statement without care and regard for its truth or falsity commits a fraud'. *Derry & Others v Peek*, HL 1889, 14 AC 337.

[29.2] In a non-tax case, a company and its managing director were convicted of conspiracy to defraud another company. The company appealed to the CCA, which dismissed the appeal, holding that 'the facts proved were amply sufficient to justify a finding' that the managing director's actions were 'the acts of the company' and that fraud committed by the director was fraud by the company. *R v ICR Haulage Ltd*, CCA [1944] 1 All ER 691. (*Note*. For HMRC's interpretation of this decision, see Enquiry Manual, para EM4830.)

Whether sufficient evidence to justify inference of fraud

[29.3] The Revenue issued estimated assessments on a partnership which operated a gaming club, after discovering that two of the partners had deposited deed boxes with a bank under false names, and that evidence suggested that the boxes contained a substantial amount of concealed takings. The Special Commissioners upheld the assessments in reduced amounts. The partnership appealed, contending that the evidence did not justify the Commissioners' inferences of fraud. The Ch D and CA unanimously rejected this contention and upheld the Commissioners' decision, except with regard to one minor amount. Nourse LJ held that 'an inference of fact drawn by the Commissioners can only be displaced by the court if it cannot be justified by the primary facts. But before an inference which involves fraud or other criminal conduct can be justified, the primary facts must have a probative value which weighs up to the gravity of the offence.' The two essential questions for the Commissioners were whether the deed boxes contained cash and, if so, whether the cash represented takings of the club. There was 'ample material from which the Commissioners could infer that the cash in the deed boxes represented the fruits of a joint venture between (the partners) which they were determined to conceal'. The evidence justified 'the Commissioners' inferences of fraudulent extraction of club takings' by the partners. *Les Croupiers Casino Club v Pattinson*, CA 1987, 60 TC 196; [1987] STC 594.

Finding of fraud in absence of appellant

[29.4] The Revenue raised assessments on a butcher covering 1963/64 to 1975/76 inclusive. The butcher appealed. The appeals were listed for hearing before the General Commissioners in May 1977, and were adjourned until 16 June. On 14 June the butcher wrote a letter requesting a further adjournment on the ground that he had consulted a QC. The Revenue opposed the request and the Commissioners proceeded to hear the appeals. On the evidence put forward by the Revenue, they found that there had been fraud, and confirmed the assessments. The butcher appealed to the Ch D, contending that the Commissioners had acted unfairly in refusing a further adjournment. Fox J accepted this contention, holding that 'the refusal of an adjournment prevented the appellant from putting his case and may have caused him serious injustice'. In the circumstances of this case, 'the Commissioners should have granted an adjournment. It could have been for a short time and it could have been made plain that no further time would be given.' The case was remitted for hearing by different Commissioners. *Ottley v Morris*, Ch D 1978, 52 TC 375; [1978] STC 594; [1979] 1 All ER 65.

No finding of fraud for basis year—assessment discharged

[29.5] A greengrocer began trading in 1966 and also opened an off-licence in 1972. From 1972 he made regular purchases from two wholesalers. These purchases did not appear in his accounts. In 1983 the Revenue raised assessments under *TMA, s 36* for the years 1966/67 to 1976/77 inclusive. The General Commissioners discharged the assessments for 1966/67 to 1971/72 inclusive, but confirmed the assessments for 1972/73 to 1976/77 inclusive and made a finding of fraud for those years. The trader appealed against the confirmation of the assessment for 1972/73, as this was based on his accounts ending in 1971/72 and the Commissioners had not found him guilty of fraud in 1971/72. The Ch D upheld this contention and discharged the 1972/73 assessment. *Verdon v Honour*, Ch D 1988, 61 TC 413; [1988] STC 809.

Whether fraud by employee may be imputed to company

[29.6] In 2000 a company discovered that a senior employee (HI) had fraudulently diverted payments, which were intended for HMRC, to himself. HI was subsequently convicted of theft. In 2004 HMRC began a compliance review into the company, and formed the opinion that forms P35 which it had submitted had understated the amount of tax and NIC due. Subsequently HMRC issued determinations to recover the tax and NIC due. The company appealed, contending that the underdeclarations were attributable to HI and that the determinations had been issued outside the statutory time limits. The First-tier Tribunal upheld the determinations, finding that the forms P35 which the company had submitted to HMRC understated the amount of tax due and that HI had prepared different forms P35 for the company's managing director, which had not been submitted to HMRC. Judge Blewitt held that, applying the principles laid down by the CA in *Bilta (UK) Ltd v Nazir & Others*, [2013] STC 2298, 'attribution of fraud to a company is appropriate in circumstances where a company would suffer loss by compensating HMRC for a loss of tax which was properly due'. On the evidence here, the actions of HI should be attributed to the company, so that 'the element of fraud has been established and the extended time limit in respect of PAYE and NIC liabilities applied'. *Isocom Ltd v HMRC*, FTT [2014] UKFTT 571 (TC), TC03696. (*Note*. The case was heard with *Tahmosybayat v HMRC*, **22.142** EMPLOYMENT INCOME.)

Whether onus on Revenue to prove fraud

[29.7] See *Brady v Group Lotus Car Companies*, **4.209** APPEALS.

Fraudulent conduct

Whether director guilty of fraudulent or negligent conduct

[29.8] A UK company (R) was incorporated in 1983. It obtained supplies of evening primrose seeds from a Netherlands company (G), and arranged for evening primrose oil to be extracted from those seeds. In 1985 G agreed to supply the seeds to a newly-incorporated Swiss company, which arranged to extract the oil and to supply the oil to R. The Inland Revenue formed the opinion that one of R's directors (Y), who owned 40% of the shares in R, 'had fraudulently arranged for (the Swiss company) to be inserted in the chain of supply of the evening primrose oil as a device to extract money from R without paying tax in the UK', and that the profits of the Swiss company (which was owned by Y's family) had been applied for the benefit of Y and of the principal shareholder (S) in a Canadian company which owned the remaining 60% of the shares in R. The Revenue issued assessments on the basis that the payments which R made to the Swiss company were excessive, and that part of the payments was not allowable in computing R's profits. The Revenue also issued assessments under *ICTA 1988, s 419* and *ICTA 1988, s 160* on the basis that, from those retained profits, R had made loans or advances to Y and S. Additionally, the Revenue issued alternative assessments under *ICTA 1988, s 209* and *ICTA 1988, s 20* on the basis that R had made distributions to Y. Of the total of 39 assessments which the Revenue issued, only three were issued within the normal six-year time limit. The remaining 36 assessments were issued on the basis that there had been 'fraudulent or negligent conduct' on the part of Y. R and Y appealed, contending firstly that there had been no 'fraudulent or negligent conduct' on the part of Y, and additionally, with regard to the three assessments which had been issued within the normal time limits, that the payments which R had made to the Swiss company had been wholly and exclusively for the purpose of its trade and were allowable deductions. The Special Commissioner reviewed the evidence in detail and allowed all the appeals, observing that the relations between R and S had become 'strained', and that the allegation that the payments to the Swiss company had been excessive derived from information supplied by S. The Commissioner found that S was 'an unsatisfactory witness' and, where the evidence of S and Y conflicted, 'preferred that of (Y)'. The Commissioner found on the evidence that the Swiss company had been formed as a finance company and that it had performed the commercial function of helping to finance the desired purchases from G. The price which the Swiss company charged R for the evening primrose oil 'was not an unreasonable price, bearing in mind all the relevant factors'. The Commissioner found that 'some of the statements made on behalf of (Y) were incorrect', but expressed the view that in this appeal, the making of inaccurate statements 'must be considered within the context of the whole investigation. This is not a case where a taxpayer has refused to provide any information or to co-operate with the Inland Revenue's enquiries over a long period'. The evidence was 'not sufficiently clear and cogent' to justify a finding of fraudulent conduct. Furthermore, 'if the allegations made by the Inland Revenue in this appeal had been proved, then the correct finding would be one of fraudulent conduct; the evidence does not support a finding of negligent conduct'. *Rochester (UK) Ltd v Pickin; York v Pickin*, Sp C [1998] SSCD 138 (Sp C 160).

Accountant—whether guilty of fraudulent conduct

[29.9] A chartered accountant (R) made substantial claims for loan interest relief. The Revenue discovered that the interest was payable on loans made to a company (N), and formed the opinion that R was not entitled to relief. They issued assessments to recover the tax, outside the normal six-year time limit, on the basis that R had been guilty of 'fraudulent or negligent conduct', within *TMA, s 36(1)*. R appealed, contending firstly that he was entitled to the relief claimed since N was acting as a nominee for him, and alternatively that he had not been guilty of 'fraudulent or negligent conduct'. The Special Commissioners reviewed the evidence in detail, rejected R's contentions, and dismissed the appeal. The Commissioners observed that 'there was no statutory basis for the claim' to interest relief. They found that all nine of the specific allegations made by the Revenue were 'substantiated by the evidence'. On the evidence, N had been trading and had not been acting as a nominee, and R had not believed that N was acting as a nominee. The Revenue had discharged the burden of showing that R had made the claims for interest relief when he knew that he was not entitled to do so. That was 'fraudulent conduct as it involved dishonesty and the appellant knew what he was doing'. R appealed to the Ch D, which upheld the Commissioners' decision. Lloyd J observed that R's 'standing as a professional man renders the more grave the finding of dishonesty against him'. However, the transcripts of the hearing indicated that 'some of his evidence was shown to be, at the least, problematical'. There was clearly 'material on which the Special Commissioners could come to the conclusion that (R's) evidence was not reliable'. Although it was 'a serious matter' to make a finding of fraudulent conduct in relation to a chartered accountant, the Commissioners' 'finding in favour of the Revenue was inevitable'. *Rowland v Boyle (aka Chartered Accountant v HM Inspector of Taxes)*, Ch D 2003, 75 TC 693; [2003] STC 855; [2003] EWHC 781 (Ch).

Doctor—whether guilty of fraudulent conduct

[29.10] HMRC discovered that a doctor (E) had failed to declare income arising from offshore bank accounts. Following an enquiry, they formed the opinion that E had significantly underdeclared his income for several years. They issued discovery assessments and imposed penalties at the rate of 50% of the potential lost revenue. The First-tier Tribunal reviewed the evidence in detail and found that E 'was attempting to conceal information from HMRC: this was not merely negligent conduct, but fraudulent conduct'. The Tribunal also found that 'HMRC were justified in regarding the disclosed deposits of undeclared business income as merely examples of what was likely to be a more widespread practice'. The Tribunal upheld all the assessments and penalties. *Dr S Easow v HMRC (and related appeals)*, FTT [2013] UKFTT 493 (TC), TC02882. (*Note*. The Tribunal also upheld assessments, and penalties at the rate of 42.5%, on a company of which E was the controlling director, and which had failed to account for tax under what is now *CTA 2010, s 455*.)

Trader—whether guilty of fraudulent conduct

[29.11] See *Corcoran v HMRC*, 44.101 PENALTIES.

Criminal conduct (Proceeds of Crime Act 2002)

Assessments following confiscation order under POCA 2002

[29.12] In a Northern Ireland case, an individual (M) was convicted in 2007 of several offences relating to dealing in counterfeit and contraband cigarettes. In February 2009 the court made a confiscation order of £35,316 under *Proceeds of Crime Act 2002, s 6*. In August 2009 HMRC issued discovery assessments charging income tax totalling £382,687 on M's income from self-employment. M appealed, contending that the confiscation order should be treated as extinguishing the tax liability on his income. The First-tier Tribunal rejected this contention and dismissed his appeal. Judge Huddleston held that 'in certain circumstances it may be the case that the proceedings under the Proceeds of Crime Act does indeed encompass an assessment of all of the tax liability which may or may not be due in particular circumstances, but that can only be determined after the assessment process has been undertaken'. However that was not the case here. The appropriate course of action was to confirm the assessments, leaving the amount M had paid under the confiscation order to be set against the tax liability. *J Martin v HMRC*, FTT [2012] UKFTT 304 (TC), TC01990.

[29.13] A similar decision was reached in *M Nugent v HMRC (and related appeal)*, FTT [2012] UKFTT 329 (TC), TC02015.

Assessments under Proceeds of Crime Act 2002, s 317

[29.14] In a Northern Ireland case, the Director of the Assets Recovery Agency issued assessments on an individual (H) for 1995/96 to 2002/03, under the provisions of *Proceeds of Crime Act 2002, s 317*. The assessments were issued on the basis that H had failed to declare 'details of income derived from his involvement in dealing in counterfeit goods, illegally imported tobacco and alcohol and proceeds of others' criminal activity'. H appealed, contending that the assessments were excessive. The Special Commissioners reviewed the evidence in detail and determined the assessments, finding that 'the conditions authorizing the raising of the assessments are satisfied'. *Harper v Director of the Assets Recovery Agency*, Sp C [2005] SSCD 874 (Sp C 507).

[29.15] In 2001 an individual (K) was charged with 'money-laundering' offences. The prosecution alleged that he had 'acted as a courier of money arising from drug trafficking and other criminality'. In 2003 the proceedings were halted, after the judge accepted K's contention that he was in poor health, and that 'to put (him) through a trial would involve an unacceptably high risk of heart attack'. In 2004 the Director of the Assets Recovery Agency issued assessments on K for 1998/99 to 2001/02, under the provisions of *Proceeds of Crime Act 2002, s 317*. K appealed, contending as a preliminary point that the assessments were invalid, and that the proceedings contravened the *European Convention on Human Rights*. The Special Commissioners rejected these contentions, holding that *PCA 2002, s 317(1)* did not require 'proof of criminal conduct but a genuine suspicion which is reasonable viewed objectively'. The proceedings were within *Article 1* of the *First Protocol of the European Convention*, which specifically provided that it did not 'in any way impair the right of a State to enforce such laws as it deems necessary to control the use of property in accordance with the general interest or to secure the payment of tax or other contributions and penalties'. *Khan v Director of the Assets Recovery Agency*, Sp C [2006] SSCD 154 (Sp C 523).

[29.16] The Director of the Assets Recovery Agency issued assessments on an individual (R), on the basis that he was carrying on a trade of dealing in drugs. R appealed, contending that he was not carrying on a trade of dealing in drugs. The Special Commissioner allowed his appeal, finding 'on the balance of probabilities' that he was not carrying on such a trade. The Director appealed to the Ch D, where it was agreed that there 'were undeclared profits from an ironing trade'. The Ch D remitted the case to the Special Commissioner 'to determine the quantum of the undeclared profits and to adjust the assessments accordingly'. At a subsequent hearing, the Special Commissioner found that four cheques represented proceeds of sales of jewellery which were not taxable income. The Commissioner adjourned the appeal in the hope that the parties could agree the amount of the assessments. *JG Rose v Director of the Assets Recovery Agency (No 2)*, Sp C 2007, [2008] SSCD 48 (Sp C 620).

[29.17] The Norfolk police received complaints that an individual (F) had been obtaining money by deception, by taking money from investors, paying it into a Jersey bank account, and using it for personal expenditure. The Director of the Assets Recovery Agency issued assessments on F for 1995/96 to 2003/04 inclusive. F appealed. The Special Commissioner upheld the assessments for 1995/96 and 1996/97, but allowed the appeals against the later assessments, finding that there was 'no evidence that any deposits were obtained after 1996/97 from the fraudulent activity' and that it appeared that 'the efforts of the police put a stop to any further criminal enterprise similar to the activities of 1995/96 and 1996/97'. *MP Forbes v Director of the Assets Recovery Agency (No 1)*, Sp C 2006, [2007] SSCD 1 (Sp C 566). (*Note*. For subsequent developments in this case, see **4.444** APPEALS.)

[29.18] In the case noted at **29.21** below, the Serious Organised Crime Agency had issued discovery assessments and imposed penalties under *TMA, s 95* on an individual (F) who had been the controlling shareholder of a company which bought and sold building materials, although he was not a director. F appealed. The First-tier Tribunal dismissed the appeals, finding on the evidence that F had been involved in fraudulent mortgage applications, had been convicted for handling stolen property and had been charged with the theft of bricks and roof tiles. Judge Demack observed that F had 'made no attempt whatsoever to run his companies' businesses or his business with regard to accepted, indeed essential, accounting and administrative principles'. The evidence pointed 'to his having treated his affairs and those of the companies as interchangeable, and as having been arranged with the intention of evading tax, and to ensure that the tax authorities would have the greatest difficulty in finding, let alone tracing, any audit trail'. *GM Fenech v Serious Organised Crime Agency (No 2)*, FTT [2013] UKFTT 555 (TC), TC02944.

[29.19] The Serious Organised Crime Agency discovered that a former café proprietor (L) had more than £270,000 in cash at his home. Following an investigation, the National Crime Agency (which succeeded the Serious Organised Crime Agency in 2013) issued assessments on him. The First-tier Tribunal dismissed L's appeals, finding that the requirements of *PCA 2002, s 317(1)* (as amended by the *Crime and Courts Act 2013*) were satisfied, and that L had not 'provided proof of any grounds to justify reduction of any of the assessments'. *T Lynch v National Crime Agency*, FTT [2014] UKFTT 1088 (TC), TC04177.

Proceeds of Crime Act, s 317—'freezing order'

[29.20] A company director (M) was charged with attempted murder. During his trial, he stated in cross-examination that he had income of about £300,000 p.a., which he had not declared to the Revenue. The Assets Recovery Agency subsequently obtained a 'freezing order' under *PCA 2002, s 317*. M appealed to the QB, contending that the order was invalid because HMRC had not yet quantified the unpaid taxes under *TMA, s 29(1)*. The QB rejected this contention, holding that the order was valid. Pitchers J held that there was 'an existing cause of action in respect of unpaid tax' even though the exact amount had not yet been quantified. *Director of Assets Recovery Agency v McCormack*, QB [2007] EWHC 908 (QB); [2008] STC 1097.

[29.21] The Serious Organised Crime Agency began an investigation into the tax affairs of an individual (F), who had been the controlling shareholder of a company which bought and sold building materials, although he was not a director. They formed the opinion that F had failed to declare the full extent of his income, and issued assessments covering the years 2004/05 to 2008/09. They also seized more than £200,000 in cash, and applied for a 'freezing order' under *PCA 2002, s 317*. The QB granted the order, finding that there was 'abundant evidence' of 'a risk of dissipation'; that F had 'failed to properly account to HMRC in relation to his or his companies' tax responsibilities', and that the evidence suggested that there had been 'fraudulent conduct'. *SOCA v GM Fenech (No 1)*, QB [2011] EWHC 10 (QB). (*Note*. For subsequent developments in this case, see **29.18** above.)

Proceeds of Crime Act 2002, s 335—'appropriate consent'

[29.22] A bank (L) made an application under *PCA 2002, s 335* for consent to carry out a banking mandate of a customer (C) dealing with funds held on trust for a New Zealand company (U). The Serious Organised Crime Agency refused to grant consent. U applied for judicial review of the Agency's decision. The CA granted the application (reversing the QB decision). Ward LJ observed that the refusal had 'caused significant harm' to U's customers, and held that 'if the proper balance is to be struck between undue interference with personal liberties and the need constantly to fight crime, then the least that can be demanded of SOCA is that they do not withhold consent without good reason'. On the evidence, 'the proper course was to grant permission to apply for judicial review but send the matter back to the Administrative Court. The parties will then have a less frenzied opportunity to consider their positions, put in their evidence, and call for production of documents and consider any public interest immunity. Important issues may arise and it is better that they are described properly rather than hastily. It is preferable that the Administrative Court decide these questions in the usual way, so that the short-cut offered to the Court of Appeal by CPR 52.15 is no longer the appropriate route for taking these decisions.' Sedley LJ held that 'in setting up the Serious Organised Crime Agency, the State has set out to create an Alsatia – a region of executive action free of judicial oversight. Although the statutory powers can intrude heavily, and sometimes ruinously, into civil rights and obligations, the supervisory role which the court would otherwise have is limited by its primary obligation to give effect to Parliament's clearly expressed intentions. However, except where the statute specifically prevented it, the scheme should also accommodate 'the justice of the common law'. *R (oao UMBS Online Ltd) v Serious Organised Crime Agency*, CA [2007] EWCA Civ 406; [2008] 1 All ER 465.

Proceeds of Crime Act, s 340(3)—definition of 'criminal property'

[29.23] The RCPO took criminal proceedings against the owner of a 'money transfer' business (SK), his son, and two other individuals, one of whom (M) was the proprietor of a grocery business. The prosecution alleged that M had substantially underdeclared his business profits over a period of several years, and that SK had helped M to transfer the underdeclared profits to Pakistan. The case was referred to the CA, which unanimously held that the proceeds of a legitimate business could constitute 'criminal property' within *PCA 2002, s 340(3)*, where those proceeds had not been declared to the Revenue. Dyson LJ held that 'a person who cheats the Revenue obtains a pecuniary advantage as a result of criminal conduct' within the meaning of *PCA 2002, s 340(6)*. On the evidence, the prosecution had made out a *prima facie* case of cheat. *R v K*, CA Criminal Division 2007, [2008] STC 1270; [2007] EWCA Crim 491.

Whether assessments precluded by agreement with SOCA

[29.24] During an investigation into money-laundering, the Assets Recovery Agency raided the premises of an individual (P). In 2007 they began legal proceedings against P in the High Court. In 2009 SOCA (which had succeeded the ARA) agreed not to proceed with any criminal cases against P. In 2011 SOCA issued assessments on P, covering the years 1998/99 to 2005/06 and charging tax of more than £3,000,000. P appealed, contending as a preliminary point that the effect of the agreement reached in 2009 was that the assessments were invalid. The First-tier Tribunal rejected this contention and held that the assessments were valid. Judge Cannan held that the 2009 agreement precluded SOCA from taking criminal proceedings against P, but did not prevent them from raising assessments to recover the tax due, as 'there was no agreement to compromise (P's) potential tax liabilities'. *BG Pepper v SOCA*, FTT [2013] UKFTT 654 (TC), TC03038.

Wilful default

NOTE

TMA, s 36, which originally referred to 'fraud or wilful default', was substituted by *FA 1989, s 149(1)* with effect from 27 July 1989 and the reference to 'fraud or wilful default' was replaced by a reference to 'fraudulent or negligent conduct'. In *Hurley v Taylor*, **29.47** below, Park J observed that the change in question 'was a change of terminology rather than of substance', and that 'the large body of case law about fraud, wilful default or neglect is applicable to the new concepts of fraudulent or negligent conduct'. *TMA, s 36* was again amended by *FA 2008* with effect from 1 April 2010, to refer to a 'loss of tax brought about carelessly or deliberately'. For HMRC's interpretation of what constitutes 'culpability', see Enquiry Manual, para EM5101 *et seq*.

Cases held to constitute wilful default

Persistent failure to make returns—whether wilful default

[29.25] A trader (B) who carried on business as a 'general dealer' made a return for 1939/40 showing income of £70, but did not make any returns for 1940/41 to 1947/48, or notify the Revenue that he was liable to tax. The Revenue subsequently issued additional assessments for 1939/40 to 1952/53 inclusive. The Commissioners held that B 'had committed fraud and/or wilful default' and confirmed the assessments, except two which they reduced and one which they increased. The Ch D upheld their decision. Wynn-Parry J held that the Commissioners were 'justified in concluding that he had made no explanation which was acceptable as to why no returns had been made, and that consequently they must conclude that he had done so deliberately, in which case he was guilty either of fraud or at least wilful default'. *Barney v Pybus*, Ch D 1957, 37 TC 106.

[29.26] A similar decision was reached in a subsequent case in which the appellant had submitted no returns for 14 years. Vinelott J held that there was 'ample material on which the Commissioners could have concluded that (the) failure to make returns was deliberate and accordingly wilful'. The CA unanimously upheld this decision. *Kovak v Morris*, CA 1985, 58 TC 493; [1985] STC 183.

[29.27] The Revenue issued estimated assessments for 1979/80 to 1983/84 on a trader (B) who carried on a business of selling sewing machines, and had made no returns since 1970. B appealed, contending that he had been trading at a loss. The Commissioners rejected this contention, found that B had 'been guilty of wilful default', and confirmed the assessments. The Ch D upheld their decision. *Barnes-Sherrocks v McIntosh*, Ch D 1989, 62 TC 675; [1989] STC 674.

Undisclosed profits of jeweller—whether wilful default

[29.28] The Revenue issued estimated assessments on a jeweller. Five of the assessments were made outside the normal time limits, on the basis that she had committed fraud or wilful default. The Commissioners held that she 'had been guilty of wilful default or fraud', and determined the assessments on the basis that she had understated her profits for 1940/41 to 1955/56. The Ch D upheld their decision. *Amis v Colls*, Ch D 1960, 39 TC 148. (*Note*. The appellant made an unsuccessful application for an order of *certiorari*—see *R v Great Yarmouth Commrs (ex p. Amis)*, **4.211** APPEALS.)

Undisclosed profits of farmer—whether wilful default

[29.29] The Revenue issued additional assessments on a farmer (W) under the extended time limits for fraud or wilful default. The Commissioners found that there had been wilful default, and determined the assessments on the basis that certain amounts paid into private bank accounts represented undisclosed profits. The Ch D upheld the Commissioners' decision, except with regard to two specific amounts paid into an account held by W's wife, for which Buckley J held there was no evidence that they were taxable receipts. *Woodrow (Woodrow's Executor) v Whalley*, Ch D 1964, 42 TC 249.

Assessments on amounts received by director/shareholder

[29.30] Following an investigation, the Revenue issued assessments on a company's controlling shareholder (H), on the basis that he had received undeclared income which represented undisclosed remuneration from the company. Four of the assessments were under the extended time limits for fraud or wilful default. H appealed, contending that 'his neglect did not amount to wilful default'. The Commissioners rejected this contention, held that he had been guilty of wilful default, and determined the appeals accordingly. The Ch D upheld their decision, holding that 'the Commissioners were entitled to draw the inference of wilful default'. *Hudson v Humbles*, Ch D 1965, 42 TC 380.

[29.31] In 1956 an ironmonger transferred his business to a family company, of which he became a director and shareholder. Subsequently, following an investigation, the Revenue issued estimated assessments for 1946/47 to 1960/61, on the basis that he had received undeclared income and that, for the years from 1956/57 onwards, this represented undisclosed remuneration from the company. The Commissioners held that there had been wilful default for each of the years assessed, and determined the assessments. The Ch D upheld their decision, observing that there were a 'considerable number of unexplained receipts' and holding that the Commissioners were entitled to conclude that 'the unexplained receipts were remuneration'. *James v Pope*, Ch D 1972, 48 TC 142.

Undisclosed profits of hairdresser—whether wilful default

[29.32] The Revenue issued estimated assessments on a hairdresser, covering the years from 1942/43 to 1960/61, after discovering that she had received undeclared bank interest. The Commissioners found that she had been 'guilty of wilful default'. They determined the assessments in the figures proposed by the Revenue's capital statements, except that they reduced the Revenue's proposed figures for living expenses by 25%. The CS upheld their decision. *Hillenbrand v CIR*, CS 1966, 42 TC 617.

Wilful default attributed to accountant

[29.33] A haulage contractor had been assessed on the basis of accounts and returns submitted on his behalf by an accountant. Following the accountant's death, the Revenue began an investigation and issued assessments for 1943/44 to 1948/49 under the extended time limits for wilful default. The Commissioners upheld the assessments, finding that the accountant had had sufficient information 'to enable him to make correct returns' and holding that the accountant 'was guilty of wilful default committed on behalf of the appellant'. The contractor appealed, contending that the assessments should be discharged because he had not authorised the accountant to submit incorrect returns. The Ch D upheld the Commissioners' decision. Cross J observed that Parliament had intended that the extended time limits should apply 'to cases where the fraud or wilful default was committed by an agent and it could not be proved that the taxpayer was privy to it'. *Clixby v Pountney*, Ch D 1967, 44 TC 515; [1968] Ch 719; [1968] 1 All ER 802.

[29.34] In 1981 the Revenue issued an assessment on an architect for 1972/73 after discovering that his accounts, prepared by an accountancy firm on his behalf, had included deductions for private expenditure in computing his business profits. The Commissioners upheld the assessment, finding that, while the architect had not been personally guilty of wilful default, the accountants had been 'guilty of committing wilful default on behalf of the appellant'. The Ch D upheld their decision. *Pleasants v Atkinson*, Ch D 1987, 60 TC 228; [1987] STC 728.

Understated company profits—whether wilful default

[29.35] The Revenue issued estimated assessments on a company (F) for 1952/53 to 1957/58 under the extended time limits for fraud or wilful default. The Commissioners found that there had been wilful default and determined the assessments. F appealed, contending firstly that there was no evidence of wilful default by its secretary, and alternatively, that the findings of fact amounted to a finding of fraud and that, if it was guilty of fraud, it could not also be guilty of wilful default. The CA unanimously rejected these contentions and dismissed the appeal. Salmon LJ observed that 'the Commissioners were abundantly justified in coming to the conclusion that the evidence laid before them and the facts which they found established wilful default'. *Frederick Lack Ltd v Doggett*, CA 1970, 46 TC 524. (*Note*. For another issue in this case, see **4.70** APPEALS.)

Barrister's clerk—whether 'guilty of fraud or wilful default'

[29.36] The Revenue issued assessments on a barrister's clerk, for the years 1946/47 to 1960/61 inclusive, on the ground of fraud or wilful default. He appealed to the General Commissioners but chose not to give evidence. However, he cross-examined the inspector, using an account book which was not proved in evidence. The Commissioners found that he 'was guilty of fraud or wilful default', confirmed the assessments for 1946/47 to 1959/60 inclusive, and increased the 1960/61 assessment to the amount indicated by the account book. The Ch D and CA unanimously upheld their decision, holding that there was ample evidence to support the Commissioners' findings. Walton J (in the Ch D) observed that the legislation 'throws upon the taxpayer the onus of showing that the assessments are wrong. It is the taxpayer who knows and the taxpayer who is in a position (or, if not in a position, who certainly should be in a position) to provide the right answer, and chapter and verse for the right answer, and it is idle for any taxpayer to say to the Revenue, "Hidden somewhere in your vaults are the right answers: go thou and dig them out of the vaults." That is not a duty on the Revenue. If it were, it would be a very onerous, very costly and very expensive operation, the costs of which would of course fall entirely on the taxpayers as a body. It is the duty of every individual taxpayer to make his own return and, if challenged, to support the return he has made, or, if that return cannot be supported, to come completely clean, and if he gives no evidence whatsoever he cannot be surprised if he is finally lumbered with more than he has in fact received. It is his own fault that he is so lumbered.' Orr LJ observed that it was not surprising 'that the Commissioners, having found striking discrepancies in the figures for certain years, were prepared to infer that there had been fraud or wilful default in all the years going back to 1946'. *Nicholson v Morris*, CA 1977, 51 TC 95; [1977] STC 162.

Undisclosed profits of market trader—whether wilful default

[29.37] The Revenue issued estimated assessments on a market trader for 1957/58 to 1969/70 inclusive, after discovering that he had received bank interest which he had not declared in his returns. The Commissioners held that there had been wilful default, and determined the assessments. The Ch D upheld their decision. *Read v Rollinson*, Ch D 1982, 56 TC 41; [1982] STC 370.

Understated rental income—whether wilful default

[29.38] In the case noted at 5.100 ASSESSMENTS, the Commissioners held that the persistent understatement of rental income constituted wilful default. The Ch D upheld their decision. *Honig & Others (Honig's Administrators) v Sarsfield*, Ch D 1984, 59 TC 337; [1985] STC 31.

Undisclosed profits of garage proprietors—whether wilful default

[29.39] General Commissioners held that two garage proprietors had been guilty of wilful default. The CA upheld their decision. *Fletcher & Fletcher v Harvey (and related appeal)*, Ch D 1989, 63 TC 539; [1989] STC 826.

Undisclosed profits of ice-cream salesman—whether wilful default

[29.40] Following an investigation, the Revenue issued further assessments on an ice-cream salesman for 1968/69 to 1982/83 inclusive. The Commissioners held that there had been wilful default, and determined the assessments on the basis of capital statements submitted by the inspector. The Ch D upheld their decision. *Rea v Highnam*, Ch D 1990, 63 TC 287; [1990] STC 368.

Acceptance of inadequate estimated assessment—whether wilful default

[29.41] An individual (N) had purchased a dilapidated building in 1979 for £3,360. After making improvements, he sold it for £25,000 in 1984. On his 1985/86 return, he disclosed the disposal of the property but gave no details of figures, stating only that the chargeable gain was 'to be agreed'. The inspector issued an estimated CGT assessment, showing a chargeable gain of £10,000. N did not appeal, and paid the tax charged by the assessment. In July 1988, after discovering the actual cost and sale price, the inspector issued a further assessment. The General Commissioners confirmed the assessment and found that there had been 'wilful default or neglect'. The Ch D upheld their decision and dismissed N's appeal, holding that the Commissioners were entitled to make a finding of wilful default. *Nuttall v Barrett*, Ch D 1992, 64 TC 548; [1992] STC 112.

Undisclosed profits of guest house—whether wilful default

[29.42] The Revenue issued assessments, covering the years 1973/74 to 1986/87 inclusive, on a guest house proprietor (K). K appealed. The Special Commissioners heard his appeals in 1991, reviewed the evidence in detail, found that the proprietor had been guilty of wilful default for 1973/74 (and neglect for the eight subsequent years), and determined the appeals. The proprietor appealed to the CA, which heard his appeal in 1995 and upheld the Commissioners' decision (see **4.9** APPEALS). The proprietor subsequently appealed against determinations of interest and penalties. (The penalties imposed were 80% of the tax lost.) The Special Commissioners dismissed the appeals and the Ch D upheld their decision. Jacob J observed that K had put forward 'near-preposterous, varied and mutually inconsistent stories about improbable partnerships' and that 'there was no room whatever for any other finding than wilful default or neglect'. Furthermore, the imposition of the penalty did not give rise to any breach of the *European Convention on Human Rights*, and the Commissioners were entitled to uphold penalties of 80% of the tax lost. *King v Walden (No 2)*, Ch D 2001, 74 TC 45; [2001] STC 822; 3 ITLR 682. (*Notes.* (1) The Commissioners also held that further assessments, issued after the original Commissioners' decision, had been made 'to make good a loss of tax attributable to the wilful default or negligent conduct of the appellant'. For the validity of these assessments, see **5.85** ASSESSMENTS. (2) The CA dismissed K's application to lodge a further appeal against the Ch D decision—see [2001] EWCA Civ 1518. K subsequently appealed to the ECHR—see **31.32** HUMAN RIGHTS.)

Cases held not to constitute wilful default

Undisclosed profits of wife's business—whether wilful default

[29.43] A married woman carried on business as an innkeeper. An investigation revealed that she had substantial savings, and in 1957 the Revenue issued additional assessments on her husband (under the law then in force) for 1936/37 to 1948/49, on the basis that the savings represented concealed profits of the business and that there had been fraud or wilful default. The husband appealed, contending that the savings came from gifts to his wife from her late mother and that he had been unaware of them. The Commissioners found that the savings came from business profits, and confirmed the assessments. The Ch D allowed the husband's appeals, holding that there was ample evidence to justify the finding that the savings represented profits of the wife's trade, but that there was no evidence to warrant the conclusion of wilful default by the husband. Wilberforce J defined 'wilful default' as 'some deliberate or intentional failure to do what the taxpayer ought to have done, knowing that to omit to do so was wrong'. *Wellington v Reynolds*, Ch D 1962, 40 TC 209.

Case remitted to Commissioners to explain their findings

[29.44] Following an investigation, the Revenue issued additional assessments on a farmer (P) for 1944/45 to 1952/53. The assessments for 1944/45 to 1948/49 were made under the extended time limits, on the basis that there had been wilful default. P (who was a former jockey) appealed, contending that the increase in his assets was attributable to gambling winnings. The Commissioners dismissed his appeals against the assessments for 1949/50 to 1952/53, but discharged the assessments for 1944/45 to 1948/49, finding that 'no fraud or wilful default had been committed'. Both sides appealed. The Ch D dismissed P's appeal against the later assessments, but remitted the case to them to explain their decision on the earlier assessments. Cross J observed that 'the facts expressly found all tell in favour of wilful default'. *Brimelow v Price (and cross-appeal)*, Ch D 1965, 49 TC 41. (*Note*. There was no further public hearing of the appeals.)

Commissioners confirming assessment but no finding of wilful default

[29.45] The Revenue issued CGT assessments on an individual (H) for 1973/74 and 1974/75. The assessment for 1974/75 was made within the normal six-year time limit but that for 1973/74 was not. H appealed, contending that the assessments were invalid because he had ceased to be resident in the UK in 1971. The Commissioners rejected this contention, finding that he had not become non-resident until after February 1976. H appealed to the Ch D. In the Stated Case, the Commissioners set out their findings with regard to the question of H's residence, but made no finding of fraud, wilful default or neglect. The Ch D allowed H's appeal against the 1973/74 assessment, holding that the Commissioners' decision was clearly 'open to objection in the absence of a proper finding of fraud, wilful default or neglect'. However, the Ch D dismissed the appeal for 1974/75, since it was clear that that assessment had been made under the normal time limits. *Hawkins v Fuller*, Ch D 1982, 56 TC 49; [1982] STC 468.

Negligent conduct

NOTE

TMA, s 36, which originally referred to 'fraud or wilful default', was substituted by *FA 1989, s 149(1)* with effect from 27 July 1989 and the reference to 'fraud or wilful default' was replaced by a reference to 'fraudulent or negligent conduct'. In *Hurley v Taylor*, **29.47** below, Park J observed that the change in question 'was a change of terminology rather than of substance', and that 'the large body of case law about fraud, wilful default or neglect is applicable to the new concepts of fraudulent or negligent conduct'. *TMA, s 36* was again amended by *FA 2008* with effect from 1 April 2010, to refer to a 'loss of tax brought about carelessly or deliberately'. For HMRC's interpretation of what constitutes 'culpability', see Enquiry Manual, para EM5101 *et seq*.

Definition of 'negligence'

[29.46] In a non-tax case, Baron Alderson defined 'negligence' as 'the omission to do something which a prudent and reasonable man would do'. *Blyth v Birmingham Waterworks Co*, Ex D 1856, 11 Ex 781. (*Note*. This dictum is frequently cited by the Revenue, and has been applied in many subsequent cases. However, in the 2011 case of *Verma v HMRC*, **44.165** PENALTIES, Judge Berner held that 'reliance on a 19th century authority on negligence in a civil claim can hardly be regarded as authoritative in the context of the interpretation of a statutory provision for tax penalties enacted by the *Finance Act 2007*'.)

Whether Commissioners' findings sufficient to support assessment

[29.47] The Revenue issued assessments on a trader (H) covering the years from 1983/84 to 1992/93 inclusive. The assessments for 1987/88 to 1992/93 inclusive were made under the normal time limits of *TMA, s 34*, while the assessments for 1983/84 to 1986/87 were made under the extended time limits of *TMA, s 36*, on the basis that H had been guilty of 'fraudulent or negligent conduct'. The Commissioners confirmed all the assessments in reduced amounts, stating that they were 'not satisfied' with H's explanations. The CA upheld the Commissioners' decision as a finding of fact, which could only be reversed if it was unreasonable, which was not the case here. Furthermore, H was not entitled to introduce additional evidence before the High Court or have the case remitted to the Commissioners, since he had failed to submit that evidence to the Commissioners. *Hurley v Taylor (and cross-appeal)*, CA 1998, 71 TC 268; [1999] STC 1.

Application for judicial review of assessments under TMA, s 36

[29.48] The Revenue issued further assessments for 1985/86 to 1989/90 inclusive, under the provisions of *TMA, s 36*, on an individual (N). He appealed, and, at the hearing of the appeals, he cross-examined the inspector and made representations concerning the assessments. The Commissioners held that the Revenue had had the right to make the further assessments, and adjourned the hearing of the appeals. At a subsequent hearing, which N did not attend, they confirmed the assessments. N applied for judicial review, contending that the Commissioners' decision was unfair and irrational. The QB rejected this contention and dismissed his application. *R v North London General Commrs (ex p. Nii-Amaa)*, QB 1999, 72 TC 634; [1999] STC 644.

Accountant—whether guilty of negligent conduct

[29.49] An accountant (H) submitted a 1996/97 return showing a net profit of £9,908. Following the submission of accounts, it became clear that the true net profit was £20,017. The Revenue issued an assessment under *TMA, s 29*. H appealed, contending that there had been no 'negligent conduct' within *TMA, s 29(4)*. The Special Commissioner rejected this contention and dismissed the appeal, holding on the evidence that H's return 'was positively misleading' and that 'the reasonable competent taxpayer, to whom the services of the Inland Revenue telephone enquiry lines were available, could and would have reached the right answer'. H's 'standards of compliance fell below the standards reasonably expected of the competent taxpayer; his conduct amounted to negligence'. *Hancock v CIR*, Sp C [1999] SSCD 287 (Sp C 213). (*Note*. The Commissioner also dismissed appeals against assessments for 1994/95 and 1995/96, holding that the inspector had made a 'discovery' within *TMA, s 29*.)

[29.50] An accountant (M) failed to submit accounts for the two years ending 5 April 1987 in time, and the Revenue issued estimated assessments. In 1990 he submitted accounts showing that his profits had substantially exceeded the amounts assessed. The Revenue investigated his accounts and ascertained that there were unexplained bankings of about £100,000. Further information, obtained as a result of M divorcing his wife, indicated that M had accumulated substantial capital, including property purchases, which could not have been financed from his declared income. In 1996 the Revenue made further assessments, under *TMA, s 36*, covering 1976/77 to 1985/86 inclusive. The Special Commissioners dismissed M's appeal, finding that he had never made a 'full and frank disclosure' and had refused to co-operate with the Revenue. There was a loss of tax which was attributable 'at least' to M's negligent conduct, within *s 36*. *Mashood v Whitehead (and related appeals)*, Sp C [2002] SSCD 166 (Sp C 308). (*Notes*. (1) The Commissioners imposed a penalty of £250 on M—see **44.338** PENALTIES. (2) The Commissioners also determined appeals against estimated assessments for subsequent years, including assessments on an associated partnership and three associated companies, in the amounts requested by the Revenue.)

Errors in return—whether 'negligent conduct'

[29.51] The trustees of a retirement benefit scheme submitted a return for 2006/07 containing several incorrect entries. Following the submission of the return, HMRC issued a calculation of the scheme's tax liability in which tax was only charged at the basic rate. In December 2009, following an enquiry into a subsequent return, HMRC issued a discovery assessment charging tax at the higher rate attributable to trusts. The First-tier Tribunal upheld the assessment and dismissed the trustees' appeal, holding that the trustee who had submitted the return had been negligent. *EA & A Manisty (Trustees of the EA Manisty FURBS Trust) v HMRC*, FTT [2011] UKFTT 507 (TC), TC01354.

Failure to notify chargeability—whether 'negligent conduct'

[29.52] Two partners operated an Indian restaurant, but did not notify the Revenue. The Revenue issued assessments on the partnership under the extended time limits of *TMA, s 36*. The General Commissioners upheld the assessments, finding that the partners' failure to notify the Revenue was 'negligent conduct'. The Ch D upheld this decision. *The Last Viceroy Restaurant v Jackson*, Ch D 2000, 73 TC 322; [2000] STC 1093.

[29.53] A landscape gardener (S) failed to notify the Revenue that he was chargeable to income tax. In 2009 HMRC issued discovery assessments for

2003/04 to 2005/06. The First-tier Tribunal dismissed S's appeal, holding that his failure to notify chargeability constituted 'negligent conduct'. *D Stanley v HMRC*, FTT [2011] UKFTT 169 (TC), TC01038.

Failure to notify disposal of shares—whether 'negligent conduct'

[29.54] In the case noted at **71.355** CAPITAL GAINS TAX, the Special Commissioner held that the failure to notify a disposal of shares constituted 'negligent conduct'. *Billows v Hammond*, Sp C [2000] SSCD 430 (Sp C 252).

Failure to notify gain on shares—whether 'negligent conduct'

[29.55] In January 2000 a woman (R) disposed of some shares. She did not declare the gain on her 1999/2000 tax return. In May 2006, following an enquiry into R's return for a subsequent year, HMRC issued a discovery assessment. R appealed, contending that she had reinvested the proceeds of the share sale in April 2001, and her accountant (M) had told her that this would qualify for rollover relief. The First-tier Tribunal upheld the assessment, holding that M had been negligent. Judge Berner observed that 'even if an ordinarily competent accountant and tax adviser had not been familiar with the law in this respect, he would have been able to ascertain very readily, from the legislation itself and other published materials, that shares were not included amongst the assets that would qualify for business asset rollover relief'. *Mrs K Rotberg v HMRC*, FTT [2014] UKFTT 657 (TC), TC03780.

Failure to notify gain on exercise of share option

[29.56] In *Employee v HMRC*, **22.324** EMPLOYMENT INCOME, an employee (E) made substantial gains on the exercise of share options in 2000/01. He failed to include these on his tax return. The Revenue subsequently began an enquiry into E's affairs, and issued an assessment in 2005, charging tax on the gains. The Special Commissioner upheld the assessment, observing that the effect of the decision in *Ball v Phillips*, **22.323** EMPLOYMENT INCOME, was that 'income tax is chargeable on the exercise of the right to acquire shares even when the shares are retained and not sold'. On the evidence, E's accountant had been aware of the law, but had made a deliberate decision 'to submit the self-assessment return on the incorrect basis'. The Commissioner observed that 'the standards of compliance shown by the appellant and his advisers fell below the standards reasonably expected of the competent taxpayer and adviser and such conduct amounted to negligent conduct. The Revenue must be entitled to assume that a professionally prepared tax return has been prepared competently.' There had been 'a loss of tax attributable to negligent conduct on the part of the appellant or his advisers', within *TMA, s 29(4)*.

Failure to declare gain on overseas bond

[29.57] In *Anderson v HMRC*, **5.53** ASSESSMENTS, the First-tier Tribunal held that the failure to declare a gain on the encashment of an overseas bond constituted 'negligent conduct'.

Failure to notify disposal of interests in partnerships

[29.58] An individual (J) had been a member of two partnerships which carried on insurance business. In 2002 he sold his interests in these partnerships to one of the other partners. He did not declare the disposals on his tax return. HMRC issued a discovery assessment. The First-tier Tribunal dismissed J's appeal, finding that he had made the disposals in question and holding that his failure to declare them constituted 'negligent conduct'. *M Jones v HMRC (No 1)*, FTT [2011] UKFTT 149 (TC), TC01023.

Claim to be non-resident—whether 'negligent conduct'

[29.59] In *Hankinson v HMRC*, 48.20 RESIDENCE, where a company director had claimed that he had not been resident in the UK during 1998/99, the First-tier Tribunal held that this constituted 'negligent conduct'.

[29.60] In March 2000 a banker (D) realised a large capital gain. He submitted a 1999/2000 tax return claiming to have been resident outside the UK. HMRC subsequently formed the opinion that D had remained resident in the UK, and issued a discovery assessment charging tax on the gain. D appealed, contending firstly that he had been working full-time in Belgium in 1999/2000 and alternatively that he had not been negligent. The First-tier Tribunal rejected these contentions and dismissed his appeal, finding that although D had worked in Belgium in 1999/2000, he had not been working there full-time and had remained resident in the UK. Judge Nowlan observed that 'if the taxpayer thinks and decides that there are doubts, and perhaps major doubts, and he files the return on the basis of a hope that HMRC will fail to open enquiries, then that conduct comes closer to fraud than negligence'. *P Daniel v HMRC (No 2)*, FTT [2014] UKFTT 173 (TC), TC03312. (*Notes*. (1) For a preliminary issue in this case, see **4.322** APPEALS. (2) For subsequent developments in this case, see **4.126** APPEALS.)

Appellant claiming capital loss on endowment policy

[29.61] In 1999/2000 an individual (C) sold some shares, realising capital gains of more than £2,000,000. He approached an accountancy firm with the aim of reducing his CGT liability. In his return, he claimed that he had also made a capital loss of more than £2,000,000 relating to the acquisition and disposal of an endowment policy. The Revenue subsequently began an enquiry and formed the opinion that C had never actually acquired such an endowment policy and that the transactions which he claimed to have taken part in were sham transactions. They issued an assessment under *TMA, s 29*. The Special Commissioners reviewed the evidence in detail and dismissed C's appeal, finding that C had 'never truly acquired the endowment trust policy', so that 'he cannot have disposed of it or made a loss on that disposal'. Furthermore, 'it could not be said that these transactions gave rise to a real loss constituting a loss on a disposal within the meaning of the Act'. The conditions of *TMA, s 29(4)* were satisfied. *DR Collins v HMRC*, Sp C [2008] SSCD 718 (Sp C 675).

Incorrect claim to rollover relief—whether 'negligent conduct'

[29.62] A trader (M) claimed roll-over relief to which he was not entitled. When the Revenue discovered this, they issued an assessment under the extended time limits of *TMA, s 36*. The General Commissioners upheld the assessment, finding that the information and computations supplied by M's accountants 'were incomplete, inaccurate and misleading'. The Ch D dismissed M's appeal. Park J held that, on the evidence found by the Commissioners, 'the accountants did not apply a proper degree of care to the preparation of the computation'. He observed that 'an inspector of taxes is entitled to assume that a professionally prepared tax computation has been prepared properly'. The Commissioners had been entitled to find that 'there had been negligent conduct on (M's) behalf'. *McEwan v Martin*, Ch D [2005] STC 993; [2005] EWHC 714(Ch).

Company director found to be conducting parallel trade

[29.63] The Revenue formed the opinion that a company director (S) had been selling items of fabric which had been purchased by the company, and paying the proceeds into his private bank account. They issued estimated assessments, under the extended time limits of *TMA, s 36*, on the basis that S had been conducting a parallel trade to that carried on by the company. The Special Commissioner upheld the assessments, holding that S had been 'at least' guilty of negligent conduct. *PM Smith v HMRC*, Sp C [2005] SSCD 772 (Sp C 498).

Plasterer—whether 'negligent conduct'

[29.64] The Revenue formed the opinion that a plasterer (G) had understated his profits for 2002/03, and issued an notice of amendment to his return. They also issued assessments for 2000/01 and 2001/02, on the basis that G had committed 'negligent conduct'. G appealed. The Special Commissioner reviewed the evidence in detail and found that G's records indicated that he had received regular income during 2000/01 and 2001/02, but that there were periods during 2002/03 for which no income was recorded, although there were claims for business expenditure. The Commissioner found that G had understated his income for 2002/03, and upheld the Revenue's notice of amendment for that year. However the Commissioner allowed G's appeals for the two previous years, finding that 'the Revenue have not discharged the burden of proving that there was a loss of tax in the two years ending on 5 April 2001 and 5 April 2002'. Since G's records declared regular income for that year, 'there could be no presumption that the understatement in 2003 also applied to 2001 and 2002'. *Gaughan v HMRC*, Sp C [2007] SSCD 148 (Sp C 575).

Underdeclaration of income—whether 'negligent conduct'

[29.65] The Revenue formed the opinion that a restaurant proprietor (R) had substantially underdeclared his takings. They issued estimated assessments for 1995/96 and 1996/97 on the basis that R had been guilty of 'negligent conduct', within *TMA, s 36*. (They also issued amendments to R's self-assessment returns for the six subsequent years.) The General Commissioners upheld the assessments and amendments, finding that 'the failure to maintain complete and reliable records amounted to negligence'. The CS unanimously dismissed R's appeal. Lord Osborne held that the effect of *TMA, s 50(6)* was that 'the general onus to show an overcharge lay upon the appellant'. On the evidence, 'the Commissioners were quite entitled to conclude that they were not satisfied that the assessments made by the respondents were excessive'. *MA Rouf v HMRC*, CS 2009, 79 TC 736; [2009] STC 1307; [2009] CSIH 6.

[29.66] A married couple traded in partnership until 1987, when they transferred the business to a limited company. HMRC received information suggesting that the couple had consistently underdeclared their income (and that underdeclared takings from 1987 onwards had been advanced to the directors, and invested in overseas accounts). They issued assessments covering the period from 1982/83 to 2000/01. The First-tier Tribunal dismissed the couple's appeals, finding that the husband was not 'a credible witness', and that 'there had been underdeclared cash sales for many years'. Judge Kempster held that it was 'self-evident that submitting returns which fail to report cash sales or overseas income or gains constitutes at least negligent conduct'. *J & C Cooksey v HMRC*, FTT [2009] UKFTT 275 (TC), TC00221.

[29.67] See also *TSD Design Development Engineering Ltd v HMRC*, **44.171** PENALTIES.

Musician—whether 'negligent conduct'

[29.68] See *Duffy v HMRC*, **49.9** RETURNS AND INFORMATION.

Assessments to make good loss of tax (TMA, s 29(4))

Assessment issued within normal six-year time limit

[29.69] A taxpayer had received income from Australia which he had not declared on his returns. In April 1960 the Revenue issued assessments on this income for 1947/48 to 1953/54 inclusive. The taxpayer appealed, contending that the assessments were outside the statutory time limits then in force because there was no evidence that the 1953/54 assessment had been made for the specific purpose of making good a loss of tax attributable to fraud, wilful default or neglect. The General Commissioners rejected this contention and dismissed his appeal, and the Ch D upheld their decision, applying *dicta* of Pennycuick J in *Hudson v Humbles*, **29.30** above. Plowman J held that 'what matters is not the purpose of the assessor but of the assessment', so that the statutory conditions were met if the assessment did in fact result in making good a loss of tax through fraud, wilful default or neglect, and the test was an objective test and not a subjective one. Plowman J specifically declined to follow the decision of Lowry J in *O'Mullan v Walmsley*, QB(NI) 1965, 42 TC 573. *Thurgood v Slarke*, Ch D 1971, 47 TC 130; [1971] 3 All ER 606. (*Notes*. (1) There have been substantial amendments to the relevant legislation. The case concerned *FA 1960, s 51*. This became *TMA, s 37*, which was repealed by *FA 1989, s 149(2)* with effect from 27 July 1989. (2) The case also concerned the date on which the 1953/54 assessment was made. The notice of assessment was issued on 7 April 1960, but the Commissioners accepted evidence by the inspector that the assessment was actually made on 4 April, and the Ch D upheld their decision as one of fact.)

Whether notice of assessment should specify neglect

[29.70] The Revenue issued assessments covering 1954/55 to 1961/62 on an individual (R). He appealed. The Special Commissioners issued a decision in principle that R was trading and that the relevant profits were trading income, without formally determining the assessments. R applied to the QB for orders to quash the assessments and prohibit the Commissioners from proceeding. The QB rejected the application and the CA unanimously dismissed R's appeal, holding that the assessments had been issued to recover tax lost through R's neglect and that there was no requirement for the notices of assessment to state this. Orr LJ observed that the case should have been 'left to the ordinary processes of appeal' and disapproved 'the use of the prerogative procedure adopted by the appellant'. *R v Special Commrs (ex p. Rogers)*, CA 1972, 48 TC 46.

Surtax assessments made outside normal time limit

[29.71] In 1955 the Revenue issued estimated assessments for 1952/53 to 1955/56 inclusive on a cattle dealer (K) who had not submitted accounts. After a prolonged investigation, the General Commissioners determined the assessments in 1968 in higher aggregate amounts than the profits shown by capital statements submitted by K's accountant. Since the relevant assessments had been issued within the normal time limits, the question of fraud or wilful default was not raised at the appeal hearing. In 1970 the Revenue obtained leave from a Special Commissioner to raise surtax assessments outside the normal time limits. K appealed against the assessments, contending that they were invalid since they should have been raised within the normal time limits. The Special Commissioners rejected this contention and dismissed the appeals and the CA unanimously upheld their decision. Stamp LJ held that, since K had failed to make a correct return, there had been a 'loss of tax' within what is now *TMA, s 36*, and that loss was attributable to K's wilful default. *Knight v CIR*, CA 1974, 49 TC 179; [1974] STC 156. (*Note*. K made a subsequent unsuccessful application for an order of prohibition—see *R v Havering Commrs (ex p. Knight)*, **44.86** PENALTIES.)

Tax paid shortly before issue of assessment

[29.72] In 1970 the Revenue issued assessments for 1965/66 to 1969/70 inclusive, charging tax of more than £200,000, on the trustees of two settlements, who had not submitted returns. Shortly before the issue of the assessments, the trustees paid £80,000 on account of the liability. The Revenue applied to the General Commissioners for certificates that the assessments had been made for the purpose of making good 'a loss of tax attributable to the trustees' wilful default or neglect'. The Commissioners found that the trustees were guilty of wilful default, and granted the certificates. The trustees applied to the QB for orders to quash the Commissioners' decision, contending that, since they had made a payment on account before the issue of the assessments, they could not have been made 'to make good a loss of tax'. The QB rejected this contention and dismissed the applications, applying the principles laid down by the CA in *Knight v CIR*, **29.71** above. Lord Widgery CJ held that the expression 'loss of tax' included 'tax the payment of which was ultimately secured but the payment of which was delayed for an unreasonable time owing to the default of the taxpayer'. *R v Holborn Commrs (ex p. Rind Settlement Trustees)*, QB 1974, 49 TC 656; [1974] STC 567; [1975] QB 517; [1975] 1 All ER 30. (*Note.* The procedure whereby General Commissioners were responsible for the issue of interest certificates has now been superseded, but the case remains relevant with regard to the definition of a 'loss of tax'.)

Permission from Commissioner to raise late assessment

[29.73] The Revenue obtained permission from a General Commissioner, as required by the legislation then in force, to raise assessments on a hotel proprietor (D) outside the normal time limits. The Commissioners subsequently held that there had been 'neglect tinged with wilful default', and determined the assessments. D appealed, contending firstly that he should have had a right to be heard at the meeting at which the Commissioner gave permission for the assessments, and secondly that the Commissioners' decision was invalid because one of the Commissioners who determined the appeal had been present when the permission was granted (although he had not been a party to the decision). The CA unanimously rejected these contentions and dismissed D's appeal. *Day v Williams*, CA 1969, 46 TC 59. (*Note.* The provisions requiring the Revenue to seek a Commissioner's permission for the issue of assessments outside the normal time limits were consolidated into *TMA, s 41*, which was repealed by *FA 1989, s 149(2)* with effect from 27 July 1989.)

[29.74] The decision in *Day v Williams*, **29.73** above, was approved by the HL in a similar subsequent case. The HL held that the Commissioner's function in giving leave was administrative rather than judicial, and that there was no injustice in the taxpayer's not being heard as he had the right of appeal against the assessments. *Pearlberg v Varty*, HL 1972, 48 TC 14; [1972] 1 WLR 534; [1972] 2 All ER 6. (*Note.* See now the note following *Day v Williams*, **29.73** above.)

[29.75] In the case noted at **5.111** ASSESSMENTS, a Special Commissioner granted the Revenue leave under *TMA, s 41* to make a late assessment on a company (S). S applied for judicial review of the decision. The CA allowed the application. Ackner LJ held that S had 'an arguable case'. *R v Special Commr, ex p. Stipplechoice Ltd (No 1)*, CA [1985] STC 248; [1985] 2 All ER 465. (*Note.* See now the note following *Day v Williams*, **29.73** above. For subsequent developments, see **29.76** below.)

[29.76] Following the leave granted by the CA in the case noted at **29.75** above, S applied to the QB for an order to quash the permission given for a late assessment by the Special Commissioner. The Commissioner had meanwhile filed an affidavit disclosing the information supplied to her by the Revenue and giving her reasons for granting leave for the assessment. The QB dismissed S's application. Nolan J held that, on the evidence, the Commissioner 'would have been failing in her plain duty had she declined to give leave'. *R v Special Commr, ex p. Stipplechoice Ltd (No 2)*, QB 1986, 59 TC 396; [1986] STC 474. (*Note*. For subsequent developments in this case, see **5.111** ASSESSMENTS.)

[29.77] The Revenue formed the opinion that a company director (M) had omitted certain income from his 1978/79 return. They applied to a Special Commissioner, under *TMA, s 41*, for leave to raise an assessment outside the normal time limits. M applied for judicial review. The QB(NI) rejected the application and the CA unanimously upheld this decision. Carswell LCJ observed that 'the obligation upon the inspector is to provide the Commissioner with such information as is necessary to enable him to perform his statutory function of making a judgment'. On the evidence, 'the inspector fulfilled his duty in providing the Commissioner with material when making the application'. M and his advisers had 'created a skein of transactions which made it exceptionally difficult for the Revenue to unravel them', and had then 'obstructed all attempts by the Revenue to unravel the true facts'. Furthermore, the Revenue was not required to give an account of its reasons for not having raised an assessment in time. At the time when the normal six-year time limit expired, 'it was a matter of judgment how the Revenue should best proceed in the state of knowledge which it possessed', and the inspector had been entitled to form the opinion that he did not have sufficient information to justify the issue of an assessment. The CA specifically disapproved *dicta* of Lowry J in *J O'Mullan & Co v Walmsley*, QB(NI) 1965, 42 TC 573. *Re McGuckian, R v Dickinson (HM Inspector of Taxes) (ex p. McGuckian)*, CA(NI) 1999, 72 TC 343; [2000] STC 65. (*Note*. See now the note following *Day v Williams*, **29.73** above.)

Other cases

[29.78] There have been many cases in which the Special Commissioners or the First-tier Tribunal have dismissed appeals against assessments issued under *TMA, s 29(4)*. In the interest of space, such cases are not summarised in this book.

Onus of proof

Onus of proof—general principles

[29.79] In a Malaysian case, the Privy Council upheld assessments covering 20 years, which had been confirmed by the Special Commissioners and the Malaysian courts on the basis that the onus of proving fraud or wilful default rested on the Revenue, but that once fraud or wilful default had been proved, the onus of proving that the assessments were excessive or erroneous rested on the taxpayer. *Arumugam Pillai v Director-General of Inland Revenue (Malaysia)*, PC [1981] STC 146.

[29.80] See also *Brady v Group Lotus Car Companies plc*, 4.209 APPEALS, and *Hurley v Taylor*, 29.47 above.

Formal submission by appellant of no case to answer

[29.81] The Revenue issued assessments on a trader (M) under what is now *TMA, s 36*. He appealed. At the hearing of the appeals, the Revenue opened the case, and M contended that the Revenue had not shown adequate grounds for issuing the assessments, and that there was no case to answer. The Commissioners rejected this contention. M applied to the QB for an order requiring the Commissioners to determine whether the Revenue's evidence showed that there had been fraud or wilful default. The QB dismissed the application and the CA unanimously dismissed M's appeal. Applying the principles laid down by the CA in *Alexander v Rayson*, CA 1935, [1936] 1 KB 169, the Commissioners could not be required 'to express any opinion upon the evidence until the evidence is completed'. *R v Special Commrs (ex p. Martin)*, CA 1971, 48 TC 1. (*Note.* Under the legislation in force at the relevant time, the Revenue required a Commissioner's permission for the issue of the assessments. The relevant provisions were consolidated into *TMA, s 41*, which was repealed by *FA 1989, s 149(2)* with effect from 27 July 1989. See the note following *Day v Williams*, 29.73 above.)

Onus of proof—appellant choosing not to give evidence

[29.82] See *Nicholson v Morris*, 29.36 above.

Onus where most assessments made within normal time limit

[29.83] As a result of an investigation, the Revenue issued assessments for the years 1957/58 to 1964/65 on a company's managing director and controlling shareholder (J) on the basis that he had received undisclosed remuneration from the company. The 1957/58 assessment was made outside the normal time limits but the other assessments were made within the normal time limit. The Special Commissioners allowed J's appeal for 1957/58, holding that the Revenue had not established wilful default, but upheld the other assessments. J appealed to the Ch D, contending that the onus fo proof was on the Revenue. The Ch D rejected this contention and dismissed his appeal. Walton J held that J had 'not discharged the onus which lay upon the taxpayer of showing that the additional assessments were wrong'. *Jonas v Bamford*, Ch D 1973, 51 TC 1; [1973] STC 519.

Amendments of partnership statements (TMA, s 30B)

[29.84] A firm of solicitors undertook several items of unsuccessful personal litigation on behalf of its senior partner (S). In one of these cases, S was required to pay costs to the successful party. The firm paid £160,000 (in six half-yearly instalments) in respect of these costs. It also paid several disbursements, totalling more than £160,000. It claimed a deduction for this expenditure in computing its profits. When the Revenue discovered this, they issued amendments to the partnership statements, under *TMA, s 30B*. The partnership appealed, contending that S had been advised by an accountant that the expenditure was deductible. The Special Commissioners reviewed the evidence in detail and found that they were 'not satisfied' that the accountant 'was given all the relevant facts nor was he asked the right question'. The Commissioners upheld the amendments and dismissed the partnership's appeal, finding that S 'did not avoid the conflicts which arose between his own personal interests on the one hand and the interests of the firm and the Revenue on the other'. The costs and disbursements had not been 'wholly and exclusively expended' for the purposes of the partnership's profession. S was a practising solicitor and 'should have known that the only sums which could be deducted from the profits of the firm were sums which were wholly and exclusively laid out for the purposes of the profession of the firm. He knew that at the time of the payment of £160,000 the firm had no liability and that the liability was his personally. He had gone out of his way to engineer a state of affairs designed to make the appellant firm pay the costs while the actual liability had remained with him. He should have known that the discharge of a personal liability of his was not deductible from the profits of the firm from which it follows that, in claiming the deduction, he engaged in negligent conduct.' On the evidence, there had been 'negligent conduct on the part of the representative partner', within *TMA, s 30B(5)*. *Stockler Charity (a firm) v HMRC (aka AB v HMRC)*, Sp C [2007] SSCD 99 (Sp C 572). (*Note.* The firm appealed to the Ch D, but the appeal was settled by an agreement under *Civil Procedure Rules 1998 (SI 1998/3132), rule 36*, under which the firm agreed to pay the full amount of tax charged by the amendments. For subsequent proceedings in this case, see 44.187 PENALTIES.)

Assessments on personal representatives (TMA, s 40)

Death of partner

[29.85] In 1962 the Revenue made assessments under what is now *TMA, s 36* on a firm of two partners, one of whom had died in 1957. The Commissioners held that the assessments had been made outside the time limit of what is now *TMA, s 40(2)*, and the Revenue appealed. The CA held that the assessments were valid against the surviving partner, but were invalid insofar as they sought to make the executors of the deceased partner liable. Harman LJ held that the Revenue were entitled to take proceedings 'in the partnership name, though the partnership has been dissolved, in respect of events happening while it was a going concern'. A judgment in the partnership name would 'enure against the partnership assets, if there be any at this date', and against the survivor of the joint debtors. Winn LJ held that 'the joint obligation to pay tax attracted by profits earned in any year by a partnership rests on the shoulders of any person or persons who was or were then partner or partners so long only as he or they may live; should one of them die, no obligation to the Crown, joint or several, in respect of such tax passes to his estate in any case where he was not charged with it by a competent assessment in his lifetime'. The case was remitted to the Commissioners to restore the assessments, but to strike out the references in them to the executors. *Harrison v Willis Bros*, CA 1965, 43 TC 61; [1966] Ch 619; [1965] 3 All ER 753.

TMA, s 40—whether assessment made before notice served

[29.86] See *Honig & Others v Sarsfield*, 5.100 ASSESSMENTS.

Reasonable excuse (TMA, s 118)

Whether a 'reasonable excuse' for failing to deliver returns

[29.87] The Revenue issued determinations charging interest in respect of CGT assessments for 1974/75 to 1984/85 inclusive. The Special Commissioner confirmed the determinations, holding that the appellant (K) had been guilty of neglect in failing to deliver returns, and that he had no reasonable excuse within *TMA, s 118(2)*. K appealed to the Ch D, contending that if he had requested and been granted an adjournment, he could have produced evidence that information had previously been supplied to the inspector. The Ch D upheld the Commissioner's decision and rejected K's application to remit the Case to the Commissioner. *Kingsley v Billingham*, Ch D 1992, 65 TC 133; [1992] STC 132.

Whether a 'reasonable excuse' for omission from return

[29.88] An individual (N) submitted a tax return on which he failed to disclose that he had received a dividend, or that he had sold a quantity of shares, giving rise to a chargeable gain. The Revenue subsequently discovered the omission and issued a determination charging interest. N appealed, contending that he had a reasonable excuse in that he had relied on his previous accountant (who had ceased to act for him before the omission was discovered). The Special Commissioner dismissed the appeal, observing that it was doubtful whether N's reliance on his accountant could be regarded as a reasonable excuse, and holding that since N had failed to correct the omission 'without unreasonable delay', the conditions of *TMA, s 118(2)* were not satisfied. *Nunn v Gray*, Sp C [1997] SSCD 175 (Sp C 123).

[29.89] For cases concerning 'reasonable excuse' and not involving fraudulent or negligent conduct, see **44.247** *et seq* PENALTIES.

Assessments on understated profits

Cases where the appellant was successful

Assessments not made with 'due care and diligence'—appeal allowed

[29.90] In December 1994 the Revenue issued further assessments, for 1988/89 to 1994/95 inclusive, on a couple who operated a restaurant. The couple appealed, contending that their accounts were correct and that there had been no discovery within *TMA, s 29*. The Special Commissioner accepted this contention and allowed the appeal. Applying *R v St Giles & St George Commrs (ex p. Hooper)*, 5.20 ASSESSMENTS, an inspector made a 'discovery' where he came to a conclusion 'honestly and *bona fide* after due care and diligence'. On the evidence here, the inspectors responsible for the assessment had not acted with 'due care and diligence' and there had been 'no honest *bona fide* discovery'. The first inspector concerned in the investigation had prepared an incorrect business economic exercise because he did not recall the contents of a letter from the traders' accountants. The second inspector had failed to read the correspondence file and, in another business economics exercise, had failed to add columns of figures correctly. The Commissioner found that the District Inspector had betrayed a prejudicial attitude to the trader's accountant after that accountant had complained to Inland Revenue Head Office. The Commissioner also found that the traders' business records were complete and that the accounts prepared from them accurately reflected the trading results, and expressed the view that the accountant had 'represented his clients in a proper and fair manner throughout this long and difficult investigation'. The Revenue had failed to find any bankings or expenditure which had not been accounted for. The Revenue's assessments rested on business economic exercises which were 'inaccurate or just plain wrong'. The Commissioner observed that 'business economic exercises alone can rarely if ever justify the sort of attack mounted by the Inland Revenue in these appeals'. The Revenue had 'acted wholly unreasonably' and had 'shown bad faith'. *Scott (Mr & Mrs) (t/a Farthings Steak House) v McDonald*, Sp C [1996] SSCD 381 (Sp C 91). (*Note*. Costs were awarded to the taxpayers.)

Cases where the appellant was partly successful

[29.91] The Revenue issued assessments on the controlling director of a company which operated an Indian restaurant, on the basis that he had received undeclared income which represented undisclosed remuneration from the company. The assessments included rent which the company had paid on behalf of the director, benefits in kind, and amounts in respect of takings which the Revenue considered had been abstracted by the director without appearing in the company's records. The director appealed, accepting that he was liable to tax on the rental income and the benefits in kind, but contending that there had been no undeclared takings. The Commissioners upheld the assessments in principle but reduced them in amount, finding that there had been undeclared takings but that the amount assessed was excessive. The Commissioners determined the amount of undeclared takings by applying a mark-up to the amount of meat which the company had purchased, and determined the amount of undeclared remuneration in amounts varying from £15,000 for 1992/93 to £71,000 for 1998/99. The director appealed to the Ch D, which upheld the assessments in principle but reduced the amount of each assessment by £5,000. *Khawaja v Etty*, Ch D 2003, 75 TC 774; [2004] STC 669. (*Note.* For subsequent developments in this case, see **44.191** PENALTIES.)

[29.92] A trader carried on a business of repairing gaming machines. The Revenue examined his return and accounts for 2000/01, and discovered that his business records were inadequate. They issued 'discovery' assessments for 1992/93 to 1999/2000 inclusive. These assessments were computed on the basis that the trader had suppressed £22,572 for 2000/01, and adjusting this for earlier years by reference to the retail price index. The trader appealed, accepting that he had underdeclared his income by £22,572 for 2000/01, but contending that the assessments for earlier years were excessive. The Special Commissioner reviewed the evidence in detail and upheld the assessments in principle, holding that there had been 'a loss of income tax attributable to the appellant's fraudulent or negligent conduct'. However the Commissioner directed that the assessments for 1992/93 to 1999/2000 should be recomputed by taking the percentage increase in the declared profits for 2000/01 and applying the same percentage increase to the profits returned for earlier years. The Commissioner observed that 'this implies that the appellant has been suppressing the same proportion of profits throughout which seems to me to be more probable than to say that he has suppressing £22,572 per annum (adjusted for the cost of living index) throughout'. *Hall v Couch*, Sp C [2004] SSCD 353 (Sp C 417).

[29.93] The Revenue formed the opinion that a married couple, who carried on a retail business in partnership, had submitted accounts which understated their takings and significantly overstated their closing stock. They issued estimated assessments, covering the years from 1987/88 to 1994/95. The couple appealed. The Special Commissioner reviewed the evidence in detail and found that there was 'no direct reliable evidence of contemporary records of stock valuations, stock takes, or records from which to derive reliable stock values'. He accepted the Revenue's view that 'the accounts and returns submitted were little better than guesses'. However, he also observed that the assessments for the later years were significantly higher than the assessments for the earlier years, and concluded that they were 'little better than guesses – or were intended to force an appeal', and were far in excess of the likely actual profits. On the evidence, the Commissioner concluded that 'the gross profit margin basis of analysis is the form of analysis that is most probably going to generate a sound figure on which to base the profits of the business'. He confirmed the assessments for 1987/88 and 1988/89, and determined the appeals for subsequent years on the basis of a gross profit margin of 43% (with the effect of increasing the assessments for 1989/90 to 1990/91, and reducing the assessments for 1991/92 to 1994/95). *R & JM Pooley v HMRC*, Sp C [2006] SSCD 221 (Sp C 525). (*Note.* The Commissioner also rejected the appellants' contention that the proceedings contravened *Article 6* of the *European Convention on Human Rights*.)

[29.94] See also *Marsden & Marsden (t/a Seddon Investments) v Eadie*, **63.214** TRADING PROFITS.

Cases where the appellant was unsuccessful

NOTE

The following cases are appeals, to the High Court unless otherwise stated, by taxpayers against assessments covering previous years, where the Commissioners have determined the appeals on the basis contended for by the Revenue. Decisions by the Special Commissioners and the First-tier Tribunal on appeals against estimated assessments have not been summarised unless the decision appears to raise a point of particular importance.

[29.95] A father and son traded in partnership as hosiery manufacturers. The Revenue discovered that the partners had substantial amounts of money in private bank accounts, and issued estimated assessments. The firm appealed, contending that most of the money derived from betting winnings. The Commissioners rejected this contention and determined the appeals on the basis that profits had been understated by a total of £28,000 over a period of six years. The Ch D upheld their decision. *G Deacon & Sons v CIR; G Deacon & Sons v Roper*, Ch D 1952, 33 TC 66.

[29.96] The Revenue issued estimated assessments on the director and controlling shareholder of a company dealing in leather goods, on the basis that he had also carried on a similar business as a sole trader. He appealed, contending that the increases in his wealth derived from the sale of furniture and jewellery, and from betting winnings. The Commissioners rejected this contention, and determined the appeals on the basis that he had made undeclared profits of more than £11,000 over a period of seven years. The Ch D upheld their decision. *Horowitz v Farrand*, Ch D 1952, 33 TC 221.

[29.97] The Revenue issued estimated assessments on a clothing manufacturer. He appealed, contending that the increases in his wealth derived from jewellery and foreign currency brought into the UK from Germany (where he had previously lived). The Commissioners rejected this contention, and determined the appeals on the basis that he had made undeclared profits of more than £39,000 over a period of seven years. The Ch D and CA unanimously upheld their decision. *Moschi v Kelly*, CA 1952, 33 TC 442. (*Note*. For another issue in this case, see **63.174** TRADING PROFITS. For a sequel to this case, see *Moschi v CIR*, **6.2** BANKRUPTCY AND PERSONAL INSOLVENCY.)

[29.98] The Revenue issued additional assessments on a hairdresser. He appealed, contending that the increases in his wealth derived from betting winnings. The Commissioners rejected this contention, and confirmed the assessments. The Ch D upheld their decision as one of fact. *Kilburn v Bedford*, Ch D 1955, 36 TC 262.

[29.99] The Revenue issued estimated assessments on a farmer. He appealed, contending that the increases in his wealth derived from betting winnings. The Commissioners rejected this contention, and determined the assessments on the basis that he had made underdeclared profits of £10,000 over a period of 11 years. The Ch D upheld their decision. *Roberts v McGregor*, Ch D 1959, 38 TC 610.

[29.100] A raincoat manufacturer submitted accounts indicating that he had introduced capital of more than £36,000 into his business over a period of less than four years. The Revenue issued additional assessments on the basis that this money should be treated as trading income. The trader appealed, contending that it represented betting winnings. The Commissioners rejected this contention, and determined the assessments on the basis that £34,267 should be treated as trading income. The Ch D upheld their decision. *Chuwen v Sabine*, Ch D 1959, 39 TC 1.

[29.101] The Revenue issued estimated assessments on a company trading as car dealers, after discovering that its managing director had made a cash payment of £8,000 (in 1949) in connection with a purchase of shares. The Commissioners found that the company's records were 'rudimentary', and determined the assessments on the basis that the company's profits had been understated by £8,000. The Ch D upheld their decision. *Erddig Motors Ltd v McGregor*, Ch D 1961, 40 TC 95.

[29.102] A trader carried on business as a restaurant proprietor and a potato merchant. The Revenue issued estimated assessments on profits as a 'dealer'. He appealed, contending that the increases in his wealth derived from betting winnings and from the sale of furniture. The Commissioners found that 'the majority of the capital increases in issue were derived from dealing' and that 'the most that could reasonably be ascribed to betting was about £200 in any one year'. They determined the assessments accordingly. The Ch D upheld their decision. *Hellier v O'Hare*, Ch D 1964, 42 TC 155.

[29.103] The Revenue issued estimated assessments on a second-hand clothes dealer. She appealed, contending that she had received £12,000 from non-taxable sales of private jewellery. The Commissioners rejected this contention and determined the assessments in the figures proposed by the inspector's capital statements (which allowed £1,000 for income from such sales). The Ch D upheld their decision. *Hurley v Young*, Ch D 1966, 45 ATC 316.

[29.104] The Revenue issued estimated assessments on a builder and decorator. He appealed, contending that the increases in his wealth derived from betting winnings of more than £30,000 (he owned a number of greyhounds). The Commissioners determined the assessments on the basis that he had had betting winnings of £19,500, which he had used for general living expenses. The CA upheld the Commissioners' decision and dismissed the builder's appeal. *Anson v Hill*, CA 1968, 47 ATC 143. (*Note*. See **4.180** APPEALS for another point in this case.)

[29.105] A married woman operated a haulage business. Her husband failed to declare the profits from this, and the Revenue began an enquiry. He submitted accounts for his wife's business, and the Revenue issued assessments accordingly. However, the inspector drew up capital statements disclosing significant increases in the couple's wealth, and issued estimated assessments on the basis that they arose from the wife's business. The husband appealed, contending that the assessments were excessive, and that the increases in their wealth derived from betting winnings of more than £15,000. The Commissioners determined the assessments on the basis that he had had betting winnings of £5,300, and that the remainder of the increases shown by the capital statements arose from the wife's business. The Ch D upheld their decision. *Hope v Damerel*, Ch D 1969, 48 ATC 461.

[29.106] A shopkeeper began trading in 1961 and moved to a different shop in 1964. He ceased trading in 1971. Following an investigation, the Revenue issued estimated assessments for the entire period of trading. The Special Commissioners discharged the additional assessments for 1961/62 to 1964/65 inclusive, but determined the assessments for the subsequent years on the basis that profits had been understated by £300pa. The CS unanimously upheld their decision. *Driver v CIR*, CS 1977, 52 TC 153.

[29.107] In a Mauritius case, a trader appealed against assessments for 1976/77 to 1981/82, contending that the increase in his wealth derived from eight separate lottery winnings. The Mauritius Tribunal rejected this contention and confirmed the assessments, finding that the trader 'must have purchased winning tickets after the respective draws from *bona fide* winners in order to camouflage his taxable business profits'. The Privy Council dismissed the trader's appeal (by a 4-1 majority, Lord Ackner dissenting). Lord Templeman observed that the trader had 'decided not to produce any evidence that his business transactions were conducted and recorded in a manner which might give a touch of verisimilitude to a bald and unconvincing narrative of his lottery transactions'. *Fon Teen Kission v Mauritius Commr of Income Tax*, PC 1988, [1989] BTC 26.

[29.108] In another Mauritius case, the Privy Council upheld estimated assessments covering 13 consecutive years of assessment. *Jauffur v Mauritius Commr of Income Tax*, PC [2006] UKPC 32.

[29.109] Following an investigation, the Revenue issued assessments on the managing director and controlling shareholder of a family company for 1972/73 to 1985/86, on the basis that he had received undeclared income which represented undisclosed remuneration from the company. The Commissioners discharged the assessments for 1972/73 to 1977/78 inclusive, but confirmed the assessments for 1978/79 to 1985/86 in reduced amounts. The CA unanimously upheld the Commissioners' decision and dismissed the director's appeal. *Billows v Robinson (and related appeal)*, CA 1991, 64 TC 17; [1991] STC 127.

[29.110] In a Trinidad & Tobago case, a trader appealed against assessments for 1971 to 1975. The assessments had been computed on the basis of capital statements, as the trader stated that his records had been destroyed in a fire. The Trinidad & Tobago Court of Appeal upheld the assessments and the Privy Council unanimously dismissed the trader's appeal. *Juman v Trinidad & Tobago Board of Inland Revenue*, PC [1991] STC 525.

[29.111] Following an investigation, the Revenue issued estimated assessments on a taxi driver for 1985/86 to 1989/90 inclusive. The assessments were computed by reference to the amount of petrol which the driver had used. The Commissioners upheld the assessments in principle, but slightly reduced them to allow for private use of the taxi. The Ch D upheld their decision and dismissed the driver's appeal. *Kudehinbu v Cutts*, Ch D [1994] STC 560.

[29.112] The Revenue issued assessments on the director of a construction company, on the basis that the company had received undeclared income which had been passed to the director as undisclosed remuneration. The Commissioners determined the assessments in the amounts requested by the inspector. The Ch D upheld their decision and dismissed the director's appeal. *MacEachern v Carr*, Ch D 1996, 68 TC 196; [1996] STC 282.

[29.113] Following an investigation, the Revenue issued estimated assessments on a family partnership which operated a restaurant. The General Commissioners found that the partnership had not declared the true takings, and upheld the assessments in principle but reduced them in amount. The Ch D upheld the Commissioners' decision as one of fact. *Momin & Others v HMRC*, Ch D [2007] EWHC 1400 (Ch).

[29.114] The Revenue began an investigation into a company, and formed the opinion that its chairman (S) had received significant benefits in kind and that there were unexplained deposits totalling more than £400,000 in his bank account. They issued assessments for 1992/93 to 1998/99 inclusive, on the basis that the unexplained deposits represented trading profits. (S had previously traded as a wine dealer.) S appealed. The Special Commissioner reviewed the evidence in detail and dismissed the appeals, finding that 'the unexplained monetary deposits in the appellant's bank account and the appellant's personal expenditure incurred on the employer's credit card constituted taxable income upon which the appellant had not declared and paid income tax'. *PM Smith v HMRC (No 2)*, Sp C [2008] SSCD 779 (Sp C 680).

[29.115] See also *Duhra v HMRC*, **44.151** PENALTIES.

Revenue investigations—negotiated settlements

Validity of negotiated settlement

[29.116] The Revenue agreed a negotiated settlement with a shipbroker (C) in respect of excess profits duty, without issuing a formal assessment. C paid the amount in question, but subsequently sought to reopen the settlement, contending that it was unlawful. The Special Commissioners rejected this contention and the CA unanimously dismissed C's appeal. Slesser LJ held that 'there is nothing in the machinery and the scheme of the Income Tax Acts to prevent a subject paying, if he will, an amount in settlement of the liability which the Act imposed upon him, without an assessment'. *Sir Walter Cockerline (t/a WH Cockerline & Co) v CIR*, CA 1930, 16 TC 1.

Whether penalty may be compounded without formal proceedings

[29.117] A trader had incurred penalties for making incorrect returns. In 1921 he agreed to pay the Revenue a total of £3,000 in instalments, in consideration of proceedings not being taken against him. He failed to pay the last two instalments, and the Revenue took proceedings to recover the amount due. The KB gave judgment for the Revenue. Rowlatt J observed that it was 'very advantageous' for people to 'be able to come to the Commissioners of Inland Revenue and put their cards on the table and make an arrangement with them to pay something in respect of the penalties on account of the injustice which they have inflicted on the other taxpayers'. The effect of what is now *TMA, s 102* was that 'a fine or penalty which the Commissioners honestly think the facts may support may be compounded by them without taking any proceedings'. *A-G v Johnstone*, KB 1926, 10 TC 758.

[29.118] The decision in *A-G v Johnstone*, **29.117** above, was applied in the similar subsequent case of *CIR v Richards*, KB 1950, 33 TC 1.

[29.119] Following an investigation into his returns, an individual (N) signed an agreement with the Revenue in 1985, by which he undertook to pay the Revenue £15,000 in consideration of the Revenue taking no proceedings against him in respect of income tax, penalties or interest for the years 1977/78 to 1979/80. He paid £5,000 under the agreement but failed to pay the balance of £10,000. The Revenue issued a writ for that amount, and subsequently sought summary judgment. N sought leave to defend, contending that the agreement was *ultra vires* and invalid. The CA rejected this contention and gave judgment for the Revenue. *TMA, s 105* provided that the Revenue could accept pecuniary settlements. The Revenue had the power under *IRRA 1890, ss 1, 35*, to enter into negotiated agreements, and this power was not overridden by the specific provisions of *TMA, s 54*. Parker LJ held that the Revenue had the power 'to enter into an agreement to compromise an overall situation consisting partly in outstanding tax, partly in a potential liability to culpable interest, and partly in a potential liability to pay penalties if by that means they consider they can best recover and manage the tax which is committed to their care'. *CIR v Nuttall*, CA 1989, 63 TC 148; [1990] STC 194; [1990] 1 WLR 631.

Death of taxpayer after settlement—liability of executor

[29.120] Following an investigation into his affairs, a company director (M) made an offer in settlement of underpaid duties and penalties. The Revenue accepted the offer, but M died without paying the full amount offered. The company which acted as his executor paid a sum in respect of the assessed tax, but refused to pay the balance. The Attorney-General brought an action for payment of the balance, and the KB gave judgment against the company. Singleton J held that, since the action was on a contract, M's death did not extinguish it. The agreement had been made for consideration, and was therefore enforceable. The Revenue could accept a sum in composition for penalties even if they had not taken proceedings to recover them. *A-G v Midland Bank Executor & Trustee Co Ltd (Marsh's Executor)*, KB 1934, 19 TC 136.

Executor seeking to resile from settlement

[29.121] The owner of a farm died in 2005. His executors valued the farm for IHT purposes at £650,000. The farm was sold in 2006 for £800,000. HMRC subsequently sought to charge CGT on the sale, and the executors made a claim under *IHTA 1984, s 191* that the sale proceeds should be substituted for the probate value. Following negotiations, it was agreed that the farm should be valued at £740,000 at the date of death. In 2010 the executors agreed to pay £26,612 in respect of tax, penalties and interest. Subsequently one of the executors, and one of the beneficiaries, lodged an appeal with the First-tier

Tribunal, seeking to resile from the agreed valuation of the farm. The First-tier Tribunal struck out the appeal, holding that it had no jurisdiction. Judge Cannan held that 'a contract settlement takes effect outside the statutory regime of assessments and appeals to the FTT. In so far as HMRC wish to enforce a contract settlement, they must do so by proceedings in debt. In so far as a taxpayer wishes to challenge the enforceability of such a contract, he or she must do so in defending such proceedings.' *Mrs DM Morris & Mrs J Gregson v HMRC*, FTT [2014] UKFTT 993 (TC), TC04098.

Negotiated settlement remaining unpaid—bankruptcy order

[29.122] Following an investigation, the Revenue agreed a settlement with a car dealer in 1994, under which the dealer agreed to pay £25,000 in instalments. He failed to pay any of this, and in 1999 a bankruptcy order was made against him. In February 2000 the CA dismissed his application for leave to appeal against the order. The dealer subsequently applied for annulment of the order. The Ch D dismissed the application, holding that there was no basis for reopening the case and no grounds for annulling or rescinding the bankruptcy order. *Newsam v CIR*, Ch D 22 May 2002 unreported.

[29.123] The Ch D reached a similar decision in a subsequent appeal by the same appellant. *Newsam v HMRC*, Ch D 24 June 2005 unreported.

Negotiated settlement—further investigation by Revenue

[29.124] A partnership traded from 1998 to 2002, when it sold its business to a limited company. The Revenue began an investigation into the partnership. In May 2004 the partners agreed to pay the Revenue £525,000 in respect of tax, interest and penalties. In October 2004 an inspector wrote to the partners stating that he intended to open an enquiry into their returns, and the partnership return, for the year ending 5 April 2003. The partners appealed to the General Commissioners, who held that the effect of the May 2004 agreement was that it was not possible for the Revenue to open a further enquiry for the year ending April 2003. The Revenue applied to the QB for an order quashing the Commissioners' decision. The QB granted the Revenue's application, holding that the true interpretation of the May 2004 agreement was that the sum of £525,000 was payable in respect of liabilities and potential liabilities which were specified in a schedule to the agreement. In respect of the two partners, the liability specified under the schedule was all their actual or potential liabilities for the tax years between 1998/99 and 2001/02. However for the year 2002/03 the liability under the agreement was restricted to actual or potential liabilities arising from the affairs of two specific named companies. *R (oao HMRC) v Berkshire Commrs*, QB 2007, [2008] STC 1494; [2007] EWHC 871 (Admin). (*Note*. For subsequent developments in this case, see *R & S Thomas v HMRC (Nos 2 & 3)*, **4.99** and **4.380** APPEALS.)

[29.125] The Revenue began an investigation into a Scottish company (S), covering the period from 1998 to 2001. This investigation was settled by a contract settlement in early 2004, under which S paid tax of £525,000. Later in 2004 HMRC began an enquiry into S's returns for 2002 and 2003 (in which

S claimed relief for amortisation of goodwill). In 2006 HMRC also began an enquiry into S's returns for 2004 and 2005 (in respect of which S had submitted a covering letter claiming terminal loss relief). In 2011 HMRC issued closure notices rejecting S's claims. S appealed, contending as a preliminary point that its claim to terminal loss relief had become final and conclusive. Judge Mosedale rejected this contention, finding that HMRC had issued a closure notice rejecting the claim, and the Upper Tribunal dismissed S's appeal against this decision. Warren J upheld Judge Mosedale's decision that there should be a further hearing before the First-tier Tribunal to consider the substantive appeals against the notices. *Spring Salmon & Seafood Ltd v HMRC (No 2)*, UT [2014] UKUT 488 (TCC). (*Notes.* (1) For a preliminary issue in this case, see **49.77** RETURNS AND INFORMATION. (2) For subsequent developments in this case, see **29.126** below.)

[29.126] In the case noted at **29.125** above, HMRC discovered that the company (S) had failed to account for PAYE and NIC on a retrospective bonus of £900,000 which it had awarded to its controlling directors (or on smaller bonuses awarded to their wives), and issued determinations under *reg 80* of the *Income Tax (PAYE) Regulations (SI 2003/2682)*. The First-tier Tribunal upheld the determinations. Judge Reid held that 'there has been a loss of tax deliberately brought about by the company'. With regard to the NIC determinations, he held that the time limits of *TMA, s 36* did not apply, but that the effect of the *Prescription & Limitation (Scotland) Act 1973, s 7* was that the relevant time limit was 20 years. *Spring Salmon & Seafood Ltd v HMRC (No 3)*, FTT [2014] UKFTT 887 (TC), TC04002.

[29.127] HMRC began an enquiry into the tax returns submitted by a contractor (H), and formed the opinion that he had understated his profits. They agreed a settlement covering income tax and Class 4 national insurance contributions. The officer conducting the enquiry observed that H had failed to deduct tax from certain payments to subcontractors, and told H that this would be dealt with separately. Subsequently HMRC issued determinations under *Income Tax (Construction Industry Scheme) Regulations 2005 (SI 2005/2045), reg 13*, and imposed penalties under *TMA, s 98A*. H appealed against the determinations and penalties, contending that these liabilities should have been included in the negotiated settlement which had previously been agreed. The First-Tier Tribunal rejected this contention and dismissed H's appeal, noting that the wording of the negotiated settlement made it clear that it dealt with H's personal income tax and national insurance contributions. Judge Blewitt observed that 'it would be an affront to common sense to interpret the wording as including liabilities arising under a wholly separate regime, governed by different legislation, which had not been the subject of the enquiry, which had played no part in negotiations between the parties and to which no reference is made within the document'. The settlement did not preclude HMRC 'from taking any further action in respect of separate tax outstanding'. *S Hughes v HMRC*, FTT [2010] UKFTT 589 (TC), TC00839.

HMRC seeking to resile from negotiated settlement

[29.128] In February 2002 a company director (C) was offered the opportunity to invest in a property development company (S). He borrowed

£1,000,000 from a finance company (T) and subscribed for a £1,000,000 loan note in S. On 5 April 2002 C made a payment of £899,995 to T, which was described as a prepayment of interest due on the loan (which had been expressed as lasting for 30 years). On his 2001/02 tax return, he claimed tax relief on the basis that this was a payment of interest. HMRC rejected the claim on the basis that the payment was partly of capital rather than interest, and issued an amendment to C's return. C appealed. In the meantime, C had entered into a similar transaction and made a similar payment, also described as a prepayment of interest, in March 2003. C claimed relief for this payment in his 2002/03 return, and HMRC began an enquiry. Following negotiations, a meeting took place between C, his professional advisers, and two HMRC officers in November 2005. One of the HMRC officers proposed a compromise agreement whereby relief should be given for 50% of the disputed payments in the tax years in which they were made, with relief for the remaining 50% being spread over the life of the loans. Later that month HMRC sent a draft agreement, on these lines, to C's solicitors. In December 2005 C sent a signed copy of the agreement to HMRC, and paid £404,258 to HMRC in accordance with the agreement. HMRC formally accepted C's offer in November 2007. Meanwhile, C had entered into similar transactions in 2006/07, and had made a payment of £2,594,028, again as a prepayment of interest due on a 30-year loan, on 4 April 2007. On his 2006/07 tax return, C claimed tax relief on the basis that this was a payment of interest. HMRC began a further enquiry into this return. They subsequently issued a closure notice rejecting the claim, and in January 2009 they issued discovery assessments for 2001/02 to 2005/06 under *TMA, s 36*, resiling from the previous agreement on the grounds that there had been a 'material non-disclosure'. C appealed, contending firstly that the payments were genuine prepayments of interest, and alternatively that the effect of the agreement reached in December 2005 was that the discovery assessments were invalid. The First-tier Tribunal reviewed the evidence in detail, accepted both these contentions and allowed C's appeals. Judge Berner accepted C's contention that he had decided to make the prepayments 'on investment grounds, whilst appreciating that tax is an element in calculating the value of any investment decision'. The payments were of interest rather than capital, and were not paid at 'a rate in excess of a reasonable commercial rate'. Furthermore, the 'discovery assessment' for 2001/02 was invalid because the assessment for that year had been settled by an agreement under *TMA, s 54*. The liability for subsequent years had not been agreed under *s 54*, but HMRC were still bound by the settlement agreement which they had reached in December 2005 relating to the transactions in April 2002 and March 2003. The December 2005 agreement had not included any requirement for C to give any undertaking not to enter into similar subsequent transactions, and C's failure to mention that he was contemplating entering similar transactions in the future did not mean that the agreement could be treated as void. *GP Curran v HMRC (No 1)*, FTT [2012] UKFTT 517 (TC), TC02194. (*Note*. For the award of costs in this case, see **4.427** APPEALS.)

Whether settlement permissible during bankruptcy

[29.129] See *Re Hurren*, 6.35 BANKRUPTCY AND PERSONAL INSOLVENCY.

Negotiated agreement—joint and several liability

[29.130] Following an investigation, in 1986 the Revenue entered into an agreement with three companies and a director of those companies, whereby the companies and the director became jointly and severally liable to pay a sum in settlement of tax, interest and penalties by instalments. After a small amount had been paid, the companies went into administrative receivership. The Revenue did not claim as a preferential creditor of the companies, but took proceedings to recover the balance of the amount due from the director. The QB granted judgment for the Revenue, and the director appealed, contending that he was a surety and that the Revenue's failure to make a preferential claim was prejudicial to his interests. The CA dismissed the director's appeal. The making of the agreement gave the Revenue the right to sue for the sums due under that agreement, rather than for the tax previously assessed on the companies. Since the sums due under the agreement were not tax assessed on the companies, the Revenue could not rank as a preferential creditor in respect of them, and was obliged to seek recovery from the director. *CIR v Woollen*, CA 1992, 65 TC 229; [1992] STC 944.

Miscellaneous

Payment to informer

[29.131] The Revenue made an ex gratia payment of £250 to an informer in accordance with *IRRA 1890, s 32*. He alleged that a senior Revenue inspector had agreed that he should be paid 10% of any sums recovered by the Revenue as a result of his information, and brought an action claiming a further £29,750. The CS dismissed his action (by a 3-1 majority, Lord Clyde dissenting). Lord Blackburn held that *IRRA 1890* did not give the Revenue the power 'to enter into a bargain with an informer *ab ante* that he should be awarded a percentage of the sums which might be recovered eventually'. *Riach v Lord Advocate*, CS 1931, 18 TC 18.

[29.132] The Revenue made ex gratia payments totalling £7,465 to an informer in accordance with *IRRA 1890, s 32*. He applied for judicial review, contending that he should have received a further payment as a reward for giving further information. The QB dismissed his application. Munby J held that the Revenue's policy with regard to informers complied with 'the requirements of rationality and reasonableness'. The applicant had no grounds for any 'legitimate expectation' that he would receive a larger reward. *R (oao Churchhouse) v CIR*, QB 2003, 75 TC 231; [2003] STC 629; [2003] EWHC 681 (Admin).

New evidence advanced in High Court

[29.133] See *R v Great Yarmouth Commrs (ex p. Amis)*, 4.211 APPEALS, and *Frowd v Whalley*, 4.212 APPEALS.

Admissibility of Revenue capital statements as evidence

[29.134] See *Johnson v Scott*, 4.54 APPEALS.

Appellant seeking remission of Case Stated for amendment

[29.135] See *Fen Farming Co Ltd v Dunsford*, 4.200 APPEALS, and *Hurley v Taylor*, 29.47 above.

Application for prerogative order following new evidence

[29.136] See *R v Great Yarmouth Commrs (ex p. Amis)*, 4.211 APPEALS.

Additional assessments—whether any discovery

[29.137] See *Young v Duthie*, 5.79 ASSESSMENTS.

Whether inspector entitled to review nominal ledger

[29.138] In an Irish case, an inspector asked to see a taxpayer's accounting records, including any nominal ledger. The accountant refused to produce the nominal ledger, contending that it was a working paper belonging to him and was not in the power or possession of the taxpayer. Carroll J held that the inspector was entitled to review the nominal ledger, and the Irish Supreme Court upheld this decision. In writing up the ledger, the accountant was acting as an agent of the taxpayer, rather than as an auditor. The accountant was not entitled to regard the ledger as his private property. The nominal ledger was 'within the possession or power' of the taxpayer, and in the circumstances of the case no reasonable person could come to a conclusion about the taxpayer's liability in the absence of records which would show what adjustments had been made in preparing the accounts, and why such adjustments had been made. *Quigley v Burke*, SC(I) 1995, 5 ITR 265.

Validity of action under TMA, s 20C

[29.139] See the cases noted at 49.63 to 49.65 RETURNS AND INFORMATION.

Failure to notify liability under CTA 2010, s 455

[29.140] See *Earlspring Properties Ltd v Guest*, 11.4 CLOSE COMPANIES; *Joint v Bracken Developments Ltd*, 11.5 CLOSE COMPANIES, and *Khera's Emporium Ltd v Marshall*, 11.7 CLOSE COMPANIES.

FA 1998, Sch 18 para 24—Revenue enquiry into company return

[29.141] See *R (oao Spring Salmon & Seafood Ltd) v CIR*, 49.72 RETURNS AND INFORMATION.

30

Higher Rate Liability

The cases in this chapter are arranged under the following headings.

GENERAL NOTE

From 1909/10 to 1973/74 income tax was charged at a standard rate, and supertax or surtax was charged on additional income above a certain amount. The legislation was radically amended with effect from 1973/74 by *FA 1971*, to allow for income tax to be charged at a basic rate, and at higher rates on income above certain limits. The majority of the cases in this chapter are appeals against assessments to supertax or surtax which do not fall under any other heading in this book and which appear to be applicable, *mutatis mutandis*, to higher rate liability. For surtax appeals under other headings, see in particular **2** ANNUAL PAYMENTS, **3** ANTI-AVOIDANCE, **19** DECEASED PERSONS and **56** SETTLEMENTS. For the additional rate imposed by *ITA 2007, s 479* on certain discretionary trust income, see **56.101** *et seq.* SETTLEMENTS.

Taxable income

General

Bonus issue of shares

[30.1] The Revenue issued supertax assessments on shareholders who had received bonus issues of shares. The Special Commissioners allowed the shareholders' appeals and the HL upheld this decision (by a 3–2 majority, Lords Dunedin and Sumner dissenting), holding that a bonus issue of shares by a public company was not income of the shareholders. *CIR v Blott; CIR v Greenwood*, HL 1921, 8 TC 101; [1921] 2 AC 171. (*Note*. See now *CTA 2010, ss 1022, 1023* for bonus issues following a repayment of share capital.)

[30.2] The decision in *CIR v Blott*, **30.1** above, was applied in a subsequent case in which a shareholder received a bonus in the form of debentures. Lord Cave observed that the company had 'elected definitively and irrevocably not to distribute the fund as income, but to impound and apply it as income-producing capital', and that election was binding on the shareholders. *CIR v Fisher's Executors*, HL 1926, 10 TC 302. (*Note*. *Obiter dicta* of Lord Sumner were disapproved in the subsequent case of *Aykroyd v CIR*, **3.56** ANTI-AVOIDANCE.)

[30.3] A similar decision, also applying *CIR v Blott*, **30.1** above, was reached in *Whitmore v CIR*, KB 1925, 10 TC 645.

[30.4] The decision in *CIR v Blott*, **30.1** above, was applied in a similar subsequent case in which the shareholder had an option to receive cash rather than bonus shares, but chose to receive bonus shares. *CIR v Wright*, CA 1926, 11 TC 181.

Distributions from reserves of private company

[30.5] A private company made distributions from a reserve fund to its directors' loan accounts. The Revenue issued assessments charging supertax on the amounts distributed. The KB upheld the assessments, holding that the distributions were income of the directors. *CIR v Doncaster*, KB 1924, 8 TC 623.

Capital distributions on company liquidation

[30.6] Several family companies were put into voluntary liquidation, and the Revenue issued assessments charging supertax on the amounts distributed to the shareholders. The Special Commissioners allowed the shareholders' appeals, holding that the distributions were capital rather than income, and the CA upheld this decision. *CIR v Burrell (and related appeal)*, CA 1924, 9 TC 27.

Shares in subsidiary distributed to shareholders in parent company

[30.7] The shares in a subsidiary company were distributed among the shareholders in the parent company (N). One of the shareholders appealed against a supertax assessment, contending that the distribution was capital. The Special Commissioners held that, to the extent that N had acquired the shares out of accumulated profits, they were income liable to supertax. The KB upheld this decision. *Wilkinson v CIR*, KB 1931, 16 TC 52.

[30.8] A similar decision was reached in *Briggs v CIR*, KB 1932, 17 TC 11.

[30.9] In a Trinidad and Tobago case, a company went into voluntary liquidation in 1976. In 1978 its controlling shareholder received substantial payments out of the proceeds of the liquidation, most of which represented the realisation of work in progress. He appealed against income tax assessments in respect of these payments, contending that they were distributions of capital and were not taxable. The Privy Council rejected this contention and dismissed his appeal. Lord Millett observed that 'it is a commonplace that what is capital in the hands of the payer may be income in the hands of the recipient'. *Singh v Trinidad & Tobago Board of Inland Revenue*, PC [2000] STC 255; [2000] 1 WLR 1421.

Income applied to repay a loan

[30.10] A married woman borrowed money from an insurance company and gave as security a life policy, shares which she had purchased from her husband with the loan, and her life interest under her marriage settlement. Her husband appealed against a supertax assessment, contending that he was only liable to supertax on the dividends on the shares to the extent that they exceeded the aggregate of the premium on the policy and the interest and capital repayments due under the terms of the loan. The CA unanimously rejected this contention and upheld the assessment. *CIR v Paterson*, CA 1924, 9 TC 163.

[30.11] A shareholder appealed against a supertax assessment, contending that income which he had applied in reducing a mortgage on shares should be excluded from his income. The Special Commisioners rejected this contention and dismissed his appeal, and the KB upheld their decision. *Perkins' Executor v CIR*, KB 1928, 13 TC 851.

Income applied in payment of insurance premiums

[30.12] Lord Wolverton mortgaged the income from property of which he was life tenant, giving life insurance policies, the premiums on which were to be first charges on the income, as security. The Revenue issued a supertax assessment charging tax on the amounts applied in payment of the premiums. The CA allowed Lord Wolverton's appeal (by a 2–1 majority), and the HL upheld this decision. *Lord Wolverton v CIR*, HL 1931, 16 TC 467.

Taxed interest for period spanning date of sale of securities

[30.13] Registered Notes in a company were sold on the day before the half-yearly interest was payable. The vendor received the interest but passed it to the purchaser under Stock Exchange rules. The KB held that the whole of the interest was income of the purchaser. *CIR v Oakley*, KB 1925, 9 TC 582. (*Note*. The case was heard with *Wigmore v Thomas Summerson & Sons Ltd*, 52.14 SAVINGS AND INVESTMENT INCOME.)

Dividends on shares—transfer delayed

[30.14] A shareholder's will left some shares to his son (H), but there was a delay in transferring them. Meanwhile, dividends on the shares had been paid to the executors, who paid them to H when the shares were transferred. The Revenue issued supertax assessments on the basis that the dividends which the executors had received were H's income. The KB upheld the assessments. *CIR v Hawley*, KB 1927, 13 TC 327; [1928] 1 KB 578.

Dividends on shares contingently subject to transfer

[30.15] A company's controlling shareholder (P) instituted a scheme to give certain employees a closer interest in the company. Shares which P owned were transferred to the employees when dividends on the shares, plus any payment made by the employees, equalled the par value of the shares. The CA held that the dividends were income of P until the actual transfer of the shares to the employees. *CIR v Parsons*, CA 1928, 13 TC 700.

Dividends on shares sold and later recovered

[30.16] A shareholder (S) contracted to sell certain shares and transferred them to the purchaser (C). S subsequently alleged that C had been guilty of fraudulent misrepresentation, and obtained a court order under which the shares were transferred back to S, with an amount equal to the dividends which C had received while the shares were in his name. The Revenue included the dividends in surtax assessments on S. The CS unanimously upheld the assessments. *Spence v CIR*, CS 1941, 24 TC 311.

Interim dividend—date on which assessable

[30.17] On 31 March 1965 a company's directors declared an interim dividend, which was paid in May 1965. The Revenue included the amount of the dividend in surtax assessments for 1965/66. Two of the shareholders appealed, contending that the dividends should be treated as income for 1964/65, rather than for 1965/66. The Special Commissioners dismissed the appeals and the Ch D upheld their decisions, holding that a resolution to pay an interim dividend did not create a debt before the dividend was paid. *Potel v CIR*; *Poteliakhoff v CIR*, Ch D 1970, 46 TC 658.

Patent royalties

[30.18] An engineer had granted a company (C) a licence to use certain patent rights. He appealed against surtax assessments on the royalties he received from C. The CA unanimously dismissed his appeals. *Kirke v CIR*, CA 1944, 26 TC 208. (*Note*. See also *ITA 2007, s 844*.)

Balancing charge on sale of plant

[30.19] A farmer sold his farm, together with its plant and machinery. The Revenue included a balancing charge on the sale of the plant in a surtax assessment on him. The Ch D upheld the assessment. *CIR v Lloyds Bank Ltd & Another (Scott's Executors)*, Ch D 1963, 41 TC 294.

Sale of shares with promise of dividends

[30.20] A shareholder (B) held 96% of the ordinary shares of a company (E), which was in a position to declare a dividend of £100,000 out of accumulated profits. In March 1933 he sold the shares for £75 each, with a promise that a dividend would be paid. (He could fulfil this promise as he controlled E by virtue of voting rights attached to preference shares which he held.) On 28 March 1933 a dividend of £50 per share was declared for the year ended 30 April 1932, and a similar dividend was declared on 18 April 1933 for the year ended 30 April 1933. The Revenue included the dividends on the transferred shares in a surtax assessment on B for 1932/33. The KB allowed B's appeal, holding that he had no beneficial interest in the dividends. *Bilsland v CIR*, KB 1936, 20 TC 446; [1936] 2 KB 542; [1936] 2 All ER 616.

ITEPA 2003, s 225—payment to barrister ceasing practice

[30.21] A barrister with an extensive practice agreed to take employment with a company (G). He covenanted to cease his practice, and G covenanted to pay him £40,000 as an inducement to him to give up his status as a practising barrister. The Revenue accepted that the payment was not taxable on him as income from his new employment, but assessed him to surtax on the basis that what is now *ITEPA 2003, s 225* applied. The Ch D allowed his appeal, holding that *s 225* did not apply, since the payment had been made to induce him to accept the professional and social consequences flowing from his taking up employment. It was not in respect of his undertaking to cease practice, for that was inevitable under the Bar's professional code of conduct. *Vaughan-Neil v CIR*, Ch D 1979, 54 TC 223; [1979] STC 644; [1979] 1 WLR 1283; [1979] 3 All ER 481.

Ownership of income in dispute

[30.22] A married couple separated, and disputed the ownership of certain securities deposited with a bank. Eventually, one half was transferred to each, together with one half of the income which had accumulated during the dispute. The Revenue issued surtax assessments on the wife's share of the accumulated income. The Special Commissioners and the KB upheld the assessments. *Shenley v CIR*, KB 1945, 27 TC 85.

Partnership profits held in suspense pending future contingency

[30.23] A member of a partnership (FF), who had been entitled to 14% of the partnership profits, died in 1918 and nominated his son (AF) as his successor. Under the partnership agreement, the allocation of this 14% of the profits after FF's death depended on whether the other partners agreed to accept AF as a partner. They reached no decision on this until 1926, when they decided not to accept AF. The Revenue then made supertax assessments on two of the partners on their shares of the 14%, for the years in which the profits had been earned. The KB allowed their appeals and discharged the assessments. Rowlatt J held that, before 1926, the partners' entitlement to the income had been subject to a future contingency. *Franklin v CIR; Swaythling's Executors v CIR*, KB 1930, 15 TC 464.

Income due but not received

Mortgage interest due but not received—borrower in receivership

[30.24] In 1926 an individual (L) lent money to a firm, which gave him a mortgage over some land which it leased as security for the loan. The firm did not pay any mortgage interest after 1929, and went into receivership in March 1931. The Revenue issued a surtax assessment on L for 1930/31, charging tax on the full amount of interest due under the mortgage agreement. The KB allowed L's appeal. Finlay J held that, as none of the interest had been paid, none of it should be included in the computation of L's total taxable income. *Lambe v CIR*, KB 1933, 18 TC 212; [1934] 1 KB 178.

Interest paid in arrear

[30.25] An individual (L) purchased mortgage bonds issued by a Canadian company, on which no interest had been paid for several years. The interest was subsequently paid in arrears. The Revenue issued a supertax assessment on the basis that the arrears of interest formed part of L's total income for the year in which he received them. The Special Commissioners upheld the assessment and the KB dismissed L's appeal. *Leigh v CIR*, KB 1927, 11 TC 590.

[30.26] A private company had failed to pay interest on debentures which it had issued. In 1920, the holders agreed to the cancellation of the debentures and entered into an arrangement under which arrears of interest should be paid if the company's funds permitted. In 1929/30, a debenture-holder (C) received a payment from which tax was deducted at the rate of tax in force at the time, representing arrears of interest for periods back to 1910. The Revenue assessed C to surtax on the amount for 1929/30. His executors appealed. The Special Commissioners upheld the assessment and the CA unanimously dismissed the executors' appeal, holding that the interest became payable in 1929/30 under the terms of the arrangement made in 1920. *Champneys' Executors v CIR*, CA 1934, 19 TC 375.

Income exigible but not claimed

[30.27] An individual (D) was bequeathed a substantial legacy under his uncle's will. Part of his legacy was not paid. He was entitled by law to interest on the unpaid amount but, for the relevant years, had neither received any interest nor elected whether or not to claim it. The Revenue issued an assessment charging surtax on the interest to which D was entitled. The KB allowed his appeal and the CA unanimously upheld this decision, holding that, as D had not received any interest, it could not be included in his total income. Romer LJ held that 'the truth of the matter here is that no one owes a duty to the State to maintain his assessment for surtax at the highest possible figure. If a subject thinks proper so to do he assuredly may get rid of an income-bearing security for the purposes of avoiding the addition of the income from that security to his assessment for surtax purposes.' *Dewar v CIR*, CA 1935, 19 TC 561; [1935] 2 KB 351.

[30.28] A company's controlling director (W) sold some property to the company, receiving an annuity as part of the consideration. From 1928/29 to 1930/31 he did not call on the company to pay the annuity in full, although it had ample funds with which to pay it. The Revenue issued surtax assessments on the basis that W was taxable on the full amount of the annuity. The KB allowed W's appeal, applying the principles laid down in *Dewar v CIR*, **30.27** above. Lawrence J held that W was only assessable to surtax on the amounts which he actually received. *Woodhouse v CIR*, KB 1936, 20 TC 673.

[30.29] One of the members of a partnership, which carried on a manufacturing business, died in 1907. A share of the partnership profits was payable to his trustees, and by them to his widow (L). The payments by the partnership fell into arrear. The Revenue issued a surtax assessment on L for 1938/39, charging tax on an amount representing the share of the profits due to her for that year, which had not actually been paid. She appealed. The Special Commissioners allowed her appeal and the CA unanimously upheld their decision, holding that she was not a partner and that her share of the profits did not form part of her income for surtax until it was paid to her. *CIR v Lebus's Executors*, CA 1946, 27 TC 136; [1946] 1 All ER 476.

Interest on unpaid moneys—purchaser defaults

[30.30] See *St Lucia Usines & Estates Co Ltd v Colonial Treasurer of St Lucia*, 52.23 SAVINGS AND INVESTMENT INCOME.

Interest paid by cheque—period for which assessable

[30.31] See *Parkside Leasing Ltd v Smith*, 52.37 SAVINGS AND INVESTMENT INCOME.

Shareholder refusing to accept dividends tendered

[30.32] A company (C) made a successful takeover bid for the stock of another company (B). One of B's stockholders (D) objected to the takeover. She was compelled to transfer her stock to C, but she refused to accept the consideration (cash and shares in C) or subsequent dividends from C. These were accordingly allotted or paid to B, which held them in trust for her and credited the cash it received to a deposit account in her name. The Revenue issued surtax assessments on D, including the dividends and interest credited to her. The Special Commissioners upheld the assessments, holding on the evidence that D had not 'alienated her title to the capital or the dividends in dispute'. The Ch D dismissed D's appeal. *Dreyfus v CIR*, Ch D 1963, 41 TC 441. (*Note*. The appellant appeared in person.)

Deductions in computing total income

CROSS-REFERENCE

For annual payments deductible from total income, see **2.1** et seq. ANNUAL PAYMENTS.

General

[30.33] A solicitor claimed that 'short interest', paid to a company which was not carrying on a banking business, should be allowed as a deduction in computing his total income for surtax purposes. The HL unanimously rejected this contention, holding that the interest was not deductible. *CIR v Frere*, HL 1964, 42 TC 125; [1965] AC 402; [1964] 3 All ER 796.

Amounts borrowed to make good deficiency in residuary income

[30.34] An individual (B) died in 1924. He bequeathed his residuary estate to trustees, directing them to pay an annuity his widow, and to hold the residue in trust for his two sons. The income of the estate proved insufficient to meet the annuity and the trustees borrowed from a bank to meet the deficiency. One of B's sons claimed that his share of the amounts borrowed should be deducted in computing his total income for surtax. The CA unanimously rejected his claim, holding that the amount was not deductible. Lord Wright observed that the son was under no 'personal liability of any sort or kind' to make the payments. *Bowen v CIR*, CA 1937, 21 TC 93; [1937] 1 All ER 607.

Expenses of curator bonis

[30.35] The Court of Session appointed a *curator bonis* to look after the affairs of a ward of court (an *incapax*). The Revenue assessed the *curator bonis* to surtax on the ward's income. He claimed a deduction for his administration expenses. The CS unanimously rejected the claim, holding that the ward retained his vested interest in his income, and that the *curator bonis* was merely administering the estate on his behalf. Lord Clyde held that 'the fees and charges incurred in managing the estate do not fall to be considered in ascertaining the income of the *incapax* for surtax purposes'. *CIR v McIntosh (curator bonis to McMillan)*, CS 1955, 36 TC 334.

Non-residents

Liability of non-resident on UK income

[30.36] A married woman had separated from her husband and lived outside the UK from 1908 to 1914, when she returned to England after the outbreak of the First World War. The Revenue issued a supertax assessment for 1911/12 on her UK income. She appealed, contending that she was not liable to supertax for that year because she had not been resident in the UK. The Special Commissioners rejected this contention and dismissed her appeal, and the CA unanimously upheld their decision. *Brooke v CIR*, CA 1917, 7 TC 261; [1918] 1 KB 257.

31

Human Rights

The cases in this chapter are arranged under the following headings.

The *European Convention for the Protection of Human Rights* was adopted in 1950, as a treaty of the Council of Europe. (This body predates, and is entirely separate from, the European Community which originates from the 1957 Treaty of Rome.) *Article 1* of the *First Protocol of the European Convention* provides that 'every natural or legal person is entitled to the peaceful enjoyment of his possessions' but goes on to add that 'the preceding provisions shall not . . . in any way impair the right of a State to enforce such laws as it deems necessary to control the use of property in accordance with the general interest or to secure the payment of tax or other contributions and penalties'. The Convention is recognised as part of European Community law by *article 6* of the *1997 Treaty of Amsterdam*. For discussions of the *Convention* and its impact on UK tax law, see the article by Christopher Wallworth in 'Taxation', 15 June 2000, pp 284–287, and the detailed article by Philip Baker in British Tax Review 2000, pp 211–377.

The right to life (Article 2)

Distraint proceedings—whether any breach of Convention

[31.1] In a Polish case, a trader (L) paid outstanding social security contributions in 1994. However, the local tax office subsequently continued to threaten collection proceedings. On 29 January 1996 two bailiffs visited his flat, spoke to L's wife, and threatened to seize his property. The bailiffs subsequently left without executing distraint, and on the following day L visited the tax office and proved that he had paid the outstanding contributions. On 25 February L's wife died. L complained to the District Prosecutor, claiming that 'his wife's death had resulted from the stress caused by the actions of the bailiffs'. The District Prosecutor rejected the complaint, finding that 'it was impossible to establish the existence of a causal link between the bailiffs' actions and the death of (L's) wife'. L lodged an application with the ECHR, contending that the bailiffs' visit had been a breach of *Article 2* of the *European Convention on Human Rights*. The ECHR rejected this contention and dismissed the application, finding that the evidence 'did not show the existence of a causal link between the actions of the bailiffs and the death of the applicant's wife'. *Lewandowski v Poland*, ECHR Case 43457/98, 15 June 1999 unreported.

The prohibition of torture and degrading punishment (Article 3)

Whether company director assaulted by tax inspector

[31.2] In a Ukrainian case, a company director (K) was required to visit a senior tax inspector. He took a tape recorder to the meeting. K alleged that when the inspector discovered this, he assaulted him and broke the tape recorder. K was subsequently treated in hospital for head injuries. The Regional Prosecutor's Office began a criminal investigation into the alleged incident, but the investigation was ended on the grounds that there was insufficient evidence as to whether the inspector was responsible for K's injuries. K subsequently lodged an application with the ECHR, contending that his treatment by the tax inspector had contravened *Article 3* of the *European Convention on Human Rights* (which provides that 'no one shall be subjected to torture or to inhuman or degrading treatment or punishment'). The ECHR held (by a 6-1 majority) that K had not proved 'beyond reasonable doubt' that the inspector had caused his injuries, so that there had been 'no violation of the substantive limb of *Article 3*'. However the ECHR also held that the Ukrainian authorities had failed to instigate 'an effective official investigation' into K's complaints, so that there had been 'a violation of the procedural limb of *Article 3*'. The ECHR ordered the Ukrainian government to pay K compensation of €2,000 plus costs and expenses of €237. *Kozinets v Ukraine*, ECHR Case 75520/01; 6 December 2007 unreported.

Imprisonment of tax evader—prison conditions

[31.3] In a Romanian case, an individual (P) was convicted of tax evasion and forgery, and was sentenced to six and a half years' imprisonment. After some breaches of prison discipline, he was transferred to a high security prison for prisoners deemed to be dangerous, and was kept in a dormitory which he shared with 53 other prisoners. After his release, he lodged a complaint with the ECHR, contending that the conditions of his imprisonment had constituted a breach of *Article 3* of the *European Convention on Human Rights*. The ECHR granted the application, observing that it had 'frequently found a violation of *Article 3* of the *Convention* on account of the lack of personal space afforded to detainees'. Although there was 'no indication that there was a positive intention of humiliating or debasing the applicant', the absence of any such purpose could not 'exclude a finding of a violation of *Article 3*'. The ECHR ordered the Romanian government to pay P compensation of €3,000. *Petrea v Romania*, ECHR Case 4792/03; 29 April 2008 unreported.

The prohibition of forced labour (Article 4)

Obligation to deduct PAYE—whether a breach of Convention

[31.4] In an Austrian case, four companies applied to the ECHR, contending that the obligation to deduct PAYE from their employees' salaries contravened *Article 4* of the *European Convention on Human Rights*. The ECHR rejected this contention and dismissed the applications, holding that the operation of PAYE was 'part of normal civic obligations'. *Companies W, X, Y and Z v Austria*, ECHR Case 7427/76; 7 ECDR 148.

Penalties for failure to comply with notice under TMA 1970, s 19A

[31.5] See *Murat v CIR*, 44.346 PENALTIES.

Penalties for failure to comply with notice under TMA 1970, s 20

[31.6] In the case noted at 44.355 PENALTIES, General Commissioners imposed a penalty on an individual (P) who had failed to comply with a notice under *TMA 1970, s 20C*. P appealed to the CA, contending that the imposition of the penalty was a breach of *Article 4* of the *European Convention on Human Rights*. The CA unanimously rejected this contention and dismissed the appeal. Peter Gibson LJ described P's contentions as 'wholly fanciful'. *Patrick v CIR (No 2)*, CA [2002] EWCA Civ 1649.

The right to liberty and security (Article 5)

Imprisonment for failure to pay council tax

[31.7] Several UK citizens, who had served terms of imprisonment for failure to pay council tax, applied to the ECHR, contending that their imprisonment had been a breach of *Article 5* of the *European Convention on Human Rights*. The ECHR reviewed the evidence in detail and accepted this contention, holding that 'a period of detention will in principle be lawful if it is carried out pursuant to a court order. A subsequent finding that the court erred under domestic law in making the order will not necessarily retrospectively affect the validity of the intervening period of detention. For this reason, the Strasbourg organs have consistently refused to uphold applications from persons convicted of criminal offences who complain that their convictions or sentences were found by the appellate courts to have been based on errors of fact or law.'

However, on the evidence, in several of the cases concerned the magistrates had acted in excess of their jurisdiction. In some cases, the magistrates had failed to make any enquiry into the applicants' ability to pay the tax. In two cases, they had failed to ensure that people aged under 21 had been given the opportunity to be legally represented. In several cases, the magistrates had committed applicants to prison in their absence, without adequate evidence that the applicants had received proper notice of the hearing. There had therefore been breaches of *Article 5(1)* of the *Convention*. Furthermore, the fact that there was 'no enforceable right to compensation in domestic law' meant that there had also been breaches of *Article 5(5)*. The ECHR ordered the UK Government to pay them compensation ranging from €5,000 to €9,000. *Lloyd & Others v United Kingdom*, ECHR Case 29798/96; [2005] All ER (D) 17 (Mar).

Imprisonment of suspected tax evader

[31.8] In a Czech case, an individual (F) was charged with tax evasion in May 1996, and was remanded in custody. He remained in custody until May 1998, when he was convicted of tax evasion and sentenced to 18 months' imprisonment. Since he had already spent two years in custody, he was released. He applied to the ECHR for a ruling that the length of time in which he had been held in custody before his trial had been unreasonable, and had been a breach of *Article 5* of the *European Convention on Human Rights*. The ECHR granted his application, holding that there was insufficient reason to justify the length of time for which F had been held in custody, and that there had been a breach of *Article 5(3)* and *(4)*. *Fešar v Czech Republic*, ECHR Case 76576/01; [2008] ECHR 1436.

[31.9] In a Polish case, an individual (G) was charged with tax evasion in April 2005, and was remanded in custody. He remained in custody until April 2008, when he was released on bail on payment of 300,000 Polish zlotys. He applied to the ECHR for a ruling that the length of time in which he had been held in custody before his trial had been unreasonable, and had been a breach of *Article 5* of the *European Convention on Human Rights*. The ECHR granted his application, holding that there was insufficient reason to justify the length of time for which he had been held in custody, and that there had been a breach of *Article 5(3)*. The ECHR awarded G damages of €2,000. *Godysz v Poland*, ECHR Case 46949/07; 28 April 2009 unreported.

[31.10] In *OAO Neftyanaka Kompaniya Yukos v Russia*, **31.111** below, the Russian tax authority formed the opinion that an oil company (N) had a large tax liability for 2000, and ordered it to pay tax arrears of more than €1,000,000,000 and a penalty of more than €500,000,000. N failed to pay, and the Moscow City Commercial Court gave judgment for the tax authority. One of N's directors (L) was arrested, charged with tax evasion and remanded in custody. He was convicted at a trial in 2005 and sentenced to eight years' imprisonment. While in prison, he took proceedings in the ECHR, contending that his conviction and treatment was a breach of *Article 5* of the *European Convention on Human Rights*. The ECHR held that there had been a breach of *Article 5* with regard to the manner in which L had been detained after September 2004, but rejected other complaints made by L, and rejected

L's application for damages. *PL Lebedev v Russia*, ECHR Case 13772/05; 25 July 2013 unreported. (*Note*. The case was heard with *MB Khodorkovskiy v Russia (No 2)*, **31.58** below.)

Imprisonment for removing distrained asset

[31.11] In a Swedish case, the tax authority levied distraint on a mobile sawmill belonging to a trader (G) who owed €27,300 in tax. G subsequently removed the sawmill and refused to disclose its location. The Swedish Court of Appeal imprisoned G for failing to comply with an injunction. He was released after 42 days. He applied to the ECHR, contending that his imprisonment had been a breach of *Article 5* of the *European Convention on Human Rights*. The ECHR rejected this contention and dismissed his application, holding that his imprisonment had been 'proportionate to the legitimate aim to induce him to fulfil his legal obligation to cooperate with the authorities and give them the necessary information about his property so that they could secure the payment of his tax debt'. *Göthlin v Sweden*, ECHR Case 8307/11; 16 October 2014 unreported.

The right to a fair trial (Article 6)

Cases where the application was dismissed

Prosecution for tax evasion—whether any breach of Convention

[31.12] In a French case, a company's managing director (B) was convicted of evasion of tax. The court found that B had 'deliberately decided, with the aim of evading tax on part of the company's receipts, to conceal about 25% of the company's turnover by not entering it in the company's books'. B applied to the ECHR for a ruling that the conduct of the prosecution had been a breach of *Article 6* of the *European Convention on Human Rights*. The ECHR rejected this contention and dismissed the application, holding that 'having regard to the large number of offences of the kind referred to', Contracting States 'must be free to empower the Revenue to prosecute and punish them, even if the surcharges imposed as a penalty are large ones. Such a system is not incompatible with *Article 6* of the *Convention* so long as the taxpayer can bring any such decision affecting him before a court.' *Bendenoun v France*, ECHR Case 12547/86; 18 EHRR 54.

[31.13] In a Netherlands case, an individual (H) was arrested on suspicion of tax fraud in December 1983, and detained for four days. In 1985 he was charged with tax fraud and forgery. He appealed to the Amsterdam courts and subsequently to the Netherlands Supreme Court, which dismissed his appeal in June 1989. The criminal proceedings began in October 1989. In January 1990 H was convicted on three charges, fined, and given a suspended prison sentence. He again appealed, firstly to the Court of Appeal and subsequently to the Netherlands Supreme Court, which dismissed his appeal in June 1993. He then applied to the ECHR for a ruling that the proceedings had not been concluded within a reasonable time, and that this was a breach of *Article 6* of the *European Convention on Human Rights*. The ECHR rejected this contention, finding that the case had been 'complex' and that, by objecting to the indictment, H had contributed 'to the overall length of the proceedings to a considerable extent'. Accordingly, there had been no violation of H's 'right to a hearing within a reasonable time' and no breach of the *Convention*. *HH v Netherlands*, ECHR Case 23229/94; 1 July 1997 unreported.

[31.14] In a Finnish case, a company director was convicted of four charges of 'aggravated tax fraud', and sentenced to four years' imprisonment. He applied to the ECHR for a ruling that the conduct of the prosecution had been a breach of *Article 6* of the *European Convention on Human Rights*. The ECHR rejected this contention and dismissed the application. *K Uoti v Finland*, ECHR Case 21422/02; 25 October 2007 unreported.

[31.15] In a Swedish case, a taxi driver was convicted of tax evasion and sentenced to two months' imprisonment. The tax authority also imposed surcharges. The driver applied to the ECHR, contending that he had been punished twice for the same offence, and that this had been a breach of *Article 6* of the *European Convention on Human Rights*. The ECHR rejected this contention and dismissed the application, holding that his conviction for keeping incorrect records had required a finding of 'intent or negligence', and that 'these subjective elements are not a condition for the imposition of tax surcharges'. Accordingly, the court held that 'the two offences in question were sufficiently separate for it to conclude that the applicant was not punished twice for the same offence'. *K Carlberg v Sweden*, ECHR Case 9631/04; 27 January 2009 unreported.

[31.16] In a German case, an individual (S) was convicted of tax evasion and sentenced to nine months' imprisonment. The court specifically stated that the length of the sentence had been reduced to take account of a delay in bringing the case to trial. S applied to the ECHR, contending that the length of the proceedings had constituted a breach of *Article 6* of the *European Convention on Human Rights*. The ECHR rejected this contention and dismissed his application, finding that 'the domestic authorities have acknowledged the violation of the *Convention* and have provided sufficient redress by reducing the prison sentence in an express and measureable manner'. *Stein v Germany*, ECHR Case 12895/05; 7 July 2009 unreported.

[31.17] A Finnish citizen (E) lived in Sweden. He was convicted of aggravated tax fraud and sentenced to five years' imprisonment. He failed to pay the outstanding tax, and the Swedish authorities requested the assistance of the Finnish authorities. The Finnish authorities distrained a Mercedes car. E was subsequently convicted of fraud in Finland and sentenced to a further nineteen months' imprisonment. E applied to the ECHR, contending that the investigation by the Finnish authorities had contravened *Article 6* of the *European Convention on Human Rights*. The ECHR rejected this contention and dismissed the application. *K Elomaa v Finland*, ECHR Case 37670/04; 13 April 2010 unreported.

[31.18] See also *R v Allen*, 51.8 REVENUE PROSECUTIONS.

Penalties for failure to comply with notice under TMA 1970, s 19A

[31.19] See *Sharkey v De Croos*, 44.347 PENALTIES.

Penalty for failure to make returns—whether any breach of Convention

[31.20] In a Swedish case, the ECHR held that the imposition of penalties for failure to make tax returns did not involve any breach of *Article 6(1)* of the *European Convention on Human Rights. Rosenquist v Sweden*, ECHR Case 60619/00; 7 ITLR 270.

[31.21] See also *Mrs ME Pipe v HMRC*, 44.13 PENALTIES.

Surcharge—whether any breach of Convention

[31.22] In an Austrian case, the ECHR held that the imposition of a surcharge did not involve any breach of *Article 6* of the *European Convention on Human Rights. L Popovici v Austria*, ECHR Case 49598/07; 4 October 2011 unreported.

Investigation of company director—whether any breach of Convention

[31.23] In a Netherlands case, the tax authorities began enquiring into the affairs of two companies in 1981. The managing director of the companies was interrogated in 1984, and arrested on suspicion of fraud in 1985. After a prolonged investigation, he was convicted on five counts of fraud in 1989 and sentenced to a period of imprisonment. He appealed to the Court of Appeal, which upheld his conviction on three of the counts but acquitted him on the other two, and reduced the period of imprisonment to which he had been sentenced. He appealed again to the Supreme Court, which rejected his appeal in 1992. He lodged an application with the European Commission of Human Rights, contending that the length of the investigation had been unreasonable and was a breach of *Article 6* of the *European Convention on Human Rights.* The case was referred to the European Court of Human Rights, which held (by a 7-2 majority) that the length of the proceedings had not been unreasonable in the circumstances of the case, and that there had been no breach of the Convention. The Court observed that the judicial investigation appeared to have lasted 'a disturbingly long time'. However, the investigating judge had been 'confronted with the task of unravelling a network of interlocking companies and accounts which had been created in such a way as to make it as difficult as possible for the authorities to detect fraudulent tax and social security practices. To mount a case against the applicant the authorities had to take evidence from a substantial number of witnesses and collect and examine a very significant volume of materials. The undoubted scale and complexity of the investigation were further compounded by the involvement of other suspects in the fraud.' *Hozee v The Netherlands*, ECHR Case 21961/93, 22 May 1998 unreported.

[31.24] In a German case, a company director was accused of tax evasion by failing to declare commission payments relating to a deal for the sale of arms to Saudi Arabia. He was convicted and sentenced to five years' imprisonment. He applied to the ECHR, contending that the proceedings had been a breach of *Article 6* of the *European Convention on Human Rights*, in that he had been denied access to a file relating to alleged tax evasion by the company of which he was a director. The ECHR reviewed the evidence in detail and rejected his application, finding that 'the public prosecution authorities have taken into account the interests of the defence and the accused in their respective decisions and weighed them against the necessity to keep the file in the preliminary investigations secret'. The ECHR concluded that 'the rights of the defence were not restricted to an extent that is incompatible with the guarantees provided by *Article 6* of the *Convention*'. *Massmann v Germany*, ECHR Case 11603/06; 3 June 2010 unreported.

Investigation of dentist—whether any breach of Convention

[31.25] In a German case, the tax authorities discovered that a dentist (HM) had transferred substantial amounts of money to Luxembourg. In March 1996 they began criminal proceedings against her, and in October 1996 they ordered the provisional attachment of some of her goods. HM moved abroad, and her lawyer applied to the ECHR, contending that the investigation was a breach of *Article 6* of the *European Convention on Human Rights*. The ECHR rejected this contention and dismissed the application, observing that 'it is entirely imputable to the applicant that the criminal proceedings could not be pursued. She had fled and gone into hiding abroad by the end of 1996 in order to prevent being arrested and convicted. German law does not allow a criminal trial of the nature in question to be conducted in the applicant's absence.' Consequently the length of the proceedings could not be considered unreasonable. *HM v Germany*, ECHR Case 62512/00; 8 ITLR 206.

Delay in determining appeals—whether any breach of Convention

[31.26] In an Italian case, two assessments were served on a company in 1987. The company appealed. The hearing of the appeals was delayed for several years, and the District Tax Commission eventually dismissed them in 1999. In the meantime, the company's controlling director lodged an application with the ECHR, contending that the length of the proceedings had been a breach of *Article 6(1)* of the *European Convention on Human Rights*. The ECHR rejected this contention and dismissed the application (by 11 votes to 6), holding that *Article 6(1)* did not apply, since 'tax disputes fall outside the scope of civil rights and obligations'. (It was accepted that the proceedings did not concern a 'criminal charge'.) The ECHR ruled that 'tax matters still form part of the hard core of public authority prerogatives' and observed that *Article 1* of the *First Protocol* 'reserves the right of States to enact such laws as they deem necessary for the purpose of securing the payment of taxes'. *Ferrazzini v Italy*, ECHR Case 44759/98; [2001] STC 1314.

[31.27] In *Pooley v HMRC*, 29.93 FURTHER ASSESSMENTS: LOSS OF TAX, and *Fullarton & Others v CIR*, 71.35 CAPITAL GAINS TAX, the Special Commissioners held that delay in determining appeals did not involve any breach of the *European Convention on Human Rights*.

[31.28] In a German case, the ECHR held that a delay of eight years in hearing an appeal concerning the taxability of certain bonds did not involve any breach of the *European Convention on Human Rights*. *Remy v Germany*, ECHR Case 70826/01; 7 ITLR 270.

EC Directive 91/308/EEC—whether any breach of Convention

[31.29] In a Belgian case, the ECJ held that 'the obligations of information and of cooperation with the authorities responsible for combating money laundering', laid down in *Article 6(1)* of *Council Directive 91/308/EEC* on the prevention of the use of the financial system for the purpose of money laundering, did not infringe the right to a fair trial as guaranteed by *Article 6* of the *Convention for the Protection of Human Rights. Ordre des barreaux francophones et germanophone v Conseil des Ministres (and related appeals)*, CJEC Case C-305/05; [2007] All ER (EC) 953.

Cases where the application was partly successful

[31.30] In a Swedish case, the tax authority formed the opinion that the proprietor of a taxi firm (J) had underdeclared business takings and employer's contributions. The authority issued assessments and surcharges in December 1995. J appealed on 8 March 1996, and did not pay the assessments or surcharges. On 29 March the relevant Enforcement Office began bankruptcy proceedings. In June 1996 J was declared bankrupt, and in October 1997 he was sentenced to ten months' imprisonment for tax fraud. In February 1999 the tax authority rejected the appeals which J had lodged in March 1996. J appealed to a county court, which dismissed his appeals in December 2001. In the meantime, J applied to the ECHR, seeking a declaration that the delay in determining his appeals, and the bankruptcy proceedings, were a breach of *Article 6* of the *European Convention on Human Rights*. The ECHR allowed his application in part, holding that the delay in determining the appeals was a breach of *Article 6(1)* of the *Convention*. However, the ECHR also held that neither the imposition of the surcharges, nor the bankruptcy proceedings, were a breach of *Article 6*. The Court observed that 'a system of taxation principally based on information supplied by the taxpayer would not function properly without some form of sanction against the provision of incorrect or incomplete information, and the large number of tax returns that are processed annually, coupled with the interest in ensuring a foreseeable and uniform application of such sanctions, undoubtedly require that they be imposed according to standardised rules'. *Janosevic v Sweden*, ECHR Case 34619/97, 23 July 2002 unreported.

[31.31] A similar decision was reached in *Västberga Taxi Aktiebolag v Sweden*, ECHR Case 36985/97; 5 ITLR 65.

[31.32] In the case noted at **29.42** FURTHER ASSESSMENTS: LOSS OF TAX, where penalties were imposed on the proprietor of a guest house, the proprietor appealed to the ECHR, contending that the case had not been resolved within a reasonable time, and claiming damages. The ECHR rejected the claim for damages, finding that the majority of the proprietor's complaints were 'manifestly ill-founded' and 'without substance'. The ECHR observed that 'the right not to incriminate oneself is primarily, though not exclusively, concerned with respecting the will of an accused person to remain silent in the context of criminal proceedings and the use of compulsorily obtained information in criminal prosecutions'. It did not 'act as a prohibition on the use of compulsory powers to require taxpayers to provide information about their financial affairs. Indeed, the obligation to make disclosure of income and capital for the purposes of the calculation and assessment of tax is a common feature of the tax systems of Member States and it would be difficult to envisage them functioning effectively without it.' The ECHR observed that the length of the proceedings 'was not without beneficial effect on the real value of the applicant's eventual liabilities. The domestic courts in that context noted that the applicant had not suffered any prejudice.' The ECHR observed that 'the applicant contributed to their difficulty due to his failure to disclose properties and assets', and by a number of 'unmeritorious appeals'. For the period from 1997 to 2001, the delays were primarily attributable to the applicant's illness. However, the Special Commissioners had been responsible for a delay of eight months in producing a Stated Case in 1992. The Revenue had been responsible for a delay of nine months in issuing penalty determinations in 1994. The clerk to the General Commissioners had been responsible for a delay of two years in transferring some of the appeals to the Special Commissioners between 1995 and 1997. While there had been 'deliberate time-wasting by the applicant', the authorities had also contributed to the fact that the proceedings had not been concluded within a 'reasonable time', so that there had been a violation of *Article 6(1)*. However, the ECHR held that in the circumstances of the case there were no grounds for compensation, and that the finding of a violation was 'in itself just satisfaction for any non-pecuniary damage sustained by the applicant'. *King v United Kingdom (No 3)*, ECHR Case 13881/02; 76 TC 699; [2005] STC 438; 7 ITLR 339.

[31.33] A Russian tax inspector was charged with extorting a bribe, and was convicted of fraud. She was dismissed from her post and fined approximately €5,000. The Presidium of the Supreme Court of the Russian Federation found that the offence 'had not been brought to completion', so that the inspector was guilty of attempted fraud rather than actual fraud, but confirmed the sentence. The inspector applied to the ECHR, contending that the conduct of the proceedings had contravened *Article 6* of the *European Convention on Human Rights*, and claiming more than €900,000 in compensation. The ECHR found that 'the proceedings before the Presidium of the Supreme Court of the Russian Federation did not comply with the requirements of fairness', so that there had been a breach of *Article 6(1)*. However, after reviewing the facts of the case, the ECHR rejected the inspector's claim for substantial compensation and awarded her damages of €1,000. *Aldoshkina v Russia*, ECHR Case 66041/01; 12 October 2006 unreported.

Cases where the application was successful

Tax penalties imposed on heirs of evader

[31.34] In a Swiss case, an individual (P) was found to have evaded substantial amounts of tax. He subsequently died, and the tax authorities imposed penalties on his widow and children, as his heirs. They applied to the ECHR for a ruling that this was a breach of *Article 6(2)* of the *European Convention on Human Rights*. The ECHR accepted this contention, holding that it was 'a fundamental rule of criminal law that criminal liability does not survive the person who has committed the criminal act'. Accordingly there had been a breach of *Article 6(2)*. *AP, MP and TP v Switzerland*, ECHR Case 19958/92; 26 EHRR 541.

Penalty for failure to produce information

[31.35] In a Swiss case, the tax authorities discovered that an individual (B) had made certain investments which had not been reflected in his tax returns.

In 1989 they imposed a fine, which B paid. They also formally required B to submit all documents which he had concerning these investments. B refused to submit the documents, and the tax authorities imposed two further fines. The case was eventually cleared by a negotiated settlement in 1996. While negotiations were in progress, B applied to the ECHR for a ruling that the requirement to disclose information was a breach of the right to remain silent and thus a breach of the right to a fair trial under *Article 6(1)* of the *European Convention on Human Rights*. The ECHR accepted this contention and granted the application, finding that the penalties were not 'intended as pecuniary compensation' but were 'essentially punitive and deterrent in nature' and amounted to 'the determination of a criminal charge'. The ECHR held that 'although not specifically mentioned in *Article 6* of the *Convention*, the right to remain silent and the privilege against self-incrimination are generally recognised international standards which lie at the heart of the notion of a fair procedure under *Article 6(1)*'. There had been 'a violation of the right under *Article 6(1)* of the *Convention* not to incriminate oneself'. *JB v Switzerland*, ECHR Case 31827/96; 3 ITLR 663.

Prosecution for tax evasion—whether any breach of Convention

[31.36] In an Austrian case, a tax consultant had claimed substantial losses for 1985 to 1987. In December 1989, after discovering that some of his clients had been charged with fraud, he withdrew his claims. Two weeks later the Salzburg Tax Office told him that he was being investigated for suspected tax evasion. In February 1995 the Public Prosecutor's Office issued a bill of indictment charging him with tax evasion. He was convicted and appealed, contending that he should not have been tried or convicted because he had made a voluntary disclosure. The Supreme Court rejected this contention and dismissed his appeal, holding that he had not made a true voluntary disclosure because the tax authorities had already obtained information indicating that he had been involved in tax fraud. He then applied to the ECHR for a ruling that the proceedings had not been concluded within a reasonable time, and that this was a breach of *Article 6* of the *European Convention on Human Rights*. The ECHR accepted this contention (by a 6-1 majority), observing that 'the applicant's case concerned merely three financial transactions, for which he had given information already in 1989 and the amount of which had been uncontested throughout the proceedings'. The case was not 'particularly complex', and there was no justification for the delays between 31 January 1990, when he replied to a letter from the Salzburg Tax Office, and February 1995, when the bill of indictment was issued. *Hennig v Austria*, ECHR Case 41444/98; 2 October 2003 unreported.

[31.37] In a Finnish case, a company (X) went into liquidation in 1990. The police subsequently began investigating X's affairs. In 1994 X's managing director (K) was charged with tax fraud. He was convicted by a district court in 1995, and sentenced to two years' imprisonment. He appealed to the Finnish Court of Appeal, which referred the case back to the district court for reconsideration. In 1996 the district court upheld his conviction but reduced the prison sentence by two months. K again appealed to the Finish Court of Appeal, which upheld his conviction and sentence in February 1998. K subsequently applied to the ECHR for a declaration that the length of the proceedings had been a breach of *Article* 6 of the *European Convention on Human Rights*. The ECHR granted his application, holding on the evidence that 'the pre-trial investigation and the district court proceedings were excessive in length'. *Kangasluoma v Finland*, ECHR Case 48339/99; 20 January 2004 unreported.

[31.38] In a German case, a civil servant (U) was charged with tax evasion in 1990. He was subsequently also charged with fraud. He was convicted of both charges in 1995, and sentenced to two and a half years' imprisonment. He appealed, and his sentence was reduced to a suspended sentence of 21 months. The public prosecutor appealed against the leniency of this sentence, but it was confirmed in 1999. U then lodged a complaint with the ECHR, contending that the length of the proceedings had been a breach of *Article* 6 of the *European Convention on Human Rights*. The ECHR granted his application, finding that the case was 'not particularly complex' and that there had been substantial 'delays caused by the judicial authorities especially during the preliminary investigations'. The ECHR also held that 'the finding of a violation constitutes in itself sufficient just satisfaction for any non-pecuniary damage sustained by the applicant'. *Uhl v Germany*, ECHR Case 64387/01; 10 February 2005 unreported.

[31.39] In an Austrian case, an accountant (G) admitted to a tax inspector in December 1989 that he had made false statements in his tax returns. In May 1994 the Salzburg tax authority began criminal proceedings against him. In June 1996 he was convicted of 'intentional tax evasion', and fined €50,900. In September 1996 G filed a complaint concerning the conduct of the proceedings with the Salzburg administrative court. In September 2000 the court dismissed his complaint and ordered him to pay the costs. G lodged a complaint with the European Court of Human Rights, contending that the proceedings had not been concluded within a 'reasonable time'. The ECHR granted the application, finding that there had been a 'significant period of delay' on the part of the Austrian authorities between December 1996 and September 2000. The ECHR awarded G compensation of €4,500, and costs of €2,000. *Geyer v Austria*, ECHR Case 69162/01; 7 July 2005 unreported.

[31.40] In a Hungarian case, the tax authority discovered that a trader (K) had failed to pay tax on his income. In 1998 the authority imposed a fine of €4,384 plus interest. K applied for judicial review. In 2002 the regional court dismissed the application. K appealed to the Court of Appeal, which dismissed his appeal in 2004. K then lodged a complaint with the ECHR, contending that the length of the proceedings had been a breach of *Article* 6 of the *European Convention on Human Rights*. The ECHR granted this application, finding that the length of the proceedings had been 'excessive', and awarded K damages of €1,200. *Kovács v Hungary*, ECHR Case 8174/05; 17 July 2008 unreported.

[31.41] In a Finnish case, a woman was questioned by the police in 1995, on suspicion of fraud. After a prolonged investigation into her affairs, she was convicted of tax fraud in May 2000, and was sentenced to 22 months' imprisonment. In 2002 the Court of Appeal dismissed her appeal against conviction, and in April 2003 the Supreme Court refused her application for leave to appeal against that decision. She subsequently applied to the ECHR for a ruling that the length of the proceedings had been a breach of *Article 6* of the *European Convention on Human Rights*. The ECHR granted this application, holding that the length of the proceedings had been 'excessive', and awarded her damages of €3,300. *Eloranta v Finland*, ECHR Case 4799/03; 9 December 2008 unreported.

[31.42] A similar decision was reached in *Seppala v Finland*, ECHR Case 45981/08; 11 January 2011 unreported.

[31.43] In a Danish case, a stockbroker (H) was arrested in September 1995 and charged with tax fraud. He was held in custody for three months. After a prolonged investigation, he was convicted in April 2001 and sentenced to two years' imprisonment. He appealed. In September 2004, after a delay caused by H suffering from illness, the High Court dismissed his appeal. He applied to the Supreme Court for leave to appeal against this decision. In June 2006 the Supreme Court dismissed his application, and he subsequently applied to the ECHR for a ruling that the length of the proceedings had been a breach of *Article 6* of the *European Convention on Human Rights*. The ECHR granted this application, holding that the length of the investigation and of the court proceedings up to September 2004 had been reasonable, but that the delay which had taken place between September 2004 and June 2006, in deciding whether H should be granted leave to appeal, had been unreasonable and had been a breach of *Article 6(1)*. The ECHR awarded damages of €2,000. *Hasslund v Denmark*, ECHR Case 36244/06; 11 December 2008 unreported.

[31.44] A similar decision was reached in another case involving a Danish stockbroker (in which the facts were similar except that the initial arrest took place in February 1998). *Petersen v Denmark*, ECHR Case 32848/06; 11 December 2008 unreported.

[31.45] In a Ukrainian case, a bank's controlling shareholder (F) was arrested and charged with tax evasion. He was held in custody pending the trial. During the trial, the presiding judge gave an interview to a Ukrainian newspaper in which he criticised F's lawyers. F was convicted of tax evasion and embezzlement, and sentenced to nine years' imprisonment (which was subsequently reduced to five years' imprisonment). F applied to the ECHR, contending that the proceedings had been a breach of the *European Convention on Human Rights*. The ECHR granted the application, holding that the judge had showed a 'lack of impartiality', and awarded damages of €8,000. *Feldman v Ukraine*, ECHR Case 76556/01; 8 April 2010 unreported.

[31.46] See also *Doroshenko v Ukraine*, **31.116** below.

Failure to hold oral hearing

[31.47] In a Finnish case, the tax authority formed the opinion that a company had underdeclared its income, and that the underdeclared income had effectively been paid to its controlling director (L) as disguised dividends. They issued assessments and imposed surcharges. L appealed to the Administrative Court, which refused to hold an oral hearing and dismissed the appeal. L subsequently lodged a complaint with the ECHR, contending that the failure to hold an oral hearing had been a breach of *Article 6* of the *European Convention on Human Rights*. The ECHR accepted this contention and granted the application, declining to follow the majority decision in the VAT case of *Jussila v Finland*, ECHR Case 73053/01; [2009] STC 29; 9 ITLR 662. The ECHR awarded L damages of €3,000. *H Lehtinen v Finland*, ECHR Case 32993/02; 22 July 2008 unreported.

[31.48] A similar decision was reached in *Kallio v Finland*, ECHR Case 40199/02; 22 July 2008 unreported.

[31.49] In a Hungarian case, the tax authority formed the opinion that a woman (P) had underdeclared her income. They issued assessments and imposed surcharges at the rate of 50%. The Hungarian Supreme Court upheld the surcharges, on the basis of written submissions and without holding an oral hearing. P applied to the ECHR, contending that this was a breach of the *European Convention on Human Rights*. The ECHR granted her application, holding that the severity of the surcharges indicated that P had been 'charged with a criminal offence' and that the failure to hold an oral hearing was a breach of *Article 6*. *Pakozdi v Hungary*, ECHR Case 51269/07; 25 November 2014 unreported.

Repeated prosecution of customs officer

[31.50] In an Ukrainian case, a customs officer (S) was charged with smuggling and tax evasion, but was acquitted of both these charges in November 2000. The president of the regional court demanded a review of the decision. The case was reheard in January 2001. S was convicted of aiding and abetting in smuggling, but acquitted of tax evasion. The president of the regional court again demanded a review, and the case was heard for the third time in October 2001, when S was convicted of tax evasion and sentenced to five years' imprisonment. S appealed to the Ukrainian Supreme Court, which directed that he be acquitted of smuggling and tax evasion, but convicted of 'negligent performance of his professional duty', and reduced his sentence to two years' imprisonment. S applied to the ECHR, contending that the repeated demands for a review of his acquittal of tax evasion was a breach of *Article 6* of the *European Convention on Human Rights*. The ECHR accepted this contention, finding that 'the grounds for re-opening the proceedings were based neither on new facts, nor on serious procedural defects, but rather on the personal disagreement of the President of the Regional Court' with the decisions of the lower courts. Accordingly, there had been a violation of *Article 6*. *Savinsky v Ukraine*, ECHR Case 6965/02; 28 February 2006 unreported.

Court refusing to hear appeal without payment of court fee

[31.51] In an Armenian case, a company (P) failed to pay the tax charged by an assessment. The tax authority took proceedings to recover the tax. The Commercial Court gave judgment for the tax authority. P lodged an appeal with the Court of Cassation. Under Armenian legislation, companies were required to pay a 'State fee' for 'lodging appeals and cassation appeals against court judgments and decisions'. P failed to pay the 'State fee', claiming that it could not afford to do so. The court refused to hear the appeal, and P applied to the ECHR for a declaration that the relevant Armenian legislation was a breach of *Article 6* of the *European Convention on Human Rights*. The ECHR accepted this contention, holding that the right to a court could be subject to limitations, but that 'the limitations applied must not restrict the access left to the individual in such a way or to such an extent that the very essence of the right is impaired'. On the evidence, 'the Court of Cassation was prevented from making any assessment of the applicant company's ability to pay by the express provisions of the law'. This had been a breach of *Article 6(1)*. *Paykar Yev Haghtanak Ltd v Armenia*, ECHR Case 21638/03; 20 December 2007 unreported.

Trader taking court proceedings against tax authority

[31.52] In a Ukrainian case, the tax inspectorate began criminal proceedings against a trader (S) in 1999. These proceedings were subsequently terminated, and in November 2000 S began civil proceedings against the tax inspectorate, claiming compensation. In June 2004 the Kerch City Court dismissed the claim. S appealed to the Court of Appeal, which remitted the case to the City Court for rehearing. Meanwhile S had lodged an application with the ECHR, contending that the delays in hearing the case were a breach of *Article 6* of the *European Convention on Human Rights*. The ECHR accepted this contention, noting that the substantive proceedings were still awaiting determination after more than eight years, and awarded S damages of €2,000. *Smirnov v Ukraine*, ECHR Case 1409/03; 30 July 2009 unreported.

No punishment without law (Article 7)

[31.53] In an Estonian case, the police instigated criminal proceedings against a company's managing director (P) in August 1995, charging him with tax offences committed from 1993 to 1995, including falsification of documents. P was convicted and sentenced to four years' imprisonment. He appealed, contending that part of the relevant Estonian Criminal Code had not come into force until January 1995, so that in applying this legislation to the offences which he had committed in 1993, the court had acted retrospectively. The Estonian Supreme Court dismissed his appeal, and he applied to the ECHR for a ruling that the retrospective application of the relevant legislation constituted a breach of *Article 7* of the *European Convention on Human Rights*. The ECHR granted his application, finding that under the relevant section of the Estonian Criminal Code as in force prior to January 1995, a criminal conviction could be imposed only if a person had been previously subjected to an administrative punishment for a similar offence. This condition was not satisfied in P's case. On the evidence, the Estonian authorities had 'applied retrospectively the 1995 law to behaviour which did not previously constitute a criminal offence'. This was a breach of *Article 7* of the *European Convention on Human Rights*. *Puhk v Estonia*, ECHR Case 55103/00; 10 February 2004 unreported.

[31.54] In *Khodorkovskiy v Russia (No 2)*, **31.58** below, the applicant contended that 'his conviction was based on an unforeseeable interpretation of the criminal law', which was a breach of *Article 7* of the *European Convention on Human Rights*. The ECHR rejected this contention.

The right to respect for private life (Article 8)

Search of lawyer's office—whether any breach of Convention

[31.55] In the case noted at 49.66 RETURNS AND INFORMATION, the Revenue formed the opinion that a US attorney (T), practising in London, had helped one of his clients to evade UK taxation by diverting commission and bonus payments offshore. They obtained warrants under *TMA 1970, s 20C*, authorising them to enter and search T's offices. T applied to the ECHR, contending that the search of his offices was a breach of *Article 8* of the *European Convention on Human Rights*. The ECHR dismissed the application, holding that the search complied with the requirements of *Article 8*, since it was 'in accordance with the law', and was undertaken in the interests of the prevention of crime. The search 'was not disproportionate to the legitimate aims pursued', and 'adequate safeguards attached to the procedure'. The interference with T's rights was 'necessary in a democratic society'. *Tamosius v United Kingdom*, ECHR Case 62002/00; [2002] STC 1307.

[31.56] The Ukrainian tax authorities were investigating a company (K), which they suspected of tax evasion. A district court ordered the seizure of certain documents belonging to K, which were in the possession of its lawyer (U). In 2002 tax police officers entered U's offices, searched him and accompanied him to the tax office. Subsequently the officers also searched U's home and offices. U subsequently lodged a complaint with the ECHR, contending that the searches had been a breach of *Article 8* of the *European Convention on Human Rights*. The ECHR rejected the application, holding that the evidence did not 'disclose any appearance of a violation of the rights and freedoms set out in the Convention'. *Ulyanov v Ukraine*, ECHR Case 16472/04; 9 November 2010 unreported.

Trader with tax debts prevented from leaving country

[31.57] A Bulgarian woman (R) moved to Austria in 1985. She subsequently married an Austrian, and in 1989 she obtained Austrian nationality. However she returned to Bulgaria in 1991 and carried on business there. She failed to pay substantial amounts of Bulgarian tax. In 1995 she attempted to travel from Bulgaria to Greece, but was prevented from leaving Bulgaria because of her tax debts. She applied to the ECHR for a declaration that this contravened *Article 8* of the *European Convention on Human Rights*. The ECHR reviewed the evidence in detail and allowed the application in part, holding that the Bulgarian authorities had been justified in preventing R from leaving the country in 1995, but that the ban had been maintained in force for too long. The Bulgarian courts had found that R 'owed a significant amount in taxes'. Accordingly, 'the prohibition against the applicant leaving Bulgaria had legal basis in Bulgarian law' and 'the aim of the interference with the applicant's right to leave Bulgaria was to secure the payment of considerable amounts in taxes, owed by her'. The ECHR observed that *Article 1* of the *First Protocol* 'reserves the right of States to enact such laws as they deem necessary for the purpose of securing the payment of taxes'. Unpaid taxes could be 'a ground for restrictions on the debtor's freedom of movement', where the purpose of such restrictions was the 'maintaining of public order and protection of the rights of others'. Accordingly, 'the travel ban imposed on the applicant had a legitimate aim'. However, 'even where a restriction on the individual's freedom of movement was initially warranted, maintaining it automatically over a lengthy period of time may become a disproportionate measure violating the individual's rights. It follows from the principle of proportionality that a restriction on the right to leave one's country on grounds of unpaid debt can only be justified as long as it serves its aim – recovering the debt.' Consequently the authorities were 'not entitled to maintain over lengthy periods restrictions on the individual's freedom of movement without periodic reassessment of their justification in the light of factors such as whether or not the fiscal authorities had made reasonable efforts to collect the debt through other means and the likelihood that the debtor's leaving the country might undermine the chances to collect the money. In the applicant's case it does not appear that the fiscal authorities actively sought to collect the debt.' (R had also made a request to renounce her Bulgarian citizenship. The Bulgarian authorities had rejected this request in view of R's tax debts. The ECHR held that this refusal did not contravene *Article 8* of the *Convention*.) *Riener v Bulgaria*, ECHR Case 46343/99; 9 ITLR 1013.

Imprisonment of suspected tax evader

[31.58] In *OAO Neftyanaka Kompaniya Yukos v Russia*, **31.111** below, the Russian tax authority formed the opinion that an oil company (N) had a large tax liability for 2000, and ordered it to pay tax arrears of more than €1,000,000,000 and a penalty of more than €500,000,000. N failed to pay, and the Moscow City Commercial Court gave judgment for the tax authority. In 2003 one of N's principal shareholders (K) was arrested, charged with tax evasion and remanded in custody. He was convicted at a trial in 2005, was sentenced to nine years' imprisonment, and was imprisoned in Krasnokamensk. While in prison, he took proceedings in the ECHR, contending that his imprisonment had been a breach of *Article 8* of the *European Convention on Human Rights*. The ECHR ruled that there had been a violation of *Article 8* in that K had been imprisoned in a very remote area of Russia, and awarded K damages of €10,000. *MB Khodorkovskiy v Russia (No 2)*, ECHR Case 11082/06; 25 July 2013 unreported.

[31.59] The ECHR reached a similar decision in *Lebedev v Russia*, **31.10** above.

Police intercepting trader's correspondence

[31.60] In a Ukrainian case, a trader was accused of tax evasion. He was not remanded in custody, and despite obtaining a warrant for his arrest, the police were unable to locate him. In an effort to trace him, the police issued an order for the interception of the correspondence of his mother and his brother. They subsequently applied to the ECHR for a declaration that the interception of their correspondence contravened *Article 8* of the *European Convention on*

Human Rights. The ECHR granted the declarations and awarded each of the applicants damages of €1,000. *Volokhy v Ukraine*, ECHR Case 23543/02; 2 November 2006 unreported.

Freedom of thought, conscience and religion (Article 9)

Use of taxation—whether a breach of Article 9

[31.61] A member of the Religious Society of Friends applied to the ECHR for a ruling that the UK Government's use of taxation to fund military expenditure violated his religious beliefs and contravened *Article 9* of the *European Convention on Human Rights*. The ECHR rejected this contention and ruled that the application was inadmissible, holding that *Article 9* 'does not confer on the applicant the right to refuse, on the basis of his convictions, to abide by legislation, the operation of which is provided for by the Convention, and which applies neutrally and generally in the public sphere, without impinging on the freedoms guaranteed by *Article 9*. If the applicant considers the obligation to contribute through taxation to arms procurement an outrage to his conscience, he may advertise his attitude and thereby try to obtain support for it through the democratic process.' *C v United Kingdom*, ECHR Case 10358/83; 37 ECDR 142.

[31.62] See also *R (oao Boughton & Others) v HM Treasury*, **4.320** APPEALS, and *Oxley v Raynham*, **43.7** PAYMENT OF TAX.

Taxpayer identification number—whether a breach of Article 9

[31.63] In 1999 the Russian tax authorities issued taxpayers with taxpayer identification numbers, consisting of twelve digits. A woman (S), who was a practising Christian, was issued with a twelve-digit number which included the digits 666. She applied for her number to be cancelled, contending that in Christian teaching, 666 was 'the mark of the Antichrist' (see the Book of Revelation, chapter 13, verses 15 to 18). The tax authority rejected her request, and she applied to the ECHR for a ruling that the allocation of this taxpayer identification number affronted her religious beliefs and was a breach of *Article 9* of the *European Convention on Human Rights*. The ECHR rejected this contention and dismissed her application, holding that 'general legislation which applies on a neutral basis without any link whatsoever with an applicant's personal beliefs cannot in principle be regarded as an interference with his or her rights under *Article 9* of the *Convention*'. The ECHR observed that the reference number which had been allocated to S was 'merely an incidental effect of generally applicable and neutral legal provisions', and that 'the contents of official documents or databases cannot be determined by the wishes of the individuals listed therein'. *T Skugar v Russia*, ECHR Case 40010/04; 23 December 2009 unreported.

Obligation to deduct PAYE—whether a breach of Convention

[31.64] A religious society was required to deduct PAYE from its employees' salaries. In accounting for PAYE to the Revenue, the society withheld about 12% of the tax due. The Revenue took court proceedings to recover the money. Two members of the society made applications to the ECHR, contending that the 12% which they had withheld corresponded to the proportion of the tax which the UK Government would spend for military purposes, and that requiring them to pay tax for such purposes was a breach of their religious principles and contravened *Article 9* of the *European Convention on Human Rights*. The ECHR rejected this contention and ruled that their application was inadmissible, holding that 'the obligation to pay taxes is a general one which has no specific conscientious implications in itself. Its neutrality in this sense is also illustrated by the fact that no taxpayer can influence or determine the purpose for which his or her contributions are applied, once they are collected. Furthermore, the power of taxation is expressly recognised by the Convention system and is ascribed to the State by *Article 1 of the First Protocol*.' *Hibbs v United Kingdom; Birmingham v United Kingdom*, ECHR Case 11991/86, 18 July 1986 unreported.

Allocation of tax to religion—whether a breach of Convention

[31.65] Under Italian law, 0.8% of income tax revenue is allocated to the State, to the Catholic church, or to one of the representative institutions of five other religions (Union of Seventh-Day Adventist Churches, Assemblies of God of Italy, Union of Methodist and Waldensian Churches, Evangelical Lutheran Church and Union of Jewish Communities of Italy). Taxpayers are required to indicate their choice for the allocation of the relevant percentage of income tax when they fill in their tax return. If no option is indicated, the sum is divided between the State, the Catholic church and the institutions representing the other religions, in proportion to the choices made by all taxpayers. An Italian lawyer (S) applied to the ECHR, contending that this obliged him 'to manifest his religious beliefs when completing his income tax return', and that this contravened *Article 9* of the *European Convention on Human Rights*. The ECHR rejected S's contentions, observing that 'taxpayers are entitled not to make any choice as to the allocation of the eight thousandths of their income tax. Accordingly, the provision in question does not entail an obligation to manifest one's religious beliefs'. *C Spampinato v Italy*, ECHR Case 23123/04; 29 April 2010 unreported.

Freedom of expression (Article 10)

Injunction against newspaper identifying alleged tax evader

[31.66] An Austrian newspaper published an article reporting that the managing director of a well-known company was under investigation after being accused of tax evasion. It published a picture of the director. The Austrian Supreme Court granted an injunction against the company prohibiting it from publishing any picture of the director 'in the context of reports on charges of tax evasion'. The company applied to the ECHR, contending that the injunction was a breach of *Article 10* of the *European Convention on Human Rights*. The ECHR granted the application, observing that 'the press fulfils an essential function in a democratic society. Although the press must not overstep certain bounds, in particular in respect of the reputation or the rights of others its duty is nevertheless to impart – in a manner consistent with its obligations and responsibilities – information and ideas on all matters of public interest.' The ban on publishing any picture of the director 'in the context of reporting on the investigations against him on the suspicion of tax evasion was not proportionate to the legitimate aim pursued. It follows that the interference with the applicant company's right to freedom of expression was not "necessary in a democratic society".' *Verlagsgruppe News GmbH v Austria (No 2)*, ECHR Case 10520/02; 14 December 2006 unreported.

Prosecution of journalist and newspaper publicising alleged fraud

[31.67] In a Finnish case, a magazine published an article about criminal proceedings which were taking place against a businesswoman (X) who had been accused of tax fraud. X subsequently took proceedings against the magazine and the journalist who had written the article. The Helsinki Court of Appeal dismissed the proceedings, but X appealed to the Supreme Court, which held that the magazine and the journalist had violated X's right to privacy, and ordered them to pay damages to X. Between the Court of Appeal decision and the Supreme Court decision, X had been convicted of tax fraud and sentenced to 22 months' imprisonment. The magazine, the journalist and the editor of the magazine took proceedings in the ECHR, contending that the Supreme Court decision had been a breach of *Article 10* of the *European Convention on Human Rights*. The ECHR accepted this contention, holding that 'from the point of view of the general public's right to receive information about matters of public interest, and thus from the standpoint of the press, there were justified grounds supporting the need to encourage public discussion of the matter'. The Finnish Supreme Court had not shown sufficient grounds 'to justify the interference with the applicants' right to freedom of expression'. The ECHR awarded the magazine €9,179 in respect of pecuniary damages, and awarded both the journalist and the editor €5,000 in respect of non-pecuniary damages. *Eerikäinen & Others v Finland*, ECHR Case 3514/02; 10 February 2009 unreported.

Prosecution of tax adviser for defamation of inspector

[31.68] A Finnish tax adviser (M) had given evidence for a defendant who was convicted of tax fraud. M subsequently published a book in which she accused a senior tax inspector of having 'committed perjury fully knowingly and intentionally', and accused another inspector of having acted dishonestly with regard to the case. She was charged with 'aggravated defamation', convicted and given a suspended sentence of four months' imprisonment. She was also ordered to pay legal costs of €33,390, and compensation of €4,000 to the inspectors. She applied to the ECHR, contending that her conviction and imprisonment had been a breach of *Article 10* of the *European Convention on*

Human Rights. The ECHR reviewed the evidence and held that M's prosecution 'pursued the legitimate aim of protecting the reputation or rights of others', within *Article 10(2)*. However, the imposition of a prison sentence for a 'defamation offence' was only compatible with the Convention 'in exceptional circumstances, notably where other fundamental rights have been seriously impaired, as, for example, in the case of hate speech or incitement to violence'. The ECHR noted that the European Parliament had 'urged those Member States which still provide for prison sentences for defamation, even if they are not actually imposed, to abolish them without delay'. Accordingly, the sentence had been a violation of *Article 10*. The ECHR noted that M had claimed damages of more than €400,000. It found that this claim was excessive, and awarded €33,390 in payment of pecuniary damages and a further €6,000 as compensation. *Mariapori v Finland*, ECHR Case 37751/07; 6 July 2010 unreported.

Effective remedy (Article 13)

[31.69] In a Ukrainian case, a tax police squad visited a shopkeeper who had failed to submit tax returns. However the shopkeeper and his employees prevented the tax police from accessing his records. One of the employees (T) alleged that she had been punched by a tax officer, and lodged a complaint with the police. The local prosecutor's office held an investigation and concluded that there was insufficient evidence to prosecute the officer. T subsequently applied to the ECHR, contending that the failure to prosecute the officer was a breach of *Article 13* of the *European Convention on Human Rights*. The ECHR rejected the application, finding that 'the available materials do not demonstrate any violent behaviour on the part of the tax police officers, given that the applicant's allegation of having been punched in her face was not confirmed by any independent evidence, including the medical examinations, which did not reveal any injuries on the applicant's face. It is important to note that the applicant did not try to explain such a discrepancy between her version of events and the results of a medical examination that was conducted within hours of the incident.' *OS Terletskaya v Ukraine*, ECHR Case 18773/05; 3 November 2011 unreported.

Prohibition of discrimination (Article 14)

Capital taxation—whether a breach of European Convention

[31.70] Iceland imposed a special capital tax of 15% on taxpayers with capital exceeding a certain level. An Icelandic resident applied to the ECHR for a ruling that this was a breach of *Article 14* of the *European Convention on Human Rights*. The ECHR rejected this contention and dismissed his application, holding that the legislation was authorised by *Article 1 of the First Protocol* of the *Convention*. *Gudmundsson v Iceland*, ECHR Case 511/59; 4 ECCD 1.

IHTA 1984, s 18—whether any breach of Convention

[31.71] Two elderly sisters lived together in a jointly-owned house on land which they had inherited from their parents. They lodged a complaint with the ECHR, contending that the provisions of *IHTA 1984, s 18* (as amended by the *Tax and Civil Partnership Regulations 2005*) were a breach of *Article 14* of the *European Convention on Human Rights*, because when one of them died, the survivor would be required to pay IHT on her sister's share of their home, whereas no IHT would have been charged if they had lived together as a registered lesbian civil partnership. The case was referred to the Fourth Section of the ECHR, which rejected their application (by a 4-3 majority), holding that the inheritance tax exemption for married and civil partnership couples 'pursues a legitimate aim, namely to promote stable, committed heterosexual and homosexual relationships by providing the survivor with a measure of financial security after the death of the spouse or partner'. The United Kingdom's decision 'to treat differently for tax purposes those who were married or who were parties to a civil partnership from other persons living together, even in a long-term settled relationship' was within the 'margin of appreciation' available to national authorities. The Grand Chamber upheld this decision (by a 15-2 majority), holding that 'the relationship between siblings is qualitatively of a different nature to that between married couples and homosexual civil partners' and that 'the fact that the applicants have chosen to live together all their adult lives, as do many married and *Civil Partnership Act* couples, does not alter this essential difference between the two types of relationship.' The absence of 'a legally binding agreement between the applicants' rendered 'their relationship of co-habitation, despite its long duration, fundamentally different to that of a married or civil partnership couple'. Accordingly, 'the applicants, as co-habiting sisters, cannot be compared for the purposes of *Article 14* to a married or *Civil Partnership Act* couple. It follows that there has been no discrimination and, therefore, no violation of *Article 14*'. *Burden & Burden v United Kingdom*, ECHR Case 13378/05; [2008] STC 1305; 10 ITLR 772.

[31.72] In 1984 two homosexuals (C and S) purchased a property as joint tenants. They lived there until S died in January 2005. The Revenue issued a determination that IHT was chargeable on S's share of the property. C applied to the ECHR for a ruling that the provisions of *IHTA 1984, s 18* (prior to their amendment by the *Tax and Civil Partnership Regulations 2005*) were a breach of *Article 14* of the *European Convention on Human Rights*. The ECHR rejected the application, holding that 'notwithstanding social changes, marriage remains an institution that is widely accepted as conferring a particular status on those who enter it' and that 'the promotion of marriage, by way of limited benefits for surviving spouses, cannot be said to exceed the margin of appreciation afforded to the respondent Government'. *Courten v United Kingdom*, ECHR Case 4479/06; [2008] ECHR 1546.

[31.73] See also *Holland (Holland's Executor) v CIR*, 72.21 INHERITANCE TAX.

ICTA 1988, s 259—whether any breach of Convention

[31.74] A married woman (M), whose husband was severely disabled and confined to a wheelchair, claimed additional personal allowance for 1994/95. The Revenue rejected the claim on the basis that, under the wording of *ICTA 1988, s 259* (as originally enacted), the allowance was available to a married man whose wife was totally incapacitated, but not to a married woman whose husband was totally incapacitated. M applied to the ECHR for a ruling that the relevant provisions of *ICTA 1988, s 259* were a breach of *Article 14* of the *European Convention on Human Rights*. The ECHR ruled that the application was admissible. *MacGregor v United Kingdom*, ECHR Case 39548/96, 3 December 1997 unreported. (*Note*. *ICTA 1988, s 259* was subsequently amended by *FA 1998, s 26*, with retrospective effect for 1997/98 *et seq*, to end the discrimination in question. The Government agreed to pay M £1,000 in respect of the tax years 1994/95 to 1996/97— ECHR 1 July 1998 unreported.)

ICTA 1988, s 262—whether a breach of Convention

[31.75] A married woman, with an eight-year old daughter, died in 1996. Her husband continued his employment but had to employ a childminder. The Revenue informed him that, although a married woman whose husband died would be entitled to widow's bereavement allowance under *ICTA 1988, s 262*, there was no corresponding tax allowance for widowers. He applied to the ECHR for a ruling that the provisions of *ICTA 1988, s 262* were a breach of *Article 14* of the *European Convention on Human Rights*. The UK Government initially resisted the claim, and the ECHR made a preliminary ruling that the application was 'admissible, without prejudging the merits of the case'. Subsequently the UK Government agreed to pay him compensation of £14,573, plus legal costs of £5,000. *Fielding v United Kingdom*, ECHR Case 36940/97, 29 January 2002 unreported. (*Notes*. (1) *ICTA 1988, s 262* was repealed by *FA 1999* with effect for deaths occurring after 5 April 2000. (2) See also *Crossland v United Kingdom*, **31.76** below. Despite the agreement to pay compensation in this case, the UK Government did not offer compensation in other cases where claimants continued in employment following the death of their wives. See Simon's Tax Intelligence 2000, pp 1374–1377, and *R (oao Wilkinson) v CIR*, **31.77** below.)

[31.76] A married woman, with three young children, died in 1995. Her husband gave up his employment to care for the children, and began self-employment. The Revenue informed him that, although a married woman whose husband died would be entitled to widow's bereavement allowance under *ICTA 1988, s 262*, there was no alternative tax allowance for widowers. He applied to the ECHR for a ruling that the provisions of *ICTA 1988, s 262* were a breach of *Article 14* of the *European Convention on Human Rights*. The UK Government decided not to contest the application, and agreed to pay him compensation of £575, representing the amount that he would have been paid if widow's bereavement allowance had been available to men at the date his wife died, together with legal costs of £3,692. *Crossland v United Kingdom*, ECHR Case 36120/97, 9 November 1999 unreported. (*Notes*. (1) *ICTA 1988, s 262* was repealed by *FA 1999* with effect for deaths occurring after 5 April 2000. (2) Despite the decision in this case, the UK Government did not offer compensation in cases where claimants continued in employment following the death of their wives. See Simon's Tax Intelligence 2000, pp 1374–1377, and *R (oao Wilkinson) v CIR*, **31.77** below.)

[31.77] Following the settlement of the appellant's claim in *Crossland v United Kingdom*, **31.76** above, another widower (W) submitted a claim for a sum equivalent to the amount of widow's bereavement allowance. The Revenue rejected the claim, and W applied for judicial review. The QB dismissed the application and the HL unanimously dismissed the widower's appeal. Lord Hoffmann held that *ICTA 1988, s 262* could not be construed as including widowers. The Revenue were not authorised 'to concede, by extra-statutory concession, an allowance which Parliament could have granted but did not grant, and on grounds not of pragmatism in the collection of tax but of general equity between men and women'. Furthermore, if Parliament 'had paid proper regard to *Article 14*, it would have abolished the allowance for widows. (W) would not have received an allowance and no damages are therefore necessary'. *R (oao Wilkinson) v CIR*, HL 2005, 77 TC 78; [2006] STC 270; [2005] UKHL 30; [2006] 1 All ER 574. (*Note*. For the Revenue's powers of extra-statutory concession, see now *FA 2008, s 160*.)

[31.78] Following the settlement of the appellant's claim in *Crossland v United Kingdom*, **31.76** above, four more widowers applied to the ECHR for a ruling that the provisions of *ICTA 1988, s 262* were a breach of *Article 14* of the *European Convention on Human Rights*. The ECHR held that there had been a violation of *Article 14* but that there was 'no reason to remedy the inequality of treatment by "levelling up" and awarding the value of tax benefits which had been found to be unjustified'. It also rejected the appellants' claims that they had been 'caused real and serious emotional damage as a result of being denied a tax allowance'. *Hobbs & Others v United Kingdom*, ECHR Case 63684/00 (and related applications); [2008] STC 1469.

[31.79] Similar decisions have been reached in a large number of subsequent cases. In the interests of space, such decisions are not summarised individually in this book.

ITA 2007, s 454—whether a breach of Convention

[31.80] An unmarried couple had a daughter in 1991, and separated in 1997. The father agreed to make maintenance payments of £25 per week. He claimed a deduction for these in computing his tax liability. The Revenue rejected the claim on the ground that he had never married the child's mother, and that *ICTA 1988, s 347B* (see now *ITA 2007, s 454*) only allowed such a deduction where the couple had been married. He applied to the ECHR, contending that the restriction of tax relief to couples who had been married was a breach of *Article 14* of the *European Convention on Human Rights*. The ECHR accepted this contention, holding that 'as a general rule unmarried fathers, who have established family life with their children, can claim equal rights of contact and custody with married fathers'. The applicant had 'been acknowledged as the father' and had 'acted in that role'. Accordingly, there was 'no reason for treating him differently from a married father, now divorced and separated from the mother, as regards the tax deductibility of those payments.

The purpose of the tax deductions was purportedly to render it easier for married fathers to support a new family; it is not readily apparent why unmarried fathers, who undertook similar new relationships, would not have similar financial commitments equally requiring relief.' The ECHR awarded him damages of €292, plus costs of €7,900. *PM v United Kingdom*, ECHR Case 6638/03; [2005] STC 1566; 7 ITLR 970.

Taxation of Jehovah's Witnesses—application of Article 14

[31.81] The Austrian *Inheritance and Gift Tax Act 1955* provided that certain donations to religious institutions were exempt from inheritance and gift tax. However, the Austrian Jehovah's Witnesses were not included in the list of qualifying institutions until 2009. They began proceedings in the ECHR, contending that this had been a breach of *Article 14* of the *European Convention on Human Rights*. The ECHR accepted this contention. *Jehovahs Zeugen in Österreich v Austria*, ECHR Case 27540/05; 25 September 2012 unreported.

Taxation of witches—application of Article 14

[31.82] See *Rongen v Inspecteur der Directe Belastingen Leeuwarden*, 63.242 TRADING PROFITS.

The right to peaceful enjoyment of possessions (First Protocol, Article 1)

Cases where the application was dismissed

'Profit-sharing' tax—whether a breach of Convention

[31.83] A Swedish company applied to the ECHR for a ruling that the imposition of a new 'profit-sharing' tax contravened the *European Convention on Human Rights*. The ECHR dismissed the application, holding that it was 'for the national authorities to decide what kind of taxes or contributions are to be collected' and that 'the decisions in this area will commonly involve the appreciation of political, economic and social questions which the Convention leaves within the competence of the Contracting States. The power of appreciation of the Contracting States is therefore a wide one'. *Svenska Managementgruppen AB v Sweden*, ECHR Case 11036/84; 45 ECDR 211.

'Windfall' tax

[31.84] A Swedish life insurance company applied to the ECHR for a ruling that the imposition of a new 'windfall' tax contravened the *European Convention on Human Rights*. The ECHR rejected this contention and dismissed the application. *Wasa Liv Ömsesidigt v Sweden*, ECHR Case 13013/87; 58 ECDR 163.

Gift tax

[31.85] A Czech company applied to the ECHR for a ruling that the imposition of a 'gift tax' contravened the *European Convention on Human Rights*. The ECHR rejected this contention and dismissed the application. *CBC-Union SRO v Czech Republic*, ECHR Case 68741/01, 8 ITLR 224.

Real estate transfer tax

[31.86] In another Czech case, a company applied to the ECHR for a ruling that the imposition of a 'real estate transfer tax' contravened the European Convention on Human Rights. The ECHR rejected this contention and dismissed the application, which it described as 'manifestly ill-founded'. *Agro-B Spol sro v Czech Republic*, ECHR Case 740/05; 15 February 2011 unreported.

Health insurance contributions

[31.87] A Slovakian trader applied to the ECHR for a ruling that the imposition of flat-rate health insurance contributions contravened the *European Convention on Human Rights*. The ECHR rejected this contention and dismissed the application. *Fratrik v Slovakia*, ECHR Case 51224/99; 7 ITLR 173.

Repeal of legislation granting favourable tax treatment

[31.88] In 1992 Ukraine enacted the *Foreign Investments Act*, which granted favourable tax treatment to companies which were at least 20% owned by a foreign shareholder. This legislation was repealed in 2000 by the *National Property and Assets (Termination of Discrimination) Act*. A Ukrainian company director, who held a 50% shareholding in a company which had benefited from the *Foreign Investments Act*, took court proceedings, contending that his company should be held to be immune from the change in legislation. The Ukrainian Supreme Court rejected his claim and he applied to the ECHR, contending that the change in the tax treatment of his company contravened the *European Convention on Human Rights*. The ECHR rejected this contention and dismissed the application, holding that 'as a general rule, shareholders of a company, including the majority shareholders, cannot claim to be victims of an alleged violation of the company's rights under the Convention'. *Ketko v Ukraine*, ECHR Case 31223/03; [2008] ECHR 1314.

Right of pre-emption

[31.89] In 1976 a German woman (J) inherited some agricultural land in Saxony (which was then part of the German Democratic Republic). The land had been expropriated from its previous owners in 1945, when Saxony was in Soviet occupation. In 1990 Saxony (along with the rest of the German Democratic Republic) became part of the Federal Republic of Germany. In 1994 J decided to sell the land. The Saxony Department of Agriculture opposed the sale and registered a right of pre-emption in favour of the tax authorities. J appealed. The German courts dismissed J's appeal, and she applied to the ECHR for a declaration that the exercise of the right of pre-emption was a breach of the *European Convention on Human Rights*. The ECHR rejected this contention, holding that 'in the unique context of

German reunification, the lack of any compensation does not upset the "fair balance" which has to be struck between the protection of property and the requirements of the general interest.' *Jahn & Others v Germany*, ECHR Case 46720/99; 30 June 2005 unreported.

Seizure of goods

[31.90] A German company (G) sold a concrete-mixer to a Netherlands company (J). The sale agreement included a clause providing that G retained ownership until J had made payment in full. J failed to pay its tax liabilities and bailiffs acting on behalf of the Collector of Taxes seized all its goods. J was subsequently declared bankrupt. G applied to the ECHR for a ruling that the seizure of the concrete-mixer contravened the *European Convention on Human Rights*. The ECHR rejected this contention, holding (by 6 votes to 3) that there had been no violation of *Article 1 of the First Protocol*. The ECHR observed that the second paragraph of the *Article* 'explicitly reserves the right of Contracting States to pass such laws as they may deem necessary to secure the payment of taxes'. In passing such laws, 'the legislature must be allowed a wide margin of appreciation, especially with regard to the question whether — and if so, to what extent — the tax authorities should be put in a better position to enforce tax debts than ordinary creditors are in to enforce commercial debts. The Court will respect the legislature's assessment in such matters unless it is devoid of reasonable foundation.' *Gasus Dosier- und Fördertechnik GmbH v Netherlands*, ECHR Case 15375/89; 20 EHRR 403.

Seizure of company funds

[31.91] The Czech tax authorities charged the controlling shareholder of a company (B) with tax evasion. In 2001 the prosecuting authorities seized more than €300,000 which had been deposited in B's bank accounts. The money was returned to B in 2008. B applied to the ECHR, contending that the length of the seizure was a breach of the *European Convention on Human Rights*. The ECHR rejected the application, finding that 'the prosecuting authorities were faced with an alleged crime that was highly sophisticated and extensive', and holding that there had been no breach of the *Convention*. *Benet Czech Spol sro v Czech Republic*, ECHR Case 31555/05; 21 October 2010 unreported.

Ecclesiastical taxation

[31.92] A married couple owned the freehold of a farm in Warwickshire, and were therefore lay rectors of the parish, with an obligation under common law and *Chancel Repairs Act 1932* to maintain the chancel of the parish church. The parochial church council (PCC) served a notice on the couple calling upon them to repair the chancel. The couple disputed liability, and the PCC took proceedings to recover more than £95,000. The HL found in favour of the PCC, holding that it was not a 'public authority' for the purposes of *Human Rights Act 1998, s 6*. Applying the principles laid down in *Holy Monasteries v Greece*, ECHR 1995, 20 EHRR 1 and *Hautanemi v Sweden*, ECHR 1996, 22 EHRR 155, an ecclesiastical body was a 'non-governmental organisation' for the purposes of *Article 34* of the *Convention*. *Aston Cantlow and Wilmcote with Billesley Parochial Church Council v Wallbank & Wallbank*, HL [2003] UKHL 37; [2003] 3 WLR 283; [2003] 3 All ER 1213.

TMA 1970, s 33—whether a breach of Convention

[31.93] See *Monro v HMRC*, **24.4** ERROR OR MISTAKE RELIEF.

FA 1991, s 53—whether a breach of Convention

[31.94] In *R v CIR (ex p. Woolwich Equitable Building Society)*, **7.1** BUILDING SOCIETIES, the HL held that the *Income Tax (Building Societies) Regulations 1986 (SI 1986/482)* were unlawful. Following the HL decision, Parliament enacted *FA 1991, s 53* to give retrospective validity to the provisions, and enacted *F (No 2) A 1992, s 64* to retrospectively validate the Treasury Orders which had set the composite rate tax for 1986/87 and following years. In 1993 three building societies applied to the European Commission of Human Rights, contending that the provisions in question were a violation of the *European Convention on Human Rights*. The European Court of Human Rights rejected this contention, holding that the retrospective measures which Parliament had adopted did not upset the balance between the societies' rights to restitution and the public interest in securing the payment of taxes. *National & Provincial Building Society v United Kingdom (and related appeals)*, ECHR 1997, 69 TC 540; [1997] STC 1466.

SSCBA 1992, ss 6(2), 122—whether a breach of Convention

[31.95] Under *SSCBA 1992, s 6(2)*, workers in the UK who were below the 'state pension age' were required to pay Class 1 NICs on their earnings. Under *SSCBA 1992, s 122*, the 'state pension age' was set at 65 for men and 60 for women. A male worker (W) applied to the ECHR for a declaration that this was a breach of *Article 14* of the *European Convention on Human Rights*. The ECHR rejected this contention and dismissed his application, holding that 'the linkage of NICs to the notional end of working life or state pensionable age must be regarded as pursuing a legitimate aim and as being reasonably and objectively justified'. The UK's decision to defer equalisation of the pension age for men and women until 2020 was within the 'margin of appreciation' available to national authorities. *Walker v United Kingdom*, ECHR Case 37212/02; [2008] STC 786.

TCGA 1992, s 171—whether any breach of Convention

[31.96] In the case noted at **71.269** CAPITAL GAINS TAX, the HL dismissed an appeal by a company (N) concerning the tax consequences of a share exchange. The relevant disposal took place in 1985, and the relevant legislation had subsequently been amended with effect from 1988, to reverse the 1987 CA decision in *Westcott v Woolcombers Ltd*, **71.268** CAPITAL GAINS TAX. (See now *TCGA, s 171(3)* for the legislation as amended.) At the time of the share exchange, the *Woolcombers* case had only proceeded as far as the General Commissioners, and the Revenue had appealed to the Ch D. N applied to the ECHR, contending that the change in the legislation should have had retrospective effect, and that the Revenue's failure to inform it of the Commissioners' decision in the *Woolcombers* case was a breach of the *European Convention on Human Rights*. The ECHR rejected these contentions and dismissed the application, holding that 'on the basis that the decision of the General Commissioners in the *Woolcombers* case could not have been anticipated', there was 'no reason why the Revenue should have informed (N) in particular or taxpayers generally about what it must have regarded as a maverick decision.' The UK Government had been entitled 'not to give retroactive effect to the amending legislation' on the basis that 'it would not be fair to individuals who had arranged their affairs subsequent to the *Woolcombers* decision if the effects of that decision were nullified retroactively'. *NAP Holdings UK Ltd v United Kingdom*, ECHR Case 27721/95, 12 April 1996 unreported.

FA 2008, s 58—whether any breach of Convention

[31.97] See *R (oao Huitson) v HMRC*, 21.43 DOUBLE TAX RELIEF.

Increase in air passenger duty

[31.98] A group of companies providing package holidays applied to the QB for a declaration that an increase in air passenger duty contravened the *European Convention on Human Rights*. The QB and CA unanimosly rejected. Waller LJ held that air passenger duty was 'a tax on flight operators, by reference to the passengers they carry, the justification for which in general terms would not be susceptible of challenge under *Article 1* of the *First Protocol*'. *R (oao Federation of Tour Operators) v HM Treasury*, CA [2008] STC 2524; [2008] EWCA Civ 752.

Assessment and penalty on company failing to comply with regulations

[31.99] The accounts and tax computations of a Czech company failed to comply with the relevant statutory regulations. The tax authority issued an assessment and imposed a penalty on the company. The company appealed, contending that the relevant regulations had not been adequately publicised and should not be treated as legally binding, and that the assessment and penalty were a breach of the *European Convention on Human Rights*. The ECHR rejected this contention, holding that the regulations were 'adequately accessible', and that the assessment and penalty were authorised by *Article 1 of the First Protocol*. *Spacek sro v Czech Republic*, ECHR Case 26449/95; 9 November 1999 unreported.

Delay in resolving tax appeals—whether any breach of Convention

[31.100] Two Belgian companies appealed against corporation tax assessments issued between 1989 and 1997, and applied for payment of the tax charged to be postponed. The tax authority accepted the postponement applications. In 2006, while the appeals were still pending, the companies applied to the ECHR for a ruling that the delay in resolving the appeals was a breach of *Article 1* of the *First Protocol of the European Convention on Human Rights*. The ECHR rejected this contention and dismissed the application. *Optim & Industerre v Belgium*, ECHR Case 23819/06; 11 September 2012 unreported.

Penalty for late return

[31.101] See *Bysermaw Properties Ltd v HMRC*, 44.194 PENALTIES.

Surcharges

[31.102] In a Swedish case, the tax authority began a detailed audit of a company (P) which had claimed a substantial loss. The authority formed the opinion that P's accounts did not comply with the legislation, and levied additional taxes and surcharges (at the rate of 40% of the additional tax charged). The Swedish courts upheld the assessments and surcharges, and P appealed to the ECHR, contending that the surcharges were disproportionate. The ECHR rejected this contention, holding that 'having regard to the State's need to secure an effective system of taxation', the taxes and surcharges could not be considered disproportionate. *Provectus i Stockholm AB v Sweden (and related application)*, ECHR Case 19402/03; 16 January 2007 unreported.

[31.103] See also *Gladders v Prior*, **43.39** PAYMENT OF TAX, and *Auntie's Café Ltd v HMRC*, **44.69** PENALTIES.

Cases where the application was successful

French tax authorities exercising right of pre-emption

[31.104] A married couple bought 6,766 square metres of land in France in 1979. In 1980 the French tax authority exercised a right of pre-emption over the property. The couple appealed, but the French court dismissed their appeal. The wife then applied to the ECHR for a ruling that the exercise of the right of pre-emption was a breach of *Article 1 of the First Protocol* of the *European Convention on Human Rights*. The ECHR accepted this contention, holding (by 5 votes to 4), that there had been a breach of *Article 1 of the First Protocol*. *Hentrich v France*, ECHR Case 13616/88; 18 EHRR 440. (*Note*. The ECHR observed that the right of pre-emption did 'not seem to have any equivalent in the tax systems of the other States parties to the Convention'. It is understood that, since 1987, the French authorities have ceased to exercise pre-emption.)

Retrospective legislation—whether any breach of Convention

[31.105] In 1988 Belgian law was amended, with retrospective effect, to restrict claims for damages arising from collisions involving ships. The ECHR held that the retrospective nature of the law was a breach of the *European Convention on Human Rights*, and that the need to protect the public finances 'could not justify legislating with retrospective effect with the aim and consequence of depriving the applicants of their claims for compensation'. *Pressos Compania Naviera SA v Belgium*, ECHR Case 17849/91, 21 EHRR 301.

[31.106] In May 2011 the Hungarian Parliament enacted legislation which provided that payments of severance pay exceeding 2,000,000 Hungarian forints, paid to public sector workers after 1 January 2010, should be taxed at 98%. A woman, who had been made redundant from the civil service in May 2011, lodged an application with the European Court of Human Rights. The ECHR held that the legislation was a breach of *Article 1 of the First Protocol* of the *European Convention on Human Rights*, finding that it was disproportionate and had deprived the applicant 'of the larger part of a statutorily guaranteed, acquired right'. It awarded the applicant damages of €11,000 and costs of €6,000. *NKM v Hungary*, ECHR Case 66529/11; [2013] STC 1104.

[31.107] The ECHR reached a similar decision in *Gall v Hungary*, ECHR Case 48570/11; 25 June 2013 unreported.

French tax authorities taking charge over property

[31.108] The French tax authorities took a charge over nine properties, with a total value of about 1,000,000 francs, to guarantee a payment of taxes of around 80,000 francs. The debtor applied to the ECHR for a ruling that the charge was disproportionate and was a breach of the *European Convention on Human Rights*. The ECHR accepted this contention, holding that there had been a breach of *Article 1 of the First Protocol*. *Lemoine v France*, ECHR Case 26242/95, 9 June 1999 unreported.

Tax authority exercising power of 'attachment' over house

[31.109] In a Swedish case, a company director (R) failed to submit his 2001 tax return. The tax authority issued an estimated assessment and imposed a surcharge. R failed to pay, and in May 2003 the tax authority exercised the power of attachment over R's house. R appealed to the District Court, which dismissed his appeal. In September 2003 R's house was sold at auction. R refused to leave the house, and was forcibly evicted in October 2003. R subsequently applied to the ECHR for a ruling that his eviction was disproportionate and was a breach of the *European Convention on Human Rights*. He died before the ECHR had delivered judgment, but his widow pursued the application and the ECHR held that there had been a violation of *Article 1 of the First Protocol*. It awarded R's widow damages of €80,000 plus costs of €8,300. *Rousk v Sweden*, ECHR Case 27183/04; 25 July 2013 unreported.

Hungarian tax authority exercising power of 'attachment'

[31.110] A Hungarian company (M) owed 10,000,000 forints in tax. In 1997 the tax authority exercised the power of 'attachment' over M's shareholding in another company. This shareholding had a nominal value of more than 103,000,000 forints. The attachment prevented M from raising funds by selling the shareholding. In 1999 the tax authority released the power of attachment. However, by this time the shareholding had become worthless. M began court proceedings against the tax authority, seeking compensation. The Hungarian Supreme Court dismissed his appeal, and M applied to the ECHR for a ruling that the exercise of the power of attachment had been unduly prolonged and disproportionate, and had contravened *Article 1 of the First Protocol* of the *European Convention on Human Rights*. The ECHR accepted this contention, finding that under Hungarian law, the tax authority should have held an auction to sell the shareholding within two months of the attachment, but had not done so. The ECHR awarded M damages of €5,000. *Metalco BT v Hungary*, ECHR Case 34976/05; [2011] STC 675.

Russia—tax authority seizing company's assets

[31.111] A Russian oil company (N), originally owned by the State, had been privatised in 1996. In 2003 the tax authority carried out a detailed tax inspection and formed the opinion that N had a large tax liability for 2000, in that it had purported to trade through sham companies registered in low-tax areas of Russia such as Mordoviya and Kalmykiya. The tax authority ordered

N to pay tax arrears of more than €1,000,000,000 and a penalty of more than €500,000,000. N failed to pay, and the tax authority took proceedings in the Moscow City Commercial Court. The court gave judgment for the tax authority, and the Federal Commercial Court upheld this decision, holding that the court had been entitled to find that 'the applicant company was the effective owner of all goods traded by the sham companies registered in low-tax areas, that the transactions of these entities were in fact those of the applicant, that neither the company nor the sham entities were eligible for the tax exemptions and that the applicant company had received the entirety of the resulting profits'. The Supreme Commercial Court upheld this decision. In 2004, before the appeal to the Supreme Commercial Court had been decided, bailiffs seized some of N's assets, including shares in one of its principal production subsidiaries (Y), in order to enforce the earlier judgment of the Moscow City Commercial Court. Most of the shares in Y were sold at auction. Subsequently the tax authority also took proceedings to collect tax from N for 2001 to 2003. N applied to the ECHR for a ruling that the proceedings had constituted a breach of the *European Convention on Human Rights*, contending that it had adopted a 'tax optimisation scheme' which had previously been tolerated. The ECHR reviewed the evidence in detail and rejected this contention, finding that 'the Court has little doubt that the factual conclusions of the domestic courts in the tax assessment proceedings 2000-2003 were sound. The factual issues in all of these proceedings were substantially similar and the relevant case files contained abundant witness statements and documentary evidence to support the connections between the applicant company and its trading companies and to prove the sham nature of the latter entities.' However, the ECHR granted N's application, holding (by a 5-2 majority) that, in pursuing the enforcement proceedings, 'the domestic authorities failed to strike a fair balance between the legitimate aims sought and the measures employed'. *OAO Neftyanaka Kompaniya Yukos v Russia*, ECHR Case 14902/04; [2011] STC 1988; 14 ITLR 229. (*Notes.* (1) At a subsequent hearing, the ECHR awarded N damages of €1,866,104,634 and costs of €300,000 — ECHR Case 14902/14; 31 July 2014 unreported. (2) For a case involving one of N's principal shareholders, see *Khodorkovskiy v Russia*, 31.58 above.)

Failure to implement EC Directive—whether any breach of Convention

[31.112] *Article 13B(a)* of the *EC Sixth Directive on VAT* exempted insurance and insurance-related transactions from VAT with effect from 1 January 1978. France failed to implement this Directive, and continued to charge VAT on such transactions. On 30 June 1978 the *EC Ninth Directive on VAT* gave France until 1 January 1979 in which to implement *Article 13B(a)*. A French company (D) claimed reimbursement of the tax which it had been charged from January 1978 to June 1978, contending that the *Ninth Directive* did not have retrospective effect so that, under EC law, the transactions were exempt for that period. The French authorities rejected the claim and the Conseil d'Etat dismissed D's appeal. D then applied to the ECHR, contending that the decision of the Conseil d'Etat contravened *Article 1 of the First Protocol of the European Convention on Human Rights*. The ECHR granted the application, holding that there was no justification for 'the Conseil d'Etat's refusal to give effect to a directly applicable provision of Community law'. The decision breached the company's 'right to the peaceful enjoyment of its possessions'. The interference was 'disproportionate', since 'both the negation of the applicant company's claim against the State and the absence of domestic procedures affording a sufficient remedy to ensure the protection of the applicant company's right to the peaceful enjoyment of its possessions upset the fair balance that must be maintained between the demands of the general interest of the community and the requirements of the protection of the individual's fundamental rights'. *SA Dangeville v France*, ECHR Case 36677/97; [2003] STC 771; 5 ITLR 604.

[31.113] A similar decision was reached in *SA Cabinet Diot v France, ECHR Case 49217/99; SA Gras Savoye v France*, ECHR Case 49218/99; 22 July 2003 unreported.

Government taking court proceedings to quash previous court decision

[31.114] In a Romanian case, three former soldiers received allowances from the Ministry of Defence. The Ministry deducted tax from the payments, and the recipients took court proceedings, contending that the allowances were not subject to tax. In January 2001 the Romanian Court of First Instance gave judgment in favour of the recipients. In March 2001 this decision was upheld on appeal. In September 2001 the Romanian Procurator-General applied to the Romanian Supreme Court of Justice to quash the judgments in favour of the recipients, contending that the lower courts had 'committed serious errors of law'. In January 2002 the Supreme Court accepted this contention and quashed the previous judgments. The recipients applied to the ECHR for a declaration that the decision of the Romanian Supreme Court of Justice contravened *Article 1 of the First Protocol of the European Convention on Human Rights*. The ECHR accepted this contention and granted the applications, holding that the decisions of the lower courts 'had become *res judicata*'. The ECHR held that 'no party is entitled to seek a review of a final and binding judgment merely for the purpose of obtaining a rehearing and a fresh determination of the case' and that 'were that not the case, the reversal of final decisions would result in a general climate of legal uncertainty, reducing public confidence in the judicial system and consequently in the rule of law.' The Procurator-General had not been a party to the previous proceedings, and his intervention had upset 'the fair balance that must be struck between the protection of property and the requirements of the general interest'. Accordingly, there had been a violation of *Article 1 of the First Protocol. Stere & Others v Romania*, ECHR Case 25632/02; 8 ITLR 636.

Whether Presidential Decree overrides Parliamentary legislation

[31.115] In 1992 the Ukrainian Parliament approved a Ministerial Decree providing for certain income to be taxed at a flat rate of 20%. In 1994 the Ukrainian President issued a Presidential Decree providing that such income should be taxed at progressive rates. In 2002 a Ukrainian national (S) began proceedings in the Ukrainian courts, contending that the Presidential Decree was invalid and that his income should only be taxed at 20%. The Ukrainian Supreme Court rejected this contention and dismissed his appeal. S applied to the ECHR for a declaration that the Ukrainian Presidential Decree contravened *Article 1* of the *First Protocol of the European Convention on Human*

Rights. The ECHR accepted this contention and granted the application, finding that under the Ukrainian Constitution, the Ukrainian President was 'empowered to issue decrees in the field of economic reforms if the relevant matters were not covered by the laws of Parliament'. However the rates of taxation were covered by the laws of Parliament, so that the Presidential Decree purporting to increase the relevant rate of tax was unlawful and breached *Article 1 of the First Protocol*. *Shchokin v Ukraine*, ECHR Case 23759/03; [2011] STC 401.

The right to freedom of movement (Fourth Protocol, Article 2)

[31.116] In a Ukrainian case, the tax authorities formed the opinion that a businessman (D) had been guilty of tax evasion, and began criminal proceedings. In June 2001 he was required to give a written undertaking not to abscond, implying that he could not leave his home town, without the investigators' permission. While the criminal proceedings were awaiting trial, D began civil proceedings against the tax authorities. In 2007 D was convicted of tax evasion and sentenced to five years' imprisonment, suspended on probation. D applied to the ECHR, contending that the requirement that he should undertake not to abscond was a breach of *Article 2* of the *Fourth Protocol of the European Convention on Human Rights*. The ECHR rejected this contention, holding that 'the measure applied to the applicant was not disproportionate'. *Doroshenko v Ukraine*, ECHR Case 1328/04; 26 May 2011 unreported. (*Note*. The ECHR held that the length of the proceedings had been a breach of *Article 6* of the *Convention*, and awarded token damages of €1,200.)

Double jeopardy (Seventh Protocol, Article 4)

[31.117] In a Finnish case, the tax authority formed the opinion that a company director (H) had received disguised dividends, which he had failed to declare. They imposed surcharges for 2004 and 2005. H did not appeal. Subsequently, but before the time limit for appealing had expired, H was charged with aggravated tax fraud. He was convicted, and sentenced to 31 months' imprisonment. He appealed to the Finnish Supreme Court, which dismissed his appeal, finding that in view of the extended time limits for appeals, the civil proceedings had not become final before the criminal proceedings started. H also applied to the ECHR, contending that the proceedings were a breach of *Article 4* of the *Seventh Protocol of the European Convention on Human Rights*. The ECHR rejected this contention and dismissed his application, finding that 'the present case concerns two parallel and separate sets of proceedings' and that the civil proceedings had not become final until December 2010 whereas the criminal proceedings had become final in June 2010. *Hakka v Finland*, ECHR Case 758/11; 20 May 2014 unreported.

[31.118] In another Finnish case, where the tax authority had imposed surcharges on a company, and criminal proceedings were subsequently taken against its major shareholder, the ECHR held that 'the two impugned sets of proceedings did not constitute a single set of concrete factual circumstances arising from identical facts or facts which were substantially the same'. *Pirttimaki v Finland*, ECHR Case 35232/11; 20 May 2014 unreported.

[31.119] The ECHR reached a contrasting decision in a case where the facts were broadly similar to those in *Hakka v Finland*, **31.117** above, but where civil proceedings had become final in April 2009 and the applicant had been sentenced to ten months' imprisonment in March 2010. The ECHR held that 'as the second set of proceedings was not discontinued after the first set of proceedings became final', there had been a violation of *Article 4* of the *Seventh Protocol*. *Nykanen v Finland*, ECHR Case 11828/11; 20 May 2014 unreported.

[31.120] The ECHR reached a similar decision in a case where civil proceedings had become final in January 2010 and the applicant had been sentenced to 32 months' imprisonment in October 2010. *Glantz v Finland*, ECHR Case 37394/11; [2014] STC 2263.

[31.121] In a Swedish case, the tax authority formed the opinion that a couple who operated a restaurant had underdeclared their income, and imposed surcharges on them. The wife was also charged with false accounting. In January 2009 she was convicted of false accounting and ordered to perform community service. In October 2009 the Supreme Court refused her leave to appeal against the surcharges. She applied to the ECHR, contending that the proceedings were a breach of *Article 4* of the *Seventh Protocol of the European Convention on Human Rights*. The ECHR granted her application and awarded her compensation of €2,000. *Mrs L Dev v Sweden*, ECHR Case 7356/10; 27 November 2014 unreported.

[31.122] See also *Carlberg v Sweden*, **31.15** above.

32

Interest on Overpaid Tax

Application for repayment supplement

[32.1] The Ch D held that a German bank was exempt from paying UK tax on interest which it received under the 1946 UK/USA double taxation convention as then in force. It ordered the repayment to the bank of overpaid tax of £4.2 million. The bank applied for repayment supplement. The Revenue refused to pay any repayment supplement, considering that the supplement was not payable to taxpayers who were not resident in the UK, and that the bank had not been discriminated against by virtue of its non-residence, since, if the bank had been resident in the UK, the tax would not have been repaid in the first place. The bank applied for judicial review. The QB referred the case to the ECJ, which held that the residence requirement laid down by the UK legislation was incompatible with the *EC Treaty*, and that the fact that the exemption from tax which gave rise to the refund was available only to non-resident companies could not justify a rule of a general nature withholding the benefit. Accordingly, the bank was entitled to repayment supplement. *R v CIR (ex p. Commerzbank AG)*, ECJ 1993, 68 TC 252; [1993] STC 605; [1994] 2 WLR 128; [1993] 4 All ER 37. (*Notes.* (1) The exemption from UK tax was removed by *Article 11* of the 1980 UK/USA double taxation agreement. (2) For the Revenue's practice following this decision, see the Revenue Press Release dated 23 July 1993. (3) The application was concluded by a consent order in the QB—see 68 TC 278.)

[32.2] In March 1989 a company (S) effected a purchase of its own shares which constituted a distribution for corporation tax purposes with a consequential liability for ACT. Since this ACT exceeded the company's prospective liability for the accounting period in which the distribution had taken place, the result was that S had surplus ACT available to be carried back and set against CT liability for earlier accounting periods. Assessments in respect of earlier periods remained open, some of the tax charged having been postponed under *TMA 1970, s 55*. S made revised postponement applications, to which the Revenue agreed, and repayments were made in April 1989. S claimed repayment supplement under *ICTA 1988, s 825*, but the Revenue rejected the claim, considering that no supplement was due by virtue of *ICTA 1988, s 825(4)(a)*. Subsequently, following the issue of the assessment for its accounting period ending in March 1989, S submitted a formal claim for the carry-back of its surplus ACT, and issued a summons seeking a declaration that the repayments made to it in April 1989 should be increased by repayment supplement. The Ch D dismissed the summons and the CA unanimously dismissed S's appeal, holding that the letter in which S had submitted a revised postponement application was also a claim to carry back surplus ACT, and it followed that the effect of *ICTA 1988, s 825(4)(a)* was that no repayment supplement was due. *Savacentre Ltd v CIR*, CA 1995, 67 TC 381; [1995] STC 867.

[32.3] A company (J) which operated the Japanese postal service was accepted as being 'an arm of the Japanese government' and thus as entitled to sovereign immunity from UK tax. It received dividends from UK companies, and was repaid tax credits relating to these dividends. It claimed repayment supplement under *ICTA 1988, s 824*. The Revenue rejected the claim and the QB dismissed J's appeal. Collins J held that there was nothing in *s 824* which entitled J to repayment supplement. *Japan Post v HMRC (and related appeals)*, QB [2008] STC 3295; [2008] EWHC 1511 (Admin).

Application by building society

[32.4] In the case noted at **7.1** BUILDING SOCIETIES, the QB had held that the *Income Tax (Building Societies) Regulations 1986 (SI 1986/482)* were unlawful with regard to the period prior to April 1986. Before that date the Revenue had obtained some £56 million from the society in reliance on those regulations. After the QB decision, the money was repaid to the society with interest from the date of the decision but not from before that date. The society brought an action to claim interest on the payments from the date they were made to the date of the decision. The HL upheld the society's claim (by a 3–2 majority, Lord Keith of Kinkel and Lord Jauncey dissenting). As a matter of principle, 'money paid by a citizen to a public authority in the form of taxes or other levies paid pursuant to an *ultra vires* demand by the authority is *prima facie* recoverable by the citizen as of right'. There had been no lawful basis for the Revenue's demands for tax in this case. Since the Revenue had acted *ultra vires*, the society was entitled to redress under the principle of 'unjust enrichment'. *Woolwich Equitable Building Society v CIR*, HL 1992, 63 TC 265; [1992] STC 657; [1992] 3 WLR 366; [1992] 3 All ER 737.

Compounding of interest

[32.5] In the case noted at **25.18** EUROPEAN LAW, the ECJ held that the provisions of *ICTA 1988, s 247* contravened what is now *Article 49* of the the TFEU. The companies claimed compensation. The Revenue agreed to pay interest computed on a simple basis. One of the companies applied to the Ch D for a ruling that the interest should be paid on a compound basis. The Ch D held that interest for the period between the payment of the ACT to the date upon which it was set off against mainstream corporation tax should be computed on a compound basis, but that interest for the post-utilisation period (the period from when the cause of action accrued until the date of judgment) arose under UK domestic law rather than under EC law, and the effect of *Supreme Court Act 1981, s 35A* was that such interest should be computed on a simple basis. The Revenue appealed to the HL, which largely upheld the Ch D decision (by a 3-2 majority, Lord Scott of Foscote and Lord Mance dissenting), subject to a variation in the rate of interest to be used. Lord Hope of Craighead held that 'the time has come to recognise that the court has jurisdiction at common law to award compound interest where the claimant seeks a restitutionary remedy for the time value of money paid under a mistake'. Simple interest was 'an artificial construct which has no relation to the way money is obtained or turned to account in the real world.' In this case, the company's claim for restitution 'ought to be measured by an award of interest at conventional rates calculated by reference to the rates of interest and other terms applicable to borrowing by the Government in the market during the relevant period'. Lord Nicholls of Birkenhead observed that 'we live in a world where interest payments for the use of money are calculated on a compound basis. Money is not available commercially on simple interest terms.' For the law to 'achieve a fair and just outcome when assessing financial loss, it must recognise and give effect to this reality'. *CIR v Sempra Metals Ltd*, HL [2007] STC 1559; [2007] UKHL 34; [2007] 4 All ER 657.

33

Interest Payable

The cases in this chapter are arranged under the following headings.

CROSS-REFERENCES

See 52 SAVINGS AND INVESTMENT INCOME generally for interest receivable, and 63.278 *et seq.* TRADING PROFITS for the allowance of interest in computing business profits.

Yearly interest (ITA 2007, s 874)

NOTE

The deduction of tax from interest is now governed by *ITA 2007, s 874* and the principal type of interest payment now affected is one of yearly interest (other than bank interest) made by a company or local authority. Cases which are relevant in construing 'yearly interest' in *ITA 2007, s 874* are included in this section, notwithstanding that the payment involved would not now be subject to deduction of tax.

Bank interest—whether 'yearly interest'

[33.1] A banking firm arranged with its customers to deduct tax from interest on loans for a specified period of less than a year, treating it as 'yearly interest' within *ITA 1853, s 40* (compare now *ITA 2007, s 874*). It appealed against an assessment on its trading income, contending that the interest should be excluded from its taxable trading profits. The Special Commissioners rejected this contention and dismissed the appeal, and the CA unanimously upheld their decision, holding that the interest was not 'yearly interest'. *Goslings & Sharpe v Blake*, CA 1889, 2 TC 450; 23 QBD 324. (*Note.* The substantive issue has been overtaken by later legislation, but the case remains of importance in relation to the meaning of 'yearly'.)

Interest on judgment debt

[33.2] The CA held that interest on a judgment debt was not within the definition of 'yearly interest'. *Re Cooper*, CA [1911] 2 KB 550.

Current account interest—whether yearly

[33.3] The Special Commissioners held that interest on a charity's current bank account, calculated on the daily balance, was not 'yearly interest' (and therefore not exempt in the hands of the charity). The KB upheld their decision. *Garston Overseers for the Poor v Carlisle*, KB 1915, 6 TC 659; [1915] 3 KB 281.

Fluctuating interest—whether yearly

[33.4] Solicitors lent money to a baronet over a period of several years, without security or any written agreement. The amounts varied and interest was charged annually, at a rate which fluctuated in accordance with the rate charged by Scottish banks on overdrafts. The baronet appealed against a super-tax assessment, contending that the interest was 'yearly interest' (and was therefore deductible in computing his total income for super-tax). The Special Commissioners accepted this contention and allowed his appeal, and the CS unanimously upheld their decision. *CIR v Sir Duncan Hay*, CS 1924, 8 TC 636.

Compound interest on compensation payment—whether yearly

[33.5] An individual (B) established a settlement in favour of his children. In 1923 he reinvested the settled funds in unauthorised securities, which subsequently fell in value. The other trustees objected to this as a breach of trust. In 1930 B agreed to repay this money to the trustees, with compound interest. He appealed against surtax assessments, contending that the compound interest was 'yearly interest' and was deductible in computing his income for surtax. The KB accepted this contention and allowed his appeal. *Barlow v CIR*, KB 1937, 21 TC 354.

Loan interest—whether yearly

[33.6] A finance company took proceedings for possession of property which was the subject of a secured loan. The borrower defended the proceedings, contending that the interest payable on the loan was yearly interest from which he was required to deduct tax under the legislation then in force, so that he was not in arrears with the payments. The CA unanimously accepted this contention and gave judgment for the defendant. *Corinthian Securities Ltd v Cato*, CA 1969, 46 TC 93; [1970] 1 QB 377; [1969] 3 All ER 1168.

[33.7] A company (M) had a substantial overdraft. Its parent company (S) extinguished the overdraft by paying £270,000 into M's bank account. A loan account was opened in the books of S and M, but there was no formal agreement as to the terms on which the loan was made. In April 1986 entries were made in the loan accounts crediting S and debiting M with interest at a commercial rate for the accounting periods ending 30 September 1983 and 1984. M appealed against a corporation tax assessment for 1985/86, contending that the interest should be allowed as a deduction in computing its trading profits. The Special Commissioner dismissed M's appeal, holding that the interest was yearly interest and had not been paid within the meaning of what is now *CTA 2010, s 189*. The Ch D upheld this decision. The Commissioner had found as a fact that the loan was in the nature of a long-term loan, and it followed that the interest was yearly interest. Although in some circumstances a book entry could constitute payment, the interest in this case had been compounded and had not been paid within the meaning of *s 189*. *Minsham Properties Ltd v Price; Lysville Ltd v Price*, Ch D 1990, 63 TC 570; [1990] STC 718.

Payments in respect of expenditure incurred by recipient

[33.8] A bank (K) acquired rights under a building agreement from another company (E). E was required to make payments, described as 'interest', to K. It did not withhold tax from the payments. Subsequently K took winding-up proceedings against E for arrears of rent, and E lodged a counterclaim that it should have withheld tax from the payments of 'interest' to K under what is now *ITA 2007, s 874*, so that there were no grounds for the petition. The Ch D rejected this contention and dismissed E's counterclaim, holding that the payments were not 'yearly interest of money'. Megarry J held that, for a payment to amount to 'interest of money', there must be a sum of money, due to the person entitled to receive the interest, 'by reference to which the payment which is said to be interest is to be ascertained'. The sums by reference to which the payments here were ascertained were units of calculation, rather than loans due to K. The payments were not interest on loans but were compensation for E's 'delay in performance of other obligations'. *Re Euro Hotel (Belgravia) Ltd*, Ch D 1975, 51 TC 293; [1975] STC 682; [1975] 3 All ER 1075.

[33.9] Two oil groups (BP and C) each held the licence to operate two separate tracts of a North Sea oil field. It was agreed that, in the exploration and development of the field, the two tracts should be dealt with as a single unit. Most of the relevant work was done by a company in C's group, with BP contributing to the cost. Its contribution was based on the estimated oil in the respective two tracts, with periodic adjustments either way as more accurate information became available as to the expected yield. For the purpose of each periodic adjustment, a statement was prepared showing the total expenditure in each month to date, with 'interest factors' added to each monthly amount, calculated at prescribed rates from the middle of the month. The aggregate, including the interest factors, was apportioned between the parties to arrive at the appropriate adjustment between the parties. Because of an increase in its estimated share of the yield, a substantial sum became due from BP following a periodic adjustment. On paying it, BP treated tax as deductible from the interest factors. C applied to the Ch D for a ruling on whether this was correct. The Ch D gave judgment for BP, holding that the 'interest factors' were interest of money from which tax was deductible. Sir Robert Megarry V-C held that 'if in its nature a sum is "interest of money"', it retained that nature 'even if the parties to a contract provides for it to be wrapped up with some other sum and the whole paid in the form of a single indivisible sum. The wrappings may conceal the nature of the contents, but they do not alter them.' *Chevron Petroleum (UK) Ltd and Others v BP Petroleum Development Ltd and Others*, Ch D 1981, 57 TC 137; [1981] STC 689.

Payment under avoidance scheme—whether annual interest

[33.10] An individual (C) was employed by the Rossminster group of companies, which specialised in tax avoidance schemes (see **49.63** RETURNS AND INFORMATION for a HL decision involving the group). In 1974 C borrowed £37,740 from a subsidiary of the group. Under a written agreement, the loan was to last for two years with interest of 13% payable in advance. On the same day he gave the company a cheque for £5,000, stated to be the interest. Four days later he entered into an arrangement under which he was released from his liability to repay the £37,740, and paid £32,740 to another Rossminster subsidiary which agreed to stand in his shoes as debtor. He claimed tax relief on the £5,000 on the basis that it was 'annual interest'. The Revenue rejected the claim and the CA unanimously dismissed C's appeal. Firstly, applying the HL decision in *WT Ramsay Ltd v CIR*, **71.285** CAPITAL GAINS TAX, the transactions 'lacked all reality'. Sir John Donaldson observed that C 'neither paid a fee nor incurred any expenses', and 'at the end of a series of connected and intended transactions, his financial position was precisely as it was at the beginning'. Accordingly the payment did not constitute 'interest'. Furthermore, even if the payment had constituted interest, it would have been short interest rather than annual interest, since the loan to C 'was never intended to last for more than a few days'. *Cairns v MacDiarmid*, CA 1982, 56 TC 556; [1983] STC 178. (*Note.* See also *CTA 2009, s 443*, deriving from *FA 1976*.)

Whether interest arising in the UK

[33.11] A company director (P), who was resident and domiciled in the UK, borrowed some money from an Isle of Man company. The loan was paid into an Isle of Man bank account in P's name. The agreement provided that P was required to pay interest at 4.75% pa. P paid this from his Isle of Man bank account, without deducting tax under *ITA 2007, s 874*. HMRC issued assessments under *ITA 2007, s 963*, on the basis that the interest had arisen in the UK, where P was resident. P appealed, contending that the interest had arisen in the Isle of Man, so that *s 874* did not apply. The First-tier Tribunal rejected this contention and dismissed P's appeal. Judge Hellier observed that 'the country from or in which (P's) obligations to pay would be contemplated to be enforced or would substantively originate' was the UK. Therefore the interest had arisen in the UK, and was within *s 874*. *AC Perrin v HMRC*, FTT [2014] UKFTT 223 (TC); [2014] SFTD 919, TC03363; 16 ITLR 856.

[33.12] A UK company (C) paid interest of more than £5,000,000 to two Gibraltar trusts and to two companies incorporated in the British Virgin Islands, without deducting tax under *ITA 2007, s 874*. HMRC issued assessments under *ITA 2007, s 957*, on the basis that the interest had arisen in the UK. C appealed, contending that the interest should be treated as having arisen outside the UK, so that *s 874* did not apply. The First-tier Tribunal rejected this contention and dismissed the appeal. Judge Brooks observed that 'the United Kingdom, in addition to being the source or origin of the funds for payment, would be the place of enforcement of the debt'. Therefore the interest had arisen in the UK. *Ardmore Construction Ltd v HMRC*, FTT [2014]

UKFTT 453 (TC); [2014] SFTD 1077, TC03580; 16 ITLR 992. (*Note*. For another issue in this case, see **4.146** APPEALS.)

Relief for interest payable (ITA 2007, s 383–410)

NOTE

The cases noted at **33.13** to **33.16** below relate to claims under *ITA 1918, s 36*. This provision was abolished from 1969/70, but the cases may still be of some relevance with regard to the provisions now contained in *ITA 2007, s 383–410* (which derive from *FA 1972*). Relief for mortgage interest was abolished with effect from April 2000 by *FA 1999, s 38, Sch 4*. The cases in this section should be read in the light of the changes in the legislation.

Interest paid by guarantors

[33.13] Two individuals, who had guaranteed a company's bank overdraft, paid an amount to the bank to clear the overdraft and claimed relief under *ITA 1918, s 36* insofar as the payment represented unpaid interest debited to the overdraft. The CA rejected the claim and the HL unanimously dismissed the guarantors' appeal. Viscount Dunedin held that 'interest payable on an advance from a bank means interest on an advance made to the person paying. The guarantor does not pay on an advance made to him, but pays under his guarantee.' *CIR v Holder and Holder*, HL 1932, 16 TC 540. (*Note*. Overdraft interest no longer qualifies for relief, but the case remains relevant as showing that payment of loan interest by a guarantor does not qualify for relief.)

Interest paid to Guernsey branch of UK bank

[33.14] The KB held that interest debited on an overdrawn account at a Guernsey branch of a UK bank was payable in the UK for the purposes of *ITA 1918, s 36*. *Maude v CIR*, KB 1940, 23 TC 63; [1940] 1 KB 548; [1940] 1 All ER 464. (*Note*. Overdraft interest no longer qualifies for relief, but the case remains relevant with regard to the place of payment of interest.)

Interest debited by bank—no payment by borrower

[33.15] The HL held that interest debited to a bank account, for a year in which nothing had been paid into the account, had not been paid to the bank for the purposes of relief under *ITA 1918, s 36*. Lord Macmillan held that 'the fact that the banks treat the accrued and accumulated interest in this fashion as an item of income in their income tax accounts' did not 'necessarily lead to the view that the customer has paid this interest within the statutory meaning'. *Paton (Fenton's Trustee) v CIR*, HL 1938, 21 TC 625; [1938] AC 341; [1938] 1 All ER 786.

Discount on promissory notes discounted with bank

[33.16] In a Northern Ireland case, an individual (T) gave promissory notes to a firm of solicitors, who endorsed them and passed them to a bank for a discounting. T claimed relief under *ITA 1918, s 36* on the difference between the face value of the notes and their discounted value. The Revenue rejected the claim and the Special Commissioners and the KB dismissed T's appeal, holding that the discounts charged by the bank did not constitute payment of interest. Best LJ held that 'when a banker discounts a bill for a customer, giving him credit for the amount of the bill and debiting him with the discount, there is a complete purchase of the bill by the banker'. *Torrens v CIR*, KB(NI) 1933, 18 TC 262.

Interest on overdraft secured by deeds of property

[33.17] An individual held a current account with a bank, with overdraft facilities secured by on the deeds of a house. He claimed relief on the interest he paid to the bank. The Revenue rejected the claim and the Ch D dismissed his appeal, holding that the interest was ordinary overdraft interest, and that the effect of what is now *ITA 2007, s 384(1)(a)* was that it was not eligible for relief. *Walcot-Bather v Golding*, Ch D 1979, 52 TC 649; [1979] STC 707.

ITA 2007, s 384(1)—relief claimed on overdraft interest

[33.18] A property developer financed his expenditure by overdrawing on bank current accounts. He subsequently transferred the overdrawn balances to a new loan account, and claimed relief for the interest charged on the loan account. The Ch D rejected the claim, holding that since relief for interest on the overdrawn current accounts was prohibited by what is now *ITA 2007, s 384(1)(a)*, it followed that no relief was available for the replacement loan. *Lawson v Brooks*, Ch D 1991, 64 TC 462; [1992] STC 76.

[33.19] The decision in *Lawson v Brooks*, **33.18** above, was applied in the similar subsequent case of *W Green v HMRC*, FTT [2011] UKFTT 660 (TC), TC01502.

Interest paid under guarantee of overdraft of close company

[33.20] A married couple controlled a company (B) and had guaranteed its overdraft. B ceased trading and the couple sold its business premises (which they had owned), using the proceeds to pay off the overdraft and the interest on it, in accordance with the guarantee. The husband claimed relief on the interest under what is now *ITA 2007, s 392*. The Ch D rejected the claim, holding that the interest was not on a loan to an individual within the meaning of the legislation. *Hendy v Hadley*, Ch D 1980, 53 TC 353; [1980] STC 292; [1980] 2 All ER 554.

Whether house occupied as 'main residence'

[33.21] A publican (F) was the tied tenant of an inn in Essex. The brewery could terminate the tenancy on giving 12 months' notice, and one of its terms required F to live on the premises, In March 1976 F and his wife purchased and furnished a house in Wales with a building society mortgage. They had not previously owned a house, and thereafter they regarded it as their home, one or both of them spending 'several days' in it each month. F claimed relief on the mortgage interest for 1975/76 and 1976/77. The Revenue rejected the claim but the Commissioners allowed F's appeal and the Ch D upheld their decision as one of fact. Nourse J held that 'if someone lives in two houses the question, which does he use as the principal or more important one, cannot be determined solely by the way in which he divides his time between the two'. Applying *dicta* of Lord Denning in *Fowell v Radford*, CA 1969, [1970] RVR 82, 'very often a couple have two residences, a town residence and a country residence, so that it is almost impossible to say which is the main residence. In such a case, the judge has to come down on one side of the line'. *Frost v Feltham*, Ch D 1980, 55 TC 10; [1981] STC 115; [1981] 1 WLR 452.

House resold without being lived in

[33.22] An individual, who owned and lived in a house in Chester, bought a house in Liverpool with the intention of making it his main residence and selling his Chester house. He obtained a bridging loan from a bank, but was unable to sell his Chester house, and sold the Liverpool house instead. He claimed relief on the interest on his bridging loan. The Ch D rejected the claim, holding that, since he had not used the Liverpool house as his main residence, he was not entitled to relief. *Hughes v Viner*, Ch D 1985, 58 TC 437; [1985] STC 235; [1985] 3 All ER 40. (*Note*. For a preliminary issue in this case, see **4.189** APPEALS.)

Relief for loan to close company

[33.23] A company (W) received a substantial loan from its chairman (T), who had financed this by a loan from another company. T claimed relief under what is now *ITA 2007, s 392* for the interest he paid on the loan to him. HMRC rejected the claim on the basis that the loan did not meet the statutory conditions, because W had lent the money to an associated Canadian company (WA), rather than using it for its own business. T appealed, contending that W's loan to WA should be treated as part of W's business. The First-tier Tribunal accepted this contention and allowed the appeal. *JS Torkington v HMRC*, FTT [2010] UKFTT 441 (TC), TC00706.

[33.24] An individual (N) agreed to lend £100,000 to a company (V) of which he was a director. He financed this by increasing the mortgage on his house, and claimed relief under what is now *ITA 2007, s 392* for the additional interest he had to pay. HMRC rejected the claim on the grounds that although N was a director of V, he did not own any shares in V and thus did not have a material interest in V, within what is now *ITA 2007, s 394*. N appealed. The First-tier Tribunal allowed N's appeal, finding that he had a 50% interest in a company (P) which was associated with V, whose controlling director was a major shareholder in P and was P's main creditor, entitling him to receive the greater part of P's net assets if it were to be wound up. Judge Geraint Jones held that the effect of what is now *s 394(4)* was that N should be treated as having a material interest in V, as he was a significant loan creditor and was therefore a 'participator' in V within what is now *CTA 2010, s 454*. *A Nowosielski v HMRC*, FTT [2012] UKFTT 212 (TC), TC01907.

Whether loan used to buy interest in close company

[33.25] An accountant (C) acquired a 50% shareholding in a company (B) which dealt in motor cars. B suffered financial difficulties and C made various loans to it. He also obtained a loan of £70,200 from a building society (H) to finance his purchase of a flat which his mother owned and continued to occupy. His mother subsequently repaid £46,000 to him, and he made further loans, in excess of that amount, to B. He claimed relief under what is now *ITA 2007, s 392* for the interest which he paid to H. The Revenue rejected the claim on the ground that the money had been used to purchase the flat, rather than for lending to B. The Special Commissioner dismissed C's appeal. *Cohen v Petch*, Sp C [1999] SSCD 207 (Sp C 199).

ITA 2007, s 398—relief for loan to buy into partnership

[33.26] A married couple purchased a 189-acre estate. In May 1987 they signed a contract stating that they had been operating the estate as a partnership (the S partnership) since June 1986. Two days previously they had entered into an agreement with a finance company (C), under which C lent them £450,000 to enable them to buy a farm from two individuals who had operated it in partnership. In June 1987 S and one of the vendors of the farm (HM) entered into a contract of partnership (the WM partnership) to operate the farm. In December 1988 and June 1989 the couple borrowed further money from C. The couple claimed relief under what is now *ITA 2007, s 398* on the interest payable on the loans from C (except for that relating to a small proportion of the loans which had been retained as working capital). The Revenue rejected the claim on the basis that the loans had been made to S, whereas the relevant trade of farming was carried on by WM. The couple appealed, contending that the loans had been applied by S for the purposes of a trade of farming which was carried on in partnership by S and HM, and that the relevant interest qualified for relief. The Special Commissioner accepted this contention and allowed the couple's appeal, observing that there was 'no reason why (S) should not carry on the business of farmers in partnership with a third party'. The Ch D upheld this decision. *Major v Brodie & Brodie (aka Badger & Badger v Major)*, Ch D 1998, 70 TC 576; [1998] STC 491.

[33.27] In 1990 L, the senior partner in an accountancy firm, arranged for the firm to pay a cheque for £30,000 to his wife. On the same day his wife paid a cheque for £30,000, drawn on a joint account in the couple's name, to the firm. Subsequently L claimed interest relief of £3,000 p.a. for 1992/93 to 1995/56 under what is now *ITA 2007, s 383* and *ITA 2007, s 398*, relating to interest which he claimed to have paid to his wife with regard to this transaction. The Revenue rejected the claim and the Special Commissioner dismissed L's appeal, observing that the transaction was 'pre-arranged' and noted that the interest which L's wife claimed to have received from her husband was almost entirely covered by her personal allowance. The effect of what is now *CTA 2009, s 443* was that interest relief was not due 'if a scheme has been effected or arrangements have been made' with the aim that 'the sole or main benefit that might be expected to accrue to that person from the transaction' was a reduction in tax liability. On the evidence, there was 'no other financial benefit in the entire arrangement', so that the effect of *s 443* was that no relief was due. Furthermore, the transaction was not within *s 398*, since 'the true net result of the circular transaction was that no money was contributed or advanced to the partnership which it did not already have'. *Lancaster v CIR*, Sp C [2000] SSCD 138 (Sp C 232).

Bank interest payable by property dealing company

[33.28] A property-dealing company (F) was taxable under Schedule A in respect of rent from property, and under Schedule D on its profits from its property sales. The Revenue treated loan interest, paid by the company on a loan to acquire a property for trading purposes, as a deduction in the Schedule D computation. F appealed, contending that the interest should be dealt with as a charge on income. (The interest would then have been set against its Schedule A income, the consequent increase in its Schedule D profits being covered by otherwise unused trading losses available for carry-forward.) The Ch D rejected this contention, holding that the interest was 'deductible' under what is now *CTA 2010, s 189(2)*. Nourse J held that the word 'deductible' did not import a requirement for a formal claim for deduction. The interest was paid in respect of a loan to acquire trading stock. It was therefore properly deductible in the Schedule D computation, following the ordinary principles of commercial trading, and hence not deductible as a charge on income. *Wilcock v Frigate Investments Ltd*, Ch D 1981, 55 TC 530; [1982] STC 198.

Interest on loan to purchase overseas property let

[33.29] See *Ockenden v Mackley*, 28.24 FOREIGN INCOME.

Miscellaneous

Payment of accrued interest—whether genuine

[33.30] A property-holding company (W) suffered financial difficulties and was loaned substantial sums of money by its major shareholder (a pension fund). Subsequently it obtained further interest-free loans from the same source and paid accrued interest on the earlier loans. It claimed that these payments should be treated as charges on income. The Revenue rejected the claim, considering firstly that W did not qualify as an investment company, secondly that the accrued interest had not been paid for the purposes of what is now *CTA 2010, s 189*, and alternatively that even if the interest were held to have been paid, the payment was not wholly and exclusively for the purpose of W's business. The Special Commissioners allowed W's appeal, holding that W was an investment company within what is now *CTA 2009, s 1218* and that the payments of interest were genuine, had been made for the purpose of W's business, and were effective for the purpose of *s 189*. The HL upheld the Commissioners' decision. The payments of money borrowed from the pension fund constituted payments of interest for the purposes of *s 189*, and the Commissioners were entitled to find that they had been made wholly and exclusively for the purpose of W's business. Lord Nicholls observed that 'the source from which a debtor obtains the money he uses in paying his debt is immaterial'. Lord Hoffmann observed that 'the only apparent reason for the insistence on payment of yearly interest is that payment gives rise to an obligation to deduct tax. In the present case, (W) complied with that obligation. The Crown's real complaint is that the scheme, as an exempt fund, was able to reclaim the tax. But this cannot be remedied by giving the word "paid" a different meaning in the case of a payment to an exempt lender. The word must mean the same, whatever the status of the lender.' Lord Hutton observed that 'the obligation undertaken by (W) to pay interest on the sums it had been lent by the scheme trustees was a genuine one which existed in the real world'. Furthermore, the anti-avoidance provisions of what is now *CTA 2009, s 443* did not apply. *MacNiven v Westmoreland Investments Ltd*, HL 2001, 73 TC 1; [2001] STC 237; [2001] 2 WLR 377; [2001] 1 All ER 865. (*Notes*. (1) For another issue in this case, see **4.384** APPEALS. (2) *Obiter dicta* of Lord Hoffmann were strongly criticised by Lord Millett in *Hong Kong Collector of Stamp Revenue v Arrowtown Assets Ltd*, **75.13** STAMP DUTY LAND TAX. In the subsequent case of *Mawson v Barclays Mercantile Business Finance Ltd*, **8.101** CAPITAL ALLOWANCES, the HL (which included Lord Hoffmann) delivered a composite judgment stating that the relevant part of Lord Hoffmann's judgment was not 'intended to provide a substitute for a close analysis of what the statute means. It certainly does not justify the assumption that an answer can be obtained by classifying all concepts *a priori* as either "commercial" or "legal".')

Discharge of liability for accumulated interest

[33.31] See *CIR v Oswald (Cosier's Settlement Trustee)*, **20.11** DEDUCTION OF TAX.

34

Life Assurance

The cases in this chapter are arranged under the following headings.

Calculation of profits (FA 1989, ss 82–89A)

FA 1989, s 82—calculation of profits

[34.1] A life assurance company claimed that, in computing the profits of its pension business, it was entitled to a deduction under *FA 1989, s 82(1)* for foreign tax expended on behalf of holders of pension policies in respect of amounts for which it had secured credit. The Special Commissioners rejected this contention, holding that it was not entitled to such a deduction. The Commissioners observed that the company's contention was 'anomalous', since it was claiming that there should be 'both a deduction and a credit for the same foreign tax'. The purpose of *FA 1989, s 82* was 'to separate the tax referable to policyholders from the tax referable to the shareholders and to give a deduction for the former'. The Commissioners held that 'the credit treatment of the foreign tax must be taken into account in order to decide whether such foreign tax has been expended on behalf of policyholders'. The Ch D dismissed the company's appeal against this decision. Evans-Lombe J held that the words 'there shall be taken into account as an expense' (in *FA 1989, s 82(1)(a))* should be construed 'so as to exclude amounts which have been recouped by other means or which it is anticipated will be recouped'. *Legal & General Assurance Society Ltd v HMRC (aka Legal & General Assurance Society Ltd v Thomas (No 2))*, Ch D 2006, 78 TC 321; [2006] STC 1763; [2006] EWHC 1770 (Ch); 8 ITLR 1124. (*Notes*. (1) For another issue in this case, see **21.40** DOUBLE TAX RELIEF. (2) *FA 1989, s 82* was repealed by *FA 2012* for accounting periods beginning on or after 1 January 2013.)

FA 1989, s 83—receipts to be taken into account

[34.2] A large life insurance company (S) claimed that it had made Case I losses of more than £1,000,000,000 following its demutualisation. HMRC began an enquiry into S's returns and ascertained that amounts which S had described as 'transfers from capital reserve' had not been taken into account in the computation. The case was referred to the Special Commissioners under *FA 1998, Sch 18 para 31A*. The Commissioners upheld HMRC's contention that the effect of *FA 1989, s 83* was that the 'transfers from capital reserve' had to be taken into account as receipts in computing the loss. Both sides appealed to the Supreme Court, which unanimously dismissed S's appeal and allowed HMRC's cross-appeal, holding that the amounts to be brought into account as receipts for the computation of profits or losses for tax purposes under *FA 1989, s 83(2)(b)* were the amounts shown in line 15 of Form 40. *Scottish Widows plc v HMRC (and cross-appeal)*, SC 2011, 80 TC 796; [2011] UKSC 32; [2011] STC 2171; [2012] 1 All ER 379. (*Note. FA 1989, s 83* was subsequently substantially amended by *FA 2007, Sch 9*, and was repealed by *FA 2012* for accounting periods beginning on or after 1 January 2013. See Simon's Taxes, para D7.5100.)

FA 1989, s 83A—accounts to be 'brought into account'

[34.3] HMRC began an enquiry into the returns submitted by a large life insurance company. HMRC and the company were unable to agree on which of the company's revenue accounts were 'required to be prepared' for the purposes of *FA 1989, s 83A(2)(b)*. The First-tier Tribunal found in favour of the company, holding that the revenue accounts which were 'recognised' for the purposes of *s 83A(2)* were 'the revenue account in respect of the whole of the long term business; the revenue account in respect of the Life and Annuity business; the revenue account in respect of the Permanent Health Insurance business; and the revenue account in respect of the Capital Redemption Business; but not the memorandum Form 40 in respect of the with-profits part of the Life and Annuity business'. The Upper Tribunal upheld this decision, holding that 'for a memorandum Form 40 to be recognised for the purposes of *section 83* would be inconsistent with the scheme of the legislation'. *Legal & General Assurance Society Ltd v HMRC (No 2)*, UT [2010] STC 2741. (*Note. FA 1989, s 83A* was repealed by *FA 2012* for accounting periods beginning on or after 1 January 2013.)

Miscellaneous

Recovery of tax under SI 1978/1159, reg 10

[34.4] A life insurance company made annual deficiency claims in respect of periods ending from December 1984 to December 1991. The Revenue formed the opinion that the company had claimed relief in respect of policies which had not been effected until after 13 March 1984, and thus did not qualify for relief. It indicated that it intended to recover any overpayments of deficiencies under *Income Tax (Life Assurance Premium Relief) Regulations 1978 (SI 1978/1159), reg 10(6)*. The company applied to the Ch D seeking declarations that the Revenue could only recover any deficiencies by assessments issued under *TMA 1970*. (For 1984 to 1990, the Revenue had not issued such assessments within the normal six-year time limit.) The Ch D rejected the company's contentions and dismissed the application. The effect of *reg 10(6)* was that the Revenue had an immediate enforceable statutory right to recover overpayments of deficiencies without issuing assessments. *United Friendly Insurance plc v CIR*, Ch D 1998, 70 TC 627; [1998] STC 621.

Application for certification of policy under ICTA 1988, Sch 15

[34.5] A life insurance company (M) submitted to the Revenue a draft of an unusual form of with-profits ten-year term life assurance policy, requesting that it should be certified as a 'qualifying policy' under *ICTA 1988, s 267* and *Sch 15*. The policy included, *inter alia*, an option for a new policy on the expiration of the ten-year period, with a right to carry forward, to the new policy, the reversionary bonuses declared on the original policy. The Revenue declined to certify the policy as a 'qualifying policy', and M applied for judicial review. The QB dismissed the application and the CA unanimously dismissed M's appeal, holding that the policy failed to meet the statutory test. Robert Walker LJ observed that 'it is of the essence of a term policy that it is worthless if the life assured is still living when the term expires'. The policy in question was not worthless after the end of the ten-year period. Furthermore, the Revenue could not be required to certify a policy where there was 'real doubt as to its legal effect'. *R (oao Monarch Assurance plc) v CIR*, CA 2001, 74 TC 346; [2001] STC 1639.

Financial futures transactions—whether within CTA 2009, ss 296–301

[34.6] Five life assurance companies entered into 'financial futures' transactions with derivatives dealers, intended to cover the element of risk in index-linked bonds which the companies issued. Under the agreements, most of the transactions were to be settled in shares, but with an option to take cash instead, The Revenue issued assessments on the basis that the transactions fell within the 'loan relationships' provisions of what is now *CTA 2009, ss 296–301*. The companies appealed, contending that the transactions were not within the scope of these provisions. The Special Commissioners accepted this contention and allowed the appeals, holding that 'from any commercial perspective none of the transactions involved loans. None of the parties regarded themselves as lenders or borrowers or intended to be.' *HSBC Life (UK) Ltd v Stubbs (and related appeals)*, Sp C 2001, [2002] SSCD 9 (Sp C 295). (*Note*. The Commissioners also held that the *Ramsay* principle—see 58.6 TAX PLANNING AND AVOIDANCE—did not apply to the transactions.)

Life assurance companies—double taxation relief

[34.7] See *Legal & General Assurance Society Ltd v Thomas (No 1)*, **21.40** DOUBLE TAX RELIEF.

Life assurance companies—mutual business

[34.8] See *Styles v New York Life Insurance Co*, **40.1** MUTUAL TRADING, and *CIR v Cornish Mutual Assurance Co Ltd*, **40.3** MUTUAL TRADING.

Life assurance company—bonuses to policy-holders

[34.9] See *Last v London Assurance Corporation*, **68.60** TRADING PROFITS.

Life assurance companies—untaxed interest

[34.10] See *Clerical Medical & General Life Assurance Co v Carter*, 53.13 SCHEDULE D, and *Revell v Edinburgh Life Insurance Co*, 53.14 SCHEDULE D.

Life assurance companies—annuities

[34.11] See *Gresham Life Assurance Society v Styles*, 68.62 TRADING PROFITS.

Life assurance company—discount on premiums

[34.12] See *North British & Mercantile Insurance Co v Easson*, 68.67 TRADING PROFITS.

Overseas life assurance companies

[34.13] See *Ostime v Australian Mutual Provident Society*, 68.69 TRADING PROFITS; *Sun Life Assurance Company of Canada v Pearson*, 68.70 TRADING PROFITS; *The Manufacturers' Life Assurance Co Ltd v Cummins*, 68.71 TRADING PROFITS, and *General Reinsurance Co Ltd v Tomlinson*, 68.72 TRADING PROFITS.

ICTA 1988, s 266—life assurance premium relief—individuals

[34.14] See the cases noted at 1.6 to 1.12 ALLOWANCES AND TAX RATES—INDIVIDUALS.

35

Loss Relief

The cases in this chapter are arranged under the following headings.

CROSS-REFERENCES

See **18.79** *et seq.* CORPORATION TAX for losses carried forward on company reconstructions or on the change in ownership of a company; **21.37** DOUBLE TAX RELIEF for the interaction of that relief and losses; and **61.38** *et seq.* TRADING INCOME for whether a trade has been continuous for loss relief carry-forward. For the treatment of interest and dividends received in computing business profits, see **64.35** *et seq.* TRADING PROFITS.

Trade losses (ITA 2007, ss 60–101)

Trade loss relief against general income (ITA 2007, ss 64-65)

Interaction of ITA 2007, ss 64 and 72

[35.1] An individual (H) began trading in 1978/79. Because of capital allowances, he made a trading loss for that year of some £41,000. He had employment income for that year of more than £46,000. He claimed loss relief under both of what is now *ITA 2007, s 64* and *s 72*, and contended that he was entitled to use only £35,000 of the loss in the *s 64* claim and to set the balance against his 1975/76 income under *s 72*. The Ch D rejected this contention, holding that a claim under *s 64* 'must be a claim for relief of an amount of the taxpayer's income equal to the amount of the loss, not an amount equal to such part of the loss as may be specified by the taxpayer'. Where a trader claimed relief first under *s 64*, the whole amount of the loss had to be set against the income of that year before considering any claim under *s 72*. *Butt v Haxby*, Ch D 1982, 56 TC 547; [1983] STC 239.

Interaction of ITA 2007, ss 64 and 83

[35.2] A pensioner (D) carried on a small picture framing business, which consistently made losses. He appealed against an amendment to a self-assessment, contending that he should be allowed to carry forward these losses against non-trading income for subsequent years. The First-tier Tribunal rejected this contention and dismissed his appeal, holding that trading losses could only be set against non-trading income for the same year under *ITA 2007, s 64* or carried forward against subsequent trading profits under *ITA 2007, s 83*. There was 'no provision to carry forward unrelieved losses to set against general income in future years'. *G Duckett v HMRC*, FTT [2010] UKFTT 57 (TC), TC00370.

Claim to carry back loss under ITA 2007, s 64—effect of TMA 1970, Sch 1B

[35.3] An individual (N) had substantial income tax liability for 1998/99, having exercised a number of share options. In January 2000 he became a member of a partnership which had been set up to finance films. In March 2000 N's advisers wrote to the Revenue stating that the partnership would make a loss for its accounting period ending 5 April 2000, and that N would like to use this loss to extinguish his tax liability for 1998/99. On 2 November 2000 N's advisers gave details of the loss and lodged a claim for it to be carried back to 1998/99 under what is now *ITA 2007, s 64*. The Revenue treated this claim as effective from 2 November 2000, but charged interest on the 1998/99 liability from 31 January 2000 to 2 November 2000. N appealed, contending that the claim should be treated as fully retrospective and that there should be no liability to interest. The Special Commissioner rejected this contention and dismissed N's appeal, observing that the tax had become due on 31 January 2000 and holding that 'where a person anticipated that a loss might arise in a later year but it had not arisen at the relevant time, the liability to income tax was not reduced because of such anticipation. The tax was still due.' The letter which N's advisers had sent in March 2000 could not be treated as a valid claim for loss relief, since 'the losses for the accounting period had not arisen as the accounting period had not ended'. The loss relief had not been claimed until 2 November 2000. The effect of *TMA 1970, Sch 1B* was that the loss relief should be granted by set-off from the date of the claim. However interest remained due until the date of the claim. *Norton v Thompson*, Sp C [2004] SSCD 163 (Sp C 399).

[35.4] Two individuals claimed to have incurred substantial losses in a trade of film financing, and claimed that they should be permitted to set these losses against income of earlier years. HMRC formed the opinion that the claimed losses were excessive, and began enquiries into the relevant partnerships, which were settled by agreement with the partnerships, under which the partnership losses were agreed at substantially reduced figures. HMRC subsequently amended the claimants' returns to reduce the amount of loss relief in accordance with the partnership agreements. The claimants applied for judicial review. The Upper Tribunal dismissed their applications. Sales J held that 'as a result of the restatement of the partnership losses under the partnership settlement agreement, the claimants did lose the right to carry back to earlier years the higher (pre-amendment) losses which had been claimed'. The effect of *TMA 1970, Sch 1B* was that 'the focus in the case of a carry-back claim such as those in issue here is on the later year, ie the year in which the partnership losses actually arose and were allocated to the partners'. The fact that the claimants had 'included claims to set off their shares of the partnership losses in later years in their individual returns for earlier years' was 'simply a convenient way of intimating to HMRC that they would wish to set off those losses (which would only in fact arise in the later years) against their income in the earlier years'. Applying the principles laid down by Lord Hodge in *HMRC v Cotter*, 35.51 below, 'where an entry which is the foundation for carry-back relief is made in the taxpayer's return for a particular year (here, the entry showing the partnership losses included in the claimants' returns for the later years), an appropriate (if not, in fact, *the* appropriate) means of challenge by HMRC to that entry and in that respect to the claim for carry-back relief is by way of a enquiry into the return itself, rather than an enquiry under *Sch 1A*. This was the means of challenge which HMRC has employed in the present case.' He concluded that 'a taxpayer cannot expect to be immune from a challenge to a claim for carry-back relief while still vulnerable to having relevant entries in his tax return for the later year corrected pursuant to a challenge to that return brought in proper time'. *R (oao De Silva) v HMRC (and related application)*, UT [2014] UKUT 170 (TCC); [2014] STC 2088.

Loss carried back under ITA 2007, s 64—whether penalty due

[35.5] On 24 January 2012 an accountant notified HMRC that his client (R) had incurred 'current year losses', which he wished to set against his profits for 2010/11. In May 2012 R submitted his 2011/12 return. In the meantime, HMRC had imposed a penalty for failure to pay the 2010/11 tax by the due date of 31 January 2012. The First-tier Tribunal dismissed R's appeal against the penalty. Judge Cornwell-Kelly held that *TMA 1970, s 42(1A)* required a claim to be quantified. Therefore the letter of 24 January 2012 could not be treated as a claim. *ME Robins v HMRC*, FTT [2013] UKFTT 514 (TC), TC02902.

Loss relief claim outside statutory time limit

[35.6] In 1991 a trader (R) claimed that he had incurred losses between 1981 and 1985, and that he was entitled to relief against subsequent profits. The Revenue rejected the claim on the grounds that it had been made outside the statutory time limit. The General Commissioners dismissed R's appeal and the Ch D upheld this decision. *Richardson v Jenkins*, Ch D 1994, 67 TC 246; [1995] STC 95.

[35.7] A similar decision was reached in *Privet v CIR*, Sp C [2001] SSCD 119 (Sp C 279).

[35.8] The decision in *Privet v CIR*, 35.7 above, was applied in the similar subsequent case of *C Watts v HMRC*, FTT [2010] UKFTT 574 (TC), TC00824.

Limited partner—whether ITA 2007, s 64 loss relief limited to capital contribution

[35.9] See *Reed v Young*, 41.47 PARTNERSHIPS.

Upkeep of properties—whether a 'trade loss'

[35.10] A landlord claimed loss relief in respect of the upkeep of several properties. HMRC rejected the claim and she appealed, contending that she had purchased the properties with the intention of selling them at a profit within a short period. The First-tier Tribunal dismissed her appeal. Judge Staker observed that 'the purchase of properties, followed by tenanting them for several years, is not typical of a trade in real estate'. *Ms P Azam v HMRC (No 2)*, FTT [2011] UKFTT 50 (TC), TC00928.

Restriction on relief for uncommercial trades (ITA 2007, s 66)

[35.11] An accountant (K), who was also a keen runner, was made redundant in 1989. While seeking new employment, he began a small business selling running kit. He opened a shop in 1990. The shop consistently made net losses, for which K claimed relief against his employment income. For 2009/10 HMRC rejected his claim on the basis that K had not met the conditions of *ITA 2007, s 66(2)(b)*, since he was not trading 'with a view to the realisation of profits'. K appealed, contending that the business would be profitable if he could achieve a turnover of more than £28000, which he still hoped to do. The First-tier Tribunal dismissed K's appeal. Judge Cannan held that *s 66* should be construed so that 'a taxpayer is not permitted relief where it is anticipated that at some future date the way in which the business is carried on will or may change, enabling profits to be generated in the future'. He expressed the view that the evidence did not indicate that a turnover of £28000 was 'reasonably achievable', that K 'must have known that the business could not make a profit until he was able to devote more time to the business', and that K had operated the shop because 'it offered an exit strategy from his job as an accountant'. *S Kitching v HMRC*, FTT [2013] UKFTT 384 (TC), TC02781.

[35.12] An individual (M) submitted tax returns for 2007/08 to 2010/11 claiming substantial losses from a trade as a breeder and trainer of racehorses. Following an enquiry, HMRC issued a closure notice denying relief on the basis that the trade had not been carried on on a commercial basis. The First-tier Tribunal dismissed M's appeal, finding that he 'did not demonstrate sufficiently that his activities were carried out on a commercial basis with a view to the realisation of a profit of a trade'. *R Murray v HMRC*, FTT [2014] UKFTT 338 (TC), TC03474.

[35.13] The First-tier Tribunal reached a similar decision in *Ms J Thorne v HMRC*, FTT [2014] UKFTT 730 (TC), TC03851.

[35.14] A social worker (P) submitted tax returns claiming losses in respect of two separate trades, one of running cookery workshops and one of selling Indian art. HMRC issued an amendment to P's 2009/10 return, and discovery assessments for previous years, on the basis that the trades had not been carried on on a commercial basis. The First-tier Tribunal dismissed P's appeals, finding that his 'real motivation was not profit, but the enjoyment he got from working with people and conveying his passion for cookery and photography'. He 'was not carrying on the trades with a view to the realisation of profits'. *D Patel v HMRC*, FTT [2015] UKFTT 0013 (TC), TC04225.

Restriction on relief for farming (ITA 2007, ss 67–70)

[35.15] A surveyor (H) purchased a herd of deer in 1990. He disposed of the deer in 2004. In 2002 he claimed that he had made losses in a trade of deer farming which should be set against his income as a surveyor. Following an enquiry, HMRC issued a closure notice stating that the restriction laid down by what is now *ITA 2007, s 67* applied, and that no loss relief was due for 1996/97 and subsequent years. The First-tier Tribunal dismissed H's appeal against the notice, finding that the farming trade had never been profitable, so that 'the restrictions on the use of farming losses therefore apply for the tax year 1996/97 and subsequent years'. *M Howes v HMRC (No 1)*, FTT [2012] UKFTT 179 (TC), TC01874.

[35.16] A farmer died in 1961. His son (F) inherited the farm and operated it as a dairy farm in partnership with his wife. After 1998 it ceased to be profitable, and in 2000 the couple sold their cattle. They subsequently let the farm to a neighbouring farmer, who began arable farming on the land. F and his wife resumed operating the farm in 2004, but continued to make losses. For 2008/09 to 2010/11 the couple claimed to set these losses against their other income (derived from letting buildings on the farm). HMRC rejected the claim on the basis that relief was precluded by *ITA 2007, s 67*, but the First-tier Tribunal allowed the couple's appeal. Judge Nowlan held that the couple had ceased trading between 2001 and 2004, and observed that the couple's losses had diminished between 2008 and 2011, and that the farm had made a profit in 2011/12. He held that the couple's operation of the farm satisfied the requirements of *ITA 2007, s 68(3)*, which was intended 'to preclude a farmer from enjoying the sideways and carry-back offset for farming losses only if the actual farmer has been slower in anticipating profit than "the notional competent farmer"'. *CJ & Mrs MA French v HMRC*, FTT [2014] UKFTT 940 (TC), TC04053.

Early trade losses relief (ITA 2007, ss 72–74)

[35.17] A partnership began trading on 1 May 1990, and made a loss in its first year of trading. For 1990/91, one of the partners (G) claimed relief under what is now *ITA 2007, s 72* on $^{340}/_{365}$ of his share of the loss made in the year ending 30 April 1991. The Revenue accepted this claim, and the loss was set against G's income for 1987/88. In May 1993 G claimed relief in respect of the remaining $^{25}/_{365}$ of his share of the loss made in the year ending 30 April 1991. The Revenue rejected this claim, since the partnership had made a profit in its accounting year ending 30 April 1992 and in the fiscal year 1991/92, and loss relief under what is now *ITA 2007, s 72* was only due on an actual basis, such losses being computed by reference to the whole year of assessment with appropriate apportionments being made where a trader's accounting period was not coterminous with the end of a year of assessment. (The Revenue accepted that G could carry the balance of his share of the loss forward under what is now *ITA 2007, s 83* for relief against future profits of the trade.) The Special Commissioner dismissed G's appeal, holding that what is now *s 72* gave relief for actual losses in the actual years of assessment in which they were sustained. The Ch D upheld the Commissioner's decision. *Gascoine v Wharton*, Ch D 1996, TL 3498; [1996] STC 1481.

[35.18] An individual (G) began trading in May 1984. His first accounts, for the year ending 20 May 1985, showed a loss, for which he claimed relief under what is now *ITA 2007, s 72*. The Revenue set the loss against his 1981/82 income and made a repayment accordingly. G appealed, contending that the loss should also be set against his income for 1982/83 and 1983/84, and that he was also entitled to repayments for those years. The Special Commissioner rejected this contention, holding that 'the relief is limited to an amount of income equal to the amount of the loss which means that the relief is given once only; as the relief is given against income for an earlier year, that also makes it clear that it is not given against income for each of the three preceding years'. The Ch D dismissed G's appeal against this decision. *Gamble v Rowe*, Ch D 1998, 71 TC 190; [1998] STC 1247. (*Note.* The Special Commissioner allowed appeals against estimated assessments, finding that it was 'very improbable that the appellant made business profits, either of the amounts estimated in the assessments, or at all'.)

Letting of furnished holiday accommodation

[35.19] See *Walls v Livesey*, 47.19 PROPERTY INCOME, and *Brown v Richardson*, 47.20 PROPERTY INCOME.

Farming—whether profits 'could reasonably be expected'

[35.20] In April 1994 a married couple formed a partnership to carry on a trade of farming. They claimed substantial loss relief for 1994/95 to 1997/98 inclusive. The Revenue rejected the claim on the basis that the trade had not begun until 1995/96, and was not being conducted in such a way that profits could reasonably be expected within a reasonable time, as required by what is now *ITA 2007, s 74*. The couple appealed. The Special Commissioner dismissed their appeal, observing that the only income shown in the couple's accounts for 1994/95 was 'bunker rental' of £170, which was not trading income. Accordingly, there was 'insufficient evidence that a farming trade had actually started' in that year. The accounts for the three subsequent years showed losses ranging from £54,000 to £85,000, and the available evidence indicated that 'no commercial profit could be made until at least after 2000'. It appeared from the evidence that 'the farm was too small to be viable when it could not be run by the owner in person'. *Walsh & Walsh v Taylor*, Sp C 2003, [2004] SSCD 48 (Sp C 386).

Commodities dealing

[35.21] An individual (W), who had previously been employed as a commodities trader, left his employment and began dealing on his own account. He made losses and claimed loss relief. The Revenue rejected his claim on the basis that his dealings in commodities did not constitute trading, or alternatively that, even if they were regarded as trading, they were not 'carried on on a commercial basis', so that the effect of what is now *ITA 2007, s 74* was that no relief was due. The Special Commissioner dismissed W's appeal, finding that the case was very close to the borderline with regard to the definition of a trade, and holding that 'a case which is so close to the trading borderline because of its lack of commercial organisation was bound to be on the wrong side' of the borderline for the purposes of *s 74*. The Ch D upheld this decision as one of fact. *Wannell v Rothwell*, Ch D 1996, 68 TC 719; [1996] STC 450.

Saw doctors

[35.22] In April 1990 a married couple began trading in partnership as saw doctors, offering the service of sharpening saws and other cutting implements to the general public. The couple claimed loss relief for 1990/91 to 1996/97 inclusive. The Revenue rejected the claim, accepting that the partnership was trading but considering that the trade was not 'carried on on a commercial basis', so that the effect of what is now *ITA 2007, s 74* was that no relief was due. The Special Commissioner allowed the partnership's appeal, observing that the partnership had made a small profit in the year ending April 1998 and appeared set to make a larger profit in the following year, and finding that the trade was being carried on 'in order to produce income', rather than as a hobby. *Delian Enterprises v Ellis*, Sp C [1999] SSCD 103 (Sp C 186).

Beautician

[35.23] A married woman was a qualified beautician. She had given up work in order to have children, but subsequently began to give manicures and pedicures from the matrimonial home. Her husband (J), who was an employee, submitted tax returns claiming loss relief against his employment income. HMRC began an enquiry and rejected the loss claims on the basis that it did not appear that the couple were carrying on any trade, and if they were, it was not being conducted on a commercial basis. They issued assessments for 2003/04 to 2005/06, and amendments to J's self-assessments for 2006/07 to 2008/09. J appealed, contending that he was the proprietor of the trade, that his wife was his employee, that he paid her wages which were covered by her personal allowance, and that the trade had the effect of benefiting 'his wife's self-esteem, in that she earns her own income and does not need to ask him for support'. The First-tier Tribunal reviewed the evidence in detail and found that the expenditure on cosmetic supplies had been very similar to the total amounts received from customers, so that 'the business had never made a profit'. The tribunal held that the trade was being carried on by J's wife, rather than by J himself. Judge Poole observed that 'she gave all the treatments, dealt with all the bookings, bought most of the relevant supplies, had insurance in her own name and insofar as any promotion of the business was involved, it was promoted in her name as her business'. Furthermore, the trade was not being conducted on a commercial basis. Accordingly, the tribunal dismissed J's appeals against the assessments and amendments for 2004/05 to 2008/09 inclusive. (The tribunal allowed the appeal against the 2003/04 assessment, finding that in October 2004 J had given an HMRC officer sufficient information to enable the officer to conclude that the trade had not been conducted on a commercial basis for 2003/04, while he had been ill and his wife had been looking after him. Accordingly the issue of the 2003/04 assessment had been precluded by *TMA, s 29(5)*. However, J had not made it clear that the trade would continue to be conducted on a non-commercial basis for subsequent years, and the officer had warned J that HMRC would review the 2004/05 accounts in due course to assess profitability. Accordingly the tribunal found that 'no officer of HMRC could have been reasonably expected, on the basis of the information made available to him before 31 January 2006, to be aware of the insufficiency in the appellant's self-assessment for the year 2004/05'.) *JCL Agnew v HMRC*, FTT [2010] UKFTT 272 (TC), TC00566.

Exploitation of historic house

[35.24] In September 2006 an individual (K) took a lease of a historic house, built in 1380, from the National Trust. He began repairing the property and restoring the gardens, and in October 2006 he opened the house to visitors. In his 2006/07 tax return he claimed that he had made a substantial trading loss which should be set against his other income. HMRC rejected the claim, considering firstly that his exploitation of the property did not amount to a trade, and alternatively that if it did amount to a trade, it had not been carried on on a commercial basis. K appealed. The First-tier Tribunal allowed his appeal in principle (subject to agreement as to figures). Judge Radford found that K had shown an intention 'to run the property as a business charging admission fees to non-National Trust members and opening the property for events', and that 'the anticipated activities when carried on as a trade would clearly be and were commercial'. *AW Kerr (t/a Grantham House) v HMRC*, FTT [2011] UKFTT 40 (TC), TC00917.

Yacht chartering

[35.25] A blacksmith (C) submitted returns for 2007/08 to 2009/10, claiming that he had made losses on a trade of yacht chartering which should be set against his other income. HMRC rejected the claims on the basis that it appeared that the trade had not been conducted on a commercial basis. C appealed. The First-tier Tribunal reviewed the evidence in detail and allowed the appeal in part. Judge Tildesley held that the trade had not been conducted on a commercial basis in 2007/08 or 2008/09, but had been conducted on a commercial basis in 2009/10, when C had relocated the business to Plymouth and had had 'a reasonable expectation of making a profit'. *C Atkinson v HMRC*, FTT [2013] UKFTT 191 (TC), TC02606.

Restrictions on sideways relief for capital allowances (ITA 2007, ss 75-79)

[35.26] In 2001 an individual (F), who was employed under PAYE, also began a boat chartering business. For 2002/03 to 2005/06 he claimed that losses, including capital allowances, which he had incurred in this business should be set against his employment income. HMRC subsequently issued 'discovery' assessments disallowing the losses on the basis that substantially the whole of F's time was not given to carrying on the trade, as required by what is now *ITA 2007, s 75*. F appealed, accepting that he did not devote substantially all his time to the trade, but contending that his business was not simply a leasing business, since more than 40% of the charters of the boat included the provision of a skipper, which was the provision of a service rather than simply the lease of an asset. The First-tier Tribunal accepted this contention and allowed the appeal in part. Judge Khan held that where the boat was leased without a skipper, this was the hire of an asset and the losses were not available to be set against F's other income. However, where the boat was hired with a skipper, this could not be described as the leasing of plant and machinery and F was entitled to set off the losses. (The tribunal also held that the assessments had been made within the time limits of *TMA 1970, s 29.*) *GB Forbes v HMRC*, FTT [2011] UKFTT 425 (TC); [2011] SFTD 1143, TC01278.

[35.27] In 2003 an individual (J), who was employed under PAYE, also began a yacht chartering business. He claimed that losses, including capital allowances, which he had incurred in this business should be set against his employment income. In 2010 HMRC issued assessments for 2003/04 to 2006/07 inclusive, disallowing the losses on the basis that substantially the whole of J's time was not given to carrying on the trade, as required by what is now *ITA 2007, s 75*. J appealed, contending that he should be regarded as providing services rather than simply leasing the yacht. The First-tier Tribunal rejected this contention and upheld the assessments for 2004/05 to 2006/07 inclusive (but allowed J's appeal against the 2003/04 assessment on the grounds that it had been issued outside the statutory time limit.) *C Johnson v HMRC*, FTT [2012] UKFTT 399 (TC), TC02094.

[35.28] See also *Salmon v HMRC*, **5.52** ASSESSMENTS.

Carry-forward trade loss relief (ITA 2007, ss 83-88)

[35.29] An accountant began to practice on 1 June 1929 and made up his accounts to 31 March. For the ten months to 31 March 1930 he made a loss of £61, and for the year to 31 March 1931 he made a profit of £142. For his first twelve months his actual loss was therefore £37, i.e. the £61 less one-sixth of the £142 profit (£24), producing a nil assessment for 1930/31. He appealed against an assessment for 1931/32, contending that he should be entitled to loss relief of £98 (i.e. the £61 loss of the first ten months plus the 'actual' loss of £37 of 1930/31). The CS unanimously rejected this contention, holding that the loss available for carry-forward under what is now *ITA 2007, s 83* was £37, i.e. the £61 loss of the first ten months less the £24 used in arriving at the nil assessment for 1930/31. (Lord Clyde described the accountant's contentions as 'preposterous'.) *CIR v Scott Adamson*, CS 1932, 17 TC 679.

[35.30] A television company (W) began trading on 1 August 1960. Its first accounts were for a period of nine months (ending in the second year of assessment under the legislation then in force), and showed a loss of £132,107. The next accounts showed a profit of £165,572. The assessments for 1961/62 and 1962/63 (W's second and third years of trading) were based on the profits of the first twelve months, which were agreed to be nil (comprising the loss of £132,107 from the first nine months and an apportioned profit of £41,393 from the next three months). The Special Commissioners held that, applying the decision in *CIR v Scott Adamson*, **35.29** above, £82,786 of the initial loss had been used in computing W's assessments for 1961/62 and 1962/63 and thus was not available for carry-forward. The CA unanimously upheld this decision. *Westward Television Ltd v Hart*, CA 1968, 45 TC 1; [1969] Ch 201; [1968] 3 All ER 91.

Change in trade—losses incurred in old trade

[35.31] See *Gordon & Blair Ltd v CIR*, **61.46** TRADING INCOME.

Company director claiming relief for company's losses

[35.32] A company which had promoted three concerts made a loss and went into liquidation. One of its four directors also carried on business as a builder, and claimed loss relief for the losses which the company had incurred. HMRC rejected his claim and the First-tier Tribunal dismissed his appeal. *L Agus v HMRC*, FTT [2010] UKFTT 425 (TC), TC00696.

Claim for non-trading losses to be carried forward

[35.33] In a case where the facts are not fully set out in the decision, the Revenue treated an individual (F) as having begun trading in 1995. He appealed to the General Commissioners, claiming that he had incurred losses in 1992/93. The General Commissioners found that he had incurred losses, but held that these were not trading losses. F subsequently claimed relief for these losses against his trading income for 2000/01. The Revenue rejected his claim and the Special Commissioner dismissed his appeal, holding that the non-trading losses 'cannot be set against trading profits'. *Francis v HMRC*, Sp C [2005] SSCD 692 (Sp C 490).

Corporation tax losses (CTA 2010, ss 36–96)

Whether accounts should be time-apportioned

[35.34] A company (C) incurred a loss, after capital allowances, of £309,721 in its accounting period ending 31 March 1998. It claimed to set $^{92}/_{365}$ of the loss against its profits for its accounting periods ending in 1995 and 1996. The Revenue rejected the claim, on the basis that £308,630 of the loss was attributable to first-year allowances on acquisitions which had taken place after 2 July 1997 (the date on which the carry-back period was reduced from three years to twelve months, by virtue of *F(No 2) A 1997, s 39*). C appealed, contending that the loss should be time-apportioned. The Special Commissioner rejected this contention and dismissed the appeal, holding on the evidence that C's time-apportionment of the loss would be 'unjust or unreasonable'. The Commissioner upheld the Revenue's contention that 'time-apportionment gave an arbitrary result which may be the most reasonable solution if there is no more accurate way of identifying which losses were incurred which side of the 2 July dividing line. Where, however, it was possible to allocate particular losses to one or other side of the dividing line, that course should be followed, given that the purpose of the statutory provisions was to ascertain the part of the loss attributable to the pre-commencement period. In this case there was a more accurate means of allocating losses to either side of the dividing line which was to allocate the losses arising from the acquisition of the printing presses on which first-year allowances were available to the time of acquisition, which was in all four cases after 2 July 1997.' In this case, the first-year allowances should not be included in the loss for the purposes of time-apportionment, so that only a loss of £275 (i.e. $^{92}/_{365}$ × (£309,721 – £308,630)) was available for carry-back for more than twelve months. *Camcrown Ltd v McDonald*, Sp C [1999] SSCD 255 (Sp C 208).

Application of CTA 2010, s 44

[35.35] A company (G) which operated a football club submitted returns claiming losses, which it claimed to surrender to its holding company. HMRC issued discovery determinations refusing the claims on the grounds that G's business had not been carried on 'so as to afford a reasonable expectation of gain', within what is now *CTA 2010, s 44*. The First-tier Tribunal reviewed the evidence in detail and dismissed G's appeal. Judge Walters observed that the directors' report had 'indicated that the accounts had been prepared on a going concern basis only by reference to the directors' and shareholders' indication of their intention to continue to support the club'. *Glapwell Football Club Ltd v HMRC*, FTT [2013] UKFTT 516 (TC); [2014] SFTD 485, TC02904.

[35.36] A company (B), which carried on a property business, purchased a luxury yacht in 1998 and began a separate business of yacht chartering. It submitted returns claiming losses for the three years ending 31 March 2000, declaring profits for the two years ending 31 March 2002, and claiming losses for the following ten years. HMRC accepted the returns for the years up to and including 31 March 2008, but rejected the loss claims for the next four years on the grounds that the yacht chartering business had not been carried on 'so as to afford a reasonable expectation of gain', within *CTA 2010, s 44*. The First-tier Tribunal allowed B's appeal, finding that the business had been conducted on a commercial basis and that there was 'a realistic possibility or reasonable expectation of the company making a profit or gain from its chartering activities in the future'. *Beacon Estates (Chepstow) Ltd v HMRC*, FTT [2014] UKFTT 686 (TC), TC03808.

Application of CTA 2010, s 45

[35.37] See *Willis v Peeters Picture Frames Ltd*, **18.76** CORPORATION TAX; *Robroyston Brickworks Ltd v CIR*, **61.41** TRADING INCOME, and the cases noted at **18.79** to **18.88** CORPORATION TAX.

Application of CTA 2010, s 54

[35.38] See *Boote v Banco do Brasil SA*, **21.41** DOUBLE TAX RELIEF.

CTA 2010, s 60—contribution to limited liability partnership

[35.39] A company (H) was established to develop and run a golf course. It claimed loss relief in relation to losses made by a limited liability partnership of which it was a member. HMRC rejected the claim on the basis that *ICTA 1988, s 118ZC* (which has subsequently been replaced by *CTA 2010, s 60*) limited the relief to the contribution H had made to the limited liability partnership, which was nil. H appealed, contending that since the partnership agreement provided that it had a one-third share in the capital of the partnership, this should be included in the amount that it was liable to contribute to the assets of the limited liability partnership in the event of the partnership being wound up. The First-tier Tribunal accepted this contention and allowed the appeal (by the casting vote of the chairman, Judge Raghavan). *Hamilton & Kinneil (Archerfield) Ltd v HMRC*, FTT [2014] UKFTT 350 (TC); [2014] SFTD 1008, TC03485. (*Note.* HMRC have appealed to the Upper Tribunal against this decision. The Upper Tribunal is scheduled to begin hearing HMRC's appeal in February 2015.)

Losses on disposal of shares (ITA 2007, ss 131–149)

[35.40] In 1993/94 an individual (H) incurred a loss on the disposal of shares in a trading company. In August 1994 he claimed relief under what is now *ITA 2007, s 131*. In April 1995 he claimed that the part of the loss which had not been relieved against his 1993/94 income should be set against his income for 1992/93. The Revenue rejected the claim on the basis that the unrelieved loss could be carried forward and relieved against H's income for 1994/95, but could not be carried back and relieved against H's income for 1992/93. The Special Commissioner dismissed H's appeal against this decision. *Hobart v Williams*, Sp C [1997] SSCD 330 (Sp C 144).

[35.41] In June 1994 an individual (M) acquired the entire share capital of a newly-formed company (G). G agreed to purchase the entire share capital of another company (S) for £225,000. In December 1994 S went into liquidation. Its liquidators sold its assets to a newly-incorporated company with a similar name. M became a director of this new company. In his 1994/95 tax return, M stated that he had disposed of his shares in G for no consideration. In 1996 he claimed relief under what is now *ITA 2007, s 131* in respect of his shares in G. The Revenue rejected the claim on the grounds that, despite the statement in his tax return, M had not actually disposed of the shares in G. M appealed, contending that the shares should be treated as having become worthless, within *TCGA, s 24(2)*. The Special Commissioner dismissed the appeal, holding that in order to establish an allowable loss, 'there must be either a disposal or a deemed disposal'. On the evidence, M had not disposed of the shares during 1994/95. *Marks v McNally*, Sp C [2004] SSCD 503 (Sp C 428).

[35.42] In January 2005 two company directors agreed to purchase shareholdings in another company (T). They soon discovered that there were 'serious deficiencies' in T's accounting records. T subsequently went into liquidation. The directors claimed that since their shares in T had become of 'negligible value', they should be entitled to relief for this loss against their income. HMRC rejected this claim on the basis that what is now *ITA 2007, s 131* stipulated that such relief was only due where an investor had subscribed for new shares, and was not available where an investor had purchased existing shares. The First-tier Tribunal upheld HMRC's ruling and dismissed the directors' appeals. *S Joyce v HMRC (and related appeal)*, FTT [2010] UKFTT 566 (TC), TC00817.

[35.43] An individual (M) acquired 18 shares in a company (G), paying £46,000. The shares subsequently became worthless, and M claimed loss relief under *ITA 2007, s 131*. HMRC rejected the claim on the basis that M had purchased the shares from another shareholder (W), so that the conditions of *s 131(2)(a)* were not satisfied. M appealed, contending that W had originally subscribed for the shares on his behalf, because he had been divorcing his wife, and that he had subsequently reimbursed W for the subscription, so that he should be treated as having acquired the shares by subscription rather than by purchase. The First-tier Tribunal accepted this contention and allowed his appeal. Judge Gammie observed that 'HMRC acknowledge that shares subscribed by a nominee satisfy the requirements of *section 135(2)*' and held that 'this must extend to a case in which money is advanced to an individual to permit subscription but the shares are issued to another as security for the advance'. *N McLocklin v HMRC*, FTT [2014] UKFTT 042 (TC), TC03182.

[35.44] An individual (F) held shares in a company which ceased to trade during 2004/05. He was granted loss relief for 2004/05 against his employment income for that year, leaving a balance of unused relief. He subsequently submitted a 2005/06 return claiming to carry forward this unused relief against his employment income for 2005/06. HMRC initially made the repayments claimed, but subsequently issued amendments, on the basis that the relevant legislation (see now *ITA 2007, s 132*) only permitted such relief to be carried back and did not permit it to be carried forward, and additionally that the shares had originally been issued to F's father and that F was not entitled to relief because he had not 'subscribed for' the shares as required by what is now *ITA 2007, s 131(2)*. The First-tier Tribunal upheld the amendments and dismissed F's appeal. Judge Walters commented that 'we regard HMRC's policy of making repayments of tax against claims which have not been checked for their validity as extraordinary, and in need of immediate high-level review, in the light of the country's current well-known financial difficulties. This appellant is an honest man. A dishonest taxpayer in the same situation might have absconded with the excessive repayments.' *F Fard v HMRC*, FTT [2011] UKFTT 63 (TC), TC00941.

[35.45] A company (M) ceased trading in 2004 and subsequently went into liquidation. Two of its directors submitted claims for loss relief, contending that they had subscribed for shares in M, and that the shares had become worthless. However they failed to provide share certificates in support of their claims, and HMRC rejected the claims on the grounds that the directors had not shown that they had subscribed for shares in the company. The First-tier Tribunal dismissed the directors' appeals against this decision. *J Halnan v HMRC (and related appeal)*, FTT [2011] UKFTT 580 (TC), TC01423.

[35.46] The decision in *Halnan v HMRC*, **35.45** above, was applied in the similar subsequent case of *P Saund v HMRC*, FTT [2012] UKFTT 740 (TC), TC02400.

[35.47] See also *Leadley's Executors v HMRC*, **19.23** DECEASED PERSONS, and *Mrs R & Mrs S Thomas v HMRC*, **44.104** PENALTIES.

ITA 2007, s 134—qualifying trading companies

[35.48] A couple claimed loss relief in respect of the disposal of shares in a Canadian company. HMRC rejected the claim on the grounds that what is now *ITA 2007, s 134* stipulated that the company must have 'carried on its business wholly or mainly in the United Kingdom'. The First-tier Tribunal dismissed the couple's appeal against this decision. *Professor Sir P Lachmann v HMRC (and related appeal)*, FTT [2010] UKFTT 560 (TC), TC00811.

ITA 2007, s 137—whether company met 'trading requirement'

[35.49] In 2002 an individual (B) subscribed for shares in a company (IR). The shares became worthless, and B claimed to set the capital loss on them against his income for 2004/05 under what is now *ITA 2007, s 131*. HMRC rejected the claim on the basis that IR had not met the 'trading requirement' of what is now *ITA 2007, s 137*. The First-tier Tribunal dismissed B's appeal against this decision. Judge Poole observed that IR's accounts had stated that its principal intended activity had been 'to act as a provider of residential mortgages', which was not a qualifying trade for the purpose of *s 137*. *I Branagan v HMRC*, FTT [2014] UKFTT 1100 (TC), TC04188.

Miscellaneous

Underwriting losses

[35.50] An underwriter made a loss in 1989, and claimed loss relief under what is now *ITA 2007, s 72*. The Revenue ruled that the effect of *ICTA 1988, s 454(4)* was that part of the loss had to be set against a deemed withdrawal from the underwriter's Special Reserve Fund. The underwriter appealed, contending that the inspector had not been required to certify any part of the loss under *ICTA 1988, s 453*, and that the whole of the loss should be relieved under *s 72*. The Special Commissioners rejected this contention and dismissed the appeal, holding that the inspector had been obliged to certify the loss under *s 453* and that this obligation was not affected by the *s 72* claim. The effect of *ICTA 1988, s 454(4)* was that the loss relief had to be set against the deemed withdrawal from the Special Reserve Fund before it could be set against any other income. *Peterson v De Brunner*, Sp C 1995, [1996] SSCD 91 (Sp C 64). (*Note. ICTA 1988, ss 453, 454* were repealed by *FA 1993* with effect from 1992/93. However, the principle established by this case may still be relevant with regard to underwriters' claims for loss relief. See Simon's Taxes, para E5.623.)

ITA 2007, s 128—relief for losses in employment

[35.51] An individual (C) submitted a 2007/08 tax return showing a significant liability. In January 2009 he submitted an amendment to the return, stating that he had made a loss in an employment for 2008/09 and claiming that he should be allowed to set this loss against his income for 2007/08 under *ITA 2007, s 128(2)*. HMRC began an enquiry into the loss claim, on the basis that it arose from an avoidance scheme, and subsequently began county court proceedings to collect the tax shown in C's original return. C defended the proceedings, and the case was referred to the Ch D, which gave judgment for HMRC. David Richards J held that C's claim for loss relief was not a defence to HMRC's claim for payment of the tax originally shown as due for 2007/08.

The CA reversed this decision but the Supreme Court unanimously restored it. Lord Hodge held that the effect of *TMA 1970, Sch 1B* was that 'the relief is quantified on the basis that the tax liability in year 1 has already been assessed' and that 'whatever rights the claim for relief might have given the taxpayer in relation to a payment to account for 2008/09, if the Revenue had accepted its validity, it did not affect his obligation to pay the tax payable for 2007/08'. In calculating C's 2007/08 tax liability, HMRC were 'entitled to treat as irrelevant to that calculation information and claims, which clearly do not as a matter of law affect the tax chargeable and payable in the relevant year of assessment'. Income tax was an annual tax, and 'disputes about matters which are not relevant to a taxpayer's liability in a particular year should not postpone the finality of that year's assessment'. Accordingly, 'the claim for relief based on an employment-related loss in 2008/09 did not provide a defence to the Revenue's demand for the payment of the tax assessed for 2007/08'. *HMRC v MD Cotter*, SC [2013] UKSC 69; [2013] STC 2480; [2014] 1 All ER 1.

36

Maintenance Payments

The cases in this chapter are arranged under the following headings.

Qualifying maintenance payments (ITA 2007, ss 453–456)

[36.1] A couple who had divorced executed a deed of agreement whereby the ex-husband (J) agreed to pay maintenance of £30 per week to the daughter of the marriage (who was aged five at the date of the agreement). J actually made the payments to his ex-wife, who had care and control of the daughter. J claimed that the payments should be treated as qualifying maintenance payments under what is now *ITA 2007, s 453*. The Revenue rejected the claim on the grounds that the agreement had not stipulated that the payments should be made to the ex-wife, as required by what is now *ITA 2007, s 454*. The Ch D upheld the Revenue's ruling. The payments had been covenanted to be made to the daughter, and therefore remained J's income for tax purposes. *Billingham v John*, Ch D 1997, 70 TC 380; [1998] STC 120.

[36.2] A married couple had purchased a house in 1984 with the aid of a mortgage from a bank. In 1991 they separated and the husband moved out of the house. He continued to make the remaining payments due to the bank under the mortgage agreement, and cleared the outstanding balance in 1993. He subsequently claimed relief for these payments under what is now *ITA 2007, s 453*. The Revenue rejected the claim, and he appealed. The Special Commissioner dismissed his appeal, holding that the payments had not been made 'to or for the benefit of' the wife, as required by what is now *ITA 2007, s 454*. They were paid by the husband to discharge a joint and several liability which he had entered into with the bank in 1984. The Commissioner observed that 'just as periodical payments to or for the benefit of a child will not qualify for relief unless they are paid under a written agreement', so payments under a written agreement would not qualify 'unless that agreement provides for them to be made to the other party to the marriage'. *Otter v Andrews*, Sp C [1999] SSCD 67 (Sp C 181).

[36.3] A married couple, with one daughter, divorced in 1984. The wife subsequently remarried, but divorced again. In 1996 the Child Support Agency ordered her first husband (E) to pay maintenance to his ex-wife for the benefit of their daughter. He claimed tax relief under what is now *ITA 2007, s 453*. The Revenue rejected his claim, on the grounds that the effect of what is now *ITA 2007, s 454* was that the payment was not a 'qualifying maintenance payment', as the wife had subsequently remarried. The Ch D upheld the Revenue's rejection of the claim. Park J held that there was no ambiguity in the legislation. The fact that E's former wife had remarried meant that the conditions of what is now *ITA 2007, s 454* were not satisfied. The condition specifically required that the wife 'has not remarried', not that she 'is not remarried'. Accordingly, the fact that she had subsequently divorced her second husband was irrelevant. *Norris v Edgson*, Ch D 2000, 72 TC 553; [2000] STC 494.

ITA 2007, s 454—European Convention on Human Rights

[36.4] See *PM v United Kingdom*, 31.80 HUMAN RIGHTS.

Miscellaneous

Payments to divorced wife for maintenance of children

[36.5] Under a divorce court order, a taxpayer (T) was required to pay his ex-wife specified amounts for the maintenance and education of the children of the marriage. The Revenue issued assessments on the basis that the payments were income of the children (so that T was not entitled to child allowance). The General Commissioners allowed T's appeal and the CA unanimously upheld their decision, holding that the payments were income of the mother rather than the children. Clauson LJ held that the effect of the order was 'to increase the income of the mother so as to enable her to discharge the duty of maintenance laid upon her by the court' *Stevens v Tirard*, CA 1939, 23 TC 321; [1940] 1 KB 204; [1939] 4 All ER 186. (*Note.* For HMRC's practice following this decision, see Relief Instructions, para RE1164.)

[36.6] Under a divorce court order, a taxpayer (S) was required to make annual payments 'free of tax' to his ex-wife for the maintenance of the children. The Revenue issued an assessment on the basis that the payments were 'annual payments' from which S was required to account for tax. S appealed. The General Commissioners dismissed his appeal and the KB upheld their decision, holding that the payments were subject to deduction of tax and should be grossed up at the standard rate. *Spencer v Robson*, KB 1946, 27 TC 198.

Scottish divorce action—aliment for children payable to mother

[36.7] In a Scottish divorce action, the husband was ordered to pay his wife aliment for each of the children of the marriage, in her capacity as *tutrix* of the children. The CS held that these payments of aliment were income of the children for tax purposes. *Huggins v Huggins*, CS [1981] SLT 179. (*Note.* Compare the English case of *Stevens v Tirard*, 36.5 above.)

[36.8] The decision in *Huggins v Huggins*, 36.7 above, was applied in a similar subsequent case where the husband was ordered to pay his wife an interim aliment of £25 per week for each of the two children of the marriage, in her capacity as *tutrix* of the children. He deducted tax from the aliment. The mother sought an order requiring the aliments to be paid in full. The Inner

House of the CS granted the order, holding that the payments should be treated as payments to the children. *Finnie v Finnie*, CS [1984] STC 598.

Sheriff Court decree—whether a variation of a previous agreement

[36.9] A married couple separated in April 1981. The husband agreed to make weekly payments for the two children of the marriage from the date of separation. The agreement stated that they were to be paid to the children direct or 'in such a way that the said amounts are treated by the Inland Revenue as being the income of each of the said children respectively, and not the income of the wife'. The husband deducted tax from the payments. On 23 April 1982 the wife obtained a decree from the Sheriff Court, stating that each child was entitled to weekly payments of similar amounts payable 'commencing as from 26 April 1981'. She claimed repayment of the tax deducted from the payments during 1981/82. The Revenue rejected the claim on the basis that the effect of the legislation relating to settlements was that those payments were income of the husband for tax purposes. The wife appealed, contending that the effect of the Sheriff Court decree was that the payments should be treated as income of the children. The CS unanimously rejected this contention, holding that the wife was not entitled to the repayment which she had claimed. The husband had made the payments in implementation of his contractual obligations under the 1981 agreement. The 1982 decree had no bearing on them; it did not, and could not, revoke or modify the 1981 agreement. *CIR v Craw*, CS 1985, 59 TC 56; [1985] STC 512.

Variation of maintenance order—whether any retrospective effect

[36.10] In divorce proceedings in 1969, a husband was ordered to pay his former wife (M) £2.50 per week for the maintenance of her son. The Revenue issued assessments on M charging tax on these payments. In 1980 M, wishing to avoid tax on the payments, obtained by consent a variation of the order, whereby the payments were to be treated as income of her son. She appealed against the assessments for 1975/76 to 1979/80, contending that the effect of the variation of the order was that the maintenance payments should not be treated as her income. The General Commissioners rejected this contention and dismissed her appeal, and the CA unanimously upheld their decision. Oliver LJ held that although the court could exercise its power of variation by substituting a new payee, it could not change the fiscal consequences of what had previously taken place. The sums had been paid to M under an obligation in force at the time of payment, and remained her income for tax purposes. Sir Denys Buckley held that the court had 'no power to reopen concluded transactions by means of a retroactive variation'. *Morley-Clarke v Jones*, CA 1985, 59 TC 567; [1985] STC 660; [1985] 3 WLR 749; [1985] 3 All ER 193.

Divorce—application by father for order against himself

[36.11] In divorce proceedings, the father obtained custody of the three children of the marriage. He applied for an order under the *Matrimonial*

Causes Act 1973 against himself to pay each child such amounts as, after deduction of tax, equalled the child's school fees, the payments to be made to the school as agent for the child. It was admitted that he sought the order for the sole purpose of enabling him to deduct the grossed-up payments from his income and allowing the children's tax allowances to be set against the payments. The HL unanimously granted the order (reversing the CA decision). Lord Brandon observed that, if the children had lived with the mother, she would have been granted an order against the father to make the proposed payments. The order would benefit the children by increasing 'the amount of income available for their maintenance and education'. *Sherdley v Sherdley*, HL [1987] STC 217; [1987] 2 WLR 1071; [1987] 2 All ER 54.

Supplementary benefit payments by husband

[36.12] A woman who was separated from her husband received supplementary benefit payments to enable her to maintain the two children of the marriage. The husband was ordered to pay £16 per week to the Secretary of State for Social Services, under *Supplementary Benefits Act 1976*, in respect of the children. He claimed that the payments should be treated as deductible in computing his total income. The Ch D rejected this contention, holding that these payments were not chargeable to income tax, and that they were therefore not 'annual payments' deductible in computing the husband's income. Peter Gibson J observed that 'the money went to the wife in non-taxable form, in contrast to the ordinary situation which would apply if there were a Court order requiring maintenance payments to be made directly to the wife'. *McBurnie v Tacey*, Ch D 1984, 58 TC 139; [1984] STC 347; [1984] 1 WLR 1019. (*Note.* Supplementary benefit was subsequently superseded by income support, payable under the *Social Security Contributions and Benefits Act 1992*. The effect of *ITEPA 2003, s 666* is that income support which is attributable to a child maintemance bonus is not taxable: see Simon's Taxes, para E4.328.)

Court order following divorce—whether settlement created

[36.13] See *Yates v Starkey*, **56.61** SETTLEMENTS.

Car provided by company director for former wife

[36.14] See *Gibson v HMRC*, **22.133** EMPLOYMENT INCOME.

Alimony and maintenance payments—other cases

[36.15] For other cases dealing with alimony or maintenance payments, see *Watkins v CIR*, **2.7** ANNUAL PAYMENTS; *Peters' Executors v CIR*, **2.8** ANNUAL PAYMENTS; *Bingham v CIR*, **2.10** ANNUAL PAYMENTS; *Keiner v Keiner*, **2.41** ANNUAL PAYMENTS; *Spilsbury v Spofforth*, **2.55** ANNUAL PAYMENTS; *Jefferson v Jefferson*, **2.58** ANNUAL PAYMENTS; *Butler v Butler*, **20.45** DEDUCTION OF TAX; *Stokes v Bennett*, **39.38** MISCELLANEOUS INCOME, and *Johnstone v Chamberlain*, **56.92** SETTLEMENTS.

37

Married Couples

The cases are arranged under the following headings.

GENERAL NOTE

The taxation of married couples was substantially amended with effect from 1990/91, with the introduction of independent taxation by *FA 1988, s 32, Sch 14 Part VIII*. For cases concerning the married couple's allowance (*ITA 2007, ss 45, 46*), see **1.1** to **1.5** ALLOWANCES AND TAX RATES. The cases in this chapter should be read in the light of the changes in the legislation.

Married persons 'living together' (ITA 2007, s 1011)

[37.1] In a case concerning assessment provisions which have subsequently been superseded, the HL unanimously held that a husband and wife, who had been living apart for three years while the husband was on war service abroad, should be treated for tax purposes as living together and not as separated. *Nugent-Head v Jacob*, HL 1948, 30 TC 83.

[37.2] In the case noted at **1.2** ALLOWANCES AND TAX RATES, the Ch D held that a married couple were living 'as separate households under the same roof', and were not living together for tax purposes. *Holmes v Mitchell*, Ch D 1990, 63 TC 718; [1991] STC 25.

Miscellaneous

ITA 2007, s 836—jointly held property

[37.3] A married couple held joint bank accounts, on which interest arose. The husband (L) failed to declare any of this interest on his tax returns. HMRC issued amendments to his self-assessments, and discovery assessments for previous years, on the basis that L was taxable on 50% of this income. L appealed, contending that the interest should be treated as belonging solely to his wife. The First-tier Tribunal rejected this contention and dismissed his appeal, observing that L and his wife could have made a declaration of unequal beneficial interests under what is now *ITA 2007, s 837*, but had failed to do so. *PA Lorber v HMRC (No 1)*, FTT [2011] UKFTT 101 (TC), TC00977. (*Note*. For another issue in this case, see **56.35** SETTLEMENTS.)

[37.4] HMRC discovered that a married couple had received rental income from several properties. They issued discovery assessments and imposed penalties. The couple appealed, and the husband contended that because his wife managed the properties, all the income should be treated as accruing to her. The First-tier Tribunal rejected this contention and dismissed the appeals. Judge Khan held that the effect of *ITA 2007, s 836* was that, as the couple had not lodged an election under *s 837*, 'the rental income is to be jointly assessed on both appellants'. *D & Mrs M Koshal v HMRC*, FTT [2013] UKFTT 410 (TC), TC02806.

[37.5] See also *Professor AK Halpin v HMRC*, **52.25** SAVINGS AND INVESTMENT INCOME.

Annulment of marriage

[37.6] See *Dodworth v Dale*, **1.1** ALLOWANCES AND TAX RATES.

Divorce—time when spouses cease to be connected

[37.7] In *Aspden v Hildesley*, **71.22** CAPITAL GAINS TAX, the Ch D held that spouses who were divorced by decree nisi remained connected persons for tax purposes until the divorce was made absolute.

Gift by husband to wife—CGT liability

[37.8] See *Godfrey v HMRC*, **71.134** CAPITAL GAINS TAX, and *Jolaoso v HMRC*, **71.136** CAPITAL GAINS TAX.

Gift by wife to husband about to become non-resident

[37.9] See *R v Inspector of Taxes (ex p. Fulford-Dobson)*, **71.135** CAPITAL GAINS TAX.

IHTA, s 18—whether applicable to transfers to common law wife

[37.10] See *Holland (Holland's Executor) v CIR*, **72.21** INHERITANCE TAX.

Married woman—election not to pay Class 1 NICs

[37.11] See *Newnham v Clatworthy*, **73.59** NATIONAL INSURANCE CONTRIBUTIONS; *Whittaker v HMRC*, **73.62** NATIONAL INSURANCE CONTRIBUTIONS, and *Gutteridge v HMRC*, **73.63** NATIONAL INSURANCE CONTRIBUTIONS.

38

Mining Rents and Royalties (CTA 2009, ss 270–276)

The cases in this chapter are arranged under the following headings.

CROSS-REFERENCE

For the computation of profits of mines, oil wells, etc. see 68.96 *et seq.* TRADING PROFITS.

Mining rents (CTA 2009, ss 270, 271)

Royalties in kind

[38.1] Under a mining lease, the lessor was entitled to a certain quantity of free coal in addition to rent or royalties in cash. The Revenue issued an assessment on the lessor, charging tax on the value of the free coal. The CS unanimously upheld the assessment. Lord Morison held that 'the coal under this lease formed part of the consideration or rent'. *CIR v Baillie*, CS 1936, 20 TC 187.

Payments for right to withdraw surface support

[38.2] A colliery company paid a minimum yearly rent to the surface owner of its mine, for the right to work the mine notwithstanding any subsidence of the surface. The company claimed that these payments should be allowed as a deduction in computing its trading profits. The CA rejected the claim (by a 2-1 majority, Romer LJ dissenting). Slesser LJ held that the payments were 'in respect of benefits over or derived from land', and that they were not deductible in computing the trading profits. *CIR v New Sharlston Collieries Co Ltd*, CA 1936, 21 TC 69; [1937] 1 KB 583; [1937] 1 All ER 86. (*Note*. The decision was approved by the HL in *Earl Fitzwilliam's Collieries Co v Phillips*, 38.4 below.)

[38.3] A colliery company made tonnage payments to the surface owner of its mine for the right to lower the surface. The Revenue included these payments in a surtax assessment on the owner. The CS unanimously upheld the assessment. *CIR v Hope*, CS 1937, 21 TC 116.

[38.4] Under mining leases, a colliery company was empowered to withdraw surface support in working coal under the land leased. The leases required it to pay half-yearly certain fixed sums per acre of the seams worked 'as liquidated damages in respect of the overlying surface'. The company claimed that these payments should be allowed as deductions in computing its profits. The Special Commissioners rejected this contention and the HL dismissed the company's appeal (by a 4-1 majority, Lord Romer dissenting). *Earl Fitzwilliam's Collieries Co v Phillips*, HL 1943, 25 TC 430; [1943] AC 570; [1943] 2 All ER 346.

Short-term agreements

[38.5] In two cases heard together, the KB held that tonnage payments by a sand and gravel merchant to remove sand and gravel from certain land for three years with an option for renewal, and payments by a colliery to remove coal for two years from specified seams, were within what is now *CTA 2009, s 271(1)* (and were not payments for stock). *Stratford v Mole & Lea*; *Old Silkstone Collieries Ltd v Marsh*, KB 1941, 24 TC 20.

Payments to remove shingle

[38.6] A contractor (G) made payments to a landowner (D) for the right to remove shingle. The payments were based on the quantity of shingle removed. G withheld tax from the payments, and D took proceedings against G, claiming that the payments should have ben made in full. The CS unanimously gave judgment for D, holding that the payments were not subject to deduction of tax because there was no 'concern' within *ITA 1918, Sch A III rules 1-3* (which was similar to what is now *CTA 2009, s 39(4)*). *Duke of Fife's Trustees v George Wimpey & Co Ltd*, CS [1943] SC 377. (*Note. CTA 2009, s 39(4)(a)* differs from the *ITA 1918* provisions in specifically including 'gravel pits, sand pits and brickfields'. It is thought that these differences do not affect the decision in this case.)

Payments to work spoil banks

[38.7] A company (C) which operated a quarry took stone from the quarry and three adjoining spoil banks. The agreement for working the spoil banks was a separate one, and under it C paid the landowner 9d per ton for the material removed. C claimed that these payments were for the purchase of stock and should be allowed as deductions in computing its profits. The CS unanimously rejected this contention, holding that the payments were rent within what is now *CTA 2009, s 271*. *Craigenlow Quarries Ltd v CIR*, CS 1951, 32 TC 326.

Mineral royalties (CTA 2009, ss 273–276)

[38.8] Trustees of various family settlements had granted rights to various mining companies, to extract coal and to disturb other minerals for the purpose of mining coal. The companies made payments to the beneficiary of the settlements. In his tax returns, he treated the payments as falling within *ICTA 1988, s 122*, so that half of them were taxable as income and half of them were taxable as a capital gain under *TCGA 1992, s 201*. The Revenue issued assessments on the basis that the whole of the payments were taxable as income. The Special Commissioner reviewed the evidence in detail and allowed the beneficiary's appeal, holding that the payments should be treated as relating to 'the winning and working of minerals', within *s 122(5)(b)*. The CS unanimously upheld this decision. Lord Osborne held that coal was a 'mineral' for the purposes of *s 122*. He observed that 'not only were the periodical payments related to the winning and working of the mineral coal, but the making of those payments was a necessary precondition of any entitlement on the part of the miner to carry on the activities'. *HMRC v J Bute* , CS 2009, 80 TC 1; [2009] STC 2138; [2009] CSIH 42. (*Note. ICTA 1988, s 122(5)* became *ITTOIA 2005, s 341(2)*, which was subsequently repealed by *FA 2012*.)

Payments to work old mining dumps

[38.9] A mineral merchant made payments, on a tonnage basis, to a farmer for material which he excavated and removed from old lead mining dumps on the farm. The Revenue issued income tax assessments on the farmer, charging tax on the basis that the receipts were mineral royalties. The Commissioners allowed the farmer's appeal and the Ch D upheld this decision. Stamp J held that the payments were not mineral rents within what is now *ITTOIA 2005, ss 335–338*, and were not chargeable to income tax. The dumps were part of the land and the excavation was not a mine. *Rogers v Longsdon*, Ch D 1966, 43 TC 231; [1967] Ch 93; [1966] 2 All ER 49.

[38.10] See also *Shingler v Williams & Sons*, 68.107 TRADING PROFITS.

39

Miscellaneous Income (ITTOIA 2005, ss 574–689)

The cases in this chapter are arranged under the following headings.

Receipts from intellectual property (ITTOIA 2005, ss 578–608)

CROSS-REFERENCE

See 68.1 *et seq.* TRADING PROFITS for the assessment of authors, etc.

Non-trading income from intellectual property (ITTOIA 2005, ss 579–582)

Payments for use of diaries

[39.1] The will of a First World War military commander authorised his trustees to publish his war diaries at their discretion. They arranged for a biography of him to be written and published using material in the diaries. It was agreed that the author and the trustees would share the profits equally. The publisher paid the author advance royalties of £10,000. The author also received payments from a newspaper in return for the right to publish extracts from the book. The Revenue issued assessments on the trustees, charging income tax on the amounts that they received under the agreement. They appealed, contending that the receipts were capital rather than income. The CS accepted this contention and allowed their appeal. Lord Normand held that the receipts were 'capital payments in return for the partial realisation of an asset'. *Trustees of Earl Haig v CIR*, CS 1939, 22 TC 725.

Payment for permission to issue further edition of book

[39.2] A barrister (C) wrote a standard history of the courts in 1899. In 1935 the publishers paid him £150 for permission to issue a further edition. C retained the copyright, and made very few changes to the text of the previous edition. The Revenue issued an assessment charging tax on the £150. The

General Commissioners allowed C's appeal, holding that it was a capital receipt. The KB upheld their decision as one of fact. Macnaghten J observed that it was accepted that the book had needed 'very little revision', and that the £150 'should be treated as having been paid merely for permission to publish the edition'. *Beare v Carter*, KB 1940, 23 TC 353; [1940] 2 KB 187.

Fee for newspaper articles

[39.3] A retired solicitor's clerk (H) sold the serial rights of his life story to a newspaper for £1,500, payable in instalments. The newspaper published a series of articles compiled from his dictation. The Revenue issued assessments charging tax on these payments. H appealed, contending that the £1,500 should be treated as capital. The Special Commissioners rejected this contention and dismissed his appeal, and the KB upheld this decision. Lawrence J held that 'the true nature of the transaction was the performance of services'. *Hobbs v Hussey*, KB 1942, 24 TC 153; [1942] 1 KB 491; [1942] 1 All ER 445.

[39.4] A jockey agreed to the publication of newspaper articles under his name, written by a representative of the newspaper and 'vetted' by him. He received £750. The Revenue issued an assessment charging tax on this amount. The Ch D upheld the assessment. Harman J held that 'the major object and effect of the agreement was that he was paid a sum of money for services to be rendered'. *Housden v Marshall*, Ch D 1958, 38 TC 233; [1959] 1 WLR 1; [1958] 3 All ER 639.

[39.5] The wife of a man who had been convicted for his part in a major robbery agreed to supply information to a UK newspaper. She was temporarily resident in Canada at the time she supplied the information, and the newspaper paid £39,000 to her solicitors in the UK. The Revenue issued an assessment charging tax on this, and she appealed, contending firstly that it was a capital receipt, and alternatively that it arose from services rendered in Canada. The Special Commissioners rejected these contentions and dismissed her appeal, holding that the money which she received was income rather than capital, and arose from a UK contract. The CA unanimously upheld their decision, holding that the payment had been correctly assessed for 1967/68 (the year in which the information was supplied and the money was paid to her solicitors), although she did not receive the money from her solicitors until 1973. Lord Denning observed that the payment arose from 'a chose in action in England', and was therefore taxable in the UK. *Alloway v Phillips*, CA 1980, 53 TC 372; [1980] STC 490; [1980] 1 WLR 888; [1980] 3 All ER 138. (*Note*. For the territorial scope of *ITTOIA 2005, Part 5* ('miscellaneous income'), see now *ITTOIA 2005, s 577*.)

Sale of film rights

[39.6] In 1897 a dramatist (N) obtained the rights to produce a play based on a book by a well-known author (K). In 1914, K agreed to pay her one-third of the receipts from any film version of the book or play. He died in 1936, and in 1939 his widow assigned the film rights for ten years for £8,000, of which £2,666 was paid to N. The Revenue issued assessments charging tax on the £2,666. She appealed, contending that it was a capital receipt for the sale of copyright. The CA accepted this contention and allowed her appeal, and the HL unanimously upheld this decision. Viscount Simon held that N had 'made a partial assignment of her copyright and ceased to be the owner of the portion assigned'. This amounted 'to a sale of property by a person who is not engaged in the trade or profession of dealing in such property'. It was 'a sum in the nature of untaxable capital and not in the nature of taxable revenue'. *Nethersole v Withers*, HL 1948, 28 TC 501; [1948] 1 All ER 400.

Receipts from exploitation of film

[39.7] An American (M) had acquired the sole rights to exploit a Swiss film in the USA and the UK. An actress (R), who had appeared in the film, paid M £1,000 for the rights to exploit the film in the UK, under an agreement whereby M and R would share the receipts. She restored some scenes which had been deleted from the American version. The Revenue issued assessments on R, charging tax on her receipts from the film. She appealed, contending that they were capital. The CA unanimously rejected this contention and upheld the assessments, holding that the receipts were 'annual payments' within the charge to income tax. (The Revenue accepted that the receipts did not arise from her trade, profession or vocation.) *Mitchell v Rosay*, CA 1954, 35 TC 495.

Payments relating to development of inhaler

[39.8] An individual (B) invented a type of dry powder inhaler. He entered into a deed with a company (L), whereby the intellectual property in the inhaler was assigned to L, and L agreed to make regular royalty payments to B, the amounts of these payments being dependent on L's income from sales of the inhaler. In his tax returns, B treated 50% of the payments under this deed as belonging to his wife. The Revenue issued discovery assessments, charging tax on the basis that the full amount of the royalty payments was taxable income of B. The Special Commissioner upheld the assessments and dismissed B's appeal, holding that the effect of the deed was that the payments belonged to B alone. (The Commissioner commented that it appeared that B had been badly advised by the solicitors who acted for him at the time the deed was drawn up.) *PW Braithwaite v HMRC*, Sp C [2008] SSCD 707 (Sp C 674).

Copyright royalties paid to authors resident outside UK

[39.9] A company acted as literary agents and paid copyright royalties to authors who were resident outside the UK. The Revenue issued assessments charging tax on the royalties, without allowing any deduction for the company's incidental expenses. The Commissioners allowed the company's appeal in part, holding that the royalties were taxable but that the company's expenses should be allowed as deductions. The KB upheld this decision. *Curtis Brown Ltd v Jarvis (and cross-appeal)*, KB 1929, 14 TC 744. (*Note*. HMRC accept this case as establishing the principle that, in computing assessments on miscellaneous income, the rules governing trade profits should be followed, 'so far as they are applicable': see Business Income Manual, BIM100155.)

Sales of patent rights (ITTOIA 2005, ss 587–599; CTA 2009, ss 911–923)

Payments for patents—whether capital

[39.10] Two people held patent rights in respect of some disinfecting apparatus. They agreed to assign the rights in return for royalties of 10% for ten years. One of them appealed against a supertax assessment, contending that the royalties were capital. The Special Commissioners rejected this contention and dismissed his appeal, and the KB upheld their decision. *WJ Jones v CIR*, KB 1919, 7 TC 310; [1920] 1 KB 711.

[39.11] A company agreed to make monthly payments to the owner of some patents. The Revenue issued assessments charging tax on the owner. He appealed, contending firstly that the payments were capital, and alternatively that they could not be assessed on the recipient under the legislation then in force. The KB rejected these contentions and upheld the assessments. Rowlatt J held that the payments were royalties. *Wild v Ionides*, KB 1925, 9 TC 392.

[39.12] After the First World War, the Royal Commission on Awards to Inventors awarded two people a total of £85,000 for the use of certain patents during the war. Tax was deducted from the payments. One of the recipients appealed, contending that the payments were capital and that tax should not have been deducted. The HL unanimously rejected this contention and dismissed the appeal. Viscount Cave held that the payments were 'royalty in respect of the successive uses of the invention', from which tax was deductible. *Constantinesco v R*, HL 1927, 11 TC 730.

[39.13] The Royal Commission on Awards to Inventors made an award of £27,750 to the inventor of a type of bomb. The Revenue issued surcharges (under the legislation then in force) charging tax on the award. The inventor appealed, contending that the award was capital. The Commissioners rejected this contention and dismissed the appeal, and the HL unanimously upheld their decision as one of fact. *Mills v Jones*, HL 1929, 14 TC 769.

[39.14] A company was formed in 1906 to acquire and exploit patents. Its only assets were certain patents from which it derived royalty income. In 1917 it sold some of these patents. The Revenue issued assessments charging tax on the proceeds. The company appealed, contending that they were capital. The Special Commissioners rejected this contention and dismissed the appeal, holding that the payments were trading receipts. The HL unanimously upheld their decision as one of fact. *Rees Roturbo Development Syndicate Ltd v Ducker; Rees Roturbo Development Syndicate Ltd v CIR*, HL 1928, 13 TC 366; [1928] AC 132.

[39.15] A trader carried on a business of selling machines which used a process, which he had patented, for dyeing cotton. In some instances the sale was accompanied by an agreement giving the buyer the right to use the process in return for a lump sum payment. The Revenue issued assessments charging tax on the payments, and the trader appealed, contending that the lump sums were capital. The Special Commissioners rejected this contention and dismissed the appeals, holding that the lump sums were trading receipts. The KB upheld their decision as one of fact. *Brandwood v Banker; Brandwood v CIR*, KB 1928, 14 TC 44.

[39.16] A company received £3,000 in return for the grant of a licence to use a patent. The Revenue issued an assessment charging excess profits tax on this amount. The company appealed, contending firstly that the £3,000 was capital, and alternatively that it was investment income and not chargeable to excess profits tax (see **39.19** below). The CA unanimously rejected these contentions and upheld the assessment. Lord Greene observed that 'the time during which the licence is to continue is limited to the time required for the application of the process to the contractual number of boxes'. He held that 'the fact that the parties call the £3,000 a capital sum cannot make it a capital sum if it is not. The word capital is a mere label attached to the £3,000 with an eye, no doubt, to tax considerations. The fact that the agreement separates the £3,000 from the royalties is nothing more than a drafting necessity'. The division of the price into the two separate elements did not 'necessarily produce the result that the sum down must be regarded for tax purposes as a capital receipt.' *CIR v Rustproof Metal Window Co Ltd (and cross-appeal)*, CA 1947, 29 TC 243; [1947] 2 All ER 454.

[39.17] See also *International Combustion Ltd v CIR*, **2.32** ANNUAL PAYMENTS; *Desoutter Bros Ltd v JE Hanger & Co Ltd and Artificial Limb Makers Ltd*, **20.35** DEDUCTION OF TAX, and *CIR v British Salmson Aero Engines Ltd*, **20.36** DEDUCTION OF TAX.

Payment by company to managing director—year for which assessable

[39.18] In 1919 the managing director of a company which manufactured aircraft assigned his rights in certain inventions to the company. In 1923/24 the company was awarded £39,000 by the Royal Commission on Awards to Inventors. In 1927 the company passed £30,483 of the award to the director. The Revenue issued an assessment on the director for 1923/24, charging tax on the award. The CA allowed his appeal and the HL upheld this decision. Lord Tomlin held that the director had 'a definite contractual right against the company' under the 1919 agreement, but had no right to a specific share of the award made by the Royal Commission for 1923/24. Accordingly he could not be taxed on the award for 1923/24. *Handley Page v Butterworth*, HL 1935, 19 TC 328.

Patent royalties—whether investment income

[39.19] The charge to profits tax and excess profits tax was on the profits of a 'trade or business' as defined (see as to this **59.1** TRADING INCOME). For profits tax, certain 'income received from investments or other property' was excluded from the profits, and there was a similar exclusion for excess profits tax of certain 'income from investments'. A number of cases reached the courts in which the question was whether certain royalties were investment income for these purposes. The income tax treatment of the royalties was not in issue—in most cases the royalties were received under deduction of tax—and the decision was based on the particular facts. The cases are, therefore, not summarised individually. Patent royalties were held to be investment income in *CIR v Rolls-Royce Ltd (No 1)*, KB 1944, 29 TC 14. Patent royalties were held not to be investment income in *CIR v Anglo-American Asphalt Co Ltd*, KB 1941, 29 TC 7; *CIR v Rolls-Royce Ltd (No 2)*, KB 1944, 29 TC 137; *CIR v Desoutter Bros Ltd*, CA 1945, 29 TC 155; [1946] 1 All ER 58; and *CIR v*

Tootal Broadhurst Lee Ltd, HL 1949, 29 TC 352; [1949] 1 All ER 261. In *Tootal Broadhurst Lee Ltd*, Lord Normand held that 'the meaning of investment is not its meaning in the vernacular of the man in the street but in the vernacular of the business man. It is a form of income-yielding property which the business man looking at the total assets of the company would single out as an investment.'

Receipts from director relating to patents

[39.20] In a Northern Ireland case, a company allowed its managing director to use its premises, materials and staff to develop certain patents. After negotiations, the director agreed to pay the company more than £200,000 for this. The Revenue issued assessments on the company, charging excess profits duty on the payments. The company appealed, contending that the payments were not trading receipts. The Special Commissioners rejected this contention and dismissed the appeal, and the CA upheld their decision. Lord MacDermott held that 'the agreements provided for the future exploitation of the plough as a commercial profit-earning enterprise and for a division of the profits of this enterprise between the parties until the company's share of those profits had reached an agreed total'. Accordingly, 'the relevant payments were income and not capital in the hands of the company'. *Harry Ferguson (Motors) Ltd v CIR*, CA (NI) 1951, 33 TC 15.

Patent rights—sale not implemented

[39.21] A company agreed to purchase certain patent rights for £1,500, to be paid in instalments of £1,000 and £500. The company paid the £1,000 but did not complete the other terms of the sale agreement. The vendor took proceedings against the company, and received damages of £1,500 and the return of the patent rights. The Revenue issued assessments charging tax on the £1,000 (less expenses of £209). The vendor appealed, contending that the £1,000 constituted damages and was not taxable. The Ch D rejected this contention and upheld the assessments. Danckwerts J held that the £1,000 was 'part of the purchase price of the invention'. *Green v Brace*, Ch D 1960, 39 TC 281.

Annual payments not otherwise charged (ITTOIA 2005, ss 683–686)

Assessment of recipient where tax not deducted

[39.22] The Revenue issued an assessment on a body of magistrates, charging tax on certain bank interest. They appealed, contending that, as a judicial body, they could not be assessed and that the bank should account for the tax under *CIRA 1888, s 24(3)* (the origin of *ITA 2007, ss 899-901*). The KB dismissed their appeal, holding that where tax had not been deducted, the legislation did not preclude assessment of the recipient. *Quarter Sessions for the County of Glamorgan v Wilson*, KB 1910, 5 TC 537; [1910] 1 KB 725.

[39.23] The National Coal Board paid in full rent due under an 81-year lease, from which it was entitled to deduct tax under *ITA 1952, s 177*. The Revenue issued an assessment on the company (G) which received the rent. G appealed, contending that the effect of what is now *ITA 2007, ss 899–901* was that the tax had to be assessed on the payer. The Special Commissioners rejected this contention and dismissed the appeal, and the CA upheld this decision (by a 2-1 majority, Harman LJ dissenting). *Grosvenor Place Estates Ltd v Roberts*, CA 1960, 39 TC 433; [1961] 1 All ER 341. (*Note*. Although *ITA 1952, s 177* is no longer in force, the case remains relevant in relation to *ITA 2007, ss 899–901* and *s 961*. The judgment of Donovan LJ contains a useful review of the origins of what are now *ITA 2007, ss 899–901*.)

Assessment on recipient of 'annual payment'

[39.24] A settlement provided for the payment to an individual (P) of £1,000 per annum out of the capital of a trust fund, the income of which was to be accumulated and added to the capital. Two payments were made out of the accumulated net income. The Revenue issued an assessment on P, charging tax on the payments, but the Ch D allowed P's appeal, holding held that the payments were annual payments and that the assessments were invalid under the legislation then in force. *Postlethwaite v CIR*, Ch D 1963, 41 TC 224. (*Notes*. Prior to 1973/74, the legislation provided that no assessment to income tax (other than surtax) should be made on the person entitled to an annual payment within what is now *ITA 2007, s 899*. This provision was repealed by *FA 1971*.)

Payments to trustees 'as remuneration'

[39.25] Under a deed of settlement, each trustee was entitled to £100 per annum as 'remuneration for his services'. The trustees made the payments out of the income of the trust, and deducted tax. The Revenue assessed one of the trustees on the basis that the payments to him were income of his profession. The KB allowed his appeal, holding that the payments were 'annual payments' (within Schedule D Case III under the legislation then in force). *Baxendale v Murphy*, KB 1924, 9 TC 76; [1924] 2 KB 494.

[39.26] Two of the trustees of a settlement were paid annual remuneration. The Revenue issued assessments charging tax on them, on the basis that the payments were income from an office. The Special Commissioners allowed the trustees' appeals and the KB upheld their decision, holding that the payments were annual payments within what is now *ITA 2007, s 899*. *Hearn v Morgan*; *Pritchard v Lathom-Browne*, KB 1945, 26 TC 478; [1945] 2 All ER 480.

Quarterly payments for use of partnership name

[39.27] The senior partner of a firm died. Under the partnership agreement, the surviving partners had to pay his executors £500 per quarter for five years for the use of the firm's name, goodwill, etc. AT first the partners made the payments in full, but subsequently they treated them as annual payments and deducted tax. The Revenue issued a supertax assessment on the deceased partner's widow. She appealed, contending that the payments were capital and were not taxable. The Special Commissioners rejected this contention and dismissed her appeal, and the KB upheld their decision. *Mackintosh v CIR*, KB 1928, 14 TC 15.

Payments as compensation for delay in fulfilling obligation

[39.28] In 1905 the Clyde Navigation Trustees acquired Renfrew Harbour from the Renfrew Town Council, under an agreement whereby the Trustees undertook to construct a quay at Renfrew within twelve years. Completion was delayed, and in 1925 the Trustees agreed to pay £2,000 annually to the Council as compensation until the quay was completed. The Trustees did not deduct tax from these payments, and claimed them as deductions in computing their trading profits. The Revenue issued assessments on the Council, charging tax on the payments. The Council appealed, contending that the payments should be treated as capital. The Special Commissioners rejected this contention and dismissed the appeal. The CS unanimously upheld this decision, holding that the payments were annual payments and were taxable on the Council. Lord Clyde held that the compensation was for 'a loss due to an injury continuing from year to year and therefore *prima facie* a revenue rather than a capital loss'. *Renfrew Town Council v CIR*, CS 1934, 19 TC 13. (*Note*. The Council would now be exempt by virtue of *CTA 2010, s 984*.)

Will trust—payments out of capital

[39.29] Under a will, a trust fund was established from which the trustees could at their discretion make payments to the beneficiaries out of capital. The Revenue issued assessments on a beneficiary, charging tax on such payments. She appealed, contending that the payments were loans. The Special Commissioners rejected this contention and dismissed her appeal, holding that the payments were annual payments within the charge to income tax. The HL unanimously upheld their decision. *Williamson v Ough*, HL 1936, 20 TC 194; [1936] AC 384.

[39.30] The trustees of a will were empowered to make payments out of capital for the maintenance of the liferentrix of the estate. The Revenue issued an assessment on the basis that payments purporting to be loans to her were annual payments within the charge to income tax. The Commissioners upheld the assessments and the CS unanimously upheld their decision. *Esdaile v CIR*, CS 1936, 20 TC 700.

[39.31] See also *Cunard's Trustees v CIR* and *McPheeters v CIR*, **20.24** DEDUCTION OF TAX.

Residuary estate insufficient to meet annuities

[39.32] Under a will, the residuary estate was charged with certain annuities. The income of the estate was insufficient to meet the annuities, and the annuitants were therefore entitled to the estate proportionately to the value of their annuities. The Revenue issued surtax assessments on payments made to the testator's widow, and she appealed, contending that the payments were capital rather than income. The Special Commissioners accepted this contention and allowed her appeal, and the KB upheld this decision. *CIR v Lady Castlemaine*, KB 1943, 25 TC 408; [1943] 2 All ER 471.

Compensation for war injuries

[39.33] An American soldier (C) had been wounded in the First World War. He was discharged from the US Army in 1919. Subsequently, while visiting relatives in the UK, he was certified insane and detained in an asylum in Scotland. His *curator bonis* (L) applied to the US authorities for compensation for C's injuries, and was awarded monthly payments for twelve years. The Revenue issued assessments charging income tax on these payments, and L appealed. The CS allowed his appeal. Lord Clyde held that the sums received were 'instalments of a capital sum' rather than income. *Laird (curator bonis to Christie) v CIR*, CS 1929, 14 TC 395.

Disability payments under insurance policies

[39.34] A dentist (F) was disabled in an accident and received disability payments from two insurance societies. The Revenue issued assessments charging tax on the payments, and F appealed. The Special Commissioners dismissed his appeal, holding that the payments were 'annual payments' within the charge to income tax. The KB upheld their decision. *Forsyth v Thompson*, KB 1940, 23 TC 374; [1940] 2 KB 366; [1940] 3 All ER 465.

Payments in lieu of superannuation

[39.35] A doctor (L) opted not to participate in the NHS pension scheme and instead to receive an amount equal to 8% of his NHS remuneration, described as a contribution towards the maintenance of life assurance policies which he held. The Revenue issued assessments charging tax on the payments, and L appealed. The Special Commissioners dismissed his appeal, holding that the amounts received were 'annual payments' within the charge to income tax. The Ch D upheld their decision. *Leahy v Hawkins*, Ch D 1952, 34 TC 28; [1952] 2 All ER 759. (*Note.* The Revenue had also issued alternative assessments on the basis that the payments were professional receipts. The Commissioners discharged these assessments and the Ch D upheld their decision.)

Statutory payments following premature retirement

[39.36] A local government officer (S) had worked for many years for the Borough of Southall. Following the *London Government Act 1963*, that borough ceased to exist. He was transferred to the Borough of Ealing, but was made redundant two years later. He received statutory periodical payments, described as 'long-term compensation'. The Revenue issued assessments charging tax on the payments, and S appealed, contending that they were compensation for the loss of his employment, and were therefore exempt from tax. The Ch D rejected this contention and upheld the assessments. Ungoed-

Thomas J held that the payments were 'annual payments' within the charge to income tax (and were not within the definition of a 'pension'). *McMann v Shaw*, Ch D 1972, 48 TC 330; [1972] 1 WLR 1578; [1972] 3 All ER 732.

Payment as compensation for inaccurate advice about pension

[39.37] On reaching the age of 50, an employee (J) decided to consider early retirement. His employer (G) informed him that he would receive a pension of £43,000 pa. He therefore retired. A year later, G informed him that the pension calculation was incorrect, that the pension to which he was entitled was only £38,000 pa, and that he would be paid this reduced amount from the following month. J took legal advice, and began court proceedings against G. Subsequently G agreed to pay J compensation of £5,000 pa, in monthly instalments. J accepted this, and declared the payments on his tax returns. Subsequently, on the advice of an accountant, he ceased to declare the payments. The Revenue issued amendments to his self-assessments, and he appealed, contending that the payments should be treated as capital. The Special Commissioner rejected this contention and dismissed his appeal, holding that the payments were 'annual payments' within the charge to income tax. *Joyce v HMRC*, Sp C [2005] SSCD 696 (Sp C 491).

Annual payments by non-resident to resident

[39.38] A divorced woman (S) was entitled to maintenance payments of £22 per month free of tax under a court order. Her former husband continued making the payments after he ceased to be resident in the UK, but there was no evidence that he purported to deduct tax, had any income subjected to income tax, or had accounted for any tax deducted under what is now *ITA 2007, s 963*. The Revenue issued assessments on S, charging tax on the amounts she received. The Ch D allowed her appeal, holding that the payments could not be assessed on her under the legislation then in force. Upjohn J held that S's former husband was entitled to withhold tax, that *s 963* applied to non-residents as well as residents, and that it was up to the Revenue to collect the tax from the former husband if it could. *Stokes v Bennett*, Ch D 1953, 34 TC 337; [1953] 3 WLR 170; [1953] 2 All ER 313. (*Note*. See now *ITTOIA 2005, s 686*.)

Payments by company to executors of deceased director

[39.39] In 1938 a company agreed to make a series of payments to its chairman (or his executors or administrators) up to 1958. He died in 1941 and the Revenue issued assessments on his executors, charging tax on the payments which they received in accordance with the agreement. The Special Commissioners dismissed the executors' appeal, and the Ch D upheld this decision. Vaisey J held that the payments were 'annual payments arising under a contract', and were therefore chargeable to income tax. *Westminster Bank Ltd (McCurdy's Trustee) v Barford*, Ch D 1958, 38 TC 68; [1958] 1 WLR 406; [1958] 1 All ER 829.

Payments of 'interim income' under Coal Industry Act 1946

[39.40] Under the *Coal Industry Act 1946*, the assets of various colliery companies were transferred to the National Coal Board, and payments of 'interim income' were made to the companies as compensation. In a case concerning the provisions for the apportionment of the income of closely-controlled companies (see **11.1** CLOSE COMPANIES), the HL held (by a 4-1 majority, Lord Radcliffe dissenting) that these payments were 'annual payments' and were chargeable to income tax. Viscount Simonds held that the payments were 'received as pure profit income' and were 'of a recurring character'. *CIR v Whitworth Park Coal Co Ltd (and related appeals)*, HL 1959, 38 TC 531; [1961] AC 31; [1959] 3 All ER 703.

Shares sold for yearly instalments—whether income or capital

[39.41] A shareholder (V) sold some shares, valued at £2,000,000, to the trustees of a family settlement for £5,500,000, expressed to be payable in 125 yearly instalments of £44,000. The Revenue issued surtax assessments for 1956/57 and 1957/58 on the basis that the instalments receivable in those years were part of V's total income. The Special Commissioners held that the payments should be divided into capital and interest and that each of them other than the first contained an interest element, to be calculated on the method laid down in *Scoble v Secretary of State for India*, **2.28** ANNUAL PAYMENTS. The Ch D upheld their decision. *Vestey v CIR*, Ch D 1961, 40 TC 112. (*Note*. Some of the reasoning in this decision was disapproved by the HL in *CIR v Church Commissioners*, **2.21** ANNUAL PAYMENTS.)

Income not otherwise charged (ITTOIA 2005, ss 687–689)

Commission for guaranteeing overdraft

[39.42] Two directors of a company guaranteed its bank overdraft in return for the company paying them commission of 2% of the amount guaranteed. The guarantee was for one year but was renewed, on similar terms, for a further year. The Revenue issued assessments charging tax on the commissions. The KB upheld the assessments. *Ryall v Hoare; Ryall v Honeywill*, KB 1925, 8 TC 521; [1923] 2 KB 447.

[39.43] A solicitor received £500 for guaranteeing an overdraft. The Revenue issued an assessment charging tax on this. The Special Commissioners dismissed the solicitor's appeal, and the KB upheld their decision. *Sherwin v Barnes*, KB 1931, 16 TC 278.

Commission for negotiating sale of shares

[39.44] The controlling director of a company (K) paid an employee (G) commission of £11,245 for negotiating the sale of shares in K. G was also given some shares in a company associated with the purchaser. He sold these shares two years later for £1,750. The CA held that the £11,245 was chargeable to income tax, but that the £1,750 was not taxable. *Grey v Tiley (and cross-appeal)*, CA 1932, 16 TC 414.

Commission received by architect

[39.45] An architect (B) became aware that a landowner (C) wished to sell an estate (T). B introduced C to the principal director of a company (D), which purchased T for £12,000. D asked B for help in reselling T at a profit, and agreed to pay him 25% of its net profits. D subsequently sold T for £33,000, and paid £4,740 to B in accordance with the agreement. The Revenue issued an assessment charging income tax on this. The Special Commissioners dismissed B's appeal, and the CA unanimously upheld their decision. *Brocklesby v Merricks*, CA 1934, 18 TC 576.

Commission from insurance company

[39.46] A company secretary (H) became an agent of an insurance company (P) in 1937. From 1937 to 1952 the only commission which he received from P arose from premiums on his own life policies (the commission being set against the amount of the premiums). In 1952 he negotiated a policy with P on behalf of the company of which he was secretary. P paid him commission of £750. The Revenue issued an assessment charging tax on this. The Special Commissioners dismissed H's appeal, and the Ch D upheld their decision. *Hugh v Rogers*, Ch D 1958, 38 TC 270.

[39.47] The Revenue issued assessments on an insurance agent (W). He appealed, contending that he was not taxable on commission relating to one of his clients (M) because he had passed part of the commission to M. The Ch D rejected this contention, holding that W remained taxable on the commission even though he had voluntarily passed part of it to M. The CA unanimously dismissed W's appeal against this decision. (The Ch D also held that W was not taxable on commission relating to premiums paid through him by a company of which he was a director and his wife was the controlling shareholder. The Revenue did not lodge a cross-appeal against this decision.) *Way v Underdown (No 2)*, CA 1975, 49 TC 648; [1975] STC 425; [1975] 2 All ER 1064. (*Note*. See **4.169** APPEALS for preliminary proceedings in this case.)

Sale of cotton futures

[39.48] Two partners in a firm of cotton brokers dealt in cotton futures on their own. The Revenue issued assessments charging tax on their profits. The CA unanimously upheld the assessments. *Cooper v Stubbs*, CA 1925, 10 TC 29; [1925] 2 KB 753.

[39.49] A manufacturer made profits from dealing in cotton futures. The Revenue assessed him on the profits and he appealed. The KB upheld the assessments. *Townsend v Grundy*, KB 1933, 18 TC 140.

Shares allotted as consideration for guarantee

[39.50] A company (N) received shares in an associated company (F), in return for guaranteeing certain dividends payable by F. N subsequently went into liquidation. The Revenue issued an assessment to the liquidator (T), charging tax on the value of the shares. The KB allowed T's appeal, holding that N had acquired the shares as a capital asset. *Trenchard (as liquidator of National United Laundries (Greater London) Ltd) v Bennet*, KB 1933, 17 TC 420.

Mining finance development scheme—shares allotted to members

[39.51] A company (S) which prospected for precious metals acquired land and sold it to development companies, receiving shares in return. S's activities were partly financed by subscribers, who received shares in the development companies in return for their subscriptions. The Revenue assessed some of the subscribers on the excess of the par value of the shares they received over the amounts of their subscriptions. The KB allowed the subscribers' appeals, holding that their profits were 'of a capital nature' and were not chargeable to income tax. *Whyte v Clancy (and related appeals)*, KB 1936, 20 TC 679; [1936] 2 All ER 735.

Amounts paid for arranging loans to finance property deals

[39.52] A solicitor (M) lent money to a building company (C) to finance two property purchases, and also arranged for clients to make a further such loan. C repaid the loans on the resale of the properties, and paid M sums of £500 and £300 out of its profit on the transactions. The Revenue issued assessments charging income tax on these payments. M appealed, contending that the payments were capital. The KB rejected this contention and upheld the assessments, holding that the payments were income. *Wilson v Mannooch*, KB 1937, 21 TC 178; [1937] 3 All ER 120.

Premiums on repayments of loan to overseas company

[39.53] A UK company (T) lent money to an Indian company under an agreement which provided for interest at 3% per annum and for certain premiums on the repayment or partial repayment of the loan. The Revenue issued assessments charging tax on the premiums and T appealed, contending that they were capital. The CS unanimously rejected this contention and upheld the assessments, holding that the premiums were within the charge to income tax. *CIR v Thomas Nelson & Sons Ltd*, CS 1938, 22 TC 175.

Stallion fees

[39.54] A syndicate purchased a stallion. Members of the syndicate were entitled to one free nomination to the stallion per season. Two members of the syndicate sold some of their nominations, and the Revenue assessed them on the proceeds. The KB upheld the assessments, holding that the receipts were not trading income but were chargeable to income tax (within Schedule D Case VI under the legislation then in force). *Benson v Counsell; Leader v Counsell*, KB 1942, 24 TC 178; [1942] 1 KB 364; [1942] 1 All ER 435. (*Note*. Compare *Malcolm v Lockhart*, 59.37 TRADING INCOME, and *Lady Zia Wernher v CIR*, 59.40 TRADING INCOME, where stallion fees were held to be trading income.)

Ex gratia payment for services

[39.55] In an Irish case, an individual (F) gave advice and assistance to a company (X). There was no agreement that he would be remunerated for his services. X was then dissolved by statute and a new company was set up, with F as its general manager. Shortly before its dissolution, X made an *ex gratia* payment to M. The Revenue issued an assessment charging tax on this. The Special Commissioner allowed F's appeal, holding that the payment was a gratuity which was not chargeable to income tax. The HC(I) upheld this decision as one of fact. *McGarry v EF*, HC(I) 1953, 3 ITC 103; [1954] IR 64.

Introduction fee

[39.56] A company (T) produced ice-skating shows. An ice-skating judge (M) paid T £1,000 for a 50% interest in a forthcoming show. M also paid £9,000 to T's controlling director. The Revenue issued an assessment on the director, charging tax on the £9,000. The General Commissioners allowed his appeal, holding that the £9,000 was a capital receipt and was not taxable. The Ch D upheld this decision. *Bradbury v Arnold*, Ch D 1957, 37 TC 665.

Payment to solicitor following take-over negotiations

[39.57] A solicitor (B) helped a large retail company (L) to purchase the share capital of a small trading company. L paid B £1,950 for his work. The Revenue issued an assessment on B, charging tax on the £1,950. He appealed, contending that he had no enforceable right to the payment and that it was 'a gratuitous gift'. The Ch D accepted this contention and allowed his appeal. *Bloom v Kinder*, Ch D 1958, 38 TC 77.

Racehorses let for share of prize moneys

[39.58] A farmer and racehorse breeder (E) let racehorses on terms whereby the lessee bore the racing expenses and E received half of any prize money from racing the horses. The Revenue issued assessments charging tax on the amounts which E received. The Ch D upheld the assessments. Buckley J observed that the money arose from 'a businesslike transaction entered into between (E) and the lessees' and did not 'arise merely from a recreational activity'. *Norman v Evans*, Ch D 1964, 42 TC 188; [1965] 1 WLR 348; [1965] 1 All ER 372.

Payment of share of profits to retired partner

[39.59] H and M were in partnership as solicitors. H retired in 1956. M became entitled to the partnership assets and undertook to pay one-quarter of the profits to H for 15 years, during which time H agreed to provide such assistance and advice as M might reasonably require. For 1961/62, the Revenue assessed H on the payment which he received under the agreement. The Commissioners dismissed H's appeal and the Ch D upheld their decision. *Hale v Shea*, Ch D 1964, 42 TC 260; [1965] 1 WLR 290; [1965] 1 All ER 155.

Payment to estate agent for relinquishing claim to development

[39.60] In 1959 Bristol Corporation leased a site to a development company (P). P paid £36,000 to a local co-operative society (B), which had previously been negotiating to acquire the site (and which had begun legal proceedings against the Corporation in connection with its negotiations). P also paid £39,000 to an estate agent (R) who had acted for B. The Revenue issued an assessment on R, charging tax on the £39,000. He appealed, contending that the £39,000 was a capital receipt, in settlement of his claim to an interest in the site. The Special Commissioners accepted this contention and allowed his appeal, and the CA unanimously upheld their decision. Russell LJ held that the £39,000 was paid 'for the withdrawal by (R) of his claim to be entitled to an interest in an investment in the development' of the site. This was 'not a legally enforceable claim', but 'was considered a strong non-legal claim which was well worth the substantial payment made for its withdrawal'. *Scott v Ricketts*, CA 1967, 44 TC 303; [1967] 1 WLR 828; [1967] 2 All ER 1009.

Payment linked with sale of land

[39.61] Following the death of a farmer (W), a bank acted as trustee of his estate, which included 240 acres of farmland. The bank sold this land to a gravel company (C) for £100,000. C also paid £10,000 to K, the husband of W's grand-daughter, who had advised the bank to accept C's offer. The Revenue issued an assessment on K, charging tax on the £10,000. The General Commissioners allowed K's appeal, finding that he had given no consideration for the payment and that there was no enforceable contract. The Ch D upheld their decision as one of fact. Pennycuick J observed that 'the critical factor in the case is that the General Commissioners accepted without qualification' K's evidence, even though this must have given ground for 'deep suspicion'. *Dickinson v Abel*, Ch D 1968, 45 TC 353; [1969] 1 WLR 295; [1969] 1 All ER 484.

Receipts from service agreement with actress

[39.62] An actress (C) entered into a service agreement with a company (R), whereby she gave R her exclusive services for a seven-year period for an agreed salary. R agreed that C should perform her services for or at the direction of another company (G), which was the trustee of a settlement. The income from that settlement was to be held by a third company (B) as trustee of a discretionary trust, of which C was one of the beneficiaries. Under complex agreements, it was intended that C's financial advisers should receive 32.5% of the profits derived from her services as their commission for devising the scheme, with the remaining 67.5% being retained by B as trustee of the discretionary trust. The Revenue issued assessments on B, charging tax on the sums it received from exploiting C's services. The Special Commissioners upheld the assessments, holding that the sums were chargeable to income tax as profits of C's profession. B appealed to the Ch D, contending that C had ceased to carry on her profession when she began her seven-year service agreement with R, and that the payments it received were not taxable since they were repayments of money which it had lent to another company (S), which was controlled by C's advisers. The Ch D dismissed the appeal. Templeman J accepted that C had ceased to carry on her profession but held that the sums were chargeable to income tax. He observed that the companies involved in the scheme were all attempting to procure that part of the profits 'would devolve and be held upon the trusts declared by the settlement of which (B) were the trustees. This simple object was achieved in a complicated manner in the hope that the moneys thus received and held by (B) upon those trusts would escape tax. But complications are not trading, and tax avoidance, whether successful or unsuccessful, is not by itself trading.' The sums which B received were annual profits or gains, arising from contracts entered into by R for the exploitation of C's services, and taxable on B as the company in receipt of them. *Black Nominees Ltd v Nicol (and cross-appeal)*, Ch D 1975, 50 TC 229; [1975] STC 372. (*Note*. See also now *ITA 2007, ss 773–789*.)

Letting of grazing rights

[39.63] See *McKenna v Herlihy*, 27.1 FARMING.

Payment received by hedge fund manager

[39.64] In April 2001 a hedge fund manager (M) took up employment with a Luxembourg bank (D). D's directors agreed to pay M an 'investment bonus' as consideration for M introducing certain business to D. However, in November 2001 D made M redundant without paying him the promised 'investment bonus'. M began legal action against D. The action was settled out of court, and D agreed to pay M compensation for the loss of the 'investment bonus' (in addition to the redundancy payment which M had already received). In his 2002/03 return, M treated the compensation payment as a capital receipt. Following an enquiry, HMRC issued a closure notice treating it as chargeable to income tax. The First-tier Tribunal dismissed M's appeal, holding that the agreed 'investment bonus', and thus the compensation payment, was a reward for the part which M had paid in enabling D to acquire additional business, and was not a capital sum. *P Manduca v HMRC*, FTT [2013] UKFTT 234 (TC), TC02648.

40

Mutual Trading

The cases in this chapter are arranged under the following headings.

Mutual insurance

[40.1] A mutual life insurance company had no members other than holders of participating policies. It also carried on business with non-members. The HL held (by a 4–2 majority, Lords Halsbury and Fitzgerald dissenting) that the surplus arising from the excess of the premiums paid by the participating policy-holders over the cost of their insurance was not taxable. *Styles v New York Life Insurance Co*, HL 1889, 2 TC 460; 14 App C 381. (*Note. Obiter dicta* of Lord Watson were unanimously disapproved by the HL in the subsequent case of *CIR v Cornish Mutual Assurance Co Ltd*, **40.3** below.)

[40.2] Several colliery owners formed an association (incorporated as a company limited by guarantee) to provide them with mutual insurance against liability for compensation in respect of fatal accidents to their employees. The association raised funds by making 'calls' on its members. The Revenue issued an assessment charging tax on the surplus of the association's calls over its expenditure in meeting claims. The association appealed, contending that this surplus did not constitute profits arising from a trade. The Special Commissioners accepted this contention and allowed the appeal. The KB, CA and HL all unanimously upheld this decision. Viscount Cave observed that at some time 'the whole of the association's receipts must go back to the policy-holders as a class, though not precisely in the proportions in which they have contributed to them, and the association does not in any true sense make a profit out of their contributions'. *Jones v The South-West Lancashire Coal Owners Association Ltd*, HL 1927, 11 TC 790; [1927] AC 827. (*Note.* See *Thomas v Richard Evans & Co Ltd*, **63.192** TRADING PROFITS, for the deductibility of payments by members.)

[40.3] The Revenue issued assessments on the basis that a company (C) which carried on a mutual insurance business, its members being the persons insured, was carrying on a 'trade or business' for corporation profits tax purposes. The CA upheld the assessments and the HL unanimously dismissed C's appeal. (The charge to corporation profits tax differed from that to income tax and extended to the surplus of a mutual trading concern from transactions with its members. Hence the case was not concerned with C's liability to income tax on its surplus but is of interest because the HL unanimously disapproved *obiter dicta* of Lord Watson in *Styles v New York Life Insurance*, **40.1** above.) *CIR v Cornish Mutual Assurance Co Ltd*, HL 1926, 12 TC 841; [1926] AC 281.

[40.4] A company (M) had been formed by the representatives of various local authorities primarily for mutual fire insurance, which the Revenue accepted as not being taxable. M also carried on employers' liability and miscellaneous business. The Revenue issued assessments charging tax on the surplus from these activities. The Special Commissioners upheld the assessments, and M appealed, contending that insofar as the surplus on such business was attributable to business with its fire policy holders, it should not be treated as taxable. The KB rejected this contention and dismissed the appeal, holding that this disputed surplus did not arise from mutual insurance, and was taxable. The CA and HL unanimously upheld this decision. *Municipal Mutual Insurance Ltd v Hills*, HL 1932, 16 TC 430.

[40.5] Following the decision in *Municipal Mutual Insurance Ltd v Hills*, **40.4** above, Parliament enacted *FA 1933, s 31*, which provided that the surpluses of a mutual insurance company from transactions with its members should be treated as if the transactions had been with non-members. A mutual insurance company appealed against an assessment for 1935/36 on its surpluses from such transactions. The CS allowed the company's appeal and the HL upheld this decision. Lord Macmillan held that 'it is not membership or non-membership which determines immunity from or liability to tax, it is the nature of the transactions. If the transactions are of the nature of mutual insurance the resultant surplus is not taxable whether the transactions are with members or with non-members'. Lord Simonds observed that 'the language of the section fails to achieve its apparent purpose', and the court could not 'insert words or phrases which might succeed where the draftsman failed'. Lord Normand observed that 'no tax can be imposed on the subject without words in an Act of Parliament clearly showing an intention to lay a burden on him'. *Ayrshire Employers Mutual Insurance Association Ltd v CIR*, HL 1946, 27 TC 331; [1946] 1 All ER 637. (*Note. FA 1933, s 31(1)* became *ICTA 1970, s 345(1)*, which was subsequently amended by *FA 1987, Sch 16* to repeal the disputed provision. This remains an important case on the attitude of the courts where legislation has failed to achieve its objective, although, where legislation is ambiguous, the judgments here should now be read in the light of the subsequent case of *Pepper v Hart*, **22.171** EMPLOYMENT INCOME.)

[40.6] The Ch D held that an incorporated association, providing mutual insurance for its members against employers' liability and workmen's compensation claims, was a mutual concern and not assessable to income tax in respect of surpluses arising from business done with its members. Upjohn J held that the fact 'that the time has not yet arrived when any part of the surplus can safely be returned to the members' did not prevent the transactions from constituting mutual trading. *Faulconbridge v National Employers' Mutual General Insurance Association Ltd*, Ch D 1952, 33 TC 103.

[40.7] For a case concerning the application of a double taxation agreement to a mutual assurance society, see *Ostime v Australian Mutual Provident Society*, **68.69** TRADING PROFITS.

Miscellaneous

Corn exchange

[40.8] An association was incorporated with the objects of protecting the interests of the corn trade and providing a corn exchange and other facilities for persons engaged in the trade. Members were required to acquire a share in the company, and pay an entrance fee and an annual subscription. Non-members could also subscribe. The association made certain charges on members or others using its facilities. The Revenue issued an assessment on the basis that its surplus represented trading income. The association appealed, contending that it was not trading. The Special Commissioners rejected this contention and dismissed the appeal, holding that the association was carrying on a trade within the charge to income tax, and that any profit from its transactions with its members and their entrance fees and subscriptions should be included in the profits. The KB upheld this decision. *Liverpool Corn Trade Association Ltd v Monks*, KB 1926, 10 TC 442; [1926] 2 KB 110.

Co-operative society

[40.9] In a corporation profits tax case, a registered co-operative society purchased milk from members and sold it to non-members. The Revenue issued an assessment on the basis that the society was required to account for tax on its surplus. The KB upheld the assessment. *CIR v Sparkford Vale Co-operative Society Ltd*, KB 1925, 12 TC 891.

Co-operative tea planting

[40.10] In an Indian case, a UK co-operative society, the only members of which were two other UK co-operative societies, grew tea in Assam, substantially all of it being sold to its members. Its operating expenses were met by loans from the members who were debited with the market value of tea sold to them. The Privy Council held that it was liable to tax on its surplus, distinguishing *Styles v New York Life Insurance Co*, **40.1** above. Lord Normand held that for trading to constitute mutual trading, there had to be a common fund with complete identity between the contributors to the fund and the participators in it. This was not the case here. *English & Scottish Co-Operative Wholesale Society Ltd v Assam Agricultural Income Tax Commissioner*, PC [1948] AC 405.

Members' clubs

[40.11] See 70 VOLUNTARY ASSOCIATIONS.

41

Partnerships

The cases in this chapter are arranged under the following headings.

Whether a partnership exists

Cases held to constitute a partnership

Joint cotton transactions

[41.1] A UK firm trading as cotton merchants and brokers, based in Liverpool, sold cotton which had been purchased in the USA by an American firm which also traded as cotton merchants and brokers. The profits and losses on the transactions were shared by the two firms equally, after crediting certain commission to each. The Revenue issued assessments on the basis that the two firms were trading in partnership. The firms appealed, contending that the transactions did not amount to a partnership, that the money paid by the UK firm to the US firm was an expense incurred in earning the profits rather than a distribution of the profits, and that the profits of the US firm were earned outside the UK and were outside the scope of UK tax. The Special Commissioners rejected these contentions and dismissed the appeals, finding that the firms were trading in partnership. The CA unanimously upheld their decision as one of fact. *Morden Rigg & Co and RB Eskrigge & Co v Monks*, CA 1923, 8 TC 450.

Temporary joint coal merchanting during strike

[41.2] During a coal strike, a Glasgow coal merchant and a London company which traded as coal importers entered into an informal arrangement involving the importation and merchanting of coal. The Revenue assessed the profits on them jointly. They appealed, contending that they were not trading in partnership and should not be assessed jointly. The Special Commissioners dismissed the appeal, finding that the arrangement constituted a partnership, and the CS unanimously upheld their decision as one of fact. *Gardner and Bowring Hardy & Co Ltd v CIR*, CS 1930, 15 TC 602.

Joint crop growing

[41.3] A farming firm and a firm trading as agricultural merchants agreed to grow carrots on land occupied by the farmers. Each firm contributed certain expenses, being reimbursed out of the proceeds of the crop, the balance of which was divided equally between them. The Revenue issued assessments on the basis that the arrangement constituted a partnership between the two firms. The farmers appealed, contending that the agreement did not constitute a partnership and that each of the firms should be separately assessed on its profits from the transaction. The Commissioners rejected this contention and dismissed the appeal, and the Ch D upheld their decision. *George Hall & Son v Platt*, Ch D 1954, 35 TC 439.

Passenger transport business—whether children partners

[41.4] An individual (R) purchased a bus in January 1926, and used it to operate a passenger transport business. In October 1927 he entered into a partnership agreement with five of his children (two of whom were below the age of majority). The agreement stated that the partnership should be treated as commencing in January 1926. The Revenue issued assessments for 1925/26 to 1928/29 on the basis that R was the sole proprietor of the business, and R appealed. The CS held (by a 3-1 majority, Lord Morison dissenting) that the business had been operated in partnership from the date of the partnership agreement, but held that the agreement did not have retrospective effect, so that R had been the sole proprietor of the business from January 1926 to October 1927. (Lord Clyde's judgment includes the observation that 'no man in this country is under the smallest obligation, moral or other, so as to arrange his legal relations to his business or to his property as to enable the Inland Revenue to put the largest possible shovel into his stores'.) *Ayrshire Pullman Motor Services & Ritchie v CIR*, CS 1929, 14 TC 754. (*Note*. For whether children below the age of majority can be partners, compare the cases noted at **41.13** to **41.19** below.)

Purchase and development of land—whether a partnership

[41.5] An individual (F) wished to purchase and develop some land, but lacked the necessary finance. He entered into an agreement with another individual (S), under which S purchased the land and F assisted him in its development and sale. The agreement (which was drawn up by S) provided for F to be paid half of any profits on the sale, and stated that the arrangement did not constitute a partnership. The Revenue assessed F to income tax. He appealed, contending that, notwithstanding the provisions of the written agreement, the transactions constituted a partnership. The KB accepted this contention and allowed his appeal. Wrottesley J held that the written disclaimer could not 'change the character of what is in essence a partnership'. *Fenston v Johnstone*, KB 1940, 23 TC 29.

Purchase and sale of flat—whether a partnership

[41.6] HMRC discovered that an individual (J) had purchased a flat for £109,000 and sold it 11 months later for £151,000. They issued a discovery assessment, and J appealed, contending that he had purchased the flat in partnership with a friend who had contributed £50,000. The First-tier

Tribunal accepted this contention and directed that the assessment should be reduced accordingly. *A Al-Jibouri v HMRC*, FTT [2014] UKFTT 010 (TC), TC03151.

'Salaried partner'—whether a partner or an employee

[41.7] One of the two members of an accountancy partnership died in 1967. The surviving partner (E) engaged another accountant (S) as an employee later that year. S wished to become a partner rather than remain as an employee, and in 1968 it was agreed that he should be described as a 'salaried partner', but that E should continue to be the sole owner of the partnership capital. Following this agreement, S was paid a fixed salary without deduction of tax, and was described as a partner on the firm's notepaper. Subsequently relations between S and E deteriorated, and in 1970 S left the firm. He began an action against E, seeking a declaration that a partnership had existed between the two but had been dissolved in 1970, and an order that the affairs of the partnership should be wound up. The Ch D held that there had been a partnership between E and S. It was stated in *Pollock's 'The Law of Partnership' (1952 edn)*, that 'a salaried partner is a true partner notwithstanding that he is paid a fixed salary irrespective of profits and that as between himself and his co-partner he is not liable for the partnership debts'. Megarry J observed that 'perhaps "salaried partner" is not really an apt term for someone who is entitled not to a fixed salary but to the profits (if any) up to a fixed limit'. On the evidence here, although E had been the sole owner of the partnership capital, the agreement reached in 1968 was a partnership agreement. The parties had been 'carrying on business in common with a view of profit', within *Partnership Act 1890, s 1*. On the evidence, the partnership had been terminated by mutual agreement in 1970. However, since S had held no interest in the partnership capital, there was no reason to justify an order to wind up the partnership. *Stekel v Ellice*, Ch D 1972, [1973] 1 WLR 191; [1973] 1 All ER 465. (*Notes*. (1) The decision here was distinguished in the subsequent case of *Nationwide Building Society v Lewis & Williams*, **41.28** below. (2) For HMRC's current views on the tax status of 'salaried partners', see Business Income Manual, BIM82025.)

[41.8] In a case where a bankruptcy order had been made against the senior partner in a solicitors' firm, it was accepted by both the Revenue and the senior partner that two 'salaried partners' were partners (as in *Stekel v Ellice*, **41.7** above) and not employees (as in *Nationwide Building Society v Lewis & Williams*, **41.28** below). *CIR v Bielecki*, Ch D [2001] BPIR 975.

[41.9] A similar decision, also applying *Stekel v Ellice*, **41.7** above, was reached in *Gross Klein & Co v Braisby*, **41.43** below.

Limited liability partner—whether a partner or an employee

[41.10] In a non-tax case, the CA held that a member of a limited liability partnership, who was entitled only to a guaranteed fixed share of the profits, was a partner rather than an employee. *Tiffin v Lester Aldridge*, CA [2011] IRLR 105.

Engineering consultant—whether a partner or an employee

[41.11] An engineering consultant (E), who was resident but not domiciled in the UK, appealed against assessments on income from work in Singapore, contending that he was an employee of his brother (who was a management consultant). The Special Commissioner observed that there was a business bank account in the brothers' joint names, which E was able to operate. The Commissioner held that the two brothers were trading in partnership, and determined the assessments accordingly. *Engineer v CIR*, Sp C [1997] SSCD 189 (Sp C 124).

Restaurant—agreement terminated before commencement of trading

[41.12] In a non-tax case, a waiter and chef wanted to open a restaurant, but lacked the necessary finance. They approached an acquaintance (K) and agreed that they would form a partnership, with K providing most of the initial capital. They acquired premises and arranged for builders to undertake the necessary conversion work. However, before the restaurant opened, K's relationship with the other partners broke down. The other partners began operating the restaurant. K subsequently took legal proceedings, contending that he was entitled to a 50% share in the partnership. Rich J made a declaration accordingly, and the HL unanimously upheld his decision as one of fact. Lord Millett held that 'there is no rule of law that the parties to a joint venture do not become partners until actual trading commences. The rule is that persons who agree to carry on a business activity as a joint venture do not become partners until they actually embark on the activity in question. It is necessary to identify the venture in order to decide whether the parties have actually embarked upon it, but it is not necessary to attach any particular name to it. Any commercial activity which is capable of being carried on by an individual is capable of being carried on in partnership.' Furthermore, Rich J had been entitled to find that, since K had 'put up the bulk of the money', he was entitled to a 50% share in the partnership. *Khan v Miah & Others*, HL 2000, [2001] 1 All ER 20.

Cases held not to constitute a partnership

Whether young children were partners

[41.13] A farmer appealed against an assessment on him, contending that he was in partnership with his children. The Commissioners rejected this contention and dismissed his appeal, and the KB upheld their decision as one of fact. *Hawker v Compton*, KB 1922, 8 TC 306.

[41.14] A similar decision was reached in *Dickenson v Gross*, KB 1927, 11 TC 614.

[41.15] A farmer appealed against assessments on him, contending that he was in partnership with his sons. The CS unanimously rejected this contention and upheld the assessments, holding that the facts did not justify the inference that a partnership existed. Lord Clyde held that 'the only proof that a partnership exists is proof of the relations of agency and of community in losses and profits and of the sharing in one form or another of the capital of the concern' and that 'you do not constitute or create or prove a partnership by saying that there is one'. *CIR v Williamson*, CS 1928, 14 TC 335.

[41.16] A farmer (S) appealed against assessments for seven years ending in 1930/31, contending that he had transferred his interest in the farm to a partnership comprising his children (and that he was not himself a member of the partnership). A partnership deed had been drawn up in July 1928 and stated that the partnership should be considered to have begun in 1920 (when S was 74 years old). However, S had remained the owner and the rated occupier of the land, and there had been no tenancy agreement and no payment of rent. The KB upheld the assessments. Finlay J held that there was no evidence 'upon which the Commissioners could find that the occupier was anybody other than (S)'. *Calder v Allanson*, KB 1935, 19 TC 293.

[41.17] A farmer appealed against an assessment, contending that he was not the sole proprietor of the farm, but was in partnership with his son. The Commissioners rejected this contention and dismissed the appeal, finding that there was no written partnership agreement. The KB upheld their decision as one of fact. *Taylor v Chalklin*, KB 1945, 26 TC 463.

[41.18] A mother and her two children traded in partnership as wine and spirit merchants. In 1972 they invited two granddaughters, then aged 15 and 14, to become partners. A partnership deed was subsequently signed by the five in 1974. The partnership appealed against a 1972/73 assessment, contending that the two granddaughters had been partners during that year. The Commissioners rejected this contention and dismissed the appeal, holding that the granddaughters were not partners in 1972/73 in view of their 'inexperience and immaturity'. The CS upheld their decision, applying the principles laid down by Lord Clyde in *CIR v Williamson*, **41.15** above. *Alexander Bulloch & Co v CIR*, CS 1976, 51 TC 563; [1976] STC 514.

[41.19] A family partnership submitted returns claiming that four of the senior partner's grandchildren (aged between 7 and 10) were partners. The Revenue issued amendments to the returns on the basis that the grandchildren were not partners. The Special Commissioner dismissed the partnership's appeal, finding that there was 'no evidence that the grandchildren acted as partners'. *Peter Eley Partnership v HMRC*, Sp C [2008] SSCD 1168 (Sp C 705).

Solicitor—whether partnership agreement retrospective

[41.20] A solicitor informed his son on 31 December 1928 that he intended to take him into partnership from that date. The partnership agreement was not executed until 11 May 1929, but was expressed to be effective from 1 January. The solicitor appealed against an assessment for 1929/30, contending that the partnership had begun on 1 January 1929. The Commissioners rejected this contention and dismissed his appeal, holding that there had not been a partnership until 11 May. The KB upheld their decision. *Waddington v O'Callaghan*, KB 1931, 16 TC 187.

Repair business—whether wives partners

[41.21] Two individuals (S and P) had traded in partnership for many years, repairing agricultural machinery. They appealed against assessments for

1973/74 and 1974/75, contending that their respective wives had become partners on 6 April 1973. The General Commissioners dismissed the appeals, finding that no partnership deed had been signed until June 1975, and that, although the wives had been credited with shares of profits in the partnership accounts from April 1973, they had not drawn any of the sums credited and there was no evidence as to when the accounts had been drawn up. The Ch D upheld the Commissioners' decision, holding that the partnership agreement could not have retrospective effect. *Saywell & Others (t/a Eaton Tractor Co) v Pope*, Ch D 1979, 53 TC 40; [1979] STC 824.

Landscape gardening business—whether wife a partner

[41.22] A married couple had carried on a landscape gardening business in partnership for many years. This business ceased in September 2002 when the couple separated. The husband (V) moved abroad, and the wife (P) subsequently moved to Yorkshire. V returned to the UK in 2003 and moved into P's new house. In early 2004 V resumed working as a landscape gardener, without making any tax returns. When HMRC discovered this, they formed the opinion that V and P had resumed trading in partnership, and issued assessments on this basis. P appealed. The First-tier Tribunal reviewed the evidence and allowed her appeal. Judge Nowlan observed that 'many wives, even semi-estranged wives, will support the work and activities of their husbands in minor ways without that occasioning any serious contention that the two are in partnership', and found that '(V's) past unfaithfulness had irretrievably undermined the relationship between (V) and the appellant', so that 'even though they might live under the same roof, they were unlikely to live again as a normal couple'. *Mrs P Valantine v HMRC*, FTT [2011] UKFTT 808 (TC), TC01644.

'Joint' property dealing

[41.23] See *Dodd & Tanfield v Haddock*, 67.50 TRADING PROFITS—PROPERTY DEALING.

Société en nom collectif—whether a partnership

[41.24] A 'société en nom collectif' (a business organisation under French law) was directed and controlled in France, and carried on business in several countries including the UK. The Revenue treated its UK profits as trading income, and issued supertax assessments on two members of the société in respect of their share of the profits. They appealed, contending that the société was not a partnership but was a legal person distinct from the persons comprising it, so that their share of the profit did not form part of their total income for supertax purposes. The KB accepted this contention and allowed the appeals, and the CA unanimously upheld this decision. Lawrence LJ observed that the members of the société 'may be likened more or less to that of shareholders in a limited company or unlimited company in England'. *Dreyfus v CIR (and related appeal)*, CA 1929, 14 TC 560.

Sale of medical practice—vendor continues to assist

[41.25] See *Pratt v Strick*, 61.26 TRADING PROFITS.

Furniture manufacturer—whether trading in partnership with companies

[41.26] A furniture manufacturer (R) appealed against various assessments, contending that he had previously been trading in partnership with two companies which he controlled, and was entitled to loss relief brought forward from previous years. The General Commissioners rejected these contentions and dismissed his appeal, finding that there had been no partnership and that the losses in question could not be set against R's income since they had been incurred by the companies. The Ch D upheld their decision as one of fact. *Rigby v Samson*, Ch D 1997, 71 TC 153; [1997] STC 524.

Accountant—whether trading in partnership with limited company

[41.27] An accountant (C) agreed with a financial training company (X) that he would provide some financial training in Slovakia. The Slovakian tax authority treated the training as being carried out by a branch of X. However C claimed double tax relief on the basis that he had actually been trading in partnership with X. The Revenue rejected his claim and the Special Commissioner dismissed his appeal, finding that C had worked for X under a profit-sharing agreement rather than a partnership agreement. *Training Consultant v HMRC*, Sp C [2007] SSCD 231 (Sp C 584).

'Salaried partner'—whether a partner or an employee

[41.28] A solicitor (L), who practised as 'L & Co', invited another solicitor (W) to join his practice as a 'salaried partner'. W accepted the offer, and was named as a partner on notepaper in the name of 'L & Co', although he was not entitled to a share of profits. Subsequently a building society, for which L had acted in the name of 'L & Co', took legal proceedings for negligence against both L and W. W contended that he had not in fact been a partner and was not liable for any negligence by L (who had subsequently been declared bankrupt and had ceased to practise). The Ch D held that the relationship between L and W was that of 'master and servant', and that W had not in fact been a partner, distinguishing *Stekel v Ellice*, **41.7** above. *Nationwide Building Society v Lewis & Williams*, Ch D [1997] 3 All ER 498. (*Note*. The Ch D held that, because W had acquiesced in being named as a partner on the notepaper issued in the name of 'L & Co', he remained liable for any negligence. The CA reversed this decision (CA [1998] 2 WLR 915; [1998] 3 All ER 143), holding on the evidence that W was not liable. The building society accepted the Ch D decision that W was not a partner.)

Rotary Club—whether a partnership

[41.29] See *Blackpool Marton Rotary Club v Martin*, **70.8** VOLUNTARY ASSOCIATIONS.

Computation of partnership profits (ITTOIA 2005, ss 849–856)

Removal expenses of partner moved in interests of firm

[41.30] A large firm of chartered accountants, with numerous offices, comprised nearly 100 partners and employed almost 1500 staff. In the interests of the firm, partners or employees were on occasion asked to move from one office to another. They were not moved against their wishes but they mostly agreed to move when asked. The firm contributed to the expenses of a partner who was moved, by paying various removal and ancillary expenses including a subsistence allowance while house-hunting and a disturbance allowance. The firm appealed against an income tax assessment, contending that this expenditure should be allowed as a deduction in computing its taxable profits. The HL unanimously rejected this contention, holding that a partnership could not be treated as a separate legal entity from its individual partners in considering the purpose of expenditure it had incurred. Lord Oliver of Aylmerton observed that 'a partner working in the business or undertaking of the partnership is in a very different position from an employee'. The question of whether a partner's removal expenses could be said to be expended for the purposes of the partnership could not 'be answered simply by ascertaining what was the motive with which the move was undertaken'. It was fallacious to confuse the purpose of the expenditure with the motives of the partners. The removal expenditure served the personal purposes of the partners concerned in establishing their private residences, and consequently was not deductible. *MacKinlay v Arthur Young McClelland Moores & Co*, HL 1989, 62 TC 704, [1989] STC 898; [1989] 3 WLR 1245; [1990] 1 All ER 45. (*Note*. With regard to the distinction between motive and purpose, see also *Smith's Potato Estates Ltd v Bolland*, **63.156** TRADING PROFITS.)

Partnership salaries

[41.31] A partnership appealed against income tax assessments, claiming that salaries paid to two of the partners should be allowed as deductions in computing the partnership profits. The Special Commissioner rejected this contention and dismissed the appeals. Partners' salaries were an apportionment of the partnership profit, rather than an operational expense. Furthermore, it was not open to partners to inflate loss claims by payment of a 'salary' to one or more of their number. *PDC Copyright (South) v George*, Sp C [1997] SSCD 326 (Sp C 141).

Partnership asking partners to leave

[41.32] A large accountancy firm asked two of its partners to withdraw from the firm. It paid them each more than £300,000. The firm did not claim deductions for these payments in computing its profits. In their relevant tax returns, one of the recipients initially treated his payment as a share of the partnership profits, but subsequently submitted an amended return claiming that it should be treated as a non-taxable ex gratia payment. HMRC issued rulings that these payments were profits which were chargeable to income tax. The recipients appealed, contending that the payments did not constitute a share of the firm's taxable income and should not be subjected to tax. The First-tier Tribunal rejected this contention and dismissed the appeals, holding that 'what an individual partner receives out of the partnership funds is part of his share of the profits unless he can demonstrate that it represents a payment to him in reimbursement of sums expended by him on partnership purposes or an entirely collateral payment made to him otherwise that in his capacity as a partner'. On the evidence, the payments 'were made to the appellants in their capacity as partners', and were chargeable to income tax. *G Morgan v HMRC; H Self v HMRC*, FTT [2009] UKFTT 78 (TC); [2009] SFTD 160, TC00046.

[41.33] An accountant (AB) became a partner in a large firm of accountants. Following a period of ill-health, she retired from the partnership in November 2007. She received a payment of £191,532. She accepted that £63,333 of this was taxable, but considered that the balance of £128,199 represented non-taxable compensation. In July 2008 she became a partner in a smaller firm. However, her relations with a senior partner were unsatisfactory, and in February 2009 she was asked to leave. She subsequently received payment of £205,250. She accepted that £102,500 of this was taxable, but considered that the balance of £102,750 represented non-taxable compensation. HMRC issued amendments to her returns, charging tax on the payments of £128,199 and £102,750 which she had treated as non-taxable. AB appealed, contending that she had been discriminated against on the basis of her gender, and the payments were compensation for this. The First-tier Tribunal reviewed the evidence in detail and allowed her appeal in part. Judge Bishopp held that the payment which AB had received in 2007 represented her share of profits, and was taxable accordingly. However, on the evidence, there was 'no real doubt' that she had been treated badly by the firm which she joined in 2008, and it appeared that the partners in that firm recognised she 'had been treated unfairly, and that compensation had to be paid'. Accordingly the tribunal dismissed her appeal with the payment with regard to the £128,199 which she had received from the first firm, but allowed her appeal with regard to the £102,750 which she had received from the second firm. *AB v HMRC*, FTT [2011] UKFTT 685 (TC), TC01527.

Deductibility of rents paid by partnership to a partner

[41.34] See *Heastie v Veitch*, 63.40 TRADING PROFITS.

Partnership—costs of legal action for individual partner

[41.35] See *Stockler Charity v HMRC*, 29.84 FURTHER ASSESSMENTS: LOSS OF TAX.

Interest paid by partnership on money lent by it to a partner

[41.36] A family partnership borrowed £120,558 from a bank at interest. It lent this amount to one of the partners interest-free. That partner used the loan to buy land in his name. The partnership claimed that the bank interest paid was deductible in computing its profits. The Revenue rejected the claim. Twenty-six months later the partnership applied for judicial review. The QB refused the application. Peter Gibson J held that Inland Revenue Statement of Practice SP 4/85, on which the partnership relied, did not apply in cases where a loan was made to a partnership and the money then made available to one of the partners. Furthermore, although it was strictly unnecessary to consider the point, the delay of 26 months in making the application was inexcusable. *R v HM Inspector of Taxes (ex p. Brumfield & Others)*, QB 1988, 61 TC 589; [1989] STC 151.

Payment under guarantee entered into by deceased partner

[41.37] See *Bolton v Halpern & Woolf*, 63.146 TRADING PROFITS.

Payments to executor of deceased partner

[41.38] See *CIR v Ledgard*, 2.5 ANNUAL PAYMENTS; *CIR v Hogarth*, 2.6 ANNUAL PAYMENTS; *CIR v Hunter*, 2.13 ANNUAL PAYMENTS, and *McCash & Hunter v CIR*, 62.26 TRADING PROFITS.

Partnership meetings—whether expenditure deductible

[41.39] See *Watkis v Ashford Sparkes & Harward*, 63.208 TRADING PROFITS.

Married couple trading in partnership—expenses claims

[41.40] See *Marsden & Marsden (t/a Seddon Investments) v Eadie*, 63.214 TRADING PROFITS.

Apportionment between partners

NOTE

The rules for the assessment of partnerships were changed by *FA 1994*, when *ICTA 1988, s 111* was substituted by *FA 1994, s 215*. See now *ITTOIA 2005, s 848*.

[41.41] One of the three partners in a firm, who had been entitled to 9/32 of the partnership profits, retired in October 1921. It was agreed that he should be paid £1,500 in 'full satisfaction' of his share of the partnership profits for the calendar year 1921, £200 in respect of work in progress, and a further £500 in respect of profits of the first year of retirement (of which £250 was to be payable to him in 1921/22, the balance being payable in 1922/23), with similar payments reducing from £400 to £100 over the next four years. The firm's assessable profits for 1921/22 (computed, under the legislation then in force, on the average of the three calendar years 1919, 1920 and 1921) were £5,440. The Revenue issued supertax assessments for 1922/23 (based on the firm's assessable profits for 1921/22) apportioning the £5,440 between the partners on the basis that the retiring partner was entitled to $^{9}/_{32} \times {}^{7}/_{12}$ of the assessable profits for the period to October (i.e. £892) and to $^{5}/_{12}$ of £500 for the period to 5 April 1923 (i.e. £208), so that the balance of £4,340 was divisible between the continuing partners. One of the continuing partners appealed, contending that, as the retiring partner had actually received £1,950 during 1921/22, that amount should be attributed to him, so that only £3,490 was divisible between the continuing partners. The Special Commissioners rejected this contention and upheld the Revenue's assessments, and the CS unanimously upheld their decision. *Rutherford v CIR*, CS 1926, 10 TC 683.

[41.42] For supertax purposes, the Revenue allocated the statutory income of the partnership among the partners by, firstly, allocating to each partner the appropriate salary, interest on capital or commission to which he was entitled for that year and then dividing the balance among the partners in the proportions to which the partnership deed entitled them. One of the partners appealed, contending that the computation of each partner's profits should be made by first ascertaining the share of the firm's actual income to which each partner was entitled for the year in question (regardless of whether this represented salary, commission or share of profit), then taking such share as a percentage of the whole, and finally dividing the statutory income for the year according to these percentages. The Special Commissioners rejected this contention and dismissed his appeal, and the CA unanimously upheld their decision. *Lewis v CIR*, CA 1933, 18 TC 174; [1933] 2 KB 557.

[41.43] An accountancy firm had four partners, one of whom was a 'salaried partner' entitled to a specific amount of the profits (as in *Stekel v Ellice*, **41.7** above). For 1989/90, the firm had total profits of £133,506. Its assessable profits (under the 'preceding year' basis of assessment) were £189,929. It was agreed that one of the partners (L) was entitled to a fixed salary of £27,175, and another partner (R) was entitled to a salary of £15,558, plus a 15% share of the partnership profits. In its tax computation, the firm allocated its actual profits of £133,506 as £46,234 to the senior partner (G); £28,731 to a second partner (K); £27,175 to the salaried partner (L); and £31,366 to the fourth partner (R). For tax purposes, it allocated its taxable profits of £189,929 as £75,574 to G; £47,350 to K; £27,175 to L; and £39,830 to R. R lodged an appeal, contending that he should only have been taxed on £33,503 rather than on £39,830. The Special Commissioner reviewed the computations, rejected R's computation, and upheld the computation as submitted by the senior partner. *Chartered Accountants' Firm v Braisby (aka Gross Klein & Co v Braisby)*, Sp C [2005] SSCD 389 (Sp C 463).

Partnership change during year—apportionment of assessment

[41.44] A new partner was admitted to a firm of stockbrokers in February 1938. The firm applied for an order of prohibition to prevent the Commissioners from apportioning the 1937/38 assessment under the legislation then in force. (The purpose of the application was that, if no apportionment were made, the whole of the assessment would be reduced on an alteration from a 'preceding year' basis to an 'actual' basis, whereas, if the assessment were apportioned, only that part relating to the period from February 1938 to 5 April 1938 would be reduced.) The KB rejected the application and the HL upheld this decision (by a 4–1 majority, Lord Russell of Killowen dissenting). Lord Wright observed that, on a partnership change, 'the old business is superseded by a new business, with a different division of property ownership, of powers of agency and representative capacity, of rights on dissolution and of all the incidents of partnership, including joint liability'. Although a partnership was not a person in English law, the relevant legislation should be construed in a way which treated a partnership as a person, to prevent differences in the treatment of English and Scottish partnerships. Lord Macmillan observed that 'the Income Tax Acts are Imperial Statutes equally applicable both sides of the border, and the language which they employ ought to be construed so as to have, as far as possible, uniform effect in England and Scotland alike'. *R v City of London Commissioners (ex p. Gibbs & Others)*, HL 1942, 24 TC 221; [1942] AC 402; [1942] 1 All ER 415. (*Note*. The substantive issue has been superseded following *FA 1953*, but the HL judgments remain important as a discussion of the differing nature of partnerships under English and Scottish law, and the implications of this in construing tax legislation. However, certain *dicta* of Lord Macmillan were subsequently disapproved by Lord Denning in *Harrison v Willis Bros*, 29.85 FURTHER ASSESSMENTS: LOSS OF TAX.)

Limited partnerships (ITA 2007, ss 103B–106)

Limited partnership engaged in film financing—capital allowances

[41.45] See *Ensign Tankers (Leasing) Ltd v Stokes*, 8.100 CAPITAL ALLOWANCES.

Limited partnership engaged in film financing—loss relief

[41.46] See *Ensign Tankers (Leasing) Ltd v Stokes*, 59.85 TRADING INCOME.

Whether loss relief limited to capital contribution

[41.47] In a case before the introduction of what is now *ITA 2007, s 104–107* (which derives from *FA 1985*), the HL held that a limited partner's share of the firm's loss for the purposes of relief under what is now *ITA 2007, s 64* was not limited to his or her capital contribution under the *Limited Partnership Act 1907, s 4(2)*. (The partner's capital contribution was £10,068 and she successfully claimed relief under *s 64* on £41,423, her share of the relevant partnership loss under the partnership agreement.) *Reed v Young*, HL 1986, 59 TC 196; [1986] STC 285; [1986] 1 WLR 649.

Tax treatment of Jersey limited partnership

[41.48] Two major UK accountancy partnerships asked the Revenue to rule on whether Jersey limited liability partnerships would be treated as partnerships or companies for tax purposes. The Revenue advised the partnerships that, in the event that a UK partnership registered as a Jersey limited liability partnership, the Jersey partnership and its members would be taxed in the UK as if the Jersey partnership were a company. One member of each of the UK partnerships applied to the QB, seeking a declaration that there would continue to be a partnership in English law if they registered as Jersey limited liability partnerships. The QB dismissed the applications. Dyson J held that it would not be appropriate to grant any form of declaratory relief in this case. Firstly, as Parliament had made a limited intervention in the area of pre-transaction rulings, the courts 'should be extremely slow to entertain challenges to pre-transaction advisory opinions by the Revenue'. Parliament had 'been very cautious in permitting challenges to pre-transaction responses by the Revenue' and the courts 'should be very slow to make a massive move into territory into which Parliament had made (one assumes deliberately) only the most limited incursions'. Secondly, the dispute was based to a significant degree on hypothetical facts, and the courts normally refused to answer abstract questions. Thirdly, it was not appropriate in judicial review proceedings to resolve disputes of foreign law. *R v CIR (ex p. Bishopp) (p.p. Pricewaterhouse Coopers); R v CIR (ex p. Allan) (p.p. Ernst & Young)*, QB 1999, 72 TC 322; [1999] STC 531.

Partnership mergers and demergers

Merger of businesses on formation of partnership

[41.49] See *George Humphries & Co v Cook*, **61.62** TRADING INCOME.

Partnership demerger—whether continuation election permissible

[41.50] See *C Connelly & Co v Wilbey*, **61.64** TRADING INCOME.

Overseas partnerships

US partnership purchasing goods in UK for sale in USA

[41.51] See *Sulley v Attorney-General*, **60.33** TRADING INCOME.

Overseas partnership to exploit talents of UK television entertainer

[41.52] See *Newstead v Frost*, **53.12** SCHEDULE D—SUPERSEDED LEGISLATION.

Joint trading by UK and US partnerships

[41.53] See *Morden Rigg & Co and RB Eskrigge & Co v Monks*, **41.1** above.

Miscellaneous

TMA 1970, s 31—right of appeal against partnership assessments

[41.54] In a case where the facts were complex and disputed, HMRC formed the opinion that two architects (B and P) had been carrying on business in partnership from 1998 to 2003, although there was no written partnership agreement. The business relationship came to an end when P took legal proceedings against B. These proceedings were eventually settled by a Tomlin order. HMRC issued assessments on the partnership. In correspondence with HMRC, B accepted that there had been a partnership and submitted partnership accounts. P denied that there had been a partnership, although he had previously claimed that there was a partnership in the course of his legal proceedings against B. Following an enquiry, HMRC issued various assessments on P. P appealed. At a preliminary hearing, the First-tier Tribunal reviewed the evidence in detail and held that B and P had been carrying on business in partnership. Judge Mosedale observed that they had shared net profits, and that this was 'prima facie evidence of the existence of a partnership between them'. She also held that, although B had been the 'nominated partner' under *TMA 1970, s 12AA*, P had a right of appeal against the partnership assessments, since *TMA 1970, s 31* did not 'limit the right of appeal to the nominated partner'. Since an amendment to a partnership return would lead to amendments to the partners' personal returns, it followed that any partner could 'exercise the right of appeal under *s 31* against assessments of the partnership or amendments to partnership returns'. Judge Mosedale expressed the hope that the parties could agree the amount of the assessments in the light of this decision, failing which the case would revert to the tribunal to 'consider the correctness of the actual amendments and assessments which were made'. *RJ Phillips v HMRC*, FTT 2009, [2010] SFTD 332; [2009] UKFTT 335 (TC), TC00276. (*Note.* HMRC initially appealed to the Upper Tribunal against this decision, but subsequently withdrew their appeal. The decision here was not followed in the subsequent case of *Mcashback Software 6 Llp v HMRC*, **41.55** below.)

[41.55] HMRC began an enquiry into the return submitted by a limited liability partnership (M), which had made a substantial claim for capital allowances. They also began an enquiry into the return submitted by one of M's partners (W). In 2011 HMRC issued a closure notice amending the partnership statement and rejecting the claim for first-year capital allowances. M did not appeal against this amendment, but W lodged an appeal, without the agreement of some of the other partners. HMRC contended that W had no locus standi to pursue the appeal. The First-tier Tribunal considered this issue at a preliminary hearing, and held that W did have a right of appeal and that he should be substituted as the appellant. Judge Cannan held that *TMA 1970, s 31* should be construed as providing that an individual partner did not have the right to appeal against a 'consequential amendment of a personal return whether the amendment is under *section 28B(4)* or *30B(2)*. If an individual partner is to have an opportunity to ensure that he pays the right amount of tax it could only be through an appeal against an amendment to the partnership return'. *Mcashback Software 6 Llp v HMRC*, FTT [2013] UKFTT 679 (TC); [2014] SFTD 510, TC03061.

[41.56] See also *Sutherland & Partners v Gustar*, 4.255 APPEALS.

Penalties for non-compliance with TMA 1970, s 20(1)

[41.57] See *Wan & Others v Doncaster Commrs & CIR*, 44.357 PENALTIES.

TMA 1970, s 30B—amendments of partnership statements

[41.58] See *HMRC v Lansdowne Partners Limited Partnership*, 5.69 ASSESSMENT, and *AB (a firm) v HMRC*, 29.84 FURTHER ASSESSMENTS: LOSS OF TAX.

Assessments—liability of executors of deceased partner

[41.59] See *Harrison v Willis Bros*, 29.85 FURTHER ASSESSMENTS: LOSS OF TAX.

Partnership dissolution—liability for unpaid tax

[41.60] See *Conway v Wingate*, 43.81 PAYMENT OF TAX; *Stevens v Britten*, 43.82 PAYMENT OF TAX, and *Barber v Eppell*, 43.83 PAYMENT OF TAX.

Insolvent partnership—partners applying for administration order

[41.61] See *DKLL Solicitors v HMRC*, 6.39 BANKRUPTCY AND PERSONAL INSOLVENCY.

Trustee continuing business of insolvent partnership

[41.62] See *Armitage v Moore*, 59.43 TRADING INCOME.

Arrears of profits payable to widow of deceased partner

[41.63] See *CIR v Lebus's Executors*, 30.29 HIGHER RATE LIABILITY.

Partnership deed—whether a settlement

[41.64] See *O'Dwyer v Cafolla & Co*, 56.100 SETTLEMENTS.

Assignment of share in partnership—income tax liability

[41.65] A partner in a New Zealand accountancy firm established a trust with his wife and child as the principal beneficiaries. He then assigned to the trustees 40% of his share in the partnership. He was assessed on the whole of his income from the partnership, and appealed, contending that the effect of the assignment was that he was not liable in respect of 40% of the income assessed. The Privy Council dismissed his appeal (upholding the decisions of the New Zealand courts). The assignment did not have the effect of shifting liability to income tax from the accountant to the assignees. *Hadlee & Another v New Zealand Commissioner of Inland Revenue,* PC 1993, 65 TC 663; [1993] STC 294; [1993] 2 WLR 696.

Payment on termination of partnership

[41.66] Three people entered into a deed of partnership in 1996. One of the partners died in 2003. Following her death, a dispute arose between the other two partners (H and W). H claimed that he had not received some of the money which he was entitled to under the partnership deed, and took legal proceedings against W. The dispute was settled in 2006 by a Tomlin order under which W agreed to pay H £55,000 in full and final settlement. In 2009 a HMRC officer formed the opinion that £35,000 of this represented shares of partnership profits which should have been charged to income tax, and issued discovery assessments for 1996/97 to 2003/04 inclusive. H appealed, contending that the £55,000 was a capital receipt and that the assessments were invalid because the HMRC officer had not made any discovery. The First-tier Tribunal accepted these contentions and allowed the appeal. Judge Hacking observed that 'it is quite clear that the Revenue received the tax properly due from each of the partners in the business for each of the years in question. An additional charge to tax arising out of a quite different set of circumstances occurring after the periods concerned would have the effect of providing the Revenue with tax receipts in excess of that justified by the income actually received by the partners.' *D Howell v HMRC*, FTT [2011] UKFTT 179 (TC), TC01048.

ITA 2007, s 398—relief for loan to buy into partnership

[41.67] See *Major v Brodie & Another*, 33.26 INTEREST PAYABLE, and *Lancaster v CIR*, 33.27 INTEREST PAYABLE.

Whether partnership managed and controlled outside UK

[41.68] See *Mark Higgins Rallying v HMRC*, 48.67 RESIDENCE.

Legal costs relating to partnership dispute—capital gains tax

[41.69] See *Lee v Jewitt*, 71.103 CAPITAL GAINS TAX.

42

Pay As You Earn

The cases in this chapter are arranged under the following headings.

NOTE

See also 16 CONSTRUCTION INDUSTRY: CONTRACTORS AND SUBCONTRACTORS and 22 EMPLOYMENT INCOME. The *Income Tax (Employments) Regulations 1993 (SI 1993/744)* were replaced by the *Income Tax (PAYE) Regulations 2003 (SI 2003/2682)* with effect from 6 April 2004. The cases in this chapter should be read in the light of the changes to the regulations.

Scope of PAYE (ITEPA 2003, s 684)

The territorial limitation of PAYE

[42.1] An overseas company was engaged, through a Belgian branch, in installing pipelines, etc. in the North Sea, including the UK sector. It also had a permanent establishment on the mainland UK. For this purpose it had some 400 employees working from barges based in the UK sector but sometimes towed into other sectors. The employees were paid in US dollars by cheques posted by the company's Brussels headquarters. The company accepted corporation tax liability in respect of its North Sea activities, but did not deduct or account for any tax under PAYE from the remuneration of its employees on the barges. The Revenue issued a determination under what is now *reg 80* of the *Income Tax (PAYE) Regulations 2003 (SI 2003/2682)*, charging tax of £2,030,000. The company appealed. The HL upheld the determination (by a 3-2 majority, Lords Edmund-Davies and Lowry dissenting), holding that the company had a sufficient 'tax presence' in the UK to justify the imposition of what is now *ITEPA 2003, s 684*. Lord Scarman held that 'the only critical factor, so far as collection is concerned, is whether in the circumstances it can be made effective. A trading presence in the United Kingdom will suffice. Upon the facts of this case a trading presence is made out.' Accordingly the company was liable to operate PAYE in respect of emoluments within what is now *ITEPA 2003, s 41(1)*. *Clark v Oceanic Contractors Incorporated*, HL 1982, 56 TC 183; [1983] STC 35; [1983] 2 WLR 94; [1983] 1 All ER 133.

[42.2] Two directors of a UK company (S), which was a subsidiary of a Maryland company, became aware that that company was seeking to sell S to a third party. In December 1986 they signed agreements whereby, if the Maryland company were to sell S to a third party, they would receive compensation payments from a Delaware company which was also a subsidiary of the Maryland company. In January 1987 the Maryland company sold S, and in February 1987 the directors received payments of more than £175,000 each from the Delaware company. PAYE was not applied to the payments, and the Revenue assessed them under Schedule E. The directors appealed, contending firstly that the payments were not 'emoluments' and alternatively that the Delaware company should have accounted for PAYE. The Special Commissioner rejected these contentions and dismissed the appeals. The payments were 'emoluments' and the Delaware company did not have sufficient 'tax presence' in the UK for PAYE to apply to it. It was not carrying on a trade in the UK, and had no address for service. Any PAYE liabilities would effectively be unenforceable. The mere fact that the directors would have been deemed to be its employees under what are now the *Income Tax (PAYE) Regulations*, if those regulations applied, did not bring it within them. *Bootle v Bye*; *Wilson v Bye*, Sp C 1995, [1996] SSCD 58 (Sp C 61).

Whether benefits in kind within PAYE

[42.3] An employee had the use of a company car. The taxable benefits were taken into account in his codings for 1978/79 to 1980/81, by deduction from his allowances. He appealed, contending that only monetary payments could be dealt with under PAYE. The General Commissioners dismissed his appeal, and he applied by way of judicial review for orders quashing the decision and ordering the inspector not to make the deductions in his coding. The CA unanimously rejected his application, holding that the notices of coding were correct, and that the reference to 'income' in what is now *ITEPA 2003, s 684* and the *Income Tax (PAYE) Regulations* was wide enough to cover all emoluments, including benefits in kind. *R v Walton Commrs (ex p. Wilson)*, CA [1983] STC 464.

Garage allowance to employee—whether within PAYE

[42.4] See *Beecham Group Ltd v Fair*, 42.38 below.

Profit on sale of shares to parent company

[42.5] An employee (H) negotiated a contract whereby he was entitled to purchase shares in his employing company and would also have the right to sell those shares to the parent company. He made a profit of about £380,000 on the sale of the shares, on which capital gains tax was assessed and paid. The Revenue subsequently raised income tax assessments on the amount by which the sale proceeds of the shares exceeded their cost. H appealed, contending that, if any liability arose, the tax should have been deducted and paid by the parent company under PAYE. The HL rejected this contention and upheld the assessments, holding that, since only part of the amounts paid to H were emoluments assessable to income tax, neither what is now *ITEPA 2003, s 684* nor the *Income Tax (PAYE) Regulations* obliged the payer to deduct income tax from such a payment. The income tax due was therefore assessable on the payee. *CIR v Herd*, HL 1993, 66 TC 29; [1993] STC 436; [1993] 1 WLR 1090; [1993] 3 All ER 56. (*Note.* For the Revenue's practice following this decision, see Revenue Tax Bulletin August 1993, p 85.)

Company awarding employees units in unit trust

[42.6] A company (G) awarded four of its directors a substantial bonus, in the form of units in an authorised unit trust. It was accepted that these units were taxable emoluments. The Revenue issued assessments charging tax on the gross value of the units. The directors appealed, contending that G should have deducted PAYE under what is now *ITEPA 2003, s 684*. The Special Commissioner accepted this contention and allowed the appeals. On the evidence, G's chairman had made a binding commitment to remunerate the directors, and G should have deducted tax before providing the units. Furthermore, the units in the unit trust could be turned into money, and were therefore emoluments within what is now *ITEPA 2003, s 62(2)*. *Black v HM Inspector of Taxes (and related appeals)*, Sp C [2000] SSCD 540 (Sp C 260).

Share option gain following MBO—whether within PAYE

[42.7] A woman (T) was employed by a company (E), and in 2005 became a member of its SAYE share option scheme. In 2007 E was the subject of a management buy-out, following which it ceased to be a listed company and, by virtue of *ITEPA 2003, Sch 3 para 19*, could no longer operate an approved SAYE share option scheme. T exercised her share options and sold her shares to the company (K) which was conducting the management buy-out. T realised a gain of £8,410. Since this took place within three years of the grant of the option, this gain was liable to income tax. On her 2007/08 tax return, T declared that she had made a gain but did not declare any tax as due. HMRC began an enquiry in 2009. In 2011 they issued an amendment to T's return charging income tax on the gain. T appealed, contending that the tax due should have been deducted under PAYE and should be treated as having been deducted at source under *SI 2003/2682, reg 185(6)*. The First-tier Tribunal accepted this contention and allowed T's appeal, holding on the evidence that the offer by which K acquired the shares from the 'non-management' employees who were not involved in the management buy-out was 'not an offer to acquire the whole of the issued ordinary share capital of (E) or to acquire all the shares in (E) which are of the same class of the shares in question' for the purposes of *ITEPA 2003, Sch 3 para 37*. Therefore *ITEPA 2003, s 701(2)(c)* did not apply, and E should have deducted tax from the gain under PAYE. Judge Brannan held that, since 'PAYE should have been deducted by (E) in respect of the option gain but was not so deducted, the appellant cannot be assessed on that gain under the self-assessment rules'. *Miss H Tailor v HMRC*, FTT [2013] UKFTT 199 (TC); [2013] SFTD 945, TC02614. (*Note.* See now the amendments to *ITEPA 2003, Sch 3* enacted by *FA 2013*. The amendments were intended to 'confirm that a qualifying "general offer" can take place where shares in the company are already held by the person making the offer (so that the shares are not included within the general offer to acquire the remaining shares), or if the offer is made to some shareholders in a different manner'.)

Company awarding director bonus in form of land

[42.8] See *Paul Dunstall Organisation Ltd v Hedges*, 42.43 below.

Company awarding directors interests in overseas trusts

[42.9] See *DTE Financial Services Ltd v Wilson*, 42.44 below.

Workers supplied by agencies (ITEPA 2003, ss 44–47)

Services of sales promotion workers provided by agency

[42.10] The proprietor of a business which supplied fashion models and sales promotion workers (mainly to a company in the tobacco industry) did not account for PAYE on payments to the workers. The Revenue issued a determination under what is now *Income Tax (PAYE) Regulations 2003, reg 80 (SI 2003/2682)*, and the proprietor appealed. The Ch D upheld the determination, holding on the evidence that there was a relevant contract within the meaning of what is now *ITEPA 2003, s 44(1)(b)*, and that the proprietor was required to deduct tax from the payments. *Brady v Hart (t/a Jaclyn Model Agency)*, Ch D 1985, 58 TC 518; [1985] STC 498.

[42.11] A company (T) provided temporary staff for companies which sold cosmetics at duty-free shops at airports. It did not account for PAYE or NICs on the amounts paid to the staff, which it referred to as 'consultants'. HMRC issued assessments totalling more than £3,600,000, on the basis that the effect of *ITEPA 2003, ss 44-47* was that T should have accounted for tax and NICs. T appealed. The First-tier Tribunal allowed the appeal, finding that there was 'no framework contract' between T and the consultants, and that there were no written contracts between T and the cosmetics companies. The tribunal found that the consultants had 'an unfettered right of substitution', that there was no 'contract of service', and that there was 'no obligation to render (or provide) personal service(s) within the legislation'. The Upper Tribunal upheld this decision as one of fact. *Talentcore Ltd (t/a Team Spirits) v HMRC*, UT [2011] UKUT 423 (TCC); [2011] STC 2377.

Remuneration of doctor from agency engagements

[42.12] A doctor (B) had obtained several locum jobs through medical agencies. The Revenue issued an assessment on his earnings from these agencies, on the basis that what is now *ITEPA 2003, s 44* applied. B appealed, contending firstly that he was self-employed and should not be taxed as an employee, and alternatively that, even if he were taxed as an employee, amounts which he had paid to his wife as wages for secretarial services, and his travelling expenses between his home and the hospital he was assigned to, should be treated as allowable deductions. The Commissioners rejected these contentions and dismissed his appeal, holding that the conditions of *s 44* were satisfied and finding that his duties did not begin until his arrival at the hospital, so that the expenses were not allowable. The Ch D upheld their decision. Knox J observed that 'the question of liability for professional negligence is an entirely separate one from the question whether there is a right to control the manner in which services are rendered'. There was a 'statutory hypothesis that (B) should be treated as though he was an employed person'. *Bhadra v Ellam*, Ch D 1987, 60 TC 466; [1988] STC 239.

Company supplying staff to police force

[42.13] A company (S) supplied the services of various staff (mostly former police officers) to the Bedfordshire Police. HMRC issued determinations charging tax under *Income Tax (PAYE) Regulations 2003, reg 80 (SI 2003/2682)*. S appealed, contending that the workers were performing 'excluded services', within *ITEPA 2003, s 47(2)(b)(ii)*, so that it was not required to account for PAYE. The First-tier Tribunal allowed the appeal in respect of 'project managers' and staff who took witness statements or worked from home on various projects, but dismissed the appeal in respect of disclosure officers, indexers, exhibit officers and 'scene of crime' officers who 'were required to carry out their duties as required by the nature of the services'. *Serpol Ltd v HMRC*, FTT [2011] UKFTT 174 (TC), TC01043. (*Note*. The First-tier Tribunal subsequently approved the issue of a notice under *FA 2008, Sch 36 para 1*—FTT [2013] UKFTT 105 (TC), TC02523.)

Security guards for building sites

[42.14] A security guard (GO) provided other security guards to work at building suites. HMRC issued assessments on the basis that the guards were agency workers, within *ITEPA 2003, s 44*, so that GO was required to account for PAYE and NIC. The First-tier Tribunal allowed GO's appeal, holding that the guards were not within *s 44*. Judge Nowlan held that *s 44* was 'designed essentially to deal with the position of agency workers who are neither employed by the agency, nor the client to which they are provided (in the latter case largely because there will probably be no contractual relationship at all between the worker and the client), but nevertheless the workers fit into the infrastructure of the client, albeit possibly only on a temporary basis, and work under the control of the client rather as if they were employees. Accordingly an essential part of the test quoted above is that the worker must be subject to the control or right of control of some person (either the agency or the client) as to how he performs his functions.' This was not the case here, where neither GO nor the clients 'had control or the right of control over how the work was done'. *G Oziegbe v HMRC*, FTT [2014] UKFTT 608 (TC), TC03733.

Recovery of tax from employee (Income Tax (PAYE) Regulations 2003, Reg 72)

Reg 72(4)—whether a 'wilful' failure to deduct

[42.15] A company director (C) received remuneration for several years without deduction of tax. The Revenue made a direction under what is now the *Income Tax (PAYE) Regulations 2003 (SI 2003/2682), reg 72* that C should account for the tax. He applied for an order to quash the direction, contending that, while he acknowledged that tax had not been deducted, the material before the Revenue did not indicate that the company's failure was 'wilful'. The QB rejected the application. McNeill J held that 'wilful' means 'intentional' or 'deliberate'. He observed that 'this was not an isolated payment of a single week or a short period'. C 'was receiving his full emoluments without deduction', and it was 'difficult to conceive of a man receiving his emoluments in that way without knowing that that was precisely what was happening'. On the evidence, the persistent failure to deduct tax must have been wilful. *R v CIR (ex p. Chisholm)*, QB 1981, 54 TC 722; [1981] STC 253; [1981] 2 All ER 602.

[42.16] The decision in *R v CIR (ex p. Chisholm)*, **42.15** above, was applied in a similar subsequent case in which a company had failed to account for tax on bonuses voted to its directors. One of the directors subsequently applied for an order quashing the direction, contending that the bonuses which had been voted to him had been credited to his loan account net of tax. The QB rejected this contention and dismissed his application. May J held that there had been 'no deduction in the normal sense of a deduction constituted by the payment of a net sum against a pre-existing entitlement to gross pay'. It would be 'a misuse of language to say that the bookkeeping and accounting alone, without actual payment, and without any of the procedures which the (*regulations*) require, constituted a deduction of tax from the gross payment. There was, on the contrary, a wilful failure to do anything relating to tax obligations, beyond making some internal paper entries which the company proceeded to ignore for tax accounting purposes.' *R v CIR (ex p. McVeigh)*, QB 1995, 68 TC 121; [1996] STC 91.

[42.17] A company (B) failed to deduct tax under PAYE from emoluments paid to one of its directors (S), who held one-third of its shares. Subsequently B went into receivership and the Revenue issued a direction under what is now the *Income Tax (PAYE) Regulations 2003 (SI 2003/2682), reg 72*. S applied by way of judicial review for an order to quash the direction. The QB rejected his application. Schiemann J observed that S had been involved with B's PAYE system, and had signed the relevant form P35. On the evidence, he 'must have known, and did know' that there had been a failure to deduct tax. *R v CIR (ex p. Sims)*, QB 1987, 60 TC 398; [1987] STC 211.

[42.18] A similar decision was reached in a case where the Revenue had made directions covering two company directors for the years 1976/77 to 1981/82 inclusive. Nolan J held that 'the Revenue had reasonable grounds for forming the opinion that the two directors did wilfully procure the company to pay their remuneration without deduction of tax, knowing the tax should have been deducted'. *R v CIR (ex p. Cook and Keys)*, QB 1987, 60 TC 405; [1987] STC 434.

[42.19] The Revenue discovered that a builder (M) had received payments from three companies of which he was a director, and that the companies did not appear to have operated PAYE on these payments. They issued directions under what is now the *Income Tax (PAYE) Regulations 2003 (SI 2003/2682), reg 72*, on the basis that the companies had wilfully failed to deduct tax, and issued assessments on M under *TMA 1970, s 29*. M appealed, contending that the amounts he had received should be treated as being net of tax, and that he should be given credit for the tax due on such payments. The Special Commissioner rejected this contention and dismissed M's appeals, finding that none of the companies had accounted for PAYE in respect of any of the payments in question. M had failed to show 'on the balance of probabilities that he should be given credit for the tax he alleged was deducted from his employment earnings with the three companies for the years in question'. The provisions of *TMA 1970, s 29* were satisfied. *MJ Moran v HMRC*, Sp C [2008] SSCD 787 (Sp C 681).

[42.20] HMRC discovered that a company (E) had not accounted for PAYE or NIC on amounts which it paid to its directors. They issued directions under the *Income Tax (PAYE) Regulations 2003 (SI 2003/2682), reg 72*, and assessments under *TMA 1970, s 29*. The directors appealed, contending that they had relied on their accountants and had not known that the amounts due had not been paid. The First-tier Tribunal dismissed the appeals. Judge Porter found that the principal director had 'acted negligently and that he knew that the company had wilfully failed to deduct the appropriate PAYE and NIC'. *DS & Mrs CA Pinion v HMRC*, FTT [2011] UKFTT 525 (TC), TC01372.

[42.21] A married couple were directors of a company (S) which had traded for many years, but began to suffer financial difficulties, ceased paying its PAYE and NIC liability to HMRC, and subsequently went into liquidation. HMRC issued directions under *Income Tax (PAYE) Regulations 2003 (SI 2003/2682), reg 72*. The couple appealed, contending that they had relied on S's accountants, had received their net salaries after deduction of tax, and had not been aware that the PAYE was not being paid to HMRC. Judge Kempster accepted this contention and allowed their appeals, specifically distinguishing the earlier decisions in *R v CIR (ex p. McVeigh)*, **42.16** above, and *Moran v HMRC*, **42.19** above. *J & Mrs LA Prowse v HMRC*, FTT [2014] UKFTT 491 (TC), TC03617.

Reg 72(4)—whether payments were emoluments or dividends

[42.22] A married couple were directors of a company (P) which traded as a recruitment consultancy, and which went into liquidation in 2009. HMRC formed the opinion that P had failed to deduct PAYE from emoluments it had paid to the couple, and issued directions under *Income Tax (PAYE) Regulations 2003 (SI 2003/2682), reg 72(4)*. The couple appealed, contending that the payments were interim dividends rather than emoluments. Judge Cannan accepted their evidence and allowed the appeal. *R & Mrs J Jones v HMRC*, FTT [2014] UKFTT 1082 (TC), TC04171.

Whether motives of directors to be imputed to company

[42.23] In a non-tax case, Lord Denning held that 'a company may in many ways be likened to a human body. They have a brain and a nerve centre which controls what they do. They also have hands which hold the tools and act in accordance with directions from the centre. Some of the people in the company are mere servants and agents who are nothing more than hands to do the work and cannot be said to represent the mind or will. Others are directors and managers who represent the directing mind and will of the company, and control what they do. The state of mind of these managers is the state of mind of the company and is treated by the law as such.' *HL Bolton (Engineering) Co Ltd v TJ Graham & Sons Ltd*, CA [1956] 3 All ER 624. (*Note*. Although this was not a tax case, it has been cited by some commentators as an authority on the question of whether an employer can be deemed to have 'wilfully failed to deduct' tax: see *Income Tax (PAYE) Regulations 2003, reg 72(4)*.)

HMRC making direction under reg 72(5)—appeal by employee

[42.24] In July 2003 a company (D) began employing a part-time driver (B) and deducted tax at the basic rate. From September 2005 to January 2006 B worked for another company (H), which gave him a form P45 indicating that his tax code with H was 489L. He remained on D's books and resumed working for D in January 2006. For the rest of 2005/06 D continued to deduct tax from B's wages at the basic rate, but for 2006/07 D began using code 503L. The use of this code led to an underpayment in 2006/07 and 2007/08. HMRC initially sought to recover the additional tax due from D, but subsequently issued a direction under *Income Tax (PAYE) Regulations 2003, reg 72(5)* requiring B to pay the tax. He appealed, contending that D had not taken reasonable care. Judge Mitting allowed the appeal, finding that D had adopted 'a careless approach to the payroll'. *TJ Blanche v HMRC (No 2)*, FTT [2011] UKFTT 863 (TC), TC01697.

[42.25] In November 2008 a company (AM) took on a new employee (S), who produced his P45 from his previous employer (T), which showed his tax code as 375L but failed to give details of S's earnings from T. AM deducted PAYE as if S had had no previous earnings in 2008/09, instead of adopting a 'month 1' basis. This resulted in an underpayment. HMRC initially sought to recover the additional tax due from AM, but subsequently issued a direction under *Income Tax (PAYE) Regulations 2003, reg 72(5)* requiring S to pay the tax. He appealed, contending that AM had not taken reasonable care. The First-tier Tribunal accepted this contention and allowed his appeal. *T Sparrey v HMRC*, FTT [2014] UKFTT 823 (TC), TC03940.

[42.26] A company (IL) paid one of its shareholders (W), who owned 65% of its share capital but was not a director, without deducting PAYE and NIC. IL subsequently went into liquidation, and HMRC issued a direction under *Income Tax (PAYE) Regulations 2003, reg 72(5)*, requiring W to pay the tax and NIC. The First-tier Tribunal dismissed W's appeal, finding that he had been a 'shadow director' and that he had known that IL had 'wilfully failed to deduct the amount of tax which should have been deducted from the payments'. *MO Williams v HMRC*, FTT [2012] UKFTT 302 (TC), TC01988.

[42.27] HMRC discovered that a company (F) had made payments to its managing director (M) without deducting PAYE and NIC. They made a direction under *Income Tax (PAYE) Regulations 2003, reg 72(5)*, and issued assessments on M. The First-tier Tribunal dismissed M's appeal, finding that he had 'received payment from (F) of the sums at issue in this appeal knowing that (F) wilfully failed to deduct the amount of tax and NIC which should have been deducted from those payments'. *MJ Febrey v HMRC*, FTT [2014] UKFTT 401 (TC), TC03530.

[42.28] See also *Deluca v HMRC*, 4.438 APPEALS.

Application of Income Tax (PAYE) Regulations, reg 101(2)

[42.29] See also *Clifton v HMRC*, 42.101 below.

Employer requesting direction (Income Tax (PAYE) Regulations 2003, reg 72A)

[42.30] A company (E) was asked to deduct tax from one of its employees using a code with a prefix K. E did not operate the code correctly, and did not deduct sufficient tax. HMRC sought to recover the tax from E under *Income Tax (PAYE) Regulations 2003 (SI 2003/2682), reg 68*. E made a request under *reg 72A* that HMRC should make a direction under *reg 72(5)*. HMRC rejected the request and E appealed. The First-tier Tribunal dismissed E's appeal, finding on the evidence that E 'did not take reasonable care to comply with the Regulations'. *Equinox Gifted Thoughts Ltd v HMRC*, FTT [2010] UKFTT 173 (TC), TC00478.

[42.31] In July 2002 an employer (S) took on an employee (C) whose P45 indicated that his tax code was 702H. S deducted tax using this code. In June 2003 the Revenue advised employers (including S) that codes with H suffixes were no longer being used, and employers who were using H codes should contact their tax office to request a new code number. S failed to contact his tax office, and continued to employ C until 2007/08, using codes of 715H, 730H, 744L and 763L. The use of these codes led to a significant underdeduction of tax. HMRC subsequently sought to recover the tax for 2004/05 to 2007/08 inclusive from S under *Income Tax (PAYE) Regulations 2003 (SI 2003/2682), reg 68*. S made a request under *reg 72A* that HMRC should make a direction under *reg 72(5)*. HMRC rejected the request and the First-tier Tribunal dismissed S's appeal, observing that S was in breach of *regulation 21* in having unilaterally adopted codes 744L and 763L when he had never been instructed to use such a code. Additionally, S had failed to contact his tax office when he had been informed that H codes were no longer valid. Judge Staker observed that 'where the employer has been given clear notice that the previous tax code is no longer valid, and that it is necessary for the employer to contact HMRC to obtain the correct tax code', it would 'defeat the purpose of these provisions of the PAYE Regulations if the employer could be entitled simply to ignore that notice'. On the evidence, S had failed to take reasonable care to comply with the Regulations. *J Sasin v HMRC*, FTT [2010] UKFTT 354 (TC), TC00636.

[42.32] HMRC sent a company (P) a coding notice instructing it to deduct tax from one of its employees using code 46L. P failed to apply this code, and deducted insufficient tax. HMRC sought to recover the tax from P under *Income Tax (PAYE) Regulations 2003 (SI 2003/2682), reg 68*. P made a request under *reg 72A* that HMRC should make a direction under *reg 72(5)*. HMRC rejected the request and the First-tier Tribunal dismissed P's appeal, finding that P had failed to demonstrate that it had taken reasonable care to comply with the Regulations. *Portslade Dental Care Ltd v HMRC*, FTT [2013] UKFTT 341 (TC), TC02744.

[42.33] In 2004 an employer (O) employed a new driver (E). E, who was a widower, produced a form P46 indicating that he was in receipt of a pension. However, O deducted tax for 2004/05 using code 474L instead of code BR, and continued to use the equivalent code for 2005/06 and 2006/07. HMRC did not discover the error until October 2007. O made a request under *Income Tax (PAYE) Regulations 2003 (SI 2003/2682), reg 72A* that HMRC should make a direction under *reg 72(5)*. HMRC rejected the request on the grounds that O had not taken sufficient care to comply with the regulations, as required by *reg 72(3)*. The First-tier Tribunal dismissed O's appeal for 2004/05 but allowed his appeal for 2005/06 and 2006/07, finding that O had failed to take reasonable care when he first employed E in 2004, but that O should not be treated as having made a similar failure for 2005/06 and 2006/07. Judge Williams held that he could 'not accept that a failure to take reasonable care in one tax year automatically means that the effect of the failure in that year continues without more to make the conduct of the employer unreasonable in later years. Each year must be considered separately as a matter of fact.' He found that 'HMRC was aware from November 2004 of the failure by the appellant to operate the correct code, but did nothing about this when it was informed in a timely way that the appellant continued to operate the incorrect code in 2005/06 and 2006/07'. *DP Owens (t/a Buses Rhiwlas) v HMRC*, FTT [2011] UKFTT 645 (TC), TC00926.

Determinations of tax payable by employer (Income Tax (PAYE) Regulations 2003, reg 80)

Director's bonus credited but not drawn

[42.34] In 1964/65 a company (N) voted bonuses totalling £31,000 to each of its two directors and controlling shareholders, and credited these sums to their accounts with N. In fact, each drew only £7,500 in the year. N did not account for PAYE on the undrawn bonuses, and the Revenue issued determinations under what is now *SI 2003/2682, reg 80*. The Ch D upheld the determinations. Walton J held that 'the placing of the money unreservedly at the disposal of the directors as part of their current accounts with the company' was equivalent to payment. *Garforth v Newsmith Stainless Ltd*, Ch D 1978, 52 TC 522; [1979] STC 129; [1979] 1 WLR 409; [1979] 2 All ER 73. (*Note*. See also now *ITEPA 2003, s 686*, deriving from *FA 1989*.)

Company awarding retrospective bonus to director

[42.35] See *Spring Salmon & Seafood Ltd v HMRC (No 3)*, **29.126** FURTHER ASSESSMENTS: LOSS OF TAX.

Company failing to operate PAYE on payments to director

[42.36] See *David A Marshall Jeweller Ltd v HMRC*, **44.239** PENALTIES.

Payment to accountant on taking up employment

[42.37] An engineering company (G) appointed an accountant as financial director. It paid him £10,000 on taking up the appointment, and failed to deduct tax under PAYE. The Revenue issued a determination under what is now *SI 2003/2682, reg 80*. The Special Commissioners dismissed G's appeal and the Ch D upheld their decision, holding that the payment was an inducement to the accountant to change his job, and was therefore an emolument from which G should have deducted tax. *Glantre Engineering Ltd v Goodhand*, Ch D 1982, 56 TC 165; [1983] STC 1; [1983] 1 All ER 542.

Garage allowance to salesmen with company car

[42.38] A company (B) provided its salesmen with company cars, and required them to hold significant amounts of stock. It required them to keep the cars and stock in a garage overnight, and paid them an allowance of £2 per week for this. B failed to deduct PAYE from the payments, and the Revenue issued a determination under what is now *SI 2003/2682, reg 80*. The Commissioners dismissed B's appeal and the Ch D upheld their decision, holding that the payments were emoluments from which B should have deducted tax. *Beecham Group Ltd v Fair*, Ch D 1983, 57 TC 733; [1984] STC 15.

Mileage allowances

[42.39] Several associated companies carried on businesses as employment bureaux. They paid allowances to employees to cover travelling expenses. In 1998 a Revenue officer granted a dispensation under which the companies were not required to account for PAYE and NICs. HMRC subsequently formed the opinion that the dispensation should have not been granted, and in 2006 they revoked it. The companies continued to pay the allowances without accounting for PAYE, and in 2007 HMRC issued determinations under *SI 2003/2682, reg 80*. The companies appealed. The First-tier Tribunal dismissed the appeals, holding that the allowances were payments of earnings, intended to reimburse ordinary commuting expenses. The Upper Tribunal upheld this decision. *Reed Employment plc v HMRC (No 4) (and associated appeals)*, UT [2014] UKUT 160 (TCC); [2014] STC 1982. (*Note*. For an application for judicial review, see **4.155** APPEALS.)

Potato pickers and graders—by whom emoluments paid

[42.40] A company (S) carried on business as potato merchants. It engaged an individual (N) to supply workers. N had no formal contract, but only worked for S. N selected up to five workers and drove them to the site in his van, the cost of petrol being shared between them. S supplied the machinery and equipment for the work. S did not pay any holiday pay, and did not make any payment if work was prevented by bad weather. S decided the time, place and nature of the work. S paid N in cash, and N divided the amount paid equally between himself and the other workers. S never supplied N with any written statement of the amount of the earnings, and did not give any indication that any tax had been deducted or national insurance paid. The Revenue issued determinations on N under what is now *SI 2003/2682, reg 80*, on the basis that N should have deducted tax from the payments under PAYE. N appealed, contending that he was an employee of S and was not the employer of the other workers. The Ch D accepted this contention and allowed N's appeal, observing that he exercised no control over where and how the work was to be carried out, and his work, like that of the other workers, was subject to the supervision of S. N worked alongside the other workers, did not pay their wages, and exercised no power over them. Any determination under *regulation 80* should have been served on S rather than on N. *Andrews v King*, Ch D 1991, 64 TC 332; [1991] STC 481.

Restaurant

[42.41] A company operated a restaurant. Tips collected from customers were placed in a box, totalled each day, and kept in envelopes signed by one of the directors. At the end of each week a director opened the envelopes and divided the contents among the waiters and other staff. No troncmaster was formally appointed and no records were kept of the tips. The Revenue issued determinations to the company under what is now *SI 2003/2682, reg 80*, on the basis that the company was required to deduct and account for tax on the tips. The company appealed, contending that the arrangements amounted to a tronc and that what is now *SI 2003/2682, reg 100* applied. The General Commissioners rejected this contention and dismissed the appeal, and the CA upheld their decision. *Regulation 100* had no application where emoluments in the form of a share of gratuities were paid to employees by the employer. *Regulation 100* only applied where payments were made by a troncmaster other than the employer, which was not the case here. *Figael Ltd v Fox*, CA 1991, 64 TC 441; [1992] STC 83.

[42.42] An appeal against a *regulation 80* determination on the proprietor of a restaurant was dismissed in *A Kahim (t/a Balti Nite) v HMRC*, FTT [2012] UKFTT 263 (TC), TC01956.

Company awarding director bonus in form of land

[42.43] A company (P) owned land, which it was in the course of negotiating to sell, and for which an unrelated purchaser had offered £1,450,000 (at a time when property prices were rising rapidly). In 1988 P awarded its controlling director (D) a bonus of £800,000, to be paid in the form of a proportion of the site, and agreed to sell him the remainder of the site for £680,000. One day later D contracted to sell the site to the prospective purchaser for £1,500,000. The contract was completed two days later, the purchaser paying £820,000 to D and £680,000 to P. P did not account for PAYE on the bonus. The Revenue issued a notice of determination under what is now *SI 2003/2682, reg 80*, on the basis that P should have accounted for tax on the bonus of £800,000. P appealed, contending that, as there had been no monetary payment, the liability was that of D . The Special Commissioners rejected this contention and dismissed the appeal, holding that P had placed a 'perquisite or profit' at D's disposal. The obligation to deduct tax from payments of emoluments was not restricted to the payment of emoluments in money, but included cases where the emoluments took the form of perquisites or profits. Payment could be made in money's worth by the delivery of goods or securities, or by transferring the title to land. The bonus of £800,000 was paid to the director, and tax should have been deducted accordingly. (The Commissioners noted that, when the transaction was planned, the market value of the site was taken to be £1,480,000, although the site had actually been sold for £1,500,000. The Revenue did not dispute the valuation, so that the additional £20,000 which D received was held to be a capital gain attributable to the increase in property prices. The Commissioners also held that the transactions were 'pre-ordained', within the scope of the *Ramsay* principle—see **58.6** TAX PLANNING AND AVOIDANCE.) *Paul Dunstall Organisation Ltd v Hedges (and related appeal)*, Sp C 1998, [1999] SSCD 26 (Sp C 179).

Company awarding directors interests in overseas trusts

[42.44] The three directors of a financial services company (D) agreed to pay themselves bonuses of £40,000 each. D wished to avoid liability to national insurance contributions on the payments. It accordingly implemented a pre-arranged avoidance scheme under which it purchased interests in overseas trusts, and assigned these interests to the directors. (D paid £40,600 for each of the interests. The directors realised their interests for £40,000 each, the balance of £600 per director being shared equally by two overseas companies which helped to implement the scheme.) The Revenue issued a notice of determination under what is now *SI 2003/2682, reg 80*, on the basis that D should have accounted for tax. The CA unanimously dismissed D's appeal and upheld the determination. Jonathan Parker LJ held that the *Ramsay* principle (see **58.6** TAX PLANNING AND AVOIDANCE) was applicable to 'the concept of "payment" in the context of the statutory provisions relating to PAYE', since 'in the context of the PAYE system the concept is a practical, commercial concept'. For the purposes of the PAYE system, payment 'ordinarily means actual payment: i.e. a transfer of cash or its equivalent'. There had been a composite transaction consisting of a decision by D that a bonus of £40,000 should be paid, coupled with the payment of that amount to each of the directors by the trustees. The payment was 'a payment of assessable income'. (Jonathan Parker LJ also observed that 'for those employers who operate the PAYE system in a straightforward manner, and who do not resort to the complexities of tax avoidance schemes, there will be neither confusion nor uncertainty; whereas for those employers who choose to operate such schemes the effect of applying the *Ramsay* principle is to restore the certainty which the legislature intended'.) *DTE Financial Services Ltd v Wilson*, CA 2001, 74 TC 14; [2001] STC 777; [2001] EWCA Civ 455.

Payments to personal service companies

[42.45] A football club (S) recruited two players who had previously played for Italian clubs. It was accepted that the players' salaries were emoluments which were liable to PAYE. In addition, S entered into agreements with two personal service companies (Y and Z), under which it paid for promotional and consultancy services to be provided by the players. The Revenue issued a notice of determination under what is now *SI 2003/2682, reg 80*, on the basis that S should have accounted for PAYE on the payments which it made to Y and Z. The Special Commissioners allowed S's appeal, holding that the agreements were 'genuine commercial agreements', as the players were 'established stars' and 'capable of earning very substantial sums each year from commercial contracts'. The agreements were not 'a smokescreen for the payment of additional remuneration'. The payments were not emoluments from the players' employments, and accordingly S was not required to deduct PAYE. *Sports Club v HM Inspector of Taxes (and related appeals)*, Sp C [2000] SSCD 443 (Sp C 253). (*Notes*. (1) The Commissioners also allowed appeals by the players against income tax assessments, holding additionally that the payments were not benefits in kind or retirement benefits. (2) See now *ITEPA 2003, ss 48–61* where services are provided through an intermediary.)

[42.46] A company (L) provided computer consultancy services. It entered into a series of agreements with another company (T) for the provision of services to a third company (M). L subsequently provided the services of its controlling director (B) to M. The Revenue issued a determination under *SI 2003/2682, reg 80*, on the basis that the arrangements were within what is now *ITEPA 2003, ss 48–61*, and that L should have deducted PAYE and paid Class 1 National Insurance Contributions on the basis that the payments it received under the relevant contract were emoluments which it paid to B. The General Commissioners allowed L's appeal but the Ch D held that they had erred in law and remitted the case to a different body of Commissioners for rehearing. Sir Donald Rattee observed that, applying the principles laid down by Robert Walker LJ in *R v CIR (oao Professional Contractors Group Ltd and Others)*, **22.41** EMPLOYMENT INCOME, the purpose of the legislation was 'to ensure that individuals who ought to pay tax and NIC as employees cannot, by the assumption of a corporate structure, reduce and defer the liabilities imposed on employees by the United Kingdom's system of personal taxation'. On the evidence, the Commissioners had misdirected themselves in relation to their consideration of the questions of 'control' and 'mutuality of obligation'. They had failed to apply the principles laid down by Lord Parker CJ in *Morren v Swinton & Pendlebury Borough Council*, **22.3** EMPLOYMENT INCOME, and had overlooked the fact that B had been required to work during M's 'core hours'. *HMRC v Larkstar Data Ltd*, Ch D [2008] EWHC 3284 (Ch); [2009] STC 1161.

Cash withdrawals from company treated as remuneration

[42.47] The Revenue formed the opinion that a company which manufactured clothing had claimed deductions on the basis of false invoices, and that the money had actually been paid as undisclosed remuneration. They issued determinations under what is now *SI 2003/2682, reg 80*. The General Commissioners upheld the determinations, and the Ch D upheld their decision as one of fact. *New Fashions (London) Ltd v HMRC*, Ch D [2005] EWHC 1628 (Ch); [2006] STC 175.

Overseas company operating in UK sector of North Sea

[42.48] See *Clark v Oceanic Contractors Incorporated*, 42.1 above.

Proprietor of agency within ITEPA 2003, s 44

[42.49] See *Brady v Hart*, 42.10 above.

Payments to employees—whether emoluments or dividends

[42.50] A company (U) failed to account for PAYE and NIC on the amounts which it paid to its employees. HMRC issued determinations under *SI 2003/2682, reg 80*. U appealed, contending that it had entered into an arrangement whereby the employees had agreed to receive only the national minimum wage as their emoluments, and that the bulk of the payments represented dividends paid to them as shareholders. The First-tier Tribunal rejected this contention and dismissed the appeal, holding that the payments which the employees received arose from their employment and were taxable accordingly. *Uniplex (UK) Ltd v HMRC*, FTT [2010] UKFTT 422 (TC), TC00698.

Payments to directors—whether emoluments or dividends

[42.51] A company appealed against determinations under *SI 2003/2682, reg 80*, contending that certain payments which it had made to its directors, and declared on its forms P35, should have been treated as dividends rather than emoluments. The First-tier Tribunal rejected this contention and dismissed the appeal. Judge Connell observed that it was 'difficult to understand how the directors could possibly have allowed their returns to have been incorrectly submitted over such an extended period'. *Key Recruitment (UK) Ltd v HMRC*, FTT [2014] UKFTT 755 (TC), TC03874.

Payments to employee benefit trusts

[42.52] A company (M) entered into a tax avoidance scheme, described as a 'discounted options scheme', with the aim of providing additional remuneration to seven of its employees without incurring liability to PAYE or NIC. The scheme involved payments into an employee benefit trust, which acquired 15 Isle of Man companies, and which purported to settle nominal sums on family benefit trusts for the relevant employees and to grant each of the family benefit trusts share options in one of the Isle of Man companies. The intention of the scheme was that there would be no UK tax charge on the cash held in the Isle of Man company until the cash was brought back to the UK (for example, by dividend or liquidation). HMRC issued determinations under *SI 2003/2682, reg 80*. M appealed, contending firstly that the arrangements did not amount to a payment of income to the employees, and alternatively that if there were any tax liability, it should be recovered from the employees rather than M. The CS unanimously rejected these contentions and dismissed M's appeal. Lord Gill held that 'our concern is with the reality rather than with any simulation of reality that may be achieved by the interposition of a company, the issue of shares and the oversight of compliant directors'. On the evidence, it was 'obvious that the employee had complete control of the company and had immediate access to its cash. The money box company was simply a conduit between the EBT and the employee. The directors' purpose was that of compliance with the objective of the scheme.' Applying the principles laid down in *WT Ramsay Ltd v CIR*, **71.285** CAPITAL GAINS TAX, the transfer of shares to the employee was a 'payment'. *Aberdeen Asset Management plc v HMRC*, CS [2013] CSIH 84; [2014] STC 438.

[42.53] A company (MG) provided management services to a group of companies which included a major football club. In 2001 the group established an employees' remuneration trust, which was administered in Jersey, for the benefit of employees and their families. Group companies paid money into the trust, with a direction to the trustees to establish and fund a sub-trust for the benefit of the family of a particular employee, and make a loan facility available to the employee. HMRC issued determinations under *SI 2003/2682, reg 80* on the basis that the various payments were emoluments of the employees' employment, and were liable to PAYE and NIC. MG, and four associated companies, appealed. The First-tier Tribunal allowed the appeals in principle (by a 2-1 majority). Judge Mure held that, in the majority of the cases under appeal, 'the acceptance of loans in the circumstances of the present appeal' did not amount to payment of remuneration, since 'the employees benefiting did not obtain an absolute legal entitlement to the monies'. While there was 'a degree of orchestration in the arrangements made with employees', these did not amount to 'an absolute transfer of funds to the employee'. However, on the evidence, 'advances in favour of certain players are taxable and liable to NIC'. It followed that 'the assessments made fall to be reduced substantially'. Judge Mure expressed the hope that the parties could 'settle the sums due for the limited number of cases mentioned without further reference to the tribunal'. HMRC appealed to the Upper Tribunal, which substantially upheld the majority First-tier decision. Lord Doherty held that the tribunal had been entitled to find that 'the end result was that the employees received loans, not earnings'. *HMRC v Murray Group Holdings Ltd (and related appeals)*, UT [2014] UKUT 292 (TCC); [2015] STC 1. (*Note*. See now the anti-avoidance provisions introduced by *FA 2011, Sch* 2.)

[42.54] See also *Sempra Metals Ltd v HMRC*, **63.267** TRADING PROFITS, and *Scotts Atlantic Management Ltd v HMRC*, **63.270** TRADING PROFITS.

Payments derived from employee benefit funds

[42.55] For 2000/01 to 2002/03, a company (P) entered into complex arrangements under which it paid certain employees bonuses in the form of dividends, which were financed from a capital contribution to P from employee benefit funds which in turn were derived from P. The Revenue imposed determinations under *SI 2003/2682, reg 80*. The CA unanimously upheld the determinations. Moses LJ held that the court 'should focus on the character of the receipt in the hands of the recipients'. The payments 'arrived in the hands of employees, as they were intended to do, as bonuses'. Since the payments 'were emoluments in the hands of (P's) employees, they could not be dividends or distributions in the hands of those employees'. The inserted steps 'which created the form of dividends or distributions did not deprive the payments of their character as emoluments', and 'had no fiscal effect'. *HMRC v PA Holdings Ltd (and cross-appeal)*, CA [2011] EWCA Civ 1414; [2012] STC 582. (Note. For a preliminary issue in this case, see **4.10** APPEALS.)

[42.56] The decision in *HMRC v PA Holdings Ltd*, **42.55** above, was applied in the similar subsequent case of *Manthorpe Building Products Ltd v HMRC*, FTT [2012] UKFTT 82 (TC), TC01778.

Award of shares to employees—whether emoluments

[42.57] The principles laid down in *HMRC v PA Holdings Ltd*, **42.55** above, were applied in a subsequent case where four company directors were awarded shares in two companies which were subsequently liquidated. The First-tier Tribunal upheld HMRC's contention that the provision of shares was 'nothing more than the mechanism for delivery of bonuses', and held that the liquidated companies were 'merely money-box companies serving an essentially mechanical purpose'. Accordingly, the payments were liable to PAYE and NIC. *Sloane Robinson Investment Services Ltd v HMRC*, FTT [2012] UKFTT 451 (TC); [2012] SFTD 1181, TC02132.

[42.58] See also the cases noted at **22.306** to **22.309** EMPLOYMENT INCOME.

Determinations on trustees of pension fund

[42.59] See *HMRC v Barclays Bank plc*, **46.17** PENSION SCHEMES.

Payments by pension scheme on early retirement

[42.60] See *Venables and Others v Hornby*, **46.19** PENSION SCHEMES.

Payments in lieu of notice

[42.61] See *EMI Group Electronics Ltd v Coldicott*, **15.25** COMPENSATION FOR LOSS OF EMPLOYMENT.

Payments to redundant employees

[42.62] See *Mimtec Ltd v CIR*, **15.37** COMPENSATION FOR LOSS OF EMPLOYMENT.

Construction workers

[42.63] HMRC issued a determination under *SI 2003/2682, reg 80* on the basis that a civil engineering contractor (W) was acting as an employer. W appealed, contending that the workers were self-employed. The First-tier Tribunal upheld HMRC's determination but the Upper Tribunal remitted the case for rehearing for a different judge. *PJ Wright v HMRC (No 5)*, UT [2013] UKUT 481 (TCC).

[42.64] A partnership carried on a business of installing windows, doors and curtain walling in commercial buildings. It treated its workers as self-employed subcontractors, and operated the Construction Industry Scheme. The Revenue issued determinations under *SI 2003/2682, reg 80* on the basis that the partnership should have treated the workers as employees. The Special Commissioner allowed the partnership's appeal, holding that the partnership 'did not exercise control over the workers', so that the contracts were contracts for services rather than contracts of service. *J & C Littlewood (t/a JL Window & Door Services) v HMRC (and related appeal)*, Sp C [2009] SSCD 243 (Sp C 733).

[42.65] A property development company (E) did not account for PAYE or NIC on the amounts which it paid to a labourer (F) who worked for it. HMRC issued determinations under *SI 2003/2682, reg 80*. The First-tier Tribunal dismissed E's appeal, holding that F was employed under a contract of service. *Eric Newman Developments Ltd v HMRC*, FTT [2012] UKFTT 111 (TC), TC01807.

[42.66] See also *Lewis (t/a MAL Scaffolding) & Others v HMRC*, **73.39** NATIONAL INSURANCE CONTRIBUTIONS, and *Castle Construction (Chesterfield) Ltd v HMRC*, **73.40** NATIONAL INSURANCE CONTRIBUTIONS.

Hotel maintenance worker

[42.67] A married couple operated a hotel in partnership. They arranged for an individual (M) to undertake maintenance work at the hotel. They treated M as self-employed. The Revenue issued a determination under *SI 2003/2682, reg 80* on the basis that the partnership should have treated M as an employee. The partnership and M appealed. The Special Commissioner reviewed the evidence in detail and allowed their appeals, holding that M was not an 'employee' or an 'employed earner', so that the partnership was not required to deduct PAYE or NIC. *Parade Park Hotel v HMRC; P May v HMRC*, Sp C [2007] SSCD 430 (Sp C 599).

Hotel workers

[42.68] HMRC discovered that a partnership which operated a hotel had failed to account for PAYE on payments to eight employees. They issued a determination under *SI 2003/2682, reg 80*. The First-tier Tribunal dismissed the partnership's appeal. *Cruachan Hotel v HMRC*, FTT [2014] UKFTT 071 (TC), TC03211.

Flying instructors at club

[42.69] A company (S) operated a flying club. It arranged for flying instructors to provide tuition at the club. It treated the instructors as self-employed contractors. In 2007 HMRC issued determinations under *SI 2003/2682, reg 80* on the basis that S should have treated the instructors as employees. The Special Commissioner allowed S's appeal, holding that the instructors were self-employed subcontractors who were 'in business in their own account, although in a relatively modest way'. *Sherburn Aero Club Ltd v HMRC*, Sp C, [2009] SSCD 450; [2009] UKFTT 65 (TC), TC00006.

Driver

[42.70] A company (E) operated a vehicle recovery service. HMRC formed the opinion that it should have accounted for PAYE on payments it had made to a driver (M), who had his own recovery vehicle and had done some work for it. They issued determinations under *SI 2003/2682, reg 80*. E appealed, contending that M had been a self-employed contractor and had not been an employee. The First-tier Tribunal accepted this contention and allowed the appeal. *EMS (Independent Accident Management Services) Ltd v HMRC*, FTT [2014] UKFTT 891 (TC), TC04006.

Company marketing 'weight loss' programme

[42.71] A company (W) marketed a 'weight loss' programme. Customers were asked to attend weekly meetings, where they were weighed. W paid women to lead these meetings. It failed to account for PAYE or NIC on the amounts it paid to the women to lead these meetings. HMRC issued determinations under *SI 2003/2682, reg 80*. W appealed, contending that the women should be treated as self-employed. The First-tier Tribunal rejected this contention and dismissed the appeal, and the Upper Tribunal upheld this decision. Briggs J held that 'the fact that one group of a company's employees are less integrated into a typical modern employment structure than another group is of no significant weight towards a conclusion that the first group are not employees at all'. *Weight Watchers (UK) Ltd v HMRC (and related appeals)*, UT [2011] UKUT 433 (TCC); [2012] STC 265.

Cleaners

[42.72] A company (R) which operated a cleaning business failed to account for PAYE on the amounts it paid to the cleaners who worked for it. HMRC issued determinations under *SI 2003/2682, reg 80*. R appealed, contending that the cleaners were self-employed. The First-tier Tribunal rejected this contention and dismissed the appeals, holding that the cleaners were employees. *Red Apple Cleaning Management Ltd v HMRC*, FTT [2010] UKFTT 618 (TC), TC00860.

[42.73] The First-tier Tribunal reached a similar decision in *M Keenan (t/a Real Clean) v HMRC*, FTT [2013] UKFTT 610 (TC), TC02997.

Car wash business

[42.74] The First-tier Tribunal dismissed an appeal by the proprietor of a car wash business, against determinations under *SI 2003/2682, reg 80*, in *A Ibrahim v HMRC*, FTT [2014] UKFTT 081 (TC), TC03221.

Sandwich bar

[42.75] HMRC discovered that the proprietors of a sandwich bar had failed to account for PAYE on payments to employees. They issued determinations under *SI 2003/2682, reg 80*. The partnership appealed, contending that the determinations were excessive because most of the employees were young women who worked less than 16 hours per week and whose earnings were below the PAYE and NIC thresholds. The First-tier Tribunal allowed the appeal in part, and adjourned the appeal for three months in the hope that the parties could reach an agreement as to figures. *A & V Khanna (t/a The Fresh Sandwich Bar) v HMRC*, FTT [2011] UKFTT 198 (TC), TC01067.

Takeaway food shop

[42.76] HMRC discovered that the proprietor of a shop selling takeaway food had failed to account for PAYE on payments to employees. They issued determinations under *SI 2003/2682, reg 80*. The First-tier Tribunal upheld the determinations in principle but reduced them in amount. *S Hussain v HMRC*, FTT [2011] UKFTT 620 (TC), TC01462.

[42.77] A similar decision was reached in *KY Lai & YY Lau (t/a Gourmet House)*, FTT [2014] UKFTT 402 (TC), TC03531.

[42.78] HMRC formed the opinion that the proprietor of a takeaway restaurant should have accounted for PAYE in respect of two workers, and issued *regulation 80* determinations. The proprietor appealed, contending that one of the workers, who delivered meals for him, was self-employed. The First-tier Tribunal accepted this contention and allowed the appeal in part. *YW Liu v HMRC*, FTT [2014] UKFTT 1022 (TC), TC04118.

Publicans

[42.79] HMRC discovered that a married couple who operated a public house had failed to account for PAYE on payments to part-time bar staff. They issued determinations under *SI 2003/2682, reg 80*. The First-tier Tribunal upheld the determinations in principle but reduced them in amount, finding that some of the employees had not been liable to tax. *Mr & Mrs Brown (t/a Gamekeeper Inn) v HMRC*, FTT [2013] UKFTT 222 (TC), TC02636.

[42.80] See also *Moran*, **44.238** PENALTIES.

Validity of determination

[42.81] A company (W) made substantial payments to companies controlled by three of its directors, describing the payments as 'management charges'. The Revenue formed the opinion that these payments were taxable emoluments of the directors, and issued notices of determination under *SI 2003/2682, reg 80*. W appealed, contending that the notices were invalid. The Special Commissioner rejected this contention and dismissed the appeal. *Westek Ltd v HMRC*, Sp C 2007, [2008] SSCD 169 (Sp C 629).

[42.82] Determinations under *SI 2003/2682, reg 80* were also upheld in *Harrison News Ltd v HMRC*, FTT [2011] UKFTT 251 (TC), TC01115.

[42.83] See also *Pawlowski (Collector of Taxes) v Dunnington*, **43.12** PAYMENT OF TAX.

Miscellaneous

Cash set aside for PAYE tax stolen from employer

[42.84] A hairdresser did not pay the Collector of Taxes the PAYE which she had deducted from her employees. The Revenue took proceedings to recover the money, which the hairdresser stated had been stolen from her premises. The KB upheld the Revenue's claim, holding that the hairdresser remained liable to pay the money to the Revenue. Croom-Johnson J held that 'if a person who is liable to pay interest on an annuity or anything of that sort, and is under a duty to deduct tax at the source, chooses to put the money in a bureau or a chest of drawers or a safe or any other receptacle and the money is lost, it is absurd for him to say that the money is at the risk of the Revenue. The answer is that it is not.' *A-G v Jeanne Antoine*, KB 1949, 31 TC 213; [1949] 2 All ER 1000.

Failure by employer to deduct tax

[42.85] A company (B) paid remuneration to a director (S) without deducting tax under PAYE. The Revenue claimed the tax from B, which in turn claimed an equivalent amount from S (who had left B in the meantime), contending that he was party to the payment in full and held the amount overpaid to him as trustee for S. The KB rejected S's claim, holding that its failure to deduct tax had not arisen because of a mistake but in breach of its obligations under the PAYE regulations. *Bernard & Shaw Ltd v Shaw*, KB 1951, 30 ATC 187.

[42.86] A company (P) failed to deduct PAYE from earnings paid to one of its directors (T). P subsequently ceased making payments to T. T began court proceedings against P's controlling shareholder (S). S defended the proceedings, contending that P should have deducted PAYE and had already paid T more than the net amount he was entitled to. Judge Mackie accepted this contention and gave judgment for S. Judge Mackie held that S had 'in principle and subject to the facts as they later emerge, a right to claim reimbursement for past sums which should have been deducted but were not'. *Telfer v Sakellarios*, QB [2013] EWHC 1556 (Comm); [2013] STC 2413.

[42.87] See also *Companies W, X, Y and Z v Austria*, **31.4** HUMAN RIGHTS, and *Hibbs v United Kingdom*, **31.64** HUMAN RIGHTS.

Cost to employer of complying with PAYE requirements

[42.88] A solicitor failed to account for tax due from him under the PAYE Regulations. He was summoned to appear before the local magistrates, where he contended firstly that he should be entitled to deduct an amount for work done in operating PAYE, and alternatively that the Regulations were *ultra vires* in not providing for remuneration for such work. The magistrates rejected these contentions and the QB upheld their decision. *Meredith v Hazell*, QB 1964, 42 TC 435. (*Note.* See *Meredith v Roberts*, **63.159** TRADING PROFITS, for a sequel to this case.)

Agreement to pay remuneration 'without any deductions and taxes'

[42.89] A company agreed to pay an employee (J) remuneration of £36 per month, 'without any deduction and taxes, which will be borne by' the employer. Despite the agreement, the company subsequently deducted income tax from the payments, so that J received less than £36. J took proceedings against the company, claiming that he was entitled to receive a net payment of £36. The CA unanimously gave judgment for J, holding that the agreement was for such remuneration as would leave the specified amount of £36 after deduction of tax under PAYE. Somervell LJ observed that 'an intention that any employee or annuitant should get a certain sum, irrespective of variations in income tax, is common'. (The CA also held that *TMA, s 106(2)** did not apply as payments of remuneration are not 'annual payments' and, in any case, it did not apply where deduction of tax is mandatory.) *Jaworski v Institution of Polish Engineers in Great Britain Ltd*, CA 1950, 29 ATC 385; [1951] 1 KB 768.

Agreement to reimburse tax as expenses—whether enforceable

[42.90] An employee sued his employer for arrears of salary and expenses under a contract which provided for the payment of a weekly salary and for the reimbursement to him as 'expenses' of the tax deducted from the salary under PAYE. The CA held that no action lay to recover the arrears, since the whole contract was illegal as contrary to public policy. The agreement to pay the salary was not severable from the rest of the contract. *Miller v Karlinski*, CA 1945, 24 ATC 483.

[42.91] A similar decision was reached in a case where an employee sued his former employer for salary in lieu of notice of dismissal. Denning LJ observed that 'the insertion of a fictitious figure for expenses in order to defraud the Inland Revenue is illegal. It vitiates the whole remuneration, and disentitles the servant from recovering any part of it.' *Napier v National Business Agency Ltd*, CA 1951, 30 ATC 180; [1951] 2 All ER 264.

Payments from third party—whether within PAYE Regulations

[42.92] In June 1988 a company (M) agreed with B, a potential employee of an associated company (P), that it would pay B certain monetary benefits in certain defined circumstances, including the ending of his employment with P. B began employment with P in July 1988, and his employment ended in September 1991. M paid B the monetary benefits as agreed, but deducted basic rate tax in accordance with the *Income Tax (PAYE) Regulations**. B took legal proceedings against M, contending that, since he had never been an employee of M, M was not entitled to deduct tax. The QB dismissed B's claim, holding that the *regulations* required M to deduct tax from the payments. *Booth v Mirror Group Newspapers plc*, QB [1992] STC 615. (*Note*. The decision discusses the detailed provisions of the *Income Tax (Employments) Regulations 1993 (SI 1993/744)*. These were revoked with effect from 6 April 2004 and replaced by the *Income Tax (PAYE Regulations) 2003 (SI 2003/2682)*. However it seems to be generally accepted that the courts would reach the same decision with regard to the current regulations.)

Determination of PAYE code

[42.93] In February 2002 a Lloyd's underwriter (K) wrote to the Revenue, asking them to amend his PAYE code for the year 2002/03, to take account of losses of more than £400,000 which he anticipated being declared in the 2003 underwriting year, and which would substantially exceed his pension income. The Revenue rejected the claim on the grounds that K's entitlement to loss relief could not be established until the end of the underwriting year in which the loss had been sustained. The CA unanimously upheld the Revenue's rejection of the claim. Carnwath LJ held that the right to relief arose under *ICTA 1988, s 380*, and was triggered when a taxpayer sustained a loss in any year of assessment. Losses declared in May 2003 were 'sustained' in the year of assessment 2003/04. In February 2002, when K made the claim, 'there was as yet no right to the relief, since the losses had not yet been "sustained"'. The effect of what is now *Income Tax (PAYE) Regulations 2003 (SI 2003/2328), reg 14* was that relief was only due where an employee had established title to the relief at the time of the determination. Carnwath LJ observed that 'there would be no purpose in a specific provision, restricting reliefs to those to which title has been established, if it can be overridden by a general discretion to make a provisional deduction at an earlier time'. Furthermore, if the Commissioners 'were given a free hand to make provisional allowances for prospective losses, it would add a further layer of complication and uncertainty to the already complex task of preparing PAYE codes'. *Blackburn v Keeling*, CA 2003, 75 TC 608; [2003] STC 1162; [2003] EWCA Civ 1221.

[42.94] An airline pilot (F), who was resident in the UK but worked for a Hong Kong airline, appealed against his PAYE coding, contending that because he worked for a Hong Kong airline, he should be issued code NT. The First-tier Tribunal rejected this contention and dismissed his appeal. Judge Raghavan observed that because F was resident in the UK, he was subject to UK tax on his salary. *R Fryett v HMRC*, FTT [2014] UKFTT 220 (TC); [2014] SFTD 979, TC03360.

Employer deducting tax at basic rate

[42.95] An employee (B) began a new employment in February 2001. In his previous employment, he had been liable to the higher rate of tax. However his new employer deducted tax at the basic rate. Since B was liable to the higher rate of tax, this meant that he had underpaid tax for 2000/01. The Revenue issued an assessment to collect the underpayment. B appealed, contending that the underpayment was the fault of his employer and that he should not be required to pay it. The First-Tier Tribunal rejected this contention and dismissed his appeal. Judge Berner found, on the balance of probabilities, that B had not given a form P45 to his new employer. Therefore, in deducting tax at the basic rate, that employer had complied with *Income Tax (PAYE) Regulations 2003 (SI 2003/2328), reg 31*, and B was liable for the underpayments of tax. The Upper Tribunal upheld this decision, holding that '*regulations 101* and *101A* do not provide relief to the employee for all failures by employers (or HMRC) under the Regulations. The relief is limited to the difference between the amount actually deducted and the amount which the employer was liable to deduct. For these Regulations to be brought into play, there must be a "difference" between these two figures. Breaches of the Regulations which do not give rise to a "difference" do not give rise to any relief from tax.' *M Burton v HMRC*, UT [2010] SFTD 2410; [2010] UKUT 252 (TCC). (*Note*. The CA rejected an application for leave to appeal against this decision—[2011] EWCA Civ 176.)

[42.96] In 2010 a doctor (G) began working for a NHS trust. The trust did not deduct tax in accordance with the code issued by HMRC, but only deducted tax at the basic rate. After G submitted his 2010/11 tax return, HMRC discovered that there had been an underpayment of more than £6,000. HMRC failed to make a direction under the *Income Tax (PAYE) Regulations 2003 (SI 2003/2682), reg 72* or *81*, but issued a closure notice requiring G to pay the tax. G appealed, contending that the underpayment was the fault of his employer and the tax should be collected by adjusting his PAYE code. The First-tier Tribunal allowed his appeal. Judge Hellier held that the effect of *TMA, s 59B* and *SI 2003/2682, reg 185* was that, where HMRC had not made a direction under *reg 72* or *reg 81*, 'the amount of tax which is to be treated as having been deducted from (G's) income is the amount which the employer was liable to deduct from the relevant payments, not the amount actually deducted'. *Dr A Gayen v HMRC*, FTT [2013] UKFTT 127 (TC), TC02556.

Income Tax (PAYE) Regulations—whether retrospective

[42.97] A company (D) made substantial payments to certain employees and former employees for the release of share options. It did not deduct PAYE from these payments. The Revenue issued a determination under what is now *Income Tax (PAYE) Regulations 2003 (SI 2003/2682), reg 80*. D appealed, contending that at the time that the payments were made, it was under no duty to deduct PAYE. The Special Commissioners accepted this contention and allowed D's appeal, finding that the payments had been made before *FA 1998, s 67* and the *Income Tax (Employments) Regulations 1993, reg 80ZA* (which derived from *Income Tax (Employments) (Notional Payments) (Amendment) Regulations 1998 (SI 1998/1891)*) came into force. The Commissioners held that the wording of *s 67* did not impose 'any obligation on an employer to deduct tax from a payment made before 1 August 1998'. *Demon Internet Ltd v Young*, Sp C 2004, [2005] SSCD 233 (Sp C 449). (*Note*. The decision here was specifically disapproved in the subsequent case of *Clifton v HMRC*, 42.101 below.)

Application of Income Tax (PAYE) Regulations, reg 78

[42.98] See *R (oao Valentines Homes & Construction Ltd) v HMRC*, 4.440 APPEALS.

Income Tax (PAYE) Regulations, reg 79

[42.99] A company (H) employed a number of scaffolders. Some of these employees became entitled to tax rebates. H failed to pay the rebates, and some of the employees complained to HMRC. HMRC began investigating H's records, issued certificates under *Income Tax (PAYE) Regulations 2003 (SI 2003/2682), reg 79*, and took court proceedings to recover the amounts in question. The Ch D gave judgment for HMRC. David Richards J found that H had provided in its payroll records for rebates of income tax payable to employees, had deducted those rebates from the PAYE payments which it made to the Revenue, but had not in fact paid them to the employees. The certificates which HMRC had issued were valid. Furthermore, no notice of the certificate needed to be given and there was no procedure set out in the Regulations for challenging the certificate as a statement of the liability due, as opposed to defending the proceedings. There was no proper legal reason for H having subtracted from the figure for total tax deducted a sum for 'tax repaid to the employee', which had not in fact been repaid. Accordingly H was obliged to pay the sums in question to HMRC. *Bulley (HMRC) v Hemmer Investments Ltd*, Ch D [2010] EWHC 938 (Ch); [2010] STC 1779.

Income Tax (PAYE) Regulations, reg 81

[42.100] See *R v CIR (ex p. McVeigh)*, 42.16 above; *Pawlowski (Collector of Taxes) v Dunnington*, 43.12 PAYMENT OF TAX, and *Rangos v HMRC*, 43.13 PAYMENT OF TAX.

Application of Income Tax (PAYE) Regulations, reg 101(2)

[42.101] Following the decision in *Demon Internet Ltd v Young*, 42.97 above, the Revenue issued amendments to the employees' self-assessment returns, charging tax on the payments they had received. The employees appealed, contending that notwithstanding the previous decision, the tax should have been paid by their employer and was not taxable on them. The Special Commissioner (Mr. Hellier) rejected this contention and dismissed their appeals. Mr. Hellier specifically disapproved Mr. Gammie's reasoning in the previous case, and expressed the view that D 'was liable to account for tax on the option release payments'. However, *Income Tax (PAYE) Regulations 2003 (SI 2003/2682), reg 101(2)* provided that 'if the tax payable under the assessment exceeds the total net tax deducted from the employee's emolument during the year less any subsequent repayments made, the inspector may require the person concerned to pay the excess to the Collector'. Under self-assessment, 'the employee is liable for the difference between the tax on his income and the tax which was actually or which should have been deducted as PAYE together with the amounts for which the employer accounted under (*ICTA 1988, s 203J*)'. *R Clifton v HMRC (and related appeals)*, Sp C [2007] SSCD 386 (Sp C 597).

Succession to a business—Income Tax (PAYE) Regulations, reg 102

[42.102] A woman (H) had been the proprietor of a business with about 90 employees. She sold the business in March 2010, and transferred all the computer records to the new owner (W). In September 2010 HMRC imposed a penalty on H for not submitting a 2009/10 form P35. H appealed, contending that since W had succeeded to the business, it was his responsibility to submit the P35. The First-Tier Tribunal accepted this contention and allowed the appeal. Judge Redston held that the effect of *Income Tax (PAYE) Regulations 2003 (SI 2003/2682), reg 102(4)* was that 'the obligation to complete and submit the 2009/10 P35 rested with (W), not with (H)'. *Mrs J Harmsworth v HMRC*, FTT [2011] UKFTT 814 (TC), TC01650.

Application of Income Tax (PAYE) Regulations, reg 196

[42.103] HMRC discovered that an employer (MU) had failed to apply the correct PAYE code for one of its employees, and issued a determination under *SI 2003/2682, reg 80*. MU appealed, contending that it had not received an email from HMRC advising it of the correct code number. The First-tier Tribunal dismissed the appeal, finding that MU had registered to receive electronic communications from HMRC in 2005, and had not opted to continue receiving paper notifications; and that HMRC had delivered the coding notification in accordance with *SI 2003/2682, reg 196*. Judge Cornwell-Kelly observed that *regulation 196(1)(b)* 'deems communications of which there is an official computer record of their being sent to have been delivered to the taxpayer "unless the contrary is proved". The burden of proof of non-delivery is on the taxpayer.' *The Mothers' Union v HMRC*, FTT [2014] UKFTT 275 (TC), TC03414.

Application of Income Tax (PAYE) Regulations, reg 205

[42.104] See *Mike Haynes Ltd v HMRC*, 44.222 PENALTIES.

Revenue directing company to use correct PAYE reference number

[42.105] A company provided an 'administrative and financial outsourcing service' for various clients. It accounted for PAYE on behalf of its clients. When it did this, it used its own PAYE reference number instead of the clients' PAYE reference numbers. (It also admitted that it had made significant underpayments of PAYE due.) The Revenue issued a direction instructing the company that, when it accounted for PAYE on behalf of its clients, it should use the clients' PAYE references (so that the Revenue could allocate the payments made to the correct companies, and ascertain the company to which any underpayments related). The company lodged an appeal with the Special Commissioners, contending that it found it more convenient to use a single PAYE reference. The Special Commissioner dismissed the appeal, holding that the Commissioners had no statutory jurisdiction to hear an appeal against the disputed decision. *Oriel Support Ltd v HMRC (No 3)*, Sp C 2007, [2008] SSCD 292 (Sp C 641).

[42.106] Following the Special Commissioners' decision at **42.105** above, the company applied for judicial review of the Revenue's direction. The QB dismissed the application, holding that the person who 'should as a general rule account to HMRC for PAYE in respect of a relevant payment to an employee' was 'the person who employs that employee and who was obliged, under the contract of employment, to make the relevant payment to the employee in his or her capacity as an employee of that person'. An employer could not 'shift liability to account for PAYE to enterprises that were in substance no more than payroll agents'. The CA unanimously upheld this decision. Moses LJ held that the company was paying the employees 'as an intermediary on behalf of the labour provider. The payment is therefore to be treated, for the purposes of PAYE, as a payment of income by the labour provider'. *R (oao Oriel Support Ltd) v HMRC*, CA [2009] STC 1397; [2009] EWCA Civ 401.

Application for incentive payments under SI 2003/2494

[42.107] A chartered accountant incorporated 500 companies and acted as their company secretary. His wife was the sole shareholder of each company. Each of the companies submitted online PAYE returns for 2004/5 and 2005/6 stating that they had paid director's remuneration of £1. They each claimed an 'incentive payment' of £250 for each year under *Income Tax (Incentive Payments for Voluntary Electronic Communication of PAYE Returns) Regulations (SI 2003/2494)*. The Revenue made 33 such payments, but rejected the remainder of the claims. The Special Commissioner dismissed the companies' appeals, finding that none of the companies carried on any business and that 'the petty cash sheets were compiled as an attempt to conjure up a movement of money when none existed'. Accordingly, none of the companies was required to complete or maintain deductions working sheets within *SI 2003 No 2494, reg 1(4)* and none of them qualified as a 'small employer' within *SI 2003 No 2494, reg 3(2)*. *ZXCV 1 Ltd v HMRC (and related appeals)*, Sp C [2008] SSCD 1171 (Sp C 706).

P800 tax calculation—whether a right of appeal

[42.108] See *Prince v HMRC*, **4.94** APPEALS.

43

Payment of Tax

The cases in this chapter are arranged under the following headings.

Collection of tax by Revenue

Time limits for summary proceedings

[43.1] A Collector of Taxes began summary proceedings on 19 December 1929 for the second instalment of Schedule D tax, which had become due on 1 July 1929. A preliminary application for payment had been made on 12 June, and the defendant contended that the proceedings were outside the six-month time limit. The KB rejected this contention, holding that the six-month limit ran from 1 July. *Mann v Cleaver*, KB 1930, 15 TC 367.

Time limits for Court proceedings in Scotland

[43.2] In a Scottish case, the Revenue began Court proceedings on 4 April 1989 in respect of tax which had become due on 26 March 1984. The defendant contended that the proceedings were invalid in view of the five-year time limit provided by the *Prescription and Limitation (Scotland) Act 1973, s 6*. The CS rejected this contention and gave judgment for the Revenue, holding that the defendant's liability to account for tax and interest thereon did not fall within the scope of that *section*. *Lord Advocate v Hepburn*, CS 1989, [1990] BTC 250.

[43.3] In another Scottish case, the Revenue began Court proceedings against the former partners of a firm in October 1989, to recover unpaid Schedule D tax and Class 4 National Insurance contributions for 1979/80 to 1981/82 inclusive. The relevant assessment for 1979/80 had been confirmed by Commissioners and the assessments for the other two years had been settled by agreement under *TMA, s 54*. The partners defended the proceedings, contending that the *Prescription and Limitation (Scotland) Act 1973, s 6* applied. The Inner House of the CS gave judgment for the Revenue. By virtue of *TMA, s 69*, interest on tax due was treated as if it were tax charged and due under the assessment to which it related. Thus, notwithstanding the *Prescription and Limitation (Scotland) Act*, all interest on the tax in question, whenever it accrued, was recoverable. *Lord Advocate v Butt & Others*, CS 1991, 64 TC 471; [1992] STC 122. (*Note*. Compare, with regard to England and Wales, the

Limitation Act 1980, of which *s 37(2)(a)* provides that it does not apply to any proceedings by the Crown for the recovery of any tax, duty or interest thereon.)

Validity of assessments questioned in collection proceedings

[43.4] The Revenue began High Court proceedings to recover unpaid tax. The defendant contended that the underlying assessments were incorrect. The CA granted judgment for the Revenue. Denning LJ held that the defendant should have challenged the assessments 'by appeal to the Commissioners in the way provided by the Income Tax Acts; and, as he did not raise the matters by way of appeal, he is not allowed to raise them now'. He observed that 'questions of fact and law on tax assessments' had been 'decided to the general satisfaction for a great many years now by the Commissioners, with an appeal on points of law by Case Stated to the High Court. That is the proper remedy.' He held that 'all issues on the merits of these cases, as to fact or law, should have been determined by appeal to the Commissioners and cannot be raised at this stage. If there has been no appeal to the Commissioners the debts become absolute and conclusive, and their legal effect cannot be denied.' *CIR v Pearlberg*, CA 1953, 34 TC 57; [1953] 1 WLR 331; [1953] 1 All ER 388.

[43.5] The decision in *CIR v Pearlberg*, **43.4** above, was applied in a subsequent case where General Commissioners had confirmed six assessments. The QB gave judgment for the Revenue, and the defendant appealed to the CA, contending that the income assessed did not belong to him but to his trustee in bankruptcy. The CA dismissed the appeal, holding that the effect of the Commissioners' decision was that the assessments were final and conclusive. Bridge LJ held that 'it is not open to the taxpayer to dispute his liability in proceedings brought by the Commissioners to enforce the assessments against him'. *CIR v Soul*, CA 1976, 51 TC 86.

[43.6] In another case where the Revenue took High Court proceedings to recover unpaid tax under *TMA, s 68*, the Ch D gave judgment for the Revenue. Warren J found that the defendant was 'not being full and frank', and that there was 'a justified fear of dissipation as a result of his dishonesty'. He also granted a 'freezing injunction' against the defendant. *HMRC v Ali*, Ch D [2011] EWHC 880 (Ch); [2012] STC 42.

[43.7] The Revenue began county court proceedings to recover unpaid tax. The defendant contended that he had withheld the tax as a matter of principle in accordance with *Article 9* of the *European Convention on Human Rights*. The court gave judgment for the Revenue, observing that the defendant was obliged to 'render unto Caesar the things which are Caesar's'. *Oxley v Raynham*, Weston-super-Mare County Court 1983, 54 TC 779.

[43.8] A company, the registered office of which was in Scotland, appealed against an assessment to corporation tax. It applied to have payment of the tax postponed under *TMA, s 55(3)*. Its application was rejected by a Special Commissioner, and the Revenue began proceedings in the Court of Session to recover the tax. The company contended that the proceedings should be halted, as it had made an application for judicial review of the Special Commissioner's decision in the High Court. The CS granted judgment in favour of the Revenue. Lord Wylie held that since the company's registered office was in Scotland, the Special Commissioner's decision was 'subject to the supervisory jurisdiction of the Scottish court'. No proceedings for judicial review had been raised in the CS, and the Revenue was entitled to proceed for payment of the tax assessed. *Lord Advocate v RW Forsyth Ltd*, CS 1986, 61 TC 1. (*Note*. For the proceedings for judicial review in the QB, see **4.396** APPEALS.)

[43.9] Assessments on a prostitute had been settled by agreement under *TMA, s 54*. However, she did not pay the tax charged by the assessments, and the Revenue sought to recover the tax under *the Rules of the Supreme Court 1965* as then in force. The prostitute sought leave to defend the proceedings, contending that the assessments had been *ultra vires*. The QB entered judgment for the Revenue and the CA unanimously dismissed the prostitute's appeal. Fox LJ held that the agreement under *TMA, s 54* was a binding agreement and was enforceable as such. It had the force of a determination by Commissioners, and was final and conclusive. Applying the decisions in *CIR v Pearlberg*, **43.4** above, and *CIR v Soul*, **43.5** above, the validity of the assessments could not be disputed in collection proceedings. *CIR v Aken*, CA 1990, 63 TC 395; [1990] STC 497; [1990] 1 WLR 1374. (*Notes*. (1) For another issue in this case, see **59.73** TRADING INCOME—DEFINITION OF TRADING. (2) The *Rules of the Supreme Court 1965* have now been replaced by the *Civil Procedure Rules 1998 (SI 1998/3132)*, of which *rule 24* deals with applications for summary judgment.)

[43.10] General Commissioners determined assessments on a restaurant proprietor. The proprietor failed to pay the tax charged, and the County Court gave judgment for the Revenue. The CA unanimously dismissed the proprietor's appeal. Jonathan Parker LJ held that 'the statutory machinery for appeal against a notice of assessment is exclusive' and that 'the county court has no appellate jurisdiction in respect of determinations of the General Commissioners'. The effect of *TMA, s 70* was that the County Court was required to accept the certificates submitted by the Revenue as evidence of the debt. *Ahluwalia v McCullough*, CA [2004] STC 1295; [2004] EWCA Civ 889.

[43.11] However, in a Scottish case where the allocation of payments on account was disputed, Lady Paton held that certificates under *TMA, s 70* 'are "sufficient" evidence, but are not necessarily "conclusive" evidence. If a defender offers contradictory averments and evidence, the court must take that evidence into account.' (The case was adjourned for further argument.) *Advocate-General for Scotland v Montgomery*, CS 2006, [2009] STC 2387; [2006] CSOH 123.

*Determination under Income Tax (PAYE) Regulations 2003, reg 81**

[43.12] The Revenue discovered that a company was failing to deduct PAYE from a director's emoluments. The Revenue therefore issued determinations under what is now *Income Tax (PAYE) Regulations 2003, reg 80**. The company failed to pay the tax determined, and subsequently went into liquidation. The Revenue then made a direction under *reg 81** that the tax should be recovered from the director. (The Revenue also made a direction under *reg 72** covering previous years.) The director failed to pay the tax demanded, and the Collector of Taxes took proceedings in the Wigan County Court. The County Court judge ruled that the Collector had failed to prove that the director knew that the company had not been deducting PAYE. The Revenue appealed to the CA, which allowed the appeal and remitted the case to the County Court for rehearing. Simon Brown LJ observed that the County Court judge had approached the case in 'the wrong way' and had 'dismissed the claim on an impermissible basis'. The Collector did not have to prove that the director knew that the company had not been deducting PAYE, but simply had to show that there was material on which the Board could properly have formed such an opinion. (The CA also held that a defendant was entitled to raise a public law defence in collection proceedings of this kind, rejecting the Revenue's contention that the directions could only be challenged by judicial review. The decisions in *CIR v Pearlberg*, **43.4** above, *CIR v Soul*, **43.5** above, and *CIR v Aken*, **43.9** above, were distinguished, on the grounds that they concerned appeals against assessments, where 'statutory machinery exists for appealing' and was 'the exclusive machinery by which an assessment could be contested'. Simon Brown LJ observed that there were 'practical disadvantages which flow from raising a public law challenge like this by way of defence instead of judicial review' but held that 'the Revenue's solution to the problem raised by the present case is a simple one: they should confer on taxpayers a right of appeal against directions comparable to that which arises on assessment'.) *Pawlowski (Collector of Taxes) v Dunnington*, CA [1999] STC 550.

[43.13] Five companies, which traded in tickets for various events, went into liquidation. The Official Receiver formed the opinion that all five companies had been under the control of an individual (R), who had been a director of one of the companies and had acted as a 'shadow director' of the other companies. HMRC issued determinations under *Income Tax (PAYE) Regulations 2003 (SI 2003/2682), reg 80*, and issued a notice of direction under *reg 81(4)* requiring R to pay the tax in question. R appealed, denying that he had been a shadow director of two of the companies. The First-tier Tribunal reviewed the evidence in detail and upheld the direction in principle, finding that R had been 'a shadow director and thus an employee' of the two companies in question. (However, the tribunal reduced the amounts assessed from £525,808 to £324,600.) *M Rangos v HMRC*, FTT [2012] UKFTT 198 (TC), TC01893.

[43.14] See also *R v CIR (ex p. McVeigh)*, **42.16** PAY AS YOU EARN.

County court proceedings to collect Class 1 NICs

[43.15] On the advice of an accountancy firm (G), a company (H) paid substantial bonuses to its directors and employees in gold coins, and failed to pay Class 1 National Insurance Contributions. In May 2002 the Revenue began proceedings in the Tameside county court. H applied for the proceedings to be adjourned pending the hearing of an appeal to the Special Commissioners. Subsequently a district judge struck out the Revenue's claim. The Revenue appealed to the CA, contending that the appeal should be reinstated. The CA unanimously accepted this contention and ordered that the action should be reinstated in the county court. Waller LJ strongly criticised the Revenue for failing to respond to communications from the county court. However, on the evidence, he held that 'it would be unfair to hold the Revenue guilty of intentionally not complying with a court order'. The administration of justice required the reinstatement of the case in the county court. Lloyd LJ held that 'while the court is perfectly entitled to enquire as to the progress of the appeals whose outcome the collection proceedings must await', it would 'be altogether disproportionate to refuse to reinstate the claim'. He also observed that H, 'having taken advantage of the scheme which appears to have been devised by (G), cannot properly dissociate itself from the conduct of that firm in launching the various appeals and in dealing with the Revenue as regards the conduct of the appeals generally'. *HMRC v Hyde Industrial Holdings Ltd*, CA [2006] EWCA Civ 502; [2006] All ER (D) 281 (Apr).

[43.16] See also *HMRC v Benchdollar Ltd & Others*, 73.17 NATIONAL INSURANCE CONTRIBUTIONS.

Application for summary judgment—whether an arguable defence

[43.17] See *CIR v Napier*, 4.245 APPEALS.

Cheque submitted for less than full amount of liability

[43.18] A married woman (F) owed the Revenue more than £120,000. Her accountants advised the Revenue that she had no assets, but that her husband was willing to pay the Revenue £5,000 in full settlement of her liability. The Revenue rejected this offer, and the Revenue Enforcement Office warned that, if an offer to pay the full amount by instalments was not made, they would consider bankruptcy proceedings. On 20 May 1999 the husband sent a cheque for £10,000 to the Enforcement Office, with an accompanying letter stating that the cheque was offered 'in full and final settlement', and that encashment would be taken as 'acceptance of our offer'. The letter and the cheque were separated at the Enforcement Office's cashiers' section, and the cheque was banked. On 28 May the Enforcement Office telephoned the husband stating that the cheque had been banked but that the offer in his letter was not accepted. Subsequently the Revenue took proceedings against F for the balance of the liability. She defended the proceedings, contending that the banking of her husband's cheque meant that her liability had been extinguished. The Ch D rejected this contention and gave judgment for the Revenue. Jacob J held that the only reasonable conclusion was that there was no agreement and no contract. A reasonable observer 'would know that the Revenue must receive thousands of cheques a day. Obviously they should be banked as soon as possible. It would not be possible to do that if every time there was a letter it had to be read by a case officer.' The Revenue's cashing of the cheque gave rise to 'no more than a rebuttable presumption of acceptance of the accompanying letter. That presumption is fully rebutted here.' *CIR v Fry*, Ch D [2001] STC 1715.

[43.19] Following the decision in *Foulser & Foulser v MacDougall*, **71.260** CAPITAL GAINS TAX, the case was remitted to the First-tier Tribunal to consider the amount of the assessment. The appellant (F) raised an alternative contention that he had sent a cheque to HMRC with a covering letter indicating that it was 'in full and final settlement' of his liability, and that since HMRC had cashed this cheque, this should be treated as an agreement of the appeal under *TMA, s 54*. The First-tier Tribunal rejected this contention, applying the principles laid down by Jacob J in *CIR v Fry*, **43.18** above. Judge Berner observed that a statement of account that HMRC had sent to F clearly indicated that the cheque represented payment of the amount that had not been postponed under *TMA, s 55*. He held that 'the statement of account negated any possible inference from the banking of the cheque that there had been a settlement'. *BG Foulser v HMRC*, FTT [2014] UKFTT 483 (TC), TC03609.

Recovery of tax under SI 1978/1159

[43.20] See *United Friendly Insurance plc v CIR*, **34.4** LIFE ASSURANCE.

Distraint

Liquidation of company before sale of goods levied on

[43.21] A Collector of Taxes levied distraint on a company's goods under *TMA, s 61*, entering into a 'walking possession' agreement with the company. Within three months of the distraint, and before the goods had been sold, the company went into voluntary liquidation. The HL unanimously held that the Collector was entitled to complete the distraint by selling the goods, and that distrained assets were not assets of the company available for distribution by the liquidator. *Herbert Berry Associates Ltd v CIR*, HL 1977, 52 TC 113; [1977] 1 WLR 1437; [1978] 1 All ER 161.

[43.22] The decision in *Herbert Berry Associates Ltd v CIR*, **43.21** above, was applied in the similar subsequent case of *Brenner v HMRC (re Jet Support Centre Ltd)*, Ch D 2005, [2006] STC 808; [2005] EWHC 1611 (Ch).

Perishable items

[43.23] It was held that perishable items (such as food), which could not be restored in the same condition as when they were distrained upon, were exempt from distraint. *Morley v Pincombe*, Ex D 1848, 2 Ex D 101.

Tools of trade

[43.24] A Collector of Taxes levied distraint on a piano which the debtor's wife used to give music lessons. The debtor claimed damages, contending that distraint could not be levied on a trader's tools. The KB rejected this contention and dismissed the claim. Bray J held that the tools of a debtor's trade were only exempt from distraint for rent, and were not exempt from distraint for tax. *MacGregor v Clamp & Son*, KB 1913, [1914] 1 KB 288.

Entry to premises

[43.25] The QB held that a bailiff was entitled to enter premises through an open window, and may also further open a window which was already partly open. *Nixon v Freeman*, QB 1860, 5 H & N 647.

[43.26] The QB held that a bailiff was not entitled to open a window catch in order to enter premises without a warrant authorising him to 'break open' the premises. *Hancock v Austin*, QB 1863, 14 CBNS 634.

[43.27] The QB held that a bailiff was entitled to enter premises through a partially opened skylight. *Miller v Tebb*, QB 1893, 9 TLR 515.

[43.28] The QB held that a bailiff had no right to break into premises without a warrant, but was entitled to climb over a wall or fence from adjoining premises. *Long v Clarke*, QB [1894] 1 QB 119.

'Walking possession' agreement

[43.29] A Collector of Taxes visited a trader who owed tax of 13s 4d. The only person on the premises was the trader's teenage daughter. The Collector levied distraint on some of the trader's goods, and the daughter signed a 'walking possession' agreement. The trader subsequently paid the tax but refused to pay the costs of the distraint. The Revenue took court proceedings to recover the tax. The trader contended that the Collector had abandoned the distraint by leaving the premises. The CA rejected this contention and gave judgment for the Revenue. Chitty LJ held that the signature of the 'walking possession' agreement showed the Collector's intention 'not to abandon the possession, but to retain it'. *Lumsden v Burnett*, CA [1898] 2 QB 177.

Tax demands sent to office address—distraint at home address

[43.30] See *Berry v Farrow*, 5.103 ASSESSMENTS.

Application for judicial review during distraint proceedings

[43.31] In 1993 the Revenue levied distraint on the goods of a trader. The trader applied to the County Court for an order that the distraint should be stayed, but this application was rejected. He then applied for leave for judicial review. The QB dismissed the application, holding that it had been unduly delayed. Hutchison J observed that judicial review must 'be sought promptly and in any event within three months' and that 'time can only be extended if good reason for the delay is shown'. The trader should have exercised his right of appeal against the decision of the County Court. *R v HM Inspector of Taxes (ex p. Uchendu)*, QB 1993, 67 TC 487.

Distraint proceedings—whether a breach of Convention on Human Rights

[43.32] See *Lewandowski v Poland*, **31.1** HUMAN RIGHTS.

Surcharges on tax paid late (TMA, s 59C)

Cases where the appeal was dismissed

[43.33] The Revenue issued an assessment to an individual (M). He paid the assessed tax 29 days after the due date. The Revenue imposed a surcharge under *TMA, s 59C*. M appealed, contending that the effect of *s 59C(2)* was that he was not liable to a surcharge, since he had paid the tax 'on the day following the expiry of 28 days from the due date'. The Ch D rejected this contention and upheld the surcharge. Ferris J held that the effect of *s 59C(2)* was that a taxpayer was liable to a surcharge if the tax remained unpaid at the beginning of the day in question, i.e. the 29th day. *TMA, s 59C(2)* did not require that the tax remained unpaid throughout the day in question. *Thompson v Minzly*, Ch D 2001, 74 TC 340; [2002] STC 450. (*Note*. For the Revenue's practice following this decision, see Revenue Tax Bulletin, December 2001, p 904.)

[43.34] On 28 February 2000 two solicitors, who practised in partnership, posted a cheque for the tax which had become due on 31 January. The Revenue received the cheque on 29 February, and imposed a surcharge under *TMA, s 59C*. The solicitors appealed. The Special Commissioner dismissed their appeal, holding that there was no reasonable excuse for the late payment. The Commissioner observed that the solicitors 'were playing brinkmanship in paying tax on the last possible date but they had not read the rules properly'. *Bancroft & Bancroft v Crutchfield*, Sp C [2002] SSCD 347 (Sp C 322).

[43.35] HMRC imposed a surcharge on a woman (W) in respect of the tax due on 31 January 2009, on the basis that they had not received her payment until 2 March 2009. She appealed, contending that she had initiated the payment on 27 February 2009, which was within the statutory time limit. The First-Tier Tribunal dismissed her appeal, observing that HMRC's guidance stated that 'it normally takes three working days for payment to reach HMRC', and holding that the payment had not been 'made' until HMRC had received the funds. *Mrs L West v HMRC*, FTT [2010] UKFTT 442 (TC), TC00707. (*Note*. Similar decisions have been reached in a large number of VAT cases concerning default surcharges: see Tolley's VAT Cases, chapter 18.)

[43.36] A similar decision was reached in *M West v HMRC*, FTT [2010] UKFTT 443 (TC), TC00708.

[43.37] A taxpayer who had failed to pay his 2008/09 tax liability until 10 March 2010 appealed against the resulting surcharge, contending that he had a reasonable excuse because HMRC had failed to provide him with a payslip and he had not wished to pay online because he was concerned about the security of online payments. The First-Tier Tribunal dismissed his appeal, noting that he had eventually paid by post with a covering letter, and holding that the circumstances did not constitute a reasonable excuse. *J Orrock v HMRC*, FTT [2010] UKFTT 523, TC00778.

[43.38] An Irish landlord (J) was not resident in the UK, but received income from property, and interest, which was taxable in the UK. In January 2010 his new accountants informed HMRC that he had neither received nor filed a tax return for 2008, although he had taxable UK income in 2007/08. J submitted the return, and paid the tax due, later that month. HMRC imposed a surcharge, and J appealed, contending that he had a reasonable excuse because he had not received a tax return. The First-Tier Tribunal dismissed his appeal. Judge Hellier held that, since J's UK income was 'substantial', there was no reasonable excuse for 'not having considered his UK obligations at an earlier date'. *S Jones v HMRC*, FTT [2011] UKFTT 650 (TC), TC01492.

[43.39] An individual appealed against two surcharges under *TMA, s 59C* and two penalties under *TMA, s 93*, contending that he objected to direct taxation since it was a means 'of raising monies for the propagation of war'. The Special Commissioner dismissed his appeals, holding that his political views did not constitute a reasonable excuse, and that the imposition of taxes was authorised by *Article 1 of the First Protocol* of the *European Convention on Human Rights*. *Gladders v Prior*, Sp C [2003] SSCD 245 (Sp C 361).

[43.40] An individual (C) submitted his 2007/08 tax return in October 2008, but did not pay the tax due until 14 April 2009. HMRC imposed a surcharge, and C appealed, contending that he had a reasonable excuse because HMRC's original calculation of the tax due had been incorrect. The First-Tier Tribunal rejected this contention and dismissed C's appeal. Judge Gandhi observed that C knew 'that he would have to pay some tax' and 'did have an approximate idea of what he owed'. *N Chudusama v HMRC*, FTT [2010] UKFTT 81 (TC), TC00393.

[43.41] A medical practitioner appealed against several surcharges, contending that he had a reasonable excuse for late payment because his marriage had broken down, causing him to suffer from stress. The First-Tier Tribunal dismissed his appeal, holding that the circumstances did not constitute a reasonable excuse. *M Bodani v HMRC*, FTT [2011] UKFTT 61 (TC), TC00939.

[43.42] A retired civil servant (K) submitted a 2009/10 return showing a tax liability of £1842. He failed to pay this amount by 31 January 2011, and HMRC imposed a surcharge. K appealed, contending that the tax due should have been deducted under PAYE. HMRC produced a copy of K's return, in which K had put an X in the box marked 'if you owe tax for 2009/10 and have a PAYE code we will try to collect the tax up to £2000 unless you put an X in the box'. The First-tier Tribunal dismissed K's appeal, observing that the X which K had entered in the box had been a valid objection to the tax being collected through his PAYE code, and he therefore had no reasonable excuse for not paying the tax by the due date. *D Knowles v HMRC*, FTT [2012] UKFTT 523 (TC), TC02199.

[43.43] Appeals against surcharges under *TMA, s 59C* have also been dismissed in a large number of subsequent cases, none of which appear to raise any point of general importance. In the interests of space, such cases are not summarised individually in this book. For details of such cases decided up to and including 31 December 2011, see Tolley's Tax Cases 2012.

Cases where the appeal was allowed

'Reasonable excuse'

[43.44] A woman (R) realised a very large capital gain in 1999/2000, with the result that a large tax payment would become due on 31 January 2001. Her accountants advised her that she would have a large partnership loss to set against the gain, and only needed to make a relatively small balancing payment. She paid the amount recommended by her accountants. However the Revenue did not agree the loss claim submitted by R's accountants, and imposed a surcharge on R under *TMA, s 59C*. R appealed, contending that she had a reasonable excuse within *s 59C(9)*. The Special Commissioner accepted her contention and allowed her appeal, holding that 'it was reasonable for (R) to rely on her then accountants and it was this reliance that led to the underpayment'. He observed that the corresponding VAT legislation specifically provided that where 'reliance is placed on any other person to perform any task, neither the fact of that reliance nor any dilatoriness or inaccuracy on the part of the person relied on is a reasonable excuse'. However, there was 'no equivalent provision that reliance on a third party is not a reasonable excuse for direct tax purposes'. *Rowland v HMRC*, Sp C [2006] SSCD 536 (Sp C 548).

[43.45] In April 2007 an individual (R) asked his accountants to inform HMRC that he was receiving income from self-employment as a website manager. The accountants did not do so until April 2008, and then received no reply from HMRC. In April 2010 the accountants submitted an online form CWF1, and also submitted returns for 2006/07 to 2009/10. HMRC imposed surcharges for 2007/08 and 2008/09. R appealed, contending that he had relied on his accountants. The First-Tier Tribunal accepted R's evidence and allowed his appeal. Judge Aleksander found that R had provided details of his income to his accountants in time for them 'to prepare tax computations and returns by the statutory time limits', and that there was 'no reason for (R) to think that his accountants would fail to notify HMRC of his chargeability to income tax within the statutory time limit'. Applying the principles laid down in *Rowland v HMRC*, **43.44** above, the circumstances constituted a reasonable excuse. *S Rich v HMRC*, FTT [2011] UKFTT 533 (TC), TC01380.

[43.46] A woman (C) sent a cheque for her balancing payment for 2009/10 to HMRC on 24 February 2011, by first-class post. HMRC did not receive the cheque until 2 March 2011, and imposed a surcharge. The First-Tier Tribunal allowed C's appeal, holding that she had 'exercised reasonable foresight by allowing three working days for delivery of the letter containing the payment', so that the circumstances constituted a reasonable excuse. *Mrs L Coghill v HMRC*, FTT [2011] UKFTT 7 (TC), TC01706.

[43.47] An employee (W) had significant investment income. In April 2008 he received a P810 tax review form, requesting him to provide details of his income for 2007/08 by 30 September 2008. He completed this form on

25 September. HMRC did not respond until 13 January, when they wrote to him advising that 'due to the level of his investment income he would need to complete a self-assessment return', which HMRC would issue 'shortly'. HMRC issued this form on 22 January, advising him that he must submit the form within three months, and must pay any tax due by 31 January 2009 (ie within nine days of the issue of the return). HMRC did not enclose a form SA102 which should have accompanied the return. W returned the tax return on 13 April 2009. In June 2009 HMRC wrote to him advising him that he had underpaid tax of £4,390 for 2007/08. W made an appointment with his nearest tax office to clarify the situation, but 'was told by an officer there at the interview that HMRC could not look into any of his tax affairs or calculations as HMRC's computer "was down".' After consulting an accountant, W paid the tax due on 20 June. HMRC imposed a surcharge, and W appealed. The First-Tier Tribunal allowed his appeal, holding that the circumstances constituted a reasonable excuse for his late payment of the tax due. Judge Vellins observed that 'the appellant prior to 2007/08 had completed forms P810 on which he had been able to provide details of his income, and where if an underpayment of tax had occurred then this could be collected through his following year's PAYE code'. The tax return which HMRC had issued had wrongly stated that W must pay the tax due by 31 January 2009, although *TMA, s 59B(3)* allowed three months after the date of issue of the return to pay the tax due. W had expected HMRC 'to send him a statement of account and calculation of tax due from him, in addition to the tax that he had already paid under the PAYE scheme. HMRC did not explain to the appellant that he had to calculate his own relevant tax to meet deadlines.' W had 'telephoned the helpline of HMRC who were unable to help, and he arranged an appointment with an officer at HMRC's tax office in Hull. When he attended at that appointment no help or assistance was given to him. No explanation of calculations were made to him. The computer at HMRC's premises at Hull was not functioning. The Appellant still did his best to attempt to understand the calculation of tax by going to see an accountant, and, within five days of the date of the interview at Hull on 15 June 2009 with HMRC, he had paid the tax.' The circumstances amounted to a reasonable excuse. *A Waddington v HMRC*, FTT [2010] UKFTT 114 (TC), TC00425.

[43.48] A self-employed massage therapist appealed against surcharges for 2002/03 to 2007/08 inclusive, contending that she had a reasonable excuse because she had been badly injured in a robbery in February 2003, as a result of which she had been unable to work for some time and had suffered serious financial difficulties. The tribunal allowed her appeal in part, holding that the circumstances constituted a reasonable excuse for the defaults for 2002/03 to 2005/06 inclusive, but not for the defaults for 2006/07 or 2007/08. *Ms AZ v HMRC*, FTT [2010] UKFTT 225 (TC), TC00526.

[43.49] A sole trader failed to pay his 2007/08 tax liability by the due date, and HMRC imposed a surcharge. He appealed, contending that he had a reasonable excuse because he had been suffering from peptic ulcers. The First-Tier Tribunal allowed his appeal. Judge Gort commented that she was 'not very impressed with HMRC's approach to reasonable excuse in this case'. *P Atkinson v HMRC*, FTT [2011] UKFTT 32 (TC), TC00909.

[43.50] In a case where a company director gave evidence that she had been suffering from prolonged ill-health, the First-Tier Tribunal accepted her contention that this constituted a reasonable excuse for the late payment of tax. *Mrs K O'Carroll v HMRC*, FTT [2011] UKFTT 43 (TC), TC00920.

[43.51] Similar decisions were reached in *I Bond v HMRC*, FTT [2013] UKFTT 761 (TC), TC03140, and *GA Wedgwood v HMRC*, FTT [2014] UKFTT 1055 (TC), TC04148.

[43.52] An individual (H) sent a self-assessment return to HMRC on 15 January 2010. HMRC imposed a surcharge. H appealed, contending that he had a reasonable excuse because he had intended to file the return online, and had not realised until January that he did not have the necessary software. The First-Tier Tribunal accepted his evidence and allowed his appeal. Judge Geraint Jones commented that 'HMRC is actively encouraging taxpayers to file returns and many other documents on line. It is clear that they wish to move away from paper filing. There may be excellent reasons for so doing. Nonetheless, if HMRC seek to achieve that result, it must be for HMRC to facilitate online filing and to give accurate information relating thereto.' H had 'trust and pension income to be taken into account which resulted in him being unable to use the online filing facility provided by HMRC without going to the trouble and risk of installing third-party software on his computer'. Judge Geraint Jones concluded that 'it is not reasonable to expect a taxpayer to have to procure third-party software, which may or may not be reliable, before being able to use the much advertised online filing facility'. *C Humphreys v HMRC*, FTT [2011] UKFTT 98 (TC), TC00974.

[43.53] An appeal against a surcharge was allowed in a case where the tribunal found that an appellant had been caring for his elderly parents, and his father had been admitted to hospital with a serious illness. *C Sanders v HMRC*, FTT [2011] UKFTT 131 (TC), TC01005.

[43.54] An individual (B) was employed by a bank, but left his employment in December 2007. The bank only deducted basic rate tax from its final payment to B, although he was liable to tax at the higher rate. HMRC subsequently imposed surcharges, and B appealed, contending that he had a reasonable excuse because he had believed that the bank had deducted all the tax that was due, and had not realised that there had been an underpayment. The First-Tier Tribunal accepted B's evidence and allowed his appeal. *Y Budiadi v HMRC*, FTT [2011] UKFTT 233 (TC), TC01098.

[43.55] A company director (K) failed to pay his tax liability for 2007/08 by the due date, and failed to keep an instalment agreement which he agreed with HMRC. HMRC imposed surcharges. K appealed, contending that he had a reasonable excuse because he had been working for an Irish company which had failed to pay him, causing him significant financial difficulty and forcing him to remortgage his house. The tribunal accepted his evidence and allowed his appeal, applying the principles laid down by Nolan LJ in the VAT case of *C & E Commrs v JB Steptoe*, CA [1992] STC 757. *G Knapper v HMRC*, FTT [2011] UKFTT 365 (TC), TC01220.

[43.56] An employee (B) was paid more than £100,000pa, but his employer only deducted the basic rate of tax. B informed HMRC in January 2010, and was sent tax returns for 2006/07 to 2008/09 in February 2010. B submitted the returns in April 2010. HMRC processed them in June 2010, and sent B calculations showing significant underpayments for all three years. In August 2010 HMRC imposed surcharges. B paid the underpayments in September 2010, and appealed against the surcharges. The First-Tier Tribunal allowed his appeal. Judge Redston found that B 'had always relied on his employer to deduct the correct tax from his earnings before receipt and that as a result he was unaware of the shortfall in his income tax until January 2010'. Accordingly he had a reasonable excuse for the late payment of the tax due. *J Brady v HMRC*, FTT [2011] UKFTT 415 (TC), TC01268.

[43.57] A similar decision was reached in *M Styles v HMRC*, FTT [2013] UKFTT 184 (TC), TC02599.

[43.58] A woman (B), who received rental income, failed to make a payment of tax for 2008/09 by the due date of 31 January 2010. HMRC imposed a surcharge. The First-Tier Tribunal allowed B's appeal. Judge Geraint Jones found that 'as a result of damage and default by a former tenant at one of her let properties, she found herself with an empty damaged house over the winter of 2009/2010 and had to spend significant sums on repairs and maintenance so as to ensure that further damage was not caused by such things as pipes freezing and then splitting, allowing water damage to occur'. He held that this constituted a reasonable excuse. *Miss M Barron v HMRC*, FTT [2011] UKFTT 482 (TC), TC 01329.

[43.59] A trader appealed against a surcharge of £155 for 2009/10, contending that he had entered into an instalment arrangement to pay £60 per month, and had assumed that this would avoid any surcharge. The First-Tier Tribunal accepted his evidence and allowed his appeal. Judge Geraint Jones held that 'an honest belief in a given state of affairs can amount to a reasonable excuse at least until such time as the person holding that belief is given proper cause to believe that the belief is incorrect'. *S Stuart-Turner v HMRC*, FTT [2011] UKFTT 702 (TC), TC01539.

[43.60] A woman (L) received a share dividend in 2009/10, which gave rise to a CGT liability. She informed HMRC of this on 10 January 2011. HMRC sent her a tax return on 3 February 2011. She completed the return on 3 March 2011 and paid the CGT on 7 March. HMRC imposed a surcharge but the First-tier Tribunal allowed L's appeal, observing that she had previously been outside the self-assessment system and that there had been a delay in HMRC issuing a UTR and sending her a return. Judge Staker held that the circumstances constituted a reasonable excuse for the late payment of the tax. *Mrs JM Lyons v HMRC*, FTT [2012] UKFTT 121 (TC), TC01816.

[43.61] A woman submitted a cheque for her 2009/10 tax liability, but her bank failed to honour the cheque. She subsequently paid her liability by debit card after the due date. HMRC imposed a surcharge and she appealed, contending that she had a reasonable excuse because she had had sufficient money to pay the tax liability in a different account, and had been under the impression that her bank would automatically transfer money between the accounts in order to honour her cheques. Judge Geraint Jones accepted her evidence and allowed her appeal. *Mrs H Chichester v HMRC*, FTT [2012] UKFTT 397 (TC), TC02081.

[43.62] The First-tier Tribunal allowed an appeal against a surcharge in a case where the appellant had underpaid tax under PAYE, and the tribunal found that HMRC had failed to send subsequent correspondence to his correct address. *A Dowson v HMRC*, FTT [2012] UKFTT 654 (TC), TC02326.

[43.63] In 2012 HMRC began an enquiry into the 2009/10 return submitted by a trader (S) who owned a yacht chartering business. While the enquiry was in progress, HMRC issued a protective estimated assessment for 2007/08. S did not pay the tax charged by the assessment, and HMRC imposed a surcharge, against which S appealed. The First-tier Tribunal allowed his appeal. Judge Redston observed that, since the tax liability had not been finalised, S could have applied for postponement of the tax, and held that the circumstances constituted a reasonable excuse. *A Salmon v HMRC (No 1)*, FTT [2013] UKFTT 306 (TC), TC02711. (*Note*. For subsequent proceedings in this case, see 5.52 ASSESSMENT.)

[43.64] A subcontractor (K) submitted accounts on an earnings basis, so that his 2009/10 accounts included work which he had carried out for a contractor (C), but for which C had not paid him until 2010/11. K did not pay the full amount of his 2009/10 tax by the due date, and HMRC imposed surcharges. K appealed, contending that he had a reasonable excuse because the surcharges related to the work for which he had not been paid until 2010/11, and in respect of which C had accounted for tax under the CIS scheme. The First-tier Tribunal allowed K's appeal. Judge Redston found that K 'knew by January 2011 that the CIS tax deducted by the contractor exceeded the 2009/10 income tax actually due on 31 January 2011, and thus believed he had overpaid tax for that year'. *J O'Kane v HMRC*, FTT [2013] UKFTT 307 (TC), TC02712.

[43.65] The First-tier Tribunal allowed an appeal against a surcharge in a case where Judge Khan accepted the appellant's evidence that he considered that the surcharge should have been eliminated by the carry-back of a trading loss from a subsequent period. *S Thorp v HMRC*, FTT [2014] UKFTT 207 (TC), TC03347.

FA 2009, s 108—suspension of surcharges—deferred payment agreement

[43.66] An individual (S) who was employed by a cleaning business appealed against a surcharge of £66, contending that his employer should have deducted all the necessary tax. The First-Tier Tribunal reviewed the evidence in detail and allowed the appeal. Judge Redston observed that S had requested time to pay any arrears of tax, and that the effect of *FA 2009, s 108* was that no surcharge was due where a 'time to pay' agreement was in force. She also observed that the underpaid tax derived from S's employment income, and that S's employer had failed to provide payslips in spite of being asked to do so. She held that 'to the extent that the tax shortfall arises from this employment, (S) appears to be protected from assessment by *reg* 72: he clearly did not receive his wages "knowing that the employer wilfully failed to deduct the amount of tax which should have been deducted from those payments"'. *M Savage v HMRC*, FTT [2011] UKFTT 816 (TC), TC01652.

[43.67] An individual (W), who had been employed under PAYE, appealed against surcharges for 2008/09 and 2009/10, contending that he had requested a deferred payment agreement. HMRC contended that 'no time-to-pay arrangement was ever formally concluded with (W)' and that any payment arrangement which W had made under the PAYE system had been cancelled when his agent submitted details of his expenses. The First-tier Tribunal rejected HMRC's contentions and allowed W's appeal, finding that he had agreed a 'time-to-pay arrangement' with HMRC by telephone, and rejecting HMRC's contention that the agreement 'would have been automatically cancelled' when W was brought into the self-assessment system. Judge Aleksander held that 'the time-to-pay arrangement is a contractual arrangement for payment of tax concluded with HMRC under their broad powers of collection and management. Unless there was an express term included in the time-to-pay arrangement which provided for its termination on the transfer of (W) to self-assessment, the arrangement would remain valid and continue, notwithstanding the transfer.' *D Wilmot v HMRC*, FTT [2012] UKFTT 653 (TC), TC02325.

[43.68] A solicitor appealed against a surcharge for 2009/10, contending that she had a reasonable excuse because she had separated from her husband and had requested a 'time to pay' arrangement in February 2011. The First-Tier Tribunal allowed her appeal. Judge Blewitt held that the appellant 'had acted as a prudent and diligent taxpayer in attempting to agree a time to pay agreement prior to the surcharge trigger date'. *Mrs S Cornes v HMRC*, FTT [2012] UKFTT 2 (TC), TC01701.

[43.69] Following the decision in *Metcalfe v HMRC (No 1)*, **71.295** CAPITAL GAINS TAX, HMRC imposed a surcharge on the basis that the appellant had failed to pay the tax due within 30 days of the tribunal's determination. He appealed, contending that he had requested a 'time to pay' arrangement within 30 days of receiving the determination. The tribunal accepted his evidence and allowed his appeal. *A Metcalfe v HMRC (No 2)*, FTT [2012] UKFTT 97 (TC), TC01793.

[43.70] A married couple appealed against surcharges relating to a substantial CGT liability, contending that they had been seeking to raise funds by selling shares and had requested a deferred payment agreement. The First-tier Tribunal accepted their evidence and allowed their appeals. Sir Stephen Oliver found that HMRC had received the couple's application but had failed to reach a decision, and that the couple had 'had reasonable grounds for expecting that a time to pay agreement would be reached'. *G & Mrs L Kofteros v HMRC*, FTT [2013] UKFTT 286 (TC), TC02692.

[43.71] Judge Huddleston reached a similar decision in *R Campbell v HMRC*, FTT [2014] UKFTT 501 (TC), TC03628.

[43.72] An individual (P) appealed against a surcharge, contending that he had entered into a 'time to pay' arrangement with HMRC. The First-tier Tribunal allowed his appeal. Judge Brannan observed that HMRC had cancelled the agreement but had 'failed to inform the appellant', so that the circumstances constituted a reasonable excuse. *P Procter v HMRC*, FTT [2012] UKFTT 530 (TC), TC02206.

[43.73] An individual (J) appealed against a surcharge under *TMA, s 59*, contending that he had suffered financial problems which constituted a reasonable excuse, and had entered into a deferred payment agreement in February 2011. The First-tier Tribunal accepted his evidence and allowed his appeal. Judge Gammie observed that HMRC had cancelled the deferred payment agreement in July 2011, and held that J 'had a reasonable excuse throughout the period of default'. *T James v HMRC*, FTT [2013] UKFTT 109 (TC), TC02527.

HMRC imposing surcharge—tax paid before due date

[43.74] An individual (M) failed to submit his 2006/07 return within the statutory time limit, but paid the tax due on 30 January 2008. HMRC repaid the tax to him on 15 August 2008. M filed the tax return on 8 December 2008. HMRC then imposed a surcharge under *TMA, s 59C*. M appealed, contending that no surcharge was due because he had paid the tax on 30 January. The First-Tier Tribunal accepted this contention and allowed the appeal. Judge Aleksander held that the relevant dates for the purposes of *TMA, s 59C(2)* and *(3)* were 29 February 2008 and 1 August 2008. On those dates, 'the tax had been paid and had not been refunded. Therefore there was no default by the taxpayer, and HMRC should not have levied a surcharge'. *SW McMullan v HMRC*, FTT [2009] UKFTT 367 (TC), TC00305.

HMRC imposing surcharge—tax paid on due date

[43.75] A woman appealed against a surcharge, contending that she had paid the tax on 28 February 2011, which was the due date for the purpose of *TMA, s 59C*. The First-Tier Tribunal accepted her evidence and allowed her appeal. *Ms J Jackson v HMRC*, FTT [2012] UKFTT 23 (TC), TC01722.

Surcharges—whether a 'criminal charge'

[43.76] A pensioner appealed against a surcharge of £1256, contending that she had sent her payment in time. Judge Geraint Jones allowed her appeal, expressing the opinion that the effect of the ECHR decision in Jussila v Finland, **31.47** HUMAN RIGHTS, was that the penalties were criminal in nature. *Mrs J Cox v HMRC*, FTT [2012] UKFTT 407 (TC), TC02084. (*Note*. Judge Geraint Jones' decision fails to refer to the Ch D decision in *HMRC v Khawaja*, **44.191** PENALTIES, where Mann J reviewed the previous case law and held that 'the civil standard of proof applied to the income tax regime'.)

Miscellaneous

Interest on overdue tax—TMA, s 86

[43.77] An individual failed to pay his tax liability by the due date. The Revenue imposed surcharges under *TMA, s 59C* and interest under *TMA, s 86*. He appealed. The General Commissioners found that he had a reasonable excuse for late payment, and allowed his appeal against the surcharges. Following their decision, he refused to pay the interest, and the Revenue applied for summary judgment. The QB gave judgment for the Revenue.

Hallett J held that there was no provision whereby the defendant could be relieved of his liability to pay interest on unpaid tax. *Duffy v CIR*, QB [2003] EWHC 382 (QB).

[43.78] In the case noted at **46.25** PENSION SCHEMES, HMRC issued assessments under *ICTA 1988, s 647*, charging tax on a couple who had arranged for their pension funds to be transferred to Guernsey schemes. HMRC also imposed penalties. The First-tier Tribunal dismissed the couple's appeals against the assessments but allowed their appeals against the penalties, holding that they had not been negligent because they had been misinformed by a fraudulent financial adviser. In the First-tier Tribunal, Judge Khan also directed that the couple should not have to pay interest on the tax. HMRC appealed to the Upper Tribunal against this part of Judge Khan's decision. The Upper Tribunal allowed HMRC's appeal. Judge Herrington observed that 'there is nothing in the First-tier Tribunal's decision to indicate the basis on which it had concluded that it was appropriate to determine that there should be no interest payable on the tax which it had concluded was properly payable pursuant to the assessments made by HMRC. Nor does it appear from the decision that any submissions were made by either party on this issue.' The wording of *TMA, s 86* clearly stated that income tax 'shall carry interest' and the First-tier Tribunal had no discretion or jurisdiction to determine that interest should not be payable. *HMRC v N & Mrs S Gretton (No 2)*, UT [2012] UKUT 261 (TCC); [2012] STC 2061.

[43.79] See also *R v CIR (ex p. Barker & Beresford)*, **4.304** APPEALS.

TMA, s 59B—procedure where tax not deducted under PAYE

[43.80] See *Gayen v HMRC*, **42.96** PAY AS YOU EARN.

Partnership dissolution—liability for outstanding tax

[43.81] A partner retired from a partnership under an agreement whereby the remaining partners undertook to pay 'all liability (including that of the vendor personally) for income tax' of and relating to the partnership. The CA held that this did not include surtax assessed on the retiring partner in respect of his share of the partnership income. Morris LJ observed that 'the partnership, as such, is not liable to surtax' so that 'having regard to the context, there is a clear indication that the phrase "income tax" is used in its limited sense and not as including surtax'. *Conway v Wingate*, CA 1952, 31 ATC 148; [1952] 1 All ER 782.

[43.82] Two people (S and B) had carried on business in partnership. S retired, and B continued the business as a sole trader. The partnership was dissolved under an agreement whereby B agreed to take over 'all debts and liabilities of the said partnership'. However he only paid half of the partnership's tax liability for 1950/51. S paid the other half to the Revenue, and took proceedings against B to recover the amount he had paid. The CA unanimously gave judgment for S, holding that the income tax was a partnership liability, and that the effect of the agreement was that B had accepted responsibility for paying the partnership income tax. *Stevens v Britten*, CA 1954, 33 ATC 399; [1954] 1 WLR 1340; [1954] 3 All ER 385.

[43.83] In another case where a partnership had been dissolved, the QB held that tax on partnership profits, rents received by the partnership, and a capital gain accruing to the partnership, were within the definition of 'outstanding loans or liabilities' in the dissolution agreement, but that a partner's surtax liability was not within the definition. *Barber v Eppell*, QB 24 February 1981 unreported.

Income tax—whether a liability of a business sold

[43.84] A company purchased a business from an individual under an agreement whereby it undertook to discharge the debts and liabilities of the business. The CA held that the liabilities included income tax on the business profits up to the date of completion, but excluded the tax due under *ITTOIA 2005, s 173** (valuation of trading stock on discontinuance). *Hollebone v WJ Hollebone & Sons Ltd (re Hollebone's Agreement)*, CA 1959, 38 ATC 142; [1959] 1 WLR 536; [1959] 2 All ER 152.

Claim by appellant for set-off of tax allegedly repayable

[43.85] An individual appealed against two assessments on untaxed interest, contending that he was entitled to repayments of income tax which should be set against the amount assessed. The Commissioners dismissed the appeals, holding that the possibility of a set-off was outside their jurisdiction, and the Ch D upheld their decision. *Collis v Cadle*, Ch D 1955, 36 TC 204. (*Note*. The appellant appeared in person.)

Whether tax payable affected by subsequent loss claim

[43.86] On 10 July 1985 General Commissioners imposed penalties of £9,000 under *TMA, s 95(1)* on a partnership for 1980/81 to 1982/83. The partners appealed, contending that the penalties should be reduced because they had claimed loss relief in respect of another business. (The first accounts of this other business had been submitted in May 1985, and the claim to loss relief had been made on 8 July.) The Ch D dismissed their appeal. Harman J held that the tax due under an assessment becomes due and payable on the prescribed date, and that the amount due is not affected by a subsequent claim to loss relief. If the loss relief claims were validated, the Revenue could mitigate the penalties under *TMA, s 102*. *Khan & Ather v First East Brixton Commrs & CIR*, Ch D 1986, 59 TC 242; [1986] STC 331.

Overseas tax—whether enforceable in UK

[43.87] The Australian revenue authorities assessed a UK company (L) to Australian tax. In order to collect the tax, they directed another company (B), managed and controlled in Australia but incorporated in the UK, to deduct the tax from certain dividends which it paid to L. B withheld the tax from the dividends, and L took proceedings against B in the Ch D, contending that the dividends were not assessable to Australian income tax. The Ch D gave judgment for L. Tomlin J held that the dividend was an English debt payable under an English contract, that the Australian Government had no power to tax it, and that B was not entitled to deduct Australian income tax from dividends payable to English shareholders. *London & South American Investment Trust Ltd v British Tobacco Co (Australia) Ltd*, Ch D 1926, 5 ATC 633; [1927] 1 Ch 107. (*Note.* For a discussion of the principle that the UK courts will not enforce tax debts due to other countries, see Simon's Taxes, para A2.103.)

[43.88] The Government of India claimed capital gains tax from the liquidator of a UK company which had carried on business in India. The liquidators rejected proofs for the tax. The Indian Government appealed against the rejection. The HL unanimously dismissed the appeal, holding that the liquidators had acted correctly. Viscount Simonds held that there was 'a rule of law which precludes a foreign state from suing in England for taxes due under the law of that state'. *In re Delhi Electric Supply & Traction Co Ltd, Government of India v Taylor & Hume*, HL 1955, 34 ATC 10; [1955] AC 491; [1955] 1 All ER 292.

[43.89] A married couple, resident in the USA, sent certain goods by ship to their son-in-law (B) in England. The US Government sent a levy to the company which owned the ship, claiming possession of the goods on the grounds that the couple had not paid US taxes. The company complied with the levy and did not deliver the goods to B. B and his mother-in-law (S) took legal proceedings in the UK against the company and the US government, contending that the levy was invalid and that the company was required to deliver the goods to B. The CA gave judgment for B and S, holding that the US levy was not enforceable in the UK. Lord Denning held that 'it is well established in English law that our courts will not give their aid to enforce, directly or indirectly, the revenue law of another country'. *Brokaw & Shaheen v Seatrain UK Ltd and United States Government*, CA 1971, 50 ATC 95; [1971] 2 All ER 98.

[43.90] A number of Danish companies went into compulsory liquidation, owing substantial amounts to the Danish tax authorities. The companies began legal action in the UK against their former controlling director, who was resident in the UK. In the QB, Sullivan J struck the action out, applying *Government of India v Taylor*, **43.88** above. The CA dismissed the companies' appeals against this decision. Applying *dicta* of Kingsmill Moore J in the Irish case of *Peter Buchanan Ltd and Macharg v McVay*, HC(I) [1954] IR 89; [1955] AC 516, 'the whole object of the suit is to collect tax for a foreign revenue'. The liquidator was, in substance, 'a nominee for a foreign State' and was seeking 'to give extra-territorial effect to that state's revenue law'. *QRS 1 ApS & Others v Frandsen*, CA 1999, 71 TC 515; [1999] STC 616; [1999] 1 WLR 2169; [1999] 3 All ER 289.

[43.91] A Canadian company (IE) claimed a substantial deduction for a payment to another company (EH), which it described as expenditure on research and development. The Canadian tax authorities formed the opinion that the payment had been wrongly described and had been made in order to confer a benefit on EH's controlling director (who was the brother of IE's controlling director). While the Canadian authorities were investigating IE's affairs, IE's controlling director (H) left Canada, and subsequently moved to the UK. The Canadian Government sought his extradition. H appealed to the QB, contending that he had not committed any offence under *Extradition Act 2003, s 137(2)(b)*. The QB accepted this contention and allowed H's appeal. Laws LJ held that the Canadian Government had failed to prove 'that the conduct alleged, if transposed to the United Kingdom, would involve or generate a charge to tax whose concealment by the appellant would then amount to the offence of cheating the Revenue'. *W Hertel v Government of Canada*, QB [2010] EWHC 2305 (Admin).

[43.92] The South Africa Revenue Service (SARS) obtained judgment for more than £200,000,000 (including penalties and interest) against a company (B) which was registered in the British Virgin Islands. SARS formed the opinion that B's assets had been transferred to another British Virgin Islands company (M), and that more than £7,000,000 of this money was held in a London bank account. SARS asked HMRC for help in recovering the amounts due, in accordance with *Article 25A* of the Double Tax Convention between the UK and South Africa. In February 2012 HMRC and SARS obtained freezing orders against B, M, and a Guernsey company (H) which was the registered holder of the shares in B and M. The companies appealed, and the Ch D allowed the appeal by H, but dismissed the appeals by B and M. B and M appealed to the CA, contending that *FA 2006, s 173* should not be treated as having retrospective effect and that SARS' claim was unenforceable in the English courts. The CA unanimously rejected these contentions and dismissed the appeals. Lloyd Jones LJ held that the tax claims which HMRC and SARS were seeking to enforce fell within *Article 25A* of the Double Tax Convention, and that there was 'no unfairness in *Article 25A* permitting the enforcement of pre-existing tax liabilities'. The tax enforcement arrangements were authorised by *FA 2006, s 173*. *Ben Nevis (Holdings) Ltd v HMRC (and related appeals)*, CA [2013] EWCA Civ 578; [2013] STC 1579; 15 ITLR 1003.

44

Penalties

The cases in this chapter are arranged under the following headings.

GENERAL NOTE

Proceedings for penalties in courts below the High Court (or Court of Session) are outside the scope of this book and are therefore excluded. See also **29** FURTHER ASSESSMENTS: LOSS OF TAX for compositions of penalties and for assessments involving fraud, wilful default or neglect (including fraudulent or negligent conduct). For appeals against penalties under *IHTA, ss 245–249*, see *Robertson v CIR*, **72.171** INHERITANCE TAX; *HMRC v Evans*, **72.177** INHERITANCE TAX, and *Cairns v HMRC*, **72.179** INHERITANCE TAX. For appeals against stamp duty penalties, see the cases noted at **75.14** STAMP DUTY LAND TAX to **75.27** STAMP DUTY LAND TAX.

Penalties for failure to give notice of liability (TMA, s 7(8))

[44.1] A trader (C) purchased an off-licence in 1996, but failed to notify the Revenue that he was liable to income tax. He ceased the business in 2003 when he became an employee. HMRC subsequently discovered that he had failed to give notice of liability to income tax for 1996/97 to 2002/03 inclusive. They imposed penalties under *TMA, s 7(8)*, at the rate of 45% of the evaded tax. The First-tier Tribunal upheld the penalties in principle but reduced them to 30% of the evaded tax. *N Chauhan v HMRC*, FTT [2011] UKFTT 412 (TC), TC01265.

Penalties in relation to returns or accounts

Failure to make returns (TMA, s 93; FA 2009, Sch 55)

Penalties awarded while assessments open

[44.2] In an Irish case where the relevant legislation was similar to that now in *TMA, s 93*, a solicitor failed to make a return. Estimated assessments were made on him against which he appealed. Before the appeals had been determined, penalties were awarded against him for his failure to make his return. The Irish Supreme Court held that the action for penalties should not have been brought before the assessments had become final. *A-G for Irish Free State v White*, SC(I) 1931, 38 TC 666. (*Note.* The decision was approved by Lord Keith of Avonholm in the English case of *CIR v Hinchy*, HL 1960, 38 TC 625—the decision in which has been overtaken by subsequent changes in the legislation.)

Penalties reduced on appeal

[44.3] General Commissioners imposed maximum penalties under *TMA, s 93** at a hearing at which the taxpayer was not represented. The Ch D held that there was no ground for interfering with the imposition of penalties, but reduced the penalties by 50% to take account of the taxpayer's means. *Wells v Croydon Commrs*, Ch D 1968, 47 ATC 356.

[44.4] General Commissioners imposed penalties of £1,198 under *TMA, ss 93* and *95* on a market trader, following an investigation covering several years. The Ch D reduced the penalties to £1,000 (with costs of £75 awarded to the Revenue). *Taylor v Bethnal Green Commrs & CIR*, Ch D 1976, [1977] STC 44.

[44.5] The Revenue took penalty proceedings against an undischarged bankrupt (S) who had failed to make two returns. S did not attend the hearing, and the inspector gave a history of the case, stating that S had not made returns for 15 years, but not stating that S was an undischarged bankrupt and that it had been agreed not to press for returns for previous years. The Commissioners awarded continuing penalties at the maximum rate of £10 per day (totalling £960) for each return. S appealed. The Ch D allowed the appeal in part, finding that the inspector's evidence had been misleading and holding that the Commissioners had been wrong to impose the maximum penalties. Each award was reduced to £50, but S was ordered to pay £250 towards the Revenue's costs as he had made the appeal necessary by not writing to the Commissioners to explain his position. *Stableford v Liverpool Commrs*, Ch D 1982, [1983] STC 162.

[44.6] A woman (G), who was employed by Devon County Council, received mileage expenses. HMRC sent her a 2009/10 tax return, which she failed to submit in time. HMRC imposed a penalty of £100. G appealed, contending that the penalty was excessive because her additional tax liability was only £15.80. Judge Geraint Jones accepted this contention and reduced the penalty accordingly. *Ms N Geyko-Bisson v HMRC*, FTT [2012] UKFTT 406 (TC), TC02083.

Penalties upheld on appeal

[44.7] General Commissioners imposed penalties against a taxpayer for failure to submit returns. He appealed, contending that he did not have all the necessary information to submit an accurate return. The Ch D dismissed his appeal. Goulding J observed that the taxpayer's responsibility was to declare 'that the return is to the best of his knowledge correct and complete', and that it was open to a taxpayer to include an estimated figure 'if he has done his best' and providing that 'he puts in a genuine estimate and, if necessary, explains that it is not very reliable'. *Dunk v Havant Commrs*, Ch D 1976, 51 TC 519; [1976] STC 460. (*Note.* For the Revenue's interpretation of the principles laid down in this case to returns under self-assessment, see Revenue Tax Bulletin October 1998, pp 594–596.)

[44.8] The decision in *Dunk v Havant Commrs*, **44.7** above, was applied and approved in the similar case of *Alexander v Wallington Commrs & CIR*, CA 1993, 65 TC 777; [1993] STC 588.

[44.9] General Commissioners imposed penalties under *TMA, s 93* on an individual (M) who had failed to make returns. M subsequently sent in returns which did not specify his sources of income or their amounts but referred to a letter in which he had named companies, the returns of which would cover his income. The Revenue took proceedings for further penalties. M failed to attend the hearing and the Commissioners imposed maximum daily penalties from the date of the previous meeting. The Ch D upheld the penalties and dismissed M's appeal. Goulding J observed that the penalty arises under *s 93* 'not because a person has delivered no return but because he has failed to comply with a notice under *s 8*, and the notice requires "a return of his income, computed in accordance with the Income Tax Acts and specifying each separate source of income and the amount from each source"'. *Moschi v Kensington Commrs & CIR*, Ch D 1979, 54 TC 403; [1980] STC 1.

[44.10] For another case where penalties under *TMA, s 93* were imposed in respect of incomplete returns, see *Cox v Poole Commrs (Nos. 1 & 2)*, **49.2** and **49.3** RETURNS AND INFORMATION.

[44.11] A painter and decorator failed to submit tax returns for 1998/99, 1999/2000 and 2000/01. In 2005 the Revenue imposed penalties of £490 under *TMA, s 93* for each of the three returns. The Special Commissioner upheld the penalties, observing that they were 'some 58.3% of the maximum' and holding that this was 'appropriate in all the circumstances of the case'. *P Adkins v HMRC*, Sp C [2007] SSCD 323 (Sp C 590).

[44.12] An individual (T) failed to submit a return (on form SA100) for 2003/04. The Revenue imposed a penalty of £100 under *TMA, s 93(2)*. T appealed, contending firstly that he had submitted the relevant information on a form R40, and alternatively that the notice requiring him to submit a return was invalid because it did not specify the name of the officer who had issued it. The General Commissioners rejected this contention and dismissed T's appeal, and the Ch D upheld their decision. Henderson J held that a notice under *TMA, s 8* simply had to be given by 'an officer', and did not require that officer to be named. *TMA, s 113(1A)* provided for a notice to be 'issued in the name of the area officer by a junior official', or 'in the name of the Board as a whole'.

He observed that T had received income from self-employment, and had also received significant investment income. He held that even though T had completed a form R40, the Revenue were entitled to require him 'by notice under *section 8* to deliver a further return, since the form R40 was 'in no way a substitute for a proper return, except in cases where the Revenue decides that it is prepared to accept it as a substitute'. *D Tomlinson v HMRC*, Ch D 2007, 79 TC 271; [2007] EWHC 2966 (Ch).

[44.13] A woman (P), and two members of her family, failed to submit tax returns for 1996/97 to 2002/03 inclusive. The Revenue imposed penalties under *TMA, s 93(2)*. They also applied to the General Commissioners for a direction under *s 93(3)* imposing further penalties. The Commissioners granted the Revenue's application, and the Revenue imposed penalties of £840 for each year on P. She appealed, contending that the relevant penalty notices were invalid because they did not correctly identify the actual days to which the penalties related. The Commissioners rejected this contention and dismissed her appeal, holding that 'the imposition of the penalties was not invalidated by the date error on the penalty notices' and that *TMA, s 114* applied. The Ch D upheld this decision. Henderson J held that *TMA, s 114(2)(b)* 'provided that the determinations were not to be "impeached or affected" by reason of the discrepancy between the dates specified in the penalty notices and the dates for which the determinations were actually made'. He also held that the imposition of the penalties did not contravene the *European Convention on Human Rights*. *Mrs ME Pipe v HMRC (and related appeals)*, Ch D [2008] STC 1911; [2008] EWHC 646 (Ch).

[44.14] A woman (M) failed to submit her 2010/11 tax return on time, and HMRC imposed a penalty. She appealed, contending that the notice requiring her to file her return was invalid because it had only stated one of her two initials. The First-tier Tribunal dismissed her appeal. Judge Redston noted that M had completed a previous return which had been addressed in the same way, and held that the effect of *TMA, s 114(1)* was that the omission of one of M's initials did not invalidate the notice. *Mrs HB McGuinness v HMRC*, FTT [2013] UKFTT 88 (TC), TC02506.

[44.15] An individual (B) failed to submit tax returns, and HMRC imposed penalties under *TMA, s 93(3)*. B appealed, contending that the UK Parliament had acted illegally when it ceded sovereignty to the EC by passing the *European Communities Act 1972*, and that as a result he should no longer be required to comply with Acts passed by Parliament. The First-tier Tribunal rejected this contention and dismissed his appeal. Judge Aleksander observed that 'Parliament cannot fetter itself, and Parliament remains free to repeal the *European Communities Act* and withdraw from the EU'. *IK Bell v HMRC*, FTT [2009] UKFTT 270 (TC), TC00216.

[44.16] An individual (H) appealed against a penalty for the late submission of his 2012/13 return, contending that he had a reasonable excuse because he had relied his agent to submit the return, and the agent had had to request an activation code, which HMRC had issued by post. The First-tier Tribunal dismissed the appeal. Judge Connell observed that H could have submitted the return himself, and had 'had ample time to arrange for his return to be filed online prior to 31 January 2014'. *Z Hegedus v HMRC*, FTT [2014] UKFTT 1049 (TC), TC04142.

[44.17] Two individuals did not submit their returns by the due date. HMRC imposed penalties of £100 each under *FA 2009, Sch 55 para 3*, and daily penalties under *FA 2009, Sch 55 para 4*. They appealed against the penalties imposed under *Sch 55 para 4*, contending that HMRC had failed to give them the notice 'specifying the date from which the penalty is payable', as required by *Sch 55 para 4(1)(c)*. The Upper Tribunal unanimously rejected this contention and upheld the penalties, holding that the forms SA326D which HMRC had issued fulfilled the conditions of *para 4(1)(c)*. *HMRC v K Donaldson (and related appeal)*, UT [2014] UKUT 536 (TCC).

[44.18] Appeals against penalties under *TMA, s 93* or *FA 2009, Sch 55* have also been dismissed in a large number of subsequent cases, none of which appear to raise any point of general importance. In the interests of space, such cases are not summarised individually in this book. For details of such cases decided up to and including 31 December 2011, see Tolley's Tax Cases 2012.

Alleged non-receipt of notice of hearing at which penalty awarded

[44.19] General Commissioners imposed penalties of £1 per day under *TMA, s 93* on an employee (K) who had failed to make returns. K appealed, contending that he had not received notice of the hearing at which the penalties were imposed. The Ch D dismissed his appeal, finding that the notice had been posted to him and holding that this was a matter which could only be raised on an application for *certiorari* and could not be raised on the appeal. *Kenny v Wirral Commrs & CIR*, Ch D 1974, 50 TC 405; [1975] STC 61.

Paper return filed late—online return submitted within extended time limit

[44.20] An individual (D) submitted his 2010/11 tax return, on paper, in December 2011. HMRC imposed a penalty of £100. In January 2011 D's agent submitted the return electronically, and appealed against the penalty, contending that no penalty was due because he had submitted the electronic return before 31 January. The First-tier Tribunal dismissed the appeal. Judge McKenna held that 'if a paper tax return is filed late, it is not possible to avoid a penalty by filing a further tax return online before 31 January'. *G Dajani v HMRC*, FTT [2012] UKFTT 514 (TC), TC02191.

[44.21] Judge Baird reached a similar decision in *Ms K Lainchbury v HMRC*, FTT [2014] UKFTT 033 (TC), TC03174.

[44.22] Judge Sheppard reached a contrasting decision in a case where an individual (L) had submitted a paper return for 2012/13 in early January 2014 (ie after the deadline for paper returns), and his agent subsequently submitted an electronic return on 22 January (ie within the extended deadline for electronic returns). HMRC imposed a penalty and L appealed, contending that he had submitted the paper return in error and had not realised that his agent had intended to submit the return electronically. Judge Sheppard allowed the appeal, specifically rejecting HMRC's contention 'that the submission of the return electronically after submission of the paper return was done for the purpose of avoiding a penalty. The more likely explanation is that submitted by the appellant that this was a simple mistake being a result of a lack of communication between the appellant and his agent.' *A Lorimer v HMRC*, FTT [2014] UKFTT 797 (TC), TC03914.

Award of penalties during bankruptcy

[44.23] See *Re Hurren*, **6.35** BANKRUPTCY AND PERSONAL INSOLVENCY.

Appeal against penalties allowed

[44.24] HMRC imposed penalties totalling £560 on an individual (F), for failing to submit his income tax returns for 2004/05 and 2005/06 until 2009. F appealed, contending that he had previously submitted the returns in question, and that the returns which he had filed online in 2009 had been duplicates. The tribunal observed that HMRC's records showed that they had received F's 2004/05 return in January 2006, but had returned it to F on the grounds that it was incomplete. HMRC had written to F at a farm although F had written to HMRC from a flat in a town. HMRC had failed to explain why they had continued writing to F at an address which differed from the one which he had given them in correspondence. F's evidence had 'a ring of truth about it' and HMRC had not proved that he had failed to submit the returns by the due date. *P Frossell v HMRC*, FTT [2010] UKFTT 80 (TC), TC00392.

[44.25] A trader ceased self-employment in March 2009, when he became a full-time employee. He did not submit the return which he had been sent for 2009/10, and HMRC imposed a penalty. On receipt of the penalty notice he telephoned HMRC. Following the telephone conversation, HMRC sent him a paper return, which he completed and returned within seven days. He appealed against the penalty, contending firstly that he had assumed that, because he was no longer self-employed, he would not need to submit the 2009/10 return, and additionally that when he telephoned HMRC, he had been told that provided that he submitted the paper return within 14 days, no penalty would be charged. The First-tier Tribunal accepted his evidence and allowed his appeal. Judge Redston held that the appellant's behaviour in ignoring the return did not constitute a reasonable excuse. However, it appeared that when he telephoned HMRC, the officer to whom he spoke had agreed to exercise HMRC's power under *TMA, s 102* to discharge the penalty. *D Archer v HMRC*, FTT [2011] UKFTT 717 (TC), TC01554.

[44.26] HMRC imposed a penalty of £100 on an individual (C) who had not submitted his 2009/10 tax return. C appealed, contending that he had not received the notice requiring him to file a return. The First-tier Tribunal accepted his evidence and allowed the appeal. Lady Mitting held that 'a taxpayer's obligation is to deliver a return of his income when required to do so by being sent a notice to file. The obligation arises out of receipt of the notice'. *S Chard v HMRC*, FTT [2011] UKFTT 753 (TC), TC01590.

[44.27] Similar decisions were reached in *A Charleson v HMRC*, FTT [2011] UKFTT 759 (TC), TC01596; *J Hart v HMRC*, FTT [2012] UKFTT 185 (TC), TC01880; *D Preece v HMRC*, FTT [2012] UKFTT 192 (TC), TC01887; *D Marshall v HMRC*, FTT [2012] UKFTT 237(TC), TC01931; *G Zadra v HMRC*, FTT [2012] UKFTT 292 (TC), TC01980; *TC Draper v HMRC*, FTT [2013] UKFTT 239 (TC), TC02653, and *Armstrong v HMRC*, **4.135** APPEALS.

[44.28] HMRC imposed a penalty of £100 on an individual (S) who had not submitted a 2012/13 tax return. S appealed, contending that his income 'was below the tax threshold', and that although he had received a notice requiring him to file a return, he had not received a return form. Judge Rankin allowed his appeal, holding that the circumstances constituted a reasonable excuse. *EJ Smith v HMRC*, FTT [2014] UKFTT 761 (TC), TC03881.

[44.29] Judge Sheppard reached a similar decision in *SM South v HMRC*, FTT [2014] UKFTT 807 (TC), TC03924.

TMA, s 93(8)—whether a 'reasonable excuse'

[44.30] See *Gladders v Prior*, 43.39 PAYMENT OF TAX, and the cases noted at 44.247 to 44.322 below.

Failure to make partnership return (TMA, s 93A; FA 2009, Sch 55 para 3)

Whether TMA, s 93(7) applicable

[44.31] A partnership submitted its tax return for the year ending 31 January 2008 on 13 January 2009. HMRC imposed penalties of £100 on each partner, on the basis that the due date for the return was 31 October 2008. The partnership appealed, contending that it had a reasonable excuse because HMRC's website stated that 'if all the tax due has been paid by 31 January the penalty notice will be issued in the sum of nil; as the penalty cannot exceed the amount of tax outstanding at 31 January'. The First-tier Tribunal allowed the appeal. Judge Mosedale held that the information on HMRC's website was incorrect , because *TMA, s 93(7)* only applied to personal returns and not to partnership returns, and was 'only applicable where the liability on the return is less than the standard penalty and does not apply to situations where the liability to tax is greater than the standard penalty but the taxpayer has discharged it on or before 31 January'. However reliance on HMRC's website was a reasonable excuse, since 'HMRC has responsibility for gathering the correct amount of tax and it must be reasonable for a taxpayer to rely on HMRC's guidance as a correct statement of the law. Further, it is actually HMRC who impose the penalty: HMRC must therefore ensure that they do not mislead taxpayers into mistaken actions which incur a penalty'. *B & J Shopfitting Services v HMRC*, FTT [2010] UKFTT 78 (TC), TC00390.

[44.32] A partnership failed to file its return by the due date, and HMRC imposed a penalty of £100 on the representative partner. She appealed, contending *inter alia* that since the partnership had no tax liability, the effect of *TMA, s 93(7)* was that the penalty should be reduced to nil. The First-tier Tribunal rejected this contention, holding that *s 93(7)* only applied to personal tax returns and that 'there are no provisions in (*TMA, s 93A*) which limit the penalties in relation to partnership returns in a similar way'. (The tribunal also held that there was no reasonable excuse for the late submission of the return.) *SM Fleming (Paul Kingston Furniture) v HMRC*, FTT [2010] UKFTT 94 (TC), TC00405.

Whether TMA, s 93A(1) applicable

[44.33] HMRC imposed a penalty under *TMA, s 93A* on a partnership which had not submitted a return. The representative partner (S) appealed. The First-tier Tribunal allowed the appeal, finding that S had never received a notice requiring him to file a partnership return. Judge Powell observed that S had 'taken some considerable care to submit his individual return properly and on time' and had 'dealt promptly with the penalty notice and all subsequent correspondence'. *J Stirling v HMRC*, FTT [2012] UKFTT 143 (TC), TC01838.

[44.34] A similar decision was reached in *A Cornish (Kittiwake Partnership) v HMRC*, FTT [2012] UKFTT 203 (TC), TC01898.

[44.35] HMRC imposed a penalty under *TMA, s 93A* on a partnership which had not submitted a return. The representative partner appealed, contending that he had never received a notice requiring him to file a partnership return. The First-tier Tribunal dismissed the appeal. Judge Walters held that 'the burden of proof is on the appellant to show that on the balance of probabilities the notice was not given to the appellant'. *F Parker v HMRC*, FTT [2012] UKFTT 447 (TC), TC02128.

Whether TMA, s 93A(5) applicable

[44.36] A limited liability partnership appealed against penalties under *TMA, s 93A*, contending that it had submitted the relevant return within the statutory time limit. The First-tier Tribunal initially dismissed the appeal, with Judge Petherbridge finding that the representative partner had not provided 'a shred of evidence that that was, in fact, the case. No copy of the partnership return has been produced and no evidence of it having been posted has been produced.' The partnership appealed to the Upper Tribunal, which remitted the case for rehearing by a different First-Tier Tribunal judge. At the rehearing Judge Gammie accepted the partnership's evidence and allowed the appeal. *Eamas Consulting Llp v HMRC (No 2)*, FTT [2012] UKFTT 323 (TC), TC02009.

[44.37] An appeal was allowed in a similar subsequent case where Judge Geraint Jones accepted the partnership's evidence that it had submitted its return within the statutory time limit. *The Source Partnership v HMRC*, FTT [2012] UKFTT 458 (TC), TC02137.

[44.38] A similar decision was reached in C *Newton v HMRC*, FTT [2013] UKFTT 108 (TC), TC02526.

PDF—whether a valid return

[44.39] In January 2011 a firm of solicitors submitted its partners' returns electronically, and attached a PDF file with the partnership return. HMRC formed the opinion that the submission of an electronic PDF did not comply with the notice given under *TMA, s 12AA*, and imposed penalties under *TMA, s 93A*. The First-tier Tribunal allowed the firm's appeal. Judge Hellier held that 'the documents produced by HMRC do not prescribe the use of third-party software as the only way to make an electronic return. The best that can be said is that they prescribe the making of a return via the internet as constituting an electronic return'. Accordingly, the PDF which the firm had submitted 'was an electronic return for the purpose of *section 12AA*'. *Fitzpatrick & Co (Solicitors) v HMRC*, FTT [2012] UKFTT 238 (TC); [2012] SFTD 816, TC01932.

Paper return filed late—online return submitted within extended time limit

[44.40] A partnership submitted its 2010/11 tax return, on paper, in November 2011. On 1 December it submitted the return electronically. On 6 December HMRC imposed a penalty of £300. The partnership appealed, contending that no penalty was due because it had submitted the electronic return before 31 January. The First-tier Tribunal dismissed the appeal. Judge McKenna held that 'if a paper tax return is filed late, it is not possible to avoid a penalty by filing a further tax return online before 31 January'. *Cox Partnership v HMRC*, FTT [2012] UKFTT 516 (TC), TC02193.

Right of appeal—application of TMA, s 93A(6)

[44.41] A married couple carried on business in partnership, with the husband as the representative partner. They failed to submit their 2009/10 partnership return, and HMRC imposed penalties. The wife lodged appeals, contending firstly that the returns had been posted and additionally that because of ill-health, she had not taken an active part in the business during 2009. The First-tier Tribunal struck out the appeal. Judge Brannan held that the effect of *TMA, s 93A(6)(a)* was that only the representative partner had the right to bring an appeal. *Mrs L Jarvis v HMRC*, FTT [2012] UKFTT 483 (TC), TC02160.

Whether TMA, s 93A(7) applicable

[44.42] A partnership failed to file its return by the due date, and HMRC imposed penalties of £100 on each of the partners. The partnership appealed, contending that it had a reasonable excuse because its representative partner had intended to file the return electronically, in the same way that he had filed his personal tax return, and had not realised that he did not have the appropriate software to file a partnership return electronically. The First-tier Tribunal accepted this contention and allowed the appeal. *Davies Software Services v HMRC*, FTT [2010] UKFTT 117 (TC), TC00428. Compare the subsequent case of *Assessor Analysis Services v HMRC*, **44.52** below, in which similar circumstances were held not to constitute a reasonable excuse.)

[44.43] A similar decision was reached in *Simply Birth v HMRC*, FTT October 2009, TC/2009/10674. (*Note*. The Tribunal Centre has not yet publicly issued this decision, although it has been cited in argument in subsequent cases.)

[44.44] Two people began trading in partnership in December 2009. HMRC sent them a partnership return on 6 April 2010, but they did not receive it. They did both complete their individual self-assessment returns, including the partnership pages. In February 2011 HMRC imposed a penalty of £100 for failure to file the 2009/10 partnership return. They appealed, contending that they had a reasonable excuse because they had not realised that they had to submit a partnership return as well as their own individual returns. The First-tier Tribunal accepted this contention and allowed their appeal. Lady Mitting found that they had visited their local tax office and that the officer to whom they spoke had not told them that they would have to submit a separate partnership return. Since they had not received such a return, and had submitted one within a few days of receiving the penalty notice, the circumstances constituted a reasonable excuse. *H & N Singh (t/a Candlestick Company) v HMRC*, FTT [2011] UKFTT 736 (TC), TC01573.

[44.45] A partnership submitted its 2009/10 tax return in paper format on 31 January 2011, and HMRC imposed a penalty. The partnership appealed, contending that it had a reasonable excuse because it had intended to file its return online, but did not have the appropriate software. Judge Geraint Jones accepted the partnership's evidence and allowed its appeal. Judge Geraint Jones observed that HMRC required a partnership to 'purchase software that would allow it to file online', although individual taxpayers 'are provided with a comprehensive online filing service by the respondent and do not need to go into the commercial market to buy specialised software to allow online filing to take place'. HMRC had not explained 'why it discriminates between taxpayers in that way. It does not explain why it fails to provide a comprehensive online filing facility for some but not for others.' Accordingly, the fact that HMRC 'had failed to make available a suitable and comprehensive online filing facility' constituted a reasonable excuse. *St Georges Bricklayers v HMRC*, FTT [2011] UKFTT 800 (TC), TC01636. (*Note*. Compare the cases noted at **44.49** to **44.53** below, none of which are referred to in Judge Geraint Jones' decision.)

[44.46] Judge Geraint Jones reached a similar decision in *Mike's News v HMRC*, FTT [2011] UKFTT 849 (TC), TC01683.

[44.47] Judge Khan reached a similar decision in *P & A Galbraith (t/a Galbraith Ceramics) v HMRC*, FTT [2013] UKFTT 225 (TC); [2013] SFTD 857, TC02639.

[44.48] A partnership did not submit its 2009/10 return until May 2011, and HMRC imposed penalties of £100 on each partner. The partnership appealed, contending that it had a reasonable excuse because it had not received a paper return and did not receive its UTR until January 2011. The First-tier Tribunal accepted the partnership's evidence and allowed the appeal. *Oracle Fieldwork v HMRC*, FTT [2012] UKFTT 9 (TC), TC01708.

[44.49] A partnership failed to file its return by the due date, and HMRC imposed penalties of £100 on each of the partners. The partnership appealed, contending that it had a reasonable excuse because its accountant had intended to file the return electronically, and had not realised that he did not have the appropriate software to file a partnership return electronically. The First-tier Tribunal dismissed the appeal, holding that this did not constitute a reasonable excuse. *RG & Mrs B Beebe v HMRC*, FTT [2010] UKFTT 265 (TC), TC00559.

[44.50] Similar decisions were reached in *T & S Arnold (t/a Wood Chalet & Caravan Park) v HMRC*, FTT [2011] UKFTT 73 (TC), TC00951; *Pet Essentials v HMRC*, FTT [2011] UKFTT 161 (TC), TC01030; *D & T Jewiss (t/a The Amelie Partnership)*, [2011] UKFTT 163 (TC), TC01032; *H & Y Colbran v HMRC*, FTT [2011] UKFTT 175 (TC), TC01044; *SC Services v HMRC*, FTT [2011] UKFTT 227 (TC), TC01092; *A & C Akin v HMRC*, FTT [2011] UKFTT 291 (TC), TC01153; *A Koyeni Efreeitems v HMRC*, FTT [2012] UKFTT 13 (TC), TC01712; *Colana Office Cleaning v HMRC*, FTT [2012] UKFTT 88 (TC), TC01784; *GL & CL Wilson (t/a Frosty Fingers) v*

HMRC, FTT [2012] UKFTT 208 (TC), TC01903, and *D & M Flooring v HMRC*, FTT [2012] UKFTT 735 (TC), TC02395.

[44.51] An appeal was dismissed in a case where Judge Blewitt observed that 'the fact that third party software is required, and must be purchased, is widely publicised by HMRC, not least on the front of the partnership return itself'. She held that 'where the choice is made to file online, the lack of the necessary software cannot amount to a reasonable excuse'. *B Peck & Ms J Wilson v HMRC*, FTT [2011] UKFTT 859 (TC), TC01693.

[44.52] A partnership failed to file its return by the due date, and HMRC imposed penalties of £100 on each of the partners. The partnership appealed, contending that it had a reasonable excuse because its representative partner had intended to file the return electronically, in the same way that he had filed his personal tax return, and had not realised that he did not have the appropriate software to file a partnership return electronically. The First-tier Tribunal dismissed the appeal, holding that this did not constitute a reasonable excuse. *Assessor Analysis Services v HMRC*, FTT [2010] UKFTT 529 (TC), TC00783.

[44.53] Similar decisions were reached in *David Owen & Son v HMRC*, FTT [2011] UKFTT 223 (TC), TC01088; *Ms C McKendrick v HMRC*, FTT [2012] UKFTT 376 (TC), TC02060, and *Alfa Biuro Partnership v HMRC*, FTT [2012] UKFTT 598 (TC), TC02274.

[44.54] Appeals against penalties for failure to file partnership returns have been dismissed in a large number of subsequent cases, which appear to raise no point of general importance. In the interests of space, such cases are not summarised individually in this book. For a list of cases decided up to 31 December 2012, see Tolley's Tax Cases 2013.

Failure to make corporation tax return (TMA, s 94; FA 1998, Sch 18)

TMA, s 94—penalty for late submission of corporation tax return

[44.55] An appeal against a penalty for the late submission of a corporation tax return and accounts was dismissed by the Special Commissioner in *S Mashood Insurance Agency Ltd v Hudson*, Sp C [1996] SSCD 265 (Sp C 80). (*Note. TMA, s 94* was repealed by *FA 1998* with effect for accounting periods ending after 30 June 1998, and replaced by *FA 1998, Sch 18, paras 17–19*.)

FA 1998, Sch 18 para 17(2)—penalty for late submission of return

[44.56] A company's corporation tax return for the year ending December 2008 was not delivered until February 2010. HMRC imposed a penalty of £100 under *FA 1998, Sch 18 para 17(2)*. The company appealed. The First-tier Tribunal dismissed the appeal, observing that 'it is the company's responsibility to ensure that relevant tax regulations are observed and that returns are filed by their due date'. *RL Mallinson (Heating Engineers) Ltd v HMRC*, FTT [2010] UKFTT 575 (TC), TC00825.

[44.57] Similar decisions were reached in *Troup Curtis & Co Ltd v HMRC*, FTT [2011] UKFTT 170 (TC), TC01039; *Somercombe OTS No 39 Ltd v*

HMRC, FTT [2011] UKFTT 244 (TC), TC01108; *GR8 Green Ltd v HMRC*, FTT [2011] UKFTT 536 (TC), TC01383, and *World of Enterprise Ltd v HMRC*, FTT [2011] UKFTT 719 (TC), TC01556; *Business Womens Coaching v HMRC*, FTT [2012] UKFTT 549 (TC), TC02226, and *Teesdale West Durham CIC v HMRC*, FTT [2014] UKFTT 034 (TC), TC03175.

[44.58] A company did not post its corporation tax return for the year ending 31 May 2009 until 27 August 2010. HMRC did not receive the return until 6 September 2010. HMRC imposed a penalty of £200 under *FA 1998, Sch 18 para 17(2)(b)*. The company appealed, contending that the return had been submitted within three months of the filing date, so that the penalty should only be £100 (under *FA 1998, Sch 18 para 17(2)(a)*). The First-tier Tribunal rejected this contention and dismissed the appeal, observing that the effect of *Sch 18 para 17(2)(a)* was that the penalty was only £100 provided that the return was delivered within three months of the filing date. Judge Brooks held that, since the return had not been posted until Friday 27 August 2010, and the following Monday had been a bank holiday, the company could not have had a reasonable expectation that HMRC would receive the return by Tuesday 31 August 2010. *GV Cox Ltd v HMRC*, FTT [2011] UKFTT 311 (TC), TC01172.

[44.59] A company submitted two corporation tax returns after the due date. HMRC imposed penalties of £200 for each return under *FA 1998, Sch 18 para 17(2)*. The First-tier Tribunal dismissed the company's appeals, holding that there was no reasonable excuse for the delays. *Afshin Safa Ltd v HMRC*, FTT [2010] UKFTT 609 (TC), TC00850.

[44.60] Similar decisions were reached in *Company of the Plumed Horse Ltd v HMRC*, FTT [2011] UKFTT 417 (TC), TC01270, *Horseshoe Inn & Lodge Ltd v HMRC*, FTT [2011] UKFTT 418 (TC), TC01271; *St Loan Rilsky Chudotworec Ltd v HMRC*, FTT [2012] UKFTT 338 (TC), TC02024; *Cothelstone Property Ltd v HMRC*, FTT [2012] UKFTT 554 (TC), TC02231; *Sharing The Truth Ltd v HMRC*, FTT [2014] UKFTT 073 (TC), TC03213, and *Crestdata IT Ltd v HMRC*, FTT [2014] UKFTT 340 (TC), TC03476.

[44.61] A company (P) had used its accountant's address as its registered office. During 2007 the accountant ceased to act for P, and in April 2008 P changed its registered office to the address of its controlling director (H). In the meantime, in September 2007 HMRC had issued P with a notice requiring it to file a corporation tax return for the period ending 30 August 2007. P's former accountant failed to forward this notice to H. In September 2008 HMRC imposed a penalty of £100. Since P had not informed HMRC that it had changed its registered office, HMRC sent the penalty notice to P's former registered office. At some time in 2008 Companies House informed HMRC that P had changed its registered office, and HMRC began sending correspondence to P's new registered office. P appealed against the penalty which HMRC had imposed in September 2008, and against subsequent penalty notices. The First-tier Tribunal allowed P's appeal. Judge Redston rejected HMRC's contention that the effect of *TMA, s 115(2)(a)* was that the notice had been validly served by being sent to P's last known registered office, and held that the phrase 'usual or last known place of residence' was only applicable to sole traders and partners, and did not include companies. She held that, although it was 'possible validly to serve a notice by delivering it to the company's registered office, to its place of business, or by effectively communicating the notice in some other way', a notice was 'not served on a company merely by delivering it to its "last known" registered office'. She also expressed the view that it was likely that Companies House had informed HMRC of P's change of registered office before the issue of the penalty notice, although HMRC had not updated their records until after the issue of the notice. On the evidence, she found that while the notice to file the return had been validly served (by being sent to the accountant's address which was P's registered office at the time of issue), the penalty notice had not been validly served because it had been sent to P's old registered office. *Partito Media Services Ltd v HMRC*, FTT [2012] UKFTT 256 (TC), TC01949.

Company submitting unsigned accounts—HMRC imposing penalty

[44.62] A company (C) submitted two CT returns. HMRC rejected the returns on the grounds that they were incomplete because the accounts and directors' report had not been signed. C subsequently submitted the returns online, after the prescribed filing dates. HMRC imposed penalties of £100 for each return under *FA 1998, Sch 18 para 17(2)*. C appealed, contending firstly that no penalty was due because it had originally submitted the returns within the statutory time limits (and alternatively that it had a reasonable excuse because it had not been aware that HMRC would reject the returns). The First-tier Tribunal accepted C's first contention and allowed the appeal. Judge Staker held that 'in the absence of any evidence or authority having been submitted by HMRC in support of the contention that the appellant was required specifically to submit the relevant documents in signed format, the tribunal finds that HMRC has failed to discharge the burden of proving that the appellant did not submit valid returns within the applicable deadline'. *Codu Computer Ltd v HMRC*, FTT [2011] UKFTT 186 (TC), TC01055.

FA 1998, Sch 18 para 17(3)—penalty for late submission of returns

[44.63] A company submitted three successive corporation tax returns after the due date. Following the first failure, the Revenue imposed a penalty under *TMA, s 94*. Following the second failure, they imposed a penalty of £200 under *FA 1998, Sch 18 para 17(2)* (which had replaced *TMA, s 94* with effect for accounting periods ending after 30 June 1999). Following the third failure, they imposed a penalty of £1,000 in accordance with *FA 1998, Sch 18 para 17(3)*. The company appealed, contending that because the first failure had been penalised under the earlier provisions of *TMA, s 94*, the penalty for the third failure should only be £200 (by virtue of *FA 1998, Sch 18 para 17(2)*) rather than £1,000 (by virtue of *para 17(3)*). The Special Commissioner rejected this contention and dismissed the company's appeal. *Lessex Ltd v Spence*, Sp C 2003, [2004] SSCD 79 (Sp C 391).

[44.64] A company submitted three successive corporation tax returns after the due date. Following the third failure, the Revenue imposed a penalty of £1,000 in accordance with *FA 1998, Sch 18 para 17(3)*. The company appealed, contending that the provisions of *Sch 18* were unreasonable. The General Commissioners reduced the penalty to £200, but the Ch D reversed their decision. Lindsay J held that *Sch 18 para 17* did not give the Commissioners any discretion 'to lessen the penalty by reference to some unexpressed yardstick such as reasonableness or unreasonableness'. *HMRC v La Senza Ltd*, Ch D 2006, [2007] STC 901; [2006] EWHC 1331 (Ch).

[44.65] A company submitted four successive corporation tax returns late. The Revenue imposed penalties of £1,000 under *FA 1998, Sch 18 para 17(3)*. The company appealed, contending that the provisions of *Sch 18* contravened the *European Convention on Human Rights*. The Special Commissioner rejected this contention and dismissed the appeal. *Auntie's Café Ltd v HMRC*, Sp C [2007] SSCD 306 (Sp C 588).

[44.66] An appeal against penalties under *FA 1998, Sch 18 para 17(3)* was also dismissed in *Tamar Enterprises Ltd v HMRC*, FTT [2012] UKFTT 626 (TC), TC02302.

[44.67] A company (M) submitted its corporation tax returns for the periods ending 30 April 2011 and 30 April 2012 after the due date. HMRC imposed a penalty of £1,000 under *FA 1998, Sch 18 para 17(3)*. The First-tier Tribunal allowed M's appeal in part. Judge Lyons held that there was no reasonable excuse for M's failure to submit the returns. However she observed that the penalty of £1,000 under *para 17(3)* only applied where there was a 'third successive failure'. HMRC had not shown that M had failed to submit a return for the period ending 30 April 2010, so that the return for the period ending 30 April 2012 was the second failure rather than the third failure. It followed that M was only liable to a penalty of £200 under *para 17(2)*, rather than to the penalty of £1,000 under *para 17(3)* which HMRC had imposed. *Mint Business Solutions Ltd v HMRC*, FTT [2014] UKFTT 383 (TC), TC03516.

Company submitting accounts without directors' report—HMRC imposing penalty

[44.68] A company (G) submitted accounts without including a directors' report. HMRC imposed penalties under *FA 1998, Sch 18 paras 17(3)* and *18*, on the basis that G had failed to comply with the *Companies Act*. G appealed, contending firstly that no penalty was due, and alternatively that it had a reasonable excuse for not having realised that its returns were insufficient. The First-tier Tribunal rejected these contentions and dismissed the appeals. Judge Raghavan observed that *Sch 18 para 11* permitted HMRC to require that accounts should be accompanied by 'such documents as are required to be prepared under the *Companies Act*'. This included a directors' report, the preparation of which was required by the *Companies Act* even for small companies which were not required to file such reports with the Registrar of Companies. *Goodtime Print & Design Ltd v HMRC*, FTT [2012] UKFTT 609 (TC), TC02286.

FA 1998, Sch 18 para 18(2)—penalty for late submission of return

[44.69] A company failed to submit its CT return for the period ending 31 July 2006 until 25 March 2009. The return showed CT due of £430,850. HMRC imposed a penalty of £82,940 under *FA 1998, Sch 18 para 18(2)*. The First-tier Tribunal dismissed the company's appeal. Judge Trigger held that the company had not 'demonstrated a responsible attitude to the requirement placed upon it by the legislation to submit a return on time'. There was no reasonable excuse for the long delay in filing the return. *ASI Properties Ltd v HMRC*, FTT [2011] UKFTT 105 (TC), TC00981.

[44.70] Similar decisions were reached in *ESA Films Ltd v HMRC*, FTT [2011] UKFTT 248 (TC), TC01112; *Torbensrichard Ltd v HMRC*, FTT [2012] UKFTT 99 (TC), TC01795; *Sterling Developments (London) Ltd v HMRC*, FTT [2012] UKFTT 282 (TC), TC01970; *Wardside House Ltd v HMRC*, FTT [2012] UKFTT 445 (TC), TC02126; *TJS Consulting Ltd v HMRC*, FTT [2012] UKFTT 665 (TC), TC02336, and *SR Derivatives Ltd v HMRC*, FTT [2013] UKFTT 301 (TC), TC02706.

[44.71] A company (W) failed to submit its CT return for the period ending August 2008 until 23 August 2010. HMRC imposed a penalty under *FA 1998, Sch 18 para 18(2)*. W appealed, contending that it had a reasonable excuse because its accountant had been ill. The First-tier Tribunal dismissed the appeal, holding that since the accountant's illness had lasted for some time, the circumstances did not constitute a reasonable excuse. *WG & TN Garrad Ltd v HMRC*, FTT [2012] UKFTT 524 (TC), TC02200.

[44.72] HMRC did not receive a company's return for the period ending 30 November 2007 until June 2009. They therefore imposed a penalty under *FA 1998, Sch 18 para 18(2)*. The company appealed, contending that it had submitted the return on time. The First-tier Tribunal reviewed the evidence, rejected this contention and dismissed the appeal. *Globalnet Resources Ltd v HMRC*, FTT [2011] UKFTT 498 (TC), TC01345.

Company submitting computations in PDF rather than iXBRL—HMRC imposing penalty

[44.73] In March 2012 HMRC imposed a penalty on a company (S) which had not submitted its CT return for the period ending 31 March 2011. S submitted the return in June 2012, but HMRC refused to accept it as the accompanying computations were in PDF format rather than iXBRL format. S did not submit a corrected return until April 2013, and HMRC imposed a penalty under *FA 1998, Sch 18 para 18*. S appealed, contending that 'it was wrong for HMRC to insist that taxpayers must purchase certain software to enable them to submit returns'. The First-tier Tribunal rejected this contention and dismissed the appeal, observing that directions issued under *SI 2003/282* specifically provided that where a company chose not to use HMRC's integrated accounts template, the accounts must be delivered in iXBRL format. *Systems Plus Ltd v HMRC*, FTT [2014] UKFTT 762 (TC), TC03882.

Failure to make trust return (FA 2009, Sch 55)

[44.74] In April 2011 HMRC issued a company (C) with a trust and estate tax return. C submitted the return, on paper, in November 2011. HMRC imposed a penalty of £100 under *FA 2009, Sch 55*. C appealed, contending that it had a reasonable excuse because its agent had not told it that it was required to submit the return. The First-tier Tribunal dismissed the appeal, holding that this was not a reasonable excuse. *Chatsworth (Bournemouth) Management Ltd Sinking Fund v HMRC*, FTT [2012] UKFTT 513 (TC), TC02190.

[44.75] In April 2011 HMRC issued a trust and estate tax return to the trustee of a settlement. HMRC received the completed return on 20 December 2011. They imposed a penalty of £100 under *FA 2009, Sch 55*. The trustee appealed, contending that the penalty was unfair because he had intended to file the return online, but did not have the appropriate software and considered that it was unreasonable to expect him to purchase third party software. The First-tier Tribunal rejected this contention and dismissed the appeal, applying the principles laid down in *Peck & Wilson v HMRC*, **44.51** above. *Trustee of the Georgia Vickery, Franki and Mia Settlement v HMRC*, FTT [2013] UKFTT 282 (TC), TC02688.

[44.76] In April 2011 HMRC issued a trust and estate tax return to the trustees of a settlement. HMRC received the completed return on 1 November 2011, one day after the deadline for paper returns. They imposed a penalty of £100. The trustees appealed, contending that they had posted the return on Friday 28 October. The First-tier Tribunal dismissed the appeal, holding that this was not a reasonable excuse. Judge McKenna observed that it was not 'the action of a reasonable and prudent taxpayer to post a return on the very last day before a deadline, especially with an intervening weekend'. *Derek Evans Settlement v HMRC*, FTT [2012] UKFTT 553 (TC), TC02230.

[44.77] HMRC imposed penalties totalling £500 on an executor who did not submit a 2012/13 trust and estate return until March 2014. The First-tier Tribunal dismissed the executor's appeal, holding that there was no reasonable excuse for the delay. *J Groves v HMRC*, FTT [2014] UKFTT 858 (TC), TC03974.

[44.78] In March 2012 HMRC issued trust returns for 2008/09 to 2010/11 to the executors of a shareholder who had died in 2005. The executors did not submit the returns until 28 February 2013. The 2010/11 return declared a substantial CGT liability. HMRC imposed penalties totalling £10,666 for the late filing of the returns (including daily penalties under *FA 2009, Sch 55 para 4*, totalling £900, in respect of the 2010/11 return). They also imposed surcharges and penalties totalling £13,995 for late payment of the tax due. The executors appealed. The First-tier Tribunal dismissed the appeals and upheld the penalties in principle, holding that there was no reasonable excuse for the delay. (However, the Tribunal adjourned the appeals against the penalties under *Sch 55 para 4* pending the release of the Upper Tribunal decision in *HMRC v Donaldson*, **44.17** above). *Verdegaal's Executors v HMRC*, FTT [2014] UKFTT 878 (TC), TC03994.

[44.79] In April 2011 HMRC issued a trust and estate tax return to the trustee of a settlement. HMRC received the completed return on 2 November 2011, two days after the deadline for paper returns. They imposed a penalty of £100 under *FA 2009, Sch 55*. The trustee appealed, contending that he had posted the return on 26 October. The First-tier Tribunal accepted the trustee's evidence and allowed his appeal. Judge Hellier held that 'HMRC have produced no evidence of the date of delivery' and held that a letter posted on 26 October could normally be expected to be received by 28 October. *Trustee of the De Britton Settlement v HMRC*, FTT [2013] UKFTT 106 (TC), TC02524.

[44.80] In April 2012 HMRC sent a tax return to an executor. HMRC received the completed return form on 14 January 2013,and imposed a penalty. The executor submitted an online return on 24 January 2013, and appealed against the penalty. Judge Brannan allowed the appeal, holding that since HMRC had not submitted the paper return in evidence, and there was no proof that it had been signed, it should not be treated as a valid return for the purposes of *TMA, s 8A*. Accordingly the online return should be treated as the valid return, so that no penalty was due. *T Rosenbaum's Executor v HMRC*, FTT [2013] UKFTT 408 (TC), TC02804. (*Note*. For subsequent proceedings in this case, see **4.127** APPEALS.)

Incorrect return or accounts (TMA, s 95; FA 2007, Sch 24)

Penalty imposed after trader's death—means of widow

[44.81] The Revenue began an investigation into the returns submitted by a trader (D). D died before the investigation was completed. It was accepted that D had submitted incorrect accounts and had been guilty of fraud. His widow, who was his executrix and sole beneficiary, paid the underpaid tax of £11,200 with interest. The Commissioners imposed a penalty of £6,000, taking into account the widow's financial position. She appealed, contending that the penalty was excessive. The Ch D rejected this contention and dismissed her appeal. *Dawes v Wallington Commrs & CIR; R v Wallington Commrs (ex p. Dawes)*, Ch D 1964, 42 TC 200; [1965] 1 All ER 258.

Appeal against penalties—whether relevant assessments excessive

[44.82] General Commissioners awarded a penalty against a trader under *TMA, s 95**. The trader appealed, contending that the inspector had used excessive estimates of his domestic expenditure in arriving at the relevant assessments. The CA unanimously dismissed the appeal. Lord Donovan observed that the Commissioners had determined the relevant assessments and that it was not the court's function to conduct an accountancy investigation. *Salmon v Havering Commrs & CIR*, CA 1968, 45 TC 77.

[44.83] The Revenue discovered that an employee (W) had received commissions which he had omitted from his returns, and issued assessments. W appealed, and the assessments were determined by General Commissioners. Subsequently, the Special Commissioners imposed maximum penalties under *TMA, s 95*. W appealed, producing a letter from the alleged payer of the commissions, stating that the amounts paid were lower than the amounts assessed. The Ch D dismissed his appeal. Walton J held that there was no ground for disturbing the Commissioners' conclusion and 'no reason why they should have awarded less than the maximum penalty'. He also observed that 'there can be no question at all as to the nature of these payments and as to their liability to income tax'. *Williams v Special Commrs & CIR*, Ch D 1974, 49 TC 670; [1975] STC 167.

Appeal against penalty—error of fact in Commissioners' findings

[44.84] A trader appealed against a penalty awarded by General Commissioners. In their Note of Findings, the Commissioners referred to the trader's failure to explain the omission from his accounts and returns of the profits of a second business. The Revenue subsequently accepted that his accounts did in fact refer to this business. The Ch D held that the finding against him appeared to be derived at least in part from this error, and quashed the Commissioners' determination. *Collins v Croydon Commrs & CIR*, Ch D 1969, 45 TC 566.

Proceedings for penalties—jurisdiction of Commissioners

[44.85] Following an investigation into a trader's returns, the Revenue took penalty proceedings under *TMA, s 95**. The trader appealed to the CA, contending that the proceedings were invalid because the Commissioner who had granted permission to raise the assessments was not authorised by *TMA, Sch 3**. The CA unanimously rejected this contention and dismissed the appeal, holding firstly that *Sch 3** did not apply to the proceedings in question, and furthermore that *Sch 3* was directory rather than mandatory. *CIR v Adams*, CA 1971, 48 TC 67. (*Note.* The provisions whereby the Revenue required a Commissioner's permission for certain assessments were consolidated into *TMA, s 41*. This was repealed by *FA 1989, s 149(2)* with effect from 27 July 1989, but still applies to assessments for 1982/83 and earlier years. Under *TMA, s 36*, the latest date for raising an assessment for 1982/83 was 31 January 2004.)

[44.86] The Revenue began penalty proceedings against a cattle dealer under *TMA, s 95*. The relevant income tax assessments had been settled but the surtax assessments remained open pending the outcome of *Knight v CIR*, **29.71** FURTHER ASSESSMENTS: LOSS OF TAX. At the hearing, the dealer objected to the jurisdiction of the Commissioners on the ground that, although he had resided in the Division in the relevant years, his trade (which had since ceased) had not been carried on in the Division. The Commissioners overruled the objection and the dealer applied for an order prohibiting the Commissioners from proceeding. The CA unanimously rejected the application. *R v Havering Commrs (ex p. Knight)*, CA 1973, 49 TC 161; [1973] STC 564; [1973] 3 All ER 721.

Whether penalties imposed affected by subsequent loss claim

[44.87] See *Khan v First East Brixton Commrs*, **43.86** PAYMENT OF TAX.

Penalties reduced on appeal

[44.88] The General Commissioners imposed penalties, mitigated by 30%, on an individual (W) whose returns had understated his profits. W appealed to the Ch D, contending that the proceedings before the Commissioners had not been conducted in a judicial manner. The Ch D rejected this contention but reduced the penalties from 70% to 40% of the statutory maximum. *Willey v CIR & East Dereham Commrs*, Ch D 1984, 59 TC 640; [1985] STC 56. (*Note.* W was ordered to pay 50% of the Revenue's costs.)

[44.89] General Commissioners imposed penalties of £10,000 on a doctor who had submitted several incorrect returns. The doctor appealed, contending that the amount imposed was excessive. The Ch D reduced the penalties by 20%. Scott J observed that the maximum penalty had been £10,300 and that the award seemed to be out of line with other reported cases such as *Willey v*

CIR & East Dereham Commrs, **44.88** above, where the Commissioners had discounted the maximum penalties by 30%, and *Lear v Leek Commrs*, **44.91** below, where the Commissioners had discounted the maximum penalties by 60%. Although some variation was inevitable, it was 'desirable that the penalties awarded by different panels of General Commissioners in different parts of the country should, in relation to similar cases, bear some resemblance to one another'. *Brodt v Wells Commrs*, Ch D 1987, 60 TC 436; [1987] STC 207.

[44.90] See also *Taylor v Bethnal Green Commrs & CIR*, **44.4** above, and *Coll & Coll v HMRC*, **71.206** CAPITAL GAINS TAX.

Penalties upheld on appeal

[44.91] General Commissioners imposed penalties of £1,500 (approximately 40% of the maximum) on a trader for incorrect returns. The trader appealed, contending that the amount imposed was excessive. The Ch D rejected this contention and dismissed the appeal. Vinelott J held that the court should only interfere with an award 'where the penalty was plainly disproportionate to any possible fault'. *Lear v Leek Commrs*, Ch D 1986, 59 TC 247; [1986] STC 542.

[44.92] Penalties in relation to returns or accounts imposed by Commissioners were upheld in the following cases, none of which appears to raise any general point of importance. *Turton v Birdforth Commrs*, Ch D 1970, 49 ATC 346; *Garnham v Haywards Heath Commrs*, Ch D 1977, [1978] TR 303; *Napier v Farnham Commrs*, CA [1978] TR 403; *Sweeney v Maidstone Commrs*, Ch D 1984, 60 TC 113; [1984] STC 334; *Jolley v Bolton Commrs & CIR*, Ch D 1986, 65 TC 242; [1986] STC 414; *Walsh v Croydon Commrs*, Ch D 1987, 60 TC 442; [1987] STC 456; *Montague v Hampstead Commrs & Others*, Ch D 1989, 63 TC 145; [1989] STC 818.

Determination of penalties by Special Commissioners

[44.93] In the case noted at **29.42** FURTHER ASSESSMENTS: LOSS OF TAX, the Special Commissioners upheld penalties which had been imposed at the rate of 80% of the tax lost, and the Ch D upheld their decision. *King v Walden (No 2)*, Ch D [2001] STC 822.

[44.94] An individual (C) did not submit his 1991/92 tax return until January 1996. The Revenue issued a determination under *TMA, s 100*, imposing a penalty of £5,160, calculated at the rate of 15% of the relevant tax. C appealed. The Special Commissioner upheld the penalty in principle, but reduced it to 10% of the relevant tax. The Commissioner referred to the published guidelines for mitigation set out in Revenue Pamphlet IR 73, and allowed mitigation of 20% for disclosure, 40% for co-operation and 30% for gravity. *Caesar v HM Inspector of Taxes*, Sp C 1997, [1998] SSCD 1 (Sp C 142).

[44.95] An individual (S) submitted incorrect returns for 1986/87 to 1997/98 inclusive. The Revenue imposed penalty determinations. The penalties were imposed at 65% of the relevant tax, allowing mitigation of 5% for disclosure, 15% for co-operation, and 15% for 'size and gravity'. S appealed, contending that the penalties were excessive. The Special Commissioner rejected this contention and dismissed the appeal, holding that 'the inspector's abatements seem entirely reasonable'. *Shaw v Thatcher*, Sp C 2002, [2003] SSCD 25 (Sp C 343).

[44.96] The Revenue imposed a penalty on a contractor (S) who had failed to declare rental income on his returns. The penalty was imposed at the rate of 30% of the tax lost. S appealed, contending that the penalty should be reduced to 15%. The Special Commissioner rejected this contention and dismissed the appeal, holding that the penalty had been 'fixed in a reasonable manner and in accordance with standard procedures', and that the abatement of 70% was 'fairly generous'. *MP Singh v HMRC*, Sp C [2008] SSCD 1055 (Sp C 697).

Determination of penalties by First-tier Tribunal

Penalty imposed at 65%

[44.97] HMRC began an enquiry into the returns submitted by a trader (E) who bought, refurbished and sold motor vehicles. They formed the opinion that E had significantly understated his profits, and issued amendments to his self-assessments and imposed penalties at the rate of 70% of the evaded tax (with abatements of 20% for seriousness and 10% for co-operation). E appealed. The First-tier Tribunal upheld the penalties in principle but reduced them to 65% of the evaded tax (with abatements of 30% for seriousness but only 5% for co-operation). *R Evans v HMRC*, FTT [2014] UKFTT 078 (TC), TC03218.

Penalty imposed at 60%

[44.98] HMRC formed the opinion that a trader (D) had underdeclared his profits and income from property. They issued discovery assessments and imposed penalties under *TMA, s 95*, at the rate of 60% of the evaded tax. The First-tier Tribunal slightly reduced the amount of the assessments but upheld the penalties, finding that D had 'deliberately destroyed primary records of the shop takings'. *DS Dosanjh v HMRC*, FTT [2014] UKFTT 973 (TC), TC04085.

Penalty imposed at 50%

[44.99] HMRC imposed penalties under *TMA, s 95* on a partnership which operated a nursing home, at the rate of 50% of the evaded tax. The First-tier Tribunal dismissed the partners' appeal, finding that the appropriate abatements were 30% for co-operation, 15% for size and gravity, and 5% for disclosure, so that the overall penalty of 50% was appropriate. *B Malhi & KJ Kaur v HMRC*, FTT [2011] UKFTT 220 (TC), TC01085.

[44.100] HMRC formed the opinion that a building contractor had significantly underdeclared his profits. They issued discovery assessments and imposed penalties under *TMA, s 95* at the rate of 50% of the evaded tax (giving abatements of 20% for co-operation, 20% for size and gravity, and 10% for disclosure. The First-tier Tribunal upheld the assessments and the penalties. *J Trodden v HMRC*, FTT [2012] UKFTT 413 (TC), TC02090.

[44.101] HMRC discovered that an individual (C) had failed to declare substantial amounts of interest arising from an Isle of Man bank account. They issued discovery assessments and imposed penalties at 50% of the evaded tax. The First-tier Tribunal dismissed C's appeal, finding that his evidence had been 'untruthful' and that 'his deliberate decision to exclude the Isle of Man interest from his returns was fraudulent'. Judge Barlow held that the reduction of the penalty to 50% was 'at least as generous as (C) could expect'. *A Corcoran v HMRC*, FTT [2014] UKFTT 104 (TC), TC03244.

[44.102] HMRC formed the opinion that a company director (D) had failed to declare benefits and had underdeclared other income. They issued assessments (and amendments to D's self-assessments), and imposed penalties at the rate of 50% of the tax allegedly evaded. D appealed. The First-tier Tribunal reviewed the evidence in detail and upheld the assessments in principle but reduced them in amount. The tribunal upheld the imposition of penalties at 50% in respect of the majority of the undeclared income and benefits (but directed that the penalty relating to the use of a motorboat should be reduced to 45% of the evaded tax, and that the penalty relating to the CGT due on the sale of a flat should be reduced to 35% of the evaded tax). *RWG Denny v HMRC (No 1)*, FTT [2013] UKFTT 309 (TC), TC02714.

[44.103] Following the decision noted at **44.102** above, the parties failed to agree figures, and at a subsequent hearing the tribunal upheld its original decision with regard to the penalties. *JM Williams (RWG Denny's Trustee in Bankruptcy) v HMRC (No 2)*, FTT [2014] UKFTT 200 (TC), TC03340.

[44.104] The wives of two company directors submitted returns claiming share loss relief under *ITA 2007, s 131*. HMRC began an enquiry and formed the opinion that the conditions of *ITA 2007, s 131* were not satisfied, because the company which had issued the shares had been restored to the register and there had been no loss of an asset within *TCGA 1992, s 24(1)*. HMRC also formed the opinion that the women had treated certain gross interest, which they had received from companies of which their husbands were directors, as if it had been received net of tax. They issued discovery assessments and imposed penalties under *TMA, s 95*, at the rate of 50% of the evaded tax (allowing abatements of 5% for disclosure, 20% for co-operation, and 25% for gravity). The First-tier Tribunal reviewed the evidence in detail and upheld the assessments and the penalties. Judge Redston held that the abatement for co-operation was 'generous' and that 'the appellants' negligence was serious, both in amount and by reason of the total lack of evidence supporting either the share loss relief claim or the tax deduction on the interest. Had the discovery assessments not been made, both appellants would have received repayments of over £30,000. Instead, the true position is that they owed over £30,000 of tax.' *Mrs R & Mrs S Thomas v HMRC*, FTT [2014] UKFTT 980 (TC), TC04092.

[44.105] A farmer (RH) had a Swiss bank account, which he had not declared to HMRC. In March 2009 he transferred this account, containing £443,669, to one of his sons (CH). RH died in October 2009, leaving the bulk of his estate to CH. RH's executors submitted a form IHT 400 which did not refer to any lifetime gifts. HMRC subsequently became aware of the account, issued a determination to CH charging IHT, and imposed a penalty on him under *FA 2007, Sch 24 para 1A*, at the rate of 50% of the potential lost revenue. CH appealed against the penalty, contending that RH's executors had not asked him about lifetime gifts. The First-tier Tribunal dismissed the appeal, finding that the executors had asked the beneficiaries about lifetime gifts, both at a meeting and in writing, and that CH had given 'inconsistent and incompatible explanations for his failure to disclose the account'. *C Hutchings v HMRC*, FTT [2015] UKFTT 0009 (TC), TC04221.

[44.106] See also *Easow v HMRC*, **29.10** FURTHER ASSESSMENTS: LOSS OF TAX.

Penalty imposed at 45%

[44.107] HMRC formed the opinion that a taxi driver (S) had underdeclared his profits. They issued an amendment to his 2005/06 return, issued discovery assessments covering four years, and imposed penalties at the rate of 45%. S appealed. The First-tier Tribunal dismissed his appeals, holding that there were no grounds for any further mitigation. *KM Sudhan v HMRC*, FTT [2011] UKFTT 78 (TC), TC00956.

[44.108] HMRC formed the opinion that a newsagent, who also sold confectionery and tobacco, had understated his profits. They issued amendments to his returns, and imposed penalties at 45%. The First-tier Tribunal dismissed the newsagent's appeals. Judge Shipwright observed that the penalties were 'considerably less than HMRC could have sought to levy'. *M Budi v HMRC*, FTT [2011] UKFTT 776 (TC), TC01610.

[44.109] HMRC imposed penalties for 1996/97 to 2003/04 under *TMA, s 95*, at the rate of 45% of the evaded tax, on an MC who had failed to maintain full records of his income. The First-tier Tribunal upheld the assessments and the penalties (but allowed appeals against estimated assessments for years before 1996/97). The MC appealed to the Upper Tribunal, which dismissed his appeal, holding that there was 'no basis to disturb the Tribunal's decision'. *C Reid v HMRC*, UT [2012] UKUT 338 (TCC); [2013] STC 959. (*Note*. The CA dismissed an application for leave to appeal against this decision—CA [2014] EWCA Civ 236.)

[44.110] HMRC discovered that two associated companies had failed to declare all the payments which they had made to directors and employees. They imposed penalties at the rate of 45% of the evaded tax. The companies appealed. The First-tier Tribunal upheld the penalties, finding that the companies' director was 'not a credible witness' and that 'both companies failed to keep proper records and this amounted to more than mere carelessness'. Judge King held that the abatements made by HMRC were generous and that a penalty of 45% was appropriate. *St Peters Travel Ltd v HMRC (and related appeal)*, FTT [2011] UKFTT 422 (TC), TC01275.

[44.111] HMRC formed the opinion that a newsagent, who also sold confectionery and tobacco, had understated his profits. They issued discovery assessments, and imposed penalties under *TMA, s 95* at the rate of 65% of the evaded tax. The First-tier Tribunal upheld the assessments but reduced the penalties from 65% to 45% of the evaded tax. Judge Clark held that the appropriate abatements were 15% for disclosure, 20% for co-operation, and 20% for seriousness. *AH Chowdhury v HMRC*, FTT [2012] UKFTT 630 (TC), TC02306.

[44.112] Following an enquiry, HMRC formed the opinion that a civil engineer had underdeclared his income by more than £70,000. They issued an amendment to his self-assessment, and imposed a penalty under *TMA, s 95*, at the rate of 60% of the evaded tax. The First-tier Tribunal upheld the penalty in principle but directed that it should be reduced to 45% of the evaded tax. Judge Tildesley observed that 'the Tribunal is entitled to take an overall view of the appropriate penalty, and not obliged to follow HMRC's approach of giving abatements for various categories of conduct'. *Dr J Kohal v HMRC*, FTT [2013] UKFTT 487 (TC), TC02870.

Penalty imposed at 40.75%

[44.113] HMRC formed the opinion that a restaurant proprietor had significantly understated his profits. They issued discovery assessments and imposed penalties under *FA 2007, Sch 24*, at the rate of 40.75% of the potential lost revenue. The First-tier Tribunal slightly reduced the amount of the assessments but upheld the penalties, holding that there was 'no reason to disturb the percentage rates calculated by HMRC'. *KM Pang v HMRC*, FTT [2014] UKFTT 964 (TC), TC04076.

Penalty imposed at 40%

[44.114] HMRC formed the opinion that a family partnership, which operated a general grocery store, had underdeclared its income for many years. They issued amendments to the partnership profits for the years 1996/97 to 2004/05 inclusive. They also imposed penalties on the partners, at the rate of 40% of the evaded tax. The partners appealed. The First-tier Tribunal reviewed the evidence in detail and dismissed the appeals, holding that the penalty of 40% was 'appropriate'. *Seafield General Store & Post Office v HMRC*, FTT [2010] UKFTT 18 (TC), TC00333.

[44.115] HMRC formed the opinion that a self-employed salesman (H) had underdeclared his income for several years. They issued assessments and imposed penalties under *TMA, s 95*, at the rate of 40% of the evaded tax. H appealed. The tribunal dismissed his appeal, holding that 'the 60% reduction of the penalty is appropriate in the circumstances'. *WC Harbron v HMRC*, FTT [2010] UKFTT 127 (TC), TC00438.

[44.116] A former tax inspector (E) was appointed as Clerk to three divisions of the General Commissioners. In his returns, he claimed significant deductions for travelling and secretarial assistance (provided by his wife). In 2005 HMRC began an investigation into his returns, and formed the opinion that E had significantly overstated his expenses. They issued discovery assessments under *TMA, s 29* and imposed penalties under *TMA, s 95*, at the rate of 35% of the evaded tax. E appealed. the First-tier Tribunal reviewed the evidence in detail and observed that E had failed to produce documentary records and 'surprisingly, given his background, did not co-operate fully with the enquiry'. The Tribunal held that, despite E's failure to discharge 'the burden of proof on him in relation to the figures', he should be allowed a deduction of £500pa for travel expenses and of £11,000pa for secretarial assistance (both figures being slightly higher than those conceded by HMRC). With regard to the penalty, the Tribunal held that E had been negligent and that 'the abatement given in relation to co-operation is generous'. Accordingly the Tribunal directed that the penalty should be increased to 40% of the evaded tax. *J Evans v HMRC*, FTT [2010] UKFTT 140 (TC), TC00446.

[44.117] HMRC imposed penalties under *TMA, s 95* on a trader who had submitted accounts and returns which understated her profits. The penalties were imposed at 40% of the evaded tax. The First-tier Tribunal dismissed the trader's appeal, finding that 'this abatement is generous' and that 'HMRC would have been justified in making a significantly smaller abatement than 60%'. *KD Agnihotri v HMRC*, FTT [2010] UKFTT 230 (TC), TC00531.

[44.118] HMRC imposed a penalty, at the rate of 40% of the evaded tax, on the proprietor of a kebab shop who had underdeclared his profits. The First-Tier Tribunal upheld the penalty. Judge King held that 'the imposition of tax-geared penalties at 40% is appropriate on these amounts of tax'. *H Hassan v HMRC*, FTT [2012] UKFTT 222 (TC), TC01917.

[44.119] HMRC imposed a penalty, at 40% of the evaded tax, on the proprietor of a kiosk selling confectionery at an underground station. The First-tier Tribunal upheld the penalty. *M Khagram v HMRC*, FTT [2012] UKFTT 494 (TC), TC02171.

[44.120] HMRC imposed a penalty, at 40% of the evaded tax, on a woman who failed to declare profits from sales of cars on her return. The First-tier Tribunal upheld the penalty. Judge Walters observed that the abatement given by HMRC was 'generous rather than harsh'. *Mrs L Hurd v HMRC*, FTT [2013] UKFTT 414 (TC), TC02808.

[44.121] HMRC began an investigation into a trader (S) who had bought and sold plant and machinery, and had opened a Guernsey bank account, which he disclosed in 2007. They issued discovery assessments, and imposed penalties at the rate of 40% in respect of underdeclared trading profits, and at 25% in respect of underdeclared bank interest. S appealed. The First-tier Tribunal reviewed the evidence in detail and dismissed the appeals (apart from reducing the assessment for 2001/02), finding that the penalty rates imposed by HMRC were 'appropriate'. *JR Swanston v HMRC*, FTT [2014] UKFTT 210 (TC), TC03350.

[44.122] HMRC formed the opinion that a bookmaker (B) had significantly underdeclared his profits. They issued discovery assessments, and imposed penalties at the rate of 50% (giving abatements of 10% for disclosure, 20% for co-operation and 20% for seriousness). The First-tier Tribunal upheld the assessments and penalties in principle, but directed that the penalties should be imposed at the rate of 40% rather than 50% (increasing the abatement for co-operation to 30%). *R Brown v HMRC*, FTT [2014] UKFTT 302 (TC), TC03439.

[44.123] HMRC formed the opinion that a woman (M), who traded via the internet, had underdeclared her income and had overclaimed expenses. They imposed a penalty under *TMA, s 95*, at the rate of 40% of the evaded tax. The First-tier Tribunal dismissed M's appeal, holding that she had been negligent. *Mrs CG Martin v HMRC*, FTT [2014] UKFTT 1021 (TC), TC04117.

[44.124] HMRC formed the opinion that a mortgage broker and landlord had substantially underdeclared his income. They issued discovery assessments and amendments to his self-assessments, and imposed penalties under *TMA, s 95*, at the rate of 40% of the evaded tax. The First-tier Tribunal upheld the assessments, amendments and penalties. *I Osbourne v HMRC*, FTT [2015] UKFTT 0003 (TC), TC04215.

Penalty imposed at 35%

[44.125] HMRC imposed penalties under *TMA, s 95* on a trader who had failed to declare commission income from financial transactions. The penalties were imposed at 35% of the evaded tax. The First-tier Tribunal upheld the penalties and dismissed the trader's appeal. *AH Moosa v HMRC*, FTT [2010] UKFTT 248 (TC), TC00543.

[44.126] HMRC imposed a penalty, at the rate of 40% of the evaded tax, on a trader who had underdeclared his profits. The First-tier Tribunal upheld the penalty in principle but reduced it to 35% of the evaded tax. *R Mysliwek v HMRC*, FTT [2011] UKFTT 550 (TC), TC01395.

[44.127] HMRC formed the opinion that a subcontractor (K) had underdeclared his profits by substantially over stating his expenses. They issued assessments and imposed penalties at the rate of 35% of the evaded tax. The First-tier Tribunal dismissed K's appeal, finding that K 'had no reasonable basis on which to make the claims' and had acted negligently, and holding that '35% of the tax due is a reasonable and proportionate amount'. *G Kay v HMRC*, FTT [2012] UKFTT 255 (TC), TC01948.

[44.128] The First-tier Tribunal reached a similar decision in a case where it found that a partnership had persistently overclaimed expenses. *KLS Electrical Contracting v HMRC*, FTT [2015] UKFTT 0004 (TC), TC04216.

[44.129] HMRC imposed a penalty, at the rate of 35% of the evaded tax, on a taxi driver (L) who had understated his income. The First-tier Tribunal upheld the penalty, finding that L 'was not credible' and had been 'irresponsible'. *R Larkin v HMRC*, [2012] UKFTT 401 (TC), TC02096.

[44.130] HMRC imposed penalties, at the rate of 35% of the evaded tax, on a doctor (S) who practised as a weight loss consultant, and had failed to keep adequate business records. The First-tier Tribunal dismissed the doctor's appeals. Judge Aleksander found that S 'must have known that the amount of taxable income shown on the return was less than her actual income', and held that HMRC had been generous in only imposing penalties at 35%. *Dr BR Subbrayan (t/a Swiss Cottage Diet Clinic) v HMRC*, FTT [2013] UKFTT 161 (TC), TC02577.

[44.131] HMRC discovered that a trader (G) had failed to declare a gain from a sale of land. They issued an amendment and imposed a penalty at the rate of 35% of the evaded tax. The First-tier Tribunal dismissed G's appeal. Judge Barlow held that the reduction of 65% was 'generous in the circumstances'. *B Gabriel v HMRC*, FTT [2014] UKFTT 105 (TC), TC03245.

[44.132] HMRC formed the opinion that a window cleaner (G) had underdeclared his profits. They issued assessments and imposed penalties at the rate of 35% of the evaded tax. The First-tier Tribunal dismissed G's appeal. Judge Connell held that 'the penalty has been assessed entirely in line with the legislation which ensures that the amount of a penalty is proportionate to the inaccuracy'. *W Green v HMRC*, FTT [2014] UKFTT 259 (TC), TC03398.

[44.133] In the case noted at **71.306** CAPITAL GAINS TAX, the First-tier Tribunal had upheld two CGT assessments on a company director (R) who had failed to declare gains on the disposal of shares. HMRC also imposed penalties under *TMA, s 95*. At a subsequent hearing, the First-tier Tribunal dismissed R's appeal against the penalties. *John Regan v HMRC (No 2)*, FTT [2014] UKFTT 390 (TC), TC03523.

[44.134] HMRC discovered that a partnership had failed to deduct PAYE or NIC from three employees. They imposed penalties under *FA 2007, Sch 24*, at the rate of 35% of the tax and NIC due. The First-tier Tribunal dismissed the partnership's appeal, describing the reduction to 35% as 'being generous to the appellant'. *S Ahmed & J Iqbal (t/a Al Badar) v HMRC*, FTT [2014] UKFTT 919 (TC), TC04033.

[44.135] See also *Khawaja v HMRC (No 2)*, **44.191** below.

Penalty imposed at 30.6%

[44.136] In the case noted at **71.18** CAPITAL GAINS TAX, the First-tier Tribunal upheld a CGT assessment on a property developer who had failed to declare a substantial gain on a disposal of shares. HMRC had issued an assessment charging tax of £744,000, and imposed a penalty of 35% of this amount – ie £260,400. The tribunal subsequently determined that the tax due had been £849,449, and increased the assessment accordingly. The tribunal upheld the penalty in its original amount, equating to about 30.6% of the tax due. Judge Bishopp held that the tribunal should be 'reluctant to increase penalties save in clear cases'. *OI Iny v HMRC (No 2)*, FTT [2012] UKFTT 540 (TC), TC02216.

Penalty imposed at 30%

[44.137] In the case noted at **46.24** PENSION SCHEMES, HMRC imposed a penalty, mitigated by 70%, on a financial adviser who had failed to declare an unauthorised pension fund transfer on his tax return. The First-tier Tribunal upheld the penalty. Judge Mosedale observed that HMRC had been 'generous' in mitigating it by 70%. *BJ Kent v HMRC*, FTT [2009] UKFTT 358 (TC), TC00296.

[44.138] HMRC imposed a penalty, at the rate of 30% of the maximum chargeable, on an individual (K) who had made an incorrect claim to gift aid relief. The First-tier Tribunal upheld the penalty and dismissed K's appeal. *V Karnani v HMRC*, FTT [2011] UKFTT 627 (TC), TC01469.

[44.139] A builder (F) had entered into a joint venture agreement with another individual (C). F submitted a return in which he claimed a deduction for a payment of £40,000 to a friend of C, which he described as interest. HMRC formed the opinion that the £40,000 was not a payment of interest, but was a distribution of partnership profits. They issued an amendment to F's self-assessment and imposed a penalty at the rate of 30% of the potential lost revenue. The First-tier Tribunal dismissed F's appeals, finding that his return had been negligent. *TA Fraser v HMRC*, FTT [2012] UKFTT 350 (TC), TC02036.

[44.140] An individual (S) disposed of two flats, but failed to declare the gains on his tax return. When HMRC discovered this, they issued an assessment under *TMA, s 29* and imposed a penalty, at 70% of the culpable tax. S appealed against the penalty, contending that he had relied on his accountant (M). Judge Geraint Jones reviewed the evidence in detail and found that M was not 'a satisfactory or reliable witness' and that he knew 'that the appellant has not resided in either flat for any period of time whatsoever'. If M had told S that no CGT was due on the sale of the flats, such advice 'was obviously wrong' and S 'ought to have realised that it was obviously wrong or so potentially obviously wrong that it called for further explanation or justification'. However, since S had 'been ill served by his professional adviser', the penalty should be reduced to 30%. *W Shakoor v HMRC*, FTT [2012] UKFTT 532 (TC); [2012] SFTD 1391, TC02208.

[44.141] HMRC discovered that a market trader (P) had failed to disclose small amounts of income from four different employers. They imposed a penalty at the rate of 30% of the potential lost revenue. The First-tier Tribunal dismissed P's appeal. Judge Connell held that 'the penalty has been assessed entirely in line with the legislation which ensures that the amount of a penalty is proportionate to the inaccuracy'. *F Pirzada v HMRC*, FTT [2014] UKFTT 260 (TC), TC03399.

[44.142] Penalties at the rate of 30% of the evaded tax were also upheld in *Woods v HMRC*, **10.25** CLAIMS TO RELIEF OR REPAYMENT, where the appellant had made a false claim to rent-a-room relief.

Penalty imposed at 25%

[44.143] HMRC imposed a penalty under *FA 1998, Sch 18, para 20* on a company which operated a pharmacy, and had underdeclared its profits. The penalty was computed at the rate of 25% of the evaded tax. The company appealed to the First-tier Tribunal. At the hearing, HMRC indicated that they were willing to reduce the penalty to 20% of the evaded tax. The tribunal reviewed the evidence in detail and held that 'a 25% penalty is appropriate'. Judge Mosedale observed that *TMA, s 100B* gave the tribunal the power to increase the penalty. *Soka Blackmore Ltd v HMRC*, FTT [2010] UKFTT 161 (TC), TC00466.

[44.144] HMRC imposed penalties under *TMA, s 95* on an individual (M) who had underdeclared bank interest. The penalties were imposed at the rate of 55% of the evaded tax. The First-tier Tribunal upheld the penalties in principle, finding that M had been negligent, but reduced the penalties to 25% of the evaded tax. The Upper Tribunal dismissed M's appeal against this decision. *C Moore v HMRC*, UT [2011] UKUT 239 (TCC); [2011] STC 1784.

[44.145] HMRC formed the opinion that a plumber had understated his trading profits. They amended his self-assessments and imposed penalties under *TMA, s 95*, at the rate of 25% of the evaded tax. The First-tier Tribunal dismissed the plumber's appeals. *A Goudie v HMRC*, FTT [2010] UKFTT 552 (TC), TC00805.

[44.146] A woman (L) inherited a house in 2000 and let it to tenants until 2004, when she sold it. HMRC formed the opinion that she had underdeclared her rental income, and imposed penalties under *TMA, s 95*, at the rate of 25% of the evaded tax. The First-tier Tribunal dismissed L's appeal, finding that she had failed to keep the records required by *TMA, s 12B*. *Mrs S Larkin v HMRC*, FTT [2012] UKFTT 293 (TC), TC01981.

[44.147] A company (C) had acquired four properties from its principal director (S). It disposed of one of the properties in the year ending 31 May 2007. In its return, it claimed that it had incurred expenditure of £360,000 on improving the properties, so that it had incurred a loss on the disposal. HMRC formed the opinion that the claim was fraudulent, and imposed a penalty at the rate of 25% of the evaded tax. The First-tier Tribunal dismissed C's appeal, finding that 'the claim was indeed fraudulent'. Judge Nowlan expressed the view that the mitigation had been excessive, but declined to 'disturb the quantum of the penalty', as S was in poor health. *Clarisa Ltd v HMRC (and related appeals)*, FTT [2014] UKFTT 778 (TC), TC03896. (*Note*. The tribunal also upheld assessments on S and his wife in respect of private use of a car owned by C.)

[44.148] The First-tier Tribunal upheld penalties under *TMA, s 95*, at the rate of 25% of the evaded tax, in *E Freeman v HMRC*, FTT [2013] UKFTT 608 (TC), TC02995.

Penalty imposed at 20%

[44.149] HMRC imposed a penalty under *TMA, s 95*, at the rate of 20% of the evaded tax, on a taxi driver who had understated his profits. The First-tier Tribunal upheld the penalty and dismissed the driver's appeal. *A Majid v HMRC*, FTT [2010] UKFTT 459 (TC), TC00724.

[44.150] HMRC formed the opinion that a dentist had underdeclared his profits. They issued discovery assessments under *TMA, s 29*, and imposed penalties under *TMA, s 95*, at the rate of 20% of the evaded tax. The First-tier Tribunal upheld the assessments and penalties, and dismissed the dentist's appeals. *Dr I Syed v HMRC*, FTT [2011] UKFTT 315 (TC), TC01176.

[44.151] HMRC formed the opinion that a couple who operated a taxi rental business had underdeclared their profits. They issued discovery assessments under *TMA, s 29* covering the years 1998/99 to 2005/06 inclusive, and imposed penalties at the rate of 40% of the tax allegedly evaded. The First-tier Tribunal reviewed the evidence in detail, upheld the assessments for 1998/99 to 2002/03 inclusive in reduced amounts, allowed the appeals for 2003/04 to 2005/06 inclusive, and reduced the penalties to 20% of the evaded tax. *KS & PK Duhra v HMRC*, FTT [2011] UKFTT 322 (TC), TC01182.

[44.152] HMRC formed the opinion that an electrical contractor (F) had underdeclared his profits. They issued assessments and imposed penalties at the rate of 30% of the tax allegedly evaded. The First-Tier Tribunal reviewed the evidence in detail and upheld the assessments but reduced the penalties to 20% of the amounts allegedly evaded. *S Farid v HMRC*, FTT [2012] UKFTT 268 (TC), TC01961.

[44.153] HMRC formed the opinion that a company director (R) had acted negligently in failing to declare various benefits on his tax returns. They issued discovery assessments, and imposed penalties at the rate of 35% of the tax due. R appealed. The First-tier Tribunal upheld the assessments in principle, finding that R had been negligent and had failed to declare car and fuel benefits, the transfer of a Mercedes and a Volvo at an undervalue, and a beneficial loan. However the Tribunal reduced the amount of the penalties from 35% to 20% of the tax due. With regard to the beneficial loan, the Tribunal found that R had not been negligent in failing to declare this for 2004/05, but that he had been negligent in failing to declare this for 2005/06. The Tribunal held that there should be abatements of 20% for disclosure, 40% for co-operation and 20% for seriousness. *R Rhodes v HMRC (and related appeal)*, FTT [2013] UKFTT 431 (TC), TC02825. (*Note.* The Tribunal also upheld a penalty of 20% on the company of which R was a director, which had failed to declare liability under what is now *CTA 2010, s 455*, but allowed the company's appeal against a decision under *SSCTFA 1999, s 8* for 2000/01 to 2003/04, holding that it had been issued outside the statutory time limit.)

[44.154] In 2001 an employee (S) acquired 250 shares in his employer (G). In 2006 G was taken over by a consortium. S surrendered the shares to G, receiving payment of £382,748, from which G deducted PAYE. In his 2006/07 tax return, S claimed a refund of the tax deducted under PAYE. Following an enquiry, HMRC rejected S's claim for a refund and imposed a penalty under *TMA, s 95*, at the rate of 20% of the potential lost revenue. S appealed. The First-tier Tribunal dismissed S's appeal, holding that the sale of the shares was liable to income tax under *ITEPA 2003, s 423*, and that S had acted negligently when submitting his return claiming a repayment. *P Stratton v HMRC*, FTT [2013] UKFTT 578 (TC), TC02967.

[44.155] HMRC discovered that an individual had failed to declare a gain on the sale of a property. They issued an assessment charging tax on the gain, and imposed a penalty at the rate of 20%. The First-tier Tribunal upheld both the assessment (in a slightly reduced amount) and the penalty. *L Meikle v HMRC*, FTT [2014] UKFTT 941 (TC), TC04054.

Penalty imposed at 18.75%

[44.156] HMRC discovered that an employee had underdeclared his income, and formed the opinion that he had overclaimed expenses relating to his employment. They imposed a penalty, calculated at the rate of 18.75% of the potential lost revenue. The First-tier Tribunal dismissed the employee's appeal, finding that he had been careless in understating his income and had 'failed to explain how individual purchases were incurred wholly, exclusively and necessarily in the performance of the duties of his employment'. *P Anghel v HMRC*, FTT [2014] UKFTT 689 (TC), TC03809.

Penalty imposed at 15.75%

[44.157] HMRC discovered that a company (E) had overlooked the requirements of *CTA 2009, s 931W*, and had overclaimed loss relief as a result. They imposed a penalty under *FA 2007, Sch 24*, at the rate of 15.75% of the potential lost revenue. The First-tier Tribunal dismissed E's appeal. Judge Clark held that 'it would not be appropriate to suspend the penalties'. *Elsina Ltd v HMRC*, FTT [2015] UKFTT 0014 (TC), TC04226.

Penalty imposed at 15%

[44.158] On his 2008/09 tax return, an employee (F) overstated the amount of tax deducted by his previous employer. HMRC imposed a penalty under *FA 2007, Sch 24*, at the rate of 15% of the evaded tax. The First-tier Tribunal dismissed F's appeal, holding that F had been 'careless' and that there were no grounds for suspending the penalty under *Sch 24 para 14*. *A Fane v HMRC*, FTT [2011] UKFTT 210 (TC), TC01075.

[44.159] The decision in *Fane*, **44.158** above, was applied in the similar subsequent cases of *JPL Cobb v HMRC*, FTT [2012] UKFTT 40 (TC), TC01738; *Mrs B Hackett v HMRC*, FTT [2012] UKFTT 122 (TC), TC01817, and *R Summersell v HMRC*, FTT [2013] UKFTT 47 (TC), TC02467.

[44.160] HMRC formed the opinion that a trader (C) who owned a garden centre, and also received rental income from several properties, had underdeclared his income. They issued amendments to C's returns, and imposed penalties under *TMA, s 95*, at the rate of 40% of the evaded tax. The First-tier Tribunal held that C had been negligent, finding that he 'was disorganised and simply failed to discharge the burden of showing us how he financed the apparent cash shortfall'. However, the tribunal reduced the penalties to 15% of the evaded tax (allowing abatements of 20% for disclosure, 30% for co-operation and 35% for seriousness). *G Carter v HMRC (No 2)*, FTT [2013] UKFTT 247 (TC), TC02661.

[44.161] A woman (S) had carried on business as a camera operator, but transferred her business to a limited company (H) in 2008. Following an enquiry, HMRC formed the opinion that S's tax return for 2007/08 had understated her income and overclaimed her expenses (including a claim for membership of a gym). They imposed a penalty under *TMA, s 95*, at the rate of 15% of the evaded tax. S appealed, accepting that some of her income had been incorrectly credited to H, but contending that her inaccuracies were attributable to her accountants. The First-tier Tribunal dismissed her appeal. Judge Walters held that S 'should have noticed, and queried, and rejected, a reallocation of almost £30,000 of turnover (two-thirds of the total) from her sole trader activity in that year to a limited company acquired by her midway through the following tax year'. He also held that HMRC had acted reasonably by imposing the penalty at 15%. *Ms H Sheard v HMRC*, FTT [2014] UKFTT 913 (TC), TC04027. (*Notes*. (1) Appeals against smaller penalties under *FA 2007, Sch 24*, for 2008/09 and 2009/10, were also dismissed. (2) For proceedings involving S's accountants, see *R (oao Lunn) v HMRC*, **50.42** REVENUE ADMINISTRATION.)

[44.162] HMRC formed the opinion that a doctor (M) had overclaimed expenses and had failed to declare income from overseas. They issued amendments to M's self-assessments, and imposed penalties at the rate of 15% of the potential lost revenue. The First-tier Tribunal dismissed M's appeals against the amendments and the penalties. *Dr S Madhusudhan v HMRC*, FTT [2014] UKFTT 996 (TC), TC04099.

[44.163] HMRC imposed a penalty, at the rate of 15% of the evaded tax, on an employee (C) who had failed to declare benefits in kind on his return. The

Tribunal upheld the penalty, observing that C's employer had given him a form P11D setting out the benefits in question. *D Collis v HMRC*, FTT [2011] UKFTT 588 (TC), TC01431.

[44.164] A similar decision was reached in *C Rayburn v HMRC*, FTT [2014] UKFTT 968 (TC), TC04080.

[44.165] A bank employee (V) failed to declare various items of income from his current and previous employer on his 2008/09 return. When HMRC discovered this, they imposed a penalty under *FA 2007, Sch 24*, at the rate of 15% of the potential lost revenue. V appealed, contending that the penalty contravened the *European Convention on Human Rights*. The First-tier Tribunal rejected this contention and dismissed the appeal. *S Verma v HMRC*, FTT [2011] UKFTT 737 (TC), TC01574.

[44.166] A woman (H) who had received a bonus payment from a previous employer failed to declare this on her tax return. When HMRC discovered this, they imposed a penalty under *FA 2007, Sch 24*, at the rate of 15% of the potential lost revenue. The First-tier Tribunal upheld the penalty and dismissed H's appeal. *Ms R Hook v HMRC*, FTT [2011] UKFTT 739 (TC), TC01576.

[44.167] A similar decision was reached in *Ms J Ashton v HMRC*, FTT [2013] UKFTT 140 (TC), TC02538.

[44.168] An employee (P) had three different employers during 2008/09, one of whom failed to deduct tax from his earnings. In his 2008/09 return, P overstated the total amount of tax deducted from his earnings. When HMRC discovered this, they imposed a penalty under *FA 2007, Sch 24*, at the rate of 15% of the potential lost revenue. The First-tier Tribunal upheld the penalty and dismissed P's appeal. *D Parker v HMRC*, FTT [2011] UKFTT 829 (TC), TC01665.

[44.169] An employee (M) changed jobs at the end of September 2009. On his 2009/10 tax return, he only declared his income from the second employer, and only declared his benefits from his first employer. When HMRC discovered this, they imposed a penalty under *FA 2007, Sch 24*, at the rate of 15% of the potential lost revenue. The First-tier Tribunal upheld the penalty and dismissed M's appeal. *S McHale v HMRC*, FTT [2012] UKFTT 664 (TC), TC02335.

[44.170] An employee (H) was made redundant in 2008. He received a redundancy payment of £329,415, which he failed to disclose on his tax return. When HMRC discovered this, they imposed a penalty at the rate of 15% of the potential lost revenue. The First-tier Tribunal upheld the penalty and dismissed H's appeal. *M Hearn v HMRC*, FTT [2012] UKFTT 782 (TC), TC02433.

[44.171] A married couple controlled a small engineering company: the husband was the managing director while his wife was the company secretary. HMRC formed the opinion that the company had underdeclared profits which the couple had extracted from the business. They issued assessments and imposed penalties at the rate of 15% of the evaded tax. The company appealed. The First-tier Tribunal reviewed the evidence in detail and dismissed the appeal. Judge King observed that 'it is clear from the cases that a default by directors can and should be assessed to tax in a company'. *TSD Design Development Engineering Ltd v HMRC*, FTT [2012] UKFTT 247 (TC), TC01941.

[44.172] A large accountancy firm terminated the contract of one of its employees (H), and paid him an ex gratia severance payment of £109,793. H failed to declare this on his tax return. When HMRC discovered this, they issued an amendment to H's self-assessment and also imposed a penalty under *FA 2007, Sch 24*, at the rate of 15% of the potential lost revenue. H appealed against the penalty, contending that he had had reasonable grounds for believing that the payment was not taxable. The First-tier Tribunal rejected this contention and dismissed his appeal, and the Upper Tribunal upheld this decision, observing that 'the notes accompanying his Short Tax Return should have prompted him to make a full self-assessment return to include the payment or at least indicate that he had received a payment, but that he did not consider it was liable to tax'. *T Harding v HMRC*, UT [2013] UKUT 575 (TCC); [2014] STC 891.

Penalty imposed at 11.25%

[44.173] In 2009 a company (N) made a payment of £25,000, described as a loan, to a new employee (B). In 2011 N wrote off the loan, and included this as a taxable benefit on B's P11D. However B failed to declare this on his tax return. When HMRC discovered this, they imposed a penalty under *FA 2007, Sch 24*, at the rate of 15% of the potential lost revenue. B appealed. The First-tier Tribunal allowed his appeal in part, holding that there were no grounds for suspending the penalty, but that there were special circumstances within *Sch 24 para 11*, and that the amount of the penalty should be reduced by 25% (ie to 11.25% of the potential lost revenue). *F Berrier v HMRC*, FTT [2014] UKFTT 457 (TC), TC03584. (*Note*. Judge Aleksander also found that the accountant who represented B at the hearing had acted unreasonably by misleading the tribunal, and gave HMRC leave to apply for an award of costs.)

Penalty imposed at 10%

[44.174] An employee (E) submitted tax returns claiming expenses amounting to 40% of his income. HMRC formed the opinion that this was grossly excessive, and imposed penalties under *TMA, s 95*, at the rate of 10% of the evaded tax. The First-tier Tribunal upheld the penalties. Judge Hellier observed that 'the expenses claimed in (E's) return were not merely a little wrong but clearly excessive. To claim so much more than is allowable is not something a reasonable man would have done. The return was delivered negligently.' *E Eze v HMRC*, FTT [2010] UKFTT 610 (TC), TC00851.

[44.175] A university paid one of its employees (W) relocation expenses of £14,617. £8,000 of this was exempt from tax under *ITEPA 2003* but the remaining £6,617 was taxable. W failed to include this on his tax return. When HMRC discovered this, they imposed a penalty under *TMA, s 95*, at the rate of 10% of the evaded tax. W appealed. The First-tier Tribunal dismissed his appeal, finding that W had been negligent and that the amount of the penalty was reasonable. *D Wald v HMRC*, FTT [2011] UKFTT 183 (TC), TC01052.

[44.176] In 2004/05 an individual (L) disposed of some shares, incurring a CGT liability. He entered into a capital redemption scheme, similar to that used in *Drummond v HMRC*, **71.84** CAPITAL GAINS TAX, which was designed to incur a tax loss which could be set against this liability, but which the CA subsequently ruled was ineffective. HMRC imposed a penalty at the rate of 25% of the tax due, and L appealed. The First-tier Tribunal directed that the penalty should be reduced to 10% of the tax due (allowing abatements of 20% for disclosure, 40% for co-operation, and 30% for seriousness). *BP Litman v HMRC (and related appeal)*, FTT [2014] UKFTT 089 (TC), TC03229.

Penalty imposed at 7.5%

[44.177] In his 2008/09 tax return, an employee (D) only declared his employment income from his current employer, and failed to declare his employment income from a previous employer. His return claimed a repayment of tax of £4,184, whereas he had actually underpaid tax of £503. When HMRC discovered this, they imposed a penalty under *FA 2007, Sch 24*, at the rate of 15% of the difference. The First-tier Tribunal upheld the penalty in principle but reduced it to 7.5% of the difference (ie from £703 to £351). *G Davis v HMRC*, FTT [2011] UKFTT 391 (TC), TC01246.

[44.178] A woman (R) was made redundant in 2008, and received a redundancy payment of £194.748. She failed to declare this on her 2008/09 tax return, and HMRC imposed a penalty under *FA 2007, Sch 24*, at the rate of 15% of the potential lost revenue. The First-tier Tribunal upheld the penalty in principle, finding that R had been careless, but reduced it to 7.5% of the potential lost revenue. *Ms S Roche v HMRC*, FTT [2012] UKFTT 333 (TC), TC02019.

Penalty imposed at 6%

[44.179] A woman (W) was made redundant in 2009, and received a redundancy payment of £53,988. She failed to declare this on her 2009/10 tax return, and HMRC imposed a penalty under *FA 2007, Sch 24*, at the rate of 15% of the potential lost revenue. The First-tier Tribunal upheld the penalty in principle, finding that W had been careless, but reduced it to 6% of the potential lost revenue. *Ms PB White v HMRC*, FTT [2012] UKFTT 364 (TC), TC02050.

Penalty imposed at 2.5%

[44.180] A bank made one of its employees (H) redundant in July 2008. He received two redundancy payments, totalling more than £1,000,000, in October and December 2008. He failed to declare these payments on his 2008/09 tax return. HMRC imposed a penalty at the rate of 15% of the evaded tax. The First-tier Tribunal upheld the penalty in principle, finding that H had been careless, but reduced the penalty to 2.5% of the evaded tax. *T Hardy v HMRC*, FTT [2011] UKFTT 592 (TC), TC01435.

Penalty suspended by First-Tier Tribunal

[44.181] In his 2008/09 tax return, an individual (B) wrongly claimed an exemption of £30,000 in respect of a redundancy payment. HMRC imposed a penalty at the rate of 15% of the potential lost revenue. B appealed, asking for the penalty to be suspended. HMRC rejected this request but Judge Geraint Jones issued a direction under *FA 2007, Sch 24 para 17(4)* that the penalty should be suspended for two years, on the condition that B's returns were completed and certified by a chartered or certified accountant. *P Boughey v HMRC*, FTT [2012] UKFTT 398 (TC), TC02082.

[44.182] Judge Poole reached a similar decision in *D Testa v HMRC*, FTT [2013] UKFTT 151 (TC); [2013] SFTD 723, TC02549.

Tax avoidance scheme—whether appellants negligent

[44.183] A married couple and their son entered into a marketed tax avoidance scheme, of the type which was subsequently held to be ineffective in *Drummond v HMRC*, **71.84** CAPITAL GAINS TAX, in an attempt to avoid CGT liability on the disposal of shares. HMRC imposed penalties under *TMA, s 95*, but the First-tier Tribunal allowed their appeal, holding that HMRC had not shown that they had acted negligently. *R Gardiner v HMRC (and related appeals)*, FTT [2014] UKFTT 421 (TC), TC03550.

Whether online return incomplete

[44.184] HMRC imposed a penalty under *FA 2007, Sch 24* on the basis that an employee (B) had failed to declare his employment income on his tax return. B appealed, contending that he had included this income in his online return and it appeared that HMRC's computer had failed to capture the data correctly. The First-tier Tribunal accepted this contention and allowed B's appeal, finding on the balance of probabilities that B had submitted these details. *A Banks v HMRC*, FTT [2014] UKFTT 465 (TC), TC03592.

Penalties—relevant assessments dealt with by different Commissioners

[44.185] The West Brixton Commissioners imposed penalties under *TMA, s 95(1)* for incorrect returns. The relevant assessments had been determined by the Launceston Commissioners. The Ch D upheld the penalties. Fox J held that the assessments at Launceston were evidence of the understatement of profits under *TMA, s 101* and were sufficient evidence to support the award of penalties by the West Brixton Commissioners. *Sparks v West Brixton Commrs*, Ch D [1977] STC 212.

Award of penalties during bankruptcy

[44.186] See *Re Hurren*, **6.35** BANKRUPTCY AND PERSONAL INSOLVENCY.

Penalties—effect of agreement under Civil Procedure Rules

[44.187] In the case noted at **29.84** FURTHER ASSESSMENTS: LOSS OF TAX, the Special Commissioners held that a firm of solicitors had been guilty of 'negligent conduct', within *TMA, s 30B(5)*. The Revenue subsequently issued a penalty determination under *TMA, s 95*, imposing a penalty of 70% of the 'culpable tax'. The solicitors applied to the Ch D for a declaration that because their appeal against the Commissioners' decision had been settled by an agreement under *Civil Procedure Rules 1998 (SI 1998/3132), rule 36* (under which they had agreed to pay the full amount of tax sought by the Revenue), the Revenue should be precluded from seeking penalties. The Ch D rejected this contention and dismissed the application. Warren J observed that the Revenue had explicitly stated, in a letter accompanying their acceptance of the *rule 36* offer, that their acceptance was 'entirely without prejudice to any penalty determination which may follow'. He also observed that there was 'no provision which in fact allows an adjustment of this nature, following a decision on an appeal to the Special Commissioners, to be made to a return by agreement between the taxpayer and HMRC'. Figures could be changed following the determination of an appeal to reflect the decision, but 'the actual decision of the Special Commissioners determined that the amendments which had been made to the partnership return by HMRC should stand.' *Stockler Charity (a firm) v HMRC (No 2)*, Ch D 2007, [2008] STC 2070; [2007] EWHC 2967 (Ch).

[44.188] Following the Ch D decision noted at **44.187** above, the senior partner (S) made a further appeal to the Special Commissioners, contending *inter alia* that the imposition of the penalty was not authorised by *TMA, s 95*. The Special Commissioner held a preliminary hearing to determine this issue and rejected the partner's contentions, observing that 'the amount which the taxpayer is actually required to pay can be arrived at by way of a contract settlement or some other agreement with similar effect', and holding that *TMA, s 95* gave the Revenue the power to raise a penalty determination. The CA upheld the Commissioner's decision (by a 2–1 majority, Lloyd LJ dissenting). Sir Mark Waller held that *TMA, s 101* should not 'be construed so as to allow (S) to rely on the result of the compromise to effectively contradict the terms of the compromise itself'. Mummery LJ held that 'the fact that the compromise creates a contractual debt and that there are no amended returns is irrelevant in the context of *section 95(2)*, which is solely concerned with the process of calculating the ceiling on the amount of the penalty that can be imposed on the taxpayer'. *W Stockler v HMRC*, CA [2010] STC 2584; 80 TC 412; [2010] EWCA Civ 893. (*Note.* The Supreme Court rejected the solicitor's application for leave to appeal against this decision.)

[44.189] Following the CA decision noted at **44.188** above, the First-tier Tribunal held a further hearing to consider the amount of the penalty. Judge Clark held that the penalty should be at the rate of 70% of the 'culpable tax' (with no abatement for disclosure, an abatement of 10% for co-operation, and an abatement of 20% for 'size and gravity'). *W Stockler v HMRC (No 2)*, FTT [2012] UKFTT 404 (TC), TC02099.

Interaction of TMA, ss 50(6) and 95

[44.190] A married couple stated on their 1997/98 tax return that they were not resident in the UK. The Revenue held information suggesting that this was incorrect, and that they had substantial CGT liability in the UK. The Revenue imposed penalties under *TMA, s 95*. The couple appealed against the penalties and against the related closure notices. At a preliminary hearing, they contended that, since the burden of proof in the penalty appeals was on the Revenue (i.e. to show that the conditions of *s 95* were satisfied), the burden of proof in the appeals against the closure notices was also on the Revenue (i.e. to show that the returns were incorrect, ie reversing the normal burden of proof under *TMA, s 50(6)*). The Special Commissioners rejected this contention and the Ch D upheld their decision. Patten J held that 'there is nothing of substance in this point' and that 'the determination of these matters is unlikely to be affected by the incidence of the burden of proof'. *Morris & Morris v HMRC (No 3)*, Ch D 2007, 79 TC 184; [2007] EWHC 1181 (Ch). (*Notes.* (1)

For preliminary issues in this case, see 4.443 APPEALS; 44.358 below, and 55.41 SELF-ASSESSMENT. (2) The Ch D observed that the hearing of the substantive appeals was scheduled to begin on 4 June 2007. However, there was no further public hearing.)

Penalties under TMA, s 95—standard of proof

[44.191] In the case noted at 29.91 FURTHER ASSESSMENTS: LOSS OF TAX, the General Commissioners and the Ch D found that a company which operated a restaurant had underdeclared its takings, and that the company's controlling director (K) had failed to declare income from property and had received substantial amounts of underdeclared remuneration. Following this decision, the Revenue imposed penalties totalling £41,332 on K under *TMA, s 95*. K appealed to the General Commissioners, who upheld the penalties in principle but reduced them to £6,000, holding that they should apply the criminal standard of 'proof beyond reasonable doubt', and finding that although the Revenue had shown that K had negligently understated income from property and benefits in kind, the Revenue had not proved that he 'negligently understated income in respect of remuneration'. The Revenue appealed to the Ch D, contending that the Commissioners had misdirected themselves as to the standard of proof, and should have applied the normal civil standard of the balance of probabilities. The Ch D accepted this contention and remitted the case to the Commissioners for rehearing. Mann J declined to apply *obiter dicta* of Lord Jauncey in *CIR v Ruffle*, CS [1979] SC 371, observing that Lord Jauncey's *dicta* had subsequently been implicitly disapproved by the CS in the VAT case of *First Indian Cavalry Club Ltd v C & E Commrs*, CS 1997, [1998] STC 293. He observed that in 1983, the Keith Report of the Committee on the Enforcement Powers of Revenue Departments had 'assumed that a civil penalty system for dishonesty in relation to income tax required proof only to the civil standard', and that this reasoning had been applied in subsequent VAT cases in which 'it was plainly assumed that the civil standard of proof applied to the income tax regime'. It was 'sensible that the same standard of proof should apply' to income tax and VAT, and 'for the reasons given in the Keith Report and referred to in the cases, that standard should be the civil standard'. *HMRC v Khawaja*, Ch D [2008] STC 2880; [2008] EWHC 1687 (Ch). (*Notes*. (1) The CA rejected an application by K for leave to appeal against this decision—[2009] EWCA Civ 399. (2) Following this decision, the First-tier Tribunal reheard K's appeals against the penalties relating to suppressed takings and directed that they should be imposed at the rate of 40% of the evaded tax. K appealed to the Upper Tribunal, which allowed his appeal in part, directing that the penalties should have been imposed at 35% of the evaded tax and that there should be a further reduction of 10% to reflect the fact that K's appeal had not been heard 'within a reasonable time', resulting in total penalties of £18,347—*TI Khawaja v HMRC (No 2)*, UT [2013] UKUT 353 (TCC); [2014] STC 150.)

Penalty under FA 2007, Sch 24—definition of 'reasonable care'

[44.192] In 2008/09 an individual (H) disposed of some loan notes, giving rise to a substantial CGT liability. In his return he completed Box 20, indicating that he was making a claim for relief, but without giving details of the relief. HMRC began an enquiry and, after correspondence, H accepted that he was not entitled to relief under *TCGA 1992, s 135*. HMRC imposed a penalty under *FA 2007, Sch 24*. H appealed, contending that he had relied upon his accountants who had told him that he was entitled to relief, and he had therefore taken 'reasonable care' within *FA 2007, Sch 24, para 18*. The First-tier Tribunal accepted this contention and allowed the appeal. Judge Cannan held that 'the effect of *paragraph 18* is to remove the liability of a taxpayer to a penalty where a return is completed and lodged by an agent, and an inaccuracy in the return is the result of something done or omitted by the agent, but the taxpayer took reasonable care to avoid that inaccuracy'. He held that 'a taxpayer cannot simply leave everything to his agent', and 'must satisfy himself that the agent has not made any obvious error'. On the evidence, H's accountants had been careless, but H had 'had no reason to doubt their competence or their advice that relief was available'. *JR Hanson v HMRC*, FTT [2012] UKFTT 314 (TC), TC02000.

[44.193] On his 2009/10 tax return, an individual (J) claimed relief for a capital loss in both box 5 and box 12, with the result that he claimed and received a repayment. When HMRC discovered this, they imposed a penalty under *FA 2007, Sch 24*, at the rate of 15% of the potential lost revenue. J appealed, contending that the penalty was unreasonable as he had been abroad for ten years and found the return confusing. The First-tier Tribunal allowed his appeal. Judge Radford found that J 'had made a mistake despite taking reasonable care in completing his tax return and had therefore not been careless'. *D Jones v HMRC*, FTT [2013] UKFTT 249 (TC), TC02663.

Special penalties for certain returns (TMA, ss 98, 98A)

CIS returns

Cases where the appellant was unsuccessful

[44.194] A company failed to file its annual subcontractors' return for 2001/02 by the due date. The Revenue imposed penalties under *TMA, s 98A(2)*. The company appealed, contending that since it had only engaged one subcontractor during the year, the penalty was disproportionate and contravened the *Human Rights Act 1998*. The Special Commissioner rejected this contention and dismissed the appeal, observing that 'the imposition of penalties as a means of encouraging compliance with the obligation to file a particular tax return represents a legitimate interference with the appellant's rights under *Article 1* of the *First Protocol*'. The amount of the penalty was stipulated by *TMA, s 98A*, which had been enacted following the recommendations of the Keith Committee on Enforcement Powers of the Revenue Departments. There was no breach of *Human Rights Act 1998, s 6*, because the effect of *HRA 1998, s 6(2)*, as interpreted by the HL in *R (oao Wilkinson) v CIR*, **31.77** HUMAN RIGHTS, was that the Revenue were required to give effect to the provisions of *TMA, s 98A*. The penalty did not breach the principle of proportionality. *Bysermaw Properties Ltd v HMRC*, Sp C 2007, [2008] SSCD 322 (Sp C 644). (*Note*. This decision was approved and applied by the Upper Tribunal in *HMRC v Hok Ltd*, **44.215** below.)

[44.195] The decision in *Bysermaw Properties Ltd v HMRC*, 44.194 above, was applied by the First-tier Tribunal in the similar subsequent case of *Y Koleychuk v HMRC*, FTT [2012] UKFTT 224 (TC), TC01918.

[44.196] HMRC imposed penalties totalling £54,100 on a contractor (B) who had failed to make 18 monthly CIS returns by the due dates. B appealed, contending that he had posted the returns in time and had not received the penalty notices. The First-tier Tribunal rejected these contentions, finding that B was not a credible witness and holding that there was no reasonable excuse for his failure to submit the returns. However Judge Aleksander expressed the view that the fixed monthly penalties of £100 per month per return were disproportionate. HMRC appealed to the Upper Tribunal, which reversed Judge Aleksander's decision on this point, holding that the penalties did not infringe the European Convention on Human Rights and were not disproportionate. *A Bosher v HMRC*, UT [2013] UKUT 579 (TCC); [2014] STC 617. (*Note*. The Upper Tribunal gave B permission to raise a new contention concerning the interpretation of *TMA, s 100(1)*, and directed that consideration of this contention should be adjourned pending the decision in the similar case of *Barrett v HMRC* (FTT 2013, not yet reported).)

[44.197] A company filed its form CIS 36 (subcontractors' return) more than three months late. HMRC imposed a penalty of £400, and the company appealed. The First-tier Tribunal dismissed the appeal, holding that the company had not shown that it had a reasonable excuse for the late return. *Leeds Lifts Ltd v HMRC*, FTT [2009] UKFTT 287 (TC), TC00231.

[44.198] Similar decisions were reached in *Century Builders Ltd v HMRC*, FTT [2010] UKFTT 415 (TC), TC00685; *M Mitchell v HMRC*, FTT [2010] UKFTT 485 (TC), TC00745; *GT Plasterers v HMRC*, FTT [2010] UKFTT 492 (TC), TC00750; *C Lawton v HMRC*, FTT [2010] UKFTT 507 (TC), TC00762; *Timar (Road Planning) Ltd v HMRC*, FTT [2010] UKFTT 640 (TC), TC00879; *RP Building Services Ltd v HMRC*, FTT [2011] UKFTT 53 (TC), TC00931; *J O'Brien v HMRC*, FTT [2011] UKFTT 152 (TC), TC01026; *C Crooks v HMRC*, FTT [2011] UKFTT 246 (TC), TC01110; *Champion Scaffolding Ltd v HMRC*, FTT [2011] UKFTT 375 (TC), TC01230; *Peacock Developments Ltd v HMRC*, FTT [2011] UKFTT 491 (TC), TC01338; *D Ireton v HMRC*, FTT [2011] UKFTT 639 (TC), TC01481; *AE Joiners v HMRC*, FTT [2011] UKFTT 672 (TC), TC01514; *Westwood Houses Ltd v HMRC*, FTT [2012] UKFTT 166 (TC), TC01862; *SR & CDE Iles (t/a Purbeck Plumbing Heating & Drainage) v HMRC*, FTT [2012] UKFTT 389 (TC), TC02073; *Masters At Carpentry Ltd v HMRC*, FTT [2012] UKFTT 510 (TC), TC02187, and *C Dunn v HMRC*, FTT [2012] UKFTT 550 (TC), TC02227.

[44.199] HMRC did not receive a partnership's CIS return until 22 April 2010, three days late. They imposed a penalty of £100. The partnership appealed, contending that it had posted the return on 9 April 2010. The tribunal dismissed the appeal, finding that the partnership had failed to provide proof of posting and that it 'held no record to corroborate its assertion that the return was posted on 9 April 2010'. *Holland Kitchen & Bathroom Design v HMRC*, FTT [2010] UKFTT 541 (TC), TC00794.

[44.200] Similar decisions were reached in *Hi Tech Paints Ltd v HMRC*, FTT [2010] UKFTT 591 (TC), TC00841; *E Heatley v HMRC*, FTT [2011] UKFTT 41 (TC), TC00918; *KD Ductworks Installations v HMRC*, FTT [2011] UKFTT 76 (TC), TC00954; *Expo Decor Ltd v HMRC*, FTT [2011] UKFTT 195 (TC), TC01064; *Tony Bacon Decorators v HMRC*, FTT [2011] UKFTT 497 (TC), TC01344; *PG Glazing Ltd v HMRC*, FTT [2011] UKFTT 562 (TC), TC01407; *John Regan v HMRC (No 1)*, FTT [2012] UKFTT 21 (TC), TC01720, and *First In Service Ltd v HMRC*, FTT [2012] UKFTT 250 (TC), TC01944.

[44.201] A contractor (K) failed to file 21 consecutive monthly CIS returns by the due date. HMRC imposed 150 separate penalties under *TMA, s 98A*, totalling £17,600. K appealed, contending that the penalties were disproportionate. The First-tier Tribunal rejected this contention and dismissed the appeals. *R King v HMRC*, FTT [2010] UKFTT 79 (TC), TC00391.

[44.202] Similar decisions were reached in *J Sillitoe v HMRC*, FTT [2010] UKFTT 409 (TC), TC00679; *AJ Flack Ltd v HMRC*, FTT [2011] UKFTT 279 (TC), TC01141; *Castledale Building Services v HMRC*, FTT [2011] UKFTT 301 (TC), TC01163; *M & J Plumbing v HMRC*, FTT [2011] UKFTT 337 (TC), TC01197, and *M & J Plumbing v HMRC*, FTT [2011] UKFTT 819 (TC), TC01655.

[44.203] For cases where there was held to be no reasonable excuse for failure to submit a CIS return, see **44.257** et seq below.

Cases where the appellant was partly successful

[44.204] A construction company failed to file 22 consecutive monthly CIS returns. HMRC imposed 205 separate penalties under *TMA, s 98A*, totalling £41,900. The First-tier Tribunal upheld the penalties in principle but reduced each penalty to £100, giving a total penalty of £20,500. *Bells Mills Developments Ltd v HMRC*, FTT [2009] UKFTT 390 (TC), TC00349.

[44.205] A contractor (L) failed to file 12 consecutive monthly CIS returns. HMRC imposed 133 separate penalties under *TMA, s 98A*, totalling £37,400. The First-tier Tribunal upheld the penalties in principle but reduced each penalty to £100, giving a total penalty of £13,300. *B Lewis v HMRC*, FTT [2010] UKFTT 327 (TC), TC00612.

[44.206] A builder (B), who normally worked alone, engaged two subcontractors for the period from August to November 2007. He accounted for tax under the CIS scheme, and submitted a return for September 2007. From December 2007 he resumed working alone and did not use any subcontractors until August 2008, when he telephoned HMRC to inform them that he had engaged a subcontractor again. He did not file CIS returns for the periods from December 2007 to August 2008. HMRC sent him some blank CIS returns in November 2008. In December 2008 B submitted these returns for August to November 2008, and paid the tax due. He also telephoned HMRC to inform them that he had again stopped using a subcontractor. In early 2009 HMRC imposed 134 penalties under *TMA, s 98A*, totalling £20,300 and covering the period from August 2007 to December 2008 (but excluding the periods for which returns had been made). B appealed, contending *inter alia* that he had told an HMRC officer in April 2008 that he was no longer using subcontractors. The First-tier Tribunal reviewed the evidence in detail and observed that 'the failures were generally in respect of months in which he had no contractors working for him, and for which the returns would thus have been nil returns'. Judge Hellier noted that *FA 2004, s 70* provided for regulations to require returns from people 'who make payments under construction contracts'. He held that 'if a person is merely a contractor, but not a person who "makes payments" then the Regulations cannot make, and cannot be treated as making, any provision requiring him to make returns'. On the evidence, B had never submitted a return for October, November or December 2007. There was no reasonable excuse for his initial failure to do so, but his telephone conversation with an HMRC officer in April 2008 did constitute a reasonable excuse from the date of the telephone call. For the periods from January 2008 to July 2008, the tribunal held that B was no longer a person who made payments within scope of *FA 2004, s 70*, and could not therefore be required to deliver returns. For the periods from August 2008 to October 2008, B had been required to deliver returns but had a reasonable excuse because he had not received the blank return forms from HMRC. The December 2008 return had been submitted late and there was no reasonable excuse for this. The tribunal therefore reduced the total penalties from £20,300 to £1,900. *G Bushell v HMRC*, FTT [2010] UKFTT 577 (TC), TC00827.

[44.207] A partnership which had submitted CIS returns electronically changed its accountants in January 2010 (without notifying HMRC). HMRC did not receive an electronic return for the month ended 5 February 2010 and issued a penalty notice. They issued similar notices for the following four months. The partnership appealed, contending that its new accountants had submitted paper returns for the months in question. The First-tier Tribunal allowed the appeal against the initial penalty, holding that there was a reasonable excuse for the partnership having relied on its new accountants to submit that return. However there was no reasonable excuse for the four subsequent returns, since the issue of the penalty notice should have made the partnership aware that its new accountants were not submitting electronic returns. Judge Clark observed that *SI 2005/2045, reg 4* stipulated that CIS returns must be made 'in a document or format approved by the Commissioners'. The partnership had produced copies of the paper returns which its accountants claimed to have sent, and it was clear that they did not comply with the guidance in the HMRC guide CIS340. *Contour Business Interiors v HMRC*, FTT [2011] UKFTT 300 (TC), TC01162.

[44.208] A company (P) failed to submit five CIS returns by the due date, and HMRC imposed penalties. P appealed, contending that the penalties were excessive because it had requested duplicate returns in August 2009 but HMRC had not supplied them until October. The First-tier Tribunal accepted P's evidence and directed that the penalties should be reduced accordingly. *Project Developments (South Wales) Ltd v HMRC*, FTT [2012] UKFTT 322 (TC), TC02008.

Cases where the appellant was successful

[44.209] A small company in the construction industry failed to file its forms CIS 36 (subcontractors' returns) by the due date. HMRC imposed penalties totalling £2,800 under *TMA, s 98A*. The company appealed to the First-tier Tribunal. At the hearing, Judge Walters expressed doubt as to whether the provisions of *TMA, s 98A* complied with the principle of 'proportionality', and directed that the case should be listed for further argument on this point. *SKG (London) Ltd v HMRC (No 1)*, FTT [2009] UKFTT 341 (TC), TC00282. (*Note*. Following this decision, HMRC withdrew the penalties and at a subsequent hearing the tribunal formally allowed the company's appeal—FTT [2010] UKFTT 89 (TC), TC00400. Judge Walters stated that HMRC had no power 'to mitigate the penalty', but this statement appears to be incorrect: see *TMA, s 102*.)

[44.210] HMRC did not receive a company's CIS return until three days after the due date. They imposed a penalty of £100. The company appealed, contending that it had posted the return well before the due date. The First-tier Tribunal accepted the company's evidence and allowed its appeal. *Heronslea Ltd v HMRC*, FTT [2011] UKFTT 102 (TC), TC00978.

[44.211] Similar decisions were reached in *H Gibson v HMRC*, FTT [2011] UKFTT 113 (TC), TC00989; *Lilystone Homes Ltd v HMRC*, FTT [2011] UKFTT 185 (TC), TC01054; *AT Davies v HMRC*, FTT [2011] UKFTT 303 (TC), TC01165; *M McGillen (t/a McGillen Building Services) v HMRC*, FTT [2011] UKFTT 486 (TC), TC01333; *MEM Industrial Roofing Ltd v HMRC*, FTT [2011] UKFTT 604 (TC), TC01447, and *CM Oddy v HMRC*, FTT [2014] UKFTT 673 (TC), TC03796.

[44.212] HMRC imposed penalties totalling £2,600 under *TMA, s 98A* on a company (T), on the basis that it had submitted several CIS returns after the due date. T appealed. The First-tier Tribunal allowed the appeal (on the basis of written submissions and without a formal hearing). Judge Geraint Jones held that the effect of the ECHR decision in *Jussila v Finland*, **31.47** HUMAN RIGHTS, was that the penalties were criminal in nature. He held that HMRC's statement of case was not sufficient proof of the alleged defaults, and expressed the view that 'if HMRC wishes to prove its case, in judicial proceedings, it is up to it to adduce evidence in respect of its allegations and all and any facts that it needs to prove. It might seek to do that by putting in one or more witness statements from a person or persons who can speak to the relevant facts from their own knowledge or from knowledge gained by them personally perusing the relevant record-keeping system or systems. If appropriate, the appellant then has a witness who can be cross-examined.' He held that 'HMRC has not discharged the onus of proof upon it'. *TDG Carpentry & Joinery Ltd v HMRC*, FTT [2011] UKFTT 695 (TC), TC01537. (*Note*. Judge Geraint Jones' decision fails to refer to the Ch D decision in *HMRC v Khawaja*, **44.191** above, where Mann J reviewed the previous case law and held that 'the civil standard of proof applied to the income tax regime'.)

[44.213] HMRC imposed penalties under *TMA, s 98A* and *FA 2007, Sch 24*, totalling £7,381, on a builder (L) who had failed to submit monthly CIS returns. The First-tier Tribunal allowed L's appeal, finding that all three of

L's subcontractors held certificates allowing them to be paid gross, so that the returns would have been nil returns. Judge Porter observed that *TMA, s 102* gave HMRC 'a specific power to mitigate penalties', and that HMRC had used that power in this case, where one of the penalties had been originally imposed at £21,600 and had been mitigated by two-thirds. However he held that the manner in which HMRC had assessed the mitigated penalty had been incorrect, and also held that L had a reasonable excuse, because his accountant had not told him that it was necessary to submit nil returns. *G Laithwaite v HMRC*, FTT [2014] UKFTT 759 (TC), TC03879.

[44.214] For another case where there was held to be a reasonable excuse for failure to submit a CIS return, see *Stone v HMRC*, **44.303** below.

PAYE returns

Cases where the appellant was unsuccessful

[44.215] A company (H) had only one employee, who ceased employment during 2009/10. H did not submit its P35 for 2009/10 by the due date of 19 May. On 27 September HMRC imposed a penalty of £400 (at £100 per month for four months). H appealed, contending that the amount of the penalty was unreasonable because HMRC should have warned it earlier that it was still required to submit a P35 even though its only employee had left. The First-tier Tribunal allowed the appeal in part but the Upper Tribunal reversed this decision and restored the penalty which HMRC had imposed. The tribunal (Warren J and Judge Bishopp) held that 'the First-tier Tribunal does not have any judicial review jurisdiction', and specifically disapproved the reasoning of Judge Geraint Jones in *Foresight Financial Services Ltd v HMRC*, FTT [2011] UKFTT 647 (TC), TC01489. The UT held that the First-tier Tribunal could not 'give effect to common law principles in order to override the clear words of a statute', and could not 'arrogate to itself a jurisdiction which Parliament has chosen not to confer on it. Parliament must be taken to have known, when passing the 2007 Act, of the difference between statutory, common law and judicial review jurisdictions. The clear inference is that it intended to leave supervision of the conduct of HMRC and similar public bodies where it was, that is in the High Court, save to the limited extent it was conferred on this tribunal. It follows that in purporting to discharge the penalties on the ground that their imposition was unfair, the tribunal was acting in excess of jurisdiction, and its decision must be quashed.' The UT also commented that 'there was no evidence before the tribunal' which could justify Judge Geraint Jones' statement that HMRC's delay in issuing penalty notices was deliberate. This statement had been based on his belief that because 'he assumed (and it was no more than assumption) a penalty notice could have been sent out within a month, the fact that it was sent later meant that HMRC deliberately delayed. He appears to have made no enquiry of HMRC about the justification or reasons for the practice' and had not given HMRC 'an opportunity to make representations before condemning their conduct as unfair, even unconscionable. Against that background, in our judgment, the tribunal's comments to that effect were not appropriate'. *HMRC v Hok Ltd*, UT [2012] UKUT 363 (TCC); [2013] SFTD 225.

[44.216] The Upper Tribunal decision in *HMRC v Hok Ltd*, **44.215** above, was applied in the similar subsequent cases of *Kudos Software Ltd v HMRC*, FTT [2013] UKFTT 246 (TC), TC02660; *I Normington v HMRC*, FTT [2013] UKFTT 508 (TC), TC02897; *Fountayne International Supplies Ltd v HMRC*, FTT [2013] UKFTT 538 (TC), TC02927; *Gipping Press Ltd v HMRC*, FTT [2013] UKFTT 539 (TC), TC02928; *Simon Tubb Painter & Decorator Ltd v HMRC*, FTT [2013] UKFTT 540 (TC), TC02929; *Amber Clearflow Ltd v HMRC*, FTT [2013] UKFTT 541 (TC), TC02930; *Beauxfield Ltd v HMRC*, FTT [2013] UKFTT 543 (TC), TC02932; *Croft House Associates Ltd v HMRC*, FTT [2013] UKFTT 546 (TC), TC02935; *Winster Homes Ltd v HMRC*, FTT [2013] UKFTT 547 (TC), TC02936; *Lewis Groundworks Ltd v HMRC*, FTT [2013] UKFTT 548 (TC), TC02937; *Capmark Ltd v HMRC*, FTT [2013] UKFTT 558 (TC), TC02947; *Regen Ltd v HMRC*, FTT [2013] UKFTT 559 (TC), TC02948; *Stuart Edwards Landscapes Ltd v HMRC*, FTT [2013] UKFTT 560 (TC), TC02949; *Duffin Transport v HMRC*, FTT [2013] UKFTT 561 (TC), TC02950; *M Birch (t/a the Woodman Inn) v HMRC*, FTT [2013] UKFTT 562 (TC), TC02951; *M Brown (t/a Heavenly Beauty Salon) v HMRC*, FTT [2013] UKFTT 565 (TC), TC02954; *Mytton Williams Ltd v HMRC*, FTT [2013] UKFTT 591 (TC), TC02980; *Aubrey Brocklebank & Associates Ltd v HMRC*, FTT [2013] UKFTT 615 (TC), TC03002; *S Andrew v HMRC*, FTT [2013] UKFTT 623 (TC), TC03010; *Gantholme Co Ltd v HMRC*, FTT [2013] UKFTT 624 (TC), TC03011, and *The Square Orange Cafe Bar Ltd v HMRC*, FTT [2013] UKFTT 667 (TC), TC03049.

[44.217] An employer (C) failed to submit forms P14 for his two employees, and HMRC imposed penalties under *TMA, s 98A*. The First-tier Tribunal upheld the penalties and dismissed C's appeal. Judge Porter observed that C had 'been in business for some time and is aware of his obligations to complete the forms'. *M Currier v HMRC*, FTT [2010] UKFTT 322 (TC), TC00609.

[44.218] A company failed to submit its 2008/09 employer's return by the due date, and HMRC imposed a penalty of £500 under *TMA, s 98A*. The First-tier Tribunal upheld the penalty and dismissed the company's appeal. *La Mancha Ltd v HMRC*, FTT [2010] UKFTT 638 (TC), TC00877.

[44.219] An appeal by a pension fund against a penalty under *TMA, s 98A* was dismissed in a case where Judge Blewitt observed that 'there is no statutory obligation on HMRC to remind taxpayers of their legal duties'. *Resources for Learning Pension Fund v HMRC*, FTT [2011] UKFTT 844 (TC), TC01678.

[44.220] HMRC imposed a penalty on a company for failing to submit its P35 by the due date. The company appealed, contending that it had posted the return. The First-tier Tribunal dismissed the appeal, finding that the company had failed to provide proof of posting. *Speed Enterprise Ltd v HMRC*, FTT [2012] UKFTT 31 (TC), TC01729.

[44.221] Similar decisions were reached in *Hardakers (Horsforth) Ltd v HMRC*, FTT [2012] UKFTT 164 (TC), TC01859, and *Voice Technology Ltd v HMRC*, FTT [2014] UKFTT 652 (TC), TC03775.

[44.222] A company (M) failed to submit its 2010/11 P35 until December 2011, and HMRC imposed penalties under *TMA, s 98A*. M appealed, contending that the online return was a duplicate and it had submitted a paper return as it had not had internet access. The First-tier Tribunal dismissed the appeal. Judge Cornwell-Kelly observed that HMRC had no record of receiving a paper return from M, but held that even if M had submitted such a return, 'a paper return is not a valid return for the purposes of *regulation 73*'. The effect of *SI 2003/2682, reg 205* was that it was 'mandatory to file the employer's annual return electronically'. *Mike Haynes Ltd v HMRC*, FTT [2014] UKFTT 279 (TC), TC03418.

[44.223] For cases where there was held to be no reasonable excuse for failure to submit an employer's return, see **44.260** et seq below.

[44.224] Appeals against penalties under *TMA, s 98A*, for failure to submit employers' returns, have also been dismissed in a large number of subsequent cases, none of which appear to raise any point of general importance. In the interests of space, such cases are not summarised individually in this book. For details of such cases decided up to and including 31 December 2011, see Tolley's Tax Cases 2012.

Cases where the appellant was partly successful

[44.225] In a case where HMRC had imposed penalties totalling £900, Judge Pritchard observed that 'HMRC's guidance states that notification will be sent out "shortly" after 19 September in any year', but that they had apparently failed to notify the appellant until February 2010, and reduced the penalties to £400. *DL Cavanagh v HMRC*, FTT [2011] UKFTT 676 (TC), TC01518.

[44.226] In a similar case where HMRC had imposed penalties totalling £800, Judge Short reduced the penalties to £400. *HB & Mrs E Davenport v HMRC*, FTT [2011] UKFTT 746 (TC), TC01583.

[44.227] In a case where a partnership had failed to submit two forms P35 by the due date, and HMRC had imposed penalties of £1200 for each year, Judge King reduced the penalties to £100 for each year. *Mr & Mrs MacDonald (t/a Cafe View) v HMRC*, FTT [2011] UKFTT 809 (TC), TC01645.

[44.228] In a case where a partnership failed to submit its 2009/10 P35 until January 2011, HMRC imposed a penalty of £800 but Judge Poole reduced the penalty to £500. *Dennis Burrows Insurance Brokers v HMRC*, FTT [2011] UKFTT 851 (TC), TC01685.

[44.229] In a case where a partnership failed to submit its 2009/10 P35 until February 2011, HMRC imposed a penalty of £900 but Judge Geraint Jones reduced the penalty to £700. *Hilltop Syndicate Shoot v HMRC*, FTT [2012] UKFTT 26 (TC), TC01725.

[44.230] Penalties under *TMA, s 98A* were also reduced in *P Stump v HMRC*, FTT [2012] UKFTT 27 (TC), TC01726; *Atlas Industrial Services Ltd Pension Scheme v HMRC*, FTT [2012] UKFTT 39 (TC), TC01737; *Midshire Décor Ltd v HMRC*, FTT [2012] UKFTT 115 (TC), TC01811; *DA Dent (t/a Tony's Meats) v HMRC*, FTT [2012] UKFTT 139 (TC), TC01834, and *Moh Properties Ltd v HMRC*, FTT [2012] UKFTT 597 (TC), TC02273.

Cases where the appellant was successful

[44.231] In October 2008 HMRC imposed a penalty determination under *TMA, s 100*. The determination was issued in the name of an HMRC area director (C) who had retired on 31 August 2008. HMRC indicated in evidence that 'the print run for penalty notices was not immediately changed to reflect the new appointment'. The First-tier Tribunal discharged the penalty, holding that the determination was invalid. Judge Mosedale observed that C 'could not have been an officer of the Board authorised by the Board' at the time when the penalty was stated to be imposed, since 'he had retired from employment as an officer of HMRC before the date the penalty was issued'. *HJ Ashenford v HMRC*, FTT [2010] UKFTT 311 (TC), TC00598.

[44.232] HMRC imposed a penalty under *TMA, s 98A* on the basis that an association (B) had failed to submit its form P35 by 19 May 2010. B appealed, contending that it had submitted the P35 online on 26 April 2010. The First-tier Tribunal accepted B's evidence and allowed its appeal. Judge Geraint Jones found that 'the P35 was submitted online, notwithstanding that, for whatever reason, it may not have become lodged or located in HMRC's computer'. *Ballysillan Community Forum v HMRC*, FTT [2011] UKFTT 257 (TC), TC01121.

[44.233] Similar decisions were reached in *Consult Solutions v HMRC*, FTT [2011] UKFTT 429 (TC), TC01282; *Hicharms (UK) Ltd v HMRC*, FTT [2011] UKFTT 432 (TC), TC01285; *HMD Response International v HMRC*, FTT [2011] UKFTT 472 (TC), [2011] SFTD 1017, TC01322; *Walton Kiddiwinks Private Day Nursery v HMRC*, FTT [2011] UKFTT 479 (TC), TC01326; *Rushworths Furniture Ltd v HMRC*, FTT [2011] UKFTT 480 (TC), TC01327; *TAH Management Services Ltd v HMRC*, FTT [2011] UKFTT 537 (TC), TC01384; *Key Interiors Creative Associates Ltd v HMRC*, FTT [2011] UKFTT 591 (TC), TC01434; *Bridge Utilities Ltd v HMRC*, FTT [2011] UKFTT 683 (TC), TC01525; *Oz Build Construction Ltd v HMRC*, FTT [2011] UKFTT 735 (TC), TC01572; *Gavin Alexander Partnership v HMRC*, FTT [2011] UKFTT 837 (TC), TC01673, and *J Marshall v HMRC*, FTT [2012] UKFTT 34 (TC), TC01732.

[44.234] HMRC imposed a penalty under *TMA, s 98A* on the basis that a company (N) had failed to submit its form P35 by the due date. N appealed, contending that it had never received a copy of the form P35. The First-tier Tribunal accepted this contention and allowed the appeal. Judge Geraint Jones held that the fact that N's accountants had submitted its 2006/07 form P35 online did not absolve HMRC from the requirement to send a paper copy of the return. *NA Dudley Electrical Contractors Ltd v HMRC*, FTT [2011] UKFTT 260 (TC), TC01124.

[44.235] The decision in *NA Dudley Electrical Contractors Ltd v HMRC*, 44.234 above, was applied in the similar subsequent case of *Buxton Rugby Union Football Club v HMRC*, FTT [2011] UKFTT 428 (TC), TC01281.

[44.236] A company did not submit its 2009/10 P35 until 11 October 2010, and HMRC imposed a penalty of £500. The company appealed, contending that the penalty was unduly harsh, since its total PAYE and NIC for the year was only £1045, and it had submitted the return within a few days of receiving an initial reminder notice from HMRC. The First-tier Tribunal accepted the company's evidence and allowed its appeal. Judge Poole held that there was no reasonable excuse for the failure, but observed that 2009/10 had been 'the first year in which HMRC did not send out paper P35s to employers', and held that 'a penalty of £500 in the circumstances we have outlined for late delivery of a form with no associated outstanding tax liability was not merely harsh but plainly unfair'. Accordingly the penalty was 'disproportionate'. Judge Poole observed that 'HMRC cannot be surprised to be faced with a proportionality argument if they delay notifying a penalty to a defaulter until a penalty which Parliament has fixed at £100 per month is allowed to escalate to £500 while HMRC apparently sit on their hands. If the delivery of the return is so important that it merits a fine at such a level, it seems surprising (to put it at the very lowest) that they should take no steps for over four months to chase it.' *AST Systems Ltd v HMRC*, FTT [2011] UKFTT 802 (TC), TC01638. (*Note*. HMRC initially appealed to the Upper Tribunal against this decision, but subsequently withdrew their appeal. Compare the Special Commissioner's decision in *Bysermaw Properties Ltd v HMRC*, **44.194** above, which was not referred to in Judge Poole's decision.)

[44.237] For cases where there was held to be a reasonable excuse for failure to submit an employer's return, see **44.304** et seq below.

Failure to account for PAYE

[44.238] HMRC discovered that a publican had failed to account for PAYE on payments to various bar staff. They issued determinations under *Income Tax (PAYE) Regulations 2003 (SI 2003/2682), reg 80*, and imposed penalties under *TMA, s 98A*, at the rate of 45% of the evaded tax. The First-tier Tribunal upheld the determinations and the penalties. Judge Aleksander held that the penalty abatement of 55% was 'generous'. *A Moran v HMRC*, FTT [2011] UKFTT 577 (TC), TC01420.

[44.239] In 2006/07 a company paid its controlling director more than £300,000 without accounting for PAYE. HMRC issued a determination under *Income Tax (PAYE) Regulations 2003 (SI 2003/2682), reg 80*, and imposed a penalty under *TMA, s 98A*, at the rate of 10% of the evaded tax. The First-Tier Tribunal upheld the determination and the penalty. Sir Stephen Oliver held that the fact that the director had declared the income in his personal return did not absolve the company of its liability to account for tax. *David A Marshall Jeweller Ltd v HMRC*, FTT [2012] UKFTT 262 (TC), TC01955.

[44.240] HMRC formed the opinion that a property development company (S) had failed to account for PAYE and NIC on substantial payments to employees, and had failed to deduct tax from payments to subcontractors. They issued determinations under the PAYE and CIS regulations and *SSCTFA 1999*, and imposed penalties under *TMA, s 98A(4)*, mitigated by 50%. S appealed. The First-tier Tribunal reviewed the evidence in detail and observed that two accountancy firms had resigned as S's auditors and had qualified their opinions concerning S's accounts. Judge Berner observed that 'in a case of this nature, where so little underlying information has been provided by the taxpayer, it is of course the case that the assessments made by HMRC will not be correct. They are merely estimates. But that does not mean they must be discharged. They are valid and must be upheld except to the extent that the taxpayer satisfies the tribunal as to the correct, or more nearly correct, figures.' He also held that HMRC had been 'over-generous' in mitigating the penalty by

50%. He observed that S had failed to prepare a disclosure report, had not given access to its primary records, and had 'been engaged throughout in a campaign of delay and obstruction'. It appeared that 'not only have a large number of employees been omitted from the annual P35 returns, resulting in a substantial underdeclaration and payment of tax and NICs, but the remainder of the workforce have not been returned on any CIS returns'. In the circumstances, there should only be an abatement of 5% for disclosure, and there should be no abatement for co-operation or seriousness. The tribunal therefore increased the penalty from 50% to 95% of the statutory maximum. *Seacourt Developments Ltd v HMRC*, FTT [2012] UKFTT 522 (TC), TC02198.

Penalty under SI 2001/1004, reg 81

[44.241] A company submitted its 2009/10 P35 in May 2010 but did not submit the appropriate forms P11D until March 2011. HMRC imposed a penalty of £900 under *Social Security (Contributions) Regulations 2001 (SI 2001/1004), reg 81*. The company appealed, contending that the penalty was unduly harsh since it represented approximately 84% of its Class 1A national insurance liability for the year. The First-tier Tribunal dismissed the appeal. Judge Blewitt held that there was no reasonable excuse for the late submission, and that the tribunal had no power to mitigate the penalty. *Rowland May Ltd v HMRC*, FTT [2011] UKFTT 846 (TC), TC01680.

[44.242] A similar decision was reached in *Trade Tec Services Ltd v HMRC*, FTT [2014] UKFTT 606 (TC), TC03731.

[44.243] A company failed to submit its 2010/11 P11D(b) until March 2012, and HMRC imposed a penalty under *Social Security (Contributions) Regulations 2001 (SI 2001/1004), reg 81*. The company appealed, contending that it had a reasonable excuse because it had attempted to submit the P11D(b) with its P35 in April 2011, but its software had been inadequate. The First-tier Tribunal dismissed the appeal. Judge Cornwell-Kelly concluded 'that the confusion apparently experienced by the appellant does not amount to a reasonable excuse and that the instructions for operating the system were adequate'. *Agriemach Ltd v HMRC*, FTT [2013] UKFTT 530 (TC), TC02918.

[44.244] A family company, which was controlled by a married couple (Mr & Mrs S), failed to submit forms P11D for 2005/06 to 2008/09 inclusive, and HMRC imposed penalties. The First-tier Tribunal upheld the penalties for 2005/06 to 2007/08 inclusive, but allowed the appeal against the penalty for 2008/09, observing that the couple's daughter had been diagnosed with breast cancer in January 2009, and that Mrs S had had to help look after her daughter's two young children, leaving Mr S to run the company single-handedly. Judge Connell held that this was a reasonable excuse for the failure to submit the 2008/09 P11D. *Renown Services (UK) Ltd v HMRC*, FTT [2013] UKFTT 503 (TC), TC02892.

[44.245] See also *Lifescience Products Ltd v HMRC*, **44.290** below.

Time limits (TMA, s 103)

Date of 'final determination of the amount of tax'

[44.246] The Revenue issued estimated assessments on a company for each of the three years ending 30 June 1974. The company did not appeal, and belatedly submitted accounts in 1978, showing that further tax of £40,157 was chargeable. The company paid the tax. The inspector wrote to the company in June 1979, enclosing a computation which agreed with that submitted by the company, subject to the production of statements of assets from the company's directors, and inviting the company to make an offer to the Revenue in respect of interest and penalties. The company did not make an offer, and in 1983 the Revenue took penalty proceedings. The General Commissioners awarded penalties of £18,000. The company appealed, contending that there had been a final determination of the liability in June 1979 and that the proceedings had not been taken 'within three years after the final determination of the amount of tax', as required by *TMA, s 103*. The CS unanimously rejected this contention and dismissed the appeal, holding that the amount of the tax chargeable had not been finally determined in 1979. Furthermore, having regard to the delay in the production of the accounts, there was no reason to interfere with the amount of the penalties. *Carco Accessories Ltd v CIR*, CS 1985, 59 TC 45; [1985] STC 518. (*Note. TMA, s 103* was substituted by *FA 1989* with effect from 27 July 1989. See now *TMA, s 103(4)*.)

Reasonable excuse (TMA, s 118(2); FA 2009, Sch 55 para 23)

Cases where the appellant was unsuccessful

Company tax return

[44.247] A company's CT200 for the period ending 30 April 1994 was not received by its inspector until 3 May 1995, and the relevant accounts were not submitted until 24 May. A penalty of £100 was imposed. The company appealed, contending that it had a 'reasonable excuse' within *TMA, s 118(2)*, as the original form CT200 had been posted on 18 March and its director had not realised that he should also have submitted the company's accounts. The Special Commissioner dismissed the appeal, finding 'on the balance of probabilities' that the CT200 had not been posted 'until much later than 18 March' and holding that there was no reasonable excuse for only sending a return when accounts were also required. *Creedplan Ltd v Winter*, Sp C [1995] SSCD 352 (Sp C 54).

[44.248] A company failed to submit its corporation tax return by the due date, and HMRC imposed a penalty of £200 under *FA 1998, Sch 18 para 17(2)*. The company appealed, contending that it had a reasonable excuse because its accountants had been unable to file the return online. The First-tier Tribunal dismissed the appeal, finding that the accountants had 'experienced difficulties in online registration' but had not shown 'that they took active steps to overcome these difficulties despite the lengthy default period'. *Animals At Home (North Wilts) Ltd v HMRC*, FTT [2014] UKFTT 378 (TC), TC03511.

[44.249] Similar decisions were reached in *Harris Greenlees Design Ltd v HMRC*, FTT [2014] UKFTT 379 (TC), TC03512, and *Onesmart Solutions Ltd v HMRC*, FTT [2014] UKFTT 380 (TC), TC03513.

Individual tax return

[44.250] A woman (H) failed to submit her 2007/08 tax return by the due date, and HMRC imposed a penalty of £100. H appealed, contending that she had a reasonable excuse because this was the first occasion on which she had attempted to file her return online, and her activation PIN had not worked. The First-tier Tribunal dismissed her appeal, finding that the reason the PIN had not worked was that H 'had not used the PIN within 28 days of it being issued so it had expired'. Judge Gandhi observed that 'this is clearly written on the letter sent to her with her PIN both in the text of the letter and in bold and capitals at the very top of the letter as well as this information being available on HMRC website' (*sic*). Accordingly the circumstances did not constitute a reasonable excuse. *F Haque v HMRC*, FTT [2010] UKFTT 82 (TC), TC00394.

[44.251] An individual (N) did not submit his 2012/13 tax return until June 2014, and HMRC imposed a penalty. N appealed, contending that he had forgotten his User ID and had written to HMRC requesting a reminder of it, but had not received a reply and had eventually submitted the return on paper. The First-tier Tribunal dismissed his appeal, holding that the circumstances did not constitute a reasonable excuse. *BA Newman v HMRC*, FTT [2014] UKFTT 861 (TC), TC03977.

[44.252] An individual (G) appealed against penalties imposed for failing to submit his 2009/10 tax return by the due date, contending that he had attempted to file the return online on 31 January, and had assumed that HMRC had received it. The First-Tier Tribunal dismissed the appeal. Judge Hacking found that the return had not been submitted successfully, and held that the circumstances did not constitute a reasonable excuse. *A Garnsworthy v HMRC*, FTT [2012] UKFTT 332 (TC), TC02018.

[44.253] A similar decision was reached in *AJ Miles v HMRC*, FTT [2012] UKFTT 383 (TC), TC02067.

[44.254] A woman did not submit her 2007/08 tax return until December 2009. HMRC imposed a penalty under *TMA, s 93*. She appealed, contending that she had a reasonable excuse because her father had been very ill (and had died in July 2009). The First-tier Tribunal dismissed her appeal, observing that her return had been submitted more than twelve months late and holding that her father's illness did not constitute a reasonable excuse for such a prolonged delay. *Ms J Naylor v HMRC*, FTT [2010] UKFTT 576 (TC), TC00826.

[44.255] A woman (H) failed to submit her tax return by the due date, and HMRC imposed a penalty of £100. She appealed, contending that she had 'relied on her accountant to submit the Return to HMRC on her behalf within the statutory time limit'. The First-tier Tribunal dismissed her appeal, holding that the circumstances did not constitute a reasonable excuse. Judge Brooks observed that 'the responsibility for filing a self-assessment tax return remains that of the individual taxpayer even where, as in this case, an accountant has been instructed to prepare and submit the self-assessment return to HMRC on his client's behalf'. *Mrs SH Heaney-Irving v HMRC*, FTT [2011] UKFTT 785 (TC), TC01619.

[44.256] Judge Connell reached a similar decision in *Ms A Nolan v HMRC*, FTT [2014] UKFTT 508 (TC), TC03635.

CIS returns

[44.257] A contractor failed to file his 2005/06 CIS return by the due date. HMRC imposed a penalty under *TMA, s 98A*, and he appealed, contending that he had a reasonable excuse because he had changed his accountant. The First-tier Tribunal dismissed his appeal, holding that this did not constitute a reasonable excuse. *M Smith v HMRC*, FTT [2010] UKFTT 185 (TC), TC00489.

[44.258] A company failed to file 20 monthly CIS returns by the due date. HMRC imposed penalties under *TMA, s 98A*, and the company appealed, contending that it had a reasonable excuse because it had not received the blank return forms. The First-tier Tribunal dismissed the appeal, observing that 'it would appear that the appellant waited 16 months to inform HMRC that sub-contractors were being employed within the CIS scheme'. The circumstances did not constitute a reasonable excuse. *Apex Design & Build Ltd v HMRC*, FTT [2010] UKFTT 216 (TC), TC00517.

[44.259] A contractor failed to submit 20 monthly CIS returns by the due date. HMRC imposed penalties under *TMA, s 98A*, and the contractor appealed, contending that he had a reasonable excuse because he was dyslexic. The First-tier Tribunal dismissed the appeal, holding that this was not a reasonable excuse. *G Austin v HMRC*, FTT [2010] UKFTT 312 (TC), TC00599.

Employers' returns

[44.260] An employer (B) did not file his P35 for 2007/08 until 19 September 2008. HMRC imposed penalties totalling £400 under *TMA, s 98A*. B appealed, contending that he had a reasonable excuse because his accountant had been ill. The First-tier Tribunal dismissed his appeal, holding that this did not amount to a reasonable excuse, since the accountant 'should have had in place arrangements for his practice to have continued whilst he was unfit through illness'. *MR Brookes v HMRC*, FTT [2010] UKFTT 112 (TC), TC00423.

[44.261] A company failed to submit three successive P35 annual returns, and HMRC imposed penalties under *TMA, s 98A*. The company appealed, contending that it had had a reasonable excuse because it had relied on its company secretary. The First-tier Tribunal dismissed the appeal, holding that this was not a reasonable excuse. *Third Stone Ltd v HMRC*, FTT [2010] UKFTT 234 (TC), TC00533.

[44.262] A company (K) submitted its P35 after the due date and HMRC imposed a penalty under *TMA, s 98A*. The First-tier Tribunal dismissed K's appeal. Judge Staker held that 'reliance on a dilatory bookkeeper cannot be a reasonable excuse'. *Khalil Opticians Ltd v HMRC*, FTT [2011] UKFTT 605 (TC), TC01448.

[44.263] Similar decisions were reached in *The Cove Fish & Chip Restaurant Ltd v HMRC*, FTT [2011] UKFTT 625 (TC), TC01467; *HS French Flint Ltd v HMRC*, FTT [2011] UKFTT 857 (TC), TC01691; *Nonstop International Ltd v HMRC*, FTT [2014] UKFTT 020 (TC), TC03161, and *Ms TT Le v HMRC*, FTT [2014] UKFTT 193 (TC), TC03333.

[44.264] A parish council had one employee (its clerk). The council failed to submit its P35 by the due date, and HMRC imposed a penalty. The council appealed, contending that it had a reasonable excuse because its clerk had found it impossible to submit the return online, and had submitted the required details by post. The First-tier Tribunal dismissed the council's appeal, finding that HMRC had not received the letter in question, and holding that there was no reasonable excuse for the failure to submit the return. *Dalton Piercy Parish Council v HMRC*, FTT [2010] UKFTT 478 (TC), TC00739.

[44.265] Similar decisions were reached in *Greatham Parish Council v HMRC*, FTT [2010] UKFTT 479 (TC), TC00740; *Dent Parish Council v HMRC*, FTT [2010] UKFTT 782 (TC), TC01616; *BRFM Ltd v HMRC*, FTT [2014] UKFTT 093 (TC), TC03233, and *Associated management Ltd v HMRC*, FTT [2014] UKFTT 100 (TC), TC03240.

[44.266] An accountancy firm failed to submit its 2007/08 P35 by the due date, and HMRC imposed a penalty of £1200. The firm appealed, contending that its senior partner had attempted to file the return online in April 2008, and had assumed that HMRC had received it. The First-tier Tribunal dismissed the appeal, finding on the balance of probabilities that the return had not been filed online, and holding that the circumstances did not constitute a reasonable excuse. *DJ Windsor & Co v HMRC*, FTT [2011] UKFTT 558 (TC), TC01403.

[44.267] Similar decisions were reached in *K Lau v HMRC*, FTT [2011] UKFTT 560 (TC), TC01405; *The Wallis Company v HMRC*, FTT [2011] UKFTT 623 (TC), TC01465; *Hotline Cars Ltd v HMRC*, FTT [2011] UKFTT 629 (TC), TC01471; *Urban Illustrate Ltd v HMRC*, FTT [2011] UKFTT 779 (TC), TC01613; *Homega Ltd v HMRC*, FTT [2011] UKFTT 783 (TC), TC01617; *Little Comberton Parish Council v HMRC*, FTT [2012] UKFTT 241 (TC), TC01935; *Rennie Smith & Co v HMRC (No 1)*, FTT [2013] UKFTT 505 (TC), TC02894; *IY Macintyre v HMRC*, FTT [2013] UKFTT 590 (TC), TC02979; *Michael Young Plumbing & Heating Engineers Ltd v HMRC*, FTT [2013] UKFTT 710 (TC), TC03090; *Sceptre Associates Ltd v HMRC*, FTT [2014] UKFTT 036 (TC), TC03177; *Quality Meat Scotland v HMRC*, FTT [2014] UKFTT 119 (TC), TC03259; *Michael Dabb Design Services Ltd v HMRC*, FTT [2014] UKFTT 120 (TC), TC03260; *Paintball Challenge Ltd v HMRC*, FTT [2014] UKFTT 136 (TC), TC03276; *Dalkeith Private Bowling Club v HMRC*, FTT [2014] UKFTT 137 (TC), TC03277; *Bletchingley Skills Centre v HMRC*, FTT [2014] UKFTT 253 (TC), TC03392; *Agentronic Ltd v HMRC*, FTT [2014] UKFTT 255 (TC), TC03394; *Keith Dennis Associates v HMRC*, FTT [2014] UKFTT 285 (TC), TC03424; *Carryduff Building Supplies Ltd v HMRC*, FTT [2014] UKFTT 288 (TC), TC03427; *Avon Lee Lodge v HMRC*, FTT [2014] UKFTT 463 (TC), TC03590; *D Osher (t/a Marathon Motors) v HMRC*, FTT [2014] UKFTT 509 (TC), TC03636; *London School of Economics v HMRC*, FTT [2014] UKFTT 619 (TC), TC03744; *Nantyffyllon Rugby Club v HMRC*, FTT [2014] UKFTT

827 (TC), TC03945; *Miss PJ Newton (t/a Pammy's Cleaning) v HMRC*, FTT [2014] UKFTT 859 (TC), TC03975, and *Refina Ltd v HMRC*, FTT [2014] UKFTT 860 (TC), TC03976.

[44.268] A similar decision was reached in a case where Judge Long observed that 'it was unsafe and unreasonable, without more, to rely on an unfamiliar software package which had not demonstrated evidence of despatch or receipt'. *Capricorn Film Productions Ltd v HMRC*, FTT [2011] UKFTT 598 (TC), TC01441.

[44.269] HMRC imposed a penalty on the basis that a company (W) had failed to submit its P35 within the statutory time limit. W appealed, contending that it had a reasonable excuse because HMRC had treated its online submission as a test submission. The First-tier Tribunal dismissed W's appeal, finding that W's payroll agent had 'sent the return as a test submission on 13 May 2010, and that a live submission was not made until 20 October 2010'. Judge Staker declined to follow the decision in *Writtle College Services Ltd v HMRC*, **44.320** below, and accepted HMRC's evidence that 'HMRC's own system does not have a "test" facility but that many commercial software packages do, and that the operator has to actively access the "test" mode and that the screen clearly shows that it is in the "test" mode'. He held that 'it ought to be apparent to a person submitting a return whether the system is in "test" mode or "live" mode, and that while the confirmation message may be the same in either case, the operator of the system should know whether the submission being confirmed was sent in test mode or in live mode'. Accordingly, 'a payroll agent exercising due diligence would not have made this mistake'. *Westbeach Apparel UK Ltd v HMRC*, FTT [2011] UKFTT 561 (TC), TC01406.

[44.270] Judge Clark reached a similar decision in *TL Watson (t/a Kirkwood Coaches) v HMRC*, FTT [2013] UKFTT 553 (TC), TC02942.

[44.271] Judge Manuell reached a similar decision in *R Patterson & S Blair (t/a Dirtbuggy NI) v HMRC*, FTT [2013] UKFTT 683 (TC), TC03065.

[44.272] Judge Connell reached a similar decision in *Quality Asset Management Ltd v HMRC*, FTT [2014] UKFTT 526 (TC), TC03653.

[44.273] Judge Coverdale reached similar decisions in *Aurum Healthcare Ltd v HMRC*, FTT [2014] UKFTT 664 (TC), TC03787 and *Bishops Printers Ltd v HMRC*, FTT [2014] UKFTT 665 (TC), TC03788.

[44.274] A dentist (H) ceased his practice in September 2010. He gave his employees P45s and paid the PAYE due. However he did not submit a form P35, and HMRC subsequently imposed a penalty. Judge Mure dismissed H's appeal, holding that the circumstances did not constitute a reasonable excuse. *Heslop v HMRC*, FTT [2014] UKFTT 062 (TC), TC03202.

[44.275] Judge Connell reached a similar decision in *Tummy Gym/Gymphobics Hucknall Ltd v HMRC*, FTT [2014] UKFTT 238 (TC), TC03378.

[44.276] A partnership did not submit its 2008/09 P35 until 30 October 2009, and HMRC imposed a penalty. The partnership appealed, contending that it had a reasonable excuse because it had not received the blank form P35 until October. The First-tier Tribunal dismissed the appeal, finding that the blank P35 which HMRC had sent on 13 October 2009 was a duplicate which had been issued at the partnership's request, and holding that the circumstances did not constitute a reasonable excuse. *Ian Barlow Builders v HMRC*, FTT [2013] UKFTT 583 (TC), TC02972.

[44.277] A company (G) did not submit its 2010/11 form P35 until 26 May, and HMRC imposed a penalty. G appealed, contending that it had a reasonable excuse because it had requested the necessary activation code on 16 May, and had not been aware that this code would be issued by post. The First-tier Tribunal dismissed the appeal. Judge Rankin observed that 'HMRC's guidance notes indicate that the activation code will be sent by post and will take up to a week to arrive'. He held that G 'should have applied for the activation code much earlier and cannot rely on the delay in receiving the code as a reasonable excuse'. *Geno Services Ltd v HMRC*, FTT [2014] UKFTT 656 (TC), TC03779.

Cases where the appellant was partly successful

Company tax return

[44.278] A company (S) failed to submit its corporation tax return by the due date, and HMRC imposed a penalty of £200 under *FA 1998, Sch 18 para 17(2)*. S appealed, contending that it had a reasonable excuse because it had been unable to file the return online, and had submitted a paper return instead, which HMRC had refused to accept. The First-tier Tribunal reduced the penalty to £100. Judge Lyons held that 'the paper return was not an "approved form of electronic communication" as required by the regulations'. She also held that the difficulties in filing an online return constituted a reasonable excuse for not filing the return within three months of the due date, but that there was no reasonable excuse for the subsequent failure to submit an online return. *Springfield China Ltd v HMRC*, FTT [2014] UKFTT 375 (TC), TC03508.

Partnership tax return

[44.279] A married couple who carried on business in partnership did not submit their returns for 2008/09 and 2009/10 until October 2012, and did not submit their 2010/11 return until November 2012. HMRC imposed penalties, and the couple appealed, contending that they had a reasonable excuse because the wife's mother had been suffering from cancer (and had died in 2010), and the wife had suffered from illness after her mother's death. The First-tier Tribunal allowed their appeal in part. Judge Mitting held that there was a reasonable excuse for the late submission of the 2008/09 and 2009/10 returns, but that there was no reasonable excuse for the late submission of the 2010/11 return. *D & Mrs K Breen (t/a Redmires Lodge Nursery & Pre-School) v HMRC*, FTT [2014] UKFTT 544 (TC), TC03670.

Individual tax return

[44.280] A woman (F) failed to submit her 2008/09 tax return until December 2010, and HMRC imposed two penalties of £100 each. F appealed, contending that she had a reasonable excuse because she had tried to submit her return online during January 2010 but that the access codes which HMRC had sent her did not work. The First-tier Tribunal accepted her evidence and allowed her appeal against the first penalty but dismissed her appeal against the second penalty, holding that the problems with HMRC's website constituted a reasonable excuse for her failure to file the return by 31 January 2010 but not for her failure to file the return by 31 July 2010. *Ms L Fernandez v HMRC*, FTT [2011] UKFTT 259 (TC), TC01123.

[44.281] On 29 April 2011 HMRC issued a 2009/10 return to a taxpayer (E) who had tax deducted under PAYE. E submitted the return on 18 August. HMRC imposed a penalty of £100. The First-tier Tribunal allowed E's appeal, finding that the return did not make it clear that it should be submitted within three months, and holding that this constituted a reasonable excuse. *RW Eadie v HMRC*, FTT [2012] UKFTT 544 (TC), TC02221. (*Note.* There was, however, found to be no reasonable excuse for the late submission of E's 2010/11 return.)

CIS returns

[44.282] HMRC imposed six penalties of £100 each on a company which had failed to submit its monthly construction industry scheme returns by the due date. The company appealed, contending that it had a reasonable excuse, within *TMA, s 118(2)*. The First-tier Tribunal allowed the appeal in part, holding that the unexpected absence of the company's accountant constituted a reasonable excuse for the first default, but that there was no reasonable excuse for the remaining five defaults. *Jonathan David Ltd v HMRC*, FTT [2009] UKFTT 289 (TC), TC00233.

[44.283] HMRC imposed penalties totalling £2,200 on a civil engineer (T), with one subcontractor, who had failed to submit his CIS returns by the due date. The First-tier Tribunal reviewed the evidence in detail and reduced the penalties to £1,400, holding that there was no reasonable excuse for 14 of the 22 penalties, but that there was a reasonable excuse for eight of the penalties, because HMRC had been slow in responding to a letter from T's accountants. *T Turner v HMRC*, FTT [2010] UKFTT 483 (TC), TC00743.

Employers' returns

[44.284] A company (T) did not submit its 2008/09 P35 until 10 March 2010. HMRC imposed penalties totalling £1000. T appealed, contending that it had a reasonable excuse because its accountant had had a hip operation in May 2009. The First-tier Tribunal allowed the appeal in part. Judge Geraint Jones held that the accountant's unavailability amounted to a reasonable excuse until 30 August 2009, but was no longer a reasonable excuse from 31 August onwards, with the result that the penalty was reduced from £1000 to £600. *Tower Perkins Products & Services Ltd v HMRC*, FTT [2011] UKFTT 481 (TC), TC01328.

[44.285] For 2009/10 a company (T) was required to submit a form P35 for itself and a form P35(TAS) for a taxed award scheme. HMRC issued a manual form P35 for the award scheme, but T incorrectly submitted this return on 27 April 2010 with its own details. HMRC telephoned T on 27 May and informed it that it was required to submit its own return online. T did not do so until 9 August 2010, and HMRC imposed a penalty. T appealed, contending that it had attempted to submit the return online on 16 June 2010. The First-tier Tribunal allowed T's appeal in part. Judge Gandhi found that HMRC had sent a P35 rather than a form P35(TAS) for the award scheme. Accordingly there was a reasonable excuse for T having treated this form as its own P35 and submitting it manually. However T had been informed in May 2010 that it would need to submit its P35 online, and had failed to do so until August. Judge Gandhi observed that 'a reasonably diligent taxpayer would have been aware that the P35 is not received by HMRC unless a successful transmission report had been generated because they would have read the relevant documentation. The company ought to have contacted HMRC when notification of successful transmission was not received.' Therefore, although 'initially there was a reasonable excuse for the correct P35 not to be filed', that excuse ceased from 16 June 2010, and 'the P35 was not thereafter filed without "unreasonable delay"'. The penalty was therefore reduced from £300 to £200. *Tower Leasing Ltd v HMRC*, FTT [2011] UKFTT 487 (TC), TC01334.

[44.286] HMRC imposed penalties of £900 on the basis that a company (L) had failed to submit its 2011/12 P35 within the statutory time limit. L appealed, contending that its principal director had attempted to file the return online in May 2012, and had assumed that HMRC had received it. The First-tier Tribunal allowed the appeal in part. Judge Barrett held that the circumstances constituted a reasonable excuse for the period from May 2012 to August 2012, but not for the period after August 2012, and reduced the penalties from £900 to £500. *Littlewood Hire Ltd v HMRC*, FTT [2013] UKFTT 586 (TC), TC02975.

[44.287] Judge Sheppard reached a similar decision in *Smart Polymers Ltd v HMRC*, FTT [2013] UKFTT 600 (TC), TC02987.

[44.288] Judge Lyons reached similar decisions in *G Redfern & Sons v HMRC*, FTT [2014] UKFTT 381 (TC), TC03514, and *G & S Billett (t/a Hill Farm Caravan Park) v HMRC*, FTT [2014] UKFTT 407 (TC), TC03536.

[44.289] A company (N) did not submit its 2010/11 P35 until 22 January 2012, and HMRC imposed penalties of £900. N appealed, contending that it had a reasonable excuse because it had not received any reminders from HMRC. The First-tier Tribunal allowed the appeal in part. Judge Lyons held that there was no reasonable excuse for the period from May to September 2011, but found that N would have submitted the return if it had received a reminder in September 2011, and held that this was a reasonable excuse for the period from 26 September 2011 to January 2012. She therefore reduced the penalty from £900 to £500. *Nightingale Knitwear Centre Ltd v HMRC*, FTT [2014] UKFTT 471 (TC), TC03598.

[44.290] Judge Connell reached a similar decision in *Ms L Awdry v HMRC*, FTT [2014] UKFTT 791 (TC), TC03908.

[44.291] A company (L) submitted its 2012/13 P35 in April 2013, and submitted its forms P11D in June 2013, but did not submit the completed form P11D(b) until October 2013. HMRC imposed a penalty of £300 under *Social*

Security (Contributions) Regulations 2001 (SI 2001/1004), reg 81. L appealed, contending that it had a reasonable excuse because it had submitted the forms P11D within the statutory time limit and the reminder which it had received from HMRC did not make it sufficiently clear that it must also submit a form P11D(b). The First-tier Tribunal allowed the appeal in part. Judge Lyons found that a reminder issued by HMRC on 16 June 2013 was insufficiently clear, but that a letter issued by HMRC on 22 July was sufficiently clear to have alerted L to the need to file the return. She therefore held that there was a reasonable excuse for the failure to submit the return before 2 August, but that there was no reasonable excuse for the subsequent failure, and reduced the penalty from £300 to £200. *Lifescience Products Ltd v HMRC*, FTT [2014] UKFTT 474 (TC), TC03601.

Cases where the appellant was successful

Company tax return

[44.292] In October 1995 the Revenue sent a company a return form (CT200) for its accounting period ending 30 September 1994. The company returned the CT200 seven days after receiving it, indicating that it had no tax liability for the period in question. However, the company did not submit its accounts, which had not been completed. In January 1996 the Revenue returned the CT200 to the company with a covering form CT214, advising the company that its return was incomplete and requesting a copy of its accounts. The company again returned the CT200 to the Revenue, but its accountants did not submit the relevant accounts until 17 April 1996, by which time the Revenue had again returned the CT200. The company resubmitted the CT200 on 24 April 1996, but the Revenue failed to link the accounts with it, and returned the CT200 to the company on 29 April. The company resubmitted the CT200 on 8 May, but the Revenue again failed to link it with the accounts. On 14 May the Revenue returned the accounts to the company's accountants and on 15 May the Revenue returned the form CT200 to the company. On 28 May the company resubmitted the form CT200 with the accounts. The Revenue imposed a penalty of £200 under *TMA, s 94(1)(b)*. The company appealed, contending that it had a reasonable excuse within *TMA, s 118(2)* because its principal director had suffered a stroke in October 1995 and its company secretary had been in poor health, which had delayed the preparation of the accounts in question. The Special Commissioner accepted the company's evidence and allowed the appeal. *Akarimsons Ltd v Chapman*, Sp C [1997] SSCD 140 (Sp C 116).

Partnership tax return

[44.293] An accountancy firm submitted a partnership tax return on 9 October 2013. The return contained an arithmetical error. On 5 November HMRC sent the return to the representative partner for correction (without notifying the accountancy firm which had actually submitted the return). The partnership did not submit a corrected return, and in February 2014 HMRC imposed a penalty under *FA 2009, Sch 55, para 25* on the basis that the partnership had failed to submit a return. The First-tier Tribunal allowed the partnership's appeal. Judge Sheppard held that since HMRC had failed to notify the accountancy firm that they had rejected the initial return, there was a reasonable excuse for the partnership's failure to submit a corrected return. *Peter Haigh Partnership v HMRC*, FTT [2014] UKFTT 796 (TC), TC03913. (*Note.* The Tribunal did not consider an alternative contention that since the partnership had submitted a return in October 2013, albeit one which included an arithmetical error, any penalty which HMRC sought to impose should have been for submitting an incorrect return, rather than for failing to submit a return. Compare *Frossell v HMRC*, **44.24** above.)

Individual tax return

[44.294] A hairdresser's 1996/97 tax return was delivered by hand on the morning of Monday 2 February 1998. The Revenue imposed a penalty under *TMA, s 93*. The hairdresser appealed, contending that she had a reasonable excuse because her accountant had had to complete a large number of returns and had been advised by the local tax office that returns would be accepted if delivered 'at any time prior to Monday morning opening'. The Special Commissioner accepted this evidence and allowed the appeal, observing that the period of default was Sunday 1 February and, throughout that day, the hairdresser had a reasonable excuse because her accountant had been told that 'the acceptable deadline for returns hand-delivered after closure of the tax office on Saturday 31 January would in practice be the time on which the letterbox of that tax office was opened on Monday 2 February'. The Commissioner observed that 'reliance on Inland Revenue advice as to the practical extension of a deadline, if unequivocally given, is as reasonable an excuse as can be found'. *Steeden v Carver*, Sp C [1999] SSCD 283 (Sp C 212). (*Note.* For the Revenue's practice following this decision, see Revenue Tax Bulletin December 1999, pp 705, 706, and Revenue Tax Bulletin, Special Edition, April 2000, p 8. The Revenue stated that 'where a return required to be filed by the 31 January is delivered after that date the enquiry window is extended to the 30th April in the following year. That will be the position in future years. However, for returns filed or treated as filed on the 1 February 2000, following the 31 January 2000 deadline, we will not open enquiries in the three months to 30 April 2001. This is because we did not warn taxpayers about the implications of late filing for the enquiry window'.)

[44.295] A trader (P) ceased self-employment in 2008, when he became a full-time employee. He informed HMRC of this in October 2010, when he belatedly submitted his 2008/09 tax return. He did not submit the return which he had been sent for 2009/10, and HMRC imposed a penalty. P appealed, contending that because he had told HMRC that he had ceased self-employment in 2008, he had assumed that he would not need to submit the 2009/10 return. The First-tier Tribunal allowed his appeal. Lady Mitting held that the circumstances constituted a reasonable excuse. *N Pickles v HMRC*, FTT [2011] UKFTT 678 (TC), TC01520.

[44.296] A pensioner (B) submitted his 2009/10 tax return on 3 February 2011, ie three days after the due date. The return showed a tax liability of £93, and HMRC imposed a penalty of this amount. B appealed, contending that he had a reasonable excuse because he could not afford to arrange for an accountant to deal with his return, and had asked to visit an HMRC office at the end of January to ensure that he had completed the form correctly, but HMRC had arranged the appointment for 3 February. The First-tier Tribunal allowed the appeal, holding that the circumstances constituted a reasonable excuse. *J Bentley v HMRC*, FTT [2012] UKFTT 233 (TC), TC01927.

[44.297] A woman (L) submitted her 2009/10 tax return, on paper, on 17 January 2011. HMRC imposed a penalty and she appealed, contending that the penalty was unreasonable because she had not realised that she was required to submit a return until she received a letter from HMRC on 10 January informing her of this. She had telephoned HMRC on the same day and had received a paper return in response to that telephone call. The First-tier Tribunal accepted her evidence and allowed her appeal. Judge Geraint Jones observed that HMRC had 'given no explanation as to why one of its personnel should have offered to send out a paper return when, on its case, the deadline for using a paper return had expired and, thereafter, only online filing would be acceptable. Similarly, it has given no explanation for why a member of its staff desisted from informing the appellant that it was too late for her to file a paper tax return and, instead, must now file online.' It appeared that HMRC had waived the requirement for a return submitted between 31 October and 31 January to be submitted online, rather than on paper. Furthermore, it appeared that, if L had been told that she would have to submit her return online, she would have done so. There was a reasonable excuse for her failure to submit the return online. *Ms K Lomas v HMRC*, FTT [2012] UKFTT 324 (TC), TC02010.

[44.298] A German woman worked as a dentist in the UK between January and April 2010, and then returned to Germany. HMRC sent her a 2009/10 tax return on 25 January 2011. She did not submit it until October 2011, and HMRC imposed a penalty. She appealed, contending that she had a reasonable excuse because she had had to ask her German tax adviser to complete the return, and he did not have sufficient knowledge of the UK tax system, so that she had required the help of a UK tax adviser. The First-tier Tribunal allowed her appeal. Judge Blewitt observed that the case 'involved the understanding of two wholly separate and distinct tax systems and was therefore a matter in which the appellant understandably required specialist assistance which caused delay'. *Ms R Theurer v HMRC*, FTT [2012] UKFTT 593 (TC), TC02270.

[44.299] An individual (F) appealed against a penalty imposed for failure to submit his 2009/10 tax return, contending that he had submitted it online on 27 January 2011. Judge Khan allowed his appeal, observing that F had given the precise time and day of filing and that 'it was clear that he had used HMRC's computers to calculate his tax liability on the same day'. He had 'received replies which related to his online filing which suggested to him that the filing was completed'. It appeared 'possible that the error lay with HMRC's online computer facility dealing with online filing'. F 'genuinely and honestly believed that he had completed the online filing', so that the circumstances constituted a reasonable excuse. *R Fergus v HMRC*, FTT [2013] UKFTT 32 (TC), TC02452.

[44.300] Judge Sheppard reached a similar decision in *SJ Varma v HMRC*, FTT [2014] UKFTT 006 (TC), TC03147.

[44.301] In February 2012 HMRC issued a taxpayer (G) a notice to file a 2010/11 return. G's accountant filed the return in June (and paid the outstanding tax the following day). HMRC imposed a penalty for the late submission of the return. G appealed, contending that his accountant had tried to submit the return earlier but HMRC had allocated him a new reference number, and his accountant had not been aware of the new number. Judge Lyons accepted G's evidence and allowed his appeal. *A Goodall v HMRC*, FTT [2014] UKFTT 029 (TC), TC03170.

[44.302] A woman (M) submitted a 2010/11 tax return in which she claimed that a loss on rental income should be set against her earned income. HMRC rejected the claim and imposed a penalty. M appealed, contending that she had not been negligent as her tax adviser had completed the return on her behalf. The First-tier Tribunal allowed M's appeal against the penalty. Judge Geraint Jones held that 'if the advice of a professional, in the sphere of tax matters usually an accountant, is negligently provided, that negligence is not to be imputed to the taxpayer'. This contrasted with the position where an accountant was merely acting as an agent, for the purpose of filing a return. He concluded that 'if a taxpayer claims that his accountant has been negligent, for example, by failing to meet a deadline for filing a return or undertaking some or other administrative task, then the negligence of the accountant will not usually provide a defence to a penalty because the accountant is simply acting as the taxpayer's agent or functionary in filing the document that needs to be filed by a particular deadline. In other words, he is acting as a mere agent or functionary for his principal; but not as an independent professional adviser. However, in a situation where a professional adviser is not retained simply to act as a functionary, but is retained to give professional advice based upon the best of his skill and professional ability, he is not then a functionary or agent for his principal.' In such cases, 'reliance upon properly provided professional advice, absent reason to believe that it is wrong, unreliable or hedged about with substantial caveats, will usually lead to the conclusion that a taxpayer has not been negligent if she has taken and acted upon that advice'. *Mrs E Mariner v HMRC*, FTT [2013] UKFTT 657 (TC); [2014] SFTD 504, TC03039.

CIS returns

[44.303] HMRC imposed penalties totalling £31,800 on a roofing contractor (S) who had failed to submit his CIS returns by the due date. S appealed, contending that he had a reasonable excuse because he had been receiving dialysis treatment following the failure of a transplanted kidney, and had relied on a bookkeeper while he had been recovering from the treatment. Furthermore, HMRC had not sent him the CIS forms until they had been requested to do so by an accountant whom he had engaged to replace his former bookkeeper. The First-tier Tribunal accepted S's evidence and allowed his appeal, finding that S had 'been stoical in running or attempting to run his business, so as to avoid becoming a burden on the State, at a time when he has suffered very substantial medical difficulties'. *M Stone v HMRC*, FTT [2010] UKFTT 414 (TC), TC00684.

Employers' returns

[44.304] A company (M) failed to submit its P35 by the due date, and HMRC imposed a penalty. M appealed, contending that it had a reasonable excuse because it had applied for the necessary activation codes, and that

HMRC had been slow in issuing them. The First-tier Tribunal accepted M's evidence and allowed its appeal. *The Management & Design Co Ltd v HMRC*, FTT [2011] UKFTT 574 (TC), TC01417.

[44.305] Similar decisions were reached in *Palewell Interims Ltd v HMRC*, FTT [2011] UKFTT 734 (TC), TC01571; *Corballon Ltd v HMRC*, FTT [2011] UKFTT 798 (TC), TC01634, and *Beauxfield Ltd v HMRC*, FTT [2013] UKFTT 545 (TC), TC02934.

[44.306] A company failed to submit its 2007/08 P35 by the due date, and HMRC imposed a penalty. The company appealed, contending that it had a reasonable excuse because it had attempted to submit the P35 online on 19 May 2008, but the Government Gateway had crashed; it had telephoned HMRC and had been advised to submit a paper return; it had submitted a paper return which HMRC had not received; and it had not discovered this until after the due date, and had then submitted a duplicate paper return. The First-tier Tribunal accepted the company's evidence and allowed its appeal. *A & B Fencing Ltd v HMRC*, FTT [2014] UKFTT 592 (TC), TC03717.

[44.307] A village rugby club, with one employee, attempted to file its P35 online on 26 May 2010 (seven days after the due date). HMRC did not receive the return, but the club treasurer did not realise this. HMRC subsequently imposed penalties. The club appealed, contending that it had a reasonable excuse because it had thought that the P35 had been successfully transmitted on 26 May. The First-tier Tribunal accepted this contention and allowed the appeal. *Pontyberem Rugby Football Club v HMRC*, FTT [2011] UKFTT 511 (TC), TC01358.

[44.308] Similar decisions were reached in *JW Hardy (t/a Benwell Garage) v HMRC*, FTT [2011] UKFTT 716 (TC), TC01553; *P & D Needham v HMRC*, FTT [2011] UKFTT 752 (TC), TC01589; *W Seddon & S McMinn (t/a Bridge House Bar & Dining Room) v HMRC*, FTT [2011] UKFTT 784 (TC), TC01618; *B Purveur v HMRC*, FTT [2011] UKFTT 850 (TC), TC01684; *Ms S Marshall (t/a Friday Field Stables) v HMRC*, FTT [2012] UKFTT 15 (TC), TC01714; *Send Project v HMRC*, FTT [2012] UKFTT 78 (TC), TC01774; *KJ Bellchambers v HMRC*, FTT [2012] UKFTT 204 (TC), TC01899; *Wayne Watkins Oil Burner Services Ltd v HMRC*, FTT [2013] UKFTT 195 (TC), TC02610; *Eclipse Generic Ltd v HMRC*, FTT [2013] UKFTT 248 (TC), TC02662; *DJ Porter v HMRC*, FTT [2013] UKFTT 519 (TC), TC02907; *David Wake-Walker Ltd v HMRC*, FTT [2013] UKFTT 717 (TC), TC03097; *Took Us A Long Time Ltd v HMRC*, FTT [2014] UKFTT 026 (TC), TC03167, and *Hogg Joinery Ltd v HMRC*, FTT [2014] UKFTT 286 (TC), TC03425.

[44.309] A company (T) did not submit its 2010/11 P35 until 31 January 2012. HMRC imposed a penalty, and T appealed, contending that it had a reasonable excuse because its managing director had been suffering from prolonged illness. Judge Mitting accepted this contention and allowed the appeal. *TW Clark Holdings Ltd v HMRC*, FTT [2013] UKFTT 231 (TC), TC02645.

[44.310] Prolonged illness suffered by a publican was held to constitute a reasonable excuse in *R Howard (t/a the Albion Inn) v HMRC*, FTT [2013] UKFTT 587 (TC), TC02976.

[44.311] Prolonged illness suffered by a vet was held to constitute a reasonable excuse in *P Collins v HMRC*, FTT [2014] UKFTT 479 (TC), TC03606.

[44.312] A church failed to submit its 2010/11 P35 until February 2012, and HMRC imposed a penalty. The church appealed, contending that it had a reasonable excuse because its treasurer had been suffering from stress. Judge Sheppard accepted this contention and allowed the appeal. *Peebles Baptist Church v HMRC*, FTT [2014] UKFTT 064 (TC), TC03204.

[44.313] A company (R) failed to submit its 2010/11 P35 until December 2011, and HMRC imposed a penalty. R appealed, contending that it had a reasonable excuse because its company secretary had been pregnant and had suffered unexpected complications. The First-tier Tribunal accepted this contention and allowed the appeal. *Rockwell Management Ltd v HMRC*, FTT [2014] UKFTT 470 (TC), TC03597.

[44.314] A trader (F) sold his business in July 2008. He gave his employees P45s and paid the PAYE due. However he did not submit a form P35, and HMRC subsequently imposed a penalty. F appealed, contending that he had phoned HMRC in 2008 and had been told that he simply needed to send a letter explaining that he had ceased trading and paid all PAYE due, and that he had not been told that he would also need to submit a form P35. The First-tier Tribunal accepted F's evidence and allowed his appeal. Judge Geraint Jones found that F had been given 'misleading or incomplete information which led him reasonably to believe that he had done all that he was required to do upon closing or selling his business', and held that this constituted a reasonable excuse. *TJ Fisher (t/a The Crispin) v HMRC*, FTT [2011] UKFTT 235 (TC), TC01100.

[44.315] Similar decisions were reached in *P McStay v HMRC*, FTT [2012] UKFTT 48 (TC), TC01746; *Hott Joint Carvery v HMRC*, FTT [2013] UKFTT 230 (TC), TC02644; *L Howard v HMRC*, FTT [2014] UKFTT 013 (TC), TC03154, and *Gray Publishing v HMRC*, FTT [2014] UKFTT 113 (TC), TC03253.

[44.316] A parish council failed to submit two forms P35 by the due date, and HMRC imposed penalties. The council appealed, contending that it had not received the necessary forms although its clerk had informed HMRC that she had changed her address. The First-tier Tribunal accepted the council's evidence and allowed its appeal, holding that the circumstances constituted a reasonable excuse. *Mayfield Parish Council v HMRC*, FTT [2012] UKFTT 3 (TC), TC01702.

[44.317] An employer (L) failed to submit his P35 by the due date, and HMRC imposed a penalty. L appealed, contending that he had a reasonable excuse because he had thought that his accountant would submit the return. Judge Geraint Jones accepted this contention and allowed L's appeal. *A Leachman (t/a Whiteley & Leachman) v HMRC*, FTT [2011] UKFTT 261 (TC), TC01125.

[44.318] Judge Cornwell-Kelly reached a similar decision in *Yellow Crown Ltd v HMRC*, FTT [2013] UKFTT 527 (TC), TC02915.

[44.319] A company (P) failed to submit its 2010/11 P35 by the due date, and HMRC imposed a penalty. P appealed, contending that it had relied on its accountant to submit the P35, but he had failed to do so, and it had subsequently appointed a new accountant. The First-tier Tribunal allowed the appeal, applying the principles laid down in *Rowland v HMRC*, **43.44** PAYMENT OF TAX. Judge Sheppard observed that 'the standard of service provided by the former agent was significantly below that expected of a chartered accountant'. *Providence Health Consultants Ltd v HMRC*, FTT [2013] UKFTT 601 (TC), TC02988.

[44.320] A company (W) attempted to submit its 2009/10 P35 online on 8 April 2010, but inadvertently failed to remove the tick from the box marked 'test submission'. HMRC subsequently imposed a penalty of £400 on the basis that W had not submitted its P35. W appealed. The First-tier Tribunal allowed its appeal. Judge Redston stated that 'the default position is that a P35 filing is treated as a test rather than a live submission', and that 'HMRC have not provided any evidence to the tribunal which shows that taxpayers were warned of the significance of this tick box'. She held that 'it was reasonable for the company to have thought that the P35 had been filed correctly online'. *Writtle College Services Ltd v HMRC*, FTT [2011] UKFTT 478 (TC), TC01325.

[44.321] Judge Redston reached similar decisions in *Global Legalisation Services Ltd v HMRC*, FTT [2011] UKFTT 587 (TC), TC01430 and *Lifesmart Ltd v HMRC*, FTT [2012] UKFTT 137 (TC), TC01832.

[44.322] Judge Tildesley reached a similar decision in *Comprehensive Management Consultants Ltd v HMRC*, FTT [2013] UKFTT 238 (TC), TC02652.

[44.323] Judge Staker reached a similar decision in *G West (t/a Dishforth Nursery Gardens) v HMRC*, FTT [2013] UKFTT 485 (TC), TC02868.

[44.324] Similar decisions were reached in *TRM Electronics Ltd v HMRC*, FTT [2013] UKFTT 602 (TC), TC02989, and *Valley Centre v HMRC*, FTT [2014] UKFTT 118 (TC), TC03258.

Penalties in relation to notices (including 'precepts')

Notices issued by Commissioners

Failure to comply with precepts—illness alleged in mitigation

[44.325] In December 1973 General Commissioners issued a notice to a taxpayer (S) under *TMA, s 51** requiring certain information. In February 1974 S submitted medical certificates indicating that he was suffering from a chest infection. On 13 March the Commissioners imposed a penalty of £50 for non-compliance with the notice, and on 10 April they imposed a further penalty of £280. S appealed to the Ch D, which dismissed his appeal, holding that there was no ground for interfering with the Commissioners' decision. Goulding J observed that S's illness was not such 'as would make it impossible to produce any information at all'. *Shah v Hampstead Commrs & CIR*, Ch D

1974, 49 TC 651; [1974] STC 438. (*Note. TMA, s 51* was subsequently repealed by *SI 1994/1813*. See *General Commissioners (Jurisdiction and Procedure) Regulations 1994 (SI 1994/1812), reg 10.*)

[44.326] An individual appealed against a penalty of £25 imposed for non-compliance with a precept, contending that he had been unable to attend the hearing because of hay fever. The Ch D dismissed his appeal. Walton J observed that the Commissioners had not imposed the maximum penalty. *Chapman v Sheaf Commrs & CIR*, Ch D 1975, 49 TC 689; [1975] STC 170.

[44.327] In January 1981 General Commissioners issued a notice to an individual (S) under *TMA, s 51*. He did not supply the information requested, and the Commissioners imposed a £2 per day penalty from May 1981 to March 1982. S appealed to the Ch D, contending that he had been seriously ill in hospital, and had entrusted his accountant with the work of supplying the information. The Ch D dismissed the appeal. Warner J observed that the Commissioners had not imposed the maximum penalty of £10 per day, nor had it been for the whole of the period in which there had been a failure to comply with the precept. Taking all the circumstances into account, the penalty was lenient. *Sen v St Anne Westminster Commrs*, Ch D [1983] STC 415.

Precepts requiring balance sheets—whether unreasonable

[44.328] General Commissioners imposed penalties at the maximum rate of £10 per day on two brothers, and six companies of which they were directors, for failure to comply with notices under *TMA, s 51*. They appealed, contending that the notices were *ultra vires* since they called for balance sheets. The Ch D rejected this contention and dismissed the appeals. Templeman J held that 'companies are under a statutory duty to keep accounts and if they have no balance sheets they must make them. When these notices were served, if there were copies of balance sheets in existence they should have been supplied, and if there were not then the accounts should have been brought up to date and then supplied'. *Toogood & Others v Bristol Commrs (No 2)*, Ch D 1976, 51 TC 634; [1977] STC 116.

[44.329] General Commissioners issued precepts requiring a landlord to produce balance sheets. He failed to do so, and the Commissioners imposed penalties. He appealed to the Ch D, contending that he should only be required to produce a profit and loss account, and should not have been required to produce balance sheets. The Ch D rejected this contention and dismissed his appeal. *Khan v Newport Commrs & CIR*, Ch D 1994, 70 TC 239; [1994] STC 972. (*Note.* The CA rejected an application to make a late appeal against this decision—see 4.229 APPEALS.)

Precepts requiring information within 50 days—whether unreasonable.

[44.330] At a hearing on 11 December 1990, General Commissioners issued four precepts under *TMA, s 51(1)* requiring two companies to deliver accounts and specified documents and information within 50 days. The companies failed to comply with the notices, and at a subsequent hearing on 5 February 1991 the Commissioners imposed an initial penalty of £50 in respect of each precept, and adjourned the hearing for 60 days. At the next hearing, on 23 April, the companies produced information to satisfy two of the precepts, but failed to supply the information required by the remaining two. The Commissioners awarded a penalty of £2,000 against each company. The companies appealed against the penalties, contending that they were excessive. The Ch D dismissed the appeals, holding that the fact that the Commissioners had not awarded the maximum penalties showed that they were aware of the difficulties faced by the companies. *Delapage Ltd v Highbury Commrs & CIR (and related appeal)*, Ch D 1992, 64 TC 560; [1992] STC 290.

Effect of non-receipt of notice of hearing at which penalties imposed

[44.331] General Commissioners imposed a penalty of £50 on an individual (C) for non-compliance with a notice issued under *TMA, s 51*. C appealed, contending that the penalty was unreasonable since he had not received notice of the hearing at which it was imposed. The Ch D dismissed his appeal, holding that this could not be considered on appeal but only by way of an application for a prerogative order. Templeman J observed that C had failed 'to take any steps to attempt to comply with the Commissioners' notice'. *Campbell v Rochdale Commrs & CIR*, Ch D 1975, 50 TC 411; [1975] STC 311; [1975] 2 All ER 385.

Precept issued after purported withdrawal of appeal

[44.332] A solicitor (B) appealed against an estimated assessment. Two days before the hearing of his appeal, B wrote to the Commissioners and the Revenue purporting to withdraw it. The Revenue refused to agree to the withdrawal, and at the hearing the Commissioners issued a notice under *TMA, s 51*. B failed to comply with the notice, and the Commissioners subsequently imposed a penalty of £50. B appealed against the penalty, contending that, because he had withdrawn his appeal against the assessment, the Commissioners had no jurisdiction to issue the notice. The Ch D rejected this contention and dismissed the appeal, observing that the effect of *TMA, s 54(4)(b)* was that the Revenue was entitled to refuse to agree to the withdrawal of an appeal. *Beach v Willesden Commrs & CIR*, Ch D 1981, 55 TC 663; [1982] STC 157. (*Note.* Various other contentions raised by the solicitor, who conducted his appeal in person, were also rejected.)

Penalties upheld on appeal—other cases

[44.333] Penalties in relation to Commissioners' precepts were upheld in the following cases, none of which appears to raise any point of general importance. *Toogood & Others v Bristol Commrs (No 1)*, Ch D 1976, 51 TC 634; [1976] STC 250; *Galleri v Wirral Commrs*, Ch D [1979] STC 216; *QT Discount Foodstores Ltd v Warley Commrs & CIR*, Ch D 1981, 57 TC 268; [1982] STC 40; *Rujaib v Kensington Commrs & CIR*, Ch D 1981, 57 TC 268; [1982] STC 40; *Stoll v High Wycombe Commrs & CIR (No 1)*, Ch D 1992, 64 TC 587; [1992] STC 179 and *Stoll v High Wycombe Commrs (No 2)*, Ch D 1994, 67 TC 490; [1995] STC 91.

Penalty imposed while assessment under appeal

[44.334] General Commissioners issued a notice under *TMA, s 51*, requiring an Individual (B) to deliver to them details of an account with a Geneva bank, into which he had transferred more than £200,000, including the names of the people beneficially entitled to the funds in the account. B provided part of the required information, but the Commissioners did not accept as credible his explanation of the reasons why he was unable to supply the further information required. They held that he had failed to comply with the notice and awarded a penalty against him. The Ch D allowed B's appeal against the penalty, holding that, as he had not had the opportunity to give evidence in support of his contention and his appeal against the assessment had not been determined, the award of a penalty effectively prejudged the issue. *Boulton v CIR & Poole Commrs*, Ch D 1988, 60 TC 718; [1988] STC 709.

Appeal against penalties—respondent wrongly named

[44.335] In 1985 the Special Commissioners awarded penalties against a company. The company appealed but wrongly named the Kensington General Commissioners as respondents. Although the company was advised of the error in June 1985, its solicitors did not apply to amend the proceedings until 13 months later. The Ch D dismissed the company's appeal and its application for extension of time, observing that the appellants had themselves to blame and had disregarded an opportunity to correct their error. *Wardman Paul Ltd v Kensington Commrs & CIR*, Ch D 1986, 59 TC 416; [1986] STC 545.

Company struck off register before hearing of appeal

[44.336] General Commissioners imposed penalties (at the rate of two-thirds of the permitted maximum), on an individual and on a number of companies which he controlled, for failure to comply with precepts. The Ch D dismissed appeals against the penalties, holding that the Commissioners had been justified in imposing them. One of the companies had been struck off the Register of Companies after the imposition of the penalties but before the appeal to the Ch D. The Ch D awarded costs against the solicitors purporting to act for the company, holding that, in purporting to act for a defunct company, they were in breach of a warranty of authority given by holding out that their client existed. *Wilson & Others v Leek Commrs & CIR*, Ch D 1993, 66 TC 537; [1994] STC 147.

Appeal against penalty for failure to comply with witness summons

[44.337] General Commissioners imposed a penalty of £25 for failure to comply with a witness summons. The witness appealed, but his appeal was outside the 30-day time limit. The Ch D dismissed his application for an extension of the time limit. *R v Rochford Commrs (ex p. Bales)*, Ch D 1964, 42 TC 17.)

SI 1994/1811—penalty for non-compliance

[44.338] In the case noted at 29.50 FURTHER ASSESSMENTS: LOSS OF TAX, the Special Commissioners imposed a penalty of £250 on an accountant who had failed to comply with a direction. *Mashood v Whitehead (and related appeals)*, Sp C [2002] SSCD 166 (Sp C 308).

[44.339] A similar decision was reached in *Doshi v Andrew*, Sp C [2005] SSCD 427 (Sp C 469). (*Note.* At a subsequent hearing, the Commissioner determined the accountant's profits at £494,994 for 1996/97 and £538,905 for 1997/98—*Doshi v Andrew (No 2)*, Sp C [2005] SSCD 680 (Sp C 487).)

[44.340] In the case noted at **71.102** CAPITAL GAINS TAX, the Special Commissioner imposed a penalty of £500 under *Special Commissioners (Jurisdiction and Procedure) Regulations 1994 (SI 1994/1811), reg 24* for failure to comply with directions. *Foxton v HMRC*, Sp C July 2005 (Sp C 485).

SI 1994/1812—penalty for non-compliance

[44.341] General Commissioners served a notice under *General Commissioners (Jurisdiction and Procedure) Regulations 1994 (SI 1994/1812), reg 10* on a married couple who traded in partnership, requiring them to make certain books, accounts and other documents available for inspection. The husband replied that the documents would be available at his house at 11.59 p.m. on a specified date, and subsequently refused access to the house and the documents. The Commissioners imposed a penalty of £200 on both the husband and the partnership for non-compliance with the notice. The couple appealed, contending that they had made the documents available at a specified time. The Ch D dismissed the appeals, holding that they were obliged to make the documents available for inspection at a reasonable time, but had set conditions which were 'totally unreasonable', and thus had failed to comply with the notice. The CA upheld this decision. *Johnson v Blackpool Commrs & CIR (and related appeal)*, CA 1997, 70 TC 1; [1997] STC 1202.

[44.342] General Commissioners imposed two penalties of £4,000 each on an individual (P) who had failed to comply with notices served under the *General Commissioners (Jurisdiction and Procedure) Regulations 1994 (SI 1994/1812), reg 10*. The Ch D upheld the penalties and dismissed P's appeals. *Phipps v New Forest West Commrs & CIR*, Ch D [1997] STC 797.

[44.343] Seven companies, each of which were 'small companies' within *Companies Act 1985, s 247*, submitted abbreviated accounts, without external verification, in support of appeals against estimated assessments. An inspector visited the companies' premises and formed the opinion that the records were inadequate. Subsequently the General Commissioners served notices under the *General Commissioners (Jurisdiction and Procedure) Regulations 1994 (SI 1994/1812), reg 10*. The companies failed to comply with the notices, and the Commissioners imposed penalties totalling £3,450. The Ch D dismissed the companies' appeals. Lightman J held that the privileges and exemptions conferred on 'small companies' under *Companies Act 1985* did not extend to excusing them 'from the obligation to prepare and retain accounting records'. The Commissioners could not be required to take the companies' figures on trust. They were entitled to require 'satisfaction that the figures shown in accounts have a proper basis in fact' and 'to require a profit and loss account in one of the four formats appropriate to a small company'. On the evidence, 'if the level of penalties imposed is to be criticised at all, that criticism would be rather that they are too low than that they were too high'. The companies' defaults had been 'deliberate, of longstanding and inexcusable'. *Slater Ltd & Others v Beacontree Commrs*, Ch D 2001, 74 TC 471; [2002] STC 246.

[44.344] A similar decision was reached in a subsequent case involving the same seven companies. *Slater Ltd & Others v Beacontree Commrs (No 2)*, Ch D 2002, [2004] STC 1342; [2002] EWHC 2676(Ch).

Notices issued by Revenue

Penalties for failure to comply with notice under TMA, s 12AC

[44.345] See *Flaxmode Ltd v HMRC (No 1)*, **49.12** RETURNS AND INFORMATION.

Penalties for failure to comply with notice under TMA, s 19A

[44.346] In *Murat v HM Inspector of Taxes*, **49.24** RETURNS AND INFORMATION, an accountant was ordered to comply with a notice under *TMA, s 19A*. He failed to do so, and the Revenue subsequently imposed penalties under *TMA, s 97AA*, at the rate of £30 per day laid down by *s 97AA(2)*. The accountant appealed, contending that the penalty notices were invalid. The Special Commissioner rejected these contentions and dismissed the appeal in principle, but reduced the amount of the penalties under *TMA, s 100B(2)(b)*, observing that the penalties totalled £4,260, which was 'very substantial' by comparison with the accountant's tax liability. The Commissioner directed that the penalties should be reduced by one-third to £20 per day. The accountant appealed to the QB and also applied for judicial review, contending that he should not have been required to produce a balance sheet, and that the imposition of the penalties contravened *Articles 3 and 4* of the *European Convention on Human Rights*. The QB rejected these contentions and dismissed the appeal and application. Moses J held that the effect of *TMA, s 19A(11)* was that the Commissioner's decision in *Murat v HM Inspector of Taxes*, **49.24** RETURNS AND INFORMATION, was final and conclusive. Furthermore, the work necessary to comply with the notices was a 'civic obligation' which was authorised by *Article 4* of the *Convention*. *Murat v CIR (aka Murat v Ornoch); R v CIR (oao Murat)*, QB 2004, 77 TC 122; [2005] STC 184; [2004] EWHC 3123 (Admin).

[44.347] An individual (S) failed to comply with a notice under *TMA, s 19A*. The Revenue imposed a penalty of £50 under *TMA, s 97AA(1)(a)*. S appealed, contending that the imposition of the penalty contravened *Article 6* of the *European Convention on Human Rights*. The Special Commissioner rejected this contention and dismissed the appeal, and the QB upheld this decision. Etherton J held that although there was an 'element of punishment' in the penalty, its primary function was 'to procure the production of the documents requested by the Revenue'. The charge was not 'a criminal charge' within *Article 6(1)*, so that there was no scope for any complaint that S's 'privilege to remain silent and not to incriminate himself' had been infringed. Since neither prosecution or 'evasion penalties' were under consideration, the provisions of *Police and Criminal Evidence Act 1984, s 66* did not apply. Furthermore, the Commissioner had not shown any bias in favour of the Revenue. *Sharkey v HMRC (aka Sharkey v De Croos)*, Ch D 2006, 77 TC 484; [2006] STC 2026; [2006] EWHC 300 (Ch). (*Note*. In the report at 77 TC 484, the judge's name is wrongly given as 'Etherington J': this is an error by the TSO editor.)

[44.348] The Revenue issued four penalty notices to a hairdresser who had failed to comply with notices under *TMA, s 19A*. The hairdresser appealed. The Special Commissioner reviewed the evidence in detail and allowed the appeals against two of the notices, finding that their wording was defective because they stated 'two different figures for the penalty: £340 at the beginning and £340 per day for 34 days at the end'. The Commissioner held that the other two notices were valid but that the amounts of the penalties were excessive in relation to the tax liability, and reduced each of these penalties from £510 to £255 (ie 20.5% of the tax liability for the earlier year and 12.5% of the tax liability for the later year). *Austin v Price*, Sp C [2004] SSCD 487 (Sp C 426).

[44.349] In one of the cases listed at **49.21** RETURNS AND INFORMATION, where a landlord had failed to comply with two notices issued under *TMA, s 19A*, the Revenue subsequently imposed penalties under *TMA, s 97AA*. The landlord appealed, contending that the penalties should be discharged because his ability to deal with the notices had been seriously affected by his religious duties as an Islamic imam. The Special Commissioner dismissed the appeal, holding that the penalties were 'reasonable and proportionate in all the circumstances'. *M Afsar v HMRC (No 2)*, Sp C 2007, [2008] SSCD 348 (Sp C 645).

[44.350] In the case noted at **49.20** RETURNS AND INFORMATION, an individual (S) had failed to comply with a notice under *TMA, s 19A*. HMRC imposed a penalty of £50 under *TMA, s 100(1)*. The First-tier Tribunal allowed S's appeal against the penalty, holding that the notice was invalid because it had specified the wrong date. Judge Berner also held that, because S had appealed to the High Court, and had applied for leave to appeal to the Court of Appeal, he had a reasonable excuse for not complying with the notice 'up to the time his possibilities of appeal were legally exhausted'. *AO Sokoya v HMRC (No 2)*, FTT [2009] SFTD 480; [2009] UKFTT 163 (TC), TC00125.

[44.351] A company failed to comply with several notices under *TMA, s 19A*, and HMRC imposed penalties under *TMA, s 97AA*, covering the years 2003/04 to 2005/06 inclusive. The company appealed, contending *inter alia* that the penalties amounted to a criminal charge within *Article 6* of the *European Convention on Human Rights*. The First-tier Tribunal rejected this contention and dismissed the appeal, applying the principles laid down by Etherton J in *Sharkey v HMRC*, **44.347** above, and declining to follow *obiter dicta* of Henderson J in *Pipe v HMRC*, **44.13** above. Furthermore, the penalty determinations complied with *TMA, s 100*, and the company did not have a reasonable excuse for the failure to comply with the notices. *Flaxmode Ltd v HMRC (No 2)*, FTT [2010] SFTD 498; [2010] UKFTT 28 (TC), TC00342. (*Note*. For a previous appeal by the same company, see **49.12** RETURNS AND INFORMATION.)

[44.352] HMRC issued notices under *TMA, s 19A*, for 2001/02 to 2006/07 inclusive, to a landlord (H). H did not respond to the notices, and HMRC subsequently imposed penalties under *TMA, s 97AA*. H appealed against the penalties, contending that he had already produced all the documents which he had. The First-tier Tribunal rejected this contention and dismissed his appeals, finding that 'only some of the information requested had been supplied' and that 'the documents sought were clearly in the possession and power'. *S Habashi v HMRC*, FTT [2010] UKFTT 531 (TC), TC00785.

[44.353] A solicitor failed to comply with a notice under *TMA, s 19A*. HMRC imposed penalties under *TMA, s 97AA*. The First-tier Tribunal upheld the penalties and dismissed the solicitor's appeal. *MJ Rayner v HMRC*, FTT [2012] UKFTT 694 (TC), TC02363. (*Note*. Appeals against discovery assessments were also dismissed.)

[44.354] See also *Jacques v HMRC (No 2)*, **55.18** SELF-ASSESSMENT.

Penalty for non-compliance with TMA, s 20(1)

[44.355] The Revenue issued a notice under *TMA, s 20(1)* to an individual who had failed to submit any tax returns since moving to the UK. He failed to comply with the notice, and the General Commissioners imposed a penalty of £300 under *TMA, s 100C*. The Ch D upheld the penalty. Lloyd J held that there was 'ample material before the Commissioners' to justify their conclusion that 'it was appropriate to impose a penalty'. *Patrick v CIR*, Ch D 2002, 74 TC 700. (*Note*. For subsequent proceedings in this case, see **31.6** HUMAN RIGHTS.)

[44.356] In October 2000 a married couple disposed of some shares. The Revenue issued a notice under *TMA, s 20(1)* to the husband (J), requesting certain documents relating to this disposal. J failed to produce the documents, and the General Commissioners imposed a penalty of £300 under *TMA, s 98*. The Ch D upheld their decision. Morgan J held that this was 'a proper case for the imposition of a penalty', and that there were no grounds for interfering with the amount. *MA Johnson v HMRC*, Ch D [2008] STC 2179; [2008] EWHC 412 (Ch).

[44.357] A partnership failed to comply with a notice issued under *TMA, s 20(1)*. The General Commissioners imposed penalties of £300 on each of the partners. They appealed, contending that the penalty should have been charged on the partnership, rather than on the individual partners. The Ch D rejected this contention and dismissed the appeal. Norris J observed that 'in English law, a partnership has no separate legal identity or existence'. Under *Partnership Act 1890, s 24*, 'each individual partner has an immediate right of access to all books and records'. Accordingly the Commissioners were entitled to hold 'that the penalty should be imposed on the individual partners'. *Wan & Others v Doncaster Commrs & CIR*, Ch D 2004, 76 TC 211.

[44.358] A married couple stated on their 1997/98 tax return that they were not resident in the UK. The Revenue held information suggesting that this was incorrect, and that they had substantial CGT liability in the UK. Accordingly the Revenue issued a notice under *TMA, s 20(1)*, requesting particulars of the days which the couple had spent in the UK from 6 April 1996 to 5 April 1998. The couple failed to comply with the notice, and the Revenue imposed penalties under *TMA, s 100*. The couple appealed against the penalties, contending that they now accepted that they were resident in the UK for tax purposes so that the information required was 'no longer relevant'. The Special Commissioner dismissed their appeal, holding that 'the inspector is entitled, perhaps bound, to determine residence as a matter of fact and law regardless of any concession by the appellants'. The Commissioner observed that there appeared to be a tax liability of about £7,000,000, and held that there were no grounds for mitigating the penalties. *Morris & Morris v Roberts*

(No 1), Sp C [2004] SSCD 245 (Sp C 407). (*Notes.* (1) Costs were awarded to the Revenue—see **4.443** APPEALS. (2) For subsequent developments in this case, see **44.190** above.)

[44.359] An individual (W) submitted a 2004/05 tax return claiming a capital loss of £2,000,000. The Revenue entered these figures on their computer, but subsequently lost the return. They subsequently asked W for a copy of the return, so that they could ascertain whether W had disclosed any information with regard to the claimed loss. W failed to produce a copy of the return, and the Revenue issued a notice under *TMA, s 20(1)*. W still failed to submit a copy of the return, and the Revenue issued a summons under *TMA, s 100C*. The Special Commissioner imposed a penalty of £300, holding that the return contained information relevant to W's tax liability, and the fact that the Revenue had received the original return did not prevent them from requiring a copy. *HMRC v MI Wilson*, Sp C 2008, [2009] SSCD 130 (Sp C 724).

[44.360] HMRC issued a notice under *TMA, s 20(1)*, requiring an individual (D) to provide bank statements. D failed to comply with the notice, and the First-tier Tribunal imposed a penalty of £300 under *TMA, s 98*. The tribunal observed that 'the maximum penalty is modest compared with the tax which is in issue'. *HMRC v AL Deadman (and related applications)*, FTT [2009] UKFTT 76 (TC), TC00044. (Note. The tribunal also dismissed appeals by D, and a partnership of which he was a member, against notices under *TMA, s 19A*, and applications for closure notices under *TMA, s 28A*.)

[44.361] HMRC issued notices under *TMA, s 20(1)* requiring three settlors to provide various documents relating to the trusts they had established. They provided some of the information requested, but failed to provide all the relevant information, and HMRC applied for penalties. The First-tier Tribunal imposed penalties of £200 on two of the settlors, and imposed a penalty of £250 on the third settlor. Judge Mosedale observed that it was 'improbable that a settlor would destroy such documents particularly in respect of a trust in which he and his close family are the only beneficiaries'. *HMRC v P Parissis (and related applications)*, FTT [2011] UKFTT 218 (TC); [2011] SFTD 757, TC01083.

[44.362] See also *B & S Displays Ltd v Special Commrs*, **49.30** RETURNS AND INFORMATION, and *Kempton v Special Commrs & CIR*, **49.38** RETURNS AND INFORMATION.

Penalty for non-compliance with TMA, s 20(3)

[44.363] The Revenue issued a notice under *TMA, s 20(3)* to an accountant (F), requiring him to produce certain files relating to one of his clients. F failed to comply with the notice, and the Commissioners imposed a penalty. F appealed, contending that the penalty was unreasonable, as he had moved the relevant records to a depository and was unable to trace the documents in question. The Ch D rejected this contention and dismissed the appeal. Jacob J held that there was a *prima facie* expectation that an accountant would hold the documents in question. The onus was therefore on F to demonstrate that he did not have them. In view of the information which F had provided, the inspector and the Commissioners were entitled to decline to accept that the documents could not be traced. *Fox v McKay; Fox v Uxbridge Commrs*, Ch D 2001, 75 TC 42; [2002] STC 455.

Validity of action under TMA, s 20C

[44.364] See *R v CIR (ex p. Rossminster Ltd & Others)*, 49.63 RETURNS AND INFORMATION.

Penalties for non-compliance with TMA, s 22*

[44.365] An individual (J) failed to comply with notices issued under *TMA, s 22** covering a period of nine years. The Revenue sued for penalties of £50 per year, alleging that J 'without reasonable excuse has failed to furnish the particulars required'. He submitted a defence stating that he denied 'that he failed to furnish any such particulars without reasonable cause'. The CA ordered J to provide further details of the excuse alleged. Pearce LJ observed that 'the only object of the defendant in seeking to avoid giving these particulars is admittedly to prevent the Crown knowing before the trial what the defendant's case is and thus to give the defendant the advantage of surprise. That is an unmeritorious object and would probably lead to an inconvenient adjournment of the case in the middle of the hearing.' *CIR v Jackson*, CA 1960, 39 TC 357; [1960] 1 WLR 873; [1960] 3 All ER 31. (*Note.* The *Rules of the Supreme Court 1965 (SI 1965/1776)*, and their precursors, refer to 'particulars'. With effect from 26 April 1999, these rules have largely been replaced by the *Civil Procedure Rules 1998 (SI 1998/3132)*, which refer instead to 'information'.)

Penalties for failure to comply with notices under ITA 2007, s 748*

[44.366] The Special Commissioners imposed penalties of £200 on an individual (M) for failure to comply with notices to him under *ITA 2007, s 748**, together with further penalties totalling £5,760 for his continued failure to comply. M appealed, contending that he had a reasonable excuse because he had relied on his accountant. The Ch D dismissed his appeal, holding that the circumstances did not constitute a reasonable excuse and that the penalties were not excessive. Foster J observed that 'it was lucky for (M) that the Crown did not ask me to increase the penalties to the full amount of £10 per day, which I have power to do'. *Mankowitz v Special Commrs & CIR*, Ch D 1971, 46 TC 707.

Penalties for failure to comply with notice under FA 1998, Sch 18 para 27

[44.367] A company's accounts showed disposals of fixed assets, which were not reflected in its tax computations. The Revenue requested further information. The company failed to respond to a letter from the Revenue, and in May 2003 the Revenue issued a notice under *FA 1998, Sch 18 para 27*. The Revenue still did not receive the requested information, and the Revenue imposed penalties of £20 per day (totalling £620). The company appealed, contending that its accountant had sent a letter to the Revenue in June 2003. The Special Commissioner found 'on the balance of probability' that the letter had been sent but had not been received by the Revenue. However the Commissioner noted that the letter failed to provide much of the information requested by the Revenue's notice, and found that the company had 'made no serious attempt to reply to the notice by providing the inspector with information necessary to check the computation'. The Commissioner reduced the penalty from £620 to £310. *Alan Porter Ltd v HM Inspector of Taxes*, Sp C [2004] SSCD 147 (Sp C 398).

[44.368] A company (R) submitted a return claiming tax relief for expenditure on research and development. HMRC began an enquiry into the return, and requested further information. R did not produce the information, and HMRC issued notices under *FA 1998, Sch 18 para 27*. R failed to comply with the notices, and HMRC imposed penalties under *Sch 18 para 29*. R appealed, contending that it had a reasonable excuse because it had asked its accountants to produce the information. The First-tier Tribunal accepted this contention and allowed the appeal, observing that the notices required R 'to produce a detailed explanation of its research and development tax relief claim with reference to the research and development legislation'. Judge Brooks held that since this legislation was complex and would not be easily understood by 'those not generally acquainted with tax law', it was reasonable for R to have relied on its accountants to provide the information to HMRC. *The Research & Development Partnership Ltd v HMRC*, FTT [2009] UKFTT 328 (TC), TC00271.

[44.369] A company (H) submitted a return claiming group relief. HMRC began an enquiry into the return, and requested further information. H did not produce the information, and HMRC issued notices under *FA 1998, Sch 18 para 27*. H failed to comply with the notices, and HMRC imposed penalties under *Sch 18 para 29*. H appealed, contending that it had a reasonable excuse because it had asked its accountants to produce the information. The First-tier Tribunal rejected this contention and dismissed the appeal, holding that the information and documents required by the notices was 'straightforward and easily understood'. Accordingly it was 'not reasonable' for H to rely on its accountants to provide this 'when it should have been able to comply with the notices itself'. *Huntley Solutions Ltd v HMRC*, FTT [2009] UKFTT 329 (TC), TC00272.

[44.370] HMRC began an enquiry into the returns submitted by two associated companies (one of which owned a large caravan site). The companies failed to comply with notices under *FA 1998, Sch 18 para 27*, and HMRC imposed penalties of £5,150 on each company under *Sch 18 para 29*. The companies appealed, contending that they were unable to comply with the notices because they were unable to retrieve the requisite records from their former accountant. The First-tier Tribunal rejected this contention and dismissed the appeals. Judge Tildesley observed that 'the appellants as a matter of law are prevented from questioning the contents of the notices for production in penalty proceedings. The appellants had their opportunity to challenge the notices in their appeal before the General Commissioners. The appellants did not attend the two meetings of the General Commissioners which had been set up to hear their appeal.' On the evidence, the appellants had 'been deliberately obstructive since HMRC opened its enquiry into their tax affairs'. *Tallington Lakes Ltd v HMRC (and related appeal)*, FTT [2011] UKFTT 402 (TC), TC01257.

Penalties for failure to comply with notices under FA 2008, Sch 36 para 1

[44.371] A couple carried on business in partnership. HMRC began an enquiry into their return, and issued notices under *FA 2008, Sch 36 para 1*, seeking copies of bank statements in an attempt to verify the origin of capital allegedly invested in the partnership. The couple failed to comply with the notices, and HMRC imposed penalties of £300 on each of them under *FA 2008, Sch 36 para 39*. The tribunal upheld the penalties and dismissed the couple's appeals. *CV & Mrs J Carden (t/a Platinum World Travel) v HMRC*, FTT [2011] UKFTT 23 (TC), TC00900.

[44.372] In October 2007 HMRC began an enquiry into a return submitted by an individual (C). In March 2010 HMRC issued a notice under *FA 2008, Sch 36 para 1* to C, requiring him to produce certain invoices, plus a reconciliation and print-out of his nominal ledger. C failed to comply with the notice, and HMRC imposed a penalty of £300 under *Sch 36 para 39*. C appealed, contending that he could not comply with the notice because the invoices were in his loft, and he was suffering from osteoporosis and could not access them. The First-tier Tribunal dismissed the appeal, observing that C had given no explanation of his failure to produce a reconciliation and print-out of his nominal ledger. Accordingly there was no reasonable excuse and no grounds for any mitigation of the penalty. *PC Clarke v HMRC (No 2)*, FTT [2011] UKFTT 427 (TC), TC01280.

[44.373] HMRC began an enquiry into the returns submitted by an accountant (P), and issued a notice under *FA 2008, Sch 36 para 1*. P failed to comply with the notice, and HMRC imposed penalties of £1020 (102 days at £10 per day). The First-tier Tribunal upheld the penalties and dismissed P's appeal. *D Parker v HMRC*, FTT [2011] UKFTT 581 (TC), TC01424.

[44.374] A retailer (W) began trading in October 2003, but did not submit any tax returns until March 2008. In January 2009 HMRC began an enquiry into his returns, and in September 2009 they sent a notice under *FA 2008, Sch 36 para 1*, requiring documents and information including bank statements. In April 2010 HMRC imposed penalties at the rate of £10 per day (totalling £1340). W appealed, contending that he had supplied all the necessary information. The First-tier Tribunal rejected this contention and dismissed his appeal, finding that W had failed to provide statements for three bank accounts. *T Wan v HMRC*, FTT [2011] UKFTT 442 (TC), TC01295.

[44.375] HMRC began an enquiry into a return submitted by a dentist (H), and issued a notice under *FA 2008, Sch 36 para 1*, requiring details of certain payments which H had claimed as deductions. H failed to comply with the notice, and HMRC imposed a penalty of £300 under *Sch 36 para 39*, and further penalties of £40 per day under *Sch 36 para 40*. The First-tier Tribunal upheld the penalties in principle but reduced the amount of the daily penalties from £40 per day to £20 per day. *Dr RM Hughes v HMRC*, FTT [2014] UKFTT 747 (TC), TC03866.

[44.376] Appeals against penalties for failure to comply with notices under *FA 2008, Sch 36 para 1* were also dismissed in *R v Hirani v HMRC (and related appeals)*, FTT [2011] UKFTT 775 (TC), TC01609; *M & J Ivison v*

HMRC, FTT [2011] UKFTT 830 (TC), TC01666; *J Beckwith v HMRC*, FTT [2012] UKFTT 181 (TC), TC01876; *F Dawaf v HMRC*, FTT [2012] UKFTT 415 (TC), TC02092; *Ms J Burton v HMRC (and related appeal)*, FTT [2012] UKFTT 473 (TC), TC02150; *R Davidson v HMRC*, FTT [2012] UKFTT 757 (TC), TC02414; *D Amin v HMRC*, FTT [2013] UKFTT 130 (TC), TC02559; *WY Chan v HMRC (No 3)*, FTT [2013] UKFTT 133 (TC), TC02562; *Community v HMRC*, FTT [2014] UKFTT 041 (TC), TC03181; *WY & SY Lam v HMRC (No 2)*, FTT [2014] UKFTT 359 (TC), TC03494; *D Pittack v HMRC*, FTT [2014] UKFTT 670 (TC), TC03793; *W Kernahan v HMRC*, FTT [2014] UKFTT 872 (TC), TC03988, and *Singh v HMRC*, **49.99** RETURNS AND INFORMATION.

[44.377] In 2010 an individual (T) was sentenced to five years' imprisonment for fraud. In 2013 HMRC sent him a notice under *FA 2008, Sch 36 para 1*. T did not comply with the notice, and HMRC imposed penalties under *Sch 36 paras 39 and 40*. T appealed, contending that he could not provide the requested information because the police had not returned his papers. The First-tier Tribunal allowed his appeal, holding that T had a reasonable excuse for not complying with the notice. Judge Cornwell-Kelly observed that 'the terms of the information itself were vague and unlimited in point of time' and that 'any further information notice would need to be more precise'. *V Tee v HMRC*, FTT [2014] UKFTT 977 (TC), TC04089.

Penalties for failure to comply with notices under FA 2008, Sch 36 para 5

[44.378] HMRC issued 20 notices under *FA 2008, Sch 36 para 5* to a company director (B), requiring information about several companies. B failed to provide the required information about five of the companies, and HMRC issued penalties of £300 under *Sch 36 para 39*. HMRC also formed the opinion that B had provided inaccurate information in relation to a further notice, and imposed a penalty of £2,000 under *Sch 36 para 40A*. B appealed against all six of the penalties. The First-tier Tribunal dismissed his appeals, finding that B had been careless and that the penalty of £2,000 was appropriate. Judge Demack observed that since the information which B had provided had contained two inaccuracies, the effect of *Sch 36 para 40A(6)* was that HMRC could have imposed a maximum penalty of £6,000. *J Backhouse v HMRC*, FTT [2014] UKFTT 247 (TC), TC03386.

Penalties for failure to make payments (FA 2009, Sch 56)

Cases where the appellant was unsuccessful

[44.379] A company (D) regularly paid its PAYE and NIC after the due dates. HMRC imposed penalties under *FA 2009, Sch 56*. D appealed. The First-tier Tribunal dismissed the appeal. Judge Berner held that the penalties were proportionate and did not contravene the European Convention on Human Rights. *Dina Foods Ltd v HMRC*, FTT [2011] UKFTT 709 (TC), TC01546.

[44.380] Similar decisions were reached in *Agar Ltd v HMRC*, FTT [2011] UKFTT 773 (TC), TC01625; *M & B Precision Engineering (Leicester) Ltd v HMRC*, FTT [2011] UKFTT 853 (TC), TC01687; *St John Patrick Publishers Ltd v HMRC*, FTT [2012] UKFTT 20 (TC), TC01719; *Meteor Capital Group Ltd v HMRC*, FTT [2012] UKFTT 101 (TC), TC01797; *SLBT Ltd v HMRC*, FTT [2012] UKFTT 422 (TC), TC02104; *McTear Contracts Ltd v HMRC*, FTT [2012] UKFTT 535 (TC), TC02211; *Falkirk Football & Athletic Club Ltd v HMRC*, FTT [2012] UKFTT 585 (TC), TC02262; *P & H Cleaning Co Ltd v HMRC*, FTT [2013] UKFTT 669 (TC), TC03051; *Denwis Ltd v HMRC*, FTT [2013] UKFTT 745 (TC), TC03123; *Clarity Copiers (Western) Ltd v HMRC*, FTT [2013] UKFTT 750 (TC), TC03129, and *P Wall v HMRC*, FTT [2014] UKFTT 139 (TC), TC03279.

[44.381] A company persistently paid its PAYE and NIC after the due dates, and HMRC imposed penalties under *FA 2009, Sch 56*. The company appealed, contending that the penalties were excessive because payments which it had made should have been allocated to its liability for the current tax month, rather than to its liability for the previous tax month. The First-tier Tribunal rejected this contention and dismissed the appeal. Applying *dicta* of Lord Macnaghten in *Cory Bros & Co Ltd v Turkish SS Mecca*, HL [1897] AC 286, 'when a debtor is making a payment to his creditor he may appropriate the money as he pleases, and the creditor must apply it accordingly. If the debtor does not make any appropriation at the time when he makes the payment, the right of application devolves on the creditor'. On the evidence, the company had chosen to make its payments a month late, and to allocate its payments to the debt for the previous month. *AJM Mansell Ltd v HMRC*, FTT [2012] UKFTT 602 (TC), TC02279.

[44.382] A limited liability partnership made several payments of PAYE and NIC after the due dates, and HMRC imposed penalties under *FA 2009, Sch 56*. The partnership appealed, contending that payments which it had made should have been allocated to its liability for the current tax month, rather than to its liability for the previous tax month. The First-tier Tribunal rejected this contention and dismissed the appeal. Judge Raghavan specifically declined to follow Judge Radford's decision in *Kelcey & Hall Solicitors v HMRC*, **44.395** below, accepting HMRC's contention that the guidance in DMBM210105, which Judge Radford had quoted, referred to 'an exceptional circumstance, not to a regular monthly payment that is governed by the PAYE Regulations'. *Bilaman Management Services Llp v HMRC*, FTT [2014] UKFTT 270 (TC), TC03409.

[44.383] The First-tier Tribunal reached a similar decision in a subsequent Scottish case in which Judge Sheppard applied the principles laid down in *Devaynes v Noble (Clayton's Case)*, RC 1816, 35 ER 767, and held that 'unless there is a clear specification otherwise, an amount received should be applied to reduce the earliest debt'. *C & DDH Ltd v HMRC*, FTT [2014] UKFTT 688 (TC), TC03810.

[44.384] A company (P) regularly paid its PAYE and NIC after the due dates. HMRC imposed penalties, calculated at 4% of the relevant tax, under *FA 2009, Sch 56*. P appealed contending that it had a reasonable excuse because it was suffering from a shortage of funds. The First-tier Tribunal dismissed the appeal. Judge Blewitt observed that 'the legislation specifically excludes cash-flow difficulties as a reasonable excuse unless attributable to events outside of the appellant's control'. *PA Dunwell Transport Ltd v HMRC*, FTT [2011] UKFTT 786 (TC), TC01620.

[44.385] Similar decisions were reached in *N Sign Ltd v HMRC*, FTT [2012] UKFTT 16 (TC), TC01715; *Aquila Processing Ltd v HMRC*, FTT [2012] UKFTT 142 (TC), TC01837; *Xtreme Business Solutions Ltd v HMRC*, FTT [2012] UKFTT 230 (TC), TC01924, and *Byre Theatre of St Andrews Ltd v HMRC*, FTT [2012] UKFTT 555 (TC), TC02232.

[44.386] An individual (B) failed to pay his 2011/12 CGT liability by the due date, and HMRC imposed a penalty under *FA 2009, Sch 56*. B appealed, contending that he had requested a deferred payment arrangement under *FA 2009, s 108*. The First-tier Tribunal dismissed his appeal, finding that HMRC had rejected B's initial proposals for deferred payment, and that no agreement under *s 108* had been reached until May 2013, which was after the due date for payment and the imposition of the penalty. *R Briggs v HMRC*, FTT [2014] UKFTT 161 (TC), TC03299.

[44.387] A similar decision was reached in *N King v HMRC*, FTT [2014] UKFTT 192 (TC), TC03332.

[44.388] An individual (H), who lived in Spain, had owned a nursing home in the UK, but sold it in 2011/12. His accountants submitted his 2011/12 tax return on 31 January 2013, and he did not pay the CGT due until March 2013. HMRC imposed a penalty under *FA 2009, Sch 56*, and H appealed, contending that he had claimed entrepreneurs' relief and had not known the amount of his CGT liability. The First-tier Tribunal dismissed his appeal, observing that H's accountants had calculated the tax liability when they filed the return, and holding that there was no reasonable excuse for the delay in payment. *JW Hall v HMRC*, FTT [2014] UKFTT 346 (TC), TC03482.

[44.389] See also *Verdegaal's Executors v HMRC*, **44.78** above.

[44.390] Appeals against penalties under *FA 2009, Sch 56* have been dismissed in a large number of other cases. In the interests of space, such cases are not summarised individually in this book. For a list of such cases decided up to 31 December 2012, see Tolley's Tax Cases 2013.

Cases where the appellant was partly successful

[44.391] During 2010/11 a solicitor consistently paid his PAYE and NIC after the due date, and HMRC imposed penalties under *FA 2009, Sch 56*. The solicitor appealed, contending that the penalty was unfair and that he had a reasonable excuse because the Legal Services Commission had consistently paid his invoices late. The First-tier Tribunal rejected these contentions and upheld the penalty in principle. Judge Hellier observed that 'a firm of lawyers which always paid late should itself have taken all reasonable steps itself to ensure that that practice did not incur penalties and should not be relieved of its liability by reason of a lack of warning in a particular notice'. However he directed that the penalty should be recomputed because a late payment of PAYE and NIC, due on 19 April 2011, had been taken into account in the computation of the penalty, which should not have been the case, since it was outside the 2010/11 tax year. *R Warren (t/a Rodney Warren & Co) v HMRC*, FTT [2012] UKFTT 57 (TC), TC01754.

[44.392] In 2010/11 a company (S) made eleven of its 12 payments of PAYE and NIC after the due dates. HMRC imposed a penalty of £7,418, calculated at 4% of the relevant tax, under *FA 2009, Sch 56*. S appealed, contending that it had a reasonable excuse because it was suffering from a shortage of funds as a result of the economic recession. The First-tier Tribunal reviewed the evidence in detail and allowed the appeal in part, holding that there was a reasonable excuse for non-payment of the amounts due on 19 May 2010 but finding that the company had had sufficient funds to have made the subsequent payments. Judge Poole also observed that the late payment of 2010/11 PAYE and NIC, due on 19 April 2011, had been taken into account in the computation of the penalty. He held that the effect of *Sch 56 para 6(3)* was that this should not be taken into account, since it was outside the 2010/11 tax year. He directed that the penalty should be imposed at 3% and reduced to £5,494. *Stone Manor Hotels Ltd v HMRC*, FTT [2011] UKFTT 774 (TC), TC01626.

[44.393] A similar decision was reached in a case where the tribunal held that a company had a reasonable excuse for one late payment, because a major customer had gone into liquidation, but that there was no reasonable excuse for nine other late payments. *Trio Offset Ltd v HMRC*, FTT [2012] UKFTT 60 (TC), TC01757.

[44.394] A similar decision was reached in *Franco Vago UK Ltd v HMRC*, FTT [2012] UKFTT 722 (TC), TC02386.

[44.395] A firm of solicitors persistently paid its PAYE and NIC after the due dates, and HMRC imposed penalties under *FA 2009, Sch 56*. The firm appealed, contending that it had a reasonable excuse because it had not received money due from the Legal Services Commission, and that the penalties were excessive because payments which it had made should have been allocated to its liability for the current tax month, rather than to its liability for the previous tax month. Judge Radford allowed the appeal in part, finding that HMRC had failed to observe the practice laid down at DMBM210105, which instructs HMRC staff that 'where exceptionally you feel the customer's allocation would not be in their best interests, for example because a different debt is about to be enforced, you can suggest to the customer that it would be in their best interests to allocate differently'. *Kelcey & Hall Solicitors v HMRC*, FTT [2012] UKFTT 662 (TC), TC02333. (*Note*. Judge Radford's decision fails to refer to the earlier decision in *AJM Mansell Ltd v HMRC*, **44.381** above. See also the subsequent decision in *Bilaman Management Services Llp v HMRC*, **44.382** above.)

[44.396] In 2010/11 a company (S) consistently paid its PAYE and NIC after the due dates. HMRC imposed a penalty under *FA 2009, Sch 56*. S appealed, contending that it had a reasonable excuse because its bank had unexpectedly reduced its overdraft facility in March 2010. The First-tier Tribunal allowed the appeal in part, holding that this constituted a reasonable excuse for the first three months but not for subsequent months. *Shine Telecom Ltd v HMRC*, FTT [2012] UKFTT 448 (TC), TC02129.

[44.397] A similar decision was reached in *Bale Group Ltd v HMRC*, FTT [2013] UKFTT 139 (TC), TC02568.

[44.398] An appeal against a penalty under *FA 2009, Sch 56* was allowed in part in a case where the tribunal found that a company's turnover had been severely reduced by unusually bad weather in January 2011. Judge Brannan held that this constituted a reasonable excuse for the late payment of the PAYE due in that month, but that there was no such excuse for previous late payments. *Rogers Concrete Ltd v HMRC*, FTT [2012] UKFTT 482 (TC), TC02159.

[44.399] A family company appealed against penalties under *FA 2009, Sch 56*, contending that it had a reasonable excuse because the daughter of its controlling directors had been diagnosed with a brain tumour in March 2010 and had died in October 2010. The First-tier Tribunal allowed the appeals in part, holding that this constituted a reasonable excuse for the first eight months of the 2010/11 tax year, but not for subsequent defaults. *Frost Group Ltd v HMRC*, FTT [2012] UKFTT 678 (TC), TC02349.

[44.400] A similar decision was reached in a case where a company's director had been suffering from cancer (and had died in March 2011). The First-tier Tribunal held that this constituted a reasonable excuse for the first six months of 2010/11, but was not a reasonable excuse for subsequent defaults, as the company should have made alternative arrangements. *Four Colours Print Services Ltd v HMRC*, FTT [2012] UKFTT 685 (TC), TC02356.

[44.401] Similar decisions were reached in *Mullany's Coaches Ltd v HMRC*, FTT [2012] UKFTT 763 (TC), TC02420, and *All Day Recruitment Services Ltd v HMRC*, [2013] UKFTT 293 (TC), TC02699.

[44.402] During 2010/11 a company (C) consistently paid its PAYE and NIC after the due dates, and HMRC imposed penalties under *FA 2009, Sch 56*. The First-tier Tribunal allowed C's appeal in respect of the first two months, finding that there was no reasonable excuse but that there were 'special circumstances' within *FA 2009, Sch 56 para 9*, because C's managing director was recovering from a heart attack which he had suffered in September 2009. *Claygold Property Ltd v HMRC*, FTT [2013] UKFTT 314 (TC), TC02717.

[44.403] A trader (C) regularly paid her PAYE and NIC after the due date, and HMRC imposed penalties under *FA 2009, Sch 56*. C appealed, contending that the penalties were excessive and that four of the monthly payments had been posted within the statutory time limits. The First-tier Tribunal allowed her appeal with regard to these four payments, holding that postal delays constituted a reasonable excuse, but dismissed her appeal with regard to the remaining payments. *Mrs S Crowson (t/a MacKenzies Smoked Products) v HMRC*, FTT [2011] UKFTT 789 (TC), TC01623.

[44.404] Similar decisions were reached in *Visual Packaging (Plastics) Ltd v HMRC*, FTT [2012] UKFTT 496 (TC), TC02173; *Browns CTP Ltd v HMRC*, FTT [2012] UKFTT 566 (TC), TC02244; *TBD Morris Environmental Ltd v HMRC*, FTT [2012] UKFTT 622 (TC), TC03009, and *Elite Elevators Ltd v HMRC*, FTT [2014] UKFTT 025 (TC), TC03166.

[44.405] HMRC imposed penalties under *FA 2009, Sch 56* on the basis that a company had made twelve successive payments of PAYE and NIC after the due dates. The First-tier Tribunal upheld the penalties in principle but found that the two final payments had been posted within the time limit, and reduced the penalties accordingly. *RA & JC Atkinson Ltd (t/a Minster Cleaning Services) v HMRC*, FTT [2012] UKFTT 140 (TC), TC01835.

[44.406] Similar decisions were reached in *Metokote UK Ltd v HMRC*, FTT [2012] UKFTT 592 (TC), TC02269; *Core Technology Systems (UK) Ltd v HMRC*, FTT [2012] UKFTT 629 (TC), TC02305, and *Mackintosh Ltd v HMRC*, FTT [2012] UKFTT 689 (TC), TC02360.

[44.407] HMRC imposed penalties under *FA 2009, Sch 56* on a company (P) which had made five payments of PAYE and NIC after the due dates. The First-tier Tribunal allowed P's appeal with regard to one of the payments, finding that it had problems with its computer software, but dismissed the appeal with regard to the other four payments. *The Partnership (UK) Ltd v HMRC*, FTT [2013] UKFTT 122 (TC), TC02551.

[44.408] HMRC imposed six penalties under *FA 2009, Sch 56* on a company (C) which had made several payments of PAYE and NIC after the due dates. Penalties were not imposed in respect of two months which had been covered by a deferred payment agreement under *FA 2009, s 108*. C appealed, contending that it had believed that the deferred payment agreement covered four months rather than two. The First-tier Tribunal allowed C's appeal in part, finding that there was no evidence that HMRC had given C written details of the deferred payment agreement, and holding that the misunderstanding over the terms of the agreement constituted a reasonable excuse. The tribunal upheld penalties in respect of the four later periods. *Cornwallis Care Services Ltd v HMRC*, FTT [2012] UKFTT 724 (TC), TC02388.

[44.409] HMRC imposed six penalties under *FA 2009, Sch 56* on a company (R) which had made several payments of PAYE and NIC after the due dates. R appealed, contending that it had entered into an informal deferred payment agreement under *FA 2009, Sch 56 para 10*. The First-tier Tribunal allowed the appeal against the first four penalties, finding that they were covered by such an agreement, but dismissed the appeal against the other two. *RJ Herbert Engineering Ltd v HMRC*, FTT [2013] UKFTT 753 (TC), TC03132.

[44.410] HMRC imposed penalties under *FA 2009, Sch 56* on a partnership (B) which had made several payments of PAYE and NIC after the due dates. B appealed, contending that it had a reasonable excuse because it had not received a warning letter. The First-tier Tribunal allowed the appeal in part. Judge Radford held that this constituted a reasonable excuse for two defaults but not for subsequent defaults. *Broome Park Nursing Home v HMRC*, FTT [2012] UKFTT 756 (TC), TC02413.

[44.411] Judge Radford reached a similar decision in *Heirtrace Ltd v HMRC*, FTT [2013] UKFTT 192 (TC), TC02607.

[44.412] In April 2010 a company (E) began making its PAYE payments electronically, but used a reference number which related to its corporation tax liability instead of using its PAYE reference. When HMRC informed E that it had not received its payments, E queried this, and stopped making the payments. HMRC subsequently imposed penalties under *FA 2009, Sch 56*. E appealed, contending that the incorrect allocation of its payments constituted a reasonable excuse. The First-tier Tribunal allowed the appeal in part, holding that E had a reasonable excuse for having withheld three months' payments but that there was no reasonable excuse for subsequent late payments. *Eurobulk Ltd v HMRC*, FTT [2012] UKFTT 755 (TC), TC02412.

[44.413] A company director (H) filed his 2010/11 tax return in October 2011. When HMRC calculated the tax due, it showed that there had been an underpayment. H failed to pay this by the due date, and HMRC imposed a penalty under *FA 2009, Sch 56*. H appealed, contending that he had expected any underpayment to be collected by adjusting his PAYE code. The First-tier Tribunal held that this did not constitute a reasonable excuse within *Sch 56 para 16*, since the underpayment exceeded £2,000. However, Judge Mosedale noted that the company of which H was a director had gone into administration in April 2012, and H had subsequently been unemployed. H was 'a high earner whose employment income suddenly ceased two weeks into the tax year, since when he has been on benefits'. It seemed likely that the tax which had been deducted from his salary in April 2012 would not only exceed his 2012/13 liability but would also exceed his 2010/11 underpayment. This constituted 'special circumstances' within *Sch 56 para 9*. The tribunal directed that the penalty should be stayed until H's 2012/13 tax liability was known, and that any 2012/13 overpayment should be set against the 2010/11 underpayment, with the penalty only being upheld to the extent that the 2010/11 underpayment exceeded the 2012/13 overpayment. *C Horne v HMRC*, FTT [2013] UKFTT 177 (TC), TC02592.

[44.414] An individual (S) disposed of some shares in 2011/12. On his tax return he indicated that he had a realised a capital gain, but did not declare the amount. He subsequently submitted schedules, and in January 2013 HMRC sent him a computation showing tax payable of £40,655. S paid this in March 2013 and HMRC imposed a penalty under *FA 2009, Sch 56*, at the rate of 5% of the unpaid tax. S appealed, contending that he had not received HMRC's computation until March. The First-tier Tribunal allowed his appeal in part. Judge Hellier observed that S 'knew that he had a CGT liability and he knew its amount. In January he rather complacently sat back and waited for a calculation from HMRC. He could and should have been more active.' Therefore the circumstances did not constitute a reasonable excuse. However, he directed that the penalty should be reduced from 5% to 4% under *Sch 56 para 9*. *G Seaborn v HMRC*, FTT [2014] UKFTT 086 (TC), TC03226.

[44.415] A woman (P) failed to pay the whole of her tax liability for 2010/11 and 2011/12 by the due date, and HMRC imposed penalties under *FA 2009, Sch 56*. P appealed, contending that she had requested the tax due to be collected via the PAYE system. The First-tier Tribunal allowed P's appeal in part, holding that there was a reasonable excuse for her initial belief that the tax would be collected by PAYE. However, in May 2013 she had received a letter from an HMRC officer clarifying that the tax would not be collected by PAYE because her returns had not been filed in time. Therefore P should have been aware, from the date of receiving this letter, that the underpayment 'would not be collected via PAYE and thus that she had to pay the balance owing to HMRC by other methods, such as cheque or bank transfer'. *Mrs C Perrin v HMRC*, FTT [2014] UKFTT 488 (TC), TC03614. (*Note*. Appeals against penalties for the late filing of returns were adjourned pending the Upper Tribunal decision in *K Donaldson v HMRC*, **44.17** above.)

Cases where the appellant was successful

[44.416] An individual (B) sold some land to a property developer in 2010, incurring a CGT liability for 2010/11. However the developer failed to pay the agreed amount. In February 2012 B asked HMRC for additional time to pay the CGT due. HMRC rejected this request, and subsequently imposed a penalty under *FA 2009, Sch 56*. The First-tier Tribunal allowed B's appeal, holding that the circumstances constituted a reasonable excuse. *S Brand v HMRC*, FTT [2012] UKFTT 783 (TC), TC02434.

[44.417] A woman (W) paid the balance of her 2009/10 tax liability in March 2011. HMRC imposed a penalty under *FA 2009, Sch 56*. W appealed, contending that she had been suffering from cancer and had had major surgery followed by chemotherapy and radiation treatment. The First-tier Tribunal allowed her appeal, holding that the circumstances constituted a reasonable excuse. *Ms J Woolf v HMRC*, FTT [2014] UKFTT 024 (TC), TC03165.

[44.418] An individual (C) sold some shares in April 2011, realising a substantial CGT liability. He did not pay the tax until October 2013, and HMRC imposed a penalty under *FA 2009, Sch 56*. C appealed, contending that he had a reasonable excuse because he had been suffering financial difficulties which had been aggravated by the breakdown of his marriage in March 2012. The First-tier Tribunal accepted this contention and allowed the appeal. *T Cooke v HMRC*, FTT [2014] UKFTT 506 (TC), TC03633.

[44.419] An employee (J) retired in September 2012. He filed his 2010/11 tax return on 9 January 2012. This showed a tax underpayment of £13,841, because J's employer had only deducted basic rate tax from a payment of severance pay awarded to him on his retirement. J did not pay the tax due until 23 March, and HMRC imposed a penalty under *FA 2009, Sch 56 para 3(2)*. The First-tier Tribunal allowed J's appeal, finding that J had 'believed that the appropriate tax had been deducted by his employer under the PAYE provisions', so that he had a reasonable excuse for the late payment. *JB Jackson v HMRC*, FTT [2013] UKFTT 28 (TC), TC02448.

[44.420] In August 2012 HMRC sent a 2009/10 tax return to an employee (DU) who had income of more than £100,000 and had had insufficient tax deducted under PAYE (for reasons which are not fully set out in the tribunal decision). In February 2013 HMRC sent DU a tax calculation showing an underpayment of £8595. They also imposed a penalty under *FA 2009, Sch 56*. The First-tier Tribunal allowed DU's appeal against the penalty. Judge Sheppard held that 'it was understandable that the appellant did not realise that the PAYE deductions by his employer had created a shortfall that could not be collected by adjustment of his tax code'. *D Urwin v HMRC*, FTT [2014] UKFTT 004 (TC), TC03145.

[44.421] A former schoolteacher began receiving rental income in 2011/12. She did not inform HMRC of this until February 2013. HMRC sent her a return in March 2013, which she submitted in May 2013. HMRC imposed a penalty under *FA 2009, Sch 56* for failure to pay the tax due by 31 January 2013. Judge Sheppard allowed her appeal, criticising HMRC for providing insufficient information and finding that 'she may have been adequately and correctly advised about her filing and payment responsibilities but crucially she was not advised that if tax due she needed to make a payment of that tax urgently in order to avoid a penalty'. He held that the circumstances constituted a reasonable excuse. *MC Armitage v HMRC*, FTT [2014] UKFTT 055 (TC), TC03195.

[44.422] In 2011/12 a woman (S) received a lump sum pension payment from the Department for Work and Pensions. The DWP advised her that this was being paid after deduction of tax, and S completed her 2011/12 return accordingly. HMRC subsequently informed S that the payment was taxable, and amended her self-assessment. S did not pay the tax attributable to this payment until September 2013, and HMRC imposed a penalty. S appealed, contending that she had a reasonable excuse because of the misleading information that she had received from the DWP. The First-tier Tribunal accepted this contention and allowed her appeal against the penalty. *Ms PD Spink v HMRC*, FTT [2014] UKFTT 524 (TC), TC03651.

[44.423] A company (D) made several payments of PAYE and NIC after the due dates, and HMRC imposed a penalty under *FA 2009, Sch 56*. D appealed, contending that it had a reasonable excuse because it was having difficulties with its bank, which had insisted on reducing its overdraft and imposing a discounting arrangement which increased its bank charges and reduced its working capital. The First-tier Tribunal accepted D's evidence and allowed its appeal. Judge Geraint Jones found that D 'was doing all that it could to collect in its debts and to renegotiate its facilities with its bankers, on commercially acceptable terms, as swiftly as it could manage'. *Dudman Group Ltd v HMRC*, FTT [2011] UKFTT 771 (TC), TC01608.

[44.424] A similar decision was reached in *Cuco Ltd v HMRC*, FTT [2013] UKFTT 121 (TC), TC02550.

[44.425] A company (N) made several payments of PAYE and NIC after the due dates, and HMRC imposed a penalty under *FA 2009, Sch 56*. N appealed, contending that it had a reasonable excuse because it had only one customer, a large company (T) which had delayed paying it, causing severe cash-flow difficulties. The First-tier Tribunal accepted N's evidence and allowed its appeal. *Northern Bulk Transport Ltd v HMRC*, FTT [2011] UKFTT 787 (TC), TC01621.

[44.426] Similar decisions were reached in *HCM Electrical Ltd v HMRC*, FTT [2011] UKFTT 852 (TC), TC01686; *Anaconda Equipment International Ltd v HMRC*, FTT [2014] UKFTT 388 (TC), TC03521, and *PSC Photography Ltd v HMRC*, FTT [2014] UKFTT 926 (TC), TC04039.

[44.427] HMRC imposed a penalty under *FA 2009, Sch 56* on a company (N) which had repeatedly paid its PAYE and NIC after the due date. N appealed, contending that it had a reasonable excuse because one of its major customers had gone into liquidation, owing it £300,000, and this had caused it financial problems. It had agreed a deferred payment agreement under *FA 2009, s 108* with HMRC for 2009/10, and had assumed that this agreement would continue for 2010/11. The First-tier Tribunal allowed the appeal, observing that N had also been awaiting a VAT repayment, and holding that the circumstances constituted a reasonable excuse. *NAP Anglia Ltd v HMRC*, FTT [2013] UKFTT 163 (TC), TC02579.

[44.428] HMRC imposed a penalty under *FA 2009, Sch 56* on a company (ID) which had repeatedly paid its PAYE and NIC after the due date. ID appealed, contending that it had a reasonable excuse because it had suffered from unusually high worker absenteeism, which had prevented it from completing some contracts on time and had adversely affected its cash-flow. The First-tier Tribunal accepted ID's evidence and allowed its appeal. Judge Khan held that 'the underlying reason for the late payment and insufficiency of funds within the company did amount to a reasonable excuse'. *ID Machinery Ltd v HMRC*, FTT [2013] UKFTT 175 (TC), TC02590.

[44.429] HMRC imposed a penalty under *FA 2009, Sch 56* on the basis that an individual (F) had failed to pay his 2010/11 tax liability by the due date. F appealed, contending that he had sent a cheque for the liability but that HMRC had allocated against this against arrears for previous years, rather than against his 2010/11 liability. The First-tier Tribunal allowed F's appeal. Judge Khan held that F had 'a reasonable excuse for assuming that HMRC would allocate the payments to the current liability rather than to the oldest debt due. The practice of the Commissioners does not appear to be covered in the legislation but rather in the Debt Management and Banking Manual (paras 210105 and 210120). It does not appear that these were brought to the notice of the taxpayer. In the circumstances therefore a taxpayer should be able to ask the Commissioners to reallocate the payments.' *J Francis v HMRC*, FTT [2013] UKFTT 477 (TC), TC02860.

[44.430] A solicitor (B) did not pay his 2010/11 tax liability until May 2012. HMRC imposed a penalty under *FA 2009, Sch 56*. B appealed, contending that he had telephoned HMRC in February 2012 to state that he would not be able to pay until 26 March, and had assumed that this conversation amounted to a deferred payment agreement under *FA 2009, Sch 56 para 10*. HMRC contended that this conversation had simply amounted to an informal agreement 'to withhold recovery action for a short period'. Judge Connell held that the misunderstanding of the telephone conversation constituted a reasonable excuse. *G Brown v HMRC (No 1)*, FTT [2014] UKFTT 208 (TC), TC03348. (*Note*. The appellant unsuccessfully applied for costs—see **4.423** APPEALS.)

[44.431] HMRC imposed penalties under *FA 2009, Sch 56* on the basis that a company (C) had made ten successive payments of PAYE and NIC after the due dates. The First-tier Tribunal allowed C's appeal, finding that the payments had been posted within the time limit. *CED Ltd v HMRC*, FTT [2013] UKFTT 219 (TC), TC02633.

[44.432] A similar decision was reached in *Kestrel Guards Ltd v HMRC*, FTT [2014] UKFTT 184 (TC), TC03324.

[44.433] The Upper Tribunal allowed a company's appeal against a penalty under *FA 2009, Sch 56* in *Novair Ltd v HMRC*, UT June 2013, FTC/73/2013 unreported. (*Note*. At the time of writing, the Upper Tribunal has not released the full text of this decision.)

45

Pension Income (ITEPA 2003, ss 565-654)

The cases in this chapter are arranged under the following headings.

Tax on pension income (ITEPA 2003, ss 566–568)

ITEPA 2003, s 567—amount of income pension charged to tax

[45.1] In September 1955 a local government pensioner (B), who had retired in 1950, exercised a statutory option under the *Local Government Superannuation (Benefits) Regulations 1954*. As a result, his pension was reduced from £987 to £768, but he received further benefits including a non-taxable retirement grant of £152. (If the Regulations had been in force at the time of his retirement, he would have received a pension of £768 and a non-taxable lump sum of £1,229.) The Revenue issued an assessment for 1954/55 (i.e. before the exercise of the option) charging tax on the £987 which he received. B appealed, contending that the assessment should be reduced to £768 and that the balance of the pension should be treated as non-taxable. The Ch D rejected this contention and upheld the assessment. Harman J held that the reduction in B's pension had not been retrospective, so that the whole of the £987 which he had received in 1954/55 was taxable. *Cooke v Burton*, Ch D 1957, 37 TC 478.

UK pensions: general rules (ITEPA 2003, ss 569-572)

ITEPA 2003, s 570—definition of 'pension'*

[45.2] A chaplain's salary was paid by trustees appointed by the will of the Duke of Newcastle. The chaplain retired in 1931. Following his retirement, the Duke's trustees paid him an annual pension of £250, from which they deducted tax. The Revenue issued assessments charging tax on the pension (under Schedule E under the legislation then in force). The chaplain appealed, contending that the payments which he received should be treated as annual payments within Schedule D, Case III. The KB rejected this contention and dismissed the appeal. Finlay J held that the payments were within the definition of a 'pension'. Kemp *(Hawkins' Executor) v Evans*, KB 1935, 20 TC 14.

'Temporary pension' under pension scheme

[45.3] The employees of a company normally retired at the age of 62. The company's pension scheme provided for the normal pension plus a 'temporary pension' until the pensioner attained 65. A pensioner who received a 'temporary pension' appealed against an assessment, contending that it was not taxable. The Commissioners rejected this contention and dismissed his appeal, and the CA unanimously upheld this decision. *Esslemont v Estill*, CA 1980, 53 TC 663; [1980] STC 620. (Note. The appellant appeared in person.)

Pension scheme rules amended after retirement of taxpayer

[45.4] The appellant in the case noted at **45.3** above appealed against subsequent assessments charging tax on payments which he received from a company pension scheme, contending that, because the rules of the scheme had been amended since his retirement, the payments were not taxable. The General Commissioners rejected this contention and dismissed his appeal, holding that the payments were within the definition of a 'pension' and were taxable accordingly. The CA unanimously upheld their decision. *Esslemont v Marshall*, CA 1996, 68 TC 596; [1996] STC 1086.

Monthly payments of disability benefit from pension fund

[45.5] An employee was absent from his employment for a year through illness, and was declared redundant before returning to work. He was thereafter paid a monthly disability benefit by the trustees of his employer's pension fund. The Revenue issued an assessment charging tax on the payments and he appealed, contending that they were termination payments within what is now *ITEPA 2003, s 401 et seq*, and therefore eligible for relief under the legislation then in force. The Commissioners rejected this contention and dismissed his appeal, holding that the payments were within the definition of a 'pension', and were taxable accordingly. The Ch D upheld their decision. Morritt J held that the fact that the employee had not yet finally retired did not prevent the payments from being classified as a pension, and the fact that the payments were made on account of his disability, rather than on account of his past services, was immaterial. *Johnson v Holleran*, Ch D 1988, 61 TC 428; [1989] STC 1.

[45.6] The appellant in the case noted at 45.5 above appealed against assessments on the same source of income for subsequent years. The General Commissioners again dismissed his appeals, and the Ch D upheld their decision, awarding costs to the Revenue 'to discourage the taxpayer from pursuing hopeless appeals in future'. *Johnson v Farquhar*, Ch D 1991, 64 TC 385; [1992] STC 11.

Payment as compensation for shortfall in widow's pension

[45.7] In March 1999 a company (J) announced that it would stop paying contributions in respect of widows' pensions. Its managing director died later that year. Under the company pension scheme, his widow (F) received a substantial lump sum and a pension of just over £12,000 pa. She asked for her pension to be increased, since in April 1998 her husband had been given a reserved benefit statement indicating that if he had died in service, she would receive a pension of more than £40,000 pa. In 2001 J agreed to pay F £2,600 per month, with arrears backdated to January 2000. She did not declare these payments as taxable income on her returns. The Revenue issued amendments to her self-assessments, and she appealed, contending that the payments should be treated as capital. The Special Commissioner rejected this contention and dismissed the appeal, holding that the payments were within the definition of a 'pension' and were taxable accordingly. *Mrs JA Ford v HMRC*, Sp C 2007, [2008] SSCD 226 (Sp C 634).

Foreign pensions: general rules (ITEPA 2003, ss 573-576)

ITEPA 2003, s 573—foreign pension

[45.8] A South African civil servant retired in 1929. The South African Government awarded him a pension of £229 in South African pounds. In March 1931 he moved to London, and his pension was paid in the UK. In 1931/32 he received the sterling equivalent of £268, from which was deducted £51 in respect of certain unsuccessful litigation which he had taken against the South African Government. The Revenue issued an assessment charging tax on the pension. He appealed, contending firstly that the legal costs of £51 should be deducted from the taxable amount, and secondly that the £39 which was attributable to the fluctuation in the exchange rate was not taxable, so that he should only be taxed on £178. The General Commissioners rejected these contentions and held that he was taxable on £268. The KB upheld their decision. *Magraw v Lewis*, KB 1933, 18 TC 222. (Notes. (1) The appellant appeared in person. (2) The South African currency was changed in 1961, when the rand replaced the pound as legal tender.)

Application of ITEPA 2003, s 575(2)

[45.9] A woman (E) was born in Switzerland in 1944. She lived and worked in Switzerland until 1967, when she moved to France. In 1968 she married a British diplomat. She subsequently acquired dual nationality and became resident in the UK. Between 1995 and 2009 she made voluntary contributions to her Swiss personal Old Age and Survivors Insurance pension. She claimed relief for these contributions against her UK income. HMRC rejected the claim, and she appealed. The First-tier Tribunal dismissed her appeal, holding that the contributions failed to qualify for relief. Judge Walters observed that 'voluntary national insurance contributions do not attract tax relief in the UK'. He also held that the effect of *ITEPA 2003 s 575(2)* was that only 90% of E's income from her Swiss pension was liable to UK tax, observing that HMRC had failed to explain why tax had been charged on the full amount. *Mrs E Haseldine v HMRC*, FTT [2012] UKFTT 480 (TC), TC02157.

UK social security pensions (ITEPA 2003, ss 577-579)

Husband arranging for pension to be paid to wife

[45.10] A married man instructed the Department of Social Security to pay his State Retirement Pension into his wife's bank account. He appealed against assessments on the pension, contending that he had disclaimed the pension so that it was income of his wife, rather than himself. The Special Commissioner rejected this contention and dismissed his appeal, holding that he had assigned rather than disclaimed the income, so that it remained taxable on him. *Meredith-Hardy v McLellan*, Sp C [1995] SSCD 270 (Sp C 42).

Approved retirement benefit schemes (ITEPA 2003, ss 580-589)

ITEPA 2003, s 582—person entitled to pension

[45.11] A married man (S) received an occupational pension from his former employer. In his tax returns, he treated half of the pension as his income and half of it as his wife's income (so that some of it was offset by his wife's personal allowance). The Revenue issued amendments on the basis that the whole of the pension remained S's income for tax purposes. S and his wife appealed. The Special Commissioner dismissed their appeals, holding that S 'was the person both receiving and entitled to the pension he received'. By virtue of *ITEPA 2003, s 582*, he was 'liable to income tax on the whole of it'. *A & Mrs M Stubbs v HMRC*, Sp C 2007, [2008] SSCD 265 (Sp C 638).

[45.12] A police officer (R) retired in 1998 and received an occupational pension. In his 1998/99 tax return, he only declared half of this pension as his income. The Revenue began an enquiry and issued an amendment on the basis that the whole of the pension was R's income for tax purposes. R appealed, contending that half of it should be treated as income of his wife, and that treating the whole of it as his income discriminated against 'the institution of marriage' and contravened the *European Convention on Human Rights*. The First-Tier Tribunal rejected these contentions and dismissed R's appeal. *T Rockliff v HMRC*, FTT, [2009] UKFTT 162 (TC), TC00124. (*Note*. The appellant appeared in person.)

46

Pension Schemes (FA 2004, ss 149–284)

The cases in this chapter are arranged under the following headings.

General principles (FA 2004, ss 149–152)

Withdrawal of approval of pension scheme

[46.1] A Singapore company (T) was the trustee of a pension scheme (R). In November 2006 HMRC recognised R as a 'qualifying recognised overseas pension scheme' within *FA 2004, s 150(8)*. In January 2008 HMRC withdrew that recognition, on the basis that R's application had given incorrect information and that R did not satisfy the statutory conditions. T subsequently took proceedings in the Ch D, which dismissed the proceedings and gave judgment for HMRC. HHJ Hodge QC held that the *Singapore Income Tax Act 1948, s 5*, provided a system for the approval or recognition of Singapore pension schemes by the Singapore Inland Revenue Authority. It appeared that R failed to meet the requirements of that system, so that it was not entitled to recognition as a 'qualifying recognised overseas pension scheme' within *s 150(8)*, and HMRC had been entitled to withdraw its recognition. The CA unanimously upheld this decision. *TMF Trustees Singapore Ltd (aka Equity Trust Singapore Ltd) v HMRC*, CA [2012] EWCA Civ 192; [2012] STC 998. (*Notes*. (1) The Supreme Court dismissed the company's application for leave to appeal against this decision. (2) For subsequent developments in this case, see *R (oao Gibson) v HMRC*, **4.336** APPEALS.)

Registered pension schemes: tax charges (FA 2004, ss 204–242)

Application for late election under SI 2006/3261

[46.2] In 1992 an individual (S) retired from his post as a full-time director of a large life insurance company, and took up an occupational pension. In 1994 S invested in a second pension, into which he paid premiums from 1994 to 2004. In 2010 he advised this pension provider that he wished to take his benefits under the policy. He was informed that his pension would be affected by the 'lifetime allowance charge' introduced by *FA 2004, s 214* with effect from 6 April 2006. In September 2010 he submitted a claim to make a late election under the *Registered Pension Schemes (Enhanced Lifetime Allowance) Regulations 2006 (SI 2006/3261)*. HMRC rejected the claim on the basis that the time limit laid down by *SI 2006/3261* had expired on 5 April 2009. S appealed, contending that he had not previously been aware of the changes to the taxation of pension benefits, and that this should be treated as a reasonable excuse within *SI 2006/3261, reg 12*. The First-Tier Tribunal dismissed his appeal. Judge Tildesley observed that 'prior to and after 6 April 2006 HMRC put extensive advice in the public arena on the changes to the taxation of pension savings, which was accessible at different entry levels'. The changes had also been publicised in the national newspapers, and their consequences had been 'tempered by the three-year period after its implementation in which an individual could secure protection against the change'. On the evidence, S had been 'aware of the changes to pension benefits but for some inexplicable reason did not perceive the relevance of those changes to his personal situation'. He 'could reasonably have been expected to discover the need to apply for protection of his pension benefits by 5 April 2009', and 'his ignorance of the legal provisions dealing with protection of pension benefits had no rational basis, and did not constitute a reasonable excuse'. *H Scurfield v HMRC*, FTT [2011] UKFTT 532 (TC), TC01379.

[46.3] A similar decision was reached in a case where the tribunal found that the appellant's former employer had sent him details of the forthcoming deadline in December 2008, but the appellant had failed to read the advice. *A Platt v HMRC*, FTT [2011] UKFTT 606 (TC), TC01449.

[46.4] The decision in *Platt v HMRC*, **46.3** above, was applied in the similar subsequent case of *M Hargrove v HMRC*, FTT [2014] UKFTT 921 (TC), TC04035.

[46.5] In 1999 a company director (C) set up a personal pension plan. By April 2006 the value of the plan exceeded £4,000,000. In 2010 he decided to change the trustee of his pension plan. The new trustee advised him that he should have submitted an election under the *Registered Pension Schemes (Enhanced Lifetime Allowance) Regulations 2006 (SI 2006/3261)*. C subsequently discovered that the previous trustee had failed to do this. In September 2010 he submitted a late election. HMRC rejected the claim on the basis that the time limit laid down by *SI 2006/3261* had expired on 5 April 2009. C appealed, contending that he had a reasonable excuse because he had relied on the company (UB) which had been acting as the trustee of his pension plan to make the necessary application. The First-tier Tribunal accepted this contention and allowed his appeal, specifically distinguishing the previous decisions in *Scurfield v HMRC*, **46.2** above, and *Platt v HMRC*, **46.3** above. Judge Walters observed that in September 2004 C had specifically requested UB for an explanation of the changes to the taxation of pensions, that in 2006 he had met an employee of UB and had been given the impression that UB would make the necessary application, and that he had subsequently made a formal complaint about UB's handling of his case. In the light of his meeting and correspondence with UB, it had been reasonable for him to rely on UB 'to make the necessary notification in time on his behalf'. *C Irby v HMRC*, FTT [2012] UKFTT 291 (TC), TC01979.

Compliance (FA 2004, ss 250–274A)

FA 2004, s 255—assessment on scheme administrator

[46.6] In 2006 a pension scheme made an unauthorised payment of £100,000 to one of its members. HMRC issued an assessment on the scheme administrator (W) under *FA 2004, s 255*. The First-tier Tribunal dismissed W's appeal against the assessment. Judge Cannan noted that W was a chartered accountant and a chartered tax adviser. W had failed to observe the statutory reporting requirements and 'had delegated day-to-day control of the schemes for which he was the scheme administrator to another individual'. Judge Cannan observed that 'one of the reasons for the tax charges which arise where a pension scheme makes unauthorised payments is to safeguard the tax-relieved funds in the scheme for the provision of retirement benefits. In relation to loans, the provisions seek to ensure that funds are not loaned in circumstances where there is a risk they might not be repaid.' *FA 2004, s 268(7)* provided relief for a scheme administrator in certain circumstances where he 'reasonably believed that the unauthorised payment was not a scheme chargeable payment'. However it was implicit in *s 268(7)* 'that the scheme administrator should have systems in place whereby he is aware that payments are going to be made by the trustees'. W 'had no systems in place to identify whether unauthorised payments were being made', and 'had no systems to identify in advance any payments being made'. Furthermore, the charge was not disproportionate and did not contravene the *European Convention on Human Rights*. *SC Willey v HMRC*, FTT [2013] UKFTT 328 (TC), TC02731.

Special annual allowance charge (FA 2009, s 72, Sch 35)

[46.7] In January 2011 a woman (L) made a payment of £30,000 into her self-invested personal pension. HMRC subsequently issued a notice of amendment to her 2010/11 self-assessment, ruling that this payment gave rise to a tax charge of £3,000 under *FA 2009, Sch 35*. The First-tier Tribunal dismissed

L's appeal, holding that 'on the facts her contribution fell within the legislation' and was subject to the charge. *Mrs CV Lott v HMRC*, FTT [2014] UKFTT 947 (TC), TC04060.

Superseded legislation (ICTA 1988, ss 590–655)

GENERAL NOTE

The taxation of pensions was radically altered by *FA 2004, ss 149-284, Schs 28-36*, which introduced a new tax regime with effect from 6 April 2006. The cases noted at **46.8** *et seq.* below relate to the pre-2006 legislation, but may still be of some relevance as illustrating points of principle.

Approval of schemes (ICTA 1988, ss 590–591D)

ICTA 1988, s 591B—withdrawal of approval of pension scheme

[46.8] A company (W) was the trustee of an approved pension scheme for the benefit of its controlling director (R) and his wife. The grant of approval of the scheme contained a condition that the funds of the scheme were to be used for the purchase of an annuity, which would then provide the pension. In July 1995 another company (L) established a new scheme with UK-resident trustees including R, and sought Revenue approval. R requested W to transfer his retirement benefits from the old scheme to the new scheme. On 1 August 1995 R ceased to be a paid director of W and ceased to be in pensionable employment for the purposes of the old scheme. On 24 August 1995 the value of R's retirement benefits was transferred from the old scheme to the new scheme, the UK-resident trustees were replaced by trustees resident in Guernsey, and the Guernsey trustees amended the scheme in such a way that it became incapable of approval. The Revenue exercised their discretion under *ICTA 1988, s 591B* to withdraw their approval of the old scheme with effect from 24 August 1995, giving rise to a charge to income tax on W (as the trustee of the old scheme) under *ICTA 1988, s 591C*. W applied for judicial review, but the QB dismissed the application. Tucker J observed that where, as in the instant case, a tax avoidance scheme comprising a number of separate transactions had been implemented, the Revenue and the courts were not limited to considering the genuineness or otherwise of each individual step or transaction in the scheme, but could consider the scheme as a whole. On the evidence, 'the real and effective purpose of the new scheme was that it was to be an unapproved scheme so as to provide a vehicle for the release of (R's) pension funds from the inhibitions formerly placed upon them'. The Revenue were justified in withdrawing their approval of the old scheme. *R v CIR (ex p. Roux Waterside Inn Ltd)*, QB 1997, 70 TC 545; [1997] STC 781. (*Note. ICTA 1988, ss 591B, 591C* were repealed by *FA 2004* with effect from 6 April 2006, subject to certain transitional provisions.)

[46.9] An approved pension scheme had three trustees: a UK company and a married couple who were the only two beneficiaries of the scheme. On 5 November 1996 the couple were replaced as trustees by a Guernsey company. On the same day, the trustees authorised a substantial transfer of funds to another pension scheme, the original UK trustees of which were (also on the same day) replaced by new trustees resident outside the UK. The Revenue discovered this in April 2000, and issued a notice under *ICTA 1988, s 591B*, withdrawing their approval of the scheme with effect from 5 November 1996. The husband applied for judicial review, but the QB dismissed the application. Sullivan J observed that the couple had been removed as trustees 'because they wanted to be removed, and that (the Guernsey company) replaced them as trustees because that is what they wished to happen'. On the evidence, 'this was a chain of actions that was preplanned from the outset.' The transfer of the funds had been made at the couple's request. The husband's witness statement had been 'deliberately misleading' and had not given a 'true and full picture of all the facts'. There had been a deliberate plan 'to export funds out of an approved scheme into another scheme that, whilst it was approved at the moment of transfer, would, immediately the money was transferred, be effectively rendered unapprovable'. The Revenue were clearly justified in withdrawing their approval from the scheme. *R (oao Mander) v CIR*, QB 2001, 73 TC 506; [2002] STC 531; [2001] EWCA 358 (Admin). (*Notes.* (1) See the note following *R v CIR (ex p. Roux Waterside Inn Ltd)*, **46.8** above. (2) For subsequent developments in this case, see **46.12** below.)

ICTA 1988, s 591C—assessment following withdrawal of approval of scheme

[46.10] A retirement benefit scheme was established in 1980. In August 1997 the company which had acted as the 'pensioneer trustee', as required by *Retirement Benefits Schemes (Restriction on Discretion to Approve) (Small Self-Administered Schemes) Regulations 1991 (SI 1991/1614), reg 9*, gave notice of resignation. The trustees failed to submit a deed of appointment to the Revenue, notifying the appointment of a new 'pensioneer trustee'. The Revenue subsequently issued a notice under *ICTA 1988, s 591B*, withdrawing their approval of the scheme, and issued an assessment on the trustees under *ICTA 1988, s 591C*. The trustees appealed, contending that the withdrawal of approval was unjustified. The Special Commissioner rejected this contention and dismissed the appeal, observing that the trustees had failed to comply with the requirements of the trust deed. The Revenue was 'legally entitled to withdraw approval from the scheme even though it was *bona fide* established and administered for the sole purpose of providing retirement benefits'. The Commissioners had no jurisdiction to hear an appeal against such a decision, which could only be challenged by way of judicial review. The assessment was in accordance with *ICTA 1988, s 591C*, which was mandatory. The Commissioner held that 'the fact that the scheme administrator has not evaded or avoided tax nor has distributed the funds improperly is simply irrelevant to the legislation. Payment of the tax is in effect the automatic sanction for withdrawal of approval.' The trustees had 'a personal liability to pay 40% of the funds by way of tax under Schedule D'. *Lambert & Others (Administrators of the CID Pension Fund) v Glover*, Sp C [2001] SSCD 250 (Sp C 292). (*Note.* See the note following *R v CIR (ex p. Roux Waterside Inn Ltd)*, **46.8** above.)

[46.11] An individual (T) was the administrator and sole remaining member of a small self-administered pension scheme. In 1998 he withdrew £200,000 from the scheme. The Revenue withdrew their approval from the scheme under *ICTA 1988, s 591B(1)*, and issued an assessment on T in his capacity as the scheme administrator under *ICTA 1988, s 591C*. T appealed, contending that he had been entitled to wind up the scheme by virtue of the decision in *Saunders v Vautier*, **71.137** CAPITAL GAINS TAX. The Special Commissioner rejected this contention and dismissed T's appeal, holding that the decision in *Saunders v Vautier* only entitled beneficiaries to wind up a trust where they were '*sui juris* and are together entitled to the whole beneficial interest in the trust property'. It was 'fundamental to the application of the rule that the beneficiaries must be together entitled to the whole of the beneficial interest'. Accordingly, 'the rule can have no application where there are potential beneficiaries not yet in existence, however remote their interests might be'. T appealed to the Ch D and CA, which unanimously upheld the assessment, holding that T's withdrawal of the fund was unauthorised, so that tax was due under *s 591C*. Lloyd LJ observed that 'the withdrawal of the funds in direct contravention of the rules of the scheme, after a deliberate series of actions designed to achieve this' fully justified the Revenue's withdrawal of their approval from the scheme. *H Thorpe v HMRC*, CA [2010] STC 964; [2010] EWCA Civ 339. (*Note*. The Revenue also issued an assessment on T under *ICTA 1988, s 596A*, charging tax on the payments he had received. The Ch D conditionally allowed T's appeal against this assessment—see **46.18** below.)

[46.12] Following the decision noted at **46.9** above, the Revenue issued an assessment under *ICTA 1988, s 591C* on the company which acted as the administrator of the scheme. The company appealed, contending that the assessment was invalid and unenforceable. The First-Tier Tribunal rejected this contention and dismissed the appeal. Judge Mosedale observed that 'the purpose of the 40% charge on assets leaving an approved scheme is to re-coup the tax advantages the funds enjoyed while in an approved scheme. If a scheme member does not wish to abide by the rules, and in particular accept the limitations on what can be done with the funds in an approved scheme, then he is not entitled to the tax benefits, and it seems quite reasonable for the Government to seek to recoup them.' She held that the effect of *ICTA 1988, s 658A* was that 'all administrators from the moment the deemed charge arises onwards are liable, as the charge arises during their control of the funds, although the assessment must be in the name of the administrator at the time of the assessment'. The effect of the legislation was that 'on becoming administrator, the new administrator becomes responsible for the scheme's affairs and liable to discharge its accumulated liabilities. It was not intended by Parliament that changing administrator would relieve the fund of liability to pay an assessment to tax under *s 658A*.' Accordingly, 'current and future administrators are jointly and severally liable', and tax charged under *s 591C* 'can be recovered in full from any single relevant person (unless they ceased to be a relevant person before the events in question) on the basis that the assessment of only a single relevant person in the name of the administrator of the scheme establishes joint and several liability of all relevant persons. The liability which is joint and several extends to relevant persons not in existence at the time of the assessment.' The Upper Tribunal upheld this decision. Vos J observed that 'there is no reason on earth why the legislation should be read as meaning that HMRC was unable to seek the tax from the trustees in post as administrator at the time when the withdrawal notice was served, if they had chosen to resign before the assessment was served. The suggestion that HMRC must issue repeated assessments on the trustees serving as the current administrator however often they change is a construction that would be unwieldy and often unworkable. Ultimately it might even lead to the time limits operating to prevent collection of the tax at all.' The trustees appealed to the CA, raising an alternative contention that the assessment should have been raised for 1996/97 (the year in which the scheme made a transfer of funds) rather than for 2000/01 (the year in which the Revenue issued a notice under *ICTA 1988, s 591B*). The CA unanimously rejected this contention and dismissed the appeal. Moses LJ held that, for the purposes of *s 591C(1)*, the relevant date was 'the date when approval of the scheme is withdrawn and not the date specified in the notice from which approval ceases to continue'. *John Mander Pension Trustees Ltd v HMRC*, CA [2013] EWCA Civ 1683; [2014] STC 2136.

Tax reliefs (ICTA 1988, ss 592–594)

ICTA 1988, s 592(3)—exemption for underwriting commissions

[46.13] Three approved pension schemes received income from sub-underwriting commissions. The Revenue issued assessments on the basis that these commissions were chargeable under Schedule D, Case I. The trustees of the schemes appealed, contending that the income was within Schedule D, Case VI, and was therefore exempt from tax by virtue of *ICTA 1988, s 592(3)*. The Special Commissioners accepted this contention and allowed the appeals, finding that the relevant activities 'were regarded as incidental and ancillary to investment'. The CA unanimously upheld their decision as one of fact. *British Telecom Pension Scheme Trustees v Clarke (and related appeals)*, CA 2000, 72 TC 472; [2000] STC 222. (*Notes.* (1) The Commissioners rejected two alternative contentions raised by the trustees, holding that the transactions were not 'options contracts' within *ICTA 1988, s 659A*, and were also not within *ITA 2007, s 479**. (2) *ICTA 1988, s 592* was repealed by *FA 2004* with effect from 6 April 2006, subject to certain transitional provisions.)

ICTA 1988, s 594—additional voluntary contributions

[46.14] An employee (N) had regularly paid additional voluntary contributions into an approved pension scheme. During 2000, the company (E) to which he had made such payments suffered financial difficulties. On the advice of his employer, he decided to make subsequent payments to a different company (S). However, because of various 'administrative errors' on the part of S and of N's employer, there was a significant delay in transferring the relevant fund from E to S. In the interim, N was unable to pay further AVCs until September 2002. He then gave S cheques representing the AVCs which he had wished to pay from January 2001 to August 2002. Consequently, the total AVCs which N actually paid during 2002/03 exceeded 15% of his salary. The Revenue issued a ruling that the effect of *ICTA 1988, s 594(2)* was that he was not entitled to relief for the excess. N appealed, contending that most of the payment which he had made in September 2002 should be treated as relating to 2000/01 and 2001/02. The Special Commissioner rejected this contention and dismissed his appeal, observing that '*section 594* contains no form of "carry back" provision, in the way that several other pension relief provisions do'. *Col IG Nason v HMRC*, Sp C [2007] SSCD 125 (Sp C 573). (*Note. ICTA 1988, s 594* was repealed by *FA 2004* with effect from 6 April 2006, subject to certain transitional provisions.)

Charge to tax (ICTA 1988, ss 595–603)

Payments by sports club to personal service companies

[46.15] See *Sports Club v HM Inspector of Taxes (and related appeals)*, **42.45** PAY AS YOU EARN.

ICTA 1988, s 596A—benefits under non-approved schemes

[46.16] An individual (M) had been an employee of the Scottish Transport Group, which was privatised under the *Transport (Scotland) Act 1989*, and was dissolved some years later. He had also been a member of one of the group's pension schemes, which had more funds than was needed to meet its liabilities. In 2002 he received an 'ex gratia' payment from the Government, representing part of the pension scheme surplus on privatisation. Basic rate tax was deducted from the payment. On his tax return, M did not declare this payment as taxable, but stated in Box 23.5 that he had received the sum, that he considered that it 'should not be subject to tax', and that he was seeking repayment of the tax deducted. The Revenue issued an amendment to charge tax on the payment under *ICTA 1988, s 596A*. M appealed, contending firstly that the amendment to his self-assessment was invalid and secondly that the payment was not taxable under *s 596A*. The Special Commissioner rejected these contentions and dismissed M's appeal, holding that the payment 'satisfied the criteria for the charge to tax provided by *s 596A*'. M had received a payment of 'relevant benefits' under a 'retirement benefits scheme'. *Moffat v HMRC*, Sp C [2006] SSCD 380 (Sp C 538). (*Note. ICTA 1988, s 596A* was repealed by *ITEPA 2003, s 722* with effect from 6 April 2003. See now *ITEPA 2003, ss 393–400*.)

[46.17] A group of companies had arranged for certain pensioners to receive benefits such as free help with their tax affairs. The group decided to withdraw these benefits, and made voluntary payments to the affected pensioners as compensation. The Revenue issued determinations on the trustees of the group pension fund, charging tax on these payments under what is now *Income Tax (PAYE) Regulations 2003 (SI 2003/2682), reg 80*. The Ch D and CA unanimously upheld the determinations, holding that the payments were made 'in connection with past service' and were 'relevant benefits' within *ICTA 1988, s 596A* and *s 612(1)*. Arden LJ held that 'a connection may be indirect for the purpose of the definition of relevant benefits' and observed that 'it is difficult to think of a case where a benefit made available to persons chosen for their connection with an occupational pension scheme is not given in connection with their service'. *Barclays Bank plc v HMRC (No 3) (and related appeal)*, CA 2007, 79 TC 18; [2008] STC 476; [2007] EWCA Civ 442. (*Note. ICTA 1988, s 596A* was repealed by *ITEPA 2003, s 722* with effect from

6 April 2003, and *s 612* was repealed by *FA 2004* with effect from 6 April 2006. See now *ITEPA 2003, ss 393–400.*)

[46.18] In the case noted at **46.11** above, the Revenue issued an assessment under *ICTA 1988, s 596A* on an individual (T), who was the administrator and sole remaining member of a small self-administered pension scheme, charging tax on £200,000 which he had withdrawn from the scheme. The Ch D held that, by sanctioning an unauthorised payment, T had committed a breach of trust. Accordingly, he held the £200,000 as a constructive trustee for the fund. Thus, even though the money had in fact been paid into a private account in T's name, as a matter of law the money should be treated as never having left the trusts of the pension scheme. It followed that neither *ICTA, s 596A* nor *ICTA, s 600* applied to the payments. Sir Edward Evans-Lombe specifically declined to follow *obiter dicta* of Chadwick LJ in *Venables and Others v Hornby*, **46.19** below, observing that since the HL had reversed the CA decision on another issue in that case, Chadwick LJ's judgment could not be treated as forming part of the *ratio decidendi*. Sir Edward Evans-Lombe held that the effect of this reasoning was that T's appeal against the assessment under *s 596A* should be allowed 'subject to being able to satisfy myself, by means of undertakings or otherwise, that the fund held by (T) has been returned into the control of the original trustees of the scheme including the pensioneer trustee'. He also observed that the scheme remained unapproved, and that while that was the case, any pension payments made by the scheme would be subject to tax. *H Thorpe v HMRC*, Ch D [2009] EWHC 611 (Ch); [2009] All ER (D) 283 (Mar).

ICTA 1988, s 600—unauthorised payments to employee

[46.19] V, who had been the controlling director of a property company, retired as chairman of the company in June 1994, when he was aged 53. He became a non-executive director and continued to be the company's major shareholder. The company's pension scheme could authorise an immediate award of a pension to a scheme member who retired 'in normal health at or after the age of 50'. V received three substantial payments from the company's pension scheme. The Revenue issued assessments charging tax on the payments under *ICTA 1988, s 600*, on the basis that the payments were not authorised by the terms of the scheme, since V had continued to be a director, and had therefore not retired. V appealed, contending that he had retired in June 1994 even though he had continued as a non-executive director. The HL accepted this contention and allowed his appeal (by a 4-1 majority, Lord Walker of Gestingthorpe dissenting). Lord Millett held that 'it does not follow from the fact that the word "employee" is defined to include a director that an employee who is also a director must retire from both his employment and his office as director before he can be said to "retire" within the meaning of the trust deed'. Accordingly, it was 'not necessary that a member who is an employee and a director should retire from both positions' and 'the fact that the taxpayer has remained in his non-pensionable occupation as a non-executive director cannot affect his right to benefit on retiring from his only pensionable occupation'. *Venables and Others v Hornby*, HL 2003, 75 TC 553; [2004] STC 84; [2003] UKHL 65; [2004] 1 All ER 627. (*Notes.* (1) The HL also allowed an appeal against a determination on the trustees, under what is now *regulation 80* of the *Income Tax (PAYE) Regulations 2003 (SI 2003/2682)*. (2) V raised an alternative contention that the payments were in breach of trust and thus should not be treated as having been 'made' for the purposes of *ICTA 1988, s 600*. The HL refrained from deciding this issue. Lord Millett commented that 'it depends on whether it is sufficient that the payments were made to the recipient for his own use and benefit and were valid to pass the legal title to the money, or whether they must also have been received free from any legal or equitable obligation on the part of the recipient to make restitution. In short, it may depend on whether the determining factor is the payment or the receipt.' V's alternative contention was subsequently approved by the Ch D in *Thorpe v HMRC*, **46.18** above. (3) *ICTA 1988, s 600* was repealed by *ITEPA 2003, s 722* with effect from 6 April 2003. See now *ITEPA 2003, ss 583–585*.)

[46.20] An individual (D), who was born in 1959, had accrued pension benefits in an approved occupational pension scheme (L), under which he would be entitled to a pension when he reached the age of 60. In 2001 these benefits were transferred to another scheme (H). The Revenue issued an amendment to D's self-assessment, charging tax on the transfer under *ICTA 1988, s 600*, on the basis that D was not an employee of H, so that the transfer was not authorised by the rules of the scheme. D appealed. The Special Commissioner dismissed his appeal, finding that H had been 'incorporated for the sole purpose of assisting people to gain access to accrued pension benefits in advance of their retirement'. The purported employment was 'a sham, operating as a cover to enable (D) to draw out pension benefits in advance of his retirement'. *CJ Dunne v HMRC*, Sp C [2008] SSCD 422 (Sp C 654). (*Notes.* (1) *ICTA 1988, s 600* was repealed by *ITEPA 2003, s 722* with effect from 6 April 2003. See now *ITEPA 2003, ss 583–585*. (2) Following this decision, D made an application for it to be set aside under *Special Commissioners (Jurisdiction and Procedure) Regulations 1994 (SI 1994/1811), reg 19*. The application was dismissed—Sp C [2008] SSCD 527 (Sp C 662).)

ICTA 1988, s 601—charge to tax on payments to employers

[46.21] A company (H) had acquired the shares in a company (F), the pension scheme of which was in surplus. The trustees of F's pension scheme paid its assets to the company (P) which was the trustee of H's pension scheme. P in turn paid the surplus assets to H, subject to the payment to the Revenue of the charge to tax under *ICTA 1988, s 601*. Some members of F's pension scheme complained to the Pension Ombudsman that the transfer of the scheme's surplus assets to H was in breach of trust and was invalid. The QB upheld this complaint and directed H to return the gross amount of the payment, including the tax to the extent that it was recovered from the Revenue, to P for the benefit of the members of F's pension scheme. P and H claimed repayment of the tax paid under *ICTA 1988, s 601*. The Revenue rejected the claim on the ground that, under *ICTA 1988, s 601(1)*, tax had been due on the payments and there were no grounds for repaying it. The companies took proceedings to recover the tax from the Revenue. Arden J upheld the companies' claims, holding that 'there is no reason in the present case why Parliament should seek in *ICTA 1988, s 601* to tax a payment which was not effectively made'. Accordingly, *ICTA 1988, s 601* did not apply to the payments by P to H, and the companies were entitled to recover the tax paid. *Hillsdown Holdings plc & Another v CIR*, Ch D 1999, 71 TC 356; [1999] STC 561. *ICTA 1988, s 601* was repealed by *ITEPA 2003, s 326* with effect from 6 April 2003.)

Retirement annuities (ICTA 1988, ss 618–629)

ICTA 1988, s 623(2)(c)—underwriting by external name

[46.22] An external Lloyd's underwriter, who spent no more than four hours per week on his Lloyd's affairs, claimed retirement annuity relief against his underwriting income. The Revenue rejected his claim, considering that the underwriting income did not constitute 'relevant earnings', as the underwriter was not personally carrying on a trade, as required by *ICTA 1988, s 623(2)(c)*. The Special Commissioner dismissed the underwriter's appeal, holding that the trade was carried on by the underwriting agents, rather than by the external Name. The CA unanimously upheld this decision. *Koenigsberger v Mellor*, CA 1995, 67 TC 280; [1995] STC 547.

Personal pension schemes (ICTA 1988, ss 630–655)

Payment to recover benefit of annuities from trustee in bankruptcy

[46.23] An individual (B) was made bankrupt in 1995. Among his assets were certain retirement annuity policies, the premiums on which had qualified for income tax relief. These policies passed to B's trustee in bankruptcy under *Insolvency Act 1986, s 306*. B was discharged from bankruptcy in 1998. Subsequently he arranged to pay his trustee £24,000 to recover the right to receive future income from the retirement annuity policies. He borrowed £25,800 for this purpose. He claimed tax relief for this payment under *ICTA 1988, s 639*. The Revenue rejected the claim and the Special Commissioner dismissed B's appeal, holding that such payments would attract relief under *s 639* only if they were made for 'approved personal pension arrangements', as defined in *s 630*. The Board of Inland Revenue had not approved any personal pension arrangements in respect of B, so that B was not entitled to relief on the payment. *Borchert v Cormack*, Sp C [2006] SSCD 500 (Sp C 545).

ICTA 1988, s 647—unauthorised payments

[46.24] A financial adviser (K) had funds in two authorised personal pension schemes. In 2001/02 he transferred his funds out of these schemes into another pension plan, administered by a limited company (H) and only open to employees of H. Following an enquiry, HMRC issued an amendment to K's return on the basis that K had never been an employee of H, so that the transfer was an 'unauthorised' transfer, within *ICTA 1988, s 647*. They also issued a direction that K, rather than the pension schemes, should be liable for the tax which should have been deducted; and they imposed a penalty on K under *TMA, s 95* for negligently delivering an incorrect return. (The penalty was mitigated by 70%.) K appealed, contending that he had been employed by H as a 'sales associate'. The First-Tier Tribunal reviewed the evidence in detail and dismissed all three appeals, finding that K was 'an unreliable witness'. The tribunal found that H appeared to have been established 'with the object of taking a commission on pension fund liberation', and the scheme was intended to persuade 'persons who wished to realise their pension funds before their retirement age to become sham employees of (H)'. The participators would be left with '80% of the value of their pension fund as cash in hand at the current date rather than with 100% tied up in an pension fund inaccessible until they reached retirement age'. On the evidence, the tribunal found as a fact that K was not an employee of H. The relevant written agreement was 'a sham' and 'lacked the "irreducible minimum of mutual obligation necessary to create a contract of service" required by law'. Since K was not an employee of H, the transfer of funds from the two authorised pension schemes was an 'unauthorised transfer' and K was liable to tax under *ICTA 1988, s 647(3)*. The tribunal also considered that HMRC had been 'generous' in mitigating the penalty by 70%. *BJ Kent v HMRC*, FTT [2009] UKFTT 358 (TC), TC00296.

[46.25] In 1996 a couple arranged for their pension funds to be transferred to Guernsey schemes. They leased a property in Alderney (which is part of the Bailiwick of Guernsey), but never occupied it. When the Revenue discovered what had happened, they issued assessments on the basis that the transfers had not met the criteria set out in the Reciprocal Arrangement between Guernsey and the UK, and were 'unauthorised' transfers, within *ICTA 1988, s 647*. They also imposed penalties under *TMA, s 95* (mitigated by 55%). The couple appealed, contending that they had acted in good faith and had been told that they were entering into a legitimate tax avoidance scheme. The First-Tier Tribunal reviewed the evidence in detail and dismissed the appeals against the assessments but allowed the appeals against the penalties. The tribunal noted that the pension planning scheme which the couple had adopted had been designed by a financial adviser who was 'a convicted fraudster' and 'perhaps did not act in their best interest'. The transfer had not complied with the scheme rules and the couple were obliged to account for tax on the transfers. However, since the couple had believed that they were acting in 'a correct manner', it was questionable whether they had been negligent, and it would not be appropriate to impose a penalty. *N & Mrs S Gretton v HMRC*, FTT [2010] UKFTT 521 (TC), TC00776. (*Note*. For another issue in this case, taken to the Upper Tribunal, see **43.78** PAYMENT OF TAX.)

ICTA 1988, s 655(1)(b)—definition of 'unused relief'

[46.26] For 1993/94 a taxpayer (B) had net relevant earnings of £16,499. She paid retirement annuity premiums of £4,100 (and personal pension contributions of £3,000). Under *ICTA 1988, s 619(2)* as then in force, she was entitled to retirement annuity relief of 20% of her net relevant earnings (i.e. £3,300). She had had unused relief of £2,012 for previous years, but had paid a personal pension contribution of £2,000 in 1992/93. Accordingly, the Revenue issued a ruling that her 'unused relief' as defined by *ICTA 1988, s 655(1)(b)* was £12 (i.e. £2,012 minus £2,000), so that for 1993/94 she was entitled to retirement annuity relief of £3,312. The Special Commissioner upheld the Revenue's ruling and dismissed B's appeal, accepting the Revenue's contention that the 'overall purpose of the legislation is to ensure extra relief is not available for those with both retirement annuity contracts and personal pension arrangements' and holding that the statutory purpose of *ICTA 1988, s 655(1)(b)* was 'to avoid double relief where an individual has a retirement annuity contract and a personal pension scheme'. *Brock v O'Connor*, Sp C [1997] SSCD 157 (Sp C 118).

[46.27] A barrister claimed relief for retirement annuity premiums and personal pension contributions. The Revenue restricted the relief under *ICTA 1988, s 655(1)(b)*. The barrister appealed, contending that the unused relief brought forward should not be reduced by her current year's contributions. The General Commissioners rejected this contention and dismissed her appeal, and the Ch D and CA unanimously upheld their decision. Mummery LJ held that 'the natural and ordinary reading of the language of *section 655(1)*' was that the expression 'the individual's unused relief for any year' in *subsection (1)(b)* 'includes both unused retirement annuity relief carried forward from the previous years and the unused relief arising in the current year. The unused retirement annuity relief is reduced by the amount of personal pension payments paid by the taxpayer in that year under the approved personal pension arrangements. The balance left after the deductions is the amount of relief which the taxpayer can carry forward to the next year, when the same calculation is made.' *Lonsdale v Braisby*, CA 2005, 77 TC 358; [2005] STC 1049; [2005] EWCA Civ 709. (*Note*. For another issue in this case, not taken to the CA, see **4.234** APPEALS.)

47

Property Income (ITTOIA 2005, ss 260–364)

The cases in this chapter are arranged under the following headings.

Profits: basic rules (ITTOIA 2005, ss 268–275)

Sale of colliery dross bings

[47.1] A landowner agreed to sell colliery dross bings, which had been lying on the land for several years. The Revenue issued assessments charging income tax on the proceeds, and the landowner appealed, contending that they were capital receipts and not chargeable to income tax. The Commissioners accepted this contention and allowed the appeal, and the CS unanimously upheld their decision. *Roberts v Lord Belhaven's Executors*, CS 1925, 9 TC 501. (*Note*. See also *Rogers v Longsdon*, 38.9 MINING RENTS AND ROYALTIES.)

Receipts from contractors for use of land

[47.2] A landowner received £72,125 from contractors under two agreements licensing them to enter 25 acres of land to deposit subsoil. He also received £4,000 under a licence to fill in a disused railway cutting. (The Commissioners found as a fact that, following the fulfilment of the agreements, there was no further prospect of tipping on the land.) The Revenue issued an assessment charging tax on these receipts. The Commissioners allowed the landowner's appeal and the Ch D upheld their decision, holding that the receipts were capital. They were for the realisation of assets and were received on capital account because there was a once and for all disposal of a right or advantage appertaining to the land. *McClure v Petre*, Ch D 1988, 61 TC 226; [1988] STC 749; [1988] 1 WLR 1386.

Receipts from sales of turf

[47.3] See *Lowe v JW Ashmore Ltd*, 27.12 FARMING.

Periodic payments—whether rent or instalments of purchase price

[47.4] A landlord (M) owned a number of houses, most of which were divided into flats. He entered into agreements with the occupiers whereby they paid him monthly amounts purporting to be instalments of the purchase price of the properties. The Revenue issued assessments charging income tax on the basis that the payments were actually rent. The Commissioners upheld the assessments, finding that 'no person has become the owner of one of (M's) properties' and that M 'was to all intents and purposes letting his properties at monthly rentals'. The Ch D dismissed M's appeal, applying the principles laid down by the CA in *Martin v Davies*, CA 1952, 42 TC 114 (a case in which M had sought to recover possession of one of his houses from a tenant who had defaulted on the agreement). *Martin v Routh*, Ch D 1964, 42 TC 106.

Amounts paid to company by shareholders—whether rent

[47.5] A married couple purchased a large house, which was used by a company of which they were sole shareholders. The company made various payments to the couple. These payments were shown in the company's accounts as rent and in the husband's returns as income from property. The Revenue issued assessments on the husband, charging tax on the payments. He appealed, contending that his returns were incorrect. The Ch D rejected this contention and upheld the assessments. Walton J held that the evidence clearly showed that the payments had been in respect of the company's occupation of the property. *Jeffries v Stevens*, Ch D 1982, 56 TC 134; [1982] STC 639.

Rents from surplus premises sublet—excess profits tax cases

[47.6] See *CIR v Broadway Car Co (Wimbledon) Ltd*, **64.51** TRADING PROFITS—RECEIPTS; *CIR v Buxton Palace Hotel Ltd*, **64.52** TRADING PROFITS—RECEIPTS, and *Albert E Reed & Co Ltd v CIR*, **64.53** TRADING PROFITS—RECEIPTS.

Repairs to let property

[47.7] An individual (W) claimed a deduction of £43,665 for substantial repairs to an old building which he let to tenants. HMRC issued an amendment disallowing the deduction on the grounds that this was capital expenditure. W appealed. The First-Tier Tribunal allowed his appeal, applying the principles laid down in *Conn v Robins Bros Ltd*, **63.91** TRADING PROFITS, and finding that 'the disputed work undertaken was one of essential repair'. *C Wills v HMRC*, FTT [2010] UKFTT 174 (TC), TC00479.

Capital element of mortgage repayments

[47.8] A woman (C) purchased a house with the aid of a mortgage, and let part of it to tenants. She submitted returns in which she claimed a deduction for the whole of the amounts payable under the mortgage. HMRC issued amendments on the basis that C was only permitted to deduct the interest element of the repayments, and that the part of the repayments that represented a repayment of the capital was not deductible. The First-tier Tribunal dismissed C's appeal, holding that 'the only amounts which are deductible are the amounts of interest'. *Mrs S Chinyanga v HMRC*, FTT [2014] UKFTT 516 (TC), TC03643.

Lease premiums, etc. (ITTOIA 2005, ss 276–307)

ITTOIA 2005, s 281—variation of lease*

[47.9] The tenant of two shops sublet them, in breach of the terms of the lease. The landlord threatened to take proceedings against the tenant, and the tenant paid the landlord £3,000 as compensation. The HL held (by a 4-1 majority, Lord Morris of Borth-y-Gest dissenting) that the payment had been made for the waiver or variation of the terms of the lease, within *ITTOIA 2005, s 281**. Lord Hailsham held that 'the primary meaning of the word "waiver" in legal parlance is the abandonment of a right in such a way that the other party is entitled to plead the abandonment by way of confession and avoidance if the right is thereafter asserted'. *Banning v Wright*, HL 1972, 48 TC 421; [1972] 1 WLR 972; [1972] 2 All ER 987. (*Note.* For another issue in this case, see **5.80** ASSESSMENTS.)

Application for rectification of tenancy agreement

[47.10] A bank held a tenancy of a house in London, which was occupied by one of its senior employees. Under a tenancy agreement dated August 1996, it agreed to pay rent totalling £345,000 covering the period to 1 June 1998. It subsequently applied to the Ch D for rectification of the agreement, by substituting the word 'premium' for 'rent', in order to reduce the tax liability under the legislation then in force (*ICTA 1988, s 145*). The landlords agreed to the rectification, but the Revenue opposed it. The Ch D reviewed the evidence in detail and granted the bank's application in part, accepting the bank's evidence that 'the parties intended to create a tenancy in consideration of a premium and with no rent', and that the sum of £345,000 was 'far too large to be rent; there is only any commercial sense in the transaction if it is to be regarded as a premium'. However, the Ch D also held that the first payment (of £32,500) fell to be treated as rent, on the grounds that 'it represented advance payment under a subsisting lease at a rent' and 'cannot retrospectively be recategorised (in particular for tax purposes) as part of a premium'. *Toronto-Dominion Bank v Oberoi & Others*, Ch D 2002, 75 TC 244; [2004] STC 1197.

Furnished lettings (ITTOIA 2005, s 308)

House let furnished—cost of alternative accommodation

[47.11] A woman owned a house in North Berwick. She let it to a tenant, and rented another house in Aberfeldy. The Revenue issued an assessment on her profits from letting her house in North Berwick. She appealed, claiming that the rent she paid to live in the Aberfeldy house should be allowed as a deduction. The General Commissioners rejected this contention and dismissed her appeal, and the CS unanimously upheld their decision. *Wylie v Eccott*, CS 1912, 6 TC 128.

[47.12] An Army officer let his house while he was stationed away from home. The Revenue assessed him on the profits from the letting and he appealed, contending that part of the cost of living in billets should be allowed as a deduction. The KB rejected this contention and upheld the assessment. Atkinson J held that any claim for the cost of living in billets should be made against the assessment on his Army income. *Smith v Irvine*, KB 1946, 27 TC 381.

Furnished letting of cinema

[47.13] A property-dealing company (S) acquired the freehold of a cinema and let it to a tenant, together with fittings, fixtures and furnishings. The KB held that S was chargeable to income tax on the proportion of the rent attributable to the furniture and fittings comprised in the lease. *Shop Investments Ltd v Sweet*, KB 1940, 23 TC 38; [1940] 1 All ER 533. (*Note*. The substantive point at issue was the extent to which the rent was covered by the Schedule A assessment on the cinema under the law in force at the time. This is no longer relevant.)

[47.14] See also *Windsor Playhouse Ltd v Heyhoe*, 64.50 TRADING PROFITS—RECEIPTS.

Computation of income from furnished lettings

[47.15] A landlord appealed against estimated assessments on furnished lettings. The Commissioners determined the assessments and the Ch D upheld their decision as one of fact. *Abidoye v Hennessey*, Ch D 1978, [1979] STC 212. (*Note*. The landlord appeared in person. The judgment is of interest in approving the Revenue's allowance of 10% of the rents as a deduction to cover wear and tear of furniture, etc. Walton J observed that 'this is the first time, I think, I have ever had any appellant in my court complaining that the inspector of taxes had treated him more generously than he was strictly entitled to'. Compare Revenue Pamphlet IR 131, SP A19.)

Furnished letting for public entertainments

[47.16] See *Governors of Rotunda Hospital Dublin v Coman*, 9.83 CHARITIES.

Furnished letting abroad—deductibility of interest

[47.17] See *Ockendon v Mackley*, 28.24 FOREIGN INCOME.

Expenditure on sea walls (ITTOIA 2005, s 315)

[47.18] A landowner arranged for the construction of a new embankment to reclaim a salt marsh by preventing it from being flooded at high tide. He claimed relief for the cost under *ITTOIA 2005, s 315**. The Revenue rejected the claim and the CA unanimously dismissed the landowner's appeal, holding that the relief extends only to expenses incurred in preserving or protecting lands in their existing state. *Hesketh v Bray*, CA 1888, 2 TC 380; 21 QBD 444.

Furnished holiday accommodation (ITTOIA 2005, ss 322–328)

*Whether letting 'on a commercial basis' —ITTOIA 2005, s 323(2)**

[47.19] An individual (W) purchased three flats in an old castle in Cornwall, at a total cost of £343,000, of which he borrowed £276,000 from a bank. He let the flats as furnished holiday accommodation, but the income from them was significantly less than the interest which he had to pay to the bank. He claimed loss relief under *ITA 2007, s 72** in respect of the lettings. The Revenue rejected the claim, on the grounds that the accommodation was not let 'on a commercial basis and with a view to the realisation of profits', as required by *ITTOIA 2005, s 323(2)**. W appealed, contending that when he had purchased the flats he had anticipated that interest rates would fall and that the lettings would become profitable within three years. The Special Commissioner allowed his appeal, holding that the test in *ITTOIA 2005, s 323(2)** was a subjective test, whereas the test for loss relief purposes in *ITA 2007, s 74** was an objective test. The Commissioner held on the evidence that W clearly satisfied the subjective test in *ITTOIA 2005, s 323(2)**, and also held 'on balance' that he satisfied the objective test of *ITA 2007, s 74**. Accordingly he was entitled to loss relief. *Walls v Livesey*, Sp C [1995] SSCD 12 (Sp C 4). (*Notes.* (1) This decision was distinguished in the subsequent case of *Brown v Richardson*, **47.20** below. (2) For the Revenue's interpretation of this decision, see Revenue Tax Bulletin October 1997, pp 472–473.)

[47.20] An accountant purchased a three-bedroomed bungalow in Cornwall. He let the bungalow as furnished holiday accommodation, but the income from it was less than the mortgage interest which he had to pay. He claimed loss relief under *ITA 2007, s 72** in respect of the lettings. The Revenue rejected the claim, on the grounds that the accommodation was not let 'on a commercial basis and with a view to the realisation of profits', as required by *ITTOIA 2005, s 323(2)**. The Special Commissioner dismissed the accountant's appeal, distinguishing *Walls v Livesey*, **47.19** above, and holding on the evidence that the accountant had bought the bungalow as a holiday home. Although the cottage had been let on a commercial basis, it had been let 'with a view to generating revenue to offset costs rather than with a view to the realisation of profits'. *Brown v Richardson*, Sp C [1997] SSCD 233 (Sp C 129). (*Note.* For the Revenue's practice following this decision, see Revenue Tax Bulletin October 1997, pp 472–473.)

Definition of 'qualifying holiday accommodation'—ITTOIA 2005, s 325

[47.21] See *Horner v HMRC*, **71.332** CAPITAL GAINS TAX.

Definition of a lease (ITTOIA 2005, s 364)

[47.22] In a non-tax case, the CA held that an agreement by which an employer granted an employee exclusive occupation of a house, but was specifically stated not to create a tenancy, was a lease rather than merely a licence (so that the tenant was protected by the *Rent Restriction Acts*). Somervell LJ held that 'if, looking at the operative clauses in the agreement, one comes to the conclusion that the rights of the occupier, to use a neutral word, are those of a lessee, the parties cannot turn it into a licence by saying at the end "this is deemed to be a licence"; nor can they, if the operative paragraphs show that it is merely a licence, say that it should be deemed to be a lease'. *Facchini v Bryson*, CA [1952] 1 TLR 1386.

[47.23] The decision in *Facchini v Bryson*, **47.22** above, was approved and applied by the HL in a subsequent case where an agreement which granted exclusive occupation, but was expressed to be a licence, was held to have created a tenancy. Lord Templeman held that 'in the case of residential accommodation there is no difficulty in deciding whether the grant confers exclusive possession. An occupier of residential accommodation at a rent for a term is either a lodger or a tenant. The occupier is a lodger if the landlord provides attendance or services which require the landlord or his servants to exercise unrestricted access to and use of the premises. A lodger is entitled to live in the premises but cannot call the place his own.' However, if residential accommodation was 'granted for a term at a rent with exclusive possession, the landlord providing neither attendance nor services, the grant is a tenancy; any express reservation to the landlord of limited rights to enter and view the state of the premises and to repair and maintain the premises only serves to emphasise the fact that the grantee is entitled to exclusive possession and is a tenant.' He observed that 'parties cannot turn a tenancy into a licence merely by calling it one. The circumstances and the conduct of the parties show that what was intended was that the occupier should be granted exclusive possession at a rent for a term with a corresponding interest in the land which created a tenancy.' *Street v Mountford*, HL [1985] 1 AC 809; [1985] 2 All ER 289.

48

Residence, Ordinary Residence and Domicile

The cases in this chapter are arranged under the following headings.

CROSS-REFERENCES

See *Fry v Burma Corporation Ltd*, **61.66** TRADING PROFITS, for the application of the basis period rules when a person first becomes a UK resident.

Residence

Mariner with home in UK

[48.1] The Commissioners held that a master mariner, who had a house in Glasgow where his wife and family lived, but was in the UK for only 88 days in the relevant year, was resident in the UK. The Court of Exchequer upheld their decision. *In re Young*, CE 1875, 1 TC 57.

[48.2] The decision in *Re Young*, **48.1** above, was applied in a subsequent case where a mariner had a home in the UK but was wholly abroad in the relevant year. Lord Glencorse held that 'every sailor has a residence on land' and that 'he is not a bit the less a resident in Great Britain because the exigencies of his business have happened to carry him away for a somewhat longer time than usual during this particular voyage.' *Rogers v CIR*, CE 1879, 1 TC 225.

Merchant seaman

[48.3] An individual (F) was employed as a merchant seaman. In August 2003 he began working for a Norwegian company. This employment continued until September 2005. HMRC issued assessments for 2003/04 to 2005/06 on the basis that he was resident in the UK in those years. F appealed, contending that other taxpayers in similar employment had been accepted as non-resident. The First-Tier Tribunal dismissed his appeal, finding that F had kept his home in the UK and had not established a home elsewhere. He had visited the UK for 85 days in 2003/04 and 97 days in 2004/05. Accordingly, as a matter of law, he remained resident in the UK. Judge Radford observed that

F 'had produced evidence to show that he had not been treated in the same way as other taxpayers in exactly the same position as him'. It was arguable that he had a 'legitimate expectation that he be treated as the other taxpayers in his position', and suggested that he should 'consider referring his case to the Revenue Adjudicator'. *D Farquhar v HMRC*, FTT [2010] UKFTT 231 (TC), TC00532.

Trader abroad with residence in UK

[48.4] A trader (L) carried on business in Italy, but owned a castle in Scotland, where he stayed with his family from July to October 1883. The Revenue issued an assessment on the profits of the Italian trade, on the basis that L was resident in the UK for 1883/84. The Commissioners upheld the assessment and the Court of Exchequer dismissed L's appeal. Lord Glencorse held that the words 'residing in the United Kingdom' included 'a person who is not for a time actually residing in the United Kingdom, but who has constructively his residence there because his ordinary place of abode and his home is there, although he is absent for a time from it, however long continued that absence can be'. *Lloyd v Sulley*, CE 1884, 2 TC 37.

[48.5] A trader carried on a business in Madras where he normally resided. His wife owned a house in the UK which he and his family visited in most years, and in which his children had lived in the relevant year of assessment. The Court of Exchequer held that he was not resident in the UK. *Turnbull v Foster*, CE 1904, 6 TC 206. (*Note*. See now *ITA 2007, s 830*.)

US citizen with residence in UK

[48.6] An American, ordinarily resident in New York, rented a house and shooting rights in Scotland for a period of three years, spending about two months each year in the house. He was held to be resident in the UK. *Cooper v Cadwalader*, CE 1904, 5 TC 101. (*Note*. See now *ITA 2007, s 831*.)

US citizen living on yacht anchored in UK

[48.7] An American had for many years lived on board a yacht he owned which had been anchored throughout the period within the port of Colchester. The General Commissioners held that he was resident in the UK, and the CA unanimously upheld their decision. *Bayard Brown v Burt*, CA 1911, 5 TC 667.

Belgian with hunting box in UK

[48.8] A Belgian with a residence in Brussels visited the UK for periods not exceeding six months in any one year. While in the UK he had the use of a hunting box in Leicestershire, owned by a UK company which he controlled. The KB held that he was resident in the UK. *Loewenstein v De Salis*, KB 1926, 10 TC 424.

South African with house in UK

[48.9] An airline pilot (G) had been born in South Africa in 1952. His parents had moved to Kenya when he was a child, and he had become a naturalised British citizen. He moved to the UK in 1986 and began to work for a British airline (which was subsequently taken over by British Airways). He purchased a house in Horley, near Gatwick Airport. In 1997 he bought a house in Cape Town. He continued to work for British Airways and to own the house in Horley, where he stayed for about two or three days before and after long-haul flights to and from the UK. The Revenue issued a determination that he had continued to be resident and ordinarily resident in the UK from 1997/98 to 2002/03 inclusive. G appealed, contending that he had ceased to be resident in the UK in 1997. The First-Tier Tribunal rejected this contention and dismissed G's appeal. Judge Mosedale reviewed the evidence in detail and found that, for the years from 1998/99 to 2001/02 inclusive, G had never spent less than 114 days in the UK, and, over the period as a whole, he had spent almost as much time in the UK as he had in South Africa. Accordingly he had never ceased to be resident in the UK, but had simply changed 'from being a person resident in one country to being a person resident in two'. *LD Grace v HMRC (No 2)*, FTT [2011] UKFTT 36 (TC); [2011] SFTD 669, TC00913.

British subject living in hotels

[48.10] A British subject had worked in the Indian Civil Service and lived in India, generally in hotels, for most of his life. Two years before retiring, he left India (on two years' leave) and since then had lived in hotels in the UK, Belgium and France. His visits to this country were to visit friends. The Revenue issued an assessment charging UK tax on his Indian pension, and he appealed, contending that he was not resident in the UK. The Commissioners accepted this contention and allowed his appeal, and the KB upheld their decision. *CIR v Zorab*, KB 1926, 11 TC 289.

[48.11] A British subject had worked in the Indian Civil Service and lived in India for many years. In 1893 he retired, and moved to the UK, where he acquired a house. In 1918 he relinquished the house and thereafter lived in hotels, mainly in France, but spending about three months each year in the UK. The Revenue issued an assessment charging UK tax on his Indian pension, and he appealed, contending that he was not resident in the UK. The Special Commissioners accepted this contention and allowed his appeal, and the KB upheld their decision as one of fact. *CIR v Brown*, KB 1926, 11 TC 292.

Irish resident staying in UK hotels for business purposes

[48.12] An individual (L) was born in England of Irish parents. He lived in England until 1919, and became managing director of a UK company. In 1919 he retired from his post as managing director, while continuing to act as an 'advisory director', and sold his property in the UK. From 1920 he lived with his family in the Irish Free State. For 1922/23 and 1923/24 he visited the UK for business purposes for 101 and 94 days respectively, usually staying at a hotel. He claimed that he was not resident in the UK for these years. The Special Commissioners rejected his claim, holding on the evidence that he remained resident in the UK for both years. The HL upheld their decision as one of fact (by a 4-1 majority, Viscount Cave dissenting). Viscount Sumner held that 'it does not follow that keeping up a permanent establishment abroad and having none here is incompatible with "being resident here" if there is other sufficient evidence of it'. Lord Warrington held that 'the question of residence or ordinary residence is one of degree'. There was 'no technical or special meaning attached to either expression for the purposes of the Income Tax Act, and accordingly a decision of the Commissioners on the question is a finding of fact'. *Lysaght v CIR*, HL 1928, 13 TC 511; [1928] AC 234.

British subject, temporarily employed abroad, visiting UK

[48.13] A British subject (C), whose ordinary residence had hitherto been in the UK, took a three-year apprenticeship with an American firm. During those three years he had no place of abode in the UK, but visited it occasionally, staying at hotels, for the purpose of his employment. The Revenue issued an assessment charging tax on his remuneration, on the basis that his visits abroad had been for occasional residence only, within the meaning of *ITA 2007, s 829(1)**. The Commissioners allowed his appeal, holding that he was not resident in the UK, and the CS upheld their decision. Lord Clyde held that C's 'business and residential headquarters were permanently in New York throughout the three years'. *CIR v Combe*, CS 1932, 17 TC 405.

Stockbroker returning to UK after working abroad

[48.14] A British subject (K) had been a partner in a firm of stockbrokers. He had been resident in the UK from 1994 until September 1997, when the firm posted him to an office in Japan. He continued to work in Japan until he resigned from the partnership on 11 July 2005. He returned to the UK on 17 July and stayed at his mother's house in Kent until 30 July, when he went to Italy on holiday. He remained in Italy until 28 August. While he was in Italy, he disposed of a significant holding of shares. HMRC issued a ruling that CGT was chargeable on the disposal, on the basis that K had become resident in the UK when he returned from Japan on 17 July. K appealed, contending that he should be treated as not having become resident in the UK until he returned from his Italian holiday on 28 August. The First-tier Tribunal rejected this contention and dismissed the appeal, finding that while K was in Kent, and before he travelled to Italy, he had agreed to lease a property in Norfolk. Judge Nowlan concluded that 'at some time before 30 July, even if not on 17 July, the appellant formed the intention to stay in the UK permanently and then became resident'. *R Kimber v HMRC*, FTT [2012] UKFTT 107 (TC), TC01803.

British actress temporarily living abroad—short visit to UK

[48.15] In 1931 a British actress agreed to act in a play in the USA. She stayed in the USA from November 1931 to April 1933, and from September 1933 to July 1934, when she returned to the UK. Between April and September 1933 she spent sixteen weeks in the UK (staying in rented accommodation) and eight weeks on holiday abroad. The Revenue issued assessments charging income tax on her professional earnings for 1932/33 and 1933/34. She appealed, contending that she had not been resident in the UK for those years. The Commissioners accepted this contention and allowed her appeal, and the KB upheld their decision as one of fact. *Withers v Wynyard*, KB 1938, 21 TC 722.

Residence in UK on military service

[48.16] The heir to an Irish peerage lived in England from 1921. He succeeded to the estate in 1929 on the death of his father, but continued to live in England. In August 1939 he was called up for military service. His mother, who had continued to live in the family home in Ireland, died in June 1940. In February 1942 he was released from military duty, and in April 1942 he took up permanent residence in the family home in Ireland. He claimed exemption from UK income tax for 1940/41 and 1941/42, contending that he should be treated as having ceased to be resident in the UK on the death of his mother. The Special Commissioners rejected this contention and dismissed his appeal, and the CA unanimously upheld their decision as one of fact. *Lord Inchiquin v CIR*, CA 1948, 31 TC 125.

Musician ordinarily resident in UK but absent for entire tax year

[48.17] A British musician (C) was ordinarily resident in the UK, where he owned a house which he occupied with his parents. However, he spent considerable time in the USA promoting his recordings. In December 1977 he received a substantial advance payment for copyright. He was advised that he could avoid paying tax on this by not being resident in the UK in 1978/79 (when his 1977 profits would have been taxed under the 'preceding year' basis of assessment then in force). He therefore left the UK on 3 April 1978 and did not return until 2 May 1979. During the intervening period he lived in California. The Revenue issued assessments on him for 1978/79 on the basis that he had continued to be resident in the UK, and alternatively that he was chargeable under *ITA 2007, s 829(1)** as he had only left the UK for the purposes of occasional residence abroad. The Special Commissioners allowed his appeal and the Ch D upheld their decision. Nicholls J held that the Commissioners had been entitled to find that C had not been resident in the UK during 1978/79, and that his presence in California amounted to more than 'occasional residence'. *Reed v Clark*, Ch D 1985, 58 TC 528; [1985] STC 323; [1985] 3 WLR 142.

British subject with house in Seychelles—whether resident in UK

[48.18] An individual (G) was born in England in 1937. In 1975 he bought a house in the Seychelles. In 1976 he moved to Canada and let his Seychelles house to tenants. In 1979 he married and moved to California. This marriage was dissolved in 1986. In 1988 a Panamanian company which G controlled bought a large house in Berkshire, where he lived when visiting the UK. In

1993 he married a woman who had been born in the Seychelles but who had lived in the UK since 1977. In 1998 they had a son, who was born in the UK. G appealed against various assessments, contending as a preliminary issue that he had acquired a domicile of choice in the Seychelles in 1976, and that for 1993/94 onwards he was neither resident, ordinarily resident or domiciled in the UK. The Special Commissioners reviewed the evidence in detail and rejected these contentions, finding that G travelled very frequently on business but that for 1993/94 to 2000/01 he had been in the UK for at least 110 days each year. His wife and son both lived in the UK. Accordingly he had remained resident, ordinarily resident and domiciled in the UK. The Ch D upheld the Commissioners' decision as one of fact. *R Gaines-Cooper v HMRC*, Ch D 2007, [2008] STC 1665; [2007] EWHC 2617 (Ch); 10 ITLR 255. (*Notes*. (1) The CA dismissed an application by G for leave to appeal against the Ch D decision. Rimer LJ described the application as 'an illegitimate attempt to reargue the facts' (CA 2008, TL 3839). (2) For HMRC's practice following the Commissioners' decision, see HMRC Brief 01/07, issued on 5 January 2007. See also *FA 2008, s 24*, which introduced a new statutory test for determining days of residence. (3) G subsequently made an unsuccessful application for judicial review—see **4.324** APPEALS.)

Company director spending most of year outside UK

[48.19] An individual (B) was born in Canada in 1957, but moved to the UK at the age of two and was educated in the UK. He subsequently became a director of a UK company, and in 1998 was awarded a bonus of more than £2,000,000. He did not declare this on his UK tax return. The Revenue issued an amendment charging tax on it, and B appealed, contending that he had not been resident in the UK during 1998/99. The Special Commissioner reviewed the evidence in detail, rejected this contention and dismissed the appeal. The Commissioner found that B had been in the UK on 6 April 1998, and that although he had spent much of 1998/99 outside the UK, he had visited the UK on at least eleven subsequent occasions during that year, spending a total of at least 45 days in the UK. His partner and sons had continued to live in the UK in a house which he owned, and to which his post was sent. The Commissioner observed that 'there was no evidence of a distinct break in the pattern of (B's) life'. Accordingly B remained resident in the UK for 1998/99. *L Barrett v HMRC*, Sp C 2007, [2008] SSCD 268 (Sp C 639).

[48.20] A company director (H), who was born in the UK, became the managing director of a UK company (B) in 1982. In 1985 he arranged a management buy-out and in 1987 he transferred his shares in B to family trusts resident outside the UK. He remained a director of B and became its chairman in 1992. In 1997 his family trusts sold their holdings in B to a venture capital fund, and realised substantial capital gains, but retained an interest in B. In February 1998 H began working for M, a Netherlands subsidiary of B, while continuing to be chairman of B. In March 1999 the capital gains which H's family trusts had realised in 1997 were crystallised. H submitted a 1998/99 tax return stating that he had not been resident or ordinarily resident in the UK, and that he had been working in the Netherlands during that year. In 2004/05 HMRC issued a 'discovery assessment, charging CGT of more than

£30,000,000 on the basis that H had been resident and ordinarily resident in the UK in 1998/99. H appealed. The First-Tier Tribunal reviewed the evidence in detail and dismissed his appeal, finding that during 1998/99 H had spent 130 days in the Netherlands and 82 days in the UK. (He had also spent 113 days in Barbados, where he had travelled on holiday and had remained on medical grounds after being taken ill.) The tribunal held that he had been resident and ordinarily resident in the UK in 1998/99, finding that his move to the Netherlands was no more than 'occasional residence abroad'. His work for M 'was not full-time', and some of his visits to the UK had been for the purposes of his duties as B's chairman. *DW Hankinson v HMRC (No 2)*, FTT [2009] UKFTT 384 (TC), TC00319. (*Note*. For preliminary issues in this case, see **4.14** and **4.321** APPEALS. For another issue in this case, taken to the CA, see **5.25** ASSESSMENTS.)

Company director with house in Jersey

[48.21] A company director (O) had lived in Jersey since 1988. In 2002 his son became seriously ill and was admitted to hospital in the UK. In October 2002 he was dismissed from his directorship following a change of company ownership, and received a substantial termination payment. He did not include this on his tax return. HMRC issued an amendment charging tax on it, and O appealed, accepting that he had spent more than 183 days in the UK in 2002/03, but contending that he had only done so because of his son's illness, and that he should not be treated as resident in the UK. The First-Tier Tribunal rejected this contention and dismissed his appeal. *N Ogden v HMRC*, FTT [2011] UKFTT 212 (TC), TC01077.

Company director with apartment in Monaco

[48.22] A company director (G) had been born in the UK in 1949. In 2004 he acquired an apartment in Monaco, and moved there on 5 April 2005. However he retained the house in London where he had lived from 1993 to 2005. During 2005/06 he visited that house on 22 occasions, although none of the visits lasted for more than two days. HMRC issued a ruling that G had remained resident in the UK in 2005/06, and was therefore liable to UK tax on his UK dividend income. The First-tier Tribunal allowed G's appeal. Judge Nowlan found that G 'had a genuine home in Monaco, that much of his way of life revolved around life in Monaco', and that he 'had purposes broader and more genuine for being in Monaco than simply camping abroad to avoid tax'. He held that G had effected 'a distinct break', and had not been resident in the UK in 2005/06. *J Glyn v HMRC*, FTT [2013] UKFTT 645 (TC), TC03029.

Woman with apartment in Spain—whether resident in UK

[48.23] A woman (Y) was born in England in 1955. In March 2000 she began renting an apartment in Spain. She appealed against capital gains tax assessments for 2003/04 to 2006/07 inclusive, contending that she had been resident in Spain and had not been resident in the UK. The First-tier Tribunal reviewed the evidence in detail and dismissed her appeal, finding that she had spent 72 days in the UK in 2003/04 and had spent 108 days in the UK in 2006/07. She had retained her UK bank account, and had continued to receive incapacity benefit from the Department of Work and Pensions. Judge Walters held that, although she had been resident in Spain during the years in question, she had not 'made a distinct break in the pattern of her life for the purpose of relinquishing her status as UK-resident'. Her personal and economic relations continued to be centred in the UK, and she had remained resident in the UK. *Ms LD Yates v HMRC*, FTT [2012] UKFTT 568 (TC), TC02220; 15 ITLR 205.

Couple with house in Portugal—whether resident in UK

[48.24] A company director and his wife had both been born in England in 1956. In 1997 they moved into a property in Cheshire. In June 2001 they took possession of a flat in Belgium, and were granted residence status under Belgian law. They subsequently purchased a house in Portugal, and in 2002 they were granted residence status under Portuguese law. In their 2001/02 tax returns, they claimed that they had become non-resident in the UK from 4 April 2001. HMRC subsequently began an enquiry and issued amendments to their 2001/02 self-assessments charging tax on the basis that they had continued to be resident in the UK for that year. They also issued discovery assessments for 2002/03, 2003/04 and 2004/05. The couple appealed, contending that they had ceased to be resident in the UK. The First-tier Tribunal reviewed the evidence in detail, rejected this contention and dismissed the appeals in principle, finding that the couple had continued to occupy their Cheshire property as their family home after April 2001, and had 'remained resident in the UK during 2001/02 and 2002/03'. Furthermore, they had failed to satisfy the tribunal 'that they ceased to be resident in the UK during 2003/04 and 2004/05'. *SN & Mrs PM Rumbelow v HMRC*, FTT [2013] UKFTT 637 (TC), TC03022.

Woman emigrating from UK to Portugal—whether resident in UK

[48.25] A woman (K) was born in Tanzania in 1953 and moved to the UK in 1968. She was a student in the UK until 1977, and subsequently worked as a pharmacist. In 1989 she purchased two buildings which she operated as care homes. In 1991 she transferred this business to a company (T) of which she was the controlling director. From 2000/01 she began spending most of her time in Portugal. In November 2003 she sold her shares in T for £250,000. She also sold two other properties which she had acquired one of which she had let to tenants and one of which had been used as her residence while she was in the UK. HMRC subsequently issued an assessment under *TMA, s 29*, charging CGT on the gains. She appealed, contending firstly that she was not resident in the UK, and alternatively that if she was held to be resident in the UK, her residence was only 'temporary', so that the effect of *TCGA, s 9(3)* was that no CGT was due. The First-Tier Tribunal reviewed the evidence in detail, rejected these contentions and dismissed her appeals. The tribunal found that it appeared that in 2002/03 K had spent 121 days in the UK and in 2003/04 she had spent 84 days in the UK. The dates of arrival and departure indicated that 'her visits to the UK were frequent and generally of at least several days' duration'. Until November 2003 K had had 'a settled abode' in the UK, where she had lived for a long time. She had spent 'a significant amount of time in the UK'. The fact that she may also have been resident in Portugal was irrelevant. Accordingly she was resident in the UK for 2003/04, and her residence had not been 'temporary'. Judge Hellier also held that K had been negligent in not declaring the gains on her tax return, since 'it was clear that (K) was within the residence criteria' of *TCGA, s 9*, and this was not 'a borderline case'. *N Karim v HMRC*, FTT [2009] UKFTT 368 (TC), TC00306.

Whether doctor resident in UK

[48.26] A doctor (B) was born in England in 1949, and was resident in the UK until 1977 and from 1980 onwards. He married in 1989 but divorced in 1999. He disposed of two properties in 2000/01, but failed to declare the gains on his tax return. Following an enquiry, HMRC issued a jeopardy amendment charging tax on the gains. B appealed, contending that he had ceased to be resident in the UK after his divorce. The First-Tier Tribunal reviewed the evidence in detail, rejected this contention, and dismissed his appeal, finding that he had purchased a property in France in April 2000 but had made several return visits to the UK. Judge Connell noted that B had subsequently sold his French property and had told the French revenue authorities that 'he considered himself to be a non-resident for the purposes of French regulations in force and that his primary residence was in England'. Although B had owned a property in France, he had not paid any French income tax, and there was no evidence that he 'became, or ever intended to declare to the French authorities that he had become, resident in France'. *Dr P Broome v HMRC*, FTT [2011] UKFTT 760 (TC), TC01597.

Banker working for part of year in Belgium

[48.27] See *Daniel v HMRC*, **29.60** FURTHER ASSESSMENTS: LOSS OF TAX.

Whether individual resident in UK for 'six months'

[48.28] In 1947 an individual (W), who was domiciled in Scotland but had no place of abode in the UK, arrived in the UK at 2 p.m. on 2 June and left at 10 a.m. on 2 December. He subsequently claimed repayment of UK tax deducted from a foreign dividend. The Revenue rejected his claim, considering that he had resided in the UK for six months during 1947/48. The Ch D allowed his appeal. Donovan J held that 'six months' meant six calendar months and that hours could be taken into account. Hence W had not resided in the UK for six months of 1947/48. *Wilkie v CIR*, Ch D 1951, w32 TC 495; [1952] Ch 153; [1952] 1 All ER 92. (*Note*. The reference to 'six months' which appeared in *ITA 1918* has subsequently been replaced by a reference to 183 days. See now *ITA 2007, s 831(1)* and *FA 2008, s 24*.)

Residence for part of year

[48.29] For the meaning of 'resident in the UK for a year of assessment' where the individual was so resident for part only of the year, see *Neubergh v CIR*, 5.16 ASSESSMENTS. See also Extra-Statutory Concession A11.

Ordinary residence

[48.30] A woman who had been born in Scotland left the UK in July 1919 and lived in hotels abroad until June 1920. She then stayed at a hotel in London until October 1920, when she left the UK until the summer of 1921. She held a bank account in London, and stored her personal effects with a sister in the UK. The Special Commissioners held that she remained ordinarily resident in the UK for 1919/20 and 1920/21. The CS unanimously upheld their decision as one of fact. *Reid v CIR*, CS 1926, 10 TC 673.

[48.31] From December 1919 to January 1925, a British subject had no fixed abode but lived in hotels, spending between four and five months each year in the UK. The Commissioners held that he remained resident and ordinarily resident in the UK, and the HL unanimously upheld their decision. Viscount Sumner observed that L had 'left the United Kingdom for the purpose of occasional residence only' and 'was a bird of passage of almost mechanical regularity'. *Levene v CIR*, HL 1928, 13 TC 486; [1928] AC 217.

[48.32] A widow, with no fixed place of abode, lived in hotels both in the UK and abroad. From 1921/22 to 1927/28, she was in the UK for periods varying from 40 to 177 days each year, mainly because her son was being educated in England. For 1924/25, the Special Commissioners had held that she was neither resident nor ordinarily resident in the UK. The Revenue accepted this decision for 1925/26 and 1926/27. However, for 1927/28, they issued a ruling that she was liable to income tax on her income from securities, on the basis that she was ordinarily resident in the UK. The Special Commissioners dismissed her appeal, finding that 'having regard to the continuance through the years of the regular and lengthy visits to the United Kingdom, the circumstances were different from those under consideration when the appeal for the year 1924/25 was heard'. The KB upheld their decision as one of fact. *Kinloch v CIR*, KB 1929, 14 TC 736.

[48.33] A British subject, with business interests in both Egypt and the UK, had houses in both countries. From 1921/22 to 1924/25 he spent an average of 139 days in the UK each year. The Special Commissioners held that he was ordinarily resident in the UK, and the CS unanimously upheld their decision. *Peel v CIR*, CS 1927, 13 TC 443.

[48.34] A British subject (E), who had lived outside the UK for several years, married an American woman in April 1925. They travelled to the UK in May 1925, and spent most of 1925/26 in the UK, supervising the formation of a school, which they opened in September 1926. The Special Commissioners held that E and his wife were ordinarily resident in the UK for 1925/26 to 1927/28, and the KB upheld their decision as one of fact. *Elmhirst v CIR*, KB 1937, 21 TC 380; [1937] KB 551; [1937] 2 All ER 349.

[48.35] An airline pilot (S), who was born and domiciled in the UK, purchased a flat in Cyprus in October 1998. He claimed that he was not ordinarily resident in the UK for 1999/2000. The Revenue rejected the claim and S appealed. The Special Commissioner dismissed his appeal, finding that during 1999/2000 he had spent 80 days in the UK, 77 days in Cyprus, 180 days flying in the course of his employment, and 28 days holidaying elsewhere. While in the UK, he had stayed in the house which he shared with his wife. The Commissioner held that 'the absences of (S) after October 1998 were temporary absences from the United Kingdom as were his absences when flying in the course of his duties'. S's time in Cyprus was only 'occasional residence abroad', within *ITA 2007, s 829(1)(a)**. The Ch D upheld the Commissioner's decision as one of fact. *Shepherd v HMRC*, Ch D 2006, 78 TC 389; [2006] STC 1821; [2006] EWHC 1512 (Ch).

[48.36] An individual (T) was born in Scotland in 1951. He lived and worked in the UK until 1979, when he began to work for an international oil company (S). He retained ownership of a house in the UK, and was posted back to the UK in February 1997. He left S in October 1998, and in 2001 he accepted a three-year contract to work in the USA, with effect from 1 July. However he was made redundant in October 2002. In December 2002 he leased a property in Monaco. During 2002/03 he spent a total of 140 days in the UK, 22 of which were attributable to the death of his mother. HMRC issued a determination that T was ordinarily resident in the UK for both 2001/02 and 2002/03. T appealed. The First-Tier Tribunal dismissed his appeal for 2001/02, but allowed his appeal for 2002/03, holding on the evidence that he had 'continued his previous ordinary residence in the UK from 6 April 2001 to around 1 July 2001 and there was then a distinct break in his residence'. Although he had returned to the UK in late 2002 before moving to Monaco, this had been 'a time of transition' during which he did not have 'a regular order of life anywhere'. *PG Turberville v HMRC*, FTT [2010] UKFTT 69 (TC), TC00381.

Visitor certified insane and remaining in asylum

[48.37] In an estate duty case, the Ch D held that an Australian woman, who was certified as insane in 1885 while on a temporary visit to England, and who had remained in an asylum in England until her death in 1939, was ordinarily resident in the UK. Morton J observed that 'it might seem strange if the court were to hold that a lady who spent the last 54 years of her life continuously in this country was not ordinarily resident in the United Kingdom'. *In re Mackenzie decd.*, Ch D 1940, 19 ATC 399; [1941] Ch 69; [1940] 2 All ER 310.

Foreign refugee remaining at school in UK

[48.38] A Dutch national (M), who was born in 1933, came to the UK in 1939 with his father as a refugee. His father left for Switzerland in 1946, but M remained at boarding school in the UK until July 1951. M claimed that he was not ordinarily resident in the UK for 1947/48 to 1951/52. The Special Commissioners rejected his claim, and the Ch D and CA unanimously upheld their decision as one of fact. *Miesegaes v CIR*, CA 1957, 37 TC 493.

Italian citizen working in UK

[48.39] In 1987 an Italian citizen (G) began working for an American bank. In 1990 he was posted to London, where he stayed until 1995, when he was made redundant. He found a new job with a Swiss bank and worked in Switzerland from 1995 to 1998, when he was again posted to London, where he remained for more than ten years. At first he lived in a rented flat, but in the autumn of 2001 he began looking to buy a house in London (and completed the purchase in 2002). The Revenue issued an assessment on the basis that he was ordinarily resident in the UK for 2001/02 (and thus was liable to income tax under Case I of Schedule E under the legislation then in force). G appealed, accepting that he was resident in the UK for that year, but contending that he could not be considered to have become 'ordinarily resident' (and thus was taxable under Case II rather than Case I of Schedule E). The Special Commissioner reviewed the evidence in detail and dismissed G's appeal, finding that G 'was ordinarily resident in the UK from the end of September 2001', since by that time he 'had been living with his family in the London flat under successive short-term tenancies for three years' and throughout that period he had 'been working for the same banking group'. The Commissioner held that 'this was sufficient to establish the habitual nature of the residence by that stage'. *FM Genovese v HMRC*, Sp C [2009] SSCD 373 (Sp C 741).

Overseas students living in UK for further education

[48.40] The *Education Act 1962* required local educational authorities to make certain awards to persons who, *inter alia*, were 'ordinarily resident in the area of the authority'. Five overseas students, each of whom had entered the UK at least three years earlier and obtained an educational qualification at their own expense, applied for an award for a course of further education. The local authorities rejected their applications on the ground that they were not ordinarily resident in the area, as required by the legislation. The CA allowed the appeal by one of the students (N) but dismissed the other four. The HL unanimously upheld the decision in N's appeal and allowed the appeals by the other four students. Lord Scarman held that the words 'ordinarily resident' should have their natural and ordinary meaning 'that the person must be habitually and normally resident here, apart from temporary or occasional absences of long or short duration'. The term should be construed as referring to a man's abode in a particular place or country which he has adopted voluntarily and for settled purposes as part of the regular order of his life for the time being, whether of short or long duration'. *Barnet London Borough Council v Nilish Shah (and other appeals)*, HL 1982, [1983] 2 WLR 16; [1983] 1 All ER 226.

Austrian banker working in UK

[48.41] An individual (T) was born in Austria in 1971. He became an investment banker. In July 1997 he began working for a bank in London. Initially he lived in rented accommodation, but in May 1998 he purchased a house in Notting Hill. On his tax returns for 1998/99 to 2000/01 he declared that he was resident in the UK, but not ordinarily resident in the UK. On his

2001/02 tax return he declared that he was ordinarily resident in the UK. In 2002 HMRC began an enquiry into his residence status, and subsequently issued a notice of determination that he had been ordinarily resident in the UK for 1998/99 to 2000/01 inclusive. T appealed, contending that he should only be treated as being ordinarily resident for 2001/02 onwards. The First-Tier Tribunal reviewed the evidence in detail, rejected this contention and dismissed T's appeal, holding that he had been ordinarily resident in the UK from 1998/99. Judge Clark held that, applying the principles laid down by Lord Scarman in *Barnet London Borough Council v Nilish Shah*, 48.40 above, 'the determination of ordinary residence status requires objective examination of immediately past events, and not intention or expectation for the future'. The key question was at what point in time 'did the purpose of (T) living where he did (ie in the UK) have a sufficient degree of continuity to be described as settled'. On the evidence, T had 'become ordinarily resident during 1998/99' when he had chosen 'to remain in London for a settled purpose, namely his employment, and adopted a pattern of living which in fact continued until 2002 (and, with certain changes, subsequently)'.The Upper Tribunal upheld this decision as one of fact. Roth J observed that 'for an individual to be 'ordinarily resident' in a country does not require that he intends to stay there permanently or for an indefinite period'. *A Tuczka v HMRC*, UT [2011] UKUT 113 (TCC); [2011] STC 1438.

Nigerian working in UK

[48.42] A Nigerian (M) moved to the Irish Republic in 1999 and married an Irishwoman. In May 2001 he began working as a mariner, based in Aberdeen. In February 2002 his wife moved to Aberdeen to join him. M claimed foreign earnings deduction on the basis that he had become resident and ordinarily resident in the UK from May 2001. HMRC accepted that M had become ordinarily resident in the UK from February 2002, but issued a ruling that he had not been ordinarily resident in the UK between May 2001 and February 2002 (and thus did not qualify for foreign earnings deduction). The First-Tier Tribunal dismissed M's appeal against this decision, finding that M 'did not dwell permanently in the UK between May 2001 and February 2002 but returned to Ireland when on leave from his ship to be with his wife'. Accordingly he had not been ordinarily resident in the UK until February 2002 when his wife moved to the UK. *S Megwa v HMRC*, FTT [2010] UKFTT 543 (TC), TC00796.

Person unlawfully resident in UK—whether ordinarily resident

[48.43] In a non-tax case, the HL unanimously held that a woman, who had been resident in the UK unlawfully, was ordinarily and habitually resident in the UK. Baroness Hale of Richmond held that residence 'need not be lawful residence. The question of whether the residence is habitual is a factual one which should be answered by applying the test, derived from the 1928 tax cases, laid down by Lord Scarman in *Shah* (see 48.40 above). It is possible that the legality of a person's residence here might be relevant to the factual question of whether that residence is "habitual". A person who was on the run after a deportation order or removal directions might find it hard to establish a habitual residence here. But such cases will be rare, compared with the large numbers of people who have remained here leading perfectly ordinary lives here for long periods, despite having no permission to do so.' She also observed that 'there is no reason in principle why a person whose presence here is unlawful cannot acquire a domicile of choice in this country'. *Mark v Mark*, HL [2005] UKHL 42; [2005] All ER (D) 370 (Jun).

Domicile

NOTE

Domicile is a concept of general law particularly important in relation to wills, intestacies and inheritance tax, but now of limited importance in income tax. The determination of a person's domicile normally entails a review in some detail of his life history. The summaries below give the facts only in broad outline. Unless otherwise shown, the case relates to a claim to be assessed on the remittance basis under *ICTA 1988, s 65(4)(5)* or similar earlier legislation. The judgments in *CIR v Bullock*, **48.59** below, give a useful review of the law of domicile.

Jurisdiction of Courts in relation to determination of domicile

[48.44] In an Irish case, the Special Commissioners had held that an appellant had not given up his domicile of origin. The Supreme Court held that domicile was a question of fact and the Commissioners' decision, if one of fact, could not be reviewed by the Courts. However, in this case the Special Commissioners had approached the question as one of law and had misconstrued the law. The case was remitted to them to determine the question of domicile as one of fact. *Earl of Iveagh v Revenue Commrs*, SC(I) 1930, 1 ITC 316; [1930] IR 431. (*Note*. See now, for the jurisdiction of Courts on questions of fact, *Edwards v Bairstow & Harrison*, **4.238** APPEALS. See also the judgment of Russell LJ in *Steiner v CIR*, **48.57** below.)

English domicile of origin retained

[48.45] An individual (C) was born in England in 1860, but lived in Australia from 1878 to 1910. From 1911 to 1933 he spent most of his time in the UK but did not have a permanent residence. The Revenue issued a ruling that for 1931/32 and 1932/33 he was liable to tax on his income from Australian investments on the basis that he was domiciled in England. He appealed, contending that he had acquired a domicile of choice in Australia and had not abandoned it. The Special Commissioners accepted this contention but the KB reversed their decision. Finlay J held that C had retained his English domicile of origin. On the evidence, his 'physical connection with Australia' had ceased 'as soon as his business connection with Australia closed', and from then on 'his connection, his base, has been English'. *CIR v Cohen*, KB 1937, 21 TC 301.

[48.46] An individual (C) had been born in the UK in 1904, the son of a refugee from Lithuania. He left the UK in February 1977, and was provisionally accepted by the Revenue as not resident or ordinarily resident in the UK.

He owned property in France and Israel, and in 1978 he acquired an apartment in Monaco. He established a Jersey settlement in February 1979, and died in London five months later. The Revenue claimed CTT on his free estate outside the UK, and on the assets of the settlement, on the basis that he was still domiciled in England when he made the settlement and at his death. The Ch D upheld the Revenue's claim. Warner J held on the evidence that C's father had been domiciled in England when he was born, so that his domicile of origin was England, and that he had not established a domicile of choice elsewhere, so that he retained his English domicile of origin. He observed that 'in these days of air travel and sophisticated systems of communication, it is not unusual for wealthy people to own several properties and to have business and sporting interests in several parts of the world'. *Re Clore (decd.) (No 2), Official Solicitor v Clore and Others*, Ch D [1984] STC 609.

[48.47] A woman (P) was born in London, of English parents, in 1965. When she was aged 15, her mother and a sister went to live in Guernsey with her grandmother. From then she continued her education in England, but spent most weekends and holidays in Guernsey. She claimed that for 1983/84 and 1984/85 she was domiciled in Guernsey. The Special Commissioners rejected her claim, holding that she had not become an 'inhabitant' of Guernsey in the years of claim and therefore could not be said to have acquired a domicile of choice in Guernsey. The Ch D upheld their decision. Hoffmann J held that a person who kept a residence in his domicile of origin could only acquire a domicile of choice in another country if the residence established there was his or her chief residence. On the facts, the Commissioners were entitled to conclude that P had not yet settled in Guernsey and therefore had not acquired a domicile of choice there. *Plummer v CIR*, Ch D 1987, 60 TC 452; [1987] STC 698; [1988] 1 WLR 292; [1988] 1 All ER 97.

[48.48] An individual, who had been born in England, moved to Hong Kong in 1960. He left Hong Kong in September 1989 and returned to the UK. In 1996 he appealed against a determination to IHT, contending that he had acquired a domicile of choice in Hong Kong. The Special Commissioner rejected this contention and dismissed his appeal, finding on the evidence that he had never established a domicile of choice in Hong Kong. Furthermore, even if he had acquired such a domicile of choice, his departure from Hong Kong, with the intention of never returning, would have resulted in the immediate revival of his English domicile of origin. *Civil Engineer v CIR*, Sp C 2001, [2002] SSCD 72 (Sp C 299). (*Note*. For another issue in this case, see 9.100 CHARITIES.)

[48.49] See also *Gaines-Cooper v HMRC*, 48.18 above.

Foreign domicile of choice acquired

[48.50] In an estate duty case, a testator had been born in 1871 with an English domicile, but had lived abroad from about 1890 onwards. He died in 1955. The Ch D held that was he domiciled in France on his death, notwithstanding a declaration in his will (made in 1948) that he had not abandoned his English domicile of origin. *In re Lawton*, Ch D 1958, 37 ATC 216.

[48.51] A surveyor had been born in England in 1958. He moved to Hong Kong in 1986, and married in 1990. In 1997 he and his wife received a 'right of permanent abode' in Hong Kong. In 1999 he established a discretionary trust in Jersey, for the benefit of his wife and children. He transferred £247,500 to the trustees. The Revenue issued a notice of determination that this was a chargeable transfer. He appealed, contending that he had lost his English domicile of origin and acquired a domicile of choice in Hong Kong (so that the money transferred to the trust was excluded property within *IHTA, s 6(1)*). The Special Commissioner accepted this contention and allowed his appeal, finding that at the date of the transfer, he 'had the intention to reside permanently in Hong Kong'. *Surveyor v CIR*, Sp C [2002] SSCD 501 (Sp C 339).

[48.52] A woman (J) had been born in England in 1922. She married in 1953 and spent most of the next 30 years outside the UK, with her husband who worked for an oil company. In 1982 J's husband retired and the couple settled in Spain. J's husband died in late 1996, and J stayed with her half-sister in England until she died. She lived there until her death in early 2002, although she continued to own the house in Spain which she had previously occupied with her husband. The Revenue issued a notice of determination charging IHT on her estate. Her executors appealed, contending that she had acquired a domicile of choice in Spain and had not subsequently lost that domicile despite spending the last five years of her life in England. The Special Commissioner accepted this contention and allowed her appeal, holding that 'an existing domicile is presumed to continue until it is proved that a new domicile has been acquired'. On the evidence, J 'retained the intention of returning to live in her home in Spain if and when the circumstances permitted'. *Allen & Hately (Johnson's Executors) v HMRC*, Sp C [2005] SSCD 614 (Sp C 481).

Foreign domicile of choice lost

[48.53] An individual (F) was born in England in 1896 and moved to the USA in 1928. He married a US citizen in 1935, but returned to England in 1943. In 1947 he became a director of a UK company. The Special Commissioners held that he had acquired a US domicile of choice when he married, but that he had lost that domicile by about 1947, whereupon his English domicile of origin revived. The Ch D upheld their decision as one of fact. *Fielden v CIR*, Ch D 1965, 42 TC 501.

Husband's domicile retained on widowhood

[48.54] A woman (W) was born in France, but married a German in 1906. The couple moved to England in 1939. They both died in England in 1943. W (who did not leave a will) survived her husband by a few days. W's cousin took court proceedings against the Treasury Solicitor, claiming that W had regained her French domicile of origin when her husband died. The court rejected this contention. Hodson J held that W had acquired her husband's German domicile when she married, that W's husband had subsequently acquired an English domicile of choice, and that when W became a widow, she retained her late husband's English domicile of choice. Her domicile of origin had not revived on her husband's death, and she remained domiciled in England. *In re Wallach decd., Weinschenck v Treasury Solicitor*, PDA 1949, 28 ATC 486; [1950] 1 All ER 199.

Domicile of choice retained on dissolution of marriage

[48.55] An Australian woman, born in 1905, married a Frenchman in 1934. In 1949 they moved to England and her husband acquired a domicile of choice in England. The marriage was dissolved and she remained in England. The Special Commissioners held that she was domiciled in the UK for the relevant years, and the Ch D upheld their decision. Cross J held that 'one cannot abandon a domicile of choice simply by becoming dissatisfied with it without actually leaving it'. *Faye v CIR*, Ch D 1961, 40 TC 103.

Effect of Matrimonial Proceedings Act 1973

[48.56] A woman, who was born in Canada, married an Englishman in 1948 and acquired her husband's English domicile by dependence. She lived in England with her husband, but had a house in Canada which she visited annually and where she intended to live on her husband's retirement or death. The Ch D held that, by virtue of the *Matrimonial Proceedings Act 1973*, she retained her English domicile as a deemed domicile of choice, and that her visits to Canada did not amount to an abandonment of that domicile. *CIR v Duchess of Portland*, Ch D 1981, 54 TC 648; [1982] STC 149; [1982] 2 WLR 367; [1982] 1 All ER 784.

Whether English domicile of choice acquired

[48.57] An individual (S) was born in 1889 in what is now Slovakia but was then part of the Austrian Empire. He moved to Berlin in 1906 and established a textile business there. He came to England in 1939 to escape Nazi persecution, and in 1947 he successfully applied for British nationality. He subsequently appealed against assessments charging UK tax on his German income, contending that he was domiciled in Germany. The Special Commissioners rejected this contention and dismissed his appeal, holding that he had acquired an English domicile of choice. The CA unanimously upheld their decision as one of fact. *Steiner v CIR*, CA 1973, 49 TC 13; [1973] STC 547.

[48.58] A South African, born in 1921, moved to England at the age of seven. He subsequently lived in India for several years, but returned to England in 1952 and married an Englishwoman in 1961. In 1968 he visited South Africa and purchased a property there. The Revenue issued assessments for 1961/62 to 1967/68 charging tax on the basis that he had acquired an English domicile of choice. The CA allowed his appeal, holding on the evidence that he had not acquired an English domicile of choice. *Buswell v CIR*, CA 1974, 49 TC 334; [1974] STC 266; [1974] 1 WLR 1631; [1974] 2 All ER 520.

[48.59] A Canadian (B) married an Englishwoman in 1946 and came to live in the UK. By 1966, he had given up any idea of returning to Canada during his wife's lifetime. The Special Commissioners held that he had not acquired an

English domicile of choice for the relevant years (1971/72 and 1972/73), and the CA upheld their decision. Buckley LJ observed that B had 'always maintained a firm intention to return to Canada in the event of his surviving his wife'. *CIR v Bullock*, CA 1976, 51 TC 522; [1976] STC 409; [1976] 1 WLR 1178; [1976] 3 All ER 353.

[48.60] An individual (F) was born in the USA in 1883 but came to England in 1887. After completing his education in England he took up employment in America, where he married an American. In 1923, originally on medical advice, he came with his family to England, where his wife purchased a farm which remained the matrimonial home until he died in 1963, aged 80. From 1950 onwards he said that he would remain at the farm so long as he was able to do physical work there; he remained so able until his death. His executor applied for a declaration of his domicile for estate duty purposes, and the Ch D held that he had acquired an English domicile of choice. *In re Furse decd., Furse v CIR*, Ch D [1980] STC 596; [1980] 3 All ER 838.

[48.61] An individual (B) was born in 1931 in Mauritius, which was then a UK colony. He moved to the UK in 1960. In 1968, when Mauritius became independent, he applied to retain British citizenship rather than take out Mauritian citizenship. The CA held that he had acquired a domicile of choice in England. Chadwick LJ held that B's 'decision, taken at the time when Mauritius became independent, to obtain a British passport and to take British nationality, (was) a clear pointer to the deceased's intention at that time that he would make his home in England'. *Re Bheekhun deceased*, CA 2 December 1998 unreported.

[48.62] An Iranian, born in 1930, came to the UK in 1949 for further education. He returned to Iran in 1960. In 1969 he sent his children to the UK to be educated. He continued to be based in Iran, but in 1979, following a change of regime there, he visited Germany on business and did not return to Iran. He was subsequently granted leave to remain in the UK, and in 1982 he successfully applied for naturalisation as a UK citizen, stating in his application that he was stateless and intended to live in the UK. He died in 1992, while visiting the USA, and was buried in England. The Revenue issued a notice of determination that he had acquired a domicile of choice in England. His executors appealed, contending that he had never lost his Iranian domicile of origin. The Special Commissioners accepted this contention and allowed the appeal, holding on the evidence that the deceased had 'never integrated into English life' and had 'never lost his wish to return to Iran and to resume permanent residence there' The Commissioners noted that he 'had never created a business or opened a professional office in the UK, never registered with a British doctor, and never attempted to transfer funds from Iran to England'. The fact that he had been naturalised as a British citizen did not necessarily mean that he had changed his domicile, applying *dicta* of the HL in *Wahl v Attorney-General*, HL 1932, 147 LT 382. The Commissioners found that the statements which the deceased had made in his application for naturalisation were untrue, since 'he was desperate to obtain a document which would permit him to travel freely around the world and it is apparent that he was willing to say almost anything in order to obtain that document'. *Mrs F and S2 (Personal Representatives of F deceased) v CIR*, Sp C 1999, [2000] SSCD 1 (Sp C 219).

[48.63] A US citizen (M), born in Missouri, moved to the UK in 1991 and acquired a property in London. He lived in the UK until his death in 1997, although he continued to use a US passport. He left two wills, a US will leaving his US assets to two individual beneficiaries, and an English will, disposing of his non-US assets to a wide range of beneficiaries. The Revenue issued a notice of determination that he had acquired a domicile of choice in England. The executors of his English will appealed. The Special Commissioners allowed the appeal, observing that M had remained a US citizen and taxpayer, and holding on the evidence that 'his living solely in London had been determined more by ill-health than by a desire to make England his permanent home'. *Moore's Executors v CIR*, Sp C [2002] SSCD 463 (Sp C 335).

Scotsman resident in England at time of death

[48.64] An individual (R) was born in Scotland in 1909. He lived in Scotland until 1974, when he sold his property in Scotland and moved to Cornwall. A few months after moving, he suffered a serious heart attack. He died in 1982, having lived in Cornwall for eight years and leaving his widow as his executrix. Following her subsequent death, the Revenue considered that R had acquired a domicile of choice in England. Her executor (who was R's son) appealed, contending that R had retained his domicile of origin in Scotland. The Special Commissioner accepted this contention and allowed the appeal, observing that there was 'an inherent improbability in a 65-year-old Scotsman, who has lived in Scotland all his life, abandoning his roots and intending to acquire a domicile of choice in England'. There was 'nothing inconsistent with an elderly Scottish gentleman acquiring a residence in the south of England at his retirement without having any firm intention to acquire a domicile in England'. *Anderson (Anderson's Executor) v CIR*, Sp C 1997, [1998] SSCD 43 (Sp C 147).

Whether English peer was domiciled in UK

[48.65] Baron Wrottesley was born in Dublin in 1968, and inherited an English peerage in 1977. He subsequently married a Swiss woman, and owned properties in both Switzerland and London. HMRC issued determinations charging tax for 2000/01 to 2007/08 on the basis that Baron Wrottesley was domiciled in the UK. He appealed, contending that he was not domiciled in the UK, and applied for a preliminary hearing to determine his domicile of origin. The First-tier Tribunal dismissed his application, holding that his domicile of origin did not necessarily determine the question of his domicile for 2000/01 to 2007/08, and holding that there should be a full hearing of the appeal 'to determine all the matters in dispute'. *Baron Wrottesley v HMRC*, FTT [2014] UKFTT 972 (TC), TC04084.

Whether unlawful residence can give rise to domicile of choice

[48.66] See *Mark v Mark*, 48.43 above.

Partnership residence

[48.67] A rally driver (H) was domiciled in the Isle of Man. In 1991 he formed a partnership with a Manx solicitor (D) to exploit his skills as a driver. In 1993 H became resident in the UK. HMRC issued assessments charging UK income tax on the partnership income for 1998/99 to 2004/05. The partnership appealed, contending that it was wholly managed and controlled outside the UK, so that H's share of its non-UK income was only taxable on the remittance basis. The First-Tier Tribunal accepted this contention and allowed the appeal, finding that 'the high level decisions of the partnership were made outside the UK, because those were determined by the views of (D), as the commercial brains of the partnership'. *Mark Higgins Rallying v HMRC*, FTT [2011] UKFTT 340 (TC); [2011] SFTD 936, TC01200.

Company residence

Overseas State bank—shareholders' meetings in London

[48.68] The Imperial Ottoman Bank was the State bank of Turkey and was created under Turkish law. It carried on banking business in London and its shareholders' meetings were held, and its dividends declared, there, although under its statutes the meetings could be held wherever its committee of management might fix. It was held that the bank was not resident in the UK, and was liable to UK income tax only on its profits from its business carried on in the UK. *A-G v Alexander*, Ex D 1874, LR 10 Ex 20.

Trading activities abroad—directors' meetings in London

[48.69] A company, registered in England, carried on the business of spinning and manufacturing jute, using mills in India. Its directors' and shareholders' meetings were in England. It was held to be resident in the UK and liable to UK income tax in respect of the whole of its profits. *Calcutta Jute Mills Co Ltd v Nicholson*, Ex D 1876, 1 TC 83; [1876] 1 Ex D 428. (*Note*. This is an important early case establishing that a company has a residence for tax purposes and that the centre of control determines that residence.)

[48.70] A similar decision was reached in a case which the Court heard with *Calcutta Jute Mills Co Ltd v Nicholson*, 48.69 above. *Cesena Sulphur Co Ltd v Nicholson*, Ex D 1876, 1 TC 88; [1876] 1 Ex D 428.

[48.71] The decision in *Cesena Sulphur Co Ltd v Nicholson*, 48.70 above, was followed in a subsequent case where the facts were similar. *Imperial Continental Gas Association v Nicholson*, Ex D 1877, 1 TC 138.

Overseas company held to be effectively managed from UK

[48.72] A company registered in South Africa worked diamond mines there. Its head office and shareholders' general meetings were held in South Africa. Directors' meetings took place in both South Africa and the UK, although the majority of the directors lived in the UK. The company appealed against assessments charging UK income tax, contending that it was not resident in the UK. The Commissioners rejected this contention and upheld the assessments, and the HL unanimously dismissed the company's appeal, holding that the company was resident in the UK for tax purposes and that all its profits were chargeable to UK income tax. Lord Loreburn observed that a company was resident 'where the central management and control actually abides'. *De Beers Consolidated Mines Ltd v Howe*, HL 1906, 5 TC 198; [1906] AC 455.

[48.73] A New Zealand shipping company had a New Zealand board of directors and a separate London board. The New Zealand board managed the business and negotiated most freight contracts independently. However, some contracts of major importance were entered into in London, where all important questions of policy were decided. The Commissioners held that the company was resident in the UK, and the CA unanimously upheld their decision as one of fact. *New Zealand Shipping Co Ltd v Stephens*, CA 1907, 5 TC 553.

[48.74] The HL reached a similar decision in a subsequent appeal by the same company. *New Zealand Shipping Co Ltd v Thew*, HL 1922, 8 TC 208.

[48.75] A company (L) was incorporated in Netherlands. From 1992 to August 1996 its controlling director was a German national (B), who was resident in the UK, where he owned a house. HMRC issued assessments on L, covering the periods from 1993 to 1996, on the basis that its effective place of management was in the UK. L appealed to the First-Tier Tribunal, which reviewed the evidence in detail and dismissed the appeal, finding that B 'carried out activities of the appellant of a strategic and policy nature and managed the business of the appellant, and that he did so to a substantial extent in the UK'. On the evidence, the 'central control and management of the appellant was exercised in the UK'. The tribunal also found that, from August 1996 to December 1996, the company's remaining director (T) was acting on B's instructions 'without considering the merits of them'. There was 'no change in the way the appellant was managed' after B had ceased to be a director. L was 'resident in the UK during the time after (B) ceased to be a director on 30 August 1996 until at least 31 December 1996', since B's activities 'constituted the real top level management (or the realistic positive management) of the appellant and (T's) activities were limited to signing documents when told to do so and dealing with routine matters such as the accounts. As such the place of effective management was in the UK.' *Laerstate BV v HMRC*, FTT [2009] SFTD 551; [2009] UKFTT 209 (TC), TC00162. (*Note*. The company initially appealed to the Upper Tribunal, which struck out the apepal on 1 March 2011 on the grounds that the company had failed to comply with directions.)

UK company with overseas board

[48.76] A UK company incorporated an American subsidiary which manufactured cotton thread in the USA. Three of its seven directors were required to live in the USA and formed an executive committee to direct its current business. Regular meetings of the directors were held in the USA, but extraordinary meetings were held in London to deal with important matters. The Commissioners held that the company was resident in the UK and was liable to UK income tax, and the HL unanimously upheld their decision as one of fact. *American Thread Co v Joyce*, HL 1913, 6 TC 163.

[48.77] A company registered in the UK owned and ran two hotels in Egypt. In the relevant period, its affairs in Egypt, including the running of the hotels, were under the control of an Egyptian board of directors independent of the London board. The London board controlled the share capital and fixed the remuneration of directors including the Egyptian directors. The annual accounts as approved by the London board were adopted by an AGM in London. The Revenue issued assessments charging tax on the company's trading profits. The CA allowed the company's appeal, holding that the matters within the control of the London board did not extend to the control of the company's trade. Hence, although the company was resident in the UK, its trade was only assessable under Schedule D Case V under the legislation then in force. The Revenue appealed to the HL where, unusually, the case was heard by four judges rather than the usual five. The HL was equally divided and upheld the CA decision. *Egyptian Hotels Ltd v Mitchell*, HL 1915, 6 TC 542; [1915] AC 1022.

[48.78] A UK company carried on a business of mining in Bolivia. Its Bolivian activities were under the control and management of a local board, the duties of the London directors being confined to the declaration of dividends and the normal business necessary for its continuance as a company. However, all the products of its mines were sold in the UK through agents. The KB held that it was resident in the UK and liable to UK income tax on its profits, and the HL unanimously upheld this decision. *Eccott v Aramayo Francke Mines Ltd (and related appeals)*, HL 1925, 9 TC 445; [1925] AC 634. (*Note*. The appeal also concerned two actions relating to an assessment of the same profits made on the Bolivian local board as agents of the company. The HL held that this assessment was invalid.)

Company incorporated in UK—activities in UK formal only

[48.79] A company registered in the UK and carrying on business in Egypt altered its Articles of Association in order to remove its control and management to Cairo where all the meetings of directors and of the company were held and all books and records were kept. A London secretary was appointed to comply with the requirements of the *Companies Acts*. The Commissioners held that the company was not resident in the UK, and the HL unanimously upheld their decision. Viscount Sumner held that incorporation under the *Companies Acts*, and the arrangements necessary to comply with them, did not alone render a company resident in the UK. *Todd v Egyptian Delta Land & Investment Co Ltd*, HL 1928, 14 TC 119; [1929] AC 1.

Company registered in Northern Ireland and USA

[48.80] A company which sold linen goods was registered in both Northern Ireland and the USA. Most of its sales were in the USA, where its only director resided, but it purchased its raw materials in Scotland and Ireland, bleached them in Northern Ireland, and kept the finished goods in a warehouse in Belfast. The Special Commissioners held that the company was resident in Northern Ireland, and liable to UK income tax on the whole of its profits. The KB upheld this decision. *John Hood & Co Ltd v Magee*, KB(I) 1918, 7 TC 327.

Company with dual residence

[48.81] A UK company constructed a railway in Sweden which it subsequently leased to a Swedish concern. Its Articles of Association were altered and as a consequence its management and control were transferred to Sweden where most of its shareholders resided and where all its directors' and shareholders' meetings were held. It retained its registered office in London where its secretary resided and certain administrative matters were handled. The Commissioners held that, although the company was resident in Sweden, it was also resident in the UK and hence liable to tax on the rent it received under the lease. The HL upheld their decision (by a 4-1 majority, Lord Atkinson dissenting). Viscount Cave observed that a company's central management and control 'may be divided, and it may "keep house and do business" in more than one place; and if so, it may have more than one residence'. *Swedish Central Railway Co Ltd v Thompson*, HL 1925, 9 TC 342; [1925] AC 495.

[48.82] Two companies appealed against profits tax assessments, contending that they were 'ordinarily resident outside the United Kingdom' within the meaning of the relevant legislation, on the grounds that they were ordinarily resident in South Africa as well as in the UK. The CA dismissed the appeals, accepting that the companies were ordinarily resident in both countries, but holding that they did not qualify as 'ordinarily resident outside the United Kingdom' for the purposes of the relevant legislation, since the words in question should be construed as 'not ordinarily resident in the United Kingdom'. The HL unanimously upheld this decision. *Union Corporation Ltd v CIR (and related appeals)*, HL 1953, 34 TC 207; [1953] 3 WLR 615; [1953] 1 All ER 729.

Overseas subsidiaries of UK parent—whether resident in UK

[48.83] A UK company had three subsidiaries registered and carrying on business in East Africa, the Articles of Association of which provided for their management and control to be in the hands of their directors, who could not meet in the UK. The companies did not prosper and in 1950 the parent company decided to take over their management and control. There was no formal agreement with the subsidiaries, but thereafter the parent company made all important decisions and the East African directors did not meet as boards. The parent company claimed that the subsidiaries were resident in the UK for the relevant years (so that it was entitled to deduct certain 'subvention payments' in computing its profits). The Special Commissioners accepted this contention and the HL unanimously upheld their decision. *Bullock v The Unit Construction Co Ltd*, HL 1959, 38 TC 712; [1960] AC 351; [1959] 3 All ER 831.

[48.84] A UK company had several subsidiaries, including one which was incorporated in Jersey and carried on business in Bermuda and one which was both incorporated and managed in the Channel Islands. The Revenue issued assessments for accounting periods up to 31 March 1987 on the basis that these two subsidiaries were resident in the UK. The companies appealed, contending that their central management and control had been overseas so that they were resident overseas. (It was accepted that the Bermuda company had become resident in the UK after March 1987, when three UK directors were appointed and it was resolved to hold future board meetings in the UK.) The Special Commissioners accepted the companies' contentions and allowed the appeals. Applying *dicta* in *Cesena Sulphur Co Ltd v Nicholson*, **48.70** above, the burden of proof with regard to company residence was on the Revenue. The residence of a company was the place where the directors met, transacted their business and exercised the powers conferred upon them. On the evidence, the directors of the subsidiary companies were 'exercising central management and control' outside the UK, in Bermuda and Sark respectively. *Untelrab Ltd v McGregor (and related appeals)*, Sp C 1995, [1996] SSCD 1 (Sp C 55). (*Note*. The decision was approved by the Ch D in *Wood & Wood v Holden*, **48.85** below.)

Netherlands subsidiary of British Virgin Islands company

[48.85] A married couple entered into a sophisticated scheme, devised by an accountancy firm, with the aim of avoiding CGT on a share disposal by taking advantage of *TCGA, s 171*. As part of the scheme, the shares were transferred to a company (C) which was registered in the British Virgin Islands, and then transferred again to a subsidiary company (E) which was incorporated in the Netherlands. The Revenue issued assessments on the basis that *TCGA, s 171* did not apply because the 'central management and control' of E was exercised in the UK, by or on behalf of the husband. The couple appealed, contending that E was resident in the Netherlands. The Ch D accepted this contention and allowed their appeal, holding that the only tenable conclusion on the evidence was that E was resident in the Netherlands, since its 'central management and control' was in Amsterdam, where its board meetings were held. The CA unanimously upheld this decision. Chadwick LJ held that 'the only conclusion open to the Special Commissioners, on the facts which they had found, was that (E) was resident in the Netherlands'. He distinguished *Bullock v The Unit Construction Co Ltd*, **48.83** above, on the grounds that E's directors 'were not by-passed nor did they stand aside since their representatives signed or executed the documents'. *Holden v Wood & Wood (aka Mr & Mrs R v Holden)*, CA 2006, 78 TC 1; [2006] STC 443; [2006] EWCA Civ 26; [2006] 1 WLR 1393.

Proof of company residence under double tax agreement

[48.86] A company claimed relief from tax under the UK/Barbados Double Tax Agreement. The Revenue rejected the claim, considering that the company was not resident in Barbados. The company appealed to the Special Commissioners, and tendered as evidence statements by its secretary that it was managed and controlled in Barbados, and by the Barbados Deputy Commissioner of Inland Revenue that it was resident there. The Special Commissioners dismissed the appeal, finding that 'such evidence as there is in favour of the company's Barbados residence is weakened not only by the company's refusal to provide the further information for which the Inland Revenue had (in our view quite reasonably) asked but also by its decision to rely solely on evidence which we have held to be inadmissible without calling those with personal knowledge of the facts, who could have testified thereto and been cross-examined . . . the company has failed to discharge the onus of satisfying us that it was resident in Barbados at the relevant time.' The Ch D upheld this decision as one of fact. *Forth Investments Ltd v CIR*, Ch D 1976, 50 TC 617; [1976] STC 399. (*Note.* For another issue in this case, see **4.43** APPEALS.)

Company registered in Guernsey

[48.87] The income of a company registered in Guernsey was treated as the income of a UK taxpayer by virtue of *ITA 2007, s 721**. The Special Commissioners upheld the assessments, holding on the evidence that the company was both resident and domiciled in Guernsey (notwithstanding that it may also have been resident in the UK). The KB upheld their decision. Macnaghten J held that 'a company has a domicile—an English domicile if registered in England and a Scottish domicile if registered in Scotland'. *Gasque v CIR*, KB 1940, 23 TC 210; [1940] 2 KB 80. (*Note.* The substantive issue has been overtaken by legislation now in *ITA 2007, s 718(2)*.)

TCGA, s 179—whether vendor company resident in UK*

[48.88] See *News Datacom Ltd v Atkinson*, **71.283** CAPITAL GAINS TAX.

Residence of trusts

[48.89] A settlement was created in December 1981. There were two trustees, of whom one was resident in the Republic of Ireland and the other was resident in the UK. The settlor had held a majority shareholding in a UK trading company, which he wished to sell. Following a reconstruction of the company's share capital, he renounced a letter of allotment and transferred the shares covered by the letter to the trustees. They sold the shares in January 1982. The Revenue issued a CGT assessment on the sale. The trustees appealed against the assessment, and claimed relief under *Article 4* of the UK/Ireland Double Taxation Agreement (see *SI 1976/2151*), contending that the place of effective management of the settlement was in the Republic of Ireland, so that under the Agreement they were only liable to Irish tax, rather than to UK CGT. The Revenue rejected the claim on the grounds that the place of effective management of the settlement was not in the Republic of Ireland, and that by virtue of *TCGA, s 69(1)**, the trustees were to be treated as resident in the UK. The Special Commissioner upheld the Revenue's contention and dismissed the trustees' appeals, holding on the evidence that the settlement was effectively managed from the UK, that the Irish trustee 'was a trustee in name rather than in reality' and that the fact that the trustees had operated a bank account in the

Republic of Ireland was not conclusive. *Wensleydale's Settlement Trustees v CIR*, Sp C [1996] SSCD 241 (Sp C 73). (*Note*. See also *TCGA, s 169*, deriving from *FA 1986*.)

[48.90] In 1989 an individual (S) had established a trust, over which he had the power to appoint new trustees. The trust assets included shares which had increased in value. From 1994 to December 2000 a Jersey company acted as the trustee. In December 2000 S appointed a Mauritius company as the new trustee. In January 2001 the trustees sold the shares, realising a substantial gain. In March 2001 S appointed himself and his wife (both resident in the UK) as trustees. The Revenue began enquiries, and issued closure notices to S and the trust, amending the relevant returns on the basis that S had made a chargeable gain of more than £6,800,000, and was liable to pay CGT of more than £2,700,000 under *TCGA, s 77(1)*. S and the trustees appealed, contending that at the time the shares were sold, the trust had been resident in Mauritius and the effect of the UK/Mauritius Double Taxation Agreement was that the gains were not taxable in the UK. The Special Commissioners rejected this contention and dismissed the appeals, finding that the trust had not been solely resident in Mauritius during the tax year in question and that its 'place of effective management' had been in the UK, so that the effect of Article 4 of the UK/Mauritius Double Taxation Agreement was that the gain was taxable in the UK. The CA upheld this decision (by a 2-1 majority, Patten LJ dissenting). Hughes LJ held that the Commissioners had been entitled to find that the place of effective management of the trust was in the UK. He observed that 'it was integral to the scheme that the trust should be exported to Mauritius for a brief temporary period only and then be returned, within the fiscal year, to the United Kingdom, which occurred. (S) remained throughout in the UK. There was a scheme of management of this trust which went above and beyond the day to day management exercised by the trustees for the time being, and the control of it was located in the United Kingdom.' *HMRC v T Smallwood (Settlor of the Trevor Smallwood Trust) (and related appeal)*, CA 2010, 80 TC 536; [2010] EWCA Civ 778; [2010] STC 2045; 12 ITLR 1002. (*Notes*. (1) (*Note*. The Supreme Court rejected the solicitor's application for leave to appeal against this decision. (2) See also *ICTA 1988, s 815AZA*, introduced by *FA 2008, s 59*.)

49

Returns and Information

The cases in this chapter are arranged under the following headings.

CROSS-REFERENCES

See 44 PENALTIES for penalties for failure to make returns, etc.

Returns of income and gains (TMA, ss 7–12B)

Exemption claimed—whether liable to make return

[49.1] An engineer was served with a notice requiring him to make a return of his profits for excess profits duty. He refused to make the return and brought an action seeking a declaration that he was exempt from excess profits duty and under no obligation to make the return. The Ch D dismissed the action, holding that the question of whether the engineer's business was exempt should be decided by the normal appeal procedure. *Smeeton v A-G*, Ch D 1919, 12 TC 166; [1920] 1 Ch 85.

Return endorsed 'details to follow'—whether a completed return

[49.2] An employee submitted two tax returns endorsed 'details to follow'. The General Commissioners imposed penalties against him for failure to make returns. He appealed, contending that by submitting the returns thus endorsed he had complied with *TMA, s 8*. The Ch D rejected this contention and dismissed his appeals. Knox J held that a return has to specify 'each separate source of income and the amount from each source'. *Cox v Poole Commrs & CIR*, Ch D 1987, 60 TC 445; [1988] STC 66.

[49.3] The appellant in the case noted at **49.2** above submitted a subsequent tax return endorsed 'as returned by employer'. The Commissioners held that this did not comply with *TMA, s 8*, and imposed a penalty of £500. The Ch D upheld their decision. *Cox v Poole Commrs & CIR (No 2)*, Ch D 1989, 63 TC 277; [1990] STC 122.

[49.4] The decision in *Cox v Poole Commrs & CIR (No 2)*, **49.3** above, was applied in a subsequent case where the First-Tier Tribunal dismissed an appeal against a penalty imposed on an individual who had failed to provide details of a capital gain. *GG Twinn v HMRC*, FTT [2012] UKFTT 67 (TC), TC01763.

TMA, s 9ZA(2)—time limit for amendment of return

[49.5] An individual (R) had submitted a return for the year ending 5 April 2001 in which he declared a substantial capital gain and claimed loss relief to be carried back from the following year. In December 2002 his accountants advised him that it would be more advantageous if he carried the loss forward, and that he should submit an amendment to his 2000/01 return. The Revenue subsequently rejected the amendment on the basis that it had been made more than twelve months after the 'filing date' of 31 January 2002. R appealed, contending that his accountant had delivered the amendment by hand to an HMRC office in Woking on the evening of 31 January 2003. The Special Commissioner accepted the accountant's evidence and allowed R's appeal. *M Ransom v HMRC*, Sp C [2008] SSCD 1192 (Sp C 708).

[49.6] A woman (W) began trading in February 2007. In February 2008 her accountant submitted a return form purporting to show a profit for the accounting period from 21 February 2007 to 31 March 2008 (although that period had not yet ended) and declaring a small profit for 2006/07. W subsequently appointed a new accountant. In January 2011 her new accountant submitted a 2006/07 return claiming a small loss for a revised accounting period of 21 February 2007 to 31 March 2007, and submitted a 2007/08 return claiming a loss for the accounting period from 1 April 2007 to 31 March 2008. HMRC began an enquiry into the 2007/08 return, and subsequently issued a closure notice determining that W had made a profit of £93,600 for 2007/08. The First-tier Tribunal allowed W's appeal. Judge Staker held that the return submitted in January 2011 should be treated as an amendment to the return submitted in February 2008, holding that the time limit laid down by *TMA, s 9ZA(2)* did not apply, on the basis that *s 9ZA* only applied where HMRC had issued a notice under *TMA, s 8* requiring a return, and did not apply where a taxpayer had submitted an unsolicited return, as was the case here. He held that the 'unsolicited return' which W's first accountant had submitted in 2007 should be treated as a notice of chargeability under *TMA, s 7*, rather than as a return under *s 8*. He also held that 'the basis of calculation of the figures in the appellant's 2007/08 tax return is more reliable than the basis of calculation of the figures in the HMRC closure notice'. *Mrs F Weerasinghe v HMRC*, FTT [2013] UKFTT 144 (TC), TC02542.

TMA, s 9A—notice of enquiry into return—whether valid

[49.7] In December 1997 a restaurant proprietor (L) signed a self-assessment for the year ending 5 April 1997. The Revenue posted a notice of inquiry, under *TMA, s 9A*, dated 27 January 1999, also sending a copy to L's accountant. L appealed, contending that the notice was invalid, because he had not received it until Tuesday 2 February 1999, and his accountant had not received his copy until Monday 1 February 1999, whereas the time limit laid down by *TMA, s 9A* expired at midnight on 30 January. The Special Commissioner accepted this contention and allowed the appeal. The Commissioner accepted that the notice had been posted on 27 January. However, it had been posted by second-class post. By virtue of *Interpretation Act 1978, s 7*, the service of the notice was deemed 'to have been effected at the time at which the letter would be delivered in the ordinary course of post'. A practice direction issued by the Queen's Bench Division on 8 March 1985 had ruled that, in the case of second-class mail, this was taken to be the fourth working day after posting (working days being Monday to Friday inclusive). The Royal Mail Code of Practice promised delivery of 98% of letters within three working days after posting. Accordingly, the service of the notice could not be deemed to have been effected until 1 February at the earliest, and the notice was, therefore, invalid. *Wing Hung Lai v Bale*, Sp C [1999] SSCD 238 (Sp C 203). (*Note.* The Revenue set out their practice following this decision in an annex to the Revenue Tax Bulletin, Special Edition, April 2000 (never published in hard copy but previously available on the old Revenue website). The Revenue stated that they 'now accept that, for returns filed on time, an enquiry is valid only if the notice is delivered no later than 30 January'. They also stated that 'where we are satisfied that the notice was received late we will accept that an "enquiry" was never opened. However, where we have substantial doubts about the evidence, the matter will need to be decided by the Commissioners or the Courts.')

[49.8] In October 1997 a married couple submitted their self-assessment returns for the year ending 5 April 1997. The Revenue posted notices of enquiry, under *TMA, s 9A*, on 25 January 1999 by second-class post. The Revenue subsequently issued notices under *TMA, s 19A*. The couple appealed, contending that the notices under *s 9A* were invalid because they had not received them until 3 February, after the expiry of the statutory time limit. The Special Commissioner accepted their evidence and allowed their appeals, holding that 'where a time limit is stated in the legislation, then the effect of the second part of (*Interpretation Act 1978, s 7*) is that service is effected at the time the document would be received or, if proved, the time of actual receipt'. *Holly & Laurel v HM Inspector of Taxes*, Sp C [2000] SSCD 50 (Sp C 225). (*Note.* See the note following *Wing Hung Lai v Bale*, **49.7** above.)

[49.9] The Revenue sent a notice under *TMA, s 9A* to a musician (D), opening an enquiry into his 2002/03 tax return. Subsequently the Revenue issued assessments for 1999/2000 to 2003/04 inclusive on the basis that D's returns had underdeclared his income. D appealed, contending that the original notice of enquiry had been invalid, and that the assessments were also invalid. The Special Commissioner rejected this contention and dismissed the appeals, finding that D had been guilty of 'negligent conduct'. *T Duffy v HMRC*, Sp C [2007] SSCD 377 (Sp C 596).

[49.10] See also *Rigby v Jayatilaka*, **4.372** appeals; *Siwek v CIR (No 1)*, **49.19** below, and *Bensoor v Devine*, **55.16** SELF-ASSESSMENT.

TMA, s 12AA—partnership return sent as PDF—whether valid

[49.11] See *Fitzpatrick & Co (Solicitors) v HMRC*, 44.37 PENALTIES.

TMA, s 12AC—notice of enquiry into partnership return

[49.12] The Revenue issued two letters, which they treated as notices under *TMA, s 12AC*, to a company which was a member of a trading partnership. In March 2007 they issued notices under *TMA, s 19A* for the years 2003/04 and 2004/05. The company did not comply with the notices, and the Revenue imposed penalties under *TMA, s 97AA*. The company appealed, contending that the original letters had not been valid notices under *s 12AC*. The Special Commissioner rejected this contention and dismissed the appeal, observing that *s 12AC* did not require 'particular formality about the giving of notice'. The notice was intended 'to warn the taxpayer that an enquiry is under way so that he knows questions may be asked and that time limits may be affected, and to provide a mechanical activation of the enquiry procedure. This does not require something formal: all that is needed is something in writing which informs the taxpayer that an enquiry is under way.' The Commissioner held that 'a letter which announces that "I intend enquiring into" a tax return is sufficient to be a notice for the purposes of *section 12AC*'. *Flaxmode Ltd v HMRC (No 1)*, Sp C [2008] SSCD 666 (Sp C 670). (*Note*. For a subsequent appeal by the same company, see 44.351 PENALTIES.)

[49.13] HMRC decided to enquire into the self-assessment return of a partnership. They served a notice under *TMA, s 12AC*. The partnership appealed, contending that the notice was invalid because it had not been received until 4 November 2009, which was one day later than the prescribed time limit. HMRC gave evidence that the notice had been delivered by hand on the morning of 3 November 2009, which was the last day of the relevant period. The First-Tier Tribunal accepted HMRC's evidence and dismissed the partnership's appeal, observing that 'the reason why the enquiry notice was hand delivered by a special car journey rather than posted was that HMRC realised that 3 November 2009 was the last date on which the notice could be given, and that mail strikes at the time made the mail unreliable'. *The Sandrock Hotel v HMRC*, FTT [2010] UKFTT 484 (TC), TC00744.

Other returns (TMA, ss 13–19)

Returns under TMA, s 13—underwriting agents

[49.14] A firm of underwriting agents was served with a notice under *TMA, s 13** requiring a list of the underwriters for which it acted and of the profits accruing to each. The firm failed to comply with the notice. The CS unanimously held that the firm was obliged to submit the required information, and imposed a penalty for the failure to comply. *Lord Advocate v Gibb*, CS 1906, 5 TC 194.

Returns under TMA, s 13—bank as nominee, etc

[49.15] A bank was served with a notice under *TMA, s 13** requiring details of War Loan, etc. interest which it received as trustee or as nominee or where it held the stock as security. The bank refused to comply with the notice. The KB held that the bank was obliged to submit the information in question. *A-G v National Provincial Bank Ltd*, KB 1928, 14 TC 111.

Returns under TMA, s 13—company trading as auctioneers

[49.16] A company traded as auctioneers of livestock. The Revenue issued notices under *TMA, s 13*, calling for a return for certain years of all persons on whose behalf it had received any money, value, profit or gains chargeable to income tax. The company did not comply with the notices, and the inspector laid an information before the Special Commissioner, claiming that the company was liable to penalties under *TMA, s 98*. The Commissioner dismissed the information, considering that *TMA, s 13* imposed a reporting obligation only where an agent received the balance of profits of another person, and that no such obligation could be imposed on an agent who received the gross receipts of another person. The CA allowed the Revenue's appeal against this decision and made a declaration that the company had been liable to comply with the notices. Millett LJ observed that there was no good reason why Parliament should have intended *s 13* to have such a limited effect as the Commissioner had ascribed to it. *TMA, s 13* derived from *ITA 1842*, in which the expression 'profits or gains' was commonly used to describe pure income receipts. *Fawcett v Special Commissioners and Lancaster Farmers' Auction Mart Co Ltd*, CA 1996, 69 TC 279; [1997] STC 171.

Production of accounts, etc. (TMA, ss 19A–21)

Power to call for documents (TMA, ss 19A, 20)

Notices by officers (TMA, s 19A)

Notice under TMA, s 19A—whether valid

[49.17] An inspector issued a notice under *TMA, s 19A*, requiring the production of certain information within 30 days from the date of issue of the notice. The recipient appealed, contending that the notice was invalid as, under *TMA, s 19A(2)*, the notice should have allowed a period of 30 days from the date of receipt. The Special Commissioner accepted this contention and allowed the appeal. *Self-Assessed v HM Inspector of Taxes*, Sp C [1999] SSCD 253 (Sp C 207). (*Note*. For the Revenue's practice following this decision, see Revenue Tax Bulletin, Special Edition, April 2000, p 8. The Revenue stated that future notices 'will give the taxpayer a minimum of 30 days from receipt of the notice to produce the documents or particulars' and that they 'have decided to discharge' any penalties raised under *TMA, s 97AA* after 14 December 1998 following failure to comply with an invalid notice.)

[49.18] An inspector issued a notice under *TMA, s 19A* to an individual (M), requesting, *inter alia*, all books and records, including paying-in books and chequebook stubs, relating to a property management business, together with dividend counterfoils. M appealed, contending that it was unreasonable to require the production of all her books and records, as she acted as a managing agent for a number of companies, and that there was no authority to require production of paying-in books and chequebook stubs. The Special Commissioner rejected these contentions and dismissed M's appeal, holding that 'with regard to records of the taxpayer's business which may reveal information concerning other taxpayers, such documents must nevertheless be supplied, providing as little information concerning other taxpayers as is compatible with the requirement to produce documents relating to the taxpayer's business'. Furthermore, 'in relation to missing dividend counterfoils, the taxpayer must attempt to obtain replacement copies from the companies concerned at her own expense. If the companies concerned cannot comply, and she can show evidence of this to the inspector, no further action on her part will be required as the missing documents will no longer be in her possession or power.' *Mother v HM Inspector of Taxes*, Sp C [1999] SSCD 279 (Sp C 211).

[49.19] In June 2001 the Revenue issued a notice of enquiry under *TMA, s 9A* to an individual (S) who had submitted a return for 1999/2000 claiming a repayment. S subsequently failed to provide information which the Revenue had requested, and in October 2001 the Revenue issued a notice under *TMA, s 19A* requiring him to produce certain documents and information. S appealed, contending that the notices should be held to be invalid. The Special Commissioner rejected this contention and dismissed the appeal, holding that both notices were valid. *Siwek v CIR*, Sp C [2002] SSCD 247 (Sp C 314). (*Note*. For subsequent developments in this case, see **55.2** SELF-ASSESSMENT and **73.3** NATIONAL INSURANCE CONTRIBUTIONS.)

[49.20] An individual (S) submitted a 2004/05 tax return declaring employment income of £4,650, and no other income. The Revenue issued a notice under *TMA, s 19A* requiring him to produce bank statements, credit and debit card statements, documents relating to property sales and a statement of his income and outgoings. S appealed, contending that this information was not 'reasonably required'. The Special Commissioner rejected this contention and dismissed the appeal, and the Ch D upheld this decision. Floyd J observed that the Revenue were entitled to make enquiries into the accuracy of 'nil' entries on a tax return. *Sokoya v HMRC (No 1)*, Ch D [2008] STC 3332; [2008] EWHC 2132 (Ch). (*Notes*. (1) The appellant appeared in person. (2) The CA rejected an application for leave to appeal against this decision—CA, 28 January 2009 unreported. (3) For subsequent developments in this case, see **44.350** PENALTIES.)

[49.21] Notices under *TMA, s 19A* were also upheld in *Murphy v Gowers*, Sp C 2004, [2005] SSCD 44 (Sp C 434); *Baltrusaitis v Byrne*, Sp C 2004, [2005] SSCD 188 (Sp C 445); *Guest House Proprietor v Kendall*, Sp C [2005] SSCD 280 (Sp C 454); *Low v HMRC (No 1)*, Sp C 2005, [2006] SSCD 21 (Sp C 510); *Low v HMRC (No 2)*, Sp C [2006] SSCD 67 (Sp C 516); *Commane v HMRC*, Sp C [2006] SSCD 81 (Sp C 518); *Afsar v HMRC (No 1)*, Sp C [2006] SSCD 625 (Sp C 554); *Mr A v HMRC (No 1)*, Sp C 2007, [2008] SSCD 380 (Sp C 650); *A Humphreys v HMRC*, FTT [2010] UKFTT 204 (TC), TC00506;

PC Opara v HMRC, FTT [2010] UKFTT 480 (TC), TC00741; *Sharkey v De Croos*, **44.347** PENALTIES, and *HMRC v Deadman*, **44.360** PENALTIES.

[49.22] The Revenue issued notices under *TMA, s 19A* to a partnership which operated a restaurant, and to the individual partners. The Special Commissioner upheld the notices in principle but set aside specific parts of the notices which called for details of 'who maintains the business records' and 'should any of the expenditure be unvouched, please say what evidence is available to support the expenditure claimed'. The Commissioner held that these specific requirements were not 'reasonably required', within *TMA, s 19A(2)*. *Z Uyar v HMRC (and related appeals)*, Sp C [2008] SSCD 609 (Sp C 667).

[49.23] HMRC issued notices under *TMA, s 19A* to a married couple who operated a property lettings business. The notices required the production of bank statements and statements of money market transactions. The First-tier Tribunal upheld the requirement to produce bank statements. Judge Kempster observed that the couple's business was 'run through a bank account that also includes items of personal expenditure', and held that 'details of the transactions in that bank account are reasonably required by HMRC, as they relate at least in part to transactions of the letting business'. However he allowed the appeal against the requirement to produce money market statements, finding that 'it would be unduly onerous to require the appellants to provide those other documents'. *I & Mrs P Phillips v HMRC*, FTT [2013] UKFTT 354 (TC), TC02756.

TMA, s 19A—Revenue requiring accountant to produce documents

[49.24] The Revenue began an enquiry into an accountant's return for 1996/97. The inspector issued a notice under *TMA, s 19A* requiring the accountant to produce statements, paying-in books and chequebooks for all his bank and building society accounts, together with a balance sheet. The accountant appealed, contending that it was unreasonable to require him to produce documents relating to the accounts which he used as client accounts, and that it was unreasonable to require him to produce a balance sheet. The Special Commissioner rejected these contentions and dismissed the appeal, holding that it was reasonable for the Revenue to require the accountant 'to produce documents relating to his personal and undesignated clients' bank and building society accounts'. The accountant was 'being required to produce documents in his capacity as taxpayer'. Although *TMA, s 19A(2)(a)* was 'limited to existing documents', *s 19A(2)(b)* did not contain the words 'in the taxpayer's possession or power', so that the effect of that subsection was that a taxpayer could 'be requested to prepare accounts such as income and expenditure accounts or balance sheets and also to furnish particulars which may not necessarily be contained in existing documents'. The Commissioner observed that 'if an inspector is to enquire into a return it would seem reasonable for his enquiries not to be limited to existing documents'. Furthermore, it was reasonable for the Revenue to require the preparation of a balance sheet, since 'a balance sheet would assist the Inspector in determining whether the return is incomplete or incorrect because it will indicate movements in capital assets'. *Murat v HM Inspector of Taxes (aka Accountant v HM Inspector of Taxes)*, Sp C [2000] SSCD 522 (Sp C 258). (*Note*. The decision here was approved by the QB in a subsequent case involving the same accountant—see *Murat v CIR*, **44.346** PENALTIES.)

[49.25] The decision in *Accountant v HM Inspector of Taxes*, **49.24** above, was applied and approved in the subsequent case of *Parto v Bratherton*, Sp C [2004] SSCD 339 (Sp C 414).

[49.26] The Revenue issued a notice under *TMA, s 19A* to an accountant, requiring him to produce certain documents and information. The accountant appealed, contending firstly that the notice had been issued unreasonably and vindictively, and alternatively that the notice could not require him to produce documents which did not previously exist. The Special Commissioner reviewed the evidence in detail, rejected these contentions and dismissed the appeal. The Commissioner held that the Revenue were entitled to have formed the opinion that the accountant's claimed expenses were unusually high in relation to his declared turnover. Furthermore, applying the decision in *Accountant v HM Inspector of Taxes*, **49.24** above, *TMA, s 19A(2)(b)* 'may be used to impose an obligation to create certain documents'. *PC Clarke v HMRC (No 1)*, Sp C [2009] SSCD 278 (Sp C 735). (*Note*. For a subsequent appeal by the same accountant, see **44.372** PENALTIES.)

TMA, s 19A—Revenue requiring solicitor to produce documents

[49.27] The Revenue issued a notice under *TMA, s 19A* to a solicitor, requiring him to produce his clients ledger, his clients cash book, and supporting records. The solicitor appealed, contending that the documents were confidential and privileged and that it was unreasonable for the Revenue to require them. The Special Commissioner rejected this contention and dismissed the appeal, holding that the information requested was 'reasonably required', that the provisions of *TMA, s 19A* 'override the contractual duty of confidence owed by a solicitor to his clients', and that 'the rule of legal professional privilege is excluded because it is not expressly preserved by *s 19A*'. Furthermore, the disclosure of the documents would not contravene either the *Human Rights Act 1998* or the *Data Protection Act 1998*. *Guyer v Walton*, Sp C [2001] SSCD 75 (Sp C 274).

Notice under TMA, s 19A requiring details of private expenditure

[49.28] The Revenue issued a notice under *TMA, s 19A* to a taxi driver. He appealed, contending that the notice was unreasonable. The Special Commissioner allowed the appeal in part, holding that the notices were valid in 'so far as the documents and information specified in the notices relate to the taxpayer's income and allowable deductions'. However. the Commissioner also held that the inspector's request was 'intrusive' and that 'the taxpayer should not be required to divulge details of his personal expenditure if that could be avoided'. The Commissioner directed that the inspector could 'restore the appeal for further argument in order that a decision may be made whether the taxpayer is required to comply with any additional part of the notices'. *Taylor v Bratherton*, Sp C 2004, [2005] SSCD 230 (Sp C 448).

Notice under TMA, s 19A requiring details of 'Gift Aid' payments

[49.29] An individual (E) submitted a 2003/04 return claiming relief for Gift Aid payments, most of which was to be related back to 2002/03. The Revenue began an enquiry into the return and asked for evidence of the payments. E admitted that the figures in his return had been incorrect and submitted revised figures, but refused to provide evidence of the amounts to be related back. The Revenue issued a notice under *TMA, s 19A*, and E appealed, contending that the Revenue were not entitled to ask for details of the amounts to be related back. The Special Commissioner rejected this contention and dismissed the appeal, observing that 'the total gift aid payments made in the year were contained in the return and so the enquiry extends to them'. *AJ Eder v HMRC*, Sp C [2007] SSCD 334 (Sp C 592).

Notices by inspectors (TMA, s 20)

Whether notice may cover period for which no return issued

[49.30] The Special Commissioners imposed penalties on six associated companies for non-compliance with notices under *TMA, s 20* (as originally enacted). The companies appealed, contending firstly that the normal six-year time limit applied and that the notices were invalid since they related to years outside that limit, and alternatively that four of the nine notices were invalid since they called for information for a period which included years for which no returns had been issued. The Ch D rejected the first of these contentions, holding that the normal six-year time limits did not apply. However, the Ch D accepted the companies' alternative contention and allowed the appeals relating to four of the notices, holding that notices calling for information for a period which included years for which no returns had been required were invalid. *B & S Displays Ltd and Others v Special Commrs*, Ch D 1978, 52 TC 318; [1978] STC 331. (*Note. TMA, s 20* was subsequently substituted by *FA 1976*.)

Application for order of discovery

[49.31] A solicitor was required by a notice under *TMA, s 20(2)*, to deliver certain documents to an inspector. He applied for an order of *certiorari* to quash the notice (for which see **49.32** below). He also applied to the QB for an order of discovery of a submission and report made to the Board of Inland Revenue by the inspector examining his affairs prior to the issue of the notice. The CA rejected his application for discovery, holding that the submission was subject to legal professional privilege, and the solicitor had not produced evidence suggesting that the decision to issue a notice was unreasonable. *R v CIR (ex p. Taylor)*, CA 1988, 62 TC 562; [1988] STC 832; [1989] 1 All ER 906. (*Note*. The *Rules of the Supreme Court 1965 (SI 1965/1776)* referred to 'discovery' of documents. With effect from 26 April 1999, these rules were largely replaced by the *Civil Procedure Rules 1998 (SI 1998/3132)*, which refer instead to 'disclosure' of documents.)

Application for order of certiorari

[49.32] In the case noted at **49.31** above, a solicitor applied for an order of *certiorari*, contending firstly that a notice under *TMA, s 20(2)* should not be issued in a case where assessments were under appeal, and secondly that the documents in question were protected by legal professional privilege. The CA rejected these contentions and dismissed the application, holding that the issue of the notice had not been shown to be unreasonable, and the Revenue had not acted irrationally or unlawfully. *R v CIR (ex p. Taylor) (No 2)*, CA 1990, 62 TC 578; [1990] STC 379; [1990] 2 All ER 409. (*Note.* The decision here was approved by the HL in the subsequent case of *R (oao Morgan Grenfell & Co Ltd) v Special Commissioner*, **49.33** below, but *obiter dicta* of Bingham LJ were disapproved. Lord Hoffmann held that the solicitor 'would have been entitled to refuse to produce documents in respect of which he personally was entitled to legal professional privilege, such as legal advice from counsel about his own tax affairs'.)

Notice under TMA, s 20—whether documents subject to legal privilege

[49.33] In 1999 a Special Commissioner gave consent for a notice to be issued to a company under *TMA, s 20(1)*. The company applied for judicial review of the Commissioner's decision, contending that some of the documents were subject to legal professional privilege. The QB rejected this contention but the HL allowed the company's appeal. Lord Hoffmann held that the principle of legal professional privilege was 'absolute' and was 'based not merely upon the general right to privacy but also upon the right of access to justice'. Applying the New Zealand case of *New Zealand Commissioner of Inland Revenue v West-Walker*, NZSC [1954] NZLR 191, legal professional privilege was 'a substantive right founded on an important public policy'. Furthermore, when the relevant provisions (which derived from *FA 1976*) were debated in the House of Commons, the Chief Secretary to the Treasury had stated that 'the purpose of this part of the schedule is not to require privileged and confidential documents to be handed over to the Inland Revenue'. *R (oao Morgan Grenfell & Co Ltd) v Special Commissioner*, HL 2002, 74 TC 511; [2002] STC 786; [2002] UKHL 21; [2002] 3 All ER 1. (*Notes.* (1) For another issue in this case, not taken to the HL, see **49.47** below. (2) See also *TMA, Sch 1AA para 5*, introduced by *FA 2000*.)

[49.34] The Revenue applied to a Special Commissioner for consent to serve a notice under *TMA, s 20(3)* on a public company and a notice under *TMA, s 20(1)* on a subsidiary. The companies objected to the notices, contending that some of the documents consisted of advice from its accountants which should be treated as subject to legal privilege. The Special Commissioner rejected this contention and granted the Revenue's application, observing that *TMA, Sch 1AA para 5* specifically confined legal privilege to 'communications between a professional legal adviser and his client'. While it was 'difficult in theory to make any valid distinction between advice about tax matters given to a client by a tax agent and similar advice given by solicitors', only Parliament could provide 'equality between different types of adviser'. *HMRC v Plc and Subsidiary (re application to serve TMA, s 20 notices)*, Sp C 2007, [2008] SSCD 358 (Sp C 647).

[49.35] A Special Commissioner gave consent for notices under *TMA, s 20* to be issued to two associated insurance companies which had engaged in a tax avoidance scheme, promoted by a large accountancy firm. The companies applied for judicial review, contending that some of the documents were subject to legal professional privilege, and that some of the material sought was not relevant to any tax liability. The QB rejected these contentions and dismissed the applications. Charles J held that 'for legal professional privilege to apply to legal advice and assistance, it has to be given by a member of the legal profession, with exceptions or extensions when the right or privilege arises in litigation, or when litigation is contemplated'. The Supreme Court upheld this decision (by a 5-2 majority, Lords Clarke and Sumption dissenting). Lord Neuberger observed that 'where a common law rule is valid in the modern world, but it has an aspect or limitation which appears to be outmoded, it is by no means always right for the courts to modify the aspect or remove the limitation. In any such case, the court must consider whether the implications of the proposed modification or removal are such that it would be more appropriate to leave the matter to Parliament.' He held that the question of whether legal professional privilege 'should be extended to cases where legal advice is given from professional people who are not qualified lawyers raises questions of policy which should be left to Parliament'. *R (oao Prudential plc) v Special Commissioner (and related applications)*, SC [2013] UKSC 1; [2013] STC 376; [2013] 2 All ER 247.

Revenue losing original return—notice under TMA, s 20 requesting copy

[49.36] See *HMRC v Wilson*, **44.359** PENALTIES.

Notice under TMA, s 20(3)—whether ultra vires

[49.37] An inspector served a notice under *TMA, s 20(3)* on a firm of stockbrokers, requiring them to deliver certain documents relating to seven client companies and a former employee in connection with enquiries into the latter's tax affairs. The firm applied for judicial review, contending that there was no connection between six of the companies and the former employee, and that they had already supplied all relevant information concerning the seventh company. The HL unanimously upheld the validity of the notice, reversing the majority decision of the CA and restoring that of the QB. Under *TMA, s 20(7)*, an independent Commissioner was entrusted by Parliament with the duty of supervising the exercise of the power conferred by *s 20(3)*. The Commissioner had been satisfied that the inspector was justified in proceeding under *s 20*. The presumption that the Commissioner was right to be satisfied could be displaced only by positive evidence. The Commissioner was in a much better position to make a just appraisal than a court conducting a judicial review. The applicants had not proved that the inspector's opinion that they had possession of relevant documents was unreasonable. *R v CIR (ex p. TC Coombs & Co)*, HL 1991, 64 TC 124; [1991] STC 97; [1991] 2 WLR 682; [1991] 3 All ER 623.

Notice under TMA, s 20—whether unreasonable

[49.38] In 1988 the Revenue began an enquiry into the tax affairs of a company director (K). He died in 1989, before having been interviewed. In 1990 the Revenue issued a notice under *TMA, s 20* to K's widow and executrix, requiring details of K's assets, liabilities, income and expenditure for 1985 to 1989 inclusive. She failed to comply with the notice and the Revenue began penalty proceedings. K's widow appealed to the Ch D, contending firstly that the notice had been unreasonable, secondly that the inspector could not reasonably have come to the opinion that the information sought might be relevant to K's tax liability, and thirdly that the Commissioner had acted wrongly in ruling as inadmissible a statement by a former Revenue officer, which she had sought to have admitted as expert advice. The Ch D rejected these contentions and dismissed the appeal. On the evidence, the Commissioner had been entitled to conclude that it was reasonable for the inspector to have considered that the information called for by the notice was required to ascertain K's tax liability. There was no evidence that the inspector had failed to take account of the likely costs of compliance. Furthermore, the Commissioner had read the proof submitted by the former Revenue officer, and had correctly ruled that it was not admissible as expert evidence since it sought to answer the very matter for the Commissioner's decision, and this was a question for which the witness was not qualified as an expert. Accordingly, the Commissioner had been entitled to exclude the testimony under *Civil Evidence Act 1972, s 5(3)*. *Kempton v Special Commrs & CIR*, Ch D 1992, 66 TC 249; [1992] STC 823.

[49.39] The Revenue sent draft notices under *TMA, s 20(3)* to a bank, requiring it to deliver documents containing information relating to 'sundry parties' accounts'. The bank applied for leave to bring proceedings for judicial review of the draft notices. The CA dismissed the application, holding that it was premature since the draft notices had not yet been considered by the Special Commissioner, as required by *s 20*. It was for the Special Commissioner to consider whether the proposed notices were justified. The CA specifically disapproved *dicta* of Ferris J in *R v O'Kane & Clarke (ex p. Northern Bank Ltd)*, QB 1996, 69 TC 187; [1996] STC 1249, and held that the proposed notices complied with the provisions of *TMA, s 20(8A)*. Morritt LJ observed that *TMA, s 20(8D)* referred to documents 'specified or described'. The word 'described' was 'appropriately used for the indication of classes or categories of documents as opposed to a single document'. It could not have been the intention of Parliament 'to restrict the description permissible in a notice under (*TMA, s 20(3) or (8A)*) to one which excludes classes or categories of document or documents which are not known to exist or to be in the possession or power of the recipient of the notice and which are to that extent conjectural'. Simon Brown LJ observed that 'it is difficult to think that there could ever hereafter be a proper judicial review challenge to a precursor notice'. *R v CIR (ex p. Ulster Bank Ltd)*, CA 1997, 69 TC 211; [1997] STC 832.

[49.40] The Revenue were enquiring into the tax affairs of an individual (M), and a company of which he was a director. A General Commissioner gave consent, under *TMA, s 20(7)*, to the Revenue serving notices under *TMA, s 20(3)* on M's bank. M applied for judicial review, contending that the inspector had failed to put all the relevant information before the Commissioner, since the company was dependent on financial support from the bank, which might be prejudiced by the issue of the notices. Kay J reviewed the evidence in detail and dismissed the application, observing that it must have been 'self-evident to the Commissioner that the issue of notices of this kind would have the sort of effect that (M) was concerned about'. The Revenue were justified in investigating M's affairs, and there was nothing 'to overturn the presumption of regularity both on the part of the Revenue and on the part of the Commissioner'. *R v CIR and Connolly (ex p. Mohammed and Electrowide Ltd)*, QB 1998, 73 TC 128; [1999] STC 129.

[49.41] The Revenue issued notices under *TMA, s 20(3)* (and also under *ICTA 1988, s 767C*) on a Luxembourg bank which had provided finance for corporate tax avoidance schemes. The bank applied for an order of *certiorari* to quash the notices. The QB dismissed the application, holding that there was ample justification for the issue of the notices. Lightman J observed that 'the size and sophistication of the tax avoidance schemes in question and what appears to the inspector to have been the dubious (if not dishonest) character of the devices employed required him to take the immediate remedial action which the legislature in (*s 20*) provided for in this situation'. *R v CIR (ex p. Banque Internationale a Luxembourg SA)*, QB 2000, 72 TC 597; [2000] STC 708.

[49.42] Following the decision noted at **51.3** REVENUE PROSECUTIONS, the Revenue issued a notice under *TMA, s 20* relating to a company director who was serving a sentence of four years' imprisonment. He applied for judicial review, contending that it was unreasonable to issue the notice while he was in prison, or to expect him to comply while he was subject to a restricted parole licence. The Ch D rejected this contention and dismissed the application, observing that the director had 'adopted a stance of taking every opportunity he can to avoid answering the reasonable requests which have been made'. The CA upheld the decision, holding that the issue of the notice had not been unreasonable. *R (oao Werner) v CIR*, CA [2002] STC 1213; [2002] EWCA Civ 979.

[49.43] In 2005 an individual (P) submitted a tax return claiming a capital loss of more than £2,600,000. HMRC subsequently received information suggesting that P had engaged in a tax avoidance scheme of the type considered in *R (oao Paulden Activities Ltd & Others) v HMRC*, **49.48** below, and that the claimed loss did not meet the requirements of *TCGA, s 37*. In 2007 an inspector issued a notice under *TMA, s 20(1)*. P applied for judicial review, contending that the notice was unreasonable. The CS rejected this contention and dismissed the application. Lord Ballantyne held that there was nothing unreasonable in the decision to issue the notice. Applying the principles laid down in *Veltema v Langham*, **5.48** ASSESSMENTS, P's return did not contain sufficient information to have alerted an inspector to 'an insufficiency in tax'. *N Pattullo v HMRC (No 1)*, CS 2009, [2010] STC 107; [2009] CSOH 137. (Note. The First-tier Tribunal subsequently dismissed P's appeal against a discovery assessment—see **5.61** ASSESSMENTS.)

[49.44] Notices under *TMA, s 20* were also upheld in *R (oao Johnson & Others) v Branigan*, QB [2006] EWHC 885 (Admin); *R (oao Parissis & Others) v Grinyer*, QB 2009, [2010] STC 891; [2009] EWHC 3734 (Admin), and *Fox v McKay & Another*, **44.363** PENALTIES.

Company engaging in share option scheme—whether within TMA, s 20(3)

[49.45] The managing director and secretary of a company (C) held options to acquire shares in that company. They agreed with another company (M) to exchange those options for options to acquire shares in Isle of Man companies, with the aim of deferring their income tax liability until a gain accrued in respect of their new options. The inspector considered that documents in the possession of M might show that there was also an assignment for value giving rise to a taxable gain by virtue of the transaction, and served notices on M under *TMA, s 20(3)*, requiring it to produce the documents. M refused to comply with the notices, and the Revenue took penalty proceedings. The Special Commissioner imposed nominal penalties, and M appealed, contending *inter alia* that it was not subject to *s 20(3)*. The Ch D rejected this contention and dismissed the appeal. *Monarch Assurance Co Ltd v Special Commrs*, Ch D 1986, 59 TC 594; [1986] STC 311. (*Note*. The case also concerned the application of *TMA, s 20(4)*, which was deleted by *FA 1989*.)

Consent by Commissioner (TMA, s 20(7)–(8H))

TMA, s 20(7)—whether application to be heard ex parte (without notice)

[49.46] The Revenue informed a taxpayer's solicitors that they intended to lodge an application under *TMA, s 20(7)* for the issue of a notice under *TMA, s 20(1)*. The solicitors wrote to the Clerk to the Special Commissioners, requesting that the Commissioner hearing the application should admit argument *inter partes*. The Special Commissioner rejected this contention, observing that one would not expect an application for leave to carry out 'an administrative act on the part of an inspector to garner information' to be heard *inter partes* 'when it is to be expected that the taxpayer would object to the inspector adopting the course he has in a sense been compelled to adopt'. It was 'inherent that the application should be made *ex parte* and not only should be made *ex parte* but cannot sensibly be made *inter partes*'. *Taxpayer v Inspector of Taxes*, Sp C [1996] SSCD 261 (Sp C 79). (*Note*. The *Rules of the Supreme Court 1965 (SI 1965/1776)* referred to applications being made 'ex parte' or 'inter partes'. With effect from 26 April 1999, these rules were largely replaced by the *Civil Procedure Rules 1998 (SI 1998/3132)*, which refer instead to applications being made 'without notice' or 'on notice'.)

[49.47] The Revenue issued a 'precursor notice' under *TMA, s 20B(1)* to a company which provided financial facilities. The company's solicitors wrote to the Presiding Special Commissioner, requesting him to allow an *inter partes* hearing if and when the Revenue lodged an application under *TMA, s 20(7)* for the issue of a notice under *TMA, s 20(1)*. The Special Commissioner rejected the application, holding that the company had no right to attend the hearing and the Commissioner had no discretion to permit its attendance. The QB and the CA unanimously upheld this decision. Buxton LJ observed that 'in sensitive cases, such as those involving informers, it would be impossible for the Commissioner to give acceptable reasons for not exercising his discretion without effectively giving the game away'. Blackburne J held that 'the possibility of an oral hearing is excluded by the nature of the process in question'. *R (oao Morgan Grenfell & Co Ltd) v Special Commissioner*, CA 2001, 74 TC 511; [2001] STC 497; [2001] EWCA Civ 329; [2002] 1 All ER 776. (*Notes*. (1) For the Revenue's practice following the Commissioner's decision, see Revenue Tax Bulletin, April 2000, pp 743–746. (2) For another issue in this case, taken to the HL, see **49.33** above. (3) See the note following *Taxpayer v Inspector of Taxes*, **49.46** above.)

TMA, s 20(7)—whether Commissioner justified in giving consent

[49.48] The Revenue were investigating an avoidance scheme, devised by a solicitor resident in the isle of Man, which sought to use capital redemption policies to avoid capital gains tax. They issued notices under *TMA, s 20*, requiring information from fourteen companies with the same registered office. The companies applied for judicial review, contending that the General Commissioner had not been justified in giving consent to the issue of the notices. The CS rejected this contention and dismissed the applications, applying the principles laid down by Lord Lowry in *R v CIR (ex p. TC Coombs & Co)*, **49.37** above. *R (oao Paulden Activities Ltd & Others) v HMRC*, CS 2009, TL 3820; [2009] STC 1884; [2009] CSOH 55. (*Note*. For previous proceedings involving the solicitor, see *R v CIR (ex p. Taylor) (Nos 1 and 2)*, **49.31** and **49.32** above.)

TMA, s 20(8A)—whether application 'authorised by order of the Board'

[49.49] An inspector applied to a Special Commissioner for consent to issue a notice under *TMA, s 20(3)* requiring a bank to produce certain documents. The inspector produced a signed authorisation under *TMA, s 20(8A)* from the director of the Board's Special Compliance Office. However, the Commissioner (Mr. Wallace) considered that *s 20(8A)* required the Board to give the necessary authorisation itself, rather than by an officer exercising delegated authority. The Revenue applied for judicial review, and the QB reversed the Commissioner's decision, holding that the Commissioner had erred in law. Dyson J held that the effect of *IRRA 1890, s 4A* was that the Board could delegate any of its functions to one of its officers unless that section was disapplied by specific words or by necessary implication, which was not the case here. Accordingly, on the evidence accepted by the Commissioner, the application had been properly authorised. *R v Special Commissioner (ex p. CIR); R v CIR (ex p. Ulster Bank Ltd) (No 2)*, QB 2000, 73 TC 209; [2000] STC 537.

TMA, s 20(8A)—notice without naming taxpayers

[49.50] The Revenue applied to a Special Commissioner for consent to issue a notice under *TMA, s 20* requiring a financial institution (F) to produce information about credit card customers with UK addresses whose cards were associated with offshore bank accounts (mostly in the Channel Islands and the Isle of Man). The Commissioner reviewed the evidence in detail and granted the application, finding that it appeared that only 19% of the relevant customers had made UK tax returns, and that only 18% of those had declared any income from outside the UK. The information submitted by the Revenue indicated that there was a potential tax yield of more than £300,000,000. The notice was not onerous and the information requested was in F's 'possession or power'. The Revenue were not engaged in a 'fishing expedition', and the evidence suggested that a significant percentage of the customers in question were in 'default in complying in tax obligations'. The Commissioner observed that if the customers had 'associated their credit card with a UK bank account, the UK bank would automatically give the Revenue information about interest earned on that account'. The Revenue were 'pursuing a legitimate purpose, which the information so far obtained shows they are right to pursue'. The information already obtained by the Revenue 'raises serious questions that merit investigation and cannot be investigated by any other means'. *HMRC v Financial Institution*, Sp C [2006] SSCD 71 (Sp C 517).

[49.51] Following the decision noted at **49.50** above, the Revenue made a second application relating to the same financial institution (and two UK subsidiaries), seeking information about customers with UK addresses and non-UK bank accounts. The Commissioner reviewed the evidence in detail and granted the application. *HMRC v Financial Institution (No 2)*, Sp C [2006] SSCD 360 (Sp C 536).

[49.52] Similar decisions were reached in *Financial Institution No 1 v HMRC*, Sp C [2007] SSCD 202 (Sp C 580); *Financial Institution No 2 v HMRC*, Sp C [2007] SSCD 208 (Sp C 581); *Financial Institution No 3 v HMRC*, Sp C [2007] SSCD 216 (Sp C 582); *Financial Institution No 4 v HMRC*, Sp C [2007] SSCD 222 (Sp C 583); *HMRC v Financial Institution No 5*, Sp C [2009] SSCD 488; [2009] UKFTT 68 (TC), TC00009; *HMRC v Financial Institutions Nos 6 and 7*, Sp C [2009] SSCD 493; [2009] UKFTT 69 (TC), TC00010, and *HMRC v Financial Institution No 8*, Sp C [2009] SSCD 498; [2009] UKFTT 70 (TC), TC00011.

[49.53] The Revenue formed the opinion that a number of traders, who were resident in the UK, had evaded tax by trading in shares through a nominee company registered in the British Virgin Islands, using a UK investment bank as the 'prime broker'. They applied to a Special Commissioner for consent to issue a notice to the bank under *TMA, s 20(8A)*. The Commissioner granted the application, observing that the relevant individuals were clients for whom the bank 'acted as prime broker who are UK-resident individuals and who conduct share transactions via a company registered in a tax haven enjoying institutional investor status'. This was 'certainly not in the nature of a fishing expedition by the Revenue'. There were 'reasonable grounds for believing' that some of the people concerned had 'seriously failed to comply with their tax obligations', and that 'the tax yield will be of the order of £35m'. *Tax Haven Company v HMRC*, Sp C [2006] SSCD 310 (Sp C 533).

[49.54] The Revenue made a similar application with regard to a financial institution which was acting as a broker, but not as the 'prime broker', with regard to share transactions using a 'tax haven' company. The Commissioner granted the Revenue's application, observing that 'while it is possible that there is avoidance rather than evasion', there were 'reasonable grounds for believing that fraud is more probable'. *HMRC v Financial Institution (re a Tax Haven Company)*, Sp C [2006] SSCD 376 (Sp C 537).

[49.55] HMRC issued a notice under *TMA, s 20(8A)* to a company (R) which had marketed capital redemption policies. R appealed, contending that the notice was unduly onerous. The First-Tier Tribunal rejected this contention and dismissed the appeal. The tribunal noted that the company's accounts indicated that at March 2006 it had had a capital redemption fund of more than £37,000,000, and that this had been reduced to less than £20,000,000 in the following twelve months. The tribunal concluded that it seemed probable that the company had been issuing policies for 'sizeable sums'. On the evidence, the tribunal held that 'the notice is not onerous'. *Rincham Ltd v HMRC*, FTT [2010] UKFTT 502 (TC), TC00757.

TMA, s 20(8E)—failure to provide summary of reasons for notices

[49.56] An inspector who was investigating the affairs of two individuals obtained the consent of a General Commissioner to issue notices under *TMA, s 20(3)* requiring a bank to deliver documentary information regarding accounts held by two companies. The Commissioner accepted the inspector's contention that, by virtue of *TMA, s 20(8G)*, a written summary of the reasons for the notices need not be issued either to the individuals or to the companies, since it might identify informants. The companies applied for judicial review, contending that the inspector had been required to give a written summary of his reasons by *TMA, s 20(8E)*, and that the failure to do so rendered the notices invalid. Tucker J dismissed the applications. The inspector had erred in law in failing to provide a written summary of his reasons in accordance with *TMA, s 20(8E)*. However, this failure did not invalidate the notices. The effect of *TMA, s 20(8G)* was that any information which might identify informants could be omitted from the summary of reasons, so that the inspector could have issued a bland summary which would not have assisted the companies. Tucker J held that this was 'not a case where relief should or need be granted', since the failure to fulfil the requirements of *s 20(8E)* was a technical breach 'from which no harm had resulted'. *R v CIR (ex p. Continental Shipping Ltd & Atsiganos SA)*, QB 1996, 68 TC 665; [1996] STC 813. (*Note*. The Revenue were only awarded 50% of their costs.)

Direction under TMA, s 20(8G)—application for judicial review

[49.57] The Revenue issued notices under *TMA, s 20*, requiring information, including capital statements and bank reconciliations, from two companies in the timeshare industry, and from their controlling director (H). The Commissioner issued a direction under *TMA, s 20(8G)* that the Revenue were not required to disclose certain information leading to the issue of the notices. H and the two companies applied for judicial review, contending firstly that they should not be required to disclose details relating to overseas clients, and secondly that the Revenue had not given adequate reasons for the issue of the notices, as required by *TMA, s 20(8E)*, and that the Commissioner's direction had not been reasonable. Carnwath J rejected the applicants' first contention but accepted their second contention and granted the application. On the first issue, the Revenue had been entitled to form the opinion that they required to inspect the accounts in question, even though the money held in them was not beneficially owned by the applicants, since there were reasonable grounds for believing that the accounts might contain information relevant to the applicants' tax liability. The details of the client accounts were therefore within *TMA, s 20*, as were capital statements and bank reconciliations. However, with regard to the specific direction issued by the Commissioner, Carnwath J noted that the Revenue had failed to show the Commissioner a letter which had been received from the applicants' tax adviser, giving reasons for objecting to the proposed notices. As a matter of fairness, the inspector should have shown this letter to the Commissioner. Although the applicants were not entitled to see full details of the inspector's submissions to the Commissioner, they were entitled to receive a statement dealing with the main issues. The brief covering letters which the Revenue had issued to the applicants were not an adequate summary of the reasons for issuing the notices. Accordingly, there was 'sufficient doubt as to the fairness of the procedure to justify quashing the relevant parts of the notices'. Carnwath J also observed that 'in principle the inspector is entitled to the particulars he seeks', and that 'the only issue is as to how the information can be most expeditiously and economically provided'. *R v MacDonald & CIR (ex p. Hutchinson & Co Ltd and Others)*, QB 1998, 71 TC 1; [1998] STC 680.

Restrictions on powers (TMA, s 20B)

Whether 'reasonable grounds for suspecting the taxpayer of fraud'

[49.58] The Revenue were investigating the affairs of a number of offshore companies. A General Commissioner authorised the service of notices under *TMA, s 20(3)* on the companies' UK bank and UK broker, requiring them to deliver or make available certain documents. The Commissioner also directed, under *TMA, s 20B(1B)*, that copies of the notices need not be given to the companies, on the grounds that he was satisfied that the inspector had reasonable grounds for suspecting the companies of fraud. The companies applied for judicial review. Scott-Baker J dismissed the applications, observing that the General Commissioner was an independent third party and that his decision was final. On the evidence, there was nothing to suggest that either the inspector or the Commissioner had not discharged their duties appropriately. There was no evidence before the court to suggest any irregularity on the part of the Revenue. *R v CIR (ex p. Archon Shipping Corporation & Others)*, QB 1998, 71 TC 203; [1998] STC 1151.

TMA, s 20B(3)—whether Revenue officer acting as delegate of Board

[49.59] The Revenue's Special Compliance Office in Solihull issued a notice under *TMA, s 20(3)* to a firm of solicitors, requiring them to produce certain documents. The firm applied for judicial review, contending firstly that the effect of *TMA, s 20B(3)* was that the notice was invalid, and alternatively that the notice was unduly onerous. The QB rejected these contentions and dismissed the application, holding that the director of the Special Compliance Office had acted as the delegate of the Board for the purposes of *s 20B(3)*. In giving the notice, he had been exercising the powers of the Board, rather than the powers of an inspector. Accordingly the notice was valid. Furthermore, in the circumstances of the case, the notice was not unduly burdensome or oppressive. *R v CIR (ex p. Davis Frankel & Mead)*, QB 2000, 73 TC 185; [2000] STC 595.

TMA, s 20B(3)—whether Revenue required to give reasons for notice

[49.60] The Revenue issued a notice under *TMA, s 20B(3)* to a solicitor requiring delivery of certain documents concerning his client's tax liability. The solicitor applied for judicial review, contending that the notice was invalid because the Revenue had not provided a summary of its reasons for issuing the notice. The QB rejected this contention and dismissed the application. Munby J held that an inspector who gave a notice under *TMA, s 20(3)* was required to give a summary of his reasons, but there was no such requirement with regard to a notice issued by the Board under *TMA, s 20B(3)*. *R (oao Cooke) v HMRC*, QB 2007, TL 3797; [2007] EWHC 81 (Admin); [2007] All ER (D) 269 (Jan).

Claim to legal professional privilege—TMA, s 20B(8)

[49.61] A barrister was served with a notice under *TMA, s 20(3)*, requiring him to deliver or make available to the Revenue certain copies of documents in his possession which had been sent to him by a US attorney for legal advice. He refused to comply with the notice and the Revenue began penalty proceedings. The barrister applied for judicial review. The QB granted the application and declared that the documents were subject to legal professional privilege within *TMA, s 20B(8)*. *R v CIR (ex p. Goldberg)*, QB 1988, 61 TC 403; [1988] STC 524. (*Note*. The decision was subsequently disapproved by the CA in *Dubai Bank Ltd v Galadari*, CA [1989] 3 WLR 1044; [1989] 3 All ER 769.)

[49.62] The Revenue sought to issue notices under *TMA, s 20(3)* to two banks, requiring them to disclose correspondence relating to the financial affairs of a solicitor (L). L applied for judicial review, contending firstly that the inspector had failed to put all the relevant information before the Commissioner, and secondly that some of the correspondence related to clients and that the documents were subject to legal professional privilege within *TMA, s 20B(8)*. The QB rejected these contentions and dismissed the application. On the evidence, there was no 'material incompleteness or inadequacy' in the material which the inspector had put before the Commissioner. Secondly, legal professional privilege only extended to lawyers in their professional capacity, and did not cover the situation where notices were directed against them in their capacity as a taxpayer. *R v CIR (ex p. Lorimer)*, QB 2000, 73 TC 276; [2000] STC 751.

Entry with warrant (TMA, s 20C)

NOTE

TMA, s 20C was repealed by *FA 2007* with effect from 1 December 2007, and has been superseded by equivalent powers under *Police and Criminal Evidence Act 1984, s 114*.

Validity of action under TMA, s 20C

[49.63] Acting under warrants issued by a circuit judge in accordance with *TMA, s 20C*, Revenue officers entered the offices of two companies, the home of the managing director of one of the companies, and the home of an accountant who had acted for the company. The Revenue officers seized a very large quantity of documents. The warrants were worded generally, following the wording of the relevant parts of the section and not specifying the suspected fraud or the documents to be seized. The Revenue refused to divulge this information to the persons whose premises were entered. They applied for judicial review of the seizure and for the warrants to be quashed, contending that to be lawful the warrants must specify the suspected offence and that the volume of the documents taken was such that the Revenue could not, at the time of the seizure, have had reasonable grounds for believing they might be required as evidence. The HL rejected these contentions and held (by a 4–1 majority, Lord Salmon dissenting) that the warrants were valid. *TMA, s 20C* did not require the suspected fraud to be specified, and, on the evidence, the applicants had failed to establish that the Revenue officials had acted unlawfully in seizing the documents in question. *R v CIR & Quinlan (ex p. Rossminster Ltd & Others)*, HL 1979, 52 TC 160; [1980] STC 42; [1980] 2 WLR 1; [1979] 3 All ER 385. (*Notes.* (1) For contempt of court proceedings which arose following this decision, see *CIR v Tucker*, CA 1980, 52 TC 219. (2) See also the amendments to *TMA, s 20C* made by *FA 1989* with effect from 27 July 1989.)

[49.64] The Revenue obtained warrants under *TMA, s 20C(1)* to enter a company's premises and seize documents held there. Subsequently two directors of the company were charged with conspiracy to cheat the public revenue. One of the directors (S) pleaded guilty to an amended charge of cheating the revenue, and the charges of conspiracy against him were not proceeded with. The second director (H) was convicted of conspiracy and was sentenced to eight years' imprisonment. He appealed against his conviction, contending *inter alia* that the warrants were unlawful because they did not name the Revenue officers who were to enter the company's premises. The CA dismissed his appeal, holding that it was not necessary for warrants issued under *TMA, s 20C(1)* to name the Revenue officers who were to carry out the operation. *Obiter dicta* of Lord Diplock in *R v CIR (ex p. Rossminster Ltd)*, **49.63** above, were not followed (and were implicitly disapproved). (The CA also rejected various alternative contentions raised by the director, holding *inter alia* that the charge sufficiently identified the conduct alleged to amount to the common law offence of cheating the revenue.) *R v Hunt*, CA 1994, 68 TC 132; [1994] STC 819. (*Note.* For an unsuccessful application for judicial review of the conviction, see **50.23** REVENUE ADMINISTRATION.)

[49.65] The Revenue were investigating the tax affairs of two individuals, and obtained warrants from a circuit judge, in accordance with *TMA, s 20C*, to search the premises of their accountants. During the search, the accountants made an emergency application for judicial review, and at about 5 p.m. the QB granted an injunction by telephone, halting the search pending a hearing which was arranged for the following morning. However, the Revenue officer conducting the search continued it until 9 p.m. that day. At the subsequent hearing, Buxton J observed that the Revenue's action in continuing the search had been 'a plain breach of the Court's order', and noted that the Deputy Chairman of the Board of Inland Revenue had subsequently apologised for the Revenue having acted in contempt of Court. Buxton J also strongly criticised the Revenue officer in charge of the search for failing to understand the legal position. *R v CIR & Others (ex p. Kingston Smith)*, QB 1996, 70 TC 264; [1996] STC 1210.

[49.66] The Revenue formed the opinion that a US attorney, practising in London, had helped one of his clients to evade UK taxation by diverting commission and bonus payments offshore. They obtained warrants under *TMA, s 20C*, authorising them to enter and search the attorney's offices. Under *TMA, s 20C(3)*, they were then entitled to seize and remove documents. The attorney applied for judicial review of the decision to apply for the search warrants. The QB rejected the application, holding that the warrants were valid and that the seizure and removal of the documents was legal, applying the principles laid down in *R v CIR (ex p. Rossminster Ltd)*, **49.63** above. With regard to the attorney's claim that some of the seized documents were subject to legal professional privilege, the QB held that it was 'for the courts to determine whether the documents in fact seized and removed were subject to such privilege' and that there was as yet 'no evidence that any of the documents seized and removed was privileged'. As a measure of protection, the Revenue had arranged for the material which had been seized to be reviewed by counsel nominated by the Attorney-General. Moses J observed that, in cases such as these, the presence of counsel 'was to be encouraged'. *R v CIR and Middlesex Guildhall Crown Court (ex p. Tamosius & Partners)*, QB [1999] STC 1077; [2000] 1 WLR 453. (*Note.* The attorney subsequently made an unsuccessful application to the ECHR—see **31.55** HUMAN RIGHTS.)

[49.67] The Revenue were investigating the affairs of an individual (H) and obtained a warrant under *TMA, s 20(C)*, to enter and search his house. When they executed the warrant, H was on holiday in France, but his father-in-law gave the officers access to the house. The officers removed a computer in order to copy the contents of the hard drive. The computer was returned to H after the copying had taken place. H applied for judicial review, contending that *TMA, s 20C* did not authorise the Revenue to copy the entire contents of the hard drive. The QB rejected this contention and dismissed the application. Stanley Burnton J held that if a Revenue officer executing a warrant under *s 20C* found a computer, and had reasonable cause to believe that the data on the computer's hard drive might be required as evidence for the purpose of criminal proceedings, he could seize and remove that computer even though it also contained irrelevant material. The effect of *s 20C* was that the seizure and removal of the computer had been lawful. *R (oao H) v CIR*, QB 2002, 75 TC 377; [2002] STC 1354; [2002] EWHC 2164 (Admin).

[49.68] The Revenue obtained warrants from two Crown Court judges under *TMA, s 20C*, authorising them to enter and search the premises of a company (M) which provided tax consultancy services. The company applied for judicial review. The QB granted the application. Underhill J held that the information available to the Revenue showed 'reasonable ground to suspect that there were serious flaws in the implementation' of a tax avoidance scheme which M had marketed. However, a Revenue officer had given evidence to the Crown Court suggesting that M had concealed certain details from its clients, which was not in fact the case. Accordingly, the Crown Court had been 'misled' in a material respect. Underhill J also commented that this had been 'something of a borderline case for the deployment of the nuclear weapon of an application under *s 20C*. If HMRC were to persuade the court that this was a proper case for the issue of search warrants (covering not only business premises but the private homes of over twenty individuals) on an *ex parte* basis, it was incumbent on them to put their case with scrupulous accuracy and in such a way that the judge was able to make a fair assessment of the grounds for suspicion being put forward. That did not occur.' *R (oao Mercury Tax Group Ltd) v HMRC*, QB 2008, [2009] STC 743; [2008] EWHC 2721 (Admin).

Company tax returns (FA 1998, Sch 18)

FA 1998, Sch 18 para 11—documents accompanying returns

[49.69] See *Goodtime Print & Design Ltd v HMRC*, 44.68 PENALTIES.

FA 1998, Sch 18 para 17—fixed penalties for late returns

[49.70] See the cases noted at 44.56 to 44.68 PENALTIES.

FA 1998, Sch 18 para 18—tax-geared penalties for late returns

[49.71] See the cases noted at 44.69 to 44.71 PENALTIES.

FA 1998, Sch 18 para 24—Revenue enquiry into company return

[49.72] The Revenue gave a company notice in March 2002, under *FA 1998, Sch 18 para 24*, that they intended to enquire into the company's tax return. The company did not supply the requested information, and in November 2003 the Revenue issued a notice of amendment, under *FA 1998, Sch 18 para 30*. The company subsequently applied for judicial review of the notice, contending that it was invalid because it had been sent to a business address and not to its registered office. The CS rejected this contention and dismissed the application. Lady Smith held that the effect of *TMA, s 115(2)(a)* was that a notice of enquiry could be served at a company's place of business. She also observed that *s 115* was not 'prescriptive' and that there was 'no reason why, for instance, effective intimation would not be achieved by handing a notice of enquiry to a company director in the course of a meeting'. *Spring Salmon & Seafood Ltd v Advocate-General for Scotland*, CS 2004, 76 TC 609; [2004] STC 444. (*Note*. For subsequent developments in this case, see 49.77 below.)

[49.73] In August 2003 a company (F) submitted a return for the year ending 31 July 2002, declaring estimated profits of £20,000. In February 2004 F submitted an amended return, claiming that it had actually made a loss of more than £70,000. The Revenue began an enquiry into the amended return. They discovered that F's records were incomplete, and formed the opinion that they were unreliable. They issued a notice of amendment to reinstate the original declared profit of £20,000. F appealed. The Special Commissioner dismissed the appeal, observing that it was 'difficult to accept that (F's) customers are all willing to pay substantial sums for the construction of extensions at their homes but do not require invoices setting out the nature of the work undertaken and the price paid for it'. The Commissioner also observed that 'a trader who does not keep accounting records to a reasonable standard can scarcely complain if his claims to have produced accurate and reliable annual accounts are doubted'. *Ferriby Construction (UK) Ltd v HMRC*, Sp C 2007, [2008] SSCD 234 (Sp C 635).

[49.74] In 2012 HMRC issued a notice of enquiry under *FA 1998, Sch 18 para 24* into a company's tax return. The company appealed. HMRC applied for the appeal to be struck out on the grounds that there was no right of an appeal against the opening of an enquiry under *Sch 18 para 24*. The First-tier Tribunal accepted this contention and struck out the appeal. Judge Mosedale observed that 'there is no right of appeal against a notice opening an enquiry. This is not surprising as one is not needed: the notice of enquiry is nothing more than an opening of enquiries to check the correctness of the return.' *Spring Capital Ltd v HMRC*, FTT [2013] UKFTT 41 (TC); [2013] SFTD 570, TC02461.

[49.75] HMRC issued a notice of enquiry under *FA 1998, Sch 18 para 24* to a company (D), which they delivered by hand exactly 12 months after the date on which D filed its return. D appealed, contending that the notice had been issued one day outside the time limit. The First-tier Tribunal rejected this contention and dismissed the appeal. Judge Clark held that the word 'from' in *FA 1998, Sch 18 para 24(2)* excluded the day when the return was filed, so that the notice was within the 12-month time limit. *Dock And Let Ltd v HMRC*, FTT [2014] UKFTT 943 (TC), TC04056.

FA 1998, Sch 18 para 27—notice to produce documents

[49.76] The Revenue began an enquiry into the affairs of a UK company (M) which provided investment advisory services to its Bermudan parent company and to two other clients. They issued a notice under *FA 1998, Sch 18 para 27*, requesting M to produce certain documents. M appealed, contending *inter alia* that it was unable to obtain much of the requested information from its Bermudan parent company. The Special Commissioner reviewed the evidence in detail and dismissed the appeal, holding that the Revenue's requests for information were relevant and reasonable, and that the evidence indicated that the documents were 'in (M's) *de facto* power or possession'. *Meditor Capital Management Ltd v Feighan*, Sp C [2004] SSCD 273 (Sp C 409).

[49.77] In the case noted at 49.72 above, the Revenue issued two notices under *FA 1998, Sch 18 para 27*, requesting the company to produce certain documents relating to the acquisition of the business of an associated partnership, in respect of which it had claimed relief under *FA 2002, Sch 29*. The company appealed. Its registered office was in Edinburgh, but its trading premises were in Berkshire. The appeal was set down for hearing by a Special Commissioner in London, and the company applied for the appeal to be transferred to Edinburgh. The Special Commissioner reviewed the evidence in detail, dismissed the company's application for the appeal to be transferred, and upheld the Revenue's notices in principle, subject to the exclusion of any documents and information subject to legal professional privilege. The Commissioner observed that the documents and information in question were 'relevant to ascertaining whether the transaction was solely or mainly motivated for tax avoidance reasons, whether the transaction was made on arm's length terms and whether (the partners) were related parties in relation to the sale'. The information available gave rise to 'a potential reasonable concern' that the material transactions were between related parties within *FA 2002, Sch 29 para 95*, that the transactions might not have been at arm's length, that the transactions were tax-motivated and that 'the valuation of the trade and assets and/or the goodwill was manipulated for tax purposes'. With regard to hearing of the appeal in London, the Commissioner observed that ' the jurisdiction of the Special Commissioners is a UK-wide jurisdiction.' The Commissioner (who was qualified in Scots law as well as in English law) observed that 'London was the appropriate location for this hearing', since the evidence indicated that the company's trading premises were in England, and neither of its directors lived in Scotland. *Spring Salmon & Seafood Ltd v HMRC (No 1)*, Sp C [2005] SSCD 830 (Sp C 503). (*Notes*. (1) *FA 2002, Sch 29 para 95* has subsequently been replaced by *CTA 2009, s 835*. (2) For subsequent developments in this case, see **29.125** FURTHER ASSESSMENTS: LOSS OF TAX.)

[49.78] In *Vodafone 2 v HMRC*, **3.85** ANTI-AVOIDANCE, the Special Commissioners upheld the Revenue's contention that a letter sent by the inspector conducting the enquiry did not constitute a formal notice to produce documents under *FA 1998, Sch 18 para 27*.

[49.79] See also *Alan Porter Ltd v HM Inspector of Taxes*, **44.367** PENALTIES.

FA 1998, Sch 18 para 32—completion of enquiry

[49.80] In November 2005 HMRC issued a notice of enquiry into the return submitted by a company (B) for the period ending 31 March 2004. On 31 October 2007 HMRC mistakenly issued two closure notices, which did not include a substantial adjustment which the officer (H) who was responsible for the enquiry wished to make to B's profits. On the same day H sent an email to B, informing it that the notices had been issued in error. On 8 November H wrote to B, stating that the notices had statutory effect under *FA 1998, Sch 18 para 32* but that he proposed to amend B's returns under *Sch 18 para 34*. In April 2008 H again wrote to B, purporting to withdraw the closure notices, and in February 2010 he purported to issue revised new closure notices. B appealed, contending as a preliminary point that the closure notices issued in October 2007 were final and that HMRC had no power to amend its returns under *Sch 18 para 34*. The Upper Tribunal accepted this contention and allowed the appeal. Peter Smith J held that 'the closure notices were effective with the result that it is not open to HMRC to investigate further the derivative issues in respect of the year ending 31 March 2004'. *Bristol & West plc v HMRC*, UT [2014] UKUT 073 (TCC); [2014] STC 1048. (*Note*. For another issue in this case, see **18.15** CORPORATION TAX.)

FA 1998, Sch 18 para 33—application for closure notice

[49.81] In June 2004 the Revenue began an enquiry into a return submitted by a company which operated a Chinese restaurant. The company's principal director refused to attend a meeting with the Revenue, and in December 2005, after protracted correspondence, the company applied for a closure notice under *FA 1998, Sch 18 para 33*. The Special Commissioner reviewed the evidence in detail and found that there was 'nothing unreasonable' about the Revenue's concerns about the company's accounts. The cash balances were 'remarkably high' and the Revenue were 'understandably concerned as to the true level of drawings by the directors'. However, the Commissioner observed that 'if the Revenue amend the return under *paragraph 34(2)* and the appellant company appeals, then unless the appellant satisfies the tribunal that it is overcharged, the assessment will stand good under (*TMA, s 50(6)*). The burden of proof will be on the appellant.' He held that 'provided this matter is given proper priority, four months is adequate.' Accordingly, the Commissioner directed that the enquiry into the return be closed within four months. *Jade Palace Ltd v HMRC*, Sp C [2006] SSCD 419 (Sp C 540).

[49.82] The Revenue began an enquiry into a company's returns for the years ending 31 October 1999 to 2002 inclusive. They formed the opinion that some of the deductions claimed by the company were not allowable, and in 2005 they issued assessments, against which the company appealed. In 2008, while the appeals were awaiting hearing, the company applied for a closure notice under *FA 1998, Sch 18 para 33*. The Special Commissioner dismissed the application, holding that 'the corporation tax enquiry depends on the result of the appeals' and that the Revenue had 'reasonable grounds for not giving a closure notice while those appeals remain to be determined'. *ECL Solutions Ltd v HMRC*, Sp C 2008, [2009] SSCD 90 (Sp C 721).

[49.83] In December 2009 HMRC began an enquiry into a return submitted by a company (E), whose accounts showed a turnover of £187,000 and directors' salaries of £116,500. A meeting took place in May 2010, and the officer responsible for the enquiry formed the opinion that the salaries shown in E's accounts were insufficient to meet its directors' living expenses. E applied for a closure notice, contending that it had already supplied information about its own income and could not be required to provide information about its directors' personal affairs. The First-Tier Tribunal granted the application. Judge Clark held that there was no 'basis for continuing to make further enquiries into the level of the remuneration'. *Estate 4 Ltd v HMRC*, FTT [2011] UKFTT 269 (TC), TC01131.

[49.84] HMRC began enquiries into the returns submitted by a company (F) which had made claims for cross-border group loss relief. In May 2010 F applied for closure notices. The First-Tier Tribunal reviewed the evidence in detail and dismissed the applications. Judge Kempster observed that F's international group structure was complicated, and had varied over different accounting periods. Accordingly, it was 'reasonable that HMRC should need to gather detailed information on specific points they require to be clarified'. *Finnforest UK Ltd v HMRC (and related appeals)*, FTT [2011] UKFTT 342 (TC); [2011] SFTD 889, TC01202.

[49.85] See also *Vodafone 2 v HMRC*, 3.85 ANTI-AVOIDANCE.

Miscellaneous

Application under Bankers' Books Evidence Act 1879

[49.86] For the purpose of preparing its case against a man accused of fraud, the Revenue wanted to see entries in the account of a Manx company with a Manx branch of Barclays Bank Ltd, and obtained an appropriate order from the High Court under the *Bankers' Books Evidence Act 1879, s 7* to inspect the account. Barclays took a neutral stance in the matter, but the Manx company appealed against the order to the CA, which allowed the appeal. The judiciary's discretionary power under the legislation must be used with great caution, and there was no reason why the Manx branch of a UK bank should be treated differently from such a branch of an overseas bank. The Manx branch should be regarded as a separate unity and it would not be right for the confidence of its Manx customers to be broken for UK proceedings. *R v Grossman*, CA [1981] Crim LR 396.

TMA, s 28ZA—referral of questions during enquiry

[49.87] See *Retirement Care Group Ltd v HMRC*, **56.105** SETTLEMENTS.

Revenue application under Family Proceedings Rules 1991

[49.88] During proceedings in the Family Division, the judge hearing the case (Wilson J) concluded that an offshore company which owned the matrimonial home was controlled by the husband. The judge inferred from the evidence that the reason that the husband had interposed the offshore company in the purchase of the property was to evade tax. Through an administrative error, a copy of the transcript was supplied to the wife's brother, although he was not a party to the proceedings. A copy was subsequently forwarded to the Revenue. The Revenue applied to the court, under the *Family Proceedings Rules 1991 (SI 1991/1247)*, to keep the transcript, and to inspect the affidavits and documents filed in court. Wilson J rejected the application, observing that tax evasion was 'greedy and anti-social', but noting that the finding of evasion in the present case was an inference of 'the most general character'. None of the relevant documents directly established that there had been evasion, other than inferentially. Furthermore, the evasion had taken place at least nine years ago, the proceedings had been concluded, and the husband had left the UK and had 're-ordered his affairs'. *S v S (No 2)*, Fam D 1997, TL 3518; [1997] STC 759; [1997] 1 WLR 1621; [1997] 2 FLR 774. (*Note*. This case was distinguished in the subsequent cases of *A v A*, **49.90** below, and *R v R*, **50.21** REVENUE ADMINISTRATION, but was applied in the 2012 case of *HMRC v Charman*, **49.89** below.)

[49.89] Following divorce proceedings, a woman applied for ancillary relief against her former husband (C), who had moved from the UK to Bermuda. The Family Division awarded her more than £40,000,000. HMRC subsequently issued assessments on C, charging substantial amounts of income tax. HMRC applied to the Family Division for transcripts of certain documents relating to the date on which C ceased to be resident in the UK. Coleridge J rejected the application, applying the principles laid down by Wilson J in *S v S (No 2)*, **49.88** above. The subsequent decision in *A v A*, **49.90** below, was distinguished on the grounds that in that case there had been 'a clear finding by the court of tax evasion', whereas in the present case there was 'no suggestion that the husband is guilty of tax evasion or criminal conduct'. *HMRC v Charman*, Fam D [2012] EWHC 1448 (Fam); [2012] STC 2076.

Family Division proceedings—disclosure of details to Revenue

[49.90] Two women took divorce proceedings against their husbands, who were in business together. The women ascertained that their husbands, who were the beneficial owners of several companies, had attempted to conceal substantial assets and income. They obtained *Mareva* injunctions, following which the husbands lodged affidavits admitting that they had failed to declare their true tax liabilities to the Revenue. Charles J held, *inter alia*, that if the husbands 'had not volunteered full information to the Revenue', the court could not have ignored 'the clear and explicit nature of the material' indicating that there had been 'evasion or non-payment of tax', and that he would have ordered that the affidavits and a copy of his judgment should be sent to the Revenue. *A v A; B v B*, Fam D [2000] 1 FLR 701; [2000] All ER (D) 109. (*Note*. Under the *Civil Procedure Rules 1998 (SI 1998/3132)*, which largely took effect from 26 April 1999, '*Mareva*' injunctions are now referred to as 'freezing injunctions'.)

Civil Procedure Rules—disclosure of details to HMRC

[49.91] A company (SU) purchased a shareholding in another company (E). Subsequently it formed the opinion that the vendors had provided false information about E's financial position, and that E had made substantial cash payments and had significant tax liabilities which had not been disclosed. SU took proceedings against the vendors, and obtained orders requiring the seizure of certain documents, under terms whereby SU agreed not to disclose the contents of the documents. HMRC subsequently began an investigation into E's affairs. SU applied to the QB, under *Civil Procedure Rules (SI 1998/3132), rule 32.11*, for an order permitting it to disclose documents and information to HMRC. The QB granted the application. *Sita UK Group Holdings Ltd & Another v Serruys & Others*, QB [2009] STC 1595; [2009] EWHC 869 (QB).

*Validity of notice under ICTA 1988, s 745**

[49.92] See *Royal Bank of Canada v CIR*, 3.72 ANTI-AVOIDANCE, and *Clinch v CIR*, 3.73 ANTI-AVOIDANCE.

*Validity of notice under ICTA 1988, s 778**

[49.93] See *Essex v CIR*, 3.79 ANTI-AVOIDANCE.

Validity of notice under FA 2003, Sch 10

[49.94] See *Coolatinney Developments Ltd v HMRC*, 75.9 STAMP DUTY LAND TAX.

Form R40—whether a 'return'

[49.95] See *Osborne v Dickinson*, **5.22** ASSESSMENTS, and *Tomlinson v HMRC*, **44.12** PENALTIES.

Whether return made 'in accordance with prevailing practice'

[49.96] See *HMRC v Household Estate Agents Ltd*, **5.71** ASSESSMENTS.

FA 2008, Sch 36 para 1—power to obtain information

[49.97] HMRC issued a notice under *FA 2008, Sch 36 para 1* to an individual (W) who had sold a substantial shareholding in a public company, and had claimed that he was not resident in the UK. W appealed, contending that the notice was onerous and unreasonable. The First-Tier Tribunal rejected this contention and dismissed the appeal. Judge Shipwright observed that 'HMRC has the right to check the position and in particular to see original documents'. He held that W 'has not shown as a matter of fact that the information or documents are not reasonably required by the officer for the purpose of checking the taxpayer's tax position'. He also held that 'the request is not disproportionate or onerous in the particular circumstances of the case'. *P Whight v HMRC*, FTT [2011] UKFTT 60 (TC), TC00938.

[49.98] The First-Tier Tribunal also upheld the validity of notices under *FA 2008, Sch 36 para 1* in *J Oduntan v HMRC*, FTT [2011] UKFTT 54 (TC), TC00932; *D Midgley & Sons Ltd v HMRC (and related appeal)*, FTT [2011] UKFTT 187 (TC), TC01056; *WY Chan v HMRC (No 2)*, FTT [2011] UKFTT 462 (TC), TC01312; *WY & SY Lam v HMRC (No 1)*, FTT [2012] UKFTT 118 (TC), TC01813; *K D'Souza v HMRC*, FTT [2012] UKFTT 210 (TC), TC01905; *Mrs P Lee v HMRC (No 1)*, FTT [2012] UKFTT 312 (TC), TC01998; *BN Alkadhi v HMRC*, FTT [2012] UKFTT 741 (TC), TC02401; *Mrs E Thompson v HMRC*, FTT [2013] UKFTT 103 (TC), TC02521; *M Jarvis v HMRC*, FTT [2013] UKFTT 132 (TC), TC02561; *NJ Cowan v HMRC*, FTT [2013] UKFTT 604 (TC), TC02991; *HA & K Patel v HMRC*, FTT [2014] UKFTT 167 (TC), TC03305; *Whitefields Golf Club v HMRC (and related appeals)*, FTT [2014] UKFTT 458 (TC), TC03585; *C Jordan v HMRC*, FTT [2014] UKFTT 895 (TC), TC04010; *K Mawji v HMRC*, FTT [2014] UKFTT 899 (TC), TC04014; *Spring Capital Ltd v HMRC (No 2)*, FTT [2015] UKFTT 0008 (TC), TC04220; *Nijjar Dairies Ltd v HMRC*, **5.73** ASSESSMENTS; *Serpol Ltd v HMRC (No 2)*, **42.13** PAY AS YOU EARN, and *Carden & Carden v HMRC*, **44.371** PENALTIES.

[49.99] HMRC began an enquiry into an individual (S), who worked as a taxi driver and received income from renting properties. During the enquiry, they issued a notice under *FA 2008, Sch 36 para 1*, requesting details of the source of various payments into his wife's bank and building society accounts. He appealed, contending that some of the payments were gifts or loans from friends and relatives. The First-tier Tribunal upheld the notice in principle, holding that it was reasonable for HMRC to request the names and full postal addresses of the people whom S claimed had made the relevant payments. However the Tribunal also held that S should not be required to explain 'the nature of his stated friendship or his exact familial relationship' with the people in question. *S Singh v HMRC*, FTT [2013] UKFTT 171 (TC), TC02586. (*Note.* At a subsequent hearing, the Tribunal dismissed S's appeal against penalties imposed for failing to comply with the notice—[2014] UKFTT 299 (TC), TC03436.)

[49.100] HMRC began an enquiry into a trader's 2009/10 tax return. In January 2013 they issued a notice under *FA 2008, Sch 36 para 1*. The First-tier Tribunal upheld the notice in principle but extended the deadline for compliance from 28 February 2013 to 19 July 2013. *M Deegan v HMRC*, FTT [2013] UKFTT 338 (TC), TC02741.

[49.101] A company director (B) submitted a tax return claiming not to be resident or ordinarily resident in the UK after March 2008. HMRC sought further information from B, and subsequently issued a notice under *FA 2008, Sch 36 para 1* seeking the production of bank, building society and credit card statements. B appealed. The First-tier Tribunal allowed his appeal, finding that the requirements of *FA 2008, Sch 36 para 21* had not been satisfied. Judge Perez held that HMRC had not given a formal notice of enquiry under *para 21(4)*, and that, although B had drawn a substantial dividend during 2008/09, there was no reason to suspect that 'an amount that ought to have been assessed to relevant tax for the chargeable period' had not been assessed, under *para 21(6)*. *K Betts v HMRC*, FTT [2013] UKFTT 430 (TC), TC02824.

[49.102] HMRC issued a notice under *FA 2008, Sch 36 para 1* to an individual (B). B appealed, contending that some of the documents which HMRC had sought were subject to legal professional privilege, within *Privileged Communications Regulations 2009 (SI 2009/1916)*. The First-tier Tribunal allowed his appeal in part. Judge Mosedale held that a report relating to 'trust arrangements', prepared by a firm of solicitors, was subject to privilege, as was part of an engagement letter from the solicitors. *EC Behague v HMRC (No 1)*, FTT [2013] UKFTT 596 (TC), TC02983. (*Note.* A subsequent appeal was dismissed—FTT [2013] UKFTT 647 (TC), TC03031.)

[49.103] HMRC issued a notice under *FA 2008, Sch 36 para 1* to an employee (L). L appealed, contending that certain correspondence between his solicitor and his employers was subject to 'litigation privilege' (as distinguished from 'legal advice privilege': see the judgment of Lord Rodger of Earlsferry in *Three Rivers District Council v Governor & Company of the Bank of England (No 6)*, HL [2004] UKHL 48). The First-tier Tribunal rejected this contention and upheld the notice. Judge Sinfield observed that 'litigation privilege does not protect documents created for the purpose of settling litigation and provided to the other party'. *M Lewis v HMRC*, FTT [2013] UKFTT 722 (TC), TC03012.

[49.104] HMRC began an enquiry into a return submitted by a doctor (L) who provided cosmetic treatments. They issued a notice under *FA 2008, Sch 36 para 1*, requiring L to produce her business appointments diary. L appealed, contending that this diary provided no financial information, but contained confidential clinical information about her clients. The First-tier Tribunal accepted L's evidence and allowed her appeal. Judge Reid held that the diary was not 'reasonably required in order to check the taxpayer's position', since it was 'not necessarily an accurate record of patients seen and services provided or charged for' and there was 'no way of correlating the numbers of patients with the turnover generated'. *Dr K Long v HMRC*, FTT [2014] UKFTT 199 (TC), TC03339.

[49.105] HMRC began an enquiry into a return submitted by a company (R). They issued a notice under *FA 2008, Sch 36 para 1*, requiring two documents and two items of additional information. R produced the documents but appealed against the requirement to provide additional information, contending that the notice was 'defective in asking for subjective information, which was not lawfully required to be provided'. The First-tier Tribunal accepted this contention and allowed the appeal. Judge McKenna held that 'information notices should be expressed in clear terms' and that 'it should be a straightforward matter for both parties to know whether an information notice has been complied with. That is why HMRC guidance states that the information notice should request facts and not opinion. In this case, the built-in assumptions on which the requests for information were based made it impossible for the parties to know whether the notice had been complied with because the accuracy of the assumptions was disputed'. *RD Utilities Ltd v HMRC*, FTT [2014] UKFTT 303 (TC), TC03440.

FA 2008, Sch 36 para 3—approval of third party notices

[49.106] The Australian Taxation Office made a request to HMRC for assistance in accordance with the exchange of information procedure under *Article 27* of the Double Taxation Agreement between the UK and Australia. HMRC applied to the First-tier Tribunal, under *FA 2008, Sch 36 para 3*, for approval of the issue of certain third party notices under *FA 2008, Sch 36 para 2(2)*. The First-tier Tribunal approved the notices. Judge Berner held that the effect of *FA 2006, s 173(8)* was that Australian tax was 'relevant foreign tax' within *FA 2008, Sch 36 para 63*. Furthermore, the issue of the notices did not contravene the *European Convention on Human Rights*, since a taxpayer who was aggrieved by a notice under *Sch 36* could apply for judicial review. *Application by HMRC (re Certain Taxpayers)*, FTT [2012] UKFTT 765 (TC), TC02424.

[49.107] Following the decision noted at **49.106** above, 24 of the companies which had appealed to the First-tier Tribunal applied for judicial review. The QB dismissed the applications. Simler J held that that the courts should 'be careful to avoid giving by the avenue of judicial review what is, in reality, an appeal against the tribunal's decision. It is only exceptionally or for clearly identifiable reasons that the court will interfere to set aside a notice.' She also held that the issue of the notices did not contravene the *European Convention on Human Rights. R (oao Derrin Brother Properties Ltd) v HMRC (and related applications)*, QB [2014] EWHC 1152 (Admin); [2014] STC 2238.

[49.108] The First-tier Tribunal approved the issue of notices under *FA 2008, Sch 36 para 3*, relating to more than 300 participants in tax avoidance schemes. (For one of the schemes in question, see *E Flanagan v HMRC*, **59.100** TRADING INCOME.) Three of the participants applied to the First-tier Tribunal for the decisions to be set aside, contending that there had been a procedural irregularity in that HMRC's applications had been dealt with on an 'ex parte' basis. The First-tier Tribunal dismissed the applications and upheld the issue of the notices. Judge Cannan observed that the applicants had been made aware that HMRC were intending to apply for the notices, and had been given the opportunity to make representations. He held that, 'if the applicants have reason to believe that there was no justification for the notices to be approved, so that *paragraph 3(3)(b)* was not satisfied, then their means of challenge would be through judicial review rather than an appeal'. The hearing at which the notices were approved had complied with *Tribunal Procedure (First-tier Tribunal) (Tax Chamber) Rules (SI 2009/273), rule 19*, and there had been no procedural impropriety. *Dr AM Skelly v HMRC (and related applications)*, FTT [2014] UKFTT 478 (TC), TC03605.

[49.109] In hearing an ex parte application by HMRC for the issue of a notice under *FA 2008, Sch 36 para 3*, Judge Berner gave specific guidance as to the application of *Sch 36 para 3(4)*. He observed that 'an example of a case where an application under *para 3(4)* might be made is where the reasons for HMRC wishing to obtain information and/or documents include reasons arising from intelligence obtained by HMRC by virtue of the *Proceeds of Crime Act 2002*. Under that Act, certain bodies, including banks, solicitors and accountants, are required to make "suspicious activity reports" in certain circumstances. HMRC may have access to such materials subject to the information being treated in such a manner that the content of the suspicious activity reports and the identity of those who have made them is protected.' He concluded that 'in considering an application for such a dispensation under *para 3(4)*, the tribunal will have regard to the question of prejudice to the whole system of the administration and collection of tax. That system recognises, by statute, the value of whistle-blowing in certain areas, including tax evasion. Any requirement for reports to be made of suspicious activity carries with it a need for confidentiality, both for the protection of the reporter and to prevent "tipping off".' *HMRC v A Taxpayer*, FTT [2014] UKFTT 931 (TC), TC04044.

FA 2008, Sch 36 para 5—power to obtain information

[49.110] HMRC applied to the First-Tier Tribunal, under *FA 2008, Sch 36 para 5*, for the approval of notices requiring 308 financial institutions to give details of customers with UK addresses and offshore accounts. The tribunal granted the applications, observing that *Article 58* of the *EC Treaty* authorised Member States 'to take all requisite measures to prevent infringements of national law and regulations, in particular in the field of taxation'. The tribunal held that the notices were 'requisite measures', and that the documents were reasonably required 'for the purpose of checking the UK tax position of a class of taxpayers whose individual identities are not known'. *HMRC v Financial Institution (and related applications)*, FTT [2009] SFTD 780; [2009] UKFTT 224 (TC), TC00174.

[49.111] HMRC applied to the First-Tier Tribunal, under *FA 2008, Sch 36 para 5*, for the approval of a notice requiring a financial institution to give details of 89 customers with offshore accounts. The tribunal granted the application, finding that 'of the persons with foreign bank accounts for which

HMRC have previously obtained information from other financial institutions the number making notifications under the offshore disclosure facility or otherwise being investigated that resulted or are expected to result in a tax loss was 20% of cases'. *HMRC v Financial Institution No 9*, FTT [2009] UKFTT 195 (TC), TC00148.

[49.112] A similar decision was reached in *HMRC v Financial Institution No 10*, FTT [2009] UKFTT 196 (TC), TC00149.

[49.113] See also *Backhouse v HMRC*, **44.377** PENALTIES.

Box 23.5 of return—information to be included

[49.114] In the case noted at **46.16** PENSION SCHEMES, the Special Commissioner held that 'in completing a self-assessment tax return, a taxpayer must be at liberty to state circumstances which may or may not have given rise to a liability to tax and, at the same time or in the next breath, deny that tax is or was due. The whole point of self-assessment is that one discloses the circumstances in which one is, or might be, liable for tax, and specifies one's view of the resultant liability, which may be non-existent or nil.' He also held that 'the Revenue were entitled to repair the contents of the return to produce the conclusion as to the tax due contained in the closure notice'. *Moffat v HMRC*, Sp C, [2006] SSCD 380 (Sp C 538).

50

Revenue Administration

The cases in this chapter are arranged under the following headings.

CROSS-REFERENCES

See also 49 RETURNS AND INFORMATION.

Estoppel

Whether estoppel may be claimed against Revenue

[50.1] For the purpose of excess profits duty, a distinction was drawn between assets held as capital employed in a company's business, and assets held as investments. A company which needed to invest to finance rebuilding purchased a large number of government securities. The Inland Revenue had advertised in public notices that these securities were capable of being regarded as capital employed in business. Nevertheless, the Revenue issued EPD assessments on the basis that, in the circumstances of the case, these particular securities were being held as investments. The KB dismissed the company's appeal. Rowlatt J held that 'the Commissioners of Inland Revenue have no power to bind the Crown by a general declaration of what the law is in particular circumstances beforehand'. *Liberty & Co Ltd v CIR*, KB 1924, 12 TC 630.

[50.2] In the case noted at 20.21 DEDUCTION OF TAX, an Inland Revenue officer had told the trustees of a settlement that no income tax would be claimed on sums paid to a beneficiary. An inspector who reviewed the case later realised that there was a tax liability and issued assessments accordingly. The KB dismissed the trustees' appeal. Finlay J held that the doctrine of estoppel could not be invoked to prevent a claim for tax which was lawfully due, and that incorrect representations by officials could not bind the Crown. *Brodie's Trustees v CIR*, KB 1933, 17 TC 432.

[50.3] An individual (R) claimed a deduction for travelling expenses. The Revenue rejected the claim and he appealed, contending that he had previously telephoned a Revenue office and had been told that the expenses would be allowable. The General Commissioners dismissed his appeal, finding that there was no record of the alleged telephone conversation and that R had not produced any evidence to corroborate his case. The Ch D upheld the Commissioners' decision, applying the principles laid down by Bingham LJ in *R v CIR (ex p. MFK Underwriting Agencies Ltd & Others)*, **50.32** below. Pelling J also held that any question of 'legitimate expectation' should be dealt with by judicial review, rather than by the statutory appeal procedure. *Refson v HMRC*, Ch D 2008, [2009] STC 64; [2008] EWHC 1759 (Ch).

[50.4] For another case concerning an alleged telephone conversation, see *R v CIR (ex p. J Rothschild Holdings plc) (No 2)*, **50.29** below. For other cases concerning the principle of estoppel, see *Caffoor & Others (Abdul Gaffoor Trustees) v Colombo Income Tax Commr*, **4.77** APPEALS; *Murphy v Elders*, **4.82** APPEALS; *Bolands Ltd v CIR*, **4.233** APPEALS; *Lonsdale v Braisby*, **4.234** APPEALS; *Bye v Coren*, **5.10** ASSESSMENTS; *CIR v Fry*, **43.18** PAYMENT OF TAX, and *JH Clarke & Co Ltd v Musker*, **63.261** TRADING PROFITS.

Confidentiality of information

General principles

[50.5] The CS held that a public department cannot be compelled by a court of law to produce confidential documents in its possession coming from third parties, if the effect would be to discourage similar communications being made in future. *Brown's Trustees v Hay*, CS 1897, 3 TC 598.

[50.6] In a case concerning *Companies Act 1862, s 115* (which gave the Court discretionary power to order the production of documents during a winding-up), the liquidator of a company applied for copies of some balance sheets which had been sent to the Revenue. The Ch D rejected the application. Wright J observed that tax returns may contain confidential matters, and that 'it may be of the utmost importance to the public service that persons should be able to be certain that returns made by them for those purposes should in no case be disclosed'. It was 'a matter of public concern that persons should have confidence in the secrecy of that procedure'. The CA unanimously upheld this decision. *In re Joseph Hargreaves Ltd*, CA 1900, 4 TC 173; [1900] 1 Ch 347.

[50.7] In a case relating to legislation which is now obsolete, an appellant (S) sought production of confidential reports on his affairs made to the Board of Inland Revenue by their officers. The Commissioners accepted claims of Crown privilege, supported by an affidavit on behalf of the Board that the reports should be kept secret in the interests of the efficient administration of the collection of taxes. S appealed, contending that the Commissioners should be asked to reconsider their findings, on the ground that the claim of privilege had not been considered by a Minister. The CA rejected this contention and dismissed his appeal. *Soul v Irving & Another*, CA 1963, 41 TC 517.

[50.8] In a case where a former police officer had sued a police superintendent, claiming damages for malicious prosecution, the Home Secretary rejected a request to disclose certain documents, considering that they should remain confidential. The case was referred to the HL, which held that the documents should be produced for inspection, distinguishing *In re Joseph Hargreaves Ltd*, **50.6** above. Lord Reid observed that 'if the State insists on a man disclosing his private affairs for a particular purpose, it requires a strong case to justify that disclosure being used for other purposes'. *Conway v Rimmer & Another, HL*[1968] 1 All ER 874.

[50.9] In a case concerning the infringement of patent rights, the holders of the rights applied for discovery of certain documents held by Customs, relating to goods which had been imported in breach of the patents. The HL granted the application. Lord Reid held that where someone 'through no fault of his own gets mixed up in the tortious acts of others so as to facilitate their wrong-doing, he may incur no personal liability, but he comes under a duty to assist the person who has been wronged by giving him full information and disclosing the identity of the wrongdoers'. *Norwich Pharmacal Co v C & E Commrs, HL 1973*, [1974] AC 133; [1973] 2 All ER 943.

[50.10] At the request of Tynwald (the representative assembly of the Isle of Man), the Governor of the Isle of Man established a Commission of Inquiry to investigate a decision taken by a Manx Planning Committee, authorising the development of an area of land. The Commission of Inquiry asked the Assessor of Income Tax to produce certain files relating to three associated companies involved in the development. The companies applied for an order restraining the Commission from examining the material, contending that the disclosure of the files would breach their right to confidentiality. The Isle of Man High Court rejected the companies' claims and held that the Commission was entitled to retain and examine the material which it had requested. The Privy Council dismissed the companies' appeals. Lord Walker of Gestingthorpe held that it would be wrong 'to impose any conditions on the use which the Commission makes of material disclosed to it. The Commission will of course respect the confidentiality of documents produced to it so far as is consistent with its public duty to report.' *Mount Murray Country Club Ltd & Others v Macleod & Others*, PC 2003, 75 TC 197; [2003] STC 1525.

[50.11] A company director, who had been involved in a number of insolvent companies, was convicted of three offences of cheating the public revenue, and sentenced to 18 months' imprisonment. He appealed against his conviction, contending that the Official Receiver should not have passed certain information to the Inland Revenue. The CA rejected this contention and dismissed his appeal. Tuckey LJ held that, where the Official Receiver was satisfied that relevant material was 'required by another prosecuting authority for the purpose of investigating crime, it should be free to disclose it without an order of the court or notice to the person who provided it. It is self-evidently in the public interest that the appropriate prosecuting authority should have such material to aid its investigation'. Accordingly the disclosure of the information was lawful, and there had been no abuse of power. *R v Brady, CA Crim Div*, [2004] All ER (D) 234 (Jun).

[50.12] A barrister requested details of legal advice which HMRC had obtained in relation to proposed legislation which was subsequently enacted in *FA 2006*. HMRC rejected the request on the grounds that the information was subject to legal professional privilege, within *Freedom of Information Act 2000, s 42(1)*. The Information Commissioner upheld the Revenue's ruling, and the barrister appealed to the Information Tribunal. The Tribunal unanimously dismissed his appeal, holding that 'the public interest in maintaining the exemption outweighs the public interest in favour of disclosure'. *Kessler v Information Commissioner; Kessler v HMRC*, Information Tribunal EA 2007/0043; 29 November 2007 unreported.

[50.13] A UK company sold a 'telebetting' business to an associated Gibraltar company. HMRC assessed the shareholders on the basis that there had been a transfer of assets abroad, within what is now *ITA 2007, ss 714–751*. The shareholders appealed, and applied for disclosure of various documents held by HMRC. The First-tier Tribunal rejected the application with regard to the majority of the documents in issue, but allowed the application with regard to correspondence and notes of meetings with the Betting Office Licensees Association. Judge Mosedale observed that the shareholders were engaged in 'a fishing exercise to catch fish that are most unlikely to be of any interest to the tribunal hearing the substantive appeal'. (The tribunal also rejected an application by HMRC that the shareholders should disclose notes of a conference with a well-known QC, holding that the notes were privileged.) *PAD Fisher v HMRC (and related appeals)*, FTT [2012] UKFTT 335 (TC), TC02021.

[50.14] See also *R v CIR (ex p. J Rothschild Holdings plc)*, **4.330** APPEALS, and *R v CIR (ex p. Taylor)*, **49.31** RETURNS AND INFORMATION.

Alleged breach of confidentiality by senior HMRC official

[50.15] In 2012 a senior HMRC official (H) held a meeting with two journalists, in which H alleged that a company (IM) and its chief executive (PM) were promoting tax avoidance schemes. IM and PM were subsequently named in a national newspaper. They applied for judicial review, contending that the disclosures which H had made were unlawful and were a breach of confidentiality. The QB dismissed their applications. Sales J held that 'there was a rational connection between the function of HMRC to collect tax in an efficient and cost-effective way and the disclosures made by (H) in the course of the briefing, and his decision to make the limited revelations that he did was based on a judgment which fell well within the lawful parameters' of *CRCA 2005, s 18(2)(b)*. Sales J also held that 'the attitude of disapproval and scepticism which HMRC adopted in relation to use of film investment schemes, and the decision to seek to inform the public about that attitude in order to influence their behaviour, fell well within the wide margin of appreciation applicable to decisions of state authorities in the field of tax policy'. *R (oao Ingenious Media Holdings plc) v HMRC (and related application)*, QB [2013] EWHC 3258 (Admin); [2014] STC 673.

Admissibility in appeals of information relating to other taxpayers

[50.16] See *Gamini Bus Co Ltd v Colombo Income Tax Commr*, **4.42** APPEALS.

[50.17] In the case noted at 6.32 BANKRUPTCY AND PERSONAL INSOLVENCY, a building contractor sought the disclosure of a Revenue file relating to another taxpayer. The Ch D rejected his application. *Woodward v CIR*, Ch D 2001, TL 3641.

Application for disclosure of copies of tax returns

[50.18] In a civil case, the CS refused to order the production of income tax returns, on the grounds of confidentiality and public interest. *Shaw v Kay*, CS 1904, 5 TC 74.

[50.19] A public company (L) began legal proceedings against some individuals, contending that they had deliberately and fraudulently misrepresented their financial position. L sought an order for disclosure of a number of documents, including copies of the defendants' tax returns. The QB granted the order sought, and the CA dismissed the defendants' appeal against this decision. Sir Thomas Bingham MR observed that documents in the hands of the Revenue were normally prevented from disclosure. However, public interest immunity did not necessarily apply to documents which were in the possession of a taxpayer, rather than of the Revenue. Furthermore, the principle of confidentiality of documents could be overridden by the public interest in the administration of justice, applying the principles laid down in *Conway v Rimmer*, 50.8 above, and distinguishing *Joseph Hargreaves Ltd*, 50.6 above, and *H v H*, 50.20 below. *Lonrho plc v Fayed & Others (No 4)*, CA 1993, 66 TC 220; [1994] STC 153; [1994] 2 WLR 209; [1994] 1 All ER 870.

Family proceedings—disclosure of documents

[50.20] A woman applied for financial provision against her husband, and applied for an order requiring the Capital Taxes Office to produce estate duty affidavits relating to her husband's late grandfather. Balcombe J rejected her application, applying the principles laid down in *Joseph Hargreaves Ltd*, 50.6 above, and *Conway v Rimmer*, 50.8 above, and observing that 'people who file an Inland Revenue affidavit on the occasion of a death, because they are by statute compelled to do so, should be entitled to assume that the information contained in that document should not go further than the Inland Revenue'. *H v H*, Fam D 1980, 52 TC 454.

[50.21] In a case concerning a woman's application for ancillary relief against her ex-husband (R), the judge (Wilson J) found that R had not disclosed all his income to the Revenue. Subsequently the Revenue issued assessments on R, and R applied to the court for a reduction of the payments which he had been ordered to make to his ex-wife. Wilson J ordered the Revenue to produce all correspondence between the ex-wife and the Revenue concerning R's financial affairs. The Revenue applied to have the order set aside on the grounds of confidentiality, and R applied for a further order that the Revenue should deliver any copies which it held of the judgment made in the course of his ex-wife's application for ancillary relief. Wilson J dismissed both applications. On the evidence, it appeared that somebody had irregularly disclosed to the Revenue part of a transcript of a judgment delivered in chambers. There was a *prima facie* case that R's ex-wife, or her accountant, had caused the judgment to be sent to the Revenue. Accordingly, it was desirable 'to see what else, if anything, has been said to the Revenue by the wife about the husband's affairs'. With regard to R's application, the finding that he had underdeclared his income was based on substantial evidence. It was in the public interest that all tax due should be paid, and that action should be taken against evaders of tax. Accordingly, an order should be made specifically regularising the Revenue's possession of the relevant pages of the judgment. The decision in *S v S*, **49.88** RETURNS AND INFORMATION, was distinguished on the basis that, in that case, the finding that the husband had evaded tax was 'a finding of a most general character', based on inference rather than on detailed evidence. *R v R*, Fam D 1997, 70 TC 119; [1998] STC 237; [1998] 1 FLR 922.

Revenue refusing to disclose identity of informant

[50.22] The Revenue received information concerning an individual (D), who had received bank interest which had not been declared on his returns. The nature of this information was disclosed in questions put to D, but the identity of the informant was not disclosed. D complained to the Revenue Adjudicator's Office about the use of the information. The Adjudicator rejected the complaint, finding that the Revenue had considered the information carefully, had used it with caution, and had not accepted it without testing its credibility. D applied for judicial review, but the QB rejected the application. Turner J observed that there was a very strong public interest in enabling a citizen, who was aware or suspected that another person was evading his tax liabilities, to supply that information to the Revenue in confidence. If it became known that the identity of an informant might be disclosed without his consent, it was likely that sources of information, which were vital for the proper policing of tax liabilities, would disappear. There was 'nothing to indicate that the adjudicator treated the informant's allegations as factual' and nothing unreasonable 'in the withholding of the identity of the informer by the adjudicator from the appellant'. *R v Revenue Adjudicator's Office (ex p. Drummond)*, QB 1996, 70 TC 235; [1996] STC 1312.

Applications for judicial review

Cases where the application was unsuccessful

Tax amnesty

[50.23] In 1978 the Revenue offered an amnesty, on certain conditions, to casual workers in the newspaper industry who had been evading tax by using fictitious names. A federation of small businessmen applied for a declaration that the amnesty was unlawful. The HL held that the federation did not have a sufficient interest in the matter to support the application. The action taken by the Revenue had been 'genuinely in the care and management of the taxes, under the powers entrusted to them'. *R v CIR (ex p. National Federation of*

Self-Employed and Small Businesses Ltd), HL 1981, 55 TC 133; [1981] STC 260; [1981] 2 WLR 722; [1981] 2 All ER 93.

HMRC accused of unduly lenient settlement with large company

[50.24] In the case noted at **73.73** NATIONAL INSURANCE CONTRIBUTIONS, HMRC issued a ruling to a company (GSI) that the exercise of certain options to employees gave rise to a liability to national insurance contributions. GSI appealed, contending that the staff were supplied by an associated company (GSL), and applied for a preliminary hearing to determine whether it could be treated as the employer of the employees who had exercised the options (see **4.18** APPEALS). The First-Tier Tribunal held a preliminary hearing, reviewed the evidence in detail, and determined the preliminary issue in favour of HMRC, finding that GSL 'did not have a place of business in Great Britain at any time relevant to these appeals', and holding that GSL was a 'foreign employer' within *Social Security (Categorisation of Earners) Regulations 1978 (SI 1978/1689), r 1(2)*, with the result that GSI was the 'host employer' within *SI 1978/1689, Sch 3 para 9*, and was the 'secondary contributor' for the purposes of *SSCBA 1992, s 7*. GSI appealed to the Upper Tribunal, but the appeal was subsequently settled by an agreement which was strongly criticised by the House of Commons Public Accounts Committee for waiving the interest which was legally chargeable on the unpaid tax. Another company (UKU) applied to the QB for judicial review of the agreement between HMRC and GSI, contending that the settlement breached HMRC's duty of fairness to the general body of taxpayers. The QB dismissed the application. Nicol J observed that, although UKU had criticised the written evidence given by a senior Commissioner of HMRC, it had not applied to cross-examine him. Applying the principles laid down by Stanley Burnton J in *R (oao S) v Airedale NHS Trust*, QB [2002] EWHC 1780 (Admin), 'it is a convention of our litigation that in general the evidence of a witness is accepted unless he is cross-examined and is thus given the opportunity to rebut the allegations made against him'. On the evidence, Nicol J found that 'the settlement with (GS) was not a glorious episode in the history of the Revenue. The HMRC officials who negotiated it had not been briefed by the lawyers who were litigating against (GS). They relied on their belief or recollection that there was a barrier to the recovery of interest on the unpaid NICs. That was erroneous. HMRC now accepts that there was no such barrier.' However, 'maladministration and illegality are separate issues', and the settlement had not been unlawful. *R (oao UK Uncut Legal Action Ltd) v HMRC*, QB [2013] EWHC 1283 (Admin); [2013] STC 2357.

Revenue action under ITA 2007, s 684*

[50.25] An accountant (P) made certain claims for tax relief. In 1978 an inspector from the Revenue Special Investigation Section discussed his returns with him, and he withdrew the claims. The inspector wrote recording the withdrawal and saying that he did 'not intend to raise any further enquiries on your tax affairs'. In 1979 the Revenue raided his employers' offices (see *R v CIR, ex p. Rossminster Ltd*, **49.63** RETURNS AND INFORMATION), and subsequently obtained information (not from P) that he had purchased and sold shares in two companies in the course of avoidance schemes, and that the sale price in respect of one of the companies had been arrived at on an asset basis with no provision for tax on the company's profits. In 1982 the Revenue notified P, under *ITA 2007, s 695**, that they had reason to believe that *s 684** applied to his transactions in these shares. P then applied for an order prohibiting the Revenue from taking further action. The CA rejected the application and the HL unanimously dismissed P's appeal. Lord Templeman held that it would be improper 'for the Commissioners to absolve a taxpayer from a tax liability of which the Commissioners were unaware'. The information which P had given in 1978 'was woefully inadequate', and the Revenue had been entitled to raise further assessments. *R v CIR (ex p. Preston)*, HL 1985, 59 TC 1; [1985] STC 282; [1985] 2 WLR 836; [1985] 2 All ER 327.

'Forward tax agreement' with non-domiciled taxpayer

[50.26] A wealthy businessman (F) was resident in the UK, and the Revenue accepted that he was not domiciled in the UK. He was therefore chargeable to UK income tax on his overseas income on the remittance basis, so that it was to his advantage to ensure that he remitted capital, rather than income, to the UK. He had substantial amounts of capital overseas, mostly in Switzerland. In 1990 the Revenue made a 'forward tax agreement' with him and his two brothers that they should pay £200,000 per annum for 1991/92 to 1996/97 inclusive 'in full and final settlement' of their UK income tax and CGT liability. In 1997 the Revenue reached a similar agreement for payment of £240,000 p.a. for 1997/98 to 2002/03 inclusive. However, in 2000 the Revenue wrote to F's solicitors stating that they were not willing to continue the agreement for 2000/01 and subsequent years, and would require F to complete tax returns for 2000/01 onwards. F applied for judicial review of the Revenue's decision to resile from the 1997 agreement. The CS dismissed the application. Lord Cullen held that it was unlawful for the Revenue 'to make a concession where it would be in conflict with their statutory duty'. The Revenue 'had no power to enter into a forward tax agreement'. The 1997 agreement had been *ultra vires*, and the Revenue 'did not have any discretion to continue to abide by the agreement once they knew that it was *ultra vires*'. In revoking the agreement, the Revenue 'were pursuing a legitimate aim, namely to apply the tax system fairly between taxpayers. A fair balance was struck between the interests of the community and the protection of the petitioners' rights. Such interference as there was, was justified and was not therefore disproportionate'. *Fayed & Others v Advocate-General for Scotland and CIR*, CS 2004, 77 TC 273; [2004] STC 1703. (*Note*. For a separate application for judicial review made by the same applicant, see 50.27 below.)

Revenue investigation

[50.27] In the case noted at 50.26 above, the Revenue Special Compliance Office wrote to F's accountants in June 2000, stating that they wished to conduct a 'detailed examination' of the tax returns of F and his two brothers, and various companies with which he was concerned. F applied for judicial review, contending that the proposed investigation was unreasonable. The CS rejected this contention and dismissed the application. Lord Reed held that 'the ability of the Revenue to carry out effective investigation of suspected tax evasion or tax avoidance is a matter of public importance' and that 'effective investigation of tax avoidance is essential in the public interest and to ensure fairness as between taxpayers'. He observed that F 'works as a director of major companies but does not appear to be paid a salary. He lives in expensive accommodation, but he does not appear to own or rent it'. It appeared that private aircraft, domestic staff and 'other trappings of wealth' were 'provided by a variety of companies, most of which are located offshore, in such jurisdictions as Liechtenstein and Jersey'. The natural inference from the evidence was that 'a great deal of effort and ingenuity has gone into creating networks of offshore companies, trusts and other entities in order to minimise liability to tax. In the face of such opaque and sophisticated arrangements, it is important that the Revenue should be able to ensure that UK tax liabilities are accurately assessed and accounted for. The ordinary taxpayer is entitled to expect that the Revenue will exercise its powers when necessary to obtain any information which it reasonably requires for that purpose.' On the evidence, 'the decision to investigate was taken fairly and in good faith for the purpose of fulfilling the Revenue's statutory responsibility for the collection of taxes, and not for any ulterior, extraneous or improper purpose'. *Fayed & Others v Advocate-General for Scotland and CIR (No 2)*, CS 11 May 2004 unreported.

Validity of assessments

[50.28] In a Hong Kong case, two companies applied for judicial review of property tax assessments. The Hong Kong courts rejected the applications, and the Privy Council dismissed the companies' appeals, holding that they should have adopted the statutory appeal procedure. Lord Jauncey of Tullichettle observed that 'where a statute lays down a comprehensive system of appeals procedure against administrative decisions, it will only be in exceptional circumstances, typically an abuse of power, that the courts will entertain an application for judicial review'. *Harley Development Inc v Hong Kong Commr of Inland Revenue*, PC [1996] STC 440; [1996] 1 WLR 727.

Revenue refusing to implement alleged concession

[50.29] In a stamp duty case, a company sought judicial review of the Revenue's refusal to implement an alleged concession. The company had claimed that certain transactions were exempt from capital duty, but the Revenue considered that the exemption was not available because the qualifying percentage of shares was not satisfied. The company alleged that a solicitor acting for it had previously telephoned the Revenue's stamp duty office and had been advised that the transactions would be exempt. The Revenue had no record of any such conversation. The Ch D rejected the company's application, holding that the company had not shown that it was entitled to the exemption. Furthermore, the solicitor could not have been given the necessary assurance by anyone authorised to deal with telephone enquiries and, in any event, the company could not rely on an answer given in a telephone conversation as founding an estoppel against the Revenue. *R v CIR (ex p. J Rothschild Holdings plc) (No 2)*, Ch D 1987, 61 TC 188; [1988] STC 645.

[50.30] A merchant bank had for many years valued its trading stock (which consisted of investments) at the lower of cost or market value. In 1986 it became a member of a group which included two stockbrokers which used the 'mark to market' basis of stock valuation, and adopted the same basis. The effect of this change was to increase its stock valuation by more than

£4,000,000. The Revenue treated this as a taxable profit. The bank applied for judicial review, contending that the increase should be treated as an adjustment to reserves rather than as a taxable profit, since a 1962 Statement of Practice had permitted a tax-free uplift in stock valuation following a change from one valid basis of valuation to another. The QB dismissed the application, holding that the Revenue's decision had been 'wholly reasonable', and the bank should have proceeded by appealing to the Commissioners, rather than by judicial review. *R v (ex p. SG Warburg & Co Ltd)*, QB 1994, 68 TC 300; [1994] STC 518.

[50.31] See also *R v Inspector of Taxes (ex p. Brumfield & Others)*, **41.36** PARTNERSHIPS.

Company allegedly misled by informal statements by Revenue officers

[50.32] Between 1986 and October 1988, there were more than 60 issues of index-linked bonds which were denominated in Canadian and US dollars. The Revenue received several enquiries from people wishing to clarify whether the indexation uplift, reflected in the sale price or redemption values of the securities, would be taxed as capital or as income. In three cases enquirers were told that they would be taxed as capital, and the Revenue proceeded accordingly. However, in several other cases the Revenue did not give an unequivocal reply until October 1988, when it issued a circular declaring that the indexation uplift was taxable as income. Five applicants (all Lloyd's underwriting syndicates or managing agents) sought judicial review of the Revenue's decision. The QB rejected the applications. Bingham LJ held that the Revenue could not be held to be bound by anything less than a clear, unambiguous and unqualified representation. In the five cases in question, the Revenue had neither promised nor indicated that it would follow a particular course and accordingly there had been no abuse of power. *R v CIR (ex p. MFK Underwriting Agencies Ltd & Others)*, QB 1989, 62 TC 607; [1989] STC 873; [1990] 1 All ER 91; [1990] 1 WLR 1545.

Withdrawal of assurance based on inadequate disclosure of information

[50.33] A company (M) sponsored a scheme which was designed to take advantage of the availability of industrial buildings allowances in designated enterprise zones. The sale price of the buildings which were the subject of the scheme was expressed to be £95 million, but the vendor of the buildings was to receive only £8 million, most of the balance being paid to a subsidiary of M. Under the scheme, 67.5% of the price payable by potential investors would be covered by loans from a merchant bank, so that the investors would make no net contribution. The loans themselves would be repaid under special 'exit arrangements', so that the investors would assume no significant risk. In July 1993 M's solicitors submitted a letter giving some details of the scheme to an inspector of taxes, who agreed that the payments would qualify for industrial buildings allowances. Subsequently the Revenue received further information concerning the scheme, and in October 1993 the Revenue Financial Institutions Division wrote to M informing it that the scheme appeared to fall within the decision in *Ensign Tankers (Leasing) Ltd v Stokes*, **8.100** CAPITAL ALLOWANCES, that the assurances made by the inspector had been wrongly given, and that it was not bound by them. M applied for judicial review. The

HL unanimously dismissed the application, holding that the information submitted by M had been 'inaccurate and misleading'. Lord Jauncey observed that 'the proposed sale by the receiver of the property for £8m was a card of critical importance in the exercise which the applicant asked the Revenue to carry out and was never placed on the table'. The Revenue were therefore entitled to withdraw the clearance. Lord Browne-Wilkinson and Lord Griffiths observed that M had been aware that the Revenue required applications for clearance to be made to its Financial Institutions Division, so that a clearance by a local inspector was not to be treated as binding. *R v CIR (ex p. Matrix Securities Ltd)*, HL 1994, 66 TC 587; [1994] STC 272; [1994] 1 WLR 334; [1994] 1 All ER 769.

Withdrawal of agreement reached by inexperienced officer

[50.34] An airline company (M) had agreed a 'flat-rate expense allowance' scheme with the Revenue. In 2004 it sought to renegotiate the allowances available under the scheme. The Revenue delegated the negotiation to an inexperienced compliance officer (S), who wrote to the company in June 2004 agreeing certain figures, backdated for six years. A substantial number of M's employees subsequently claimed refunds of tax in accordance with this agreement. The Revenue formed the opinion that the agreement was unusually generous by comparison with other companies in the same industry. In November 2004 they wrote to M, resiling from the agreement. One of M's employees (B) applied for judicial review. The QB dismissed the application. Lindsay J observed that it had been the Revenue's practice for flat-rate agreements not to be backdated beyond the current year. The agreement which S had reached 'was quite exceptional in permitting not only some retrospectivity but a retrospectivity of some six years' duration'. There was 'a public interest in the Revenue not permitting and not being seen to permit' an agreement that was 'so out of accord with its general practice'. Furthermore, the amounts granted by the agreement represented a deal that was 'of unusual generosity in comparison with similar deals made for employees of other airlines'. Accordingly there was 'a substantial public interest' in allowing the Revenue to resile from the agreement which S had reached. *R (oao Bamber) v HMRC (No 1)*, QB 2005, [2006] STC 1035; [2005] EWHC 3221 (Admin).

[50.35] The applicant in the case noted at 50.34 above subsequently submitted a claim for damages. The QB dismissed his application. Lindsay J observed that B had enjoyed the benefit of his expenditure, and reiterated that there had been 'a substantial public interest pointing towards the Commissioners being entitled to resile from the June agreement'. *R (oao Bamber) v HMRC (No 2)*, QB 2007, [2008] STC 1864; [2007] EWHC 798 (Admin).

Taxation of pension

[50.36] A former British Airways pilot, born in the UK, had retired to Jersey. The Revenue issued a ruling that his pension from BA was chargeable to UK tax. He applied for judicial review, contending that he had previously been told by the relevant tax office that UK tax would not be charged. The QB dismissed his application. Davis J held that as a matter of UK law, UK tax was deductible from the pension. The applicant had not shown that there had been any specific representation by the Revenue that his pension would not be chargeable to UK tax, and the evidence showed that the relevant tax office 'considered the case of each BA employee by reference to his or her individual circumstances'. Furthermore, the courts 'would ordinarily be slow to promote into a policy, available to the entire class of relevant taxpayer, an asserted practice which a particular branch had allowed to develop acting under a mistake or misapprehension.' The Revenue was entitled and required to assess the applicant to UK tax on his BA pension. *R (oao Esterson) v HMRC*, QB 2005, 77 TC 629; [2005] EWHC 3037 (Admin).

Application for disclosure of documents in judicial review proceedings

[50.37] See *R v CIR (ex p. Taylor)*, **49.31** RETURNS AND INFORMATION.

Revenue revoking direction that dividend payable gross

[50.38] See *R v CIR (ex p. Camacq Corporation)*, **18.90** CORPORATION TAX.

Application for judicial review of criminal prosecution

[50.39] See *R v CIR (ex p. Mead & Cook)*, **51.18** REVENUE PROSECUTIONS, and *R v CIR (ex p. Allen)*, **51.19** REVENUE PROSECUTIONS.

Revenue refusing to disclose identity of informant

[50.40] See *R v Revenue Adjudicator's Office (ex p. Drummond)*, **50.22** above.

Cases where the application was successful

Revenue resiling from established administrative procedure

[50.41] A large group of companies had regularly submitted its detailed computations, including loss claims, more than two years after the end of the relevant accounting period. The Revenue had established an administrative procedure whereby it had sent the group a non-statutory document each year seeking a provisional estimate of its likely taxable profits, and had subsequently allowed the claims to loss relief. This procedure had been followed for more than 20 years, but the Revenue rejected such claims for the periods ending in 1986 to 1988 inclusive on the grounds that they had been submitted outside the statutory time limit. Two of the companies in the group applied for judicial review, contending firstly that the documents which it had completed each year should be treated as loss relief claims, and alternatively that the Revenue's decision had been unreasonable as there had been a long-standing practice of allowing the claims even though they were submitted outside the time limits. The QB granted the application and the CA upheld this decision. The documents in question did not themselves constitute loss relief claims, applying the decision in *Gallic Leasing Ltd v Coburn*, **18.61** CORPORATION TAX. However, there had been a 'consensual procedure' which had 'operated harmoniously for years'. Sir Thomas Bingham MR held that the Revenue's rejection of the claims, 'without clear and general advance notice, (was) so unfair as to amount to an abuse of power'. The Revenue's conduct had been 'so unreasonable as to be, in public law terms, irrational'. *R v CIR (ex p. Unilever plc) (and related application)*, CA 1996, 68 TC 205; [1996] STC 681.

HMRC declining to deal with accountant suspected of fraud

[50.42] An unqualified accountant (L) was made bankrupt in 1995 and discharged from bankruptcy in 1998. He continued to practise as an accountant after his discharge, and significantly increased his client base. In 2008 HMRC wrote to him, expressing significant concerns about the accuracy of the returns which he, and a company (C) of which he was the controlling director, was submitting. In 2009 HMRC's Criminal Investigation Unit began a criminal investigation of L. They formed the conclusion that L 'had systematically committed fraud'. In June 2010 HMRC applied for, and were granted, search warrants under the *Police and Criminal Evidence Act 1984*. Later that month L and his son were arrested on suspicion of cheating the public revenue contrary to common law, false accounting and offences contrary to the *Fraud Act 2006*, and were interviewed under caution in the presence of a solicitor. They declined to answer most of the questions. In November 2010 HMRC terminated L's status as an 'authorised agent'. L and C applied for judicial review of this decision. Kenneth Parker J reviewed the evidence in detail and held that L 'should have been given the opportunity to make representations before the challenged decision was made and was communicated to it'. Although L had declined to answer questions at his meetings with HMRC in June 2010, he should have been given a further opportunity 'to set out a reasonably detailed response to the serious allegations that were being advanced'. He directed that 'the challenged decision should be quashed on account of the unlawful procedural failure, and that the matter should be remitted to the Commissioners for reconsideration in the light of the terms of this judgment'. *R (oao Lunn) v HMRC (and related application)*, QB [2011] EWHC 240 (Admin); [2011] STC 1028. (*Note*. Following this decision, HMRC initially restored L's status as an 'authorised agent', but withdrew it again on 25 July 2011: see Taxation, 28 July 2011.)

Political organisation seeking information about export controls

[50.43] An organisation (P) with political objectives was campaigning against a UK company (G) which had exported various goods to overseas governments. P requested HMRC to disclose information about its export controls. HMRC rejected the request on the grounds that this would breach its duty of confidentiality under *CRCA 2005, s 18*. P applied for judicial review. Green J granted the application, holding on the evidence that HMRC had failed to give sufficient consideration as to the way in which G's products were allegedly being used. *R (oao Privacy International) v HMRC*, QB [2014] EWHC 1475 (Admin).

Miscellaneous

Binding effect of extra-statutory agreements

[50.44] In a case which is otherwise no longer of current interest, the Ch D held that an alleged agreement between the inspector and a company as to the amounts on which the company was to be assessed for future years would, if made, be invalid and *ultra vires* as regards the inspector and the Board. *Gresham Life Assurance Co Ltd v A-G*, Ch D 1916, 7 TC 36; [1916] 1 Ch 228.

[50.45] See *CIR v Peter McIntyre Ltd*, **62.5** TRADING PROFITS, as to the authority of an extra-statutory arrangement between the Board and a professional body.

Validity of extra-statutory concessions

[50.46] In the 1979 case of *Vestey & Others v CIR* (see **3.57** ANTI-AVOIDANCE), Walton J expressed the view that 'one should be taxed by law, and not untaxed by concession'. However, in the 1987 case of *R v Inspector of Taxes (ex p. Fulford-Dobson)*, **71.135** CAPITAL GAINS TAX, McNeill J held that the Revenue's policy of issuing extra-statutory concessions were 'within the concept of good management or of administrative common sense' and 'within the proper exercise of managerial discretion'. In the 2003 case of *R (oao Wilkinson) v CIR*, **31.77** HUMAN RIGHTS, Lord Phillips MR held that 'one of the primary tasks of the Commissioners is to recover those taxes which Parliament has decreed shall be paid. (*TMA 1970, s 1*) permits the Commissioners to set about this task pragmatically and to have regard to principles of good management. Concessions can be made where those will facilitate the overall task of tax collection.' See also *FA 2008, s 160*.

Alleged misdirection by Revenue

[50.47] In the case noted at **28.20** FOREIGN INCOME, the taxpayer claimed before the General Commissioners that he had been misinformed by a Revenue officer that a pension would not be taxable, and that because of this he had decided to buy a house in the UK. The Commissioners made no findings of fact on this matter, as it was not relevant to the issue before them. In the CA he was represented by counsel, who contended that the matter should be remitted to the Commissioners to find the facts. The CA refused to do this, holding that, even if the taxpayer's claims were correct, the Commissioners could take no action on them. Whether there had been an abuse of power was a matter for which the only remedy was by way of judicial review, which was exclusively within the jurisdiction of the High Court. *Aspin v Estill*, CA 1987, 60 TC 549; [1987] STC 723.

[50.48] A self-employed radio presenter (S) claimed deductions for expenditure on clothing, cosmetics, hairdressing, and subsistence expenses. HMRC issued amendments to her returns for 2006/07 to 2008/09 disallowing the deductions. S appealed, contending that when she began self-employment in 2001, she had been informed by a HMRC officer (C) that she could claim a deduction where she spent money for the specific purpose of making public appearances, and that she could claim subsistence expenses if she was working at least five miles away from her normal place of work. The First-tier Tribunal accepted S's evidence, holding that as a matter of law, the expenditure was not deductible, applying the principles laid down in *Mallalieu v Drummond*, **63.216** TRADING PROFITS, and *Caillebotte v Quinn*, **63.209** TRADING PROFITS, but finding that S had been given incorrect advice by an HMRC officer. Judge Cannan expressed the view that he 'would expect HMRC to amend the review decision to allow (S's) claim under these headings for 2006/07'. However, by the time S came to complete her returns for 2007/08 and 2008/09, she was aware that HMRC had queried the claims which she had made for 2006/07, and she had been told by the officer conducting the enquiry that 'the wardrobe costs and subsistence expenses were not allowable for tax purposes'. Therefore S was no longer entitled to rely on the incorrect advice which C had given her. Judge Cannan observed that 'it would be unfair on taxpayers generally if (S) were able to insist on entitlement to relief where none would otherwise be available in the absence of clear unambiguous advice to the contrary'. *Ms L Stones v HMRC*, FTT [2012] UKFTT 110 (TC), TC01806. (*Note*. In a subsequent decision, the First-tier Tribunal upheld HMRC's amendments for 2007/08 and 2008/09, rejecting S's claim that she should be allowed further deductions for expenses. Judge Cannan held that 'it is now too late to challenge the amendments on a completely different basis'—[2013] UKFTT 26 (TC), TC02446.)

Whether Revenue's statutory powers discretionary or mandatory

[50.49] In a case concerning legislation in *FA 1972* which has subsequently been superseded, the substantive issue was whether the word 'may' in *FA 1972, Sch 16 para 3(1)* was discretionary (as the company contended) or mandatory (as the Revenue contended). The CA upheld the company's contention, holding that the wording of the legislation conferred a general discretion rather than a mandatory duty. *R v Inspector of Taxes and Others (ex p. Lansing Bagnall Ltd)*, CA 1986, 61 TC 112; [1986] STC 453.

[50.50] The decision in *R v HM Inspector of Taxes & Others (ex p. Lansing Bagnall Ltd)*, **50.49** above, was distinguished and not followed in *Baylis v Roberts & Roberts*, **53.20** SCHEDULE D—SUPERSEDED LEGISLATION, in which the Revenue's powers to issue increased assessments on the cessation of a business were held to be mandatory rather than discretionary.

[50.51] In the case noted at **11.1** CLOSE COMPANIES, the QB held that *CTA 2010, s 451** conferred a discretionary power rather than a mandatory duty, but that that power had to be exercised in a way which would identify a company as being a close company, if that were possible. Accordingly, in the circumstances of the case, the Revenue had been bound to exercise their power under *CTA 2010, s 451** and to find that both companies were under common control. *R v CIR (ex p. Newfields Development Ltd)*, QB 1999, TL 3581; [1999] STC 373.

[50.52] See also *Scofield v HMRC (No 2)*, **16.38** CONSTRUCTION INDUSTRY, where the First-Tier Tribunal held that *FA 2004, s 66(1)* was discretionary rather than mandatory, and *CIR v Adams*, **44.85** PENALTIES, where the CA held that *TMA 1970, Sch 3* was mandatory rather than discretionary.

Request for determinations under SI 1973/334

[50.53] A roofing business, which was originally operated by a sole trader but was subsequently incorporated, engaged the services of a part-time bookkeeper whom the Revenue accepted as self-employed. The proprietors of the business subsequently formed the view that the bookkeeper had been an employee and that PAYE ought to have been applied. They appealed to the Special Commissioners, contending that the Revenue should be required to make determinations under the *Income Tax (Employments) Regulations 1973 (SI 1973/334)* in respect of the sums paid to the bookkeeper. The Special Commissioner rejected this contention and dismissed the appeals, and the Ch D upheld this decision. An allegation that the Revenue had connived at a deception perpetrated by the bookkeeper was not a matter which could be raised on an appeal or by way of Case Stated. The relevant regulation was permissive rather than obligatory, and any appeal against a decision not to invoke the regulation could only be pursued by way of an application for judicial review. *Wright v Field; Devon Flat Roofing Ltd v Field*, Ch D 1990, 63 TC 707; [1991] STC 18. (*Note*. The *Income Tax (Employments) Regulations 1973* have subsequently been replaced by the *Income Tax (PAYE) Regulations 2003 (SI 2003/2682)*.)

51

Revenue Prosecutions

The cases in this chapter are arranged under the following headings.

Making false statements

Prosecution for fraud

[51.1] A farmer had submitted false accounts and a false certificate of disclosure. He was convicted on charges of making false statements to the prejudice of the Crown and the public revenue with intent to defraud, and was fined. He appealed against the convictions, contending that the offence charged was not one known to the law. The CCA rejected this contention and upheld the convictions, holding that 'all frauds affecting the Crown and public at large are indictable as cheats at common law'. The jury had been entitled to find that the documents which the farmer had submitted were 'false and fraudulent', and that the farmer had submitted them 'for the purpose of avoiding the payment of tax, and that is defrauding the Crown and defrauding the public'. The farmer had committed a common law offence. *R v Hudson*, CCA 1956, 36 TC 561; [1956] 2 QB 252; [1956] 1 All ER 814.

Prosecution for forgery

[51.2] In 1969 an accountant sent a document to the Revenue, purporting to be a copy of a resolution passed at a general meeting of a company in 1966. He subsequently admitted that there had never been any such meeting, and that the document was a forgery, submitted in the hope of persuading the Revenue to stop enquiring into the company's affairs. He was convicted of 'uttering a forged instrument with intent to defraud'. He appealed, admitting that the document was a forgery but contending that there was no intent to defraud, because he had genuinely (although mistakenly) believed that the company should have no further tax liability. The CA dismissed his appeal. Orr LJ observed that 'the law of forgery can be applicable as much to a false document put forward to bolster up a good claim as to a false document put forward to bolster up a false claim'. *R v Patel*, CCA 1973, 48 TC 647.

Tax avoidance scheme—criminal prosecution for false accounting

[51.3] A company, which operated a holiday time-share business, paid very large sums in respect of invoices submitted to it by another company. The

Revenue formed the opinion that the invoices did not represent genuine transactions, but had been intended to reduce the company's corporation tax liability and enable its controlling shareholders to avoid income tax on the income in question. In 1997 the company made an offer of payment in respect of tax, interest and penalties, which the Revenue accepted. At the time this offer was made, the Crown Prosecution Service had already instigated criminal proceedings against the company's shareholders, alleging conspiracy to account falsely and conspiracy to defraud. At a preparatory hearing under *Criminal Justice Act 1987*, the shareholders contended that, in view of the settlement between the company and the Revenue, the Crown could not prosecute them. The Crown Court judge rejected this contention and ruled that the Crown was entitled to prosecute. The shareholders applied to the CA for leave to appeal, but the CA rejected their application. Firstly, the CA had no jurisdiction under *Criminal Justice Act 1987* to entertain an appeal at the preparatory stage, and the application was 'akin to an application to quash the indictment'. Furthermore, under the *Prosecution of Offences Act 1985, s 3(2)(a)*, the Crown Prosecution Service had a power and a duty 'to take over the conduct of all criminal proceedings' instituted 'on behalf of a police force'. The Revenue's power and duty to collect taxes was separate and distinct. It included the power to negotiate a settlement and impose penalties, but the exercise of those powers had nothing to do with the criminal process. The Revenue's power of prosecution under common law was 'ancillary to, supportive of, and limited by' its duty to collect taxes. However, the statutory duty of the Crown Prosecution Service to take over and conduct criminal proceedings was free-standing and reflected 'much wider public interests, concerns and objectives'. Accordingly, 'the power in the Crown Prosecution Service to prosecute remains separate and distinct, and is uninhibited by the Revenue's exercise of their power to compound proceedings'. There was 'no necessary dichotomy or logical inconsistency in the Crown's position if the Crown Prosecution Service prosecute in circumstances where the Revenue have decided not to'. *R v Werner & Clarke (aka R v W & Another)*, CA Criminal Division [1998] STC 550; [1998] BTC 202. (*Notes.* (1) See also the Parliamentary Written Statement by the Attorney-General on 8 April 1998, published in Hansard, col. 230–231. The Attorney-General stated that 'proceedings brought by the Crown Prosecution Service will ordinarily encompass charges relating to tax evasion only in circumstances where that evasion is incidental to allegations of non-fiscal criminal conduct'. (2) For the Revenue's interpretation of the implications of this decision, see Revenue Tax Bulletin, June 1998, p 544. (3) For subsequent developments in this case, see **49.42** RETURNS AND INFORMATION.)

False evidence under oath before Commissioners—whether perjury

[51.4] See *R v Hood Barrs*, **4.40** APPEALS.

Cheating the public revenue

'Cheating the public revenue'—definition

[51.5] The controlling director of a number of companies was convicted of cheating the public revenue in relation to PAYE and NIC. Hardy J held that 'the common law offence of cheating the public revenue does not necessarily require a false representation either by words or conduct. Cheating can include any form of fraudulent conduct which results in diverting money from the Revenue and in depriving the Revenue of the money to which it is entitled.' The CA unanimously approved this definition and dismissed the director's appeal against his conviction. *R v Less*, CA 12 March 1993, Times 30.3.1993.

Tax avoidance scheme—criminal prosecution

[51.6] Four individuals (three accountants and a barrister), who had been involved in tax avoidance schemes, were charged with cheating the public revenue, and were convicted and sentenced to terms of imprisonment. Under one of the schemes, a Jersey company was established to purchase goods from overseas suppliers and sell them to UK companies at a higher price. Under the other scheme, a Jersey company received commission from UK companies for services rendered (the value of the services in question being regarded by the Revenue as being substantially less than the price paid). Some of the directors of some of the purchasing companies involved in the schemes had been asked by Revenue officers in writing whether any transactions had been 'omitted from or incorrectly recorded in the books of the company'. After consulting the barrister who was subsequently prosecuted, they had replied in the negative, although it was accepted at the trial that they should have replied in the affirmative. The prosecution and the convictions were on the basis that the defendants were guilty of 'falsely representing' that some of the transactions in question were *bona fide* commercial transactions, and that the barrister had been 'a party to deceiving the Revenue'. The defendants appealed against their convictions, contending that the schemes as proposed were legitimate tax avoidance (while accepting that the directors of some of the companies involved in implementing the scheme had acted dishonestly and that some of the companies had failed to give the notice of chargeability required by *TMA, s 10*). The barrister contended that he had been 'protecting his clients from any oppressive enquiries', and had not known that the answers which he had advised the directors to give were incorrect. The CA dismissed all the defendants' appeals against their convictions. Farquharson LJ observed that 'for the scheme to be tax effective for the purpose of the UK revenue legislation', the Jersey company 'had to be controlled and administered in Jersey by directors who were not resident in the UK', whereas in fact, its management and control remained in the hands of the UK company's directors. With regard to the accountant who had devised the scheme, Farquharson LJ observed that it was 'difficult to reconcile' his contention that he did not know that the schemes 'were applied dishonestly with the fact that all the schemes were mis-applied in the same way'. With regard to the barrister,

Farquharson LJ observed that the issue was 'whether he was party to (the) fraud on the one hand or that he was acting energetically in his clients' best interest on the other'. The CA held that there was sufficient evidence of his participation in the fraud attempted by one of the directors to support his conviction. The jury had 'ample opportunity to assess his credibility', and 'plainly they did not believe him'. The jury had been entitled to find that, in view of 'the nature and content of the correspondence he engaged in', he had been 'a party to deceiving the Revenue'. With regard to the sentences of imprisonment, Farquharson LJ observed that 'the Revenue not only have to rely on the taxpayer's good faith, but more especially on the professional advisors they appoint to act for them and, accordingly, when professional advisors are found to have acted dishonestly towards the Revenue, it is almost inevitable that sentences of imprisonment must follow'. *R v Cunningham, Charlton, Wheeler & Kitchen*, CA Criminal Division 1995, 67 TC 500; [1996] STC 1418.

[51.7] An individual, who was resident in Jersey, controlled a company which provided financial services, including the formation and administration of offshore companies. He was convicted of conspiracy to cheat the public revenue, and was sentenced to 18 months' imprisonment. He appealed against his conviction, contending *inter alia* that because the company's income was within *ITA 2007, s 720** for income tax purposes, the profits did not need to be declared on the company's corporation tax return. The HL unanimously rejected this contention and dismissed his appeal, holding that, in view of the history of the legislation, no distinction should be drawn between company transferees and individual transferees. *R v Dimsey*, HL 2001, 74 TC 263; [2001] STC 1520; [2001] UKHL 46; [2001] 4 All ER 786. (*Note.* The case was heard in the CA and HL with *R v Allen*, **51.8** below.)

[51.8] The Revenue obtained information that an individual, who was resident in the UK, had failed to disclose profits made by offshore companies which were managed and controlled by him in the UK. He was convicted on 13 counts of conspiracy to cheat the public revenue, and sentenced to seven years' imprisonment. The court also made a confiscation order under *Criminal Justice Act 1988*. He appealed against his conviction, contending firstly that, because the companies' income was within *ITA 2007, s 720** for income tax purposes, the profits did not need to be declared on the companies' corporation tax returns; secondly that, as a 'shadow director' of the companies, he was not liable to tax on benefits which fell within *ITEPA 2003, ss 97–113**; and thirdly that the proceedings had breached his right to a fair trial under the *European Convention on Human Rights*. The HL unanimously rejected all these contentions and dismissed his appeal. Lord Hutton held that it was the intention of Parliament that 'accommodation and benefits in kind received by a shadow director should be taxed in the same way as those received by a director'. The effect of *ITEPA 2003, s 67(1)** was that 'a shadow director is taken to be a director'. Accordingly, 'it follows that living accommodation and benefits received by him should be treated as emoluments'. Furthermore, the proceedings had not involved any breach of the *European Convention on Human Rights*. Lord Hutton observed that 'to the extent that there was an inducement contained in the Hansard statement, the inducement was to give true and accurate information to the Revenue'. However, the accused 'did not respond to that inducement and instead of giving true and accurate information gave false information'. *R v Allen*, HL 2001, 74 TC 263; [2001] STC 1537; [2001] UKHL 45; [2001] 4 All ER 768. (*Notes*. (1) The case was heard in the CA and HL with *R v Dimsey*, **51.7** above. (2) For a preliminary issue in this case, see **51.19** below. (3) For an unsuccessful appeal against the confiscation order, see **51.9** below. (4) For the Revenue's practice following this decision, see Revenue Tax Bulletin, December 2002, pp 979–981.)

[51.9] The defendant in the case noted at **51.8** above appealed against the confiscation order, contending that he had not obtained a 'pecuniary advantage' within *Criminal Justice Act 1988, s 71(5)*, because he remained liable to pay the tax which he had evaded. The CA dismissed his appeal and upheld the order. Laws LJ held that 'the ordinary and natural meaning of "pecuniary advantage" must surely include the case where a debt is evaded or deferred'. The fact that the tax remained due did not mean that its evasion did not confer a pecuniary advantage. Applying dicta of Lord Reid in *Director of Public Prosecutions v Turner*, HL 1973, [1974] AC 357; [1973] 3 All ER 124, 'evasion does not necessarily mean permanent escape'. The validity of the order was also not affected by the fact that some of the tax liability related to offshore companies. The courts had repeatedly stated that 'the corporate veil may fall to be lifted where companies are used as a vehicle for fraud'. Furthermore, the sentences were not excessive, since the offences 'were conducted in a determined and sophisticated manner over a long period of time and involved colossal sums of money'. *R v Allen*, CA Criminal Division 1999, [2000] 3 WLR 273; [2000] 2 All ER 142.

[51.10] A barrister controlled a number of companies. The Revenue formed the opinion that he had arranged for the companies to evade the payment of corporation tax by an elaborate scheme involving bogus transactions. He was convicted on two counts of cheating the public revenue, and sentenced to 4½ years' imprisonment. Fingret J found that the barrister had 'arranged for the creation of false documents'. He held that 'the appropriate range of sentences for large-scale efforts to cheat the Revenue is between four and eight years'. The CA upheld both the conviction and the sentence. *R v Stannard*, CA Criminal Division 13 February 2002 unreported. (*Notes*. (1) For a discussion of the scheme in question, written after the barrister's conviction but before the CA decision, see the article by James Kessler in Taxation, 7 June 2001, p 234. (2) For subsequent developments in this case, see **51.16** below.)

Charges dismissed by judge without reference to jury

[51.11] An individual (L), who was resident in Switzerland, arranged for companies which he controlled to purchase a number of UK companies, which had substantial cash reserves and corporation tax liabilities. Following the purchases, the companies claimed substantial corporation tax repayments, on the basis that they had made large profits from foreign exchange transactions but had incurred significant interest liabilities and declared substantial dividends. The claims depended on some of the companies changing their residence from the UK to Guernsey. The Revenue formed the opinion that the scheme was dishonest, in that some of the transactions apparently carried out by the companies were shams, that the purported Guernsey directors were nominees of L, and that, following the purchases, the true centre of management and control of the companies was Switzerland rather than Guernsey. They charged a partner in a large accountancy firm, who had advised L in the course of the transactions in question, with conspiracy to defraud the Revenue. The partner applied for the charges to be dismissed, contending that the scheme would have been legal if the transactions had been carried out correctly, and that he had not known that some of the transactions purportedly carried out by L were not genuine, or that L had submitted false documents to the Revenue. Hucker J accepted this contention and dismissed the charges, holding that 'the evidence does not provide the necessary inference' so that 'it would not be safe' to leave the case to a jury. 'They could only convict on the basis of speculation and prejudice.' The Revenue applied to the QB for judicial review of Hucker J's decision. The QB dismissed the application, holding that it could only reverse Hucker J's decision if it was 'perverse'. On the evidence, it could not be said that Hucker J's decision was 'perverse or one that he could not reasonably have arrived at'. *R (oao CIR) v Kingston Crown Court*, QB [2001] STC 1615; [2001] EWHC Admin 581; [2001] 4 All ER 721.

Whether interview evidence admissible

[51.12] Two brothers traded in partnership as clothing manufacturers. The Revenue began investigating their affairs, and in March 1995 Revenue officers interviewed the brothers under the 'Hansard' procedure, as set out in a Parliamentary Statement by the then Chancellor of the Exchequer (John Major) in 1990. At the interviews, the brothers each stated that no transactions had been omitted from their records, and that their accounts and records were correct. The brothers were subsequently charged with cheating the public revenue. At their trial, the Revenue introduced evidence of the interviews which had taken place in 1995. The trial judge ruled that the evidence was admissible. The brothers were convicted and sentenced to imprisonment. They appealed against their convictions, contending that the judge should have ruled that the interview evidence was inadmissible. The CA unanimously dismissed their appeals, holding that there was no ground for overturning the convictions. Clarke LJ held that the effect of the *Police and Criminal Evidence Act 1984* was that the brothers should have been formally cautioned, and the interview should have been tape-recorded. However, the fact that this had not taken place did not mean that 'evidence of everything said by the appellants at the meeting must be excluded'. On the evidence, the brothers had given false answers at the interviews, and even if they had previously been cautioned, it was unlikely that they 'would have done anything different'. The evidence of the interviews had not had 'any adverse effect on the fairness of the proceedings'. The brothers 'chose to tell lies' and 'had every opportunity at the trial to explain why they had answered as they did'. The jury had been 'correctly directed as to the correct approach', and 'there was nothing unsafe about the convictions'. *R v Gill & Gill*, CA [2003] STC 1229; [2003] EWCA Crim 2256; [2003] 4 All ER 681.

[51.13] In the course of divorce proceedings, an individual (K) disclosed that he had various bank accounts and investments in Switzerland and Liechtenstein. He was subsequently charged with cheating the public revenue. In a preliminary hearing under the *Criminal Procedure and Investigations Act 1996, s 29(1)*, he contended that some of the admissions that he had made should not be admitted in evidence. The CA reviewed the evidence in detail and accepted this contention in part. Moore-Bick LJ held that 'the privilege against self-incrimination remains an important protection against oppression and it is not lightly to be inferred that Parliament has chosen to abrogate it, especially where it has not made its intention clear by the use of express language'. On the evidence, statements which K had made at a meeting in October 2001 were not admissible as evidence against him at his trial, but statements which he had made at a subsequent meeting in April 2002 were admissible. *R v K (No 2)*, CA Criminal Division [2009] STC 2553; [2009] EWCA Crim 1640.

Amount of confiscation order

[51.14] A market trader (M), who had underdeclared his income for many years, pleaded guilty to cheating the public revenue, and was sentenced to nine months' imprisonment. Daniel J made a confiscation order of £190,000, being the amount of the tax underpaid plus interest. The Attorney-General applied for leave to appeal against the amount of the order, contending that it was unduly lenient and that the whole of M's undeclared profits (£386,584) should have been confiscated. The CA rejected this contention and upheld Daniel J's order. *R v Moran (Attorney-General's Reference No 25 of 2001)*, CA Criminal Division, [2001] STC 1309; [2001] EWCA Crim 1770; [2002] 1 WLR 253. (*Note.* This decision was distinguished in the subsequent case of *R v Foggon*, **51.15** below.)

[51.15] A company director had pleaded guilty to defrauding the Inland Revenue by diverting more than £1,000,000 of company money into a hidden bank account. The Crown Court made a confiscation order in the sum of £1,068,441, which reflected the total amount of money diverted, rather than simply the amount of tax and interest evaded. The CA unanimously upheld this decision, holding that the effect of *Criminal Justice Act 1988, s 71(4)* was that the benefit received by the director was the total amount diverted, and distibguishing *R v Moran*, **51.14** above, on the grounds that it related to a sole trader rather than a company director. Jack J held that 'where a person misappropriates money from a company as an essential part of a fraud on the Inland Revenue, and is convicted of that fraud, he is liable to a confiscation order in the amount of the monies which he has misappropriated on the ground that the monies are property obtained as a result of or in connection with the fraud'. *R v Foggon*, CA Criminal Division, [2003] STC 461; [2003] EWCA Crim 270. (*Note.* For the Revenue's practice, see Revenue Press Release CC12/01, issued on 31 August 2001.)

[51.16] Following the decision noted at **51.10** above, the Southwark Crown Court made a confiscation order of £1,678,954 against the barrister. He appealed to the CA, contending firstly that he had obtained no pecuniary advantage because he was merely the beneficiary of a discretionary trust, and secondly that the order should be reduced in view of his 'actual realisable assets'. The CA unanimously rejected these contentions and dismissed the appeal. Pill LJ held that, applying *dicta* of Laws LJ in *R v Dimsey*, **51.7** above, 'the corporate veil may fall to be lifted where companies are used as a vehicle for fraud'. On the evidence, the court had been entitled to find that this was a case where 'it is appropriate to lift the corporate veil'. *R v Stannard (No 2)*, CA Criminal Division, [2005] EWCA Crim 2717; [2005] All ER (D) 14 (Nov).

[51.17] A trader (S) who had failed to notify his liability to tax was convicted of cheating the public revenue. The Cardiff Crown Court found that S had been involved in 'criminal activity', and imposed a confiscation order of £707,200. S appealed to the CA, which unanimously dismissed his appeal and upheld the confiscation order. Moses LJ observed that S had been 'unable to show the extent to which the assets he held and the expenditure he had incurred were derived either from tax which he ought to have paid but which he had not paid, or his criminal activities, or his legitimate activities'. *R v Steed*, CA Criminal Division [2011] EWCA Crim 75.

Applications for judicial review

[51.18] Following an investigation into the tax affairs of an accountant, criminal charges were brought against the accountant and two of his clients. The clients applied for judicial review of the decision to prosecute, contending that they had been unfairly treated because other clients of the accountant had not been prosecuted. The QB dismissed the application. Although a decision to prosecute was within the scope of judicial review, the circumstances in which judicial review could be successfully invoked would be extremely rare. The Revenue operated a selective policy of prosecution, for three main reasons. Firstly, its main objective was the collection of tax, rather than the punishment of offenders. Secondly, it had inadequate resources to prosecute everyone who had dishonestly evaded payment of tax. Thirdly, it was necessary to prosecute in some cases because of the deterrent effect of prosecutions on the general body of taxpayers. The applicants' case had been considered fairly and dispassionately on its merits, and the decision to prosecute had been taken in good faith. The policy of selective prosecution was rational and was 'probably the only workable policy'. *R v CIR (ex p. Mead & Cook)*, QB 1992, 65 TC 1; [1992] STC 482; [1993] 1 All ER 772.

[51.19] The Revenue were investigating the affairs of an individual (A), who was involved in a number of overseas companies. From 1992 to 1994, the Revenue had treated the case as one in which they would settle for a monetary settlement, but in 1994 the Revenue's Enquiry Branch discovered new evidence which suggested that the proposed settlement would have been inadequate, and that A might have been involved in a conspiracy to defraud the Revenue. In February 1995 the Revenue notified A that the investigation was now being treated as a criminal investigation, and in August 1995 A was interviewed under caution and charged. In June 1996 he applied for judicial review of the decision to prosecute him, contending that it was contrary to established Revenue practice. The QB rejected this contention and dismissed his application. What is now *Civil Procedure Rules 1998 (SI 1998/3132), Sch 1, RSC Order 53, rule 4* provided that an application for judicial review should be made within three months, whereas A had delayed his application until the proceedings were ten months old. Furthermore, nothing which had occurred during the investigation had amounted to an assurance or representation, or had given rise to any legitimate expectation, that A would remain free from criminal prosecution if the Revenue were later to conclude, in the light of further evidence and information, that criminal proceedings were appropriate. The decision to prosecute was in accordance with the guidelines laid down in the Revenue's Enquiry Branch Manual, since the Revenue had not been aware of all the relevant facts when A had been led to believe that the case could be settled by way of monetary penalties. At no stage had A been told, either directly or indirectly, that he would not be prosecuted. As time passed without any settlement and without any noticeable co-operation from A, but with increasing evidence of his criminality, it remained open to the Revenue to review the position and to decide to prosecute. *R v CIR (ex p. Allen)*, QB 1997, 69 TC 442. (*Note.* A was subsequently convicted and sentenced to seven years' imprisonment—see **51.8** above.)

[51.20] The Revenue discovered that a company director had failed to declare the receipt of building society interest on his tax returns. In 1995 the director signed a certificate that he had made a complete disclosure of his income, and the enquiry into his building society interest was closed by means of a 'back duty' settlement. in 1996, following information from the French tax authorities, the Revenue discovered that the director had drawn more than £700,000 in cash from the company, and paid this into bank accounts in Monaco. In 1999 the Revenue decided to prosecute the director for cheating the public revenue. He applied for judicial review of the decision to prosecute him. The QB dismissed his application. Lightman J observed that 'it is inconceivable that the applicant was not advised by his accountant and did not appreciate that the deliberate omission of the substantial receipts from the company might lead to a prosecution'. On the evidence, 'the tax fraud was both serious and substantial'. Applying the decision in *R v CIR (ex p. Allen)*, **51.19** above, 'a decision to prosecute can only be challenged in the most exceptional circumstances'. Lightman J held that 'there is nothing exceptional in this case save perhaps its total hopelessness'. *R v CIR (ex p. Hunt)*, QB 5 November 1999 unreported.

[51.21] In the case noted at **49.64** RETURNS AND INFORMATION, a company director was convicted of conspiracy to cheat the Revenue, and was sentenced to eight years' imprisonment. He subsequently applied to the Criminal Cases Review Commission to refer his case to the Court of Appeal. The Commission declined to do so, and he applied for judicial review of the Commission's decision. The QB dismissed his application, holding *inter alia* that the Revenue had an unrestricted power to conduct a prosecution in the Crown Court, and there was no requirement for the Revenue to obtain consent from the Attorney-General. The Revenue had a common law power to prosecute in support of their overall duty to collect taxes. *R (oao Hunt) v Criminal Cases Review Commission*, QB 2000, 73 TC 406; [2000] STC 1110; [2001] 2 WLR 319.

Miscellaneous

Tax avoidance scheme—prosecution for fraudulent trading

[51.22] An accountant set up a bank in Nauru (a small island in the Pacific). He bought 13 companies and then claimed that these businesses had taken out large loans from the bank. The 'interest payments' for these loans were offset against tax owed. He claimed that the loans were used to make profitable exchange deals through his brokerage business. Bogus dividends were then used to reclaim corporation taxes paid by the companies' former owner. He was convicted of 13 charges of fraudulent trading. The judge at Southwark Crown Court found that he had made a net profit of £22 million and sentenced him to 12½ years in prison. The CA unanimously upheld the conviction but reduced the sentence to ten years' imprisonment. *R v Leaf*, CA Criminal Division, [2007] EWCA Crim 802. (*Note*. The Southwark Crown Court subsequently made a confiscation order of £16,250,000.)

Proceeds of Crime Act, s 340(3)—definition of 'criminal property'

[51.23] See *R v K*, 29.22 FURTHER ASSESSMENTS: LOSS OF TAX.

Validity of search warrants where fraud suspected—TMA, s 20C

[51.24] See *R v CIR (ex p. Rossminster Ltd)*, 49.63 RETURNS AND INFORMATION.

Whether any breach of European Convention of Human Rights

[51.25] See *Hozee v The Netherlands*, 31.23 HUMAN RIGHTS.

Successful defence of charge—deductibility of costs

[51.26] See *Spofforth & Prince v Golder*, 63.160 TRADING PROFITS.

52

Savings and Investment Income (ITTOIA 2005, ss 365–573)

The cases in this chapter are arranged under the following headings.

Interest (ITTOIA 2005, ss 369–371)

Charge to tax on interest (ITTOIA 2005, s 369)

Guarantee payments on capital

[52.1] A company formed to build and work a railway in Brazil raised capital by issuing 5% debentures. The Brazilian Government guaranteed it 7% of its capital, the guarantee payments to be applied in paying the debenture interest and forming a sinking fund to pay off the debentures. The CA held that the payments were interest and chargeable to income tax. *Blake v Imperial Brazilian Railway Co*, CA 1884, 2 TC 58.

[52.2] The decision in *Blake v Imperial Brazilian Railway Co*, 52.1 above, was applied in the similar subsequent case of *Nizam's Guaranteed State Railway Co v Wyatt*, QB 1890, 2 TC 584; 24 QBD 548.

Interest element in building society repayments

[52.3] Loans made by a building society were repayable by weekly amounts covering both interest and capital. The Revenue issued assessments charging tax on the interest element of the repayments which it received. The Special Commissioners dismissed the society's appeal and the CA upheld their decision. *Leeds Permanent Benefit Building Society v Mallandaine*, CA 1897, 3 TC 577; [1897] 2 QB 402.

Interest on unpaid instalments of purchase price of land abroad sold

[52.4] A company which owned substantial land in Canada sold some of the land on terms whereby part of the purchase price was to be paid by instalments over a period of years, with interest on the purchase price unpaid. (The CA had held that the sales were not trading transactions—see 67.17 TRADING PROFITS.) The Revenue assessed the company on the basis that the interest was taxable in the UK. The company appealed, contending that the interest was not taxable. The KB rejected this contention and upheld the assessments. *Hudson's Bay Co v Thew*, KB 1919, 7 TC 206; [1919] 2 KB 632.

Interest under court decree

[52.5] In 1911, a court decree awarded £1,040 to trustees with interest from 1902. The sum was paid to them in 1913/14 with £462 representing eleven years' interest on the £1,040 and two years' interest on their costs. The CS held that the £462 was assessable on the trustees for 1913/14. *Schulze v Bensted (No 1)*, CS 1915, 7 TC 30.

[52.6] The decision in *Schulze v Bensted*, 52.5 above, was applied in a subsequent Scottish case where the CS held that interest which formed part of a court award following litigation was chargeable to income tax. *Sweet v Macdiarmid (aka Henderson)*, CS 1920, 7 TC 640.

[52.7] A bank was required to pay interest of £10,028 on damages awarded under the *Law Reform (Miscellaneous Provisions) Act 1934*. The bank withheld tax from the interest, as required by *ITA 1918, Rule 21*. The payee contended that the £10,028 should not be treated as interest for tax purposes, so that the bank should not have withheld tax. The HL held that the interest was 'interest of money' within the charge to income tax (so that the bank had acted correctly in deducting tax). Lord Wright held that 'the essence of interest is that it is a payment which becomes due because the creditor has not had his money at the due date. It may be regarded either as representing the profit he might have made if he had had the use of the money, or, conversely, the loss he suffered because he had not that use. The general idea is that he is entitled to compensation for the deprivation.' *Westminster Bank Ltd v Riches*, HL 1947, 28 TC 159; [1947] AC 390; [1947] 1 All ER 469. (*Note*. The substantive issue is no longer relevant, but the case remains an important authority on the definition of 'interest'.)

Interest element in arbitration award

[52.8] Following arbitration, a firm was awarded damages together with an amount described as interest up to the date of payment. The CS held that the award was substantially one of damages and that the 'interest' was part of the damages and not chargeable to income tax. *CIR v Ballantine*, CS 1924, 8 TC 595.

[52.9] Following court proceedings, an individual (B) was awarded £877,250 by a court referee. The referee's order described the payment as 'a single capital sum', but the supporting computation showed that £433,059 of the total represented compound interest. The Revenue issued assessments charging tax on the interest. B appealed, contending that the interest was 'damages or compensation' which was outside the scope of income tax and supertax. The

CA unanimously rejected this contention and dismissed the appeal. Lord Wright MR held that the referee's use of the words 'a single capital sum' should be construed as 'referring to the manner of payment, and not to its character'. *CIR v Barnato*, CA 1936, 20 TC 455; [1936] 2 All ER 1176.

Interest on refund of insurance premiums

[52.10] In 1994 an individual (S) purchased an insurance policy. In 2004 the insurer changed the terms of the policy. S complained to the Financial Services Authority. In 2008, following prolonged negotiations involving the Financial Ombudsman Service, the insurer agreed to refund S's premiums with interest at 8% pa. The insurer deducted tax from the interest. S appealed to the First-Tier Tribunal, contending that the whole of the repayment, including the interest, should be treated as capital. The tribunal rejected this contention and dismissed the appeal. *R Sutton v HMRC*, FTT [2011] UKFTT 679 (TC), TC01606. (*Note*. The appellant appeared in person. The Upper Tribunal dismissed an application for leave to appeal against this decision.)

[52.11] The decision in *R Sutton v HMRC*, **52.10** above, was applied in a similar case in which the First-tier Tribunal struck out an appeal by S's wife. *Mrs P Sutton v HMRC*, FTT [2014] UKFTT 044 (TC), TC03184.

Compensation for interest lost

[52.12] See *Simpson v Bonner Maurice Executors*, **28.18** FOREIGN INCOME.

Bank interest arising during liquidation

[52.13] In an Irish case, interest credited to a deposit account, into which the liquidator of a company had paid receipts from disposing of the assets, was held to be chargeable to income tax. *Irish Provident Assurance Co Ltd v Kavanagh*, HC(I) 1924, 4 ATC 115.

Accrued interest on sale of securities

[52.14] A company sold War Stock, with the right to accrued interest. The Revenue issued an assessment charging tax on the accrued interest to the date of sale. The Commissioners allowed the company's appeal and the KB upheld their decision. Rowlatt J held that the sale proceeds could not be divided between capital and accrued interest. *Wigmore v Thomas Summerson & Sons Ltd*, KB 1925, 9 TC 577.

[52.15] The principles laid down by *Wigmore v Thomas Summerson & Sons Ltd*, **52.14** above, were applied in a subsequent case where an investor purchased 6% Treasury Loan Stock in May 1974 and received half-yearly interest in August 1974. The Revenue issued an assessment charging tax on this, and the investor appealed, contending that part of it should be assessed on the vendor. The Commissioners rejected this contention and dismissed his appeal, and the CA unanimously upheld their decision. Shaw LJ observed that 'those who venture into the stock market without knowledge, guidance or advice lay themselves open to unlooked for disadvantages'. *Schaffer v Cattermole*, CA 1980, 53 TC 499; [1980] STC 650.

[52.16] See also *CIR v Oakley*, **30.13** HIGHER RATE LIABILITY.

Interest element in loan repayments after death of moneylender

[52.17] A moneylender (B) made loans repayable in instalments covering both capital and interest. He died and his business ceased. His administrator collected the instalments which fell due after B's death. The Revenue issued assessments charging tax on the interest element in these instalments. The administrator appealed, contending that the payments should be treated as trading income (and as not taxable under the legislation then in force) and not as 'interest'. The Commissioners rejected this contention and dismissed the appeal, and the KB upheld their decision. Rowlatt J held that 'when you are dealing with what is interest and nothing but interest you cannot say it is in the nature of business, because it is payment by time for the use of money'. *Bennett v Ogston*, KB 1930, 15 TC 374.

Money lent to builder repaid by creation of ground rents

[52.18] A company (R) lent a building company £15,000 at interest of 6% to finance the construction by the building company of 255 houses. The loan was to be repaid by the transfer to R of ground rents of £6 per annum to be created on the sale of the houses. For this purpose, each ground rent was to be valued at $^{1}/_{255}$th of £15,000. In three years, 249 ground rents were so transferred and the building company was then released from any further liability. The value of the ground rents considerably exceeded £15,000 and the Revenue assessed R on the excess. The Special Commissioners upheld the assessments, holding that the excess was taxable interest. The CA unanimously dismissed R's appeal. *Ruskin Investments Ltd v Copeman*, CA 1943, 25 TC 187; [1943] 1 All ER 378. (*Note*. Although the CA were unanimous in dismissing the appeal, Scott LJ expressed the view that the excess was 'miscellaneous income' taxable under Schedule D Case VI under the legislation then in force, rather than interest taxable under Schedule D Case III.)

Premium on repayment of convertible notes

[52.19] A UK company issued £500,000 registered convertible notes at par, not bearing interest but repayable after six years at a premium of 30%. The Revenue issued assessments charging tax on the premiums. The KB upheld the assessments, holding that the premium on repayment was interest within the charge to income tax. *Davies v Premier Investment Co Ltd; Hewetson v Carlyle*, KB 1945, 27 TC 27; [1945] 1 All ER 681.

Promissory note in satisfaction of arrears of interest

[52.20] A woman (L) owned $100,000 mortgage bonds issued by an American company, on which she was owed interest of $36,000. Under an agreement to facilitate the sale of the mortgaged property, the mortgage bonds were cancelled, a promissory note of $100,000 was issued to L in 1942, and the $36,000 was paid in two instalments, in 1943 and 1944. The Revenue issued assessments charging tax on the interest. L appealed, contending that it was not taxable since it represented income from a source (the bonds) which she no longer possessed. The Special Commissioners rejected this contention and upheld the assessments. The HL unanimously dismissed L's appeal, holding that the $36,000 retained its character of interest and remained taxable despite the cancellation of the bonds. *Lilley v Harrison*, HL 1952, 33 TC 344.

Interest on sums deposited in support of guarantee

[52.21] See *Dunmore v McGowan*, 52.46 below.

Interest retained by bank as security for debt

[52.22] See *Peracha v Miley*, 52.48 below.

Income charged (ITTOIA 2005, s 370)

Interest due but not received—whether assessable

[52.23] In a St. Lucia case, a company sold property in 1920, part of the purchase price being payable on 30 November 1921 with interest from 19 November 1920. The purchaser defaulted and, after legal action, the company received the interest after 1921. It was assessed for 1921 on the interest due for payment in that year. The PC allowed the company's appeal, holding that since the company had not received the 'income arising or accruing' during 1921, it was not assessable under the relevant legislation. *St. Lucia Usines & Estates Co Ltd v Colonial Treasurer of St. Lucia*, PC 1924, 4 ATC 112; [1924] AC 508.

Interest credited on closure of account

[52.24] In March 1990 a company deposited money at a bank, on terms that interest would be credited quarterly. After the first credit had been made, the company agreed with the bank that further credits would be deferred. The account was closed on 18 December 1992 and the interest was credited at that time. The Revenue assessed the company on the basis that some of the interest had arisen in 1990 and 1991. The company appealed, contending that none of the interest credited when the account was closed arose until the date of closure, so that it was assessable in 1992. The Special Commissioners accepted this contention and allowed the appeal, and the Ch D upheld this decision. Although the interest was an accruing debt, it did not constitute income until it was paid, applying the principles laid down in *St. Lucia Usines & Estates Co Ltd v Colonial Treasurer of St. Lucia*, 52.23 above, and *Dewar v CIR*, 30.27 HIGHER RATE LIABILITY, and distinguishing *Dunmore v McGowan*, 52.46 below. Neuberger J observed that the agreement in question was not 'artificial', and did not involve an attempt to convert income into capital. The effect of the agreement was merely to defer the date on which income would arise. *Girvan v Orange Personal Communications Services Ltd*, Ch D 1998, 70 TC 602; [1998] STC 567.

Interest credited to joint account

[52.25] A professor (H) did not declare any interest on his 2006/07 return, although interest of more than £5,000 had been credited to a joint account held by H and his wife. HMRC issued an assessment on the basis that 50% of the interest credited to the account was assessable on H. He appealed, contending that none of the interest should be taxed until it had been withdrawn by one of the account-holders. The First-Tier Tribunal rejected this contention and dismissed the appeal. Judge Clark held that the effect of *ITTOIA 2005, s 370* was that tax was charged on 'the full amount of interest arising in the tax year', and that 'interest arises when it is credited to an account'. Therefore the interest which was credited to the joint account in 2006/07 was taxable in that year; and the effect of *ICTA 1988, s 282A* (see now *ITA 2007, s 836*) was that H was taxable on 50% of that interest. *Professor AK Halpin v HMRC*, FTT [2011] UKFTT 512 (TC), TC01359.

Overdraft interest calculated by reference to current account balances

[52.26] A company (C), which was a member of a group, had an overdrawn current account. However, some of its branches had surplus funds. These were deposited in the same bank as C's overdrawn current account, and it was agreed that the credit balances 'would be aggregated on a daily basis and would be set off against any net borrowings on current account by (C)'. The Revenue issued assessments on C, charging tax on the interest on the credit balances. C appealed, contending that the arrangement in force from April 1990 to December 1992 (when the terms of the agreement were changed) did not provide for it to receive interest, but provided for its obligation to pay interest to be reduced. The Special Commissioners reviewed the evidence and accepted this contention. The effect of the agreement in force up to December 1992 was that the rate ascribed to the credit balances was 'relevant only to the calculation of interest on (C's) borrowings'. It served 'only to abate the interest on the amounts overdrawn' and was 'not a separate stream of interest due from the bank to (C)'. *Cooker v Foss*, Sp C [1998] SSCD 189 (Sp C 165). (*Note*. C originally also appealed against assessments for subsequent years, but withdrew these appeals before the hearing, accepting that the revised agreement which took effect from December 1992 gave rise to liability to income tax.)

Interest accrued before, but receivable after, death

[52.27] See *Reid's Trustees v CIR*, 19.2 DECEASED PERSONS, and *CIR v Henderson's Executors*, 19.3 DECEASED PERSONS.

Accrued annuity to date of death of annuitant

[52.28] See *Bryan v Cassin*, 19.4 DECEASED PERSONS.

Accrued interest on death of life tenant

[52.29] See *Wood v Owen*, 19.5 DECEASED PERSONS.

Payment less tax made in arrear—year for which income of payee

[52.30] See *CIR v Crawley and Others*, 20.44 DEDUCTION OF TAX.

Interest on foreign bonds paid by guarantor

[52.31] See *Westminster Bank Executor & Trustee Co (Channel Islands) Ltd v National Bank of Greece SA*, 20.47 DEDUCTION OF TAX.

Mortgage interest not received

[52.32] See *Lambe v CIR*, 30.24 HIGHER RATE LIABILITY.

Interest received in arrear

[52.33] See *Leigh v CIR*, 30.25 HIGHER RATE LIABILITY, and *Champneys' Executors v CIR*, 30.26 HIGHER RATE LIABILITY.

Payments under building agreement described as 'interest'

[52.34] See *Re Euro Hotel (Belgravia) Ltd*, 33.8 INTEREST PAYABLE.

Notional interest payments under 'Ponzi' scheme

[52.35] An individual (M) had life savings of about £140,000. An accountant (L) persuaded him to 'invest' his savings by making a series of short-term loans to a company (DL) which traded in firearms, and of which L was the managing director. DL (which subsequently went into liquidation) issued M with documents indicating that he had been credited with interest totalling £304,505 over three years, all of which had been reinvested. HMRC issued assessments charging tax on this interest, and M appealed. The First-Tier Tribunal reviewed the evidence in detail and allowed M's appeal. Judge Nowlan held that 'in reality, the arrangement had all the attributes of a fluctuating loan where, in cash terms, the appellant would extract nothing from the arrangements unless and until the loans could ultimately be repaid in full'. In these circumstances, it was 'appropriate to ignore the fictitious form of the individual transactions under which each loan, and each receipt of interest, was treated as a separate transaction. The realistic analysis is that the high interest was only paid to lure investors to re-advance everything transiently repaid and paid, and that the appellant should only be treated as receiving interest, after full repayment of the principal advanced. Since at no time in the cycle of loans and further loans, did the Appellant ever in net terms get his £140,000 back and since, at the end of the day, he lost everything, we conclude that in realistic terms, no interest was received.' Judge Nowlan observed that it was not suggested that 'the tax liability on interest received by an individual would be eliminated merely because the interest is reinvested and subsequently lost'. However, the position might differ 'if the transactions are always part of a scam, in which the borrower has a manifest plan, always to lure investors in to re-advance virtually everything repaid and paid under earlier transactions, particularly where in reality the borrower must know that the likelihood of being able to discharge any of the mushrooming debts at the end of the day is virtually zero'. On the evidence, L had deliberately misrepresented the potential tax liability to M, and had 'proceeded on a basis of quite improper concealment', so that 'from the very outset it was of the essence of the plan that the profits given to investors would be pure paper profits, and that invariable reinvestment was always contemplated, and indeed utterly vital'. Accordingly, it was 'appropriate to ignore the fictitious form of the individual transaction under which interest was paid in theory, but inevitably reversed by the investors being lured into reinvesting virtually everything received'. Judge Nowlan concluded that 'utterly fictitious receipts of interest, invariably matched by reinvestments, when the borrower knows that the borrower company is inevitably heading for a catastrophic collapse in which the investors will never receive any return and will probably lose everything, all in a Ponzi-style transaction, are not relevant receipts of interest for tax purposes'. *J Mazurkiewicz v HMRC*, FTT [2011] UKFTT 807 (TC), TC01643.

[52.36] The decision in *Mazurkiewicz v HMRC*, 52.35 above, was distinguished in a subsequent case in which the appellant (R) had invested funds with the same fraudster (L), but where the tribunal found that R had 'received a profit, or surplus, in excess of the principal sums invested which has been demonstrated by the cleared cheques through his bank accounts'. Since R had received 'a positive balance', that balance was within the definition of 'interest'. *R Rusling v HMRC*, FTT [2014] UKFTT 692 (TC), TC03813.

Interest paid by cheque—whether received when cheque received

[52.37] A company had given up its trade as a haulage contractor when its premises were compulsorily purchased. On 9 April 1979 it received a cheque for compensation for disturbance and for interest, the amount of the interest being £44,070. On 10 April 1979 it began a new trade of leasing and incurred allowable losses. The Revenue issued an assessment on the basis that the interest was received on 9 April, which meant that it was included in an accounting period in which there were no allowable losses. The company appealed, contending that the interest was not received until the cheque was cleared. The Ch D accepted this contention and allowed the appeal. Scott J held that 'it is the receipt of the proceeds, whether as cash or by the crediting of the sum to an account of the payee, that places the proceeds at the disposal of the payee' and 'attracts the liability to tax'. *Parkside Leasing Ltd v Smith*, Ch D 1984, 58 TC 282; [1985] STC 63; [1985] 1 WLR 310.

Interest on tax paid late—whether deductible from interest received

[52.38] Trustees appealed against an income tax assessment, contending that interest which they had paid on unpaid estate duty should be deducted in computing their income tax liability. The Commissioners rejected this contention and dismissed the appeal, and the CS upheld their decision. *Lord Inverclyde's Trustees v Millar*, CS 1924, 9 TC 14; [1924] AC 580.

'Lunacy percentage'—whether deductible

[52.39] A woman's affairs were administered by a committee in accordance with the *Lunacy Act 1890*. The committee was required to pay a 'lunacy percentage' of 4% of the woman's income to the Crown. The committee appealed against an income tax assessment on war loan interest, contending that the 4% should be deducted in computing the tax liability. The Special Commissioners rejected this contention and dismissed the appeal, and the KB upheld their decision. *Tax Committee of AB (a lunatic) v Simpson*, KB 1928, 14 TC 29. (*Note*. Following the *Mental Health Act 1959*, the terms 'lunacy' and 'lunatic' are no longer used in the general legislation dealing with mental health, but the term 'lunatic' is still used in *TMA, s 118*.)

Claim to deduct expenses from assessment on savings income

[52.40] The widow of a teacher appealed against assessments on Trustee Savings Bank account interest, claiming that the expenses which she had incurred in voluntary work for a pensioners' association should be deducted from the interest assessable. The Commissioners rejected her claim and the Ch D upheld their decision. *Shaw v Tonkin*, Ch D 1987, [1988] STC 186.

Person liable (ITTOIA 2005, s 371)

Assessment on shipbroker as agent

[52.41] A shipbroker acting as agent for a Danish company received substantial amounts owing to the company which could not be remitted because of wartime conditions. He deposited them in a bank account earmarked for his principal. The Revenue assessed him in his capacity as agent for the Danish company on the interest credited to the account. The KB upheld the assessment. *Scales v Atalanta Steamship Co of Copenhagen*, KB 1925, 9 TC 586.

Interest paid under life insurance policy

[52.42] See *Pope v HMRC*, 26.13 EXEMPT INCOME.

Income not claimed by legatee—whether taxable

[52.43] See *Dewar v CIR*, 30.27 HIGHER RATE LIABILITY.

Liability of estate agent on interest derived from clients' moneys

[52.44] An estate agent deposited moneys derived from rents collected for clients in a bank account. The Revenue assessed him on the interest. He appealed, contending that the interest belonged to his clients and should not be treated as his income. The Ch D rejected this contention and dismissed the appeal. Megarry J held that the estate agent was taxable under *ITTOIA 2005, s 371** as the person receiving the income. *Aplin v White*, Ch D 1973, 49 TC 93; [1973] STC 322; [1973] 1 WLR 1311; [1973] 2 All ER 637.

Solicitor—interest on accounts in joint names

[52.45] A solicitor (B) opened bank and building society accounts in the joint names of him and his wife, and subsequently opened further accounts in the joint names of him and one or more of his three children. In his tax returns, he initially declared only a proportion of the interest received on these joint accounts, treating the majority of the interest as accruing to his wife and children. Subsequently he did not declare any of the interest on his personal return, apportioning the whole of it between his wife and children. HMRC issued assessments for 1996/97 to 2009/10, and imposed penalties, on the basis that all the interest accruing on these joint accounts was taxable on B, as the person 'receiving or entitled to' the interest. B appealed, contending that he had transferred a beneficial interest in the accounts to his wife and children. The First-tier Tribunal upheld the assessments in principle. Judge Hacking found that B had intended 'to establish a jointly held fund accessible to all family members'. The fact that B had remained a signatory to the accounts was 'inconsistent with a transfer of a beneficial interest in the fund'. Accordingly, B remained liable 'to account to the revenue for the whole of the interest earned on the jointly held bank accounts'. Furthermore, even if there had been a transfer of the beneficial interest, the transfer would have fallen within the 'settlement' provisions of *ITTOIA 2005, ss 619, 620*. (However, the tribunal allowed B's appeal against the assessments for 1996/97 to 2004/05 as they had been issued outside the normal time limits, and B had not acted negligently as he 'had an honestly held but incorrect belief that he was properly entitled to apportion the interest earned on the accounts according to what he believed were the relevant beneficial interests of his family members'. Judge Hacking also observed that 'enquiry by the Revenue into the underlying beneficial interests in jointly held bank accounts' appeared to be unusual, so that this was not 'a suitable case for the imposition of penalties'.) *AJ Bingham v HMRC*, FTT [2013] UKFTT 110 (TC); [2013] SFTD 689, TC02528.

Liability of guarantor on interest on sums deposited to support guarantee

[52.46] A solicitor (D) deposited sums with a bank in support of his guarantee of a loan by the bank to a company for which he acted professionally. Eventually the loan was repaid and the deposits were released with interest which had been credited. The Revenue issued an assessment charging tax on the interest, and he appealed, contending that the interest was held by the bank as trustee during the existence of the guarantee and that he had not received or been entitled to it. The General Commissioners rejected this contention and dismissed his appeal and the CA unanimously upheld their decision. Stamp LJ held that 'the interest was received or "got" when it was credited to the deposit account, an account of money which was at all times owed by the bank to the taxpayer'. D was the person entitled to the interest even though he was unable to draw it. *Dunmore v McGowan*, CA 1978, 52 TC 307; [1978] STC 217; [1978] 1 WLR 617; [1978] 2 All ER 85.

Capital sum and interest charged to bank to secure debts of third party

[52.47] An individual (M) deposited £10,000 with a bank in 1972 in a special account, to secure sums owed to the bank by a company (R). The bank could refuse to pay money out of the account while the balance was below the amounts which R owed to the bank. Interest was credited to the account half-yearly. In the event the balance, with accumulated interest, was always less than the amounts which R owed to the bank. R was wound up in 1979, and the bank retained the whole of the balance on the account. The Revenue issued assessments on M, charging tax on the accumulated interest. M appealed, contending that he was not taxable on the interest because he had never received or become entitled to it. The Ch D accepted this contention and allowed his appeal, distinguishing *Dunmore v McGowan*, **52.46** above. Vinelott J held that M did not at any time receive or become entitled to the interest. *Macpherson v Bond*, Ch D 1985, 58 TC 579; [1985] STC 678; [1985] 1 WLR 1157.

Interest retained by bank as security for a debt

[52.48] An individual (P) made a deposit with the London branch of a foreign bank which had lent money to P's family company. P signed a 'letter of lien and authority for advances' authorising the bank to retain the deposit as part security for the loans. Subsequently the company, which had been taken over by a Bangladesh government body, was released from its obligations and P became the principal debtor for the amount of the loans, although the bank had at the time of the hearing taken no steps to recover the money. The Revenue assessed P on the interest accumulated in the account, and P appealed. The Special Commissioner dismissed his appeal and the CA unanimously upheld this decision, applying the principles laid down in *Dunmore v McGowan*, **52.46** above. Dillon LJ held that P was taxable under *ITTOIA 2005, s 371**. He had benefited to the extent that his liability to repay the loans was reduced by the interest credited to the account, and he could secure the repayment of the deposit and the accrued interest if he himself repaid the original loans. *Peracha v Miley*, CA 1990, 63 TC 444; [1990] STC 512.

[52.49] In 2007 an individual (C), who was resident in the UK, agreed to buy a property (which had not yet been built) in Cyprus. To finance the purchase, he borrowed a large sum of money (in Swiss francs) from a Cyprus bank. He exchanged these for Cypriot pounds, which he deposited in an account with the same bank. He was credited with interest on this deposit account. He subsequently became dissatisfied with the delay in building the property and stopped repaying the loan. The bank then froze the deposit account which he had opened. When HMRC discovered this, they issued discovery assessments charging tax on the interest which had been credited to the deposit account. C appealed, contending that he should not be taxed on the interest as he had never received it. The First-tier Tribunal rejected this contention and dismissed his appeal, holding that he was taxable on the interest under *ITTOIA 2005, s 371*. *N Coxon v HMRC*, FTT [2013] UKFTT 112 (TC), TC02530.

[52.50] The decision in *Coxon*, **52.49** above, was applied in the similar subsequent case of *Mrs R Thomas v HMRC*, FTT [2014] UKFTT 281 (TC), TC03420.

Other income taxed as interest (ITTOIA 2005, ss 372–381)

Discounts (ITTOIA 2005, s 381)

Treasury Bill discounts

[52.51] A private company (not carrying on a trade) purchased Treasury Bills, some of which were held until maturity, some sold during their currency and the rest converted into War Loan. The HL held that the difference between the cost and the sum realised on maturity, sale or conversion was income of the year of realisation. *National Provident Institution v Brown*, HL 1921, 8 TC 57; [1921] 2 AC 222. (*Note*. The case also involved the basis period rules for Schedule D Case III under the legislation then in force. The decision here, which was by a 3-2 majority, has been overtaken by subsequent changes in the legislation, originating with *FA 1926, ss 22, 29, 30*. The majority of the HL held that there was a general principle that income could not be assessed for a year in which the taxpayer did not possess the source. This principle was questioned by Lord Atkin in the 1944 case of *Absalom v Talbot*, **68.43** TRADING PROFITS. It was applied by Lord Oliver in the 1989 case of *Bray v Best*, **54.20** SCHEDULE E—SUPERSEDED LEGISLATION, but it was strongly criticised by Lord Hoffmann eleven years later in the case of *The Centaur Clothes Group Ltd v Walker*, **5.14** ASSESSMENTS, where Lord Hoffmann held that it was 'no longer true to say that liability to income tax depends upon the existence during the year of assessment of a source within the charge'. However the 'source doctrine' was subsequently applied by the Ch D in the 2007 case of *HMRC v Bank of Ireland Britain Holdings Ltd*, **3.3** ANTI-

AVOIDANCE, where counsel for HMRC apparently failed to draw the judge's attention to the HL decision in *Centaur Clothes Group Ltd v Walker*.)

Promissory notes received for cash consideration

[52.52] Under arrangements with four Canadian companies, an individual (W) received a series of 120 promissory notes from each, payable quarterly. The face value of the promissory notes was approximately 4% greater than the expressed consideration paid by W. The Revenue issued assessments charging tax on the excess. The KB upheld the assessments in principle, holding that the promissory notes included an element of taxable income, to be calculated according to the method approved in *Scoble v Secretary of State for India*, **2.28** ANNUAL PAYMENTS. *Lord Howard de Walden v Beck*, KB 1940, 23 TC 384. (*Note*. For another appeal relating to the same transactions, see *Lord Howard de Walden v CIR*, **3.51** ANTI-AVOIDANCE.)

Discount and premiums on loan to overseas company

[52.53] A UK company (P) which manufactured newsprint formed a Finnish company (T), controlled in Finland, to secure a supply of wood pulp. It lent £319,600 to T. Under arrangements to regulate the repayment of the loan, T gave P 680 notes of an aggregate face value of £340,000 expressed to be issued at 94%, i.e. for an aggregate amount equal to the amount of the advance. The notes carried interest at a commercial rate and on repayment at specified times carried a premium of 20%. The Revenue issued assessments charging tax on the 6% 'discount' and the premiums received on repayment of the notes. The Commissioners allowed P's appeal, holding that the discount and premiums were capital sums. The CA unanimously upheld their decision. Lord Greene MR held that there was 'no difference between writing down the capital value of an existing debt and writing down the capital value of a new debt which is what is done where a company makes an ordinary issue of debentures at a discount or repayable at a premium'. Furthermore, it was 'impossible to suppose that the legislature intended to include under the one word "discounts" two such entirely different commercial transactions as the discounting of a bill of exchange or a Treasury Bill (which normally are short-dated and carry no interest) and a subscription for debentures issued at a discount. The issue of debentures or other obligations by companies was unknown in 1805 when profits on "discounts" were for the first time expressly subjected to income tax.' Where a loan was made 'at or above such a reasonable commercial rate of interest as is applicable to a reasonably sound security, there is no presumption that a "discount" at which the loan is made or a premium at which it is payable is in the nature of interest. The true nature of the "discount" or the premium, as the case may be, is to be ascertained from all the circumstances of the case and, apart from any matter of law which may bear upon the question (such as the interpretation of the contract), will fall to be determined as a matter of fact by Commissioners.' *Lomax v Peter Dixon & Son Ltd*, CA 1943, 25 TC 353; [1943] 1 KB 671; [1943] 2 All ER 255.

Issue of promissory note for an amount not carrying interest

[52.54] The trustees of a settlement were major shareholders of a company (B). B had acquired certain shares and, as part consideration for them, gave a promissory note, dated 1969, for £2,399,000, payable on 1 February 1973 and not carrying interest. In 1970 the trustees sold their shares in B, using the proceeds to purchase (with others) the promissory note for £1,779,631 from a merchant bank which had acquired it and which guaranteed payment of 75% of the face value on maturity. The trustees retained the note until maturity and it was honoured in full. The Revenue assessed them on the basis that the profit was a 'discount'. They appealed, contending that the profit was capital. The CA rejected this contention and upheld the assessment, holding that 'all discounts' (see now *ITTOIA 2005, s 381(1)*) should be defined as covering 'profits arising from discounts received on discounting transactions'. Here the purchase of the note by the trustees was a discounting transaction. Where, as here, no interest was payable as such, a 'discount' would normally, if not always, be chargeable to income tax. Furthermore, the trustees' profit in a period of three years represented a return of about 11% per annum, and the only proper conclusion on the evidence was that the profit was of an income nature. *Ditchfield v Sharp & Others*, CA 1983, 57 TC 555; [1983] STC 590; [1983] 3 All ER 681.

Floating rate notes stripped of interest—profit on sale

[52.55] An individual (H) purchased certain floating rate notes, marketed by a bank and described as 'flexi-notes', which had been stripped of interest for a certain period. At the end of the period, H sold the notes, making a total profit of £8,680,000. HMRC issued amendments to H's self-assessment, treating the profits which he had made on the sale of the notes, as discounts which were chargeable to income tax under what is now *ITTOIA 2005, s 381*. H appealed, contending that the flexi-notes were qualifying corporate bonds and that his profits were capital rather than income. The First-tier Tribunal rejected this contention and dismissed H's appeal, applying the principles laid down by the HL in *National Provident Institution v Brown*, **52.51** above. Sir Stephen Oliver observed that the marketing brochure which advertised the notes 'stresses that the product was designed to give an enhanced after-tax return significantly in excess of interest on fixed-term deposits. Moreover, the brochure offers the flexi-note package as a suitable investment for individuals and their trustees. The trustees would, if there were competing claims between income and capital beneficiaries, be bound to treat the profit on the discount, or a large part of it, as income.' *M Healey v HMRC*, FTT [2013] UKFTT 176 (TC); [2013] SFTD 861, TC02591. (*Note*. For HMRC's practice following this decision, see their News Release issued on 18 April 2013.)

Corporate bonds stripped of interest—profit on sale

[52.56] In 2004 an individual (S) purchased certain corporate bonds, marketed by a bank, which had been stripped of interest for a certain period. At the end of the period, S sold the bonds. HMRC issued amendments to his self-assessment, treating the profits which he had made on the sale of the notes as discounts, which were chargeable to income tax under what is now *ITTOIA 2005, s 381*. The First-tier Tribunal dismissed S's appeal, applying the principles laid down by the HL in *National Provident Institution v Brown*, **52.51** above. *P Savva v HMRC (and related appeals)*, FTT [2013] UKFTT 211 (TC), TC02625. (*Notes*. (1) See also now *ITTOIA 2005, ss 452A-452G*. (2) For HMRC's practice following this decision, see their News Release issued on 18 April 2013.)

Dividends from UK companies, etc. (ITTOIA 2005, ss 382–401C)

Charge to tax—ITTOIA 2005, s 383

[52.57] A UK company (R) and a Jersey company (T) had the same controlling shareholder (C). R lent £120,000 to T, which only repaid £35,000 of the loan, the remaining £85,000 being written off. T incurred expenditure of £103,600 on acquiring a property, which it transferred to C for a stated consideration of £60,000. However, C never paid this sum. The Revenue assessed C on the basis that the £85,000 outstanding on the loan from R to T, and the £103,600 which T had spent on the property which had been transferred to C, were distributions. The Ch D upheld the assessments. On the facts found by the Commissioners, C had not made any repayment of the sums in question and there were no grounds for discharging the assessments. *Cassell v Crutchfield (No 2)*, Ch D 1996, 69 TC 259; [1997] STC 423. (*Notes.* (1) Appeals against CGT and Schedule E assessments were also dismissed. (2) For a preliminary issue in this case, see **4.38** APPEALS.)

Qualifying distributions—interpretation of ITTOIA 2005, s 399

[52.58] A UK resident (S) was the life tenant and beneficiary of two settlements, one of which was established in the Republic of Ireland and one of which was established in the Isle of Man. The settlements received dividend income from several non-UK companies, and paid the dividend income to S. In his tax returns for 2005/06 to 2008/09, S claimed a tax credit in respect of this dividend income. HMRC rejected the claims and S appealed, contending that the effect of *ITTOIA 2005, s 399* was that he should be treated as if he had paid tax on the distributions, so that he was entitled to the credit which he had claimed. The First-tier Tribunal accepted this contention and allowed his appeals, specifically declining to follow obiter dicta of Lord Simon of Glaisdale in *Farrell v Alexander*, HL [1977] AC 59 (a non-tax case which HMRC had cited as an authority on the interpretation of a statute which consolidated previous legislation). Judge Aleksander observed that 'it is not possible to ascertain a consistent and logical basis in the legislation for the taxation of dividends. Whilst there might have been some sort of logical underpinning to the basis of taxation of dividends in the early 1970s, when the partial imputation system was introduced (with ACT and tax credits), any such logic had long disappeared as a result of the many amendments to dividend legislation in the period leading to the enactment of *ITTOIA*.' *P Shirley v HMRC*, FTT [2014] UKFTT 1023 (TC), TC04119.

Distributions by overseas companies (ITTOIA 2005, ss 402–404)

Distribution of surplus funds

[52.59] An American company, in which a UK investment company was a stockholder, distributed part of its accumulated surplus funds by way of special dividend on its stock, satisfied partly by the transfer of stock it held in another American company. The UK company sold the stock transferred to it and the Revenue issued an assessment charging tax on the proceeds. The company appealed, contending that the distribution should be treated as a capital receipt which was not chargeable to income tax. The KB rejected this contention and upheld the assessment. Sankey J observed that 'the so-called dividend was severed from the capital, was not added to it and never became part of it, but was received by the company for its separate use, benefit and disposal'. *Pool v Guardian Investment Trust Co Ltd*, KB 1921, 8 TC 167; [1922] 1 KB 347.

Certificates of indebtedness in satisfaction of a dividend

[52.60] A US corporation declared a dividend on its stock, satisfying the dividend by the issue of certificates of indebtedness redeemable at a future date. The Revenue issued an assessment on a UK company which was a substantial stockholder in the corporation, charging tax on the sums which it received from the redemption of the certificates. The company appealed, contending firstly that the redemption of the certificates represented the discharge of a capital obligation, and alternatively that, if the issue of the certificates represented a receipt of income, the income arose when they were issued and not when they were redeemed. The Special Commissioners rejected these contentions and dismissed the appeal, and the Ch D and CA unanimously upheld their decision, holding that the dividend was income which arose when the certificates of indebtedness were redeemed. *Associated Insulation Products Ltd v Golder*, CA 1944, 26 TC 231; [1944] 2 All ER 203.

Capital dividends

[52.61] The trustees of a settlement received a dividend from a South African company 'payable from capital profits' made by the company out of the profit from the sale of certain of its premises. The Revenue issued an assessment charging tax on the dividend. The trustees appealed, contending that the dividend was capital. The HL unanimously rejected this contention and upheld the assessment. Lord Simonds observed that 'what may be capital in the hands of the payer may yet be income in the hands of the payee'. On the evidence, the dividend was 'income in the hands of the shareholders'. Lord Reid held that 'if a foreign company chooses to distribute its surplus profits as dividend, the nature and origin of those profits do not and cannot be made to affect the quality of the receipt by the shareholder for the purpose of income tax'. *CIR v Reid's Trustees*, HL 1949, 30 TC 431; [1949] AC 361; [1949] 1 All ER 354.

Distribution of assets

[52.62] A company (L) held shares in a Maryland company (C) which sold part of its business to another US company (B) in exchange for shares in B. C distributed the shares to its own shareholders, the distribution being capital under Maryland law. The Special Commissioners held that the shares which L received were received as capital and were not chargeable to income tax. The HL upheld their decision as one of fact, distinguishing *CIR v Reid's Trustees*, **52.61** above, on the grounds that the Commissioners here had specifically found that the relevant Maryland law differed from English law. *Rae v Lazard Investment Co Ltd*, HL 1963, 41 TC 1; [1963] 1 WLR 555. (*Note. Dicta* of Lord Reid with regard to the distinction between income and capital were not followed, and were implicitly disapproved, in the subsequent case of *Sinclair v Lee & Another*, **56.142** SETTLEMENTS.)

Distribution from share premium reserve

[52.63] A UK company held shares in an Italian company and received a substantial distribution from a share premium reserve, which was treated as a return of capital under Italian law. The Revenue issued an assessment charging tax on the distribution, but the Ch D allowed the company's appeal. Buckley J held that 'under Italian law this distribution from the share premium reserve was a return of capital; it was not distributable as profit'. *Courtaulds Investments Ltd v Fleming*, Ch D 1969, 46 TC 111; [1969] 1 WLR 1683; [1969] 3 All ER 1281.

Stock dividends

[52.64] The trustees of a Californian trust fund received stock dividends on shares in American companies forming part of the fund. Under Californian law, the stock dividends were income of the trust, and half of the proceeds of them was paid to a married woman, resident in the UK, who was the life tenant of half of the trust fund. The Revenue issued an assessment (on her husband under the legislation then in force) charging tax on the dividends. The Ch D allowed the husband's appeal. Foster J held that there was 'no element of recurrence' in the issue of the stock dividends, so that they were not within the definition of 'income'. *Lawson v Rolfe*, Ch D 1969, 46 TC 199; [1970] Ch 612; [1970] 1 All ER 761.

Stock dividends from UK-resident companies (ITTOIA 2005, ss 409–414)

ITTOIA 2005, s 414(1)—income tax treated as paid

[52.65] See *Howell & Morton (Robin Settlement Trustees) v Trippier*, **56.107** SETTLEMENTS.

Release of loan from participator in close company (ITTOIA 2005, ss 415–421)

*Release from liability to repay loan—ITTOIA 2005, s 417**

[52.66] Two directors (C and G) of a close company owed the company £79,000. They agreed to sell all their shares in the company to another director (B) for £200,000. Under the agreement, the company released C and G from their debts to it up to a limit of £68,000. B agreed to take over these debts, and subsequently paid the company £79,000. C and G paid B the balance of £11,000. The Revenue issued assessments on C and G on the basis that, by substituting B for C and G as the debtor, the company had released C and G from their liability to repay the loans. Accordingly, by virtue of *ITTOIA 2005, s 417**, the grossed-up equivalent of the £68,000 released should be treated as income of C and G in computing their liability to higher rate tax. C and G appealed, contending that, since B had taken over the debts, the transactions should not be treated as being within *ITTOIA 2005, s 417**. The Special Commissioner rejected this contention and dismissed their appeals, and the Ch D and CA unanimously upheld this decision. C and G had received £68,000 from the company by way of a loan, which the company had subsequently released. The facts that the company's assets had not been depleted, and that consideration had been given for the release, did not alter the fact that the release of the debt was within *ITTOIA 2005, s 417**. *Collins v Addies; Greenfield v Bains*, CA 1992, 65 TC 190; [1992] STC 746.

Purchased life annuity payments (ITTOIA 2005, ss 422–426)

Purchased annuities

[52.67] In order to finance his children's education, a clergyman (P) took out annuity policies, under each of which an annual payment was to be made to him for a specified period if a named child survived. If the child died in the period, the premiums were returnable with interest, less the payments actually made to him. The sums payable under the policies were calculated so that, if the children survived, the 'annuity' payments would equal the premiums paid plus 3% compound interest. In the event, the children survived the relevant years, and the Revenue issued assessments on P, charging tax on the full amounts he received. The KB allowed P's appeal in part, holding that the liability was limited to the interest element in the payments. The CA unanimously upheld this decision. Lawrence LJ held that the courts should 'look at the real nature of the transaction, whatever may be the form in which it is expressed', and 'if the circumstances warrant it dissect a payment, even though it be called an annuity, so as to prevent so much of it as represents capital from being charged with income tax'. *Perrin v Dickson*, CA 1929, 14 TC 608; [1930] 1 KB 107. (*Note.* The decision was distinguished (and implicitly disapproved) in the subsequent case of *Sothern-Smith v Clancy*, 52.68 below.)

[52.68] An individual had purchased a life annuity from an overseas life assurance society. He died before the total payments to him had reached the sum he paid for the annuity and, under the annuity contract, the annuity continued to be payable to his sister until the total payments reached that sum. The Revenue issued assessments charging tax on the payments she received. She appealed, contending that they were payments of capital. The CA unanimously rejected this contention and upheld the assessments. The decision in *Perrin v Dickson*, 52.67 above, was distinguished, on the grounds that 'in that case the company's liability could never exceed the amount of the premiums with the compound interest at 3%, while in the present case the contract involved the company in a possible liability which, if (the appellant) lived for an unexpected number of years, might exceed the original payment and a reasonable rate of interest thereon by a very large figure'. *Sothern-Smith v Clancy*, CA 1940, 24 TC 1; [1941] 1 KB 276; [1941] 1 All ER 111.

Purchased annuity—determination of capital element

[52.69] An individual (R) purchased an annuity. The Revenue determined the capital element in the annuity by reference to the tables prescribed in *SI 1956/1230 para 6*. R appealed, contending that the tables used were out of date and that the capital element had been determined at too low a figure. The Special Commissioners rejected this contention and dismissed his appeal, holding that the capital element had to be determined in accordance with the tables prescribed by Statutory Instrument. The Ch D upheld their decision. *Rose v Trigg*, Ch D 1963, 41 TC 365. (*Note*. The appellant appeared in person.)

Purchased life annuities—tax deducted

[52.70] See *Allchin v Corporation of South Shields*, 20.8 DEDUCTION OF TAX.

Profits from deeply discounted securities (ITTOIA 2005, ss 427–460)

[52.71] In 2001/02 two individuals entered into a tax avoidance scheme, promoted by a large accountancy firm, under which they claimed substantial losses on transactions in 'relevant discounted securities', within *FA 1996, Sch 13*. Under the scheme, the claimants lent money to a trust in which they had a life interest, in return for a security issued by a company which was one of the trustees. They subsequently redeemed the securities at a substantial loss, while the amount of the loan continued to be held by the trust, for their benefit. The Revenue issued amendments to the claimants' tax returns, rejecting the claims. The claimants appealed. The Special Commissioner dismissed the appeals, holding that the securities were not within the definition of 'relevant discounted securities', because the terms under which they might theoretically be redeemed at a 'deep gain' would never occur. The Commissioner observed that 'the scheme is entirely artificial and the appellants had no commercial purposes in entering into it other than generating an artificial loss to set against taxable income'. On the evidence, it was 'a practical certainty' that the securities would be sold or redeemed at a loss within two months. The Commissioner held that 'a purposive construction of the definition of relevant discounted security must have regard to real possibilities of redemption, not ones written into the document creating the security that the parties know, and any reasonable person having the knowledge available to the parties knows, will never occur.' The difference between the issue price and the redemption price 'must give rise to a possibility of making a gain that can be objectively seen to exist.' The CA unanimously upheld the Commissioner's decision. Arden LJ held that *FA 1996, Sch 13, paras 2, 3* 'must receive a purposive interpretation. That purpose was that there should be a real possibility of a deep gain' if losses incurred on a relevant discounted security were to be capable of set-of for income tax purposes. In this case, the relevant terms of issue had 'no practical reality' and the securities did not meet the statutory requirements to qualify as relevant discounted securities. *Astall v HMRC; Edwards v HMRC*, CA 2009, 80 TC 22; [2010] STC 137; [2009] EWCA Civ 1010. (*Notes.* (1) *FA 1996, Sch 13* was repealed by *ITTOIA 2005* with effect from 6 April 2005, and replaced by *ITTOIA 2005, ss 427–460*, which deals with 'profits from deeply discounted securities'. (2) The Supreme Court rejected applications to appeal against this decision.)

[52.72] An individual (B) claimed that in 2003/04 he had made a loss of £400,000 as a result of certain transactions in discounted securities ('gilt strips'). HMRC issued an amendment to his self-assessment rejecting the claim. B appealed. The First-Tier Tribunal reviewed the evidence in detail and dismissed his appeal, finding that B had entered into a 'scheme' which was 'self-cancelling'. On the evidence, 'no loss was sustained by (B); nor was any amount paid by him for the gilt strips, nor was there any transfer of the strips'. The Upper Tribunal upheld this decision, applying the principles laid down by the CA in *Astall v HMRC*, **52.71** above. *A Berry v HMRC*, UT [2011] UKUT 81 (TCC); [2011] STC 1057. (*Note.* See also the note following *Astall v HMRC*, **52.71** above.)

Loss claim—purchase price of discounted security

[52.73] An individual entered into a tax avoidance scheme, marketed by an accountancy firm, under which he transferred his house (which was valued at £1,800,000) and £250,000 in cash to a family trust in return for a loan note. He subsequently submitted a tax return claiming that he had made a tax loss of more than £2,000,000 on the disposal of a 'relevant discounted security'. HMRC rejected his claim and the First-Tier Tribunal dismissed his appeal, applying the principles laid down by the CA in *Astall v HMRC*, **52.71** above. The terms of the loan note 'were artificial' and only £35,700 of the alleged consideration was actually paid for the acquisition of the loan note. *R Audley v HMRC*, FTT [2011] UKFTT 219 (TC); [2011] SFTD 597, TC01084.

[52.74] In February 2003 a barrister (B) acquired six loan notes from a company (O) for their face value of £500,000. The notes carried the right of early redemption for the first 14 days at their issue price or very slightly less.

After 14 days, they were redeemable at the noteholder's option for 5% of the issue price (ie £25,000). B granted a call option over the notes to a trust, of which he was the settlor, the life tenant and one of the trustees. This trust exercised the call option, received £499,500 from O, and was substituted for O as the issuer of the notes. On the same day B gave the notes to a second trust, of which he was the settlor and a trustee (but was not the life tenant), so that at the end of 2002/03, the first trust held £499,500 while the second trust held the loan notes, which could be redeemed for £25,000. In 2004 B submitted an amendment to his 2002/03 tax return, claiming that the loan notes were 'relevant discounted securities', and that he had incurred a loss of £475,000 on his transactions in them. HMRC began an enquiry and rejected the claim. B appealed, contending inter alia that his reason for putting his assets into a trust was not tax avoidance, but was 'to avoid potential creditors'. The First-tier Tribunal dismissed his appeal. Judge Mosedale observed that, if B's only concern had been asset protection, he could have transferred the £500,000 directly into a trust, and found that 'the loan notes transactions were undertaken solely for tax avoidance reasons'. She found that O 'did not require a loan of £500,000' and its 'grant of the call option and its issue of the loan notes was done solely to facilitate (B's) tax avoidance scheme'. Furthermore, 'the main purpose of the 14-day redemption clause was tax avoidance and in particular to establish that the loan notes were issued at full value. The scheme was pre-planned and the dramatic drop in value from £499,500 to £25,000 on day 15 was engineered on the face of the documents.' There had been a series of transactions, under which B had transferred money to a family trust. Viewed realistically, B had acquired the notes for £25,000 and had not made a loss on them. *GR Bretten v HMRC*, FTT [2013] UKFTT 189 (TC); [2013] SFTD 900, TC02604.

Loss claim—whether loan stock was a relevant discounted security

[52.75] On 28 March 2000 an individual (P) purchased a newly-incorporated company. On 31 March 2000 he paid £6,000,000 for loan stock in the company. On 5 April 2000 he transferred the loan stock to a newly-created trust of which he and his wife were trustees. He subsequently submitted a tax return claiming that he had made a loss of more than £3,400,000 on a relevant discounted security. HMRC rejected the claim and P appealed, contending that the loan stock had had a market value of £2,600,000 when he transferred it to the trust. The First-tier Tribunal dismissed his appeal, finding that 'the transactions at issue in this appeal were part of a scheme of tax avoidance' and that P had 'intended to realise a loss for income tax purposes'. Judge Mosedale held that 'to avoid absurdity some of the language used by the drafters must be given a purposive rather than a literal reading'. It had been 'asymmetrical for the legislation to have an open market rule on transfers between connected parties without having the same open market value for grants and issues between connected parties'. The additional sum intended to be paid to P on the redemption of the loan stock should be treated as interest, even though it was not payable periodically. Accordingly, the loan stock was not a 'relevant discounted security'. The Upper Tribunal and the CA unanimously upheld this decision as one of fact, holding that the First-tier Tribunal had been entitled to find that the additional payment was interest. *N Pike v HMRC*, CA [2014] EWCA Civ 824; [2014] STC 2549. (*Note.* See also *FA 1996, Sch 13, para 9A*, introduced by *FA 2002* with effect from 25 March 2002 with the intention of ensuring that no loss relief could be claimed in a situation where the issue of the loan stock was at a price in excess of the market value and the issuer and creditor were connected parties.)

Gains from contracts for life insurance, etc. (ITTOIA 2005, ss 461–546)

Annual partial surrenders of single premium insurance policy

[52.76] An individual (S) entered into a policy with a Luxembourg insurance company, under which he paid a single premium of £200,000. At the commencement of the policy, he decided to effect annual partial surrenders of about £20,000. The Revenue issued assessments charging tax on these surrenders. S appealed, contending that they were capital payments and that the first £10,000 of each payment was tax-free under the legislation then in force (*ICTA 1988, ss 539–554*). The Special Commissioner accepted this contention and allowed the appeal. *Sugden v Kent*, Sp C [2001] SSCD 158 (Sp C 283).

Partial surrenders of life insurance policies

[52.77] In March 2006 an individual (S) paid £150,000 to purchase 50 overseas life insurance policies. In March 2007 he surrendered approximately one-third of the rights under the policies and withdrew £50,000. HMRC issued an assessment charging tax under *ITTOIA 2005, s 461 et seq*, treating £42,000 of the amount withdrawn as taxable income. The First-Tier Tribunal upheld the assessment and dismissed S's appeal. Judge Nowlan observed that S 'had not entirely understood the tax implications of making the partial surrenders', and that there would have been no charge to income tax if S had made total surrenders of 16 or 17 of the policies, rather than partial surrenders of all 50. *C Shanthiratnam v HMRC*, FTT [2011] UKFTT 360 (TC), TC01215.

[52.78] A similar decision was reached in a subsequent case in which Judge Poole observed that 'when parties are advised to invest in complex financial products for tax planning purposes, the outcome illustrates all too clearly the fact that full advice needs to be given as to all the implications of that decision and where any associated traps and pitfalls may lie'. *MH Rogers v HMRC*, FTT [2011] UKFTT 791 (TC), TC01627.

[52.79] The decisions in *Shanthiratnam v HMRC*, **52.77** above, and *MH Rogers v HMRC*, **52.78** above, were applied in the similar subsequent case of *RJ Anderson v HMRC*, FTT [2013] UKFTT 126 (TC), TC02555.

[52.80] In March 2002 an individual (C) had invested £66,000 in an Isle of Man life insurance policy. During 2002/03 he withdrew £24,300, and he made further withdrawals in the next two years. HMRC subsequently issued assessments under *ITTOIA 2005, s 498*. The First-Tier Tribunal upheld the assessments and dismissed C's appeal. *Capt S Cleghorn v HMRC*, FTT [2011] UKFTT 488 (TC), TC01335.

[52.81] In 2006 a Dutchman (L), who was working in the UK, invested $1,400,000 in life assurance policies. In the next two years he withdrew most of his investment by making a partial surrender of each policy. He did not declare this on his tax returns, and HMRC issued assessments charging tax under *ITTOIA 2005, s 461 et seq*, treating $560,000 as taxable income. The First-tier Tribunal dismissed L's appeal. Judge Hellier commented that the legislation produced an outrageously unfair result', but held that there was 'no way to give a different interpretation to the legislation'. *J Lobler v HMRC*, FTT [2013] UKFTT 141 (TC), TC02539.

[52.82] The decision in *Lobler v HMRC*, **52.81** above, was applied in the similar subsequent case of *R Downward v HMRC*, FTT [2013] UKFTT 517 (TC), TC02905.

Claim for deficiency relief

[52.83] An individual (M) claimed that he was entitled to a deduction for 'deficiency relief' of more than £1,800,000 for 2003/04, as a result of certain payments into and out of life insurance policies which had been assigned to him and which he had subsequently surrendered. As part of the scheme, additional premiums were added to the policies on 7 March 2003 and the amounts of those premiums were withdrawn 24 days later. HMRC rejected M's claim, considering that the part of the scheme whereby additional premiums were added and withdrawn in quick succession should be disregarded, applying the principles laid down in *WT Ramsay Ltd v CIR*, **71.285** CAPITAL GAINS TAX. M appealed. The Ch D allowed his appeal (reversing the decision of the Special Commissioner) and the CA upheld this decision. Mummery LJ held that the decision in *WT Ramsay Ltd v CIR* 'did not lay down a special doctrine of revenue law striking down tax avoidance schemes on the ground that they are artificial composite transactions and that parts of them can be disregarded for fiscal purposes because they are self-cancelling and were inserted solely for tax avoidance purposes and for no commercial purpose. The *Ramsay* principle is the general principle of purposive and contextual construction of all legislation. ICTA is no exception and is not immune from it. That principle has displaced the more literal, blinkered and formalistic approach to revenue statutes often applied before *Ramsay*. The essence of the principle applicable to this case is that the ICTA provisions on the taxation of life insurance policies are to be given a purposive construction in order to determine the nature of the transaction to which they were intended to apply.' On the facts of this case, 'although the corresponding deficiency was created solely to save tax, that alone does not entitle the court to disregard the fiscal consequences of payment of premium and the partial surrender which led to its creation'. The court could not 'as a matter of construction, deprive those events of their fiscal effects under ICTA'. Toulson LJ observed that the relevant legislation 'creates a complex set of rules for determining when a gain is to be treated as arising in connection with a life insurance policy. Inherent in the scheme is the possibility of a disconnection between what would be regarded as a gain on an ordinary commercial view and what is to be treated as a gain for the purposes of the statute. In some cases a taxpayer may be liable for a gain which the statute requires him to be treated as having made, although the chargeable event giving rise to the deemed gain has not caused him to make an equivalent gain in real terms.' In the present case, however, the deviser of the scheme had 'found a clever way of making the legislative structure work to HMRC's disadvantage by devising a series of steps giving rise to a chargeable event and a corresponding deficiency, albeit that the taxpayer was no worse off commercially'. *HMRC v D Mayes*, CA [2011] EWCA Civ 407; TL 3840; [2011] STC 1269. (*Notes*. (1) M also claimed a capital loss on his surrender of the bonds. The Ch D held that the Special Commissioner had not determined 'what the purchase consideration or its constituent elements were given for', and remitted the case to the First-Tier Tribunal for rehearing. The CA upheld this decision. (2) Thomas LJ observed that 'the higher rate taxpayers with large earnings or significant investment income who have taken advantage of the scheme have received benefits that cannot possibly have been intended and which must be paid for by other taxpayers. It must be for Parliament to consider the wider implications of the decision as it relates to the way in which revenue legislation is structured and drafted'. (3) The Supreme Court rejected HMRC's application for leave to appeal against the CA decision.)

53

Schedule D—Superseded Legislation

The cases in this chapter are arranged under the following headings.

NOTE

The provisions charging income tax under Schedule D were abolished with regard to individuals by the *Income Tax (Trading and Other Income) Act 2005* and with regard to corporation tax by the *Corporation Tax Act 2009*. Consequently, the cases noted in this chapter are now of historical interest only. For detailed coverage of the changes, see Tolley's Income Tax.

Scope of Schedule D (ICTA 1988, s 18)

Trade carried on abroad—basis of assessment

[53.1] A UK resident was a partner in an Australian firm, the business of which was carried on in Australia. He did not take any active part in the partnership business. He was assessed under Schedule D Case I on the full amount of his share of the profits of the business. The HL held that his partnership interest was a possession within Schedule D Case V, assessable on the remittance basis under the legislation then in force. *Colquhoun v Brooks*, HL 1889, 2 TC 490; 14 AC 493. (*Note*. This case was of historical importance in establishing that the charge under Case I did not extend to trades controlled and carried on abroad, although its practical importance was diminished by *ICTA 1988, s 112*, deriving from *FA 1914*. See now *ITTOIA 2005, s 6(1)*, which provides that profits of a trade arising to a UK resident are chargeable to tax wherever the trade is carried on. For non-trading income, see *ITTOIA 2005, ss 368, 577*.)

Profits from letting unfurnished premises with services

[53.2] In two cases heard together in the HL, two estate companies let buildings in rooms and suites as unfurnished offices to numerous tenants. In addition to the rents, they derived profits from the provision of lighting, cleaning, caretaking and other services, and accepted Schedule D liability in respect of these profits. The Revenue issued Schedule D Case I assessments on the basis that the companies were carrying on a trade and that all their receipts, including their rental profits (reduced by the amounts of the Schedule A assessments on the buildings under the law in force at the time), were within Case I. The CA allowed the companies' appeals, and the HL upheld this decision. The rents were covered by the Schedule A assessments and could not be brought into any Schedule D assessment. *Salisbury House Estate Ltd v Fry; City of London Real Property Co Ltd v Jones*, HL 1930, 15 TC 266; [1930] AC 432.

[53.3] The decision in *Salisbury House Estate Ltd v Fry*, 53.2 above, was applied in a subsequent case where a company owned an aerodrome licensed for public use. It received rents and other income from the occupation or use of its buildings by private flying clubs, and from garage rents, housing and landing fees, and other sources. It was assessed under Schedules A and B (under the law in force at the time) in respect of the land, and under Schedule D in respect of the profit from its various sources of revenue. The CA held (by a 2–1 majority, du Parcq LJ dissenting) that the company's liability to tax was exhausted by the Schedule A and B assessments. *Sywell Aerodrome Ltd v Croft*, CA 1941, 24 TC 126; [1942] 1 KB 317, [1942] 1 All ER 110.

Annuity to retired clergyman

[53.4] In a Scottish case, an annuity which was granted to a minister of the Church of Scotland, on condition that he retired from the parish, was held to be assessable under Schedule D Case III. *Duncan's Executors v Farmer*, CE 1909, 5 TC 417. (*Note*. Under the legislation in force at the time, the annuity was not assessable under Schedule E because it was granted after the office had ceased, and thus could not be said to have arisen from it. However, since the clergyman had given consideration, in that he covenanted to resign, the income was held to be assessable as an annuity under Schedule D. The annuity would probably now be treated as a pension within *ITEPA 2003, ss 565–608*.)

Assessment issued under wrong Case of Schedule D

[53.5] An individual (P), who had a family home in England, agreed to work in Nigeria for two years as an agent for a UK company. The company paid him commission. The Revenue assessed the agent under Schedule D Case V under the legislation then in force. P appealed. The KB allowed his appeal and the HL unanimously upheld this decision, holding that the source of income was not wholly abroad, so that the liability was under Schedule D Case II rather than Case V. The HL declined to remit the appeal to the Commissioners to treat the assessment as one under Case II, since the Revenue had been aware of the full facts and had deliberately chosen to proceed under Case V. *Pickles v Foulsham*, HL 1925, 9 TC 261; [1925] AC 458.

[53.6] A company had sold land to the War Department at the beginning of the Second World War, subject to a right to repurchase it at market value. In July 1962 it contracted to repurchase the land for £42,000, and in August 1962 it contracted to sell it for £113,000. The Revenue assessed the profit under Schedule D Case VII. The company appealed, contending that the assessment was invalid because the transaction was an adventure in the nature of trade, so that the gain should have been assessed under Case I. The Special Commissioners rejected this contention and dismissed the appeal, holding that the assessment was valid. The Ch D upheld this decision, holding that, where an assessment had been raised under the wrong Case of Schedule D, the court had a discretion to deal with it under the correct Case, and that it should exercise such a discretion in this instance because the company had misled the Revenue by not supplying all the relevant facts. Walton J observed that 'any other conclusion than the one to which I have come in this case would place an absolutely intolerable strain upon Inspectors of Taxes; they would either have to spend so much time considering what alternative assessments might possibly be applicable if the facts were not as they had been told by the taxpayer that the whole business of their offices would grind to a near halt, or else they would automatically have to duplicate assessments under every conceivable Case, thus straining the resources of their offices and making life extremely difficult for the taxpayer.' (However, he also held that, for the purpose of computing the profits of the adventure, the cost of acquiring the land included the value of the pre-emption rights which the company had obtained when it first sold the land. Accordingly, he remitted the case to the Commissioners to establish the value of the pre-emption rights.) *Bath & West Counties Property Trust Ltd v Thomas*, Ch D 1977, 52 TC 20; [1978] STC 30; [1977] 1 WLR 1423; [1978] 1 All ER 305.

ICTA 1988, s 18(3)—income from overseas investments*

[53.7] The income of a fire insurance company included interest on American securities forming a reserve, as required by US law, in respect of business in America. The interest was retained in America, but brought to account in the company's books. The QB held that the interest was part of its profits within Case I and not within Case IV, and that, even if it had been within Case IV, it had been remitted to the UK. (Under the law then in force, the remittance basis applied to Case IV.) *Norwich Union Fire Insurance Co v Magee*, QB 1896, 3 TC 457.

[53.8] The income of an insurance company included income from investments abroad which had not been remitted to this country, and accordingly was not assessable under Case IV or V (under the law in force at the time). The HL held that the income was part of the receipts of the business which fell, at the Revenue's option, to be included in the Case I assessment. The HL also held that the Revenue could not be compelled to proceed under Case IV or V if it preferred to proceed under Case I. *Liverpool & London & Globe Insurance Co v Bennett (and related appeals)*, HL 1913, 6 TC 327; [1913] AC 610.

ICTA 1988, s 18(3)—sale of properties*

[53.9] An individual (P), who had worked for several years in the building industry, firstly as an employee and later as a company director, bought seven properties in the years 1920 to 1924 and sold four of them in that period. The Revenue issued Schedule D assessments. On appeal, the Revenue defended the assessments under Case I or, alternatively, under Case VI. The Commissioners determined the appeals on the basis that there was liability under Case VI. The KB held that, as a matter of law, the profits could not be within Case VI, and remitted the case to the Commissioners to consider whether the transactions constituted a trade within Case I. *Pearn v Miller*, KB 1927, 11 TC 610. (*Note*. The outcome of the remission to the Commissioners was not reported. Compare *Leeming v Jones*, **53.10** below, in which the KB made a similar remission to the Commissioners.)

[53.10] A syndicate, comprising two partnerships, a solicitor and one other person (L), acquired options over two rubber estates and assigned its rights to a public company, the promotion of which was arranged by the solicitor. The Revenue assessed L under Schedule D on his share of the syndicate's profit, and appealed. The Revenue defended the assessment under Case I or, alternatively, under Case VI. The Commissioners initially confirmed the assessment under Case VI but the KB remitted the case to them, holding that the profits could not be within Case VI. The Commissioners then produced a Supplementary Case, accepting L's contention that the transaction was not a concern in the nature of trade, following which the KB allowed L's appeal. The CA and HL unanimously upheld this decision. Lord Buckmaster approved *dicta* of Lawrence LJ that in the case of an isolated transaction 'there is really no middle course open. It is either an adventure in the nature of trade, or else it is simply a case of sale and resale of property'. *Leeming v Jones*, HL 1930, 15 TC 333; [1930] AC 415.

ICTA 1988, s 18(3)—letting of rooms to students*

[53.11] Two chartered accountants derived income from the furnished letting, mainly to students, of more than 180 rooms in properties they had acquired in Bristol. The Revenue assessed them on the basis that the profits were assessable under Case VI. They appealed, contending that the profits were assessable under Schedule D Case I as trading profits. The Ch D rejected this contention and upheld the Case VI assessments. Vinelott J held that it was a cardinal principle of tax law that income derived from the exercise of property rights was not from carrying on a trade. *Griffiths v Jackson; Griffiths v Pearman*, Ch D 1982, 56 TC 583; [1983] STC 184. (*Note*. The income would now be assessable under *ITTOIA 2005, s 308*. See **46** PROPERTY INCOME for cases concerning this provision.)

ICTA 1988, s 18(3)—income from overseas partnership*

[53.12] A television entertainer (F), resident in the UK, was assessed under Schedule D Case II. In 1967, in order to minimise his tax liabilities on overseas earnings, he entered into partnership with a Bahaman company to carry on the business of exploiting television artistes outside the UK. The profits of the partnership arose from F's appearances on US television. The day-to-day management of the business was in the hands of the Bahaman company and partnership decisions were by a majority, the company having two votes and the taxpayer one. The company received 5% of the profits and F received 95%. None of this was remitted to the UK in the relevant years. The Revenue considered that the partnership was not valid for tax purposes, and included F's share of the partnership profits in Case II assessments on him. He appealed, contending that the work which he carried out for the overseas partnership was distinct from the self-employed work which he carried on in the UK, and that his income from the partnership was only assessable under Case V. (Under the law then in force, the Case V liability was on the remittance basis.) The General Commissioners allowed F's appeal and the Ch D, CA and HL unanimously upheld this decision. Viscount Dilhorne held that the partnership was not a sham, but was carrying on a trade of helping to exploit F's talents. It had been formed with a view to making profits, and the fact that it also had the object of avoiding tax did not render it invalid. *Newstead v Frost*, HL 1980, 53 TC 525; [1980] STC 123; [1980] 1 WLR 135; [1980] 1 All ER 363.

Life assurance company—untaxed interest

[53.13] A life assurance company was assessed under Schedule D Case III on its untaxed interest. It appealed, contending that the interest formed part of its profits and could not be separately assessed. (Its overall profits, taking into account its taxed income and the untaxed interest, were less than the amount of its taxed income.) The Commissioners rejected this contention and dismissed the company's appeal, and the CA unanimously upheld their decision. *Clerical Medical & General Life Assurance Co v Carter*, CA 1889, 2 TC 437; 22 QBD 444.

[53.14] A similar decision was reached in a subsequent Scottish case. *Revell v Edinburgh Life Insurance Co*, CE 1906, 5 TC 221.

Interest payable on loan to Netherlands company

[53.15] An individual lent £1,500,000 to a Netherlands company, repayable by instalments. The CA unanimously held that the interest on the loan was taxable under Schedule D Case V (rather than under Schedule D Case IV). *Lord Manton's Trustees v Steele*, CA 1927, 11 TC 549.

Shares in overseas company resident in the UK

[53.16] See *Bradbury v English Sewing Cotton Co Ltd*, 28.12 FOREIGN INCOME.

Avoidance scheme—payments under lease agreements

[53.17] Under a series of transactions forming part of a complex avoidance scheme, in 1995 and 1996 a company (P) agreed to lease a number of properties to its parent company (C). The properties covered by the 1996 agreement were within *Landlord and Tenant (Covenants) Act 1995*, but the properties covered by the 1995 agreement were not. In August 1996 P sold all its assets to another group company (G), under an agreement whereby it would retain a payment of rent due from C two weeks later. C then sold P to an outside purchaser. It was intended to create a tax saving which would be shared between C and the purchaser. However (for reasons which are not fully set out in the decision), it was subsequently 'accepted that the proposed tax avoidance scheme to create a deduction did not work'. The Revenue issued corporation tax assessments on P, charging tax on the 'retained rent payment'. P appealed, contending that this payment was not taxable because, in the accounting period in which it received the payment, it had no interest in land. The Special Commissioners reviewed the evidence in detail and held that part of the payment, relating to those properties affected by the *Landlord and Tenant (Covenants) Act 1995*, was taxable under Schedule D Case VI since it arose from 'a contractual right against (G)'. The Commissioners held that the payment in question 'is not rent and it has no legal connection with land because the effect of the 1995 Act is that it is not possible to retain such an interest in land'. However, the Commissioners held that the part of the payment relating to the properties covered by the 1995 agreement, to which the *Landlord and Tenant (Covenants) Act 1995* did not apply, was not taxable because it arose from a Schedule A source which was not possessed in the period when the right to it arose. The Commissioners' decision records that it was 'common ground that the source doctrine applies to Schedule A' and that an estate or interest in or right over land 'must be possessed in the relevant accounting period'. *Property Company v HM Inspector of Taxes*, Sp C 2004, [2005] SSCD 59 (Sp C 433). (*Note*. The 'source doctrine' was laid down by the majority HL decision in the 1921 case of *National Provident Institution v Brown*, **52.51** SAVINGS AND INVESTMENT INCOME. However, the decision in question was not followed by the HL in the 2000 case of *The Centaur Clothes Group Ltd v Walker*, **5.14** ASSESSMENT: see in particular the leading judgment of Lord Hoffmann. The Special Commissioners' decision in *Property Company v HM Inspector of Taxes* fails to make any reference to the 2000 HL decision in *Centaur Clothes Group Ltd v Walker*, which counsel for the Revenue apparently failed to cite as an authority.)

Cases I and II—'Preceding year' basis of assessment (ICTA 1988, ss 60–63 as originally enacted)

NOTE

The rules governing the basis of assessment under Schedule D, Cases I and II, were radically altered by *FA 1994*. *ICTA 1988, ss 60–63* were substituted by *FA 1994, ss 200–204*. The new rules generally apply with effect from 1996/97, except for trades, etc. beginning after 5 April 1994, when they apply from commencement. The cases noted at **53.18** to **53.22** below relate to periods before the enactment of *FA 1994*, and should be read in the light of these changes. For detailed coverage of the changes, see Tolley's Income Tax.

Change of accounting date

[53.18] A company changed its accounting date from 31 January to 30 April, its first accounts to the new date being those for the 15 months to 30 April 1965. Following standard practice, the Revenue fixed the basis periods as the year to 30 April 1964 for 1965/66 and the year to 30 April 1963 for 1964/65, with the consequence that the profits of the nine months to 31 January 1963

(£78,798) entered into the basis periods of both 1963/64 and 1964/65, and that, under the provisions of *FA 1965*, the company's profits became liable to corporation tax from 1 May 1964 rather than from 1 February 1965 as they would have done if there had been no change of accounting date. The company appealed, contending that there had been a double assessment which should be remedied by reducing the 1964/65 assessment by the £78,798. The HL unanimously rejected this contention and upheld the assessments, holding that the impact of corporation tax was irrelevant and there was no basis for relief. Lord Wilberforce held that 'any supposed hardship arising from the overlap in the financial year 1964/65 of corporation tax and income tax is inherent in the nature of that tax and is common in some degree to all trading companies. The courts cannot regard as an injustice that which merely flows from the nature of a tax as devised by Parliament.' *CIR v Helical Bar Ltd*, HL 1972, 48 TC 221; [1972] AC 773; [1972] 1 All ER 1205.

Commencement of new trade

[53.19] In the case noted at 59.91 TRADING INCOME, the Special Commissioner had upheld an author's contention that he had begun a separate trade of publishing in 1993/94. Following this decision, the Revenue issued income tax assessments under Schedule D Case I accordingly (with the result that the profits attributable to the publishing trade in 1993/94 were assessed for both that year and the following year, under the basis of assessment rules then in force). The author appealed, contending that the profits could not be assessed again, since they had been included in the 1994/95 Case II assessment on him as an author. The Special Commissioner rejected this contention, holding that the effect of *TMA, s 32* was that the amount in question should be taken out of the Case II assessment and assessed under Case I. (The Commissioner observed that 'if this results in the figure of £2,025 apparently being assessed more than once under the rules applicable to new trades, that is simply the result of those rules, and of the appellant's insistence that he was carrying on such a trade'.) *Salt v Fernandez (No 2)*, Sp C [1998] SSCD 176 (Sp C 162).

Further assessments on cessation—whether discretionary

[53.20] A husband and wife traded as greengrocers until 1985. Following the cessation of the trade, the Revenue raised further assessments for 1983/84 and 1984/85. The couple appealed, contending that the issue of such further assessments was discretionary and that the inspector had followed mandatory instructions from the Revenue and had not exercised his discretion. The General Commissioners allowed the appeals but the Ch D reversed their decision. On a true construction of the legislation then in force, taking into account its history commencing with *FA 1926*, the inspector did not have a general discretion as to whether or not to make the further assessments. *Baylis v Roberts & Roberts*, Ch D 1989, 62 TC 384; [1989] STC 693.

Discontinuance rules—balancing charges

[53.21] The KB upheld an assessment issued on the discontinuance of a company's trade, holding that a balancing charge arising under legislation which has subsequently been repealed was not part of the profits or gains of the year for which it was assessed. *Townsend v Electrical Yarns Ltd*, KB 1952, 33 TC 166; [1952] 1 All ER 918.

[53.22] A company, which made up its accounts to 31 December each year, carried on an electricity undertaking in Madras until 29 August 1947, when it was purchased by the Madras Government. The company's profits had been assessed under Schedule D Case I, and the Revenue assessed a balancing charge on the company for 1947/48 on the basis that the Madras Government had succeeded to the company's trade, that the basis period for the 1947/48 assessment was the period from 6 April 1947 to 29 August 1947, and that the sale of the company's undertaking occurred in that basis period. The company appealed, contending that the person succeeding to its trade was the Crown, and that its basis period for 1947/48 was the year ending 31 December 1946, and not the period in which the sale occurred. The Ch D, CA and HL unanimously rejected this contention and upheld the assessment. *Boarland v Madras Electric Supply Corporation Ltd*, HL 1955, 35 TC 611; [1955] AC 667; [1955] 1 All ER 753.

Cases I and II—'Current year' basis of assessment (FA 1994, ss 200–205)

Change of accounting period—apportionment of accounts

[53.23] A firm of architects prepared accounts for the 12 months from 1 May 1995 to 30 April 1996, and for the 12 months from 1 May 1996 to 30 April 1997. It then changed its accounting date to 31 March, so that its next accounts were prepared for the 11 months from 1 May 1997 to 31 March 1998, and its 1997/98 basis period was the 23 months from 1 May 1996 to 31 March 1998. *FA 1994, Sch 20 para 2(4)* required that the profits or gains of the basis period for 1997/98 which arose before 6 April 1997 should be calculated and treated as an 'overlap profit' for the purposes of *ICTA 1988, s 63A*. One of the partners submitted a 1997/98 return, computing the 'overlap profit' on the basis that it was necessary to time-apportion the profits for the 23-month period from 1 May 1996 to 31 March 1998 (700 days), and take $^{340}/_{700}$ of the profits for this period as the overlap profit. The Revenue issued a ruling that the overlap profit should be calculated by taking $^{340}/_{365}$ of the profits for the twelve months ending after 30 April 1997. The Special Commissioner upheld the Revenue's ruling and dismissed the architect's appeal, holding that the Revenue's method of apportionment was in accordance with the wording of *ICTA 1988, s 72*, avoided anomalies and produced a consistent result which 'bears a truer relationship to the actual profits arising before 6 April 1997' and was 'consistent with the principle underlying the current year basis of assessment'. *Lyons v Kelly*, Sp C [2002] SSCD 455 (Sp C 334).

1996/97 assessment—application of FA 1994, Sch 20 para 2

[53.24] A dentist appealed against assessments for 1995/96 and 1996/97. The 1995/96 assessment was computed on the 'preceding year' basis as required by the legislation then in force (*ICTA 1988, s 60*), and the 1996/97 assessment was computed in accordance with *FA 1994, Sch 20 para 2(2)*. The dentist appealed, contending that his 1996/97 assessment should be computed on an 'actual year' basis, rather than in accordance with *Sch 20 para 2(2)*. The General Commissioners rejected this contention and upheld the assessments, and the Ch D dismissed the dentist's appeal. *Chauhan v Wilson*, Ch D 2004, [2005] STC 1786; [2004] EWHC 3364 (Ch). (*Note*. The dentist appeared in person.)

Case III—basis of assessment (ICTA 1988, s 64 as originally enacted)

NOTE

The basis of assessment under Schedule D Case III was amended *by FA 1994. ICTA 1988, s 64* was substituted by *FA 1994, s 206*, to provide for assessment to be on a 'current year' basis. The cases in this section should be read in the light of this change.

The 'commencing years' rules

[53.25] An individual received bank interest which first arose in 1974/75. Accordingly, under the legislation then in force, the assessments on him for 1975/76 and 1976/77 were both based on the interest which arose in 1975/76. He appealed against the 1976/77 assessment, contending that the interest had already been assessed for 1975/76. The Ch D dismissed his appeal. *Beese v Mackinlay*, Ch D [1980] STC 228. (*Note*. The appellant appeared in person. It was not to his advantage to claim the 'current year' basis for 1976/77.)

[53.26] An individual received interest on a Government security without deduction of tax. He was assessed on the current year basis for the first three years, and appealed against preceding year basis assessments for the fourth and fifth years, contending that he was being assessed on the same income twice and that he was being required to pay tax before he had received the full interest in the year of assessment. The Commissioners dismissed his appeal and the Ch D upheld their decision. *Moore v Austin*, Ch D 1985, 59 TC 110; [1985] STC 673.

Government securities including Exchequer Bonds

[53.27] A widow received interest in full on three different types of Government securities, including a holding of 6% Exchequer Bonds which were redeemed in February 1920. She was assessed for 1920/21 on the whole of the interest which she had received in 1919/20 on Government securities, including the interest on the 6% Exchequer Bonds. She appealed, contending that the interest on the Bonds was a separate source of income and should not be included in the assessment. The Commissioners accepted this contention and allowed her appeal, and the Ch D and CA unanimously upheld their decision, applying the principles laid down in *National Provident Institution v Brown*, **52.51** SAVINGS AND INVESTMENT INCOME. *Grainger v Maxwell's Executors*, CA 1925, 10 TC 139; [1926] 1 KB 430.

Interest waived—whether source ceased

[53.28] An individual (C) was a major shareholder in a small bank. He held a deposit account with the bank, to which interest had been credited for several years . For 1930/31 he agreed to waive interest on the account. The Revenue assessed C under Case III for 1930/31 on the interest credited in 1929/30, on the preceding year basis. C appealed, contending that the source had ceased. The Commissioners rejected this contention and upheld the assessment, and the KB upheld their decision. *Cull v Cowcher*, KB 1934, 18 TC 449.

Substantial addition to deposit account—whether new source

[53.29] An individual (S) had for many years kept a bank deposit account. Interest was calculated on a day-to-day basis and credited on 20 June and 20 December. On 17 March 1951, he paid £2,000,000 into the account. The Revenue issued Case III assessments for 1951/52 and 1952/53 on a current year basis. S appealed, contending that the assessments should have been under a preceding year basis under the legislation then in force. The Ch D rejected this contention and upheld the assessments, holding that a new source or addition to a source was acquired on 17 March 1951. The CA unanimously upheld this decision. *Hart v Sangster*, CA 1957, 37 TC 231; [1957] Ch 329; [1957] 2 All ER 308.

Cases IV and V—Basis of assessment (ICTA 1988, s 65 as originally enacted)

NOTE

The basis of assessment under Schedule D, Cases IV and V, was amended by *FA 1994*. *ICTA 1988, s 65* was amended by *FA 1994, s 207*, to provide for assessment to be on a 'current year' basis. The cases in this section should be read in the light of this change.

New resident

[53.30] An individual took up permanent residence in the UK on 7 April 1927. While resident abroad, he had received income from non-UK stocks and shares. Income from the same sources continued after his coming to England. The Revenue issued assessments on the basis that the source should be regarded as beginning when he became resident in the UK, so that the income was assessable on a current year basis. He appealed, contending that the income first arose before he became resident in the UK, and was therefore assessable on a preceding year basis under the legislation then in force. The KB rejected this contention and upheld the assessments. *Back v Whitlock*, KB 1932, 16 TC 723; [1932] 1 KB 747.

[53.31] A doctor who had been in partnership in a South African practice for several years came to the UK in June 1948 and remained here. The South African partnership ceased in December 1949. For 1949/50, he was resident, but not domiciled, in the UK and he was assessed for that year on remittances of his South African profits including a sum received in March 1950. He appealed, contending that this amount should be excluded from the profits. The Special Commissioners rejected this contention and dismissed the appeal, and the Ch D upheld their decision. *Joffe v Thain*, Ch D 1955, 36 TC 199.

Differing interests under foreign will—whether separate source

[53.32] An American woman (V) died in 1950. Under her will, her daughter, who had married an English peer and become resident in the UK, was entitled to 25% of the income of the estate. V's husband died in January 1955, and the daughter became entitled to the whole of the income, and also, under a codicil, to 1% of the capital on each of the first twenty anniversaries of her mother's death. The percentage payments were treated as capital under the relevant American law. The Revenue issued assessments (on V's son-in-law under the legislation then in force) on the basis that they should be treated as income, and that the payments under the codicil were from a new source and were assessable on the current year basis. He appealed, contending firstly that they should be treated as capital, and alternatively that the will and codicil constituted a single source of income rather than three separate sources (so that the 1954/55 and 1955/56 assessments should be on the preceding year basis). The Ch D upheld the assessments in principle, but allowed the appeals in part, holding firstly that the percentage payments were income, and secondly that the will and codicil constituted a single source of income rather than three separate sources. *Lord Inchyra v Jennings*, Ch D 1965, 42 TC 388; [1966] Ch 37; [1965] 2 All ER 714.

Miscellaneous

CTA 2009, s 1307(1)—whether accounts 'drawn up'*

[53.33] The accounts of a company presented to its shareholders in annual general meetings were for the year to 30 June, but half-yearly accounts, to 31 December and 30 June, were regularly prepared for the board of directors. The Revenue issued excess profits tax assessments on the basis that the accounting periods were the successive years to 30 June, and that the half-yearly accounts were not 'made up' for the business within the meaning of the relevant excess profits tax legislation. The Special Commissioners upheld the assessments and dismissed the company's appeal, and the CA unanimously upheld their decision. *Jenkins Productions Ltd v CIR*, CA 1944, 29 TC 142; [1944] 1 All ER 610.

[53.34] The decision in *Jenkins Productions Ltd v CIR*, 53.33 above, was applied in an Irish case where the facts and the relevant legislation were similar. *Revenue Commissioners v R Hilliard & Sons Ltd*, SC(I) 1948, 2 ITC 410.

[53.35] In a case involving an appeal against a surtax direction, a company had sold its business, carrying it on until 30 January 1937 (a Saturday). Its auditor made up accounts for the seven months to 31 January 1937, which were submitted to the Special Commissioners but were not signed by the directors nor formally approved. The company contended that its accounts had not been 'made up' within the meaning of *FA 1922*. The Special Commissioners rejected this contention and dismissed the appeal, holding that the accounts had been 'made up', and the KB upheld their decision. *BFP Holdings v CIR*, KB 1942, 24 TC 483.

Apportionment of accounts—whether time basis obligatory

[53.36] See *Marshall Hus & Partners Ltd v Bolton*, 18.89 CORPORATION TAX.

ICTA 1988, s 74—whether expenditure deductible*

[53.37] A firm of solicitors found it convenient to discuss business affairs with clients at lunch. It claimed the cost of such lunches as deductions in computing its profits. The Revenue rejected the claim but the CA allowed the firm's appeal, holding on the evidence that the business purpose was the sole purpose of the lunches, and that the fact that the nature of the activity necessarily involved an incidental benefit (food and drink for the partner entertaining the client) was not conclusive. *Bentleys Stokes & Lowless v Beeson*, CA 1952, 33 TC 491; [1952] 2 All ER 82. (*Note*. The decision has subsequently been overtaken by the entertainment expenses legislation of *ITTOIA 2005, ss 45–47*, but is still occasionally cited as an authority on the 'wholly and exclusively' rules of *ICTA 1988, s 74(1)(a)* and *ITTOIA 2005, s 34*. However, Romer LJ's *dicta* on the 'purpose' of expenditure should be read in the light of Lord Brightman's judgment in *Mallalieu v Drummond*, 63.216 TRADING PROFITS.)

FA 1989, s 43 as originally enacted—employee benefit trust

[53.38] Six associated companies claimed deductions for payments which they made to an employee benefit trust. The Revenue rejected the claims, considering that the payments were 'potential emoluments' within *FA 1989, s 43(11) as originally enacted*, so that no deduction was allowable until the relevant employees were taxed on the fund as an emolument. The companies appealed, contending that the payments should not be treated as 'potential emoluments' within *s 43(11)*. The HL unanimously rejected this contention and dismissed the companies' appeals. Lord Hoffmann held that 'in the ordinary use of language, the whole of the funds were potential emoluments. They could be used to pay emoluments.' He observed that this was 'the result of an arrangement into which the taxpayers have chosen to enter. Any untoward consequences can be avoided by segregating the funds held on trust to pay emoluments from funds held to benefit employees in other ways.' *Dextra Accessories Ltd & Others v MacDonald*, HL 2005, 77 TC 146; [2005] STC 1111; [2005] UKHL 47; [2005] 4 All ER 107. (*Notes.* (1) See now *ITTOIA 2005, ss 36, 37* and *CTA 2009, ss 1288, 1289. FA 1989, s 43* was amended by *FA 2003, Sch 24* with effect from 27 November 2002, and was substituted by *ITEPA 2003, s 722* with effect for accounting periods ending after 5 April 2003. The changes were intended to provide that any contributions into an employee benefit trust will only attract corporation tax relief for the sponsoring company when payments subject to income tax and NICs have been made to the underlying employees. See Inland Revenue Budget Notice BN27, reproduced at SWTI 2003, pp 737–738. (2) For appeals against assessments on the employees, see *Caudwell & Others v MacDonald*, **22.169** EMPLOYMENT INCOME.)

[53.39] See also *HMRC v Household Estate Agents Ltd*, **5.71** ASSESSMENT, and *Sempra Metals Ltd v HMRC*, **63.267** TRADING PROFITS.

FA 1996, Sch 13—relevant discounted securities

[53.40] A wealthy investor (C) entered into a complex scheme, devised by a bank, which was intended to give rise to an income tax loss which would offset an anticipated gain on the exercise of certain share options. Following the implementation of the scheme, he claimed loss relief of £2,483,100 in respect of the transfer of some loan notes to his wife. The Revenue rejected the claim on the basis that the purpose of the scheme was to produce a loss, and that the effect of the HL decision in *WT Ramsay Ltd v CIR*, **71.285** CAPITAL GAINS TAX, was that the relevant transactions should be disregarded. C appealed, contending that the loan notes were a 'relevant discounted security', within *FA 1996, Sch 13*, and that there was 'a commercial objective to invest' as well as 'a tax motive'. The Special Commissioners reviewed the evidence in detail and allowed his appeal, finding that he had a commercial purpose in subscribing for the loan notes, but that his decision to give them to his wife was 'wholly tax-motivated'. The Commissioners held that 'the circumstances in which a person sustains a loss from the discount on a relevant discounted security and the amount of such loss are specifically articulated in *paragraph 2* of *Schedule 13*, subject to *paragraph 8* when the transfer is to a connected person. The appellant sustained a loss under the express terms of the statute. The concept of sustaining a loss in *paragraph 2* is an artificial construct which encompasses situations such as gifts which would not either in ordinary parlance or in a commercial sense be regarded as giving rise to a loss. The decided cases do not support the implication of an additional condition that the transactions resulting in the loss should not have been for the sole purpose of producing a loss or otherwise avoiding tax.' *Campbell v CIR*, Sp C [2004] SSCD 396 (Sp C 421). (*Notes.* (1) *FA 1996, Sch 13 para 2* was repealed by *FA 2003* with regard to securities transferred or redeemed on or after 27 March 2003. (2) The Revenue accepted that C had paid a subscription of £3,750,000 for the loan notes. The decision here was distinguished in the subsequent case of *Audley v HMRC*, **52.73** SAVINGS AND INVESTMENT INCOME, where the First-Tier Tribunal specifically rejected the appellant's claim that he had paid more than £2,000,000 for loan notes. A similar decision was reached in

Bretten v HMRC, 52.74 SAVINGS AND INVESTMENT INCOME, where Judge Mosedale specifically criticised HMRC's conduct of the *Campbell* case for having mistakenly accepted that the loan notes had been issued at full value.)

[53.41] See also *Astall v HMRC*, 52.71 SAVINGS AND INVESTMENT INCOME.

54

Schedule E—Superseded Legislation

The cases in this chapter are arranged under the following headings.

GENERAL NOTE

From *ITA 1842* to *FA 1922*, income from 'public offices or employments' was assessed under Schedule E, but income from other employments was assessed under Schedule D. Following the HL decision in *Great Western Railway Co Ltd v Bater*, 22.23 EMPLOYMENT INCOME, the scope of Schedule E was extended to include employments which had previously been assessed under Schedule D, Case II. Employment income continued to be assessed under Schedule E until 5 April 2003. The *Income Tax (Earnings and Pensions) Act 2003* received Royal Assent on 6 March 2003, with the result that the previous provisions whereby income tax on earned income was charged under Schedule E therefore no longer have effect for 2003/04 and subsequent years. For details, see Tolley's Income Tax. The cases in this chapter are those which are primarily of historical interest. For summaries of cases relating to years up to and including 2002/03, which appear to remain relevant to the new legislation, see 22 EMPLOYMENT INCOME. For cases concerning deduction of tax by employers, see 42 PAY AS YOU EARN.

Scope of Schedule E (ICTA 1988, s 19)

[54.1] In a case where the substantive issue has been superseded by subsequent legislation, Lord Macnaghten held that the charge under Schedule E extended 'only to money payment or payments convertible into money' and that a taxpayer was chargeable 'not on what saves his pocket, but on what goes into his pocket'. Lord Field held that, under the legislation then in force, the appellant was not taxable on benefits which 'could not in any way be converted by him into money or money's worth'. *Tennant v Smith*, HL 1892, 3 TC 158; [1892] AC 150. (*Note*. The case concerned the provision of living accommodation, which is now chargeable to tax under *ICTA 1988, ss 145–146A* and *ITEPA 2003, ss 97–113*. However, HMRC accept that the 'money's worth' principle established in this case continued to apply in respect of other benefits in kind: see Employment–Related Securities Manual, para ERSM22030.)

[54.2] A company arranged for its male employees to be supplied with clothing up to a cost of £15 as a Christmas present. The employees were given a letter to be presented to a local tailor. The tailor then invoiced the company for the cost of the clothing. The CA held that, under the provisions of *ITA 1952* as then in force, the assessable amount was the second-hand value of the clothing, rather than its cost. *Wilkins v Rogerson*, CA 1960, 39 TC 344. (*Note*. The substantive issue is now governed by *ICTA 1988, s 141* and *ITEPA 2003, ss 73–96*, so that the assessable amount would now be the cost of the clothing. However, the case is still occasionally cited as an authority on the principles of what constitutes an emolument.)

[54.3] In a case concerning provisions relating to the basis of assessment which are now obsolete, Rowlatt J held that the question 'whether there are two separate employments or two activities in one employment' was 'a pure question of fact, and in a case like this it may be one way or the other'. *Elliott v Guastavino*, KB 1924, 8 TC 632. (*Note.* Despite the subsequent changes in the legislation, this case is still occasionally cited as an authority on the question of 'whether a person is exercising two employments or vocations or merely two activities of one employment or vocation'. See, for example, Simon's Taxes, para E4.222.)

Benefits in kind (ICTA 1988, ss 154–165)

[54.4] A public company established an educational trust fund for the benefit of its employees. The trustees made discretionary awards to children of two of the company's employees. It was accepted that, in the hands of the children, the awards were scholarship income, within the exemption of *ICTA 1988, s 331**. The Revenue issued assessments on the parents, on the basis that the awards were taxable benefits within *ICTA 1988, s 154**. The HL allowed the parents' appeals, holding that the awards were provided 'at the cost' of the employer within *ICTA 1988, s 154(3)**, but (by a 4-1 majority, Lord Templeman dissenting) that they were exempt from income tax under *ICTA 1988, s 331**. *Wicks v Firth; Johnson v Firth*, HL 1982, 56 TC 318; [1983] STC 25; [1983] 2 WLR 34; [1983] 1 All ER 151. (*Note.* See now *ICTA 1988, s 165*, deriving from *FA 1983*, and *ITEPA 2003, ss 211–215*. The effect of this is that such payments no longer qualify for exemption in the hands of a parent, but the case remains of significance in showing that such payments are taxable benefits.)

ICTA 1988, s 157—computation of car benefit*

[54.5] An employee was provided with a car by his employer, but wanted a more expensive car. He agreed to pay his employer £5,800, in monthly instalments, in return for being provided with such a car. The Revenue included the appropriate scale charge for the car, as laid down by *ICTA 1988, s 157* and *Sch 6*, in his 1992/93 assessment. He appealed, contending that the payment which he had made should be deducted from the scale charge. The Special Commissioner dismissed his appeal, holding that there was 'no provision for a reduction in the cash benefit in the event of the employee paying to the employer a sum of money in order to obtain a better car than the employer was prepared to provide'. *Brown v Ware*, Sp C [1995] SSCD 155 (Sp C 29). (*Note. ICTA 1988, Sch 6* was substituted by *FA 1993, Sch 3* with effect from 1994/95, and was radically amended by *FA 2000, Sch 11* with effect from 2002/03. See now *ITEPA 2003, s 121*.)

Reduction for business travel—ICTA 1988, Sch 6 para 2

[54.6] An employee (C) was provided with a Citroen by his employer. In August 1993 his employer replaced the Citroen with a Ford. In computing C's car benefit for 1993/94, the Revenue apportioned the threshold of 2,500 miles (see *ICTA 1988, Sch 6 para 2**) on a time basis, so that a threshold of 836 miles was allocated to the period for which C had had the Citroen and a threshold of 1,664 miles was allocated to the period for which he had had the Ford. On this basis, C had comfortably exceeded the threshold for the period in which he had had the Citroen, but had failed to reach the threshold for the period in which he had had the Ford. C appealed, contending that, since his total business mileage for the year had exceeded 2,500 miles (which the Revenue accepted), he should be treated as having exceeded the threshold for the year as a whole. The Ch D rejected this contention and upheld the Revenue's assessment. Ferris J held that the effect of *Sch 6* was that the cars had to be treated separately. *Henwood v Clarke*, Ch D 1997, 69 TC 611; [1997] STC 789. (*Note. ICTA 1988, Sch 6 para 2* was substituted by *FA 2000, Sch 11* with effect from 2002/03.)

Beneficial loan to employee of building society

[54.7] In 1993 a building society granted one of its employees (C) a loan at a reduced rate of interest. In 1994 the loan was transferred, at C's request, to a two-year fixed-rate scheme which was available to the public. The Revenue assessed C for 1994/95 on the cash equivalent of the benefit of the loan, calculated by reference to the difference between the 'official rate' of interest and the lower rate payable under the fixed-rate scheme. C appealed, contending that the effect of *ICTA 1988, s 161(1A)* was that the cash equivalent of the benefit should not be treated as an emolument of his employment, since comparable fixed-rate loans were available to the general public. The Ch D rejected this contention and upheld the assessment. Lindsay J held that, for the purposes of *ICTA 1988, s 161(1A)*, the loan had been made in 1993. The transfer to the fixed-rate scheme did not amount to the making of a new loan. *ICTA 1988, s 161(1A)* required a comparison to be made between the loan to the employee and loans to the public at the time when the loan was first made, not at a time when its terms were varied. The cash equivalent of the benefit received by C in 1994/95 was, therefore, an emolument of his employment, within *ICTA 1988, s 160(1)*. (Lindsay J observed that C had 'paid genuine high street rates of interest' and that it was 'difficult to read the ability to fix the "official rate" for the purposes of *ICTA 1988, s 160* as intended to lead to an arbitrary new tax on the difference between a commercial rate actually paid and whatever higher rate which the Treasury might care to specify'.) *West v Crossland (and related appeal)*, Ch D 1999, 71 TC 314; [1999] STC 147. (*Note. ICTA 1988, s 161(1A)* was subsequently repealed by *FA 2000, Sch 10*.)

Miscellaneous

ICTA 1988, s 167(2)—definition of 'higher-paid' employment

[54.8] A woman was employed by an accountancy firm, and was paid an annual salary of less than £8,500. She also had the use of a car, and was able to buy petrol for the car with a credit card provided by her employer. The Revenue issued Schedule E assessments for 1998/99 to 2000/01 (under the legislation then in force) on the basis that the effect of *ICTA 1988, s 167(2)* was that she was a 'higher-paid' employee. The Special Commissioner upheld the assessments, holding that *s 167(2)* 'requires there to be taken into account both the value of the notional car fuel allowance and the value of payments actually made by the employer for the car fuel used'. The Commissioner expressed the view that 'there is no justification as a matter of policy' for this double charge, and hoped 'that this anomaly will be quickly addressed'. *Allcock v King*, Sp C [2004] SSCD 122 (Sp C 396). (*Note.* See now Extra-Statutory Concession A104, issued on 5 July 2004. For the current definition of 'lower-paid employment', see *ITEPA 2003, ss 217–219* as amended by *FA 2007, s 61*.)

ICTA 1988, s 178—profit-related pay—cancellation of registration

[54.9] A company (D) had instituted a profit-related pay scheme with effect from 1 January 1997. In an attempt to circumvent the provisions of *FA 1997, s 61* (which provided for the phasing-out of profit-related pay by reducing the limit on relief for periods beginning on or after 1 January 1998), it arranged for a subsidiary company (S) to register a new scheme on 11 December 1997. The scheme was intended to run from 31 December 1997, and S would take over the employment and management of D's employees with effect from 1 January 1998. On 22 December 1997 the Revenue gave notice of cancellation of the new scheme under *ICTA 1988, s 178*. S appealed. The Special Commissioner dismissed S's appeal, finding on the evidence that the sole reason for the arrangements 'was to retain the £4,000 cap in the profit-related pay scheme. A tax advantage was sought and there was no genuine commercial reason for the institution of the scheme.' The transfer of D's employees to S was admitted to be 'an artificial transaction serving no commercial purpose whatever'. The Commissioner held that 'not only was this a pure tax avoidance scheme, it was very close to sham'. Applying the principles laid down in *Furniss v Dawson*, **71.288** CAPITAL GAINS TAX, as interpreted in *Craven v White*, **71.289** CAPITAL GAINS TAX, the artificial interposition of S as the employer could be disregarded. The manipulation of dates which had taken place was prohibited by *ICTA 1988, s 178*, and the Revenue had been entitled to cancel the new scheme. The Commissioner observed that S had attempted to implement 'an unmeritorious scheme to benefit financially at the expense of the main body of taxpayers'. *Colours Ltd (formerly Spectrum Ltd) v CIR*, Sp C [1998] SSCD 93 (Sp C 156). (*Note.* See also *FA 1998, s 62*.)

Share options

[54.10] In October 1954, the secretary of a company acquired for £20 a non-transferable option (lasting for ten years) to be allotted 2,000 shares in the company at their then market price of 68s 6d. In March 1956, he acquired 250 shares under the option. The market price was then 82s. The Revenue issued a Schedule E assessment for 1955/56 charging tax on the excess of this market price of the shares over their cost, less an appropriate proportion of the cost of the option. The secretary appealed. The HL allowed his appeal (by a 3-2 majority, Lord Keith of Avonholm and Lord Denning dissenting), holding that the relevant perquisite was the granting of the option in 1954/55, and that the subsequent increase in the price of the shares was not a perquisite of his office. *Abbott v Philbin*, HL 1960, 39 TC 82; [1961] AC 352; [1960] 2 All ER 763. (*Notes*. (1) The decision was subsequently superseded by *FA 1966* with regard to employees within Schedule E, Case I—see Employee Share Schemes User Guide, para ESSUM 39300—but continued to govern the grant of options to employees within Case II and III. For the current legislation governing share options, see *ITEPA 2003, ss 471–484*. (2) For another issue in this case, see **4.240** APPEALS.)

Termination payment received while payee not resident in UK

[54.11] An individual (N) had been employed by a UK company for many years. His employment ended on 6 April 1984. He left the UK on 1 April 1984 to take up employment in Jamaica, his employer having given him leave of absence until the termination of his employment. He remained in Jamaica until 14 April 1985. He received a termination payment of some £60,000. The Revenue issued a 1984/85 assessment charging tax under *ICTA 1988, s 148** on the payment. N appealed, contending that since he was neither resident nor ordinarily resident in the UK for 1984/85 (which the Revenue accepted), none of the payment was taxable in the UK. The Commissioners dismissed his appeal, and the CA upheld their decision, holding that the effect of *ICTA 1988, s 148** was that the payment was assessable under Schedule E whether or not the taxpayer was within Case I, II or III of Schedule E. *Nichols v Gibson*, CA 1996, 68 TC 611; [1996] STC 1008.

Termination payment—whether exempt under ICTA 1988, s 188

[54.12] A tax consultant retired from his employment with an accountancy firm at the age of 58, and received a severance payment of £90,000. He appealed against a Schedule E assessment, contending that the payment should be treated as exempt under *ICTA 1988, s 188*, since it had been made on account of mental disability brought about by the pressure of campaigning against the Inland Revenue. The Special Commissioner rejected this contention and dismissed his appeal, holding that there was no evidence that the appellant had suffered from a medical condition which had disabled or prevented him from carrying out the duties of his employment. The Ch D upheld this decision. *Horner v Hasted*, Ch D 1995, 67 TC 439; [1995] STC 766. (*Notes*.

(1) *ICTA 1988, s 188* was repealed by *FA 1998, s 165* with effect from 6 April 1998. (2) Various other contentions raised by the appellant, who conducted his appeal in person, were also rejected.)

Airline pilot—whether within Schedule E, Case I

[54.13] A pilot lived in Hertfordshire and worked for a Netherlands airline. His base was in Amsterdam, to which he commuted by air. He flew mainly on scheduled flights, none of which started from the UK but some of which called at the UK. In the relevant period, 38 of his 811 take-offs and landings were in the UK. The Revenue assessed him under Schedule E, Case I. He appealed, contending that what he did in the UK was incidental to the performance of his duties outside the UK, and that he should be treated as not resident in the UK. The Special Commissioners rejected this contention and dismissed his appeal, and the Ch D upheld their decision. Sir John Pennycuick V-C held that the words 'merely incidental to' were 'apt to denote an activity (here the performance of duties) which does not serve any independent purpose but is carried out in order to further some other purpose'. *Robson v Dixon*, Ch D 1972, 48 TC 527; [1972] 1 WLR 1493; [1972] 3 All ER 671. (*Note*. For HMRC's interpretation of this decision, see Revenue Tax Bulletin April 2005, pp 1201, 1202, and Employment Income Manual, para EIM40203.)

Non-domiciled employee—whether within Schedule E, Case I

[54.14] See *Carvill v Frost*, 4.434 APPEALS.

Payment made by employer under 'tax equalisation' scheme

[54.15] A US citizen (P), who worked for a large accountancy firm, was seconded to an associated UK firm in July 1997, and became a UK resident. For 1997/98, her emoluments from the date she became UK-resident were apportioned on the basis of working days, so that $^{137}/_{245}$ was attributable to UK duties and $^{108}/_{245}$ to non-UK duties. In accordance with her contract of employment, the firm also made a 'tax equalisation' payment of £18,601, which was intended to provide that 'US employees working overseas will pay no more income tax as a result of relocating overseas than they would have paid if they stayed at home'. It was accepted that this was a taxable emolument, but in completing her 1997/98 self-assessment return, P treated $^{108}/_{245}$ of the payment as attributable to non-UK duties. The Revenue issued a ruling that the whole of the equalisation payment was 'in respect of duties performed in the UK'. The Special Commissioner dismissed P's appeal, observing that 'the tax was only payable because of the performance of duties in the United Kingdom and the amount of the tax depended on the proportion of her emoluments attributable to those duties'. The payment was in respect of the performance of her duties in the UK. *Perro v Mansworth*, Sp C [2001] SSCD 179 (Sp C 286). (*Note*. For the Revenue's practice, see Revenue Tax Bulletin, June 2002, pp 931–934.)

Schedule E, Case III—whether emoluments received in UK

[54.16] In 1960 a South African, employed by two associated South African companies, became resident in the UK. Before arriving in the UK, he arranged for two companies (A and L) to be formed in South Africa. He controlled one of the companies (A), but had no shareholding in L, which was controlled by trusted business associates with substantial interests in the companies which employed him. He arranged for £20,000 of his salary to be applied in subscribing for shares in A, which lent the £20,000 to L, which then lent the £20,000 to him in London. The Revenue issued assessments under Schedule E, Case III charging tax on the money he received from L. The Special Commissioners dismissed his appeal and the Ch D upheld their decision. Templeman J observed that 'one does not need to strip aside the corporate veil if you find that emoluments, which mean money, come in at one end of a conduit pipe and pass through certain traceable pipes until they come out at the other end to the taxpayer'. *Harmel v Wright*, Ch D 1973, 49 TC 149; [1974] STC 88; [1974] 1 WLR 325; [1974] 1 All ER 945.

[54.17] See also *Grimm v Newman & Another*, 58.46 TAX PLANNING AND AVOIDANCE.

Relief for earnings abroad—'qualifying period'

[54.18] An employee left the UK on 13 August 1979 to take up a one-year contract abroad. He spent a total of 30 days in the UK during November 1979 and March 1980, which did not exceed the limits for the qualifying period. He was dismissed from his employment on 19 June, and returned to the UK on 26 June pending an appeal. Between 28 June and 4 August he was on holiday in the Republic of Ireland. He was reinstated in his employment and his contract extended to September 1980, but he was not required to work abroad again. The Ch D held that, as the qualifying period in which he had performed his duties abroad consisted of less than the 365 days required by *FA 1977, Sch 7 para 1(1)(b)*, the 100% relief was not due. *Robins v Durkin*, Ch D 1988, 60 TC 700; [1988] STC 588. (*Note. FA 1977, Sch 7 para 1(1)* became *ICTA 1988, s 193(1)*, which was repealed by *FA 1998, s 63* with effect from 17 March 1998.)

ICTA 1988, s 193—aggregation of qualifying periods

[54.19] An employee lived and worked in Asia from June 1987 to February 1993 and was accepted as non-resident in the UK for 1987/88 to 1992/93 inclusive. He appealed against a Schedule E assessment for 1993/94, contending that his six-year absence from the UK should be taken into account for the purpose of computing a 'qualifying period' of non-residence under *ICTA 1988, s 193(1)*, so that he was entitled to foreign earnings deduction for 1993/94. The Ch D rejected this contention and upheld the assessment. Hart J held that 'the question whether somebody is at a particular moment absent from the United Kingdom must be answered by reference to the current status of the person in relation to which the question is asked'. This required 'absence' in the sense of not being physically present in the place of residence.

Carstairs v Sykes, Ch D 2000, 73 TC 225; [2000] STC 1103. (*Note. ICTA 1988, s 193(1)* was repealed by *FA 1998, s 63* with effect from 17 March 1998.)

Distribution of trust assets for benefit of employees

[54.20] A public company (F) took over another company (G) in 1977 and became the employer of G's employees from 1 April 1979. Before 1977, G had established two trusts to enable the trustees to acquire shares in it, to be held for the benefit of the employees. In anticipation of the takeover, the trustees took steps to distribute the funds to the eligible employees as fairly as they could, applying a formula which took into account the length of service and level of salary of the employee. The merits of the beneficiaries as individuals were not considered. In 1979/80 B, who had been employed by G since 1958, received in two amounts a total of £18,111 allocated to him under the distribution. He was assessed under Sch E on these amounts, apportioned over the years 1958/59 to 1978/79, and appealed. The Special Commissioner allowed the appeals, finding that the amounts assessed were emoluments from the taxpayer's former employment but holding that, under the legislation then in force, they could not be attributed to 1978/79 or apportioned between years back to 1958/59. The HL upheld this decision as one of fact. *Bray v Best*, HL 1989, 61 TC 705; [1989] STC 159; [1989] 1 WLR 167; [1989] 1 All ER 969. (*Note.* See now *ITEPA 2003, s 17*, deriving from *FA 1989, s 36*.)

Interpretation of ICTA 1988, Sch 11

[54.21] A bank manager took early retirement in 1995, at the age of 52. He received a lump sum payment, which was assessed under *ICTA 1988, s 148*. He appealed, contending that the payment was made in pursuance of an obligation incurred before 10 March 1981, and was therefore eligible for 'top-slicing relief' by virtue of *ICTA 1988, Sch 11 as originally enacted*. The Special Commissioner rejected this contention and dismissed his appeal. On the evidence, it was accepted that the payment fell within *ICTA 1988, s 148*, rather than *ICTA 1988, s 19*. It followed that 'the payment cannot therefore have been made on the basis of an obligation all along contained in the appellant's contract of employment'. *O'Brien v Williams*, Sp C [2000] SSCD 364 (Sp C 245). (*Note.* 'Top-slicing relief' was abolished by *FA 1988*, except where payments were made in pursuance of an obligation incurred before 10 March 1981. *ICTA 1988, s 148* and *Sch 11* were substituted by *FA 1998* for payments or benefits received after 5 April 1998.)

Auctioneer—use of home

[54.22] An auctioneer, employed by a firm of chartered surveyors, was required to do some work at home. In his tax returns, he claimed that part of his salary was attributable to his provision of office accommodation for his employer, and was assessable under Schedule A rather than Schedule E. The Revenue amended his self-assessments on the basis that the entire salary was assessable under Schedule E, with an appropriate deduction for expenses. The auctioneer appealed. The Special Commissioner dismissed his appeal, holding that the use of his home as an office was incidental to his employment, and the whole of his salary was assessable under Schedule E. *Ainslie v Buckley*, Sp C [2002] SSCD 132 (Sp C 304).

55

Self-Assessment

The cases in this chapter are arranged under the following headings.

Completion of Enquiry into Return (TMA 1970, ss 28A, 28B)

TMA, s 28A(2)—amendment following Revenue enquiry

[55.1] An individual (W) had operated a video hire business from 1981 to 1994. Assessments covering this business became final and conclusive. However, in his self-assessment for 1996/97, W claimed a repayment on the basis that he had overpaid tax of at least £2,500 during this period of trading. The Revenue issued a notice of amendment under *TMA, s 28A*, and W appealed. The Special Commissioner dismissed W's appeal, holding on the evidence that 'it is not now possible to reopen the assessments covering the taxpayer's period of trading, which have all become final by one means or another'. *Wadhams v Mitchell*, Sp C [1999] SSCD 277 (Sp C 210).

[55.2] The Revenue issued an enquiry into a company director's tax return. Following the enquiry, they issued a notice under *TMA, s 28A*, showing additional tax due. The director appealed. The Special Commissioner upheld the notice and dismissed the appeal, finding that the director had 'misconstrued the correspondence on a number of occasions and has generally done everything he could to be obstructive, to procrastinate, to obfuscate and delay producing relevant information properly requested and latterly properly required'. *Siwek v CIR (No 2)*, Sp C [2004] SSCD 493 (Sp C 427). (*Notes*. (1) The appeal was heard with *Siwek Ltd v CIR*, 73.3 NATIONAL INSURANCE CONTRIBUTIONS. (2) Following this decision, the director made an application for it to be aside under *Special Commissioners (Jurisdiction and Procedure) Regulations 1994 (SI 1994/1811), reg 19*. He did not attend the hearing of this application, which was duly dismissed— Sp C 2004, [2005] SSCD 163 (Sp C 442).)

[55.3] A company director received bank and building society interest, but failed to include it in his tax return. Following an enquiry, HMRC issued an amendment to the director's self-assessment charging tax on this income at the upper dividend rate. The First-Tier Tribunal upheld the amendment and dismissed the director's appeal. *R Farrell v HMRC*, FTT [2011] UKFTT 182 (TC), TC01051.

[55.4] The Revenue received information that a building contractor had significantly understated his income in his 2003/04 tax return. Following an enquiry, they issued a notice under *TMA, s 28A*, showing additional tax due.

The Special Commissioner upheld the notice and dismissed the contractor's appeal. *J Bryant v HMRC*, Sp C 2007, [2008] SSCD 85 (Sp C 623).

[55.5] The Revenue began an enquiry into a builder's self-assessment for 2003/04. The builder failed to provide his business records, and the Revenue formed the opinion that he had overstated his expenditure. They issued an amendment to disallow the disputed expenditure, and the builder appealed. The Special Commissioner dismissed the appeal, holding that the effect of *TMA, s 50(6)* was that the burden of proof was on the appellant. *ME Walsh v HMRC*, Sp C [2008] SSCD 742 (Sp C 676).

[55.6] Similar decisions were reached in *DO Needham v HMRC*, FTT [2010] UKFTT 571 (TC), TC00822; *JA Draper (t/a JA Draper Joinery) v HMRC*, FTT [2011] UKFTT 137 (TC), TC01011; *J Boak v HMRC*, FTT [2012] UKFTT 123 (TC), TC01818; *J Verschueren v HMRC*, FTT [2012] UKFTT 184 (TC), TC01879, and *K Okeke v HMRC*, FTT [2013] UKFTT 568 (TC), TC02957.

[55.7] The Revenue began an enquiry into the returns submitted by a restaurant proprietor. They formed the opinion that he had understated his profits, and issued 'jeopardy amendments' and closure notices. The Special Commissioner dismissed the proprietor's appeal, observing that 'the burden of proof is on the appellant to displace them and he has done nothing to do so'. *S Aumchareon (t/a Bangkok Thai Restaurant) v HMRC*, Sp C [2008] SSCD 905 (Sp C 691).

[55.8] Similar decisions were reached in *RD Richards v HMRC*, Sp C [2008] SSCD 1200 (Sp C 709); *A Ouerradi v HMRC*, FTT [2009] UKFTT 339 (TC), TC00280; *R Auksoriatus v HMRC*, FTT [2010] UKFTT 547 (TC), TC00800; *B Njoku v HMRC*, FTT [2010] UKFTT 553 (TC), TC00806; *PA Maloney (t/a Advanced Property Services) v HMRC*, FTT [2010] UKFTT 588 (TC), TC00838; *AJ Segal v HMRC*, FTT [2011] UKFTT 99 (TC), TC00975; *RGA Sentence v HMRC*, FTT [2011] UKFTT 578 (TC), TC01421; *G Mohammed & N Arshad (t/a Diamond News) v HMRC*, FTT [2012] UKFTT 239 (TC), TC01933; *J Ebrill v HMRC*, FTT [2012] UKFTT 240 (TC), TC01934, and *A Latif v HMRC*, FTT [2012] UKFTT 419 (TC), TC02101.

[55.9] An individual (C) formed the opinion that he had underclaimed expenses in 2001/02 and 2002/03. He sought to correct this by claiming the expenses in question in his return for 2006/07. Following an enquiry, HMRC issued a closure notice and amended C's self-assessment by disallowing the retrospective expenses claim. The First-Tier Tribunal dismissed C's appeal against this decision. *M Cassin v HMRC*, FTT [2010] UKFTT 515 (TC), TC00770.

[55.10] An individual (JO) submitted four tax returns declaring income from property development. HMRC began an enquiry into the returns and formed the opinion that JO 'could provide no credible evidence to substantiate the figures for either turnover or expenditure'. They subsequently issued amendments to JO's returns, accepting his declared turnover figures but disallowing some of the claimed expenditure. JO appealed, contending that he had submitted false returns and accounts in the hope of obtaining a bank loan. The Upper Tribunal accepted JO's evidence and allowed his appeal (reversing the

First-tier decision). Arnold J held that 'there is simply no credible evidence that (JO) carried on any business or trade as either a property developer or a builder during the four years in question' and that 'in the absence of any challenge to (JO's) evidence to the tribunal that he had not developed, refurbished or redecorated any properties other than his own residence, it was not open to the tribunal to disbelieve that evidence'. *J Okolo v HMRC*, UT [2012] UKUT 416 (TCC); [2013] STC 906.

[55.11] HMRC began an enquiry into a return submitted by a woman (H) who owned a minicab business. They issued a notice of amendment on the basis that H had underdeclared her income by £42,000. The First-tier Tribunal reviewed the evidence in detail and allowed H's appeal in part, directing that her declared income should be increased by £25,000. *Mrs QJ Haleem v HMRC*, FTT [2013] UKFTT 402 (TC), TC02798.

[55.12] HMRC began an enquiry into the returns submitted by a minicab driver (W). They issued notices of amendment on the basis that W had underdeclared his turnover. The First-tier Tribunal reviewed the evidence in detail and allowed W's appeal. *G Whittle v HMRC*, FTT [2014] UKFTT 254 (TC), TC03393.

[55.13] HMRC began an enquiry into the return submitted by a married couple who traded in partnership, and issued a closure notice substantially increasing the partnership profits. The First-tier Tribunal allowed the partners' appeal, finding that there had been no underdeclaration of profits. *H & Mrs I Newell (t/a Tanya's Takeaway) v HMRC*, FTT [2013] UKFTT 742 (TC), TC03120.

[55.14] The First-tier Tribunal reached a similar decision in *I Cardazzone (t/a Mediterranean Ices) v HMRC*, FTT [2014] UKFTT 357 (TC), TC03492.

[55.15] See also *Rigby v Jayatilaka*, **4.372** APPEALS; *Singh v Williams*, **22.276** EMPLOYMENT INCOME; *Rouf v HMRC*, **29.65** FURTHER ASSESSMENTS: LOSS OF TAX; *Jackman v Powell*, **63.202** TRADING PROFITS; *Silk v Fletcher*, **63.291** TRADING PROFITS, and *Wildin & Co v Jowett*, **64.8** TRADING PROFITS.

TMA, s 28A(4)—application by taxpayer for closure notice

[55.16] A trader (B) submitted his 2002 tax return in January 2003. In January 2004 the Revenue issued a notice under *TMA, s 9A*, making an enquiry into a claim for loan interest relief. In April 2004 the Revenue Capital Taxes Shares Valuation Office wrote to B's accountants, requesting information relating to the transfer of a business from B to a limited company. Following further correspondence, B applied to the Commissioners, under *TMA, s 28A(4)*, for the issue of a closure notice, contending *inter alia* that the notice under *s 9A* was invalid because it had been issued by a Revenue executive below the rank of inspector. The Special Commissioner rejected this contention and dismissed the application, holding that the executive responsible for the notice was 'an officer of the Board', within *IRRA 1890, s 39* and *TMA, s 9A*. The Commissioner observed that 'Parliament could not have intended the inconvenient results in relation to self-assessment returns of a requirement that the person issuing the *section 9A* notice must be a higher grade officer such as an inspector'. Furthermore, there was 'no basis within the legislation for questioning the scope of any form of enquiry commenced under *section 9A*'. There were also no grounds for any 'complaint concerning the transfer of the work relating to the return from Norwich 1 District to the City of London Area Compliance Office. The self-assessment legislation does not tie work on a taxpayer's return to a particular district'. *Bensoor v Devine*, Sp C [2005] SSCD 297 (Sp C 456). (*Note*. An appeal against a notice under *TMA, s 19A* was also dismissed.)

[55.17] A trader carried on business from a market stall, adapting Sony Playstations and DVD players to enable them to play counterfeit Playstation games and DVDs. He submitted his 2000/01 tax return in January 2002. The Revenue subsequently became aware that he had purchased a property in Florida in July 2001, began an enquiry into the figures declared on his return. In 2005, while the enquiry was still continuing, the trader made an application under *TMA, s 28A(4)* for the issue of a closure notice. The Special Commissioner dismissed the application, finding that the trader 'has kept, or at least has produced, virtually no business records. His income and expenditure have been reconstructed in a manner which raises as many questions as it answers. The opening of the enquiry was entirely reasonable in the circumstances. Since the enquiry has been opened the taxpayer has provided minimal information in a vague and unsatisfactory form, usually with such lack of specification as to make the Revenue justifiably suspicious and request further information. This process has been continuing since the enquiry opened.' The Commissioner observed that 'the underlying suspicion must be that the taxpayer's income is very substantially greater than it appears to be, that he hopes the Revenue will run out of patience and issue an assessment based on current information which he will then pay, in the knowledge that the assessment understates his true tax liability to a significant extent'. Furthermore, 'the economic well-being of the country plainly requires that the Revenue should not be disabled from pursuing their legitimate enquiries where, despite lengthy correspondence, they reasonably consider that they do not yet have enough information to draw a reasonable conclusion as to the amount of tax which should be contained in the taxpayer's self-assessment'. Accordingly, there were no grounds for issuing a closure notice. *Doyle v HMRC*, Sp C [2005] SSCD 775 (Sp C 499).

[55.18] A trader's return for 2002/03 declared a taxable profit of £1,875. In February 2004 the Revenue began an enquiry into the return, and requested certain documents. In May 2004 the trader submitted a notice of amendment declaring a taxable profit of £22,540. However he failed to produce the requested documents. In August 2004 the Revenue issued a notice under *TMA, s 19A*. The trader still failed to produce the documents, and made an application under *TMA, s 28A(4)* for the issue of a closure notice. The Special Commissioner (Mr. Shipwright) dismissed the application, holding that, because of 'the magnitude of the discrepancy between the original and revised accounts', it would be unreasonable to conclude the enquiry without the production of the documents. The trader's accountant had agreed to let HMRC officers inspect the records for one day. The Commissioner held that this did not constitute production of the records, holding that production of the records 'means allowing sufficient unrestricted use of all the documents in question to HMRC for HMRC to do such work, tests and other things (such as photocopying) in relation to those documents as is reasonable for HMRC to do'. *Jacques v HMRC (No 2)*, Sp C [2007] SSCD 166 (Sp C 577). (*Notes.* (1) The Commissioner also dismissed an appeal against penalties for failure to comply with the notice under *TMA, s 19A*. (2) For a preliminary issue in this case, see **4.26** APPEALS. The trader's accountant accused the previous Special Commissioner (Dr. Avery Jones) of having made an untrue statement in that decision. Mr. Shipwright described the accountant's allegations as 'unfounded, unsubstantiated, unsupported by evidence and as typical of his approach to the whole of this matter'.)

[55.19] A married couple operated a taxi business in partnership. The Revenue began an enquiry into their return. They discovered that the accounts contained estimated figures for takings and drawings, and that there were no prime records of takings. The inspector asked the partnership to provide certain information. The partners provided some of the information, but refused to provide details of private expenditure and refused to attend a meeting with the inspector. The partnership applied for a closure notice. The Special Commissioner dismissed the application, observing that 'while an investigation into their private expenditure is an interference into their private life, it is in accordance with the law and is necessary in a democratic society in the economic well-being of the country that such investigation should be permitted for the purpose of establishing the true taxable profit. If the applicants had kept better records such investigation would not have been necessary, but I can see no other way of verifying the accounts.' *GR & Mrs HA Gould (t/a Garry's Private Hire) v HMRC*, Sp C [2007] SSCD 502 (Sp C 604).

[55.20] In October 2005 the Revenue began an enquiry into the 2003/04 return submitted by a roofing contractor (F). A month later F admitted that he had failed to declare rental income and a capital gain. In January 2007 the Revenue began an enquiry into F's 2004/05 return. In June 2007 the Revenue informed F that they were considering applying for a notice under *TMA, s 20*. In July 2007 F applied for the issue of closure notices, under *TMA, s 28A(4)*. The Special Commissioner dismissed the applications, finding that there were 'unanswered queries relating to deposits into three bank accounts'. On the evidence, the Revenue was 'justified in pursuing a *section 20* notice'. The Commissioner observed that 'if the applicant wants to put a stop to the enquiry he will have to meet the inspector's concerns in a way that goes beyond what he and his wife have already done'. *KC Floyd v HMRC*, Sp C 2007, [2008] SSCD 353 (Sp C 646).

[55.21] The Revenue began an enquiry into a finance company (M), which had acted on behalf of four overseas companies which had engaged in more than 200 property transactions in the UK. They also began enquiries into two of M's directors. M and the directors applied for closure notices under *TMA, s 28A(4)*. The Special Commissioner dismissed the applications, finding that one of the directors (K) had paid more than £200,000 into his private bank accounts during 2002/03. The Commissioner observed that 'it is wholly unclear why the affairs of the (overseas) companies, particularly payments to tradesmen working on the properties, should have been handled through (K's) personal accounts rather than directly through (M's) accounts or even the (overseas) accounts themselves, and the activities of (M) cannot be described as simple'. M's directors had persistently failed 'to disclose details of the identity of the persons they dealt with from the (overseas) companies, assuming there are such persons, and of the nature of the instructions received'. The Revenue had requested a further six months to complete their enquiries, and 'at least that length of time is reasonable'. *F Kilbride v HMRC (and related appeals)*, Sp C [2008] SSCD 517 (Sp C 660).

[55.22] In December 2006 the Revenue issued a notice under *TMA, s 9A* in respect of a return submitted by a married woman (L). In 2008 L applied for a closure notice under *TMA, s 28A(4)*. The Special Commissioner dismissed the application, observing that 'HMRC, since the merger of the two separate direct and indirect tax departments, properly may use information about investigations about possible failures to comply with the requirements of value added tax law (or PAYE provisions or other tax matters) as relevant to possible failures to comply with the obligation to make a full return for income tax purposes.' There was 'relevant evidence of test purchases within the period relevant to this return', and there was evidence that L's 'original return for this year was not fully in accordance with the statements she signed at the end of the return with regard to trading income'. Furthermore, L had failed to produce information which the Revenue had requested, and the Revenue were entitled not to be satisfied that L had 'disclosed all relevant bank accounts and similar records and any relevant savings'. The Commissioner concluded that 'it would not be right at present to impose any timetable' on the Revenue's conduct of the enquiry. *KC Lee v HMRC (and related appeals)*, Sp C 2008, [2009] SSCD 1 (Sp C 715).

[55.23] Applications for closure notices were also dismissed in *SH Khan v HMRC (and related appeals)*, FTT [2010] UKFTT 19 (TC), TC00334; *BJH Building & Plumbing v HMRC*, FTT [2010] UKFTT 60 (TC), TC00373; *WY Chan v HMRC (No 1)*, FTT [2011] UKFTT 84 (TC), TC00961; *Mrs SK Huan v HMRC (No 1)*, FTT [2011] UKFTT 626 (TC), TC01468; *TWL (GB) Ltd v HMRC*, FTT [2011] UKFTT 682 (TC), TC01524; *R & S Thomas v HMRC (No 1)*, FTT [2011] UKFTT 826 (TC), TC01662; *Mrs SK Huan v HMRC (No 2)*, FTT [2012] UKFTT 62 (TC), TC01759; *M Sheppard & K McGrath v HMRC*, FTT [2014] UKFTT 333 (TC), TC03469, and *B Khan v HMRC*, FTT [2014] UKFTT 1050 (TC), TC04143.

[55.24] An individual (C) claimed that he had made a tax loss of more than £400,000 in 1998/99 as a result of certain transactions in securities. In January 2001 the Revenue began an enquiry into C's return. In September 2009 C applied to the First-Tier Tribunal for a closure notice. The tribunal granted his application, and directed that HMRC should issue a closure notice within 30 days. Judge Shipwright observed that 'nine years is a considerable time to wait to know whether a Government Department will or will not allow your claim. If the claim is denied it is not until a closure notice has been issued that an appeal can be lodged. It could be some time then before the case is heard and a decision reached. The longer the period from the time the actual transactions took place the harder it is to find documents and reliable evidence. Witnesses cease to be available and memories fade. This makes it harder for there to be a fair trial in a reasonable time.' *HH Collinson v HMRC*, FTT [2010] UKFTT 165 (TC), TC00470.

[55.25] A company director (G) submitted a 2006/07 return claiming that he had made a loss in a business venture. HMRC began an enquiry. Within a week of the enquiry being opened, G applied for it to be closed. The General Commissioners rejected his application, and G applied for judicial review. The QB dismissed this application. Behrens J observed that it would be highly unusual 'for a closure notice to be issued within a week of an enquiry being opened when none of the information requested had been formally supplied', and held that there was 'a perfectly reasonable explanation for the enquiry'. *R (oao Golding) v General Commissioners*, QB [2011] EWHC 2435 (Admin); [2012] STC 381.

[55.26] An individual (P) claimed that he had made a tax loss of more than £1,500,000 in 2005/06, following certain transactions which fell within the *Tax Avoidance Schemes (Information) Regulations 2004 (SI 2004/1864), reg 7* (subsequently superseded by *Tax Avoidance (Prescribed Description of Arrangements) Regulations 2006 (SI 2006/1543)*). HMRC began an enquiry, and asked P to produce certain documents. In March 2011 P applied for a closure notice. The First-tier Tribunal dismissed his application, finding that more than 400 other people had participated in similar transactions, and that six of these (of whom P was not one) had been selected as 'informal lead cases' by HMRC and the promoters of the scheme. Following P's application, HMRC had requested further documents, which P had only provided two days before the hearing. Judge Mosedale observed that P's advisers were aware that 'both parties had been proceeding (even though there was no formal agreement) on the basis that HMRC would enquire in detail into the tax returns of the sample taxpayers who had implemented similar tax planning to the applicant. In particular, the applicant's representatives had made detailed disclosure on those three other enquiries and were well aware when applying for the closure notice that they had not made a similar disclosure in relation to (P's) affairs. P was entitled 'to decide that he no longer wished to sit behind a sample case and he wanted his enquiry brought to an end', but HMRC were entitled to a reasonable time to examine the documents which P had only provided two days before the hearing. Accordingly, it would be premature to order the issue of a closure notice. *S Price v HMRC (No 1)*, FTT [2011] UKFTT 624 (TC), TC01466.

[55.27] In January 2010 HMRC began an enquiry into the 2008 tax return submitted by a pensioner (B) who owned several properties. In 2013 B applied for the enquiry to be closed, contending that he had supplied all the relevant information and that the enquiry had been unreasonably protracted. Judge Blewitt directed that HMRC should issue a closure notice within 30 days. *KW Bloomfield v HMRC*, FTT [2013] UKFTT 593 (TC), TC02982.

[55.28] In 2011 HMRC began an enquiry into a return submitted by an accountant (K) who had substantial income from property. In 2013 K applied for a closure notice. HMRC opposed the application on the grounds that K had not provided all the information which they had requested. Judge Cornwell-Kelly reviewed the evidence in detail and found that K's 'disclosures or responses to the Revenue's requests and notices have frequently not been adequate or timely'. He held that 'the Revenue must not be constrained to close an enquiry when there is genuinely significant information which needs to be provided', but observed that 'there is unlikely to be any ultimate prejudice to the public interest in placing a reasonable limit on the extent of the enquiry, since in any eventual amendment to his self-assessment return the taxpayer has an unrestricted right of appeal in regard to everything relevant to the year under enquiry, and he bears the burden of displacing the Revenue's assessment'. He directed that HMRC should issue a closure notice within nine months. *A Khan v HMRC*, FTT [2014] UKFTT 018 (TC), TC03159.

[55.29] HMRC began an enquiry into the return submitted by a company (E) for the year ending 31 March 2011. The officer (L) who conducted the enquiry received information suggesting that E had not recorded all its purchases, and concluded that it was likely to have failed to record the corresponding sales. He issued a closure notice amending E's return accordingly. He also issued a discovery assessment for the year ending 31 March 2012 on the basis that there had been a similar underdeclaration. E appealed against the assessment. The appeal was reviewed by a different HMRC officer (M), who formed the opinion that there was 'insufficient evidence to support the amount assessed in this year'. He agreed to withdraw the assessment. Shortly afterwards L wrote to E opening an enquiry into its return for the year ending 31 March 2012. E applied to the First-tier Tribunal for a closure notice, contending that since M had agreed to withdraw the initial discovery assessment for the year ending 31 March 2012, HMRC could not begin a subsequent enquiry into that year. The Tribunal rejected this contention and dismissed the application. Judge Hellier held that the manner in which M had withdrawn the assessment had constituted the agreement of E's initial appeal, within *TMA, s 54*. However, the scope of that agreement was simply 'that a presumption of continuity did not justify the additional assessment'. M had not agreed 'that the company's profits were precisely those shown on the return or that profits had not been suppressed'. *Easinghall Ltd v HMRC*, FTT [2014] UKFTT 677 (TC), TC03800.

[55.30] See also *HMRC v Deadman*, **44.360** PENALTIES.

TMA, s 28B—completion of enquiry into partnership return

[55.31] A limited liability partnership entered into a complex series of transactions in relation to the licensing and distribution of film rights. The partners made substantial claims to tax relief under *ICTA 1988, s 353*. In October 2007 HMRC began an enquiry into the partnership's tax return for 2006/07. In August 2008 the partnership applied to the Special Commissioners for a closure direction under *TMA, s 28B*. At a hearing in 2009, the Special Commissioner reviewed the evidence in detail and directed HMRC to issue a closure notice within three months. The Commissioner observed that the partnership 'has given every assistance to the Commissioners in the enquiry, consistent with its desire to have matters resolved as speedily as possible, so that it is concluded, or can proceed to an appeal and to a final determination by that route. It has volunteered documents and information from the outset and has for the most part responded fully and promptly to subsequent requests'. The Commissioner expressed the view that HMRC had 'sufficient information to enable them to make an informed judgment as to the matter they have identified as relevant to the tax return of the applicant, namely whether or not it was, in the three days to 5 April 2007, carrying on a trade with a view to a profit'. *Eclipse Film Partners No 35 Llp v HMRC (No 1)*, Sp C [2009] SSCD 293 (Sp C 736). (*Note*. Following this decision, HMRC issued a closure notice in May 2009, determining that the partnership had not been carrying on a trade, so that the partners were not entitled to the tax relief which they had claimed. For subsequent proceedings in this case, see **4.113** APPEALS and **59.108** TRADING INCOME.)

[55.32] The decision in *Eclipse Film Partners No 35 Llp v HMRC (No 1)*, 55.31 above, was applied in the similar subsequent case of *Vaccine Research Llp v HMRC*, FTT October 2009, TC00274. (*Note*. For subsequent proceedings in this case, see **8.108** CAPITAL ALLOWANCES.)

Miscellaneous

TMA, s 9A—notice of enquiry into return—whether valid

[55.33] See *Wing Hung Lai v Bale*, **49.7** RETURNS AND INFORMATION, and *Holly & Laurel v HM Inspector of Taxes*, **49.8** RETURNS AND INFORMATION.

TMA, s 9A—procedure for disputing loss claims

[55.34] See *Cotter v HMRC*, **35.51** LOSS RELIEF.

Notice under TMA, s 19A—whether valid

[55.35] See *Self-Assessed v HM Inspector of Taxes*, **49.17** RETURNS AND INFORMATION, and *Mother v HM Inspector of Taxes*, **49.18** RETURNS AND INFORMATION.

TMA, s 19A—whether any grounds for proceeding with appeal

[55.36] In December 1998 the Revenue issued a notice under *TMA, s 19A*. The taxpayer appealed, but produced the information required by the notice. At the hearing of the appeal, the taxpayer declined to withdraw her appeal, but the Revenue contended that the appeal should be dismissed without a full hearing, since there was no live issue between the parties. The Special Commissioner accepted this contention and dismissed the appeal. Applying the HL decision in *R v Secretary of State for the Home Department (ex p. Salem)*, HL [1999] 2 WLR 483; [1999] 2 All ER 42, 'academic appeals should not be heard unless there was a good reason in the public interest for so doing'. On the evidence, there was 'no longer any dispute between the parties' and there was therefore 'no basis for the continuation of this appeal'. *Self-Assessed v HM Inspector of Taxes (No 2)*, Sp C [2000] SSCD 47 (Sp C 224).

Additional assessment issued after submission of return

[55.37] See *Langham v Veltema*, **5.48** ASSESSMENTS.

Errors in return—whether 'negligent conduct' within TMA, s 29(4)

[55.38] See *Hancock v CIR*, 29.49 FURTHER ASSESSMENTS: LOSS OF TAX.

TMA, s 31—scope of appeal against closure notice

[55.39] See *Tower Mcashback LLP1 v HMRC*, 4.22 APPEALS.

Claim under TMA, s 33 after agreement of self-assessment

[55.40] See *Wall v CIR*, 24.8 ERROR OR MISTAKE RELIEF.

TMA, s 34—whether applicable to notices under TMA, s 28A

[55.41] In the case noted at 44.190 PENALTIES, counsel acting for the appellants contended that the time limit for assessments laid down by *TMA, s 34* should also be treated as applying to closure notices under *TMA, s 28A*. The Special Commissioners rejected this contention and the Ch D upheld their decision. Patten J held that it was 'unlikely that Parliament would have wished to protect the Revenue's power to recover an overpayment of tax from the time limit under *s 34* but not to have given equal treatment to an inquiry designed to recover undeclared tax'. He observed that the time limit under *s 34* 'would have expired in this case solely due to the delaying tactics of (the appellants) and the Revenue, in order to serve the closure notices, would have to rely on allegations of negligence and fraud'. This was 'an unlikely structure for Parliament to have adopted'. *Morris & Morris v HMRC (No 3)*, Ch D [2007] EWHC 1181 (Ch).

FA 1998, Sch 18 para 24—application for judicial review of enquiry

[55.42] See *R (oao Spring Salmon & Seafood Ltd) v CIR*, 49.72 RETURNS AND INFORMATION.

FA 1998, Sch 18 para 27—notice to produce documents

[55.43] See *Alan Porter Ltd v HM Inspector of Taxes*, 44.367 PENALTIES; *Meditor Capital Management Ltd v Feighan*, 49.76 RETURNS AND INFORMATION, and *Spring Salmon & Seafood Ltd v HMRC*, 49.77 RETURNS AND INFORMATION.

FA 1998, Sch 18 para 33—company applying for closure notice

[55.44] See the cases noted at 49.81 to 49.84 RETURNS AND INFORMATION.

Box 23.5 of return—information to be included

[55.45] See *Moffat v HMRC*, 49.114 RETURNS AND INFORMATION.

56

Settlements

The cases in this chapter are arranged under the following headings.

Liability of trustees

Interest accrued before death—assessment on trustees

[56.1] See *Reid's Trustees v CIR*, 19.2 DECEASED PERSONS, and *CIR v Henderson's Executors*, 19.3 DECEASED PERSONS.

Overseas income of UK trust paid to non-resident beneficiary

[56.2] The trustees of an English trust were resident in the UK. As trustees, they were registered owners of shares in a foreign company, the dividends on which were, under mandate of the trustees, paid direct to the beneficiary, who was resident and domiciled out of the UK. The Revenue issued assessments charging tax on the trustees, on the basis that whether or not the remittance basis applied depended on the residence and domicile of the trustees rather than those of the beneficiary, so that the dividends were assessable on the arising basis rather than on the remittance basis. The Special Commissioners allowed the trustees' appeals and the HL upheld this decision. Viscount Cave held that 'the person charged with tax is neither the trustee nor the beneficiary as such, but the person in actual receipt and control of the income which it is sought to reach'. *Williams v Singer & Others*, HL 1920, 7 TC 387; [1921] 1 AC 65. (*Notes.* (1) For HMRC's interpretation of this decision, see International Tax Handbook, para INTM367730. (2) For details of the background to the case, see the article 'The Singer Family and their Tax Cases' by David Parrott and John Avery Jones in British Tax Review 2008, pp 56–94.)

Liability of trustees where no ascertainable beneficiary

[56.3] A UK resident was trustee under an American will of a fund for the benefit of her sister, also resident in the UK, who was an incapacitated person within *TMA, s 72**. The will provided for sums to be applied for the maintenance of the sister but under the relevant American law she had no specific right to any of the investments of the fund which comprised mainly American securities and shares. The trustee had been assessed on amounts remitted to the UK for the maintenance of the sister. Further assessments were made on her on the full amount of the income of the American securities and shares of the fund less the amounts expended for the sister's maintenance. The CA upheld the assessments, holding that tax was chargeable on the trustee. The decision in *Williams v Singer*, 56.2 above, was distinguished on the grounds that there was no ascertainable beneficiary entitled to the balance of the income of the trust fund. *Kelly v Rogers (Willmer's Trustee)*, CA 1935, 19 TC 692; [1935] 2 KB 446. (*Note.* The case also turned on the application of machinery provisions which are now obsolete.)

Special dividend received by trustees of settlement

[56.4] A family settlement received a special dividend of £240,000 from a family company following a reorganisation of its share capital. The trustees failed to account for tax on this, and HMRC issued an amendment to the trust return. The trustees appealed, contending that the dividend should be treated as capital rather than income. The First-Tier Tribunal rejected this contention and dismissed the appeal. Judge Berner observed that 'as a general rule profits of a company that are distributed by the company by way of dividend are received by trustees as trust income'. A special dividend was 'trust income unless in substance the transactions amount to something other than a distribution'. The dividend here was a cash dividend rather than a capitalisation. *Raymond Taube Discretionary Trust (Trustees) v HMRC*, FTT [2010] UKFTT 473 (TC); [2011] SFTD 153, TC00735. (*Note.* An appeal by a similar family settlement was allowed on the ground that that income was only taxable at the Schedule F ordinary rate of 10%, and that liability 'would be entirely franked or offset by the tax credit attaching to the dividend'. An appeal by the beneficiary against an assessment on him was dismissed.)

Income accumulated below age of majority

[56.5] See *CIR v Pakenham & Others*, 56.79 below.

Definition of 'settlement' (ITTOIA 2005, s 620)

Cases held to constitute a settlement

Settlement of shares on godchildren

[56.6] An individual (S) transferred some shares into the joint names of himself and another individual (B), who was the father of S's godchildren. Later on the same day a dividend was declared on the shares. On the following day S executed a deed settling the shares on the godchildren, with himself and B as trustees of the settlement. The trustees claimed repayment of the tax deducted from the dividend, contending that it was income of the godchildren. The Revenue rejected the claim but the KB allowed the trustees' appeal. Rowlatt J held that a valid trust had been created and the dividend was income of the godchildren. *Brennan Minors' Trustees v Scanlan*, KB 1925, 9 TC 427. (*Note*. The KB rejected an application by the trustees for interest on the tax repayable, holding that *TMA, s 56(9)(a)** applies only to tax assessed directly. See now *ICTA 1988, ss 824, 825* as to interest on tax repayable.)

Shares allotted to trustee

[56.7] A married couple transferred certain assets to a company, the purchase price being satisfied by the allotment of 233,000 preference shares to them and of 75,000 ordinary shares to the trustees of settlements which they executed on the same day in favour of their children. Each share carried one vote, so that the couple controlled the company. The Revenue assessed the husband to surtax on the excess of the company's income over the preference dividends, on the basis that the whole transaction was a settlement which the couple could determine by virtue of their control of the company. The CS upheld the assessment (by a 3–1 majority, Lord Moncrieff dissenting on the grounds that he considered that the settlement was irrevocable). *CIR v Morton*, CS 1941, 24 TC 259. (*Note*. The decision here was followed in *Dalgety v CIR*, **56.8** below. With regard to whether the settlement was revocable or irrevocable, Lord Moncrieff's dissenting judgment was subsequently approved by Lord Macmillan in *Chamberlain v CIR*, **56.26** below, and by Lord Morton of Henryton in *Lord Vestey's Executors & Vestey v CIR*, **56.40** below. The case remains an authority on the definition of a 'settlement'.)

[56.8] The decision in *CIR v Morton*, **56.7** above, was applied by the KB in the similar subsequent case of *Dalgety v CIR*, KB 1941, 24 TC 280.

Covenant to pay annual sum to company controlled by covenantor

[56.9] In 1937 an individual (B) formed a company, and covenanted to make annual payments to the company of an amount equal to 75% of the dividends payable on certain shares. In January 1938 the share capital of the company was increased by the creation of a number of deferred ordinary shares. On the same day B settled £2,000 on irrevocable trusts for the benefit of his children. The trustees invested £1,000 of this in the purchase of deferred ordinary shares in the company. In March 1938 B made a net annual payment of £32,195 to the company under the covenant executed in 1937. The Revenue issued a surtax assessment on B on the gross amount payable under the covenant. The

Special Commissioners dismissed B's appeal, holding that the transactions constituted an arrangement which was deemed to be a settlement. The KB upheld their decision in principle, but remitted the case to them to reconsider the amount of the assessment. *Burston v CIR (No 1); Halperin v CIR*, KB 1942, 24 TC 285; [1945] 2 All ER 61. (*Note*. The Commissioners subsequently upheld the assessment, and B failed to request a Stated Case within the statutory time limit—see *Burston v CIR (Supplemental Case)*, CA 1946, 28 TC 123.)

Reorganisation of shares

[56.10] An individual (P) held all the preference shares and most of the ordinary shares of a company. He sold the ordinary shares to the trustees of a settlement made by his father for the benefit of P's children. Subsequently, the preference shares were converted into ordinary shares, and the ordinary shares were converted into preference shares carrying special rights for five years and thereafter carrying rights normal for 5% preference shares. As a result of these special rights, the trustees received certain dividends which absorbed nearly all the income of the company. The KB held that the transactions together constituted an 'arrangement', and therefore a settlement of which P was a settlor (with the result that the dividends in excess of 5% were assessable to surtax as P's income). *CIR v Prince-Smith*, KB 1943, 25 TC 84; [1943] 1 All ER 434.

Preference shares issued to wives of company directors

[56.11] The controlling directors and sole shareholders of a trading company arranged for preference shares in the company to be issued to their wives. The company subsequently declared substantial dividends to the holders of the preference shares. The Revenue issued assessments on the basis that the transactions amounted to an 'arrangement', and hence to settlements in which the settlors retained an interest. The Ch D upheld the assessments, holding that the transactions were within the statutory definition of a settlement and that the preference dividends fell to be treated as income of the settlors. *Young v Pearce; Young v Scrutton*, Ch D 1996, 70 TC 331; [1996] STC 743.

Allotment of 'B' shares to wife of company director

[56.12] The controlling director of an engineering company wished to retire. He and his family held 85 of the 100 issued shares, with the remaining 15 being held by the other director (P). In January 2000 P purchased 83 of the 85 shares, giving him a 98% shareholding, while his wife purchased the other two shares. (The share purchase was funded by a mortgage on a house which was jointly owned by P and his wife.) In March 2000 these 100 shares were renamed A shares, and a further 10 B shares were issued and allotted to P's wife. Between April 2000 and September 2002 dividends totalling £141,000 were paid on the 100 A shares, while dividends totalling £79,000 were paid on the 10 B shares held by P's wife. HMRC subsequently issued amendments to P's self-assessments, charging tax on the basis that the dividend income paid to P's wife was income arising under a settlement, and was taxable on P (at the higher rate of tax). P appealed, contending that the share structure had been intended to protect P's wife from some of the risk inherent in the company, but to enable her to have a 'fair share' of the dividends. The

First-Tier Tribunal reviewed the evidence in detail and held that there had been a settlement but that HMRC's amendments were excessive. Judge Mosedale held that the issue of the B shares was not a 'settlement', because P's wife had contributed half of the capital to buy the 85 A shares but had only received two of those 85 shares. However, the payment of dividends on the B shares was within the definition of a 'settlement', since 'a decision by the controlling shareholder to only issue a dividend on one class of shares rather than another (B shares in this case in preference to A shares) can be an arrangement'. Judge Mosedale expressed the view that in view of the capital contribution which P's wife had made to the purchase of the A shares, she should be entitled to 42.5% of the total dividends paid by the company, and directed that HMRC's amendments should be altered to reflect this. *DT Patmore v HMRC*, FTT [2010] SFTD 1124; [2010] UKFTT 334 (TC), TC00619.

Gift of ordinary share to wife of company director

[56.13] See *Garnett v Jones (re Arctic Systems Ltd)*, 56.50 below.

Settlement of rents receivable under determinable lease

[56.14] See *Lord Vestey's Executors & Vestey v CIR*, 56.40 below.

Settlement and associated mortgage of settlor's property

[56.15] By a deed dated 30 June 1950, a taxpayer settled £60,000 in trust for her grandson. By a deed dated 3 July 1950, she mortgaged certain properties to the trustees for £60,000 with interest at 5% per annum. Cheques for £60,000 were exchanged. She appealed against surtax assessments, claiming that the mortgage interest which she paid should be allowed as a deduction. The Ch D upheld the assessments, holding that the two deeds constituted an 'arrangement', and that the mortgage interest was not deductible. *CIR v Pay*, Ch D 1955, 36 TC 109.

Settlement by grandparent and associated transactions

[56.16] An actor (H) entered into a service agreement with a company for £50 per week and expenses when required. Subsequently, 98 of the 100 shares in the company were acquired by the trustees of a settlement made by H's father-in-law in favour of H's children (who were below the age of majority). In the relevant period, H acted in a film and the company received £25,000 for his services, paying him £900 and paying to the trustees of the settlement an interim dividend of £500 free of tax. H claimed repayment, on behalf of his children, of the tax deducted from the dividend. The Revenue rejected the claim, holding that the formation of the company, the service agreement, and the deed of settlement together constituted an 'arrangement' and hence a settlement, and that H had indirectly provided funds for the purposes of the settlement. H appealed, contending that the transactions were not an 'arrangement', because the deed of settlement did not exist when H entered into the service agreement. The CA rejected this contention, holding that there had been an 'arrangement', so that the dividend was income of H and no repayment was due. Donovan LJ observed that it was not essential 'that the whole of the eventual arrangement must be in contemplation from the outset'. The whole arrangement was 'conceived and in being' within the same tax year, and there was 'sufficient unity about the whole matter to justify it being called an "arrangement"'. Pearce LJ observed that a settlor cannot 'avoid liability by merely giving his solicitors carte blanche to effect some scheme for the benefit of his family and refusing to concern himself with its precise form'. *Crossland v Hawkins*, CA 1961, 39 TC 493; [1961] Ch 537; [1961] 2 All ER 812.

[56.17] L's mother executed a settlement under which L, his wife and his son had discretionary interests. Following various transactions, the trust fund comprised £34,000 lent by the trustees to L at 6% interest and re-lent by him free of interest to a company in which he was interested. The income arising to the trustees was applied for the benefit of L's son, who was below the age of majority. The Revenue included this income in surtax assessments on L. The Ch D upheld the assessments, holding that the arrangements constituted a settlement of which L was a settlor, and that he had provided income for the purposes of the settlement. *CIR v Leiner*, Ch D 1964, 41 TC 589.

Shares given to charity subject to grant of purchase option to third party

[56.18] An individual (V) was the managing director and controlling shareholder of an engineering company. In 1952 he had transferred 100,000 non-voting shares in the company to a bank as security. In 1958 the bank released the shares and V arranged for them to be transferred to a charity, subject to the charity granting a trustee company an option to purchase the shares within five years. Substantial dividends were paid to the charity in 1958/59 and 1959/60, and the Revenue assessed V to surtax on the basis that the transactions constituted an 'arrangement' and hence a settlement. The Special Commissioners confirmed the assessments and the HL upheld their decision (by a 3–2 majority, Lords Reid and Donovan dissenting). Lord Upjohn observed that 'the intention was that the trustee company should hold on such trusts as might thereafter be declared'. *Vandervell v CIR*, HL 1966, 43 TC 519; [1967] 2 AC 291; [1967] 1 All ER 1.

Guarantee of trustees' overdraft by settlor

[56.19] Under a trust for the benefit of the settlor's children, the trustees held shares purchased by means of a bank overdraft guaranteed by the settlor (and later by a company which he and his wife wholly owned). The overdraft was secured by the settlor (and later the company) depositing an equivalent amount with the bank. The deposit earned no interest, and interest of 1% was charged on the overdraft. As the overdraft was paid off, corresponding amounts of the deposit were released. In the relevant years, dividends which the trustees received were paid to the bank, and the settlor was assessed to surtax on the basis that he retained an interest in the settlement. The Ch D upheld the assessments, holding that the arrangements with the bank, together with the settlement deed, was within the definition of an 'arrangement' and hence a settlement. The settled fund included the shares and the dividends which the settlor had provided directly or indirectly. Accordingly the income was deemed to be his. *CIR v Wachtel*, Ch D 1970, 46 TC 543; [1971] Ch 573; [1971] 1 All ER 296.

Actress aged 14—whether a settlor

[56.20] In 1960 M, an actress aged 14 at the time, entered into an agreement with a company (S) to render her exclusive services as an artiste to it for five years, for a salary of £400 per year. On the same day, her father, who had formed the company, settled the shares in it to be held in trust for her until she reached the age of 25. In 1961, M, S and a film company entered into an agreement under which M's services as an actress were made available to the film company for five years, in return for payments to S ranging from $30,000 in the first year to $75,000 in the fifth year. The bulk of S's income was paid to the trustees by way of dividend, and none of the income paid to them was distributed. The Revenue assessed M to surtax on the basis that she should be deemed to be the settlor of an 'arrangement', so that the undistributed income of the settlement fell to be treated as hers. She appealed, contending that even if there was an 'arrangement', the settlor of the deemed arrangement was her father. The HL unanimously rejected this contention and upheld the assessments. Viscount Dilhorne held that all the relevant arrangements, including the 1960 service agreement and the 1961 agreement with the film company, constituted a settlement of which M was a settlor and for which she had indirectly provided funds. The facts that M's father could also be held to be a settlor, and that M was below the legal age of discretion, were not conclusive. *Mills v CIR*, HL 1974, 49 TC 367; [1974] STC 130; [1975] AC 38; [1974] 1 All ER 722.

Allotment of shares to children

[56.21] See *Copeman v Coleman*, 56.55 below; *Hood Barrs v CIR*, 56.56 below, and *Butler v Wildin*, 56.58 below.

Post Office Savings Bank deposits

[56.22] See *Thomas v Marshall*, 56.60 below.

Court Order following divorce

[56.23] See *Yates v Starkey*, 56.61 below.

Deed of separation

[56.24] See *Harvey v Sivyer*, 56.62 below.

Deed of appointment

[56.25] See *EG v MacShamhrain*, 56.66 below.

Cases held not to constitute a settlement

Shares of company controlled by settlor held in trust

[56.26] In 1935 an individual (C) established an investment company (S), to which he transferred certain assets in return for preference shares. In March 1936 he executed a deed of settlement and paid trustees £3,500 to be held on trust for his wife and his four young children. The money was invested in ordinary shares in S. In December 1936 the capital structure of S was altered by dividing the ordinary shares into five classes, and C executed four identical deeds of settlement in favour of his children. The money settled was invested in shares in S, the result being that the trustees of each of the five settlements held a separate class of ordinary shares in S, the whole of the capital of which was held by C and the trustees. The Revenue assessed C to surtax on the excess of S's income over the amount distributed to him by way of dividends on his preference shares. The HL allowed C's appeal, holding that the formation and structure of S and the five settlements did not constitute an 'arrangement', and the only sums settled were the funds provided for the purpose of the settlements. Although S was controlled by C, it did not hold its assets as part of the provisions settled on the children, and its assets did not constitute 'property comprised in the settlement'. *Chamberlain v CIR*, HL 1943, 25 TC 317; [1943] 2 All ER 200. (*Note. Obiter dicta* of Lord Macmillan were disapproved by Lord Greene in the subsequent case of *Hood Barrs v CIR*, 56.56 below.)

[56.27] The decision in *Chamberlain v CIR*, **56.26** above, was applied by the CA in the similar subsequent case of *Clark v CIR*, CA 1944, 28 TC 55. (*Note.* The case also involved the application of legislation which was subsequently repealed by *FA 1972*.)

Arrangements to prevent takeover of company

[56.28] A number of shareholders in a public company (B) discovered that another company was attempting to acquire a majority shareholding in B. In an effort to prevent this, they entered into an arrangement involving the sale of their shares to a newly-formed company (Y) at undervalue with an option to repurchase. The Revenue issued surtax assessments charging tax on the dividends on the shares transferred to Y, on the basis that the transactions constituted a settlement. The Ch D allowed the shareholders' appeals against the assessments. Sir John Pennycuick held that the transactions had been entered into for *bona fide* commercial reasons, without any element of bounty, and were not within the definition of a settlement. *Bulmer & Others v CIR*, Ch D 1966, 44 TC 1; [1967] Ch 145; [1966] 3 All ER 801.

Money lent to company by director on commercial terms

[56.29] The controlling director of a company lent the company £3,330,000 in May 1973. In October 1973 the company repaid an amount to cover the loan, as well as £110,000 owing to him from earlier small loans. During the interval the company had invested the amount by deposit in a merchant bank, for use in connection with its business. The Revenue assessed the director on the income which the company derived from its investment of the money lent, on the basis that the loan was a settlement. The Special Commissioners allowed his appeal and the Ch D upheld their decision. Nourse J held that there must be an element of bounty to bring a loan within the definition of a 'settlement'. On the evidence, the loan in question was a commercial transaction with no element of bounty. *CIR v Levy*, Ch D 1982, 56 TC 68; [1982] STC 442.

Calculation of income (ITTOIA 2005, s 623)

Covenanted payments—whether investment income of covenantor

[56.30] A married couple covenanted to make payments aggregating £2,200 per annum to their respective parents (resident overseas). They accepted that the covenants were 'settlements'. Apart from a small amount of building society interest, the couple's only income, from which the payments could be made, was earned income. The Revenue assessed the husband for 1974/75 on the basis that the £2,200 was investment income, liable to the investment income surcharge then in force. He appealed, contending that there had been a gift of earned income which remained earned income. The General Commissioners rejected this contention and dismissed the appeal, and the Ch D upheld their decision. Walton J held that for tax purposes the income arising under the settlement was not earned income. *Ang v Parrish*, Ch D 1980, 53 TC 304; [1980] STC 341; [1980] 1 WLR 940; [1980] 2 All ER 790.

Retained interests (ITTOIA 2005, ss 624–628)

Income where settlor retains an interest (ITTOIA 2005, ss 624, 625)

Annual payments to company controlled by settlor

[56.31] In March 1938 an individual (P) covenanted to make weekly payments to a company he controlled for the remainder of his life or until the company was put into liquidation. In October 1938 it was resolved that the company should be wound up. P claimed repayment of the tax which he had withheld from the payments he had made under the covenant. The Revenue rejected the claim, considering that the covenant was a revocable settlement so that the payments remained P's income, and no repayment was due. The Ch D and CA unanimously upheld this contention and dismissed P's appeal. *CIR v Payne (and related appeal)*, CA 1940, 23 TC 610.

[56.32] Three settlors covenanted to make annual payments of an amount equal to the dividends which they received from a company which one of them controlled. The controlling shareholder was assessed to surtax. He appealed, contending that the payments were deductible from his income for surtax proposes. The KB allowed his appeal and the HL unanimously upheld this decision, holding that the effect of the relevant deed was that the settlor had no power to revoke the settlement, so that the payments were not to be treated as his income under the legislation then in force. (Lord Simonds observed that 'it is not the function of a court of law to give to words a strained and unnatural meaning because only thus will a taxing section apply to a transaction which, had the legislature thought of it, would have been covered by appropriate words'.) *Wolfson v CIR*, HL 1949, 31 TC 141; [1949] 1 All ER 865.

Settlor assigning life insurance policies to trustees

[56.33] A woman (T) executed a deed of settlement by which she assigned to trustees two policies on her life, but retained the power to revoke the trusts with the consent of the trustees, and to create new trusts in favour of any person except herself. She covenanted to pay the trustees each year a sum which, after deduction of income tax, would equal the premiums payable on the policies. She appealed against surtax assessments, contending that the annual payments under the deed should be treated as deductible in computing her income for surtax purposes. The KB rejected this contention and upheld the assessments. Lawrence J held that T had retained the power to revoke the settlement and to appoint new trusts in favour of a future husband, and that she therefore had an interest in income arising under the settlement. *CIR v Tennant*, KB 1942, 24 TC 215.

Settlement in favour of grandchildren

[56.34] A taxpayer executed a deed of settlement in favour of his two grandsons. The Revenue assessed him to surtax for 1938/39 on the basis that, under the terms of the settlement in question, the income from the settlement might become payable to the settlor if his grandchildren predeceased him, so that he retained an interest in the settlement. The settlor died in April 1939 and his executors appealed against the surtax assessment. The Special Commissioners dismissed the appeal and the CS upheld their decision. *Barr's Trustees v CIR*, CS 1943, 25 TC 72. (*Note*. The decision is chiefly concerned with the application of trust law to the interpretation of the settlor's wishes as regards the ultimate disposal of the trust assets.)

[56.35] Two young children received income from several building societies. HMRC issued assessments on their father (L) on the basis that he had settled the relevant capital on his children. L appealed, contending that the funds derived from the children's grandfather, for whom he held a power of attorney (and who had died before the hearing of the appeal). The First-Tier Tribunal accepted this contention and allowed the appeals, finding that the grandfather had been the settlor. *PA Lorber v HMRC (No 1)*, FTT [2011] UKFTT 101 (TC), TC00977. (*Note*. For another issue in this case, see **37.3** MARRIED COUPLES.)

Settlement income applied in reduction of loan from settlor

[56.36] Two individuals made irrevocable settlements on their children in 1934. They lent money to the trustees of the settlements, who used the loans to acquire shares in companies controlled by the settlors, applying dividends received on the shares in 1936/37 and 1937/38 towards partial repayment of the loan. The CA held that the effect of the transactions was that the settlor had an interest in the income of the settlements. *Jenkins v CIR; Mason v CIR*, CA 1944, 26 TC 265; [1944] 2 All ER 491. (*Note*. The appeal against the assessment for 1936/37 was successful, as the provisions charging tax on settlements in which the settlor retained an interest were introduced by *FA 1938, s 38* with effect from 1937/38. Before 22 April 1936, settlements on children below the age of majority were not 'caught' if the settlement was irrevocable. The CA held that the settlements were 'irrevocable' and thus did not fall within *FA 1936, s 21*. The decision on this point was subsequently disapproved by the HL in *Jamieson v CIR*, **56.126** below. For other cases concerning the provisions of *FA 1936, s 21*, see **56.51** to **56.53** below.)

Supplemental Deed—whether settlor retaining an interest

[56.37] In 1936 an individual (T) executed a deed of covenant. In 1938 he revoked this covenant and executed a further deed, which reserved a power of revocation, but provided that this power could not be exercised until more than six years after the execution of the 1936 deed. Under a further deed in 1939, it was provided that the 1938 deed should be modified to provide for payment of a net sum after deduction of income tax (whereas the original deeds had provided for payment of a gross sum free of tax). By a supplemental deed in 1940, it was provided that the power of revocation could not be exercised before April 1946. T claimed that, in computing his income for surtax purposes, the additional sum covenanted to be paid under the 1939 deed as representing income tax should be allowed as a deduction. The Revenue rejected the claim, on the basis that the payments had been made under a settlement which could be revoked within six years, so that the income fell to be treated as that of the settlor. The Special Commissioners dismissed T's appeal, and the KB and CA unanimously upheld their decision. The first additional payment arose under the 1939 deed and was paid under a covenant which could be revoked within six years, so that the income fell to be treated as that of the settlor. The supplemental deed created a new settlement, so that the subsequent payments were also paid under a covenant which could be revoked within six years and the income fell to be treated as that of the settlor. *Taylor v CIR*, CA 1946, 27 TC 93.

[56.38] A woman made payments under a deed of covenant in favour of a charitable trust. The deed provided that it could not be revoked for seven years. By a supplemental deed, executed shortly before the expiration of the seven years, she postponed her power of revocation for a further three years. The trustees reclaimed tax in respect of payments made under the supplemental deed. The Ch D held that no repayment was due, since the supplemental deed was a new settlement which could be revoked within six years of having been made. *CIR v Nicolson & Bartlett*, Ch D 1953, 34 TC 354; [1953] 1 WLR 809; [1953] 2 All ER 123.

Unexercised power of appointment jointly held by settlor and beneficiary

[56.39] Under a settlement executed in 1907, various investments were held in trust for an individual (G) and his son for life. In 1928 G executed a deed of resettlement surrendering his life interest and providing for the investments to be held upon such trusts as he and his son should jointly appoint. If no appointment were made, the investments were to be accumulated until G's son (who was then aged 21) reached the age of 35 (or the age of 31 if he had married with G's consent), or died. The power of appointment was not exercised and the investments were accumulated. The Revenue issued surtax assessments on G for 1937/38 to 1939/40 on the basis that he had retained an interest in the settlement by virtue of the joint power of appointment. The Special Commissioners dismissed G's appeal and the KB upheld their decision. *Glyn v CIR*, KB 1948, 30 TC 321; [1948] 2 All ER 419.

Settlement of rents receivable under determinable lease

[56.40] Two brothers (W and E) leased certain properties abroad to a UK company, the rents to be paid to trustees resident in Paris. (The treatment of the rents in relation to the company was considered in *Union Cold Storage Co Ltd v Adamson*, 63.38 TRADING PROFITS.) The lease was determinable at six months' notice by either the lessors or the lessee. On the following day, W and E settled the rents payable to the trustees on trust to invest and accumulate the income (with wide powers to W and E to direct how the rents were to be invested). The trust fund comprising the investments and accumulated income was to be divided into two parts, to be held on trust for the children and remoter issue of W and E respectively as either might appoint by deed or will. Power was reserved to each of them to appoint by will in favour of his widow, although E subsequently executed a deed relinquishing this power. In 1942 the Revenue issued income tax and surtax assessments on E and on the executors of W (who had died in 1940), on the basis that the lease and settlement together constituted a revocable settlement, and also issued additional or alternative assessments on the basis that *ITA 2007, ss 714–751** (transfer of assets abroad) applied. The HL unanimously allowed the appeals against all the assessments, holding that the 'property comprised in the settlement' was only the rental income, rather than the leased properties. Accordingly, the power to determine the lease was not a power to determine the settlement. Lord Morton also held that the right to direct investment was merely a fiduciary power, rather than a right which conferred any benefit upon its holders, so that neither W nor E had an interest in the settlement. *Lord Vestey's Executors & Vestey v CIR; Lord Vestey's Executors & Vestey v Colquhoun*, HL 1949, 31 TC 1; [1949] 1 All ER 1108.

Trust income paid to be charities nominated by settlor

[56.41] A married couple created a settlement. Part of the trust income was paid as an annuity to their daughter (who was below the age of majority). The trust deed did not provide directions as to how the remainder of the income was disposed of, but it was paid to charities nominated by the husband. The Revenue issued a surtax assessment on the basis that the husband retained an interest in the trust income. The Special Commissioners dismissed the husband's appeal and the CS unanimously upheld their decision. Lord Clyde observed that the trust deed 'made no provision for the disposal of income not required for children's annuities'. Accordingly, the settlor retained an interest in that 'surplus income'. *Hannay's Executors v CIR*, CS 1956, 37 TC 217.

Bermudan settlement of income from UK securities

[56.42] A woman who was neither resident nor ordinarily resident in the UK settled UK securities to the value of £700,000 on trusts for the benefit of herself and her issue. The trustees were empowered to hold in trust for the settlor any part of the trust fund up to the value of £60,000 in any triennial period. The trustees were not resident in the UK, and the settlement was executed in Bermuda and expressed to be subject to Bermudan law. The Revenue issued surtax assessments on the basis that the income of the settlement fell to be treated as that of the settlor. She appealed, contending firstly that she was not assessable since neither she nor the trustees was resident in the UK, and alternatively that the settlement was irrevocable. The HL unanimously rejected these contentions and upheld the assessments, holding that the settlor was assessable since the income arose from property in the UK, and that the settlement was not irrevocable, as the trust fund could be exhausted during the settlor's lifetime. The HL specifically declined to follow the previous decision in *Astor v Perry*, HL 1935, 19 TC 355 (which the appellant had cited as an authority), observing that case had been decided on the wording of *FA 1922, s 20*, and that the legislation had subsequently been amended by *FA 1938, s 38* 'precisely to overcome the difficulties to which that case had given rise'. *CIR v Countess of Kenmare*, HL 1957, 37 TC 383; [1958] AC 267; [1957] 3 All ER 33.

Accumulation settlement—whether any statutory power of advancement

[56.43] Under a settlement, income was to be accumulated during the lifetime of the settlor (B). After his death, two-thirds of the fund was to be held for the benefit of a woman (T), and the remaining one-third was to be held for the benefit of any children which they might have. B and T subsequently married, and the Revenue assessed B to surtax on the basis that there was a statutory power of advancement in favour of T under *Trustee Act 1925, s 32*, so that he retained an interest in the settlement. B appealed. The Special Commissioners allowed his appeal, and the Ch D and CA unanimously upheld their decision, holding that the trust for accumulation under the terms of the settlement was inconsistent with the statutory power of advancement, which was therefore inapplicable. *CIR v Bernstein*, CA 1960, 39 TC 391; [1961] Ch 399; [1961] 1 All ER 320.

Settlement with power of revocation—whether power extinguished

[56.44] An individual executed a settlement under which he had a life interest and the trustees had power, at their discretion and at his request, to pay to him the whole or any part of the settled property. In March 1967 he executed a deed of release, in which no reference was made to this power, by which he surrendered his life interest in part of the settled property with the intent that this part was to be held under the settlement as if he were dead. The Revenue assessed him to surtax for 1967/68 to 1969/70 on the income arising under the settlement. He appealed, contending that the deed of release should be construed as extinguishing the trustees' discretionary power, so that the settlement had become irrevocable. The CA unanimously rejected this contention and upheld the assessments. *CIR v Cookson*, CA 1977, 50 TC 705; [1977] STC 140; [1977] 2 All ER 331.

Dividend waiver

[56.45] The controlling director of a company owned 9999 of the 10000 shares in it. His wife (who was not a director) owned the remaining share. The director waived his entitlement to a dividend in respect of his 9999 shares, so that his wife received an enhanced dividend in respect of her share. The Revenue issued an amendment to the director's self-assessment, charging tax on the basis that the basis that the dividend waiver constituted a 'settlement', so that the income represented by the waived dividends was treated as belonging to the director for tax purposes. The director appealed. The Special Commissioner dismissed the appeal, holding that 'a definite plan, including a relatively simple one, to use a company's shares to divert income falls within the meaning of an arrangement'. The Commissioner observed that 'there was no commercial purpose for either of the waivers and it would surely not have taken place on an arm's length basis'. The director had retained an interest in 'the property from which the dividend arose'. *SR Buck v HMRC*, Sp C 2008, [2009] SSCD 6 (Sp C 716).

[56.46] The two directors of a company (V) each owned 40% of the shares in V. Their wives each owned 10% of the shares. The directors waived their rights to a dividend, so that their wives (who were liable to tax at the basic rate) received enhanced dividends. HMRC issued discovery assessments on the basis that the dividend waivers constituted a settlement, in which the settlors retained an interest. The First-tier Tribunal dismissed the directors' appeals against these decisions. Judge Blewitt observed that 'there was no commercial purpose for the waivers' and they 'would not have taken place at arm's length'. *P Donovan v HMRC (and related appeal)*, FTT [2014] UKFTT 048 (TC), TC03188.

Trust income deriving from settlor

[56.47] In 1985 an individual (R) established a trust, of which he was one of the beneficiaries. In 2001 the company which was the trustee of the settlement lent R £1,000,000. R subsequently paid interest to the trustee. HMRC issued assessments charging income tax on these payments. The First-Tier Tribunal upheld the assessments and dismissed R's appeal, applying the principles laid down in *Ang v Parrish*, 56.30 above .*O Rogge v HMRC (and related appeals)*, FTT [2012] UKFTT 49 (TC), TC01747.

ITTOIA 2005, s 625(5)*—definition of 'related property'

[56.48] See *Trennery v West*, **71.183** CAPITAL GAINS TAX.

Cross-references

[56.49] See also *Muir v CIR*, **4.247** APPEALS; *Burston v CIR (No 1)*, **56.9** above; *CIR v Wachtel*, **56.19** above; *Mills v CIR*, **56.20** above, and *Watson v Holland*, **56.68** below. For other cases concerning whether a settlement was revocable or irrevocable, see *CIR v Morton*, **56.7** above; *Taylor v CIR*, **56.37** above; *CIR v Warden*, **56.51** below; *CIR v Lord Delamere*, **56.52** below; *Eastwood v CIR*, **56.53** below; *Hood Barrs v CIR (No 3)*, **56.57** below, and *Jamieson v CIR*, **56.126** below.

Exception for outright gifts between spouses (ITTOIA 2005, s 626)

[56.50] A consultant (J) purchased a newly-incorporated company. He retained one of the two shares, and gave the other to his wife. J was appointed as the company's sole director, while his wife was appointed company secretary. The company began to carry on an information technology consultancy business. J carried out the consultancy work, while his wife carried out some administrative work, totalling about four or five hours per week. On the advice of J's accountants, the company paid him and his wife small salaries but significant dividends. The Revenue formed the opinion that the amounts paid to J's wife were out of line with her contribution to the business, and that the company had distributed its profits by way of dividend rather than salary in an attempt to ensure that much of the couple's income was attributed to the wife and taxed at a lower rate than would have been applicable if it had been paid to J as salary. They issued a notice of amendment on the basis that the arrangements constituted a 'settlement'. J appealed, contending firstly that the distribution of the company's profits did not amount to a 'settlement', and alternatively that the transfer of the share to his wife had been an outright gift to his wife, within the exception in *ITTOIA 2005, s 626**. The HL rejected the first contention but unanimously accepted the latter contention. Lord Hoffmann held that the arrangements were not 'a normal commercial transaction between two adults' and that 'it would not have been an arrangement into which (J) would ever have entered with someone with whom he was dealing at arm's length.' The arrangements contained the 'necessary element of bounty' to constitute a settlement. However the transfer of the share to his wife had been an 'outright gift between spouses', within *s 626**, so that the charging provision in *s 624** did not apply. Lord Hope of Craighead observed that 'an arrangement by which one spouse uses a private company as a tax-efficient vehicle for distributing to the other income which its business generates is likely to constitute a "settlement" on the other spouse'. However, 'so long as the shares from which that income arises are ordinary shares, and not shares carrying contractual rights which are restricted wholly or substantially to a right to income, the settlement will fall within the exception' (in *s 626**). *Garnett v Jones (re Arctic Systems Ltd)*, HL 2007, 78 TC 597; [2007] STC 1536; [2007] UKHL 35; [2007] 4 All ER 857. (*Note.* For HMRC's practice following this decision, see HMRC Trusts Settlements and Estates Manual, para TSEM4001 *et seq.* See also the Ministerial Statement by the Exchequer Secretary on 26 July 2007. She stated that 'the case has brought to light the need for the Government to ensure that there is greater clarity in the law regarding its position on the tax treatment of "income splitting". Some individuals use non-commercial arrangements (arrangements that they would not reasonably enter into with an arms-length third party) to divert income (which would, in the absence of those arrangements have flowed to them) to others. That minimises their tax liability, and results in an unfair outcome, increasing the tax burden on other tax payers and putting businesses that compete with these individuals at a competitive disadvantage. It is the Government's view that individuals involved in these arrangements should pay tax on what is, in substance, their own income and that the legislation should clearly provide for this. The Government will therefore bring forward proposals for changes to legislation to ensure this is the case.' Despite the Exchequer Secretary's statement, no such legislation has yet been brought forward.)

Unmarried children (ITTOIA 2005, ss 629–632)

Pre-1936 settlement in favour of children—whether irrevocable

[56.51] A settlor claimed repayments of income tax in respect of payments made under a settlement established in 1935 in favour of (amongst others) his daughter, who was below the age of majority. The trustees had power to cancel the obligations under the trust deeds without the consent of the settlor or of the beneficiaries. The Revenue rejected his claim, and he appealed, contending that the settlement was irrevocable, so that the tax was repayable under the legislation then in force (*FA 1936, s 21*). The CS unanimously rejected this contention, holding that the settlement was not irrevocable. Lord Normand held that 'a deed is revocable if it is terminable either by the truster or by persons appointed by the truster with power to terminate'. *CIR v Warden*, CS 1938, 22 TC 416. (*Note*. The relevant legislation was repealed by *FA 1995* with effect from 1995/96.)

[56.52] In 1932 a taxpayer made a settlement on his children with discretionary powers in favour of, *inter alia*, himself and his wife. *FA 1936* introduced provisions charging tax on such settlements, except where the settlement was irrevocable. The settlor was assessed to surtax for 1936/37 in respect of the settlement, and appealed, contending that the settlement was 'irrevocable'. The KB rejected this contention and upheld the assessment. *CIR v Lord Delamere*, KB 1939, 22 TC 525; [1939] 2 KB 667; [1939] 3 All ER 386.

[56.53] The decision in *CIR v Lord Delamere*, **56.52** above, was approved by the CA in the similar subsequent case of *Eastwood v CIR*, CA 1943, 25 TC 100; [1943] 1 KB 314; [1943] 1 All ER 350.

[56.54] The provisions of *FA 1936, s 21* were also considered in *Jenkins v CIR*, **56.36** above, but the decision on this point was subsequently disapproved by the HL in *Jamieson v CIR*, **56.126** below.

Allotment of shares to children of company directors

[56.55] A company controlled by a married couple created 25 preference shares of £200 each. They were issued for £10 on allotment, leaving £190 uncalled. Later a dividend of £40 per share free of tax was declared, and by the same resolution a call of £40 was made on each share. One share had been allotted to each of two children of the controlling directors. The husband submitted a repayment claim on behalf of the children (who were below the age of majority). The KB held that no repayment was due, since there had been an arrangement of assets constituting a settlement, rather than a *bona fide* commercial transaction. *Copeman v Coleman*, KB 1939, 22 TC 594; [1939] 2 KB 484; [1939] 3 All ER 224. (*Note*. The decision here was approved by the HL in *Mills v CIR*, **56.20** above.)

[56.56] A company director transferred shares in the company to his two daughters. The CA unanimously held that the transfer was a settlement. Lord Greene specifically disapproved *obiter dicta* of Lord Macmillan in *Chamberlain v CIR*, **56.26** above. *Hood Barrs v CIR*, CA 1946, 27 TC 385; [1946] 2 All ER 768. (*Note*. The settlor was convicted of perjury with regard to some of his evidence before the Special Commissioners—see **4.40** APPEALS.)

[56.57] In a subsequent case involving the same settlement, the Special Commissioners held that the settlement in question was within the definition of a revocable settlement, and that the settlor was liable to surtax on certain dividends paid to one of his daughters. The CA unanimously upheld this decision. *Hood Barrs v CIR (No 3)*, CA 1960, 39 TC 209. (*Note*. See **4.241** APPEALS for a preliminary point in this case.)

[56.58] Two brothers bought the shares of an 'off-the-shelf' limited company in 1980. The £100 issued share capital was initially allotted or transferred to the brothers and their four young children, 12 shares to each brother and 19 shares to each child. A fifth child born subsequently received his father's 12 shares and 7 shares from his uncle, and a sixth child born to the other brother received her father's 5 remaining shares and 11 shares from the other children. Dividends were declared in 1985 and paid to each of the shareholders. They claimed repayment of the tax credit attaching to the dividends. The Revenue rejected the claims on the basis that the dividends represented income derived from the parents, and that the arrangements by which the children acquired the shares amounted to a settlement. The Ch D upheld the Revenue's ruling with regard to 88 of the 100 shares. Vinelott J held that the allotment of shares to the four older children was a settlement. The brothers had together arranged for all the steps which had taken place, and they had taken all the risks in providing the company with the opportunity to become profitable, so that the necessary element of bounty existed. It could not, however, be inferred that these arrangements extended to the provision of shares to the two youngest children. The 12 shares provided to the fifth child by his father were also within the settlements legislation, as there was no direct evidence that the child had given full value for the shares. The 7 shares he had received from his uncle could, however, be disregarded, as, on the evidence, they were not paid under any reciprocal arrangement; and there was also no such arrangement with regard to the shares transferred to the sixth child by the older children. With regard to the 5 shares transferred to the sixth child by her father, the Revenue had conceded that they were transferred for full value, so that there was no settlement. *Butler v Wildin*, Ch D 1988, 61 TC 666; [1989] STC 22. (*Note*. An appeal and a cross-appeal against this decision were dismissed by the CA on terms agreed between the parties. The decision that the allotment of shares to the older children constituted a 'settlement' was approved by the HL in the subsequent case of *Garnett v Jones (re Arctic Systems Ltd)*, **56.50** above.)

[56.59] A married couple each owned 50% of the shares in a family company. In 1995 the company made a further issue of shares, as a result of which the couple each owned 20% of the shares and each of their three daughters, who were below the age of majority, also owned 20% of the shares. The Revenue issued amendments to their self-assessments, on the basis that the dividend income which the company paid to their daughters was income arising under a settlement. The couple appealed. The Special Commissioner dismissed the appeal, applying the principles laid down in *Garnett v Jones (re Arctic Systems Ltd)*, **56.50** above, and *Butler v Wildin*, **56.58** above. The Commissioner observed that 'the use of a corporate structure to provide an income stream to a minor child, thereby reducing higher rates of tax, is a typical situation where the taxation of settlor legislation can and does apply'. *PA & Mrs FJ Bird v HMRC*, Sp C 2008, [2009] SSCD 81 (Sp C 720). (*Note*. The Revenue had also issued 'extended time limit' assessments for 1995/96 to 1997/98 inclusive. The Commissioner allowed the couple's appeals against these assessments, holding that there had not been any 'negligent conduct' on the part of the couple, since the notes which the Revenue had sent with the 1995 tax returns did not make it sufficiently clear that they should declare the daughters' dividends as their income.)

Post Office Savings Bank deposits—whether a settlement

[56.60] A father made payments into Post Office Savings Bank accounts in the names of his children (who were below the age of majority), and purchased Defence Bonds in their names. The Revenue issued assessments charging tax on the interest, on the basis that the payments were settlements. The HL unanimously upheld the assessments. *Thomas v Marshall (and cross-appeal)*, HL 1953, 34 TC 178; [1953] AC 543; [1953] 1 All ER 1102. (*Note.* Under the legislation then in force, the provisions did not apply where the aggregate amount of the income paid to, or for the benefit, of the child in question did not exceed £5. The corresponding figure in *ITTOIA 2005, s 629(3)* is £100. The HL held that the exemption limit applied only when the aggregate income of all settlements in favour of a particular child was below the limit, rejecting the appellant's contention that there should be a separate limit for the income of each individual settlement.)

Court order following divorce—whether settlement created

[56.61] Under a court order following divorce proceedings, the husband was required to pay to his former wife 'the annual sum of £100 less tax in trust for each of the three children issue of the marriage'. The CA allowed his claim to child allowances, holding that the order created a settlement and that the sums payable under the order must be treated as his income. *Yates v Starkey*, CA 1951, 32 TC 38; [1951] Ch 465; [1951] 1 All ER 732.

Deed of separation—whether settlement created

[56.62] The decision in *Yates v Starkey*, **56.61** above, was applied in a case where a husband made payments to his children under a deed of separation. The wife had custody of the children and the husband covenanted to pay a monthly sum to each of them. The Ch D held that the covenant was a settlement and the payments to the children were income of the husband. Although he was compelled by parental obligation to make the payments, the natural relationship between parent and young child was one of such deep affection and concern that there must always be an element of bounty by the parent. Nourse J held that it was 'now well established that the legal effect of the provisions embodied in this kind of consent order is derived from the order itself and does not depend on any anterior agreement between the parties.' *Harvey v Sivyer*, Ch D 1985, 58 TC 569; [1985] STC 434; [1985] 3 WLR 261; [1985] 2 All ER 1054.

ITTOIA 2005, s 629(7)(a)*—definition of 'stepchild'

[56.63] An individual (R) married in 1938 and separated in 1948. Following the separation he made a settlement, the income from which was paid to his wife's daughter by a previous marriage. That marriage had been ended by divorce, and his wife's former husband was still alive. The Revenue issued surtax assessments on the basis that the income from the settlement should be treated as R's income for tax purposes, on the basis that his wife's daughter was his 'stepchild'. He appealed, contending that the daughter was not his stepchild because her father was still alive. The CS rejected this contention and upheld the assessments. Lord Clyde held that 'remarriage of the parent and not the death of one or other of the parents is the qualification for falling into the category of stepchild'. *CIR v Russell*, CS 1955, 36 TC 83.

Partnership Deed with children below age of majority

[56.64] In an Irish case, a café proprietor (C) entered into a deed of partnership on 29 March 1944 with three of his sons, hitherto full-time employees in the business, and his mother-in-law, aged 80, who took no part in the business. The deed gave him extensive powers which conferred upon him a commanding position in the partnership and the conduct of its business. On 3 April 1944 his mother-in-law executed a deed irrevocably assigning her interest in the partnership to C in trust for his other four children. The Revenue issued partnership assessments for 1944/45 and 1945/46, at the beginning of which all seven children were unmarried and were below the age of majority, on the basis that the whole of the income was income of C. The Special Commissioner allowed the partnership's appeals, finding that the partnership was a *bona fide* commercial transaction. The SC(I) upheld his decision (by a majority) as one of fact. *O'Dwyer v Cafolla & Co*, SC(I) 1948, 2 ITC 374; [1949] IR 210.

Release of life interest—whether a settlement

[56.65] Under the will of a testator who died in 1927, a fund was settled on his son (G) for life, with remainder to G's daughter (D) for life, with remainder to any children of D. In 1948 G and D surrendered their interests to D's children, who were below the age of majority. D's first husband, who was the father of the children, had been killed in the Second World War, and in 1948 she married B. The Revenue assessed B to surtax for 1949/50 and 1950/51 on the basis that the surrender of D's interest was a 'disposition' and hence a settlement, so that the income paid to the children was deemed to be his. He appealed, contending that the will had been a settlement, so that neither he nor his wife had been the settlor of the funds from which the income arose. The CA rejected this contention and upheld the assessments. *CIR v Buchanan*, CA 1957, 37 TC 365; [1958] Ch 289; [1957] 2 All ER 400.

Whether Deed of Appointment a settlement

[56.66] In an Irish case, income under a settlement was appointed, in accordance with a power in the settlement, to an unmarried daughter of the settlor. The daughter was below the age of majority. It was held that the Deed of Appointment was a settlement for the purposes of the relevant Irish legislation. *EG v MacShamhrain*, HC(I) 1957, 3 ITC 217; [1958] IR 288.

Whether income paid to children under a disposition

[56.67] Under a settlement made by her father in 1934, a married woman (D) was entitled to a life interest in a settled fund should her sister die without issue. The sister died without issue in 1963. Meanwhile, in 1959, D had released her contingent life interest and subsequently, under powers in the 1934 settlement, made appointments in favour of her children (who were below the age of majority). The Special Commissioners held that D had made a disposition of this income and that the income paid to the children fell to be treated as her husband's income. The Ch D upheld their decision, applying the principles laid down by *CIR v Buchanan*, **56.65** above. *D'Abreu v CIR*, Ch D 1978, 52 TC 352; [1978] STC 538.

Settlements for benefit of children—whether exhaustive

[56.68] An individual (W) had made two similar settlements, with one of his two children as the principal beneficiary of each. The principal beneficiary had no entitlement to the trust capital. The Revenue issued assessments on the basis that the trusts were not exhaustive and the settlement income was to be treated as the settlor's. The Special Commissioners upheld the assessments but the Ch D allowed W's appeal, holding that the trusts were exhaustive and there was no resulting trust in favour of the settlor, so that he was not assessable under the legislation then in force. *Watson v Holland*, Ch D [1984] STC 372; [1985] 1 All ER 290.

'Capital sums' to be treated as income (ITTOIA 2005, ss 633–640)

Director selling shares in company to trustees of settlement

[56.69] A settlor sold to the trustees of the settlement all but one of the shares in a company of which he was the principal director. It was accepted that the company was associated with the settlement. The settlor held a current account with the company, to which amounts paid by the company to him or on his behalf were debited, and to which his remuneration was credited. The account became substantially overdrawn, but he paid off the balance in December 1940. He subsequently died, and the Revenue issued surtax assessments on his executors for 1939/40 and 1940/41, on the basis that the payments to third parties which were debited to the account were loans to him, and were therefore capital sums within *ITTOIA 2005, s 634(1)**. The HL allowed the executors' appeals (by a 4-1 majority, Lord Morton dissenting), holding that the sums were not paid directly or indirectly to him by the trustees, and were not within *ITTOIA 2005, s 634**. *Potts' Executors v CIR*, HL 1950, 32 TC 211; [1951] AC 443; [1951] 1 All ER 76. (*Note. Obiter dicta* of Lord Simonds were subsequently disapproved by Judge Mosedale in *Aspect Capital Ltd v HMRC*, **11.13** CLOSE COMPANIES.)

Repayment of money lent to trustees by settlor's wife

[56.70] One of the trustees of a settlement was the wife of the settlor. She lent £7,000 to the trustees in 1957 to acquire certain shares. The loan was repaid in two amounts within twelve months. The Revenue issued surtax assessments on the settlor, on the basis that the repayments were capital sums within *ITTOIA 2005, s 634**. The HL unanimously upheld the assessments. Lord Reid observed that 'there is no suggestion that either the appellant or his wife was trying to evade tax, and the transaction which has attracted tax liability was one which would never suggest that possibility to anyone unless he was familiar with income tax law. But the Revenue do not and probably should not have any discretion to remit tax legally due on the ground that the innocent taxpayer has fallen into a trap.' *CIR v De Vigier*, HL 1964, 42 TC 24; [1964] 1 WLR 1073; [1964] 2 All ER 907.

Shares settled—payments by company to clear settlor's overdraft

[56.71] A company director settled shares in the company in trust for his children. The trustees received no income from the shares before 1953/54, but received income totalling £9,969 for the years 1953/54 to 1955/56, which was accumulated. Each April from 1950 to 1954, the company cleared the director's bank overdraft by paying sums of at least £8,000 into his bank account, including a cheque of £9,100 paid on 5 April 1954. The Revenue issued surtax assessments for 1953/54 to 1955/56 on the basis that the company was connected with the settlement and that the sums paid by the company were capital sums within *ITTOIA 2005, s 634**. The HL unanimously upheld the assessments, holding that the company was connected with the settlement for 1953/54 and that the payment of £9,100 was a capital sum within *ITTOIA 2005, s 634**. *CIR v Bates*, HL 1966, 44 TC 225; [1968] AC 483; [1967] 1 All ER 84.

Shares purchased with overdraft guaranteed by settlor

[56.72] See *CIR v Wachtel*, 56.19 above.

Loan of securities to settlor

[56.73] Trustees of a settlement lent securities valued at £45,000 to the settlor. The Revenue issued a surtax assessment on the basis that this was a 'capital sum' within *ITTOIA 2005, s 634**. The settlor appealed, contending that the £45,000 was not a 'capital sum' because it was paid by the transfer of securities, rather than by cash. The Special Commissioners rejected this contention and dismissed the appeal, and the CS unanimously upheld their decision. *McCrone v CIR*, CS 1967, 44 TC 142.

Transactions involving connected companies—life policy premiums

[56.74] In a case in which the facts were complex, a married couple had each made identical discretionary settlements; the husband (P) had transferred certain shares to his settlement, and the trustees of both settlements had transferred sums to a close company which was not connected with the settlements. The Revenue issued surtax assessments on P on the basis that both the withdrawals and the transfers were repayments of loans to him within *ITTOIA 2005, s 634**. P appealed. The Ch D allowed his appeal in part. Slade J held that the sums which P had withdrawn from a running account with a company connected with the settlement were capital sums within *s 634** (and could not be offset by sums which P had paid to the company), but that transfers by a connected company of funds deposited by P to a close company which was not connected with the settlement, but with which trust funds were deposited, were not within the scope of *s 634**. Slade J also held that premiums on a policy on the settlor's life, payable by the trustees, were capital payments (if not in breach of trust) and thus were not deductible in arriving at the available income. *Piratin v CIR*, Ch D 1981, 54 TC 730; [1981] STC 441.

Power to obtain information (ITTOIA 2005, s 647)

Definition of 'party to a settlement'

[56.75] The Revenue served a notice on one of several trustees of a settlement, requiring, *inter alia*, a copy of the settlement. He applied to the QB for a declaration that the notice was invalid, contending that, as one of several joint trustees, he was not within the definition of a 'party to a settlement'. The QB rejected this contention and dismissed the application, holding that the trustee was within the definition of a 'party to a settlement'. *Cutner v CIR*, QB 1974, 49 TC 429; [1974] STC 259.

Validity of notice requiring information

[56.76] The Revenue served a notice on a company (W) in its capacity as the trustee of a declaration of trust. Having supplied part of the information asked for, W applied to the Ch D for a declaration that it was under no obligation to supply the remainder, contending that the questions asked were too wide and were oppressive. The Ch D rejected this contention, dismissed the application and awarded a penalty against W for failure to comply with the notice. The CA unanimously dismissed W's appeal against this decision, holding that a request for information concerning what a trustee had done in relation to a trust could not be regarded as oppressive. Stamp LJ observed that the courts should not 'assist a taxpayer to obstruct a fair and proper exercise of the powers with which the officers of the Revenue are armed for the performance of their duty to collect taxes which are exigible'. *Wilover Nominees Ltd v CIR*, CA 1974, 49 TC 559; [1974] STC 467; [1974] 3 All ER 496.

Income arising under a settlement (ITTOIA 2005, s 648)

Income apportioned to foreign company

[56.77] A UK citizen (W) was the controlling shareholder of a Canadian company which had six subsidiary companies. He transferred 60% of his shareholding to settlements, retaining an interest in the income. The Revenue issued assessments charging surtax. The Special Commissioners allowed W's appeal against the assessments, holding that income which was apportioned or sub-apportioned to a foreign company was not 'income arising under a settlement' within the meaning of *ITTOIA 2005, s 648**. The HL unanimously upheld this decision. *Lord Howard de Walden v CIR (and cross-appeal)*, HL 1948, 30 TC 345; [1948] 2 All ER 825.

Income of beneficiaries (ITTOIA 2005, ss 649–682)

Income applied in reducing charges

[56.78] An individual (W) settled shares on trust for the income to be paid to him for life with remainders over. If the yield on the shares exceeded a certain amount in any year, the trustees were directed to apply the excess in reducing two charges on the trust funds. The CS held that the excess did not form part of W's income for supertax. *CIR v Wemyss*, CS 1924, 8 TC 551. (*Note*. A decision in the same case on another point was subsequently disapproved by the HL in *Lady Miller v CIR*, **56.90** below.)

Income accumulated below age of majority

[56.79] In 1915, a 12-year-old boy (L) became tenant of certain estates under an 1899 settlement. In 1918 he became tenant of estates under an 1862 settlement. The respective trustees paid sums to him for his maintenance and accumulated the balance of the income. His mother, as his guardian, was assessed to supertax for 1916/17 on the income of the 1899 settlement; the trustees of the 1899 settlement were assessed for the years 1917/18 to 1919/20 on the income of both settlements; and L himself (while still below the age of majority then in force) was assessed for 1920/21 on the income of both settlements. The KB held that the income of both settlements was L's income and was assessable on him year by year as it accrued. The HL held that L's guardian could not be assessed to supertax in respect of L's income, and that trustees of a settlement could not be assessed to supertax in respect of the income of a beneficiary. *CIR v Countess of Longford*; *CIR v Pakenham and Others*; *CIR v Earl of Longford*, HL 1928, 13 TC 573; [1928] AC 252.

[56.80] Under a will, landed estates were devised to a young woman, the income to be accumulated until she attained 21 or married, and the residue to be left to her absolutely if she attained 21 or married. She became 21 in 1919 and was subsequently assessed to supertax for 1916/17 to 1918/19 on the whole income arising from the property and the residuary estate in those years. The KB upheld the assessments. *Gascoigne v CIR*, KB 1926, 13 TC 573; [1927] 1 KB 594.

[56.81] An individual (M) died in 1919. His son, who was born in 1903, was entitled to a share of an estate under a power of appointment exercised by M's will, under which the income was to be accumulated for 20 years from M's death. The Special Commissioners held that the accumulated income was the son's income for supertax, and the HL unanimoulsy upheld their decision. *Stern v CIR*, HL 1930, 15 TC 148.

[56.82] A testator's will left a vested life interest in certain estates to his son (S), who was below the age of majority. The trustees applied part of the income for S's maintenance while he was below the age of majority. S became absolutely entitled to the accumulated balance on reaching the age of 21, and was assessed to surtax on amounts including the accumulated income. The CA unanimously allowed his appeal, holding that his interest in the accumulated income was only contingent. *Stanley v CIR*, CA 1944, 26 TC 12; [1944] KB 255; [1944] 1 All ER 230.

[56.83] An individual (W) covenanted to pay £150 per annum for eight years to C, on trust for the absolute benefit of such of the children of W's son then living, or born during the period, as C should think fit and with the son's consent. In the relevant years, the son had only one child, who was below the age of majority. C paid the premiums on a policy on the child's life and on an educational endowment policy and accumulated the balance of the trust income. He claimed repayment of tax deducted from the income on behalf of the child, contending that it was income of the child who was entitled to child allowance. The Commissioners rejected the claim, holding that the child had only a contingent interest in the income and did not have a vested interest. The Ch D dismissed C's appeal,. Harman J held that even if the child's interest were vested, it was liable to be divested, so that the income was never indefeasibly the income of the child and he was not entitled to relief. *Cornwell v Barry*, Ch D 1955, 36 TC 268.

Life tenant of trust—deductibility of management expenses

[56.84] The life tenant of a trust claimed a repayment of tax deducted from the gross income of the trust. The Revenue agreed to repay the tax deducted from the net income after deducting the prior charges and management expenses of the trust. She appealed, contending that the prior charges and management expenses should not be deducted in computing the repayable amount. The General Commissioners dismissed her appeal and the CS unanimously upheld their decision. Lord Clyde observed that 'the total revenue which arose from the residuary estate was not the income of any of the liferent beneficiaries in the residuary estate', but was 'income of the trustees who were administering the residuary estate'. *Murray v CIR*, CS 1926, 11 TC 133.

[56.85] The decision in *Murray v CIR*, **56.83** above, was applied in the subsequent case of *MacFarlane v CIR*, CS 1929, 14 TC 532.

Trustees providing residence and paying expenses

[56.86] In accordance with their powers under a will, trustees permitted the grandson of the testator to occupy a mansion. The trustees paid the rates on the mansion and the occupier's supertax. The Revenue issued supertax assessments on the occupier on the basis that the amounts paid by the trustees formed part of his total income. The Special Commissioners dismissed the occupier's appeal and the KB upheld their decision. *Lord Tollemache v CIR*, KB 1926, 11 TC 277.

[56.87] Under a marriage settlement, a widow was entitled for life to the use and enjoyment of a house, the repairs, insurance, rates, etc. of which were paid by the trustees. The CS unanimously held that the amounts so paid, with the income tax appropriate thereto, were assessable to supertax. *Donaldson's Executors v CIR*, CS 1927, 13 TC 461.

[56.88] Under a will, the widow and daughter of the testator jointly occupied a house and received £2,000 per annum towards its upkeep and expenses. The Revenue assessed the daughter to supertax on the basis that one-half of the £2,000 and of the annual value of the house was her income. The Special Commissioners upheld the assessments and the CA unanimously upheld their decision. *Shanks v CIR*, CA 1928, 14 TC 249; [1929] 1 KB 342. (*Note*. The decision was approved by the HL in *Lady Miller v CIR*, 56.90 below.)

[56.89] Under a will, an individual (S) was entitled for life 'to occupy, use and enjoy' a house and lands and to be responsible for the expenses of keeping up the house and lands as a residence. The Revenue issued supertax assessments on the basis that the amounts so paid by the trustees, with the appropriate addition for income tax, were S's income. The Special Commissioners dismissed S's appeal and the CA unanimously upheld their decision. *Sutton v CIR*, CA 1929, 14 TC 662.

[56.90] Under a trust disposition and settlement, the testator's widow was entitled to occupy and possess a mansion house and lands for life 'free of rent or taxes', while the trustees paid out of the income of the trust the feu duties, rates and taxes, repairs and upkeep expenses and foresters' wages. The Revenue assessed the widow to supertax on a sum including the amount (grossed-up for income tax) of the rates paid by the trustees. The HL unanimously upheld the assessment (reversing the majority decision of the CS). *Lady Miller v CIR*, HL 1930, 15 TC 25; [1930] AC 222.

[56.91] A father (W) and his sons, who resided together, settled £50,000 on certain trusts in favour of the sons, subject to payments to W out of the trust income 'as a contribution towards the cost of maintaining the joint establishment'. The Revenue issued surtax assessments on W on the basis that the sums paid to him (which in the relevant years comprised the whole of the income of the trust) were his income for surtax purposes. The Special Commissioners dismissed W's appeal against the assessments, and the KB upheld their decision. *Waley Cohen v CIR*, KB 1945, 26 TC 471.

Payments to father for maintenance of children

[56.92] The trustees of a marriage settlement had discretionary power to make payments to and on behalf of the children of the marriage. Their father

(J) claimed child relief. The Revenue formed the opinion that the payments were income of the children, so that J was not entitled to child relief under the legislation then in force, and issued assessments to recover the sums which J had claimed. He appealed, contending that the children's rights under the contract were contingent and that the sums paid by the trustees were not income of the children in their own right. The KB rejected this contention and dismissed the appeal, holding that the payments which the trustees made to J for the children's maintenance were income of the children. (Certain procedural matters were also involved, but the relevant procedure is no longer in force.) *Johnstone v Chamberlain*, KB 1933, 17 TC 706.

Payment from capital for maintenance of beneficiary

[56.93] See *Stevenson v Wishart & Others (Levy's Trustees)*, 56.108 below.

Shares allotted in consideration of arrears of dividends

[56.94] The holders of preference shares in a company surrendered their rights to arrears of dividend in return for the allotment to them of ordinary shares. Some of the shares were held by trustees of a settlement, who applied for an originating summons to determine whether the shares allotted to them were held as income or as capital. The Ch D held that the shares were income of the trust fund. *In re MacIver's Settlement, MacIver v Rae*, Ch D 1935, 14 ATC 571.

[56.95] The decision in *MacIver v Rae*, 56.94 above, was applied in the similar subsequent case of *In re Smith's Will Trust, Smith v Melville*, Ch D 1936, 15 ATC 613.

Whether interest under will contingent

[56.96] Under a will, the residue was held on trust for the testator's son (K) on terms whereby half of the capital would be paid to him on attaining the age of 25 and the remaining half on attaining 30, conditional on his becoming proficient in German and French, passing a Civil Service examination and travelling abroad for a year. The testator died in 1931, when K was four years old. The Revenue issued surtax assessments on K's tutors for 1933/34 and 1934/35, on the basis that K had a vested interest in the residue. The Special Commissioners allowed the tutors' appeal and discharged the assessments, holding that his interest was contingent only, and the CS upheld their decision. *CIR v Kidston & Another (Kidston's Tutors)*, CS 1936, 20 TC 603.

Whether interest under a settlement contingent

[56.97] Under a settlement for the benefit of the two children of the settlor, the income of the share of the trust fund settled on each was directed to be accumulated until they became 22. The share vested absolutely on their reaching 30, which both of them did. The Revenue assessed them to surtax on the basis that they had a vested interest in the income which was accumulated between their 21st and 22nd birthdays. They appealed, contending that their interests were contingent rather than vested. The CA unanimously rejected this contention and upheld the assessments. *Brotherton v CIR*; *Mears v CIR*, CA 1978, 52 TC 137; [1978] STC 201; [1978] 1 WLR 610; [1978] 2 All ER 267.

Release of accumulated income on termination of trust

[56.98] Investments were held on trust for the income to be accumulated during the life of the settlor and then, in the event, on trust absolutely for his eldest son (H) as 'tenant in tail male' of certain property. H became 21 in 1928 and was then entitled in law to put an end to the trust. He did not do this until January 1939, when he became entitled to investments representing the accumulated income of the trust from 1928 to January 1939. H died in 1940, and the Revenue issued a surtax assessment on his executors for 1938/39, charging tax on the whole of this accumulated income. In the High Court, the Revenue conceded that the assessment could not be supported to the extent that it included income accumulated before 6 April 1938. The CA held that the trust income from 6 April 1938 to January 1939 was income of H and was taxable on the executors. *Hamilton-Russell's Executors v CIR*, CA 1943, 25 TC 200; [1943] 1 All ER 474.

Entitlement to income applied by trustees

[56.99] A trust was set up as part of a complicated arrangement to enable the managing director of a company to acquire shares in it. The Revenue assessed the director to surtax on the basis that certain income applied by the trustees was his income. The Special Commissioners dismissed the director's appeal and the Ch D upheld their decision. Romer LJ held that 'the interests purchased by the trustees represented immediate money's worth to the appellant, notwithstanding that his right to shares in the company was at all material times future and contingent'. *Curtis-Willson v CIR*, Ch D 1950, 31 TC 422.

Income of investments transferred invalidly

[56.100] The trustees of a 1932 settlement transferred the investments to another settlement in 1952, with the consent of the life tenants (who were the granddaughters of the settlor), in purported exercise of the statutory power of advancement. The effect of the decision in *Pilkington v CIR*, **56.125** below, was that the advancement was invalid and the investments were still held on the trusts of the 1932 settlement. The life tenants were assessed to surtax for 1955/56 to 1959/60 on the income of the settlements. They appealed, contending that, because of certain other proceedings, the assessments were barred by *estoppel per rem judicatum*. The Special Commissioners rejected this contention and dismissed their appeals, and the Ch D upheld this decision. Megarry J held that the income became income of the life tenants as soon as it was received by the trustees. *Spens v CIR; Holdsworth Hunt v CIR*, Ch D 1970, 46 TC 276; [1970] 1 WLR 1173; [1970] 3 All ER 295.

Trustees' accumulated or discretionary income (ITA 2007, s 479)

Dividends from UK companies

[56.101] A company (R) which was resident in Jersey was the trustee of a discretionary trust and was assessed under *ITA 2007, s 479**. The income assessed included dividends from UK companies. R appealed, contending that, as it could not be assessed at the basic rate in respect of the dividends under the legislation then in force (see *FA 1972, s 87(5)*), it could not be charged at the additional rate. The Ch D rejected this contention and upheld the assessments. *CIR v Regent Trust Co Ltd*, Ch D 1979, 53 TC 54; [1980] STC 140; [1980] 1 WLR 688.

Application of power to accumulate

[56.102] A married couple settled funds for the benefit of their son. The capital was to vest in the son when he reached the age of 45. Until then, he was entitled to a life interest in the income, subject to the trustees having power to accumulate it. In the relevant years all the income was accumulated, and the Revenue assessed it on the trustees under *ITA 2007, s 479**. They appealed, contending that the income accrued to the son as it arose and was not within their discretion. The Ch D rejected this contention and upheld the assessments. Vinelott J held that the intention of Parliament was clearly 'to impose additional rate tax on income which would otherwise not have attracted additional rate tax when it arose to the trustees as part of the total income of a beneficiary'. *CIR v Berrill & Gumb (Kent Settlement Trustees)*, Ch D 1981, 55 TC 429; [1981] STC 784; [1981] 1 WLR 1449; [1982] 1 All ER 867.

Copyright royalties received by trustees—rate of tax

[56.103] In 2004 a company (C) produced a stage musical, based on a children's book written in the 1930s. From 2004/05 to 2008/09, copyright royalties from the musical were paid to the trustees of a settlement created on the death of the author of the book (T). The trustees submitted tax returns on the basis that these royalties were only liable to the basic rate of income tax. HMRC issued a ruling that these royalties were taxable at the higher rate applicable to trust income, by virtue of what is now *ITA 2007, s 479*. The trustees appealed. The First-tier Tribunal allowed the appeal in part, holding that the effect of *Law of Property Act 1925, s 164* (which has subsequently been repealed) was that these royalties were taxable at the higher trust rate insofar as they derived from an exclusive copyright licence which T had granted to C two years before her death, but not insofar as they derived from a later assignment of the relevant copyright by the trustees. *Trustees of the Mrs PL Travers Will Trust v HMRC*, FTT [2013] UKFTT 436 (TC); [2014] SFTD 265, TC02830.

Assurance premiums and advisers' fees—whether capital

[56.104] In two cases heard together, settlement trustees had paid premiums on assurance policies on the settlor's lives. The Revenue issued assessments under *ITA 2007, s 479**, and the settlors appealed, contending that the premiums, and (in one of the cases) fees charged by investment advisers, should be allowed as deductions. The Special Commissioners rejected this contention and dismissed the appeals, and the HL upheld their decision (by a 4-1 majority, Lord Diplock dissenting). Lord Templeman held that it was an established principle that 'expenditure incurred for the benefit of the whole estate is a capital expense'. Applying *dicta* of Warrington J in *Re Sherry*, Ch D [1913] 2 Ch 508, life assurance premiums were 'paid for the preservation of an item of the testator's property, the benefit of which goes to capital'. The advisers' fees were also capital expenditure. *Carver v Duncan; Bosanquet v Allen*, HL 1985, 59 TC 125; [1985] STC 356; [1985] 2 WLR 1010; [1985] 2 All ER 645. (*Note*. The appeal also concerned the provisions of *FA 1973, s 16(2)(d)*, which became *ICTA 1988, s 686(2)(d)* and was subsequently repealed by *FA 1997* with effect from 1996/97.)

ITA 2007, s 480(1)(a)—service charge income held by trusts*

[56.105] A company received service charge income which it held as a trustee in accordance with *Landlord and Tenant Act 1987, s 42* (prior to its amendment by the *Commonhold and Leasehold Reform Act 2002*). The Revenue issued a ruling that this income was taxable at the rate applicable to trusts, and the question was referred to the Special Commissioner under *TMA, s 28ZA*. The Commissioner upheld the Revenue's ruling, holding that 'any trust income "which is to be accumulated" is to be treated as within the charge and therefore liable to tax at the rate applicable to trusts. There is no basis for implying any other limitation of the categories of trust.' *Retirement Care Group Ltd v HMRC*, Sp C [2007] SSCD 539 (Sp C 607).

ITA 2007, s 484—management expenses*

[56.106] The trustees of a large discretionary trust made payments in respect of management expenses which related partly to income and partly to capital. They claimed a deduction for part of the payments on the basis that they related to income. The Revenue rejected much of the claim, and the trustees appealed. The Special Commissioners reviewed the evidence in detail and allowed the appeal in part, holding that a proportion of the expenses in issue should be charged to income, but that the investment management fees were 'predominantly attributable to capital'. Both sides appealed to the Ch D, which allowed the Revenue's appeal in part. Lindsay J held that 'trustees' expenditure incurred for the benefit of the whole estate 'had to be regarded as a capital expense'. He also held that the Commissioners had been correct 'in treating the totality of investment management fees as properly chargeable to capital', and in holding that 'the accruals basis adopted here is a proper way of allocating expenses to a particular year of assessment'. (The Revenue had argued for the cash basis.) The trustees appealed to the CA, which allowed their appeal in part, holding that certain professional fees, including a fee paid to non-executive trustees, could be apportioned. However the effect of the HL decision in *Carver v Duncan*, **56.104** above, was that 'once the trustees had resolved to accumulate the income, the monies to be accumulated ought properly to be regarded as capital; so that the expenses incurred in connection with the investment of those monies could not be said to be chargeable to income'. *Trustees of the Peter Clay Discretionary Trust v HMRC*, CA 2008, 79 TC 473; [2009] STC 469; [2008] EWCA Civ 1441; [2009] 2 All ER 683.

Stock dividend paid to trustees of discretionary trust—rate of tax

[56.107] The trustees of a settlement held a number of shares in a limited company. In July 1999 they elected to receive a dividend in the form of further shares, rather than in the form of cash. In submitting their 1999/2000 tax return, they accepted that the market value of the stock dividend should be treated as taxable income, but treated it as taxable at the Schedule F ordinary rate of 10%. The Revenue issued an amendment on the basis that the effect of *ITA 2007, s 479** was that it was taxable at the Schedule F trust rate of 25%. The trustees appealed, contending that *s 479** did not apply because it was restricted to sums which were income under trust law, whereas the 'bonus' shares were capital. The CA unanimously rejected this contention and dismissed the trustees' appeal, holding that the 'bonus' shares were deemed to be received as income by virtue of *ITTOIA 2005, s 414(1)**. Neuberger LJ observed that the trustees' interpretation would produce an anomalous result in relation to the taxation of bonus shares 'where they are issued to trustees of an accumulation or discretionary settlement, and where the shares are capital receipts in their hands'. *Howell & Morton (Robin Settlement Trustees) v Trippier (aka Red Discretionary Trustees v HM Inspector of Taxes)*, CA 2004, 76 TC 415; [2004] STC 1245; [2004] EWCA Civ 885. (*Notes*. (1) The HL refused an application by the trustees for leave to appeal against the CA decision. (2) For the Revenue's practice following this decision, see Revenue Tax Bulletin, February 2005, pp 1178–1179.)

Payments for maintenance of beneficiary under discretionary trust

[56.108] An elderly woman (H), who was a beneficiary under a discretionary trust, went into a nursing home in 1978 and died in 1981. During this period the trustees made payments out of capital totalling £114,250 to defray her medical and nursing home expenses. The trust beneficiaries also included charities and, in the relevant years, the whole of the trust income was distributed to charity. The Revenue issued assessments on the trustees, charging tax on the payments to H under *ITA 2007, s 496**. The Special Commissioner allowed the trustees' appeal, and the CA upheld his decision. Fox LJ held that 'the "reality" of the matter' was that the payments were 'emergency expenditure of very substantial amounts which would be quite outside normal income resources'. They were 'wholly of a capital nature'. *Stevenson v Wishart & Others (Levy's Settlement Trustees)*, CA 1987, 59 TC 740; [1987] STC 266; [1987] 1 WLR 1204; [1987] 2 All ER 428.

Superseded legislation

Claims for personal allowances on accumulated income (ITA 1952, s 228)

NOTE

The cases under this heading relate to claims to relief under *ITA 1952, s 228* or its precursor, *ITA 1918, s 25*. The relief was withdrawn by *FA 1969* with regard to income for the years after 1968/69. The cases may however still be of some relevance as illustrating matters of general principle.

Whether entitlement contingent

[56.109] The KB held that a transfer of Consols was an absolute gift, and not contingent, with the result that there was no entitlement to relief in respect of income from the Consols which was accumulated while the donee was below the age of majority. *Roberts v Hanks*, KB 1926, 10 TC 351.

[56.110] Stock was transferred to two trustees, to accumulate the dividends and transfer the stock to a young woman when she became 21. She claimed relief on reaching that age. The Commissioners rejected her claim, holding that her interest in the stock was vested rather than contingent, and the KB upheld their decision. *Edwardes Jones v Down*, KB 1936, 20 TC 279.

Contingent interest as life tenant

[56.111] A woman, on reaching the age of 21, became entitled under a settlement to a life interest in trust funds, including the income from them which had been accumulated while she was below the age of majority. She claimed relief under *ITA 1918, s 25*. The Commissioners granted her claim and the CA unanimously upheld their decision, holding that the income had been accumulated for her benefit within the meaning of the legislation although her interest was that of a life tenant only. *Dale v Mitcalfe*, CA 1927, 13 TC 41; [1928] 1 KB 383.

[56.112] The decision in *Dale v Mitcalfe*, **56.111** above, was applied in a similar subsequent case in which the trust was a protective trust rather than a discretionary trust. Ungoed-Thomas J held that 'protective trusts, comprising a protected life interest and supplementary discretionary trusts designed for her greater benefit and well recognised as such and established for that reason' should also be treated as qualifying for relief. *Lynch v Davies*, Ch D 1962, 40 TC 511.

Title to repayment

[56.113] Following the decision in *Dale v Mitcalfe*, **56.111** above, a life tenant under a will trust obtained repayment of tax deducted from income accumulated while she was below the age of majority. The trustees applied to the Ch D for a declaration as to whether the repayment was an accretion to the life tenant's share of the trust fund. The Ch D held that the right to claim relief under *ITA 1918, s 25* was a personal one and that the life tenant was absolutely entitled to the repayment. *In re Fulford (dec'd); Fulford v Hyslop*, Ch D 1929, 8 ATC 588; [1930] 1 Ch 71.

Whether income vested on a contingency provided for by the legislation

[56.114] Under a will, the surplus income of the residuary estate was to be accumulated until the youngest of three granddaughters attained the age of 30 (which took place in August 1918), when the capital and accumulated income were to be held on trust for the three equally, but the interest of each of them was vested at the age of 21 or marriage and settled on her for life. One of the granddaughters, who had married in 1906, claimed relief after 1918. The KB held that for her the 'contingency' happened in 1906, so that her claim had been made after the three-year time limit and she was not entitled to the relief. *Stoneley v Ambrose*, KB 1925, 9 TC 389.

[56.115] Under a will, investments were held in trust for 20 years, during which the income was to be accumulated, and thereafter divided between the surviving children of a particular marriage. In the event, there was only one child of the marriage. He received the accumulated fund in 1925, and claimed repayment under *ITA 1918, s 25* of the tax incurred on the trust income throughout the 20-year period. The KB rejected his claim, holding that he was not entitled to relief since the relevant contingency was not the attainment of a specified age, as required by *s 25*. *White v Whitcher*, KB 1927, 13 TC 202.

[56.116] Under a will, the residuary estate was held in trust equally for the children the testator's sister (R), including any child born to her after the will, to vest in and be divided among them when the youngest became 21. R died in 1925, leaving five children of whom the youngest had become 21 in 1921. The income had been accumulated until her death. The CS held that the children were not entitled to relief, since there was no presumption in law that R was incapable of bearing further children after 1921, and the children's entitlement to the income remained contingent until their mother's death. This was not a contingency for which the legislation provided. Lord Blackburn observed that 'it may well be that the testator did not realise that would be the full legal effect of including among the beneficiaries the unborn issue of his sister'. *CIR v Bone & Others*, CS 1927, 13 TC 20.

[56.117] Under a marriage settlement, a fund was held in trust for such of the children of the marriage as the parents jointly (or the survivor alone) should appoint, and in default of appointment equally for such of the children of the marriage as attained 21, or, being females, married under that age. In the event, there were three children of the marriage. The wife died in 1913. In 1922 the husband appointed the fund equally to the three children absolutely. All three were then below the age of majority. One became 21 in 1929 and claimed relief on his share of the income accumulated up to 1922. The Commissioners allowed his claim and the KB upheld their decision. Finlay J held that during the period between the death of his mother and the appointment of the fund, the income was being accumulated for his benefit, contingently on his reaching the age of 21. *Chamberlain v Haig Thomas*, KB 1933, 17 TC 595.

[56.118] In exercise of their discretionary powers, the trustees of a settlement paid accumulated income to a contingent beneficiary on his attaining the age of 23. However, none of the contingencies under which he would become entitled to the trust fund and accumulated income had happened. The KB held that he was not entitled to relief. *Dain v Miller*, KB 1934, 18 TC 478.

[56.119] A father settled stocks on trust in equal shares on his three children. The income of each child's share was to be accumulated until the child attained the age of 25 (subject to powers of advancement and maintenance) whereupon each child became entitled to the income on the capital and accumulations for life, subject to an absolute discretion to the trustees to restrict the income to such lower figure as they should consider proper, and to accumulate the balance or apply it for the benefit of other specified persons. One of the children became 25 in 1940, and claimed repayment under *ITA 1918, s 25* of the tax incurred on the accumulated income. The CS unanimously rejected the claim, holding that the effect of the trustees' discretionary powers was that the relief was not due. *CIR v Maude-Roxby*, CS 1950, 31 TC 388.

Whether any accumulation of income

[56.120] Under a will, the residuary estate was held on trust equally for such of the children of the testator as attained 21, subject to an annuity to the widow. In fact, the widow spent the whole of the income insofar as it exceeded the annuity. The Commissioners held that there had been no accumulation of income to qualify for relief, and the KB upheld their decision. *Cusden (JC, SH & GM) v Eden*, KB 1939, 22 TC 435.

Dispositions for short periods (ICTA 1988, ss 660–662)

NOTE

ICTA 1988, ss 660–662, which originated from *FA 1922, s 20*, were repealed by *FA 1995* with effect from 1995/96. The provisions of *ICTA 1988, ss 660–662* had effectively become obsolete following the changes introduced by *FA 1988*, which provided that deeds of covenant executed after 14 March 1988 (other than those providing for payments to charity, or for *bona fide* commercial reasons in connection with the payer's trade, profession or vocation) were ineffective for tax purposes.

[56.121] A company's controlling directors covenanted to pay annuities to the company, to maintain its level of income until the payments reached a total of £100,000. The total was reached within two years, and the Revenue issued surtax assessments on the basis that the effect of *FA 1922, s 20* (the origin of *ICTA 1988, s 660*) was that the payments were not allowable deductions for surtax. The Commissioners allowed the directors' appeals and the CA unanimously upheld their decision, holding that the payments were not 'caught' by the legislation, since the annuities were potentially payable for a period which could have exceeded six years. *CIR v RW & CW Black*, CA 1940, 23 TC 715; [1940] 4 All ER 445.

[56.122] By a deed dated 14 March 1958, an individual (V) covenanted to pay a yearly sum for seven years from the date of the deed, the first payment to be made on that date and subsequent payments on 1 March each year. The Revenue issued a surtax assessment on the basis that the effect of the deed was that the last payment would be made on 1 March 1964, so that the income was payable for a period which could not exceed six years, and thus was not allowable as a deduction. The Special Commissioners allowed V's appeal, holding that the deed provided for eight payments, the last of which was due on 1 March 1965 (and hence the payments were for a period exceeding six years). The CA unanimously upheld the Commissioners' decision. Donovan LJ observed that it was 'very probable that the settlor here intended to make himself liable for seven payments of £2,000 only, but if the language he has used when fairly construed makes him liable for eight, effect must be given to the language'. *CIR v Verdon-Roe*, CA 1962, 40 TC 541.

[56.123] See also *CIR v The Trustees of the Hostel of St Luke*, 9.88 CHARITIES.

Extension of period by supplemental deed

[56.124] See *CIR v Nicolson & Bartlett*, 56.38 above.

Power of advancement or appointment

Trustee Act 1925, s 32—power of advancement

[56.125] By the will of a testator, who died in 1925, a fund was bequeathed in trust for his nephews and nieces. In 1959 the trustees of the will issued an originating summons to determine whether they were entitled to advance part of the share of one nephew, with his consent, to his daughter (who was below the age of majority), by paying it to the trustees of a new settlement. The Revenue objected to the proposed advancement, considering that it was not authorised by *Trustee Act 1925, s 32* (and that its main purpose was the avoidance of death duties and surtax). The HL held that the trustees were entitled to exercise the power of advancement in favour of the daughter, by applying money to form a trust for her benefit, but that for the purpose of the rule against perpetuities, the power of advancement was analogous to a special power of appointment, and that some of the proposed trusts were void under this rule. Lord Reid observed that 'if it is thought that the power which Parliament has conferred is likely to be used in ways of which Parliament does not approve, then it is for Parliament to devise appropriate restrictions of the power'. *Pilkington & Another v CIR & Another*, HL 1962, 40 TC 416; [1962] 3 WLR 1051; [1964] AC 612; [1962] 3 All ER 622. (*Note.* The *Rules of the Supreme Court 1965 (SI 1965/1776)* referred to the use of an 'originating summons'. With effect from 26 April 1999, these rules were largely replaced by the *Civil Procedure Rules 1998 (SI 1998/3132)*, which refer instead to 'alternative procedure'.)

Power of appointment—whether a power of determination

[56.126] In two cases where settlements were held on trust for such persons as the trustees should appoint, the HL unanimously held that the power of appointment was a power of determination, and that the settlements were revocable, so that the income was deemed to be income of the settlor under the legislation then in force (*ITA 1952, s 399 as originally enacted*). Lord Reid and

Lord Hodson specifically disapproved *dicta* of Lord Greene in *Jenkins v CIR*, **56.36** above. *Jamieson v CIR; Wills v CIR*, HL 1963, 41 TC 43; [1964] AC 1445; [1963] 2 All ER 1030. (*Note. ITA 1952, s 399* was subsequently amended by *FA 1958*, and was the origin of *ICTA 1988, s 665*, which was repealed by *FA 1995* with effect from 1995/96.)

Exercise of power of advancement—whether invalid

[56.127] In an estate duty case, a settlement had been created in 1947. In 1958 the trustees exercised their power of advancement to transfer £50,000 from this settlement to another family settlement, in order to create an indefeasible life interest in possession in the money transferred (thus avoiding estate duty on that amount on the death of the first settlor). However, the effect of the decision in *Pilkington & Another v CIR & Another*, **56.125** above, was that all the beneficial interests created by the advancement, apart from the immediate life interest, were void for perpetuity. The first settlor died in 1964, and the Revenue sought to charge estate duty on his death, on the basis that the trustees' exercise of the power of advancement had been invalid, so that the fund remained subject to the 1947 settlement. The Ch D accepted this contention but the CA allowed the executors' appeal, holding that the exercise had been valid. Buckley LJ held that where, by the terms of a trust, 'a trustee is given a discretion as to some matter under which he acts in good faith, the court should not interfere with his action notwithstanding that it does not have the full effect which he intended', unless 'what he has achieved is unauthorised by the power conferred upon him'. *Hastings & Others v CIR (re Hastings-Bass deceased)*, CA [1974] STC 211; [1975] Ch 25; [1974] 2 All ER 193. (*Note. Obiter dicta* of Buckley LJ were unanimously disapproved by the Supreme Court in the subsequent case of *Futter & Cutbill v HMRC*, **56.128** below. Lord Walker observed that the *Hastings-Bass* decision was concerned with the scope of the fiduciary power held by trustees, 'rather than the nature of the decision-making process which led to it being exercised in a particular way', and held that Buckley LJ's statement was 'open to criticism for the generality of its reference to unintended consequences'.)

[56.128] The trustees of two discretionary trusts exercised powers of advancement, with the intention of transferring assets out of the settlements in such a way as to avoid incurring a charge to CGT. However, the trustees and their solicitors had overlooked the provisions of *TCGA 1992, s 2(4)* (which provides that allowable losses cannot be set off against gains attributed to beneficiaries in specified circumstances). The trustees applied to the Ch D for declarations that the exercise of the power of advancement had been invalid. Norris J accepted this contention but HMRC appealed to the CA, which unanimously reversed Norris J's decision and held that the exercise of the power had been valid. Lloyd LJ observed that 'if the problem to be resolved is what is the effect on an operation such as an advancement of the failure of some of the intended provisions, because of external factors such as perpetuity, it is not useful to ask what the trustees would have thought and done if they had known about the problem. The answer to that question is almost certainly that they would have done something different, which would not have run into the perpetuity or other difficulty. It is for that reason that the test has to be objective, by reference to whether that which was done, with all its defects and consequent limitations, is capable of being regarded as beneficial to the intended object, or not.' He held that 'in a case where the trustees' act is within their powers, but is said to be vitiated by a breach of trust so as to be voidable, if the breach of trust asserted is that the trustees failed to have regard to a relevant matter, and if the reason that they did not have regard to it is that they obtained and acted on advice from apparently competent advisers, which turned out to be incorrect, then the charge of breach of trust cannot be made out.' An exercise of the power vested in trustees was 'voidable if, and only if, it can be shown to have been done in breach of fiduciary duty'. On the facts here, 'the enlargement and the advancements are not only not void, because they were within the relevant powers of the trustees, but they are also not voidable, because no breach of fiduciary duty was committed in the process of making them'. The Supreme Court unanimously dismissed the trustees' appeal against this decision. Lord Walker held that a court should intervene when trustees had acted in such a way as to amount to a breach of their fiduciary duty. It was not sufficient to show that the trustees' deliberations had fallen short of the highest possible standards, or that the court would, on a surrender of discretion by the trustees, have acted in a different way. It would be contrary to principle and authority to impose a form of strict liability on trustees who conscientiously obtain and follow, in making a decision which is within the scope of their powers, apparently competent professional advice which turns out to be wrong. On the facts here, the trustees' exercise of the power of advancement had been valid and there were no grounds for the court to intervene. *Futter & Cutbill v HMRC (aka Futter & Cutbill v Futter & Others)*, SC [2013] UKSC 26; [2013] STC 1148. (*Note*. The CA and the Supreme Court heard the case with *Pitt & Others v HMRC*, **56.138** below.)

Deed of appointment—whether invalid

[56.129] The decision in *Hastings v CIR (re Hastings-Bass deceased)*, **56.127** above, was distinguished in a subsequent case where the Ch D held that three deeds of appointment exercised by the trustees of a discretionary trust were invalid. Mervyn Davies J held that 'the court can put aside the purported exercise of a fiduciary power, if satisfied that the trustees never applied their minds at all to the exercise of the discretion entrusted to them.' *Turner & Others v Turner & Others*, Ch D [1983] 1 All ER 745.

[56.130] The decision in *Hastings v CIR (re Hastings-Bass deceased)*, **56.127** above, was applied in a subsequent case where the Ch D held that a deed of appointment made by trustees of a pension scheme was valid. Warner J held that, on the evidence, it was possible that the trustees would still have exercised the deed in question if they had received additional advice concerning its effects. *Mettoy Pension Trustees Ltd v Evans*, Ch D [1990] 1 WLR 1587; [1991] 2 All ER 513. (*Note*. *Obiter dicta* of Warner J were subsequently disapproved the CA and the Supreme Court in *Futter & Cutbill v HMRC*, **56.128** above.)

[56.131] The decision in *Mettoy Pension Trustees Ltd v Evans*, **56.130** above, was distinguished in a case where trustees had purported to execute a deed of appointment one day after their powers to do so had expired. They applied to the Ch D for the deed to be treated as valid, but the Ch D rejected their application. Park J observed that 'it cannot be right that, whenever trustees do something which they later regret and think that they ought not to have done, they can say that they never did it in the first place'. There was 'a very big difference between, on the one hand, the courts declaring something which the trustees have done to be void, and, on the other hand, the courts holding that a trust takes effect as if the trustees had done something which they never did at all'. Park J also held that there were no grounds for treating a previous deed of appointment as invalid, since 'it would be astonishing, and to my mind unacceptable', for the *Hastings-Bass* principle to be capable of being invoked in an attempt to upset some action by trustees which may have been taken decades ago (as in this case), and on the basis of which many intervening decisions and actions have been taken'. *Breadner & Others v Granville-Grossman & Others*, Ch D [2000] 4 All ER 705.

[56.132] Trustees of a settlement exercised a deed of appointment without realising that this gave rise to considerable IHT liability. They subsequently applied to the Ch D for the deed to be treated as invalid. The Ch D accepted this contention. Mann J held that the trustees had not given 'full and proper consideration' to the fiscal implications of the deed, and that 'had they done so they would not have acted as they did'. Accordingly the court was justified in treating the deed as invalid. *Burrell & Another v Burrell & Others*, Ch D [2005] STC 569; [2005] EWHC 245 (Ch).

[56.133] In a similar subsequent case in which a deed of appointment was held to be of no effect, Lloyd LJ held that 'where trustees act under a discretion given to them by the terms of the trust, in circumstances in which they are free to decide whether or not to exercise that discretion, but the effect of the exercise is different from that which they intended, the court will interfere with their action if it is clear that they would not have acted as they did had they not failed to take into account considerations which they ought to have taken into account, or taken into account considerations which they ought not to have taken into account'. *Sieff & Others v Fox & Others*, Ch D [2005] EWHC 1312 (Ch); [2005] 3 All ER 693.

[56.134] The decision in *Sieff & Others v Fox & Others*, **56.133** above, was applied in the similar subsequent case of *Jiggens & Another v Low & Another*, Ch D [2010] STC 1899; [2010] EWHC 1566 (Ch).

[56.135] In 1991 a UK resident established a settlement with a company (T) resident outside the UK as trustee, creating life interests in income in favour of the settlor and his wife, with a charity as the default beneficiary. A scheme was subsequently embarked upon to avoid a CGT liability arising on the settlor (albeit recoverable from T) under *TCGA 1992, s 86*, on the maturity in July 1998 of loan notes held by a company whose shares were included in the trust assets. The scheme's effectiveness depended upon there being no disposal of the loan note or shares before 6 April 1998. However, T executed a deed of appointment transferring the shares to the charity on 3 April 1998. T applied to the Ch D for a declaration that the deed of appointment should be treated as void. The Ch D granted the application (which the charity had opposed). Patten J held that the execution of the deed of appointment had been 'a breach of duty' by T, which had been obliged to ensure that it 'did not nullify the financial and fiscal effect of the earlier dispositions' which had been made at a time when T owed 'a fiduciary duty to the settlor and the other family beneficiaries'. Accordingly, the exercise of the power of appointment should be held to be 'invalid and of no effect'. *Abacus Trust Co (Isle of Man) Ltd v National Society for the Prevention of Cruelty to Children*, Ch D [2001] STC 1344.

Miscellaneous

Application for transfers of assets into settlements to be set aside

[56.136] In April 2003 an individual (G) granted a deferred lease of his property to a settlement, and transferred his shares in a company to a short-term discretionary trust. In February 2004 he transferred his reversionary interest in the shares to a third settlement. Later that year he was diagnosed as suffering from cancer. He died in April 2005, so that the transfers became chargeable to IHT. His executors applied to the Ch D for the transfers to be set aside. The Ch D granted the application in part. Lewison J declined to set aside the April 2003 transfers, as medical evidence indicated that it was 'extremely unlikely' that G had been suffering from cancer at that time. Applying the principles laid down in *Ogilvie v Allen*, HL 1899, 15 TLR 294, 'a donor can only obtain back property which he has given away by showing that he was under some mistake of so serious a character as to render it unjust on the part of the donee to retain the property given to him'. However the evidence suggested that G had already been suffering from cancer in February 2004, so that his chances of surviving for three years were very remote. If G had been aware of this, he would not have transferred his reversionary interest in the shares. Accordingly the Ch D exercised its discretion to set aside the February 2004 transfer. *Ogden & Hutchinson (Griffiths' Executors) v Trustees of the RHS Griffiths 2003 Settlement & Others*, Ch D [2008] STC 776; [2008] EWHC 118 (Ch). (*Note*. The decision to set aside the 2004 transfer was doubted by Lloyd LJ in the 2011 case of *HMRC v Futter & Others*, **56.128** above. Lloyd LJ noted that 'there was no adversarial argument on the law or the facts'.)

[56.137] In 2004, on the advice of a solicitor, a widow transferred her interest in the house in which she lived, and which she had inherited from her late husband, into a trust for the benefit of her children. She subsequently applied for the relevant deeds to be rescinded. The Ch D granted the application, applying *dicta* of Millett J in *Gibbon v Mitchell*, Ch D [1990] 3 All ER 338. *Bhatt v Bhatt & Others*, Ch D [2009] STC 1540; [2009] EWHC 734 (Ch).

[56.138] In 1990 an individual (P) suffered serious head injuries in a road accident. He was rendered permanently incapable of managing his own affairs, and his wife was appointed as his receiver. In 1994 P was awarded substantial damages. On the advice of solicitors, P's wife put these payments into a settlement. The form of settlement gave rise to significant liability to inheritance tax (under *IHTA 1984, s 237*). P's wife did not discover this until 2003.

She applied to the Ch D for a declaration that she should be entitled to unravel the settlement and a related assignment. The CA rejected this contention but the Supreme Court unanimously allowed P's appeal, holding that a voluntary disposition could be set aside on the grounds of equity where there had been a mistake which was sufficiently serious to satisfy the conditions laid down by the HL in *Ogilvie v Littleboy*, HL 1897, 13 TLR 399. Lord Walker held that the court was required to make an evaluative judgment as to whether it would be unconscionable or unjust to leave the mistake uncorrected, and form a judgment about the justice of the case. On the facts here, P's wife had an incorrect conscious belief, or made an incorrect tacit assumption, that the proposed settlement had no adverse tax effects. The settlement could have been framed so as to comply with the statutory requirements for relief under *IHTA 1984, s 89* without any artificiality or abuse of that statutory relief. It was precisely the sort of trust to which Parliament intended to grant relief under *s 89*. Accordingly the settlement should be set aside. *Pitt & Others v HMRC (aka Pitt & Shores v Holt)*, SC [2013] UKSC 26; [2013] STC 1148. (*Note*. The Supreme Court heard the case with *Futter & Cutbill v HMRC*, 56.128 above.)

Whether settlement void for perpetuity or uncertainty

[56.139] There are a number of tax cases where the substantive issue was whether a settlement was void for perpetuity or uncertainty. As they do not turn on any point of tax law they are not summarised individually in this book. The cases include *Aked v Shaw*, KB 1947, 28 TC 286; *CIR v Broadway Cottages Trust*, CA 1954, 35 TC 577; [1955] Ch 20; [1954] 3 All ER 120; *Innes v Harrison*, Ch D 1954, 35 TC 594; *In re Hooper's 1949 Settlement*, Ch D 1955, 34 ATC 3; *In re Hooper's 1934 Settlement*, Ch D 1955, 34 ATC 9 and *Haworth v CIR*, Ch D 1974, 49 TC 489. See also *Muir v CIR*, **4.247** APPEALS, and *Pilkington v CIR*, **56.125** above, where an issue was whether a settlement was void for uncertainty. The HL considered the question of whether a settlement was void for uncertainty in the non-tax case of *McPhail & Others v Doulton & Others*, HL 1970, [1971] AC 424; [1970] 2 All ER 228 (and partly overruled the decision in *CIR v Broadway Cottages Trust*).

Expenses of administering trust—not deductible in assessments

[56.140] The trustees of a deceased person were assessable (on a remittance basis) on the income from certain foreign possessions which comprised the greater part of the trust income. They claimed that the expenses incurred in this country in administering the trust should be allowed as a deduction. The CE unanimously rejected the claim. *Aikin v Macdonald Trustees*, CE 1894, 3 TC 306.

Whether shares to be held as income or capital

[56.141] In a non-tax case, the PC held that shares received by trustees following a direct demerger were received as income rather than as capital, because as a matter of company law they took the form of a dividend paid out of the accumulated profits of the distributing company. *Hill v Permanent Trustee Co of New South Wales*, PC [1930] AC 720. (*Note*. For the Revenue's interpretation of this decision, see Revenue Tax Bulletin October 1994, p 163.)

[56.142] The decision in *Hill v Permanent Trustee Co of New South Wales*, 56.141 above, was distinguished in a subsequent case in which a holding of shares in a public company was held by trustees, with income passing to the settlor's widower as life tenant and with the remainder of the estate held for the settlor's son. The public company undertook a demerger, under which it allotted some shares to the trustees. The trustees sought a declaration as to whether they should hold the new shares as income (belonging to the life tenant) or as capital (to pass to the remainderman). The Ch D held that the shares should be held as capital. Sir Donald Nicholls observed that the commercial purpose of the transaction was not that the public company should part with some of its assets to its shareholders, but was to replace a single 'head company' with two head companies. He hedl that to view such a transaction as a distribution of profits 'would be to exalt form over commercial substance to an unacceptable extent', and would be to produce a result 'manifestly inconsistent with the presumed intention of the testator'. *Sinclair v Lee & Another*, Ch D [1993] 3 WLR 498; [1993] 3 All ER 926.

Application for declaration of beneficial ownership of settlement

[56.143] The Revenue had issued substantial income tax assessments on an individual (S) who had business interests in Nigeria. He was also a trustee of several settlements. S died in 2005. His widow made claims against the trustees of six of the settlements under *Inheritance (Provision for Family and Dependants) Act 1975, s 10*, claiming that S had been the beneficial owner of the assets held by the settlements, and that she was therefore entitled to a substantial share of the settlement assets. In 2006 the Revenue issued notices of determination charging IHT on the basis that S had been the settlor of each settlement, within *IHTA 1984, s 44*. The trustees of the six settlements took proceedings in the Ch D, seeking a declaration that S had not been the beneficial owner of the assets transferred into these settlements, and that the assets had been beneficially owned by a Nigerian (K), who had had business connections with S. The Revenue applied for the proceedings to be struck out on the grounds that the beneficial ownership of the settlements was a matter to be determined by the Special Commissioners under the normal statutory appeal procedure, applying the principles laid down in the 1964 case of *Argosam Finance Co Ltd v Oxby & CIR*, **4.271** APPEALS. The Ch D dismissed the Revenue's application. Warren J declined to follow the *Argosam* decision on the grounds that the 'beneficial ownership issue goes not only to the trustees' liabilities to inheritance tax but also to whether HMRC can obtain effective enforcement for a completely different liability – the liability of (S) and his estate for income tax – which has nothing at all to do with the possible inheritance tax liability of the trustees'. He held that 'if a dispute or potential dispute arises between a person and HMRC which is independent of the tax appeal under consideration, the exclusive jurisdiction principle does not render that dispute or potential dispute non-justiciable in the High Court simply because the same, or a very similar, issue will be relevant to, or perhaps even determinative of, both that dispute and the tax appeal.' *Stow & Others v Stow & Others*, Ch D 2008, 79 TC 561; [2008] STC 2298; [2008] EWHC 495 (Ch).

Whether trust resident in UK

[56.144] See *Wensleydale's Settlement Trustees v CIR*, 48.89 RESIDENCE, and *Smallwood (Settlor of the Trevor Smallwood Trust) v HMRC*, 48.90 RESIDENCE.

57

Statutory Bodies

Harbour board

[57.1] A harbour board was empowered by Act of Parliament to levy dock dues, etc. Its surplus income, after paying interest, was directed to be applied in forming a sinking fund to extinguish the debt incurred in the construction of the docks. The HL held that the surplus income constituted profits which were chargeable to income tax, notwithstanding the requirements as to their application. *Mersey Docks & Harbour Board v Lucas*, HL 1883, 2 TC 25; 8 AC 891. (*Note*. The appeal related to an assessment under Schedule A provisions which are now obsolete. This remains an important case on what constitutes profits: see Simon's Taxes, para B1.415.)

[57.2] The HL decision in *Mersey Docks & Harbour Board v Lucas*, 57.1 above, was applied in a subsequent case where the Port of London Authority appealed against excess profits duty assessments. The CA unanimously upheld the assessments in principle (remittimg the case to the Special Commissioners to consider their amount.) *Port of London Authority v CIR*, CA 1920, 12 TC 122; [1920] 2 KB 612.

Harbour mooring commissioners

[57.3] An Act of Parliament authorised harbour mooring commissioners to levy dues on ships using a 'cut' from the Wash to King's Lynn. The dues were to be paid to a local authority (the King's Lynn Corporation), which had contributed to the cost of making the cut. The QB held that the dues were taxable (reversing the General Commissioners' decision). *Sowrey v King's Lynn Harbour Mooring Commissioners*, QB 1887, 2 TC 201. (Note. The QB rejected the Revenue's application for costs. Smith J observed that the General Commissioners were 'creatures of the Crown, and have gone wrong'.

River conservancy board

[57.4] The receipts of a river conservancy board included statutory annual contributions from four railway companies and a canal company. The Revenue issued assessments charging tax on these contributions, and the board appealed. The Special Commissioners dismissed the appeal and the KB upheld this decision, holding that the contributions were part of the board's income for tax purposes. *Humber Conservancy Board v Bater*, KB 1914, 6 TC 555; [1914] 3 KB 449.

[57.5] The Forth Conservancy Board had been established by statute to carry out the customary duties of conservators over a stretch of the River and Firth of Forth. It was empowered to levy shipping dues. The Revenue issued assessments under provisions corresponding to *ITTOIA 2005, s 12(4)*. The HL unanimously held that the Board was outside the scope of these provisions. *CIR v Forth Conservancy Board (No 1)*, HL 1928, 14 TC 709; [1929] AC 213. (*Note*. For subsequent developments in this case, see 57.6 below.)

[57.6] Following the decision noted at 57.5 above, the Revenue issued income tax assessments (under the provisions of Schedule D Case VI), charging tax on the surplus revenues of the Forth Conservancy Board. The HL unanimously upheld the assessments, holding that the obligation on the Board to use the dues for the purposes of river conservation was not a reason for not taxing them. *CIR v Forth Conservancy Board (No 2)*, HL 1931, 16 TC 103; [1931] AC 540.

[57.7] In an Irish case, the receipts of a statutory river conservancy board consisted mainly of rates but also included receipts from fishing licences, fines and bank interest. In the relevant years its receipts exceeded its expenses. The Revenue issued an assessment charging tax on the proportion of this surplus which its receipts other than rates bore to its total receipts. Martin Maguire J allowed the board's appeal and the SC(I) unanimously upheld his decision, holding that if the rates which it levied exceeded its net expenditure, the overall surplus was available to reduce future rates and was not liable to income tax. *Moville District of Conservators v Ua Clothasaigh*, SC(I) 1949, 3 ITC 1; [1950] IR 301.

Fishery board

[57.8] The Revenue issued assessments on a fishery board, set up by statute to maintain the fisheries in its district and empowered to issue licences for fees, etc. The KB allowed the board's appeal. Rowlatt J held that the board was not trading. *Severn Fishery District Conservators v O'May*, KB 1919, 7 TC 194; [1919] 2 KB 484. (*Note*. Rowlatt J's decision was disapproved by Lord Thankerton in the subsequent case of *CIR v Forth Conservancy Board (No 2)*, 57.5 above.)

Council of veterinary surgeons

[57.9] In an Irish case, a statutory body whose functions included the maintenance of a register of veterinary surgeons was assessed to income tax on the excess of its receipts (registration fees and proceeds of sales of register) over its expenditure. The HC(I) allowed its appeal, holding that its activities were not analogous to carrying on a trade and its surplus was not income. *The Veterinary Council v Corr*, HC(I) 1950, 3 ITC 59.

Statutory body to operate insurance scheme

[57.10] In an Irish case, a Board had been set up by statute to carry into effect a scheme for the compulsory insurance of livestock shipped to Britain. The shippers paid levies to the Board to form a Fund out of which were to be met claims under the scheme, the Board's expenses and 'no other moneys'. The Board appealed against assessments on its surpluses, accepting that it was carrying on a trade, but contending that its receipts were earmarked to meet its expenses and claims on it, and that the relevant Act did not contemplate that it was a profit-making business. The SC(I) unanimously rejected this contention and dismissed the appeal, holding that the provision in the Act as to the application of its receipts did not preclude assessment of its surpluses. (Whether there should be any provision for unexpired risks was not considered.) *The Exported Live Stock (Insurance) Board v Carroll*, SC(I) 1951, 3 ITC 67; [1951] IR 286.

British Broadcasting Corporation

[57.11] The Revenue issued assessments on the BBC, charging tax on its surplus income from its broadcasting services as well as its profits from its publications, etc. The BBC appealed against the assessment for 1958/59, and the CA unanimously allowed the appeal, holding that the surplus income from its broadcasting services was not chargeable to income tax, because it had ultimately to be returned to the Postmaster-General who provided the finance for its services. Danckwerts LJ held that 'if a man provides a sum of money for the carrying out of a certain purpose which proves more than is required, and receives back the surplus, it is not a profit but a return of his money'. (However, the BBC's profits from its publications, etc. were held to be taxable, applying the principles laid down in *Carlisle and Silloth Golf Club v Smith*, **13.1** CLUBS AND SOCIETIES.) *British Broadcasting Corporation v Johns*, CA 1964, 41 TC 471; [1965] Ch 32; [1964] 1 All ER 923. (*Note*. The CA also held that the BBC was not entitled to Crown exemption, and that if its surplus from its broadcasting services had been chargeable to income tax, its additional subscriptions to BCINA—see **64.70** TRADING PROFITS—would have been deductible.)

58

Tax Planning and Avoidance

The cases in this chapter are arranged under the following headings.

GENERAL NOTE

This chapter brings together references to the general approach of the courts to tax planning, including tax avoidance schemes, and cases involving allegations of professional negligence. Where, as in most cases, the substantive issue on which a case was decided is still relevant, the main reference to the facts of the case will be found in the appropriate chapter. Cases dealing with the specific anti-avoidance provisions are dealt with at **3** ANTI-AVOIDANCE.

General principles

Judicial attitudes to tax planning

[58.1] In the 1929 case of *Ayrshire Pullman Motor Services & Ritchie v CIR*, **41.4** PARTNERSHIPS, Lord Clyde observed that 'no man in this country is under the smallest obligation, moral or other, so to arrange his legal relations to his business or to his property as to enable the Inland Revenue to put the largest possible shovel into his stores'. A taxpayer was 'entitled to be astute to prevent, so far as he honestly can, the depletion of his means by the Revenue.' In the 1949 case of *Lord Vestey's Executors & Vestey v CIR*, **56.14** SETTLEMENTS, Lord Normand held that 'tax avoidance is an evil, but it would be the beginning of much greater evils if the courts were to overstretch the language of the statute in order to subject to taxation people of whom they disapproved'.

[58.2] However, in the 1941 case of *Lord Howard de Walden v CIR*, **3.51** ANTI-AVOIDANCE, Lord Greene MR observed that 'for years a battle of manoeuvre has been waged between the Legislature and those who are minded to throw the burden of taxation off their own shoulders on to those of their fellow subjects. In that battle the Legislature has often been worsted by the skill, determination and resourcefulness of its opponents.' Therefore, 'it would not shock us in the least to find that the Legislature has determined to put an end to the struggle by imposing the severest of penalties. It scarcely lies in the mouth of the taxpayer who plays with fire to complain of burnt fingers.' In the

1971 case of *Greenberg v CIR*, **3.20** ANTI-AVOIDANCE, Lord Reid observed that 'plain words are seldom adequate to anticipate and forestall the multiplicity of ingenious schemes which are constantly being devised to evade taxation. Parliament is very properly determined to prevent this kind of tax evasion and, if the courts find it impossible to give very wide meanings to general phrases, the only alternative may be for Parliament to do as some other countries have done, and introduce legislation of a more sweeping character which will put the ordinary well-intentioned person at much greater risk than is created by a wide interpretation of such provisions as those which we are now considering'.

The 'Duke of Westminster' principle

[58.3] In *Duke of Westminster v CIR*, **2.3** ANNUAL PAYMENTS, Lord Tomlin stated that 'every man is entitled if he can to order his affairs so that the tax attaching under the appropriate Acts is less than it would otherwise be'. The decision in the *Duke of Westminster* case was a majority one, and the extent to which Lord Tomlin's principle should be treated as applicable to complex tax avoidance schemes was questioned by Lord Roskill in the 1984 case of *Furniss v Dawson*, **71.288** CAPITAL GAINS TAX. In the 1992 case of *Ensign Tankers (Leasing) Ltd v Stokes*, **8.100** CAPITAL ALLOWANCES, Lord Templeman observed that 'subsequent events have shown that, though this *dictum* is accurate so far as tax mitigation is concerned, it does not apply to tax avoidance'. In the 1997 case of *CIR v McGuckian*, **3.64** ANTI-AVOIDANCE, Lord Steyn observed that while Lord Tomlin's words 'still point to a material consideration, namely the general liberty of the citizen to arrange his financial affairs as he thinks fit, they have ceased to be canonical as to the consequence of a tax avoidance scheme'. In the same case, Lord Cooke of Thorndon observed that the '*Ramsay* principle' (see **58.6** below) was 'more natural and less extreme' than the majority decision in the *Duke of Westminster* case, and specifically refrained 'from speculating about whether a sharper focus on the concept of "wages" in the light of the statutory purpose and the circumstances of the case would or would not have led to a different result in the *Duke of Westminster* case'.

'Dividend-stripping'

[58.4] The basic 'dividend-stripping' device involved acquiring a company with substantial undistributed profits, taking out these profits as a dividend on the shares, and selling the shares, reduced in value and often virtually worthless following the payment of the dividend. If the purchase and sale of the shares were trading transactions, the loss on their sale could be used in support of a claim to repayment of the tax deemed to have been deducted from the dividend by virtue of *ITA 1952, s 184*. Legislation was introduced from 1955 onwards to counter dividend-stripping, which was finally ended by the introduction of Schedule F by *FA 1965*. In *JP Harrison (Watford) Ltd v Griffiths*, HL 1962, 40 TC 281; [1963] AC 1, the HL held by a 3–2 majority (Lords Reid and Denning dissenting) that a dividend-stripping operation had been in the course of a trade of dealing in shares. For subsequent cases concerning 'dividend-stripping', see **59.54** to **59.57** TRADING INCOME. In *Lupton v FA & AB Ltd*, **59.56** TRADING INCOME, Viscount Dilhorne specifically declined to follow Viscount Simonds' reasoning in *JP Harrison (Watford) Ltd v Griffiths*, and expressed the view that that case had been wrongly decided. Lord Donovan expressed a similar view, while Lord Morris upheld *dicta* of Megarry J that 'neither fiscal elements nor fiscal motives will prevent what is in substance a trading transaction from ranking as such. On the other hand, if the greater part of the transaction is explicable only on fiscal grounds, the mere presence of elements of trading will not suffice to translate the transaction into the realms of trading'. In *Coates v Arndale Properties Ltd*, **71.271** CAPITAL GAINS TAX, Fox LJ stated that Viscount Simonds' *dicta* in *JP Harrison (Watford) Ltd* could no longer be considered an accurate statement of the law. The decision and reasoning in *Lupton* were applied in *Ensign Tankers (Leasing) Ltd v Stokes*, **59.85** TRADING INCOME.

Sale of companies with capital losses—interpretation of contracts

[58.5] In 1990 two Swedish companies sold the shares in two UK companies, which had allowable capital losses, to an unrelated UK company (IMD). The sale price was geared to the tax capable of being saved by the use of the losses, so that IMD became liable to pay 50% of the tax saved, or capable of being saved, in December 1995. However, IMD did not use the losses immediately, and in March 1993 a change in the law (see *TCGA, Sch 7A*, introduced by *FA 1993*) meant that IMD could not use the losses. IMD failed to pay the sale price agreed in the contract, and the Swedish companies took action against IMD. The CA gave judgment for the Swedish companies, holding that on the wording of the contract, IMD was required to pay the specified consideration to the Swedish companies. Neither the obligation to pay, nor the amount payable, was altered by the change in the law which took place in 1993. The effect of the change was that the agreement made in 1990 'turned out to be less advantageous (to IMD) than it had hoped at the time when it had made it'. *Bromarin AB & Another v IMD Investments Ltd*, CA [1999] STC 301.

Avoidance schemes

Composite transactions—the 'Ramsay principle'

[58.6] In *WT Ramsay Ltd v CIR*, **71.285** CAPITAL GAINS TAX, Lord Wilberforce stated that a finding that a document is genuine does not preclude the Commissioners from considering whether, on the facts, what is in issue is a composite transaction or a number of independent transactions. The Commissioners are not 'bound to consider individually each separate step in a composite transaction intended to be carried through as a whole'. Lord Wilberforce observed that 'while the techniques of tax avoidance progress and are technically improved, the courts are not obliged to stand still. Such immobility must result either in loss of tax, to the prejudice of other taxpayers, or to Parliamentary congestion or (most likely) to both. To force the courts to adopt, in relation to closely integrated situations, a step by step, dissecting, approach which the parties themselves may have negated, would be a denial rather than an affirmation of the true judicial process.' In the 1997 case of *CIR v McGuckian*, **3.64** ANTI-AVOIDANCE, in which the '*Ramsay* principle' was applied and an assessment under *ICTA 1988, s 739** was upheld, Lord Steyn observed that 'during the last 30 years there has been a shift away from literalist to purposive methods of construction. Where there is no obvious meaning of a statutory provision, the modern emphasis is on a contextual approach designed to identify the purpose of a statute and to give effect to it'. The *Ramsay* approach 'was not invented on a juristic basis independent of statute' but 'was founded on a broad purposive interpretation, giving effect to the intention of Parliament'.

[58.7] In 1995 a bank (C) and a company (S) initiated a series of transactions, admittedly designed as a 'tax avoidance scheme', under which each party granted a call option to the other party. The scheme was designed to take advantage of the provisions of *FA 1994, ss 147A, 150A* and produce a deemed net loss of £20,000,000. The Revenue issued an assessment on the basis that the relevant transactions should be treated as a single composite transaction having no commercial purpose, and giving rise to no gain or loss. The HL unanimously upheld the assessment, observing that 'the purpose of the transaction was to create a tax loss, not a real loss or profit'. The Special Commissioners had found that 'there was an outside but commercially real possibility that circumstances might occur in which the two options would not be exercised so as to cancel each other out'. Nevertheless, this did not require the Commissioners to treat the options as separate transactions. The HL unanimously distinguished the majority decision in the 1988 case of *Craven v White*, **71.289** CAPITAL GAINS TAX, and held that 'it would destroy the value of the *Ramsay* principle of construing provisions such as (*FA 1994, s 150A(1)*) as referring to the effect of composite transactions if their composite effect had to be disregarded simply because the parties had deliberately included a commercially irrelevant contingency, creating an acceptable risk that the scheme might not work as planned. We would be back in the world of artificial tax schemes, now equipped with anti-*Ramsay* devices. The composite effect of such a scheme should be considered as it was intended to operate and without regard to the possibility that, contrary to the intention and expectations of the parties, it might not work as planned.' The scheme was a 'single composite transaction' which 'created no entitlement to gilts', so that 'there was therefore no qualifying contract'. *CIR v Scottish Provident Institution*, HL 2004, 76 TC 538; [2005] STC 15; [2004] UKHL 52; [2005] 1 All ER 325.

[58.8] In a Jamaican case in which the Privy Council upheld an assessment to 'transfer tax', Lord Hoffmann held that 'revenue statutes in particular are concerned with the characterisation of transactions which have a commercial unity rather than the individual steps into which such transactions may be divided. This approach does not deny the existence or legality of the individual steps but may deprive them of significance for the purposes of the characterisation required by the statute.' He also observed that 'any uncertainty is likely to be confined to transactions into which steps have been inserted without any commercial purpose. Such uncertainty is something which the architects of such schemes have to accept.' *Carreras Group Ltd v Jamaican Stamp Commissioner*, PC [2004] STC 1377; [2004] UKPC 16.

[58.9] See also the 2011 Supreme Court decision in *HMRC v Tower Mcashback LLP1*, 8.79 CAPITAL ALLOWANCES.

Application of Ramsay principle to stamp duty

[58.10] See *Ingram v CIR*, 75.12 STAMP DUTY LAND TAX, and *Hong Kong Collector of Stamp Revenue v Arrowtown Assets Ltd*, 75.13 STAMP DUTY LAND TAX.

Application of Ramsay principle to national insurance contributions

[58.11] The *Ramsay* principle was applied in a case where, on the advice of its accountants, a company paid its directors substantial bonuses in platinum sponge rather than cash, in an attempt to avoid Class 1 national insurance contributions. Langley J observed that 'national insurance contributions are very closely analogous to a tax', and held that the *Ramsay* principle entitled the Secretary of State to characterise 'the cash receipts the directors in fact obtained as payments in cash and not in kind within the meaning of the relevant provisions'. *NMB Holdings Ltd v Secretary of State for Social Security*, QB 2000, 73 TC 85. (*Note.* The decision was approved by Lord Hoffmann in *MacNiven v Westmoreland Investments Ltd*, 33.30 INTEREST PAYABLE.)

Distinction between avoidance and mitigation

[58.12] In a New Zealand case heard by the PC, and relating to New Zealand legislation which has no counterpart in UK legislation, Lord Templeman discussed the distinction between 'tax avoidance' and 'tax mitigation'. He defined tax mitigation as occurring 'where the taxpayer obtains a tax advantage by reducing his income or by incurring expenditure in circumstances in which the taxing statute affords a reduction in tax liability'. Tax avoidance takes place 'when the taxpayer reduces his liability to tax without involving him in the loss or expenditure which entitles him to that reduction. The taxpayer engaged in tax avoidance does not reduce his income or suffer a loss or incur expenditure but nevertheless obtains a reduction in his liability to tax as if he had.' *New Zealand Commr of Inland Revenue v Challenge Corporation Ltd*, PC [1986] STC 548; [1987] 2 WLR 24; [1987] AC 155.

[58.13] The decision in *New Zealand Commr of Inland Revenue v Challenge Corporation Ltd*, 58.12 above, was applied by the HL in the 1992 case of *Ensign Tankers (Leasing) Ltd v Stokes*, 8.100 CAPITAL ALLOWANCES and 59.85 TRADING INCOME, in which expenditure incurred for a commercial purpose, but with a subjective fiscal motive, was held to qualify for capital allowances. It was also adopted by Lord Nolan in the 1997 case of *CIR v Willoughby & Another*, 3.44 ANTI-AVOIDANCE. He held that 'the hallmark of tax avoidance is that the taxpayer reduces his liability to tax without incurring the economic consequences that Parliament intended to be suffered by any taxpayer qualifying for such a reduction in his tax liability. The hallmark of tax mitigation, on the other hand, is that the taxpayer takes advantage of a fiscally attractive option afforded to him by the tax legislation and generally suffers the economic consequences Parliament intended to be suffered by those taking advantage of the option'.

[58.14] In an insurance premium tax case, the tribunal defined tax avoidance as 'where a person follows an artificial series of transactions, the whole and only purpose of which is the reduction of a liability to tax, without incurring the economic consequences of the transactions'. The tribunal defined tax mitigation as 'where a person adopts a fiscally attractive option provided by the taxing statutes and genuinely suffers the economic consequences'. *GIL Insurance Ltd v C & E Commrs (and related appeals)*, LON/99/9003 (IPT6). (*Note*. The case in question was subsequently referred to the CJEC—CJEC Case C-308/01; [2004] All ER (EC) 954. The CJEC gave judgment in favour of Customs, but without specifically ruling on the distinction between tax avoidance and tax mitigation.)

Distinction between avoidance and evasion

[58.15] In *Furniss v Dawson*, **71.288** CAPITAL GAINS TAX, Lord Scarman held that the courts could not 'attempt anything so ambitious as to determine finally the limit beyond which the safe channel of acceptable tax avoidance shelves into the dangerous shallows of unacceptable tax evasion'.

CGT avoidance scheme—whether documents shams

[58.16] In a case where the facts were complex, a family which owned 463 acres of agricultural land entered into a scheme intended to avoid CGT liability by converting capital sums, representing the realisation of the development value of the land, into income. The Revenue issued CGT assessments on the basis that the deviser of the scheme had acted as an agent of the family, and held the proceeds of the realisation on a bare trust for the family. The Special Commissioners upheld the assessments, holding that two documents relied upon by the appellants were shams and had no legal effect, applying *dicta* of Diplock LJ in *Snook v London & West Riding Investments Ltd*, CA [1967] 2 QB 786; [1967] 1 All ER 518. The CA upheld this decision. Arden LJ held that 'it is of the essence of this type of sham transaction that the parties to a transaction intend to create one set of rights and obligations' but intend to give third parties 'the appearance of creating different rights and obligations'. On the evidence, the Commissioners were entitled to conclude that the documents were shams, and that 'the real arrangements between the parties transcended and transformed those documents'. Furthermore, the fact that the first clause in a deed was valid and effective did not prevent the second clause in that deed from being a sham. *Hitch & Others v Stone*, CA 2001, 73 TC 600; [2001] STC 214; [2001] EWCA Civ 63. (*Note*. For subsequent developments in this case, see **4.210** APPEALS.)

Tax avoidance scheme—criminal prosecution for false accounting

[58.17] See *R v Werner & Clarke*, 51.3 REVENUE PROSECUTIONS.

Avoidance scheme—prosecution for cheating the public revenue

[58.18] See *R v Cunningham, Charlton, Wheeler & Kitchen*, 51.6 REVENUE PROSECUTIONS.

Transfer of assets from approved pension scheme to unapproved scheme

[58.19] See *R v CIR (ex p. Roux Waterside Inn Ltd)*, 46.8 PENSION SCHEMES, and *R (oao Mander) v CIR*, 46.9 PENSION SCHEMES.

Disclosure of tax avoidance schemes

[58.20] See *HMRC v Mercury Tax Group Ltd (No 2)*, 3.94 ANTI-AVOIDANCE.

Tax avoidance arrangements—whether trading

[58.21] See *Ransom v Higgs*, 59.99 TRADING INCOME.

Football club—avoidance scheme involving Jersey settlement

[58.22] See *O'Leary v McKinlay*, 22.80 EMPLOYMENT INCOME.

New Zealand avoidance scheme—investors misled by company

[58.23] In a New Zealand case, a film production company persuaded investors to finance the production of two films. The company required the investors to make substantial payments, some of which had to be borrowed from a specific lender (which was associated with the production company). The amount which the investors were required to pay exceeded the true cost of the films, the balance being recycled to the lender. The investors claimed tax relief on the full amounts which they had paid. The Revenue only agreed to grant relief on the true cost of the films, considering that the excess which the investors had been required to pay was not deductible by virtue of the relevant New Zealand anti-avoidance legislation (*New Zealand Income Tax Act 1976, s 99*). The PC allowed the investors' appeal (by a 3-2 majority, Lords Bingham and Scott dissenting). Lord Millett held that, on the evidence as found by the New Zealand Taxation Review Authority, the investors had entered into a contractual obligation to make payments to the production company. The relevant costs were those incurred by the investors, not those incurred by the production company. The fact that the production company had engaged in a 'deceitful inflation of the costs of production', and had made a profit at the expense of the investors, did not prevent the investors' expenditure from qualifying for tax relief. (Lord Millett also observed that such expenditure would not qualify for relief if 'loans were made on uncommercial terms such that no commercial lender would advance money unless it received some additional consideration for doing so'.) *Peterson & Others v New Zealand Commissioner of Inland Revenue*, PC [2005] STC 448; [2005] UKPC 5. (*Note*. In the subsequent UK case of *HMRC v Tower Mcashback LLP1*, **8.79** CAPITAL ALLOWANCES, Lord Hope implicitly criticised the majority decision in this case and held that it should be confined 'to its own facts'.)

Russian avoidance scheme involving low-tax areas

[58.24] See *OAO Neftyanaka Kompaniya Yukos v Russia*, **31.111** HUMAN RIGHTS.

IHT avoidance scheme—whether transaction may be set aside

[58.25] See *Wolff & Wolff v Wolff & Others*, **72.183** INHERITANCE TAX.

Tax indemnities

Sale of shares—payments made on account of tax liabilities

[58.26] In October 1989 the five shareholders in a family company (W) agreed to sell their shares to a public company (C). W was the subject of an investigation by the Inland Revenue Enquiry Branch, and the sale agreement included a standard deed of tax indemnity, under which the vendors agreed to pay C an amount equal to any tax liability of W, or its subsidiaries, arising out of events occurring, or income or profits earned, before December 1989. The agreement also provided for a portion of the sale proceeds to be paid into bank accounts in the vendors' names, but secured in favour of C. Between September 1988 and July 1989 W had made payments to the Revenue, totalling £500,000, on account of the Enquiry Branch investigation. In November 1989 W paid a further £400,000 to the Revenue. The sale was completed in May 1990, and on the following day C recouped £900,000 from the secured bank accounts established under the sale agreement. The vendors subsequently began proceedings against C, claiming that C had only been entitled to withdraw £400,000. The Ch D reviewed the evidence in detail and dismissed the proceedings, holding that C had been entitled to withdraw the full £900,000. *JW Rosedale Investments Ltd and Others v Corus UK Ltd*, Ch D [2000] All ER (D) 2137. (*Note*. For a discussion of the decision, see British Tax Review 2001, pp 164–171.)

Professional negligence

NOTE

For a recent discussion of professional negligence in relation to tax advisers, see the article by Joseph Howard in Taxation, 28 October 2010, pp 14-16.

Whether Limitation Act 1980 applicable

[58.27] In a non-tax case, in which the Ch D rejected a contention by a firm of solicitors that proceedings alleging professional negligence had been brought outside the time limit of the *Limitation Act 1939* (which has subsequently superseded by the *Limitation Act 1980*), Oliver J held that 'the test is what the reasonably competent practitioner would do having regard to the standards normally adopted in his profession'. *Midland Bank Trust Co Ltd v Hett Stubbs & Kent*, Ch D [1979] Ch 384.

[58.28] In 1984 an individual (M) undertook a scheme marketed by a life assurance company, which the company claimed would avoid liability to capital transfer tax (subsequently renamed inheritance tax). However, the scheme failed to take account of *IHTA, s 3(3)**, so that the whole of M's free estate became liable to IHT on her death (on 4 March 1991). On 3 March 1997 M's executors issued a writ against the life assurance company, alleging that it owed a duty of care to ensure that its brochure was accurate and pointed out any CTT risks inherent in the scheme. The company defended the action, contending that the writ had been issued outside the six-year time limit laid down by *Limitation Act 1980*. The Ch D rejected this contention and held that the writ had been issued within the six-year period. The cause of action had accrued when M died. Her executors were not suing in respect of a lost opportunity suffered by M in her lifetime; they were suing in respect of the IHT liability which arose on her death, and which did not exist until she died. Liability for IHT was payable by M's estate, and was not imposed on the deceased. M's executors were suing for a loss or damage which did not exist until M's death. *Macaulay & Another v Premium Life Assurance Co Ltd*, Ch D 29 April 1999 unreported.

[58.29] In 1989 a woman (D) consulted a solicitor with the aim of mitigating inheritance tax on her estate. The solicitor put forward a scheme under which she transferred the freehold of the property where she lived to her son, but continued to live in the property, thus giving rise to an inheritance tax liability under *FA 1986, s 102*, dealing with gifts with reservation. D died in 1998, and the Revenue charged IHT on her estate on the basis that there had been a reservation of benefit in relation to the property. D's executor accepted that the Revenue's charge to tax was correct, and began proceedings against the solicitor, contending that he had been negligent. The solicitor defended proceedings on the basis that any negligence (which he did not admit) had occurred in 1989 when he gave the relevant advice, so that the effect of the *Limitation Act 1980* was that any claim would have been brought no later than 1995. The CA accepted this contention and gave judgment for the solicitor. Dyson LJ held that 'the true detriment suffered by (D) was that the defendant's negligence frustrated her wish to confer on her son the benefit of a reduction in the inheritance tax liability of her estate. But that is not a detriment recognised by our law as damage which is capable of assessment in money terms'. Furthermore, if D had had a claim in negligence during her lifetime, then 'it must have arisen at the time when she relied on the defendant's advice and did not take steps which would have ensured that the transfer was an exempt transfer'. *Daniels v Thompson*, CA [2004] EWCA Civ 307; [2004] All ER (D) 357 (Mar).

[58.30] The decision in *Daniels v Thompson*, 58.29 above, was distinguished in a subsequent case in which an individual (R) took proceedings against a firm of solicitors, claiming that the estate of his late mother had incurred unnecessary IHT liabilities as a result of negligent advice from the solicitors. The solicitors applied for the claim to be struck out, contending that it was excluded by the *Limitation Act 1980*. The Ch D rejected this contention and dismissed the solicitors' application. Morgan J held that it was arguable that the limitation period should be held to run from the date of R's death. He also held that a resolution of the issue as to the existence of a duty of care 'depends upon a detailed investigation of the facts which can only be conducted at a trial'. *Rind v Theodore Goddard*, Ch D [2008] EWHC 459 (Ch); [2008] All ER (D) 134 (Mar).

[58.31] In 1997 an individual (B) sold a successful business and received $150,000,000 in loan notes as consideration. On 2 April 1998 he subscribed the $150,000,000 for shares in a newly-incorporated company (P). He claimed reinvestment relief (which was abolished for acquisitions made after 5 April 1998 by *FA 1998, s 165, Sch 27*). However P was unable to reinvest the full amount of B's investment within the statutory time limit. Furthermore, P reinvested much of the investment by buying controlling shareholdings in trading companies. Much of the value of these businesses lay in the goodwill they had built up before the acquisition by P. When the assets of the business were 'hived up' to P, the base cost at which P was taken to acquire those assets for the purposes of corporation tax on capital gains was the original base cost to the acquired business. Since the goodwill had been built up by the acquired business itself, it had not paid anything for it. Thus the value of the goodwill (for which P had paid) did not form part of the base cost to the acquired business. When P then came to sell those assets, with their accompanying goodwill, its gain fell to be calculated as the excess of the sale price over the original base cost to the acquired business (not the gain over the purchase price paid by P). This had the consequence that if P were to sell one of the businesses for less than the amount that it itself had paid for it, but more than that base cost, it would still be making a capital gain for tax purposes and would be liable to corporation tax on that gain. If P had bought the assets of the target companies (including their goodwill) instead of buying shares in them, it would only have been liable to pay tax on a gain over and above the whole price that it paid for the assets. And if P had acquired the businesses through subsidiary companies, it would have been able to dispose of an acquired business by a sale of its shares in the subsidiary without triggering a liability for tax on capital gains (save insofar as it made an actual gain on the sale). In 2005 B and P took proceedings against the accountants who had acted for B, claiming damages for negligence, on the basis that the accountants 'knew or ought to have known' that relief would have been available if P 'had incorporated and funded subsidiaries to make purchases and to hive the businesses up to those subsidiaries', rather than to P itself. The accountants defended the proceedings, contending that they had not been acting for P, and that any damage which B had suffered had occurred before 1999, so that the claims were outside the statutory time limit. The Ch D accepted these contentions and dismissed the applications, holding that the damage which B had suffered had been sustained at the date of the share issue, in April 1998, and B's claim was outside the statutory six-year time limit. The CA unanimously upheld this decision. *Bradbury v Ernst & Young; Pegasus Management Holdings SCA v Ernst & Young*, CA [2010] STC 1461; [2010] EWCA Civ 181; [2010] 3 All ER 297.

Cases where the practitioner was held to be negligent

Solicitors advising on property transaction

[58.32] A company (H) undertook a property transaction whereby it purchased a lease of business premises and granted a sub-lease of the premises. The transaction was structured in a way which exposed H to a charge under *ICTA 1988, s 34(1)* on a proportion of the premium, and to associated costs. The charge could have been avoided if the transaction had been structured in a different way. H took legal action against the solicitors who had acted for it in connection with the transaction, claiming damages for breach of the contractual duty of care and for negligence. The Ch D gave judgment in favour of H, ordering the solicitors to pay the amount claimed, plus interest. Lightman J observed that the partner who had dealt with the case had admitted that he had 'next to no knowledge of tax law' and had no appreciation 'of the tax risks involved in the transaction'. He should have appreciated that H 'needed his advice and services to avoid any unnecessary tax risk', and he 'owed a duty to advise how the transaction should be structured', and to advise that the structure in fact adopted exposed him to the tax charge which 'by alterations to the form rather than the substance of the transaction could have been avoided'. *Hurlingham Estates Ltd v Wilde & Partners*, Ch D 1996, [1997] STC 627.

Tax advice by accountant—whether accountant negligent

[58.33] A trader (P) was also the majority shareholder in a company, to which he devoted most of his working time. He wished to retire and, on the advice of his accountants, he caused the company to realise the value of his shares by paying an interim dividend. Subsequently he took legal action against the accountants, contending that they had been negligent in that they should have advised him to realise the value of his shares by a capital distribution, so that he could have claimed retirement relief. The accountants contended, *inter alia*, that P had not been a 'full-time working officer or employee' of the company as required by *TCGA, s 163(5)*. The CA accepted P's contentions (by a 2-1 majority, Nourse LJ dissenting) and ordered the accountants to pay P damages. Aldous LJ held that, since P worked for the company for 42.5 hours each week, he qualified as a 'full-time working officer or employee' of the company, within *s 163(5)*. The fact that he also worked for a separate business for 7.5 hours each week was irrelevant. *Palmer v Maloney; Palmer v Shipleys*, CA 1999, 71 TC 502; [1999] STC 890. (*Note.* For HMRC's interpretation of the phrase 'full-time working officer or employee', see Capital Gains Manual, para CG63619. For the Revenue's practice following the Ch D decision in this case, see Revenue Tax Bulletin, April 1999, p 653.)

[58.34] A company carried on an estate agency business. One of its directors resigned, and the other directors agreed to purchase his shares. They sought advice from an accountancy firm. The firm proposed a scheme involving the company repurchasing the shares, which overlooked the CGT 'pooling' provisions. When it became apparent that that scheme had failed, the firm proposed another scheme which overlooked the effect of *TCGA, s 18** (dealing with transactions between connected persons). Subsequently the directors took proceedings against the firm, contending that its advice had been negligent, and that it should have given specific advice about the timing and structure of the repurchase. The QB gave judgment for the plaintiffs, holding on the evidence that the firm had been negligent. The firm should have advised on the timing of the repurchase. As a result of the firm's negligence, the plaintiffs had incurred a tax liability which could have been avoided. The firm appealed to the CA, which upheld the QB decision, and increased the amount of the award to the plaintiffs. *Little and Others v George Little Sebire & Co*, CA [2001] STC 1065; [2001] EWCA Civ 894.

[58.35] In 1995 a major accountancy firm approached a university, offering to help it to establish a 'profit-related pay' scheme under the rules of *ICTA 1988, ss 169–184* (which were repealed by *FA 1997*). The university accepted the offer. However, the scheme which the firm implemented did not fulfil the conditions of *ICTA 1988, Sch 8 para 8*. The auditors were unable to certify the scheme accounts, and the Revenue subsequently cancelled the schemes. The university took proceedings against the accountancy firm, claiming damages for negligence. Hart J reviewed the evidence in detail and gave judgment for the university, holding that the accountancy firm had been negligent. He ruled that the university was entitled to damages of more than £1,600,000, comprising the net tax it had to pay as a result of the cancellation of the schemes; 80% of the savings which would have been achieved by schemes successfully implemented for each of the relevant years, and the professional fees incurred in extricating itself from the scheme; plus interest on the moneys of which the university had been deprived (at base rate minus 1%). The firm appealed to the CA, accepting that its advice had been negligent but contending that its terms of engagement excluded liability for 'failure to realise anticipated savings or benefits and a failure to obtain registration of the scheme'. The CA rejected this contention and dismissed the appeal. Arden LJ held that the relevant clause should be construed as meaning that the firm 'did not guarantee that a particular saving would be made if that saving was dependent, for example, on the level of take-up by employees of the client'. However, the firm 'should not be wholly free from the consequences of their negligence if that resulted in the client losing a tax saving it would otherwise have achieved'. *Price Waterhouse v University of Keele*, CA [2004] EWCA Civ 583; [2004] All ER (D) 264 (May).

[58.36] In 1995 a US bank posted one of its employees (S), who was a citizen of the Republic of Ireland, to work in its London branch. Because S became resident in the UK, but was not ordinarily resident, he was liable to pay UK tax on all his earnings for work carried out in the UK, but was only liable to pay UK tax on earnings for work done outside the UK on the 'remittance' basis. However, S was not aware of this, and asked his employers to pay the whole of his earnings into a UK bank account. S consulted a UK accountancy firm, which prepared his tax returns on the basis that he was not liable to pay UK tax in respect of his earnings for work carried out abroad (and obtained substantial refunds for 1996/97 and 1997/98 on this basis). When the Revenue discovered that the relevant income had been paid into the UK, they demanded payment of the tax due, plus interest. S then took proceedings against the accountancy firm, claiming damages for professional negligence, on the basis that the firm should have advised him to arrange for his earnings to be paid into a Jersey bank account, so that he would not have had to pay UK tax on earnings for work done outside the UK. The Ch D gave judgment for S, holding that the accountants' failure 'even to alert (S) to the potential benefits of offshore payment' was 'a lapse which ought not to have been made'. S's accountants 'fell below the standard to be expected of a reasonably careful and competent tax accountant'. They had failed to suggest 'what on the evidence should have been the obvious solution in his position as someone resident but not ordinarily resident in the United Kingdom who often worked abroad, ie the opening of a Channel Islands bank account into which his earnings could be paid'. As a result, S had incurred a substantial tax liability for 1996/97 and 1997/98 which could easily have been avoided. For 1996/97, the Ch D awarded damages of the whole of the relevant tax and interest (£123,900). However, for 1997/98, the Ch D reduced the award by 50% (from £146,380 to £73,190) on the basis that S had failed to query the refund which he had received for 1996/97, and that this constituted 'contributory negligence' by S. *Slattery v Moore Stephens*, Ch D [2003] STC 1379; [2003] EWHC 1869 (Ch).

[58.37] A company (B) designed and produced computer software. It sought taxation advice from a company (S) which specialised in financial planning. Subsequently B took proceedings against S, contending that it had been negligent in not advising it of the possibility of making claims for tax relief under *FA 2000, Sch 20*. S defended the proceedings, accepting that its failure to notify B of these provisions 'constituted a breach of their retainer and negligence', but contending that B had suffered no loss because its activities did not qualify for relief under *FA 2000*. The Ch D accepted this contention and dismissed B's claim for damages. Evans-Lombe J held that since B had not been entitled to tax relief, it had not 'suffered damage as a result of (S's) breach of duty'. *BE Studios Ltd v Smith & Williamson Ltd*, Ch D 2005, [2006] STC 358; [2005] EWHC 1506 (Ch). (*Note.* In subsequent proceedings, the Ch D awarded S 80% of its costs, and ordered that these costs should be paid by one of B's directors—*BE Studios Ltd v Smith & Williamson Ltd (No 2)*, Ch D [2005] EWHC 2730 (Ch); [2006] 2 All ER 811.)

Tax advice by solicitor—solicitor subsequently suspended by Law Society

[58.38] A solicitor (B) gave advice in relation to setting up arrangements for making loans from a pension fund in such a way as to avoid liability to UK tax. Following his advice, sums of money were paid into his client account and then distributed. The security given for the payments transpired to be worthless. The trustees of the pension scheme were unable to recover the sums, and took legal proceedings. The Ch D found that B had given a reference to a major bank in connection with the transactions, stating that an individual (N) was 'a person of integrity and good standing', when in fact he was guilty of fraud. Etherton J held that B had failed to give 'any proper explanation for a letter by a solicitor, apparently in connection with Money Laundering Regulations', which gave the impression and 'was intended to give the impression, that one or more people in the firm had met and dealt with (N) personally'. Following these proceedings, the Law Society took proceedings against B, alleging that he was guilty of 'conduct unbefitting a solicitor'. The Solicitors' Discipline Tribunal observed that 'people who are not qualified as solicitors are able to recognise that it is improper to give a reference on behalf of a person that they do not know. Solicitors know that they can only properly give references which are truthful in all respects.' The tribunal found that B 'gave a false reference indicating that the person he referred to was a person of good standing when he neither knew nor had any opportunity to know whether that was accurate'. To write 'such a false reference was both improper and a serious breach of a solicitor's professional duty. In writing such a letter the respondent had been at the very least extraordinarily reckless with regard to this professional duty.' Such behaviour on the part of a solicitor was 'wholly unacceptable'. The tribunal directed that B should be suspended for three years. B appealed, contending that the order of suspension was excessive. The CA unanimously rejected this contention and dismissed B's appeal. Sir Igor Judge observed that the tribunal had a duty to maintain 'the collective reputation of the profession and continued public confidence in its integrity'. B had known that the bank was seeking a reference 'in the context of money laundering regulations', and that 'the reference was critical to the proper discharge of the bank's duties'. On the evidence, B had been guilty of 'reprehensible behaviour' and had displayed 'extraordinary recklessness'. *Baxendale-Walker v Law Society*, CA [2007] EWCA Civ 233; [2007] 3 All ER 330. (*Note.* B was subsequently struck off the Roll of Solicitors: see *Baxendale-Walker v Middleton & Others*, QB [2011] EWHC 998 (QB).)

Legal advice on creation of settlement—whether negligent

[58.39] In 1988 a woman (E) set up a discretionary settlement, on the advice of a firm of solicitors, who in turn had consulted a barrister. The creation of the settlement was not reported to the Revenue, although E transferred 500 shares to the settlement a month later. E died in 1994. Subsequently her executors, and the trustees of the settlement, brought actions against the solicitors and barrister, contending that they had been negligent, since they should have advised E to set up an interest in possession trust, rather than a discretionary settlement, in order to avoid the inheritance tax liability which had arisen when E had transferred the shares to the settlement. The Ch D upheld this contention, observing that the solicitors had failed to do any independent research, but had relied solely on the barrister's advice. The barrister had failed to make it clear that the gift of shares to a discretionary settlement would be an immediately chargeable transfer. Arden J held that the fact that he had believed that this was self-evident 'does not justify not mentioning such a significant point'. The solicitor had lacked 'basic knowledge', and had wrongly believed that the transfer of shares to the discretionary settlement was a potentially exempt transfer. This was 'not some obscure point of tax law' but 'was a basic principle of IHT'. On the evidence, 'a reasonably competent barrister would have considered an interest in possession trust'. By setting up a discretionary settlement, rather than an interest in possession trust, an inheritance tax liability of £170,000 had been incurred, which could have been avoided. Accordingly, both the solicitors and the barrister had been negligent. *Estill & Others v Cowling Swift & Kitchin; Estill & Others v Carswell*, Ch D [2000] WTLR 417.

Sale of shares in company—failure to meet conditions of TCGA, s 163(3)

[58.40] An individual (J), who was aged over 50, was a director, shareholder and employee of a trading company. He decided to resign from his employment and sell his shares back to the company. If he had still been a full-time working officer or employee of the company when he sold the shares, he would have been entitled to retirement relief under *TCGA, s 163*. However, he resigned from his employment before selling the shares, and thus lost his entitlement to relief. He subsequently took proceedings against his accountants, contending that they had been negligent in failing to advise him of the conditions of *s 163(3)*. The accountants defended the proceedings, contending that J had only asked them to act in relation to income tax and had not asked them to act in respect of the share sale. The CA unanimously rejected this contention and gave judgment for J. Sir Martin Nourse held that the documentary evidence clearly showed that the accountants had been acting for J and had given him 'negligent advice'. *Joel v Langley & Partners*, CA [2002] EWCA Civ 523; [2002] All ER (D) 191 (Apr).

Unsuccessful avoidance scheme—action alleging misrepresentation by promoter

[58.41] A chartered accountant (H) invested in a scheme, marketed by a partnership, which claimed to take advantage of the legislation providing tax relief for film production (see now *CTA 2009, ss 1180–1216*). He claimed a repayment of income tax from HMRC. Following an enquiry, HMRC issued a ruling that the scheme was ineffective and required H to return the amount of the repayment, together with interest. H took proceedings against the partner who had persuaded him to enter the scheme, alleging fraudulent misrepresentation. The QB gave judgment for H. Judge Seymour found that the partner 'knew perfectly well that she was not a specialist in film tax investment schemes', and 'knew perfectly well that the representations which were made' were false. He also held that H had begun the proceedings within the extended time limit of *Limitation Act 1980, s 32(1)*. The CA unanimously upheld this decision. *Allison v Horner*, CA [2014] EWCA Civ 117.

Unsuccessful avoidance scheme—action alleging negligence by promoters

[58.42] See *Macaulay & Another v Premium Life Assurance Co Ltd*, 58.28 above.

Cases where the practitioner was held not to be negligent

Solicitors failing to advise of ways of avoiding IHT

[58.43] A testator died in December 1986, bequeathing his residuary estate to his sister. She died in May 1988, naming seven charities as residuary beneficiaries. The charities brought an action seeking damages from her solicitors, contending that the solicitors had been negligent in failing to advise her to make a deed of arrangement under *IHTA, s 142*. The Ch D rejected this contention and dismissed the action, holding that the solicitors had not been in breach of their duty of care. Harman J observed that a legatee was entitled to 'consider that tax avoidance is something rather unattractive, to be indulged in by sharp people with connections in the City of London who use various arcane devices to get out of their proper obligations to the Crown'. In the present case, the legatee had been entitled to take the view that she should retain her late brother's estate in her own hands. In any event, 'there was no duty in law upon the solicitors' to advise about possible tax avoidance. The decision in *White v Jones*, HL [1995] 2 AC 207; [1995] 1 All ER 691, was distinguished. The sister's executor was also under no duty to take steps to reduce the tax burden on the residuary legatees, since 'the duties imposed by the law upon an executor' could not include a duty to facilitate 'the entry into a scheme of tax avoidance'. *Cancer Research Campaign and Others v Ernest Brown & Co and Others*, Ch D [1997] STC 1425.

Unsuccessful avoidance scheme—whether solicitors negligent

[58.44] A company had adopted a tax avoidance scheme, devised by an accountant, with the object of claiming capital allowances on a deemed sale price which was substantially more than the amount actually paid to the vendor of the buildings in question. The Revenue issued a ruling that the scheme was ineffective, and the company applied for judicial review. The HL dismissed the application (see **50.33** REVENUE ADMINISTRATION), and the company took legal action against the solicitors and counsel who had advised it in connection with the implementation of the scheme, contending that they had been negligent. The Ch D rejected this contention and dismissed the action, holding that neither the solicitors nor the counsel had been in breach of their duties to the company. On the evidence, it was apparently the decision of the company, rather than the advice of the counsel, to send a key letter to a local tax district rather than to Inland Revenue Head Office—a decision which had been strongly criticised by the House of Lords. Applying *dicta* of Lord Diplock in *Saif Ali v Sidney Mitchell & Co*, HL 1978, [1980] AC 198; [1978] 3 All ER 1033, there was no liability for damage resulting from an error of judgment by any person practising a profession, 'unless the error was such as no reasonably well-informed and competent member of that profession could have made'. *Matrix Securities Ltd v Theodore Goddard; Matrix Securities Ltd v Goldberg*, Ch D 1997, [1998] STC 1.

Unsuccessful avoidance scheme—whether accountants negligent

[58.45] In 1995 an individual (W) sold her shareholding in a company to another company. On the advice of her accountants, W adopted a scrip dividend scheme, designed to incur a charge to income tax at 25%, rather than a charge to CGT at 40%. Subsequently W took legal action against the accountants, contending that they had been negligent in failing to advise her of alternative ways of mitigating her tax liability (such as taking part of the consideration in guaranteed loan notes). The Ch D dismissed her action, holding on the evidence that she had failed to prove that the accountants had been negligent. Rattee J observed that he 'did not find (W) a convincing witness' and that 'on various issues of fact she has convinced herself of the truth of what she would like to believe in the interests of her case'. *Wedderburn v Grant Thornton*, Ch D 14 May 1999 unreported.

Claim against accountants—advice held to be correct in law

[58.46] In 1991 a US citizen (G), who had been resident in the UK for several years, sought advice from an accountancy firm with regard to purchasing property in the UK for him and his fiancée. The couple married later in the year, and G made his wife a substantial gift. The accountants advised G that the transactions did not give rise to UK tax liability. The Revenue later began investigating G's affairs and claimed that the gift represented a remittance of foreign emoluments, so that tax was due under Schedule E Case III, applying the principles laid down in *Harmel v Wright*, **54.16** SCHEDULE E. On counsel's advice, G reached a financial settlement. He subsequently began legal proceedings, alleging professional negligence, against the accountants who had advised him. The Ch D gave judgment for G, holding that 'a reasonably skilful and careful accountant tax adviser' should have recognised that the scheme 'ran a high risk of being challenged by the Inland Revenue and stood a significant prospect of giving rise to a charge to tax'. The CA allowed the accountants' appeal against this decision, holding that the accountants had not been negligent (by a 2-1 majority, Carnwath LJ dissenting). Sir Andrew Morritt V-C held that the advice given by the accountants 'was correct as a matter of law', and that the gift was not assessable, applying the principles laid down in *Carter v Sharon*, **28.6** FOREIGN INCOME, and distinguishing *Harmel v Wright*, **54.16** SCHEDULE E. The gift to G's wife had been 'perfected in the United States at the time the transfers to her were made'. *Grimm v Newman & Another*, CA, [2002] STC 1388; [2002] EWCA Civ 1621. (*Note*. The Revenue were not represented. Sir Andrew Morritt V-C observed that 'those who may read this judgment must bear in mind that we have not heard any argument from the Inland Revenue and the conclusion we reach relates to the efficacy of advice given in 1991. They must consider for themselves the extent to which they may safely rely on our decision in arranging their affairs now.')

Client dying shortly after share sale—whether solicitors negligent

[58.47] A company's chairman and controlling shareholder (S), who was 61 years old, overweight and had previously suffered a heart attack, sought the advice of a solicitors' firm with regard to the sale of his shares. Less than three weeks after the sale, S died unexpectedly during a hospital operation. S's daughters and executors subsequently began proceedings against the solicitors, alleging that they should have advised S to defer the sale of his shares until after the hospital operation, since if he had still held the shares at the time of his death, they would have qualified for business property relief and the IHT liability on S's death would have been substantially lower. The Ch D reviewed the evidence in detail and dismissed the claim, finding that S had been aware that he needed to survive seven years in order that any gifts should qualify for IHT exemption, and the solicitors had not been given any information which would suggest that S might die within a few weeks of the share sale. They had learnt about the operation 'essentially by chance' and 'the information they received did not suggest that the procedure was other than a routine one'. The CA unanimously upheld this decision. *Swain, Mason & Others v Mills & Reeve*, CA [2012] EWCA Civ 498; [2012] STC 1760.

Accountants not advising client on CGT avoidance scheme

[58.48] The controlling shareholders of a clothing company sold their shares for £22,000,000 in early 2005. The sale gave rise to significant CGT liability. One of the shareholders (M) had been born in Iran, although he had moved to the UK at the age of 12. He subsequently took proceedings against the accountants (HB) who had acted for him in relation to the sale, contending that they should have taken steps to take advantage of his non-UK domicile and should have taken advice from a large accountancy firm, who might have advised him to adopt an avoidance scheme known as the 'bearer warrant scheme' which would involve converting the shares from registered shares to bearer shares, and then relocating them outside the UK. (Such schemes were subsequently blocked by what is now *TCGA 1992, s 275A*.) The CA unanimously rejected this contention, holding that HB had not been negligent. Patten LJ held that a prudent tax adviser would have been 'cautious about recommending the bearer warrant scheme where no obvious marker in the securities existed in the foreign situs at the date of transfer'. HB had not been 'under a general roving duty to have regard to and to advise on all aspects of the claimant's affairs absent a request to do so'. On the evidence, M had never specifically asked HB 'to give him tax planning advice on possible ways of minimising or eliminating the already low rate of CGT applicable to his disposal' of the shares. HB had been asked to provide 'routine tax advice', but had not been asked to advise on 'the much more sophisticated form of tax planning exemplified by the bearer warrant scheme which often involves a reformulation of the transaction in order to bring about particular tax consequences rather than a mitigation of the tax liability which the transaction will otherwise produce'. M's non-UK domicile did not give rise to any tax advantages on the disposal of shares in a UK company, and there were no grounds for finding that HB 'should have known and advised (M) that it would or might be possible to change the situs of the shares without triggering a charge to CGT in the process'. *Mehjoo v Harben Barker (and related appeal)*, CA [2014] EWCA Civ 358; [2014] STC 1470; [2014] 4 All ER 806.

Miscellaneous

Admissible evidence

Civil Evidence Act 1972, s 3—evidence of 'expert witness'

[58.49] Following an investigation, a charity paid the Revenue more than £2,000,000 in respect of tax, interest and penalties. The charity took proceedings against a barrister who had advised it with regard to the requirements for charitable exemption under *ICTA 1988, s 505(1)(e)*, contending that he had given advice which no 'reasonably competent' barrister could have given, and had been 'negligently optimistic about the likely outcome of the Inland Revenue investigation'. G sought to call another barrister (F) from the same chambers, whom he had known for many years, as an 'expert witness' in his defence. The charity objected to this evidence, contending that an expert witness was required to be independent, and that F was not independent. The Ch D accepted this contention and ruled that the evidence was inadmissible. Evans-Lombe J held that, where it was demonstrated that there was a relationship between the proposed expert and the party calling him, which a reasonable observer might think was capable of affecting the views of the expert so as to make them unduly favourable to that party, the witness could not qualify as an expert witness within *Civil Evidence Act 1972, s 3*. In the present case, the closeness of the relationship between F and G made F unsuitable, on grounds of public policy, to be called as an expert witness in support of G's case. *Liverpool Roman Catholic Archdiocesan Trustees Incorporated v Goldberg (No 2)*, Ch D [2001] 1 WLR 2337; [2001] 4 All ER 950. (*Note*. The proceedings were subsequently settled by an out-of-court agreement.)

Accountants held to be in breach of duty but no award of damages

Effect of CTA 2009, s 1263

[58.50] A company (AG), which was a member of a limited liability partnership, took court proceedings against a large accountancy firm (B), contending that B had failed to advise it on the implications of the enactment of *CTA 2009, s 1263*, and that if B had provided sufficient advice, it would have implemented a restructuring scheme to avoid the tax consequences of *s 1263*. B defended the proceedings, accepting that it had been in breach of duty but contending that AG had not suffered any loss, since AG would not have implemented the restructuring scheme which it had subsequently considered, and alternatively that even if AG had implemented such a scheme, the scheme would have been ineffective as a matter of law and would have been successfully challenged by HMRC. The Ch D accepted B's first contention, finding that there was no evidence that such a scheme had ever been successfully implemented, and gave judgment for B. *Altus Group (UK) Ltd v Baker Tilly Tax & Advisory Services Llp*, Ch D [2015] EWHC 12 (Ch).

59

Trading Income—Definition of Trading

The cases in this chapter are arranged under the following headings.

CROSS-REFERENCES

See **9.81** *et seq.* CHARITIES for trading by charities; **11** CLOSE COMPANIES for whether a close company is trading; and **67** TRADING PROFITS—PROPERTY DEALING for property dealing.

'Trade or Business'—general

Definition of 'business'

[59.1] *ITTOIA 2005, Part 2 (ss 3–259)* deals with 'trading income' and charges tax on 'trade profits'. Elsewhere in the legislation the word 'business' is frequently used (see, for example, *ICTA 1988, ss 12, 13*) so that it may be necessary to decide whether a 'business' as distinct from a 'trade' is being carried on. For a relatively recent decision on this point, see *Jowett v O'Neill & Brennan Construction Ltd*, **59.20** below. In *American Leaf Blending Co v Director-General of Inland Revenue*, **59.17** below, Lord Diplock observed that ' "business" is a wider concept than "trade"'. A number of older tax cases turned on the question of whether the taxpayer was carrying on a 'trade or business' within the charge to excess profits duty (EPD), corporation profits tax, excess profits tax or profits tax (formerly national defence contribution), but in which the position under income tax was not in issue. The cases in question are summarised at **59.2** to **59.16** below.

Company receiving royalties

[59.2] In an EPD case, the KB held that a company which received patent royalties and distributed dividends was not carrying on a trade or business. *CIR v Marine Steam Turbine Co Ltd*, KB 1919, 12 TC 174. (*Note. Dicta* of Rowlatt J were disapproved by Atkin LJ in the subsequent case of *CIR v Korean Syndicate Ltd*, **59.3** below.)

[59.3] In an EPD case, a company had been formed in 1905 for the purpose of acquiring 'concessions, rights and privileges of any and every kind'. From

1915 to 1917 its activities were confined to receiving bank interest and royalties, paying premiums on a sinking fund policy, and making distributions to its shareholders. The CA unanimously held that it was carrying on the business for which it was incorporated of acquiring concessions and turning them to account, and was therefore liable to EPD. Atkin LJ held that 'there is nothing in the Act which says that the business must be actively carried on'. *CIR v Korean Syndicate Ltd*, CA 1921, 12 TC 181. (*Note*. The decision was approved by the HL in *CIR v South Behar Railway Co Ltd*, **59.10** below.)

Inventor receiving royalties

[59.4] An individual granted a company, which he had promoted, licences to use certain inventions which he had patented. The KB held that the royalties which he received under the licences were income from property, and that he was not carrying on a trade or business. *CIR v Sangster*, KB 1919, 12 TC 208.

Oil company receiving royalties

[59.5] A company (B) was incorporated with the object of acquiring an oilfield. In 1915 it transferred its rights to another company in return for royalties. The KB held that B was carrying on a trade or business and was liable to EPD. *CIR v Budderpore Oil Co Ltd*, KB 1921, 12 TC 467.

Speculative purchase and resale of brandy

[59.6] In an excess profits duty case, three members of different firms in the wine trade jointly acquired a quantity of South African brandy in 1916 as a speculation. Most of it was shipped to the UK where it was blended by their firms with French brandy, re-casked and sold in numerous lots over a period ending in September 1917. The CA held that the transactions amounted to a 'trade or business'. *Cape Brandy Syndicate v CIR*, CA 1921, 12 TC 358; [1921] 2 KB 403.

Company holding lease of theatre

[59.7] A company held the lease of a theatre. Its income consisted of rent and interest. The KB held that it was carrying on a trade or business and was liable to EPD. *CIR v Birmingham Theatre Royal Estate Co Ltd*, KB 1923, 12 TC 580.

Property-holding company

[59.8] A company was incorporated to acquire some freehold property with the object of managing it in the interest of the beneficiaries of the wills of two brothers who had previously owned the property. The company's income consisted of rent. The CA unanimously held that it was carrying on a trade or business, within the charge to corporation profits tax. *CIR v Westleigh Estates Co Ltd*, CA 1923, 12 TC 657.

Purchase and resale of whisky in bond

[59.9] In an Irish case, a publican had for many years bought considerable quantities of whisky in bond from a distillery company. Apart from a small amount used in his public house, he resold it to the distillery after four or five years at varying terms, but generally at cost plus an amount for 'interest'. He was free to sell the whisky to others but did not do so. The Commissioners held that he had been carrying on a business for excess profits duty purposes, and the KB upheld their decision. *Representatives of PJ McCall (decd.) v CIR*, KB(I) 1923, 1 ITC 31; 4 ATC 522.

Railway company receiving annuity and interest

[59.10] From 1895 to 1906, a company had owned a railway in India. In 1906 it relinquished possession of the railway to the Secretary of State for India. It received an annuity, which it distributed to its shareholders. Its other income consisted of interest. The HL unanimously held that it was carrying on a trade or business, within the charge to corporation profits tax. Lord Sumner observed that 'the old business still continues of getting some return for capital embarked in the line'. There had not been a complete 'termination of the business formerly carried on'. *CIR v South Behar Railway Co Ltd*, HL 1925, 12 TC 657.

[59.11] The HL decision in *CIR v South Behar Railway Co Ltd*, 59.10 above, was applied by the CS in a subsequent case in which a company, which obtained rent from a railway which it owned and leased, was held to be carrying on a trade or business. *CIR v Edinburgh & Bathgate Railway Co*, CS 1926, 12 TC 895.

[59.12] A similar decision was reached in the Irish case of *CIR v Dublin & Kingstown Railway Co*, HC(I) 1926, 5 ATC 721; 1 ITC 131; [1930] IR 317.

Company deriving income from tramway

[59.13] A company (T) which had owned and operated a tramway sold it to another company for 80 annual payments of £70,660. T subsequently went into liquidation, and its right to receive the annual payments was transferred to a new company (C) with the same shareholders. The KB held that C was carrying on a trade or business. *CIR v City of Buenos Ayres Tramways Co (1904) Ltd*, KB 1926, 12 TC 1125.

Shipping company receiving interest

[59.14] A shipping company had owned five ships. It sold one of these and lost the other four during the First World War. After 1917 (when it received substantial insurance money) its income consisted entirely of interest. The KB held that it was carrying on a trade or business within the charge to corporation profits tax. *CIR v Dale Steamship Co Ltd*, KB 1924, 12 TC 712.

[59.15] In an Irish case, a company which had sold all its ships, but received investment income and made an annual payment under an agreement concluded while it was trading, was held to be carrying on a trade or business. *City of Dublin Steam Packet Co v CIR*, HC(I) 1926, 1 ITC 118; [1926] IR 438.

[59.16] The company in the case noted at **59.15** above subsequently went into liquidation. It was held that, notwithstanding the liquidation, it was still carrying on a trade or business within the charge to corporation profits tax. *City of Dublin Steam Packet Co (in liquidation) v CIR*, HC(I) 1930, 1 ITC 285; [1930] IR 217.

Company ceasing to trade but receiving rental income

[59.17] In a Malaysian case, a company had traded in tobacco, but this proved unprofitable. In 1964 it ceased its tobacco trade and began letting out its factory and warehouse for rent. It subsequently claimed that the losses it had incurred in its trade should be carried forward and set against its rental income. The Malaysian Inland Revenue rejected the claim on the basis that the company was not carrying on any business. The PC allowed the company's appeal (reversing the decision of the Malaysian Federal Court and restoring that of the Special Commissioners). The PC distinguished *Salisbury House Estate Ltd v Fry*, **53.2** SCHEDULE D—SUPERSEDED LEGISLATION, on the grounds that '"business" is a wider concept than "trade"'. Lord Diplock held that 'in the case of a company incorporated for the purpose of making profits for its shareholders any gainful use to which it puts any of its assets prima facie amounts to the carrying on of a business'. He also observed that the carrying on of a business 'usually calls for some activity on the part of whoever carries it on, though, depending on the nature of the business, the activity may be intermittent with long intervals of quiescence in between'. On the evidence, there had been 'activity in and about the letting of its premises by the company during each of the five years that had elapsed since it closed down its former tobacco business'. There had been three successive lettings of the warehouse to different tenants, while the factory had been let to another tenant. The Commissioners had been entitled to find that the company was carrying on a business. *American Leaf Blending Co v Director-General of Inland Revenue (Malaysia)*, PC [1978] STC 561; [1978] 3 WLR 985; [1978] 3 All ER 1185.

[59.18] A company (M) ceased trading but continued to own some former business premises, which it had let to a tenant since 1966, receiving rental income. An associated company (S) claimed small companies' relief. The Revenue restricted the relief under *CTA 2010, ss 24, 25**. S appealed, contending that M was not carrying on a 'trade or business' during the period in question, and should therefore be disregarded, by virtue of *s 25**. The Commissioner allowed S's appeal, holding that M was no longer carrying on a 'trade or business'. The Ch D upheld this decision as one of fact. Lawrence Collins J observed that the case was 'not in any sense an artificial arrangement to take advantage of small companies' rate'. *HMRC v Salaried Persons Postal Loans Ltd*, Ch D [2006] STC 1315; [2006] EWHC 763 (Ch).

Investment company letting out property

[59.19] A company (L) appealed against a corporation tax assessment, contending that it was entitled to small companies' relief. The Revenue rejected the claim on the basis that L had an associated company (C), so that the effect of *CTA 2010, ss 24, 25* was that relief was not due. C was an investment company, which derived rental income from a tenanted residential freehold property. It also made and held investments, made loans, and received dividends, rents and bank interest. It paid administration and other expenses, and distributed its profits to shareholders. L appealed, contending that C's activities did not amount to carrying on business, so that the effect of *s 25** was that it should be disregarded. The Special Commissioner rejected this contention and dismissed L's appeal, holding that C was carrying on business. *Land Management Ltd v Fox*, Sp C [2002] SSCD 152 (Sp C 306).

Company receiving bank interest—whether carrying on a business

[59.20] A company (N) appealed against a corporation tax assessment, contending that it was entitled to small companies' relief. The Revenue rejected the claim on the basis that N had an associated company (W), so that the effect of *CTA 2010, ss 24, 25** was that relief was not due. N appealed, contending that W was not carrying on a 'trade or business' during the period in question, so that the effect of *s 25** was that it should be disregarded. It was accepted that W had carried on no trading activity during the period in question, although it had substantial sums of money in a bank account and had received interest accordingly. The Special Commissioner allowed N's appeal, holding on the evidence that W was 'in a state of suspended animation and carried on no trade or business' during the relevant period. The receipt of interest did not in itself mean that W was carrying on a business of investment. The Ch D upheld this decision as one of fact. *Jowett v O'Neill & Brennan Construction Ltd*, Ch D 1998, 70 TC 566; [1998] STC 482.

Company owning property in France

[59.21] A company (J) appealed against a corporation tax assessment, contending that it was entitled to small companies' relief. The Revenue rejected the claim on the basis that J had an associated company (P), so that the effect of *CTA 2010, ss 24, 25** was that relief was not due. J appealed, contending that P was not carrying on a 'trade or business' during the period in question, so that the effect of *s 25** was that it should be disregarded. P owned a property in France, which was used by the companies' controlling director and his family. The property was not let and the director paid all expenses personally. The Special Commissioner allowed J's appeal, holding that the mere acquisition and holding of a property did not amount to a 'trade or business'. *John M Harris (Design Partnership) Ltd v Lee*, Sp C [1997] SSCD 240 (Sp C 130).

Film production

[59.22] A limited liability partnership (M) claimed that it had made a substantial loss on a trade of exploitation of films, including a loss of more than £13,000,000 on film production and a payment of more than £1,600,000 to a company for 'film consultancy services'. HMRC rejected the claim, considering firstly that M was not trading, since it had effectively sold the master negative of the film in question to a distribution company (P); secondly that because the film had not been completed until after June 2005, any relief to which M was entitled was for 2005/06 rather than 2004/05; and thirdly that the relief due should be restricted under *FA 2005, s 60*. The CA allowed M's appeal in part, holding that M had been carrying on a trade or business of exploiting the film even though it no longer held the ownership of the master negative. Sir Andrew Morritt held that 'the value in a film susceptible of exploitation lies in the copyright, not the physical embodiment of the sequence of images'. (However, the CA upheld HMRC's contention that the relief due should be restricted under *FA 2005, s 60*.) *Micro Fusion 2004-1 Llp v HMRC*, CA 2010. 80 TC 475; [2010] STC 1541; [2010] EWCA Civ 260. (*Notes*. (1) *FA 2005, s 60* was subsequently repealed by *FA 2006, s 178*. (2) The Supreme Court rejected an application by HMRC for leave to appeal against this decision. (3) The decision here was not followed in the subsequent case of *Samarkand Film Partnership No 3 v HMRC*, 59.106 below, on the grounds that it related to superseded legislation which specifically referred to a trade or business, rather than to a trade.)

Income from letting of property—whether a 'business'

[59.23] See also *Rashid v Garcia*, 73.90 NATIONAL INSURANCE CONTRIBUTIONS.

Husbandry—whether a business

[59.24] See *Wernher v CIR*, 59.40 below.

VATA 1994, s 94(4)—definition of 'business' for VAT purposes

[59.25] See *Customs & Excise Commrs v Morrison's Academy Boarding Houses Association*, CS 1977, [1978] STC 1 and *Customs & Excise Commrs v Lord Fisher*, QB [1981] STC 238; [1981] 2 All ER 147. However, although the UK legislation refers to 'business', the relevant EC legislation (*Article 4* of the *EC Sixth Directive*) refers to an 'economic activity'. For VAT cases concerning the definition of 'business' and 'economic activity', see the relevant chapter of Tolley's VAT Cases.

Isolated or speculative transactions

CROSS-REFERENCE

For profits and losses on sales, etc. of investments, see 62.82 *et seq*. TRADING PROFITS.

Purchase and resale of war surplus linen

[59.26] An agricultural machinery merchant, with no previous connection with the linen trade, bought a Government surplus stock of 44,000,000 yards of linen. Negotiations for its resale direct to linen manufacturers fell through, and, to bring pressure on them, he set up an organisation to advertise and sell the linen. As a result, the whole of the linen was sold within a year to numerous purchasers. The Revenue issued an assessment charging tax on the profits. He appealed, contending that the profits were not 'annual profits or gains' within the meaning of the legislation then in force (which became *ICTA 1988, s 18(1)(a)*), because they were made within a single year. The HL unanimously rejected this contention and dismissed his appeal. *Martin v Lowry*, HL 1926, 11 TC 297; [1927] AC 312.

Purchase, conversion and resale of ship

[59.27] Three individuals, not connected in business, jointly purchased a cargo vessel, had it converted into a steam-drifter and sold it at a profit. They had never previously bought a ship. The Revenue assessed them on the profit, and the CS unanimously upheld the assessment. *CIR v Livingston & Others*, CS 1926, 11 TC 538.

Purchase and resale of cotton mills

[59.28] An individual (P) was a member of four different syndicates involved in buying and selling cotton-spinning mills. The syndicate acquired shares in a mill-owning company, liquidated it and sold its assets at a profit to a new company. The Revenue assessed him on his share of the profits of each syndicate. The CA upheld the assessments. *Pickford v Quirke*, CA 1927, 13 TC 251.

[59.29] Two individuals purchased some cotton-spinning plant and resold it in five lots, at a profit. The Revenue assessed them on the profit. The General Commissioners allowed their appeals, finding that there was no trade or adventure in the nature of trade. The HL unanimously allowed the Revenue's appeal and restored the assessments, holding that the only reasonable conclusion on the evidence before the Commissioners was that there had been an adventure in the nature of trade. *Edwards v Bairstow & Harrison*, HL 1955, 36 TC 207; [1956] AC 14; [1955] 3 All ER 48. (*Note*. This is the leading case concerning when the Courts will disturb a finding of fact by Commissioners—see 4.238 APPEALS.)

Purchase and resale of paper

[59.30] The CS held that a profit on an isolated purchase and resale of a large quantity of toilet paper was chargeable to income tax as being from 'an adventure in the nature of trade'. *Rutledge v CIR*, CS 1929, 14 TC 490.

Purchase and illegal resale of whisky

[59.31] Three people acquired a quantity of rye whisky and exported it to the USA, involving a violation of US law and a deception of the UK Customs authorities. The Revenue assessed them on their profits, and the CS upheld the assessment. *Lindsay, Woodward & Hiscox v CIR*, CS 1932, 18 TC 43.

Purchase and resale of whisky in bond

[59.32] The CS held that an isolated purchase and resale of whisky in bond was taxable as an adventure in the nature of trade (reversing the decision of the General Commissioners). *CIR v Fraser*, CS 1942, 24 TC 498.

[59.33] See also *Representatives of PJ McCall (decd.) v CIR*, 59.9 above.

Purchase, repair, and resale of stills

[59.34] A company director bought two stills for £80 each, put them in working order and sold them for £3,750 each, one to each of two companies he controlled. The Revenue assessed him on the profit. The General Commissioners allowed his appeal, holding that this was not an adventure in the nature of trade. The CA upheld their decision as one of fact. *Jenkinson v Freedland*, CA 1961, 39 TC 636. (*Note*. There were unusual circumstances. The judgments indicate that, if the sale had been at arm's length, the profit would have been taxable.)

Purchase and sale of bullion

[59.35] An actor made a profit from the purchase and sale of silver bullion. The Revenue assessed him on the profit. The CA upheld the assessment, holding that the profit was from an adventure in the nature of trade. *Wisdom v Chamberlain*, CA 1968, 45 TC 92; [1969] 1 WLR 275; [1969] 1 All ER 332.

Speculative dealing in commodities

[59.36] See *Wannell v Rothwell*, 35.21 LOSS RELIEF.

Stallion fees

[59.37] A farmer owned a stallion for breeding purposes. The stallion served the mares of other farmers for service fees as well as serving his own mares. The General Commissioners held that the service fees were trading income and chargeable to income tax. The HL unanimously upheld this decision. *Malcolm v Lockhart*, HL 1919, 7 TC 99; [1919] AC 463. (*Note*. This decision was distinguished in the subsequent case of *Lord Glanely v Wightman*, 59.38 below, on the grounds that the services of the stallion in *Malcolm v Lockhart* were sometimes supplied outside the owner's farm, whereas the services of the stallions in *Lord Glanely v Wightman* were only supplied at the owner's stud farm.)

[59.38] The decision in *Malcolm v Lockhart*, 59.37 above, was distinguished in a subsequent case in which no mare was served outside the stud farm. The HL held that, since all the services were supplied at the owner's farm, the fees were part of the farming profits, and were assessable under Schedule B under the legislation then in force. The HL disapproved the decision in the Irish case of *McLaughlin v Bailey*, CA(I) 1920, 7 TC 508. *Lord Glanely v Wightman*, HL 1933, 17 TC 634; [1933] AC 618.

[59.39] In two unrelated appeals which were heard together in the KB, the Revenue had issued assessments on racehorse-owners who had their own breeding establishments. In each case the stallions, as well as serving the owner's mares, served other mares in return for stallion fees. The owners appealed, contending that the stallion fees were the incidental receipts of a non-commercial enterprise. The Special Commissioners dismissed the appeals, holding that the profits from the fees were chargeable to income tax. The KB upheld their decision as one of fact. *Earl of Jersey's Executors v Bassom; Earl of Derby v Bassom*, KB 1926, 10 TC 357.

[59.40] In an appeal against a national defence contribution (profits tax) assessment, the Commissioners found that the letting of the services of stallions was taxable as a separate business from the activity of breeding racehorses for recreational purposes. The KB upheld their decision. The KB also held that husbandry was a business within the charge to national defence contribution (profits tax). *Lady Zia Wernher v CIR*, KB 1942, 29 TC 20; [1942] 1 KB 399.

[59.41] See also *Benson v Counsell*, 39.54 MISCELLANEOUS INCOME, and *Blaney v HMRC*, 71.10 CAPITAL GAINS TAX.

Stallions—whether qualifying for capital allowances

[59.42] See *Earl of Derby v Aylmer*, 8.53 CAPITAL ALLOWANCES, in which stallions were held not to be 'plant'.

Liquidators, etc. and personal representatives

Receiver discontinuing spinning but continuing to supply power

[59.43] A firm which carried on a business of worsted spinning and supplying power to sub-tenants of parts of its premises became insolvent and its assets were assigned to a trustee for the benefit of the creditors. The trustee discontinued the spinning but continued the supplying of power. The QB held that he was carrying on a business and was assessable on the profits, even though they were required to be applied for the benefit of the creditors. *Armitage v Moore*, QB 1900, 4 TC 199; [1900] 2 QB 363. (*Note*. The report of the case does not specifically state whether the assessments were on the basis that the trustee was continuing to carry on the trade of the insolvent firm. However, it is believed that this was the case.)

Sale of stock of whisky by liquidator

[59.44] In a Northern Ireland case, a whisky-distilling company went into liquidation in August 1920. The liquidator ceased distilling operations in March 1921, but continued to sell off the stock until March 1923. The Recorder held that the liquidator was not trading from April 1921. The KB upheld this decision as one of fact. *CIR v 'Old Bushmills' Distillery Co Ltd*, KB(NI) 1927, 12 TC 1148. (*Note*. For a previous appeal by the same company, see **4.74** APPEALS.)

Completion by liquidator of contracts of film company

[59.45] A company which carried on business as film distributors went into liquidation. The liquidator transferred its assets to two new companies but retained the benefit of contracts made, or about to be made, for exhibiting films in hand at the liquidation. It was agreed that the new companies were to carry out the contracts, paying the liquidator 90% of the proceeds as regards existing contracts, and 80% as regards new contracts. The Special Commissioners held that the arrangements amounted to trading by the liquidator, through the new companies as agents. The KB upheld their decision. *Baker v Cook*, KB 1937, 21 TC 337; [1937] 3 All ER 509.

Receiver continues trading—whether new trade set up

[59.46] See *CIR v Thompson*, **61.65** TRADING INCOME.

Winding-up of business by trader's personal representatives

[59.47] A wholesale jeweller died in June 1927. His sisters acted as his executrices. They were unable to sell the business as a going concern, and sold the stock over a period of nine months. The Revenue issued assessments on the basis that the executrices were trading. The Special Commissioners upheld the assessments and the KB dismissed the executrices' appeal. *Weisberg's Executrices v CIR*, KB 1933, 17 TC 696.

[59.48] A testator's will directed his executors to wind up his trawling and other businesses within three years of his death. Vaisey J held that the winding up of the businesses amounted to trading (reversing the decision of the Commissioners). *Wood v Black's Executor; CIR v Black's Executor*, HC 1952, 33 TC 172.

[59.49] A tenant farmer and cattle dealer and feeder died in November 1951. His trustees completed contracts he had entered into for the winter feeding of cattle on the farm. The Revenue issued assessments charging tax on their profits. The trustees appealed, contending that they were not trading but realising the deceased's estate to its best advantage. The CS rejected this contention and upheld the assessments, holding that the activities amounted to trading. *Pattullo's Trustees v CIR*, CS 1955, 36 TC 87.

[59.50] A farmer, whose sole farming interest was a pedigree herd of Aberdeen Angus cattle, died in March 1955. The Special Commissioners held that the activities of his testamentary trustee up to May 1956, including the sale of the herd, were directed to disposing of the herd and farm and did not constitute the carrying on of the trade of farming. The CS upheld their decision as one of fact. *CIR v Donaldson's Trustees*, CS 1963, 41 TC 161.

Completion and sale of vessel under construction at death

[59.51] In a case where the facts were unusual, the CA held that executors were not liable to excess profits duty on the profit from their sale of a ship which was being built for the deceased but was not completed until after his death. *Cohan's Executors v CIR*, CA 1924, 12 TC 602.

Property dealers—sales after death of partner

[59.52] See *Marshall's Executors & Others v Joly*, 67.58 TRADING PROFITS, and *Newbarns Syndicate v Hay*, 67.59 TRADING PROFITS.

Dealing in shares

'Dividend-stripping'

[59.53] A solicitor took part in an elaborate 'dividend-stripping' scheme, involving the setting up of a chain of companies, which purported to declare a dividend out of a capital reserve created by a sum of money which passed along the chain, and the manufacture of an alleged dealing loss of almost £3,000,000. The CA held that the transactions did not amount to trading (so that the alleged loss could not be set against the tax deemed to have been deducted from the dividend). Donovan LJ described the transactions as 'a cheap exercise in fiscal conjuring and book-keeping phantasy, involving a gross abuse of the *Companies Act* and having as its unworthy object the extraction from the Exchequer of an enormous sum which the appellant had never paid in tax and to which he has no shadow of a right whatsoever'. Lord Evershed expressed 'great regret that the engineer of this extraordinary scheme should be a member of the profession of solicitor'. *Johnson v Jewitt*, CA 1961, 40 TC 231.

[59.54] In a subsequent case, the HL unanimously held that shares which were held for five years after the 'dividend-stripping' operations were not held as trading stock. Lord Morris observed that the shares 'were not acquired for the purposes of dealing with them. In no ordinary sense were they current assets. For the purpose of carrying out the scheme which was devised the shares were to be and had to be retained.' *Finsbury Securities Ltd v Bishop*, HL 1966, 43 TC 591; [1966] 1 WLR 1402; [1966] 3 All ER 105.

[59.55] The decision in *Finsbury Securities Ltd v Bishop*, 59.54 above, was applied in a subsequent case where the Ch D upheld the Revenue's contention that 'dividend-stripping' operations did not constitute trading. *Cooper v Sandiford Investments Ltd*, Ch D 1967, 44 TC 355; [1967] 1 WLR 1351; [1967] 3 All ER 835.

[59.56] The decision in *Finsbury Securities Ltd v Bishop*, 59.54 above, was also applied in another subsequent case where the HL unanimously held that 'dividend-stripping' operations did not constitute trading. Lord Morris upheld *dicta* of Megarry J that 'neither fiscal elements nor fiscal motives will prevent what in substance is a trading transaction from ranking as such. On the other hand, if the greater part of the transaction is explicable only on fiscal grounds, the mere presence of elements of trading will not suffice to translate the transaction into the realms of trading. In particular, if what is erected is predominantly an artificial structure, remote from trading and fashioned so as to secure a tax advantage, the mere presence in that structure of certain elements which by themselves could fairly be described as trading will not cast the cloak of trade over the whole structure.' Viscount Dilhorne and Lord Donovan held that *JP Harrison (Watford) Ltd v Griffiths*, HL 1962, 40 TC 281; [1963] AC 1, had been wrongly decided. *Lupton v FA & AB Ltd*, HL 1971, 47 TC 580; [1972] AC 634; [1971] 3 All ER 948. (*Note*. The reasoning in this case was applied by the HL in *Ensign Tankers (Leasing) Ltd v Stokes*, 59.85 below.)

[59.57] A similar decision was reached in *Thomson v Gurneville Securities Ltd*, HL 1971, 47 TC 633; [1972] AC 661; [1971] 3 All ER 1071.

Losses on stock exchange transactions by company

[59.58] A company trading as fruit and vegetable dealers began buying and selling shares through the Stock Exchange, and in so doing carried out numerous transactions. This activity gave rise to losses on which the company claimed relief. The Revenue rejected the claim but the Ch D allowed the company's appeal (reversing the decision of the Special Commissioners). Pennycuick J observed that the company was prohibited from gambling by its Articles of Association, and held that the only reasonable conclusion on the evidence was that the company was carrying on the trade of a dealer in securities. *Lewis Emanuel & Son Ltd v White*, Ch D 1965, 42 TC 369. (*Note*. See now *CTA 2010, ss 36–44*, deriving from *FA 1991*.)

[59.59] In 1961 a company, which had been treated as an investment company for tax purposes since 1953, made a substantial loss on the sale of shares in a hire-purchase company. It claimed loss relief on the basis that it was carrying on a trade of dealing in securities. The Revenue rejected the claim. The Commissioners dismissed the company's appeal and the Ch D upheld their decision. *Halefield Securities Ltd v Thorpe*, Ch D 1967, 44 TC 154.

[59.60] In 1976 a company which carried on business as footwear manufacturers made substantial investments in gilts. It made 13 purchases and sales between April and December 1976 but, because of a fall in the gilts market, they resulted in an overall loss of £96,587. The company claimed that the loss arose from a separate trade, and was available for set-off against its profit from its main trade. The General Commissioners allowed the claim and the Ch D upheld their decision as one of fact. *Cooper v C & J Clark Ltd*, Ch D 1982, 54 TC 670; [1982] STC 335.

Losses on share transactions by individual

[59.61] An individual (S) speculated on the Stock Exchange, made a loss, and claimed relief under *ITA 2007, s 64**. The Revenue rejected his claim and the Commissioners dismissed his appeal, holding that his transactions did not constitute a trade. The Ch D upheld their decision as one of fact. *Salt v Chamberlain*, Ch D 1979, 53 TC 143; [1979] STC 750.

[59.62] The decision in *Salt v Chamberlain*, **59.61** above, was applied in the similar subsequent case of *Dr KMA Manzur v HMRC*, FTT [2010] UKFTT 580 (TC), TC00830.

Sale of shares held as capital asset

[59.63] In a Hong Kong case, a company (B) was incorporated to develop certain properties. It was jointly-owned by two other Hong Kong companies. It acquired shares in another company (R), which in turn owned more than 52% of the shares in a company owning valuable land. B sold its shares in R five months later, making a large profit. The Hong Kong Revenue assessed this as a trading profit but the PC allowed B's appeal. Lord Keith observed that B had not been incorporated for the purpose of dealing in shares. The shares had been held as a capital asset, which had been sold after the receipt of 'a fortuitous offer at a very good price'. *Beautiland Co Ltd v Hong Kong Commr of Inland Revenue*, PC [1991] STC 467.

[59.64] In a New Zealand case, a company (R) had been incorporated in 1937. It consistently made long-term investments in shares and, on occasion, made substantial profits on their disposal. Until 1983 the Revenue accepted that these profits were capital gains, but they issued assessments charging tax on the disposal of shares acquired after March 1983, on the basis that R was carrying on a business of dealing in shares. R appealed, contending that there had been no change in its policy and that the profits should continue to be treated as capital gains. The High Court allowed the appeal, holding that R was not carrying on a business of dealing in shares (except with regard to three specific transactions which were held to be taxable on the grounds that the shares had been purchased for resale at a profit). The Privy Council upheld this decision. Applying *dicta* of Hill J in the Australian case of *Federal Commissioner of Taxation v Radnor Property Ltd*, [1991] 102 ALR 187, 'the question whether the respondent was carrying on a business of dealing in shares is a question of fact and degree'. Applying *dicta* of Viscount Radcliffe in *Edwards v Bairstow & Harrison*, **59.29** above, 'it could not be said to be wrong to arrive at a conclusion one way or the other'. *Rangatira Ltd v New Zealand Commissioner of Inland Revenue*, PC 1996, [1997] STC 47.

Insurance company—profits from sale of investments

[59.65] See *Northern Assurance Company v Russell*, **68.64** TRADING PROFITS.

Investment trust company—whether dealing in shares

[59.66] See *Scottish Investment Trust Company v Forbes*, 62.82 TRADING PROFITS.

Purchase and sale of shares in associated company

[59.67] A company (N) was incorporated in July 1991 as a subsidiary member of a group. In October 1991 it acquired a substantial number of shares in a fellow-subsidiary (B). These shares had a large in-built chargeable gain which would, *prima facie*, become taxable on an actual or deemed disposal of the shares. They were purchased from other companies in the group, and N had to borrow the purchase price of £54,000,000 from its holding company. Five days later N sold the shares to an outside purchaser. The Revenue issued an estimated assessment on the gain. N appealed, contending that it had acquired the shares as trading stock and had subsequently acquired a number of government securities and four freehold properties as trading stock, with the result that it was entitled to set losses on the freehold properties against the gain on the shares. (The freehold properties had been acquired from other companies in the group between eight and nine months after the sale of the shares.) The Special Commissioners rejected N's contentions and dismissed the appeal (subject to agreement as to figures). On the evidence, the transactions had been conceived for the 'special purpose' of fragmenting the shareholding in B. The shares in B had not been transferred to N as trading stock. The government securities had been purchased for the fiscal purpose of keeping N's accounting period in order to shelter the gain on the shares in B, but their purchase was in the nature of an investment rather than as part of a trade. At the time the freehold properties were acquired, N was not trading in government securities. The fact that N's transactions in such securities subsequently increased to a point where they might qualify as trading was not material. The transfer of the properties to N was 'dictated by purely fiscal considerations, namely the need to shelter the gain on the B shares by acquiring loss-bearing assets'. Accordingly, the properties had not become trading stock in N's hands. (The Commissioners also observed that, even if N had been held to be trading in the properties, the effect of *ICTA 1988, s 12(3)* was that the relevant losses would have been deemed to be realised in an accounting period after that in which N had made the gain on the shares.) *N Ltd v HM Inspector of Taxes*, Sp C [1996] SSCD 346 (Sp C 90).

Miscellaneous activities

Cases held to constitute trading

Systematic betting

[59.68] The QB held that profits from systematic and habitual betting on horse racing were from carrying on a vocation, and taxable. Denman J held that 'in my opinion, if a man carried on a systematic business of receiving stolen goods and made by it £2,000 a year, the Income Tax Commissioners would be right in assessing him thereon'. *Partridge v Mallandaine*, QB 1886, 2 TC 179; [1886] 18 QBD 276. (*Note*. The assessment was on two people in partnership, and the appellants stated that 'they attended race courses as bookmakers or betters on horse racing' but that 'they did not take commissions for betting'. Presumably they were recognised bookmakers who did not take off-course bets.)

Newspaper articles based on betting systems

[59.69] A racing tipster devised a system of horse race betting and received payments from newspapers for articles based on the system. The Revenue issued assessments on the payments. He appealed, contending that the effect of the decision in *Graham v Green*, **59.93** below, was that they were not taxable. The KB rejected this contention and upheld the assessments. *Graham v Arnott*, KB 1941, 24 TC 157.

Illegal trading

[59.70] During the 1920s the Province of Ontario, unlike the rest of Canada, prohibited the sale of alcohol. A trader who sold alcohol ('bootlegging') in Ontario was assessed to Canadian excess profits tax. He appealed, contending that his profits were not assessable because his activities were illegal under Ontario legislation. The Privy Council rejected this contention and upheld the assessments. Lord Haldane held that 'once the character of a business has been ascertained as being in the nature of a trade, the person who carried it out cannot found upon the elements of illegality to evade the tax'. *Canadian Minister of Finance v Smith*, PC 1926, 5 ATC 621; [1927] AC 193.

[59.71] A trader carried on a business of operating automatic machines on piers, etc. He also made profits from selling and hiring 'fruit' machines, the use of which was illegal in this country at the time. He was assessed on the profits and appealed, contending that the profits were not chargeable since they were from an unlawful business. The KB rejected this contention and upheld the assessments, holding that the profits were chargeable to income tax. *Mann v Nash*, KB 1932, 16 TC 523; [1913] 1 KB 752.

[59.72] The KB held that the profits of a bookmaker, derived solely from forms of betting which were illegal under the law at the time, were chargeable to income tax. *Southern v AB*, KB 1933, 18 TC 59; [1933] 1 KB 713.

Prostitution—whether trading

[59.73] In the case noted at **43.9** PAYMENT OF TAX, a prostitute contended her profits from prostitution were not taxable. The CA unanimously rejected this contention and dismissed her appeals, holding that prostitution was a trade, and that the provision of services for money was within the charge to income tax. *CIR v Aken*, CA 1990, 63 TC 395; [1990] STC 497; [1990] 1 WLR 1374.

Committee operating golf course owned by town council

[59.74] A committee consisting of representatives of a town council and local golf clubs managed and maintained a golf course which the council owned. The CS unanimously held that the committee was carrying on a trade and was taxable on the surplus of its receipts over its expenses. *Carnoustie Golf Course Committee v CIR*, CS 1929, 14 TC 498.

Recreation ground

[59.75] Under a private Act of Parliament, trustees managed a recreation ground with tennis and bowls facilities. Users were charged for admission. The CS held that the trustees were trading. *CIR v Stonehaven Recreation Ground Trustees*, CS 1929, 15 TC 419.

Greyhound breeding

[59.76] A farmer had bred dogs for many years, for the purpose of his hobby of coursing greyhounds. Before 1945, he gave away or destroyed unwanted puppies. However, from 1945 to 1950 (when he gave up breeding) he sold all healthy surplus puppies. The Revenue issued assessments for 1946/47 to 1948/49 charging tax on the profits. He appealed, contending that he had bred the puppies as a hobby. The Commissioners upheld the assessments, holding that the sale of puppies had become an adventure in the nature of trade. The Ch D upheld their decision as one of fact. *Hawes v Gardiner*, Ch D 1957, 37 TC 671.

Company promotion

[59.77] A stockbroker (K) incorporated a private company (O) for the purpose of promoting a public company. The Revenue issued assessments on O, charging tax on its profits from the purchase and sale of shares. O appealed, contending that it was acting as an agent for K. The Commissioners dismissed the appeals, holding that O was trading. The KB upheld their decision. *OK Trust Ltd v Rees*, KB 1940, 23 TC 217.

Exploitation of derelict gold mines by promotion of mining companies

[59.78] See *Murphy v Australian Machinery & Investment Co Ltd*, **60.30** TRADING INCOME.

Purchase and resale of mining claim

[59.79] In a Rhodesian case, a UK company acquired a mining claim in Rhodesia and, after spending £2,000 on its development, sold it shortly afterwards to another associated UK company. The PC held that the profit was a trading profit (and was chargeable to Rhodesian tax even though the relevant contracts had been made in London). *Rhodesia Metals Ltd (in liquidation) v Commissioner of Taxes*, PC 1940, 19 ATC 472; [1940] AC 774; [1940] 3 All ER 422.

Sale of purchased endowment policies

[59.80] Between 1937 and 1939 a mathematician purchased a large number of endowment policies on other people's lives, having chosen the dates of maturity with the aim of providing an income of £7,000 a year for personal expenditure until 1960. In 1942 he decided to settle in India, and sold all the unmatured policies except for a small number which he gave away. The Revenue issued assessments for 1938/39 to 1942/43, charging tax on the profits from the maturity or sale of the policies. The CA unanimously upheld the assessments, holding that they were from a concern in the nature of trade. *Smith Barry v Cordy*, CA 1946, 28 TC 250; [1946] 2 All ER 396. (*Note*. The decision was questioned in the HL in *Ransom v Higgs*, **59.99** below.)

Purchase and resale of amusement equipment

[59.81] A trader appealed against estimated assessments, contending that much of his profits had resulted from the purchase and resale of certain amusement equipment. The Commissioners held that these profits were from an adventure or concern in the nature of trade, and were chargeable to income tax. The KB upheld their decision. *Crole v Lloyd*, KB 1950, 31 TC 338.

Sale of boats previously used for passenger services

[59.82] A company carried on a business of shipbuilding and repairing. It also operated passenger services, although these were temporarily ceased in 1939 when its boats were requisitioned by the Admiralty. After the end of the Second World War some of the boats were returned by the Admiralty, and the company purchased others so that it could recommence the passenger services. It subsequently sold twelve boats, two of which had never been used in the passenger services, at a profit. The Commissioners held that the profits from the sales should be included in the income tax assessments on the company. The CA unanimously dismissed the company's appeal, holding that the Commissioners were entitled to find that the profits were trading receipts. *J Bolson & Son Ltd v Farrelly*, CA 1953, 34 TC 161.

Promotion of driving schools

[59.83] Between 1955 and 1959 a trader started 30 driving schools. Once the schools were in operation, he transferred them to companies, partly for cash and partly for shares. He accepted the Special Commissioners' decision that the consideration which he received was taxable as trading income, except with regard to the first transaction, which he contended was capital. The Ch D dismissed his appeal, holding that the Commissioners were entitled to take the subsequent 29 transactions into account in throwing light on the first transaction. *Leach v Pogson*, Ch D 1962, 40 TC 585.

Dormant company selling debts and securities—whether trading

[59.84] A banking company (W) had made substantial loans, secured on property. Because of the poor state of the property market, its parent company decided that it would be desirable to take the debts and securities out of W's books, and in 1974 and 1975 they were transferred at face value to an associated company (T), which was then more or less dormant. Most of the securities were sold in the year to 31 March 1978, at a substantial loss. T claimed that the loss was a trading loss, which could be surrendered to its parent company as group relief. The Revenue rejected the claim but the Ch D allowed the appeals. Harman J held that T had undertaken the transactions in the hope of a profit, and that was trading. *Torbell Investments Ltd & Others v Williams*, Ch D 1986, 59 TC 357; [1986] STC 397.

Financing of film production—whether trading

[59.85] In the case noted at 8.100 CAPITAL ALLOWANCES, the Revenue contended that two limited partnerships, set up to finance film production, were not trading, since the transactions in question had tax avoidance as their motive. The appellant company contended that the transactions into which the partnerships had entered constituted trading, and that the presence of a subjective fiscal motive could not affect the objective nature of the transactions. The HL held that since the production and exploitation of a film was a trading activity, expenditure for the purpose of producing and exploiting a commercial film was incurred for a commercial purpose. Where the objective purpose of expenditure was a trading purpose, the fact that the subjective motive underlying the transaction may have been fiscal, rather than trading, did not render the expenditure disallowable. *Ensign Tankers (Leasing) Ltd v Stokes*, HL 1992, 64 TC 617; [1992] STC 226; [1992] 2 WLR 469; [1992] 2 All ER 275. (*Note*. See also, with regard to the distinction between motive and purpose, the judgment of Lord Simonds in *Smith's Potato Estates Ltd v Bolland*, **63.156** TRADING PROFITS.)

Commercial agent

[59.86] A commercial agent received income (salary and commission) from five firms. He appealed against an excess profits tax assessment, contending that he was an employee of each of the firms, and was not carrying on any trade or business. The Special Commissioners rejected this contention and dismissed his appeal, and the KB upheld their decision. *Marsh v CIR*, KB 1943, 29 TC 120.

Video and television technician—whether a trader or an employee

[59.87] An individual (B) notified the Revenue that he was self-employed as a video and television technician. The Revenue accepted this and issued assessments, which were settled by agreement under *TMA, s 54*. Subsequently the Revenue discovered that B had received undisclosed income from work carried out for a partnership, and issued further assessments charging tax on this income. B appealed, contending that he should be treated as an employee of the partnership. The General Commissioners rejected this contention and dismissed his appeal, finding that B had chosen 'to be a self-employed technician' and holding that 'the relationship between the parties was one providing a contract for services'. The Ch D upheld their decision as one of fact. *Barnett v Brabyn*, Ch D 1996, 69 TC 133; [1996] STC 716.

Builder refurbishing clinic—whether an employee of doctor

[59.88] A doctor arranged for a builder (C) to refurbish the clinic from which he practised. C did not include the income from this work in his accounts. Following an enquiry, HMRC issued assessments charging tax on this income. C appealed, contending that he should be treated as an employee of the doctor. The First-tier Tribunal rejected this contention and dismissed his appeal. *T Coffey (t/a Coffey Builders) v HMRC*, FTT [2012] UKFTT 193 (TC), TC01888.

Toolmaker—whether a trader or an employee

[59.89] HMRC issued a discovery assessment charging tax on an individual who worked as a toolmaker at a car plant. He appealed, contending that he should be treated as an employee. The First-tier Tribunal rejected this contention and dismissed his appeal. *LC Meynell-Smith v HMRC*, FTT [2013] UKFTT 113 (TC), TC02531.

Catering by stewardess at golf club—whether trading

[59.90] A golf club employed a stewardess, who was required to provide catering services. The Revenue issued an assessment charging tax on her profits from this. She appealed, contending that she had been an employee of the club. The General Commissioners rejected this contention and dismissed her appeal, and the Ch D upheld their decision. On the evidence, the stewardess had been carrying on the catering business on her own account. The club had no entitlement to, or participation in, the receipts or profits of the catering business, and did not even have any right to know their amount. *McManus v Griffiths (and related appeal)*, Ch D 1997, 70 TC 218; [1997] STC 1089.

Lecturer—whether carrying on trade of publishing

[59.91] In 1983 a lecturer (S) published a book which he had written himself. In 1994 he published, in booklet form, a lecture which had been given more than 80 years previously. The Revenue issued assessments on the basis that S was acting as a professional author. S appealed, contending that, in addition to being a professional author, he had begun a separate trade of publishing when he published the lecture. The Special Commissioner accepted this contention and allowed his appeal in principle, applying *CIR v Maxse*, **62.1** TRADING PROFITS. *Salt v Fernandez*, Sp C [1997] SSCD 271 (Sp C 135). (*Note.* For subsequent developments in this case, see **53.19** SCHEDULE D.)

Sub-underwriting commissions received by pension scheme trustees

[59.92] See *Clarke v The Trustees of British Telecom Pension Scheme*, **46.13** PENSION SCHEMES.

Cases held not to constitute trading

Systematic betting

[59.93] A professional gambler (G) habitually bet on horse races from his house. He was not a bookmaker and did not attend race meetings. The Revenue issued an assessment charging tax on his winnings. The KB allowed G's appeal, holding that his winnings were not taxable. Rowlatt J observed that, if gambling winnings were held to be taxable, 'a gentleman earning a profit in some recognised form of industry but having the bad habit of frequently, persistently, continuously and systematically betting with bookmakers, might set off the losses by which he squandered the fruits of his industry, for Income Tax purposes, against his profits'. *Graham v Green*, KB 1925, 9 TC 309; [1925] 2 KB 37.

Illegal sweepstakes

[59.94] In an Irish case, a turf commission agent was assessed on his profits from promoting two large sweepstakes. Under the law then in force, the carrying on of the sweepstakes was a criminal offence, although they were extensively advertised and the State took no steps against them. The Irish Supreme Court held that the profits were not taxable, on the grounds that the Revenue cannot, unless expressly authorised, tax profits from activities which the State has declared to be unlawful. The decision in *Canadian Minister of*

Finance v Smith, 59.70 above, was distinguished as in that case the tax had been imposed by the Dominion and the activities were declared unlawful by the Province. *Hayes v Duggan*, SC(I) 1928, 1 ITC 269; [1929] IR 406. (*Note.* The decision was referred to but not followed in the UK cases of *Mann v Nash*, 59.71 above, and *Southern v AB*, 59.72 above.)

Realisation of war surplus stocks of wool

[59.95] In an Australian case, the PC held that a company, which had been set up in accordance with an agreement between the British and Australian Governments for the sale of surplus wool acquired by the British Government under wartime arrangements, was realising capital assets and was not trading. *Australian Commissioner of Taxes v British Australian Wool Realisation Association Ltd*, PC 1930, [1931] AC 224.

Extraction of timber from land being developed as oil palm plantation

[59.96] See *Mamor Sdn Bhd v Malaysian Director-General of Inland Revenue*, 61.61 TRADING INCOME.

Engineer—whether a trader or an employee

[59.97] An engineer acted as a representative in the London area for two companies, one based in Devon and one in Manchester. He appealed against an excess profits tax assessment, contending that he was an employee of each of the companies and was not carrying on any trade or business. The General Commissioners accepted this contention and allowed his appeal. The KB upheld their decision as one of fact. *CIR v Turnbull*, KB 1943, 29 TC 133.

Administration of scheme for holidays with pay

[59.98] A company (B) administered a scheme for holidays with pay for employees in the building and civil engineering contracting industries. Under the scheme, the employers paid B for stamps, which B redeemed on the presentation of stamped cards. B accumulated a substantial surplus from unpresented stamps. The Revenue issued an assessment charging tax on the surplus, but the Ch D allowed B's appeal. Danckwerts J held that it was not carrying on a trade. *Building & Civil Engineering Holidays Scheme Management Ltd v Clark*, Ch D 1960, 39 TC 12.

Tax avoidance arrangements—whether a trade

[59.99] H and his wife held the shares of companies (the H companies) which owned undeveloped land which cost £87,000 but which, on development, could be expected to yield a profit of about £200,000. They also held the shares of a development company, C. On the advice of X, a finance company, in which they held no interest, a partnership was set up between Mrs H and two X subsidiaries in which Mrs H had a 90% interest. She settled this interest on discretionary trusts for the benefit of herself, her husband and her issue. The partnership then bought the land from the H companies for £87,000, the trustees of the settlement sold their partnership interest to X for £170,000 and the partnership sold the land to an X company for a small profit. The X group then appointed C as its agent to develop and sell the land. If the profit exceeded

£200,000, C was to keep the excess; if it was less, C was to make it up to that figure. The result was that X derived a certain profit of £30,000 from the transactions and any further profit on the development remained with H and his wife, of which up to £170,000 reached the trustees. The Revenue assessed H on the basis that the £170,000 was the profit of a trade carried on by him and made an alternative assessment on the trustees as the persons in receipt of the profits of the trade. The Special Commissioners held that H was trading but the HL reversed their decision, holding that, by merely procuring others to enter into a scheme which involved trading by some of those others on their own account, H did not himself engage in any trade. Lord Reid defined a trade as 'operations of a commercial character by which the trader provides to customers for reward some kind of goods or services'. Lord Simon of Glaisdale held that 'where an appeal lies only on a point of law, the appellate tribunal ought only to interfere with a decision falling within "the no-man's land" of fact and degree if a plain error shows that the instance tribunal must have misdirected itself in law'. However, on the evidence, the only reasonable conclusion was that H was not trading. *Ransom v Higgs (and associated appeals)*, HL 1974, 50 TC 1; [1974] STC 539; [1974] 1 WLR 1594; [1974] 3 All ER 949.

[59.100] An individual (F) entered into a tax avoidance scheme, notified under *FA 2004, Part 7*. In his 2006/07 return he claimed that he had begun self-employment as a car dealer, with no turnover and a tax loss of £5,000,284, largely attributable to finance charges. HMRC began an enquiry and issued an amendment to F's return, rejecting the loss claim. F appealed. The First-tier Tribunal dismissed his appeal. Judge Bishopp held that this was not 'a trade seriously pursued with a view to profit', since 'the supposed traders care nothing about the profit and, moreover, have not in reality put any money at risk'. From F's perspective, 'this was not a trade but a means of securing tax relief'. *E Flanagan v HMRC (and related appeals)*, FTT [2014] UKFTT 175 (TC); [2014] SFTD 881, TC03314. (*Note*. See also now *ITA 2007, ss 74A-74D*, introduced by *FA 2008*.)

Overseas partnership to exploit talents of television entertainer

[59.101] See *Newstead v Frost*, 53.12 SCHEDULE D.

Company providing finance for restaurant

[59.102] A company, which was a member of a group, provided finance for another member of the group which operated a restaurant. It appealed against corporation tax assessments, contending that it was carrying on a trade and that the advances which it made to its fellow-subsidiary were deductible in computing its profits. The Commissioners dismissed its appeal, holding on the evidence that none of the advances made by the company were made in the course of any trade of banking or money-lending, and that the company was not carrying on any trade. The Ch D upheld the Commissioners' decision. *Stone & Temple Ltd v Waters; Astrawall (UK) Ltd v Waters*, Ch D 1994, 67 TC 145; [1995] STC 1.

British Olympic Association

[59.103] The Revenue issued assessments on the British Olympic Association, computed on the basis that the Association was carrying on a trade. The Special Commissioner allowed the Association's appeal, holding that its 'activities as a whole are uncommercial and do not constitute a trade'. The fact that the Association sought commercial sponsorship was not conclusive. *British Olympic Association v Winter*, Sp C [1995] SSCD 85 (Sp C 28).

Management of golfers

[59.104] A pharmacist (M) had two sons, who were both professional golfers. He submitted tax returns claiming loss relief on the basis that he was carrying on a trade of managing professional golfers. HMRC rejected the claim and the First-tier Tribunal dismissed M's appeal, finding that his activities were aimed at fostering his sons' careers, and did not constitute 'a trading venture'. *PI Murtagh v HMRC*, FTT [2013] UKFTT 352 (TC), TC02754.

Reinsurance broker—whether trading

[59.105] An individual (S) was employed by a company as a reinsurance broker. He submitted tax returns claiming that he was also carrying on a separate trade as a 'reinsurance and business consultant', and that he had incurred losses in this trade. Following an enquiry, HMRC issued amendments to S's returns on the basis that he was not carrying on any trade. The First-tier Tribunal dismissed S's appeal, finding that he had not shown that he was 'conducting any trade or profession'. *J Shah v HMRC*, FTT [2014] UKFTT 432 (TC), TC03561.

Sale and leaseback of films—whether trading

[59.106] Two partnerships claimed that they had incurred substantial losses from the sale and leaseback of films. HMRC rejected the claims on the grounds that the partnerships had not been trading. The partnerships appealed. The First-Tier Tribunal reviewed the evidence in detail and dismissed the appeals, declining to follow the earlier decision in *Micro Fusion 2004-1 Llp v HMRC*, 59.22 above, on the grounds that the legislation at issue in that case had specifically referred to a 'trade or business', rather than simply to a trade. Judge Hellier held that the partnerships were not trading, and that 'the partners were not entitled to sideways loss relief because the businesses of the partnerships were not carried on on a commercial basis with a view of profit'. *Samarkand Film Partnership No 3 v HMRC (and related appeals)*, FTT [2011] UKFTT 610 (TC); [2012] SFTD 1, TC01453.

Purchase and sale of film rights—whether trading

[59.107] A bank marketed a tax avoidance scheme whereby, in a complex series of transactions, a film company (GF) sold the rights in two films to a hedge fund manager (D) for a nominal price of £21,900,000. D was only required to pay £4,800,000 of this, as the balance of £17,100,000 was lent to him by a company associated with GF. Later on the same day D assigned the rights to GD (another company associated with GF) for £881,000. D claimed the difference as a trading loss. HMRC rejected the claim on the basis that D was not trading, and that the aim of the transactions was not to make profits but to 'generate artificial tax losses for the participants'. D appealed, contending that he was carrying on a trade of acquiring and exploiting film distribution rights. The First-tier Tribunal rejected this contention and dismissed D's appeal, holding that D was not carrying on a trade. Judge Blewitt held that 'the sole purpose of the scheme, and therefore the sole purpose of (D's) participation therein, was to shelter his taxable income'. *P Degorce v HMRC*, FTT [2013] UKFTT 178 (TC); [2013] SFTD 806, TC02593.

Licensing and distribution of film rights—whether trading

[59.108] A limited liability partnership (E) entered into a complex series of transactions in relation to the licensing and distribution of film rights. The partners made substantial claims to tax relief under *ICTA 1988, s 353*. HMRC began an enquiry into E's tax return for 2006/07, and subsequently issued a closure notice, determining that E had not been carrying on a trade, so that the partners were not entitled to the tax relief which they had claimed. The First-tier Tribunal reviewed the evidence in detail and dismissed E's appeal against this decision, observing that 'the profit over a twenty-year period, year by year, is determined at the outset, and is determined without any reference to the success or otherwise of the exploitation of the rights sub-licensed. In these circumstances we cannot realistically regard the profit as the speculative profit of a trading venture consisting of the exploitation of film rights'. The transactions which E had entered into 'did not have the speculative aspect which we would expect to see in trading transactions'. Its activities amounted to a 'non-trade business', within *ITTOIA 2005, s 609*. E appealed to the Upper Tribunal, which upheld the First-tier decision. Sales J observed that the main income streams from the films involved 'no prospect of loss or gain'. He held that 'an element of speculation in the sense of conducting an activity which might result in a profit or a loss is strongly indicative of that activity being capable of having the character of trading, and the absence of such an element is strongly indicative that it is not a trading activity'. *Eclipse Film Partners No 35 Llp v HMRC (No 4)*, UT [2013] UKUT 639 (TCC); [2014] STC 1114. (*Notes*. (1) For preliminary issues in this case, see **4.113** APPEALS and **55.31** SELF-ASSESSMENT. (2) For the award of costs, see **4.456** APPEALS. (3) For HMRC's practice following this decision, see the HMRC Notice issued on 28 March 2014.)

Ownership of racehorse

[59.109] A doctor (M) submitted a tax return claiming loss relief on the ownership of a racehorse. HMRC rejected the claim on the basis that this did not amount to trading. The First-tier Tribunal dismissed M's appeal against this decision. *Dr ELJ McMorris v HMRC*, FTT [2014] UKFTT 1116 (TC), TC04204.

[59.110] See also *Norman v Evans*, **39.58** MISCELLANEOUS INCOME.

Speculative dealing in commodities

[59.111] See *Wannell v Rothwell*, **35.21** LOSS RELIEF.

Leaseback transaction—whether trading

[59.112] See *CIR v Richmond & Jones (re Loquitur Ltd)*, 13.9 COMPANY LIQUIDATION AND RECEIVERSHIP.

Underwriting—external name—whether carrying on a trade

[59.113] See *Koenigsberger v Mellor*, 46.22 PENSION SCHEMES.

60

Trading Income—Territorial Scope (ITTOIA 2005, s 6)

The cases in this chapter are arranged under the following headings.

Individuals resident in the UK

Trade managed abroad but controlled from UK

[60.1] An individual living in Aberdeen owned a merchanting business in Canada, which was managed by Canadians on his behalf. The Revenue issued an assessment charging tax on the profits. He appealed, contending that the income was income from overseas, within Schedule D Case V under the legislation then in force, so that he should only be taxed on any amounts which he remitted to the UK, applying the principles laid down in *Colquhoun v Brooks*, 53.1 SCHEDULE D—SUPERSEDED LEGISLATION. The CE rejected this contention and upheld the assessment. Lord Stormonth Darling held that the 'head and brain of the trading adventure' was in Aberdeen. *Ogilvie v Kitton*, CE 1908, 5 TC 338.

UK resident acting as overseas agent

[60.2] An individual acted as an agent, on a commission basis, for several UK manufacturers for the sale of their products abroad. For this purpose he was frequently abroad, but when he was in this country he lived with his wife and children in a house which his wife owned. The General Commissioners held that the whole of the profits of his business were chargeable to UK income tax, and the KB upheld their decision. *Spiers v Mackinnon*, KB 1929, 14 TC 386.

Companies resident in the UK

NOTE

In the cases below the company assessed was admitted to be resident in the UK and the issue was whether the trade assessed was within the charge to UK income tax (under Schedule D Case I under the legislation then in force). Cases where the residence of the company assessed was in dispute are included at **48.68** et seq. RESIDENCE.)

UK bank with branches in UK and abroad

[60.3] The CA unanimously upheld the Revenue's contention that a bank registered and controlled in the UK, with branches in the UK and abroad, carried on a single business in the UK and the whole of its profits were chargeable to UK income tax. *London Bank of Mexico v Apthorpe*, CA 1891, 3 TC 143; [1891] 2 QB 378.

Company resident and controlled in UK—trading activities abroad

[60.4] A company registered and controlled in the UK operated a railway in Brazil, with a salaried superintendent who was resident there. The HL held that the whole of its profits were chargeable to UK income tax as trading income, under Schedule D Case I. *San Paulo (Brazilian) Railway Co Ltd v Carter*, HL 1895, 3 TC 407; [1896] AC 31.

[60.5] The decision in *San Paulo (Brazilian) Railway Co Ltd v Carter*, **60.4** above, was applied in a subsequent case where a company registered and controlled in the UK operated a hotel in the USA under a salaried manager. *Denver Hotel Co Ltd v Andrews*, CA 1895, 3 TC 356.

[60.6] The decision in *San Paulo (Brazilian) Railway Co Ltd v Carter*, **60.4** above, was applied in a subsequent case where a company registered and controlled in the UK operated oil wells in Austria. *Grove v Elliots & Parkinson*, QB 1896, 3 TC 481.

US brewery operated through local committee of management

[60.7] The decision in *San Paulo (Brazilian) Railway Co Ltd v Carter*, **60.4** above, was applied by the CA in relation to a company registered and controlled in the UK which acquired a brewery in Illinois (USA), operating it through an American committee of management. The brewery had previously been carried on by an Illinois company and because of local laws preventing alien corporations from holding real property in Illinois, the Illinois company was kept in existence, the UK company holding all but three of its shares. *Apthorpe v Peter Schoenhofen Brewing Co Ltd*, CA 1899, 4 TC 41.

[60.8] Similar decisions were reached in *Frank Jones Brewing Co Ltd v Apthorpe*, QB 1898, 4 TC 6; *United States Brewing Co Ltd v Apthorpe*, QB 1898, 4 TC 17 and *St Louis Breweries Ltd v Apthorpe*, QB 1898, 4 TC 111.

UK company assessed on profits of foreign subsidiary

[60.9] A UK company (K) owned 98% of the shares in a US subsidiary. The Revenue assessed K on the profits of the subsidiary. The KB allowed K's appeal and the CA unanimously upheld this decision. On the evidence, the subsidiary was not a 'sham' and the control which K exercised was control as shareholder. *Kodak Ltd v Clark*, CA 1903, 4 TC 549; [1903] 1 KB 505.

[60.10] A UK company had a wholly-owned German subsidiary. The Revenue issued an assessment charging tax on the whole of the profits of the subsidiary. The company appealed, contending that it was only liable on its dividends from the subsidiary. The KB accepted this contention and allowed the appeal, and the CA unanimously upheld this decision, holding that the subsidiary was not merely the agent of its parent. *Gramophone & Typewriter Ltd v Stanley* , CA 1908, 5 TC 358; [1908] 2 KB 89.

UK company—power of attorney to non-resident director

[60.11] A UK company carried on business as insurance brokers in London and Paris. It gave a director, who was resident in France, power of attorney to conduct its Paris business from an office in Paris. The Commissioners held that the Paris business was a separate trade, but that it was controlled from London and was chargeable to UK income tax (under Schedule D Case I). The KB dismissed the company's appeal, holding that the control of the Paris trade was with the London board and that their authority was not divested by the power of attorney. *BW Noble Ltd v Mitchell*, KB 1926, 11 TC 372. (*Note*. For another issue in this case, see **63.301** TRADING PROFITS.)

Non-residents with agents or branches in the UK

Non-resident held to be trading in the UK

Danish telegraph company with agency and offices in UK

[60.12] A Danish telegraph company had an agency and offices in the UK to deal with calls received in the UK. The Revenue assessed the company on the net profit derived from its receipts here. The relevant contracts were made in the UK. The Commissioners upheld the assessment, and the company's agent appealed. The CA unanimously dismissed the company's appeal. *Erichsen v Last*, CA 1881, 4 TC 422; 8 QBD 414.

French wine merchant selling through UK agent

[60.13] The Revenue assessed a French firm of wine growers and merchants, with an office in the UK, on its profits from its sales in the UK. Some of the wine so sold was consigned to the firm's UK agent. The QB upheld the assessment, holding that the power to assess an agent (under legislation which became *TMA, s 78*) did not debar the Revenue from assessing the principal when he could be served with proper notices. *Tischler v Apthorpe*, QB 1885, 2 TC 89. (*Note*. *TMA, s 78* was repealed by *FA 1995* for 1996/97 *et seq*.)

[60.14] A French firm sold wine through a UK agent. The QB held that it was exercising a trade within the UK, and upheld an assessment on the agent on its profits from its UK sales. *Pommery & Greno v Apthorpe*, QB 1886, 2 TC 182. (*Note*. The decision was approved and applied by the CA in *Werle & Co v Colquhoun*, **60.15** below.)

[60.15] A French firm (W) sold wine in England through London agents. The Commissioners held that W's profits from the sales were the profits of a trade exercised in the UK and were assessable on the agents. The CA unanimously upheld their decision. *Werle & Co v Colquhoun*, CA 1888, 2 TC 402; 20 QBD 753.

Ship owned in Norway but managed by Glasgow agent

[60.16] A company registered and controlled in Norway operated a ship. The chartering of the ship, and all receipts and disbursements, were dealt with by agents in Glasgow. It was held that the company was not resident in the UK, but exercised a trade within the UK, the profits of which were assessable on the Glasgow agents. *James Wingate & Co v Webber*, CE 1897, 3 TC 569.

Commission agent selling in own name

[60.17] An American firm sold lard and bacon in the UK through UK agents, who were remunerated by commission. The agents sold the goods in their own name and collected the sale proceeds for the firm. The Revenue issued assessments to the agents, charging tax on the profits. The QB upheld the assessments, holding that the American firm was exercising a trade within the UK. *Watson v Sandie & Hull*, QB 1897, 3 TC 611; [1898] 1 QB 326.

Sales by agent subject to principal's approval—goods consigned to agent

[60.18] An American manufacturing company (R) effected its UK sales through a UK company (T). T obtained R's authority before accepting offers for R's goods. The goods were then consigned to T, for delivery to the customer. The Revenuie issued an assessment on T, charging tax on the profits. The Commissioners upheld the assessment and the QB dismissed T's appeal, holding that the contracts for sale were made in the UK and that R exercised a trade in the UK through T. *Thomas Turner (Leicester) Ltd v Rickman*, QB 1898, 4 TC 25.

[60.19] A Belgian manufacturer (P) sold yarn in the UK through a UK agent (M). M accepted offers after approval by P. The goods were consigned to M for delivery to the customer, and M collected the sale proceeds, accounting for them to P. The CS unanimously held that P exercised a trade within the UK, the profits of which were assessable on M. *MacPherson & Co v Moore*, CS 1912, 6 TC 107.

Sales by UK company of goods manufactured by Netherlands company

[60.20] A UK company (W) sold gas mantles manufactured by a Netherlands company (R). The Revenue issued assessments on W, charging tax on the profits. The Commissioners upheld the assessments and the CA unanimously upheld their decision, holding that the terms of the arrangement were such that R was exercising a trade within the UK and that W was acting as its agent. *Weiss, Biheller & Brooks Ltd v Farmer*, CA 1922, 8 TC 381; [1923] 1 KB 226.

Commission agent selling subject to principal's approval

[60.21] An Egyptian firm of cotton merchants sold cotton through an agent in Manchester. The agent made the contracts of sale after obtaining the firm's authority either to accept a particular offer, or to offer specified quantities of cotton for sale on specified terms. The firm shipped the cotton, collected the sale proceeds, and paid the agent commission. The Revenue issued assessments, and the firm appealed, contending that it was not carrying on a trade in the UK. The CA unanimously rejected this contention and upheld the assessments. *Wilcock v Pinto & Co*, CA 1924, 9 TC 111; [1925] 1 KB 30.

[60.22] A Java firm sold various Asian goods, mainly sugar, in London, through an associated London firm which acted as its agent. The sales were effected in a variety of ways. The HL unanimously held that the Java firm exercised a trade within the UK with regard to those sales (the majority of them) where the contract was made in the UK. *Maclaine & Co v Eccott*, HL 1926, 10 TC 481; [1926] AC 424. (*Note*. The case also concerned the application of *ITA 1915, s 31*, which became *TMA, s 82*, and was repealed by *FA 1995* for 1996/97 *et seq.*)

[60.23] An Italian firm appointed a UK resident (B) as sole agent for the UK, Canada and Australia, for the sale of the majority of its products. He solicited orders, which were accepted only after approval by the firm, which normally consigned the goods direct to the customer. The Revenue issued assessments on B. The Special Commissioners upheld the assessments and the CA unanimously dismissed B's appeal, holding that the firm exercised a trade within the UK, the profits of which were assessable on B. *Belfour v Mace*, CA 1928, 13 TC 539.

Whether agent an authorised person carrying on regular agency

[60.24] In two cases where non-residents sold goods through UK agents, the KB held that the non-residents were exercising a trade within the UK, the profits of which were assessable on the agents who were regarded as 'authorised persons' carrying on the regular agency of the non-residents. *Gavazzi (E & P) v Mace*; *TL Boyd & Son Ltd v Stephen*, KB 1926, 10 TC 698.

[60.25] Two UK companies, which traded as shipping agents and shipbrokers, acted as agents for a Danish shipping company in relation to the conveyance from English to Danish ports of goods consigned by English customers. The Revenue assessed them on the profits, and they appealed, contending firstly that the Danish company was not trading in the UK, and secondly that they were not agents of the company. The Special Commissioners rejected these contentions and dismissed the appeals, holding that the Danish company was exercising a trade within the UK, the profits of which were assessable on the agents, who were authorised persons carrying on the regular agency of the non-resident person. The HL upheld this decision. *Nielsen Andersen & Co v Collins; Tarn (for Thomas Wilson Sons & Co Ltd) v Scanlan*, HL 1927, 13 TC 91; [1928] AC 34.

[60.26] A similar decision was reached in a case involving two Netherlands companies, which the CA and HL heard with *Nielsen Andersen & Co v Collins*, 60.25 above. *WH Muller & Co (London) Ltd v Lethem*, HL 1927,

13 TC 126; [1928] AC 34. (*Note*. The case also concerned the application of *ITA 1915, s 31*, which became *TMA, s 82*, and was repealed by *FA 1995* for 1996/97 *et seq*.)

[60.27] A trader (R) was a member of the Liverpool Produce Exchange. He sold bacon and ham produced by an American company, receiving bids and transmitting their acceptance to the buyers after ratification by the company. Generally, he had no further involvement with the transaction, but sometimes he sold produce consigned to him. The Revenue issued assessments on R, charging tax on the basis that the company was exercising a trade in the UK through R as its authorised agent. The Special Commissioners upheld the assessments and the KB dismissed R's appeals. *Rowson v Stephen*, KB 1929, 14 TC 543.

[60.28] A US company established a UK subsidiary which manufactured tyres. The UK subsidiary fulfilled orders obtained by European agents of the parent company. The purchasers paid the UK company, which credited the parent company with the sale price less its own costs plus 5%. The Special Commissioners held that the US company was trading in the UK and that the UK subsidiary was correctly assessed as its agent. The Ch D, CA and HL unanimously upheld their decision. *Firestone Tyre & Rubber Co Ltd (as agents for Firestone Tire & Rubber Co of USA) v Lewellin*, HL 1957, 37 TC 111; [1957] 1 WLR 464; [1957] 1 All ER 561.

[60.29] The business of a UK company (L) consisted mainly of importing meat, etc. from New Zealand through a New Zealand company and selling it in London on behalf of a South African company. All three companies were controlled by the same shareholders. The Revenue assessed L as agents of the South African company in respect of the profits from the sales. L appealed, contending that it was a broker or general commission agent. The Ch D rejected this contention and upheld the assessments. *Fleming v London Produce Co Ltd*, Ch D 1968, 44 TC 582; [1968] 1 WLR 1013; [1968] 2 All ER 975. (*Note*. For another issue in this case, see **5.106** ASSESSMENTS.)

Exploitation of derelict gold mines by promotion of mining companies

[60.30] An Australian company acquired interests in some derelict gold mines, and transferred them to a number of Western Australian companies formed for the purpose in return for fully paid-up shares in those companies. Subsequently, it sold the shares at intervals through a UK agent. The Revenue issued assessments on the basis that the company carried on a trade in the UK, taxable through its agent. The CA unanimously upheld the assessments, holding that, in computing the profits, the cost of the shares in the Western Australian companies should be taken as the value of the mining interests at the time of their sale to those companies. *Murphy v Australian Machinery & Investment Co Ltd*, CA 1948, 30 TC 244.

Jersey company employing UK consultant

[60.31] In the case noted at **3.58** ANTI-AVOIDANCE, the Ch D held that a Jersey company, which employed a UK-resident chartered surveyor, was trading in the UK through a branch or agency. *Brackett v Chater*, Ch D 1986, 60 TC 134, 639; [1986] STC 521.

Non-resident held not to be trading in the UK

Commission agent transmits orders for execution by principal

[60.32] A French wine merchant (R) sold wine in England with the help of an English partnership (G), which was paid on a commission basis, and transmitted orders to R. The Revenue issued assessments charging tax on G. The HL allowed G's appeal (by a 4–1 majority, Lord Morris dissenting), holding that R did not exercise a trade within the UK. *Grainger & Son v Gough*, HL 1896, 3 TC 462; [1896] AC 325.

US partnership purchasing goods in the UK for sale in the USA

[60.33] A US partnership purchased goods in the UK for export to the USA, where they were sold. One of the partners was resident in the UK and he was assessed on the profits accruing to the partnership. The Court held that he was only liable in respect of his share of the profits. The purchase of goods in the UK for resale abroad did not amount to trading in the UK. *Sulley v A-G*, Ex D 1860, 2 TC 149.

Overseas bank floating loan issue in London market

[60.34] A Japanese bank (IB), which did not have an office in the UK, employed a London bank (Y) to float loan stock issues in the London market for its Japanese clients. The Revenue issued assessments charging tax on Y. The KB allowed Y's appeal, holding that IB was not trading in the UK. *Yokohama Specie Bank Ltd v Williams*, KB 1915, 6 TC 634.

Danish firm with UK sales agent

[60.35] A Danish firm selling cement-making machinery had an office in London in the charge of an employee who met prospective UK purchasers to discuss their requirements, and reported to the firm. All contracts were negotiated from, and made in, Denmark. The Revenue issued assessments charging UK tax but the KB allowed the firm's appeal, holding that the firm did not exercise a trade within the UK. The CA and HL unanimously upheld this decision. *FL Smidth & Co v Greenwood*, HL 1922, 8 TC 193; [1922] AC 417.

Tickets issued by shipping company paid for in advance abroad

[60.36] A UK shipping company carried on business in Ireland through an Irish branch office, and had agents in the USA. It operated a scheme to facilitate the emigration of Irish citizens to the USA. Under the scheme, someone in the USA (e.g. a relative of a would-be emigrant) could purchase a prepaid certificate in the USA which entitled the would-be emigrant to a ticket from the company's Irish agents for the journey to America. If the would-be emigrant did not take up the ticket, the US purchaser of the certificate was refunded his money, less a cancellation fee. The company was assessed to Irish tax on its profits from these transactions. The Court allowed the company's appeal, holding that the passenger's ticket was not issued under an Irish contract and hence there was no liability to Irish tax on the profit from its issue. *Cunard Steamship Co Ltd v Herlihy*, SC(I) 1931, 1 ITC 373; [1931] IR 307.

UK company operating ship owned by French company

[60.37] A UK company (B) held shares in a French company (M) of which its managing director (P) was a director. In 1940 France was occupied by German troops, and P arranged for B to operate a fishing trawler belonging to M, which was in UK waters at the time of the occupation. In 1945, B accounted to M for the profits from the ship. The Revenue assessed B on the profits for 1940/41 to 1944/45, on the basis that it had acted as an agent of M. The Ch D allowed B's appeal, holding that it had not been an authorised agent. Harman J observed that 'at the time the acts were done the French company was an alien enemy at common law'. *Boston Deep Sea Fishing & Ice Co Ltd v Farnham*, Ch D 1957, 37 TC 505; [1957] 1 WLR 1051; [1957] 3 All ER 204.

61

Trading Income—Commencements and Cessations

The cases in this chapter are arranged under the following headings.

The date of commencement or cessation

Preliminary activities—whether trading

[61.1] In an excess profits duty case, a company carried on the business of processing and marketing butchers' by-products. From June to October 1913 its directors secured premises and plant and arranged for the supply of by-products etc. A works manager was taken on in August, and the actual processing began in October. The Commissioners found that the trade began in October, and the KB upheld their decision. *Birmingham & District Cattle By-Products Co Ltd v CIR*, KB 1919, 12 TC 92. (*Note*. The decision was questioned by Lord Millett in the subsequent case of *Khan v Miah & Others*, 41.12 PARTNERSHIPS.)

[61.2] During 1992 and 1993 an individual (M) investigated the development of motorway service areas. He helped to negotiate agreements between two landowners and an Isle of Man company which he controlled. The agreements were signed on 15 April 1994. Later in 1994 another overseas company which M controlled received £50,000 from a major oil company in relation to the site which was the subject of the agreements. M subsequently received a further £250,000 in relation to the site. The Revenue issued assessments on the basis that M had begun carrying on a trade in 1994/95. M appealed, accepting that he had carried on a trade but contending that he had begun trading before April 1994. (This would have been to his advantage because of the changes to the basis of assessment introduced by *FA 1994*.) The Special Commissioner dismissed the appeal, finding that M's trade had not begun until after 5 April 1994. *Mansell v HMRC*, Sp C [2006] SSCD 605 (Sp C 551).

Electronic engineer—date of commencement

[61.3] An electronic engineer had been self-employed, and assessed under Schedule D under the legislation then in force, until 1976. From 1976 to May 1980 he was an employee. He was then unemployed until May 1981, when he began working under a contract for services. The Revenue issued assessments on the basis that his business had commenced in May 1981. He appealed, contending that he had recommenced self-employment in May 1980. The Special Commissioner rejected this contention and dismissed his appeal, and the CA upheld this decision as one of fact. *Napier v Griffiths*, CA 1990, 63 TC 745; [1991] STC 55. (*Note*. For a preliminary issue in this case, see **4.166** APPEALS. For a subsequent appeal against summary judgment, see **4.245** APPEALS.)

Farming—date of commencement of trade

[61.4] See *Walsh & Walsh v Taylor*, **35.20** LOSS RELIEF.

Whether de facto succession before sale agreement

[61.5] A company (J) acquired the trade of another company, the formal contract being dated 16 April 1928. The KB held that this was the date of succession, rejecting J's contention that there had been a *de facto* succession earlier. *Todd v Jones Bros Ltd*, KB 1930, 15 TC 396.

[61.6] A partnership decided to transfer its business to a company with effect from 31 March 1950. A company was formed for this purpose on that date, but the sale agreement was not signed until June 1950. The Special Commissioners held that there had been a *de facto* transfer of the trade on 1 April 1950, and the Ch D upheld their decision as one of fact. *Angel v Hollingworth & Co*, Ch D 1958, 37 TC 714.

Sale of stock after retirement announced

[61.7] A firm of wine and spirit merchants announced early in 1916 that they intended to retire, but continued selling during 1917, mainly from existing stock but partly from spirits acquired from distillers under running contracts. The Special Commissioners held that their trade continued during 1917, and the HL unanimously upheld their decision. *J & R O'Kane & Co v CIR*, HL 1922, 12 TC 303.

[61.8] A whisky broker (N) was in poor health and wished to retire. On 15 July 1937 he closed his business bank account and gave his accountant a mandate to wind up his business. On the following day his customers and creditors were notified of his retirement. On 27 July one of the customers bought N's stock and office equipment, paying £130,000. The Revenue issued an assessment on the basis that the £130,000 was a trading receipt. N appealed, contending that his trade had ceased on 15 July, so that the £130,000 was not taxable under the legislation then in force. The Special Commissioners accepted this contention and allowed his appeal, and the CS upheld their decision as one of fact. *CIR v Nelson*, CS 1939, 22 TC 716. (*Note*. See now *ITTOIA 2005, s 173 et seq.*)

New partnership—old partnership completes open contracts

[61.9] A partnership of four people, carrying on business as grain merchants, terminated on 31 March 1926. Two of them formed a new partnership to carry on a similar business. The old partnership held grain to fulfil existing forward contracts with customers and acquired further grain for this purpose. The Revenue assessed the old partnership for 1926/27 on the profits from the fulfilment of contracts in that year. The Commissioners upheld the assessment, finding that the old partnership was trading during 1926/27. The CA unanimously upheld their decision. *Hillerns & Fowler v Murray*, CA 1932, 17 TC 77.

Whether trading continued after newspaper merger

[61.10] Following the merger of two newspapers, the company (M) which had previously owned one of them had no premises or staff and its only receipts were monthly payments, based on the circulation of the joint newspaper, from the company which owned the continuing newspaper. The Revenue issued assessments charging tax on the payments. M appealed, contending that it was continuing to trade (and hence was entitled to relief on its previous unrelieved losses). The Commissioners rejected this contention and dismissed the appeal, and the KB upheld their decision. *Morning Post Ltd v George*, KB 1940, 23 TC 514.

Musician—whether trade continuing

[61.11] A self-employed musician had had a reasonable income during the 1990s, but his income declined after 2001 and he subsequently began working as a music teacher. In his 2006/07 tax return he claimed a loss of £6,181. HMRC began an enquiry and discovered that 94% of his trading income derived from his work as a music teacher. They issued an amendment disallowing much of the expenses which M had claimed, on the basis that he was no longer trading as a musician and should be treated as a teacher. M appealed, contending that he was continuing to trade as a musician despite the decline in his income. The First-tier Tribunal accepted this contention and allowed his appeal in part. Judge Brooks held that 'despite the significant fall in his income, he had not ceased to be a musician and become a teacher'. On the evidence, he held that the majority (but not all) of the expenditure which M had claimed was allowable (reducing the loss from £6,181 to £2,489). *TJ Moore v HMRC*, FTT [2011] UKFTT 526 (TC), TC01373.

Sole trader transferring business to company

[61.12] An individual (C), who traded as a merchant and commission agent, sold his business to a company (H) on terms whereby H would complete any order not executed at the sale, retaining 25% of the profits or commissions and paying the balance to C. The KB held that the amounts which C received were profits of a new trade which he carried on through the agency of H. The CA unanimously upheld this decision. *Southern v Cohen's Executors*, CA 1940, 23 TC 566; [1940] 3 All ER 439.

[61.13] An individual (P) sold his business of selling musical instruments, etc., mainly on hire-purchase terms, to a company. He retained the benefit of hire-purchase agreements outstanding at the transfer, and the company collected instalments for him. The Special Commissioners held that, on the transfer, P began a new trade of carrying through outstanding hire-purchase agreements. The KB upheld their decision. *Parker v Batty*, KB 1941, 23 TC 739.

[61.14] An individual (S) sold his business to a company (K) in 1940. K completed all unexecuted contracts of the business. S appealed against income tax assessments, contending that he was continuing to trade. The Commissioners rejected this contention and dismissed his appeals, and the KB upheld their decision. *Sethia v John*, KB 1947, 28 TC 153.

[61.15] See also *Keyl v HMRC*, 8.73 CAPITAL ALLOWANCES.

Coal mining continued under licence after nationalisation

[61.16] A firm (D) had operated a coal mine. On the nationalisation of the coal industry, the assets of the mine were vested in the National Coal Board in January 1947. However, D continued to operate the mine under a temporary licence from the NCB until March 1949. The CS unanimously upheld the Revenue's contention that D continued to trade until March 1949. *CIR v Daniel Beattie & Co*, CS 1955, 36 TC 379.

Trade of hiring aircraft—time of cessation

[61.17] A trader (B) hired two aircraft to a company (F) of which he was managing director. One of the aircraft was destroyed in a crash on 12 March 1950. B was informed shortly afterwards and left immediately for the scene of the crash, after giving instructions for the other aircraft to be grounded. He terminated the hiring by a letter to F, dated 12 March and signed on 13 March. The Revenue assessed a balancing charge on B on the basis that the aircraft had been destroyed before the trade of hiring ceased. B appealed, contending that the trade ceased at the moment the aircraft crashed. The Commissioners rejected this contention and dismissed his appeal, and the HL unanimously upheld their decision. *Bennett v Rowse*, HL 1958, 38 TC 476. (*Note*. The substantive issue was overtaken by subsequent legislation.)

Date of cessation—premises closed at relevant times

[61.18] An individual formed a company on 25 March 1953 to take over the manufacturing business of another company he controlled. There was no formal assignment or other contemporary written evidence as to the date the business was transferred. The factory was closed from 1 to 6 April 1953. The Ch D upheld the Commissioners' decision that the succession was on 1 April. *Aeraspray Associated Ltd v Woods*, Ch D 1964, 42 TC 207.

Doctor—date of cessation of trade or profession

[61.19] A doctor (B), who had carried on an employment agency for locum doctors, was suspended by the General Medical Council in 1998, and was erased from the register of medical practitioners in 2006. He submitted a tax return for 2008/09 declaring that he had no income and claiming a loss of £8785. HMRC rejected the claim on the basis that B was no longer carrying on a trade or profession as a doctor. B appealed, contending that he had been actively continuing to challenge the GMC decision (see *Bhadra v General Medical Council*, CA [2009] EWCA Civ 317). The First-Tier Tribunal dismissed B's appeal. Judge Staker held that B had not been carrying on a trade during 2008/09. *T Bhadra (t/a Admirals Locums) v HMRC*, FTT [2011] UKFTT 573 (TC), TC01416. (*Note*. An appeal against discovery assessments for 2006/07 and 2007/08 was allowed, on the grounds that B had made a full disclosure in his returns for those years, so that HMRC had not made any discovery.)

Dealing in mobile phones—whether trade ceased

[61.20] Between 2000 and 2006 an individual (K) bought and sold large numbers of mobile telephones, mostly as an agent for a Singapore company but also as an independent principal. In 2010 he submitted a 2006/07 tax return claiming terminal loss relief of £24,234,078, on the basis that his trade had ceased in 2006. HMRC rejected the claim and K appealed. The First-tier Tribunal dismissed his appeal, observing that he had remained registered for VAT and had resumed active trading in 2009, and finding that he 'did not in fact cease trading in 2006/07'. (The Tribunal also held that K was carrying on a single trade, regardless of whether he was acting as an agent or as an independent principal.) *D Kishore v HMRC*, FTT [2013] UKFTT 465 (TC), TC02855.

Closure of museum—date of cessation

[61.21] See *Marriott v Lane*, 71.249 CAPITAL GAINS TAX.

Whether a succession

NOTE

A 'succession' takes place on a change in the persons carrying on a business. The term is still sometimes used by tax practitioners and is therefore used below. However, it is derived from pre-1928 legislation and is no longer in the relevant legislation.

Assets acquired by a person not already trading

Sale of steamer

[61.22] In a Scottish case, the acquisition of a tramp steamer, without books, accounts or a list of customers, was held not to amount to a succession to the trade of the vendors. *Watson Bros v Lothian*, CE 1902, 4 TC 441.

Transfer of order books

[61.23] In an excess profits duty case, the owner of a millinery business retired when the lease of the premises expired. She handed over certain order books to five of her saleswomen, who formed a company (M) to carry on a similar business nearby. The Commissioners held that M had not succeeded to the old business, and the KB upheld their decision. *Mills from Emelie Ltd v CIR*, KB 1919, 12 TC 73.

Transfer of business temporarily closed

[61.24] A company had carried on the business of a waxworks exhibition. Because of a disastrous fire, the exhibition was closed in 1925 and not re-opened until 1928. Meanwhile, the undertaking had been transferred to another company in 1926. The new company appealed against tax assessments, contending that it had succeeded to the old company's business. The Special Commissioners accepted this contention and allowed the appeal, and the KB upheld their decision as one of fact. *Wild v Madame Tussaud's (1926) Ltd*, KB 1932, 17 TC 127.

Purchase of rubber plantations

[61.25] A company (P) acquired the rubber plantations of another company (M), including its plantation employees, but not its selling organisation or its book debts. The Commissioners held that there had been a 'succession', and the KB dismissed P's appeal against their decision. *Malayalam Plantations Ltd v Clark*, KB 1935, 19 TC 314.

Medical practice

[61.26] A doctor (P) purchased a medical practice in July 1929. Under the purchase agreement, the vendor assisted him until 30 September 1929, and they shared the receipts and expenses for the intervening period. The Revenue issued an assessment on the basis that P had succeeded to the vendor's practice. P appealed, contending that he had begun a new business in July 1929. The KB accepted this contention and allowed his appeal, holding that P had not succeeded to the vendor's practice, and that the arrangement for the period from July to September 1929 did not amount to a partnership between them. *Pratt v Strick*, KB 1932, 17 TC 459.

Company reconstruction during receivership

[61.27] A company (WD) went into receivership. Some of its activities were taken over by a new company (WM) with the same directors and shareholders. The Ch D held that WM had succeeded to WD's trade of the old, with the result that there was a company reconstruction within *FA 1954, s 17*—see now *CTA 2010, ss 940A-953*—and WM was entitled to relief in respect of

WD's unused losses. *Wadsworth Morton Ltd v Jenkinson*, Ch D 1966, 43 TC 479; [1967] 1 WLR 79; [1966] 3 All ER 702.

Assets or existing trade acquired by a person already trading

Acquisition of new branch by bank

[61.28] A bank, with 199 branches, acquired the business of another bank with only one branch, which it merged with its own business. The CA unanimously upheld the Revenue's contention that there had been a 'succession' to the business acquired. *Bell v National Provincial Bank of England Ltd*, CA 1903, 5 TC 1; [1904] 1 KB 149.

Acquisition of share of second ship

[61.29] A shipping company (S), trading with a single steamship, acquired a 92% share in a second ship. The KB upheld the Revenue's contention that, since S only owned part of the second ship, its profits from that ship must be assessed separately. *Farrell v Sunderland Steamship Co Ltd*, KB 1903, 4 TC 605.

'Single ship' company replacing its ship

[61.30] A steamship company could, by virtue of its memorandum of association, own only one vessel at a time. It lost its first ship in April 1906 and replaced it by a ship which made its first voyage in October 1906. The KB upheld the Revenue's contention that its trade had been continuous throughout. *Merchiston Steamship Co Ltd v Turner*, KB 1910, 5 TC 520; [1910] 2 KB 923.

Acquisition of further sawmill

[61.31] A partnership, which traded as timber importers and sawmillers, needed new premises and purchased another sawmill to use as their base. The Special Commissioners upheld the Revenue's contention that the partnership had succeeded to the vendor's business. The CS unanimously dismissed the partnership's appeal against this decision. *Thomson & Balfour v Le Page*, CS 1923, 8 TC 541.

Acquisition of second foundry

[61.32] A company (F) which operated a foundry acquired a second foundry. The Special Commissioners found that F had set up a new business at the second foundry (and had not succeeded to the business previously carried on there, as the Revenue contended, nor extended its existing business, as F contended). The CS upheld the Commissioners' decision as one of fact. *Fullwood Foundry Co Ltd v CIR*, CS 1924, 9 TC 101.

Change of cinemas

[61.33] A company (H) sold two cinemas which it had operated in Hampshire, and opened a new cinema in London. The Special Commissioners upheld the Revenue's contention that H had began a new trade was set up when it opened the London cinema was opened. The KB upheld their decision as one of fact. *H & G Kinemas Ltd v Cook*, KB 1933, 18 TC 116.

Shoe retailer taking over manufacturing from subsidiaries

[61.34] A company (F), which sold shoes, obtained some of its supplies from two wholly-owned manufacturing subsidiaries. It wound up the subsidiaries, took over their staff and factories and other assets, and thereafter manufactured shoes itself at the factories. The CA accepted F's contention that it had not succeeded to the trades of the subsidiaries, since F was trading as a retailer and they had been trading as wholesalers. *Laycock v Freeman Hardy & Willis Ltd*, CA 1938, 22 TC 288; [1939] 2 KB 1; [1938] 4 All ER 609.

Steel manufacturer taking over tinplate manufacture from subsidiaries

[61.35] A group of companies manufactured tinplate. The parent company (B) produced steel bars which it supplied to subsidiaries who used it for manufacturing. Following a group reconstruction, B took over the assets of the subsidiaries and thereafter manufactured the tinplate. itself. The CA unanimously held that B had succeeded to the trades of the subsidiaries, distinguishing the earlier decision in *Laycock v Freeman Hardy & Willis Ltd*, **61.34** above. The essence of the subsidiaries' trades was the sale of the tinplate, and this continued. *Briton Ferry Steel Co Ltd v Barry*, CA 1939, 23 TC 414; [1940] 1 KB 463; [1939] 4 All ER 541.

Food distributor acquiring similar businesses

[61.36] A company (W) which carried on a substantial business of distributing foodstuffs acquired two similar businesses from unrelated companies, and claimed stock relief in respect of its increased stock. The Revenue rejected W's claim, considering that it had succeeded to the trade of the two businesses, so that the stock relief had to be restricted. W appealed, contending that it had not continued the trades previously carried on by the other two companies. The Special Commissioners allowed W's appeal, holding that the two businesses had been merged with W's existing business and had ceased to exist as separate entities. The CS unanimously upheld the Commissioners' decision. *CIR v Watson & Philip Ltd*, CS 1984, 57 TC 587; [1984] STC 184.

Owners of fish and chip shop acquiring second shop

[61.37] The owners of a fish and chip shop acquired a second shop, five miles away, as a going concern. The Revenue issued assessments on the basis that the second shop constituted a separate trade, which was to be treated as recommencing on the date of the change of ownership. The owners appealed, contending that the acquisition of the second shop should be treated as the expansion of their existing trade, so that their total profits from the two shops should be assessed on a preceding year basis. The General Commissioners allowed their appeal, holding that the owners had 'continued an existing and enlarged trade, rather than succeeding to a new one'. The Ch D upheld their decision as one of fact. *Maidment v Kibby & Kibby*, Ch D 1993, 66 TC 137; [1993] STC 494.

Changes in activities of existing trades, etc.

NOTE

In some of the cases below the substantive issue was the entitlement of companies to loss relief in circumstances where *CTA 2010, ss 672–676* may now apply.

Fishing vessel requisitioned

[61.38] In an excess profits duty case, the owner of a steamship used it for fishing until 1915, when it was compulsorily requisitioned by the Admiralty. The Special Commissioners held that the shipowner continued to carry on the same trade of employing a ship for profit, and the CS unanimously upheld this decision. *Sutherland v CIR*, CS 1918, 12 TC 63.

Resumption of active trading

[61.39] A contracting company (K) closed its premises in 1913. From 1914 to February 1920 it had no works and no plant, although its directors made persistent unsuccessful attempts to obtain new contracts. In 1920, following a change of shareholders and an injection of new capital, it agreed some new contracts and obtained new plant. The KB held that K's trade had continued throughout the period (reversing the decision of the Commissioners). *Kirk & Randall Ltd v Dunn*, KB 1924, 8 TC 663. (*Note.* The decision was questioned by Park J in the 1998 case of *Jowett v O'Neill & Brennan Construction Ltd*, 59.20 TRADING INCOME.)

[61.40] A local council requisitioned a company's premises in 1939. The company ceased active trading, realised all its assets, and remained dormant for several years, except that in 1941 it made an unsuccessful application for a licence to resume business. In 1944, following a change of shareholding, it acquired new premises and commenced active trading operations, mainly similar to those it had carried on up to 1939. The Ch D accepted the Revenue's contention that the company's 1944 trade was not a continuation of its old trade (reversing the decision of the Commissioners). *Goff v Osborne & Co (Sheffield) Ltd*, Ch D 1953, 34 TC 441.

[61.41] A brick-manufacturing company (R) closed its works in March 1968, selling its stock and plant and paying off its employees. In August its shares were acquired by another company (C). Thereafter R manufactured bricks at premises leased to it by C, using C's plant and employees. R claimed that losses incurred up to March 1968 should be relieved under *CTA 2010, s 45(1)** against its profits after August 1968. The Revenue rejected the claim but the CS allowed R's appeal (by a 2–1 majority, Lord Avonside dissenting). Lord Emslie held that the trade had been continuous despite the break in manufacturing. *Robroyston Brickworks Ltd v CIR*, CS 1976, 51 TC 230; [1976] STC 329.

Boilermaker commencing shell-making

[61.42] A company trading as boilermakers manufactured shells during the 1914/18 War, using premises and plant which it had acquired for the purpose. The Commissioners held that the shell-making was an extension of the existing business. The CS unanimously upheld their decision as one of fact. *Howden Boiler & Armaments Co Ltd v Stewart*, CS 1924, 9 TC 205.

Drift coal-mining pending sinking of pits

[61.43] A coal-mining company (C) began drift-mining in 1908, pending the sinking of pits, which was completed in late 1911. C appealed against assessments to excess profits duty, contending that it had commenced a new business in June 1912. The Special Commissioners rejected this contention and dismissed the appeal, and the KB upheld this decision. *Cannop Coal Co Ltd v CIR*, KB 1918, 12 TC 31.

Shipbrokers commencing management for Ministry of Shipping

[61.44] In an excess profits duty case, a firm of shipbrokers, who were normally remunerated by commission, also managed ships for the Ministry of Shipping for a fixed annual remuneration. The CA unanimously upheld the Revenue's contention that the firm's management for the Ministry was not a separate business. *CIR v Turnbull Scott & Co*, CA 1924, 12 TC 749.

Flour miller and baker—flour milling partly discontinued

[61.45] In an Irish case, a company carried on business as flour millers (at two mills) and bread bakers, about half of the flour it milled being used in its bakeries. After making losses, the mills were closed in August 1922, but one was re-opened in April 1923, mainly to supply the bakeries. The Special Commissioners held that it had carried on a single trade throughout. The KB upheld their decision as one of fact. *Bolands Ltd v Davis*, KB(I) 1925, 1 ITC 91; 4 ATC 532.

Brewing ceased—beer selling continued

[61.46] A brewing company (G) ceased brewing but continued to sell beer, purchasing it from another company. The Special Commissioners upheld the Revenue's contention that G had ceased its trade of brewing and begun a new trade of selling beer, so that its unrelieved losses from the brewing trade could not be set against profits from the new trade. The CS unanimously upheld this decision. *Gordon & Blair Ltd v CIR*, CS 1962, 40 TC 358.

Confectionery company beginning to sell sugar

[61.47] A company (T), which had manufactured and sold confectionery, closed its factory and its two shops, and began to supply its parent company (F) with sugar. The Ch D upheld the Revenue's contention that T had begun a new trade of selling sugar. (T continued to supply factored confectionery to F's canteen, and the case was remitted to the Commissioners to decide whether this amounted to a continuation of its old trade.) *Seaman v Tucketts Ltd*, Ch D 1963, 41 TC 422.

Gas cooker manufacturer commencing assembling food mixers

[61.48] A company (C) manufactured gas cookers, etc. for sale to companies in the same group. It began assembling electric food mixers for retail sale. TheSpecial Commissioners upheld the Revenue's contention that the new activity was an extension of C's existing trade, and the Ch D upheld their decision. *Cannon Industries Ltd v Edwards*,Ch D 1965, 42 TC 625; [1966] 1 WLR 580; [1966] 1 All ER 456. (*Note*. For another issue in this case, see **4.213** APPEALS.)

Similar goods sold continuously but acquired differently

[61.49] A company (J), which manufactured and sold rubber surgical goods, traded at a loss for several years. A receiver was appointed, and in September 1961 its plant was sold and its factory closed. From then until June 1962, J sold similar goods made by an associated company. In June 1962, after a change in shareholding, J began making similar goods, but using plastic instead of rubber, and using plant and factory space obtained from its new parent company. Throughout this time, it sold the goods under its own brand name. J claimed loss relief on the basis that it had carried on a continuous trade. The Special Commissioners rejected the claim, holding that the old trade was permanently discontinued in September 1961, that a new trade was begun in June 1962, and that the intervening merchanting was a separate trade. The CA unanimously upheld their decision, holding that the fact that J sold surgical goods continuously did not necessarily mean that it had carried on a continuing trade. Lord Donovan held that there was 'an organic unity about a trade'. *JG Ingram & Son Ltd v Callaghan*, CA 1968, 45 TC 151; [1969] 1 WLR 456; [1969] 1 All ER 433.

Computer software company providing IT consultancy services

[61.50] A company had carried on a business of dealing in computers and computer software. It made losses, and ceased trading in 1995. In 1998 it began a new activity of providing IT consultancy services and associated computer software. It claimed that the losses incurred up to 1995 should be set against the profits for 1998. The Revenue rejected the claim on the basis that the company had carried on two separate trades. The Special Commissioners dismissed the company's appeal. Applying *dicta* of Lord Donovan in *JG Ingram & Son Ltd v Callaghan*, **61.49** above, there was no 'organic unity' about the company's activities. *Kawthar Consulting Ltd v HMRC*, Sp C [2005] SSCD 524 (Sp C 477). (*Note*. The appeal was heard with *Netlogic Consulting Ltd v HMRC*, **63.272** TRADING PROFITS.)

Building and decorating partnership—building activities transferred

[61.51] A partnership traded as builders and decorators. From 1971 its building activities were transferred to and carried on by a limited company controlled by the partners. The Revenue issued assessments on the basis that the partnership had continued to trade. The partnership appealed, contending that it had ceased trading in 1971. The General Commissioners rejected this contention and dismissed the appeal, and the Ch D upheld their decision. *Watts & Others v Hart*, Ch D 1984, 58 TC 209; [1984] STC 548. (*Note*. For a preliminary issue in this case, see **4.204** APPEALS.)

Barrister becoming KC

[61.52] Two barristers were appointed as King's Counsel. The Revenue assessed them on the basis that they were carrying on a continuing profession. They appealed, contending that they had set up a new profession on appointment as King's Counsel. The KB rejected this contention and upheld the assessments. *Seldon v Croom-Johnson; Seldon v Thomas*, KB 1932, 16 TC 740; [1932] 1 KB 759.

Television producer

[61.53] An individual (E) had been employed as a part-time television producer. In April 1990 he began working on a freelance basis. His freelance work occupied about 60% of his working time and his employment occupied the remaining 40%. His employment ended in June 1992 and from then E worked as a freelance producer on a full-time basis. His freelance profits increased significantly after June 1992, and the Revenue issued assessments on the basis that E had begun a new profession in 1992/93. E appealed, contending that his profession had begun in April 1990. The Ch D accepted this contention and allowed E's appeal. On the evidence, E had provided the same services as a self-employed television producer before and after June 1992. Applying the principles laid down by *Seldon v Croom-Johnson*, **61.52** above, the intensification of his freelance activities could not have effected a discontinuance of his previous business and the commencement of a new business. *Edmunds v Coleman*, Ch D 1997, 70 TC 322; [1997] STC 1406.

Optician—change from franchisee to locum

[61.54] An optician (HA) worked as a franchisee until 3 April 2009. He made a loss in his final period of trading, part of which was carried back to his profit for the previous year. He subsequently began working as a freelance locum optician, and claimed that the balance of his loss for 2008/09 should be set against his income from this source in 2010. HMRC rejected the claim on the basis that HA's trade as a freelance locum optician was a different trade from his previous trade as a franchisee dispensing optician. The First-tier Tribunal dismissed HA's appeal. Judge Cornwell-Kelly held that 'the facts very clearly indicate the cessation of one business activity and the commencement of another'. *HL Amah v HMRC (No 2)*, FTT [2014] UKFTT 1084 (TC), TC04173. (*Note*. For a preliminary issue in this case, see **4.137** APPEALS.)

Miscellaneous matters

Railway company operating steamships—whether one trade

[61.55] A railway company (H) fell to be assessed for 1883/84 on its profits for the year to 31 August 1882, during which it sold two steamships which it had operated at a loss. In determining H's profits of the year to 31 August 1882, the Special Commissioners excluded the loss from operating the steamships in that year. The Court allowed H's appeal, holding that the assessment should be based on its net profit from its whole undertaking. *Highland Railway Co v Special Commrs*, CE 1885, 2 TC 151.

Chemical manufacturing company also occupying farm

[61.56] A company (W) manufactured and sold chemical products. For this purpose, it occupied a farm to grow herbs for distillation. The KB upheld W's contention that its farming was a separate trade or business for excess profits duty purposes, and therefore was not within the charge to EPD (which did not extend to husbandry). *CIR v William Ransom & Son Ltd*, KB 1918, 12 TC 21; [1918] 2 KB 709. (*Note*. For income tax, the farming profits were within Schedule B under the law then in force.)

Shipowning and underwriting—whether separate trades

[61.57] A family partnership had carried on a shipowning business. Two of the four partners (G and S) also acted as Lloyd's underwriters. The partnership transferred its activities to a company (T). G and S continued their underwriting on behalf of T. (At the relevant time, a company could not be admitted as a 'name' at Lloyd's.) S retired in 1919 and G died in 1920. T claimed that its underwriting was a separate trade which ceased on G's death. The Commissioners accepted this contention and the KB upheld their decision as one of fact. *Scales v George Thompson & Co Ltd*, KB 1927, 13 TC 83.

Selling and letting railway wagons—whether separate trades

[61.58] A company (N) sold railway wagons. It also hired wagons to customers, but discontinued this on the nationalisation of the railways in 1948. N appealed against assessments for 1947/48 and 1948/49, contending that hiring wagons to customers had been a separate trade. The Commissioners rejected this contention and upheld the assessments, and the CA unanimously dismissed N's appeal. *North Central Wagon & Finance Co Ltd v Fifield*, CA 1953, 34 TC 59; [1953] 1 WLR 110; [1953] 1 All ER 1009.

Electronics business—whether one trade or several trades

[61.59] A company carried on an electronics business, organised through six separate divisions. It closed two of its UK factories. It claimed terminal loss relief on the basis that each of its divisions constituted a separate trade. The

Revenue rejected the claim on the basis that the company was carrying on a single trade. The Special Commissioners dismissed the company's appeal, finding that the company was carrying on 'a single global trade'. *Electronics Ltd v HM Inspector of Taxes*, Sp C [2005] SSCD 512 (Sp C 476).

Timber plantation—whether timber extraction a separate business

[61.60] In a Malaysian case, a company (R) was engaged commercially in the extraction of timber and in the management of a plantation in Borneo. The Revenue issued assessments on the basis that R carried on two separate businesses: a plantation business (which would include timber extraction necessary to clear an estate for plantation), and a business of timber extraction in forest areas where there was no planting. (The practical importance of the issue was certain special plantation allowances which R wished to set off against income from its timber operations.) The PC upheld the assessments and dismissed R's appeal. *River Estates Sdn Bhd v Malaysian Director General of Inland Revenue*, PC 1983, [1984] STC 60.

Company developing jungle as oil palm plantation

[61.61] In another Malaysian case, a company (M) entered into an agreement with the Johore government under which, in return for a capital payment, it was granted 7,000 acres of jungle for development as an oil palm plantation at the rate of 1,000 acres a year. It was licensed, subject to royalty payments, to sell timber from the land as it was cleared. The Revenue issued assessments on the basis that the receipts from the sale of the timber were chargeable as 'gains or profits from a business' within the meaning of the relevant legislation. The Malaysian Special Commissioners upheld the assessments but the PC allowed M's appeal. The agreement had to be looked at as a whole, and the felling and extraction of timber was a necessary and obligatory step inseparable from the process of developing the area as an oil palm plantation. The timber was part of the capital asset acquired by payment of a capital sum and the sums received on the sale of the timber were in mitigation of capital expenditure in developing the asset. M was not carrying on a business of timber operators. *Mamor Sdn Bhd v Malaysian Director-General of Inland Revenue*, PC [1985] STC 801.

Merger of businesses on commencement of partnership

[61.62] A trader (H) carried on the business of contracting for the processing of films. The actual processing was done for him by another trader (T), who carried on a separate business of film processing. H and T entered into partnership and thereafter the two businesses were merged. The Commissioners held that the merged business was an entirely new business, and not a continuation of either or both of the businesses merged. The KB upheld their decision as one of fact. *George Humphries & Co v Cook*, KB 1934, 19 TC 121.

Union of building societies

[61.63] Under arrangements authorised by *Building Societies Act 1962*, two building societies united as a single society. They retained their certificates of incorporation, and no such certificate was issued to the new society. However, the united society (NR) thereafter conducted the affairs of the two in its own name with the same directors and staff and in the premises of one of them. The Special Commissioners held that NR was a separate person which had carried on the trades previously carried on by its constituent societies. The Ch D upheld this decision. *Northern Rock Building Society v Davies*, Ch D 1969, 46 TC 98; [1969] 1 WLR 1742; [1969] 3 All ER 1310.

Dissolution of accountancy partnership

[61.64] A firm of chartered accountants comprised two main equity partners, each operating from one of two independently-run offices. A dispute arose between the partners, and the partnership was dissolved in April 1983. Each of the former partners continued to operate from the same office as a sole practitioner. The Revenue issued an assessment to recover stock relief, and the partners appealed, contending that the assessment was invalid because they had lodged a continuation election. The Commissioners dismissed the appeal, holding that a continuation election could not be made where a trade was split into substantive parts. The Ch D upheld the Commissioners' decision, holding that neither of the practices could be treated as a continuation of the trade which had previously been carried on by the partnership. *C Connelly & Co v Wilbey*, Ch D 1992, 65 TC 208; [1992] STC 783. (*Note*. For another issue in this case, see **63.162** TRADING PROFITS.)

Trading by receiver

[61.65] A company's business was carried on by a receiver appointed by its debenture holder. The KB held that he had not succeeded to the trade (but was taxable on the profits as the person 'receiving or entitled to the income' under legislation which has subsequently been repealed. *CIR v Thompson*, KB 1936, 20 TC 422; [1937] 1 KB 290; [1936] 2 All ER 651. (*Note*. *Dicta* of Lawrence J, with regard to whether the income was 'received' by the receiver, were subsequently disapproved by Lightman J in *CIR v Piacentini & Others*, **13.23** COMPANY LIQUIDATION AND RECEIVERSHIP.)

Non-resident trader becoming resident

[61.66] An overseas company, previously not within the charge to UK tax, became resident here from 1 July 1925, and chargeable to UK income tax in respect of the mining business it had been carrying on since its incorporation in 1919. The Revenue contended that the 1925/26 assessment should be on the basis that a new trade was 'set up or commenced' on 1 July 1925. The HL held that the assessment should be on the basis that there had been no commencement in 1925/26 (and should be based on the average of the three preceding years under the rules then in force). *Fry v Burma Corporation Ltd*, HL 1930, 15 TC 113; [1930] AC 321. (*Notes*. (1) See now *ITTOIA 2005, s 17*. (2)

HMRC treat this case as authority for the proposition that 'the relocation of a local business, if substantial enough in nature, will give rise to the permanent discontinuance of one trade and the commencement of a new and different one': see Business Income Manual, BIM70605.)

Transfer of right to receive post-cessation receipts

[61.67] See *Brewin v McVittie*, 65.61 TRADING PROFITS.

*Post-cessation receipts—effect of ITTOIA 2005, s 257**

[61.68] See *Gilmore v Inspector of Taxes*, 65.63 TRADING PROFITS.

62

Trading Profits—Basic Rules (ITTOIA 2005, ss 24–31)

The cases in this chapter are arranged under the following headings.

Professions and vocations (ITTOIA 2005, s 24)

NOTE

Paragraphs **62.1** to **62.11** below relate to claims to exemption from excess profits duty or excess profits tax. For a useful discussion of the ordinary meaning of 'profession', see the judgment of du Parcq LJ in *Carr v CIR*, **62.7** below.

Journalist

[62.1] The owner of a monthly political magazine wrote a large part of the contents himself. The CA held that, for excess profits duty purposes, he carried on a separate profession of journalist and editor, and that a reasonable allowance for his services should be made in arriving at the profits of his publishing business. Scrutton LJ held that 'a "profession" in the present use of language involves the idea of an occupation requiring either purely intellectual skill, or if any manual skill, as in painting or sculpture, or surgery, skill controlled by the intellectual skill of the operator, as distinguished from an occupation which is substantially the production, or sale, or arrangements for the production or sale of commodities'. Therefore 'a journalist whose contributions have any literary form, as distinguished from a reporter, exercises a "profession"'. *CIR v Maxse*, CA 1919, 12 TC 41; [1919] 1 KB 647. (*Note*. For a recent case in which this decision was applied, see *Salt v Fernandez*, **59.91** TRADING INCOME.)

Photographer

[62.2] The KB held that a freelance photographer was not carrying on a profession. *Cecil v CIR*, KB 1919, 36 TLR 164.

Tax consultant

[62.3] The Commissioners held that the business of an income tax repayment agent was not a profession, and the CA unanimously upheld their decision. *Currie v CIR*,CA 1921, 12 TC 245; [1921] 2 KB 332. (*Note*. The case was heard in the CA with *Durant v CIR*, 62.4 below.)

Insurance broker

[62.4] The Commissioners held that the business of an insurance broker was not a profession, and the CA unanimously upheld their decision. *Durant v CIR*, CA 1921, 12 TC 245; [1921] 2 KB 332. (*Note*. The case was heard in the CA with *Currie v CIR*, 62.3 above.)

Auctioneering company

[62.5] The CS held that a company which carried on business as auctioneers was not carrying on a profession, on the grounds that a company could not have the 'personal qualifications' necessary to bring it within the exemption. *CIR v Peter McIntyre Ltd*, CS 1926, 12 TC 1006. (*Note*. The company also contended that it was entitled to the benefit of an arrangement between the Inland Revenue and the Auctioneers' Institute which the Revenue refused to apply to it. The CS held that the arrangement could not and did not grant an exemption not conferred by the Finance Acts.)

Optician

[62.6] The KB held that an ophthalmic optician was not carrying on a profession, but was carrying on the business of selling spectacles. The eye-testing was ancillary and the receipts from eye-testing did not qualify for exemption. *Webster v CIR*, KB [1942] 2 All ER 517.

[62.7] In a subsequent case, the Commissioners held that an optician was carrying on a profession and the CA upheld their decision as one of fact. Du Parcq LJ observed that 'before one can say that a man is carrying on a profession, one must see that he has some special skill or ability, or some special qualifications derived from training or experience. Even there one has to be very careful, because there are many people whose work demands great skill and ability and long experience and many qualifications who would not be said by anybody to be carrying on a profession'. He held that 'it must be the intention of the legislature, when it refers to a profession, to indicate what the ordinary intelligent subject, taking down the volume of the statutes and reading the section, will think that "profession" means'. *Carr v CIR*, CA [1944] 2 All ER 163.

[62.8] In another case concerning an optician, the General Commissioners found that £750 of the profit of £2,902 was derived from the carrying on of a profession. The CA reversed their decision, holding that there was no evidence of the existence of two separate businesses, so that none of the profit qualified for exemption. *Neild v CIR*, CA 1948, 27 ATC 328.

[62.9] In *Amah v HMRC (No 2)*, 61.54 TRADING INCOME, the First-tier Tribunal held that an optician was carrying on a trade rather than a profession.

Dance band leader

[62.10] The KB held that the leader and conductor of a well-known dance band was not carrying on a profession. *Loss v CIR*, KB [1945] 2 All ER 683.

Estate agents

[62.11] The KB held that a firm carrying on business as land and estate agents, auctioneers and valuers was carrying on a profession (reversing the decision of the Commissioners). *Escritt & Barrell v CIR*, KB 1947, 26 ATC 33.

Dramatist

[62.12] A former barrister wrote and sold a successful play, after having written several plays in his spare time without selling them. The Special Commissioners held that he had been carrying on the vocation of dramatist, and that his receipts from the successful play were receipts of that vocation. The KB upheld their decision. *Billam v Griffith*, KB 1941, 23 TC 757.

Solicitor—fees for professional services as trustee

[62.13] A solicitor acted as trustee under certain wills and a deed of settlement, under which he was entitled to charge for any professional service rendered. The KB held that his charges were part of the profits of his profession and were chargeable to income tax. *Jones v Wright*, KB 1927, 13 TC 221.

[62.14] A practising solicitor was one of two trustees of certain property, of which he beneficially owned four-ninths. He charged his normal fees for his professional services to the trust, and appealed against an assessment, contending that four-ninths of these fees should be excluded from his profits on the ground that he effectively bore this proportion as his own client. The Special Commissioners rejected this contention and dismissed his appeal, holding that the full fees were assessable. The CA unanimously upheld their decision. *Watson & Everitt v Blunden*, CA 1933, 18 TC 402.

Doctor—whether profession continuing after deregistration

[62.15] See *Bhadra (t/a Admirals Locums) v HMRC*, 61.18 TRADING INCOME.

Payments to trustees as 'remuneration'

[62.16] See *Baxendale v Murphy*, 39.25 MISCELLANEOUS INCOME, and *Hearn v Morgan*, 39.26 MISCELLANEOUS INCOME.

Application of cash basis to professions

[62.17] See the cases noted at 62.24 *et seq.* below.

Generally accepted accounting practice (ITTOIA 2005, s 25; CTA 2009, s 46)

General

The relevance of accountancy principles

[62.18] The courts have consistently accepted that where there is no explicit guidance in the legislation, the way the profits are arrived at under the principles of commercial accounting is important. For examples of the relevance of accountancy principles, see *Willingale v International Commercial Bank Ltd*, 62.47 below; *Threlfall v Jones*, 62.56 below; *Herbert Smith v Honour*, 62.80 below; *BSC Footwear Ltd v Ridgway*, 65.23 TRADING PROFITS; *Mars UK Ltd v Small*, 65.24 TRADING PROFITS, and *William Grant & Sons Distillers Ltd v HMRC*, 65.25 TRADING PROFITS. In the latter case Lord Hope of Craighead observed that 'accounting principles have moved on since 1961. What may have been regarded as unacceptable then need not be regarded as unacceptable now. The golden rule is that the profits of a trading company must be computed in accordance with currently accepted accounting principles.'

Whether accounts may be reopened

[62.19] In a case where the substantive issue has been overtaken by subsequent legislation (see now *ITTOIA 2005, s 97* and *CTA 2009, s 94*), the HL held that accounts could not be reopened to take account of the fact that a debt had subsequently been written off. *British Mexican Petroleum Co Ltd v Jackson*, HL 1932, 16 TC 570. (*Note*. Despite the subsequent changes to the legislation, the Revenue for many years accepted this case as establishing that written-back trade debt need not be credited to the profit and loss account. However, in 2001 they announced that they 'no longer consider' that the decision is applicable, and they had reached the view that 'the correct computation of profits chargeable to tax under Schedule D, Cases I and II should include the credit to profit and loss account of a trade debt write-back': see Revenue Tax Bulletin, December 2001, p 901, and Business Income Manual, BIM40265.)

[62.20] For other cases concerning retrospective adjustments to accounts, see *Isaac Holden & Sons Ltd v CIR*, 62.33 below; the cases noted at 62.35 to 62.39 below; *New Conveyor Co Ltd v Dodd*, 62.43 below; *North v Spencer's Executors*, 62.46 below, and *Bernhard v Gahan*, 62.52 below.

Whether profit may be determined by current cost accounting method

[62.21] Income tax in New Zealand is charged on 'assessable income' elaborately defined. In 1973 the definition was extended to include profits or gains from the sale of land under an undertaking or scheme involving the development or division into plots of the land, where the undertaking or scheme was commenced within ten years of the acquisition of the land by the taxpayer. In a New Zealand case, the taxpayers had purchased land in 1961 and decided in 1963 to divide it into plots for development and sale as housing sites. In 1973/74 they sold six plots for $29,366. The cost of the plots was $13,800 and they were assessed on the difference of $15,566. They appealed on the ground that the profit they derived was not the $15,566 based on historic cost accounting but a lesser figure based on a current cost accounting method which would reflect the effect of inflation between 1961 and 1973. The PC dismissed the appeals (upholding the decision of the New Zealand courts). Lord Templeman observed that 'this appeal must however be determined not by fashionable theories but by practice and law. It is clear that by the practice and law of New Zealand, a profit or loss for income tax purposes can only be measured in the present circumstance by the difference between dollars expended and dollars received'. *Lowe & Others v Inland Revenue Commr*, PC [1983] STC 816.

[62.22] In an Irish case, it was held that accounts for tax purposes must prepared on the historical cost accounting convention, and that current cost accounting was not acceptable. *Carroll Industries plc and PJ Carroll & Co Ltd v O'Culachain*, HC(I) 2 December 1988 unreported.

Cash basis

NOTE

Following *FA 1998, s 42*, the cash basis is no longer permitted for tax purposes (except for barristers or advocates in the early years of practice).

Consultant—whether cash basis permissible

[62.23] A consultant began self-employment in May 1984. In his first year of trading he issued invoices totalling £18,245 for work carried out, but he did not receive payment until his subsequent year of account. He produced accounts on a cash basis, which indicated that he had made a loss in the opening year of trading. The Revenue issued assessments on the basis that the accounts should have been drawn up on an earnings basis, so that the £18,245 should have been included as income in the opening accounts. The consultant appealed, contending that he was entitled to use a cash basis. The Special Commissioner rejected this contention and dismissed the appeal. Applying *dicta* of Sir Thomas Bingham MR in *Gallagher v Jones*, **62.56** below, the profits had to be determined using the accepted principles of commercial accountancy. Accordingly, the accounts should have been drawn up on an earnings basis. *Walker v O'Connor*, Sp C [1996] SSCD 218 (Sp C 74). (*Note*. For another issue in this case, see **63.249** TRADING PROFITS.)

Change from earnings to cash basis—treatment of 'overlapping' receipts

[62.24] A civil engineer was, at his request, assessed on the 'cash basis' for 1928/29. He had previously been assessed on the earnings basis. He contended that amounts which he had earned before 6 April 1927 but not received until the year ending 5 April 1928 (which was his basis period for 1928/29 under the legislation then in force) should be excluded from his 1928/29 assessment. The CS rejected this contention. *CIR v Morrison*, CS 1932, 17 TC 325.

Whether earnings basis appropriate

[62.25] The assessments on a firm of accountants for 1954/55 to 1957/58 were on an earnings basis and under appeal. For previous years the assessments had been on a cash basis and the 1958/59 assessment, not under appeal, was also on a cash basis. The firm contended that the assessments under appeal should also be on that basis. The Ch D rejected this contention, holding that the assessments under appeal were properly made on the earnings basis. Any objection to the change back to the cash basis for 1958/59 could have been dealt with only by way of an appeal for that year. *Wetton, Page & Co v Attwooll*, Ch D 1962, 40 TC 619; [1963] 1 WLR 114; [1963] 1 All ER 166.

Cash basis in force—receipts paid to executors of deceased partner

[62.26] A partner in a firm of solicitors died. The assessments on the firm's profits were on a cash basis and were computed on the basis that there had been no discontinuance at the partner's death. The firm appealed, contending that amounts which it paid to the executors in respect of profits earned before, but received after, the death (in compliance with the terms of the partnership agreement) were not part of the firm's income after the death or, alternatively, were deductible as an expense. The CS rejected these contentions and dismissed the appeals. *McCash & Hunter v CIR*, CS 1955, 36 TC 170. (*Note*. See also *CIR v Hunter*, **2.12** ANNUAL PAYMENTS.)

Whether Revenue can revert to earnings basis

[62.27] A firm of civil and mining engineers had been assessed for many years on the cash basis. The business was discontinued in 1944/45. A first assessment was made for 1944/45 on the earnings basis, and additional assessments were made for 1942/43 and 1943/44 to cover substantial fees earned in those years but not received until after the discontinuance. The CS held that the 1944/45 assessment could properly be on the earnings basis, but that the original cash basis assessments for 1942/43 and 1943/44 exhausted the liability for those years. (The cash basis assessments for those years on the 'preceding year' basis exceeded the actual profits on the cash basis.) *D & GR Rankine v CIR*, CS 1952, 32 TC 520. (*Note*. The fees would now be assessable under *ITTOIA 2005, ss 242–245* ('charge to tax on post-cessation receipts'), deriving from *FA 1960*.)

Receipts and expenses (ITTOIA 2005, s 27)

The date a receipt arises

NOTE

Some of the cases below are excess profits duty appeals, relating to sums received after the period for which excess profits duty was charged, but which the Revenue considered should be included in the profits of that period.

Long-term contract

[62.28] A company (J) agreed to supply sets of certain control gear, to be manufactured for it by a subcontractor. The purchase price was invoiced on delivery. The CA held that the profit should be included in the periods in which the sets were delivered (and not, as J contended, in the period in which the contract was made). *JP Hall & Co Ltd v CIR*, CA 1921, 12 TC 382; [1921] 3 KB 152.

Variation of long-term contract

[62.29] A company (F) had agreed to supply two customers with ironstone under a long-term contract with provision for negotiated price variation. It reached a provisional agreement that it would increase its prices with effect from 1919. However, the agreements were not signed until 1925. They were then deemed to have come into operation at the end of 1920 (for one customer) and from 1921 (for the other customer). F subsequently received payments totalling more than £70,000 from the customers, backdated to 1919 and paid in instalments. F appealed against assessments on these payments, contending firstly that they were capital receipts and not taxable, and alternatively that they were only taxable when they were received. The Special Commissioners rejected these contentions and the KB dismissed F's appeal, holding that the payments were trading receipts and were taxable for the periods in which the relevant ironstone was delivered. *Frodingham Ironstone Mines Ltd v Stewart*, KB 1932, 16 TC 728.

Progress payments under long-term contracts of architects

[62.30] See *Symons v Weeks*, 65.43 TRADING PROFITS.

Cancellation of contracts for sale of goods

[62.31] See *Jesse Robinson & Sons v CIR*, 66.19 TRADING PROFITS.

Whether forward contracts cancelled

[62.32] A company (W) sold yarn under forward contracts. In January 1921 a customer requested to be invoiced for the difference between the contract price in certain uncompleted contracts and the current market value (which was substantially lower). The customer agreed to pay the difference (£4,107) as the yarn was taken up. The Revenue assessed W to excess profits duty on the basis that the £4,107 was assessable in its accounting period ending in February 1921. The KB allowed W's appeal, holding that the original contracts had not been cancelled, and that the £4,107 was not a trading receipt when it was invoiced. *Wright Sutcliffe Ltd v CIR*, KB 1929, 8 ATC 168. (*Note*. See *JH Young & Co v CIR*, **62.65** below, as to the treatment of a similar arrangement in the accounts of the purchaser.)

Retrospective variation of commission rate

[62.33] While the wool trade was subject to wartime controls, a company was engaged in woolcombing for the Government on a commission basis. The rate of commission for 1918 was not finally agreed until July 1919. The Special Commissioners held that, in arriving at the company's profits to 30 June 1918, the commission should be credited at the rate eventually agreed. The KB upheld this decision. *Isaac Holden & Sons Ltd v CIR*, KB 1924, 12 TC 768.

Refund of Government levy

[62.34] A company (E), which manufactured dairy products, was required to obtain a licence from the Food Controller to purchase the milk it required, paying the Controller 2d per gallon. In the year to 30 April 1920 it paid £8,236. The legality of the levy was disputed. Subsequently it was accepted that the levy had been illegal, and the £8,236 was refunded to E in 1924. The Special Commissioners upheld the Revenue's contention that the refund should be treated as a receipt of the year to 30 April 1920, and the KB upheld this decision. *English Dairies Ltd v Phillips*, KB 1927, 11 TC 597.

Retrospective award for requisition of trading stock

[62.35] In 1918, the Admiralty, acting under wartime regulations, requisitioned part of the stocks of rum held by a brewery company (N). It paid N £10,315 for the rum. N accepted this without prejudice to its claim to a further amount, and credited it in its accounts for the year ending October 1918. In 1921 a War Compensation Court awarded N an additional £5,309. The Revenue issued an EPD assessment on the basis that this was a trading receipt and was taxable for N's accounting year ending October 1918. The KB upheld the assessment and the HL unanimously dismissed N's appeal. *CIR v Newcastle Breweries Ltd*, HL 1927, 12 TC 927.

Delayed closing of 'pooling' arrangement

[62.36] During the First World War, the coaling of ships at Gibraltar took place under a wartime pooling agreement between the coal merchants and the Ministry of Shipping. This ended in 1919, and it was found that the actual closing coal stock of the pool considerably exceeded the figure in the pool accounts. Lengthy negotiations ensued between the merchants and the Ministry, during which certain commission which had been credited to the merchants was carried to a suspense account. The matter was settled in 1923, the merchants receiving amounts representing their share of the commission and of the value of the surplus stock. The CA upheld assessments issued on the basis that these amounts were trading receipts and were taxable for the period during which the pool was in existence. *Lambert Bros Ltd v CIR*, CA 1927, 12 TC 1053.

Delayed compensation for detention of ships

[62.37] During a coal strike in 1920, the Government ordered that two ships owned by a company (E) should be temporarily detained in port. After prolonged negotiations, the Government paid E compensation in 1924 for its loss of the use of the ships. The CA held that the compensation was a trading receipt, to be brought into E's profits for 1920. *Ensign Shipping Co Ltd v CIR*, CA 1928, 12 TC 1169.

Shipbuilder—compensation received on cancellation of order

[62.38] See *Short Bros Ltd v CIR*, **66.15** TRADING PROFITS.

Insurance recovery for stock—retrospective variation of contract

[62.39] The KB held that insurance recoveries in respect of the accidental destruction of stock were taxable in the year of destruction and that certain additional receipts under the variation of a contract were taxable when they became ascertainable. *Rownson Drew & Clydesdale Ltd v CIR*, KB 1931, 16 TC 595. (*Note*. For another issue in this case, see **62.53** below.)

Accrued whisky storage charges

[62.40] A distillery company (D) sold its whisky as soon as possible after distillation, and generally then stored it for the purchaser in its bonded warehouses. By law, the whisky could not be sold for consumption before three years. The storage charges were not due or payable until the whisky was removed or transferred, and were subject to an allowance for leakage. Before 1928/29 the charges had been treated as assessable when they were paid, but for 1928/29 the Revenue claimed that they should be brought in as they accrued during the period of storage. The CS allowed D's appeal (by a 3–1 majority, Lord Morison dissenting), holding that the accrued charges could not be included in the profits. *Dailuaine-Talisker Distilleries Ltd v CIR*, CS 1930, 15 TC 613. (*Note*. This decision was subsequently disapproved by Lord Normand and Lord Simonds in *CIR v Gardner Mountain & D'Ambrumenil Ltd*, **62.44** below.)

[62.41] See also *CIR v Oban Distillery Co Ltd*, **68.28** TRADING PROFITS.

Acquisition of accrued whisky storage charges

[62.42] A distillery company (B) purchased the assets of a similar company (M), including bonded warehouses where whisky which M had sold to customers was stored. The storage charges were payable by customers when they removed the whisky. B paid M £5,000 for the right to receive the accrued charges which M had agreed with the customers. The Revenue issued assessments charging tax on the amounts which B subsequently received from M's customers but the Commissioners allowed B's appeal and the CS upheld this decision. Lord Normand observed that B 'had bought ascertained book debts', so that 'these book debts as they came to be paid to the respondents were not subject to income tax'. *CIR v Arthur Bell & Sons Ltd*, CS 1932, 22 TC 315.

Retrospective revision of 'cost-plus' prices

[62.43] A company (N) manufactured doors for two other companies which supplied them to the War Office on a 'cost-plus' basis. Following a revision of the costings, N became entitled to further payments. The KB held that these were trading receipts of the years in which the doors were delivered. *New Conveyor Co Ltd v Dodd*, KB 1945, 27 TC 11.

Underwriting commission

[62.44] A company acted as an agent for Lloyd's underwriters, and was paid salary and commission. As a consequence of the special method used at Lloyd's for ascertaining underwriting profits, its commission on policies underwritten in year 1 was not ascertained and paid until after the end of year 3. The HL unanimously upheld the Revenue's contention that the commissions were earned in the year in which the policies were underwritten, and should be brought into account accordingly. *CIR v Gardner Mountain & D'Ambrumenil Ltd*, HL 1947, 29 TC 69; [1947] 1 All ER 650.

[62.45] A self-employed insurance agent acted for a major insurance company, receiving initial commission and renewal commission. His right to full initial commission depended on policies being kept up for up to four years. He was paid on 'indemnity terms', under which (in his case) 50% of the initial commission was paid to him before the periodic premiums were received from the assured person. On average, 13% of the policies which he had arranged lapsed. He appealed against an assessment, contending that the sums which he had received on indemnity terms should only be brought into account to the extent to that his entitlement was vested, with no potential liability to repay. The Special Commissioners rejected this contention and dismissed his appeal, holding that 'the correct principle of commercial accounting practice to be applied in the light of the facts and circumstances of this case is the "up-front" method' (i.e. recognising advances when received, with any necessary provision for lapses). *Robertson v CIR*, Sp C [1997] SSCD 282 (Sp C 137).

Retrospective awards to doctors

[62.46] A doctor (S) took his brother into partnership in 1950, and died two years later. In 1953, following an award of retrospective remuneration to doctors in the National Health Service, payments were made to his executors and his brother, covering the years 1948/49 to 1952/53 inclusive. The Revenue included the payments in additional assessments on the executors (for 1949/50 and 1950/51) and on the executors and S's brother (for 1950/51 to 1952/53). The Ch D upheld the assessments. *North v Spencer's Executors & CH Spencer*, Ch D 1956, 36 TC 668.

Discount on Bills of Exchange

[62.47] A bank was formed to provide medium-term finance to commercial companies. It operated by discounting or purchasing bills, etc. for periods up to ten years. The bills were usually held until maturity and in its accounts, its discount, i.e. the excess of the amount of the bill over its cost, was spread over the period of the bill. The Revenue issued an assessment on the basis that its profits should be arrived at similarly. The Commissioners allowed the bank's appeal, holding that for tax purposes the discount could not be anticipated before the maturity of the bill. The HL upheld their decision (by a 3-2 majority, Lord Diplock and Lord Russell of Killowen dissenting). Lord Salmon held that 'a profit may not be taxed until it is realised. This does not mean until it has been received in cash but it does mean until it has been ascertained and earned'. It followed that 'corporation tax cannot be levied in respect of the bank's transactions until the fiscal year in which the bank sells the bill or, if the bank holds it until maturity, until the fiscal year in which it matures'. Lord Fraser of Tullybelton held that 'the bank's accounts prepared for commercial purposes are drawn up on the principle of anticipating future profits' and were 'not a proper basis for assessing the bank's liability to corporation tax'. *Willingale v International Commercial Bank Ltd*, HL 1977, 52 TC 242; [1978] STC 75; [1978] 2 WLR 452; [1978] 1 All ER 754. (*Note.* For HMRC's interpretation of this decision, see Business Income Manual, BIM40090. They state that the case 'is a specialised one and it is unlikely that the decision is of any general application outside the financial sector'.)

Farmer—sale of growing crops

[62.48] See *Gunn v CIR*, 27.8 FARMING.

Collateral deposits by builder

[62.49] See *John Cronk & Sons Ltd v Harrison*, 68.40 TRADING PROFITS.

The date an expense is deductible

General

Rubber planting—preliminary expenditure before rubber reaped

[62.50] A UK company (V) carried on a business of rubber planting in Federated Malay States. Rubber trees do not yield rubber until they are about six years old. The Revenue contended that only one-seventh of V's expenditure on superintendence, weeding, etc. for any year was deductible in computing the profits of that year, and that the remaining six-sevenths was not deductible as it was capital expenditure which wsa not referable to a profit reaped within the year. The Court allowed V's appeal, holding that the whole of the expenditure was deductible. *Vallambrosa Rubber Co Ltd v Farmer*, CE 1910, 5 TC 529. (*Note.* This has been viewed by some commentators as a leading case, but in the 1993 case of *Threlfall v Jones*, **62.56** below, Sir Thomas Bingham MR held that the decision here did not lay down 'any general overriding principle'.)

Repairs expenditure—whether deductible when repairs accrued

[62.51] Because of a strike, a colliery company (N) was compelled to close its mines from 1 April to 2 July 1921. It incurred unusually high expenditure in making good the damage to the mines during the closure, and claimed that this expenditure should be deducted from the profits of its accounting period ending 30 June 1921. The Special Commissioners rejected the claim and the

HL unanimously dismissed N's appeal, holding that the expenditure could not be deducted until the repairs were actually undertaken. *Naval Colliery Co Ltd v CIR*, HL 1928, 12 TC 1017.

Re-opening of accounts—estimated liability later revised

[62.52] An exporter (B) financed his shipments by borrowing from a bank, using bills drawn on the buyers as security. One of the buyers could not meet its liabilities and, in his accounts to March 1921, B claimed a deduction of £22,410 for his estimated liability to the bank. The Revenue initially accepted these accounts, but the bank subsequently accepted £8,000 in full settlement of its claim, and the Revenue issued assessments to substitute a deduction of £8,000 for the £22,410 previously. The Special Commissioners dismissed B's appeal and the CA unanimously upheld their decision. *Bernhard v Gahan*, CA 1928, 13 TC 723.

Retrospective variation of selling agreement

[62.53] A company (R) claimed a deduction in 1920 for an accrued loss on a contract which was still running and was subsequently varied retrospectively. The Revenue rejected the claim and the KB dismissed R's appeal. *Rownson Drew & Clydesdale Ltd v CIR*, KB 1931, 16 TC 595. (*Note*. For another issue in this case, see **62.39** above.)

Deductibility of wages of footballers for non-playing period

[62.54] In 1948 the Scottish Football League instructed its members to make their agreements with their players to run from 1 August to 31 July, instead of from 1 May to 30 April as previously. Accordingly, a club made its agreements for 15 months to 31 July 1949 to effect the transition. It appealed against income tax and profits tax assessments, contending that, as its accounts to 31 March 1949 covered eight of the nine months of the 1948/49 playing season, eight-ninths of its payments to players for the two non-playing periods of May to July 1948 and 1949 should be treated as deductible in computing its profits of the year to 31 March 1949. The Special Commissioners rejected this contention and upheld the assessments, holding that the payments to players were deductible as and when they became due and payable. The HL unanimously upheld this decision. Lord Porter observed that the payments for May to July were 'more naturally attributable to the following season and not to the preceding one'. *Albion Rovers Football Club Ltd v CIR*, HL 1952, 33 TC 331.

Damages awarded by court but later compounded

[62.55] In 1955 a bank obtained judgment against a company and a solicitor who had acted for it. The company paid part of the amount, leaving £28,521 payable by the solicitor. In 1958 the bank agreed to accept £3,000 in settlement of its claim. The Revenue agreed to allow a deduction for the £3,000. The solicitor appealed against an income tax assessment for 1958/59, contending that the whole of the £28,521 should be allowed as a deduction. The Special Commissioners rejected this contention and the Ch D dismissed the solicitor's appeal. Megarry J observed that the accounts should show 'the true amount of that debt which has ultimately been established'. *Simpson v Jones*, Ch D 1968, 44 TC 599; [1968] 1 WLR 1066; [1968] 2 All ER 929.

Whether leasing payments deductible when incurred

[62.56] In 1989 two individuals began leasing boats, in order to carry on a trade of hiring them out on a short-term basis. The leases were for a primary period of 24 months, and provided for a substantial initial payment, followed by 17 monthly payments and five months in which no payment was due. After the end of the primary period, the boats were to be rented at £5 p.a. for a secondary period of 21 years. In their first accounts, the taxpayers claimed a deduction for the whole amount which they had paid under the leases in that basis period (thereby creating a substantial trading loss for which they claimed relief under *ICTA 1988, s 381*). The Revenue rejected the claims, considering that, under accountancy principles, the total payments due in the first 24 months of the agreements should be spread evenly over the 24 months in question. The Special Commissioner dismissed the taxpayers' appeals and the CA unanimously upheld the Commissioner's decision. The way to ascertain the profits or losses of a business was to apply accepted principles of commercial accountancy. The accounts submitted had not been drawn up in accordance with such principles, and gave 'a completely misleading picture' of the taxpayers' trading results. The fact that trading expenditure had been incurred in a given period did not necessarily mean that it automatically fell to be deducted in that period. *Threlfall v Jones*; *Gallagher v Jones*, CA 1993, 66 TC 77; [1993] STC 537; [1994] 2 WLR 160; [1994] Ch 107. (*Note*. For the Revenue's practice following this decision, see Revenue Tax Bulletin February 1995, pp 189–193.)

Contribution to pension scheme—whether deductible when paid

[62.57] A company made a special contribution of £186,200 to an approved pension scheme. It claimed a deduction for this in the year of payment. The Revenue issued a direction under *FA 1970, s 21(3)* that the expense should be spread over five years. The Commissioners determined the appeal on the basis that the expense should be allowed in full in the year of payment, but the Ch D reversed their decision. Arden J held that the Revenue had been entitled to exercise its discretion under *ICTA 1988, s 592(6)**, and the Commissioners did not have the power to review the exercise of that discretion. *Kelsall v Investment Chartwork Ltd*, Ch D 1993, 65 TC 750; [1994] STC 33. (*Note. FA 1970, s 21(3)* subsequently became *ICTA 1988, s 592(6)*, which was repealed by *FA 2004* with effect from 6 April 2006.)

Retrospective claim for deduction of interest previously capitalised

[62.58] In a Hong Kong case, a company (S) was incorporated to undertake property development. It incurred significant interest charges. For 1988 to 1990 it capitalised these by treating them as part of the cost of the development. However, in its 1991 accounts, it claimed to deduct the total interest capitalised in the three previous years from the proceeds of its sales of flats in 1991. The Hong Kong Board of Review rejected the claim, and the Final Court of Appeal upheld this decision. Lord Millett observed that S's accounts for 1998 to 1990 had given 'a true and fair view of its profits or losses for each of these years. Any increase in the cost of work in progress, whether resulting from the incurring of further construction costs or the payment of interest, was matched by a corresponding increase in the value of property under development and gave rise to neither profit nor loss. Thus the exclusion of both figures from the profit and loss account did not affect the final balance on the account. The two figures would have cancelled each other out, reflecting the fact that the acquisition of an asset at a cost equal to its value produces neither a profit nor a loss.' If S had continued to adopt this accounting policy, 'it would have obtained relief for its interest payments by treating them as part of the cost of sales and deducting an appropriate proportion of the total from the proceeds of sales made in the current year'. Instead, it had 'elected to rewrite its accounts retrospectively' in order to set the whole of the interest charges for the earlier years, as well as the interest charge in the current year, against the proceeds of sales made in the current year. S's accounts for 1998 to 1990 had been 'properly prepared in accordance with ordinary accounting principles' and 'showed a true and fair view of the taxpayer's losses. In the computation of these losses interest was properly deducted by being debited and then set off against the corresponding increase in the value of property under development.' However, in its 1991 accounts, S had claimed 'to bring forward losses which, because it capitalised the interest, it did not sustain. These fictitious losses arise from double counting. The process involves charging the interest to the development cost account in order to prevent the increased value of property under development creating a trading profit for the year to be carried into the profit and loss account, and at the same time charging it to the profit and loss account in order to increase the loss for the year.' *Hong Kong Commissioner of Inland Revenue v Secan Ltd; Hong Kong Commissioner of Inland Revenue v Ranon Ltd*, FCA(HK) 2000, 74 TC 1. (*Note*. For the Revenue's practice following this decision, see Revenue Tax Bulletin, June 2002, pp 936–937.)

Services performed by associated company

[62.59] In his accounts for the year ending 30 April 2006, a landscape gardener (C) claimed a deduction of £110,000 for services allegedly carried out by an associated company (W). HMRC began an enquiry, and discovered that W had only been incorporated on 15 March 2006. It had invoiced C for £59,000 on 30 April 2006 and for £51,000 on 1 May 2007. HMRC issued an amendment on the basis that the £59,000 should be spread over the period from 15 March 2006 to 30 April 2007 (so that only a small proportion of it was deductible in the year ending April 2006), and that the £51,000 was deductible in the year ending April 2008. C appealed. The First-Tier Tribunal dismissed the appeal, holding that the effect of *FA 1998, s 42* was that C's accounts should have been prepared on the basis of generally accepted accounting practice, which meant that any services he had received from W 'should be treated as expenses in the periods to which they relate and this should be, as far as possible, in the periods when the services were received'. Judge Reid observed that it appeared that the invoices had been 'an attempt to transfer to (W) income already earned by the appellant in order to take advantage of reduced rates of corporation tax. That, unfortunately for the appellant, is a tax avoidance or mitigation manoeuvre which does not work.' C had provided no evidence which would justify varying the straight-line apportionment which HMRC had allowed. *W Craig v HMRC*, FTT [2012] UKFTT 90 (TC), TC01786.

Future and contingent liabilities

Provision for future expenditure

[62.60] A local authority acquired a gas works which was in poor condition, and claimed a deduction of £500 as a provision for future repairs. The QB rejected the claim. *Clayton v Newcastle-under-Lyme Corporation*, QB 1888, 2 TC 416.

[62.61] A retail company (J), which traded from a historic building, claimed a deduction for £2,060,000 for a specific provision for repairs to premises. The Revenue rejected the claim on the grounds that, at the end of the accounting period in question, the contracts for the necessary work had not been concluded, the repairs had not been carried out, and none of the amount had actually been paid. The Special Commissioners allowed J's appeal, holding that the inclusion of the provision 'accorded with sound principles of commercial accountancy'. *Jenners Princes Street Edinburgh Ltd v CIR*, Sp C [1998] SSCD 196 (Sp C 166). (*Note.* For the Revenue's practice following this decision, see Revenue Tax Bulletin, December 1999, pp 707–709, and Business Income Manual, BIM46550.)

[62.62] For provisions by insurance companies for unexpired risks, etc., see 68.55 et seq. TRADING PROFITS.

Cemetery company—liability for future maintenance of graves

[62.63] A cemetery company received lump sum payments in return for undertaking to maintain graves. The KB held that a deduction should be allowed for the estimated future expenditure on maintaining the graves. *London Cemetery Co v Barnes*, KB 1917, 7 TC 92; [1917] 2 KB 496.

Forward purchases contracts—'loss' arising from subsequent fall in prices

[62.64] A company (E) agreed to purchase trading materials. Prices subsequently fell, and E claimed a deduction for the excess of the contract price over the market value at the end of its accounting year. The CS rejected the claim, holding that the loss was only an apprehended future one which had not been suffered in the year. Lord Clyde observed that the provision of a reserve 'has no effect on the true amount of the profits actually made', and did not prevent the whole of the profits from being 'taken into computation in the year in question for purposes of assessment'. *Edward Collins & Sons Ltd v CIR*, CS 1924, 12 TC 773.

[62.65] A partnership had agreed to purchase yarn. Prices subsequently fell. In March 1921 it asked the vendors to send it an invoice, showing the difference between the agreed price and the current market price, to be paid when the yarn was received. It claimed to deduct this in its accounting period ending March 1921. The Special Commissioners rejected the claim and the CS upheld their decision. Lord Cullen described the invoice as 'an artificial transaction'. *JH Young & Co v CIR*, CS 1925, 12 TC 827.

[62.66] A company (B) had agreed to purchase more than 200,000 bags at 9d each. The market price fell heavily, and in March 1921 B wrote to the supplier (M) cancelling the contract. M claimed damages. In August 1921 B and M agreed that B should take delivery of the remaining bags at a price which exceeded the market price by £4,733. B claimed a deduction for the £4,733 in its accounts to June 1921. The Revenue rejected the claim on the basis that the loss did not arise until August 1921. The Recorder of Belfast allowed B's appeal, holding that the loss arose in March 1921. The case was heard in the KB by two judges who took opposite views, so that the Recorder's decision stood (see **4.243** APPEALS). *CIR v Hugh T Barrie Ltd*, KB(NI) 1928, 12 TC 1223. (*Note.* For a preliminary issue in this case, see **4.186** APPEALS.)

Provision for future 'loss' because of fall in charter hire rates

[62.67] A firm hired a number of ships under long-term contracts. In its 1920 accounts, it claimed a deduction for the amount by which the future hire payments which it was committed to make under unexpired contracts exceeded the amounts which would have been payable if it had been able to renegotiate the contracts at current market rates. (The rates had fallen because of a depression in the shipping industry.) The Commissioners rejected the claim and the CS dismissed the firm's appeal. Lord Clyde observed that the firm was seeking to 'include future anticipated losses'. Lord Sands observed that 'it would lead to great confusion if such haphazard and speculative estimates were to enter into the business of the collection of the public revenue'. *Whimster & Co v CIR*, CS 1925, 12 TC 813.

Provision for disputed liability

[62.68] A company trading as grain merchants claimed that, in computing its profits, a provision should be deducted for a claim against it which it disputed and which was subsequently abandoned. The Special Commissioners dismissed the appeal, holding that the provision was not deductible since it was only a contingent liability, and the KB upheld their decision. *H Ford & Co Ltd v CIR*, KB 1926, 12 TC 997.

[62.69] A company contended that, in computing its profits for 1945, a provision should be deducted for its liability in respect of accidents among its workers which had taken place before the end of that year, but where compensation had not been paid or admitted. The Special Commissioners rejected the claim, holding that no liability arose for tax purposes until it was admitted by the firm or, if disputed, determined by a court. The CS unanimously upheld this decision. *James Spencer & Co v CIR*, CS 1950, 32 TC 111.

[62.70] In 1889 a railway company (R) agreed to allow a coal company (N) to use some wagons. In 1944 a new agreement was made, under which R withdrew certain claims against N. N had not admitted liability, but had provided for the claims in its accounts. The provision had not been allowed as a deduction for tax purposes. N appealed against a 1945/46 assessment, contending that £17,815 should be allowed as a deduction in computing its profits. The CS rejected this contention, holding that this was not an allowable deduction. *CIR v Niddrie & Benhar Coal Co Ltd*, CS 1951, 32 TC 244.

Provision for future expenditure on renewals of utensils

[62.71] A catering company (P) operated factory canteens, and agreed that it would replace crockery, cutlery and utensils provided by the factory owners.

Because of wartime conditions, it was unable to obtain all the necessary replacements. It provided in its accounts for the cost of such replacements when they could be obtained, and claimed the provision as a deduction in computing its profits. The Commissioners rejected the claim and the CA dismissed P's appeal. *Peter Merchant Ltd v Stedeford*, CA 1948, 30 TC 496.

Liability for future leaving payments to employees

[62.72] Under Peruvian law, a company (S) was required to make compensation payments to employees leaving its service, the amount being dependent on the length of service and the rate of pay on leaving. S claimed to deduct an amount representing the accrued compensation each year. The HL rejected the claim, holding that there was no rule of law preventing the deduction if a sufficiently accurate estimate could be made, but that S's calculation was not sufficiently accurate. *Owen v Southern Railway of Peru Ltd*, HL 1956, 36 TC 602; [1957] AC 334; [1956] 2 All ER 728.

[62.73] In 1971 a UK company (T), trading in India, became liable to make statutory leaving gratuities to some of its employees, calculated by reference to their salary and length of service at the time of leaving. In its 1971 accounts it made a provision of £221,619 for this liability, of which £23,547 was referable to the employees' 1971 service. The Revenue only agreed to allow the £23,547 as a deduction, and T appealed, contending that the full £221,619 was allowable. The Special Commissioners accepted this contention and allowed the appeal, and the CS upheld their decision, holding that the liability did not emerge until 1971, and was revenue expenditure rather than capital expenditure. *CIR v Titaghur Jute Factory Ltd*, CS 1978, 53 TC 675; [1978] STC 166.

Provision for payment in commutation of right to annuity

[62.74] In 2001 a company acquired a solicitors' practice from a partnership. One of the former partners (P) was entitled to an annuity. The company decided that it would be preferable to make a lump sum payment in commutation of P's right to an annuity. It entered into negotiations with P, and in 2004 it made a provision of £1,150,000 in its accounts, which it claimed as a deduction in computing its profits. HMRC rejected the claim and the First-Tier Tribunal dismissed the company's appeal, finding that the company had assumed the obligation to pay P's annuity as part of the consideration for its acquisition of the partnership business. Accordingly it was capital expenditure rather than revenue expenditure. *Parnalls Solicitors Ltd v HMRC*, FTT 2009, [2010] SFTD 284; [2009] UKFTT 318 (TC), TC00261.

Provision for future expenditure on abandonment of North Sea oil wells

[62.75] A company (R) had a 25% interest in a consortium which obtained a licence to exploit an oilfield in the North Sea. The consortium hired a drilling rig for conversion into a drilling platform. It faced considerable costs in reconverting the rig when the field was exhausted, and would also be required to cap the wells and remove the well heads and certain installations such as mooring buoys which could constitute a hazard for navigation and fishing. R claimed a provision of £734,000 in its accounts for the estimated future expenditure. The Special Commissioners rejected the claim and the Ch D dismissed R's appeal, holding that the expenditure was capital rather than revenue. *RTZ Oil & Gas Ltd v Elliss*, Ch D 1987, 61 TC 132; [1987] STC 512.

Provision for future overhaul of jet aircraft

[62.76] A company (B) which operated a charter airline made provisions in its accounts for the future overhaul of jet aircraft. It did so by taking the average cost of overhauling the last ten engines, calculating the average cost per flying hour in the light of the earlier history of that engine, and charging a provision in its accounts arrived at by multiplying the average cost by the hours flown by each engine in the accounting period. The Revenue issued assessments on the basis that the provision was not an allowable deduction for tax purposes. The Special Commissioners allowed B's appeal, holding that the provision gave a true and fair view of B's trading position, and that there was no rule of law which prevented the provision from being taken into account in computing profits for tax purposes. The Ch D upheld their decision, holding that the accounts were prepared in accordance with accepted principles of commercial accountancy and that the Commissioners had not erred in law. *Johnston v Britannia Airways Ltd*, Ch D 1994, 67 TC 99; [1994] STC 763. (*Note*. With regard to the 'accepted principles of commercial accountancy', see FRS12 'Provisions, Contingent Liabilities and Contingent Assets', issued by the Accounting Standards Board in 1998. This stipulates that no provision should be made unless 'an entity has a present obligation (legal or constructive) as a result of a past event' and specifically states that, where 'an airline is required by law to overhaul its aircraft once every three years, there is no present obligation (and thus) no provision is recognised'. The Revenue took the view that the effect of FRS12 was that the provision made in this case 'no longer accords with generally accepted accounting practice' and 'will no longer be acceptable for tax purposes'. See Revenue Tax Bulletin, February 1999, p 624.)

Moneylender

[62.77] A company (M) carried on business as moneylenders, its loans being repaid in instalments consisting of both interest and capital. It claimed a deduction for the estimated future cost of collecting the capital element of future repayments. The Commissioners rejected the claim and the Ch D dismissed M's appeal. *Monthly Salaries Loan Co Ltd v Furlong*, Ch D 1962, 40 TC 313.

Sale of motor vehicles—provision for liabilities under unexpired warranties

[62.78] In a New Zealand case, a company (M) sold motor vehicles with the benefit of a warranty against defects appearing within a year of delivery or until the vehicle had been driven for 20,000 kilometres. In computing its profits for tax purposes, it claimed a deduction in respect of anticipated liabilities under warranties which were unexpired at the end of its accounting year. The New Zealand High Court allowed the deduction and the PC upheld this decision. On the evidence, 63% of the vehicles which M had sold in 1988 were returned for some kind of work under the warranty. Normal commercial practice therefore required that a reasonable estimate of the anticipated liabilities should be brought into account as a deduction. *New Zealand Commr of Inland Revenue v Mitsubishi Motors New Zealand Ltd*, PC [1995] STC 989; [1995] 3 WLR 671.

Provision for future operating loss

[62.79] A company (M) which supplied processed meats to various retailers claimed a deduction for a provision of £670,000 for an anticipated future operating loss. (In Ms profit and loss account, this was described as a 'bad debt provision', but M subsequently accepted that this was not an accurate description.) The Revenue refused to allow the deduction, and the Special Commissioners dismissed M's appeal, holding that the provision 'did not accord with best accounting practice', and that for tax purposes, neither a profit nor a loss should be anticipated. *Meat Traders Ltd v Cushing*, Sp C [1997] SSCD 245 (Sp C 131).

Provision for future rents

[62.80] A firm of solicitors appealed against two assessments, claiming that a substantial provision for future rents, which it was obliged to pay in respect of premises which it was vacating, should be allowed as a deduction. The Ch D accepted this contention and allowed the appeal. Lloyd J held that the provision was required by the concept of 'prudence', in accordance with the generally accepted principles of commercial accountancy. There was a general rule that 'accounts prepared according to generally accepted principles of commercial accounting are, in general, the guide to the amount of those profits'. There was no 'general exception prohibiting the deduction of sums entered in the debit side of the accounts by way of a provision in accordance with the prudence concept as set out in paragraph 14(d) of SSAP 2'. The firm's accounts should be accepted for tax purposes as a true statement of the firm's profits for the relevant period. *Herbert Smith (a firm) v Honour*, Ch D 1999, 72 TC 130; [1999] STC 173. (*Note.* For the Revenue's practice following this decision, see Revenue Press Release 137/99, issued on 20 July 1999, and Revenue Tax Bulletin December 1999, pp 707–709.)

Landfill site—provision for future restoration expenditure

[62.81] A company (D) operated a landfill site. In its accounts, it claimed a deduction of more than £600,000 for a provision for future expenditure on reinstating the site. The Revenue rejected the claim and the Special Commissioner dismissed D's appeal. *Dispit Ltd v HMRC*, Sp C [2007] SSCD 194 (Sp C 579).

Profits and losses on sales, etc. of investments

CROSS-REFERENCES

See **59.53** to **59.60** TRADING INCOME for dealing in shares; **64.63** and **64.64** TRADING PROFITS for periodic receipts linked with the sale of shares; **65.31** to **65.37** TRADING PROFITS for acquisitions or disposals of shares not at arm's length; and **68.62** to **68.66** TRADING PROFITS for sales of investments by insurance companies.

Investment trust company with power to deal

[62.82] In a Scottish case, an investment trust company was held to be chargeable to income tax on its net gains from realisations of its securities, and to be unable to deduct a fall in the book value of its unsold securities. (A factor here was the powers given to the company in its Memorandum of Association to deal, etc. with its investments.) *Scottish Investment Trust Co v Forbes*, CE 1893, 3 TC 231.

Losses on investments acquired by architect to secure contracts

[62.83] An architect sought contracts in connection with the erection of cotton mills. In order to improve his chances of obtaining such contracts, he took up shares in the companies granting the contracts. He subsequently sold such shares in order to finance the acquisition of shares in other companies for the same purpose, and claimed that his net losses on the sales should be allowed as deductions in computing his profits. The Commissioners held that the losses were capital losses and were not allowable deductions, and the KB upheld their decision. *Stott v Hoddinott*, KB 1916, 7 TC 85.

Trading company—loss relating to shares in subsidiary

[62.84] A trading company (J) owned two-thirds of the shares in another company (H) which sold its goods overseas. The shares issued were only partly paid-up. H went into liquidation and the liquidator required J to pay £8,000, the uncalled capital on the shares it held. The Special Commissioners held that the £8,000 was a capital loss, and the KB upheld their decision. *M Jacobs Young & Co Ltd v Harris*, KB 1926, 11 TC 221.

Sale of investments earmarked for reserve fund

[62.85] In an Irish case, a gas company established under a private Act of Parliament was empowered to set up a dividend equalisation fund. It claimed a deduction for the loss on realising some of the investments. The claim was rejected. The loss was not connected with, or arising out of, its trade; the Act did not impose a duty on the company to create the fund. *Alliance & Dublin Consumers' Gas Co Ltd v Davis*, HC(I) 1926, 5 ATC 717; 1 ITC 114; [1926] IR 372.

Share dealer—profits on investments acquired before dealing commenced

[62.86] A company (D), which carried on business as moneylenders, extended its business in 1943 to include dealing in shares. From 1944 to 1946 it sold, at a profit, shares which it had acquired from its managing director in 1940. The Revenue issued assessments charging tax on these profits. The Ch D allowed D's appeal, holding that the sales were realisations of investments. *The Dunn Trust Ltd v Williams*, Ch D 1950, 31 TC 477.

Investment sales by company formed to provide credit for farmers, etc

[62.87] In an Irish case, a company was established by statute to give credit to persons engaged in agriculture and facilitate borrowing by farmers on the security of their farms. It was accepted as carrying on a banking business, and the Revenue assessed it on the basis that its profits less losses on the realisation of its investments were part of its trading profits. In the two relevant years, there were respectively ten and six sales, mostly of Government securities. The Commissioners found that the gains or losses were part of the company's trading receipts, and the HC(I) upheld their decision. *Agricultural Credit Corporation Ltd v Vale*, HC(I) 1935, 2 ITC 46; [1935] IR 681.

Statutory reduction of company capital—fall in value of investment

[62.88] In an Irish case, a bank held stocks in a railway, and it was accepted that any profit or loss on the realisation of these stocks should be brought into the computation of its profits. The stocks were reduced by the *Irish Railways Act 1933*, under which stockholders received new stock certificates in place of the old. The market value of the bank's investments in the railway company fell as a result, and the bank claimed that it should be allowed to deduct this fall in computing its profits. The SC(I) rejected the claim, holding that there had been no realisation or conversion of an investment. *Davis v Hibernian Bank Ltd*, SC(I) 1936, 2 ITC 111.

Sale of investments by bank

[62.89] In an Indian case, the PC held that a bank's profits on its sales of investments (mainly Indian Government securities) were taxable as being derived from a normal part of the business of banking. *Punjab Co-operative Bank Ltd v Lahore Income Tax Commissioner*, PC 1940, 19 ATC 533; [1940] AC 1055; [1940] 4 All ER 87.

[62.90] A company (W), which was a wholly-owned subsidiary of a Hong Kong bank, purchased 150,000,000 shares in one of the bank's customers (H), a large trading company which was in financial difficulties. The shares were shown as capital assets in W's accounts. H subsequently merged with another company and W received 180,000,000 shares in the successor company. It sold half of these at a profit in 1979. The profit was assessed as a trading profit and W appealed, contending that it was a capital profit and thus not assessable to Hong Kong profits tax. The PC accepted this contention and allowed W's appeal, holding that the shares had been held as a capital investment. *Waylee Investment Ltd v Hong Kong Commissioner of Inland Revenue*, PC 1990, 63 TC 684; [1990] STC 780.

Bank—profit on sale of shares of associated company

[62.91] In 1948 and 1952 a small bank purchased a number of shares in an associated company. In 1958 it sold the shares at a profit. The Special Commissioners held that the shares had been bought and sold in the course of the bank's trade, so that the profit was chargeable to income tax. The HL unanimously upheld their decision. *Frasers (Glasgow) Bank Ltd v CIR*, HL 1963, 40 TC 698.

Whether unsold investments may be valued as stock-in-trade

[62.92] In an Irish case, a company which dealt in stocks and shares was assessed on the basis that its unsold investments should be brought in at their cost. The company appealed, contending that they should be brought in at market value if that was lower than cost. The HC(I) rejected this contention and upheld the assessments, applying *Davis v Hibernian Bank Ltd*, **62.88** above. *AB Ltd v MacGiolla Riogh*, HC(I) 1960, 3 ITC 301.

Bank purchasing debentures with interest shortly before redemption

[62.93] See *CIR v Kleinwort Benson Ltd*, 3.19 ANTI-AVOIDANCE.

Sale of shares associated with property transaction

[62.94] A property-dealing company (L) and an individual (H) formed a new company (P), each owning 50% of the share capital. L then sold some land which it owned to P for development. There was an agreement between L and H that either could purchase, on certain terms, the other's interest in the building to be erected on the land. Shortly after the sale of the land, L sold its shares in P to H for £25,500, including the resultant profit of £25,450 in its accounts as part of its profits from 'sales in connection with land'. The Revenue issued an assessment charging tax on the profit and L appealed, contending that the profit arose not from the sale of the land but from the sale of its shares in P, and was a capital profit. The Commissioners dismissed the appeal, holding that the profit was part of L's trading profits. The CA unanimously upheld their decision. *Associated London Properties Ltd v Henriksen*, CA 1944, 26 TC 46.

Property-dealing company—loss on liquidation of wholly-owned subsidiary

[62.95] A property-dealing and development company (F) acquired the shares of another company (G) in order to be in a position to develop a building site of which G held the lease. It paid £22,634 for the shares, most of this being attributable to the value of the site. The development was completed, the plots were sold, and G was put into voluntary liquidation. F received £11,447 in the liquidation, and claimed that it had made a trading loss of £11,187, contending that it had acquired the shares as trading stock of its trade as an estate developer. The Commissioners rejected the claim, holding that the shares had not been acquired as trading stock. The Ch D upheld their decision. *Fundfarms Developments Ltd v Parsons*, Ch D 1969, 45 TC 707; [1969] 1 WLR 1735; [1969] 3 All ER 1161.

Sale of shares in hotel company to provide finance for expansion

[62.96] See *Lim Foo Yong Sdn Bhd v Comptroller-General of Inland Revenue*, 67.24 TRADING PROFITS.

Payment to secure release of option over trading investment

[62.97] See *Walker v Cater Securities Ltd*, 63.131 TRADING PROFITS.

Loss on disposal of secured loans held by subsidiary company

[62.98] See *Torbell Investments Ltd v Williams*, 59.84 TRADING INCOME.

Interest (ITTOIA 2005, s 29)

Interest—whether trading income

[62.99] A company's business consisted of lending money on security in the USA. It claimed that the interest which it received was trading income. The

Revenue rejected the claim and the CE dismissed the company's appeal (holding that the interest was within Schedule D Case IV under the legislation then in force). *Scottish Mortgage Co of New Mexico v McKelvie*, CE 1886, 2 TC 165.

[62.100] The decision in *Scottish Mortgage Co of New Mexico v McKelvie*, **62.99** above, was distinguished in a subsequent case where a company which carried on a wool-broking business made temporary loans in Australia, secured by second mortgages or by wool or produce. The amount of the loans fluctuated as the produce was realised. The Commissioners held that the interest was trading income and the CE upheld their decision, holding that in view of the transitory nature of the advances, and their close connection with the wool-broking, the company should be treated as analogous to a banker.) *Smiles v Australasian Mortgage & Agency Co Ltd*, CE 1888, 2 TC 367.

[62.101] A UK company carried on the business of lending money on security in Egypt. It was accepted that the company was resident in the UK but that its business was controlled in Egypt and that its trading income was not taxable in the UK. The CA unanimously held that the loan interest which the company received was not trading income (and was taxable in the UK under Schedule D Case IV under the legislation then in force). *Butler v Mortgage Co of Egypt Ltd*, CA 1928, 13 TC 803.

63

Trading Profits—Deductions (ITTOIA 2005, ss 32–94; CTA 2009, ss 53–92)

The cases in this chapter are arranged under the following headings.

NOTE

See also 8 CAPITAL ALLOWANCES. For cases concerning the time at which an expense is deductible, see 62.50 *et seq*. TRADING PROFITS.

Capital expenditure (ITTOIA 2005, s 33; CTA 2009, s 53)

Payments to associated companies

Manufacturing company—payment to support associated company

[63.1] Two companies (S and W) carried on similar manufacturing businesses. W agreed to allow S to nominate the majority of its directors, in return for S agreeing to make up W's profits to a specified amount (to enable it to meet its preference dividends). In 1904 S paid W £841 under this agreement, and claimed a deduction for this payment in computing its profits. The Revenue refused to allow the deduction, considering that the payment was an allocation of profits, rather than an expense incurred in earning profits. The Commissioners allowed S's appeal, holding that the payment was deductible, and the CS upheld their decision as one of fact. *Moore v Stewarts & Lloyds Ltd*, CS 1905, 6 TC 501.

Zinc smelter—loans to supplier of ore

[63.2] A company which carried on the business of zinc smelting formed a subsidiary to acquire and operate blende ore mines, since it needed such ore for its zinc smelting. It made loans to the subsidiary to finance its acquisition and development of mines, but the venture failed and the loans became irrecoverable. The company claimed the loss as a bad debt. The Special Commissioners held that the loss was capital and not an allowable deduction, and the KB upheld their decision. *English Crown Spelter Co Ltd v Baker*, KB 1908, 5 TC 327.

Paper-maker—advance to supplier of wood pulp

[63.3] In 1916, a paper-making company (C) entered into a ten-year agreement with a Canadian company (H) for the supply of wood pulp, advancing £30,000 to that company to be repaid by setting off £1 against the purchase price of each ton of pulp supplied. The British Government subsequently prohibited the import of wood pulp, so that H was unable to make the intended deliveries. H disclaimed any liability to repay the advance, and C claimed a deduction for the £30,000 in its accounts to 30 September 1917. The Special Commissioners rejected the claim, holding that the advance was capital and the loss was not deductible. The KB upheld their decision. *Charles Marsden & Sons Ltd v CIR*, KB 1919, 12 TC 217.

Publishing company—trading loss of subsidiary written off

[63.4] A printing and publishing company carried out work for a wholly-owned subsidiary, charging for it at full trade prices. For 1933, the subsidiary made a loss, and the parent company wrote off an equivalent amount from the amount owing from the subsidiary. (There had been similar writings-off in other years but these were not in dispute.) The Special Commissioners held that the writing-off was not an allowable deduction, and the HL unanimously upheld their decision as one of fact. *Odhams Press Ltd v Cook*, HL 1940, 23 TC 233; [1940] 3 All ER 15.

Guarantee of indebtedness of associated company

[63.5] A UK company had guaranteed loans to an associated Irish company (not a subsidiary) with which it had close trading connections. It paid £20,048 under the guarantee. The Ch D held that the payment was capital expenditure and was not an allowable deduction. *Milnes v J Beam Group Ltd*, Ch D 1975, 50 TC 675; [1975] STC 487.

[63.6] See also *Garforth v Tankard Carpets Ltd*, **63.138** below.

Cash injection into subsidiary company

[63.7] A company (J), which dealt in precious metals, owned a number of subsidiary companies. One of these subsidiaries (B), which operated a banking business, suffered financial difficulties. J informed the Bank of England that B would have to be wound up. The Bank of England offered to purchase B's share capital for the nominal sum of £1 on condition that J injected cash of £50 million into B before the sale. J anticipated that, if B were to be wound up, J itself would be forced into receivership, and therefore accepted the Bank's offer. It claimed that the £50 million was deductible in computing its profits. The Revenue rejected the claim, considering that the payment was capital expenditure, since it was made to dispose of a capital asset. The Commissioners allowed J's appeal and the HL unanimously upheld their decision. Lord Goff of Chieveley held that whether a payment was capital expenditure or revenue expenditure did not depend on the motive or purpose of the taxpayer, but on what was procured by the expenditure. If this was the transfer of the shares, the expenditure was capital. If it was the removal of the threat to J's continuation in business, it was revenue. The Commissioners were entitled to conclude on the evidence that the payment was not made simply to procure the disposal of J's shares in B, but was made to remove the threat of insolvency and to enable J itself to remain in business. Accordingly it was revenue expenditure. *Lawson v Johnson Matthey plc*, HL 1992, 65 TC 39; [1992] STC 466; [1992] 2 WLR 826; [1992] 2 All ER 647.

Purchase of premises from subsidiary company

[63.8] In 2001 a company (B) agreed to purchase the freehold of a hospital from a subsidiary company (L), paying part of the purchase price immediately and the remainder in three instalments from 2005 to 2007. In 2005 B and L modified the agreement and described £400,000 of the amount due from B to L as a 'premium'. B claimed a deduction for this amount in computing its profits. HMRC issued a closure notice rejecting the claim on the basis that the expenditure was capital. The First-Tier Tribunal dismissed B's appeal against this decision. Judge Cornwell-Kelly observed that the terms of the agreement 'were evidently not typical of a bargain made at arms' length and were in fact devised with VAT avoidance in mind'. He held that 'on the face of it, any payment under a sale agreement must in the hands of the payer be presumed to be in the nature of capital, unless it is clearly otherwise'. The payment was a capital payment for the acquisition of a capital asset. *Bluesparkle Ltd v HMRC*, FTT [2012] UKFTT 45 (TC), TC01743.

Newspaper companies—payments to holding company

[63.9] A group of companies published several regional newspapers. Several subsidiary companies assigned unregistered trade mastheads to their parent company, and then paid a lump sum to the parent company to license the trade marks for a fixed term. The purpose of these transactions was described as being 'to reduce reported profits in the newspaper subsidiaries, since the levels of profit become common knowledge and could lead to union claims'. The subsidiaries claimed a deduction for the payments they had made to the parent company, although the parent company treated the payments it received as outside the scope of corporation tax. HMRC rejected the subsidiaries' claims and the First-tier Tribunal dismissed the companies' appeals. Judge Walters held that it was a principle of common law that unregistered trade marks 'were not assignable in gross, but only assignable in connection with the goodwill of the business concerned in the goods to which the mark was referable'. Applying the principles laid down by Fry LJ in *Pinto v Badman*, CA 1891, 7 TLR 317, an unregistered trade mark 'cannot be assigned independently of the business to which it relates because such an assignment would enable the transferee to represent that it was part of the goodwill of the business, which it could not be if it were independently assigned out of the ownership of the owner of the business'. On the facts here, the purported assignments 'were assignments in gross and were void for mistake as to the assignability of the subject matter of the purported assignments'. *Iliffe News & Media Ltd v HMRC (and related appeals)*, FTT [2012] UKFTT 696 (TC); [2013] SFTD 309, TC02365. (*Note*. For HMRC's reaction to the case, see their Press Release dated 14 November 2012.)

Biscuit manufacturer—purchases at overvalue from subsidiary

[63.10] See *CIR v Huntley & Palmers Ltd*, 63.133 below.

Applications of profits

Cross-references

[63.11] See *Mersey Docks & Harbour Board v Lucas*, **57.1** STATUTORY BODIES (surplus of harbour board taxable although applicable to form sinking fund); *Exported Live Stock (Insurance) Board*, **57.10** STATUTORY BODIES (surplus of statutory insurance fund taxable); *Armitage v Moore*, **59.43** TRADING INCOME (receiver taxable although income applicable for benefit of creditors); *Young v Racecourse Betting Control Board*, **63.107** below (payments to promote horse racing not deductible), and *Hutchinson & Co v Turner*, **63.259** below (profits from publication for benevolent fund taxable). There are a number of older cases, which are not summarised individually in this book because the substantive issue has been overtaken by subsequent changes in the law, but which considered the question of whether the application of profits precludes their assessment. These include *Paddington Burial Board v CIR*, QB 1884, 2 TC 46 (surplus income of Board taxable although applicable in aid of poor rates); *Dublin Corporation v M'Adam*, Ex(I) 1887, 2 TC 387 (surplus of water undertaking taxable although applicable to reduce indebtedness); *Webber v Glasgow Corporation*, CE 1893,

3 TC 202 (local authority profits taxable although applicable for public purposes); *Brighton College v Marriott*, HL 1925, 10 TC 213 (profits of school taxable although applicable for charitable purposes).

Payments towards statutory sinking fund

[63.12] In an Irish case, a company issued debenture stock to finance its carrying out a Government contract, and was required to set aside part of its receipts to establish a sinking fund to repay the debentures. The Special Commissioners held that the sums set aside in this way were not allowable deductions. The KB upheld their decision, applying the principles laid down in *Mersey Docks & Harbour Board v Lucas*, **57.1** STATUTORY BODIES. *City of Dublin Steam Packet Co v O'Brien*, KB(I) 1912, 6 TC 101.

Share of profits paid under terms of railway concession

[63.13] In an Indian case, a railway company obtained a concession to build and operate a railway in what was then French territory on terms whereby half the profits should be paid to the French Government. The PC held that its profits from the concession were part of the profits of its business but that the payments to the French Government were not allowable deductions as they were 'not incurred solely for the purpose of earning' its profits (the relevant statutory test). *Pondicherry Railway Co Ltd v Madras Commissioner of Income Tax*, PC 1931, 10 ATC 365.

Share of commission payable on acquiring agency

[63.14] In an Indian case, a company (A) acted as agent for another company (B). B obtained loans through the agent under agreements whereby A passed on to the lenders a quarter of the commission which it received from B. The amounts which A paid were accepted as deductions in computing its profits. Subsequently, a third company (C) took over the agency on similar terms. The PC held that C Ltd was not entitled to the allowance, on the ground that it had incurred the liability to hand over a share of the commission in exchange for the right to conduct the business, rather than 'solely for the purpose of earning' the profits (the relevant statutory test). *Tata Hydro-Electric Agencies Ltd (Bombay) v Bombay & Aden Income Tax Commissioner*, PC 1937, 16 ATC 54; [1937] AC 685; [1937] 2 All ER 291.

Share of profits payable under agreement for transfer of business

[63.15] In an Indian case, a company agreed in 1932 to transfer the control and operation of its business to another company until 1944. The transferee agreed to pay one-half of the net profits to the transferor. The PC held that the amounts so paid were not allowable deductions in computing the transferee's profits, as they had not been incurred 'solely for the purpose of making or earning' the profits (the relevant statutory test). *Indian Radio & Cable Communication Co Ltd v Bombay & Aden Income Tax Commissioner*, PC 1937, 16 ATC 333; [1937] 3 All ER 709.

Share of profits as partial consideration for loan

[63.16] See *AW Walker & Co v CIR*, **63.281** below.

Legal and professional expenses

Expenditure held not to be allowable

Expenses of debenture issue

[63.17] A company (T), which lent money on mortgages, issued debentures to raise additional funds. The Commissioners held that the expenses of issuing the debentures were not deductible in computing its profits, and the QB dismissed T's appeal against this decision. *Texas Land & Mortgage Co v Holtham*, QB 1894, 3 TC 255.

Expenses of reducing share capital

[63.18] A company incurred legal costs and related expenses in obtaining a reduction of its capital. The CS held that this expenditure was not allowable in computing the company's profits, since they were incurred for the purpose of distributing its profits to its shareholders, rather than for the purpose of its business. *Archibald Thomson Black & Co Ltd v Batty*, CS 1919, 7 TC 158.

Expenses of share flotation

[63.19] A company, which was in financial difficulties, raised funds through a flotation on the Stock Exchange in 1994. It claimed that its expenditure on professional fees relating to this flotation should be allowed as a deduction. The Revenue rejected the claim and the company appealed, contending that the expenditure had been incurred wholly and exclusively for the purpose of repaying its existing loan finance. The Special Commissioner rejected this contention and dismissed the appeal, holding on the evidence that 'the company had more than one purpose when deciding to raise funds by means of a flotation'. On the evidence, 'the repayment of debt (was) only one of the purposes' behind the flotation. The company did not simply wish to repay its debts, but also wished 'to provide finance for expansion and acquisitions'. *Focus Dynamics plc (formerly Eurovein plc) v Turner*, Sp C [1999] SSCD 71 (Sp C 182).

Expenses of formation of holding company

[63.20] In an Irish case, the shareholders of three companies in the bacon trade set up a new holding company, exchanging their shares for shares in the new company. The expenses of forming the company were shared between two of the companies, one of which claimed its share of the expenses as a deduction in computing its profits. The Irish High Court held that the expenses were not allowable as deductions, holding firstly that they were capital expenditure rather than revenue expenditure, and secondly that they were not incurred wholly or exclusively for the purposes of the company's trade. *Kealy v O'Mara (Limerick) Ltd*, HC(I) 1942, 2 ITC 265; [1942] IR 616.

Expenses of capital reorganisation

[63.21] In a Canadian case, the PC held that legal costs and other expenses, incurred by a company in replacing a large bond issue by bonds on more favourable terms, were not allowable deductions. The expenses were not incurred 'wholly, exclusively and necessarily' for the purpose of earning the income (the relevant statutory test). *Montreal Coke & Manufacturing Co v Minister of National Revenue*, PC [1944] AC 126; [1944] 1 All ER 743.

Legal expenses relating to liability assumed by company on formation

[63.22] In an Irish case, a group of people contracted with a builder for the construction of a cinema, with a view to forming a company to take it over. The cinema was completed and opened for business in November 1947, and a company was registered in January 1948, taking over all the assets and liabilities of the cinema business on the same day. The balance due to the builder had not been settled, and the matter reached the High Court, which awarded the builder £650 with costs, which the company duly paid. The company accepted that the £650 was capital but claimed a deduction for the legal expenses which it had incurred in connection with the court action. The Irish High Court held that the expenses were capital expenditure, having been made in relation to a capital liability and being 'solely referable to the capital structure of the company'. *Casey v AB Ltd*, HC(I) 1964, TL(I) 104; 2 ITR 500.

Brewery—expenses of unsuccessful application for licences

[63.23] The KB held that the expenses incurred by a brewery company in unsuccessful applications for licences for new public houses were capital expenditure and not allowable deductions. (The company accepted that the expenses of successful applications were capital.) *Southwell v Savill Bros Ltd*, KB 1901, 4 TC 430; [1901] 2 KB 349.

Brewery—costs of applying for transfer of licence

[63.24] A brewer claimed deductions for legal expenses incurred in obtaining the transfer of a licence to different premises, and compensation paid to the previous tenants who were displaced as a result of the transfer. The Revenue rejected his claim and the KB dismissed his appeal, holding that the expenditure was capital and was not an allowable deduction. *Morse v Stedeford*, KB 1934, 18 TC 457.

[63.25] The Ch D held that the legal costs incurred by a brewery company in obtaining the removal of excise licences to new premises, mainly as a result of development plans, were capital expenditure and not allowable deductions. *Pendleton v Mitchells & Butlers Ltd*, Ch D 1968, 45 TC 341; [1969] 2 All ER 928.

Costs of unsuccessful application for variation of carrier's licence

[63.26] A road haulage company incurred legal costs in an unsuccessful application for its public carrier's licence to be varied to cover seven vehicles instead of four. The Ch D held that the costs were not an allowable deduction, and the CA dismissed the company's appeal. *Pyrah v Annis & Co Ltd*, CA 1956, 37 TC 163; [1957] 1 WLR 190; [1957] 1 All ER 196.

Costs of promoting private Bills

[63.27] A partnership which owned a colliery was dissatisfied with the facilities offered by an existing railway, and incurred expenditure in promoting two Bills for the construction of a new railway line. The Bills were dropped following an undertaking by the existing railway to improve its facilities.

The Commissioners held that the cost of promoting the Bills was not an allowable deduction, and the CS upheld their decision (by a 2–1 majority, Lord Johnston dissenting). *AG Moore & Co v Hare*, CS 1914, 6 TC 572.

Costs of replacing bond on premises

[63.28] In a Scottish case, a trader's business premises were subject to certain bonds. The Commissioners held that the legal costs of replacing one of these on the bondholder's death were capital expenditure, and were not an allowable deduction. The CS upheld their decision (by a 2–1 majority, Lord Salvesen dissenting). *Small v Easson*, CS 1920, 12 TC 351.

Costs of application for planning permission

[63.29] A company made an unsuccessful claim for planning permission to extract sand and gravel from certain sites, which, if successful, would have enabled it to pursue its activities at the sites for more than 30 years. The Special Commissioners held that the cost of the unsuccessful application was capital expenditure, and the Ch D upheld their decision. Brightman J observed that 'unchallenged evidence, or a finding, that a sum falls to be treated as capital or income on principles of correct accountancy practice is not decisive of the question whether in law the expenditure is of a capital or income nature'. *ECC Quarries Ltd v Watkis*, Ch D 1975, 51 TC 153; [1975] STC 578; [1977] 1 WLR 1386. (*Note.* See now HMRC Pamphlet IR 131, SP 4/78.)

Expenditure held to be partly allowable

Flotation of building society as public limited company

[63.30] A large building society (H) decided to incorporate and convert itself into a public limited company. It claimed that the associated costs should be allowed as a deduction in computing its profits. The Revenue rejected the claim, accepting that the trade continued after the conversion but considering that the expenditure was capital in nature (and also contending that it was not wholly and exclusively for the purpose of H's business). The Special Commissioners allowed H's appeal in part, holding that all the expenditure in question had been incurred for the purposes of H's business. With regard to the question of whether the costs were capital or revenue, the Commissioners held that expenditure relating to statutory cash bonuses paid to investing members of the building society was capital in nature. The bonuses were dealt with as an item deducted from the profit and loss reserves in H's balance sheet. Accordingly, 'the accountancy treatment indicates that the statutory cash bonuses were capital in nature'. Additionally, the bonuses were 'capital withdrawn from the trade'. However, the Commissioners held that the remainder of the expenditure was revenue in nature, noting that it was treated as an ordinary expense in H's profit and loss account. Although 'the lack of an asset on the balance sheet does not necessarily mean that the expenditure is of a revenue nature', in this case the expenditure was not incurred to acquire any capital asset. The Commissioners held that 'the business was carried on in the same way, and by the same people, before and after the conversion. The advantage obtained by the payment of the conversion costs was not a new asset but the ability to continue to trade in the same way but with fewer restrictions.' *Halifax plc v Davidson*, Sp C [2000] SSCD 251 (Sp C 239).

[63.31] Similar decisions were reached in *Woolwich plc v Davidson*, Sp C [2000] SSCD 302 (Sp C 240); *Northern Rock plc v Thorpe*, Sp C [2000] SSCD 317 (Sp C 241) and *Alliance & Leicester plc v Hamer*, Sp C [2000] SSCD 332 (Sp C 242).

Costs of application for planning permission

[63.32] A company (M) operated an indoor market at a site in Cornwall. The relevant planning permission only allowed it to trade at weekends. M applied for planning permission to allow it to trade on weekdays. The council granted planning permission to trade on ten weekdays. M subsequently breached the terms of this permission by trading from the site each Wednesday. The council issued an enforcement notice, against which M appealed. The QB dismissed this appeal. In its tax return, M claimed a deduction for the legal and professional fees incurred in applying for planning permission and in appealing against the enforcement notice issued by the council. HMRC issued an amendment disallowing the deduction on the basis that this was capital expenditure. M appealed. The First-tier Tribunal dismissed the appeal but the Upper Tribunal remitted the case for rehearing. Judge Avery Jones held that 'there should be an apportionment on the analogy of expenditure on a building that is partly an improvement and partly repairs'. *Markets South West (Holdings) Ltd v HMRC*, UT [2011] STC 1469.

Expenditure held to be allowable

Costs of promoting private Bills

[63.33] In an Irish case, a gas undertaking was carried on by a committee constituted by a private Act. On modernisation of the works, a number of the employees became redundant and the committee promoted a private Bill (which was eventually passed) to enable it to pay pensions to its former employees. It claimed a deduction for the cost of promoting the Bill. The Special Commissioners allowed the deduction, and the Irish High Court upheld their decision as one of fact. *McGarry v Limerick Gas Committee*, HC(I), 1 ITC 405; [1932] IR 125.

Costs of defending title to land used by overseas branch

[63.34] A UK company (B) had a wholly-owned American subsidiary (P). For UK tax purposes, P's business was treated as a branch of B's trade. B owned land near Los Angeles, which P used in its trade. The City of Los Angeles took legal action against B and P in the American courts, disputing the validity of their title to the land. B incurred substantial legal costs in defending the action and claimed that they should be allowed as deductions in computing its profits. The Revenue rejected the claim but the Commissioners allowed B's appeal and the KB upheld their decision. *Southern v Borax Consolidated Ltd*, KB 1940, 23 TC 597; [1941] 1 KB 111; [1940] 4 All ER 412.

Costs of defending ownership of business

[63.35] Two brothers operated a small shop in partnership. Their sister (R) began High Court proceedings, claiming that she was also a partner. The High Court dismissed the claim. The partnership claimed a deduction for the cost of defending the proceedings. HMRC rejected the claim on the basis that it was capital expenditure and related to a partnership dispute. The First-tier Tribunal allowed the partnership's appeal, specifically distinguishing *C Connelly & Co v Wilbey*, **63.162** below (which HMRC had cited as an authority), on the grounds that that case related to a dispute between two partners, whereas in the present case the court had found that R had never been a partner. Judge Kempster observed that the High Court proceedings had been 'a failed claim by an outsider (R) against the assets and profits of the firm' and the partners had been resisting 'an unjustified claim in order to preserve the assets of the business'. *Linslade Post Office & General Store v HMRC*, FTT [2012] UKFTT 457 (TC), TC02136.

Moneylender—costs of successful defence of action

[63.36] In an Indian case, a moneylender (S) lent money to a company in which he was a shareholder and successfully sued the company for its recovery. Subsequently, other shareholders in the company took legal action against S, alleging conspiracy, misrepresentation and breach of contract in connection with a transaction of which the loan formed part. S died during the action and his son, who took over his business, defended the proceedings. The defence was successful and the PC held that the legal costs were deductible in computing the profits of the moneylending business, as the legal action had been taken against S in his capacity as a moneylender. Lord Thankerton held that 'the expenditure in question was incurred solely for the purpose of earning the profits or gains of the moneylending business'. *Bihar & Orissa Income Tax Commissioner v Maharaja Sir Rameshwar Singh of Dharbanga*, PC 1941, 20 ATC 337; [1942] 1 All ER 362.

Chartered company—costs of obtaining variation of charter

[63.37] A company (C) had been incorporated in 1773 by charter, which hampered it by restricting its borrowing powers and preventing the setting-up of a modern management structure. It petitioned for, and obtained, a supplementary charter to modernise the existing charter, but in so doing incurred substantial legal and other expenses in overcoming the opposition of two shareholders. C claimed that these expenses should be allowed as deductions in computing its profits. The Revenue rejected the claim, considering that the expenditure was capital. The Special Commissioners allowed C's appeal, holding that the expenditure was of an income nature, and the HL unanimously upheld this decision. *CIR v Carron Co*, HL 1968, 45 TC 18.

Rent, etc

Rent subject to abatement dependent on profits

[63.38] In a case where the circumstances were complex and unusual, a company (C) occupied premises abroad under a lease which included a provision for the rent to be abated if its profits fell below certain limits. C claimed that the full amount of the rent which it paid should be allowed as a deduction in computing its profits. The Revenue rejected the claim, considering that the payments under the lease were not rents, but a distribution of profits. The KB allowed C's appeal and the HL upheld this decision. *Union Cold Storage Co Ltd v Adamson*, HL 1931, 16 TC 293.

Rent payable for premises no longer required

[63.39] A company rented a warehouse for the purposes of its business. It ceased to occupy the warehouse before the lease had expired, and sublet parts of the warehouse. It claimed a deduction for the rent payable, less the rents received from the sub-tenants. The Commissioners allowed the claim and the CS upheld their decision. *CIR v Falkirk Iron Co Ltd*, CS 1933, 17 TC 625.

Rent paid by partnership to a partner

[63.40] An accountancy partnership practised from premises owned by the senior partner and paid him rent. The CA held that the rent was deductible, and that the firm had correctly been allowed error or mistake relief for years in which it had failed to claim the deduction. (The substantive issue was whether, under the law in force at the time, the deduction should be the rent or the annual value of the premises.) *Heastie v Veitch & Co*, CA 1933, 18 TC 305; [1934] 1 KB 535.

Rent for building acquired to control access to works and sublet

[63.41] A newspaper company (N) rented a building from a subsidiary. It occupied a small part of the building for its trade but most of it was sublet when possible. The site had been acquired, and the building erected, so that N could control the access to its main printing works. It claimed a deduction for the rent it paid, less the rents which it received from the subletting. The Revenue rejected the claim but the KB allowed N's appeal and the CA upheld this decision. *Allied Newspapers Ltd v Hindsley*, CA 1937, 21 TC 421; [1937] 2 All ER 663.

Rent of unprofitable branch closed

[63.42] A tailor (L) carried on business at several shops in London. One of them made losses and was closed in 1935. L held it under a lease at an annual rent of £3,500 with nearly 29 years remaining. L sub-let it for the remaining period of the lease at £2,500 per annum, and claimed that the difference of £1,000 should be allowed as a deduction in computing his profits. The Revenue rejected the claim but the Special Commissioners allowed L's appeal and the KB upheld their decision. *Hyett v Lennard*, KB 1940, 23 TC 346; [1940] 2 KB 180; [1940] 3 All ER 133.

Rentcharges payable for reversions—whether capital

[63.43] A company (L) leased properties from the Church Commissioners. The Church Commissioners conveyed their interests in the properties to L in return for rentcharges totalling £96,000 per annum for ten years. The rents payable under the leases had been smaller, but for longer periods. L appealed against profits tax assessments, contending that the rentcharges should be allowed as deductions. The HL unanimously rejected this contention, holding that the rentcharges were the cost of acquiring capital assets, and were not allowable deductions. *CIR v Land Securities Investment Trust Ltd*, HL 1969, 45 TC 495; [1969] 1 WLR 604; [1969] 2 All ER 430.

Additional rent for acquisition of freehold—whether capital

[63.44] A trading company (L) occupied premises owned by a charity (M) under a lease with 88 years to run, at a rent of £23,444 pa. The rackrental value was about £60,000 pa. Following a series of transactions, a subsidiary of L became the freeholder, subject to a 22-year lease to M at a nominal rent, and L became a sub-lessee of M under a 22-year lease at an annual rent of £42,450. L claimed that its additional rental liability of £19,006 should be allowed as a deduction. The Special Commissioners rejected this contention and the CA unanimously upheld their decision, holding that the liability had been incurred in order to acquire a capital asset, namely the freehold which L acquired through its subsidiary. *Littlewoods Mail Order Stores Ltd v McGregor*, CA 1969, 45 TC 519; [1969] 1 WLR 1241; [1969] 3 All ER 855.

Cost of obtaining release from mining lease

[63.45] A company wished to surrender its leases of certain coal seams, which had several years still to run. It agreed to pay lump sums to the landowners as compensation. The CA held that the payments were capital expenditure and were not allowable as deductions, as they had been made to get rid of fixed capital assets. *Mallett v Staveley Coal & Iron Co Ltd*, CA 1928, 13 TC 772; [1928] 2 KB 405.

Payments for cancellation of lease of unprofitable branch

[63.46] A company (R) trading as fishmongers carried on a business at several branches. One branch, held under a lease expiring in 1923, made losses and was closed in 1916. R surrendered its lease, paying £1,812 in annual instalments of £250. In 1921, when £1,125 had been paid off, it paid £600 in satisfaction of its outstanding liability. The KB held that the £600 was not deductible. *Cowcher v Richard Mills & Co Ltd*, KB 1927, 13 TC 216. (*Note.* Rowlatt J also considered that the instalments were not allowable. However, these had already been allowed by agreement and the Revenue did not seek to reopen the matter.)

Payment to secure cancellation of lease no longer required

[63.47] A company (C) made a payment of £6,000 to secure the cancellation of a 40-year lease (with ten years to run) of premises which it no longer required for the purposes of its trade. It claimed that the payment should be allowed as a deduction in computing its profits. The Special Commissioners rejected this contention and the KB dismissed C's appeal, holding that the payment was not wholly and exclusively for the purposes of C's trade, and was capital expenditure. *Union Cold Storage Co Ltd v Ellerker*, KB 1938, 22 TC 547; [1938] 4 All ER 692.

[63.48] In 1950 a company (S), which promoted speedway racing, agreed to rent a stadium until 1957 for £2,500 pa. The stadium was unsuccessful, and in 1952 S paid £4,000 (including rent arrears of £625) to be released from the agrement. The Ch D held that the balance of £3,375 was capital expenditure and was not an allowable deduction. *Dain v Auto Speedways Ltd*, Ch D 1959, 38 TC 525.

[63.49] A company (S) occupied leased premises, but failed to comply fully with its repairing obligations under the terms of the lease. S agreed to assign the lease to another company (W), and paid a 'reverse premium' of £150,000 plus VAT to W. S also took an underlease, from W, of premises which it occupied. S claimed that the payment should be allowed as a deduction in computing its profits. The Revenue rejected the claim on the basis that the payment was capital expenditure. The Special Commissioner dismissed S's appeal, holding that the payment was made to ensure the disposal of a disadvantageous capital asset (and incidentally to acquire a less disadvantageous capital asset).' *Southern Counties Agricultural Trading Society Ltd v Blackler*, Sp C [1999] SSCD 200 (Sp C 198).

[63.50] In 1988 a company (B) took a ten-year lease of business premises at a rent of £550,000 pa. In 1992 it decided that it wished to surrender the lease, and paid the landlord £550,000 for this. It claimed that this payment should be allowed as a deduction in computing its profits. The Revenue rejected the claim, on the basis that the payment was capital expenditure. The Special Commissioner dismissed B's appeal, holding that the lease was a capital asset and that the payment was capital expenditure. *Bullrun Inc v HM Inspector of Taxes*, Sp C [2000] SSCD 384 (Sp C 248).

Lease premium

[63.51] The CS held that a premium paid to obtain a five-year renewal of a lease of business premises was capital expenditure. *MacTaggart v B & E Strump*, CS 1925, 10 TC 17. (*Note*. See now *ITTOIA 2005, ss 60–67*. The case remains of interest in establishing the principle that a premium is capital. It may be relevant, for example, in cases where the premises are overseas.)

Payment to modify terms of lease

[63.52] A company (G) had agreed to rent a motorway service area from the Ministry of Transport. The lease was not assignable, and had 40 years to run. The rent was partly calculated by reference to G's gross takings, which included excise duty on sales of tobacco. G paid the Ministry £122,220 in return for the tobacco duty being excluded from its takings in computing the rent. G claimed that this payment should be allowed as a deduction in computing its profits. The Ch D rejected the claim and the HL dismissed G's appeal (by a 4-1 majority, Lord Salmon dissenting), holding that the payment was capital expenditure, as it made a capital asset (the lease) more advantageous. *Tucker v Granada Motorway Services Ltd*, HL 1979, 53 TC 92; [1979] STC 393; [1979] 1 WLR 683; [1979] 2 All ER 801.

Premises destroyed—payment for cancellation of lease

[63.53] A company (W) rented business premises in West Africa which were destroyed by an earthquake, with 12 years of the lease remaining. The landlord (G) claimed that, under the terms of the lease, W must restore the premises and pay rent for the remainder of the term. Eventually W paid G £2,753 to be released from its obligations. The Special Commissioners held that this was a capital payment and was not deductible in computing W's profits. The KB upheld their decision. *West African Drug Co Ltd v Lilley*, KB 1947, 28 TC 140.

Duplicand

[63.54] In a Scottish case, a company which operated a school paid a duplicand, at intervals of 21 years, to the owners of its playing fields. The CS held that the duplicand was capital expenditure, paid as a condition of ownership of land and not as an expense of carrying on the school. *Dow v Merchiston Castle School Ltd*, CS 1921, 8 TC 149.

Periodical payments in respect of capital expenditure by landlord

[63.55] A trader (E) operated a hotel under a 60-year lease providing for a low yearly rent and 50 half-yearly payments, described as being mixed repayments of capital and interest, in respect of expenditure which the landlord had incurred on structural improvements to the hotel. The KB held that these payments were capital expenditure, and were not deductible in computing E's profits. *Ainley v Edens*, KB 1935, 19 TC 303.

Private accommodation on business premises

[63.56] The rateable value of a public house, with residential accommodation included, was increased because of an increase in sales of beer. The Revenue considered that two-thirds of the rates were allowable as a deduction, and the publican appealed, claiming a deduction for the whole of the increase, plus two-thirds of the rates payable before the increase. The Commissioners dismissed his appeal but the Ch D remitted the case for rehearing. Roxburgh J held that more than two-thirds of the rates should be allowed as a deduction. *Wildbore v Luker*, Ch D 1951, 33 TC 46.

[63.57] A brewery required the tenant of a public house to live on the premises. He claimed that the whole of his expenditure on rent, rates, lighting, heating and insurance should be allowed as a deduction in computing in his profits. The General Commissioners held that only five-sixths of the expenditure in question was allowable as a deduction, and the Ch D upheld their decision. *McLaren v Mumford*, Ch D 1996, 69 TC 173; [1996] STC 1134.

Business carried on from home—allowance for rates, etc

[63.58] A freelance draughtsman carrying on business from his home claimed a deduction for 25% of his home expenses (rates, heat and lighting). His gross receipts in the relevant years were £125 and £136. The Commissioners held that only £10 was allowable and the Ch D upheld their decision. *Thomas v Ingram*, Ch D 1978, 52 TC 428; [1979] STC 1. (*Note.* Appeals against estimated assessments on undeclared bank interest were also dismissed.)

Repairs and renewals

CROSS-REFERENCES

See *Hinton v Maden & Ireland Ltd*, 8.32 CAPITAL ALLOWANCES for allowances for loose tools, etc. under *ITTOIA 2005, s 68** and *Caledonian Railway Co v Banks*, 8.94 CAPITAL ALLOWANCES for renewals allowances for plant.

Expenditure held not to be allowable

NOTE

In many of the cases listed, the disputed expenditure might now qualify for relief by means of capital allowances.

Improvements to railway line

[63.59] Expenditure by a railway company, on improving a section of its track, was held to be capital expenditure. *Highland Railway Co v Balderston*, CE 1889, 2 TC 485. (*Note*. Compare *Rhodesia Railways Ltd v Collector of Tax of the Bechuanaland Protectorate*, **63.87** below.)

Dredging of channel to shipbuilders' works

[63.60] A shipbuilding company (V) was based on the Walney Channel in Furness. Between 1896 and 1911 the channel became obstructed with silt, preventing V from delivering a ship which it was building. In 1912 V and the harbour authorities contributed to the cost of dredging the channel. The KB held that V's contribution was capital expenditure. *Ounsworth v Vickers Ltd*, KB 1915, 6 TC 671; [1915] 3 KB 267.

Repairs to newly-purchased second-hand ship

[63.61] A shipping company (L) purchased a second-hand ship, which was awaiting its periodical Lloyd's survey, for £97,000. The survey took place six months later, and revealed that the ship needed extensive repairs. L spent £51,558 on repairs and claimed the whole of this as a deduction in computing its profits. The Commissioners allowed £12,000 as being attributable to the period during which L had operated the ship, but disallowed the balance on the grounds that it was part of the cost of acquiring the ship, and was capital expenditure. The CS upheld their decision, holding that the cost of the arrears of repairs with which the ship was burdened was part of the cost of acquisition, since the ship would not have been seaworthy had the repairs not been carried out. Lord Clyde observed that 'the sellers would have demanded and obtained a higher price than they actually did, but for the immediate necessity of repairs to which the ship was subject'. *Law Shipping Co Ltd v CIR*, CS 1923, 12 TC 621.

Repairs to ship released from wartime detention

[63.62] A company (G) owned a single steamship, which was seized by the German Government in 1914 and returned in a state of disrepair at the end of 1918. Extensive repairs were carried out in early 1919. G claimed most of the cost of the repairs from the German Government. The CS held that the cost of the repairs was capital expenditure. (The claim against the German Government for the cost of the repairs was eventually settled. Lord Blackburn held that the expenditure was also disallowable on the ground that it should be set against the amount recovered from the German Government, which had been accepted as a capital receipt.) *CIR v Granite City Steamship Co Ltd*, CS 1927, 13 TC 1.

Rebuilding of premises

[63.63] In an Irish excess profits duty case, the cost of rebuilding premises which had been destroyed in the Easter Rising of 1916, and of adapting temporary premises, was held to be capital expenditure and not allowable as a deduction. *Fitzgerald v CIR*, SC(I) 1925, 1 ITC 100; 5 ATC 414; [1926] IR 585.

[63.64] In an Irish case, a company carried on business from a 300-year-old building. It was in very bad condition and the company was advised that it was not feasible to put it in a state of good repair. It was therefore demolished except for the rear wall and part of a side wall, and was replaced by a modern two-storey shop at a total cost of £6,509, of which the architect allocated £4,919 to 'repairs'. The company claimed to deduct the £4,919. The Irish High Court rejected the claim, holding that this was capital expenditure. *Curtin v M Ltd*, HC(I) 1957, 3 ITC 227; [1960] IR 97.

[63.65] A company (M) arranged for building work at its premises which involved substantial alterations and improvements. It claimed a deduction for the cost of this work. Following an enquiry, HMRC issued an amendment on the basis that £34,000 of the expenditure should be treated as capital. M appealed, contending that the expenditure should be treated as a repair. The First-tier Tribunal rejected this contention and dismissed the appeal. Applying dicta of Buckley LJ in the (non-tax) case of *Lurcott v Wakely & Wheeler*, CA [1911] 1 KB 905, 'repair is restoration by renewal or replacement of subsidiary parts of a whole. Renewal, as distinguished from repair, is reconstruction of the entirety, meaning by the entirety not necessarily the whole but substantially the whole subject-matter under discussion.' *Moonlight Textiles Ltd v HMRC*, FTT [2010] UKFTT 500 (TC), TC00755.

Repairs to premises acquired in dilapidated condition

[63.66] A company took a 14-year lease of premises in a bad state of repair at a peppercorn rent for the first year, and thereafter at a rent increasing from £700 to £1,200 a year. It claimed a deduction for expenditure of £2,295, incurred in accordance with a covenant in the lease to reinstate the premises. The Ch D rejected the claim, holding on the evidence that this was capital expenditure. *Jackson v Laskers Home Furnishers Ltd*, Ch D 1956, 37 TC 69; [1957] 1 WLR 69; [1956] 3 All ER 891.

Replacement of furnishings of recently-acquired hotel

[63.67] A trader (B) took over a hotel and, in his first year of trading, spent £169 on replacing floor coverings and pillows. The Commissioners held that this was capital expenditure, and the Ch D dismissed B's appeal. *Bidwell v Gardiner*, Ch D 1960, 39 TC 31.

Conversion of plant and buildings for different use

[63.68] A manufacturing company incurred expenditure in converting plant and buildings to adapt them for another process. The Commissioners held that this expenditure was capital, and the CS upheld their decision. Lord Clyde observed that in computing the 'balance of profits and gains', it was necessary to consider the 'ordinary principles of commercial accounting' and that 'where these ordinary principles are not invaded by statute, they must be allowed to prevail'. He also held that 'expenditure does not change its nature according to whether it be successful or unsuccessful'. *Lothian Chemical Co Ltd v Rogers*, CS 1926, 11 TC 508.

Replacement of factory chimney

[63.69] A colliery company (B) built a factory chimney at a cost of £3,067. After several years it became unsafe, and B demolished it and built another, improved, chimney near the site of the old one. It claimed £287 of the cost as repairs. The KB held that the whole cost was capital expenditure. The replacement was of an 'entirety'. *O'Grady v Bullcroft Main Collieries Ltd*, KB 1932, 17 TC 93. (*Note.* Compare *Samuel Jones & Co (Devondale) Ltd v CIR*, 63.89 below, where a chimney was an integral part of the factory.)

Replacement of reservoir—whether 'notional repairs' allowable

[63.70] A water company built a ferro-concrete water tower to increase the water pressure, and a reservoir to replace one not worth repairing, about double the size of the old one and on a different site. It claimed that the tower was plant (for the purposes of wear and tear deductions under the law then in force), and that part of the cost of the reservoir should be allowed as a deduction. The KB held that the tower was not plant and that the expenditure on the reservoir was capital. *Margrett v The Lowestoft Water and Gas Co*, KB 1935, 19 TC 481. (*Note.* The decision has subsequently been overruled with regard to the definition of 'plant'—see *CIR v Barclay Curle & Co Ltd*, **8.34** CAPITAL ALLOWANCES.)

Building reconstructed—replacement of roof

[63.71] A manufacturing firm (L) rebuilt its premises, replacing the original building by another which was about 20% larger. The old roof had been in poor condition and L claimed that five-sixths of the cost of the new roof should be treated as expenditure on repairs, and allowed as a deduction. The Commissioners rejected the claim and the CS dismissed L's appeal, holding that the expenditure was capital. *William P Lawrie v CIR*, CS 1952, 34 TC 20.

[63.72] A spinning company (T) owned a three-storey building. The roof and top storey were in a dangerous condition. T rebuilt the premises, increasing their height and building a new roof at a cost of £15,372. The Commissioners held that this was capital expenditure, and the Ch D upheld their decision. *Thomas Wilson (Keighley) Ltd v Emmerson*, Ch D 1960, 39 TC 360.

Retail shops—fixtures and fittings

[63.73] A company (E) traded as retail butchers, through a large number of shops. E claimed a deduction for the amount by which the cost of fixtures and fittings of new shops exceeded the amount realised from the sale of the fixtures and fittings of shops it had closed. The Commissioners rejected the claim and the HL unanimously upheld their decision, holding that the expenditure on the new shops was capital. *Eastmans Ltd v Shaw*, HL 1928, 14 TC 218.

Shop fittings

[63.74] A retail partnership closed two of its shops and opened another nearby. It claimed a deduction for the cost of the fittings of the new shop.

The Commissioners rejected the claim and the CS upheld their decision. *Messrs Hyam v CIR*, CS 1929, 14 TC 479.

Improvement of sanitation

[63.75] In an Irish case, a company carried on business as woollen manufacturers. Following the installation of a new water and sewerage scheme in the locality of its mill, and in compliance with orders made by the local authority, it replaced the earthen privies at its mill, housed in various sheds detached from the mill building, by water closets in a concrete structure attached to the mill building. The Irish Supreme Court held that the expenditure was capital, and was not an allowable deduction. *Vale v Martin Mahony & Bros Ltd*, SC(I) 1946, 2 ITC 331; [1947] IR 30, 41.

Barrier as protection against coastal erosion

[63.76] A company, which owned a café at a beach, erected a barrier of wooden piles and brushwood in front of the café, as protection against erosion by the sea. The Commissioners held that the cost was capital expenditure, and the Ch D upheld their decision. *Avon Beach & Café Ltd v Stewart*, Ch D 1950, 31 TC 487.

Replacement of canal embankment

[63.77] The Ch D held that the cost of replacing an embankment between a factory and a canal was not a repair of the factory, and was capital expenditure. *Phillips v Whieldon Sanitary Potteries Ltd*, Ch D 1952, 33 TC 213.

New access road to premises

[63.78] A company (C) traded from warehouses, access to which was through a residential road. To meet complaints by residents, C constructed a new access road. The Ch D held that the cost was capital expenditure and was not an allowable deduction. *Pitt v Castle Hill Warehousing Co Ltd*, Ch D 1974, 49 TC 638; [1974] STC 420; [1974] 1 WLR 1624; [1974] 3 All ER 146.

Expenditure on cattle ring forming part of cattle mart

[63.79] A company (B) traded as auctioneers at a cattle mart. B spent £8,605 on the cattle ring, replacing the original walls, roofing it and concreting an area which had previously been earth. The Ch D held that this was capital expenditure, and was not an allowable deduction. *Wynne-Jones v Bedale Auction Ltd*, Ch D 1976, 51 TC 426; [1977] STC 50.

Replacement of stand at football ground

[63.80] A stand at a football club's ground was found to be unsafe. It had been built in 1912 and was of wood and steel with a brick wall at the back. It was demolished and replaced by a concrete stand of modern design, nearer the pitch and of approximately the same capacity, and containing office and other accommodation not provided by the old stand. The club claimed that the cost of the new stand should be allowed as a deduction. The Ch D rejected the claim, holding that the replacement was not a repair, and that the cost was capital expenditure and not an allowable deduction. *Brown v Burnley Football*

& Athletic Co Ltd, Ch D 1980, 53 TC 357; [1980] STC 424; [1980] 3 All ER 244. (*Note*. The Ch D also held that the grandstand was not plant and did not qualify for capital allowances—see **8.63** CAPITAL ALLOWANCES.)

Repairs to grandstand at racecourse

[63.81] In an Irish case, the proprietors of a racecourse incurred expenditure on renovating the grandstand. The Circuit Court Judge held that the work on the part of the stand which was retained constituted revenue expenditure. The HC(I) allowed the Revenue's appeal in part, holding that repairs to the walls constituted revenue expenditure, but that the replacement of the roof, and alterations to the terracing, were improvements and constituted capital expenditure. *O'Grady v Roscommon Race Committee*, HC(I) 6 November 1992 unreported. (*Note*. For another issue in this case, see **8.43** CAPITAL ALLOWANCES.)

Gas company—insertion of polyethylene pipes into network

[63.82] In a New Zealand case, a gas company began a programme of inserting polyethylene pipes into its network, in an attempt to prevent gas leakage. It claimed that the expenditure on this should be deducted in computing its profits. The Revenue rejected the claim on the grounds that the expenditure was capital. The company appealed, contending that it should be treated as a repair of the existing network. The PC rejected this contention and dismissed the appeal, holding that the work changed the character of the existing gas distribution system and was work of a capital nature. Lord Nicholls held that 'the speed or slowness with which the work was carried out cannot affect its nature or, hence, its proper characterisation'. Furthermore, 'the desire to solve a maintenance problem is not inconsistent with carrying out work of a capital nature'. *Auckland Gas Co Ltd v New Zealand Commissioner of Inland Revenue*, PC 2000, 73 TC 266; [2000] STC 527; [2000] 1 WLR 1783.

Provisions for future expenditure on repairs and renewals

[63.83] See *Naval Colliery Co Ltd v CIR*, **62.51** TRADING PROFITS (repairs to mine following national stoppage); *Clayton v Newcastle Corporation*, **62.60** TRADING PROFITS (depreciation reserve for dilapidated assets), and *Peter Merchant Ltd v Stedeford*, **62.71** TRADING PROFITS (provision for renewals deferred because of wartime conditions).

Expenditure on property transferred to director

[63.84] In 1998 a company (L) purchased a property for £850,000. It incurred expenditure on repairing and improving the property, and then transferred it to its controlling director, as a bonus. It claimed that its expenditure on repairs and improvements should be allowed as a deduction in computing its profits. The Revenue rejected the claim on the basis that the expenditure was capital. The First-tier Tribunal dismissed L's appeal against this decision. *Lion Co v HMRC*, FTT [2009] UKFTT 357 (TC); [2010] SFTD 454, TC00295.

Repairs to flat above business premises

[63.85] See *Mason v Tyson*, **63.225** below.

Expenditure held to be allowable

Renewal of harbour moorings

[63.86] Money which harbour mooring commissioners borrowed to replace chain moorings by screw moorings was held to be allowable (as expenditure on renewals). *In re King's Lynn Harbour Mooring Commissioners*, Ex D 1875, 1 TC 23.

Repair of railway line

[63.87] In a Bechuanaland case, the Privy Council held that expenditure on the repair and renewal of railway tracks was an allowable deduction, distinguishing *Highland Railway Co v Balderston*, **63.59** above. *Rhodesia Railways Ltd v Collector of Tax of the Bechuanaland Protectorate*, PC 1933, 12 ATC 223; [1933] AC 368.

Harbour board—removal of wreck

[63.88] A harbour board incurred expenditure on the removal of a wreck. The General Commissioners held that this was an allowable deduction and the CA unanimously upheld their decision as one of fact. *Whelan v Dover Harbour Board*, CA 1934, 18 TC 555.

Replacement of factory chimney

[63.89] The CS unanimously held that the cost of replacing a factory chimney was an allowable deduction, distinguishing the KB decision in *O'Grady v Bullcroft Main Collieries Ltd*, **63.69** above, on the grounds that the chimney in that case had been an 'entirety', whereas the chimney here was 'physically, commercially and functionally an inseparable part of an "entirety" which was the factory'. *Samuel Jones & Co (Devondale) Ltd v CIR*, CS 1951, 32 TC 513.

Replacement of weighbridge building

[63.90] In an Irish case, a company (P) trading as leather manufacturers had a small building housing weighbridge machinery and also providing some workshop and storage accommodation. Following severe storm damage, the building was demolished and replaced by a smaller building, housing only the weighbridge machinery. A new building was also erected for workshop and storage accommodation. P accepted that the cost of the latter building was capital expenditure, but claimed that the cost of demolishing the old building and of erecting the replacement building for the weighbridge machinery should be allowed as a deduction. The Irish Supreme Court accepted the claim. *Hodgins v Plunder & Pollak (Ireland) Ltd*, SC(I) 1955, 3 ITC 135; [1957] IR 58.

Repairs and structural alterations to old premises

[63.91] Part of a company's premises was more than 400 years old. The company spent £2,736 on replacing a slate roof, strengthening a floor and replacing the shop front. The General Commissioners held that this expenditure was on essential repairs and was an allowable deduction, and the Ch D upheld their decision as one of fact. *Conn v Robins Bros Ltd*, Ch D 1966, 43 TC 266.

Repairs to cinemas deferred because of wartime conditions

[63.92] During and immediately after the Second World War, a company which operated a large number of cinemas acquired several which, because of wartime restrictions on building work, were in need of repair and redecoration. Their state of disrepair had not affected their purchase price, nor did it restrict their use for public showing. The company carried out the repairs over a period of several years, and the Revenue considered that the proportion of the cost which was referable to years before the cinemas were acquired was capital expenditure. The CA held that the whole of the expenditure was allowable, distinguishing *Law Shipping Co Ltd v CIR*, **63.61** above, since in that case the ship could not have been used without the necessary repairs and the purchase price had taken this into account, whereas here the cinemas remained usable despite their state of disrepair. *Odeon Associated Theatres Ltd v Jones*, CA 1971, 48 TC 257; [1973] Ch 288; [1971] 1 WLR 442; [1972] 1 All ER 681.

Resurfacing of farm drive

[63.93] A farming partnership claimed a deduction for the cost of resurfacing the driveway at its farm. HMRC rejected the claim on the basis that this was capital expenditure, but the First-tier Tribunal allowed the partnership's appeal, holding that it was revenue expenditure rather than capital expenditure. *G Pratt & Sons v HMRC*, FTT [2011] UKFTT 416 (TC), TC01269.

Resurfacing of caravan park

[63.94] A partnership operated a caravan park. It claimed a deduction for the cost of resurfacing part of the park, replacing the previous grass surface with a hardcore surface. HMRC rejected the claim on the basis that the expenditure was capital. The First-tier Tribunal allowed the partnership's appeal. Judge Reid observed that the new surface had less aesthetic appeal, was not suitable as a recreational area for children, and had generated customer complaints. He held that the expenditure should be treated as revenue rather than capital. *Cairnsmill Caravan Park v HMRC*, FTT [2013] UKFTT 164 (TC), TC02580.

Work on industrial estate

[63.95] A company (H) traded from a site on an industrial estate. It claimed deductions for expenditure on relaying and resurfacing a carriageway, resiting its car park, reinstating a footpath and diverting telecommunications cables. HMRC rejected the claims on the basis that the expenditure was capital, but the First-tier Tribunal allowed H's appeal, holding that the expenditure was revenue expenditure. *Hopegar Properties Ltd v HMRC*, FTT [2013] UKFTT 331 (TC), TC02734.

Gas company—insertion of polyethylene into network of metallic pipes

[63.96] A gas company (T) began a programme of inserting polyethylene pipes into its existing network of steel and iron pipes, in an attempt to prevent gas leakage. It claimed that the expenditure on this should be deducted in computing its profits. The Revenue rejected the claim and issued corporation tax assessments on the basis that the expenditure was capital. T appealed, contending that since it was not replacing whole areas of pipes, but only the areas between two joints in a metallic pipe, the expenditure should be treated as revenue rather than capital. The Special Commissioners accepted this contention and allowed the appeals, observing that 'what was done was a mere replacement of parts of the pipeline that were defective and the renewal of those parts'. The work 'did not alter the character of the network' and the expenditure should be treated as revenue expenditure. *Transco plc v Dyall*, Sp C [2002] SSCD 199 (Sp C 310).

Miscellaneous

Expenditure held not to be allowable

Cost of land with deposits of raw materials

[63.97] A company manufactured nitrates, iodine, etc. It obtained the raw material from nitrate deposits on land which it owned in Chile, and claimed a deduction for an amount representing the exhaustion of the deposits. The Commissioners rejected the claim and the HL unanimously upheld their decision, holding that the cost of the land and deposits was capital. *Alianza Co Ltd v Bell*, HL 1905, 5 TC 172; [1906] AC 18.

Removal expenses

[63.98] A company which sold granite moved to larger premises. The removal expenses were held to be capital, and not allowable deductions. *Granite Supply Association Ltd v Kitton*, CE 1905, 5 TC 168.

Business acquired as going concern—payment for unexpired contracts

[63.99] A coal merchant, who died in March 1915, had entered into contracts to purchase coal for periods up to December 1915. His son acquired the business, paid £30,000 for the benefit of the unexpired contracts, and claimed this as a deduction in computing his profits for excess profits duty. The Revenue rejected the claim and the HL dismissed his appeal. Despite their short duration, the contracts were fixed capital rather than circulating capital, so that the payment to acquire them was capital expenditure. *John Smith & Son v Moore*, HL 1921, 12 TC 266; [1921] 2 AC 13.

Payments by carting contractor for right to deposit material

[63.100] A carting contractor paid £3,200, payable in instalments over eight years, for the right to deposit waste material on certain land. The CS held that the £3,200 was capital expenditure. *CIR v Adam*, CS 1928, 14 TC 34.

Purchase of tipping sites by waste disposal company

[63.101] A waste disposal company (W) purchased several sites and claimed that the purchases were revenue expenditure, on the grounds that it had acquired the land in order to use the airspace above it. The Ch D rejected this contention, holding that the expenditure was capital. Harman J observed that 'it is quite plain that airspace is not something which even the most ingenious conveyancer of Lincoln's Inn has ever dealt with as an item of property unrelated to the ground over which it lies'. The CA dismissed W's appeal, holding that the sites were capital assets. *Rolfe v Wimpey Waste Management Ltd*, CA 1989, 62 TC 399; [1989] STC 454.

Loan by company to protect agency

[63.102] A company (M) lent money to another company (C), in return for a verbal assurance that it would retain a selling agency for three companies associated with C. M lost the agency and £6,100 of the loan. The KB held that the £6,100 was a capital loss and was not deductible in computing M's profits. *Henderson v Meade-King Robinson & Co Ltd*, KB 1938, 22 TC 97.

Payment to retiring director following dispute

[63.103] One of the two directors and shareholders of a company (D) resigned. D paid him £450 and released him from a debt of £150, which was recorded in the minutes as the purchase price of his 'assets'. D appealed against an assessment, contending that the £600 should be allowed as a deduction in computing its profits. The KB rejected this contention and dismissed the appeal, holding that the payment was capital expenditure. *Deverell Gibson & Hoare Ltd v Rees*, KB 1943, 25 TC 467.

Loss on sale of temporary residence provided for employee

[63.104] To ensure the continued service of a valued employee, a firm of solicitors paid for a bungalow to be built for him to live in and bought a house for him to occupy while the bungalow was being built. When the bungalow was finished, the firm sold the house at a loss of £422, and claimed this as a deduction from its profits. The Ch D held that the claim was not allowable, as it was capital expenditure. *Owen & Gadsdon v Brock*, Ch D 1951, 32 TC 206.

Quarry abandoned—payment in commutation of liability for electricity

[63.105] A partnership abandoned a quarry, but remained liable to pay £75 per quarter to the electricity authority for four years. It paid £600 to the authority in commutation of this liability, and claimed this as a deduction in computing its profits. The CS held that the payment was not an allowable deduction. It was capital expenditure, and had been made for the purpose of abandoning part of the trade rather than for the purpose of carrying it on. *CIR v William Sharp & Son*, CS 1959, 38 TC 341.

Payment to NCB in return for undertaking not to work coal

[63.106] To safeguard against subsidence on its factory site, a company paid £40,000 to the National Coal Board in five annual instalments, in return for an undertaking by the Board not to work any coal seam under the factory. The CA held that the payments were capital expenditure. *Bradbury v The United Glass Bottle Manufacturers Ltd*, CA 1959, 38 TC 369.

Payments by Betting Board to promote horse racing

[63.107] The Racecourse Betting Control Board operated totalisators at racecourses. It used its funds to make various payments for the benefit of horse-breeding and horse-racing. It claimed these payments as deductions in computing its profits. The HL rejected the claim, holding that the payments were appropriations of profits that had been earned, rather than expenses incurred for the purposes of the Board's trade of operating totalisators. Viscount Simonds observed that 'though the appropriations may benefit the

Board, it is no part of its trade to assist racecourse executives or to encourage racing in other ways. That is the object to which, under the control of the Secretary of State, the profits of its trade may be devoted'. *Young v Racecourse Betting Control Board*, HL 1959, 38 TC 426; [1959] 1 WLR 813; [1959] 3 All ER 215.

Purchase price paid in instalments

[63.108] Three partners bought a restaurant for £6500, paying £1950 as a lump sum and the balance by instalments of £25 per week. They claimed that these payments should be deducted in computing their profits. The CS rejected the claim, holding that the payments were capital expenditure. *CIR v Pattison & Others*, CS 1959, 38 TC 617.

Grant of sisal estates for payments based on production

[63.109] The Government of Tanganyika granted a company (R) the right to occupy sisal estates for 99 years for a premium of £311,000 and monthly payments based on sisal production up to a total of £174,000. R paid the £174,000 within two years. The PC held that the £174,000 was capital expenditure. *Ralli Estates Ltd v East Africa Income Tax Commissioner*, PC 1961, 40 ATC 9; [1961] 1 WLR 329.

Farmer—visit to Australia with a view to farming there

[63.110] A Gloucestershire farmer visited Australia with a view to emigrating and buying a farm there. The Ch D held that the cost of the journey was not an allowable deduction in computing his profits, since it was capital expenditure. *Sargent v Eayrs*, Ch D 1972, 48 TC 573; [1973] STC 50; [1973] 1 WLR 236; [1973] 1 All ER 277.

Payments for technical information

[63.111] An Irish company (S) and a UK firm (W) carried on similar businesses. W agreed to supply S with technical information, and to grant an exclusive licence in the Republic of Ireland of any patents which it held, for ten years. In return S agreed to pay W £15,000 in instalments over a six-year period. The payments by S were held to be capital expenditure, and not deductible in computing its profits. *S Ltd v O'Sullivan*, HC(I) 1972, TL(I) 108.

Payment to remove onerous terms of loan

[63.112] A company (T), which carried on a manufacturing business in Wiltshire, had acquired additional premises in Scotland. In 1975 it had to borrow £80,000 from a finance company (C) at 17.5% pa, repayable in instalments over nine years and secured by a debenture creating a fixed or floating charge over all its assets. The terms of the loan gave C an option to become a 15% shareholder in T. In 1978 T paid £20,000 to C to secure the cancellation of the debenture. The CA held that the £20,000 was capital expenditure and was not an allowable deduction. *Whitehead v Tubbs (Elastics) Ltd*, CA 1983, 57 TC 472; [1984] STC 1.

Payment for right to operate sub-post office

[63.113] An individual (D) was appointed as a subpostmaster, and was required to make an introductory payment, in four instalments, to Post

Office Counters Ltd. He was permitted to operate a retail business from the sub-post office. The Revenue issued assessments covering D's income from the retail business and his salary as subpostmaster. He appealed, contending that the introductory payment should be allowed as a deduction. The Special Commissioner rejected this contention and dismissed his appeal, holding that the payment was capital expenditure rather than revenue expenditure. The Commissioner also observed that although the Revenue had included D's Post Office salary in the assessment on his retail profits (in accordance with an unpublished concession), the salary was strictly assessable under the separate rules of Schedule E under the legislation then in force. The introductory payment had not been made wholly and exclusively for the purposes of D's retail trade. *Dhendsa v Richardson*, Sp C [1997] SSCD 265 (Sp C 134).

Payment for goodwill of shop including sub-post office

[63.114] In 1997 a trader (D) purchased a shop which included a sub-post office. He paid £110,000, of which £45,000 was attributed to goodwill. In 2008 the sub-post office was closed. In his tax return, D claimed a deduction for the £45,000 which he had paid for the purchase of the goodwill (resulting in a trading loss). HMRC began an enquiry and issued an amendment disallowing the deduction. The First-tier Tribunal dismissed D's appeal, holding that the payment was capital expenditure. *S Devaraj v HMRC*, FTT [2014] UKFTT 713 (TC), TC03834.

Transfer of business—vested or contingent liabilities to employees

[63.115] In a New Zealand case, a company (N) agreed to acquire the assets and undertaking of a forestry research business which had been operated by a Government department. It also agreed to take over some of the department's contractual obligations to its employees, including their vested or contingent entitlements to paid leave attributable to their service with the department. N claimed that the subsequent payment of these sums should be treated as deductible in computing its profits. The Revenue rejected the claim on the grounds that the payments were capital expenditure. The PC upheld the Revenue's rejection of the claim. Lord Hoffmann held that the payments were capital expenditure, observing that 'the discharge of the vendor's liability to a third party, whether vested or contingent, can be part of the purchase price. It does not matter that the payment is not made at once but pursuant to an arrangement whereby the purchaser agrees to be substituted as debtor to the third party.' *New Zealand Commissioner of Inland Revenue v New Zealand Forest Research Institute Ltd*, PC 2000, 72 TC 628; [2000] STC 522; [2000] 1 WLR 1755.

Transfer of business—depreciation charges

[63.116] A company (S) had carried on a substantial business involving the repair of computers. It sold its repair business to a newly-formed company (T). T paid S £7,800,000 as consideration. In its accounts it treated this as capital expenditure, but it subsequently submitted a claim under *TMA, s 33* that the part of the payment which it charged each year as 'depreciation' should be treated as deductible in computing its profits. The Revenue rejected the claim on the grounds that the payment was capital expenditure. The Special Commissioners dismissed T's appeal, observing that 'the mechanism for spreading the payment here has been to capitalise it and then to depreciate the capital over the seven year period'. T's counsel had failed to 'cite any case where expenditure was correctly treated as capital for accountancy purposes, but was nevertheless a revenue expense for tax purposes'. The payment was a capital payment which had been made 'with a view to bringing into existence an asset or an advantage for the enduring benefit of a trade'. *Triage Services Ltd v HMRC*, Sp C [2006] SSCD 85 (Sp C 519).

Purchase of additional milk quota

[63.117] A family partnership owned a herd of cows for the production and sale of milk. They claimed a deduction for the cost of purchasing additional milk quota. The Revenue rejected the claim on the basis that it was capital expenditure rather than revenue expenditure. The Special Commissioner dismissed the partnership's appeal, holding that the partnership had 'purchased and retained an asset which gives an enduring benefit to the trade'. *Terry & Terry v HMRC*, Sp C [2005] SSCD 629 (Sp C 482).

Training and examination fees

[63.118] A freelance tutor (D) trained for a diploma in law, and claimed a deduction for his examination fees. The Revenue rejected the claim on the basis that this was capital expenditure rather than revenue expenditure. The Special Commissioner dismissed D's appeal, finding that D had undertaken the course with the aim of gaining a new qualification. The Ch D upheld this decision as one of fact. *Dass v Special Commissioner*, Ch D 2006, [2007] STC 187; [2006] EWHC 2491 (Ch).

Consultancy fee paid regarding major contract

[63.119] A trader (B) operated a cleaning business. He claimed a deduction for £11,000, described as a consultancy fee, which he had paid to an American who had helped him win a major contract. HMRC rejected the claim on the grounds that the payment was capital expenditure. The First-tier Tribunal dismissed B's appeal. Judge Tildesley observed that the projected turnover under the contract exceeded B's current annual turnover, and was intended to secure 'an enduring benefit for the appellant's business'. *G Bowman (t/a The Janitor Cleaning Co) v HMRC*, FTT [2012] UKFTT 607 (TC), TC02284.

Interest payments held to be capital expenditure

[63.120] See *European Investment Trust Co Ltd v Jackson*, 63.282 below; *Ward v Anglo-American Oil Co Ltd*, 63.283 below; *EJ & WH Bridgwater v King*, 63.285 below, and *Wharf Properties Ltd v Hong Kong Commissioner of Inland Revenue*, 63.286 below.

Expenditure held to be partly allowable

Guarantee payments under finance lease agreement

[63.121] A company (C) leased a paper mill from a leasing company (L). It was accepted that the rental payments which C made under the lease were allowable deductions in computing its profits. However, L also required C to enter into a guarantee agreement with a number of banks. Under this agreement, C was required to pay an initial management fee and make yearly payments of guarantee fees. C claimed that these lease guarantee payments should be allowed as deductions, and claimed loss relief accordingly. The Revenue rejected the claim, on the basis that these payments constituted capital expenditure rather than revenue expenditure. C appealed. The Special Commissioners allowed the appeal in part, holding that the initial management fee was capital expenditure but that the yearly guarantee payments were revenue expenditure. *Caledonian Paper plc v CIR*, Sp C [1998] SSCD 129 (Sp C 159).

Expenditure held to be allowable

Hire-purchase payments

[63.122] A coal company (D) acquired its railway wagons under hire-purchase agreements. In its accounts it treated the payments as revenue expenditure, and in its tax computations it apportioned the payments between revenue expenditure and capital expenditure. The Revenue issued assessments on the basis that none of the payments were deductible in computing D's profits for tax purposes. D appealed, contending that a part of the payments should be allowed as a deduction. The CS unanimously allowed the appeal, holding that the payments under the agreement should be split between amounts for hire, which were allowable, and payments for the eventual purchase, which were capital. *Darngavil Coal Co Ltd v Francis*, CS 1913, 7 TC 1. (*Note.* In practice it is now usual to allow as interest the excess of the aggregate of the hire-purchase payments over the cash price.)

Share of profits for hire of ships

[63.123] In 1910 and 1911 a shipping company (G) chartered two vessels, agreeing to pay the owner a fixed sum for depreciation plus a share of the net profits, if any, of each voyage. In computing G's 'standard profits' for excess profits duty purposes, the Revenue treated these payments as allowable deductions. G appealed, contending that the payments should be treated as distributions of profits rather than as deductions. The KB rejected this contention, holding that the whole of the payments were allowable deductions. *George Thompson & Co Ltd v CIR*, KB 1927, 12 TC 1091. (*Note.* See 64.57 TRADING PROFITS for another point at issue in this case.)

Purchase of dumps of tailings

[63.124] A gold-mining company sold its business, but retained the right to work five dumps of 'tailings' (residual material left after the extraction of gold from gold ore), from which gold could be extracted by a re-treatment process, for ten years. It assigned this right to a new company (G) for £122,750. G claimed a deduction for the cost of the tailings actually processed in computing its profits. The Revenue rejected the claim, considering that the payment was capital expenditure. The CA allowed G's appeal, holding that it was operating 'a manufacturing business applied to raw material already won and gotten', and that the payment was revenue expenditure rather than capital expenditure. *Golden Horse Shoe (New) Ltd v Thurgood*, CA 1933, 18 TC 280; [1934] 1 KB 548.

Yearly payments for goodwill

[63.125] A company (M) was assigned an underlease of a cinema and equipment for 13 years at an annual rent of £500. Under a supplementary deed, the assignor granted M the goodwill of the cinema business in return for further payments of £500 pa, with an option to M to purchase the headlease and the goodwill for £3,500. M claimed a deduction for the payments of £500 pa in computing its profits. The Revenue accepted that the rent was an allowable deduction, but rejected the claim with regard to the payments under the supplementary deed, considering that they were capital expenditure. The Special Commissioners allowed M's appeal and the KB upheld their decision, holding that the payments were revenue expenditure. *Ogden v Medway Cinemas Ltd*, KB 1934, 18 TC 691.

Payments of share of profits in return for technical assistance

[63.126] A company (B) agreed to pay to two other companies a specified percentage of its net profits for eight years 'in consideration of their giving to the company the full benefit of their technical and financial knowledge and experience'. It claimed a deduction for payments made under this agreement in computing its taxable profits. The Revenue rejected the claim, considering that the payments were distributions of profits rather than an expense incurred in earning the profits. The CA allowed B's appeal, holding that the payments were revenue expenditure and were deductible in computing B's profits. *British Sugar Manufacturers Ltd v Harris*, CA 1937, 21 TC 527; [1938] 2 KB 220; [1938] 1 All ER 149. (*Note*. The case also turned on whether there had been a 'discovery'. Here, the KB found for the Revenue, applying *Williams v Grundy's Trustees*, **5.29** ASSESSMENTS. The CA did not pass judgment on this issue. For cases concerning whether there has been a 'discovery', see **5.19** *et seq*. ASSESSMENTS.)

Payments for use of totalisator calculated by reference to cost

[63.127] A racecourse company built a totalisator and gave the exclusive use of it for 21 years to the Racecourse Betting Control Board, in return for payment of an annual amount equal to 12.5% of the cost, with a minimum of 12.5% of £23,000 and a maximum of 12.5% of £27,000. The agreement expressly declared that the payments were for the right to use the totalisator and in repayment by yearly instalments of the cost of its construction. The Control Board claimed that the payments were deductible in computing its profits. The Revenue rejected the claim, considering that the payments should be apportioned and that part of the payments represented capital expenditure. The KB allowed the Control Board's appeal, holding that the payments were revenue expenditure and were deductible in full. Macnaghten J held that the fact that the payments would cover almost the whole of the cost of construction was not conclusive. *Racecourse Betting Control Board v Wild*, KB 1938, 22 TC 182; [1938] 4 All ER 487.

Business sold as going concern—purchaser paying liabilities of vendor

[63.128] A partnership purchased a business as a going concern, under an agreement whereby the vendor agreed to discharge all outstanding liabilities. He failed to do so, and the partnership subsequently made the necessary payments, in order to preserve the goodwill of the business and to ensure continuity of supplies of materials, etc. The partnership claimed that the payments were allowable deductions in computing its profits. The Revenue rejected the claim, considering that the payments were capital expenditure. The Commissioners allowed the partnership's appeal, holding that the payments were revenue expenditure, and the KB upheld their decision as one of fact. *Cooke v Quick Shoe Repair Service*, KB 1949, 30 TC 460.

Cropping of leaves for cigarette manufacturer

[63.129] In an Indian case, a firm manufactured cigarettes rolled in tendu leaves. It entered into contracts with owners of tendu trees to enable it to tend the trees and crop the leaves. The Privy Council held that payments under the contracts were allowable deductions in computing the firm's profits. They were payments for raw materials of the trade, and were revenue expenditure rather than capital expenditure. *Mohanlal Hargovind of Jubbulpore v Central Provinces & Behar Commissioner of Income Tax*, PC 1949, 28 ATC 287; [1949] AC 521.

Industrial and provident society—rebates

[63.130] A registered industrial and provident society carried on a trade of grading and distributing eggs, most of its produce being brought from its members. Members were allotted 'bonuses' on their transactions with the society, and the society's rules allowed part of these bonuses to be allocated towards the purchase of fully paid-up shares in the society. The society claimed these sums as deductions in computing its profits. The Revenue rejected the claim, but the CA allowed the society's appeal, holding that the amounts allocated in this way were deductible under what is now *CTA 2009, s 132*. *Staffordshire Egg Producers Ltd v Spencer*, CA 1963, 41 TC 131.

Payment to secure release of option over trade investment

[63.131] A company (C) held a 19.5% shareholding in another company (J). J's controlling shareholder held an option to purchase these shares at par or a fair value. J became C's principal customer, and C decided to attempt to obtain the release of the option. It paid £10,000 for this, and claimed the payment as a deduction in computing its profits. The Revenue rejected the claim, considering that the payment was capital expenditure, and C appealed. The Commissioners allowed the appeal and the Ch D upheld this decision, holding that the payment was a revenue payment. It was made for the purpose of preserving C's goodwill, and did not result in the acquisition of any asset. *Walker v Cater Securities Ltd*, Ch D 1974, 49 TC 625; [1974] STC 390; [1974] 1 WLR 1363; [1974] 3 All ER 63.

'Wholly and exclusively' and 'losses' rules (ITTOIA 2005, s 34; CTA 2009, s 54

General principles

Whether expenditure wholly and exclusively for the purposes of the trade—leading cases

[63.132] There have been a very large number of cases concerning the question of whether expenditure has been 'wholly and exclusively' for the purposes of the trade. Among the leading cases (in chronological order) are *Strong & Co of Romsey Ltd v Woodifield* (1906, **66.70** TRADING PROFITS); *Smith's Potato Estates Ltd v Bolland* (1948, **63.156** below); *Morgan v Tate & Lyle Ltd* (1954, **63.239** below); *Mallalieu v Drummond* (1983, **63.216** below), and *McKnight v Sheppard* (1999, **66.73** TRADING PROFITS). For the application of the 'dual purpose' rule to professional partnerships, see *MacKinlay v Arthur Young McClelland Moores & Co*, **41.30** PARTNERSHIPS.

Payments to associated companies

Biscuit manufacturer—purchase of tin boxes at overvalue from subsidiary

[63.133] A company (H) which manufactured biscuits purchased a subsidiary company's entire stock of tin boxes and tinplate. The price paid exceeded the market value, and the stock was brought into H's accounts at market value. H claimed the difference as a trading expense. The KB rejected the claim, holding on the evidence that the object of the transactions was to finance the subsidiary. *CIR v Huntley & Palmers Ltd*, KB 1928, 12 TC 1209.

Loans to company under same control

[63.134] A company (M) made loans to another company (W). M's managing director owned all except one of the shares in W, and he and his wife also controlled M. W ceased trading and most of the loans proved to be irrecoverable. M claimed that the irrecoverable amount should be allowed as a deduction in computing its profits. The KB rejected this contention, holding that the financing of W was not part of M's business, and that the loss was not allowable in computing M's profits. *Baker v Mabie Todd & Co Ltd*, KB 1927, 13 TC 235.

[63.135] A similar decision was reached in a case where a company wrote off arrears of rent which it was owed by an associated company. *Sere Properties Ltd v HMRC*, FTT [2012] UKFTT 778 (TC), TC02429.

Estate development company—guarantee of indebtedness of builder

[63.136] A development company (H) guaranteed the indebtedness of a building firm to solicitors who financed the builders' construction of houses on land which H owned. (H's consideration for the sale of the land took the form of chief rents created on the sale of the houses.) H paid the solicitors £3,105 under the guarantee, and claimed that this should be allowed as a deduction in computing its profits. The Commissioners rejected this contention, holding that the payment was not allowable, and the KB upheld their decision. *Homelands (Handforth) Ltd v Margerison*, KB 1943, 25 TC 414.

Payments to meet operating expenses of agent/subsidiary

[63.137] A UK company (M) formed a US subsidiary to act as its agent and agreed to pay to it a minimum annual sum of $25,000 towards its operating expenses, these payments to be treated as on account of agency commission payable to the subsidiary. From 1950 to 1952, the payments exceeded the commission earned and M claimed a deduction for the excess. The Revenue rejected the claim and the Ch D dismissed M's appeal, holding that the payments were made to finance the subsidiary and were not wholly and exclusively for the purpose of M's trade. *Marshall Richards Machine Co Ltd v Jewitt*, Ch D 1956, 36 TC 511.

Guarantee of indebtedness of associated company

[63.138] A manufacturing company (TC) gave security for the liability of an associated property-owning company (TP), which in turn had given security for loans by a bank to its parent company (J). J handled TC's products and provided it with raw materials and administrative services. The Ch D held that the payments which TC made under the guarantee were not deductible in computing its profits, since they were part of an arrangement in the interest of all three companies, and therefore could not have been incurred wholly and exclusively for the purposes of TC's trade. *Garforth v Tankard Carpets Ltd*, Ch D 1980, 53 TC 342; [1980] STC 251.

[63.139] A company which carried on an electroplating business had acquired two subsidiary companies with similar businesses. The group borrowed a large sum of money from a bank, which required the three companies to guarantee each other's liabilities to the bank. Subsequently the bank demanded payment from the companies. The parent company made payment under the guarantee and claimed loss relief on the basis that the payment was an allowable deduction in computing its profits. The Revenue rejected the claim on the grounds that the expenditure had not been incurred wholly and exclusively for the purposes of the parent company's business. The Special Commissioners dismissed the company's appeal, finding that the guarantee given by the parent company 'was not given for the purposes of its own trade'. *Redkite Ltd v HM Inspector of Taxes*, Sp C [1996] SSCD 501 (Sp C 93).

Contribution to legal costs incurred by parent company

[63.140] Two brothers (SB and DB) controlled a Delaware corporation (BC). They, and BC, each owned one-third of the shares in a UK company (BL), which owned 95% of the shares in another UK company (P). In 2000 the US government began legal proceedings against BC, SB and DB, for supplying goods to Cuba in violation of the *Trading With the Enemy Act 1917* and the *Cuban Assets Control Regulations*. BC, DB and SB were convicted on some of the charges against them: BC was fined $250,000, while DB and SB were each fined $10,000. P made a contribution of £3,807,294 to the legal costs which BC had incurred, and claimed that this should be allowed as a deduction in computing its profits. HMRC rejected the claim on the basis that the expenditure had not been wholly and exclusively incurred for the purpose of

P's business. The First-tier Tribunal dismissed P's appeal against this decision. Judge Clark held that there had been a 'duality of purpose' and that '(P's) expenditure in making a contribution to the legal costs was not wholly and exclusively for the purposes of its trade'. *Purolite International Ltd v HMRC*, FTT [2012] UKFTT 475 (TC), TC02152.

Banking company—loans to leasing subsidiary

[63.141] A banking company, with capital and reserves of more than £1,000,000,000, acquired a majority shareholding in a leasing company (J). It made loans to J totalling £57,000,000. J suffered financial difficulties, and the bank eventually sold its shareholding, making a loss of about £30,000,000 on the loans. It claimed loss relief in respect of this as a trading expense. The Revenue rejected the claim, on the basis that the bank had made the loan in its capacity as a shareholder, rather than for the purposes of its business. The Special Commissioners reviewed the evidence in detail and allowed the bank's appeal, holding on the evidence that 'the actions of the bank were those of a banker acting as a banker; it had wanted to enter what it saw as a lucrative and expanding market, and the way it had chosen to do so was by making loans to (J)'. *AB Bank v HM Inspector of Taxes*, Sp C [2000] SSCD 229 (Sp C 237).

Loans or guarantees by solicitors or accountants for clients

Loan held not to be allowable

[63.142] An Edinburgh firm of Writers to the Signet lent money to a company formed by clients. The loan became irrecoverable and the firm claimed that the loss should be allowed as a deduction. The CS rejected the claim and the HL unanimously upheld this decision. Lord Buckmaster held that the moneylending had been 'a separate venture from that of Writers to the Signet and even if undertaken in the hope and expectation that it would help their business, it was none the less no part of their true profession'. *CIR v Hagart & Burn-Murdoch*, HL 1929, 14 TC 433; [1929] AC 286.

[63.143] A Scottish firm of solicitors which also acted as insurance agents, factors and stockbrokers, regularly lent money to clients. The Commissioners held that losses incurred on two such advances were not allowable deductions, and the CS upheld their decision. *WA & F Rutherford v CIR*, CS 1939, 23 TC 8.

[63.144] A firm of solicitors claimed a deduction for a loss on a loan to a builder and the estimated cost of entertaining clients, etc. The Special Commissioners held that both items were inadmissible, and the Ch D upheld this decision. *Bury & Walkers v Phillips*, Ch D 1951, 32 TC 198. (*Note*. For entertaining expenses see now *ITTOIA 2005, ss 45–47*.)

Payment under guarantee allowed

[63.145] A firm of solicitors guaranteed a client's overdraft. The client became bankrupt, and the firm paid the bank £412 under the guarantee. The Commissioners held that this was an allowable deduction in computing the firm's profits, and the Ch D upheld this decision. Pennycuick J observed that 'it is the practice of some solicitors to give guarantees to their clients'. *Jennings v Barfield & Barfield*, Ch D 1962, 40 TC 365; [1962] 1 WLR 997; [1962] 2 All ER 957.

Payment by partnership under guarantee by deceased partner

[63.146] In 1964 an accountant (H) guaranteed the overdraft of an important client company. In 1965 he took his son (D) into partnership. H died in 1967 and shortly afterwards D took another accountant into partnership. In 1969 the bank appointed a receiver for the company and called on the firm to pay £14,000 under the guarantee. The firm accepted the liability, paid the £14,000, and claimed this as a deduction. The Commissioners allowed the deduction, finding that the payment had been wholly and exclusively for the purposes of the practice, and the CA unanimously upheld their decision as one of fact. *Bolton v Halpern & Woolf*, CA 1980, 53 TC 445; [1981] STC 14.

Losses on other advances or guarantees

Losses by brewery company on loans to customers

[63.147] See *Reid's Brewery Co Ltd v Male*, 68.20 TRADING PROFITS.

Balance due from deceased controlling director

[63.148] A family company (J) was run informally under the sole control of its managing director, who prepared its accounts. Following his death, J's shareholders asked accountants to investigate its affairs. They prepared a balance sheet showing that the director owed J £14,584, attributable to private transactions which had been passed through J's books. The debt proved to be irrecoverable and J claimed that it should be allowed as a deduction in computing its profits. The KB rejected this contention, holding that the loss was not allowable, since it was not attributable not to J's trade but to the director's freedom to do as he pleased. *Curtis v J & G Oldfield Ltd*, KB 1925, 9 TC 319.

Commission drawn in advance

[63.149] A company (R) allowed its managing director (M) to draw amounts in anticipation of future commission. M was subsequently declared bankrupt, owing money which R was unable to recover. The CS held that the loss was not an allowable deduction in computing R's profits. *Roebank Printing Co Ltd v CIR*, CS 1928, 13 TC 864.

Misappropriation by director

[63.150] A company's finance director (N), who held 50% of its shares, misappropriated £15,000 belonging to the company, diverting it to another company which he controlled. N was subsequently declared bankrupt. The company was unable to recover the £15,000, and claimed that it should be allowed as a deduction in computing its profits. The Ch D rejected the claim, holding that the £15,000 was not an allowable deduction. *Bamford v ATA Advertising Ltd*, Ch D 1972, 48 TC 359; [1972] 1 WLR 1261; [1972] 3 All ER 535.

[63.151] The decision in *Bamford v ATA Advertising Ltd*, **63.150** above, was applied in the similar subsequent case of *Mirror Image Contracting Ltd v HMRC*, **11.11** CLOSE COMPANIES.

Exhibition guarantee

[63.152] A firm trading as asphalt contractors paid £375 under a guarantee to the 1923 British Empire Exhibition. It claimed that the payment should be allowed as a deduction in computing its profits, since it had made the guarantee in the hope of securing contracts for work at the Exhibition. The Commissioners allowed the claim and the CA upheld their decision as one of fact. *Morley v Lawford & Co*, CA 1928, 14 TC 229.

Film writer—guarantee of indebtedness of film company

[63.153] A film writer (W) purchased the film rights for a novel and formed a company (F) to produce the film. He lent F £1500 and guaranteed its overdraft. The film made a loss. W was unable to recover the £1500, and had to pay £1253 to the bank under the guarantee. He claimed these sums as deductions in computing his profits. The Commissioners allowed the claim and the KB upheld their decision as one of fact. *Lunt v Wellesley*, KB 1945, 27 TC 78.

Legal and professional expenses

Costs of successful defence of ownership of business

[63.154] In a Ceylon case, the purchaser of a business successfully defended an action against him alleging that he had purchased it as agent for a syndicate, the members of which were entitled to share in the profits. The PC held that his legal expenses were not deductible as they related to an issue affecting only his share of the profits, rather than the amount of the profits. *Ceylon Commissioner of Inland Revenue v Appuhamy*, PC 1962, 41 ATC 317.

Costs of appeals before Commissioners

[63.155] A partnership, which had successfully appealed to the Special Commissioners, claimed that the fees charged by its solicitors and counsel should be allowed as a deduction in computing its profits. The KB rejected this contention. Finlay J held that this was an application 'of profits after they have been earned and was not an expenditure necessary to earn the profits'. *Allen v Farquharson Bros & Co*, KB 1932, 17 TC 59.

[63.156] A company (S) incurred legal and accountancy expenses in connection with a successful excess profits tax appeal (which concerned the deductibility of increased remuneration paid to a senior employee). It claimed that the expenses should be allowed as a deduction in computing its profits. The Special Commissioners rejected this contention and S appealed, contending that it had pursued the appeal in order to retain the services of the employee concerned. The HL dismissed S's appeal (by a 3–2 majority, Viscount Simon and Lord Oaksey dissenting). Lord Simonds held that 'neither the cost of ascertaining taxable profit, nor the cost of disputing it with the Revenue authorities, is money spent to enable the trader to earn profit in his trade'. As a matter of principle, the cost of contesting a tax claim was not a deductible expense, and the fact that S had an ulterior motive for contesting the claim could not make it deductible. *Smith's Potato Estates Ltd v Bolland (and related appeal)*, HL 1948, 30 TC 267; [1948] AC 508; [1948] 2 All ER 367. (*Note*. On the distinction between motive and purpose, drawn by Lord Simonds in this case, see also *MacKinlay v Arthur Young McClelland Moores & Co*, **41.30** PARTNERSHIPS.)

[63.157] The decision in *Smith's Potato Estates Ltd v Bolland*, **63.156** above, was applied in the similar case of *Rushden Heel Co Ltd v Keene*, HL 1948, 30 TC 298; [1948] 2 All ER 378.

Costs of reviewing settled tax liabilities

[63.158] In 1925, a company (W) engaged a firm of accountants to review its excess profits duty assessments for the seven years to September 1920, which had already been settled and agreed with the Revenue. As a result, W obtained a substantial EPD repayment, paying the accountants 15% as their fee. The Commissioners held that the fee was not an allowable deduction, and the CA unanimously upheld their decision. *Worsley Brewery Co Ltd v CIR*, CA 1932, 17 TC 349.

Costs of disputing PAYE liability as employer

[63.159] In *Meredith v Hazell*, **42.88** PAY AS YOU EARN, a solicitor unsuccessfully opposed a demand for tax which he had failed to deduct under PAYE from his employees' emoluments. He appealed against a subsequent assessment, contending that the costs of the litigation should be allowed as a deduction. The Special Commissioners rejected this contention and dismissed his appeal, and the Ch D upheld their decision. *Meredith v Roberts*, Ch D 1968, 44 TC 559.

Partnership—successful defence of partner charged with conspiracy

[63.160] One of the two partners in a firm of accountants received a summons to defend a criminal charge for conspiracy to defraud the Revenue. The summons was dismissed. At the hearing, counsel held a watching brief for the other partner. The Commissioners held that the resultant legal expenses were not allowable deductions in computing the firm's profits, and the KB upheld their decision. (A small part of the total expenses, relating to legal advice concerning a letter to the firm from the Solicitor of Inland Revenue, stating that he wished to take evidence from employees of the firm, were allowed.) *Spofforth & Prince v Golder*, KB 1945, 26 TC 310; [1945] 1 All ER 363.

Partnership—costs of defending criminal prosecution

[63.161] A married couple traded in partnership as haulage contractors. The husband was convicted of polluting a tributary of a river with insecticide (causing the death of more than 100,000 fish). The partners claimed the costs of defending the criminal proceedings as a deduction. HMRC issued amendments to the partnership statements, disallowing the deductions, and the partners appealed. The First-tier Tribunal dismissed the appeals. Judge Long observed that the prosecution had been against the husband as an individual, rather than against the partnership. On the evidence, 'there was a personal motivation in incurring the expenditure as well as a business one'. *MA & Mrs BC Raynor v HMRC*, FTT [2011] UKFTT 813 (TC), TC01649.

Legal costs of dissolution of partnership

[63.162] An accountancy partnership was dissolved after a dispute between the partners. The partners appealed against an assessment for their final period of trading, contending that the legal expenses of dissolving the practice should be allowed as a deduction. The Commissioners dismissed their appeal and the Ch D upheld this decision. The legal expenses had not been wholly or exclusively laid out for the purposes of the partnership trade, but had been incurred to protect the interests of one of the partners. *C Connelly & Co v Wilbey*, Ch D 1992, 65 TC 208; [1992] STC 783. (*Note*. For another issue in this case, see **61.64** TRADING INCOME.)

Partnership—unsuccessful legal action on behalf of partner

[63.163] See *AB v HMRC*, **29.84** FURTHER ASSESSMENTS: LOSS OF TAX.

Legal costs incurred by stockbroker

[63.164] See *McKnight v Sheppard*, **66.73** TRADING PROFITS.

Legal costs incurred by solicitor

[63.165] A solicitor (V) was a member of an English limited liability partnership (S), and also worked in the London office of a German law firm (H). H ceased to trade, owing substantial sums to a German bank (B). Following negotiations, V agreed to pay B €300,000 in full settlement of all claims against him. He claimed this as a deduction from his income from S. HMRC issued a notice of amendment disallowing the claim on the grounds that V had a dual purpose in making the payment, but the First-tier Tribunal allowed V's appeal. Judge Brooks held on the evidence that V's purpose in making the payment was 'to preserve and protect his professional career'. *P Vaines v HMRC*, FTT [2013] UKFTT 576 (TC), TC02965.

Sole trader—costs of defending manslaughter charge

[63.166] A sole trader (D) operated a vehicle transport business. In 2002 one of his lorries killed a pedestrian. D was charged with manslaughter and attempting to pervert the course of justice. He was subsequently convicted of attempting to pervert the course of justice, but was acquitted of manslaughter. In his returns, he claimed a deduction for the legal costs of defending himself. HMRC issued amendments disallowing the deductions, and D appealed. The First-tier Tribunal dismissed his appeal, holding that the expenses were not wholly and exclusively incurred for the purposes of D's trade. Judge Connell held that D's 'main purpose in incurring significant expenditure on legal and other professional fees was to defend the manslaughter charge for the purpose of protecting his liberty and personal reputation'. The Upper Tribunal upheld this decision as one of fact. *P Duckmanton v HMRC*, UT [2013] UKUT 305 (TCC); [2013] STC 2379.

Company—costs of defamation proceedings

[63.167] A company (K) carried on a consultancy business. Its controlling director (S) was also a shareholder in another company (AG). In February 2008 S sent an email, to several recipients, proposing that AG's chairman should be removed from the board. AG's chief executive (P) subsequently sent a letter to various shareholders in AG, stating that certain assertions in S's email were 'wholly untrue'. S and K then began legal proceedings against AG and P, claiming that P's letter had been defamatory. The proceedings went to court but were settled by an agreement under which each side paid its own costs and AG withdrew 'any suggestion that (S) did not act honestly in his earlier communications with (AG's) shareholders'. K claimed that the costs of bringing these proceedings should be allowed as a deduction. HMRC rejected 50% of the claim on the basis that, since K was not a shareholder in AG, the proceedings had been primarily brought for S's personal purposes and had not been wholly for the purpose of K's business. (However, HMRC did agree to allow 50% of the expenditure under *CTA 2009, s 54(2).*) K appealed, contending that its 'ability to operate successfully depended on (S's) reputation being cleared of the accusation allegedly made by the letter'. The First-tier Tribunal accepted this contention and allowed the appeal. Judge Staker accepted S's evidence that he had not instigated the proceedings 'merely to vindicate his own personal hurt feelings' and found 'on the particular facts of this specific case that the sole purpose of bringing the defamation proceedings was to protect the business reputation of (K)'. *Key IP Ltd v HMRC*, FTT [2011] UKFTT 715 (TC); [2012] SFTD 305, TC01552.

Remuneration, etc

Remuneration considered excessive

[63.168] A worsted spinner employed his two sons. Their remuneration comprised salary and commission, the commission being a percentage of the profits. For several years the commission had been 5% but it was increased to 10% for 1915 to 1917 and to 33⅓% for 1918 and 1919. The father's health broke down in June 1918. The sons became partners from 1 January 1920. The Special Commissioners held that the 1918 and 1919 commission was not on a commercial basis and that only 10% was deductible. The KB upheld their decision. *Stott & Ingham v Trehearne*, KB 1924, 9 TC 69.

[63.169] A trader employed his three adult sons. Until 1909, each received wages of £150 a year, but he agreed in 1910 to pay each of them 25% of the net profits. The profits increased substantially and by 1916 the amount paid to each had risen to £1,803. In appeals against excess profits duty assessments for the years 1914–1916, the Commissioners held that only £250 pa of the remuneration paid to each son was allowable as a deduction. The KB upheld their decision as one of fact. *Johnson (t/a Johnson Bros & Co) v CIR*, KB 1919, 12 TC 147; [1919] 2 KB 717.

[63.170] A family company (W) traded as pig-dealers. Among the directors were two children of the controlling shareholder—his daughter aged 17 and his son aged 23. For the year ending April 1938, each was voted remuneration of £2,600 pa, with the result that W made a loss of some £300 for that year.

The son only drew £277 of his remuneration and the daughter only drew £70. W appealed against an assessment, contending that the full amount of the remuneration which had been voted should be allowed as a deduction, so that it had made no profit for the year in question. The Revenue only agreed to allow £350 in respect of the son and £78 in respect of the daughter, considering that the balance of the remuneration had not been paid wholly or exclusively for the purpose of W's trade. The General Commissioners held that they could not interfere with W's decision to pay such remuneration as it considered appropriate, and the Revenue appealed to the KB. Lawrence J observed that 'it may very well be that there are sums which are paid to the directors as remuneration for their services in accordance with the articles of association and in accordance with a resolution of the company, but it does not necessarily follow in the least that they are sums which are wholly and exclusively laid out for the purposes of the trade'. He therefore remitted the case to the Commissioners 'to find as a fact whether the sums in question were wholly and exclusively laid out for the purpose of the company's trade, and if they were not, to find how much of such sums was wholly and exclusively laid out for the purposes of the company's trade'. *Copeman v William Flood & Sons Ltd*, KB 1940, 24 TC 53; [1941] 1 KB 202.

[63.171] A property company (E) paid much of its income to its controlling director, a married woman. The Revenue considered that, since she did very little work for E (the consultancy work and rent collection being undertaken by her husband), the payments were not made wholly and exclusively for the purposes of E's business, and were not deductible in computing its profits. The General Commissioners held that only 5% of E's taxable profits could be treated as a trading expense, and the Ch D upheld this decision. *Earlspring Properties Ltd v Guest*, Ch D 1993, TL 3367; [1993] STC 473. (*Note*. For another issue in this case, taken to the CA, see **11.5** CLOSE COMPANIES).

Payments to children—whether remuneration

[63.172] A married couple farmed 165 acres in partnership and were helped by their four children, aged 14, 11, 9 and 7 respectively, doing odd jobs round the farm. For the year ending September 1977, each child was paid £2 per week and was bought £250 National Savings Certificates. The partnership claimed deductions for all the payments in computing the farm profits. The Revenue rejected the claim, and the couple appealed. The General Commissioners allowed the £104 paid to the eldest child but disallowed the rest as in the nature of pocket money, observing that it would have been illegal to employ the three younger children. The Ch D upheld their decision as one of fact. *Dollar & Dollar v Lyon*, Ch D 1981, 54 TC 459; [1981] STC 333.

Wife's wages—whether payments made for business purposes

[63.173] A trader claimed wife's earned income relief on the basis that he had paid her a wage to assist him in his business. He had not appealed against the relevant assessments on his business, and had not claimed, or been allowed, a deduction for his wife's wages in arriving at the profits. The wages were not in the wages book. The Commissioners rejected the claim and the KB upheld their decision. *Thompson v Bruce*, KB 1927, 11 TC 607. (*Note*. Wife's earned income relief was abolished for 1990/91 *et seq*. by *FA 1988, s 33*.)

[63.174] The Revenue was dissatisfied with the accounts submitted by a manufacturer (M), and issued estimated assessments. He appealed, contending that the Revenue should have accepted his accounts, which included claims for deductions for wages (increasing from £500 pa to £1,500 pa) allegedly paid to his wife. The Revenue refused to allow the deductions claimed. The Commissioners dismissed the appeals, holding on the evidence that the amounts were 'not an allowable deduction for taxation purposes'. The CA upheld their decision. Somervell LJ observed that the sums 'were merely book entries, and the amounts had not been paid to her but had been credited to the appellant's drawing account. In those circumstances (the Commissioners) were plainly entitled to disallow them'. *Moschi v Kelly*, CA 1952, 33 TC 442. (*Note*. M's accounts were found to be inaccurate—see **29.97** FURTHER ASSESSMENTS: LOSS OF TAX. For a sequel to this case, see **6.2** BANKRUPTCY AND PERSONAL INSOLVENCY.)

[63.175] A trader submitted a claim under *TMA, s 33*, contending that, in computing his profits, £10,000 should be deducted in respect of wages paid to his wife. The Revenue rejected the claim and the Special Commissioner dismissed the trader's appeal, applying the CA decision in *Moschi v Kelly*, **63.174** above. It was accepted that the wife had carried out some work for the business. However, no payments to her were shown in the business records, and the trader had not operated PAYE. The original accounts had not claimed a deduction for wages, and the trader's accountants had indicated that the wages had not been drawn by the trader's wife. *Abbott v CIR*, Sp C 1995, [1996] SSCD 41 (Sp C 58).

Dividends—whether remuneration

[63.176] A company claimed that dividends on shares held by two directors (the controlling shareholders) should be allowed as deductions in computing its profits, on the ground that they were part of their remuneration. The CS rejected the claim. *Eyres v Finnieston Engineering Co Ltd*, CS 1916, 7 TC 74.

Shares allotted to employees—whether remuneration

[63.177] A trader transferred his business to a limited company, and claimed a deduction for the face value of shares which he had promised to allocate to employees, to recognise their increased work in his business during the First World War. The CS rejected the claim. *CIR v Bell*, CS 1927, 12 TC 1181.

Shares allotted to employees at undervalue

[63.178] Some of a company's employees were entitled to be issued with shares in the company at their face value. The market value of the shares considerably exceeded their face value, and the company claimed the excess as a deduction in computing its profits. The HL rejected the claim (by a 3–2 majority, Lords Wright and Romer dissenting). Viscount Caldecote held that 'the cost to the company of earning its trading receipts was not increased by the issue of these shares at less than their full market value'. *Lowry v Consolidated African Selection Trust Ltd*, HL 1940, 23 TC 259; [1940] AC 648; [1940] 2 All ER 545.

Payment to director on change of duties because of ill-health

[63.179] A company's managing director agreed to resign because of ill-health, but continued to act as an advisory director at a much lower salary. The company paid him compensation of £75,000 for relinquishing his rights under his previous agreement. The Special Commissioners held that the £75,000 was deductible in computing the company's profits, and the KB upheld their decision. *Wilson v Nicholson Sons & Daniels Ltd*, KB 1943, 25 TC 473; [1943] 2 All ER 732. (*Note*. The KB also held that the payment was assessable on the director—see *Wilson v Daniels*, 15.5 COMPENSATION FOR LOSS OF EMPLOYMENT).

Payment of share of profits following sale of shares

[63.180] A company's controlling shareholders wished to retire from the business, and sold their shares to the other directors at £2 per share. In addition, the purchasers agreed to pay the vendors 50% of the fees and commissions received by the company, above a fixed limit, in each of the next five years. The company claimed these payments as deductible remuneration. The Ch D held that the payments were not deductible. *Faulconbridge v Thomas Pinkney & Sons Ltd*, Ch D 1951, 33 TC 415.

Payment to director on variation of terms of service

[63.181] A company's Articles of Association, and the service agreement of its controlling director (H), provided for an annuity of £1,000 to be paid to H's widow. H accepted £4,500 from the company to release it from its obligation. The Special Commissioners held that the £4,500 was not deductible in computing the company's profits, and the KB upheld this decision. *Alexander Howard & Co Ltd v Bentley*, KB 1948, 30 TC 334.

Salary of employee seconded to overseas subsidiary

[63.182] A company (S), which manufactured and marketed chemical intermediates and synthetic resins, increased its shareholding in a French subsidiary company and seconded one of its employees (F) to manage the subsidiary and provide it with the necessary technical and marketing expertise. S continued to pay F's remuneration and expenses for six months, following which he became managing director of, and was paid by, the subsidiary. Some of S's specialist products, sold to an arm's length French customer, could be used only with basic products supplied by the French subsidiary. The General Commissioners found that the rescue operation had been undertaken to further S's business in France and Europe, and held that the remuneration was deductible in computing its profits. The CA unanimously upheld their decision. *Robinson v Scott Bader & Co Ltd*, CA 1981, 54 TC 757; [1981] STC 436; [1981] 1 WLR 1135; [1981] 2 All ER 1116.

Payment to retiring director following dispute

[63.183] See *Deverell, Gibson & Hoare Ltd v Rees*, 63.103 above.

Loss on sale of temporary residence provided for employee

[63.184] See *Owen & Gadsdon v Brock*, 63.104 above.

Transfer of business—payments by purchaser to employees

[63.185] See *New Zealand Commissioner of Inland Revenue v New Zealand Forest Research Institute Ltd*, 63.115 above.

Trade association contributions

Apportionment of subscriptions by reference to expenses of association

[63.186] A colliery company (L) was a member of a coal owners' association, which imposed certain levies. L claimed that the levies should be allowed as a deduction in computing its profits. The Special Commissioners rejected the claim and L appealed to the CS. The parties prepared an agreed analysis of the association's expenses, and the CS held that the levies were allowable insofar as the expenses which the association met out of the levies would have been allowable if they had been incurred by the members themselves. *Lochgelly Iron & Coal Co Ltd v Crawford*, CS 1913, 6 TC 267. (*Note*. See now *ITTOIA 2005, s 34*. Most trade associations now enter into a special arrangement with HMRC. The case is of importance in establishing the position if there is no arrangement.)

[63.187] The Special Commissioners refused to allow a deduction for levies paid to a trade association (the object of which was to maintain prices) without production of the association accounts. The CS upheld their decision. *Grahamston Iron Co v Crawford*, CS 1915, 7 TC 25.

[63.188] A shipping company was a member of a shipowners' mutual insurance association which was in turn a member of a trade association. The General Commissioners refused to allow the company a deduction for calls made on it by the mutual insurance association, in the absence of evidence as to how the trade association applied the contributions. The CS upheld their decision. *Adam Steamship Co Ltd v Matheson*, CS 1920, 12 TC 399.

[63.189] In a case involving a subscription by a colliery company to a coal owners' association, the Commissioners allowed only part of the subscription, and the CA unanimously upheld their decision. *Thomas Merthyr Colliery Co Ltd v Davis*, CA 1932, 17 TC 519; [1933] 1 KB 349.

Association to indemnify members for losses because of strikes, etc

[63.190] A company which operated a colliery paid a subscription to a coalowners' association, formed to indemnify its members in the event of loss of output caused by strikes, etc. The Commissioners held that the subscription was not for the purposes of the company's trade and therefore not allowable. The QB upheld this decision. *Rhymney Iron Co Ltd v Fowler*, QB 1896, 3 TC 476; [1896] 2 QB 79.

Association to maintain prices

[63.191] The KB held that a company's net contributions to a trade protection association, formed mainly to keep up prices, were an allowable deduction. *Guest Keen & Nettlefolds Ltd v Fowler*, KB 1910, 5 TC 511; [1910] 1 KB 713.

Payments to mutual insurance society

[63.192] A colliery company made payments to an association for the mutual insurance of its members against liability for compensation in respect of fatal accidents to their employees. The company claimed that the payments should be allowed as a deduction in computing its profits. The Revenue rejected the claim on the grounds that the payments were partly applied in accumulating a fund which might in certain events be returned to members. The Special Commissioners allowed the company's appeal and the HL upheld their decision. *Thomas v Richard Evans & Co Ltd*, HL 1927, 11 TC 790; [1927] 1 KB 33. (*Note.* See *Jones v The South-West Lancashire Coal Owners Association Ltd*, 40.2 MUTUAL TRADING as to the assessability of the association.)

War surplus stocks purchased by association

[63.193] A company paid certain sums to a trade association for the purpose of purchasing and selling war surplus stocks of metal. The KB held that the payments were allowable deductions in computing the company's profits. *Charles Clifford & Son Ltd v Puttick*, KB 1928, 14 TC 189.

Payments towards closing down of business of rival company

[63.194] A firm of boilermakers made payments to the Association of Shell Boiler Makers towards its expenses in acquiring and closing down the business of a non-member, and making a grant to a member to acquire the shares of a non-member company. The KB held that the payments were capital expenditure. *Collins v Joseph Adamson & Co*, KB 1937, 21 TC 399; [1938] 1 KB 477; [1937] 4 All ER 236.

Subscriptions by association to Economic League

[63.195] A trade association within the shipbuilding industry made contributions to the Economic League, a political organisation which distributed anti-socialist literature. The Revenue issued additional assessments on a shipbuilding company, disallowing the part of its payments to the trade association which were attributable to the contributions to the Economic League. The Commissioners dismissed the company's appeal and the Ch D upheld their decision. *Joseph L Thompson & Sons Ltd v Chamberlain*, Ch D 1962, 40 TC 657.

Breweries

[63.196] See *Cooper v Rhymney Breweries Ltd*, 68.33 TRADING PROFITS, for contributions by a brewery to a trade association to obtain local polls on Sunday opening.

Travelling and subsistence expenses

Barrister—travelling between home and London chambers

[63.197] A barrister did the greater part of his work in his London chambers when the courts were sitting, but at other times he worked at home with only an occasional journey to his London chambers. He claimed the expenses of travelling between his home and his chambers during both term-time and vacation-time. The CA held that none of the expenses could be allowed as a deduction. Lord Denning held that 'a distinction must be drawn between living expenses and business expenses. In order to decide into which category to put the cost of travelling, you must look to see what is the base from which the trade, profession, or occupation is carried on. In the case of a tradesman, the base of his trading operation is his shop. In the case of a barrister, it is his chambers. Once he gets to his chambers, the cost of travelling to the various courts is incurred wholly and exclusively for the purposes of his profession. But it is different with the cost of travelling from his home to his chambers and back. That is incurred because he lives at a distance from his base. It is incurred for the purposes of his living there and not for the purposes of his profession, or at any rate not wholly or exclusively; and this is so, whether he has a choice in the matter or not. It is a living expense as distinct from a business expense. Romer LJ held that 'the object of the journeys, both morning and evening, is not to enable a man to do his work but to live away from it'. *Newsom v Robertson*, CA 1952, 33 TC 452; [1953] 1 Ch 7; [1952] 2 All ER 728.

Solicitor—overseas trip partly for holiday

[63.198] A solicitor visited North America partly as a holiday and partly to attend two professional conferences there, mainly on foreign law. He claimed his expenses of the visit. The Ch D rejected the claim. Since the expenses were admitted to be for the dual purpose of a holiday and to attend the conferences, they were not wholly and exclusively for the purposes of the solicitor's business. *Bowden v Russell & Russell*, Ch D 1965, 42 TC 301; [1965] 2 All ER 258.

Accountant—attendance at professional conference abroad

[63.199] An accountancy firm sent one of its partners to an international congress of accountants in New York. The Commissioners held that his return air fare, conference fee and living expenses during the six days of the congress were an allowable deduction, and the Ch D upheld their decision. *Edwards v Warmsley Henshall & Co*, Ch D 1967, 44 TC 431; [1968] 1 All ER 1089.

Bricklayer—travelling between home and building sites

[63.200] A bricklaying subcontractor (H), who was accepted as self-employed, travelled daily between his house and the building sites at which he was engaged. He mostly worked at each site for three weeks or so. His contracts were all verbal and with the same main contractor. He wrote up his books and kept his tools at home. The CA held that his travelling expenses between his home and the sites were allowable. Stamp LJ observed that H 'had no place which you could call his place of business except his home'. *Horton v Young*, CA 1971, 47 TC 60; [1972] Ch 157; [1971] 3 All ER 412.

Electrician—travelling between home and sites

[63.201] A self-employed electrician (M), who worked for various building contractors, claimed a deduction for the cost of driving from his home to the sites where he worked. HMRC rejected his claim but the First-Tier Tribunal allowed his appeal in principle (subject to agreement as to figures), applying the principles laid down in *Horton v Young*, 63.200 above. Judge Powell observed that M could not 'have coordinated his business activities without having somewhere to receive the electrical drawings which allowed him to make quotes'. *P Mellor v HMRC*, FTT [2011] UKFTT 29 (TC), TC00906.

Self-employed milk roundsman—travelling between home and depot

[63.202] In 1997 a milk roundsman (P), who had previously been employed by a dairy, entered into a franchise agreement with the dairy, under which he was treated as self-employed. Each day he travelled about 26 miles to a depot, owned by the dairy, to collect his float and milk, which he then delivered on his 'round'. In his 1998/99 self-assessment, he claimed a deduction for the cost of travelling between his home and the depot. The Revenue issued a notice of amendment disallowing the claim. P appealed, contending that he used his home as his office, and that the cost of travelling from his home to the depot was incurred wholly and exclusively for the purposes of his trade. The Ch D rejected this contention and upheld the Revenue's notice. Lewison J observed that P ordered and received his supplies of milk at the depot, where he kept his float and tools. Accordingly the expenditure was not deductible. *Jackman v Powell*, Ch D 2004, 76 TC 87; [2004] STC 645; [2004] EWHC 550 (Ch).

Self-employed flying instructor—travelling between home and airfields

[63.203] A self-employed flying instructor (W) claimed a deduction for the cost of travelling between his home and the two airports at which he gave lessons. HMRC issued discovery assessments rejecting the claims, and the First-tier Tribunal dismissed W's appeal. Judge Sinfield held that the travelling expenses 'were not incurred wholly and exclusively for the purposes of his profession as a flying instructor and examiner but also as a result of his decision to live away from the airports'. *N White v HMRC*, FTT [2014] UKFTT 214 (TC), TC03354.

Market trader

[63.204] A market trader (M) claimed a deduction for motoring expenses, including the cost of travel between his home and his market stall. HMRC rejected the claim on the basis that the market stall was M's place of business. M appealed, contending that his place of business was where he stored his trailer and stock (at an industrial unit which was four miles from his home). The tribunal rejected this contention and dismissed his appeal. *M Manders v HMRC*, FTT [2010] UKFTT 313 (TC), TC00600.

Business call en route when travelling between home and business

[63.205] A dentist travelled by car daily between his home and his surgery, about ten miles apart, calling *en route* at his dental laboratory, a mile from his home, to collect dentures. The Ch D held that the cost of the journeys was not an allowable deduction. Although the journeys were necessary to collect the dentures, they were not wholly and exclusively for the purposes of the business, as they included the private purpose of travelling from home to work. *Sargent v Barnes*, Ch D 1978, 52 TC 335; [1978] STC 322; [1978] 2 All ER 737.

Doctor—motoring expenses

[63.206] A doctor (J) claimed that 50% of his motoring expenses should be allowed as a deduction in computing his profits. HMRC issued an amendment to his self-assessment on the basis that only 10% of his motoring expenses were deductible. The First-tier tribunal dismissed J's appeal. *Dr AS Jolaoso v HMRC*, FTT [2011] UKFTT 44 (TC), TC00921. (Note. For another issue in this case, see **71.136** CAPITAL GAINS TAX.)

[63.207] A doctor (S), who was employed by a NHS trust, also did some private work at two hospitals. The NHS trust provided him with a permanent office at the NHS hospital where he carried out most of his work. He also maintained some office facilities at his home, although he never saw patients there. He claimed a deduction for travelling expenses from his home, and from his NHS hospital, to the two hospitals where he did private work. HMRC rejected the claims and the First-tier Tribunal dismissed S's appeal, applying the principles laid down in *Newsom v Robertson*, **63.197** above, and distinguishing *Horton v Young*, **63.200** above, as in that case the appellant's home was his only place of business. Judge Poole observed that there was an 'important distinction between travelling in the course of a business and travelling to get to the place where the business is carried on'. The Upper Tribunal upheld this decision. Arnold J held that the journeys between S's home and the private hospitals were 'partly for the purpose of conducting his private practice at the hospitals and partly for the purpose of enabling him to enable him to maintain his home (the place where he lives and conducts his private life) at a location of his choosing'. *Dr S Samadian v HMRC*, UT [2014] UKUT 13 (TC); [2014] STC 763.

Food and drink provided at partners' meetings

[63.208] A firm of solicitors practising in Devon, with 19 partners and four offices, claimed a deduction for the cost of food and drink consumed by the partners at weekly or fortnightly lunch-time meetings at two of its offices to discuss business matters, and at evening meetings attended by all the partners, some at a hotel and others in one of its offices, at which matters affecting the firm as a whole were discussed. The Ch D held that this expenditure was not an allowable deduction, since the meals were provided at times when the partners would normally have eaten lunch or dinner and the expenditure was not wholly and exclusively for business purposes. However, expenditure on providing food, drink and accommodation for the partners at the firm's annual weekend conference at a hotel was an allowable deduction, since what was being provided for the partners was a method of enabling them to continue their discussion over the weekend. *Watkis v Ashford Sparkes & Harward*, Ch D 1985, 58 TC 468; [1985] STC 451; [1985] 2 All ER 916.

Excess cost of eating lunch away from home

[63.209] A subcontractor, who was accepted as self-employed, claimed a deduction for the excess cost of eating lunch away from home. The Ch D rejected the claim. Templeman J held that 'a Schedule D taxpayer, like any other taxpayer, must eat in order to live; he does not eat in order to work'. Furthermore, because the claim was for the excess cost only, the cost could not be exclusively for the purposes of the trade. The cost of a meal could not be apportioned. *Caillebotte v Quinn*, Ch D 1975, 50 TC 222; [1975] STC 265; [1975] 1 WLR 731; [1975] 2 All ER 412.

Ceiling fixer—subsistence expenses

[63.210] A self-employed ceiling fixer, who worked in the London area from 1984 to 1988 but used his father's home in Bournemouth as a postal address, claimed a deduction for subsistence expenses while working in London, and for part of the cost of his accommodation in London. The Ch D rejected his claim, holding that the expenditure which he had incurred on food and accommodation was not wholly or exclusively for the purposes of his trade. *Prior v Saunders*, Ch D 1993, 66 TC 210; [1993] STC 562.

Self-employed pipe fitter—travelling and subsistence

[63.211] A self-employed pipe fitter lived in Cheshire, but most of his work was carried out for a large brewery company (B), based in Greenwich. He claimed deductions for his travelling and subsistence expenses. HMRC rejected the claims and he appealed. The First-Tier Tribunal allowed his appeal in part. Judge Porter held that the subsistence expenses were not deductible, but his travelling expenses were allowable, because he had worked for other clients in addition to B, and his 'base of operations' was his home in Cheshire. *A Kenyon v HMRC*, FTT [2011] UKFTT 91 (TC), TC00968.

Self-employed scaffolder—travelling and subsistence

[63.212] A self-employed scaffolder (R) lived in Grimsby, but most of his work was carried out in the Birmingham area, where he usually stayed during the week. He claimed deductions for his travelling and subsistence expenses. HMRC rejected the claims but the First-tier Tribunal allowed his appeal. Judge Trigger found that R's 'base of operations' was in Grimsby, and held that the subsistence expenses which he had claimed 'were wholly, exclusively and necessarily incurred in the course of his business'. *S Reed v HMRC*, FTT [2011] UKFTT 92 (TC), TC00969.

Self-employed subcontractor—travelling and subsistence

[63.213] A self-employed subcontractor lived in Coventry, but worked for a single contractor at Dungeness in Kent. He stayed at Dungeness during the week, and claimed deductions for his travelling and subsistence expenses. HMRC rejected the claims and the First-Tier Tribunal dismissed his appeal, specifically distinguishing *Horton v Young*, **63.200** above, as the appellant there had worked at several different sites, whereas H had been 'full-time working in one place for a period of years'. *TD Hanlin v HMRC*, FTT [2011] UKFTT 213 (TC), TC01078.

Married couple trading in partnership—claims for hotel expenses

[63.214] A married couple traded in partnership, manufacturing and selling toys and gifts. They claimed a deduction for expenditure on meals, hotel expenses and petrol. The inspector rejected the claim for meals and part of the claim for hotel expenses and petrol. The couple appealed. The Commissioner allowed the appeal in relation to the expenditure on petrol, but dismissed it in relation to the claims for meals and hotel expenses, holding that 'expenditure of traders, whether sole traders or partners, in keeping themselves fed is not deductible'. There was 'a dual motive in providing oneself with food, i.e. to keep oneself alive as well as to defray the additional cost of eating away from home in the course of carrying on a trading activity'. With regard to the claim for hotel expenses, the couple had failed to show that some of the accommodation was occupied for the purposes of the business; and where expenditure had been incurred for business purposes, the couple were only entitled to deduct the amount actually spent, where this was less than the civil service subsistence allowance which they had used as the basis of their claim. *Marsden & Marsden (t/a Seddon Investments) v Eadie*, Sp C [1999] SSCD 334 (Sp C 217).

Farmer—visit to Australia with a view to farming there

[63.215] See *Sargent v Eayrs*, 63.110 above.

Miscellaneous

Expenditure not 'wholly and exclusively' for the business

Clothing—court dress of female barrister

[63.216] A female barrister wore in court and chambers (and travelling there) black dresses, suits, tights and shoes and white shirts or blouses. She claimed that £564, spent in replacing and laundering such clothing, should be allowed as a deduction in computing her profits. The Revenue rejected the claim on the ground that the expenditure had been for the dual purpose of meeting the appellant's professional requirements and of enabling her to be warmly and decently clothed. She appealed, contending that she was required to wear such clothing to conform with notes for guidance on Court dress issued by the Bar Council. The Commissioners dismissed her appeal and the HL upheld their decision (by a 4–1 majority, Lord Elwyn-Jones dissenting). Lord Brightman observed that the object of the expenditure must be distinguished from its effect, and if a private advantage is an unavoidable effect of expenditure incurred for the purposes of a business, the expenditure may nevertheless be allowable. However, the conscious motive of the taxpayer at the time of the expenditure is not the only purpose which the Commissioners are entitled to find to exist. On the facts here it was an inescapable conclusion that the taxpayer purchased the clothing in question partly with the object of meeting her personal needs. The Commissioners were entitled to reach the conclusion that the object of the expenditure was both to serve the purposes of her profession and also to serve her personal purposes, and it would have been 'impossible to reach any other conclusion'. *Mallalieu v Drummond*, HL 1983, 57 TC 330; [1983] STC 665; [1983] 2 All ER 1095.

Medical expenses—illness said to be due to working conditions

[63.217] A self-employed shorthand writer claimed a deduction for medical expenses, etc., contending that they had been incurred because of his poor working conditions. The CA rejected the claim. Lord Greene MR held that medical expenses, like food and clothing, were not wholly and exclusively laid out for the purposes of a trade, profession or vocation, because they were partly laid out for the benefit of the taxpayer as a human being. *Norman v Golder*, CA 1944, 26 TC 293; [1945] 1 All ER 352. (*Note*. For another issue in this case, see **4.172** APPEALS.)

Medical expenses—business carried on from nursing home

[63.218] A trade-mark agent went into a private nursing home for medical treatment, and while there carried on his business from his room. He claimed 60% of his nursing home expenses as business expenses. The Ch D held that none of the expenses in question were allowable. *Murgatroyd v Evans-Jackson*, Ch D 1966, 43 TC 581; [1967] 1 All ER 881.

Medical expenses—guitarist—operation on finger

[63.219] A professional guitarist (P) suffered a finger injury. This hampered his guitar playing, and he underwent an operation to restore the flexibility of the finger. He claimed a deduction for the cost of the operation. The Revenue rejected the claim, considering that the expenditure had partly been incurred for private purposes. P appealed to the Commissioners, but admitted in evidence that he also played the guitar as a hobby. The Commissioners dismissed his appeal and the Ch D upheld their decision. Pennycuick J held that, as the expenditure was admittedly for the dual purpose of P's profession and his hobby, none of the expenditure was deductible. *Prince v Mapp*, Ch D 1969, 46 TC 169; [1970] 1 All ER 519.

Counselling expenses

[63.220] The proprietor of a beauty salon claimed a deduction for counselling expenses. HMRC rejected the claim, and she appealed, contending that she had undertaken the counselling in order to help her deal with 'issues such as those where she needed to confront her staff'. The First-tier Tribunal dismissed her appeal, finding that she had incurred the expenditure with a dual purpose, part of which 'was to enhance her own wellbeing'. Accordingly the expenditure was not exclusively for the purposes of her business. *Mrs P Azam v HMRC*, FTT [2011] UKFTT 18 (TC), TC00895.

Insurance premiums on premises used by associated company

[63.221] A company carried on a trade of cold storage in the UK. It owned premises, plant and machinery in China, Russia and Argentina. It agreed that these assets should be used by an associated company, incorporated in the USA. The UK company claimed capital allowances on the plant and machinery, and a deduction for insurance of the premises, in arriving at its profits. The Revenue rejected the claims on the grounds that the assets had not been formally let to the US company, and had not been used for the purposes of the trade of the UK company. The CA dismissed the company's appeal. Pollock MR held that 'you must look at what is the direct concern and direct purpose for which the money is laid out, and I do not think that you can go to the remoter or indirect results for which it may be possibly useful to lay out money'. *Union Cold Storage Co Ltd v Jones*, CA 1924, 8 TC 725.

Subscription to hospital

[63.222] A company had for several years made annual subscriptions of up to £50 to a local hospital. In 1919 and 1920 it made payments of £1,050 to the hospital and claimed these as deductions in computing its profits. The Special Commissioners held that the payments were not deductible and the KB upheld their decision. *Bourne & Hollingsworth Ltd v Ogden*, KB 1929, 14 TC 349.

Overseas taxes

[63.223] A company (D) resident in the Irish Republic, had two UK branches. It claimed that, in computing the profits of its UK branches for excess profits tax, a proportion of the tax which it paid in the Irish Republic should be allowed as a deduction. The HL held that none of the tax paid in the Irish Republic was wholly and exclusively expended for the purposes of D's UK trade, so that none of it was deductible. *CIR v Dowdall O'Mahoney & Co Ltd*, HL 1952, 33 TC 259; [1952] AC 401; [1952] 1 All ER 531.

Expenditure on political propaganda

[63.224] Three associated companies circulated a pamphlet described as 'Chairman's Supplementary Remarks at Annual General Meeting', attacking the policy and actions of Her Majesty's Government. They claimed that the expenses thus incurred should be allowed as a deduction in computing their profits. The Ch D rejected this contention, holding that the expenditure in question had not been incurred wholly and exclusively for the purposes of the companies' trades. *Boarland v Kramat Pulai Ltd (and related appeals)*, Ch D 1953, 35 TC 1; [1953] 2 All ER 1122.

Repairs to flat above business premises

[63.225] A chartered surveyor, who worked in Hackney and lived in Kensington, often found it necessary to work late. He therefore acquired a flat above his office so that he could sleep there after working late. He claimed that, in computing his profits, £270 spent on repairs and redecorations to the flat should be allowed as a deduction. The Commissioners rejected this claim, holding that it was not incurred wholly and exclusively for the purposes of his profession. The Ch D upheld their decision. *Mason v Tyson*, Ch D 1980, 53 TC 333; [1980] STC 284. (*Note*. His claim to capital allowances on furniture for the flat also failed—see **8.64** CAPITAL ALLOWANCES.)

Sponsorship of horse-riding school

[63.226] A company (E) carried on a recruitment business. The wife of its controlling shareholder (T) owned a riding school. She had two teenage children, who rode horses which she owned in horse shows and equestrian events. E made payments to her, which it described as sponsorship, and claimed these payments as deductions in computing its profits. The Revenue rejected the claim on the basis that the expenditure had not been wholly and exclusively for the purpose of E's business. The Special Commissioners dismissed E's appeal, holding on the evidence that 'personal benefit played a part in the decision to make the sponsorship payments' and that the desire to confer a benefit on T's wife and children was a 'conscious motive' of T and was 'one of the objects for incurring the sponsorship expenditure'. *Executive Network (Consultants) Ltd v O'Connor*, Sp C 1995, [1996] SSCD 29 (Sp C 56).

Sponsorship of rugby club

[63.227] A company which carried on business in the fishing industry made substantial sponsorship payments to a rugby club. It claimed that these should be allowed as deductions in computing its profits. HMRC rejected the claims on the grounds that the payments were not wholly and exclusively for the purpose of the company's business, but were partly made because the company's controlling director was very keen on rugby and wanted to strengthen the club. The First-tier Tribunal dismissed the company's appeal against this decision, finding that the payments had been made with a dual purpose. Both the Upper Tribunal and the CA unanimously upheld this decision as one of fact. Moses LJ observed that the Tribunal had found two purposes, 'and one of those purposes was not the purpose of the taxpayer's trade: there is no warrant for distinguishing between the two purposes by assessing one as being intermediate or subordinate to the other'. *Interfish Ltd v HMRC*, CA [2014] EWCA Civ 876; [2015] STC 55.

Sponsorship of motor rallying company

[63.228] A company (P) carried on business in the construction industry. It claimed deductions for significant payments to a company (M) which took part in motor rallies. P's controlling director was an experienced rally driver who had driven for M. HMRC issued discovery assessments and amendments to P's self-assessments, disallowing the expenditure on the grounds that it had not been wholly and exclusively incurred for the purpose of P's business. The First-Tier Tribunal dismissed P's appeal against this decision, applying the principles laid down in *Executive Network (Consultants) Ltd v O'Connor*, 63.226 above. *Protec International Ltd v HMRC*, FTT [2010] UKFTT 628 (TC), TC00867.

Childcare expenses

[63.229] A sole trader, who worked from home, claimed a deduction for childcare expenses. The Revenue rejected her claim, and she appealed, contending that she had incurred the expenditure in order to prevent clients being distracted by interruptions from her children, and to enable her to work without distraction. The Special Commissioner dismissed her appeal, holding that she had incurred the expenditure with a dual purpose, and one of her purposes had been 'to have the children properly looked after while she worked'. Accordingly, the expenditure had not been incurred wholly and exclusively for the purposes of her trade, and was not allowable as a deduction. *Carney v Nathan*, Sp C 2002, [2003] SSCD 28 (Sp C 347).

Musician

[63.230] A self-employed musician (M) claimed a deduction for expenses of £18,000, although his income for the relevant year was only £635. HMRC rejected most of the expenses claimed, on the basis that they had not been incurred wholly and exclusively for the purpose of M's business. The tribunal dismissed M's appeal, finding that HMRC had been 'more than reasonable'. *AI Muhammad v HMRC*, FTT [2009] UKFTT 319 (TC), TC00262.

Sole trader operating separate businesses—claim for set-off of expenditure

[63.231] The Revenue accepted that a writer (S) was carrying on three separate businesses: one as an author, one as a researcher, and one as a publisher. In his 1997/98 return, S claimed a deduction of £2,200 from the profits of each of his businesses as an author and publisher, in respect of payments purportedly made to his business as a researcher. The Revenue rejected the claim and the Special Commissioner dismissed S's appeal, finding that there was no 'documentary record showing the transfer of money between the businesses' and that a purported agreement which S had produced was 'merely a means of enabling (S) to claim that he has transferred between his various businesses such arbitrarily chosen sums as may justify his making whatever claims for tax allowances suit his convenience'. *Salt v Buckley*, Sp C [2001] SSCD 262 (Sp C 293). (*Note.* A claim to capital allowances was also dismissed—see **8.110** CAPITAL ALLOWANCES.)

Removal expenses of partner moved in interests of partnership

[63.232] See *MacKinlay v Arthur Young McClelland Moores & Co*, **41.30** PARTNERSHIPS.

Payment for right to operate sub-post office

[63.233] See *Dhendsa v Richardson*, **63.113** above.

Expenditure held to be partly allowable

Service company of professional firm

[63.234] In December 1960 the partners in an accountancy firm established a company (B) to provide services (staff, premises, etc.) for the firm. For the year to 30 November 1961, it was verbally agreed that the firm should pay B £47,000, which was considerably more than the cost of the services, on the understanding that the charge for later years would be reduced so as to secure for B, over the long term, a nominal profit only. (For tax purposes, there had been a deemed cessation and commencement of the firm's business following the death of a partner, so that the firm's profits of the year to 30 November 1961 fell to be taken into account for more than one basis period under the legislation then in force.) The Revenue refused to allow the whole of the £47,000 as a deduction in computing the firm's profits, considering that only £32,000 (the cost of the services) was deductible. The Commissioners allowed the firm's appeal but the Ch D reversed this decision. Pennycuick J observed that 'the £15,000 was not in truth a profit charge at all, but an allocation of part of the actual cost of the services for the subsequent period of account'. He held that, 'upon the ordinary principles of commercial accountancy', the deductible amount must be restricted to £32,000 plus a 'nominal profit' for B. *Stephenson v Payne Stone Fraser & Co*, Ch D 1967, 44 TC 507; [1968] 1 WLR 858; [1968] 1 All ER 524.

Accountant practising from home

[63.235] An accountant appealed against assessments, claiming that he should be allowed to deduct 50% of his total expenditure in maintaining, heating and lighting his private residence. One of the three bedrooms at the house was used exclusively as a library, and another was used for storage of files. He worked at home for some of the time to be free from interruption and also entertained at least 30 clients or potential clients each year. The Revenue agreed to allow a deduction of 20% of the expenditure in question, but rejected the appellant's claim for a deduction of 50%. The Special Commissioner held on the evidence that no more than 20% of the expenditure was deductible. The Commissioner noted that the annual running costs of the house totalled almost £16,000, and observed that the Revenue's agreement to allow £3,200 of this was 'not unreasonable'. *Gazelle v Servini*, Sp C [1995] SSCD 324 (Sp C 48). (*Note.* The accountant also claimed deductions for estimated travelling expenses, and for amounts found to be set aside as a reserve for repairs and renewals. The Commissioner held that the amounts in question were not deductible.)

Stunt performer

[63.236] An individual (P) worked as a self-employed stunt performer in films and television productions. In his tax returns, he claimed deductions for the cost of a knee operation, for chiropractic treatment, for sports massage, for dental treatment and for the cost of maintaining 'health and fitness'. HMRC issued assessments disallowing the deductions, and P appealed. The First-tier Tribunal reviewed the evidence in detail and allowed the appeal in part. Judge Staker observed that P had injured his knee while performing a stunt, and needed the operation to continue performing similar work. On the evidence, 'in a physically less demanding job he could have carried on working in the meantime', and 'it was only because of the particular demands of the kind of work that he does that he could not carry on working until the operation was done'. The same reasoning applied to the chiropractic treatment and to the massage, which were needed because he had injured his back while working. The tribunal accepted P's evidence that 'he would not have incurred the expenses for these services but for his work'. Similarly, the dental treatment 'all related to injuries to the appellant's teeth sustained in the course of his work', and 'it was necessary for him to have the dental treatment in order to continue working'. However, the tribunal held that the cost of maintaining P's health and fitness were not allowable as a deduction, since the expenditure was not related 'directly and specifically' to maintaining the 'specialised skills that the appellant must have to remain on the stunt register'. The expenditure appeared to be related to 'maintaining the standard of fitness generally that is required in order for the appellant to be able to perform this type of work'. Judge Staker observed that 'maintaining health and fitness is a general human need, even if it also serves the purposes of the trade or profession'. Accordingly this expenditure had a dual purpose, and was not allowable as a deduction. *DS Parsons v HMRC*, FTT [2010] UKFTT 110 (TC), TC00421.

Exploitation of intellectual property rights

[63.237] Several limited liability partnerships entered into various agreements for the acquisition and exploitation of certain intellectual property rights. The partnerships submitted returns claiming to have incurred substantial losses in their first accounting periods. HMRC began an enquiry and issued closure notices rejecting the claims and amending the partnership returns, on the basis that the great majority of the expenditure which had given rise to the supposed losses had not been incurred wholly and exclusively for the purposes of the partnerships' trades. The partnerships appealed. The First-tier Tribunal reviewed the evidence in detail and substantially dismissed the appeals, applying the principles laid down by the Upper Tribunal in *Icebreaker1 Llp v HMRC*, **63.323** below. Judge Bishopp found that prospective partners 'had no verifiable information about the possible revenues from the projects, yet they all put a fairly substantial amount of their own money at risk'. On the evidence, 'no serious and even moderately sophisticated investor, or one with a competent adviser, genuinely seeking a profit', would have chosen to join one of the appellant partnerships. He held that the partnerships had participated in a tax avoidance scheme under which 'the aim was to secure sideways relief for the members, and to inflate the scale of the relief by unnecessary borrowing, coupled with the illusion that the borrowed money was available for use in the exploitation of intellectual property rights by the device of the purported payment of a large production fee offset by the equally purported payment of a fee for a share of the resulting revenue'. Furthermore, 'the sums borrowed by the members of all the appellant partnerships were not used for the purposes of the partnerships' trades, but in the purchase of a capital asset'; and 'none of the appellant partnerships' trades were carried on on a commercial basis and with a view to profit'. However, he also held that a small part of the expenditure which HMRC had disallowed should be treated as deductible revenue expenditure. *Acornwood Llp v HMRC (and related appeals)*, FTT [2014] UKFTT 416 (TC); [2014] SFTD 694, TC03545.

Expenditure held to be allowable

Exempt income—whether associated expenses may be deducted

[63.238] A New Zealand bank was chargeable to UK income tax on the profits of its London branch, the business receipts of which included interest on securities which was exempt under the law in force at the time. The HL rejected the Revenue's claim to assess the interest as part of the trading profits, but upheld the bank's claim for the allowance of interest on money borrowed to finance the purchase of the securities. The HL held that an exemption conferred on income could not be removed on the ground that it is a trading receipt, and that the deductibility of a trading expense did not require the presence of a taxable receipt. *Hughes v Bank of New Zealand*, HL 1938, 21 TC 471; [1938] AC 366; [1938] 1 All ER 778. (*Note.* The law was subsequently amended by *FA 1940, s 60* to provide that such interest would no longer be exempt unless specified by the Treasury. Subsequent issues of UK Government securities were issued subject to the condition that the exemptions for non-residents did not 'exclude the interest from any computation for taxation purposes of the profits of any trade or business carried on in the United Kingdom'. For a case in which the Revenue's interpretation of this condition was upheld, see *The Manufacturers' Life Assurance Co Ltd v Cummins*, **68.71** TRADING PROFITS. Despite the changes in the legislation, HMRC accept this case as establishing the principle that 'a trade receipt may be excluded by specific provision from computations of profit, but related expenses may still be deductible in the business accounts': see Business Income Manual, BIM42150.)

Expenditure on protection of assets against threat of nationalisation

[63.239] A sugar-refining company incurred expenditure in launching a publicity campaign against proposals to transfer the sugar-refining industry to public ownership. It claimed that the cost of this campaign was deductible in computing its profits. The Revenue rejected the claim, considering that the expenditure was not wholly and exclusively for the purpose of the company's business. The General Commissioners allowed the company's appeal and the HL upheld their decision (by a 3–2 majority, Lord Tucker and Lord Keith of Avonholm dissenting). Lord Morton held that 'the only purpose for which this money was expended was to prevent the seizure of the business and assets of the company'. If the money had been spent to defend the existing shareholders' ownership of their shares, it would not have been allowable, since 'money laid out merely for the purpose of preventing a change in the identity of the stockholders could not be regarded as being laid out for the purposes of the trade'. However, on the evidence, the expenditure had been found to have been spent to defend the company's ownership of its assets, and was therefore allowable. *Morgan v Tate & Lyle Ltd*, HL 1954, 35 TC 366; [1955] AC 21; [1954] 2 All ER 413.

Technical education

[63.240] A farmer employed his sons as labourers, and paid fees for them to attend an agricultural course at a technical college. He claimed that the payments should be allowed as deductions in computing his profits. The Revenue rejected the claim, considering that the payments had been made for personal reasons. The Commissioners allowed the farmer's appeal, holding that the payments were allowable deductions. The Ch D and the CA unanimously upheld their decision. *Wickwar v Berry*, CA 1963, 41 TC 33; [1963] 1 WLR 1026; [1963] 2 All ER 1058.

Motor rallying—whether incurred for advertising purposes

[63.241] The proprietor of a coach business was also an amateur rally driver. In 1998 he decided to use motor rallying as a way of advertising his business. He purchased a new rally car for this purpose and competed in several events. He claimed capital allowances on the car and claimed related expenditure as advertising expenses. The Revenue discovered this in 2002 and issued discovery assessments on the basis that the expenditure had not been wholly and exclusively incurred for the purposes of the business. The Special Commissioner allowed the proprietor's appeal, finding that the expenditure had been incurred for the purpose of promoting the business and 'getting the names and liveries into the public awareness'. Although the proprietor gained some personal satisfaction from competing in rallies, his 'preferred leisure activity' was sailing rather than rallying, and 'the private satisfaction of success on the rally circuit' was an incidental benefit of the expenditure, rather than its purpose. *RS McQueen v HMRC*, Sp C [2007] SSCD 457 (Sp C 601). (*Note.* The Commissioner rejected an alternative contention that the assessments had been raised outside the statutory time limit, holding that the rallying expenditure had not been adequately disclosed in the proprietor's tax returns, so that the assessments had been within the statutory time limits.)

Witch—expenditure on professional training

[63.242] In a Netherlands case, a woman sold various items relating to witchcraft by means of the internet. She claimed a deduction for the cost of professional training in witchcraft. The tax authority rejected her claim but the court allowed her appeal. It was accepted that ministers of the Christian religion could offset their expenditure on their training against their income from their vocation. To deny similar relief to practising witches would be a breach of *Article 14* of the *European Convention on Human Rights*. *Rongen v Inspecteur der Directe Belastingen Leeuwarden*, Leeuwarden District Court, 23 September 2005 unreported.

Bad and doubtful debts (ITTOIA 2005, s 35)

CROSS-REFERENCES

The cases below relate to trading debts for goods and services supplied. See **63.147** to **63.153** above for losses on advances and guarantees. For allowances to builders for amounts outstanding on properties sold, see *John Cronk & Sons Ltd v Harrison*, **68.40** TRADING PROFITS; *Lock v Jones*, **68.42** TRADING PROFITS, and *Absalom v Talbot*, **68.43** TRADING PROFITS. The judgments in *Absalom v Talbot* are an important review of the treatment of trading debts. For the future cost of collecting debts see *Monthly Salaries Loan Co Ltd v Furlong*, **62.77** TRADING PROFITS. For accounting principles, see SSAP 17 (Accounting for Post-Balance Sheet Events).

Whether allowance can be withdrawn if circumstances change

[63.243] A company (AH) which manufactured cotton made supplies to a subsidiary company (H) on credit. The Revenue agreed that most of the amount which H owed could be allowed in computing AH's profits for 1921 and 1922. AH continued to supply cloth to H in the ensuing five years and H, while reducing its other indebtedness, increased its indebtedness to AH. In 1929 the Revenue issued additional assessments on AH to neutralise the deductions given in the 1921 and 1922 computations. The KB allowed AH's appeal, holding that there was no evidence that the deductions were wrongly allowed by reference to the circumstances at the time, and that the additional assessments were not justified. *Anderton & Halstead Ltd v Birrell*, KB 1931, 16 TC 200; [1932] 1 KB 271.

Debtor still in business—whether bad debt allowable

[63.244] In an Indian case, a firm of agents claimed an allowance for an amount owing by its principal, a company which was still in business but was unable to meet the liability. The Bombay High Court rejected the claim on the ground that, for a debt from a company to be allowable, the company should no longer be a going concern. The PC held that this reasoning was wrong in law, and remitted the case for the claim to be reconsidered in the light of all the available evidence. *Dinshaw v Bombay Commissioner of Income Tax*, PC 1934, 13 ATC 284.

Goods supplied to subsidiary—debt subsequently written off

[63.245] From 1987 to 1993 a company (S) supplied goods to a subsidiary company (E). In 1990 S made an interest-free loan to E. E made eight payments to S towards repayment of the loan, and then ceased trading owing money to S for goods supplied. S took over E's trading stock and credited its value to the loan account. S also paid some of E's creditors. In its accounts, S claimed deductions for the debt owed to it by E for goods supplied, and for the amounts which it had paid to E's creditors. The Revenue rejected these claims (and also rejected consequential claims to loss relief and group relief). S appealed. The Special Commissioner allowed the appeal in part, holding that the value of the stock which S had originally supplied to E, and had subsequently recovered, should have been credited to the trade account rather than to the loan account. However, the balance of the trading debt written off was an allowable deduction; the loss on the goods which S had supplied to E while E was making loan repayments was a loss 'connected with or arising out of the trade', and the money which S had paid to E's creditors was wholly and exclusively for trading purposes. *Sycamore plc v Fir (and related appeal)*, Sp C 1996, [1997] SSCD 1 (Sp C 104).

Loss on unusual trading transaction

[63.246] A company (C) traded as timber merchants. In 1930 it was asked by another timber company (L) to take over a certain amount of timber, and agreed to sell the timber on behalf of L at a guaranteed commission. In 1933 L became insolvent, owing C £74,000. C released L from the debt in return for its principal shareholder (S) agreeing to pay it (with 5% interest until the date of payment), and providing as security his shares in a German company and a debt owing to him by that company. The German company owned property which was mortgaged, and in 1934, when the mortgages were called in, C paid them to preserve its security. S died in 1939 and, though his estate in Germany was sufficient to pay his debts, it was impossible for C to realise his estate. Accordingly, it wrote the debt off over the four years 1937/38 to 1940/41, and claimed the amounts written off as a deduction from its profits. The Revenue rejected the claim but the CS allowed C's appeal, holding on the evidence that the original debt was a trading debt, and that the subsequent arrangements did not alter its character. *Calders Ltd v CIR*, CS 1944, 26 TC 213.

Loan by architect to company—whether bad debt allowable

[63.247] An architect (T) lent £150,000 to a building company, under an agreement whereby the loan was to be repaid after twelve months. However, the company subsequently went into receivership and none of the loan was repaid. T claimed the £150,000 as a bad debt in his accounts. The Revenue rejected the claim and T appealed. The Special Commissioner dismissed the appeal, finding that the loan had been backed by a personal guarantee from the chairman of the company, who had stated in evidence that he hoped 'to make some repayment in due course'. Accordingly, the debt was not a bad debt within *ITTOIA 2005, s 35**. Furthermore, the loan was a capital investment and had not been made wholly and exclusively for the purposes of the architect's business. *Taylor v Clatworthy*, Sp C [1996] SSCD 506 (Sp C 103).

Debts owed by associated company—whether bad debt allowable

[63.248] A sole trader (W), who owned a skip hire business, claimed a deduction for bad debts allegedly owed by a company (M) which was owned by his father. HMRC rejected the claim on the grounds that the loans had not been incurred wholly and exclusively for the purpose of W's business. The First-tier Tribunal dismissed W's appeal, observing that W was managing M on behalf of his father and had not submitted any evidence 'as to how the debts have been incurred'. *J White v HMRC*, FTT [2014] UKFTT 046 (TC), TC03186.

Debts paid late—provision not allowable

[63.249] In the case noted at 62.23 TRADING PROFITS, a consultant claimed a provision for doubtful debts which had not been paid at the end of his first accounting period. The Special Commissioner rejected the claim, observing that although the debts were unpaid at the end of the accounting period, they had been paid by the time the accounts were submitted. *Walker v O'Connor*, Sp C [1996] SSCD 218 (Sp C 74). (*Note*. The appellant appeared in person.)

Accountant—claim for bad debt relief

[63.250] See *Thompson v CIR*, 24.7 ERROR OR MISTAKE RELIEF.

Employee benefit contributions (ITTOIA 2005, ss 38–44; CTA 2009, ss 1288–1297)

Initial contribution to staff pension fund

[63.251] A company set up a contributory pension fund for its staff, making an initial lump sum contribution of the actuarially ascertained amount necessary to enable past service of existing staff to rank for pension. The HL held (by a 3-2 majority, Lords Carson and Blanesburgh dissenting) that the payment was capital expenditure and was not an allowable deduction. Viscount Cave held that expenditure was normally capital if it was 'made, not only once and for all, but with a view to bringing into existence an asset or an advantage for the enduring benefit of the trade'. *Atherton v British Insulated & Helsby Cables Ltd*, HL 1925, 10 TC 155; [1926] AC 205.

Long service ex gratia payment

[63.252] In accordance with its usual practice, a company gave a gratuity of £1,500 to an employee on his retirement after long service. The Commissioners held that the gratuity was deductible in computing the company's profits, and the KB upheld their decision. *Smith v Incorporated Council of Law Reporting for England & Wales*, KB 1914, 6 TC 477; [1914] 3 KB 674.

Purchase of annuity to replace pension

[63.253] In 1905 a company (G) granted its secretary a retirement pension of £666 pa. In 1913, G paid an assurance society £4,994 for an annuity in commutation of the pension. The Special Commissioners held that the £4,994 was deductible in computing G's profits. The KB upheld their decision, holding that the payment was the actuarial equivalent of the pension and was identical in character; it was not a capital payment. *Hancock v General Reversionary & Investment Co Ltd*, KB 1918, 7 TC 358; [1919] 1 KB 25.

Insurance policy to meet costs of pensions

[63.254] A company (M) habitually paid voluntary pensions to its retired employees. It paid £23,100 to an insurance company (E), in return for which E agreed to pay M annuities equal to the pensions of the then surviving pensioners. The Special Commissioners held that the payment was capital expenditure and the KB upheld their decision. *Morgan Crucible Co Ltd v CIR*, KB 1932, 17 TC 311; [1932] 2 KB 185.

Commutation of premiums under staff assurance scheme

[63.255] In 1944, a company (C) introduced a 'staff assurance scheme', and paid additional premiums in respect of certain long-serving employees. In 1946, C paid the insurance company £9,320 in commutation of these additional premiums. The Special Commissioners held that the £9,320 was an allowable deduction, and the KB upheld their decision. *Green v Cravens Railway Carriage & Wagon Co Ltd*, Ch D 1951, 32 TC 359.

Premiums to secure directors' pensions

[63.256] A family company (S) paid premiums to an insurance company to make pension provision for two of its directors. The Commissioners held that the payments were not deductible in computing S's profits, and the Ch D upheld this decision. Harman J held that the Commissioners had been entitled to find that this was 'not a proper business expense' and that the directors had authorised the expenditure for their own advantage 'and not for that of the company'. *Samuel Dracup & Sons Ltd v Dakin*, Ch D 1957, 37 TC 377.

Premiums for directors' life insurance

[63.257] A company (B) paid premiums on life assurance policies for its principal directors. It claimed that these payments should be allowed as a deduction in computing its profits. The Revenue rejected the claim and the Special Commissioner dismissed B's appeal, holding that the payments were not wholly and exclusively for the purpose of B's trade. *Beauty Consultants Ltd v HM Inspector of Taxes*, Sp C [2002] SSCD 352 (Sp C 321).

Lump sum payment to employees' benevolent fund

[63.258] A company (R) paid £50,000 to trustees for a benevolent fund, the income of which was to be used for the relief of sickness or incapacity among its employees. The Special Commissioners held that the payment was capital expenditure, and was not deductible in computing R's profits. The CA upheld their decision. *Rowntree & Co Ltd v Curtis*, CA 1924, 8 TC 678.

Publisher—payments to printing trade benevolent fund

[63.259] A publishing company produced publications for a charity and paid the profits to the charity. It also paid for some of its employees to become life members of the charity. The Ch D held that the payments were not allowable deductions. *Hutchinson & Co (Publishers) Ltd v Turner*, Ch D 1950, 31 TC 495; [1950] 2 All ER 633.

Transfer of investments from unapproved fund to approved fund

[63.260] In 1928 the trustees of a company's staff benefit fund transferred investments with a market value of £78,303 to form the nucleus of a superannuation fund. The superannuation fund was approved under the legislation then in force, whereas the benefit fund had not been. The Special Commissioners held that the £78,303 was a contribution by the company to the superannuation fund, and was therefore an allowable deduction. The CA unanimously upheld their decision. *Lowe v Peter Walker (Warrington) and Robert Cain & Sons Ltd*, CA 1935, 20 TC 25.

Spreading of lump sum payment to superannuation scheme

[63.261] A partnership (in which a company had a 98% interest) set up a staff pension fund in 1950 which was approved by the Revenue. The Revenue agreed that an initial lump sum could be allowed by spreading equally over the next ten years. However, a few days after the approval and the payment of the lump sum, the company took over the business from the partnership, the takeover being treated as a notional discontinuance and commencement of the trade. The company claimed a deduction for the amount which the partnership would have deducted under the spreading agreement. The Special Commissioners held that the deduction was not allowable and that the spreading agreement did not give rise to an estoppel. The Ch D upheld their decision. *JH Clarke & Co Ltd v Musker*, Ch D 1956, 37 TC 1.

Payments to trustees to purchase shares for benefit of employees

[63.262] A company (P), carrying on business as consulting engineers, with professionally qualified staff, undertook to pay 10% of its annual profits, subject to a minimum of £5,000, to a trust set up to give its staff the opportunity of acquiring shares in P and to remove the possibility of its coming under the control of outside shareholders. The Special Commissioners held that the payments were allowable deductions, having been made for the purposes of the trade and being revenue expenditure rather than capital expenditure. The CA unanimously upheld their decision. *Heather v P-E Consulting Group Ltd*, CA 1972, 48 TC 293; [1973] Ch 189; [1973] 1 All ER 8.

[63.263] A company (C) set up a trust for the purchase of its shares, the income from the dividends to be distributed to its employees. The trust deed provided for the shares to be sold and the proceeds paid to C after 80 years, or on C's winding-up, or on C's giving one year's notice to the trustees. The Ch D held that payments which C made to the trustees were capital expenditure and were not allowable deductions. Each payment gave rise to a corresponding asset of a durable nature. *Rutter v Charles Sharpe & Co Ltd*, Ch D 1979, 53 TC 163; [1979] STC 711; [1979] 1 WLR 1429.

[63.264] In 1978 a company (R) set up a trust fund for the benefit of its employees. The company which acted as trustee was required to invest any money received from R in purchasing its shares, and to hold the trust fund and income for the benefit of the employees. It was envisaged that R would contribute 5% of its profits to the fund, and in 1980 it paid £35,000 to the fund as one of a series of such payments. The Special Commissioners held that the payment was an allowable deduction, and the Ch D upheld their decision. The payment was intended as one of a series and could not be said to have created or acquired an asset or enduring advantage of a capital nature. *Jeffs v Ringtons Ltd*, Ch D 1985, 58 TC 680; [1985] STC 809; [1986] 1 WLR 266; [1986] 1 All ER 144.

[63.265] The shares in a trading company (E) were held by two elderly directors and their wives. To meet employees' fears that E would cease trading when the directors died, a trust was set up with the object of ensuring that E's share capital should be held by trustees for the benefit of the employees. E made an initial payment of £2,500, and further payments of £2,224 and £1,000, to the trustees to enable them to acquire 5% of the share capital from the directors. It appealed against corporation tax assessments, contending that the payments should be allowed as deductions. The Ch D accepted this contention and allowed the appeal, holding on the evidence that the payments had been incurred wholly and exclusively for the purposes of E's trade. *E Bott Ltd v Price*, Ch D 1986, 59 TC 437; [1987] STC 100.

[63.266] In 1993 a company (M) established an employee trust to purchase shares held by its controlling director (K), on his anticipated retirement in 1998. It claimed that payments made to the trust should be treated as allowable deductions in computing its profits. The Revenue rejected the claims and the Special Commissioner dismissed M's appeals. Firstly, the payments were capital expenditure, since their 'purpose was to build up a fund with the view of making a capital purchase of (K's) shares on his retirement'. Furthermore, 'the money was not laid out wholly and exclusively to provide a smooth succession on (K's) retirement. The primary object was to enable (K) to sell his shares without trouble when he retired.' *Mawsley Machinery Ltd v Robinson*, Sp C [1998] SSCD 236 (Sp C 170).

Payments to employee benefit trusts

[63.267] A company (S) appealed against corporation tax assessments, claiming a deduction for payments to an employee benefit trust (before 2003) and a family benefit trust (from 2003 to 2005). The Special Commissioners dismissed the appeals, holding that although the payments were made for the purposes of S's trade, the effect of *CTA 2009, ss 1288, 1289** was that the payments to the employee benefit trust were not deductible for the purposes of corporation tax. Furthermore, the payments to the family benefit trust were not deductible by virtue of *CTA 2009, ss 1290–1297**. The Commissioners observed that the effect of *CTA 2009, s 1290** was that 'employee benefit contributions are not deductible unless and until they give rise to an employment income tax charge and a liability to pay national insurance contributions'. On the evidence, the family benefit trust was within the definition of an 'employee benefit scheme' in *CTA 2009, s 1291(2)**. The employees 'benefited both indirectly because of the financial payments to their families, and directly in those cases where the loans by the trustee to the nominated beneficiaries were paid into joint accounts with the employee or to discharge loans on jointly owned property'. Accordingly, the payments to the trust were not deductible when they were paid. *Sempra Metals Ltd v HMRC*, Sp C [2008] SSCD 1062 (Sp C 698). (*Note*. The Commissioners allowed appeals against notices of determination under *Income Tax (PAYE) Regulations 2003 (SI 2003/2682), reg 80*, holding that the payments to the trusts did not constitute the payment of emoluments or earnings to its employees, and also held that S was not liable to pay Class 1 national insurance contributions in respect of the payments.)

[63.268] The decision in *Sempra Metals Ltd v HMRC*, **63.267** above, was applied in the similar subsequent case of *BW Male & Sons Ltd v HMRC*, FTT [2012] UKFTT 719 (TC), TC02383.

[63.269] A company (J) appealed against a corporation tax assessment for the accounting period ending December 1997, contending that it was entitled to a deduction for a payment of £3,000,000 to an employee benefit trust, The First-Tier Tribunal rejected this contention and dismissed the appeal. Applying the principles laid down by the HL in *Dextra Accessories Ltd & Others v MacDonald*, **53.38** SCHEDULE D—SUPERSEDED LEGISLATION, the payment was a 'potential emolument' and could therefore only be deducted from taxable profits if it was paid within nine months of the end of the accounting period in which the deduction was claimed. *JT Dove Ltd v HMRC*, FTT [2011] UKFTT 16 (TC); [2011] SFTD 348, TC00893.

[63.270] Two associated companies, which promoted film financing schemes, claimed deductions for substantial payments to employee benefit trusts in favour of their controlling directors. HMRC rejected the claims, considering that in reality the payments were distributions of profits, rather than expenses incurred for the purpose of earning profits. The companies appealed. The First-tier Tribunal reviewed the evidence in detail and dismissed the appeals. Judge Nowlan found that the companies had engaged in a 'highly contrived scheme' in the hope of 'achieving the precisely opposite corporation tax treatment for the EBT contributions than the result intended by Parliament'. He observed that 'the deliberate and all-pervading objective of achieving a corporation tax deduction makes it impossible to treat the corporation tax result sought for the contributions as the "ordinary, intended or realistically expected outcome" of making salary, bonus or equivalent payments'. He also found that one of the company directors (an accountant who had subsequently been declared bankrupt) had 'admitted that he had lied to the tribunal' when giving evidence as to the date of certain documents, and appeared also to have fabricated evidence and forged certain documents. *Scotts Atlantic Management Ltd v HMRC (and related appeals)*, FTT [2013] UKFTT 299 (TC); [2014] SFTD 210, TC02704. (*Note*. The First-tier Tribunal allowed the companies' appeals against PAYE determinations, distinguishing the Upper Tribunal decision in *Aberdeen Asset Management plc v HMRC*, 42.52 PAY AS YOU EARN.)

Business entertaining (ITTOIA 2005, ss 45–47; CTA 2009, ss 1298–1300)

Publishing company—whether CTA 2009, s 1299 applicable*

[63.271] A newspaper publishing company incurred entertainment expenditure through its journalists to obtain material for publication from potential contributors, etc. It included this expenditure in a claim for loss relief. The Revenue rejected the claim, considering that the deduction was prohibited by what is now *CTA 2009, s 1298*. The company appealed, contending that the expenditure should be treated as allowable under what is now *CTA 2009, s 1299(2)* as being of a kind which it was its trade to provide. The CA and HL rejected the claim, holding that that provision referred to a trade of providing entertainment or hospitality, or to the provision of free samples. *Fleming v Associated Newspapers Ltd*, HL 1972, 48 TC 382; [1973] AC 628; [1972] 2 All ER 574.

Room hire and catering

[63.272] A company (N) organised a function for customers and potential customers. It spent £681 on the hire of the room, and £1,800 on hospitality and catering. It claimed that these payments should be allowed as deductions. The Revenue rejected the claim on the basis that the function was 'business entertainment'. N appealed. The Special Commissioners allowed the appeal in part, holding that the £1,800 related to 'business entertainment' and was not deductible, but that the £681 spent on the hire of the room should be allowed as a deduction. *Netlogic Consulting Ltd v HMRC*, Sp C [2005] SSCD 524 (Sp C 477). (*Note*. The appeal was heard with *Kawthar Consulting Ltd v HMRC*, 61.50 TRADING INCOME.)

Sponsorship of powerboat grand prix

[63.273] A UK company invited some of its clients to attend a powerboat grand prix in Tunisia. It claimed a deduction for the cost of this. HMRC issued an assessment disallowing the claim on the basis that the expenditure constituted 'business entertainment'. The First-tier Tribunal dismissed the company's appeal against the assessment. *Aeroassistance Logistics Ltd v HMRC*, FTT [2013] UKFTT 214 (TC), TC02628.

Entertaining expenditure—definition of 'business entertainment'

[63.274] The definition of 'business entertainment' has been considered in several VAT cases, including *Customs & Excise Commrs v Shaklee International & Another*, CA [1981] STC 776; *Thorn EMI plc v Customs & Excise Commrs*, CA [1995] STC 674 and *Celtic Football & Athletic Club Ltd v Customs & Excise Commrs*, CS [1983] STC 470. See Tolley's VAT Cases for summaries of these.

Car or motor cycle hire (ITTOIA 2005, ss 48–50; CTA 2009, ss 56, 57)

Company hiring leased cars to customers

[63.275] A company (B) owned a subsidiary company (AL), which carried on a trade of hiring motor cars. AL obtained its cars under finance leases. In 1998 B sold AL to another company (S), and in 2000 S in turn sold AL to a third company (LU). The sale agreement included a number of tax warranties. Subsequently LU ascertained that AL's previous tax returns had failed to apply the restrictions of *CTA 2009, s 56** to the vehicles which it hired to its customers. LU considered that the restrictions of *CTA 2009, s 56** should have been applied to the payments which AL made to the finance lessors, thus reducing the amount which could be deducted in computing its profits for tax purposes, and that this gave rise to a claim against S under the tax warranties. S resisted the claim, and LU took legal proceedings against S, seeking a declaration that *CTA 2009, s 56** applied to the payments. The Ch D granted the declaration. Sir Andrew Morritt V-C held that the transactions concerned were 'hirings', to which *CTA 2009, s 56** applied and the fact that AL was 'an intermediate lessor' was 'immaterial'. B, which had been joined as a defendant in the proceedings, appealed to the CA, which upheld the Ch D decision. Dismissing a separate point raised by B, Jonathan Parker LJ observed that 'expenditure which is brought into account in computing gross profits is just as much expenditure "deducted in computing for the purposes of tax the profits of the trade" as expenditure which is deducted from gross profits once computed. In each case, the expenditure is brought into account as a deduction in the computation of taxable profits.' *Britax International GmbH v CIR (aka Lloyds UDT Finance Ltd v Chartered Finance Trust Holdings plc and Others)*, CA 2002, 74 TC 662; [2002] STC 956; [2002] EWCA Civ 806.

Carpenter using vehicle owned by mother

[63.276] A self-employed carpenter claimed a deduction of £8,400 in respect of the use of a vehicle which was owned by his mother. HMRC rejected the claim and he appealed. The First-tier Tribunal dismissed his appeal, finding that the appellant had failed to show either that he had actually paid his mother the amount claimed or that any such payment was wholly and exclusively for the purpose of his trade. *S Moulton v HMRC*, FTT [2011] UKFTT 111 (TC), TC00987. (*Note*. The appellant appeared in person.)

Patent royalties (CTA 2009, s 59)

Payments for use of patents and technical assistance

[63.277] An engineering company (P) made payments to an American company for the use of certain patents and trade marks owned by the American company and for details of secret processes, etc. It claimed that these payments should be deducted in computing its profits. The Revenue rejected the claim, considering that the payments were patent royalties and not deductible under the legislation then in force. The KB allowed P's appeal in part, holding that part of the payments were royalties and therefore disallowable, but that part of the payments were not for the use of patents and were allowable. The KB remitted the case to the Commissioners to determine how much of the payments was allowable. *Paterson Engineering Co Ltd v Duff*, KB 1943, 25 TC 43.

Interest payments (ITTOIA 2005, s 52)

Bonus (premium) on repayment of mortgage

[63.278] A company borrowed money by way of mortgage, on terms that it could opt to repay the loan before the end of the term of the mortgage on payment of a bonus (premium) of 10%. It was held that the bonus was not deductible in computing its profits. *Arizona Copper Co v Smiles*, CE 1891, 3 TC 149.

London branch of German company—interest on short-term loans

[63.279] The London branch of a German company borrowed on short-term loans from foreign banks. The QB held that the interest on the loans was not deductible. *Anglo-Continental Guano Works v Bell*, QB 1894, 3 TC 239.

Interest on fluctuating loans from overseas banks

[63.280] An investment-dealing company financed its purchase of certain American investments by fluctuating loans from its New York bankers on the security of the investments. The CS held that the interest on the bank advances was deductible, and the HL unanimously upheld this decision. *Scottish North American Trust Ltd v Farmer*, HL 1911, 5 TC 693; [1912] AC 18.

Share of profits as partial consideration for loan

[63.281] A company borrowed £4,000, and agreed to pay the lender £200 pa plus up to 15% of its profits (not exceeding £300). The KB held that these payments were distributions of profits and were not allowable deductions. *AW Walker & Co v CIR*, KB 1920, 12 TC 297; [1920] 3 KB 648.

Finance company—interest on advances from overseas parent

[63.282] A hire-purchase finance company was partly financed by fluctuating advances from its American parent company, paying interest on the daily balances at rates fluctuating with the American bank rate. The Commissioners held that the advances were capital and that the interest was not deductible. The CA unanimously upheld their decision. *European Investment Trust Co Ltd v Jackson*, CA 1932, 18 TC 1.

Borrowings to acquire shares of another company

[63.283] An oil company borrowed money in order to finance its purchase of shares in another company (thereby acquiring control of that company). The KB held that the interest, the expenses of the borrowing, and associated exchange losses, were capital expenditure and not deductible in computing the company's profits. *Ward v Anglo-American Oil Co Ltd*, KB 1934, 19 TC 94.

Commission paid under loan guarantees

[63.284] A Netherlands company (N) guaranteed the trading liability of a subsidiary UK company (G) in return for commission of 3% pa. N's parent company guaranteed a loan of £150,000 to G for a similar commission, holding debenture stock as security. G claimed that the commission payments should be allowed as deductions. The Special Commissioners held that the commission on the first guarantee was deductible in computing G's profits but that the commission on the second guarantee was not. The KB upheld this decision. *Ascot Gas Water Heaters Ltd v Duff*, KB 1942, 24 TC 171.

Estate developer—premium on loan to finance development

[63.285] A firm which carried on business as an estate developer borrowed £15,000 to finance a development. The terms of the loan provided for the payment of a premium of £6,500 and for repayment by instalments. The lender wished to obtain earlier repayment and agreed to accept a repayment of the balance with a premium of only £4,000. The Special Commissioners held that the premium was capital expenditure and was not deductible in computing the firm's profits. The KB upheld this decision. *EJ & WH Bridgwater v King*, KB 1943, 25 TC 385.

Property development company—interest paid on loans

[63.286] In a Hong Kong case, a property development company (W) borrowed substantial sums of money in order to acquire and redevelop an old tramway depot. It claimed that the interest which it paid on the loans should be deducted in computing its taxable profits. The Commissioner rejected the claim and the Privy Council dismissed W's appeal, holding that the interest was capital expenditure. *Wharf Properties Ltd v Hong Kong Commissioner of Inland Revenue*, PC [1997] STC 351; [1997] 2 WLR 334.

Interest on loan applied to redeem share capital

[63.287] In an Irish case, a company (R) had issued 11,500,000 redeemable preference shares to finance the purchase of a number of shops. It subsequently decided to redeem some of the preference shares, and borrowed £6,000,000 from a bank. It claimed that the interest on the loan should be allowed as a deduction in computing its profits. The Revenue rejected the claim on the basis that the interest should be treated as capital expenditure. The Circuit Court allowed R's appeal, and the SC(I) upheld this decision. Geoghegan J held that 'the ongoing interest payments were necessarily part and parcel of the trading of the company'. *MacAonghusa v Ringmahon Company*, SC(I) [2001] IESC 44.

Company carrying on two trades—purposes for which interest paid

[63.288] Prior to *FA 1969*, annual interest paid wholly and exclusively for the purposes of a trade, but not paid out of profits or gains brought into charge for tax, created losses available for carry-forward against future profits of that trade. A company (E) had purchased a ship in 1961 by means of a loan from its parent, and began a trade of chartering the ship, which ceased in February 1967. E had also carried on a separate manufacturing trade which it continued to carry on after 1967, and it claimed that losses created by the payment of the interest could be used for set-off against future profits of the manufacturing trade. The Special Commissioners rejected the claim, holding that, as the loan had been for the purposes of purchasing the ship, the losses could not be carried forward against profits of the manufacturing trade. E appealed, contending that the interest had been paid for the purposes of both trades and should be apportioned. The Ch D rejected this contention and dismissed the appeal. *Olin Energy Systems Ltd v Scorer (and cross-appeal)*, Ch D 1982, 58 TC 592; [1982] STC 800. (*Note*. For another issue in this case, taken to the HL, see **5.81** ASSESSMENTS.)

Interest relating to subsidiary companies

[63.289] The parent company of a group of insurance companies claimed loss relief on the basis that interest which it paid on a number of loans should be allowed as a deduction. The Revenue rejected the claim, considering that the interest was partly for the purpose of the separate trades carried on by the subsidiary companies, and thus was not wholly and exclusively for the purpose of the parent company's trade. The Commissioners dismissed the company's appeal and the Ch D upheld their decision. *Commercial Union Assurance Co plc v Shaw*, Ch D 1998, 72 TC 101; [1998] STC 386. (*Note*. For another issue in this case, taken to the CA, see **21.39** DOUBLE TAX RELIEF.)

Bank interest paid by property-dealing company

[63.290] See *Wilcock v Frigate Investments Ltd*, **33.28** INTEREST PAYABLE.

Interest paid by accountant

[63.291] An accountant (S) claimed a deduction for loan interest of £59,000 in computing his profits for 1995 and 1996. The Revenue issued an amendment under *TMA, s 28A(4)*, on the basis that only 33.2% of the amount claimed was allowable as a deduction, since S's capital account was substantially overdrawn and his drawings exceeded his profits, so that some of the loans to S were being used to fund private expenditure. (According to S's balance sheet, the overdrawn capital account represented 66.8% of the total loans to him.) S appealed, contending firstly that his capital account should be adjusted by adding back the consideration which he had paid for goodwill when he had set up in practice, and secondly that it should be adjusted by adding back an amount of cumulative depreciation. The Special Commissioner reviewed the evidence in detail and upheld the Revenue amendment in principle but reduced it in amount. On the evidence, when S had left his previous partnership and begun as a sole practitioner, he had 'received the goodwill which attached to the clients that he took with him, (but) he made no payment, and he did not give any other consideration for it, to the firm'. Any goodwill which S had received from the firm 'was not purchased; no sum of money was paid for it'. Accordingly, there were no grounds for adjusting the capital account in respect of goodwill. However, the Commissioner accepted that the account should be adjusted by adding back an amount in respect of cumulative depreciation, reduced by the excess of debtors over creditors. *Silk v Fletcher*, Sp C [1999] SSCD 220 (Sp C 201). (*Note*. For subsequent developments in this case, see **63.292** below.)

[63.292] Following the decision in the case noted at **63.291** above, the parties were unable to agree the amount of the final adjustment. S contended that the figure for creditors should include loan repayments due within the next twelve months. The Special Commissioner rejected this contention and found that 'none of the loans upon which interest was paid was used to acquire goodwill'. The Commissioner reduced the amount of the disallowance from £20,172 to £12,382. *Silk v Fletcher (No 2)*, Sp C [2000] SSCD 565 (Sp C 262).

Newsagent—mortgage interest

[63.293] A trader (D) purchased a newsagency business and a house which adjoined the premises, with the aid of a mortgage. He claimed a deduction for the whole of the mortgage interest. The Revenue issued discovery assessments on the basis that only 50% of the interest was deductible as a trading expense, the remaining 50% being attributable to the house which D occupied as his private residence. D appealed. The Special Commissioner reviewed the evidence in detail and allowed the appeal in part, holding that 'the apportionment should be based on the value of the residential property against the purchase price of the whole package'. On the evidence, the Commissioner directed that 35% of the interest should be attributed to D's private residence and that the remaining 65% of the interest was deductible. *Dixon v HMRC*, Sp C 2005, [2006] SSCD 28 (Sp C 511). (*Note*. At a subsequent hearing, the Commissioner formally determined the relevant assessments—Sp C [2006] SSCD 295 (Sp C 531).)

Shopkeeper—mortgage interest

[63.294] The proprietor of a fish and chip shop purchased a house with the aid of a mortgage. In his tax returns, he treated the mortgage interest as a deduction from his profits. HMRC issued discovery assessments on the basis that the interest was not an allowable deduction. The First-tier Tribunal upheld the assessments, finding that 'there was no business purpose element to the mortgage'. *PT Stavrou v HMRC*, FTT [2011] UKFTT 59 (TC), TC00937.

Incidental costs of obtaining finance (ITTOIA 2005, s 58)

[63.295] In 1989 a Japanese company (K), which was not resident in the UK, purchased a large commercial property in the UK for £130,000,000. In order to finance the purchase, it had borrowed £95,250,000 from the UK branch of a Japanese bank. The loan was at a variable rate, dependent on the rate of exchange between yen and sterling. Following changes in the exchange rate, the interest rate became higher than the rental yield from the property. K therefore repaid the loan before the scheduled date, and became liable to pay the bank about £21,000,000 under an indemnity agreement. Since K was not resident in the UK for tax purposes, it was agreed that its rental income was chargeable to UK income tax rather than corporation tax. It claimed that the indemnity payment should be allowed as a deduction, giving it substantial losses available for carry forward. The Revenue issued closure notices on the basis that the effect of what is now *ITTOIA 2005, s 58(4)* was that the indemnity payment was not deductible. K appealed. The Special Commissioner reviewed the evidence in detail and held that the payment had to be apportioned. The effect of *ITTOIA 2005, s 58(1)** was that the payment, although capital in nature, was deductible in principle by virtue of being an 'incidental cost of obtaining finance'. However the effect of *ITTOIA 2005, s 58(4)** was that part of the payment was not deductible, since it was a sum 'paid because of losses resulting from movements in the rate of exchange between different currencies'. On the available evidence, the Commissioner expressed the view that £3,242,727 of the payment was deductible as an indemnity payment, but that the remainder of the payment (almost £18,000,000) was 'caused solely by a change in the rate of exchange between yen and sterling and so is not deductible'. *Kato Kagatu Co Ltd v HMRC*, Sp C [2007] SSCD 412 (Sp C 598).

Payments for restrictive undertakings (ITTOIA 2005, s 69; CTA 2009, s 69)

[63.296] The managing director and another director of a cement company (P), both with considerable knowledge of the cement industry, announced their intention to retire. P paid them £20,000 and £10,000 respectively in return for covenants by them not to engage in the manufacture or sale of cement after retirement, except with P's consent of the company. The Special Commissioners held that the payments were capital expenditure and not deductible in computing P's profits. The CA unanimously upheld this decision. Lord Greene observed that P had bought off two 'dangerous potential competitors', and had thereby increased the value of its goodwill. P could not crown its 'success in acquiring these solid advantages by passing on to the general taxpayer the privilege of paying for a large part of the expense so incurred'. *Associated Portland Cement Manufacturers Ltd v Kerr*, CA 1945, 27 TC 103; [1946] 1 All ER 68.

Redundancy payments (ITTOIA 2005, ss 76–80; CTA 2009, ss 76–81)

Payment on termination of service following sale of business

[63.297] An insurance company (R) acquired the business of another insurance company (Q). It agreed to retain Q's manager at a salary of £4,000 pa, with an option to terminate his service on paying him a sum (calculated from annuity tables) in commutation. Shortly after the transfer, R exercised the option and paid the manager £55,000 in accordance with the agreement. The HL unanimously held that this amount was capital expenditure, being part of the consideration for the business acquired, and was not an allowable deduction in computing R's profits. *Royal Insurance Co v Watson*, HL 1896, 3 TC 500; [1897] AC 1.

Redundancy payments on cessation of trading

[63.298] A company (AB) ceased trading in November 1921. Subsequently, under arrangements agreed by its directors in March 1921, it made payments in compensation for loss of office to some of its employees, and awarded pensions, later commuted for lump sums, to others. AB claimed that the payments should be treated as deductions in computing its profits for the year ending 31 March 1921. The KB held that the payments were not deductible in computing AB's profits, since they were for the purpose of winding up the trade rather than for the purpose of carrying it on, and were not made in the year ending March 1921. *CIR v Anglo Brewing Co Ltd*, KB 1925, 12 TC 803. (*Note*. HMRC regard this case as establishing the proposition that 'payments to go out of business are not allowed'; see HMRC Busines Income Manual, para BIM38310.)

[63.299] A printing company (S) ceased trading in 1978 and, in addition to making statutory redundancy payments, was obliged to make further payments totalling £8,085 to its employees in lieu of adequate notice of termination of their employment. It claimed a deduction for this amount in computing its profits for the final period of trading. The Revenue rejected the claim on the basis that the £8,085 was linked with the cessation of the business and was capital expenditure, but the Special Commissioners allowed S's appeal, finding that the £8,085 was paid 'for the purpose of achieving the orderly conduct of its business prior to the date of cessation'. The Ch D upheld this decision as one of fact. *O'Keeffe v Southport Printers Ltd*, Ch D 1984, 58 TC 88; [1984] STC 443.

[63.300] In a Hong Kong case, a manufacturing company (C) closed its factory in 1991 and made its employees redundant. It was obliged to make redundancy payments to employees with at least two years' service. It claimed a deduction for these payments in computing its profits for the final period of trading. The Revenue rejected the claim, on the basis that the payments had been made for the purpose of closing the business rather than for the purpose of carrying on the business. C appealed. The Hong Kong Board of Review allowed the appeal, and the PC upheld this decision. The payments had been made in accordance with a statutory obligation which had been incurred as a necessary condition of retaining the services of the employees concerned. *Hong Kong Commr of Inland Revenue v Cosmotron Manufacturing Co Ltd*, PC 1997, 70 TC 292; [1997] STC 1134; [1997] 1 WLR 1288. (*Note*. For the Revenue's practice following this decision, see Revenue Tax Bulletin February 1999, pp 630–631.)

Redundancy payments following change of ownership

[63.301] Following a change of ownership, two associated companies made some of their directors and employees redundant, and paid them compensation. The companies claimed that the payments should be deducted in computing their profits, but the Revenue rejected the claim on the grounds that the payments were capital expenditure. The Ch D held that none of the payments were allowable deductions. On the evidence, the payments were not made exclusively for the purposes of the companies' trades. Wilberforce J observed that 'there was a mixture of motives in the decision which led to the payment of the compensation'. *George Peters & Co Ltd v Smith*; *Williams v JJ Young & Son Ltd*, Ch D 1963, 41 TC 264.

Payment to manager in anticipation of sale of business

[63.302] A company (W) employed a manager (P) under a contract which entitled him to six months' notice. In anticipation of the sale of the business, W gave P notice of termination in March 1958 and paid him £1,900, representing his estimated remuneration for the six months to September 1958. W sold the business on 31 March 1958. The Ch D held that the £1,900 was not paid for the purpose of carrying on W's trade, and was not an allowable deduction. The CA unanimously upheld this decision. *Godden v A Wilson's Stores (Holdings) Ltd*, CA 1962, 40 TC 161.

Payment to secure resignation of director appointed for life

[63.303] The directors of a private insurance company (B) were appointed for life, with provisions for dismissal on bankruptcy or misconduct. The majority of the directors suspected one of their colleagues of misconduct, and sought to obtain his retirement. Following negotiations, the continuing directors purchased his shares for their par value of £300 (although they were worth considerably more) and B agreed to pay him £19,200 as compensation in five annual instalments. B claimed a deduction for the instalments in computing its profits. The Revenue rejected the claim but the Special Commissioners allowed B's appeal and the CA unanimously upheld their decision. *Mitchell v BW Noble Ltd*, CA 1927, 11 TC 372. (*Note*. For another issue in this case, not taken to the CA, see **60.11** TRADING INCOME.)

[63.304] L, H and T were life directors and sole shareholders of an advertising company (G). Following disagreements between them, T paid L and H £3,000 for their shares, while G paid £5,000 to L, and £500 to H, as compensation for loss of office on resigning as directors. G claimed that the £5,500 should be allowed as a deduction in computing its profits. The Revenue rejected the claim and the Commissioners dismissed G's appeal, holding that G had 'failed to establish' that the £5,500 had been expended wholly and exclusively for the purposes of its trade. The Ch D upheld this decision. *George J Smith & Co Ltd v Furlong*, Ch D 1968, 45 TC 384; [1969] 2 All ER 760.

Compensation for loss of office linked with sale of shares

[63.305] The directors and sole shareholders of a company disposed of their shares. Immediately before the sale, a resolution was passed at an extraordinary meeting of the company, voting them £3,000 as compensation for loss of office. The KB held that the £3,000 was a distribution of profits, and was not deductible in computing the company's profits. *Overy v Ashford Dunn & Co Ltd*, KB 1933, 17 TC 497.

[63.306] Following a dispute among members of a family holding all the shares of a company (B), the shares were sold to an outside purchaser on condition that ten of the employees (all but one of whom was a member of the family) should receive sums on cancellation of their service agreements. The Special Commissioners held that the compensation was part of the share transaction and was not deductible in computing B's profits. The KB upheld this decision. *Bassett Enterprise Ltd v Petty*, KB 1938, 21 TC 728.

[63.307] Under an agreement for the sale of the shares in a company (J), its directors and auditor were required to resign and were paid compensation for loss of office. The Commissioners held that the payments were not an allowable deduction in computing J's profits. The CA unanimously upheld this decision. Sir Raymond Evershed MR observed that J's 'motives or purposes in this matter must have been mixed'. *James Snook & Co Ltd v Blasdale*, CA 1952, 33 TC 244.

Company takeover—directors' service agreements terminated

[63.308] Following a takeover of a group of companies, the service agreements of the managing directors of three subsidiary companies were terminated, the subsidiaries being subsequently liquidated. The companies made payments to the managing directors, expressed to be in lieu of notice in one case and in satisfaction of rights to future remuneration in the other two, and claimed these as deductions in computing their profits. The Revenue rejected the claim but the Commissioners allowed the companies' appeals, finding that the payments were not made as part of the agreement for the sale of the shares in the company. The CS upheld the Commissioners' decision as one of fact. *CIR v Patrick Thomson Ltd (and related appeals)*, CS 1956, 37 TC 145.

Compensation voted to director following sale of part of business

[63.309] A company (R) sold part of its business in the year ended 31 May 1995. It claimed a deduction for a payment of £30,000 as compensation to the director who had been responsible for the relevant part of the business, and for a payment of £160,000 to his pension fund. The Revenue rejected the claims on the basis that R had not actually made the payments in question in the year ended 31 May 1995, and that the compensation payment did not qualify for relief in any event as it was a gratuitous payment which was made for the purpose of winding up the trade rather than for the purpose of carrying it on. The Special Commissioner dismissed R's appeal, observing that 'a gratuitous payment made on the cessation of business would not qualify for relief'. *Relkobrook Ltd v Mapstone*, Sp C 2004, [2005] SSCD 272 (Sp C 452).

Prospective liability for future leaving payments to employees

[63.310] See the cases noted at 62.72 *et seq.* TRADING PROFITS.

Expenses of foreign trades (ITTOIA 2005, ss 92–94)

Loss on foreign exchange

[63.311] A UK company (R) carried amounts to a suspense account to cover the exchange loss on a trading balance due to its US parent company (the loss being attributable to a fall in the value of sterling). R's profit and loss accounts were made up on a sterling basis, but it subsequently submitted a claim to error or mistake relief, contending that the amounts carried to the suspense account should be allowed as deductions in computing its profits. The KB accepted this contention and allowed the claim, and the CA unanimously upheld this decision. *Radio Pictures Ltd v CIR*, CA 1938, 22 TC 106.

[63.312] A US corporation set up an Irish subsidiary (L) in 1947. L's accounts were made up to 31 December. Immediately after the end of each year, L's auditors were told the cost in dollars of goods sent to L from the USA and the proportion of the corporation's expenses charged to L in the year, with their sterling equivalent at the year-end rate. The aggregate amount so notified for the two years to 31 December 1948 was $24,300 (Irish equivalent £6,075). The $24,300 was not remitted to the USA. The £6,075 was allowed as a deduction in arriving at L's taxable profits. The Irish pound was devalued in September 1949 and in the 1949 accounts, the £6,075 was revalued at the new rate, increasing it by £2,603. L claimed that this £2,603 should be deducted in computing its 1949 profits. The Irish Supreme Court rejected the claim, holding that the deductions in the 1947 and 1948 computations concluded the matter. *Revenue Commissioners v L & Co*, SC(I) 1956, 3 ITC 205.

[63.313] A US company set up a UK subsidiary (F) in 1922. In 1931 F'ss total indebtedness to its parent, amounting to almost $5,000,000, was treated in its accounts as a fixed loan, converted into sterling at the then exchange rate of $4.86. There were two minor repayments of the fixed loan, the resultant exchange differences being agreed at the time as 10% revenue and 90% capital. In 1965, F repaid the balance of the fixed loan, incurring an exchange loss of £568,489. The Special Commissioners found that 90% of the loss was capital expenditure and was not an allowable deduction in computing Fs profits. The Ch D upheld their decision as one of fact. *Firestone Tyre & Rubber Co Ltd v Evans*, Ch D 1976, 51 TC 615; [1977] STC 104.

[63.314] A US company set up a UK subsidiary (M) in 1971 to carry on an international banking business. M derived its profits from the interest differentials in its lendings and borrowings, which were mainly in dollars; it did not speculate in currency. In its accounts and books it revalued its currency assets and liabilities into sterling, using the balance sheet date exchange rates. Its dollar liabilities included loan stock of $15m issued, on its formation, to two fellow-subsidiaries. The proceeds of the issue became part of its dollar funds, used to make loans to its customers. In 1976 the stock was repaid out of dollar funds. Because of a fall in the value of sterling, the sterling equivalent of the $15m was £6m when the stock was issued but £8.6m when it was repaid. In its trading M aimed to ensure that its liabilities in each currency were matched by its assets and to minimise the need for forward currency deals to close an open position. In arriving at its dollar position, the loan stock was treated as a dollar liability. The CA allowed M's appeal against corporation tax assessments and the HL unanimously upheld this decision, holding that there were no relevant currency conversions. M's only profit was the differential between the interest it paid to the loan stock holders and the interest it received from customers to whom it lent the $15m. Had there been any relevant currency conversions, any resultant exchange profit or loss would have entered into the tax profits 'as incidents in the company's currency transactions in the course of carrying on a commercial banking business'. *Pattison v Marine Midland Ltd*, HL 1983, 57 TC 219; [1984] STC 10; [1984] 2 WLR 11. (*Note.* For HMRC's current practice concerning exchange rate fluctuations, see Revenue Statement of Practice 2/02, issued on 30 September 2002.)

[63.315] A company (W) entered into two loans in June 1971 and February 1972, each for 50m Swiss francs and for five years, repayable earlier at the option of the company subject to payment of a graduated premium. It repaid the first loan in January 1976, six months before the due date, and the second on the due date in February 1977, buying Swiss francs out of general funds. The exchange transactions gave rise to losses of about £11.4m, which W claimed as a deduction in computing its profits. The Revenue rejected the claim, considering that the losses were on capital account and therefore not allowable. The HL unanimously upheld the Revenue's view. Lord Templeman held that the question of whether the transactions were of a revenue or capital nature was a question of law. A trader who borrowed 100m Swiss francs for a fixed period of five years increased the capital employed in the trade. W had obtained an asset or advantage which endured for five years and such an asset was a capital asset. A loan was only a revenue transaction if it was part of the ordinary day-to-day incidence of carrying on the business, which was not the case here. The loss which W had incurred was in connection with a capital transaction and therefore was not an allowable deduction. *Beauchamp v FW Woolworth plc*, HL 1989, 61 TC 542; [1989] STC 510; [1989] 3 WLR 1.

[63.316] In 1965 four leading UK shipowners formed a company (OCL) to conduct a container shipping trade for them. In 1967 OCL placed contracts with German shipyards for five container ships for the founding companies. The price was payable in Deutschmarks by stage instalments and the shipbuilders made loans to OCL for the construction. In 1969 OCL formed a subsidiary company (F) to handle its financial activities. Later in that year, when a devaluation of sterling was widely anticipated, the loans to OCL were novated so as to become loans to F, and F lent OCL equivalent sums in sterling at commercial rates of interest, repayable in instalments as the German loans were repayable. In December 1969 F entered into further long-term loans in Deutschmarks for the construction of more ships for two of the founding companies, and made loans in sterling to those companies. These two batches of transactions resulted in exchange losses of £39.2m. Net exchange losses in a number of smaller transactions increased the loss to £42.2m, while F received £27.7m net interest, resulting in an overall net loss of £14.5m. F appealed against corporation tax assessments, contending that this loss arose from trading transactions. The Special Commissioners rejected this contention and dismissed the appeal, holding that the losses were not from trading transactions. The CA upheld this decision, holding on the evidence that the interposition of F between OCL and the German lenders served no commercial purpose. Its only purpose was to attempt to transmute an exchange loss on capital account into a revenue loss. For a transaction to constitute trading, it was necessary for there to be a commercial purpose. Where, considering the group as a whole, the sole purpose of a transaction was to obtain a fiscal advantage, it was logically impossible to postulate the existence of any commercial purpose. *Overseas Containers (Finance) Ltd v Stoker*, CA 1989, 61 TC 473; [1989] STC 364; [1989] 1 WLR 606.

[63.317] See also *Ward v Anglo-American Oil Co Ltd*, 63.283 above.

Overseas capital tax

[63.318] Under Argentinian law, companies were required to pay annually a 'substitute tax' of one per cent of their capital. The tax extended to foreign companies trading in the Argentine with a commercial establishment known as an '*empresa estable*'. A UK company (H), which owned a large retail store in Buenos Aires, was required to pay the tax, and claimed it as a deduction in computing its profits. The Revenue rejected the claim but the Ch D allowed H's appeal and the CA unanimously upheld this decision, holding that the payment was wholly and exclusively for the purposes of H's trade and was deductible. *Harrods (Buenos Aires) Ltd v Taylor-Gooby*, CA 1964, 41 TC 450.

Remediation of contaminated land (CTA 2009, ss 1143–1179)

[63.319] A company constructed a marina at Portland in Dorset. It incurred expenditure on the construction of a sea wall, the construction of a plinth to enable buildings to be constructed, and the construction of floodwater drainage systems. It claimed relief under *FA 2001, Sch 22* on the basis that this constituted 'qualifying land remediation expenditure'. HMRC rejected the claim on the grounds that 'the land in respect of which the expenditure was incurred was not in a contaminated state within the terms of the relief'. The company appealed. The First-tier Tribunal allowed the appeal in part, holding that the company was entitled to relief for work carried out on the foreshore. However, the construction of a breakwater on the seabed, and work carried out on land above the tidal high-water mark, failed to qualify for relief. (Judge Sadler observed that the law relating to land remediation relief was amended with effect from 1 April 2009 to provide that 'land is now in a contaminated state only if the contaminating substance is present as a result of industrial activity, and not by reason of natural processes'. The company would not now be entitled to relief, since its claim was based on land having been contaminated by seawater.) *Dean & Reddyhoff Ltd v HMRC*, FTT [2013] UKFTT 367 (TC), TC02767.

Film production (CTA 2009, ss 1180–1216)

Whether films 'qualifying British films'

[63.320] A group of companies produced more than 8,500 short films. They wished to claim relief for the production costs, and applied to the Secretary of State to have more than 4,000 of the films certified as 'qualifying British films' under *Films Act 1985, Sch 1*. The Secretary of State rejected the applications, on the grounds that she was not satisfied that 'at least 70% of the total expenditure incurred in the production of the film was incurred on film production activity carried out in the United Kingdom', as required by *Films Act 1985, Sch 1 para 4(3)*. The QB dismissed the companies' appeals. Lawrence Collins J observed that the films were 'a remarkable business venture', since 'although more than 8,500 of these films have been made, it would seem that none of them has been commercially shown or exploited'. It was 'within the powers of the Secretary of State to refuse to grant certificates to applications which are not based on the real costs incurred in production'. There was 'abundant material in the correspondence, and in the evidence' to justify the Secretary of State's conclusions, so that she had been entitled to reject the applications. *Peakviewing (Interactive) Ltd and Others v Secretary of State for Culture Media and Sport*, QB [2002] STC 1226; [2002] EWHC 1531 (Admin). (*Notes*. (1) The CA subsequently dismissed an application to appeal against this decision—see [2002] EWCA Civ 1864. (2) The principal director of the group was subsequently sentenced to five and a half years' imprisonment for VAT fraud—*R v Matthews*, Bristol Crown Court 15 June 2007 unreported.)

Date trade began—whether film consultancy fees deductible

[63.321] A limited liability partnership (H) claimed a loss of more than £14,000,000 relating to expenditure on three films, including a payment of more than £1,800,000 to a company (L) for 'film consultancy services'. HMRC rejected the claim, considering firstly that the effect of *FA 2002, s 101* was that no relief was due; secondly that H had begun trading in December 2003 (rather than March 2003), so that the relief claimed for 2003/04 was excessive; and thirdly that the amount claimed was excessive and that the payment to L was not allowable as a deduction. The Special Commissioners reviewed the evidence in detail and allowed H's appeal in principle on the first issue, holding that H was entitled to relief on the whole of the expenditure, and that *FA 2002, s 101* did not preclude the relief claimed. The fees which it had paid to L were also allowable as a deduction, since they were revenue expenditure and had been arrived at 'on an arm's length basis'. However the Commissioners also held that H had not begun trading until 9 December 2003, when it had entered into sale and leaseback transactions in relation to the master negatives of the three films. The Ch D and CA unanimously upheld the Commissioners' decision. *HMRC v Halcyon Films Llp*, CA 2010. 80 TC 475; [2010] STC 1125; [2010] EWCA Civ 261. (*Notes.* (1) *FA 2002, s 101* was repealed by *FA 2005* with effect from 2 December 2004. Davis J's judgment includes the observation that 'from time to time Parliament grants special tax reliefs and incentives with a view to promoting financing for British films: and then, when the implications in terms of lost revenue are fully realised and the capacity for the exploitation of loopholes in the statutory drafting is brought home, seeks from time to time to modify or withdraw the previous legislation'. (2) The Ch D and CA heard the appeal with *HMRC v Micro Fusion 2004–1 Llp*, 59.22 TRADING INCOME. (3) The Supreme Court rejected an application by HMRC for leave to appeal against this decision.)

[63.322] See also *Micro Fusion 2004-1 Llp v HMRC*, 59.22 TRADING INCOME.

Film distribution—claim for substantial losses

[63.323] A limited liability partnership was formed in February 2004 with the aim of conducting a trade of film distribution. On 5 April 2004 it admitted six new partners who contributed capital totalling £1,520,000, of which 70% (£1,064,000) had been funded by non-recourse loans advanced by a Scottish bank. The partnership submitted accounts for a one-day accounting period (5 April 2004) indicating that it had begun trading on that date, had made payments equal to virtually its entire capital and resources, and had made a very substantial trading loss (£1,491,816) that its members could set against their other income. HMRC began an enquiry and formed the opinion that a major element of the payments which the partnership had made 'had nothing to do with its trade but simply generated guaranteed receipts, basically inserted into the structure to ramp up the apparent spending on trading items in order to increase the initial tax relief available' to the partnership and its members. HMRC issued a closure notice on the basis that the partnership should be treated as having made a trading loss of only £11,900. The partnership appealed. The Upper Tribunal reviewed the evidence in detail and allowed the appeal in part. Vos J held that a payment of £1,064,000 under a 'distribution agreement' and funded by the non-recourse bank loans was not allowable on the basis that it was not wholly and exclusively expended for the purpose of the partnership's trade. However, he accepted the partnership's contention that a further payment of £209,866 made to the same recipient was an allowable deduction. Of the £170,000 which the partnership had paid to a management company, he held that £50,000 paid under an 'advisory agreement' was not deductible because it was a prepayment for future services, but £120,000 paid under an 'administration agreement' was an allowable deduction. *Icebreaker 1 Llp v HMRC*, UT [2011] STC 1078; [2010] UKUT 477 (TCC).

[63.324] A partnership was formed in 2001 to produce a film. In its first accounting period, ending 5 April 2002, it claimed to have made a loss of £1,920,529. Its return claimed significant deductions for 'deferred amounts' payable to members of the cast and production crew. HMRC began an enquiry and formed the opinion that these amounts were not properly deductible in the period ending 5 April 2002. They issued an amendment disallowing these amounts and reducing the loss to £597,300. The partnership appealed. The First-tier Tribunal reviewed the evidence in detail and dismissed the appeal. Sir Stephen Oliver observed that 'expenditure incurred on the production of a film is deductible as soon as there is an unconditional obligation to pay it'. In the present case, the financial statement which the partnership had submitted 'failed to comply with generally accepted accounting practice in the UK'. It 'should have been corrected to remove the provision for deferred payments to cast and crew before being used as a starting point for the calculation of the taxable profit or loss of the partnership'. At the time the financial statement was signed, the 'deferred cast and crew amounts' were unascertainable, and the partnership had not yet incurred the expenditure it had claimed. *Alchemist (Devil's Gate) Film Partnership v HMRC*, FTT [2013] UKFTT 157 (TC), TC02573.

Film production—tax avoidance scheme—whether promoter fraudulent

[63.325] See *Allison v Horner*, 58.41 TAX PLANNING AND AVOIDANCE.

64

Trading Profits—Receipts (ITTOIA 2005, ss 95–106)

The cases in this chapter are arranged under the following headings.

NOTE

For cases concerning the time at which a receipt arises, see **62.34** *et seq*. TRADING PROFITS.

Capital receipts (ITTOIA 2005, s 96)

General principles

[64.1] In a case where the substantive issue (concerning the interpretation of *CIRA 1888, s 24*) has been superseded by subsequent changes in the legislation, Lord MacNaghten observed that 'income tax, if I may be pardoned for saying so, is a tax on income. It is not meant to be a tax on anything else. It is one tax, not a collection of taxes essentially distinct.' *Attorney-General v London County Council*, HL 1899, 4 TC 265. (*Note*. This *dictum* has been applied in many subsequent cases. In the CA, Smith LJ had expressed the view that 'tax under Schedule D is a tax upon "gains and profits"'. Lord MacNaghten specifically disapproved this *dictum* of Smith LJ.)

[64.2] In *Trustees of Earl Haig v CIR*, **39.1** MISCELLANEOUS INCOME, Lord Moncrieff held that trading profits 'are profits which have an "income" and not a "capital" nature'. In *Beauchamp v FW Woolworth plc*, **63.315** TRADING PROFITS, Lord Templeman held that 'the expression "annual profits" confirms that income tax is to be charged on profits of an income nature as opposed to capital profits'.

Profits on foreign exchange transactions

[64.3] A company (H) which traded as a stonemerchant contracted to supply a quantity of marble, and received an advance of £20,000 from the customer to finance the purchase of the marble from Italy. Pending purchase of the marble, the greater part of the £20,000 was converted into lire and, because of a rise in the lira, H made an exchange profit of £6,707. The Revenue included this in the assessment on H's trading profits. The Special Commissioners allowed H's appeal, holding that the profit was not a trading receipt but merely an appreciation of a temporary investment. The KB upheld this decision. *McKinlay v HT Jenkins & Son Ltd*, KB 1926, 10 TC 372.

[64.4] A UK company (S) sold and distributed petroleum products in China. It engaged about 600 Chinese agents, requiring them to deposit sums with it. The deposits were repayable at the end of the agency. The deposits and repayments were normally in Chinese dollars, and S maintained equivalent dollar deposits in Chinese banks. In 1937 war broke out between China and Japan. During the next 12 months S transferred its deposits into sterling and banked them in the UK. As the result of a fall in the Chinese dollar, S made a substantial exchange profit on repayment of the agency deposits. The Revenue included the amount of the profit in an assessment on S. S appealed, contending that the deposits were part of its fixed capital and that the exchange profit was a capital profit. The Special Commissioners allowed the appeal, and the CA unanimously upheld their decision. Jenkins LJ held that the profit 'was simply the equivalent of an appreciation in a capital asset not forming part of the assets employed as circulating capital in the trade'. *Davies v The Shell Co of China Ltd*, CA 1951, 32 TC 133.

Periodic payments to reimburse capital expenditure

[64.5] A District Council which operated a water undertaking entered into a 30-year agreement with a colliery company (W), under which W agreed to supply water to the Council and erect the necessary buildings and plant, and the Council agreed to pay W an annual sum equal to one-thirtieth of the cost of the works (in addition to payments for the water which W supplied). The Revenue assessed W on the payments. W appealed, contending that the annual payments for the cost of the works were capital receipts. The Commissioners accepted this contention and allowed W's appeal, and the CA unanimously upheld their decision. *Boyce v Whitwick Colliery Co Ltd*, CA 1934, 18 TC 655. (*Note*. The CA also held that the payments were capital expenditure by the Council. However, the Council would not now be liable to tax.)

Lump sum receipts under restrictive covenants

[64.6] A company (T) carried on the business of renovating motor tyres under a process for which it held the patent. In the course of this business it would install plant in premises provided by a motor trader in which it would renovate tyres, invoicing them to the trader at less than the list price. T undertook not to install another plant, nor canvass for orders direct, in a prescribed area, and received lump sum payments from the traders as consideration for this undertaking. The Commissioners held that the lump sums were capital receipts, and the KB upheld their decision. *Margerison v Tyresoles Ltd*, KB 1942, 25 TC 59.

Debts released (ITTOIA 2005, s 97; CTA 2009, s 94)

Bad debt recoveries

[64.7] During the Spanish Civil War, a company (W) wrote off several debts owed by Spanish customers. These were allowed as deductions in the company's accounts for 1937/38 and 1938/39. W subsequently recovered some of the debts, and the Revenue sought to include the amounts recovered as trading receipts of the years in which they were recovered. The KB upheld the Revenue's contentions and the CA unanimously dismissed W's appeal. Lord Greene held that W's appeal was 'singularly devoid of merit'. *Bristow v William Dickinson & Co Ltd*, CA 1946, 27 TC 157; [1946] KB 321; [1946] 1 All ER 448. (*Note.* HMRC regard this case as establishing the proposition that 'where a deduction for a bad or doubtful debt has been made and the taxpayer subsequently recovers the debt or an amount in excess of its written-down value, the amount recovered or the excess should be brought into credit in the year of recovery'. See Business Income Manual, BIM42730.)

Amount of debt released

[64.8] An accountancy partnership entered into a service contract with a limited company. The company subsequently went into liquidation. The partnership calculated that it owed the company £208,090 at the date of liquidation, but claimed a set-off of £194,533, and paid the balance of £13,557 to the liquidator. The liquidator did not accept the claimed set-off, and took proceedings against the partnership. A consent order was subsequently agreed whereby the senior partner (W) agreed to pay £120,000 in instalments. The Revenue issued an amendment to the partnership's self-assessment (under *TMA, s 28B(3)*), to the effect that the balance of £88,090 was a taxable release of a debt under *ITTOIA 2005, s 97**. The partnership appealed, contending firstly that it was entitled to credit for the £13,557 which it had already paid to the liquidator, and secondly that further payments of £43,574 should be deducted in respect of creditors of the company for which the senior partner had accepted liability. The Special Commissioner held that there had been a release of £74,533 (ie £88,090 – £13,557), but that this amount should be reduced by any further payments under the consent order. The Commissioner observed that the Revenue had 'not had the opportunity of verifying the figure of £43,574 as the amount of the additional creditors of the company'. Accordingly, the Commissioner directed that the amount of £74,533 which had been released should be reduced 'by £43,574 or whatever amount is determined to be the final amount of the additional creditors' for which W was liable under the consent order. *Wildin & Co v Jowett*, Sp C

[2002] SSCD 390 (Sp C 327). (*Note*. An alternative contention by the partnership, that the debt had been assigned to the senior partner rather than released, was rejected.)

Acquisition of trade: receipts from transferor's trade (ITTOIA 2005, s 98; CTA 2009, s 95)

[64.9] A self-employed salesman (R) had carried on business selling life assurance products, etc. devised by one major company (D). Following a heart attack, he decided to retire, and in June 1996 he sold his practice to a company (F) which was a subsidiary of D. In October 1996 F resold the practice to another salesman (S). The Revenue issued a 'discovery' assessment on R, charging tax on commission which arose from his trade before the sale, and which F received after the sale. R appealed. The Special Commissioners allowed his appeal, finding that R's trade 'did not cease on the transfer to (F) and there was a succession by (F) to the appellant's trade'. The Commissioners distinguished the 1998 decision in *Brewin v McVittie*, **65.61** TRADING PROFITS, holding that the sale to F was 'a genuine transaction' and that 'a motive of mitigating tax' should not 'invalidate the transaction'. Applying the principles laid down by the HL in *Mawson v Barclays Mercantile Business Finance Ltd*, **8.101** CAPITAL ALLOWANCES, it would not 'be in accordance with the statutory purpose to impose a tax charge in these circumstances on the Appellant, and not (F)'. Accordingly, the effect of *ITTOIA 2005, s 98** was that 'the part of the consideration for the transfer of the trade which represents fees and commissions is not taxable on the appellant but is taxable instead on (F)' because the trade 'was treated as permanently discontinued by reason of a change in the persons carrying it on and the right to receive the renewal commissions was transferred to (F)'. *Rafferty v HMRC*, Sp C [2005] SSCD 484 (Sp C 475).

Government grants and subsidies (ITTOIA 2005, s 105; CTA 2009, s 102)

Grants from Unemployment Grants Committee

[64.10] A dock company (S) received Government grants from the Unemployment Grants Committee, calculated by reference to its liability to pay interest on money which it had borrowed to finance a dock extension. The grants were made periodically over a number of years, and the Revenue issued assessments charging tax on them. The CA allowed S's appeal, holding that the grants were not profits or gains of S's trade. The HL unanimously upheld this decision. *Seaham Harbour Dock Co v Crook*, HL 1931, 16 TC 333.

Ex gratia payment—1926 Irish Grants Committee

[64.11] See *Robinson v Dolan*, **66.45** TRADING PROFITS.

Sugar manufacturer—subsidies linked with production

[64.12] Under a 1925 Act, sugar manufacturers were entitled to subsidies for the ten years to September 1934, based on their sugar production from beet grown in Great Britain. Under a 1931 Act, they were entitled to weekly 'advances' during the year ending September 1932, based on their sugar production and linked with the price of sugar. The Act provided that, if prices rose in the two years ending September 1934, the advances under the 1931 Act would be repaid by deduction from the subsidies under the 1925 Act, but otherwise they were not repayable unless the manufacturer was wound up before October 1934. A company which had received such advances appealed against assessments on them, accepting that the subsidies under the 1925 Act were taxable but contending that the advances under the 1931 Act were not taxable. The CA rejected this contention and upheld the assessments, holding that the advances under the 1931 Act were trading receipts of the year in which they were received. The HL unanimoously upheld this decision. *Smart v Lincolnshire Sugar Co Ltd*, HL 1937, 20 TC 643; [1937] AC 697; [1937] 1 All ER 413.

'Interest relief grant' under Industry Act 1972

[64.13] Under powers in the *Industry Act 1972*, which provided for financial assistance 'to provide, maintain or safeguard employment in any part of the assisted areas', the Department of Trade and Industry paid £18,000 pa to a company (S) building a new factory. The DTI described the payments as an 'interest relief grant towards the interest costs of finance obtained from commercial sources'. S made trading losses which it surrendered to its parent company (T) as group relief. In their computations, S and T treated the payments from the DTI as non-taxable capital receipts. The Revenue rejected the claims on the basis that the payments were trading receipts. The Ch D upheld the Revenue's rejection of the claims, holding that the payments were trading receipts since they were designed to relieve S from paying interest which it would otherwise have had to pay. *Burman v Thorn Domestic Appliances (Electrical) Ltd*, Ch D 1981, 55 TC 493; [1982] STC 179.

[64.14] The Ch D reached a similar decision in the similar subsequent case of *Ryan v Crabtree Denims Ltd*, Ch D 1987, 60 TC 183; [1987] STC 402.

Wartime arrangements for flour-milling—'miller's remuneration'

[64.15] During the First World War, flour-milling was controlled by the Ministry of Food. Millers who had been trading before the war were entitled to a standard profit from their mill, described as the 'miller's remuneration', paying the Ministry any excess of their profit over the standard and receiving from the Ministry any deficiency. The Revenue issued assessments on the basis that 'remuneration' which the Ministry paid to a partnership under these provisions was a trading receipt. The CA unanimously dismissed the partnership's appeal. *Charles Brown & Co v CIR*, CA 1930, 12 TC 1256.

[64.16] A trader (D) had ceased flour-milling in 1929, and thus was not within the terms of arrangements introduced in 1939, which were similar to those described at **64.15** above. D resumed milling in 1941 but transferred the business to a company in September 1945. In 1942 D had been informed that the position of millers who were not trading in 1939 was under consideration, and 1949 he received payments from the Ministry on the basis laid down by the wartime arrangements. The Revenue included these payments in assessments on D's trading profits for 1944/45 and 1945/46. D appealed, contending firstly that the payments were gratuitous and not trading receipts, and alternatively that the accounts could not be re-opened. The Ch D rejected these contentions and upheld the assessments, holding that the payments were trading receipts, since at the time D ceased trading the question of whether he would be paid such remuneration was unsettled, and that his final accounts must be re-opened to include the payments as trading receipts. *Severne v Dadswell*, Ch D 1954, 35 TC 647; [1954] 1 WLR 1204; [1954] 3 All ER 243.

Property dealer—payments under War Damage Act

[64.17] A property-dealing company (L) received payments under the *War Damage Act 1943* in respect of some of its properties which had been damaged or destroyed by enemy action. The CA held that the payments were trading receipts, and the HL unanimously dismissed L's appeal against this decision. *London Investment & Mortgage Co Ltd v Worthington*, HL 1958, 38 TC 86; [1959] AC 199; [1958] 2 All ER 230.

Subsidies under Employment and Training Act 1973

[64.18] A manufacturing company (G) received a subsidy under the *Employment and Training Act 1973*, to enable it to retain employees instead of making them redundant. The Ch D held that the subsidy was a trading receipt. Walton J observed that the subsidy was to be used or employed in G's business, either as an undifferentiated receipt or as a contribution to reduce one of its ordinary trading expenses, the payment of wages. *Poulter v Gayjon Processes Ltd*, Ch D 1985, 58 TC 350; [1985] STC 174.

Grants to farmers

[64.19] See *Higgs v Wrightson* (ploughing grants), **27.3** FARMING; *Watson v Samson Bros* (grants towards rehabilitation of flood-damaged land), **27.4** FARMING; *White v Davies*, **66.56** TRADING PROFITS and *CIR v Biggar*, **66.57** TRADING PROFITS (payments under EC scheme for changing to meat production).

Insurance recoveries (ITTOIA 2005, s 106)

Payment for stock destroyed by fire and not wholly replaced

[64.20] A company (J) traded as a timber merchant. Most of its stock was destroyed by fire. The stock was valued in J's books at its cost (£160,824), but

J recovered £477,838 from its insurers. In fact, J only replaced part of the timber because the current demand was for timber of a different character. The KB held that the £477,838 was a trading receipt, and the HL unanimously upheld this decision. *Green v J Gliksten & Son Ltd*, HL 1929, 14 TC 364; [1929] AC 381.

Stock destroyed—date insurance recoveries should be credited

[64.21] See *Rownson Drew & Clydesdale Ltd v CIR*, 62.39 TRADING PROFITS.

Recovery under insurance against loss of profits

[64.22] In a Canadian case, a company's plant and premises were destroyed by fire. It recovered £43,000 under an insurance policy, and claimed that part of the recovery should be excluded from its profits as it exceeded the actual loss of profits. The PC rejected this contention, holding that the full amount was taxable. *R v British Columbia Fir & Cedar Lumber Co Ltd*, PC [1932] AC 441.

[64.23] In an Irish case, a baker's premises were destroyed by fire in 1942. He was able to continue trading in temporary premises, but with reduced turnover and increased costs. In November 1944 he received £1,300 under an insurance policy, having incurred professional expenses of £130 in settling his claim. Maguire J held that the £1,170 was a taxable trading receipt of the year ending April 1945. *Corr v Larkin*, HC(I) 1949, 3 ITC 13; [1949] IR 399.

Recovery under insurance against accidents to employees

[64.24] A company (G) received £937 under an insurance policy after the death of an employee (W). It paid £38 to W's widow to defray funeral expenses, etc. The Special Commissioners held that the £937 was a trading receipt and that the £38 was not an allowable deduction. The KB upheld this decision. *Gray & Co Ltd v Murphy*, KB 1940, 23 TC 225.

Abdication of Edward VIII—recovery under insurance policy

[64.25] A company which manufactured paper decorations had expected large orders for the coronation of Edward VIII. Following his abdication, it received £4,950 under an insurance policy. The Special Commissioners held that the £4,950s was a trading receipt, and the KB upheld their decision. *Mallandain Investments Ltd v Shadbolt*, KB 1940, 23 TC 367.

Assignment of endowment policy to doctor

[64.26] A hospital had taken out an endowment policy on the life of one of its doctors. In 1948, following the introduction of the National Health Service, the policy was assigned to the doctor. The Revenue assessed the surrender value on the doctor. The Ch D upheld the assessment. *Temperley v Smith*, Ch D 1956, 37 TC 18; [1956] 1 WLR 931; [1956] 3 All ER 92.

Recovery under insurance against death of engineer

[64.27] A company (K) secured a contract to construct a dam, having given an assurance that the work would be directed by a specific engineer (G). G died soon after the work had started, and K received £50,000 under an insurance policy. The Special Commissioners held that the £50,000 was a taxable receipt of K's trade. The CS unanimously upheld their decision. *Keir & Cawder Ltd v CIR*, CS 1958, 38 TC 23.

Life insurance policy on company director

[64.28] Between 1990 and 1993 a company (G) took out six life insurance policies on one of its directors. The director was diagnosed with cancer in 1997, and died in 1999. G recovered £585,999 under the insurance policies. The Revenue issued a corporation tax assessment on the basis that this was a taxable receipt of G's trade. The Special Commissioner allowed G's appeal, finding that the policies had been taken out at the request of one of G's shareholders (T), as a condition of agreeing to guarantee its bank overdraft. On the evidence, the policies had been 'taken out as a requirement of (T) entering into the agreement to provide funds'. Accordingly G 'had a capital purpose' in taking out the policies, and 'the policy moneys therefore were not part of the trading profits'. *Greycon Ltd v Klaentschi*, Sp C [2003] SSCD 370 (Sp C 372).

Recovery under insurance against late delivery of ships

[64.29] A shipping company (B) agreed to buy seven newly-built ships and took out insurance policies against delays in their delivery. The Special Commissioners held that the sums recovered under the policies were capital receipts. The Ch D upheld this decision. Buckley J observed that B did not own the ships when it took out the insurance, which was related to the acquisition of the ships. *Crabb v Blue Star Line Ltd*, Ch D 1961, 39 TC 482; [1961] 1 WLR 1322; [1961] 2 All ER 424.

Recovery of insurance against damage to jetty

[64.30] See *London & Thames Haven Oil Wharves Ltd v Attwooll*, **66.39** TRADING PROFITS.

Donations

Gift to professional jockey

[64.31] The owner of the winner of the 1921 Irish Derby gave the winning jockey (W) a present of £400. The Special Commissioners held that the £400 was a taxable receipt of W's vocation. The the Irish Supreme Court upheld their decision (by a 2–1 majority). Kennedy CJ observed that the payment was made 'for successfully accomplishing the object of his professional engagement, and that it was in the nature of a bonus or voluntary addition to the prescribed fee'. Fitzgibbon J observed that 'the voluntary character of the payment, viewed from the standpoint of the donor, does not necessarily exempt it from liability to assessment in the hands of the recipient'. *Wing v O'Connell*, SC(I) 1926, 1 ITC 170; [1927] IR 84.

Donation to ice rink from associated club

[64.32] A company operated an ice rink on a commercial basis, and provided facilities for curling to members of the public who paid admission charges. The company also leased rooms at a commercial rent to a club, the members of which were admitted at preferential rates. The charges which the company made for curling did not cover the cost of providing the quality of ice surface required, and the club made a donation of £1,500 to the company, fearing that otherwise the company might have to discontinue the provision of curling facilities. The company appealed against a corporation tax assessment, contending that the £1,500 should not be taxable. The CS unanimously rejected this contention, holding that the £1,500 was a trading receipt of the company. It was made to be used in the company's business, to supplement its trading revenue and to preserve its ability to continue to provide curling facilities. *CIR v Falkirk Ice Rink Ltd*, CS 1975, 51 TC 42; [1975] STC 434.

Foreign exchange gains

[64.33] A partnership which carried on business as fur merchants was appointed sole commission agent of a company dealing in furs exported from the USSR. The partnership paid the company a proportion of the value of the furs when they were imported, and deducted such payments, together with the agreed commission, from the sale proceeds. The transactions between the partnership and the company were in US dollars and, because of a fall in sterling when Britain abandoned the gold standard, the partnership derived a substantial exchange profit on the repayment of the sums which it had advanced. The Special Commissioners held that the exchange profit was part of the partnership's trading receipts, and the KB upheld their decision. *Landes Brothers v Simpson*, KB 1934, 19 TC 62.

[64.34] A tobacco company accumulated dollars to finance purchases of tobacco leaves from the USA. Because of wartime restrictions, the company was left with surplus dollars which it was required to sell to the Treasury. The sale resulted in an exchange profit. The Special Commissioners held that this was part of the company's trading profits, and the CA unanimously upheld this decision. Lord Greene observed that the acquisition of the dollars was 'an essential part of a contemplated commercial operation'. *Imperial Tobacco Co (of Great Britain and Ireland) Ltd v Kelly*, CA 1943, 25 TC 292; [1943] 2 All ER 119.

Interest and dividends

CROSS-REFERENCES

See 62.99 et seq. TRADING PROFITS for overseas interest and dividends ancillary to a business, and the cases noted at 68.56, 68.59 and 68.60 TRADING PROFITS for interest and dividends received by insurance companies.

Interest in arrear satisfied by debentures

[64.35] A company (S) held 5% debentures in another company (W), which was unable to pay the interest due. Following a reconstruction of W, S surrendered the debentures in exchange for similar 5% debentures in a new company (N), and surrendered the unpaid interest coupons in exchange for 7% debentures in N, of a face value equal to the amount of the unpaid interest. The Revenue included 75% of the face value of the 7% debentures in an assessment on S's trading profits (on the basis that their market value was only 75% of their face value). The CS unanimously dismissed S's appeal. *Scottish & Canadian General Investment Co Ltd v Easson*, CS 1922, 8 TC 265.

Current account interest

[64.36] A trading company received substantial interest on the current bank accounts which it held at its head office and its various branches. The Revenue issued a profits tax assessment charging tax on the basis that the interest was trading income. The company appealed, contending that it was investment income and was therefore not chargeable to profits tax. The Special Commissioners accepted this contention and allowed the appeal, and the KB upheld their decision. *CIR v Imperial Tobacco Co (of Great Britain & Ireland) Ltd*, KB 1940, 29 TC 1; [1940] 2 KB 287; [1940] 3 All ER 248.

Contango—payments in lieu of dividends

[64.37] A company (M) entered into contango operations on the Stock Exchange, profits or losses on which fell to be brought into its trading profits. In certain circumstances, it would be credited in its contango accounts with amounts equal to net dividends. The Revenue issued asessments on the basis that these amounts were trading receipts and not dividends. The KB dismissed M's appeal. *Multipar Syndicate Ltd v Devitt*, KB 1945, 26 TC 359; [1945] 1 All ER 298. (*Note*. The KB also held that there had been a 'discovery'—see 5.37 ASSESSMENTS.)

Underwriter—interest on securities deposited with Lloyd's

[64.38] A Lloyd's underwriter, neither resident nor ordinarily resident in the UK, received the interest on certain securities in full. The Revenue issued assessments on the basis that the interest formed part of his business profits. The Ch D upheld the assessments. *Owen v Sassoon*, Ch D 1950, 32 TC 101.

Whether taxed dividends can be included in trading profits

[64.39] A share-dealing company (F) made a large loss following a dividend-stripping operation (prior to *FA 1960*). The Revenue made a surtax direction on the basis that F's income consisted mainly of investment income. F appealed, contending that the stripped dividends were trading receipts. The HL unanimously rejected this contention and upheld the direction. *FS Securities Ltd v CIR*, HL 1964, 41 TC 666; [1965] AC 631; [1964] 3 All ER 691.

Shipping company—income from investments

[64.40] A shipping company (B) invested substantial amounts in a fund to finance replacement of its ships. It claimed loss relief on the basis that the income from the investments was trading income. The Special Commissioners rejected the claim and the CS unanimously dismissed B's appeal. *Bank Line Ltd v CIR*, CS 1974, 49 TC 307; [1974] STC 342.

Interest from funds to be used for paying trade liabilities

[64.41] A company (N) carried on the business of generating electricity from nuclear fuel. Its nuclear reactors had a life of about 30 years, after which they had to be shut down and decommissioned. It set funds aside to meet these future liabilities. It appealed against a corporation tax assessment, contending that its investment income from these funds should be treated as trading income, so that trading losses carried forward from previous years could be set against it. The Special Commissioners upheld the assessment, and the HL dismissed N's appeal. Lord Jauncey held that 'whether income from investments held by a business is trading income must ultimately depend upon the nature of the business and the purpose for which the fund is held'. The business of the appellant company was to produce and supply electricity, and the making of investments was not a part of that business. The investments which it had made had not been employed in the business of producing electricity during the year of assessment. The income from its investments could not be treated as trading income. *Nuclear Electric plc v Bradley*, HL 1996, 68 TC 670; [1996] STC 405; [1996] 1 WLR 529.

Interest received by solicitors

[64.42] A firm of solicitors received interest on short-term funds held in a clients' account. In its tax return, the firm treated this interest as trading income. HMRC issued an amendment on the basis that the interest could not be treated as trading income, but had to be taxed as savings income. The First-tier Tribunal allowed the firm's appeal. Judge Bishopp held that 'the interest was earned in the course of the solicitors' trading, and as an integral part of the trading activities'. On the evidence, 'the interest is properly to be regarded as part of the solicitor's trading income, because it was understood between solicitor and client that the interest would form part of the total fee'. *Barnetts v HMRC*, FTT [2010] SFTD 1074; [2010] UKFTT 286 (TC), TC00575. (*Note*. For a discussion of this case, see Taxation, 18 November

2010, p 21. Mike Truman commented that 'this case was very much decided on its particular facts' and that 'it would seem that in the normal day-to-day work of solicitors and other professional firms where interest arises on client accounts, this will continue to be treated as investment rather than earned income'.)

Bank interest received by estate agent

[64.43] See *Aplin v White*, 52.44 SAVINGS AND INVESTMENT INCOME.

Discount on bills

[64.44] See *Willingale v International Commercial Bank Ltd*, 62.47 TRADING PROFITS.

Prepayments and deposits

Unclaimed 'deposits' paid by customers

[64.45] The Ch D held that unclaimed 'deposits', paid for goods ordered but not collected by customers of a company trading as retail tailors, were trading receipts of the year in which they were received. *Elson v Prices Tailors Ltd*, Ch D 1962, 40 TC 671; [1963] 1 WLR 287; [1963] 1 All ER 231.

[64.46] A company (G) sold chemicals in returnable containers. It required customers to pay a refundable deposit in respect of these containers. Some customers did not return the containers or reclaim the deposits. Initially G accounted for tax on the basis that these deposits were trading receipts of the year in which they were received, in accordance with the decision in *Elson v Prices Tailors Ltd*, 64.45 above. However, following the decision in *Anise Ltd v Hammond*, 64.79 below, it submitted an error or mistake claim on the basis that it should not have treated the deposits as trading receipts. The Revenue rejected the claim and G appealed. The Special Commissioner dismissed G's appeal, applying the principles laid down in *Elson v Prices Tailors Ltd* and distinguishing *Anise Ltd v Hammond*. The Commissioner held that since about 20% of the deposits were not repaid, it was 'impossible to say that the appellant is merely holding the deposit for the customer. The straightforward analysis is that the deposit is a trading receipt just as the payment for the goods is a trading receipt but with the difference that about 80% of the deposits will have to be repaid, for which it is right to make a provision.' *Gower Chemicals Ltd v HMRC*, Sp C [2008] SSCD 1242 (Sp C 713).

Overpayments by customers

[64.47] A company (P) operated recruitment agencies which provided staff to its customers. Some customers made overpayments. P returned some of these overpayments to the customer, or set them against other liabilities. However, in some cases, P did not refund the overpayments, At the end of each financial year, P included these overpayments as receipts in its profit and loss account. Initially P treated these overpayments as taxable receipts. Subsequently it submitted claims for error or mistake relief on the basis that the effect of the decision in *Morley v Tattersall*, **64.77** below, was that these payments were not its property and that it should not be required to account for tax on them. HMRC rejected the claims and the First-Tier Tribunal dismissed P's appeal, distinguishing *Morley v Tattersall* on the grounds that in that case, the firm had held the funds 'in a fiduciary capacity', which was not the case here. The Upper Tribunal upheld this decision. Arnold J observed that obiter dicta of Sir Wilfrid Greene in *Morley v Tattersall* were 'a classic example of a judicial statement which is broader than was necessary for disposition of the case at hand and subsequently requires qualification.' He also specifically disapproved the Special Commissioners' decision in *Anise Ltd v Holland*, **64.79** below, observing that the Inspector who represented the Revenue in that case had failed to cite some important precedents. He concluded that 'the fact that a payment is made in circumstances such that the payer has a restitutionary claim to repayment of that sum does not mean that the recipient is not legally entitled to receive it. On the contrary, the recipient is legally entitled to receive and keep the money unless and until a claim for repayment is made.' On the evidence here, 'the mistaken payments are the property of (P), albeit that the customers have a claim for restitution'. *Pertemps Recruitment Partnership Ltd v HMRC*, UT [2011] STC 1346.

Prepayments for vehicle hire retained on sale of business

[64.48] A company had carried on a business of vehicle hire. It required its customers to make advance payments up to one year before the actual hire took place. These sums were included in its balance sheet as 'creditors (accruals and deferred income)' and were included in the profit and loss account as income in the following year, when the hiring actually took place. The company sold its business in October 1993. At that date, it held prepayments totalling £5,189,609, which it retained, in accordance with the terms of the sale agreement. In its accounts for the accounting period ending 31 July 1994, it declared a net loss of £1,556,670 on the sale of its business. For this purpose, the prepayments, together with a payment of £200,000 for goodwill, were netted off against a loss of £6,946,279 on the disposal of fixed assets. The Revenue included the prepayments in the assessment on the company's trading profits. The company appealed, contending that the amount of the prepayments did not represent 'profits arising or accruing' from its trade, and were not taxable. The Ch D rejected this contention and dismissed the appeal. Hart J held that the sale of the business removed any possible justification for deferring recognition of the profit earned by the relevant trade contracts. By virtue of this agreement, the profit 'could be both quantified and treated as made in the relevant accounting period'. Accordingly, it arose from the company's trade. *Tapemaze Ltd v Melluish, Ch D 2000*, 73 TC 167; [2000] STC 189.

Mauritius company—deposits received from customers

[64.49] A Mauritius company (T) sold liquefied petroleum gas in portable metal bottles. It required customers to pay a deposit for the bottles. The tax authority issued assessments charging tax on the basis that the deposits were trading receipts, and T appealed. The Mauritius Supreme Court upheld the assessments but the Privy Council allowed T's appeal, holding that 'sums received from, or for the benefit of, a customer that are to be held and ultimately paid to the customer without reduction fall to be treated as if they belong to the customer and are not trading receipts. The supplier has the use of the deposits and will be taxed on the profits earned by such use, but this does not make them trading receipts.' *Total Mauritius Ltd v Mauritius Revenue Authority*, PC [2011] UKPC 40; [2012] STC 100.

Rents received

Furnished letting of cinema

[64.50] A company (W) built and equipped a cinema with a cafe, and operated it successfully for a few months before letting it to another company for 21 years. The Revenue issued assessments on the basis that the whole of the rent receivable under the lease constituted trading income. The Commissioners upheld the assessments, and the KB dismissed W's appeal. *Windsor Playhouse Ltd v Heyhoe*, KB 1933, 17 TC 481.

Rents from surplus premises

[64.51] A company (B) sublet part of its premises which became surplus to its requirements. The Revenue issued assessments charging excess profits tax on the rent. The CA unanimously allowed B's appeal, holding that the rent was investment income. *CIR v Broadway Car Co (Wimbledon) Ltd*, CA 1946, 29 TC 214; [1946] 2 All ER 609.

[64.52] A company owned a hotel, which was requisitioned on the outbreak of war. It received an annual sum as compensation under the relevant legislation. The Special Commissioners held that the sums received were income from property and were not chargeable to national defence contribution. The KB upheld this decision. *CIR v Buxton Palace Hotel Ltd*, KB 1948, 29 TC 329.

[64.53] Two stockrooms of a paper manufacturing company (R) became surplus to its requirements following wartime restrictions on the manufacture of paper. One was let and the other was requisitioned by the Admiralty, whioch paid rent to R. The Revenue issued assessments charging excess profits tax on the rent, and R appealed, contending that it was investment income and was outside the scope of excess profits tax. The Special Commissioners rejected this contention and dismissed the appeal, holding that the rents were not investment income, since the letting was only temporary. The CA upheld this decision as one of fact. *Albert E Reed & Co Ltd v CIR*, CA 1948, 27 ATC 352.

Miscellaneous receipts

Receipts held to be taxable

Cemetery—lump sums in commutation of future charges

[64.54] A cemetery company received lump sums in commutation of its annual charge for the upkeep of grave spaces. It appealed against an assessment on these sums, contending that they should be treated as capital. The court rejected this contention and dismissed the appeal, holding that they were trading receipts. *Paisley Cemetery Co v Reith*, CE 1898, 4 TC 1.

Purchase and sale of wagons by colliery agents

[64.55] A company (T) carried on business as an agent for colliery companies, and bought railway wagons for its clients. Foreseeing a rise in prices, it purchased several wagons on its own behalf and subsequently sold them to a colliery company at a profit. The Special Commissioners held that the profit was part of T's business profits, chargeable to income tax, and the KB upheld their decision. *T Beynon & Co Ltd v Ogg*, KB 1918, 7 TC 125.

Company manufacturing and selling railway wagons

[64.56] A company (G) had manufactured railway wagons for many years, either selling them or hiring them out. The wagons which it hired out were capitalised in its accounts at cost plus a 'manufacturing profit' and depreciated year by year, the depreciation being allowed for tax purposes. G decided to discontinue hiring and sold those wagons for amounts considerably in excess of their depreciated value. The Special Commissioners held that the excess was a trading receipt, and the HL unanimously upheld their decision. Lord Dunedin observed that the wagons were not machinery or plant. Their sale was in the course of G's business of selling wagons, even though they had been hired out in the meantime. *Gloucester Railway Carriage & Wagon Co Ltd v CIR*, HL 1925, 12 TC 720; [1925] AC 469.

Consumable stores—contract assigned

[64.57] The Australian Government requisitioned some of the vessels of a shipping company (G) in 1916. Before this, G had already entered into a contract for the delivery to it of a large quantity of bunker coal, which would be surplus to G's requirements as a result of the requisition. G agreed to transfer this contract to another company (S) at a premium calculated on a tonnage basis. The Special Commissioners held that the amounts so received were part of G's trading profits, and the KB upheld their decision. *George Thompson & Co Ltd v CIR*, KB 1927, 12 TC 1091. (*Note.* See **63.123** TRADING PROFITS for another point at issue in this case.)

Railway sidings—allowances from railway company

[64.58] A railway company (G) constructed sidings at a quarry, the cost being borne by the company (H) which owned the quarry. G made an allowance to H of a proportion (up to 10%) of its receipts from traffic to and from the sidings. H appealed against assessments on its trading profits, contending that the sums which it received from G were capital receipts (and that the traffic charges which it paid to G were allowable deductions). The KB upheld the assessments, holding that, in computing H's assessable profits, the sums which it received from G should be set off against the traffic charges which it paid to G. *Westcombe v Hadnock Quarries Ltd*, KB 1931, 16 TC 137.

Credit draper

[64.59] A credit draper employed a number of 'travellers' to sell clothing for him in defined areas (or 'rounds'). The KB held that he was chargeable to income tax on certain receipts from 'rounds' which he had contracted to sell to three of his employees, but where they had not completed the purchase. *Bonner v Frood*, KB 1934, 18 TC 488.

Trading stamp scheme operator—sales of unredeemed stamps

[64.60] The proprietor of a trading stamp scheme sold stamps to retailers for distribution to their customers, who could 'redeem' them for 'gifts'. He appealed against assessments on his trading profits, contending that they should be calculated by reference to stamps redeemed, with the sale price (to the retailer) of unredeemed stamps being carried to a reserve. The Commissioners rejected this contention and determined the assessments on the basis that the sale proceeds should be included in his profits, less a provision of 2% for the redemption of unredeemed stamps. The CS unanimously upheld their decision. *Cowen (t/a Ideal Trading Stamp Co) v CIR; Cowen's Ideal Trading Stamp Co (Glasgow) Ltd v CIR*, CS 1934, 19 TC 155.

Defalcations made good by auditor

[64.61] From 1928 to 1934, two employees at a slate quarry misappropriated money by falsifying the wage accounts. After discovering the defalcations, the auditors admitted negligence by their staff and made good the full amount of the defalcations except for a small amount attributable to the period before they became auditors. The refund was made in 1934 and the KB held that it was a trading receipt of that year. *Gray v Lord Penrhyn*, KB 1937, 21 TC 252; [1937] 3 All ER 468.

Co-operative society 'dividends' on purchases

[64.62] A restaurant proprietor received a cash rebate (described as a 'dividend') from a co-operative society in respect of his purchases of meat from the society. The KB held that this was a trading receipt. *Pope v Beaumont*, KB 1941, 24 TC 78; [1941] 2 KB 321; [1941] 3 All ER 9.

Receipts linked with sales of shares

[64.63] An investment company (H) sold the shares of a trading company (R) in return for certain payments which were accepted as being capital, augmented by additional payments based on R's sales. These additional payments were to continue indefinitely, subject to an option to the purchaser of the shares (not exercised in the relevant periods) to commute them by paying a lump sum. The CA held that these additional payments were income of H. *CIR v 36/49 Holdings Ltd*, CA 1943, 25 TC 173.

[64.64] A steamship company (L) sold shares to an oil company (C) on terms whereby C agreed to pay L 50% of its commission on fuel and diesel oil supplied to L until the amounts so paid, together with the expressed consideration for the shares, equalled their par value. L appealed against an income tax assessment, contending that these payments were capital receipts for the sale of the shares. The Special Commissioners rejected this contention and dismissed the appeal, holding that the payments were trading receipts. The CA upheld this decision. *Lamport & Holt Line Ltd v Langwell*, CA 1958, 38 TC 193.

Sale of brine baths

[64.65] A company (H) had been formed to acquire and develop an estate in Lancashire. It had undertaken a variety of activities, which had been treated as a single composite trade for tax purposes. Its activities included running brine baths which it had bought in 1930. These baths were sold in 1935 at a substantial profit which was included in the assessment on H. H appealed, contending that the profit was capital. The Commissioners rejected this contention and dismissed the appeal, holding that the profit arose in the course of H's trade and was chargeable to income tax. The KB upheld their decision. *Hesketh Estates Ltd v Craddock*, KB 1942, 25 TC 1.

Pawnbroker—sale of unredeemed pledges

[64.66] A pawnbroking company could sell unredeemed pledges, but the surplus of the sale proceeds over the amount due to it was payable to the holder of the pawn ticket, if claimed by him within three or six years (dependent on the amount of the loan). The Special Commissioners held that the unclaimed surpluses were trading receipts, taxable at the end of the three or six years, and the KB upheld their decision. *Jays The Jewellers Ltd v CIR*, KB 1947, 29 TC 274; [1947] 2 All ER 762.

Shares allotted as consideration for sale of mining concessions

[64.67] A company (G), which dealt in gold concessions, transferred concessions which it had acquired to public companies formed for the purpose, being allotted shares in the companies at par as consideration for the concession transferred. The HL held that, in computing G's profits, the value of the shares at the time of the allotment should be brought in, both where the concession was held and transferred by G itself and where it was held and transferred by a company in which G held a controlling interest. The value to be credited was the 'money value' of the shares. The HL remitted the case to the Commissioners to determine this. *Gold Coast Selection Trust Ltd v Humphrey*, HL 1948, 30 TC 209; [1948] AC 459; [1948] 2 All ER 379.

Financial intermediary—receipt of exclusivity payment

[64.68] A company (C) carried on business as a financial intermediary. It received £25,000,000 from a life insurance company in return for entering into an exclusivity agreement. In its corporation tax return, it treated this £25,000,000 as a capital receipt. HMRC issued an amendment charging corporation tax on the basis that it was a trading receipt. C appealed. The First-tier Tribunal dismissed the appeal, holding that C had not disposed of 'anything in the nature of a capital asset'. The Upper Tribunal upheld this decision. Sales J held that the disputed payment was 'income earned by the appellant from use of its goodwill, not a capital sum received by it in return for giving up any part of its goodwill'. *Countrywide Estate Agents FS Ltd v HMRC*, UT [2011] UKFTT 470 (TCC); [2012] STC 511.

Sale of goods—repayment subsequently claimed by purchaser

[64.69] In a Ceylon case, an individual (S) arranged for a quantity of goods to be sold to a Chinese company, and received commission on the sale. The Chinese company subsequently discovered that some of the documents supplied by the vendor were forgeries, and claimed repayment from S. (In the event, none of the money was repaid to the Chinese company.) S appealed against an assessment on the commission which he had received, contending that the amounts which he had received were not legally his 'property' and thus were not assessable on him. The Privy Council rejected this contention and upheld the assessment. S had received the amount assessed, and the Ceylon Court had found as a fact that the money would not be repaid. *Ceylon Commissioner of Inland Revenue v Savundranayagam*, PC 1957, 67 TC 239.

Newsfilm service—payments from principal subscribers

[64.70] A company (B) was set up to provide a newsfilm service for subscribers. Its two principal shareholders and subscribers were the BBC and a company (R), who each agreed to make good 50% of any operating deficit of B by way of additional subscription. For this purpose they entered into a deed of covenant to make the payments annually. R deducted tax from its payment and B claimed repayment of the tax. The Special Commissioners rejected the claim, holding that the payment was a trading receipt and was not an annual payment subject to deduction of tax. The HL unanimously dismissed B's appeal. Lord MacDermott observed that 'both in substance and in form', it was a payment made to a trading company 'as a supplement to its trading revenue and in order to preserve its trading stability'. *British Commonwealth International Newsfilm Agency Ltd v Mahany*, HL 1962, 40 TC 550; [1963] 1 WLR 69; [1963] 1 All ER 88. (*Note*. See *British Broadcasting Corporation v Johns*, **57.11** STATUTORY BODIES, as to the deductibility of the additional subscription by the BBC.)

Card winnings of club proprietor

[64.71] The proprietor of a club, which provided a card-room for gambling by members, appealed against an assessment, contending that he regularly played cards with members and was invariably successful, and that the amounts of his winnings should be excluded from the assessment. The Commissioners dismissed his appeal, holding that his card winnings were part of his profits from the trade of running the club. The Ch D upheld their decision. *Burdge v Pyne*, Ch D 1968, 45 TC 320; [1969] 1 WLR 364; [1969] 1 All ER 467.

Research grants to medical practitioner

[64.72] A trading company made payments to a medical practitioner (W) to enable him to undertake research in radiaesthesia The Ch D held that the payments were receipts of W's profession. *Duff v Williamson*, Ch D 1973, 49 TC 1; [1973] STC 434.

Bookmaker—profits from transactions in sweepstakes tickets

[64.73] In an Irish case, a bookmaker had regularly purchased shares in Irish Hospitals Sweepstakes tickets which had drawn horses. Some of the races were run in Ireland and some in England. In his accounts, he included his winnings and losses relating to Irish races but not those relating to English races. The Revenue issued assessments on his estimated profits from transactions relating to English races. He appealed, contending that, as he did not attend English races and had no influence over the odds, his profits from English races were a separate activity from his business as a bookmaker. The HC(I) rejected this contention and dismissed his appeal, holding that he was carrying on a trade which included the purchase of sweepstakes tickets relating to races run in England, and that the profits were taxable. The SC(I) upheld this decision. *HH v Forbes*, SC(I) 1977, TL(I) 113.

Solicitor—amount owed by firm set against amount owed to firm

[64.74] A firm of solicitors discovered that one of its partners (D) had arranged for £90,000 to be withdrawn from the firm without authorisation. The firm took legal action against D, and required him to retire from the firm. D was also struck off the Roll of Solicitors by the Law Society. D had been entitled to a share of the firm's profits for 2004/05 and 2005/06. Rather than paying this to D, the firm set most of this against the amounts it was owed by D (which included legal costs as well as the original unauthorised withdrawal). D did not include the amounts which the firm had retained on his 2005/06 tax return. Following an enquiry, HMRC issued an amendment charging tax on the amounts in question. D appealed. The First-tier Tribunal dismissed his appeal, holding that he was chargeable to tax under *ITTOIA 2005* 'because he was entitled to the money irrespective of whether he received it'. *D Demetriou v HMRC*, FTT [2011] UKFTT 394 (TC), TC01249.

Exclusion of VAT in computing taxable receipts

[64.75] The Special Commissioners confirmed assessments on a certified accountant, finding that he had omitted some items of income from his accounts. The accountant appealed, contending *inter alia* that some of the fees which the Commissioners had included in his taxable receipts had included VAT. The CA remitted the case to the Commissioners to adjust the assessments by excluding the payments of VAT. (Certain other contentions by the accountant, who conducted his appeal in person, were rejected.) *Franklin v Holmes*, CA 1993, 66 TC 147; [1993] STC 720.

Repayments of amounts wrongly paid as VAT

[64.76] Four companies, which acted for VAT purposes as the representative members of large groups which carried on business as retailers, had accounted for VAT on amounts which were subsequently accepted not to be due, and had received substantial repayments, together with statutory interest. They treated these repayments as outside the scope of corporation tax. HMRC issued amendments to their self-assessments charging corporation tax on the repayments, and the companies appealed. The First-tier Tribunal dismissed the appeals, holding that 'the VAT repayments received by each of the appellants were trading receipts', and that 'the interest payments are chargeable to corporation tax under Case III of Schedule D'. The Upper Tribunal and the CA unanimously upheld this decision, holding inter alia that the fact that the companies had subsequently transferred the trades in the course of which the repayments had been made to a successor company did not mean that the receipts escaped the charge to corporation tax. *Shop Direct Group v HMRC (and related appeals)*, CA [2014] EWCA Civ 255; [2014] STC 1383.

Receipts held not to be taxable

Racehorse auctioneers—unclaimed balances

[64.77] A partnership (T) carried on the business of selling racehorses by auction. A condition of the terms of sale (dating back to 1847) was that the proceeds of sale would be sent only by post, and only on receipt of a written order. In the course of time, substantial unclaimed balances accumulated. Under the terms of the partnership agreement, balances not claimed within six years were credited to the partners. The Revenue issued assessments charging income tax on these amounts. T appealed, contending that, despite the treatment of these balances in its accounts, it regarded itself as liable to repay them whenever they were claimed. The CA allowed the appeal, holding that the unclaimed balances were not taxable as receipts of the business. They were not trading receipts when paid by the purchasers of the horses, and did not change their character on being credited to the partners. They remained the property of the customers. *Morley v Tattersall*, CA 1938, 22 TC 51; [1938] 3 All ER 296. (*Note*. This decision was distinguished in the subsequent cases of *Elson v Prices Tailors Ltd*, **64.45** above; *Pertemps Recruitment Partnership Ltd v HMRC*, **64.47** above; *Jays The Jewellers Ltd v CIR*, **64.66** above, and *Ceylon Commissioner of Inland Revenue v Savundranayagam*, **64.69** above.)

Share-dealing company—exercise of option to purchase

[64.78] A finance company (B) engaged in share-dealing, and its profits or losses on sales of shares were included in its trading profits. As part of a complex operation, B lent £200,000 and was given an option to acquire 100,000 shares in a mining company at £1 per share. It exercised the option, the option price of £100,000 being set against the loan of £200,000. The market value of the shares when the option was exercised exceeded their cost by £117,500, and the Revenue considered that this should be included in B's trading profits. The HL allowed B's appeal (by a 4-1 majority, Lord Guest dissenting), holding that no profit or loss arose until the shares were sold. *Varty v British South Africa Company*, HL 1965, 42 TC 406; [1966] AC 381; [1965] 2 All ER 395.

Advertising services—accidental overpayments by customers

[64.79] Four associated companies supplied advertising services. In some cases customers made accidental overpayments (for example, as a result of not cancelling bank standing orders). In many cases, the companies did not repay these amounts. Until 1993, they treated them in their accounts as creditors for six years, and then transferred them to the profit and loss accounts as 'exceptional items'. In 1993, they decided to reduce the period for which they were treated as creditors from six to two years (so that five years' worth of overpayments were transferred to their profit and loss accounts in the same year). The Revenue issued corporation tax assessments on the basis that these amounts should be treated as trading receipts. The companies appealed, contending that they were not trading receipts. The Special Commissioners accepted this contention and allowed the appeals in principle, applying the CA decision in *Morley v Tattersall*, **64.77** above, and observing that 'there is no suggestion that the member companies were conducting their business so as to receive the overpayments'. The Commissioners distinguished *Jays The Jewellers Ltd v CIR*, **64.66** above, on the grounds that in that case 'the surpluses did arise directly from the trading activities' and 'the retention of the surpluses was the most profitable part of the business and was fully authorised by law'. *Anise Ltd v Hammond (and related appeals)*, Sp C [2003] SSCD 258 (Sp C 364). (*Note*. This decision was disapproved by the Upper Tribunal in the subsequent case of *Pertemps Recruitment Partnership Ltd v HMRC*, **64.47** above. Arnold J observed that the Inspector who represented the Revenue had apparently failed to cite all the relevant precedents.)

65

Trading Profits—Miscellaneous Provisions (ITTOIA 2005, ss 107–259)

The cases in this chapter are arranged under the following headings.

Valuation of stock and work in progress (ITTOIA 2005, ss 173–186; CTA 2009, ss 162–171)

Valuation of trading stock on cessation (ITTOIA 2005, s 173; CTA 2009, s 162)

[65.1] In *Bradshaw v Blunden (No 1)*, 67.79 TRADING PROFITS, the Ch D held that a builder had ceased his business in 1945/46, and had retained certain houses as investments rather than as trading stock. The Ch D remitted the case to the General Commissioners to adjust the 1945/46 assessment. The builder contended that, as the assessment had initially been based on the preceding year's profits, it should continue to be so based. The Revenue contended that, since the Ch D had held that the business ceased in 1945/46, the assessment must be based on the actual year's profits, and that the closing trading stock must now be valued at its open market value. The Commissioners accepted the Revenue's contention and called for fresh evidence on the market value of the closing stock. The Ch D held that the assessment must be based on the actual profits and that the closing stock must be valued at its actual market value, but held that the Commissioners were not entitled to hear new evidence. *Bradshaw v Blunden (No 2)*, Ch D 1960, 39 TC 73. (*Note*. See **4.242** APPEALS for a preliminary point in this case.)

Goods subject to hire-purchase agreements

[65.2] A company (L) which sold furniture, etc. on hire-purchase agreements sold its business. The consideration included £225,717 for the 'hire-purchase debts'. The Revenue considered that this was a trading receipt. L appealed, contending that only part of the payment represented the value of the goods subject to hire-purchase agreements, which was trading stock, and that part of the payment represented the value of the right to receive future payments from the hirers, which was not taxable. (The purchaser contended that the whole of the payment related to trading stock.) The Special Commissioners upheld the purchaser's contention but the CS allowed L's appeal (by a 2-1 majority, Lord Carmont dissenting). *Lions Ltd v Gosford Furnishing Co Ltd & CIR*, CS 1961, 40 TC 256. (*Note*. The CS did not consider the value to be placed on the goods, or L's contention before the Commissioners that the part of the £225,717 not referable to the goods would not be a trading receipt. There was no further public hearing of the appeal.)

What constitutes stock (ITTOIA 2005, s 174; CTA 2009, s 163)

CROSS-REFERENCES

See **67** TRADING PROFITS for cases concerning whether property was held as trading stock. For whether assets were acquired as trading stock for the purposes of *TCGA, s 173**, see *Coates v Arndale Properties Ltd*, **71.271** CAPITAL GAINS TAX, and *Reed v Nova Securities Ltd*, **71.272** CAPITAL GAINS TAX.

Purchase of unwon oil

[65.3] An oil company (B) took over the assets of an Indian subsidiary. The consideration included £70,000 for the unwon oil in the wells of the subsidiary, which B credited to a 'Crude Oil Suspense Account'. As oil was produced, it debited an amount equal to two rupees per barrel to its revenue account. It claimed to deduct the amount so charged in the relevant year, as the cost of stock produced. The KB held that the £70,000 was capital expenditure and that none of it was deductible. *Hughes v British Burmah Petroleum Co Ltd*, KB 1932, 17 TC 286.

Greyhounds kept by company holding race meetings

[65.4] A company carried on the business of holding greyhound race meetings, maintaining a kennel of greyhounds to provide runners if there were insufficient entries by private owners. The KB held that the greyhounds were not trading stock and that the cost of their acquisition (other than replacements) was not an allowable deduction. *Abbott v Albion Greyhounds (Salford) Ltd*, KB 1945, 26 TC 390; [1945] 3 All ER 308. (*Note*. Wrottesley J also held that, although the greyhounds were fixed capital, they did not qualify as plant or machinery—see **8.54** CAPITAL ALLOWANCES.)

Brick manufacturer—cost of blaes

[65.5] A company (B) manufactured bricks from blaes or pit refuse obtained from colliery bings. It agreed to pay £1,475 for the materials forming two bings, paying a nominal rent for the land on which they stood. In its accounts it charged the £1,475 to capital, and debited an amount each year for the cost of the blaes actually used. The Commissioners held that the amount debited was deductible in computing B's profits, and the CS unanimously upheld their decision. *CIR v Broomhouse Brick Co Ltd*, CS 1952, 34 TC 1.

Purchase of unworked sand and gravel deposits

[65.6] A company (S) trading as sand and gravel dealers purchased two unworked deposits lying on certain land. It appealed against income tax assessments, contending that the deposits should be treated as trading stock. The CA unanimously rejected this contention, holding that S had acquired a capital asset rather than trading stock. *Stow Bardolph Gravel Co Ltd v Poole*, CA 1954, 35 TC 458; [1954] 1 WLR 1503; [1954] 3 All ER 637.

[65.7] Other cases involving payments for sand, gravel, minerals, etc., in which the question of whether the payments were for trading stock was implicitly or explicitly in dispute, include *Stratford v Mole & Lea* and *Old Silkstone Collieries v Marsh*, **38.5** MINING, ETC. RENTS AND ROYALTIES (short-term agreements); *Craigenlow Quarries Ltd v CIR*, **38.7** MINING, ETC. RENTS AND ROYALTIES (payments to work spoilbanks); *Alianza Co Ltd v Bell*, **63.97** TRADING PROFITS (purchase of nitrate deposits), and *Golden Horse Shoe (New) Ltd v Thurgood*, **63.124** TRADING PROFITS (purchase of dumps of tailings).

Goods subject to hire-purchase agreements

[65.8] In a stamp duty case, a company which sold goods on hire-purchase sold its business, including the benefit of its outstanding hire-purchase agreements. The KB held that the amount of the sale consideration attributable to the sale of goods (and accordingly exempt from stamp duty under the law then in force) should be estimated by reference to the likelihood of the goods being returned to the vendors. *Drages Ltd v CIR*, KB 1927, 46 TC 389.

Publican—whisky and spirits in bond

[65.9] The executors of a deceased publican continued the business until they sold the premises. The KB upheld the Revenue's contention that wine and spirits in bond which the publican had purchased were part of the stock belonging to the trade. *CIR v Smith's Executors*, KB(NI) 1951, 33 TC 5.

Standing timber

[65.10] In a case where the substantive issue has been superseded by subsequent changes in the legislation, the Ch D held that standing timber, owned by a company which managed woodlands, was not within the definition of 'trading stock'. *Coates v Holker Estates Company*, Ch D 1961, 40 TC 75.

[65.11] See also *Hood Barrs v CIR (No 2)*, **68.130** TRADING PROFITS, and *Hopwood v Spencer Ltd*, **68.131** TRADING PROFITS.

Unsold investments of share-dealing company

[65.12] A share-dealing company transferred certain investments to a subsidiary company. The Ch D upheld the Revenue's contention that the securities had been 'trading stock' of the parent company. *Alherma Investments Ltd v Tomlinson*, Ch D 1970, 48 TC 81; [1970] 1 WLR 466; [1970] 2 All ER 436. (*Note*. The case was heard with *General Reinsurance Co Ltd v Tomlinson*, 68.72 TRADING PROFITS.)

[65.13] See also *AB Ltd v MacGiolla Riogh*, 62.92 TRADING PROFITS.

Payments by cigarette manufacturer for cropping trees

[65.14] See *Mohanlal Hargovind of Jubbulpore v Central Provinces & Behar Commissioner of Income Tax*, 63.129 TRADING PROFITS.

Excess profits duty—trading stock-in-hand

[65.15] *FA 1921* gave relief from excess profits duty for 'trading stock-in-hand'. The legislation contained special provisions for forward contracts, and was considered in three cases. In *JW Greene & Co (Cork) Ltd v Revenue Commrs*, SC(I) 1926, 1 ITC 142, grain purchased for future delivery was held not to be within the relief as not being in the actual possession or under the control of the purchaser). A similar decision was reached in *Revenue Commrs v Latchford & Sons Ltd*, HC(I) 1928, 1 ITC 238. In *Benjamin Smith & Sons v CIR*, HL 1928, 7 ATC 135, grain bought by an importer under c.i.f. or 'ex-ship' contracts and sold while the cargoes were at sea was held not to qualify for the relief.

Basis of valuation of trading stock (ITTOIA 2005, s 175; CTA 2009, s 164)

Textile merchant—market value

[65.16] The KB held that, in valuing the stock of a textile merchant, 'market value' meant the price at which the merchant could purchase the goods in the market. If there were no spot market, this should be the price ruling at the time when contracts would have required to be made for delivery at the balance sheet date. (The case also involved the valuation of certain defective or potentially defective goods. The KB held that these should be valued at cost.) *Brigg Neumann & Co v CIR*, KB 1928, 12 TC 1191.

Assessment to rectify undervaluation of stock

[65.17] In an Indian case, a cotton mill had regularly shown in its accounts that its stock was valued at below cost or market value (without specifying the amount of the undervaluation). Its assessments up to and including 1926/27 had been based on the accounts. However, on ascertaining that the undervaluation at the end of 1925 (the basis period for 1926/27) was 63% of the true value, the tax authority made a supplementary assessment for 1926/27 on the amount of the undervaluation. On appeal, the Bombay High Court held that, in arriving at the 1926/27 assessments, any undervaluation in the opening stock should also be corrected. The PC upheld this decision. *Bombay Commissioner of Income Tax v Ahmedabad New Cotton Mills Co Ltd*, PC 1929, 8 ATC 574.

Whether all stock should be valued at either cost or market value

[65.18] In an excess profits tax case, a company (C) trading as wine and spirit merchants valued part of its stock at cost and part at market value (which was lower than cost). The Revenue issued an assessment on the basis that the whole of the stock should be valued at cost, the aggregate cost being lower than the aggregate market value. The Commissioners allowed C's appeal, holding that its method of valuation was acceptable, and the KB upheld this decision. *CIR v Cock Russell & Co Ltd*, KB 1949, 29 TC 387; [1949] 2 All ER 889.

Cotton industry—payments under special wartime arrangements

[65.19] Under wartime arrangements, a company trading as cotton spinners paid £55,087 to the Cotton Controller, this being the amount by which the current value of cotton which it held, and required to meet existing yarn contracts, exceeded the amount which it had paid for the cotton. It was agreed that the £55,087 was an allowable deduction in computing the company's profits, but the Revenue assessed the company on the basis that it was an addition to the cost of the cotton, to be taken into account in valuing its trading stock. The Special Commissioners allowed the company's appeal, holding that the payment was not an addition to the cost of the cotton, and the HL upheld this decision. *Ryan v Asia Mill Ltd*, HL 1951, 32 TC 275.

Cotton spinner—whether base stock system permissible

[65.20] A cotton-spinning company used in its accounts the 'base stock' system under which certain cotton, including cotton on the machines, was included in the accounts at a fixed price, which, with some modification, was accepted for tax purposes up to 1947/48. For 1948/49, however, the Revenue issued assessments on the basis that all stocks should be valued at cost (market value being higher). The CA upheld the assessments, holding that the base stock system did not correctly ascertain the full amount of the profits or gains, and that the stock should be included at cost (being lower than market value). *Patrick v Broadstone Mills Ltd*, CA 1953, 35 TC 44; [1954] 1 WLR 158; [1954] 1 All ER 163.

Whether LIFO or FIFO to be used

[65.21] In a Canadian case, a manufacturing company, which used metals as its raw materials, had valued its stock for many years by the FIFO method. For 1947, when the prices of the metals which it used greatly increased, it valued its stock by the LIFO method. The Privy Council held that the LIFO method was not appropriate for tax purposes and the fact that a method was appropriate for commercial accountancy purposes was not conclusive of its suitability for tax purposes. *Minister of National Revenue v Anaconda American Brass Co Ltd*, PC 1955, 34 ATC 330; [1956] AC 85; [1956] 1 All ER 20.

Whether overheads must be included in valuation of cost

[65.22] A manufacturing company (D) included its work in progress in its accounts at direct cost (materials and labour) only. The Revenue issued assessments on the basis that indirect costs (a proportion of indirect factory and office expenses) should be taken into account. The Special Commissioners found that the accountancy profession permitted either method, but held that, for tax purposes, factory overheads (although not other overheads) must be taken into account. The Ch D allowed D's appeal, holding that the Commissioners' findings did not justify a requirement to change from the direct cost method, which was not inconsistent with income tax rules. The HL upheld this decision. Lord Reid observed that 'whatever method is followed, it must be applied consistently'. The real question was 'what method best fits the circumstances of a particular business. And if a method has been applied consistently in the past, then it seems to follow that it should not be changed unless there is good reason for the change sufficient to outweigh any difficulties in the transitional year.' *Duple Motor Bodies Ltd v Ostime*, HL 1961, 39 TC 537; [1961] 1 WLR 739; [1961] 2 All ER 167.

Shoe retailer—market value—selling expenses

[65.23] A company (B) which sold shoes valued its stock at replacement value less cost, taking as replacement value the estimated retail price less its overall gross profit margin. The Revenue issued an assessment on the basis that the stock should have been valued at the lower of cost and market value, treating market value as the expected retail price. The HL dismissed B's appeal. Lord Reid observed that the application of the principles of commercial accounting was 'subject to one well-established though non-statutory principle. Neither profit nor loss may be anticipated.' A trader may have 'made such an improvident contract in year 1 that he will certainly incur a loss in year 2, but he cannot use that loss to diminish his liability for tax in year 1'. *BSC Footwear Ltd v Ridgway*, HL 1971, 47 TC 495; [1972] AC 544; [1971] 2 All ER 534.

Confectionery manufacturer—depreciation of stock

[65.24] A company (M) manufactured confectionery. In its tax computation, it claimed a deduction for the cumulative depreciation of its stock. The Revenue issued an assessment to cancel the deduction, and the company appealed. The Special Commissioners allowed the appeal and the HL unanimously upheld their decision. Lord Hoffmann held that treating an increase in stock value as if it was revenue 'may have been the only practical method when record-keeping was not sufficiently sophisticated to enable one to make a meaningful attribution of costs in one year to sales in some future year. It is not, however, the philosophy of SSAP 9, which permits the cost of unsold stock to be carried over into future years and set against future sales.' Nothing in the relevant legislation should be construed as preventing 'depreciation (or any other cost) being deducted in a subsequent year if that is calculated to give a true and fair view of the profits'. *Mars UK Ltd v Small*, HL 2007, 78 TC 442; [2007] STC 680; [2007] UKHL 15; [2007] 2 All ER 440. (*Note*. For HMRC's revised practice following this decision, see Business Income Manual, BIM33190.)

Whisky distiller—depreciation of stock

[65.25] A company distilled whisky, which it retained in stock for up to 18 years while it matured. In its tax computations, it claimed deductions for the cumulative depreciation of its stock. For 1995 to 2001, the Revenue agreed to allow deductions. However, in 2002 the Revenue ruled that the deduction was not allowable for tax purposes. The company appealed. The Special Commissioners allowed the appeal and the HL unanimously upheld their decision. Lord Hope of Craighead implicitly disapproved *obiter dicta* of Lord Reid in *Duple Motor Bodies Ltd v Ostime*, 65.22 above. He observed that 'accounting principles have moved on since 1961. What may have been regarded as unacceptable then need not be regarded as unacceptable now. The golden rule is that the profits of a trading company must be computed in accordance with currently accepted accounting principles.' *William Grant & Sons Distillers Ltd v HMRC*, HL 2007, 78 TC 442; [2007] STC 680; [2007] UKHL 15; [2007] 2 All ER 440. (*Note*. The HL heard the case with *Mars UK Ltd v Small*, 65.24 above. For HMRC's revised practice following this decision, see Business Income Manual, BIM33190.)

Change in treatment of unfinished contracts

[65.26] See *Pearce v Woodall-Duckham Ltd*, 65.42 below.

Sale of stock to unconnected person (ITTOIA 2005, s 176; CTA 2009, s 165)

[65.27] A building company (R) ceased trading and sold its stock (consisting of two blocks of flats) to another company at less than market value. The Revenue issued an assessment on the basis that the value of the stock should be brought into account, applying the principles in *Sharkey v Wernher*, 65.29 below. R appealed, contending that the stock should be valued at the agreed sale price. The Special Commissioners accepted this contention and allowed R's appeal, and the Ch D upheld their decision. *Moore v RJ Mackenzie & Sons Ltd*, Ch D 1971, 48 TC 196; [1972] 1 WLR 359; [1972] 2 All ER 549.

Sale of stock to connected person (ITTOIA 2005, s 177; CTA 2009, s 166)

Chick hatchery—credit for chicks transferred to separate poultry farm

[65.28] A partnership carried on a chick hatchery and a poultry farm. It was accepted that the two activities were separate businesses. The chicks were advertised for sale at specified prices but only about 50% were sold in this way. The rest were transferred to the farm's brooder houses or sold by auction. At the relevant time, the cost of the chicks was 7d each but they fetched only 4d on average at auction. The Revenue considered that in computing the profits of the hatchery, the price of the chicks transferred to the farm should be treated as the production cost of 7d per chick. The KB allowed the partnership's appeal, holding that the price should be treated as the market price of 4d per chick. *Watson Bros v Hornby*, KB 1942, 24 TC 506; [1942] 2 All ER 506.

Stud farm—credit for horses withdrawn for private purposes

[65.29] A woman carried on a stud farm, which was accepted as being a trade. She owned a horse racing stables, which was not treated as a trading activity. Five horses were transferred from the stud farm to the racing stables. The market value of the horses considerably exceeded the cost of breeding them. The HL held that the market value should be credited in the stud farm profits (by a 4-1 majority, Lord Oaksey dissenting). *Sharkey v Wernher*, HL 1955, 36 TC 275; [1956] AC 58; [1955] 3 All ER 493. (*Note.* This is the leading case establishing the principle that, where trading stock is disposed of otherwise than by way of trade, the market value should be included for tax purposes. For the Revenue practice in the light of this decision, see Revenue Pamphlet IR 131, SP A32, 18 June 1979. See also *FA 2008, s 37*)

Goods acquired from controlling shareholder at undervalue

[65.30] A UK company, formed in 1936, sold goods imported from its sole shareholder (a German trading in Berlin). He died in 1938. The company claimed that it had purchased the goods from him at an undervalue (to avoid controls imposed by the Nazi Government on German exports) and it claimed (by way of error or mistake relief) to substitute the market value in the company's accounts. The Special Commissioners rejected the claim and the KB dismissed the company's appeal. *Julius Bendit Ltd v CIR*, KB 1945, 27 TC 44.

Consideration partly satisfied by allotment of shares

[65.31] A newly-formed company (S) acquired stock, with other assets, from its managing director (H) in return for a cash payment of £10,500 and the allotment of shares with a par value of £29,997. The stock and other assets in question had previously belonged to a company which had gone into receivership, and H had purchased it from the receiver for £2,493. The cash payment of £10,500 was apportioned on the basis that £2,493 related to the stock and the remaining £8,007 was attributed to land and buildings, plant and machinery, fixtures and fittings and goodwill. S appealed against an estimated assessment, contending that it should be allowed to deduct £21,868 as the market value of the stock. The Revenue considered that S could only deduct the cash paid of £2,493. The Special Commissioners held that S was entitled to treat the value of the shares allotted to H as part of the consideration for the stock, and fixed the market value of the stock as £10,000. The CA upheld their decision as one of fact. *Osborne v Steel Barrel Co Ltd*, CA 1942, 24 TC 293; [1942] 1 All ER 634. (*Note.* For a sequel to this case, see *Steel Barrel Co Ltd v Osborne (No 2)*, **5.31** ASSESSMENTS.)

Share-dealing company—acquisition of shares from associated company

[65.32] As part of the reconstruction of the estate of a deceased person, an investment-dealing company (F) was formed to take over some of the unsold investments of another investment-dealing company (S) which had suffered financial difficulties and was being wound up. The investments were acquired for £1,029,958, which had been their cost to S. The purchase price was satisfied by the issue to S of fully paid-up shares of £620,030 in F, and the taking over by F of liabilities of £409,928 of S. The Revenue issued an assessment on the basis that, in computing F's profits, the debit for the investments should be £363,173 (which was the Revenue's estimate of their market value) or, alternatively, that the £409,928 was the true consideration for them. The Commissioners allowed F's appeal and the HL upheld their decision, holding that the Revenue had failed to establish that the value of the investments was less than the nominal value of their cost to F, so that the £1,029,958 should be debited as their cost. (Lord Greene observed that the bargain between the two companies was not 'in any way colourable or a device to circumvent the Revenue'.) *Craddock v Zevo Finance Co Ltd*, HL 1946, 27 TC 267; [1946] 1 All ER 523.

Share-dealing company—disposal of shares at undervalue

[65.33] As part of a complex dividend-stripping operation, a share-dealing company (P) sold to its parent company for £205,000 investments forming part of its trading stock and having a realisable market value of £835,505, and sold War Loan to a fellow-subsidiary (B) for £10,000 four days after it had purchased it for £105,525. The Revenue considered that the sales of the investments which had been held as stock were not trading transactions and, applying the principles laid down in *Sharkey v Wernher*, **65.29** above, their market value should be substituted for the agreed sale price. With regard to the sale of the War Loan, neither the purchase nor the sale was a trading transaction and the relative figures should be eliminated from the computation of P's profits. The Special Commissioners upheld the Revenue's contentions and the CA dismissed P's appeal. *Petrotim Securities Ltd v Ayres*, CA 1963, 41 TC 389; [1964] 1 WLR 190; [1964] 1 All ER 269.

Share-dealing company—acquisition of securities at undervalue

[65.34] In *Petrotim Securities Ltd v Ayres*, **65.33** above, a share-dealing company (B) purchased War Loan from an associated company for £10,000 and sold it shortly afterwards in the open market for £104,918. B's parent company (R) claimed that the result of this transaction was that B had made a profit out of which it could declare a dividend. The Special Commissioners rejected this contention and the Ch D dismissed R's appeal. Applying the decision in *Petrotim Securitiesv Ayres*, **65.33** above, and the principles laid down in *Sharkey v Wernher*, **65.29** above, the acquisition of War Loan should be brought into the computation at its market value (with the result that there was no profit). *Ridge Securities Ltd v CIR*, Ch D 1963, 44 TC 373; [1964] 1 WLR 479; [1964] 1 All ER 275.

Property-dealing company—profit on sale of property

[65.35] A company (J) was incorporated in May 1959. Two months previously, its controlling shareholder (R) had agreed to purchase a hotel and an adjoining property for £88,000, and had paid a deposit of £8,800 (of which £7,000 was agreed as relating to the hotel). In September 1959 he authorised the vendors to convey the hotel to J for £72,000. J paid the vendors the balance of £65,000. It subsequently cleared the site, and sold it for £155,000 in February 1960. The Revenue issued an assessment charging income tax on the profit. J appealed, contending that it should be treated as having acquired the property from R at a market value of £150,000, rather than at its actual cost of £72,000. The Special Commissioners rejected this contention and dismissed the appeal, and the Ch D upheld their decision. Plowman J observed that the transaction 'was not a gift or a sale by (R) to the company at an undervalue, but a purchase by the company of trading stock at a price which had been fairly negotiated between (R) and the vendors'. *Jacgilden (Weston Hall) Ltd v Castle*, Ch D 1969, 45 TC 685; [1969] 3 WLR 839; [1969] 3 All ER 1110.

Land-dealing company—sale of land to parent company at undervalue

[65.36] A company (W) acquired the share capital of a land-dealing company (B). Later the same day B sold to W, for £4,175, land which it had acquired for £3,575, and W resold the land for £40,000. When the Revenue became aware that W had resold the land at a substantial profit, they raised further assessments on the basis that B should be treated as having disposed of the land for its market value of £40,000, rather than for the actual price of £4,175. The Ch D upheld the further assessments, holding on the evidence that the sale to W was not in the course of B's trade. *Skinner v Berry Head Lands Ltd*, Ch D 1970, 46 TC 377; [1970] 1 WLR 1441; [1971] 1 All ER 222. (*Note*. For another issue in this case, see **5.78** ASSESSMENTS.)

Tax avoidance scheme—purchase from associated company at overvalue

[65.37] A company (D) owned development rights in an estate. Its controlling director entered into a tax avoidance scheme (similar to the scheme in *Ransom v Higgs*, **59.99** TRADING INCOME) with the object of siphoning £60,000 of the profits from the development into the hands of trustees. The scheme involved the sale of the rights by D for £2,250 and their re-acquisition by K, a development company also controlled by D's controlling director, for £77,250. K appealed against the relevant assessment, contending that the £77,250 should be allowed as a deduction in computing its profits. The Special Commissioners rejected this contention and dismissed the appeal, and the HL unanimously upheld this decision. On the evidence, the £77,250 was a price dictated by the tax avoidance scheme, rather than a price paid by K as a free agent acting from commercial motives in its own interest. Therefore it was not paid wholly and exclusively for the purposes of K's trade. *Kilmorie (Aldridge) Ltd v Dickinson (and associated appeals)*, HL 1974, 50 TC 1; [1974] STC 539; [1974] 1 WLR 1594; [1974] 3 All ER 949. (*Note*. The case was heard with *Ransom v Higgs*, **59.99** TRADING INCOME.)

Manufacturing company—purchase at overvalue from subsidiary

[65.38] See *CIR v Huntley & Palmers Ltd*, **63.133** TRADING PROFITS.

Purchase from associated Swiss company—whether at overvalue

[65.39] See *Rochester (UK) Ltd v Pickin*, **29.8** FURTHER ASSESSMENTS: LOSS OF TAX.

Sale of property at undervalue

[65.40] See *CIR v Spencer-Nairn*, **72.14** INHERITANCE TAX.

Valuation of work in progress (ITTOIA 2005, ss 182–185)

Payment for right to complete unfinished contracts

[65.41] A company (C) acquired the business of a firm of public works contractors as a going concern for £180,000, and claimed a deduction for £80,000 of this in computing its profits, as representing the cost of the right to complete the unfinished contracts of the business acquired. The Commissioners rejected the claim and the CA unanimously dismissed C's appeal, holding that the whole of the £180,000 was capital expenditure. *City of London Contract Corporation Ltd v Styles*, CA 1887, 2 TC 239.

Accrued profit on long-term contracts

[65.42] A company (W) was engaged in construction work under long-term contracts. Before 1969, it had included work in progress on unfinished contracts in its accounts at cost, but in 1969 it decided to bring in the estimated accrued profit on these contracts and elected to be assessed to tax accordingly. It appealed against its corporation tax assessment for that year, contending that the accrued profit before 1969, amounting to £579,874, on its opening work in progress should not be treated as taxable. The Ch D rejected this contention, holding that the £579,874 was a taxable receipt of 1969, the year in which it was first revealed and brought into account. The CA unanimously upheld this decision. *Pearce v Woodall-Duckham Ltd*, CA 1978, 51 TC 271; [1978] STC 372; [1978] 1 WLR 832; [1978] 2 All ER 793. (*Note*. For HMRC's interpretation of this decision, see Business Income Manual, BIM34005.)

Progress payments under long-term contracts of architects

[65.43] An architects' practice was transferred from a firm to an unlimited company in 1975. The practice involved mainly long-term contracts relating to large buildings, under which the firm was entitled to, and received, substantial 'progress payments' at various stages of the contracts. The Revenue having objected to accounts on the cash basis, the accounts submitted were on an earnings basis. Under a formula generally accepted for architects, the work in progress included a fraction of the estimated profit from uncompleted contracts, this fraction never being more than 40% even at the later stages. The progress payments on uncompleted contracts were not credited to profit and loss. As a result, in the final accounts showed closing work in progress of £2.9m, excluding accumulated progress payments of £5.1m which were not included in the profits. (The uncompleted contracts were subsequently completed by the company which took over the practice.) The Revenue considered that the progress payments should be credited for tax purposes as they became due, and that, as the final accounts were not submitted until 1979, it was not bound by them until then, and that they should be re-written in the light of the more accurate information then available as to the profits on the contracts uncompleted at 1975. The partnership contended that the accounts, having been drawn up on correct accountancy principles, provided the proper measure of the profits or losses for tax purposes and that the assessments should be determined accordingly. The Special Commissioners accepted the partnership's contention and the Ch D upheld their decision. Warner J held that, since the accounts had been drawn up on the correct principles of commercial accounting, the Revenue were not entitled to treat them as still open for as long as it might take to ascertain whether subsequent events proved or disproved the accuracy of estimated items in them. Warner J also rejected the Revenue's contention that the accounts anticipated losses, holding that the purpose of drawing up architects' accounts in the way done was to avoid anticipating profits which had not yet been earned and ascertained. *Symons v Weeks (as personal representative of Lord Llewelyn-Davies) & Others*, Ch D 1982, 56 TC 630; [1983] STC 195.

Building contractor

[65.44] Following an enquiry, HMRC formed the opinion that the accounts submitted by a building contractor (S) seriously understated the value of his work in progress, and issued 'discovery' assessments covering the years 1994/95 to 2001/02. S appealed. The First-tier Tribunal was 'not impressed' by the evidence given by S's accountant, who had stated that he had 'in general not included work in progress in the accounts'. The tribunal noted that this ignored the requirements of SSAP9 and FRS5, and held that this was 'negligent conduct' within *TMA, s 29(4)*. The tribunal reviewed the evidence in detail and allowed the appeals in part, reducing the assessments for 1997/98 to 2001/02 and discharging the assessments for 1994/95 to 1996/97. The Upper Tribunal dismissed S's appeal against this decision. Arnold J held that the First-tier Tribunal had been entitled to conclude that S's accounts did not comply with standard accounting practice; that income should have been brought into account when S made an application for payment; and that S's accountant had been guilty of 'negligent conduct'. *L Smith v HMRC*, UT [2011] UKUT 270 (TCC); [2011] STC 1724.

Payment for benefit of contract with suppliers

[65.45] See *John Smith & Son v Moore*, **63.99** TRADING PROFITS.

Completion of contracts after sale, etc. of business

[65.46] See *Southern v Cohen's Executors*, **61.12** TRADING INCOME; *Parker v Batty*, **61.13** TRADING INCOME, and *Sethia v John*, **61.14** TRADING INCOME.

Determinations by Commissioners (ITTOIA 2005, s 186; CTA 2009, s 171)

[65.47] A business was sold, and the vendor appealed against assessments for his final years of trading. At the hearing of the appeal, the General Commissioners purported to determine the value to be placed on the closing stock. The purchaser was not a party to the hearing. The CS unanimously upheld the Revenue's contention that, since the purchaser had not been party to the proceedings, the Commissioners' decision was not a valid determination under what is now *ITTOIA 2005, s 186*. *CIR v Barr (No 2)*, CS 1955, 36 TC 455.

[65.48] The CS held that a determination by General Commissioners under what is now *CTA 2009, s 171* was one of fact and there was no ground for interfering with it. *Kirkcaldy Linoleum Market Ltd v Duncan & CIR*, CS 1965, 44 ATC 66.

Disposal and acquisition of know-how (ITTOIA 2005, ss 192–195)

[65.49] In an excess profits duty case, a UK company (B) agreed with an American company to exchange information as to patents and secret processes, the agreement specifying the respective territories in which each should exploit such patents and processes. B was to receive £25,000 per annum for ten years, provided that information it supplied enabled the American company to manufacture a satisfactory product. The Revenue issued assessments on the basis that the annual sums were profits of B's trade. B appealed, contending that they were instalments of a capital sum for the sale of an asset. The Special Commissioners rejected this contention and dismissed the appeal, and the CA unanimously upheld their decision. *British Dyestuffs Corporation (Blackley) Ltd v CIR*, CA 1924, 12 TC 586.

[65.50] A company (E) with a worldwide trade manufacturing pharmaceuticals carried on business in Burma through an agency. It agreed to assist the Burmese Government in setting up an industry there. It provided certain services for an annual fee, which was accepted as subject to tax, and also agreed to disclose secret processes and other information in return for a 'capital sum of £100,000'. The Revenue included this £100,000 in an assessment on E's trading profits. The HL allowed E's appeal, holding (by a 3–2 majority, Lords Morton and Keith dissenting) that the £100,000 was a capital receipt. *Evans Medical Supplies Ltd v Moriarty*, HL 1957, 37 TC 540; [1958] 1 WLR 66; [1957] 3 All ER 718.

[65.51] A company (R) entered into several different agreements with companies in various countries for the sale of information relating to the manufacture of aero-engines. The CA held that the sums which R received under the agreements were trading receipts, and the HL unanimously upheld their decision. *Jeffrey v Rolls-Royce Ltd*, HL 1962, 40 TC 443; [1962] 1 WLR 425; [1962] 1 All ER 801.

[65.52] The decision in *Jeffrey v Rolls-Royce Ltd*, **65.51** above, was applied in the similar subsequent case of *Musker v English Electric Co Ltd*, HL 1964, 41 TC 556.

[65.53] A company (ICI) granted licences or sub-licences to seven overseas companies for the use of certain patents relating to man-made fibres, including one patent of which it was itself a licensee from another company (C). The agreements provided that ICI would provide technical assistance and that, in return for lump sums payable in instalments, ICI and C would not sell or manufacture similar fibres in the licensees' territories for a stipulated period . ICI appealed against assessments on its trading profits, contending that the lump sum payments in respect of the covenants against competition were capital receipts. The Special Commissioners accepted this contention and allowed the appeal, and the CA unanimously upheld their decision. The covenants against competition, being ancillary to patent licences granted for the term of the respective patents, were part and parcel of transactions which, taken as a whole, constituted dispositions by ICI of part of its fixed capital. *Murray v Imperial Chemical Industries Ltd*, CA 1967, 44 TC 175; [1967] Ch 1038; [1967] 2 All ER 980.

[65.54] A company (W), which manufactured power tools, had a considerable export trade. Under threat of Indian legislation to restrict imports, an Indian company (R) was set up to manufacture power tools there. W subscribed for 9,000 of the 20,000 shares in R, supplying plant and equipment as consideration for 5,375 of these and supplying drawings and 'know-how', etc. as consideration for the remaining 3,625. The Revenue issued an assessment on W on the basis that the market value of the 3,625 shares was a trading receipt. The Ch D allowed W's appeal, holding that the transaction was capital. *Wolf Electric Tools Ltd v Wilson*, Ch D 1968, 45 TC 326; [1969] 2 All ER 724.

[65.55] A company received £68,000 for the sale of 'know-how' to an overseas consortium. It appealed against corporation tax assessments, contending that the £68,000 was a capital receipt. The Special Commissioners rejected this contention and dismissed the appeal, holding that it was a trading receipt, and the Ch D upheld this decision. *Coalite & Chemical Products Ltd v Treeby*, Ch D 1971, 48 TC 171.

[65.56] A UK company manufactured caravans. Following the cessation of its export business, it helped to form a Belgian company (R) to make and sell caravans abroad. It supplied relevant information in return for 25% of the shares in R. It appealed against assessments for the relevant periods, contending that the shares were a capital receipt. The Commissioners rejected this contention, holding that the value of the shares was a trading receipt, and the CS upheld their decision. *Thomsons (Carron) Ltd v CIR*, CS 1976, 51 TC 506; [1976] STC 317.

[65.57] A company director (X) invented a specialist product (the details of which are not fully set out in the tribunal decision). He licensed the product to a company (U) of which he was the managing director and his wife was the controlling shareholder. U sold the product to the US Government Department of Defence, and paid X sums which were described as 'licence fees'. The First-Tier Tribunal upheld assessments on X charging tax on the basis that these payments were trading income, applying the principles laid down in *Jeffrey v Rolls-Royce Ltd*, **65.51** above, and finding that 'the beneficial ownership of all the IP rights remained throughout with (X) as inventor'. (The tribunal allowed appeals against alternative assessments which HMRC had issued on the basis that the fees were employment income rather than trading income, and against assessments issued on the basis that the payments were 'annual payments' within *ICTA 1988, s 349*.) *XX v HMRC (and related appeals)*, FTT [2010] UKFTT 419 (TC); [2011] SFTD 72, TC00689. (*Note*. For another issue in this case, taken to the Upper Tribunal, see **5.107** ASSESSMENT.)

Time receipts arise

[65.58] A UK company (J) sold secret processes and know-how to an Italian company (B) for 410,000,000 lire, payable in instalments. Most of the consideration was to be used in purchasing shares in B. (The consideration had originally been intended to take the form of fully-paid shares in B, and the arrangements made were entered into because of certain requirements of

Italian law which would have applied if the consideration for the shares had not been cash.) The Special Commissioners held that the consideration was a trading receipt, and that the cash instalments were taxable when they became due. The CA unanimously dismissed J's appeal. *John & E Sturge Ltd v Hessel*, CA 1975, 51 TC 183; [1975] STC 573.

Basis periods (ITTOIA 2005, ss 196–220)

Apportionment of profits—whether time basis obligatory

[65.59] See *Marshall Hus & Partners Ltd v Bolton*, 18.89 CORPORATION TAX.

Averaging profits of farmers and creative artists (ITTOIA 2005, ss 221–225)

Application of ITTOIA 2005, s 221

[65.60] A farmer (D) made a trading profit of £20,244 in 2005/06, and a trading loss of £10,315 in 2006/07. He claimed that the profit of these two years should be averaged under *ITTOIA 2005, s 221*. HMRC issued a ruling that the result of this claim was that D had taxable profits of £10,122 for 2005/06, and that £10,122 of the trading loss could be set against the averaged profit of £10,122 for 2006/07, leaving a small loss of £193 to be carried forward to 2007/08. D appealed, contending that as his total profit for the two years had been £9,929, he should be treated as having a taxable profit of £4,964.50 for each of 2005/06 and 2006/07. The Upper Tribunal rejected this contention and dismissed his appeal. *PG Donaghy v HMRC*, UT [2012] UKUT 148 (TCC); [2012] STC 1931.

Post-cessation receipts (ITTOIA 2005, ss 241–257; CTA 2009, ss 188–200)

Payment for transfer of right to receive post-cessation receipts

[65.61] A self-employed financial planning consultant (B) had carried on business selling life assurance products, etc. devised by one major company (D). In January 1995 she decided to retire, and agreed to sell the goodwill of her practice to another individual (Y) for £8,000. In April 1995 she entered into an agreement purporting to sell her practice to a company in D's group, and to continue to run the practice on behalf of that company for a period of about three months. The consideration for the sale was expressed as £33,415 payable immediately, £11,138 payable one year later, and whatever sum the company received for the resale of the practice (less a £250 deduction). In

August 1995 the company resold the practice to Y for the agreed goodwill of £8,000, and paid B £7,750 in accordance with the agreement. The Revenue issued a 1995/96 assessment, charging tax on the payment of £33,415 under what is now *ITTOIA 2005, s 251*. B appealed, contending that the payment was not taxable. The Special Commissioner rejected this contention and dismissed the appeal, holding on the evidence that B had 'no business purpose' in the transactions which took place in April 1995. Her only object could have been tax avoidance. (The Special Commissioner also held that the company which devised the transactions had 'no relevant business purpose' when agreeing to employ B as its agent for the period from April to August 1995.) *Brewin v McVittie*, Sp C 1998, [1999] SSCD 5 (Sp C 176).

VAT repayment following transfer of trade to successor company

[65.62] See *Shop Direct Group v HMRC*, 64.76 TRADING PROFITS.

Effect of election under ITTOIA 2005, s 257

[65.63] An accountant (G) ceased to practise on 30 April 1994. He received contingent fees of £50,000 in August 1996, and made an election under what is now *ITTOIA 2005, s 257* for these fees to be carried back to 1994/95. The Revenue issued an assessment charging tax accordingly, but G appealed, contending that the £50,000 should be treated as if it were a receipt in the year ending 30 April 1994, and that only $^{25}/_{365}$ of the sum was chargeable. The Special Commissioner rejected this contention and dismissed the appeal, holding that the election did not affect the 'calculation of the amount chargeable' and that 'what is being carried back is the sum that has already been calculated as chargeable'. *Gilmore v HM Inspector of Taxes*, Sp C [1999] SSCD 269 (Sp C 206).

66

Trading Profits—Compensation And Damages

The cases in this chapter are arranged under the following headings.

Compensation receipts on the termination of offices, etc. ancillary to a business

Compensation to managers on liquidation of shipping company

[66.1] A partnership acted as managers of a shipping company (S), their remuneration being a percentage of S's profits, including its substantial investment income. S went into voluntary liquidation and in a general meeting it authorised the liquidator to transfer £50,000 5% National War Bonds to the managers as compensation for loss of office (the Articles of Association having been altered shortly before the winding-up commenced to enable this to be done). Subsequently, S's business was transferred to a new company with the same shareholders, and the firm became managers of the new company. The Commissioners held that the £50,000 was not taxable and the KB upheld their decision. *Chibbett v Joseph Robinson & Sons*, KB 1924, 9 TC 48.

Finance company—resignation as agent linked with sale of shares

[66.2] A company (AF) provided agency and secretarial services for a number of companies. One of its clients (K), in which it held a substantial shareholding, was taken over by another company (P). Under the terms of the takeover, AF resigned as secretary of K, receiving compensation of £20,000 from P of which, in the event, it retained £16,138. The Commissioners held that the £16,138 was a trading receipt, and the CA unanimously upheld their decision. *Anglo-French Exploration Co Ltd v Clayson*, CA 1956, 36 TC 545; [1956] 1 WLR 325; [1956] 1 All ER 762.

Cancellation of agreement to provide secretarial services

[66.3] A company (C) which carried on a merchant banking business entered into a three-year agreement to provide secretarial services. A dispute arose and the agreement was terminated. C received £15,000 as compensation. The Ch D held that the £15,000 was a trading receipt. *Blackburn v Close Bros Ltd*, Ch D 1960, 39 TC 164.

Compensation for loss of auditorship, etc

[66.4] An accountant was auditor of a group of companies for which he also did accountancy work, and received fees in addition to his audit fees. All these fees were included in his professional receipts for income tax purposes. Following a difference of opinion with the directors of the group, he relinquished the auditorships, and received compensation of £1,500. The Special Commissioners held that £375 was attributable to his general accountancy work and was a trading receipt. The balance was attributable to the loss of the auditorships, taxable under Schedule E under the legislation then in force (and exempt by virtue of what is now *ITEPA 2003, s 403(1)*)). The Ch D upheld their decision. *Ellis v Lucas*, Ch D 1966, 43 TC 276; [1967] Ch 858; [1966] 2 All ER 935.

[66.5] Following a reorganisation of a group of companies, an accountancy firm relinquished the auditorship, which it had held for several years, of six companies in the group. Later the firm was given an unsolicited *ex gratia* payment of £2,567 'as *solatium* for the loss of the office of auditors'. The Special Commissioners held that the payment was not chargeable to income tax, and the Ch D upheld their decision. Pennycuick J held that ordinary commercial principles did not require including in profits voluntary payments which were not consideration for past services, but were made as recognition of past services or consolation for the termination of a contract. *Walker v Carnaby Harrower Barham & Pykett*, Ch D 1969, 46 TC 561; [1970] 1 WLR 276; [1970] 1 All ER 502.

Loss of office as secretary, etc

[66.6] Partners in a firm of advocates in Aberdeen derived a considerable part of their income from acting as secretaries and/or registrars of companies. Following the takeover of one such company and its subsidiary, the firm gave up their registrarships but continued to act as secretaries. They were paid £2,500 in compensation for the termination. The Special Commissioners held that the registrarships were offices, taxable under Schedule E under the legislation then in force, and that the £2,500 was exempt by virtue of what is now *ITEPA 2003, s 403(1)*. The CS and the HL unanimously upheld their decision. *CIR v Brander & Cruickshank*, HL 1970, 46 TC 574; [1971] 1 WLR 212; [1971] 1 All ER 36.

Author—cancellation of agreement as script writer

[66.7] See *Household v Grimshaw*, **68.11** TRADING PROFITS.

Cancellation of agreement exploiting services of actor

[66.8] See *John Mills Productions Ltd v Mathias*, 68.17 TRADING PROFITS.

Compensation receipts on the termination of agencies

[66.9] A manufacturing company (G) entered into an agreement whereby it appointed a partnership as agents for selling its products in Scotland. The agreement was for three years, but G decided to terminate it after two years, and paid the partnership £1,500 as compensation. The Commissioners held that the £1,500 was a trading receipt, and the CS upheld their decision. The compensation could not be regarded as capital, since the partnership held several similar agencies. *Kelsall Parsons & Co v CIR*, CS 1938, 21 TC 608.

[66.10] A company (F) acted as agents for several manufacturers. One agency, which F had held for many years and accounted for 30% to 45% of its earnings, was terminated and F was paid £5,320 as compensation for the loss of the agency. The CS held that the compensation was a trading receipt. *CIR v Fleming & Co (Machinery) Ltd*, CS 1951, 33 TC 57.

[66.11] A company (J) held several agencies, including one for the manufacturer of a toy typewriter invented by a director who had founded J's business. This agency was cancelled, and J received £16,000 as compensation. The Ch D held that the compensation was a trading receipt. *Elson v James G Johnston Ltd*, Ch D 1965, 42 TC 545.

[66.12] A partnership (D) which sold engineering products acted as an agent for several manufacturers. One of these (C) decided to cancel the agreement. D claimed commission on orders not completed at the termination, and one year's commission as compensation in lieu of notice. C agreed to pay D £1,000 in settlement of the claim. The CS held that the £1,000 was a trading receipt. *CIR v David MacDonald & Co*, CS 1955, 36 TC 388.

Agent dismissed—damages for breach of contract

[66.13] In 1942 a manufacturing company (G) appointed an individual (W) as its sole sales agent. In 1948 G cancelled the agreement. W began legal action against G, claiming damages for breach of contract. G paid W £4,000 to settle the action. The Commissioners held that the £4,000 was a taxable receipt of W's business. The CA unanimously dismissed W's appeal, observing that the £4,000 represented profit which W would or might have earned if the agreement had not been broken. *Wiseburgh v Domville*, CA 1956, 36 TC 527; [1956] 1 WLR 312; [1956] 1 All ER 754.

Sum received for grant of sub-agency

[66.14] A company (B) traded as a wholesale distributor of sewing machines, including those made by a German company (P) for which it had the sole UK agency, and which formed the greater part of its business. Another company paid B £12,500 for a sub-agency for P's machines, and subsequently distributed the German machines in competition with B. The Ch D held that the £12,500 was a trading receipt. *Fleming v Bellow Machine Co Ltd*, Ch D 1965, 42 TC 308; [1965] 1 WLR 873; [1965] 2 All ER 513.

Compensation receipts for cancellation or variation of other trading agreements

Shipbuilder—cancellation of order for ships

[66.15] In February and March 1920, a shipbuilding company contracted to build two ships. In November 1920 it agreed to the cancellation of the contracts in return for compensation of £100,000. The Commissioners held that the compensation was a trading receipt, to be brought into the profits of the year to June 1921. The KB and CA unanimously upheld their decision. *Short Bros Ltd v CIR*, CA 1927, 12 TC 955.

[66.16] A similar decision was reached in a case which the KB heard with *Short Bros Ltd v CIR*, **66.15** above. *Sunderland Shipbuilding Co Ltd v CIR*, KB 1926, 12 TC 955.

Cancellation of long-term contract for supply of chalk, etc

[66.17] A company (N) which owned a chalk quarry had entered into a long-term contract for the supply of chalk and the building of a wharf at which the chalk could be loaded. The contract was cancelled and N received £3,000 as compensation. The KB held that the compensation was a trading receipt. *CIR v Northfleet Coal & Ballast Co Ltd*, KB 1927, 12 TC 1102.

Cancellation of agreement to supply cattle to subsidiary

[66.18] The Irish Ministry of Agriculture ceased to supply cattle to a company, and paid compensation to the company's parent. The Special Commissioners held that the compensation was not a trading receipt, and the HC(I) upheld their decision as one of fact. *O'Dwyer v Irish Exporters and Importers Ltd*, HC(I) 1942, 2 ITC 251; [1943] IR 176. (*Note.* For another issue in this case, see **4.173** APPEALS.)

Cancellation of contracts for sale of goods

[66.19] A partnership trading as worsted spinners received compensation on the cancellation of contracts for the sale of yarn. The Special Commissioners held that the amounts received were trading receipts of the year in which the contracts were cancelled, and the KB upheld their decision. *Jesse Robinson & Sons v CIR*, KB 1929, 12 TC 1241.

Termination of profit-sharing arrangement

[66.20] In 1908, a UK company (V) entered into a profit-sharing agreement with a competing Netherlands company (J), intended to last until 1940. V's payments and receipts under the agreement were treated as trading receipts and expenses. The agreement could not be implemented during the 1914/18 War. It was amended in 1920, but the two companies were unable to agree as to the amounts payable by each for the period 1914 onwards. V claimed that, up to 1922, it was owed £449,042 by J, and credited this amount in its accounts. J claimed that it was a net creditor. After an abortive attempt to resort to arbitration, the two companies agreed in 1927 to withdraw all claims and counterclaims up to 1927 and to terminate the pooling arrangement, with J agreeing to pay £450,000 to V 'as damages'. V appealed against an income tax assessment, contending that the payment was capital and was not taxable. The HL unanimously accepted this contention and allowed the appeal. Lord Macmillan observed that 'the nature of a receipt may vary according to the nature of the trade. The price of the sale of a factory is ordinarily a capital receipt, but it may be an income receipt in the case of a person whose business it is to buy or sell factories'. He held that the pooling arrangement 'related to the whole structure of the company's profit-making apparatus', and formed 'the fixed framework within which its circulating capital operated'. *Van den Berghs Ltd v Clark*, HL 1935, 19 TC 390; [1935] AC 431.

Cancellation of contract for purchase of goods

[66.21] A company trading as chemical merchants received compensation for the cancellation of a contract to purchase agricultural chemicals. The Commissioners held that the compensation was a trading receipt, and the KB upheld their decision. *Bush Beach & Gent Ltd v Road*, KB 1939, 22 TC 519; [1939] 2 KB 524; [1939] 3 All ER 302.

Surrender of lease of greyhound track

[66.22] A company (G) was the lessee of a greyhound racing track under a lease with several years to run. It had hired the track to another company (E) for the remainder of the lease. E subsequently went into liquidation, and G agreed to cancel the hiring agreement under an agreement whereby the track was let to a third company (at a lower rent) and E paid G £15,640, representing the value on an actuarial basis of the difference between the new and the old rents. The Special Commissioners held that the £15,640 was a trading receipt, and the KB upheld their decision. *Greyhound Racing Association (Liverpool) Ltd v Cooper*, KB 1936, 20 TC 373; [1936] 3 All ER 742.

Variation of estate development agreement

[66.23] A building company (S) was developing a housing estate on land owned by an Oxford college. The college subsequently decided to make other use of some of the land, and paid S £5,000 as compensation. The KB held that the £5,000 was a trading receipt. *Shadbolt v Salmon Estate (Kingsbury) Ltd*, KB 1943, 25 TC 52.

Car distributor—variation of agreement with manufacturer

[66.24] A company (L) carried on business as a distributor for a company (AM) in the motor industry, under annual agreements containing a 'continuity clause' giving L a renewal option. In 1953, following its amalgamation with other car manufacturers, AM made certain alterations in the agreement, including a material variation and weakening of the continuity clause. AM paid L £7,000 as compensation for any loss resulting from the alterations. The Special Commissioners held that the payment was a capital receipt, and the CA upheld their decision. *Sabine v Lookers Ltd*, CA 1958, 38 TC 120.

Cancellation of commission agreement

[66.25] A company (D), through its managing director, introduced another company (C) to a third company (R). Following this introduction, C agreed to pay commission to D on orders which C received from R. Subsequently, the agreement was cancelled and C paid compensation of £1,500 to D. The KB held that the £1,500 should be included in D's profits. *Shove v Dura Manufacturing Co Ltd*, KB 1941, 23 TC 779.

Cancellation of royalty agreement

[66.26] A company, incorporated in 1912, had engaged in various activities including oil prospecting. Since 1935 its principal source of income had been royalties received under an agreement reached in 1922 for the sale of an oil concession which it had acquired. In 1964 it surrendered its rights under this agreement for £900,000. The Ch D held that the £900,000 was a capital receipt. *British-Borneo Petroleum Syndicate Ltd v Cropper*, Ch D 1968, 45 TC 201; [1968] 1 WLR 1701; [1969] 1 All ER 104.

Termination of agreement as ship-managers

[66.27] The business of a company (C) consisted almost entirely of managing ships for another company (S) under a long-term agreement. S went into liquidation when the agreement had about eight years to run, and paid S compensation. The CS held that the compensation was a capital receipt, observing that C had lost almost its entire business. *Barr Crombie & Co Ltd v CIR*, CS 1945, 26 TC 406.

Cancellation of consultancy agreement

[66.28] An accountant entered into a consultancy agreement with a US company, for a three-year period from 1 January 1992. The agreement was terminated by mutual consent at the end of 1993, the company paying the accountant $2,000,000 as compensation. He appealed against a 1993/94 assessment, contending that the compensation was a capital receipt. The Special Commissioner rejected this contention and dismissed his appeal, finding that the cancellation of the agreement 'did not affect "the whole structure of the (taxpayer's) profit-making apparatus"', and holding that the compensation which he had received was revenue rather than capital. *Consultant v HM Inspector of Taxes*, Sp C [1999] SSCD 63 (Sp C 180).

Breach of contract for goods

[66.29] The Ministry of Supply contracted to sell certain war surplus material to a company (K) but, in breach of that contract, sold some of the material in the open market. In the meantime, K had sold its business to another company (S). The Ministry paid compensation of £50,000 to K, which handed the cheque to S. The Special Commissioners held that the £50,000 was a trading receipt of S, and the Ch D upheld their decision. *Sommerfelds Ltd v Freeman*, Ch D 1966, 44 TC 43; [1967] 1 WLR 489; [1967] 2 All ER 143.

Damages following discontinuance of contract for goods

[66.30] A company (L) had manufactured hats, most of its sales being to a major retailer (M). In 1961 M decided to discontinue selling hats, and offered to assist L to produce other types of clothing. L accepted the offer and, after installing new machinery and engaging specialist staff, began making clothing for M while continuing to make hats for other customers. In 1963 M ceased buying goods from L and offered it an *ex gratia* payment of £5,000. L relected this offer and began legal action against M. The action was settled by an agreement under which M paid L £22,500 for 'loss of goodwill'. The Ch D held that the £22,500 was a trading receipt. *Creed v H & M Levinson Ltd*, Ch D 1981, 54 TC 477; [1981] STC 486.

Compensation receipts relating to capital assets

CROSS-REFERENCE

See 64.20 et seq. TRADING PROFITS for cases concerning insurance recoveries.

Compensation for expropriation of undertaking

[66.31] During the Boer War, the British Government expropriated a South African railway, and subsequently paid compensation to the company which owned it. The Commissioners held that the compensation was a trading receipt, and the CA upheld this decision. *Pretoria-Pietersburg Railway Co Ltd v Elwood*, CA 1908, 6 TC 508.

Compensation for not working fireclay bed

[66.32] A company (G), which manufactured fireclay goods, owned a bed of fireclay which ran underneath a railway. The railway issued a statutory order requiring G not to work the bed underlying the railway line, and paid it compensation. The HL held that the compensation was a capital receipt, paid for the sterilisation of a capital asset. Lord Dundas held that 'the compensation was paid for the loss of a capital asset' and could 'not be described as profits arising from the appellant's trade or business'. (G had included the compensation in its profits for income tax purposes and had paid tax on them. Its appeal was against excess profits duty assessments, where the Revenue contended that the compensation was capital and should be excluded from G's 'standard profit' for excess profits duty. Another issue, concerning other compensation which G had received from the railway, was settled by agreement before the case reached the HL.) *Glenboig Union Fireclay Co Ltd v CIR*, HL 1922, 12 TC 427.

[66.33] See also *Thomas McGhie & Sons Ltd v British Transport Commission*, 14.7 COMPENSATION, ETC.—'GOURLEY' PRINCIPLE.

Compensation for detention of ships during coal strike

[66.34] In an Irish case, a gas company owned two ships to carry coal to its works. They were compulsorily detained in England during the 1920 coal strike. The company received compensation from the UK Government in 1924. The Special Commissioners held that this was a trading receipt, and the HC(I) dismissed the company's appeal. *Alliance & Dublin Consumers' Gas Co v McWilliams*, HC(I) 1927, 1 ITC 199; [1928] IR 1.

[66.35] See also *Ensign Shipping Co Ltd v CIR*, 62.37 TRADING PROFITS.

Compensation for delay in completing overhaul of ship

[66.36] Two companies jointly purchased a second-hand ship, which was immediately sent for repair, for overhaul by a specified date. The repairers were late in completing the overhaul, and the owners claimed damages calculated by reference to their estimated loss of profits as a result of the delay. Each company received £1,500 as compensation. One of the companies appealed against an income tax assessment, contending that the £1,500 was not taxable. The Special Commissioners rejected this contention and dismissed the appeal, and the CS unanimously upheld their decision. *Burmah Steam Ship Co Ltd v CIR*, CS 1930, 16 TC 67.

Compensation for requisition of mining land

[66.37] The Ministry of Works requisitioned some land which was leased by a colliery company (W), for opencast mining. The Ministry paid W compensation for the profit it would have derived from working the coal. The Special Commissioners held that this compensation was a trading receipt, and the KB upheld their decision. *Waterloo Main Colliery Co Ltd v CIR (No 1)*, KB 1947, 29 TC 235.

Compensation on release of requisitioned vessel

[66.38] The Ministry of War Transport requisitioned a fishing vessel for war service. It was returned in defective condition, and the owners accepted £3,686 in full settlement of their claims against the Ministry. They appealed against an income tax assessment, contending that the £3,686 was a capital receipt and was not taxable. The Special Commissioners accepted this contention and allowed the appeal, and the CS upheld their decision. *CIR v West & Others*, CS 1950, 31 TC 402. (*Note*. Other cases heard at the same time related to balancing charges where the decisions have been overtaken by subsequent changes in the legislation.)

Compensation for loss of jetty while under repair

[66.39] A company (L) operated an oil storage installation. A jetty which it owned was damaged by a tanker. L received £77,875 from its insurers, and compensation of £26,738 from the owners of the tanker. Taken together, these amounts exceeded the cost of repairing the jetty by £21,404. The Special Commissionrs held that the £21,404 was compensation for loss of profits and was a trading receipt. The CA unanimously upheld their decision. *London & Thames Haven Oil Wharves Ltd v Attwooll*, CA 1966, 43 TC 491; [1967] Ch 772; [1967] 2 All ER 124.

Damages for unlawful occupation of premises

[66.40] In a Singapore case, the tenants of a building unlawfully retained possession for six years after their lease expired, paying the same rent as before. The owner was awarded damages computed by reference to the rent received and that which could have been received had he been able to re-let the building. The PC held that the damages were taxable as being income in respect of 'rents, royalties, premiums and any other profits arising from property' (the relevant statutory test). *Raja's Commercial College v Gian Singh & Co Ltd*, PC [1976] STC 282; [1977] AC 312; [1976] 2 All ER 801.

Compensation for temporary loss of land

[66.41] A water company (N) obtained a compulsory purchase order in respect of some land owned by an unrelated company (L). N subsequently vacated the site and the order was rescinded. The Lands Tribunal awarded L compensation of £2,185,000. In its tax computations, L treated this as a capital receipt. The Revenue issued a notice of amendment treating the compensation as taxable income. The General Commissioners dismissed L's appeal and the Ch D and CA unanimously upheld their decision. Moses LJ observed that there had been only a 'temporary interruption' to L's use of its land. Therefore the compensation was income rather than capital. *Able (UK) Ltd v HMRC*, CA 2007, 78 TC 790; [2008] STC 136; [2007] EWCA Civ 1207.

Compensation on compulsory acquisition of premises

[66.42] See *West Suffolk County Council v W Rought Ltd*, **14.13** COMPENSATION, ETC.—'GOURLEY' PRINCIPLE, and *Stoke-on-Trent Council v Wood Mitchell*, **14.4** COMPENSATION, ETC.—'GOURLEY' PRINCIPLE.

Premises destroyed—compensation for 'loss of profit'

[66.43] See *Lang v Rice*, 71.49 CAPITAL GAINS TAX.

Other compensation and damages receipts

Retrospective award for wartime requisition of trading stock

[66.44] See *CIR v Newcastle Breweries Ltd*, 62.35 TRADING PROFITS.

1926 Irish Grants Committee—ex gratia payment

[66.45] In 1926 the UK Government set up an Irish Grants Committee to consider claims from British subjects who had suffered hardship or loss because of their support of the Government before the partition of Ireland. A trader (R) claimed an award of £29,469 for losses sustained or profits lost and £11,437 for loss of goodwill. The Government, on the recommendation of the Committee, made an *ex gratia* payment of £14,000 in two instalments in the two years to 31 January 1930. The Irish Revenue assessed R on the basis that the instalments were trading receipts of the years in which they were received. The HC(I) allowed R's appeal, holding that the payments were not trading receipts. *Robinson (t/a James Pim & Son) v Dolan*, HC(I) 1934, 2 ITC 25; [1935] IR 509.

Damages for breach of licence to produce play

[66.46] A theatrical company (P) held a five-year licence to produce a play in the UK. Contrary to the terms of the licence, a film based on the play was extensively shown in the UK. P was awarded damages of £5,000 for breach of contract. The KB held that the £5,000 was a trading receipt, as it was computed by reference to P's loss of profit from the breach of contract. *Vaughan v Archie Parnell & Alfred Zeitlin Ltd*, KB 1940, 23 TC 505.

Compensation under Restriction of Ribbon Development Act

[66.47] A development company received compensation under the *Restriction of Ribbon Development Act 1935*. The CA unanimously held that the compensation was a trading receipt of the year in which it was received. *Johnson v WS Try Ltd*, CA 1946, 27 TC 167; [1946] 1 All ER 532.

Compensation for disruption caused by construction of tramway

[66.48] A solicitor (L) occupied premises on the route of the Edinburgh Tramway. He received compensation of £4,000 for possible disruption caused by the construction of the tramway. HMRC issued a ruling that this was a trading receipt. The First-tier Tribunal dismissed L's appeal. Judge Mure observed that 'the inclusion within the scheme of businesses, but not private individuals, suggests that it is a surrogatum for business turnover'. *J Lints v HMRC*, FTT [2012] UKFTT 491 (TC), TC02168.

Compromise damages

[66.49] A company (W) began proceedings against two former shareholders, claiming damages for unlawful diversion of its business. W received £11,000 in settlement of the action. The Ch D held that the payment was a trading receipt. *Roberts v WS Electronics Ltd*, Ch D 1967, 44 TC 525.

Voluntary payment on termination of wartime trading arrangements

[66.50] In 1939 the UK and Australian Governments entered into arrangements under which Australian wool growers were required to sell their wool clip to the Australian Government for resale to the UK Government. Any profit made by the sale of the wool by the UK Government outside the UK was to be shared between the two Governments, as a result of which the Australian Government received large amounts and, in 1948, passed an Act under which amounts were to be paid to the growers proportionate to the value of the wool they supplied. A company received £22,851 under this Act in 1949, and was assessed to Australian tax on the basis that this was a trading receipt. The PC upheld the assessment, holding that it was a trading receipt notwithstanding its voluntary nature. *Australian Commissioner of Taxation v Squatting Investment Co Ltd*, PC [1954] AC 182; [1954] 1 All ER 349.

Voluntary payment to insurance broker on loss of client

[66.51] A company (J) which carried on business as insurance brokers lost an important company client (C) following a change in C's ownership. C agreed to pay J £5,000 by annual instalments of £1,000, in recognition of the long period during which J had acted for it. J appealed against a corporation tax assessment, contending that the £5,000 was not taxable. The Special Commissioners accepted this contention and allowed the appeal, and the CA unanimously upheld their decision. On the evidence, the payments were gifts, rather than an additional reward for services rendered, and were not assessable. The payments were 'unsolicited and unexpected'. *Simpson v John Reynolds & Co (Insurances) Ltd*, CA 1975, 49 TC 693; [1975] STC 271; [1975] 1 WLR 617; [1975] 2 All ER 88.

Payment to estate agents for failure to obtain letting agency

[66.52] A firm of estate agents (S) negotiated the purchase of a site for a client for development, charging their normal scale fee for their services, and expecting that, as was customary, they would be given the letting agency when the site was developed. The client sold the site to a development company (C), for which S did not act, so that it did not get the agency. S protested to C, which agreed to make an *ex gratia* payment of £2,500 to S. The Ch D held that the payment was a taxable business receipt since, although it was voluntary, it had been solicited by S and was referable to work done by S. (It was assessed as a receipt of the year in which C promised to make the payment, which was several years after S had negotiated the sale of the site. The Ch D upheld the assessment on this point also, holding that admissions made before the Commissioners prevented S from contending for a different year.) *McGowan v Brown & Cousins (t/a Stuart Edwards)*, Ch D 1977, 52 TC 8; [1977] STC 342; [1977] 1 WLR 1403; [1977] 3 All ER 844.

Voluntary payments to caterers on giving up tenancies

[66.53] A company (G) carried on the business of running licensed catering establishments, mainly public houses with restaurants attached. It had been formed in 1929 by two former senior employees of a major brewing company (W). By 1968 it had 36 establishments, of which 31 were held on tied tenancy agreements from W. W decided to take back 13 of these and made *ex gratia* payments to G, calculated by reference to the rateable values of the premises. The Special Commissioners held that the payments were not trading receipts, and the CA unanimously upheld their decision. *Murray v Goodhews*, CA 1977, 52 TC 86; [1978] STC 207; [1978] 1 WLR 499; [1978] 2 All ER 40. (*Note*. The Ch D rejected W's claim to deduct the payments — see *Watneys London Ltd v Pike*, **68.27** TRADING PROFITS.)

Non-contractual compensation for loss of prospective customer

[66.54] The Diamond Trading Corporation only sold diamonds to clients, approved by the Corporation, of one of a small number of recognised brokers. Approval of a client could entail years of 'lobbying' by a broker, who was not paid for this work but received commission on purchases by the client, when he was approved. After a broker (N) had been working diligently to obtain approval of a client (G), G decided to go to another broker (H). N complained to H and they agreed to refer the matter to a third broker for informal arbitration. The arbitration was not legally binding but H paid N the recommended amount of £15,000. R was assessed on the basis that the £15,000 was a trading receipt. The CA unanimously upheld the assessment, holding on the evidence that the payment had been made to compensate R for his otherwise unremunerated work or loss of anticipated profits. *Rolfe v Nagel*, CA 1981, 55 TC 585; [1982] STC 53.

Compensation received for agent's failure to oppose rent increase

[66.55] A company (D) traded from leased premises. The landlord, in accordance with rent review provisions in the lease, served notice of an increase in the rent from £5,000 per annum to £12,500 per annum. D was advised by an estate agent that a proper market rent would be about £7,500 per annum. It instructed the agent to serve an appropriate counter-notice on the landlord and to try to negotiate a market rent. The agent failed to serve the counter-notice and the landlord then demanded the rent of £12,500 per annum. A settlement was agreed under which the landlord accepted a rent of £11,500 per annum and the agent agreed to pay D £14,000 as damages and to pay the costs. D appealed against a corporation tax assessment, contending that the £14,000 was a capital receipt. The Special Commissioners rejected this contention and dismissed the appeal, and the CA upheld their decision. The compensation was paid because D would have to incur increased revenue expenditure. It was therefore paid on revenue account, and fell to be taxed as a trading receipt. *Donald Fisher (Ealing) Ltd v Spencer*, CA 1989, 63 TC 168; [1989] STC 256.

Payment to farmers under EEC scheme

[66.56] A family partnership which had traded as dairy farmers entered into an EEC scheme, aimed to induce farmers to change from dairy to beef cattle. They undertook to cease selling milk products over four years and, while maintaining their livestock numbers, to reduce their dairy cow herds to a certain figure. In return, they received a premium, payable in instalments, from the Ministry of Agriculture, Fisheries and Food. The Ch D held that the premium was a trading receipt. *White v G & M Davies*, Ch D 1979, 52 TC 597; [1979] STC 415; [1979] 1 WLR 908.

[66.57] The decision in *White v G & M Davies*, **66.56** above, was applied in the similar Scottish case of *CIR v W Andrew Biggar (a firm)*, CS 1982, 56 TC 254; [1982] STC 677.

Payments to accountants on departure from partnership

[66.58] See *Morgan & Self v HMRC*, **41.32** PARTNERSHIPS, and *AB v HMRC*, **41.33** PARTNERSHIPS.

Other compensation payments

Payment as compensation for cancellation for order of ship

[66.59] A shipping company, which owned only one ship, contracted for the construction of another at a price of £226,000. However, because of a slump in the shipping industry, it decided to cancel the contract, paying compensation of £30,000 (and forfeiting its £30,000 deposit) to the shipbuilder. The Commissioners held that the £60,000 was capital expenditure, and the KB upheld their decision. *'Countess Warwick' Steamship Co Ltd v Ogg*, KB 1924, 8 TC 652; [1924] 2 KB 292.

[66.60] In 1919 a company (D) which carried on a mutual marine insurance business had entered into contracts for the construction of four ships. Because of a slump in the shipping industry, it cancelled two of the contracts, paying compensation of £70,000. (It took delivery of the other two ships and subsequently sold them to its parent company.) It claimed that the £70,000 should be allowed as a deduction in computing its profits, on the basis that it had begun a new trade of dealing in ships in 1919. The Revenue rejected the claim and the KB dismissed D's appeal, holding that D's only trade was that of mutual marine insurance and that the £70,000 was not an allowable deduction. *Devon Mutual Steamship Association v Ogg*, KB 1927, 13 TC 184.

Compensation for termination of agency

[66.61] A company (P) appointed another company (S) as its agent in Central Asia under an agreement for 10 years from 1 January 1914, with provision for its continuation. Subsequently, P decided that its affairs in Central Asia would be best managed by its own organisation and, after negotiation, it was agreed that the agency would terminate at the end of 1922 and that P would pay £300,000 to S as compensation. P claimed that the £300,000 should be allowed as a deduction in computing its profits. The Revenue rejected the claim but the KB allowed P's appeal and the CA upheld this decision. Lord Hanworth MR observed that the expenditure 'ought to be debited to the circulating capital rather than to the fixed capital'. *Anglo-Persian Oil Co Ltd v Dale*, CA 1931, 16 TC 253; [1932] 1 KB 124.

[66.62] A company (C) had been incorporated to build and operate a hotel on a site which it leased from a Borough Council. In 1981 it appointed another company (H) to operate the hotel as its agent under a 20-year management agreement. In 1990 it terminated the agreement and paid H about £2,000,000 as compensation. It claimed that the compensation was an allowable deduction in computing its profits. The Revenue rejected the claim, considering that the payment was capital rather than revenue, but the Special Commissioners allowed C's appeal. On the evidence, 'the appropriate accounting treatment for the compensation payment was to charge the full cost to the profit and loss account in the year of payment'. The agreement was an 'ordinary commercial contract' and was not a 'capital asset'. The termination payment 'did not have the effect of enlarging the scope of (C's) trade or enabling it to embark on a different enterprise', but 'merely effected a change in (C's) business methods and internal organisation, leaving its fixed capital untouched'. *The Croydon Hotel & Leisure Co Ltd v Bowen*, Sp C [1996] SSCD 466 (Sp C 101).

Compensation payments by brewer on termination of tenancies

[66.63] See *Watneys London Ltd v Pike*, 68.27 TRADING PROFITS.

Building of factory—payment to settle compensation claim

[66.64] In an Irish case, a manufacturing company decided to move to another site and to build a new factory there for the purpose. It received all the requisite planning approvals, but while the factory was under construction, tenants of adjacent houses began proceedings against it, alleging that the factory would infringe their rights to light and air. The company settled the action, paying the tenants £225 as compensation and £75 for costs, and claimed these amounts as deductions in computing its profits. The SC(I) accepted the claim. The expenditure was paid to defend its assets, was wholly and exclusively for the purposes of its trade, and was not capital expenditure. *Davis v X Ltd*, SC(I) 1946, 2 ITC 320; [1947] ILTR 157.

Compensation payment to associated company

[66.65] In a Rhodesia & Nyasaland case, a group of three independent copper mining companies (with overlapping directorates) decided to cut production by 10% because of a fall in prices. To achieve this, one of the three agreed to cease production for a year in return for compensation from the other two. One of these (N) paid £1,384,569 under the agreement and claimed that this should be allowed as a deduction. The PC accepted the claim. *Commissioner of Taxes (Rhodesia & Nyasaland) v Nchanga Consolidated Copper Mines Ltd*, PC [1964] AC 948; [1964] 1 All ER 208.

Payment to cancel agreement for payment of share of profits

[66.66] A company (V) had two subsidiaries, one of which operated a cellular mobile telephone network and one of which sold such telephones. 80% of V's shares were owned by another UK company, and 15% of them were owned by a US company. In 1983 V agreed to pay 10% of its pre-tax profits to the US company for 15 years in return for the supply of know-how and technical support. In 1986 V cancelled the agreement, paying the US company $30,000,000 as compensation. It claimed loss relief on the basis that the payment was an allowable deduction from its profits. The Revenue rejected the claim, considering firstly that the payment was capital, and secondly that it was not wholly and exclusively for the purpose of V's business, since it was also for the purposes of other members of the group. The CA allowed V's appeal, holding that the payment was revenue rather than capital and that it was wholly and exclusively for the purpose of V's trade. On the evidence, V's directors had intended the expenditure to rid the group of a trading liability owed to a third party. The liability in question was a liability of V alone. Accordingly, the payment was intended 'exclusively to serve the purposes' of V's trade. The fact that the expenditure also benefited the two subsidiaries was not conclusive. *Vodafone Cellular Ltd v Shaw*, CA 1997, 69 TC 376; [1997] STC 734.

Payment to effect closure of rival business

[66.67] A company (J) operated a credit card scheme. It entered into an agreement with an international credit card organisation (EI), under which its cards could be used in EI's retail outlets. Subsequently both J and EI's UK subsidiary (E) became members of a scheme (the 'Interbank scheme') operated by another international credit card organisation. E published a pamphlet addressed to its retailers in connection with the forthcoming change. J was advised that this pamphlet amounted to an unlawful attempt to encroach on its business. Following negotiations, J and EI agreed that, in return for J paying £75,000 to E, E would phase out its existing retailer agreements, cease trading in credit cards and terminate its licence under the Interbank scheme. J appealed against a corporation tax assessment, contending that the £75,000 should be allowed as a deduction. The Ch D rejected this contention, holding that the £75,000 and ancillary legal expenses were capital payments. They had produced two permanent results, namely that J would be the unchallenged UK member of Interbank, and that its goodwill would be protected by the closure of E's rival business. *Walker v The Joint Credit Card Co Ltd*, Ch D 1982, 55 TC 617; [1982] STC 427.

Annual payments to compensate for delay in completion of quay

[66.68] See *Renfrew Town Council v CIR*, **39.28** MISCELLANEOUS INCOME.

Damages for breach of contract—date deductible

[66.69] See *CIR v Hugh T Barrie Ltd*, **62.66** TRADING PROFITS.

Damages and penalties payments

Payment of damages for injuries to guest at inn

[66.70] A brewery company which owned several licensed houses incurred damages and costs of £1,490 after a guest at one of its houses was injured by the collapse a chimney. The Commissioners held that the £1,490 was not deductible in computing its profits, and the HL unanimously upheld their decision. Lord Davey held that 'it is not enough that the disbursement is made in the course of, or arises out of, or is connected with, the trade, or is made out of the profits of the trade. It must be made for the purpose of earning the profits.' *Strong & Co of Romsey Ltd v Woodifield*, HL 1906, 5 TC 215; [1906] AC 448.

Penalty for breach of wartime regulations

[66.71] A company (E), which traded as oil merchants, shipped some oil to Norway and, as a result, was sued for a penalty for breach of certain wartime regulations. The action was settled by agreement and E paid a mitigated penalty of £2,000. E claimed that this, and its legal costs of defending the action, should be allowed as deductions. The KB rejected the claim. *CIR v EC Warnes & Co Ltd*, KB 1919, 12 TC 227; [1919] 2 KB 444.

[66.72] The decision in *CIR v EC Warnes & Co Ltd*, **66.71** above, was approved and applied by the CA in another case where the circumstances were similar. Lord Sterndale MR observed that there was 'a difference between a commercial loss in trading and a penalty imposed on a person or a company for a breach of the law which they have committed in that trading'. *CIR v Alexander von Glehn & Co Ltd*, CA 1920, 12 TC 232; [1920] 2 KB 553.

Stockbroker—fines imposed by professional regulatory body

[66.73] The Stock Exchange Council imposed fines totalling £50,000 on a stockbroker for breaches of the rules and regulations of the Stock Exchange. The stockbroker claimed to deduct the amount of the fines, and his associated legal costs, in computing his profits. The inspector rejected the claim and the stockbroker appealed, contending that the expenditure had been incurred in order to prevent his suspension or expulsion from the Stock Exchange and thus to protect his business. The Special Commissioner held that the fines were not deductible, since they were 'not connected with or arising out of the trade'.

The payment of such a fine was not an ordinary commercial loss, since there was a difference between a commercial loss incurred in trading and a penalty imposed for a breach of the rules committed in that trading. However, the Commissioner also held that the associated legal costs were deductible. The Commissioner accepted the stockbroker's evidence that he was 'wholly unconcerned' with his personal reputation, holding that it was not 'inescapable' that the protection of his reputation was an object of the expenditure. On the evidence, the Commissioner found that the costs had been incurred with the 'sole object' of preserving the existence of the stockbroker's business, so that they were deductible. The HL upheld the Commissioner's decision. Lord Hoffmann held that the reason why a fine was not deductible 'relates to the particular character of a fine or penalty. Its purpose is to punish the taxpayer, and a court may easily conclude that the legislative policy would be diluted if the taxpayer were allowed to share the burden with the rest of the community by a deduction for the purposes of tax.' However it did not follow that the costs were not deductible, since it was 'fundamental that everyone, guilty or not guilty, should be entitled to defend themselves'. To refuse to allow a deduction for the legal expenses 'would in effect be an additional fine or penalty for which the regulatory scheme does not provide'. *McKnight v Sheppard*, HL 1999, 71 TC 419; [1999] STC 669; [1999] 1 WLR 1133; [1999] 3 All ER 491.

Motor racing company—fine imposed by governing body

[66.74] The FIA, which is the governing body for Formula 1 motor racing, imposed a penalty of £32,000,000 on a company (M) which had broken the rules of the FIA's International Sporting Code by obtaining information belonging to a rival company (F). M claimed that this penalty should be allowed as a deduction in computing its profits. HMRC rejected the claim, and M appealed. The First-tier Tribunal allowed the appeal (by Judge Hellier's casting vote), but the Upper Tribunal reversed this decision, holding that 'a deliberate activity which is contrary to contractual obligations and the rules and regulations governing the conduct of the trade, which is not an unavoidable consequence of carrying on a trade and which could lead to the destruction of the trade is not an activity carried on in the course of that trade'. Although the payment of the fine was a commercial necessity, one of its purposes was the satisfaction of a legal obligation arising out of activities which were not in the course of M's trade. Therefore it was not deductible. *HMRC v McLaren Racing Ltd*, UT [2014] UKUT 269 (TCC); [2014] STC 2417.

Damages for libel of Government officials

[66.75] A sugar broker (F) libellously accused a Ministry of Food official of abusing his office to further the interests of a sugar-producing company, to the detriment of a company for which F acted. The official obtained damages for the libel and F claimed the damages and his costs as deductible in computing his profits. The Special Commissioners held that the payments were not deductible and the KB upheld their decision, applying *dicta* in *Strong & Co of Romsey Ltd v Woodifield*, **66.70** above. Macnaghten J observed that it would 'be preposterous if the appellant were allowed to deduct these sums and thus be enabled to share equally with the public revenue the loss to which he was condemned in the judgment'. *Fairrie v Hall*, KB 1947, 28 TC 200; [1947] 2 All ER 141.

Damages for breach of US 'anti-trust' law

[66.76] A UK subsidiary of an American company incurred fines and expenses arising out of alleged infringements of American 'anti-trust' law. The UK company agreed to submit to the jurisdiction of an American court to facilitate the negotiation by its parent company of a compromise settlement. The KB held that the fines and expenses were not allowable deductions (except with regard to £28 incurred in obtaining legal advice in the UK). *Cattermole v Borax & Chemicals Ltd*, KB 1949, 31 TC 202.

Payments to secure withdrawal of action by director

[66.77] The three directors of a company (S) acquired a controlling interest in another company (B). One of B's directors (T), who was a minority shareholder in B, issued a writ against S and its directors, claiming that they had made an invalid issue of debentures, and seeking damages. The directors then issued a writ against T, alleging defamation. A compromise settlement was subsequently agreed. However, one of S's three directors (H) was reluctant to withdraw the defamation proceedings against T. The directors agreed that S should pay H £7,500 as compensation for damage to his reputation. S appealed against an income tax assessment, contending that the £7,500 (and associated legal costs) should be allowed as a deduction. The KB accepted this contention and allowed the appeal, holding that the expenditure had been incurred for the purposes of S's trade (to get rid of a disadvantageous trading relationship) and was therefore deductible. The CA upheld this decision. *G Scammell & Nephew Ltd v Rowles*, CA 1939, 22 TC 479; [1939] 3 All ER 337.

Company promoter—payment to settle actions for damages

[66.78] A company (G) formed, or helped to form, three companies in the gold-mining industry. Later, civil actions were taken against it in connection with the formations. G paid £25,000 to settle the actions. The Special Commissioners held that the £25,000 and the legal costs were allowable deductions, and the Ch D upheld their decision as one of fact. *Golder v Great Boulder Proprietary Gold Mines Ltd*, Ch D 1952, 33 TC 75; [1952] 1 All ER 360.

Solicitor—damages for breach of contract as employee

[66.79] A solicitor (P), who had previously been an employee, set up practice on his own. His former employer (S) took legal proceedings against him, alleging a breach of his contract of employment in undertaking business for one of S's clients. P was ordered to pay damages and costs. The Ch D held that the damages and costs were not deductible in computing P's profits. *Knight v Parry*, Ch D 1972, 48 TC 580; [1973] STC 56.

Sole trader—damages for breach of contract as employee

[66.80] An individual (M) had been employed as a recruitment consultant by a company (Q). In April 2007 he left Q and became self-employed. Subsequently Q began legal proceedings against him, claiming that he had breached an undertaking not to contact or canvass any of Q's clients. The proceedings were settled by a 'Tomlin order', under which M agreed to pay Q £100,000 in settlement of Q's claims. In his 2007/08 tax return, M claimed a deduction for this payment, together with his legal costs. HMRC rejected the claim on the basis that the expenditure had not been wholly and exclusively incurred for the purpose of M's business. The First-tier Tribunal dismissed M's appeal. Judge Cannan held that the expenditure had a dual purpose, and that one of the purposes had arisen out of M's contract of employment. Accordingly the expenditure was not wholly and exclusively for the purpose of M's business. *P McMahon v HMRC*, FTT [2013] UKFTT 403 (TC), TC02799.

Compromise settlement of action by former director

[66.81] A former director of an engineering company (H) began legal action against H, its directors and some of its shareholders. H paid £5,938 to settle the action, and claimed a deduction for the payment in computing its profits. The Special Commissioners rejected the claim, holding that the payment was not made wholly and exclusively for the purposes of H's trade, and the Ch D upheld their decision as one of fact. *Hammond Engineering Co Ltd v CIR*, Ch D 1975, 50 TC 313; [1975] STC 334.

Prospective liability for damages not formally admitted

[66.82] See *James Spencer & Co v CIR*, **62.69** TRADING PROFITS.

Damages awarded later compounded—amount deductible

[66.83] See *Simpson v Jones*, **62.55** TRADING PROFITS.

67

Trading Profits—Property Dealing

The cases in this chapter are arranged under the following headings.

Property sales by companies other than builders

Profits held to be trading profits

Purchase and resale of copper-bearing land

[67.1] A newly-formed company (C) purchased copper-bearing land for £24,000 in 1901 and sold it to another company (F) in two lots for £300,000 in 1902 and 1903, the purchase price being satisfied by fully-paid shares in F. The Commissioners held that C was taxable on the difference between the purchase price and the value of the shares received on sale. Their decision was upheld. *Californian Copper Syndicate Ltd v Harris*, CE 1904, 5 TC 159. (*Note*. It is apparent from the Stated Case that the Revenue accepted as the value of the shares an amount considerably below their par value, but this valuation was not in issue.)

Land acquired under concession

[67.2] A UK company acquired certain concessions in what is now Namibia (which was largely unexploited at the time) including mineral rights, railway rights and the right to the freehold of 3,000,000 acres of land to be selected by it. From time to time, it sold land to settlers or to other companies. The KB held that profits on sales of the land were taxable as trading profits, and the CA unanimously upheld this decision. *Thew v South West Africa Co Ltd*, CA 1924, 9 TC 141.

Land acquired from trustees

[67.3] A company (C) was formed in 1882, to handle the interests of the UK holders of bonds issued by the State of Alabama, on which the State had defaulted. C acquired interests in land in Alabama, which it subsequently sold. The Revenue issued assessments charging tax on the basis that C was trading. The Special Commissioners dismissed C's appeal, and the KB upheld this decision. *Alabama Coal, Iron, Land & Colonization Co Ltd v Mylam*, KB 1926, 11 TC 232.

[67.4] Under a will, some land was assigned to trustees, who transferred it to a newly-formed company (B), receiving shares in B as consideration. The trustees assigned most of the shares to the beneficiaries under the will. Shortly after its incorporation, B acquired further land, financing the purchase by borrowing. Some years later, it sold some of the land which it had acquired from the trustees and the whole of the additional land which it had purchased. The CS held that B was carrying on a trade and was taxable accordingly. *Balgownie Land Trust Ltd v CIR*, CS 1929, 14 TC 684.

[67.5] A company acquired 1,200 acres of land. It developed part of the land as building sites, selling them as opportunities arose. The Commissioners held that the profits on the sales were chargeable to income tax, and the KB upheld their decision. *St Aubyn Estates Ltd v Strick*, KB 1932, 17 TC 412.

[67.6] In 1946, a company (T) acquired land with development value from trustees. It retained most of the land for several years, but sold significant parts of it from 1964 onwards. The Revenue assessed the profits from some of these sales as trading profits. The Commissioners dismissed T's appeals and the Ch D upheld their decision as one of fact. *Tempest Estates Ltd v Walmsley*, Ch D 1975, 51 TC 305; [1976] STC 10.

Property sold after period of letting

[67.7] A company (R) purchased some land, houses and garages in 1938 and 1943. It was treated as an investment company up to 1945/46. Between July 1945 and August 1947, it sold some of its properties. The Revenue issued assessments for 1946/47 and 1947/48 on the basis that R was trading. The Commissioners upheld the assessments, and the CA unanimously dios-missed R's appeal. *Rellim Ltd v Vise*, CA 1951, 32 TC 254.

[67.8] A company (T) purchased some shops and tenements in 1942. It sold them at a profit in 1946 and 1949, having previously let them. The CS unanimously held that T's profits were chargeable to income tax. *CIR v Toll Property Co Ltd*, CS 1952, 34 TC 13.

[67.9] A company (F) purchased properties which had been built by its shareholders, and sold them as and when they fell vacant. The General Commissioners held that F was trading, and the CA unanimously upheld their decision. *Forest Side Properties (Chingford) Ltd v Pearce*, CA 1961, 39 TC 665.

[67.10] In a Hong Kong case, a company (R) purchased several properties in 1972. It sold two of these in 1973 and a third, in two parts, in 1976 and 1978. R accepted that the profits on all four sales should be treated as trading profits. In 1980 it sold another of the properties, which it had previously let to tenants. It appealed against an assessment on this sale, contending that this property was a capital asset. The Hong Kong Board of Review rejected this contention and upheld the assessment, finding that the property had been held as trading stock. The PC dismissed R's appeal, holding that this was a legitimate conclusion from the primary facts. *Richfield International Land & Investment Co Ltd v Hong Kong Commr of Inland Revenue*, PC [1989] STC 820.

Estate acquired by ship management company

[67.11] A company, which managed several steamships, purchased a landed estate in 1915 for £153,000. Between 1918 and 1937 it granted a contractor options to build houses on part of the estate, granted numerous feus to purchasers of such houses, and spent £90,000 on the construction of roads, etc. From 1935 to 1937, it sold feu duties and undeveloped land for £201,000. The Commissioners held that the profits from these sales were chargeable to income tax, and the CS unanimously upheld their decision. *Cayzer Irvine & Co Ltd v CIR*, CS 1942, 24 TC 491.

Profits on sales carried to capital reserve

[67.12] Two associated companies made profits from numerous purchases and resales of properties. In their accounts, they allocated the profits to a capital reserve fund. The Revenue issued assessments on the basis that the profits were trading income. The Commissioners dismissed the companies' appeals, and the Ch D upheld their decision as one of fact. *Emro Investments Ltd v Aller*; *Lance Webb Estates Ltd v Aller*, Ch D 1954, 35 TC 303.

Development project abandoned—land compulsorily acquired

[67.13] A company (P) purchased land in 1934 for development as a suburb, but abandoned the project in 1936. It sold part of the land, but most of it remained undeveloped and was let for farming or grazing. In 1961, under threat of compulsory acquisition, P sold all its properties to Hull Corporation and went into voluntary liquidation. The Revenue issued income tax (and profits tax) assessments on the basis that the proceeds of the sale to the Corporation were trading receipts. The Commissioners dismissed P's appeal, holding that the land had been acquired as trading stock and remained trading stock when sold. The Ch D upheld their decision. *Orchard Parks Ltd v Pogson*, Ch D 1964, 42 TC 442.

Development of industrial estate—disposals of land by sub-letting

[67.14] A building company (F) acquired a 150-year lease of some land. It transferred the lease to an associated company (P), which developed the land as an industrial estate, installing services, etc. and dividing it into twelve plots. Several of the plots were sublet for the remainder of the headlease (less one day). F built factories on the plots. One of these was built for P, which let it for ten years, and the others were built for the sub-lessees. The Special Commissioners held that P's activities amounted to trading, and that the leasing of the factory was in the course of that trade. The Ch D upheld their decision. *Parkstone Estates Ltd v Blair*, Ch D 1966, 43 TC 246.

Sale of woodland by housing society

[67.15] A housing society (H) sold some woodland, which it had owned for many years, to a builder. The Revenue issued an assessment charging income tax on the profit. The Special Commissioners dismissed H's appeal and the Ch D upheld their decision. *Haywards Heath Housing Society Ltd v Hewison*, Ch D 1966, 43 TC 321.

Acquisition of land from associated company during resale negotiations

[67.16] A company (B) owned some agricultural land. The County Council wished to purchase 15 acres of the land in order to build a school on the site. While negotiations were in progress, B sold the land to an associated company (S). S subsequently sold the land to the County Council at a substantial profit. The Revenue issued an assessment on S, charging income tax on the profit. The CA upheld the assessment (by a 2–1 majority, Willmer LJ dissenting). *Eames v Stepnell Properties Ltd*, CA 1966, 43 TC 678; [1967] 1 WLR 593; [1967] 1 All ER 785.

Profits held not to be trading profits

Land acquired under Royal Charter

[67.17] A company (H) had been granted extensive land in what is now Canada by Royal Charter. It surrendered the land to the Crown in 1869, receiving in exchange the right to claim a 5% share in some of the land within 50 years as and when it was settled. It sold this land over a period of several years. The Revenue issued an assessment charging tax on the profits. The CA unanimously allowed H's appeal, holding that it was not trading in land. *Hudson's Bay Co Ltd v Stevens*, CA 1909, 5 TC 424.

Purchase and resale of rubber estates

[67.18] A company acquired rubber estates in Malaysia. After planting a considerable acreage, but before producing any rubber, it sold its estates at a profit. It was held that the profit was a capital profit and not taxable. *Tebrau (Johore) Rubber Syndicate Ltd v Farmer*, CE 1910, 5 TC 658.

Land acquired held in trust

[67.19] A company (L) was formed to acquire land in Vancouver which was held in trust for various persons, to manage and develop it with a view to its ultimate sale. The KB held that L was not taxable on its surplus from the sale of portions of the land, since its function was to realise the capital value of the nterests in the land under the trust. *Rand v Alberni Land Co Ltd*, KB 1920, 7 TC 629.

Property sold after period of letting—whether an investment

[67.20] Between 1920 and 1926, a company sold 16 of 40 flats it had held and let since 1900. The CS upheld the Commissioners' decision that it was realising capital and not trading. *CIR v Hyndland Investment Co Ltd*, CS 1929, 14 TC 694.

[67.21] A company (G) sold properties which it had acquired from an associated building partnership. The Revenue issued assessments charging income tax but the CS allowed G's appeal (by a 2–1 majority, Lord Russell dissenting). *Glasgow Heritable Trust Ltd v CIR*, CS 1954, 35 TC 195.

[67.22] A company (L) trading as timber merchants controlled a building company which had ceased active building, but had retained and let some houses it had built. As part of an arrangement to help the subsidiary resume building, L acquired the houses and subsequently sold some of them. The Revenue issued assessments charging income tax but the Ch D allowed L's appeal, holding that the transactions were not trading. *Lucy & Sunderland Ltd v Hunt*, Ch D 1961, 40 TC 132; [1962] 1 WLR 7; [1961] 3 All ER 1062.

Sales resulting from change of circumstances

[67.23] A company and two of its subsidiaries went into liquidation and sold nine properties. The Revenue issued assessments on the basis that the proceeds were trading income. The liquidator appealed, contending that the properties had been acquired as investments and had been sold as a result of the introduction of CGT by *Finance Act 1965*. The HL allowed the appeals (by a 4-1 majority, Lord Scarman dissenting). Lord Wilberforce held that the properties had not been acquired as trading stock, and that the sales by the liquidator were the forced realisations of investments. *Simmons (as liquidator of Lionel Simmons Properties Ltd) v CIR (and related appeals)*, HL 1980, 53 TC 461; [1980] STC 350; [1980] 1 WLR 1196; [1980] 2 All ER 798.

Sale and leaseback of hotel to finance expansion

[67.24] In a Malaysian case, a family company (L) built a hotel with the aid of a secured loan and let it to a subsidiary (M). To finance further expansion, a complex series of transactions was entered into in 1963 and 1964 involving the sale and leaseback of the hotel and land with an agreement to re-purchase in ten years, the assignment of the lease and repurchase rights to another company (H) in return for shares in H, the sale of L's shares in M to H (again for shares in H), and the subsequent sale of some of L's shares in H to various members of the public. L appealed against assessments on its profits from these transactions. The PC allowed the appeals. Applying *dicta* of Lord Wilberforce in *Simmons v CIR*, 67.23 above, a company may hold both trading stock and investment assets, and an investment does not turn into trading stock simply because it is sold. Here the whole tenor of the lease-back agreement indicated that L intended to retain the hotel as a profit-earning asset. *Lim Foo Yong Sdn Bhd v Comptroller-General of Inland Revenue*, PC [1986] STC 255.

Leaseback arrangement—exercise of option

[67.25] A company (C) wished to raise finance. One of its subsidiary companies (W) owned six freehold properties. C approached an unrelated company (H), which carried on business as an asset finance company. H had a wholly-owned subsidiary (R), which carried on investment business. In 1989 C and H negotiated a transaction whereby W granted R a lease of the six properties for 999 years. In return R paid W a premium of £39,722,000. On the same day R granted W an underlease of the properties for 35 years at an escalating rent. Also on the same day, R granted another of C's subsidiaries (L) a call option, exercisable in 1994, to acquire the lease for £48,659,000. In 1994 L exercised the call option and paid R the £48,659,000. The Revenue issued a CT assessment on the basis that this was a trading transaction, and that the receipt was taxable. R appealed, contending that it had acquired the properties as an investment and that the £48,659,000 was not trading income. The Special Commissioners accepted this contention and allowed R's appeal, holding on the evidence that the transaction 'was a transaction in land and was not the provision of short-term finance'. As a matter of law, it had been undertaken by R, and could not be treated as having been undertaken by H. Furthermore, 'the participation of (R) in the transaction was not by way of trade but by way of investment'. *Rosemoor Investments v HM Inspector of Taxes*, Sp C [2002] SSCD 325 (Sp C 320).

Property purchases and sales by individuals

Profits held to be trading profits

[67.26] A motor engineer (R) was also a partner in a land development scheme. It was accepted that the partnership was trading. In 1932 R purchased a farm. He resold it in the same year to a development company. He carried out a similar purchase and resale in 1934. The Revenue issued assessments charging income tax on R's profits. The KB upheld the assessments. *Reynolds' Executors v Bennett*, KB 1943, 25 TC 401.

[67.27] The Revenue issued assessments on a retired pharmacist (H), charging income tax on his profits from four property transactions in the years 1924 to 1931. The Commissioners found that three of them were trading transactions, within the charge to income tax, and the KB upheld this decision. H had purchased other property and contended that, if he was held to be trading, his remaining property should be brought into account as stock-in-trade. The KB accepted this contention in principle and remitted the case to the Commissioners to determine which of his unsold properties were part of his trading stock. The Commissioners found that only the property which was the subject of the three trading transactions constituted trading assets, the remaining properties being investments. H accepted this decision and his appeal was dismissed by consent. *Hudson v Wrightson*, KB 1934, 26 TC 55.

[67.28] A builder (B) transferred his business to a company of which he and his father were shareholders and directors. The Revenue issued assessments charging income tax on certain subsequent transactions in land entered into respectively by B, by B and his father, and by three different syndicates of which B and his father were members. The KB upheld the assessments, holding that the transactions amounted to trading. *Broadbridge v Beattie (and associated appeals)*, KB 1944, 26 TC 63.

[67.29] A builder and a grocer jointly purchased a farm and adjoining land in 1930 and 1932, and sold them to estate companies (one of which they controlled) in 1935 and 1936. The Revenuie issued assessments charging income tax on their profits. The KB upheld the assessments. *Gray & Gillitt v Tiley*, KB 1944, 26 TC 80.

[67.30] Two brothers purchased an area of land and arranged for a company which they controlled to build houses on it. They sold some of the houses, and also purchased and resold other land. The Revenue issued income tax assessments. They appealed, contending that some of the sales had been carried out in order to finance an unsuccessful film-manufacturing venture in which they were interested, which should be treated as part of a composite trade including the land transactions. The Special Commissioners rejected this contention and dismissed their appeal, and the KB upheld this decision. *Laver & Laver v Wilkinson (and related appeal)*, KB 1944, 26 TC 105.

[67.31] Between 1943 and 1948 two sisters purchased and resold two houses, a hotel and a block including a hotel and shops, etc. The sisters lived in two of the properties during the period of their ownership. The Revenue issued assessments charging income tax on their profits. The CS upheld the assessments. *MacMahon & MacMahon v CIR*, CS 1951, 32 TC 311.

[67.32] Between 1943 and 1949 a former builder sold some houses which he had built and others which he had bought. The Revenue issued assessments on the basis that he was trading as a property dealer. The Ch D upheld the assessments. *Foulds v Clayton*, Ch D 1953, 34 TC 382.

[67.33] A carpenter built and sold two bungalows, without using outside labour. He lived in each bungalow before selling it. He appealed against income tax assessments, contending firstly that he was not trading, and alternatively that his profit should be spread over the period of building. The Commissioners allowed his appeal in part, holding that tax was not chargeable on the sale of the first bungalow, but that his profit on the second bungalow was chargeable in the year of sale. The Ch D upheld their decision as one of fact. *Page v Pogson*, Ch D 1954, 35 TC 544.

[67.34] A partnership carried on business as window cleaners and dealers in army surplus stores. Between 1930 and 1948, they had acquired 299 houses which were let. They sold 58 of them between 1946 and 1952. The Commissioners held that the profits on the sales were chargeable to income tax, and the CA upheld this decision. *Mitchell Bros v Tomlinson*, CA 1957, 37 TC 224.

[67.35] Five individuals purchased an estate and sold it within six months. The Revenue issued income tax assessments on the profits. The Ch D upheld the assessment. *Burrell & Others v Davis*, Ch D 1948, 38 TC 307.

[67.36] A solicitor (C) purchased an area of land which had planning permission. He sold part of the land in 23 building plots, and sold a further part to a development company. The Revenue issued income tax assessments, and the Ch D dismissed C's appeal. *Cooke v Haddock*, Ch D 1960, 39 TC 64.

[67.37] In a Ceylon case, an individual purchased some land which was near the school attended by his children, built a house for his family, and sold the remainder of the land. The PC held that there had been an adventure in the nature of trade. *Iswera v Ceylon Commr of Inland Revenue*, PC [1965] 1 WLR 663.

[67.38] A farmer (T) purchased an area of land, part of which had planning permission for building. He obtained planning permission for the remainder of the land and sold it, in two lots, a few months later. The Revenue issued income tax assessments, and the Ch D dismissed T's appeal. *Turner v Last*, Ch D 1965, 42 TC 517.

[67.39] Under a will, trustees held an area of land for the testator's son and daughter. The son purchased his sister's interest and arranged for the development and sale of the land. The Revenue issued an income tax assessment and he appealed, contending that he was simply realising inherited property. The Special Commissioners rejected this contention and dismissed his appeal, and the CA upheld their decision. *Pilkington v Randall*, CA 1966, 42 TC 662.

[67.40] A building company (P) wished to sell some undeveloped land with planning permission. One of its employees (H) offered to help find a purchaser. In March 1962 he agreed to sell the land to a company for £25,000. Eight days later he purchased the land from P for £15,000. The Revenue issued an income tax assessment. The Ch D upheld the assessment. Goff J observed that H 'had actually contracted to sell the land before the agreement to purchase it'. *Johnston v Heath*, Ch D 1970, 46 TC 463; [1970] 1 WLR 1567; [1970] 3 All ER 915.

[67.41] A company purchased some property for £26,500 in May 1960. In December 1960 it sold the property for £28,000 to a syndicate of three people, which included its controlling director. The syndicate sold the property for £81,000 in January 1961. The Revenue issued an income tax assessment on the syndicate. The Ch D upheld the assessment. (The syndicate had attempted to avoid tax by a contrived succession and cessation to take advantage of the basis period rules then in force, but the attempt failed.) *Reeves v Evans Boyce & Northcott Syndicate*, Ch D 1971, 48 TC 495.

[67.42] During the Second World War, a farmer (C) sold his farm to the Air Ministry for conversion into an airfield. In 1963 the Government offered to sell it back to him for £14,250. He repurchased it and sold it at auction in 1964 for £39,000. The Revenue issued an assessment charging income tax on the profit. The Ch D dismissed C's appeal, holding that the transaction constituted an adventure in the nature of trade. *Clark v Follett*, Ch D 1973, 48 TC 677; [1973] STC 240.

[67.43] In a Trinidad and Tobago case, a woman agreed in 1969 to buy six parcels of land. In 1973 and 1974 she sold two of these. The PC upheld the decision of the Trinidad and Tobago CA that the transactions amounted to trading, and held that the profit was taxable in the year the land was conveyed, when the right to receive payment arose. *Eckel v Board of Inland Revenue (Trinidad and Tobago)*, PC 1989, 62 TC 331; [1989] STC 305.

[67.44] In 1991 a bricklayer purchased a plot of land and built a property comprising two flats. He obtained a bank loan of £40,000 to help finance the building work. It was agreed that this loan would be cleared when the first flat was sold. In August 1992 he granted a 99-year lease of one of the flats for a premium of £41,500 and a peppercorn rent. The Revenue issued an income tax assessment. The bricklayer appealed, contending that the profit should be treated as a capital gain. The Special Commissioner rejected this contention and dismissed the appeal, holding on the evidence that the transaction was 'a typical trading transaction'. *Lynch v Edmondson*, Sp C [1998] SSCD 185 (Sp C 164).

[67.45] In a Mauritius case, a group of people had purchased some agricultural land and had obtained planning permission for residential development.

The Mauritius government acquired some of the land under the *Land Acquisition Act 1973*. The owners of the land received compensation. The tax authority issued assessments charging income tax on basis that the owners had acquired the land 'in the course of a business the main purpose of which was the acquisition and sale of immoveable property'. The PC upheld the assessments, holding that 'by purchasing the land the taxpayers had invested money in a business venture with profit in mind'. The land had been trading stock, so that the compensation was chargeable to income tax. *Lutchumun & Others v Director-General of the Mauritius Revenue Authority*, PC 2008, [2009] STC 444; [2008] UKPC 53.

[67.46] See also *Parkin v Cattell*, 5.34 ASSESSMENTS (sale of houses let at controlled rents as they fell vacant).

Profits held not to be trading profits

[67.47] Two company directors jointly purchased undeveloped land and gave it to their respective wives. The wives then sold the land at a profit to development companies controlled by their husbands. The Revenue issued income tax assessments on the profits. The Special Commissioners discharged the assessments, holding that the transactions did not amount to trading. The KB upheld their decision as one of fact. *Williams v Davies (and related appeal)*, KB 1945, 26 TC 371; [1945] 1 All ER 304.

[67.48] In 1924 a farmer and a solicitor purchased a farm, which they subsequently let. Between 1930 and 1940 they purchased and developed five trading estates. In 1938 they sold the farm. The Revenue issued an income tax assessment on the sale of the farm. They appealed, accepting that their purchase and development of the five trading estates had been chargeable to income tax, but contending that the farm had been purchased as an investment. The KB accepted this contention and allowed their appeal. *Cooksey & Bibby v Rednall*, KB 1949, 30 TC 514.

[67.49] A company director (R) bought four houses in January 1945 and let them to tenants until December 1947, when he sold them at a profit. The Revenue issued an assessment charging income tax on the profit. R appealed, and the case was heard by four General Commissioners, who were equally divided and allowed the appeal. The CS unanimously upheld this decision. Lord Keith held that an intention to resell at a profit does not in itself establish that a purchase and resale amounts to trading. The fact that the properties had been let justified the Commissioners' decision as one with which the court should not interfere. *CIR v Reinhold*, CS 1953, 34 TC 389.

[67.50] In 1948 a solicitor (T) purchased a property which had been badly damaged during the Second World War. In 1951 he sold it, with the help of a tax inspector (D), with whom he had agreed to share the profit. The Revenue issued an income tax assessment on D and T, but the Ch D allowed their appeal. Buckley J held that the evidence did not justify a finding that T had been engaged in a joint venture, or that he was trading. *Dodd & Tanfield v Haddock*, Ch D 1964, 42 TC 229.

[67.51] In 1955 three people bought a freehold property with its plant and machinery for £59,000. Immediately afterwards they sold the plant and machinery for £56,490, and they also contracted to resell part of the premises for £18,000. Prior to completion of the contract, one of the three arranged for the property to be conveyed to a friend (W), subject to W paying the two co-purchasers £7,000 each. In 1959 W sold a further part of the property for £16,000. The Revenue issued an assessment on W, charging income tax on the profit. The Ch D allowed W's appeal, holding that W had no beneficial interest in the part sold in 1956, and the facts did not justify a conclusion that the 1959 sale was trading. *Wrigley v Ward*, Ch D 1967, 44 TC 491.

[67.52] In an Australian case, a brother (S) and sister (M) each inherited a half share in land with development potential. S wished to sell the land but M wished to retain it. After negotiations, M purchased S's share. In order to finance the purchase, she sold a substantial part of the land (while retaining the part with most development potential). The Privy Council allowed her appeal against an income tax assessment, holding (by a 3–2 majority, Lord Pearson and Lord MacDermott dissenting) that the transaction was not an adventure in the nature of trade. *McClelland v Australian Commissioner of Taxation*, PC 1970, [1971] 1 All ER 969.

[67.53] A grocer (T) purchased a large country house at auction for £5,100. He considered using it as a residence but his wife refused to live in it. He therefore applied for, and obtained, planning permission for its demolition and the erection of 90 dwellings on the site. He then sold it to a developer for £54,500. The Revenue issued an assessment charging income tax on the profit. In the courts, the Revenue conceded that the purchase had not been by way of trade, but contended that the property had subsequently been appropriated to trading stock. The CA allowed T's appeal, holding that, on the facts found or conceded, there was no evidence of an adventure in the nature of trade. *Taylor v Good*, CA 1974, 49 TC 277; [1974] STC 148; [1974] 1 WLR 556; [1974] 1 All ER 1137.

[67.54] Four brothers bought some land, for which planning permission had been granted, in June 1977 for £65,000. They had not previously invested in land. In September 1977 they sold the land for £100,000 following an unsolicited offer. The Revenue issued an assessment charging income tax on the profit. The brothers appealed, contending that they had intended to hold the land as an investment. The Commissioners accepted their evidence and allowed their appeals, and the Ch D upheld their decision as one of fact. *Marson v Morton (and related appeals)*, Ch D 1986, 59 TC 381; [1986] STC 463; [1986] 1 WLR 1343.

[67.55] A demolition and plant hire contractor (K) purchased a site on which he had worked, and used part of the site as an office and to store materials. He subsequently obtained planning permission to build a large dwelling-house on the site. After building the house, he sold the whole site and carried on the business from other premises. The Revenue issued an assessment charging income tax on the profit. K appealed, contending that he had acquired the site as a capital asset. The CA allowed his appeal (by a 2–1 majority, Ralph Gibson LJ dissenting). Nourse LJ held that K's principal purpose in buying the site had been to obtain office and storage space for his business. Applying the principles laid down in *Simmons v CIR*, **67.23** above, the site had therefore been acquired as a capital asset, rather than as trading stock. *Kirkham v Williams*, CA 1991, 64 TC 253; [1991] STC 342; [1991] 1 WLR 863.

[67.56] An individual (H) purchased a house in September 2001, let it to tenants, and sold it in December 2005. HMRC issued an assessment charging CGT on the gain. H appealed, contending that he should be treated as carrying on a trade of dealing in property. The First-tier Tribunal rejected this contention and dismissed his appeal. Judge Walters found that H's acquisition of the house 'was motivated to a significant extent by the prospect of the rental income to be derived from it (an investment motive)', and that he had continued to hold the house as an investment until he sold it. *A Headley v HMRC*, FTT [2013] UKFTT 382 (TC), TC02779.

[67.57] See also *Pearn v Miller*, 53.9 SCHEDULE D, and *Leeming v Jones*, 53.10 SCHEDULE D.

Sales by partnerships

[67.58] A partnership of three people (M, H and R) carried on the business of dealing in land (all sales being to a company which they and their families controlled), developing land and building houses for sale. H died in July 1930 and his executors required the surviving partners to realise the unsold land, all of which was sold in blocks by October 1933. Meanwhile, M had died in 1932. The Revenue issued assessments for 1930/31 to 1933/34 on the basis that the partnership trade had continued until October 1933. The executors and R appealed, contending that the partnership trade had ceased in July 1930 and that the subsequent sales were not sales in the course of exercising a trade but were realisations of assets after the trade had ceased. The KB accepted this contention and allowed the appeals. *Marshall's Executors & Others v Joly*, KB 1936, 20 TC 256; [1936] 1 All ER 851.

[67.59] In 1916 four people formed a syndicate to purchase land and sell it at a profit. In 1921 one member of the syndicate (B) died. Some of the land was sold in 1930, and the Revenue issued an assessment charging income tax, on the basis that B's executor (H) had continued the trade with the three surviving members. The CA unanimously upheld the assessment. Sir Wilfrid Greene MR observed that 'things went on exactly as before, so far as the machinery and personnel of the partnership are concerned, and they went on, not with (H) outside in the position of a mere executor, but with (H) inside, as one of the persons taking part in the management of this affair'. *Newbarns Syndicate v Hay*, CA 1939, 22 TC 461.

[67.60] A partnership acquired land for investment. It transferred some of the land to an associated company for development, and sold one plot to a local authority. The Revenue issued an income tax assessment on the partnership. The Special Commissioners allowed the partnership's appeal, holding that the partnership was not trading. The CS unanimously upheld their decision as one of fact. *CIR v Dean Property Co*, CS 1939, 22 TC 706.

Sales by limited liability partnership

[67.61] See *Albermarle 4 Llp v HMRC*, 5.68 ASSESSMENTS.

Sales by partners after cessation of partnership

[67.62] Two brothers traded in partnership as builders. In 1949 they transferred the building business to a company, but retained some of the houses which they had built as investments. They sold the houses between 1955 and 1958. The Revenue issued income tax assessments but the Ch D allowed the partnership's appeal, holding that the trade had ceased in 1949, and the CA unanimously upheld this decision. *Seaward & Others v Varty*, CA 1962, 40 TC 523.

Property sales by builders (individuals or companies)

Profits held to be trading profits

Extension of activities

[67.63] A company, which for many years had confined itself to building houses for customers, extended its activities to include erecting buildings which it let and subsequently sold, and the redevelopment and sale of buildings and property. The Special Commissioners held that it had carried on a single trade throughout, and that the profits on the sale of the properties which it had purchased were part of its trading profits. The KB upheld their decision. *Spiers & Son Ltd v Ogden*, KB 1932, 17 TC 117.

Transactions entered into because of ill-health

[67.64] A builder contemplated retiring for health reasons and taking up poultry farming as a hobby. He purchased some land for this purpose. His health deteriorated, and he abandoned the project of poultry farming and sold the land at a profit. The Commissioners found that the profit arose in the course of his business as a builder, and the KB upheld their decision. *Sharpless v Rees*, KB 1940, 23 TC 361.

Sale of site—development project abandoned

[67.65] A building company (H) purchased a site with a view to erecting three blocks of flats on it for sale or letting. Subsequently, H's directors abandoned the project and sold the site at a profit. The Ch D held that the only reasonable conclusion on the evidence was that the purchase and sale were trading transactions. *Shadford v H Fairweather & Co Ltd*, Ch D 1966, 43 TC 291.

Sale of land surplus to requirements

[67.66] A building company (R) bought a house, suitable for conversion into flats, and five acres of adjoining land. It converted the house into flats, which it sold, and sold the land to a developer. The Revenue issued an assessment charging tax on the sale of the land. R appealed, accepting that the sales of the flats were trading but contending that the sale of the land was a capital transaction. The Ch D rejected this contention and upheld the assessment, holding that the profit was within the charge to income tax, since the acquisition of the land had been incidental to the acquisition of the house. *Snell v Rosser Thomas & Co Ltd*, Ch D 1967, 44 TC 343; [1968] 1 WLR 295; [1968] 1 All ER 600.

Sale of houses after long period in which let

[67.67] Between 1927 and 1953, a family building partnership built or bought 53 houses, of which 17 were sold. Those not sold were let. The partnership appealed against an assessment on the sale of a house built in 1929 and not sold until 1953, contending that the house should be treated as an investment. The Ch D rejected this contention and dismissed the appeal. *J & C Oliver v Farnsworth*, Ch D 1956, 37 TC 51.

[67.68] Between 1945 and 1953 a company (J) sold several houses which it had built before the Second World War and had let to tenants. The Revenue issued assessments chatrging income tax. J appealed, contending that the houses were investments. The Ch D rejected this contention and upheld the assessments. *James Hobson & Sons Ltd v Newall*, Ch D 1957, 37 TC 609.

Sale of factory after having been let

[67.69] A building company (W) built a factory in 1951 and let it to a manufacturing subsidiary (R). The factory became unsuitable and was sold in 1963, after W had built another factory for R. The Revenue issued an assessment charging income tax on the sale of the factory. The Ch D upheld the assessment. *WM Robb Ltd v Page*, Ch D 1971, 47 TC 465.

Sale of land in wife's name

[67.70] In 1957, a builder (S) and a friend (G) contracted to buy some farmland, which was conveyed to S's wife and G in equal shares. The deeds of the land were deposited in S's bank to secure his overdraft. The land had building potential, of which S was aware, and in 1973 the land was sold to the Warrington Development Corporation for £750,000. The Revenue assessed S on the basis that half the land was part of his trading stock. He appealed, contending that he had no beneficial interest in the land. The Special Commissioners rejected this contention and dismissed his appeal, holding that the land was trading stock in his wife's name as nominee or bare trustee. The Ch D upheld their decision. *Smart v Lowndes*, Ch D 1978, 52 TC 436; [1978] STC 607.

Sale of land acquired with business

[67.71] A builder (D) transferred his business to a company (R) in 1957. The assets transferred included a parcel of land which D had acquired in 1955 and subsequently let. R treated it as a fixed asset in its accounts, and sold it in 1966 at a substantial profit. The Ch D held that R had acquired the land as a trading asset, and its sale was chargeable to income tax. *Bowie v Reg Dunn (Builders) Ltd*, Ch D 1974, 49 TC 469; [1974] STC 234.

Whether houses acquired by builder as private residence

[67.72] The Revenue assessed a builder (K) to income tax in respect of the sale of three properties that he had built or improved. He appealed, contending that he had not purchased or sold the first property as part of his trade, and that each of the properties had been acquired with the intention of occupying them as a private residence. The General Commissioners dismissed his appeal, finding that the size of the properties was substantially larger than would have been necessary for K's sole occupation, and that the periods of occupancy were short, and holding that the profits on the sales of the properties were chargeable to income tax. The Ch D upheld their decision as one of fact. *Kirkby v Hughes*, Ch D 1992, 65 TC 532; [1993] STC 76.

[67.73] A builder (H) purchased a house in 1996, built an extension, and sold it a profit in January 2000. He then purchased another house (P) for £200,000, and sold it in July 2002 for £550,000. In September 2002 he purchased another house (G), which was in poor condition, for £170,000, demolished and rebuilt it, and sold it in February 2004 for £650,000. In January 2004 he purchased another house for £335,000, demolished and rebuilt it, and advertised it for sale for £975,000 in 2005, although he did not find a buyer. H did not declare the profits on the sales of P and G on his tax returns. HMRC issued a discovery assessment for 2002/03, and an amendment to H's self-assessment for 2003/04, charging income tax on the sales of P and G. H appealed, contending that he had occupied both P and G as his private residence. The First-tier Tribunal reviewed the evidence in detail and allowed his appeal against the 2002/03 assessment but dismissed his appeal for 2003/04, holding that 'his purchase, reconstruction and sale of (G) were carried out in the course of trade'. *TA Hartland v HMRC*, FTT [2014] UKFTT 1099 (TC), TC04187.

Sales after cessation of building

[67.74] A company (G) developed two estates, building about 250 houses, the last of which was sold in 1939 (except for one which was let). In most of the sales, the purchasers obtained building society mortgages, and G gave the society collateral guarantee for part of the advance. If the purchaser defaulted, G could repurchase the house. G did in fact repurchase some houses, two of which it resold. It did no more building after 1939. The Revenue issued an income tax assessment on G for 1945/46. G appealed, contending that it had ceased trading. The Special Commissioners rejected this contention and dismissed the appeal, holding that G was continuing to carry on its original trade. The KB upheld their decision. *Gladstone Development Co Ltd v Strick*, KB 1948, 30 TC 131.

[67.75] A builder disposed of his plant and materials in 1941 and did no active building afterwards, except rebuilding four of his own houses for the War Damage Commission. He retained several houses, which he had built and let. He appealed against income tax assessments on him as a builder for 1957/58 to 1960/61. The Commissioners found that he had continued trading after 5 April 1957, but ceased on 5 April 1961 (when there were 24 houses remaining unsold). The Ch D and the CA upheld this decision as one of fact. *Andrew v Taylor*, CA 1965, 42 TC 557.

[67.76] A builder (S) gave up active building in 1949 but retained unsold houses and land. He sold some of the houses and land in 1958/59 and 1964/65. The Revenue issued assessments charging income tax on the profits. S appealed, contending that he haad ceased to trade in 1949. The Special Commissioners rejected this contention and upheld the assessments, and the KB upheld their decision as one of fact. *Speck v Morton*, Ch D 1972, 48 TC 476.

[67.77] A building company (G) built a house in 1938. From 1942 it treated the house as a capital asset in its accounts. It sold the house in 1950. The Revenue issued an assessment charging tax on the profit, and G appealed. The Commissioners dismissed the appeal, holding that the house was trading stock, and the Ch D upheld their decision as one of fact. *Granville Building Co Ltd v Oxby*, Ch D 1954, 35 TC 244.

Profits held not to be trading profits

Sales after cessation of building

[67.78] In 1946 and 1948 a builder (H) sold shops which he had built in 1927 and subsequently let, and a house which he had built in 1939 for his foreman to live in. The Revenue issued assessments charging income tax on the profits. H appealed, contending that the sales were realisations of investments. The Ch D accepted this contention and allowed his appeal. *Harvey v Caulcott*, Ch D 1952, 33 TC 159.

Sale of houses retained on transfer of business

[67.79] In 1945 a builder (B) formed a company (H) to take over his business, retaining some houses which H did not require. The Revenue issued assessments charging income tax on the subsequent sale of some of these, on the basis that they were trading stock of B's business. B appealed, contending that he had ceased trading in 1945 and had retained the houses as investments rather than as trading stock. The Ch D accepted this contention and remitted the case to the Commissioners to determine the assessments accordingly. *Bradshaw v Blunden (No 1)*, Ch D 1956, 36 TC 397. (*Note*. See **65.1** TRADING PROFITS for a sequel to this case concerning the assessment for 1945/46.)

Retired builder—houses built for letting

[67.80] A builder (W) gave up active building in 1942. In 1946 he held 2,495 houses which he had built between 1933 and 1941. Of these, 2,208 had been built as investments for letting and 287 for eventual sale. From 1946, he began to sell houses of either category as they fell vacant or as suitable offers were made by sitting tenants. The Revenue issued assessments charging income tax on the profits of all W's sales. The Ch D allowed W's appeal in part, holding that the houses which had been built for eventual sale remained trading stock of his business, but that the majority of the houses, having been built for letting, were investments and that the profits on their sales were not taxable. *West v Phillips*, Ch D 1958, 38 TC 203.

Builder selling house previously used as private residence

[67.81] A builder (K) purchased old bungalows, renovated them, and sold them at a profit. However in 1989 he began suffering financial difficulties, after the renovation of a dilapidated bungalow (HR) proved more expensive than he had anticipated. He attempted to raise funds by selling his private residence

(HW), but was not successful. In 1990 K and his wife moved out of HW and into HR. From 1990 to 1998 HW was let to tenants. During 1999 K incurred significant further expenditure on renovating HW, which he sold in 2000. The Revenue issued assessments charging tax on the income which K had received from letting HW. He appealed, contending that HW had become trading stock of his business when he and his wife moved out of it, so that the mortgage interest was allowable as a deduction from the rental income. The Special Commissioner reviewed the evidence in detail and rejected this contention, finding that there was 'no persuasive evidence' that supported a change of intention 'to transfer the property to trading stock'. Accordingly the Commissioner held that HW had never become trading stock of K's business, so that only a proportion of the mortgage interest was allowable against the rental income. *Kings v King (and related appeal)*, Sp C [2004] SSCD 186 (Sp C 402). (*Note*. The Commissioner allowed an appeal by K's wife against alternative assessments on her, holding on the evidence that she had surrendered her entitlement to the rental income, so that it was solely assessable on K.)

68

Trading Profits—Specific Businesses

The cases in this chapter are arranged under the following headings.

Authors and artistes

Actress

[68.1] An actress (B) appealed against income tax assessments, contending that she was an employee. The KB rejected this contention and upheld the assessments, holding that B was taxable on the the whole of her professional income, including income from performances in the USA. *Davies v Braithwaite*, KB 1933, 18 TC 198.

British actress temporarily living abroad—short visit to UK

[68.2] See *Withers v Wynyard*, 48.15 RESIDENCE.

Actor—temporary accommodation

[68.3] A professional actor (H), who lived in Cheshire with his wife, accepted a role in a play at a London theatre. He rented a flat which was just over a mile from the theatre. He claimed a deduction of £32,503 in respect of the rent of the flat, and also claimed deductions of £8,174 in respect of travelling (by taxi) and subsistence (meals in restaurants). HMRC rejected the claim and H appealed. The First-tier Tribunal held that the expenditure on restaurant meals was not wholly and exclusively for the purpose of his profession, and H had not submitted sufficient evidence in support of his claim for taxi fares, so these items were not deductible. With regard to the rent of the flat, Judge King allowed H's appeal but the Upper Tribunal remitted the case for rehearing, observing that 'the FTT needed to consider whether in all the circumstances of the case, the sole purpose for renting the flat was in order to carry on his profession of an actor'. If that had been H's sole purpose, the expenditure would be deductible, but if H had had a dual purpose, the expenditure would not be deductible. *HMRC v Healy*, UT [2013] UKUT 367 (TCC); [2014] STC 384.

Singer—advance payments for royalties on gramophone records

[68.4] A professional singer appealed against an income tax assessment, contending that £1,500 which he had received from a gramophone company was a loan and was not taxable. The KB rejected this contention and upheld the assessment, holding that the £1,500 was an advance payment of royalties on gramophone records. *Taylor v Dawson*, KB 1938, 22 TC 189.

Dramatist—only one successful play

[68.5] See *Billam v Griffith*, 62.12 TRADING PROFITS.

Author—lump sums in commutation of future royalties

[68.6] An author entered into certain publishing agreements, receiving royalties on the books sold. After some years the agreements were cancelled and instead she received lump sums from the publisher for the publishing rights. The Revenue issued assessments charging income tax on these receipts, and she appealed, contending that they were capital. The KB rejected this contention and upheld the assessments, holding that the lump sums were revenue receipts of her vocation. *Glasson v Rougier*, KB 1944, 26 TC 86; [1944] 1 All ER 535.

Author—sale of film rights

[68.7] An author sold the film rights in two of her books, in return for fixed sums which were paid in instalments over a period of several years. The Ch D held that the amounts in question were receipts of her vocation and were chargeable to income tax. *Howson v Monsell*, Ch D 1950, 31 TC 529; [1950] 2 All ER 1239.

Actress—receipts from exploitation of film

[68.8] See *Mitchell v Rosay*, 39.7 MISCELLANEOUS INCOME.

Actor—payment for restrictive covenant

[68.9] An actor (L) gave his services to a film company (T) as producer, director and actor in a film. T paid L a fixed sum, plus a proportion of the net profits from the film. In 1945 T agreed to pay L a further £15,000 not to engage in any film for any other person for 18 months. The Special Commissioners held that the £15,000 was a capital receipt and not chargeable to income tax, and the CA upheld their decision. *Higgs v Olivier*, CA 1952, 33 TC 136; [1952] Ch 311.

Author—sales of copyright in novels written when non-resident

[68.10] An author sold the copyright in novels which he had written when he was not resident in the UK. He was assessed on the proceeds, and appealed, contending firstly that the sale proceeds were capital receipts and alternatively that, if they were held to be income receipts, expenses incurred when writing the books should be deducted. The General Commissioners rejected these contentions and dismissed his appeal, and the CA upheld their decision. *Mackenzie v Arnold*, CA 1952, 33 TC 363.

Author—payment on cancellation of contract with film company

[68.11] An author (H) entered into a three-year contract with a film company (M), by which H agreed to work for M as a script writer, and M received options to film rights in some books written by H. After a few months the contract was cancelled by an agreement under which M paid H £3,000 and acquired certain film rights options. The Special Commissioners held that the £3,000 was a taxable receipt of H's profession, and the Ch D upheld their decision. *Household v Grimshaw*, Ch D 1953, 34 TC 366; [1953] 1 WLR 710; [1953] 2 All ER 12.

Film writer—guarantee of indebtedness of film company

[68.12] See *Lunt v Wellesley*, **63.153** TRADING PROFITS.

Actor—purchase and resale of film rights in novel

[68.13] An actor (S) acquired the film rights in a novel and resold them to a film company at a profit of £2,300. The Revenue issued an assessment charging income tax on the profit. The Ch D allowed S's appeal, holding that he had realised an investment and that the profit was not taxable. *Shiner v Lindblom*, Ch D 1960, 39 TC 367; [1961] 1 WLR 248; [1960] 3 All ER 832.

Author—gift of copyright to father

[68.14] An author (H) assigned to his father the rights in a novel shortly before its publication. The Revenue included the market value of the rights in an income tax assessment on H. The Special Commissioners allowed his appeal, holding that the rights were not trading stock and that the principle laid down in *Sharkey v Wernher*, **65.29** TRADING PROFITS, did not apply to professions. The CA upheld their decision. *Mason v Innes*, CA 1967, 44 TC 326; [1967] Ch 1079; [1967] 2 All ER 926.

Author—sale of working papers

[68.15] A professional author sold his working papers to a university for £25,000, payable in three instalments. The Revenue included the amount of the first instalment in his 1987/88 income tax assessment. The Special Commissioners dismissed the author's appeal, and the Ch D upheld their decision.

The working papers had been created in the course of his activities as an author. What he sold was part of the fruits of his profession as an author. The exploitation by an author of anything produced in the course of his profession was within the charge to income tax. *Wain's Executors v Cameron*, Ch D 1995, 67 TC 324; [1995] STC 555.

Author—claim for expenses

[68.16] A freelance journalist and author (H) decided to write a book entitled 'A Year on a Pontoon'. He claimed a deduction for expenses incurred in moving a boat which he owned to southern France and living there for a year. HMRC rejected the claim on the basis that the expenditure had not been wholly and exclusively incurred for the purpose of his profession as an author, but was partly incurred for personal reasons. H appealed. The First-tier Tribunal allowed the appeal in part, holding that the cost of transporting the boat to France, and the cost of purchasing maritime charts, were allowable deductions. However, expenditure on repairs, improvements, mooring fees and insurance was not allowable, since the evidence indicated that H would have owned a boat even if he had not written the book, so that his ownership of the boat was not wholly and exclusively for the purpose of his profession as an author. *C Huhtala v HMRC (No 2)*, FTT [2012] UKFTT 79 (TC), TC01775.

Company formed to exploit services of actor

[68.17] A company (J) was formed to exploit the services of an actor. In 1947 J entered into an agreement giving a film company (R) his exclusive services for seven years. In 1951 R paid £50,000 to cancel the agreement. The Special Commissioners held that the £50,000 was a trading receipt, and the Ch D upheld their decision. *John Mills Productions Ltd v Mathias*, Ch D 1967, 44 TC 441.

Theatrical artiste

[68.18] See *Fall v Hitchen*, 22.4 EMPLOYMENT INCOME.

Entertainers on cruise ships

[68.19] HMRC issued discovery assessments on two people who worked as entertainers on cruise ships. They appealed, contending that they should be treated as employees of the company which operated the ships (and as entitled to seafarers' earnings deduction). The First-tier Tribunal rejected this contention and dismissed their appeals, observing that the appellants 'earn their living by entering into a series of separate engagements with a number of different cruise lines in a similar way to actors but with far shorter engagements than normally for actors'. Accordingly they were self-employed. The Upper Tribunal upheld this decision as one of fact. *P Matthews v HMRC (and related appeal)*, UT [2012] UKUT 229 (TCC); [2014] STC 297.

Breweries, distilleries, publicans, etc

Losses on loans to customers

[68.20] A brewery company habitually acted as banker for, and lent money to, its customers. The QB held that the company's banking activities were ancillary to its brewing business, and that losses on the loans were deductible in computing its profits. *Reid's Brewery Co Ltd v Male*, QB 1891, 3 TC 279; [1891] 2 QB 1.

Compensation Fund levies—whether deductible

[68.21] The *Licensing Act 1904* imposed an annual levy on licensees to form a Compensation Fund where a licence was not renewed. Where the licensee was a tenant, a proportion varying according to the length of the lease was deductible from the rent. A brewery claimed a deduction for the levy borne by it in respect of its tied houses. The CA held, by a 2-1 majority, that the deduction was allowable. The HL was equally divided, and because of the equal division of opinion, the CA decision stood. Lord Atkinson held that the company had acquired the premises in question 'for the sole and exclusive purpose of increasing the volume of their sales and securing for their goods a higher price than they could otherwise obtain'. *Smith v Lion Brewery Co Ltd*, HL 1910, 5 TC 568; [1911] AC 150.

Breweries—licence applications, etc

[68.22] See *Southwell v Savill Bros*, 63.23 TRADING PROFITS; *Morse v Stedeford*, 63.24 TRADING PROFITS, and *Pendleton v Mitchells & Butlers*, 63.25 TRADING PROFITS.

Brewery—expenditure on repairs of tied houses

[68.23] A brewery company claimed a deduction for its expenditure on repairs to its tied houses (and for the amount by which its Schedule A assessment on the tied houses exceeded the rents which it received from the tenants). The KB allowed the claim. *Youngs Crawshay & Youngs Ltd v Brooke*, KB 1912, 6 TC 393.

Brewery—tied houses—excess of rents paid over rents received

[68.24] The HL held that a brewery company was entitled to deduct its expenditure on the repairs, insurance premiums, and rates and taxes of its tied houses, together with certain legal expenses referring to the tied houses, and the excess of the rents it paid (in the case of leasehold houses) over the rents which it received from its tenants. *Usher's Wiltshire Brewery Ltd v Bruce*, HL 1914, 6 TC 399; [1915] AC 433. (*Note*. See now *ITTOIA 2005, s 19* and *CTA 2009, s 42*.)

[68.25] The HL held that, in arriving at a deficiency of rent allowance permitted under the decision in *Usher's Wiltshire Brewery v Bruce*, 68.24

above, each tied house should be considered separately, and that lease premiums received from the tied tenants should be taken into account. *Collyer v Hoare & Co Ltd*, HL 1932, 17 TC 169; [1932] AC 407. (*Note*. See now *ITTOIA 2005, s 19* and *CTA 2009, s 42* with regard to '*Usher*' allowances. See *ITTOIA 2005, ss 277–283* and *CTA 2009, s 217* with regard to lease premiums.)

Brewery—expenditure on rehabilitation of licensed houses

[68.26] A brewery entered into an extensive programme of altering and improving some of its licensed premises. It accepted that most of its expenditure was capital, but claimed certain expenditure as revenue on the ground that it was extra expenditure incurred to keep the houses open during rehabilitation. The Special Commissioners held that the disputed expenditure was capital, and the KB upheld their decision. *Mann Crossman & Paulin Ltd v Compton*, KB 1947, 28 TC 410; [1947] 1 All ER 742.

Brewery—compensation payments on termination of tenancies

[68.27] As part of a general expansion scheme, a brewery group was increasing the proportion of its managed houses. This involved terminating the tenancies of a number of houses let to tied tenants, and two of the companies in the group made *ex gratia* payments to the displaced tenants. There was considerable opposition by the group tenants to the scheme, including the formation of a tenants' association to organise the opposition, and the compensation payments, although voluntary, were made on the basis of a scale and scheme regarded as acceptable by the association. The Special Commissioners held that the payments were capital, as an essential part of obtaining possession of the tied houses, and that in any event they were not wholly and exclusively for the purposes of the brewing companies' trades as the intention was for the management company to manage the houses. The Ch D upheld their decision. *Watneys London Ltd v Pike; Watney Combe Reid & Co Ltd v Pike*, Ch D 1982, 57 TC 372; [1982] STC 733. (*Note*. For the treatment of such payments in the hands of the displaced tenants, see *Murray v Goodhews*, 66.53 TRADING PROFITS.)

Distillery—whisky storage rents

[68.28] A whisky-distilling company (D) was voluntarily wound up, and its business was taken over by another company (S), which had acquired its shares. S paid the liquidator an amount representing the accrued rents for whisky sold and stored in bonded warehouses. The CS held that the accrued rents were profits of D, and were assessable on the liquidator. *CIR v Oban Distillery Co Ltd*, CS 1932, 18 TC 33.

[68.29] See also *Dailuaine-Talisker Distilleries v CIR*, 62.40 TRADING PROFITS, and *CIR v Arthur Bell & Sons*, 62.42 TRADING PROFITS.

Licensed premises—monopoly value payments

[68.30] A restaurant proprietor was granted a renewal of his licence for three years, subject to paying £75 in three annual instalments for 'monopoly value'. The KB held that the payments were capital expenditure. *Kneeshaw v Albertolli*, KB 1940, 23 TC 462; [1940] 2 KB 295; [1940] 3 All ER 500.

[68.31] A company operated a licensed hotel. It was required by the lease to make 'monopoly value' payments in instalments. The KB held that the payments were capital expenditure and were not allowable deductions. The CA unanimously upheld this decision. *Henriksen v Grafton Hotels Ltd*, CA 1942, 24 TC 453; [1942] 2 KB 184; [1942] 1 All ER 678.

Whisky liqueur—commission received for sale of trade mark, etc.

[68.32] A firm sold the trade mark, the manufacturing formula and the goodwill of a brand of whisky liqueur which it manufactured. Under the agreement it also sold certain materials, in return for acommission on sales of whisky liqueur manufactured from the materials. The Revenue included the commission in income tax and excess profits tax assessments, and the firm appealed, contending that the commission was a capital receipt. The Commissioners rejected this contention and dismissed the appeal, and the Ch D upheld their decision. *Orchard Wine & Spirit Co v Loynes*, Ch D 1952, 33 TC 97.

Brewery—expenditure to obtain poll on Sunday opening

[68.33] The *Licensing Act 1961* permitted local polls on the question of whether public houses in Wales and Monmouthshire could be opened on Sundays. The polls were to be held if they were requested under a specified procedure. A brewery company (R) contributed £5,500 towards the expenses of a trade association in obtaining signatures requesting polls, and claimed that the £5,500 should be deducted in computing its profits. The Revenue rejected the claim on the grounds that it was capital expenditure, but the Special Commissioners allowed R's appeal and the Ch D upheld their decision. *Cooper v Rhymney Breweries Ltd*, Ch D 1965, 42 TC 509; [1965] 1 WLR 1378; [1965] 3 All ER 416.

Brewing ceased—beer selling continued—whether a new trade

[68.34] See *Gordon & Blair Ltd v CIR*, 61.46 TRADING INCOME.

Builders

Property sales—whether trading profits

[68.35] See 67.63 *et seq.* TRADING PROFITS for certain property sales by builders where the issue was whether the profits were trading profits.

Sale of houses subject to ground annuals

[68.36] A building partnership built houses on land which it had acquired, creating ground annuals over the houses and the attached land, and selling the houses subject to the ground annuals, which it retained. The HL held that the realisable value of the ground annuals should be included in arriving at the partnership's profits. (The ground annuals represented money's worth readily measurable by reference to the current market price of ground annuals.) *CIR v John Emery & Sons*, HL 1936, 20 TC 213; [1937] AC 91.

[68.37] A building company (B) granted 99-year leases of houses it built, on land it owned, in return for a premium and an annual ground rent. The Revenue considered that the premiums and the market value of the ground rents should be brought into account in computing B's profits. The CA allowed B's appeal in part, holding that the premiums were trading receipts but that the ground rents could only be brought in at the lower of their cost or market value. The HL upheld this decision, distinguishing *CIR v John Emery & Sons*, **68.36** above, as B retained the freehold subject to the ground rent. The HL held that B could not be taxed on the excess of the market value over the cost. *BG Utting & Co Ltd v Hughes*, HL 1940, 23 TC 174; [1940] AC 463; [1940] 2 All ER 76.

[68.38] The decision in *BG Utting & Co Ltd v Hughes*, **68.37**, was applied in a Scottish case where a builder had sold houses subject to feu duties. *McMillan v CIR*, CS 1942, 24 TC 417.

[68.39] The decision in *BG Utting & Co Ltd v Hughes*, **68.37** above, was also applied in a case where a building firm had created ground rents and increased such rents when it sold houses on long leases. The KB held that the formula in *CIR v John Emery & Sons*, **68.36** above, should be used in arriving at the cost of the ground rents. *Heather v Redfern & Sons*, KB 1944, 26 TC 119.

Part of sale proceeds left with building society as security

[68.40] A building company (J) sold houses on terms whereby it deposited part of the sale proceeds with building societies as collateral security for its guarantee of part of the advance by the society to the purchaser. The Revenue issued assessments on the basis that the full amount of the sale proceeds was taxable on J at the time of the sales. J appealed, contending that the amounts deposited with the building societies should not be treated as taxable until the societies released them. The HL held that the amounts in question were taxable at the time of sale, but only at an actuarial valuation to take account of the risk of the purchaser defaulting, rather than at their face value. If an actuarial valuation were impracticable, the amounts deposited should not be assessed until the societies released them. *John Cronk & Sons Ltd v Harrison*, HL 1936, 20 TC 612; [1937] AC 185; [1936] 3 All ER 747.

Collateral securities repaid to liquidator

[68.41] A building company (H) had deposited sums with a building society, as collateral security on sales of houses it built. The amounts deposited were not included in the computation of the profits of the years of sale. H went into voluntary liquidation in November 1946. Prior to that date, the building society had told H that it would repay the deposits if it were asked to do so, but H made no such request. The deposits were later repaid to H's liquidator. The CA held that the deposits were taxable in full in 1946/47, since they were worth their face value and the building society would have repaid them if requested. *Chibbett v Harold Brookfield & Son Ltd*, CA 1952, 33 TC 467; [1952] 2 QB 677; [1952] 2 All ER 265.

Profit on sale lent to purchaser—loan becoming irrecoverable

[68.42] In 1935 a builder and property dealer (L) sold property at a profit of £12,500 to a company which he and two others had formed for the purpose. It was hoped that the company would quickly resell the property at a profit, and it was agreed that the £12,500 should remain with the company as a loan, repayable on the resale of the property. In the event, the hopes for a quick resale were not realised; the property remained on the company's hands and the loan was not repaid. The Revenue included the £12,500 in L's profits for the year to 7 March 1936 (assessed for 1936/37). The Commissioners dismissed L's appeal, finding that there was no evidence that the value of the debt at 7 March 1936 was less than £12,500. The KB upheld their decision. *Lock v Jones*, KB 1941, 23 TC 749.

Builder selling houses and lending part of proceeds to purchasers

[68.43] A builder sold numerous houses under terms whereby part of the sale price was treated as a loan to the purchaser. The loans carried interest and were repayable by instalments over a number of years, and were secured by a second mortgage or by promissory notes. The Revenue considered that the full sale price should be brought into the accounts less any permissible allowance for bad or doubtful debts. The builder appealed against the relevant assessments, contending that the sums receivable under the second mortgages and promissory notes should be valued at their actual value at the time of the sale of the houses, and that if a valuation were impracticable, the amounts assessable in any year were only the amounts repaid in that year. The HL accepted this contention and allowed the appeal (by a 3-2 majority, Viscount Simon and Lord Porter dissenting), holding that the sums due under the second mortgages or promissory notes should be brought in at their value. The case was remitted to the Commissioners to make a valuation. (Viscount Simon and Lord Russell expressed the view that, if valuation proved impracticable, the debts should be brought in as the instalments were received.) *Absalom v Talbot*, HL 1944, 26 TC 166; [1944] AC 204; [1944] 1 All ER 642.

Commercial occupation of land (ITTOIA 2005, s 10; CTA 2009, ss 37, 38)

Hire of Town Hall

[68.44] The Middlesbrough Corporation hired out its Town Hall for meetings, organised public dances in it and provided roller skating facilities in the crypt. The Revenue issued assessments on the basis that the whole of the activities amounted to trading. The Corporation appealed, contending that the assessment should be limited to its profits from the provision of chattels and services (with the consequence that, under the law then in force, its other profits would be covered by assessments under Schedule A). The Ch D rejected this contention and held that the whole of the activities amounted to trading. *Jennings v Middlesbrough Corporation*, Ch D 1953, 34 TC 447; [1953] 1 WLR 833; [1953] 2 All ER 207.

Letting of petrol station

[68.45] A company (C) owned various properties, which it let on licence. It granted a licence to an associated company to use a site which it owned as a petrol station. The licensee began, but discontinued, legal action against certain oil companies. C paid the costs of this action, and claimed the payment as a deduction in computing its profits for corporation tax. The Ch D rejected the claim, holding that C was not carrying on a trade of letting properties, so that the payment was not an allowable deduction. The exploitation of rights in land did not amount to trading. *Webb v Conelee Properties Ltd*, Ch D 1982, 56 TC 149; [1982] STC 913.

Unfurnished letting—whether a trade

[68.46] In an Irish case, a woman let unfurnished a shop and a number of flats. She provided no services, but negotiated the lettings and supervised the properties herself. She claimed earned income relief, contending that the letting amounted to a trade. Her claim was rejected. *Pairceir v EM*, HC(I) 1971, TL(I) 107.

Farming company selling one of two farms—unrelieved losses

[68.47] See *Bispham v Eardiston Farming Co (1919) Ltd*, 27.9 FARMING.

Land planted with coniferous trees

[68.48] See *Jaggers (t/a Shide Trees) v Ellis*, 27.13 FARMING.

Garage proprietors

Exclusivity payments

[68.49] A garage proprietor entered into an exclusivity agreement with a petrol wholesale company, under which the company undertook to refund his expenditure on sales promotion up to a maximum of £115 per year for ten years. The Ch D held that the payments which he received under the agreement were trading receipts. *Evans v Wheatley*, Ch D 1958, 38 TC 216. (*Note.* Similar payments had previously been held to be revenue expenditure by the wholesale company—see *Bolam v Regent Oil Co Ltd*, 68.120 below.)

[68.50] A garage proprietor entered into a ten-year exclusivity agreement with a petrol wholesale company under which he received a contribution towards certain capital expenditure on extending his premises. The CS held that the amount received was a capital receipt, distinguishing *Evans v Wheatley*, 68.49 above. Lord Patrick held that 'a sum of money which a trader receives to enable him to obtain valuable assets of a capital nature, a sum which he can only obtain if he does so add to his capital assets, and in return for which he parts with a valuable asset of a capital nature, cannot properly be described as a trading profit'. As a matter of principle, 'such a transaction should be properly entered in a capital account and not an account of the annual profits, gains and losses of the trader'. *CIR v Coia*, CS 1959, 38 TC 334.

[68.51] Under a five-year exclusivity agreement, a petrol wholesale company paid a garage proprietor sums which, apart from small payments for repainting and advertising, were used to meet expenditure on improvements to his premises. The Ch D held that the payments, other than the amounts for repainting and advertising, were capital receipts and were not taxable . *McLaren v Needham*, Ch D 1960, 39 TC 37.

[68.52] A company (W) operated a petrol station. In 1951 the local Council served a compulsory purchase order on it, forcing it to seek new premises. In 1954, before it had moved into new premises, it entered into a 20-year exclusivity agreement with a petrol wholesale company (R) under which R was to pay to W a maximum of £20,000 in reimbursement of expenditure on sales promotion, etc. The full £20,000 was eventually paid in four amounts, partly to W and partly on W's behalf to contractors carrying out work at the new premises. The Ch D held that the payments were capital receipts. *Walter W Saunders Ltd v Dixon*, Ch D 1962, 40 TC 329.

[68.53] A company (T) operated a petrol filling station and also sold towing brackets from separate premises. It entered into a five-year exclusivity agreement with a petrol wholesale company (E), whereby E paid T £300,000 in 1990 and £100,000 in 1991. T appealed against corporation tax assessments, contending that the payments which it had received were capital rather than revenue. The Special Commissioner rejected this contention and dismissed T's appeal, holding on the evidence that the payments were trading receipts rather than capital receipts. The Commissioner noted that, since T's business was 'not limited to' the filling station which was the subject of the agreement, the agreement did not affect the 'whole structure' of T's business. *Tanfield Ltd v Carr*, Sp C [1999] SSCD 213 (Sp C 200).

[68.54] A partnership purchased a petrol filling station. Immediately before completing the purchase, they entered into a five-year exclusivity agreement with a petrol wholesale company (S), whereby S agreed to make four payments to the partnership, totalling £405,000. Initially the partnership treated these payments as trading receipts. However, the partnership's accountant subsequently formed the opinion that the effect of the agreement between the partnership and S was that two of the payments, totalling £145,000, should have been treated as capital receipts. The partnership therefore lodged a claim to error or mistake relief under *TMA, s 33*. The Revenue rejected the claim, and the partnership appealed. The Special Commissioner allowed the appeal, holding that the agreement showed that S had intended the £145,000 to 'be used for the purpose of acquiring the business'. It was therefore a capital receipt, applying *Walter W Saunders Ltd v Dixon*, **68.52** above, and distinguishing *Evans v Wheatley*, **68.49** above. *McClymont & McClymont v Jarman; McClymont & McClymont v Glover*, Sp C 2003, [2004] SSCD 54 (Sp C 387).

Insurance companies

Unearned premiums and unexpired risks

[68.55] A fire insurance company was refused a deduction from its profits on account of 'unearned premiums'. *Imperial Fire Insurance Co v Wilson*, Ex D 1876, 1 TC 71. (*Note*. The decision was approved by the HL in *General Accident Fire & Life Assurance Ltd v M'Gowan*, **68.57** below.)

[68.56] In a Scottish case, it was held that the untaxed interest of an insurance company should be included in its profits, and that the profit of the company's life insurance branch could only be ascertained by actuarial valuation, rather than by the balance of the receipts and expenses of the year. The decision in *Imperial Fire Insurance Co v Wilson*, **68.55** above, was distinguished. *Scottish Union & National Insurance Co v Smiles*, CE 1889, 2 TC 551. (*Notes*. (1) It was also held that the life and fire insurance branches should be assessed as one. The decision here has been overtaken by legislation now in *ICTA 1988, s 431G*. (2) The case was heard with *Northern Assurance Co v Russell*, **68.64** below.)

[68.57] A company carrying on the business of fire, sickness, accident and guarantee insurance claimed a deduction of 33⅓% of its premium receipts in respect of unexpired risks. The HL rejected the claim, holding that the deduction claimed was not a sufficiently accurate estimate of the 'real value' of the unexpired risks. Lord Loreburn observed that the Revenue method, approved by the Commissioners, of allowing expenses and losses actually incurred was 'a good working rule in the present instance'. *General Accident Fire & Life Assurance Ltd v M'Gowan*, HL 1908, 5 TC 308; [1908] AC 207.

[68.58] A fire insurance company allocated 40% of its premium receipts to a reserve for estimated losses on unexpired risks, and claimed a deduction for this. The HL allowed the claim, distinguishing *General Accident Fire & Life Assurance Ltd v M'Gowan*, 68.57 above. *Sun Insurance Office v Clark*, HL 1912, 6 TC 59; [1912] AC 443.

[68.59] A Fijian company (S) was incorporated to carry on the business of underwriting general insurance. In its accounts for the year to June 1979 it claimed a deduction of $85,000 for claims incurred but not yet reported, basing the figure on an examination of claims made in the period from 1974 to 1978. The Fijian Commissioner disallowed the deduction and the Fijian Court of Review dismissed S's appeal, finding that 17.94% of claims were unsuccessful. The Privy Council allowed 82.06% of the amount claimed, holding that since 82.06% of claims were successful, that percentage of the total amount claimed was a permissible deduction in calculating S's profits. *Southern Pacific Insurance Co (Fiji) Ltd v Fijian Commr of Inland Revenue*, PC [1986] STC 178.

Bonuses to policy-holders

[68.60] In a case where the substantive issue has been overtaken by legislation now in *ICTA 1988, s 431G*, the HL held (by a 2–1 majority) that bonuses paid by an insurance company to policy-holders participating in profits ('with-profits' policy-holders) had to be included in the calculation of the company's profits assessable to income tax. The payment of the bonuses was a distribution of profits, rather than an expense incurred in earning profits. *Last v London Assurance Corporation*, HL 1885, 2 TC 100. (*Note.* For the Revenue's practice following this decision, see HMRC Statement of Practice 4/95.)

Life assurance company—untaxed interest

[68.61] See *Clerical Medical & General Life Assurance Co v Carter*, **53.13** SCHEDULE D, and *Revell v Edinburgh Life Insurance Co*, **53.14** SCHEDULE D.

Life assurance company—annuities

[68.62] A life assurance company (G) carried on general annuity business. It claimed that the annuities which it paid were deductible in arriving at its profits. The Revenue rejected the claim on the grounds that the annuities were distributions of profit, rather than expenses in earning profits, but the HL allowed G's appeal. Lord Halsbury held that 'this particular commercial adventure consists in selling annuities, and that which they pay therefore is to them the cost of the article supplied'. *Gresham Life Assurance Society v Styles*, HL 1890, 3 TC 185; [1892] AC 309.

Life assurance company—income from overseas investments

[68.63] See *Norwich Union Fire Insurance Co v Magee*, **53.7** SCHEDULE D, and *Liverpool & London & Globe Insurance Co v Bennett*, **53.8** SCHEDULE D.

Profits on sale of investments

[68.64] In a Scottish case, it was held that the surpluses derived by an insurance company from realising investments in the course of its business were part of its profits. *Northern Assurance Co v Russell*, CE 1889, 2 TC 551.

Loss on conversion of investments—whether allowable

[68.65] An insurance company (R) held investments in British railways for the purpose of its fire, accident and general insurance business. The railways were amalgamated into four large companies in 1921, and R was required to take new railway stocks in place of those held. The market value of the new stocks was below the cost of the old. R claimed that the difference should be allowed as the equivalent of a loss on realisation. The KB accepted this contention and allowed R's appeal. *Royal Insurance Co Ltd v Stephen*, KB 1928, 14 TC 22. (*Note*. See now, however, *CTA 2009, s 129*.)

Profit on realisation of investments out of surplus funds

[68.66] The Commissioners found that the profits of a general insurance company on its realisation of investments made out of surplus funds were not trading profits. The CS upheld their decision as one of fact. *CIR v Scottish Automobile & General Insurance Co Ltd*, CS 1931, 16 TC 381.

Discount on premiums—whether an expense of management

[68.67] A life assurance company (N) entered into an agreement with an association of civil servants under which members of the association could obtain a discount of 15% on premiums on policies effected with N. The CS held that the discounts were not management expenses of N, within what is now *CTA 2009, ss 1219–1231*. *North British & Mercantile Insurance Co v Easson*, CS 1919, 7 TC 463.

Whether annuity business carried on

[68.68] In a stamp duty case, the CS upheld the Revenue's contention that a private investment trust company which covenanted to pay a shareholder an annuity in consideration of a capital payment, and had previously granted one similar annuity, was not carrying on a business of granting annuities on human life. *Stevenston Securities Ltd v CIR*, CS 1959, 38 TC 459.

Overseas mutual assurance society—double tax convention

[68.69] An Australian mutual assurance society carried on business through a UK branch. Under the UK/Australia double tax convention then in force, the UK tax on the 'industrial or commercial profits' of the UK 'permanent establishment' of an Australian enterprise was limited to tax on the profits which might be expected to arise if the establishment were independent. The Revenue considered that, being mutual, the society had no 'industrial or commercial profits' or, alternatively, that any relief could be given only against trading profits. The society appealed, contending that relief should be allowed against its Case III assessment. The Special Commissioners accepted this contention and allowed the appeal, and the HL upheld their decision (by a 4–1 majority, Lord Denning dissenting). The purpose of the relevant legislation (which has subsequently been superseded) was to attribute to a foreign life assurance society a reasonable profit in respect of business done in the UK, and the rule was superseded by the double tax convention. *Ostime v Australian Mutual Provident Society*, HL 1959, 38 TC 492; [1960] AC 459; [1959] 3 All ER 245.

[68.70] A Canadian life assurance company (S) carried on business in the UK through a branch. It appealed against assessments for its accounting periods from 1972 to 1977, contending that the assessments were inconsistent with certain provisions of the relevant UK/Canada Double Taxation Conventions. The Ch D rejected this contention and upheld the assessments in principle, and the CA dismissed S's appeal. *Sun Life Assurance Co of Canada v Pearson*, CA 1986, 59 TC 250; [1986] STC 335. (*Note*. Other issues in the case have been overtaken by changes in the relevant legislation.)

Overseas insurance company holding Government securities

[68.71] A Canadian life insurance company carried on business in the UK through a UK branch. It received substantial amounts of interest on UK Government securities which it held as investments. It appealed against corporation tax assessments for accounting periods up to September 1995, contending that this interest should be treated as exempt from tax under *ICTA 1988, s 47(1)*. The Ch D rejected this contention and dismissed the appeal. The Treasury prospectus relating to such securities clearly stipulated that the exemption for non-residents did not 'exclude the interest from any computation for taxation purposes of the profits of any trade or business carried on in the United Kingdom'. The company here was carrying on business in the UK, and its computation of profits on the 'I minus E' basis was a 'computation for taxation purposes of the profits of any trade or business'. Neuberger J observed that 'it would be anomalous if a non-resident mutual life assurance company carrying on business in the United Kingdom enjoyed a significant tax advantage, and therefore a substantial competitive edge, over (UK-resident) life assurance companies'. Accordingly, the interest did not qualify for exemption. *The Manufacturers' Life Assurance Co Ltd v Cummins*, Ch D 2000, TL 3622; [2001] STC 316. (*Note. ICTA 1988, s 47* was repealed by *FA 1996* for accounting periods ending after 31 March 1996.)

London branch of overseas insurance company—investment sales

[68.72] A company (G), resident in the Netherlands with a London branch, carried on reinsurance business. Under the relevant double tax convention, the profits of the branch were to be taken as the profits it might be expected to derive if it had been an independent enterprise dealing at arm's length with the Netherlands company. The London branch had a portfolio of investments. The Ch D held that profits on realisation of investments in the portfolio and income from them were part of G's reinsurance profits. *General Reinsurance Co Ltd v Tomlinson*, Ch D 1970, 48 TC 81; [1970] 1 WLR 566; [1970] 2 All ER 436. (*Note*. The case was heard with *Alherma Investments Ltd v Tomlinson*, **65.12** TRADING PROFITS.)

Overseas insurance companies operating in London through committee

[68.73] An unincorporated association of 15 American insurance companies carried on fire and marine insurance in the UK from premises in London and in the names of two of its members. All members of the association participated in receipts and expenses in agreed proportions. The Revenue issued income tax assessments on the association. The Special Commissioners upheld the assessments and the Ch D dismissed the association's appeal. *American Foreign Insurance Association v Davies (and related appeals)*, Ch D 1950, 32 TC 1.

Management expenses

[68.74] See **18.31** *et seq*. CORPORATION TAX for cases concerning management expenses, including management expenses of insurance companies.

Mutual insurance

[68.75] See the cases noted at **40.1** to **40.6** MUTUAL TRADING.

Manufacturing businesses

Payments to secure closure of rival business

[68.76] A railway company (L) had operated a steel works. It agreed with two steel companies (U and B) to close its steel works and purchase certain steel products from U and B. They paid L compensation of £180,000 in 120 monthly instalments of £1,500. U and B arranged for part of L's requirements to be met by outside manufacturers, which made tonnage payments to U and B, shared between them in the proportion in which they paid the £180,000. The Special Commissioners held that the instalments of the £180,000 were capital payments, and that the payments which U and B received from the outside manufacturers were trading receipts. The CA upheld their decision. *United Steel Companies Ltd v Cullington (No 1)*, CA 1939, 23 TC 71.

Manufacturing company—payments from railway company

[68.77] A railway company built sidings for the works of a brick-manufacturing company (F). F paid for the sidings, which became its property. The agreement, however, provided for the railway to pay to F a certain proportion of its receipts from the traffic to and from the works, and that when these payments in aggregate equalled the cost of the sidings, the ownership of the sidings was to pass to the railway. The Revenue issued assessments on F, charging income tax on the payments. F appealed, contending that they were capital receipts. The Special Commissioners accepted this contention and allowed the appeal, and the KB upheld their decision. Lawrence J held that 'the substance of the transaction embodied by the agreement' was 'equivalent to a sale and resale of a capital asset'. *Legge v Flettons Ltd*, KB 1939, 22 TC 455; [1939] 3 All ER 220.

Payments based on by-products of manufacture of chemicals

[68.78] A company (M) was engaged in the manufacture of magnesium, which needs large quantities of chlorine. M proposed to build a plant to produce the chlorine which it needed. An important by-product of making chlorine is caustic soda. A major chemical manufacturer (ICI), which derived substantial income from the sale of caustic soda, was anxious to avoid competition. After negotiations, M and ICI agreed that M should obtain its chlorine from ICI for ten years at a basic price of £10 per ton. Under a separate agreement signed on the same day, M undertook not to make chlorine or caustic soda itself, and ICI agreed to pay M £7 10s for each ton of chlorine supplied by ICI, expressed to be 'in respect of' the caustic soda which M would have produced if it had made the chlorine itself. The Revenue assessed M on the basis that the payments of £10 per ton which it made were allowable deductions but the payments of £7 10s per ton which it received were trading receipts. M appealed, contending that the payments which it received from ICI were not trading receipts. The CA rejected this contention and upheld the assessment, holding that the two agreements formed a composite arrangement to enable M to obtain its chlorine requirements. *Thompson v Magnesium Elektron Ltd*, CA 1943, 26 TC 1; [1944] 1 All ER 126.

Company manufacturing gramophone records

[68.79] A company manufacturing gramophone records, in which it held the copyright, received fees and other receipts from the use of its records in public. It appealed against assessments to excess profits tax, contending that the receipts were income from investments and therefore outside the scope of excess profits tax (see **39.19** MISCELLANEOUS INCOME). The HL rejected this contention and upheld the assessments, holding that the receipts were not income from investments. *Electric & Musical Industries Ltd v CIR*, HL 1950, 29 ATC 156.

Sugar manufacturer—subsidies linked with production

[68.80] See *Smart v Lincolnshire Sugar Co Ltd*, **64.12** TRADING PROFITS.

Paper manufacturer—recovery under insurance policy

[68.81] See *Mallandain Investments Ltd v Shadbolt*, **64.25** TRADING PROFITS.

Paper manufacturer—income from letting surplus premises

[68.82] See *Albert E Reed & Co Ltd v CIR*, 64.53 TRADING PROFITS.

Receipts for disclosure of details of manufacturing processes

[68.83] See the cases noted at 65.49 to 65.58 TRADING PROFITS.

Payments for disclosure of technical information

[68.84] See *British Sugar Manufacturers Ltd v Harris*, 63.126 TRADING PROFITS, and *Paterson Engineering Co Ltd v Duff*, 63.277 TRADING PROFITS.

Company manufacturing railway wagons—sale of wagons

[68.85] See *Gloucester Railway Carriage & Wagon Co Ltd v CIR*, 64.56 TRADING PROFITS.

Manufacturing company—purchase at overvalue from subsidiary

[68.86] See *CIR v Huntley & Palmers Ltd*, 63.133 TRADING PROFITS.

Guarantee of indebtedness of associated company

[68.87] See *Garforth v Tankard Carpets Ltd*, 63.138 TRADING PROFITS.

Payments to directors for restrictive covenants

[68.88] See *Associated Portland Cement Manufacturers Ltd v Kerr*, 63.296 TRADING PROFITS.

Salary of employee seconded to overseas subsidiary

[68.89] See *Robinson v Scott Bader & Co Ltd*, 63.182 TRADING PROFITS.

Conversion of plant and buildings for different use

[68.90] See *Lothian Chemical Co Ltd v Rogers*, 63.68 TRADING PROFITS.

Manufacturing firm—replacement of roof

[68.91] See *William P Lawrie v CIR*, 63.71 TRADING PROFITS.

Manufacturing company—expenditure on premises

[68.92] See *Vale v Martin Mahony & Bros Ltd*, 63.75 TRADING PROFITS; *Phillips v Whieldon Sanitary Potteries Ltd*, 63.77 TRADING PROFITS, and *Hodgkins v Plunder & Pollak (Ireland) Ltd*, 63.90 TRADING PROFITS.

Cost of land with deposits of raw materials

[68.93] See *Alianza Co Ltd v Bell*, 63.97 TRADING PROFITS.

Manufacturing company—payment to National Coal Board

[68.94] See *Bradbury v The United Glass Bottle Manufacturers Ltd*, 63.106 TRADING PROFITS.

Cigarette manufacturer—payments for cropping of leaves

[68.95] See *Mohanlal Hargovind of Jubbulpore v Central Provinces & Behar Commissioner of Income Tax*, 63.129 TRADING PROFITS.

Mines, quarries, etc. (ITTOIA 2005, s 12; CTA 2009, s 39)

CROSS-REFERENCES

See also chapter 38 MINING RENTS AND ROYALTIES.

Pit-sinking, etc.

[68.96] In a Scottish case, a partnership which operated a colliery claimed a deduction for a percentage of the original cost of sinking its pits, and for depreciation of buildings and machinery. The Exchequer Court rejected the claim, holding that the expenses were chargeable to capital and were not allowable deductions for income tax. *In re Robert Addie & Sons*, CE 1875, 1 TC 1, 12 SLR 274. (*Note*. The decision has been largely overtaken by the modern capital allowances system but the case, the first in the Official Reports of Tax Cases, is of importance as an early statement of the principle that capital expenditure is not allowable in computing profits.)

[68.97] The HL reached a similar decision in *Coltness Iron Co v Black*, HL 1881, 1 TC 287; 6 AC 315.

[68.98] A tin-mining company claimed a deduction for the cost of deepening a main shaft. The KB rejected the claim, holding that this was capital expenditure and was not an allowable deduction. *Bonner v Basset Mines Ltd*, KB 1912, 6 TC 146.

Shortworkings

[68.99] Under the terms of its mining lease, a company (B) which operated a colliery paid royalties with a minimum dead rent. Any excess of the dead rent over royalties could be recovered from subsequent surpluses of royalties over dead rent. B claimed to deduct these amounts in arriving at its profits. The Special Commissioners rejected the claim, holding that the amount to be deducted was the amount actually paid after setting off the excess brought forward. The QB upheld this decision and dismissed B's appeal. *Broughton & Plas Power Coal Co Ltd v Kirkpatrick*, QB 1884, 2 TC 69; 14 QBD 491.

[68.100] The KB reached a similar decision in an appeal by a mining company against an excess profits tax assessment. *CIR v Cranford Ironstone Co Ltd*, KB 1942, 29 TC 113.

Cost of 'de-watering' seam

[68.101] A mining company deepened a pit to reach a lower seam. It took a small quantity of coal from the seam but then discontinued working it and allowed the water to rise in the pit up to the level of the upper seams which it continued to work. Some years later, when the upper seams were nearing exhaustion, it 'de-watered' the pit in order to work the lower seam. The Special Commissioners held that the cost of the de-watering was capital expenditure, and the CS unanimously upheld their decision. *United Collieries Ltd v CIR*, CS 1929, 12 TC 1248.

Cost of obtaining release from mining lease

[68.102] See *Mallett v Staveley Coal & Iron Co Ltd*, 63.45 TRADING PROFITS.

Surface damage—lump sum payment

[68.103] In 1919 a company terminated a mineral lease dating from 1891, entered into a new lease, and, in accordance with an option under the original lease, paid the lessor £6,104 for surface damage up to 1919. The Special Commissioners held that the payment was capital expenditure, and the CS unanimously upheld their decision. *Robert Addie & Sons' Collieries Ltd v CIR*, CS 1924, 8 TC 671.

Surface damage—periodic payments

[68.104] Under its mining lease, a colliery company made periodic payments to the lessor based on the acreage worked, in indemnification of its liabilities for surface damage. The Special Commissioners held that the payments were allowable deductions, and the KB upheld their decision. *O'Grady v Bullcroft Main Collieries Ltd*, KB 1932, 17 TC 93.

Periodic payments for right to withdraw surface support

[68.105] See *CIR v New Sharlston Collieries Co Ltd*, 38.2 MINING RENTS AND ROYALTIES; *CIR v Hope*, 38.3 MINING RENTS AND ROYALTIES, and *Earl Fitzwilliam's Collieries Co v Phillips*, 38.4 MINING RENTS AND ROYALTIES.

Sales of slag

[68.106] A colliery company (W) sold quantities of slag, mainly from heaps which it had acquired on its incorporation but partly from slag arising as the result of its activities, since discontinued, of manufacturing iron and steel. The Revenue sought to include the proceeds in the income tax assessment on Ws profits. The Commissioners allowed W's appeal, holding that W had not carried on any trading activity in relation to the disposal of the slag heaps, and that the receipts from the sale of slag were not receipts arising from any of its trading operations and were not taxable. The KB upheld their decision as one of fact. *Beams v Weardale Steel, Coal & Coke Co Ltd*, KB 1937, 21 TC 204.

[68.107] A partnership ceased trading in 1911 but was not dissolved. Its assets included a field covered with slag, which was regarded at the time as practically worthless, but which later became of value for road-making. In 1925 it granted a contractor the right to take away the slag in return for certain payments on a royalty basis. The Revenue issued an assessment on the basis that the payments were trading receipts. The partnership appealed, contending that it was not trading. The Special Commissioners accepted this contention and allowed the appeal, and the KB upheld their decision as one of fact. *Shingler v Williams & Sons*, KB 1933, 17 TC 574. (*Note*. The case preceded the introduction by *FA 1934* of what is now *CTA 2009, s 271*. See *Craigenlow Quarries Ltd v CIR*, 38.7 MINING RENTS AND ROYALTIES, and *Rogers v Longsdon*, 38.9 MINING RENTS AND ROYALTIES.)

Payment by instalments towards drainage improvement scheme

[68.108] A colliery company (D) discontinued mining a particular seam, because to continue would have led to subsidence damaging the drainage system, involving it in expenditure on 'remedial works' under a local drainage Act. Some years later it agreed to pay a drainage board £39,000, in 60 half-yearly instalments, towards the cost of a general drainage improvement scheme for the district, which would avoid the need for remedial works. The HL held that the payments to the drainage board were capital payments, and were not deductible in computing D's profits. *Bean v Doncaster Amalgamated Collieries Ltd*, HL 1946, 27 TC 296; [1946] 1 All ER 642.

Compensation for requisition of mining area

[68.109] See *Waterloo Main Colliery Co Ltd v CIR*, 66.37 TRADING PROFITS.

Opencast coal-mining

[68.110] A partnership carried on the trade of opencast coal-mining and purchased land for £2,000 for this purpose. The conveyance required them to reinstate the land, and the vendor to repurchase the land for £500, after mining was ended. The Ch D upheld the Revenue's contention that the payment of the £2,000 and the receipt of the £500 were capital transactions. *Knight v Calder Grove Estates*, Ch D 1954, 35 TC 446.

[68.111] A company carrying on the business of opencast coal-mining made two payments to the owners of the land on which it was operating, one for the right to enter upon the land and one as compensation for the diminution in the value of the land. The Ch D upheld the Revenue's contention that the payments were capital expenditure. *HJ Rorke Ltd v CIR*, Ch D 1960, 39 TC 194; [1960] 1 WLR 1132; [1960] 3 All ER 359.

Colliery houses—whether industrial buildings

[68.112] See *CIR v National Coal Board*, 8.22 CAPITAL ALLOWANCES.

Payments to work old mining dumps

[68.113] See *Rogers v Longsdon*, 38.9 MINING RENTS AND ROYALTIES.

Drift coal-mining pending sinking of pits—date trade commenced

[68.114] See *Cannop Coal Co Ltd v CIR*, 61.43 TRADING INCOME.

Quarry—cost of removal of topsoil

[68.115] A company worked a limestone quarry, using the limestone mainly to produce limestone flour. To ensure the purity of the flour, the topsoil had to be removed before blasting the limestone from the side of the quarry. The Irish Supreme Court held that the cost of removing the top soil was an allowable deduction, as it was part of the cost of manufacture of the marketable product. *Milverton Quarries Ltd v Revenue Commissioners*, SC(I) 1959, 3 ITC 279; [1960] IR 224.

Payments to remove shingle

[68.116] See *Duke of Fife's Trustees v George Wimpey & Co Ltd*, 38.6 MINING RENTS AND ROYALTIES.

Harbour boards

[68.117] See *Mersey Docks & Harbour Board v Lucas*, 57.1 STATUTORY BODIES, and *Port of London Authority v CIR*, 57.2 STATUTORY BODIES.

River conservancy boards

[68.118] See *Humber Conservancy Board v Bater*, **57.4** STATUTORY BODIES; *CIR v Forth Conservancy Board (No 1)*, **57.5** STATUTORY BODIES; *CIR v Forth Conservancy Board (No 2)*, **57.6** STATUTORY BODIES, and *Moville District of Conservators v Ua Clothasaigh*, **57.7** STATUTORY BODIES.

Oil extraction (CTA 2010, ss 270–357)

[68.119] See *RTZ Oil and Gas Ltd v Elliss*, **62.75** TRADING PROFITS (future expenditure on terminating North Sea oil exploration); *Golden Horse Shoe (New) Ltd v Thurgood*, **63.124** TRADING PROFITS (purchase of tailings), *Hughes v British Burmah Petroleum Co Ltd*, **65.3** TRADING PROFITS (payment for unwon oil), and **74** PETROLEUM REVENUE TAX (PRT cases).

Petrol marketing companies

Exclusivity payments by petrol companies

[68.120] A petrol marketing company (R) entered into exclusivity agreements with several retailers under which R reimbursed the retailer for certain expenditure on repairs, etc, based on the retailer's sales of petrol. The agreements were originally for a year or less, but later, to counter proposals by competitors, were for longer periods. The Special Commissioners held that the payments were allowable deductions, finding that they were made to preserve R's goodwill and did not create capital assets. The Ch D upheld their decision. *Bolam v Regent Oil Co Ltd*, Ch D 1956, 37 TC 56.

[68.121] A petrol company (R) entered into exclusivity agreements with garages whereby the garage proprietor leased his premises to R for a premium (computed by reference to the expected gallonage of petrol he would take) and a nominal rent, and R sub-leased the premises to the garage proprietor, for the same period less three days, at a nominal rent. The HL held that the premiums were capital payments and not allowable deductions. *Strick v Regent Oil Co Ltd*, HL 1965, 43 TC 1; [1966] AC 295; [1965] 3 All ER 174.

[68.122] In an Australian case, a petrol company entered into exclusivity agreements with retailers under which it paid lump sums, described as 'development allowances', to be used by the retailer 'to defray the cost of advertising and other merchandising expenses, alterations and/or improvements'. The amount of petrol sold was one of the factors taken into account in fixing the amount of the allowances. The PC held that the payments were deductible in computing the company's profits. *BP Australia Ltd v Australian Commissioner of Taxation*, PC 1965, 44 ATC 312; [1966] AC 224; [1965] 3 All ER 209. (*Note*. The judgment includes a useful review of relevant cases in UK and Commonwealth courts. The judgments in this case and in *Strick v Regent Oil Co Ltd*, **68.121** above, and *Mobil Oil Australia Ltd v*

Australian Commissioner of Taxation, **68.123** below, were delivered on the same day and the Law Lords were also the members of the Judicial Committee of the PC.)

[68.123] In another Australian case, the PC held that exclusivity payments were allowable deductions. The agreements were of two types. Under one, a loan was made to the retailer repayable monthly and the payments to him were monthly amounts equal to the repayments. Under the other, there were yearly payments. (The case also involved whether the agreements contravened certain Australian anti-avoidance legislation and the decision here was also in favour of the company.) *Mobil Oil Australia Ltd v Australian Commissioner of Taxation*, PC 1965, 44 ATC 323; [1966] AC 275; [1965] 3 All ER 225.

[68.124] In an Irish case, in which the exclusivity payments were similar to those considered in *BP Australia Ltd v Australian Commissioner of Taxation*, **68.122** above, the SC(I) held, by a 4-1 majority, that the payments where the agreement was for a period not exceeding 10 years (as were most of the agreements) were of a revenue nature and allowable and, by a 3–2 majority, that there was no ground for according different treatment to payments where the agreement was for more than 10 years. *Dolan v AB Co Ltd*, SC(I) 1968, TL(I) 109.

[68.125] See the cases noted at **68.49** to **68.53** above for the assessability of exclusivity payments in the hands of the retailer.

Whether payments wholly for purchase of trading stock

[68.126] In a New Zealand case, an independent petrol marketing company (E) obtained its petrol from an international oil group (G) under complex arrangements. G was prepared to supply the petrol at 2.5 US cents below the 'posted prices' but not by way of a straightforward discount. Arrangements were agreed whereby E paid G the posted price, and G paid a refining fee of about 5 cents a gallon on petrol which E supplied to a Bahamas company (P), which had been set up for the purpose and was jointly-owned by subsidiaries of E and G. P was required to distribute all its profits, so that E would eventually get the benefit of 2.5 cents per gallon of its purchases via the dividends which one of its subsidiaries received from P. The PC held (by a 3–2 majority, Lord Donovan and Viscount Dilhorne dissenting) that the payments were not incurred exclusively to produce assessable income (the relevant statutory test) and were not deductible. Lord Wilberforce observed that there was a 'single interrelated complex of agreements' and E's purchasing contract could not be looked on in isolation. On the evidence, 2.5 cents per gallon of the payments under this contract were to secure the benefit of the 2.5 cents received and were not for petrol. *New Zealand Commissioner of Inland Revenue v Europa Oil (NZ) Ltd*, PC 1970, 49 ATC 282; [1971] AC 760.

[68.127] From 1964 onwards the company (E) in the case noted at **68.126** above obtained its petrol from semi-refined products of crude oil ('feedstocks') refined for it in a New Zealand co-operative refinery in which it had an interest. The previous contracts with G were replaced by new contracts under which E's feedstocks requirements were met by G under basically similar arrangements, with the group of which E was part receiving the equivalent of

2.5 cents a gallon in the form of dividends from P. There were, however, significant modifications. The purchases from G were made by R, a company which was associated with E but was neither a subsidiary, a parent, or a fellow-subsidiary. E purchased its feedstocks from R but was under no contractual obligation to do so. The arrangement under which P got its 5 cents per gallon profit was protected by a covenant by G to R's parent. The PC held (by a 4-1 majority, Lord Wilberforce dissenting) that the whole of the price paid by E to R was for 'feedstocks' and was an allowable deduction. *Europa Oil (NZ) Ltd v New Zealand Commissioner of Inland Revenue*, PC [1976] STC 37; [1976] 1 WLR 464; [1976] 1 All ER 503.

Timber merchants

[68.128] In 1940 a timber merchant purchased two timber plantations. He sold them in 1947 without having felled any of the timber. He appealed against income tax assessments, contending that the purchase and sale were capital transactions. The CS unanimously rejected this contention and dismissed his appeal. *Murray v CIR*, CS 1951, 32 TC 238.

[68.129] In 1949 a company, which traded as a timber merchant, purchased an area of woodland. It sold it at a profit later that year. It appealed against an income tax assessment, contending that the purchase and sale were capital transactions. The Ch D accepted this contention and allowed the appeal. *McLellan Rawson & Co Ltd v Newall*, Ch D 1955, 36 TC 117.

[68.130] A timber merchant (H) agreed to make substantial payments to a company (C), of which he was a director and shareholder, in return for an indefinite right to enter C's land and select, fell and remove a specified number of trees of various types. He appealed against income tax assessments, contending that these payments should be allowed as deductions. The CS dismissed his appeals, holding that the payments were capital expenditure. The HL upheld this decision (by a 4-1 majority, Lord Oaksey dissenting). Lord Cohen held that what H had acquired 'was not goods or stock-in-trade but an enduring interest in the land and the natural increment of the trees of the nature of a capital asset'. *Hood Barrs v CIR (No 2)*, HL 1957, 37 TC 188; [1957] 1 WLR 529; [1957] 1 All ER 832.

[68.131] A company, which traded as a sawmiller and timber merchant, purchased a wood of mature trees near its sawmill to provide a reserve of timber for its business. It appealed against income tax assessments, contending that this was a purchase of trading stock. The Special Commissioners accepted this contention and allowed the appeal, and the Ch D upheld their decision. *Hopwood v CN Spencer Ltd*, Ch D 1964, 42 TC 169.

Timber plantation—whether timber extraction a separate business

[68.132] See *River Estates Sdn Bhd v Director General of Inland Revenue*, 61.60 TRADING INCOME.

Jungle developed as oil palm plantation—sale of timber

[68.133] See *Mamor Sdn Bhd v Director General of Inland Revenue*, **61.60** TRADING INCOME.

Visiting performers (ITTOIA 2005, ss 13, 14; ITA 2007, ss 965–970)

Income paid by non-resident companies to non-resident sportsman

[68.134] An American tennis player (P), who was neither resident nor domiciled in the UK, received some UK prize money. In addition, two sportswear companies (N and H) paid substantial endorsement income to a US company (E) which P controlled. Both N and H were resident outside the UK, but the amount of endorsement which they paid to E was partly dependent on P's performance in various tournaments, including tournaments in the UK. P submitted a UK tax return claiming a UK loss of £63,869. This was computed on the basis that £42,961 of the total endorsement income which N and H paid to E was taxable in the UK, basing the relevant percentage of the endorsement income on the number of days which P had spent in the UK during the year. The Revenue issued a notice under *TMA, s 28A(5)* on the basis that the relevant percentage should be arrived at on the basis of the number of days taken up by UK tournaments in which P participated, divided by the total number of days taken up by tournaments in which he participated. On this basis, the Revenue computed £125,908 of P's endorsement income as taxable in the UK, so that he had made a UK profit and was liable to UK tax. P appealed, contending that his return had been incorrectly computed and that the income which N and H paid to E should be treated as outside the scope of what is now *ITTOIA 2005, s 13*. The HL rejected this contention and upheld the Revenue's notice (by a 4-1 majority, Lord Walker of Gestingthorpe dissenting). Lord Scott of Foscote held that the purpose of the legislation was 'to subject foreign entertainers or sportsmen to a charge to tax on profits on gains obtained in connection with their commercial activities in the United Kingdom. Payments to foreign companies controlled by them are to be treated as payments to them. The infrequent or sporadic nature of their commercial activities and presence in the United Kingdom and the difficulty of collecting from them' was one of the reasons why a new collection regime had been introduced in 1988. To treat the statutory provisions as including 'a limitation preventing the collection regime from applying where the payer is a foreign entity with no UK presence and thereby relieving the foreign entertainer/sportsman from the charge to tax' could not 'possibly be justified on the basis of a presumed legislative intention'. Accordingly, 'the statutory language should be given its natural meaning.' Lord Mance held that 'there is no incongruity about a primary tax charge being levied on a sportsman or entertainer who performs an activity within the United Kingdom and receives or is treated as receiving a payment from whatever source for that activity. But it would be incongruous if a primary tax charge for payment in respect of a United Kingdom activity depended on whether the payment was or was not made by a person present here.' *Agassi v Robinson (aka Set v Robinson)*, HL 2006, 77 TC 686; [2006] STC 1056; [2006] UKHL 23; [2006] 3 All ER 97. (*Notes.* (1) For another issue in this case, not taken to the HL, see **4.409** APPEALS. (2) *ICTA 1988, s 556* and *ITTOIA 2005, s 13* were subsequently amended by *ITA 2007, Sch 1*. The changes were intended 'to make explicit that these sections will have effect regardless of whether there is a duty to deduct income tax': see the Explanatory Notes to the Income Tax Bill.)

[68.135] An American tennis player (D), who was neither resident nor domiciled in the UK, received endorsement income from two companies which were resident outside the UK. She received prize money in the UK, and in her UK tax returns, she declared a proportion of the endorsement income received by a US company on her behalf. The Revenue issued notices under *TMA, s 28A(5)*, charging UK tax on a significantly larger share of D's endorsement income (adopting the same method as in *Agassi v Robinson*, **68.134** above). She appealed, contending that her return had been incorrectly computed and that the income from companies outside the UK was outside the scope of what is now *ITTOIA 2005, s 13*. The Special Commissioners rejected this contention and dismissed her appeal in principle, holding that what is now *ITTOIA 2005, s 13* applied to payments made to non-residents by non-resident companies. With regard to the computation, the Commissioners rejected the basis used in D's tax return and upheld the Revenue method in principle, subject to the proviso that 'if an appellant is (say) knocked out in the first round of Wimbledon, why should the rest of Wimbledon count into the UK proportion'. They suggested that 'an apportionment based on the number of days played in tournaments might be a better measure but we are not deciding this as we did not hear any argument on it'. *Deuce v Robinson*, Sp C [2003] SSCD 382 (Sp C 373); 6 ITLR 52.

[68.136] A South African tennis player (B), who was neither resident nor domiciled in the UK, received endorsement income from two companies, one of which was resident outside the UK. Some of this income was paid to him personally, and some was paid to a UK company which he controlled. B received prize money in the UK, and in his UK tax returns, he declared a proportion of the endorsement income. The Revenue issued notices under *TMA, s 28A(5)*, charging UK tax on a significantly larger share of B's endorsement income (adopting the same method as in *Agassi v Robinson*, **68.134** above). B appealed, contending that his return had been incorrectly computed; that the income from the company outside the UK was outside the scope of what is now *ITTOIA 2005, s 13*, and that the payments by the UK company were outside the scope of the *Income Tax (Entertainers and Sportsmen) Regulations 1987 (SI 1987/530)*. The Special Commissioners rejected these contentions and dismissed his appeal in principle. The Commissioners held that the relevant income was within *SI 1987/530, reg 6(2)*, since when B played at a tournament in the UK, this was 'an activity performed within the United Kingdom by an entertainer in his character as entertainer on or in connection with a commercial occasion or event'. The money paid to B personally was taxable in the UK since 'when playing at Wimbledon (B) is exercising his trade within the United Kingdom'. With regard to the computation, the Commissioners rejected the basis used in B's tax return and upheld the Revenue method in principle (subject to the proviso quoted in *Deuce v Robinson*, **68.135** above). *Ball v Robinson*, Sp C [2003] SSCD 382 (Sp C 373); 6 ITLR 52.

69

Underwriters

The cases in this chapter are arranged under the following headings.

Income tax

Underwriting commission—year in which assessable

[69.1] See *CIR v Gardner Mountain & D'Ambrumenil Ltd*, 62.44 TRADING PROFITS.

Underwriting commission—whether taxable

[69.2] A company director received commission for underwriting an issue of shares. He was not involved in any other underwriting in the relevant period. The Special Commissioners held that the commission was taxable under Schedule D Case VI, under the legislation then in force. The KB upheld their decision, applying the principles laid down in *Ryall v Hoare*, 39.42 MISCELLANEOUS INCOME. *Lyons v Cowcher*, KB 1926, 10 TC 438.

Damages awarded against managing agent

[69.3] See *Deeny & Others v Gooda Walker & Others*, 14.4 COMPENSATION, ETC.—'GOURLEY' PRINCIPLE.

Underwriter—interest on securities deposited with Lloyd's

[69.4] See *Owen v Sassoon*, 64.38 TRADING PROFITS.

Underwriting losses—claims for relief

[69.5] See *Peterson v De Brunner*, 35.50 LOSS RELIEF.

External name—whether retirement annuity relief due

[69.6] See *Koenigsberger v Mellor*, 46.22 PENSION SCHEMES.

Returns under TMA, s 13—underwriting agents

[69.7] See *Lord Advocate v Gibb*, 49.14 RETURNS AND INFORMATION.

Voluntary payments—whether taxable emoluments

[69.8] See *McBride v Blackburn*, 22.63 EMPLOYMENT INCOME.

Corporation tax

Group relief—whether FA 1994, s 227A applicable

[69.9] A company (S), which was owned by a consortium, carried on business as a corporate Lloyds underwriter, and made losses. It was subsequently acquired, as a wholly-owned subsidiary, by one of the consortium members. It sought to surrender, by way of group relief, underwriting losses which had been deferred by elections under *FA 2000, s 107(4)*. HMRC rejected the claims on the basis that the effect of *FA 1994, s 227A* was that the losses were not available for surrender. S appealed, contending that the existence of a consortium relationship between the companies during the period in which the losses arose satisfied the 'group relief continuity condition' of *FA 1994, s 227A(5)*, so that the restriction in *s 227A* did not apply. The First-tier Tribunal accepted this contention and allowed the appeal. *Standfast Corporate Underwriters Ltd v HMRC*, FTT [2014] UKFTT 182 (TC); [2014] SFTD 957, TC03322.

Inheritance tax

IHTA, s 110(b)—definition of 'assets used in the business'

[69.10] See *Mallender & Others (Drury-Lowe's Executors) v CIR*, 72.79 INHERITANCE TAX.

IHTA, s 110(b)—liabilities incurred for the purposes of the business

[69.11] See *Hardcastle & Hardcastle (Vernede's Executors) v CIR*, 72.80 INHERITANCE TAX.

70

Voluntary Associations

The cases in this chapter are arranged under the following headings.

Facilities for non-members

[70.1] A members' golf club was required by the terms of its lease to permit non-members to use its course, in return for payment of green fees. The KB held that the activity of providing facilities for non-members was severable from the club's other activities, and that the club was taxable on the green fees, less the expenses referable to them. The CA unanimously upheld this decision. *Carlisle & Silloth Golf Club v Smith*, CA 1913, 6 TC 198; [1913] 3 KB 75.

Members' holiday camp admitting visitors

[70.2] An association of local government employees ran a holiday camp to which both members and non-members were admitted. The Revenue assessed the association on the whole of the profits of the camp. The KB allowed the club's appeal, applying the principles laid down in *Carlisle & Silloth Golf Club v Smith*, 70.1 above, and holding that it was liable only on the profits derived from non-members. *National Association of Local Government Officers v Watkins*, KB 1934, 18 TC 499.

Members' social club

[70.3] A company, limited by guarantee, operated a members' social club. The CA held that it was not carrying on a trade or business within the charge to corporation profits tax (reversing the KB decision). Warrington LJ observed that the club's objects were 'immune from every taint of commerciality'. *CIR v Eccentric Club Ltd*, CA 1923, 12 TC 657; [1924] 1 KB 390. (*Note*. The company had never been assessed to income tax and the income tax position was not in issue. However, as the corporation tax charge extended to 'any trade or business, or any undertaking of a similar character, including the holding of investments', the company was effectively also held not to be carrying on a trade within the charge to income tax.)

Members' football supporters' club

[70.4] A members' club had been established to provide 'social intercourse and recreation for the members, support for Glentoran Football Club and interest in football generally'. It had two categories of members: ordinary members and associate members. Associate members had no voting rights, and were not eligible for election to the club committee, but both ordinary and associate members paid the same level of subscriptions. The Revenue accepted that profits derived from business with ordinary members were not assessable by virtue of the 'mutuality' principle, but issued assessments on the basis that profits derived from business with associate members were trading profits and chargeable to income tax. The club appealed, contending that the 'mutuality' principle should also apply to transactions with associate members. The Special Commissioner accepted this contention and allowed the appeal, holding that 'equality of voting rights is not a basic essential' and that, on the evidence, there was 'no real difference between the ordinary and associate members'. *Westbourne Supporters of Glentoran Club v Brennan*, Sp C [1995] SSCD 137 (Sp C 22).

Bathing club—facilities for 'hotel members'

[70.5] In a Jamaican case, a members' club owned a bathing beach. The facilities of the beach were open to guests at local hotels if the hotel was a 'hotel member' of the club. A hotel member paid a small annual subscription plus two shillings per head in respect of its guests in a specified period. The PC upheld an assessment on the club on the amount of its profits attributable to its receipts from hotel members. The relationship between the club's ordinary members and the hotels was not 'truly one of mutuality' but was 'of a trading character'. *Fletcher (for Trustees & Committee of Doctor's Cave Bathing Beach) v Jamaica Income Tax Commissioner*, PC 1971, [1972] AC 414; [1971] 3 All ER 1185.

Stock exchange—whether a club

[70.6] In a case concerning Hong Kong profits tax, a company of stockbrokers, limited by guarantee with no share capital, provided premises for use as a stock exchange by its members. The Hong Kong CA held that the company was not a club but was a trade association, and the PC upheld this decision. The company existed to aid the profit-making activities of its members and could not properly be called a club. The activities of stockbrokers were within the definition of a 'trade'. *Kowloon Stock Exchange Ltd v Hong Kong Commissioner of Inland Revenue*, PC [1984] STC 602; [1985] 1 WLR 133; [1985] 1 All ER 205.

Conservative Party—whether an association

[70.7] The Revenue assessed the Conservative Party Central Office (CPCO) to corporation tax on its investment income. CPCO appealed, contending that the Conservative Party was not an unincorporated association, and that it did not hold the relevant funds on behalf of an unincorporated association. (The applicable rate of income tax was substantially lower than the rate of corporation tax.) The CA accepted this contention and held that the relevant income was chargeable to income tax rather than corporation tax. Lawton LJ held that an 'unincorporated association' was 'two or more persons bound together for one or more common purposes, not being business purposes, by mutual undertakings, each having mutual duties and obligations, in an organisation which has rules which identify in whom control of it and its funds rests and on what terms and which can be joined or left at will. The bond of union between the members of an unincorporated association has to be contractual.' *Conservative & Unionist Central Office v Burrell*, CA 1981, 55 TC 671; [1982] STC 317; [1982] 1 WLR 522; [1982] 2 All ER 1.

Assessability of Rotary Club

[70.8] A Rotary Club, founded in 1972, raised funds for charities and also acted as a social club for its members. It appealed against estimated corporation tax assessments on bank interest, contending that it was a partnership and accordingly not liable to corporation tax. The Special Commissioner rejected this contention and determined the assessments in the agreed figures, and the Ch D upheld this decision. Hoffmann J held that the only duty of Club members was to pay a subscription and to comply with Club rules, with no entitlement to profits or liability for losses. The Club was thus clearly not a partnership but an unincorporated association. *Blackpool Marton Rotary Club v Martin*, Ch D 1988, 62 TC 686; [1988] STC 823. (*Note.* For another issue in the case, taken to the CA, see **4.365** APPEALS.)

Assessability of members' sports club

[70.9] In 1926 a rugby club, which was an unincorporated members' society, had acquired some land and registered it in the names of trustees. It sold the land in 1977 and 1978. The Revenue made CGT assessments on the trustees, and alternative corporation tax assessments on the club. The Ch D upheld the corporation tax assessments, holding that the club was liable to corporation tax on the gains. Peter Gibson J observed that an unincorporated association is an entity for income tax and corporation tax purposes. It was common ground that the trustees were bare trustees. Applying the *Interpretation Act 1889, s 19*, a 'person' in what is now *TCGA, s 60(1)* included an unincorporated association. Hence the club was absolutely entitled to the land as against the trustees, and had to be treated as 'a person which can itself acquire, own and dispose of assets, including land'. *CIR v Worthing Rugby Football Club Trustees (and cross-appeal)*, Ch D 1984, 60 TC 482; [1985] STC 186; [1985] 1 WLR 409. (*Notes.* (1) The case also involved the development land tax on the disposals. The club appealed to the CA against the DLT assessments, but accepted the Ch D decision with regard to the corporation tax assessments. The CA dismissed the club's appeal—see [1987] STC 273; [1987] 1 WLR 1057. (2) The *Interpretation Act 1889* has subsequently been superseded. See now *Interpretation Act 1978, Sch 1*.)

71

Capital Gains Tax

The cases in this chapter are arranged under the following headings.

NOTE

Corporation Tax and Schedule D, Case VII (short-term gains) decisions relevant to capital gains tax are included in this chapter.

Allowable losses (TCGA 1992, s 2)

TCGA 1992, s 2(2)—losses carried forward

[71.1] In 1975/76 gains of £3,405 accrued to the trustees of a non-resident settlement in 1975/76, and it was accepted that these had to be attributed to a beneficiary (M). However, in 1974/75 losses of £41,536 had accrued to the trustees. M's husband appealed against the 1975/76 assessment, contending that the 1974/75 losses should be set off against the gains. The Special Commissioners accepted this contention and allowed the appeal, and the Ch D upheld this decision. Nourse J held that what is now *TCGA 1992, s 2(2)* provided for a deduction of any losses accruing to the trustees in any year of assessment, so far as it had not been already allowed as a deduction. The loss of £41,536 that had accrued to the trustees in 1974/75 was not to be deprived in the following year of the status that it enjoyed in 1974/75. *Ritchie v McKay*, Ch D 1984, 57 TC 719; [1984] STC 422.

Claim for carry-back of losses—effect of TCGA 1992, s 2(3)

[71.2] An individual (B) disposed of a property in 2005/06. HMRC formed the opinion that his computation of the chargeable gain on this disposal had been incorrect, and issued an amendment to B's return. B appealed. The computation of the gain was subsequently agreed, but B proceeded with his appeal, contending that he intended to sell some shares at a loss, and that he should be allowed to carry this loss back to set it against the gain for 2005/06. The First-tier Tribunal rejected this contention and dismissed B's appeal, holding that the effect of *TCGA 1992, s 2(3)* was that capital losses could not be set against chargeable gains accruing in earlier years. *H Barnett v HMRC*, FTT [2010] UKFTT 39 (TC), TC00353.

Taper relief (TCGA 1992, s 2A)

NOTE

This relief was withdrawn for disposals after 5 April 2008 by *FA 2008, s 8, Sch 2 paras 23, 25*.

Rate of relief

[71.3] In May 1999 a woman (S) sold a share in a close company for more than £1m. She declared this on her 1999/2000 return, and subsequently sent the Revenue an amended return claiming taper relief of 75%. The Revenue queried the amended return, and subsequently issued a notice of amendment allowing taper relief at 15% in accordance with *TCGA 1992, s 2A(5) as enacted by FA 1998*. The Special Commissioner upheld the Revenue's amendment and dismissed S's appeal. Although S had held the share for many years, the effect of *TCGA 1992, s 2A(8)* was that the 'holding period' was two years (ie one complete year after 5 April 1998, plus one additional year in accordance with *TCGA 1992, s 2A(8)(b)*). The Commissioner observed that S had originally acquired the share for £1, and commented that 'the case illustrates the sharp distinction in result that can occur between the provision of relief by tapering the gain from a disposal as against provision by indexing the original acquisition cost'. The Ch D upheld the Commissioner's decision. Lawrence Collins J held that the Commissioner was 'plainly right to decide that taper relief was to be granted on the basis of a qualifying period of one year, plus one year under *section 2A(8)(b)*, the "bonus year".' He also observed that 'it would be anomalous if both indexation allowance and taper relief were available for the same period'. *O'Sullivan v Philip*, Ch D [2005] STC 1712; [2005] EWHC 2130 (Ch). (*Note. TCGA 1992, s 2A(5)* was subsequently amended by *FA 2000* and *FA 2002*. Taper relief of 75% is due for business assets with a two-year holding period which are disposed of from 6 April 2002 to 5 April 2008. The corresponding rate was 15% for disposals from 6 April 1998 to 5 April 2000, and 25% for disposals from 6 April 2000 to 5 April 2002.)

Sale of share in non-trading partnership

[71.4] Two individuals (C and D) agreed to form a consortium for property ventures in which each would have a 50% interest. C subsequently agreed to sell 10% of his 50% interest (ie 5% of the consortium) to a company (S), in return for £500,000. C subsequently submitted a self-assessment return claiming business taper relief. The Revenue issued an amendment rejecting the claim and charging tax on the £500,000. C appealed. The Special Commissioner dismissed the appeal, finding that the consortium was a partnership and that what C had sold was 'a partnership share or interest'. However the partnership had not yet acquired any assets and therefore had not begun trading, since 'it is impossible to commence a trade without acquiring trading assets'. The partnership interest which C had sold was 'a capital asset liable to capital gains tax', but was not 'an asset that was being used for the purposes of a trade carried on at the time of the disposal by a partnership of which the appellant was a member'. Accordingly the sale did not qualify for business taper relief. *CM Chappell v HMRC*, Sp C 2008, [2009] SSCD 11 (Sp C 717). (*Note*. For a preliminary issue in this case, see **4.23** APPEALS.)

Sale of property—whether a business asset

[71.5] In 1984 a woman gave a house to her son and daughter. They held the house as joint tenants. They divided the house into bedsits, which they let to tenants. In 2005 they sold the house. In their tax returns, they treated the sale as qualifying for business asset taper relief. HMRC issued amendments to their self-assessments on the basis that the house was not a business asset. The vendors appealed, contending that an inspector of taxes had previously agreed that their income from letting the bedsits qualified as 'earned income'. The First-tier Tribunal dismissed their appeals, applying the principles laid down in *Griffiths v Jackson*, **53.11** SCHEDULE D. Judge Connell held that the income which the vendors had received from letting the bedsits was not trading income and the house did not qualify as a business asset. Furthermore, 'there has to be a clear and unambiguous representation by the Revenue upon which the appellant has relied before it can be held that it is unfair for the Revenue to undertake its tax collection obligations under legislation'. There were 'long-standing authorities for the proposition in relation to direct tax matters that there is no estoppel against the Crown'. *MG Jones v HMRC (and related appeal)*, FTT [2009] UKFTT 312 (TC), TC00256.

[71.6] A couple sold two properties, which they had previously let. They claimed business asset taper relief. HMRC issued amendments to their self-assessments, charging tax on the basis that the properties failed to qualify for business asset taper relief. The First-tier Tribunal dismissed the couple's appeal against this decision. *G & Mrs R Sahota v HMRC*, FTT [2010] UKFTT 587 (TC), TC00837.

[71.7] A similar decision was reached in *S & L McCaughern v HMRC*, FTT [2013] UKFTT 294 (TC), TC02700.

[71.8] A couple traded in partnership as printers. In 1998 they purchased a four-bedroomed house. They sold the house in 2006. In their tax returns, they claimed business asset taper relief, on the basis that the house had partly been used for storage and partly as accommodation for specialist workers and for nurses. Following an enquiry, HMRC accepted that the house had qualified for business asset taper relief for two years when it had been used to accommodate specialist workers, but rejected the remainder of the claim. The First-tier Tribunal dismissed the couple's appeal against this decision. *A & Mrs H Mateides v HMRC*, FTT [2013] UKFTT 347 (TC), TC02750.

[71.9] A restaurant proprietor (M) purchased a house in 1995 and sold it in 2006. He claimed business asset taper relief. HMRC rejected the claim but the First-tier Tribunal allowed M's appeal, finding that the house had been used to provide accommodation for workers employed in M's restaurant business. *SC Mak v HMRC*, FTT [2013] UKFTT 417 (TC); [2013] SFTD 1250, TC02811.

[71.10] A builder (B), who owned some horses, sold an interest in some agricultural land. In his tax return he claimed business asset taper relief. HMRC issued an amendment on the basis that the land had not been a business asset. B appealed, contending that he had used the land for a business of breeding horses. The First-tier Tribunal rejected this contention and dismissed his appeal, finding that although B had been breeding horses, this had been on 'a small scale' and he 'was not carrying on a trade of horse breeding'. *E Blaney v HMRC*, FTT [2014] UKFTT 1001 (TC), TC04013.

Interaction of taper relief and EIS deferral relief

[71.11] An accountant (D) claimed EIS deferral relief under *TCGA 1992, Sch 5B*, and taper relief under *TCGA 1992, s 2A(5)*. The Revenue computed his liability on the basis that the EIS deferral relief had to be deducted from the chargeable gains accruing in the year of assessment before taper relief was applied. D appealed, contending that taper relief should be applied before EIS deferral relief. The Special Commissioner rejected this contention and dismissed his appeal. *Daniels v HMRC*, Sp C [2005] SSCD 684 (Sp C 489).

[71.12] An individual (S) disposed of several properties, some of which had been used for business purposes , some of which had been used partly for business purposes, and some of which had not been used for business purposes. He claimed EIS deferral relief under *TCGA 1992, Sch 5B* and taper relief under *TCGA 1992, s 2A(5)*, and claimed that the EIS relief should be set firstly against the gains on the non-business properties and secondly against the non-business parts of the 'mixed use' properties. HMRC accepted that the relief could be set firstly against the gains on the properties that had never been used for business purposes, but issued a ruling that where a property had been used for both business and non-business purposes, the EIS relief had to be treated as diminishing a single gain (so that it was split between the business and non-business elements on a pro rata basis). The Upper Tribunal upheld HMRC's ruling (reversing the First-tier decision). David Richards J held that there was nothing 'in the legislation which deems for the purposes of EIS relief the gain on the disposal of a single mixed-use asset to be two separate gains'. *HMRC v M Stolkin*, UT [2014] UKUT 165 (TCC); [2014] STC 2672.

Taper relief—interaction with private residence relief

[71.13] A married couple sold a large house, 65% of which they had used as their private residence and 35% of which they had used as a hotel. The total gain was £576,945. It was agreed that 65% of the gain (ie £375,014) was covered by private residence relief, leaving a total gain (before taper relief) of £201,931. In their returns, the couple treated the whole of this £201,931 as qualifying for business asset taper relief. HMRC issued amendments on the basis that only 35% of the £201,931 should be treated as qualifying for business asset taper relief. The couple appealed, contending that there was no requirement to apportion the £201,931 into business and non-business gains before the application of taper relief, since an apportionment between business and non-business use had already been made for the purposes of private residence relief. The First-tier Tribunal accepted this contention and allowed the couple's appeal. Judge Short held that it was 'axiomatic' that the gains of £201,931 were 'gains relating to the part of the asset which is treated for PRR purposes as being used for exclusively for business purposes'. HMRC's contentions would 'have the result of producing gains from this asset which are outside the scope of both PRR and business asset taper relief'. *TCGA 1992, Sch A1, para 9* required a 'just and reasonable apportionment'. It could not be 'just and reasonable' to treat only 35% of the £201,931 as qualifying for business asset taper relief. *IS & LA Jefferies v HMRC*, FTT [2009] UKFTT 291 (TC); [2010] SFTD 189, TC00235.

Non-resident with UK branch or agency (TCGA 1992, s 10)

Sale of partnership property—application of TCGA 1992, s 10

[71.14] A married couple operated a restaurant in partnership. They emigrated to France in 1985/86, leaving the business under the day-to-day management of their son, whilst themselves retaining financial control. They sold the restaurant in the following year. The Revenue issued CGT assessments, and the husband appealed, contending that he was not chargeable on the grounds that he was neither resident nor ordinarily resident in the UK in the year of sale. The Special Commissioner dismissed his appeal, holding that he was chargeable by virtue of what is now *TCGA 1992, s 10*, since he was carrying on a trade in the UK through his son who was acting as his agent. *White v Carline*, Sp C [1995] SSCD 186 (Sp C 33). (*Note*. The Revenue also issued an assessment on the couple's son, considering on the available evidence that he was also a partner. The Commissioner allowed the son's appeal, holding on the evidence that he was not entitled to any share in the partnership assets.)

Sale of residential home—application of TCGA 1992, s 10

[71.15] The Revenue issued a CGT assessment charging tax on the sale of a residential home. The proprietor appealed, contending that he was not chargeable since he was not resident in the UK. The Special Commissioner rejected this contention and upheld the assessment in principle, holding that the proprietor was trading in the UK through a 'branch or agency', and was therefore chargeable to CGT by virtue of what is now *TCGA 1992, s 10*. *Puddu v Doleman*, Sp C [1995] SSCD 236 (Sp C 38).

The computation of gains and losses (TCGA 1992, ss 15–57)

Disposals and acquisitions treated as made at market value (TCGA 1992, s 17)

Acquisition of shares—whether TCGA 1992, s 17 applicable

[71.16] A company (B) acquired two 25% shareholdings in a publishing company, from different vendors, for a total of £25,000. It subsequently lodged a claim that what is now *TCGA 1992, s 17* should be treated as applying to the acquisitions, so that its acquisition cost should be treated as market value rather than as £25,000. The Revenue rejected the claim and the Special Commissioner dismissed B's appeal, holding on the evidence that the shares had been acquired at arm's length and the consideration of £25,000 appeared to be 'a full and fair price'. Accordingly, what is now *TCGA 1992, s 17* did not apply. The Ch D upheld this decision, applying the principles laid down in *Edwards v Bairstow & Harrison*, **4.238** APPEALS. *Bullivant Holdings Ltd v CIR*, Ch D 1998, 71 TC 22; [1998] STC 905.

Acquisition of shares under share option scheme—TCGA 1992, s 17

[71.17] An employee (J) was granted options to acquire shares in his employer's parent company. He was not resident in the UK at the time he was granted these options, but subsequently became UK-resident, exercised the options, and then sold the shares. The Revenue issued CGT assessments on the basis that the base value of the shares was the sum of the price paid for the shares on the exercise of the options and the market value of the options when they were originally granted (which was treated as nil). J appealed, contending that the base value of the shares was their market value when the options were exercised. The Special Commissioner accepted this contention and allowed the appeal, and the Ch D and CA upheld this decision. Chadwick LJ held that the acquisition of the shares was clearly 'an incident of the taxpayer's employment', and was therefore within what is now *TCGA 1992, s 17(1)(b)*. In the CGT computation, the cost of acquisition of the shares was 'the market value of the underlying asset' at the time when the options were exercised. *Mansworth v Jelley*, CA 2002, 75 TC 1; [2003] STC 53; [2002] EWCA Civ 1829. (*Note.* For the Revenue's practice following this decision, see the Revenue Technical Notes issued on 8 January 2003 and 17 March 2003, and Revenue Tax Bulletin October 2003, pp 1061–1063. See also *TCGA 1992, s 144ZA*, introduced by *FA 2003, s 158* for options exercised after 9 April 2003, and intended to restore 'the tax treatment of capital gains and losses on the exercise of options to that which was generally understood to apply before the judgment'.)

Disposal of shares—TCGA 1992, s 17

[71.18] In 1993 a property developer acquired the shares in a newly incorporated UK company. In October 1994 he sold the shares to a Bahamian company. The consideration was expressed to be £20,000. The vendor did not declare a gain on his tax return. The Revenue subsequently issued an assessment on the basis that the disposal was not at arm's length, so that the shares should be valued at their market value. The vendor appealed, contending that the disposal should be treated as having been at arm's length. The First-tier Tribunal reviewed the evidence in detail and rejected this contention, finding that the vendor's evidence was 'implausible' and that 'his memory was selective'. Accordingly the tribunal dismissed the appeal in principle (subject to agreement as to figures). *OI Iny v HMRC*, FTT [2010] UKFTT 457 (TC), TC00722. (*Note*. The Tribunal subsequently increased the tax charged by the assessment, and upheld a penalty of £260,400—see **44.136** PENALTIES.)

Gain on assigned debt—whether TCGA 1992, s 17(1)(b)* applicable

[71.19] In May 1986 a Netherlands company obtained judgment against a UK company for £124,223. In July 1986 the Netherlands company assigned the debt to the two directors of the UK company for £3,000. The directors each recovered £50,000 from the company in 1986/87, and recovered the balance of the debt in the two following years. One of the directors appealed against a CGT assessment on the gain, contending that his remuneration had been reduced in consequence of the assignment of the debt, and that the effect of what is now *TCGA 1992, s 17(1)(b)* was that there was no CGT liability. The General Commissioners rejected this contention and dismissed his appeal. The Ch D upheld their decision. Vinelott J held that the evidence fell 'far short of establishing any relevant connection' between the assignment and a diminution of the director's emoluments. Furthermore, even if what is now *s 17(1)(b)* had applied, the director had not adduced evidence to show that the market value of the debt differed from the sums which he had received. *Whitehouse v Ellam*, Ch D 1995, 68 TC 377; [1995] STC 503.

Transactions between connected persons (TCGA 1992, s 18)

[71.20] A company (K) was a UK-resident subsidiary of a US parent company (HC). K acted as a holding company for a number of UK subsidiaries. As part of a corporate reorganisation, a new company (HU) purchased the share capital of two of K's subsidiaries. HU was a subsidiary of another US company (HG), which in turn was a subsidiary of HC. K made a substantial capital loss on the sale. It claimed that this could be set against subsequent chargeable gains. The Revenue rejected the claim on the basis that HU and K were 'connected persons', within *TCGA 1992, s 18*. K appealed, contending that the effect of *TCGA 1992, s 28* was that the disposal did not take place until the agreement became unconditional, by which time the shares in K's two former subsidiaries had been distributed to the shareholders in K's parent company (HC), so that K and HU should not be treated as being 'connected'. The Special Commissioner rejected this contention and dismissed K's appeal, finding that 'one could identify a collection of shareholders who owned the greater part of the share capital' of both the relevant parent companies. Therefore K and HU were connected with each other.' The Ch D and the CA unanimously upheld this decision. The effect of *TCGA 1992, s 28(2)* was that the disposal was made at the time the relevant contract was satisfied, which was when the distribution was effected. The word 'group' in *TCGA 1992, s 286(5)(b)* should be given its natural meaning. Its effect was that K and HU were connected at the time of the share sale. Smith LJ observed that 'in its ordinary and natural meaning, "group" must mean a collection of people'. There was 'no warrant at all for the suggestion that the word implies some kind of common purpose'. *Kellogg Brown & Root Holdings Ltd v HMRC*, CA [2010] STC 925; [2010] EWCA Civ 118.

[71.21] See also *Corbally-Stourton v HMRC*, 5.49 ASSESSMENTS, and *Foulser & Foulser v MacDougall*, 71.260 below.

Transfer of assets under Court Order on divorce

[71.22] In 1964 a married couple became the joint owners of a house, which neither of them lived in as their main residence. They separated in 1970 and were divorced by a 'decree nisi' order in 1976. The order provided for the husband's half share of the house to be transferred to the wife. The Revenue issued a CGT assessment on the husband for 1975/76 on the basis that he had disposed of his share in the property and that, since the transaction was between connected persons, the consideration was to be taken as the market value. He appealed, contending that he had made no gain on the transfer. The Ch D rejected this contention and upheld the assessment. The husband's interest in the property had been transferred at the time of the divorce, the court order being an unconditional contract for the transfer. As the decree was not then absolute, the parties were still married and the transfer fell to be treated as having been made at market value. *Aspden v Hildesley*, Ch D 1981, 55 TC 609; [1982] STC 206; [1982] 1 WLR 264; [1982] 2 All ER 53.

Definition of an 'asset' (TCGA 1992, s 21)

Guarantee payment—whether chargeable asset acquired

[71.23] An investment company (C) guaranteed the bank overdraft of an associated company (F) and paid £27,351 under the guarantee. It claimed that this was an allowable loss for CGT purposes, contending that it had acquired the bank's rights as a creditor of F, and that these rights were an asset for CGT purposes, the value of which had become negligible within what is now *TCGA 1992, s 24(2)*. The Revenue rejected this claim and the CS dismissed C's appeal, holding that C's acquisition of the bank's worthless claim was merely an incidental consequence of its discharge of its obligation to the bank. *Cleveleys Investment Trust Co v CIR (No 2)*, CS 1975, 51 TC 26; [1975] STC 457.

Payment from employee for release from service agreement

[71.24] A holding company (H) acquired the share capital of a trading company and entered into a seven-year service agreement with B, the sales director of the trading company. After two years in which B carried out his duties with conspicuous success, he asked to be released from the agreement. He paid £50,000 to H as compensation. The Revenue assessed this as a chargeable gain, and H appealed, contending that the rights were not assets within the charge to CGT because they had no market value. The HL unanimously rejected this contention and upheld the assessment, holding that although the rights were not assignable, they could be turned to account in the hands of the employer and were an asset within the general scheme of the legislation. The fact that the rights had no market value did not prevent them from constituting assets within the charge to CGT. *O'Brien v Benson's Hosiery (Holdings) Ltd*, HL 1979, 53 TC 241; [1979] STC 735; [1979] 3 WLR 572; [1979] 3 All ER 652.

Right to sue—whether an asset—when acquired

[71.25] See *Zim Properties Ltd v Proctor*, 71.37 below.

Compensation for nationalisation of asset by foreign government

[71.26] See *Davenport v Chilver*, 71.41 below.

Annual payments under covenant—TCGA 1992, s 237(c)

[71.27] A company (R) held a licence from another company (X) to make use of the 'xerographic' process in certain areas. It surrendered this licence to X in return for a 'royalty' of 5% of certain sales by X in those areas. The relevant agreements to pay the 'royalties' were made under seal. Subsequently, R distributed the 'royalty' rights in specie to its shareholders, who in turn surrendered them to X for consideration. R appealed against a corporation tax assessment on its gain from the disposal, contending that the 'royalties' were annual payments due under a covenant within what is now *TCGA 1992, s 237(c)*. The HL unanimously rejected this contention and upheld the assessment. Lord Wilberforce held that 'annual payments under a covenant' should be construed as referring to payments under 'a unilateral and voluntary enforceable promise as distinguished from an "agreement" supported by consideration'. He observed that 'as a matter of substance it is impossible to detect any reason of fiscal policy why the affixing of a seal to an agreement should have any relevance to the imposition of the tax'. *Rank Xerox Ltd v Lane*, HL 1979, 53 TC 185; [1979] STC 740; [1979] 3 WLR 594; [1979] 3 All ER 657. (*Note*. For a preliminary point in this case, see **4.174** APPEALS.)

Sale of new lease—whether a continuation of old lease

[71.28] A trader had held his business premises under a 14-year lease. This expired in December 1974 and, following proceedings under the *Landlord and Tenant Act 1954*, he was granted a new lease. He disposed of the new lease in 1976 and was assessed on the gain, on the basis that the new lease was a separate asset from the old. He appealed, contending that the new lease was a continuation of the old and that the straight-line basis over the period from 1960 should be used by virtue of what is now *TCGA 1992, Sch 2 para 16*. The Ch D rejected this contention and upheld the assessment, holding that the two leases were separate assets, and the second lease was not derived from the first within the meaning of what is now *TCGA 1992, s 43*. *Bayley v Rogers*, Ch D 1980, 53 TC 420; [1980] STC 544.

Disposal of business lease and goodwill—whether separate assets

[71.29] In February 1965 a trader (B) was granted a 21-year lease of a shop. He began to trade there on 6 April 1965. In 1970 he sold the business for £3,000, of which £2,500 was attributed to the goodwill, £250 to the lease and £250 to the fixtures and fittings. The Revenue issued a CGT assessment on the basis that the lease and goodwill were separate assets, so that an election for valuation at 6 April 1965 was not available for the goodwill (as it was not in existence before that date), while any loss on the disposal of the lease fell to be disregarded by virtue of what is now *TCGA 1992, Sch 2 para 17(2)*. B appealed, contending that the lease and goodwill constituted an indivisible asset acquired before 6 April 1965. The Commissioners dismissed his appeal, finding that the lease and goodwill were separate assets. The Ch D upheld their decision. *Butler v Evans*, Ch D 1980, 53 TC 558; [1980] STC 613.

Loan for payment of shares—incorporeal rights

[71.30] An investment company (C) lent £25,000 to another company (F), which undertook to reconstruct its share capital and give C a 51% shareholding. The £25,000 was to be used to acquire the shares. F went into voluntary liquidation before its capital had been reconstructed and C did not recover the £25,000. It appealed against a corporation tax assessment, contending that the £25,000 was an allowable loss. The CS accepted this contention and allowed the appeal (by a 3–1 majority, Lord Migdale dissenting). *Cleveleys Investment Trust Co v CIR (No 1)*, CS 1971, 47 TC 300.

Repayment of loan waived as condition of sale of shares

[71.31] A company sold its shares in a subsidiary for £250,000, a condition of the sale being that it waived repayment of unsecured loans of £500,000 it had made to the subsidiary. It was assessed on its gain from the sale of the shares, with no allowance for the £500,000, and appealed, contending *inter alia* that the loans were a 'debt on a security' within what is now *TCGA 1992, s 251(1)*. The HL rejected this contention, but allowed the appeal in part, holding (by a 3-2 majority, Viscount Dilhorne and Lord Russell of Killowen dissenting) that the waiver of the loan was part of the consideration for the £250,000. Lord Wilberforce held that, where a bundle of assets had been sold together, it was necessary to consider each disposal separately, in the light of the rules which applied to that asset. The HL remitted the case to the Special Commissioners to make an appropriate apportionment. *Aberdeen Construction Group Ltd v CIR*, HL 1978, 52 TC 281; [1978] STC 127; [1978] 2 WLR 648; [1978] 1 All ER 962.

Consideration for non-competition covenant

[71.32] A holding company (T) held the shares of another company (M). In 1977 T, M and an American corporation (G) reached an agreement whereby T procured the sale to G of three subsidiaries of M, and signed a covenant that it and its subsidiaries would not engage in any competing business in the UK before 1983. G paid consideration of $1,730,000, of which $575,000 was apportioned to the covenant. The CA held that the $575,000 gave rise to a chargeable gain, being a capital sum derived from T's goodwill. *Kirby v Thorn EMI plc*, CA 1987, 60 TC 519; [1987] STC 621; [1988] 1 WLR 445; [1988] 2 All ER 947. (*Note*. Nicholls LJ expressed the opinion that the case should be remitted to the Special Commissioners to value the goodwill, but the CA subsequently agreed that the case should not be remitted and that the Commissioners' determination should be varied in specified terms set out in a schedule of 'terms of compromise'—see 1988 STI 90.)

Compromise agreement for sale of defendant's property

[71.33] A Norwegian company obtained judgment against another company. The defendant company appealed, but a compromise agreement was reached whereby the defendant's premises, plant and machinery were to be sold and the proceeds divided between the parties. The defendant subsequently went into voluntary liquidation, and the property was sold a year later. The Ch D upheld the plaintiff's contention that the compromise agreement effected a part disposal of the property by the defendant to the plaintiff, and that each company subsequently disposed of its interest to the ultimate purchaser. *Anders Utkilens Rederi AS v OY Lovisa Stevedoring Co AB & Another*, Ch D 1984, [1985] STC 301.

Loan evidenced by statutory declaration—whether a 'debt on a security'

[71.34] See *WT Ramsay Ltd v CIR*, 71.285 below.

Sale of fishing vessel with licence and quota—whether separate assets

[71.35] A partnership operated a fishing vessel. It agreed to sell this, including the relevant licence and 'quota', for £1,300,000. It subsequently agreed with the purchaser that £900,000 of the purchase price should be allocated to the vessel and that £400,000 should be allocated to the licence and quota. However, in the partnership's 1997/98 tax return, the whole of the £1,300,000 was allocated to the vessel. The Revenue issued a notice of amendment to treat £900,000 as attributable to the sale of the vessel and £400,000 as attributable to the licence and quota. The partnership appealed. The Special Commissioners dismissed the appeal, finding that 'in the sale of the vessel, its licence and quote, three separate assets were involved, each of which were capable of a separate value'. Where a 'bundle of assets' had been sold together, it was necessary to consider each disposal separately, in the light of the rules which applied to that asset. *Fullarton & Others v CIR (re MV Endeavour)*, Sp C [2004] SSCD 207 (Sp C 403).

The location of property

[71.36] See *Young v Phillips*, 71.383 below, and the cases noted at 72.149 *et seq*. INHERITANCE TAX.

Capital sums derived from assets (TCGA 1992, s 22)

Amount received as part of out-of-court settlement

[71.37] In July 1973 a company (Z) contracted to sell three properties. The date of completion was fixed for July 1974. However, the sale of the properties was not completed, because the original conveyance to one of them had been lost and Z was unable to provide proof of ownership. The purchaser refused to complete and successfully sued Z for the return of its deposit. Z issued a writ against its solicitors, claiming damages of more than £100,000. Following negotiations, Z agreed to accept payment of £69,000 in two instalments, in settlement of its claim. The Revenue included the amount of the first instalment as a chargeable gain in a CT assessment. Z appealed, contending that the gain was not chargeable since it had not been derived from an asset.

The Special Commissioners upheld the Revenue's contention that the £69,000 was a capital sum derived from Z's right against its solicitors, and upheld Z's contention that the right had been acquired otherwise than by way of an arm's length agreement, so that its market value was deductible. The Ch D upheld this decision (against which both sides had appealed) and remitted the case back to the Commissioners for figures to be agreed. *Zim Properties Ltd v Proctor (and cross-appeal)*, Ch D 1984, 58 TC 371; [1985] STC 90. (*Note*. See now Extra-Statutory Concession D33.)

Amount received for release of put option

[71.38] 25% of the shares in an investment company (B) were owned by an employee (K). K entered into an agreement with B under which he could require B to purchase his shareholding. In 1969 B paid him £5,000 to relinquish his rights under this agreement. The Revenue included the £5,000 in a CGT assessment on K for 1968/69. He appealed, contending that there had been no disposal of any asset. The Ch D rejected this contention and upheld the assessment. Vinelott J held that a sum paid to a person who had the right to call on another person to buy property from him (a put option) was a capital sum derived from an asset. What is now *TCGA 1992, s 144* provided that the exercise of a put option would not be treated as a disposal for the purpose of creating allowable losses, but it did not exempt a gain made from such a transaction. *Golding v Kaufman*, Ch D 1985, 58 TC 296; [1985] STC 152.

[71.39] In 1961 a company (W) acquired an option to participate in a property development. In 1971 it began proceedings to enforce its option, but these were settled by consent in 1974. W received £2,000,000 in return for agreeing to 'release and abandon' the option. The Revenue assessed the amount as a chargeable gain and W appealed, contending that the surrender of the option did not constitute the disposal of an asset. The CA rejected this contention and upheld the assessment, holding that what is now *TCGA 1992, s 144* did not confer any exemption from the chargeable disposal which arose under what is now *TCGA 1992, s 22(1)* when W received a capital sum for the surrender of the option. *Powlson v Welbeck Securities Ltd*, CA 1987, 60 TC 269; [1987] STC 468.

Consideration for a covenant linked with sale of shares

[71.40] See *Kirby v Thorn EMI plc*, 71.32 above.

Compensation for confiscation of asset—application of TCGA 1992, s 22(1)

[71.41] In 1940 the USSR nationalised private property in Latvia. Following the *Foreign Compensation (USSR) Order 1969 (SI 1969/735)*, a woman who was resident in the UK made a claim in respect of such property in Latvia, some of which she had held in her own right and some of which had been held by her mother. In 1972/73 she received a payment in respect of the claim. She appealed against a CGT assessment on the payment. The Ch D held that the compensation for the loss of the assets she had held was within what is now *TCGA 1992, s 22(1)(a)*, and that the compensation for the assets her mother had held was within what is now *TCGA 1992, s 21*. The case was remitted to the Special Commissioner for figures to be determined. *Davenport v Chilver*,

Ch D 1983, 57 TC 661; [1983] STC 426; [1983] 3 WLR 481. (*Note*. See now *TCGA 1992, s 17* and *TCGA 1992, s 268B*.)

Deferred sale consideration—application of TCGA 1992, s 22(1)

[71.42] Under an agreement made in 1970, shares in a private company (J) were sold for an immediate payment of £750 per share, plus a further amount to be calculated by reference to the quoted price of shares representing them on the first dealing day following J's proposed flotation. The relevant dealing day was 5 December 1972 and the further consideration was agreed at £2,825 per share. It was accepted that, in arriving at the gain on the disposal of the shares, the £750 and the value at 15 September 1970 of the contingent right to further consideration were to be taken into account. The Revenue issued a 1972/73 assessment on the basis that the right to receive the further consideration, being a chose in action, was an asset from which a capital sum was derived on 5 December 1972; that there was a deemed disposal under what is now *TCGA 1992, s 22(1)*; and that this right was not a debt within what is now *TCGA 1992, s 251(1)*. The HL unanimously upheld the assessment, and specifically disapproved the decision of Walton J in *CIR v Montgomery*, Ch D 1974, 49 TC 679; [1975] STC 182. *Marren v Ingles (and related appeals)*, HL 1980, 54 TC 76; [1980] STC 500; [1980] 1 WLR 983; [1980] 3 All ER 95.

Compensation for revocation of licence—whether within TCGA 1992, s 22(1)

[71.43] See *Pennine Raceway Ltd v Kirklees Metropolitan Borough Council*, 14.16 COMPENSATION, ETC.—'GOURLEY' PRINCIPLE.

Payment for termination of merger agreement

[71.44] A company (B) owned 20% of the share capital in another company (M). In 1996 B and M agreed a merger, under which B would take over the remaining 80% of M's share capital. However a third company (W) subsequently made a higher offer for M's share capital. W paid B $450,000,000 for agreeing to withdraw from its merger agreement. The Revenue issued a ruling that the $450,000,000 was within *TCGA 1992, s 22(1)*. The Special Commissioner allowed B's appeal, holding that the payment was not within *s 22(1)*, since the effect of the agreements was that B 'was being paid for supporting the (W) merger and in consequence for being relieved from an obligation, not for giving up any asset'. *British Telecommunications plc v HMRC*, Sp C [2006] SSCD 347 (Sp C 535).

Statutory compensation for disturbance on surrender of agricultural lease

[71.45] A farmer (P) surrendered some land whch he leased to the Milton Keynes Development Corporation, receiving compensation of £5,971 from the Corporation. This included £591 representing compensation for disturbance under *Agricultural Holdings Act 1948*, and £2,366 which the Revenue accepted was not chargeable by virtue of *Agricultural (Miscellaneous Provisions) Act 1968*. The Revenue issued a CGT assessment on the £591. The Commissioners allowed P'ss appeal and the Ch D upheld their decision, holding that no gain could be made out of a sum of money given to compensate for loss or expense which was unavoidably incurred after the lease has gone. The £591 was not a capital sum 'derived from' the lease or received in return for surrender of rights and was not liable to capital gains tax. *Davis v Powell*, Ch D 1976, 51 TC 492; [1977] STC 32; [1977] 1 WLR 258; [1977] 1 All ER 471.

[71.46] The decision in *Davis v Powell*, 71.45 above, was applied in a subsequent case in which a farmer had surrendered an agricultural tenancy to his landlord under an agreement providing for payment of £455,180 as compensation for disturbance under *Agricultural Holdings Act 1986, s 60*, and £520,000 as additional compensation. The Revenue issued an assessment charging CGT on both payments. The farmer appealed, accepting that the £520,000 was chargeable to CGT but contending that the £455,180 was not taxable. The Special Commissioners accepted this contention and allowed the appeal, holding that the payment was statutory compensation under *Agricultural Holdings Act 1986*, and was therefore not taxable. The Commissioners held that 'the notice to quit need not necessarily be the sole or proximate cause of the termination of a tenancy: it may be sufficient for the notice to quit to be one of a number of links in a chain of causal events'. The Revenue's contention that the tenancy had been terminated by agreement was rejected. *Davis v Henderson*, Sp C [1995] SSCD 308 (Sp C 46). (*Note*. For the Revenue's practice following this decision, see Revenue Tax Bulletin, April 1996, p 303.)

[71.47] A similar decision was reached in *Pritchard v Purves*, Sp C [1995] SSCD 316 (Sp C 47).

Compensation for disturbance on termination of tenancy of premises

[71.48] A solicitor had carried on practice for many years in premises leased to him by a bank. The bank required the premises for the purposes of its own business and gave him notice under *Landlord and Tenant Act 1954* that it would oppose a renewal of his lease. He did not oppose the notice and received compensation of £31,384 under *Landlord and Tenant Act 1954, s 37*. The Special Commissioners allowed his appeal against a CGT assessment on this sum, and the CA upheld their decision. The right to the compensation was a statutory one. There was no entitlement to it under the lease and it was therefore not derived from the lease. The compensation was not for the loss of an asset. The lease had expired, but it was never 'lost'. *Drummond v Brown*, CA 1984, 58 TC 67; [1984] STC 321; [1984] 3 WLR 381; [1984] 2 All ER 699.

Business ceased following destruction of premises—compensation

[71.49] A trader (R) had carried on business from two bars in Belfast, rented on short leases. Both were bombed, the premises being destroyed, and R did not restart business at either. He claimed compensation from the Northern Ireland Office and was paid compensation which included £5,113 for 'consequential loss'. The amount represented 18 months' net profit and in the claim was described as being for 'loss of profit, i.e. goodwill'. The loss adjusters for the Northern Ireland Office accepted that 18 months was a valid estimate of the time it would have taken to rebuild the premises, and the Northern Ireland Office, although aware that the business would not be restarted, confirmed that the payment 'was in respect of the temporary loss of profit whilst awaiting repairs to be carried out'. The Revenue issued a CGT assessment on the basis that the payment was for loss of goodwill. The Special Commissioners allowed R's appeal and the CA(NI) upheld their decision, holding that the payment was of a revenue nature, arrived at on the basis of the loss of profits for a defined period estimated at 18 months. The fact that R did not recommence trading did not convert a revenue profit into a capital gain. *Lang v Rice*, CA(NI) 1983, 57 TC 80; [1984] STC 172.

Consideration under development agreement

[71.50] Under a development agreement made in 1987, a company (P) received 'money's worth' in the form of site works. The works were not completed until 1991. The Revenue considered that the effect of what is now *TCGA 1992, s 28* was that the consideration was taxable in 1987, by reference to the date of the contract. P appealed, contending that the consideration was a capital sum derived from an asset, within what is now *TCGA 1992, s 22*, so that it was not taxable until the period in which it was received. The Ch D rejected this contention and upheld the assessment, holding that the consideration was taxable in 1987. *Chaloner v Pellipar Investments Ltd*, Ch D 1996, 68 TC 238; [1996] STC 234.

Assets lost, destroyed or of negligible value (TCGA 1992, s 24)

Whether assets dissipated within TCGA 1992, s 24(1)

[71.51] In 1973/74 an individual (L) made a substantial gain on the disposal of shares. Shortly after the disposal, he and his wife invested in two companies, the shares in which had become of negligible value by 5 April 1974. L did not declare the gain on his 1973/74 tax return, and the Revenue did not issue an assessment on it until 1978. L appealed, claiming relief under what is now *TCGA 1992, s 24(2)*. The General Commissioners heard the appeal in 1979 and allowed the claim in principle, adjourning the appeal for the value of the shares to be agreed. The appeal was not restored for hearing until 1984. In the meantime, *Williams v Bullivant*, 71.53 below, had been decided in the Ch D, and the Commissioners accepted the Revenue's contention that the effect of that decision was that since the claim for relief had not been made until 1978/79, the relief could not be given against the 1973/74 assessment. L appealed to the Ch D, contending firstly that the Commissioners should not have permitted their 1979 decision in his favour to be reopened, and secondly that, since the shares in the companies in which he and his wife had invested had lost their value by April 1974, they had by then been dissipated within what is now *TCGA 1992, s 24(1)*. The Ch D rejected both contentions and dismissed the appeal. There had been no final decision on any matter raised at the 1979 hearing, as the value of the shares was unsettled. L had not been prejudiced by the delay, because if the final decision had been in his favour, the Revenue could, and no doubt would, have appealed to the Ch D. Although the relevant assets had become valueless, they remained in existence, and a loss in value of an asset (as distinct from the loss or extinction of an asset itself) fell under *TCGA 1992, s 24(2)* rather than under *TCGA 1992, s 24(1)*. *Larner v Warrington*, Ch D 1985, 58 TC 557; [1985] STC 442.

Shares in company restored to Register after being struck off

[71.52] See *Mrs R & Mrs S Thomas v HMRC*, 44.104 PENALTIES.

Claim for relief under TCGA 1992, s 24(2)

[71.53] In 1973/74 an individual (B) had disposed of various shares, giving rise to chargeable gains which were assessed in 1977. In 1978, he made a claim under what is now *TCGA 1992, s 24(2)* for relief to be given against the assessment for certain shares owned by his wife which, it was agreed, had become of negligible value in February 1974. The Revenue rejected the claim on the grounds that, since the claim had not been made until 1977/78, relief could not be granted for any year earlier than 1975/76. The Ch D accepted the Revenue's contentions and upheld the assessment. *Williams v Bullivant*, Ch D 1982, 56 TC 159; [1983] STC 107. (*Note*. See now, with regard to time limits under *TCGA 1992, s 24(2)*, Extra-Statutory Concession D28.)

[71.54] An individual (D) was allotted 30,000 £1 shares in a company, in consideration of future services to the company. Shortly after being allotted these shares, he was appointed a director of the company. The company's liabilities exceeded its assets, and it subsequently became insolvent. After correspondence, the Revenue accepted for Schedule E purposes that the shares had a nil market value at the time of their allotment. Three years later, D submitted a claim for relief under *TCGA 1992, s 24(2)* in respect of the shares. The Revenue rejected this claim and the Special Commissioner dismissed D's appeal. Under *TCGA 1992, s 17*, the shares were deemed to have been acquired for a consideration equal to their market value, which was clearly nil. Since the shares had a market value of nil when they were acquired, they were not capable of *becoming* of negligible value, within *s 24(2)*. (The Commissioner observed that D had 'sought both to have his cake and to eat it'.) *Director v HM Inspector of Taxes*, Sp C [1998] SSCD 172 (Sp C 161).

[71.55] A property developer (H) acquired some shares in a company in June 2002, and acquired a further batch of shares in December 2003. In 5 April 2004 he claimed a loss on the basis that the shares had become of 'negligible value', within *TCGA 1992, s 24(2)*. HMRC rejected the claim on the basis that the shares had already been of negligible value when he acquired them. The First-tier Tribunal dismissed H's appeal against this decision, finding that in June 2002 the company was 'in considerable financial difficulty'. The burden of proof was on H, and he had failed to show that the company had any 'positive value' at that time. *D Harper v HMRC*, FTT [2009] UKFTT 382 (TC), TC00317.

[71.56] In October 2007 a couple acquired some shares in a company which their daughter controlled. In 2009 they claimed a loss on the basis that the shares had become of 'negligible value', within *TCGA 1992, s 24(2)*. HMRC rejected the claim on the basis that the shares had already been of negligible value when the couple acquired them. The First-tier Tribunal reviewed the evidence in detail and dismissed the couple's appeal against this decision. Judge Cornwell-Kelly observed that 'the company was effectively worthless at the time of the investment'. *R & Mrs J Dyer v HMRC*, FTT [2013] UKFTT 691 (TC), TC03073.

[71.57] In December 2000 three individuals acquired shares in a company (D), at a total cost of £3,333,333 to each of the three. D subsequently made significant losses, and entered a creditors' voluntary agreement in March 2002. The shareholders subsequently claimed relief under *TCGA 1992, s 24(2)* on the basis that the shares had become of negligible value by 5 April 2001. HMRC rejected the claims, considering that the shares still had some value at that date, and the shareholders appealed. The First-tier Tribunal reviewed the evidence in detail and allowed the appeals, finding that D had made substantial losses during the first three months of 2001, and concluding that 'each of the appellants' shareholdings would in all probability have been unsaleable at 5 April 2001 in the open market in a sale by private treaty at arm's length'. Accordingly they were of negligible value at that date. *S Barker v HMRC (and related appeals)*, FTT [2011] UKFTT 645 (TC); [2012] SFTD 244, TC01487.

[71.58] The decision in *Barker v HMRC*, **71.57** above, was applied in the similar subsequent case of *R Brown v HMRC*, FTT [2013] UKFTT 740 (TC), TC03118.

[71.59] See also *Marks v McNally*, **35.41** LOSS RELIEF, and *Cleveleys Investment Trust Co v CIR (No 2)*, **71.23** above.

Land occupied by squatter—effect of Limitation Act

[71.60] In a non-tax case, the CA held (by a 2–1 majority, Willmer LJ dissenting) that an individual who had used a shed for twelve years without permission had obtained a new and separate 'squatter's title' under what is now the *Limitation Act 1980*. The *Limitation Act* destroyed the leaseholder's title to the land on which the shed stood, but did not vest it in the squatter, so that the freeholder of the land was entitled to possession. There had been an involuntary transfer and the asset was 'entirely lost' to the leaseholder. *St Marylebone Property Co Ltd v Fairweather & Another*, CA 1961; [1963] AC 510; [1961] 3 All ER 560. (*Note*. HMRC accept that the effect of this decision is that a leaseholder in this situation could claim relief for the loss of his interest in the asset under *TCGA 1992, s 24(1)*. See Capital Gains Manual, para CG13139.)

The date of disposal (TCGA 1992, s 28)

[71.61] In 1965 a shareholder (J) agreed to sell certain shares. The date of completion was fixed for 1970, but in fact completion did not take place until 1971/72. The Revenue issued a 1971/72 CGT assessment and J appealed, contending that, by virtue of what is now *TCGA 1992, s 28(1)*, the date of disposal was in February 1965. The Ch D rejected this contention and dismissed his appeal, holding that the words 'where an asset is disposed of under a contract' in *s 28* apply to a disposal after 5 April 1971 under a contract entered into after that date, but not to a disposal after that date under a contract entered into before that date. *Johnson v Edwards*, Ch D 1981, 54 TC 488; [1981] STC 660.

[71.62] In September 1978 a company (M) exchanged contracts for the sale of a factory to another company (J) for £1,400,000. Completion was arranged for February 1979, but for financial reasons J was unable to complete the purchase, and forfeited its deposit. Meanwhile, M had gone into voluntary liquidation in December 1978. The liquidator did not rescind the contract of sale, but arranged for M to acquire an 'off-the-shelf' company (S), to which it assigned its beneficial interest under the contract on 6 July 1979. Three days later certain variations in the contract were agreed, including a reduction of the purchase price to £1,150,000 and a new completion date of 9 October 1979. On the same day S exchanged contracts with a fourth company (B) for the sale of the factory on terms practically identical with those in the original contract as varied. B duly completed. The Revenue issued an assessment on the basis that the disposal had taken place after M had gone into liquidation. M appealed, contending that the disposal had taken place in September 1978 (so that trading losses of that accounting period could be set against the gain). The Special Commissioners dismissed M's appeal, and the CA upheld their decision. The disposal to B was not under the 1978 contract, but under a new contract made in July 1979. Furthermore, the interposition of S was part of an artificial avoidance scheme which could be disregarded, applying the principles laid down in *Furniss v Dawson*, **71.288** below. *Magnavox Electronics Co Ltd (in liquidation) v Hall*, CA 1986, 59 TC 610; [1986] STC 561.

[71.63] In 1987 a married couple signed a contract to dispose of three plots of land. The sale of the first plot was not completed until 1990, and the sale of the final plot was not completed until 1992. Meanwhile, in 1989, the couple had assigned half of their beneficial interests in the land to the trustees of two Bermudan settlements which they had created. The Revenue issued a CGT assessment on the basis that the effect of what is now *TCGA 1992, s 28* was that the couple had disposed of the whole of their interests in the land in 1987/88. The husband (J) appealed, contending that the disposal in 1987/88 should be treated as being limited to the half of the beneficial interests which they still held when the sales were completed, and should not be treated as also covering the half of the beneficial interests which they had assigned in 1989. The HL accepted this contention and allowed the appeal. Lord Hoffmann observed that the draftsman responsible for *s 28 (1)* 'did not think about what should happen in the situation which has arisen in this case'. He held that it would be wrong 'to attribute to Parliament an intention to impose a liability to tax upon a person who would not be treated as having made a disposal under the carefully constructed scheme for taxing the disposals of assets held on trust'. What is now *s 28 (1)* should be treated as 'concerned solely with fixing the time of disposal by a person whose identity is to be ascertained by other means. It follows that the disposal under the conveyance to the purchasers was made by the Bermudian trustees', and not by Mr and Mrs J. Lord Walker of Gestingthorpe observed that the legislation created 'an obvious problem for a taxpayer who has entered into a contract to sell an asset, with completion postponed until a later tax year. Should he assume that the contract will be duly completed and, on that assumption, return a chargeable gain accruing on the date of the contract? The Revenue acknowledge that this is a flaw in the capital gains tax legislation. Good legislative practice requires that a taxpayer should not be left in doubt as to whether or not he has incurred a tax charge.' *Jerome v Kelly*, HL 2004, 76 TC 147; [2004] STC 887; [2004] UKHL 25; [2004] 2 WLR 835.

[71.64] In a Scottish case, a married couple owned a farm. In May 1991 they accepted an offer to sell the farm to a company (B) for £400,000. In August 1991 they executed a disposition in favour of B. The Revenue issued a 1991/92 CGT assessment charging tax on the disposal. The couple appealed, contending that because one of the conditions in the disposition had not been strictly complied with, the sale should not be treated as having been completed until October 1999. The Special Commissioner rejected this contention and dismissed their appeals, holding that the effect of what is now *TCGA 1992, s 28* was that the disposal had taken in place in 1991/92. *Smith v CIR (and related appeal)*, Sp C 2003, [2004] SSCD 60 (Sp C 388; Sp C 389).

[71.65] In 1992 a company director (B) purchased a holding of shares in the company. Following disagreements with the other directors, he resigned his directorship in 1997 and agreed to sell his shares to the company for £245,000. However, the company was unable to pay this amount, and in February 1999 B agreed to sell the shares for the reduced price of £139,000. He received this amount in August 1999. In his tax return he treated the gain on the shares as covered by retirement relief, on the basis that he had disposed of the shares in 1997/98. Following an enquiry, the Revenue issued a closure notice on the basis that the disposal had taken place in 1999/2000, so that it did not qualify for retirement relief. The Special Commissioner allowed B's appeal, holding that B appeared to have given a gratuitous undertaking 'to forego the difference between the originally agreed sum of £245,000 and the sum of £139,000 that he eventually received. That did not mean, however, that the original agreement no longer subsisted'. The original agreement reached between B and the company in 1997 'was neither novated nor rescinded and replaced, either by the exchange of letters in February and March 1999 or by the conduct of the parties subsequent to that exchange. The original contract continued to subsist and it was in pursuance of this original contract that the shares were eventually disposed.' Therefore the effect of *TCGA 1992, s 28* was that the disposal must be treated as having taken place in 1997/98, so that B was entitled to claim retirement relief against the gain on his disposal of the shares. *JG Burt v HMRC*, Sp C [2008] SSCD 814 (Sp C 684).

[71.66] See also *Kellogg Brown & Root Holdings Ltd v HMRC*, **71.20** above; *Chaloner v Pellipar Investments Ltd*, **71.50** above, and *Hatt v Newman (No 1)*, **71.246** below.

Consideration for disposal paid in instalments

[71.67] In 1979/80 a taxicab proprietor (P) contracted to sell some of his cabs together with their licences. Under the contract for each, the purchase price was £6,000, payable in instalments of £40 over 150 weeks. The contract provided that the licence would not be transferred until 'payment of all monies hereunder'. The Revenue issued an assessment on the basis that the cabs had been disposed of in 1979/80. P appealed, contending that the sales had been conditional, within what is now *TCGA 1992, s 28(2)*, so that the disposal had not taken place until the date on which the final instalment was paid. The Ch D rejected this contention and upheld the assessment. By virtue of the *Town Police Clauses Act 1847*, it was not possible to sever the licences from the taxicabs. The contracts as a whole were not conditional, and the full amount of the consideration was chargeable in 1979/80. *Lyon v Pettigrew*, Ch D 1985, 58 TC 452; [1985] STC 369.

Value-shifting (TCGA 1992, ss 29–34)

Arrangements to reduce liability—interpretation of TCGA 1992, s 29(2)

[71.68] It had been arranged that, subject to contract, the share capital of a company (M) would be sold (at a substantial profit to the shareholders) to a US company (K). F and his two sons-in-law, who together controlled M, carried out a scheme under which they transferred their shares in M to W, a company set up for the purpose, in exchange for preferred shares in W; W sold the shares in M to K for cash; a Cayman Islands company (D) acquired a relatively insignificant holding of preferred shares in W; following a rights issue, open to all preferred shareholders but accepted only by D, D became the sole ordinary shareholder in W; W went into liquidation and, because of the differing rights attached to the two classes of shares, D became entitled to six-sevenths of the assets of W. The result was that most of the proceeds of sale of the shares in M reached D. The Revenue issued a CGT assessment on F, on the basis that he should be treated as having disposed of his shares to K. The Special Commissioners upheld the assessment and the HL dismissed F's appeal, holding that what is now *TCGA 1992, s 29* applied (by a 4-1 majority, Lord Wilberforce dissenting). Viscount Dilhorne held that value had passed out of the shares in W, within the meaning of *s 29(2)*, and that F was taxable accordingly, since 'person' in *s 29(2)* should be taken as including the plural, and F and his sons-in-law had exercised their control, notwithstanding that two of them had not voted on the resolution to wind up W. *Floor v Davis*, HL 1979, 52 TC 609; [1979] STC 379; [1979] 2 WLR 830; [1979] 2 All ER 677. (*Notes*. (1) See also *TCGA 1992, ss 30–34*, deriving from *FA 1989*. (2) In the CA, Eveleigh LJ had held in favour of an alternative Revenue contention, that F had should be treated as having disposed of his shares in M to K. The HL did not consider this point, but Eveleigh LJ's judgment was specifically approved in the subsequent case of *Furniss v Dawson*, **71.288** below.)

[71.69] See also *Young v Phillips*, 71.383 below.

Whether TCGA 1992, s 30 applicable

[71.70] A company (L) entered into a series of transactions between March and September 2003, disposing of nine shares which it had acquired in 1969 and reacquiring them six months later. The transactions were intended to exploit a perceived loophole in *TCGA 1992, s 106* and create a capital loss for tax purposes of £200,000,000. HMRC rejected the claims on the basis that the value-shifting provisions of *TCGA 1992, s 30* applied to diminish the loss. L appealed. The Upper Tribunal dismissed the appeal. Roth J held that, for the purpose of *s 30(9)*, the 'relevant acquisition of the asset' was the reacquisition of the shares in September 2003, rather than their original acquisition in 1969, so that this was 'a case in which the disposal of an asset precedes its acquisition'. *TCGA 1992, s 30(5)* required 'an increase to be made to the consideration for the disposal on 31 March 2003'. There was 'no logic to a partial adjustment to consideration', and 'in the circumstances of this case, having regard to the scheme undertaken by (L) and the tax-free benefit which the scheme delivered and which enabled (L) to claim the loss in question', the requisite adjustment was 'to increase the consideration for the disposal of the nine shares to the extent necessary to eliminate the loss'. *Land Securities plc v HMRC*, UT [2013] UKUT 124 (TCC); [2013] STC 1043. (*Note. TCGA 1992, s 106* was subsequently repealed by *FA 2006*.)

[71.71] See also *HBOS Treasury Services plc v HMRC*, **18.14** CORPORATION TAX.

Assets held at 6 April 1965 (TCGA 1992, s 35, Sch 2)

TCGA 1992, Sch 2 para 9—whether land 'reflecting development value'

[71.72] In 1972 a farmer sold 22 acres of farmland, which he had inherited, to a developer. The local planning authority had previously published a proposal to allow residential development of the land, and the Revenue issued an assessment under what is now *TCGA 1992, Sch 2 para 9* on the basis that the land had development value, although conditional planning permission was not granted until July 1973. The HL unanimously upheld the assessment, holding that the land had development value even though formal planning permission had not been granted. *Watkins v Kidson*, HL 1979, 53 TC 117; [1979] STC 464; [1979] 1 WLR 876; [1979] 2 All ER 1157.

[71.73] In 1948 an individual (G) acquired an interest in land which had an agreed value of £15,545. In 1984 the land was sold to the British Airports Authority for £160,000, with the condition that, should the Authority obtain planning permission within 30 years, a further sum of up to £350,000 would be payable. The Revenue issued an assessment on the basis that the consideration received on disposal included development value and that therefore what is now *TCGA 1992, Sch 2 para 9* applied. G appealed, contending that the conditions of *Sch 2 para 9(1)(b)* were not satisfied, and that the assessment should be computed on a straight-line apportionment basis. The Ch D rejected this contention and upheld the assessment. There was a clear finding of fact that the sale price included an element of 'hope value', which was equivalent to anticipated development value. That being so, the provisions of what is now *TCGA 1992, Sch 2 para 9* had to be applied. *Morgan v Gibson*, Ch D 1989, 61 TC 654; [1989] STC 568. (*Note*. For a preliminary issue in this case, see *Gibson v Stroud Commissioners & Morgan*, **4.188** APPEALS.)

TCGA 1992, Sch 2 para 9—whether applicable where land acquired by gift

[71.74] In 1950 a woman gave her daughter (P) some land. P sold part of the land in 1976 for consideration which reflected its potential for development. The Revenue issued an assessment under what is now *TCGA 1992, Sch 2 para 9*, computed on the basis that the land should be treated as having been sold on 6 April 1965 and re-acquired at its market value on that date. P appealed, contending that, since the land had been acquired by gift, *Sch 2 para 9(1)(a)* was not satisfied and the gain should be time-apportioned over the whole period from 1960 to 1976. The CA unanimously rejected this contention and upheld the assessment, holding that the reference in *Sch 2 para 9* to 'expenditure incurred' should be construed as including deemed expenditure. *Mashiter v Pearmain*, CA 1984, 58 TC 334; [1985] STC 165.

Election for 6 April 1965 valuation—TCGA 1992, Sch 2 para 17

[71.75] In 1973 an individual (W) disposed of land which he had acquired in 1957. The market value at 6 April 1965 was slightly above the disposal figure, but W had not made an application for a 6 April 1965 valuation under what is now *TCGA 1992, Sch 2 para 17(1)* within the statutory time limit, and an extension of the time limit had been refused. If he had made such an application in time, there would have been a no loss/no gain situation as a result of *Sch 2 para 17(2)*. The Revenue issued an assessment on the gain computed on the time-apportionment basis, and W appealed, contending that it was unnecessary to make an election for a 6 April 1965 valuation where it would produce a no loss/no gain result. The Special Commissioners rejected this contention and dismissed his appeal, and the Ch D upheld their decision, holding that *Sch 2 para 17(2)* has effect only if there has been an election under *Sch 2 para 17(1)*. *Whitaker v Cameron*, Ch D 1982, 56 TC 97; [1982] STC 665.

TCGA 1992, Sch 2 para 17—whether land subject to a tenancy

[71.76] In 1975 a married woman (K) sold land which she had held for many years. From 1961 to 1972 it had been farmed by a company (R) which she controlled, and from then until the sale she had farmed it in partnership. R had originally paid an annual rental of £2,000, but this was waived in 1966. K elected under what is now *TCGA 1992, Sch 2 para 17(1)* for the land to be valued at 6 April 1965. The Revenue issued a CGT assessment to the executors of K's husband, charging tax on the disposal on the basis that the land had been subject to a tenancy at 6 April 1965. The executors appealed, contending that the valuation of the land at 6 April 1965 should be on the basis of vacant possession. The Ch D rejected this contention and upheld the assessment. On the evidence, at 6 April 1965 the land had been subject to a tenancy. *Henderson v Karmel's Executors*, Ch D 1984, 58 TC 201; [1984] STC 572.

Assets held at 31 March 1982 (TCGA 1992, s 35, Sch 2)

TCGA 1992, s 35—Revenue refusing to allow late election

[71.77] An individual (L) held shares in three associated companies at 31 March 1982. In 1986 he exchanged these shares for shares in the parent company of the group. In 1991 he sold some shares in an unrelated company (R), which he had acquired in 1976. This sale gave rise to a chargeable gain which was below the annual exemption limit. In April 1992 the parent company of the group went into receivership, so that its shares became worthless. As a result of the disposal of the shares in R, the time limit for making an election under *TCGA 1992, s 35(5)*, to treat the value of the shares in the three associated companies at 31 March 1982 as their cost of acquisition, expired on 5 April 1994. L failed to make such an election within the statutory time limit, but in March 1995 he applied for an extension of the time limit under *s 35(6)(b)*. The Revenue rejected the application. L applied for judicial review, contending that the sale of his shares in R should not be regarded as a relevant disposal, and that the Revenue's refusal to allow a late election was unreasonable. The CS rejected this contention and dismissed the application. Lord Eassie observed that the circumstances did not fall within Inland Revenue Statement of Practice SP 4/92, or within the scope of a Ministerial Statement issued in December 1985 in relation to the extension of time limits. Furthermore, there was 'a clear distinction between disposals upon which the gain, irrespective of amount, will not be chargeable and those which will give rise to a chargeable gain, which may possibly not give rise to actual liability to tax by virtue of the exemption afforded by (*TCGA 1992, s 3*). The chartered accountants acting for the petitioner effectively invited the Board to alter or erase that boundary. In its response the Board adhered to its analysis by emphasising that chargeable gains remained chargeable even in the event that their net amount is sufficiently low to come within the annual exempt amount.' The Revenue had been entitled to take the view that 'oversight by the professional advisers was not a sufficient reason for their granting an extension of the time limit.' *Liddell v CIR*, CS 1997, 72 TC 62. (*Note*. The Ministerial Statement in question was previously contained in HMRC Capital Gains Manual, para 13802, but appears to have been removed from the current version of the Manual.)

Valuation of house at 31 March 1982

[71.78] An individual (N) sold a house in 1995. He had held a 50% share in the house at 31 March 1982. The Revenue valuation officer considered that the value of his half-share of the house at that date had been £29,250 (computed on the basis that the valuation of the house had been £64,750, but that 10% should be deducted from this to take account of the difficulty in selling a half-share). N appealed, contending that the value of his half-share had been between £42,000 and £45,000, and that the 10% deduction was inappropriate. The Lands Tribunal reviewed the evidence in detail, rejected N's contentions, and upheld the Revenue's valuation. *Hatt v Newman (No 2)*, Lands Tribunal 2001, [2002] 4 EG 175.

[71.79] An individual (B) purchased a three-storey house in Harrow in 1970. He converted it into offices and used it as such for many years, although it was subsequently reconverted into flats. He sold the house for £482,000 in 2006. In his 2006/07 self-assessment, he computed the gain on the basis that, at 31 March 1982, the value of the property had been £200,000. HMRC issued an amendment reducing the value to £100,000. B appealed. The Upper Tribunal reviewed the evidence in detail and allowed the appeal in part, holding that at 31 March 1982 the rental value of the property had been £11,000 pa and that this should be multiplied by 12.5, giving a value at that date of £137,500. *MB Blum v HMRC*, UT [2013] UKUT 304 (LC).

Valuation of leasehold interest at 31 March 1982

[71.80] Two people, who carried on business in partnership, purchased a short leasehold interest in a dilapidated house for £2,950 in 1979. In September 1982 one of the partners (C) purchased the freehold for £40,000. In 2002 he sold the freehold for £1,300,000. HMRC issued a determination that at 31 March 1982, the value of C's 50% leasehold interest had been £1,450. C appealed, contending that the value had been £275,000. The Lands

Tribunal reviewed the evidence in detail and held that the value of the leasehold interest had been £7,032, and that the value of C's 50% interest should be reduced by 10% 'to reflect the disadvantages of owning an undivided share', so that the value of C's interest had been £3,164. *N Chakravorty v HMRC*, UT [2014] UKUT 184 (LC).

Valuation of accountancy practice at 31 March 1982

[71.81] An accountant (W) disposed of the goodwill of his practice in 2003. HMRC issued a CGT assessment on the basis that he had made a gain of £230,759. W appealed, contending that the value of his practice at March 1982 should have been calculated on the basis of applying a multiple of 3.5 to his gross recurring fees, giving a gain of £21,505. The First-tier Tribunal allowed his appeal in part, accepting his contention that the goodwill of an accountancy firm should be ascertained by applying a multiple to the gross recurring fees, without deducting the value of the net assets of the practice (as HMRC had contended), but holding that the appropriate multiple should be 1.625. However Judge Short also held that W's computation, which HMRC had initially agreed to, had undervalued the goodwill of the practice at the date of disposal, resulting in an increase in the CGT liability (for reasons which are not fully set out in the decision). *GM Wildin v HMRC (No 2)*, FTT [2014] UKFTT 459 (TC), TC03586. (*Note.* For a preliminary issue in this case, see **4.148** APPEALS.)

Whether asset held at 31 March 1982

[71.82] In a Northern Ireland case, a company (P) carried on business as sand merchants, extracting sand from Lough Neagh. When P was formed, it took over a licence, originally granted in 1965, to extract such sand. A new licence was granted in 1993 and was replaced by another licence in September 1998. In November 1998 P sold its business to another company. P appealed against a CT assessment, contending that the licence was part of its goodwill and that the computation of chargeable gains should include a deduction for the value of the licence as at March 1982. The First-tier Tribunal rejected this contention and dismissed the appeal, holding that 'the asset disposed of by the appellant in 1998 was the right to extract sand pursuant to the 1998 licence'. *P & J McCann (Toomebridge) Ltd v HMRC*, FTT [2013] UKFTT 204 (TC), TC02619.

Allowable deductions (TCGA 1992, ss 37–43)

Consideration chargeable to tax on income (TCGA 1992, s 37)

Amounts taken into account in computing balancing charge

[71.83] In 1980 a company (C) sold for £715,967 some looms which it had purchased for £545,930. The sale gave rise to a balancing charge under what is now *CAA 1990, s 24*. The Revenue issued an assessment on the overall gain of £170,037. C appealed, contending that the effect of what is now *TCGA 1992, s 37(1)* was that the acquisition cost of the looms should be excluded from the disposal consideration, since it had been taken into account in computing the balancing charge. The Ch D rejected this contention and upheld the assessment. Vinelott J held that the acquisition cost was not to be excluded from the disposal consideration. Where legislation was ambiguously worded, it was necessary to have regard to the context and scheme of the Act under consideration, and to strive to find an interpretation which avoided injustice or absurdity. The words 'taken into account' in *s 37(1)* should be read as referring to sums which had to be brought directly into the computation. The purpose of the limitation of the disposal value to the cost of acquisition was to avoid double taxation of any profit on disposal. It would be paradoxical to find that the cost of acquisition was itself to be deducted from the disposal consideration, thereby ensuring that the gain escaped altogether the charge to tax. *Hirsch v Crowthers Cloth Ltd*, Ch D 1989, 62 TC 759; [1990] STC 174.

Application of TCGA 1992, s 37 to transactions in life assurance policies

[71.84] On 4 April 2001 an individual (D) contracted to purchase five life assurance policies for a stated consideration of £1,962,233. On the following day he asked the vendor to surrender the policies. The surrender value was £1,751,376. In his tax return, D claimed that the effect of this was that he had made an allowable loss of £1,962,233 for CGT purposes. HMRC rejected the claim and D appealed, contending that the effect of *TCGA 1992, s 37* was that the 'surrender value' could be excluded from the computation of the gain or loss on the disposal. The Ch D reviewed the evidence in detail, rejected this contention, and rejected D's claim. Norris J observed that for income tax purposes the surrender had given rise to a 'chargeable event gain' of £1,351; and that the transactions had cost D £210,857. He held that this £210,857 represented professional fees which had not been 'wholly and exclusively expended in the acquisition of the policies'. Accordingly, for CGT purposes, the disposal had produced a loss of £1,351, being the amount chargeable to income tax and the only amount which fell to be excluded from the consideration charged to CGT by virtue of *TCGA 1992, s 37*. The CA unanimously upheld this decision. Rimer LJ held that 'the interpretation of legislation involves more than black letter literalism. In a case such as the present, in which there is a question as to which of limbs (i) and (ii) applies, it is necessary to give the statute a purposive construction'. The purpose of *TCGA 1992, ss 37-39* was 'to prevent the double taxation that might otherwise arise from the circumstance that the disposal of an asset will or may give rise to a charge to income tax and also be a disposal for CGT purposes'. It was 'not their purpose to enable the creation of an imaginary loss that the taxpayer can set against a real gain and so reduce a CGT liability'. *J Drummond v HMRC*, CA 2009, 79 TC 793; [2009] STC 2206; [2009] EWCA Civ 608.

[71.85] The decision in *Drummond v HMRC*, **71.84** above, was applied in the similar subsequent cases of *RJ Smith v HMRC*, Sp C 2008, [2009] SSCD 132 (Sp C 725); *Abbeyland Ltd v HMRC*, FTT [2013] UKFTT 287 (TC); [2013] SFTD 1212, TC02693, and *Pattullo v HMRC (No 2)*, **5.61** ASSESSMENTS.

Acquisition and disposal costs (TCGA 1992, s 38)

Acquisition cost of shares

[71.86] In September 1972 a company (D) agreed to acquire investments from an insurance company for £3,937,632, to be paid by means of 2,461,226 shares in D at their issue price of 160p per share. The agreement was conditional on permission being obtained for the shares to be dealt in on the Stock Exchange. The agreement became unconditional on 11 October, when the shares were issued. On 12 October, when they were first quoted on the Stock Exchange, their middle market price was 125p per share. Subsequently D sold some of the investments it had acquired from the insurance company. The Revenue issued an assessment on the gains, in which the cost of the investments was computed on the basis that the shares in D should be valued at 125p each. D appealed, contending that the shares should be valued at 160p each. The CA accepted this contention and allowed D's appeal, and the HL unanimously upheld this decision. There had been an honest arm's length agreement in which the shares had been valued at 160p, and there was no reason for going behind this agreed value. Market value was only relevant where no agreed value was available. *Stanton v Drayton Commercial Investment Co Ltd*, HL 1982, 55 TC 286; [1982] STC 585; [1982] 3 WLR 214; [1982] 2 All ER 942.

[71.87] In 2006 an individual (M) entered into an avoidance scheme, intended to create a large tax loss. He exercised an option to buy some shares in a trading company (S) for a nominal price of £6,000,000. This nominal price was payable to a discretionary trust of which M was the principal beneficiary, and whose assets consisted mainly of that debt. Accordingly, the economic effect of the scheme was to transfer almost £6,000,000 of M's assets into that discretionary trust. A few days later M sold the shares for £552. On his 2005/06 tax return, he claimed that he had made a tax loss of £5,999,448 on the transaction, which would be available for offset against his income (under *ICTA 1988, s 574*). HMRC issued an amendment rejecting the claim. The First-tier Tribunal substantially dismissed M's appeal. Judge Hellier observed that *TCGA 1992, s 38(1)* provided that there should be a deduction for consideration given 'wholly or exclusively for the acquisition of the asset'. On the evidence and in the context of the scheme, M had not paid £6,000,000 wholly and exclusively for the shares in S. He held that the only sum given wholly and exclusively for those shares was their redemption value of £600. That was their acquisition cost for tax purposes, so that M had only made a loss of £48, rather than the amount claimed. *J Myers v HMRC; S Price v HMRC (and related appeal)*, FTT [2013] UKFTT 297 (TC), TC02703.

Expenses of obtaining confirmation (probate)

[71.88] The Revenue issued an assessment on executors, charging CGT on their gains from disposals of investments forming part of the estate. They appealed, claiming a deduction for part of the fees paid to solicitors for valuing the estate, paying the estate duty, obtaining confirmation, etc. and for commission paid to them for their work done in disposing of the investments. The Commissioners allowed their appeal and the HL upheld this decision (by a 3–2 majority, Lord Morris and Lord Upjohn dissenting). *CIR v Richards' Executors*, HL 1971, 46 TC 626; [1971] 1 WLR 571; [1971] 1 All ER 785.

Insurance premium paid as part of trust variation

[71.89] An elderly widow (W) had been the principal beneficiary under a settlement. To avoid estate duty, the settlement was varied by agreement and much of the trust fund became absolutely vested in her daughter (M). The trustees required M to effect an insurance policy in their favour, to insure against her predeceasing W. W died in 1966, survived by M. The Revenue issued an assessment on M's husband, charging CGT on the gain on the trustees' sale of certain investments which had been appropriated to M. He appealed, contending that the insurance premium should be allowed as a deduction. The Ch D rejected this contention and upheld the assessment, holding that the premium did not fall within what is now *TCGA 1992, s 38(1)*. *Allison v Murray*, Ch D 1975, 51 TC 57; [1975] STC 524; [1975] 1 WLR 1578; [1975] 3 All ER 561.

Assignment of lease—whether arrears of rent deductible

[71.90] A company (C) ceased trading and went into voluntary liquidation. Its liquidator paid the landlord arrears of rent on the premises it leased, including £6,131 for the period of liquidation after trading had ceased. C appealed against a CT assessment, claiming to deduct the £6,131 in arriving at the gain on the assignment of the leases. The CA unanimously rejected the claim, holding that the £6,131 was not within what is now *TCGA 1992, s 38(1)(b)*, and that the deduction was precluded by what is now *s 39(2)*. *Emmerson v Computer Time International Ltd*, CA 1977, 50 TC 628; [1977] STC 170; [1977] 1 WLR 734; [1977] 2 All ER 545.

Own labour on enhancement of asset—whether value deductible

[71.91] An individual (J) purchased a derelict cottage for £2,250 in 1968. He carried out extensive work in restoring and improving it, much of the work being done himself with the help of his son and friends. In 1975 he sold it for £11,500. He appealed against an assessment on the gain, claiming a deduction of £1,700 for the estimated value of his personal labour in improving the property. The Ch D rejected his claim, holding that in a revenue context 'expenditure' means primarily 'monetary expenditure' and secondly expenditure in 'money's worth'. J's expenditure of time and labour was not expenditure within the meaning of what is now *TCGA 1992, s 38(1)*. *Oram v Johnson*, Ch D 1980, 53 TC 319; [1980] STC 222; [1980] 1 WLR 558; [1980] 2 All ER 1.

Deductible monetary liability replaced by non-monetary obligation

[71.92] An individual (C) had owned a house, which his mother-in-law (W) occupied as a protected tenant. He was offered £7,200 for the house subject to the tenancy but refused it. Subsequently he agreed that, if W would vacate the house, he would compensate her by paying her half the difference between the tenanted value and the actual sale price. He sold the house for £26,000. Before completion he and W agreed that he would provide her with rent-free accommodation for life if she released him from his obligation to pay her £9,400 under their previous agreement. She subsequently lived in an extension to C's own residence, built for £25,000. The Revenue assessed C's gain from the disposal of the house, and he appealed, contending that the £9,400 should be allowed as a deduction. The Ch D allowed the appeal in part. If the £9,400 had been paid, it would have been deductible under what is now *TCGA 1992, s 38(1)(b)*. The obligation to pay this sum was replaced by an obligation which was capable of being valued in monetary terms. The case was remitted to the Commissioners to determine the deductible amount. *Chaney v Watkis*, Ch D 1985, 58 TC 707; [1986] STC 89.

Requirements of TCGA 1992, s 38(1)(b)

[71.93] In 1983 the trustees of a settlement acquired all the shares in an American company for £661. They made capital contributions of more than £1,500,000 to the company. Despite this investment, they disposed of the shares for the nominal sum of $1 in 1994. They claimed a capital loss of more than £1,500,000. The Revenue rejected the claim on the basis that the capital contributions were not 'reflected in the state or nature of the asset at the time of disposal', as required by *TCGA 1992, s 38(1)(b)*, so that the allowable loss was limited to the original acquisition cost of £661. The Special Commissioners upheld the Revenue's ruling and dismissed the trustees' appeal. *Trustees of the FD Fenston Will Trusts v HMRC*, Sp C [2007] SSCD 316 (Sp C 589).

[71.94] An individual (B) held a substantial shareholding in a successful publishing company (BH). In 2003 he entered into an agreement with another company (T), under which T paid B £1,000,000 in return for B, inter alia, agreeing to support T in attempting a takeover of BH. In 2006, after a US company (JW) had expressed interest in acquiring BH, T agreed to release B from this obligation in return for payment of £25,000,000. In 2007 JW acquired control of BH. In his tax return, B declared the gain on the disposal of his shares but claimed a deduction for the payment of £25,000,000. HMRC issued an amendment rejecting the claim, and B appealed. The First-tier Tribunal allowed his appeal in part. Judge Barlow specifically declined to follow the Special Commissioners' decision in *Trustees of the FD Fenston Will Trusts v HMRC*, **71.93** above, and held that the payment fell within *TCGA 1992, s 38(1)(b)*, as it enhanced the value of B's shares by enabling him to support JW's offer. However, £7,500,000 of the payment had been directly funded by JW (which had reduced its total offer to take this into account), so that B was only entitled to a deduction for £17,500,000. *J Blackwell v HMRC*, FTT [2014] UKFTT 103 (TC), TC03243.

Residuary legatee paying deficiency to executor to secure transfer of asset

[71.95] A woman died in 1965 owning a house worth £6,000. However, because of debts and specific legacies, the residuary estate was only worth £3,610. Her son (P), who was the residuary legatee, wished to acquire the house, and paid the deficiency of £2,390 to the executor to do so. In 1969 P sold the house for £9,000. The Revenue issued an assessment allowing a deduction of £6,000 under what is now *TCGA 1992, s 38(1)*. P appealed, contending that the acquisition cost should be taken as £8,390. The Special Commissioners rejected this contention and dismissed his appeal, and the CA upheld their decision. *Passant v Jackson*, CA 1986, 59 TC 230; [1986] STC 164.

Sale of cottage—claim to deduct replacement value

[71.96] An individual (N) sold a holiday cottage and was assessed to CGT on the resulting gain. He appealed against the assessment, contending that the value of replacing the cottage (which he estimated at £160,000) should be taken into account as a deduction in the computation, as should the value of a number of chattels which he had inherited and which had been stolen from the cottage. The General Commissioners rejected this contention and dismissed his appeal, and the CA upheld their decision. There was no basis for allowing the estimated replacement value of the cottage as a deduction in the computation. Since N had not produced evidence to indicate that any of the stolen chattels had had a market value in excess of £2,000 when he inherited them, no allowable loss had arisen on their disposal. *Neely v Ward*, CA 1993, 65 TC 567; [1993] STC 196. (*Note*. The appellant appeared in person.)

Sale of property—claim to deduct 'gifted deposit'

[71.97] An individual (S) purchased a property in 2007 and sold it in 2008. In his tax return, he claimed a deduction for £60,040 which he described as a 'gifted deposit' and had paid to a company of which his son was a director, which had acted as an intermediary. HMRC issued a closure notice disallowing the deduction, and the First-tier Tribunal dismissed S's appeal. *H Symonds v HMRC*, FTT [2012] UKFTT 197 (TC), TC01892.

Sale of property—claim to deduct cost of building work

[71.98] Following an enquiry, HMRC issued an amendment to a return submitted by a woman (W) who had sold a residential property, charging CGT on the sale. W lodged a late appeal, claiming that she should be allowed a deduction for building work carried out on the property. The First-tier Tribunal dismissed the appeal, finding that she had not shown that an invoice, which she had submitted, related to the property in question. *Ms JB Williams v HMRC*, FTT [2014] UKFTT 1051 (TC), TC04144.

Sale of property purchased in instalments

[71.99] In 1983 two individuals (B and C) each purchased 50% of a house, each paying £5,000. In 1999 C bought B's 50% share for £26,000. In 2006 C sold the house for £147,500. In his 2006/07 tax return, he claimed a deduction for £52,000 (the market value of the house when he purchased B's share). HMRC issued an amendment reducing the deduction to £31,000 (the amount C had actually paid). The First-tier Tribunal dismissed C's appeal. *BS Chahal v HMRC*, FTT [2013] UKFTT 373 (TC), TC02772.

Costs of appealing against valuation of unquoted shares

[71.100] In the share valuation case noted at **71.360** below, the administrators of a deceased's estate contended that the costs of their appeal qualified as incidental costs of disposal. The Ch D rejected this contention and the CA dismissed the administrators' appeal. Morritt LJ held that, although the costs of an initial valuation were deductible, a liability to tax could not be diminished (or even extinguished altogether) by contesting it. If such expenses were to be treated as deductible, there 'would be a positive deterrent to reaching a sensible agreement with the Revenue as to the quantum of liability'.

Applying *Smith's Potato Estates Ltd v Bolland*, **63.156** TRADING PROFITS, there was a distinction between the costs of producing accounts from which to compute profits and the conduct of a tax controversy with the Revenue. The costs and expenses which a taxpayer might deduct under what is now *TCGA 1992, s 38(2)(b)* were limited to those incurred in complying with the requirements of *TMA 1970, s 12*, and did not extend to costs incurred in negotiating over, or contesting, the tax liability arising from a disposal. *Caton's Administrators v Couch*, CA 1997, 70 TC 10; [1997] STC 970.

Sale of milk quota—whether part of cost of land deductible from gain

[71.101] A farmer (C) owned 56.68 acres of land and was entitled to 120,000 litres of milk quota. In 1991 he sold 60,000 litres of milk quota to a company (T). On the same day, but under separate agreements, he granted T a tenancy of 10.39 acres of his land for a ten-month period, and T appointed him as its agent to enter into occupation of that part of the land. The Revenue issued a CGT assessment on the gain. C appealed, contending that the sale of the milk quota should be treated as a part disposal of his land, so that part of the acquisition cost of the land should be allowed as a deduction. The Special Commissioners rejected this contention and dismissed C's appeal. The milk quota was a separate asset from the land. Although milk quota corresponded to a holding of land, it did not 'correspond to any particular parcel of land in that holding'. Milk quota did not derive from the occupier's land, but was 'an advantage derived from the context of the common organisation of the market in milk'. Milk quota was a valuable asset, and those holding it had the right (subject to restrictions laid down in EC law) to dispose of it for profit. The sale of the milk quota was not a part disposal of C's land within what is now *TCGA 1992, s 21(2)(b)*, and was not a capital sum derived from the land within *s 22(1)*. Since the value of the quota did not derive from the holding, what is now *TCGA 1992, s 43* did not apply. *Cottle v Coldicott*, Sp C [1995] SSCD 239 (Sp C 40).

[71.102] The decision in *Cottle v Coldicott*, **71.101** above, was applied in the similar subsequent case of *Foxton v HMRC*, Sp C [2005] SSCD 661 (Sp C 485). (*Note*. A penalty of £500 was imposed on the appellant for failure to comply with directions.)

Legal costs relating to partnership dispute

[71.103] In 1981 an accountancy partnership admitted three new partners. The new partners paid a total of £150,000 to the original partners. In the relevant agreements, the payment was attributed to the purchase of 20% of the partnership goodwill. Following disagreements, the new partners took legal proceedings, seeking a dissolution of the partnership and the repayment of the £75,000 paid to one of the two original partners (L). L incurred legal costs of some £13,000 in defending the proceedings. The Ch D ordered that the partnership should be dissolved, but rejected the claim for repayment. L subsequently disposed of his share of the goodwill, and the Revenue issued a CGT assessment on him in respect of the disposal. L appealed, contending that the legal costs should be allowed as a deduction. The Special Commissioner accepted this contention and allowed the appeal. *Lee v Jewitt*, Sp C [2000] SSCD 517 (Sp C 257).

Transfer of building society business to banking company

[71.104] A building society transferred its business to a banking company. Shareholders and depositors were paid lump sums of £500 and percentage bonus payments calculated by reference to the balance on their accounts. Two shareholders appealed against CGT assessments, contending that they had made a complete disposal of their existing assets and that there was no chargeable gain. The Special Commissioner accepted this contention and allowed the appeals in principle, holding that there had been a total disposal of the relevant assets. With regard to the share accounts, the amount of the credit balance on each account was allowable expenditure within *TCGA 1992, s 38*. With regard to the deposit accounts, the effect of *TCGA 1992, s 251* was that there was no chargeable gain. Furthermore, since payments were made to shareholders and depositors alike, none of the expenditure could be attributed to the shareholders' equity rights. *Foster v Williams; Horan v Williams*, Sp C [1997] SSCD 112 (Sp C 113). (*Note*. For the Revenue's practice following this decision, see the Revenue Press Release issued on 27 March 1997.)

Expenditure allowed in computing income (TCGA 1992, s 39)

[71.105] A woman (R) acquired a house in 1976. She lived in it until 1985, and then let it to tenants until April 2006. She sold it in September 2006. In her 2006/07 tax return, she claimed that various expenses (including service charges, furniture clearance and council tax) should be allowed as deductions in computing the capital gain on the sale. HMRC rejected the claim and the First-Tier Tribunal dismissed R's appeal, holding that the expenses were 'expenditure which would be allowable in computing income', so that the effect of *TCGA 1992, s 39(1)* was that they were not allowable in the CGT computation. *Mrs M Raha v HMRC*, FTT August 2010, TC00590.

[71.106] See also *Emmerson v Computer Time International Ltd*, 71.90 above.

Restriction of losses by reference to allowances (TCGA 1992, s 41)

Losses on disposal of units in enterprise zone unit trust

[71.107] In 1989 an individual (S) invested £10,000 in an enterprise zone unit trust. The trustees used the funds to acquire land and buildings, and claimed capital allowances. S was credited with some of these allowances under the *Income Tax (Definition of Unit Trusts Schemes) Regulations 1988 (SI 1988/267)*. Subsequently the property was disposed of and S received distributions, which were treated for CGT purposes as part disposals of S's units. S claimed that these disposals gave rise to allowable losses. The Revenue rejected the claim on the basis that the effect of *TCGA 1992, s 41(2)* was that S's allowable expenditure had to be restricted by the capital allowances. S appealed, contending that *s 41(2)* did not apply because it was the trustees' expenditure, rather than his expenditure, which gave rise to capital allowances. The Special Commissioner accepted this contention and allowed S's appeal, holding that 'once the step has been taken of treating the unit trust as a company and the rights of the unitholders as shares in that company', then for CGT purposes 'the computation of gains on disposals of units must be treated in the same way as the computation of gains on disposals of shares'. Accordingly, the reference in *TCGA 1992, s 41(2)* to the extent to which any capital allowance 'has been or may be made in respect of' any expenditure had to be construed as referring to 'expenditure comprised in the consideration given wholly and exclusively for the acquisition of the relevant asset, i.e. the £10,000 given by (S) for his units. Capital allowances were not given in respect of that expenditure. Thus *section 41(2)* does not apply.' The CA unanimously upheld this decision. Lawrence Collins LJ held that the effect of *TCGA 1992, s 99* was 'that there are two levels of capital gains tax. First, gains made by the trustee in respect of trust assets are taxed as if they were gains of a company (except that the tax paid would not be corporation tax but capital gains tax). Any tax on these gains is assessed on the trustee. Second, each unit holder is treated on a disposal of his units as if they were shares in a company, his gains or losses on units being taxed as if they were gains or losses on shares.' *HMRC v C Smallwood*, CA 2007, 78 TC 560; [2007] STC 1237; [2007] EWCA Civ 462.

Assets derived from other assets (TCGA 1992, s 43)

[71.108] See *Bayley v Rogers*, 71.28 above, and *Cottle v Coldicott*, 71.101 above.

Options

Option payment contingently repayable

[71.109] A farmer (R) granted a gravel company an option to purchase some land for £100,000. He received £25,000 for the option. The agreement included a proviso that R would repay the £25,000 to the company if, after ten years, the company had not obtained planning permission to extract sand and gravel from the land. The Revenue assessed the £25,000 to CGT for the year in which the option was granted. The Ch D allowed R's appeal in part, holding that the consideration should not be the full amount of the £25,000, but that the £25,000 should be brought in at a valuation taking the contingency into account. (The contingency was not within what is now either *TCGA 1992, s 48* or *49*.) *Randall v Plumb*, Ch D 1974, 50 TC 392; [1975] STC 191; [1975] 1 All ER 734. (*Note.* This decision was distinguished in the subsequent case of *Garner v Pounds Shipowners & Shipbreakers Ltd*, 71.110 below.)

Option to purchase land—payment for release of restrictive covenants

[71.110] A company (P) granted an option to purchase freehold land which was subject to certain restrictive covenants. The purchaser paid £399,750 for the option, this amount being held by P's solicitors as stakeholders pending the release of the covenants. P subsequently paid £90,000 to obtain the release of the covenants. The Revenue issued an assessment charging tax on the consideration of £399,750 without allowing a deduction for the £90,000. The HL unanimously dismissed P's appeal and upheld the assessment. Lord Jauncey held that 'no payment by the company to a third party can alter the value of the cash sum of £399,750 paid by (the purchaser) in terms of the agreement as a consideration for the disposal, i.e. the grant of the option'. Furthermore, the £90,000 was not allowable expenditure within what is now

TCGA 1992, s 38. The implementation of the obligation to obtain the release of the covenants was 'not a prerequisite of the option being exercised'. Accordingly, the expenditure was not 'wholly and exclusively incurred by (P) in providing' the option. Additionally, the expenditure referred to in *s 38(1)* 'must be expenditure which is extraneous to the asset rather than part of it'. *Garner v Pounds Shipowners & Shipbreakers Ltd (and related appeal)*, HL 2000, 72 TC 561; [2000] STC 420; [2000] 1 WLR 1107; [2000] 3 All ER 218.

Grant of option to purchase land

[71.111] Four brothers owned some agricultural land and their mother owned some adjoining land. They granted a company an option, exercisable within 10 years, to purchase the land on prescribed terms. (In the event, the option was not exercised.) The company paid £125,000 for the option, and the Revenue issued assessments on the brothers charging CGT on the amount each received. They appealed, contending that, by virtue of what is now *TCGA 1992, s 144(2)**, no assessment should be raised until the option was exercised or abandoned. The Ch D rejected this contention and upheld the assessments, holding that *s 144* was not intended to supersede what is now *TCGA 1992, s 21*, but provided how the chargeable gain on the grant of an option was to be computed. Accordingly, the whole amount of the option price, less the costs of granting it, was a chargeable gain under the general provisions of *s 144(1)*. Furthermore, the part disposal rules were not applicable to the grant of an option. *Strange v Openshaw (and related appeals)*, Ch D 1983, 57 TC 544; [1983] STC 416.

[71.112] In 1982 a landowner (N) conveyed an area of farmland to his two sons as trustees. Two days later he and his sons granted a building company (W) an option to purchase most of the land. Under the option agreement, W covenanted to 'use all reasonable endeavours' to obtain the inclusion of the land 'in any relevant local plan or planning policy document for the area as land suitable for residential development'. In 1985 W assigned the benefit of the option to two other companies (M and C). Later that year the local council granted outline planning permission for residential development on 11.3 hectares of land. M and C subsequently exercised the option in respect of those 11.3 hectares, and paid £680,000 to N and his children in accordance with the agreement. In 1986 N and his sons released C from some of its obligations under the option agreement in return for a payment of £175,000. The Revenue issued CGT assessments on N's sons, against which they appealed. The Special Commissioners dismissed their appeals, holding that the date of disposal for CGT purposes was the date on which the option was exercised, and that the value of the right to receive further consideration must be added to the cash actually received on the disposal. The effect of what is now *TCGA 1992, s 60* was that N's sons were chargeable to CGT. *Newman v Pepper; Newman v Morgan*, Sp C [2000] SSCD 345 (Sp C 243). (*Notes*. (1) The appellants appeared in person. (2) Appeals against assessments under *ICTA 1988, s 776* were also dismissed (except that an assessment on one of N's sons was discharged by agreement). (3) The Commissioners also found that N and his sons had submitted a hold-over election under *FA 1980, s 79* (which has since been repealed), rejecting a contention by one of N's sons that their signatures had been forged.)

Attempt to establish CGT loss by transaction involving option

[71.113] In 1990 an individual (U) purchased some land for £1,400,000. In April 1993 he contracted to sell the land to a company (R) for £400,000. On the same day R gave him an option to repurchase the land for £400,000 plus 10% of any subsequent increase in its value. In November 1994 R contracted to sell the land to U for £420,000. On the same day U contracted to sell the property to a company (B) which he controlled. U appealed against CGT assessments for 1993/94 and 1994/95, contending that the April 1993 transactions had resulted in a CGT loss which could be set against gains he had made on the disposal of certain shares. The Special Commissioners, the Ch D and the CA unanimously rejected this contention and dismissed his appeal. Lawrence Collins LJ held that 'there was no event which resulted in a disposal of the property by (U) to (R) under the 1993 contract or an acquisition by (R) of the property under that contract'. This was not a 'bed and breakfast' transaction in which 'the owner of the asset disposes of it and then re-acquires it' since, on the evidence, the beneficial interest in the property had never been transferred to R. *PJ Underwood v HMRC*, CA 2008, 79 TC 631; [2009] STC 239; [2008] EWCA Civ 1423.

[71.114] In 2002/03 an individual (S) realised a substantial capital gain on the disposal of some loan notes. However, in his tax return, he claimed that he had made a loss of more than £11,000,000 on the disposal of a 'put' option. He had purchased the option on 7 February 2003, along with a corresponding 'call' option, and disposed of it on 4 April 2003. (He disposed of the 'call' option on 7 April 2003, by which time he had become resident in Spain, so that the gain on this disposal was outside the scope of UK CGT.) HMRC rejected the claim and S appealed. The First-Tier Tribunal dismissed his appeal, holding on the evidence that the options 'were inextricably linked with each other to form a continuous process which could be viewed commercially as a single or composite transaction'. The transactions had no commercial purpose, and their sole aim was to avoid tax. The Upper Tribunal and the CA unanimously upheld this decision, applying the principles laid down by Lord Fraser in *WT Ramsay Ltd v CIR*, **71.285** below. Sir Andrew Morritt held that 'the relevant transaction was the four options together and such a transaction does not constitute a disposal' within *TCGA 1992, ss 1, 2*. Hallett LJ held that 'the relevant transaction here is plainly the scheme as a whole: namely a series of interdependent and linked transactions, with a guaranteed outcome. Under the scheme as a whole, the options were created merely to be destroyed. They were self cancelling. Thus, for capital gains purposes, there was no asset and no disposal. There was no real loss and certainly no loss to which the TCGA 1992 applies. There is in truth no significant difference between this scheme and the scheme in *Ramsay*, other than the nature of the "asset".' *HP Schofield v HMRC*, CA [2012] EWCA Civ 97; [2012] STC 2019. (*Note*. The Supreme Court has dismissed an application for leave to appeal against this decision.)

Amount received for release of put option

[71.115] See *Golding v Kaufman*, **71.38** above, and *Powlson v Welbeck Securities Ltd*, **71.39** above.

Wasting assets (TCGA 1992, ss 44–47)

Application of TCGA 1992, s 45 where capital allowances withdrawn

[71.116] In 1973 a company (W), which published regional newspapers, agreed to purchase a printing press. The purchase price was paid by instalments beginning in 1973 and ending in 1977. The press was not delivered until 1976, by which time it was surplus to W's requirements. It was never used in W's trade, and was kept in storage until 1978 when it was sold to a Netherlands company at a profit of more than £650,000. W had been given first-year allowances on the instalments of the purchase price, but these were subsequently withdrawn under *FA 1971, s 41(2)*. The Revenue included the profit on the sale of the press in a CT assessment on W. W appealed, contending that the press was a wasting asset within what is now *TCGA 1992, s 45* and had not qualified in full for a capital allowance within the meaning of *s 45(2)(b)*, so that the gain was exempt under *s 45(1)*. The Special Commissioner accepted this contention and allowed the appeal, and the Ch D upheld this decision. The expenditure on the press had not fulfilled the necessary conditions to attract a capital allowance, so that *s 45(2)(b)* did not apply. *Burman v Westminster Press Ltd*, Ch D 1987, 60 TC 418; [1987] STC 669.

Lease—whether a wasting asset

[71.117] On the death of their mother in 1982, a brother and sister inherited the freehold interest in a house. The house was subject to a lease, for a term of 99 years from 1904, in favour of their father. He died in 1985 and the brother and sister then acquired the lease as his executors. Neither of them lived in the house, and in 1987 they sold the freehold and leasehold interests to the same purchaser. The Revenue issued a CGT assessment in which the value of the house was apportioned between the leasehold and freehold interests. In the assessment the lease was treated as a wasting asset, so that its value at the date of acquisition was written down in accordance with what is now *TCGA 1992, Sch 8*. The executors appealed, contending that, by virtue of *Leasehold Reform Act 1967*, the lease should not be treated as a wasting asset. The General Commissioners rejected this contention and dismissed the appeal, and the Ch D upheld this decision. The lease as granted did not contain any express term providing for its extension beyond 2003. The rights conferred by the *Leasehold Reform Act* did not constitute a provision 'for the extension of the lease beyond a given date' within the meaning of *Sch 8 para 8(5)*. Furthermore, the executors' father had not given notice of any desire to extend the lease and the executors had no power to extend the lease either in their capacity as executors or as the heirs of his estate. Accordingly, the lease was a wasting asset and the assessment had been computed on the correct basis. *Lewis v Walters*, Ch D 1992, 64 TC 489; [1992] STC 97.

Painting—whether a wasting asset

[71.118] In 2001 executors sold a painting for £9,400,000. They declared the gain on their return, but subsequently sought to amend the return on the basis that the sale of the painting was exempt under *TCGA 1992, s 45*. HMRC issued a closure notice stating that CGT was chargeable on the disposal. The executors appealed, contending that since the painting had been displayed at a large 18th-century house, which was open to the public as part of a trade, it was 'plant' and was therefore deemed to be a wasting asset. The Upper Tribunal accepted this contention and allowed the appeal, and the Court of Appeal unanimously upheld this decision. Briggs LJ observed that the reference to 'plant and machinery' in what is now *TCGA 1992, s 44(1)(c)* was introduced by *FA 1965* 'to prevent those disposing of plant and machinery from seeking to argue that, because it had a predictable life of more than 50 years, the computation of gains or losses on its disposal should admit the deduction of the full acquisition cost, rather than the written-down cost attributable to wasting assets'. Rimer LJ observed that the exemption for wasting assets, contained in what is now *TCGA 1992, s 45*, had been introduced by *FA 1968* and 'was probably not so much with a view to benefiting taxpayers with a new exemption on gains on the disposal of tangible movables as to foreclose their opportunity of achieving allowable losses on such disposals'. He held that 'once an item qualifies as "plant", it is in every case deemed by *section 44(1)(c)* to be a wasting asset; and for HMRC to argue that an item of plant enjoying unusual longevity is not plant at all is to advance an argument that the section expressly excludes'. *HMRC v Lord Howard of Henderskelfe's Executors*, CA [2014] EWCA Civ 278; [2014] STC 1100; [2014] 3 All ER 50.

Deferred consideration (TCGA 1992, s 48)

Deferred sale consideration—whether TCGA 1992, s 48 applicable

[71.119] In March 1965 an individual (M) agreed to sell to a development company 47 acres of land with development possibilities. The consideration was £47,040 payable immediately, together with future payments of £7,500 for each acre developed and provision for compensation to the taxpayer should the land be compulsorily purchased from the company. In the event, the company developed the land in 1975/76 and paid £348,250 to M in settlement of the agreement. The Revenue issued a CGT assessment for 1975/76 on the basis that the £348,250 was a taxable receipt. M appealed, contending that, by virtue of what is now *TCGA 1992, s 48*, the consideration could have been brought into account in March 1965 and was not assessable for 1975/76. The Ch D rejected this contention and upheld the assessment, holding that the provision for compensation should the land be compulsorily purchased meant that the future consideration was not ascertainable in 1965 and the transaction did not fall within *s 48*. Fox J held that *s 48* covered cases where the right to receive consideration was contingent, but did not cover cases where the amount of the consideration was 'wholly uncertain'. *Marson v Marriage*, Ch D 1979, 54 TC 59; [1980] STC 177.

Exchange rate fluctuations—whether TCGA 1992, s 48 applicable

[71.120] In 1985 a company (L) sold various assets under a lease-purchase agreement for $38,610,000. The Revenue issued an assessment on the basis that the sterling equivalent of the disposal proceeds, at the then exchange rate, was £33,313,000. As a result of subsequent fluctuations in the exchange rate, L only received £23,853,000. It claimed relief under what is now *TCGA 1992, s 48* for the balance of £9,500,000. The Ch D upheld the Revenue's rejection of the claim, and the CA dismissed L's appeal, holding that the consideration 'brought into account' was the contractual consideration, rather than its sterling equivalent. The tax computation merely involved a valuation exercise, rather than an actual conversion of dollars into sterling. L had anticipated receiving $38,610,000 and had received that amount. The exchange loss of £9,500,000 was not irrecoverable consideration within the meaning of *s 48*. *Loffland Bros North Sea Inc v Goodbrand (aka Poseidon Inc v HM Inspector of Taxes)*, CA 1998, 71 TC 57; [1998] STC 930.

Contingent liabilities (TCGA 1992, s 49)

Payment to settle court proceedings—whether within TCGA 1992, s 49(1)(c)

[71.121] In 2000 a public company (G) acquired the share capital of another public company (P). P's chairman (M) had owned a substantial shareholding in P, and following the takeover, he received consideration valued at more than £33,000,000. In 2002 M transferred much of this consideration (shares and loan notes) into a trust, giving rise to a CGT liability. Meanwhile G had formed the opinion that a profit forecast which M had provided during the takeover negotiations had been misleading. G began court proceedings against M, alleging fraudulent misrepresentation and seeking damages of £132,000,000. In 2006 M and G agreed an out-of-court settlement under which M paid G £12,000,000. M claimed that this payment should be deducted from his CGT liability for 2002/03. HMRC rejected the claim and M appealed, contending that the payment related to a 'contingent liability in respect of a warranty or representation made on a disposal', within *TCGA 1992, s 49(1)(c)*, and was deductible under *s 49(2)*. The Upper Tribunal rejected this contention but the CS unanimously allowed M's appeal and remitted the case to the First-tier Tribunal to reconsider 'whether the whole, or if not what part, of the settlement payment made by the appellant was attributable to representations made by the appellant giving rise to the contingent liability'. *Sir AF Morrison v HMRC (aka Nevis v HMRC)*, CS [2014] CSIH 113. (*Note*. The First-tier Tribunal decision had been anonymised. The Upper Tribunal rejected an application for its hearing of the appeals to take place in private. Lord Glennie held that 'the court will not depart from the principle of open justice simply to save one or other party from embarrassment'.)

Indexation allowance (TCGA 1992, ss 53–57)

NOTE

For disposals after 5 April 2008, this allowance only applies for corporation tax. See *TCGA 1992, s 52A*, introduced by *FA 2008, s 8, Sch 2*.

Indexation allowance—interaction with time-apportionment

[71.122] A woman had acquired two chattels in 1952. She sold them in 1987. Her chargeable gain fell to be time-apportioned in accordance with what is now *TCGA 1992, Sch 2 para 16(2)*. The Revenue deducted the indexation allowance from the unindexed gain before time-apportionment. She appealed, contending that the indexation allowance should be deducted only from the amount of the post-1965 gain. The HL unanimously rejected this contention and upheld the assessment. The issue had to be determined by construing the relevant statutory provisions against the underlying philosophy of the legislation, rather than by detailed consideration of hypothetical examples producing apparently anomalous results. The effect of the legislation was that the indexation allowance had to be applied to the gross gain before time-apportionment, and could not be set only against that part of the gain apportioned to the period after 6 April 1965. *Smith v Schofield*, HL 1993, 65 TC 669; [1993] STC 268; [1993] 1 WLR 398.

Indexation allowance—business expansion scheme—TCGA 1992, s 150

[71.123] An individual (C) had purchased a number of shares which entitled him to relief under the business expansion scheme. He subsequently sold the shares at a loss. The Revenue issued CGT assessments on the basis that indexation allowance only applied to the cost of the shares as reduced by *TCGA 1992, s 150(3)*. C appealed, contending that the effect of *TCGA 1992, s 53* and *s 150* was that indexation allowance should be applied to the original purchase price of the shares. The Ch D rejected this contention and upheld the assessments (reversing the decision of the Special Commissioner). Lightman J observed that the purpose behind *TCGA 1992, s 150(3)* was that a taxpayer should not have the benefit of a loss on the disposal of his shares to the extent that he had already had the benefit of BES relief on the acquisition cost. Having regard to the interrelationship of the relevant statutory provisions, indexation should only be applied to the cost as reduced by *s 150(3)*. *Quinn v Cooper*, Ch D 1998, 71 TC 44; [1998] STC 772.

Miscellaneous

Gain due to inflation

[71.124] An individual who had disposed of some shares appealed against an assessment on the gain, contending that inflation should be taken into account. The Commissioners rejected this contention and dismissed his appeal, and the Ch D upheld their decision. *Secretan v Hart*, Ch D 1969, 45 TC 701; [1969] 1 WLR 1159; [1969] 3 All ER 1196. (*Note*. The case related to a period before the introduction of the indexation allowance or taper relief. See now *TCGA 1992, s 2A* for taper relief and *TCGA 1992, ss 53–57* for indexation allowance. For cases concerning taper relief, see **71.3** to **71.13** above. For cases concerning indexation allowance, see **71.122** and **71.123** above.)

Rate of exchange where gain realised abroad

[71.125] Under German law, two sisters became equally entitled to real property in Germany under the intestacy of their father, who had died in October 1967, resident and domiciled in Israel. Following the issue of the German equivalent of Letters of Administration, the sisters were entered in the German Land Registry in July 1972 as tenants in common of the property. The property was sold in July 1973, the sisters receiving their shares of the net proceeds in Deutschmarks. The Revenue assessed the husband of one of the sisters on her share of the gain taken as the difference between the Deutschmark value of her share of the property at her father's death, converted into sterling at the then ruling exchange rate, and the Deutschmarks she received on the sale, converted into sterling at the rate ruling at the date of sale. The husband appealed, contending that the date of acquisition was the date his wife was entered in the Land Registry, and that the gain was the difference between the two Deutschmark figures converted at the rate at the time of disposal. The Commissioners rejected this contention and dismissed the appeal, and the Ch D upheld their decision. On the evidence, under German law, the appellant's wife became absolutely entitled on her father's death. This was the date of acquisition by virtue of what is now *TCGA 1992, s 62(1)(a)*. The unit of account for assessment was sterling and the market value of the deemed acquisition on the death must be arrived at using the exchange rate at the time. *Bentley v Pike*, Ch D 1981, 53 TC 590; [1981] STC 360.

[71.126] The decision in *Bentley v Pike*, **71.125** above, was applied in a subsequent case where a company (C) had made a loss on the disposal of shares in a Canadian company. The shares had been purchased and sold for Canadian dollars, and the Revenue computed the resulting loss by translating the dollar purchase price and the dollar sale price into sterling at the spot rates prevailing at, respectively, the date of purchase and the date of sale, and deducting the sterling equivalent of the sale price from the sterling equivalent of the purchase price. C appealed, contending that the loss should be computed by deducting the dollar sale price from the dollar cost, and translating the resulting sum into sterling at the spot rate prevailing at the date of disposal. The Special Commissioner rejected this contention and dismissed the appeal, and the CA unanimously upheld this decision. For the purpose of tax on capital gains, foreign currency was not money but was an asset. Therefore, when the company acquired the Canadian shares for Canadian dollars, it gave a consideration in money's worth which fell to be valued in sterling at that time. *Capcount Trading v Evans*, CA 1992, 65 TC 545; [1993] STC 11; [1993] 2 All ER 125.

Transactions in US dollars —whether to be taxed separately

[71.127] In May 1982 a company borrowed some US dollars to finance an investment (the rate of interest on the dollar loan being less than the company could have obtained on a sterling loan). It simultaneously entered into a forward contract to purchase sufficient dollars to repay the loan when it matured some ten months later. During the intervening ten months the pound sterling depreciated substantially against the dollar. The Revenue treated the two transactions as separate, with the result that the company had made a loss on the dollar loan which was not allowable for CGT purposes, and had made a chargeable gain on the disposal of its rights under the forward contract. The CA upheld the Revenue's contentions (by a 2–1 majority, Aldous LJ dissenting). Nourse LJ held that the loan and the forward contract had to be considered separately. Additionally, the fact that the subject matter of the forward contract was currency did not mean that the company had acquired a 'debt' within what is now *TCGA 1992, s 251*. The forward contract was in substance no different from any contract for the sale of real or personal property with a deferred date for completion. With regard to the computation of the amount of the gain, in the absence of any specific provision to the contrary, it would be wrong in principle to value the acquisition cost of an asset on any date other than the actual date of acquisition. The cost of acquiring the US dollars had to be valued at May 1982 and their cost to the company was the value of its promise to repay them in March 1983, together with interest during that period. *Whittles v Uniholdings Ltd (No 3)*, CA 1996, 68 TC 528; [1996] STC 914. (*Notes*. (1) Nourse LJ rejected a contention by the company that the effect of the *Ramsay* principle (see **58.6** TAX PLANNING AND AVOIDANCE) was that the liability was confined to the amount by which its gain on the contract exceeded its loss on the loan, holding that the *Ramsay* principle had 'no application' to the facts of this case. (2) For preliminary issues in this case, see **4.195** and **4.196** APPEALS.)

Sale coupled with mortgage to purchaser

[71.128] A married woman agreed to sell some land for £20,000. She mortgaged the land to the purchaser for £20,000 and conveyed the equity on the following day, in return for a release from her obligation to repay the £20,000. The Revenue assessed her husband on the basis that the land had been sold for £20,000. He appealed, contending that the actual conveyance was for the equity of redemption of a nil market value. The Ch D rejected this contention and upheld the assessment, holding that the two transactions together constituted a conveyance on sale of the property free of the legal charge. *Thompson v Salah*, Ch D 1971, 47 TC 559; [1972] 1 All ER 530.

[71.129] An individual (C) agreed to sell land for £3,750, of which £2,250 would be lent to the purchaser on a mortgage at 9% interest, repayable over ten years. Accordingly, a transfer of the property to the purchaser, acknowledging receipt of £3,750, was executed on the same day as a legal charge charging the property with £2,250 acknowledged to have been lent by C. In fact the only cash which then passed was the balancing sum of £1,500 due from the purchaser. The Revenue assessed C on the basis that he had disposed of the land for a lump sum of £3,750. He appealed, contending that there was a single transaction and that the repayments of the mortgage were instalments of the purchase price. The Commissioners rejected this contention and dismissed his appeal, and the Ch D upheld their decision. Ungoed-Thomas J held that where two cross-demands 'are honestly set off against each other without the formality of handing the money over and handing it back again', each set-off constitutes payment in cash. *Coren v Keighley*, Ch D 1972, 48 TC 370; [1972] 1 WLR 1556.

Gain on disposal by way of gift

[71.130] An individual gave some shares to his children and was assessed on the basis that he had disposed of them at their market value at the time. He appealed, contending that in giving the shares away he had suffered a capital loss, and that it was contrary to natural justice to treat him as having made a capital gain. The Commissioners rejected this contention and dismissed his appeal, and the CA unanimously upheld their decision, holding that the gift was a disposal within what is now *TCGA 1992, s 21*. *Turner v Follett*, CA 1973, 48 TC 614; [1973] STC 148.

Part of consideration paid to religious charity

[71.131] In 1999 a company (S) purchased the shares of another company (G). S gave the vendors consideration totalling £3,500,000, most of which was paid in shares and loan notes rather than cash. In addition, S's holding company paid £200,000 to a religious charity (X) of which one of the vendors (C) was a member. The Revenue formed the opinion that this £200,000 was part of the consideration for C's shares, and issued a CGT assessment. C appealed, contending that the £200,000 was simply a donation and was not part of the consideration for the shares. The Special Commissioner reviewed the evidence in detail, rejected this contention and dismissed the appeal. The Commissioner observed that if the £200,000 was excluded, the amount per share paid to C was less than the amount per share paid to another shareholder (Y) who was not connected with X. The Commissioner concluded that 'the commercial reality of the transaction was that the purchase price for the shares was £3,700,000; that figure did not change; however, part of the purchase price was by agreement diverted to (X)'. The 'donation' of £200,000 was 'a commercial expedient to push through the deal' and 'was part of the overall commercial consideration'. *Crusader v HMRC*, Sp C 2007, [2008] SSCD 281 (Sp C 640).

Consideration for sale of shares

[71.132] The shareholders of a company (R) agreed to sell all their shares to another company (B). One of R's principal shareholders (C) wished to retire. Under the agreement for the sale of the shares, B paid C £15,267 and also paid £95,179 to R, while R made a pension contribution of £120,480 on behalf of C, and also paid £25,301 to C. In his tax return, C treated the payments of £15,267 and £25,301 as chargeable to CGT. The Revenue issued a ruling that C was also liable to account for CGT in respect of the £95,179 which B had paid to R. The Ch D upheld the Revenue's ruling. Henderson J held that the effect of the agreement was that the £95,179 was part of the consideration for C's disposal of his shares. The fact that the sum was not payable to C himself, but to R at his direction, was irrelevant. *HMRC v TM Collins*, Ch D 2009, 79 TC 524; [2009] STC 1077; [2009] EWHC 284 (Ch).

Appellant claiming capital loss on endowment policy

[71.133] See *DR Collins v HMRC*, **29.61** FURTHER ASSESSMENTS: LOSS OF TAX.

Husband and wife (TCGA 1992, s 58)

[71.134] In 1968 a solicitor inherited a property, which was valued at £40,000. In 2005 he gave a half share in the property to his wife (G). The value at the date of transfer was declared as £450,000. In 2006 the property was sold for £465,000. On her 2006/07 tax return, G calculated the capital gain on the basis that her acquisition cost was £225,000. HMRC opened an enquiry and issued an amendment on the basis that the effect of *TCGA 1992, s 58* was that G should have been treated as acquiring the asset at a value which produced neither a gain or loss for the transferor, ie at £20,000. The First-tier Tribunal upheld the amendment and dismissed G's appeal. Judge Brannan observed that *TCGA 1992, s 58* 'expressly provides that in a transfer between a husband and wife the transferee takes over, so to speak, the acquisition cost of the transferor. The intention of the provision is to prevent capital gains arising on transactions between spouses. It operates to defer a gain arising until the transferee spouse disposes of the asset. It is not the intention of *section 58* to make part of the gain disappear from the charge to tax.' G's husband had 'paid capital gains tax on his share of the disposal proceeds of the property and it would be a strange conclusion indeed if the appellant were not similarly liable.' *Mrs A Godfrey v HMRC*, FTT [2010] UKFTT 611 (TC), TC00852.

Gift by wife to husband about to become non-resident

[71.135] A married woman had inherited a farm, which she was actively considering selling. On 18 August 1980 her husband (F), who had been unemployed for several months, entered into a contract of employment in Germany, under which he was required to begin work there on 15 September. Acting on professional advice, and with the admitted intention of taking advantage of Inland Revenue Extra-Statutory Concession D2, his wife transferred the ownership of the farm to him on 29 August. On 13 September F left the UK and became resident in Germany, having previously been resident and ordinarily resident in the UK. On 17 September the farm was sold at auction. The Revenue assessed F to CGT for 1980/81 on the gain on the sale. He applied for judicial review to quash the assessment, contending that the Revenue should have applied Extra-Statutory Concession D2. The QB rejected this contention and dismissed the application, holding that the Revenue had been entitled to refuse to apply the concession. It was clearly stated inside the front cover of Revenue Pamphlet IR1, listing the extra-statutory concessions in operation, that a 'concession will not be given in any case where an attempt is made to use it for tax avoidance'. *R v Inspector of Taxes (ex p. Fulford-Dobson)*, QB 1987, 60 TC 168; [1987] STC 344; [1987] 3 WLR 277. (*Note*. For the circumstances in which the Revenue will refuse to apply ESC D2, see Revenue Capital Gains Manual, para CG25980 *et seq*.)

Half of consideration paid to wife

[71.136] A doctor sold a flat in 2006. He only declared half of the gain on his tax return. HMRC issued an amendment to his self-assessment, charging CGT on the whole of the gain. The doctor appealed, contending that he had given half of the proceeds to his wife, so that he should only be taxed on the half which he had retained. The First-tier Tribunal rejected this contention and dismissed his appeal, finding that he had been the sole owner of the flat so that the whole of the gain was taxable on him. *Dr AS Jolaoso v HMRC*, FTT [2011] UKFTT 44 (TC), TC00921. (*Note*. For another issue in this case, see **63.206** TRADING PROFITS.)

Settlements (including trusts under a will)

'Absolutely entitled as against the trustee' (TCGA 1992, s 60)

Conventional trust with only one beneficiary

[71.137] Stock was left to trustees to accumulate the interest until the beneficiary (V) reached the age of 25. When V reached 21 he claimed the whole fund on the basis that he had a vested interest and the accumulations were for his benefit only. The QB upheld this contention. Lord Langdale MR held that 'where a legacy is directed to accumulate for a certain period, or where the payment is postponed, the legatee, if he has an absolutely indefeasible interest in the legacy, is not bound to wait until the expiration of that period, but may require payment the moment he is competent to give a valid discharge', in other words, at the age of majority. *Saunders v Vautier*, QB 1841, 4 Beav 115. (*Notes*. (1) For HMRC's interpretation of this decision, see Capital Gains Manual, para CG34430. (2) For an income tax case where this decision was distinguished, see *Thorpe v HMRC*, **46.11** PENSION SCHEMES.)

Scottish law—trust in favour of future wife and children

[71.138] In a Scottish case, the CS held that where a settlor created a trust in favour of a future wife and children, it was a trust for administration only and the property was fully at his disposal. *Scott v Scott*, CS [1930] SC 903. (*Note*. For HMRC's interpretation of this decision, see Capital Gains Manual, para CG34454.)

Trust for benefit of children below age of majority

[71.139] A settlor (K) had settled a trust fund for such of his children as should attain 21 or marry. In 1965/66, the trustees of the fund disposed of some of the assessments. All K's children were below the age of majority, and were unmarried. The Revenue assessed the trustees and they appealed, contending that the children were assessable by virtue of what is now *TCGA 1992, s 60(1)* (in which case the rate of tax under *FA 1965, s 21* would have been nil). The CA rejected this contention and upheld the assessment, holding that *s 60(1)* should be construed as if it had read 'or for any person who would be absolutely entitled against the trustee if he were not under disability and so not able to demand a transfer or give a receipt'. *Tomlinson v Glyn's Executor & Trustee Co Ltd*, CA 1969, 45 TC 600; [1970] Ch 112; [1970] 1 All ER 381. (*Note*. *FA 1965, s 21* was repealed for years after 1977/78.)

Sale of shares—whether residuary legatee absolutely entitled

[71.140] A testator domiciled in Scotland left his estate to his executors in trust, to convey the residue to his son (C) absolutely. The executors sold certain shares (to pay debts and meet a legacy) and the Revenue assessed them on the gains on the sales. The executors appealed, contending that C was 'absolutely entitled as against the trustee' to the assets and so the liability fell on C under what is now *TCGA 1992, s 60(1)*. (C would not have been effectively liable, as he was not resident and not ordinarily resident in the UK at the material times.) The Special Commissioners rejected this contention and upheld the assessment, and the CS unanimously upheld their decision. It was for the executors to decide what assets should be realised and the son never had any right to those sold. *Cochrane's Executors v CIR*, CS 1974, 49 TC 299; [1974] STC 335.

Application of TCGA 1992, s 60 to freehold property

[71.141] Trustees under a will held freehold property on trust to sell and hold the proceeds on certain trusts for the benefit of five children of the testator and their issue. The property was sold in 1969/70 and the trustees were assessed on the gain. Meanwhile, two of the children had died, their shares of the trust fund devolving on their children absolutely. The Ch D upheld the assessment in principle. Goff J held that since the trust fund comprised freehold land, the issue of the deceased children could not direct the trustees how to deal with their respective shares, and they were therefore not 'absolutely entitled as against the trustees'. *Crowe v Appleby*, Ch D 1975, 51 TC 457; [1975] STC 502; [1975] 1 WLR 1539; [1975] 3 All ER 529. (*Note*. Another issue in this case was taken to the CA and heard with *Pexton v Bell*, **71.179** below.)

Interpretation of 'jointly' in TCGA 1992, s 60(1)

[71.142] In an appeal against an assessment on executors, on their disposal of the deceased's half share of certain freehold land, the substantive issue was the interpretation of 'jointly' in what is now *TCGA 1992, s 60(1)*. The Ch D upheld the Revenue's contention that the word was to be given its ordinary meaning of 'concurrently' or 'in common' and not its technical meaning in English real property law. *Kidson v Macdonald & Another*, Ch D 1973, 49 TC 503; [1974] STC 54; [1974] Ch 339; [1974] 1 All ER 849.

[71.143] Under a will, several houses were vested in H and his sister as trustees for sale, for the benefit of themselves as tenants in common. After having been let for several years, the houses were sold. The Revenue assessed H on his share of the gain and he appealed, contending firstly that the disposal was of an interest in a settlement within what is now *TCGA 1992, s 76(1)* and alternatively that the management of the properties was a family business qualifying for retirement relief under what is now *TCGA 1992, s 163*. The Commissioners rejected these contentions and dismissed his appeal, and the Ch D upheld their decision. The disposal was not of an interest in a settlement and the lettings did not amount to a business. *Harthan v Mason*, Ch D 1979, 53 TC 272; [1980] STC 94.

Shares transferred to trustees under pooling agreement

[71.144] Twelve shareholders in a family company agreed to transfer some of their shares to trustees. This was done so that they and their families could retain effective control of the company if its shares were traded on the Stock Exchange. The agreement was for 15 years but could be determined earlier by shareholders who, between them, held 75% of the transferred shares. The broad effect of the agreement was that the shares were pooled. The participants received the trust income proportionate to the shares they transferred and they were able to direct the trustees how to exercise the votes attaching to the shares. Provisions ensured that, should a participant die or wish to sell, the shares would remain in the family. The Revenue issued CGT assessments on the basis that the shares had been transferred to a settlement. The Ch D allowed an appeal by one of the shareholders, and the CA upheld this decision. The shareholders collectively had power to end the trust, and although their interests in their shares were subject to restraints, they did not lose their beneficial interests. They were absolutely entitled to their shares as against the trustees, within what is now *TCGA 1992, s 60(1)*, so that the transfer to the trustees was not a chargeable disposal. *Booth v Ellard*, CA 1980, 53 TC 393; [1980] STC 555; [1980] 1 WLR 1443; [1980] 3 All ER 569.

Deed of rearrangement distributing settled property

[71.145] A farmer (B) and his five children conveyed parcels of land totalling some 1680 acres, which had been in their separate ownership, to trustees for the purpose of 'pooling' the family farms. Under the terms of the deed of settlement B and his children received undivided and unequal percentage shares in the trust fund, these shares being intended to correspond to the value of the property that each had contributed. It was accepted that they were absolutely entitled to the settled property as against the trustees. After B's death, three of the children wished to have the land that they had contributed taken out of trust and returned to them. Accordingly a deed of rearrangement was executed to unscramble the trust. By the deed, identified areas of land were segregated from the settled property and distributed to the three beneficiaries; the remainder of the trust property was to continue to be held, in revised unequal shares, for the other two beneficiaries. The Revenue issued assessments on the basis that the execution of the deed of rearrangement constituted a disposal of assets. The General Commissioners allowed the beneficiaries' appeals and the Ch D upheld their decision. Applying *Booth v Ellard*, **71.144** above, there was no disposal for tax purposes because the measure of the beneficial interests of the settlors had remained unaffected by the trust. *Jenkins v Brown; Warrington v Brown (and related appeals)*, Ch D 1989, 62 TC 226; [1989] STC 577; [1989] 1 WLR 1163.

TCGA 1992, s 71(1)—whether beneficial entitlement required

[71.146] Trustees of a 1955 settlement declared that the whole of the settled property should be held on the trusts of a 1972 settlement, made for the purpose by the same settlor with the same trustees. The Ch D upheld the Revenue's contention that the 'new' trustees had become absolutely entitled to settled property as against the old. Brightman J held that 'absolutely entitled' in what is now *TCGA 1992, s 71(1)* does not imply beneficial ownership, but whether an advancement is a continuance of the existing trust or a new trust is a question of fact and degree. *Hart v Briscoe & Others*, Ch D 1977, 52 TC 53; [1978] STC 89; [1979] Ch 10; [1978] 1 All ER 791. (*Notes.* (1) See also *Roome v Edwards*, **71.154** below. (2) For a preliminary point in this case, see **5.94** ASSESSMENTS.)

[71.147] A similar decision was reached in a case where trustees used a power of advancement in a settlement to declare trusts of assets advanced. *Hoare Trustees v Gardner*, Ch D 1977, 52 TC 53; [1978] STC 89; [1979] Ch 10; [1978] 1 All ER 791. (*Note.* The case was heard in the Ch D with *Hart v Briscoe & Others*, **71.146** above.)

Trust fund subject to annuities—whether beneficiaries absolutely entitled

[71.148] Under a will, a fund was held in trust for such of the testator's grandchildren who should attain 21 years, subject to the payment of annuities to three daughters during widowhood. There were two grandchildren, both of whom had attained 21 before 1969, when a deed of family arrangement provided that a fund was appropriated for the annuities and money was advanced to the grandchildren to purchase further income for the daughters with the intention that the balance of the trust fund, mainly comprising shares, should be transferred to the grandchildren. The Revenue assessed the trustees for 1968/69 on the basis that there had been a notional disposal under what is now *TCGA 1992, s 71(1)*, the grandchildren having become 'absolutely entitled as against' the trustees when the deed of family arrangement was entered into. The trustees appealed, contending that the annuities were 'outgoings' within what is now *TCGA 1992, s 60(2)*, with the result that the grandchildren had become absolutely entitled when the younger attained 21. The Ch D rejected these contentions and upheld the assessment. *Stephenson v Barclays Bank Trust Co Ltd*, Ch D 1974, 50 TC 374; [1975] STC 151; [1975] 1 WLR 882; [1975] 1 All ER 625.

[71.149] See also *Prest v Bettinson*, 71.187 below.

Appointment of loan notes by trustees to beneficiary

[71.150] An individual (M) acquired some loan notes in 2002. In an attempt to avoid CGT on their disposal, he established a settlement in February 2003 and transferred the loan notes to the trustees of the settlement. On 6 March 2003 the trustees made a deed of appointment, relating to the loan notes, in favour of a beneficiary (G) who was domiciled outside the UK. On the following day the trustees disposed of the loan notes. Following an enquiry, HMRC issued an amendment charging tax on M. He appealed, contending that the effect of *TCGA 1992, s 71(1)* was that G had become absolutely entitled to the loan notes and that the disposal had been by G. The First-tier Tribunal accepted this contention and allowed the appeal. Judge Shipwright held that 'a transaction whereby a person gains a beneficial interest in effect at the expense of the trustee is one that answers to the statutory language and purpose'. He observed that HMRC had accepted that the transactions involving G were not a 'sham', and specifically rejected HMRC's contention that 'the anti-*Ramsay* device of not looking for a purchaser until a late stage in the planning can be ignored'. *JA McLaughlin v HMRC*, FTT [2012] UKFTT 174 (TC); [2012] SFTD 1003, TC01870.

Land disposed of before completion of administration of deceased estate

[71.151] In a development land tax case, the CS upheld the Revenue's contention that the residuary beneficiaries of an estate were not absolutely entitled to land comprised in the estate immediately before the trustees disposed of it. It was the duty of the trustees to realise the estate and to divide the proceeds of the disposal between the beneficiaries. They had no power to deal with the assets of the estate by taking a decision which irrevocably conferred on the residuary beneficiaries the exclusive right to direct how the land should be dealt with. *CIR v Matthew's Executors*, CS 1984, 58 TC 120; [1984] STC 386.

Unincorporated members' society—whether absolutely entitled to land

[71.152] See *CIR v Worthing Rugby Football Club Trustees*, 70.9 VOLUNTARY ASSOCIATIONS.

Date on which beneficiaries absolutely entitled

[71.153] In 1963 the trustees of a settlement made an appointment whereby certain investments and income should be held 'upon trust for such of the children (of the settlor) now living or hereafter to be born' as should attain the age of 21. In 1964 the settlor, who had four children, was paralysed from the chest down in a hunting accident, leaving no realistic possibility that he could beget any more children. The settlor's youngest child became 21 in 1977 and the settlor died in 1990. The Revenue issued a CGT assessment on the surviving trustee for 1990/91 on the basis that the children had become absolutely entitled as against the trustee when the settlor died. The trustee appealed, contending that, in view of the settlor's paralysis, all the children had been absolutely entitled from 1977, when the youngest child became 21. The Special Commissioner rejected this contention and dismissed the appeal, and the Ch D upheld this decision. Blackburne J held that it was an established legal principle that a court could not normally inquire into whether it was practically impossible for a person to have future children. *Figg v Clarke*, Ch D 1996, 68 TC 645; [1997] STC 247; [1997] 1 WLR 603.

Powers of appointment

Whether exercise of power of appointment creates a new settlement

[71.154] Under a 1944 marriage settlement, the trust fund was held on trust for the wife for life, with remainder to the husband for life, with remainder to two daughters (born in 1948 and 1951) absolutely in equal shares. In 1955 investments in the fund worth about £13,000 were appointed in trust for the elder daughter absolutely on attaining 25. In 1972 the beneficiaries of the 1944 fund assigned their respective interests to two Cayman Islands companies for sums totalling £868,000. The trustees of the 1944 fund were replaced by Cayman Islands trustees, and in April 1972 one of the companies assigned its interests to the other which, as a consequence, became absolutely entitled to the 1944 fund. There was no similar transaction regarding the 1955 fund, which was administered separately from the 1944 fund by trustees resident in the UK. The 1972 transactions gave rise to a substantial gain under what is now *TCGA 1992, s 71(1)*. The Revenue assessed this gain on the trustees of the 1955 fund, on the basis that the effect of what is now *TCGA 1992, s 69(3)* was that the two sets of trustees should be treated as a single body, of which the UK members could be assessed under what is now *TCGA 1992, s 65(1)*. The HL unanimously upheld the assessment, holding that there was a single settlement. Lord Wilberforce observed that the CGT legislation had 'attached the liability to pay capital gains tax to the trustees of settlements, not to funds held on distinct trusts', and had 'not concerned itself with questions of incidence of the tax between beneficiaries or funds within a settlement'. Lord Roskill observed that people who accepted appointment as trustees of settlements 'have only themselves to blame if they accept the obligations of trustees in these circumstances without ensuring that they are sufficiently and effectively protected whether by their beneficiaries or otherwise for fiscal or other liabilities which may fall upon them personally as a result of the obligations which they had felt able to assume'. *Roome & Denne v Edwards*, HL 1981, 54 TC 359; [1981] STC 96; [1981] 2 WLR 268; [1981] 1 All ER 736.

[71.155] In 1972 the trustees of a discretionary settlement, which had been established in 1961, executed two deeds to allocate part of the settled property. The allocated funds continued to be held by the trustees of the main settlement and were subject to the administrative powers of that settlement. The trustees were assessed on the basis that there had been a deemed disposal under what is now *TCGA 1992, s 71(1)*. The Special Commissioners allowed their appeal and the CA upheld this decision, distinguishing *Roome v Edwards*, 71.154 above. Slade LJ held that there was a distinction between powers to alter the trusts of a settlement which expressly or implicitly authorise the trustees to remove assets altogether from the original settlement (without rendering any person absolutely entitled to them), and powers which do not confer such authority on the trustees. The relevant powers here were of the latter type. *Bond v Pickford*, CA 1983, 57 TC 301; [1983] STC 517.

[71.156] See also *Hart v Briscoe*, 71.146 above.

Exercise of power of appointment—whether a deemed disposal

[71.157] The trustees of a settlement executed a deed of appointment by which the trust fund was divided into two parts. One part of the fund was appointed to the settlor's daughter. The second part was placed on trust, the income to be paid to the daughter for life. It was accepted that the absolute appointment to the daughter gave rise to a deemed disposal of that part of the trust fund under what is now *TCGA 1992, s 71(1)*, and CGT was assessed and paid accordingly. The Revenue issued a further CGT assessment on the basis that there had also been a new and separate settlement of the appointed fund, which constituted a deemed disposal. The principal trustee appealed, contending that the exercise of the power of appointment had not created a new settlement of the fund and had not amounted to a deemed disposal under *s 71(1)*. The Special Commissioner accepted this contention and allowed the appeal, and the Ch D upheld this decision. On the evidence, the assets of the appointed fund remained subject to the trusts of the original settlement as varied by the deed of appointment, and had not become subject to the trusts of a new settlement. Accordingly, the trustees' exercise of the power of appointment had not amounted to a deemed disposal under *TCGA 1992, s 71(1)**. *Swires v Renton*, Ch D 1991, 64 TC 315; [1991] STC 490.

[71.158] See also *Ewart v Taylor*, 71.175 below and *Eilbeck v Rawling*, 71.286 below.

Exercise of power of appointment in favour of grandchildren of settlor

[71.159] In 1975 the trustees of a settlement made in 1959 exercised their power of appointment in favour of the settlor's three grandchildren, and thereafter held the trust fund contingently for the grandchildren contingently on their reaching the age of 21. The eldest grandchild became 21 in 1990, and thus became absolutely entitled to a one-third share of the settled property.

The Revenue issued a 1990/91 assessment on one of the trustees, charging CGT on the deemed disposal to the grandchild in accordance with what is now *TCGA 1992, s 71*. The trustee appealed, contending that the gain should be held over by virtue of an election made under what is now *TCGA 1992, s 260(2)(d)*. The Ch D rejected this contention and upheld the assessment. The disposal could not be held over under *s 260(2)(d)*, because the grandchild had become entitled to an interest in possession in her share of the settled property in 1987, when she reached the age of 18. Before the exercise of the power of appointment, the grandchild had had only a revocable interest in the trust property. Her relevant interest arose from the power of appointment. Since this had been exercised in 1975, it fell within the provisions of *Family Law Reform Act 1969* (which had reduced the age of majority to 18 with effect from January 1970), even though the original settlement had been made before the date on which that act took effect. *Begg-McBrearty v Stilwell (Trustee of the GE Coke Settlement)*, Ch D 1996, 68 TC 426; [1996] STC 413; [1996] 1 WLR 951; [1996] 4 All ER 205. (*Note*. For the Revenue's practice following this decision, see the Revenue Press Release dated 30 September 1996.)

Non-resident settlements

Non-resident settlement established through deed of family arrangement

[71.160] K's father-in-law (B) died in 1977, resident and ordinarily resident in Jersey. Half of B's personal estate was bequeathed to K's wife, who was a UK resident. By a deed of family arrangement in 1978 she settled her share of the estate on Jersey trustees, to be held on discretionary trusts for herself and her family. The administration of the estate was not completed until 1979 and the assets were at no time vested in K's wife. Between 1981 and 1985 the settlement trustees made capital payments to K's wife. The Revenue issued assessments under what is now *TCGA 1992, ss 87–98**. K appealed, contending that, by virtue of what is now *TCGA 1992, s 62(6)*, B should be deemed to be the settlor of the trusts, so that, since he had been neither resident nor ordinarily resident in the UK, there was no CGT liability. The HL unanimously rejected this contention and upheld the assessments. The arrangement did not settle any specific assets comprised in the estate, but settled the legatee's half-share in the residuary estate, which had not by then been constituted. The property settled by the legatee constituted a separate chose in action, being her right to have the estate of the deceased duly administered. Where a legatee varied her entitlement under a will by means of a family arrangement, the making of the variation was deemed not to be a disposal in itself. However, *s 62(6)* did not have the further effect of treating the assets vested in the legatee as acquired from the deceased at the date of death. Accordingly, the legatee was the settlor of the arrangement for the purposes of *s 87*. *Marshall v Kerr*, HL 1994, 67 TC 56; [1994] STC 638; [1994] 3 WLR 299; [1994] 2 All ER 106.

Interaction of TCGA 1992, ss 77 and 87(2)*

[71.161] In 1989 the trustees of two non-resident settlements, which had been established in 1982 by a UK resident, sold the trust funds and resolved to pay the whole amount realised to the settlor. The Revenue raised an assessment on the settlor under what is now *TCGA 1992, s 87(2)*, charging CGT on the amount on which the trustees would have been chargeable to tax if they had been resident or ordinarily resident in the UK. The settlor appealed, contending that the effect of what is now *TCGA 1992, s 77* was that the gains of the settlements were not to be treated as accruing to the trustees and that the assessment should be reduced to nil. The Special Commissioners rejected this contention and dismissed his appeal, and the CA upheld their decision. *TCGA 1992, s 77* did not apply, since it dealt with cases where trustees were in fact chargeable to tax on realised gains. In a case within *TCGA 1992, s 87(2)*, gains were to be computed on the amount on which the trustees would have been chargeable to tax if they had been resident or ordinarily resident in the UK. That provision did not make the trustees themselves chargeable to tax, and the gains so computed were to be treated as chargeable gains accruing to the beneficiary. *De Rothschild v Lawrenson*, CA 1995, 67 TC 300; [1995] STC 623.

Application of TCGA 1992, ss 77

[71.162] See also *Smallwood (Settlor of the Trevor Smallwood Trust) v HMRC*, **48.90** RESIDENCE, and the cases noted at **71.183** to **71.186** below.

Whether TCGA 1992, s 86 applicable

[71.163] In 1994 an Isle of Man company purchased some land in Cornwall for £725,000. £700,000 of this was provided by a wealthy individual (C). The company subsequently sold the land to a developer for £2,200,000. In 2001 the shares in the company were transferred to an Isle of Man settlement of which C and his wife were the only beneficiaries. The Revenue issued a CGT assessment on C under *TCGA 1992, s 86*. The General Commissioners upheld the assessment and C appealed to the Ch D, contending that he was not within the definition of a 'settlor' in *TCGA 1992, Sch 5 para 7*. The Ch D accepted this contention and allowed the appeal. Sir Donald Rattee held that the land which the company had disposed of was not 'settled property' because it was never held in trust for the 2001 settlement. The disposal was outside the scope of *TCGA 1992, s 86*. *Coombes v HMRC*, Ch D 2007, [2008] STC 2984; [2007] EWHC 3160 (Ch). (*Note*. For a preliminary issue in this case, see **4.157** APPEALS.)

[71.164] In 1994 a UK resident (B) established a settlement with an Isle of Man company as the sole trustee. B subsequently gave a shareholding to the settlement, and the trustee transferred the shares to an Isle of Man company (BH) which the trustee controlled. In 1998 BH exchanged those shares for loan notes in another company (J). In March 1999 B established another settlement with two UK-resident trustees and with himself as life tenant. Later that month the trustee of the 1994 settlement appointed £1,386,000 to the trustees of the 1999 settlement. On 1 April 1999 the trustee of the 1994 settlement excluded B, and his wife and children, from the class of beneficiaries of that settlement. In 1999/2000 BH redeemed the loan notes in J and went into liquidation. The proceeds of BH's liquidation were paid to the trustee of the 1994 settlement. The Revenue issued an amendment to B's self-assessment for 1999/2000, charging CGT in respect of the gains which the trustee of the 1994 settlement had realised, on the basis that B was still interested in the 1994 settlement because money borrowed by that settlement had subsequently been appointed to the 1999 settlement. The First-tier Tribunal allowed B's appeal, holding that in 1999/2000 B did not have an interest in the 1994 settlement within *TCGA 1992, s 86(1)(d)* or *Sch 5 para 2(1)*. (The tribunal also considered the potential application of *TCGA 1992, s 87*, in respect of which the judges disagreed. Judge Wallace held that when the money was transferred from the first settlement to the settlement, B should be treated as receiving a capital payment within *TCGA 1992, s 87(4)*; but that there was not an outright payment of money, so that the effect of *TCGA 1992, s 97(4)* was that the value of the capital payment was to be treated as 'the value of the benefit conferred by it', which was nil. Judge Shipwright expressed the view that B should not be treated as receiving a capital payment within *s 87(4)*.) *E Burton v HMRC (and related appeals)*, FTT [2009] STC 682; [2009] UKFTT 203 (TC), TC00156.

[71.165] See also *Abacus Trust Co (Isle of Man) Ltd v National Society for the Prevention of Cruelty to Children*, **56.135** SETTLEMENTS.

Trustees making loans to settlor—whether TCGA 1992, s 87(4) applicable

[71.166] In 1987 a UK resident (C) established a settlement, the trustees of which were resident in Switzerland and the Cayman Islands. The trustees made a number of interest-free loans, repayable on demand, to C. The Revenue issued CGT assessments on the basis that C should be treated as having received capital payments, within *TCGA 1992, s 87(4)*, from the trustees of the settlement, the amount of such payments being the interest that would have been payable had the loans from the trustees been made on a commercial basis. C appealed, contending that, while there had been a nominal payment of capital when each initial loan was made, there was no further capital payment while that loan remained outstanding. The Ch D rejected this contention and upheld the assessments. Lloyd J held that, when the trustees had made a loan which was repayable on demand, they conferred a benefit on C 'by leaving the loan outstanding for any period, even for a single day'. The effect of *TCGA 1992, s 97* was that the benefits were to be treated as capital payments for the purposes of *TCGA 1992, s 87(4)*. The CA unanimously dismissed C's appeal against this decision. Applying *dicta* of Viscount Simon LC in *Nokes v Doncaster Amalgamated Collieries Ltd*, HL [1940] AC 1014; [1940] 3 All ER 549, 'if the choice is between two interpretations, the narrower of which would fail to achieve the manifest purpose of the legislation, we should avoid a construction which would reduce the legislation to futility and should rather accept the bolder construction based on the view that Parliament would legislate only for the purpose of bringing about an effective result'. Robert Walker LJ held that 'the whole scheme of the legislation requires the court to see what benefit a beneficiary actually receives, in cash or in kind, otherwise than as income or under an arm's length transaction. Any pre-existing beneficial interest belonging to the beneficiary is irrelevant.' *Cooper v Billingham; Fisher v Edwards*, CA 2001, 74 TC 139; [2001] STC 1177.

Indirect receipt of capital payments—TCGA 1992, s 97(5)

[71.167] In 1990 an individual (H) created a non-resident settlement of which his family were beneficiaries. In February 2002 he and his wife created a UK-resident settlement of which he and his wife were beneficiaries and trustees. Later that month the trustees of the 1990 settlement appointed substantial assets (cash, Treasury stock and the benefit of an unsecured loan) to the trustees of the 2002 settlement. In March 2002 the trustees of the 2002 settlement appointed all of the trust assets to H and his wife. The Revenue issued amendments to their self-assessments on the basis that the trust gains for 2001/02, including the 'stockpiled' gains of the 1990 settlement, were to be treated as chargeable gains accruing to H and his wife in that year. They appealed. The Special Commissioner reviewed the evidence in detail and dismissed the appeals, observing that the 2002 settlement had been established 'in order to implement a capital gains tax avoidance scheme', and to take advantage of a perceived loophole in *FA 2000*. The Commissioner held that H and his wife had indirectly received capital payments from the trustees of the 1990 settlement, within *TCGA 1992, s 97(5)(a)*, thus giving rise to a charge to capital gains tax. *DP & Mrs B Herman v HMRC*, Sp C [2007] SSCD 571 (Sp C 609). (*Note*. See also *FA 2003, s 163*, introduced in order to counter the type of avoidance scheme used in this case.)

[71.168] The decision in *Herman v HMRC*, 71.167 above, was applied in the similar subsequent case of *C Bowring v HMRC (and related appeal)*, FTT [2013] UKFTT 366 (TC); [2014] SFTD 347, TC02766.

Non-resident settlement—whether deed of appointment invalid

[71.169] In 1990 the trustees of a non-resident settlement executed a deed of appointment, settling part of the assets of the settlement on accumulation and maintenance trusts for the benefit of a granddaughter of the testator. For CGT purposes, the effect of the appointment was that the settlement and the accumulation and maintenance trusts constituted a single composite settlement, and that because five of the ten trustees were resident in the UK, the settlement lost its non-resident status. The trustees subsequently applied for a declaration that the 1990 deed should be held to be invalid. The Ch D granted the declaration, applying *dicta* of Warner J in *Mettoy Pension Trustees Ltd v Evans*, 56.130 SETTLEMENTS. *Green & Others v Cobham & Others*, Ch D 2000, [2002] STC 820; [2000] WTLR 1101. (*Note*. The relevant *dicta* of Warner J were subsequently disapproved by the Supreme Court in *HMRC v Futter & Others*, 56.128 SETTLEMENTS.)

Place of residence of settlement

[71.170] See *Wensleydale's Settlement Trustees v CIR*, 48.89 RESIDENCE.

Application of FA 1965, s 42

NOTE

The cases noted at 71.171 to 71.176 below turn on the application of *FA 1965, s 42*, which was subsequently replaced by *CGTA 1979, s 17*. *CGTA 1979, s 17* was itself repealed from 1981/82 and replaced by the provisions now contained in *TCGA 1992, ss 87 et seq*.

Whether shares sold held under non-resident settlement

[71.171] Under a 1960 settlement, shares in L Ltd, a public quoted company, were held on discretionary trusts. A scheme was subsequently carried out with the aim of avoiding CGT. The existing (resident) trustees were replaced by non-resident trustees, and a series of transactions were effected on the same day. With the settlor's permission, 184,500 of the shares held by the trustees were appointed to each of two brothers, discretionary beneficiaries under the trust, contingently on their surviving three days; each brother assigned his contingent interest to a Jersey company for £352,705, and that company contracted to sell each brother 184,500 shares in L Ltd for £355,162 (their then market value), the contract to be completed three days later. The brothers survived the three days, with the result that they had acquired the shares for their full price, the cost being financed by their disposal of their contingent interests (exempt under what is now *TCGA 1992, s 76(1)*). The Revenue assessed the brothers on the basis that *FA 1965, s 42(2)* applied. They appealed. The Special Commissioners dismissed their appeals and the HL unanimously upheld this decision. The scheme was an arrangement within the definition of 'settlement' in *FA 1965, s 42(7)*. There had been an act of bounty in favour of the sons. The settlor's bounty was incomplete when he divested himself of the shares settled. *Chinn v Collins*; *Chinn v Hochstrasser*, HL 1980, 54 TC 311; [1981] STC 1; [1981] 2 WLR 14; [1981] 1 All ER 189.

Whether beneficiaries had 'interests in the settled property'

[71.172] A UK settlor (L) had established a discretionary trust with a Bermuda trustee. The income was to be accumulated with power to the trustees at their discretion to apply it for the benefit of L's grandchildren and their families. At the expiration of a defined period, the trust fund vested equally between the settlor's issue '*per stirpes*' but, in a letter of intent to the trustees, L said they should regard the settlement as 'existing primarily for the grandchildren in equal shares'. At the relevant times there were five grandchildren, all below the age of majority and resident in the UK. Capital gains accrued to the trustee. The Revenue apportioned the gains equally to the five under *FA 1965, s 42(2)* and assessed them on their fathers (as their guardians). The HL unanimously upheld the assessments, holding that the discretionary beneficiaries had 'interests in the settled property', that apportionment on a just and reasonable basis was a question of fact, and that the apportionment here was reasonable . (The question of whether the beneficiaries could recover the tax from the trustee was considered but not formally decided. The majority of the HL reserved decision on this point. Lord Scarman considered that recoupment was permissible, applying the decision in the estate duty case of *In re Latham decd.*, Ch D [1961] 3 All ER 903.) *Leedale v Lewis*, HL 1982, 56 TC 501; [1982] STC 835; [1982] 1 WLR 1319; [1982] 3 All ER 808. (*Note.* The appeal taken to the HL related to three of the grandchildren. Other related appeals were not taken higher than the CA.)

[71.173] In a case where the facts were complex, capital gains which had accrued to the trustees of a non-resident discretionary trust were apportioned between two UK-resident beneficiaries. The Ch D upheld the assessments, applying the HL decision in *Leedale v Lewis*, **71.172** above. *Bayley v Garrod (and related appeal)*, Ch D 1983, 56 TC 695; [1983] STC 287.

[71.174] A UK trust was transferred to Guernsey in February 1973 to avoid a future charge to CGT. In June 1973 the UK-resident beneficiaries assigned their interests in the settlement to a Guernsey company in return for a payment of £248,647. On the following day the trustees sold the trust investments for a cash sum which (with interest) amounted to more than £750,000 at the termination of the trust on 2 July 1973, and was paid to the company at that date. The Revenue issued assessments on the basis that the gain realised by the trustees on the sale of the trust fund for cash should be apportioned between the three UK-resident beneficiaries. The Special Commissioner allowed the beneficiaries' appeals, and the Ch D upheld this decision. The relevant time was 2 July 1973 when the settlement came to an end. At that time the beneficiaries no longer had any interest in the settlement, since they had previously assigned their interests to the Guernsey company. *Jones v Lincoln-Lewis & Others*, Ch D 1991, 64 TC 112; [1991] STC 307.

Year for which gains apportioned to beneficiaries should be assessed

[71.175] A UK settlor had established a trust for the benefit of her three daughters (E, F and V). In 1969 the trustees transferred the trust fund to the trustees of a Jersey discretionary settlement, set up for the purpose. In 1976 the trustees of the Jersey settlement carried out a series of transactions, designed to distribute the trust property without incurring CGT liability. The trust fund then comprised cash of £534,000 and shares valued at £461,000. The transactions carried out included (in date order) borrowing the requisite money from a Jersey bank; appointing a total of £640,000 absolutely to E and F, and a further £314,000 to themselves to be held on trusts for the benefit of V's children; and selling the shares at valuation equally to E and F. The remaining cash was used or required for expenses and costs. In the period from 1969 to 1975 the trustees had realised gains of £379,000, which had not been apportioned to beneficiaries, and the 1976 sale of the shares to E and F had resulted in gains of £395,000. All the beneficiaries were resident in the UK. The Revenue issued assessments for 1976/77 on the basis that all the gains, including the pre-1976 gains, were assessable on the beneficiaries for that year by virtue of *FA 1965, s 42*. The beneficiaries appealed. The Ch D allowed the appeal with regard to the gains from 1969 to 1975, but dismissed the appeal with regard to the 1976 gains. Vinelott J held that, under *FA 1965, s 42(2)*, the pre-1976 gains were assessable for the years in which they arose. *FA 1965, s 42(3)(b)* did not operate to make them assessable for 1976/77, as the beneficiaries who received the capital payments in 1976 were the beneficiaries among whom the gains were apportionable for the years in which they arose. Applying *Roome v Edwards*, **71.154** above, the appointment to V's children's fund created a separate settlement. It was part of a scheme for the distribution of the trust fund and bringing the Jersey settlement to an end. *Ewart v Taylor (and related appeals)*, Ch D 1983, 57 TC 401; [1983] STC 721.

Treatment of previous losses of trustees

[71.176] See *Ritchie v McKay*, **71.1** above.

Miscellaneous

The general treatment of disposals to trustees

[71.177] In March 1972 an individual (B) transferred shares to a Guernsey company (G) as bare trustee. On 4 April 1972 he entered into an agreement with G and a Jersey company (J), described as a deed of settlement, whereby J paid £14,500 and B's beneficial interest in the shares in G was transferred into a life interest, with remainder to J absolutely. On 6 April 1972 B sold his life interest in the shares to a Bahaman company for £130,753 (the market value). His wife made similar arrangements in respect of shares which she owned. The Revenue assessed B on the basis that he had disposed of the shares on 4 April 1972. He appealed, contending that on 4 April there had been a disposal of the reversionary interest only, and that on 6 April there had been a disposal of the life interest, the gain on which was exempt under what is now *TCGA 1992, s 76(1)*. The Special Commissioners rejected these contentions and dismissed the appeal, and the HL unanimously upheld their decision. B had disposed of the shares to G on 4 April, and G had acquired the shares by an agreement which was not at arm's length, so that CGT was chargeable on the market value. *Berry v Warnett*, HL 1982, 55 TC 92; [1982] STC 396; [1982] 1 WLR 698; [1982] 2 All ER 630.

Application to vary trusts to avoid taxation

[71.178] In 1964, an individual (W) settled shares in a UK company on his sons under two settlements made in England with English trustees. In 1966, following the introduction of CGT by *FA 1965*, and with the aim of avoiding CGT and estate duty, he bought a house in Jersey, where he subsequently lived with his wife and sons. In 1967 he applied under *Trustee Act 1925, s 41* and *Variation of Trusts Act 1958, s 1* for the approval of the appointment of Jersey trustees in place of the UK trustees, and for the trusts to be varied to give the trustees powers to transfer the trust assets to new trusts made in Jersey. The CA unanimously rejected his application, observing that it was not clear that W's children would remain resident in Jersey, and holding that approval of the transfer of the trusts to Jersey would not be justified. Lord Denning observed that 'the avoidance of tax may be lawful, but it is not yet a virtue. The Court of Chancery should not encourage or support it.' *In re Weston's Settlements*, CA 1968, [1969] 1 Ch 223; [1968] 3 WLR 786; [1968] 3 All ER 338.

Death of life tenant of share of trust fund

[71.179] A testator who died in 1929 had settled his residuary estate upon trusts for his children. A daughter (R), who was entitled to a life interest in one-quarter of the trust fund, died in 1968/69. None of the investments of the trust fund had been appropriated among the will beneficiaries. The Revenue assessed the trustees for 1968/69 on the basis that, on R's death, there had been a deemed disposal of the whole of the trust fund. They appealed, contending that R's life interest in a fractional part of the fund was to be treated as a separate settlement, and that they should be deemed to have disposed of only one-quarter of the fund. The Commissioners accepted this contention and allowed the appeal, and the CA unanimously upheld their decision. *Pexton v Bell & Colbourne*, CA 1976, 51 TC 457; [1976] STC 301; [1976] 1 WLR 885;

[1976] 2 All ER 914. (*Note*. The charge on a deemed disposal on the death of a life tenant was abolished by *FA 1971* for deaths after 30 March 1971. See now *TCGA 1992, s 72 et seq*.)

[71.180] The CA reached a similar decision in *Crowe v Appleby*, **71.141** above.

TCGA 1992, s 69—whether 'trustees' include 'trustees de son tort'

[71.181] In 1982 the trustees of a settlement purported to resign, leaving an Irish bank as one of the two remaining trustees. In 1987 the bank purported to resign its trusteeship, appointing another non-resident company as trustee. In 2002 a UK company (J) was appointed as a trustee. Subsequently J and the other current trustees took proceedings against the solicitors who had advised the previous trustees in 1982, contending that the purported resignations of the trustees in 1982 had been ineffective, because *Trustee Act 1925, s 37(1)(c)* required two individuals to be trustees. The Ch D accepted this contention, holding that the purported resignations had been ineffective. Mann J also held that the subsequent changes in the composition of the trustees had been ineffective, that the trustees purportedly appointed after 1982 had been 'executors *de son tort*', and that for the purposes of *TCGA 1992, s 69*, 'trustees of the settlement' did not include 'executors *de son tort*'. He observed that it was not 'necessary to allow or require trustees *de son tort* to be trustees of the settlement in order to make the tax regime work. Any tax chargeable on disposals by the *de facto* trustees would prima facie be chargeable as against them because they are the persons who made the gains'. Furthermore, 'anyone holding property as a trustee *de son tort* would be obliged to transfer it to the actual trustees when called upon to do so'. Accordingly the actual trustees were within *TCGA 1992, s 60*, and 'where there are actual trustees who are not in fact acting, but one or more trustees *de son tort* who are, then the disposals made by the latter will generate a charge to tax attributable to the former. If the actual trustees have to pay it they can get hold of the trust assets to enable them to do so'. *Jasmine Trustees Ltd v Wells & Hind*, Ch D [2007] STC 660; [2007] EWHC 38 (Ch).

Expenses of terminating trust

[71.182] Under a marriage settlement, a fund was settled on the wife for life with remainder to the issue of the marriage. The husband (C) subsequently died, leaving only one child. In 1968 arrangements were made under which the trust was terminated and the trust fund vested absolutely in C's widow and daughter. The Revenue issued an assessment under what is now *TCGA 1992, s 71(1)*. The trustee appealed, contending that the cost of legal expenses (including fees to counsel for advice), stamp duty and other expenses should be allowed as deductions, as having been necessarily incurred to bring about the chargeable occasion under *s 71(1)*. The Commissioners accepted this contention and allowed the deduction, and the CS unanimously upheld their decision. *CIR v Chubb's Trustee*, CS 1971, 47 TC 353.

TCGA 1992, s 77—whether settlor benefiting from 'derived property'

[71.183] A company director (T) held 10,000 shares in an unquoted company. He executed a scheme designed to 'avoid and reduce' the CGT liability on his disposal of these shares. Under the scheme, on 4 April 1995 he transferred 8,000 shares to a settlement which he had executed a few days earlier, and in which he was a beneficiary. On the same day the trustees borrowed cash, using the shares as security, and advanced the cash to a second settlement, in which T had an interest. On 5 April 1995 the trustees of the first settlement executed a deed of exclusion, excluding T and his wife from being beneficiaries of the first settlement, leaving other beneficiaries (their children) with an interest in possession. On 13 April 1995, the trustees of the first settlement sold the shares. The Revenue issued a CGT assessment for 1995/96, on the basis that T had benefited from 'derived property', within *TCGA 1992, s 77*. The HL unanimously upheld the assessment. Lord Millett observed that the purpose of *s 77* was 'to prevent taxpayers from obtaining the benefit of the lower rate of tax by transferring assets pregnant with capital gains into a settlement in which they retain an interest before procuring the trustees to dispose of them'. The effect of *s 77(2)* was that T was to be regarded as having had an interest in the first settlement during 1995/96. The trust funds of the second settlement, and the income paid to T, were 'derived property' within *s 77(8)*. Lord Millett also observed that 'the fact that the settlor obtained his right to income under the trusts of the second settlement is immaterial if the income represented the income of the proceeds of property comprised in the first settlement'. *Trennery v West (and related appeals) (aka Tee v HM Inspector of Taxes)*, HL 2005, 76 TC 713; [2005] STC 214; [2005] UKHL 5; [2005] 1 All ER 827. (*Note*. See also *TCGA 1992, Sch 4B*, introduced by *FA 2000, s 92* with effect from 21 March 2000, and designed to counter the scheme used in this case.)

Application of TCGA 1992, ss 77

[71.184] In 1991 an individual (D) established a trust, of which he was the life tenant. In 1998/99 the trust realised a substantial capital gain on the disposal of some loan notes. On his self-assessment return, D claimed a capital loss to set against this gain. HMRC subsequently discovered that this alleged loss was attributable to a 'scheme' which had been intended to take advantage of the provisions of *TCGA 1992, s 71(2)* by providing for a loss to be incurred by a UK resident while a corresponding gain accrued to trustees who were resident outside the UK, for non-resident UK beneficiaries. They issued an amendment to D's self-assessment disallowing the loss claim. D appealed, accepting that the scheme was ineffective (following the decision in *Corbally-Stourton v HMRC*, 5.49 ASSESSMENTS), but contending that because HMRC had not issued a notice of enquiry to the trustees within the statutory time limit, they were too late to assess the gain under *TCGA 1992, s 77*. The First-tier Tribunal rejected this contention and dismissed D's appeal. Judge Khan held that *TCGA 1992, s 77* was directed at D 'as the person who has the liability to tax given his interest in the trust. The expression "would" be chargeable to tax only means that one looks at what the trustees would be assessed on before making an assessment to the settlor.' Since the claimed losses were not available, HMRC were entitled to claim the requisite tax from D as the chargeable person, rather than from the trustees. *P Duke v HMRC*, FTT [2010] UKFTT 306 (TC), TC00593.

[71.185] See also *Smallwood (Settlor of the Trevor Smallwood Trust) v HMRC*, 48.90 RESIDENCE.

Interpretation of TCGA 1992, s 77(2) as originally enacted

[71.186] Three people had carried on business in partnership. In 1979 the business was transferred to a newly-formed company. Each of the partners received shares in the company, and became a director of the company. In 1984 one of the directors (U), who was 60 years of age, executed a discretionary trust, from which he was excluded from benefit, and to which he gave some of his shares. In 1991 the company was taken over, and the trustees of the settlement which U had created made a capital gain on the sale of their shares. The Revenue issued a CGT assessment on the basis that U had an interest in the settlement, by virtue of *TCGA 1992, s 77(2)* as originally enacted, since the terms of the settlement did not exclude any future spouse of the settlor from becoming a beneficiary. U appealed, contending that he should not be deemed to have an interest in the settlement, since he was homosexual, had never married, and had no intention of ever marrying. The Special Commissioner dismissed U's appeal and upheld the assessment, holding that it was clear on the face of the settlement that any future spouse of U could be added as a beneficiary. Applying *dicta* in *CIR v Tennant*, **56.33** SETTLEMENTS, the possibility of a settlor marrying in the future should be taken into account, so that the possibility of a future spouse benefiting was within *s 77(2)*. Although it was accepted that U was in a stable homosexual relationship, it was not impossible that at some time in the future he might marry for companionship, or (for example) to give a right of residence to someone who was not an EU citizen. The possibility of U marrying could not be ignored on *de minimis* grounds. *Unmarried Settlor v CIR*, Sp C [2003] SSCD 274 (Sp C 345). (*Note. TCGA 1992, s 77* was subsequently substituted by *FA 1995* with effect from 1995/96. See now *TCGA 1992, s 77(3)*.)

Charities included in residuary legatees of estate subject to annuities

[71.187] Under a will the residuary estate was held on trust for the benefit of five institutions, equally and absolutely, subject to certain annuities. Four of the residuary legatees were charities. The income was more than sufficient to cover the annuities and no annuity fund was set up. Assets of the estate were sold, so permitting capital distributions to the residuary legatees, and the Revenue assessed the gains on the trustee. He appealed, contending that as four-fifths of the gains accrued to charities, that proportion should be treated as exempt. The Ch D rejected this contention and upheld the assessment. *Prest v Bettinson (Dodd's Trustee)*, Ch D 1980, 53 TC 437; [1980] STC 607. (*Note.* Compare now, however, the subsequent SDLT decision in *Pollen Trustee Co Ltd v HMRC*, **75.6** STAMP DUTY LAND TAX.)

Shares and securities (TCGA 1992, ss 104–151B)

Share pooling, identification, etc. (TCGA 1992, ss 104–114)

Interaction of TCGA 1992, ss 30 and 106

[71.188] See *Land Securities plc v HMRC*, 71.70 above.

Whether a deemed disposal within TCGA 1992, s 106A

[71.189] Trustees of a settlement sold a substantial number of shares, became resident in Mauritius, and then purchased shares of the same class within 30 days. The Revenue issued a notice of amendment on the basis that there had been a deemed disposal of the shares, within *TCGA 1992, s 106A*, when the trustees became non-resident. The settlor appealed, contending that there was no such deemed disposal and that the shares sold before the trustees became non-resident could not be identified with the shares which they had subsequently acquired. The Special Commissioners accepted this contention and allowed the settlor's appeal. The Commissioners held that 'the result of our decision cannot have been intended by Parliament and had there been an alternative interpretation reasonably open to us we might have preferred it'. However, this was 'simply a case where Parliament failed to consider the combined effect of *s 106A* in so far as it negates "bed and breakfast" transactions and the deemed disposal on emigration of trustees.' The Ch D upheld the Commissioners' decision. Park J held that *s 106A* was 'a computational provision and not a deeming provision'. *Davies v Hicks*, Ch D 2005, 78 TC 95; [2005] STC 850; [2005] EWHC 847 (Ch). (*Note*. See now, however, *FA 2006, s 74*, which was intended to reverse the effect of this decision with effect from 22 March 2006.)

TCGA 1992, s 108—identification of relevant securities

[71.190] Between March and April 1964 an individual (M) bought 6.000 shares in a company (P). He bought a further 6,000 shares in M on 11 September, the delivery date for which was 22 September. However on 14 September he sold 6,000 shares in M, the delivery date being 14 October. The Revenue issued an assessment (under Schedule D, Case VII) on the basis that the shares disposed of should be identified with those acquired on 11 September, resulting in a loss of £20. M appealed, contending that the shares sold should have been matched with those first purchased, producing a loss of £3,702. The Special Commissioners rejected this contention and dismissed his appeal, and the Ch D upheld their decision. *MacPherson v Hall*, Ch D 1972, 48 TC 210. (*Note*. Schedule D, Case VII was abolished with effect from April 1971, but the wording of the relevant legislation is identical to *TCGA 1992, s 108(4)(b)*.)

Gilt-edged securities and qualifying corporate bonds (TCGA 1992, ss 115–117B)

Avoidance scheme—whether TCGA 1992, s 116 applicable

[71.191] A married couple held the entire share capital of a company (B). In 2000 they sold the shares to another company (L), receiving loan notes as consideration. The terms of issue of the loan notes included a provision enabling the noteholders to require repayment in US dollars, which prevented the loan notes from constituting qualifying corporate bonds within *TCGA 1992, s 117*. The sale agreement also included provision for further consideration depending on the subsequent performance of B's business. In 2001 the couple received further loan notes under this provision. These further notes initially also included a provision enabling the noteholders to require repayment in US dollars, but that provision was removed by deeds of variation in 2002, with the result that these further notes did constitute qualifying corporate bonds. In May 2003 the couple exchanged both their QCB and non-QCB holdings of loan notes for further loan notes, which constituted qualifying corporate bonds, and which were redeemed in June 2003. HMRC issued assessments charging CGT under *TCGA 1992, s 116*. The couple appealed, contending that *s 116* did not apply where a holding which consisted partly but not wholly of qualifying corporate bonds was exchanged for a holding of qualifying corporate bonds, as was the case with regard to their exchange of loan notes in May 2003, so that their gain on the loan notes which had not been qualifying corporate bonds was rolled over into the notes which they had acquired in May 2003; and that their redemption of the loan notes in June 2003 was exempt from CGT under *TCGA 1992, s 115(1)*, since those notes were qualifying corporate bonds. Judge Berner accepted these contentions and allowed their appeal, observing that 'there appears to be an unfortunate mismatch between the introductory provisions of *s 116(1)(b)* on the one hand, and the definitional provisions of *s 116(3)* and *(4)* which feed into the operative provisions'. *TCGA 1992, s 116(1)* appeared to envisage 'a situation where either the original shares or the new holding would not consist entirely of a QCB, but would include both a QCB and a non-QCB'. He held that although 'Parliament cannot have intended to allow the non-QCB element of a conversion of securities into QCBs to escape taxation', that was 'the effect of the clear words of *s 116(1)(b)*'. He also observed that the anti-avoidance provisions of *TCGA 1992, s 137* were limited to exchanges and reconstructions which fell within *ss 135* and *136* and did not 'apply to other reorganisations, including conversions'. *A & Mrs TL Hancock v HMRC*, FTT [2014] UKFTT 695 (TC); [2014] SFTD 1163, TC03816.

TCGA 1992, s 116(10)—market value of loan notes on conversion

[71.192] Following a company reorganisation in 1999, an individual (B) exchanged some shares for some loan notes in a public company. In February 2004 B entered into two deeds of variation with the company which had issued the loan notes, removing an option to redeem them in a foreign currency, and thus converting them into qualifying corporate bonds. In March 2004 B redeemed the notes for a total of £328,860. In his 2003/04 tax return, he claimed that he had made a capital loss on the redemption, computed on the basis that the loan notes had a value of £9,866 at the time of their conversion in February 2004. Following an enquiry, HMRC formed the opinion that the redemption had given rise to a capital gain, and issued a CGT assessment. B appealed. The First-tier Tribunal reviewed the evidence in detail and dismissed the appeal, holding that the deeds of variation which converted the loan notes into qualifying corporate bonds did not have the effect of depressing their value in the way that B had contended. The tribunal observed that there was no 'likelihood that any relevant noteholder intended or was likely to transfer the loan notes during the second relevant period. The intention was simply temporarily to drive down the market value of the loan notes at the time when they were converted from NQCBs to QCBs.' The tribunal held that the reference to 'market value' in *TCGA 1992, s 116(10)* should not be construed as referring 'to a value or price which has been artificially manipulated, solely for tax purposes, in a wholly uncommercial fashion to produce a temporarily depressed value. There was no commercial or economic reason why the value of the loan notes should have been reduced to £9,866. The value thus manipulated is not the value or the price which the relevant statutory provisions, construed purposively, envisage.' Accordingly the tribunal concluded that the deeds of variation did not have the effect of reducing the market value of the loan notes, and that 'the "frozen" gain which arose on this conversion must be calculated without reference to the artificial depression in value attempted by the deeds of variation'. *W Blumenthal v HMRC*, FTT [2012] UKFTT 497 (TC); [2012] SFTD 1264, TC02174. (*Note*. The tribunal also held that the assessment was authorised by *TMA 1970, s 29* and was not precluded by *s 29(5)*, applying the principles laid down in *Veltema v Langham*, 5.48 ASSESSMENTS.)

TCGA 1992, s 117—definition of qualifying corporate bonds

[71.193] An individual (J) held a number of shares in a company (P). In 1984 P was taken over by another company (M), and J exchanged his shares in P for loan stock in M. He sold some of this stock in 1985 and 1986. In 1987 M converted the loan stock into non-voting stock in its parent company. J sold some of his holding of this stock between 1990 and 1992. The Revenue issued CGT assessments on the disposals. J appealed, contending that *FA 1989, s 139(1)* should be treated as applying to all disposals after 13 March 1989, required stock such as the loan stock in M to be treated as qualifying corporate bonds within what is now *TCGA 1992, s 117* (with retrospective effect), and had the effect that the disposal was not chargeable to CGT. The Special Commissioner rejected this contention and dismissed the appeal, and the Ch D upheld this decision. Neuberger J observed that J's contentions produced 'an undoubted anomaly which is contradictory to the evident purpose of the relevant statutory provisions'. It was necessary to construe the legislation in such a way as to avoid an unreasonable result. Accordingly, *s 139(1)* must be construed as not creating a disposal before 14 March 1989. The exchange which had taken place in 1987 could not be retrospectively treated as a disposal. The purpose of the second part of *s 139(1)* was to ensure that, in a case where corporate bonds, which had been received in the context of a reorganisation before 14 March 1989 in exchange for shares and which became qualifying corporate bonds on 14 March 1989, had been sold on or before that date, any gain which had actually been enjoyed on the shares should not be exempted from charge. *Jenks v Dickinson*, Ch D 1997, 69 TC 458; [1997] STC 853. (*Note. FA 1989, s 139(1)* was not re-enacted in the 1992 consolidation of *TCGA 1992*.)

[71.194] A company director (W) entered into a series of transactions, including the creation of a settlement, designed to reduce the CGT liability on the sale of his shares in the company. As one of the transactions, the trustees of the settlement sold a holding of loan notes. W did not declare any capital gain in respect of this disposal. The Revenue issued an amendment to his self-assessment on the basis that the trustees were liable to CGT on their disposal of the loan notes, and that W was taxable on his share of the gain made by the trustees. W appealed, contending that the loan notes were 'qualifying corporate bonds' within *TCGA 1992, s 117*, and thus were exempt from CGT. The Special Commissioner rejected this contention and dismissed his appeal, and the CA unanimously upheld this decision. Chadwick LJ held that 'the relevant question is whether the underlying loan carries any right to conversion into shares'. Since the loan notes carried the right of conversion into shares, it followed that they were not 'qualifying corporate bonds' within *s 117*. The fact that this right was indirect, and could not be exercised immediately, did not take the notes outside the scope of what is now *CTA 2010, s 162*. *Weston v Garnett (aka Businessman v HM Inspector of Taxes)*, CA 2004, 77 TC 650; [2005] STC 1134; [2005] EWCA Civ 742. (*Note*. For an unsuccessful application for judicial review, see **4.299** APPEALS.)

Interpretation of TCGA 1992, s 117(1)(b)

[71.195] In January 1995 a company director (H) exchanged some shares in a UK company for loan notes issued by a German company. The notes contained an option for redemption in a currency other than sterling, if the holder made an election to this effect within ten days. It was accepted that the effect of this condition was that the loan notes were not qualifying corporate bonds, within *TCGA 1992, s 117*, when they were issued. H did not make such an election, and in July 1995 he redeemed the loan notes for sterling. The Revenue issued an assessment charging CGT on the gain. H appealed, contending that the loan notes should be treated as qualifying corporate bonds when he disposed of them, so that the gain was not taxable. The Special Commissioner, Ch D and the CA unanimously rejected this contention and dismissed the appeal. Lawrence Collins LJ observed that 'it could not have been intended that the language of *section 117(1)(b)* should have the effect that a rolled-over gain should disappear altogether from tax'. He held that the loan notes were not securities 'in respect of which no provision is made for conversion into, or redemption in, a currency other than sterling', within *TCGA 1992, s 117(1)(b)*. Provision had been made for their conversion, even though the right could not be exercised. The word 'provision' should be construed as 'a reference to the terms of the agreement, and not simply to subsisting rights'. Accordingly the gain on the disposal of the loan notes was subject to CGT. *NJ Harding v HMRC*, CA 2008, 79 TC 885; [2008] STC 3499; [2008] EWCA Civ 1164.

Interpretation of TCGA 1992, s 117(2)(b)

[71.196] An investor made a gain on the disposal of certain bonds which were denominated in sterling, but had been issued with a provision for their conversion into euros if the UK were to adopt the euro. In his tax return, he treated this gain as exempt from CGT. HMRC formed the opinion that the provision for conversion into euros prevented the bonds from constituting qualifying corporate bonds, within *TCGA 1992, s 117*. The case was referred to the First-tier Tribunal for a ruling under *TMA 1970, s 28ZA*. Judge Mosedale held that the effect of *TCGA 1992, s 117(2)(b)* was that the relevant provision did not prevent the bonds from constituting qualifying corporate bonds. She observed that 'the redemption value of the bonds in this appeal cannot vary by reference to another currency because the euro redemption value is fixed at the moment of conversion. The effect of the redenomination in euros would be no more than to permit the bonds to be redeemed in euros but at the rate of exchange which prevails at the date of redemption (which must be the same rate as prevails at the date of conversion).' *TCGA 1992, s 117(2)(b)* should be interpreted on the basis that 'the QCB exemption was intended to extend to bonds issued in sterling even if there was provision to convert them to another currency, as long as such conversion did not mean that on redemption any change in value of that other currency was reflected in the value of that bond'. *NMF Trigg v HMRC*, FTT [2014] UKFTT 967 (TC), TC04079.

Capital distributions (TCGA 1992, ss 122–123)

Capital distribution—whether TCGA 1992, s 122 applicable

[71.197] An individual (B) held a large number of shares in a company (C). The total allowable expenditure on any disposal of those shares was £214,000. Under a merger agreement between C and a public company, B exchanged his shares for 840,000 shares in the public company and 75,000 shares in a subsidiary company (the market value of these being £246,000). The transfer of the shares in the subsidiary company to B was treated as a capital distribution, and thus as a partial disposal of his shares in C. The Revenue issued a CGT assessment in which the total allowable expenditure was apportioned in accordance with what is now *TCGA 1992, s 42*. B appealed, contending that, since the total allowable expenditure was less than the value of the shares in the subsidiary, he was entitled to elect that the amount of the distribution should be reduced by the total allowable expenditure, in accordance with what is now *TCGA 1992, s 122(4)*. The CA rejected this contention and upheld the assessment. The words of *s 122(4)* were ambiguous, and in the circumstances the court should give effect to the presumed intention of the legislature by inserting words into the subsection. B could not make an election under *s 122(4)* unless the distribution was 'small', within *s 122(2)*. The capital distribution here (which amounted to 15.58% of the total expenditure) was not small for the purposes of *s 122(2)*. *O'Rourke v Binks*, CA 1992, 65 TC 165; [1992] STC 703.

Reorganisations of share capital, etc. (TCGA 1992, ss 126–140L)

TCGA 1992, s 126—definition of 'reorganisation of company's share capital'

[71.198] In 1967 all the shares in a private company (S) were exchanged for shares in another company (L). A shareholder (B) disposed of 100,000 of these shares in 1974. They had fallen in value since 1967. The Revenue issued a CGT assessment on the basis that the exchange of shares had constituted a 'reorganisation of a company's share capital' (see now *TCGA 1992, s 126*), so that what is now *TCGA 1992, Sch 2 para 19(3)* applied, and there was a capital gain. B appealed, contending that *Sch 2 para 19(3)* did not apply, because the shares in S had been subject to a restriction on transfer to which those in L were not subject, and consequently were not 'of the same class as the original shares'. The Commissioners accepted this contention and allowed B's appeal, and the CS upheld their decision. The CS also held that *TCGA 1992, Sch 2 para 19(3)* was inapplicable in any event, as a 'reorganisation of a company's share capital' could not be construed to cover an amalgamation of two companies. *CIR v Beveridge*, CS 1979, 53 TC 178; [1979] STC 592.

[71.199] A company (U) had acquired all the ordinary shares in a subsidiary company (B) before April 1965. On 29 April 1965 B's share capital was the subject of a Scheme of Arrangement which involved the cancellation of all its preference shares, leaving only the ordinary shares. Before the Scheme of Arrangement, U had held 62% of the voting rights in B; after the Scheme, it held 100% of the voting rights. U sold its ordinary shares in B, at a loss, in 1992. It sought to set this loss against a subsequent gain, and contended that the shares should be treated as having been acquired at market value on 29 April 1965, on the basis that they had been concerned in a 'reorganisation' on that date, within what is now *TCGA 1992, s 126*. The Revenue rejected the claim on the basis that the ordinary shares had not been concerned in a 'reorganisation', so that the loss should be computed on the basis of a straight-line apportionment since the actual acquisition. The Special Commissioners dismissed the company's appeal, and the Ch D and CA upheld this decision. Jonathan Parker LJ held that the cancellation of the preference shares did not amount to a 'reorganisation', since it did not 'alter the rights attaching either to the ordinary shares or to the preference shares'. *Unilever (UK) Holdings Ltd v Smith*, CA 2002, 76 TC 300; [2003] STC 15; [2002] EWCA Civ 1787.

[71.200] A company (Y) carried on an engineering business. In 1977 it acquired for £16,100 the 1,000 issued £1 shares of a company (J) with a similar business. Shortly afterwards it joined a large group; one of the shares in J was registered in the name of a fellow-subsidiary (T), the remainder being registered in its own name. J was not trading profitably. By March 1979 it had incurred debts of £200,911 to other companies in the group, mainly to Y, and it was decided to sell it. An arm's length purchaser was found, and J issued a further 200,000 £1 shares on 12 June 1979. These were allotted to Y for £200,000 cash, which was promptly repaid to Y to clear its indebtedness. On 29 June an agreement was completed between Y, T and the purchaser for the sale of the 201,000 shares for £38,000. Y appealed against a CGT assessment, contending that the issue of the further 200,000 shares constituted a reorganisation of J's capital within what is now *TCGA 1992, ss 126, 128*, with the consequence that the new shares should not be treated as a separate acquisition and that the £200,000 should be treated as having been given for the original 1,000 shares, making their cost £216,100 and giving rise to a capital loss of £178,100. (The Revenue accepted that there was a capital loss but considered that, since the shares had not been acquired at arm's length, the effect of *FA 1965, s 22(4)* was that the amount of the loss was the original acquisition cost of £16,100.) The Special Commissioner accepted Y's contentions and allowed its appeal, and the CA upheld this decision, holding that the phrase 'reorganisation of a company's share capital' in what is now *TCGA 1992, s 126* included an increase in a company's share capital and the allotment of the new shares to its parent company for cash. *Dunstan v Young Austen Young Ltd*, CA 1988, 61 TC 448; [1989] STC 69. (Note. *FA 1965, s 22(4)* became *CGTA 1979, s 19(3)*, which was repealed by *FA 1981*. See now *TCGA 1992, s 128(2)*.)

[71.201] See also *Dugan-Chapman's Executors v HMRC*, 72.76 INHERITANCE TAX.

TCGA 1992, s 132—'conversion of securities'

[71.202] In 1993 an individual (K) sold some shares as part of a reorganisation of a company's share capital, within *TCGA 1992, s 126*. He received shares and loan notes as part of the consideration. At the time they were issued, the loan notes contained a provision whereby the company (R) which issued them could convert them into dollars. However, in October 1995, the terms of the loan note instrument were altered so that R's right to convert them into dollars was cancelled. Shortly afterwards K redeemed the notes. On his 1995/96 tax return, K treated his disposal of the notes as exempt from CGT. The Revenue issued an assessment charging CGT on the gain, and K appealed. The First-Tier Tribunal reviewed the evidence in detail and dismissed the appeal, holding that the transactions by which R lost its right to convert the loan notes into dollars constituted a conversion of securities, so that the latent chargeable gains were crystallised at that time and CGT was chargeable when the notes were redeemed. The Upper Tribunal upheld this decision, holding that the ordinary meaning of the word 'conversion' included 'a change in character, nature, form or function'. *MR Klincke v HMRC*, UT [2010] STC 2032; [2010] UKUT 230 (TCC).

Whether TCGA 1992, s 135 applicable

[71.203] Two large companies (RD and S) decided to merge and form a new company (RDS). Shareholders in RD received two shares in RDS for each share they had held in RD. One of the shareholders (H) submitted a tax return claiming relief under *TCGA 1992, s 135*. HMRC subsequently opened an enquiry into the return, and issued a ruling that relief under *s 135* was not applicable. H appealed. The First-Tier Tribunal reviewed the arrangements in detail and dismissed his appeal, holding that the transactions did not qualify for relief under *s 135*, since the conditions of *s 135(2)* were not satisfied. *P Hadfield v HMRC*, FTT [2010] UKFTT 261 (TC), TC00555. (*Note*. The appellant appeared in person.)

Company partition—whether a 'scheme of reconstruction'

[71.204] A company (F) had carried on business through two divisions. In 1979 its directors decided, for commercial reasons, that each division should be carried on through a separate company, each company being owned by a different group of F's shareholders. To achieve this, a number of transactions were carried out on or about 1 April 1980. F was placed in members' voluntary liquidation, and its shareholders received shares in one of the two new companies. In 1987 one of the shareholders (M) sold a substantial number of shares in one of the new companies (L). The Revenue issued a CGT assessment, computed on the basis that the transactions carried out in April 1980 fell within what is now *TCGA 1992, s 136*, so that the acquisition cost of the shares in L was the original acquisition cost of the shares in F. M appealed, contending that the transactions did not fall within *s 136*, so that the acquisition cost of the shares in L was the market value of the shares in F at 1 April 1980. The Ch D accepted this contention and allowed the appeal. Park J held that the transactions in question constituted a partition, and were not a 'scheme of reconstruction'. Accordingly *s 136* did not apply. *Fallon & Kersley (Morgan's Executors) v Fellows*, Ch D 2001, 74 TC 232; [2001] STC 1409. (*Note*. See now *TCGA 1992, ss 284A, 284B*, introduced by *FA 1999, s 76*; and the changes enacted by *FA 2002, Sch 9*. The Economic Secretary explained in the Finance Bill Standing Committee on 21 May 2002 that *FA 2002, Sch 9* was intended 'to restore the position to what it was before the court decision'.)

Application of TCGA 1992, s 137

[71.205] An individual (S) held 91% of the shares in a company. In December 1996 he exchanged these shares for three different types of loan stock. In April 1997 he emigrated to the Isle of Man, and subsequently redeemed the loan stock. He did not declare the gain on the disposal of the shares in his tax return for 1996/97. The Revenue issued an amendment to the return, charging CGT on the gain. S appealed, contending that the effect of *TCGA 1992, s 135* was that the gain should be deferred until the redemption of the loan stock, and was not chargeable to UK tax because he was not resident in the UK at the time of the redemption. The Special Commissioners rejected this contention and dismissed his appeal, holding that the effect of *TCGA 1992, s 137* was that *s 135* did not apply. The Commissioners observed that S had previously considered moving to Jersey but had been advised that he was not sufficiently wealthy, and found that he 'always had the purpose' of becoming non-resident before redeeming the loan notes. On the evidence, the transactions formed 'part of a scheme or arrangements of which the main purpose, or one of the main purposes, is avoidance of liability to capital gains tax or corporation tax'. The Commissioners also observed that S 'wanted loan stock for tax reasons and would not have agreed to cash'. The Ch D upheld the Commissioners' decision. Sir Andrew Morritt held that 'the exchange was part of a scheme or arrangements of which a main purpose was the avoidance of liability to capital gains tax'. *Snell v HMRC*, Ch D 2006, 78 TC 294; [2007] STC 1279; [2006] EWHC 3350 (Ch).

[71.206] In November 1997 a couple sold their shares in a company for £2,500,000. The consideration took the form of guaranteed unsecured variable loan notes. The couple did not redeem the notes until 1998/99, by which time they had ceased to be resident in the UK. The couple's 1997/98 tax returns incorrectly stated that the transaction had received clearance from the Revenue under *TCGA 1992, s 138*, although in fact the Special Commissioners had rejected their clearance application. The Revenue subsequently began investigating the couple's affairs, and discovered that this statement was incorrect. They issued CGT assessments on the basis that the couple had made a chargeable disposal for tax purposes. The Special Commissioner reviewed the evidence in detail and upheld the assessments, finding that the exchange formed part of a 'scheme or arrangement', and that 'the main purpose of the arrangements was to avoid liability to capital gains tax', so that *TCGA 1992, s 137* applied. The Upper Tribunal upheld this decision, holding on the evidence that the Commissioner had been entitled to conclude that 'the exchange was part of a scheme and that a main purpose of the scheme was avoidance of capital gains tax'. *JP & Mrs M Coll v HMRC*, UT [2010] STC 1849; [2010] UKUT 114 (TCC). (*Note.* The Revenue also imposed penalties under *TMA, s 95(1)*. The Special Commissioner upheld the penalties in principle but reduced them from 85% of the tax due to 30% of the tax due, finding that the returns had been drawn up by the couple's accountants, and holding that the couple had acted negligently rather than fraudulently in making the incorrect statement on their 1997/98 return.)

Whether election made under TCGA 1992, s 138A

[71.207] In 1999 the controlling shareholder of an unquoted company disposed of his shares. His 1999/2000 return declared that he had received deferred consideration of £913,572. The Revenue subsequently issued an assessment charging tax on the 'deferred consideration'. The shareholder appealed, contending that he had submitted an election under *TCGA 1992, s 138A*. The First-Tier Tribunal accepted this contention and allowed the appeal, applying the principles laid down by Lord Oliver in *Gallic Leasing Ltd v Coburn*, **18.61** CORPORATION TAX, and observing that 'any officer with sufficient knowledge of the law who received the return with the computation could not have been under any misapprehension that the appellant wished *section 138A* to apply'. *D Adams v HMRC*, FTT [2009] SFTD 184; [2009] UKFTT 80 (TC); TC00048.

Miscellaneous provisions (TCGA 1992, ss 141–151G)

TCGA 1992, s 143(2)—definition of 'qualifying option'

[71.208] In 1994 an investment company (C) purchased two options from an associated banking company. The combined effect of the two options was that a pre-determined amount was payable on their exercise. The options matured in 1996. The Revenue assessed the gains and C appealed, contending that the options were 'qualifying options' within *TCGA 1992, s 143(2)*. The Special Commissioners accepted this contention and allowed the appeal, holding on the evidence that the options had to be considered separately and that 'the fact that the two options were intended to have effect together does not make them a single composite transaction'. They were qualifying options within *s 143(2)*, rather than simply a loan. The Ch D upheld this decision, distinguishing *WT Ramsay Ltd v CIR*, **71.285** below. Patten J observed that there was 'a real difference between the taxpayer who sets out to utilise a tax avoidance scheme in order to reduce or eliminate an already existing tax liability and one who makes a legitimate choice between investment options having regard to his own fiscal and financial position'. The *Ramsay* principle did not apply 'to transactions of the kind in question which have a clear commercial purpose, contain no artificial steps and were entered into for full market value on recognised terms'. *Griffin v Citibank Investments Ltd*, Ch D 2000, 73 TC 352; [2000] STC 1010.

TCGA 1992, Sch 5B—reinvestment in enterprise investment scheme

[71.209] A company was incorporated in 1998 to operate a sports club. It made several issues of shares to its controlling director (B). He claimed EIS deferral relief in respect of these shares. The Revenue rejected the claim on the basis that some of the shares were not issued in order to raise money for the purpose of a qualifying business activity, as required by what is now *TCGA 1992, Sch 5B para 1(2)*, and that the other shares failed to qualify because they were caught by the 'value received' provisions of *Sch 5B para 13*. The director and the company appealed. The Special Commissioner allowed the appeals in relation to 450,000 of the shares. The CA held that a further 590,000 shares qualified for relief, but that the initial allotment of 149,998 shares failed to qualify, since that share issue failed to meet the requirements of *Sch 5B para 1(2)(f)*. *HMRC v Blackburn (and related appeal)*, CA 2008, [2009] STC 188; [2008] EWCA Civ 1454.

[71.210] In October 2001 a company (D) issued ordinary shares to 12 people in return for cash. On the same day it issued shares of the same class to one of its directors (M) as consideration for providing a guarantee, and issued further shares to M and his wife (among others) in order to convert certain loan notes into shares. D claimed enterprise investment relief in respect of these share issues. The Revenue rejected the claim on the basis that not all the shares had been issued for the purpose of D's qualifying business activity, within *TCGA 1992, Sch 5B para 1* (and additionally that the shares issued to M and his wife were not 'eligible shares' because M and his wife had received value from D, within *TCGA 1992, Sch 5B para 13*). D appealed. The Special Commissioner dismissed the appeal, distinguishing the earlier decision in *Blackburn v HMRC*, **71.209** above. The Commissioner held that the shares issued to M and his wife had not been issued in order to raise money for D's trade, and it followed that 'the condition for the relief contained in *paragraph 1(2)(f)* is not satisfied in relation to any of the ordinary shares issued on that day'. Furthermore, M and his wife had received value from D, within *TCGA 1992, Sch 5B para 13*. *Domain Dynamics (Holdings) Ltd v HMRC*, Sp C [2008] SSCD 1136 (Sp C 701).

[71.211] A family company (H) was incorporated in 2001. It became a partner in a trading partnership, the other four partners being its shareholders. H raised money by issuing shares and increased its interest in the partnership (the money effectively being paid out to the other partners). It applied to HMRC for authority to issue EIS certificates in respect of the shares. HMRC rejected the claim on the basis that the conditions of *TCGA 1992, Sch 5B, para 1(2)* were not satisfied, as the money raised by the share issue had not been 'employed wholly for the purposes' of a qualifying business activity. The

First-tier Tribunal dismissed H's appeal against this decision. Judge Hellier held that 'the monies raised were not employed in the activities of the qualifying trade', as 'there was no evidence that they were used for anything other than to pay for changing the partners' interests in the partnership'. Furthermore, 'there was no evidence that the monies were raised with the intention that the money would be employed in the activities of the trade' and 'all the evidence showed that the monies were intended to be employed in giving the money to the other partners'. *Harvey's Jersey Cream Ltd v HMRC*, FTT [2013] UKFTT 663 (TC); [2014] SFTD 599, TC03045.

[71.212] See also *GC Trading Ltd v HMRC (No 1)*, **23.8** ENTERPRISE INVESTMENT SCHEME.

TCGA 1992, Sch 5B para 1—Revenue refusing to extend three-year time limit

[71.213] In 1997 an individual (D) disposed of some assets, giving rise to a substantial capital gain. In 2001 he asked the Revenue to extend the three-year time limit provided by *TCGA 1992, Sch 5B para 1* for reinvestment in the enterprise investment scheme. The Revenue rejected this request, and D applied for judicial review. The QB rejected his application. Moses J reviewed the evidence in detail and observed that if D had wished to take advantage of the relief in question, 'he should have started earlier and possibly investigated more companies'. *R (oao Devine) v CIR*, QB 2003, 75 TC 679.

TCGA 1992, Sch 5B para 13—return of value to subscribers

[71.214] A company (S) had a subsidiary company (B) which operated a football club and had suffered financial difficulties. In 1999 S's controlling shareholder (O) subscribed for further shares in S. S applied for authority to issue EIS certificates to O. HMRC rejected the application on the grounds that B owed money to O, that S's subscription had been used to repay that debt, and that the subscription was an arrangement within *TCGA 1992, Sch 5B, para 13*. S appealed, contending that payments which had previously been described as loans should instead be treated as having been made on capital account. The First-Tier Tribunal reviewed the evidence in detail, rejected this contention, and dismissed the appeal, finding that O had previously made significant loans to B. Although certain payments by B to O were repayments of sums which had been misappropriated by a former employee of B, the relevant payment made by B to O in December 1999 had been a repayment of the loans and was 'a repayment of debt' which fell within *Sch 5B, para 13(2)(b)*. The tribunal specifically rejected S's contention that the payment should be apportioned, observing that 'there was only one subscription for and issue of shares. All the shares comprised in that single issue are "the" shares to which *paragraph 13(2)(b)* refers.' The Upper Tribunal upheld this decision, observing that 'Parliament should be taken to have wished to legislate such a strict set of conditions to be satisfied in order to claim EIS reinvestment relief. Use of such conditions greatly simplifies and facilitates the policing by the revenue authorities of the proper use of the relief and operates as a clear safeguard against the possibility of abuse.' *Segesta Ltd v HMRC*, UT [2012] UKUT 176 (TCC); [2012] STC 1847. (*Note*. For subsequent developments in this case, see **4.305** APPEALS.)

[71.215] See also *Optos plc v HMRC*, 23.7 ENTERPRISE INVESTMENT SCHEME; *Blackburn v HMRC*, 71.209 above, and *Domain Dynamics (Holdings) Ltd v HMRC*, 71.210 above.

Rollover relief (TCGA 1992, ss 152–162)

Rollover relief: general (TCGA 1992, s 152)

Project to build factory abandoned

[71.216] A trading company (V) bought a site on which it proposed to build a factory, but after getting planning permission, it realised that the site had disadvantages and purchased another site. It sold the first site a year later and claimed rollover relief under what is now *TCGA 1992, s 152*. The Ch D rejected the claim, holding that the site had not been used and occupied for the purposes of V's trade. *Temperley v Visibell Ltd*, Ch D 1973, 49 TC 129; [1974] STC 64.

Whether land occupied for purposes of trade

[71.217] A farmer (L) obtained planning permission for the building of 11 houses on part of his farm. He sold nine building plots and retained the remaining two, on which houses were built at a cost of £23,000. These houses were occupied by L's two sons, who had been employed by him full-time on the farm, and were subsequently taken into partnership. The Revenue issued an assessment on the gain from the sale of the land, and L appealed, claiming rollover relief. The Revenue rejected the claim, considering that although the houses were used for the purposes of the farming business (and therefore qualified for capital allowances) they were not *occupied* for the purposes of the business. The Ch D upheld the assessment, holding that it was not essential for the sons to occupy the houses in order for them to work on the farm, and they were not contractually required to do so. Accordingly, the houses were not occupied for the farming business. *Anderton v Lamb*, Ch D 1980, 55 TC 1; [1981] STC 43. (*Note*. L appealed to the CA, where the action was stayed on terms agreed between the parties—see 1982 STI 179.)

[71.218] In 1990 a trading company (P) purchased a farm, which it used it as its premises until 2000. It then sold the farm for £600,000 and purchased a replacement property for £354,900. P's directors moved into the new property, and P claimed rollover relief in respect of part of its gain on the sale of the farm. Following an enquiry, HMRC issued a closure notice on the basis that 95% of the new property was used for non-trading purposes, so that only 5% of the purchase price (ie £17,745) could be treated as qualifying for rollover relief. P appealed. The First-Tier Tribunal reviewed the evidence and allowed the appeal in part, finding that most of the property was occupied by P's directors, and that P was only the occupier of that part of the house which was used as an office, and of various outbuildings which were used for storage and packing. The effect of *TCGA 1992, s 156* was that only those parts of the house 'which were actually used for selling are to be treated as both used and occupied by the company for the purposes of its trade'. *TCGA 1992, s 152(11)* required an apportionment of the purchase price in order 'to estimate what would have been paid for the separate parts of the property'. On the evidence, the tribunal held that £270,000 of the purchase price was attributable to the house and that only 10% of that could be treated as attributable to the part which P used as an office. Additionally, £40,000 of the purchase price should be attributed to the outbuildings which P used for storage and packing. The result was that £67,000 qualified for rollover relief. *PEMS Butler Ltd v HMRC*, FTT [2012] UKFTT 73 (TC), TC01769.

New asset used partly for business and only partly owned by claimant

[71.219] An accountant (M) sold part of the goodwill of his practice for a chargeable gain of £155,688. Two months later he and his wife entered into partnership to carry on a hotel business, at a house being purchased in their joint names. The partnership agreement stated that the business was to be carried on in the part of the premises 'attributable to the share provided by' M. The total cost of the property with the furniture and fittings and expenses was £209,093. It was accepted that 75% of this (i.e. £156,820) was provided by M, and that the premises were used as to 75% for business purposes. The property was transferred to a settlement, to be held for M and his wife as tenants in common, expressed as 75% for M and 25% for his wife. The Revenue issued a CGT assessment allowing rollover relief of £117,615 (i.e. 75% of £156,820). M appealed, contending that he was entitled to relief of £156,820. The Ch D rejected this contention and upheld the assessment. Since M and his wife, as tenants in common, were entitled to an interest in every part of the property, the relief due was restricted to 75% of M's contribution to the cost. *Tod v Mudd*, Ch D 1986, 60 TC 237; [1987] STC 141.

Purchase of land by associated company

[71.220] Two associated companies (C and W) disposed of some land in Sunderland. Their controlling director purchased a farm in France, and transferred its ownership to a French company, all the shares in which were owned by C and W. C and W claimed rollover relief. The Revenue rejected the claim on the grounds that the disposals and acquisition had not been by the same person, and that neither the land in Sunderland, nor the farm in France, had been used for the purpose of the trades of C and W, as required by what is now *TCGA 1992, s 152*. The Commissioners dismissed the companies' appeals and the Ch D upheld their decision. *Joseph Carter & Sons Ltd v Baird; Wear Ironmongers & Sons Ltd v Baird*, Ch D 1998, 72 TC 303; [1999] STC 120.

Whether business transferred as a going concern

[71.221] A farmer (G) entered into an agreement with his wife to farm an estate in partnership. Five days later the partnership agreed to transfer its business to an unlimited company (N) which G and his wife had formed in the previous month. The Revenue issued a CGT assessment charging tax on the transfer of the business to N. G appealed, contending that the business had been transferred as a going concern, so that rollover relief was available. The CS accepted this contention and allowed his appeal. Although contracts for the sale of the estate to an outside purchaser had been exchanged by the time when N took over the farming of the estate, no such sale had been agreed at the time when the partnership had agreed to transfer the estate to N. Accordingly, N could have continued to operate the business if it had so wished. Furthermore, N subsequently continued to farm an estate elsewhere, using machinery and cattle transferred to it from the partnership. Lord Hope held that 'a planned move of the entire assets of a business from one place to another is not inconsistent with the continuation of its trade'. On the evidence, N had received the whole assets of the business as a going concern. *Gordon v CIR*, CS 1991, 64 TC 173; [1991] STC 174. (*Note*. For another issue in this case, see 4.160 APPEALS.)

Whether new premises used for trading purposes 'on' acquisition

[71.222] A music publishing company (C) sold its trading premises in 1984, and moved into the premises of its parent company. In January 1986 it purchased the freehold of another property, but was unable to obtain vacant possession because the property was occupied by lessees. In 1986 C's parent company purchased the leasehold interest. C then moved into the property and began using it for trading purposes. C claimed rollover relief in respect of the gain on the sale of its previous premises. The Revenue rejected the claim, considering that the premises had not been taken into trade use 'on the acquisition', as required by what is now *TCGA 1992, s 152(1)*, and that the acquisition into which the gain could have been rolled over was the purchase of the leasehold interest, which had been carried out by the parent and not by C. The General Commissioners dismissed C's claim and the CA upheld their decision. The premises had not been used for the purposes of C's trade on the acquisition of the freehold, and neither could the acquisitions of the freehold and leasehold interests by different legal persons be regarded as one transaction. Accordingly relief was not due. *Campbell Connelly & Co Ltd v Barnett*, CA 1993, 66 TC 380; [1994] STC 50.

Leasehold shop remaining closed for eleven months after acquisition

[71.223] An individual (M) was a partner in a launderette business and in a hotel business. The hotel was sold in March 1990. In August 1991 M purchased a leasehold shop. He was granted planning permission to convert the shop into a launderette. However, he subsequently discovered that the gas supply was inadequate and formed the opinion that by opening a launderette in the shop he would damage his existing partnership business. In July 1992 he reopened the shop for a partnership business of selling second-hand goods. He claimed rollover relief in respect of his share of the gain on the share of the hotel. The Revenue rejected the claim on the basis that the leasehold shop had not been taken into use for the purposes of a trade 'on the acquisition', as required by what is now *TCGA 1992, s 152(1)*. M appealed, contending that 'on the acquisition' should be construed as meaning 'as a result of the acquisition'. The Special Commissioner rejected this contention and dismissed the appeal, holding that 'there must be some link between the acquisition of the new assets and their being taken into use'. If M had proceeded with his plan to use the shop as a launderette, the conditions of *s 152(1)* might have been satisfied. However, there was 'an appreciable lapse of time' before M 'managed to decide on the trade he wished to carry on'. For *s 152(1)* to be satisfied, 'the taking into use and the acquisition must be reasonably proximate to one another'. *Milton v Chivers*, Sp C 1995, [1996] SSCD 36 (Sp C 57).

Interaction of TCGA 1992, s 152 and TCGA 1992, s 50

[71.224] In 1995 a rugby club sold some land for £315,105, resulting in a chargeable gain of £204,165. The club used the proceeds of the land to build a new clubhouse. The clubhouse cost £600,459. The club received a grant of £409,000 from the Sports Council (which was accepted as a 'public authority' within *TCGA 1992, s 50*). The club claimed rollover relief in respect of the total cost of the new clubhouse. The Revenue ruled that the effect of *TCGA 1992, s 50* was that rollover relief could only be given in respect of the net cost (of £191,459) after deducting the Sports Council grant. The General Commissioners allowed the club's appeal, holding that *TCGA 1992, s 50* would only apply to any gain on any subsequent disposal of the clubhouse and did not apply to its acquisition. The Ch D upheld this decision. Ferris J held that there was nothing in *s 152* which required *s 50* to be applied before giving effect to rollover relief, and 'no words in *section 50* itself which are capable of producing this result'. *Wardhaugh v Penrith Rugby Union Football Club*, Ch D 2002, 74 TC 499; [2002] STC 776; [2002] EWHC 918 (Ch).

TCGA 1992, s 152(3)—three-year time limit

[71.225] A publican sold his business in October 1986. In February 1988 he purchased a barge, which he intended to convert into a wine bar and restaurant. Between December 1989 and November 1994 he incurred substantial expenditure on the barge. He eventually began to trade from it in August 1995. He claimed rollover relief. The Ch D rejected his claim (reversing the General Commissioners' decision). Sir Richard Scott V-C held that the Commissioners were not entitled to extend the three-year time limit laid down by *s 152(3)*. The Revenue's power to extend the time limit was not reviewable by the Commissioners, and could only be challenged by judicial review. Additionally, the Commissioners had no discretion to consider whether the Revenue should have invoked Extra-Statutory Concession D24, and the only reasonable conclusion on the evidence was that the trades were not carried on 'successively', as required by *TCGA 1992, s 152(8)*. *Steibelt v Paling*, Ch D 1999, 71 TC 376; [1999] STC 594.

[71.226] The Revenue rejected a claim to rollover relief on the grounds that it had been made outside the three-year time limit of *TCGA 1992, s 152(3)*. The claimant applied for judicial review. The QB rejected the application, holding that the Revenue had been entitled to exercise their discretion to refuse to extend the time limit. *R (oao Barnett) v CIR*, QB 2003, 75 TC 796; [2004] STC 763.

Purchase of single property followed by sale of part of property

[71.227] In 1988 a trader purchased some business premises. In 1989 he sold part of the premises at a profit. The Revenue issued a CGT assessment and he appealed, contending that he was entitled to treat the proceeds of sale as having been used in acquiring the balance of the premises, so that he was entitled to rollover relief under what is now *TCGA 1992, s 152*. The CA rejected this contention and upheld the assessment. The disposal had been a part disposal of the original asset. The premises had been acquired as 'one single asset for an undivided consideration', and continued to constitute a single asset until the part disposal. Accordingly relief was not due. *Watton v Tippett*, CA 1997, 69 TC 491; [1997] STC 893.

Relevant classes of assets (TCGA 1992, s 155)

TCGA 1992, s 155—claim for relief on machinery

[71.228] A civil engineering partnership sold some earth-moving vehicles at a profit and reinvested the proceeds in two similar machines. The partners appealed against a CGT assessment on the gain, claiming rollover relief. The Ch D dismissed their appeals. Nourse J held that what is now *TCGA 1992, s 155, Class 1, Head B* confined the relief to fixed plant and fixed machinery. The relief did not extend to moveable machinery. *Williams v Evans (and related appeals)*, Ch D 1982, 59 TC 509; [1982] STC 498; [1982] 1 WLR 972.

TCGA 1992, s 155—attribution of consideration to 'goodwill'

[71.229] A company (B) owned part of two franchised restaurant businesses. The franchisor (P) wished to purchase the businesses and operate them itself. B agreed to sell its interests to P. It attributed most of the consideration to goodwill, on which it claimed rollover relief. The Revenue rejected the claim on the basis that the goodwill already belonged to P, and that most of the consideration represented compensation for the early termination of the franchise agreements. B appealed. The Special Commissioner reviewed the evidence in detail and allowed the appeal in principle, holding that the goodwill had belonged to B, and that the consideration for the goodwill qualified for relief. The Commissioner observed that 'goodwill distinguishes an established business from a new business and is built up by years of honest work and investment in the business'. He also specifically criticised the Revenue's Capital Gains Tax Manual, firstly for applying a 'zoological definition of goodwill which was considered to be of limited value in *Whiteman Smith Motor Co v Chaplin*, CA [1934] 2 KB 35', and secondly for its claim that the goodwill of a franchised business always belonged to the franchisor. The Commissioner held that 'the ownership of goodwill between franchisor and franchisee is primarily a question of fact'. On the evidence, P was not 'a well-known brand' at the time B acquired the business, and B had 'established the reputation of their restaurants, which was based principally on the service they provided to their customers'. *Balloon Promotions Ltd v Wilson; Vela-Castro & Others v Wilson (No 1)*, Sp C [2006] SSCD 167 (Sp C 524). (*Notes*. (1) For HMRC's interpretation of this decision, see Revenue Tax Bulletin, Issue 83, June 2006. HMRC state that 'we accept the finding of the Special Commissioner that the question of whether a franchisee owns goodwill is principally a question of fact. Where a franchised business is disposed of as a going concern the question of whether there has been a disposal of goodwill will be determined in the light of the relevant facts. These will include a detailed consideration of the terms of the franchise agreement, the extent of control exercised by the franchisor and the terms and conditions relating to the sale. Therefore, we do not consider that the decision in these appeals is of general application to other cases involving the sale of franchised businesses.' (2) A subsequent application for costs was dismissed—see **4.421** APPEALS.)

[71.230] In a stamp duty case, in which the goodwill of a German business was held not to be chargeable with stamp duty, Lord MacNaghten defined goodwill as being the 'benefit and advantage of the good name, reputation, and connection of a business. It is the attractive force which brings in custom. It is the one thing which distinguishes an old-established business from a new business at its first start.' He also observed that 'if there is one attribute common to all cases of goodwill it is the attribute of locality'. *CIR v Muller & Co (Margarine) Ltd*, HL [1901] AC 217. (*Note*. This definition has been cited in several subsequent cases, including *Kirby v Thorn EMI plc*, **71.28** above.)

[71.231] A company (M) had carried on a business of selling Mercedes cars. In 2003 it sold this business in return for consideration of £1,705,502. M claimed rollover relief on the basis that the gain arose from the disposal of its goodwill. HMRC disallowed 50% of the claim on the basis that only 50% of the consideration should be treated as attributable to goodwill and that 50% was compensation for the loss of M's agreement with the car manufacturer, which did not qualify for relief under *TCGA 1992, s 155*. The CA unanimously dismissed M's appeal. Patten LJ observed that part of the payment (described as a 'territory release payment') 'became payable under a variation of the franchise agreement which reserves the right to control the use of the Mercedes mark'. On the evidence, he held that this could not 'have been the subject of a claim for compensation by (M) as a result of the termination of the franchise and, for that reason, the territory release payment cannot be treated as a payment derived from an asset belonging to (M)'. M could not 'assert an interest of its own in the goodwill which it was surrendering on the termination of the agreement. The compensation for both aspects of the dealership was therefore, on the face of the agreement, calculated as the amount of lost profit attributable to the period in question.' Therefore the territory release payment was 'compensation for the loss of the right to trade under the dealership agreement' and was taxable accordingly. *Mertrux Ltd v HMRC*, CA [2013] EWCA Civ 821; [2013] STC 2199.

Sale of shares

[71.232] Two individuals claimed rollover relief in respect of the sale of shares. The Revenue rejected the claim on the basis that shares were not included in the 'relevant classes of assets' as defined by *TCGA 1992, s 155*. The vendors appealed, contending that one should 'look beyond the shares in the company to the company's own assets'. The Special Commissioner rejected this contention and dismissed the appeals. *Buckley & Buckley v HMRC*, Sp C [2005] SSCD 860 (Sp C 505).

[71.233] In *Rotberg v HMRC*, **29.55** FURTHER ASSESSMENTS: LOSS OF TAX, the First-tier Tribunal held that shares failed to qualify for rollover relief.

Trade carried on by personal company (TCGA 1992, s 157)

TCGA 1992, s 157—definition of 'personal company'

[71.234] A married couple owned some chicken farms, which they let to a company (C). 99.87% of the shares in C were held by another company (H).

The husband (B) held 50.02% of the shares in H, while his wife held the remaining 49.98%. During 2001 and 2002 the couple sold some farms and mills and acquired replacement properties, which they also let to C. B claimed rollover relief under *TCGA 1992, s 152*. The Revenue rejected the claim on the basis that C did not qualify as B's 'personal company' within *TCGA 1992, s 157*. The Special Commissioner dismissed B's appeal, holding that it would be 'far too wide a construction of the expression "voting rights which are exercisable in a company" to hold that it can attribute such rights to any person who is able, as a matter of fact, to exercise voting rights on behalf of another person, whether by a one-stage or a two-stage process. Such a construction would sever the ties of ownership between the "personal company" and the individual whose "personal company" it is', which was 'essential in the scheme of rollover relief'. The definition of a 'personal company' could not 'be construed so as to allow relief in the case of gains accruing on the disposal of assets owned by an individual and used for the purposes of a trade carried on by a company in which that individual had no (or no sufficient) degree of ownership, but over which he as a matter of fact exercises influence short of ownership.' *Boparan v HMRC*, Sp C [2007] SSCD 297 (Sp C 587).

Transfer of a business to a company (TCGA 1992, s 162)

[71.235] A married woman (R) had acquired a large house in Belfast, which was divided into flats and let to tenants. In 2004 she transferred the house to a company. She claimed relief under *TCGA 1992, s 162*. Following an enquiry, HMRC issued a ruling that no relief was due, on the grounds that the property was an investment and was not a business. The Upper Tribunal allowed R's appeal (reversing the First-tier decision). Judge Berner held that the activity which R had undertaken in respect of the property outweighed 'what might normally be expected to be carried out by a mere passive investor' and was sufficient in nature and extent to amount to a business for the purpose of *TCGA 1992, s 162*. *Mrs EM Ramsay v HMRC*, UT [2013] UKUT 226 (TCC); [2013] STC 1764.

[71.236] A married couple had traded in partnership, carrying on a business of managing residential projects such as extensions and loft developments. However the partnership turnover declined from 2003, and the business ceased in April 2006. In 2003 the husband (R) had become a director of a limited company (G) which owned a commercial property. In May 2006 G made an issue of shares to R. Subsequently HMRC formed the opinion that these shares represented consideration for the disposal of a business asset by R, namely an agreement with a contractor (P) relating to landfill, so that he was required to pay CGT on the value of the shares. R appealed, contending that he had transferred a property development consultancy business, rather than simply an asset, and was entitled to relief under *TCGA 1992, s 162*. The First-tier Tribunal accepted this contention and allowed the appeal, finding that R had been developing his business from 2003, that it was separate from the partnership business, and that he had transferred it to G as a going concern. On the evidence, the issue of the shares had not been solely as consideration for the contract with P, but had also been 'in return for the transfer of the entire business'. *P Roelich v HMRC*, FTT [2014] UKFTT 579 (TC), TC03704.

Retirement relief (TCGA 1992, ss 163, 164)

NOTE

This relief was abolished for 2003/04 and subsequent years of assessment by *FA 1998, s 140, Sch 27*. See Tolley's Capital Gains Tax.

Whether claimant had 'retired on ill-health grounds'

[71.237] A greengrocer (M) sold his market stall business and subsequently began trading from a shop. He claimed retirement relief on ill-health grounds in relation to the disposal of his market stall. The Revenue rejected the claim and the Special Commissioner dismissed M's appeal, finding that he did not satisfy the statutory conditions. *Mayes v Woods*, Sp C [1997] SSCD 206 (Sp C 126).

[71.238] A woman who had been a partner in a newsagent's business claimed retirement relief, contending that she was suffering from depression. The Special Commissioner dismissed her appeal, finding that she was 'unlikely to remain permanently incapable of engaging in work of the kind which she previously undertook'. Accordingly, the effect of *TCGA 1992, Sch 6 para 3(1)* was that she did not qualify for relief. *Palmer v Richardson*, Sp C [2005] SSCD 418 (Sp C 467).

Whether a 'material disposal of business assets'

[71.239] A farmer, aged 68, had farmed 35 acres for more than 10 years. He sold 4.8 acres, for which he had obtained planning permission for building development. The Revenue issued an assessment charging CGT on the gain and the farmer appealed, claiming retirement relief. The Ch D rejected the claim, holding that 'the sale did not constitute a disposal of any part of the business'. *McGregor v Adcock*, Ch D 1977, 51 TC 692; [1977] STC 206; [1977] 1 WLR 864.

[71.240] A farmer, who had farmed 89 acres, sold nine of them. He was assessed and claimed retirement relief, contending that the sale was a disposal of part of his business. The Ch D rejected his claim, holding that no relief was due. *Atkinson v Dancer*, Ch D 1988, 61 TC 598; [1988] STC 758.

[71.241] A similar decision was reached in a case where a farmer, who had farmed 78 acres, sold 35 of them in 1984. *Mannion v Johnston*, Ch D 1988, 61 TC 598; [1988] STC 758. (*Note*. The case was heard in the Ch D with *Atkinson v Dancer*, 71.240 above.)

[71.242] A farmer (D) had owned 113 acres of land, on which he had reared and grazed cattle, for several years. He gradually ceased to rear cattle, and sold

83 acres in 1986. In 1987 he obtained planning permission in respect of a covered cattle yard comprising 0.6 acres, which he sold in 1988. Thereafter his only activity was cattle grazing. The Revenue issued a CGT assessment on the sale of the cattle yard. D appealed, contending that he was entitled to retirement relief. The Ch D rejected this contention and upheld the assessment. On the evidence, D had changed the nature of his activities from rearing cattle to grazing them in preparation for the sale of the yard. Following this change, the yard was no longer used for his business, so that its sale did not constitute a disposal of a part of that business. *Pepper v Daffurn*, Ch D 1993, 66 TC 68; [1993] STC 466.

[71.243] A farmer (R) owned 64 acres with a milking parlour and yard, and had a dairy herd of 34 animals. In 1988 he sold the parlour and yard, and during the next three months he sold 14 of the animals. He transferred most of the remaining animals to a farm three miles away which belonged to his wife. He ceased dairy farming and used his land for rearing and finishing store cattle, although he retained and leased the milk quota. The Revenue issued an assessment charging CGT on the sale of the parlour and yard. R appealed, claiming retirement relief. The Commissioners allowed his appeal and the Ch D upheld their decision. Knox J held that the Commissioners were entitled to find that the dairy farming was a separate business from the rearing and finishing of store cattle. *Jarmin v Rawlings*, Ch D 1994, 67 TC 130; [1994] STC 1005.

Sale of milk quota following cessation of dairy farming

[71.244] In 1988 a dairy farmer (B) sold his entire herd. In 1989, having reached the age of 60, he sold his milk quota. He appealed against a CGT assessment, claiming retirement relief. The Ch D upheld the assessment, holding that the milk quota was simply an asset and that its disposal was not the disposal of part of a business. The relevant business activity had ceased in 1988 when B sold the herd. *Wase v Bourke*, Ch D 1995, 68 TC 109; [1996] STC 18.

Surrender of tenancy—farming continued under temporary licence

[71.245] In 1990 a tenant farmer (P) received £120,000 from his landlord as compensation for surrendering his agricultural tenancy. He was allowed to continue to farm the land, under a temporary licence, for 18 months. The Revenue assessed the compensation to CGT for 1989/90. P appealed, contending that it qualified for retirement relief. The Ch D rejected this contention and upheld the assessment, holding that the payment was not made for the disposal of the whole or part of P's business, since he had been able to continue farming the land in question for two summers under the temporary licence. *Barrett v Powell*, Ch D 1998, 70 TC 432; [1998] STC 283.

Sale of property partly let to tenants

[71.246] A married couple purchased a property in 1967. They let parts of the property, furnished, to tenants, and sold the property in 1995. They claimed retirement relief. The Revenue rejected the claim and the husband (H) appealed. The Special Commissioner dismissed the appeal, and the Ch D upheld this decision. The letting of furnished rooms was not a trade. Although H had carried on business as a contractor, that business had ceased in 1990. The occasional use of parts of the property for the purposes of H's haulage business did not mean that it was an asset of that business, and even if it were accepted that it was, the period between the cessation of the business and the disposal of the property exceeded the one-year time limit of *TCGA 1992, s 163*. *Hatt v Newman (No 1)*, Ch D 2000, 72 TC 462; [2000] STC 113. (*Notes*. (1) The Ch D also upheld the Revenue's contention that, by virtue of *TCGA 1992, s 28*, the disposal took place in 1994/95 when the contract was made, rather than in 1995/96 when the contract was completed. For cases concerning the date of disposal, see **71.61** to **71.67** above. (2) For subsequent developments in this case, see **71.78** above.)

Sale of premises nine months before sale of business

[71.247] The proprietor of a coach and a minibus service wished to retire. In March 1990 he sold the freehold of his business premises to a company which owned a nearby petrol station. The company agreed to lease the premises back to him for three years, and he continued to carry on the business until December 1990, when he sold it to a business colleague. He claimed retirement relief in respect of the sale of the business, including the premises. The Revenue accepted the claim in respect of the business sold in December 1990, but rejected the claim in respect of the earlier sale of the premises. The Ch D upheld the Revenue's ruling. Blackburne J held that the two sales could not be treated as a single transaction. The sale of the premises in March could not be treated as part of the sale of the business in December. *Purves v Harrison*, Ch D 2000, 73 TC 390; [2001] STC 267.

Sale of land leased to family company

[71.248] In 1988 an individual (H), who was 60 years of age, disposed of 163 acres of land which had been used by a trading company of which he was a director and shareholder. The company, which had paid rent to H for the use of the land, qualified as H's 'family company' under *FA 1985, s 69*. The Revenue issued a CGT assessment, and H's personal representatives appealed, contending that the sale of the land qualified for retirement reliefThe CA accepted this contention and allowed the appeal, holding that where there was a disposal of assets in a discontinued business, it was not essential that the business must have been owned by the individual making the disposal. *Plumbly & Others (Harbour's Personal Representatives) v Spencer*, CA 1999, 71 TC 399; [1999] STC 677.

TCGA 1992, s 163(4)(c)—date of cessation of business

[71.249] An individual (M) owned land and buildings which were used as an aircraft museum by a company (T) of which he was the controlling director. The museum closed in 1988. In 1989 the premises were sold to a subsidiary company which had been incorporated to undertake the residential development of the site. The Revenue issued an assessment charging CGT on the disposal. M appealed, claiming retirement relief. The Ch D allowed his appeal, holding that since the museum had never in fact reopened, the fact that T had originally hoped to reopen it was not conclusive. Sir Richard Scott observed that 'if trade is closed down on a basis intended to be only temporary but that becomes in the event permanent', the date when the trade ceased to be carried on 'is the date on which the trade was closed down'. Accordingly, the business should be treated as having ceased in 1988, and M qualified for retirement relief. *Marriott v Lane*, Ch D 1996, 69 TC 157; [1996] STC 704; [1996] 1 WLR 111.

TCGA 1992, s 163(5)—definition of 'personal company'

[71.250] From 1986 to 1991 an individual (N) was a full-time working director of a trading company (FH), but was not a shareholder in FH. In 1991 FH's business was taken over by another company (FC). N was a full-time working director and majority shareholder in FC. In 1996 N reached the age of 50, and sold his majority shareholding in FC. He claimed retirement relief. The Revenue computed the relief on the basis that the qualifying period applicable to the disposal was five years, ie the period from 1991 to 1996 during which FC was carrying on the trade, so that the 'appropriate percentage' for the purposes of *TCGA 1992, Sch 6 para 13* was 50%. N appealed, contending that the period during which the trade was carried on by FH should be treated as part of the 'qualifying period', so that the 'appropriate percentage' was 100%. The Commissioner rejected this contention and dismissed the appeal, holding that although FC qualified as N's 'personal company' within *TCGA 1992, s 163(5)*, FH did not qualify as N's 'personal company' because he had not held 5% of the voting rights in it, as required by *Sch 6 para 1(2)*. The Commissioner held that the legislation required that the 'personal company' test must be satisfied in relation to any company 'which, at any time during a putative extended qualifying period, owned the business which is assumed to be the same business as the business at retirement by *subparagraph 14(2)* of *Schedule 6*'. *N Fraser v HMRC*, Sp C [2006] SSCD 285 (Sp C 530).

TCGA 1992, s 164—associated disposals

[71.251] A company (K) was incorporated in 1954 to take over a retail business which had previously been carried on by a father (F) and son (M) in partnership. F acquired 50.01% of the company's shares, and M acquired the remaining 49.99%. In 1988, when M was aged 60, contracts were exchanged for the sale of premises which K occupied (and in which M had a 25% interest) to an unrelated company. On 25 January 1989 F died, bequeathing his shareholding to M. On 31 January the sale of the property was completed. On 28 February 1989 K ceased trading. In 1990 M transferred his original 49.99% shareholding in K to his children. He claimed retirement relief. The Revenue rejected the claim, on the grounds that the statutory conditions were not satisfied, since K had ceased to occupy the property four weeks before the date on which it ceased trading. The Commissioners allowed M's appeal, holding that the disposal of the shares was a 'material disposal', that the disposal of the property was an 'associated disposal', and that, although K had ceased to occupy the property four weeks before it ceased trading, the property qualified as having been used by K 'immediately before' the cessation of the business. The Ch D upheld this decision. Evans-Lombe J held that the words 'immediately before' could be construed as meaning 'sufficiently proximate in time to the material disposal or cessation so as to justify the conclusion that the transaction in question formed part of it'. *Clarke v Mayo*, Ch D 1994, 66 TC 728; [1994] STC 570.

[71.252] A married couple carried on a farming business in partnership. They had a 70% interest in some land which was used for grazing as part of the partnership business, the other 30% of the land being owned by their three children. They agreed to sell some of the land to a building company. On the same day they gave each of their children a 20% interest in the partnership. They claimed retirement relief on the sale of the land. The Revenue rejected the claim but the Special Commissioner allowed the couple's appeal, holding that they had made a 'material disposal' of partnership assets, within *TCGA 1992, s 163*, and that the sale of the land to the building company was an 'associated disposal', within *TCGA 1992, s 164*. *Todd & Todd v Fawcett*, Sp C 2004, [2005] SSCD 97 (Sp C 438).

TCGA 1992, Sch 6 para 1(2)—voting rights not exercised

[71.253] A company (W) had an issued share capital of 100 shares. One of these was owned by its principal director (S), one was owned by S's wife, one was owned by another director (B), and the remaining 97 were owned by an associated company (IB), which had never appointed a representative to exercise the voting rights carried by the shares. W ceased to trade and transferred the business to a partnership comprising S and B. S subsequently retired from the partnership. He appealed against a CGT assessment, contending that W had qualified as his 'family company' for the purposes of *FA 1965, s 34*, as he had held one-third of the voting rights actually exercised. The Ch D rejected this contention, holding that W did not qualify as S's 'family company' as he had only held 1% of the exercisable voting rights. The fact that the majority shareholder (IB) had never exercised its voting rights was not conclusive. *Hepworth v Smith*, Ch D 1981, 54 TC 396; [1981] STC 354.

TCGA 1992, Sch 6 para 12(2)—definition of 'chargeable business asset'

[71.254] An accountant (D) retired from an accountancy firm. He had held 11.11% of the shares in the firm's service company, and disposed of these on his retirement. He claimed retirement relief. The Revenue rejected his claim and the Special Commissioner dismissed D's appeal, holding that the shares were not 'chargeable business assets'. *Durrant v CIR*, Sp C [1995] SSCD 145 (Sp C 24).

Reinvestment relief (TCGA 1992, ss 164A–164N)

NOTE

This relief was abolished for acquisitions made after 5 April 1998 by *FA 1998, s 165, Sch 27*. See Tolley's Capital Gains Tax.

Application of TCGA 1992, s 164A

[71.255] See *Bradbury v Ernst & Young*, 58.31 TAX PLANNING AND AVOIDANCE.

TCGA 1992, s 164G—definition of 'qualifying company'

[71.256] A married couple carried on a holiday business in partnership, owning a hotel and six apartments. The partnership sold shares in a property company (K) and reinvested the gain in another company (H). H purchased three apartments from the partnership and began a business of providing serviced holiday accommodation. The couple claimed reinvestment relief under *TCGA 1992, s 164A*. The Revenue rejected the claim on the basis that H was not a 'qualifying company' within *TCGA 1992, s 164G*. The Special Commissioner dismissed the couple's appeal, holding that 'income derived from the commercial letting of furnished accommodation, whether for a short or long period, is not generally regarded as income derived from carrying on a trade, even although this activity may properly be described as the carrying on of a business. "Business" is a wider concept than "trade".' On the evidence, 'the services provided by the company are typical of the services provided under a holiday letting arrangement'. The company's income 'was derived from payments by holidaymakers for the use of the apartments'. That was a 'licence fee' within *TCGA 1992, s 164I(2)(d)*. *DS & Mrs LM MacLean v HMRC*, Sp C [2007] SSCD 350 (Sp C 594).

Whether TCGA 1992, s 164L applicable

[71.257] In June 1995 M, the controlling shareholder of four companies, sold 51% of the shares in three of the companies for total consideration of £375,000. These shares had no base value. M reinvested the consideration by subscribing for new shares in the company (P) of which he had retained 100% ownership. M paid the £375,000 to P on 30 June 1995, but P did not actually issue the shares until March 1996. P then used this money to repay a loan which it had previously received from one of the companies which M had sold. The Revenue issued a CGT assessment on the basis that M had realised chargeable gains of £375,000 in 1995/96, and that the effect of *TCGA 1992, s 164L(3)* was that M was not entitled to reinvestment relief. M appealed, contending that the anti-avoidance provisions of *TCGA 1992, s 164L* did not apply, and that he was entitled to reinvestment relief under *TCGA 1992, ss 164A–164N*. The Special Commissioners accepted this contention and allowed M's appeal, finding that M 'intended the payment on 30 June 1995 to be a subscription for shares to be issued rather than a loan'. Between that date and 29 March 1996, when the shares were issued, P was indebted to M. However, the repayment of the debt by P was 'outside of the mischief of the return of value provisions in *section 164L(3)*.' The Commissioners held that 'the repayment of a debt, where the debt itself only arises as an incidence of the share acquisition, which does not involve the utilisation, by the reinvestor, of any part of the funds which she uses to acquire the eligible shares, and which leaves him with a net increased investment in the qualifying company of an amount equal to the chargeable gain he seeks to relieve, is in our judgment outside the scope of *section 164L(3)*'. *Inwards v Williamson*, Sp C [2003] SSCD 355 (Sp C 371).

[71.258] In 1995 an individual (W) sold shares in two companies (V and C), making substantial capital gains. He and his wife were the only shareholders in two other companies (B and R). During 1996 R had made payments to W totalling more than £500,000, and it made further payments in 1997 and 1998. In March 1997 B passed a resolution substantially increasing its share capital. In June 1997 W invested £600,000 in additional shares in B, and in March 1998 he invested a further £500,000 (partly deriving from a payment of £300,000 made to him by R). He claimed reinvestment relief under *TCGA 1992, ss 164A–164N* in respect of the total investment of £1.1m. The Revenue rejected the claims on the basis that the transactions had constituted arrangements for the return of part of the value of his investment, within *TCGA 1992, s 164L(1)*, so that relief was not due. The Special Commissioners dismissed W's appeal against this decision, finding that his purchases of shares were partly funded by the payments from R. The Commissioners held that there had been 'arrangements' within *TCGA 1992, s 164L(1)*, and a 'return of value' within *s 164L(3)*, involving connected persons within *s 164L(9)*. Accordingly relief was not due. *Wakefield v HM Inspector of Taxes*, Sp C [2005] SSCD 439 (Sp C 471).

Gifts of business assets (TCGA 1992, ss 165–169G)

Transfer of business to company—claim under TCGA 1992, s 165

[71.259] Two individuals (C and H) carried on a business in partnership until 1999, when they transferred the business to a company of which they were the sole shareholders and directors. The company subsequently submitted accounts indicating that it had paid £250,000 for the goodwill of the partnership business, although neither C nor H had declared such a receipt on their tax returns. The Revenue issued amendments to their self-assessments, charging tax on the payments. They appealed, claiming that they should be entitled to retirement relief. The Revenue rejected this claim as they were below the statutory age, and their accountants then claimed that the original company accounts had been incorrect and that they had 'gifted' the goodwill under *TCGA 1992, s 165*. The Special Commissioner reviewed the evidence in detail, rejected this contention, and dismissed the appeals. The Commissioner held that C and H had not shown that the original company accounts were incorrect. On the evidence, the accountants had treated the transaction as a transfer of the goodwill at a market value of £250,000. The purported 'revision of the accounts took place only after queries had been raised about the earlier accounts by the inspector'. The Commissioner observed that 'accounts cannot just be rewritten at whim'. *Colley & Hillberg v Clements*, Sp C [2005] SSCD 633 (Sp C 483). (*Note.* For subsequent developments in this case, see **71.347** below.)

TCGA 1992, s 167—gifts to foreign-controlled companies

[71.260] A UK resident (F) held 51% of the shares in a private company (BG). His wife owned 9% of the shares. They entered into a complex scheme designed to avoid CGT on the disposal of their shares in BG. They each set up an Isle of Man settlement; the trustees of each of the settlements acquired two 'off-the-shelf' Isle of Man companies; Mr & Mrs F each took out an insurance bond issued by a Republic of Ireland company (IL), and assigned their bond to one of the Isle of Man companies under the settlement; and IL acquired two 'off-the-shelf' companies (L and M) within the bond. Mr & Mrs F then gave their shares in BG to L and M, and claimed relief under *TCGA 1992, s 165* on the gift of the shares. The Revenue issued a ruling that Mr & Mrs F and IL were 'connected persons acting together to secure or exercise control of the donee company', within *TCGA 1992, s 167(3)*, so that *TCGA 1992, s 167* applied and relief under *s 165* was not available. The Special Commissioner upheld the Revenue's contentions and the shareholders appealed to the CA, contending firstly that IL should not be treated as 'connected' to the shareholders, and alternatively that *TCGA 1992, s 167* contravened *Article 43EC* of the *EC Treaty*. The CA unanimously rejected these contentions and dismissed the appeals. Chadwick LJ held that the effect of *TCGA 1992, s 286(7)* was that there was 'a relevant connection between (IL) and the persons making the disposal of the (BG) shares'. The effect of *s 167* was to 'deter those United Kingdom taxpayers who see a bond-based scheme with a non-United Kingdom resident insurance company as a means of avoiding a potential charge to capital gains tax from entering into arrangements which enable them to remain in control of the factors affecting the underlying value of the asset which is to be transferred under that scheme'. That was not a restriction on the right to 'freedom of establishment' under *Article 43EC*. *Foulser & Foulser v MacDougall*, CA [2007] STC 973; [2007] EWCA Civ 8. (*Notes.* (1) The CA also criticised the appellants for seeking to raise new points in the courts which they had failed to raise before the Special Commissioner. (2) For subsequent developments in this case, see **4.115** APPEALS and **43.19** PAYMENT OF TAX.)

Entrepreneurs' relief (TCGA 1992, ss 169H–169S)

Material disposal of business assets—TCGA 1992, s 169I

[71.261] A trader (G) had carried on a business of selling food on commission, representing nine different suppliers. In 2008 he agreed to sell part of his business to one of the suppliers (F), under an agreement whereby he agreed to have no further contact with F's customers. He made a gain of £285,000 on this disposal. In his tax return, he claimed entrepreneurs' relief, reducing the gain by four-ninths. HMRC rejected the claim on the basis that G had not disposed of 'an identifiable part of the business'. G appealed, contending that his business had comprised nine different parts (ie one part for each of the suppliers he represented), and that he had disposed of one of those parts. The First-Tier Tribunal accepted this contention and allowed his appeal, finding that G had sold part of his business as a going concern. Judge Radford held that 'what characterises a sale as a going concern is a sale of goodwill where it exists'. G had sold the goodwill and had 'also sold his customer database, a crucial asset in distinguishing a sale of a going concern from a mere sale of assets'. *M Gilbert (t/a United Foods) v HMRC*, FTT [2011] UKFTT 705 (TC), TC01542.

Disposal of land

[71.262] Three brothers had inherited some farmland, which they farmed in partnership. In 2009 they disposed of about 35% of the land, but continued to farm the remainder. One of the brothers (R) claimed entrepreneurs' relief in respect of his share of the gain on the disposal. HMRC rejected the claim on the basis that the disposal was simply the disposal of a business asset, rather than the disposal of part of the partnership business, and did not qualify as a material disposal under *TCGA 1992, s 169I*. The First-tier Tribunal dismissed R's appeal, applying the principles laid down by Fox J in *McGregor v Adcock*, **71.239** above, and Lightman J in *Barrett v Powell*, **71.245** above. *WSG Russell v HMRC*, FTT [2012] UKFTT 623 (TC), TC02299.

Requirements of TCGA 1992, s 169I(4)(b)

[71.263] A trader (R) had sold second-hand cars. In 2008 he sold the premises from which he had traded to a property developer. He claimed entrepreneurs' relief on the disposal. HMRC rejected the claim on the basis that a letter from R's accountant had stated that R had ceased to trade more than three years before the date on which he sold the premises, so that the disposal failed to meet the requirements of *TCGA 1992, s 169I(4)(b)*. R appealed, contending that the information in the letter from his accountant had been incorrect. Judge Brannan accepted R's evidence and allowed his appeal. *J Rice v HMRC*, FTT [2014] UKFTT 133 (TC), TC03273.

Requirements of TCGA 1992, s 169I(6)(b)

[71.264] A company (K) purchased the shares in another company (OI) in October 2009. A woman (SC), who had previously been employed by OI, and whose husband (MC) was a director of OI, claimed entrepreneurs' relief on the sale of her 1500 shares. HMRC rejected the claim on the grounds that SC had ceased to be employed by OI in February 2009, and had therefore not been an employee of OI for the whole of the year ending with the disposal, as required by *TCGA 1992, s 169I(6)(b)*. SC appealed, contending that although she had been removed from OI's payroll in February 2009, because K had a clear policy of not employing directors' wives, she had in fact continued to work for OI, which had increased MC's salary to compensate for not paying SC. The First-tier Tribunal accepted this contention and allowed her appeal, finding that 'the motivation for removing (SC) from the payroll at the end of February 2009 was to keep her out of sight of the potential purchaser because of (K's) sensitivity to the employment of spouses of senior executives'. *Mrs S Corbett v HMRC*, FTT [2014] UKFTT 298 (TC), TC03435.

[71.265] A company (W) carried on a business of arranging corporate finance. In December 2007 one of its directors (H) resigned. H sold his shares in W in July 2009. In his 2009/10 tax return, he claimed entrepreneurs' relief. HMRC rejected the claim on the grounds that H had not been either an officer or an employee of W during the year ending with the disposal of his shareholding, so that the conditions of *TCGA 1992, s 169I(6)(b)* were not satisfied. H appealed, contending that he had continued to act as a *de facto* director of W despite his formal resignation, although it had not been considered appropriate for him to be acknowledged as a director as he had been facing criminal charges. (He had been convicted of assault, but acquitted of other charges.) The First-tier Tribunal allowed H's appeal. Judge Kempster held that H had been acting as a 'significant shareholder', rather than as a *de facto* director, during the period in question. However he had been 'entitled to commissions for the introduction of new business' and there had been 'an employment relationship' between W and H. Therefore he met the conditions of *s 169I(6)(b)* and qualified for relief. *R Hirst v HMRC*, FTT [2014] UKFTT 924 (TC), TC04038.

Groups of companies (TCGA 1992, ss 170–181)

Transactions within groups (TCGA 1992, ss 171–175)

Transfers within a group—interpretation of TCGA 1992, s 171(2)

[71.266] A company (F) went into liquidation in 1961. Its parent company (W) received a capital distribution of shares in a public quoted company (C), which had a market value of 13s 4d each. The value fell to 6s 3d by 6 April1965, although this still exceeded their cost to F. W made various sales of the shares and the Revenue issued assessments on the gains, treating the consideration for the shares as 6s 3d each. W appealed, contending that the cost should be taken as 13s 4d each. The Ch D rejected this contention and upheld the assessments. The reference in what is now *TCGA 1992, s 171(2)* to what is now *TCGA 1992, s 122* applied to W's disposal of its shares in F, but not to the shares in C which it acquired on F's liquidation. *Innocent v Whaddon Estates Ltd*, Ch D 1981, 55 TC 476; [1982] STC 115.

Avoidance scheme—whether TCGA 1992, s 171 applicable

[71.267] A company (H) owned the share capital of a subsidiary company (B) and was itself wholly owned by a parent company (BC). BC agreed, subject to contract, to sell B to an unconnected company (S). To avoid the chargeable gain which would have arisen on a direct sale, a scheme was carried out whereby a new company (V) was formed with capital of 76 £1 participating preference shares held by H and 24 £1 ordinary shares held by S. Another company (Z) was formed with share capital owned by V. Z bought the shares in B from money lent to it by S. V then went into liquidation, and the liquidator transferred its shares in Z to S as the ordinary shareholder of V. The

Revenue assessed H on the basis that it had sold the shares in B to S, considering that the interposition of V and Z should be ignored as they had acted as nominees or agents for S. H appealed, contending that the sale to Z was within what is now *TCGA 1992, s 171*. The Special Commissioners accepted this contention and allowed the appeal, and the Ch D upheld their decision. *Burman v Hedges & Butler Ltd*, Ch D 1978, 52 TC 501; [1979] STC 136; [1979] 1 WLR 160. (*Note*. The definition of a group of companies was amended by *FA 1989* with effect from 13 March 1989. See now *TCGA 1992, s 170*.)

Transfer of assets within a group in exchange for shares

[71.268] In 1965 a company (H) acquired the issued share capital of three companies for £1.27m. In 1966 it transferred this to a wholly-owned subsidiary (T) in exchange for ordinary shares in T, credited as fully paid. In December 1971 T sold the shares in the three companies to an associated company (W), which was also wholly-owned subsidiary of H, for £601,235. On 7 January 1972 the three companies went into voluntary liquidation. W received assets with a market value of £601,235 on the distribution. It appealed against a corporation tax assessment for the period to 31 March 1972, contending that the effect of *FA 1965, Sch 13* was that the cost of the shares should be treated as the £1.27m which H had paid for them. The General Commissioners accepted this contention and allowed W's appeal. The CA upheld this decision, holding that the policy of *Sch 13* was to ignore transactions in a group and compute gains and losses by comparing the consideration paid when the asset came into the group with the consideration received when it left the group. *Westcott v Woolcombers Ltd*, CA 1987, 60 TC 575; [1987] STC 600. (*Note*. See now *TCGA 1992, s 171(3)*, deriving from *FA 1988*.)

[71.269] The decision in *Westcott v Woolcombers Ltd*, **71.268** above, was approved by the HL in a subsequent case in which the appellant company (N) had made a substantial gain in 1985 on the disposal of shares which it had acquired from its holding company (O) in 1983 as part of a share exchange. The Revenue issued an assessment on the basis that the original price paid by O for the shares should be treated as N's acquisition cost. N appealed, contending that its acquisition cost should be taken to be the market value of the shares at the time it acquired them from O. The Special Commissioner rejected this contention and dismissed the appeal. The HL upheld the Commissioner's decision (by a 4-1 majority, Lord Lloyd dissenting). Lord Keith held that, in relation to a group of companies, 'gains and losses should be computed by reference to the consideration paid when an asset comes into the group and the consideration received when it goes out'. Lord Jauncey observed that the 'underlying philosophy' of the legislation was 'to secure that shareholders in companies which are involved in reorganisations of share capital or which are the subject of amalgamations or take-overs do not incur chargeable gains on disposals over which they have little or no control'. *NAP Holdings UK Ltd v Whittles*, HL 1994, 67 TC 166; [1994] STC 979. (*Notes*. (1) See now *TCGA 1992, s 171(3)*, deriving from *FA 1988*. (2) For subsequent proceedings in this case, see *NAP Holdings UK Ltd v United Kingdom*, **31.96** HUMAN RIGHTS.)

Joint election under TCGA 1992, s 171A—whether effective

[71.270] In 1998 a company (D), which was a member of a group, sold its shares in a New Zealand subsidiary in exchange for loan notes which were qualifying corporate bonds, so that the gain on the sale was held over until D disposed of the loan notes. D's holding company (B) had realised significant capital losses. B and D entered into a series of transactions with the aim of setting B's capital losses against some of D's held-over gains. In November 2003 D redeemed the loan notes. In December 2003 D and an associated company (G) made an election under *TCGA 1992, s 171A* as then in force, deeming the disposal of the loan notes to have been made by G rather than D, with the intention that the held-over gain would accrue to G rather than to D and could be set against the capital losses (which had accrued to G by virtue of an election under *TCGA 1992, s 179*). HMRC began an enquiry into the transactions, and issued a ruling that the election under *s 171A* was not effective, so that D was required to account for the CGT due on the redemption of the loan notes. (HMRC accepted that, if D had transferred the loan notes to G before their redemption, then that transfer would have fallen within *s 171(1)*.) D appealed, contending inter alia that the satisfaction of a debt should be treated as a disposal of the debt to the debtor by the creditor. The Upper Tribunal rejected this contention and dismissed D's appeal. Rose J held that, on the facts here, 'it is not possible to identify someone to whom the debt is disposed of when it is satisfied', and that the repayment of the loan notes did not constitute a disposal of either the debt or the loan notes for the purposes of *s 171A*. *Dmwshnz Ltd v HMRC*, UT [2014] UKUT 98 (TCC); [2014] STC 1440. (*Note. TCGA 1992, s 171A* was subsequently amended by *FA 2009, s 31*. See now *TCGA 1992, s 171A(4)*, which enables two group companies to make a joint election.)

Avoidance scheme—whether TCGA 1992, s 173(1) applicable

[71.271] A company (S) had acquired and developed property at a cost of £5,313,822. By 1973, its market value had fallen to £3,100,000, and S assigned the property to an associated company (P) for £3,090,000. On the same day, P assigned the property to an associated investment company (T) for £3,100,000. P then made a purported election under what is now *TCGA 1992, s 161(3)* whereby the transfer from S to P would give rise to no loss or gain for CGT purposes, and in computing P's trading profits it could treat the cost of the property as its market value plus the CGT loss which would have accrued under *s 161(1)* if the election had not been made. The Revenue assessed P on the basis that the election was invalid, considering that P had not acquired the property as trading stock within the meaning of what is now *TCGA 1992, s 173(1)*. The HL unanimously upheld the assessment, holding that P had not acquired the lease as trading stock. The transfer of the lease from S to P and from P to T was procured with the object of obtaining group relief, and did not change the lease from a capital asset to a trading asset. P had never had any intention of trading with the lease. *Coates v Arndale Properties Ltd*, HL 1984, 59 TC 516; [1984] STC 637; [1984] 1 WLR 1328; [1985] 1 All ER 15.

[71.272] In March 1973 a company (L) acquired a company (N) which traded in shares and securities. In August 1973 L sold shares in a German company, and debts owed by two associated overseas companies, to N for their market value of £30,000. These assets had cost L almost £4,000,000, and had not been part of L's trading stock. N purported to make an election under what is now *TCGA 1992, s 161(3)* in respect of the assets acquired, and appealed against a CT assessment, contending that the effect of the election was that it had made a loss of more than £3,900,000. The HL held that the election was valid with regard to the debts, as the Commissioners had been entitled to find that N had acquired the debts as trading stock. However the election was not valid with regard to the shares, which 'were not commercially saleable at any price'. *Reed v Nova Securities Ltd*, HL 1985, 59 TC 516; [1985] STC 124; [1985] 1 WLR 193; [1985] 1 All ER 686. (*Note.* The CA heard this case with *Coates v Arndale Properties Ltd*, 71.271 above, but the HL heard the cases separately.)

[71.273] See also *Mr & Mrs R v Holden*, 48.85 RESIDENCE.

Transfer of properties within a group—whether within TCGA 1992, s 173

[71.274] On 13 November 1996 a company (N), which was a member of a group, acquired nine properties from other companies in the same group. The properties had previously been held as investments. Between 18 November 1996 and March 1997 it sold all but one of the properties. In its corporation tax return for the period ending 31 December 1996, it claimed that it had acquired the properties as trading stock, within *TCGA 1992, s 173*, and that the market value of the properties on 13 November 1996 should be increased by the amount of the loss which would have arisen if they had been sold at market value on that date, within *TCGA 1992, s 161*. Subsequently the Revenue issued a notice of determination that the properties had not been acquired as trading stock, so that the claimed loss was not available for group relief. The CA allowed N's appeal. Jonathan Parker LJ held that 'fiscal considerations (whether they be described in terms of motive, purpose or object) must be put entirely on one side in considering whether an asset was acquired "as trading stock" for the purposes of *section 173(1)*'. On the evidence, he held that N had acquired the properties as 'trading stock' within *s 173(1)*, since they 'were assets of a kind which were sold in the ordinary course of (N's) trade' and were acquired by N 'for the purposes of that trade, with a view to resale at a profit'. *New Angel Court Ltd v Adam*, CA 2004, 76 TC 9; [2004] STC 779; [2004] EWCA Civ 242; [2004] 1 WLR 1988.

Leaseback arrangement—claim to rollover relief under TCGA 1992, s 175

[71.275] See *CIR v Richmond & Jones (re Loquitur Ltd)*, 13.9 COMPANY LIQUIDATION AND RECEIVERSHIP.

Losses attributable to depreciatory transactions (TCGA 1992, ss 176–177B)

Depreciatory transaction within a group—TCGA 1992, s 176

[71.276] On 11 February 1991 S was a subsidiary company of H, which in turn was a subsidiary of T. On 12 February H sold S to T for well below its market value. This sale had the effect of reducing the market value of H from more than £1,000,000,000 (the actual value had not been agreed) to about

£2,000,000. On 14 February T sold H to an unrelated company for about £40,000,000 (this price reflected ACT prospectively recoverable by the purchaser). Subsequently T appealed against an assessment on chargeable gains, contending that the effect of indexation allowance (based on the value of H at 31 March 1982) was that it had made an allowable loss of some £740,000,000 on the sale of H. (T had claimed that H's market value at 31 March 1982 was about £1,200,000,000, the indexation allowance on which was £778,000,000.) The Revenue rejected the claim, considering that the loss on the sale of H was eliminated by what is now *TCGA 1992, s 176*. The Special Commissioners dismissed T's appeal and the Ch D upheld their decision, holding that *s 176* had to be applied to the allowable loss after indexation, rather than to the unindexed loss before indexation. Sir Richard Scott VC observed that the purpose of *s 176* was 'to prevent allowable losses being produced by depreciatory transactions'. *Tesco plc v Crimmin*, Ch D 1997, 69 TC 510; [1997] STC 981.

[71.277] P was a subsidiary company of W. In 1987 and 1988 W disposed of P's assets, at less than market value, to another member of the same group. In 1990 W disposed of P's share capital at a loss. W subsequently sought to set this loss against chargeable gains on a later disposal. It was accepted that, for the purposes of what is now *TCGA 1992, s 176(5)*, there had been a diminution of value of £3,212,740, which was attributable to the depreciatory transactions in 1987 and 1988. The Revenue issued a CT assessment on the basis that the effect of *s 176(4)* was that the allowable loss should be further reduced by £923,569 (being an amount equal to indexation allowance on £3,212,740 between the dates of the depreciatory transactions and the date of the ultimate disposal in 1990). W appealed. The Special Commissioner upheld the assessment and dismissed W's appeal, holding that it was 'just and reasonable to adjust the values of the depreciatory transactions to take account of inflation'. The purpose of *s 176(5)* was to ensure 'that the allowable loss on the ultimate disposal of the shares does not reflect any diminution in value of the company's assets which was attributable to the depreciatory transaction. If the adjustment were not made, then the allowable loss on the ultimate disposal of the shares would not adequately reflect the diminution of assets which were (*sic*) attributable to the depreciatory transactions, as the allowable loss on the ultimate disposal would include the indexation allowance up to the date of the ultimate disposal on that part of the base cost of the shares which represented assets previously disposed of in the depreciatory transactions.' *Whitehall Electric Investments Ltd v Owen*, Sp C [2002] SSCD 229 (Sp C 312).

TCGA 1992, Sch 7A—restriction on set-off of pre-entry losses

[71.278] In May 2001 a public company (T) acquired a group of companies (D). Six companies in the group had incurred capital losses, totalling more than £4,000,000, before T had taken control of the group. The companies claimed that these losses could be set against capital gains made by another company in the group between May 2001 and March 2002. The Revenue issued notices of amendment, ruling that the effect of *TCGA 1992, Sch 7A* was the losses were 'pre-entry losses' which could not be set off in this way. The Special Commissioner (Dr. Avery Jones) upheld the Revenue's notices and dismissed the companies' appeals. The Commissioner upheld the Revenue's interpretation of *Sch 7A, para 1(6)*, observing that 'the purpose of the provision deeming the company to have become a member of the relevant group at the time of the merger of the groups must be in order to deal with a loss accruing before that time'. *Five Oaks Properties Ltd v HMRC (and related appeals)*, Sp C [2006] SSCD 769 (Sp C 563).

[71.279] A company (C) had incurred substantial capital losses. On 26 September 2000 its parent company (AU) transferred C's share capital to two of AU's other subsidiary companies (L and P) for a nominal consideration of £1 each. On the following day AU sold its shares in L and P for £4,000,000 to an unrelated company (GL). L and P each claimed losses of more than £113,000,000 in their returns for the accounting period ending 30 September 2000. In their returns for the two subsequent accounting periods, they claimed that some of these losses should be set against gains by other companies in GL's group. The Revenue rejected the claims on the basis that the effect of *TCGA 1992, Sch 7A* was the losses were 'pre-entry losses' which could not be set off in this way. L and P appealed, contending that because GL had become part of a larger group in December 2000, the effect of *Sch 7A, para 1(6)(b)* was that the losses were available for set-off. The Ch D rejected this contenton and upheld the Revenue's rejection of the claims. Blackburne J held that *Sch 7A, para 1(6)* 'requires two separate conditions to be fulfilled if it is to apply and the operation of *section 170(10)* is to be modified. The first, set out in *sub-paragraph (a)*, is that there has at some time been a takeover of the first group by the second group so that the two groups are treated as the same by virtue of *section 170(10)*. The second, set out in *sub-paragraph (b)*, is that "the second group, together in pursuance of *section 170(10)* with the first group, is the relevant group"'. *Sch 7A, para 1(6)* was directed at losses which were 'pre-entry in relation to the second group' rather than at losses which were 'pre-entry in relation to the first group'. It should be construed as operating 'to put losses accruing to companies in a group which is subsequently taken over by another group on the same footing as losses accruing to a single company which is subsequently taken over by a group'. The reference to 'the relevant group' in *para 1(6)(b)* should be construed 'as confined to losses of the acquired (the first) group which are not pre-entry losses in relation to that group immediately before its acquisition by the acquiring (second) group'. The CA unanimously upheld this decision. Mummery LJ held that the losses claimed by the companies were 'not within the category of pre-entry losses identified on the hypothesis of *paragraph 1(6)(b)* of *Schedule 7A*. *Prizedome Ltd v HMRC; Limitgood Ltd v HMRC*, CA [2009] STC 980; [2009] EWCA Civ 177.

[71.280] The CA decision in *Prizedome Ltd v HMRC*, **71.279** above, was applied in the similar subsequent case of *Greathey Investments Ltd v HMRC (and related appeals)*, FTT [2013] UKFTT 461 (TC), TC02851.

Transfers of shares and properties to subsidiary company—whether trading

[71.281] See *N Ltd v HM Inspector of Taxes*, **59.67** TRADING INCOME.

Companies leaving groups (TCGA 1992, ss 178–181)

Principal group company becoming non-resident

[71.282] In May 1978 D, which had been the principal member of a group of companies, became non-resident. The Revenue issued an assessment on the basis that what is now *TCGA 1992, s 179* applied, so that D was deemed to have sold and immediately re-acquired shares in a subsidiary company, which it had acquired from another group member in March 1978. The Special Commissioners upheld the assessment, observing that the change of residence was 'an appropriate point at which to bring to an end the deferral of any gain or loss'. The Ch D and the CA dismissed D's appeal against this decision. Chadwick LJ observed that the object of *s 179* was 'to prevent the transferee company from taking the asset out of the group in circumstances in which the gain will not crystallise on a subsequent disposal — because there will be no subsequent disposal'. *Dunlop International AG v Pardoe (aka Lion Ltd v HM Inspector of Taxes)*, CA 1999, 72 TC 71; [1999] STC 909. (*Note*. See also *TCGA 1992, s 185*, deriving from *FA 1988*.)

Whether vendor company resident in UK

[71.283] On 1 July 1992 a group of companies (N) acquired control of a company (S) which was incorporated in Hong Kong. On 7 July S acquired a UK subsidiary (L). On 8 July S transferred its business assets to L, and on 9 July S disposed of L to another UK company in the N group. Subsequently the Revenue issued an assessment on L under what is now *TCGA 1992, s 179*. L appealed, contending *inter alia* that S had not been resident in the UK at the time it disposed of its business, so that the disposal did not give rise to a charge to UK tax. The Special Commissioners reviewed the evidence in detail, accepted this contention, and allowed the appeal in principle, finding that the relevant meetings of S's board had taken place in the USA, and that S had not been resident in the UK at the time it disposed of its business. (The Commissioners specifically declined to find whether S should be treated as resident in the USA or in Hong Kong.) *News Datacom Ltd v Atkinson (and related appeal)*, Sp C [2006] SSCD 732 (Sp C 561). (*Note*. L also contended that the effect of *TCGA 1992, s 178(10)* was that the assessment had been made outside the statutory time limit. The Commissioners rejected this contention, holding that the assessment had been made within the time limit laid down by *TMA, s 34*.)

Interpretation of TCGA 1992, s 179(2)

[71.284] A company (G) was a member of a group, the ultimate parent company being M. In 1997 G acquired a newly-incorporated company (H). On the same day H made a large rights issue of shares to G. Another company in the M group (P) sold its shares in certain subsidiary companies to H. The effect of *TCGA 1992, s 171* was that this was treated for tax purposes as producing no gain or loss to P. However, because H and P did not by themselves form a group, they did not fall within the definition of 'associated companies' in *TCGA 1992, s 179(10)*. Following this sale, P paid a dividend to its immediate parent company (R) within a group election under *ICTA 1988, s 247*. Following the payment of this dividend, R sold its shares in P to H. Again, the effect of *TCGA 1992, s 171* was that this was treated for tax purposes as producing no gain or loss to R. In 1998 G sold its shares in H to an outside purchaser (Y). H and its subsidiaries (including P) then ceased to be a member of the M group. The Revenue issued an assessment on H, charging tax under *TCGA 1992, s 179* in respect of the subsidiaries which it had acquired from P when both companies were members of the M group. H appealed, contending that since H and P had been associated when they both left the M group, the effect of *s 179(2)* was that no tax was due. The Special Commissioner rejected this contention and upheld the assessment in principle, holding that the exemption under *s 179(2)* only applied where both companies were associated, within *s 179(10)(a)*, at the time of the intra-group transfer. In this case, H and P had been associated within *s 179(10)(a)* when they left the group in 1998, but had not been associated within *s 179(10)(a)* at the time of the intra-group transfer in 1997. Accordingly they did not qualify for exemption and tax remained due. The CA dismissed H's appeal (by a 2-1 majority, Toulson LJ dissenting). Sir John Chadwick observed that the object of the legislation was 'to prevent the transferee from taking the asset out of the group without crystallising the gain (and the liability to tax) which would have arisen (had the transferor and transferee not been members of the same group) at the time that the transferee acquired the asset'. Tuckey LJ held that the word 'associated' was included in *s 179(2)* 'as part of the test to be applied as at the time of the acquisition', and was 'addressing the question whether the companies in question were associated as at the time of the acquisition'. *Johnston Publishing (North) Ltd v HMRC*, CA [2008] STC 3116; [2008] EWCA Civ 858. (*Note.* For HMRC's practice following this decision, see HMRC Brief 59/08, issued on 17 December 2008.)

Avoidance schemes—the Ramsay principle

NOTE

The HL decisions in *WT Ramsay Ltd v CIR*, **71.285** below, *Eilbeck v Rawling*, **71.286** below, and *Furniss v Dawson*, **71.288** below, clarified the attitude of the judiciary to artificial avoidance schemes. The HL approach to 'composite transactions' is commonly referred to as the *Ramsay* principle. See **58.6** to **58.11** TAX PLANNING AND AVOIDANCE for other cases in which the principle has been invoked.

Artificial avoidance scheme—whether a nullity for tax purposes

[71.285] A company (W), which had made a substantial gain on the sale of a farm, carried out several share and loan transactions with the object of creating a large tax loss. The loss emerged as one of about £175,000 on shares it subscribed for in a newly-formed company (C). The success of the scheme depended on W establishing that a loan to C, sold at a profit of about £173,000, was not a debt on a security within what is now *TCGA 1992, s 251(1)*. The acceptance of the offer of the loan was evidenced by a statutory declaration by a director of the borrowing company. The CA held that the loan, being evidenced by the statutory declaration, which represented a marketable security, was a debt on a security. The scheme therefore failed. W appealed to the HL, and the Revenue advanced the new argument that the scheme should be treated as a fiscal nullity producing neither loss nor gain. The HL accepted this approach and dismissed W's appeal. Lord Wilberforce held that although the *Duke of Westminster* principle (see **2.3** ANNUAL PAYMENTS) prevented a court from looking behind a genuine document or transaction to some supposed underlying substance, it did not 'compel the court to view a document or transaction in blinkers, isolated from any context to which it properly belongs'. The court was required 'to ascertain the legal nature of any transaction to which it is sought to attach a tax or a tax consequence and if that emerges from a series or combination of transactions, intended to operate as such, it is that series or combination which may be regarded'. The Commissioners were not 'bound to consider individually each separate step in a composite transaction intended to be carried through as a whole'. In such cases, the Commissioners 'should find the facts and then decide as a matter (reviewable) of law whether what is in issue is a composite transaction or a number of independent transactions'. Turning to the facts here, it was clear that the scheme was for tax avoidance with no commercial justification, and that it was the intention to proceed through all its stages to completion once set in motion. It would therefore be wrong to consider one step in isolation. The true view was that, regarding the scheme as a whole, there was neither a gain nor a loss. (The HL also upheld the CA decision that the relevant debt was a 'debt on a security'.) *WT Ramsay Ltd v CIR*, HL 1981, 54 TC 101; [1981] STC 174; [1981] 2 WLR 449; [1981] 1 All ER 865.

[71.286] An individual (R) made a chargeable gain of £355,094 in 1974/75 as to which there was no dispute. Later in the same year he entered into a chain of transactions with the object of creating a commensurate allowable loss, at a cost to him of only £370 apart from the fees, etc. paid for the scheme, which was an 'off-the-peg' avoidance device obtained from a Jersey company. The central feature of the scheme involved his acquiring reversionary interests in two trust funds, one held by Jersey trustees and the other by Gibraltar trustees. Under a special power of appointment, the Gibraltar trustees advanced £315,000 to the Jersey trustees to be held on the trusts of the Jersey settlement. R then sold both reversionary interests, making a gain on the sale of his interest under the Jersey settlement (claimed to be exempt under what is now *TCGA 1992, s 76(1)*) and a matching loss of £312,470 on the sale of his interest under the Gibraltar settlement (claimed as an allowable loss). The Revenue issued a CGT assessment on the chargeable gain with no allowance for the alleged loss on the sale of R's interest under the Gibraltar settlement. R appealed. The CA upheld the assessment, holding, *inter alia*, that the exercise of the power of appointment did not take the £315,000 outside the Gibraltar settlement; hence the sale of his reversionary interest in the £315,000 was a part sale of his interest under the Gibraltar settlement. R appealed to the HL, which heard the appeal with *WT Ramsay Ltd v CIR*, **71.285** above, and dismissed it for the same general reason that the scheme should be looked at as a composite transaction under which there was neither gain nor loss apart from the £370. Furthermore, the HL upheld the CA decision that the sale of the reversionary interest in the £315,000 was a sale of part of R's reversionary interest in the Gibraltar settlement. *Eilbeck v Rawling*, HL 1981, 54 TC 101; [1981] STC

174; [1981] 2 WLR 449; [1981] 1 All ER 865. (*Note*. The schemce would also now be caught by the value-shifting provisions of *TCGA 1992, s 30*.)

[71.287] A company (H), which was a member of a group, was dormant but owned stock with a market value substantially less than its acquisition cost. Its parent company (B) carried out a series of transactions including a capital reorganisation and the loan of £160,000,000 to H via another company in the same group. At the end of these transactions, B held the stock previously held by H, which had been put into liquidation. B appealed against a CT assessment, contending that it had made a loss of £160,000,000 on the disposal of its shareholding in H. The HL unanimously rejected this contention, holding that the transactions had 'no commercial purpose apart from the avoidance of a liability to tax', and should be disregarded. *CIR v Burmah Oil Co Ltd*, HL 1981, 54 TC 200; [1982] STC 30.

[71.288] The shareholders in two family companies wished to dispose of their shares, and found an unconnected company (W) willing to acquire the shares at an agreed price. Before disposing of the shares, they exchanged them for shares in a Manx company which in turn sold them to W. The Revenue issued assessments on the basis that the shares should be treated as having been disposed of directly to W, since the interposition of the Manx company had been designed solely to take advantage of the law then in force with regard to company reconstructions and amalgamations. The HL unanimously upheld the assessments, holding that the transactions should be regarded as a single composite transaction. Lord Bridge of Harwich observed that 'the distinction between form and substance' could 'usefully be drawn in determining the tax consequences of composite transactions'. Lord Brightman held that the *Ramsay* principle applied in cases where there was a 'pre-ordained series of transactions' or 'one single composite transaction' and steps were 'inserted which have no commercial (business) purpose apart from the avoidance of a liability to tax—not "no business effect". If these two ingredients exist, the inserted steps are to be disregarded for fiscal purposes. The court must look at the end result.' *Furniss v Dawson*, HL 1984, 55 TC 324; [1984] STC 153; [1984] 2 WLR 226; [1984] 1 All ER 530. (*Notes*. (1) See also *TCGA 1992, s 137*. (2) Although the decision was unanimous, there was implicit disagreement as to the continuing validity of the *Duke of Westminster* principle—see **58.3** TAX PLANNING AND AVOIDANCE. Lords Bridge and Scarman indicated that the principle still applied, but Lord Roskill specifically refrained from endorsing the *Westminster* decision. For subsequent developments, see the judgment of Lord Templeman in *Ensign Tankers (Leasing) Ltd v Stokes*, **59.85** TRADING INCOME, and the judgments of Lord Steyn and Lord Cooke in *CIR v McGuckian*, **3.64** ANTI-AVOIDANCE.)

[71.289] Three members of a family owned all the shares in a UK company (Q), which owned a number of shops. From 1973 they conducted negotiations with various other companies with a view to selling Q or merging it with a similar business. In 1976, at a time when they were negotiating with two unconnected companies, they exchanged their shares for shares in an Isle of Man company (M). Nineteen days later M sold the shares in Q to one of the two companies with which negotiations had been in progress at the time of the share exchange. The sale proceeds were paid by M to the shareholders over a period of five years. The Revenue issued CGT assessments on the basis that the disposal of the shares to M and their subsequent sale by M should be treated as a single composite transaction and that the transfer of the shares to M was a fiscal nullity. The Special Commissioners reduced the assessments, holding that the transfer could not be treated as a fiscal nullity but that the shareholders were assessable on the amounts they had received from M at the time of receipt. The HL upheld this decision (by a 3-2 majority, Lord Templeman and Lord Goff dissenting). Lord Oliver held that the principles adopted in *WT Ramsay Ltd v CIR*, **71.268** above—that the Commissioners are not bound to consider individually each step in a composite transaction intended to be carried through as a whole—applied only where there was a 'pre-ordained series of transactions' or 'one single composite transaction' and where steps were inserted which had no commercial purpose apart from the avoidance of a liability to tax. In this case, however, the transactions that the Revenue sought to reconstruct into a single direct disposal were not pre-ordained since, at the time of the share exchange, it was not certain what the ultimate destination of the property would be. Lord Jauncey considered that 'a step in a linear transaction which has no business purpose apart from the avoidance or deferment of tax liability will be treated as forming part of a pre-ordained series of transactions or of a composite transaction if it was taken at a time when negotiations or arrangements for the carrying through as a continuous process of a subsequent transaction which actually takes place had reached a stage when there was no real likelihood that such subsequent transaction would not take place and if thereafter such negotiations or arrangements were carried through to completion without genuine interruption'. Lord Oliver concurred with this definition. *Craven v White*, HL 1988, 62 TC 1; [1988] STC 476; [1988] 3 WLR 423; [1988] 3 All ER 495. (*Note*. With regard to Lord Oliver's endorsement of the *Duke of Westminster* principle, compare now the judgments of Lord Steyn and Lord Cooke in the 1997 case of *CIR v McGuckian*, **3.64** ANTI-AVOIDANCE. Lord Cooke of Thorndon described *Craven v White* as 'a difficult case, partly because of the differences of opinion in (the) House'.)

[71.290] A company (C) entered into negotiations to acquire another company (P). P's controlling director (G), and his associates set up a Manx company to exchange their shares in P with shares in the Manx company. C ended the negotiations, but the share exchange was proceeded with. No further steps were taken to sell P for 14 months, until a third company (H) became interested in it. Eventually, the Manx company sold the shares in P to H. The Revenue issued CGT assessments on the basis that G should be treated as having sold the shares to H, ignoring the interposition of the Manx company. The Special Commissioners allowed G's appeals and the HL upheld their decision, holding that the transactions were not a 'pre-ordained series of transactions'. *Baylis v Gregory (and related appeal)*, HL 1988, 62 TC 1; [1988] STC 476; [1988] 3 WLR 423; [1988] 3 All ER 495. (*Notes*. (1) For another issue in this case, see **5.108** ASSESSMENTS. (2) The HL heard the case with *Craven v White*, **71.273** above.)

[71.291] The trustees of an unapproved pension scheme disposed of a substantial shareholding for more than £9,000,000. They subsequently entered into a tax avoidance scheme with the aim of creating a capital loss. They borrowed some money, subscribed for shares in a company at a premium, received a similar sum back as a dividend, repaid the amount they had borrowed, and then (five months later) sold the shares for a small sum representing the assets left in the company reduced by a small amount for the purchaser. Since the dividend was received as income, the trustees claimed that it should be ignored in computing the capital loss on the shares of the difference between the subscription price and the sale price. The Revenue rejected the loss claim, and the Special Commissioner dismissed the trustees' appeal, finding that the transactions had no commercial purpose, but were undertaken for 'the sole purpose of creating a capital loss'. The Commissioner held that the fact that the purchaser had not been identified in advance was 'a commercially irrelevant condition that should be ignored', since 'a purchaser for a company containing cash would be found who would be given a turn so that it was effectively buying cash at a discount'. The decision in *Craven v White*, **71.289** above, was distinguished, since that case concerned 'the genuine sale of a trading company to a third party', which was not the case here. The transactions formed a self-cancelling single composite transaction, so that for the purposes of the CGT legislation 'there was neither an acquisition of shares, nor a dividend, nor a disposal of shares'. There was 'no difficulty in treating the dividend, which is outside the capital gains tax computation, as effectively cancelling the acquisition cost of the shares'. Accordingly there was no capital loss. *Trustees of the Eyretel Unapproved Pension Scheme v HMRC*, Sp C 2008, [2009] SSCD 17 (Sp C 718).

[71.292] See also *Schofield v HMRC*, **71.114** above.

Private residences (TCGA 1992, ss 222–226)

Relief on disposal of private residence (TCGA 1992, s 222)

Farmhouse inhabited by claimant for only 32 days

[71.293] A company (S) had exchanged contracts for the purchase of a farm, which included a nine-bedroomed farmhouse. It agreed that, following completion of the purchase, it would sell the farmhouse to one of its directors (G). S completed the purchase of the farmhouse on 7 March 1985, and completed the sale to G on 1 April. G, who was in the process of separating from his wife, had already instructed estate agents with regard to the sale of the farmhouse, but moved into it immediately. On 3 April G completed the purchase of a small cottage, and on 11 April he advertised the farmhouse for sale. He continued to live in the farmhouse until 3 May, when he completed the sale of the farmhouse and moved into the cottage. He appealed against a CGT assessment, contending that the gain on the sale of the farmhouse was eligible for relief under what is now *TCGA 1992, s 222*. The General Commissioners rejected this contention, finding that G had not intended to occupy the farmhouse as his permanent residence, and the Ch D and CA upheld their decision as one of fact. *Goodwin v Curtis*, CA 1998, 70 TC 478; [1998] STC 475.

Whether flat used as principal private residence

[71.294] A market trader (F) purchased a flat in 1999. He transferred it to his son in 2003. HMRC issued an assessment charging CGT on the disposal, and F appealed, contending that he was entitled to principal private residence relief as he had occupied the flat as his residence during 2001 after temporarily splitting up with his partner, but had resumed living with her later in the year (and had subsequently married her). The First-tier Tribunal dismissed the appeal, finding that he had not shown that he had lived in the flat as his principal residence. *P Favell v HMRC*, FTT [2010] UKFTT 360 (TC), TC00642.

[71.295] Similar decisions were reached in *A Metcalfe v HMRC (No 1)*, FTT [2010] UKFTT 495 (TC), TC00753; *Miss A Bradley v HMRC*, FTT [2011] UKFTT 49 (TC), TC00927, and *Dr S Iles & Dr D Kaltsas v HMRC*, FTT [2014] UKFTT 436 (TC), TC03565.

Whether house used as principal private residence

[71.296] An individual (M) purchased a terraced house, which was in poor condition, in 1999. He renovated it, and sold it in 2004. HMRC issued an assessment charging CGT, and M appealed, contending that he should be entitled to principal private residence relief because he had lived at the property for two months while he had been renovating it. The First-tier Tribunal reviewed the evidence and dismissed the appeal, finding that M's fiancée had refused to live in the property and that M had never occupied it as his main residence. *JT Moore v HMRC*, FTT [2010] UKFTT 445 (TC), TC00710.

[71.297] An individual (S) was divorced in 1997. He sold his former matrimonial home in 1998 and began staying with his brother. In 1999 he purchased a house which was in very poor condition. He began renovating it, and in 2000 he let it to students. He sold it in 2005. HMRC formed the opinion that the house had never been S's principal private residence, and issued an amendment to S's self-assessment for 2005/06. The First-tier Tribunal dismissed S's appeal, finding that he had 'failed to discharge the burden of proof' that he had occupied the house as his residence. Judge Brannan observed that the electricity bills had been minimal, there had been no cooking facilities, and 'the gas had been switched off until March 2000 with the result that there was no hot water available for washing'. To the extent that S had occupied the house, 'he did so for the purpose of renovating the property rather than occupying it as his home which he expected to occupy with some degree of continuity'. *M Springthorpe v HMRC*, FTT [2010] UKFTT 582 (TC), TC00832.

[71.298] Similar decisions were reached in *D Lowrie v HMRC*, FTT [2011] UKFTT 309 (TC), TC01170; *P Gibson v HMRC*, FTT [2013] UKFTT 636 (TC), TC03021, and *Miss A Clarke v HMRC*, FTT [2014] UKFTT 949 (TC), TC04062.

[71.299] An individual (B), who was married and worked as a tiler in the construction industry, purchased a dilapidated house for £124,000 and sold it six months later for £175,000. HMRC issued a CGT assessment and B appealed, contending that he had used the house as his principal private residence while he had been temporarily separated from his wife. The First-tier Tribunal rejected this contention and dismissed the appeal, finding that B's post had continued to be delivered to the matrimonial home and he had admitted that he had continued to have baths and showers there. The electricity bills indicated that very little electricity had been consumed during the six months in which B owned the house. B had told the local council that the house was empty and that he was still living at the matrimonial home (so that he had been granted exemption from council tax). Although it was accepted that B had spent some nights at the house, 'there was not sufficient assumption of permanence or degree or expectation of continuity to turn such occupation into residence'. The tribunal also noted that B's wife had given birth to a son in November, so that B had 'not discharged the burden of proof required to demonstrate that he was separated from his wife in such circumstances that the separation was likely to be permanent'. *M Benford v HMRC*, FTT [2011] UKFTT 457 (TC), TC01309.

[71.300] A couple purchased a house in 1976 and moved into it in 1977. In 1996 one of them (L) purchased a second house, which was in poor condition. He renovated it and subsequently began letting it. In 2007 he sold it. HMRC subsequently issued a closure notice charging CGT on the sale. L appealed, contending that he had occupied the second house as his principal private residence for 16 months in 1997 and 1998, at a time when his relationship with his partner had temporarily deteriorated. The First-tier Tribunal reviewed the evidence in detail and dismissed L's appeal, finding that 'there was no independent evidence to show that his occupation of the property amounted to residence there with some degree of permanence, some degree of continuity or expectation of continuity'. *W Llewellyn v HMRC*, FTT [2013] UKFTT 323 (TC), TC02726.

[71.301] A financial adviser (M) purchased a two-bedroomed house (110H) in 2002. He let it to tenants until November 2006, when he moved into it after separating from his wife. However he arranged for correspondence to be sent to the house of his new partner (J), with whom he purchased another house in July 2007 (and whom he subsequently married after divorcing his first wife). In August 2007 M sold 110H. HMRC issued an amendment to his self-assessment, charging CGT on the gain. The First-tier Tribunal dismissed M's appeal, finding that M's occupation of the house 'did not have any degree of permanence or expectation of continuity' and that he had 'an expectation of being able to move from (110H) and set up home by buying a house jointly with (J)'. M had never envisaged 110H as a long-term home, so that his occupation of it did not constitute 'residence' for the purposes of *TCGA 1992, ss 222, 223*. *P Moore v HMRC*, FTT [2013] UKFTT 433 (TC), TC02827.

[71.302] A doctor (E) agreed to purchase a house in December 2006, completed the purchase in March 2007, but sold the house in May 2007, realising a gain of £550,000. HMRC issued an assessment on charging CGT on the gain. The First-tier Tribunal dismissed E's appeal, observing that EO 'had chosen (or been advised) not to attend or give evidence'. *Dr A Eghbal-Omidi*, FTT [2013] UKFTT 449 (TC), TC02841.

[71.303] A married couple had lived together, with their two daughters, on a farm. The wife began an affair, and in July 2002 the husband (C) purchased a nearby house, and moved into it with his elder daughter. He obtained planning permission to build a second house on part of the land. In March 2003 he sold the house for financial reasons, but retained the land for which he had obtained planning permission, and built a new house on the site. He moved into the new house in July 2003 (having stayed at his mother's house for the intervening four months). In July 2005 he moved back to the farm with his wife, and in October 2005 he sold the house which he had built in 2003. C and his wife subsequently divorced, and he moved into another house with his daughters. In 2009 HMRC issued assessments charging capital gains tax on the disposals of the houses which C had sold in March 2003 and October 2005. C appealed, contending that he was entitled to principal private residence relief for both houses. The First-tier Tribunal allowed his appeal, finding that at the time C moved into the houses, 'he intended to live there permanently'. *AJ Clarke v HMRC*, FTT [2011] UKFTT 619 (TC), TC01461.

[71.304] A married couple lived together in a house which they had owned for several years. The husband (H) had also inherited a house from his father, which his stepmother occupied as her residence until she died in May 2007. H subsequently gave his wife a joint interest in this house. In October 2007 the couple sold it to the owner of a neighbouring property. They claimed private residence relief. HMRC issued an amendment charging CGT on the sale, and the First-tier Tribunal dismissed the couple's appeal. Judge Staker observed that 'occupation of a property, or merely staying in a property, is not sufficient on its own to make the property a residence for PRR purposes. It must be occupied in such a manner that it becomes a person's home.' *MJ & Mrs BA Harte v HMRC*, FTT [2012] UKFTT 258 (TC), TC01951.

[71.305] A woman (B) lived in a house (AR) which she owned jointly with her husband. She also owned a flat and a second house (ER), both of which had been let to tenants. In 2007 she separated from her husband and moved into the flat. In April 2008, after her tenants had moved out, she moved into ER but in November 2008 she moved back into AR with her husband. In January 2009 she sold ER. HMRC issued an assessment charging CGT on the gain. The First-tier Tribunal dismissed B's appeal, observing that she had already advertised ER for sale before she began living there and finding that 'it was always only ever going to be a temporary home, and therefore it was never her residence'. *Mrs S Bradley v HMRC*, FTT [2013] UKFTT 131 (TC), TC02560.

[71.306] A married couple purchased a house in May 2000. In February 2003 they agreed to sell that house to a company, which intended to demolish it to make way for a new access road. They purchased the house next door (No 93), which needed complete modernisation. They installed a new bathroom and kitchen, and moved into No 93 in June 2003. They lived there until May 2004, when they moved into another house in the same town. They subsequently added an extension to No 93, and in 2006 they sold it. HMRC issued an assessment charging CGT on their gain on the sale. The First-tier Tribunal allowed the couple's appeal, finding that they had occupied No 93 as their principal private residence. *J & Mrs S Regan v HMRC*, FTT [2012] UKFTT 569 (TC), TC02246. (*Note*. For another issue in this case, see **44.133** PENALTIES.)

[71.307] An individual (R) purchased a house in 1994. He renovated the house and took in a married couple as lodgers. In 1998 he purchased a house with his girlfriend, and moved into it. He sold his old house to his parents in 2000. HMRC issued an assessment charging CGT on the gain on the sale. The First-tier Tribunal allowed R's appeal, finding that he had occupied the house as his principal private residence. *D Regan v HMRC*, FTT [2012] UKFTT 570 (TC), TC02247.

[71.308] In 2001 a man (M), who was engaged to be married, agreed to purchase a house. Shortly before the completion of the purchase, his fiancée ended the engagement. M moved into the house on 15 June and moved out on 30 August. He rented the house to tenants from then until March 2006. He then moved back into the house, but sold it four months later. HMRC issued an assessment charging tax on the gain. M appealed, contending that the house had qualified as his principal private residence. The First-tier Tribunal accepted this contention and allowed his appeal. Judge Gort held that, when M moved into the house, 'it was his intention to make it his permanent residence'. *D Morgan v HMRC*, FTT [2013] UKFTT 181 (TC), TC02596.

Part of garden retained on sale of house and subsequently sold

[71.309] An individual (L) owned and occupied a house and garden (of less than one acre). He sold the house and part of the garden in June 1971. In May 1972 he sold the rest of the garden, for which he had meanwhile obtained planning permission, at a substantial profit. The Revenue issued an assessment charging CGT on the gain. The Ch D upheld the assessment, holding that what is now *TCGA 1992, s 222(1)(b)* related only to the actual moment of disposal of the land. *Varty v Lynes*, Ch D 1976, 51 TC 419; [1976] STC 508; [1976] 1 WLR 1091; [1976] 3 All ER 447.

Sale of field inherited with bungalow

[71.310] A woman (W) had inherited a bungalow and a nearby field in 1969. The bungalow was about 10 yards from the field, but was separated from it by a cottage in separate ownership. W and her family used the field for many years but sold it, in two plots, in 1987 and 1988. The Revenue issued assessments charging tax on the gains. The Special Commissioner allowed W's appeal, holding that the distance between the bungalow and the field was not sufficient to disqualify the field from qualifying as 'garden or grounds' for the purposes of what is now *TCGA 1992, s 222(1)(b)*. On the evidence, the field had been used for many years as part of the 'garden or grounds'. *Wakeling v Pearce (aka Wakeling v Maidment)*, Sp C [1995] SSCD 96 (Sp C 32). (*Note*. For the Revenue's practice following this decision, see Revenue Tax Bulletin August 1995, p 239.)

Sale of land adjoining house

[71.311] A woman (D) owned a house with a large garden and grounds. In 2007 she sold part of the land, with planning permission for the construction of four houses, to a company (L), of which she was a director, for £300,000. In her tax return she claimed that the sale qualified for relief under *TCGA 1992, s 222*. HMRC rejected the claim on the basis that the land was already under development at the date when contracts were exchanged. The First-tier

Tribunal allowed D's appeal. Judge Connell found that L had been 'allowed onto the land disposed of to start foundation work on an informal basis', and held that the land had 'retained its character as "garden or grounds" within the meaning of *s 222(1)(b)* until the time of its disposal on 27 July 2007 when contracts were exchanged'. *Mrs A Dickinson v HMRC*, FTT [2013] UKFTT 653 (TC), TC03037.

[71.312] A woman and her son owned a house with 1.54 acres of adjoining land. They sold the house and land to a developer in one transaction for £725,000. They attributed £325,000 of this to the house, and as qualifying for relief under *TCGA 1992, s 222*, and £400,000 to the land, which they accepted as not qualifying for relief. HMRC issued a determination that only £170,000 should be attributed to the house, and that £555,000 was attributable to the land. The Upper Tribunal allowed the vendors' appeal, holding that 'the figure to be apportioned to the house could not be less than the £325,000 for which the appellants contend'. *R & Mrs D Oates v HMRC*, UT [2014] UKUT 409 (LC).

Whether caravan a dwelling-house

[71.313] An engineer had purchased some land on which to build a house. While construction was in progress, he lived with his family in a wheeled caravan jacked up and resting on bricks on the land, with water, electricity and telephone installed. Before completing the house, he sold the site, with the caravan. The Revenue assessed him on the gain but the Ch D allowed his appeal, holding that the caravan qualified for relief under what is now *TCGA 1992, s 222*. *Makins v Elson*, Ch D 1976, 51 TC 437; [1977] STC 46; [1977] 1 WLR 221; [1977] 1 All ER 572.

[71.314] In 1973 a couple (M and JM) purchased a farmhouse, which needed extensive renovation. M purchased a caravan which was towed onto the courtyard of the farmhouse, and where he stayed while renovating the farmhouse. In 1976 the couple separated. In 1977 JM and her children stayed for two weeks in the caravan, and she continued to stay there for short periods while working on the farmhouse. In 1978 she purchased M's share in the farmhouse, and wrote to the Revenue, purporting to elect that the farmhouse had been her main residence since 1974. In 1979 she sold the farmhouse (which she had never lived in) and the caravan. The Revenue issued a CGT assessment, and the Ch D dismissed JM's appeal. Millett J observed that JM's occupation of the caravan was 'sporadic and occasional'. *Moore v Thompson*, Ch D 1986, 61 TC 15; [1986] STC 170.

Bungalow separated from main house—whether part of house

[71.315] An individual (W) owned a house in Marlborough, built on 1.1 acres of land, but lived with his family in a London flat during the week, returning to the house at weekends. He had elected under what is now *TCGA 1992, s 222(5)* for the house to be treated as his main residence. After a burglary, he had a bungalow built on the land, which was occupied by a farmworker who acted as a caretaker. In 1974 W began living in the house on a full-time basis and, no longer needing a caretaker, sold the bungalow with 0.2 acres of land. The Revenue issued a CGT assessment but the General Commissioners allowed W's appeal, finding that the bungalow had qualified as part of W's dwelling-house, and holding that the occupation by the caretaker amounted to occupation by W as part of his residence. The CA upheld the Commissioners' decision as one of fact. *Batey v Wakefield*, CA 1981, 55 TC 550; [1981] STC 521; [1982] 1 All ER 61. (*Note*. *Dicta* of Fox LJ were subsequently disapproved by the CA in *Lewis v Rook*, **71.318** below.)

[71.316] In 1951 a woman had purchased a four-acre estate with a main house and outbuildings 130 metres from the main entrance gates. In 1963 she sold this to her daughter (S), who had acquired 9 acres of adjoining land in 1956. In 1965 S built a three-bedroom bungalow by the entrance gates, with a quarter-acre garden, which was occupied rent-free by a gardener and housekeeper. In 1980 S sold the whole estate, including the bungalow, to a single purchaser. The Revenue issued a CGT assessment on the sale of the bungalow. The Ch D upheld the assessment, distinguishing *Batey v Wakefield*, **71.315** above, and holding that the bungalow was not part of S's residence. *Markey v Sanders*, Ch D 1987, 60 TC 245; [1987] STC 256; [1987] 1 WLR 864.

[71.317] In 1956 a barrister (M) purchased a small estate in Sussex comprising a main house with 4 acres of garden and land and a lodge at the entrance of the estate, about 200 metres from the house. The house became his main residence and the lodge was occupied by a married couple (L and his wife) whom he employed as caretaker/gardener and domestic help. In 1976 M sold the main house and estate, but retained the lodge and allowed L to continue living in it. L died in 1979 and M then sold the lodge to the purchaser of the main house. The Revenue issued a CGT assessment but the General Commissioners allowed M's appeal, finding that from 1956 to 1976 the lodge had been part of M's only or main residence. The Ch D upheld this decision as one of fact. *Williams v Merrylees*, Ch D 1987, 60 TC 297; [1987] STC 445. (*Note*. *Dicta* of Vinelott J were subsequently disapproved by the CA in *Lewis v Rook*, **71.318** below.)

[71.318] In 1968 a woman (R) purchased a large house, ten acres of land, and two cottages. In 1979 she sold one of the cottages, which was 190 yards from her house and had been occupied by a gardener. The Revenue issued a CGT assessment on the gain. The CA unanimously upheld the assessment, holding that the cottage was not part of R's residence, since it was some way from the main building and separated by a large garden. *Lewis v Rook*, CA 1992, 64 TC 567; [1992] STC 171; [1992] 1 WLR 662.

Whether self-contained flat formed part of dwelling-house

[71.319] The owner of four separate flats, located in separate buildings in the same square within 95 yards of each other, sold one of them, which had been used to provide occasional bedroom accommodation for his children and guests and, on rare occasions, sleeping accommodation for him and his wife. (The square contained 32 houses, most of which were divided into flats.) The Revenue issued a CGT assessment on the gain. The Ch D upheld the assessment. The flat was a separate dwelling-house, which could not be regarded as part of a common entity with the flat in which the owner and his wife lived. The fact that the owner had sometimes used it to accommodate his children or guests did not make it a part of his private residence. *Honour v Norris*, Ch D 1992, 64 TC 599; [1992] STC 304.

Whether land 'required for the reasonable enjoyment' of the house

[71.320] In a case concerning a compulsory purchase order, du Parcq J held that the word 'required' did not 'mean merely that the occupiers of the house would like to have it, or that they would miss it if they lost it, or that anyone proposing to buy the house would think less of the house without it than he would if it was preserved to it'. The word 'required' should be construed as meaning that 'without it there will be such a substantial deprivation of amenities or convenience that a real injury would be done to the property owner'. *In Re Newhill Compulsory Purchase Order, Payne's Application*, KB 1937, [1938] 2 All ER 163.

[71.321] An individual (L) separated from his wife in 1990 and moved out of the matrimonial home, which was a farmhouse including stables and 18.68 acres (7.56 hectares) of land. In 1995 the couple divorced, and L disposed of his beneficial interest in the property to his former wife. The Revenue issued a CGT assessment on the basis that only 2.61 of the 18.68 acres of land qualified for private residence relief under *TCGA 1992, s 222(3)*. (It was accepted that L was entitled to relief by virtue of Extra-Statutory Concession D6, although he had not lived in the property since 1990.) L appealed, contending that all 18.68 acres had been 'required for the reasonable enjoyment of' the house. The Special Commissioner rejected this contention and dismissed the appeal, and the Ch D upheld this decision. Evans-Lombe J held that *s 222(3)* imposed an objective test, and that 'it is not objectively required, i.e. necessary, to keep horses at a house in order to enjoy it as a residence'. *Longson v Baker*, Ch D 2000, 73 TC 415; [2001] STC 6.

TCGA 1992, s 222(5)—notice of determination of main residence

[71.322] An individual (C), who owned a house in Stockwell, acquired a house in Winchester in August 1985. In July 1986 he sold his house in Stockwell and bought another house in Clapham. In January 1988 he submitted a notice under what is now *TCGA 1992, s 222(5)* declaring that the house in Winchester should be treated as his main residence. In January 1989 he sold that house, realising a capital gain. The Revenue issued a CGT assessment on the basis that 11/41 of the gain was chargeable, considering that the period from August 1985 to June 1986 was not covered by the notice submitted in January 1988, since that notice was for the purpose of determining whether the Winchester house or the Clapham house should be treated as the taxpayer's main residence, and any notice determining whether the Stockwell house or the Winchester house had been the taxpayer's main residence would have had to have been lodged within two years of the taxpayer's acquisition of the Winchester house in August 1985. C appealed, contending that the notice should be treated as effective from January 1986, so that only 5/41 of the gain was chargeable. The Ch D rejected this contention and upheld the assessment. The two-year period of *s 222(5)(a)* began to run from the time when it first became necessary to determine which of two specific residences should be treated as a taxpayer's main residence. C had made no election covering the period when he owned a house in Stockwell as well as the house in Winchester. The election which he had made in January 1988 was an election between his house in Clapham and the house in Winchester. Since he had not acquired the house in Clapham until July 1986, the notice could not cover any period before that time. (Vinelott J observed that *s 222(5)* derived from *FA 1965*, and that during the relevant Parliamentary debates the Financial Secretary had stated that the intention of the clause was so that a taxpayer could 'exercise a choice within two years from the time when he acquires the second house'.) *Griffin v Craig-Harvey*, Ch D 1993, 66 TC 396; [1994] STC 54.

[71.323] A married couple purchased a property in 1999. They let it to tenants until August 2004. In October 2004 they submitted an election under *TCGA 1992, s 222(5)* that the property should be treated as their main residence. In March 2005 they sold the property at a profit. Subsequently HMRC issued assessments on the basis that the property had not qualified for relief under *s 222*. The couple appealed. At the hearing of the appeal, HMRC stated that they 'accepted that the property was a residence used by the taxpayers' but contended that 'the nature and extent of the use made of the property did not permit of the conclusion that it was their main residence'. The First-tier Tribunal allowed the couple's appeal. Judge Geraint Jones held that 'the respondents can challenge the assertion made by a taxpayer that a particular property is a residence used/occupied by him, but once it is proved or accepted that a particular property is a residence used/occupied by the taxpayer, the respondents cannot argue that as a matter of fact and degree that residence is not the taxpayer's main residence if an election has been made in favour of that property under *section 222(5)*'. *Mrs PA Ellis v HMRC (and related appeal)*, FTT [2012] UKFTT 775 (TC); [2013] SFTD 144, TC02426.

Amount of relief (TCGA 1992, ss 223, 224)

TCGA 1992, s 223(1)—land acquired before construction of house

[71.324] A married couple purchased 2.66 acres of land in 1982, with planning permission for the construction of one house. In 1991 they began building a house on the land. The construction was completed in 1993, and the couple then moved into the house. In 1995 they obtained planning permission for the construction of two more houses on the land. They subsequently sold two plots of land, each of which comprised 0.54 acres. The Revenue issued assessments charging CGT on the gain. The couple appealed, contending that the whole of the disposal qualified for relief under *TCGA 1992, s 222*. The Special Commissioner reviewed the evidence in detail and upheld the assessments in principle, holding that the sales of the two plots were each part disposals within *TCGA 1992, s 21(2)*. In relation to these part disposals, expenditure which was attributable to the land (rather than to the construction of the house) had to be apportioned under *TCGA 1992, s 42*. Additionally, the couple had purchased the land in 1982, but had only used the house as their principal private residence since 1993. The house had not been their 'only or main residence' throughout their period of ownership of the land, so that *TCGA 1992, s 223(1)* did not apply and an apportionment was required under *s 223(2)*. The Commissioner observed that it would have been 'particularly odd if Mr and Mrs (H) could have continued to qualify for private residence relief in respect of their two previous owner-occupied properties while benefiting at the same time from the same relief in respect of their unbuilt plot', since 'the overall scheme of the legislation is to provide a single exemption.' *Mr*

& Mrs AJ Henke v HMRC, Sp C [2006] SSCD 561 (Sp C 550). (*Note.* The Commissioner also held that the assessments were valid, applying the earlier decision in *Osborne v Dickinson*, 5.22 ASSESSMENTS.)

Private residence partly used as guest house

[71.325] A married couple had carried on a private guest house business from premises they owned and lived in. They had occupied different parts of the premises at different times of the year in such a way that every part of the premises had, at some time during their period of ownership, constituted their main residence. When the property was sold, it was agreed that one-third of the gain was exempt under what is now *TCGA 1992, ss 222* and *223(2)*. The husband appealed against an assessment on the gain, contending that further relief was due under what is now *TCGA 1992, s 223(4)*. The CA accepted this contention and allowed his appeal. The phrase 'let by him as residential accommodation' in *s 223(4)* did not, directly or by association, mean premises let which were likely to be occupied as a home. It referred to living accommodation as distinct, for example, from office accommodation. The lettings undertaken by the couple were within the words 'residential accommodation'. *Owen v Elliott*, CA 1990, 63 TC 319; [1990] STC 469; [1990] 3 WLR 133.

Mansion house—whether wings of mansion part of residence

[71.326] In 1975 an auctioneer (G) sold a mansion house and grounds which he had acquired in 1971. The building comprised a central block with 33 rooms, and two wings, which were connected to the central block by corridors but which had separate entrances. Some work of reconstruction and redecoration had been carried out, during which G, various members of his family and others had occupied parts of the central block (although many of the 33 rooms had remained empty), while a self-contained flat had been made in one of the wings for a gardener. The Revenue issued a CGT assessment and G appealed, contending that the whole of the gain was within the private residence exemption. The General Commissioners held that the two wings were not part of the residence and that the gain on their sale did not qualify for exemption. With regard to the main block, they applied what is now *TCGA 1992, s 224(2)*, adjusting the relief in respect of a 'change in what is occupied as the individual's residence', and allowed relief on one-third of the gain. The CS allowed G's appeal in part, holding on the evidence that the Commissioners had not been entitled to adjust the relief under *s 224(2)*, since there was 'no finding that there was any change in the rooms normally used for ordinary family living, or that reconstruction or redecoration after entry to the mansion house in any way affected the family's occupation thereof'. Accordingly, the whole of the gain on the sale of the central block and grounds qualified for relief. However, whether the wings were part of the residence was a question of fact for the Commissioners, and their decision was not inconsistent with the evidence. Accordingly, the appeal failed with regard to the gain on the sale of the wings. *Green v CIR*, CS 1982, 56 TC 10; [1982] STC 485.

Loss on sale of property—whether TCGA 1992, s 224(3) applicable

[71.327] In 1988 an accountant (J) and his wife purchased a house for more than £120,000. They subsequently incurred considerable expenditure on improvements, but, following a general fall in house prices, sold the house for £97,000 in 1993. J had other capital gains in the year of disposal, and claimed that the loss on the house should be set against such gains. The Revenue rejected the claim, on the basis that the house had been the couple's private residence, so that the effect of *TCGA 1992, ss 16, 223(1)* was that the loss was not allowable. J appealed, contending that the house had been purchased 'wholly or partly for the purpose of realising a gain', within *TCGA 1992, s 224(3)*, so that *TCGA 1992, s 223* did not apply. The Special Commissioner rejected this contention and dismissed the appeal. On the evidence, the couple's purpose in buying the house was to use it as their home. Their hope that they would be able to make a profit on its eventual sale 'was not a purpose within *s 224(3)*'. *Jones v Wilcock*, Sp C [1996] SSCD 389 (Sp C 92).

Residence occupied under terms of settlement (TCGA 1992, s 225)

Occupation of residence under discretionary trust

[71.328] The trustees of a discretionary trust permitted certain beneficiaries to occupy a house subject to the trust as their residence. The house was exchanged and the Revenue assessed the gain on the beneficiaries. They appealed, contending that the gain qualified for relief under what is now *TCGA 1992, s 225*. The Ch D upheld this contention and allowed their appeal. Brightman J held that, while the beneficiaries were in occupation with the trustees' permission, they were 'entitled to occupy it under the terms of the settlement'. The fact that they had no absolute right under the terms of the settlement did not prevent their occupation from qualifying for relief. *Sansom & Another (Ridge Settlement Trustees) v Peay*, Ch D 1976, 52 TC 1; [1976] STC 494; [1976] 1 WLR 1073; [1976] 3 All ER 375.

Whether ownership of a flat was subject to a trust

[71.329] A woman (BW) purchased a flat in 1990. In 1996 she sold the flat to her son (SW) and daughter-in-law (VW), subject to an agreement whereby she could continue to live in the flat until her death or remarriage. In 2005 BW was injured in a fall, and in 2006 she moved into a single-storey home. In 2007 SW and VW sold the flat. They declared the gain on their tax returns, but subsequently submitted a claim for relief under *TCGA 1992, s 225*, on the basis that their ownership of the flat had been subject to a trust and that the flat was settled property. The First-tier Tribunal accepted this contention and allowed their appeal. Judge Gammie held that 'in acquiring the flat on terms that included the agreement, the appellants were assuming the role of trustees' and 'did not become at that time absolutely entitled to the flat, with the exclusive right to direct how the flat should be dealt with'. *S & Mrs V Wagstaff v HMRC*, FTT [2014] UKFTT 043 (TC), TC03183.

Leases (TCGA 1992, ss 240–241, Sch 8)

Grant of lease of freehold property after development

[71.330] In 1978 a company (M), which carried on a property investment and development business, entered into an agreement with contractors for the development of a freehold site which it owned. In 1979 it signed an 'agreement for a lease' with another company (N), under which N agreed to reimburse M's expenditure on the development, on completion of which M was to grant N a long lease of the property at a rent below the market value, the formula for which was directly related to N's payments in reimbursement of M's development expenditure. The Revenue issued an assessment on the basis that the reimbursement of the expenditure was a premium within what is now *TCGA 1992, Sch 8 para 2(1), 10(2)*. M appealed, contending that it had been reimbursed the expenditure in its capacity of property developer and not in its capacity of landlord, and that the reimbursement was not a premium. The Ch D rejected this contention and upheld the assessment. Walton J held that the only reasonable conclusion on the evidence was that M had developed the site for itself and not for N, which was not a party to the development contracts. *Clarke v United Real (Moorgate) Ltd*, Ch D 1987, 61 TC 353; [1988] STC 273.

Lease—whether a wasting asset

[71.331] See *Lewis v Walters*, 71.117 above.

TCGA 1992, s 241—furnished holiday lettings

[71.332] In September 2004 a couple purchased a property which they intended to let as holiday accommodation. Their first letting of the property did not begin until 9 July 2005. During the twelve months from 9 July 2005 to 8 July 2006, the property was only let for 64 days. The final letting ceased on 9 December 2006 and the couple sold the property in June 2007. HMRC issued assessments charging CGT on the sale. The couple appealed, contending that the property should be treated as qualifying for business asset taper relief for their entire period of ownership. The First-tier Tribunal rejected this contention and dismissed the appeal, holding that although it was accepted that the property had qualified as a business asset for 2006/07, it had not done so for 2005/06. Judge Rankin observed that *TCGA 1992, s 241* provided that property used for furnished holiday lettings only qualified as a business asset for taper relief purposes where the property was 'commercially let as holiday accommodation', within the definition in *ITTOIA 2005, s 325*. Since the couple had not let the property during 2004/05, the 'relevant period' for 2005/06, as defined by *ITTOIA 2005, s 324(2)*, had been the 12 months from 9 July 2005 to 8 July 2006, during which the property had only been let for 64 days. *D & Mrs E Horner v HMRC*, FTT [2013] UKFTT 80 (TC), TC02498.

Debts (TCGA 1992, ss 251–255)

Dollar floating rate notes—whether debts 'on a security'

[71.333] In July 1986 a US company issued its UK parent company (T) twelve loan notes of $5,000,000 each. The notes could only be transferred with the prior consent of the issuing company, which could be refused without any reason being given, and the issuing company could redeem them at any time. They were redeemed at par in December 1987. Because of the fall in value of the dollar, T made a loss of more than £6,000,000. It claimed that this loss should be allowed against its chargeable gains. The Revenue rejected the claim, considering that the effect of what is now *TCGA 1992, s 251(1)* was that there was no chargeable gain or allowable loss. T appealed, contending that the loans were debts 'on a security', so that the loss was allowable. The Special Commissioners rejected this contention and dismissed the appeal. The distinguishing feature of a debt on a security was that it is 'in the nature of an investment which can be dealt in as such'. The loan notes in this case were not in the nature of investments, since they could only be transferred with the prior consent of the issuing company and that company could redeem them at any time. *Tarmac Roadstone Holdings Ltd v Williams*, Sp C [1996] SSCD 409 (Sp C 95).

Loan to overseas subsidiary secured on property

[71.334] In 1984 a company (T) gave a promissory note for $15,193,000, repayable on demand, to a US subsidiary. The loan in question was repaid in two stages, in 1986 and 1992. Because of the fall in the value of the dollar, the company made a loss on the loan. T appealed against an assessment for its accounting period ending in 1992, contending that the loan was a 'debt on a security' and that the loss could be set against its chargeable gains. The Special Commissioners dismissed the appeal, holding that the loan was not a 'debt on a security', and the CA unanimously upheld their decision. Peter Gibson LJ held that 'Parliament could not have intended that the existence of any security, however inadequate, for any debt, however impermanent, should without more turn the debt into a debt on a security'. On the evidence, the debt here was 'not a marketable security in any realistic sense'. *Taylor Clark International Ltd v Lewis*, CA 1998, 71 TC 226; [1998] STC 1259.

Loan with conversion rights—whether a 'debt on a security'

[71.335] In an Irish case, the HC(I) held that a loan which was subject to a right of conversion into company shares, at a predetermined price, was a 'debt on a security' (so that an ensuing loss was allowable). Morris J held that 'the essence of a loan on a security' must be whether the additional 'bundle of rights', acquired with the granting of the loan, enhanced the loan 'so as to make it marketable and potentially more valuable than the value of the repaid loan upon repayment. This potential increase in value must not be illusory or theoretical. It must be realistic at the time of the loan'. *Mooney v McSweeney*, HC(I) 1997, 5 ITR 163; [1997] 3 IR 424.

[71.336] The decision in *Mooney v McSweeney*, 71.335 above, was distinguished in a subsequent Irish case whether the SC(I) held on the evidence that 'the conversion rights, such as they are, added nothing to the value or marketability of the debt', so that the debt was not a 'debt on a security'. *O'Connell v Keleghan*, SC(I) [2001] IESC 42. (*Note*. For another issue in this case, see 22.85 EMPLOYMENT INCOME.)

'Debt on a security'—other cases

[71.337] For other cases concerning the definition of a 'debt on a security', see *Aberdeen Group Construction Ltd v CIR*, 71.31 above, and *WT Ramsay Ltd v CIR*, 71.285 above.

Loss on certificate of deposit—effect of TCGA 1992, s 251(1)

[71.338] An individual (W) claimed relief for capital losses on the basis that a certificate of deposit, issued to him by an overseas bank, had become of negligible value. HMRC rejected his claim on the basis that the certificate of deposit represented a debt, so that the effect of *TCGA 1992, s 251(1)* was that no chargeable gain or allowable loss could accrue to him on its disposal. W appealed, contending that the certificate of deposit should be treated as a foreign currency bank account, within *TCGA 1992, s 252*. The First-tier Tribunal rejected this contention and dismissed his appeal. *GL Weston v HMRC*, FTT [2013] UKFTT 011 (TC), TC03152.

Capitalisation of loan—whether TCGA 1992, s 251(3) applicable

[71.339] A woman (F) had lent a substantial sum of money to a company of which she was a shareholder. In May 2003 she capitalised £50,000 of the loan, receiving shares with restricted rights in return. In 2005 the company went into liquidation, and F claimed that she had incurred a capital loss of £50,000. The Revenue rejected the claim on the basis that the shares had been worthless at the time of the capitalisation of the debt, so that the effect of *TCGA 1992, s 251(3)* was that there was no allowable loss. The Special Commissioner reviewed the evidence in detail and allowed F's appeal. The Commissioner noted that HMRC Capital Gains Manual para CG53516A explicitly stated that where shares were issued as part of a reorganisation of a company's share capital, *s 251(3)* could not apply. On the evidence, the capitalisation of the loan in 2003 had taken place as part of a reorganisation of the company's share capital, within *TCGA 1992, s 126*. The Commissioner also found that, notwithstanding the subsequent liquidation of the company, its shares had had 'a very significant value' in May 2003. The Commissioner specifically distinguished *CIR v Burmah Oil Co Ltd*, 71.287 above, finding that this was not a case where 'worthless debt was swapped for shares in the tax hope of turning an admitted and non-allowable loss on the debt into an allowable tax loss on shares'. *JE Fletcher v HMRC*, Sp C [2008] SSCD 1219 (Sp C 711).

TCGA 1992, s 253(1)—definition of 'qualifying loan'

[71.340] A bank granted a company a loan, to replace its existing overdraft. The company's controlling director gave the bank legal charges over two properties which he owned as security. One of the properties was sold a year later. Part of the sale proceeds were credited to the company's loan account. The director claimed relief under *TCGA 1992, s 253*. The Revenue rejected the claim on the basis that the loan was not a 'qualifying loan' within *TCGA 1992, s 253(1)*. The director appealed. The General Commissioners dismissed his appeal, finding that it was difficult to disentangle the director's personal affairs from those of the company, and holding that the loan had not been used wholly for the purposes of the company's trade. The CA unanimously upheld their decision. Neuberger LJ held that 'where money lent is used to repay an existing indebtedness, the purpose served by the use of that money is characterised by the existing indebtedness'. A 'refinancing exercise' did not convert a non-qualifying loan into a qualifying loan. On the evidence, the Commissioners had been entitled to find that the money concerned had been spent for the purpose of benefiting the director, rather than for the purposes of the company's trade. *Robson v Mitchell*, CA 2005, TL 3757; [2005] STC 893; [2005] EWCA Civ 585.

Claim for relief under TCGA 1992, s 253(3)

[71.341] An individual (R) claimed relief against investment income for an irrecoverable loan under *TCGA 1992, s 253(3)*. The Revenue rejected the claim and the Special Commissioner dismissed R's appeal, observing that the loan had been made in 1976, so that the effect of *TCGA 1992, s 253(15)* was that relief was not due. The Ch D upheld this decision. *Rigby v Jayatilaka*, Ch D 2000, 72 TC 365; [2000] STC 179. (*Notes*. (1) The appellant appeared in person. The Special Commissioner also rejected a claim to loss relief, finding that there was 'no loss brought forward'. (2) For another issue in this case, see **4.372** APPEALS. For a previous appeal by the same appellant, see *Rigby v Samson*, **41.26** PARTNERSHIPS.)

[71.342] In 1987 a bank (W) lent money to a trading company (E). One of E's directors (G) guaranteed the loans. In 1994 W demanded the immediate repayment of the loans. G repaid the outstanding amounts, and E was subsequently dissolved. G subsequently claimed relief under *TCGA 1992, s 253* for the payments which he had made. HMRC rejected the claim on the grounds that the loan had been irrecoverable at the outset, and had not therefore become irrecoverable. The First-tier Tribunal allowed G's appeal against this decision. Judge Raghavan observed that the bank was a commercial lender, which 'had been prepared to lend money to a company which had bought two properties and which had offers on the table for the resale of the property at a profit.' That indicated that the loans had not been irrecoverable at the outset. On the evidence, G had lent money to E to pay interest which E had incurred for the purposes of its trade. Therefore G was entitled to relief under *TCGA 1992, s 253(3)*. (However, the tribunal upheld a ruling by HMRC that the loss could not be set against G's general income under *ICTA 1988, s 574*.) *P Goldsmith v HMRC*, FTT [2012] UKFTT 521 (TC), TC02197.

[71.343] See also *Leadley's Executors v HMRC*, 19.23 DECEASED PERSONS.

TCGA 1992, s 253(4)—loss relief for payment made under guarantee

[71.344] In 1985 a company (L), and ten companies in the same group, entered into a composite joint and several guarantee with a bank whereby the liabilities to the bank of each of the companies were guaranteed by all the other ten companies as co-guarantors. In 1988 the bank sought repayment of liabilities incurred by two of the associated companies, which were no longer solvent. L made a payment of £2,115,000 to the bank, and did not seek to recover any contributions from its co-guarantors. L claimed relief for the payment under what is now *TCGA 1992, s 253(4)*. The Revenue considered that the relief should be restricted to take account of the fact that the liability was shared between L and the other companies which had acted as guarantors. The Special Commissioner found on the evidence that only three of the co-guarantors remained solvent at the time when L had made the payment in question, and held that L was entitled to relief in respect of one-third of the payment. The Ch D dismissed L's appeal against this decision. The amount of the relief had to be restricted to take account of potential contributions from the co-guarantors. (Chadwick J also observed that the Commissioner had apparently been wrong to disregard any possibility of recovery from a liquidation of the eight co-guarantors which were no longer solvent, but declined to remit the matter to the Commissioner to reconsider this point, since the Revenue had not appealed against the decision.) *Leisureking Ltd v Cushing*, Ch D 1992, 65 TC 400; [1993] STC 46.

Irrecoverable loans—whether TCGA 1992, s 253(12) applicable

[71.345] In 1988 a wealthy investor (C) purchased a majority shareholding in a company (BG) which had four subsidiaries. The group was suffering financial difficulties. From 1989 to 1992 C made loans of more than £2,000,000 to one of BG's subsidiaries (B). However, B continued to suffer financial problems, which were exacerbated by the devaluation of sterling in 1992. In 1994 BG sold its shareholding in B to another company (GD), and a week later B sold its net assets to GD. GD did not take over B's overdraft or the loans from C. C claimed relief under *TCGA 1992, s 253(3)* for his loans to B. The Revenue rejected the claim, considering that *TCGA 1992, s 253(12)* applied, on the basis that the loans had become irrecoverable as a result of an act by the lender, namely the sale of B's shares and assets. C appealed, contending that the loans had become irrecoverable as a result of the commercial situation. The Special Commissioner accepted this contention and allowed the appeal. When C had first invested in B, he believed that it had commercial potential. However, he could not be expected to fund B indefinitely. By 1994 B had become insolvent and C's loans had become irrecoverable. Accordingly C was entitled to relief. *Cann v Woods*, Sp C [1999] SSCD 77 (Sp C 183).

[71.346] Trustees of a settlement made loans totalling £250,000 to a trading company. The company suffered financial difficulties, and was sold in 1992.

Under the sale agreement, the trustees were required to waive the loans. They claimed relief for this loss in their 1992/93 tax return. The Revenue rejected the claim, considering that *TCGA 1992, s 253(12)* applied, on the basis that the loans had become irrecoverable as a result of an act by the lender. The Special Commissioners allowed the trustees' appeal, holding that the purpose of *s 253(12)* was 'to afford relief to those who, having made a loan to a trader, will not see the money, or a part of it, again'. The Commissioners held that '*subsection (12)* should be taken as an exhaustive list of the circumstances which disqualify a lender from the relief to which he would otherwise have been entitled'. The fact that the loan had been waived before the claim was made did not prevent the loan from qualifying for relief. *Crosby & Others (Crosby's Trustees) v Broadhurst*, Sp C [2004] SSCD 348 (Sp C 416).

Transfer of business to company—whether a 'qualifying loan'

[71.347] In the case noted at 71.259 above, two individuals had transferred the goodwill of a partnership business to a company of which they were the sole shareholders and directors. They subsequently claimed relief for a capital loss, contending that the transfer of the goodwill constituted a 'qualifying loan' within *TCGA 1992, s 253*. The Revenue rejected the claim and the Special Commissioner dismissed the directors' appeals. The Commissioner observed that the appellants had previously contended that they had gifted the goodwill to the company, and that they had produced no documents setting out the terms of the loan, and no board minutes recording the existence of a loan. *Colley & Hillberg v HMRC*, Sp C [2007] SSCD 236 (Sp C 585).

Gain on assigned debt

[71.348] See *Whitehouse v Ellam*, 71.19 above.

Valuation (TCGA 1992, ss 272–274)

General principles (TCGA 1992, s 272)

Value of quoted shares while secret takeover negotiations in progress

[71.349] A company director (C) disposed of some shares in the company during 1965/66. The Revenue issued a CGT assessment on the basis that their market value at 6 April 1965 was their quoted price. C appealed, contending that because takeover negotiations were in progress at that date, but had not been made public, the market value of the shares at 6 April 1965 was substantially higher than the actual quoted price. The CA upheld the assessment and the HL unanimously dismissed C's appeal, holding that the mere fact that directors of a company possessed information which, if made public, would affect the quoted prices of its shares did not constitute 'special circumstances' for the purposes of what is now *TCGA 1992, s 272(3)*, and did not justify departing from the normal principles of valuation. *Hinchcliffe v Crabtree*, HL 1971, 47 TC 419; [1972] AC 707; [1971] 3 All ER 967.

Valuation of property at 31 March 1982

[71.350] See *Hatt v Newman (No 2)*, 71.78 above, and *Blum v HMRC*, 71.79 above.

Unquoted shares and securities (TCGA 1992, s 273)

[71.351] A director (M) acquired some shares following a company liquidation. He subsequently sold the shares, and appealed against an assessment on the gain, contending that there were irregularities in the liquidation and that the prices used in calculating the gain had been incorrect. The Special Commissioners dismissed his appeal and the CS upheld their decision. *McBrearty v CIR*, CS [1975] STC 614.

[71.352] N and his wife had been directors of a company (S), but disposed of their shares and relinquished their directorships. They received a total of £30,000 (less legal costs). The Revenue issued a CGT assessment on the disposal of the shares. N appealed, contending that the £30,000 did not relate to the disposal of the shares but represented repayment of money which S owed to them. The Commissioners reviewed the available evidence and found that £18,750 was for amounts owed by S (and that legal expenses of £2,300 could be deducted). The CA unanimously dismissed N's appeal. *Neely v Rourke*, CA [1988] STC 216.

[71.353] In three appeals heard together, members of the same family disposed of shares in an unquoted Cayman Islands company (G) which was the holding company of a group which produced and sold sherry. Under G's Articles of Association, it could refuse to register the transfer of shares to anyone who was not a member of the two families which had originally formed it (and the disposals were to members of the other family). The valuation of the shares at 31 March 1982 was disputed. The Special Commissioners reviewed the evidence in detail, holding that in the particular circumstances, it was not appropriate to value the shares on an earnings basis or on a dividend basis, but that the company should be valued on an assets basis and on a turnover basis to arrive at a notional quoted value which should be uplifted by a 'control premium' of 30% to arrive at an entirety value of £46,000,000. The shares should then be valued on the basis that the two smaller shareholdings (comprising 11.09% and 9.09% of the total shares respectively) could have been acquired with a bid of two-thirds of their 'entirety value' (i.e. at £256 each) and that, for the largest shareholding (comprising 18.16% of the share capital), a 20% premium should be added to this (arriving at a value of £307 each). *Hawkings-Byass v Sassen (and related appeals)*, Sp C [1996] SSCD 319 (Sp C 88).

[71.354] 24% of the voting shares in a family company (C) were owned by its managing director (D). 74% of the voting shares were held by D's parents, and the remaining 2% were held by his brother and sister. In 1987 D resigned from C following a disagreement with his father, and in 1988 C went into liquidation. The Revenue issued CGT assessments, and D appealed. The Revenue considered that, at 31 March 1982, D's shares had been worth £18.48 each, whereas D contended that they had been worth £48.48 each. The Special Commissioner reviewed the evidence in detail and held that D's shares had been worth £26.89 each. The Commissioner found that C's assets at 31 March 1982 had been worth £598,064, producing a share value of £59.75 per share, and that, because D had only held a minority shareholding, this figure should be discounted by 55%. The Ch D upheld this decision as one of fact. *Denekamp v Pearce*, Ch D 1998, 71 TC 213; [1998] STC 1120.

[71.355] A company director (B) gave most of his shares to his two children. The Revenue issued a CGT assessment, and B appealed, contending that the shares had no value at the time of the transfer. The Special Commissioner rejected this contention and upheld the assessment in principle, holding on the evidence that the shares transferred had an open market value of £195 each. *Billows v Hammond*, Sp C [2000] SSCD 430 (Sp C 252). (*Note*. B had failed to notify the gift on his tax return and the Commissioner held that this constituted 'negligent conduct' within *TMA, s 36*. In separate proceedings, the CA had previously held that the company's accounts were unreliable—see *Billows v Robinson*, **29.109** FURTHER ASSESSMENTS: LOSS OF TAX.)

[71.356] In March 1982 a company director (M) held 66% of the company's shares. He subsequently disposed of some of the shares, so that it became necessary to determine their market value at 31 March 1982. It was agreed that the entire company should be valued, and that M's shares should be valued at 66% of this total, ie without any premium or discount. It was also agreed that the company should be valued on the 'capitalised earnings' basis, ie requiring the maintainable earnings of the business to be identified and then multiplied by an appropriate factor. The Revenue considered that the maintainable earnings should be taken as £82,000 pa, and that these should be multiplied by 10. M contended that the maintainable earnings should be taken as £148,190 pa, and that these should be multiplied by 11. The Special Commissioner reviewed the evidence in detail and held that the maintainable earnings should be taken as £95,910 pa, and that these should be multiplied by 10. *Marks v Sherred*, Sp C [2004] SSCD 362 (Sp C 418).

[71.357] In 1981 a company (S) acquired a 100% shareholding in another company (C) for £152,634. C's main asset was a leasehold property. In 1988 S sold its shares in C for £397,365. The Revenue issued a corporation tax assessment charging tax on the amount by which the value of the shareholding had risen between 31 March 1982 and the date of disposal. S appealed. The Lands Tribunal determined that at 31 March 1982, the value of the property had been £168,000. The Special Commissioner upheld the Revenue's contention that C's valuation at 31 March 1982 had been £200,257 (ie the total valuation of its net assets). The Commissioner observed that 'majority interests in investment intermediaries will usually be valued on the assets basis', and that 'capitalising dividends is not relevant in valuing a controlling interest in an unlisted property investment company', since 'the amount paid by way of dividends in any year by a company which is profitable and has significant distributable reserves' was largely 'at the whim of the controlling shareholder'. *Shinebond Ltd v Carrol*, Sp C [2006] SSCD 147 (Sp C 522).

[71.358] An individual (E) disposed of some shares which he held at 31 March 1982. HMRC issued CGT assessments on the basis that the value of each share at that date had been £1.23. E appealed, contending that the shares should be valued at £4 each. The First-tier Tribunal allowed the appeal in part, holding that the shares should be valued on the basis of a price/earnings ratio of 14.0. On this basis, each share had been worth £4.04. However, since E had held less than 2% of the shares in the company, this value should be discounted by 40% to take account of low dividend payments and the lack of marketability of the shares, giving a valuation for CGT purposes of £2.42 each. Judge Reid observed that it was not 'worthwhile or appropriate to trawl the cases comparing discounts in share valuation cases. Each case must depend on its own particular facts and circumstances; these circumstances would then have to be compared with the company in question and appropriate adjustments made none of which could be carried out scientifically. The range seems to be between 25% and 75%.' *SP Erdal v HMRC*, FTT [2011] UKFTT 87 (TC), TC00964.

[71.359] A company director (M) owned the entire share capital of two companies at 31 March 1982. He disposed of some of the shares between 2000 and 2004. HMRC formed the opinion that M's returns were incorrect as they overestimated the value of the shares at 31 March 1982. They issued amendments to M's self-assessments, valuing the two companies at £3,100,000 at that date. M appealed, contending that the companies had had a total value of £8,425,000. The First-tier Tribunal reviewed the evidence in detail and allowed the appeal in part, valuing one at £3,709,000 and the other at £443,000. *SAS Marks v HMRC*, FTT [2011] UKFTT 221 (TC), TC01086.

Valuation of unquoted shares—unpublished information about profits

[71.360] A taxpayer (C) held a 14% shareholding in a substantial unquoted company (Y). He died in September 1987. Y's accounts for the year ending 31 August 1987 (which had not been published at the time of C's death) showed pre-tax profits of £2,350,000. All of Y's share capital was sold in 1988. The Revenue issued a CGT assessment on the basis that the market value of the shares at the time of C's death was 35p each. (This valuation was computed by applying a price/earnings ratio of 12 to the earnings per share, and discounting it by 60% for unmarketability, leaving a net price/earnings ratio of 4.8.) The administrators of C's estate appealed, contending that the shares should be valued, on the basis of expected future dividends, at not less than 50p each at the date of death, so that the gain accruing on the sale of the shares should be reduced accordingly. The Special Commissioners allowed the appeal, holding on the evidence that the shares should be valued at 56p each. The Commissioner held that the effect of what is now *TCGA 1992, s 273(3)* was that the unpublished information about the company's pre-tax profits, and the information about the expected future sale of Y, should be taken into account. On the evidence, the administrators' valuation on the basis of expected future dividends was reasonable. The Revenue's valuation was defective in that it assumed both a level of earnings which was too low and a price/earnings ratio which was too low. In the circumstances of the case, the valuation should be based on the principle that a sale of Y's entire share capital would take place in the near future, and that a purchaser would pay six times the value of pre-tax profit plus the cash worth of Y (giving a valuation of £20,000,000 for the entire company and £1.12 per share) discounted by 50% 'for delay and risk', to give a valuation of 56p per share. *Caton's Administrators v Couch*, Sp C [1995] SSCD 34 (Sp C 6). (*Notes*. (1) The appeal was heard before the appeal in *Clark (Clark's Executor) v CIR*, **71.361** below, which related to a smaller shareholding in the same company, although the decision in *Clark* was published before the decision in this case. (2) For another issue in this case, taken to the CA, see **71.100** above.)

[71.361] A woman (C) held a 3.16% shareholding in a substantial unquoted company (Y). She died in September 1987. Y's accounts for the year ending 31 August 1987 (which had not been published at the time of C's death) showed pre-tax profits of £2,350,000. All of Y's share capital was sold in 1988. The Revenue issued a CGT assessment on the basis that the value of the shares at the time of C's death was 30p each. (This valuation was computed by applying a gross price/earnings ratio of 12 to the earnings per share, and discounting it by 65% for unmarketability, leaving a net price/earnings ratio of 4.2.) C's executor appealed, contending that the shares should be valued at 18p each, since the Revenue's valuation took account of unpublished information concerning Y's profits which should have been ignored. The Special Commissioner dismissed the appeal and upheld the Revenue's valuation, holding that the effect of what is now *TCGA 1992, s 273(3)* was that the unpublished information concerning Y's profits should be taken into account, and that the Revenue's valuation had been made on a reasonable basis. Although the shareholding was a small minority holding, the hypothetical purchaser was 'considering an investment of something in the region of £100,000–£169,000'. The Commissioner also considered that the Revenue's valuation was 'if anything, rather low', and noted that the valuation was significantly less than the valuation of shares in the same company in *Caton's Administrators v Couch*, **71.360** above, but observed that 'the difference between the two valuations reflects the difference in the size of the shareholdings which, in turn, reflects the amount of information assumed to be available'. (The valuation in *Caton's Administrators* was based on the assumption that the prospective purchaser would know that Y's entire share capital was likely to be sold in the near future, which was not the case here since the shareholding here was significantly smaller.) *Clark (Clark's Executor) v Green & CIR*, Sp C [1995] SSCD 99 (Sp C 5). (*Notes*. (1) The appeal was heard after the appeal in *Caton's Administrators v Couch*, **71.360** above, although the decision in *Caton* was published after the decision in this case. (2) The executor's accountant was contending for a lower valuation of the shares than that adopted by the Revenue, which would produce a greater CGT liability on the disposal of the shares. However, it was accepted that the CGT valuation would also govern the IHT payable on the death, although the appeal was not directly concerned with the valuation for IHT purposes.)

Sale of unquoted shares accompanied by waiver of debt

[71.362] A company (E) sold shares in a subsidiary (W) for £35,000 and accepted £20,969 in full satisfaction of a debt of £55,839 owed to it by W. The debt was not a 'debt on a security'. E appealed against a CT assessment, contending that the £34,870 written off should be deducted from the £35,000 it had received for the shares. The Ch D rejected this contention and dismissed the appeal. *EV Booth (Holdings) Ltd v Buckwell*, Ch D 1980, 53 TC 425; [1980] STC 578.

Consideration for sale of companies with tax losses

[71.363] In 1977 a company (V) sold shares in eight subsidiary companies to an unconnected company (M). The subsidiary companies had incurred capital losses which had not been quantified at the date of the sale. The shares were sold for their market value of £19,529, but under the agreement M provided a guarantee that each of the eight companies should pay V an amount equal to 7.5% of their allowable capital losses. In 1979 the losses in question were agreed at £19.5 million, and the subsidiaries paid V the agreed amounts. The Revenue issued a CGT assessment on V for the period ending December 1977, including the amount received by V from the subsidiaries as part of the consideration for the sale of the shares. V appealed, contending that the consideration should be restricted to the £19,529 which was agreed to be the market value of the companies in 1977. The Special Commissioner allowed V's appeal and the Ch D upheld this decision. The guarantees were terms of the sale agreements, and no additional monetary value could or should be placed on them. Further, even if they were to be regarded as part of the consideration, they were incapable of valuation for CGT purposes. *Fielder v Vedlynn Ltd*, Ch D 1992, 65 TC 145; [1992] STC 553.

Consideration for sale of company with substantial debt to bank

[71.364] A company (S) owned several subsidiaries, one of which operated a liquid chromatography business which another company (B) wished to purchase. S wished to structure the sale in such a way as to minimise its tax liability. In July 1986 one of S's wholly-owned subsidiary companies (H) declared a cash dividend of $20,000,000. It was offered an overdraft facility of this amount by a bank, the overdraft being secured by a deposit of that amount by S (so that, on payment of the dividend, the $20,000,000 effectively travelled in a circle). In September 1986 S sold some of its subsidiaries, including H, to B, and agreed not to compete with B in the liquid chromatography business. The agreement provided that B should pay $23,000,000 in total, of which $20,000,000 should be paid to the bank to clear the loan to H, and that $1,000 of the $23,000,000 related to the common stock of H. S appealed against a CT assessment, contending that the consideration which it had received for the sale of H was only $1,000. The Special Commissioners rejected this contention and dismissed the appeal, holding that the effect of the agreement was that the consideration paid for the common stock of H was $20,001,000, since S 'could and did direct how that sum should be applied'. The Ch D upheld the Commissioners' decision. Lightman J observed that, 'if the parties had intended that the sale of the shares should be for $1,000, this would have been very simple to say'. Where a holding company sold a solvent subsidiary and the purchaser agreed to discharge a debt owed by that subsidiary, 'the payment of the debt will not necessarily or indeed (perhaps) ordinarily constitute additional consideration of monetary value for the shares'. However, the parties here had specifically agreed that the amount of the debt should be allocated to the purchase price. Accordingly, in view of the wording of the specific agreements, the consideration for the common stock was $20,001,000. *Spectros International plc v Madden*, Ch D 1996, 70 TC 349; [1997] STC 114.

Issue of new shares not acquired at arm's length

[71.365] See *Dunstan v Young Austen Young Ltd*, 71.200 above.

Value determined for inheritance tax (TCGA 1992, s 274)

Valuation of unquoted shares—estate duty and inheritance tax cases

[71.366] See the cases noted at 72.134 to 72.138 INHERITANCE TAX.

Miscellaneous

Whether contract conditional

[71.367] In June 1962, the owners of some land agreed to allow a company (L) to construct a building, which was to be leased to E for 125 years. The building was completed, and the lease granted, in 1964. In July 1965, L disposed of the lease at a large gain. The Revenue assessed L on the basis that the 1962 agreement was a conditional contract and that the right to the lease had been acquired in 1964, so that the acquisition and disposal of the lease had taken place within three years and there was a charge to tax under *FA 1965, s 82*. L appealed, contending that the lease had been acquired under the 1962 agreement, so that the disposal had taken place more than three years after the acquisition. The Special Commissioners accepted this contention and allowed the appeal, holding that the 1962 agreement was a single and absolute contract, and the CA upheld their decision. *Eastham v Leigh London & Provincial Properties Ltd*, CA 1971, 46 TC 687; [1971] Ch 871; [1971] 2 All ER 811. (*Note. FA 1965, s 82* is now obsolete, but the case remains of interest on the question of whether a contract is conditional or unconditional.)

[71.368] At an auction in 1962, an individual (B) agreed to purchase a farm, but was unable to pay the agreed price, and the farm was instead sold to another purchaser (P). In 1963 P sold the farm to B. In 1965 B sold part of the farm. The Revenue assessed B under Schedule D, Case VII (a charge on short-term gains which preceded the introduction of CGT), on the basis that he had acquired the farm in 1963. He appealed, contending that he should be treated as having acquired the farm in 1962. The Commissioners rejected this contention and dismissed his appeal, and the Ch D upheld their decision. *Beattie v Jenkinson*, Ch D 1971, 47 TC 121; [1971] 1 WLR 1419; [1971] 3 All ER 495.

TCGA 1992, s 13—whether compatible with EC law

[71.369] See *European Commission v United Kingdom (No 2)*, 25.96 EUROPEAN LAW.

Sales during bankruptcy

[71.370] The properties of a bankrupt, some of which were subject to mortgages, were assigned to the Official Assignee in Bankruptcy, who applied to the court for certain directions. The QB held that the gains from sales of the properties were liable to CGT, that the sale proceeds of mortgaged property should be applied first in discharge of incumbrances, and that the tax payable was part of the costs of administration of the bankruptcy. *In re McMeekin*, QB(NI) 1973, 48 TC 725; [1974] STC 429.

[71.371] See also *Re Mesco Properties Ltd*, 13.18 COMPANY LIQUIDATION AND RECEIVERSHIP.

Beneficial ownership of asset disputed

[71.372] Three people had carried on a business in partnership. One of them (D) wished to buy out his partners. He did so, with the aid of £10,000 lent to him by a friend (K). The business was then transferred to a company which D and K had formed. The Revenue issued assessments on the basis that, immediately before the formation of the company, D was the sole beneficial owner of the business. He appealed, contending that in the negotiations to buy out his partners he had been acting as K's agent and that he had not purchased the partnership business on his own behalf. The CA(NI) accepted this contention and allowed D's appeal (by a 2-1 majority, Curran LJ dissenting). *De Pol v Cunningham*, CA(NI) 1974, 49 TC 445; [1974] STC 487.

[71.373] A company director (B) sold some shares in 1988. He appealed against CGT assessments on the gain, contending that, in return for a loan from his parents, he had agreed to pay them 60% of the sale proceeds of the shares, and that the amount in question should be excluded from the consideration. The Special Commissioner rejected this contention and upheld the assessments, finding that there was no evidence of B having completed a declaration of trust in favour of his parents, or of his having agreed to hold shares for them as nominee. The Ch D upheld the Commissioner's decision. Park J held that the fact that B was 'contractually bound' to pay some money to his parents 'does not exclude the amount so payable from the consideration for his disposal of his asset'. *Burca v Parkinson*, Ch D 2001, 74 TC 125; [2001] STC 1298.

[71.374] A married woman (L) was the legal owner of a property in Northampton which had been occupied by her daughter, but was sold in 2005. L's accountant submitted a CGT computation on the basis that L's husband was the joint beneficial owner of the property and was entitled to a half share of the gain. HMRC issued an amendment to L's self-assessment, charging CGT on the basis that L was the sole owner of the property. The First-tier Tribunal allowed L's appeal, finding that L and her husband had been joint beneficial owners of the property. *Mrs Y Lawson v HMRC*, FTT [2011] UKFTT 346 (TC), TC01206.

[71.375] In a Northern Ireland case, a trader (W) purchased a petrol station and garage in 1975. He subsequently took his wife (L) into partnership, and in 1988 the couple purchased an area of land adjoining the petrol station. In

1995 L became seriously ill, and ceased to work in the business. In 2005 the couple sold the business and the land. On their 2005/06 tax returns, 75% of the disposal proceeds were allocated to W and 25% was allocated to L. HMRC subsequently issued a CGT assessment on L on the basis that she had been entitled to a 50% beneficial interest in the land. She appealed, contending that the original tax returns had been incorrect, and that she had relinquished the whole of her beneficial interest in the land to W in 1998. The First-tier Tribunal accepted this contention and allowed her appeal. *Mrs L Watson v HMRC*, FTT [2014] UKFTT 613 (TC), TC03738.

[71.376] HMRC discovered that a trader (S) had failed to declare a capital gain on the disposal of four properties. S appealed, contending that the assessment was excessive because he had only had a beneficial interest as to one-third of the properties, and that his two brothers had each also had a beneficial interest. The First-Tier tribunal reviewed the evidence in detail and allowed the appeal in part, finding that one of S's brothers had a beneficial interest in the properties but that the other brother did not, so that S was only taxable on 50% of the gain. *T Singh v HMRC*, FTT [2011] UKFTT 584 (TC), TC01427. (*Note.* The Tribunal also found that S had underdeclared his business takings, and dismissed an appeal against an amendment to his declared profits.)

[71.377] In 1989 a married couple purchased a 20% interest in a property which was used as a nursing home. The property was sold in 2007. The couple failed to declare the disposal in their tax returns. HMRC issued assessments and the couple appealed, contending that they had disposed of their interest in the property to their son in 2001. The First-tier Tribunal rejected this contention, finding that there was no evidence of such a transfer, and dismissed their appeals. *BM & Mrs RB Patel v HMRC*, FTT [2013] UKFTT 84 (TC), TC02502.

[71.378] Three brothers had submitted tax returns indicating that they were carrying on a property business in partnership. One of the brothers appealed against a discovery assessment charging CGT on the disposal of a property, contending that he had been an employee rather than a partner. The First-tier Tribunal reviewed the evidence in detail, rejected this contention and dismissed the appeal. *IH Bhatti v HMRC*, FTT [2013] UKFTT 355 (TC), TC02757.

Whether UK resident taxable as agent for Isle of Man company

[71.379] An Isle of Man company realised a gain from the purchase and sale of land in Wales. The Revenue assessed the gain on an individual (W) who was resident in the UK, considering that he was acting as an agent of the company. The General Commissioners upheld the assessment and the Ch D dismissed W's appeal, holding on the evidence that W 'was the person through whom all the transactions of (the company) in the United Kingdom were carried out during the relevant period'. *Willson v Hooker*, Ch D 1995, 67 TC 585; [1995] STC 1142. (*Note.* The Ch D also rejected an application for the Case Stated to be remitted to the General Commissioners—see **4.200** APPEALS.)

TCGA 1992, s 210—transactions in life assurance policies

[71.380] See *Drummond v HMRC*, 71.84 above.

TCGA 1992, s 247—relief on compulsory acquisition

[71.381] A landowner acquired a right to build a restaurant on some land by a grant from the Milton Keynes Development Corporation (MKDC). In 1992, after the dissolution of MKDC, the landowner's plans for the restaurant were approved by the Commission for the New Towns, which granted him a leasehold interest in the land, and agreed to transfer the freehold for the nominal sum of £1 when the development of the restaurant was complete. However local residents objected to the proposed building, and the landowner subsequently agreed to relinquish his interest in the land on the basis that he would be granted an alternative site in Milton Keynes. In 1996 he sold his interest in the land to a company. The Revenue issued an assessment charging CGT on the gain, and the landowner appealed, contending that he was entitled to relief under *TCGA 1992, s 247*. The First-tier Tribunal rejected this contention and dismissed the appeal. Judge Walters observed that relief under *s 247* was only available where land was disposed of to an 'authority exercising or having compulsory powers'. The appellant here had disposed of the land to a limited company, which was not an 'authority exercising or having compulsory powers'. *A Ahad v HMRC*, FTT [2009] UKFTT 353 (TC), TC00291.

Foreign assets—delayed remittances—effect of TCGA 1992, s 279

[71.382] A UK resident (P) owned one-third of the share capital of a Rhodesian company (R), which would have been a close company if it had been resident in the UK. The company made gains on the sale of assets outside the UK. Under what is now *TCGA 1992, s 13*, part of the gains were treated as accruing to P, although R did not make any distributions. Regulations imposed by the *de facto* Rhodesian government (which had made a unilateral declaration of independence from the UK) prohibited R from paying dividends to shareholders resident in the UK. P claimed relief under what is now *TCGA 1992, s 279*. The Ch D rejected this claim, holding that the relief was not due, as *s 279* applied only where a gain was represented by money or money's worth in the hands of the taxpayer. P could not receive the money because R had not made any distributions, so that *s 279* did not apply. *Van Arkadie v Plunket*, Ch D 1982, 56 TC 310; [1983] STC 54.

Location of letters of allotment

[71.383] Two brothers, who were resident and ordinarily resident in the UK but domiciled in South Africa, owned equally the ordinary shares of three associated UK companies. During 1978/79 they implemented a pre-arranged avoidance scheme with the aim of 'exporting' the shares outside the UK (and so taking them outside the scope of capital transfer tax) without incurring any CGT liability. Each company created new preferred ordinary shares, capitalised the amounts credited to profit and loss, appropriated these amounts to the brothers and used them to pay up the new preferred ordinary shares, in respect of which the company issued the brothers with renounceable letters of allotment. Shortly afterwards two Jersey companies, which had been set up for the purpose (and of which the brothers had become directors), issued the brothers with shares at a premium of £1,364,216 and resolved to buy from them their preferred ordinary shares in the UK companies for the same amount. The brothers then went to Sark with their letters of allotment and issued letters of renunciation in favour of the Jersey companies. The Revenue issued CGT assessments on the basis that there had been a disposal of assets situated in the UK. The Special Commissioners dismissed the brothers' appeals, and the Ch D upheld this decision. On the evidence, the brothers had disposed of rights against the UK companies, and these rights were situated in the UK irrespective of where the letters of allotment happened to be. Nicholls J also observed that the transactions fell within the principles laid down by the HL in *WT Ramsay Ltd v CIR*, **71.268** above, and were also within what is now *TCGA 1992, s 29(2)*. Furthermore, the effect of what is now *TCGA 1992, s 137(1)* was that the transactions fell outside the relieving provisions of what is now *TCGA 1992, s 135*, since one of the main purposes of the issuing of the shares in the UK companies was the avoidance of liability to tax. *Young v Phillips (and related appeal)*, Ch D 1984, 58 TC 232; [1984] STC 520.

The situation of property

[71.384] See also the cases noted at **72.149** *et seq.* INHERITANCE TAX.

Disposal of land by unincorporated members' association

[71.385] See *CIR v Worthing Rugby Football Club Trustees*, **18.87** CORPORATION TAX.

TCGA 1992, s 62(5)—'donatio mortis causa'

[71.386] In an 1827 case, the Ch D defined a disposal by way of 'donatio mortis causa' as a gift of personal property made in 'contemplation of the conceived approach of death'. *Duffield v Elwes*, Ch D 1827, 1 BR(NS) 497.

Assessment on donee under TCGA 1992, s 282

[71.387] An individual (R) transferred three flats to his daughter (H) in 2002. R died in 2003. HMRC began an enquiry into his returns, and issued a notice of amendment in 2007. HMRC agreed the tax due with R's personal representative, but the tax remained unpaid. In 2009 HMRC sent a letter to H enclosing a notice purporting to be an assessment under *TCGA 1992, s 282* for 2002/03. H appealed, contending that the assessment should have been issued for 2009/10 rather than 2002/03, so that she should not have to pay interest attributable to her father's default. The First-tier Tribunal allowed her appeal. Judge Brooks observed that the purpose of *s 282* was 'not to determine the liability to CGT, as this has already been finally and conclusively determined by the assessment on the donor, but to protect the public purse and provide a mechanism to ensure that any outstanding CGT is paid in circumstances where the donor of a gift has, despite being liable to CGT, failed to make payment of the tax.' It followed that such an assessment 'should only apply from the date, and therefore for the year, in which it was made'. *Mrs Z Hamar v HMRC*, FTT [2011] UKFTT 697 (TC), TC01529.

TCGA 1992, Sch 7AC—'substantial shareholding' exemption

[71.388] A company (W) agreed to sell its entire shareholding in a subsidiary company (B) to another company (M) for more than £17,500,000. HMRC accepted that this sale qualified for the 'substantial shareholding' exemption under *TCGA 1992, Sch 7AC*. Under the agreement, M paid W a further sum of more than £3,700,000 in return for W agreeing to enter into a 'non-competition' agreement. HMRC issued an amendment to W's return, charging tax on the basis that this payment was a capital sum derived from a disposal of goodwill, within *TCGA 1992, s 22*, and failed to qualify for the 'substantial shareholding' exemption. W appealed, contending that the non-competition agreement had been 'an entirely artificial device with a view to enabling (M) to pay a lower price to the minority shareholders', and that the payment of £3,700,000 should also be treated as qualifying for exemption. The First-tier Tribunal accepted W's evidence and allowed the appeal, holding on the evidence that 'the consideration paid for the NCA attracted the substantial shareholdings exemption'. *Williamson Tea Holdings Ltd v HMRC*, FTT, [2010] SFTD 1101; [2010] UKFTT 301 (TC), TC00589.

CGT avoidance scheme—whether documents shams

[71.389] See *Hitch & Others v Stone*, **58.16** TAX PLANNING AND AVOIDANCE.

72

Inheritance Tax

The cases in this chapter are arranged under the following headings.

INHERITANCE TAX—GENERAL NOTE

This chapter includes not only IHT and capital transfer tax cases but also a number of others, mainly estate duty, where the principles established are still relevant to IHT. However non-IHT cases in other chapters of this book which cover common topics, such as domicile, or which make a general point that may be relevant to IHT, are not repeated here. See in particular 9 CHARITIES; 48 RESIDENCE; 56 SETTLEMENTS and 71 CAPITAL GAINS TAX. Some of the legislation interpreted in the earlier cases has been amended, repealed or replaced. Nevertheless the cumulative nature of IHT means that knowledge of the law in earlier years will continue to be necessary for some time to come.

Definition of 'estate' (IHTA, s 5)

Community property—power of appointment

[72.1] A Fiji company was liable for death duties on shares of a deceased shareholder, because it had intermeddled with his estate. The shareholder had been domiciled in California, and the Fiji shares were community property of the shareholder and his wife under Californian law. He had had the power of management, control and disposition, other than testamentary, of all community property but could not have disposed of it without a valuable consideration. The PC held that this did not amount to a general power of appointment to deal with the property as he thought fit for his own benefit (which would have meant that the whole of the shares was subject to duty). Accordingly duty was only chargeable on the husband's half interest in the shares. *Fiji Estate and Gift Duty Commissioner v Fiji Resorts Ltd*, PC [1982] STC 871. (*Note*. The case is of interest in view of the fact that *IHTA, s 5(2)* provides, broadly, that a person with a general power of appointment to deal with property as he thinks fit is treated as beneficially entitled to that property.)

Beneficial ownership of bank accounts

[72.2] An individual (J), who had been born in India, died in 1988 domiciled and resident in Iran, with substantial funds in a number of UK bank accounts. The Revenue issued a notice of determination charging IHT on the basis that J was the beneficial owner of these funds. His executors appealed, contending that much of the money belonged to a family partnership which had been established in Iran, and that the partnership had transferred the money to London because of the political situation in Iran. The Special Commissioner accepted the executors' evidence and allowed their appeal, holding that the funds were 'partnership funds in origin and remained such. Placing them in an account in the deceased's sole name did not make him the sole beneficial owner.' J had been a 'trustee or nominee' of the funds, which 'belonged beneficially to the deceased and his three sons in equal shares'. *Anand v CIR*, Sp C 1996, [1997] SSCD 89 (Sp C 107).

[72.3] An individual (O) died in 1992. In 1980 and 1984 he had opened deposit accounts in an Isle of Man bank, in the joint names of O and his daughter. He had deposited substantial sums in the accounts. The Revenue issued a notice of determination charging IHT on the basis that the whole of the amounts in the deposit accounts formed part of O's estate. O's daughter and executors appealed, contending that only 50% of the sums in the accounts should be treated as part of O's estate. The Special Commissioner rejected this contention and dismissed the appeals, holding on the evidence that O 'enjoyed the entire beneficial interest in the accounts during his lifetime'. O's daughter had not known that the accounts existed until after her father's death. The fact that O's daughter was never informed of the accounts in her father's lifetime rebutted the presumption of advancement except to the extent that it applied to the right of survivorship. While she had a beneficial right of survivorship, she did not have 'a present beneficial interest in the accounts during her father's lifetime'. Only O had been able to operate the accounts, and this *de facto* control of the accounts was 'a clear pointer to the conclusion' that he had not made a lifetime gift of an immediate interest in the accounts to his daughter. *O'Neill & O'Neill's Executors v CIR*, Sp C [1998] SSCD 110 (Sp C 154).

[72.4] In 1995 a woman (S) transferred her building society account into the names of herself and her two daughters. On her death her personal representatives treated her as having owned only one-third of the balance in the account. The Revenue issued a notice of determination that IHT was due on the whole balance in the account. The personal representatives appealed. The Special Commissioner dismissed the appeal, holding on the evidence that S retained power over the account. She was able to dispose of the balance as she thought fit, and withdrawals were made for her benefit. The effect of *IHTA, s 5(2)* was that the whole of the account formed part of her estate. *Sillars & Another v CIR*, Sp C [2004] SSCD 180 (Sp C 401).

[72.5] In 1996 a widow (B) inherited two building society accounts from her husband. She subsequently put the accounts into the joint names of herself and her brother-in-law (P). B died in 2004. The Revenue issued a notice of determination that B had been beneficially entitled to the whole of the money in these accounts. B's executrix appealed, contending that the money in the accounts should be treated as having belonged to P, and that B had simply held the accounts as a trustee. The Special Commissioner rejected this contention and dismissed the appeal, holding that B had not held the accounts as a trustee and that B had 'a general power which enabled her to dispose of the whole of the accounts'. Accordingly she had to be treated as beneficially entitled to the whole of the money in the accounts at the date of her death. *Ms S Taylor (Executrix of Mrs K Boland) v HMRC*, Sp C [2008] SSCD 1159 (Sp C 704).

[72.6] In 1999 an elderly widow, who had inherited some money from her father, transferred £94,000 from a bank account in her name to a new account in the joint names of her and her son (M). She died in 2007. HMRC issued a notice of determination charging IHT on the whole amount held in the account. The First-tier Tribunal upheld the determination and dismissed M's appeal, applying the principles laid down in *Sillars & Another v CIR*, 72.4 above. *J Matthews (Mrs MJ Matthews' Executor) v HMRC*, FTT [2012] UKFTT 658 (TC), TC02329.

Beneficial ownership of property

[72.7] A widow (MT) died in 2007. HMRC issued notices of determination that she had been beneficially entitled to the whole of the property which she and her late husband (JT) had lived in, and that that property formed part of her estate for IHT purposes. Her executors appealed, contending that the joint tenancy under which JT and MT had originally occupied the house had been severed in 2003, before JT's death, so that JT's share of the property was held on a trust under his will, and did not form part of MT's estate. The First-tier

Tribunal accepted this evidence and allowed the appeal. *P Chadda & Others (Mrs MB Tobin's Executors) v HMRC*, FTT [2014] UKFTT 1061 (TC), TC04154.

IHTA, s 5(3)—liabilities to be taken into account

[72.8] The holder of a life interest in certain sums in two settlements died in 2002. His estate was insolvent. The trustees of the settlements submitted IHT returns in which they claimed that the amount of the deficiency in the deceased's estate should be deducted from the value of each of the settlements. The Revenue rejected the claims and the trustees appealed. The Ch D dismissed the appeals. Mann J held that, for the purposes of *IHTA, s 5(3)*, 'the net liabilities are not available to reduce the estate beyond the value of the free estate's assets that are liable to meet them'. The personal estate comprised the property in it net of liabilities; 'once it is reduced to zero by those liabilities its value cannot decline further, and any additional liabilities have nothing against which they can be offset'. *St Barbe Green & Another v CIR*, Ch D [2005] STC 288; [2005] EWHC 14 (Ch); [2005] 1 WLR 1772.

Beneficial entitlement to death benefits under life insurance policy

[72.9] A company insured the life of one of its employees (L). Under the policy, L nominated his two sisters as the beneficiaries in the event of his death. L died in 2001. The Revenue issued a notice of determination charging IHT on the basis that the death benefits payable under the policy formed part of L's estate. His sisters (who were his personal representatives) appealed. The Special Commissioner dismissed their appeal, holding that 'the deceased had a general power under (*IHTA, s 5(2)*) which enabled him to dispose of the sum assured under the policy as he thought fit. That means that he was beneficially entitled to the sum assured and so it formed part of his estate and accordingly is chargeable to tax.' *Kempe & Roberts (Lyon's Personal Representatives) v CIR*, Sp C [2004] SSCD 467 (Sp C 424).

Lump sum payments received from ex-husband

[72.10] A married couple divorced in 1987. The husband agreed to make monthly maintenance payments to the wife (M). In 2001 he also made a lump sum payment of £20,000, and in May 2002 he made a similar payment of £6,000. M died in October 2002. The Revenue issued a Notice of Determination charging IHT on her estate. Her personal representative appealed, contending that the lump sum payments totalling £26,000, which M had received from her ex-husband, should be returned to him and should not be treated as part of her estate for IHT purposes. The Special Commissioner rejected this contention and dismissed the appeal. *Robertson v HMRC*, Sp C [2005] SSCD 723 (Sp C 494).

Money lent to company by shareholder

[72.11] An individual (L) died in 1999. He was a shareholder in a company (T), and T's records showed that L had lent T £107,210. HMRC issued a notice of determination including this £107,210 as part of L's estate. L's personal representative appealed, contending that the £107,210 should have been treated as a gift to T rather than a loan. The First-tier Tribunal rejected this contention and dismissed the appeal. *Mrs G Silber (MMM Lerner's Personal Representative) v HMRC*, FTT [2012] UKFTT 700 (TC), TC02369.

IHTA, s 272—definition of 'property'

[72.12] In 1993 a settlor (M) made a discretionary settlement under terms which conferred on him a general power to direct the trustees to exercise a power of appointment, and included the power to direct the trustees to transfer the whole of the trust fund to him absolutely. In 1999 the Revenue issued a notice of determination on the trustees. They appealed, contending that M's right to require them to revest all or part of the settled property on him was part of the 'rights and interests of any description' which, by virtue of *IHTA, s 272*, formed part of M's estate immediately after the settlement. The Ch D accepted this contention and allowed the appeal. Lightman J noted that the settlement had been intended 'to create a situation in which the settlor is able to make a substantial transfer of assets into a settlement which gives rise to a charge to inheritance tax in respect of the entire disposal, while at the same time ensuring that the amount of inheritance tax actually payable is negligible'. However, he held that not to treat the general power of appointment as 'property' within *s 272* would open the way 'to the artificial diminution of settlors' estates by the purchase for valuable consideration of enduring general powers of appointment under unconnected settlements'. A general power of appointment was 'something of very real value vested in the appointor'. The CA upheld this decision, holding that the effect of *s 272* was that a general power of appointment, exercisable by the holder over property, was 'property' forming part of the holder's estate. *CIR v Melville & Others*, CA 2001, 74 TC 372; [2001] STC 1271; [2002] 1 WLR 407. (*Note*. See now *FA 2002, s 119*. This was intended to ensure that, with effect from 17 April 2002, powers over trust property are to be disregarded for IHT purposes 'except where doing so would create new scope for tax avoidance'.)

Right under Administration of Estates Act 1925

[72.13] A married couple owned a bungalow as tenants in common. In 1994 the husband died intestate. His widow was entitled to apply for a grant of letters of administration of his estate, but did not do so, and continued to live in the bungalow. She died in 2000, leaving the couple's son (D) as administrator of her estate. He was advised by his solicitor that, in order to sell the bungalow, he would need letters of administration of his father's estate, which he duly obtained. The Revenue issued a notice of administration on the basis that, when D's mother died, her interest in her husband's estate (including his 50% share of the bungalow which she occupied) formed part of her estate. D appealed, contending that because his mother had not obtained letters of administration of her husband's estate, his estate (including his 50% share of the bungalow) did not form part of her estate. The Special Commissioner rejected this contention and dismissed D's appeal. Under *Administration of Estates Act 1925*, D's mother had had the right to require the whole of her husband's estate to be transferred to her. The effect of *IHTA, ss 91* and *272* was that this right formed part of her estate. *Daffodil (Daffodil's Administrator) v CIR*, Sp C [2002] SSCD 224 (Sp C 311).

Dispositions not intended to confer gratuitous benefit (IHTA, s 10)

Sale of property at undervalue—whether IHTA, s 10 applicable

[72.14] In 1976 a landowner sold a farm, several buildings on which were in need of repair and replacement, to a Jersey company for £101,350. His son was a major shareholder in the company, which was, therefore, connected with him for the purposes of both CGT and IHT. The Revenue took the view that the sale had been at undervalue, and the Lands Tribunal subsequently valued the property (for CGT purposes) at £199,000. The Revenue issued a determination on the basis that the disposition of the farm constituted a chargeable transfer of value. The landowner appealed, contending that he had not known that the purchasing company was connected with him for IHT purposes, and that he had had no intention of conferring a gratuitous benefit on the company. The Special Commissioner allowed his appeal and the CS upheld this decision. On the evidence, the tenant of the farm had not wished to purchase it and the farm was unlikely to have been of interest to institutional investors. Accordingly it was reasonable to conclude that the sale had not been intended to confer a gratuitous benefit on the Jersey company, and was a disposition which 'might be expected to be made in a transaction at arm's length'. The transaction was within what is now *IHTA, s 10(1)(b)*, and there was no chargeable transfer of value. *CIR v Spencer-Nairn*, CS 1990, [1991] STC 60.

Deferment of pension benefits—whether IHTA, s 10 applicable

[72.15] A woman was born in 1942. In 1995 she set up a discretionary trust. Later that year she took out a pension plan. It was agreed that if she died before taking her retirement benefits, then the value of those benefits would pass to her discretionary trust. In 2002, shortly before her 60th birthday, she was diagnosed as suffering with terminal cancer. She died in 2003 without having taken the available benefits. HMRC issued a determination charging IHT on the basis that, by failing to take her retirement benefits when she reached the age of 60 in 2002, she had made a disposition of value for the purposes of *IHTA, s 3(3)*. Her personal representatives appealed, contending firstly that she should not be treated as having made any such disposition, and alternatively that if she had made such a disposition, it was not 'intended to confer a gratuitous benefit', so that *IHTA, s 10(3)* applied. The First-Tier Tribunal rejected these contentions and dismissed the appeal in principle, subject to a reduction in HMRC's valuation of the disposition. Judge Clark upheld HMRC's contention that 'the concept of a "disposition" was widened by *s 3(3)* to include passive dispositions, meaning omissions which resulted in the enhancement of another person's estate or of settled property in which no interest in possession subsisted'. He rejected HMRC's contention that the deemed disposition should be treated as having taken place on her 60th birthday (which was her normal retirement date under her pension policy), holding that the disposition should be treated as having taken place on the date of her death. Her omission to exercise her rights had increased the value of the settled property, and the evidence showed that this had been intentional. Accordingly *IHTA, s 10* did not apply. With regard to the appropriate valuation, Judge Clark reviewed the evidence in detail and found that the total benefits amounted to £119,800. He directed that this should be discounted by 25%, resulting in a chargeable consideration of £89,950. *DM Fryer & Others (Personal Representatives of Ms P Arnold) v HMRC*, FTT [2010] SFTD 632; [2010] UKFTT 87 (TC), TC00398. (Notes. (1) The determinations had been made in the name of the Commissioners of Her Majesty's Revenue & Customs. Judge Clark observed that the Commissioners' statutory title was 'the Commissioners *for* Her Majesty's Revenue & Customs' (see *CRCA 2005, s 1*), and commented that 'to avoid any possible suggestion that Notices of Determination (or any other documents issued by HMRC) are invalid, it is strongly desirable for the correct title to be used'. (2) The appellants were represented by an 'independent financial adviser', rather than by a lawyer. Judge Clark observed that it would have been better for the appellants 'to be represented by counsel, or by someone else equally experienced in representing parties before the Tribunal'.)

Transfer of funds to personal pension plan—whether IHTA, s 10 applicable

[72.16] A woman (S) had been diagnosed with terminal cancer. In November 2006, at the age of 56, she transferred significant funds to a personal pension plan, under which she was entitled to draw a pension. She did not do so, and died six weeks later. HMRC issued determinations charging inheritance tax on the basis that both the transfer of the funds to a pension plan, and the failure to take her lifetime benefits, were chargeable transfers of value within *IHTA, s 3*. S's personal representatives appealed, contending that neither of the transfers were intended to confer a gratuitous benefit, so that *IHTA, s 10(3)* appealed. The First-tier Tribunal allowed the appeal in part. Judge Mosedale held that the transfer of funds to a personal pension plan was not intended to confer a gratuitous benefit, so that no IHT was chargeable on this transfer. However, her decision not to draw the pension to which she was entitled was intended to confer a gratuitous benefit and therefore was a chargeable transfer, applying the principles laid down by Judge Clark in *Fryer & Others (Arnold's Personal Representatives) v HMRC*, **72.15** above. *RWJ Parry & Others (Mrs RF Staveley's Personal Representatives) v HMRC*, FTT [2014] UKFTT 419 (TC), TC03548.

Payment by close company to FURBS for controlling shareholder

[72.17] A motor racing engineer (P) incorporated a Jersey company (L) in 1990. In 1991 L agreed to provide P's services to an Italian company (G) for £600,000 pa, and also agreed to employ P at a salary of £75,000 pa. In 1993 L paid £700,000 to a funded unapproved retirement benefits scheme for P. P died in 1999, aged 55. Subsequently the Revenue issued a notice of determination that the payment of £700,000 was a transfer of value within *IHTA, s 94*. P's executors appealed, contending that the payment was a disposition not intended to confer gratuitous benefit, within *IHTA, s 10*. The Special Commissioners reviewed the evidence in detail, accepted this contention and allowed the appeal. The Commissioners observed that the fees paid by G to L were 'in line with the cost of the services of comparable motor racing engineers'. By contrast, 'the basic salary paid by (L) to (P) was very low for a person of his standing'. The payment of £700,000 was not unreasonable or gratuitous, since 'if (P) had contributed at the maximum allowable level to an approved UK scheme until he was 60 and his salary of £75,000 had increased with inflation, the pension which he would have obtained was about the same as that which the £700,000 would secure'. Furthermore, 'the fact that on legal analysis the payment was for past consideration does not mean that it was made with the intention of conferring a gratuitous benefit'. *Postlethwaite's Executors v HMRC*, Sp C 2006, [2007] SSCD 83 (Sp C 571).

Grant of protected life interest in valuable paintings

[72.18] See *Macpherson & Another v CIR*, 72.206 below.

Dispositions for maintenance of family (IHTA, s 11)

[72.19] A spinster (D) lived with her widowed mother (M), who was 85 years old, blind and in poor health. D, who owned two houses, was told that she was suffering from terminal cancer. In early 2003 D gave the houses to M. D died in 2005 and M died in 2007. The Revenue issued a notice of determination, charging IHT on D's gift of the houses to M (the combined value of the houses being agreed as £169,000). D's executor appealed, contending that D had given the houses to M so that they could be sold in order to pay for nursing care, so that they were exempt transfers within *IHTA, s 11(3)*. The Special Commissioner reviewed the evidence in detail and allowed the appeal in part, finding that it had been reasonable for D to have assumed that M 'would require nursing care in a residential setting'. The Commissioner held that, in order to determine what amount had been 'reasonably required' for M's care, 'the approach adopted in personal injury cases is appropriate'. On the evidence, he held that it would be reasonable to have assumed that M would have required paid nursing care for 5.5 years, and that this care would have cost £21,000 pa, leading to a basic sum of £115,500. He also held that a further £25,000 should be added 'to cover the contingency of (M's) admission to a home', so that 'reasonable provision at the time the transfers were made amounted in all to £140,500'. The Commissioner concluded that £140,500 of the transfers qualified as exempt within *IHTA, s 11* while the balance of £28,500 was a chargeable transfer within *IHTA, s 3A(4)*. *R McKelvey (personal representative of DV McKelvey) v HMRC*, Sp C [2008] SSCD 944 (Sp C 694).

[72.20] See also *Phizackerley v HMRC*, 72.224 below.

Exempt transfers (IHTA, ss 18–42)

IHTA, s 18—exemption for transfers between spouses

[72.21] An individual (H) separated from his wife in 1965 (and subsequently divorced). In 1968 he began living with another woman (K). They did not marry, but had two children together, and continued to live together until his death in 2000. H left his entire estate to K. The Revenue issued a notice of determination charging IHT. K appealed, contending that she should be entitled to the inter-spouse exemption of *IHTA, s 18*. The Special Commissioners rejected this contention and dismissed her appeal, holding that 'the word "spouse" in (*IHTA, s 18*) means a person who is legally married and does not include a person who has lived with another as husband and wife'. The Commissioners noted that, during the Parliamentary debates on the 1975 Finance Bill, an amendment to include a 'common law wife' in the definition of a 'spouse' had been considered and rejected. The relevant debate had 'highlighted the difficulty of defining exactly who should benefit and raised the question as to whether those in very brief liaisons should be included'. *Holland (Holland's Executor) v CIR*, Sp C 2002, [2003] SSCD 43 (Sp C 350). (*Note*. The Commissioners also held that this did not contravene the *Human Rights Act 1998*, since 'persons who live together as man and wife without being married are not in an analogous situation to married persons'.)

IHTA 1984, s 18—European Convention on Human Rights

[72.22] See *Burden & Burden v United Kingdom*, 31.71 HUMAN RIGHTS, and *Courten v United Kingdom*, 31.72 HUMAN RIGHTS.

Gifts to sons—whether exempt under IHTA, s 21

[72.23] Under a will, the shares in a family company were held on trust, with the income from the shares and the residuary estate being paid to the testator's widow for her life and thereafter to the testator's three sons. The trustees sold the shares in 1987, as a result of which the income of the trust was greatly increased. The testator's widow was 87 years of age and had a settled lifestyle. She authorised the trustees to distribute equally between her three sons such of the trust income for each accounting year as was surplus to her financial requirements. In February 1989 the trustees paid £9,300 to each of the sons, and on 5 February 1990 they paid £60,000 to each of the sons. The widow died suddenly on 20 February 1990. The Revenue issued determinations that the payments to the sons were chargeable to IHT. The sons appealed, contending that the gifts were exempt from IHT under *IHTA, s 21(1)* as 'part of the normal expenditure of the transferor'. The Ch D accepted this contention and allowed the appeals. (The appeals were heard by the Ch D under *IHTA, s 222(3)*, without being referred to the Special Commissioners.) Lightman J held that ' "normal expenditure" connotes expenditure which at the time it took place accorded with the settled pattern of expenditure adopted by the transferor'. For an expenditure to be viewed as 'normal', there was 'no fixed minimum period during which the expenditure shall have occurred. All that is necessary is that on the totality of evidence the pattern of actual or intended payments shall have been established and that the item in question conforms with that pattern.' The pattern need not be immutable, but t must be established that the pattern 'was intended to remain in place for more than a nominal period and indeed for a sufficient period (barring unforeseen circumstances) fairly to be regarded as a regular feature of the transferor's annual expenditure. Thus a "death bed" resolution to make periodic payments "for life" and a payment made in accordance with such a determination will not suffice.' n the evidence, the widow had adopted 'a pattern of expenditure in respect of the surplus, and the payments to the sons were made in accordance with this pattern'. *Bennett & Others v CIR*, Ch D 1994, [1995] STC 54. (*Note.* The Ch D ordered the appellant to pay part of the Revenue's costs, holding that the hearing had been prolonged by the failure of counsel for the appellant to comply with the *Rules of the Supreme Court 1965*—see **4.455** APPEALS.)

Irregular payments to close relatives—whether within IHTA, s 21

[72.24] An elderly spinster (P) died in 1995. During the years before her death, she had made a number of irregular payments to close relatives. The Revenue issued a notice of determination charging IHT on the basis that the gifts made in the seven years before P's death were transfers of value. Her executor appealed, contending that the gifts were exempt from IHT under *IHTA, s 21* as 'part of the normal expenditure of the transferor'. The Special Commissioner rejected this contention and dismissed the appeal. *IHTA, s 21* required a pattern of expenditure to be established either by proof of the existence of a prior commitment or by reference to a sequence of payments. On the evidence, the payments in question were abnormal expenditure rather than normal expenditure, and thus failed to qualify for exemption. *Nadin v CIR*, Sp C [1997] SSCD 107 (Sp C 112).

Whether IHTA, s 23 applicable

[72.25] A testator left the residue of his estate to the town council of North Berwick for use in connection with the North Berwick sports centre or for 'some purpose in connection with sport'. The Revenue issued a determination to capital transfer tax, against which the executor appealed, contending that the bequest was charitable under the *Recreational Charities Act 1958, s 1*, and was therefore exempt from CTT by virtue of what is now *IHTA, s 23(1)*. The HL accepted this contention and allowed the executor's appeal, approving *dicta* of Bridge LJ in *CIR v McMullen & Others*, **9.16** CHARITIES, and disapproving *dicta* of Walton J in the same case. The facilities at the sports centre were provided with the object of improving the conditions of life of the community generally. The phrase 'some similar purpose in connection with sport' implied a bequest which would display the leading characteristics of the sports centre, which lay in the nature of the facilities provided there and the fact that they were available to the public at large. *Guild v CIR*, HL [1992] STC 162; [1992] 2 WLR 397; [1992] 2 All ER 10.

[72.26] Under a will, a testator established a trust fund to be used for the assistance of 'the poor and needy' of defined classes of his relatives. The fund was to be distributed among such beneficiaries after 21 years, 'and in the event of there being no such persons eligible to benefit then upon trust for such charitable institutions or societies' as the trustees should think fit. The Revenue issued a determination that, because the testator had only included some of his relatives in the list of defined classes of potential beneficiaries, the disposition was a gift to poor people rather than a gift for the relief of poverty, and thus was not exclusively for charitable purposes and did not constitute an exempt transfer within *IHTA, s 23*. The executors appealed. The Ch D allowed the appeal, applying *dicta* of Jenkins LJ in *Re Scarisbrick*[1951] Ch 622, and holding that the disposition was an exempt transfer. Since the class of those eligible to benefit was not closed upon the testator's death, the testator's intention 'must be taken to have been the relief of poverty amongst the class of which they would become members'. Accordingly, the gift fell 'on the charitable side of the line, wherever that line has to be drawn'. *White & Segelman (Segelman's Executors) v CIR*, Ch D 1995, [1996] 2 WLR 173; [1995] 3 All ER 676.

[72.27] In 1985 an individual (K), who was domiciled in the UK, established a Jersey settlement, of which he was the life tenant. He died in 2001. Within twelve months of his death, the trustees of the settlement appointed 25% of the trust property to each of two charities. They appealed against a determination charging IHT on K's death, contending that the appointments should be treated as exempt transfers under *IHTA, s 23* with effect from the date of K's death. The Special Commissioner rejected this contention and dismissed the appeals, holding that the settled property had to be treated as passing from K to the trustees on his death. The subsequent appointment to the charities could not 'turn what would otherwise be chargeable transfers of value into exempt transfers'. *Bailhache Labesse Trustees Ltd & Others v HMRC*, Sp C [2008] SSCD 869 (Sp C 688).

[72.28] A woman (C), who died in 2007, left the residue of her estate to a Jersey trust, to be used in providing homes and hospice care for elderly people in a Jersey parish. HMRC issued notices of determination charging IHT on her UK estate. C's executors appealed, contending that the gift qualified for exemption under *IHTA, s 23*. The Ch D rejected this contention and dismissed the appeal. Rose J held that the trust failed to qualify for exemption under *IHTA, s 23(6)* because it was governed by Jersey law rather than UK law. She held that the words 'held on trust for charitable purposes' (in *s 23(6)*) required 'not only that the charitable purposes be UK law charitable purposes but that the relevant trust be subject to the jurisdiction of the United Kingdom courts as well'. *Routier & Venables (Coulter's Executors) v HMRC*, Ch D [2014] EWHC 3010 (Ch).

IHTA, s 33(3)—definition of 'proceeds of the sale'

[72.29] For the purpose of an estate duty provision which charged duty on previously exempt 'heritage' property, the Ch D held that 'proceeds of sale' was to be interpreted as being the net proceeds after deducting the expenses of sale. *Tyser v A-G*, Ch D [1938] Ch 426; [1938] 1 All ER 657. (*Note.* The equivalent IHT provision, *IHTA, s 33(3)*, also uses the term 'proceeds of the sale'.)

IHTA, s 35A—variation of undertakings

[72.30] The Revenue had agreed that the owners of certain valuable works of art should have the benefit of 'conditional exemption' from IHT in respect of those items, in return for the owners having entered into undertakings, within *IHTA, s 31*, that there would be 'reasonable access to the public'. The owners required members of the public who wished to view the items to make appointments before doing so. Subsequently the Revenue made applications, under *IHTA, s 35A*, to vary the undertakings so as to give wider publicity to the existence of the items, and wider access to them. The Special Commissioner reviewed the evidence in detail and dismissed the Revenue's applications, holding that 'the accumulated burdens placed on the particular owner' would 'so outweigh the benefit to the public as to make it neither just nor reasonable for me to direct that the proposals take effect'. There would be 'a serious intrusion into the family lives of the owners', and 'the increased risks of theft and damage to the owners' possessions' would go 'beyond what Parliament had in mind when empowering the inclusion of extended access requirements and publication requirements'. *Re Applications to Vary the Undertakings of 'A' and 'B'*, Sp C 2004, [2005] SSCD 103 (Sp C 439).

IHTA, s 41—allocation of exemptions

[72.31] A woman left half of her estate to two relatives and the other half to be held on trust for four charities. Her executors issued an originating summons seeking the court's declaration as to the correct method of administering the net residuary estate. The Ch D held that the half shares were to be calculated before payment of the IHT due in respect of the relatives' share (so that the net amount received by the relatives would be less than the net amount received by the charities). Blackburne J held that an equal division of disposable residue between relatives and charities inevitably meant that the IHT attributable to the relatives' share had to be borne by that share, since to subject the charities' share to any part of that burden was prohibited by *IHTA, s 41(b)*. *Holmes & Another v McMullan & Others (re Ratcliffe deceased)*, Ch D [1999] STC 262. (*Note.* Blackburne J declined to follow the earlier decision in *Lockhart v Harker & Others (re Benham's Will Trusts)*, Ch D 1994, [1995] STC 210. Although the decisions are both by the Ch D, it is settled law that 'where there are two conflicting decisions of courts of co-ordinate jurisdiction, the later decision is to be preferred, if it is reached after full consideration of the earlier decision' (per Denning J in *Minister of Pensions v Higham*, KB [1948] 1 All ER 863).)

Excluded property (IHTA, s 48)

Discretionary settlement—whether excluded property

[72.32] A trust fund was held on discretionary trusts for the benefit of the settlor's two children and two UK charities. In 1976 the trustees purchased a large quantity of exempt government securities and appointed them to the settlor's two children, neither of whom was resident or domiciled in the UK. The Revenue issued a notice of determination that the appointment was to be treated as giving rise to a capital distribution under *FA 1975, Sch 5 para 6(2)*. The CA allowed the trustees' appeal, holding that the question of whether settled property was excluded property for the purposes of *para 6(2)* depended on the state of affairs which existed immediately before the appointment, and that the exempt securities were excluded property before the appointment by virtue of what is now *IHTA, s 48(4)(b)*. Bridge LJ observed that, since 'no payment out of a discretionary trust in favour of a charity attracts capital transfer tax', it would be 'paradoxical that the mere possibility of such a payment being made out of a particular discretionary trust should deprive that trust from the immunity from taxation which it would otherwise enjoy'. *Von Ernst & Cie SA and Others v CIR*, CA 1979, CTTL 6; [1980] STC 111; [1980] 1 WLR 468; [1980] 1 All ER 677.

UK settlor transferring securities via Jersey company

[72.33] In 1977 a woman (B), who was resident and domiciled in the UK, transferred £40,000 to her non-resident, non-domiciled daughter (R), using a scheme which involved exempt government securities and a settlement on a Jersey company (C), of which B was the sole shareholder. B assigned C an interest in possession in the exempt securities. C assigned its interest to R. The Revenue issued a notice of determination on the basis that tax was chargeable as if B had made a direct gift of £40,000 to R. B appealed, contending that the property which had been transferred qualified as excluded property. The Ch D rejected this contention and upheld the determination, holding that the effect of what is now *IHTA, s 101(1)* was that B was to be treated as the person entitled to the interest in possession, and the securities were thus not excluded property. *CIR v Brandenburg*, Ch D 1982, CTTL 10; [1982] STC 555.

Trust fund invested in government securities—beneficiaries abroad

[72.34] The trust fund of a 1970 settlement was invested in a single holding of 1976 Treasury Loan Stock. This stock was exempt from taxation so long as it was in the beneficial ownership of persons neither domiciled nor ordinarily resident in the UK. The settlor's daughter (W) made a similar settlement in 1976. The settlor, trustees and beneficiaries were all domiciled outside the UK but the trust was to be governed by English law. The trustees of the two settlements transferred the 1970 settlement trust fund to themselves as trustees of the 1976 settlement, to be held on trusts for the exclusive benefit of W's four children and their issue. On the following day the trustees executed a deed of appointment whereby each child became entitled to an interest in possession of one quarter of the trust fund. The Revenue raised assessments on the ground that the making of the appointment constituted a deemed capital distribution. The Ch D dismissed the trustees' appeals. There was a possibility that the fund might benefit people domiciled in the UK. The trusts of the 1976 settlement were not exclusively for the benefit of W's four children, but might also benefit W's grandchildren. Accordingly there were resulting trusts to persons who might be resident in the UK and thus the trust fund was not excluded property. *Montagu Trust Co (Jersey) Ltd and Others v CIR*, Ch D [1989] STC 477.

Interests in possession (IHTA, ss 49–54B)

Definition of interest in possession

[72.35] Under a 1964 settlement, property was held upon trust in equal shares absolutely for the three daughters of the settlor upon their attaining the age of 21, subject to the trustees having an overriding power of appointment and power to accumulate income. In 1976 the trustees appointed the income of £16,000 to one of the daughters, F. The Revenue determined that F had become entitled to an interest in possession in the £16,000 and that CTT became payable accordingly. The HL upheld the Revenue's determination (by a 3-2 majority, Lords Salmon and Russell dissenting). The trustees' power of accumulation prevented the interests which the daughters obtained upon reaching 21 from being interests in possession. Viscount Dilhorne distinguished between trustees' administrative powers, such as those to pay duties and taxes, and their dispositive power to dispose of the net income of the trust fund. He held that a mere administrative power would not prevent an interest from being in possession. *Pearson & Others v CIR*, HL 1980, CTTL 5; [1980] STC 318; [1980] 2 All ER 479; [1980] 2 WLR 872.

[72.36] In an estate duty case, the HL held that the beneficiaries of a discretionary trust, who were not entitled either individually or collectively to receive any part of the trust income in any year, did not have interests or interests in possession in the trust fund within the meaning of the relevant estate duty provisions. Lord Reid held that an 'interest in possession' must mean an interest which enables a person 'to claim now whatever may be the subject matter of the interest'. *Gartside v CIR*, HL 1967, [1968] 2 WLR 277; [1968] 1 All ER 121; [1968] AC 553.

[72.37] Property was held on trust for an individual (H) with remainder to his brother if he should die without issue before the age of 21. The trustees were to receive the income arising while H was below the age of 21, and were to accumulate the surplus on trust for H if he should attain 21 or, if he should not, for the persons who should ultimately become entitled to the property. H died before reaching 21. The KB held that he had never become entitled to an interest in possession in the property, as he had never had any entitlement to the income from the property. *A-G v Power & Another*, KB [1906] 2 IR 272.

[72.38] A married woman (W) died in 1999, having owned a house which was divided into two flats. She had let the ground-floor flat to tenants, and had lived in the first-floor flat with her husband. By her will, she gave the house to trustees (her children by a previous marriage), but gave her husband the right to live in it 'and use it as his principal place of residence'. However, following her death, her husband stayed with his daughter for just over three weeks, before being admitted to hospital, where he died two months later. The Revenue issued a notice of determination to W's executors, ruling that her husband had not acquired an interest in possession in the house. They appealed. The Special Commissioner reviewed the evidence in detail and allowed the appeal in part, holding that the husband had acquired an interest in possession in the first-floor flat but not in the ground-floor flat. *Cook & Daw (Watkins' Executors) v CIR*, Sp C [2002] SSCD 318 (Sp C 319).

[72.39] A married woman (E) acquired a fully vested interest in her father's trust estate in 1940. She died in 1982. The Revenue issued a determination charging CTT on the basis that E had been entitled to an interest in possession in the whole of the funds then held by the trustees. The trustees appealed, contending that E's enjoyment of the trust funds was at their discretion and accordingly she had not been entitled to an interest in possession in the whole of the trust fund. The CS rejected this contention and dismissed the appeal, holding that the powers given to the trustees were administrative and not dispositive and that E had had an interest in possession in the whole fund. *Miller & Others v CIR*, CS 1986, [1987] STC 108.

Sole object of discretionary trust

[72.40] A settlor (T) directed that income from certain trust funds was to be held upon protective trusts during his life, and that the trustees were to pay or apply the income to himself or to any wife or children he might have as they in their discretion saw fit. When he died he was unmarried and childless. The Revenue issued a determination on the basis that the settlement had created a protected life interest and T had been beneficially entitled to an interest in possession in the trust funds immediately before his death. The Ch D allowed the trustees' appeal, holding that the settlement had created an immediate discretionary trust. The fact that T was the sole existing object of the discretionary trust did not give him an interest in possession. The possibility that another discretionary beneficiary might come into existence was sufficient to prevent T from having the necessary immediate entitlement to trust income as it arose. *Moore & Osborne v CIR (in re Trafford's Settlements)*, Ch D 1984, CTTL 20; [1984] STC 236; [1984] 3 WLR 341; [1984] 1 All ER 1108.

Date on which interest in possession arose

[72.41] In 1970 trustees appointed income from a trust fund to a woman (R) absolutely, although the provisions of the trust prevented R's right to the income from vesting until 1976, when her eldest child became 21. The Revenue issued a determination on the basis that R's interest under the 1970 appointment took effect only in 1976, with the result that she had had no interest in possession in the fund before then and that a capital distribution equal to the value of the fund was deemed to have been made in 1976. The trustees appealed, contending that the appointment to R had taken effect as an appointment of income in the fund subject to the vesting event occurring and to her then being alive, that consequently the trustees were obliged to pay the intermediate income of the fund to her, and that that obligation had given R a right to the enjoyment of the income and thus an interest in possession in the fund in 1970, with the result that there was no capital distribution in 1976. The Ch D accepted this contention and allowed the appeal, holding that R's interest in possession had arisen in 1970. *Swales & Others v CIR*, Ch D 1984, CTTL 24; [1984] STC 413; [1984] 3 All ER 16.

Avoidance scheme—interest in possession

[72.42] Trustees of a settlement, in which there was no interest in possession, made appointments granting interests in possession to two people (J and S) contingent upon their surviving the 'designated person for the specified period', with the interests then taking effect as from the death of the designated person. The specified period was one day. The designated person was the first person whose death on 29 November 1975 was reported in the death column of The Times on 1 December 1975, or, failing The Times, in The Daily Telegraph. The Revenue issued notices of determination that the effect of the appointments was that J and S had become absolutely entitled to the specified property in the funds and that capital distributions were to be treated as having been made out of the property comprised in those funds. The CA unanimously upheld the determinations, holding that the interest did not depend on the survival of a specified person, since there was no real possibility that the contingency would not be satisfied. The interests depended not on the death of any individual, but on the publication of The Times or The Daily Telegraph. *CIR v Trustees of Sir John Aird's Settlement (No 1)*, CA 1983, CTTL 18; [1983] STC 700; [1984] 2 WLR 178; [1983] 3 All ER 481.

Shares received as consideration for life interest in settlement

[72.43] In 1941 an individual (P) sold to a close company his life interest under a settlement for 25,000 £1 shares in the company. In 1964 he reacquired from the company his life interest in part of the settled property. His interest in the remainder of the settled property continued to be vested in the company, which was therefore entitled to an interest in possession in this part. In 1982 he held 8,993 of the 46,000 shares in the company. He gave 2,999 of the shares to a charity. Accordingly, under what is now *IHTA, s 101(1)*, he was treated as having been entitled to a part ($^{993}/_{46}$) of the interest in possession in the part of the settled property retained by the company. Following the transfer, he was treated as being entitled to $^{994}/_{46}$ of the interest in possession in question. The Revenue issued a notice of determination on the basis that he had made a transfer of value equal to ($^{999}/_{8} \times {}^{993}/_{46}$) of the settled property vested in the company. The Ch D dismissed P's appeal. The provisions of what is now *IHTA, s 101(1)* required the interest in possession held by the close company to be treated as vested in the participators in that company. Accordingly, on the disposal of the shares, part of P's interest in possession had come to an end within *IHTA, s 52(1)*. Additionally, the effect of *IHTA, s 56(3)* was that the deemed transfer of part of the settled property was not exempted by *s 23(1)*. *Powell-Cotton v CIR*, Ch D [1992] STC 625.

Life interest in matrimonial home

[72.44] A married couple lived together as tenants in common. The wife died in 1989. By her will, she appointed a trustee and bequeathed her 50% share in the matrimonial home to the trustee, directing that her husband should be permitted to continue to live there until his death, and that her share should then pass to their daughter. The husband continued to live in the property until his death in 1993. The Revenue issued a notice of determination, charging IHT on the basis that the deemed transfer of value on the husband's death included the entire interest in the property, as his wife's will had given him an interest in possession in her 50% share of the property. The trustee appealed, contending that the will did not confer an interest in possession. The Ch D rejected this contention and upheld the notice of determination. Lightman J held that the purpose and effect of the will had been to confer upon the husband a life interest in his wife's share of the property. His own rights had not been enough to entitle him to exclusive occupation for the rest of his life, and for this purpose he required the rights which had attached to his wife's share. The will granted him a determinable life interest which was an 'interest in possession' for the purpose of *IHTA, s 49(1)*. *CIR v Lloyds Private Banking Ltd*, Ch D [1998] STC 559.

[72.45] In 1980 a widower (R), with no children, made a will allowing a friend (H) and his wife 'or the survivor of them for the time being still living' to live in his house 'and have the use of the furniture as long as he she or they so wish'. R died in 1981 and the couple duly moved into the house. H died in 1998 (having outlived his wife) and the house was sold later that year. The Revenue issued a notice of determination to R's surviving trustee, on the basis that H's right of occupation had been an interest in possession in settled property, within *IHTA, s 49(1)*. The Special Commissioner upheld the notice, holding that H had had an interest in possession in the whole of the house. *Faulkner (Adams' Trustee) v CIR*, Sp C [2001] SSCD 112 (Sp C 278).

Whether testator's will conferred interest in possession

[72.46] A woman (W) was widowed in 2000. Her husband's will gave his house to trustees, with a declaration that they should allow W to occupy the house 'for such period or periods as they shall in their absolute discretion think fit'. W continued to occupy the house until her death in 2003. The Revenue issued a notice of determination on the basis that her husband's will had given her an interest in possession in the house. Her personal representatives appealed. The Special Commissioner allowed their appeal, holding that the effect of W's husband's will was that she 'had no right to occupy the property but the trustees were given a discretion (but not a duty) to allow her to occupy'. Accordingly W did not have an interest in possession in the property. *Judge & Judge (Walden's Personal Representatives) v HMRC*, Sp C [2005] SSCD 863 (Sp C 506). (*Note*. Compare Revenue Statement of Practice 10/79.)

[72.47] The will of a company director (J) gave two freehold properties to trustees, with directions to pay the trust income to his widow for her lifetime and thereafter to his three children in equal shares. One of the freehold properties was occupied by the company, and J's will directed that the trustees should not require the company to pay any rent. J's widow died in 2000, and the Revenue issued a notice of determination that IHT was chargeable on her interest in possession in the premises which were occupied by the company. Her personal representatives appealed, contending that J's will had conferred an interest in possession on the company, and that his widow did not have an interest in possession. The Special Commissioner accepted this contention and allowed the appeal, holding that J had intended that his will should protect the position of the company and preserve its use and occupancy of the premises. The will gave the company a right to occupy the premises, and that right arose 'solely under the will'. The right in question was 'a present right to present enjoyment of property' and was an 'interest in possession' within *IHTA, s 49(1)*. *Oakley & Hutson (Jossaume's Personal Representatives) v CIR*, Sp C [2005] SSCD 343 (Sp C 460).

Whether 'inter vivos' trust conferred interest in possession

[72.48] In a Scottish case, an individual (D) transferred certain securities and investments to trustees in 1962. The income arising from the trust was treated for tax purposes as income of the settlor under *FA 1958, s 22* (see now *ITTOIA 2005, ss 624–628*). D died in 1981. His wife died in 2002. The Revenue issued a notice of determination on the basis that she had had an interest in possession in the settled property. The trustees appealed. The Special Commissioner dismissed the appeal, finding that D's widow had effectively enjoyed 'a power of veto: the whole of the free annual income of the trust fund had to be paid or applied to her or for her benefit from year to year unless or until she should concur with a consideration by the trustees that it was proper and expedient for a lesser amount to be so paid or applied'. Accordingly the trust deed had conferred an interest in possession. *Trustees of the Douglas Trust (for Mrs I Fairbairn) v HMRC*, Sp C [2007] SSCD 338 (Sp C 593).

IHTA, s 50(5)—interest in part of property

[72.49] GW's will left his house to his two sons as trustees, and directed that it should not be sold as long as any of his three children wished to live in it. One of his sons (EW) had already moved out when GW died, and his daughter moved out the following year. However, his other son (AW) continued to live in the house until he died in 1997. The Revenue issued a notice of determination on the basis that, when AW died, he had a beneficial interest in the whole of the house. His personal representative appealed, contending that he only had such an interest in one half of the house, as his brother (EW) had a beneficial entitlement to the other half. (Their sister had died in 1971.) The Special Commissioner accepted this contention and allowed the appeal in part, holding that the effect of the will was that, in 1997, both AW and EW 'had the right to claim to occupy the house jointly with the other'. Accordingly, when AW died, his interest in possession subsisted in only half of the house, within *IHTA, s 50(5)*. *Woodhall (Woodhall's Personal Representative) v CIR*, Sp C [2000] SSCD 558 (Sp C 261).

IHTA, s 52(1)—effect of deed of partition

[72.50] A testator (P) left his widow a life interest in his residuary estate, with the remainder passing to his two children (by a previous marriage). In July 2000 the trustees executed a deed of partition under which the widow assigned two-thirds of the trust fund under P's estate to the reversioners, and received an absolute interest in the remainder. In December 2000 the widow died. The Revenue issued a notice of determination on the basis that the deed of partition had resulted in a transfer of value under *IHTA 1984, s 52(1)*. The executors appealed, contending that the deed of partition should not be treated as giving rise to a transfer of value. The Special Commissioner rejected this contention and dismissed the appeal. *Mrs Patch's Executors v HMRC*, Sp C [2007] SSCD 453 (Sp C 600).

Accumulation and maintenance trusts (IHTA, s 71)

Power of revocation—interpretation of IHTA, s 71(1)(a)

[72.51] Under a 1964 appointment, property was held on trust for those of B's children who attained 21 or married under that age, subject to powers of revocation and reappointment, and with interim powers of accumulation and maintenance. In May 1975 B's eldest child became 21, and in March 1976 the trustees released their power of revocation. The Revenue issued notices of determination charging CTT, and the trustees appealed, contending that the transfers were exempt under what is now *IHTA, s 71*. The CA unanimously rejected this contention and dismissed the trustees' appeals, holding that the trust had failed to meet the condition in what is now *s 71(1)(a)* that the beneficiaries 'will' become beneficially entitled to an interest in possession. The trust had been subject to a power of revocation and reappointment, under which the beneficiaries' interest could have been extinguished at the absolute discretion of the trustees. The word 'will' implied a degree of certainty inconsistent with such a power. *Lord Inglewood & Another v CIR*, CA 1982, CTTL 16; [1983] STC 133; [1983] 1 WLR 366.

Deed of appointment executed by trustees

[72.52] The trustees of a discretionary settlement executed a deed of appointment with the intention of establishing an accumulation and maintenance settlement. The appointment was declared to be conditional on the power of accumulation being valid under the *Trusts (Scotland) Act 1961*, and provided that if the accumulations were contrary to law, the appointment should be void. The Revenue refused to accept the deed as establishing an accumulation and maintenance settlement, considering that the conditions of what is now *IHTA, s 71(1)(a)* were not satisfied. The CS allowed the trustees' appeal, holding that the word 'will' in *s 71(1)(a)* did not require absolute certainty. Both the Revenue and the trustees agreed that there was no illegality, and the fact that a third party might question this in future did not prevent *s 71(1)(a)* being satisfied. The deed was not *ultra vires*, and the fact that the trustees might not safely make any distribution to the primary beneficiaries until the doubt as to the law was resolved did not prevent the settlement from qualifying as an accumulation and maintenance settlement within *IHTA, s 71*. *Maitland's Trustees v Lord Advocate*, CS [1982] SLT 483.

Assignation of interest in trust fund

[72.53] An individual (B) was born in 1969. He was due to become entitled to an interest in a trust fund, created under a 1954 settlement, on reaching the age of 21. In 1989, when he was 19 years old, he assigned the whole of his prospective interest to the trustees of a discretionary trust in which there was no interest in possession. The Revenue issued a notice of determination on the basis that the assignation of B's interest gave rise to a charge to IHT under *IHTA, s 71(3)*. The trustees of the 1954 settlement appealed. The Special Commissioner allowed the appeal, holding that *IHTA, s 71(3)* did not apply because 'immediately after the assignation, the trust comprised exactly the same property as immediately before the assignation; and viewing matters as at the date the assignation took effect, one or more persons "will" on or before attaining the age of 21 become beneficially entitled to an interest in possession in it. The conditions set forth in *section 71(1)* were met immediately after the assignation took effect in the same way they were met immediately before the assignation took effect. It cannot therefore be said that settled property ceased to be property to which *section 71* applied by virtue of the effect of the assignation. It follows that the assignation did not give rise to a charge to tax under *section 71(3)*.' *Crawford Settlement Trustees v HMRC*, Sp C [2005] SSCD 457 (Sp C 473).

Business property relief (IHTA, ss 103–114)

Definition of 'business' (IHTA, s 103)

IHTA, s 103(3)—business 'carried on otherwise than for gain'

[72.54] An individual (M) died in 1986, owning substantial shareholdings in two companies. Each of the companies had purchased property which was occupied by shareholders. The Revenue issued notices of determination charging IHT on the value of shares in the companies. M's executors appealed, contending that the shares qualified for business property relief. The Special Commissioner rejected this contention and dismissed the appeal, holding that the effect of *IHTA, s 103(3)* was that the shares did not qualify for relief, because the companies had used their funds to purchase land for occupation by their shareholders, so that their businesses had been carried on 'otherwise than for gain'. *Grimwood-Taylor & Mallender (Mallender's Executors) v CIR*, Sp C 1999, [2000] SSCD 39 (Sp C 223).

The nature of the relief (IHTA, s 104)

Transfer of farmland with development value

[72.55] In 2002 a farmer transferred some farmland, which had development value, to the trustees of a family settlement. The Revenue issued a ruling that 'none of the value transferred was attributable to the value of relevant business property'. The trustees appealed. The Special Commissioner allowed the appeal, specifically disapproving passages in Dymond's Capital Taxes and Foster's Inheritance Tax which suggested that the transfer of business assets (as distinct from the transfer of a business itself) would not qualify for relief. The Commissioner (Dr. Avery Jones) held that 'everything turns on the loss in value to the donor's estate, rather than what is given or how the loss to the estate arises, except where the identity of the recipient is crucial to a particular exemption'. He held that business property relief was 'much more concerned with values than property. Although the attribution is to the net value of the business as a whole, this does not imply that the value transferred must relate to the whole business. Indeed the exclusion for value attributed to excepted assets in *s 112* shows that the value transferred may need to be attributed to the value of particular business assets (although that would equally be the case if the relief were restricted to transfers of the whole business). Presumably the attribution to the net value of the business is to put a ceiling on the relief to prevent a transferor giving away the total assets of the business, claiming business relief for them, while retaining the liabilities and paying them out of other assets (although that seems to be possible for agricultural relief as the relief is given in terms of attribution to the agricultural value of agricultural property).' *IHTA, s 104* should be construed as meaning that 'all that is required is that the value transferred by the transfer of value is attributable to the net value of the business'. Accordingly the transfer of the farmland qualified for 100% business property relief. The Ch D upheld this decision. Sales J held that 'the general principle governing the operation of the *IHTA* is the loss to donor principle, which directs attention to changes in the value of the transferor's estate rather than in that of the transferee', and that 'any charge to tax does not turn upon what happens to property transferred when it is in the hands of the transferee'. *HMRC v Nelson Dance Family Settlement Trustees*, Ch D 2009, 79 TC 605; [2009] STC 802; [2009] EWHC 71 (Ch).

Relevant business property (IHTA, s 105)

IHTA, s 105(1)(a)—whether retired partner retained interest in business

[72.56] A woman (H) and her daughter (B) had carried on business in partnership for many years until H retired in 1993. B then continued the business as sole proprietor. H died in 1997, having retained an interest in the business through her capital account. The Revenue issued a notice of determination charging IHT on the amounts owed by B to H at H's death. B appealed, contending that the amounts in question were 'relevant business property' within *IHTA, s 105(1)(a)*. The Special Commissioner rejected this contention and dismissed the appeal. For the purposes of *IHTA, s 105*, H's interest in the business 'ceased when she retired from the partnership'.

Following H's retirement from the business, her rights 'were simply those of a creditor of the business'. *Beckman v CIR*, Sp C [2000] SSCD 59 (Sp C 226).

IHTA, s 105(1)(b)—shares in unquoted company

[72.57] See *Walding & Others v CIR*, 72.219 below.

IHTA, s 105(1)(d)—land used by company

[72.58] See *Walker's Executors v CIR*, 72.220 below.

IHTA, s 105(1)(e)—land used for business purposes

[72.59] In 1977 the life tenant of settled land, who had used that land in his farming and forestry business, died. The Revenue issued a notice of determination charging CTT, and the trustees appealed, contending that the value of the settled land qualified for business property relief. The CA accepted this contention and allowed the appeal (by a 2-1 majority, Dillon LJ dissenting). Oliver LJ held that, athough the land itself was not relevant business property, the life interest in the land was an asset used in the business. For CTT purposes the asset had to be valued as if the deceased was beneficially entitled to the land itself. It therefore qualified for business property relief. *Fetherstonhaugh, Finch & Others v CIR*, CA 1984, CTTL 21; [1984] STC 261; [1984] 3 WLR 212.

IHTA, s 105(3)—whether a business of 'making or holding investments'

Cases held to qualify for relief

[72.60] An individual (B), who owned a 99% shareholding in an unquoted UK company (G), died in 1986. G had operated a nightclub, but had sold this in 1985. The proceeds of the sale were held on short-term deposit pending re-investment in similar premises, but no such premises had been acquired at the time of B's death. The executors claimed that B's shareholding qualified for business property relief. The Revenue rejected the claim on the basis that G's business consisted wholly or mainly of making or holding investments. The executors appealed, contending that until B's death, G had been actively seeking alternative sites to open a new nightclub, and accordingly it should not be treated as an investment-holding company. The Special Commissioner accepted the executors' evidence and allowed the appeal. *Brown's Executors v CIR*, Sp C [1996] SSCD 277 (Sp C 83).

[72.61] A father and son operated a holiday caravan park in partnership. The park was licensed for 218 static caravans and 8 touring caravans. Permanent residence at the park was not permitted, and caravans were not allowed to be occupied during February. Less than 50% of the park's profits was derived from the rents for the sites for static caravans, and a significant percentage of the income came from the sale of caravans. The father died in 1996, and the Revenue issued a determination on the basis that the park did not qualify for business property relief, since the relevant business consisted 'wholly or mainly of holding investments', within *IHTA, s 105(3)*. The Special Commissioner allowed the son's appeal, holding on the evidence that the business 'did not consist wholly or mainly of holding investments'. The maintenance of the park involved three full-time employees, as well as the majority of the partner's time, and this did not 'correspond to what one would normally expect to find in a business concerned wholly or mainly with the holding of investments'. *Hall & Hall (Hall's Executors) v CIR*, 72.69 below, was distinguished since that business 'was preponderantly one of the receipt of rents', while *Powell & Halfhide (Pearce's Personal Representatives) v CIR*, 72.70 below, was distinguished as in that case the income consisted solely of pitch fees and rent. *Furness v CIR*, Sp C [1999] SSCD 232 (Sp C 202).

[72.62] A woman (S) had owned 85% of the shares in a company (D) which operated a residential caravan park, comprising 167 mobile homes, and a country club with a licensed bar. The Revenue issued a notice of determination on the basis that her shares in the company were not 'relevant business property', because D's business consisted mainly of 'making or holding investments'. S's executors appealed. The Special Commissioner reviewed the evidence in detail and allowed the appeal, observing that D had several full-time employees and was classed as a trading company for corporation tax purposes, and finding that '72% of the site fees goes in overheads', most of which related to 'the provision of upkeep of the common parts'. D's business was 'the provision of services and not the business of holding investments'. The Ch D reversed this decision but the CA restored it. Carnwath LJ held that, on the evidence, 'the holding of property as investment was only one component of the business, and on the findings of the Commissioner it was not the main component'. Accordingly the shares in D qualified for business property relief. *George & Loochin (Stedman's Executors) v CIR*, CA 2003, 75 TC 735; [2004] STC 163; [2003] EWCA Civ 1763.

[72.63] An individual (F), who owned a farm comprising 449 acres, died in 1997. Several of the properties at the farm were surplus to the requirements of the farm, and he had let these to tenants on short leases. The farm had an agreed probate value of £3,500,000, of which £2,250,000 related to the farmhouse, farm buildings and farmland, and qualified for 100% agricultural property relief. The balance of £1,250,000 related to the properties which had been let. F's executors claimed business property relief on the basis that there was a single business which qualified for relief (accepting that, by virtue of *IHTA, s 114(1)*, the business property relief was restricted to the £1,250,000 which did not qualify for agricultural property relief). The Revenue rejected the claim and issued a notice of determination that the farm business consisted mainly of making or holding investments, within *IHTA, s 105(3)*, and therefore was not 'relevant business property'. The executors appealed, accepting that the letting of property was 'making or holding investments' but contending that F's business had consisted mainly of farming. The Special Commissioner accepted this contention and allowed the appeal, holding on the evidence that 'the overall context of the business, the capital employed, the time spent by the employees and consultants, and the levels of turnover, all support the conclusion that the business consisted mainly of farming'. The fact that the lettings were more profitable than the rest of the business was not conclusive. *Farmer & Giles (Farmer's Executors) v CIR*, Sp C [1999] SSCD 321 (Sp C 216).

[72.64] A widow had held a majority shareholding in a company (P) which lent money to related family companies. Her executors claimed business property relief. The Revenue rejected the claim on the basis that the shares were not 'relevant business property', because P's business consisted mainly of 'making or holding investments', within *IHTA, s 105(3)*. The Special Commissioner allowed the executors' appeal, finding that P was 'a banking arm for in-house transactions' and holding that 'few would regard the activities of a money-lender as investment'. On the evidence, P 'was in the business of making loans and not in the business of investing in loans'. The loans 'were not investments for their own sake but the provision of a finance facility to the other companies'. Accordingly the shares in P qualified for business property relief. *Phillips & Others (Phillips' Executors) v HMRC*, Sp C [2006] SSCD 639 (Sp C 555).

[72.65] A property development company (T) owned some land in Islington, on which it had erected some workshops which it let. T's major shareholder died in 1999. His executors claimed business property relief. The Revenue rejected the claim on the grounds that because T received significant rental income, its business consisted mainly of 'making or holding investments', within *IHTA, s 105(3)*. The executors appealed, contending that it still wished to develop the land in Islington for residential purposes but had been unable to do so because of uncertainty about proposals for a new railway line. The Special Commissioner accepted this evidence and allowed the appeal, finding that T continued to hold its land as trading stock, and holding that it was not an 'investment company' for the purposes of *IHTA, s 105*. The Commissioner also held that 'the only type of land-dealing company whose shares fail to qualify for the relief' would be 'some sort of dealing or speculative trader that does not actively develop or actually build on land'. *DWC Piercy's Executors v HMRC*, Sp C [2008] SSCD 858 (Sp C 687).

Cases held not to qualify for relief

[72.66] A widow owned a number of industrial units. On her death, the Revenue issued a notice of determination. Her executors appealed, contending that the industrial units qualified for business property relief. The Special Commissioner rejected this contention and dismissed the appeal, holding that the effect of *IHTA, s 105(3)* was that the property was not 'relevant business property', since the widow's business consisted wholly or mainly of 'making or holding investments'. The Commissioner noted that *s 105(3)* derived from *FA 1976*, and that, during the relevant Finance Bill Debates, the Chief Secretary of the Treasury had stated that the letting of land did not qualify for business property relief. *Martin & Horsfall (Moore's Executors) v CIR*, Sp C [1995] SSCD 5 (Sp C 2).

[72.67] The decision in *Martin & Horsfall v CIR*, **72.66** above, was applied in a similar case where the deceased had let four flats on shorthold tenancies. The Commissioner held that the letting of the flats was a business which was 'wholly one of making or holding investments', so that the effect of *IHTA, s 105(3)* was that business property relief was not due. *Burkinyoung (Burkinyoung's Executor) v CIR*, Sp C [1995] SSCD 29 (Sp C 3).

[72.68] An executor appealed against an IHT determination, contending that shares in a company which owned and managed an eight-acre industrial estate should be treated as qualifying for business property relief. The First-tier Tribunal rejected this contention and dismissed the appeal, holding that the business consisted wholly or mainly of 'making or holding investments', so that the shares did not qualify for relief. *J Best (AW Buller's Executor) v HMRC*, FTT [2014] UKFTT 077 (TC), TC03217.

[72.69] A widow (H) had owned a caravan park. The caravans, which were owned by their respective tenants, were let from March to October each year. The park also contained 11 chalets which were let on 45-year leases. H's executors appealed against a notice of determination, contending that the park qualified for business property relief. The Special Commissioners rejected this contention and dismissed the appeal. On the evidence, almost 84% of H's income from the park consisted of rent and standing charges. It followed that H's business had consisted 'mainly of making or holding investments', within *IHTA, s 105(3)*. *Hall & Hall (Hall's Executors) v CIR*, Sp C [1997] SSCD 126 (Sp C 114).

[72.70] The decision in *Hall & Hall (Hall's Executors) v CIR*, **72.69** above, was followed in the similar subsequent case of *Powell & Halfhide (Pearce's Personal Representatives) v CIR*, Sp C [1997] SSCD 181 (Sp C 120).

[72.71] A widow (W) had owned shares in a company which operated a residential caravan park. Most of the company's income derived from pitch fees. The Revenue issued a notice of determination on the basis that her shares in the company were not 'relevant business property', because the company's business consisted mainly of 'making or holding investments'. W's executor appealed. The Special Commissioner dismissed the appeal, applying *Hall & Hall (Hall's Executors) v CIR*, **72.69** above, and distinguishing *Furness v CIR*, **72.61** above. The Ch D upheld this decision as one of fact. *Weston (Weston's Executor) v CIR*, Ch D [2000] STC 1064.

[72.72] A woman owned a number of shares in a company (T) which owned more than 100 different properties. Her executors claimed business property relief. The Revenue rejected the claim on the basis that the shares were not 'relevant business property', because T's business consisted mainly of 'making or holding investments', within *IHTA, s 105(3)*. The executors appealed, contending that because T carried out maintenance work on the properties itself, it should not be treated as falling within *s 105(3)*. The Special Commissioner rejected this contention and dismissed the executors' appeal, holding that 'the company's maintenance activity is not the separate provision of services; it is inherent in property ownership'. On the evidence, T's business consisted 'mainly of holding investments'. *Clark & Southern (Clark's Executors) v HMRC*, Sp C [2005] SSCD 823 (Sp C 502).

[72.73] In 1983 a widow (M) inherited 33 acres of farmland on the death of her husband. She did not farm the land herself, but let it to local farmers under conacre or agistment agreements. She died in 1999. The Revenue issued a notice of determination charging IHT on her estate. Her personal representatives appealed, contending that the farmland qualified for business property relief. The Special Commissioner rejected this contention and dismissed the appeal, holding that although M was carrying on a business on the land, that business consisted mainly of making or holding investments, within *IHTA, s 105(3)*, so that the land was not 'relevant business property'. The CA (NI) unanimously upheld this decision. Girvan LJ held that 'the use by the graziers was sufficiently exclusive for the land to be shown to be used as an investment.

The agisting farmer had exclusive rights of grazing; he was entitled to exclude other graziers including the deceased; the deceased could not use the land for any purpose that interfered with the grazing and the letting for grazing was the way in which the deceased decided that the grasslands could be used and exploited as uncultivated grassland short of the creation of a lease. The deceased's business consisted of earning a return from grassland whose real and effective value lay in its grazing potential.' *PN McCall & BJA Keenan (Personal Representatives of Mrs E McClean) v HMRC*, CA(NI) 2009, 79 TC 758; [2009] STC 990; [2009] NICA 12.

[72.74] A woman, who died in 2006, had owned a 25% share in a bungalow in Suffolk, which had been let as holiday accommodation. HMRC issued a determination charging IHT on her share of the bungalow. Her personal representatives appealed, contending that the letting of the bungalow had been a business and that the bungalow had not been an investment. The Upper Tribunal rejected the latter contention and upheld the determination (reversing the First-Tier decision). Henderson J held that, on the evidence, the only reasonable conclusion was that the letting had been a business 'which was mainly that of holding the property as an investment'. There was nothing to distinguish the business 'from any other actively managed furnished letting business of a holiday property, and certainly no basis for concluding that the services comprised in the total package preponderated to such an extent that the business ceased to be one which was mainly of an investment nature'. *HMRC v Lockyer & Robertson (Mrs NV Pawson's Personal Representatives)*, UT [2013] UKUT 50 (TCC); [2013] STC 976.

[72.75] A trust held a leasehold interest in a commercial property, and also owned eleven residential properties. The trustees appealed against a charge to IHT under *IHTA, s 64*, contending that the properties qualified for business property relief. The First-tier Tribunal dismissed the appeal, holding that the trust was carrying on a business which consisted mainly of making or holding investments, within *IHTA, s 105(3)*, so that the land was not 'relevant business property'. *Trustees of David Zetland Settlement v HMRC*, FTT [2013] UKFTT 284 (TC), TC02690.

Minimum period of ownership (IHTA, ss 106, 107)

Application of IHTA, s 107

[72.76] In 1968 the Earl of Balfour inherited a liferent interest in a family estate, much of which was used for farming. In November 2002 he entered into a farming partnership with his nephew (who was his heir and intended successor). In June 2003 he died. HMRC issued a ruling that business property relief was not due. The Earl's personal representative appealed, contending that the effect of the 'replacement property' provisions in *IHTA, s 107* was that the estate qualified for business property relief. The First-tier Tribunal accepted this contention and allowed the appeal, finding that the Earl had 'appeared to manage the estate in a way that was characteristic of his generation' and 'dominated and in practice controlled the running of the estate'. On the evidence, the Earl's interest in the partnership which subsisted immediately before his death replaced the business which he had previously carried on. The tribunal also held that *IHTA, s 105(3)* did not apply, since the management of the estate comprised far more than simply 'the making or holding of investments', and had been 'mainly a trading activity' in which 'the letting side was ancillary to the farming, forestry, woodland and sporting activities. The farming activities, albeit they include agricultural tenancies, occupied by far the greater area of the estate.' Accordingly, the Earl's interest in the partnership was 'relevant business property' which qualified for relief. The Upper Tribunal upheld this decision as one of fact, holding inter alia that the fact that the Earl 'as liferenter did not have a direct interest in the capital realisations of timber from the woodlands' did not prevent the woodlands from constituting 'business property' which qualified for relief. *HMRC v AM Brander (Earl of Balfour's Personal Representative)*, UT 2010, 80 TC 163; [2010] STC 2666; [2010] UKUT 300 (TC).

IHTA, s 107(4)—identification of shares

[72.77] In December 2002 a widow (D), who was in poor health, was allotted one million shares in a family company (W). She died two days later. The Revenue issued a determination charging IHT. D's executors appealed, contending that she had been allotted the shares as part of a reorganisation of W's share capital, within *TCGA, s 126*, so that the effect of *IHTA, s 107(4)* was that the shares should be identified with shares which she already held and qualified for business property relief. The Special Commissioner rejected this contention and dismissed the appeal, holding that there had not been a reorganisation of W's share capital within *TCGA, s 126*. Accordingly the provisions of *s 107(4)* did not apply and the shares did not qualify for business property relief. *Mrs MA Vinton & Mrs JJ Green (Mrs M Dugan-Chapman's Executors) v HMRC*, Sp C [2008] SSCD 592 (Sp C 666). (*Note*. For proceedings concerning a professional negligence claim, brought following this decision, see *Vinton & Others v Fladgate Fielder*, Ch D [2010] STC 1868; [2010] EWHC 904 (Ch).

Value of business (IHTA, s 110)

IHTA, s 110(b)—historic house partly used for business purposes

[72.78] Part of a historic house was open to the public, while part was used as a private residence and not open to the public. The freeholder died in 1997. The Revenue issued a notice of determination charging IHT on 22% of the value of the house, on the basis that only 78% of the house was open to the public and thus only 78% of the house qualified for business property relief. The freeholder's executors appealed, contending that the house was a single asset and that the effect of *IHTA, s 110(b)* was that the whole of the house qualified for business property relief even though 22% of the house was not open to the public. The Special Commissioner accepted this contention and allowed the appeal, observing that *s 110* made no provision for apportionment, and holding that 'it is natural to consider a single building as a single asset where the unencumbered freehold is in single ownership'. The house was 'plainly important as a single structure and the whole building is a vital backdrop to the business carried on. The whole of the exterior is essential to the business.' *Seymour & Others (Marquess of Hertford's Executors) v CIR*, Sp C 2004, [2005] SSCD 177 (Sp C 444).

IHTA, s 110(b)—Lloyd's underwriter

[72.79] A Lloyd's underwriter (D) died in 1993. His underwriting business was supported by several bank guarantees. In consideration for the guarantees, D had indemnified the bank against all liabilities and had secured this liability by a charge over some commercial property which D owned. The Revenue issued notices of determination on the basis that the commercial property did not qualify for business property relief. D's executors appealed, contending that the effect of the charge over the commercial property was that it was within the definition of 'assets used in the business', within *IHTA, s 110(b)*. The Ch D rejected this contention and upheld the notices (reversing the decision of the Special Commissioner). Jacob J held that an asset used as a security for a guarantee was not 'relevant business property' within *IHTA, s 105(1)(a)*. The property was not itself used in the business, and did not qualify for relief. *CIR v Mallender & Others (Drury-Lowe's Executors)*, Ch D [2001] STC 514.

[72.80] A Lloyd's underwriter (V) died in 1994. It was accepted that his underwriting activities constituted a business, within *IHTA, s 105(1)(a)*, qualifying for business property relief. The Revenue issued a determination charging IHT on the basis that, when computing the net value of V's business for the purposes of business property relief, the amounts owing on accounts open at the date of his death constituted 'liabilities incurred for the purposes of the business', and should be deducted from the value of the assets used in V's business. His executors appealed, contending that the amounts owing were not 'liabilities incurred for the purposes of the business', and should therefore be deducted from the value of his other estate. The Special Commissioner accepted this contention and allowed the appeal. Applying the principles in *Van den Berghs Ltd v Clark*, **61.25** TRADING INCOME, the insurance contracts in question were 'ordinary commercial contracts made in the course of carrying on the trade' and were not 'assets used in the business' for the purposes of *IHTA, s 110*. Accordingly, the money owing on open accounts 'was not a liability incurred for the purposes of the business within the meaning of *section 110(b)*'. *Hardcastle & Hardcastle (Vernede's Executors) v CIR*, Sp C [2000] SSCD 532 (Sp C 259). (*Note*. For the Revenue's practice following this decision, see Lloyd's Market Bulletin Y2543, 8 May 2001, and the chapter on 'Lloyd's Underwriters' in Tolley's Tax Planning.)

Excepted assets (IHTA, s 112)

[72.81] A married woman (W) died in 1990. Her estate included a 50% shareholding in a family company, which held cash of about £450,000 at her death. The Revenue issued a notice of determination, accepting in principle that the shares qualified for business property relief, but computed on the basis that the company only required cash of some £150,000 for the purposes of its business, and that the balance of £300,000 was an 'excepted asset', within *IHTA, s 112(2)*, and did not qualify for relief. W's executor appealed, contending that the company had held the cash 'as a contingency measure' in case 'an appropriate business opportunity should arise', so that the cash was required for future use, within *IHTA, s 112(2)(b)*. The Special Commissioner rejected this contention and dismissed the appeal, holding on the evidence that the £300,000 was not 'required'. The Commissioner held that, for the purposes of *s 112*, 'required' did not include 'the possibility that the money might be required should an opportunity arise to make use of the money in two, three or seven years' time'. The word 'required' implied 'some imperative that the money will fall to be used upon a given project or for some palpable business purpose'. *Barclays Bank Trust Co Ltd v CIR*, Sp C [1998] SSCD 125 (Sp C 158).

Agricultural property relief (IHTA, ss 115–124B)

IHTA, s 115(2)—definition of 'agricultural property'

[72.82] A deceased estate included a 2.5 acre site containing a substantial six-bedroomed farmhouse and a number of outbuildings. The site was used as part of a moderately-sized farm, most of which was held by a farming company. The Revenue issued a notice of determination that the transfer of the site was not a transfer of 'agricultural property' within *IHTA, s 115(2)*, and thus did not qualify for agricultural property relief. The Ch D and CA unanimously dismissed the executors' appeal, holding that the site was not 'agricultural property', since it was not 'agricultural land or pasture'. *Starke & Another (Brown's Executors) v CIR*, CA [1995] STC 689; [1995] 1 WLR 1439; [1996] 1 All ER 622.

[72.83] A deceased estate included a six-bedroomed house, part of which had been built in the sixteenth century, and a number of agricultural buildings, set in about 132 acres of agricultural land. The site had been used as a farm by the same family for more than 90 years. The Revenue issued a notice of determination that the house was not 'of a character appropriate to the property' for the purposes of *IHTA, s 115(2)*, and thus did not qualify for agricultural property relief. The company which acted as the deceased's personal representative appealed. The Special Commissioner allowed the appeal, finding that the property 'was in a poor state of repair and maintenance. The result was that, even if the dwelling-house had at one time been a family home of some distinction, it had, both in appearance and in use, become a farmhouse on a working farm.' On the evidence, the house was 'a farmhouse with a farm and definitely not a house with land'. It was 'of a character appropriate to the property' for the purposes of *s 115(2)*. *Lloyds TSB plc (Antrobus' Personal Representative) v CIR*, Sp C [2002] SSCD 468 (Sp C 336). (*Note.* For subsequent developments in this case, see **72.90** below.)

[72.84] In 1954 H purchased an estate comprising 134 acres and including a large hunting lodge, built in the early nineteenth century. He farmed the estate until 1985, from when he let the farmland but continued to live in the lodge. He died in 2000, and the property was sold in 2001 for £1,150,000. The Revenue accepted that the land and agricultural outbuildings qualified for agricultural property relief, but issued a ruling that the lodge was not 'of a character appropriate to the property' for the purposes of *IHTA, s 115(2)*, and thus did not qualify for agricultural property relief. H's executors appealed. The Special Commissioner dismissed the appeal, holding that 'for the purposes of *section 115(2)* the unit must be an agricultural unit: that is to say that within the unit, the land must predominate'; and any qualifying cottages, farm buildings or farmhouses must be 'ancillary to the land'. However, in view of the price paid for the property, it was clear that 'within this particular unit it is the house which predominates, and that what we have here is a house with farmland going with it (and not vice versa)'. Accordingly, the lodge was not a 'farmhouse' for the purposes of *s 115(2)*. *Higginson's Executors v CIR*, Sp C [2002] SSCD 483 (Sp C 337).

[72.85] An individual (G) began farming in about 1945, on a small farm with 16.29 acres of agricultural land. He continued to live in the farmhouse until his death in 2007. HMRC accepted that the land qualified for agricultural property relief, but issued a notice of determination charging IHT on the house, on the basis that it was not 'of a character appropriate to the property' for the purposes of *IHTA, s 115(2)*, and thus did not qualify for relief. G's executors appealed. The First-tier Tribunal allowed the appeal, finding that the condition of the house was 'such that it would only be acceptable as a farm house', and observing that 'a working farm is not expected to be finished to the higher standards of a domestic residence'. The fact that the farm had only made small profits did not prevent the house from qualifying for relief, since G had 'relied on its produce and income to supplement what was, by any standards, a meagre income'. *Golding's Executors v HMRC*, FTT [2011] UKFTT 351 (TC), TC01211.

[72.86] P and his wife owned a farm with 41 acres of land. In 1989 they gave 39 acres to their daughter (R), who was carrying on a farming business with her husband seven miles away. P and his wife retained the farmhouse and two acres of land. Following the transfer, R and her husband farmed all 41 acres of land, including the two acres which P and his wife continued to own. P died in April 2001, and his wife died seven weeks later. The Revenue issued a notice of determination charging IHT on the farmhouse and a barn. (The Revenue accepted that the two acres of land were 'agricultural property' within *IHTA, s 115(2)*.) R appealed, contending that the farmhouse and barn qualified for agricultural property relief. The Special Commissioner allowed the appeal in part, holding that by 2001 the house was not a 'farmhouse' for the purpose of *IHTA, s 115(2)*, since its 'prime function' was 'as a retirement home'. However, the barn was 'a working farm building' and qualified for relief. *Rosser v CIR*, Sp C [2003] SSCD 311 (Sp C 368). (*Note.* The Special Commissioner expressed the view that 'the nexus between the farm buildings and the property in *s 115(2)* is that the farm buildings and the property must be in the estate of the person at the time of making the deemed disposition'. This *dictum* was disapproved by the Upper Tribunal in the subsequent case of *Hanson v HMRC*, **72.88** below.)

[72.87] A married couple had owned a small country estate comprising a large house with six acres of gardens and some domestic outbuildings, and 187 acres of land, most of which was farmland. They both died in 2003. The Revenue issued notices of determination charging IHT on the house (while accepting that 110 acres of land and a farm outbuilding qualified for agricultural property relief). The executors appealed, contending that the house was a farmhouse which also qualified for agricultural property relief, as did 11 more outbuildings on the estate. The Special Commissioner reviewed the evidence in detail and held that three of the outbuildings qualified for relief but that the main house and eight of the outbuildings did not. The Commissioner observed that the farming activities were carried on by contractors who were managed by a land agent in a nearby town. The house which the couple lived in was not 'the main dwelling from which the agricultural operations over the land were conducted and managed'. *Arnander, Lloyd & Villiers (McKenna's Executors) v HMRC*, Sp C [2006] SSCD 800 (Sp C 565).

[72.88] Under a settlement, a farmhouse was occupied by the son of the settlor until his death in 2002. HMRC issued a notice of determination charging IHT on the property. The trustee of the settlement appealed, contending that the farmhouse qualified for agricultural property relief. The First-tier Tribunal accepted this contention and allowed the appeal. Judge Walters declined to follow *obiter dicta* of the Special Commissioner in *Rosser v CIR*, 72.86 above, and held that the effect of *IHTA, s 115(2)* was that 'cottages, farm buildings and farmhouses in the third limb of the definition must be of a character appropriate to agricultural land or pasture (including woodland and any building within the second limb of the definition) in the same occupation, but that it is not required that the cottages, farm buildings and farmhouses should be in the same ownership as the agricultural land or pasture (as expanded by the second limb of the definition)'. The Upper Tribunal upheld this decision. Warren J held that there had to be some nexus to establish that the agricultural land was 'connected in a relevant way with the cottage, farm building or farmhouse'. However, the 'ownership nexus' which HMRC had propounded was not an essential condition for the relief. On the facts here, where the land and the farmhouse were both occupied by the settlor's son, there was a sufficient functional connection between the land and the farmhouse. *HMRC v JN Hanson (Trustee of the William Hanson 1957 Settlement)*, UT [2013] UKUT 224 (TCC); [2013] STC 2394.

'Broiler houses' used for intensive rearing of poultry

[72.89] A farm occupied 7.41 acres of land. Part of the land was used for three 'broiler houses', which were used for the intensive rearing of poultry. In April 2000 the owner of the farm (W) let the broiler houses, and 2.59 acres of the land, to a company (S). W died in 2001. The Revenue issued a ruling that the broiler houses, and the 2.59 acres of land which had been let to S, did not qualify as 'agricultural property' within *IHTA, s 115(2)*. W's personal representative appealed. The Special Commissioner reviewed the evidence in detail and allowed the appeal in part, holding that the effect of *s 115(2)* was that the broiler houses could only qualify for relief if they had been 'a subsidiary part of the purpose of an overall agricultural activity carried out on the land'. Since they had been let to a separate company, this was not the case. Accordingly, the broiler houses had not been 'ancillary' to the farm, within *s 115(2)*, and did not qualify for relief. However, on the evidence, the broiler houses only occupied 0.68 acres of land. The Commissioner held that the remaining 1.91 acres of land which had been let to S was within the definition of 'agricultural property' and did qualify for relief. *Williams (Williams' Personal Representative) v HMRC*, Sp C [2005] SSCD 782 (Sp C 500).

IHTA, s 115(3)—valuation of agricultural property

[72.90] Following the decision noted at 72.83 above, the Revenue issued a notice of determination that the farmhouse in question had a market value in excess of its value as agricultural property, so that IHT was payable on the amount by which the market value exceeded the agricultural value. The personal representatives appealed, contending that the agricultural value was the same as the market value. The Lands Tribunal reviewed the evidence in detail, rejected this contention and dismissed the appeal, holding that the open market value of the farmhouse should be discounted by 30% to arrive at its 'agricultural value'. *Lloyds TSB plc (Antrobus' Personal Representative) v Twiddy*, Lands Tribunal 10 October 2005 unreported.

IHTA, s 117—whether property occupied for agricultural purposes

[72.91] An individual (H) died in 1990. In 1986 he had transferred his share in a farmhouse to his son (who already owned the other share). The farmhouse had been unoccupied since 1983 and remained unoccupied until 1988, when the son moved into it following the completion of renovation work. Following H's death, the Revenue included the value of the farmhouse in an IHT assessment. H's executors appealed, contending that the farmhouse was 'agricultural property' within the meaning of *IHTA, s 115(2)* and should be treated as qualifying for relief under *IHTA, s 116*. The Special Commissioner rejected this contention and dismissed the appeal, holding that, although the farmhouse was agricultural property, it had not been occupied at all for agricultural purposes before 1988, and thus had not been agricultural property 'occupied by the transferor for the purposes of agriculture throughout the period of two years ending with the date of the transfer'. Accordingly, the conditions of *IHTA, s 117* were not satisfied and agricultural property relief was not due. *Harrold's Executors v CIR*, Sp C [1996] SSCD 195 (Sp C 71).

[72.92] An individual (W) owned a meadow, which he let to a woman who owned some horses. She used the meadow for grazing her horses, paying rent to W. W died in 1997 and the Revenue issued notices of determination charging inheritance tax. W's executors appealed, contending that the meadow qualified for agricultural property relief. The Special Commissioner rejected this contention and dismissed the appeal, holding that, although the meadow constituted 'pasture' within *IHTA, s 115(2)*, it was not 'occupied for the purposes of agriculture', as required by *IHTA, s 117*. On the evidence, the horses which grazed the meadow 'were not connected with agriculture' but were used by their owner for 'leisure pursuits'. Horses were not 'livestock' and grazing by horses would only fall within the provisions of *s 117* if the horses were connected with agriculture, which was not the case here. *Wheatley's Executors v CIR*, Sp C [1998] SSCD 60 (Sp C 149).

[72.93] A woman (B) died in 1998, owning a 60% interest in a property consisting of a cottage, garden and orchard, with a total area of 0.6 acres. B had sometimes allowed a neighbouring farmer to graze sheep on the land, and had sometimes sold damsons from the orchard. The Revenue issued a notice of determination charging IHT. B's executor appealed, contending that the property qualified for agricultural property relief. The Special Commissioner rejected this contention and dismissed the appeal, finding that the property was not 'agricultural land or pasture' but was occupied as a private residence. *Dixon v CIR*, Sp C 2001, [2002] SSCD 53 (Sp C 297).

[72.94] In 1957 a farmer (W) purchased some farmland. Initially he farmed it himself, but in 1980 he let it to a family farming partnership of which he was a member. W lived in a bungalow on the farm from 1966 until 2002, when he became ill. After leaving hospital he moved to a care home where he died in 2006. His bungalow remained unoccupied during his illness, although he occasionally visited it. His executors claimed that the bungalow qualified for agricultural property relief. HMRC rejected the claim on the basis that the bungalow had not been occupied for the purposes of agriculture throughout the seven years ending with W's death. The executors appealed. The First-Tier Tribunal allowed their appeal but the Upper Tribunal reversed this decision and upheld HMRC's ruling. On the evidence, the partnership had 'ceased to occupy the bungalow for the purposes of agriculture when (W) moved to the care home with no reasonable prospect of ever returning home'. *HMRC v Atkinson & Smith (WM Atkinson's Executors)*, UT, [2011] UKUT 506 (TCC); [2012] STC 289.

Changes in distribution of deceased's estate (IHTA, ss 142–147)

IHTA, s 142—whether more than one variation permissible

[72.95] A testator's residuary estate included a reserve fund at Lloyd's which qualified for business property relief. His executors entered into a deed of variation in 1983 and executed a further variation in 1985. The Revenue made a determination charging CTT on the basis that business property relief was not available on the first variation, and that the second variation was outside the scope of the relieving provisions in what is now *IHTA, s 142*. The executors appealed. The Ch D allowed the appeal in part, holding that business property relief was due in respect of the first variation because, on the facts of the case, the legacies in question could only be satisfied out of qualifying assets, but that the second variation was not effective for tax purposes, as what is now *s 142* did not apply to variations of dispositions which had previously been varied under that section. *Russell & Russell v CIR*, Ch D [1988] STC 195; [1988] 1 WLR 834; [1988] 2 All ER 405. (*Note.* With regard to the allocation of exemptions, see now *IHTA, s 39A*, deriving from *FA 1986*.)

IHTA, s 142—whether deed of variation effective

[72.96] A woman (S) died in November 1999. The value of her estate was less than the IHT threshold. She owned a house, in which she lived with a friend

(G). Under her will, she gave G the right to live in the house, rent-free. G died in November 2000. In an attempt to reduce the IHT due on G's death, S's executors and G's executors purported to execute a deed of variation of S's estate, under *IHTA, s 142*, removing the provision whereby G could live in the house rent-free. The Revenue issued a notice of determination that the purported deed of variation was ineffective. S's executors appealed. The Special Commissioner dismissed the appeal, observing that 'the executors of a liferentrix have nothing they can vary'. G's executors 'had neither right, title or interest to any liferent'. They 'could not have continued to receive the liferent so they had nothing to give up or vary. The liferent was not and could not be assigned to them' A purported assignation of an expired liferent had 'no reality'. *Soutter's Executry v CIR*, Sp C [2002] SSCD 385 (Sp C 325).

[72.97] A woman (G) died in 2004. Under her will, she left most of her estate to her husband. He died three months later. G's personal representatives purported to execute a deed of variation giving most of her estate (including her house) to her sister and the remainder to her nieces and nephew. The Revenue issued a notice of determination, accepting that the deed was effective but holding that its effect was that the benefit of the nil rate of IHT was to be set first against G's house rather than against the pecuniary legacies. The personal representatives appealed, contending that the deed should be construed as meaning that the house was excluded from IHT and that the nil rate band was available to be set against the pecuniary legacies. The Special Commissioner reviewed the evidence in detail and rejected this contention, holding that the first part of the deed of variation was ineffective. The Commissioner held that *IHTA, s 142* 'cannot operate to remove property from a person's estate so that it is no longer part of the estate subject to the deemed transfer of value on death under *s 4*. What *s 142* must vary is the destination of the estate on its deemed transfer under *s 4*.' In this case, the deed had purported 'to negate any disposition of the house as part of (G's) estate immediately before her death by pretending that she had transferred it immediately before the deemed *s 4* transfer of value'. However, 'nothing in *s 142* suggests that the variation that it permits should be other than a variation of the disposition on death effected by the deceased as part of the deemed transfer under *s 4* immediately before the death'. The Commissioner also held that the Revenue's notice of determination had been issued on an incorrect basis, observing that the Revenue appeared 'to have put the cart before the horse in terms of claiming to give effect to the deed and then considering its tax consequences'. The Commissioner concluded that 'the "variation" purported to be made by Clause 1 of the deed was not a variation capable of taking effect under *s 142* and, as a result of the proviso, did not therefore take effect at all'. *Glowacki's Personal Representatives v HMRC*, Sp C 2007, [2008] SSCD 188 (Sp C 631).

[72.98] An individual (L) died in October 2004. His widow (M) acted as his executrix. L left specific legacies of £665,000 to each of his two daughters and to his stepson (H), who was M's only child from a previous marriage. M was the residuary beneficiary. In July 2005 L's two daughters and H executed deeds of variation renouncing their legacies. In October 2005 M paid each of them £1,000,000. The Revenue formed the opinion that this payment represented consideration for the recipients having renounced their legacies under L's will, so that the effect of *IHTA, s 142(3)* was that the deed of variation was ineffective. They issued a notice of determination accordingly. M appealed, accepting that the deed was ineffective with regard to L's two daughters, but contending that she had given H the £1,000,000 so that he could start a business, and that her gift to H was not connected with his renunciation of his legacy. The Special Commissioner reviewed the evidence in detail, rejected this contention and dismissed M's appeal, finding that H 'was entirely dependent upon the appellant for financial support. He had been out of work for most of his adult life, and at the time of his renunciation owned no assets of significant value.' On the evidence, 'the correspondence from the Appellant's solicitors and the circumstances of the payment demonstrated a direct connection between the £1,000,000 payment and (H's) renunciation of the bequest of £665,000. The appellant's evidence denying the existence of a connection was unconvincing and utterly unpersuasive.' Accordingly, the renunciation did not meet the requirements of *IHTA, s 142(1)*, and 'was of no legal effect'. *Mrs M Lau (W Lau's Executor) v HMRC*, Sp C [2009] SSCD 352 (Sp C 740).

Appointment by trustees in favour of testator's widow

[72.99] A married man died on 14 November 1993, leaving property on a discretionary trust for the benefit of his wife and children. On 25 January 1994 the executors executed a deed of appointment, giving the deceased's widow a life interest in residue. The Revenue issued a notice of determination on the basis that the spouse exemption in *IHTA, s 18* did not apply, since the appointment had not been made by the deceased. The executors appealed, contending that the appointment should be treated as a transfer made by the deceased by virtue of *IHTA, s 143*. The Special Commissioner rejected this contention and dismissed the appeal, holding that *s 143* did not apply. Firstly, while 'in some contexts a legatee may include a trustee', the trustees here could not be treated as legatees for the purposes of *s 143*. Secondly, an appointment of property was not the same as a transfer of property. Thirdly, the Commissioner found that 'the evidence falls short of showing that the appointment was made in accordance with the deceased's wishes'. *Harding & Leigh (Loveday's Executors) v CIR*, Sp C [1997] SSCD 321 (Sp C 140).

Property settled by will—whether IHTA, s 144 applicable

[72.100] Trustees, appointed under a will, had discretion to appoint the residue among a class of beneficiaries during a period of 23 months from the testator's death. The main beneficiaries were the testator's widow (F), who was aged 81 and in poor health, and her daughter (H). There was a potentially heavy liability to CTT and the trustees undertook a number of transactions to mitigate the tax liability. On 20 December 1979, they declared that £4,000,000 should be held in trust as to both capital and income for F absolutely. On 9 January 1980 F made a gift to H of £2,000,000 net of CTT. On 14 January 1980 the trustees appointed £3,800,000 to be held on trust, subject to the income being paid to F until 15 February 1980 or her death, one half for H absolutely (the vested half) and the other half for a contingent interest. On 31 January 1980 F assigned to H, for £2,000,000, her beneficial interest in the income of the contingent half. On 5 February 1980 H settled

£1,000 on trust to pay the income to F until 15 March 1980 or her death, whichever was the earlier, and subject thereto in trust absolutely for herself. On 7 February 1980 H assigned to the trustees of her settlement her beneficial interest in the vested half of the trust established on 14 January 1980, to be accrued to the £1,000 as one fund. The Revenue served a notice of determination on the trustees, charging CTT on the basis that £4,000,000 and £3,800,000 had been appointed absolutely to F and H respectively, considering that the steps taken amounted to a single composite transaction within the principles laid down in *WT Ramsay Ltd v CIR*, **71.285** CAPITAL GAINS TAX, and that the original testator, rather than H, should be deemed to be the settlor of the settlement of the vested half made on 5 February. The trustees appealed, contending that the *Ramsay* principle did not apply, that the £4,000,000 was within what is now *IHTA, s 144* and that the gift of £2,000,000 was exempt under *FA 1976, ss 86, 87*. The Ch D allowed the trustees' appeals, and the HL upheld this decision (by a 4-1 majority, Lord Templeman dissenting). Lord Keith of Kinkel held that the steps taken in January and February 1980 could not be treated as a 'single and indivisible whole in which one or more of the steps was simply an element without independent effect'. The fact that they formed part of a 'pre-planned tax avoidance scheme' was not sufficient in itself 'to negative the application of an exemption from liability to tax which the series of transactions (was) intended to create', unless the series was 'capable of being construed in a manner inconsistent with the application of the exemption'. The series of transactions here could not be construed in such a way. Furthermore, the fact that the settled funds were historically derived from the original testator did not mean that he could reasonably be regarded as having provided property for the settlement made on 5 February 1980. *Countess Fitzwilliam & Others v CIR*, HL 1993, 67 TC 614; [1993] STC 502; [1993] 1 WLR 1189; [1993] 3 All ER 184. (*Note. FA 1976, ss 86, 87* became *IHTA, ss 148, 149*, which were repealed by *FA 1986*.)

[72.101] A married woman died on 26 September 1987, leaving property on discretionary trusts for the benefit of her husband and children. On 22 December 1987 the property was transferred to a trust, the income from which was to be paid to the deceased's husband for the duration of his life. The object of the transfer was to secure the benefit of the spouse exemption of *IHTA, s 18(1)* in respect of the charge to tax otherwise payable in respect of the death. The Revenue issued a notice of determination on the basis that the spouse exemption did not apply since the transfer had not been made by the deceased. The trustee appealed, contending that the effect of *IHTA, s 144* was that the husband's interest in possession should be treated as having arisen under the deceased's will. The CA rejected this contention and dismissed the appeal, holding that *IHTA, s 144* did not apply. The effect of *IHTA, s 65(4)* was that, since the December transfer had taken place within three months of the death, that transfer itself was not an event giving rise to a charge to tax. *IHTA, s 144* only applied where there was an event on which tax would otherwise be chargeable. The wording of *s 144* was unambiguous. Accordingly the transfer could not be treated as having been made by the deceased, and the spouse exemption did not apply. *Frankland v CIR*, CA [1997] STC 1450.

Valuation (IHTA, ss 160–198)

Market value (IHTA, s 160)

Special circumstances—definition of open market value

[72.102] A house adjoined a nurses' home. The trustees of the home wished to extend their premises, and therefore were prepared to pay more for the house than what would otherwise have been the market price. The CA held that knowledge of local conditions and requirements, including the existence of such a purchaser, were factors to be taken into account in establishing the open market value of the house. *CIR v Clay; CIR v Buchanan*, CA [1914] 3 KB 466; [1914–15] All ER 882.

Division of estate into units

[72.103] In an estate duty case, an estate comprising several blocks and totalling about 2,200 acres was sold in one lot to a speculator for £68,000. The speculator subsequently resold the estate in several lots at a profit. An estate duty referee valued the estate at £75,618. The vendor appealed to the KB, contending that the referee should have valued the estate at the actual sale price of £68,000. The KB rejected this contention and dismissed the appeal. On the evidence, the referee had been entitled to hold that 'because the property was of a miscellaneous character and not lying in a ring fence, the price paid by the single purchaser was not the true value'. *Earl of Ellesmere v CIR*, KB [1918] 2 KB 735.

[72.104] In an estate duty case, the Revenue valued a substantial estate by dividing it into 532 'natural units' for valuation purposes. The trustees appealed, accepting that 46 of the units could be sold individually but contending that the remaining 486 could only be sold within a reasonable time if they were sold as a whole to an investor or speculator, and that the price payable by such a buyer would be some 20% less than the total valuation of the individual units. The Lands Tribunal rejected this contention and dismissed the appeal, and the HL upheld this decision. The HL held that the open market value was to be determined by reference to the aggregate of the proceeds of sale in a hypothetical market of each individual unit. Lord Reid held that 'the fact that it would have taken a long time to sell separately the units of a large estate is irrelevant in so far as that delay would have been caused by the need to avoid flooding the market'. *Duke of Buccleuch & Another v CIR*, HL 1966, [1967] 1 AC 506; [1967] 1 All ER 129.

Valuation of related property

[72.105] The freeholder of a large estate had, at the time of her death, held a 92.5% interest in a partnership which farmed the land. The Revenue issued a notice of determination claiming IHT on the combined value of the deceased's freehold reversion and her interest in the partnership. The CA upheld the determination. Hoffmann LJ held that the hypothetical sale had to be supposed to have taken the course which would get the largest price provided that it did not entail 'undue expenditure of time and effort'. The freehold reversion and the partnership should be valued as one unit of property. *Gray & Others (Lady Fox's Executors) v CIR*, CA [1994] STC 360. (*Note*. For the Revenue's interpretation of this decision, see Revenue Tax Bulletin, August 1996, p 337.)

Valuation of partnership goodwill

[72.106] B was in partnership with his sons, but was not required to devote as much time to the business as his sons. On B's death his share accrued to his sons, subject to their paying his estate the value of his share, excluding any goodwill. The KB held that the sons' obligations under the partnership deed constituted full consideration for B's share of the goodwill. *A-G v Boden & Another*, KB 1911, [1912] 1 KB 539; 105 LT 247.

[72.107] In an estate duty case, the deceased held an 80% share in a partnership which owned three newspapers. The Revenue valued the partnership goodwill at £426,780. The trustees appealed. The CS held that the value should be arrived at by taking the figure of expected net profit, multiplying it by 8, and deducting the value of the tangible assets. Since the profits had been declining, the figure for expected net profit was to be taken as slightly less than the actual net profits for the previous three years. On this basis, the CS held that the value of the goodwill was £372,320. *Findlay's Trustees v CIR*, CS 1938, 22 ATC 437.

Transfer of partnership reserves

[72.108] In an estate duty case, the deceased had been a partner in a banking partnership, which held large reserves for the partnership business. The partnership deed provided that each partner's share in the reserves accrued to the remaining partners on his death or retirement. The KB held that estate duty was not payable on the deceased's interest in the reserves. There was no gift but merely an ordinary commercial transaction for full consideration. *A-G v Ralli & Others*, KB 1936, 15 ATC 523.

Joint property—value of half share

[72.109] Two women had lived in a house which they owned as tenants in common in equal shares. One of them died and the value of her half share in the house had to be ascertained for CTT purposes. It was agreed that the other co-owner would be the most likely purchaser and that this was a relevant factor in the valuation. The Lands Tribunal held that the value was half the vacant possession value, less a 15% discount to reflect the restricted demand for this type of interest. *Wight & Moss v CIR*, Lands Tribunal 1982, 264 EG 935.

[72.110] The Lands Tribunal also applied a 15% discount for joint ownership in *JDP Barrett (Barrett's Personal Representative) v HMRC*, Lands Tribunal 23 November 2005 unreported.

[72.111] The joint owner of a retail shop died in 2003. The Revenue determined the value of his interest in the shop as £175,000 (applying a 10% discount for joint ownership). His executor appealed, contending that the discount should be 15%. The Lands Tribunal rejected this contention and dismissed the appeal, applying *Cust v CIR*, KB 1917, 91 EG 11, and holding that the discount should be 10%. *St Clair-Ford (Youlden's Executor) v Ryder*, Lands Tribunal 22 June 2006 unreported.

Valuation of land

[72.112] In an Indian case concerning compensation for the compulsory purchase of land, the Privy Council held that the land should be valued not only by reference to the use to which it was actually being put at the relevant time, but also by reference to the uses to which it was reasonably capable of being put in the future. *Gajapatiraju v Revenue Divisional Officer Vizagapatam*, PC [1939] AC 302; [1939] 2 All ER 317.

Freehold interest in tenanted agricultural property

[72.113] A woman had held a freehold interest in tenanted agricultural land. The Revenue valued her interest at £45,000. Her executors appealed. The Lands Tribunal held that the valuation should be £39,000. The Tribunal rejected a strict life expectancy approach in favour of the Revenue's method of using the number of years before the holder's probable retirement at the age of 75, and held that the vacant possession value should be divided between the 'pure investment value' (taking the reversion in perpetuity) and the 'vacant possession element', adding 33% of the latter to the former on the basis that 33% was what the tenant would pay to obtain the freehold interest. *Willett and Another (Mrs Benson's Executors) v CIR*, Lands Tribunal 1982, 264 EG 257.

Renunciation of agricultural tenancy

[72.114] B and his son (DB) were joint tenants of a farm. DB died in a car accident. Three months later B renounced his tenancy in favour of his daughter-in-law and his grandson. The transferees farmed the land in partnership with B until his death. The Revenue issued a determination on the basis that B had made a chargeable transfer of the tenancy, valued at £138,000 (being 25% of the agreed vacant possession value). B's executors appealed, contending inter alia that B's interest was in only a half share of the tenancy, as the half share previously held by DB had passed to his widow rather than reverting to B. The Lands Tribunal accepted this contention and held that the amount of the chargeable transfer was £69,000. *Baird's Executors v CIR*, Lands Tribunal 1990; [1991] 1 EGLR 201.

Partnership interest in non-assignable agricultural tenancy

[72.115] The freehold of a farm was held by W and his two sons as tenants in common in equal shares. The farm was let to a partnership comprising W and one of the sons. On W's death, it was agreed that the vacant possession premium (i.e. the difference between the open market value of the freehold interest in the farm with vacant possession and that when subject to the tenancy) was £200,000. The value of tenant-right and tenants' improvements, less dilapidations, was £40,000. The Revenue issued a notice of determination, valuing the tenancy at half the vacant possession premium with a 10% discount to reflect the part interest (i.e. at £90,000), plus the net value of tenant-right and tenants' improvements, thereby giving a total value of £130,000 and valuing W's half-share at £65,000. W's executor appealed, contending that this was excessive, since it assumed an immediate purchase by the freeholders, who would not have been interested in securing the surrender of the tenancy and did not have the financial resources for such a purchase.

The Lands Tribunal accepted this evidence and allowed the appeal, holding that the realisation of the vacant possession premium was 'so far from any market expectation as to make a valuation by reference to an apportionment of the vacant possession premium wholly appropriate'. The property which was required to be valued in accordance with what is now *IHTA, s 94* was an undivided beneficial interest in the joint tenancy as a partnership asset. That tenancy could only be sold and its value realised if the terms of the partnership agreement permitted it, which they did not. The sole value of the tenancy, as a partnership asset, rested upon the extent to which its terms enhanced the partnership profits by enabling the partners to exploit the partnership assets without paying a full market rent for the farm. The Tribunal held that the value of the entire tenancy, on the assumption that the landlords could not be regarded as a hypothetical purchaser, was £12,600, so that the value of W's share was £6,300. The CA upheld this decision as one of fact. *Walton (Walton's Executor) v CIR*, CA 1995, [1996] STC 68.

Valuation of semi-detached house

[72.116] The owner of a semi-detached house in Bexley died in 2006. The Revenue issued a determination that the house should be valued at £230,000. The administratix appealed, contending that the house should be valued at £195,000. The Lands Tribunal upheld the Revenue's valuation. *Tapp (Atkinson's Administratix) v Ryder*, Lands Tribunal 5 September 2008 unreported.

[72.117] A semi-detached house was sold for £268,450 in October 2002. The purchaser (H) died in December 2005. HMRC valued the house at £275,000. H's executors appealed, contending that the house should be valued at £250,000. The Upper Tribunal accepted this contention and allowed the appeal, finding that the house had a 'relatively unattractive appearance' which would 'have resulted in reduced interest from potential purchasers'. *LF Chadwick & MC Hobart (Hobart's Executors) v HMRC*, UT [2010] UKUT 82 (LC).

Valuation of terraced house

[72.118] The owner of a terraced house in Ealing died in September 2005. Her executor (H) sold the house for £650,000 in November 2007. However, on the form IHT400, H declared the value of the house at the date of death as only £400,000. HMRC issued a determination valuing the house at £475,000. The Upper Tribunal dismissed H's appeal, finding that her evidence 'was misleading'. *LS Hatton (Hatton's Executor) v HMRC*, UT 23 June 2010 unreported.

Valuation of leasehold flat subject to covenant

[72.119] In March 1983 a woman (A) acquired a leasehold flat for £35,400 under the *Housing Act 1980*. The market value of the lease was taken to be £60,000, and the lease contained a covenant requiring A to pay the landlords a percentage of the difference of £24,600 if she should dispose of the flat within five years. A died in 1984, but her death did not constitute a disposal under the terms of the covenant. The Revenue issued a determination that the value of the lease for CTT purposes was £50,000 (allowing a deduction of

£13,000 for the potential obligation to make a payment to the landlords if the flat were sold before March 1988). A's executor appealed, contending that the deduction should be £24,600 rather than £13,000. The Lands Tribunal referred the case to the Special Commissioners, but the CA allowed the Revenue's appeal and remitted the case to the Tribunal to determine the amount which a hypothetical purchaser would be willing to pay to acquire the lease subject to the obligation to make a payment to the landlords in the event of a disposal before March 1988. *Alexander v CIR*, CA 1991, 64 TC 59; [1991] STC 112.

Valuation of a minority interest in property

[72.120] A woman (F) had held a 16.25% interest in two large buildings comprising 28 flats and 9 shops. The Lands Tribunal held that since this was a minority interest, it should be valued on an income basis, declining to follow the earlier decision in *Charkham v CIR*, Lands Tribunal 1996, [2000] RVR 7. The Tribunal assumed a net yield of 6.5% and therefore multiplied the net income of £170,000 by 15.38 to give a figure of £2,614,600 for the whole property and £425,000 (rounded to the nearest £1,000) for F's share. *HSBC Trust Co (UK) Ltd (Farmbrough's Executor) v Twiddy*, Lands Tribunal 24 August 2006 unreported.

Building society accounts—anticipated conversion into limited company

[72.121] A woman (C) died in May 1997. She had three accounts with a building society, the members of which had already voted to convert the society into a limited company. The flotation took place in July 1997. The Revenue issued a determination increasing the value of C's interest in the society by £4,250 to reflect the anticipated benefit of the conversion. C's executors appealed, contending that no value should be attributed to this, since C had nothing which could be marketed. The Special Commissioner rejected this contention and dismissed the appeal, holding that the transfer document which the society had issued to its members, giving details of the proposed conversion, conferred rights upon C which had to be valued as part of her estate. *Ward, Cook & Buckingham (Cook's Executors) v CIR*, Sp C 1998, [1999] SSCD 1 (Sp C 175).

Valuation of reserved rights to life annuity

[72.122] In 2002 a 90-year-old woman (B) paid £73,000 for a life annuity policy, issued to a trust she had created, with reserved rights to a 5% life annuity. She died five months later. The Revenue issued a determination charging IHT on the £73,000. B's executors appealed, contending that there should be a deduction of £7,800 to represent B's reserved rights to the life annuity. The Ch D rejected this contention and upheld the Revenue's determination, applying the principles laid down in *Lady Fox's Executors v CIR*, **72.105** above. *HMRC v Bower & Chesterfield (Mrs Bower's Executors)*, Ch D 2008, 79 TC 544; [2009] STC 510; [2008] EWHC 3105 (Ch). (*Note.* For the Revenue's practice following this decision, see HMRC Brief 21/09, issued on 2 April 2009.)

Valuation of retained interest in income stream

[72.123] In 2004 an 89-year-old woman (W) created a discounted gift trust in favour of her two sons (which was a potentially exempt transfer), but retained an interest in an income stream of £4,250 each three months. She died 15 months later. HMRC issued a determination charging IHT on the basis that the value of W's retained rights was only £4,250 (ie one quarterly payment). Her executors appealed, contending that the retained rights should be valued at about £49,000. The First-tier Tribunal rejected this contention and dismissed the appeal. Judge Cornwell-Kelly observed that 'the evidence adduced by the appellant shows no existing market, let alone what could be described as an open market, for the income stream to be valued, nor a market for any similar type of entitlement'. *DM Watkins & CJ Harvey (Mrs KM Watkins' Executors) v HMRC*, FTT [2011] UKFTT 745 (TC), TC01582.

Related property (IHTA, s 161)

[72.124] A married couple owned a freehold property as tenants in common. The husband (W) died in 2001. By his will, he gave his widow a life interest in his 50% share of the property, with the remainder to his daughters. In January 2002 his widow and the daughters executed a deed of variation so that W's interest in the property vested in his daughters. The Revenue issued a notice of determination that IHT was due on £275,000 (being 50% of the agreed open market value of the property). W's daughters (as his personal representatives) appealed to the Special Commissioners, contending that W's interest should be valued at less than 50% of the vacant possession value, because his widow had the right to occupy the property and not have it sold without her consent. The Commissioner accepted this contention and allowed the appeal in principle, holding that the value of W's interest should be determined in accordance with *IHTA, s 161(3)*, and making various observations concerning the effect of *s 161(3)*. The Revenue appealed to the Ch D, contending that the Commissioner had exceeded her jurisdiction and that the case should be referred to the Lands Tribunal. The Ch D accepted this contention. Gloster J held that 'the Special Commissioner was clearly entitled to conclude that, because *section 161(4)* did not apply, the value of the deceased's interest in the property was not inevitably a mathematical one-half of the vacant possession value'. However, she had exceeded her authority in purporting to determine 'that, as matter of fact, the value of his interest was indeed less than a mathematical one-half of the vacant possession value. That was properly an issue that should have been referred to the Lands Tribunal for determination by it.' *CIR v Arkwright & Sellars (Williams' Personal Representatives)*, Ch D 2004, 76 TC 788; [2004] STC 1323; [2004] EWHC 1720 (Ch); [2005] 1 WLR 1411. (*Note*. There was no subsequent hearing of the appeal, which was subsequently settled by agreement: see Tolley's Tax Digest, April 2006, p 25. For HMRC's practice following the decision, see HMRC Brief 71/2007, issued on 28 November 2007.)

[72.125] A married couple owned a freehold property as tenants in common. The wife (P) died in 1999. By her will, she left her share of the property to her children. It was agreed that if the property were to be sold as a whole, it would be valued at £1,500,000. HMRC issued a notice of determination charging

IHT on this basis. P's husband (who was also her executor) appealed, contending inter alia that the effect of *IHTA, s 161(1)* was there should be a substantial reduction in the valuation of P's half share of the property, to take account that of the fact that the property could not be sold with vacant possession. The First-tier Tribunal rejected this contention and dismissed the appeal in principle, applying the principles laid down by the CA in *Gray & Others (Lady Fox's Executors) v CIR*, **72.105** above, and holding that for the purposes of *IHTA s 161*, the 'value of the aggregate' should be taken to be 'the price which the two items of property would fetch in the open market if offered for sale at the same time'. The tribunal directed that, if the parties were unable to agree the valuation in the light of this decision, any further points of dispute should be heard by the Lands Chamber of the Upper Tribunal. *AL Price (Executor of Mrs RHP Price) v HMRC*, FTT [2010] UKFTT 474 (TC), TC00736.

Liabilities (IHTA, s 162)

[72.126] In a Scottish case where the facts are not fully set out in the decision, the Revenue issued a notice of determination in respect of a chargeable transfer of £334,771. The deceased's executor appealed, contending that the determination did not take account of a sum owed to the Italian tax authorities. The Special Commissioner dismissed the appeal, holding that the appellant had not shown that any further Italian tax was payable (and observing that, if any such tax were found to be due, double taxation relief would apply to provide a credit for the taxpayer). *Whittaker v CIR*, Sp C [2001] SSCD 61 (Sp C 272). (*Note*. The appellant appeared in person.)

Transferor's expenses (IHTA, s 164)

[72.127] The personal representative of a deceased taxpayer appealed against a notice of determination, contending that professional fees of £25,000 should be allowed as a deduction. The Revenue considered that the amount claimed was excessive, and only agreed to allow a deduction of £10,000. The Special Commissioner reviewed the evidence and allowed a deduction of £15,000. *Taylor (Sosnowski's Personal Representative) v CIR*, Sp C [2003] SSCD 254 (Sp C 363). (*Note*. Various other contentions raised by the personal representative were rejected.)

Unquoted shares and securities (IHTA, s 168)

Definition of a share

[72.128] In a case concerning the *Companies Act 1862* (which has since been superseded by the *Companies Act 1985*), Farwell J held that a share was 'the interest of a shareholder in the company measured by a sum of money' and 'made up of various rights contained in the contract, including the right to a sum of money of a more or less amount'. *Borland's Trustee v Steel Brothers & Co Ltd*, Ch D 1900, [1901] 1 Ch 279. (*Note*. HMRC regard this as the leading case on the definition of a 'share' — see Shares Valuation Division Manual, para 2.6.)

Share valuation—general principles

[72.129] In a case concerning the nationalisation of an aircraft company during the Second World War, the HL upheld the CA decision that the value of a share could not simply be arrived at by valuing the company as a whole and apportioning that valuation among the shareholders. Evershed LJ (in the CA) observed that 'shareholders are not, in the eye of the law, part owners of the undertaking. The undertaking is something different from the totality of the shareholdings.' *Short & Others v Treasury Commrs*, HL [1948] 2 All ER 509. (*Note*. The case dealt with a quoted company, and the courts upheld the Treasury decision to pay compensation on the basis of the Stock Exchange valuation. However, the principles laid down in the judgments also apply to unquoted companies — see Shares Valuation Division Manual, para 2.6.)

Value of unquoted shares by reference to balance sheet values

[72.130] In an estate duty case, a company had consistently made a loss. Its controlling shareholder, who held 998 of the 1,000 shares, died in 1922. The Revenue valued his shareholding by reference to the company's assets, at £45,908. His executors appealed, contending that because the company was making a loss, the shares should be valued at their par value of £1 each. The CS rejected this contention and dismissed the appeal. Lord Fleming observed that 'a purchaser of the shares, buying them as an ordinary investment and considering what they were worth, would certainly have been influenced by the fact that the holder of these shares would be in a position to put the company into voluntary liquidation and to realise the whole assets'. *M'Connel's Trustees v CIR*, CS 1926, [1927] SLT 14.

[72.131] In a Ceylon estate duty case, the Ceylon Supreme Court held that, in the particular circumstances of the case, it was impossible to value the company's shares by reference to average profits (since there was 'no steady trend of profits') and that they should therefore be valued by reference to balance sheet values. The Privy Council upheld this decision. Lord Reid held that 'the value of an established business as a going concern generally exceeds and often greatly exceeds the total value of its tangible assets. But that cannot be assumed to be universally true. If it is proved in a particular case that at the relevant date the business could not have been sold for more than the value of its tangible assets, then that must be taken to be its value as a going concern.' *Attorney-General of Ceylon v Mackie & Another*, PC [1952] 2 All ER 775.

Unquoted shares—valuation on basis that company would be wound up

[72.132] In an estate duty case, a director held 1,900 of the 4,000 preference shares in a company, and 2,000 of the 4,000 ordinary shares. He died in 1924. The Revenue valued his ordinary shares at £19 each. His executors appealed, contending that they should be valued at their par value of £10 each. The KB held that they should be valued at £13 each. Rowlatt J held that, in view of the size of the deceased's shareholding, the shares should be valued on the basis that the company would be wound up, and that the prospective purchaser would require 'a profit in a few years of something like 50%'. *In re Courthope deceased*, KB 1928, 7 ATC 538.

Value of unquoted shares subject to restrictions on transfer

[72.133] In an estate duty case, a company's articles of association provided that, apart from transfers of shares within the shareholder's family, 'no share shall be transferred to any person who is not a member of the company so long as any member is willing to purchase the same at its nominal value if fully paid or at a price corresponding to the amount paid up on the same'. The articles also provided that the company could resolve that any shareholder, other than one holding more than 10% of the shares and other than directors, could be required to transfer his shares. A shareholder, who held one-third of the shares in the company, died in 1926. The Revenue valued his holding at £5 10s per share. His executors appealed, contending that in view of the restrictions on transfer, the shares should be valued at their nominal value of £1 per share. The CS reviewed the evidence in detail and held that the shares should be valued at £3 each. Lord Fleming observed that 'the estimation of the value of shares by a highly artificial standard which is never applied in the ordinary share market must be a matter of opinion and does not admit of precise scientific or mathematical calculation'. *Salvesen's Trustees v CIR*, CS 1930, 9 ATC 43.

[72.134] In an estate duty case, a company's articles of association imposed restrictions on transfer, including a right of pre-emption in favour of existing shareholders. The HL held (by a 3-2 majority, Lords Russell and Macmillan dissenting) that the open market value of unquoted shares in the company was not limited to that fixed by the pre-emption clause, but should be estimated at the price obtainable in a hypothetical open market on the terms that the purchaser was registered as holder of the shares and held them subject to the same restrictions as his predecessor. *CIR v Crossman; CIR v Paulin*, HL 1936, 15 ATC 94; [1937] AC 26; [1936] 1 All ER 762.

[72.135] In an estate duty case, the articles of association of an unquoted family company prohibited the transfer of shares to non-members, if there was an existing member or a person approved by the directors, willing to purchase the shares at the valuation of the company auditor. The company directors had a general power of refusing to register transfers. A minority shareholder died in 1948. The Revenue valued his holding of ordinary shares at £1 14s per share. His executors appealed, contending that they should be valued at 11s 3d per share. The Ch D reviewed the evidence in detail and held that the shares should be valued at 19s per share. (In 1950, after the death but before the hearing of the appeal, the company had made a public issue of redeemable preference shares. Danckwerts J held that the value of the shares at the time of the death could not be affected by subsequent events.) *In re Holt*, Ch D 1953, 32 ATC 402; [1953] 1 WLR 1488.

[72.136] In an Irish estate duty case, a private company had an issued share capital of 15,000 preference shares and 50,000 ordinary shares. The company's articles of association provided that the directors could refuse to register any transfer without giving a reason. A shareholder, who had purchased 175 shares in 1938 for £1 each, died in 1950. His executor sold the shares to one of the company's directors for £1 10s each. The Revenue assessed the shares at £4 each. The Irish High Court reviewed the evidence in detail and valued the shares at £1 12s 6d each. Maguire J held that the Revenue's valuation could not 'be reconciled with the consistent history, dividend-paying policy, conservative policy as to reserves, and cautious provision for the future running through the whole of the company's accounts'. *McNamee v Revenue Commrs (Ireland)*, HC(I) [1954] IR 214.

Effect of high remuneration paid to controlling director

[72.137] In an Irish estate duty case, a company's controlling shareholder (S) died in 1928. During the previous six years, the company had paid the controlling shareholder and his son remuneration averaging about two-thirds of the company's net profits. The Revenue valued his shareholding at 22s 6d per share, on the basis that the shares gave a controlling interest, that the remuneration paid to the directors was excessive, and that if the company had paid reasonable remuneration, it could have paid dividends averaging 12%. S's executors appealed, contending that the remuneration actually paid had been reasonable, that it could only have paid dividends of about 5%, and that the shares should be valued at no more than 17s 6d per share. The HC(I) rejected this contention, upheld the Revenue's determination, and dismissed the executors' appeal. Hanna J observed that 'the profit-earning capacity of the share is the most important item'. *Smyth & Smyth (Smyth's Executors) v Revenue Commrs (Ireland)*, HC(I) [1931] IR 643.

Value of unquoted shares—effect of confidential information

[72.138] In an estate duty case, the question at issue was the price which certain unquoted shares 'would fetch if sold in the open market at the time of the death of the deceased'. At the time of the death, the company's directors were considering public flotation, and favourable confidential reports had been made to them for that purpose by a firm of accountants and a firm of stockbrokers. The HL held that although no general rule could be laid down as to the information which a hypothetical purchaser in an open market may be deemed to have, the board could not be deemed to disclose confidential information. *In re Lynall (decd.)*, HL 1971, 47 TC 375; [1972] AC 680; [1971] 3 All ER 904. (*Note*. See now *IHTA, s 168*. The substantive decision here is therefore of limited application to IHT, but the judgments include a useful review of estate duty cases dealing with the valuation of unquoted shares, and the case is frequently cited as an authority in HMRC Shares Valuation Division Manual.)

Value of unquoted shares including loans with conversion rights

[72.139] A solicitor (M) died in 1994. He held shares in three family investment companies, and had made loans to two of the companies. The Revenue issued notices of determination on the basis that these loans had given M options to acquire further shares in the companies, and were of the nature of convertible unsecured loan stock. The Revenue's determination valued the shareholdings on an assets basis. For two of the companies, where M had a majority shareholding, the Revenue allowed a discount of 12.5% to take account of lack of marketability. For the third company, where the shareholding was a minority one, the Revenue allowed a discount of 45%. M's executors appealed, contending that the conversion rights had little or no value. The Special Commissioner reviewed the evidence in detail, rejected this contention, and upheld the Revenue's determinations. The Commissioner observed that there was 'more than sufficient evidence in the form of writs of the debtor to prove the existence of the loans and conversion rights'. The unit of valuation was 'the shares in each company plus the relevant conversion rights or options which must be regarded as valid, subsisting and enforceable'. *IC McArthur's Executors v HMRC*, Sp C [2008] SSCD 1100 (Sp C 700).

Company not being conducted in a 'just and equitable manner'

[72.140] A limited company had three shareholders, one of whom (E) held 40% of the shares while the other two (who were father and son) held 60% between them. E fell out with the other two shareholders, and they voted that he should be removed from the office of director. He petitioned for an order that the company should be wound up, or that the majority shareholders should be required to purchase his shareholding at a fair valuation. The Ch D ordered that the company should be wound up, and the HL upheld this decision. Lord Wilberforce held that the Ch D had been entitled to find that the majority shareholders 'were not entitled, in justice and equity, to make use of their legal powers of expulsion' and that 'the only just and equitable course was to dissolve the association'. Lord Cross observed that 'what the minority shareholder in cases of this sort really wants' was 'to be paid a proper price for this shareholding'. *Ebrahimi v Westbourne Galleries Ltd and Others*, HL 1972, [1973] AC 360; [1972] 2 All ER 492.

[72.141] The decision in *Ebrahimi v Westbourne Galleries Ltd*, 72.140 above, was applied in a subsequent case where the CA held that a minority shareholding should be valued at its full market value, without any discount. *Re Bird Precision Bellows Ltd*, CA [1985] 3 All ER 523.

Value of unquoted shares—minority shareholding

[72.142] In an estate duty case concerning an unsuccessful avoidance scheme, the Ch D accepted the Revenue's contention that the discount on the asset value of a minority shareholding should be in the region of 15%. *Battle & Battle v CIR*, Ch D 1979, [1980] STC 86.

Value of unquoted share carrying voting control

[72.143] In a New Zealand case, a family company had a share capital of $1,000, divided into one $1 A share, which carried voting control, and 999 $1 B shares. The company had a net asset value of at least $800,000. In divorce proceedings, the High Court valued the A share at $150,000 (and the B shares at $490 each). The holder of the A share appealed, contending that it should be valued at no more than $10,000. The PC rejected this contention and dismissed the appeal. *Holt v Holt*, PC [1990] 1 WLR 1250.

Valuation of unquoted shares—evidence to be taken into account

[72.144] Trustees of a settlement appealed to a Special Commissioner against the Revenue's valuation of certain unquoted shares. The trustees called an expert witness to give evidence at the hearing. During cross-examination the Revenue asked the witness whether he, in arriving at his estimate of the value of the shares, had taken account of actual transactions in the shares in question, or of agreements on value in respect of those shares. The trustees objected to this question. The Commissioner ruled that the question was inadmissible and the Revenue appealed against this ruling under *Court of Exchequer (Scotland) Act 1856, s 17*. The CS allowed the Revenue's appeal and remitted the case to the Commissioner. As a general rule, evidence which was relevant to an issue in the case was admissible unless it was excluded by some peremptory rule of law. The effect of the Commissioner's ruling had been to prevent the Revenue from submitting evidence which, as a matter of law, was admissible. *CIR v Stenhouse's Trustees*, CS 1991, [1992] STC 103. (*Note*. There was no further public hearing of the appeal.)

Valuation of unquoted shares—capital gains tax cases

[72.145] See the cases noted at 71.351 to 71.361 CAPITAL GAINS TAX.

Sale of shares from deceased's estate (IHTA, ss 178–189)

IHTA, s 179(1)—application of twelve-month time limit

[72.146] An individual died in November 2000. In February 2002 his executors discovered that he had some investments in a unit trust, which had declined in value. They claimed relief under *IHTA, s 179*. The Revenue rejected the claim, as it had been made outside the twelve-month time limit of *IHTA, s 179(1)*. The Special Commissioner dismissed the executors' appeal. *Lee & Lee (Lee's Executors) v CIR*, Sp C 2002, [2003] SSCD 41 (Sp C 349).

Sale of land from deceased's estate (IHTA, ss 190–198)

IHTA, s 190(1)—definition of 'appropriate person'

[72.147] A woman, who owned ten freehold properties, died in 1996, leaving most of her estate to three charities, so that there was no IHT payable on her death. Accordingly, although the values of the properties were shown in the Inland Revenue Account at their market value at the date of her death, it was not necessary to agree these values for IHT purposes. Within the next three years, most of the properties were sold at prices higher than the values shown in the Inland Revenue Account. The executors made a claim under *IHTA, s 191* that the sale prices should be treated as the values of the properties for the purposes of *IHTA*. (The purpose of the claim was to enable these prices to be treated as the base value for the purposes of *TCGA, s 274*.) The Revenue rejected the claim on the basis that, since no IHT had been payable, there was no 'appropriate person' to make such a claim, within *IHTA, s 190(1)*. The Special Commissioner dismissed the executors' appeal, observing that the purpose of *s 191* was 'to grant relief from inheritance tax where there is a fall in the value of land after death. This is supported by the provision that the section only applies if a claim is made'. The legislation did not 'state in terms that it cannot apply where values increase after a death but it does state that the claim must be made by "the appropriate person".' In this case, no IHT was payable and thus there was no 'appropriate person'. *Stonor & Mills (Dickinson's Executors) v CIR*, Sp C [2001] SSCD 199 (Sp C 288).

Uncompleted contract for sale of land

[72.148] A farmer (B) died on 26 June 1988. On 25 June 1991 his administrators entered into a contract to sell the farm for £300,150. However, the contract was not completed and the farm was eventually sold for £400,000 under another contract in 1992. The probate value of the farm was agreed at £447,000, but the administrators claimed relief under *IHTA, s 191*, contending that for IHT purposes the farm should be valued at £300,150 (the price payable under the 1991 contract). The Revenue rejected the claim and the Ch D dismissed the administrators' appeal. In the context of *IHTA, s 191*, 'sold' meant 'conveyed or transferred on completion of a sale', so that the requirement of a sale within three years of B's death had not been met. Accordingly, *s 191* was not applicable and the farm had to be valued at its probate value of £447,000. *Jones & Another (Balls' Administrators) v CIR*, Ch D [1997] STC 358.

Situation of property

Registered shares

[72.149] In a Canadian case, the Privy Council held that shares issued by a Canadian company with an office in the USA were situated in the USA, where the shareholder was resident. The transfer of the shares could be registered at the company's US office, and the transferee would become legally entitled to all the rights of a shareholder. *R v Williams and Another*, PC [1942] 2 All ER 95; [1942] AC 541.

[72.150] The Privy Council reached a similar decision in *Treasurer for Ontario v Aberdein*, PC 1946, [1947] AC 24.

[72.151] A woman (P) who had been born in the UK, but had emigrated to Rhodesia (which had made a unilateral declaration of independence), had appointed a UK bank as her executor. Her assets included shares which she had purchased on the Johannesburg Stock Exchange, and which were transferable in either England or South Africa. The bank applied to the Ch D for a determination as to whether the shares were liable to estate duty. The Ch D held that the shares were situated in South Africa (and therefore not liable to duty) because that was the country in which P would have been more likely to deal with those shares. *Standard Chartered Bank Ltd v CIR*, Ch D [1978] STC 272; [1978] 1 WLR 1160.

Bearer securities

[72.152] An American citizen died in London. The Revenue charged estate duty on transferable bearer securities which he held, where the certificate of title was in the UK. His executors appealed. The HL unanimously dismissed the appeal, holding that the securities were situated in the UK and were liable to estate duty. *Winans and Another v A-G (No 2)*, HL 1909, [1910] AC 27.

Renounceable letters of allotment

[72.153] In *Young and Another v Phillips*, 71.383 CAPITAL GAINS TAX, the Ch D held that renounceable letters of allotment of shares in UK private companies were situated in the UK.

Contract debt

[72.154] The London branch of a US life insurance company had issued several policies to Germans who were resident in the UK. It applied for a ruling as to whether these policies were situated in the UK (in which case the sums payable would be liable to a charge under the *Treaty of Peace Order 1919*). The CA held that a simple contract debt was situated in the country in which the debtor resides, and that, if there was more than one country of residence, the terms of the contract may serve to localise the debt. On the facts here, the policies were situated in the UK and were liable to the charge. *New York Life Insurance Co Ltd v Public Trustee*, CA 1924, 40 TLR 430; [1924] 2 Ch 101.

[72.155] The decision in *New York Life Insurance Co Ltd v Public Trustee*, 72.154 above, was applied in a Hong Kong case where the testator had, on the day before his death, transferred assets to a Liberian company for a non-negotiable promissory note. The Privy Council held that the fact that the document recording the debt was located in Hong Kong did not alter the principle that the debt was located where the debtor, rather than the creditor, resided. There had been no suggestion by the Hong Kong Commissioner at any stage of the proceedings that the transactions carried out so close to the testator's death were a sham. Lord Oliver observed that 'it would be unwise to assume that the genuineness of similar transactions in the future will necessarily be beyond challenge'. *Kwok Chi Leung Karl (Executor of Lamson Kwok) v Commissioner of Estate Duty*, PC [1988] STC 728.

Government bonds

[72.156] The Privy Council upheld the decision of the Alberta Supreme Court that bonds issued by the Canadian government under its statutory powers were situated where they were kept, which was in Alberta. *Royal Trust Co v A-G for Alberta*, PC 1929, 46 TLR 25; [1930] AC 144.

Ships

[72.157] The Ch D upheld the Revenue's contention that, although a ship registered overseas was normally deemed to be situated outside the UK, such a ship was deemed to be situated within the UK when it was berthed within English territorial or national waters. *The Trustees Executors & Agency Co Ltd and Others v CIR*, Ch D 1972, [1973] Ch 254; [1973] 1 All ER 563.

Time of disposition

Time of gift by cheque

[72.158] In an estate duty case, an individual (O) had given a cheque to each of three relatives more than three years before his death. However, the cheques were not presented for payment until within the three-year period before O's death. The Ch D held that the gifts had been made when the cheques cleared into each donee's own account, and were therefore liable to estate duty as being gifts made within three years of the donor's death. *Owen v CIR (Re Owen)*, Ch D [1949] 1 All ER 901.

[72.159] A pensioner (P) had granted a power of attorney to a relative (C). On 21 December 2001 C issued a cheque for £6,000 on behalf of P. On 22 December 2001 P died. The cheque was not cleared until 27 December. The Revenue issued a Notice of Determination on the basis that the £6,000 was part of P's estate. C (who was P's personal representative) appealed, contending that the £6,000 did not form part of P's estate, since he had disposed of the money on the day before he died. The Special Commissioner rejected this contention and dismissed C's appeal. Applying *dicta* of Pollock MR in *Re Swinburne*, CA [1926] Ch 38, a cheque was 'nothing more than an order to obtain a certain sum of money' and 'if the order is not acted upon in the lifetime of the person who gives it, it is worth nothing'. Accordingly the £6,000 was part of P's estate when he died. *Curnock (Curnock's Personal Representative) v CIR*, Sp C [2003] SSCD 283 (Sp C 365).

Time of gift—registered shares

[72.160] In March 1943 a company director (R) transferred shares to his wife and to trustees of a settlement under seal in the form appropriate to the company's regulations, and delivered the transfer and share certificates to the transferees. The transferees did not register the shares until June 1943, and the Revenue claimed estate duty on the basis that the transfers had taken place at that time. The CA unanimously upheld the Ch D decision that the transfers had taken place in March 1943, when R had done all that he could to divest himself of his interest in the shares, and were not liable to estate duty. *Rose & Others v CIR (Re Rose)*, CA [1952] 1 All ER 1217; [1952] Ch 499.

Time of capital distribution—trustees in breach of trust

[72.161] On 8 April 1975, trustees of a discretionary trust appointed shares in the trust fund to the three daughters of the settlor. As the trustees only had power to make such an appointment to each daughter on her attaining the age of 22, and as the youngest was not yet 22, the trustees were in breach of trust. They therefore resolved that payment would not be made until all three had signed an indemnity. They applied for a declaration that they had made a capital distribution on 8 April equal to the value of the retained fund. The CS held that the interests of the daughters were severable, and that the two who were already 22 became entitled to interests in possession on 8 April 1975. However, the youngest daughter did not, as it would have been *ultra vires* the trustees to confer an absolute entitlement on her on that date. *Stenhouse's Trustees v Lord Advocate*, CS 1983, [1984] STC 195.

Disposition of interest in property

[72.162] In a stamp duty case, the HL unanimously upheld the Revenue's contention that a verbal direction that an equitable interest in property should be held on the trusts of a settlement was not a valid disposition, as it was not in writing. *Grey and Another v CIR*, HL [1959] 3 All ER 603; [1960] AC 1.

[72.163] In 1996 a woman (G), who was separated from her husband, moved into a house owned and occupied by her uncle (M). In August 2000 M, who had been diagnosed as having prostate cancer, formally transferred a 50% interest in the property to G. In April 2001 M died. His executor appealed against a subsequent Notice of Determination, contending that M had made an informal gift of the 50% interest in the property before the formal transfer. The Special Commissioner rejected this contention and dismissed the executor's appeal. *Moggs (Moggs' Executor) v CIR*, Sp C [2005] SSCD 394 (Sp C 464).

[72.164] A Scottish landowner made two dispositions of land to an accumulation and maintenance trust. The dispositions were executed on 15 March 2006. One of the dispositions was recorded in the Register of Sasines on 10 October 2006 and the other on 16 November 2006. HMRC issued a notice determining that the time of the disposition was the date when each disposition was recorded in the Register of Sasines (so that the dispositions were subject to the anti-avoidance provisions of *FA 2006*). The landowner and the trustees appealed, contending that the dispositions had taken place when they were executed, so that the anti-avoidance provisions of *FA 2006* did not apply and the transfers were potentially exempt. The CS unanimously accepted this contention and allowed the appeals, applying the principles laid down in the estate duty case of *Thomas v Lord Advocate*, CS [1953] SC 151. *Marquess of Linlithgow v HMRC (and related appeal)*, CS [2010] STC 1563; [2010] CSIH 19.

Liability (IHTA, ss 199–214)

Intermeddling—executor de son tort

[72.165] In May 1979 C, a wealthy man who had recently left the UK and was in poor health, transferred valuable land in England to S, a Jersey company, as his nominee. Two days later, S contracted to sell the land for more than £20 million. C died in July 1979. The sale was completed in September 1979, the sale proceeds being paid in Jersey. At the request of the Revenue, Dillon J granted injunctions ordering C's executors (none of whom were UK-resident) and S not to remove any of C's or S's assets from English jurisdiction. Meanwhile, the Family Division granted letters of administration of the estate to the Official Solicitor. The executors appealed, contending that the grant should have been given to them. The CA unanimously upheld the injunctions and the letters of administration, holding that the cause of action arose in England, so that the English courts had jurisdiction. S's acts in procuring payment outside England constituted an intermeddling with C's English estate within what is now *IHTA, ss 199(4), 200(4)*, and rendered S liable to pay CTT in England as an executor *de son tort*. The letters of administration had been properly granted to the Official Solicitor, since it would have been inappropriate to grant representation to executors who, as directors of S, shared responsibility for removing C's assets from the jurisdiction of the English courts and had strenuously opposed the payment by S of any tax found to be due on the English estate. Templeman LJ commented that the conduct of S and the executors 'may have been the product of a criminal conspiracy to defraud the Revenue'. *CIR v Stype Investments (Jersey) Ltd (Re Clore)*, CA [1982] STC 625; [1982] 3 WLR 228; [1982] 3 All ER 419. (*Note*. For subsequent developments in this case, see **48.46** RESIDENCE, ORDINARY RESIDENCE AND DOMICILE and **72.170** below.)

Jurisdiction—personal liability of executor

[72.166] H died in 1976, resident and domiciled in England. His executor (S) was resident in Jersey. The Revenue issued a notice of determination to capital transfer tax arising on the H's death. S did not appeal against the notice within the prescribed time limit and the Revenue issued a writ against him claiming the amount of unpaid CTT, together with interest thereon. The QB made an order for payment, and S appealed, contending that his Jersey residence made him immune from suit in England for unpaid CTT, and that he was liable for unpaid CTT only in a representative rather than in a personal capacity. The CA unanimously rejected this contention, holding that the High Court has jurisdiction to deal with a claim for CTT arising on the death of a person resident and domiciled in England, and that the CTT liability arising on death could not be a liability of the deceased but was an original, personal liability of the personal representative. *CIR v Stannard*, Ch D 1984, CTTL 22; [1984] STC 245; [1984] 2 All ER 105; [1984] 1 WLR 1039. (*Note*. For a subsequent case involving the executor, see *R v Stannard*, **51.10** REVENUE PROSECUTIONS.)

IHTA, s 200(1)—transfer on death—person liable

[72.167] A property dealer (K) had a joint bank account with a young woman (P), who lived in a property which K owned. K died in 1989, at which time there was more than £1m in the account. K's executors (a solicitor and an accountant) provided the Revenue with details of his estate, but made no reference to this bank account. In 1991 P replaced the accountant as K's personal representative. In 1995 the personal representatives (P and the solicitor) presented a bankruptcy petition, declaring that the estate was insolvent. The Revenue subsequently ascertained details of the bank account, and in 1997 they issued a notice of determination that P was liable to IHT in respect of half of the money in the account at K's death. The Special Commissioner upheld the determination and dismissed P's appeal, holding on the evidence that 'the joint account constituted a gift from (K) to the appellant of the balance for the time being in the account'. The effect of *IHTA, s 200(1)(c)* was that P was liable to account for tax on the money in question. (The Commissioner also upheld a further notice of determination, holding that in 1984 K had given P 'an irrevocable licence' to occupy the property in which she lived without paying rent.) *Perry v CIR*, Sp C [2005] SSCD 474 (Sp C 474).

[72.168] A woman (J) died in March 2003. She appointed one of her two sons (M) and his wife (S) as her executors and trustees. She left specific legacies of £5,000 each to six named grandchildren and great-grandchildren, and left the residue of her estate to be divided equally between her two sons (M and K). M and S distributed the estate, submitted an IHT return, and paid the IHT due. However the IHT return which they submitted failed to include a building society account in the joint names of J and M. The executors' solicitors disclosed this to the Revenue in June 2004. The Revenue issued Notices of Determination to M, K and S, charging IHT on the amount held in the building society account. All three appealed. The Special Commissioner reviewed the evidence in detail and partly allowed the appeals by S and K, but dismissed the appeal by M. The Commissioner observed that the executors had not divided the amount held in the building society account between M and K as if it had been formed part of J's residuary estate. Instead, M had retained the whole of the amount in question. On the evidence, it appeared that both J and M had 'considered that the interest earned in respect of the account belonged without question to the deceased whilst she was alive', and that the capital would pass to M on her death. It followed that the account been 'settled property', within *IHTA 1984, s 200(1)(d)*. Since the amount was settled property, 'the person liable for the tax attributable to it' was M 'in his capacity both as trustee and recipient of it'. The tax attributable to it was not the liability of the executors and S had no liability for it. However, 'the existence of the account will make the executors in their capacity as such to be liable for additional tax because the tax attributable to the property that was not settled increases as a result of including the value of the account in the deceased's estate for inheritance tax purposes but they do not have a liability for the tax attributable to the value of the settled property in their capacity as such'. With regard to K, the Commissioner observed that the fact that the value of the account had formed part of J's estate for IHT purposes 'will have given rise to a tax liability attributable to the property received by (K) that was not wholly discharged by the executors and he remains liable for tax to that extent'. *MB Smith v HMRC (and related appeals)*, Sp C [2009] SSCD 386 (Sp C 742).

Incidence of CTT on specific bequest of heritage

[72.169] In a Scottish case, the CS held that a specific bequest of heritage did not bear its own share of the CTT due in the absence of any direction of the testator to the contrary. *Re Dougal*, CS [1981] STC 514. (*Note*. See also *IHTA, s 211*.)

Administration and collection (IHTA, ss 215–261)

IHTA, s 216—delivery of accounts

[72.170] In 1979 an individual (C) who was domiciled in the UK, but not resident or ordinarily resident, established a settlement in which he retained a life interest. Five months later he died. The Revenue required the trustees (none of whom were resident in the UK) to deliver accounts of the trust property under what is now *IHTA, s 216*. The trustees failed to do so, and the Revenue sought an order from the High Court requiring them to comply. The Ch D granted the order sought, holding that the trustees' liability to pay tax meant that they were liable to comply with the administrative machinery of delivering accounts which normally precedes payment of tax. One of the trustees had resigned six months after C's death. Walton J held that he was required to deliver an account giving details of settlement property 'to the best of his knowledge and belief', which extended to the contents of documents in his possession, custody or power, but that he was not required to act as an information gatherer. *Re Clore (deceased) (No 3), CIR v Stype Trustees (Jersey) Ltd & Others*, Ch D [1985] STC 394; [1985] 1 WLR 1290; [1985] 2 All ER 819. (*Note*. For previous issues in this case, see **72.165** above and **48.46** RESIDENCE, ORDINARY RESIDENCE AND DOMICILE.)

IHTA, s 216(3A)—'reasonably practicable' enquiries

[72.171] A woman (S) died in October 1999. She owned a house and its contents in Scotland, and a cottage in England. Her executors, one of whom was a solicitor, wished to sell the properties as soon as possible. In November the solicitor (R) submitted an inventory of S's estate to the Capital Taxes Office, showing the Scottish house at a value of £60,000; its contents at £5,000; and the English cottage at £50,623. Although R had instructed valuers to carry out valuations of the two properties, he had not received these valuations at the time of submitting the inventory. Later that month the contents of the Scottish house were valued at £24,845, and in December the house was sold for £82,000. In January 2000 the English cottage and its grounds were valued at £315,000. R submitted a corrective inventory to the Capital Taxes Office, and paid the additional IHT due. The CTO informed him that they considered that the executors had not made 'the fullest enquiries that are reasonably practicable', as required by *IHTA, s 216(3A)*, and they proposed to charge a penalty of £9,000, under *IHTA, s 247*. The Special Commissioner reviewed the evidence and held that R was not liable to any penalty, since he had made the fullest enquiries that were reasonably practicable in the circumstances, and had acted in accordance with accepted practice. On the evidence, both executors had made a thorough examination of S's home shortly after her death, which had been 'a difficult and time-consuming task as papers were "stuffed" in drawers in various rooms, and were not in any order'. R had appreciated that a valuation of the contents would be required, and had instructed a valuation promptly. In the meantime, he had, in accordance with accepted practice, inserted estimated valuations in the inventory and had disclosed that they were estimates. He had acted 'in accordance with the common or standard practice adopted by solicitors of ordinary skill exercising ordinary care in such circumstances'. He had 'acted prudently throughout and exercised reasonable care in his capacity as executor'. The Revenue were not justified in seeking to impose a penalty. *Robertson v CIR*, Sp C [2002] SSCD 182 (Sp C 309). (*Note*. Costs were awarded to the solicitor—see **4.433** APPEALS.)

IHTA, s 221—Notices of Determination

[72.172] A woman died in 1985. There were three executors. Following the failure of the principal beneficiary to pay the CTT liability by instalments as agreed, the Revenue issued Notices of Determination under *IHTA, s 221* on each of the executors. They appealed. The Special Commissioner upheld the Notices and dismissed the appeals, observing that the fact that one of the executors had subsequently been made bankrupt, and that another was suffering from ill-health, did not provide any defence to the Notices. Applying the principles laid down by Scott J in *CIR v Stannard*, **72.166** above, 'the liability in respect of capital transfer tax for which a personal representative becomes liable' was 'necessarily an original liability which is in terms imposed on the personal representative'. *Howarth's Executors v CIR*, Sp C [1997] SSCD 162 (Sp C 119).

[72.173] Two settlors transferred certain shares in the same company to two settlements. The Revenue issued purported Notices of Determination under *IHTA, s 221* to the effect that there had been no loss to the transferors' estates. The settlors appealed, contending as a preliminary point that the Notices were premature and inappropriate, and that the Special Commissioner had no jurisdiction to decide whether there had been a transfer of a value, which was a matter to be decided in a future capital gains tax appeal. The Special Commissioner accepted this contention and held that the purported Notices of Determination were not within *IHTA, s 221* and were not appropriate. The substantive issue of whether there had been any transfer of value 'will have to be determined in any subsequent capital gains tax appeal'. *Two Settlors v CIR*, Sp C 2003, [2004] SSCD 45 (Sp C 385).

IHTA, s 225—right of appeal to High Court

[72.174] An individual (T) had been the executor of his deceased son's estate, but was declared bankrupt. A solicitor was appointed as the trustee of the estate. The Revenue issued a Notice of Determination in respect of certain shares. The solicitor appealed. T applied under *Special Commissioners (Jurisdiction and Procedure) Regulations 1994 (SI 1994/1811), reg 8* to be joined as a party to the appeal. The Special Commissioner dismissed this application, and T appealed to the Ch D, contending that the solicitor would 'not do a proper job of conducting the appeal'. The Ch D dismissed T's appeal. Laddie J held that *IHTA, s 225* provided that only a 'party to an appeal' had the right of appeal against a Special Commissioner's decision. T was not a party to the appeal. *Thorogood v HMRC*, Ch D 2005, [2006] STC 897; [2005] EWHC 1517 (Ch). (*Note*. The appellant appeared in person.)

IHTA, s 233—interest on unpaid IHT

[72.175] A personal representative failed to pay IHT of £8,000. The Revenue imposed an interest charge under *IHTA, s 233(1)(b)*. The Special Commissioner upheld the charge to interest and dismissed the personal representative's appeal. *Prosser (Jempson's Personal Representative) v CIR*, Sp C [2003] SSCD 250 (Sp C 362).

[72.176] A woman died in 2002, leaving an estate valued at £550,000. Her executrix, who was also the sole beneficiary, failed to pay the IHT due until 2007. The Revenue imposed an interest charge of more than £19,000 under *IHTA, s 233(1)(b)*. The Special Commissioner upheld the charge to interest and dismissed the executrix's appeal. *G Richardson v HMRC*, Sp C [2009] SSCD 202 (Sp C 730).

IHTA, s 245—penalty for failure to deliver accounts

[72.177] The life tenant of a settlement died in 2010. The trustee of the settlement failed to deliver an account of the settlement property, as required by *IHTA, s 216*, or to respond to any correspondence from HMRC. HMRC applied for an award of penalties under *IHTA, s 245*. The First-tier Tribunal imposed fixed penalties of £200 and a further daily penalty of £60 per day. *HMRC v R Evans*, FTT [2014] UKFTT 628 (TC), TC03759.

IHTA, s 247—penalty for incorrect information

[72.178] See also *Robertson v CIR*, 72.171 above.

IHTA, s 249—recovery of penalties

[72.179] A former Inland Revenue employee died in October 2004. He owned a house in Midlothian, which was in poor condition. The solicitor who acted as his personal representative submitted a form IHT200 in which he valued the house at £400,000. HMRC subsequently formed the opinion that this valuation was too low. They laid an information before the Special Commissioners with a summons seeking to impose a penalty of more than £33,000 on the solicitor. The Special Commissioner signed the summons in accordance with *IHTA, s 249(4)*, and the solicitor appealed. The appeal was heard by a different Special Commissioner (Mr. Reid), who dismissed the summons, holding that it was 'wholly lacking in specification'. Mr. Reid held that 'the initiating document, be it summons, summary complaint or indictment must set out the parameters of the enquiry, and the essential facts and basis in law upon which the public authority relies. If it does not do so, there is bound to be significant prejudice or the risk of such prejudice'. The solicitor was 'entitled to fair notice of the allegations being made against him and a reasonable opportunity to respond to them. Something more than the bare words of the relevant statute are required to ensure that fair notice is given'. Mr. Reid observed that when the previous Commissioner had issued the summons, that was 'a purely administrative act by which the summons reflects the material contained in the information'. It was not the responsibility of the Commissioner who signed the summons 'to make substantial revisions to the material produced and by a process of drafting create a relevant and specific summons. It might have been better in this case if the Special Commissioners had simply refused to issue a summons in terms of the draft presented to them on the grounds that the information which was reflected in the draft summons was a wholly inadequate basis upon which to commence proceedings, particularly as those proceedings appeared to involve bare allegations of fraud or negligence'. With regard to the merits of the case, Mr. Reid held that the form IHT200 should have specifically declared that the valuation of the house was 'a provisional estimate'. Accordingly 'there had been a narrow, technical failure to comply with the provisions' of *s 247(1)*. However the penalty should have been reduced to 'a nominal amount'. *GD Cairns (VDE Webb's Personal Representative) v HMRC*, Sp C [2009] SSCD 479; [2009] UKFTT 67 (TC); TC00008.

Rectification of deeds

[72.180] A testator died in November 1986, and a deed of variation was executed three months later by his widow and the trustees. However, the solicitors drew up the deed incorrectly, resulting in an increased inheritance tax liability. A second deed was subsequently executed to correct the error, but, following the decision in *Russell v CIR*, 72.95 above, the Revenue determined the liability in accordance with the original deed. The widow sought an order for the rectification of the original deed in accordance with the trustees' intentions. The Ch D granted the order, finding that there was no doubt that the original deed did not carry out the intentions of the parties, and holding that, although there was no issue before the court, this did not present an obstacle to rectification. *Lake v Lake & Others*, Ch D [1989] STC 865.

[72.181] A solicitor who had been asked to draft a deed of variation inserted a figure of £50,000 instead of the figure of £250,000 which the parties had intended. The Ch D granted an application for rectification of the error, holding that the absence of an adversarial issue between the parties was no bar to granting rectification. *Seymour & Another v Seymour*, Ch D [1989] BTC 8043.

[72.182] A deed of variation, executed within two years of the testator's death, was intended to take advantage of the spouse exemption for IHT. However, one of the clauses in the deed stated that, notwithstanding the variations set out in the rest of the deed, income should continue to devolve as if the deed had not been executed. The testator's widow and sons issued an originating summons to determine whether the deed of variation was effective. The Ch D held that, since it was obvious that a literal construction of the clause did not achieve what the parties intended, the reference to 'income' should be construed to mean income between the date of death and the date of the deed, and the deed was an effective variation of the will from the date on which it was executed. *Schnieder & Others v Mills & Another*, Ch D [1993] STC 430; [1993] 3 All ER 377.

[72.183] A married couple owned a freehold property. They sought advice from a solicitor with a view to avoiding inheritance tax. On the solicitor's advice, in 1997 they entered into a reversionary lease of the property in favour of their daughters, to begin in 2017. Subsequently they became aware that the effect of the lease was that they would have no right to remain in the property after 2017. They applied to the Ch D to set aside the reversionary lease. The Ch D granted their application. Mann J observed that the relevant deed was 'manifestly defective as a piece of drafting' and that the solicitor 'did not fully understand the implications of what he had brought about'. On the evidence, the couple 'did not know that the effect of the lease was to deprive them of their right to occupy the property in 2017'. Applying the principles laid down by Millett J in *Gibbon v Mitchell*, Ch D [1990] 3 All ER 338, 'wherever there is a voluntary transaction by which one party intends to confer a bounty on another, the deed will be set aside if the court is satisfied that the disponor did not intend the transaction to have the effect which it did'. *Wolff & Wolff v Wolff & Others*, Ch D [2004] STC 1633.

[72.184] A farmer (E) died in 2005, leaving most of his interest in the farm to his cousin (P). P wished to redirect some of his entitlement to his son (R) by way of a deed of variation under *IHTA 1984, s 142(1)*. E's solicitors prepared a deed of variation, but failed to include the statutory statement required to bring the deed within *s 142*. The solicitors subsequently noticed the omission, and R applied to the Ch D for rectification of the deed. The Ch D granted the application, applying the principles laid down in *Racal Group Services Ltd v Ashmore & Others*, **9.89** CHARITIES. Rimer J observed that 'in the absence of rectification, the deed is a lifetime potentially exempt transfer by (P). If he were to die within seven years, the transfer would result in at least significant, and possibly substantial, inheritance tax being payable. If the deed is varied as asked, the effect will be that it will not itself be a taxable disposition.' If the deed were not rectified, E's executors would 'retain a concurrent liability for any inheritance tax payable in consequence of the transfer. They will, therefore, need to retain the assets by way of security against any inheritance tax which may prove to be payable in the event of (P) dying within the seven years, whereas they will have no such need if the deed is rectified as sought.' Accordingly, there were 'real issues between the parties raised by the deed of variation'. *Wills v Gibbs & Others*, Ch D 2007, [2008] STC 808.

[72.185] A settlor (S) created a settlement for the benefit of his children, with the intention of escaping inheritance tax. Following the settlor's death, the trustees subsequently discovered that the settlement did not avoid tax, because the funds which S had transferred to them did not qualify as a potentially exempt transfer. The trustees applied for a deed of rectification, but the Ch D rejected their application and the CA unanimously upheld this decision. Mummery LJ observed that 'this case is far removed from the usual type of case in which rectification is, or might be, available. It is not a matter of correcting a mistake made in recording the settlor's intentions by inserting words or deleting words, or putting in different words because the words that are there have the wrong meaning. The claim made by the trustees involves substituting a wholly different settlement, an interest in possession settlement, in the place of the discretionary settlement, on the general ground that the substituted settlement would achieve the tax saving which the settlor intended to achieve, but failed to achieve by the document that he executed.' *Allnutt & Another (Strain's Trustees) v Wilding & Others*, CA [2007] EWCA Civ 412.

[72.186] The decision in *Allnutt & Another (Strain's Trustees) v Wilding & Others*, 72.185 above, was distinguished in a subsequent case where a married woman's will left £10,000 plus some farmland to her husband, with the residue passing to her children. The executors of the will varied it by a deed of family arrangement giving £410,000 to the children and treating the husband as the residuary beneficiary. This deed had the unintended effect of giving rise to additional inheritance tax. The husband subsequently applied to the Ch D for a deed of rectification. Judge Hodge granted the application, holding that there was an established distinction 'between a mistake as to the meaning or effect of a document (which may be amenable to rectification) and one as to its consequences (which is not)' and that 'the fact that the parties intended to use a particular form of words in the mistaken belief that it was achieving their common intention does not prevent the court from giving effect to their true intention'. On the evidence, he held that 'this is not a case where the parties merely proceeded under a misapprehension as to the true fiscal consequences of the deed of variation as actually drafted. Rather, the claimant has demonstrated a specific common intention as to how the parties' fiscal objectives were to be achieved; and he has established that, owing to a mistake in the way in which that intention was expressed in the deed of variation, effect has not been given to that intention. Underlying the parties' adoption of the deed of variation was the common intention, unarticulated and unexpressed, that the claimant should receive his entitlement under his late wife's will, as varied, free from all liability for inheritance tax, thereby replicating the position under the will as executed. There was never any intention to vary the burden of, or the incidence of the parties' liability for, inheritance tax. To the extent that the deed of variation had this effect, then it was executed under a relevant mistake, because it failed to give effect to the parties' true intention.' *Ashcroft v Barnsdale & Others*, Ch D [2010] STC 2544; [2010] EWHC 1948 (Ch).

[72.187] A woman (E) died within 19 months of her sister (H), having been the residuary beneficiary of H's estate, and also the beneficiary of a specific item of property under H's will. In an attempt to avoid inheritance tax, the solicitor who had acted as H's administratix and E's executrix executed a deed of variation which was intended to redirect E's entitlement to H's estate in favour of four charities which were the residuary beneficiaries under E's will. However the deed as executed only redirected E's entitlement to the residue of H's estate, rather than the whole of her entitlement to H's estate. The solicitor subsequently applied to the Ch D for a deed of variation to rectify the error. The Ch D granted the application, applying the principles laid down in *Racal Group Services Ltd v Ashmore & Others*, 9.89 CHARITIES, and distinguishing *Allnutt & Another (Strain's Trustees) v Wilding & Others*, 72.185 above. *Giles v RNIB & Others*, Ch D [2014] EWHC 1373 (Ch); [2014] STC 1631.

[72.188] See also the cases noted at 20.37 and 20.38 DEDUCTION OF TAX.

Rectification of deed of family arrangement

[72.189] A widow agreed with her children that her late husband's estate should be distributed in a manner different from that laid down in the *Intestacy Rules*. The deed was executed within two years of the deceased's death, as required by *IHTA, s 142*, but it contained errors of which the parties only became aware after the expiry of the two-year period. The Ch D granted the widow's application for retrospective rectification of the deed. On the evidence, the deed was clearly defective and did not reflect the proper agreement of the parties. The fact that the sole purpose of seeking rectification was the obtaining of a fiscal advantage was not a bar to granting the relief sought. *Matthews v Martin & Others*, Ch D 1990, [1991] BTC 8048.

Gifts with reservation (FA 1986, s 102, Sch 20)

General

Freehold interest transferred but equitable leasehold interest retained

[72.190] In 1987 a widow transferred a property which she owned to her solicitor, who executed declarations that he held the property as her nominee. The solicitor executed two leases giving the widow a rent-free leasehold interest on the estate for 20 years, and the land subject to the leases was transferred to a family trust. The widow continued to live at the property until her death in 1989. The Revenue treated the transfer as a gift with reservation, within *FA 1986, s 102*, and issued a notice of determination accordingly. The HL allowed the executors' appeal, applying *dicta* of Lord Simonds in *St Aubyn v Attorney-General*, HL 1951, [1952] AC 15; [1951] 2 All ER 473. Lord Hoffmann held that although *s 102*'does not allow a donor to have his cake and eat it, there is nothing to stop him from carefully dividing up the cake, eating part and having the rest. If the benefits which the donor continues to enjoy are by virtue of property which was never comprised in the gift, he has not reserved any benefit out of the property of which he disposed.' For these purposes, 'property' was 'not something which has physical existence like a house but a specific interest in that property, a legal construct, which can co-exist with other interests in the same physical object. *Section 102* does not therefore prevent people from deriving benefit from the object in which they have given away an interest. It applies only when they derive the benefit from that interest.' The policy of *s 102* was to require people to 'define precisely the interests which they are giving away and the interests, if any, which they are retaining'. The interest which the widow retained was 'a proprietary interest, defined with the necessary precision'. The gift was 'a real gift of the capital value in the land after deduction of her leasehold interest in the same way as a gift of the capital value of a fund after deduction of an annuity'. Furthermore, the leases were valid in law. Applying *Rye v Rye*, HL [1962] AC 496; [1962] 1 All ER 146, an owner of freehold property could not grant a lease to himself. However, 'a trustee in English law is not an agent for his beneficiary'. (The HL specifically declined to follow the Scottish stamp duty case of *Kildrummy (Jersey) Ltd v CIR*, CS [1990] STC 657, where the CS held that a lease granted by a landowner to a nominee acting on his behalf was equivalent to the grant of a lease to himself.) *Ingram & Palmer-Tomkinson (Lady Ingram's Executors) v CIR*, HL 1998, [1999] STC 37; [1999] 2 WLR 90; [1999] 1 All ER 297. (*Note*. See now, however, *FA 1999, s 104*, which was introduced to reverse the effect of this decision with effect from 1999/2000, and to ensure that the relevant provisions 'will work as originally intended'.)

Gift of property to trust—whether any reservation of benefit

[72.191] A woman (K) held the lease of a flat in Knightsbridge. In 1997 she granted a rent-free underlease of the flat to a company (ON), to begin in 2007 and expire in 2094. The underlease contained several covenants which reflected those included in the main lease and included a requirement to pay an amount equal to the service charge which K was required to pay under the headlease. On the same day she transferred the underlease to a newly-created settlement, the trustee of which was a company (L) in the same group as ON, and the beneficiaries of which were K's two sons. K died in 2008. HMRC issued a determination on the basis that the creation of the underlease had been a gift subject to reservation, so that the underlease of the flat was 'property to which she was beneficially entitled immediately before her death'. K's executor, L, and K's two sons, appealed to the First-tier Tribunal, contending that there had been no reservation of benefit. The CA accepted this contention and allowed the appeal. Moses LJ held that '*section 102(1)(b)* requires consideration of whether the donee's enjoyment of the property gifted is to the exclusion of any benefit to the donor. The focus is not primarily on the question whether the donor has obtained a benefit from the gifted property but whether the donee's enjoyment of that property remains exclusive. The statutory question is whether the donee enjoyed the property to the entire exclusion or virtually to the entire exclusion of any benefit to the donor.' Where the benefit to the donor had no impact on the donee's enjoyment, then the donee's enjoyment was 'to the entire exclusion of any benefit to the donor'. *M Buzzoni (Kamhi's Executor) v HMRC (and related appeals)*, CA [2013] EWCA Civ 1684. (*Note*. See now *FA 1986, s 102A*, introduced by *FA 1999* with effect for disposals on or after 27 July 1999.)

Settlor retaining powers of revocation over discretionary trust

[72.192] In 1999 a settlor (L) gave £2,700,000 to the trustees of a discretionary trust. Under the trust deed, L retained the power of revocation, and was also a potential beneficiary of the trust. During his lifetime, L received distributions totalling £15,965 from the trust. L died in 2004. Following his death, the Revenue issued a notice of determination on the basis that his transfer of the £2,700,000 to the trust was a 'gift with reservation', within *FA 1986, s 102*. The trustees, and L's personal representatives, appealed. The Special Commissioner dismissed the appeals, holding that there had been a 'reservation of benefit', within *s 102(1)(b)*. Furthermore, the manner in which the trust had been operated meant that the 'possession and enjoyment of the property' had not been 'bona fide assumed by the donee at the beginning of the relevant period', within *s 102(1)(a)*. *HD Lyon's Personal Representatives v HMRC; Trustees of the Alloro Trust v HMRC*, Sp C [2007] SSCD 675 (Sp C 616).

Relevant date for purposes of FA 1986, s 102(5)

[72.193] In 1988 a married woman (S) settled a 95% interest in a house on trust, to pay the income to her husband for life, and after his death to hold the capital and income on discretionary trusts for a class of beneficiaries which included herself and her children. S's husband died in 1992 and she died in 1998. The Revenue issued a notice of determination on the basis that, at her death, the property held by the settlement fell to be treated as her property by virtue of *FA 1986, s 102*. Her executors appealed, contending that the effect of *FA 1986, s 102(5) as originally enacted* was that no IHT was due, since the settlement had taken advantage of the exemption under *IHTA, s 18* for transfers between spouses. The Special Commissioner accepted this contention and allowed the appeal, holding that, for the purposes of *s 102(5)*, the relevant date was the date of the settlement, rather than the date of S's death. The Ch D and CA upheld this decision. Carnwath LJ held that 'the "disposal of the property by way of gift" was the transfer of the property in 1988'. This was accepted as an exempt transfer under *IHTA, s 18*. It was, therefore, outside the scope of *FA 1986, s 102*. The effect of *IHTA, s 49* was that 'in the present case, the estate of the settlor's husband is taxed on the property, but that of the settlor is not'. He observed that 'if that is of concern to the Revenue, they must look for correction to Parliament, not to the Courts.' *CIR v Eversden & Another (Greenstock's Executors) (aka Essex & Essex (Somerset's Executors) v CIR)*, CA 2003, 75 TC 340; [2003] STC 822; [2003] EWCA Civ 668. (*Note*. *FA 1986, s 102* was subsequently amended by *FA 2003, s 185* to reverse the effect of this decision with effect for disposals made after 19 June 2003. See the Inland Revenue Press Release issued on 20 June 2003.)

Estate Duty cases

NOTE

FA 1986, s 102, Sch 20 contain provisions to the effect that where, immediately before the donor's death, there is any property which, in relation to him, is property subject to a reservation then, to the extent that the property would not otherwise form part of his estate immediately before death, it is treated as property to which he was beneficially entitled at that time. The estate duty legislation contained similar, but not identical, provisions relating to gifts with reservation. The principles arising from the estate duty cases were reviewed by Lord Hoffmann in *Ingram & Palmer-Tomkinson (Lady Ingram's Executors) v CIR*, 72.190 above.

Exclusion of donor from enjoyment

[72.194] In a New South Wales case where a father had given some property to his daughter, the Privy Council held that the requirement that the gifted property should be enjoyed to the exclusion of the donor was not satisfied if, at some later date after the gift, the property or income therefrom was voluntarily applied by the donee to the donor, even if the latter was under an obligation to repay sums which he used. *Commrs of Stamp Duties of New South Wales v Permanent Trustee Co of New South Wales Ltd*, PC [1956] AC 512; [1956] 2 All ER 512; [1956] 3 WLR 152.

[72.195] In a 1911 case, the KB held that a donor may remain a guest in a house he has given away without attracting estate duty, provided that there was no agreement to this effect and it was a *bona fide* gift. *A-G v Seccombe*, KB [1911] 2 KB 688. (*Note*. Compare, however, the subsequent Privy Council decision in *Chick v Commrs of Stamp Duties of New South Wales*, 72.196

below. *A-G v Seccombe* was not cited in *Chick v Commrs of Stamp Duties of New South Wales*, but must now be regarded as being of very doubtful authority.)

[72.196] In a New South Wales case, C gave his son some property in 1934. Subsequently the property was used by a partnership of which both C and his son were members. On C's death, the New South Wales authorities charged death duty on the basis that the value of the property should be included in C's estate, since it had not been enjoyed to the entire exclusion of the donor. C's executors appealed. The Privy Council dismissed the appeal, holding that the value of the property had to be included in the dutiable estate, since the partners had been in possession and enjoyment of the property so long as the partnership subsisted, and, therefore, the son had not retained the bona fide possession and enjoyment of the property to the entire exclusion of C or of any benefit to him. *Chick & Chick v Commrs of Stamp Duties of New South Wales*, PC [1958] AC 435; [1958] 2 All ER 623; [1958] 3 WLR 93.

Exclusion of the donor from any benefit

[72.197] In a New South Wales case, the Privy Council held that a gift of land which was already subject to a lease to the donor was not a gift with reservation, as the lease was not part of the gift. *Munro v Commrs of Stamp Duties of New South Wales*, PC [1934] AC 61.

[72.198] The CA unanimously upheld the Revenue's contention that a gift of land subject to an agreement to a leaseback created at the same or a later time was a gift with reservation, since it was the grant of the whole with something reserved out of it (rather than a gift of a partial interest leaving something retained in the hands of the grantor). *Nichols v CIR*, CA [1975] STC 278; [1975] 1 WLR 534; [1975] 2 All ER 120. (*Note. Dicta* of Goff J were disapproved by Lord Hoffmann in the IHT case of *Ingram & Palmer-Tomkinson (Lady Ingram's Executors) v CIR*, 72.190 above.)

[72.199] The HL unanimously upheld the CA decision that a covenant by the donee to pay the donor's debts and funeral expenses was a benefit. *Earl Grey v A-G*, HL [1900] AC 124.

[72.200] The CA unanimously upheld the QB decision that a collated annuity to the donor, secured by a personal covenant, was a benefit. *A-G v Worrall*, CA [1895] 1 QB 99.

Settlements

[72.201] The QB held that a reservation of benefit arose where a settlor was included as a potential beneficiary under a discretionary trust. *A-G v Heywood*, QB 1887, 19 QB 326.

[72.202] The CA unanimously upheld a similar decision by Rowlatt J in *A-G v Farrell*, CA 1930, [1931] 1 KB 81.

[72.203] In a New South Wales case, the Privy Council held that a settlement of shares in favour of an child below the age of majority, with absolute gift provided he reached the age of 21 but with a resulting trust to the donor if the child failed to reach that age, was not a gift with reservation. Lord Russell of

Killowen held that '*bona fide* possession and enjoyment of the property comprised in the gift' was 'assumed by the donee immediately upon the gift and thenceforth retained to the entire exclusion of the deceased'. *Commrs of Stamp Duties of New South Wales v Perpetual Trustee Co Ltd*, PC [1943] AC 425; [1943] 1 All ER 525.

[72.204] In another New South Wales case, the Privy Council held that remuneration paid to the settlor as trustee was a benefit, but that money spent on the maintenance and education of the donor's children was not. *Oakes v Commrs of Stamp Duties of New South Wales*, PC [1954] AC 57; [1953] 3 WLR 1127; [1953] 2 All ER 1563.

[72.205] In an estate duty case, a husband (H) bequeathed his wife (L) an annuity subject to the condition that, within three months of his death, she should agree to hold a proportion of her property and income-producing investments on trust (the 'moiety fund'), to retain them for her own use during her lifetime and subsequently to bequeath them to the trustees of her will, to be held on the same trusts as those of H's residuary estate. L accepted this condition. The CA unanimously held that, since L had retained the benefit of the annuity, estate duty was payable on the moiety fund at her subsequent death. *Barclays Bank Ltd & Another v CIR (Re Lady Harmsworth deceased)*, CA [1967] 2 All ER 249.

Associated operations (IHTA, s 268)

Transactions intended 'to confer gratuitous benefit'

[72.206] On 29 March 1977, the trustees of a discretionary settlement entered into an agreement with D which meant, in effect, that D would have custody of some valuable trust paintings for 14 years. Although the agreement was on commercial terms, it reduced the value of the trustees' interest in the paintings. On the following day, the trustees appointed a protected life interest in the paintings, subject to the agreement, to D's son. The Revenue charged CTT on the reduction in value, and the trustees appealed, contending that since the transactions had not been intended to confer gratuitous benefit, they were within what is now *IHTA, s 10*. The HL unanimously rejected this contention and upheld the charge to CTT, holding that the agreement and appointment were 'associated operations' within *IHTA, s 268*, and together constituted a transaction intended to confer gratuitous benefit on D's son. *Macpherson & Another v CIR*, HL [1988] STC 362; [1988] 2 WLR 1261; [1988] 2 All ER 753.

IHTA, s 263—annuity purchased in conjunction with life policy

[72.207] In October 1996 a married couple took out three life assurance policies coupled with three annuities, and executed three 'declarations of trust' in favour of their children. The wife died in 2000 and the husband died in February 2003. The Revenue issued notices of determination that the vesting of the life assurance policies under the terms of the 'declarations of trust' was a transfer of value under *IHTA, s 263*. The executors and the beneficiaries appealed, contending that the purchase of the annuities and the making of the life assurance policies should not be treated as 'associated operations' by virtue of Revenue Statement of Practice E4. The Special Commissioner rejected this contention and dismissed the appeals, and the Ch D upheld this decision. Lightman J observed that the purpose of Statement of Practice E4 was to provide 'an effective means of protecting the Revenue from efforts made to avoid payment of inheritance tax by means of associated transactions in the form of life assurance policies and annuities. This is achieved by requiring that the life policy must be issued on the basis of the provision to the insurer of full medical evidence of the assured's health.' The information which the husband had given to the life assurance company did not constitute the 'full medical evidence' required by Statement of Practice E4. *AC Smith v HMRC (and related appeals)*, Ch D 2007, 78 TC 819; [2008] STC 1649; [2007] EWHC 2304 (Ch).

Company purchasing settled shares

[72.208] Four brothers were negotiating to sell their shares in a family company (C). Before the sale took place, they each transferred some of their shares to a discretionary trust. On the following day C purchased the shares from the trustees, and the remaining shares in C were sold to an unrelated purchaser (M). The Revenue issued notices of determination charging IHT on the transfer, on the basis that the settlement of the shares in C, and the subsequent purchase of those shares by C, were 'associated operations' (so that, by virtue of *IHTA, s 268(3)*, business property relief was not available on the transfer of the shares). The brothers appealed, contending that C's purchase of the shares 'was not a relevant associated operation because it did not contribute anything to the transfer of value', so that the transfer of the shares to the trusts qualified for business property relief. The Special Commissioners accepted this contention and allowed the appeal, finding that 'when the discretionary trusts were made, there was a real possibility that the sale to (M) would not proceed' and that 'the discretionary trusts had more than just a tax purpose' since they also had the purpose of 'benefiting the families of the settlors and charity'. Although the transfer of shares to the trusts, and C's subsequent purchase of those shares, were 'associated operations' within *IHTA, s 268*, an associated operation was relevant to a disposition 'only if it is part of the scheme contributing to the reduction of the estate'. The value of the brothers' estates 'were diminished as a result of the gift into settlement alone. The purchase of own shares contributed nothing to the diminution which had already occurred and was not therefore a relevant associated operation.' *Reynaud & Others v CIR*, Sp C [1999] SSCD 185 (Sp C 196). (*Notes*. (1) The Commissioners also held that the principles in *WT Ramsay Ltd v CIR*, **71.285** CAPITAL GAINS TAX, did not apply, finding that 'completion of the sale took place after a day of negotiations with the purchaser and there must have been a reasonable likelihood that the negotiations would fail'. Accordingly 'the two transactions were not part of a single composite transaction for the purpose of the doctrine.' Furthermore, there was no 'inserted step which could be cut out in such a way so as to transform the gift of shares into a gift of cash'. (2) The decision here was approved by the Ch D in *Rysaffe Trustee Company (CI) Ltd v CIR*, 72.209 below.)

Five settlements executed by same settlor within 35 days

[72.209] A settlor executed five settlements within a period of 35 days, and transferred shares of equal value to each settlement. The Revenue issued a notice of determination that the five holdings should be treated as a single settlement for the purposes of the charge to tax under *IHTA, s 64*. The company which acted as the trustee of the settlements appealed. The Ch D allowed the appeal, holding that there were five separate settlements for the purposes of *s 64*. Park J held that 'it is up to the settlor who places property in trust to determine whether he wishes to create one trust or several trusts, or for that matter merely to add more property to a settlement which had already been created in the past'. Each settlement was created by a 'disposition' within *IHTA, s 43*. The 'associated operations' provisions of *IHTA, s 268* did not apply, since *s 268* was 'not an operative provision which of itself imposes and inclusion of "associated operations" in the statutory description of "disposition" is not intended for cases, such as this, where there is no dispute that there was a "disposition" of property falling within *section 43(2)*. They are intended for cases where there is a dispute as to whether there was a relevant "disposition" at all.' In this case, the Revenue were 'not seeking to use the extended sense of "disposition" to determine what is to be taken as a settlement or what is the property comprised in a settlement. They are seeking to use it for the purpose of determining the different question of counting how many settlements there are in a given case. The provisions do not entitle the CIR, in the absence of clear language, to conduct the exercise of shrinking the number of settlements which satisfy the definition of a "settlement" in *s 43(2)*, or to aggregate the settled property comprised in each of the separate settlements, so as to treat, for inheritance tax purposes, property subject to discrete settlements as if it were comprised, along with other settled property, in a single settlement'. *CIR v Rysaffe Trustee Company (CI) Ltd*, Ch D [2003] STC 536; [2003] EWCA Civ 356.

Miscellaneous

IHTA, s 154—cause of death

[72.210] The Duke of Westminster, who had been wounded in the Second World War, died of cancer in 1967. The septicaemia caused by his war wound was noted on the death certificate as a significant condition contributing to the death 'but not related to the disease or condition causing it'. *FA 1952, s 71* provided exemption from estate duty for the estate of any person who was certified by the Defence Council to have died from a wound inflicted when the deceased was a member of the armed forces of the Crown 'on active service against an enemy'. The QB held that the executors were entitled to this exemption. May J held that although a wound had to be a cause of death, it did not have to be the direct or only cause. *4th Duke of Westminster's Ex-*

ecutors v Ministry of Defence (aka Barty-King & Another v Ministry of Defence), QB 1978, CTTL 2; [1979] STC 218; [1979] 2 All ER 80. (*Note*. The equivalent IHT exemption is provided by *IHTA, s 154*.)

Interpretation of IHTA, s 8A—nil rate band

[72.211] A widow (S) left a will providing for a gift to her family of her 'unused nil-rate band', with the residue of her estate to a charity (W). S's late husband had not used his nil-rate band. S's executors took the view that the effect of *IHTA, s 8A* was that S's nil-rate band was increased by the value of her late husband's nil-rate band, so that her family should receive £650,000. W objected, contending that the family should only receive £325,000, and the executors referred the question to the Ch D. The Ch D upheld the executors' contention that the effect of *s 8A* was that S's nil-rate band was £650,000, and the CA unanimously dismissed W's appeal against this decision. *The Woodland Trust v Loring & Others (Smith's Executors)*, CA [2014] EWCA Civ 1314.

Protective trusts—whether IHTA, s 44 applicable

[72.212] A woman (T) held a life interest in a trust fund under her father's will. She directed that her life interest in the fund should be held on protective trusts under *Trustee Act 1925, s 33* for three weeks, after which it would be merged with her reversionary interest. The Ch D held that this disposition did not create a separate settlement, and that *IHTA, s 44* did not apply. *Thomas & Thomas v CIR*, Ch D 1981, CTTL 8; [1981] STC 382. (*Note*. The relevant provisions of *FA 1975* were subsequently amended by *FA 1978*. For the treatment of protective trusts, see now *IHTA, ss 73, 88*.)

Protective trust—failure or determination

[72.213] By a deed of appointment dated 11 June 1979, the trustees of a settlement appointed seven farms to be held on protective trusts for M for life. By a deed of advancement dated the following day, three of the seven farms were advanced to M's eldest son, to be held in trust for him absolutely. The Revenue charged CTT on the basis that the deed of advancement ended M's protected life interest in the three farms. The trustees appealed, contending that the trust had been determined within what is now *IHTA, s 88(2)*, so that no CTT was chargeable. The Ch D rejected this contention and dismissed the appeal. Scott J held that *s 88(2)* only applied where there was a failure or determination of the protected life interest as such, rather than in relation to any particular assets. Since the protected life interest continued in relation to the other four farms, *s 88(2)* did not apply. Furthermore, the deed of appointment and the deed of advancement should be read together, so that the 'trust period' expired when the deed of advancement came into effect. *Cholmondeley & Baker (Cholmondeley's Trustees) v CIR*, Ch D 1986, CTTL 29; [1986] STC 384.

Two settlements executed on successive days—Ramsay principle

[72.214] In August 1978 C, who was terminally ill, granted a power of attorney to her daughter (H) and her solicitor. The solicitor executed a settlement which provided that a fund was to be held on trust and that the income from the fund should be paid to C until midnight on the following day or until her death, whichever was the shorter period, and that subsequently the fund was to be held for the absolute benefit of H. On the following day a settlement was executed whereby H assigned her interest under the previous settlement to trustees to pay the income to C until midnight on the following day or until C's death, whichever occurred first, and subsequently to hold the fund for the absolute benefit of H. C died nine days later. The Revenue issued notices of determination on the basis that C had effected a chargeable transfer. H appealed, contending that what is now *IHTA, s 53(3)* applied, and that no CTT was due since the property in question had reverted to her as settlor. The Special Commissioners rejected this contention and dismissed the appeal, holding that the creation of the two settlements was a 'preordained series of transactions' within the principle laid down in *WT Ramsay Ltd v CIR*, **71.285** CAPITAL GAINS TAX. Accordingly C was to be treated as the settlor of both settlements and *s 53(3)* did not apply. The Ch D upheld the Commissioners' decision. The conditions laid down by Lord Oliver in *Craven v White*, **71.289** CAPITAL GAINS TAX, were satisfied. The transactions constituted a single composite transaction whereby C had created a settlement under which she was entitled to a beneficial interest in possession in the settled property at midnight two days after the creation of the settlement. As she was then living, tax was chargeable as if she had effected a chargeable transfer at that time. (Chadwick J commented that, even if the *Ramsay* principle had not applied, C would still fall to be treated as a joint settlor of the second settlement.) *Hatton v CIR (and related appeals)*, Ch D 1992, 67 TC 759; [1992] STC 140. (*Note*. See also what is now *IHTA, s 53(5)*, introduced by *FA 1981, s 104*.)

IHTA, s 64—charge at ten-year anniversary of settlement

[72.215] The Revenue issued a notice of determination under *IHTA, s 64*, on the ten-year anniversary of a settlement without interest in possession. Following the determination, the trustees of the settlement appealed, and provided more information concerning the value of the property comprised in the settlement, which the Revenue accepted. The Commissioner upheld the determination in principle and confirmed it in the amended amount. *Henderson & Henderson (Black's Trustees) v CIR*, Sp C [2000] SSCD 572 (Sp C 263).

[72.216] HMRC issued a notice of determination charging tax under *IHTA, s 64*, on the ten-year anniversary of a settlement, including the value of assets which represented the proceeds of sales of 10,000 shares which had been issued to the trustee by way of scrip dividend. The trustee appealed, contending that these shares should be treated as income rather than capital for the purposes of trust law, so that they should not have been included in calculating the value of the 'relevant property' for the purposes of *IHTA, s 64*. The Upper Tribunal rejected this contention and dismissed the appeal, distinguishing *Howell & Morton v Tripper*, **56.107** SETTLEMENTS, on the grounds that that case had decided that shares were to be treated as notional trust income for the purposes of *ICTA 1988*, but did not require that they should also be treated as income for the purposes of general trust law. The Upper Tribunal specifically declined to follow Judge Hodge's decision in *Pierce v Wood*, Ch D [2009] EWHC 3225 (Ch) (which the trustee had cited as an authority). David Richards J held that 'the scrip dividend shares and their proceeds of sale were, both for general trust purposes and for the purposes of IHT, capital of the settlement'. *JP Gilchrist (Trustee of the JP Gilchrist 1993 Settlement) v HMRC*, UT [2014] UKUT 169 (TCC); [2014] STC 1713; [2014] 4 All ER 943.

IHTA, s 89—trusts for disabled persons

[72.217] A married couple established will trusts for the benefit of their son (E), who was a disabled person within *IHTA 1984, s 89*. The couple died in 1990 and 1995, and E died in 2005. HMRC issued a determination on the basis that the effect of *s 89* was that IHT became payable by reference to the value of the trusts' assets on E's death. The company which acted as trustee appealed. The Ch D dismissed the appeal, holding that the effect of *s 89(2)* was that E had to be treated as having beneficially entitled to an interest in possession in the settled property immediately before his death. The CA unanimously upheld this decision. Sir Andrew Morritt observed that 'the inheritance tax treatment of settlements with an interest in possession is different from the treatment of settlements where there is no such interest. In very general terms, in the case of the former the person so entitled is treated as being beneficially entitled to the property in which the interest subsists. Inheritance tax is charged on any transfers of value of such property including the termination of that limited interest. In the case of the latter, tax is charged every ten years on a percentage of value of the settled property. It is evident that the purpose of *s 89* is to include in the former category settlements for the benefit of disabled persons which, because of their disability, conferred on them something less than full interests in possession. In the latter case the disabled person is to be 'treated' as having an interest in possession so as to fall into the former category when, by definition, he did not. Such treatment avoids any depletion of the trust property in his life by the imposition of the periodic charge.' *Barclays Bank Trust Co Ltd v HMRC*, CA [2011] EWCA Civ 810.

[72.218] See also *Pitt & Others v HMRC*, **56.138** SETTLEMENTS.

IHTA, s 269(1)—whether deceased had control of company

[72.219] A woman held 45 of the 100 shares in a company at the time of her death. Of the remaining 55 shares, 24 were in the name of her four-year-old grandson. Her executors claimed that, since the grandson was not in a position to exercise the voting rights attached to his 24 shares, the deceased had had control of the company so that her shareholding qualified for business property relief. The Revenue rejected the claim and the Ch D dismissed the executors' appeal. *IHTA, s 269(1)* dealt with the ambit of the powers of voting, not the capabilities of the shareholders in whose names the shares were registered. *Walding & Others (Walding's Executors) v CIR*, Ch D 1995, [1996] STC 13. (*Note*. See also *Hepworth v Smith*, **71.253** CAPITAL GAINS TAX, in which shares were taken into account for the purposes of what is now *TCGA, s 163* although the relevant voting rights had never been exercised.)

[72.220] A married couple had formed a company (F) to operate a road haulage business and petrol station. The husband died in 1983 and the wife died in 1996. At the time of her death, she was chairman of F, with a casting vote at general meetings, and held 50% of its shares. She also owned the land from which F traded. The Revenue issued a determination charging IHT on the value of the land. Her executors appealed, contending that she had control of F by virtue of her casting vote, so that the land qualified for business property relief under *IHTA, s 105(1)(d)*. The Special Commissioner accepted this contention and allowed the appeal, holding that the casting vote had given her control of F, within *IHTA, s 269(1)*. *Walker's Executors v CIR*, Sp C [2001] SSCD 86 (Sp C 275).

Power of attorney—gifts out of deceased estate—whether valid

[72.221] In 1993 an elderly man (M) granted a deed conferring a power of attorney on his wife, and providing that if she predeceased him, the power should pass to his son-in-law. M's wife died in 1996. M's son-in-law used the power of attorney to make substantial gifts out of M's estate. M died in April 1998. His solicitors submitted an inventory to the Capital Taxes Office, accepting that gifts of £604,000 were chargeable transfers on which IHT was due, but treating gifts totalling £147,800 as exempt transfers. The Revenue issued notices of determination to M's executors, determining that these gifts were not allowable as deductions from M's estate in determining the IHT liability. The executors appealed. The Special Commissioners reviewed the evidence in detail and dismissed the appeals, holding that on a proper construction of the power of attorney, M's son-in-law had no authority to make the gifts. Applying *dicta* of Russell J in *Re Reckitt*, CA [1928] 2 KB 244, 'the primary object of a power of attorney is to enable the attorney to act in the management of his principal's affairs. An attorney cannot, in the absence of a clear power to do so, make presents to himself or to others of his principal's property.' The gifts which M's son-in-law had purported to make were *ultra vires*, and M's executors were entitled to recover them. Therefore the amounts in question formed part of M's estate at the time of his death, and were chargeable to IHT accordingly. *McDowall & Others (McDowall's Executors) v CIR (and related appeal)*, Sp C 2003, [2004] SSCD 22 (Sp C 382).

Effect of Trustee Act 1925, s 31—powers and duties of trustees

[72.222] In 1971 the trustees of a settlement executed a deed of appointment providing that the income of the settlement was to be held in trust for the settlor's six grandchildren (who were below the age of majority). In 1980 they executed a further deed of appointment, and applied to the Ch D for a determination of whether *Trustee Act 1925, s 31* applied to the capital of the trust fund. The CA held that *Trustee Act 1925, s 31* did not apply to the 1971 appointment, so that the accumulated income vested in the grandchildren as it accrued. *Re Delamere's Settlement Trusts, Kenny & Others v Cunningham-Reid & Others*, CA 1983, [1984] 1 WLR 813; [1984] 1 All ER 584.

Whether IHTA, Sch 6 para 2 applicable

[72.223] A woman (G) had been widowed in 1969. She died in 2006, leaving her two daughters as her executrices. HMRC issued a notice of determination that IHT was payable on the whole of G's estate. The executrices appealed, contending that part of the estate should be left out of account because it was settled property deriving from G's late husband, and that as estate duty had been paid when G's husband died, the property qualified for relief from IHT under *IHTA 1984, Sch 6 para 2*. The tribunal reviewed the evidence in detail, rejected this contention and dismissed the appeal, holding that there was no 'settled property' deriving from G's husband. His will had given G an absolute interest in the assets in question, so that G's estate consisted entirely of property to which she was absolutely entitled. *Mrs PJ Davies & Mrs AD Rippon (Mrs RJ Goodman's Executrices) v HMRC*, FTT [2009] UKFTT 138 (TC), TC00106.

FA 1986, s 103—treatment of certain debts

[72.224] A married woman died in 2000. Her will left an amount equal to the IHT nil rate band to a discretionary trust for her husband (P) and their children, and the residue to P. He agreed to pay £150,000 plus indexation to the discretionary trust in return for his wife's half-share in the matrimonial home. P died in 2002, and the Revenue issued a notice of determination charging IHT on his estate. His personal representative appealed, contending that the £153,222 which P owed to the discretionary trust should be deducted from the value of his estate. The Special Commissioner rejected this contention and dismissed his appeal, holding that the effect of *FA 1986, s 103* was that the debt was not deductible. The Commissioner also held that *IHTA 1984, s 11* (providing that a 'disposition for maintenance' is not a 'transfer of value') did not apply to a situation 'when a husband puts a house in joint names of himself and his wife during their marriage'. *SJ Phizackerley (Personal Representative of Dr PJR Phizackerley) v HMRC*, Sp C [2007] SSCD 328 (Sp C 591).

Ownership of property disputed

[72.225] A widow died in 1971 and bequeathed her house to her daughter (J). J died in 2002. The Revenue issued a Notice of Determination under *IHTA, s 221*, charging IHT on the value of the house. J's executor appealed, contending that despite the terms of her mother's will, J should not be treated as having been the sole owner of the house, because she had never 'signed any document accepting the title to the house'. The Special Commissioner reviewed the evidence and dismissed the appeal, finding that J was the sole owner of the house, which therefore formed part of her estate for IHT purposes. *Thomson (Thomson's Executor) v CIR*, Sp C [2004] SSCD 520 (Sp C 429).

Form R27—whether any right of appeal

[72.226] See *Taylor (Taylor's Executor) v HMRC*, **4.96** APPEALS.

73

National Insurance Contributions

The cases in this chapter are arranged under the following headings.

Decisions and appeals (SSCTFA 1999, Part II)

Whether contributions paid—jurisdiction of court

[73.1] The DHSS took proceedings against a company, claiming that it had not paid contributions in respect of two of its employees. The company defended the proceedings, contending that it had paid the contributions in question. The QB directed that the question of whether contributions had been paid should be referred to the Secretary of State for a formal ruling under the provisions of *National Insurance Act 1965, Part IV* (which have subsequently been replaced by *SSCTFA 1999, Part II*). *DHSS v Walker Dean Walker Ltd*, QB [1970] 1 All ER 757.

DHSS withdrawing proceedings against company—award of costs

[73.2] The DHSS began court proceedings against a farming company, claiming that it had failed to account for national insurance contributions in respect of some employees. The company defended the proceedings, contending that the workers were self-employed and were not employees. The question was referred to the Secretary of State under the provisions of *National Insurance Act 1965, Part IV* (which have subsequently been replaced by *SSCTFA 1999, Part II*). Following an enquiry, the Secretary of State accepted that the workers were self-employed, and the court dismissed the proceedings and awarded costs to the company. The DHSS appealed against the award of costs, contending that it was excessive. The QB accepted this contention and amended the order, holding that the DHSS should pay the costs of getting the case referred to the Secretary of State, but could not be required to pay any costs relating to the Secretary of State's enquiry. *DHSS v Envoy Farmers Ltd*, QB [1976] 2 All ER 173.

Appeal against decisions under SSCTFA 1999, s 8

[73.3] The Revenue discovered that a company had failed to pay secondary national insurance contributions in respect of its principal director. They issued notices of decision under *SSCTFA 1999, s 8*, requiring the company to pay such contributions. The Special Commissioner upheld the notices and dismissed the company's appeal. *Siwek Ltd v CIR*, Sp C [2004] SSCD 493 (Sp C 427). (*Notes.* (1) Appeals against determinations under what is now *regulation 80* of the *Income Tax (PAYE) Regulations (SI 2003/2682)* were also dismissed in principle, subject to small reductions in the amounts charged. (2) The appeal was heard with *Siwek v CIR*, **55.2** SELF-ASSESSMENT.)

[73.4] See also *Murray Group Holdings Ltd v HMRC*, **42.53** PAY AS YOU EARN; *Rhodes v HMRC*, **44.153** PENALTIES, and *Convery v HMRC*, 73.38 below.

Enforcement (Social Security Administration Act 1992, Part VI)

SSAA 1992, s 110ZA(3)—premises liable to inspection

[73.5] An inspector attempted to enter premises which were apparently being converted from a house into flats. The owner refused to allow him to enter. He was subsequently prosecuted, but a magistrate held that the onus was on the inspector to prove that the premises were no longer a private dwelling-house and that the inspector had a right of entry under what is now *SSAA 1992, s 110ZA(3)*. The inspector appealed to the QB, which remitted the case for rehearing, holding that the magistrate had erred in law and that the onus of proof was on the owner of the house to prove that it was still used as a private dwelling-house. Lord Widgery CJ held that 'the premises to be protected are premises which are the home of somebody, where a person is dwelling, but not merely a building which has the external appearance of a dwelling-house'. If 'nobody was living in the house and the builders were doing extensive work in the house, there is every reason why the inspector should go in and examine the terms of employment of those builders'. *Stott v Hefferon*, QB [1974] 3 All ER 673.

SSAA 1992, s 110ZA(5)—furnishing of information

[73.6] A musician, who had not paid national insurance contributions for 41 weeks, stated that he had been an employee but refused to tell an inspector the identity of his employer. He was charged with refusing to furnish information.

The magistrates considered that an employee was only required to disclose whether or not he was an employee, and was not required to disclose the identity of his employer. The inspector appealed to the QB, which remitted the case to the magistrates, holding that the effect of what is now *SSAA 1992, s 110ZA(5)*was to enable an inspector 'to ask the insured person whether he is employed or self-employed and the name and address of his employer if he says that he is employed'. Lord Widgery CJ observed that 'if an employee is not obliged to disclose the name of his employer, the prospect of the inspector ever discovering the identity of the person liable to make the contribution is remote'. *Smith v Hawkins*, QB 1971, [1972] 1 All ER 910.

SSAA 1992, s 116—authorisation of legal proceedings

[73.7] An officer of the Ministry of Pensions and National Insurance began legal proceedings against a farmworker (H) who had claimed sickness benefit while working. At the hearing of the prosecution, H's solicitor contended that there was no case to answer, because the prosecution had not proved that the Minister had authorised the proceedings. The QB unanimously rejected this contention. Devlin J held that '*prima facie*, the position was that the summons had been properly issued and there was no need for the prosecution to take any further step unless objection was taken'. Lord Goddard CJ held that magistrates should not 'allow an objection which has been, so to speak, kept up the sleeve until the last minute, as where the prosecution are induced to say that they have closed their case, and it is objected that they have not proved consent to the proceedings having been instituted'. *Price v Humphries*, QB [1958] 2 All ER 725. (*Note. SSAA 1992, s 116(1)* now provides that 'any person authorised by the Secretary of State in that behalf' may conduct any proceedings before a magistrates' court.)

SSAA 1992, s 119—recovery of unpaid contributions

[73.8] A self-employed person (B) failed to pay Class 2 Contributions, and an inspector took proceedings against him before the local magistrates. The magistrates declined to make an order for payment, considering that they had no jurisdiction 'to make an order for payment of a civil debt on proceedings on an information for a criminal offence'. The inspector appealed to the QB, which made a direction to the magistrates 'that it is their duty that the respondent should pay the contributions which it has been proved he has failed to pay'. *Shilvock v Booth*, QB [1956] 1 All ER 382.

[73.9] A company was prosecuted for failing to pay national insurance contributions totalling £2,904, and was convicted. The magistrates fined the company £100, but failed to order it to pay the unpaid contributions. The DHSS appealed to the QB, which held that what is now *SSAA 1992, s 119* imposed a mandatory duty on the magistrates to order the payment of the outstanding contributions. *Morgan v Quality Tools & Engineering (Stourbridge) Ltd*, QB 1971, [1972] 1 All ER 744.

SSAA 1992, s 121(4)—whether magistrates have power to mitigate

[73.10] A self-employed person (L) failed to pay Class 2 Contributions, and an inspector took proceedings against him before the local magistrates. The magistrates made an order purporting to mitigate L's arrears of contributions from £19 to £5. The inspector appealed to the QB, contending that the magistrates had no power to mitigate the arrears. The QB accepted this contention and remitted the case to the magistrates with a direction that they had no power to mitigate the arrears. *Leach v Litchfield*, QB [1960] 3 All ER 739.

SSAA 1992, s 121C—director's personal liability for company's contributions

[73.11] A company went into liquidation, having failed to pay national insurance contributions totalling more than £200,000. Its controlling director was subsequently disqualified from acting as a director under *Company Directors Disqualification Act 1986, s 7*. The Revenue issued a notice under *SSAA 1992, s 121C(2)* that the director should be personally liable for the unpaid contributions, as the failure was attributable to his 'fraud or neglect'. The director appealed, contending that he had not been guilty of any 'fraud or neglect'. The Special Commissioner rejected this contention and dismissed the director's appeal, holding on the evidence that the company's failure to pay the contributions was attributable to the director's neglect. *Inzani v HMRC*, Sp C [2006] SSCD 279 (Sp C 529).

[73.12] A company (M) failed to pay more than £60,000 in national insurance contributions for 2005/06 and 2006/07. It ceased trading in January 2007. HMRC issued a notice under *SSAA 1992, s 121C* that M's sole director (L), who was a chartered accountant, should be personally liable for the unpaid contributions. L appealed, contending that he had not been guilty of any 'fraud or neglect'. The First-tier Tribunal reviewed the evidence in detail, rejected this contention and dismissed the appeal, holding on the evidence that M's failure to pay the contributions was attributable to L's neglect. Judge Barton observed that L 'was aware that these payments were not being made; and that the responsibility for making or withholding payments rested with him'. Furthermore, it was 'significant that when funds did become available from the sale of the business, he still made no payment to HMRC but intromitted with these funds in a manner which in part was beneficial to him personally'. L should have been aware that M was 'hopelessly insolvent', and the evidence indicated that he 'was negligent in the financial management of the Company and in particular in relation to the ongoing and increasing NIC liability'. *L Livingstone v HMRC*, FTT [2010] UKFTT 56 (TC), TC00369.

[73.13] A company failed to pay more than £90,000 in national insurance contributions for its two controlling directors, and subsequently went into liquidation. Both directors were subsequently disqualified from acting as directors under *Company Directors Disqualification Act 1986*. HMRC issued notices to the directors under *SSAA 1992, s 121C* that they should be personally liable for the unpaid contributions. The directors appealed. The

First-tier Tribunal reviewed the evidence in detail and dismissed the directors' appeals. Judge Reid observed that the directors had taken 'the decision to refrain from making any payments of PAYE tax or NIC, preferring to pay their own substantial salaries'. On the evidence, it was 'clear that a pattern has developed over the years whereby a company controlled by the appellants fails to pay NIC and PAYE tax; the company becomes insolvent, with debts due to inter alios, HMRC, and then goes into liquidation; a new successor company rises phoenix-like from the ashes of the insolvent company, trades for a time, becomes insolvent, with debts due to, *inter alios*, HMRC, and then goes into liquidation; another new phoenix company starts up and trades until it becomes insolvent; and so on'. Judge Reid concluded that 'individuals such as the appellants should not be allowed to shelter behind the shield of limited liability of companies which they use to trade in order to pay themselves large salaries at the expense of ordinary business creditors who follow ordinary standards of business decency, and the general taxpayer'. *S Roberts & A Martin v HMRC*, FTT [2011] UKFTT 268 (TC), TC01130.

[73.14] Appeals against notices under *SSAA 1992, s 121C* were also dismissed in *Mrs C Roberts v HMRC*, FTT [2012] UKFTT 308 (TC), TC01994; *JP Smith v HMRC*, FTT [2012] UKFTT 428 (TC), TC02110, and *H Zubair v HMRC*, FTT [2012] UKFTT 652 (TC), TC02324.

[73.15] A company went into liquidation in 2007, having failed to pay national insurance contributions of more than £320,000. HMRC issued a notice under *SSAA 1992, s 121C* to the company's finance director, ruling that he should be liable for paying the majority of the unpaid contributions. The director appealed, contending that he had not been guilty of any 'neglect', so that the condition laid down by *s 121C(1)(b)* was not satisfied. At a preliminary hearing, the First-tier Tribunal held that 'neglect' should be construed subjectively, so that it should consider medical evidence about the director's mental capacity, but the Upper Tribunal reversed this decision. Hildyard J held that the question of 'neglect' had to be construed objectively, and remitted the case to the First-tier Tribunal for rehearing. *HMRC v CM O'Rorke*, UT [2013] UKUT 499 (TCC); [2014] STC 279.

Conviction for non-payment of contributions—imprisonment

[73.16] A self-employed person (S) failed to pay Class 2 Contributions. He was convicted, fined, and ordered to pay the arrears. He failed to do so, and the magistrates sentenced him to three months' imprisonment. The QB upheld the sentence. *R v Marlow (Bucks) Justices (ex p. Schiller)*, QB [1957] 2 All ER 783.

Employers' contributions—application of Limitation Act 1980

[73.17] Several employers had implemented avoidance schemes with the aim of minimising liability to employers' national insurance contributions by purporting to pay remuneration as payments in kind. (For an example of such a scheme, see *NMB Holdings Ltd v Secretary of State for Social Security*, **58.11** TAX PLANNING AND AVOIDANCE.) The Revenue issued determinations that NIC was chargeable on the payments in question. The employers appealed.

However, several of these appeals took a very long time to resolve, and the Revenue became concerned that they might be unable to collect the contributions because of the six-year time limit laid down by *Limitation Act 1980, s 9*. The Revenue also wished to avoid the cost of beginning county court proceedings to recover the contributions, knowing that the recovery proceedings would have to be adjourned pending the outcome of the employers' appeals to the Commissioners. The Revenue therefore asked the employers to give a formal acknowledgement of the Revenue's claims, without making any admission of liability. However, in August 2001, the Revenue received legal advice that this procedure did not have the desired effect of circumventing the statutory time limit laid down by *Limitation Act 1980, s 9*. The substantive appeals were subsequently determined in favour of the Revenue, but the employers declined to pay the contributions, and the Revenue began proceedings in the Newcastle-upon-Tyne county court. The employers defended the proceedings, contending that the effect of *Limitation Act 1980, s 9* was that they had been begun outside the statutory time limit. The county court referred the case to the Ch D for rulings on the interpretation of *Limitation Act 1980, s 9*. Briggs J reviewed the relevant correspondence in detail and held that 'the combination of a detrimental reliance by the Revenue, coupled with the obtaining by the relevant employers of the anticipated benefit of the Revenue's reliance upon the shared assumption, is sufficient to render it unfair and unjust for those employers now to advance a limitation defence in relation to NICs arising out of the 94/95 tax year. In short, in relation to NICs for that tax year, the employers are estopped by convention from asserting the ineffectiveness of the acknowledgements or part payments.' However, the Revenue had become aware of the ineffectiveness of their proposed procedure by August 2001. Therefore, with regard to claims that became statute-barred after September 2001, the Revenue should have taken alternative steps to protect its position. By failing to do so, the Revenue was 'the author of its own misfortune' and employers facing such claims were entitled to 'assert a limitation defence to those claims, arising out of the Revenue's decision not to protect them once aware of the true legal position'. *HMRC v Benchdollar Ltd & Others*, Ch D 2009, 79 TC 668; [2009] STC 2342; [2009] EWHC 1310 (Ch).

Employers' contributions—Scottish time limits

[73.18] See *Spring Salmon & Seafood Ltd v HMRC (No 3)*, **29.126** FURTHER ASSESSMENTS: LOSS OF TAX.

County court proceedings to collect contributions

[73.19] See also *HMRC v Hyde Industrial Holdings Ltd*, **43.15** PAYMENT OF TAX.

Class 1 Contributions

Employed earners (SSCBA 1992, s 2(1)(a))

Salesman—whether an 'employed earner' liable to Class 1 Contributions

[73.20] A salesman worked for a telephone company, who treated him as self-employed. Following his death, his widow took proceedings against the company, contending that he had been an employee and that the company should have paid national insurance contributions. Stable J rejected this contention and dismissed the proceedings. *Chadwick v Pioneer Private Telephone Co Ltd*, MWA [1941] 1 All ER 522.

Comedian—whether an 'employed earner' liable to Class 1 Contributions

[73.21] The Minister of National Insurance ruled that a comedian working for a company which carried on business as theatrical producers was an employee. The company appealed, contending that he should be treated as self-employed. The CS rejected this contention and dismissed the appeal. Lord Thomson observed that, under the contract, 'the artiste agrees to play in any of the management's productions and may be transferred to other managements'. *Stagecraft Ltd v Minister of National Insurance*, CS [1952] SC 288. (*Note*. For HMRC's interpretation of this decision, see Employment Status Manual, paras ESM0520, 0522.)

Actors—whether 'employed earners' liable to Class 1 Contributions

[73.22] Until November 2006 a television company (ITV) treated many actors as employed earners and accounted for Class 1 national insurance contributions on the amounts it paid them. From December 2006 it ceased to account for Class 1 NICs, treating the actors as self-employed. HMRC issued determinations charging NICs on the payments. The First-tier Tribunal issued a decision in principle that ITV was required to account for NICs in respect of most of the types of contracts, except where the actors were 'engaged to perform a specific role in a specific programme, engaged for a specific period of engagement, and received a single total inclusive fee'. The Upper Tribunal and the CA unanimously dismissed ITV's appeal against this decision. Rimer LJ analysed several different agreements, and held that they all provided for the payment of a 'salary' to the actor, within *Social Security (Categorisation of Earners) Regulations 1978 (SI 1978/1689), reg 5A*. Accordingly ITV was required to account for Class 1 NIC on the payments. *ITV Services Ltd v HMRC*, CA [2013] EWCA Civ 867; [2014] STC 325. (*Note*. For HMRC's practice following this decision, see HMRC Brief 29/13, issued on 2 October 2013, and HMRC Brief 11/14, issued on 31 March 2014.)

Trapeze artiste—whether an employee

[73.23] A woman worked for a circus, primarily as a trapeze artiste but partly as an usherette and assisting in moves. She fell off the trapeze and broke her wrist, and subsequently claimed industrial injury benefit. The Minister of Pensions and National Insurance ruled that she was not entitled to benefit on the grounds that she was self-employed. She appealed, contending that she was an employee. The QB accepted this contention and allowed her appeal. *Whittaker v Minister of Pensions and National Insurance*, QB [1966] 3 All ER 531.

Research assistant—travelling expenses exceeding salary

[73.24] A graduate, who had been crippled by polio, accepted a post as a research assistant, although, as he had to employ a chauffeur to get to and from his place of work, his travelling expenses exceeded his salary. The Minister of Pensions and National Insurance issued a ruling that he was an 'employed person' and was liable to Class 1 NICs. He appealed, contending that he should not be treated as an 'employed person', because he had not taken the post for financial gain. The QB dismissed his appeal, holding that he was 'gainfully occupied in employment' even though the employment did not produce any overall profit. *Vandyk v Minister of Pensions and National Insurance*, QB [1954] 2 All ER 723.

Lorry driver—whether an 'employed earner'

[73.25] The Ministry of Pensions and National Insurance issued a ruling that a lorry driver, who owned his own lorry, was an employee for the purposes of national insurance contributions. The company for which he drove appealed, contending that he was a self-employed contractor. The QB accepted this contention and allowed the appeal, holding on the evidence that the contract was 'a contract of carriage' rather than a contract of service. MacKenna J observed that 'freedom to do a job either by one's own hands or by another's is inconsistent with a contract of service, though a limited or occasional power of delegation may not be'. *Ready Mixed Concrete (South East) Ltd v Minister of Pensions & National Insurance*, QB 1967, [1968] 1 All ER 433.

[73.26] HMRC issued a ruling that a lorry driver was employed by a haulage contractor (T), so that T was required to deduct PAYE and NIC. T appealed, contending that the driver was self-employed. The First-tier Tribunal accepted this contention and allowed the appeal. *B Turnbull v HMRC*, FTT [2011] UKFTT 388 (TC), TC01243.

Dentist—whether an 'employed earner' liable to Class 1 Contributions

[73.27] The Greater London Council arranged for a dentist (F) to treat children in its schools on a part-time basis. It paid the dentist on a monthly basis. The payments were computed by reference to the time for which F had worked, but were described in the contract as 'fees'. The Minister of Social Security issued a ruling that F was an employee for the purposes of national insurance contributions. The GLC appealed. The QB dismissed the appeal, holding that the monthly payments were a 'salary' and that F was an employee. *Greater London Council v Minister of Social Security*, QB [1971] 2 All ER 285.

Surgeon—whether an 'employed earner' liable to Class 1 Contributions

[73.28] A cardiac surgeon (M) arranged for another surgeon (B) to assist him during operations. HMRC issued a ruling that B was an employee of M, and that M was required to account for Class 1 NICs (and deduct income tax under PAYE). The First-tier Tribunal allowed M's appeal, holding that B was not an employee, and was working under a contract for services rather than a contract of service. *I Mitchell v HMRC*, FTT [2011] UKFTT 172 (TC), TC01041.

Drivers working for plant hire company—whether 'employed earners'

[73.29] The Secretary of State issued a ruling that two drivers of earth-moving machinery, who worked for a plant hire company (G), were employees for the purposes of national insurance contributions. G appealed, contending that they were self-employed subcontractors. The QB rejected this contention and dismissed the appeal, holding that they were employees. *Global Plant Ltd v Secretary of State for Health & Social Security*, QB [1971] 3 All ER 385.

Market research interviewers—whether 'employed earners'

[73.30] A company (M) carried on a market research business. The Minister of Social Security issued a ruling that a woman, who worked for M as an interviewer, was an employee for the purposes of national insurance contributions. M appealed, contending that she should be treated as self-employed. The QB rejected this contention and dismissed the appeal. Cooke J held that 'the fundamental test to be applied is this: "is the person who has engaged himself to perform these services performing them as a person in business on his own account?" If the answer to that question is "yes", then the contract is a contract for services. If the answer is "no", then the contract is a contract of service.' *Market Investigations Ltd v Minister of Social Security*, QB [1968] 3 All ER 732.

Solicitors' clerk receiving gifts but no remuneration

[73.31] A firm of solicitors (B) employed an articled clerk (K) . Under the relevant contract, B paid K no remuneration, but the senior partner gave him a gift of £10 at Christmas 1954; a gift of £25 at Christmas 1955; and gifts totalling £100 during 1956. The Minister of Pensions and National Insurance issued a ruling that during 1956 K was an 'employed earner' within the charge to Class 1 Contributions. The QB dismissed B's appeal. *Benjamin & Collins v Minister of Pensions and National Insurance*, QB [1960] 3 WLR 430; [1960] 2 All ER 851.

Solicitors' articled clerk—whether employed by partnership

[73.32] A woman, who had worked as a clerk for a firm of solicitors, sued the firm under the *Sex Discrimination Act*. The firm defended the proceedings, contending that she had been employed by the individual solicitor to whom she had been articled, rather than by the firm. The EAT rejected this contention, holding that she had been employed by the firm. *Oliver v JP Malnick & Co*, EAT [1983] 3 All ER 795.

Musicians—whether employees

[73.33] In a case concerning breach of copyright, a company (P) which owned a dance hall engaged a band of five musicians to provide music at the hall. The KB held that the musicians were employees of P, rather than independent contractors. McCardie J observed that the relevant contract gave P 'the right of continuous, dominant and detailed control on every point, including the nature of the music to be played'. *Performing Right Society Ltd v Mitchell & Booker (Palais de Danse) Ltd*, KB [1924] 1 KB 762.

Visiting music teachers—whether liable to pay Class 1 contributions

[73.34] An independent school arranged for two visiting music teachers, who were treated as self-employed for income tax purposes, to give lessons at the school. The Secretary of State for Social Security issued a ruling that the effect of *Social Security (Categorisation of Earners) Regulations 1978 (SI 1978/1689)* was that the teachers should be treated as employees, within the charge to Class 1 national insurance contributions. The QB dismissed the school's appeal. *St John's College School Cambridge v Secretary of State for Social Security*, QB 12 June 2000 unreported.

Trade union 'sick steward'—whether an employee of the trade union

[73.35] The Minister of Pensions and National Insurance issued a ruling that a part-time 'sick steward' of a trade union was an employee of the union. The QB dismissed the union's appeal. *Amalgamated Engineering Union v Minister of Pensions and National Insurance*, QB [1963] 1 All ER 864.

Journalist—whether an employee

[73.36] In a case concerning the ownership of copyright, the Ch D held that a political journalist, who held the post of 'political correspondent' of a Sunday newspaper, was an employee of that newspaper, since her job was 'an integral part of the business'. *Beloff v Pressdram Ltd & Another*, Ch D [1973] 1 All ER 241.

Labourer—whether an employee

[73.37] A labourer, working for a building company, was injured and sued the company. The CA gave judgment for the labourer, holding (by a 2-1 majority, Lawton LJ dissenting) that he was an employee of the company. Megaw LJ held that 'a declaration by the parties, even if it be incorporated in the contract, that the workman is to be, or is to be deemed to be, self-employed, an independent contractor, ought to be wholly disregarded—not merely treated as not being conclusive—if the remainder of the contractual terms, governing the realities of the relationship, show the relationship of employer and employee'. *Ferguson v John Dawson & Partners (Contractors) Ltd*, CA [1976] 1 WLR 1213; [1976] 3 All ER 817.

[73.38] A labourer (C) was injured while renovating a building. The owner of the building (M) was a director of a demolition company (G). C claimed that he had been an employee of G. G disputed his claim, contending that he was working as a self-employed contractor under a private agreement with M. HMRC issued a formal ruling under *SSCTFA 1999, s 8* that C was not an employee of G. The First-tier Tribunal dismissed C's appeal, finding that hehad taken 'no steps to give his national insurance number to anyone' and holding that he was not an employee. *B Convery v HMRC*, FTT [2010] UKFTT 90 (TC), TC00401.

Construction workers—whether 'employed earners'

[73.39] The Revenue issued rulings that several construction industry workers, who worked for the proprietor of a scaffolding business (L), were 'employed earners' and liable to Class 1 National Insurance Contributions. They also issued determinations under *Income Tax (PAYE) Regulations 2003 (SI 2003/2682), reg 80* on L. L and the workers appealed, contending that they were independent subcontractors. The Special Commissioner reviewed the evidence in detail, accepted this contention, and allowed all the appeals. The Commissioner (Dr. Williams) specifically declined to follow an earlier decision of the Employment Tribunal, which had held that two of the workers were employees and entitled to payments in lieu of holiday at the termination of their contracts. The Commissioner observed that 'the relevant regulation has its own, extended, definition of employee for the purposes of the benefits claimed by the claimants. They could be self-employed and also entitled to holiday pay.' On the evidence, the relationship between L and the workers was 'an informal and undocumented verbal contract for services and not any form of contract of service'. *Lewis (t/a MAL Scaffolding) & Others v HMRC*, Sp C [2006] SSCD 253 (Sp C 527).

[73.40] In 2007 the Revenue issued rulings that 321 construction industry workers, who worked for a building company (C), were 'employed earners' and liable to Class 1 National Insurance Contributions. They also issued determinations under *Income Tax (PAYE) Regulations 2003 (SI 2003/2682), reg 80*. C appealed, contending that the workers were self-employed subcontractors. The Special Commissioner reviewed the evidence in detail and held that 314 of the workers (including all the bricklayers and scaffolders) were self-employed, but that the seven truck or lorry drivers were employees. The Commissioner observed that, in 2000, following a previous enquiry, the Revenue had accepted that the bricklayers working for C were self-employed subcontractors. They worked under terms that were 'reasonably common and traditional in the building industry'. The truck and lorry drivers were in a different position, since they were 'subject to more potential control'. *Castle Construction (Chesterfield) Ltd v HMRC*, Sp C 2008, [2009] SSCD 97 (Sp C 723).

Bricklayer—whether an employee

[73.41] A bricklayer (B) had submitted tax returns stating that he was self-employed. However, following an accident at work, he claimed that he should have been treated as an employee of the contractor for whom he was working. HMRC issued a ruling under *SSCTFA 1999, s 8* that B was not an employee. The First-tier Tribunal dismissed B's appeal, finding that he was working under a contract for services which 'was similar to many in the construction industry where workers move from employer to employer on short term contracts, and where the worker considers himself to be self-employed'. *PA Bell v HMRC*, FTT [2011] UKFTT 379 (TC), TC01234.

Methodist minister—whether an employee

[73.42] A Methodist minister was dismissed by the governing body of the Methodist Church. He applied to an industrial tribunal for a declaration that he had been unfairly dismissed. The CA unanimously held that the tribunal had no jurisdiction, because the minister was not an employee. *President of the Methodist Conference v Parfitt*, CA [1983] 3 All ER 747.

[73.43] The decision in *President of the Methodist Conference v Parfitt*, 73.42 above, was approved by the Supreme Court (by a 4-1 majority, Lady Hale dissenting) in the similar subsequent case of *President of the Methodist Conference v Preston*, SC [2013] UKSC 29.

Presbyterian pastor—whether an employee

[73.44] A Presbyterian pastor was dismissed from his pastorate. He applied to an industrial tribunal for a declaration that he had been unfairly dismissed. The HL held that the tribunal had no jurisdiction, because the pastor was not an employee. *Davies v Presbyterian Church of Wales*, HL [1986] 1 All ER 705.

Hotel maintenance worker—whether an 'employed earner'

[73.45] A company (D) operated a hotel. It had employed a maintenance worker (B), who retired at the age of 65. Following his retirement, B continued to do regular maintenance work at the hotel, but D treated him as self-employed. HMRC issued a ruling that he was an 'employed earner', within the charge to Class 1 national insurance contributions. The Special Commissioner dismissed D's appeal, holding that the changes which took place when B reached the age of 65 were not 'sufficient to replace the relationship of employer and employee with one between client and independent contractor'. *Demibourne Ltd v HMRC*, Sp C [2005] SSCD 667 (Sp C 486).

Service engineer—whether an 'employed earner'

[73.46] A company (SP), which manufactured and distributed soft drinks, took over the business of another company (C). C's employees continued to work for SP, and were treated as employees, with the exception of a senior service engineer (RS), whom SP treated as self-employed. RS subsequently claimed that he should also have been treated as an employee, and following an enquiry, HMRC issued a ruling that RS had been an employed earner, and that SP was required to account for Class 1 national insurance contributions. The First-tier Tribunal allowed SP's appeal, holding that RS 'was not an employed earner and was self-employed'. *Slush Puppie Ltd v HMRC*, FTT [2012] UKFTT 356 (TC), TC02042.

Club assistant manager—whether an 'employed earner'

[73.47] A company (C) appointed an assistant manager (B) at a salary of £25,000 pa. However it did not account for Class 1 national insurance contributions on this salary. HMRC issued a notice requiring C to pay contributions. C appealed, contending that B had other business interests and had asked to be treated as self-employed. The First-tier Tribunal dismissed the appeal, finding that B had occupied 'the role of an employee within the appellant company'. *The Athenaeum Club v HMRC*, FTT [2010] UKFTT 27 (TC), TC00341.

Earnings (SSCBA 1992, s 3)

Payments to employee for use of car—whether 'remuneration'

[73.48] A company required one of its employees to use his car. It paid him a salary of £17 per week, plus £5 per week towards his car expenses. It subsequently made him redundant. The QB upheld the employee's contention that the payments of car expenses had been part of his 'remuneration'. *S & U Stores Ltd v Lee*, QB [1969] 2 All ER 417.

[73.49] The decision in *S & U Stores Ltd v Lee*, 73.48 above, was distinguished, and implicitly disapproved, in a subsequent case involving similar payments of £7 per week by the same company. Sir John Donaldson held that 'any sum which is agreed to be paid by way of reimbursement or on account of expenditure incurred by the employee has to be examined to see whether in broad terms the whole or any part of the sum represents a profit or surplus in the hands of the employee'. On the evidence, the payments of £7 per week were not 'remuneration'. *S & U Stores Ltd v Wilkes*, NIRC [1974] 3 All ER 401.

[73.50] A company (C) provided the services of apprentices and trainees to employers, and supervised their training. It employed about 160 training advisors, who had to visit the trainees at their places of work. It paid these advisors a mileage allowance, plus an annual payment which was described as a 'lump sum' but was actually paid in 12 monthly instalments. Initially it accounted for national insurance contributions on these payments. Subsequently it submitted a repayment claim on the basis that the effect of *Social Security (Contributions) Regulations 2001 (SI 2001/1004), reg 22A* was that it had not been required to pay national insurance contributions on these payments. HMRC rejected the claim on the basis that the payments were not 'relevant motoring expenditure' within *reg 22A(3)*, because they were not directly linked to mileage, and were 'earnings' on which contributions were payable. The First-tier Tribunal allowed C's appeal, holding that the payments 'were paid as motoring expenditure' and 'were not paid as earnings'. The Upper Tribunal reversed this decision but the CA restored it. Etherton LJ held that the fact that the payments were not directly linked to mileage was not conclusive, since the scheme was designed to prevent staff from making a personal profit by maximising their mileage. *Cheshire Employer & Skills Development Ltd (aka Total People Ltd v HMRC)*, CA [2012] EWCA Civ 1429; [2013] STC 2121.

Payment of petrol by chargecard—whether Class 1 Contributions due

[73.51] A company issued chargecards, to be used by employees of corporate customers when purchasing petrol. The DSS issued a ruling that national insurance contributions were due on the value of all petrol provided in this way, unless the employer produced documentary evidence to prove that the petrol had been used solely for business purposes. The company applied for judicial review of the ruling, but the QB dismissed the application. Lloyd LJ held that the discharge of an employee's debt was 'the equivalent of a payment in cash, and not less so because that payment is made easier by the use of a charge card'. *R v Department of Social Security (ex p. Overdrive Credit Card Ltd)*, QB [1991] STC 129.

School fees—whether Class 1 Contributions due

[73.52] A company paid the school fees for the two sons of its controlling directors. The Revenue issued notices of determination charging Class 1 contributions on the fees. The Special Commissioner dismissed the company's appeal, holding that the liability for payment of the fees was that of the directors. The company's discharge of the liability was within the definition of 'earnings' in *SSCBA 1992, s 3*. *Ableway Ltd v CIR*, Sp C [2002] SSCD 1 (Sp C 294).

[73.53] The decision in *Ableway Ltd v CIR*, 73.52 above, was applied in a similar subsequent case in which a company paid school fees for the son of its controlling director. *Frost Skip Hire Ltd v Wood*, Sp C [2004] SSCD 387 (Sp C 420).

Payment by employer into retirement benefit scheme

[73.54] A company (T) paid bonuses to senior employees by adding short-dated securities (or 'gilts') into their retirement benefit schemes. The Revenue issued a ruling that these bonuses were liable to Class 1 NIC. The QB allowed T's appeal. Andrew Collins J held that the court 'cannot strain the language of the statutory provisions even though many might think that the reality of the situation ought to produce a different result'. The payments were not earnings 'paid to or for the benefit of' the employees, within *SSCBA 1992, s 6(1)*. *Tullett & Tokyo Forex International Ltd v State for Social Security*, QB [2000] EWHC Admin 350; [2000] All ER (D) 739. (*Note*. The payments would now be liable to Class 1A contributions.)

[73.55] A company (F) made payments to a funded unapproved retirement benefit scheme for the benefit of one of its directors. HMRC issued a determination that Class 1 national insurance contributions were due in respect of the payments. The CA upheld the determination (by a 2-1 majority, Rimer LJ dissenting), but the Supreme Court unanimously reversed this decision and allowed F's appeal, holding that sums paid into the fund were not within the definition of 'earnings'. Lord Hodge observed that 'the ordinary man on the Underground would consider it to be counter-intuitive that a person would earn remuneration both when his employer paid money into a trust to create a fund for his benefit and again when at a later date that trust fund was paid out to him'. Any payments made out of the fund to the director would be deferred earnings, but the payments which F made into the fund were not earnings. *Forde & McHugh Ltd v HMRC*, SC [2014] UKSC 14; [2014] STC 724; [2014] 2 All ER 356.

Payment by employer in French gold coins

[73.56] Several companies entered into arrangements, devised by an accountancy firm, whereby they paid their directors bonuses in the form of antique French gold coins. All the coins in question were purchased from the same broker. The companies did not account for Class 1 NIC on the bonuses. The Revenue issued rulings that the companies were required to pay secondary Class 1 NICs. The Special Commissioners reviewed the evidence in detail and dismissed the companies' appeals, holding that the arrangements were a 'mechanism to deliver cash' and the payments were not 'payments in kind' within the meaning of the *Social Security (Contributions) Regulations*. *EDI Services Ltd v HMRC (and related appeals) (No 2)*, Sp C [2006] SSCD 392 (Sp C 539). (*Note*. For a preliminary issue in this case, see **4.63** APPEALS.)

Payment by transfer of book debts to directors

[73.57] Several companies entered into arrangements, devised by an accountancy firm, whereby they paid their directors bonuses by assigning them specific book debts. The companies did not account for Class 1 NIC on the bonuses. The Revenue issued rulings that the companies were required to pay secondary Class 1 NICs. The Special Commissioners reviewed the evidence in detail and dismissed the companies' appeals, observing that the companies continued to collect the debts and that 'it was never the intention to give notice of the assignment to the debtors'. The Commissioners also held that the arrangements were a 'mechanism to deliver cash' and were not 'payments in kind' within the meaning of the *Social Security (Contributions) Regulations*. *Spectrum Computer Supplies Ltd v HMRC (and related appeals)*, Sp C [2006] SSCD 668 (Sp C 559).

Distributions derived from employee benefit funds

[73.58] See *HMRC v PA Holdings Ltd (and cross-appeal)*, 42.55 PAY AS YOU EARN.

Miscellaneous

Married woman—election not to pay Class 1 Contributions

[73.59] In July 1959 a married woman (N) elected not to pay Class 1 National Insurance Contributions. In November 1973 she divorced her husband and became liable to pay Class 1 NICs. Several years later, she became aware that her State pension would be affected by the fact that she was recorded as not having paid any NICs between July 1959 and November 1973. She wrote to the Revenue claiming that she believed that she had resumed paying Class 1 NICs when she began a new employment in 1964. The Revenue produced evidence that no such contributions had been made, and the General Commissioners dismissed N's appeal, finding that she had elected not to pay contributions in 1959, and that there was 'no evidence to support her contention that she revoked that election in 1964'. The Ch D upheld their decision as one of fact. *Newnham v Clatworthy*, Ch D 2004, 76 TC 713.

[73.60] A similar decision was reached in *Mrs PA Tarr v HMRC*, FTT [2011] UKFTT 643 (TC), TC01485.

[73.61] In 1972 a married woman completed a form CF9 electing not to pay Class 1 national insurance contributions. Many years later she realised that this would have an adverse effect on her State pension. She wrote to HMRC asking to revoke the election, with retrospective effect from 1985. HMRC rejected her application and the First-tier Tribunal dismissed her appeal. Judge McKenna observed that the regulations 'provide for prospective revocation of an election to pay reduced rate national insurance contributions but not for retrospective revocation'. *Mrs CA Slater v HMRC*, FTT [2012] UKFTT 310 (TC), TC01996.

[73.62] A woman (W) began paying Class 1 national insurance contributions in 1960. She married in 1965 and stopped paying Class 1 Contributions in 1968, when the Ministry of Pensions and National Insurance received an election, purporting to be from her, to pay the reduced rate of contributions then available to married women. In 2005 W claimed that she should be credited with payment of Class 1 Contributions for 1968/69 to 2004/05. The Revenue rejected her claim and she appealed to the Special Commissioners. The Commissioner dismissed her appeal, finding that in 1968 W had 'made a married woman's election not to pay Class 1 National Insurance Contributions'. *Whittaker v HMRC*, Sp C [2006] SSCD 271 (Sp C 528).

[73.63] A similar decision was reached in a subsequent case where the Commissioner accepted the Revenue's evidence that a woman who married in March 1968 had made an election to pay the reduced rate of contributions in March 1969 (and was therefore not entitled to a full State pension). *Gutteridge v HMRC*, Sp C [2006] SSCD 315 (Sp C 534).

[73.64] Similar decisions were reached in *Mrs MA Morgan v HMRC*, Sp C 2008, [2009] SSCD 93 (Sp C 722); *Mrs P Black v HMRC*, FTT [2009] UKFTT 54 (TC), TC00033; *Mrs LA McLaggan v HMRC*, FTT [2010] UKFTT 300 (TC), TC00588; *Mrs J McPhail v HMRC*, FTT [2011] UKFTT 369 (TC), TC01224; *Mrs CG Prochazka v HMRC*, FTT [2012] UKFTT 4 (TC), TC01703, *Mrs N Reynolds v HMRC*, FTT [2012] UKFTT 196 (TC), TC01891; *Mrs N Evans v HMRC*, FTT [2012] UKFTT 285 (TC), TC01973, and *Mrs S Bennett v HMRC*, FTT [2012] UKFTT 476 (TC), TC02153.

Tribunal accepting appellant's evidence that no election made

[73.65] A woman (S) paid Class 1 national insurance contributions from 1965 until March 1968. She married in December 1967, and from April 1968 to March 1975 she did not pay any national insurance contributions. From April 1975 to November 1987 she paid contributions at the reduced rate applicable to married women. Subsequently she discovered that she would not receive a full State retirement pension, and applied to make backdated payments of Class 1 contributions. HMRC rejected her application on the grounds that it appeared that in 1968 she had signed a declaration on form CF9 electing not to pay such contributions. S appealed, contending that she had no recollection of making such an election. The First-Tier Tribunal accepted her evidence and allowed her appeal. Judge Brooks noted that in *Gutteridge v HMRC*, **73.63** above, HMRC had produced a form RF1 with an annotation to show that the appellant had made such an election. However, in this case S's form RF1 did not contain such an annotation, and there was 'no direct evidence that she made an election by signing the declaration that she did not wish to pay national insurance contributions'. *Mrs JM Spraggs v HMRC*, FTT [2011] UKFTT 333 (TC), TC01193.

[73.66] Judge Ruthven Gemmell reached a similar decision in *Mrs JS Brown v HMRC*, FTT [2013] UKFTT 300 (TC), TC02705.

[73.67] A woman (F) married in 1967 and gave up her job. She resumed working in 1977. Subsequently she discovered that she would not receive a full State retirement pension, and applied to make backdated payments of Class 1 contributions. HMRC rejected her application on the grounds that their records showed that in 1970 she had signed a declaration on form CF9 electing not to pay such contributions (and had made a further election in 1977 electing to pay reduced-rate contributions). F appealed, contending that she had not made either of the elections. The First-tier Tribunal reviewed the evidence in detail and allowed her appeal in part. Judge Short accepted F's evidence that 'she would have had no reason for making an election in 1970 since she had no intention of working on a full or part-time basis'. This was 'sufficiently anomalous as to call into question the integrity of HMRC's records, despite their generally high standard of care'. However, the 1977 election coincided with F having resumed work. F's employer had consistently deducted contributions at the reduced rate and 'had reason to believe that (F) had made a lower rate election'. Accordingly, it was 'more likely that (F) has failed to recall that an election was made as part of the, no doubt lengthy, paperwork which she completed when she started this employment'. *Mrs P Franks v HMRC*, FTT [2012] UKFTT 438 (TC), TC02119. (*Note.* F appealed to the Upper Tribunal, which allowed her appeal regarding the 1977 election by consent.)

Polish citizen working under assumed name

[73.68] A Polish citizen (H) travelled to the UK in 1984 and worked for two months as an agricultural worker. He did the same in 1987 and 1988. When this employment ended, he remained in the UK (in breach of the conditions of his visa) and worked at a public house under an assumed name. He also worked for a short time at a 'fast food' restaurant. He left the UK in April 1989, but returned in 1995 and worked for a cleaning company for seven weeks (again in breach of the conditions of his visa), using the same name that he had used at the public house. He subsequently applied to HMRC for a certificate E205 confirming that he had paid national insurance contributions. HMRC rejected the claim on the basis that they had no records of H having paid any such contributions. H appealed. The First-tier Tribunal reviewed the evidence in detail and allowed his appeal in part, holding that H had not paid, and was not entitled to credit for, any contributions in respect of his agricultural work or his work at the 'fast food' restaurant. However the tribunal found that H had paid national insurance contributions during the two employments which he had taken under an assumed name, and was entitled to credit for these. *BM Hudziec v HMRC (No 1)*, FTT [2011] UKFTT 866 (TC), TC01700. (*Note.* At a subsequent hearing, the tribunal upheld HMRC's calculation of the contributions to be credited to H—[2012] UKFTT 618 (TC), TC02294.)

SSCBA 1992, s 4(4)—consideration for 'restrictive undertaking'

[73.69] In 1994 a company (R) terminated the employment of one of its directors (H), under an agreement whereby H agreed to a 'restrictive undertaking' not to compete with the company, in return for R making five payments to him, totalling £2,200,000. The Revenue issued a determination that R was liable to account for national insurance contributions on the payments, by virtue of *SSCBA 1992, s 4(4)*. The Special Commissioner dismissed R's appeal, holding that the effect of *SSCBA 1992, s 4(4)* was that R was required to account for national insurance contributions on the payments. The Ch D upheld this decision. Lightman J observed that 'the Special Commissioner had good and ample grounds for holding that the giving of the undertakings was clearly connected with and a direct result of (H) being an employee of (R)'. *RCI (Europe) Ltd v Woods*, Ch D 2003, 76 TC 390; [2004] STC 315; [2003] EWHC 3129 (Ch).

[73.70] In 1999 a company (E) acquired the shares of another company (K) from its controlling director (D) and his wife. D remained a director of K after the change of ownership. E and D entered into a 'non-compete agreement' under which E paid £250,000 to D in 2000/01 and a further £250,000 in 2001/02, in return for D agreeing not to enter into competition with E for a three-year period. The Revenue issued a determination that national insurance contributions were chargeable on the payments under *SSCBA 1992, s 4(4)*, and that K was liable to account for those contributions under *SSCBA 1992, s 6(4)*. K appealed. The Special Commissioner dismissed the appeal, holding that the effect of *SSCBA 1992, ss 4(4), 6(4)* was that K was required to account for national insurance contributions on the payments. *Kent Foods Ltd v HMRC*, Sp C 2007, [2008] SSCD 307 (Sp C 643).

SSCBA 1992, ss 6(1)—waiver of loan

[73.71] A close company (S) waived a loan to its controlling director (F). It was accepted that this gave rise to a charge to income tax under what is now *CTA 2010, s 455*, and that this took precedence over the employment income charge under *ITEPA 2003, s 188*. HMRC issued a ruling that the waiver of the loan gave rise to a liability to Class 1 national insurance contributions. The First-tier Tribunal dismissed S's appeal. Judge Radford observed that 'the shareholders had not been consulted on the waiving of the loans', which had been approved by S's directors. Accordingly it appeared that the waiver was in respect of F's employment rather than in respect of his shareholding. Therefore it constituted remuneration which was subject to Class 1 contributions. *Stewart Fraser Ltd v HMRC*, FTT [2011] UKFTT 46 (TC), TC00923.

SSCBA 1992, ss 6(2), 122—European Convention on Human Rights

[73.72] See *Walker v United Kingdom*, **31.95** HUMAN RIGHTS.

SSCBA 1992, s 7—interpretation of 'secondary contributor'

[73.73] HMRC issued a ruling to a company (GSI) that the exercise of certain options to employees gave rise to a liability to national insurance contributions. GSI appealed, contending that the staff were supplied by an associated company (GSL), and applied for a preliminary hearing to determine whether it could be treated as the employer of the employees who had exercised the options (see **4.18** APPEALS). The First-tier Tribunal held a preliminary hearing, reviewed the evidence in detail, and determined the preliminary issue in favour of HMRC. Judge Williams found that GSL 'did not have a place of business in Great Britain at any time relevant to these appeals'. He held that GSL was a 'foreign employer' within *Social Security (Categorisation of Earners) Regulations 1978 (SI 1978/1689), r 1(2)*, with the result that GSI was the 'host employer' within *SI 1978/1689, Sch 3 para 9*, and was the 'secondary contributor' for the purposes of *SSCBA 1992, s 7*. *Goldman Sachs International v HMRC (No 2)*, FTT [2010] SFTD 930; [2010] UKFTT 205 (TC), TC00507. (*Note*. The company subsequently appealed to the Upper Tribunal, but the appeal was reportedly settled by agreement. See **50.24** REVENUE ADMINISTRATION for subsequent developments in this case.)

PSA 1993—contracted-out employment

[73.74] An individual (W) had been in contracted-out employment from 1985 to 1991. He subsequently retired. In 2002, on reaching the age of 65, he began receiving a state retirement pension, the amount of which was reduced because he had been in contracted-out employment. He lodged an appeal to the Special Commissioners, contending that he should be treated as having paid the full rate of contributions. The Special Commissioner rejected this contention and dismissed his appeal, finding that he had paid contributions 'at the reduced rate applicable to contracted-out employment'. *GT Wilkinson v HMRC*, Sp C 2006, [2007] SSCD 9 (Sp C 567).

SI 2001/1004, reg 15—aggregation of earnings

[73.75] A company director (S) received earnings from five different companies. None of the companies accounted for any national insurance contributions, on the basis that the amounts which each company paid to S were below the relevant threshold. The Revenue issued Notices of Decision that the earnings paid to S by the five companies should be aggregated, in accordance with *SSCBA 1992, Sch 1*. One of the companies appealed, contending that they were not carrying on business in association, as required by what is now *Social Security (Contributions) Regulations 2001 (SI 2001/1004), reg 15*. The Special Commissioner rejected this contention and dismissed the appeal, holding that 'the companies were carrying on business in association on the ordinary meaning of that expression', and that it was 'reasonably practicable to make the aggregation'. *Samuels & Samuels Ltd v Richardson*, Sp C 2004, [2005] SSCD 1 (Sp C 431).

SI 2001/1004, reg 60—unpaid Class 1 contributions

[73.76] An individual (W) reached retirement age in 2006. He duly received a State pension, but did not receive a full pension on the grounds that he had not made sufficient payments of national insurance contributions. He appealed, contending that he had paid contributions between 1965 and 1975, and between 1981 and 1989, which had not been recorded on the form RF1 which HMRC had produced. The First-Tier Tribunal accepted this contention and allowed W's appeal in part. Judge Geraint Jones observed that *Social Security (Contributions) Regulations 2001 (SI 2001/1004), reg 60* provided that, where the failure to pay contributions was shown 'not to have been with the consent or connivance of, or attributable to any negligence on the part of the primary contributor', such contributions should be treated as having been paid on the due date. He accepted W's evidence that he had been employed by three specific employers between 1965 and 1975 and should be credited with contributions although HMRC had no record of the employers having accounted for contributions. For the period from 1981 to 1989, W had been a director of a limited company, but had relied on the company's accountants to account for national insurance contributions on his salary. Judge Geraint Jones found that, until December 1986, it had been reasonable for W to have relied on the accountants, so that the failure to account for contributions was not with his 'consent or connivance'. However correspondence showed that, from 1987 onwards, W should have been aware that there had been a failure to account for contributions, so that he had been negligent and was not entitled to credit for unpaid contributions from 1987 to 1989. *F Wood v HMRC*, FTT [2012] UKFTT 344 (TC), TC02030.

[73.77] An individual (T), who had been a director of several associated companies, lodged an appeal to the First-tier Tribunal, contending that he should be credited with payments of national insurance contributions which had been deducted from his salary but had not included in HMRC's records. The First-tier Tribunal reviewed the evidence and detail and dismissed T's appeal for 1981/82 to 1986/87, but allowed his appeal for 1987/88 to 1991/92. Judge Hellier found that for 1987/88 to 1991/92, the companies had employed a bookkeeper, who had had a close relationship with the companies' principal director. On the evidence, HMRC had not shown that the failure to account for contributions for those years was attributable to any negligence on the part of T, so that he should be credited with payment of Class 1 contributions. *S Tracey v HMRC*, FTT [2013] UKFTT 273 (TC), TC02681.

SI 2001/1004, reg 115—mariners

[73.78] A Scottish company (S) had a wholly-owned Jersey subsidiary (J), which employed 42 process chemists, who worked in the oil industry on various 'floating production storage offload facilities' (FPSOs) in the North Sea. J paid PAYE and primary Class 1 national insurance contributions in respect of these chemists, but did not pay secondary contributions. The Revenue were not satisfied that all the 42 chemists worked exclusively on FPSOs, and issued rulings that S was required to pay secondary Class 1 contributions in respect of the chemists' earnings. S appealed. The Special Commissioner reviewed the evidence and issued a determination that the chemists who worked on FPSOs during the relevant period were 'mariners' within *Social Security (Contributions) Regulations 2001 (SI 2001/1004), reg 115*. They were employed by a company which did not have a place of business in Great Britain, so that the condition of liability laid down by *SI 2001/1004, reg 117(c)* was not satisfied. Furthermore, there was no other statutory enactment by virtue of which S could be treated as a secondary contributor in respect of the chemists' earnings. The Commissioner formally directed the Revenue 'to inform the appellants which of the 42 chemists they dispute were deployed on FPSOs'. *Oleochem (Scotland) Ltd v HMRC*, Sp C [2009] SSCD 205 (Sp C 731).

SI 2001/1004, Sch 3 Part X para 5—gratuities

[73.79] An employee benefit trust made payments to certain employees in 2003/04. HMRC issued a ruling that Class 1 national insurance contributions were due on the payments. The Upper Tribunal upheld HMRC's ruling, disapproving the Special Commissioners' decision in *Channel 5 TV Group Ltd v Morehead*, Sp C [2003] SSCD 327 (Sp C 369), and holding that the essential feature of a gratuity was 'that it is a token of thanks for the services provided directly and personally to the donor'. A voluntary payment 'by a third party who has received an indirect benefit from the provision of the employee's services' did not amount to a gratuity. *HMRC v Knowledgepoint 360 Group Ltd*, UT [2013] UKUT 7 (TCC); [2013] STC 1690.

Class 1A Contributions

Cars provided for company directors

[73.80] A company (S) arranged for a leasing company (D) to lease two Mercedes motor vehicles to its directors. S failed to account for Class 1A national insurance contributions. HMRC issued a notice under *SSCTFA 1999, s 8* charging Class 1A contributions. S appealed against the notice, contending that it had acted as a nominee for the directors and should not be required to account for contributions. The First-tier Tribunal rejected this contention and dismissed the appeals, finding that the directors 'had not made any attempt to execute any agency or nominee arrangement'. The relevant contract had been signed between S and D, and S would have been liable to D if it had defaulted on the payments. Furthermore, 'even if there had been such an agreement, the legislation was not concerned with agency or any other law. It stipulated the correct tax treatment to be used when an employer provides a car for its employees. The contract was in the name of the company, the legislation was satisfied and so a benefit arose.' (The tribunal also dismissed appeals by the directors against closure notices charging income tax.) *Stanford Management Services Ltd v HMRC (and related appeals)*, FTT [2010] UKFTT 98 (TC), TC00409.

[73.81] A company (M) provided a car and fuel for its managing director. It failed to account for Class 1A national insurance contributions in respect of the car. HMRC issued a ruling that M was required to pay Class 1A contributions, and the First-tier Tribunal dismissed M's appeal. *McKenna Demolition Ltd v HMRC (and related appeal)*, FTT [2011] UKFTT 344 (TC), TC01204.

[73.82] Similar decisions were reached in *Autowest Ltd v HMRC*, FTT [2011] UKFTT 446 (TC), TC01299; *Time For Group Ltd v HMRC*, FTT [2012] UKFTT 214 (TC), TC01909; *Vinyl Designs Ltd v HMRC (and related appeals)*, FTT [2014] UKFTT 205 (TC), TC03345; *Yum Yum Ltd v HMRC*, **22.143** EMPLOYMENT INCOME; *Ryan-Munden v HMRC*, **22.145** EMPLOYMENT INCOME, and *Munden v HMRC*, **22.146** EMPLOYMENT INCOME.

[73.83] In April 2004 a company director (H) purchased a BMW motor car. In December 2004 he sold a 90% share in the car to the company (G). G paid for fuel, but failed to account for Class 1A national insurance contributions. HMRC issued a ruling that G was required to pay Class 1A Contributions in respect of the car and the fuel. The First-tier Tribunal dismissed G's appeal, holding that the fact that H owned 10% of the car did not avoid the liability to national insurance contributions. The Upper Tribunal upheld this decision, applying the principles laid down by Pumfrey J in *Christensen v Vasili*, **22.125** EMPLOYMENT INCOME. *GR Solutions Ltd v HMRC*, UT [2013] UKUT 278 (TCC); [2013] STC 2289.

Car provided for company secretary

[73.84] A family company (S) carried on a plumbing business. It provided its company secretary (who was the wife of the controlling director) with a BMW car, costing about £32,000. S failed to account for Class 1A national insurance contributions in respect of the car. HMRC issued a ruling that S was required to pay Class 1A contributions. The company appealed, contending that the provision of the car was 'normal commercial practice', within *ITEPA 2003, s 169(4)*. The First-Tier Tribunal rejected this contention and dismissed the appeal, finding that S had provided insufficient evidence to support its claim. *S Barnard Ltd v HMRC*, FTT [2010] UKFTT 187 (TC), TC00491.

Cars provided for employees—charge to fuel benefit

[73.85] HMRC formed the opinion that a public company (P) had failed to account for Class 1A national insurance contributions in respect of the provision of car fuel for private motoring for several employees. They issued determinations charging NICs, interest and penalties. P appealed, contending that it had not provided fuel for private motoring. The First-tier Tribunal reviewed the evidence in detail and dismissed P's appeals against the contributions and interest, finding that 'the system operated by the company was not sufficiently robust to ensure a reliable reimbursement by the employee of the cost of fuel used for private purposes'. However, the tribunal allowed P's appeal against the penalties, holding that it had not acted negligently. Judge Khan held that 'negligence in relation to tax statutes means to act in an imprudent or unreasonable manner', whereas P had 'intended to comply with the legislation and established a system' which 'had some deficiencies'. *PMS International Group plc v HMRC*, FTT [2012] UKFTT 504 (TC), TC02181.

Purchase of racehorses—whether a benefit for director

[73.86] A company (C) purchased several racehorses. HMRC formed the opinion that C had purchased the horses in order to confer a benefit on its principal director (H). They issued determinations on C, charging Class 1A national insurance contributions, and also issued income tax assessments on H. C and H appealed, contending that C had purchased the racehorses for advertising purposes and that H had no personal interest in horse racing. The First-tier Tribunal accepted this contention and allowed the appeals, observing that 'there was no evidence that (H) had entertained customers of the company in person at any racing event, or was present in any parade ring, or had been observed in any situation with racehorses'. *Chepstow Plant International Ltd v HMRC (and related appeal)*, FTT [2011] UKFTT 166 (TC), TC01035.

Benefits in kind 'made good' by directors

[73.87] A family company (M) owned a property which its directors occupied. M paid for repairs to the property. HMRC informed M that this amounted to a benefit in kind, giving rise to a charge to income tax under *ITEPA 2003, s 203*. M adjusted the directors' loan accounts in order to 'make good' the benefit in kind under *s 203(2)*. HMRC accepted that this had the effect of removing the charge to income tax under *s 203*. However HMRC issued a ruling that M was still required to pay Class 1A national insurance contributions under *SSCBA 1992, s 10*. M appealed. The First-tier Tribunal allowed the appeal. Judge Short held that 'there can be no charge to Class 1A NICs in circumstances where there is no income tax charge' and that 'the "making good" provisions at *s 203* result in any taxable benefit and therefore any income tax charge being extinguished and treated as never having arisen'. *Marcia Willett Ltd v HMRC*, FTT [2012] UKFTT 625 (TC); [2013] SFTD 65, TC02301.

Class 2 Contributions

Comedian—whether a 'self-employed person'

[73.88] A comedian agreed to appear at a theatre for one week. The contract laid down a number of regulations, prohibiting 'the use of improper words or gestures' and giving the theatre management 'the power to prohibit the whole or any part of the performance which they may reasonably consider unsuitable'. The management treated him as self-employed. He appealed, contending that in view of the nature of the contract, he should be treated as an employee and the theatre should pay employer's national insurance contributions. The KB rejected this contention and dismissed his appeal, holding that he was a 'self-employed person' and not an employee. *Gould v Minister of National Insurance*, KB [1951] 1 All ER 368.

Part-time drama teacher—whether a 'self-employed person'

[73.89] The Minister of Social Security issued a ruling that an actor, who also worked as a part-time drama teacher at a school for music and drama, was self-employed. He appealed, contending that in view of the nature of the contract, he should be treated as an employee and that the school should pay employer's national insurance contributions. The QB rejected this contention and dismissed his appeal, holding that he was a 'self-employed person' and not an employee. *Argent v Minister of Social Security*, QB [1968] 3 All ER 208.

Landlord—whether a 'self-employed earner'

[73.90] An individual (R) had carried on business as a taxi driver, and paid Class 2 national insurance contributions. He also received income from the letting of property. In 1997 he suffered a heart attack and ceased to work as a taxi driver. He continued to pay Class 2 contributions, in order to qualify for invalidity benefit. The Revenue issued a ruling that he was not a 'self-employed earner' within *SSCBA 1992, s 2(1)(b)*. The Special Commissioner dismissed R's appeal, holding on the evidence that his property income represented an investment rather than a business. *Rashid v Garcia*, Sp C 2002, [2003] SSCD 36 (Sp C 348).

Failure to pay contributions—SI 2001/769, reg 6

[73.91] An individual (T) had been self-employed, and had paid Class 2 Contributions, from 1958/59 to 1971/72. In 1972 his marriage broke up; he left his previous address and failed to inform the DHSS of his new address or to pay further Class 2 Contributions until 1986. He subsequently claimed that he should be able to make backdated payment of contributions for 1972/73 to 1982/83 inclusive, by virtue of *Social Security (Crediting and Treatment of Contributions and National Insurance Numbers) Regulations 2001 (SI 2001/769), reg* 6. The Revenue rejected the claim, on the grounds that *reg* 6 only permitted backdated payment where 'it is shown to the satisfaction of the Inland Revenue that the failure to pay the contribution before that time is attributable to ignorance or error on the part of that person and that that ignorance or error on the part of that person was not due to any failure on the part of such person to exercise due care and diligence'. The General Commissioners allowed T's appeal but the Ch D reversed their decision and upheld the Revenue's ruling. Patten J held that the relevant question was whether T's failure to pay contributions within the prescribed period was attributable to a failure to exercise due care and diligence during the material 14-year period. On the evidence, the only reasonable conclusion was that T had failed to exercise due care and diligence. Accordingly, the conditions specified in *reg* 6 had not been satisfied. Patten J also observed that, for a taxpayer to demonstrate that his was failure attributable to 'ignorance or error' for the purposes of *reg* 6, he had to 'prove total ignorance of National Insurance regulations and payments or point to circumstances existing at the time which robbed him of all knowledge and understanding that payments were due at the relevant time'. *HMRC v Thompson*, Ch D [2005] EWHC 3388 (Ch); [2007] STC 240.

[73.92] An individual (M) was born in 1943. He paid Class 1 national insurance contributions from 1958/59 to 1986/87. He began part-time self-employment in 1984/85, but failed to pay any Class 2 national insurance contributions. In 2008 he realised that, because he had not paid national insurance contributions while he was self-employed, he would not receive a full State pension. He applied to pay backdated contributions. HMRC rejected his claim for the years prior to 2002/03, on the grounds that his failure to pay contributions at the appropriate time was attributable to a failure to exercise 'due care and diligence'. The First-tier Tribunal dismissed M's appeal against this decision, applying the principles laid down in *HMRC v Thompson*, **73.91** above, and finding that M 'took no steps at all to enquire about his responsibilities as a self employed person during the relevant time'. *A Marshall v HMRC*, FTT [2010] UKFTT 608 (TC), TC00849.

[73.93] A similar decision, also applying the principles laid down in *HMRC v Thompson*, **73.91** above, was reached in *Mrs C Thacker v HMRC*, FTT [2012] UKFTT 698 (TC), TC02367.

[73.94] An individual (S) began self-employment in 1986. He paid income tax and Class 4 national insurance contributions, but failed to pay any Class 2 national insurance contributions until 2009/10. Subsequently he applied to pay backdated contributions, to enable him to qualify for a full State pension. HMRC accepted his application for 2003/04 onwards, but rejected his application for 1986/87 to 2002/03 on the grounds that his failure to pay contributions at the appropriate time was attributable to a failure to exercise 'due care and diligence'. S appealed, contending that he had been misled by the accountant who had dealt with his tax affairs and who had failed to inform the

DHSS that he was self-employed. The First-tier Tribunal accepted this contention and allowed the appeal. Judge Radford found that S had 'exercised due care and diligence by appointing an accountant to deal with all matters which arose in connection with his self-employment'. *Dr J Schonfield v HMRC*, FTT [2013] UKFTT 244 (TC), TC02658.

[73.95] The decision in *Schonfield v HMRC*, 73.94 above, was applied in the similar subsequent case of *S Murphy v HMRC*, FTT [2014] UKFTT 734 (TC), TC03855.

Reduction in rate of Class 2 NICs—whether retrospective

[73.96] An individual (M) lived and worked in the UK from 1960 to 1968, when he emigrated. He subsequently moved to Alderney. In 2009 he applied to make a backdated payment of Class 2 national insurance contributions, to enable him to qualify for a UK pension. HMRC accepted his application, and M sent a cheque which HMRC accepted as payment of 12 years' contributions. M appealed to the First-tier Tribunal, contending that, when the weekly rate of Class 2 contributions had been reduced from £6.55 to £2 in 2000, the reduction should be treated as having retrospective effect, so that the cheque which he had sent should be treated as payment of 24 years' contributions rather than 12 years' contributions. The First-tier Tribunal rejected this contention and dismissed M's appeal. *C Murfitt v HMRC*, FTT [2013] UKFTT 276 (TC), TC02684.

Failure to claim small earnings' exception

[73.97] An individual (P) registered as self-employed and paid Class 2 national insurance contributions between 2005 and 2010, although he qualified for small earnings' exception under *SSCBA 1992, s 11(4)*. In 2011 he claimed a refund of the contributions he had paid. HMRC agreed to repay the contributions which P had paid for 2009/10, but rejected his repayment claim for earlier years. The First-tier Tribunal dismissed P's appeal against this decision. *J Pugsley v HMRC*, FTT [2012] UKFTT 697 (TC), TC02366.

Class 3 Contributions

Application to pay backdated Class 3 Contributions

[73.98] A married woman, who had been born in Nigeria in 1934, paid Class 1 National Insurance Contributions from 1962 to 1968, when she exercised her right as a married woman not to pay such contributions. In 1969 she returned to Nigeria. In May 2000 she applied to pay backdated Class 3 National qualify for a UK pension. The Revenue rejected her claim on the basis that her failure to pay these contributions was attributable to her 'failure to exercise due care and diligence', within *Social Security (Contributions) Regulations 2001 (SI 2001/1004), reg 50*. She appealed, contending that she had been unaware of the relevant regulations and that it was unreasonable 'to expect an ignorant person to exercise due diligence'. The Special Commissioner dismissed her appeal, finding that she 'was not ignorant about the existence of the National Insurance Scheme and must have known the basic principle that benefits were in some way related to contributions. She had some dealings with National Insurance while she was in the United Kingdom, although her employer would have done all the work in deducting contributions. She did know enough to make a married woman's election not to pay contributions on two occasions, and to make various claims to benefits.' The Commissioner observed that 'doing nothing is not the exercise of due care and diligence. Had she made an enquiry she would have been told that there was a six-year time limit for paying contributions. Her ignorance of this was due to her failure to make enquiries, which is a failure to exercise due care and diligence.' *Adojutelegan v Clark*, Sp C [2004] SSCD 524 (Sp C 430).

[73.99] An individual (R) was born in 1935. When he was aged 64, he discovered that he would not receive a full State retirement pension, because he had been a full-time student from October 1956 to December 1964. He applied to pay backdated Class 3 National Insurance Contributions, in order to qualify for a full pension. The Revenue rejected his claim on the basis that his failure to pay these contributions was attributable to his 'failure to exercise due care and diligence', within *Social Security (Contributions) Regulations 2001 (SI 2001/1004), reg 50*. He appealed. The Special Commissioner reviewed the evidence in detail and dismissed his appeal, accepting the Revenue's evidence that, between 1956 and 1964, R had been informed of the potential consequences of not paying voluntary contributions. However R had chosen not 'to exercise due care and diligence in protecting his contribution record'. *PL Rose v HMRC*, Sp C [2007] SSCD 129 (Sp C 574).

[73.100] The decisions in *Adojutelegan v Clark*, **73.98** above, and *Rose v HMRC*, **73.99** above, were applied in the similar subsequent cases of *AA Onanuga v HMRC*, FTT [2012] UKFTT 711 (TC), TC02378, and *Mrs J Childs v HMRC*, FTT [2013] UKFTT 179 (TC), TC02594.

[73.101] A British citizen (K) was born in 1929. In 1948 he began working for the Kenyan police. He continued to work in Kenya until 1975. While he was in Kenya, he did not pay any national insurance contributions until 1971, when he was permitted to pay backdated contributions for the previous six years. He subsequently applied to pay backdated Class 3 National Insurance Contributions to cover the period from 1948 to 1965, in order to qualify for a full UK pension. HMRC rejected the claim on the basis that his failure to pay these contributions was attributable to his 'failure to exercise due care and diligence', within *Social Security (Contributions) Regulations 2001 (SI 2001/1004), reg 50*. K appealed. The General Commissioners allowed his appeal and the CA upheld their decision as one of fact. Arden LJ observed that 'the facts of this case are unusual', since K had left the UK at the age of 19, and that 'in 1948 the NIC scheme was a novel and unfamiliar concept'. *Kearney v HMRC*, CA [2010] STC 1137; [2010] EWCA Civ 288.

[73.102] The decision in *Kearney v HMRC*, **73.101** above, was applied in the similar subsequent cases of *JR Goldsack v HMRC*, FTT [2010] UKFTT 530 (TC), TC00784 and *GWM Allan v HMRC*, FTT [2011] UKFTT 115 (TC), TC00991.

[73.103] The First-tier Tribunal reached a similar decision in a case where it accepted the evidence of the appellant (an Australian citizen who had subsequently returned to Australia) that he had sent HMRC an application to make backdated payments in 2008, but had not received a reply. *WKF McPherson v HMRC*, FTT [2014] UKFTT 322 (TC), TC03456.

[73.104] An individual (C) was born in 1938. He worked in the UK, and paid Class 1 National Insurance Contributions, from 1954 to 1959. In 1959 he moved to Australia. He did not pay any further UK national insurance contributions until 2002, when he was permitted to pay backdated contributions for the previous six years. He applied to pay backdated Class 3 National Insurance Contributions to cover the period from 1959 to 1996, in order to qualify for a full UK pension. The Revenue rejected his claim on the basis that his failure to pay these contributions was attributable to his 'failure to exercise due care and diligence', within *Social Security (Contributions) Regulations 2001 (SI 2001/1004), reg 50*. The Commissioner dismissed C's appeal against this decision, holding that he could not 'reasonably expect, without making any enquiries, to receive a full British pension over 40 years after leaving Britain when he had paid only five years' contributions to the British scheme'. The Commissioner also noted that Australia had terminated its bilateral social security agreement with the UK in 2001, that C had not been resident in any of the EU Member States at any time after the UK joined the European Communities, and that 'the basic framework of international social security law, reflected in the European Union and British rules, is that individuals should become entitled to a pension in their main residence or place of work if and when they reach pensionable age there, and not in every place where they may have worked'. *NT Clements v HMRC*, Sp C [2008] SSCD 744 (Sp C 677).

[73.105] An individual (L) was born in 1930. He served in the RAF and became a police officer in the UK. From 1955 to 1967 he worked in Bechuanaland (now Botswana) and did not pay any UK national insurance contributions. He returned to the UK in 1967. In 1995 he discovered that, because he had not paid national insurance contributions from 1955 to 1967, he would not receive a full state pension. He applied to pay backdated contributions. HMRC rejected his claim on the basis that his failure to pay these contributions was attributable to his 'failure to exercise due care and diligence', within *Social Security (Contributions) Regulations 2001 (SI 2001/1004), reg 50*. L appealed. The First-Tier tribunal dismissed his appeal, observing that L 'was aware of the National Insurance scheme before he went to Bechuanaland' and holding that 'by not informing the DHSS on his return in 1967 that he had been working abroad for 12 years, even though he made enquires about "self-employed" NICs, he did not exercise due care and diligence'. *WB Langthorne v HMRC (No 1)*, FTT [2010] UKFTT 171 (TC), TC00475.

[73.106] A similar decision was reached in a subsequent appeal by the same appellant, concerning 1986/87 and 1987/88. *WB Langthorne v HMRC (No 2)*, FTT [2012] UKFTT 578 (TC), TC02255.

[73.107] A woman (M) paid Class 1 contributions from 1964 until July 1969, when she married and made an election not to pay contributions. She subsequently ceased employment, but did not make an election to pay Class 3 contributions. Some years later, she applied to pay backdated Class 3 National Insurance Contributions for the period from July 1969 to April 1978. The Revenue rejected her application on the grounds that what is now *Social Security (Contributions) Regulations 2001 (SI 2001/1004), reg 132* applied. M appealed, contending that when she had made the original election in 1969, she had not appreciated its consequences. The Ch D upheld the Revenue's ruling. Patten J held that M's 'ability to make contributions for the period from 1969 to April 1978 depends not on her personal circumstances or her state of knowledge about the effect of the election that she made, but on the proper interpretation and effect of the relevant national insurance regulations'. *HMRC v Mayor*, Ch D 2007, [2008] STC 1958; [2007] EWHC 3147 (Ch).

[73.108] The decision in *HMRC v Mayor*, **73.107** above, was applied in a similar subsequent case in which the First-tier Tribunal specifically rejected the appellant's contention that the relevant provisions of *SSCBA 1992, ss 13, 14* were inconsistent with European Community law. *Mrs S Moss v HMRC*, FTT [2010] UKFTT 295 (TC), TC00583.

[73.109] An Irishman (G) was born in Dublin in 1928. He moved to the UK in December 1948 and paid UK national insurance contributions from January 1949 until July 1950. He then left the UK and worked in the Kenyan Police Force from August 1950 until 1963. In 1963 he moved to Australia, and he subsequently lived in the Irish Republic, the Isle of Man, and Gibraltar. In January 2009 he was allowed to pay backdated UK Class 3 NICs for 1984/85 to 1992/93 (the years in which he had lived in the Irish Republic), thus qualifying for a reduced UK pension. He lodged an appeal to the First-Tier Tribunal, contending that he should also be allowed to pay such contributions for the time he had spent in Kenya. The First-tier Tribunal rejected this contention and dismissed his appeal, holding that G was not entitled to pay contributions for this period, because he had not met the requirements of the *National Insurance (Residents & Persons Abroad) Regulations 1948 (SI 1948/1275), reg 5(2)*. The Upper Tribunal upheld this decision. *JA Garland v HMRC*, UT [2013] UKUT 471 (TCC); [2013] STC 1608.

Application for repayment of Class 3 Contributions

[73.110] In 2006 the Government published a proposal that, for people reaching the state pension age on or after 6 April 2010, only 30 years of national insurance contributions should be required to earn the full basic state pension (the thresholds had previously been 44 years for men and 39 for women). This change was enacted in the *Pensions Act 2007, s 1(3)*, and came into force on 26 September 2007. An individual (F), who had paid Class 3 contributions from 2003 to 2006 in order to reach the previous 44-year limit, submitted a repayment claim under *Social Security (Contributions) Regulations 2001 (SI 2001/1004), reg 52*. HMRC rejected the claim on the basis that the contributions had not been 'paid in error'. The Ch D upheld HMRC's rejection of the claim. David Richards J held that the only circumstances in which refunds could be given were either where contributions had been made in error or where precluded contributions had been made. There was no other basis for entitlement to a refund. On the evidence, the relevant contributions had not been made in error, so that F was not entitled to a refund. *HMRC v M Fenton*, Ch D [2010] STC 2446; [2010] EWHC 2000 (Ch).

[73.111] The First-tier Tribunal heard thirteen appeals in cases where the facts were broadly similar to those in *HMRC v Fenton*, **73.110** above, reviewed the evidence in detail and allowed two of the appeals, finding that the relevant payments had been made after the publication of the Government's proposal and holding that those payments had been made 'in error'. However the tribunal dismissed the other eleven appeals, finding that the relevant payments had been made before the publication of the Government White Paper. Judge Berner held that a payment made in ignorance of 'a prospective change in law about which nobody outside the policy-making body itself is aware' could not be regarded as a payment made 'in error'. HMRC appealed to the Upper Tribunal in one of the cases where the First-tier Tribunal had allowed the appeal, and six of the unsuccessful appellants also appealed to the Upper Tribunal. The Upper Tribunal upheld the First-tier Tribunal decision in all seven cases. *C Bonner v HMRC (and related appeals)*, UT [2010] UKUT 450 (TCC); [2011] STC 538.

[73.112] The First-tier Tribunal dismissed appeals against HMRC's refusal to repay contributions, applying the Upper Tribunal decision in *Bonner v HMRC*, **73.111** above, in *Mrs J Howell v HMRC*, FTT [2012] UKFTT 75 (TC), TC01771, and *RJ Pages v HMRC*, FTT [2012] UKFTT 321 (TC), TC02007.

Application to be credited with backdated Class 3 Contributions

[73.113] From 1974 to 1979 an individual (D) worked outside the UK. He was entitled to pay Class 3 national insurance contributions, but did not do so. Accordingly, when he reached retirement age in 2008, he did not receive the full State pension. HMRC agreed that he, or his former employer, could pay the backdated contributions. D's former employer indicated that it was willing to pay the contributions, but went into receivership without doing so. D appealed to the First-tier Tribunal, contending that he should be credited with the backdated contributions without actually paying them. The First-tier Tribunal rejected this contention and dismissed his appeal, holding that it had no jurisdiction to make such an order. *D Ashworth v HMRC*, FTT [2011] UKFTT 796 (TC), TC01632.

Class 4 Contributions

[73.114] An individual (M), who was self-employed, became 65 on 19 April 2003. The Revenue issued a ruling that he was required to pay Class 4 national insurance contributions for the tax year 2003/04. M appealed, contending that it was unfair to require him to pay Class 4 contributions for the period after his sixty-fifth birthday. The Special Commissioner dismissed his appeal, holding that the charge was 'clearly in accordance with the law' and observing that 'if there is any discrimination in relation to National Insurance as a whole it is in favour of the self-employed'. *Manning v HMRC*, Sp C [2006] SSCD 588 (Sp C 552).

[73.115] A self-employed dentist subscribed for units in an enterprise zone unit trust, which had invested in a building which qualified for industrial buildings allowance. In his return, the dentist claimed that the capital allowances should be set against the profits of his dental practice for the purpose of computing his liability to Class 4 NICs. HMRC rejected the claim and the First-tier Tribunal dismissed the dentist's appeal. Judge Aleksander observed that 'there is no statutory basis on which capital allowances arising in respect of expenditure on buildings in an enterprise zone can be set against earnings from a profession'. Furthermore, the dentist had no 'legitimate expectation' that his claim would be allowed. *BJ Patel v HMRC*, FTT [2011] UKFTT 373 (TC), TC01228.

EC Regulations

EC Reg 1408/71/EC, article 1(a)(iv)

[73.116] In a Netherlands case, the ECJ held that a Catholic priest, who had worked as a missionary in Africa for 25 years before becoming ill and returning to the Netherlands, was a 'self-employed person' for the purposes of *EC Reg 1408/71/EC, article 1(a)(iv)* (and was therefore entitled to invalidity benefits). *Van Roosmalen v Bestuur van de Bedrifjsvereneging voor de Gezondheid Geestelijke en Maatschappelijke Belangen*, ECJ Case C-300/84; [1986] ECR 3097.

EC Reg 1408/71/EC, article 13(1)

[73.117] In a Netherlands case, the ECJ held that what is now *EC Reg 1408/71/EC, article 13(1)* did not 'prohibit Member States other than those in the territory of which wage-earners or assimilated workers are employed from applying their social security legislation to such persons'. However, a Member State could not require a worker who was employed in another Member State 'to contribute to the financing of an institution which would not accord him supplementary protection by way of social security in respect of the same risk and of the same period'. *Nonnenmacher v Bestuur der Sociale Verzekeringsbank*, ECJ Case C-92/63; [1964] ECR 281.

EC Reg 1408/71/EC, article 13(2)(a)

[73.118] In a Netherlands case, the ECJ held that 'a worker who is employed in the territory of one Member State but who resides in the territory of another Member State and who is conveyed at his employer's expense between his place of residence and his place of employment remains subject to the legislation of the former State'. *Bestuur der Sociale Verzekeringsbank v Van der Vecht*, ECJ Case C-19/67; [1967] ECR 345.

[73.119] In a case involving an employee who lived in the Netherlands but worked in Germany, the ECJ held that *EC Reg 1408/71/EC, article 13* prohibited 'the State of residence from requiring payment, under its social legislation, of contributions on the remuneration received by a worker in respect of work performed in another Member State and therefore subject to the social legislation of that State'. *Perenboom v Inspecteur der Directe Belastingen Nijmegen*, ECJ Case C-102/76; [1977] ECR 815.

EC Reg 1408/71/EC, article 14(2)

[73.120] A German worker held simultaneous and separate employments in both Germany and France. He suffered an accident at work and claimed benefit from a German social security agency. The agency rejected the claim, considering that what is now *EC Reg 1408/71/EC, article 14(2)* only applied where a worker was employed in two or more Member States by the same employer. The worker appealed and the case was referred to the ECJ, which allowed the worker's claim, holding that the provision applied 'independently of whether the worker is in the service of one or several employers'. *Bentzinger v Steinbruchs-Berufsgenossenschaft*, ECJ Case C-73/72; [1973] ECR 283.

EC Reg 1408/71/EC, article 45(1)—employees moving within EC

[73.121] In a case brought by an Italian citizen who took up employment in Germany, the ECJ held that *EC Reg 1408/71/EC, article 45(1)* was 'not applicable so as to determine the existence or non-existence of an obligation to effect insurance laid down by national legislation'. *Brunori v Landesversicherunganstalt Rheinprovinz*, ECJ Case C-266/78; [1979] ECR 2705; [1980] 1 CMLR 680.

EC Reg 1408/71/EC, article 71(1)—Member State of residence

[73.122] In a case brought by an Italian citizen who had worked in the UK but had then moved to Belgium without working there, the ECJ held that the concept of the Member State where the worker resides (see *EC Reg 1408/71/EC, article 71(1)*) 'must be limited to the State where the worker, although occupied in another Member State, continues habitually to reside and where the habitual centre of his interests is also situated'. For this purpose, 'account should be taken of the length and continuity of residence before the person concerned moved, the length and purpose of his absence, the nature of the occupation found in the other Member State and the intention of the person concerned as it appears from all the circumstances'. *Di Paolo v Office National de l'Emploi*, ECJ Case C-76/76; [1977] ECR 315.

EC Reg 1408/71/EC, article 71(1)(b)—unemployment benefits

[73.123] A German national was employed in the UK from October 1982 to June 1984. She then claimed and received UK unemployment benefit. In December 1984 she returned to Germany and claimed unemployment benefit. The German employment office rejected her claim and she appealed. The case was referred to the ECJ for guidance on the interpretation of *EC Reg 1408/71/EC, article 71(1)*. The ECJ held that 'a worker, other than a frontier worker, who is wholly unemployed and who resided in the territory of a Member State other than the competent one during his last employment does not lose entitlement to the unemployment benefits' under *EC Reg 1408/71/EC, article 71(1)(b)* 'by virtue of the fact that he has previously received unemployment insurance benefits from the institution of the Member State to whose legislation he was last subject'. *Knoch v Bundesanstalt für Arbeit*, ECJ Case C-102/91; [1992] 1 ECR 4341.

EC Reg 574/72/EC, article 11—issue of certificates

[73.124] In a case concerning an Irish company which placed employees in the Netherlands, the ECJ held that *EC Reg 574/72/EC, article 11* should be 'interpreted as meaning that a certificate issued by the institution designated by the competent authority of a Member State is binding on the social security institutions of other Member States in so far as it certifies that workers posted by an undertaking providing temporary personnel are covered by the social security system of the Member State in which that undertaking is established. However, where the institutions of other Member States raise doubts as to the correctness of the facts on which the certificate is based', the issuing institution 'must re-examine the grounds on which the certificate was issued and, where appropriate, withdraw it.' *Fitzwilliam Executive Search Ltd (t/a Fitzwilliam Technical Services) v Bestuur van het Landelijk Instituut Sociale Verzekeringen*, ECJ Case C-202/97; [2000] All ER (EC) 144.

Social Security Contributions (Intermediaries) Regulations 2000 (SI 2000/727)

Cases where the appeal was dismissed

[73.125] A computer analyst and programmer (B) had formed a limited company (E) to provide his services. E provided B's services to a bank for seven years. The Revenue issued a decision that the arrangements were within the *Social Security Contributions (Intermediaries) Regulations 2000 (SI 2000/727)*. The Special Commissioner dismissed B's appeal. On the evidence, B was required to work for a given number of hours per day and was paid an hourly rate, was subject to the bank's control, did not hire any employees or provide any equipment, was not subject to any financial risk or opportunity, was integrated into the structure of the bank's organisation, and provided services exclusively for the bank. Furthermore, the length of the engagement had an element of permanency. *Battersby v Campbell*, Sp C [2001] SSCD 189 (Sp C 287).

[73.126] A computer consultant (S) formed a limited company (F) to provide his services. F supplied S's services to a recruitment agency (T), which in turn supplied them to a limited company (B) for 37.5 hours per week. The Special Commissioner held that the arrangements were within the *Social*

Security Contributions (Intermediaries) Regulations 2000 (SI 2000/727). On the evidence, if the arrangements had taken the form of a contract between S and B, S 'would be regarded as employed in employed earner's employment by (B)'. *FS Consulting Ltd v McCaul*, Sp C [2002] SSCD 138 (Sp C 305).

[73.127] A computer software engineer (S) had formed a limited company (L) to provide his services. L agreed to provide G's services to another company (D) for a period of six months. The Revenue issued a ruling that the arrangements were within the *Social Security Contributions (Intermediaries) Regulations 2000 (SI 2000/727)*. L appealed. The General Commissioners dismissed the appeal, holding that if there had been a contract between S and D, it would have been a contract of service, and that the circumstances fell within *Social Security Contributions (Intermediaries) Regulations 2000, reg 6(1)*. The Ch D upheld the Commissioners' decision. Hart J observed that that the minimum hours to be worked were broadly equivalent to a normal working week, and that the only risk borne by S was the possibility of D becoming insolvent. The duration of the contract was for a fixed period rather than in relation to the completion of a particular project. S worked alongside D's employees and was sufficiently integrated with its workforce to have a line manager and to be required to comply with D's instructions. *Synaptek Ltd v Young*, Ch D 2003, 75 TC 51; [2003] STC 543; [2003] EWHC 645 (Ch).

[73.128] A company (U) provided the services of its principal director (H) to companies in the oil industry, through an employment agency (N). In May 2000 U entered into a contract with N under which H's services were to be provided to a company (B) which provided equipment for the oil industry. The Revenue issued a ruling that the arrangements were within the *Social Security Contributions (Intermediaries) Regulations 2000 (SI 2000/727)*. U appealed. The Special Commissioner dismissed the appeal, holding on the evidence that B specifically required H's services. H was expected to work B's 'core' hours and to undertake the work allocated by B in accordance with its directions. The Ch D upheld this decision. Park J held that the Commissioner had been entitled to find that, if there had been a contract between B and H, it would have been a contract of employment, rather than a contract for freelance services. *Usetech Ltd v Young*, Ch D 2004, 76 TC 811; [2004] EWHC 2248 (Ch).

[73.129] A company (F) provided the services of its controlling director (R) to a company (E) which was installing a major computer program, through an employment agency. The Revenue issued a ruling that the arrangements were within the *Social Security Contributions (Intermediaries) Regulations 2000 (SI 2000/727)*. F appealed. The Special Commissioner dismissed the appeal, holding on the evidence that E effectively controlled R's work for the duration of the relevant contract, and that if there had been a contract between R and E, R 'would have been employed rather than in business on his own account'. The Ch D upheld this decision. Sir Donald Rattee held that the Commissioner had been 'entitled to reach the conclusion that (R) was part and parcel of the organisation of (E's) business'. *Future Online Ltd v Foulds*, Ch D 2004, 76 TC 590; [2005] STC 198; [2004] EWHC 2597 (Ch).

[73.130] A company (N) was incorporated to provide the services of its controlling director (M), who was a computer programmer. N agreed with another company (R) to provide IT services to a third company (P). The initial contract was for a period of six months, but it was regularly renewed. The Revenue issued a ruling that the arrangements were within the *Social Security Contributions (Intermediaries) Regulations 2000 (SI 2000/727)*, and that N was liable to pay Class 1 National Insurance Contributions in respect of its income under the contract. The Special Commissioner upheld the Revenue's ruling and dismissed N's appeal, holding that under the 'hypothetical contract' required by the regulations, M 'would be an employee'. *Netherlane Ltd v York*, Sp C [2005] SSCD 305 (Sp C 457).

[73.131] A company (C) provided the services of its controlling director (H) to another company (S), through an employment agency, on a series of three-month contracts for a five-year computer project. The Revenue issued a ruling that the arrangements were within the *Social Security Contributions (Intermediaries) Regulations 2000 (SI 2000/727)*, and that C was liable to pay Class 1 National Insurance Contributions in respect of its income under the contract. The Special Commissioner upheld the Revenue's ruling and dismissed C's appeal, holding that under the 'hypothetical contract' required by the regulations, 'the factors predominantly point towards employment'. *Island Consultants Ltd v HMRC*, Sp C [2007] SSCD 700 (Sp C 618).

[73.132] A company (M) was incorporated to provide the services of its controlling director (E), who was a computer programmer. In 1998 M agreed to provide E's services to a company (P) which supplied contract workers. P agreed to provide E's services to another company (L). The Revenue issued a ruling that the arrangements were within the *Social Security Contributions (Intermediaries) Regulations 2000 (SI 2000/727)*, and that M was liable to pay Class 1 National Insurance Contributions in respect of its income under the contract. The Special Commissioner upheld the Revenue's ruling and dismissed M's appeal, finding that E was 'part and parcel of (L's) organisation' and holding that under the hypothetical contract required by the regulations, he would have been an employee. *MKM Computing Ltd v HMRC*, Sp C 2008 SSCD 403 (Sp C 653).

[73.133] A company (D) was incorporated to provide the services of its controlling director (B), who was a computer software engineer. In 2000 D agreed to provide B's services to an agency (DP) which in turn agreed to provide B's services to the Automobile Association. The Revenue issued a determination that the arrangements were within the *Social Security Contributions (Intermediaries) Regulations 2000 (SI 2000/727)*, and that D was liable to pay Class 1 National Insurance Contributions on the basis that the payments it received under the contract were emoluments which it paid to B. D appealed, contending that under the hypothetical contract required by the regulations, B would not have been an employee of the AA. The Special Commissioner reviewed the evidence in detail, rejected this contention and dismissed the appeal. The Commissioner observed that B 'worked fairly regular hours during each engagement' and 'had a role similar to that of a professional employee'. The Ch D upheld this decision. Henderson J observed that there were 'slight, but potentially significant differences' between the wording of the statutory test laid down for NIC purposes and that laid down for income tax purposes. He observed that 'the NIC test requires the arrangements themselves to be embodied in a notional contract, and then asks whether the circumstances (undefined) are such that the worker would be regarded as employed; whereas the income tax test directs attention in the first instance to the services provided by the worker for the client', and then asks whether 'if the services were provided under a contract directly between the client and the worker, the worker would be regarded as an employee of the client'. However, these differences did not affect the result in this case. On the evidence, the Commissioner was entitled to conclude that 'the nature and degree of the control by the AA under the hypothetical contract' pointed towards employment. *Dragonfly Consulting Ltd v HMRC*, Ch D [2008] STC 3030; [2008] EWHC 2113 (Ch).

[73.134] A company (B) had been incorporated to provide the services of its controlling director (S), who was an IT consultant. B agreed to provide S's services to a recruitment agency (C), which in turn agreed to provide them to another company (G). The Revenue issued a determination that the arrangements were within the *Social Security Contributions (Intermediaries) Regulations 2000 (SI 2000/727)*, and that B was liable to pay Class 1 National Insurance Contributions on the basis that the payments it received under the contract were emoluments which it paid to S. The Special Commissioner upheld the determination and dismissed B's appeal, finding that G 'had effectively contracted with (S) to perform the required services'. On the evidence, S 'was integrated within the IT department of (G). He worked there for seven years, doing on average 36 hours a week'. The hypothetical contract required by the regulations 'would have the necessary irreducible minimum to constitute an employment contract', and 'the picture painted of the relationship between (G) and (S) was overwhelmingly one of employment'. *Alternative Book Co Ltd v HMRC*, Sp C [2008] SSCD 830 (Sp C 685).

Cases where the appellant was partly successful

[73.135] A company (J) had been incorporated in 1994 to provide the services of its controlling director (S), who was an IT consultant. J agreed to provide S's services to a recruitment agency (H). In May 2000 H agreed to provide S's services to another company (AC), initially for six months. HMRC subsequently issued determinations that the arrangements were within the *Social Security Contributions (Intermediaries) Regulations 2000 (SI 2000/727)*, and that J was liable to pay Class 1 National Insurance Contributions on the basis that the payments it received under the contract were emoluments which it paid to S. The First-tier Tribunal reviewed the evidence in detail and allowed the appeal for the period from May 2000 until December 2003, but dismissed the appeal for the period from January 2004 to 2007. Judge Nowlan held that S's notional status had changed during the period, and that prior to the end of 2003, he 'would not have been regarded as an employee, but that from the start of 2004 onwards, he would have been regarded as an employee', finding that from the end of 2003 AC had regarded S 'as someone who they wished to engage and retain indefinitely'. *JLJ Services Ltd v HMRC*, FTT [2011] UKFTT 766 (TC), TC01603.

Cases where the appellant was successful

[73.136] A company (L) was incorporated in April 2000 to provide information technology services. Shortly after its incorporation, it entered into a contract with a company providing 'executive recruitment services', under which it provided the services of its controlling director (F) to another company (M) in relation to specific projects, including organising and managing a computer support function, new email system, organising remote access, and changing to 'Windows 2000'. The contract lasted for almost one year, but M then terminated it. The Revenue issued a ruling that the arrangements were within the *Social Security Contributions (Intermediaries) Regulations 2000 (SI 2000/727)*, and that L was liable to pay Class 1 National Insurance Contributions in respect of F's income under the contract. L appealed. The Special Commissioner reviewed the evidence in detail and allowed the appeal, observing that M contracted for particular projects, and that F 'did not work a regular pattern of hours; the hours were dictated by the requirements of the work'. L had 'suffered delays in being paid in the way that businesses do'. F 'did not work alongside any other (M) employees as part and parcel of the (M) organisation', and L Accordingly, if F had contracted directly with M, 'she would not have been employed under a contract of service; she would have been in business on her own account'. *Lime-IT Ltd v Justin*, Sp C 2002, [2003] SSCD 15 (Sp C 342).

[73.137] A company (TC) provided the services of its principal director (T) to another company (C), which in turn provided them to a large motor company (F). The Revenue issued a ruling that the arrangements were within the *Social Security Contributions (Intermediaries) Regulations 2000 (SI 2000/727)*. TC appealed. The Special Commissioner reviewed the evidence in detail and allowed the appeal, finding that 'the facts show that (C) and not (F) had operational control' of the relevant project. On the evidence, C 'was engaged as principal and acted personally in the project. It equipped itself with its own specialised personnel to discharge its own obligation to (F), either by employing them directly or by engaging outside subcontractors, such as (TC)'. F 'did not exercise control over the manner in which the (C) personnel carried out their duties. To the extent that control was exercisable over the performance of (T's) services, that lay with (C). (F) accepted suitable substitutes from (C) and (C) was obliged to accept from (TC) a suitable substitute to (T). At no time was (T) a part of (F's) business or undertaking. Those facts are inconsistent with an employer/employee relationship between (F) and (T).' *Tilbury Consulting Ltd v Gittins (No 2)*, Sp C 2003, [2004] SSCD 72 (Sp C 390).

[73.138] A company (S) was established to provide the services of its controlling director (D), who was a computer software engineer with particular expertise in 'the software elements of weapons and other defence systems'. In 2000 S entered into a contract with another company (C) for the provision of D's services. Under the contract, C arranged for D's services to be provided to a major electronics company (M) in connection with a defence project. Soon afterwards this part of M's business was taken over by another company (B), following which D continued to work for B at the same premises as before. The Revenue issued a ruling that the arrangements were within the *Social Security Contributions (Intermediaries) Regulations 2000 (SI 2000 No 727)*, and that S was liable to pay Class 1 National Insurance Contributions in respect of D's income under the contract. S appealed. The Special Commissioner reviewed the evidence in detail and allowed the appeal, holding that D 'would not have been an employee in the hypothetical contract which the IR35 legislation requires us to construct'. *Ansell Computer Services Ltd v Richardson*, Sp C [2004] SSCD 472 (Sp C 425).

[73.139] A company (F) was incorporated to provide the services of its controlling director (N), who was a computer consultant. In 2000 F agreed to provide N's services to a company (P) which provided software services to another company (R). The Revenue issued a ruling that the arrangements were within the *Social Security Contributions (Intermediaries) Regulations 2000 (SI 2000/727)*, and that F was liable to pay Class 1 National Insurance Contributions in respect of the payments which it made to N. F appealed, contending that if the services had been performed under a contract between N and R, N would not be regarded as an employee of R. The Special Commissioner reviewed the evidence in detail, accepted this contention and allowed F's appeal, finding that the relevant contract contained a right of substitution and 'the intention of the parties was that (N) was not obliged to perform the services personally'. On the evidence, N 'acted as a subcontractor, with responsibility for part only of a larger project, and not as an employee'. *First Word Software Ltd v HMRC*, Sp C [2008] SSCD 389 (Sp C 652).

[73.140] A company (D) was incorporated to provide the services of its controlling director (B), who was a computer software consultant. In 2000 D agreed to provide B's services to a company (T) which provided software services to another company (M). The Revenue issued a ruling that the arrangements were within the *Social Security Contributions (Intermediaries) Regulations 2000 (SI 2000/727)*, and that D was liable to pay Class 1 National Insurance Contributions on the basis that the payments it received under the contract were emoluments which it paid to B. D appealed, contending that if the services had been performed under a contract between B and M, B would not be regarded as an employee of M. The Special Commissioner accepted this contention and allowed the appeal, finding that there was no 'ultimate right of control on the part of (M)' and that B was 'in business on his own account and was not a person working as an employee in someone else's business on the hypothetical requirements that the legislation requires'. *Datagate Services Ltd v HMRC*, Sp C [2008] SSCD 453 (Sp C 656).

[73.141] A company (N) was incorporated to provide the services of its controlling director (B), who was an IT analyst. In 1998 N agreed to provide B's services to another company (L) which carried on an agency business, providing IT contractors to companies engaged in IT projects. L arranged for B to work for a third company (Z). HMRC issued a ruling that the arrangements were within the *Social Security Contributions (Intermediaries) Regulations 2000 (SI 2000/727)*, and that N was liable to pay Class 1 National Insurance Contributions on the basis that the payments it received under the contract were emoluments which it paid to B. N appealed, contending that if the services had been performed under a contract between B and Z, B would not be regarded as an employee of Z. The First-tier Tribunal reviewed the evidence in detail, accepted this contention, and allowed the appeal. Judge

Kempster concluded that 'the overall picture painted is one of a contract for self-employment'. *Novasoft Ltd v HMRC*, FTT [2010] UKFTT 150 (TC), TC00456.

[73.142] A company (M) was incorporated to provide the services of its controlling director (F), who was a design engineer. In 2003 M entered into a contract with another company (G), under which F's services would be provided to a large manufacturing company (AS). On the following day G entered into a contract with a fourth company (H), regulating the terms under which F was to work for AS. HMRC issued a ruling that the arrangements were within the *Social Security Contributions (Intermediaries) Regulations 2000 (SI 2000/727)*, and that M was liable to pay Class 1 National Insurance Contributions on the basis that the payments it received under the contract were emoluments which it paid to F. M appealed, contending that if the services had been performed under a contract between F and AS, F would not be regarded as an employee of AS. The First-tier Tribunal accepted this contention and allowed the appeal, holding that the arrangements appeared to be typical of a contract for services, rather than a contract of service. Judge Cornwell-Kelly observed that the terms of the relevant contract gave AS the right to cancel it without giving notice. He held that this condition was 'characteristic of a contract for services but quite foreign to the world of employment'. *MBF Design Services Ltd v HMRC*, FTT [2011] UKFTT 35 (TC); [2011] SFTD 383, TC00912.

[73.143] A company (E) provided the services of its controlling director (R) to another company (V) via an agency (B). HMRC issued determinations under *SI 2003/2682, reg 80*, and decisions under *SSC(TF)A 1999, s 8* on the basis that the arrangements were within the *Social Security Contributions (Intermediaries) Regulations 2000 (SI 2000/727)*, and that E was liable to pay Class 1 National Insurance Contributions on the basis that the payments it received under the contract were emoluments which it paid to R. E appealed, contending that if the services had been performed under a contract between R and V, R would not be regarded as an employee of V. The First-tier Tribunal accepted this contention and allowed the appeal. Judge Porter held that V had 'no control over how the work is done nor when the services are to be performed save for obvious opening times of the offices and the fact that the work had to be carried out there'. Furthermore, R had performed services for two other clients while she was working for V. On the evidence, the hypothetical contract between R and V would have been a contract for services rather than a contract of service. *ECR Consulting Ltd v HMRC*, FTT [2011] UKFTT 313 (TC), TC01174.

[73.144] A company (M) provided the services of its controlling director (H) to another company (J) via an agency (D). HMRC issued a decision under *SSCTFA 1999, s 8* that the arrangements were within the *Social Security Contributions (Intermediaries) Regulations 2000 (SI 2000/727)*, and that M was liable to pay Class 1 National Insurance Contributions on the basis that the payments it received under the contract were emoluments which it paid to H. M appealed, contending that if the services had been performed under a contract between H and J, H would be regarded as a self-employed subcontractor, rather than as an employee of J. The First-tier Tribunal accepted this contention and allowed the appeal. Judge Mitting held that there was 'no mutuality of obligation and the degree of control which would have been needed to establish a contract of employment just did not exist'. *Marlen Ltd v HMRC*, FTT [2011] UKFTT 411 (TC), TC01264.

[73.145] A company (P) provided the services of its controlling director (W), who was a computer software developer, to another company (G). HMRC issued determinations under *SI 2003/2682, reg 80*, and decisions under *SSCTFA 1999, s 8* on the basis that the arrangements were within the *Social Security Contributions (Intermediaries) Regulations 2000 (SI 2000/727)*, and that P was liable to pay Class 1 National Insurance Contributions on the basis that the payments it received under the contract were emoluments which it paid to W. P appealed, contending that if the services had been performed under a contract between G and W, W would not be regarded as an employee of G. The First-tier Tribunal accepted this contention and allowed the appeal. Judge Sadler held that 'the relationship between (G) and (W) is one of an independent and self-employed contractor, and not that of employer and employee'. *Primary Path Ltd v HMRC*, FTT [2011] UKFTT 454 (TC), TC01306.

Miscellaneous

UK-Switzerland Social Security Convention

[73.146] A UK company (P) posted three of its employees to Switzerland, to work as aircraft engineers. P applied to the DHSS for a certificate of continuing liability under which the employees would continue to pay UK social security contributions, rather than Swiss contributions. Subsequently the employees wrote to the DHSS and the Inland Revenue, objecting to the continued payment of UK contributions. The Revenue issued rulings that the employees were required to pay UK social security contributions, and they appealed. The Special Commissioner dismissed their appeals, holding that the effect of the Social Security Convention between Switzerland and the UK was that the employees were liable to pay UK contributions for the periods in question. *Stevens & Others v CIR*, Sp C [2004] SSCD 311 (Sp C 411).

Offshore worker—effect of 'artificial pay practice'

[73.147] From 1983 to 1998 an electrician (M) had been employed on drilling rigs in the North Sea. His employers reduced his monthly salary by withholding a small 'retainer', which they then paid two weeks later. For NIC purposes, his employers treated him as having two-weekly pay periods rather than four-weekly pay periods. The consequences were that the employers avoided paying NIC on the 'retainer' payments, on the basis that these payments fell below the lower limit for NICs for the notional fortnightly period, and that they paid less NIC than they would otherwise have done in respect of the balancing payments, on the basis that much of the payment exceeded the upper limit for NICs for the notional fortnightly period. Following M's retirement, he discovered that the effect of the way in which his employers had paid him was that he received a lower state pension than he would have done if his employers had paid him monthly. M lodged an appeal, contending that the amount of contributions which his employers had paid was less than the amount of contributions actually due (and that his pension should be based on the contributions which would have been due if his employers had not adopted the 'artificial pay practice' of delaying the 'retainer' payments). The First-tier Tribunal reviewed the evidence in detail and dismissed the appeal, observing that it was a common pattern of work 'to be off-shore for a two-week period, and then to have a two-week period back in Aberdeen or elsewhere on the mainland, effectively as a rest period'. In such cases, 'the workers were paid when they worked and basically not paid when they had their "weeks off"'. The Upper Tribunal upheld this decision, and held that 'it would be inappropriate to speculate, without evidence, as to the reasons or reasons why the Secretary of State did not any stage exercise his discretion to review and reform the practice in question'. *JAL Mason v HMRC (No 2)*, UT [2010] STC 2124.

Whether official record of contributions paid correct

[73.148] An individual (B) reached retirement age in 2001. He duly received a State pension, but did not receive a full pension on the grounds that he had not made the necessary payments of national insurance contributions for 44 years. He appealed, contending that he had paid contributions from 1975 to 1982, but that his contributions for these years had not been recorded. The First-tier Tribunal reviewed the evidence in detail and dismissed his appeal, finding that B had been a partner in an upholstery business from 1975 to 1978, and should have paid Class 2 contributions, but had failed to do so. With regard to the period from 1978 to 1982, B had been a director of a limited company (W), and it appeared that that company had failed to pay contributions for him. The tribunal found the contribution record submitted by HMRC was 'on the balance of probabilities the correct record'. *TJ Beamish v HMRC*, FTT [2009] UKFTT 271 (TC), TC00217.

[73.149] An individual (B) became self-employed in 1971. Between 1975 and 1996 he repeatedly failed to pay Class 2 national insurance contributions. In 2008 he lodged an appeal, contending that he had made some payments of contributions which HMRC had not recorded. The First-tier Tribunal reviewed the evidence and dismissed B's appeal, finding that there was 'no evidence of errors in the Commissioners' schedule'. *M Breen v HMRC*, FTT [2010] UKFTT 70 (TC), TC00383. (*Note.* The appellant appeared in person.)

[73.150] Similar decisions were reached in *Mrs P Register v HMRC*, FTT [2010] UKFTT 186 (TC), TC00490; *H Davies v HMRC*, FTT [2011] UKFTT 13 (TC), TC00890; *JEI Olofsson v HMRC*, FTT [2012] UKFTT 490 (TC), TC02167; *C Partridge v HMRC*, FTT [2014] UKFTT 107 (TC), TC03247, and *J Plant v HMRC*, FTT [2014] UKFTT 911(TC), TC04025.

[73.151] A woman (M) left school in 1954, but did not begin paying national insurance contributions until 1961. After she reached the age of 60, she discovered that because she had not paid contributions for several years, she would not receive a full pension. She appealed to the First-tier Tribunal, contending that she had been working for a family firm from 1954/55 to 1960/61. The tribunal reviewed the evidence in detail and dismissed her appeal, finding that the form RF1 which HMRC had produced in evidence was a correct record of her contributions. Judge Connell observed that 'the burden of proof is upon (M) to provide evidence to support her contention that she paid National Insurance contributions during the appeal period'. *Mrs J Moss v HMRC*, FTT [2011] UKFTT 448 (TC), TC01301.

[73.152] A similar decision was reached in *DK Dass v HMRC*, FTT [2011] UKFTT 632 (TC), TC01474.

[73.153] A pensioner, who was born in 1944, had been credited with 42 years' national insurance contributions, but appealed to the Tax Chamber of the First-tier Tribunal, contending that he should be credited with further contributions. The Tribunal struck out his appeal. Judge Poole held that the effect of the *First-tier and Upper Tribunal (Chambers) Order 2010, SI 2010/2655, article 6(h)* was that appeals regarding 'entitlement to be credited with earnings or contributions' were allocated to the Social Entitlement Chamber, rather than to the Tax Chamber. *AG Stewart v HMRC*, FTT [2013] UKFTT 194 (TC), TC02609.

Application of Ramsay principle to national insurance contributions

[73.154] See *NMB Holdings Ltd v Secretary of State for Social Security*, **58.11** TAX PLANNING AND AVOIDANCE.

Change of gender—effect on national insurance contributions

[73.155] An individual (M) was born in 1942 with 'the physical characteristics of a male'. He subsequently lived as a male, and married a woman. In 2004 he decided to live as a female, and in October 2004 he divorced his wife. In December 2005 he underwent gender reassignment surgery. In December 2006 the Gender Recognition Panel, established under the *Gender Recognition Act 2004*, recognised M as a female. Having been recognised as a female and having reached the age of 60, M was thus no longer required to pay national insurance contributions. HMRC issued a ruling that this change of status could not be backdated, and that M was still required to pay contributions until the issue of the certificate. M appealed, contending that her change of gender should be backdated to June 2004. The First-tier Tribunal rejected this contention and dismissed M's appeal. Judge Paines held that M 'was required to continue paying NICs until the issue to her of a gender recognition certificate under the *Gender Recognition Act 2004*'. *M v HMRC*, FTT [2010] SFTD 1141; [2010] UKFTT 356 (TC), TC00638.

74

Petroleum Revenue Tax

The cases in this chapter are arranged under the following headings.

Oil Taxation Act 1975

OTA 1975, s 3(1)—allowable expenditure

[74.1] A company conducted explorations outside, but within five kilometres of, an oilfield. It claimed that it should be allowed to deduct this exploration expenditure in computing its PRT liability, by virtue of *OTA 1975, s 3(1)*. The Revenue accepted that both the claims related to expenditure incurred within the geographical limit of *s 3(1)(a)*, but disallowed the claims on the basis that the expenditure was not incurred for a 'field purpose'. The company appealed, contending that the terms of *s 3(1)(a)* were satisfied if the exploration took place within five kilometres of the relevant field boundary for the purposes of searching for oil. The Special Commissioners accepted this contention and allowed the appeal, holding that the wording of *s 3(1)(a)* was clear and unambiguous, and the test was geographical rather than geological. The Ch D upheld this decision. Lloyd J observed that, on the Revenue's interpretation, 'there would often be difficult subjective questions of subjective intent or expectation to be answered in relation to any drilling which does not achieve its hoped for purpose'. The application of a 'purely geographical qualification' would, by contrast, be 'certain in its application'. *Amerada Hess Ltd v CIR*, Ch D 2001, 73 TC 488; [2001] STC 420.

OTA 1975, s 8—'oil allowance'

[74.2] A company (E) was a participator in an oil field, for which the first chargeable period ended on 31 December 1976. It made returns within the statutory time limits, showing the value of its oil deliveries, the authorised provisional deduction for expenditure under *OTA 1975, s 2(9)(a)*,and royalties payable. It treated the resultant net figure as its assessable profit, covered by the 'oil allowance' of *OTA 1975, s 8*, reducing its PRT liability to nil. The first expenditure claim for the field was submitted in April 1978. The Revenue allowed this in part, the amount allowed to E being £51,600,000. The Revenue formally determined E's loss for the period to 31 December 1976 at £49,900,000 (after allowing the deductible expenditure of £51,600,000) and issued assessments for the next two periods. Subsequently the Revenue issued assessments for the periods up to 31 December 1980. The assessments were in accordance with E's returns, except that the profits up to 31 December 1979 (aggregating £47,200,000) were treated as covered by the loss for the first period. The assessments for the 1980 periods were £14,500,000, of which £2,700,000 was covered by the balance of the loss and the remainder was covered by the 'oil allowance'. E appealed, contending that *OTA 1975, Sch 2 para 10(1)* required the Revenue to make an assessment as soon as it appeared to it, on receipt of a return, with figures agreed, that a profit had accrued. (The practical consequence would be that the profits would all be covered by 'oil allowances', releasing the loss for carry-forward against future profits.) The Special Commissioners rejected this contention and dismissed the appeal, and the Ch D upheld their decision, holding that the word 'shall' in *Sch 2 para 10(1)* had no temporal significance, but merely placed a duty on the Revenue to make an assessment. The only time limit was that of *TMA, s 34*, which was applicable to PRT by virtue of *OTA 1975, Sch 2 para 1*. *Amoco (UK) Exploration Co v CIR*, Ch D 1983, 57 TC 147; [1983] STC 634.

OTA 1975, s 10—gas sold to British Gas Corporation

[74.3] In 1975 a major oil company (S) entered into a contract with British Gas, which was to last until 31 October 2002. The Revenue agreed that gas sold under that contract was exempt from PRT under *OTA 1975, s 10(1)(a)*. In March 2002 S entered into a new agreement with British Gas, which took the form of amendments to the 1975 contract and which extended its term by ten years. S did not account for tax on its sales under this agreement. The Revenue issued assessments charging PRT on such sales, and S appealed. The Special Commissioners dismissed the appeal, holding that that the gas sold after 31 October 2002 failed to qualify for exemption from PRT. *Shell UK Ltd v HMRC*, Sp C 2007, [2008] SSCD 91 (Sp C 624).

OTA 1975, Sch 2 para 10—PRT assessments

[74.4] A company (F) appealed against PRT assessments for 1983 to 1988. It abandoned its appeals against the first two assessments under *OTA 1975, Sch 2 para 14(8)*, and the appeals against the other assessments were settled by agreement under *OTA 1975, Sch 2 para 14(9)*. Subsequently F applied to make further appeals out of time, on different grounds to the previous appeals. The Revenue rejected the applications and F appealed to the Special Commissioner. The Commissioner refused to hear the applications, since appeals had previously been made in time and he had no jurisdiction to hear second appeals. F applied by way of judicial review for an order of *mandamus* requiring the Commissioner to hear the applications. The QB rejected the application, holding that the abandonment of the appeals against the first two assessments, and the settlement by agreement of the remaining appeals, produced finality. The Commissioner had no jurisdiction to hear further appeals, and the assessments could only be amended if the Revenue chose to reduce the agreed profits under *OTA 1975, Sch 2 para 12*. *R v Special Commrs (ex p. Fina Exploration plc)*, QB 1991, 64 TC 358; [1992] STC 1.

OTA 1975, Sch 2 para 17—repayment interest

[74.5] Four oil companies incurred substantial PRT losses for several successive chargeable periods, following a major fire in July 1988. These losses were carried back to earlier chargeable periods, leading to repayments of PRT which the companies had previously paid. Where the losses were carried back from chargeable periods ending after 30 June 1991, the interest payable by the Revenue was restricted in accordance with *OTA 1975, Sch 2 para 17* (introduced by *FA 1990, s 121*). The companies objected to the Revenue's calculation of the interest and took proceedings in the Ch D, seeking declarations that, where a loss for one period was relieved against the profits for two periods, the full loss should be used in the calculation of the interest restriction for each of the profit periods, and that, where losses in two periods were relieved against the profits of one period, the losses of both periods should be used in the calculation of the interest restriction when the second loss was carried back. The Ch D rejected these contentions, holding that they would produce 'a result Parliament could not have intended' and one 'which is bizarre to the point of absurdity'. The Revenue had also issued assessments on the basis that *OTA 1975, Sch 2 para 17(5)* (introduced by *FA 1993, s 186*) applied to any assessments made after 27 July 1993 (the date on which *FA 1993* received Royal Assent), including two assessments for periods ending on 30 June 1993 for which the relevant loss claims had been made on 1 December 1993. The Ch D allowed appeals against these two assessments, holding that *OTA 1975, Sch 2 para 17(5)* applied only to losses in chargeable periods ending after 30 June 1993, and did not apply to losses in chargeable periods ending on or before that date, even if the loss claims had not been made until after that date. *Elf Enterprise Caledonia Ltd v CIR (and related appeals)*, Ch D 1994, 68 TC 328; [1994] STC 785.

Other legislation

FA 1982, s 134—valuation of ethane

[74.6] The PRT legislation contains provisions for arriving at the market value of oil and gas including, in *FA 1982, s 134, Sch 18*, an alternative basis of valuation for ethane used in petrochemicals, for which the oil company must make an election. This alternative had been introduced to meet representations by two major companies that they were not prepared to proceed with the construction of certain new plant without some form of Government assistance. This new plant was in competition with plant already installed by another major company (ICI). ICI applied for declarations that the acceptance by the Revenue of an election under the *FA 1982* provisions was in breach of what is now *Article 107* of the *Treaty on the Functioning of the European Union*, and that the Revenue method of valuation of ethane was unreasonable, contending that its own petrochemical activities were being discriminated against. The CA granted the declarations, holding that the Revenue's method of valuation was unreasonable where the value adopted was not determined on an arm's length basis. ICI had a standing in the matter as the only other body likely to be involved, and its complaint was not about any particular assessment made by the Revenue in relation to another taxpayer's affairs, but a complaint about a valuation made under *FA 1982*. Furthermore, a persistent misapplication of statutory provisions constituted a breach of the *Treaty*. It would be wrong in principle to deny the relief due to ICI, and retrospective declarations should be granted in a case where the Revenue had acted *ultra vires* and in breach of their statutory duties. *R v A-G (ex p. Imperial Chemical Industries plc)*, CA 1986, 60 TC 1; [1987] 1 CMLR 72.

FA 1981, s 111—expenditure supplement

[74.7] A company (M) was licensed in 1972 to prospect for oil in an oilfield in the North Sea. In 1979 it entered into an agreement with a group of companies (B) for the design and procurement of a platform, in return for a fixed fee payable in instalments and reimbursement of all costs, expenses and charges incurred in the performance of the work. Between April and June 1981 B entered into three contracts for three topside modules for the platform. *FA 1981, s 111* abolished the 'expenditure supplement' of 35%, except with regard to expenditure 'incurred before 1st January 1983 in pursuance of a contract entered into before 1st January 1981'. In its claim period ended 30 June 1982, M claimed the 35% supplement in respect of expenditure of £47,000,000. The Revenue rejected £26,000,000 of the claim on the grounds that it had been made in pursuance of the 1981 contracts. M appealed, contending that the expenditure had been incurred in pursuance of the 1979 agreement, and therefore qualified for the supplement. The Special Commissioners accepted this contention and allowed M's appeal, and the HL unanimously upheld their decision. Lord Templeman held that where the relevant language of the statute is ambiguous, the court should resolve the ambiguity by reference to the intention of Parliament as it appears from the statute. *FA 1981, s 111(7)* was intended to have the effect of preserving the supplement for expenditure to which an operator was committed before 1981, provided that the expenditure was incurred before 1983. Here the whole of the £47,000,000 was expended for one and the same purpose, bringing into existence the platform in question, and it followed that it was expended in pursuance of the agreement with B and qualified for the supplement. *CIR v Mobil North Sea Ltd*, HL 1987, 60 TC 310; [1987] STC 458; [1987] 1 WLR 1065.

[74.8] Two companies were granted licences under *Petroleum (Production) Act 1934* to search and bore for petroleum in a defined area. One of the companies (Y) acquired exclusive charge of all operations within the licensed area. The area was subsequently discovered to contain two separate oil and gas reservoirs, the smaller reservoir being discovered and developed before the larger reservoir. Y claimed expenditure supplement in respect of the development of the second reservoir, but the Revenue rejected the claim on the basis that the expenditure had been incurred after the end of the 'net profit period', so that, by virtue of *FA 1981, s 111(1)*, no supplement was due. Y appealed, contending that each development decision should be treated as having its own relevant net profit period, so that the expenditure had been incurred before the net profit period. The Special Commissioners rejected this contention and dismissed the appeal. *FA 1981, s 111* defined the net profit period as the 'earliest chargeable period ending after a development decision has been made for the field'. Once it was accepted that the two reservoirs were combined in a single oil field, there could only be one 'net profit period', and that was the earliest chargeable period ending after the development decision in relation to the first reservoir to be discovered. *Y Co Ltd v CIR*, Sp C [1996] SSCD 253 (Sp C 78).

OTA 1983, s 3(1)—allowable expenditure

[74.9] A company (BP) operated a terminal at which crude oil was loaded into ships' tanks. It incurred substantial expenditure on the installation of a marine vapour system, to extract and deal with the emission of vapours in connection with the loading of the oil. It claimed that most of this expenditure was deductible under *OTA 1983, s 3(1)*. The Revenue rejected the claim, considering that, at the time the vapours were subjected to the system, the hydrocarbons within the recovered waste were not within the definition of 'oil won from the field' in *OTA 1975, s 3(1)(g)*, so that the system was not used 'in connection with' the field for the purposes of *OTA 1983, s 3(1)*. BP appealed. The Special Commissioners allowed the appeal, holding that the emission of the vapours was 'part of the overall delivery process' and that the oil was still 'oil won from the field'. The relevant expenditure had enhanced the value of the relevant asset (the facility of which the terminal was part). *BP Exploration Operating Co Ltd v CIR*, Sp C [2000] SSCD 466 (Sp C 254).

[74.10] A company (T) was a participator in more than one oilfield. It claimed that expenditure incurred on assets to tie back wells in one of the fields to a platform in another field, in order to produce production gases in winning oil in that second field, was deductible in computing the profits of the second field under *OTA 1983, s 3(1)(a)*. HMRC rejected the claim on the basis that the expenditure was only deductible in computing the profits of the field in which the wells were actually situated, and were not allowable expenditure in respect of the second field. T appealed. The First-tier Tribunal accepted T's contentions and allowed its appeal in principle, holding that the expenditure should be apportioned between the fields in question. Judge Berner eld that the effect of *OTA 1983, s 3* was that 'it is not a requirement that the asset be acquired by a person in his capacity as a participator in the particular field in question, nor that the asset be used by that person as participator in that field'. *Talisman Energy (UK) Ltd v HMRC*, FTT [2009] SFTD 359; [2009] UKFTT 356 (TC), TC00294.

OTA 1983, s 9(1)—tariff receipts allowance

[74.11] A company (BP) owned a pipeline running from an oilfield to its processing facilities in Scotland. It transported oil and gas from an adjoining field, operated by another company, through that pipeline in return for a tariff. It processed the gas in return for further tariffs. The Revenue calculated the tariff receipts allowance by reference to the total of the sums which BP received for the whole quantity of oil and gas transported and the sums received for the processed gas. BP appealed, contending that separate allowances should be calculated for each of the sums received. The Special Commissioners rejected this contention and dismissed the appeal, and the HL unanimously upheld their decision, holding that *OTA 1983, s 9(1)* should be interpreted as providing a single allowance for each field, and not a separate allowance for each asset. *BP Oil Development Ltd v CIR*, HL 1991, 64 TC 498; [1992] STC 28.

[74.12] The participators in an oilfield (M) purchased an undivided 15% share of the pipeline and terminal of another field (N), giving them right to pass up to 150,000 barrels of oil per day from M through N's pipeline. They subsequently discovered that M was capable of producing much more oil than they were entitled to pass through the pipeline. Accordingly they negotiated an agreement with the other owners of N, under which they would be entitled to pass additional oil through N's pipeline on payment of a royalty for each additional barrel of oil. The Revenue calculated the tariff receipts allowance to the participators in N on the basis that, in the formula laid down by *OTA 1983, Sch 3 para 2*, the denominator (i.e. the amount of oil to which the qualifying tariff receipts related) was the whole amount of all the oil passed from M through N's pipeline, including oil which the participators in M were entitled to pass through the pipeline by virtue of their part ownership of the pipeline. The participators in N appealed, contending that the denominator should be restricted to the amount of oil in respect of which a tariff was paid. The Ch D accepted this contention and allowed the appeal. *Chevron UK Ltd v CIR (and related appeals)*, Ch D 1995, 67 TC 414; [1995] STC 712.

Petrol marketing companies—other cases

[74.13] For non-PRT cases involving oil or petrol marketing companies, see *Hughes v British Burmah Petroleum Co Ltd*, **65.3** TRADING PROFITS, and the cases noted at **68.95** *et seq.* TRADING PROFITS.

75

Stamp Duty Land Tax

The cases in this chapter are arranged under the following headings.

Land transactions (FA 2003, ss 43–54)

FA 2003, s 43(1)—land transaction

[75.1] In a corporation tax case, where the substantive issue was overtaken by *FA 2000, s 110*, the CA held that a deed assigning the right to receive rights was the assignment of an interest in land. *CIR v John Lewis Properties plc*, CA 2002, 75 TC 131; [2003] STC 117; [2002] EWCA Civ 1869; [2003] 2 WLR 1196.

FA 2003, s 45—transactions before completion

Transfer from company to partnership

[75.2] A company (DC), which was the principal member of a limited partnership (D), acquired some land and transferred it to D. HMRC issued a ruling that D was required to account for SDLT on its acquisition. D appealed, contending that the combined effect of *FA 2003, s 45* and *FA 2003, Sch 15 para 10* was that there was no SDLT liability. The First-tier Tribunal accepted this contention and allowed the appeal, but the CA unanimously reversed this decision and upheld HMRC's ruling. Lewison J held that the effect of *FA 2003, s 45(3)* was that, for the purposes of SDLT, DC never acquired a chargeable interest. When the contract between DC and D was completed, *FA 2003, s 44(3)* applied to D's acquisition of a chargeable interest, so that the effective date of D's land transaction was the date of completion of its contract with DC. *FA 2003, Sch 15 para 10* did not apply to the transaction, so that D was not entitled to claim exemption and was required to pay SDLT on the consideration which it gave for its own acquisition. *HMRC v DV3 RS Limited Partnership*, CA [2013] EWCA Civ 907; [2013] STC 2150.

Whether s 45(3) applicable

[75.3] A company (VT) entered into an avoidance scheme intended to take advantage of a perceived loophole in *FA 2003, s 45* to avoid a charge to stamp duty land tax on the purchase of a property. Under the scheme, VT incorporated a new unlimited subsidiary company (VP), which contracted to acquire the property from the vendor. After VP had entered into the contract to purchase the property, it reduced its share capital to a nominal amount by a special resolution, and declared a final dividend in specie of the property in favour of VT. VP claimed that its acquisition of the property was exempt from SDLT by virtue of *FA 2003, s 45(3)*, while VT claimed that its acquisition of the property from VP was exempt by virtue of *FA 2003, Sch 3 para 1*. HMRC issued a ruling that *FA 2003, s 45* did not apply to the transactions, so that VP was liable for SDLT on the purchase. (They also issued an alternative ruling that, if *s 45* was held to apply, the combined effect of *s 45(3)* and *s 44* was that VT would be liable for SDLT on the full amount of the consideration.) Both VP and VT appealed. The First-tier Tribunal reviewed the evidence in detail and dismissed VP's appeal, finding that VP had failed to comply with *Companies Act 1985, s 270*, which required the production of initial accounts in support of the declaration of a dividend in specie. It followed that the dividend was unlawful under *Companies Act 1985, s 263*, and VT 'never became entitled to call for a conveyance of the property as a result of the declaration of the dividend'. Accordingly, *s 45* did not apply and VP was liable for SDLT on its purchase. (The tribunal also observed that, if VP had complied with the *Companies Act* and the dividend had been lawful, the result would have been that VP's acquisition would have been exempt but that VT would have been liable for SDLT on the full amount of the consideration.) *Vardy Properties v HMRC (and related appeal)*, FTT [2012] UKFTT 564 (TC); [2012] SFTD 1398, TC02242. (*Note.* At a subsequent hearing, costs were awarded to HMRC—[2013] UKFTT 96 (TC), TC02514.)

[75.4] An individual (E) purchased a property in 2007. The Land Registry records (form TR1) recorded the purchase price as £2,450,000. However E submitted a form SDLT1 declaring the purchase price as £356,250. When HMRC discovered this, they issued a discovery assessment charging SDLT on the difference. E appealed, contending that he had taken advantage of a 'mitigation scheme' within *FA 2003, s 45(3)*, whereby the property had originally been purchased by a limited company (AI), and he had subsequently been substituted as the purchaser by a deed of novation. The First-tier Tribunal dismissed the appeal, applying the principles laid down in *Vardy Properties v HMRC*, 75.3 above, and holding that *s 45* did not apply. Judge Khan held that AI 'never acquired a chargeable interest in the property nor was it involved in a land transaction'. There was 'no evidence that the novation took place between the two transfers of money'. On the evidence here, E had provided the whole of the purchase price. Therefore 'the entire amount of £2,450,000 is the chargeable consideration'. *E Allchin v HMRC*, FTT [2013] UKFTT 198 (TC), TC02613.

FA 2003, s 50—chargeable consideration

[75.5] A woman purchased a house in 2010. She paid £258,000. The purchase agreement attributed £250,000 to the house and land, and £8,000 to chattels. In her SDLT return, she declared SDLT of £2,500 (at 1%). HMRC discovered that, of the amount attributed to chattels, £800 was attributable to 'fitted units' in the garage. They issued an amendment on the basis that these units were part of the land, so that the total consideration attributable to the house and land was £250,800 and the SDLT rate was 3%. The purchaser appealed. The First-tier Tribunal dismissed her appeal, finding that 'the worktop was fixed to the house' and that it was 'just and reasonable to apportion £250,800 of the consideration paid to the house and the garage worktop and units'. *Miss G Orsman v HMRC*, FTT [2012] UKFTT 227 (TC), TC01921.

Reliefs (FA 2003, ss 57–75C)

FA 2003, s 68—relief for charities

[75.6] A company (P) acquired four properties. It submitted a claim for repayment of SDLT, contending that it had made the acquisitions as a bare trustee for the beneficiaries of a trust, and that as two of those beneficiaries were UK charities, it should be entitled to relief under *FA 2003, Sch 8* in respect of the proportion of the properties which was attributable to those charitable beneficiaries. HMRC rejected the claim but the CA unanimously allowed P's appeal. Lewison LJ held that *Sch 8 para 1(1)* should be construed as providing that a land transaction was exempt from charge to the extent that the purchaser was a charity, providing that the other conditions were met. Exemption should apply to 'that proportion of the beneficial interest that is attributable to the undivided share held by the charity for qualifying charitable purposes'. Such an interpretation was 'necessary in order to give effect to what must have been Parliament's intention as regards the taxation of charities'. *The Pollen Estate Trustee Co Ltd v HMRC (and related appeal)*, CA [2013] EWCA Civ 753; [2013] STC 1479; [2013] 3 All ER 742. (*Note*. See now Clause 106 and Schedule 19 of the 2014 Finance Bill.)

FA 2003, s 74—collective enfranchisement by leaseholders

[75.7] In December 2004 a newly-incorporated company acquired the freehold interest and the headlease of a property in Bournemouth comprising 133 flats. It submitted a return claiming collective enfranchisement relief under *FA 2003, s 74*. The Revenue issued notices amending the return on the basis that the transactions did not qualify for relief. The company appealed. The Special Commissioner dismissed the appeal, observing that relief under *s 74* only applied 'where a chargeable transaction is entered into a by an RTE company in pursuance of a right of collective enfranchisement'. On the evidence, the company had not been an 'RTE company' as defined in *s 74(4)*. The Commissioner reviewed the legislation in detail and held that before the relevant provisions of *Commonhold and Leasehold Reform Act 2002* came into force, 'the existing provisions remain so that the right to collective enfranchisement can be exercised by a proportion of tenants acting through a nominee purchaser. Thus, before the provisions are brought into force, there can be no "right of collective enfranchisement exercisable by an RTE company" within the meaning of (*FA 2003, s 74(4)(b)*).' Accordingly the transactions failed to qualify for relief under *s 74*. The Ch D upheld this decision. Sir Andrew Morritt held that Parliament must be taken to have been aware that the relief would not be available until the relevant statutory provisions came into force. It therefore appeared that 'it was not the intention of Parliament that the relief for which *s 74* provided should be available before the amendments were made effective'. *Elizabeth Court (Bournemouth) Ltd v HMRC*, Ch D 2008, [2009] STC 682; [2008] EWHC 2828 (Ch). (*Note*. The relevant provisions of *Commonhold and Leasehold Reform Act 2002* are still not in force. On 12 May 2009 the Department for Communities and Local Government published a consultation on proposals to repeal the RTE company provisions. See also *FA 2009, s 80*.)

FA 2003, s 75A—anti-avoidance

[75.8] In 2007 a Guernsey company (P) agreed to purchase the freehold of a large army barracks from the Ministry of Defence. In January 2008 P entered into a sale and leaseback agreement with a Qatari financial institution (M). Two days later M and P entered into put and call options requiring or entitling P to repurchase the freehold at the end of a 'finance period' (of 999 years and 2 days); the Ministry of Defence conveyed the freehold to P; P conveyed the freehold to M, and M leased the property back to P for the 'finance period'. On the following day P granted a 999-year lease to an associated company. P failed to account for SDLT on its acquisition of the property. HMRC began an enquiry, and issued an amendment on the basis that SDLT was chargeable on consideration of £959,000,000. P appealed. HMRC subsequently issued an amendment to their Statement of Case, contending that the effect of *FA 2003, s 75A(5)* was that the chargeable consideration had in fact been £1,250,000,000 (the amount paid by M to P for the subsale of the freehold). The First-tier Tribunal upheld HMRC's amended Statement of Case, holding that the effect of *FA 2003, s 75A* was that P was chargeable to SDLT in respect of a notional land transaction, and that the chargeable consideration in respect of that notional land transaction had been £1,250,000,000. The Upper Tribunal allowed P's appeal in part, unanimously holding that P was chargeable to SDLT but holding (by the casting vote of Morgan J) that the chargeable consideration was £959,000,000. *Project Blue Ltd v HMRC*, UT [2014] UKUT 564 (TCC). (*Note*. For HMRC's response to the decision, see their Press Release dated 19 December 2014.)

Returns and administration (FA 2003, ss 76-84)

FA 2003, Sch 10 para 12—notices of enquiry

[75.9] Five companies submitted land transaction returns (forms SDLT1) declaring that they had entered into land transactions and that no SDLT was due. None of the companies filed an SDLT60 certificate in relation to any of the transactions. In August 2008 HMRC wrote to the companies stating that they intended to make enquiries into the transactions. Each of HMRC's letters wrongly stated that they intended to enquire into the 'self-certificate' rather than into the 'land transaction return'. HMRC subsequently issued notices under *FA 2003, Sch 10 para 14*, requiring the companies to produce documents and provide information. The companies appealed, contending that the letters which HMRC had issued in August 2008 were not valid notices of enquiry under *FA 2003, Sch 10 para 12*. The First-tier Tribunal rejected this contention and dismissed the appeals. Judge Berner held that it was 'abundantly clear' that HMRC had 'intended to open an enquiry into the land transaction returns and that they intended to give notice to the appellants of that intention'. This was not a case of HMRC 'seeking to change the basis on which an enquiry was opened'. The notices which HMRC had issued were 'substantially in conformity with' the relevant legislation. The companies 'would reasonably have ascertained that the intended effect was to open an enquiry into the land transaction returns, and that the reference to self certificates was a mistake'. Accordingly the notices were valid and effective. *Coolatinney Developments Ltd v HMRC*, FTT [2011] UKFTT 252 (TC), TC01116.

FA 2003, Sch 10 para 14—information notices

[75.10] A married couple purchased a property in 2006, and submitted a form SDLT1, indicating that the provisions of *FA 2003, s 45(3)* applied to the transaction. HMRC began an enquiry, sending notices under *FA 2003, Sch 10 para 12* both to the couple and to their solicitors. The couple's solicitors provided some of the information requested, but subsequently wrote to HMRC stating that the couple had never received the original notices of enquiry. In February 2009 HMRC issued notices to the couple under *FA 2003, Sch 10 para 14*. The couple appealed, contending that the notices were invalid. The First-tier Tribunal rejected this contention and dismissed the appeals, finding that 'notice of the enquiry had been sent to the appellants' agent and was received within the enquiry window'. Judge Blewitt held that the notice received by the couple's solicitors was 'valid and sufficient to satisfy the statutory requirements'. *K & R Weber v HMRC*, FTT [2011] UKFTT 437 (TC), TC01290.

FA 2003, Sch 10 para 35—right of appeal

[75.11] In 2008 a company (P) entered into an agreement for the grant of a lease. Before the lease had been formally granted, it took possession of the land and began paying rent. It filed an SDLT return and paid the SDLT due. In 2012 it entered into a deed of variation under which the extent of the land subject to the lease, and the rent payable, were reduced. It sought to amend its land transaction return and reclaim some of the SDLT which it had paid. HMRC rejected the claim on the grounds that the amendment had been made more than 12 months after the filing date. P appealed. The First-tier Tribunal dismissed the appeal, holding that 'the twelve-month time limit was specified by the legislation and must be taken as an expression of Parliament's intention to strictly limit claims to repayment of SDLT in this way'. However, the Upper Tribunal reversed this decision, holding that *FA 2003, Sch 10 para 35* should be construed as giving the Tribunal jurisdiction. The Tribunal observed that P had written to HMRC in August 2012 contending that the combined effect of *Sch 10 para 3* and *Sch 17A para 12A* was that the twelve-month time limit did not apply, that the HMRC officer dealing with the case had sought legal advice from an HMRC specialist, and that HMRC had subsequently sent two letters to P explaining why they did not accept P's contentions. Judge Herrington held that a letter of acknowledgment which HMRC had sent to P should be construed as an 'enquiry' and that the final letter which HMRC had sent to P should be construed as a closure notice, thus giving rise to a right of appeal. The case was remitted to the First-tier Tribunal 'for a substantive hearing of the arguments advanced by (P) as to why the twelve-month time limit does not apply'. *Portland Gas Storage Ltd v HMRC*, UT [2014] UKUT 270 (TCC); [2014] STC 2589. (*Note.* HMRC have applied to the Court of Appeal for leave to appeal against this decision.)

Miscellaneous

Application of Ramsay principle to stamp duty on land

[75.12] In a stamp duty appeal, a purchaser agreed to buy a freehold property for £145,500,and entered into a number of closely spaced transactions including an agreement for the property to be leased to the purchaser for 999 years for a premium of £145,000, and agreements for the freehold reversion to be sold to a company for £500 and resold by the company to the purchaser for £600. The Revenue assessed stamp duty of £1,456 (i.e. 1% of £145,600). The purchaser appealed, contending that stamp duty was only chargeable on the £600. The Ch D rejected this contention and dismissed the appeal. Applying the *Ramsay* principle, where a preordained series of transactions was entered into for the purpose of avoiding stamp duty, the court would disregard steps inserted in that series which had no business purpose, and treat the transactions as a single transaction achieving the preordained end. Here there was such a series, the preordained end being the conveyance of the unencumbered freehold interest to the appellant. The agreements for the lease and for the sale and resale of the freehold reversion had no business purpose and would be disregarded. *Ingram v CIR*, Ch D [1985] STC 835; [1986] 2 WLR 598.

[75.13] In a Hong Kong case, a company attempted to avoid the imposition of stamp duty on a sale of land by selling the land to a subsidiary company and then arranging for the issue of a number of 'B' shares that had no value. The court held that the *Ramsay* principle applied to the transactions, so that the sale of the land was within the charge to stamp duty. Ribeiro PJ held that 'the driving principle in the *Ramsay* line of cases continues to involve a general rule of statutory construction and an unblinkered approach to the analysis of the facts. The ultimate question is whether the relevant statutory provisions, construed purposively, were intended to apply to the transaction, viewed realistically.' *Hong Kong Collector of Stamp Revenue v Arrowtown Assets Ltd*, FCA(HK) 2003, 6 ITLR 454. (*Note.* This *dictum* was unanimously approved by the HL in the 2004 case of *Mawson v Barclays Mercantile Business Finance Ltd*, **8.101** CAPITAL ALLOWANCES.)

Penalty for failure to pay stamp duty

[75.14] The sale of a house was completed in September 2000. The purchasers failed to pay the stamp duty of £12,600 shown on the form TR1, so that their title to the property was not officially registered. In August 2006 they offered to pay the stamp duty so that they could register their title to the property. The Revenue imposed a penalty of £12,600 (i.e. an amount equal to the duty). The purchasers paid this amount, but lodged an appeal to the Special Commissioners, contending that the penalty was excessive. The Special Commissioners rejected this contention and dismissed the appeal, holding that there was no reasonable excuse for the delay in presenting the transfer for stamping. *IK & L De Nemethy v HMRC,* Sp C 2007, [2008] SSCD 136 (Sp C 627).

Penalty for failure to render return

[75.15] In May 2007 an individual (R) completed a lease as tenant, and became obliged to render a land transaction return under *FA 2003, s 76*. He did not render the return until June 2009 and HMRC imposed a penalty under *FA 2003, Sch 10 para 3*. R appealed, contending that he had not been aware of the obligation to make a land transaction return. The First-tier Tribunal dismissed his appeal, holding that there was no reasonable excuse for the default, and the Upper Tribunal upheld this decision. Judge Bishopp observed that 'the purpose of the legislation would be defeated if a penalty could be escaped by the expedient of placing the blame on a dilatory solicitor'. *C Ryan v HMRC*, UT [2012] UKUT 9 (TCC); [2012] STC 899.

[75.16] A company purchased five flats on 9 October 2009, and did not submit the relevant land transaction returns until 20 November 2009. HMRC imposed penalties totalling £500 under *FA 2003, Sch 10 para 3*. The Upper Tribunal dismissed the company's appeals, holding that the effect of *FA 2003, s 44(5)(b)* was that the effective date was 9 October 2009, and that the company should have submitted the returns within 30 days of that date. *Lancer Scott v HMRC*, UT [2012] UKUT 10 (TCC); [2012] STC 928.

[75.17] An individual (P) purchased 14 properties at an auction, and became obliged to render land transaction returns. HMRC did not receive the returns, and imposed penalties totalling £1,400 (ie £100 in respect of each property). P appealed, contending that he had posted the returns before the due date. The tribunal dismissed the appeal, finding that 'no evidence was led to show and/or corroborate that this letter and its enclosure had been posted'. *S Pariser v HMRC*, FTT [2010] UKFTT 460 (TC), TC00725.

[75.18] A similar decision was reached in *C Bason v HMRC*, FTT [2011] UKFTT 521 (TC), TC01368.

[75.19] Two surgeries were bought and sold in January 2010. The agents responsible for the transactions attempted to submit the land transaction returns online in February 2010. However, because of a failure in their computer system, the returns were not submitted. The agents did not realise this until March 2010, when they successfully submitted the returns. HMRC imposed penalties, and the purchasers appealed. The First-tier Tribunal dismissed the appeals, holding that the problems with the agents' computer system did not constitute a reasonable excuse. Judge Green held that 'the agent should have checked and ensured that the SDLT1 had been correctly submitted and the land transaction certificate generated. The purchaser has an obligation to ensure that a timely return is submitted.' *Sir J Oldham (Manor House Surgery Glossop) v HMRC (and related appeal)*, FTT [2011] UKFTT 236 (TC), TC01101.

[75.20] A company (S) submitted a form SDLT1 one day late, and HMRC imposed a penalty of £100. S appealed, contending that the penalty was unreasonable. The First-tier Tribunal rejected this contention and dismissed the appeal. *Shepherds Bookbinders Ltd v HMRC*, FTT [2014] UKFTT 514 (TC), TC03641.

[75.21] A couple purchased a property on 4 April 2014. Their solicitor (D) submitted a form SDLT1, with a cheque for the SDLT due, on 30 April. However D failed to complete box 4 of the return. HMRC returned the form to him on 6 May for completion. D returned the corrected form on 12 May, and HMRC imposed a penalty of £100. The First-tier Tribunal dismissed the couple's appeal, observing that D had chosen not to submit the return online, and that if he had submitted the return online, 'the built-in validation within the online submission process would have ensured that all the relevant questions on the return had been answered without omission'. *R & Mrs A Heler v HMRC*, FTT [2014] UKFTT 1002 (TC), TC04014.

[75.22] In August 2009 a woman (B) completed the purchase of a flat. She had instructed a firm of solicitors to carry out the conveyancing. However they failed to submit the relevant land transaction return to HMRC until 28 October. HMRC imposed a penalty, and B appealed, contending that she had a reasonable excuse because she had relied on her solicitors, and stating in evidence that 'the solicitors in question displayed such incompetence that the Solicitors Regulation Authority actually closed them down'. The First-tier Tribunal allowed her appeal, finding that 'the solicitors concerned were "intervened into" (i.e. closed down) by the Solicitors Regulation Authority'. Judge Brooks observed that 'although reliance on a third party is specifically precluded from being a reasonable excuse for VAT purposes' (by *VATA 1994, s 71*), *FA 2003* did not contain a similar provision with regard to SDLT. On the facts of this case, B's reliance on the solicitors constituted a reasonable excuse. *Ms C Browne v HMRC*, FTT [2010] UKFTT 496 (TC), [2011] SFTD 67; TC00754.

[75.23] In November 2009 an individual (P) completed the purchase of a property. HMRC imposed a penalty of £100 on the basis that they did not receive the relevant SDLT1 return until 18 December 2009. P appealed, contending that the solicitors acting for him had submitted the return on 30 November, which was within the statutory time limit. The First-tier Tribunal accepted his evidence and allowed his appeal. *A Pericleous v HMRC*, FTT [2011] UKFTT 52 (TC), TC00930.

[75.24] A couple purchased a property in March 2010. Their solicitors sent the form SDLT1 and appropriate cheque to HMRC. On 30 April one of the solicitors contacted HMRC because she had not received a certificate of payment (SDLT5). HMRC responded that they had not received the SDLT1 or cheque. The solicitor cancelled the original cheque, submitted a new SDLT1 electronically and paid the duty by electronic transfer. HMRC imposed a penalty but the First-tier Tribunal allowed the couple's appeal. Judge Tildesley accepted the couple's evidence and held that, despite the statement in HMRC's Stamp Duty Land Tax Manual SDLTM 86460, the fact that a return had been delayed or lost in the post could constitute a reasonable excuse. He observed that the solicitor 'had established a process which involved a prompt on her computer that the 30 day period of protection given by the official Land Registry search of the property was due to expire. This prompt alerted her to the non-receipt of the certificate of payment of the Stamp Duty Land Tax (SDLT5).' Accordingly there was a reasonable excuse, within *FA 2003, s 97*. *C Runham & Ms C Naramore v HMRC*, FTT [2011] UKFTT 55 (TC), TC00933.

Purchaser acquiring freehold and leasehold interests—whether penalty due

[75.25] In June 2010 an individual (B) acquired both the leasehold and freehold interests in a property. He submitted a land transaction return (SDLT1) showing both the freehold and leasehold title numbers, and stating that the vendor of both titles was a bank (S). HMRC issued SDLT5 certificates in respect of both purchases. However, in August 2010 the Land Registry rejected the application for registration of change of ownership of the freehold, on the grounds that the registered owner was a limited company (G) rather than S. B then submitted a replacement SDLT1 showing G as the vendor of the freehold. HMRC imposed a penalty on the grounds that the amended return had been delivered outside the statutory time limit. B appealed. The First-tier Tribunal allowed the appeal, observing that the contract of sale had stated that S was the vendor of both the leasehold and the freehold. B had delivered a land transaction return showing both the freehold and leasehold title numbers within the statutory time limit, and this return complied with the requirements of *FA 2003, s 76(1)*, so that no penalty was due. *SW Broughall v HMRC*, FTT [2011] UKFTT 193 (TC), TC01062.

Penalty for inaccurate SDLT return

[75.26] A solicitor (C) and his wife purchased a property for £763,750. They submitted an SDLT return declaring the purchase price as £100,000. When HMRC discovered this, the couple paid the SDLT due of £30,550. HMRC imposed a penalty of £16,038. The couple paid this amount. Subsequently C discovered that HMRC were proposing to disclose his identity under *FA 2009, s 94*. C applied to the First-tier Tribunal for permission to lodge a late appeal. Judge Mosedale dismissed his application, observing that the provisions of *TMA, s 54* did not apply to SDLT penalties but holding that the correspondence between C and HMRC amounted to 'a binding and lawful contract'. Therefore the tribunal had no jurisdiction to consider the application, and even if the tribunal had possessed jurisdiction, this would not be an appropriate case to admit a late appeal. Judge Mosedale observed that 'it is clear from the correspondence that the appellants were prepared to admit to deliberate misdeclaration as long as their names were not published'. It appeared that 'the main reason they want the opportunity of proving that the misdeclaration was inadvertent is in order to prevent publication of their names as deliberate defaulters'. *R & Mrs G Chan v HMRC (aka Mr & Mrs B v HMRC)*, FTT [2014] UKFTT 256 (TC), TC03395. (*Note*. For another issue in this case, see **4.151** APPEALS.)

Application for judicial review of FA 2013, s 194

[75.27] A company which had entered into a SDLT avoidance scheme applied for judicial review of *FA 2013, s 194* (which amended *FA 2003, s 45* to clarify that the scheme was ineffective). The QB dismissed the application, applying the principles laid down by the CA in *R (oao Huitson) v HMRC*, **21.43** DOUBLE TAX RELIEF. Andrews J observed that there had been 'a history of warnings and of measures being taken to close down similar artificial and abusive schemes'. She held that 'in the light of the many clear and repeated warnings given to taxpayers and their advisers, the claimants had no legitimate expectation that they would be able to acquire property of substantial value, and pay only a fraction of the SDLT which would ordinarily have been due on the transfer of that property to them, while other taxpayers who acquired land of a similar value and who abided by the spirit of the original legislation paid the SDLT in full'. It was 'a legitimate and important aim of UK public policy in fiscal affairs to ensure that everybody buying property pays their fair share of SDLT'. *R (oao St Matthews West Ltd) v HM Treasury (and related applications)*, QB [2014] EWHC 1848 (Admin); [2014] STC 2350.

Index

This index is referenced to the chapter and paragraph number.

The entries printed in bold capitals are main subject headings in the text.

B

C

D

E

F

G

H

J

K

L

M

N

Q

R

T